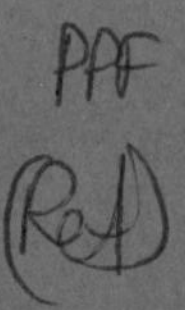

DIRECTORY OF

MUSEUMS, GALLERIES AND BUILDINGS OF HISTORIC INTEREST IN THE UNITED KINGDOM

3RD EDITION

DIRECTORY OF MUSEUMS, GALLERIES AND BUILDINGS OF HISTORIC INTEREST IN THE UNITED KINGDOM

3RD EDITION

EDITED BY KEITH W. REYNARD

11 New Fetter Lane
London EC4P 4EE
Tel: +44 (0)20 7822 4300; Fax: +44 (0)20 7822 4319
Email: edit.europa@tandf.co.uk; Internet: http://www.europapublications.com
(A member of the Taylor & Francis Group)

First edition 1993
Second edition 1996
Third edition 2003

ISBN 0 85142 473 2

A CIP record for this book is available from the British Library

Printed and bound in Great Britain by Polestar Wheatons, Exeter.

Foreword

Scope
This directory sets out to provide information useful to those wishing to visit places and to see things of beauty and historic interest, of which our country is so full. It has its origins in the Directory of Museums and Special Collections in the United Kingdom and the Aslib Directory of Information Sources in the United Kingdom.The 11th edition of the Aslib Directory of Information Sources in the United Kingdom had become as large as was reasonable to handle and several hundred entries had to be omitted for want of space. It was therefore decided to split the directory and revive the Directory of Museums and Special Collections in the United Kingdom, albeit with a different scope. The museums and other relevant records were transferred, and the new directory greatly expanded to include these and galleries and buildings of historic interest, creating what is in effect a completely new directory.

The overlap between the two previous directories was not inconsiderable so care was taken this time to minimise it. In the event only 156 of the entries and 35 cross-references out of a total of nearly 11,000 in the Aslib Directory are repeated in this Directory that has over 3200 entries.

I am especially grateful to those who completed our questionnaire and provided additional information. In particular to English Heritage, the National Trust and the National Trust for Scotland, who, when over 60 per cent of all their sites had responded, were extremely helpful in providing the additional information from their literature and, in the case of the National Trust, their database. We were permitted to construct our entries from these sources and this added to and also updated the information already received. In addition many city and county museums officers assisted in gathering information on those places for which they are responsible. Without their help this volume would be much the poorer.

Many museums are not static collections but have working machinery, they are living museums. For this reason it was decided to put all the restored railway lines into this volume. The interpretation of what was a building extended from the house, castle and cathedral to include other man-made sites such as walls, windmills and follies, and the works of those who shaped our country, our ancestors who dug Grime's Graves, or the creations of 'Capability' Brown. The more we looked the more we found.

Access
The accessibility of places and their content varies greatly, both in time and to those with some form of disability. Whereas the largest museums have sufficient permanent staff to provide year round access during regular hours, small museums of no less interest are frequently manned by volunteers and often only during holiday periods and the tourist season. Buildings vary from those like Hadrian's Wall that can be explored at any time to those that are private residences open by courtesy on a restricted basis. The layout in some places means that disabled people, such as those in wheelchairs, have limited access, though increasingly video facilities are provided so that they may see something of what is available, for example on other than the ground floor. For the partially sighted or deaf it is helpful to know that large type notices, hearing loops or tape-recorded guides are available. I asked for and have provided as much guidance as possible on the access to avoid disappointing visits by those persons with disabilities.

Opening hours
Visitors should be aware that for various reasons such as staffing, special events, holidays or hours of daylight, opening hours may vary from those listed in this book. A phone call can save a wasted journey.

Educational facilities
Increasingly schools are seeking, and places such as these are providing, facilities related to the National Curriculum. So I have asked for and provided information on the resources available. In many sites there are education officers to assist visitors, or guided tours are provided by arrangement to pre-booked parties, which may be tailored to particular audiences.

Local and family history
Very many of the places listed have resources valuable to those researching their own or the past history of other families. Strangely museums have often been overlooked in this context, whereas the

Internet resources and family history societies are well known. (The latter are covered in the Aslib Directory of Information Sources in the United Kingdom.)

The Internet
The majority of places have information, sometimes quite extensive, on their own or their parent body's website. Whilst this is helpful in finding up-to-date hours of opening and general information there is nothing to beat a personal visit. Sadly the days when one could walk round and touch the stones at Stonehenge are now gone but in many museums there are now special collections of objects that one can touch and hold.

Indexing
All entries are based on the information received from the organisations and so the indexing of this volume could only be done on the information provided. So there is some variation in the depth of indexing. Whilst it is important to include the great national museums and galleries we did not have the detailed listing of their collections and so it was not possible to index their collections to same level as some of the smaller and equally fascinating places in small towns and villages. The former are well known, and the latter have local treasures that deserve a wider audience. As with the Aslib Directory, Sarah Blair not only proofread the entries with great rigour but also marked-up the basis for the indexing which was then added to and completed with a greatly expanded thesaurus. I am very appreciative of her sterling efforts.

Support
Matthew McFarlane once again assisted with the development of the software when I ran into difficulties and Sue McFarlane pitched in at a difficult time and helped in particular with the gathering of Scottish entries. But without the support of my wife Sandra, who spent many hours on the telephone gathering information from people who were more ready to talk enthusiastically about their collections and buildings than to complete yet another questionnaire, this volume would still be some way from publication.

It has been a fascinating and rewarding time collecting this information and I hope and expect that users will discover much of what they can truly say 'not a lot of people know that'.

Keith W Reynard, Editor
12 May 2003

Contents

Main Directory

1
1 ROYAL CRESCENT
Bath, BA1 2LR

Tel: 01225 338727
Fax: 01225 481850
Acronym or abbreviation: BPT
Full name: Bath Preservation Trust
Formed: 1970

Organisation type and purpose: Registered charity, historic building, house or site, suitable for ages: all ages.
Parent body:
Bath Preservation Trust
at the same address, tel: 01225 338727, fax: 01225 481850
Other addresses:
Bath Preservation Trust (BPT)
Tel: 01225 428126

Enquiries to: Curator
Other contacts: Administrator for group bookings.
Access:
Access to staff: By letter, by telephone, by fax, visitors by prior appointment
Hours: Curator: Mon to Thu, 0900 to 1700

General description:
This was the first house to be built in John Wood the younger's Royal Crescent, in 1767. It has been restored and redecorated to look as it would have done in the late 18th century. Fine paintings and furniture in particular are well represented.
Information services:
Helpline available, tel no: 01225 428126.
Special visitor services: Guided tours.
Services for disabled people: For the visually impaired; for the hearing impaired.
Collections:
18th century Collection
Hugh Roberts Collection. Early kitchen equipment including some specifically Bath pieces.17th/18th century, some early 19th century possible, c. 250 items
A good example of a Georgian town house furnishings.
Printed publications:
Guide Book (£2)

Internet home pages:
http://www.bath-preservation-trust.org.uk

2
198 GALLERY
194-198 Railton Road, Herne Hill, London, SE24 0JT

Tel: 020 7978 8309
Fax: 020 7737 5315
Email: info@198gallery.co.uk
Formed: 1988

Organisation type and purpose: Registered charity (charity number 801614), art gallery. Multicultural visual arts.
Contemporary arts education focussing on cultural diversity.

Enquiries to: Manager/Education Co-ordinator
Direct email: lucy@198gallery.co.uk
Other contacts: Exhibition Officer
Access:
Access to staff: By letter, by email, visitors by prior appointment
Access to building, collections or gallery: No prior appointment required
Hours: Mon to Fri, 1000 to 1700; Sat, 1200 to 1600
Access for disabled people: level entry, access to all public areas, toilet facilities

General description:
Debut exhibitions of younger or emerging artists from Caribbean, Africa, Asian backgrounds, using a wide range of media including cutting edge electronic and installation work.
Education: top of the range Mac design suite offering creative IT training to disaffected and excluded young people from local schools and referral agencies, project title 'Urbanvision' after school and Saturday club.
Information services:
Library available for reference (for conditions see Access above)
Special visitor services: Materials and/or activities for children.
Education services: Group education facilities, resources for Key Stages 1 and 2, 3, 4 and Further or Higher Education..
Collections:
Slide archive of contemporary artists from different cultural backgrounds
Printed publications:
Various exhibition catalogues, past and present

Internet home pages:
http://www.198gallery.co.uk/

3
2 WILLOW ROAD
Hampstead, London, NW3 1TH

Tel: 020 7435 6166
Fax: 020 7435 6166
Email: 2willowroad@nationaltrust.org.uk
Formed: 1996

Organisation type and purpose: National organisation, registered charity (charity number 205846), museum, art gallery, historic building, house or site, suitable for ages: 12+.
Parent body:
The National Trust (South and South East Region)
Thames and Solent Regional Office, tel: 01494 528051

Enquiries to: Curator
Access:
Access to staff: By telephone, by fax, by email

General description:
The former home of Ernö Goldfinger, designed and built by him in 1939. The central house of a terrace of three, it is one of Britain's most important examples of Modernist architecture and is filled with furniture also designed by Goldfinger. The art collection includes a number of significant British and European 20th century works, Bridget Riley, Max Ernst and Henry Moore being represented, amongst others.
Information services:
Special visitor services: Guided tours.
Education services: Resources for Further or Higher Education.
Services for disabled people: For the hearing impaired.
Collections:
Goldfinger furniture designs
20th century European and British Art Collections

Internet home pages:
http://www.nationaltrust.org.uk

4
20 FORTHLIN ROAD, ALLERTON
Liverpool, L24 1YP

Tel: 0151 427 7231 (Tour booking line)
Email: 20forthlinroad@nationaltrust.org.uk

Organisation type and purpose: National organisation, registered charity (charity number 205846), historic building, house or site.
Parent body:
The National Trust (North West)
North West Regional Office, tel: 0870 609 5391

Enquiries to: Manager
Access:
Access to staff: By letter, by telephone, by email
Access for disabled people: toilet facilities
Other restrictions: Ground floor fully accessible. No access to other floors. Audiovisual/video. Adapted WC at Speke Hall.

General description:
This 1950s terraced house is the former home of the McCartney family, where the Beatles met, rehearsed and wrote many of their earliest songs. Displays include contemporary photographs by Michael McCartney and early Beatles memorabilia. The audio tour features contributions from both Michael and Sir Paul McCartney.
Information services:
Helpline available, tel no: Infoline 08457 585702 (for Speke Hall and Forthlin Road).
Audio guide.
Special visitor services: Tape recorded guides..

Internet home pages:
http://www.nationaltrust.org.uk

5
24 HOUR MUSEUM
See - Campaign for Museums

6
24TH/41ST FOOT
See - South Wales Borderers & Monmouthshire Regimental Museum

7
390TH BOMB GROUP MEMORIAL AIR MUSEUM
Parham Airfield, Parham, Woodbridge, Suffolk, IP13 9AF

Tel: 01728 621373
Formed: 1981

Organisation type and purpose: Membership association (membership is by subscription), present number of members: 200, registered charity (charity number 284146), museum, suitable for ages: 12+.
Houses the:
Museum of the British Resistance Organisation - The Auxiliary Units
at the same address

Enquiries to: Chairman
Direct tel: 01473 711275
Access:
Access to staff: By letter, by telephone
Access to building, collections or gallery: No prior appointment required
Hours: Mar to Oct: Sun, Bank Holiday Mon, 1100 to 1800
Jun to Aug: Wed, 1100 to 1600
Access for disabled people: Parking provided, ramped entry

General description:
The museum is based in a restored airfield control tower and includes many items connected with the United States Army Air Force, including aircraft engines, uniforms and mementoes; RAF and Luftwaffe; uniforms; photographs and archive material; historic DC-3 aircraft built 1939 and under restoration by museum. Artefacts from the auxiliary units and archive material. Contains material covering many aspects of military and civilian life during the period of air warfare in East Anglia, 1939 to 1945.
Collections:
Books and documents relating to operational records of 390th Bomb Group - USAAF and Auxiliary Units
Parts of Joseph Kennedy's Liberator bomber used for ill-fated 'flying bomb' missions, 1944
Catalogues:
Catalogue for library is in-house only. Catalogue for all of the collections is only available in-house.
Printed publications:
Newsletter (2 times a year for members)
Museum Guide Book
Leaflet
Auxiliary Unit Booklet

8
446TH BOMB GROUP USAAF MUSEUM
See - Norfolk & Suffolk Aviation Museum

9
A LA RONDE
Summer Lane, Exmouth, Devon, EX8 5BD

Tel: 01395 265514
Formed: 1991

Organisation type and purpose: National organisation, registered charity (charity number 205846), historic building, house or site, suitable for ages: 16+.
Small historic house and park.
Parent body:
The National Trust (South West Region)
Regional Office for Devon and Cornwall, Broadclyst, Exeter, Devon, EX5 3LE, tel: 01392 881691, fax: 01392 881954
Other addresses:
The National Trust
36 Queen Anne's Gate, London, SW1H 9AS, tel: 020 7222 9251

Enquiries to: Curator
Access:
Access to staff: By letter, by telephone
Access for disabled people: Parking provided, level entry, toilet facilities
Other restrictions: Unsuitable for wheelchairs. Ground floor accessible with assistance, narrow doorways and small rooms are difficult to access. No access to other floors. Level entrance to shop. Steps to tea-room entrance.

General description:
A unique 16-sided house built on the instructions of two spinster cousins, Jane and Mary Parminter, on their return from a grand tour of Europe. Completed c.1796, the house contains many 18th century objects and collections brought back by the Parminters. The fascinating interior decoration includes a feather frieze and shell-encrusted gallery which, due to its fragility, can only be viewed on closed-circuit television.
Information services:
Special visitor services: Guided tours, tape recorded guides.
Services for disabled people: For the visually impaired.
Collections:
Collections from a Grand Tour
Unique interior decoration using feathers and shells
Silhouettes
Ladies' amusements
Catalogues:
Catalogue for part of the collections is only available in-house.
Printed publications:
Guide Book (£2.50)

Internet home pages:
http://www.nationaltrust.org.uk/regions/devon

10
ABBEY HOUSE MUSEUM
Abbey Walk, Kirkstall, Leeds, West Yorkshire, LS5 3EH

Tel: 0113 230 5492
Fax: 0113 230 5499
Formed: 1927

Organisation type and purpose: Local government body, museum.
Housed in the:
Great Gatehouse of Kirkstall Abbey (Cistercian); one of Leeds City Museums

Enquiries to: Curator
Access:
Access for disabled people: Parking provided, ramped entry, access to all public areas, toilet facilities

General description:
Three recreated Victorian streets including The Hare to Rover Inn and an undertakers. Also visit the Victorian Leeds Gallery, the Childhood Gallery and the Kirkstall Abbey Gallery.

Information services:
Special visitor services: Materials and/or activities for children.
Education services: Group education facilities, resources for Key Stages 1 and 2, 3, 4 and Further or Higher Education.
Services for disabled people: For the visually impaired; displays and/or information at wheelchair height.
Collections:
Social history collections including toys, games and costume
Leeds and Burmantofts pottery
Printed publications:
Guide books

11
ABBEY PUMPING STATION MUSEUM OF SCIENCE AND TECHNOLOGY
Corporation Road, Leicester, LE4 5PX

Tel: 0116 299 5111
Fax: 0116 299 5125
Formed: 1973
Formerly: Leicester Museum of Technology, date of change, 1995

Organisation type and purpose: Local government body, museum, historic building, house or site, suitable for ages: all ages.
Parent body:
Leicester City Museum Service
Leicester City Council Arts and Leisure, New Wall Centre, Welford Place, Leicester, LE1 6ZG

Enquiries to: Managing Curator
Direct tel: 0116 229 5113
Direct email: warbs001@leicester.gov.uk
Access:
Access to staff: By letter, by telephone, by fax, by email, visitors by prior appointment
Hours: Mon to Sat, 0815 to 1725; Sun, 1400 to 1725
Access to building, collections or gallery: No prior appointment required
Hours: Apr to Oct: Mon to Sat, 1000 to 1700; Sun, 1400 to 1700
Nov to Mar: Mon to Sat, 1000 to 1600; Sun, 1300 to 1600
Other restrictions: Closed 24, 25, 26, 31 Dec and 1 Jan.
Access for disabled people: Parking provided, level entry, access to all public areas, toilet facilities
Other restrictions: Limited access.

General description:
Industrial history of Leicester, steam engines, buses, narrow gauge railways, sanitory and public health history.
Housed in a sewage pumping station built in 1891 and still contains four Woolf Compound Rotative beam engines, 3 are still powered by steam and one is run during special events.
Exhibitions devoted to optical science, history of Leicester trams and public health in Leicestershire; displays include interactives and hands-on interpretation.
Information services:
Helpline available, tel no: 0116 299 5111.
Special visitor services: Materials and/or activities for children.
Education services: Group education facilities, resources for Key Stages 1 and 2 and 3.
Services for disabled people: Displays and/or information at wheelchair height.
Collections:
Artefacts relating to Leicester's industrial heritage including large collection of knitting machines, machine tools, lenses and typewriters
Engines made by Gimsons of Leicester.
Working public service road vehicles, delivery lorry, fish and chip van, electric vehicles and horse-drawn vehicles
Working steam engines, narrow gauge railway (also passenger-carrying)
Extensive library to support these collections
Catalogues:
Catalogue for all of the collections is only available in-house.

Internet home pages:
http://www.leicestermuseums.ac.uk

12
ABBEYDALE INDUSTRIAL HAMLET
Abbeydale Road South, Sheffield, South Yorkshire

Tel: 0114 2367731
Fax: 0114 23653196
Formed: 1974

Organisation type and purpose: Registered charity (charity number 1042287), museum, historic building, house or site, suitable for ages: 5+.
Parent body:
Sheffield Industrial Museums Trust (SIMT)
Tel: 0114 2722106, fax: 0114 2757847

Enquiries to: Executive Director
Other contacts: (1) Executive Director (2) Collections and Access Officer (3) Education Officer (4) Operations Officer for (1) management (2) access to collections not on display (3) education queries (4) private bookings and school bookings.
Access:
Access to staff: By letter, by telephone, by fax
Hours: Museum open Easter to end Oct: Mon to Thu, 1000 to 1600; Sun, 1100 to 1645; visits can be arranged during closed season
Other restrictions: Appointments needed for curatorial services.

General description:
Waterwheels; scythe manufacture; crucible steel manufacture.
Collections:
Objects, documents, photographs (in the process of being catalogued on computer)
Catalogues:
Catalogue for part of the collections is only available in-house.

Internet home pages:
http://www.simt.co.uk

13
ABBOT HALL ART GALLERY
Kendal, Cumbria, LA9 5AL

Tel: 01539 722464
Fax: 01539 722494
Email: info@abbothall.org.uk
Formed: 1962
Formerly: Abbot Hall Art Gallery and Museum

Organisation type and purpose: Independently owned, registered charity (charity number 562980), museum, art gallery, historic building, house or site, suitable for ages: 8+.
Affiliated to:
Lakeland Arts Trust
At the same address

Enquiries to: Curator
Access:
Access to staff: By letter, by telephone, by fax, by email, visitors by prior appointment, Internet web pages
Hours: Mon to Fri, 0900 to 1700
Other restrictions: Appointment required for visitors to the library or for research of collections.
Access to building, collections or gallery: No prior appointment required
Hours: Daily, 1030 to 1700; (closes 1600 in Winter)

Other restrictions: Gallery closed Christmas and Feb.
Access for disabled people: Parking provided, level entry, access to all public areas, toilet facilities

General description:
Fine and decorative arts, identification, restoration, etc, artists and craftsmen of Cumbria, past and present. Temporary contemporary exhibitions.
Information services:
Library available for reference (for conditions see Access above)
Special visitor services: Guided tours, materials and/or activities for children.
Education services: Group education facilities, resources for Key Stages 1 and 2, 3, 4 and Further or Higher Education..
Collections:
A S Clay and M V Young Collections of watercolours, drawings and sketchbooks of John Harden
Cunliffe Bequest (35 watercolours and drawings of John Ruskin)
Important collections of watercolours, drawings and oils of Lake District views
Seven portraits by George Romney, drawings and sketchbooks by George Romney
Collections of furniture by Gillows of Lancaster, the Simpsons of Kendal, Stanley Davies and Eric Sharpe
Publications list:
is available in hard copy.
Printed publications:
Catalogue of paintings, drawings, watercolours and sculpture in the permanent collection
Catalogues for specific temporary exhibitions
Friends newsletters (quarterly)
Vision - yearly review/preview

Internet home pages:
http://www.abbothall.org.uk
Information on: Abbot Hall Art Gallery, collections, education service, visitor information, Kendal's museums, Kendal, The Lake District, Blackwell restoration project in Bowness.

14
ABBOT HOUSE HERITAGE CENTRE
Maygate, Dunfermline, Fife, KY12 7NE

Tel: 01383 733266
Fax: 01383 624908
Email: dht@abbothouse.fsnet.co.uk
Formed: 1400s

Organisation type and purpose: Independently owned, registered charity (charity number SCO 18318), museum, historic building, house or site, suitable for ages: 8+.
Heritage centre.
Educational.
Parent body:
Dunfermline Heritage Trust (DHT)

Enquiries to: Manager
Access:
Access to staff: By letter, by telephone, by fax, by email, in person, charges to non-members
Access to building, collections or gallery: No prior appointment required
Hours: Daily, 1000 to 1700
Other restrictions: Last tour 1615.
Access for disabled people: Parking provided, level entry, toilet facilities
Other restrictions: Access to ground floor and garden only.

General description:
Visit the oldest house in Dunfermline and hear its story told by the resident ghost. See history unfold before you. Feel the atmosphere within its walls. Sample fayre from the Abbot's Kitchen or stroll in the scented garden.
The displays in Abbot House span more than 1000 years of Scottish life and history from the time of the Picts to the building of the Forth Road Bridge. Originally the 15th century residence of the mighty Abbot of Dunfermline, the old house has witnessed great events and, since Dunfermline was the ancient capital of Scotland, its story and that of its folk becomes the story of the Scottish nation. The warmth of our welcome and the home baking in our café are our specialities.
Information services:
Displays/information at wheelchair height on ground floor only.
Special visitor services: Guided tours, materials and/or activities for children.
Education services: Group education facilities.
Services for disabled people: For the visually impaired; displays and/or information at wheelchair height.
Collections:
Various material of local and national interest, eg replica of Robert the Bruce's sword
Publications list:
is available on-line.
Printed publications:
House leaflet
Education packs for schools
Abbot House Guide Book

Internet home pages:
http://www.abbothouse.co.uk
Opening hours, details of exhibitions and information about contents of the house.

See also - Dunfermline Heritage Trust

15
ABBOTSFORD
Melrose, Roxburghshire, TD6 9BQ

Tel: 01896 752043
Fax: 01896 752916
Formed: 1833

Organisation type and purpose: Independently owned, historic building, house or site, suitable for ages: 8+.

Enquiries to: Owner
Access:
Access to staff: By letter, by telephone, by fax, charges made to all users
Access to building, collections or gallery: No prior appointment required
Hours: Mon to Sat, 0930 to 1700
Jun to Sep: Sun, 0930 to 1700
Mar to May and Oct: Sun, 1400 to 1700
Other restrictions: Nov to mid Mar: Groups by arrangement.
Access for disabled people: Parking provided, toilet facilities
Other restrictions: Entry via private entrance, disabled toilets on lower level accessed by terrace door.

General description:
Abbotsford - The House Sir Walter Scott, the 19th century novelist, built and lived in 1812-1832. Situated on the banks of the River Tweed. Visitors see Sir Walter Scott's study, library, drawing room and dining room where Sir Walter died on 21 September 1832, armouries and entrance hall with an impressive collection of historic relics, weapons and armour. Private chapel where Cardinal Newman said Mass on several occasions, terrace, gardens, woodland walk, gift shop and tea shop.
Information services:
Special visitor services: Guided tours.
Services for disabled people: Displays and/or information at wheelchair height.
Collections:
Sir Walter Scott. Various Scottish historical objects, including armour and weapons
Library contains:
9000 rare volumes
Bust of Sir Walter Scott by Sir Francis Chantrey (1820)
Lock of Prince Charles's Hair
Helen MacGregor's Brooch
Burns' Tumbler, with some verses scratched upon it
Montrose's sword
Rob Roy's gun, sword, dirk, sporran
Catalogues:
Catalogue for library is published.
Printed publications:
Guide Book (for purchase)
Postcards (from 20p)

Internet home pages:
http://www.scotborders.org.uk

16
ABERCONWY HOUSE
Castle Street, Conwy, Gwynedd, LL32 8AY

Tel: 01492 592246
Fax: 01492 585153

Organisation type and purpose: National organisation, registered charity (charity number 205846), museum, historic building, house or site, suitable for ages: 8+.
Parent body:
The National Trust Office for Wales
Trinity Square, Llandudno, LL30 2DE, tel: 01492 860123, fax: 01492 860233

Enquiries to: Manager
Access:
Access to staff: By letter, by telephone
Access to building, collections or gallery: No prior appointment required
Hours: Easter to November, Mon, Wed to Sun, 1100 to 1700
Other restrictions: Closed Tue

General description:
Dating from the 14th century, this is the only medieval merchant's house in Conwy to have survived the turbulent history of this walled town over nearly six centuries. Furnished rooms and an audiovisual presentation show daily life from different periods in its history.

Internet home pages:
http://www.nationaltrust.org.uk

17
ABERDEEN ART GALLERY
Schoolhill, Aberdeen, AB10 IFQ

Tel: 01224 523700
Fax: 01224 632133
Email: info@aagm.co.uk

Organisation type and purpose: Local government body, art gallery.

Enquiries to: Publications Officer
Access:
Access to staff: By letter, by telephone, by fax, by email, visitors by prior appointment
Access to building, collections or gallery: No prior appointment required
Hours: Mon to Sat, 1000 to 1700; Sun, 1400 to 1700
Access for disabled people: access to all public areas, toilet facilities

General description:
Housing an important fine art collection, with particularly good examples of 19th and 20th century works, a rich and diverse applied art collection, an exciting programme of special exhibitions, a gallery shop and a café.
Information services:
Library available for reference (for conditions see Access above)
Catalogue for all collections published.
Special visitor services: Guided tours, materials and/or activities for children.
Education services: Group education facilities..
Collections:
Pat Black Trust: Joan Eardley drawings
Joan Burnett Gift: Historical dress
Cochrane Collection: European and British Porcelain, presented through NACF
James Cromar Watt Bequest: Oriental ceramics, lacquer and metalwork and Venetian glass
Duguid Gift: Ayrshire whitework
Alexander Fleming Bequest: Ceramics
Fleming Collection: Staffordshire flatback figures
Gordon Bequest: Chinese ceramics
Miss Margaret C Hamilton Bequest: Funding
Harrower Bequest: Lace and carved wood
Miss Mary Herdman Bequest: Work by James Giles

continued overleaf

Archibald Hyslop Bequest: Paintings
Miss Margaret Cumming Innes Bequest: Funding
Sir Thomas Jaffrey Gift: Funding
Rex Nan Kivell Bequest: Etchings
Captain Harvey Loutit Bequest: Funding
Mrs Harvey Loutit Bequest: Funding
Sir Alex Lyon Trust: Funding
James McBey Bequest: Paintings and funding
Marguerite McBey Bequest: Paintings and funding
Alexander MacDonald Bequest: Paintings and funding
Sir James Murray Bequest: Paintings, plaster casts and funding
Robinson-Young Collection: Art Pottery, purchased with assistance from the National Fund for Acquisitions
Simpson Bequest: Needlework and 19th century purses
John Sparrow Bequest: Watercolours and drawings by James Giles
Vaughan Collection: Perthshire Glass, purchased with assistance from the National Fund for Acquisitions
Peggy Walker Gift: Historical dress and accessories
Alexander Webster Bequest: Paintings, china and funding
Catalogues:
Catalogue for all of the collections is published.

Internet home pages:
http://www.aberdeencity.gov.uk

18
ABERDEEN MARITIME MUSEUM
Shiprow, Aberdeen, AB11 5BY

Tel: 01224 337700
Fax: 01224 213066
Email: info@aagm.co.uk
Formed: 1984

Organisation type and purpose: Museum.
Operated by:
Aberdeen City Council
Arts and Recreation Department, St Nicholas House, Broad Street, Aberdeen
Owned by:
National Trust for Scotland

Enquiries to: Curator
Access:
Access to staff: By letter, by telephone, by fax, by email, in person, visitors by prior appointment
Hours: Mon to Fri, 0900 to 1700
Access to building, collections or gallery: No prior appointment required
Hours: Mon to Sat, 1000 to 1700; Sun, 1200 to 1500
Access for disabled people: level entry, access to all public areas, toilet facilities

General description:
The museum is housed in Provost Ross's House, which was built in 1593 and is the third oldest house in Aberdeen. It gives a wonderful insight into the rich maritime history of the city including the North Sea oil and gas industries, fishing, shipbuilding, harbour history, maritime paintings and photographs.
Information services:
Education services: Group education facilities.
Services for disabled people: Displays and/or information at wheelchair height.
Collections:
Shipbuilding Plans of Hall Russell; John Lewis; Aberdeen
Fishing equipment, 1850-1990
Ship portraits and maritime art, 1590-1994, over 150 items
Ship models and half models, 1689-1994, 225 items
Offshore oil, North Sea oil and gas industry, 1960s to the present
Catalogues:
Catalogue for all of the collections is only available in-house.

Internet home pages:
http://www.aagm.co.uk

19
ABERDEEN UNIVERSITY
Geology Department Museum, Meston Building, Kings College, Aberdeen, AB24 3UB

Tel: 01224 273448

Organisation type and purpose: University department or institute, research organisation.

Enquiries to: Curator
Direct email: n.trewin@abdn.ac.uk
Access:
Access to staff: By letter, visitors by prior appointment
Access to building, collections or gallery: Prior appointment required
Other restrictions: Access to researchers only
Access for disabled people: Parking provided, ramped entry

General description:
Geology, paleontology, mineralogy.
Collections:
Gordon collection of rocks and minerals
Nicholson collection of fossils

Internet home pages:
http://www.abdn.ac.uk/geology
General department website

20
ABERDEEN UNIVERSITY
Marischal Museum, Marischal College, Broad Street, Aberdeen, AB10 1YS

Tel: 01224 274301
Fax: 01224 274302
Email: museum@abdn.ac.uk
Formed: 1786
Formerly: Anthropological Museum, date of change, 1990

Organisation type and purpose: Museum, university department or institute.
Parent body:
University of Aberdeen

Enquiries to: Curator
Other contacts: Conservator
Access:
Access to staff: By letter, by telephone, by fax, by email, Internet web pages
Hours: Mon to Fri, 1000 to 1700; Sun, 1400 to 1700
Access to building, collections or gallery: No prior appointment required

General description:
Cultural anthropology, material culture, art and antiquities of the Ancient World, tribal art, coins, Scottish prehistory, Scottish history.
Information services:
Library available for reference (for conditions see Access above)
Special visitor services: Materials and/or activities for children.
Education services: Group education facilities, resources for Key Stages 1 and 2, 3 and 4..
Collections:
Dr James Grant (Bey) Egyptian Collection
Gordon collection of Scottish weapons and militaria
Henderson Collection of classical vases
Sir Alexander Ogston Weapon Collection
Sir William MacGregor Ethnographical Collection from Papua New Guinea
Large collection of 'Beaker' remains, Early Bronze Age, from North Scotland
Catalogues:
Catalogue for all of the collections is only available in-house.
Printed publications:
Learning with Objects (Kim Davidson, £3, free to teachers)
Magic Metal - Metal Working in NEBA (Trevor Cowie, £5)
Powerful Pots - Beakers in North East Prehistory (Ian Shepherd, £5)
Shark Tooth and Stone Blade - Pacific Art in Aberdeen University (Charles Hunt, £5)

Electronic and video products:
The Exotic Heritage (video, £10)

Internet home pages:
http://www.abdn.ac.uk/marischal_museum/

21
ABERDEENSHIRE FARMING MUSEUM
Aden Country Park, Mintlaw, Peterhead, Aberdeenshire, AB42 5FQ

Tel: 01771 622906
Fax: 01771 622884
Email: aberdeenshire.farming.museum@aberdeenshire.gov.uk
Formed: 1985
Formerly: North East of Scotland Agricultural Heritage Centre (NESAHC), date of change, 1996

Organisation type and purpose: Local government body, museum, historic building, house or site, suitable for ages: 5+.
Parent body:
Aberdeenshire Heritage
Tel: 01224 664228, fax: 01224 664615, email: heritage@aberdeenshire.gov.uk

Enquiries to: Curator
Direct email: willie.milne@aberdeenshire.gov.uk
Access:
Access to staff: By letter, by telephone, by fax, in person
Hours: Normally, Mon to Fri, 0830 to 1615
Access for disabled people: Parking provided, toilet facilities
Other restrictions: Ground floor completely accessible. Temporary exhibitions only on 1st floor.
Ground floor levels of Hareshowe Working Farm partially accessible.

General description:
Agriculture and rural life in Northeast Scotland, Aden Estate Story, Hareshowe Working Farm.
Information services:
Group education facilities: resources for all categories.
Special visitor services: Guided tours, materials and/or activities for children.
Education services: Group education facilities, resources for Key Stages 1 and 2, 3, 4 and Further or Higher Education.
Services for disabled people: Displays and/or information at wheelchair height.
Collections:
Artefacts, images, documents and associated material connected to agriculture and rural life in NE Scotland
Agriculture, social history, photographs
Catalogues:
Catalogue for all of the collections is only available in-house.

Internet home pages:
http://www.aberdeenshire.gov.uk
General description and opening hours.

22
ABERDEENSHIRE HERITAGE
Aden Country Park, Mintlaw, Peterhead, Aberdeenshire, AB42 5FQ

Tel: 01771 622906
Fax: 01771 622884
Email: heritage@aberdeenshire.gov.uk
Formed: 1996
Formed by the amalgamation of: North East of Scotland Agricultural Heritage Centre, North East of Scotland Museums Service (NESMS), date of change, 1996

Organisation type and purpose: Local government body, museum.
Parent body:
Aberdeenshire Council

Enquiries to: Curator of Local History
Direct tel: 01779 477778
Direct fax: 01771 622906
Direct email: david.bertie@aberdeenshire.gov.uk
Other contacts: Principal Curator

Access:
Access to staff: By letter, by telephone, by fax, by email, visitors by prior appointment
Hours: Mon to Fri, 0900 to 1630

General description:
Northeast Scotland local history, geology, archaeology, natural history, fishing, shipping and whaling of northeast Scotland, Banff silver, numismatics, details of museums in the north east of Scotland.

Collections:
Large photograph collection relating to the north east of Scotland
Peterhead Port Books
Some fishing boat records on microfilm

Printed publications:
Literary Families (Bertie D M, 50p)
Master and Pupil (Bertie D M, 50p)

Internet home pages:
http://www.aberdeenshire.gov.uk/ahc.htm
Details of the museums.

See also - Aberdeenshire Farming Museum; Arbuthnot Museum; Banchory Museum; Banff Museum; Brander Museum, Huntly; Carnegie Museum; Fordyce Joiner's Workshop Visitor Centre; Garlogie Mill Power House Museum; Maud Railway Museum; Sandhaven Meal Mill; Tolbooth Museum Stonehaven

23
ABERDEUNANT
Taliaris, Llandeilo, Carmarthenshire, SA19 6DL

Tel: 01558 650177
Fax: 01558 650177

Organisation type and purpose: National organisation, registered charity (charity number 205846), museum, historic building, house or site.

Parent body:
The National Trust Office for Wales
Tel: 01492 860123

Enquiries to: Manager

Access:
Access to staff: By letter, by telephone, by fax
Access to building, collections or gallery: Prior appointment required
Other restrictions: As the property is extremely small, visitor access is limited to no more than 6 people at a time. The property is administered and maintained on the Trust's behalf by a resident tenant. The gegin fawr (farm kitchen) and one bedroom are open to the public by arrangement.
Admission therefore is by guided tour only, prior booking essential.

General description:
This traditional Carmarthenshire farmhouse in an unspoilt setting provides a rare insight into an aspect of agricultural life that has all but disappeared.

Internet home pages:
http://www.nationaltrust.org.uk

24
ABERDULAIS FALLS AND TURBINE HOUSE
Aberdulais, Neath, West Glamorgan, SA10 8EU

Tel: 01639 636674
Email: aberdulais@nationaltrust.org.uk

Organisation type and purpose: Registered charity (charity number 205846), historic building, house or site.
Remains of the tinplate works.

Parent body:
The National Trust Office for Wales
Trinity Square, Llandudno, LL30 2DE, tel: 01492 860123, fax: 01492 860233

Access:
Access to staff: By letter, by telephone, by email
Access to building, collections or gallery: No prior appointment required
Hours: Easter to Nov: Mon to Fri, 1000 to 1700, Sat Sun and Bank Holidays 1100 to 1800
Nov to Christmas: Fri, Sat, Sun, 1100 to 1600
Mar to Easter: Fri, Sat, Sun, 1100 to 1600

General description:
The industrial history of Aberdulais The first manufacture of copper in 1584, to the present day remains of the tinplate works. Use of the waterfall to power the industry in the past and, in the present day, to produce environmentally friendly electicity for the property.

Information services:
Special visitor services: Tape recorded guides, materials and/or activities for children..

Collections:
Turbine House
Tinplate works

Internet home pages:
http://www.nationaltrust.org.uk

25
ABERGAVENNY MUSEUM
The Castle, Castle Street, Abergavenny, Gwent, NP7 5EE

Tel: 01873 854282
Fax: 01873 736004
Email: abergavennymuseum@monmouthshire.gov.uk
Formed: 1959

Organisation type and purpose: Local government body, museum, suitable for ages: 5+.

Enquiries to: Curator

Access:
Access to staff: By letter, by telephone, by fax, by email, in person
Hours: Curator access: Mon to Fri, 0900 to 1700
Access to building, collections or gallery: No prior appointment required
Hours: Mar to Oct: Mon to Sat, 1100 to 1300 and 1400 to 1700; Sun, 1400 to 1700
Nov to Feb: Mon to Sat, 1100 to 1300 and 1400 to 1600
Other restrictions: To view collections in store - visitors by prior appointment.
Access for disabled people: toilet facilities
Other restrictions: Access is possible to all areas with some assistance.

General description:
Local history of Abergavenny and surrounding area.

Information services:
Special visitor services: Guided tours, materials and/or activities for children.
Education services: Group education facilities, resources for Key Stages 1 and 2, 3, 4 and Further or Higher Education..

Collections:
Local history - prehistory to present day
Welsh Culture including collections relating to Llanever Estate
Father Ignatius Memorial Collection
Costume Collection
Basil Jones Collection, stock and fittings of grocer's, 1906-1988, 7000 items
3 High Street Collection, printer's proofs and stock, c. 1825, 200 to 300 items

Catalogues:
Catalogue for library is in-house only. Catalogue for part of the collections is only available in-house.

26
ABINGDON COUNTY HALL
Market Place, Abingdon, Oxfordshire

Tel: 01235 523703

Organisation type and purpose: National government body, historic building, house or site.

Parent body:
English Heritage (South East Region)
Tel: 01483 252000

Enquiries to: Manager

Access:
Access to staff: By letter
Access to building, collections or gallery: No prior appointment required
Hours: 29 Mar to 31 Oct: daliy, 1030 to 1600,1 Nov to 31 Mar: daily, 1100 to 1600
Other restrictions: Please telephone for Christmas and Bank Holiday opening.
Opening times are subject to change, for up-to-date information contact English Heritage by phone or visit the website.

General description:
This 17th century public building was constructed to house the Assize Courts.

Internet home pages:
http://www.english-heritage.org.uk

27
ACORN BANK GARDEN AND WATERMILL
Temple Sowerby, Penrith, Cumbria, CA10 1SP

Tel: 017683 61467
Fax: 017683 66824
Email: acornbank@nationaltrust.org.uk

Organisation type and purpose: Registered charity (charity number 205846), historic building, house or site, suitable for ages: 8+.

Parent body:
The National Trust (North West)
North West Regional Office, tel: 0870 609 5391

Enquiries to: Manager

Access:
Access to staff: By letter, by telephone, by fax, by email
Access for disabled people: Parking provided, level entry, toilet facilities
Other restrictions: Designated parking 50yds. 2 manual wheelchairs available. Level entrance. Level entrance to shop. Ramped entrance to tearoom. Grounds largely accessible. Recommended route map.

General description:
Ancient oaks and the high enclosing walls of this delightful garden keep out the extremes of the Cumbrian climate, resulting in a spectacular display of shrubs, roses and herbaceous borders. Sheltered orchards contain a variety of traditional fruit trees and the famous herb garden is the largest collection of medicinal and culinary plants in the North. A circular woodland walk runs along Crowdundle Beck to Acorn
Bank watermill, which although under restoration is open to visitors. The house is not open to the public.

Information services:
Braille guide.
Suitable for school groups. Children's guide.
Newt watch in June, Apple Day in Oct and lots of other events during the year.
Special visitor services: Materials and/or activities for children.
Education services: Group education facilities.
Services for disabled people: For the visually impaired.

Internet home pages:
http://www.nationaltrust.org.uk

28
ADMIRAL BLAKE MUSEUM
See - Blake Museum

29
ADVERTISING ARCHIVES
45 Lyndale Avenue, London, NW2 2QB

Tel: 020 7435 6540
Fax: 020 7794 6584
Email: library@advertisingarchives.co.uk
Formed: 1989
Formerly: The Museum of Advertising

continued overleaf

Organisation type and purpose: Independently owned, consultancy, research organisation. Commercial picture library..

Enquiries to: Managing Director
Access:
Access to staff: By letter, by telephone, by fax, by email, visitors by prior appointment
Access to building, collections or gallery: Prior appointment required
Access for disabled people: Parking provided

General description:
The largest collection of British and American press advertisements and magazine cover illustrations in Europe. Over 1 million images, dating from 1870 to the present day, catalogued for easy access.
Collections:
Original Norman Rockwell covers and advertisements, US, 1917-1970
Catalogues:
Catalogue for library is published and is on-line.

Internet home pages:
http://www.advertisingarchives.co.uk

30
AEROSPACE MUSEUM
See - Royal Air Force Museum

31
AFRICAN PEOPLE'S HISTORICAL MONUMENT FOUNDATION
See - Black Cultural Archives

32
AGRICULTURAL MUSEUM, BROOK
The Street, Brook, Ashford, Kent, TN25 5PF

Tel: 01304 824969
Formed: 1997
Formed from: Wye College Museum of Agriculture

Organisation type and purpose: Registered charity (charity number 1055879), museum, historic building, house or site, suitable for ages: 5+.
Connections with:
Wye Rural Museum Trust
(c/o Curator)
Address for correspondence:
Honorary Curator
Agricultural Museum, Brook
The Old Post Office, Slip Lane, Alkham, Dover, Kent, CT15 7DE, tel: 01304 824969

Enquiries to: Curator
Direct email: brianwimsett@hotmail.com
Access:
Access to staff: By letter, by telephone, by email, in person, visitors by prior appointment, charges made to all users
Access to building, collections or gallery: Prior appointment required
Hours: May to Sep: Wed, Sat, 1400 to 1700
Other restrictions: Other times by prior appointment only.
Access for disabled people: Parking provided, toilet facilities

General description:
Agriculture from horse-drawn days.
Information services:
Tape recording guides and hearing impaired facility - being prepared.
Special visitor services: Guided tours.
Education services: Group education facilities, resources for Further or Higher Education..
Collections:
Ploughs, seed drills, wagons, processing equipment, coopering, butter-making, reaper binder, oast house with all fittings, hundreds of small items
Catalogues:
Catalogue for library is in-house only. Catalogue for all of the collections is only available in-house.
Internet home pages:
http://www.agriculturalmuseumbrook.org.uk

33
AIKWOOD TOWER
Ettrick Valley, by Selkirk, Borders, TD7 5HJ

Tel: 01750 52253
Fax: 01750 52261

Organisation type and purpose: National organisation, registered charity, historic building, house or site.
Access:
Access to staff: By letter, by telephone, by fax
Access to building, collections or gallery: No prior appointment required
Hours: Easter weekend and May to Sep, Tue, Thu and Sun, 1400 1700
Other restrictions: Groups by appointment at other times.

General description:
Recently restored 16th century peel tower. Exhibition of the life and work of James Hogg.
Information services:
Programme of events
Temporary exhibitions of contemporary art and sculpture.
Special visitor services: Materials and/or activities for children..

Internet home pages:
http://www.scotborders.org.uk

34
AIRBORNE FORCES MUSEUM
Browning Barracks, Aldershot, Hampshire, GU11 2BU

Tel: 01252 349619
Fax: 01252 349203
Email: airborneforcesmuseum @army.mod.uk.net
Formed: 1969

Organisation type and purpose: Museum.
Affiliated to:
Ogilby Trust
South East Area Services to Museums

Enquiries to: Curator
Direct tel: 01252 349624
Access:
Access to staff: By letter, by fax, by email, visitors by prior appointment
Hours: Office: weekdays, 1000 to 1630
Other restrictions: Research weekdays only.
Access to building, collections or gallery: No prior appointment required
Hours: Mon to Fri, 1000 to 1630 (last admission 1545); Sat, Sun, Bank Holidays, 1000 to 1600
Other restrictions: No photography, no bulky bags.
Access for disabled people: Parking provided, level entry, access to all public areas

General description:
Airborne forces from 1940 to the present, Parachute Regiment, World War II campaigns (airborne involvement), campaigns since 1945, uniforms, equipment, units, personalities.
Collections:
Archives, documents, library, photographs
Printed publications:
Brochure
Printed Items

35
ALDBOROUGH ROMAN SITE
Main Street, Boroughbridge, North Yorkshire, YO5 9EF

Tel: 01423 322768

Organisation type and purpose: National organisation, advisory body, museum, historic building, house or site, suitable for ages: 5+ 8+ 12+.
Parent body:
English Heritage (Yorkshire Region)
Tel: 01904 601901

Enquiries to: Manager
Access:
Access to staff: By letter, by telephone, in person
Access to building, collections or gallery: No prior appointment required
Hours: 29 Mar to 30 Sep: daily, 1000 to 1300, 1400 to 1800,1 to 31 Oct: daily, 1000 to 1300, 1400 to 1700
Other restrictions: Opening times are subject to change, for up-to-date information contact English Heritage by phone or visit the website

General description:
The principal town of the Brigantes, the largest tribe in Roman Britain. The remains include parts of the Roman defences and two mosaic pavements. The museum displays local Roman finds.
Information services:
Education services: Group education facilities..
Collections:
A significant collection of Roman artefacts found in the Roman Town of Isurium Brigantum, includes pots, iron, copper alloy, glass and coins

Internet home pages:
http://www.english-heritage.org.uk

36
ALDEBURGH MOOT HALL
Market Cross Place, Aldeburgh, Suffolk, IP15 5DS

Tel: 01728 453295
Formed: 1911

Organisation type and purpose: Registered charity (charity number 310323), museum, historic building, house or site, suitable for ages: 8+.

Enquiries to: Curator
Other contacts: Honorary Secretary
Access:
Access to staff: By letter, by telephone
Other restrictions: Staff are all volunteers.

General description:
A 16th century building housing local history; paintings; documents; photographs and maps. There is a large collection of stuffed birds; flints; butterflies and moths; important Anglo-Saxon cemetry finds and urns, including a Bronze Age urn; fishing models and Royal National Lifeboat Institution memorabilia.
Information services:
Special visitor services: Guided tours, materials and/or activities for children..
Collections:
Snape Cemetry, urns, rivets, swords, spearheads, glass, claw beaker, etc, Anglo-Saxon
Paterson Collection of local finds: flints, fossils, 16th century forks and spoons, wig curlers etc
Charles Garrett-Jones collection of local butterflies and moths
Catalogues:
Catalogue for all of the collections is only available in-house.

37
ALDERLEY EDGE
Cheshire Countryside Office, Nether Alderley, Macclesfield, Cheshire, SK10 4UB

Tel: 01625 58442 (Cheshire Countryside Office)

Organisation type and purpose: National organisation, registered charity (charity number 205846), historic building, house or site, suitable for ages: 12+.
Parent body:
National Trust (North West Area)

North West Regional Office, tel: 0870 609 5391
Access:
Access for disabled people: Parking provided, toilet facilities
Other restrictions: One path quite level and accessible for wheelchairs with strong companion. Adapted WC in car park at Alderley Edge

General description:
This sandstone escarpment, with impressive views across Cheshire and the Peak District, is an SSSI for its geology, and has a long history of copper mining, going back to prehistoric and Roman times.
The mines are open twice a year, organised by the Derbyshire Caving Club.
There are numerous paths through the oak and beech woodlands, including a link to Hare Hill.

Internet home pages:
http://www.nationaltrust.org.uk

38
ALDERNEY RAILWAY

PO Box 75, Alderney, Guernsey, Channel Islands

Tel: 01481 822978
Formed: 1978

Organisation type and purpose: Membership association (membership is by subscription), present number of members: c. 100, voluntary organisation.
Operating the Alderney Railway.
Affiliated to:
Alderney Railway Society
at the same address
Subsidiary body:
Wickham Railcars Group

Enquiries to: Director General
Other contacts: Honorary Secretary
Access:
Access to staff: By letter, by telephone
Hours: Mon to Fri, 0900 to 1700

General description:
History of railways in the Channel Islands.
Collections:
Local Channel Islands transport history books
Printed publications:
Occasional bulletins
Timetables and information leaflet

39
ALDERNEY SOCIETY MUSEUM, THE

The Old School, High Street, Alderney, Guernsey, GY9 3TG, Channel Islands

Tel: 01481 823222 (mornings) or 822246
Fax: 01481 824979
Email: admin@alderneysociety.org
Acronym or abbreviation: Alderney Museum
Formed: 1966

Organisation type and purpose: Independently owned, voluntary organisation (charity number Guernsey 181), museum, suitable for ages: all ages.
Museum of local interest.
Originally started to try to compensate for the loss of all local records in WWII.
Connections with:
The Council of The Alderney Society
At the same address

Enquiries to: Administrator
Other contacts: Director, Guernsey Museums for Curatorial Adviser to the Alderney Society Museum.
Access:
Access to staff: By letter, by telephone, by fax, by email, in person, visitors by prior appointment
Other restrictions: Staff access - unreliable from Oct 31 to Easter.
Access to building, collections or gallery: No prior appointment required
Hours: Open Easter to end of Oct: Mon to Fri, 1000 to 1200 and 1400 to1600; Sat, Sun, 1000 to 1200
Other restrictions: Prior appointment for access to reserve collections or stores.
Access for disabled people: level entry, toilet facilities
Other restrictions: Reasonable level entry, single step before museum, 90% of displays on ground floor, and no steps.

General description:
Alderney Island life from prehistoric times, the Military Occupation 1940-45, garrisons, archaeology, geology, natural history, folklore, Island customs and traditions, domestic economy, environmental education, Elizabethan wreck material.
Information services:
Education services: Group education facilities.
Services for disabled people: For the visually impaired; displays and/or information at wheelchair height.
Collections:
A H Ewen Archive (history)
Durtnell Collection - archaeological collection and report
Early Iron Age excavation 1969-70 of pottery - collection of artefacts and report
Lukis Collection (held at Candie Gardens Museum, Guernsey)
Maps of Alderney 1750-1988, mainly for fortifications
Several exceptionally well preserved Iron Age pots and other material
The Alderney bronze hoard is kept at the Guernsey Museum, Candie Gardens
The Elizabethan Wreck artefacts
Von Hügel Collection
Catalogues:
Catalogue for library is in-house only. Catalogue for all of the collections is only available in-house.
Printed publications:
Alderney Militia
Alderney Scrapbook
Alderney (2nd edn, Coysh V)
Annual Bulletin of the Society
Birds of Alderney
Bulletins, 1966-1988 Index
Dragonflies of Alderney
Flora of Alderney
Fortress Island
Geology of Alderney
The Alderney Story

Internet home pages:
http://www.alderneymuseum.org/index.html
Catalogues, via the Guernsey Museum servers

40
ALDERSHOT MILITARY MUSEUM

Evelyn Woods Road, Queens Avenue, Aldershot, Hampshire, GU11 2LG

Tel: 01252 314598
Fax: 01252 342942
Email: musmim@hants.gov.uk
Formed: 1984
Formerly: Aldershot Military Historical Trust, date of change, 1997

Organisation type and purpose: Local government body, registered charity (charity number 280290), museum.
Parent body:
Hampshire County Council Museums Service
Chilcomb House, Chilcomb Lane, Winchester, Hampshire, SO23 8PD, tel: 01962 846304, fax: 01962 869836

Enquiries to: Curator
Access:
Access to staff: By letter, by telephone, by fax, by email, in person, Internet web pages
Access to building, collections or gallery: No prior appointment required
Hours: Mon to Sun, 1000 to 1700
Access for disabled people: Parking provided, ramped entry, access to all public areas

General description:
Military history of Aldershot, a military town since its inception in 1854. Local and social history of Aldershot and Farnborough. The daily life of both soldier and civilian as Aldershot grew up alongside the home of the British Army over the past 145 years; models, mementoes, uniforms, photographs; a Victorian barrack room, vehicle displays and early flight display.
Local history of the Rushmoor area from 1500, pottery.
Collections:
Uniforms, mementoes, photographs.
Printed publications:
Publications list is available from the Librarian, Hampshire County Council Museums Service Headquarters, Chilcomb House, Winchester, SO23 8RD

Internet home pages:
http://www.hants.gov.uk/museum/aldershot/
HMCMS web catalogue, whole collection, 100,000 plus web pages

See also - Rushmoor Local History Gallery

41
ALEXANDER FLEMING LABORATORY MUSEUM

St Mary's Hospital, Praed Street, London, W2 1NY

Tel: 020 7886 6528
Fax: 020 7886 6739
Email: kevin.brown@st-marys.nhs.uk
Formed: 1993

Organisation type and purpose: Museum.
Museum and archive service within St Mary's NHS Trust.
Parent body:
St Mary's NHS Trust
St Mary's Hospital, Praed Street, London, W2 1NY

Enquiries to: Trust Archivist and Curator
Access:
Access to staff: By letter, by telephone, by fax, by email, in person
Other restrictions: Archives subject to Provisions of Public Records Act.

General description:
A reconstruction of the laboratory, on its original site, in which Alexander Fleming discovered penicillin in 1928, with displays and exhibits covering the life of Fleming and the story of antibiotics, history of St Mary's Hospital, history of hospitals and nursing, medical history.
Information services:
Special visitor services: Guided tours.
Education services: Group education facilities, resources for Key Stages 2, 3, 4 and Further or Higher Education..
Collections:
Museum on Fleming and Penicillin with in situ reconstruction of Fleming's laboratory as it was when he discovered penicillin in 1928
Equipment used by Alexander Fleming, 1900-1955
Archives of St Mary's Hospital, St Mary's Hospital Medical School (now part of Imperial College School of Medicine), Wright-Fleming Institute and constituent hospitals associated with St Mary's Hospital
Artefacts relating to Fleming and St Mary's Hospital
Memorabilia associated with Alexander Fleming and Almoth Wright, 1881-1955
Bacteriological equipment, 1900-1930.
Catalogues:
Catalogue for library is in-house only. Catalogue for all of the collections is only available in-house.
Printed publications:
St Mary's Hospital, an illustrated history (1991, £3)

continued overleaf

St Mary's Hospital Medical School, an historical anthology (1990, £2.50)
Alexander Fleming Laboratory Museum, a guide (2000, £2.50)
Alexander Fleming and the Development of Penicillin (Alexander Fleming Laboratory Museum education resource pack, 2000, £5.50)
Hospital and Nursing, 1845-1948, a century of healthcare at St Mary's Hospital, Paddington (St Mary's Hospital Archives education resource pack, 2000, £5.50)

42
ALEXANDER KEILLER MUSEUM
High Street, Avebury, Marlborough, Wiltshire, SN8 1RF

Tel: 01672 539250

Organisation type and purpose: Registered charity (charity number 205846), museum.

Enquiries to: Visitor Services Manager
Other contacts: Curator for research visits/archaeological enquiries.
Access:
Access to staff: By letter, by telephone, by email, visitors by prior appointment
Access to building, collections or gallery: No prior appointment required
Hours: 1 Apr to 31 Oct: daily, 1000 to 1800,1 Nov to 31 Mar: daily, 1000 to 1600
Other restrictions: Closed 24 and 25 Dec.
Access for disabled people: level entry, toilet facilities
Other restrictions: Adjacent parking by arrangement.

General description:
Archaeology of the Avebury area.
Information services:
Library available for reference (for conditions see Access above)
Special visitor services: Materials and/or activities for children.
Education services: Group education facilities.
Services for disabled people: For the visually impaired; for the hearing impaired; displays and/or information at wheelchair height.
Collections:
The museum houses material relating to the major complex of prehistoric monuments in and around Avebury. The collection is mainly archaeological, although it includes records and photographs relating to research and excavation at the sites, chiefly that carried out by Alexander Keiller in the 1920s and 1930s

43
ALFORD VALLEY RAILWAY AND MUSEUM
The Station, Main Street, Alford, Aberdeenshire, AB3 8AA

Tel: 019755 62811
Formed: 1979

Organisation type and purpose: Suitable for ages: all ages.
Non-profit making company.
2ft narrow gauge passenger carrying railway.
Other addresses:
Alford Valley Railway and Museum
16 Kingsford Road, Alford, Aberdeenshire
Alford Valley Railway Association
Treasurer, Creag Mawr, Main Street, Alford, Aberdeenshire, tel: 019755 62811

Enquiries to: Chairman
Direct tel: 019755 62045
Access:
Access to staff: By letter, by telephone
Access to building, collections or gallery: No prior appointment required
Hours: Railway operating times: Apr, May, Sep weekends, 1300 to 1630; Jun, Jul, Aug, daily, 1300 to 1630
Access for disabled people: Parking provided, ramped entry, toilet facilities

General description:
2ft narrow gauge passenger railway, operating steam and diesel locomotives, linking the villages of upper Donside and Kintore junction and hence to Aberdeen. The original company was formed in 1846 and the branch line opened in 1859.
Information services:
Special visitor services: Guided tours.
Services for disabled people: For the visually impaired.
Collections:
Steam and diesel locomotives
Passenger carriages
Freight and peat bogies
Printed publications:
Available free, directly

44
ALFRED EAST GALLERY
c/o The Coach House, Sheep Street, Kettering, Northamptonshire, NN16 0AN

Tel: 01536 534274
Fax: 01536 534370
Formed: 1913

Organisation type and purpose: Local government body, art gallery, suitable for ages: 12+.
Parent body:
Kettering Borough Council (KBC)
Bowling Green Road, Kettering
Part of:
Kettering's Heritage Quarter

Enquiries to: Curator
Direct tel: 01536 534394
Direct fax: 01536 534370
Direct email: kettering.museum@excite.co.uk
Access:
Access to staff: By letter, by telephone, by fax
Hours: Mon to Sat, 0930 to 1700; Wed, 1000 to 1700
Closed Bank Holidays.
Access for disabled people: level entry, access to all public areas

General description:
Victorian and 20th century art, including works by Sir Alfred East and Symbolist Thomas Cooper Gotch. Strong collection of contemporary works. One gallery dedicated to permanent collection and two others to temporary and touring exhibitions.
Information services:
Special visitor services: Materials and/or activities for children.
Education services: Group education facilities, resources for Key Stages 3 and 4..
Catalogues:
Catalogue for all of the collections is published.
Publications list:
is available in hard copy.
Printed publications:
Available by post from the Gallery:
A5 brochures on Sir Alfred East and Thomas Cooper Gotch (£1 each)
Permanent Collection Catalogue (50p each)
Various postcards of collection (25p each)

Internet home pages:
http://www.kettering.gov.uk

45
ALFRISTON CLERGY HOUSE
The Tye, Alfriston, Polegate, East Sussex, BN26 5TL

Tel: 01323 870001
Fax: 01323 871318
Email: alfriston@nationaltrust.org.uk

Organisation type and purpose: National organisation, registered charity (charity number 205846), historic building, house or site, suitable for ages: 5+.
Parent body:
The National Trust (South and South East Region)
South East Regional Office, tel: 01372 453401

Enquiries to: Manager
Access:
Access to staff: By letter, by telephone, by fax, by email
Access to building, collections or gallery: No prior appointment required
Hours: Beg Mar to mid Mar, Sat and Sun, 1100 to 1600; 22 Mar to beg Nov, Mon, Wed, Thu, Sat, Sun, 1000 to 1700; mid Nov to 21 Dec, Wed to Sun, 1100 to 1600;
Open Bank Mondays and Good Friday

General description:
Step back into the Middle Ages with a visit to this 14th century thatched Wealden 'hall house'. Trace the history of this building which, in 1896, was the first to be acquired by the National Trust. Discover why the chalk floor is soaked in sour milk, and visit the excellent shop with its local crafts. Explore the delightful cottage garden and savour the idyllic setting beside Alfriston's parish church, with stunning views across the meandering River Cuckmere.
Information services:
Braille guide. Large-print guide. Touch list.
Suitable for school groups. Children's quiz/trail.
Special visitor services: Materials and/or activities for children.
Education services: Group education facilities.
Services for disabled people: For the visually impaired.

Internet home pages:
http://www.nationaltrust.org.uk/regions/southeast

46
ALL HALLOWS BY THE TOWER, UNDERCROFT MUSEUM
All Hallows Church, Byward Street, London, EC3R 5BJ

Tel: 020 7481 2928
Formed: 675 AD

Organisation type and purpose: International organisation, independently owned, suitable for ages: 8+.
Church of England with museum and own parish registers.

Enquiries to: Curator
Other contacts: Archivist
Access:
Access to staff: By letter, visitors by prior appointment, charges made to all users
Hours: Museum: Mon to Fri, 1030 to 1600
Other restrictions: Archives: Mon, 1400 to 1600.
Access to building, collections or gallery: No prior appointment required
Hours: Church: Mon to Fri, 0900 to 1800; Sat, Sun, 1000 to 1700
Other restrictions: During church services there is no access to museum.
Access for disabled people: ramped entry, toilet facilities
Other restrictions: Access to 80% of Church, not to Crypt museum.

General description:
A small museum of the history and development of All Hallows Church and Tower Hill in the City of London.
Information services:
Special visitor services: Guided tours, tape recorded guides.
Education services: Group education facilities, resources for Key Stage 2..
Collections:
Church Records - registers, church wardens accounts, vestry minute books
Ancient archives dating back to 10th century, 900AD to today
Roman pavement, and artefacts
Saxon artefacts. Wheelhead cross, great arch, base shaft carved
Knights Templar Altar from Castle Athlit, Palestine
William Penn Register, William Laud Register, and others.
Church Plates

Microform products:
Registers for research (microfiche)

47
ALLEN GALLERY
10-12 Church Street, Alton, Hampshire, GU34 2BW

Tel: 01420 82802
Fax: 01420 84227
Email: musmtc@hants.gov.uk
Formed: 1964

Organisation type and purpose: Local government body, museum.
Has a temporary exhibition gallery; and a herb garden.
Parent body:
Hampshire County Council Museums Service
Chilcomb House, Winchester, SO23 8RD, tel: 01962 846304, fax: 01962 869836

Enquiries to: Curator
Access:
Access to staff: By letter, by telephone, by fax, by email, in person
Access to building, collections or gallery: No prior appointment required
Hours: Tue to Sat, 1000 to 1700

General description:
Decorative art, ceramics, fine art, object painting, silver, domestic and herb garden.
Collections:
Comprehensive collection of ceramics and silver
Paintings by local artist William Herbert Allen, late 19th to early 20th century
Catalogues:
Catalogue for all of the collections is on-line.
Printed publications:
Publications list is available from the Librarian, Hampshire County Council Museums Service Headquarters, Chilcomb House, Winchester, SO23 8RD

Address for ordering publications:
Printed publications:
Registrar, Hampshire County Council Museums Service HQ

Internet home pages:
http://www.hants.gov.uk/museums/allen/allen/html
HMCMS web catalogue, whole collection, 100,000 plus web pages.

48
ALLERFORD MUSEUM
See - West Somerset Rural Life Museum

49
ALLERFORD MUSEUM
The Old School, Allerford, Minehead, Somerset, TA24 8HN

Tel: 01643 862529
Formed: 1983

Organisation type and purpose: Registered charity (charity number 1065071), museum.

Enquiries to: Secretary
Direct tel: 01398 371284
Access:
Access to staff: By letter, by telephone

General description:
Victorian life. Photographic archive of West Somerset.
A collection of vernacular items, predominantly Victorian, as used in the house and on the farm.
Features a Victorian schoolroom with original desks, forms, slates, books and toys; with 'dressing up' facilities for children.
Collections:
A large collection of early local photographs features most of the settlements.

Catalogues:
Catalogue for part of the collections is only available in-house.

Internet home pages:
http://www.allerfordwebsite.ic24.net

50
ALLHALLOWS MUSEUM OF HONITON LACE & LOCAL HISTORY
High Street, Honiton, Devon, EX14 1PG

Tel: 01404 44966
Fax: 01404 46591
Email: dyateshoniton@msn.com
Formed: 1948

Organisation type and purpose: Registered charity, museum, suitable for ages: 12+.

Enquiries to: Administrator
Direct tel: 01404 42996
Access:
Access to staff: By letter, by email, visitors by prior appointment
Access to building, collections or gallery: No prior appointment required
Hours: Mon to Fri, 1000 to 1700; Sat, 1000 to 1330
Access for disabled people: level entry
Other restrictions: Chairlift between two floors.

General description:
The museum is housed in the Ancient Chapel of Allhallows, which dates from the inauguration of the mediaeval New Town, c. 1200. It contains artefacts relating to the history of the town and surrounding countryside, with a particular emphasis on Honiton Lace.
Information services:
Demonstrations in summer.
Special visitor services: Guided tours.
Education services: Resources for Key Stages 2 and 3..
Collections:
World-class collection of Honiton lace. Examples of lace flounces, shawls, stoles, veils, dress ornaments, accessories, trimmings, bobbins, prickings, equipment, aprons, fans, etc. specifically collected since 1980. 1635-present day, 410 items
Photographs
Electoral documents
Catalogues:
Catalogue for all of the collections is only available in-house.

Internet home pages:
http://www.allhallowsmuseum.co.uk
Brochure and news.

51
ALLOA TOWER
Alloa Park, Alloa, Clackmannanshire, FK10 1PP

Tel: 01259 211701
Fax: 01259 218744

Organisation type and purpose: Museum, art gallery, historic building, house or site.
Parent body:
National Trust for Scotland (West Region)

Enquiries to: Property Manager
Access:
Access to staff: By letter, by telephone, by fax
Access to building, collections or gallery: No prior appointment required
Hours: End Mar to end Oct, daily, 1300 to 1700
Morning visits available for pre-booked groups
Access for disabled people: toilet facilities

General description:
Largest surviving 14th century keep in Scotland, retains many original medieval features including dungeon, first-floor well and magnificent roof timbers.

Collections:
Unique collection of family paintings by, amongst others, Kneller, Raeburn and Alloa artist, David Allan

Internet home pages:
http://www.nts.org.uk

52
ALMOND VALLEY HERITAGE TRUST
Millfield, Livingston, West Lothian, EH54 7AR

Tel: 01506 414957
Fax: 01506 49771
Email: almondvalley@almondvalley.co.uk
Formed: 1990

Organisation type and purpose: Museum.

Enquiries to: Director
Access:
Access to building, collections or gallery: No prior appointment required
Access for disabled people: Parking provided, ramped entry, level entry, access to all public areas, toilet facilities

General description:
Scottish shale oil industry, agriculture, local history.
Information services:
Special visitor services: Guided tours, materials and/or activities for children.
Education services: Group education facilities..
Collections:
Paraffin heaters, cookers, and other appliances, 1880-1980, 300 items
Candles, lamps and other products of the Scottish Shale oil industry, 1820-1970, 300 items

Internet home pages:
http://www.almondvalley.co.uk

53
ALMONRY HERITAGE CENTRE
Abbey Gate, Evesham, Worcestershire, WR11 4BG

Tel: 01386 446944
Fax: 01386 442348
Email: tic@almonry.ndo.co.uk
Formed: 1957

Organisation type and purpose: Local government body, museum, historic building, house or site, suitable for ages: 8+.
Parent body:
Vale of Evesham Historical Society
at the same address
Parent body:
Evesham Town Council
110/112 High Street, Evesham, Worcestershire, WR11 4EJ, tel: 01386 47070, fax: 01386 423811, email/website: fgreen@eveshamtc.ndirect.co.uk

Enquiries to: Manager
Other contacts: Town Clerk
Access:
Access to staff: By letter, by telephone, by fax, by email, in person
Access to building, collections or gallery: No prior appointment required
Hours: Mon to Sat, 1000 to 1700; Sun, 1400 to 1700
Nov to Jan: closed Sun
Other restrictions: Closed for 2 weeks Christmas/New Year.
For access to documents, photographs and other materials, contact Vale of Evesham Historical Society at the Almonry.
Access for disabled people: level entry

General description:
The home of the Evesham Abbey Almoner, with exhibits from the Abbey 701-1540, the Battle of Evesham 1265, and the Borough of Evesham 1605-1974.
Archaeology and local history of the Evesham area, and the crafts and history of the Vale.

continued overleaf

Information services:
Special visitor services: Guided tours, materials and/or activities for children.
Education services: Resources for Key Stage 1..
Collections:
Artefacts: archaeology, Saxon treasure, agriculture and horticulture, Victoriana, Evesham Abbey, militaria, costume, telephone equipment, paintings
Anglo-Saxon jewellery and weapons found in a burial site just outside the town.
Artefacts belonging to the former Evesham Abbey.
Books relating to Evesham Abbey, Simon de Montfort, Battle of Evesham, Vale of Evesham, River Avon
Publications list:
is available in hard copy.
Printed publications:
A selection of books is available from the Heritage Centre, including:
Abbey and Parish Churches
Battle of Evesham
Battle of Worecester
Evesham Official Guide 2002 (every 3-4 years)
Evesham Pocket Guide and Map (every 2-3 years)
The Almonry Museum (guide to building, 1975)

54
ALNWICK CASTLE
Alnwick, Northumberland, NE66 1NQ

Tel: 01665 510777
Fax: 01665 510876

Organisation type and purpose: Independently owned, historic building, house or site, suitable for ages: all ages.

Enquiries to: Collections Manager
Access:
Access to staff: By letter only
Access to building, collections or gallery: No prior appointment required
Hours: Easter to end Oct: daily, 1100 to 1700
Access for disabled people: toilet facilities

General description:
Fine paintings, furniture, ceramics in rich Italian Renaissance interior of mid 19th century.
Building - medieval, 18th century and 19th century additions and restorations.
Museum of Antiquities located in one of perimeter towers of castle.
Percy Tenantry Volunteer Museum located in one of perimeter towers of castle.
Information services:
Helpline available, tel no: 01665 511100.
Special visitor services: Guided tours, materials and/or activities for children.
Education services: Group education facilities, resources for Key Stages 1 and 2, 3, 4 and Further or Higher Education..
Collections:
A collection of prehistoric bronze, iron, Romano-British and Viking artefacts assembled by the Third and Fourth Dukes of Northumberland, 1826-1865
Collection of Percyana, principally made in the 19th century
Catalogues:
Catalogue for library is in-house only. Catalogue for all of the collections is only available in-house.
Printed publications:
Guide to Alnwick Castle (£4)

55
ALTON MUSEUM
See - Curtis Museum

56
AMBERLEY WORKING MUSEUM
Station Road, Amberley, Arundel, West Sussex, BN18 9LT

Tel: 01798 831370
Fax: 01798 831831
Email: office@amberleymuseum.co.uk
Formed: 1979
Formerly: Amberley Chalk Pits Museum, Amberley Museum, Chalk Pits Museum

Organisation type and purpose: Independently owned, professional body, registered charity (charity number 287722), historic building, house or site, suitable for ages: all ages.
Open air museum.
To preserve the industrial heritage of South East England.
Member of:
Association of Independent Museums
Museums Association
SE England Tourist Board
South Eastern Museums Service

Enquiries to: Administrator
Access:
Access to staff: By letter, by telephone, by fax, by email, visitors by prior appointment, Internet web pages
Access to building, collections or gallery: No prior appointment required
Hours: Opening times by telephone or the museum website.
Other restrictions: Prior appointment required for library.
Access for disabled people: Parking provided, ramped entry, toilet facilities

General description:
Situated in a 36 acre disused chalk quarry. The collection includes: industrial archaeology and social history of South East England blacksmithing; boatbuilding; pottery; printing; limeburning; concrete; narrow gauge railways; radio and telecommunications; bus transport in SE England; roads and roadbuilding; electricity supply and distribution in SE England; engineering; hand and machine tools, The Tools and Trades History Society, plus other traditional industries from the South of England.
Information services:
Library available for reference (for conditions see Access above). Helpline available, tel no: 01798 831370.
Interactive displays including traditional craftspeople, vintage bus and rail rides.
Special visitor services: Materials and/or activities for children.
Services for disabled people: For the visually impaired.
Collections:
BT Collection
Concrete, photograph albums of its use
Narrow Gauge Railway Collection
Roads and roadbuilding photographs and films
Seeboard Collection, Seeboard archive of electricity supply in SE England
The Southdown Bus Collection, Archive of Southdown Motor Services (regional bus operator)
Vintage radio and TV collection
Working machinery (demonstrated)
Catalogues:
Catalogue for library is on-line. Catalogue for part of the collections is only available in-house.
Printed publications:
General Information and School Information leaflets (free)
The Amberley Museum Narrow Gauge and Industrial Railway Collection (compiled by Cork G); Locomotive and Wagon histories (researched by Smith J, £4.95)
Museum Guide (every two years, £2.50)
The Wheelbarrow (newsletter, 6 times a year)

Internet home pages:
http://www.amberleymuseum.co.uk
Museum opening hours, prices, events, virtual tour and collections information, library catalogue.

57
AMBLESIDE ROMAN FORT
Ambleside, Cumbria

Organisation type and purpose: National organisation, advisory body, suitable for ages: .
Parent body:
English Heritage (North West Region)
Tel: 0161 242 1400
Site managed by:
National Trust

Enquiries to: Manager
Access:
Access to building, collections or gallery: No prior appointment required
Hours: Any reasonable time.

General description:
Remains of a 1st and 2nd century fort, built to guard the Roman road from Brougham to Ravenglass.

58
AMERICAN MUSEUM IN BRITAIN
Claverton Manor, Bath, BA2 7BD

Tel: 01225 460503
Fax: 01225 480726
Email: amibbath@aol.com
Acronym or abbreviation: AMIB
Formed: 1961

Organisation type and purpose: Museum.

Enquiries to: Secretary
Access:
Access to staff: By letter, by telephone, by fax, by email, visitors by prior appointment
Hours: Mon to Fri, 0900 to 1700
Access to building, collections or gallery: Prior appointment required
Access for disabled people: Parking provided, toilet facilities

General description:
American art, architecture and the decorative arts 1620-1850; textiles, maps, pewter, glass, folk art.
Collections:
The Dallas Pratt Collection of historical maps

Internet home pages:
http://www.americanmuseum.org
Brief description of all aspects of the collection.

59
AMGUEDDFA GENEDLAETHOL CYMRU
See - Museum of Welsh Life

60
ANCIENT HIGH HOUSE, THE
Greengate Street, Stafford, ST16 2JA

Tel: 01785 619131

Parent body:
Stafford Borough Council
Member of:
North Staffordshire Museums Association

Enquiries to: Heritage Manager
Other contacts: Tourist Information Centre tel: 01785 619619

General description:
The Ancient High House built in 1595 is reputedly the largest Elizabethan timber-framed house in England. The house is now a museum with displays set out as period settings to reflect its history. It contains furniture dating from the 17th century, paintings (19th century) and the period room settings from ca. 1650 to the Victorian period.

Collections:
The collection of the Staffordshire Yeomanry Museum
Catalogues:
Catalogue for part of the collections is only available in-house.

Internet home pages:
http://www.staffordbc.gov.uk

See also - ***Museum of the Staffordshire Yeomanry***

61
ANCIENT HOUSE MUSEUM, THE
26 High Street, Clare, Sudbury, Suffolk, CO10 8NY

Tel: 01787 277662
Email: clareah@btinternet.com
Formed: 1978

Organisation type and purpose: Museum.

Enquiries to: Curator
Direct tel: 01787 277520
Access:
Access to staff: By letter, by telephone, by email, in person
Hours: Thu to Sun, 1400 to 1700
May to Sep: Sat, 1100 to 1700
Bank Holidays 1100 to 1700

General description:
Clare: history of town; census information; history of houses; genealogy.
Printed publications:
Annals of Clare, 1550 to 1850 (4 booklets)

Internet home pages:
http://www.clare-ancient-house-museum.co.uk
Guide to museum contents.

62
ANCIENT HOUSE MUSEUM
21 White Hart Street, Thetford, Norfolk, IP24 1AA

Tel: 01842 752599

Parent body:
Norfolk Museums and Archaeology Service
Tel: 01603 493625, fax: 01603 493623

Enquiries to: Curator

General description:
A local history museum for Thetford and the surrounding area, located in an Early Tudor house. Wide-ranging collections including art; social history; archaeology; natural history; also flint collections featuring prehistoric and gunflint manufacture.
Collections:
Duleep Singh Collection, paintings and prints, especially portraits, 1500-1900, 1500 items

63
ANCIENT MONUMENTS SOCIETY
St Ann's Vestry Hall, 2 Church Entry, London, EC4V 5HB

Tel: 020 7236 3934
Fax: 020 7329 3677
Email: office@ancientmonumentssociety.org.uk
Acronym or abbreviation: AMS
Formed: 1924

Organisation type and purpose: National organisation, learned society (membership is by subscription), present number of members: 1900, voluntary organisation, registered charity (charity number 209605).
Study and conservation of ancient monuments, historic buildings of all ages and fine old craftsmanship.
Affiliated to:
Friends of Friendless Churches

Enquiries to: Secretary
Access:
Access to staff: By letter, by telephone, by email
Hours: Mon to Fri, 0900 to 1700
Access to building, collections or gallery: No access other than to staff

General description:
Historic buildings of all ages and types, their dating, conservation and care, new uses, planning; law as it relates to them; sources of money for their restoration.
Collections:
Historic postcards of architectural subjects
Catalogues:
Catalogue for library is in-house only.
Publications list:
is available in hard copy.
Printed publications:
Newsletters (three times per annum)
Transactions (annually latest vol. 5, 2001)

Internet home pages:
http://www.ancientmonumentssociety.org.uk

64
ANCIENT ORDER OF FORESTERS HERITAGE TRUST
12-13 College Place, Southampton, SO15 2FE

Tel: 023 8022 9655
Fax: 023 8022 9657
Email: mail@foresterers.ws
Formed: 1992

Organisation type and purpose: Independently owned, suitable for ages: 16+.
Friendly society. Informal trust run voluntarily for the Ancient Order of Foresters Friendly Society.
Preservation of records and artefacts for research purposes.
Parent body:
Ancient Order of Foresters Friendly Society at the same address

Enquiries to: Trust Co-ordinator
Direct tel: 01276 65575
Direct email: audrey@fisk72.fsnet.co.uk
Access:
Access to staff: By letter, by telephone, by email, visitors by prior appointment
Hours: By prior arrangement
Access to building, collections or gallery: Prior appointment required
Other restrictions: Archive collection only available. Collection of artefacts at present in store.

General description:
The history of the Ancient Order of Foresters Friendly Society 1834 to present day.
Collections:
Selection of branch minute and membership books in MS
Books:
Directories 1834 to present day
Foresters Miscellany, journal, from 1834 (gap in 1850s) to present day
Limited amount of documents
Catalogues:
Catalogue for library is in-house only.
Publications list:
is available in hard copy.
Printed publications:
A History of the Ancient Order of Foresters Friendly Society 1834-1984 (Cooper W G, 1984, £3)
Grandfather was a Member of the Foresters - a description of the economic and social benefits of membership and how the Order was run (Fisk A and Logan R, 1994, £2.50
Index to Archives in Manuscript (1997, £2)
By the Members for the Members (mostly data from the 1870s, Fisk A, 1997, £2.50)
Foresters Courts in Cornwall (Fisk A, 1997, £3)
Welfare & Thrift in a Country Town (Fisk A, 1998, £1.50)

65
ANDOVER MUSEUM
6 Church Close, Andover, Hampshire, SP10 1DP

Tel: 01264 366283
Fax: 01264 339152
Email: musmda@hants.gov.uk and andover.museum@virgin.net
Formed: 1981

Organisation type and purpose: Local government body, museum.
Has a temporary exhibition gallery.
Parent body:
Hampshire County Council Museums Service
Chilcomb House, Winchester, SO23 8RD, tel: 01962 846304, fax: 01962 869836

Enquiries to: Curator
Access:
Access to staff: By letter, by telephone, by fax, by email, in person
Hours: Tue to Sat, 1000 to 1700
Access to building, collections or gallery: No prior appointment required
Hours: Tue to Sat, 1000 to 1700

General description:
Local history of Andover and district, local archaeology, natural science, geology and aquarium.
Collections:
English glass
Catalogues:
Catalogue for all of the collections is on-line.
Printed publications:
Publications list is available from the Librarian, Hampshire County Council Museums Service Headquarters, Chilcomb House, Winchester, SO23 8RD

Address for ordering publications:
Printed publications:
Registrar, Hampshire County Council Museums Service HQ

Internet home pages:
http://www.hants.gov.uk/museum/andoverm/index.html
Andover Museum website.

66
ANDREW CARNEGIE BIRTHPLACE MUSEUM
Moodie Street, Dunfermline, Fife, KY12 7PL

Tel: 01383 724302
Fax: 01383 721862
Formed: 1928

Organisation type and purpose: Registered charity, museum.
Independent museum with charitable status.
To conserve, preserve and interpret the collections in the museum. To inform and educate about, and interpret, the life and work of Andrew Carnegie, and the Trusts and Foundations he created.
Adminstered by:
Carnegie Dunfermline Trust (CDT)
Abbey Park House, Dunfermline, KY12 7PB, tel: 01383 723638
Affiliated to:
Carnegie Dunfermline and Hero Funds Trust

Enquiries to: Administrator
Other contacts: Secretary of Carnegie Dunfermline Trust for administrator, works only part time.
Access:
Access to staff: By letter, by telephone, by fax, visitors by prior appointment
Hours: Mon to Fri, 1100 to 1700
Access to building, collections or gallery: No prior appointment required
Access for disabled people: Parking provided, ramped entry, toilet facilities

General description:
Andrew Carnegie 1835-1919: life and career, his association with libraries, hero funds, peace foundations and other Carnegie charitable trusts and institutions.

continued overleaf

Collections:
Freedom caskets, illuminated addresses, presentation keys
Roll of honour of The Carnegie Hero Fund
Photographs of Andrew Carnegie, family, associates and events of his life
Books and articles by and about Andrew Carnegie including handwritten drafts, typescripts and galley proofs
Printed publications:
Inventory of collection and indices available for examination
Museum guidebook and abridged version of Andrew Carnegie's autobiography available for sale

Internet home pages:
http://www.carnegiemuseum.co.uk
http://www.carnegiemuseum.com
http://www.carnegiebirthplace.com

67
ANDREW LOGAN MUSEUM OF SCULPTURE
Aquaduct Road, Berriew, Welshpool, Powys, SY21 8PJ

Tel: 01686 640689
Fax: 01686 640764
Email: info@andrewlogan.com
Acronym or abbreviation: ALMS
Formed: 1991

Organisation type and purpose: Registered charity (charity number 519865), museum, suitable for ages: all ages.
Member of:
Association of Independent Museums
Tel: 01244 373880
The Council of Museums in Wales
Tel: 029 2022 5432, fax: 029 2066 8516

Enquiries to: Director
Direct email: anne@andrewlogan.com
Access:
Access to staff: By letter only
Hours: Mon to Fri, 1000 to 1800
Access for disabled people: Parking provided, ramped entry, access to all public areas, toilet facilities

General description:
The museum houses a unique exhibition, by the internationally renowned sculptor Andrew Logan, which has been created over the past 25 years. The collection consists of sculpture; jewellery; portraits; wallpieces; and video records.
Information services:
Special visitor services: Guided tours.
Education services: Resources for Key Stages 1 and 2, 3, 4 and Further or Higher Education.
Services for disabled people: Displays and/or information at wheelchair height.
Collections:
Collection of work by artist/sculptor Andrew Logan and other works by friends, Divine, Zandra Rhodes and Bill Gibb
Catalogues:
Catalogue for library is in-house only. Catalogue for all of the collections is available in-house, part is published and part is on-line.

Internet home pages:
http://www.andrewlogan.com
A tour of the museum and information on Andrew Logan.

68
ANGEL CORNER
8 Angel Hill, Bury St Edmunds, Suffolk, IP33 1UZ

Tel: 0870 609 5388 (Regional Office)

Organisation type and purpose: National organisation, registered charity (charity number 205846), historic building, house or site.
Parent body:
The National Trust (East of England)
East Anglia Regional Office, tel: 0870 609 5388
Maintained by:
The local authority
National Trust sites:
Angel Corner
8 Angel Hill, Bury St Edmunds, Suffolk, IP33 1UZ, tel: 01284 763233

Enquiries to: Manager

General description:
A fine Queen Anne house, temporarily accommodating the National Trust East Anglia Regional office.

Internet home pages:
http://www.nationaltrust.org.uk

69
ANGLESEY ABBEY, GARDENS AND LODE MILL
Lode, Cambridge, CB5 9EJ

Tel: 01223 811200
Email: angleseyabbey@nationaltrust.org.uk

Organisation type and purpose: Registered charity (charity number 205846), historic building, house or site, suitable for ages: 5+.
Parent body:
The National Trust (East of England)
East Anglia Regional Office, tel: 0870 609 5388

Enquiries to: Manager
Direct tel: 01223 811243
Other contacts: Head Gardener for garden-related enquiries.
Access:
Access to staff: By letter, by telephone, by fax, by email, in person, visitors by prior appointment
Access for disabled people: Parking provided, ramped entry, level entry, toilet facilities
Other restrictions: Stairclimber in house for wheelchair users. 5 manual wheelchairs available, booking essential. Powered mobility vehicles for garden use: 5 singleseater, 1 two-seater, booking essential. 6-seater buggy, running from car park to house. Steps to entrance. Accessible entrance via entrance at rear of building to view two rooms. Ground floor fully accessible, Access to lower floor only in Mill. No access to other floors. Photograph album. Chairs without arms are available for resting. Photographs of all inaccessible rooms in album. Level entrance to shop and to restaurant. Grounds largely accessible. Recommended route map.

General description:
Anglesey Abbey Estate is made up of 98 acres of parkland and gardens, a manor house in the Jacobean style dating from 1600 and an 18th century watermill. The house is on the site of a 12th century Augustinian Priory. The collection today was created by the 1st Lord Fairhaven from 1926; it is an 'Aladdins' cave of treasures. Most notable are clocks, paintings, furniture and silver. The gardens have all year round interest with numerous varieties of snowdrops in late winter and fabulous dahlias during August and September.
Information services:
Helpline available, tel no: 01223 811243.
Braille guide. Touch list. Scented plants.
Frontcarrying baby slings for loan.
Children's quiz/trail. Adult study days.
Special visitor services: Guided tours, materials and/or activities for children.
Education services: Group education facilities, resources for Key Stages 1 and 2, 3, 4 and Further or Higher Education.
Services for disabled people: For the visually impaired.
Collections:
The Fairhaven Collection created by Huttleston Broughton (1st Lord Fairhaven) from 1926-1966, it contains many significant paintings (notably by Claude Lorrain, Cuyp and Bonnington)
A collection of over 50 clocks
Fine English and European silver and furniture
The Gardens contain one of the National Trust's largest sculpture collections including works by Sheermakers and Van Nost
The Collection also includes a library with c. 9000 volumes which include many interesting 18th and 19th century texts
Catalogues:
Catalogue for library is in-house only. Catalogue for all of the collections is only available in-house.
Publications list:
is available in hard copy.

Internet home pages:
http://www.nationaltrust.org.uk/angleseyabbey

70
ANGUS FOLK MUSEUM
Kirkwynd, Glamis, Forfar, Angus, DD8 1RT

Tel: 01307 840288

Organisation type and purpose: Museum, historic building, house or site.
Parent body:
National Trust for Scotland (North-East Region)

Enquiries to: Property Manager
Direct tel: 01674 810264
Access:
Access to staff: By letter, by telephone, in person
Access for disabled people: toilet facilities
Other restrictions: Access to all main rooms

General description:
Scottish rural life in the last two hundred years. Contains artefacts from everyday life in the home and on the land from the County of Angus. Features an original row of cottages, from about 1800, and a reconstructed farm steading.
Collections:
One of the finest Scottish Folk collections
A restored 19th century, black, horse-drawn 'Glenisla' hearse
Cruise lamps, candlesticks, etc. up to 1920s
Treen, luggies, quaichs, eggcups, mousetrap, up to 1920s, 60 items
Examples of Scottish and English pottery, up to 1920s, 70 items
Agricultural. Many types of implements, large and small, up to 1940, 500 items
Furniture. Bothy and box beds, chairs, up to 1920s, 25 items
Costume. Male, female and child under and outer wear, up to 1930s, 250 items

Internet home pages:
http://www.nts.org.uk
National Trust for Scolland

71
ANNE HATHAWAY'S COTTAGE
Shottery, Stratford-upon-Avon, Warwickshire, CV37 9HH

Tel: 01789 292100
Fax: 01789 205014

Organisation type and purpose: Registered charity (charity number 209302), historic building, house or site.
Parent body:
Shakespeare Birthplace Trust
Tel: 01789 204016, fax: 01789 296083

Enquiries to: Marketing & Publicity Manager
Direct tel: 01789 201807
Direct fax: 01789 263138
Direct email: info@shakespeare.org.uk
Access:
Access to staff: By letter, by telephone, by fax, by email
Access to building, collections or gallery: Prior appointment required
Hours: Nov to Mar: Mon to Sat, 1000 to 1600; Sun, 1030 to 1600
Apr to May and Sep to Oct: Mon to Sat, 1000 to 1700; Sun, 1030 to 1700

Jun to Aug: Mon to Sat, 0900 to 1700; Sun, 0930 to 1700
Access for disabled people: Parking provided, toilet facilities

General description:
Before her marriage to William Shakespeare, Anne Hathaway lived in this substantial thatched Tudor farmhouse with her family. Home to descendants of the Hathaway family until 19th century. Includes the famous Hathaway bed, courting settle and other furniture owned by her family. Traditional English cottage garden. Enjoy the tree garden, maze and sculpture park, shop and garden centre.

Internet home pages:
http://www.shakespeare.org.uk
General information on the Shakespeare Birthplace Trust.

72
ANNE OF CLEVES HOUSE MUSEUM
52 Southover High Street, Lewes, East Sussex, BN7 1JA

Tel: 01273 474610

Organisation type and purpose: Registered charity (charity number 207037), museum, historic building, house or site, suitable for ages: all ages.
Parent body:
Sussex Past
Bull House, 92 High Street, Lewes, East Sussex, BN7 1XH, tel: 01273 486260, fax: 01273 486990, email: admin@sussexpast.co.uk

Enquiries to: Manager
Access:
Access to staff: By letter, by email
Access to building, collections or gallery: No prior appointment required
Hours: Jan, Feb, Tue to Sat, 1000 to 1700; Mar to Oct, Tue to Sat 1000 to 1700, Sun, Mon and Bank Holidays, 1100 to 1700; Nov, Dec, Tue to Sat, 1000 to 1700
Other restrictions: Closed 25, 26 Dec

General description:
Covers Sussex local history, regional furniture, domestic ironwork, and the products and processes of the Wealden iron industry.
Information services:
Education services: Group education facilities, resources for Key Stage 2..
Collections:
Harmer Terracottas
Lewes Priory Stonework
Sussex Church Musical Instruments
Lewes Priory Stonework.
Sussex Pottery

73
ANTHROPOLOGICAL MUSEUM
See - Aberdeen University, Marischal Museum

74
ANTHROPOLOGY LIBRARY
British Museum Department of Ethnography, 6 Burlington Gardens, London, W1S 3EX

Tel: 020 7323 8031
Fax: 020 7323 8013
Formerly: British Museum Ethnography Library, Museum of Mankind Library, date of change, 2001

Organisation type and purpose: National government body, museum.
The Anthropology Library is a major anthropological collection with its origins in the nineteenth century. It incorporates the former library of the Royal Anthropological Institute (RAI).
Departmental library of the:
British Museum
currently housed in the former Museum of Mankind, tel: 020 7323 8031, fax: 020 7323 8013, email/website: ethnography@thebritishmuseum.ac.uk

Enquiries to: Senior Librarian
Other contacts: Reading Room Supervisor for Reading Room enquiries, appointments, bibliographical information etc.
Access:
Access to staff: By letter, by telephone, by fax, visitors by prior appointment
Hours: Mon to Fri, 0900 to 1700
Other restrictions: Visitors by prior appointment except Fellows and Junior Fellows of the RAI.
Fellows and Junior Fellows of the RAI can borrow items donated by the RAI.
Other visitors and researchers may have access, by appointment, for reference purposes only.

General description:
Its scope is worldwide and covers every aspect of anthropology: cultural anthropology, archaeology, some biological anthropology, linguistics, and related fields such as history, sociology and description and travel.
Material culture, ethnography, tribal art and anthropology of indigenous African, American, Asian, Oceanic and some European societies.
Archaeology of the New World.
Collections:
Incorporates former library of the Royal Anthropological Institute
The library includes the Henry Christy and the Sir Eric Thompson collections and a significant Pictorial Collection
The collection contains around 120,000 books and pamphlets and 4000 journal titles (of which 1450 are current)
Catalogues:
Catalogue for library is on-line.

Internet home pages:
http://www.thebritishmuseum.ac.uk
http://lucy.ukc.ac.uk/AIO.html
The Index to the Anthropology Library's journal collection is available through Anthropological Index online, a free internet service.

75
ANTONY HOUSE
Torpoint, Plymouth, Cornwall, PL11 2QA

Tel: 01752 812191
Email: antony@nationaltrust.org.uk

Organisation type and purpose: National organisation, registered charity (charity number 205846), historic building, house or site.
Parent body:
The National Trust (South West Region)
Regional Office for Devon and Cornwall, tel: 01208 74281

Enquiries to: Manager
Access:
Access to staff: By letter, by telephone, by email
Access to building, collections or gallery: No prior appointment required
Hours: Apr, May, Sep and Oct, Tue, Wed, Thu, 1330 to 1730
Jun, Jul and Aug, Tue, Wed, Thu, Sun, 1330 to 1730
Open bank Holiday Mondays.
Other restrictions: Last admission 1645. Bath Pond House can only be seen by written application to Custodian on days house is open.
Access for disabled people: toilet facilities
Other restrictions: Drop-off point. Steps to entrance. Ground floor accessible with assistance. No access to other floors. Steps to shop entrance and to tea-room entrance. Grounds largely accessible. Recommended route map.

General description:
One of Cornwall's finest early 18th century houses, faced in lustrous silvery-grey Pentewan stone, offset by colonnaded wings of red brick and set within grounds landscaped by Repton. These include the formal garden with the National Collection of Day Lilies and fine summer borders, and the superb woodland garden with its outstanding displays of rhododendrons, azaleas, camellias and magnolias (owned privately by the Carew Pole Garden Trust). Also of note is the 18th century dovecote and the 1789 Bath Pond House. Antony has been the home of the Carew family for almost 600 years.
Information services:
Services for disabled people: For the visually impaired.

Internet home pages:
http://www.nationaltrust.org.uk/regions/cornwall

76
APPLEBY CASTLE
Appleby-in-Westmorland, Cumbria, CA16 6XH

Tel: 017683 53823

Enquiries to: Property Manager
Access:
Access to staff: By letter, by telephone
Access to building, collections or gallery: No prior appointment required
Hours: Mar to Nov, daily, 1300 to 1700

General description:
A Norman keep, built on the original site of a Motte and Baily castle, and restored by Lady Anne Clifford in the 17th century.

77
APPULDURCOMBE HOUSE
Wroxall, Ventnor, Isle of Wight, PO38 3EW

Tel: 01983 852484
Fax: 01983 840188
Email: john@appuldurcombe.co.uk

Organisation type and purpose: Historic building, house or site, suitable for ages: 5+.
Parent body:
English Heritage (South East Region)
Eastgate Court, 195-205 High Street, Guildford, Surrey, GU1 3EH, tel: 01483 252000, fax: 01483 252001, email/website: www.english-heritage.org.uk

Enquiries to: Manager
Access:
Access to staff: By letter, by telephone
Access to building, collections or gallery: No prior appointment required
Hours: 2 Jan to 30 Apr: daily, 1000 to 1600,1 May to 30 Sep: daily, 1000 to 1700,1 Oct to 15 Dec: daily, 1000 to 1600
Closed 16 Dec-1 Jan 2003
Other restrictions: Last entry one hour before closing time.
Access for disabled people: Parking provided, toilet facilities
Other restrictions: Limited access due to historic site.

General description:
The shell of Appuldurcombe, which was once the grandest house on the Isle of Wight, stands in its own grounds, designed by Capability Brown. An exhibition of prints and photographs depicts the house and its history. Falconry Centre in grounds.
Collections:
Small displays of pictures, books etc, above shop (relating to the history of this historic estate)
Publications list:
is available in hard copy.
Printed publications:
Guide Books (available direct from shop)
Teachers Packs (available direct from shop)

Internet home pages:
http://www.english-heritage.org.uk

78
APSLEY HOUSE, THE WELLINGTON MUSEUM

149 Piccadilly, Hyde Park Corner, London, W1V 9FA

Tel: 020 7499 5676
Fax: 020 7493 6576
Also known as: No.1 London
Branch of: Victoria and Albert Museum

Organisation type and purpose: Registered charity, museum, suitable for ages: 5+.
Administered by:
Victoria and Albert Museum

Enquiries to: Administrator
Direct tel: 020 7495 8525
Direct fax: 020 7493 6576
Access:
Access to staff: By letter, by telephone, by fax, charges made to all users
Hours: Mon to Fri, 0900 to 1700
Access for disabled people: Parking provided
Other restrictions: 7 steps up to House, 9 steps down to lift

General description:
Apsley House holds the collection of the first Duke of Wellington, European paintings, early 19th century European ceramics, sculpture, early 19th century European silver, furniture, and costume and personal effects of the First Duke.
Information services:
Loop system for lectures, Sound Guide loop, BSL interpreters for events.
Special visitor services: Guided tours, tape recorded guides, materials and/or activities for children.
Education services: Group education facilities, resources for Key Stages 1 and 2 and Further or Higher Education.
Services for disabled people: For the visually impaired; for the hearing impaired.
Collections:
1st Duke of Wellington's collection of fine and decorative art, also memorabilia relating to his life and times
Publications list:
is available in hard copy.
Printed publications:
Duke of Wellington: pictorial survey of his life
The Wellington Museum Guide Book

Address for ordering publications:
Printed publications:
V & A Enterprises, Victoria and Albert Museum London, SW7 2RL, tel: 020 7938 8438

Internet home pages:
http://www.apsleyhouse.org.uk
General information about the museum and its collections, information on school and group visits etc.
http://www.http://www.vam.ac.uk/collections/apsley
Further information about the collection.

79
ARBEIA ROMAN FORT & MUSEUM

Baring Street, South Shields, Tyne and Wear, NE33 2BB

Tel: 0191 456 1369
Minicom no. 0191 454 4093
Fax: 0191 427 6862
Formed: 1953

Organisation type and purpose: Local government body, registered charity, museum, historic building, house or site, suitable for ages: all ages.
Roman Fort Site, reconstructed Roman buildings.
Parent body:
Tyne And Wear Museums (TWM)
Discovery Museum, Blandford Square, Newcastle Upon Tyne, tel: 0191 232 6789, fax: 0191 230 2614

Enquiries to: Office Manager
Direct tel: 0191 454 4093
Other contacts: Education Officer, tel: 0191 436 8740 for school bookings.
Access:
Access to staff: By letter, by telephone, by fax, visitors by prior appointment
Hours: Mon to Thu, 0845 to 1645; Fri, 0845 to 1615
Access to building, collections or gallery: No prior appointment required
Hours: Summer: Mon to Sat, 1000 to 1730; Sun, 1300 to 1700
Winter: Mon to Sat, 1000 to 1600
Access for disabled people: ramped entry, toilet facilities

General description:
Roman military site and archaeology, seasonal excavations, reconstructed Roman buildings, Museum with finds from site, site archive.
Arbeia combines the excavated remains of this Roman military supply base with reconstructions of the fort's buildings and stunning finds unearthed from the site.
See the reconstructed fort's West Gate, and the ongoing reconstruction of the Commanding Officer's Horse and Barracks stable.
The Museum displays site finds, some of which are amongst the most impressive found around the World Heritage Site.
Information services:
Special visitor services: Materials and/or activities for children.
Education services: Group education facilities, resources for Key Stages 1 and 2, 3, 4 and Further or Higher Education.
Services for disabled people: For the visually impaired; for the hearing impaired; displays and/or information at wheelchair height.
Collections:
Roman material from excavations on site since 1875, includes material from ongoing excavations some held on computerised databases (Modes)
Tombstones reflecting the cosmopolitan nature of Roman South Shields
Objects that would have belonged to civilians and soldiers including jewellery, weapons, Fontana ring and a ring nail suit
One of the finest collections of Roman Jet in the country
Excavated remains
Catalogues:
Catalogue for part of the collections is published.

Internet home pages:
http://www.twmuseums.org.uk
Opening hours, brief description of collection.

80
ARBERTILLERY & DISTRICT MUSEUM

The Metropole, Market Street, Abertillery, Gwent, NP13 1AR

Tel: 01495 211140
Formed: 1964

Organisation type and purpose: Independently owned (membership is by subscription), present number of members: 100, registered charity (charity number 1067213), museum, suitable for ages: all ages, research organisation.
Museum society.
Educational school visits, monthly historical lectures.

Enquiries to: Curator
Other contacts: Secretary
Access:
Access to staff: By letter, by telephone, in person
Access to building, collections or gallery: No prior appointment required
Hours: Mon to Fri, 1000 to 1300 and 1400 to 1630; Sat, 1000 to 1400
Access for disabled people: level entry, access to all public areas, toilet facilities

General description:
Domestic life, religion, music, community organisations, war, the home front, radicalism and trade unions, crafts, archaeology, farming, folklore, transport, industry, mining, costume, toys, school, sport, shops.
Information services:
Special visitor services: Guided tours.
Education services: Group education facilities, resources for Key Stages 1 and 2, 3 and 4.
Services for disabled people: Displays and/or information at wheelchair height.
Printed publications:
Newsletter (monthly)
Electronic and video products:
Oral History Series:
Voices of Abertillery, Aberbeeg & Llanhilleth (£9.99)
Abertillery & District History 2000 (£5.99)

Internet home pages:
http://www.admsonline.artshost.com

81
ARBROATH ART GALLERY

Public Library, Hill Terrace, Arbroath, Tayside, DD11 1PU

Tel: 01241 875598 (Arbroath Museum)
Fax: 01241 439263
Email: arbroath.museum@angus.gov.uk
Formed: 19th century

Organisation type and purpose: Local government body, art gallery, suitable for ages: 8+.
Parent body:
Angus Council, Leisure Services, Cultural Services

Enquiries to: Curator
Other contacts: Museums Manager for Curator who is part-time.
Access:
Access to staff: By letter, by telephone, by fax, by email, in person
Access to building, collections or gallery: No prior appointment required
Hours: Mon to Sat, 1000 to 1700
Jul and Aug: Mon to Sat, 1000 to 1700; Sun, 1400 to 1700
Access for disabled people: Parking provided

General description:
Victorian and contemporary art.
Information services:
Special visitor services: Guided tours, materials and/or activities for children.
Services for disabled people: For the hearing impaired.

Internet home pages:
http://www.angus.gov.uk

82
ARBROATH MUSEUM SIGNAL TOWER

Ladyloan, Arbroath, Tayside, DD11 1PU

Tel: 01241 875598
Email: arbroath-museum@angus.gov.uk or signal.tower@angus.gov.uk
Formed: 1843

Organisation type and purpose: Local government body, museum, historic building, house or site, suitable for ages: 5+.
Parent body:
Angus Council, Leisure Services, Cultural Services

Enquiries to: Curator
Direct tel: 01241 875998
Other contacts: Museums Manager for Curator who is part-time.
Access:
Access to staff: By letter, by telephone, by fax, by email, in person
Access to building, collections or gallery: No prior appointment required
Hours: Mon to Sat, 1000 to 1700
Jul, Aug: Mon to Sat, 1000 to 1700; Sun, 1400 to 1700
Access for disabled people: Parking provided, level entry

Other restrictions: Level entry except for one step-up.

General description:
Housed in the elegant 1813 Signal Tower Shore Station for the Bell Rock Lighthouse, this museum brings Arbroath's maritime, social and industrial history alive with a fisher street scene, smells and sounds.

Information services:
Special visitor services: Guided tours, materials and/or activities for children.
Education services: Group education facilities.
Services for disabled people: For the hearing impaired.

Collections:
Fishing - costume particularly strong
Maritime
Flax Textile Industry
Civic and Social History
Bell Rock Lighthouse
Photographs

83
ARBUTHNOT MUSEUM
St Peter Street, Peterhead, Aberdeenshire, AB42 1QD

Tel: 01771 622906
Fax: 01771 622884
Formed: 01850

Organisation type and purpose: Local government body, museum, suitable for ages: 5+.

Parent body:
Aberdeenshire Heritage
Tel: 01771 622906, fax: 01771 622884

Enquiries to: Curator

Access:
Access to staff: By letter, by telephone, by fax

General description:
Local history; Peterhead fishing, shipping, whaling; Arbuthnot coin collection; Inuit material; temporary exhibitions gallery.

Collections:
Social history, archaeology, natural history, geology, fine art, photography

Catalogues:
Catalogue for part of the collections is only available in-house.

Printed publications:
Literary Families (exhibition booklet, 1990, £0.50)
Master and Pupil (exhibition booklet, 1997, £0.50)
Various information sheets (free)

Address for ordering publications:
Printed publications:
Aberdeenshire Heritage
Aden Country Park, Mintlaw, Peterhead, Aberdeenshire, AB42 5FQ, tel: 01771 622906, fax: 01771 622884

84
ARCHAEOLOGICAL SURVEY
See - Department of the Environment for Northern Ireland

85
ARCHAEOLOGY CENTRE
4-10 London Road, Bagshot, Surrey, GU19 5HN

Tel: 01276 451181

Access:
Access to staff: By letter, by telephone, visitors by prior appointment

General description:
Contains ceramics, organics and metal objects, all of which were obtained from archaeological excavations. Covers the period Mesolithic to post-Mediaeval.

Collections:
Bagshot. English table glass and Germanic stonewares. 1600- 1640 AD. 300 plus items
Lightwater. Prehistoric and Roman lithics and ceramics. 5000 BC-400 AD. 10,000 plus items

Catalogues:
Catalogue for part of the collections is only available in-house.

86
ARCHAEOLOGY MUSEUM
See - Liverpool University, Archaeology Museum

87
ARCHITECTURE CENTRE, THE
Narrow Quay, Bristol, BS1 4QA

Tel: 0117 922 1540
Fax: 0117 922 1541
Email: architecture.centre@ukgateway.net
Formed: 1995
Formed from: Bristol Centre for the Advancement of Architecture (BCAA)

Organisation type and purpose: Independently owned, registered charity (charity number 290575), art gallery, suitable for ages: 5+, consultancy.
Principal aim of the Centre is to increase people's enjoyment and awareness of the built environment.

Enquiries to: Assistant Director
Other contacts: Retail/Information Manager for bookshop and ecological information.

Access:
Access to staff: By letter, by email, visitors by prior appointment
Hours: Tue to Fri, 1100 to 1700
Other restrictions: Retail/Information Manager: Tue to Thu, 1100 to 1700.
Access to building, collections or gallery: No prior appointment required
Hours: Tue to Fri, 1100 to 1700; Sat, Sun, 1200 to 1700
Access for disabled people: level entry, access to all public areas, toilet facilities

General description:
Architecture, visual design, ecological design, architectural consultancy.

Information services:
Education services: Group education facilities, resources for Key Stages 1 and 2, 3, 4 and Further or Higher Education..

88
ARCTIC PENGUIN MARITIME HERITAGE CENTRE
See - Inveraray Maritime Museum

89
ARDRESS HOUSE
64 Ardress Road, Portadown, Craigavon, Co Armagh, BT62 1SQ

Tel: 028 3885 1236
Fax: 028 3885 1236
Email: ardress@nationaltrust.org.uk

Organisation type and purpose: Registered charity (charity number 205846), museum, historic building, house or site, suitable for ages: all ages.

Parent body:
National Trust Office for Northern Ireland
Rowallane House, Saintfield, Ballynahinch, Co Down, BT24 7LH, tel: 028 9751 0721, fax: 028 9751 1242

Enquiries to: Manager

Access:
Access to staff: By letter, by telephone, by fax, by email
Access for disabled people: toilet facilities
Other restrictions: Three steps to ground floor rooms of house. 1 manual wheelchair available. Accessible entrance at rear of house. Ground floor fully accessible. No access to other floors. Information room: ground floor farm exhibition accessible for wheelchairs. Grounds largely accessible.

General description:
17th century farmhouse with fine plasterwork, an Adam's-style drawing room, fine furniture and paintings. Display of farm implements and livestock, including rare breeds in farmyard. Also garden, woodland walks and children's play area.

Information services:
Touch tours by arrangement, Sympathetic Hearing Scheme
School groups by arrangement.
Special visitor services: Guided tours.
Education services: Group education facilities.
Services for disabled people: For the visually impaired; for the hearing impaired.

Collections:
Collection of farm machinery from pre-tractor day farm tools
Dairy equipment
Smithy with a collection of blacksmith's tools
Small specimen orchard with types of apple formerly grown in this orchard area of Ireland.

Internet home pages:
http://www.nationaltrust.org.uk

90
ARDS ARTS CENTRE
Town Halll, Conway Square, Newtownards, Co Down, BT23 4DB

Tel: 028 9181 0803
Fax: 028 9182 3131
Email: arts@ards-council.gov.uk
Formed: 1975

Organisation type and purpose: Local government body, art gallery, suitable for ages: all ages.

Enquiries to: Manager

Access:
Access to staff: By letter, by telephone, by fax, by email
Access for disabled people: Parking provided, level entry, toilet facilities

General description:
Ards Arts aims to present an exciting, varied and attractive programme of visual arts, primarily in the two Gallery rooms at the Townhall Arts Centre. We exhibit contemporary works in a variety of styles and media by local, national and international artists in a programme that changes monthly.
Other visual art initiatives include innovative public art projects and practical art classes for adults and children at venues throughout the Borough.
Ards Arts also aims to bringing art to life in the Borough by presenting a programme of performances of dance, drama, physical theatre, concerts and talks at the Townhall Arts Centre once a month.

91
ARGORY, THE
Derrycaw Road, Moy, Dungannon, Co Armagh, BT71 6NA

Tel: 028 8778 4753
Fax: 028 8778 9598
Email: argory@nationaltrust.org.uk

Organisation type and purpose: National organisation, registered charity (charity number 205846), historic building, house or site, suitable for ages: all ages.

Parent body:
National Trust Office for Northern Ireland
Rowallane House, Saintfield, Ballynahich, Co Down, BT24 7LH, tel: 028 9751 0721, fax: 028 9751 1242

Enquiries to: Manager
Other contacts: Education Officer: 028 8778 9484

Access:
Access to staff: By letter, by telephone, in person
Access to building, collections or gallery: No prior appointment required
Hours: House: mid Mar to May, and Sep, Sat

continued overleaf

and Sun, 1200 to 1800; Jun, Jul, Aug, daily, 1200 to 1800
Grounds: Oct to Apr, daily, 1000 to 1600; May to Sep, daily
1000 to 2000
Open Bank Holidays and Good Friday; also open Bank Holidays in Northern Ireland
Other restrictions: Jun, weekdays opens 1300
Access to house by guided tour only.
Access for disabled people: Parking provided, ramped entry, toilet facilities
Other restrictions: Drop-off point. Disabled drivers may park near east door of house. Ramp at east door by arrangement at reception. 1 manual wheelchair available. Ground floor fully accessible. Photograph album. Steps to shop and to tea-room entrances. Grounds largely accessible. Recommended route map.

General description:
Set in 130 acres of wooded countryside, The Argory dates from 1824 and is substantially unchanged since the turn of the century. The cluttered interiors evoke the Bond family's Edwardian taste and interests, and include a barrel organ that is played once a month for musical house tours. Horse carriages, a harness room, the acetylene gas plant and a laundry are in the imposing stable yard. The charming sundial garden has extensive walks.
Information services:
Tours for visually impaired visitors by arrangement. Braille guide. Handling collection.
Sympathetic Hearing Scheme.
Front-carrying baby slings for loan.
Suitable for school groups. Education room/centre. Live interpretation. Hands-on activities. Children's quiz/trail.
Special events throughout the year. (phone for details)
Special visitor services: Guided tours, materials and/or activities for children.
Education services: Group education facilities.
Services for disabled people: For the visually impaired; for the hearing impaired.
Collections:
Acetylene gas plant
Horse carriages and harness

Internet home pages:
http://www.ntni.org.uk

92
ARGYLL AND SUTHERLAND HIGHLANDERS REGIMENTAL MUSEUM
The Castle, Stirling, FK8 1EH

Tel: 01786 475165
Fax: 01786 446038
Acronym or abbreviation: A and SH Museum
Formed: 1948

Organisation type and purpose: Museum, suitable for ages: all ages.

Enquiries to: Regimental Secretary
Direct email: regsec@argylls.co.uk
Access:
Access to staff: By letter, by telephone, by fax, visitors by prior appointment
Access for disabled people: Parking provided
Other restrictions: Parking on Castle Esplanade and a car courtesy service from Historic Scotland.

General description:
The museum depicts the life of the Regiment from its earliest identifiable roots, through amalgamations, wars, conflicts and peacetime, right up to the present day. This is depicted by displays of uniforms, weapons, medals, equipment and memorabilia, pictures and silver.
Collections:
Uniforms, weapons, artefacts, memorabilia and displays

Internet home pages:
http://www.argylls.co.uk

93
ARGYLL MOTOR MUSEUM LIMITED
See - Motoring Heritage Centre

94
SIR RICHARD ARKWRIGHT'S MASSON MILLS
Derby Road, Matlock Bath, Derbyshire, DE4 3PY

Tel: 01629 581001
Fax: 01629 581001
Formed: 1783

Organisation type and purpose: Museum, historic building, house or site, suitable for ages: all ages.

Enquiries to: Co-ordinator
Access:
Access to staff: By letter, by telephone, by fax, in person
Hours: Mon to Fri, 1000 to 1600
Access to building, collections or gallery: No prior appointment required
Hours: Mon to Fri, 1000 to 1600; Sat, Sun, 1100 to 1600
Access for disabled people: Parking provided, ramped entry, access to all public areas, toilet facilities

General description:
Original cotton spinning mill - 18th century complete with lire shafting, water turbines.
Weaving on old Lancashire looms 7 days a week from 1000 to 1600.
Information services:
Tearoom.
Special visitor services: Guided tours.
Education services: Group education facilities, resources for Key Stages 1 and 2, 3, 4 and Further or Higher Education.
Services for disabled people: Displays and/or information at wheelchair height.
Collections:
Textile machinery, spinning, doubling, looms, condenser mules steam engine, boiler house
Large archive collection
Bobbin-making machinery
World's largest bobbin collection - over 600,000, all different

Internet home pages:
http://www.massonmills.co.uk
Details about Sir Richard Arkwright's working textile museum, plus educational facilities.

95
ARLINGTON COURT
Arlington, Barnstaple, Devon, EX31 4LP

Tel: 01271 850296
Fax: 01271 851108
Email: arlingtoncourt@nationaltrust.org.uk
Formed: 1949

Organisation type and purpose: National organisation, registered charity (charity number 850296), historic building, house or site, suitable for ages: 8+.
Parent body:
National Trust (South West Region)
Regional Office for Devon and Cornwall, tel: 01392 881691

Enquiries to: Property Manager
Other contacts: Assistant to Property Manager
Access:
Access to staff: By letter, by telephone, by fax, in person
Hours: End Mar to beg Nov, Wed to Mon, 1030 to 1630
Beg Nov to beg Apr, Mon to Fri, 0900 to 1630
Access to building, collections or gallery: No prior appointment required
Hours: End Mar to beg Nov, Wed to Mon, 1030 to 1630
Access for disabled people: Parking provided, ramped entry, toilet facilities
Other restrictions: Accessible entrance at rear of house. Ground floor fully accessible. No access to other floors. Level entrance to shop and tearoom. Gravel paths with some slopes.

General description:
The Arlington Court estate lies in the thick wooded valley of the River Yeo. At its centre stands Arlington Court, the intimate and intriguing Victorian home of Miss Rosalie Chichester. Crowded with treasures amessed from her travels, her collections include model ships, tapestry, pewter and shells.
In the basement, from May to Sep visitors can view the comings and goings of Devon's largest colony of Lesser Horseshoe bats, via the 'batcam'. Arlington's stable block houses one of the best collections of 19th century horse-drawn vehicles in the country, and offers carriage rides around the grounds.
The gardens are largely informal, featuring a beautiful Victorian garden complete with conservatory and ornamental pond leading to a partially restored walled kitchen garden.
Information services:
Helpline available, tel no: 01271 850296.
Braille guide, audio guide.
Suitable for school groups, audio guide, family guide, children's quiz-trail.
Special visitor services: Materials and/or activities for children.
Education services: Group education facilities.
Services for disabled people: For the visually impaired.
Collections:
Horse-drawn carriages
Model ships mainly Napoleonic
Pewter
Shells

Internet home pages:
http://www.nationaltrust.org.uk/regions/devon

96
ARMADALE CASTLE
See - Museum of the Isles

97
ARMAGH COUNTY MUSEUM
The Mall East, Armagh, BT61 9BE

Tel: 028 3752 3070
Fax: 028 3752 2631
Email: catherine.mccullough-um@nics.gov.uk
Formed: 1931

Organisation type and purpose: Museum. Regional branch of a national museum.
Parent body:
Ulster Museum
Tel: 028 90 383000, fax: 028 90 383003
Part of:
National Museums and Galleries of Northern Ireland (NMGNI)

Enquiries to: Curator
Access:
Access to staff: By letter, by telephone, by fax, by email, in person, visitors by prior appointment
Other restrictions: Curatorial staff unavailable on Sat.
Access for disabled people: ramped entry, access to all public areas, toilet facilities
Other restrictions: Lift.

General description:
Prehistory, history, social history (military, railways, textile industry), natural history and art of County Armagh.
Information services:
Library available for reference (for conditions see Access above)
Guided tours for groups on request.
Special visitor services: Guided tours.
Education services: Group education facilities, resources for Key Stages 1 and 2..
Collections:
Art collections especially by George Russell (AE)
Documentary sources on (AE) including letters, manuscripts, poetry and the Blacker manuscripts
Manuscripts of T G F Paterson
Reference Library

Catalogues:
Catalogue for library is in-house only. Catalogue for all of the collections is only available in-house.
Printed publications:
Catalogue of collections - Archaeological collection only

98
ARMAGH PLANETARIUM

The Planetarium, College Hill, Armagh, BT61 9DB

Tel: 028 3752 3689
Fax: 028 3752 6187
Email: trm@armagh-planetarium.co.uk
Formed: 1968

Organisation type and purpose: Independently owned, registered charity (charity number XN 46022), museum, suitable for ages: 8+, consultancy.
To promote and educate in astronomy and earth sciences.

Enquiries to: Director
Direct tel: 028 3752 4725
Other contacts: Secretary for administration.
Access:
Access to staff: By letter, by telephone, by fax, by email, visitors by prior appointment
Access to building, collections or gallery: No prior appointment required
Hours: Mon to Fri, 1400 to 1645
Access for disabled people: Parking provided, ramped entry, access to all public areas, toilet facilities

General description:
Armagh Planetarium offers a unique visitor experience in Ireland. Start with a fascinating multimedia star show with latest digital effects, then tour our hall of astronomy and eartharium to find out more about earth and space.
Information services:
Library available for reference (for conditions see Access above), CD-ROM based services
Special visitor services: Materials and/or activities for children.
Education services: Group education facilities, resources for Key Stages 1 and 2, 3, 4 and Further or Higher Education.
Services for disabled people: For the hearing impaired; displays and/or information at wheelchair height.
Catalogues:
Catalogue for library is on-line. Catalogue for all of the collections is on-line.
Publications list:
is available in hard copy.
Printed publications:
Astronotes (monthly)
Electronic and video products:
Extensive archive library of astronomical images: VSH video, 35mm slide format, Betacam, CD-ROM

Internet home pages:
http://www.armagh-planetarium.co.uk
http://www.thestardome.co.uk

99
ARMAGH PUBLIC LIBRARY

Abbey Street, Armagh, BT61 7DY

Tel: 028 3752 3142
Fax: 028 3752 4177
Email: armroblib@aol.com
Formed: 1771

Organisation type and purpose: Registered charity, museum, public library, historic building, house or site, research organisation.

Enquiries to: Assistant Keeper
Other contacts: Administration Officer for access to cataloguing of collection.
Access:
Access to staff: By letter, by telephone, by email, visitors by prior appointment
Hours: Mon to Fri, 1000 to 1300 and 1400 to 1600
Other restrictions: Other times by prior arrangement.
Access to building, collections or gallery: No prior appointment required
Access for disabled people: ramped entry
Other restrictions: Chairlift to library.

Collections:
17th and 18th century books on theology, philosophy, classic and modern literature, voyages and travels, history, medicine, law
Medieval and 17th and 18th century manuscripts
Engravings by Piranesi, Hogarth and Bartolozzi
Catalogues:
Catalogue for library is on-line.

100
ARMITT LIBRARY & MUSEUM

Rydal Road, Ambleside, Cumbria, LA22 9BL

Tel: 015394 31212
Fax: 015394 31313
Email: info@armitt.com
Formed: 1912

Organisation type and purpose: Voluntary organisation, registered charity (charity number 526975), museum, suitable for ages: all ages. Independent library, owned by the Armitt Trust, open to all for study and research.
To provide a local centre for scholars and students.
Member of:
Association of Medical Research Charities

Enquiries to: Librarian
Other contacts: Curator
Access:
Access to staff: By letter, by telephone, by fax, by email, in person
Hours: Mon to Fri, 1000 to 1230 & 1330 to 1600
Access for disabled people: Parking provided, ramped entry, access to all public areas, toilet facilities

General description:
Information on the Lake District and on people who lived and worked in the Ambleside area, particularly in the 19th century.
Collections:
Beatrix Potter's scientific watercolours
The artefacts from Ambleside Roman Fort
Photographs of late Victorian Ambleside and surrounding area
Catalogues:
Catalogue for library is in-house only. Catalogue for all of the collections is only available in-house.
Printed publications:
Short guides and book lists to support the collection and special exhibitions (either free or for a nominal charge)

Internet home pages:
http://www.armitt.com

101
ARMY CATERING CORPS MUSEUM

See - Royal Logistic Corps Museum

102
ARMY MEDICAL SERVICES MUSEUM

Keogh Barracks, Ashvale, Aldershot, Hampshire, GU12 5RQ

Tel: 01252 868612
Fax: 01252 868832
Email: museum@keogh72.freeserve.co.uk
Acronym or abbreviation: AMS Museum
Formed: 1999
Formed from: QARANC Museum (QARANC Museum), Royal Army Dental Corps Museum (RADC Museum), Royal Army Medical Corps Historical Museum (RAMC Museum), date of change, 1999

Organisation type and purpose: Museum. Military museum.

Links with:
AMS Museum Trust
AS Museum

Enquiries to: Curator
Access:
Access to staff: By letter, by telephone, by email, in person
Hours: Mon to Fri, 1000 to 1530
Access for disabled people: Parking provided, ramped entry, toilet facilities

General description:
History of military medicine, nursing, dentistry and veterinary science from 1660 to present.
Collections:
The Muniment Room Collection (held at Wellcome Institute, London)
Catalogues:
Catalogue for library is in-house only. Catalogue for all of the collections is only available in-house.

103
ARMY PHYSICAL TRAINING CORPS MUSEUM

Army School of Physical Training, Queens Avenue, Aldershot, Hampshire, GU11 2LB

Tel: 01252 347168
Fax: 01252 370785
Acronym or abbreviation: APTC Museum
Formed: 1949
Incorporating: Army Gymnastic Staff (Past and Present), Army Physical Training Staff, Old Comrades' Association

Organisation type and purpose: Museum.
Parent body:
Army Physical Training Corps Association
Secretary:
APTC Association
at the same address, tel: 01252 347131

Enquiries to: Curator
Other contacts: Regimental Secretary
Access:
Access to staff: By letter, by telephone
Hours: Mon to Thu, 0900 to 1630; Fri, 0900 to 1230
Other restrictions: Closed during ASPT leave periods: Easter, August and Christmas. Potential visitors should telephone in advance of these periods.
Access for disabled people: Parking provided

General description:
History of the Army Gymnastic staff 1860 to 1919. History of the Army Physical Training staff 1919 to 1940. History of the Army Physical Training Corps 1940 to date.
Collections:
Books, pictures and photographs pertaining to military physical training and sport
Letters, photographs, prints, personal records and militaria from 1860
Small wartime mementoes from the Boer War onwards
Army Physical Training Corps instructors' honours and achievements in athletics, boxing, biathlon, fencing, football etc
Catalogues:
Catalogue for library is in-house only.

Internet home pages:
http://www.aptc.org.uk

104
ARNOLFINI

16 Narrow Quay, Bristol, BS1 4QA

Tel: 0117 929 9191
Fax: 0117 925 3876
Email: arnolfini@arnolfini.demon.co.uk
Formed: 1961

Organisation type and purpose: Registered charity (charity number 311504), historic building, house or site, suitable for ages: 5+. Contemporary arts centre.

Enquiries to: Marketing Manager

continued overleaf

Direct email: marketing@arnolfini.demon.co.uk
Access:
Access to staff: By letter, by telephone, by fax, by email, in person, Internet web pages
Access to building, collections or gallery: No prior appointment required
Hours: Box Office: Mon to Sat, 1030 to 2100; Sun, Bank Holiday Mon, 1230 to 2100
Gallery: Mon, Wed, Fri, Sat, 1000 to 1900; Thu, 1000 to 2100; Sun and Bank Holiday Mon, 1200 to 1900
Other restrictions: Free admission to Gallery.
Access for disabled people: Parking provided, toilet facilities
Other restrictions: Limited access to some areas. Large print brochure.

General description:
Located in Bristol's vibrant harbourside, Arnolfini is one of Europe's leading centres for the contemporary arts, with an international reputation for presenting new and innovative work in the visual arts, performance, dance and film. Based in an 1830s tea warehouse with stunning views across the water. Arnolfini also houses an arts bookshop and a stylish café/bar.
Information services:
Special visitor services: Guided tours, materials and/or activities for children.
Education services: Group education facilities..
Catalogues:
Catalogue for all of the collections is on-line.
Publications list:
is available in hard copy and online.
Printed publications:
Brochure with full programme (once every other month, free)
Catalogues of Exhibitions

Internet home pages:
http://www.arnolfini.demon.co.uk/

105
ART GALLERIES ASSOCIATION

Acronym or abbreviation: AGA
Disbanded

106
ART GALLERY, THE

34 Lisburn Street, Hillsborough, Co Down, BT26 6AB

Tel: 028 9268 9896
Fax: 028 9268 8433
Email: bill@theartgallery.freeserve.co.uk
Formed: 1994

Organisation type and purpose: Independently owned, art gallery, suitable for ages: 5+.
Retail art gallery.

Enquiries to: Director
Access:
Access to staff: By letter, by telephone, by fax, by email, in person
Access to building, collections or gallery: No prior appointment required
Hours: Mon to Sat, 1100 to 1700
Other restrictions: Or by prior appointment.

General description:
Contemporary art, paintings, drawings and prints.

Internet home pages:
http://www.theartgallery.freeserve.co.uk

107
ART SPACE GALLERY, THE

84 St Peter's Street, London, N1 8JS

Tel: 020 7359 7002
Fax: 020 7226 9533
Email: mail@artspacegallery.co.uk
Formed: 1986

Organisation type and purpose: Independently owned, art gallery, suitable for ages: 12+, consultancy, publishing house.
A commercial art gallery and consultant for private and corporate collections.

Enquiries to: Director
Access:
Access to staff: By letter, by telephone, by fax, by email, visitors by prior appointment, Internet web pages

General description:
Monthly exhibitions of contemporary art (painting, drawings, print and sculpture) specialising in painting by established and emerging artists.
Publications list:
is available in hard copy and online.
Printed publications:
From the River to the Sea (Rowlett G, £10)
1985-2002 (Kane M, £10)
Ray Atkins (£15)
Paintings of Heaven & Hell (Gopal-Chowdhury P, £10)
Mind Has Mountains (Cooper J, £15)
Electronic and video products:
CD-ROM of Gallery Artists available

Internet home pages:
http://www.artspacegallery.co.uk
Includes detailed information of past, present and future exhibitions, additional biographical information of gallery artists, and publications. The site is updated weekly.

108
ARTBANK GALLERY

114 Clerkenwell Road, London, EC1M 5SA

Tel: 020 7608 3333
Fax: 020 7608 3060
Email: info@artbank.com

Organisation type and purpose: Independently owned, art gallery.
Commercial art gallery.

Enquiries to: Managing Director
Access:
Access to staff: By email
Access to building, collections or gallery: No prior appointment required
Hours: Tue to Fri, 1130 to 1800; Sat, 1200 to 1600
Access for disabled people: level entry

General description:
Primary art business exhibiting new contemporary art and artists.

Internet home pages:
http://www.artbank.com
Online viewing of exhibitions, art for sale, delivery guarantees, gallery hire.

109
ARTLINK EXCHANGE

21 Princes Avenue, Hull, East Yorkshire, HU5 3RX

Tel: 01482 345104
Fax: 01482 345028
Email: artlink@pop3.poptel.org.uk
Formed: 1982

Organisation type and purpose: Registered charity (charity number 701335), art gallery, suitable for ages: all ages.
Community arts organisation.
Supported by:
Kingston upon Hull City Council
Yorkshire Arts

Enquiries to: Director
Access:
Access to staff: By letter, by telephone, by fax, by email, in person, visitors by prior appointment
Access to building, collections or gallery: No prior appointment required
Hours: Mon to Fri, 0900 to 1700; Sat, 1100 to 1600
Access for disabled people: level entry
Other restrictions: Access to gallery.

General description:
The region's leading community arts organisation providing quality artistic and cultiral activities.
The gallery has a programme of temporary exhibitions of local artists.
Information services:
programme of events
Outreach projects, exhibitions and information service.
Special visitor services: Guided tours..
Printed publications:
General leaflet describing the organisations aims and objectives

Internet home pages:
http://www.artlinkexchange.co.uk/

110
ARTS CENTRE, GARSTANG

See - Garstang & District Art Society

111
ARTS COUNCIL COLLECTION

Hayward Gallery, Belvedere Road, London, SE1 8XX

Tel: 020 7921 0875
Acronym or abbreviation: ACC
Formed: 1946
Formed from: Arts Council of Great Britain (ACGB); Arts Council of England (ACE), date of change, 1995

Organisation type and purpose: National government body, art gallery, suitable for ages: 12+.
Parent body:
Arts Council of England

Enquiries to: Curator
Direct tel: 020 7921 0875/8
Direct fax: 020 7401 2664
Direct email: ijohnstone@hayward.org.uk
Other contacts: Assistant Curator based at Hayward Gallery
Access:
Access to staff: By letter, by email
Access to building, collections or gallery: Prior appointment required
Hours: The Collection is rarely on view at the Hayward Gallery
Other restrictions: Loan collection work is all over UK.

General description:
The Arts Council Collection is a loan collection which is not on view in one permanent gallery but on view throughout Britain in museums, galleries and other public buildings. It is administered by the South Bank Centre, London, on behalf of the Arts Council of England. Post-war British Art.
Collections:
Post-war British paintings, sculpture, photography, artworks, prints and mixed media, 1946-present day
The Saatchi Gift
Printed publications:
Information leaflet
Various publications are distributed by Cornerhouse Publications
Electronic and video products:
ACE! Arts council Collection 1989-1995 (CD-ROM, £39.99)

Address for ordering publications:
Printed publications:
Arts Council Collection and National Touring Exhibition publications, Cornerhouse Publications
70 Oxford Street, Manchester, M1 5NH, tel: 0161 200 1503, fax: 0161 237 1504
Hayward Gallery Publications
Royal Festival Hall, London, SE1 8XX

Internet home pages:
http://www.rfh.org.uk

112
ARTS COUNCIL OF WALES
9 Museum Place, Cardiff, CF10 3NX

Tel: 029 2037 6500
Minicom no. 029 2039 0027
Fax: 029 2022 1447
Email: information@artswales.org.uk
Acronym or abbreviation: ACW
Formed: 1994
Formerly: Welsh Arts Council, date of change, 1994

Organisation type and purpose: National government body, advisory body, statutory body (membership is by election or invitation), present number of members: 18 members on ACW's Council, 150+ on panels and committees, registered charity (charity number 1034245). Distributes National Assembly for Wales and National Lottery funds for the arts in Wales.
Other addresses:
Arts Council of Wales
6 Gardd Llydaw, Jackson's Lane, Carmarthen, SA31 1QD, tel: 01267 234248, fax: 01267 233084, email/website: information@ccc-acw.org.uk
Arts Council of Wales
Cardiff, tel: 029 2037 6500, fax: 029 2022 1447, email/website: information@ccc-acw.org.uk
Arts Council of Wales
36 Prince's Drive, Colwyn Bay, LL29 8LA, tel: 01492 533440 Minicom 01492 532288, fax: 01492 533677, email/website: information@ccc-acw.org.uk

Enquiries to: Information Officer
Access:
Access to staff: By letter, by telephone, by fax, by email, Internet web pages
Hours: Carmarthen and Colwyn Bay Offices: Mon to Fri, 0900 to 1700
Cardiff Office: Mon to Fri, 0900 to 1730

General description:
Development of all art forms in Wales, funding for arts activities from National Assembly for Wales and National Lottery sources.
Catalogues:
Catalogue for library is published and is on-line.
Publications list:
is available in hard copy and online.
Printed publications:
Annual Report and Corporate Plan summary 1999-2002
Artists Notes (newsletter, quarterly, for visual artists)
ArtsFile (bi-monthly newsletter for the arts in Wales)
Crefft (quarterly newsletter for craftspeople)
Building a Creative Society - consultation paper and responses to strategic proposals to develop a practical way forward for the arts in Wales from 1999-2004
Directory of Publishers in Wales
The Arts and Young People in Wales
The Economic Impact of the Arts and Cultural Industries in Wales

Internet home pages:
http://www.artswales.org.uk

113
ARTSPACE
133 Cumberland Road, Bristol, BS1 6UX

Tel: 0117 929 2266
Fax: 0117 929 2066
Email: admin@spikeislandart.demon.co.uk

Organisation type and purpose: National organisation, registered charity (charity number 1003505), art gallery, suitable for ages: 16+. Exhibition space and 100 studio spaces.
The primary aim of Spike Island is to support the practice of artists through a range of products: Exhibitions, International Residencies, Talks Programme and provision of high quality affordable studio space.

Enquiries to: Curator
Direct email: sally@spikeislandart.demon.co.uk
Other contacts: (1) Projects Co-ordinator; (2) Director for (2) absence of above on any occasion.
Access:
Access to staff: By letter, by email, visitors by prior appointment
Access to building, collections or gallery: No prior appointment required
Hours: Tue to Sun, 1200 to 1700
Access for disabled people: Parking provided, level entry, access to all public areas, toilet facilities

General description:
Spike Island is a new model arts organisation which prioritises art production and enables innovation, experimentation and dialogue within a sympathetic setting. It is a unique environment devoted to the production and exhibition of the contemporary visual arts ranging from painting, sculpture and printmaking to multimedia and moving image arts. Spike Island combines artists studio provision with an artistic programme of exhibitions and events. Housed in the landmark Brooke Bond building, previously a tea packing factory, it contains over 80 studios, an expansive central exhibition space, visiting artists' residency studios, workshop facilities and commercial tenants.
Information services:
Hire out of studio space and also the exhibition space when not in use during exhibitions. Contact the Operations Manager for details.
Spike Island houses Artists First, see website www.artandpower.com.
Special visitor services: Guided tours..
Electronic and video products:
An extensive range of digital equipment, available for hire when not in use during exhibitions

Internet home pages:
http://www.
Under construction.
http://www.artandpower.com
Artists First website.

114
ARUNDEL CASTLE TRUSTEES LIMITED
Arundel Castle, High Street, Arundel, West Sussex, BN18 9AB

Tel: 01903 882173
Fax: 01903 884581

Organisation type and purpose: Registered charity (charity number 271833), historic building, house or site, suitable for ages: 8+.

Enquiries to: Comptroller
Other contacts: Secretary
Access:
Access to staff: By letter, by fax
Access for disabled people: Parking provided, level entry, toilet facilities
Other restrictions: Lift, access to almost all areas.

General description:
The history of Arundel Castle.
Collections:
Paintings, furniture, sculpture, tapestries, clocks
Printed publications:
Castle Leaflet (free)
Castle Guide Book

Internet home pages:
http://www.arundelcastle.org

115
ARUNDEL MUSEUM
61 High Street, Arundel, West Sussex, BN18 9AJ

Tel: 01903 882268
Formed: 1964
Formed from: Arundel Museum Society

Organisation type and purpose: Registered charity (charity number 273790), museum, suitable for ages: 8+.

Enquiries to: Curator
Access:
Access to staff: By letter only, visitors by prior appointment
Hours: Wed, 0930 to 1300
Access to building, collections or gallery: Prior appointment required
Hours: Easter to end Sep: Mon to Sat, 1030 to 1700; Sun, 1400 to 1700

General description:
History of Arundel, the Port of Arundel, rural crafts exhibits, local trades, photographs etc.
Information services:
Library available for reference (for conditions see Access above). Helpline available, tel no: 01903 885708.
Materials/activities for children from time to time.
Group education services for children by arrangement.
Special visitor services: Guided tours, materials and/or activities for children..
Collections:
Pictures, models, documents, artefacts
Collection of old tools: farming, farrier, dairy, carpenter
Catalogues:
Catalogue for library is in-house only.
Printed publications:
Arundel Voices - recollections of bygone years by local residents

116
ARUNDEL TOY & MILITARY MUSEUM
Closed

117
ASCOTT
Wing, Leighton Buzzard, Buckinghamshire, LU7 0PS

Tel: 01296 688242
Fax: 01296 681904
Email: info@ascottestate.co.uk

Organisation type and purpose: National organisation, registered charity (charity number 205846), museum, historic building, house or site.
Parent body:
National Trust (South and South East Region)
Thames and Solent Regional Office, tel: 01494 528051

Enquiries to: Manager
Access:
Access to staff: By letter, by telephone, by fax, by email
Access to building, collections or gallery: No prior appointment required
Hours: Apr and Aug to mid Sep, Tue to Sun, 1400 to 1800
Open Bank Holiday Mondays; open one day in May and one in Aug in aid of NGS
Other restrictions: Last admission one hour before closing
Access for disabled people: ramped entry, toilet facilities
Other restrictions: Drop-off point. 3 manual wheelchairs available, booking essential. Ramped entrance. Ground floor accessible with assistance. Grounds largely accessible.

General description:
Originally a half-timbered Jacobean farmhouse, Ascott was bought in 1876 by the de Rothschild family and considerably transformed and enlarged. It now houses a quite exceptional collection of fine paintings, Oriental porcelain and English and French furniture. The extensive gardens are a mixture of the formal and natural, containing specimen trees and shrubs, as well as a herbaceous walk, lily pond, Dutch garden and remarkable topiary sundial.
Information services:
Services for disabled people: For the visually impaired.

continued overleaf

Internet home pages:
http://www.nationaltrust.org.uk

118
ASHBY DE LA ZOUCH CASTLE

South Street, Ashby de la Zouch, Leicestershire, LE65 1BR

Tel: 01530 413343

Organisation type and purpose: Historic building, house or site.
Parent body:
English Heritage (East Midlands Region)
44 Derngate, Northampton, NN1 1UH, tel: 01604 735400, fax: 01604 735401
Access:
Access to staff: By letter, by telephone
Access to building, collections or gallery: No prior appointment required
Hours: Apr to Sep: daily, 1000 to 1800
Oct: daily, 1000 to 1700
Nov to Mar: Wed to Sun, 1000 to 1600
Other restrictions: Closed 24 to 26 Dec and 1 Jan
Opening times are subject to change, for up-to-date information contact English Heritage by phone or visit the website.
General description:
This late-medieval castle's ruins are dominated by the 24-metre (80-foot) Hastings Tower built between 1474 and 1483, which offers panoramic views of the countryside. Ashby was used by Sir Walter Scott for the famous jousting scene in his classic romance, 'Ivanhoe'.
Information services:
Free children's activity sheet.
Programme of guided tours.
Special visitor services: Guided tours, tape recorded guides, materials and/or activities for children..

Internet home pages:
http://www.english-heritage.org.uk

119
ASHBY-DE-LA-ZOUCH MUSEUM

North Street, Ashby-de-la-Zouch, Leicestershire, LE65 1HU

Tel: 01530 560090
Formed: 1982

Organisation type and purpose: Voluntary organisation, registered charity (charity number 513745), museum.

Enquiries to: Chairman
Other contacts: Curator for specific enquiries about holdings.
Access:
Access to staff: By letter, by telephone, visitors by prior appointment
Access for disabled people: Parking provided, ramped entry, access to all public areas, toilet facilities

General description:
Collections of local importance; changing temporary exhibitions; large archives, including very considerable photographical archive of local material; small library.
Catalogues:
Catalogue for library is in-house only. Catalogue for all of the collections is only available in-house.
Publications list:
is available in hard copy.

120
ASHDOWN HOUSE

Lambourn, Newbury, Berkshire, RG16 7RE

Tel: 01488 72584
Email: ashdownhouse@nationaltrust.org.uk

Organisation type and purpose: National organisation, registered charity (charity number 205846), historic building, house or site.
Parent body:
The National Trust (South and South East Region)
Thames and Solent Regional Office, tel: 01494 528051
National Trust sites:
Ashdown House
Lambourn, Newbury, Berkshire, RG16 7RE, tel: 01488 72584, email/website: ashdownhouse@ntrust.org.uk

Enquiries to: Manager
Access:
Access to staff: By letter, by telephone, by email
Access to building, collections or gallery: No prior appointment required
Hours: House and Garden, Apr to Oct, Wed and Sat, 1400 1700
Other restrictions: Admission to house by guided tour at 1415, 1515, 1615.

General description:
An extraordinary Dutch-style 17th century house, perched on the Berkshire Downs and famous for its association with Elizabeth of Bohemia ('The Winter Queen'), Charles I's sister, to whom the house was 'consecrated'. The interior has an impressive great staircase rising from hall to attic, and important paintings contemporary with the house. There are spectacular views from the roof over the formal parterre, lawns and surrounding countryside, as well as beautiful walks in neighbouring Ashdown Woods. Nearby Weathercock Hill and Alfred's Castle, an Iron Age defended settlement where in 871 King Alfred is rumoured to have defeated the Danes, offer fine walking.

Internet home pages:
http://www.nationaltrust.org.uk

121
ASHFORD MUSEUM

The Old Grammar School, The Churchyard, Ashford, Kent, TN23 1QG

Organisation type and purpose: Museum.

Enquiries to: Curator
Direct tel: 01233 631511
Access:
Access to staff: By letter, by telephone, by fax
Hours: Apr to Nov: Mon to Sat, 1000 to 1400

General description:
Ashford local history.A collection of exhibits and photographs portraying the social life of Ashford, mainly 19th and 20th Centuries.
Collections:
Acland collection, tokens in use in hop fields, 19th-20th century
Johnstone collection, coins and miscellaneous items
Catalogues:
Catalogue for all of the collections is only available in-house.

122
ASHLEWORTH TITHE BARN

Ashleworth, Gloucestershire

Tel: 01985 843600 (Regional office)
Email: ashleworth@nationaltrust.org.uk

Organisation type and purpose: National organisation, registered charity (charity number 205846), historic building, house or site.
Parent body:
The National Trust (South West Region)
Regional Office for Wessex, tel: 01995 843600

Enquiries to: Manager
Access:
Access to staff: By letter, by email
Access to building, collections or gallery: No prior appointment required
Hours: Apr to Oct, daily, 0900 to 1800

General description:
A 15th century tithe barn, with an immense stone-tiled roof, picturesquely located on the banks of the River Severn.

Internet home pages:
http://www.nationaltrust.org.uk/regions/wessex

123
ASHMOLEAN MUSEUM

Beaumont Street, Oxford, OX1 2PH

Tel: 01865 278000
Fax: 01865 278018
Formed: 1683

Organisation type and purpose: Museum, suitable for ages: 5+.
Parent body:
Oxford University
University Offices, Wellington Square, Oxford

Enquiries to: Administrator
Direct tel: 01865 278007
Direct email: roger.hobby@ashmus.ox.ac.uk
Other contacts: Press Officer for press and publicity.
Access:
Access to staff: By letter, by telephone, by fax, by email, in person, Internet web pages
Access to building, collections or gallery: No prior appointment required
Hours: Tue to Sat, 1000 to 1700; Sun, 1400 to 1700
Other restrictions: Check for Easter and Christmas opening.
Access for disabled people: ramped entry, toilet facilities
Other restrictions: Wheelchair available; telephone prior to visit.

General description:
A comprehensive collection of art and archaeology from Egyptian times to 20th century. Includes objects and arts from Egypt, Greece and Rome; European Medieval to Modern; also from Far East (Japan, China, Korea, India and Tibet) plus Islamic World.
Information services:
Library available for reference (for conditions see Access above)
Special visitor services: Guided tours, materials and/or activities for children.
Education services: Group education facilities, resources for Key Stages 1 and 2, 3, 4 and Further or Higher Education..
Catalogues:
Catalogue for library is in-house only. Catalogue for all of the collections is published and part is on-line.

Internet home pages:
http://www.ashmus.ox.ac.uk

124
ASHRIDGE ESTATE

Ringshall, Berkhamsted, Hertfordshire, HP4 1LT

Tel: 01442 851227 (Visitor Centre)
Fax: 01442 850000
Email: ashridge@nationaltrust.org.uk

Organisation type and purpose: National organisation, registered charity (charity number 205846), historic building, house or site, suitable for ages: all ages.
Parent body:
The National Trust (South & South East Region)
Thames & Solent Regional Office, tel: 01491 528051

Enquiries to: Warden
Direct tel: 01442 842716
Other contacts: Education officer
Access:
Access to staff: By letter, by telephone, by fax, by email
Access to building, collections or gallery: No prior appointment required
Hours: Estate: daily access throughout the year
Visitor Centre: mid Mar to mid Dec, Mon to Fri, 1300 to 1700, Sat and Sun, 1200 to 1700
Monument: end Mar to end Oct, Sat and Sun, 1200 to 1700
Other restrictions: Visitor centre and Monument open Bank Holiday Mondays & Good Fri 12

to 5
Monument: Mon to Thu by arrangement, weather permitting.
Access for disabled people: Parking provided
Other restrictions: 1 manual wheelchair available. Powered mobility vehicles: 5 single-seater, 2 two-seater. Level
entrance. Ground floor fully accessible. Visitor centre fully accessible. Level entrance to shop. Level entrance to tea-room.
Recommended route map. Adapted WC with RADAR lock.

General description:
This magnificent and varied estate runs across the borders of Herts and Bucks, along the main ridge of the Chiltern Hills. There are woodlands, commons and chalk downland supporting a rich variety of wildlife and offering splendid walks through outstanding scenery. The focal point of the area is the Monument, erected in 1832 to the Duke of Bridgewater. There are also splendid views from Ivinghoe Beacon, accessible from Steps Hill.
Information services:
Helpline available, tel no: 01494 755557 (Infoline).
A range of summer holiday activities for children and a farming weekend, inc. local farmers' market.
Workshops and activity days for children and adults. For more information please send s.a.e.
Suitable for school groups; education room/centre, hands-on activities. Adult study days.
Programme of guided walks all year.
Special visitor services: Guided tours, materials and/or activities for children.
Education services: Group education facilities.
Services for disabled people: For the visually impaired.

Internet home pages:
http://www.nationaltrust.org.uk/regions/

125
ASHTON COURT VISITOR CENTRE
Ashton Court Estate, Long Ashton, Bristol, BS18 9JN

Tel: 0117 963 9174
Formed: 1989

Organisation type and purpose: Local government body, museum.
Visitor centre.

Enquiries to: Administrator
Direct fax: 0117 953 2143
Direct email: cellan_michael@bristol-city.gov.uk
Other contacts: Ashton Court Estate Officer
Access:
Access to staff: By letter, by telephone, by email, in person
Access for disabled people: Parking provided, access to all public areas, toilet facilities

General description:
Provides an introduction to the landscape history of Ashton Court Estate and the Smyth family who lived here.

126
ASHWELL VILLAGE MUSEUM
Swan Street, Ashwell, Hertfordshire, SG7 5NY

Tel: 01462 742956
Formed: 1930

Organisation type and purpose: Registered charity, museum.

Enquiries to: Curator
Access:
Access for disabled people: level entry

General description:
The history of an English village from the Stone Age to the present day displayed in a Tudor timber-framed building. Contains archives, artefacts and photographs relating to Ashwell. New Galleries opened in 2002.

127
ASSOCIATION FOR INDUSTRIAL ARCHAEOLOGY
The Wharfage, Coach Road, Coalbrookdale, Telford, Shropshire, TF8 7DQ

Tel: 01952 432141
Fax: 01952 432237
Acronym or abbreviation: AIA
Formed: 1973

Organisation type and purpose: Advisory body, learned society (membership is by subscription), voluntary organisation, research organisation, publishing house.
Links with:
Ironbridge Gorge Museum Trust
Tel: 01952 433522
Also at:
AIA Liaison Officer
School of Archaeological Studies, University of Leicester, University Road, Leicester, LE1 7RH, tel: 0116 252 5337, fax: 0116 252 5005, email/website: aia@le.ac.uk

Enquiries to: Secretary
Other contacts: Correspondence Secretary
Access:
Access to staff: By letter, by telephone, by fax
Hours: Mon to Fri, 0900 to 1700
Access to building, collections or gallery: No prior appointment required

General description:
Industrial archaeology; conservation; preservation.
Information services:
Education services: Group education facilities, resources for Further or Higher Education..
Publications list:
is available in hard copy.
Printed publications:
IA News (4 times a year)
Industrial Archaeology Review (2 times a year)

Address for ordering publications:
Printed publications:
Sales Officer
Barn Cottage, Bridge Street, Bridgnorth, Shropshire, WV15 6AF, tel: 01746 765159

128
ASSOCIATION OF INDEPENDENT MUSEUMS, THE
Bethnal Green Museum of Childhood, Cambridge Heath Road, Bethnal Green, London, E2 9PA

Tel: 020 8983 5222
Fax: 020 8983 5225
Email: d.lees@vam.ac.uk
Acronym or abbreviation: AIM
Formed: 1977

Organisation type and purpose: Professional body, trade association (membership is by subscription), present number of members: 726, voluntary organisation.
National museum association for those institutions not directly administered by central or local government.

Enquiries to: Honorary Secretary
Access:
Access to staff: By email, by letter, by telephone, by fax
Hours: Mon to Fri, 0900 to 1700

General description:
Museum development; management; administration; fundraising; marketing; display; publications, particularly for the independent sector.
Printed publications:
AIM Bulletin (6 times a year for members)
AIM Guidelines on specific topics, generally relating to
establishment of specific roles within museums

Internet home pages:
http://www.museums.org.uk/aim

129
ASSOCIATION OF INDEPENDENT RAILWAYS AND PRESERVATION SOCIETIES

Acronym or abbreviation: AIRPS
See - Heritage Railway Association

130
ASSOCIATION OF RAILWAY PRESERVATION SOCIETIES
See - Heritage Railway Association

131
ASTLEY GREEN COLLIERY MUSEUM
Higher Green Lane, Astley, Lancashire

Tel: 01942 82812
Email: info@steamcoalcanal.co.uk

Organisation type and purpose: Registered charity (charity number 1067778), museum, historic building, house or site, suitable for ages: all ages.
Parent body:
Bridgewater Canal Linear Industrial Heritage Park
Tel: 0161 748 4414

Enquiries to: Manager
Access:
Access to staff: By letter, by telephone
Other restrictions: When closed information available from 0161 748 4414.

General description:
This is an authentic pit village with the pit head tower and engine still intact.

Internet home pages:
http://www.steamcoalcanal.co.uk

132
ASTLEY HALL MUSEUM & ART GALLERY
Astley Hall, Astley Park, Chorley, Lancashire, PR7 1NP

Tel: 01257 515555
Fax: 01257 515556
Email: astleyhall@lineone.net
Formed: 1924

Organisation type and purpose: Local government body, museum, art gallery, historic building, house or site, suitable for ages: 5+.
Parent body:
Chorley Borough Council

Enquiries to: Curator
Access:
Access to staff: By letter, by telephone, by email, visitors by prior appointment, Internet web pages
Access for disabled people: Parking provided
Other restrictions: Ground floor access only.

General description:
Large parts of the original Elizabethan Astley Hall survive despite centuries of alterations made to keep the Hall up-to-date. It was lived in by the Charnock, Brooke, Townley-Parker and Tatton families and is large enough to emphasise the wealth of the families who lived here, but small enough to retain a pleasant lived-in atmosphere.
Information services:
Special visitor services: Guided tours, tape recorded guides, materials and/or activities for children.
Education services: Group education facilities, resources for Key Stages 1 and 2, 3, 4 and Further or Higher Education.
Services for disabled people: For the visually impaired.
Collections:
Tudor/Stuart building dating from 1580
Decorative plaster ceilings

continued overleaf

Collection of Leeds pottery
Paintings
Oak furniture
Social History Collection
Printed publications:
Leaflet
Guide Book
Teachers Education Pack

Internet home pages:
http://www.astleyhall.co.uk

133
ASTON HALL MUSEUM
Trinity Road, Aston, Birmingham, B6 6JD

Tel: 0121 327 0062
Fax: 0121 327 7162
Formed: 1858

Organisation type and purpose: Local government body, museum, historic building, house or site, suitable for ages: 5+.
Parent body:
Birmingham Museums and Art Gallery (BMAG) Chamberlain Square, Birmingham, B3 3DH, tel: 0121 303 2834, fax: 0121 303 1394

Enquiries to: Curator
Access:
Access to staff: By letter, by telephone, by fax, by email, in person, visitors by prior appointment
Access for disabled people: Parking provided, level entry

General description:
Aston Hall is a Grade I listed Jacobean Mansion, and one of the most important (and little changed) examples of Jacobean architecture and decoration in the UK.
It now functions as a historic house museum, furnished as a series of period rooms depicting historic interiors from the 17th to 19th century, featuring fine furniture, textiles, paintings, silver and ceramics.
Information services:
Special visitor services: Guided tours, materials and/or activities for children.
Education services: Group education facilities, resources for Key Stages 1 and 2, 3, 4 and Further or Higher Education.
Services for disabled people: For the visually impaired; for the hearing impaired; displays and/or information at wheelchair height.
Collections:
The collections comprise Aston Hall itself which boasts superb 17th century plasterwork, joinery, stone decoration
The collections displayed at Aston include:
Furniture, arts (paintings), textiles, ceramics, silver, prints and drawings, social history material, domestic bygones
These collections are designated as being of national significance under the DCMS's Museum Designation Scheme
Catalogues:
Catalogue for part of the collections is available in-house and part is on-line.
Printed publications:
Leaflet (free)
Guidebook (available for purchase)
Detailed History Book (available for purchase)

Internet home pages:
http://www.bmag.org.uk
Birmingham Museums and Art Gallery website featuring half-a-dozen pages on Aston Hall.

134
ATHOLL COUNTRY LIFE MUSEUM
Blair Atholl, Perthshire, PH18 5SP

Tel: 01796 481232
Email: janet.cam@virgin.net
Formed: 1981

Organisation type and purpose: Museum, suitable for ages: 5+.

Enquiries to: Curator
Access:
Access to staff: By letter, by telephone
Access to building, collections or gallery: No prior appointment required
Hours: End May to end Sep: daily, 1330 to 1700;
also July and Aug: Mon to Fri, 1000 to 1700
Access for disabled people: Parking provided, ramped entry, access to all public areas, toilet facilities

General description:
A small folk museum housed in the old school, which is full of interesting exhibits of village and Glen life, including displays on the byre and stable; harness; church; school; Post Office; road and rail transport; gamekeeper; shoemaker; recreation; domestic items; dress; and smiddy.

Internet home pages:
http://www.blairatholl.org.uk
Advertisement.

135
ATKINSON ART GALLERY
Lord Street, Southport, Merseyside, PR8 1DH

Tel: 0151 934 2110
Fax: 0151 934 2109
Email: enquiries@seftonarts.co.uk
Formed: 1878

Organisation type and purpose: Local government body, art gallery, suitable for ages: 5+.

Enquiries to: Curator
Access:
Access to staff: By telephone
Access for disabled people: access to all public areas

General description:
Temporary exhibition programme, permanent collection of 19th and 20th century paintings and sculpture, including work by L S Lowry, Henry Moore and Elisabeth Frink. Every month a painting of the month talk is given about a work of art from the collection.
Collections:
18th, 19th and 20th century works of art, including oils, watercolours and sculpture
Goodison Egyptology collection, ancient Egyptian artefacts, 3100 BC-250 AD, c. 800 items
Archibald Sparke collection, 18th century drinking glasses, c. 30 items
Randell Jackson collection, 18th century drinking glasses, c. 100 items
Printed publications:
Catalogue of Twentieth Century Collection

Internet home pages:
http://www.seftonarts.co.uk
Opening hours, exhibitions, programme.

136
ATOMIC WEAPONS RESEARCH ESTABLISHMENT
See - Orford Ness National Nature Reserve

137
ATTINGHAM PARK
Shrewsbury, Shropshire, SY4 4TP

Tel: 01743 708162 (Estate Office)
Fax: 01743 708175
Email: attingham@nationaltrust.org.uk
Formed: 1947

Organisation type and purpose: Registered charity (charity number 205846), museum, suitable for ages: 8+.
Parent body:
The National Trust (West Midlands) West Midlands Regional Office, tel: 01743 708100

Enquiries to: House and Visitor Services Manager
Access:
Access to staff: By letter, by fax, by email
Access for disabled people: Parking provided, toilet facilities
Other restrictions: Access to house via lift - please telephone in advance.
Designated parking 20yds. Transfer available. 2 single-seater powered mobility vehicles. Steps to entrance. Accessible entrance different from main entrance. Ground floor fully accessible. Access to other floors via lift. Ramped entrance to shop. Steps to tea-room entrance. Seating available outside on tea-room lawn.

General description:
One of the great houses of the Midlands. The elegant mansion was built in 1785 for the 1st Lord Berwick to the design of George Steuart and has a picture gallery by John Nash. The magnificent Regency interiors contain collections of ambassadorial silver, Italian furniture and Grand Tour paintings. The park was landscaped by Repton and has attractive walks along the River Tern and through the deer park.
Information services:
Helpline available, tel no: Infoline: 01743 708123.
Free costumed introductory talks and guided tours of the house available from 1300 on house open days, except Bank Holiday Mondays. Out-of-hours tours available for booked groups at 1100; a charge is made per head (inc. NT members).
Braille guide. Large-print guide.
Frontcarrying baby slings for loan. Children's play area. Family activity room in the house.
Suitable for school groups. Education room/ centre. Live interpretation. Hands-on activities. Children's quiz/trail. Family activity packs.
Special visitor services: Guided tours, materials and/or activities for children.
Education services: Group education facilities.
Services for disabled people: For the visually impaired.
Printed publications:
Colour Guide Book (available, £3.50 plus £1 p&p)

Internet home pages:
http://www.nationaltrust.org.uk

138
AUDLEY END HOUSE AND GARDENS
Audley End House, Saffron Walden, Essex, CB11 4JF

Tel: 01799 522842 or 01799 522399 (information Line)

Organisation type and purpose: Historic building, house or site.
Parent body:
English Heritage (East of England Region) Brooklands, 24 Brooklands Avenue, Cambridge, CB2 2BU, tel: 01223 582700, fax: 01223 582701

General description:
Magnificent former home of Charles II, neoclassical architecture, 31 opulent rooms on view, the Victorian gardens, including the great walled kitchen garden. Audley End is displayed to show the house as it was in the 18th and 19th Centuries. The house retains a fine Jacobean style great hall and many fine 17th century plaster ceilings. Other treasures include the Braybrooke silver collection in the Butler's Pantry, a very fine dolls' house and Robert Adam interiors. The house is set in grounds designed by 'Capability' Brown.
Collections:
Dolls house
Furniture, glass and silver
Jacobean Screen
Paintings including some by Holbein, Lely and Canaletto
Natural History Collection

Internet home pages:
http://www.english-heritage.org.uk

139
AUGUSTUS GALLERIES, THE
St Georges Street, Tenby, Dyfed, SA70 7JB

Tel: 01834 845164 / 842204
Fax: 01834 844222
Formed: 1983

Organisation type and purpose: Independently owned, art gallery.

Enquiries to: Proprietor
Access:
Access to staff: By letter, by telephone, by fax, in person
Hours: Mon to Fri, 0900 to 1700
Other restrictions: Sat, Sun by prior appointment.
Access to building, collections or gallery: No prior appointment required
Hours: Mon to Fri, 1400 to 1630; Sat, 1030 to 1600
Other restrictions: If closed, telephone the Lock House, St Julians Street, Tenby, tel 01834 842204 for early appointment to view.

General description:
Early 19th and 20th century oil and watercolours, early Tenby and West Wales. Paintings by artists of local origins - Augustus and Evan John, Ninan Hamsett etc. Paintings, drawings, maps etc of or about West Wales. John Piper, Philip Sutton, Thos. Bush Hardy, Harry Bright, Laura Knight, Amanda Birch, Josef Herman, Alfred Munnings, T Leonard Evans.

140
AUTOMOBILIA TRANSPORT MUSEUM
Hebden Bridge

Closed

141
AVEBURY MANOR AND GARDEN
National Trust Estate Office, Avebury, Marlborough, Wiltshire, SN8 1RF

Tel: 01672 539250
Fax: 01672 539388
Email: avebury@nationaltrust.org.uk

Organisation type and purpose: Registered charity (charity number 205846), historic building, house or site, suitable for ages: 5+.
Parent body:
The National Trust (Wessex Region)
Regional Office for Wessex, tel: 01985 843600
National Trust sites:
Avebury Manor
National Trust Estate Office, Avebury, Marlborough, Wiltshire, SN8 1RF, tel: 01672 539250, fax: 01672 539388, email/website: avebury@nationaltrust.org.uk

Enquiries to: Visitor Services Manager
Access:
Access to staff: By letter, by telephone, by email
Access for disabled people: Parking provided
Other restrictions: Designated parking 300yds. Drop-off point. Grounds largely accessible.

General description:
A much-altered house of monastic origin, the present buildings date from the early 16th century, with notable Queen Anne alterations and Edwardian renovation. The garden was completely re-designed in the early 20th century by Colonel and Mrs Jenner. The topiary and flower gardens contain medieval walls, ancient box and numerous 'rooms'. Some features may be survivals of the original priory precinct.
Information services:
Special visitor services: Guided tours..

Internet home pages:
http://www.nationaltrust.org.uk/regions/wessex

142
AVEBURY
Nr Marlborough, Wiltshire, SN8 1RF

Tel: 01672 539250 (Estate Office)
Fax: 01672 538038 (Estate Office)
Email: avebury@nationaltrust.org.uk

Organisation type and purpose: National organisation, registered charity (charity number 205846), historic building, house or site, suitable for ages: all ages.
Parent body:
The National Trust (South West Region)
Regional Office for Wessex, tel: 01985 843600

Enquiries to: Manager
Access:
Access to staff: By letter, by telephone, by fax, by email, Internet web pages
Access for disabled people: toilet facilities
Other restrictions: Designated parking 200yds. Drop-off point. Largely accessible, parts of the Circle are inaccessible. Audiovisual display fitted with induction loop. Level entrance to restaurant.

General description:
One of the most important megalithic monuments in Europe and spread over a vast area, much of which is under Trust protection. The great stone circle, encompassing part of the village of Avebury, is enclosed by a ditch and external bank and approached by an avenue of stones. Many of the stones were re-erected in the 1930s by the archaeologist Alexander Keiller. The site Museum, including a new exhibition in the 17th century thatched threshing barn, presents the archaeological story of Avebury. Finds from the site and interactive and audiovisual displays are used to tell the story of the monuments and the people who have helped to reveal their past. West of Avebury, the Iron Age earthwork of Oldbury Castle crowns Cherhill Down, along with the conspicuous Lansdowne Monument. With the spectacular folds of Calstone Coombes, this area of open downland provides wonderful walking opportunities.
Information services:
Education services: Group education facilities.
Services for disabled people: For the visually impaired; for the hearing impaired; displays and/or information at wheelchair height.
Printed publications:
Walking around Avebury guide features six local walks; from property or NT Wessex office (£2.50 plus 50p p&p)

Internet home pages:
http://www.nationaltrust.org.uk

143
AVERY HISTORICAL MUSEUM
Avery Berkel, Foundry Lane, Smethwick, Warley, West Midlands, B66 2LP

Tel: 0870 903 4343 ext 2791
Fax: 0121 625 2677
Telex: 336490
Email: info@averyberkel.com
Formed: 1928
Formerly: GEC Avery

Organisation type and purpose: Museum. Historical Museum.

Enquiries to: Curator
Access:
Access to staff: By letter, by telephone, by fax, by email, in person, visitors by prior appointment
Hours: Mon, Tue, 0900 to 1700
Access for disabled people: Parking provided, access to all public areas, toilet facilities

General description:
History of the weighing machine, information on scales and weights, historical information connected with Averys.
Information services:
Special visitor services: Guided tours..

Collections:
Information on the link between Averys and the period of the industrial revolution i.e. Matthew Boulton, James Watt and William Murdoch
Old catalogues of various scale companies including some outside the UK

Internet home pages:
http://www.averyberkel.com

144
AVON VALLEY RAILWAY
Bitton Railway Station, Bath Road, Bitton, Bristol, BS30 6HD

Tel: 0117 932 5538
Fax: 0117 932 5935
Email: enquiries@avonvalleyrailway.co.uk
Full name: The Avon Valley Railway Company Limited
Formed: 1979
Formerly: The Bitton Railway Company Limited, date of change, 2001

Organisation type and purpose: Registered charity (charity number 1088545).
Preserved heritage steam railway. Registered charity: Avon Valley Railway Heritage Trust.
Parent body:
Avon Valley Railway Heritage Trust
(particularly for membership and members)

Enquiries to: Business Development Manager
Access:
Access to staff: By letter, by telephone, by fax, by email, visitors by prior appointment, Internet web pages
Hours: Mon to Fri, 0900 to 1700
Access for disabled people: Parking provided, level entry

General description:
Heritage railway, goods yard with locamotives, steam engines, carraiges and wagons at Bitton Station.

Internet home pages:
http://www.avonvalleyrailway.co.uk

145
AVONCROFT MUSEUM OF HISTORIC BUILDINGS
Stoke Heath, Bromsgrove, Worcestershire, B60 4JR

Tel: 01527 831363
Fax: 01527 876934
Email: avoncroft1@compuserve.com
Formed: 1967
Formerly: Avoncroft Museum of Buildings, date of change, 17 August 1994

Organisation type and purpose: Independently owned, membership association (membership is by subscription), present number of members: 600, registered charity (charity number 241644), museum, suitable for ages: all ages.
To rescue buildings of historic, architectural and social interest which would otherwise be destroyed, to make these buildings available to visitors, the public in general, and to schools in particular, as part of the process of education.

Enquiries to: Director
Other contacts: Education and Events Officer for education and events enquiries.
Access:
Access to staff: By letter, by telephone, by fax, by email, charges to non-members
Access for disabled people: Parking provided, toilet facilities
Other restrictions: Ramped entry to some buildings.

General description:
An open air museum of British vernacular architecture ranging from a mediaeval merchant's house to a 1946 prefab which have been rescued and reerected on a 15 acre site; building conservation; documentary evidence for

continued overleaf

the history of buildings including agricultural, industrial and domestic buildings.
Information services:
Library available for reference (for conditions see Access above)
Special visitor services: Guided tours, tape recorded guides, materials and/or activities for children.
Education services: Group education facilities, resources for Key Stages 1 and 2, 3, 4 and Further or Higher Education.
Services for disabled people: For the visually impaired; displays and/or information at wheelchair height.
Collections:
The Guestern Hall Roof. A great 14th century timber roof, originally part of the monastic complex at Worcester Cathedral. Now forming part of the exhibition hall and visitor centre.
Publications list:
is available in hard copy.
Printed publications:
Museum Mini Guide (75p)
Museum Visitor Guide (£3)
Activity Guide to Avoncroft (£1.50)
A range of study folders/resource packs

Internet home pages:
http://www.avoncroft.org.uk
General visitor information, events listing and education pages.

146
AXMINSTER MUSEUM

Church Street, Axminster, Devon, EX13 5AQ

Tel: 01297 34137
Email: axminster-museum@ukf.net
Formed: 1982

Organisation type and purpose: Registered charity (charity number 294933), museum, suitable for ages: 12+.

Enquiries to: Curator
Direct tel: 01297 32929
Other contacts: Treasurer
Access:
Access to staff: By letter, by email

General description:
Covers the local history of Axminster and surrounding area with regard to traders, agriculture, archaeology and photographic studies.
Information services:
Education services: Resources for Key Stage 2..
Collections:
Axminster Carpets; examples of designs and ephemera, 18th-20th century
Axminster's brush factories; artefacts, photographs and ephemera, 19th-early 20th century
Catalogues:
Catalogue for part of the collections is only available in-house.

147
AYCLIFFE AND DISTRICT BUS PRESERVATION SOCIETY

c/o 110 Fewston Close, Newton Aycliffe, Co Durham, DL5 7HF

Tel: 01325 317657
Acronym or abbreviation: ADBPS
Formed: 1980

Organisation type and purpose: Registered charity (charity number 512925), museum, suitable for ages: 16+.
Parent body:
NEMLAC
Newcastle Upon Tyne

Enquiries to: Secretary
Access:
Access to staff: By letter, visitors by prior appointment

General description:
A working collection of four vintage vehicles from the buses of the North East of England.

Internet home pages:
http://www.aycliffebus.org.uk

148
AYDON CASTLE

Corbridge, Northumberland, NE45 5PJ

Tel: 01434 632450

Organisation type and purpose: International organisation, advisory body, professional body, membership association (membership is by subscription), suitable for ages: all ages, training organisation, consultancy, research organisation.
Parent body:
English Heritage (North East Region)
Tel: 0191 269 1227/8, fax: 0191 261 1130

Enquiries to: Manager
Access:
Access to staff: By letter, by telephone, in person
Access to building, collections or gallery: No prior appointment required
Hours: End Mar to end Sep, daily, 1000 to 1800; Oct, daily, 1000 to 1700
Other restrictions: Opening times are subject to change, for up-to-date information contact English Heritage by phone or visit the website.

General description:
Overlooking the steep valley of the Cor Burn, Aydon Castle is one of the finest examples in England of a 13th century manor house. The house was fortified, but even so it was pillaged and burnt by the Scots in 1315, then seized by English rebels two years later, when it underwent repairs and modifications. In the 17th century, the castle was converted into a farmhouse, and remained so until 1966.

Internet home pages:
http://www.english-heritage.org.uk

149
AYSCOUGHFEE HALL MUSEUM AND GARDENS

Churchgate, Spalding, Lincolnshire, PE11 2RA

Tel: 01775 725468
Fax: 01775 762715
Email: ssladen@sholland.gov.uk
Formed: 1987

Organisation type and purpose: Local government body, registered charity (charity number 515905), museum, art gallery, suitable for ages: 5+ and all/family groups.
Charitable Trust is administered by:
South Holland District Council
as above
Funded by:
South Holland District Council (SHDC)
Priory Road, Spalding, Lincolnshire, tel: 01775 761161
Linked to:
Spalding Tourist Information Centre (fully networked).

Enquiries to: Manager
Direct tel: 01775 761161 ext 4286
Access:
Access to staff: By letter, by telephone, by fax, by email, in person, visitors by prior appointment
Access to building, collections or gallery: No prior appointment required
Hours: Mon to Fri, 0900 to 1700; Sat, 1000 to 1700; Sun and Bank Holidays, 1100 to 1700; closed at weekends Nov to Feb
Other restrictions: Prior appointments required for talks and tours.
Access for disabled people: Parking provided, level entry, toilet facilities

General description:
Local history, drainage and agriculture.
Information services:
Library available for reference (for conditions see Access above)
Special visitor services: Guided tours, materials and/or activities for children.
Education services: Group education facilities, resources for Key Stages 1 and 2..
Collections:
Ashley Maples Bird Collection - on loan from Spalding Gentlemen's Society
Dr Strong's Library - on loan from Peterborough Museum
Catalogues:
Catalogue for library is in-house only. Catalogue for all of the collections is only available in-house.
Printed publications:
4 museum leaflets supporting displays on:
History of Ayscoughfee Hall
Drainage of the Fens
Memoirs of Spalding
Matthew Flinders

150
BACUP NATURAL HISTORY SOCIETY

24 Yorkshire Street, Bacup, Lancashire, OL13 9AE

Acronym or abbreviation: BACUP 'NAT'
Formed: 1878

Organisation type and purpose: Learned society (membership is by subscription), present number of members: 70, voluntary organisation, registered charity, museum.
Has a section:
Bacup Camera Club
at the same address

Enquiries to: General Secretary
Direct tel: 01706 873042
Other contacts: Museum Curator, Tel: 01706 873961
Access:
Access to staff: By letter, in person
Hours: Mon to Fri, 0900 to 1700

General description:
Natural history - flora, fauna, fossils, local history and domestic bygones.
Collections:
Library of over 2000 books
Copies of Bacup newspapers from 1863
Some 4000 photographs of old Bacup and its mills, houses, farms, churches, public houses etc
Catalogues:
Catalogue for library is in-house only. Catalogue for part of the collections is only available in-house.

151
BADDESLEY CLINTON HALL

Rising Lane, Baddesley Clinton Village, Knowle, Solihull, West Midlands, B93 0DQ

Tel: 01564 783294
Fax: 01564 782706
Email: baddesleyclinton@nationaltrust.org.uk
Formed: 1895

Organisation type and purpose: National organisation, registered charity (charity number 205846), historic building, house or site, suitable for ages: 8+.
Parent body:
The National Trust (West Midlands)
West Midlands Regional Office, tel: 01743 708100

Enquiries to: Manager
Access:
Access to staff: By letter, by telephone, by fax, by email
Access for disabled people: Parking provided, ramped entry, level entry, toilet facilities
Other restrictions: Designated parking 10yds. 4 manual wheelchairs available. Level entrance. Ground floor fully accessible. No access to other floors. Steps to shop entrance. Ramped

entrance to restaurant. Grounds largely accessible. Braille guide, tactile route around the house.

General description:
A romantic and atmospheric moated manor house, dating from the 15th century and little changed since 1634. Home of the Ferres family for over four hundred years. The interiors reflect the house's heyday in the Elizabethan era, when it was a haven for persecuted Catholics. There are no fewer than three priest-holes. There is a delightful garden with stewponds, a lake walk and nature walk.
Information services:
Guided tours on Wed and Thur evenings by appointment. Supper can be included.
Braille guide. Touch list.
Front-carrying baby slings for loan.
Suitable for school groups. Children's guide. Children's quiz/trail.
Special visitor services: Guided tours, materials and/or activities for children.
Education services: Resources for Key Stages 1 and 2 and Further or Higher Education.
Services for disabled people: For the visually impaired; displays and/or information at wheelchair height.

Internet home pages:
http://www.nationaltrust.org.uk

152
BAIRD INSTITUTE MUSEUM
3 Lugar Street, Cumnock, Ayrshire, KA18 1AD

Tel: 01290 421701
Fax: 01290 421701

Organisation type and purpose: Local government body, museum, art gallery, suitable for ages: all ages.
Parent body:
East Ayrshire Council

Enquiries to: Curator
Access:
Access to staff: By letter, by telephone, by fax, by email, in person, visitors by prior appointment

General description:
Local history museum with collections of Cumnock Pottery, Mauchline Boxware, textiles, mining and a changing exhibition space. James Keir Hardie Exhibition (founder of the modern Labour Party).
Trace your family tree (Ayrshire) with help from experts. Reference library (local).
Information services:
Education services: Group education facilities..
Collections:
James Keir Hardie Collection
Local photographs
Library (reference), public access computers, microfilm, newspapers, documents
Catalogues:
Catalogue for library is in-house only. Catalogue for all of the collections is only available in-house.

153
BALA LAKE RAILWAY
The Station, Llanuwchllyn, Bala, Gwynedd, LL23 7DD

Tel: 01678 540666
Fax: 01678 540535
Formed: 1972

Organisation type and purpose: Private limited company.
Operator of narrow gauge railway.

Enquiries to: Manager
Access:
Access to staff: By letter, by telephone, by fax
Hours: Mon to Fri, 0900 to 1700
Access for disabled people: Parking provided, level entry

General description:
The railway was originally opened in 1868 and was operated by the Great Western. In 1868 the signal box was built and the station enlarged at Llanuwchllyn, the signal box and lever frame are still in use. The line, closed in 1965, was reopened as the Rheilffordd Llyn Tegid Cyf (Bala Lake Railway Ltd) in 1972 and continues as a passenger service for local and tourist traffic.
Collections:
Steam locomotives include:
'Holy War' built by Hunslet of Leeds in 1902 and worked in the Dinorwic Slate Quarry until 1967
'Maid Marian' a saddle tank locomotive built by Hunslet of Leeds in 1903 and also worked in the Dinorwic Slate Quarry
3 diesel locomotives and rolling stock of 9 passenger coaches

Internet home pages:
http://www.bala-lake-railway.co.uk
Timetable, news, locomotive information, fares.

154
BALFOUR LIBRARY
See - Oxford University, Balfour Library Pitt Rivers Museum

155
BALMACARA ESTATE
Lochalsh House (NTS), Balmacara, Kyle, Ross-shire, IV40 8DN

Tel: 01599 566325
Fax: 01599 566359
Email: balmacara@nts.org.uk

Organisation type and purpose: Historic building, house or site.
Parent body:
National Trust for Scotland Highlands and Islands Office (North)

Enquiries to: Property Manager
Access:
Access to staff: By letter, by telephone, by fax, by email, in person

General description:
A crofting estate.

Internet home pages:
http://www.nts.org.uk

156
BALMERINO ABBEY
Balmerino, Fife

Organisation type and purpose: Historic building, house or site.
Parent body:
National Trust for Scotland (South Region)
Enquiries to:
National Trust for Scotland (South Region)
Tel: 01721 722502

General description:
Ruins of Cistercian monastery, founded in 1229. At present, visitors may not enter the buildings, which are undergoing stabilisation work, but can view them from the grounds.

157
BAMBURGH CASTLE
Bamburgh, Northumberland, NE69 7DF

Tel: 01668 214515
Fax: 01668 214060
Email: bamburghcastle@aol.com
Formed: 1948

Organisation type and purpose: Independently owned, historic building, house or site, suitable for ages: 5+.

Enquiries to: Administrator
Access:
Access to staff: By letter, by telephone, by fax, by email, Internet web pages

Internet home pages:
http://www.bamburghcastle.com

158
BAMFORTH & CO POSTCARD MUSEUM
Picturedrome Cinema, Market Walk, Holmfirth, West Yorkshire, HD9 3DA

Tel: 01484 689759
Email: petercarr60@hotmail.com
Formed: Sep 1999
Formerly: Holmfirth Postcard Exhibition

Organisation type and purpose: Independently owned, museum, suitable for ages: 5+.
Now exhibit only in Bamforth original cinema.

Enquiries to: Owner
Access:
Access to staff: Visitors by prior appointment

General description:
This museum illustrates the history of Bamforths, a local firm who manufactured sea lantern slides, saucy seaside postcards and silent films.
Collections:
Bamforth postcards. A collection of postcards from Bamforths 1903 to present

159
BANBURY MUSEUM
Spiceball Park Road, Banbury, Oxfordshire, OX16 2PQ

Tel: 01295 259855

Organisation type and purpose: Local government body, museum, art gallery, historic building, house or site, suitable for ages: all ages.

Enquiries to: Museums Services Manager
Direct email: simon.townsend@cherwell-dc.gov.uk
Access:
Access to staff: By letter, by telephone, by email, in person
Access for disabled people: level entry, access to all public areas, toilet facilities

General description:
Collections covering the local history of the Banbury area.
Collections:
A large collection of photographs.

160
BANCHORY MUSEUM
Bridge Street, Banchory, Aberdeenshire, AB31 5SX

Tel: 01771 622906
Fax: 01771 622884
Formed: 1978

Organisation type and purpose: Local government body, museum, suitable for ages: 5+.
Parent body:
Aberdeenshire Heritage
Tel: 01771 622906, fax: 01771 622884

Enquiries to: Curator
Access:
Access to staff: By letter, by telephone, by fax
Access for disabled people: access to all public areas

General description:
Local memorabilia, Scott Skinner, Deeside silver, Royal memorabilia, natural history.
Collections:
Local history, natural history, photographs

Internet home pages:
http://www.aberdeenshire.gov.uk/banchory.htm

161
BANFF MUSEUM
High Street, Banff, AB45 1AE

Tel: 01771 622906
Fax: 01771 622884
Formed: 1828

Organisation type and purpose: Local government body, museum, suitable for ages: 5+.
Parent body:
Aberdeenshire Heritage
Tel: 01771 622906, fax: 01771 622884

Enquiries to: Curator
Access:
Access to staff: By letter, by telephone, by fax

General description:
Local history, Banff silver, Thomas Edward, James Ferguson, natural history, geology, arms and armour, archaeology.
Collections:
Social history, applied art, natural history, geology, archaeology, photography
Catalogues:
Catalogue for part of the collections is only available in-house.

162
BANGOR AND DISTRICT BUILDINGS AND AMENITY PRESERVATION TRUST, THE
Ceased to exist

163
BANK OF ENGLAND
Museum, Threadneedle Street, London, EC2R 8AH

Tel: 020 7601 5545
Minicom no. 020 7601 5491
Fax: 020 7601 5808
Email: museum@bankofengland.co.uk
Formed: 1988

Organisation type and purpose: National organisation, museum, suitable for ages: all ages. Central bank of the United Kingdom.

Enquiries to: Curator
Direct tel: 020 7601 4387
Direct fax: 020 7601 5808
Direct email: john.keyworth @bankofengland.co.uk
Other contacts: Advertising Officer
Access:
Access to staff: By letter, by telephone, by fax, by email, in person, visitors by prior appointment, Internet web pages
Hours: Mon to Fri, 1000 to 1700
Other restrictions: Closed on Bank and Public Holidays.
Access to building, collections or gallery: Prior appointment required
Access for disabled people: ramped entry, access to all public areas, toilet facilities
Other restrictions: Need prior communication before visit.

General description:
Museum and historical research, every aspect of the history of the Bank of England.
Information services:
Library available for reference (for conditions see Access above)
Special visitor services: Guided tours, tape recorded guides, materials and/or activities for children.
Education services: Group education facilities, resources for Key Stages 1 and 2, 3, 4 and Further or Higher Education.
Services for disabled people: For the visually impaired; for the hearing impaired; displays and/or information at wheelchair height.

Internet home pages:
http://www.bankofengland.co.uk

164
BANK OF SCOTLAND MUSEUM ON THE MOUND
Head Office, The Mound, Edinburgh, EH1 1YZ

Tel: 0131 529 1288
Fax: 0131 529 1307
Email: archives@bankofscotland.co.uk
Formed: 1987

Organisation type and purpose: Independently owned, museum, suitable for ages: 8+.
Other address:
Bank of Scotland
Archives Department, 12 Bankhead Terrace, Edinburgh, EH11 4DY, tel: 0131 529 1288, fax: 0131 529 1307, email/website: archives@bankofscotland.co.uk

Enquiries to: Archivist
Access:
Access to staff: By letter, by telephone, by fax, by email, visitors by prior appointment, Internet web pages
Access to building, collections or gallery: Prior appointment required
Hours: Open early Jun to early Sep: During Banking Hours
Other restrictions: Access to Archives restricted by conditions in Application for Access Agreement.

General description:
Bank of Scotland's history spans 300 years. The exhibits on display are both colourful and varied. They include old Scottish banknotes and forgeries; maps; watercolours and engravings of Old Edinburgh; early pictures and photographs of the Bank and its staff; a Victorian branch tableau; the Bank's Scottish coin collection; a 17th century bullion chest; and a variety of banking artefacts.
Information services:
Archives available for reference under certain conditions.
Special visitor services: Guided tours, materials and/or activities for children..
Collections:
Banknote collection
Coin collection
Weaponry collection
Catalogues:
Catalogue for part of the collections is only available in-house.
Printed publications:
Leaflet of the Head Office, The Mound
Leaflet of the Museum on the Mound

Internet home pages:
http://www.bankofscotland.co.uk
General description of Bank of Scotland Museum and Archives, contact details, map.

165
BANKFIELD MUSEUM
Akroyd Park, Boothtown Road, Halifax, West Yorkshire, HX3 6HG

Tel: 01422 354823
Fax: 01422 349020
Email: museums-arts@calderdale.gov.uk
Formed: 1887

Organisation type and purpose: Local government body, museum, art gallery, historic building, house or site.
Parent body:
Calderdale MBC, Museums and Arts
Piece Hall, Halifax, HX1 1RE, tel: 01422 358087, fax: 01422 349310

Enquiries to: Manager
Other contacts: Museums Officer
Access:
Access to staff: By letter, by telephone, by fax, by email, visitors by prior appointment
Other restrictions: In person subject to notification.
Access to building, collections or gallery: No prior appointment required
Hours: Tue to Sat, 1000 to 1700; Sun, 1400 to 1700; Bank Holiday Mon, 1000 to 1700
Other restrictions: Prior appointment required for access to reserve collection.
Access for disabled people: Parking provided, ramped entry, toilet facilities

General description:
Collections of international textiles and costume from Africa, Asia, Europe and the Americas, mostly 19th and 20th century including a collection of textiles collected by Edith Durham, traveller and collector in the Balkans from 1900 to 1914; related material including costume accessories; looms; spinning wheels; ethnographic material; and decorative art. Also an important basket collection and contemporary crafts. This is also the home of the Duke of Wellington's Regimental Museum of Costumes and Equipment.
Information services:
Guided tours on request.
Collections and education activities.
Special visitor services: Tape recorded guides, materials and/or activities for children.
Education services: Group education facilities, resources for Key Stages 1 and 2 and Further or Higher Education.
Services for disabled people: For the visually impaired.
Collections:
Durham collection, costume and embroideries from the Balkan States, 1850-1914
Crossley mosaics, popular Victorian textile pictures, mass produced by Crossley Carpets, Halifax, c. 1850-1890
Duke of Wellington's Regimental Museum, uniforms, related material of regiment plus personalia for Duke of Wellington, c. 1815-1980
Catalogues:
Catalogue for all of the collections is only available in-house.
Publications list:
is available in hard copy.
Printed publications:
Bread, Salt and our Hearts
Crossley Mosiacs
Handspinning and Wool Carding
Maori Mantle
Primitive Looms

Address for ordering publications:
Printed publications:
Museums Officer

Internet home pages:
http://www.calderdale.gov.uk

166
BANNOCKBURN HERITAGE CENTRE
Glasgow Road, Bannockburn, Stirling, FK7 0LJ

Tel: 01786 812664
Fax: 01786 810892

Organisation type and purpose: Historic building, house or site.
Parent body:
National Trust for Scotland (West Region)

Enquiries to: Property Manager
Access:
Access to staff: By letter, by telephone, by fax
Access to building, collections or gallery: No prior appointment required
Hours: Site, all year, daily
Heritage Centre, 20 Jan to 24 Mar and end Oct to 24 Dec, daily, 1030 to1600; 25 Mar to 27 Oct, daily, 1000 to 1800
Other restrictions: Last audio-visual show half an hour before closing
Access for disabled people: toilet facilities
Other restrictions: Access to site, Heritage Centre and audiovisual presentation, wheelchair available

General description:
King Robert the Bruce battlefield of 1314 and exhibition 'The Kingdom of the Scots'.
Information services:
Basic language tape tour for visitors with learning difficulties, Braille guidebook,

induction loop for the hard-of-hearing in audio-visual theatre, guidebook in French and German, A/V in French and German for groups.
Special visitor services: Tape recorded guides.
Services for disabled people: For the visually impaired; for the hearing impaired.

Internet home pages:
http://www.nts.org.uk

167
BAR CONVENT MUSEUM
17 Blossom Street, York, YO24 1AG

Tel: 01904 643238
Fax: 01904 631792
Email: info@bar-convent.org.uk
Formed: 1987

Organisation type and purpose: Independently owned, registered charity (charity number 294370), museum, art gallery, historic building, house or site, suitable for ages: 16+.
Guest house, conference centre, café, shop and museum.

Enquiries to: Manager
Direct tel: 01904 464901
Access:
Access to staff: By letter, by telephone, by fax, by email, in person
Access to building, collections or gallery: Prior appointment required
Hours: Mon to Fri, 0900 to 1600
Other restrictions: Artefacts and library by prior appointment.
Access for disabled people: ramped entry, toilet facilities
Other restrictions: Access to 95% of all areas.

General description:
Housed in an elegant Georgian building with a neo-classical chapel completed in 1769 by Thomas Atkinson. It has a priest hole. The museum displays the history of Christianity in North of England; Mary Ward - foundress, educator 1585-1645.
Information services:
Special visitor services: Guided tours..
Collections:
Artefacts and library by appointment
Printed publications:
History of the Bar Convent
The BC Museum
Electronic and video products:
Video available

168
BARBARA HEPWORTH MUSEUM
See - Tate St Ives

169
BARBER INSTITUTE OF FINE ARTS
University of Birmingham, University Road East, Edgbaston, Birmingham, B15 2TS

Tel: 0121 414 7333
Fax: 0121 414 7333
Email: info@barber.org.uk
Formed: 1932

Organisation type and purpose: Art gallery, university department or institute, suitable for ages: 5+.

Enquiries to: Marketing & PR Officer
Access:
Access to staff: By letter, by telephone, by email
Access to building, collections or gallery: No prior appointment required
Hours: Mon to Sat, 1000 to 1700; Sun, 1200 to 1700
Other restrictions: Closed 1 Jan, Good Friday, 24 to 26 Dec.
Reference library open by appointment.
Access for disabled people: Parking provided, level entry, toilet facilities

General description:
Outstanding collection of European art from 14th - 20th centuries, including work by Rubens, Van Dyck, Murillo, Monet and Van Gogh. Especially strong collections of Old Master and Impressionist works.
Information services:
Library available for reference (for conditions see Access above)
Special visitor services: Guided tours, materials and/or activities for children.
Education services: Group education facilities, resources for Key Stages 1 and 2, 3, 4 and Further or Higher Education..
Collections:
Art reference library of over 35,000 volumes
Coin collection, majority Roman and Byzantine
Portraits and caricatures by Edmond Kapp
Collection of European art from last 7 centuries
Prints and drawings
Sculptures
Catalogues:
Catalogue for library is in-house only. Catalogue for part of the collections is published.
Publications list:
is available on-line.
Printed publications:
Collection and exhibition catalogues

Internet home pages:
http://www.barber.org.uk
General information on collections, temporary exhibitions and public events.

170
BARBICAN HOUSE MUSEUM
See - Lewes Castle & Museums

171
BARDWELL WINDMILL
Bardwell, Suffolk

Tel: 01359 251331

Organisation type and purpose: Historic building, house or site.
Access:
Access to staff: By telephone

General description:
19th century tower mill. The sails were torm off in the 1987 storm but restoration work is in progress.

172
BARLEYLANDS FARM
Barleylands Road, Billericay, Essex, CM11 2UD

Tel: 01268 532253
Fax: 01268 290222
Email: barleyfarm@aol.com
Formed: 1984
Formerly: Barleylands Farm Museum or Animal Centre, date of change, 2000

Organisation type and purpose: Museum, suitable for ages: 5 to 18.
Farm animal centre, craft studios, glassblowing and blacksmith.

Enquiries to: Curator
Direct tel: 01268 290229
Other contacts: (1) Director (2) Director's Assistant for (1) information (2) bookings.
Access:
Access to staff: By letter, by telephone, by fax, by email
Hours: Mar to Oct: Mon to Sun, 1000 to 1700
Access to building, collections or gallery: No access other than to staff
Hours: Mon to Sun, 1000 to 1700
Other restrictions: Closed 1 Nov to 28 Feb.
Access for disabled people: level entry, toilet facilities

General description:
Barleylands Farm Museum is part of a large, modern, working arable farm. It contains over 2000 exhibits including steam engines; over 50 vintage tractors; a corn grinding mill; craft tools; agricultural implements; rural and domestic bygones; farm animals; working craft shops and a miniature steam railway. It is set in open farmland with picnic areas and farm trails.
Farming, past and present, steam railway, traction engines.
Collections:
Domestic and rural artefacts; steam ploughing engines; vintage tractors; horse-drawn implements; hand tools; photographic archives
Fowler. A set of Fowler steam ploughing engines and implements, c. 1917
Ransome. A Ransome threshing set including a steam engine and threshing machine, c. 1930.
Catalogues:
Catalogue for all of the collections is only available in-house.

173
BARLOW COLLECTION OF CHINESE ART
The University of Sussex, Falmer, Brighton, East Sussex, BN1 9QL

Tel: 01273 606755 ext 3506
Fax: 01273 678644
Formed: 1972

Organisation type and purpose: University department or institute.
Teaching and research collection.
Connected to:
University of Sussex
Falmer, Brighton, BN1 9RQ

Enquiries to: Curator
Access:
Access to staff: By letter
Hours: Tue and Thu, 1130 to 1430
Access to building, collections or gallery: No access other than to staff

General description:
The Barlow Gallery holds some 400 Chinese works of art covering every period of China's history from the 12th century BC until the 18th century AD. It includes archaic bronze vessels; pottery tomb figures and vessels; fine porcelains; jades; and Korean wares in the collection of Sir Alan Barlow.
Catalogues:
Catalogue for all of the collections is only available in-house.
Printed publications:
The Barlow Collection of Chinese Ceramics (Clunas C)
Bronzes and Jades: An Introduction (Falmer, 1997)

174
BARN GALLERY
High Street, Avebury, Marlborough, Wiltshire, SN8 1RF

Tel: 01672 539494
Formed: 2001
Formerly: Great Barn Museum

Organisation type and purpose: International organisation, national organisation, registered charity (charity number 205846), museum, historic building, house or site, suitable for ages: 5+.
Parent body:
The National Trust

Enquiries to: Manager
Access:
Access to staff: By letter, by telephone, by fax, by email
Access to building, collections or gallery: No prior appointment required
Hours: Apr to Oct: daily, 1000 to 1800
Nov to Mar: daily, 1000 to 1600
Access for disabled people: Parking provided, ramped entry, level entry, access to all public areas, toilet facilities

General description:
Archaeology of Avebury area.

continued overleaf

Information services:
Special visitor services: Materials and/or activities for children.
Education services: Group education facilities.
Services for disabled people: For the visually impaired; for the hearing impaired; displays and/or information at wheelchair height.

175
BARNARD CASTLE
Castle House, Barnard Castle, Co Durham, DL12 9AT

Tel: 01833 638212

Organisation type and purpose: Museum, historic building, house or site.
Parent body:
English Heritage (North East Region)
Tel: 0191 269 1227/8, fax: 0191 261 1130

Enquiries to: Manager
Access:
Access to staff: By telephone
Access to building, collections or gallery: No prior appointment required
Hours: End Mar to end Sep: daily, 1000 to 1800
Oct: daily, 1000 to 1700
Beg Nov to end Mar: Wed to Sun, 1000 to 1600.
Other restrictions: Closed 24 to 26 Dec and 1 Jan; closed 1300 to 1400.
Opening times are subject to change, for up-to-date information contact English Heritage by phone or visit the website.
Access for disabled people: ramped entry

General description:
One of northern England's largest medieval castles. Perched high on the edge of the steep bank overlooking the River Tees, Barnard Castle remains an imposing sight. The foundations of Barnard date back to the 12th century, when Guy de Baliol built the original fortress from wood, although it was later enclosed behind a curtain wall and divided into four enclosures creating the major castle you see today.
Information services:
Audio tours, sensory garden.
Special visitor services: Tape recorded guides.
Services for disabled people: For the visually impaired.

Internet home pages:
http://www.english-heritage.org.uk

176
BARNET MUSEUM
31 Wood Street, Barnet, Hertfordshire, EN4 9PA

Tel: 020 8440 8066
Formed: 1927

Organisation type and purpose: Museum.
Parent body:
Barnet & Dictrict Local History Society
Barnet Museum
Access:
Access to staff: By letter, by telephone
Hours: Tues to Thu, 1430 to 1630
Other restrictions: Phone calls only when Museum open.
Access to building, collections or gallery: No prior appointment required
Hours: Tues to Thu, 1430 to 1630, Sat 1030 to1230 and 1400 to 1600
Access for disabled people: level entry
Other restrictions: Wheelchair access to ground floor only.

General description:
Covers local history. There are photographs, objects and records connected with the local area, plus a costume collection.
Collections:
Watson's collection of microscopes
Catalogues:
Catalogue for library is in-house only. Catalogue for part of the collections is only available in-house.
Publications list:
is available in hard copy.
Printed publications:
A large selection of local history publications including:
Forgotten Tudor Places (Downing J)
Geoffrey de Mandeville & London's Camelot (Cobban J L)
Meanderings of a Modest Man: A Barnet childhood (Dutch D)
Opposite the Prince: The story of an East Barnet childhood in the1920s (L L Baynes)
Sixty Years of Local History (Barnet & District Local History Society)
The Barnets & Hadley in Old Photographs (Barnet & District Local History Society)
The Story of St John the Baptist's Church, Chipping Barnet: text and coloured photoghraphs (Adrian E)
800 Years of Barnet Market (Cobban J L & Willcocks D)

177
BARNSTAPLE HERITAGE CENTRE
Queen Anne's Walk, The Strand, Barnstaple, Devon, EX31 1EU

Tel: 01271 373003
Fax: 01271 373003
Email: barnstaple_town_council@northdevon.gov.uk
Formed: 1998

Organisation type and purpose: Local government body, museum, historic building, house or site, suitable for ages: 8+.
Heritage centre.
To show locals and visitors the town's rich heritage.
Other address:
Barnstaple Town Council
Barum House, The Square, Barnstaple, Devon, tel: 01271 373311

Enquiries to: Manager
Access:
Access to staff: By letter, by telephone, by fax, by email, in person, visitors by prior appointment
Access for disabled people: level entry, access to all public areas, toilet facilities

General description:
Built in the early 14th century as a chantry chapel, this charming building was used as a grammar school from the 16th century until 1910. The upper floor houses a schoolroom in which schools may have a lesson typical of the 17th century. The crypt houses an exhibition and museum of Barnstaple's heritage from Anglo-Saxon times to the 20th century.
Information services:
Colouring sheets available for 5 year olds and under.
Special visitor services: Materials and/or activities for children.
Education services: Resources for Key Stages 1 and 2, 3 and 4.
Services for disabled people: Displays and/or information at wheelchair height.
Printed publications:
Books and gifts of a local and historical nature
A selection of leaflets and booklets
Barnstaple Millennium Mosaic (book, 57 pages full colour, £3.99)
Us be goin' to Barnstaple Fair! (book, 280 pages, black & white with photographs & colour cover, £9.99)
Barnstaple in the Civil War (book, 100+ pages TBC)

Address for ordering publications:
Printed publications:
Gift Shop

178
BAROMETER WORLD & MUSEUM
Quicksilver Barn, Merton, Okehampton, Devon, EX20 3DS

Tel: 01805 603443
Fax: 01805 603444
Email: barometers@barometerworld.co.uk
Formed: 1979
Formerly: Merton Antiques

Organisation type and purpose: Independently owned, service industry, museum, suitable for ages: 16+.
Restoration of barometers also undertaken in workshops.

Enquiries to: Curator
Access:
Access to staff: By letter, by fax, by email
Access for disabled people: Parking provided, ramped entry, level entry, access to all public areas
Other restrictions: Limited toilet facilities.

General description:
Barometers; mercury and aneroid types, barographs, pocket barometers; dates and restoration, valuation.
Collections:
Houses the Banfield Family Collection of barometers with some additions
Publications list:
is available in hard copy.
Printed publications:
Antique Barometers: An Illustrated Survey (E Banfield, £4.95)
Barometers (McConnell A, £2.25)
Brass and Glass, Scientific Instrument Making Workshops in Scotland (£25)
English Barometers 1680-1860 (Sir N Goodison, £45)
The Banfield Family Collection of Barometers (E Banfield, £6.95, illustrated guide)

Internet home pages:
http://www.barometerworld.co.uk

179
BARRA HERITAGE & CULTURAL CENTRE
Dualchas, Castlebay, Isle of Barra, HS9 5XD

Tel: 01871 810413
Fax: 01871 810413
Acronym or abbreviation: CEBB
Full name: Comunn Eachdraidh Bharraidh
Formed: 1984
Formerly: Barra Cultural and Heritage Centre

Organisation type and purpose: Independently owned, registered charity (charity number SCO 23908), suitable for ages: all ages.
Heritage cultural centre.

Enquiries to: Centre Co-ordinator
Access:
Access to staff: By letter, by telephone, by fax, charges made to all users
Access for disabled people: Parking provided, ramped entry, access to all public areas, toilet facilities

General description:
Local history.
Information services:
Special visitor services: Guided tours.
Services for disabled people: For the visually impaired; for the hearing impaired; displays and/or information at wheelchair height.
Collections:
Artefacts, pictures, photographs, documents, all relate to Barra and Isles to South
Catalogues:
Catalogue for library is in-house only. Catalogue for all of the collections is only available in-house.

180
BARRACK STREET MUSEUM

Dundee

Closed
See - McManus Galleries

181
J M BARRIE'S BIRTHPLACE

9 Brechin Road, Kirriemuir, Angus, DD8 4BX

Tel: 01575 572646

Organisation type and purpose: Museum, historic building, house or site.
Parent body:
National Trust for Scotland

Enquiries to: Property Manager
Access:
Access to staff: By letter, by telephone

General description:
The birthplace of J M Barrie, playwright and author, especially known as the author of 'Peter Pan'. The upper floors are furnished as they may have been when Barrie lived there. The adjacent house, No 11, houses an exhibition - The Genius of J M Barrie - about Barrie's literary and theatrical works. The outside wash-house is said to have been his first theatre. At his death there was a proposal to remove the birthplace to the USA, but in 1937 Mr D Alves bought it and gave it to the Trust with funds for restoration.
Information services:
Audio programme
Braille information sheets, induction loop,
Explanatory text in Dutch, French, German, Italian, Japanese, Spanish, Swedish.
Special visitor services: Materials and/or activities for children.
Education services: Group education facilities.
Services for disabled people: For the visually impaired; for the hearing impaired.

Internet home pages:
http://www.nts.org.uk

182
BARRINGTON COURT

Barrington, Ilminster, Somerset, TA19 0NQ

Tel: 01460 241938
Fax: 01460 241938
Email: barringtoncourt@nationaltrust.org.uk

Organisation type and purpose: (charity number 205846), suitable for ages: all ages.
Parent body:
The National Trust (South West Region)
Regional Office for Devon and Cornwall, tel: 01392 881691

Enquiries to: Manager
Access:
Access to staff: By letter, by telephone, by fax, by email, Internet web pages
Access to building, collections or gallery: No prior appointment required
Hours: House and garden: March, Thu to Sun, 1100 to 1630; Apr to Sep, Mon and Tue, Thu to Sun, 1100 to 1730; Oct, Thu to Sun, 1100 to 1630
Access for disabled people: toilet facilities
Other restrictions: Drop-off point. Powered mobility vehicles, booking essential. Steps to entrance. Ground floor largely accessible, step up from Great Hall to mezzanine. No access to other floors. Level entrance to shop. Level entrance to restaurant. Grounds largely accessible. Recommended route map.

General description:
An enchanting formal garden, influenced by Gertrude Jekyll and laid out in a series of walled rooms, including the White Garden, the Rose and Iris Garden, and the Lily Garden. The working kitchen garden has espaliered apple, pear and plum trees trained along high stone walls.
The Tudor manor house was restored in the 1920s by the Lyle family. It is let to Stuart Interiors as showrooms with antique furniture for sale, thereby offering visitors a different kind of visit.
Information services:
Varied selection of family events. Telephone Regional box office (01985 843601) for information
Suitable for school groups. Children's quiz/trail
Braille guide, large print guide, sented plants.
Special visitor services: Materials and/or activities for children.
Services for disabled people: For the visually impaired.

Internet home pages:
http://www.nationaltrust.org.uk/regions/wessex

183
BARROW HILL ENGINE SHED SOCIETY LIMITED

266 Williamthorpe Road, Chesterfield, Derbyshire, S42 5NS

Tel: 01246 472450
Fax: 01246 472450
Acronym or abbreviation: BHESS
Formed: 1989
Formerly: Barrow Hill Roundhouse Railway Centre

Organisation type and purpose: Registered charity, historic building, house or site, suitable for ages: 5+.
Other addresses:
Barrowhill Roundhouse Railway Centre
Campbell Drive, Barrow Hill, Chesterfield, S43 2PR

Enquiries to: Manager
Access:
Access to staff: By telephone
Access to building, collections or gallery: Prior appointment required
Access for disabled people: Parking provided, ramped entry, level entry, access to all public areas, toilet facilities

General description:
Railway.
Collections:
Locomotives
Publications list:
is available in hard copy.

184
BARRY MILL

Barry, Carnoustie, Angus, DD7 7RJ

Tel: 01241 856761

Organisation type and purpose: Museum, historic building, house or site.
Parent body:
National Trust for Scotland (North-East Region)

Enquiries to: Property Manager
Access:
Access to staff: By letter, by telephone, in person
Access to building, collections or gallery: No prior appointment required
Hours: End Mar to end Oct, Thu to Mon, 1200 to 1700
Other restrictions: Milling demonstrations normally on Sat and Sun afternoons, and for pre-booked parties
Access for disabled people: toilet facilities
Other restrictions: Most parts accessible

General description:
A restored 19th century meal mill, this was the last working water-powered meal mill in Angus, producing animal feed until 1982.

Internet home pages:
http://www.nts.org.uk

185
BARTON AQUEDUCT

Barton upon Irwell, Trafford, Greater Manchester

Tel: 0161 748 4414 (Project Office)
Email: info@steamcoalcanal.co.uk

Parent body:
Bridgewater Canal Linear Industrial Heritage Park
1a Chapel Place, Barton upon Irwell, Trafford, Greater Manchester, M41 7LE, tel: 0161 748 4414

Enquiries to: Manager

General description:
Witness a feat of early engineering as a section of the Bridgewater Canal moves 800 tons of water to a different position.

Internet home pages:
http://www.steamcoalcanal.co.uk

186
BASILDON PARK

Lower Basildon, Reading, Berkshire, RG8 9NR

Tel: 0118 984 3040
Fax: 0118 984 7370
Email: basildonpark@nationaltrust.org.uk
Formed: 1895

Organisation type and purpose: National organisation, registered charity (charity number 205846), historic building, house or site, suitable for ages: 5+.
Parent body:
The National Trust (South and South East Region)
Thames and Solent Regional Office, tel: 01494 528051

Enquiries to: Administrative Assistant
Access:
Access to staff: By letter, by telephone, by fax, by email, visitors by prior appointment
Access to building, collections or gallery: Prior appointment required
Hours: End Mar to beg Nov, Wed to Sun, 1200 to 1730
Open Bank Holiday Mondays
Other restrictions: Closed for concerts and Flower Festival, check for details.
Access for disabled people: Parking provided, ramped entry, toilet facilities
Other restrictions: Designated parking 20yds. 3 manual wheelchairs available. Ground floor fully accessible, 2 steps into ground floor, ramp available. No access to other floors. Photograph album. Level entrance to shop and to restaurant.

General description:
This beautiful Palladian mansion was built in 1776-83 by John Carr for Francis Sykes, who had made his fortune in India. The interior is notable for its original delicate plasterwork and elegant staircase, as well as for the unusual Octagon Room. The house fell on hard times in the early part of the last century, but was rescued by Lord and Lady Iliffe, who restored it and filled it with fine pictures and furniture. The early 19th century pleasure grounds are currently being restored, and there are waymarked trails through the parkland. At the top of Streatley Hill 2 miles away is a car park giving access to The Holies, Lough Down and Lardon Chase, an outstanding area of downland and woodland with many beautiful walks and breathtaking views.
Information services:
Helpline available, tel no: Infoline 01494 755558.
Guided tours pre-booked.
Braille guide. Large-print guide. Touchable items.
Front-carrying baby slings for loan.
Suitable for school groups. Children's guide. Children's quiz/trail.
Special visitor services: Guided tours.
Services for disabled people: For the visually impaired.

continued overleaf

Collections:
Collection amassed in the 1950s by Lord & Lady Iliffe
Important pictures, furniture and textiles
Catalogues:
Catalogue for library is in-house only. Catalogue for all of the collections is only available in-house.
Printed publications:
Guide Book
Short Guide (30p)
Children's Guide (£1.50)
Property Leaflet (free)
Group Bookings Leaflet (free)

Address for ordering publications:
Printed publications:
National Trust Enterprises

Internet home pages:
http://www.nationaltrust.org.uk

187
BASING HOUSE HISTORIC RUIN
Basing House, Redbridge Lane, Basingstoke, Hampshire, RG24 7HB

Tel: 01256 467294
Fax: 01256 326283
Email: musmat@hants.gov.uk

Organisation type and purpose: Local government body, historic building, house or site, suitable for ages: 5+.
Parent body:
Hampshire County Council Museums Service
Chilcomb House, Winchester, SO23 8RD, tel: 01962 846304, fax: 01962 869836

Enquiries to: Curator
Access:
Access to staff: By letter, by telephone, by fax, by email, in person
Hours: Tue to Sun, 0900 to 1800
Access to building, collections or gallery: No prior appointment required
Hours: Apr to Sep: Wed to Sun and Bank Holidays, 1400 to 1800
Access for disabled people: toilet facilities
Other restrictions: Disabled parking - telephone in advance.

General description:
Personalia, Basingstoke, Hampshire.
Social history of the 16th/17th centuries, the English Civil War.
Information services:
Special visitor services: Guided tours, materials and/or activities for children.
Services for disabled people: For the visually impaired.
Collections:
Small collection of archaeological material from the site (mostly 16th/17th century)
Catalogues:
Catalogue for all of the collections is on-line.
Printed publications:
Publications list is available from the Librarian, Hampshire County Council Museums Service Headquarters, Chilcomb House, Winchester, SO23 8RD

Address for ordering publications:
Printed publications:
Registrar, Hampshire County Council Museums Service
Headquarters, tel: 01962 846304

Internet home pages:
http://www.hants.gov.uk/museums/
HMCMS web catalogue, whole collection 100,000+ web pages.

188
BASINGSTOKE MUSEUM
See - Willis Museum of Basingstoke Town and Country Life

189
BASS MUSEUM
Horninglow Street, Burton-on-Trent, Staffordshire, DE14 1YQ

Tel: 01283 511000
Fax: 01283 513509
Email: bookings@bass-museum.com

Member of:
North Staffordshire Museums Association

General description:
Museum of the history of Bass brewing and beer. Stables of the Bass Shire horses.
Information services:
Guided tours by arrangement
Special visitor services: Guided tours..
Collections:
Steam engines, vintage engines
Brewery locos
Large N gauge railway model of Burton-on-Trent
Small brewhouse
Edwardian pub

Internet home pages:
http://www.bass-museum.com

190
BATCHELORS' CLUB
Sandgate Street, Tarbolton, South Ayrshire, KA5 5RB

Tel: 01292 541940

Organisation type and purpose: Historic building, house or site.
Parent body:
National Trust for Scotland (West Region)

Enquiries to: Property Manager
Access:
Access to staff: By letter, by telephone, charges to non-members

General description:
Seventeenth century thatched house, Robert Burns and friends former debating club, period furnishings.

Internet home pages:
http://www.nts.org.uk

191
BATE COLLECTION OF MUSICAL INSTRUMENTS
See - Oxford University, Bate Collection of Musical Instruments

192
BATEMAN'S
Bateman's Lane, Burwash, Etchingham, East Sussex, TN19 7DS

Tel: 01435 882302
Fax: 01435 882811
Email: batemans@nationaltrust.org.uk
Formed: 1940

Organisation type and purpose: Registered charity (charity number 205846), historic building, house or site, suitable for ages: .
Parent body:
The National Trust
36 Queen Anne's Gate, London, SW1H 9AS, tel: 020 7222 9251, fax: 020 7222 5097

Enquiries to: Property Manager
Other contacts: Visitor Services Manager
Access:
Access to staff: By letter, by telephone, by fax, by email
Hours: Apr to Nov: Sat to Wed, 1100 to 1730
Access to building, collections or gallery: No prior appointment required
Hours: Apr to Sept, Sat to Wed, 1100 to 1700
Open Good Friday
Other restrictions: Letter and approval from regional or head office of National Trust for access to library by appointment.
Access for disabled people: Parking provided, toilet facilities
Other restrictions: Designated parking 200yds. Drop-off point. 2 manual wheelchairs available. Ground floor
accessible with assistance, one step up to dining room. No access to other floors. Virtual tour of upper floors. Steps to shop entrance. Steps to tea-room entrance. Recommended route map.

General description:
A 17th century Sussex Manor House. The home of Rudyard Kipling from 1902-36, the interior of this beautiful Jacobean house reflects the author's strong associations with the East. There are many oriental rugs and artefacts, and most of the rooms - including his book-lined study - are much as Kipling left them, reflecting Rudyard Kipling's life and times; collection of 16th century furniture; Kipling's reference library of 2000 books; 19th to early 20th century objects from India and Europe. The delightful grounds run down to the small River Dudwell, where there is a working watermill, and contain roses, wildflowers, fruit and herbs. Kipling's Rolls-Royce (1928) is also on display;
Information services:
House stewards available for guided tours.
Computerised virtual tour.
Braille guide. Large-print guide. Touch list. Scented plants.
Children's guide. Children's quiz/trail.
Special visitor services: Guided tours, materials and/or activities for children.
Services for disabled people: For the visually impaired.
Collections:
Kipling Archives kept at University of Sussex
Catalogues:
Catalogue for all of the collections is only available in-house.
Printed publications:
Various books published in conjunction with The National Trust about National Trust Houses including Bateman's

Internet home pages:
http://www.nationaltrust.org.uk

193
BATH ABBEY HERITAGE VAULTS
13 Kingston Buildings, Bath, BA1 1LT

Tel: 01225 422462
Fax: 01225 429990
Formed: 1994

Organisation type and purpose: Museum.

Enquiries to: Curator
Access:
Access to staff: By letter, by telephone, by fax, in person
Hours: Mon to Sat, 1000 to 1600
Access for disabled people: access to all public areas

General description:
An underground exhibition, housed in 18th century cellars on the south side of the Abbey, telling the story of the Abbey and the people who have used it for 1300 years. It includes some stones from the previous building on the site and a number of items collected at the Abbey over the years.
Information services:
Helpline available, tel no: 01225 422462.
Special visitor services: Guided tours, materials and/or activities for children.
Education services: Group education facilities.
Services for disabled people: For the visually impaired; displays and/or information at wheelchair height.
Collections:
The Abbey's collection of ecclesiastical silver, including the Bellott cup, a silver gilt cup and lid, made in 1619 and presented in memory of Sir Thomas Bellott, an Elizabethan benefactor. 17th-19th century

Plaster casts of the mediaeval sculptured figures on the west front taken during restoration in the 19th century. ca. 1890.
Saxon stones. Parts of carved Saxon crosses and part of a carved Saxon grave cover, plus a fenestella (small stone window). 9th-10th century
Norman stones. Stones from the Norman church, begun in 1090, and Romanesque sculpture from the same. ca. 1100-1150
Locally made encaustic tiles. ca. 1300-1400
Catalogues:
Catalogue for all of the collections is only available in-house.

194
BATH ASSEMBLY ROOMS
Bennett Street, Bath, BA1 2QH

Tel: 01225 477789
Telex: 01225 428167

Organisation type and purpose: National organisation, registered charity (charity number 205846), museum, historic building, house or site, suitable for ages: 12+.
Parent body:
The National Trust (South West Region)
Regional Office for Wessex, tel: 01985 843600

Enquiries to: Manager
Access:
Access to staff: By letter, by telephone
Access to building, collections or gallery: No prior appointment required
Hours: All year, daily, 1000 to 1700
Other restrictions: Admission free. Admission charge to Museum of Costume.
Access for disabled people: level entry, toilet facilities
Other restrictions: Drop-off point. 1 manual wheelchair available. Ground floor fully accessible, access to other floors via lift. Level entrance to shop.

General description:
Designed by John Wood the Younger in 1769, at a time when Bath was becoming fashionable among polite society, the Assembly Rooms were both a meeting place and venue for public functions. Bombed in 1942, they were subsequently restored and are now let to Bath & North East Somerset Council, which has its Museum of Costume in the basement.
Information services:
Guided tours when rooms not in use for booked functions.
Audio guide.
Suitable for school groups, audio guide, hands-on activities.
Special visitor services: Tape recorded guides..

Internet home pages:
http://www.nationaltrust.org.uk/regions/wessex

195
BATH AT WORK
Julian Road, Bath, BA1 2RH

Tel: 01225 318348
Fax: 01225 318348
Full name: Museum of Bath at Work
Formed: 1978

Organisation type and purpose: Membership association (membership is by subscription), present number of members: 350, museum.

Enquiries to: Curator
Access:
Access to staff: By letter, by telephone, by fax, by email, visitors by prior appointment
Access to building, collections or gallery: No prior appointment required
Hours: Mon to Fri, 0900 to 1700

General description:
Business and commercial records relating to Bath 1750 to present; industrial collections predominate.
The contents of a small Victorian engineering works, including a brass foundry, ironmongers, mineral water production and pattern shop; there are 80,000 items and a supporting archive comprising ca. 100,000 documents.
Collections:
Photography (print/negative), maps, documents, ephemera, books, illustrations
Cabinet making equipment, planes, patterns, etc
Equipment from Weaver and Sons, bed makers.
Photographic negatives of Stothert and Pitt Co
Timeswitches and equipment of Horstmann Gear Co
Watch and clock maker's tools and equipment
Publications list:
is available in hard copy.

Internet home pages:
http://www.bath-at-work.org.uk

196
BATH POLICE STATION MUSEUM
Central Police Station, Manvers Street, Bath, BA1 1JN

Tel: 01225 842482 or 842481
Fax: 01225 842523
Formed: 1985

Organisation type and purpose: Museum.

Enquiries to: Information Officer
Access:
Access to staff: By letter, by fax

General description:
The information held in the museum is now in store and not available to view. It covered the history of policing of the City of Bath from 1840 to the present day. Displays included records of police personnel from the last century, numerous exhibits of police memorabilia ie weapons, handcuffs etc; pictorial display of Victorian criminals and their criminal records; crime statistics for the City of Bath from 1928 to 1939, and numerous records and photographs of police activity.

Internet home pages:
http://www.avonandsomerset.police.uk

197
BATH POSTAL MUSEUM
8 Broad Street, Bath, BA1 5LJ

Tel: 01225 460333
Fax: 01225 460333
Email: info@bathpostalmuseum.org
Acronym or abbreviation: BPM
Formed: 1978

Organisation type and purpose: Independently owned, registered charity (charity number 277419), museum, suitable for ages: all ages.
To inform and entertain the general public regarding 4000 years of written communication from 'clay-mail to email'.

Enquiries to: Administrator
Access:
Access to staff: By email
Access for disabled people: ramped entry, toilet facilities
Other restrictions: Access to ground floor only.

General description:
We feature six display rooms covering 'The Story of the Post' from 'claymail to email' ie 4.000 years of written communication.
Displays regarding the above, on the Romans, Georgians and Victorians, with appropriate specially devised individual computer games.
Displays on transport (regarding transportation of mail) ie an airmail room featuring 'first flights' starting with the Wright Brothers, with specially commissioned oil painting depicting each incident and playing archive airmail video film.
Our Special Exhibition room currently features a rare collection of covers (envelopes) recovered from shipwrecks. The collector of this compiled the definitive reference book on the subject.
A room displaying a complete 1930s Post Office with appropriate displays. This is used as an interactive module for children, plus a room devoted both to education and a play area for young children.
Currently we are the only postal museum in the UK and receive postal enquiries both nationally and internationally.
Information services:
Library available for reference (for conditions see Access above)
Four specially designed computer games.
Services for adults/children with learning difficulties.
Special visitor services: Guided tours, materials and/or activities for children.
Education services: Group education facilities, resources for Key Stages 1 and 2 and 3.
Services for disabled people: For the visually impaired; displays and/or information at wheelchair height.
Collections:
Archives contain:
Complete written communication from the 18th to 19th centuries; rare documents; collection of photographs of 19th century post people
Large number of postal artefacts:
Quill pens, lenil pens, early fountain pens, inkwells, postal balances (all types) and philatelic collections (mainly postal history) donated by renowned collectors
Books on postal and coaching history eg Hendersons' Coaching Roads.
Large collection of transparencies donated by BBC
Collection of Royal Mail vehicle models
Printed publications:
A monograph of the life of 'John Palmer of Bath' (He was the iniator of horse-drawn mail coaches - a system copied throughout the Commonwealth)
Out of print currently: Monograph on 'Ralph Allen Postmaster Bath' who ran the inland postal system

Internet home pages:
http://www.bathpostalmuseum.org
Extensive coverage by navigation of the historical areas we cover, also information on all aspects.

198
BATH PRESERVATION TRUST
No 1 Royal Crescent, Bath, BA1 2LR

Tel: 01225 338727
Fax: 01225 481850
Email: admin@bptrust.demon.co.uk
Acronym or abbreviation: BPT
Formed: 1934

Organisation type and purpose: Membership association (membership is by subscription), present number of members: 1070, registered charity (charity number 203048).
Buildings preservation trust.

Enquiries to: Administrator
Other contacts: Director
Access:
Access to staff: By letter only
Hours: Mon to Fri, 0900 to 1700
Access to building, collections or gallery: Prior appointment required

General description:
The trust exists to preserve the historic character and amenities of Bath.
Printed publications:
Annual Report
Newsletter (annual)

Internet home pages:
http://www.bath-preservation-trust.org.uk

See also - 1 Royal Crescent

199
BATTLE ABBEY AND BATTLEFIELD

High Street, Battle, East Sussex, TN33 0AD

Tel: 01424 773792

Organisation type and purpose: Museum, historic building, house or site, suitable for ages: 5+.
Parent body:
English Heritage (South East Region)
Eastgate Court, 195-205 High Street, Guildford, Surrey, GU1 3EH, tel: 01483 252000, fax: 01483 252001, email: www.english-heritage.org.uk

Enquiries to: Curator
Access:
Access to staff: By letter, by telephone
Access to building, collections or gallery: No prior appointment required
Hours: Apr to 30 Sep: daily, 1000 to 1800
Oct: daily, 1000 to 1700
Nov to 31 Mar: daily, 1000 to 1600
Other restrictions: Closed 24 to 26 Dec and 1 Jan
Opening times are subject to change, for up-to-date information contact English Heritage by phone or visit the website

General description:
1066 Battle of Hastings, the defeat of the Saxons and the Norman Conquest. Life in Battle Abbey built by William the Conqueror.
Information services:
Customer services 0870 333 1181
Interactive audio tour available in English, French, German and Japanese. Also available for the visually impaired, those in wheelchairs or those with learning difficulties.
Braille guides in English only.
Interactive displays, introductory video and Family Discovery Centre
Special events
Special visitor services: Tape recorded guides, materials and/or activities for children.
Education services: Group education facilities.
Services for disabled people: For the visually impaired.
Collections:
Artefacts from the battlefield and abbey site

Internet home pages:
http://www.english-heritage.org.uk

200
BATTLE MUSEUM OF LOCAL HISTORY

The Almonry, High Street, Battle, East Sussex, TN33 0EA

Tel: 01424 772827
Formed: 1967
Formerly: Battle and District Historical Society

Organisation type and purpose: Voluntary organisation, registered charity (charity number 306336), museum, suitable for ages: all ages.
Links with:
Museum and Galleries Commission

Enquiries to: Chairman
Access:
Access to staff: By letter only
Access to building, collections or gallery: No prior appointment required
Hours: Easter to end Oct: Mon to Sat, 1030 to 1630; Sun, 1400 to 1700
Other restrictions: Summer opening only.
Prior appointment required only for the library.
Access for disabled people: level entry, access to all public areas, toilet facilities

General description:
History of Battle: prehistory, Roman, Battle of Hastings and development of the town up to end of 19th century.
Artefacts, archives, and photographs displayed.
Also Historical Society library covering history of the area, archaeological information etc.
Information services:
Library available for reference (for conditions see Access above)
Special visitor services: Guided tours.
Services for disabled people: Displays and/or information at wheelchair height.
Catalogues:
Catalogue for library is in-house only. Catalogue for all of the collections is only available in-house.

Internet home pages:
http://www.battlemuseumoflocalhistory.co.uk
Updates on special exhibitions.

201
BATTLE OF BRITAIN MEMORIAL FLIGHT VISITOR CENTRE

Royal Air Force Coningsby, Coningsby, Lincolnshire, LN4 4SY

Tel: 01526 344041
Fax: 01526 342330
Email: bbmf@lincolnshire.gov.uk
Acronym or abbreviation: BBMF
Formed: 1986

Organisation type and purpose: Local government body, museum, suitable for ages: 12+.

Enquiries to: Principal Keeper
Access:
Access to staff: By letter, by telephone
Hours: Mon to Fri, 1000 to 1700
Access to building, collections or gallery: No prior appointment required
Hours: Daily, 1030 to 1730 for guided tours
Access for disabled people: Parking provided, ramped entry, access to all public areas, toilet facilities

General description:
World War II aviation history.
Information services:
Group education services - under development.
Services for disabled people - under development.
Special visitor services: Guided tours..
Collections:
WWII artefacts, personal memorabilia, letters and medals
Airworthy aircraft including: the only flying Lancaster Bomber in Europe, a Dakota, 5 Spitfires, 2 Hurricanes and 2 Chipmunks
Catalogues:
Catalogue for all of the collections is only available in-house.

Internet home pages:
http://www.lincolnshire.gov.uk/heritage
http://www.bbmf.co.uk

202
BATTLESBRIDGE MOTORCYCLE MUSEUM

Muggeridge Farm, Maltings Road, Battlesbridge, Wickford, Essex, SS11 7RF

Tel: 01268 560866
Email: info@battlesbridge.com
Formed: 1984

Organisation type and purpose: Museum, suitable for ages: 12+.

Enquiries to: Curator
Direct email: dave@littletotham.org.uk
Access:
Access to staff: By email
Access to building, collections or gallery: Prior appointment required
Hours: Sun, 1030 to 1600
Access for disabled people: ramped entry, toilet facilities
Other restrictions: Café.

General description:
Small collection of 40+ motorcycles from 1910-1975 plus a vast quantity of automobilia. All set within an antique centre housing some 60+ dealers.

Internet home pages:
http://www.battlesbridge.com

203
BAXTER STORY, THE

Baxters Highland Village, Fochabers, Moray, IV32 7LD

Tel: 01343 820666
Fax: 01343 821790
Email: highland.village@baxters.co.uk
Formed: 1968

Organisation type and purpose: Tourist attraction.

Enquiries to: General Manager
Access:
Access to staff: By letter, by fax, by email
Access for disabled people: Parking provided, ramped entry, level entry, access to all public areas, toilet facilities

General description:
The story of a highland village.

204
BAYHAM OLD ABBEY

Lamberhurst, East Sussex

Tel: 01892 890381
Formed: 1208

Organisation type and purpose: Historic building, house or site, suitable for ages: 5+.
Parent body:
English Heritage (South East Region)
Eastgate Court, 195-205 High Street, Guildford, Surrey, GU1 3EH, tel: 01483 252000, fax: 01483 252001

Enquiries to: Curator
Access:
Access to building, collections or gallery: No prior appointment required
Hours: Apr to Sep: daily, 1000 to 1800
Oct: daily, 1000 to 1700
Nov to Mar: Sat and Sun, 1000 to 1600
Other restrictions: Closed from 24 to 26 Dec and 1 Jan.
Opening times are subject to change, for up-to-date information contact English Heritage by phone or visit the website.

General description:
Ruins of the Abbey built by the French 'White Canons' during the 13th century, and 18th century Dower House, two rooms of which are open to the public.

Internet home pages:
http://www.english-heritage.org.uk

205
BAYSGARTH HOUSE MUSEUM

Baysgarth Park, Caistor Road, Barton-upon-Humber, Lincolnshire, DN18 6AH

Tel: 01652 632318
Fax: 01652 636659

Organisation type and purpose: Local government body, museum, historic building, house or site, suitable for ages: 5+.

Enquiries to: Principal Keeper
Access:
Access to staff: By letter, by telephone, by fax
Access for disabled people: Parking provided, ramped entry

General description:
An 18th century mansion house with fine period rooms, a collection of 18th and 19th century English and Oriental pottery, and an Industrial Museum in the stable block.

Information services:
Special visitor services: Materials and/or activities for children.
Education services: Group education facilities, resources for Key Stage 1..

Internet home pages:
http://www.northlincs.gov.uk/museums/index.htm
Further information on site.

206
BEACON, THE

West Stand, Whitehaven, Cumbria, CA28 7LY

Tel: 01946 592302
Fax: 01946 599025
Email: thebeacon@copelandbc.gov.uk
Formed: 1996
Formerly: Whitehaven Museum and Art Gallery, date of change, 1996

Organisation type and purpose: Local government body, museum, art gallery, suitable for ages: all ages.

Enquiries to: Collections Officer
Direct email: gfindlay@copelandbc.gov.uk
Other contacts: Administrator
Access:
Access to staff: By letter, by telephone, by email, visitors by prior appointment
Access to building, collections or gallery: No prior appointment required
Hours: Easter to Oct: Tue to Sun, Bank Holiday and school holiday Mon, 1000 to 1730
Nov to Mar: Tue to Sun, Bank Holiday and school holiday Mon, 1000 to 1630
Other restrictions: Closed Christmas Day.
Access for disabled people: Parking provided, ramped entry, access to all public areas, toilet facilities

General description:
The Beacon is home to Whitehaven's museum and fine art collections which trace the social, industrial and maritime history of the Georgian 'gem' town and the Copeland district.
This harbourside attraction also offers panoramic views of the coast from a Met Office weather gallery, an exhibition gallery, gift shop and café.
Information services:
Education services: Group education facilities, resources for Key Stages 1 and 2, 3 and 4.
Services for disabled people: Displays and/or information at wheelchair height.
Collections:
Social history artefacts
Fine art, decorative art, archaeology, natural sciences, numismatics, photographs, prints, books
Catalogues:
Catalogue for part of the collections is only available in-house.

Internet home pages:
http://www.copelandbc.gov.uk

207
BEAD SOCIETY OF GREAT BRITAIN

See - Horniman Museum and Gardens

208
BEAMINSTER MUSEUM

Whitcombe Road, Beaminster, Dorset, DT8 3NB

Tel: 01308 863623
Email: chemeng@btinternet.com
Formed: 1987

Organisation type and purpose: Independently owned, membership association (membership is by subscription), present number of members: 100, voluntary organisation, registered charity (charity number 299616), museum, suitable for ages: 5+.

Enquiries to: Chairman
Direct tel: 01308 862880
Access:
Access to staff: By letter, by telephone, visitors by prior appointment
Hours: Tue, Thu, Sat and Bank Holiday Mon, 1030 to 1230 and 1430 to 1630; Sun, 1430 to 1630
Access for disabled people: ramped entry

General description:
Local history, Beaminster and surrounding villages; Beaminster Congregational Chapel history; Hine Cognac Family of Beaminster.
Collections:
Beaminster Congregational Chapel
History of Beaminster
Hine Cognac family of Beaminster

Internet home pages:
http://www.btinternet.com/~chemeng

209
BEAMISH: THE NORTH OF ENGLAND OPEN AIR MUSEUM

Regional Resource Centre, Beamish, Co Durham, DH9 0RG

Tel: 0191 370 4000
Fax: 0191 370 4001
Email: museum@beamish.org.uk
Acronym or abbreviation: Beamish
Formed: 1970

Organisation type and purpose: Local government body, registered charity (charity number 517147), museum, suitable for ages: all ages, research organisation.
Regional museum, administered by a consortium of 3 north-eastern county councils and 5 metropolitan districts.
To collect, study, preserve, interpret and exhibit buildings, machinery, objects and information which illustrates the development of industry, agriculture and way of life in the North East of England.

Enquiries to: Senior Keeper
Access:
Access to staff: By letter, by telephone, by fax, by email, visitors by prior appointment
Hours: Mon to Fri, 0900 to 1700
Access to building, collections or gallery: No prior appointment required
Hours: Easter to end Oct: daily 1000 to 1700
Nov to Easter: Closed Mon and Fri; other days open 1000 to 1600
Other restrictions: The photographic archive and reference library are open by appointment only.
Access for disabled people: Parking provided, level entry, toilet facilities
Other restrictions: Access to most areas.

General description:
Social history, coal mining, agriculture and industrial archaeology of the North East England region, early North East railways, advertising, folk life and trade.
Information services:
Education services: Group education facilities, resources for Key Stages 1 and 2, 3, 4 and Further or Higher Education.
Services for disabled people: For the visually impaired.
Collections:
Collection of ephemera, trade catalogues, posters and packaging
Collection of North Country quilts and coverlets
Collection of prints, books and information on the history of Shorthorn cattle
Oral recordings and sound archive
Photographic archive of some 150,000 negatives, relating to the Northern way of life
Reference library and photographic archive
Catalogues:
Catalogue for library is in-house only. Catalogue for all of the collections is only available in-house.
Publications list:
is available in hard copy.
Printed publications:
Annual Report
Guide Book (every 2 years, £2.50)
Teachers Guides
The Making of A Museum (history of Beamish £2)
North Country Quilts and Coverlets from Beamish (Allan R E, out of print)

Internet home pages:
http://www.beamish.org.uk

210
BEAR MUSEUM, THE

38 Dragon Street, Petersfield, Hampshire, GU31 4JJ

Tel: 01730 265108
Fax: 01730 266119
Formed: 1984

Organisation type and purpose: Independently owned, museum, historic building, house or site.
Privately owned museum.
To display an extensive collection of labelled examples of teddy bears. The teddy bear was created originally in late 1902 and we have examples from most periods.

Enquiries to: Curator
Access:
Access to staff: By letter, by telephone, by fax, in person
Hours: Tue to Sat, 1000 to 1630

General description:
The Museum is the world's first, devoted to teddy bears. It has one of the best labelled collections in England and has been featured in various books eg 'The Ultimate Teddy Bear Book' by DK.
Collections:
One of the best labelled collections of teddy bears in the UK
Catalogues:
Catalogue for part of the collections is on-line.
Microform products:
Film library on transparencies (at a charge)

Internet home pages:
http://www.bearmuseum.co.uk
Information for schools etc.

211
BEATRIX POTTER GALLERY, THE

Main Street, Hawkshead, Cumbria, LA22 0NS

Tel: 015394 36355
Fax: 015394 36187
Email: beatrixpottergallery@nationaltrust.org.uk
Formed: 1988

Organisation type and purpose: Registered charity (charity number 205846), art gallery, suitable for ages: 8+.
Owned by:
The National Trust (North West)
North West Regional Office, tel: 0870 609 5391

Enquiries to: Collections Manager
Access:
Access to staff: By letter, by telephone, by fax, by email
Access for disabled people: level entry
Other restrictions: Ground floor accessible with assistance, doorways too narrow for wheelchairs, but level floor means that 3 rooms could be seen by those who can walk a few steps. No access to other floors. Steep and narrow stairs mean that the pictures (upstairs) are not accessible. Level entrance to shop.

General description:
An annually changing exhibition of original sketches and watercolours painted by Beatrix Potter for her children's stories. This 17th century building, which became known as Tabitha Twitchit's shop, was once the office of Beatrix's husband, William Heelis. The interior remains substantially unaltered since his day, giving an interesting insight into a Victorian law office.

continued overleaf

Information services:
Children's guide. Children's quiz/trail.
Special visitor services: Materials and/or activities for children..
Collections:
Original illustrations and manuscripts by Beatrix Potter
Catalogues:
Catalogue for all of the collections is only available in-house.
Printed publications:
Gallery Guide Book (£2.50)

Internet home pages:
http://www.nationaltrust.org.uk

212
BEAULIEU ABBEY

John Montagu Building, Beaulieu, Brockenhurst, Hampshire, SO42 7ZN

Tel: 01590 612345
Fax: 01590 612624
Email: info@beaulieu.co.uk
Formed: c. 1906

Organisation type and purpose: Independently owned, historic building, house or site, suitable for ages: 5+.

Enquiries to: Archivist
Direct tel: 01592 614671
Direct email: susan.tomkins@beaulieu.co.uk
Access:
Access to staff: By letter, by telephone, by fax, by email, visitors by prior appointment, Internet web pages
Hours: Mon to Fri, 1000 to 1500
Access to building, collections or gallery: No prior appointment required
Hours: 1000 to 1700
Access for disabled people: Parking provided, toilet facilities

General description:
Beaulieu Abbey, Beaulieu Estate and Parish, family of Lords Montagu of Beaulieu, Buckler's Hard 18th century shipbuilding village.
Information services:
Special visitor services: Guided tours, materials and/or activities for children.
Education services: Group education facilities.
Services for disabled people: For the visually impaired.
Collections:
Archive of the Montagu family
Beaulieu Estate Archive, including Beaulieu Abbey
Catalogues:
Catalogue for all of the collections is only available in-house.
Printed publications:
Beaulieu: King John's Abbey (Hockey S F, £4.75)
The Beaulieu Record (Widnell H E R, £10.95)
An Album of Old Beaulieu and Buckler's Hard (Tomkins S A, £6.95)
Beaulieu Guidebook (£4)

Address for ordering publications:
Printed publications:
Retail Manager, Montagu Ventures Limited
John Montagu Building, Beaulieu, Brockenhurst, SO42 7ZN, tel: 01590 614639, fax: 01590 612624, email: info@beaulieu.co.uk

Internet home pages:
http://www.beaulieu.co.uk
Basic background information on Abbey and general visitor information as part of main Beaulieu site
http://www.beaulieu.co.uk/beaulieuabbey/introduction/cfm

See also - National Motor Museum

213
BEAULIEU ABBEY EXHIBITION OF MONASTIC LIFE

Beaulieu, Brockenhurst, Hampshire, SO42 7ZN

Tel: 01590 612345
Fax: 01590 612624
Email: info@beaulieu.co.uk
Formed: c. 1906

Organisation type and purpose: Museum. Private estate, leisure destination.

Enquiries to: Archivist
Access:
Access to staff: By letter, by telephone, by fax, by email, visitors by prior appointment, Internet web pages
Access for disabled people: Parking provided, toilet facilities

General description:
Beaulieu Abbey, Beaulieu estate and parish, family of Lords Montagu of Beaulieu, Buckler's Hard 18th century shipbuilding village.
Collections:
Archive of Montagu Family
Beaulieu History, including Beaulieu Abbey
Catalogues:
Catalogue for all of the collections is only available in-house.
Printed publications:
An Album of Old Beaulieu and Buckler's Hard (Tomkins S, £6.95)
Beaulieu: King John's Abbey (Hockey S F, £4.75)
Palace House/Beaulieu Abbey Guide Book (£2.50)
The Beaulieu Record (Widnell H E R, £10.95)
Wheels Within Wheels: An Unconventional Life (Lord Montagu of Beaulieu, £20)

Address for ordering publications:
Printed publications:
Shop Manager, Montagu Ventures Ltd
John Montagu Building, Beaulieu, Brockenhurst, Hampshire, SO42 7ZN, tel: 01590 614639, fax: 01590 612624, email: info@beaulieu.co.uk

214
BEAULIEU ARCHIVES

John Montagu Building, Beaulieu, Brockenhurst, Hampshire, SO42 7ZN

Tel: 01590 612345
Fax: 01590 612624
Email: info@beaulieu.co.uk
Formed: 1952

Organisation type and purpose: Museum. Montagu family & Beaulieu estate private archives.
Private estate and leisure destination.

Enquiries to: Archivist
Access:
Access to staff: By letter, by telephone, by fax, by email, visitors by prior appointment, Internet web pages
Hours: Mon to Fri, 1000 to 1500
Access for disabled people: Parking provided, ramped entry, toilet facilities
Other restrictions: Access to Archives by ramped entry and lift.

General description:
Family of Lords Montagu of Beaulieu, Beaulieu Estate & Parish Buckler's Hard 18th century shipbuilding village, Beaulieu Abbey. Ditton Park Estate, Slough, Buckinghamshire.
Collections:
Archive of the Montagu family
Beaulieu History
Catalogues:
Catalogue for all of the collections is only available in-house.
Printed publications:
40th Anniversary booklet of Palace House opening to public (£2.50)
Wheels Within Wheels: An Unconventional Life (Lord Montagu of Bealieu, £20)
An Album of Old Beaulieu & Buckler's Hard (Susan Tomkins, £6.95)
Beaulieu, King John's Abbey (S F Hockey, £4.75)
Beaulieu: The Finishing School for Secret Agents (Cyril Cunningham, £16.95)
Buckler's Hard guidebook(£2)
Buckler's Hard: a rural shipbuilding centre (A J Holland, £12.95)
John Montagu of Beaulieu (Paul Tritton, £9.50)
Palace House & Beaulieu Abbey (guidebook, £2)
The Beaulieu Record (H E R Widnell, £10.95)
The Beaulieu River goes to War, 1939-1945 (Cyril Cunningham, £6.95)

Address for ordering publications:
Printed publications:
Shops Manager, Montagu Ventures Limited
John Montagu Building, Beaulieu, Brockenhurst, Hampshire, SO42 7ZN, tel: 01590 614639, fax: 01590 612624, email: info@beaulieu.co.uk

Internet home pages:
http://www.beaulieu.co.uk

215
BEAUMARIS GAOL AND COURT

Steeple Lane, Beaumaris, Anglesey, Gwynedd, LL58 8EP

Tel: 01248 810921 or 724444
Fax: 01248 750282
Formed: 1975
Formerly: Gwynedd Archives and Museums Service

Organisation type and purpose: Museum.
Department of:
Anglesey County Council
Department of Leisure and Heritage, Council Office, Llangefni, Anglesey, LL77 7TW, tel: 01248 724444

Enquiries to: Museum Officer
Direct tel: 01248 752017
Other contacts: Museum Education Officer for educational visits or enquiries.
Access:
Access to staff: By letter, by telephone, by fax, visitors by prior appointment, charges made to all users
Hours: Mon to Fri, 0900 to 1700

General description:
Social history, mainly regarding crime and punishment, Victorian period, police history, heritage management, tourism, historic buildings.
Collections:
Police equipment
Prison equipment and furnishings
The only treadmill in situ
Victorian hospital equipment
Catalogues:
Catalogue for library is in-house only. Catalogue for all of the collections is only available in-house.
Publications list:
is available in hard copy.
Printed publications:
Leaflets and books

216
BECCLES & DISTRICT MUSEUM

Leman House, Ballygate, Beccles, Suffolk, NR34 9ND

Tel: 01502 715722
Formed: 1978

Organisation type and purpose: Voluntary organisation, registered charity, museum.

Enquiries to: Curator
Other contacts: Chairman of Trustees for financial matters.
Access:
Access to staff: By letter, by telephone
Access for disabled people: ramped entry, access to all public areas, toilet facilities

General description:
Local history, geology, archaeology, local photographs and records.
Collections:
Information files on buildings, persons, places etc
Geology (small collection)
Photographs (large and growing collection)

Internet home pages:
http://www.becclesmuseum.org.uk
Virtual tour of museum, occasional research published.

217
BECK ISLE MUSEUM OF RURAL LIFE

Bridge Street, Pickering, North Yorkshire, YO18 8DU

Tel: 01751 473653
Fax: 01751 475996
Formed: 1967

Organisation type and purpose: Local government body, voluntary organisation, registered charity (charity number L244107/2), museum.

Enquiries to: Chairman
Access:
Access to staff: By letter, by telephone, by fax
Access for disabled people: ramped entry, toilet facilities
Other restrictions: Video of upper galleries in main building, chairlifts to outside upper galleries.

General description:
Social and domestic history from the 18th century with special emphasis on Victorian times. Comprises 27 galleries showing the domestic, farming and trade life in the area over the last 200 years. The exhibits are set out as replica scenes, for example, Victorian parlour, cottage kitchen, printer's shop, photographer, cobbler's, barber's shop, costumes, nursery, gents' outfitters, hardware shop, blacksmiths, etc.
Information services:
Education services: Group education facilities..
Collections:
The Sidney Smith photographic collection, 1920-1955, c. 2000 negatives and 200 prints
The Rex Whistler Guards Paintings, (10 ft high), painted for childrens' Xmas party, 1941
Catalogues:
Catalogue for part of the collections is only available in-house.

218
BEDALE MUSEUM

Bedale Hall, Bedale, North Yorkshire, DL8 1AA

Tel: 01677 423797
Fax: 01677 425393

Organisation type and purpose: Registered charity (charity number 700687), art gallery, suitable for ages: all ages.
Rural/local history genealogy archive.
Parent body:
Bedale Hall Trust
North End, Bedale, DL8 1AA

Enquiries to: Curator
Direct tel: 01677 423272
Other contacts: Secretary, tel: 01677 423242 for research enquiries, out of hours visits.
Access:
Access to staff: By letter, by telephone, by fax, visitors by prior appointment
Hours: Curator or Secretary: Mon to Fri, 1700 to 1900
Access for disabled people: Parking provided, level entry, access to all public areas, toilet facilities

General description:
Genealogical information on local families, census records in easily accessible form from 1841, 1851, 1871 and 1891, also much information on Old Bedale 1300 onwards.
Information services:
Special visitor services: Guided tours.
Education services: Group education facilities, resources for Key Stages 1 and 2, 3 and 4.
Services for disabled people: Displays and/or information at wheelchair height.
Collections:
Probate deeds, some maps, documents and photographs (copies available at varying cost)
Artefacts dating back to prehistoric times
Bedale's Handdrawn 1748 fire engine
Radios and cameras 1900 onwards phonographs, children's toys and games
Tools of local trades
Catalogues:
Catalogue for library is in-house only. Catalogue for all of the collections is only available in-house.
Printed publications:
In-house copies of many documents, photographs etc on site

219
BEDE'S WORLD

Church Bank, Jarrow, Tyne and Wear, NE32 3DY

Tel: 0191 489 2106
Fax: 0191 428 2361
Email: visitor.info@bedesworld.co.uk
Formed: 1974
Formerly: Bede Monastery Museum

Organisation type and purpose: Registered charity (charity number 1009881), museum.
Parent body:
Jarrow 700 AD Limited
Commercial member of the:
Northumbria Tourist Board
Tel: 0191 375 3000
Association of Independent Museums
North East Museums, Libraries & Archive Council (NEMLAC)
Tel: 0191 222 1661
Supported by:
South Tyneside Metropolitan Borough Council
Tel: 0191 427 1717

Enquiries to: Visitor Services Manager
Access:
Access to staff: By letter, by telephone, by email
Access for disabled people: Parking provided, access to all public areas, toilet facilities

General description:
Early mediaeval Northumbria, especially the Monastery of Wearmouth-Jarrow, the Venerable Bede and early Christianity in Northumbria; Anglo-Saxon England in general and general knowledge of mediaeval North East and England. The growth of Jarrow as an industrial town and the occupants of Jarrow Hall; education in museums; herbs, herb gardens and history of herbalism.
Collections:
Local (Jarrow area) postcard collection
Material excavated from St Paul's Jarrow Monastic site, including sculpture, early stained glass and metalwork
Memorabilia of the occupants of Jarrow Hall (c.1800)
Printed publications:
Booklets on aspects of the Monastery of St Paul's and Early Mediaeval Life (published irregularly, for sale)
Educational Resources Teachers' Booklet (annually)
General Information Leaflet

Internet home pages:
http://www.bedesworld.co.uk

220
BEDFORD MUSEUM

Castle Lane, Bedford, MK40 3XD

Tel: 01234 353323
Fax: 01234 273401
Email: bmuseum@bedford.gov.uk
Formed: 1960

Organisation type and purpose: Local government body, museum.

Enquiries to: Curator
Access:
Access to staff: By letter, by telephone, by fax, by email, in person, visitors by prior appointment, Internet web pages
Hours: Tue to Sat, 1100 to 1700; Sun & Bank Holiday Monday, 1400 to 1700
Other restrictions: Closed Mondays.
Access for disabled people: level entry, access to all public areas, toilet facilities
Other restrictions: Parking provided by prior appointment.

General description:
Information on archaeology, social sciences, the human and natural history of Bedford and the surrounding area.
Information services:
Special visitor services: Materials and/or activities for children.
Education services: Group education facilities, resources for Key Stages 1 and 2, 3, 4 and Further or Higher Education.
Services for disabled people: Displays and/or information at wheelchair height.
Collections:
Bedfordshire sites of wildlife and geological interest
Newman collection of Bedfordshire books
North and Mid Bedfordshire archaeological site excavation archives
Hamilton Fyfe Collection of letters
Artefacts, pictures, prints, photographs, books, documents and manuscripts relating to North Bedfordshire

Internet home pages:
http://www.bedfordmuseum.org

221
BEESTON CASTLE

Tarporley, Cheshire, CW6 9TX

Tel: 01829 260464
Formed: 1226

Organisation type and purpose: National government body, historic building, house or site, suitable for ages: 5+.
Parent body:
English Heritage (North West Region)
Canada House, 3 Chepstow Street, Manchester, M1 5FW, tel: 0161 242 1400
Other addresses:
English Heritage (North West Region) (EH)
Canada House, 3 Chepstow Street, Manchester, ME1 5FW, tel: 0161 242 1400

Enquiries to: Curator
Access:
Access to staff: By telephone
Access to building, collections or gallery: No prior appointment required
Hours: 29 Mar to 30 Sep: daily, 1000 to 1800
Oct: daily, 1000 to 1700,1 Nov to 31 Mar: daily, 1000 to 1600
Other restrictions: Closed 24 to 26 Dec and 1 Jan
Opening times are subject to change, for up-to-date information contact English Heritage by phone or visit the website.
Access for disabled people: ramped entry
Other restrictions: Steep climb. No disabled access to top of the hill.

General description:
Castle built by Ranulf of Chester in 1225 on the site of a Bronze Age hill fort, commanding views across 8 counties. As a Royalist stronghold during the Civil War it withstood a year-long siege before the garrison was forced to surrender due to starvation. Currently housing the exhibition 'Castle of the Rock', which explains the castle's 4000-year history.
Information services:
Free educational visits, must be pre-booked, telephone: 01829 260464.
Castle Museum, exhibition in Victorian gatehouse.

continued overleaf

Special visitor services: Materials and/or activities for children.
Education services: Group education facilities..
Collections:
Flint tools
Fine bronze axe heads and knife
Prehistoric pottery
Post-medieval pottery
Clay pipes
Lead shot
Metal ware - Civil War
Catalogues:
Catalogue for all of the collections is published.
Printed publications:
Various books available in shop including detailed documentation of excavations done in 1968-1985

Internet home pages:
http://www.english-heritage.org.uk

222
BELFAST BOTANIC GARDENS
See - Museums and Galleries of Northern Ireland

223
BELGRAVE HALL
Church Road, off Thurcaston Road, Leicester, LE4 5PE

Tel: 0116 266 6590
Fax: 0116 261 3063
Email: marte001@leicester.gov.uk
Formed: 1937

Organisation type and purpose: Local government body, museum, historic building, house or site, suitable for ages: family and adult.
Parent body:
Leicester Museums
12th Floor, A Block, New Walk Centre, Leicester
Other addresses:
Leicester City Museums
New Walk Centre, Leicester

Enquiries to: Curator
Direct tel: 0116 226 6590
Other contacts: Deputy Curator, Gardens for historical gardens forming part of Hall.
Access:
Access to staff: By letter, by telephone, by fax, by email, in person, visitors by prior appointment, Internet web pages
Access to building, collections or gallery: No prior appointment required
Hours: Summer: daily, 1000 to 1700
Winter: daily, 1000 to 1600
Other restrictions: Stored collections off-site - prior appointment required.
Access for disabled people: Parking provided, level entry, toilet facilities
Other restrictions: Access to ground floor and gardens.

General description:
A Queen Anne house with furniture from 1650 to 1900 shown in room settings. Period and botanic gardens. History of the hall and surrounding village, domestic interiors, South Asian textiles.
Information services:
Guided tours by prior request.
Materials/activities for children on certain days.
Special visitor services: Guided tours, materials and/or activities for children.
Education services: Group education facilities, resources for Key Stages 1 and 2.
Services for disabled people: Displays and/or information at wheelchair height.
Collections:
South Asian Collection from Gujarat collected in 1985 by then Curator
Arts & Crafts, furniture - Gimson & Barnsley's Furniture 1700-1920s
Catalogues:
Catalogue for part of the collections is only available in-house.
Printed publications:
Traditional Arts and Crafts of Gujarat (Nicholson J)

Address for ordering publications:
Printed publications:
Publications, New Walk Museum
New Walk, Leicester, tel: 0116 255 4100

Internet home pages:
http://www.leicestermuseums.ac.uk
General information.

224
BELLFOUNDRY MUSEUM
Freehold Street, Loughborough, Leicestershire, LE11 1AR

Tel: 01509 233414
Fax: 01509 263305
Formed: 1986

Organisation type and purpose: World's largest working bell foundry (bell foundry started in 1784). Unique associated museum. Historical and contemporary data and exhibition of bells and artefacts.
Maintained by:
John Taylor Bell Founders Limited

Enquiries to: Curator
Access:
Access to staff: Visitors by prior appointment, charges made to all users
Hours: Tue to Sat, 1000 to 1230 and 1330 to 1630; Sun, 1330 to 1630; Mon, closed

General description:
Bell manufacture. bell founding, bell history (all forms). Manufacture of bells for worldwide market by John Taylor Bell Founders Ltd.
Collections:
Pre-war archive for internal use only
Printed publications:
Bell Founding (T S Jennings, £2.25)
Handbells (T S Jennings, £2.00)
The Development of British Bell Fittings (T S Jennings, £10.00)

225
BELMONT
Belmont Park, Throwley, Faversham, Kent, ME13 0HH

Tel: 01795 890202
Fax: 01795 890042
Email: belmontadmin@btconnect.com

Organisation type and purpose: Registered charity (charity number 280545), historic building, house or site, suitable for ages: 16+.

Enquiries to: Administrator
Access:
Access to staff: By letter, by telephone, by fax, by email, Internet web pages
Hours: Mon to Thu, 0900 to 1700
Access for disabled people: Parking provided, ramped entry, toilet facilities
Other restrictions: Access to ground floor and gardens only.

General description:
Belmont, a charming late 18th century mansion designed by Samuel Wyatt, has been the seat of the Harris family since it was acquired by General George Harris, the victor of Seringapatam in 1801. It houses the fifth Lord Harris' clock collection together with interesting mementoes of India and cricket. The history of house, family and gardens.
Information services:
Special visitor services: Guided tours..
Collections:
5th Lord Harris Clock Collection
Printed publications:
Guide Book
Clock Collection

Address for ordering publications:
Printed publications:
Administrator, Harris Belmont Charity
Belmont

Internet home pages:
http://www.belmont-house.org

226
BELPER NORTH MILL TRUST
Derwent Valley Visitors' Centre, North Mill, Bridgefoot, Belper, Derbyshire, DE56 1YD

Tel: 01773 880474
Fax: 01773 880474
Formed: 1995

Organisation type and purpose: Independently owned, registered charity (charity number 1068485), museum, historic building, house or site, suitable for ages: 8+.
Visitor centre.
Part of the:
Derwent Valley Mills World Heritage Site

Enquiries to: Manager
Access:
Access to staff: By letter, by telephone, by fax, in person, visitors by prior appointment
Access to building, collections or gallery: No prior appointment required
Hours: Wed to Sun, 1300 to 1700
Access for disabled people: Parking provided, level entry, toilet facilities

General description:
Development of cotton-spinning during Industrial Revolution, development of machine-made hosiery, building of a fireproof mill and factory community from 1776.
Information services:
Special visitor services: Guided tours, tape recorded guides, materials and/or activities for children.
Education services: Group education facilities, resources for Key Stages 1 and 2, 3 and Further or Higher Education.
Services for disabled people: For the visually impaired; for the hearing impaired; displays and/or information at wheelchair height.
Collections:
Machinery showing the development of cotton-spinning
Various types of hosiery knitting machinery
Brettle's Collection of hosiery
Printed publications:
Derwent Valley Textile Mills (£6)
Structure of North Mill
Jedediah Strutt
William Strutt
Strutt Walk Round Belper
Strutt Forfeits
Electronic and video products:
Belper Past in Pictures (video, £15)

Internet home pages:
http://www.belper-northmill.org
http://www.belpernorthmill.museum.com

227
BELSAY HALL, CASTLE AND GARDENS
Belsay, Ponteland, Northumberland, NE20 0OX

Tel: 01661 811636
Fax: 01661 881043
Formed: 1984

Organisation type and purpose: National government body, national organisation, historic building, house or site, suitable for ages: 5+.
Parent body:
English Heritage (North East Region)
Tel: 0191 269 1227/8, fax: 0191 261 1130

Enquiries to: Administrator
Access:
Access to staff: By letter, by telephone, by fax
Hours: Daily, 1000 to 1600
Access for disabled people: Parking provided, ramped entry, toilet facilities

General description:
Belsay Hall is a building of European importance. The magnificent 30-acre garden at Belsay Hall is deservedly listed Grade I in the Register of Parks and Gardens. The Castle is a

dramatic, well-preserved medieval tower house. A Jacobean manor house was added to it in 1614.
Information services:
Education services: Group education facilities, resources for Key Stages 1 and 2, 3, 4 and Further or Higher Education..

228
BELTON HOUSE
Belton, Grantham, Lincolnshire, NG32 2LS

Tel: 01476 566116
Fax: 01476 579071
Email: belton@nationaltrust.org.uk
Formed: 1685-1888

Organisation type and purpose: National organisation, registered charity (charity number 205846), historic building, house or site, suitable for ages: all ages.
House built 1685-1688; National Trust property since 1984.
Parent body:
National Trust (East Midlands Region)
East Midlands Regional Office, tel: 01909 486411

Enquiries to: Assistant to the Property Manager
Other contacts: House Manager for research information on collections.
Access:
Access to staff: By letter, by telephone, by fax, by email, Internet web pages
Access for disabled people: Parking provided, toilet facilities
Other restrictions: Telephone for information for the less-abled visitor brochure.
2 manual wheelchairs available. Powered mobility vehicles: 1 single-seater.
Ground floor accessible with assistance, 15 steps. No access to other floors. Ramped entrance to shop. Level entrance to restaurant. A number of tables have been adapted for wheelchair users. Grounds largely accessible, recommended route map.

General description:
The crowning achievement of Restoration country house architecture, Belton was built in 1685-88 and later altered by James Wyatt. The stunning interiors contain exceptionally fine plasterwork and wood-carving, as well as important collections of paintings, furniture, tapestries and silverware. There are also formal gardens, an orangery, a magnificent landscape park and a large adventure playground.
Information services:
Guided tours outside normal opening times, phone for charges.
Ghost tours
Suitable for school groups, phone 01476 577290 for information
Audio guide. Family guide.
Children's quiz/trail. Family activity packs.
Adult study days
Special visitor services: Guided tours, tape recorded guides, materials and/or activities for children.
Education services: Group education facilities, resources for Key Stages 1 and 2 and Further or Higher Education.
Services for disabled people: For the hearing impaired.
Catalogues:
Catalogue for all of the collections is only available in-house.
Printed publications:
Guide Book (for purchase)
Family Guide (for purchase)
Short Guide (for purchase)
Property Leaflet (free)
Events Leaflet (free)

Internet home pages:
http://www.nationaltrust.org.uk

229
BELVOIR CASTLE
Belvoir, Grantham, Lincolnshire, NG32 1PD

Tel: 01476 871002
Fax: 01476 870443
Email: info@belvoircastle.com

Organisation type and purpose: Historic building, house or site, suitable for ages: 5+.

Enquiries to: Manager
Access:
Access to staff: By letter, by telephone, by fax, by email, in person, visitors by prior appointment
Access for disabled people: Parking provided, level entry, toilet facilities

General description:
The ancestral home of the Duke of Rutland for nearly 1000 years.
Information services:
Special visitor services: Guided tours, tape recorded guides, materials and/or activities for children.
Education services: Group education facilities, resources for Key Stages 1 and 2..

Internet home pages:
http://www.belvoircastle.com

230
BEMBRIDGE WINDMILL
National Trust Office, Longstone Farmhouse, Strawberry Lane, Mottistone, Newport, Isle of Wight, PO30 4EA

Tel: 01983 873945 (opening hours only)

Organisation type and purpose: National organisation, registered charity (charity number 205846), historic building, house or site, suitable for ages: 5+.
Parent body:
The National Trust (South and South East Region)
Thames and Solent Regional Office, tel: 01494 528051

Enquiries to: Manager
Access:
Access to staff: By letter
Access to building, collections or gallery: No prior appointment required
Hours: Apr, May, Jun, Sep, Oct, Sun to Fri, 1000 to 1700;
Jul and Aug, daily, 1000 to 1700
Open Easter Sat

General description:
Built c.1700 and still with its original wooden machinery, the windmill is the only one surviving on the Island.
Information services:
Conducted school groups and special visits March to end Oct (but not July or Aug), by written appointment.
Braille guide.
Suitable for school groups. Children's quiz/trail.
Special visitor services: Materials and/or activities for children.
Education services: Group education facilities.
Services for disabled people: For the visually impaired.

Internet home pages:
http://www.nationaltrust.org.uk

231
BENINGBROUGH HALL AND GARDENS
Beningbrough, York, YO30 1DD

Tel: 01904 470666
Fax: 01904 470002
Email: beningbrough@nationaltrust.org.uk

Organisation type and purpose: National organisation, registered charity (charity number 205846), historic building, house or site, suitable for ages: 8+.
Parent body:
The National Trust (Yorkshire and North East)
Yorkshire Regional Office, tel: 01904 702021

Enquiries to: Manager
Access:
Access to staff: By letter, by telephone, by fax, by email
Access for disabled people: Parking provided, ramped entry, toilet facilities
Other restrictions: Designated parking 20yds. Drop-off point. 3 manual wheelchairs available. Accessible entrance to conservatory. Ground floor fully accessible. No access to other floors. Level entrance to shop and to restaurant. Servery has one or two high shelves which would be too high for those in wheelchairs, help available. Grounds largely accessible. Level paths (embedded gravel) throughout garden.
Adapted WC in stable block

General description:
York's 'country house and garden', this imposing Georgian mansion was built in 1716 and contains one of the most impressive baroque interiors in England. Exceptional wood carving, an unusual central corridor running the full length of the house and over 100 pictures on loan from the National Portrait Gallery can be found inside. There is also a fully equipped Victorian laundry, delightful walled garden and some interesting sculptures in wood.

Internet home pages:
http://www.nationaltrust.org.uk

232
BENNIE MUSEUM
9-11 Mansefield Street, Bathgate, West Lothian, EH48 4HU

Tel: 01506 634944
Email: thornton@benniemuseum.freeserve.co.uk
Formed: 1989

Organisation type and purpose: Independently owned, registered charity (charity number SCO 17071), museum, suitable for ages: 5+.

Enquiries to: Curator
Access:
Access to staff: By letter, by telephone, by email
Hours: Apr to Sep: Mon to Sat, 1000 to 1600
Oct to Mar: Mon to Sat, 1100 to 1530
Access for disabled people: level entry, access to all public areas, toilet facilities

General description:
Bennie is a small independent museum containing artefacts of social, industrial, and historical interest. It contains material covering the local history of Bathgate in photographs, postcards and artefacts.
Information services:
Education services: Group education facilities..
Collections:
Bathgate glass, collection of glass manufactured at Bathgate Glass Works, 1866-1887
Catalogues:
Catalogue for all of the collections is only available in-house.

Internet home pages:
http://benniemuseum.homestead.com/

233
BENTHALL HALL
Broseley, Shropshire, TF12 5RX

Tel: 01952 882159 (Administrator)
Email: benthall@nationaltrust.org.uk
Formed: 1962

Organisation type and purpose: Registered charity (charity number 205846), historic building, house or site, suitable for ages: 8+.
Parent body:
The National Trust
West Midlands Region, Attingham Park, Shrewsbury, SY4 4TP, tel: 01743 708100

Enquiries to: Administrator
Access:
Access to staff: By letter, by telephone

continued overleaf

Access for disabled people: Parking provided, ramped entry, toilet facilities
Other restrictions: Drop-off point. Ground floor largely accessible. No access to other floors. Steps inside. Much of the garden is accessible by wheelchairs with assistance on slopes.

General description:
Situated on a plateau above the gorge of the Severn, this 16th century stone house has mullioned and transomed windows, and a stunning interior with carved oak staircase, decorated plaster ceilings and oak panelling. There is an intimate and carefully restored plantsman's garden, old kitchen garden and interesting Restoration church.
Information services:
Booked groups Wed and Sun only.
Braille guide. Large-print guide.
Children's quiz/trail.
Special visitor services: Materials and/or activities for children.
Services for disabled people: For the visually impaired.
Catalogues:
Catalogue for part of the collections is only available in-house.
Printed publications:
Guide Book

Internet home pages:
http://www.nationaltrust.org.uk

234
BENTLEY WILDFOWL AND MOTOR MUSEUM
Harveys Lane, Halland, Lewes, East Sussex, BN8 5AF

Tel: 01825 840573
Fax: 01825 841322
Email: barrysutherland@pavilion.co.uk
Formed: 1978

Organisation type and purpose: Museum, suitable for ages: 5 to 15.
17th century farmhouse with wildfowl and car collections and gardens.
Parent body:
East Sussex County Council

Enquiries to: Manager
Access:
Access to staff: By letter, by telephone, by fax, by email, visitors by prior appointment, charges made to all users, Internet web pages
Access for disabled people: ramped entry, access to all public areas
Other restrictions: Assistance dogs not allowed in Wildfowl Reserve.

General description:
Internationally renowned collection of over 115 species of waterfowl, and motor museum with vintage vehicles including motorcycles and bicycles. Bentley House, originally a modest Tudor farmhouse, was converted into a Palladian style mansion. It has a fine collection of furniture and over 100 watercolours of wildfowl by Philip Rickman. The gardens contain a collection of old varieties of roses. The 12 acres of Glyndebourne Wood also have various dwellings built by East Sussex Archaeology and Museum Projects.
Information services:
Education and discovery centre
Exhibition and craft demonstrations
Special visitor services: Materials and/or activities for children.
Education services: Group education facilities, resources for Key Stages 1 and 2..
Collections:
Bentley through the ages
150 Watercolour paintings of wildfowl by Philip Rickman
Collection of about 60 Veteran, Edwardian and vintage cars and 25 motorcycles and bicycles
Collection of wildfowl started by the late Gerald Askew in the 1960s

Internet home pages:
http://www.bentley.org.uk

235
BENTLIF ART GALLERY

Catalogues:
Catalogue for library is in-house only.
See - Tyrwhitt-Drake Museum of Carriages

236
BERKELEY CASTLE
Berkeley, Gloucestershire, GL13 9BQ

Tel: 01453 810332

Organisation type and purpose: Registered charity (charity number 1061062).
Historic castle.
Family connection with:
Spetchley Park
Worcester

Enquiries to: Administrator
Access:
Access to staff: By letter, by telephone

General description:
England's oldest inhabited castle, the home of the Berkeleys since 1153. The State Apartments contain collections of 16th/18th century furniture of an interesting diversity, and several tapestries (Flemish and Mortlake). Also contains large collections of paintings by primarily English and Dutch masters (Stubbs, Gainsborough, Reynolds, Lely, Van Somer, Van de Velde, Tillemans, Wissing, Batoni, Hondecoeter and others).
Information services:
Special visitor services: Guided tours..

Internet home pages:
http://www.berkeley-castle.com

237
BERNEY ARMS WINDMILL
Berney Arms, Halvergate, Norwich

Tel: 01493 700605

Organisation type and purpose: Historic building, house or site, suitable for ages: all ages.
Parent body:
English Heritage (East of England Region)
Brooklands, 24 Brooklands Avenue, Cambridge, CB2 2BU, tel: 01223 582700, fax: 01223 582701
Access:
Access to staff: By letter, by telephone
Other restrictions: Letters should be addressed to English Heritage Regional Office.

General description:
Victorian windmill.

Internet home pages:
http://www.english-heritage.org.uk

238
BERRINGTON HALL
Leominster, Herefordshire, HR6 0DW

Tel: 01568 615721
Fax: 01568 613263
Email: berrington@nationaltrust.org.uk
Formed: 1781

Organisation type and purpose: National organisation, registered charity (charity number 205846), historic building, house or site, suitable for ages: 5+.
Parent body:
The National Trust (West Midlands)
West Midlands Regional Office, tel: 01743 708100

Enquiries to: Property Manager
Other contacts: Costume Curator for bookings to view Snowshill Costume Collection.
Access:
Access to staff: By letter, by telephone, by fax, by email, visitors by prior appointment
Hours: NT Office contactable all year round on 01568 615721
Other restrictions: Answerphone out of hours.
Access for disabled people: Parking provided, toilet facilities
Other restrictions: Designated parking. Space for 4 disabled drivers at house. 2 manual wheelchairs available. 1 singleseater powered mobility vehicle, booking essential. Steps to entrance. Ground floor fully accessible. Photograph album. Ramped entrance to shop. Steps to restaurant entrance. Staff will serve disabled visitors in courtyard in fine weather. Gravel paths in garden but suitable for most wheelchairs. Recommended route map.

General description:
Beautifully set above a wide valley with sweeping views to the Brecon Beacons, this elegant Henry Holland house was built in the late 18th century and is set in parkland designed by 'Capability' Brown. The rather austere external appearance belies a surprisingly delicate interior, with beautifully decorated ceilings and a spectacular staircase hall. There are good collections of furniture and paintings, as well as a nursery, Victorian laundry, Georgian dairy and an attractive garden. The walled garden contains an historic collection of old varieties of apple and pear trees.
Information services:
Braille guide. Audio guide.
Frontcarrying baby slings for loan. Hip-carrying infant seats for loan.
Outdoor orienteering course, eye spy sheet, pet sheep and peacocks.
Suitable for school groups. Audio guide. Hands-on activities. Children's quiz/trail. Adult study days.
Special visitor services: Tape recorded guides, materials and/or activities for children.
Services for disabled people: For the visually impaired; for the hearing impaired.
Collections:
Wade Costume Collection (formerly the Snowshill Costume Collection) - viewing by appointment only
NCCPG Fruit Collection - historic collection of old varieties of apples and pears in walled garden
Printed publications:
Guide Book
Short Guide
Garden Guide
Fruit Collection Leaflet
Park Walk Leaflet
Electronic and video products:
Educational CD-ROM (available from the Education Office)

Internet home pages:
http://www.nationaltrust.org.uk

239
BERRY POMEROY CASTLE
Totnes, Devon

Organisation type and purpose: National organisation, advisory body, historic building, house or site.
Parent body:
English Heritage (South West Region)
Tel: 0117 975 0700

Enquiries to: Manager
Access:
Access to staff: By letter, by telephone
Access to building, collections or gallery: No prior appointment required
Hours: 1 Apr to 30 Sep: daily, 1000 to 1800,1 to 31 Oct: daily, 1000 to 1700
Other restrictions: Opening times are subject to change, for up-to-date information contact English Heritage by phone or visit the website.
No coach access.

General description:
The romantic ruin of Berry Pomeroy Castle, built during the late 15th century, features an imposing gatehouse and defensive curtain wall. Behind the late medieval stone defences are the remains of a grand Elizabethan country house, built c.1560-1600 by the Seymours.
Information services:
Special visitor services: Tape recorded guides.

Education services: Group education facilities..

Internet home pages:
http://www.english-heritage.org.uk

240
BERSHAM IRONWORKS & HERITAGE CENTRE

Bersham Road, Wrexham, Clwyd, LL14 4HT

Tel: 01978 261529
Fax: 01978 361703
Email: bershamheritage@wrexham.gov.uk
Formed: 1983

Organisation type and purpose: Local government body, museum, historic building, house or site, suitable for ages: all ages.

Enquiries to: Manager
Access:
Access to staff: By letter, by telephone, by email
Access to building, collections or gallery: Prior appointment required
Access for disabled people: Parking provided, ramped entry, level entry, access to all public areas, toilet facilities
Other restrictions: Ironworks - limited access.

General description:
Displays about the local industrial and archaeological sites including Bersham Ironworks, Brynks Steelworks, working forge, Victorian schoolroom, temporary exhibition gallery.
Information services:
Special visitor services: Guided tours, materials and/or activities for children..
Collections:
Mainly industrial collections concentrating particularly on iron, steel and coal

241
BERWICK-UPON-TWEED BARRACKS

The Parade, Berwick-upon-Tweed, Northumberland, TD15 1DF

Tel: 01289 304493

Organisation type and purpose: National government body, museum, art gallery, historic building, house or site, suitable for ages: all ages.
Parent body:
English Heritage (North East Region)
Tel: 0191 269 1227/8, fax: 0191 261 1130

Enquiries to: Manager
Access:
Access to staff: By letter, by telephone, in person
Access to building, collections or gallery: No prior appointment required
Hours: End Mar to end Sep, daily, 1000 to 1800, Oct, daily, 1000 to 1700, Nov to end Mar
Other restrictions: Opening times are subject to change, for up-to-date information contact English Heritage by phone or visit the website

General description:
The Berwick Barracks were begun in 1717 and were among the first purpose-built barracks to be completed. These 18th century barracks house the museum dedicated to the King's Own Scottish Borderers. Besides the Barracks, you can visit the Berwick Main Guard, a Georgian Guard House near the quay. The Story of a Border Garrison Town is a permanent display of the history of the town and its fortifications. There are also the remains of the medieval castle. The Clock Block houses part of the Burrell Collection.
Information services:
Education services: Group education facilities..

Internet home pages:
http://www.english-heritage.org.uk

See also - King's Own Scottish Borderers Regimental Museum

242
BERWICK-UPON-TWEED BOROUGH MUSEUM AND ART GALLERY

The Barracks, Berwick-upon-Tweed, Northumberland, TD15 1DQ

Tel: 01289 330933

Organisation type and purpose: Museum, art gallery, historic building, house or site, suitable for ages: 5+.
Building under the Custodianship of:
English Heritage
Tel: 0191 2611585

Enquiries to: Curator
Access:
Access to staff: By letter, by telephone
Access to building, collections or gallery: No prior appointment required
Hours: Apr to Oct, Mon to Sat, 1000 to 1230, 1330 to 1800, Sun, 1000 to 1300, 1400 to 1600; Oct to Mar, Wed to Sat, 1000 to 1230, 1330 to 1600, Sun 1000 to 1300, 1400 to 1600
Other restrictions: Closed Mon and Tue from Nov to end of Mar

General description:
The museum is housed in the first purpose-built barracks.

Internet home pages:
http://www.scotborder.org.uk

243
BESSIE SURTEES HOUSE

41-44 Sandhill, Newcastle upon Tyne, NE1 3JF

Tel: 0191 269 1227/8
Fax: 0191 261 1130

Organisation type and purpose: Historic building, house or site.
Parent body:
English Heritage (North East Region)
Tel: 0191 269 1227/8, fax: 0191 261 1130

General description:
A unique group of buildings surviving from Tudor Newcastle. Originally rich merchants' houses and shops. They now house the North East Regional Office of English Heritage. There are richly decorated and elaborate plaster ceilings, 17th century panelling and important and unique fireplaces.

Internet home pages:
http://www.english-heritage.org.uk

244
BESWICK MUSEUM

Gold Street, Longton, Stoke-on-Trent, Staffordshire, ST3 2JP

Tel: 01782 291213

245
BETHLEM ROYAL HOSPITAL ARCHIVES AND MUSEUM, THE

Monks Orchard Road, Beckenham, Kent, BR3 3BX

Tel: 020 8776 4307 or 4227
Fax: 020 8776 4045
Email: museum@bethlem.freeserve.co.uk
Formed: 1967

Organisation type and purpose: Registered charity (charity number 1013523), museum, art gallery.
Archive repository and museum, psychiatric teaching hospital.

Enquiries to: Archivist and Curator
Direct tel: 020 8776 4307
Access:
Access to staff: By letter, by telephone, by email, in person, visitors by prior appointment
Hours: Mon to Fri, 0930 to 1700

General description:
History of The Bethlem Royal Hospital (the original Bedlam) and of The Maudsley Hospital, history of psychiatry in general, mentally disordered artists particularly the work of Richard Dadd, Louis Wain, William Kurelek, Jonathan Martin.
Collections:
Archives of the Bethlem Royal Hospital and the Maudsley Hospital
Guttmann-Maclay art collection and other work by artists suffering from mental disorder
Printed publications:
The Bethlem Royal Hospital: An Illustrated History (booklet, £3.50 inc p&p)
Bethlem Hospital 1247-1997 - A Pictorial Record (£12 plus p&p)
Leaflets on artists
Leaflet on the Archives and Museum Department (free)
Leaflet on the picture collection (£1.75 inc p&p)
Postcards of the picture collection

Internet home pages:
http://www.bethlemheritage.org.uk

246
BETHNAL GREEN MUSEUM OF CHILDHOOD

See - Museum of Childhood at Bethnal Green

247
BETTLES GALLERY

80 Christchurch Road, Ringwood, Hampshire, BH24 1DR

Tel: 0142 5470410
Formed: 1989

Organisation type and purpose: Independently owned, art gallery, suitable for ages: 16+.
Members of the:
Independent Craft Galleries Association (ICGA)

Enquiries to: Proprietor
Access:
Access to staff: By letter, by telephone, visitors by prior appointment
Access to building, collections or gallery: No prior appointment required
Hours: Tue to Fri, 1000 to 1700; Sat, 1000 to 1300
Other restrictions: By appointment at other times.
Access for disabled people: Parking provided
Other restrictions: 2 steps to entrance.

General description:
A small independently run gallery specialising in British studio ceramics by living artists, and contemporary paintings. All work on show individually made by leading internationally known craftsmen and artists. Approximately 8 specialist solo exhibitions each year, as well as constantly changing stock.
Printed publications:
Invitations to exhibitions (on request)

248
BEVERE VIVIS GALLERY AND PICTURE FRAMERS

Bevere Lane, Worcester, WR3 7RQ

Tel: 01905 754484
Fax: 01905 340215
Email: gallery@beverevivis.com
Formed: 1972

Organisation type and purpose: Independently owned, art gallery, suitable for ages: all ages.

Enquiries to: Manager
Access:
Access to staff: By letter, by telephone, by fax, by email, Internet web pages
Hours: Tue to Sat, 1030 to 1700
Access to building, collections or gallery: Prior appointment required
Access for disabled people: Parking provided, toilet facilities

continued overleaf

General description:
Constantly changing exhibition by local up and coming, and professional arts and crafts people.
Information services:
Education services: Group education facilities..

Internet home pages:
http://www.beverevivis.com

249
BEVERLEY MINSTER

Minster Yard North, Beverley, East Yorkshire, HU17 0DP

Tel: 01482 868540
Fax: 01482 887520
Email: minster@beverleyminster.co.uk
Formed: 1220

Organisation type and purpose: Registered charity, historic building, house or site, suitable for ages: 5+.

Enquiries to: Administrator
Direct tel: 01482 887520
Direct email: rogershaw@beverleyminster.co.uk
Access:
Access to staff: By letter, by telephone, by fax, by email, visitors by prior appointment
Access to building, collections or gallery: Prior appointment required
Access for disabled people: ramped entry, toilet facilities

General description:
Medieval Gothic architecture, Medieval, Georgian and Victorian church fittings.
Information services:
Helpline available, tel no: 01482 868540.
Special visitor services: Guided tours, materials and/or activities for children..
Printed publications:
Beverley Minster - An Illustrated History
Electronic and video products:
Beverley Minster (video)

250
BEWCASTLE CHURCH

Bewcastle, Carlisle, Cumbria, CA6 6PX

Tel: 016977 48627

Organisation type and purpose: Historic building, house or site, suitable for ages: all ages.
World Heritage Site.
Parent body:
Bewcastle Parochial Church Council

Enquiries to: Secretary
Access:
Access to staff: By letter, by telephone
Access to building, collections or gallery: No prior appointment required
Hours: Site open all hours; church open during daylight hours
Access for disabled people: Parking provided, level entry, access to all public areas
Other restrictions: Ramped entry to exhibition room

General description:
Anglican church.
Information services:
Special visitor services: Guided tours..

251
BEXHILL MUSEUM

Egerton Road, Bexhill-on-Sea, East Sussex, TN39 3HL

Tel: 01424 787950
Fax: 01424 787950
Email: museum@rother.gov.uk
Formed: 1914

Organisation type and purpose: Membership association (membership is by subscription), present number of members: 300, registered charity (charity number 286446), museum, suitable for ages: all ages.
Parent body:
Bexhill Museum Association

Enquiries to: Administrator
Access:
Access to staff: By letter, by fax, by email, in person, Internet web pages
Hours: Tue to Fri, 1000 to 1700
Access to building, collections or gallery: No prior appointment required
Hours: Feb to Dec: Tue to Fri, 1000 to 1700; Sat, Sun, 1400 to 1700
Access for disabled people: ramped entry, access to all public areas

General description:
The museum is housed in the former Egerton Park Shelter Hall built in 1903. It houses collections of local history, Egyptology, ethnography, local archaeology, general history, science, natural history, geology.
Sussex: history, archaeology, landscape etc.
General archaeology; maps and plans.
Information services:
Library available for reference (for conditions see Access above)
New interactive access centre open - as museum times.
Special visitor services: Guided tours, materials and/or activities for children.
Education services: Group education facilities.
Services for disabled people: For the visually impaired; displays and/or information at wheelchair height.
Collections:
Local history: deeds, property details etc, photographs, prints and watercolours, geology
Objects, documents, maps, books
Local archaeology: site reports, artefacts
Natural history
Ethnography: Tibet, Egypt, Africa, India, Australia
Catalogues:
Catalogue for library is in-house only. Catalogue for part of the collections is only available in-house.
Publications list:
is available in hard copy and online.
Printed publications:
Various publications available direct including:
Bexhill's Maharajah (Burl P, £2.50)
100 Years of Bexhill Motor Buses (Padgham D, £1.99)
Bexhill Voices (£5.95) and Bexhill Voices Two (Guilmant A, 1999, £6.96)
Bucking the Trend; the life and times of the 9th Earl De La Warr (Fairley A, £5)
Our Second Pilgrimage: tales of old Bexhill (Burl P, £1.99)
The Story Behind Bexhill Street Names (Bexhill Museum Association, 1996, £1.50)
Wartime Food: memories of rationing and recipes (Morrey H, 1996, £1.50)
On the Trail of the Iguanodon (Woodhams K, ISSN, £2.50)
The De La Warr Pavilion (De La Warr Pavilion Trust, illustrated, £3.50)

Internet home pages:
http://www.bexhillmuseum.co.uk
General information, opening times, history of Bexhill, museum shop.

252
BEXHILL MUSEUM OF COSTUME & SOCIAL HISTORY

Manor Gardens, Upper Sea Road, Old Town, Bexhill-on-Sea, East Sussex, TN40 1RL

Tel: 01424 210045
Acronym or abbreviation: Bexhill Costume Museum
Formed: 1972

Organisation type and purpose: Independently owned, registered charity (charity number 803577), museum, suitable for ages: 5+.
Access:
Access to staff: By letter, by telephone
Access to building, collections or gallery: No prior appointment required
Other restrictions: Prior appointment required for group bookings.
Access for disabled people: Parking provided, ramped entry, access to all public areas, toilet facilities

General description:
Contains English costume and related accessories dating from the mid-18th century. There is also an extensive collection of lace, and examples of textile design and embroidery. The social history content includes early kitchen objects; radios; gramophones; and typewriters. The displays are regularly changed.
Information services:
Special visitor services: Guided tours.
Services for disabled people: Displays and/or information at wheelchair height.
Collections:
Collection includes clothing from mid-18th century together with related accessories and artefacts
Extensive collection of Victorian, Edwardian and 1930s dresses, including a dress which formerly belonged to Queen Victoria, and was made in 1892 (this is on temporary loan)
Collections also of lace (very extensive) and toys from Victorian era

Internet home pages:
http://www.bexhillcostumemuseum.co.uk

253
BEXLEY HERITAGE TRUST

Hall Place, Bourne Road, Bexley, Kent, DA5 1PQ

Tel: 01322 526574
Fax: 01322 522921
Email: info@hallplaceandgardens.com
Formed: 1981
Formerly: Bexley Museum, date of change, 2000

Organisation type and purpose: Historic building, house or site.
Local government premises, independently managed.

Enquiries to: Director
Access:
Access to staff: By letter, by telephone, by email, visitors by prior appointment
Access to building, collections or gallery: No prior appointment required
Hours: Apr to Oct: Mon to Sat, 1000 to 1700; Sun 1100 to 1700
Nov to Mar: Tue to Sat, 1000 to 1615
Access for disabled people: Parking provided, access to all public areas, toilet facilities

General description:
Hall Place is a fine Tudor mansion built in the reign of Henry VIII for the Lord Mayor of London, Sir John Champneys. It has a panelled Tudor great hall and minstrels' gallery, gardens, topiary, herb garden, secret garden, Italianate garden and herbaceous borders. There is a sub-tropical plant house and nursery.
Temporary displays on local history themes.
Also collections of local social and industrial history; archaeology; natural sciences; costume; and ethnography, art exhibitions, Hall Place introductory gallery.
Information services:
Special visitor services: Guided tours, materials and/or activities for children.
Education services: Group education facilities..
Collections:
Willmot collection. Sewing machines. 1860s-1920s.
Boswell collection. Photographs, negatives, lantern slides and equipment. 1880s-1930s.
Packer collection. Printed ephemera. Victorian-recent.
David Evans & Co museum collection of textile, printing equipment and printed textiles
Catalogues:
Catalogue for part of the collections is only available in-house.
Printed publications:
Brochure

Internet home pages:
http://www.hallplaceandgardens.com
History of Hall Place, opening times.

254
BEXLEY LIBRARIES AND MUSEUMS DEPARTMENT

Central Library, Townley Road, Bexleyheath, Kent, DA6 7HJ

Tel: 020 8301 5151
Fax: 020 8303 7872
Email: libraries.els@bexley.gov.uk

Organisation type and purpose: Local government body, public library.
Local contact point of the:
South East Area Libraries Information Service (SEAL)

Enquiries to: Librarian
Access:
Access to staff: By letter, by telephone, by fax, by email, in person
Hours: Mon, Tue, Wed, Fri, 0930 to 1730; Sat, 0930 to 1700; Sun 1000 to 1400

General description:
General.
Collections:
British Standards
Government publications

Internet home pages:
http://www.bexley.gov.uk

255
BICTON WOODLAND RAILWAY

Bicton Park Botanical Gardens, East Budleigh, Budleigh Salterton, Devon, EX9 7BJ

Tel: 01395 568465
Fax: 01395 568374
Email: info@bictongardens.co.uk
Formed: 1998

Organisation type and purpose: Independently owned, museum, historic building, house or site, suitable for ages: all ages.

Enquiries to: Owner
Access:
Access to staff: By letter, by telephone, by fax
Access for disabled people: level entry, access to all public areas, toilet facilities

General description:
Narrow gauge railway providing 25 min ride. Countryside museum with rural memorabilia, and exhibition hall with traction engines, vintage machinery, tools and other Victorian artefacts.
Information services:
Special visitor services: Guided tours, tape recorded guides.
Education services: Group education facilities..

256
BIDDULPH GRANGE GARDEN

Biddulph Grange, Biddulph, Stoke-on-Trent, Staffordshire, ST8 7SD

Tel: 01782 517999 (Garden office)
Fax: 01782 510624
Email: biddulphgrange@nationaltrust.org.uk

Organisation type and purpose: National organisation, registered charity (charity number 205846), historic building, house or site, suitable for ages: all ages.
Parent body:
The National Trust (West Midlands)
West Midlands Regional Office, tel: 01743 708100

Enquiries to: Manager
Access:
Access to staff: By letter, by telephone, by fax, by email
Access to building, collections or gallery: No prior appointment required
Hours: Apr to Oct, Wed to Thu, 1200 to 1730, Sat and Sun, 1100 to 1730;
Nov to week before Christmas, Sat and Sun, 1200 to 1600
Open Bank Holiday Mondays, 1100 to1730
Other restrictions: Closed Good Fri. Last admission 1700 or dusk if earlier
Access for disabled people: toilet facilities
Other restrictions: Steps to entrance. Steps to shop entrance. Steps to tea-room entrance.

General description:
One of Britain's most exciting and unusual gardens with a series of connected 'compartments', designed in the mid-19th century by James Bateman to display specimens from his extensive and wide-ranging plant collection. Visitors are taken on a miniature tour of the world, featuring the Egyptian Court and imitation of the Great Wall of China, as well as a pinetum, fernery and rock gardens.

Internet home pages:
http://www.nationaltrust.org.uk

257
BIG IDEA, THE

The Harbourside, Irvine, Ayrshire, KA12 8XX

Tel: 08708 404030
Fax: 08708 403130
Email: enquiries@bigidea.org.uk
Formed: 2000

Organisation type and purpose: Independently owned, registered charity (charity number SCO 025611), suitable for ages: 5+.
Visitor attraction, science centre.

Enquiries to: Marketing Manager
Direct tel: 08708 403100
Direct email: caroline@bigidea.org.uk
Access:
Access to staff: By letter, by fax, by email
Access for disabled people: Parking provided, level entry, access to all public areas, toilet facilities

General description:
Inventors, Alfred Nobel, dynamite.
Information services:
Education services: Group education facilities.
Services for disabled people: Displays and/or information at wheelchair height.

258
BIG PIT NATIONAL MINING MUSEUM OF WALES, THE

Blaenafon, Gwent, NP4 9XP

Tel: 01495 790311
Fax: 01495 792618
Email: bigpit@nmgw.ac.uk
Acronym or abbreviation: BP
Formed: 1982
Formerly: Big Pit (Blaenafon) Trust Limited, date of change, 2001

Organisation type and purpose: National government body, registered charity, museum, suitable for ages: 5+.
Parent body:
National Museums & Galleries of Wales (NMGW)
Cathays Park, Cardiff

Enquiries to: Marketing Officer
Direct email: kathryn.stowers@nmgw.ac.uk
Access:
Access to staff: By letter, by telephone, by fax, by email, visitors by prior appointment, Internet web pages
Hours: Daily Mar 1 to Nov 30, 0930 to 1700
Access to building, collections or gallery: No prior appointment required
Hours: Mar to Nov: Mon to Sun, 0930 to 1700
Access for disabled people: Parking provided, level entry, access to all public areas, toilet facilities
Other restrictions: Please book wheelchairs for underground tours

General description:
A colliery which ceased production in 1980 now a living museum illustrating the history of coal mining.
Information services:
Special visitor services: Guided tours.
Education services: Resources for Key Stage 2.
Services for disabled people: For the visually impaired.
Collections:
Colliery headgear and winding engine
Mining machinery
Miners' tools and personal effects
Catalogues:
Catalogue for part of the collections is only available in-house.
Printed publications:
Study Pack (available to purchase)

Internet home pages:
http://www.nmgw.ac.uk/bigpit

259
BIGGAR GASWORKS MUSEUM

Gasworks Lane, Biggar, Lanarkshire, ML12 6BZ

Tel: 01899 221070
Formed: 1979

Organisation type and purpose: National government body, museum.
Part of:
National Museums of Scotland

Enquiries to: Curator
Direct tel: 01899 221050
Direct fax: 01899 221050
Direct email: margaret@bmtrust.freeserve.co.uk
Access:
Access to staff: By letter, by telephone, by fax, by email
Access for disabled people: Parking provided, level entry

General description:
The site of the Biggar Gasworks Company 1839-1973, history of the provision of gas for street lighting and private households.

260
BIGGAR MUSEUM TRUST

Moat Park Heritage Centre, Kirkstyle, Biggar, Lanarkshire, ML12 6DT

Tel: 01899 221050
Fax: 01899 221050
Email: margaret@bmtrust.freeserve.co.uk
Acronym or abbreviation: BMT
Formed: 1971
Formerly: Albion Archive, Moat Park Heritage Centre, Brownsbank Cottage, John Buchan Centre, Greenhill Farm House Museum, Gladstone Court Museum, Gas Works Museum

Organisation type and purpose: Registered charity (charity number SCO 003695), museum.
Branch museum:
Biggar Museum Trust
Brownsbank Cottage, Candymill, Biggar

Enquiries to: Manager
Access:
Access to staff: By letter, by telephone, by fax, in person
Hours: Office: Mid Oct to Easter, 0900 to 1300; Easter to Mid Oct, 0900 to 1700
Variable opening times for Museums
Access to building, collections or gallery: No prior appointment required
Hours: Office Hours for collections
Access for disabled people: ramped entry, toilet facilities

General description:
Archaeology of Clydesdale; Albion Motors; local genealogy; Scottish literature and language; geology of Clydesdale; history and pre-history of Clydesdale; local gas making; covenanters; life and work of John Buchan and Hugh MacDiarmid; Victoriana.
Information services:
Helpline available, tel no: 01899 221050.
Albion and genealogy telephone line: 01899 221497
Special visitor services: Materials and/or activities for children.
Education services: Group education facilities..
Collections:
Clydesdale archaeology, Biggar district genealogy, covenanters, local war collection, Victorian and early 20th century, local

continued overleaf

geology, costume, local Burgh; business records, paintings, photographs and slides (local provenance); school books and equipment; Albion Archive
Catalogues:
Catalogue for library is in-house only.

Internet home pages:
http://www.biggar-net.co.uk/museums/

261
BIGNOR ROMAN VILLA
Bignor, Pulborough, West Sussex, RH20 1PH

Tel: 01798 869259
Fax: 01798 869259
Email: bignorromanvilla@care4free.net
Formed: 1812

Organisation type and purpose: Museum, suitable for ages: all ages.
Roman villa site and Museum.

Enquiries to: Curator
Access:
Access to staff: By letter, by telephone, by fax, in person
Hours: Mon to Fri, 0900 to 1700

General description:
Roman villa site, construction, duration of occupation, location, habitation, utilisation, mosaic design, history, construction methods, mythology.
Collections:
Original Guide Books (1815)
Samuel Lysons (1763-1819): Reliquiae Britannico-Romanae Volume 3 (by appointment only)
Printed publications:
Guide Books (currently £1.60)
Leaflets (free)
Students Worksheets (10p)

262
BILLINGFORD CORNMILL
O.S. TM 167 786, Billingford, Norfolk

Tel: 01603 222705

Organisation type and purpose: Historic building, house or site.

General description:
Tower cornmill.

263
BILLINGHAM ART GALLERY
Queensway, Billingham, Cleveland, TS23 2LN

Tel: 01642 397590
Acronym or abbreviation: BAG

Organisation type and purpose: Art gallery.
Parent body:
Department of Education Leisure and Cultural Services
Wynyard House, Billingham Town Centre, Billingham, Teeside, TS23 2LN

Enquiries to: Museums Officer
Direct tel: 01642 358502
Other contacts: Heritage Officer, tel no 01642 393938 for Marketing and Promotions.
Access:
Access to staff: By letter
Hours: Mon to Sat, 0900 to 1700
Access to building, collections or gallery: No access other than to staff
Hours: Mon to Sat, 0900 to 1700
Other restrictions: No disabled access. Wheelchair access possible on a Saturday.

General description:
The Gallery hosts an annual programme of art and crafts exhibitions.
A small collection of fine art, but this purpose built modern art gallery is mainly devoted to a range of temporary exhibitions showing a wide range of the artistic mediums.

Internet home pages:
http://www.stockton-bc.gov.uk/

264
BILSTON CRAFT GALLERY
Mount Pleasant, Bilston, Wolverhampton, West Midlands, WV14 7LU

Tel: 01902 552507
Fax: 01902 552504
Formed: 1937
Formerly: Bilston Art Gallery and Museum, date of change, 1999

Organisation type and purpose: Local government body, art gallery, suitable for ages: 1+ (including pre-school gallery).

Enquiries to: Curator
Direct tel: 01902 552505
Other contacts: Craft Development Worker for exhibition information.
Access:
Access to staff: By letter, by telephone, by fax
Access to building, collections or gallery: No prior appointment required
Hours: Tue to Fri, 1000 to 1600; Sat, 1100 to 1600
Access for disabled people: Parking provided, ramped entry, access to all public areas, toilet facilities

General description:
A contemporary craft gallery which holds touring and short-term in-house exhibitions of contemporary craft of a local and national nature. Also features a pre-school gallery for 0-5 year olds - 'Craftplay', currently by appointment only.
Information services:
Special visitor services: Materials and/or activities for children.
Services for disabled people: For the hearing impaired; displays and/or information at wheelchair height.
Collections:
18th century Bilston enamels
Catalogues:
Catalogue for part of the collections is only available in-house.

Internet home pages:
http://www.wolverhamptonarts.org
Exhibition information.

265
BINCHESTER ROMAN FORT
Binchester, Bishop Auckland, Co Durham, DL14 8DJ

Tel: 01388 663089 or 0191 383 4225
Fax: 0191 384 1336
Email: archaeology@durham.gov.uk

Organisation type and purpose: Local government body, historic building, house or site, suitable for ages: 5+.
Parent body:
Durham County Council Cultural Services
County Hall, Durham, DH1 5TY, tel: 0191 383 3595, fax: 0191 384 1336

Enquiries to: Curator
Direct tel: 0191 383 4225
Direct fax: 0191 384 1336
Direct email: deborah.anderson@durham.gov.uk
Other contacts: County Archaeologist
Access:
Access to staff: By letter, by telephone, by email
Hours: Mon to Fri, 1100 to 1700
Access for disabled people: Parking provided, access to all public areas, toilet facilities

General description:
The best preserved Roman bathhouse in the country.
Information services:
Special visitor services: Guided tours, materials and/or activities for children.
Education services: Group education facilities, resources for Key Stages 1 and 2 and Further or Higher Education.
Services for disabled people: Displays and/or information at wheelchair height.
Collections:
Collections and excavation archives held at Bowes Museum, Barnard Castle
Printed publications:
Guide Book (direct from site)

Internet home pages:
http://www.durham.gov.uk/binchester

266
BIOLOGICAL RECORDS CENTRE & LUDLOW MUSEUM
Ludlow Museum Resource Centre, Parkway, Ludlow, Shropshire, SY8 2PG

Tel: 01584 873857
Fax: 01584 872019
Email: ludlow.museum@shropshire-cc.gov.uk
Acronym or abbreviation: SBRC
Formed: 1833

Organisation type and purpose: Museum.
Formed in 1833 as a museum.
Other addresses:
Ludlow Museum Display
Castle Street, Ludlow
Ludlow Museum Offices
Old Street, Ludlow, Shropshire, SY8 1NW, tel: 01584 873857, fax: 01584 872019, email/website: ludlow.museum@shropshire-cc.gov.uk

Enquiries to: Curator
Access:
Access to staff: By letter, by telephone, by fax, by email, in person, visitors by prior appointment
Hours: Mon to Fri, 0900 to 1300 and 1400 to 1700
Access to building, collections or gallery: Prior appointment required
Access for disabled people: Parking provided
Other restrictions: Poor disabled access in current building; level entry at rear.

Collections:
Biological and geological records
Geological, biological, social history collections
Catalogues:
Catalogue for library is in-house only. Catalogue for part of the collections is only available in-house.

Internet home pages:
http://www.shropshire-cc.gov.uk/museums.nsf

267
BIOLOGY CURATORS GROUP
North Lincolnshire Museum, Oswald Road, Scunthorpe, Lincolnshire, DN15 7BD

Tel: 01724 843533
Fax: 01724 270474
Email: steve.thompson@northlincs.gov.uk
Acronym or abbreviation: BCG

Organisation type and purpose: National organisation, advisory body, professional body, membership association (membership is by subscription), voluntary organisation.
To promote: the care knowledge and use of biology collections in the UK; and museum-based, biology-related activities.

Enquiries to: Secretary
Other contacts: Chairman
Access:
Access to staff: By letter, by telephone, by fax, by email, in person, Internet web pages
Hours: Mon to Fri, 0900 to 1700

General description:
The acquisition, long-term care and use of biological collections. The propagation of biological information to a wide range of users, and the promotion of biology.
Trade and statistical:
Nature, content and possible use of museum-based biological collections, as well as many non-museum-based collections.
Printed publications:
Biological Curator (from Feb.1994)
Journal of Biological Curation (1989-92)

Newsletter of Biology Curators Group (Pre-1994)

Internet home pages:
http://www.bcg.man.ac.uk

268
BIRDOSWALD ROMAN FORT
Gilsland, Brampton, Cumbria, CA8 7DD

Tel: 016977 47602
Fax: 016977 47605
Email: birdoswald@dial.pipex.com
Formed: 1987

Organisation type and purpose: Local government body, historic building, house or site, suitable for ages: 5+.
Interactive visitor centre and remains of Roman fort.
Parent body:
English Heritage (North West Region)
Tel: 0161 242 1400
Managed by:
Cumbria County Council
Access:
Access to staff: By letter, by telephone, by fax, by email
Access for disabled people: Parking provided, ramped entry, level entry, access to all public areas, toilet facilities

General description:
Superb stretch of Hadrian's Wall, fort, turret and milecastle can all be seen. Recent archaeological excavations have uncovered a unique basilica, or drill hall, granary buildings and the west gate to the fort with its magnificent masonry. Visitor Centre, spectacular views and countryside walks, well-stocked shop and tea-room, special events throughout the year.
Information services:
Special visitor services: Guided tours, materials and/or activities for children.
Education services: Group education facilities, resources for Key Stages 1 and 2, 3, 4 and Further or Higher Education.
Services for disabled people: Displays and/or information at wheelchair height.

Internet home pages:
http://www.birdoswaldromanfort.org

269
BIRMINGHAM AND MIDLAND MUSEUM OF TRANSPORT
Chapel Lane, Wythall, Birmingham, B47 6JX

Tel: 01564 826471
Email: enquiries@bammot.org.uk
Acronym or abbreviation: BaMMOT
Formed: 1977
Formerly: Midland Bus and Transport Museum, date of change, 1990

Organisation type and purpose: Membership association (membership is by subscription), present number of members: 150, voluntary organisation, registered charity (charity number 507191), museum, suitable for ages: 5+.

Enquiries to: Collections & Commercial Manager
Access:
Access to staff: By letter, by email, Internet web pages
Access for disabled people: Parking provided, ramped entry, level entry

General description:
100 vehicles, mostly buses and coaches, but also including fire engines and largest collection of restored battery electric road vehicles in the world; small exhibits and photographic displays. Construction, operation and restoration of vehicles.
Information services:
Events Days (generally Bank Holidays and last Sunday of the month) include museum buses and miniature steam railway offering rides.
Special visitor services: Guided tours..
Collections:
c80 Buses and Coaches, mostly built or operated in Midlands
c20 Battery Electric Vehicles
Archives of photographs, especially Metro-Cammell Bus Production, timetables, leaflets and other bus company promotional material, transport books, street furniture pertaining to transport operation, bus maintenance manuals, uniforms
Printed publications:
Museum Guide (£2.50 plus 50p p&p)
Programme of Events leaflet (free)

Internet home pages:
http://www.bammot.org.uk
Details of museum, exhibits and activities.

270
BIRMINGHAM CATHEDRAL
Colmore Row, Birmingham, B3 2QB

Tel: 0121 236 4333
Fax: 0121 212 0868

Organisation type and purpose: Suitable for ages: all ages.
Cathedral Church (C of E).

Enquiries to: Administrator
Access:
Access to staff: By letter, by telephone, in person
Other restrictions: Contact Cathedral Office on 0121 236 4333 during normal office hours.
Access to building, collections or gallery: No prior appointment required
Hours: Mon to Fri, 0900 to 1700; Sat, Sun, 1000 to 1600
Other restrictions: Access may be restricted during Cathedral services.
Access for disabled people: level entry
Other restrictions: On-street parking including designated spaces is available nearby for badge-holders.

General description:
St Philip's Church, which became the Cathedral in 1905, is a distinguished English baroque building designed by Thomas Archer and built 1708-1725. The interior includes four renowned stained glass windows by Burne-Jones.
Collections:
Historic registers and other documents are held by archives at Birmingham Reference Library
Printed publications:
Guide Book
Information Leaflets

271
BIRMINGHAM MUSEUM OF SCIENCE AND DISCOVERY
See - Thinktank - Birmingham Museum of Science and Discovery

272
BIRMINGHAM MUSEUMS AND ART GALLERY
Chamberlain Square, Birmingham, B3 3DH

Tel: 0121 303 2834
Minicom no. Textphone: 0121 303 3321
Fax: 0121 303 1394
Email: bmagenquiries@bcc.gov.uk
Acronym or abbreviation: BM&AG
Formed: 1885

Organisation type and purpose: Local government body, museum, art gallery, historic building, house or site, suitable for ages: all ages.
Parent body:
Birmingham City Council
Department of Leisure and Community Services, tel: 0121 303 3018, fax: 0121 303 1542, email: bmagenquiries@bcc.gov.uk
Other museums run by this service:
Aston Hall
Trinity Road, Birmingham, B6 7JD, tel: 0121 327 0062, fax: 0121 327 7162
Birmingham Museum and Art Gallery
Chamberlain Square, Birmingham, B3 3DH, tel: 0121 303 2834, fax: 0121 303 1394, email/website: bmagenquiries@bcc.gov.uk
Blakesley Hall
Blakesley Road, Birmingham, B25 8RN, tel: 0121 783 2193, fax: 0121 303 1394, email/website: bmagenquiries@bcc.gov.uk
Museum of the Jewellery Quarter
75-79 Vyse Street, Birmingham, B18 6HA, tel: 0121 554 3598, fax: 0121 554 9700, email/website: bmagenquiries@bcc.gov.uk
Sarehole Mill
Colebank Road, Birmingham, B13 0BD, tel: 0121 777 6612, fax: 0121 303 1394, email/website: bmagenquiries@bcc.gov.uk
Soho House
Soho Avenue, (off Soho Road), Birmingham, B18 5LB, tel: 0121 554 9122, fax: 0121 554 5929, email/website: bmagenquiries@bcc.gov.uk
Weoley Castle (currently closed to the public)
Tel: 0121 303 1675, fax: 0121 303 1394, email/website: bmagenquiries@bcc.gov.uk

Enquiries to: Curatorial Secretary
Access:
Access to staff: By letter, by telephone, by fax, by email, in person, visitors by prior appointment, Internet web pages
Access to building, collections or gallery: Prior appointment required
Hours: Mon to Thu, 1000 to 1700; Fri, 1030 to 1700; Sat, 1000 to 1700; Sun, 1230 to 1700
Access for disabled people: access to all public areas, toilet facilities
Other restrictions: Lift facility - access to all areas.

General description:
Art, fine and decorative; antiquities, Birmingham history, conservation, museum education.
Collections:
Numerous, on the subjects given above
Catalogues:
Catalogue for part of the collections is only available in-house.

Internet home pages:
http://www.bmag.org.uk
Describes museum sites and collections.

See also - Thinktank - Birmingham Museum of Science and Discovery

273
BISHOPS' HOUSE
Meersbrook Park, Norton Lees Lane, Sheffield, South Yorkshire, S8 9BE

Tel: 0114 278 2600
Fax: 0114 278 2604
Email: info@sheffieldgalleries.org.uk

Organisation type and purpose: Museum.
Parent body:
Sheffield Galleries & Museums Trust
Leader House, Surrey Street, Sheffield, S1 2LH, tel: 0114 278 2600, fax: 0114 278 2604, email: info@sheffieldgalleries.org.uk

Enquiries to: Public Relations Manager
Direct tel: 0114 278 2612
Direct email: stephanie.potts@sheffieldgalleries.org.uk
Access:
Access to staff: By letter, by telephone, by email, Internet web pages
Access to building, collections or gallery: No prior appointment required
Hours: Mon to Fri, 0900 to 1700; Sat, 1000 to 1630; Sun, 1100 to 1630

General description:
Bishops' House dating from the Tudor period has furnished rooms containing fine examples of local 17th century furniture. The house contains fine plasterwork and panelling which were added to the house in the early 17th century. A permanent exhibition explores the history of Sheffield in the Tudor and Stuart periods.
Information services:
Programme of family activities
Special visitor services: Materials and/or activities for children.
Education services: Group education facilities, resources for Key Stage 2..

continued overleaf

Internet home pages:
http://www.sheffieldgalleries.org.uk
Home page, information on all galleries opening times, collections etc.

274
BISHOP'S WALTHAM PALACE
Bishop's Waltham, Southampton

Tel: 01489 892460
Formed: 1130

Organisation type and purpose: Historic building, house or site, suitable for ages: 5+.
Parent body:
English Heritage (South East Region)
Eastgate Court, 195-205 High Street, Guildford, Surrey, GU1 3EH, tel: 01483 252000, fax: 01483 252001

Enquiries to: Curator
Access:
Access to building, collections or gallery: No prior appointment required
Hours: Apr to Sep: daily, 1000 to 1800
Oct: daily, 1000 to 1700
Other restrictions: Opening times are subject to change, for up-to-date information contact English Heritage by phone or visit the website

General description:
Bishop's Waltham Palace was one of the houses used by the medieval senior clergy of Winchester. What can be seen today are the ruins of this important medieval palace . There is an exhibition on the Winchester Bishops on the first floor of the palace.

Internet home pages:
http://www.english-heritage.org.uk

275
BL HERITAGE
See - British Motor Industry Heritage Trust

276
BLACK COUNTRY LIVING MUSEUM, THE
Tipton Road, Open Air Museum, Dudley, West Midlands, DY1 4SQ

Tel: 0121 557 9643
Fax: 0121 557 4242
Email: info@bclm.co.uk
Formed: 1976

Organisation type and purpose: Independently owned, registered charity (charity number 504481), museum, suitable for ages: all ages.
Membership support group:
Friends of Black Country Living Museum at the same address

Enquiries to: Curator
Access:
Access to staff: By letter, by fax, by email
Access to building, collections or gallery: Prior appointment required
Hours: Mar to Oct: Daily, 1000 to 1700
Nov to Feb: Wed to Sun, 1000 to 1700
Other restrictions: Proof of identity required to view reference library and reserve collections. Prior appointment required for Curatorial Department Mon to Fri, 0930 to 1630.
Access for disabled people: Parking provided

General description:
Social history; industrial history specific to the Black Country.
The regional living history museum of social and industrial history for the heart of industrial Britain. In 26 acres of open-air displays craftsmen and demonstrators recreate traditional industrial processes from coal mining to chain making. Canal and road transport and social and domestic life, including retailing compliment activities on site.
Information services:
Education services: Group education facilities, resources for Key Stage 2.
Services for disabled people: Displays and/or information at wheelchair height.
Collections:
Keith V Gale Library of Iron and Steel Industry
Kenrick Collection of Hardware and Holloware
Relocated domestic and industrial buildings and their contents
Reserve collections of screw and nail making, cooperage, and mining artefacts
The extensive transport collection includes:
trams and trolley buses
horse-drawn delivery carts and travellers' wagons
The Marston Collection of bicycles, motorbikes and locally made cars
Catalogues:
Catalogue for library is in-house only. Catalogue for all of the collections is available in-house and part is on-line.

Internet home pages:
http://www.bclm.co.uk
Some collection information; mainly opening hours; what is on Museum Village site etc.
http://www.a2a.pro.gov.uk
The archive to the Kenrick Collection (a co-operative cataloguing project).

277
BLACK CULTURAL ARCHIVES
378 Coldharbour Lane, London, SW9 8LF

Tel: 020 7738 4591
Fax: 020 7738 7168
Email: info@blackculturalarchives.org.uk
Formed: 1981
Formerly: African People's Historical Monument Foundation

Organisation type and purpose: Voluntary organisation, registered charity, museum, suitable for ages: 12+.
Archives.

Enquiries to: Director
Access:
Access to staff: By letter, by telephone, by fax, by email, in person, visitors by prior appointment
Hours: Archives: 1000 to 1600. Museum: 1000 to 1700
Access to building, collections or gallery: Prior appointment required
Access for disabled people: ramped entry, toilet facilities

General description:
Temporary exhibitions on Black People's experiences, work and life in Britain. Primary and secondary source materials on the Black presence in Britain, including photographs, newspapers, posters, objects, books, magazines, etc, and slave documents.
Printed publications:
The Windrush Legacy, Memories of Britain's post-war Caribbean Immigrants
Mary Seacole (nurse) 1805-1881 (Teacher's pack and learning resources, not currently available)

278
BLACK HILL
Lanark, South Lanarkshire

Organisation type and purpose: Historic building, house or site.
Parent body:
National Trust for Scotland

General description:
Archaeological complex with site of Bronze Age burial cairn, Iron Age hill-fort adjoined by a settlement enclosure, and field dykes which may date to the prehistoric and medieval periods.
A scheduled Ancient Monument.

279
BLACK WATCH REGIMENTAL MUSEUM
Balhousie Castle, Hay Street, Perth, Tayside, PH1 5HS

Tel: 0131 310 8530
Fax: 0131 310 8525
Email: rhq@theblackwatch.co.uk
Acronym or abbreviation: BW Museum
Formed: 1962

Organisation type and purpose: Independently owned, registered charity, museum, historic building, house or site, suitable for ages: 5+, research organisation.

Enquiries to: Curator
Access:
Access to staff: By letter, by telephone, by fax, in person, visitors by prior appointment
Access to building, collections or gallery: No prior appointment required
Hours: 1 Oct to 30 Apr: Mon to Fri, 1000 to 1530,1 May to 30 Sep: Mon to Sat, 1000 to 1630
Other restrictions: Closed 22 Dec to 6 Jan and last Sat in Jun.
Archives - prior appointment required.
Access for disabled people: Parking provided, level entry

General description:
History of the Black Watch (Royal Highland Regiment).
Information services:
Guided tours by prior appointment.
Special visitor services: Guided tours, tape recorded guides, materials and/or activities for children.
Education services: Group education facilities, resources for Key Stages 1 and 2, 3 and 4.
Services for disabled people: For the visually impaired.
Collections:
Pictures, medals, silver, weapons and other artefacts on display
Printed publications:
History of the Black Watch (Pilgrims Press)
Short History of the Black Watch (Fergusson)
Spirit of Angus - History of 5th Black Watch WWII (McGregor)
Off The Record Memoires (Lt Col Rose D)
Iron Claw - Conscripts Tale (Korea and Kenya)
Geordie & Jack Tyneside Scottish Black Watch
Black Watch and Its Movements (Sampson)

280
BLACKBURN CATHEDRAL
Cathedral Close, Blackburn, Lancashire, BB1 5AA

Tel: 01254 51491
Formed: 596

Enquiries to: Archivist

General description:
Cathedral church mentioned in the Domesday Book.
Collections:
Misericords 8 - 15th century ex Mealthey Abbey
Walker Organ incorporating Cavaille Col.
Stained Glass - Hardman, Morris -19th century
Oak pulpit by White of Norwich - 20th century
Bishop's Throne by Hunstons of Tidewell - 20th century

281
BLACKBURN MUSEUM AND ART GALLERY
Museum Street, Blackburn, Lancashire, BB1 7AJ

Tel: 01254 667130
Fax: 01254 695370
Email: stephen.whittle@blackburn.gov.uk
Formed: 1874

Organisation type and purpose: Local government body, museum, art gallery.

Parent body:
Blackburn with Darwen Borough Council

Enquiries to: Museum Manager & Curator

General description:
Fine and decorative arts, MSS and printed books, numismatics, local history and archaeology, local military history, cotton industry, South Asian arts, icons, Japanese prints.

Collections:
East Lancashire Regimental Collection
Early textile machinery models
Egyptology
Hart Collection of Greek, Roman and British coins
Hart Collection of MSS and printed books
Icon Collection
Lewis Collection of Japanese prints
Lewis Collection of Textile Machinery
Victorian oils and watercolours

Printed publications:
Handlists of Oils, Watercolours, Icons
Turner, The Origins of Genius

Internet home pages:
http://blackburnworld.gov.uk
http://www.blackburn.gov.uk/museum
Exhibitions, outline of collections, shop stock.

282
BLACKGANG SAWMILL AND ST CATHERINE'S QUAY

Blackgang Chine, Ventnor, Isle of Wight, PO38 2HN

Tel: 01983 730330
Fax: 01983 731267
Formed: 1981 & 1984

Organisation type and purpose: Independently owned, museum.

Parent body:
Vectis Ventures Limited
also runs Blackgang Chine

Enquiries to: Managing Director

Access:
Access to staff: By letter, by telephone, visitors by prior appointment
Access to building, collections or gallery: No prior appointment required
Hours: 25 Mar to 3 Nov: Daily, 1000 to 1700
Access for disabled people: Parking provided, toilet facilities

General description:
Features displays of woodworking; the uses of timber; and the general operation of a water-powered Victorian sawmill. There are examples of steam and diesel engines; country life; coastal history; the RNLI; and shipwrecks, including the skeleton of an 84 ft. fin whale.

Information services:
Education services: Resources for Key Stages 1 and 2 and 3..

Catalogues:
Catalogue for part of the collections is only available in-house.

283
BLACKWELL - THE ARTS AND CRAFTS HOUSE

Bo'ness-on-Windermere, Cumbria, LA23 3JR

Tel: 015394 46139
Fax: 015394 88486
Email: info@blackwell.org.uk
Formed: 2001

Organisation type and purpose: Independently owned, registered charity (charity number 562980), museum, art gallery, historic building, house or site, suitable for ages: 8+.

Affiliated to the:
Lakeland Arts Trust
Abbot Hall Art Gallery, Kendal, Cumbria, LA9 5AL, tel: 01539 722464, fax: 01539 722494, email/website: info@abbothall.org.uk

Enquiries to: Curator

Access:
Access to building, collections or gallery: No prior appointment required
Hours: Daily 1000 to 1700 (closing 1600 in winter)
Other restrictions: Gallery closed Christmas to Feb.
Access for disabled people: Parking provided, ramped entry, toilet facilities

General description:
Fine and decorative arts, identification, restoration, etc, artists and craftsmen of Cumbria, past and present. Temporary contemporary exhibitions, the Arts and Crafts movement.

Information services:
Library available for reference (for conditions see Access above)
Special visitor services: Guided tours, materials and/or activities for children.
Education services: Group education facilities, resources for Further or Higher Education.
Services for disabled people: For the hearing impaired.

Collections:
Roderick Gradidge Bequest through Artworkers Guild - important collection of books, magazines, printed articles, furniture and decorative arts objects from the Arts and Crafts period
Collections of furniture by the Simpsons of Kendal, Stanley Davies, Eric Sharpe and Baillie Scott

Printed publications:
Catalogues for specific temporary exhibitions
Vision - yearly review/preview

Address for ordering publications:
Printed publications:
Abbot Hall Art Gallery
Kendal, Cumbria, LA9 5AL, tel: 01539 722464, fax: 01539 722494

Internet home pages:
http://www.blackwell.org.uk
Information on Blackwell History, collections, education service, visitor information, Baillie Scott, the Lakeland Arts Trust.

284
BLAIR CASTLE

Blair Atholl, Pitlochry, Perthshire, PH18 5TI

Tel: 01796 481207
Fax: 01796 481487
Email: office@blair-castle.co.uk

Organisation type and purpose: Historic building, house or site.
Historic house, open to the public, 30 rooms to view, 18th century walled garden.

Enquiries to: Administration Office

Access:
Access to staff: By letter, by telephone, by fax, by email, visitors by prior appointment
Access for disabled people: Parking provided, level entry, toilet facilities

General description:
Dating from 1269, Blair Castle has been the home of the Atholl Family for over 700 years. Set in the dramatic scenery of Strath Garry, it commands a strategic position on the route north, welcoming guests as Scotland's most visited private home.
The skirl of pipes can be heard outside, while within, the 30 rooms on display offer an infinite variety of fine objects, beautiful plasterwork and exceptional collections of arms, china and lace, to mention just a few of the highlights of the tour.
Blair Castle is steeped in history, it is reputed to have been the last castle besieged in Britain, and is home to the only remaining private army in Europe, the Atholl Highlanders. The Castle presents a stirring picture of Scottish life from the 16th century to the present day.

Information services:
Special visitor services: Guided tours.
Services for disabled people: Displays and/or information at wheelchair height.

Internet home pages:
http://www.blair-castle.co.uk

285
BLAIRS MUSEUM, THE

South Deeside Road, Blairs, Aberdeen, AB12 5YQ

Tel: 01224 863767
Email: curator@blairs.net
Full name: Blairs Museum Trust
Formed: 2000
Formerly: Blairs College disbanded in, date of change, 1986

Organisation type and purpose: Independently owned, museum, historic building, house or site, suitable for ages: 16+.

Enquiries to: Manager

Access:
Access to staff: By letter, by telephone, in person, visitors by prior appointment
Access to building, collections or gallery: Prior appointment required
Hours: Wed to Fri, 0900 to 1600; Sat, 1000 to 1700; Sun, 1200 to 1700
Access for disabled people: Parking provided, level entry, access to all public areas, toilet facilities

General description:
Blairs College has been a sanctuary for the treasures of the Roman Catholic Church for over 170 years. This magnificent collection of paintings, gold and silver metal work, embroidered vestments and Jacobite memorabilia was one of Scotland's best-kept secrets. See them now on display in the Blairs Museum.

Information services:
Helpline available, tel no: 01224 863767.
Special visitor services: Guided tours, materials and/or activities for children.
Services for disabled people: For the visually impaired; for the hearing impaired; displays and/or information at wheelchair height.

Collections:
The Blairs Jewel - One of 4 miniature portraits of Mary Queen of Scots, painted secretly before her execution in 1587
Mary Queen of Scots Memorial Portrait - painted from the likeness on one of the 4 miniatures and presented to the Scots College in France in the early 17th century
Portrait of The Old Pretender, James III

Catalogues:
Catalogue for all of the collections is only available in-house.

Internet home pages:
http://www.blairs.net
100 of our best images.

286
BLAISE CASTLE HOUSE MUSEUM

Henbury Road, Henbury, Bristol, BS10 7QS

Tel: 0117 903 9818
Fax: 0117 903 9820
Email: info@bristol-city.gov.uk/museums
Acronym or abbreviation: BCHM
Formed: 1949

Organisation type and purpose: Local government body, museum.

Parent body:
Bristol City Museum and Art Gallery
Queens Road, Clifton, Bristol, BS8 1RL, tel: 0117 9223571, fax: 0117 9039820

Enquiries to: Curator

Access:
Access to staff: By letter, by telephone, visitors by prior appointment
Access to building, collections or gallery: No prior appointment required
Hours: 1 Apr to 31 Oct: Sat to Wed, 1000 to 1700; closed Thu, Fri;
Other restrictions: Closed 1 Nov to 31 Mar.

continued overleaf

Access for disabled people: ramped entry
Other restrictions: Access restricted to certain areas.

General description:
The house was built in 1796 by the Bristol architect William Paty (d. 1800); it now houses the museum. A museum of social history with displays of toys, costume (19th century only) and domestic equipment, eg kitchen equipment, lighting, stoves, sanitary equipment and laundry items. Also display about the history of the Blaize Castle Estate featuring Humphry Repton's Red Book.
Information services:
Library available for reference (for conditions see Access above)
Visitors may collect a key to visit King's Weston Roman Villa in Lawrence Weston.
Special visitor services: Materials and/or activities for children.
Education services: Resources for Key Stage 1..
Collections:
Model trains, dolls and toy soldiers
Victorian toilets and baths
Domestic equipment, cooking, lighting, laundering, 17th-20th century, c. 2500 items
Costumes and accessories, 1750-20th century, c. 6000 items
History of the estate
A Victorian school room
Victorian Picture Room
Friendly Society brasses, West Country, 1800-1850, c. 250 items
Keys, 15th-19th century, c. 300 items
Bristol trades cards, 1750-1850, c. 1500 items
Police truncheons, Constables' staffs, 1790-1850, c. 100 items

Internet home pages:
http://www.bristol-city.gov.uk/museums

287
BLAISE HAMLET
Henbury, Bristol

Tel: 01958 843600 (Regional Office)

Organisation type and purpose: National organisation, registered charity (charity number 205846), historic building, house or site.
Parent body:
National Trust (South West Region)
Wessex Regional Office, tel: 01958 843600

Enquiries to: Manager

General description:
A hamlet of nine different picturesque cottages, designed by John Nash in 1809 for John Harford to accommodate Blaise Estate pensioners.

Internet home pages:
http://www.nationaltrust.org.uk/regions/wessex

288
BLAKE MUSEUM
Blake Street, Bridgwater, Somerset, TA6 3NB

Tel: 01278 456127
Fax: 01278 446412
Email: museums@sedgemoor.gov.uk
Formed: 1926
Formerly: Admiral Blake Museum, date of change, 2001

Organisation type and purpose: Local government body, museum, suitable for ages: all ages.
Parent body:
Sedgemoor District Council
Tel: 01228 435435
Affiliated to:
South West Museums Council

Enquiries to: Administrative Assistant
Other contacts: Cultural Services Manager tel no: 01278 435399 for Museum Curator.
Access:
Access to staff: By letter, by telephone, by fax, by email, visitors by prior appointment
Hours: Tue to Sat, 1000 to 1600

General description:
Robert Blake and the Civil War 1642-1653; local maritime history, local Bridgwater history, Monmouth Rebellion and Battle of Sedgemoor, local industrial archaeology, brick and tile industry.
Information services:
Special visitor services: Guided tours, materials and/or activities for children.
Education services: Group education facilities, resources for Key Stages 1 and 2, 3, 4 and Further or Higher Education.
Services for disabled people: Displays and/or information at wheelchair height.
Collections:
Local history
Admiral Robert Blake
Alford, Symes and Sydenham Families Collection
John Chubb paintings and drawings
Monmouth Rebellion
Oon Smith Photograph Collection
Catalogues:
Catalogue for all of the collections is only available in-house.
Publications list:
is available in hard copy.
Printed publications:
Admiral Blake
Brick and tile industry
Bridgwater Docks and Taunton canal
Bridgwater - Old Photographs (2 volumes)
Museum guide book
Monmouth Rebellion

Internet home pages:
http://www.sedgemoor.gov.uk
Guide to the museum and contacts.

289
BLAKES LOCK MUSEUM

Closed, will reopen in a different form, see Museum of Reading, date of change, 2001
See - Museum of Reading

290
BLAKESLEY HALL
Blakesley Road, Yardley, Birmingham, B25 8RN

Tel: 0121 464 2193
Fax: 0121 464 0400
Formed: 1932 (museum)

Organisation type and purpose: Local government body, registered charity, museum, historic building, house or site, suitable for ages: 5+.
Educational and leisure venue.
Parent body:
Birmingham Museum & Art Gallery (BM&AG)
Chamberlain Square, Birmingham, B3 3DH, tel: 0121 303 2834

Enquiries to: Curatorial Manager
Direct tel: 0121 464 0364
Other contacts: Head of Community Museums, tel: 0121 303 4039 for BM&AG local sites.
Access:
Access to staff: By letter, by telephone, visitors by prior appointment
Hours: Tue to Fri, 0900 to 1600
Access to building, collections or gallery: No prior appointment required
Hours: Tue to Fri, 1300 to 1600; Sat, Sun, 1200 to 1600
Open Bank Holiday Mon
Access for disabled people: Parking provided, level entry, toilet facilities
Other restrictions: Full access to visitor centre, access to ground floor of Hall only.

General description:
Blakesley Hall is a timber-framed farmhouse built in 1590 by Richard Smallbroke. The furniture and furnishings are based on an inventory of the house's contents in 1684 and include original and reproduction material. Displays on Tudor/Stuart domestic life, displays on timber-framed construction, interactive activities for children.

Information services:
Group education services: 0121 303 3890.
Special visitor services: Guided tours, materials and/or activities for children.
Education services: Group education facilities, resources for Key Stages 1 and 2 and 3.
Services for disabled people: For the hearing impaired; displays and/or information at wheelchair height.
Collections:
Domestic items and oak furniture from 16th and 17th centuries
Catalogues:
Catalogue for all of the collections is only available in-house.

Internet home pages:
http://www.bmag.org.uk
General introduction to the site.

291
BLEDDFA CENTRE FOR THE ARTS
Bleddfa, Knighton, Powys, LD7 1PA

Tel: 01547 550377
Fax: 01547 550370
Email: enquires@bleddfacentre.com
Formerly: Bleddfa Trust, date of change, 2001

Organisation type and purpose: Registered charity, museum, art gallery, historic building, house or site, suitable for ages: 5+.

Enquiries to: Administrator
Other contacts: Artistic Director; Gallery Manager; Exhibitions Organiser
Access:
Access to staff: By letter, by telephone, by fax, by email, in person, Internet web pages
Access for disabled people: Parking provided, level entry, access to all public areas, toilet facilities

General description:
Bleddfa Centre for the Arts runs a programme of events, courses and exhibitions that focus on sustainable design. The centre has a design shop, an organic café and a secondhand bookshop. The centre is housed in a Victorian School and stone barn set in the Welsh Marches between Ludlow and Knighton.
Information services:
Education services: Group education facilities.
Services for disabled people: Displays and/or information at wheelchair height.
Collections:
Sculpture:
Tobias and the Angel by Ken Thompson
House For Stories by Tono Mirai (house made of straw and clay permanently on display, 2001)
Paper Tea House by Shigeru Ban (2001)
Printed publications:
Programme and event information (direct on request)

Internet home pages:
http://www.bleddfacentre.com
Events and exhibitions information.

292
BLENHEIM PALACE
Woodstock, Oxfordshire, OX20 1PX

Tel: 01993 811325

Organisation type and purpose: Independently owned, historic building, house or site, suitable for ages: all ages.

Enquiries to: Curator
Direct fax: 01993 813527
Direct email: administrator@blenheimpalace.com
Access:
Access to staff: By letter, by fax, by email, Internet web pages
Access to building, collections or gallery: No prior appointment required
Hours: Mid Mar to end Oct: daily, 1030 to 1730 (last admission 1645)
Access for disabled people: Parking provided, ramped entry, toilet facilities
Other restrictions: Prior enquiry essential.

General description:
18th century palace and landscaped park (Capability Brown), formal gardens.
Information services:
Special visitor services: Guided tours.
Education services: Group education facilities, resources for Key Stages 1 and 2, 3, 4 and Further or Higher Education.
Services for disabled people: Displays and/or information at wheelchair height.
Collections:
Furniture, carpets, porcelain, sculpture, paintings, tapestries
Catalogues:
Catalogue for library is in-house only. Catalogue for all of the collections is only available in-house.
Printed publications:
Guide Book (64pp full colour)
Electronic and video products:
The Blenheim Willis Organ (CD-ROM, tape)
Palace Tour (video)

Internet home pages:
http://www.blenheimpalace.com

293
BLETCHLEY PARK TRUST

The Mansion, Bletchley Park, Bletchley, Milton Keynes, Buckinghamshire, MK3 6EB

Tel: 01908 640404
Fax: 01908 274381
Email: enquiries@bletchleypark.org.uk

Organisation type and purpose: Registered charity (charity number 1012743), museum, historic building, house or site.

Enquiries to: Administrator
Access:
Access to staff: By letter, by telephone, by fax, by email, Internet web pages
Hours: Sat, Sun, 1030 to 1700
Other restrictions: Admission £6, senior citizens £5, parking free.
Access to building, collections or gallery: No prior appointment required
Hours: Sat, Sun, 1030 to 1700
Mon to Fri, public access for guided tour only at 1400, booked tour groups welcome
Access for disabled people: Parking provided, ramped entry, access to all public areas, toilet facilities

General description:
World War II, Enigma and Lorentz machines, codes, cyphers and codebreaking, history of computing, Churchill.
Information services:
Special visitor services: Guided tours.
Education services: Group education facilities, resources for Key Stages 3, 4 and Further or Higher Education..
Collections:
Churchillian memorabilia
Colossus, the world's first large electronic valve computer (rebuilt) and a collection of computers from that time onwards
More than 25 private displays of WWII memorabilia
German and Japanese codes and cyphers, messages and their decipherment
World War II electronics, wireless and radar
Publications list:
is available in hard copy.
Printed publications:
Bletchley Park Reports, a series concerning Colossus, Enigma, codebreaking
Souvenir Guide

Internet home pages:
http://www.bletchleypark.org.uk

294
BLEWCOAT SCHOOL GIFT SHOP

23 Caxton Street, Westminster, London, SW1H 0PY

Tel: 020 7222 2877
Fax: 020 7222 2877

Organisation type and purpose: National organisation, registered charity (charity number 205846), historic building, house or site.
Parent body:
The National Trust (South and South East Region)
Thames and Solent Regional Office, tel: 01494 528051

Enquiries to: Manager
Access:
Access to staff: By letter, by telephone, by fax

General description:
Built in 1709 by a local brewer to provide an education for poor children and in use as a school until 1926. It is now the National Trust London Gift Shop and Information Centre.

Internet home pages:
http://www.nationaltrust.org.uk

295
BLICKLING HALL

Blickling, Norwich, Norfolk, NR11 6NF

Tel: 01263 738030
Fax: 01263 731660
Email: blickling@nationaltrust.org.uk

Organisation type and purpose: National organisation, registered charity (charity number 205846), museum, historic building, house or site, suitable for ages: 8+.
Parent body:
The National Trust (East of England)
East Anglia Regional Office, tel: 0870 609 5388

Enquiries to: Manager
Other contacts: 0870 010 4900 (Events), 01263 738050 (Learning)
Access:
Access for disabled people: Parking provided, toilet facilities
Other restrictions: Designated car parking in main car park. 5 manual wheelchairs available, booking essential. Powered mobility vehicles: 5 singleseater, 1 two-seater, booking essential. Steps to entrance. Accessible entrance via entrance at rear of building to view two rooms. Ground floor fully accessible. Access to lower floor only in Mill. No access to other floors. Photograph album. Chairs without arms are available for resting. Photographs of all inaccessible rooms in album. Level entrance to shop and to restaurant. Grounds largely accessible. Recommended route map.

General description:
Built in the early 17th century and one of England's great Jacobean houses, Blickling is famed for its spectacular long gallery, superb plasterwork ceilings and fine collections of furniture, pictures, books and tapestries. The gardens are full of colour throughout the year, and the extensive parkland features a lake and a series of beautiful woodland and lakeside walks.
Information services:
Braille guide. Large-print guide. Touch list.
Frontcarrying baby slings for loan.
Suitable for school groups. Children's guide. Children's quiz/trail. Education groups welcome. Workshops available.
Taster tours of house at 1200 on most house open days (check on day for availability). Garden tours at 1400 on most garden open days.
Special visitor services: Guided tours, materials and/or activities for children.
Education services: Group education facilities, resources for Key Stages 1 and 2 and 3.
Services for disabled people: For the visually impaired.

Internet home pages:
http://www.nationaltrust.org.uk

296
BLISTS HILL VICTORIAN TOWN

Ironbridge Gorge Museum Trust, Coach Road, Coalbrookdale, Telford, Shropshire, TF8 7DQ

Tel: 01952 583003
Email: info@ironbridge.org.uk
Formed:
Coach Road

Organisation type and purpose: Registered charity (charity number 503717-R), museum, historic building, house or site, suitable for ages: 5+.
Open air museum.
Parent body:
Ironbridge Gorge Museum Trust
Tel: 01952 433522

Enquiries to: General Manager
Access:
Access to staff: By letter, by telephone, by email, in person
Access to building, collections or gallery: No prior appointment required
Hours: 1000 to 1700, daily
Other restrictions: Closed 24th and 25th Jan, 1st Jan.
Closes 1600 in winter. Please check for details.
Access for disabled people: Parking provided, ramped entry, toilet facilities
Other restrictions: The Museum is set on a hill and some parts are fairly steep, but much is easily accessible. Access guide for disabled visitors available on request.

General description:
An open air museum set in 52 acres with 32 different exhibits. Discover what life was really like one hundred years ago, at this recreation of a Victorian community. Working factories, shops and cottages where life is lived - and demonstrated - as it were in Victorian times. Victorian industry, crafts, customs and traditions are brought to life by the townsfolk (dressed in Victorian clothes) who will chat to you and illustrate Britain's fascinating industrial history and social life in the streets and buildings of the town. At Lloyds Bank you can change your money for 'Victorian ' token coins to spend in the shops.
Information services:
Pre-booked guided tours.
Special visitor services: Guided tours, materials and/or activities for children.
Education services: Group education facilities, resources for Key Stages 1 and 2, 3, 4 and Further or Higher Education..

Internet home pages:
http://www.ironbridge.org.uk

297
BLOXHAM VILLAGE MUSEUM

Thatchers, Church Street, Bloxham, Oxfordshire, OX15 4ET

Tel: 01295 721256
Email: peter.barwell@btinternet.com
Formed: 1981

Organisation type and purpose: Independently owned, museum, suitable for ages: 5+.
Village museum.

Enquiries to: Administrator
Other contacts: Joint Curator tel no 01295 720801
Access:
Access to staff: By letter, by email
Access for disabled people: Parking provided, level entry, access to all public areas

General description:
A small local village museum collection which reflects local village life and times throughout its history.
Printed publications:
For p&p, email for cost in first instance
Bloxham Foeffees (20p each plus p&p)

continued overleaf

Bloxham Fire Brigade (£1.50, plus p&p)
Bloxham Railway Station (£1.50, plus p&p)
Explore Old Bloxham (£5, plus p&p)
The Town of Bloxham (£7.50, plus p&p)

298
BLUEBELL RAILWAY PRESERVATION SOCIETY

Sheffield Park Station, Bluebell Railway, Uckfield, East Sussex, TN22 3QL

Tel: 01825 722370, talking timetable; 720800, enquiries, booking
Fax: 01825 720803
Email: gensec@bluebell-railway.co.uk
Acronym or abbreviation: BRPS
Formed: 1960

Organisation type and purpose: Membership association (membership is by subscription), present number of members: 8300, voluntary organisation.
Member of:
Heritage Railways Association (HRA)

Enquiries to: Honorary Secretary
Access:
Access to staff: By letter, by telephone, by fax, by email, Internet web pages

General description:
Preservation of railways, history of railways in Sussex, steam locomotives.
Collections:
Members' lending library
Printed publications:
Bluebell News (quarterly)
Bluebell Railway Historic Collection
Bluebell Railway Stock Book
Bluebell Railway: a pictorial impression
Timetable

Internet home pages:
http://www.bluebell-railway.co.uk
Information on Bluebell rolling stock, catering services, timetable and membership.

299
BOARDMAN'S DRAINAGE MILL

East bank of River Ant, O.S. TG 370 192, How Hill, Norfolk

Organisation type and purpose: , present number of members: 107, historic building, house or site.

General description:
Open-framed timber trestle drainage mill with miniature cap, sails, fantail and turbine.

300
BOARSTALL DUCK DECOY

Boarstall, Nr Aylesbury, Buckinghamshire, HP18 9UX

Tel: 01844 237488
Email: boarstall@nationaltrust.org.uk

Organisation type and purpose: National organisation, registered charity (charity number 205846), historic building, house or site, suitable for ages: all ages.
Parent body:
The National Trust (South & South East Region)
Thames & Solent Regional Office, tel: 01491 528051

Enquiries to: Warden
Access:
Access to staff: By letter, by telephone, by email

General description:
A rare survival of a 17th century decoy in working order, set on a tree-fringed lake, with nature trail and exhibition hall.

Internet home pages:
http://www.nationaltrust.org.uk/regions/

301
BOARSTALL TOWER

Boarstall, Aylesbury, Buckinghamshire, HP18 9UX

Tel: 01844 239339
Email: rob.dixon@boarstall.com

Organisation type and purpose: National organisation, registered charity (charity number 205846), historic building, house or site.
Parent body:
The National Trust (South and South East Region)
Thames and Solent Regional Office, tel: 01494 528051

Enquiries to: Manager
Access:
Access to staff: By letter, by email
Access to building, collections or gallery: No prior appointment required
Hours: Apr to Oct, Wed, 1400 to 1800
Open Bank Holiday Mondays
Other restrictions: Open Sat by prior arrangement with tenant.

General description:
The superb 14th century gatehouse (listed Grade I), and gardens with large moat, of Boarstall House (demolished 1778). John de Haudlo built 'Buckinghamshire's only complete medieval fortified building' in 1312, both as defences for his house and as an expression of his status. Although updated in 1615 for use as a banqueting pavilion or hunting lodge, and to reflect the latest taste, including handsome oriel windows and the upgrading of its fine top floor chamber, it retained its medieval belfry, crossloops, crenellations and other features, so keeping its fortified look, which was still fashionable in Jacobean times. Today, the exterior and many rooms remain virtually unchanged from that time.

Internet home pages:
http://www.nationaltrust.org.uk

302
BOAT MUSEUM, THE

South Pier Road, Ellesmere Port, Cheshire, CH65 4FW

Tel: 0151 355 5017
Fax: 0151 355 4079
Email: info@boatmuseum.freeserve.co.uk
Formed: 1976

Organisation type and purpose: Voluntary organisation, registered charity (charity number 1074541), museum.
Museum of Inland Navigation.
Parent body:
The Waterways Trust
Also part of the Trust:
The Canal Museum
Stoke Bruerne, Towcester, NN12 7SE, tel: 01604 862229
The National Waterways Museum
Llanthony Warehouse, Gloucester Docks, Gloucester, GL1 2EH, tel: 01452 318054

Enquiries to: Operations Manager
Access:
Access to staff: By letter, by telephone, by fax, by email, visitors by prior appointment, Internet web pages
Access for disabled people: Parking provided, toilet facilities

General description:
The history of canals and inland navigable waterways worldwide. The social and industrial history of inland waterways. The full story of canal building and its impact on the way of life. How families lived aboard a narrow boat, their working life and the goods they carried. Domestic life recreated in the dockworkers' cottages at 1840, 1900, 1930 and 1950. Exhibitions of canal ware, arts and crafts. The engines that revolutionised canal transport and cargo handling - still in daily use. Blacksmith's forge and stables exhibition showing how horses were used to tow the boats. Boats under restoration and fully restored boats on display.
Information services:
Special visitor services: Guided tours, tape recorded guides, materials and/or activities for children.
Education services: Group education facilities, resources for Key Stages 1 and 2, 3 and Further or Higher Education.
Services for disabled people: For the visually impaired; displays and/or information at wheelchair height.
Collections:
Library, artefacts, photographs, documents, boatbuilder's drawings, maps, periodicals, film, video, boats and boat models
De Mare Collection, 125 photographs 1945-1955
Hadfield World Canals research
IWA library
Oral archive
Michael Ware Collection, 2500 photographs 1890-1990
Printed publications:
Boat Museum Guide
Educational material for all school ages

Internet home pages:
http://www.boatmuseum.org.uk
Overview, events, education, collection, BMS.

303
BOATH DOOCOT

Auldearn, Nairn, Moray

Organisation type and purpose: Historic building, house or site.
Parent body:
National Trust for Scotland Highlands and Islands Office (North)

General description:
A 17th century doocot on the site of an ancient motte. Montrose defeated the Covenanters nearby in 1645; a battle-plan is on display.

Internet home pages:
http://www.nts.gov.uk

304
BÖD OF GREMISTA MUSEUM

Gremista, Lower Hillhead, Lerwick, Shetland, ZE1 0PX

Tel: 01595 694386
Formed: 1987

Organisation type and purpose: Museum, historic building, house or site, suitable for ages: 12+.
Other addresses:
Shetland Museum
Lower Hillhead, Lerwick, Shetland, ZE1 OEI

Enquiries to: Curator
Direct tel: 01595 695057
Access:
Access to staff: By letter only
Access for disabled people: Parking provided
Other restrictions: Access to lower floor only.

General description:
This 18th century fishing Böd on the outskirts of Lerwick, to the north, is famous for being the birthplace of Arthur Anderson, co-founder of the P and O Company. Expertly restored, this museum covers many aspects of Shetland's maritime past, with special features on Arthur Anderson.

Internet home pages:
http://www.shetland-museum.org.uk/bod/

305
BODELWYDDAN CASTLE

Bodelwyddan, Clwyd, LL18 5YA

Tel: 01745 584060
Fax: 01745 584563
Email: enquiries@bodelwyddan-castle.co.uk
Full name: Bodelwyddan Castle Trust
Formed: 1994

Organisation type and purpose: Registered charity, museum, art gallery, historic building, house or site, suitable for ages: 5+.

Enquiries to: Director
Access:
Access to staff: By letter, by telephone, by fax, by email, Internet web pages
Access to building, collections or gallery: No prior appointment required
Hours: Daily, 1030 to 1700
Winter: Closed Mon and Fri
Access for disabled people: Parking provided, ramped entry, toilet facilities

General description:
The castle is a designated outstation of the National Portrait Gallery and displays in an authentic setting over 100 portraits relevant to the Victorian era from the Gallery's collection. The portraits are supplemented by furniture from the V&A, and sculpture, chiefly of Gibson's work, from the Royal Academy of Arts.
Information services:
Special visitor services: Tape recorded guides.
Education services: Group education facilities, resources for Key Stages 1 and 2, 3, 4 and Further or Higher Education.
Services for disabled people: For the visually impaired; for the hearing impaired; displays and/or information at wheelchair height.
Collections:
Clwyd Fine Arts Trust Collection. A small collection of pictures of local relevance and by North Wales artists
Social History Collection. A small collection of artefacts relevant to the estate
Catalogues:
Catalogue for part of the collections is only available in-house.

Internet home pages:
http://www.bodelwyddan-castle.co.uk

306
BODIAM CASTLE
Bodiam, Robertsbridge, East Sussex, TN32 5UA

Tel: 01580 830436
Fax: 01580 830398
Email: bodiamcastle@ntrust.org.uk

Organisation type and purpose: National organisation, registered charity (charity number 205846), historic building, house or site, suitable for ages: 5+.
Parent body:
The National Trust (South and South East Region)
South East Regional Office, tel: 01372 453401

Enquiries to: Property Manager
Access:
Access to staff: By letter, by telephone, by fax, by email
Access to building, collections or gallery: No prior appointment required
Hours: Jan to 22 Feb, Sat and Sun, 1000 to1600; 23 Feb to end Oct, daily, 1000 to 1800; Nov to beg Feb, Sat and Sun, 1000 to1600
Access for disabled people: Parking provided, toilet facilities
Other restrictions: Designated parking by prior arrangement. Drop-off point. For alternative access tel. Property Manager in advance. Ground floor largely accessible. No access to other floors. Ramped entrance to shop. Level entrance to tea-room.

General description:
One of the most famous and evocative castles in Britain, Bodiam was built in 1385, as both a defence and a comfortable home. The exterior is virtually complete and the ramparts rise dramatically above the moat below. Enough of the interior survives to give an impression of castle life, and there are spiral staircases and battlements to explore.

Internet home pages:
http://www.nationaltrust.org.uk

307
BODMIN AND WENFORD RAILWAY PLC
Bodmin General Station, Lostwithiel Road, Bodmin, Cornwall, PL31 1AQ

Tel: 01208 73666
Fax: 01208 77963
Formed: 1986

Organisation type and purpose: Service industry.
Tourist railway.
Supported by the membership of:
Bodmin Railway Preservation Society
at the same address

Enquiries to: General Manager
Access:
Access to staff: By letter, by telephone, by fax
Hours: Daily, 0900 to 1700
Other restrictions: Trains run on selected dates, March to May, Oct to Dec; daily June to Sept.
Access to building, collections or gallery: No access other than to staff
Access for disabled people: Parking provided, level entry, access to all public areas, toilet facilities

General description:
Steam and diesel locomotives and general railway matters.
Printed publications:
Bodmin and Wenford News (3 times a year, £1.50 (2002) free to BRPS members)

Internet home pages:
http://members.aol.com/bodwenf

308
BODMIN TOWN MUSEUM
Mount Folly, Bodmin, Cornwall, PL31 2HQ

Tel: 01208 77067
Fax: 01208 79268
Email: bodmin.museum@ukonline.co.uk
Formed: 1983

Organisation type and purpose: Museum.
Local history museum.

Enquiries to: Curator
Access:
Access to staff: By letter, by telephone, by email

General description:
Early history: rocks, minerals and fossils; local history: law and order, domestic life, railways, Victoriana, agriculture, World Wars I and II, Fire Brigade, trades and occupations.
Collections:
Collection of material covering all aspects of local history. Includes displays of fossils; minerals; a Victorian kitchen; and a fire engine.

309
BOGNOR REGIS LOCAL HISTORY SOCIETY AND MUSEUM
69 High Street, Bognor Regis, West Sussex, PO21 1RY

Tel: 01243 865636
Formed: 1997
Formed from: Bognor Regis Local History Society

Organisation type and purpose: Voluntary organisation, registered charity (charity number 286590), museum, suitable for ages: 5+.
Links:
Bognor Regis Wireless Museum
at the same address

Enquiries to: Curator
Access:
Access to staff: By letter, by telephone, in person
Hours: Tue to Sun and Bank Holidays, 1030 to 1630
Access to building, collections or gallery: No access other than to staff
Hours: Tue to Sun and Bank Holidays, 1030 to 1630
Access for disabled people: level entry
Other restrictions: 90% access to all areas.

General description:
Local history, radio.
Printed publications:
Local History Newsletters
Various other publications

310
BOLLING HALL MUSEUM
Bowling Hall Road, Bradford, West Yorkshire, BD4 7LP

Tel: 01274 723057
Fax: 01274 726220
Email: abickley@legend.co.uk
Formed: 1915

Organisation type and purpose: Museum.

Enquiries to: Curator
Access:
Access to staff: By letter, by telephone, by fax, by email, in person, visitors by prior appointment
Hours: For visits: Wed to Fri, 1100 to 1600; Sat, 1000 to 1700; Sun, 1200 to 1700; Bank Holiday Mon, 1100 to 1600; Telephone: Mon to Sat, 0900 to 1700; Sun, 1200 to 1700; fax and email at all times
Other restrictions: Appointments necessary for Curatorial Staff as they are not always available during opening times.
Access to building, collections or gallery: No access other than to staff
Access for disabled people: level entry, toilet facilities

General description:
Fine example of a Yorkshire stone house; the present building was begun about 1450 and received additions and alterations in the 17th and 18th centuries. The collections and displays reflect this long history.
Information services:
Curatorial staff also have information on the history of Bradford and on English costume.
Special visitor services: Tape recorded guides.
Education services: Group education facilities, resources for Key Stages 1 and 2 and 3.
Services for disabled people: For the visually impaired; for the hearing impaired.
Collections:
Grade 1 Listed Building
Fine 17th and 18th century furniture and associated social history items
Catalogues:
Catalogue for all of the collections is only available in-house.

Internet home pages:
http://www.bradford.gov.uk/tourism/museums/bolling.htm
General information.

311
BOLSOVER CASTLE
Castle Street, Bolsover, Chesterfield, Derbyshire, S44 6PR

Tel: 01246 822844
Fax: 01246 241569

Organisation type and purpose: Historic building, house or site, suitable for ages: 5+.
Parent body:
English Heritage (East Midlands Region)
44 Derngate, Northampton, NN1 1UH, tel: 01604 735400, fax: 01604 735401

Enquiries to: Custodian
Other contacts: Switchboard at East Midlands Regional Office
Access:
Access to staff: By letter, by telephone, in person

General description:
A 17th century country house built on the site of a Norman fortress, Bolsover boasts spectacular wall paintings, rich panelling, elaborate fireplaces and painted ceilings, as well as a glorious enclosed garden in which the recently-

continued overleaf

restored Venus Fountain plays again for the first time in centuries.
Information services:
Free children's activity sheets.
School room to be pre-booked.
Audiovisual displays and interactive scale model of the little castle.
Open-air concerts, crafts and garden shows during the summer.
Special visitor services: Tape recorded guides, materials and/or activities for children.
Education services: Group education facilities..
Publications list:
is available in hard copy.

Address for ordering publications:
Printed publications:
Val Horsler, English Heritage
23 Savile Row, London, W1S 2ET

Internet home pages:
http://www.english-heritage.org.uk

312
BOLTON ABBEY
See - Priory of St Mary and St Cuthbert

313
BOLTON MUSEUMS, ART GALLERY AND AQUARIUM
Le Mans Crescent, Bolton, Lancashire, BL1 1SE

Tel: 01204 332211
Fax: 01204 332241
Email: museums@bolton.gov.uk
Formed: 1893

Organisation type and purpose: Local government body, museum, art gallery, suitable for ages: all ages.
Other addresses:
Hall i' th' Wood Museum
Green Way, off Crompton Way, Bolton, BL1 8UA, tel: 01204 332370

Enquiries to: Chief Museums Officer
Direct email: steve.garland@bolton.gov.uk
Access:
Access to staff: By letter, by telephone, by fax, by email, in person, Internet web pages
Hours: Mon to Sat, 1000 to 1700
Other restrictions: Closed Sun and Bank Holidays.
Access for disabled people: ramped entry, access to all public areas, toilet facilities

General description:
Covers British natural history; British archaeology; Egyptian antiquities; early textile collections and machinery; fine and applied art from the 18th century to the present; and 14th and 15th century buildings.
Information services:
Library available for reference (for conditions see Access above)
Special visitor services: Materials and/or activities for children.
Education services: Group education facilities, resources for Key Stages 1 and 2, 3 and Further or Higher Education.
Services for disabled people: For the visually impaired.
Collections:
Kershaw Collection, decorative panels and doors by Thomas Kershaw (1819-1898), the great Victorian grainer and marbler, born near Bolton, mid 19th century
British Drawings and Watercolours Collection, fine works by many of the masters of the 18th to 20th century, c. 800 items
Mass Observation Collection, unique group of works relating to movement which was based in Bolton in late 1930s (photographs, paintings, prints), 1930s
British Sculpture Collection, important works by Epstein, Moore, Hepworth, McWilliam, Frink, Chadwick, Paolozzi, 20th century, c. 50 items
Early Textiles, Egyptian and Sudanese textiles, c. 5000 BC to 12th century AD, c. 1500 items
Early Textile Machinery, unique spinning machinery, 18th and 19th century, 37 items
Bolton Textiles, samples of local spinning and weaving, 17th to 20th century, c. 255,000 items
Bolton Bricks, locally made bricks, tiles, sanitary ware, 18th to 20th century
Bolton Horology, locally made watches and clocks, 18th to 20th century
Skip Making, collection from local skip works 19th and 20th century, c. 500 items
Samuel Crompton, material relating to Bolton inventor, 18th to 20th century
Biological Collections, local voucher material, 1850 onwards, 10,000 items
Geological Collections, local voucher material. 1900 onwards, 1000 items
Biological Collections, type specimens, 1800 onwards, 300 items

Internet home pages:
http://www.boltonmuseums.org.uk

314
BOMBER COMMAND MUSEUM
See - Royal Air Force Museum

315
BONDGATE GALLERY
22 Narrowgate, Alnwick, Northumberland, NE66 1JG

Tel: 01665 577088

Organisation type and purpose: Registered charity (charity number 507005), art gallery, historic building, house or site.
Other address:
Honorary Secretary
Bondgate Gallery
49 Woodstead, Embleton, NE66 3XY

Enquiries to: Honorary Secretary
Direct tel: 01665 576450
Access:
Access to building, collections or gallery: No prior appointment required
Hours: Mon to Sat, 1030 to 1600
Access for disabled people: level entry, access to all public areas, toilet facilities

General description:
An art gallery run by the Alnwick and District Arts Association on a voluntary basis to stimulate an interest in contemporary arts and crafts in Alnwick and surrounding areas, and to provide facilities for artists to exhibit their work.

316
BO'NESS AND KINNEIL RAILWAY
Bo'ness Station, Union Street, Bo'ness, West Lothian, EH51 9AQ

Tel: 01506 825855
Fax: 01506 828766
Email: museum@railway.srps.org.uk
Formed: 1961
Formed from: Scottish Railway Preservation Society (SRPS)

Organisation type and purpose: Membership association, voluntary organisation, registered charity (charity number SCO 02375), museum, suitable for ages: all ages.
Steam railway.
Member of:
Heritage Railway Association (HRA)
Operators:
Scottish Railway Preservation Society (SRPS)

Enquiries to: Administrator
Direct tel: 01506 822298 (Talking Timetable)
Access:
Access to staff: By letter, by telephone, by fax, in person, Internet web pages
Access for disabled people: Parking provided, ramped entry, toilet facilities

General description:
Historic railway buildings and artefacts from Scottish Railways Passenger Services, steam and diesel traction. Operating steam and diesel trains over a 17 minute journey; extensive railway yard.
Information services:
Helpline available, tel no: 01506 822298.
Special visitor services: Materials and/or activities for children.
Education services: Group education facilities.
Services for disabled people: For the visually impaired; for the hearing impaired.
Collections:
Extensive collection of locomotives, carriages and wagons on display in the Scottish Railway Exhibition (major extension to SRE opened during 2002).
Printed publications:
Bo'ness and Kinneil Railway Guide Book
Bo'ness and Kinneil Railway Stock List
Bo'ness and Kinneil Railway 2002 Leaflet
SRPS Railtours 2002 Programme
Education Pack for Children 5-14

Internet home pages:
http://www.srps.org.uk

317
BO'NESS DEVELOPMENT TRUST
17-19 North Street, Bo'ness, West Lothian, EH51 0AQ

Tel: 01506 825855
Fax: 01506 828766
Email: johnburnie@parkave.freeserve.co.uk
Acronym or abbreviation: BDT
Formed: 1991
Formerly: Bo'ness Heritage Trust, date of change, 1991

Organisation type and purpose: Registered charity (charity number SCO 22020), museum, historic building, house or site, suitable for ages: 8+.
Operation of Birkhill Fireclay Mine as a public facility.
Other address:
Birkhill Fireclay Mine
Birkhill, By Bo'ness

Enquiries to: Chairman
Access:
Access to staff: By letter, by telephone, by fax, by email
Access for disabled people: Parking provided

General description:
There are two main collections: (i) Hamilton's Cottage - a working man's cottage from the 1920s, containing a black-lead range and various other artefacts; (ii) Birkhill Fireclay Mine, Birkhill, by Bo'ness - a unique walk-in underground experience showing how fireclay was mined and containing 300 million-year-old fossils.

318
C M BOOTH COLLECTION OF HISTORIC VEHICLES
Falstaff Antiques, 63-67 High Street, Rolvenden, Kent, TN17 4LP

Tel: 01580 241234
Formed: 1972

Organisation type and purpose: Independently owned, museum.

Enquiries to: Curator
Access:
Access to staff: By letter, by telephone, visitors by prior appointment
Access to building, collections or gallery: No prior appointment required
Hours: Mon to Sat, 1000 to 1730

General description:
A collection of 15 Morgan 3 wheel cars, 1913-1916. Other vehicles include a 1929 Ford, a 1929 Morris Van, a 1904 Humber Tricar, and a 1936 Bampton Caravan. Motorcycles include a 1911

Premier, a 1911 P and M Combination, a 1923 Levis, a 1930 Velocette, a 1941 Corgi, and a 1941 New Hudson. Bicycles include an 1880 Ordinary, an 1890 Quadrant, an 1895 Quadrant, a 1914 Sunbeam, a 1920 Sunbeam, a 1923 Dayton, a 1936 Raleigh, and a 1936 Hercules Tandem. There is much automobilia, plus toy and model cars.
Catalogues:
Catalogue for part of the collections is only available in-house.

319
BOOTH MUSEUM OF NATURAL HISTORY

194 Dyke Road, Brighton, East Sussex, BN1 5AA

Tel: 01273 292777
Fax: 01273 292778
Email: boothmus@pavilion.co.uk
Formed: 1874
Formerly: Brighton and Hove Natural History Society

Organisation type and purpose: Local government body, museum.
Parent body:
Brighton & Hove Council

Enquiries to: Keeper of Booth Museum
Direct tel: 01273 292780
Access:
Access to staff: By letter, by telephone, by fax, by email, in person
Hours: Mon to Fri, 0900 to 1700

General description:
Natural history, British birds, world butterflies, geology.
Collections:
Museum houses over half a million specimens and natural history literature and data extending back over three centuries, including British birds mounted in natural settings, world butterflies, animal skeletons and geological specimens
Extensive library (reference only)

Internet home pages:
http://www.brighton-hove.gov.uk

320
BORDER REGIMENT AND KING'S OWN ROYAL BORDER REGIMENT MUSEUM

Queen Mary's Tower, The Castle, Carlisle, Cumbria, CA3 8UR

Tel: 01228 532774
Fax: 01228 521275
Email: RHQ@kingsownborder.demon.co.uk
Formed: 1932
Formerly: Border Regiment Museum

Organisation type and purpose: Registered charity (charity number 271943), museum.
To collect, preserve & interpret material relating to the history of the Regiment from 1702 to the present day.
Governing body:
Regimental Museum Trustees
Museum supported by the:
King's Own Royal Border Regiment
MOD

Enquiries to: Curator
Access:
Access to staff: By letter, by telephone, by fax, by email, visitors by prior appointment

General description:
34th (Cumberland) Regiment and 55th (Westmorland) Regiment, 1702-1881; the Border Regiment, 1881-1959; King's Own Royal Border Regiment, 1959 to present day; Cumberland and Westmorland Militias and Rifle Volunteers; Westmorland and Cumberland Yeomanry; history, dress, personnel, documents.
Information services:
Library available for reference (for conditions see Access above)
Embryonic database established for individual soldiers' records. Information on all aspects of Regiment's history available. The Museum will deal with all enquiries and handle genealogical/family history enquiries.
Guided tours by prior arrangement.
Special visitor services: Guided tours.
Education services: Group education facilities, resources for Key Stages 1 and 2, 3, 4 and Further or Higher Education..
Collections:
Substantial archive of books, documents and photographs relating to the history of the regiment as a whole
Catalogues:
Catalogue for library is in-house only. Catalogue for all of the collections is only available in-house.
Publications list:
is available in hard copy.
Printed publications:
Catalogue of Documents available in Museum Library
Guide to the Museum
Lions of England - A Pictorial History of The King's Own Royal Regiment (Lancaster) 1680-1980 (Eastwood S, £15.00 plus p&p £2.50)
Off at Last - An Illustrated History of the 7th (Galloway) Battalion KOSB 1939-45 (Sigmund R, £20 plus p&p £3)
The Lion and The Dragon (Regimental Magazine- 2002 edn £6.00 plus p&p £1.25; back copies available)
The Little Men (Cooper K W, Burma 1945, £6.95 plus p&p)
When Dragons Flew - An Illustrated History of the 1st Battalion The Border Regiment 1939-45 (Eastwood S, Gray C and Green A, £19.95 include p&p in UK)
The Black Angel (Colin Bardgett, 1997, £8.95 plus £1 p&p)
Electronic and video products:
Cassette and Video of King's Own Royal Border regimental band available

Internet home pages:
http://www.armymuseums.org.uk
General information, hours, location, facilities.

321
BORDESLEY ABBEY

See - Forge Mill Museum & Bordesley Abbey Visitor Centre

322
BORROWDALE

Unit 2A, 13 High Hill, Keswick, Cumbria, CA12 5LU

Tel: 017687 73780 (information/shop)
Fax: 017687 74649
Email: borrowdale@nationaltrust.org.uk

Organisation type and purpose: National organisation, registered charity (charity number 205846), historic building, house or site, suitable for ages: 8+.
Parent body:
National Trust (North West Area)
North West Regional Office, tel: 0870 609 5391

Enquiries to: Property Manager
Direct tel: 017687 74649
Access:
Access for disabled people: toilet facilities
Other restrictions: Several sites and paths are accessible. Access to Friar's Crag, the Bowder Stone, Crow Park, Cat Bells Terrace, Calf Close Bay, Castlerigg Stone Circle and the shore of Derwentwater at Brandelhow; strong companions recommended at all sites for wheelchair users. Adapted WC in municipal car park.

General description:
The location of the Trust's first acquisition in the Lake District: Brandelhow Woods, on the shore of Derwentwater. Total NT protection in the area today covers 11,806ha (29,173 acres), including eleven farms, half of Derwentwater (including the main islands), the hamlet of Watendlath and well-known sites such as the Bowder Stone, Friar's Crag, Ashness Bridge and Castlerigg Stone Circle, a free-standing megalithic monument of 38 stones near Keswick.

Internet home pages:
http://www.nationaltrust.org.uk

323
BOSCOBEL HOUSE AND THE ROYAL OAK

Bewood, Bishop's Wood, Shifnal, Shropshire, ST19 9AR

Tel: 01902 850244

Organisation type and purpose: National organisation, advisory body, historic building, house or site.
Parent body:
English Heritage (West Midlands Region)
Tel: 0121 625 6820

Enquiries to: Manager
Access:
Access to staff: By letter, by telephone
Access to building, collections or gallery: No prior appointment required
Hours: 1 Mar to 30 Sep: daily, 1000 to 1800,1 to 31 Oct: daily, 1000 to 1700,1 to 30 Nov: Wed-Sun, 1000 to 1600
Other restrictions: Closed 1 Dec to 28 Feb
Opening times are subject to change, for up-to-date information contact English Heritage by phone or visit the website
Admission to house by guide tour only. Last tour one hour before closing.

General description:
Likely to have been built around 1632, the beautiful, but modest, timber-framed Boscobel House was originally intended as a hunting lodge. However, tradition holds that its true purpose was as a secret place for the shelter of Catholics in time of need, and visitors can hear tales of the 'Priest Holes' during a guided tour. Following his defeat at Worcester, the future Charles II evaded capture by sheltering in what is now known as the Royal Oak.
Information services:
Free children's activity sheets.
'Escape from Worcester' exhibition.
Special visitor services: Guided tours, materials and/or activities for children.
Education services: Group education facilities..

Internet home pages:
http://www.english-heritage.org.uk

324
BOTANIC GARDENS MUSEUM

Botanic Gardens, Southport, Merseyside, PR9 7NB

Tel: 01704 227547
Fax: 01704 224112
Email: info@seftonarts.co.uk
Formed: 1876

Organisation type and purpose: Local government body, museum, suitable for ages: 5+.

Enquiries to: Curator
Access:
Access to staff: By letter, by telephone
Access for disabled people: Parking provided, ramped entry

General description:
The museum has a temporary exhibition programme. There are two local history galleries, a natural history gallery and a Victorian room.
Information services:
Helpline available, tel no: 01704 227547.
Special visitor services: Tape recorded guides.
Services for disabled people: Displays and/or information at wheelchair height.
Collections:
Local History
Victoriana

continued overleaf

Natural History
Geology
Ceramics
Herbarium
Printed publications:
Maritime Catalogue and Guide to museum collection (available direct)

Internet home pages:
http://www.seftonarts.co.uk
Opening hours, exhibition details.

325
BOUGHTON HOUSE

The Living Landscape Trust, Boughton House, Kettering, Northamptonshire, NN14 1BJ

Tel: 01536 515731
Fax: 01536 417255
Email: llt@boughtonhouse.org.uk
Formed: 1986

Organisation type and purpose: Registered charity (charity number 292971), historic building, house or site, suitable for ages: all ages. Private house with fine arts collection.
To show the interrelationship between the Montagu family (Duke of Buccleuch & Queensbury) and its fine art collection with the surrounding traditional but modern run country estate.

Enquiries to: Director
Access:
Access to staff: By letter, by telephone, by fax, by email, visitors by prior appointment, Internet web pages
Access to building, collections or gallery: No prior appointment required
Hours: 1 Aug to 1 Sep: daily, 1300 to 1700 (house: 1400 to 1630)
Other restrictions: Prior appointment required outside public opening times.
Access for disabled people: Parking provided, ramped entry, level entry, toilet facilities

General description:
A stately home dating from 15th century monastic origins, culminating in the Versailles style of 1655. Fine arts - principally late 15th to late 18th century, English and European. Important collections of paintings, furniture, tapestries, needlework, carpets, porcelain, arms and silver.
The house is set in a Grade One listed park (500 acre).
Information services:
On-line searching
Conservation, education and countryside activities.
Special visitor services: Guided tours.
Education services: Group education facilities..
Collections:
Special Collections
Buccleuch. European fine arts. 17th and 18th century.
Catalogues:
Catalogue for library is in-house only. Catalogue for all of the collections is only available in-house.
Printed publications:
Boughton House - The English Versailles (ed Murdoch T, £100)
Guide Book
Postcards - varied selection of exteriors and collection

Internet home pages:
http://www.boughtonhouse.org.uk
Comprehensive site, over 500 pages giving full details of the House, Collection and Estate, including a virtual tour of the House.

326
BOURNE HALL MUSEUM

Spring Street, Bourne Hall, Ewell, Surrey, KT17 1UF

Tel: 020 8394 1734
Fax: 020 8786 7265
Email: j.harte@bournehall.free-online.co.uk
Formed: 1969

Organisation type and purpose: Local government body, museum, suitable for ages: all ages.

Enquiries to: Curator
Access:
Access to staff: By letter, by telephone, by email, visitors by prior appointment
Access to building, collections or gallery: No prior appointment required
Hours: Mon to Sat, 0900 to 1700; Sun, 0900 to 1200
Access for disabled people: Parking provided, ramped entry, access to all public areas, toilet facilities

General description:
The local Museum of Epsom and Ewell. Life on the London fringe of Surrey in the last two hundred years is illustrated by social history collections, especially costume, kitchenwear, tools and toys. It also includes the social history of The Derby, the Dorling Family including Isabella Beeton, 17th and 18th century wallpapers of the district, and the Roman archaeology of Ewell.
Information services:
Education services: Group education facilities, resources for Key Stages 1 and 2.
Services for disabled people: For the hearing impaired; displays and/or information at wheelchair height.
Collections:
Collections and archives relate to:
The Roman Town of Ewell
The Tudor Palace of Nonsuch
Social history, domestic science, tools, costume, canvas, local photographs and ephemera
Dorling archive, racecards for the Derby, 19th century, 50 items
Ashley Centre, clay pipes, early 18th century, 100 items
The Horton cluster of mental hospitals
Catalogues:
Catalogue for all of the collections is only available in-house.
Publications list:
is available on-line.

Internet home pages:
http://www.epsom.townpage.co.uk/bhmuseum.htm
Visitor information, guide to Museum, details of exhibitions and local history.

327
BOURNE MILL

Bourne Road, Colchester, Essex, CO2 8RT

Tel: 01206 572422

Organisation type and purpose: National organisation, registered charity (charity number 205846), historic building, house or site.
Parent body:
The National Trust (East of England)
East Anglia Regional Office, tel: 0870 609 5388

Enquiries to: Manager
Access:
Access to staff: By letter, by telephone

General description:
The mill was originally built as a fishing lodge in 1591 and features stepped 'Dutch' gables. There is a millpond, and some of the machinery, including the waterwheel, is intact and working.

Internet home pages:
http://www.nationaltrust.org.uk

328
BOURNEMOUTH AVIATION MUSEUM

Hanger 600, Bournemouth International Airport, Hurn, Christchurch, Dorset, BH23 6SE

Tel: 01202 580858
Fax: 01202 580858
Email: admin@aviation-museum.co.uk
Formed: 1998

Organisation type and purpose: Registered charity, museum, suitable for ages: all ages. Preservation and display of vintage military and civil aircraft.

Enquiries to: Manager
Access:
Access to staff: By letter, by telephone, by fax, by email, in person, Internet web pages
Access for disabled people: Parking provided, level entry

General description:
An aviation museum consisting of more than 20 different types of aircraft built mainly in the 1950s. Approximately half of the aircraft are in flying condition and include a number of first generation military jet fighters. A small percentage of the aircraft allow access to the cockpit by members of the public and the museum has a shop, model room and picnic area adjacent to the main runway at Bournemouth International Airport.
Information services:
Special visitor services: Guided tours, materials and/or activities for children..
Printed publications:
Brochure
Electronic and video products:
A CD-ROM covering all exhibits and activities of the museum (available from the shop or by post)

Internet home pages:
http://www.aviation-museum.co.uk

329
BOURNEMOUTH BEARS

See - Dorset Teddy Bear House

330
BOWES MUSEUM, THE

Barnard Castle, Co Durham, DL12 8NP

Tel: 01833 690606
Fax: 01833 637163
Email: info@bowesmuseum.org.uk
Formed: 1892
Changed to: Independent charitable trust (The Bowes Museum Company Limited), date of change, 2002
Formerly: A private museum run by trustees, date of change, 1956

Organisation type and purpose: Independently owned, registered charity (charity number 1079639), museum, suitable for ages: 5+.
Member of:
Museums Association
North of England Museums Service

Enquiries to: Marketing Assistant
Direct email: louise.stephenson@bowesmuseum.org.uk
Access:
Access to staff: By letter, by telephone, by fax, in person, charges made to all users
Access for disabled people: Parking provided, ramped entry, toilet facilities
Other restrictions: Wheelchair access except two galleries in vaults.

General description:
European painting from almost all schools from the 15th to 19th centuries; decorative arts of that range and period; archaeology of County Durham; local history of Teesdale, Durham and Yorkshire area; conservation (art and textile). Temporary exhibitions.
Information services:
Guided tours - £1.
Special visitor services: Guided tours, tape recorded guides, materials and/or activities for children.
Education services: Group education facilities, resources for Key Stages 1 and 2, 3, 4 and Further or Higher Education.
Services for disabled people: Displays and/or information at wheelchair height.

Collections:
Library of John and Josephine Bowes
Library of John Davidson, Ridley Hall
Catalogues:
Catalogue for part of the collections is on-line.
Printed publications:
Catalogue of Spanish Paintings (1988)
French Decorative Arts of the 18th Century (1986)
Guide Book to the Museum
Hoard of Bronze Age Metalwork (1983)
Selection of Twenty Quilts and Patchwork Bedcovers (1985)
Traditional Working Clothes of Northern England (1983)
Electronic and video products:
Art books on Durham County Library service database, terminals in libraries
Local history and French collections on University of Durham database

Internet home pages:
http://www.bowesmuseum.org.uk

331
BOWES RAILWAY MUSEUM
Springwell Village, Gateshead, Tyne and Wear, NE9 7QJ

Tel: 0191 416 1847/3349
Formed: 1976

Organisation type and purpose: Membership association (membership is by subscription), present number of members: 75, voluntary organisation, registered charity (charity number 511961), museum, historic building, house or site, suitable for ages: all ages.
Scheduled ancient monument.
Affiliated to:
Heritage Railway Association

Enquiries to: Curator
Direct tel: 0191 419 3349 (Mondays only)
Direct email: alison_gibson77@hotmail.com
Other contacts: Secretary, tel: 0191 487 7548 for bookings.
Access:
Access to staff: By letter, by telephone, by email, visitors by prior appointment
Hours: Wed afternoons and operating days
Access for disabled people: Parking provided, toilet facilities
Other restrictions: Restricted wheelchair access.

General description:
Victorian railway/colliery workshops, steam locomotives, operation, maintenance, history and preservation of rope-hauled railways (the last preserved standard gauge in the world), coal mining and underground colliery locomotives.
Information services:
Special visitor services: Guided tours.
Education services: Group education facilities, resources for Key Stages 1 and 2..
Collections:
Archival material: photographs, technical drawings, plans and maps, as well as tools, patten parts etc, relating to the history of Bowes Railway and connected collieries 1826 to 1974
Catalogues:
Catalogue for library is in-house only.
Printed publications:
Incline (magazine, quarterly, £1.50, free to members)
Site Guide
Electronic and video products:
Bowes Line (video on sale in shop)
CD-ROM under development

Internet home pages:
http://www.bowesrailway.co.uk

332
BOWHILL HOUSE
Selkirk, Borders, TD7 5HE

Tel: 01750 20732
Fax: 01750 22204
Email: bht@buccleuch.com

Acronym or abbreviation: BHT
Full name: Buccleuch Heritage Trust
Formed: 1974

Organisation type and purpose: Independently owned, registered charity, historic building, house or site, suitable for ages: 5+.
Education.

Enquiries to: Education Officer
Access:
Access to staff: By letter, by fax, by email
Access to building, collections or gallery: Prior appointment required
Hours: House: Jul, daily, 1300 to 1630
Country Park: mid Apr to end Aug, daily 1200 to 1700 except Fri (but open Fri in Aug)
Other restrictions: Open all year by appointment for specialist educational courses and for school and museum groups.
Access for disabled people: Parking provided, ramped entry, access to all public areas, toilet facilities

General description:
History of house and estate. History of Buccleuch collections of fine art, furniture, silver and porcelain, Education Officer on site.
Monmouth, Sir Walter Scott and Queen Victoria Relics.
Information services:
Nature trails
Audiovisual presentation
Visitors centre
Special visitor services: Guided tours, materials and/or activities for children.
Education services: Group education facilities, resources for Further or Higher Education..
Collections:
Famous artists include:
Guardi, Canaletto, Claude, Gainsborough
Display of Portrait Miniatures
17th/18th century French and 19th century British furniture and porcelain
Printed publications:
House Guide (£3)
Children's Guide (£2)
Leaflet (free)

333
BOX HILL
The Old Fort, Box Hill Road, Box Hill, Tadworth, Surrey, KT20 7LB

Tel: 01306 885502

Organisation type and purpose: National organisation, registered charity (charity number 205846), historic building, house or site, suitable for ages: all ages.
Parent body:
The National Trust (South & South East Region)
South East Regional Office, tel: 01372 453401

Enquiries to: Head Warden
Other contacts: Education Officer 01306 875030
Access:
Access to staff: By letter, by telephone, by email
Access to building, collections or gallery: No prior appointment required
Hours: Daily, throughout the year
Access for disabled people: Parking provided, toilet facilities

General description:
An outstanding area of woodland and chalk downland, long famous as a destination for daytrippers from London, but surprisingly extensive and with much to offer the rambler and naturalist. There are many beautiful walks and spectacular views towards the South Downs. On the summit there is an information centre, shop, servery and a fort dating from the 1890s (access to exterior only).

Internet home pages:
http://www.nationaltrust.org.uk/regions/

334
BRACKEN HALL COUNTRYSIDE CENTRE
Glen Road, Baildon, Shipley, West Yorkshire, BD17 5EA

Tel: 01274 584140
Fax: 01274 584140
Formed: 1981

Organisation type and purpose: Local government body, museum, suitable for ages: 5+.

Enquiries to: Countryside Interpretive Officer
Other contacts: Group Visit Officer
Access:
Access to staff: By letter, by telephone, in person
Access for disabled people: level entry, access to all public areas, toilet facilities

General description:
Displays of local and natural history, tanks of 'Pond Life' animals and an observation beehive.
Sale of natural history books; wildlife garden; children's holiday activities.
Information services:
Library available for reference (for conditions see Access above)
Special visitor services: Guided tours, materials and/or activities for children.
Education services: Resources for Key Stages 1 and 2, 3, 4 and Further or Higher Education.
Services for disabled people: Displays and/or information at wheelchair height.

335
BRADENHAM VILLAGE
Nr High Wycombe, Buckinghamshire

Tel: 01494 528051

Organisation type and purpose: National organisation, registered charity (charity number 205846), historic building, house or site.
Parent body:
National Trust (South & South East Region)
Thames & Solent Regional Office, tel: 01494 528051

Enquiries to: Manager
Access:
Access to building, collections or gallery: No prior appointment required
Hours: All year
Other restrictions: Manor house not open.

General description:
The church and 17th century manor house (not open) provide an impressive backdrop to the sloping village green. The manor was once the home of Isaac D'Israeli, father of Benjamin Disraeli, who lived nearby at Hughenden Manor.
A network of paths provides easy access for walkers to explore the delightful surrounding countryside, which includes hills, farmlands and classic Chilterns beech-woods.

Internet home pages:
http://www.nationaltrust.org.uk

336
BRADFORD ART GALLERIES AND MUSEUMS
Cartwright Hall, Lister Park, Bradford, West Yorkshire, BD9 4NS

Tel: 01274 751212
Fax: 01274 481045
Formed: 1904

Organisation type and purpose: Local government body, art gallery.
Art Collections.
Parent body:
Bradford Metropolitan District Council
Tel: 01274 752111
Funded jointly with the:
Arts Council
Museums and Galleries Commission

continued overleaf

Constituent galleries & museum:
Bolling Hall Museum
Bolling Hall Road, Bradford
Bradford Industrial Museum & Horses at Work
Moorside Road, Bradford, tel: 01274 631756, fax: 01274 636362
Cartwright Hall Art Gallery
Lister Park, Bradford, tel: 01274 751212, fax: 01274 481045
Cliffe Castle Museum
Spring Gardens Lane, Keighley, tel: 01535 618230
Manor House Museum
Castle Yard, Ilkley, tel: 01943 600066

Enquiries to: Marketing Officer
Access:
Access to staff: By letter, by telephone, by fax
Hours: Public: Tue to Sat, 1000 to 1700; Sun, 1300 to 1700

General description:
Sculpture, contemporary 19th and 20th century art and print, decorative art, printmaking, ethnic collections, art and artefacts from the Indian sub-continent.
Collections:
Collections of neo-classical paintings, British Impressionism and contemporary prints
Collections from the Sub-Continent
Printed publications:
Catalogues, leaflets and books
Electronic and video products:
Art Connections - Cultural Links (CD-ROM, £30)

Internet home pages:
http://www.bradford.gov.uk

337
BRADFORD HERITAGE RECORDING UNIT
Bradford Industrial Museum, Moorside Road, Bradford, West Yorkshire, BD2 3HP

Tel: 01274 631756
Fax: 01274 636362
Acronym or abbreviation: BHRU
Formed: 1983

Organisation type and purpose: Museum, research organisation.
Photographic and oral history archive.
Parent body:
Department of Art, Heritage and Leisure

Enquiries to: Co-ordinator
Access:
Access to staff: By letter, by telephone, by fax
Access to building, collections or gallery: No prior appointment required

General description:
Social and industrial history of the Bradford area, particularly strong collections on the textile industry, immigration and minority communities in the district.
Collections:
A collection of oral history interviews and documentary photographs which represent the memories, reflections, contemporary attitudes and images of Bradford people of all ages, races and classes.
Printed publications:
Here to Stay, Bradford's South Asian Communities (£8.95)
Home from Home, British Pakistanis in Mirpur (£7.50)
Keeping The Faith, The Polish Community in Britain (£9.95)
Tying the Knot, Bradford Weddings (£9.95)
Ukraine's Forbidden History (£13.95)

338
BRADFORD INDUSTRIAL AND HORSES AT WORK MUSEUM
Moorside Mills, Moorside Road, Eccleshill, Bradford, West Yorkshire, BD2 3HY

Tel: 01274 435900
Fax: 01274 636362
Email: paula.walsh@bradford.gov.uk
Formed: 1974

Organisation type and purpose: Local government body, museum.

Enquiries to: Education/Outreach Officer
Direct tel: 01274 435864
Access:
Access to staff: By letter, by telephone, in person
Hours: Tue to Sat, 1000 to 1700; Sun, 1200 to 1700
Other restrictions: Also open on Bank Holiday Mondays.
Access for disabled people: Parking provided, ramped entry, toilet facilities
Other restrictions: Access to most areas.

General description:
Original worsted spinning mill complete with mill-owner's cottages, mill stables (with working horses, transport gallery, all c1875) cafe and car parking. Daily demonstrations.
Information services:
Education services: Group education facilities, resources for Key Stages 1 and 2 and 3.
Services for disabled people: For the visually impaired; for the hearing impaired.
Collections:
Victorian memorabilia, steam/gas/oil engines, textile machinery, furniture

339
BRADFORD-ON-AVON MUSEUM
Bridge Street, Bradford-on-Avon, Wiltshire, BA15 1BY

Tel: 01225 863280
Formed: 1990

Organisation type and purpose: Registered charity, museum.

Enquiries to: Honorary Curator
Access:
Access to staff: By letter only
Hours: Easter to End Oct: Wed to Sat, 1030 to 1230 and 1400 to 1600; Sun, 1400 to 1600
Nov to Easter: Wed, Fri, Sun, 1400 to 1600; Sat, 1030 to 1230 and 1400 to 1600
Other restrictions: Closed Mid Dec to Mid Jan.

General description:
Local history of Bradford on Avon and surrounding villages; woollen, rubber, stone and engineering industries; pharmacy; social history.
Collections:
R T Christopher Pharmacy Collection
Local social and industrial history collections

340
BRADLEY HOUSE
Totes Road, Newton Abbot, Devon, TQ12 6BN

Tel: 01626 354513

Organisation type and purpose: National organisation, registered charity (charity number 205846), historic building, house or site, suitable for ages: 8+.
Parent body:
The National Trust (South West Region)
Regional Office for Devon and Cornwall, tel: 01392 881691
Access:
Access to staff: By letter, by telephone, visitors by prior appointment
Access to building, collections or gallery: No prior appointment required
Hours: 1 Apr to 30 Sep, Tue to Thu, 1400 to 1700
Other restrictions: 1 to 29 Oct open weekdays by prior appointment only. For appointment telephone at least one day in advance during office hours.

General description:
A small medieval manor house, set in woodland and meadows.
Information services:
Services for disabled people: For the visually impaired.

Internet home pages:
http://www.nationaltrust.org.uk/regions/devon

341
BRAIDWOOD AND RUSHBROOK MUSEUM
See - Museum of Fire

342
BRAITHWAITE HALL
East Witton, Leyburn, North Yorkshire, DL8 4SY

Tel: 01969 640287

Organisation type and purpose: National organisation, registered charity (charity number 205846), historic building, house or site.
Parent body:
National Trust (Yorkshire & North East Regional Offices)
Yorkshire Regional Office, tel: 01904 702021

Enquiries to: Manager
Access:
Access to staff: By letter, by telephone
Access to building, collections or gallery: Prior appointment required
Hours: 1st and 3rd Wed, April to Sept, 1400 to 1700
Tel. the tenant, Mrs Duffus, in advance

General description:
A remote 17th century stone farmhouse with fine original features including fireplaces, panelling and oak staircase.

Internet home pages:
http://www.nationaltrust.org.uk

343
BRAMAH TEA & COFFEE MUSEUM
40 Southwark Street, Bankside, London, SE1 1UM

Tel: 020 7403 5650
Fax: 020 7403 5650
Email: e.bramah@virgin.net
Acronym or abbreviation: Bramah Museum
Formed: 1992

Organisation type and purpose: Independently owned, registered charity (charity number 1073959), museum.

Enquiries to: Museum Director
Other contacts: Secretary for confidentiality.
Access:
Access to staff: By letter, by telephone, by fax, by email, in person, Internet web pages
Hours: Mon to Sat, 0900 to 1800
Access to building, collections or gallery: No prior appointment required
Hours: Mon to Sat, 1000 to 1700
Access for disabled people: level entry, access to all public areas, toilet facilities

General description:
The museum tells the 350 year social and commercial history of these two important commodities, expressed in a unique and colourful collection of ceramics, pictures, silver and texts.
Information services:
Education services: Group education facilities..
Collections:
Collections of tea and coffee making equipment
Teapots, large reference collection of antique and novelty teapots, 1770-1990, c. 500 items
Espresso machines, collection of Espresso coffee makers, 1920 onwards
Catalogues:
Catalogue for library is on-line. Catalogue for all of the collections is only available in-house.
Printed publications:
Coffee Makers (Edward and Joan Bramah, 1990)
Novelty Teapots (Edward Bramah, 1992)
Tea & Coffee (Edward Bramah, 1972)

Microform products:
Extensive transparency collection of exhibits and drawings, prints

Internet home pages:
http://www.bramahmuseum.co.uk

344
BRANCASTER

Brancaster Millennium Activity Centre, Dial House, Brancaster Staithe, King's Lynn, Norfolk, PE31 8BW

Tel: 01485 210719
Email: brancaster@nationaltrust.org.uk

Organisation type and purpose: National organisation, registered charity (charity number 205846), historic building, house or site, suitable for ages: 5+.
Parent body:
The National Trust (East of England Region)
East Anglia Area Office, tel: 0870 609 5388

Enquiries to: Manager
Access:
Access to staff: By letter, by telephone, by email, Internet web pages

General description:
An extensive area of saltmarsh, intertidal mud and sandflats, and including the site of the Roman fort of Branodunum.
Information services:
Suitable for school groups.
Education room/centre; residential courses for schools, from Key Stage 2 to A-level, with cutting-edge environmental technology.
Also field studies and outdoor pursuits, inc. birdwatching, coastal processes, woodlands, saltmarshes, orienteering, sailing, kayaking and cycling.
Programme for adults of both day and weekend courses in craft, sailing, birdwatching and cookery.
Family Fun weeks in school holidays. Tel. Centre for information
Education centre offers group cycling activities; all staff trained in cycle group leadership. 'Start Cycling' scheme organised for groups.
Special visitor services: Materials and/or activities for children.
Education services: Group education facilities, resources for Key Stages 2, 3, 4 and Further or Higher Education..

Internet home pages:
http://www.nationaltrust.org.uk

345
BRANDER MUSEUM, HUNTLY

The Square, Huntly, Aberdeenshire, AB54 8AE

Tel: 01771 622906
Fax: 01771 622884
Formed: 1883

Organisation type and purpose: Local government body, museum, suitable for ages: 5+.
Parent body:
Aberdeenshire Heritage
Tel: 01771 622906, fax: 01771 622884

Enquiries to: Curator
Access:
Access to staff: By letter, by telephone, by fax

General description:
General social history, George MacDonald, Anderson Bey, local ecclesiastical history.
Collections:
Social history, geology, photography
Catalogues:
Catalogue for part of the collections is only available in-house.

346
BRANGWYN GIFT

See - William Morris Gallery

347
BRANSCOMBE - OLD BAKERY, MANOR MILL AND FORGE, THE

Branscombe, Seaton, Devon, EX12 3DB

Tel: 01392 881691 (Manor Mill - Regional Office)
Fax: 01392 881954 (Regional Office)

Organisation type and purpose: National organisation, registered charity (charity number 205846), museum, historic building, house or site, suitable for ages: all ages.
Parent body:
The National Trust (South West Region)
Regional Office for Devon and Cornwall, tel: 01392 881691

Enquiries to: Property Manager
Other contacts: Tenant, Old Bakery tel: 01297 680333; Tenant, Forge tel: 01297 680481
Access:
Access to staff: By letter
Access to building, collections or gallery: No prior appointment required
Hours: Old Bakery: 31 Mar to 31 Oct, Wed to Sun, 1100 to 1700
Manor Mill: 30 Mar - 29 Jun, Sun, 1400 to 1700; 2 Jul - 31 Aug, Wed and Sun, 1400 to 1700;
7 Sep to 2 Nov, Sun, 1400 to 1700
Forge: Please telephone for details of opening times
Access for disabled people: toilet facilities
Other restrictions: Steep slope to first floor. Ground floor accessible with assistance. No access to other floors.

General description:
The Old Bakery is a stone-built and partially rendered building beneath thatch, which until 1987 was the last traditional working bakery in Devon. The old baking equipment has been preserved in the baking room and the rest of the building now serves as a tea-room.
Manor Mill, still in working order and recently restored, is a water-powered mill which probably supplied the flour for the bakery.
The forge is open daily and the blacksmith sells the ironwork he produces.

Internet home pages:
http://www.nationaltrust.org.uk/regions/devon

348
BRANTWOOD (THE HOME OF JOHN RUSKIN)

Brantwood, Coniston, Cumbria, LA21 8AD

Tel: 01539 441396
Fax: 015394 41263
Email: enquiries@brantwood.org.uk
Full name: The Brantwood Trust

Organisation type and purpose: Registered charity, historic building, house or site, suitable for ages: 8+.

Enquiries to: General Manager
Access:
Access to staff: By letter, by telephone, by fax, by email
Access to building, collections or gallery: No prior appointment required
Hours: Mid Mar to mid Nov: daily, 1100 to 1730
Mid Nov to mid Mar: Wed to Sun, 1100 to 1630
Other restrictions: Closed 25 and 26 Dec.
Access for disabled people: Parking provided, toilet facilities
Other restrictions: Limited access.

General description:
An extensive collection of watercolours by John Ruskin. Also contains Ruskin's furniture; personal memorabilia; his coach; and his boat (Jumping Jenny). Also some works by other artists e.g. Burne-Jones, Collingwood.
Information services:
Library available for reference (for conditions see Access above)
Library available for reference to members of Friends of Ruskin's Brantwood.
Guided tours of the Garden.
Special visitor services: Guided tours, materials and/or activities for children.
Education services: Group education facilities, resources for Key Stages 1 and 2, 3 and Further or Higher Education..
Collections:
The Ruskin collection. Fine watercolours by John Ruskin. 19th century. ca. 500 items
Catalogues:
Catalogue for part of the collections is only available in-house.

Internet home pages:
http://www.brantwood.org.uk

349
BRASS RUBBING CENTRE

Trinity Apse, Chalmers Close, High Street, Royal Mile, Edinburgh, EH1 1SS

Tel: 0131 556 4364

Organisation type and purpose: Local government body, museum, suitable for ages: 12+.
Parent body:
City of Edinburgh Council
Culture & Leisure Department, tel: 0131 200 2000 (main); 0131 529 7844 (Culture & Leisure Department HQ)

Enquiries to: Marketing and Sponsorship Officer
Direct tel: 0131 529 7902
Direct fax: 0131 529 3986
Access:
Access to staff: By letter, by telephone, by fax, in person
Hours: Apr to Sep: Mon to Sat, 1000 to 1700; During The Edinburgh Festival: Sun, 1200 to 1700
Other restrictions: Closed Oct to Mar.

General description:
Located in the historic Trinity Apse which was founded in 1460 by Mary of Gueldres, Consort of King James II of Scotland. The centre has an interesting collection of replica brasses from the 13th century to the early part of the 20th century from some of which brass rubbings may be made.
Collections:
Armour. Early mediaeval brasses. 13th-15th century
Celtic brasses. Illuminated manuscripts. 6th-7th century.
Civil and ecclesiastical. English - various. 14th-16th century
European. German and Belgian brasses. 15th-16th century
Family/child. Children's brasses depicted on adult brasses. 15th-16th century
Scottish stones. Pictish art. AD 500
Victorian. Artist's impressions. Early 19th century
Catalogues:
Catalogue for part of the collections is only available in-house.

Internet home pages:
http://www.cac.org.uk
Website for The City of Edinburgh Museums and Galleries Service, it contains: information on each of the 11 venues and their permanent collections; details of current temporary exhibitions; information on past temporary exhibitions; details of selected publications.

350
BRATTLE FARM MUSEUM

Brattle Farm, Five Oak Lane, Staplehurst, Kent, TN12 0HE

Tel: 01580 891222
Fax: 01580 891222
Formed: 1975

Organisation type and purpose: Museum, suitable for ages: 5+.

continued overleaf

Enquiries to: Owner
Access:
Access to staff: By letter, by telephone, by fax, in person, visitors by prior appointment
Access for disabled people: Parking provided, ramped entry, toilet facilities
Other restrictions: Access to most areas.

General description:
Agriculture, general and related trades, tractors, vintage cars, transport.
Collections:
Vintage cars and other vehicles
Vintage tractors and other implements
Hop growing
Hand sprayers and dusters
Dairywork
Blacksmith's shop
Farriery, horses and harness
Brick, tile and pipemaking
Wheelwrights and hand tools
Weights and measures
Veterinary equipment and sheep shearing
Victorian and Edwardian household equipment
Kitchen and laundry equipment
Stationary engines

351
BRAUNTON & DISTRICT MUSEUM
The Bakehouse Centre, Caen Street, Braunton, Devon, EX33 1AA

Tel: 01271 816688
Email: braunton@devonmuseums.net
Formed: 1974

Organisation type and purpose: Registered charity (charity number 1010422), museum, suitable for ages: all ages.
Also houses the Tourist Information Centre.
To preserve the history of the village for future generations.

Enquiries to: Chairman
Access:
Access to staff: By letter, by telephone, by email, Internet web pages
Access to building, collections or gallery: No prior appointment required
Hours: Mon to Sat, 0900 to 1700
Jan to Easter: Mon to Sat, 0900 to 1500
Access for disabled people: ramped entry
Other restrictions: Disabled access and stairlift

General description:
A community museum describing the life of Braunton Village, its people and their livelihoods on the land, the sea and in the home.
Information services:
Family history tracing service, census information.
Open days.
Copies of old photographs from the collection available
Out of hours group visits available by arrangement
Special visitor services: Guided tours, materials and/or activities for children..
Collections:
Approximately 3000 photographs
Model ships, Braunton pottery, tools, military uniforms, domestic and agriculture items
Catalogues:
Catalogue for part of the collections is on-line.
Publications list:
is available in hard copy and online.
Printed publications:
Various publications, available for purchase, direct, including:
Braunton Boys who went to war - WW I (Cooper R)
Braunton Great Field (Braunton Conservation Project)
Braunton Shipwrecks 1850 -1900 (Brock A and B)
Cradle to Grave - Braunton births, deaths and marriages 1850 - 1924, 7 vols (Brock A and B)
Henry Williamson - A brief look at his writings in N Devon during the 1920's / 30's (HW Society)
Recollections of Braunton during WW II, vols 1 and 2 (Elliott A)

Internet home pages:
http://www.devonmuseums.net/braunton

352
BREAMORE HOUSE AND MUSEUM
Breamore, Fordingbridge, Hampshire, SP6 2DF

Tel: 01725 512233
Fax: 01725 512858
Formed: 1952

Organisation type and purpose: Museum. Historic house.
Includes the:
Countryside Museum
Tel: 01725 512468, email/website: breamore@ukonline.co.uk
Member of:
Historic Houses Association
Southern Tourist Board

Enquiries to: Curator
Direct tel: 01725 512468
Access:
Access to staff: By letter, by telephone, by fax
Hours: Apr: Tue, Wed, Sun, 1300 to 1730
May, Jun, Jul, Sep: Tue, Wed, Thu, Sat, Sun, and all Bank Holidays, 1300 to 1730
Aug: every day, 1300 to 1730
Access to building, collections or gallery: No prior appointment required

General description:
Elizabethan manor house (c.1583); rural crafts (blacksmith's shop, wain and wheelwrights' shop, saddler and bootmaker's shop, brewery, dairy); agricultural machinery; early tools; steam engines and tractors; art; social history; agricultural heritage.
Collections:
Shops to show a village when self sufficient
Printed publications:
Booklet on Breamore House and Countryside Museum

353
BREAN DOWN
Brean, Burnham on Sea, North Somerset

Tel: 01934 844518

Organisation type and purpose: Local government body (charity number 205846), museum, historic building, house or site, suitable for ages: all ages.
Parent body:
National Trust (South West Region)
Wessex Regional Office, tel: 01958 843600

Enquiries to: Manager
Access:
Access for disabled people: toilet facilities
Other restrictions: Steps to restaurant entrance. Ground level seating available outside.

General description:
Brean Down, rich in wildlife and history, is one of the most dramatic landmarks of the Somerset coastline. At its most seaward point, a Palmerston fort built in 1865 and then re-armed in World War II, provides a unique insight into Brean's past.
Information services:
Suitable for school groups, hands-on activities
For interpretation panels and circular walk leaflet phone 01958 843601.
Special visitor services: Guided tours, materials and/or activities for children.
Education services: Group education facilities..

Internet home pages:
http://www.nationaltrust.org.uk/regions/wessex

354
BRECHIN MUSEUM
Public Library, 10 St Ninian's Square, Brechin, Angus, DD8 7AA

Tel: 01307 464123
Fax: 01307 468451
Email: the.meffan@angus.gov.uk
Formed: 1892

Organisation type and purpose: Local government body, museum.
Parent body:
Angus Council, Leisure Services, Cultural Services

Enquiries to: Museums Manager
Other contacts: Cultural Services Manager
Access:
Access to staff: By letter, by telephone, by fax, by email, in person
Access to building, collections or gallery: No prior appointment required
Hours: Mon, Wed, 0930 to 2000; Tue, 1000 to 1800; Thu, Sat, 0930 to 1800; Fri, 1000 to 1730
Access for disabled people: ramped entry
Other restrictions: Ramped entry at rear of extension to building.

General description:
The ancient trades, industries and cathedral, paintings, archaeology are all highlights of the rich local history of this ancient city.
Collections:
Brechin's archaeology, civic, religious, industrial, social and political history
David Waterson Art Collection

Internet home pages:
http://www.angus.gov.uk/history/museums/brechinmus.htm

355
BRECKNOCK MUSEUM & ART GALLERY
Captain's Walk, Brecon, Powys, LD3 7DW

Tel: 01874 624121
Fax: 01874 611281
Email: brecknock.museum@powys.gov.uk
Formed: 1928
Formerly: Brecon Museum

Organisation type and purpose: Local government body, museum, art gallery.
Connected with:
Brecknock Society and Museum Friends
c/o Brecknock Museum

Enquiries to: Curator
Access:
Access to staff: By letter, by telephone, by email, visitors by prior appointment
Hours: Mon to Fri, 1000 to 1700; Sat, 1000 to 1300 and 1400 to 1700 (4 Nov to Feb); Sun, 1200 to 1700 (Apr to Sep) under review
Access for disabled people: Parking provided, level entry, access to all public areas, toilet facilities

General description:
Archaeology and local history of Brecknock; art associated with Brecknock and environs.
Collections:
Collections of old photographs of Brecknock and archives relating to Brecknock Museum collections and members of Brecknock Society
Celtic and Roman finds
1880 Assize Court drama
Stumpwork embroidery
Rural life
Brecknock townlife
Catalogues:
Catalogue for library is in-house only. Catalogue for part of the collections is only available in-house.
Printed publications:
Guide Book
Brecon in Old Photographs

356
BRECKNOCK SOCIETY AND MUSEUM FRIENDS

Brecknock Museum, Captain's Walk, Brecon, Powys, LD3 7OW

Tel: 01874 624121
Email: brecknock.museum@powys.gov.uk
Formed: 1928
Formed from: Friends of Brecknock Museum, Brecknock Society

Organisation type and purpose: Learned society (membership is by subscription), voluntary organisation, registered charity (charity number 518041), museum, suitable for ages: all ages.
County historical and archaeological society.

Enquiries to: Secretary
Direct tel: 01874 636507
Access:
Access to staff: By letter, by telephone
Hours: Mon to Fri, 1000 to 1700
Access to building, collections or gallery: No prior appointment required
Access for disabled people: Parking provided, ramped entry, access to all public areas, toilet facilities

General description:
History and archaeology of Breconshire, place names.
Information services:
Library available for reference (for conditions see Access above)
Special visitor services: Guided tours, tape recorded guides..
Catalogues:
Catalogue for library is in-house only. Catalogue for all of the collections is only available in-house.
Printed publications:
Brycheiniog (society journal, annually)

357
BREDGAR AND WORMSHILL LIGHT RAILWAY

The Warren, Bredgar, Sittingbourne, Kent, ME9 8AT

Tel: 01622 884254
Fax: 01622 884668
Acronym or abbreviation: B&WLR
Formed: 1972

Organisation type and purpose: Independently owned, museum, suitable for ages: 12+.
Heritage railway.
Preservation of narrow guage steam locomotives.

Enquiries to: Owner

General description:
Narrow gauge steam locomotive repair, renovation and construction, their operation and driving. Narrow gauge railway construction, maintenance and repair, operations.
Information services:
Special visitor services: Guided tours..
Collections:
Twelve narrow gauge steam locomotives representing many European manufacturers, 1897-1956
British built beam engine, 1870
Vintage cars, all manufactured by the Bean Car Co, Dudley, 1920-1930
Printed publications:
Visitors Guide
Electronic and video products:
Video

Internet home pages:
http://www.bwlr.co.uk
Basic information on the collection, regular updates on locomotive rebuilding

358
BREDON BARN

Bredon, Tewkesbury, Worcestershire

Tel: 01985 843600 (Regional Office)
Email: bredonbarn@nationaltrust.org.uk

Organisation type and purpose: National organisation, registered charity (charity number 205846), museum, historic building, house or site.
Parent Body:
The National Trust (South West Region)
Wessex Regional Office, tel: 01985 843600

Enquiries to: Warden
Direct tel: 01451 844257
Access:
Access to staff: By letter, by email, Internet web pages
Access to building, collections or gallery: No prior appointment required
Hours: Beg Apr to end Nov, Wed, Thu, Sat, Sun, 1000 to 1800
Other restrictions: Closes dusk if earlier. At other times by appointment only. Not suitable for coaches.
Access for disabled people: level entry
Other restrictions: Access level but uneven, Ground floor accessible with assistance.

General description:
A 14th century barn, beautifully constructed of local Cotswold stone. Noted for its dramatic aisled interior and unusual stone chimney cowling.

Internet home pages:
http://www.nationaltrust.org.uk/regions/wessex

359
BRENZETT AERONAUTICAL MUSEUM TRUST

Ivychurch Road, Brenzett, Romney Marsh, Kent, TN29 0EE

Tel: 01797 344747 or 01233 627911
Acronym or abbreviation: BAMT
Formed: 1972

Organisation type and purpose: Independently owned, registered charity (charity number 297552), museum, suitable for ages: 8+.
15 unpaid volunteers.
Aeronautical museum.
Links with:
British Aircraft Preservation Council
Other address:
The Secretary
Brenzett Aeronautical Museum Trust
190 Hythe Road, Ashford, Kent, TN24 8PP, tel: 01233 627911

Enquiries to: Archivist
Access:
Access to staff: By letter, by telephone, in person
Hours: Mon to Fri, 1100 to 1730
Access to building, collections or gallery: No prior appointment required
Hours: Museum opens from Easter.
Mon to Fri, 1100 to 1730
Access for disabled people: level entry

General description:
A unique collection of wartime and aviation memorabilia. Includes engines; aircraft remains; two aircraft, a Canberra B2 and a D H Vampire T11; and civilian wartime memorabilia.
Collections:
Substantial research material relating to WWII

360
BRESSINGHAM STEAM MUSEUM AND GARDENS

Bressingham Hall, Thetford Road, Bressingham, Diss, Norfolk, IP22 2AB

Tel: 01379 687386
Fax: 01379 686907
Email: info@bressingham.co.uk
Formed: 1972

Organisation type and purpose: Registered charity (charity number 266374), museum, suitable for ages: 5+.
Parent body:
Bressingham Steam Preservation Company Limited
Connections with:
Souvenirs of Bressingham

Enquiries to: Chief Executive
Other contacts: (1) PR/Markting Manager; (2) Curator for (1) PR, marketing; (2) collections, health & safety.
Access:
Access to staff: By letter, by telephone, by fax, by email, in person, visitors by prior appointment, Internet web pages
Hours: Mon to Fri, 0730 to 1600 for engineering matters
Access to building, collections or gallery: No prior appointment required
Hours: Easter to end Oct: Daily, 1030 to 1730
October: Daily, 1030 to 1630
Access for disabled people: Parking provided, ramped entry, level entry, toilet facilities
Other restrictions: One gallery exhibition not accessible by wheelchair.

General description:
A comprehensive collection of steam engines of all sorts covering road and rail transport, industrial and agricultural use. Collection of 20 locomotives, operating on standard gauge and 3 narrow gauge railways. Victorian steam gallopers.
The National Dad's Army Museum with scripts and memorabilia from the Dad's Army film and series, set in a reconstruction of Walmington-on-Sea.
Two gardens, each 6 acres, displaying perennials and conifers and maintained by the 'Bloom' Family.
Information services:
Special visitor services: Guided tours, materials and/or activities for children.
Education services: Group education facilities, resources for Key Stages 1 and 2 and 3.
Services for disabled people: Displays and/or information at wheelchair height.
Collections:
Steam engines
Traction engines
Railway locomotives and coaches
Railway artefacts collection
The 'David Cooke' Dinky and Model Car Collection
The National Dad's Army Collection
Catalogues:
Catalogue for library is on-line. Catalogue for all of the collections is on-line.
Printed publications:
Souvenir guide book (£1.50)
Teachers guide to the Journey Back to Steam exhibition
Electronic and video products:
Gallopers, Gardens and Steam Giants (video)

Internet home pages:
http://www.bressingham.co.uk
Description of the museum and gardens, opening times, prices, location, events, restoration projects.

361
BREWHOUSE ARTS CENTRE

Union Street, Burton-on-Trent, Staffordshire, DE14 1AF

Tel: 01283 516030
Fax: 01283 515106
Email: info@brewhouse.co.uk
Formed: 1991

Organisation type and purpose: Registered charity (charity number 702982), art gallery, suitable for ages: all ages.
Arts Centre.

Enquiries to: General Manager
Direct tel: 01283 567720

continued overleaf

Other contacts: Sales & Marketing Officer for marketing queries.
Access:
Access to staff: By letter, by telephone, by fax, by email, in person, visitors by prior appointment, Internet web pages
Access to building, collections or gallery: No prior appointment required
Hours: Mon, closed; Tue to Sat, 1000 to 1500 and 1800 to 2000
Access for disabled people: Parking provided, level entry, access to all public areas, toilet facilities

General description:
Arts.
Catalogues:
Catalogue for all of the collections is only available in-house.
Printed publications:
Brewhouse Brochure (3 times a year, free)

Internet home pages:
http://www.brewhouse.co.uk
Online brochure and enquiry form.

362
BREWHOUSE YARD MUSEUM
Castle Boulevard, Nottingham, NG7 1FB

Tel: 0115 915 3600
Fax: 0115 915 3601
Acronym or abbreviation: BHY
Full name: The Museum of Nottingham Life At Brewhouse Yard
Formed: 1974

Organisation type and purpose: Local government body, service industry, museum, suitable for ages: 5+, research organisation.

Enquiries to: Manager
Direct tel: 0115 915 3620
Direct fax: 0115 915 3601
Direct email: anni@notmusbhy.demon.co.uk
Other contacts: Site Co-ordinator, Community Historian for museum information.
Access:
Access to staff: By letter, by telephone, by fax, by email, visitors by prior appointment, charges made to all users
Other restrictions: Prior appointment for staff. Wheelchair access on ground floor only.
Access to building, collections or gallery: No prior appointment required
Hours: Daily, 1000 to 1600 (last entry 1600).
Other restrictions: Prior appointment for groups.

General description:
Galleries: local history of Nottingham.
Collections: archaeology and history of Nottingham and in part Nottinghamshire.
Information services:
Education services: Group education facilities, resources for Key Stages 1 and 2..
Collections:
Archaeology and history of Nottingham and in part Nottinghamshire
Catalogues:
Catalogue for all of the collections is only available in-house.

363
BRIDEWELL MUSEUM
Bridewell Alley, Norwich, Norfolk, NR2 1AQ

Tel: 01603 629127
Formed: 1925

Organisation type and purpose: Local government body, museum, suitable for ages: 5+.
Connections with:
Norfolk Museums Service

Enquiries to: Curator
Direct tel: 01603 615975
Access:
Access to staff: By letter, by telephone, in person, visitors by prior appointment
Hours: Mon to Fri, 1000 to 1700

General description:
History of trade and industry in Norwich.
Information services:
Special visitor services: Guided tours, materials and/or activities for children.
Education services: Group education facilities, resources for Key Stages 1 and 2, 3 and 4..
Collections:
18th century pattern books for local textile industry
Local trade catalogues and photographs of local working life
Iron work and catalogues relating to Barnard Bishop, Barnards, Iron Founders, 1860-1930s, c. 200 items
Catalogues:
Catalogue for all of the collections is only available in-house.

364
BRIDGE HOUSE (AMBLESIDE)
See - Windermere and Troutbeck (including Bridge House)

365
BRIDGEWATER CANAL LINEAR INDUSTRIAL HERITAGE PARK
1 Chapel Place, Manchester, M41 7LE

Tel: 0161 748 4414
Email: info@steamcoalcanal.co.uk
Formed: 1996
Also known as: Steam, Coal & Canal

Organisation type and purpose: Registered charity (charity number 1067778), historic building, house or site, suitable for ages: 8+.
To create a Linear Heritage Park along a section of Britain's first canal - The Bridgewater Canal 1761.

Enquiries to: Project Co-ordinator
Access:
Access to staff: By letter, by telephone, by email, visitors by prior appointment
Hours: Hours vary as only 1 part-time member of staff is available
Access for disabled people: Parking provided, ramped entry
Other restrictions: Access to the aqueduct - not to the office.

General description:
Britain's first canal. Barton Swing Aqueduct, Worsley Delph and Astley Green Colliery Museum. The walk between these 3 sites includes many buildings of historical note as well as tracks of semi-rural land.
Information services:
Special visitor services: Guided tours..
Printed publications:
Newsletter
Booklets (in Brindley's Footstops, Worsley Village)
Leaflet

Internet home pages:
http://www.steamcoalcanal.co.uk
Details of the route and a print-out of the map can be obtained.

See also - Astley Green Colliery Museum; Barton Aqueduct

366
BRIDGNORTH CLIFF RAILWAY
Castle Terrace, Bridgnorth, Shropshire, WV16 4AH

Tel: 01746 762124
Fax: 01746 762124
Email: office@bridgnorthcliffrailway.co.uk
Full name: Bridgnorth Castle Hill Railway Company Limited
Formed: 1892

Organisation type and purpose: Independently owned, historic building, house or site, suitable for ages: all ages.

Enquiries to: Director
Access:
Access to staff: By letter, by telephone, by fax, by email
Access to building, collections or gallery: No prior appointment required
Hours: Mon to Sat, 0800 to 2000; Sun, 1200 to 2000
Closes at 1830 in Winter.

General description:
The UK's oldest and steepest inland funicular railway built in 1892 to link the High and Low Towns of Bridgnorth.
Printed publications:
Leaflet (free of charge)

Internet home pages:
http://www.bridgnorthcliffrailway.co.uk
Historical and engineering information plus general visitor information.

367
BRIDPORT MUSEUM
South Street, Bridport, Dorset, DT6 3NR

Tel: 01308 422116
Fax: 01308 458704
Email: leisure@westdorset-dc.gov.uk
Formed: 1932

Organisation type and purpose: Local government body, museum, suitable for ages: 5+.
Other addresses:
The Coach House
Gundry Lane, Bridport, tel: 01308 458703, fax: 01308 458704, email/website: s.brien@westdorset-dc.gov.uk

Enquiries to: Curator
Other contacts: Museum Administrator
Access:
Access to staff: By letter, by telephone, by fax, by email, in person, visitors by prior appointment
Access for disabled people: level entry
Other restrictions: Access to ground floor, other services by arrangment

General description:
Housed in a Tudor-façade building, the museum tells the thousand-year history of the town. Other displays show artefacts from a Roman hillfort with areas for temporary exhibitions from the reserve collections. Particular reference is made to the rope and net industry for which Bridport was world-famous.
Information services:
Special visitor services: Materials and/or activities for children.
Education services: Group education facilities, resources for Key Stages 1 and 2.
Services for disabled people: For the visually impaired; displays and/or information at wheelchair height.
Collections:
The collections cover a broad range and can be grouped as:
agriculture, fine art, geology, archaeology, firearms, costume, dolls, lace, rope and net, ephemera, natural history, photographs, numismatics and general social history
Although not all on display in the museum, the Reserve Collections are used for temporary exhibitions and can be accessed, where appropriate, by appointment
Costume, mainly female garments and accessories, 17th-20th centuries, c. 1000 items
Dolls given to the Revd Dr Donald Omand by circus folk from around the world, 19th-20th centuries, 300
Material and equipment of the rope, twine and net industry of Bridport, 18th-20th centuries, c. 500 items
Waddon Hill. Roman Hill Fort, 50-60 AD, 700 items
Photographs of local people, places, events, etc. 1850-date, 3000 items
A Local History Collection is also available for public research

Printed publications:
Local Industrial Heritage leaflets (direct, at a small charge)

368
BRIDPORT MUSEUM SERVICE
South Street, Bridport, Dorset, DT6 3NH

Tel: 01308 458703
Fax: 01308 458704
Email: sh-bridportmus@btconnect.com
Formed: 1932

Organisation type and purpose: Registered charity, museum, suitable for ages: 5+.
At the same address:
Local History Centre

Enquiries to: Curator
Other contacts: Museum Administrator for general enquiries in Curator's absence.
Access:
Access to staff: By letter, by telephone, by fax, by email, in person
Hours: Museum: Mon to Sat, 1000 to 1700
Local History Centre: Mon to Fri, 0930 to 1630
Access for disabled people: level entry

General description:
Local history for the Bridport and surrounding areas. Family history research. Rope- and net-making industries, origins and developments.
Information services:
Library available for reference (for conditions see Access above)
Special visitor services: Materials and/or activities for children.
Education services: Resources for Key Stages 1 and 2.
Services for disabled people: Displays and/or information at wheelchair height.
Collections:
Fifteen main social history collections, including rope and net and over 12,000 photographs

369
BRIGHSTONE SHOP AND MUSEUM
North Street, Brighstone, Isle of Wight, PO30 4AX

Tel: 01983 740689

Organisation type and purpose: National organisation, registered charity (charity number 205846), historic building, house or site.
Parent body:
National Trust (South and South East Region)
Thames & Solent Regional Office, tel: 01491 528051, fax: 01494 463310

Enquiries to: Manager
Access:
Access to staff: By letter, by telephone

General description:
An attractive terrace of thatched vernacular cottages, containing a National Trust shop and Village Museum (run by Brighstone Museum Trust).

Internet home pages:
http://www.nationaltrust.org.uk

370
BRIGHTLINGSEA MUSEUM
1 Duke Street, Brightlingsea, Essex, CO7 0EA

Tel: 01206 303286
Formed: 1990

Organisation type and purpose: Registered charity, museum, suitable for ages: 8+.
Parent body:
Friends of Brightlingsea Museum
9 Queen Street, Brightlingsea, Essex, CO7 0PH

Enquiries to: Museum Co-ordinator
Access:
Access to staff: By letter, by telephone
Hours: Mon to Fri, 1700 to 2130
Access to building, collections or gallery: Prior appointment required
Hours: Mon, 1400 to 1700; Sat, 1000 to 1600; Sun, 1400 to 1600
Access for disabled people: toilet facilities

General description:
Brightlingsea Museum has acquired a representative collection of objects, photographs and pictures illustrative of the social and economic history of Brightlingsea and its immediate surroundings.
Collections:
The Cinque Port Liberty of Brightlingsea. Memorabilia spanning the period 1887 to date, including artefacts and photographs.
Collection of Roman artefacts from Moveron's Farm, Brightlingsea

371
BRIGHTON AND HOVE NATURAL HISTORY SOCIETY
See - Booth Museum of Natural History

372
BRIGHTON MUSEUM AND ART GALLERY
Royal Pavilion Gardens, Brighton, East Sussex, BN1 1UE

Tel: 01273 290900
Fax: 01273 292841
Formed: 1873

Organisation type and purpose: Local government body, museum, art gallery, suitable for ages: all ages.
Parent body:
Brighton & Hove City Council

Enquiries to: Education/ Exhibition Services
Access:
Access to staff: By letter, by telephone, by fax, by email, in person
Hours: Mon to Fri, 0900 to 1700
Access to building, collections or gallery: No prior appointment required
Hours: Tue, 1000 to 1900; Wed to Sat, 1000 to 1700; Sun, 1400 to 1700
Other restrictions: Closed Mon (except public holidays) and 25, 26 Dec.
Access for disabled people: level entry, access to all public areas, toilet facilities

Information services:
Education services: Group education facilities.
Services for disabled people: For the visually impaired; for the hearing impaired; displays and/or information at wheelchair height.
Collections:
Fine Art Collection
20th century Art and Design
Mr Willett's Pottery Collection
World Art Collection
Catalogues:
Catalogue for all of the collections is only available in-house.
Printed publications:
Various catalogues available

Address for ordering publications:
Printed publications:
Commercial Services, Royal Pavilion
4/5 Pavilion Buildings, Brighton, BN1 1EE, tel: 01273 290900, fax: 01273 292871

Internet home pages:
http://www.brighton.virtualmuseum.info

373
BRIGHTON TOY AND MODEL MUSEUM
52-55 Trafalgar Street, Brighton, East Sussex, BN1 4EB

Tel: 01273 749494
Fax: 01273 749494
Email: info@brightontoymuseum.co.uk
Formed: 1991
Formerly: Sussex Toy and Model Museum, date of change, 2001

Organisation type and purpose: Voluntary organisation, registered charity (charity number 1001560), museum, suitable for ages: 5+.

Enquiries to: Public Relations Manager
Other contacts: Manager
Access:
Access to staff: By letter, by telephone, in person, Internet web pages
Access for disabled people: access to all public areas, toilet facilities

General description:
Toys, dolls and models, especially model railways.
Information services:
Education services: Group education facilities, resources for Key Stages 1 and 2..
Collections:
Catalogues and magazines relating to old toys from 1900 onwards
Panoramas of farm and country scenes, scale model aeroplanes, Victorian and modern dolls and fully furnished dolls houses, construction toys including Meccano; jigsaws and childrens puzzles, model cars, lorries and buses, ships; Napoleon's Old Guard with the armies drawn up for battle
Reference library for research purposes
Toy and model train collection covering the last 100 years and including a unique 1930s railway layout

Internet home pages:
http://www.yell.co.uk/sites/sustoymodelmuseum/

374
BRINDLEY WATER MILL & MUSEUM, THE
Mill Street, Leek, Staffordshire, ST13 8ET

Tel: 01538 483741 or 399332

Organisation type and purpose: Museum, historic building, house or site.

Enquiries to: Curator

General description:
Built in 1752 by James Brindley as a working water-powered corn mill, now with a small museum illustrating James Brindley's life and times (1716-1772).

375
BRINKBURN PRIORY
Long Framlington, Morpeth, Northumberland, NE65 8AR

Tel: 01665 570628

Organisation type and purpose: Historic building, house or site.
Parent body:
English Heritage (North East Region)
Tel: 0191 269 1227/8, fax: 0191 261 1130

Enquiries to: Manager
Access:
Access to staff: By letter, by telephone, in person
Access to building, collections or gallery: No prior appointment required
Hours: End Mar to end Sep: daily, 1000 to 1800
Oct: daily, 1000 to 1700
Other restrictions: Opening times are subject to change, for up-to-date information contact English Heritage by phone or visit the website.

General description:
Almost perfectly preserved 12th century Augustinian priory with Gothic architecture.

Internet home pages:
http://www.english-heritage.org.uk

376
BRISTOL CENTRE FOR THE ADVANCEMENT OF ARCHITECTURE
See - Architecture Centre

377
BRISTOL CITY MUSEUMS SERVICE
See - Red Lodge

378
BRISTOL INDUSTRIAL MUSEUM
Princes Wharf, City Docks, Bristol, BS1 4RN

Tel: 0117 925 1470
Fax: 0117 929 7318
Email: andy_king@bristol-city.gov.uk
Formed: 1978

Organisation type and purpose: Local government body, museum, suitable for ages: 5+.
Parent body:
Bristol City Council

Enquiries to: Curator
Access:
Access to staff: By letter, by telephone, by fax, by email, visitors by prior appointment, Internet web pages
Hours: Mon to Fri, 0900 to 1700

General description:
Bristol companies, Bristol history, engineering history, maritime history, social history, industrial history, photographs, tobacco history.
Collections:
Wills collection of tobacco antiquities
Stothert and Pitt collection of crane and engineering drawings
York collection of marine photographs

Internet home pages:
http://www.bristol-city.gov.uk/museums

379
BRISTOL MUSEUMS AND ART GALLERY
Queen's Road, Bristol, BS8 1RL

Tel: 0117 922 3571
Minicom no. 0117 922 3573
Fax: 0117 922 2047
Email: general_museum@bristol-city.gov.uk

Organisation type and purpose: Local government body, museum, art gallery, historic building, house or site, suitable for ages: 5+. Including historic houses and archaeological sites.
Parent body:
Bristol City Council

Enquiries to: Collections Manager
Direct tel: 0117 922 3600
Access:
Access to staff: By letter, by telephone, by fax, by email, in person, Internet web pages
Access for disabled people: toilet facilities
Other restrictions: Access for disabled via side entrance, lift access does not go to all floors.

General description:
Applied and fine art, geology, South Western Region archaeology, Egyptology, ethnographic collections, natural history, eastern art, social history, industrial and maritime history.
Information services:
Temporary exhibitions
Special visitor services: Materials and/or activities for children.
Education services: Group education facilities, resources for Key Stages 1 and 2, 3, 4 and Further or Higher Education..
Collections:
Assyrian reliefs
Bristol Delft and Porcelain
Bristol Herbarium and Entomology
Bristol School of Artists
Collections of objects as per disciplines listed under subjects
Eberle Collection of medals (inspection by appointment only)
Egyptology collection
Fossil reptiles collection
Library of the Bristol Naturalists Society (access by appointment with the Society only)
Schiller Collection of oriental art
Printed publications:
Diary of events and exhibitions (3 times a year)

Internet home pages:
http://www.bristol-city.gov.uk/museums
Summary of museums, exhibitions and collections.

380
BRISTOL UNIVERSITY
Theatre Collection, Department of Drama, Cantocks Close, Woodland Road, Bristol, BS8 1UP

Tel: 0117 928 7836
Fax: 0117 928 7832
Email: theatre-collection@bris.ac.uk
Formed: 1951

Organisation type and purpose: Museum, university library, university department or institute, suitable for ages: 16+, research organisation.
Research centre.
To provide resources for the study and research of theatre history.

Enquiries to: Keeper
Direct email: jo.elsworth@bris.ac.uk
Other contacts: Assistant Keeper
Access:
Access to staff: By letter, by telephone, by fax, by email, visitors by prior appointment, Internet web pages
Hours: Mon to Fri, 0915 to 1645
Other restrictions: Reference only, on Bank Holidays and Weekends.

General description:
British theatre history, dramatic theory, women's theatre, theatre design, theatre of South-west England, London and Bristol Old Vic companies, Herbert Beerbohm Tree, Welfare State International, popular entertainment.
Collections:
Collections currently being transferred onto computerised database, books online on main library system
Bristol Old Vic (on permanent loan) (1946 to present)
London Old Vic (on permanent loan) (1880s to 1997)
Eric Jones-Evans (1910s to 1980s) includes material relating to Bransby Williams
Herbert Beerbohm Tree (1880s to 1930s)
Smaller collections from theatre historians and enthusiasts, and actors, including: Kathleen Barker, Ernest Thesiger, Leon Quartermaine, Eugene Wellesley, Robert Donat
Theatre Collection of prints, photographs, original artwork, models, costumes and props, programmes, playbills and posters, reference books and periodicals (current and back copies), archive collections (primary & secondary material) (personal & business archives), audio and audiovisual recordings, slides and microfiche
Catalogues:
Catalogue for library is on-line. Catalogue for part of the collections is on-line.
Microform products:
Herbert Beerbohm Tree Archives (microfiche)
London Old Vic Archives (microfiche)

Address for ordering publications:
Microform publications:
Emmett Publishing Ltd
Glenthorne, Hill Road, Hindhead, Surrey, GU26 6QN, tel: 01428 609099

Internet home pages:
http://www.bristol.ac.uk/theatrecollection
Information about the theatre collection, its holdings and online catalogue.

381
BRITISH ASSOCIATION OF FRIENDS OF MUSEUMS
The Old Post Office, High Street, Butleigh, Glastonbury, Somerset, BA6 8SU

Tel: 01458 850520
Fax: 01458 850034
Email: bafm@templecloud.freeserve.co.uk
Acronym or abbreviation: BAFM

Organisation type and purpose: National organisation, membership association, voluntary organisation, registered charity (charity number 270253), museum, art gallery, historic building, house or site, consultancy.
To inform, encourage and support all those, whether in groups or as individuals, who wish to work in and for museums in a voluntary capacity.
Links with:
Association of Independent Museums
Museum Association
World Federation of Friends of Museums
Paris, France
Other addresses:
British Association of Friends of Museums
Manor Cottage, 25 Winsley, Bradford-on-Avon, Wiltshire, BA15 2LT, tel: 01225 723316, fax: 01225 723316

Enquiries to: Honorary Secretary
Other contacts: Administrator
Access:
Access to staff: By letter, by telephone, by fax, by email, Internet web pages
Hours: Mon to Fri, 0900 to 1700

General description:
Museums, the organisation and management of friends, groups, supporters and volunteers in museums of all kinds. Setting up a group, good practice, model constitution, contacts worldwide.
Printed publications:
The Handbook for Heritage Volunteer Managers and Administrators (£5 plus £1 p&p, 1999)
Handbook for Friends - How to set up and Run a Group of Friends for your Local Museum, Art Gallery, Theatre, Historic House, Garden or Archaeological Site (£10)
Insurance for Friends of Museums (£2)
Newsletter (3 times a year, free to members)
Information Sheets (14, free to members)

Internet home pages:
http://www.bafm.org.uk

382
BRITISH BALLOON MUSEUM AND LIBRARY
3 Chancer Road, Locks Heath, Southampton, SO31 6TF

Tel: 01489 603479
Email: tjthafb@aol.com
Acronym or abbreviation: BBM&L
Formed: 1979

Affiliated to:
British Balloon & Airship Club
Display is at this location:
West Berkshire Museum
The Wharf, Newbury, Berkshire, RG14 5AS, tel: 01635 30511, fax: 01635 38535, email/website: heritage@westberks.gov.uk

Enquiries to: Honorary Secretary

General description:
A collection of hot-air and gas balloons, with associated hardware and documentation relating to balloons and airships. Permanent displays are kept at the West Berkshire Museum. The library is housed at Cranfield University Library.
Catalogues:
Catalogue for part of the collections is only available in-house.

Internet home pages:
http://www.britishballoonmuseum.org.uk

383
BRITISH COMMERCIAL VEHICLE MUSEUM
King Street, Leyland, Lancashire, PR25 2LE

Tel: 01772 451011
Fax: 01772 623404
Acronym or abbreviation: BCVM
Formed: 1983

Organisation type and purpose: Museum, suitable for ages: all ages.

Enquiries to: Manager
Access:
Access to staff: By letter, by telephone

General description:
Commercial and passenger vehicles.
Information services:
Education services: Group education facilities, resources for Key Stages 1 and 2..
Collections:
British commercial vehicles from the close of the 19th century to the present day
500,000 glass plate negatives being computer enhanced
Displays showing the evolution of road vehicles for passenger, goods and delivery services
Exhibits from the horse-drawn era through to steam wagons and early petrol vehicles, up to the present day

384
BRITISH CYCLING MUSEUM
The Old Station, Camelford, Cornwall, PL32 9TZ

Tel: 01840 212811
Fax: 01840 212811
Formed: 1992

Organisation type and purpose: Museum.

Enquiries to: Curator
Access:
Access to staff: By letter, by telephone, by fax
Hours: Sun to Thu, 1000 to 1700
Access for disabled people: level entry, access to all public areas

General description:
Cycling history.
Collections:
A history of cycling from 1818
Over 400 examples of cycles
Over 1000 cycling medals, fobs and badges from 1881
Extensive library
Picture gallery

Internet home pages:
http://www.chycor.co.uk/cycling-museum

385
BRITISH DENTAL ASSOCIATION MUSEUM
64 Wimpole Street, London, W1M 8AL

Tel: 020 7563 4549
Fax: 020 7935 6492
Email: r.fea@bda-dentistry.org.uk
Acronym or abbreviation: BDAM
Formed: 1919

Organisation type and purpose: Professional body, museum.
Parent body:
British Dental Association (BDA)
at the same address

Enquiries to: Curator
Access:
Access to staff: By letter, visitors by prior appointment, members only
Access to building, collections or gallery: Prior appointment required

General description:
The history of the dental profession and dental industry in the United Kingdom. Two reconstructed Victorian dental surgeries; dental chairs from the 16th to 20th Centuries; dental equipment; X-ray machines; extraction tools; forceps; instruments; porcelain teeth; dentures; drills; engravings; prints; ceramics; postage stamps; toothpicks; badges; and tokens.
Collections:
Dental instruments, equipment and furniture
Small collection of dental archives
5000 images of dental history and personalities
Dental chair from Buckingham Palace
Collection of material relating to the scientific research of Sir John Tomes
Prints by T Rowlandson (1756-1827) and Boilly (1761-1845)

Internet home pages:
http://www.bda-dentistry.org.uk
General description of the collections, an image library, recent acquisitions.

386
BRITISH ENGINEERIUM, THE
The Droveway, off Nevill Road, Hove, East Sussex, BN3 7QA

Tel: 01273 559583
Fax: 01273 566403
Formed: 1976

Organisation type and purpose: Registered charity, museum, training organisation, consultancy.
Educational Charitable Trust with restoration workshops attached to the museum.
Connections with:
Industrial Continuum Limited
Tel: 01273 559583, fax: 01273 566403, email/website: info@britishengineerium.com

Enquiries to: Manager
Other contacts: Education Officer for education enquiries.
Access:
Access to staff: By letter, by telephone, by fax, by email
Hours: Mon to Fri, 0900 to 1700
Access for disabled people: Parking provided, level entry
Other restrictions: Ask for help on arrival for access to other areas.

General description:
Restoration and conservation engineering, industrial archaeology, conservation of steam engines, windmills, watermills and means of transport, museum design.
Information services:
Training courses and consultancy.
Special visitor services: Guided tours, materials and/or activities for children.
Education services: Group education facilities, resources for Key Stage 1..
Collections:
Library on all aspects of steam, including transport, engineering and hot air engines
Publications list:
is available in hard copy.
Printed publications:
Reports on above subjects

Internet home pages:
http://www.britishengineerium.com

387
BRITISH GOLF MUSEUM
Bruce Embankment, St Andrews, Fife, KY16 9AB

Tel: 01334 460046
Fax: 01334 460064
Formed: 1987

Organisation type and purpose: Museum.

Enquiries to: Curator
Direct email: kathrynbaker@randagc.org
Access:
Access to staff: By letter
Other restrictions: By appointment.
Access to building, collections or gallery: No prior appointment required
Access for disabled people: level entry, toilet facilities

General description:
History of golf in Britain and British influence abroad.
Information services:
Special visitor services: Materials and/or activities for children..
Catalogues:
Catalogue for library is in-house only. Catalogue for all of the collections is only available in-house.
Publications list:
is available on-line.
Printed publications:
All publications available from Museum Shop

Internet home pages:
http://www.britishgolfmuseum.co.uk
Location, galleries, publications, tourist information, historical information.

388
BRITISH HOROLOGICAL INSTITUTE
Upton Hall, Upton, Newark, Nottinghamshire, NG23 5TE

Tel: 01636 813795/6
Fax: 01636 812258
Email: clocks@bhi.co.uk
Acronym or abbreviation: BHI
Formed: 1858

Organisation type and purpose: Professional body, membership association (membership is by subscription), present number of members: 3000, museum, historic building, house or site, training organisation.
To protect and further the science and art of horology.
Houses the:
British Horological Federation

Enquiries to: General Secretary
Other contacts: Education Officer for education related services and facilities.
Access:
Access to staff: By letter, by telephone, by fax, by email, in person, Internet web pages
Hours: Mon to Fri, 0900 to 1700
Access to building, collections or gallery: No prior appointment required
Hours: Tue to Sat, 1100 to 1700; Sun, 1400 to 1700
Access for disabled people: Parking provided, level entry, toilet facilities
Other restrictions: Access to ground floor only.

General description:
Horology.
Collections:
Library including the Ilbert Collection
Printed publications:
Horological Journal

Internet home pages:
http://www.bhi.co.uk

389
BRITISH IN INDIA MUSEUM
1 Newtown Street, Colne, Lancashire, BB8 0JJ

Tel: 01282 870215 / 613129
Fax: 01282 870215
Formed: 1972

Organisation type and purpose: Independently owned, museum.

Enquiries to: Curator
Access:
Access to building, collections or gallery: No prior appointment required
Hours: Apr to Sep: Wed to Sat, 1400 to 1700
Other restrictions: Out of opening hours for individuals by prior appointment.
Groups min 15 by prior arrangement.

General description:
The museum contains a fascinating collection of material including model soldiers and models of the British in India at leisure, picture postcards,

continued overleaf

postage stamps, paintings, military uniforms and much more in four large rooms.
More exhibits are continually being added.

390
BRITISH LAWNMOWER MUSEUM

106-114 Shakespeare Street, Southport, Merseyside, PR8 5AJ

Tel: 01704 501336
Fax: 01704 500564
Email: museum@lawnmowerworld.co.uk
Formed: 1990
Formerly: Lawnmower Museum

Organisation type and purpose: Advisory body, museum, suitable for ages: all ages, research organisation.
To preserve and restore garden machinery of historical interest. To provide a tribute to the garden machinery industry over the last 170 years.

Enquiries to: Curator
Other contacts: Researcher, Archivist for archive information.
Access:
Access to staff: By letter, by telephone, by fax, by email, in person, visitors by prior appointment, Internet web pages
Access to building, collections or gallery: No prior appointment required
Hours: Mon to Sat, 0900 to 1730, closed Sun
Other restrictions: Guided tours by prior appointment.

General description:
Restored vintage garden machinery, safes, keys and locks.
Information services:
Helpline available, tel no: 01704 501336.
Restoration service on vintage garden machinery.
Special visitor services: Guided tours, tape recorded guides.
Education services: Group education facilities, resources for Further or Higher Education.
Services for disabled people: Displays and/or information at wheelchair height.
Collections:
300 lawnmowers, including machines made by Rolls Royce, Royal Enfield and Hawker Sidley
1830s to present day including, first Robot Mowers and those of the rich and famous
Archival books from 1799 AD, archival history on most garden machinery manufacturers
World's largest toy lawnmower collection
Catalogues:
Catalogue for library is on-line. Catalogue for all of the collections is on-line.
Publications list:
is available in hard copy.
Printed publications:
Museum brochure (free)
Electronic and video products:
Videos £19.99 each

Internet home pages:
http://www.lawnmowerworld.co.uk/
Brief history of the lawnmower, information about the Museum.

391
BRITISH LIBRARY

Philatelic Collections, 96 Euston Road, London, NW1 2DB

Tel: 020 7412 7635
Fax: 020 7412 7745
Email: philatelic@bl.uk
Formed: 1973

Organisation type and purpose: Non-departmental public body.
Access:
Access to staff: By letter, by telephone, by fax, by email, visitors by prior appointment
Hours: Mon to Fri, 0900 to 1700
Other restrictions: Reader's Pass required.
Access to building, collections or gallery: Prior appointment required
Hours: Mon to Fri, 1000 to 1600
Access for disabled people: ramped entry, toilet facilities
Other restrictions: Parking spaces for disabled people are in Midland Road.

General description:
Philately, postal history, philatelic literature, history of philately.
Collections:
Many including:
Board of Inland Revenue Stamping Department Archive
Crown Agents Philatelic and Security Printing Archive
Fletcher Collection
Foreign and Commonwealth Office Collection
Photograph Collection (of material not in the Library)
Harrison Collection
Tapling Collection (perhaps the most important and unique)
Catalogues:
Catalogue for part of the collections is only available in-house.
Printed publications:
Newsletter
Catalogue of the Crawford Library of Philatelic Literature at the British Library (Bacon Sir E, £90)
Stamps (Schoolley-West R F, 1987, £6.95)
The Care and Preservation of Philatelic Materials (Collings T J and Schoolley-West R F, £12.95)

Internet home pages:
http://www.bl.uk

392
BRITISH MOTOR INDUSTRY HERITAGE TRUST

Heritage Motor Centre, Banbury Road, Gaydon, Warwick, CV35 0BJ

Tel: 01926 641188
Fax: 01926 641555
Email: engines@heritagemotorcentre.org.uk
Acronym or abbreviation: BMIHT
Formed: 1975
Formerly: Leyland Historic Vehicles, date of change, 1979; BL Heritage, date of change, 1983

Organisation type and purpose: Registered charity (charity number 286575), museum, suitable for ages: all ages.
Conference centre, archive.

Enquiries to: Marketing Manager
Access:
Access to staff: By letter, by telephone, by fax, by email, visitors by prior appointment, Internet web pages
Hours: Mon to Fri, 0900 to 1630
Closed: 24, 25, 26 Dec
Access to building, collections or gallery: No prior appointment required
Hours: April to Oct, 1000 to 1800; Nov to Mar, 1000 to 1630
Closed: 24, 25, 26 Dec
Access for disabled people: Parking provided, ramped entry, level entry, access to all public areas, toilet facilities

General description:
All aspects of the British motor car companies and the British Motor Industry from 1896 through to today, incorporating historic documents and photographs from Riley, Rover, Land Rover, Wolseley, Austin, Morris, MG, Triumph, Standard and Mini, Austin-Healey, BMC, British Leyland and successors.
Collections:
Heritage Motor Centre Archive contains a large selection of drawings, photographs, production records, brochures and artefacts, business documents and special collections relating to Herbert Austin, William Morris, Miles Thomas and Alec Issigonis
Largest collection of British cars in the world
Lucas lamps and electrical items, 1890 to date
Photographic collection, film and still material from the factory photographic departments of Austin, Morris, Wolseley, MG, Riley, Rover, Landrover and Standard-Triumph, 1900 to 1970, some 800,000 images
Catalogues:
Catalogue for all of the collections is only available in-house.
Electronic and video products:
The large selection of videos of classic rallies and the heyday of motoring includes:
Classic Rallying Video selection includes Alpine, Monte Carlo and Tulip Rallies from 1954 to 1962
Heritage Motor Centre CD-ROM
Monte Carlo: Mini Legend (£11.95)
Le Mans 1955/64 (video)
Mini - Wizardry on Wheels (video)

Internet home pages:
http://www.heritage.org.uk
http://www.stratford.co.uk/bmiht

393
BRITISH MUSEUM (NATURAL HISTORY)

See - Natural History Museum

394
BRITISH MUSEUM ETHNOGRAPHY LIBRARY

See - Anthropology Library

395
BRITISH MUSEUM FRIENDS, THE

The British Museum, Great Russell Street, London, WC1B 3DG

Tel: 020 7323 8605 / 8195
Fax: 020 7323 8985
Email: friends@thebritishmuseum.ac.uk
Acronym or abbreviation: BMF
Formed from: British Museum Society (BMS), date of change, 1999

Organisation type and purpose: Membership association (membership is by subscription), present number of members: 14,500, registered charity (charity number 1086080), museum.
With:
The British Museum
London, WC1B 3DG, tel: 020 7323 8000

Enquiries to: Membership Officer
Other contacts: (1) Events Manager; (2) Young Friends Coordinator for BMF members' events, tel: 020 7323 8566.
Access:
Access to staff: By letter, by telephone, by fax, by email, Internet web pages
Hours: As museum opening hours via our membership desk
Access for disabled people: Parking provided, toilet facilities
Other restrictions: Limited parking; lift on forecourt; lifts to all levels.

General description:
The British Museum and its activities.
Collections:
Complete set of British Museum Magazines from 1970
Printed publications:
British Museum Friends Magazine (3 times a year, £2.50 per copy)
ReMUS (children's magazine, 3 times a year, £1 per copy (for ages 8-15))

Internet home pages:
http://www.british-museum.ac.uk

396
BRITISH MUSEUM
Great Russell Street, London, WC1B 3DG

Tel: 020 7323 8000
Minicom no. 020 7323 8920
Fax: 020 7323 8616
Email: information@thebritishmuseum.ac.uk
Acronym or abbreviation: BM
Formed: 1753
Formed from: Museum of Mankind, British Library

Organisation type and purpose: Museum. National museum.

Enquiries to: Information Officer
Direct tel: 020 7323 8299
Direct fax: 020 7323 8616
Other contacts: Visitor Information Manager
Access:
Access to staff: By letter, by telephone, by fax, by email, in person, Internet web pages
Hours: Mon to Sun, 0900 to 1730
Access for disabled people: Parking provided, ramped entry, level entry, access to all public areas, toilet facilities
Other restrictions: Pre-booking required for parking.

General description:
The history, culture and ethnography of much of the world from prehistoric times to the present day.
The collections are displayed in the following departments:
Greek and Roman Department
Ancient Near East Department
Oriental Department
Japanese Department
Prehistory and Early Europe Department
Medieval and Modern Europe Department
Coins and Medals Department
Egyptian Department
Ethnography Department
Prints and Drawings Department.
Information services:
Helpline available, tel no: 020 7323 8299.
Special visitor services: Guided tours, tape recorded guides, materials and/or activities for children.
Education services: Group education facilities, resources for Key Stages 1 and 2, 3 and 4.
Services for disabled people: For the visually impaired; for the hearing impaired.
Collections:
Records of the buildings, staff and administration, 1753 to the present day, are in the Central Archives
The departments hold manuscript records relating to the history of the collections
These include the papers of Charles Townley relating to his collection of classical antiquities, 1760-1805
Catalogues:
Catalogue for all of the collections is available in-house and part is on-line.
Publications list:
is available in hard copy.
Printed publications:
Books, children's books, scholarly titles
Full list of publications is available from the British Museum Company Limited, The British Museum Press

Address for ordering publications:
Printed publications:
British Museum Company Ltd
46 Bloomsbury Street, London, WC1B 3QQ, tel: 020 7323 1234, fax: 020 7436 7315, email: sales.products@bmcompany.co.uk

Internet home pages:
http://www.thebritishmuseum.ac.uk
General information about galleries, opening times, access for disabled visitors.
http://www.britishmuseum.co.uk
British Museum Company (retail and mail order).

397
BRITISH PIANO MUSEUM
See - Musical Museum

398
BRITISH PIANO MUSEUM EDUCATION TRUST
See - Musical Museum

399
BRITISH RED CROSS MUSEUM AND ARCHIVES
9 Grosvenor Crescent, London, SW1X 7EJ

Tel: 020 7201 5153
Minicom no. 020 7235 3159 (BRCS)
Fax: 020 7235 6456
Telex: 918657 BRCS
Email: enquiry@redcross.org.uk
Acronym or abbreviation: BRCS
Full name: British Red Cross Society
Formed: 1969
Formerly: British National Society for Aid to the Sick and Wounded in War, date of change, 1905

Organisation type and purpose: International organisation, registered charity (charity number 220949), museum, suitable for ages: 12+ 16+.
Parent body:
British Red Cross Society
9 Grosvenor Crescent, London, SW1X 7EJ
Links with:
Balfour Museum of Hampshire Red Cross History
Red Cross House, Stockbridge Road, Weeke, Winchester, tel: 01962 865174, fax: 01962 869721
London's Museums of Health and Medicine
Email/website: www.medicalmuseums.org
Registered Museum Member of:
Museums Association

Enquiries to: Curator (artefact-related enquiries)
Other contacts: (1) Archivist; (2) Information Assistant for (1) archive-related enquires; (2) general information and booking.
Access:
Access to staff: By letter, by telephone, by email, visitors by prior appointment, Internet web pages
Access to building, collections or gallery: Prior appointment required
Hours: Mon to Fri, 1000 to 1600; closed Bank Holidays
Other restrictions: Researchers meet a member of museum and archives staff (curator, archivist, information assistant). Appointments to see archivist or curator must be requested at time of booking.
Access for disabled people: ramped entry, toilet facilities
Other restrictions: Hearing loop available in meeting rooms, guided tours available.

General description:
BRCS founded in 1870. First Muniments room opened in 1969 with small display (Barnet Hill House, Guildford).
Material from the Society's national headquarters, regions, branches and centres.
Also items from people who served with or received assistance from the Society. Documents - official records of Society, personal accounts and reports.
Artefacts - textiles, equipment, medals and badges, art.
Photographs - extensive historical photographic collection.
Also access to modern collection.
Historical Reference Library.
Information services:
Library available for reference (for conditions see Access above)
Special visitor services: Guided tours.
Services for disabled people: For the hearing impaired; displays and/or information at wheelchair height.
Collections:
Changi Quilt - made by female civilian internees during WWII
1870 Flag - used by first Chairman of Society during Franco-Prussian War
Replica WWII food parcel made during WWII to illustrate contents
Toys made from fabric of Red Cross parcels - various dates
Paintings by Doris Zinkeisen
Posters - fundraising, youth, fundamental principles of BRCS
Album of Edith Maud Drummond-Hay - colour immages of WWI
WWI and WWII VAD indexes
Official reports and papers relating to National Society for Aid to Sick and Wounded in War
Catalogues:
Catalogue for library is in-house only. Catalogue for part of the collections is only available in-house.
Printed publications:
Various Medals and Badges
Historical fact sheets

Internet home pages:
http://www.redcross.org.uk/
http://www.redcross.org.uk/museums&archives
Information zone, online exhibitions.

400
BRITISH TOURIST AUTHORITY
See - English Tourist Council/British Tourist Authority

401
BROADFORD BOOKS AND GALLERY
Broadford, Isle of Skye, IV49 9AB

Tel: 01471 822748 and 01471 822011 (Gallery)
Email: enquiry@broadfordbooks.co.uk
Formed: 1988

Organisation type and purpose: Art gallery, suitable for ages: 16+.
Access:
Access to staff: By letter, by telephone, by email, in person, Internet web pages
Access for disabled people: Parking provided

General description:
Oil paintings, watercolour paintings, mixed media paintings, prints.

Internet home pages:
http://www.broadfordbooks.co.uk
http://www.skye-arts.co.uk

402
BROADWAY MAGIC EXPERIENCE
76 High Street, Broadway, Worcestershire, WR12 7AJ

Tel: 01386 858323
Fax: 01386 858323
Email: bearsanddolls@hotmail.com
Formed: 1995
Formerly: Broadway Teddybear Museum

Organisation type and purpose: Independently owned, museum, suitable for ages: all ages. Restoration of teddy bears and dolls, shop.

Enquiries to: Manager
Access:
Access to staff: By letter
Access for disabled people: Parking provided
Other restrictions: Not suitable for wheelchairs.

General description:
Museum of teddy bears and related items, covers history of teddy bears, famous bears and scenarios.
Upgraded during 2001 with many automated scenes.

403
BROCKHAMPTON HOUSE AND ESTATE
Greenfields, Bringsty, Worcester, WR6 5TB

Tel: 01885 482077 (Estate office), 01885 488099 (Lower Brockhampton)
Email: brockhampton@nationaltrust.org.uk

Organisation type and purpose: National organisation, registered charity (charity number 205846), historic building, house or site, suitable for ages: 8+.
Parent body:
The National Trust (West Midlands)
West Midlands Regional Office, tel: 01743 708100

Enquiries to: Manager
Access:
Access to staff: By letter, by telephone, by email

General description:
This 688ha (1700 acre) estate was bequeathed to the National Trust in 1946 and still maintains traditional farms and extensive areas of woodland, including ancient oak and beech. Visitors can enjoy a variety of walks through both park and woodland, which combine to form a rich habitat for wildlife such as the dormouse, buzzard and raven. A stone-flagged trail leads to the Lawn Pool and provides some access for those with disabilities. At the heart of the estate lies Lower Brockhampton House, a late 14th century moated manor house with a beautiful timber-framed gatehouse and interesting ruined chapel.
Information services:
Braille guide.
Suitable for school groups. Children's quiz/trail.
Special visitor services: Materials and/or activities for children.
Education services: Group education facilities.
Services for disabled people: For the visually impaired.

Internet home pages:
http://www.nationaltrust.org.uk

404
BRODICK CASTLE GARDEN AND COUNTRY PARK
Brodick, Isle of Arran, KA27 8HY

Tel: 01770 302202
Fax: 01770 302312
Email: brodick@nts.org.uk

Organisation type and purpose: Historic building, house or site.
Parent body:
National Trust for Scotland (West Region)

Enquiries to: Property Manager
Access:
Access for disabled people: toilet facilities
Other restrictions: Electric bus from Reception Centre to Castle, self-drive electric battery car for grounds bookable in advance from the castle, wheelchair available, Wilma's Walk nature trail suitable for disabled visitors

General description:
The ancient seat of the Dukes of Hamilton, the site was a fortress from Viking times. It has fine collections of furniture, paintings, porcelain and silver.
Collections:
Porcelain and silver
17th century furniture
Sporting pictures and trophies

405
BRODIE CASTLE
Brodie, Forres, Moray, IV36 2TE

Tel: 01309 641371
Fax: 01309 641600
Email: brodiecastle@nts.org.uk

Organisation type and purpose: Museum, art gallery, historic building, house or site.
Parent body:
National Trust for Scotland Highlands and Islands Office (North)

Enquiries to: Property Manager
Access:
Access to staff: By letter, by telephone, by fax, by email, in person
Access for disabled people: toilet facilities
Other restrictions: Access to nature trail and hides, wheelchair available

General description:
Fine 16th century Z-plan tower house with 17th and 19th century additions, home of the Brodie family for 600 years. Contains fine French furniture, English, Continental and Chinese porcelain, and a major collection of paintings, including 17th century Dutch art, 19th century English watercolours, Scottish Colourists and early 20th century works. Magnificent library holds 6,000 volumes.
Information services:
Audio tape tour, Braille guide, explanatory text in Dutch, French, German, Italian, Japanese, Spanish, Swedish.
Special visitor services: Tape recorded guides.
Services for disabled people: For the visually impaired.

Internet home pages:
http://www.nts.org.uk

406
BRODSWORTH HALL AND GARDENS
Brodsworth, Doncaster, South Yorkshire, DN5 7XT

Tel: 01302 722598

Organisation type and purpose: International organisation, advisory body, professional body, membership association (membership is by subscription), suitable for ages: all ages, training organisation, consultancy, research organisation.
Parent body:
English Heritage (Yorkshire Region)
Tel: 01904 601901

Enquiries to: Manager

General description:
One of England's most complete Victorian country houses, Brodsworth Hall was opened during 1995 following major restoration and conservation by English Heritage. Built in the Italianate style and decorated and furnished in the opulent fashion of the 1860s, much of the original scheme survives to this day, and shows how a wealthy family and their servants really lived during almost 150 years of occupation. The delightful grounds, open all year, are a mixture of formal and informal. New at Brodsworth is the magical Fern Dell in the Rock Garden, which is now open after major restoration work, and which boasts one of the largest fern collections in the north of England.
Collections:
Collections of paintings; sculpture; furniture; textiles; carpets; social history; and photographs
19th century Italian sculpture, c. 1865
Paintings by John Ward, 1810-1835

407
BROMHAM WATER MILL AND GALLERY
Bridge End, Bromham, Bedford, MK43 8LP

Tel: 01234 824330
Email: bromhmill@deed.bedfordshire.gov.uk
Formed: 1983

Organisation type and purpose: Local government body, museum, art gallery, historic building, house or site, suitable for ages: all ages. Working watermill.
Parent body:
Bedfordshire County Council
County Hall, Cauldwell Street, Bedford, MK42 9AP, tel: 01234 228330

Enquiries to: Information Officer
Access:
Access to staff: By letter, by telephone, by email, in person
Access for disabled people: Parking provided, toilet facilities

General description:
Industrial heritage, environment, art and craft, sustainability.
A collection of outmoded farming and milling equipment; there is a restored working 17th century watermill with integral machinery, and a collection of allied pieces.
Gallery with changing exhibitions every 5-6 weeks featuring local and national work.
Information services:
Picnic area and water meadow.
Special visitor services: Guided tours, materials and/or activities for children.
Education services: Group education facilities, resources for Key Stages 1 and 2 and 3..
Collections:
Working watermill with integral machinery
Printed publications:
Events Leaflets (free)

Internet home pages:
http://www.bedfordshire.gov.uk
Basic information on Mill and Gallery.

408
BROMLEY LOCAL STUDIES LIBRARY
Central Library, High Street, Bromley, Kent, BR1 1EX

Tel: 020 8460 9955
Email: localstudies.library@bromley.gov.uk

Organisation type and purpose: Local government body, public library, suitable for ages: 12+.
Parent body:
London Borough of Bromley

Enquiries to: Archivist
Access:
Access to staff: By letter, by telephone, by email, in person, Internet web pages
Hours: Mon, Wed, Fri, 0930 to 1800; Tue, Thu, 0930 to 2000; Sat, 0930 to 1700

General description:
Local history about Bromley and its surrounding areas.
Collections:
Parish records, maps, industrial records, family history resources

Internet home pages:
http://www.bromley.gov.uk

409
BROMLEY MUSEUM
The Priory, Church Hill, Orpington, Kent, BR6 0HH

Tel: 01689 873826
Email: bromley.museum@bromley.gov.uk
Full name: London Borough of Bromley Museum
Formed: 1965
Formerly: Orpington Museum, date of change, 1965

Organisation type and purpose: Local government body, museum, historic building, house or site, suitable for ages: 8+.
Parent body:
London Borough of Bromley (LBB)
Civic Centre, Stockwell Close, Bromley, BR1 3UH, tel: 020 8464 3333
Other addresses:
Crofton Roman Villa
Crofton Road, Orpington, BR6 8AD, tel: 01689 873826 or 020 8462 4737, fax: 020 8462 4737
Romano-British bath house & Anglo-Saxon cemetry
Poverest Road, Orpington

Enquiries to: Curator

Other contacts: Assistant Curator for education service enquiries.
Access:
Access to staff: By letter, by telephone, by email, in person
Hours: 1 Apr to 31 Oct, Sun to Fri, 1300 to 1700; Sat, 1000 to 1700;
Other restrictions: 1 Nov to 31 Mar:Closed Sun, Bank Holidays.
Access to building, collections or gallery: No prior appointment required
Hours: Mon to Fri 0900 to 1700
Other restrictions: Prior appointment required for items not on display.
Access for disabled people: Parking provided, ramped entry
Other restrictions: Ground floor only, accessible to wheelchair users.

General description:
Situated in attractive formal/informal gardens, the Museum is housed in an interesting medieval/post-medieval building. The displays illustrate the local history and archaeology of the London Borough of Bromley from earliest times to Domesday, and the life and work of Sir John Lubbock, 1st Lord Avebury, the man responsible for giving this country Bank Holidays. There is also a 20th century Social History Room.
Information services:
Library available for reference (for conditions see Access above)
Open for school visits each week-day morning 0900 to 1200 by appointment.
National curriculum subject based object handling boxes available for schools
Guided tours by prior appointment.
Changing displays/temporary exhibitions by the Museum and local groups throughout the year.
Special visitor services: Guided tours, tape recorded guides, materials and/or activities for children.
Education services: Group education facilities, resources for Key Stages 1 and 2, 3, 4 and Further or Higher Education..
Collections:
Most of the collections are held on computerised database (MODES)
Objects, fine art, Avebury Collection
Part of the collection of archaeology and ethnography of Sir John Lubbock, 1st Lord Avebury
Harlow Library: 18th to 20th century
Small natural history collection (not on display)
Catalogues:
Catalogue for library is in-house only. Catalogue for all of the collections is only available in-house.
Publications list:
is available in hard copy.
Printed publications:
Leaflets
Electronic and video products:
Taped Leaflets

Internet home pages:
http://www.bromley.gov.uk/museums
Basic information on all museums in London Borough of Bromley.

See also - Crofton Roman Villa; Romano-British Bathhouse

410
BRONTË PARSONAGE MUSEUM, THE

Church Street, Haworth, West Yorkshire, BD22 8DR

Tel: 01535 642323
Fax: 01535 647131
Email: bronte@bronte.org.uk
Formed: 1895
Formed from: The Brontë Society

Organisation type and purpose: Independently owned, learned society, registered charity (charity number 1232), museum, historic building, house or site, suitable for ages: 8+.

Parent body:
Brontë Society
As main address

Enquiries to: Librarian
Direct email: ann-dinsdale@bronte.org.uk
Access:
Access to staff: By letter, by telephone, by fax, by email, visitors by prior appointment, charges to non-members, Internet web pages
Hours: Mon to Fri, 1100 to 1700
Other restrictions: Prior appointment required to visit library.
Access to building, collections or gallery: No prior appointment required
Hours: Apr to Sep: daily, 1000 to 1730
Oct to Mar: daily, 1100 to 1700

General description:
History of the Brontë family and the areas associated with them; their lives, their work, their personal memorabilia.
Information services:
Library available for reference (for conditions see Access above)
Special visitor services: Materials and/or activities for children.
Education services: Group education facilities, resources for Key Stages 1 and 2, 3, 4 and Further or Higher Education.
Services for disabled people: For the visually impaired; for the hearing impaired.
Collections:
Brontë Society Collections - manuscripts, books, furniture, personal items, household objects, textiles, photographs, pictures, drawings
Bonnell Collection - manuscripts and books
Seton-Gordon Collection - manuscripts
Grolier Collection - manuscripts
Catalogues:
Catalogue for library is in-house only. Catalogue for all of the collections is only available in-house but part is published.
Printed publications:
Various publications including:
Biography
Criticism
Editions
Brontë Society Publications
Novels of the Brontës
Fiction
Children's editions
Poetry
Reference
Topography
Miscellaneous books
Electronic and video products:
Various audio tapes
Various Film Versions of the Brontë Novels (video)

Address for ordering publications:
Printed publications:
Shop Manager, Bronte Parsonage Museum

Internet home pages:
http://www.bronte.org.uk
Introduction to the museum and the society, general information about the Brontës, shop.
http://www.bronte.info.org.uk
General information

411
BROOKE ROBINSON MUSEUM

See - Dudley Museum & Art Gallery

412
BROOKLANDS MUSEUM

Brooklands Road, Weybridge, Surrey, KT13 0QN

Tel: 01932 857381
Fax: 01932 855465
Email: info@brooklandsmuseum.com
Formed: 1991

Organisation type and purpose: Museum.

Enquiries to: Curator
Other contacts: Marketing Manager for marketing, promotional, site hire and location use.

Access:
Access to staff: By letter, by fax, by email, visitors by prior appointment, Internet web pages
Hours: Summer, 1000 to 1700
Winter, 1000 to 1600
Access to building, collections or gallery: No prior appointment required
Other restrictions: Must be accompanied.
Access for disabled people: Parking provided, level entry, toilet facilities

General description:
Motoring and Aviation from 1907 (Motoring to 1939, Aviation to 1987).
Cycling, motorcycling, limited social and aviation architectural information.
Information services:
Library available for reference (for conditions see Access above)
Special visitor services: Guided tours, materials and/or activities for children.
Education services: Group education facilities, resources for Key Stages 1 and 2, 3 and 4..
Publications list:
is available on-line.
Printed publications:
Flying Start, the story of Flying Schools at Brooklands (book)
Electronic and video products:
Brooklands The Birthplace of British Aviation (video for purchase)
Brooklands The Birthplace of British Motorsport (video for purchase)

Internet home pages:
http://www.brooklandsmuseum.com

413
BROOKLANDS SOCIETY LIMITED

Rudgelands, 4 Blackstone Hill, Redhill, Surrey, RH1 6BE

Tel: 01737 217221
Fax: 01737 764401
Email: reynolds@rudgelands.prestel.co.uk
Formed: 1967

Organisation type and purpose: International organisation, learned society, membership association (membership is by subscription), present number of members: 1350, voluntary organisation.
Affiliated to:
Brooklands Museum Trust
Brooklands Museum, Brooklands Road, Weybridge, Surrey, KT13 0QN
Website management:
Brooklands Society Limited
Hartland, Copse Corner, 38 Coxheath Road, Church Crookham, Hampshire, GU13 0QC, tel: 01252 408877, fax: 01252 408878, email/website: brooklands@hartland.co.uk

Enquiries to: Assistant Secretary
Access:
Access to staff: By letter, by telephone, by fax, by email, visitors by prior appointment, Internet web pages
Hours: Mon to Fri, 0900 to 1700
Access to building, collections or gallery: Prior appointment required

General description:
Brookland motor course and airfield, history and preservation of relics.
Collections:
Large archive of films, photographs and artefacts related to the Brooklands motor course and the personalities involved for the period 1907-1987
Publications list:
is available in hard copy and online.
Printed publications:
The following are available free or for purchase direct:
Occasional Historic Publications
Quarterly Gazette
Quarterly Newsletter

Internet home pages:
http://www.brooklands.org.uk

414
BROSELEY PIPEWORKS, THE

Ironbridge Gorge Museum Trust, Coach Road, Coalbrookdale, Telford, Shropshire, TF8 7DQ

Tel: 01952 882445

Organisation type and purpose: Registered charity (charity number 503717-R), museum, historic building, house or site, suitable for ages: 5+.

Parent body:
Ironbridge Gorge Museum Trust
Tel: 01952 433522

Access:
Access for disabled people: toilet facilities
Other restrictions: Access guide for disabled visitors available on request.

General description:
Broseley, two miles from the Iron Bridge, was once home to one of the most prolific clay tobacco pipe-making factories in Britain. Production came to an end in the 1950s when the works were abandoned and left untouched. In the restoration of the works as a museum little has beeen changed since the workers left. The museum is a wonderfully preserved time-capsule of an ancient local industry.

Internet home pages:
http://www.ironbridge.org.uk

415
BROUGH CASTLE

Brough, Kirkby Stephen, Cumbria

Organisation type and purpose: National organisation, advisory body, historic building, house or site, suitable for ages: all ages.

Parent body:
English Heritage (North West Region)
Tel: 0161 242 1400

Enquiries to: Manager

Access:
Access to building, collections or gallery: No prior appointment required
Hours: Any reasonable time.

General description:
Dating from Roman times, the ruins of this 12th century keep replaced an earlier stronghold destroyed by the Scots in 1174. It was restored by Lady Anne Clifford in the 17th century.

416
BROUGHAM CASTLE

Brougham, Penrith, Cumbria, CA10 2AA

Tel: 01768 862488

Organisation type and purpose: Museum, historic building, house or site.

Parent body:
English Heritage (North West Region)
Canada House, 3 Chepstow Street, Manchester, M1 5FW, tel: 0161 242 1400

Enquiries to: Manager

Access:
Access to staff: By telephone
Access to building, collections or gallery: No prior appointment required
Hours: 29 Mar to 30 Sep: daily, 1000 to 1800,1 to 31 Oct: daily, 1000 to 1700
Other restrictions: Opening times are subject to change, for up-to-date information contact English Heritage by phone or visit the website.

General description:
Vital during the Anglo-Scottish wars and the Wars of the Roses, Brougham's military usefulness diminished after medieval times. Lady Anne Clifford finally inherited Brougham in 1643 and she restored and developed the property, making a country mansion out of an old defence structure. Today you can still see the outline of her kitchen gardens and the Countess Pillar. Also enjoy a lively exhibition of relics from the nearby Roman fort.

Internet home pages:
http://www.english-heritage.org.uk/

417
BROUGHTON CASTLE

Banbury, Banbury, Oxfordshire, OX15 5EB

Tel: 01295 276070
Fax: 01295 276070
Formed: 1306

Organisation type and purpose: Historic building, house or site, suitable for ages: 5+.

Enquiries to: Administrator

Access:
Access to staff: By letter, by fax
Access for disabled people: Parking provided
Other restrictions: Access to ground floor.

General description:
The home of Lord and Lady Saye and Sele and owned by the same family for over 600 years. It was built in 1300 and extended in 1550. It has a 3 acre moat and the rooms include a medieval Great Hall.

Collections:
Pictures, books, manuscripts
Vaulted passages, fine fireplaces, splendid plaster ceilings and panelling
Arms and armour from the Civil War and other periods
A Civil War parliamentary meeting place
Gardens and park

418
BROUGHTON HOUSE

12 High Street, Kirkcudbright, Dumfries & Galloway, DG6 4JX

Tel: 01557 330437
Fax: 01557 330437
Email: broughtonhouse@nts.org.uk

Organisation type and purpose: Museum.

Parent body:
National Trust for Scotland (NTS)
Wemyss House, 28 Charlotte Square, Edinburgh, EH2 4ET, tel: 0131 243 9300, fax: 0131 243 9301

Enquiries to: Property Manager

Access:
Access to staff: By letter, by telephone, by fax, by email, in person, charges to non-members
Access to building, collections or gallery: No prior appointment required
Hours: Apr to Jun and Sep to Oct, Mon to Sat, 1200 to 1700; Jul and Aug, Mon to Sat, 1000 to 1800, Sun, 1300 to 1700
Garden also open Feb to Mar, 1100 to 1600
Other restrictions: Exact opening and closing dates change yearly

General description:
18th century town house, the home, gallery and studio of the artist, E A Hornel, one of the 'Glasgow Boys' contains a collection of his paintings, along with paintings by other Scottish artists. There is also a notable library, particularly of local and Scottish interest (open only by application).

Collections:
Extensive collection of Scottish books including Burns' works, and local history material
Works of E A Hornel

Internet home pages:
http://www.nts.org.uk

419
BROUGHTY CASTLE MUSEUM

Castle Approach, Broughty Ferry, Dundee, DD5 2TF

Tel: 01382 436916
Fax: 01382 436951
Email: broughty@dundeecity.gov.uk
Formed: 1969

Organisation type and purpose: Museum, historic building, house or site, suitable for ages: all ages.

Parent body:
Dundee City Council Arts and Heritage
Dundee Contemporary Arts, 152 Nethergate, Dundee, DD1 4DY, tel: 01382 432321, fax: 01382 432252, email: arts.heritage@dundeecity.gov.uk

Enquiries to: Heritage Officer
Direct tel: 01382 436950

Access:
Access to staff: By letter, by email
Access to building, collections or gallery: No prior appointment required
Hours: Apr to Sep: Mon to Sat, 1000 to 1600; Sun, 1230 to 1600
Oct to Mar: Tue to Sat, 1000 to 1600; Sun, 1230 to 1600

Collections:
Local history
Whaling history
Military history
Natural history of local area

Printed publications:
Promotional Leaflet (1/3 A4 Colour)

Internet home pages:
http://www.dundeecity.gov.uk/broughtycastle
Visitor information on Broughty Castle, including opening times, access etc and images.

420
BROWNSBANK COTTAGE

See - Biggar Museum Trust

421
BROWNSEA ISLAND

Poole Harbour, Poole, Dorset, BH13 7EE

Tel: 01202 707744
Fax: 01202 701635
Email: office@brownseaisland.fsnet.co.uk

Organisation type and purpose: National organisation, registered charity (charity number 205846), historic building, house or site, suitable for ages: 8+.
Part is leased to Dorset Wildlife Trust, as a Nature Reserve.

Parent body:
National Trust (South West Region)
Wessex Regional Office, tel: 01958 843600

Enquiries to: Manager

Access:
Access to staff: By letter, by telephone, by fax, by email, Internet web pages
Access for disabled people: toilet facilities
Other restrictions: Powered mobility vehicles available, booking essential. Level entrance to shop and tea-room. Recommended route map available.

General description:
The site of the first Scout camp organised by the founder of the movement, Lord Baden-Powell. A wonderfully atmospheric island of heath and woodland, a haven for red squirrels and a rich variety of sea birds.
There are many fine walks and spectacular views of Poole Harbour.

Information services:
Nature reserve guided tours contact the Dorset Wildlife Trust Warden, 01202 709445;
Open-air theatre and other events contact the regional box office, 01985 843601;
Smugglers, young historian and explorer trails for children;
Education facilities, 01202 707744, Education centre, children's guides and quiz/trail.
Braille guide. Audio guide.
Special visitor services: Guided tours, tape recorded guides, materials and/or activities for children.
Education services: Group education facilities.
Services for disabled people: For the visually impaired.

Internet home pages:
http://www.nationaltrust.org.uk/regions/wessex

422
BRUCE CASTLE MUSEUM
Lordship Lane, London, N17 8NU

Tel: 020 8808 8772
Fax: 020 8808 4118
Email: museum.services@haringey.gov.uk
Formed: 1906
Formed from: Middlesex Regiment

Organisation type and purpose: Local government body, museum, suitable for ages: 8+.
Parent body:
Haringey Council
Haringey Libraries, Archive & Museum Service

Enquiries to: Curator
Other contacts: Education Officer for events programming.
Access:
Access to staff: By letter, by telephone, by email
Access to building, collections or gallery: No prior appointment required
Hours: Wed to Sun, 1300 to 1700
Other restrictions: Archives by prior appointment only.
Access for disabled people: Parking provided, ramped entry, level entry, access to all public areas, toilet facilities

General description:
Covers the local history of Tottenham, Wood Green and Hornsey, London Borough of Haringey; social history, costume, paintings, photographs, Roman kiln.
Information services:
Guided tours by prior appointment
Temporary art exhibitions
Regular activities for children
Special visitor services: Guided tours, tape recorded guides, materials and/or activities for children.
Education services: Group education facilities, resources for Key Stages 2 and 3.
Services for disabled people: For the visually impaired; for the hearing impaired; displays and/or information at wheelchair height.
Collections:
Local History
Social History
Photographs
Postal history, artefacts, documents, press cuttings, posters, 19th-20th century.
Borough of Haringey Archive
Publications list:
is available in hard copy.

Internet home pages:
http://www.haringey.gov.uk

423
BRUNEL ENGINE HOUSE MUSEUM
Railway Avenue, London, SE16 4LF

Tel: 020 7231 3840 (Sat & Sun only)
Email: curator@brunelenginehouse.org.uk
Formed: June 1975

Organisation type and purpose: Registered charity (charity number 1003287), museum, suitable for ages: 8+.
To educate the general public in the work of Sir Marc Brunel and Isambard Kingdom Brunel.

Enquiries to: Curator
Direct tel: 020 7231 3314
Direct email: robert.hulse@virgin.net
Access:
Access to staff: By letter, by telephone, by email, in person, Internet web pages

General description:
Located within the original engine house in Tunnel Road, Rotherhithe, London, the exhibition commemorates the world's first subaqueous tunnel built by Sir Marc and Isambard K Brunel between 1825-1843. The Brunels and the Thames Tunnel, Victorian London, engineering, tunnelling, London Underground.
Information services:
Special visitor services: Guided tours, materials and/or activities for children.
Education services: Group education facilities, resources for Key Stages 2, 3, 4 and Further or Higher Education..
Collections:
A collection of watercolours, models, memorabilia, coins and prints about Brunel
An exhibition describing the first tunnel built under a river anywhere in the world
Printed publications:
Brunel, Local History

Internet home pages:
http://www.brunelenginehouse.org.uk
General information.

424
BRUNTINGTHORPE AIRCRAFT MUSEUM
Bruntingthorpe Airfield, Lutterworth, Leicestershire, LE17 5QS

Tel: 0116 247 8030
Formed: 1993

Organisation type and purpose: Independently owned, museum, suitable for ages: 5+.

Enquiries to: Curator
Access:
Access to staff: By letter, by telephone, charges made to all users
Other restrictions: No permanent museum staff.
Access to building, collections or gallery: No prior appointment required
Hours: Sun, 1000 to 1600
Other restrictions: Groups by prior appointment at other times.
Access for disabled people: Parking provided, level entry, access to all public areas, toilet facilities

General description:
2nd World War airfield, modified for use as a USAF nuclear bomber base in the 1950s. Now in private ownership, and largely used for car storage, hence the restricted public access. Part of the former airfield is used as an aircraft museum. Aircraft on site change from time to time.
Information services:
Special visitor services: Guided tours..
Collections:
Some 30 to 40 aircraft, almost all jet and post-1945 machines
These are owned by about 14 different owners, and include fighters, bombers, trainers, tankers and transport aircraft
None fly, but nine are kept in running condition, and make simulated take-off runs in early May and early September along the 2 mile long runway
Printed publications:
Small brochure available, free

Internet home pages:
http://www.tvoc.co.uk
Progress on restoring Avro Vulcan Bomber to flying condition.

425
BRUTON GALLERY
PO Box 143, Holmfirth, West Yorkshire, HD9 1YU

Tel: 0870 747 1800
Email: art@BrutonGallery.co.uk
Formed: 1969

Organisation type and purpose: Art gallery, consultancy.

Enquiries to: Director
Access:
Access to staff: By email
Access to building, collections or gallery: Prior appointment required

General description:
French sculpture.
Publications list:
is available on-line.

Internet home pages:
http://www.BrutonGallery.co.uk

426
BT MUSEUM
Closed

427
BUCKHAVEN MUSEUM
Buckhaven Library, College Street, Buckhaven, Fife

Tel: 01592 260732

Organisation type and purpose: Local government body, museum, suitable for ages: all ages.

Enquiries to: Exhibitions Officer
Direct tel: 01592 412860
Direct fax: 01592 412870
Direct email: Dallas.Mechan@smtp5.fife.gov.uk
Access:
Access to staff: By letter, by fax
Access to building, collections or gallery: No prior appointment required
Hours: Mon, 1400 to 1700 and 1730 to 1900; Tue, 1000 to 1300 and 1400 to 1700; Thu, 1000 to 1300, 1400 to 1700 and 1730 to 1900; Fri, 1400 to 1700; Sat, 1000 to 1230
Access for disabled people: ramped entry

General description:
This display features the town's history with a focus on the fishing industry. See the stained glass windows made by local people with the help of a community artist, and a replica of a 1920s kitchen.

428
BUCKIE DRIFTER MARITIME HERITAGE CENTRE, THE
Freuchny Road, Buckie, Moray, AB56 1TT

Tel: 01542 834646
Fax: 01542 835995
Email: buckie.drifter@moray.gov.uk
Formed: 1994

Organisation type and purpose: Local government body, service industry (charity number SCO 21811), museum, art gallery, suitable for ages: all ages, training organisation. Maritime heritage centre.

Enquiries to: Museums Officer
Access:
Access to staff: By letter, by telephone, by fax, by email, in person, charges made to all users
Access for disabled people: Parking provided, level entry, access to all public areas, toilet facilities
Other restrictions: Lift, wheelchair available.

General description:
History of the herring fishing industry, steam and sailing, drifting, fishing; a recreated 1920s quayside.
Information services:
Special visitor services: Materials and/or activities for children..
Collections:
Fossils from the Moray Firth
37 foot Oakley Class lifeboat
Models of fishing boats
Catalogues:
Catalogue for part of the collections is only available in-house.

Internet home pages:
http://www.moray.org/area/bdrifter/intro.html

429
BUCKINGHAM CHANTRY CHAPEL
Market Hill, Buckingham

Tel: 01494 528051(Regional Office)

Parent body:
National Trust (South and South East Region)
Thames and Solent Regional Office, tel: 01491 528051, fax: 01372 452023

General description:
A 15th century chapel, the oldest building in Buckingham and incorporating a fine Norman doorway. Later used as a school, it was restored by Gilbert Scott in 1875.

Internet home pages:
http://www.nationaltrust.org.uk

430
BUCKINGHAMSHIRE COUNTY MUSEUM
Church Street, Aylesbury, Buckinghamshire, HP20 2QP

Tel: 01296 331441
Fax: 01296 334884
Email: museum@buckscc.gov.uk
Formed: 1854

Organisation type and purpose: Local government body, museum, art gallery.
Stores/offices:
Bucks County Museum Technical Centre
Tring Road, Halton, Aylesbury, Buckinghamshire, HP22 5PJ, tel: 01296 696012, fax: 01296 624519

Enquiries to: Head of Public Services
Access:
Access to staff: By letter, by telephone, by fax, by email
Hours: Mon to Fri, 0900 to 1700
Access to building, collections or gallery: No prior appointment required
Hours: Mon to Fri, 0900 to 1700
Other restrictions: For Technical Centre, Halton only.
Access for disabled people: Parking provided, level entry, access to all public areas, toilet facilities
Other restrictions: Parking - 2 disabled bays outside museum.

General description:
Buckinghamshire: social history; archaeology; natural history; geology; applied arts; fine art; costume.
Information services:
Library available for reference (for conditions see Access above), on-line searching
Special visitor services: Materials and/or activities for children.
Education services: Group education facilities, resources for Key Stages 1 and 2.
Services for disabled people: For the hearing impaired; displays and/or information at wheelchair height.
Collections:
Buckinghamshire lace
Costume
Studio ceramics
Topographical paintings and photographs of Buckinghamshire

Internet home pages:
http://www.buckscc.gov.uk/museum

See also - Roald Dahl Children's Gallery

431
BUCKINGHAMSHIRE RAILWAY CENTRE
Quainton Road Station, Quainton, Aylesbury, Buckinghamshire, HP22 4BY

Tel: 01296 655720
Formed: 1968
Formerly: Quainton Railway Society Limited

Organisation type and purpose: Membership association (membership is by subscription), present number of members: 1030, voluntary organisation, museum, historic building, house or site, suitable for ages: 2+.
Working steam railway.

Enquiries to: Administrator
Access:
Access to staff: By letter, by telephone, by fax, charges to non-members
Hours: Mon to Fri, 0930 to 1630
Access for disabled people: Parking provided, level entry, toilet facilities

General description:
UK railway history.
Printed publications:
Stock Book

Internet home pages:
http://www.bucksrailcentre.org.uk

432
BUCKLAND ABBEY
Yelverton, Devon, PL20 6EY

Tel: 01822 853607
Fax: 01822 855448
Email: bucklandabbey@nationaltrust.org.uk

Organisation type and purpose: National organisation, registered charity (charity number 205846), historic building, house or site, suitable for ages: 8+.
Parent body:
The National Trust (South West Region)
Devon and Cornwall Regional Office, tel: 01392 881691
Jointly managed by:
Plymouth City Museum
Drake Circus, Plymouth, Devon, PL4 8AJ, tel: 01752 304774

Enquiries to: Information Officer
Other contacts: Property Manager
Access:
Access to staff: By letter, by email, visitors by prior appointment
Access to building, collections or gallery: No prior appointment required
Hours: Mid Apr to Nov, Fri to Wed, 1030 to 1730; Nov and Dec, Sat and Sun, 1400 to 1700; mid-Feb to end Mar, Sat and Sun, 1400 to 1700
Open Bank Holiday Mondays
Open to groups off-peak seasons, phone for details
Other restrictions: Last admission 45 min before closing.
Access for disabled people: Parking provided, ramped entry, toilet facilities
Other restrictions: Designated parking 25yds. Transfer available. 2 manual wheelchairs available. Ground floor largely accessible, 1 step up and 2 steps down to chapel. Recommended route map.

General description:
Buckland was originally a small but influential Cistercian monastery. The house, which incorporates the remains of the 13th century abbey church, has rich associations with Sir Francis Drake and his seafaring rival, Sir Richard Grenville, containing much interesting memorabilia from their time. There are exhibitions on Buckland's 700-year history, as well as a magnificent monastic barn, an unusual herb garden, delightful estate walks and craft workshops. Recent developments include a hand-crafted plasterwork ceiling in the Drake Chamber, the Cot Lane rural crafts area and a new Elizabethan garden. The Abbey is managed jointly by the National Trust and Plymouth City Museum.
Information services:
Large-print guide. Touch list. Scented plants.
Independent craft workshops: variable opening (not Thur); tel. wood-turner (01364 631585), countryside artist (01752 783291).
Suitable for school groups. Education room/centre. Hands-on activities. Children's quiz/trail. Family activities in school holidays.
Front-carrying baby slings for loan.
Special visitor services: Guided tours, materials and/or activities for children.
Education services: Group education facilities, resources for Key Stage 2.
Services for disabled people: For the visually impaired.
Collections:
Plasterwork, Elizabethan (1576) and modern (1998)
Tudor Portraits
Drake's Drum (1596 - Elizabethan Side Drum)
Related artefacts to Sir Francis Drake
Printed publications:
Guide Book
Short Guide

Internet home pages:
http://www.nationaltrust.org.uk
Information on National Trust properties and research.

433
BUCKLEY LIBRARY AND HERITAGE CENTRE
The Precinct, Buckley, Flintshire, CH7 2EF

Tel: 01244 549210

Organisation type and purpose: Local government body, museum, suitable for ages: 8+.
Parent body:
Flintshire Museums Service
County Hall, Mold, Flintshire, CH7 6NW, tel: 01352 704400

Enquiries to: Information Officer

General description:
Local artefacts.
Information services:
Education services: Group education facilities, resources for Key Stages 1 and 2..
Collections:
Extensive collection of Buckley pottery, bricks, tiles and clay products.
Printed publications:
Rambles round Mold (Leslie C H, 2000, facsimile reprint of 1869 ed)
Resources for teachers/Amgueddfa Bwcle: adnoddau I athrawon (bi-lingual resource pack)
The Cambrian Popular Antiquities of Wales (Robinson P, 1994, facsimile reprint of 1815 ed)

Internet home pages:
http://www.

434
BUDE-STRATTON MUSEUM
The Castle, Bude, Cornwall, EX23 8LG

Tel: 01288 353576
Fax: 01288 353576
Email: theclerk@bude-stratton.gov.uk
Formed: 1976

Organisation type and purpose: Museum, historic building, house or site, suitable for ages: 12+.

Enquiries to: Curator
Other contacts: Archivist for extensive knowledge of collection.
Access:
Access to staff: By letter, by telephone
Access for disabled people: ramped entry, access to all public areas

General description:
Mainly a maritime museum with material on the shipwrecks in the local area. Photographs and artefacts of local trading vessels to 1920s. History of Bude, and military and social history, especially WW1 and WW2. History of Bude Canal including a working model of the inclined plane. Railway history, photographs, models, etc, plus artefacts of the Bude-Okehampton Branch Line. A well-stocked museum shop.

Collections:
Very large collection of slides/photographs on local history
Catalogues:
Catalogue for all of the collections is only available in-house.
Printed publications:
Locally produced booklets and videos on sale

Internet home pages:
http://www.budemuseum.org.uk

435
BUGATTI TRUST

Prescott Hill, Gotherington, Cheltenham, Gloucestershire, GL52 9RD

Tel: 01242 677201
Fax: 01242 674191
Email: trust@bugatti.co.uk
Acronym or abbreviation: Bugatti Trust
Full name: Bugatti Molsheim Limited
Formed: 1987

Organisation type and purpose: Membership association (membership is by subscription), present number of members: 140, registered charity (charity number 298099), museum, research organisation.
Study centre.

Enquiries to: Curator
Other contacts: Secretary for Curator is in only Thu and Fri, part-time.
Access:
Access to staff: By letter, by telephone, by fax, by email, visitors by prior appointment
Hours: Mon to Fri, 0930 to 1630
Other restrictions: Closed weekends except Prescott Speed Hill Climb weekends, Sun only; closed Bank Holidays.
Access to building, collections or gallery: No prior appointment required
Hours: Mon to Wed, 1000 to 1530; Thu, Fri, 1000 to 1700
Access for disabled people: level entry, access to all public areas, toilet facilities

General description:
All things Bugatti; extensive contemporary photograph archive; document archive; component display; car display; technical engineering drawings for virtually all Bugatti components (available to purchase to Bugatti Owners' Club Membership).
Collections:
Material associated with Ettore Bugatti 1881-1947; inventor, designer and constructor of cars, engines, railcars, etc. The collection includes drawings, photographs and historic documents relating to all aspects of Bugatti's life and work, and that of his father (Carlo), his brother (Rembrandt) and his son (Jean).
Bugatti drawings. Copies of factory drawings. 1901-1947
Hugh Conway. Documents, historical/technical. 1881-1989
Peter Hampton. Documents, historical/technical. 1901-1947
Photographs.
Catalogues:
Catalogue for library is in-house only. Catalogue for part of the collections is only available in-house.
Electronic and video products:
Videos

Internet home pages:
http://www.bugatti.co.uk
General Bugatti information.
http://www.bugatti.co.uk/trust
http://www.bugatti.co.uk/club

436
BUILDING OF BATH MUSEUM

The Countess of Huntingdon's Chapel, The Vineyards, Bath, BA1 5NA

Tel: 01225 333895
Fax: 01225 445473
Email: cathryn@bathmuseum.co.uk
Formed: 1992

Organisation type and purpose: Membership association (membership is by subscription), registered charity (charity number 291700), museum, public library, suitable for ages: all ages.

Enquiries to: Administrator
Other contacts: Curator for cultural matters.
Access:
Access to staff: By letter, by telephone, by fax
Hours: Tue to Fri 1030 to 1700
Other restrictions: Open from 15 Feb to 1 Dec.
Access for disabled people: level entry

General description:
The museum tells the story of how and why Georgian Bath was built. Exhibits explain the design, construction, decoration and lifestyle of the Georgian town house. The highlight is a huge, illuminated model of the entire city.
Georgian architecture, materials, tools, furnishings and decorative finishes; Selina, Countess of Huntingdon, Lady Huntingdon's Connection.
Information services:
Special visitor services: Guided tours, materials and/or activities for children.
Education services: Group education facilities..
Collections:
Wallpapers, 1700-1830
Prints, 1700-1830
Rare architectural books, 1650-1900
Stone carvings, 1700-1994
Plasterwork, 1700-1836
Models, 1970-1994
Tools, 1700-1860
Catalogues:
Catalogue for library is in-house only. Catalogue for all of the collections is only available in-house.
Printed publications:
Building of Bath Museum (guidebook, £3.50)
Building the King's Circus (for children, £3)
Stone - Building with Bath Stone (£3)
Windows - Sash windows and frames (£3)

Internet home pages:
http://www.bath-preservation-trust.org.uk

437
BUILDWAS ABBEY

Buildwas, Ironbridge, Telford, Shropshire, TF8 7BW

Tel: 01952 433274

Organisation type and purpose: National organisation, historic building, house or site.
Parent body:
English Heritage (West Midlands Region)
Tel: 0121 625 6820

Enquiries to: Manager
Access:
Access to staff: By letter, by telephone
Access to building, collections or gallery: No prior appointment required
Hours: 1 Apr to 30 Sep: daily, 1100 to 1700
Other restrictions: Opening times are subject to change, for up-to-date information contact English Heritage by phone or visit the website.

General description:
Set beside the River Severn, against a backdrop of wooded grounds, are the extensive remains of this Cistercian abbey founded in 1135.

Internet home pages:
http://www.english-heritage.org.uk

438
BUNGAY MUSEUM

Council Offices, Broad Street, Bungay, Suffolk, NR35 1EE

Tel: 01986 892176
Formed: 1963

Organisation type and purpose: Local government body, museum, suitable for ages: all ages.
Museum of local history.
Parent body:
Waveney District Council
Community Services Department, Mariners Street, Lowestoft, Suffolk, NR32 1JT, tel: 01502 523005

Enquiries to: Curator
Direct tel: 01986 893155
Access:
Access to staff: By letter, by telephone, in person, visitors by prior appointment
Other restrictions: Curator only available by prior appointment.
Access to building, collections or gallery: No prior appointment required
Hours: Mon to Fri, 0900 to 1300 and 1400 to 1630

General description:
The Museum provides information about life in Bungay from prehistoric times to the present day via displays of archaeology, geology, coins and social history.
Information services:
Special visitor services: Guided tours, materials and/or activities for children..
Collections:
Coin Collection: Roman to Victorian
Archaeology: Pre-historic to Roman
Geology of local significance
Programmes, posters, pamphlets and photographs illustrating the buildings of Bungay and social life in the town c1800-2000
Information about book production connected with Clays Printers
Memorabilia relating to the family of the local diarist, John Barber Scott
Catalogues:
Catalogue for part of the collections is published.
Printed publications:
Museum Guide (available direct, 60p)

439
BUNKER PRESERVATION TRUST, THE

Crown Building, Shrubland Road, Mistley, Manningtree, Essex, CO11 1HS

Tel: 01206 392271
Fax: 01206 393847
Email: info@essexsecretbunker.com
Acronym or abbreviation: BPT
Full name: Essex Secret Bunker Museum
Formed: 1995

Organisation type and purpose: Registered charity (charity number 1069916), museum, historic building, house or site, suitable for ages: all ages, research organisation.
Preservation of cold war structures, artefacts and documents for the period 1946 to 1993.

Enquiries to: Curator
Access:
Access to staff: By letter, by telephone, by fax, by email, in person, visitors by prior appointment, Internet web pages
Hours: 1 Apr to end Oct, daily 1030 to 1700
Access to building, collections or gallery: No prior appointment required
Hours: 1 Apr to end Oct, daily 1030 to 1700
Other restrictions: Research by prior appointment.
Access for disabled people: Parking provided, level entry, toilet facilities

General description:
UK cold war bunkers; UK cold war bunkers archive; video and film library; artefacts store; cold war history relating to government and emergency administration; The Royal Observer Corps; emergency (nuclear war) planning.
Collections:
The National Cold War Collection
Catalogues:
Catalogue for library is in-house only. Catalogue for all of the collections is on-line.
Publications list:
is available in hard copy and online.

continued overleaf

Printed publications:
Copies of Documents
Guide Books
Electronic and video products:
Video Films
Video film from 1946 to 1993, Emergency Planning etc

Internet home pages:
http://www.essexsecretbunker.com
Overview

440
BURGH HOUSE TRUST
New End Square, London, NW3 1LT

Tel: 020 7431 0144
Fax: 020 7435 8817
Formed: 1979

Organisation type and purpose: Registered charity (charity number 275552), museum, art gallery, historic building, house or site.
Community arts centre, historic house (Queen Anne Grade I listed building).
Rooms for hire for wedding receptions, parties and functions (fund-raising which is major source of income).
Fund-raising support group:
Friends of Burgh House
Other address:
Hampstead Museum
at the same address

Enquiries to: General Manager
Other contacts: Publicity Officer for events and general public relations aspects.
Access:
Access to staff: By letter, by telephone, by fax, in person
Hours: Wed to Sun, 1200 to 1700; Sat, by appointment
Other restrictions: Closed Christmas, New Year, Good Fri and Easter Mon; open other bank holidays 1400 to 1700.
Access for disabled people: ramped entry

General description:
Photographs, cards, books and specialist collections including local historical aspects.
Isokon furniture and part of Allingham collection, Hampstead history including Hampstead at War.
Information services:
Visually impaired - large print for displays.
Hearing impaired - hearing loop in Music Room.
Museum information at reception on ground floor.
Special visitor services: Guided tours.
Education services: Group education facilities, resources for Further or Higher Education.
Services for disabled people: For the visually impaired; for the hearing impaired.
Catalogues:
Catalogue for library is in-house only. Catalogue for all of the collections is only available in-house.
Printed publications:
Various publications available for purchase, direct
Topham & Son - a family of artists
Helen Allingham and Hampstead
D H Lawrence and his Hampstead Circle
Where they Lived in Hampstead (with map)
Hampstead in Children's Books
Stanley Spencer - a Hampstead Vision
Historic Taverns
The Rowney Family - Painting and Production in Hampstead

See also - Hampstead Museum

441
BURGHLEY HOUSE
Stamford, Lincolnshire, PE9 3JY

Tel: 01780 752451
Fax: 01780 480125
Email: info@burghley.co.uk

Organisation type and purpose: Independently owned, historic building, house or site, suitable for ages: 5+.

Enquiries to: Curator
Other contacts: Manager
Access:
Access to staff: By letter, by telephone, by fax, by email
Access for disabled people: Parking provided, toilet facilities
Other restrictions: Chair lift access to some areas, telephone for details.

General description:
One of the great stately homes of England, the house dates from 1560. Remarkable collections of Italian art, textiles, ceramics, furniture.
Information services:
Special visitor services: Guided tours, materials and/or activities for children..
Collections:
Italian oil paintings, 16th-18th century
European ceramics, 16th-20th century
Textiles
English furniture, 17th-19th century
Oriental ceramics, 16th-19th century
Catalogues:
Catalogue for part of the collections is published.
Printed publications:
Catalogues to various aspects of collections

Internet home pages:
http://www.burghley.co.uk
General.

442
BURNHAM-ON-CROUCH & DISTRICT MUSEUM
The Quay, Burnham-on-Crouch, Essex

Tel: 01621 783444

Organisation type and purpose: Independently owned, voluntary organisation, museum, historic building, house or site.
Largely funded by its own efforts.
The preservation of the local heritage.
Run by:
Burnham-on-Crouch & District Local History and Amenity Society

General description:
Archaeological and social history artefacts of the Dengie Hundred of Essex; the emphasis is on maritime and agricultural artefacts.
The premises are of great historical interest, built at the turn of the century for boat building, they were in use until 1980.
Collections:
Archive of old photographs. Particularly of sailing and topography.
Hammon collection of flints
Maritime history. Boat building, sailmaking, oyster laying, etc.
Catalogues:
Catalogue for part of the collections is only available in-house.

443
BURNS COTTAGE AND MUSEUM
Alloway, Ayr, KA7 4PY

Tel: 01292 441215
Fax: 01292 441750
Formed: 1814

Organisation type and purpose: Independently owned, registered charity (charity number SCO 09941), museum, historic building, house or site, suitable for ages: 5+.
Administering body:
Burns National Heritage Park
Murdoch's Lone, Alloway, Ayr, KA7 4PQ, tel: 01292 443700, fax: 01292 441750, email/website: info@burnsheritagepark.com

Enquiries to: Curator of Collections
Direct tel: 01292 445677
Direct email: ercburnscottage@netscapeonline.co.uk
Access:
Access to staff: By letter, by telephone, by fax, by email, in person
Access to building, collections or gallery: No prior appointment required
Hours: 1 Apr to 30 Sep: daily, 0930 to 1730,1 Oct to 31 Mar: daily, 1000 to 1700
Other restrictions: Access to library by prior appointment only.
Access for disabled people: Parking provided, ramped entry, access to all public areas, toilet facilities

General description:
Robert Burns - his life and work, his background, contemporaries and family, the influences which affected him or his work, the times in which he lived, his legacy, including associations and movements established in his honour or to spread knowledge of his work.
Information services:
Services for disabled people: Displays and/or information at wheelchair height.
Collections:
Collection of original manuscripts, many in Robert Burns' hand, including poems, songs and letters, personal items belonging to Burns, his family and connections
Extensive collection of Burns' published work and related books, artworks and artefacts reflecting his life, work and legacy
Letters from Burns to Alex Cunningham, writer, 1788-1796, 10 letters
Letters to Graham of Foray, friend and patron, 1788-1794, 24 letters and manuscripts of poems
Scots Musical Museum, collection of Burns books of Scots songs, 6 books
Printed publications:
Guide Book - Cottage, Museum, Monument (available for purchase)

444
BURNS HOUSE
See - Robert Burns House

445
BURRELL COLLECTION, THE
Pollok Country Park, 2060 Pollokshaws Road, Glasgow, G43 1AT

Tel: 0141 287 2550
Fax: 0141 287 2597
Formed: 1983

Organisation type and purpose: Local government body, art gallery, historic building, house or site, suitable for ages: all ages.
Parent body:
Glasgow Museums
Art Gallery and Museum, Kelvingrove, tel: 0141 287 2699

Enquiries to: Manager
Access:
Access to staff: By letter, by telephone, by fax, visitors by prior appointment
Access to building, collections or gallery: No prior appointment required
Hours: Mon to Thu, 1000 to 1700; Fri and Sun 1100 to 1700
Other restrictions: Closed 25, 26 Dec and 1, 2 Jan
Access for disabled people: Parking provided, access to all public areas, toilet facilities
Other restrictions: Wheelchair access and lifts to all floors

General description:
The collection was gifted to the city of Glasgow in 1944. Contains art objects from the ancient civilisations of Iraq, Egypt, Greece and Italy, from the Orient and from Mediaeval Europe. It includes paintings, sculptures, bronzes, ceramics, stained glass, metal work, arms and armour, tapestries, embroidery and furniture.
Information services:
Programme of talks.
Temporary exhibition gallery

Special visitor services: Guided tours, materials and/or activities for children.
Education services: Group education facilities..
Collections:
The Burrell Collection of some 9000 works of art.
Printed publications:
A wide range of publications; list available direct from the museum shop

Internet home pages:
http://www.colloquium.co.uk/www/glasgow/burrell.html
http://www.glasgow.gov.uk/cls

See also - Berwick-upon-Tweed Barracks

446
BURSLEDON WINDMILL MUSEUM

Windmill Lane, Bursledon, Southampton, SO31 8BG

Tel: 023 8040 4999
Formed: 1813

Organisation type and purpose: Local government body, historic building, house or site.
Parent body:
Hampshire County Council Museum Service (HCCMS)
Chilcomb House, Bar End, Winchester, Hampshire, tel: 01962 846304

Enquiries to: Curator
Access:
Access to staff: By letter, by telephone, in person
Access for disabled people: Parking provided

General description:
History of windmilling in Hampshire since the 18th century.
History of mill technology in Great Britain.
Practical stoneground flour production using wind power.
Information services:
Special visitor services: Guided tours.
Education services: Group education facilities, resources for Key Stages 1 and 2, 3, 4 and Further or Higher Education.
Services for disabled people: For the hearing impaired.
Collections:
Agricultural items from HCCMS collections relating to threshing and winnowing grain
Printed publications:
The Evolution of Windmills for Milling Grain in Hampshire (1991, direct, £2)
Harvest Home - Harvesting grain in Hampshire 1750 to present day (1993, direct, £1)
Teachers Pack (2002, direct, free)
Guide (2001, direct, 10p)
History (2002, direct, 30p)
Electronic and video products:
Windmill Video (direct, £4.25)

Internet home pages:
http://www.hants.gov.uk/museums/windmill

447
BURSLEDON WINDMILL

Windmill Lane, Bursledon, Southampton, SO3 8BG

Tel: 023 8040 4999
Email: musmgb@hants.gov.uk
Formed: 1991

Organisation type and purpose: Local government body, museum, suitable for ages: 5+.
Parent body:
Hampshire County Council Museums Service
Chilcomb House, Winchester, SO23 8RD, tel: 01962 846304, fax: 01962 869836

Enquiries to: Curator
Access:
Access to staff: By letter, by telephone, by fax, by email, in person

General description:
Restored and working windmill from 1813 to 1992, flour milling; producing stone-ground flour, the mill and displays demonstrate the relevance of wind energy to the modern age and agriculture.
Information services:
Education services: Resources for Key Stages 1 and 2 and 3.
Services for disabled people: For the hearing impaired.
Catalogues:
Catalogue for all of the collections is on-line.
Printed publications:
The following HCCMS inhouse publications for purchase from the Mill:
Burlesdon Windmill 'How it Works' (leaflet, 10p)
A Brief History (leaflet 30p)
Harvest Home (£1)
The Evolution of Windmills (£2)
A Gazeteer of Hampshire Windmills (£1)
Burlesdon Windmill Recipe Book (£1.50)
Electronic and video products:
Behind the Scenes at Burlesdon Windmill (video for purchase from the Mill)

Address for ordering publications:
Printed publications:
Registrar, Hampshire County Council Museums Service HQ
Chilcomb House, Winchester, SO23 8RD

Internet home pages:
http://www.hants.gov.uk/museums/
HMCMS web catalogue, whole collection, 100,000 plus web pages.

448
BURTON AGNES HALL

Burton Agnes, Driffield, East Yorkshire, YO25 0ND

Tel: 01262 490324
Fax: 01262 490513

Organisation type and purpose: Registered charity (charity number 272796).
Historic house.

Enquiries to: Administrator
Access:
Access to staff: By letter, by telephone, by fax
Hours: Mon to Fri, 0900 to 1300
Access for disabled people: Parking provided, ramped entry, toilet facilities

General description:
An Elizabethan house with original carving and plasterwork. Contains furnishings collected by the family over 4 centuries, with a large collection of Impressionist and Post-Impressionist paintings.
Catalogues:
Catalogue for all of the collections is only available in-house.
Printed publications:
Guide Books

449
BURTON ART GALLERY & MUSEUM

Victoria Park, Kingsley Road, Bideford, Devon, EX39 2QQ

Tel: 01237 471455
Formed: 1951

Organisation type and purpose: Museum, art gallery.
Supported by:
Friends of the Burton Art Gallery & Museum
c/o The Gallery, tel: 01237 471455

Enquiries to: Information Officer
Access:
Access to staff: By telephone
Hours: Tue to Sat, 0900 to 1700; Sun, 1400 to 1700
Access to building, collections or gallery: No prior appointment required
Hours: Summer: Tue to Sat, 1000 to 1700; Sun, 1400 to 1700
Winter: Tue to Sat, 1000 to 1600; Sun, 1400 to 1600
Other restrictions: Closed Mon except for Bank Holidays.
Access for disabled people: level entry, access to all public areas, toilet facilities
Other restrictions: Lift to first floor.

General description:
First built in 1950 by Thomas Burton, the building was almost completely rebuilt in 1993/1994. It now houses a local museum; the Coop collection of watercolours; the North Devon Slipware Collection, a craft gallery; a workshop; and visiting exhibition including examples of Henry Moore, Picasso and Paula Rego.
Information services:
Special visitor services: Guided tours, materials and/or activities for children..
Collections:
Permanent collection of oils and watercolours of 19th and 20th century
Museum artefacts relating to Bideford's history
Long Bridge model
Town Charter 1573
North Devon Slipware Collection
Napoleonic ship models
Local industry artefacts
McTaggart Short, visiting card cases, 1720-1940, c. 400 items
Art exhibitions both national touring and by local artists
Craft sales area
Catalogues:
Catalogue for part of the collections is on-line.
Printed publications:
Brochure of year's activities and exhibitions (free)
Gallery Catalogue of permanent collection and museum (£1.20 plus p&p)

Internet home pages:
http://www.burtonartgallery.co.uk
Catalogue and current exhibitions, workshops, museum, Friends Association.

450
BUS AND COACH COUNCIL

See - National Tramway Museum

451
BUSCOT OLD PARSONAGE

Buscot, Faringdon, Oxfordshire, SN7 8DQ

Tel: 01793 7622209 (Coleshill Estate Office)
Email: buscot@nationaltrust.org.uk

Organisation type and purpose: National organisation, registered charity (charity number 205846), historic building, house or site.
Parent body:
The National Trust (South and South East Region)
Thames and Solent Regional Office, tel: 01494 528051

Enquiries to: Property Manager
Access:
Access to staff: By letter, by email
Access to building, collections or gallery: Prior appointment required
Hours: Apr to Oct, Wed, 1400 to 1800
Other restrictions: Visits by appointment in writing with the tenant
Not suitable for groups.

General description:
An early 18th century house of Cotswold stone, set on the banks of the Thames and with a small garden.

Internet home pages:
http://www.nationaltrust.org.uk

452
BUSCOT PARK

Estate Office, Faringdon, Oxfordshire, SN7 8BU

Tel: 01367 240786
Fax: 01367 241794
Email: estbuscot@aol.com

continued overleaf

Organisation type and purpose: National organisation, registered charity (charity number 205846), museum, historic building, house or site.
Parent body:
The National Trust (South and South East Region)
Thames and Solent Regional Office, tel: 01494 528051
Administered on behalf of National Trust by:
Lord Faringdon
Contents of house owned by:
Faringdon Collection Trust

Enquiries to: Manager
Access:
Access to staff: By letter, by email
Access to building, collections or gallery: No prior appointment required
Hours: House and grounds: Apr to Sep, Wed, Thu, Fri, 1400 to 1800; grounds also open Mon, Tue, Apr to Sep; open weekends in season, 1400 to 1800, please check for details
Open Bank Holiday Mondays and Good Friday, times as weekends

General description:
The late 18th century neo-classical house, set in parkland, contains the fine paintings and furniture of the Faringdon Collection Trust. The grounds include various avenue walks, and an Italianate water garden, designed in the early 20th century by Harold Peto, and a large walled garden.
Information services:
Services for disabled people: For the visually impaired.

Internet home pages:
http://www.buscot-park.com

See also - Faringdon Collection Trust

453
BUSHEY MUSEUM & ART GALLERY

Rudolph Road, Bushey, Hertfordshire, WD23 3HW

Tel: 020 8420 4057
Fax: 020 8420 4923
Email: busmt@bushey.org.uk
Formed: 1983
Formed from: Bushey Museum Trust

Organisation type and purpose: Voluntary organisation, registered charity (charity number 294261), museum, art gallery, suitable for ages: all ages.
Community museum and local studies centre.
Parent body:
Bushey Museum Trust
Funded by:
Friends of Bushey Museum
Hertsmere Borough Council

Enquiries to: Curator
Access:
Access to staff: By letter, by telephone, by fax, by email, in person
Hours: Thu, Fri, 1100 to 1600
Access to building, collections or gallery: No prior appointment required
Hours: Thu to Sun, 1100 to 1600
Other restrictions: Prior appointment required for access to the local studies centre.
Access for disabled people: Parking provided, ramped entry, access to all public areas, toilet facilities

General description:
Local history of Bushey and district. Art Schools and artists in Bushey over the last 200 years, especially the Munro Circle, Herkomer Art School, Lucy Kemp-Welch and Marguerite Frobisher Schools. Local archives. Changing temporary exhibitions.
Information services:
Education services: Group education facilities, resources for Key Stages 1 and 2..

Collections:
Large fine art collection by Bushey artists, especially Hubert von Herkomer RA and his students
Local archaeological, social, commercial and industrial displays
Local records
Collections relating to famous local firms and institutions, including Cobra Polishes; Ellams Duplicators; Lotts Bricks (toys); Naturecraft models; Colne Valley Water; Royal Masonic School for Boys; and records of H T Cox and Sons (fine art printers).
Catalogues:
Catalogue for library is in-house only. Catalogue for all of the collections is only available in-house.
Publications list:
is available in hard copy and online.
Printed publications:
Local publications including:
Bushey Archive Photographs (1997)
Bushey in 1900 (2000)
Bushey Then & Now (1997)
Bushey Village Trail (1989)
Electronic and video products:
WW2 in Bushey (CD-ROM)

Internet home pages:
http://www.busheymuseum.org
Brief description, ordering publications

454
BUTE MUSEUM

7 Stuart Street, Rothesay, Isle of Bute, PA20 0EP

Tel: 01700 505067
Formed: 1872
Owned by: Buteshire Natural History Society, date of change, Formed 1872

Organisation type and purpose: Independently owned, museum, suitable for ages: 5+.
Parent body:
The Buteshire Natural History Society
at the same address

Enquiries to: Custodian
Access:
Access to staff: By letter, by telephone
Access for disabled people: ramped entry, level entry
Other restrictions: Toilet facilities - not special.

General description:
The Bute Museum Trustees collect, document, exhibit, conserve and interpret material and information relating to the Island of Bute for the local community, tourists and correspondents at home and abroad: natural history, local history, archaeology, geology, paper and photograph archives, genealogy.
Information services:
Library available for reference (for conditions see Access above)
Special visitor services: Materials and/or activities for children.
Education services: Group education facilities, resources for Key Stages 1 and 2, 3, 4 and Further or Higher Education.
Services for disabled people: For the visually impaired; displays and/or information at wheelchair height.
Collections:
Old Rothesay in photographs
4 ft scale model of the paddle steamer, Duchess of Fife, 1901-1953
Catalogues:
Catalogue for library is in-house only. Catalogue for all of the collections is only available in-house.
Publications list:
is available in hard copy.
Printed publications:
Bute: An Island history
The Piers and Ferries of Bute
Children's Guide to Bute
Nature Trails 1-7
Glimpses of Bute History
Map of the Island's Archaeology
Transactions of the Bute Natural History Society (every four years)

455
BUTTERCROSS MUSEUM

See - Ludlow Museum

456
BUTTRUM'S MILL

Woodbridge, Suffolk

Tel: 01473 583352

Organisation type and purpose: Historic building, house or site.
Access:
Access to staff: By telephone

General description:
19the century tower mill with particularly fine machinery.

Internet home pages:
http://www.tidemill.org.uk/buttmill.html

457
BUXTON MUSEUM & ART GALLERY

Terrace Road, Buxton, Derbyshire, SK17 6DU

Tel: 01298 24658
Fax: 01298 79394
Email: buxton.museum@derbyshire.gov.uk
Formed: 1891

Organisation type and purpose: Local government body, museum, art gallery, suitable for ages: all ages.
Connections with:
Derbyshire Libraries and Heritage Department
County Hall, Matlock, Derbyshire, tel: 01629 580000, email/website: libraries@derbyshire.gov.uk

Enquiries to: Museums Manager
Direct email: ros.westwood@derbyshire.gov.uk
Access:
Access to staff: By letter, by telephone, by fax, by email, in person, visitors by prior appointment
Access for disabled people: ramped entry, access to all public areas
Other restrictions: Parking available.

General description:
Archaeology: Derbyshire palaeontology, through Neolithic, to Romans and medieval.
Geology: particularly, carboniferous limestone.
Associated archives to both above by Sir William Boyd Dawkins and Dr J W Jackson.
Decorative art, especially Ashford Black Marble and Spar.
Photograph archives, especially Board collection of Buxton.
Information services:
Library available for reference (for conditions see Access above)
Special visitor services: Guided tours, materials and/or activities for children.
Education services: Group education facilities, resources for Key Stages 1 and 2, 3, 4 and Further or Higher Education.
Services for disabled people: For the visually impaired.
Collections:
W Boyd Dawkins archive, archaeology (mainly documents), 1860- 1927, c. 5000 items
J W Jackson archive, palaeontology, archaeology documents and artefacts, 1900-1970, c. 40,000 items
Catalogues:
Catalogue for part of the collections is only available in-house.

Internet home pages:
http://www.derbyshire.gov.uk/libraries

458
BWTHYN LLYWELYN
Beddgelert, Caernarfon, Gwynedd, LL55 4YA

Tel: 01766 890293 (Property)
Fax: 01766 890545

Organisation type and purpose: National organisation, registered charity (charity number 205846), historic building, house or site.
Parent body:
The National Trust Office for Wales
Tel: 01492 860123

Other contacts: Warden: 01766 890659, Education: 01766 890664
Access:
Access to staff: By letter, by telephone, by fax
Access for disabled people: ramped entry
Other restrictions: Ground floor fully accessible. Level entrance to shop.

General description:
A shop and exhibition are housed in this 17th century cottage, situated in the picturesque village of Beddgelert, near the Aberglaslyn Pass and within the Snowdonia National Park. There are superb walks in the area, including a stroll to the legendary Gelert's grave.
Information services:
Services for disabled people: For the visually impaired.

Internet home pages:
http://www.nationaltrust.org.uk

459
BYGONES MUSEUM
Holkham Park, Wells-Next-the-Sea, Fakenham, Norfolk, NR23 1AB

Tel: 01328 711383
Fax: 01328 711707
Email: s.harvey@holkham.co.uk
Formed: 1979

Organisation type and purpose: Independently owned, museum, suitable for ages: 8+.

Enquiries to: Curator
Other contacts: Assistant Curator
Access:
Access to staff: By letter, by telephone, by fax, by email, in person, Internet web pages
Access for disabled people: Parking provided, ramped entry, access to all public areas, toilet facilities

General description:
Holkham Bygones Museum is adjacent to 18th century Holkham Hall, home of the Coke Family and Earls of Leicester.
18th and 19th century farming (4-course system etc), Coke of Norfolk, late 19th century and 20th century, domestic, social and agricultural memorabilia illustrating how ordinary people lived and worked. Displays of dairy, brewing, cobbler and laundry items, and music boxes.
A selection of classic cars, tractors and some very rare steam engines.
Information services:
Services for disabled people: Displays and/or information at wheelchair height.
Collections:
A collection of vintage cars and tractors, including rate steam engines including:
1870 - Robert Tidman, steam centre engine - one of thirteen known to exist
1925 - Farmers Foundry - portable stationary steam engine - one of only two known to exist
Robinson 4 hot air engine - one of maybe two in existence
History of farming exhibition, 1750-1990
Coke of Norfolk
Catalogues:
Catalogue for all of the collections is only available in-house.

Internet home pages:
http://www.holkham.co.uk
Click on 'Bygones Museum' to find out more.

460
BYLAND ABBEY
Coxwold, North Yorkshire, YO61 4BD

Tel: 01347 868614

Organisation type and purpose: National organisation, advisory body, museum, historic building, house or site.
Parent body:
English Heritage (Yorkshire Region)
Tel: 01904 601901

Enquiries to: Manager
Access:
Access to staff: By letter, by telephone, in person
Access to building, collections or gallery: No prior appointment required
Hours: 29 Mar to 30 Sep: daily, 1000 to 1300 and 1400 to 1800,1 to 31 Oct: daily, 1000 to 1300 and 1400 to 1700
Other restrictions: Opening times are subject to change, for up-to-date information contact English Heritage by phone or visit the website.
Access for disabled people: toilet facilities

General description:
A beautiful ruin set in quiet meadows in the shadow of the Hambleton Hills. It shows the later development of Cistercian churches.

Internet home pages:
http://www.english-heritage.org.uk

461
CABINET WAR ROOMS
Clive Steps, King Charles Street, London, SW1P 3AE

Tel: 020 7930 6961
Email: cwr@iwm.org.uk
Formed: 1984

Organisation type and purpose: Museum.
Parent body:
Imperial War Museum
Lambeth Road, London, SE1 6AZ, tel: 020 7416 5000, fax: 020 7416 5374

Enquiries to: Director
Direct fax: 020 7839 5897
Direct email: preed@iwm.org.uk
Other contacts: Marketing Officer
Access:
Access to staff: By letter, by telephone, by fax, by email, visitors by prior appointment
Hours: Apr to End Sep: Mon to Sun, 0930 to 1800
Oct to End Mar: Mon to Sun, 1000 to 1700
Access to building, collections or gallery: No prior appointment required
Hours: Apr to end Sep: Mon to Sun, 0930 to 1800
Oct to end Mar: Mon to Sun, 1000 to 1700
Other restrictions: Last admission 1715 in Summer, 1630 in Winter

General description:
Winston Churchill's underground headquarters used during the Second World War. The 21 rooms housed in a former government office basement, were used by the Prime Minister, the War Cabinet, the Chiefs of Staff and Defence Committees, and numerous intelligence and ancillary staff. All the fittings and fixtures have been kept just as they were during the Second World War.
Catalogues:
Catalogue for part of the collections is only available in-house.

462
CADBURY WORLD
Linden Road, Bournville, Birmingham, B30 2LD

Tel: 0121 451 4159
Fax: 0121 451 1366
Formed: 1990

Organisation type and purpose: Museum, suitable for ages: 4+.
Visitor Centre, international public limited company.
Manufacture and marketing of confectionery and soft drinks.
Parent body:
Cadbury Trebor Bassett

Enquiries to: Archivist
Other contacts: Bookings Office tel 0121 451 4159 for reserve visits.
Access:
Access to staff: By letter, by telephone, by email
Hours: Hours vary - phone for details.
Access to building, collections or gallery: Prior appointment required
Hours: Vary around 1000 to 1600
Access for disabled people: Parking provided, ramped entry, level entry, toilet facilities
Other restrictions: Access to almost all areas.

General description:
Social history, industrial history and relations, industrial geography, business administration, marketing, ancient history through to 20th century.
Collections:
Historical examples of packaging

463
CAIY STANE
Caiystane View, Edinburgh

Organisation type and purpose: Historic building, house or site.
Parent body:
National Trust for Scotland (South Region)
Access:
Access for disabled people: Parking provided, level entry, access to all public areas
Other restrictions: Easy access on pavement.

General description:
Prehistoric cup-marked stone said to mark the site of an ancient battle.

Internet home pages:
http://www.nts.org.uk

464
CALANAIS STANDING STONES AND VISITOR CENTRE
Calanais, Isle of Lewis, HS2 9DY

Tel: 01851 621422
Fax: 01851 621446
Email: calanais.centre@btinternet.com
Acronym or abbreviation: Calanais Visitor Centre
Formed: 1995

Organisation type and purpose: Independently owned, registered charity (charity number SCO 22483), historic building, house or site, suitable for ages: 5+.
Visitor centre.
Interpretation.
Other site:
Doune Broch Visitor Centre
Caroloway, Isle of Lewis, tel: 01851 643338

Enquiries to: Manager
Access:
Access to staff: By letter, by telephone, by fax
Access for disabled people: Parking provided, level entry, access to all public areas, toilet facilities

General description:
Audiovisual interpretation about Standing Stones.
Printed publications:
Calanais Stones Guide Book (in reprint at present)
Interpretation leaflets in German, Norwegian, French.

465
CALDICOT CASTLE & COUNTRY PARK
Church Road, Caldicot, Caldicot, Monmouthshire, NP26 4HU

Tel: 01291 420241
Fax: 01291 435094
Email: caldicotcastle@monmouthshire.gov.uk
Formed: 1127

Organisation type and purpose: Local government body, historic building, house or site, suitable for ages: all ages.
Parent body:
Monmouthshire County Council
County Hall, Cwnibran, NP44 2XH, tel: 01633 644644

Enquiries to: Castle Development Officer
Access:
Access to staff: By letter, by telephone, by email, visitors by prior appointment, Internet web pages
Other restrictions: Visits by arrangement on weekdays only to staff.
Access to building, collections or gallery: No prior appointment required
Hours: Mar to Oct: Daily, 1100 to 1700
Other restrictions: Admission charges applies.
Access for disabled people: level entry, toilet facilities
Other restrictions: Staff are happy to advise on access prior to or during a visit.

General description:
Magnificent Welsh border castle set in fifty-five acres of beautiful parkland. The twelfth century keep stands on the original motte, and the castle was developed in royal hands in the fourteenth century with the addition of a tower and imposing gatehouse. The castle was restored as a family home by antiquarian Joseph Cobb, and has Victorian Room settings and tranquil gardens.
Information services:
Special visitor services: Tape recorded guides, materials and/or activities for children.
Education services: Group education facilities, resources for Key Stages 1 and 2.
Services for disabled people: For the visually impaired.
Collections:
Collections relate to the history of the castle and its restoration.

Internet home pages:
http://www.caldicotcastle.co.uk
Visitor information.

466
CALEDONIAN RAILWAY (BRECHIN) LIMITED
The Station, 2 Park Road, Brechin, Angus, DD9 7AF

Tel: 01561 377760; 01356 622992 Talking timetable
Formed: 1982

Organisation type and purpose: Membership association (membership is by subscription), present number of members: 200, voluntary organisation, registered charity, museum.
To create a working railway museum.
Subsidiary body:
Brechin Railway Preservation Society
at the same address

Enquiries to: Information Officer
Direct tel: 01561 377760
Other contacts: Marketing Director
Access:
Access to staff: By letter, by telephone
Hours: Mon to Fri, 0900 to 1700

General description:
History and operation of the Caledonian Railway, history of the line that is used, and of railways in Angus.
Printed publications:
Newsletter (free to members of the BRPS)
Internet home pages:
http://www.caledonianrailway.co.uk

467
CALEDONIAN RAILWAY ASSOCIATION
45 Sycamore Drive, Hamilton, South Lanarkshire, ML3 7HF

Tel: 01698 457777
Email: fred.landery@btinternet.com
Acronym or abbreviation: CRA
Formed: 1983

Organisation type and purpose: Voluntary organisation, research organisation.

Enquiries to: Membership Secretary
Access:
Access to staff: By letter, by telephone, by email, charges to non-members
Hours: Mon to Fri, 0900 to 1700
Other restrictions: Sample publications sent in return for two 2nd class stamps.

General description:
Research and study of former Caledonian Railway Company, including locomotive drawings, coach & wagon drawing, signal box track diagrams, industrial relations, architecture, publicity material, shipping services, tickets and history.
Printed publications:
Locomotive Drawings (quarterly)
Signal Box Track Diagrams (quarterly)
The True Line (journal, quarterly)
Timetable reprints (periodically)
Wagon Drawings (quarterly)

Address for ordering publications:
Printed publications:
Sales Officer, Caledonian Railway Association
73 Victoria Park Drive North, Glasgow, G14 9PS

Internet home pages:
http://www.crassoc.org.uk
Details of Society and publications, how to join.

468
CALKE ABBEY
Ticknall, Derbyshire

Tel: 01332 863822
Fax: 01332 865272
Email: calkeabbey@nationaltrust.org.uk

Organisation type and purpose: National organisation, registered charity (charity number 205846), historic building, house or site, suitable for ages: 5+.
Parent body:
National Trust (East Midlands Region)
East Midlands Regional Office, tel: 01909 486411

Enquiries to: Property Manager
Access:
Access to staff: By letter, by telephone, by fax, by email, in person, Internet web pages
Access for disabled people: Parking provided, level entry, toilet facilities
Other restrictions: Transfer from designated parking, 500yds, available. Drop-off point. 5 manual wheelchairs available. Ground floor accessible with assistance. No access to other floors. Audiovisual/video. Photograph album. Level entrance to shop. Level entrance to restaurant. Park: parts are accessible. Garden and church difficult for wheelchair users.

General description:
This baroque mansion, built 1701-3 and set in a stunning landscape park, has become famous as a graphic illustration of the English country house in decline. Little restored, the house contains the spectacular natural history collection of the Harpur Crewe family, as well as a magnificent 18th century state bed and interiors that are essentially unchanged since the 1880s.
The open parkland is managed for its nature conservation value, and the attractive grounds feature a beautiful walled garden and an interesting collection of garden buildings, including a newly restored orangery.
Information services:
Braille guide. Touch list
Sympathetic Hearing Scheme
Suitable for school groups. Education room/centre. Live interpretation.
Children's guide. Children's quiz/trail. Family activity packs
Open-air concert in August.
Special visitor services: Guided tours, materials and/or activities for children.
Education services: Group education facilities.
Services for disabled people: For the visually impaired; for the hearing impaired.

Internet home pages:
http://www.nationaltrust.org.uk

469
CALLENDAR HOUSE
Callendar Park, Falkirk, Strathclyde, FK1 1YR

Tel: 01324 503770
Fax: 01324 503771
Email: callendar.house@falkirk.gov.uk
Full name: Falkirk Museums
Formed: 1992
Formerly: Falkirk District Museums, date of change, 1992

Organisation type and purpose: Local government body, museum.
Parent body:
Falkirk Council
Falkirk Museums

Enquiries to: Manager
Other contacts: Archivist or Collections Manager for access to collections.
Access:
Access to staff: By letter, by telephone, by fax, by email, in person
Access to building, collections or gallery: No prior appointment required
Hours: Mon to Sat, 1000 to 1700 (all year)
Apr to Sep only: Sun, 1400 to 1700
History Research Centre: Mon to Fri, 1000 to 1230 and 1330 to 1700
Closed all public holidays
Access for disabled people: Parking provided, level entry, access to all public areas, toilet facilities

General description:
Permanent exhibitions: Story of Callendar House and William Forbes's Falkirk.
Working interpretive areas: 1825 kitchen, general store, clockmaker, printer and garden.
Specialist subjects: local history; Romans; Georgian period; archaeology; industry; social history; visual arts and crafts; archive; clocks; printing; domestic life; ironfounding; brickmaking; bookbinding; agriculture; transport; public health; environmental studies.
Information services:
Library available for reference (for conditions see Access above)
Special visitor services: Materials and/or activities for children.
Education services: Group education facilities.
Services for disabled people: Displays and/or information at wheelchair height.
Catalogues:
Catalogue for library is in-house only. Catalogue for all of the collections is only available in-house.

Internet home pages:
http://www.falkirk.net/about/callender.htm

470
CALSHOT CASTLE
Fawley, Southampton

Tel: 02380 892023
Formed: 16th Century

Organisation type and purpose: Historic building, house or site, suitable for ages: 5+.

Parent body:
English Heritage (South East Region)
Eastgate Court, 195-205 High Street, Guildford, Surrey, GU1 3EH, tel: 01483 252000, fax: 01483 252001
Access:
Access to building, collections or gallery: No prior appointment required
Hours: Apr to Oct: daily, 1000 to 1600

General description:
Coastal Fort built by Henry VIII, restored as a pre-World War I garrison.

Internet home pages:
http://www.english-heritage.org.uk

471
CAMBER CASTLE
Camber, Rye, East Sussex

Tel: 01797 223862

Organisation type and purpose: Historic building, house or site, suitable for ages: 5+.
Parent body:
English Heritage (South East Region)
Eastgate Court, 195-205 High Street, Guildford, Surrey, GU1 3EH, tel: 01483 252000, fax: 01483 252001
Managed by:
Rye Harbour Nature Reserve
Tel: 01797 223862

Enquiries to: Reserve Manager
Access:
Access to building, collections or gallery: No prior appointment required
Hours: Jul to Sep: Sat and Sun, 1400 to 1700
Other restrictions: Last entry 1630

General description:
Coastal defence fort built by Henry VIII to protect the entrance to Rye Harbour.

Internet home pages:
http://www.english-heritage.org.uk

472
CAMBORNE SCHOOL OF MINES GEOLOGICAL MUSEUM AND GALLERY
University of Exeter, Trevenson Pool, Redruth, Cornwall, TR15 3SE

Tel: 01209 714866
Fax: 01209 716977

Parent body:
University of Exeter

Enquiries to: Curator
Access:
Access to staff: By letter, by telephone, by fax

General description:
A display of rocks and minerals from Cornwall and all over the world. Features monthly exhibitions by local artists.
Collections:
Norris collection of minerals

Internet home pages:
http://geo-server.ex.ac.uk

473
CAMBRIAN RAILWAY SOCIETY LIMITED
See - Oswestry Transport Museum

474
CAMBRIDGE AND COUNTY FOLK MUSEUM
2-3 Castle Street, Cambridge, CB3 0AQ

Tel: 01223 355159
Email: info@folkmuseum.org.uk
Formed: 1936

Organisation type and purpose: Independently owned, registered charity (charity number 311309), museum.

Enquiries to: Curator
Access:
Access to staff: By letter, by telephone, by email, in person, charges to non-members, Internet web pages
Hours: Oct to Mar: Tue to Sat, 1030 to 1700: Sun, 1400 to 1700
Apr to Sep: Mon to Sat, 1030 to 1700: Sun, 1400 to 1700

General description:
Local and social history.
Information services:
Special visitor services: Guided tours, tape recorded guides, materials and/or activities for children.
Education services: Group education facilities, resources for Key Stages 1 and 2.
Services for disabled people: For the visually impaired.
Collections:
Collection of artefacts relating to history of Cambridge from the 17th century to the present day. Includes tools, childhood antiques, domestic artefacts and folklore
Printed publications:
Museum Guide
What's On in the Museum (2 times a year)
Electronic and video products:
This is your Cambridge (CD-ROM)

Internet home pages:
http://www.folkmuseum.org.uk
Museum opening times, collections and exhibitions information, events, museum history.

475
CAMBRIDGE MUSEUM OF TECHNOLOGY
The Old Pumping Station, Cheddars Lane, Cambridge, CB5 8LD

Tel: 01223 368650
Email: museumoftechnology@ic24.net
Formed: 1968

Organisation type and purpose: Independently owned, membership association (membership is by subscription), present number of members: 50, voluntary organisation, registered charity (charity number 311310), museum, historic building, house or site, suitable for ages: 5+.

Enquiries to: General Secretary
Access:
Access to staff: By letter, by telephone, visitors by prior appointment, Internet web pages
Hours: No fixed times
Access for disabled people: Parking provided

General description:
Preserved Victorian pumping station; steam, gas, oil engines; printing; Cambridge industry.
Information services:
Special visitor services: Guided tours..
Collections:
Albion, Wharfedale, Columbian, Adana printing presses
Babcock and Wilcox boilers
Gas engines
Hathorn Davey steam engine
Headley steam engines
Catalogues:
Catalogue for part of the collections is only available in-house.
Printed publications:
Guide
Museum booklets

Internet home pages:
http://www.museumoftechnology.com

476
CAMBRIDGE UNIVERSITY
Whipple Museum of the History of Science, Free School Lane, Cambridge, CB2 3RH

Tel: 01223 330906
Fax: 01223 334554
Email: hps-whipple-museum@lists.cam.ac.uk
Formed: 1944

Organisation type and purpose: Museum, university department or institute.
Museum attached to the Department of History and Philosophy of Science of the University of Cambridge.

Enquiries to: Associate Keeper of Collections
Access:
Access to staff: By letter, by fax, by email
Hours: Mon to Fri, 1330 to 1630
Other restrictions: Disabled access is via a service lift. Please phone to make arrangements.

General description:
History of science, early scientific instruments.
Exhibition: A University Within Ourselves: Sciences in Cambridge in the Eighteenth century, 'Discover' gallery.
Collections:
Cambridge Scientific Instrument Company Collection of instruments, literature and instruction manuals
Early instruments from Cambridge Colleges and Departments
Heywood Collection of early English microscopes
Hookham Collection of hand-held electronic calculators
Pollard Collection of instrument-makers' literature c. 1890-1940
R S Whipple Collection of early scientific instruments and books
Catalogues:
Catalogue for part of the collections is only available in-house.
Publications list:
is available in hard copy and online.
Printed publications:
These include:
Embryos in Wax: Models from the Ziegler studio (Hopwood N, 2002)
Your Humble Servant, John Flamsteed: Letters and writings of the first Astronomer Royal (Willmoth F, 2002)
Instruments in Print: Books from the Whipple Collection (Renzi S, 2000)
An University Within Ourselves: Sciences in Cambridge in the Eighteenth Century (1998)

Internet home pages:
http://www.hps.cam.ac.uk/whipple.html
Introduction to the museum, publications list.

See also - Fitzwilliam Museum

477
CAMERA OBSCURA AT DUMFRIES MUSEUM
Dumfries Museum & Camera Obscura, The Observatory, Church Street, Dumfries, DG2 7SW

Tel: 01387 253374
Fax: 01387 265081
Email: dumfriesmuseum@dumgal.gov.uk

Organisation type and purpose: Local government body, museum, historic building, house or site, suitable for ages: all ages.
Parent body:
Dumfries & Galloway Museum Service
Same address, tel: 01387 253374

Enquiries to: Manager
Direct email: ElaineK@dumgal.gov.uk
Access:
Access to staff: By letter, by telephone, by fax, by email, in person

General description:
The oldest working camera obscura in the UK.
Exhibitions include: Georgian astronomical and meteorological observatory;
weather station; and an exhibition of the agriculture and crafts of Dumfries.
Information services:
Suitable for school parties
Special visitor services: Materials and/or activities for children.
Education services: Group education facilities, resources for Key Stage 2..

continued overleaf

Internet home pages:
http://www.dumgal.gov.uk/museums

478
CAMERONIANS (SCOTTISH RIFLES) REGIMENTAL MUSEUM
See - Low Parks Museum

479
CAMPAIGN FOR MUSEUMS
35-37 Grosvenor Gardens, London, SW1W 0BX

Tel: 020 7233 9796
Fax: 020 7233 6770
Email: info@campaignformuseums.org.uk
Formed: 1996
Formerly: 24 Hour Museum, Museums Week

Organisation type and purpose: National organisation, registered charity (charity number 1070649).
Promoting museums and galleries to visitors and opinion-formers.

Enquiries to: Executive Director
Access:
Access to staff: By email
Access to building, collections or gallery: Prior appointment required

General description:
Marketing, promotion, awareness-raising, campaigns.
Printed publications:
Publications available via website

Internet home pages:
http://www.campaignformuseums.org.uk

480
CAMPBELTOWN MUSEUM
Campbeltown Library and Museum, Hall Street, Campbeltown, Argyll, PA28 6BS

Tel: 01586 552366
Fax: 01586 552938
Formed: 1898

Organisation type and purpose: Museum.
Parent body:
Argyll and Bute Council
Kilmory, Lochgilphead, PA31 8RT, tel: 01546 602127

Enquiries to: Museums Development Officer
Direct tel: 01369 703214
Direct fax: 01369 703214
Other contacts: Area Librarian, Mid Argyll Kintyre and Islay for Museums Development Officer if not available.
Access:
Access to staff: By letter, by telephone, by fax, in person
Hours: Tue to Sat, 1000 to 1300 and 1400 to 1700, Tue and Thu, 1730 to 1930

General description:
Local aspects of social and industrial archaeology, geology, natural history and social history.
Collections:
Beacharra ware and a jet necklace.
Important Neolithic, Bronze Age and Iron Age archaeological material from local sites.
Catalogues:
Catalogue for all of the collections is only available in-house.

Internet home pages:
http://www.argyll-bute.gov.uk

481
CANAL MUSEUM
Stoke Bruerne, Towcester, Northamptonshire, NN12 7SE

Tel: 01604 862229
Fax: 01604 864199
Full name: The Waterways Trust
Formed: 1963
Formed from: British Waterways
Formerly: Waterways Museum, date of change, 1990

Organisation type and purpose: Registered charity (charity number 1074541), museum, historic building, house or site, suitable for ages: all ages.
Museum, charitable trust associated with nationalised industry.
Part of:
The Waterways Trust
The Trust House, Church Road, Watford, Hertfordshire

Enquiries to: Manager
Access:
Access to staff: By letter, by telephone, by fax, visitors by prior appointment
Hours: Mon to Fri, 0900 to 1600
Access for disabled people: toilet facilities
Other restrictions: Ramped entry is planned.

General description:
Inland navigations past and present, with particular emphasis on Midlands-London. Social history of the waterways and colourful decoration of the narrowboats. Specialist courses in waterway crafts, specialist bookshop and souvenir outlet, general information.
Information services:
Special visitor services: Guided tours.
Education services: Group education facilities, resources for Key Stages 1 and 2, 3, 4 and Further or Higher Education..
Collections:
Displays, artefacts, pictures, documents, charting inland transport up to present day
Painted ware of the narrowboats
Social history displays
Publications list:
is available in hard copy.
Printed publications:
Constantly changing publications - apply direct
Electronic and video products:
Audio/Visual material for purchase

Internet home pages:
http://www.thewaterwaystrust.co.uk

482
CANAL MUSEUM TRUST
See - London Canal Museum

483
CANDID ARTS TRUST
3 Torrens Street, London, EC1V 1NQ

Tel: 020 7837 4237
Email: info@candidarts.com
Formed: 1995

Organisation type and purpose: Independently owned, registered charity (charity number 1051672), art gallery, suitable for ages: 16+.

Enquiries to: Manager
Access:
Access to staff: By letter, by telephone, by email, in person, Internet web pages
Hours: Mon to Fri, 1000 to 1800
Access to building, collections or gallery: No prior appointment required
Hours: Mon to Fri, 1000 to 1800

General description:
Large loft-style gallery on 3 levels. Specialising in new graduate artists and designers. Regular changing exhibitions. Galleries available for hire.

Internet home pages:
http://www.candidarts.com
Full information on all aspects of Candid Arts Trust.

484
CANDOVER GALLERY
22 West Street Gardens, Alresford, Hampshire, SO24 9AT

Tel: 01962 733200
Formed: 1984

Organisation type and purpose: Independently owned, historic building, house or site, suitable for ages: 8+.

Enquiries to: Owner
Access:
Access to staff: By telephone
Access to building, collections or gallery: Prior appointment required
Hours: Mon to Sat, 0930 to 1730
Access for disabled people: level entry
Other restrictions: Wheelchair access.

General description:
Contemporary studio ceramics and glass, many private and public collections.

485
CANONS ASHBY HOUSE
Canons Ashby, Daventry, Northamptonshire, NN1 6SD

Tel: 01327 861900
Fax: 01327 861909
Email: canonsashby@nationaltrust.org.uk

Organisation type and purpose: National organisation, registered charity (charity number 205846), historic building, house or site, suitable for ages: 5+.
Parent body:
National Trust (East Midlands Region)
East Midlands Regional Office, tel: 01909 486411

Enquiries to: Property Manager
Access:
Access to staff: By letter, by telephone, by fax, by email, in person, Internet web pages
Access for disabled people: Parking provided, toilet facilities
Other restrictions: Drop-off point; 2 manual wheelchairs available. Steps to entrance. Ground floor accessible with assistance. No access to other floors. Level entrance to shop. Steps to tea-room entrance, and ramp to tea-room garden.

General description:
The home of the Dryden family since its construction, this Elizabethan manor house has survived more or less unaltered since c.1710. The intimate and atmospheric interior contains wall paintings and Jacobean plasterwork of the highest quality. There are also a formal garden, an orchard featuring varieties of fruit trees from the 16th century, and a surprisingly grand church - all that remains of the Augustinian priory from which the house takes its name.
Information services:
Suitable for school groups. Children's quiz/trail
Guided house tours for booked school groups, April to 29 Oct, Mon to Wed mornings only, Thur/Fri all day
Special events programme
Braille guide, large print guide and audio guide available.
Special visitor services: Materials and/or activities for children.
Education services: Group education facilities.
Services for disabled people: For the visually impaired.

Internet home pages:
http://www.nationaltrust.org.uk

486
CANTERBURY CATHEDRAL
The Precincts, Canterbury, Kent, CT1 2EH

Tel: 01227 762862
Fax: 01227 865222
Email: enquiries@canterbury-cathedral.org
Formed: 597 AD

Organisation type and purpose: Registered charity, historic building, house or site, suitable for ages: 5+.
Mother Church of the Anglican Communion.

Enquiries to: Visits Office
Other contacts: Librarian for archives.

Access:
Access to staff: By letter, by telephone, by fax, by email
Hours: Mon to Fri, 0900 to 1700
Access for disabled people: ramped entry, toilet facilities
Other restrictions: Limited parking.

General description:
Romanesque 11th century Crypt, 12th century Quire, 14th century Nave. One of the oldest and most beautiful stained glass collections in the country.

Information services:
Special visitor services: Guided tours, tape recorded guides, materials and/or activities for children.
Education services: Group education facilities, resources for Key Stages 1 and 2, 3, 4 and Further or Higher Education.
Services for disabled people: For the visually impaired; for the hearing impaired.

Internet home pages:
http://www.canterbury-cathedral.org

487
CAPESTHORNE HALL
Macclesfield, Macclesfield, Cheshire, SK11 9JY

Tel: 01625 861221
Email: info@capesthorne.com

Organisation type and purpose: Independently owned, historic building, house or site.

Enquiries to: Manager
Access:
Access to staff: By letter, by telephone, by fax, by email, visitors by prior appointment
Access for disabled people: Parking provided, ramped entry, toilet facilities
Other restrictions: Access to ground floor only.

Information services:
Special visitor services: Guided tours..

Internet home pages:
http://www.capesthorne.com

488
CAPTAIN COOK & STAITHES HERITAGE CENTRE
High Street, Staithes, Saltburn-by-the-Sea, Cleveland, TS13 5BQ

Tel: 01947 841454
Formed: 1993

Organisation type and purpose: Museum.

Enquiries to: Curator
Access:
Access to staff: By letter, in person
Hours: Daily, 1000 to 1700

General description:
Captain James Cook, Staithes history, replica of a 1745 Staithes street.
Collections:
Models, maps, charts, coins
Contemporary and antique books relating to Captain Cook
John Webber's engravings from Cook's third voyage
Over 1000 photographs and many artefacts of Staithes

Internet home pages:
http://www.staithes.co.uk
http://www.captaincook.org.uk

489
CAPTAIN COOK BIRTHPLACE MUSEUM
Stewart Park, Marton, Middlesbrough, Cleveland, TS7 8AT

Tel: 01642 311211
Fax: 01642 317419
Formed: 1978

Organisation type and purpose: Local government body, museum, suitable for ages: 5+.

Enquiries to: Curator
Direct tel: 01642 515634
Direct email: jeanette_grainger @middlesbrough.gov.uk
Other contacts: Assistant Curator for Cook research.
Access:
Access to staff: By letter, by telephone, by fax, by email, visitors by prior appointment
Other restrictions: Prior appointment is required for staff, collections in store. Curatorial staff do not normally work weekends.
Access for disabled people: Parking provided, ramped entry, access to all public areas, toilet facilities
Other restrictions: Wheelchairs, hearing loop.

General description:
Main Exhibit: life, voyages and legacy of Captain James Cook. Computer and simple interactives, artefacts/database, films, special effects tell the story.
Temporary Exhibit Area: exhibitions with a Cook or maritime related theme - change every 3-4 months.
Education Suite: excellent education centre with computers, slides, maps, books, dressing-up and organised activities.
Visitor Services: café, shop, lift, babychange, wheelchairs.
Information services:
Guided tours by prior arrangement.
Special visitor services: Guided tours, materials and/or activities for children.
Education services: Group education facilities, resources for Key Stages 1 and 2 and 3.
Services for disabled people: For the visually impaired; for the hearing impaired; displays and/or information at wheelchair height.
Collections:
Ethnography - North American, Polynesia, Aboriginal etc
Personal Cook/family items
Natural history
Navigational instruments
Catalogues:
Catalogue for library is in-house only. Catalogue for all of the collections is only available in-house.
Printed publications:
Various Leaflets (free)
General Information (leaflet)
Education (leaflet)

490
CAPTAIN COOK MEMORIAL MUSEUM
Grape Lane, Whitby, North Yorkshire, YO22 4BA

Tel: 01947 601900
Fax: 01947 601900
Email: captcookmuseumwhitby@ukgateway.net
Formed: 1987

Organisation type and purpose: Independently owned, registered charity (charity number 517546), museum, historic building, house or site, suitable for ages: 8+.
To celebrate the life and achievements of Captain James Cook.
Parent body:
Cook Museum Trust
at the same address

Enquiries to: Administrator
Other contacts: Chairman of Cook Museum Trust for information about the collections.
Access:
Access to staff: By letter, by telephone, by fax, by email, Internet web pages
Access for disabled people: ramped entry, toilet facilities
Other restrictions: Wheelchair access to ground and first floors, DVD for upper floors - available shortly.

General description:
The house was the home of the Walker family and the centre of their shipping business. James Cook worked for John Walker for nine years, and lodged in the attic during his 3 year apprenticeship from 1746 to 1749. The life and voyages of Captain James Cook, his connection with Whitby, his subsequent career, his associates. Contains important models, letters, drawings and watercolours from Cook's voyages.
Information services:
Helpline available, tel no: 01947 601900.
Guided tours by prior appointment.
Special visitor services: Guided tours, tape recorded guides, materials and/or activities for children.
Education services: Group education facilities, resources for Key Stages 1 and 2, 3 and 4..
Collections:
Paintings, prints and drawings, ship models, plans and maps, manuscripts, artefacts
Tapa cloth book, Tapa cloth collected on all 3 voyages, 1728
Drawings and watercolours from all 3 voyages (originals)
Numerous original letters written by Cook, 1779
Original ships' plans
Irish loan collection, numerous items in relation to New Zealand
Models, including an outstanding model of 'Resolution'.
Catalogues:
Catalogue for all of the collections is only available in-house.

Internet home pages:
http://www.cookmuseumwhitby.co.uk
10 sections, illustrated, including full information about the house and museum, Whitby, Cook's life, the contents of the Museum and usual visitor information. Designed for A and GCSE level students, as well as visitors.

491
CAPTAIN COOK SCHOOLROOM MUSEUM
101 High Street, Great Ayton, North Yorkshire, TS9 6NB

Tel: 01642 724296
Email: Email form on website
Formed: 1928

Organisation type and purpose: Independently owned, registered charity (charity number 233623/1), museum, suitable for ages: 5+.

Enquiries to: Honorary Secretary
Direct tel: 01642 723358
Direct email: daniel.osullivan1@btinternet.com
Access:
Access to staff: By letter, by email, Internet web pages
Access for disabled people: access to all public areas

General description:
A replica of an 18th century schoolroom such as that in which Captain James Cook was educated, plus interactive displays on Cook's early life and later achievements.
Information services:
Special visitor services: Materials and/or activities for children.
Education services: Group education facilities, resources for Key Stages 2 and 3.
Services for disabled people: Displays and/or information at wheelchair height.
Catalogues:
Catalogue for all of the collections is only available in-house.
Printed publications:
The Education of Captain Cook (booklet, available direct)

Internet home pages:
http://www.captaincookschoolroommuseum.co.uk
Includes email form for further information requests.

492
CARAD CHRONICLES COMMUNITY MUSEUM, THE

CARAD, East Street, Rhayader, Powys, LD6 5ER

Tel: 01597 810192
Fax: 01597 810194
Email: office@carad.org.uk
Acronym or abbreviation: CARAD
Full name: Community Arts Rhayader and District
Formed: 1996
Formerly: Rhayader Folk Museum, date of change, 2001

Organisation type and purpose: Independently owned, registered charity, museum, suitable for ages: all ages.
Community arts and heritage organisation.
A Community Museum, and Sound and Picture Archive project which encourages wide community and visitor participation in information-gathering and practical skill-sharing activity. CARAD seeks to maximise access to The Rhayader Collections; to achieve high professional standards of care; and to broaden the interpretation of this material and its rural context.

Enquiries to: The CARAD Chronicles Development Manager
Direct tel: 01597 810800
Other contacts: CARAD Director
Access:
Access to staff: By letter, by telephone, by fax, by email, visitors by prior appointment
Other restrictions: New Community Museum building not yet open to the public. Access to parts of the Collections by arrangement. Enquiries about Sound and Picture Archives and temporary local history exhibition programme - telephone within office hours or answerphone message.

General description:
Local history of the Rhayader area - including an archive relating to the building of the Elan Valley dams by Birmingham Corporation. Some archaeology and natural history. CARAD is developing Photograph and Sound Archives, and using the museum collections within a new gallery recording Tradition and Change in this rural area.
CARAD is an innovative project for a rural area, integrating arts and heritage. Its programme of activity includes practical and accessible public workshops in traditional arts and crafts, photography, publishing, sound recording and other topics of heritage interest.
Collections:
The Rhayader Collections comprising:
The Collections of the former Rhayader Folk Museum
Local history, archaeology, natural history, photographs, topographical prints, ephemera
The Rita Morton Archive:
Material relating to the Elan Valley reservoir development
The CARAD Sound and Picture Archives

Internet home pages:
http://www.carad.org.uk
CARAD's facilities, staff, arts and heritage activities, news and what's on.

493
CARDIFF CASTLE MUSEUM

Cardiff Castle, Cardiff, CF10 3RB

Tel: 02920 222253
Email: curator@qdg.org.uk
Formed: 1987

Organisation type and purpose: Registered charity (charity number 273874), museum.

Enquiries to: Curator
Direct tel: 02920 781271
Direct fax: 02920 761384
Access:
Access to staff: By letter, by fax, by email, Internet web pages
Access to building, collections or gallery: Prior appointment required
Access for disabled people: Parking provided, ramped entry, toilet facilities

General description:
1st The Queen's Dragoon Guards Regimental Museum, 1st King's Dragoon Guards & The Queen's Boys, 2nd Dragoon Guards.

Internet home pages:
http://www.qdg.org.uk

494
CARISBROOKE CASTLE AND MUSEUM

Newport, Isle of Wight, PO30 1XY

Tel: 01983 523112
Fax: 01983 532126
Email: carismus@lineone.net
Formed: 1898

Organisation type and purpose: Independently owned, registered charity (charity number 310002), museum.
Parent body:
English Heritage (South East Region)
Tel: 01483 252000, fax: 01483 252001

Enquiries to: Curator
Access:
Access to staff: By letter, by telephone, by fax, by email, in person, visitors by prior appointment
Access to building, collections or gallery: No prior appointment required
Hours: Nov to Mar: daily, 1000 to 1600
Apr to Sep: daily, 1000 to 1800
Oct: daily, 1000 to 1700
Other restrictions: Closed 24-26 Dec and 1 Jan. Opening times are subject to change, for up-to-date information contact English Heritage by phone or visit the website.
Access for disabled people: level entry, toilet facilities
Other restrictions: Acess to grounds and lower levels only.

General description:
It has been said that whoever controlled Carisbrooke controlled the Isle of Wight. The castle has been a feature since its foundation as a Saxon camp during the 8th century. Remnants of the Saxon wall running below the Norman keep still survive to this day. During the English Civil War, Carisbrooke acted as a prison to King Charles I who twice attempted escape from the castle. Lesser prisoners were made to tread the waterwheel, drawing water up the 49 metre deep well until donkeys, still present today, were introduced in the 17th century.
Information services:
Education services: Group education facilities, resources for Key Stages 1 and 2 and 3.
Services for disabled people: For the visually impaired.
Collections:
Objects, pictures, documents relating to IoW history since 1500, including:
Civil War material
Watercolours and drawings of the Isle of Wight by the London artist John Nixon. 1755-1818, 65 items
St Dominic's Collection of ecclesiastical vestments
Artefacts regarding the poet Alfred Lord Tennyson and his residence at Farringford, Freshwater, 1856-1892
Isle of Wight Rifles collection
Material from the castle excavations
Artefacts concerning the imprisonment in the castle of Charles I and his daughter, 1647-1653
Catalogues:
Catalogue for all of the collections is only available in-house.
Printed publications:
King Charles I at Carisbrooke Castle (£2)
The Chamber Organ (20p)
The East Cowes Castle Clock (60p)
Scene Again (Isle of Wight watercolours of John Nixon and Peter Thorne) (70p)
Educational materials

Internet home pages:
http://www.carisbrookecastlemuseum.org.uk
Education materials, brief collections summary.

495
CARLISLE CASTLE

The Castle, Carlisle, Cumbria, CA3

Tel: 01228 591922
Formed: 1122

Organisation type and purpose: National organisation, historic building, house or site, suitable for ages: all ages.
Parent body:
English Heritage (North West Region)
Canada House, 3 Chepstow Street, Manchester, M1 5FW, tel: 0161 242 1400

Enquiries to: House Manager
Access:
Access to staff: By letter, by telephone
Access to building, collections or gallery: No prior appointment required
Hours: Apr to 30 Sep: daily, 0930 to 1800
Oct: daily, 1000 to1700
Nov to Mar: daily, 1000 to 1600
Other restrictions: Closed 24 to 26 Dec and 1 Jan.
Opening times are subject to change, for up-to-date information contact English Heritage by phone or visit the website.
Access for disabled people: Parking provided
Other restrictions: No wheelchair access to interior of buildings

General description:
Situated on the Anglo-Scottish border, the castle was many times under siege by both the English and the Scots as they fought over the border regions. During its 900 years it has been witness to, and used by, great historic figures. Edward I held his parliament here during his Scottish campaigns, Mary Queen of Scots was imprisoned here, Bonnie Prince Charlie's supporters were defeated and held captive in 1746 following the successful Jacobite uprising in 1745.
Information services:
Guided tours should be booked in advanvce, available Apr to Sep
Exhibitions
Special visitor services: Guided tours, materials and/or activities for children..

Internet home pages:
http://www.english-heritage.org.uk

496
CARLISLE CATHEDRAL

7 The Abbey, Carlisle, Cumbria, CA3 8TZ

Tel: 01228 535169
Fax: 01228 547049
Email: office@carlislecathedral.org.uk
Formed: 1122

Organisation type and purpose: Historic building, house or site, suitable for ages: 8+.
Supported by:
Friends of Carlisle Cathedral
Orthwaite Cottage, Orthwaite, Uldale, Wigton, CA7 1HL, tel: 016973 71562

Enquiries to: Administrative Officer
Direct tel: 01228 548071
Other contacts: (1) The Librarian; (2) Director for (1) library business; (2) Cathedral Treasury.
Access:
Access to staff: By letter, by telephone, by fax, by email, Internet web pages
Hours: Daily, 0900 to 1700
Access to building, collections or gallery: No prior appointment required
Hours: Daily, 0730 to 1830
Bank Holidays, 0930 to 1830

Access for disabled people: Parking provided, ramped entry, toilet facilities

General description:
Architecture, Christianity, history.
Information services:
Library available for reference (for conditions see Access above)
Special visitor services: Guided tours, materials and/or activities for children.
Education services: Group education facilities, resources for Key Stages 1 and 2, 3, 4 and Further or Higher Education..
Collections:
Books in Library
Church Silver in Treasury
Catalogues:
Catalogue for library is in-house only. Catalogue for all of the collections is only available in-house.
Printed publications:
Carlisle Cathedral History (Weston D W V)
Carlisle Cathedral Misericords (Grössinger C)
Aspects of Carlisle Cathedral
Carlisle Cathedral Stained Glass

Internet home pages:
http://www.carlislecathedral.org.uk

497
CARLISLE CATHEDRAL TREASURY MUSEUM
7 The Abbey, Carlisle, Cumbria, CA3 8TZ

Tel: 01228 548151
Fax: 01228 548049
Email: office@carlislecathedral.org.uk
Formed: 1990

Organisation type and purpose: Museum. The display of historic church plate for the diocese of Carlisle.
Parent body:
The Chapter, Carlisle Cathedral
Tel: 01228 548151, fax: 01228 547049, email: office@carlislecathedral.org.uk

Enquiries to: Director
Direct fax: 01228 547049
Access:
Access to staff: By letter, by telephone, by fax, by email, in person
Hours: Mon to Sun, 0900 to 1700
Access for disabled people: access to all public areas, toilet facilities
Other restrictions: Wheelchair stairlift to Treasury

General description:
Contains ecclesiastical silver; pewter; vestments; and archaeological items (coins, metalwork, pottery, etc.). All of these are illustrative of the history of Christianity in Cumbria in general and Carlisle Cathedral in particular.
Collections:
Carlisle Cathedral excavation 1985-1988. Coins, metalwork, glass, leather, ceramics, pottery, bone. The main importance of the finds was the light shed on Carlisle in the period before the Norman Conquest. Roman period onwards. Over 1500 items of pottery.
Catalogues:
Catalogue for all of the collections is only available in-house.

Internet home pages:
http://www.carlislecathedral.org.uk
General information on Cathedral.

498
CARLYLE'S HOUSE
24 Cheyne Row, Chelsea, London, SW3 5HL

Tel: 020 7352 7087 (Custodian)
Fax: 020 7352 5108
Email: carlyleshouse@nationaltrust.org.uk

Organisation type and purpose: National organisation, registered charity (charity number 205846), historic building, house or site.

Parent body:
The National Trust (South and South East Region)
Thames and Solent Regional Office, tel: 01494 528051

Enquiries to: Custodian
Access:
Access to staff: By letter, by telephone, by fax, by email
Access to building, collections or gallery: No prior appointment required
Hours: Apr to Oct, Wed, Thu, Fri, 1400 to 1700; Sat and Sun, 1100 to 1700;
Open Bank Holiday Mondays, 1100 to 1700

General description:
In a quiet and beautiful residential area of London, this Queen Anne house was the home of Thomas Carlyle, the 'Sage of Chelsea', for some 47 years until his death in 1881. The skilful Scottish home-making of his wife, Jane, is much in evidence: the Victorian period decor, the furniture, pictures, portraits and books are all still in place. As a historian, social writer, ethical thinker and powerful public speaker, Thomas is honoured in the house, while Jane's strong belief in his genius and her own brilliant wit and gift for writing are recognised in the many existing letters. Their academic and domestic lives can be experienced today in the evocative atmosphere of the house.

Internet home pages:
http://www.nationaltrust.org.uk

499
CARMARTHENSHIRE COUNTY MUSEUM
Abergwili, Carmarthen, SA31 2JG

Tel: 01267 231691
Fax: 01267 223830
Email: cdelaney@carmarthenshire.gov.uk
Formed: 1978

Organisation type and purpose: Local government body, museum.
Parent body:
Carmarthenshire County Council
Member of:
Council of Museums in Wales
Museums Association
National Museum of Wales Affiliation Scheme
Welsh Federation of Museums and Galleries
Branch museums:
Carmarthen Heritage Centre
The Quay, Carmarthen, tel: 01267 223788
Kidwelly Industrial Museum
Kidwelly, tel: 01554 891078
Museum of Speed
Pendine, tel: 01994 453488
Parc Howard Museum and Gallery
Llanelli, tel: 01554 453488

Enquiries to: Senior Museums Officer
Other contacts: Heritage Manager
Access:
Access to staff: By letter, by telephone, by fax, by email, visitors by prior appointment
Hours: Mon to Fri, 0900 to 1700

General description:
Local history, culture and environment. Museum collections.
Information services:
Special visitor services: Materials and/or activities for children.
Education services: Group education facilities, resources for Key Stages 1 and 2 and 3.
Services for disabled people: Displays and/or information at wheelchair height.
Collections:
Elements of collection on computerised database. Rest manual systems
Catalogues:
Catalogue for library is in-house only. Catalogue for all of the collections is only available in-house.
Printed publications:
Leaflets (free)

500
CARNEGIE MUSEUM
The Square, Inverurie, Aberdeenshire, AB51 3SN

Tel: 01771 622906
Fax: 01771 622884
Formed: 1883

Organisation type and purpose: Local government body, museum, suitable for ages: 5+.
Parent body:
Aberdeenshire Heritage

Enquiries to: Curator
Access:
Access to staff: By letter, by telephone, by fax

General description:
Local history, archaeology, Great North of Scotland Railway, militaria.
Collections:
Social history, archaeology, natural history, geology, photography
Catalogues:
Catalogue for part of the collections is only available in-house.

501
CARS OF THE STARS MOTOR MUSEUM
Standish Street, Keswick, Cumbria, CA12 5LS

Tel: 017687 73757
Fax: 017687 72090
Email: cotsmm@aol.com
Formed: 1989

Organisation type and purpose: Museum.
Office:
Cars of the Stars
Fitz Park House, 31 Station Street, Keswick, Cumbria, CA12 5HH, tel: 017687 72090, fax: 017687 72090

Enquiries to: Curator
Access:
Access to staff: By letter, by telephone, by fax, by email, in person, Internet web pages
Access for disabled people: level entry, access to all public areas

General description:
Features celebrity TV and film vehicles, including 'Chitty Chitty Bang Bang', The Batmobiles, FAB1 Rolls, Back To The Future, The James Bond collection, The Saint's Volvo, Laurel and Hardy's Model T and numerous other famous cars and motorcycles.
Information services:
Special visitor services: Guided tours..

502
CARTMEL PRIORY GATEHOUSE
The Square, Cartmel, Grange-over-Sands, Cumbria, LA11 6QB

Tel: 015395 36874
Fax: 015395 36636
Email: cartmelpriory@nationaltrust.org.uk
Formed: 1998
Formerly: Cartmel Priory Gatehouse

Organisation type and purpose: Registered charity (charity number 1042693), museum, historic building, house or site, suitable for ages: all ages.
Charity Name: Cartmel Village Society.
Parent body:
The National Trust (North West)
North West Regional Office, tel: 0870 609 5391
Managed by:
Cartmel Village Society

Enquiries to: Honorary Secretary
Access:
Access to staff: By letter

General description:
All that is left, apart from the church, of a 12th century Augustinian priory, which was later strengthened following devastating raids by Robert the Bruce. The dissolution of the

continued overleaf

monasteries put an end to the priory in the mid-16th century. The gatehouse later served as a grammar school from 1624 to 1790. It is managed by the Cartmel Village Society as a village heritage centre, with a newly opened exhibition catering for all ages, depicting the history of the building, Cartmel village and the Cartmel peninsula.
Information services:
Guided tours by arrangement.
Suitable for school groups. Audio guide. Hands-on activities. Family guide. Children's quiz/trail.
Special visitor services: Tape recorded guides, materials and/or activities for children..
Collections:
Artefacts, memorabilia, pictures, prints, photographs, audio-visual presentation, craft items and computer program relevant to local heritage
Printed publications:
Brochure
Local heritage publications available for purchase

Internet home pages:
http://www.nationaltrust.org.uk

503
CASTLE & REGIMENTAL MUSEUM
The Castle, Monmouth, Gwent, NP25 3BS

Tel: 01600 772175
Fax: 01600 716930
Email: curator@monmouthcastlemuseum.org.uk
Formed: 1977

Organisation type and purpose: Registered charity, museum.

Enquiries to: Administrator
Other contacts: Honorary Curator
Access:
Access to staff: By letter
Hours: Mon to Fri, 1400 to 1700
Access to building, collections or gallery: No prior appointment required
Access for disabled people: level entry, access to all public areas

General description:
Collection covering the history of the Royal Monmouthshire Royal Engineers (Militia), the Senior Reserve Regiment of the Army. There is a display of the earlier defences of Monmouth, the development of Monmouth Castle, and other local military events. Also features a small mediaeval-style herb and plant garden.
Catalogues:
Catalogue for library is in-house only. Catalogue for all of the collections is only available in-house.
Printed publications:
Militiamen & Sappers, a detailed history of the Royal Monmouthshire Royal Engineers (Militia), (Watson Dr G E, 1996, 230 pages, £15 inc p&p)

Internet home pages:
http://www.monmouthcastlemuseum.org.uk
Main website.

504
CASTLE ACRE PRIORY
Castle Acre, King's Lynn, Norfolk, PE32 2XD

Tel: 01760 755394

Organisation type and purpose: Historic building, house or site, suitable for ages: all ages.
Parent body:
English Heritage (East of England Region)
Brooklands, 24 Brooklands Avenue, Cambridge, CB2 2BU, tel: 01223 582700, fax: 01223 582701
Access:
Access to staff: By letter, by telephone

General description:
Site of a Norman settlement, ruins of the Clunic Priory with its cloister, refectory, chapter house: also the castle. These ruins span seven centuries and include a 12th century church with an elaborately decorated great west front which still rises to its full height, a 15th century gatehouse, and a porch and prior's lodging that are still fit to live in. Modern herb garden, recreated to grow both culinary and medicinal herbs.
Information services:
Audio tours also available for visually impaired visitors and those with learning difficulties.
Schools base. Exhibition.
Special visitor services: Tape recorded guides.
Education services: Group education facilities.
Services for disabled people: For the visually impaired.

505
CASTLE BROMWICH HALL GARDENS TRUST
Chester Road, Castle Bromwich, Birmingham, B36 9BT

Tel: 0121 749 4100
Fax: 0121 749 4100
Email: enq@cbhgt.swinternet.co.uk
Acronym or abbreviation: CBHGT
Formed: 1985

Organisation type and purpose: Registered charity (charity number 516855), historic building, house or site.
Historic gardens and maze.
Restoration of walled gardens to their 18th century glory.

Enquiries to: Secretary
Access:
Access to staff: By letter, by telephone
Hours: Mon to Fri, 0900 to 1700
Access for disabled people: level entry, access to all public areas, toilet facilities

General description:
Historical and horticultural. The Hall and Gardens were built in 1599 by Sir Edward Devereux who was MP for Tamworth. In 1657 the estate was purchased by Sir John Bridgeman I and later extended by his son Sir John Bridgeman II to its present boundaries. The gardens are of some 10 acres and include a 19th century holly maze.
Information services:
Lectures by special arrangement.
Special visitor services: Guided tours..
Catalogues:
Catalogue for library is in-house only.
Printed publications:
Brochure

Internet home pages:
http://www.cbhgt.swinternet.co.uk
Admission/opening hours, special events, friends' organisation, photographs and history.

506
CASTLE CARY MUSEUM
1st Floor, Market House, Market Place, Castle Cary, Somerset, BA7 7BG

Tel: 01963 350680
Formed: 1974

Organisation type and purpose: Membership association (membership is by subscription), present number of members: 45, voluntary organisation, registered charity (charity number 801319), museum, suitable for ages: 7+.
Admission free, donations appreciated.
Connected with:
Living History Society
c/o Museum

Enquiries to: Honorary Curator
Direct tel: 01963 351334 (emergency only)
Access:
Access to staff: By letter, visitors by prior appointment
Hours: Apr to Sep: Mon to Fri, 1030 to 1230 and 1430 to 1630; Sat, 1030 to 1230
Other restrictions: Telephone access available only from Apr to Sept.
Spiral and other staircase to 1st floor on which museum is housed, difficult for disabled visitors, access up 6 steps can be arranged by the curator with prior notice.
Access to building, collections or gallery: No prior appointment required
Hours: Apr to Sep: Mon to Fri, 1030 to 1230 and 1430 to 1630; Sat, 1030 to 1230
Other restrictions: Prior appointment required for serious research.

General description:
The local history of Castle Cary, in existence for 900 years, completely destroyed in 1153.
John Boyd Textiles Limited (horsehair manufacturers still in operation); Parson James Woodforde (Diary of a Country Parson); local geology; Victoriana; WWI and WWII; agricultural and domestic artefacts; a number of pottery finds, medieval, Georgian, Roman altar, Norman font. The Castle Cary Visitor 1896 to 1915.
Collections:
Parson James Woodforde
John Boyd Textiles Limited
Catalogues:
Catalogue for library is in-house only. Catalogue for all of the collections is only available in-house.
Printed publications:
Memories of Castle Cary and Ansford (book, 1998, purchase direct, £6.99)
History information sheets
Maps, including 1673 map of Castle Cary (original in the British Library)
Electronic and video products:
Video of Castle Cary (1999, purchase direct, £12.95)

Internet home pages:
http://www.ad.wtb.co.uk/castlecary

507
CASTLE COMBE MUSEUM
The Hill, Castle Combe, Chippenham, Wiltshire, SN14 7HU

Tel: 01249 782250
Fax: 01249 782250
Email: museum@castle-combe.com
Formed: 1983

Organisation type and purpose: Independently owned, registered charity, museum.

Enquiries to: Curator
Access:
Access to staff: By letter, by email

General description:
Castle Coombe is not the property of the National Trust but every building in the lower village is listed by the Department of the Environment as being of special historic or architectural interest. The museum houses the collection which is descriptive and illustrative of the local area around Castle Combe.
Information services:
Special visitor services: Materials and/or activities for children..
Collections:
Objects, photographs, displays
Catalogues:
Catalogue for all of the collections is published.
Printed publications:
Castle Combe a History and Guide

Internet home pages:
http://www.castle-combe.com
Village history.

508
CASTLE COOLE
Enniskillen, Co Fermanagh, BT74 6JY

Tel: 028 6632 2690
Fax: 028 6632 5665
Email: castlecoole@nationaltrust.org.uk

Organisation type and purpose: National organisation, registered charity (charity number 205846), historic building, house or site, suitable for ages: all ages.
Parent body:
National Trust Office for Northern Ireland
Rowallane House, Saintfield, Ballynahinch, Co Down, BT24 7LH, tel: 028 9751 0721, fax: 028 9751 1242

Enquiries to: Manager
Access:
Access to staff: By letter, by telephone, by fax, by email
Access for disabled people: Parking provided, ramped entry, toilet facilities
Other restrictions: Designated parking. Drop-off point. 1 manual wheelchair available. Ramped entrance. Ground floor fully accessible. Photograph album. Ramp is mobile. Ramped entrance to shop. All paths gravelled except main drive which is tarmac. Recommended route map.

General description:
One of the finest neo-classical houses in Ireland, built by James Wyatt in the late 18th century. It has beautiful Regency interior decoration, furnishings and furniture. Visit includes the ornate state bedroom prepared for George IV in 1821, an elegent hall, the Servant's Tunnel, the laundry house, dairy and the Belmore Private Coach.
Information services:
Booked school groups welcome, teachers' resource book available.
Special events include musical evenings and family days.
The Hall is available for private hire.
Large-print guide. Sympathetic Hearing Scheme.
Front-carrying baby slings for loan.
Special visitor services: Guided tours.
Education services: Group education facilities.
Services for disabled people: For the hearing impaired.

Internet home pages:
http://www.ntni.org.uk

509
CASTLE DOUGLAS ART GALLERY
Market Street, Castle Douglas, Kirkcudbrightshire, DG7 1BE

Tel: 01557 331643
Fax: 01557 331643
Email: davidd@dumgal.gov.uk
Formed: 1938

Organisation type and purpose: Local government body, art gallery, suitable for ages: 8+.
Parent body:
Dumfries & Galloway Museum Service
Tel: 01387 253374

Enquiries to: Curator
Access:
Access to staff: By letter, by telephone, by email
Access to building, collections or gallery: No prior appointment required
Hours: Variable according to exhibition programme.
Access for disabled people: level entry

General description:
The gallery is used for the display of a changing exhibition programme, usually comprising local art and craft exhibitions, with some touring exhibitions.

Internet home pages:
http://www.dumgal.gov.uk

510
CASTLE DROGO
Drewsteignton, Exeter, Devon, EX6 6PB

Tel: 01647 433306, 01647 433622 (Warden)
Fax: 01647 433186
Email: castledrogo@nationaltrust.org.uk

Organisation type and purpose: National organisation, registered charity (charity number 205846), historic building, house or site, suitable for ages: 5+.
Parent body:
The National Trust (South West Region)
Devon and Cornwall Regional Office, tel: 01392 881691

Enquiries to: Manager
Access:
Access to staff: By letter, by telephone, by fax, by email
Access to building, collections or gallery: No prior appointment required
Hours: Apr to Oct, Wed to Mon, 1100 to 1730
Other restrictions: Castle also open 1-23 March, Sat & Sun (pre-season guided tours only), tel. for details.
Access for disabled people: toilet facilities
Other restrictions: Transfer available. Drop-off point. 2 manual wheelchairs available. Ramped entrance. Ground floor accessible with assistance, approx 10 steps up to drawing room. Hall and library accessible. Access to other floors via lift for visitors able to transfer from a wheelchair. Steps up to green corridor rooms. Chapel and gun room accessible. Level entrance to shop. Ramped entrance to restaurant. Grounds largely accessible. Recommended route map.

General description:
This granite castle, built between 1910 and 1930 for the self-made millionaire, Julius Drewe, is one of the most remarkable works of Sir Edwin Lutyens. Perched on a moorland spur above the River Teign, it commands spectacular views of Dartmoor. The interior combines the grandeur of a medieval castle with the comfort of the 20th century. There is a delightful formal garden with roses and herbaceous borders, as well as spring flowers and many fine walks on the estate.
Information services:
Occasional guided walks on the estate.
Braille guide. Audio guide. Scented plants.
Suitable for school groups. Education room/centre. Live interpretation. Family guide.
Children's guide. Children's quiz/trail.
Hip-carrying infant seats for loan.
Special visitor services: Tape recorded guides, materials and/or activities for children.
Education services: Group education facilities.
Services for disabled people: For the visually impaired.

Internet home pages:
http://www.nationaltrust.org.uk/regions/devon

511
CASTLE FRASER
Sauchen, Inverurie, Aberdeenshire, AB51 7LD

Tel: 01330 833463
Fax: 01330 833819
Email: castlefraser@nts.org.uk

Organisation type and purpose: Historic building, house or site, suitable for ages: 12+ 16+.
Parent body:
National Trust for Scotland (North-East Region)

Enquiries to: Property Manager
Access:
Access to staff: By letter, by telephone, by fax, by email, in person
Access to building, collections or gallery: No prior appointment required
Hours: End Mar to end Jun and beg Sep to end Oct, Fri to Tue, 1200 to 1700; Jul and Aug, daily, 1000 to 1700
Access for disabled people: toilet facilities

General description:
The most elaborate Z-plan castle in Scotland, built between1575 and 1636.

Internet home pages:
http://www.nts.org.uk

512
CASTLE KEEP
Castle Garth, Newcastle upon Tyne, NE1 1RQ

Tel: 0191 232 7938
Formed: Dec 1848

Organisation type and purpose: Learned society, registered charity (charity number 230888), museum, historic building, house or site, suitable for ages: 5+.
Parent body:
The Society of Antiquaries of Newcastle Upon Tyne.

Enquiries to: Administrator
Access:
Access to building, collections or gallery: No prior appointment required
Hours: Apr to Sep: daily, 0930 to 1730
Oct to Mar: daily, 0930 to 1630
Other restrictions: Closed Good Friday, 25, 26 Dec, 1 Jan.

General description:
Local history of site from Pre-Roman to present day.
Information services:
Education services: Group education facilities..
Collections:
Local artefacts on display in small museum.
Catalogues:
Catalogue for all of the collections is only available in-house.
Printed publications:
Guide, local publications and inexpensive memorabilia (for purchase)

Internet home pages:
http://www.castlekeep-newcastle.org.uk
http://www.thekeep-newcastle.org.uk
Provides guide, timeline, bubble photo of great hall.

513
CASTLE MUSEUM, HAVERFORDWEST
See - Haverfordwest Town Museum

514
CASTLE OF ST JOHN
Castle Street, Stranraer, Wigtownshire, DG9 5RT

Tel: 01776 705544
Fax: 01776 705544
Email: johnp@dumgal.gov.uk

Organisation type and purpose: Local government body, historic building, house or site, suitable for ages: 8+.
Parent body:
Dumfries & Galloway Museum Service
Tel: 01387 253374

Enquiries to: Manager
Access:
Access to staff: By letter, by telephone, by fax, by email

General description:
A mediaeval tower house, built around 1500.

Internet home pages:
http://www.dumgal.gov.uk/museums

515
CASTLE POINT TRANSPORT MUSEUM
105 Point Road, Canvey Island, Essex, SS8 7TJ

Tel: 01268 684272

Organisation type and purpose: Voluntary organisation, registered charity, museum.

Enquiries to: Honorary Secretary
Access:
Access to staff: By letter, by telephone
Access for disabled people: Parking provided, level entry

continued overleaf

General description:
General transport history largely in Essex, public service, commercial, emergency and military vehicles.
Collections:
Over 30 vehicles, buses, coaches, commercial, emergency and military vehicles housed in a former bus garage
Eastern National, bus and coach, 1944-1968
Pictures, photographs, uniforms, documents

516
CASTLE RISING CASTLE

Castle Rising, King's Lynn, Norfolk

Tel: 01553 631330

Organisation type and purpose: Independently owned, historic building, house or site, suitable for ages: all ages.
Parent body:
English Heritage (East of England Region)
Brooklands, 24 Brooklands Avenue, Cambridge, CB2 2BU, tel: 01223 582700, fax: 01223 582701
Access:
Access to staff: By letter, by telephone
Access to building, collections or gallery: No prior appointment required
Hours: Apr to Sep: 1000 to 1800
Oct: 1000 to 1700
Nov to Mar: 1000 to 1600
Other restrictions: Closed 24 to 26 Dec and 1 Jan

General description:
One of the largest Norman buildings in the country set in twelve acres of defensive earthworks.
Information services:
Special visitor services: Tape recorded guides..

517
CASTLE WARD

Strangford, Downpatrick, Co Down, BT30 7LS

Tel: 028 4488 1204
Fax: 028 4488 1729
Email: castleward@nationaltrust.org.uk
Formed: 1952

Organisation type and purpose: National organisation, registered charity (charity number 205846), historic building, house or site, suitable for ages: all ages.
Parent body:
National Trust Office for Northern Ireland
Rowallane, Saintfield, Ballynahinch, County Down, BT24 7LH, tel: 028 9751 0721, fax: 028 9751 1242

Enquiries to: Manager
Other contacts: Education Officer: 028 4488 1543
Access:
Access to staff: By letter, by telephone, by fax, by email, charges to non-members, Internet web pages
Access to building, collections or gallery: No prior appointment required
Hours: House and Wildlife Centre: Mid Mar to mid Apr, May, Jun, Sep, Oct: Sat and Sun, 1200 to 1800;
May and Jun: Mon, Wed to Fri, 1300 to 1800
Mid Apr, Jul: daily 1200 to 1800
Grounds: All year, daily, 1000 to 2000; Oct to Apr: 1000 to 1600
Other restrictions: Access to house by guided tour only. Last tour starts at 1700.
Access for disabled people: Parking provided, toilet facilities
Other restrictions: Designated parking 50yds. Drop-off point. 2 manual wheelchairs available, booking essential. Steps to entrance. Accessible entrance still has a few steps. Ground floor accessible with assistance. Access to other floors via lift. Photograph album. Basement and tunnel not suitable for wheelchair access. Ramped entrance to shop. Level entrance to tea-room. Grounds largely accessible. Recommended route map.

General description:
Beautiful walled estate in stunning location. Fascinating mid-Georgian mansion is an architectural curiosity of its time, built inside and out in two distinct architectural styles; Classical and Gothic. Victorian laundry, playroom, cornmill, leadmine and sawmill give the full flavour of how the estate worked.
Information services:
Braille guide, touch list, scented plants, Sympathetic Hearing Scheme.
Booked school groups welcome.
Hipcarrying infant seats for loan. Victorian pastime centre; toys and dressing-up. Suitable for school groups. Education room/centre. Live interpretation. Family guide. Children's quiz/trail.
Special visitor services: Guided tours, materials and/or activities for children.
Education services: Group education facilities, resources for Key Stages 1 and 2.
Services for disabled people: For the visually impaired; for the hearing impaired.

Internet home pages:
http://www.nationaltrust.org.uk

518
CASTLEFIELD GALLERY

Hewitt Street, Knott Mill, Manchester, M15 4GB

Tel: 0161 832 8034
Fax: 0161 819 2295
Email: info@castlefieldgallery.co.uk
Formed: 1984

Organisation type and purpose: Independently owned, registered charity (charity number 515571), art gallery, suitable for ages: 12+.

Enquiries to: Administrator
Access:
Access to staff: By letter, by email
Hours: Wed to Fri, 1000 to 1800; Thu, 1000 to 2000; Sat, Sun, 1300 to 1800
Access to building, collections or gallery: No prior appointment required
Hours: Wed to Sun, 1300 to 1800; Thu, 1300 to 2000
Access for disabled people: level entry, access to all public areas, toilet facilities

General description:
Contemporary visual art by regional and national artists. Source of information and advice for emerging artists.

Internet home pages:
http://www.castlefieldgallery.co.uk

519
CASTLEGATE HOUSE GALLERY

Castlegate House, Castlegate, Cockermouth, Cumbria, CA13 9HA

Tel: 01900 822149
Fax: 01900 822149
Email: gallery@castlegatehouse.co.uk
Formed: 1987

Organisation type and purpose: Independently owned, art gallery, suitable for ages: 5+.

Enquiries to: Director
Direct email: chris@castlegatehouse.co.uk
Access:
Access to staff: By letter, by telephone, by fax, by email
Hours: Mon, Tue, Wed, Fri, Sat, 0900 to 1700; Sun, 1400 to 1700
Access to building, collections or gallery: No prior appointment required
Hours: Mon, Tue, 1030 to 1700; Wed, 1030 to 1900; Fri, Sat, 1030 to 1700; Sun, 1400 to 1700
Access for disabled people: Parking provided, level entry, access to all public areas
Other restrictions: All the above with prior notice.

General description:
This is a commercial art gallery in a beautiful Georgian house mounting 9 exhibitions a year. Sculpture in the walled Secret Garden. Mainly work by Northern and Scottish artists.

Internet home pages:
http://www.castlegatehouse.co.uk

520
CATALYST

The Gossage Building, Mersey Road, Westbank, Widnes, Cheshire, WA8 0DF

Tel: 0151 420 1121
Fax: 0151 495 2030
Email: info@catalyst.org.uk
Full name: Catalyst - Science Discovery Centre
Formed: 1987
Formed by the merger of: Halton Chemical Industry Museum Trust, Catalyst: The Museum of the Chemical Industry, date of change, 2002

Organisation type and purpose: Independently owned, registered charity (charity number 518850), museum, suitable for ages: 5+.
Science Centre.
A hands-on science centre with the theme of chemistry and the chemical industry.
Trustees for:
Halton Chemical Industry Museum Trust

Enquiries to: Director
Access:
Access to staff: By letter, by telephone, by fax, by email, visitors by prior appointment
Hours: Mon to Fri, 0900 to 1730
Other restrictions: No weekend access to archives.
Access to building, collections or gallery: No prior appointment required
Hours: Fri, 100 to 1700; Sat, Sun, 1100 to 1700
Access for disabled people: Parking provided, ramped entry, access to all public areas, toilet facilities

General description:
Chemical industry in the UK, local history of Widnes and Runcorn, industries associated to the chemical industry.
Information services:
Access to archives available by appointment.
Special visitor services: Materials and/or activities for children.
Education services: Group education facilities, resources for Key Stages 1 and 2 and 3.
Services for disabled people: For the hearing impaired; displays and/or information at wheelchair height.
Collections:
Library of books and periodicals relevant to the history of the chemical industry nationally.
Photographs have been digitised
Peter Spence Archive, photographic collection re the chemical industry in Widnes and Runcorn, other photographs include Widnes Foundry collection and local interest
Reasonable collection of general and specialist local maps
Catalogues:
Catalogue for library is in-house only. Catalogue for all of the collections is only available in-house.

Internet home pages:
http://www.catalyst.org.uk
General visitor information

521
CATER MUSEUM

74 High Street, Billericay, Essex, CM12 9BS

Tel: 01277 622023
Formed: 1960

Organisation type and purpose: Independently owned, registered charity, museum, suitable for ages: 5+.

Enquiries to: Curator

Access:
Access to staff: By letter, by telephone, visitors by prior appointment
Hours: Mon to Wed, 0900 to 1700 by telephone

General description:
Housed in an 18th century building, the museum includes three room settings of mid-Victorian furnishings and objects; walls portray the History of Billericay in photographs and portraits; a 'Billericay at War' exhibition occupies one room; and there is a substantial collection of Victorian artefacts and earlier finds from the area.

Information services:
Talks given.
Curator and loan boxes available for hands-on sessions in schools.
Special visitor services: Guided tours.
Education services: Resources for Key Stages 2, 3 and 4..

Collections:
Photographs of Billericay and the surrounding area

Printed publications:
Billericay Through The Ages (£1.50)
Christopher Martin, Great Burstead and the Mayflower (£1.50)
Billericay Town Trail (35p)
The Fate of the Zeppelin L32 (£1.50)
An Index to Billericay and Its High Street (£2)
Billericay Times (£13.99)

Address for ordering publications:
Printed publications:
Curator, The Cater Museum

522
CAUDWELL'S MILL TRUST LIMITED
Rowsley, Matlock, Derbyshire, DE4 2EB

Tel: 01629 734374
Fax: 01629 734374
Email: raymarjoram@compuserve.com
Formed: 1980

Organisation type and purpose: Manufacturing industry, registered charity (charity number 509622), museum, suitable for ages: all ages.
Preservation of historic roller flour mill (grade II*) and use as educational resource.

Enquiries to: Librarian
Direct tel: 01332 880600
Direct fax: 01332 880600
Direct email: raymarjoram@compuserve.com
Other contacts: Treasurer for finance and promotion.

Access:
Access to staff: By letter, by telephone, by fax, by email
Access for disabled people: Parking provided, toilet facilities

General description:
Art and science of flour milling and milling machinery, also provender milling machinery.
History of the Caudwell Business. Complete flour mill.

Collections:
Small collections of books on flour, flour milling, flour cookery, John Caudwell, business archives up to about 1930

Catalogues:
Catalogue for library is in-house only.

Printed publications:
Recipe book relating to our flour (£1)
Mill guides (45p)
Teachers Information Pack - History, Science and Technology (£3.50)

Internet home pages:
http://caudwellsmill.museum.com

523
CAVEHILL GALLERY
18 Old Cavehill Road, Belfast, BT15 5GT

Tel: 028 9077 6784
Fax: 028 9077 6784
Email: cavehill.gallery@virgin.net
Formed: 1986

Organisation type and purpose: Art gallery, suitable for ages: all ages.

Enquiries to: Director

Access:
Access to staff: By letter, by telephone, by fax, by email

General description:
The Cavehill Gallery holds between 3 and 5 exhibitions annually. One or two large mixed, group exhibitions; Christmas show in December is especially popular with the work of young, emerging or relatively unknown artists hanging alongside paintings by established Irish artists.
At the Belfast Festival in Oct/Nov, the gallery hosts either a solo or 2-person exhibition, occasionally showing sculpture, prints and other mixed media work that homes in on local people. Cavehill Gallery exhibits the work of Irish artists, North and South. Work is generally but not always on a domestic scale and figurative in nature.

Printed publications:
Invitations to private view and price list (free)

Internet home pages:
http://www.
Under construction.

524
CAWDOR CASTLE
Nairn, Highland, IV12 5RD

Tel: 01667 404615
Fax: 01667 404674
Email: info@cawdorcastle.com
Formed: 1976

Organisation type and purpose: Stately Home open to the public.

Enquiries to: Secretary

Access:
Access to staff: By letter, by telephone, by fax, by email
Hours: 1 May to 2nd Sun Oct: Mon to Sun, 1000 to 1730, last admission 1700
Access to building, collections or gallery: No prior appointment required
Access for disabled people: Parking provided, ramped entry, toilet facilities
Other restrictions: Access to ground floor only of castle, as well as gardens, shops, restaurant.

General description:
Said to be the most romantic castle in the Highlands, this was the 14th century home of the Thanes of Cawdor. The mediaeval tower and drawbridge are still intact, and generations of art lovers and scholars are responsible for the eclectic collection of paintings, tapestries, books and porcelain to be found in the castle.

Collections:
Tapestries, Don Quixote and biblical scenes, 17th century
Collection of family portraits by Francis Coates, Sir William Beechey, Sir Joshua Reynolds, Sir Thomas Lawrence. 18th century
Man of War, The Victory - a splendid boat to a 1:48 scale, with its original cabinet. 18th century

Printed publications:
Brochure (available for purchase, also in French, German, Italian and Japanese translation)

525
CAWTHORNE VICTORIA JUBILEE MUSEUM
Taylor Hill, Cawthorne, Barnsley, South Yorkshire, S75 4HQ

Tel: no telephone in museum
Formed: 1884

Organisation type and purpose: Voluntary organisation, registered charity (charity number 529657), museum, suitable for ages: all ages.
Visitor attraction.
Voluntary organisation providing interest to visiting members of the public.

Enquiries to: Honorary Secretary
Direct tel: 01226 790545 (private contact no)
Other contacts: Chairman (tel: 01226 790246)

Access:
Access to staff: By letter, by telephone, in person, visitors by prior appointment
Access for disabled people: ramped entry, toilet facilities
Other restrictions: Parking for 1 car provided; access to all areas except one small annex down 2 steps.

General description:
Typical village museum and collections.

Collections:
Victoriana, memorabilia, local history and industry, natural history, ethnology, souvenir china, paintings, stuffed birds, animals etc, war-time relics, ceramics, photographs, coins etc

Printed publications:
Cawthorne 1970-1990 (Jackson B, £14.95)
Aspects of Life in Old Cawthorne (Smilt DJ, £2)
Pictorial Guide of Cawthorne (30p)
Boundary Walks
Postcards (20p each)
Brief History leaflet

Internet home pages:
http://www.aboutbritain.com/cawthornemuseum.htm

526
CEFN COED COLLIERY MUSEUM
Blaenant Colliery, Neath, Glamorgan, SA10 8SN

Tel: 01639 750556
Fax: 01639 750556
Formed: 1980

Organisation type and purpose: Local government body, museum, suitable for ages: 12+.

Enquiries to: Manager

Access:
Access to staff: By letter, by telephone, by fax
Hours: Mon to Fri, 1000 to 1600
Other restrictions: Apr to Oct only by telephone.
Access for disabled people: Parking provided

General description:
The Museum is based in and around the surface buildings of the former Cefn Coed Colliery, and tells the story of coal-mining in the Neath area.

Collections:
Working machinery, tools, photographs on display

527
CENTRE FOR CONTEMPORARY ARTS
350 Sauchiehall Street, Glasgow, G2 3JD

Tel: 0141 332 7521
Fax: 0141 332 3226
Email: gen@cca-glasgow.com
Acronym or abbreviation: CCA
Formed: 1993

Organisation type and purpose: Voluntary organisation, registered charity, art gallery.
Arts centre.
To support artists in making possible the creation of original works, increasing the accessibility and strengthening the understanding of contemporary arts through a range of activities including talks, tours, writers' events, classes and workshops.

Enquiries to: Head of Administration & Resources

continued overleaf

Access:
Access to staff: By telephone, by email
Hours: Mon to Fri, 0900 to 1700
Access for disabled people: access to all public areas

General description:
Contemporary visual and performing arts especially in Scotland.
Publications list:
is available in hard copy.
Printed publications:
Catalogues for CCA commissioned or joint commissioned exhibitions 1993-1998

Internet home pages:
http://www.cca-glasgow.com

528
CENTRE FOR ENVIRONMENTAL DATA AND RECORDING
Ulster Museum, 12 Malone Road, Belfast, BT9 5BN

Tel: 028 9038 3154/3153
Fax: 028 9038 3103
Email: damien.mcferran.um@nics.gov.uk
Acronym or abbreviation: CEDaR

Organisation type and purpose: National government body, museum, university department or institute, research organisation. Grant aided by the Environment Service: Countryside and Wildlife. (Environment and Heritage Service (DoE)(NI)).

Enquiries to: Records Centre Manager
Access:
Access to staff: By letter, by telephone, by fax, by email, visitors by prior appointment
Hours: Mon to Fri, 0900 to 1700
Access to building, collections or gallery: No prior appointment required

General description:
Natural history, flora and fauna, and geology of Northern Ireland and its coastal waters.
Collections:
Databases of the location, date, vice-county, recorder, species and grid reference
Over 200,000 local natural history records
Over 1 million species and site records

Internet home pages:
http://www.ulstermuseum.org.uk/cadar

529
CENTRE FOR THE STUDY OF CARTOONS AND CARICATURE
Templeman Library, University of Kent, Canterbury, Kent, CT2 7NU

Tel: 01227 823127
Fax: 01227 823127
Email: cartoon-centre@ukc.ac.uk
Formed: 1973

Organisation type and purpose: National organisation, museum, art gallery, university department or institute, suitable for ages: 16+, research organisation, publishing house.

Enquiries to: Assistant Head
Direct email: j.m.newton@ukc.ac.uk
Access:
Access to staff: By letter, by telephone, by fax, by email, visitors by prior appointment, Internet web pages
Access for disabled people: Parking provided, access to all public areas, toilet facilities

General description:
The Centre maintains a research collection of British cartoons and caricatures, published in newspapers and magazines over the last 200 years. The emphasis is on cartoons of political and social comment, of which the Centre has a research collection of 85,000 originals. The archive also contains books and cuttings, and the online database has 80,000 images.
A small gallery has examples from the Centre's collections.

Catalogues:
Catalogue for library is on-line. Catalogue for all of the collections is available in-house and part is on-line.
Publications list:
is available in hard copy and online.
Printed publications:
Vicky (Davies R and Ottaway L, 1987, £9.99)
Vicky's Supermac: Harold Macmillan in cartoons (ed Bryant M, 1996, £9.99)
David Low (Seymour-Ure C, 1985, £9.99)
A Sense of Permanence? Essays on the Art of the Cartoon (Jensen J, Steadman R, Bell S, Harvey J, Law R, Kallaugher K, Bryant M, 1997, £9.99)
Stabbed in the Front: Post-war General Elections through political cartoons (Mumford A, 2001, £14.95)

Internet home pages:
http://library.ukc.ac.uk/cartoons
Guide to the Centre and database of 80,000 cartoons.

530
CERAMICS GALLERY
Arts Centre, University of Wales, Penglais, Aberystwyth, Ceredigion, SY23 3DE

Tel: 01970 621634 / 622887
Fax: 01970 622883
Email: mow@aber.ac.uk
Full name: Aberystwyth Arts Centre

Organisation type and purpose: Registered charity, art gallery, university department or institute.
Arts centre, theatre.

Enquiries to: Curator
Direct tel: 01970 622887
Access:
Access to staff: By letter, by telephone, by email
Access to building, collections or gallery: No prior appointment required
Hours: Daily, 1000 to 1700
Open late for theatre, cinema, café - closed Sun
Other restrictions: Collections by prior appointment.
Access for disabled people: Parking provided, ramped entry, level entry, access to all public areas, toilet facilities

General description:
Temporary exhibitions of contemporary art held throughout the year.
Information services:
Special visitor services: Guided tours, tape recorded guides, materials and/or activities for children.
Education services: Group education facilities.
Services for disabled people: Displays and/or information at wheelchair height.
Collections:
University studio ceramics collection
A collection of c. 1300 pieces of mostly studio ceramics of the inter-war years, and contemporary work. Also includes examples of British slipware, Delft plates, Chinese and Japanese pottery, and Swansea and Nantgarw porcelain.
Catalogues:
Catalogue for part of the collections is on-line.
Printed publications:
Catalogues of past exhibitions (available for purchase, direct)

Internet home pages:
http://www.aber.ac.uk

531
CEREDIGION MUSEUM
Coliseum, Terrace Road, Aberystwyth, Ceredigion, SY23 2AQ

Tel: 01970 633088
Fax: 01970 633084
Email: museum@ceredigion.gov.uk
Formed: 1972

Organisation type and purpose: Local government body, museum, art gallery, suitable for ages: 5+.

Enquiries to: Curator
Access:
Access to staff: By letter, by telephone, by fax, by email, in person, visitors by prior appointment
Hours: Mon to Sat, 1000 to 1700
Access to building, collections or gallery: No access other than to staff
Hours: Mon to Sat, 1000 to 1700
Access for disabled people: ramped entry, access to all public areas, toilet facilities

General description:
A local history museum housed in an Edwardian Theatre. The collection includes geology, archaeology, furniture, agriculture, seafaring, leadmining and folk life.
Information services:
Special visitor services: Materials and/or activities for children.
Education services: Group education facilities, resources for Key Stages 1 and 2 and 3..
Collections:
Entire collection database digitised, mostly local material
Catalogues:
Catalogue for all of the collections is only available in-house.
Printed publications:
Local History booklets
Postcards

Internet home pages:
http://www.ceredigion.gov.uk/coliseum

532
CHAIR MUSEUM
See - Wycombe Museum

533
CHALK PITS MUSEUM
See - Amberley Working Museum

534
CHANDON TRUST
See - Llandudno Museum

535
CHANNEL ISLANDS MILITARY MUSEUM
The Five Mile Road, St Ouen, Jersey, Channel Islands

Tel: 01534 723136
Formed: 1989

Organisation type and purpose: Independently owned, museum, historic building, house or site, suitable for ages: 5+.

Enquiries to: Co-owner
Access:
Access to staff: By letter only
Access for disabled people: ramped entry

General description:
The museum is housed in a restored German bunker. The collection covers the occupation years and comprises many civilian items as well as a large amount of German and British military equipment.
On display visitors can see many original German items left behind after the occupation including a rare Enigma Coding Machine, as well as many other items which have come to light in the post-war years.
Collections:
Enigma decoding machine
German uniforms, helmets, caps
German daggers, swords

Collection of German medals
Weapons - machine gun, rifles, bazooka, mortar etc
Civilian home-made items, Red Cross parcels with tinned food etc
Quantity of British/German military motorcycles.
Catalogues:
Catalogue for part of the collections is only available in-house.

536
CHAPEL MUSEUM, THE

Hillside, Chapel Bank, Mow Cop, Stoke-on-Trent, Staffordshire, ST7 3NA

Tel: 01782 522004

Organisation type and purpose: Museum, historic building, house or site.
Member of:
North Staffordshire Museums Association

General description:
A restored Victorian Chapel housing an exhibition illustrating the social, industrial and religious history of the hilltop settlement of Mow Cop. The museum was originally a Wesleyan Methodist Chapel and Sunday School, and for a time also a day school. It was built in 1852 by local colliers at a time when Mow Cop was a flourishing mining community.
Collections:
Local industrial history
Primitive Methodism and the Camp Meetings
Charles Shaw and the Chell Workhouse

537
CHARD AND DISTRICT MUSEUM

Godworthy House, High Street, Chard, Somerset, TA20 1QL

Tel: 01460 65091
Formed: 1970

Organisation type and purpose: Registered charity, museum, suitable for ages: 12+.

Enquiries to: Administrator
Direct tel: 01460 62154
Access:
Access to staff: By letter, by telephone, in person, charges made to all users
Hours: Mon to Fri, 1030 to 1630, Sat, 1000 to 1230
Jul and Aug only: Sun, 1100 to 1500
Access to building, collections or gallery: No prior appointment required
Hours: Mon to Fri, 1030 to 1630, Sat, 1000 to 1230
Jul and Aug only: Sun, 1100 to 1500
Other restrictions: Closed Nov to Apr.
Access for disabled people: ramped entry, toilet facilities

General description:
History of Chard & District, complete blacksmith forge, carpenter's and wheelwright's shops, cider-making, farm machinery, costume gallery, domestic and laundry displays. Display on John Stringfellow, inventor of first powered aircraft in 1848, James Gillingham, pioneer of artificial limbs, Margaret Bondfield, Britain's first woman cabinet minister. Lace-making machine, early garage.
Collections:
John Stringfellow - Early powered flight (including full-size replicas of 3 of his aircraft)
James Gillingham - Artificial Limbs
Blacksmith's, Wheelwright's and Carpenter's equipment, plumbing equipment
Catalogues:
Catalogue for all of the collections is only available in-house.
Printed publications:
Range of A4 leaflets relating to displays

Internet home pages:
http://www.chard.gov.uk/
Details of collections, opening times, access.
http://www.southsomerset.gov.uk/
Details of collections, opening times, access.

538
CHARLECOTE PARK

Warwick, CV35 9ER

Tel: 01789 470277
Fax: 01789 470544
Email: charlecote@nationaltrust.org.uk
Formed: 1946

Organisation type and purpose: Registered charity (charity number 205846), museum, historic building, house or site, suitable for ages: all ages.
Parent body:
The National Trust (West Midlands)
West Midlands Regional Office, tel: 01743 708100

Enquiries to: Property Manager
Other contacts: House Steward
Access:
Access to staff: By letter, by fax, by email, visitors by prior appointment, Internet web pages
Access to building, collections or gallery: No prior appointment required
Hours: House: early Mar to beg Nov, Fri to Tue, 1100 to 1700
Park and Gardens: early Mar to beg Nov, Fri to Tue, 1100 to 1800; beg Nov to 20 Dec, Sat and Sun, 1100 to 1600
Other restrictions: Prior appointment required for Wed, Thu.
Access for disabled people: Parking provided, ramped entry, toilet facilities
Other restrictions: Designated parking 200yds. Transfer available. Drop-off point. 5 manual wheelchairs available. Ground floor fully accessible. No access to other floors. Photograph album. Steps to shop entrance. Ramped entrance to restaurant. Grounds largely accessible.

General description:
The home of the Lucy family for over 700 years, the mellow brickwork and great chimneys of Charlecote seem to sum up the very essence of Tudor England. There are strong associations with both Queen Elizabeth I and Shakespeare, who knew the house well. He is alleged to have been caught poaching the estate deer. The rich early-Victorian interior contains many important objects from Beckford's Fonthill Abbey and, outside, the balustraded formal garden opens onto a fine deer park landscaped by 'Capability' Brown. Visitors can see a video film of life at Charlecote Park in the Victorian period.
Information services:
Evening guided tours for booked groups on Tuesdays, May to Sep from 1930 to 2130.
Braille guide. Large-print guide. Scented plants.
Sympathetic Hearing Scheme.
Front-carrying baby slings for loan.
Suitable for school groups. Education room/centre. Live interpretation. Children's guide. Children's quiz/trail. Adult study days. Children's activities during school holidays.
Special visitor services: Guided tours, materials and/or activities for children.
Education services: Group education facilities, resources for Key Stages 1 and 2, 3, 4 and Further or Higher Education.
Services for disabled people: For the visually impaired.
Collections:
Furniture - part of the William Beckford Collection
Rare books in library
The whole collection belonged to the family
Catalogues:
Catalogue for library is in-house only. Catalogue for all of the collections is only available in-house.
Printed publications:
Guide Book
Events leaflet
Children's Guide
Teachers' Resource Book

Internet home pages:
http://www.nationaltrust.org.uk

539
CHARLES DICKENS BIRTHPLACE MUSEUM

393 Old Commercial Road, Portsmouth, Hampshire, PO1 4QL

Tel: 023 9282 7261
Minicom no. 023 9287 6550
Fax: 023 9287 5276
Formed: 1903

Organisation type and purpose: Local government body, museum, historic building, house or site, suitable for ages: 8+.
One of six Portsmouth City museums.

Enquiries to: Keeper of Art
Other contacts: Marketing Manager for publications, enquiries, functions.
Access:
Access to staff: By letter, by telephone
Other restrictions: Museum shop closes 15 minutes before closing time.

General description:
Life style of the Dickens Family in the family home *c.* 1812, Dickens Personalia.
Information services:
Special visitor services: Materials and/or activities for children.
Education services: Group education facilities, resources for Key Stages 2, 3, 4 and Further or Higher Education..
Collections:
Charles Dickens (1812-1870), few manuscripts, letters, books, personalia, furniture and furnishings, ephemera
Printed publications:
Guide Book
Postcards, worksheets
Electronic and video products:
Video on CD

Internet home pages:
http://www.portsmouthmuseums.co.uk
Information on all our museums including Dickens Birthplace.

540
CHARLES RENNIE MACKINTOSH SOCIETY

Queen's Cross Church, 870 Garscube Road, Glasgow, G20 7EL

Tel: 0141 946 6600
Fax: 0141 945 2326
Email: info@crmsociety
Acronym or abbreviation: CRM Society
Formed: 1973

Organisation type and purpose: International organisation, advisory body, learned society (membership is by subscription), present number of members: 2000, registered charity (charity number SCO 12497), historic building, house or site, research organisation.
To promote and encourage the conservation of buildings and artefacts designed by Charles Rennie Mackintosh and his associates and to develop interest in their work. Central to our effort is the care of Queen's Cross Church.

Enquiries to: Information Officer
Other contacts: Director for comment on service provided.
Access:
Access to staff: By letter, by telephone, by fax, by email, in person, Internet web pages
Hours: Mon to Fri, 1000 to 1700; Sun 1400 to 1700

General description:
Charles Rennie Mackintosh, Margaret MacDonald Mackintosh, The Glasgow Style.

continued overleaf

Catalogues:
Catalogue for library is in-house only.
Printed publications:
Guide to Mackintosh's work: Charles Rennie Mackintosh the Glasgow Legacy (free)
CRM Society Newsletter (3 times a year, free to members, £2.50 to others)

541
CHARLESTON
Firle, Lewes, East Sussex, BN8 6LL

Tel: 01323 811265 or 01323 811626
Fax: 01323 811628
Email: info@charleston.org.uk
Formed: 1981

Organisation type and purpose: Independently owned, membership association, registered charity (charity number 279578), museum, art gallery, historic building, house or site, suitable for ages: 12+.
To preserve and maintain Charleston, the home of the Bloomsbury Group artists.

Enquiries to: Visitor Manager
Direct tel: 01323 811626
Access:
Access to staff: By letter, by telephone, by fax, by email, Internet web pages
Access for disabled people: Parking provided
Other restrictions: Access to ground floor only. Ring 01323 811626 for details and Access Information leaflet.
No dogs except guide dogs permitted.

General description:
Home of Bloomsbury Group artists Vanessa Bell and Duncan Grant from 1916. Extensive and unique collection of fine and decorative art, ceramics, furniture and textiles.
Information services:
Charleston Gallery shows a programme of exhibitions.
The Charleston Festival held in late May with talks and performances relating to Bloomsbury, literature and the arts.
Special visitor services: Guided tours.
Education services: Resources for Further or Higher Education..
Collections:
Paintings by the Bloomsbury artists
Objects from the Omega Workshops
Works by Renoir, Picasso, Matthew Smith, Sickert and Delacroix

Internet home pages:
http://www.charleston.org.uk

542
CHARNWOOD MUSEUM
Queen's Hall, Grandby Street, Loughborough, Leicestershire, LE11 3DU

Tel: 01509 233737
Fax: 01509 268140
Email: charnwood@leics.gov.uk
Formed: 1999

Organisation type and purpose: Local government body, museum, suitable for ages: 5+.

Enquiries to: Curator
Access:
Access to staff: By letter, by telephone, by email, in person
Access for disabled people: Parking provided, ramped entry, access to all public areas, toilet facilities

General description:
Exhibits reflect local history and industries.
Permanent exhibitions grouped into four areas: Coming to Charnwood, The Natural World of Charnwood, Living off the Land, and Earning a Living.
Information services:
Special visitor services: Materials and/or activities for children.
Education services: Group education facilities, resources for Key Stages 1 and 2 and 3.
Services for disabled people: Displays and/or information at wheelchair height.

Internet home pages:
http://www.leics.gov.uk/museums

543
CHART GUNPOWDER MILLS
Chart Close, off Stonebridge Way, Faversham, Kent, ME13 7SE

Tel: 01795 534542
Fax: 01795 533261
Email: faversham@btinternet.com

Organisation type and purpose: Historic building, house or site, suitable for ages: all ages.
18th century Chart Mills are the oldest of their kind in the world and made powder for Nelson at Trafalgar and Wellington at Waterloo.
Parent body:
Faversham Society
10-13 Preston Street, Faversham, Kent, ME13 8NS, tel: 01795 534542, fax: 01795 533261, email: faversham@btinternet.com
Other location:
Fleur de Lis Heritage Centre
10-13 Preston Street, Faversham, Kent, ME13 8NS, tel: 01795 534542, fax: 01795 533261, email/website: faversham@btinternet.com
Maison Dieu
Ospringe Street, Faversham, Kent, ME13 8TW, tel: 01795 534542, fax: 01795 533261, email/website: faversham@btinternet.com

Enquiries to: Honorary Director
Access:
Access to staff: By letter, by telephone, by fax, by email, in person
Access to building, collections or gallery: No prior appointment required
Hours: Easter to October, Sat, Sun and Bank Holidays, 1400-1700
Other restrictions: Admission free

General description:
The making of explosives, centre of the nation's explosives industry for 400 years.

544
CHARTWELL
Mapleton Road, Westerham, Kent, TN16 1PS

Tel: 01732 868381
Fax: 01732 868193
Email: chartwell@nationaltrust.org.uk
Formed: 1895

Organisation type and purpose: National organisation, registered charity (charity number 205846), historic building, house or site, suitable for ages: 8+.
Parent body:
The National Trust (South and South East Region)
South East Regional Office, tel: 01372 453401

Enquiries to: Visitor Services and Marketing Manager
Direct tel: 01732 868381
Direct fax: 01732 868193
Direct email: kchjss@smtp.ntrust.org.uk
Access:
Access to staff: By letter, by telephone, by fax, by email
Hours: 24 Hour Information Line: 01732 866368
Access for disabled people: Parking provided, ramped entry, toilet facilities
Other restrictions: Drop-off point. 3 manual wheelchairs available. Portable ramps. Ground floor accessible with assistance, 2 steps in hallway and 2 from library. Small lift to first floor (not accessible to powered wheelchairs); access to lower floor by stairs only. Level entrance to shop. Ramped entrance to restaurant. Grounds largely accessible. Wheelchair route includes some slopes and grassy areas.

General description:
The home of Sir Winston Churchill from 1924 until the end of his life. A delightful family home, with stunning views over the Weald, which became the place from which Sir Winston drew inspiration. The rooms and gardens remain much as they were when he lived here, with pictures, books, maps and personal mementoes strongly evoking the career and wide-ranging interests of this great statesman. The beautiful terraced gardens contain the lakes Sir Winston created, the water garden where he fed his fish, Lady Churchill's rose garden and the Golden Rose Walk, a Golden Wedding anniversary gift from their children. Many of Sir Winston's paintings can be seen in the garden studio.
Information services:
Helpline available, tel no: Infoline 01732 866368.
Guided tours by prior appointment.
Braille Guide. Large-print guide. Touch list. Scented plants
Frontcarrying baby slings for loan.
Suitable for school groups. Children's quiz/trail.
Painting days, lecture lunches, and special tours.
Special visitor services: Guided tours, materials and/or activities for children..
Collections:
Pictures, prints, photographs, books
Printed publications:
Guidebook (£4.50)
Short Guide (60p)

Internet home pages:
http://www.nationaltrust.org.uk/chartwell

545
CHASTLETON HOUSE
Chastleton, Moreton-in-Marsh, Oxfordshire, GL56 0SU

Tel: 01608 674355 (same day booking), 01494 755585 (advance booking)
Fax: 01608 674355
Email: chastleton@nationaltrust.org.uk

Organisation type and purpose: National organisation, registered charity (charity number 205846), museum, historic building, house or site, suitable for ages: 8+.
Parent body:
The National Trust (South and South East Region)
Thames and Solent Regional Office, tel: 01494 528051
National Trust sites:
Chastleton House
Chastleton, Moreton-in-Marsh, Oxfordshire, GL56 0SU, tel: 01608 674355, email/website: chastleton@ntrust.org.uk

Enquiries to: Manager
Access:
Access to staff: By letter, by telephone, by fax, by email
Access for disabled people: Parking provided
Other restrictions: Designated parking 30yds. 1 manual wheelchair available. Steps to entrance. Ground floor accessible with assistance. No access to other floors.

General description:
Chastleton House is one of England's finest and most complete Jacobean houses. It is filled not only with a mixture of rare and everyday objects, furniture and textiles collected since its completion in 1612, but also with the atmosphere of 400 years of continuous occupation by one family. The gardens have a typical Elizabethan and Jacobean layout with a ring of fascinating topiary at their heart, and it was here in 1865 that the rules of modern croquet were codified. Since acquiring the property, the Trust has concentrated on conserving it rather than restoring it to a pristine state.

Internet home pages:
http://www.nationaltrust.org.uk

546
CHATELHERAULT
Carlilse Road, Ferniegair, Hamilton, South Lanarkshire, ML3 7UE

Tel: 01698 426213
Fax: 01698 421532

Organisation type and purpose: Historic building, house or site.

Enquiries to: Curator
Access:
Access to staff: By letter
Access for disabled people: Parking provided, ramped entry, toilet facilities

General description:
Built by William Adam between the 1730s and 1740s for the 5th Duke of Hamilton as a hunting lodge, stables and banqueting rooms. Following extensive damage in the 1960s a programme of renovation was undertaken to reinstate the hunting lodge to its former splendour. A new visitor centre with displays and information is now situated behind the lodge.

547
CHATHAM DOCKYARD HISTORICAL SOCIETY
See - Museum of the Royal Dockyard

548
CHEDDLETON FLINT MILL AND MUSEUM
Leek Road, Cheddleton, Staffordshire, ST13 7HL

Tel: 01782 502907

Organisation type and purpose: Museum, historic building, house or site.
Member of:
North Staffordshire Museums Association

Enquiries to: Custodian

General description:
Twin water-wheels (20 and 22 feet diameter) on the river Churnet drive flint grinding pans. Museum collection of machinery used in the preparation of materials for the ceramic industry. This includes 100HP Robey steam engine, model Newcomen engine, edge-runner mill and the narrow boat, Vienna, moored on the Caldon Canal. Display panels explain the processes of winning and treating clays, stone and flint for the ceramic industry.

549
CHEDWORTH ROMAN VILLA
Yanworth, Cheltenham, Gloucestershire, GL54 3LJ

Tel: 01242 890256
Fax: 01242 890544
Email: chedworth@nationaltrust.org.uk
Formed: 1924

Organisation type and purpose: National organisation, registered charity (charity number 205846), museum, historic building, house or site, suitable for ages: 5+.
Parent body:
The National Trust (South West Region)
Severn Regional Office, Mythe End House, Tewkesbury, Gloucestershire, GL20 6EB

Enquiries to: Property Manager
Other contacts: Visitor Services Manager for events organiser.
Access:
Access to staff: By letter, by telephone, by fax, by email
Access to building, collections or gallery: No prior appointment required
Hours: 26 Feb to 22 Mar: daily, 1100 to 1600 Mar to 20 Oct: daily, 1000 to 1700,22 Oct to 17 Nov: daily, 1100 to 1600
Other restrictions: Open Bank Holidays.
Access for disabled people: Parking provided, ramped entry, toilet facilities
Other restrictions: Drop-off point. 1 manual wheelchair available. Audiovisual/video. Poor access to main features of site, steps to all mosaics and museum. Ramped entrance to shop.

General description:
One of the best exposed 2nd to 4th century Romano-British villa sites in Britain. It was discovered and excavated in 1864. Over one mile of walls survive and there are several fine mosaics, two bathhouses, hypocausts, a water shrine and latrine. Site museum houses objects from the villa.
Information services:
Helpline available
Short audiovisual presentation.
Audio guide. Handling collection.
Activities for children throughout school holidays. Suitable for school groups. Education room/centre. Audio guide. Live interpretation. Hands-on activities. Children's guide. Children's quiz/trail. Adult study days.
Varied programme of living history events.
Guided tours for booked groups only (these are charged for). Maximum 30 people per guide.
Special visitor services: Guided tours, tape recorded guides, materials and/or activities for children.
Education services: Group education facilities, resources for Key Stages 1 and 3.
Services for disabled people: For the visually impaired; for the hearing impaired.
Publications list:
is available in hard copy.

Internet home pages:
http://www.nationaltrust.org.uk/regions/severn
Events on at the villa.

550
CHELMSFORD CATHEDRAL
New Street, Chelmsford, Essex, CM1 1TY

Tel: 01245 294480
Fax: 01245 294499
Email: office@chelmsfordcathedral.org.uk
Full name: Cathedral Church of St Mary the Virgin, St Peter and St Cedd
Formed: 1400s

Organisation type and purpose: Historic building, house or site, suitable for ages: all ages. Cathedral.

Enquiries to: Visitors Officer
Access:
Access to staff: By letter, by telephone, by fax, by email, Internet web pages
Hours: Daily, 0800 to 1800
Access for disabled people: level entry

General description:
The present 15th century perpendicular Gothic church replaced an earlier one built in the 11th century. It became a Cathedral when the Diocese of Chelmsford was created in 1914. It has been refurbished in 1983 and 2000. It is the smallest cathedral in England, but has its own jewel-like quality. It is small, light, colourful, precious and cherished. It has a light and joyous atmosphere, and is an easy place in which to pray.
There are a number of contemporary works of art of distinction, and two new organs built by N P Mander.
Information services:
Special visitor services: Guided tours.
Education services: Group education facilities, resources for Key Stages 1 and 2..
Publications list:
is available in hard copy and online.
Printed publications:
Various publications, free and for purchase available direct from Cathedral bookstall

Internet home pages:
http://www.cathedral.chelmsford.anglican.org
Details and pictures of Cathedral, activities, services, music, education, festivals.

551
CHELMSFORD MUSEUMS SERVICE
Chelmsford Museum, Oaklands Park, Moulsham Street, Chelmsford, Essex, CM2 9AQ

Tel: 01245 615100
Fax: 01245 611250
Email: oaklands@chelmsfordbc.gov.uk
Formed: 1835
Formerly: Chelmsford & Essex Museum, date of change, 1999

Organisation type and purpose: Local government body, museum, suitable for ages: 5+.
Local museum, county regiment museum.
Parent body:
Chelmsford Borough Council
Affiliated to:
Essex Regiment Museum
Sandford Mill Museum of Science and Industry
Tel: 01245 475498, fax: 01245 475498

Enquiries to: Museums Manager
Direct tel: 01245 615121
Direct fax: 01245 611254
Direct email: nick.wickenden @chelmsfordbc.gov.uk
Access:
Access to staff: By letter, by telephone, by fax, visitors by prior appointment
Other restrictions: Professional curators Mon to Fri only.
Access for disabled people: Parking provided, ramped entry, toilet facilities
Other restrictions: No access to first floor.

General description:
Archaeology of Chelmsford and the mid-Essex area, numismatics, costume, paintings, ceramics, natural history and geology, art, military history especially Essex Regiment, social history, local history, local industries, local environment, regional art, museum development, management and administration.
Information services:
Artefact identification, family history research service.
Special visitor services: Materials and/or activities for children.
Education services: Group education facilities, resources for Key Stages 1 and 2..
Collections:
Artefact collections
Essex Regiment, Tunstill 18th century drinking glasses, 400 items
History of Chelmsford Philosophical Society
History of Museum
Local archaeological paper archives
Some archives of local industries
Printed publications:
Caesaromagus - Guide to Roman Chelmsford (1991)
Exhibition and lecture leaflets
Friends Newsletter
Information leaflets on development of Chelmsford and area, local industrial development and well-known local figures
A Celebration of Chelmsford (1999)

Internet home pages:
http://www.chelmsford.gov.uk/museums/index.shtml

See also - Essex Regiment Museum

552
CHELTENHAM ART GALLERY AND MUSEUM
Clarence Street, Cheltenham, Gloucestershire, GL50 3JT

Tel: 01242 237431
Minicom no. 01242 264264
Fax: 01242 262334
Email: artgallery@cheltenham.gov.uk
Formed: 1899

Organisation type and purpose: Local government body, art gallery, museum.

continued overleaf

Links with:
Holst Birthplace Museum

Enquiries to: Head of Art Gallery and Museum
Other contacts: (1) Information Officer (2) Administrative Officer for (1) general matters (2) publications.
Access:
Access to staff: By letter, by telephone, by fax, by email
Hours: Mon to Fri, 0900 to 1700

General description:
The English Arts and Crafts Movement (internationally significant collection). Fine and decorative arts: ceramics, glass, metalwork, Cotswold and other furniture; costume; local history and archaeology; social history; history of Cheltenham as spa and Regency town; Gloucestershire archaeology and artists.
Collections:
Berkeley Smith Collection (Chinese porcelain)
Collection of Working Drawings of Ernest Gimson and Sidney Barnsley
De Ferrieres Collection (paintings)
Hull Grundy Gift 1780s-1920s and Arts and Crafts Movement, metalwork and jewellery
Isher Bequest (pewter and treen)
The Emery Walker Library (Arts and Crafts Movement) - Printing
Trye Collection (blue and white porcelain)
Whinyates Collection (fine art, furniture, costume)
Edward Wilson, Antarctic explorer
Publications list:
is available in hard copy.
Printed publications:
Outlook (newsletter)
Catalogue of Foreign Paintings from the De Ferrieres Collection and other sources (1988, £25)
Good Citizen's Furniture: The Arts and Crafts Collection at Cheltenham
Many other publications, cards, slides, etc
Microform products:
Gimson and Barnsley Designs and Drawings in Cheltenham Art Gallery and Museum

Address for ordering publications:
Microform publications:
World Microfilms
23 North Wharf Road, London, W2 1LA
Printed publications:
Administrative Officer
at the same address

Internet home pages:
http://www.cheltenham.gov.uk/agm

553
CHERISHED CHIMNEYS
See - Stoke-on-Trent Chimney Pot Museum

554
CHERRYBURN
Station Bank, Mickley, Stocksfield, Northumberland, NE43 7DD

Tel: 01661 843276

Organisation type and purpose: National organisation, registered charity (charity number 205846), historic building, house or site, suitable for ages: 8+.
Parent body:
The National Trust (Yorkshire and North East)
North East Regional Office, tel: 01670 774691

Enquiries to: Manager
Access:
Access to staff: By letter, by telephone
Access for disabled people: level entry, toilet facilities
Other restrictions: Drop-off point. Ground floor accessible with assistance, 3 steps inside, 2 steps at rear exit. Access to event lawn via sloped cinder path. Gravel car park and drive. Cobbled farmyard. Tel. in advance for assistance. Steps to shop entrance. Lawn, borders, gravel paths, assistance required.

General description:
The birthplace of Thomas Bewick (1753-1828), Northumberland's greatest artist, wood engraver and naturalist. Cottage with farmyard, garden and play lawn. Also 19th century farmhouse, the later home of the Bewick family. Houses an exhibition on Bewick's life and work and small shop selling prints from his original wood engravings, books and gifts. Wood engraving, printing and bookbinding demonstrations in adjoining barn. Splendid views over the Tyne valley. The south bank of the River Tyne, where Bewick spent much of his childhood, is a short walk from the property.
Information services:
Services for disabled people: For the visually impaired.

Internet home pages:
http://www.nationaltrust.org.uk

555
CHERTSEY MUSEUM
The Cedars, 33 Windsor Street, Chertsey, Surrey, KT16 8AT

Tel: 01932 565764
Fax: 01932 571118
Email: enquiries@chertseymuseum.org.uk
Formed: 1965

Organisation type and purpose: Local government body, museum, suitable for ages: all ages.
Parent body:
Runnymede Borough Council

Enquiries to: Curator
Other contacts: Education Officer, Assistant Curator
Access:
Access to staff: By letter, by telephone, by fax, by email, visitors by prior appointment
Hours: Tue to Fri, 1230 to 1630; Sat, 1100 to 1600
Access to building, collections or gallery: No prior appointment required
Hours: Tue to Fri, 1230 to 1630; Sat, 1100 to 1600
Other restrictions: Prior appointment required outside given hours.
Access for disabled people: Parking provided, ramped entry

General description:
Local history, British dress, fine and decorative art, archaeology, geology, ancient Greek ceramics, horology; including material on Chertsey Abbey, and the Herring Iron Foundry.
Collections:
Local and social history, paintings, Chertsey Abbey material, photos, documents, maps
Olive Matthews Costume Collection. Fashionable dress and accessories of women, men and children. Items of lace and needlework and needlework tools. 1700-present, c. 2000 items
Tulk Bequest
Small collections of 18th century drinking glasses; Meissen porcelain; and clocks
Catalogues:
Catalogue for part of the collections is only available in-house.

556
CHESHIRE MILITARY MUSEUM
The Castle, Grosvenor Street, Chester, Cheshire, CH1 2DN

Tel: 01244 327617
Fax: 01244 401700
Email: enquiries@chester.ac.uk
Formed: 1924

Organisation type and purpose: Registered charity (charity number 272108), museum, suitable for ages: 8+, research organisation.

Enquiries to: Museum Officer
Direct tel: 01244 403933
Direct email: david.blake@chester.ac.uk
Access:
Access to staff: By letter, by telephone, by fax, in person
Hours: Museum: Mon to Sun, 1000 to 1700 (last entry 1630)
Closed Christmas

General description:
The history of four famous regiments, all raised in Chester. The Cheshire Regiment, the Cheshire Yeomanry, the 3rd Carabiniers and the 5th Royal Inniskilling Dragoon Guards. Their stories are told in an attractive and interesting way. There are special events and activities throughout the year.
Collections:
Museum: Uniforms; militaria; medals etc along with some more unusual objects
Archives: Regimental papers; photographs and personal letters; diaries; books
Captain Oates, artefacts/archive, 1913
George Jones, military artist, 1850s, 2 main paintings
Baden Powell, artefacts/archive, 1900
Sir Charles Napier
artefacts/some archival, 1850s
Catalogues:
Catalogue for part of the collections is only available in-house.
Printed publications:
Victorian Soldier; Word War I; World War II (teacher packs, available from the museum)

Internet home pages:
http://www.chester.ac.uk/militarymuseum

557
CHESHIRE MUSEUMS SERVICE
162 London Road, Northwich, Cheshire, CW9 8AB

Tel: 01606 41331 or 40394
Fax: 01606 350420
Email: cheshiremuseums@cheshire.gov.uk
Formed: 1974

Organisation type and purpose: Local government body, museum.
Administers the:
Salt Museum
Stretton Watermill

Enquiries to: Cheshire Museums Officer
Direct email: jonesgl@cheshire.gov.uk
Access:
Access to staff: By letter, by telephone, by email
Hours: Mon to Fri, 0900 to 1700
Access for disabled people: Parking provided, ramped entry, toilet facilities

General description:
Archaeology and field monuments, excavations at Northwich and Middlewich, museology, curatorship, history of the salt industry.
Collections:
Main collections relate to the industrial and social history of Mid-Cheshire with particular emphasis on salt. Material held ranges from industrial equipment, packaging, domestic items and art, to photographs, also archaeological excavation archives for Cheshire, excluding Chester district
Catalogues:
Catalogue for all of the collections is only available in-house.
Publications list:
is available in hard copy and online.

Internet home pages:
http://www.saltmuseum.org.uk

558
CHESTER ARCHIVES
See - Chester Community History & Heritage

559
CHESTER CITY RECORD OFFICE
See - Chester Community History & Heritage

560
CHESTER COMMUNITY HISTORY & HERITAGE

St Michael's Church, Bridge Street Row East, Chester, Cheshire, CH1 1NW

Tel: 01244 402110
Fax: 01244 312243
Email: s.oswald@chestercc.gov.uk
Formed: 2000
Formerly: Chester Archives, Chester City Record Office, date of change, 2000

Organisation type and purpose: Local government body, suitable for ages: all ages.

Enquiries to: Community Heritage Officer
Access:
Access to staff: By letter, by telephone, by fax, by email, in person
Hours: Mon to Thu, 1000 to 1600

General description:
Family history, local history, community history, conservation archaeology.
Information services:
Library available for reference (for conditions see Access above)
Guided tours for parties - walks and talks.
Special visitor services: Materials and/or activities for children.
Education services: Group education facilities, resources for Key Stages 1 and 2..
Collections:
General Register Office Index 1837 -1945
Census for Chester District 1841-1901,1881 census for UK
Electoral registers for Chester, IGI for Cheshire, Lancashire, Shropshire, Staffordshire, Derbyshire and Wales.
Parish registers for Chester
Local newspapers, maps
Chester photographic survey team, street by street ongoing record since 1950s with some early photographs
Local history library
Archaeological library
Printed publications:
Books, pamphlets and leaflets on Chester and surrounding district including:
Our House
History of the Roads
Tudor Chester
Millennium Trail of Chester
History of Chester (Ormerod G)
Electronic and video products:
Chester Revealed (CD-ROM)

Internet home pages:
http://www.chestercc.gov.uk/heritage/history/home.html
Chester history and heritage
http://www.chestercc.gov.uk/heritage/history/family-history.html
Internet tutorials for family history enthusiasts

561
CHESTER HERITAGE CENTRE

Closed, date of change, 1999

562
CHESTER MUSEUMS

Grosvenor Museum, 27 Grosvenor Street, Chester, Cheshire, CH1 2DD

Tel: 01244 402008
Fax: 01244 347587
Formed: 1886
Formerly: Grosvenor Museum

Organisation type and purpose: Local government body, museum.
Parent body:
Chester City Council

Enquiries to: Museums Officer
Direct tel: 01244 402012
Access:
Access to staff: Visitors by prior appointment
Hours: Mon to Fri, 0900 to 1700
Access to building, collections or gallery: No prior appointment required
Hours: Mon to Sat, 1030 to 1700; Sun, 1400 to 1700
Access for disabled people: Parking provided, toilet facilities
Other restrictions: Access via platform lifts to all changing levels on ground floor.

General description:
Chester local history and archaeology, particularly strong in Roman studies; local art and artists, Chester assayed silver, local natural history and costume.
Information services:
Library available for reference (for conditions see Access above)
Specific and detailed archaeological queries on local matters should be addresses to Chester Archaeology at the same address, tel no: 01244 402009.
Special visitor services: Guided tours, materials and/or activities for children.
Education services: Group education facilities, resources for Key Stages 1 and 2, 3 and 4.
Services for disabled people: For the visually impaired; for the hearing impaired; displays and/or information at wheelchair height.
Collections:
19th natural history reference books and specimens
Archives of excavations carried out in Chester
Publications list:
is available in hard copy.
Printed publications:
Museum Guide (£2)
Latest, and backlist, of Chester Archaeology Site Reports
Events and Exhibitions Publication (free)
Picturesque Chester - Catalogue of part of topographical arts collection (Phillimore, £15.95 inc p&p for UK)
Catalogue of Silver in The Grosvenor Museum (Phillimore, £23.95 inc p&p for UK)

Internet home pages:
http://www.chestercc.gov.uk
Home page for City Council, directs users to Museum pages giving brief description of collections and displays.

563
CHESTER TOY & DOLL MUSEUM, THE

Closed

564
CHESTERFIELD MUSEUM & ART GALLERY

Stephenson Memorial Hall, St Mary's Gate, Chesterfield, Derbyshire, S41 7TY

Tel: 01246 345727
Email: museum@chesterfieldbc.gov.uk
Formed: 1994

Organisation type and purpose: Local government body, museum, suitable for ages: 5+.
Governing body:
Chesterfield Borough Council
Town Hall, Rose Hill, Chesterfield, S40 1LP

Enquiries to: Curator
Access:
Access to staff: By letter only
Access to building, collections or gallery: No prior appointment required
Hours: Mon, Tue, Thu, Fri, Sat, 1000 to 1600
Other restrictions: See local press for Christmas Period.
Access for disabled people: ramped entry, access to all public areas, toilet facilities

General description:
Chesterfield's rich historical heritage is explored in the town's museum and art gallery. Taking 'The Story of Chesterfield' as its theme, the museum shows how the town has become the place it is today by looking at different aspects of its history. Predominantly social and industrial history, 19th and 20th centuries, relating to Chesterfield and North East Derbyshire.
Information services:
Services for hearing impaired by appointment.
Special visitor services: Guided tours.
Services for disabled people: For the hearing impaired; displays and/or information at wheelchair height.
Collections:
Social history collections relating to Chesterfield and North East Derbyshire
Industrial History, including products of Robinson & Sons Limited (Robinson Collection)
Local saltglaze pottery and pottery by studio potter, Wm Gordon, 1800-present day, c. 700 items
Collection of paintings and pastels and sketches by Joseph Syddall (Sydall Collection), 1900-1940, c. 200 items
Collection of local ephemera (Goodlad Collection)
Collection of documents relating to Old Whittington (Handford Bequest)
Mediaeval builders' windlass, 14th century
Whittington cut glass, late 18th/early 19th centuries, c. 30 items
Geology collection
Printed publications:
Advertising leaflet (free)
Children's Guide (60p)

Internet home pages:
http://www.chesterfieldbc.gov.uk

565
CHESTERHOLM MUSEUM

Bardon Mill, Hexham, Northumberland, NE47 7JN

Tel: 01434 344277
Fax: 01434 344060
Email: info@vindolanda.com
Formed: 1970

Organisation type and purpose: Registered charity (charity number 500210), museum, historic building, house or site, suitable for ages: 5+.

Enquiries to: Information Officer
Access:
Access to staff: By letter, by email
Access for disabled people: Parking provided, ramped entry, toilet facilities
Other restrictions: Limited access - telephone for further details.

General description:
Archaeology, Roman history.
Information services:
Special visitor services: Materials and/or activities for children.
Education services: Group education facilities, resources for Key Stages 1 and 2, 3, 4 and Further or Higher Education..
Publications list:
is available in hard copy.

566
CHESTERS ROMAN FORT AND MUSEUM

Chollerford, Humshaugh, Hexham, Northumberland, NE46 4EP

Tel: 01434 681379
Formed: 1896

Organisation type and purpose: National government body, museum, historic building, house or site, suitable for ages: all ages.
Parent body:
English Heritage (North East Region)
Tel: 0191 261 1585

Enquiries to: Custodian
Other contacts: Curator for enquiries relating to collections.

continued overleaf

Access:
Access to staff: By letter, by telephone, in person
Access to building, collections or gallery: No prior appointment required
Hours: Apr to Sep, daily, 1000 to 1800; Oct, daily, 1000 to 1700; Nov to Mar, Wed to Sun, 1000 to 1600
Other restrictions: Closed 24 to 26 Dec, 1 Jan. Opening times are subject to change, for up-to-date information contact English Heritage by phone or visit the website.
Access for disabled people: Parking provided, toilet facilities
Other restrictions: Limited wheelchair access.

General description:
Chesters, located between the 27th and 28th milecastles, is one of the best preserved examples of a cavalry fort. Many parts are still visible, including the barracks, a finely preserved bathhouse and remains of the headquarters. The Museum contains Roman finds from Chesters Fort, and other items from John Clayton's original collections.
Collections:
The Clayton Collection: contains non-Roman elements (including a very small amount of geology/natural history) surviving from John Clayton's original collection.
Altars and sculptures from Hadrian's Wall

Internet home pages:
http://www.english-heritage.org.uk

567
CHETHAM'S LIBRARY
Long Millgate, Manchester, M3 1SB

Tel: 0161 834 7961
Fax: 0161 839 5797
Email: librarian@chethams.org.uk
Formed: 1653

Organisation type and purpose: (charity number DG/526702C-1/E), museum, historic building, house or site.
Free public library, founded in 1653, for research and consultation.

Enquiries to: Librarian
Other contacts: (1) Archivist; (2) Senior Librarian for (1) archival enquiries; (2) systems.
Access:
Access to staff: By letter, by telephone, by fax, by email, visitors by prior appointment
Hours: Mon to Fri, 0930 to 1630
Access for disabled people: Parking provided, ramped entry

General description:
History and topography of the North West of England, rare books.
Collections:
Archival Collections re Manchester
Halliwell-Phillipps Collection of broadsides
History of Lancashire and Cheshire
Incunabula
John Byrom's Collection
Catalogues:
Catalogue for library is on-line. Catalogue for part of the collections is on-line.
Printed publications:
A Catalogue of Proclamations, Broadsides, Ballads, and Poems, presented to the Chetham Library by James O Halliwell, (Phillipps) London, privately printed, 1851
A Catalogue of the Collection of Tracts for and against Popery (published in or about the reign of James II) in the Manchester Library founded by Humphrey Chetham (Thomas Jones ed. Manchester, 1859-65, 2 vols, Chetham Society, Original Series, 48 and 64)
A Catalogue of the Library of John Byrom (Compiled by B B B R Wheatley), privately printed, 1848
A selection from the list of historical manuscripts in the Chetham Library (compiled in 1930 by Tupling G H, in Bulletin of the Institute of Historical Research, vol. X (1932-33), pp. 69-72)
Bibliothecae Chethamensis Catalogus (Manchester, 1701-1883, 6 vols)
Catalogue of the John Radcliffe Collection (compiled by Phillips C T E, Manchester, 1937)

Internet home pages:
http://www.chethams.org.uk
Archival finding aids.

568
CHICHESTER DISTRICT MUSEUM
29 Little London, Chichester, West Sussex, PO19 1PB

Tel: 01243 784683
Fax: 01243 776766
Email: districtmuseum@chichester.gov.uk
Formed: 1962
Formerly: Chichester City Museum, date of change, 1974

Organisation type and purpose: Local government body, museum, suitable for ages: 5+.
Parent body:
Chichester District Council
Department of Cultural Services, tel: 01243 785166, fax: 01243 776766
Branch museum is the:
Guildhall Museum
Chichester, tel: 01243 784683
Member of:
Museums Association
South East Museums Agency

Enquiries to: Principal Curator
Access:
Access to staff: By letter, by telephone, by email, in person
Hours: Tue to Sat, 1000 to 1730; closed Sun, Mon and Bank Holidays
Access to building, collections or gallery: No prior appointment required
Hours: Tue to Sat, 1000 to 1730
Other restrictions: Prior appointment required for:
access to reserve collection, items not on public display, for study; use of journals - museological and archaeological (in museum's reference library); access to Guildhall Branch Museum, outside seasonal opening to public (Sat, 1200 to 1600, Jun to Sep).
Access for disabled people: ramped entry
Other restrictions: Ground floor access only for wheelchairs.

General description:
Geology, fossils, archaeology prehistoric to postmediaeval, social history and local history of West Sussex, western area only, viz Chichester District administrative area.
Information services:
Guided tours by prior appointment.
Contact prior to visit to discuss individual requirements.
Special visitor services: Guided tours, materials and/or activities for children.
Education services: Group education facilities..
Collections:
Oral history
Photographic archive
Shippam Collection (food manufacturer's advertising archive 1920-1930s)
Catalogues:
Catalogue for library is in-house only. Catalogue for part of the collections is only available in-house.
Printed publications:
Books and Leaflets, etc, some for sale, some free, on local history and museum collections (published by Chichester District Museum)

Internet home pages:
http://www.chichester.gov.uk/museum
Virtual tour of museum, events, exhibitions etc, current programme.

569
CHILDREN'S DISCOVERY CENTRE
See - Discover

570
CHILLENDEN WINDMILL
Chillenden, Kent

Tel: 01304 841970

Organisation type and purpose: Historic building, house or site.
Member of:
Kent Windmills
Owned by:
Kent County Council

General description:
Built in 1868 this is one of the last 'Open-trestle' post windmills to be built in Britain. Newly restored.

571
CHILLINGHAM WILD CATTLE ASSOCIATION
Wardens Cottage, Chillingham, Alnwick, Northumberland, NE66 5NP

Tel: 01668 215250
Fax: 01668 215250
Acronym or abbreviation: CWCA
Formed: 1939

Organisation type and purpose: Registered charity (charity number 221071), suitable for ages: 5+.
Wildlife Park.
To preserve the Chillingham wild cattle.

Enquiries to: Warden
Other contacts: Secretary
Access:
Access to staff: By letter, by telephone, by fax
Access to building, collections or gallery: No prior appointment required
Hours: 1 Apr to 31 Oct: Sun, 1400 to 1700; Mon, 1000 to 1200 and 1400 to 1700; Wed to Sat, 1000 to 1200 and 1400 to 1700
Other restrictions: Closed all day Tue and Sun mornings.

General description:
The wild white cattle of Chillingham.
Information services:
Education: Science 4, history and geography to Key Stage 3.
Special visitor services: Guided tours.
Education services: Resources for Key Stages 1 and 2, 3 and 4..
Printed publications:
The Wild White Cattle of Chillingham - an introduction to this unique herd (Prof Hall, S J G, £1 incl p&p)

Internet home pages:
http://www.chillingham-wildcattle.org.uk

572
CHILTERN OPEN AIR MUSEUM
Newland Park, Gorelands Lane, Chalfont St Giles, Buckinghamshire, HP8 4AB

Tel: 01494 871117, Office; 875542, Education Dept
Fax: 01494 872774
Formed: 1976

Organisation type and purpose: Registered charity (charity number 272381), museum.
To rescue buildings of historic or architectural importance from demolition, in the Chilterns Region, and to re-erect them at the museum.
Founded by the:
Chiltern Society

Member of:
Association of Independent Museums

Enquiries to: Director
Access:
Access to staff: By letter, by telephone, visitors by prior appointment
Hours: Mon to Fri, 0900 to 1700

General description:
Buildings of historic interest and beauty from the Chilterns area rescued from demolition and re-erected on the museum site using traditional building techniques, barns, cottages, farmhouses, small town houses, farm buildings and workshops etc, reconstruction of buildings from archaeological evidence, interpretation of historic vernacular buildings. Advice on building restoration.
Collections:
Plans and photographs of the buildings re-erected at the museum
Stoke Court brick collection
The Stuart King Collection of the Chesham Woodware Industry
Printed publications:
Museum Guidebook
Teachers' Notes

Internet home pages:
http://www.coam.org.uk

573
CHIMNEY POT MUSEUM
See - Stoke-on-Trent Chimney Pot Museum

574
CHINESE ARTS CENTRE
26 Edge Street, Manchester, M4 1HW

Tel: 0116 832 7271
Fax: 0116 832 7513
Email: info@cac39.freeserve.co.uk

Organisation type and purpose: International organisation, registered charity (charity number 518992), art gallery, suitable for ages: 5+.

Enquiries to: Chief Executive
Other contacts: Project Manager
Access:
Access to staff: By letter, by telephone, by fax, by email, visitors by prior appointment
Hours: Mon to Fri, 1030 to 1630
Access to building, collections or gallery: No prior appointment required
Hours: Gallery: Mon to Fri, 1330 to 1630
Other restrictions: Gallery closed when exhibition changes.
Access for disabled people: level entry, access to all public areas, toilet facilities

General description:
The Chinese Arts Centre is the UK agency for Chinese arts and culture.
Information services:
Special visitor services: Materials and/or activities for children.
Education services: Group education facilities, resources for Key Stages 1 and 2, 3, 4 and Further or Higher Education..

Internet home pages:
http://www.cac39.freeserve.co.uk/
Forthcoming events and exhibitions, information about our education programme, funding and CAC's history.

575
CHIPPENHAM MUSEUM & HERITAGE CENTRE
10 Market Place, Chippenham, Wiltshire, SN15 3HF

Tel: 01249 705020
Fax: 01249 705025
Email: heritage@chippenham.gov.uk
Formed: 2000
Formerly: Yelde Hall Museum, date of change, 2000

Organisation type and purpose: Local government body, museum, suitable for ages: all ages.

Enquiries to: Manager/Curator
Access:
Access to staff: By letter, by telephone, by fax, by email
Access for disabled people: Parking provided, ramped entry, toilet facilities

General description:
Chippenham's museum tells the story of this historic market town. Displays focus on Saxon Chippenham, Alfred the Great, Brunel's Railway.
Information services:
Activities for children.
Special visitor services: Guided tours.
Education services: Group education facilities, resources for Key Stages 1 and 2, 3 and Further or Higher Education..
Catalogues:
Catalogue for all of the collections is only available in-house.

576
CHIRK CASTLE
Chirk, Wrexham, Clwyd, LL14 5AF

Tel: 01691 777701
Fax: 01691 774706
Email: chirkcastle@nationaltrust.org.uk

Organisation type and purpose: National organisation, registered charity (charity number 205846), museum, historic building, house or site, suitable for ages: 8+.
Parent body:
The National Trust Office for Wales
Trinity Square, Llandudno, LL30 2DE, tel: 01492 860123, fax: 01492 860233

Enquiries to: Manager
Access:
Access to staff: By letter, by telephone
Access to building, collections or gallery: No prior appointment required
Hours: Easter to beginning of October, Wed to Sun, 1200 to 1700, October 1200 to 1600
Open Bank Holidays throughout the season 1200 to 1700
Other restrictions: Last admission to garden 1hr before closing. Last admission to state rooms ½hr before closing.
Access for disabled people: toilet facilities
Other restrictions: Transfer available. Drop-off point. 3 manual wheelchairs available, booking essential. Steps to entrance. Ground floor accessible with assistance. Access to other floors via stairclimber. Advisable to contact in advance of visit if stairclimber is required. Access restricted to one wheelchair user at any one time on first floor. Steps to shop entrance. Level entrance to tea-room. Mostly accessible along gravel paths. Assistance required by most wheelchair users.

General description:
A magnificent Marcher fortress, completed in 1310. The rather austere exterior belies the comfortable and elegant state rooms inside, with elaborate plasterwork, superb Adam-style furniture, tapestries and portraits. In the formal garden are clipped yews, a rose garden and climbers on the castle wall. Further on the garden is more informal, with a thatched 'Hawk House' and rock garden. The shrub garden has a small pool and rare varieties of trees and shrubs. A terrace with stunning views leads to a classical pavilion and 17th century lime tree avenue. The beautiful 18th century parkland contains many mature trees as well as elaborate gates, made in 1719 by the Davies brothers. After 400 years of occupation, the house is still lived in by the Myddelton family.
Information services:
Pre-booked out-of-hours tours.
Braille guide. Touch list.
Front-carrying baby slings for loan. Hip-carrying infant seats for loan.
Suitable for school groups. Education room/centre. Hands-on activities. Children's guide. Children's quiz/trail. Adult study days.
Special visitor services: Materials and/or activities for children.
Education services: Group education facilities.
Services for disabled people: For the visually impaired.
Collections:
Furniture, tapestries and portaits

Internet home pages:
http://www.nationaltrust.org.uk

577
CHISENHALE GALLERY
64-84 Chisenhale Road, London, E3 5QZ

Tel: 020 8981 4518
Fax: 020 8980 7169
Email: mail@chisenhale.org.uk
Formed: 1993

Organisation type and purpose: Registered charity (charity number 1026175), art gallery. Commissions new work from contemporary visual artists for gallery's distinctive space.

Enquiries to: Director
Access:
Access to staff: By telephone
Hours: Mon to Fri, 1000 to 1800
Access to building, collections or gallery: No prior appointment required
Hours: Wed to Sun, 1300 to 1800, during advertised run of each exhibition
Access for disabled people: Parking provided, level entry, access to all public areas, toilet facilities

General description:
Contemporary visual artists, especially installation, sculpture and artists' film/video.
Publications list:
is available on-line.
Printed publications:
Various publications (available direct)

Internet home pages:
http://www.chisenhale.org.uk

578
CHISWICK HOUSE
Burlington Lane, London, W4 2RP

Tel: 020 8995 0508
Fax: 020 8742 3104

Organisation type and purpose: Historic building, house or site, suitable for ages: .
Parent body:
English Heritage (London Region)
23 Savile Row, London, W1X 1AB, tel: 020 7973 3000, fax: 020 7937 3001

Enquiries to: Curator
Access:
Access to staff: By letter, by telephone, by fax
Access to building, collections or gallery: No prior appointment required
Hours: Apr to Sep: Wed to Sun and Bank Holidays, 1000 to 1800
Oct: Wed to Sun, 1000 to 1700
Other restrictions: The House may close from 1400 on Saturdays for wedding receptions - please call in advance of visit.
Closed Nov to Mar. Exclusive group visits may be arranged during this time.
Opening times are subject to change, for up-to-date information contact English Heritage by phone or visit the website.

General description:
A fine example of 18th century British architecture, Chiswick House was designed by Lord Burlington to emulate the style and elegance of ancient Rome. Sitting in acres of spectacular Italianate gardens filled with classical temples, statues and obelisks, it is home to the sumptuous interiors of William Kent including the Blue Velvet Room with its gilded decoration and intricate ceiling paintings. It also houses a fabulous collection of paintings and furniture.

continued overleaf

Information services:
House available for corporate and private events.
Special visitor services: Tape recorded guides.
Education services: Group education facilities.
Services for disabled people: For the visually impaired.

Internet home pages:
http://www. english-heritage.org.uk

579
CHRIST CHURCH PICTURE GALLERY

Christ Church College, Oxford, OX1 1DP

Tel: 01865 276172
Fax: 01865 202429
Formed: 1968

Organisation type and purpose: Art gallery, university department or institute.

Enquiries to: Curator
Direct email: dennis.harrington@chch.ox.ac.uk
Access:
Access to staff: By letter, by telephone, by fax, by email, visitors by prior appointment, Internet web pages
Hours: Mon to Sat, 1030 to 1300 and 1400 to 1630; Sun, 1400 to 1630
Other restrictions: One week closure at Christmas and Easter.

General description:
A collection of Old Master paintings and drawings displayed in a modern gallery. Includes Quattrocento Masters; works by Tintoretto, Veronese, the Carracci, Frans Hals and Van Dyck. Art/drawing and painting: Italian 13th-18th centuries; Netherlandish 15th-17th centuries; British 16th-20th centuries. There are changing displays in the print room of works selected from over 2000 Old Master drawings. Special temporary exhibitions. Also features a collection of 18th century glass, and 18th and 19th century Russian icons.
Collections:
14th-18th century Old Master drawings, mostly Italian - one of the most important private collections in the country. Practically every major master is represented, including Leonardo, Michelangelo, Raphael and Rubens, 2000 items

Internet home pages:
http://www.chch.ox.ac.uk
Gallery opening times and access information.

580
CHRISTCHURCH MANSION AND WOLSEY ART GALLERY

Christchurch Park, Soane Street, Ipswich, Suffolk, IP4 2BE

Tel: 01473 433554
Fax: 01473 433564
Email: christchurch.mansion@ipswich.gov.uk
Formed: 1896

Organisation type and purpose: Local government body, museum, art gallery, suitable for ages: all ages.
Parent body:
Ipswich Borough Council (Museums and Galleries)
Civic Centre, Civic Drive, Ipswich
Other address:
Ipswich Museum
High Street, Ipswich, IP1 3QH, tel: 01473 433551, fax: 01473 433558, email/website: museum@ipswich.gov.uk

Enquiries to: Head of Museums Services
Direct tel: 01473 433548
Other contacts: Exhibitions Officer, tel: 01473 433554 for Art Gallery contact.
Access:
Access to staff: By letter, by telephone, by fax
Other restrictions: Visitors by prior appointment for access to Curatorial Staff.
Access to building, collections or gallery: No prior appointment required
Hours: Summer: Tue to Sat, 1000 to 1700; Sun, 1430 to 1630
Winter: Tue to Sat, 1000 to 1600; Sun, 1430 to 1600
Other restrictions: Closed Mon except Bank Holidays.
Access for disabled people: Parking provided, toilet facilities
Other restrictions: Ramped entry to some areas.

General description:
Contemporary and local fine art - comprehensive collection of Suffolk artists/Suffolk landscape. Largest collection of works by Gainsborough and Constable outside London. Touring and instigated solo and group exhibitions in the Worsley Art Gallery.
Information services:
Helpline available, tel no: 01473 433554.
Special visitor services: Guided tours, materials and/or activities for children.
Education services: Group education facilities, resources for Further or Higher Education..
Collections:
Tibenham Glass Collection
Hawstead Panel Room
Leathes Collection - Dutch Painting
Catalogues:
Catalogue for part of the collections is only available in-house.
Publications list:
is available in hard copy.
Printed publications:
David Austen - catalogue of work and selected exhibits from the Ethnographical and Natural Science collections (2001)
Elizabeth Wright (essay by the writer and curator Kate Bush, 2000)
Time and Tide: Key Works by Simon Read (2000)
Images of Man: Testaments of Human Identity (2000, essay by Dr S J Plunkett)
Freighted with Wonders (essay by Dorsett C, 1998)
John Wonnacott's East Anglian Coast (1998)
French Landscapes/Paysages Anglais (bilingual texts by Sedge J and Ambroise G, 1996)
Anthony Farrell: Paintings of People 1984-1990 (1990)
John Lessore (introduction by Peppiatt M, 1999)
The Uses of an Artist - Constable in Constable Country Now (essays by Professor C Painter, 1998)
Thomas Churchyard at Ipswich (essay by Belsey H, 1998)

Internet home pages:
http://www.ipswich.gov.uk
Brief summary of collections.

581
CHRISTCHURCH MUSEUM

See - Red House Museum and Gardens

582
CHRISTCHURCH TRICYCLE MUSEUM

Christchurch

Closed, date of change, 1999

583
CHRISTOPHER BOYD GALLERY

See - Old Gala House

584
CHUFFA TRAINS RAILMANIA MUSEUM

Whitstable

Closed, date of change, 1999

585
CHURCH FARM MUSEUM

Church Road South, Skegness, Lincolnshire, PE25 2HF

Tel: 01754 766658
Fax: 01754 898243
Email: walker@lincolnshire.gov.uk
Formed: 1976

Organisation type and purpose: Local government body, professional body, museum, suitable for ages: all ages.
Parent body:
Lincolnshire County Council
County Offices, Newland, Lincoln, LN1 1YG, tel: 01522 552222

Enquiries to: Curator
Access:
Access to staff: By letter, by telephone, by fax, by email, visitors by prior appointment
Access to building, collections or gallery: No prior appointment required
Hours: 1 Apr to 31 Oct: Mon to Sun, 1030 to 1730
Access for disabled people: Parking provided, toilet facilities
Other restrictions: 75% of museum site accessible for wheelchair users - with care.

General description:
Agriculture; rural life; social history; local history. The collections focus on the social and agrarian history of an East Lincolnshire farm around 1900.
Collections:
Material relating to Lincolnshire Mud and Stud Vernacular Buildings
Catalogues:
Catalogue for all of the collections is only available in-house.

586
CHURCH FARMHOUSE MUSEUM

Greyhound Hill, London, NW4 4JR

Tel: 020 8203 0130
Fax: 020 8359 2885
Formed: 1955

Organisation type and purpose: Local government body, museum, suitable for ages: 5+.
Parent body:
London Borough of Barnet
Tel: 020 8359 3164, fax: 020 8359 3171

Enquiries to: Curator
Other contacts: Reference, Archive and Information Adviser (tel no: 020 8359 2874) for officer in charge of London Borough of Barnet Museums and Archives.
Access:
Access to staff: By letter, by telephone, visitors by prior appointment
Access to building, collections or gallery: No prior appointment required
Hours: Mon to Thu, 1000 to 1230 and 1330 to 1700
Fri, closed
Sat, 1000 to 1300 and 1400 to 1730; Sun, 1400 to 1730
Other restrictions: Prior appointment required for reserve collections.

General description:
Local history artefacts relating to London Borough of Barnet (NB local documentary material held by London Borough of Barnet local studies and archives, housed separately). 19th and 20th century social history and domestic life.
Information services:
Special visitor services: Guided tours, tape recorded guides, materials and/or activities for children.
Education services: Group education facilities, resources for Key Stages 1 and 2.
Services for disabled people: For the hearing impaired.

Collections:
Johnsons of Hendon, objects made by, and relating to, this firm of chemical and photographic manufacturers, 1920s-1970s
Catalogues:
Catalogue for part of the collections is only available in-house.
Publications list:
is available in hard copy.
Printed publications:
London Borough of Barnet local history publications
Temporary exhibition leaflets (free)
Teachers' pack (free)

Address for ordering publications:
Printed publications:
Publications Officer, Office Services
London Borough of Barnet, Friern Barnet Lane, London, N11 3DL, tel: 020 8359 3169, fax: 020 8359 3171

Internet home pages:
http://www.barnet.gov.uk/cultural_services
Opening hours; transport arrangements; temporary exhibition information.

587
CHURCH HOUSE, THE
Widecombe in the Moor, Newton Abbot, Devon, TQ13 7TA

Tel: 01364 621321
Fax: 01364 621321

Organisation type and purpose: National organisation, registered charity (charity number 205846), historic building, house or site, suitable for ages: 8+.
Parent body:
National Trust (South West)
Devon and Cornwall Regional Office, tel: 01392 881691

Enquiries to: Manager
Access:
Access to staff: By letter, by telephone, by fax

General description:
Originally a brewhouse dating back to 1537, this former village school is now leased as a village hall. The adjacent Sexton's Cottage is a NT shop and Dartmouth National Park Information point.

Internet home pages:
http://www.nationaltrust.org.uk/regions/devon

588
CHURNET VALLEY RAILWAY
Station Road, Cheddleton, Leek, Staffordshire, ST13 7EE

Tel: 01538 360522
Fax: 01583 361848
Formed: 1992

Organisation type and purpose: Museum.

Enquiries to: Secretary
Access:
Access to staff: By letter only

General description:
The railway line runs between Cheddleton and Consall Forge via Leekbrook, about three miles along the beautiful valley of the River Churnet, with an extension of two miles to Froghall in progress. The is a museum.

589
CHYSAUSTER ANCIENT VILLAGE
Newmill, Penzance, Cornwall

Tel: 0831 757934

Organisation type and purpose: National organisation, advisory body, historic building, house or site.
Parent body:
English Heritage (South West Region)
Tel: 0117 975 0700

Enquiries to: Manager
Access:
Access to building, collections or gallery: No prior appointment required
Hours: 24 Mar to 30 Sep: daily, 1000 to 1800,1 to 31 Oct: daily, 1000 to 1700
Other restrictions: Opening times are subject to change, for up-to-date information contact English Heritage by phone or visit the website.

General description:
The original inhabitants of this deserted ancient Celtic settlement occupied the site almost 2000 years ago. The 'village' consisted of eight stone-walled homesteads known as 'courtyard houses'. Each house had an open central courtyard surrounded by a number of thatched rooms. The houses actually form one of the oldest village streets in the country.

Internet home pages:
http://www.english-heritage.org.uk

590
CIDER MUSEUM & KING OFFA DISTILLERY
The Cider Mills, 21 Ryelands Street, Hereford, HR4 0LW

Tel: 01432 354207
Fax: 01432 371641
Email: info@cidermuseum.co.uk
Formed: 1981
Formerly: Museum of Cider Limited

Organisation type and purpose: Registered charity (charity number 267034), museum.
Parent body:
Hereford Cider Museum Trust

Enquiries to: Museum Director
Access:
Access to staff: By letter, by telephone, by fax, visitors by prior appointment, charges made to all users
Other restrictions: Archive is upstairs and is not accessible to people with physical disabilities at present.
Access to building, collections or gallery: No prior appointment required
Hours: Museum: Apr to Oct: Daily, 1000 to 1730
Nov to Dec: Daily, 1100 to 1500
Jan to Mar: Tue to Sun, 1100 to 1500; Closed Mon
Other restrictions: Prior appointment required for Archive.
Access for disabled people: Parking provided, level entry
Other restrictions: Access to ground floor only.

General description:
The history of traditional cider and perry making worldwide since earliest times. How apples were harvested, milled and pressed. Collection of local and national importance, covering associated crafts/subjects: orcharding; pomology; cider and perry making, filtration, fermentation; advertising, beekeeping and propagation; wassailing; coopering; local history; advertising and marketing; production of cider brandy.
Information services:
Library available for reference (for conditions see Access above)
Special visitor services: Guided tours, tape recorded guides, materials and/or activities for children.
Education services: Group education facilities.
Services for disabled people: For the visually impaired.
Collections:
Cooper's Workshop, Pomaries (18th century books illustrating Apples and Pears), advertising, memorabilia
Books, photographs, newspaper cuttings etc from 18th century onwards
Herefordshire 'Pomonas' of 1811
Cider-making equipment, manual and hydraulic presses, bottling machinery, storage casks and vats from 17th century onwards
Catalogues:
Catalogue for all of the collections is only available in-house.
Publications list:
is available on-line.
Printed publications:
Leaflet (available direct, free)

Internet home pages:
http://www.cidermuseum.co.uk
Our main website.

591
CILGERRAN CASTLE
Cilgerran, Cardigan, Pembrokeshire, SA43 2SF

Tel: 01239 615007

Organisation type and purpose: National organisation, registered charity (charity number 205846), historic building, house or site.
Parent body:
The National Trust Office for Wales
Tel: 01492 860123
Under the guardianship of:
Cadw: Welsh Historic Monuments

Enquiries to: Manager
Access:
Access to staff: By letter, by telephone

General description:
This 13th century ruin is perched overlooking the spectacular Teifi gorge and has inspired many artists, including Turner.

Internet home pages:
http://www.nationaltrust.org.uk

592
CINEMA MUSEUM
The Master's House, The Old Lambeth Workhouse, 2 Dugard Way (off Renfrew Road), London, SE11 4TH

Tel: 020 7840 2200
Fax: 020 7840 2299
Email: martin@cinemamuseum.org.uk
Formed: 1984

Organisation type and purpose: (charity number 293285), museum.

Enquiries to: Director
Direct tel: 020 7840 2202
Other contacts: Curator
Access:
Access to staff: Visitors by prior appointment, by letter, by telephone, by fax, by email
Hours: Mon to Fri, 0900 to 1700

General description:
Cinema history, filmography of actors, directors, technicians, information on films, cinemas and projection, biographical information on actors and directors, cinema organs.
Collections:
5000 books, 750,000 film stills, 10,000 posters covering history of cinema 1895 to present, 30,000 trade magazines and year books, 2 million feet of film

593
CIRENCESTER MUSEUM
See - Corinium Museum

594
CISTERCIAN MUSEUM
Hailes Abbey, Winchcombe, Gloucestershire, GL54 5PB

Tel: 01242 602398
Email: customers@english-heritage.org.uk
Formed: 1946

Organisation type and purpose: National organisation, museum, historic building, house or site, suitable for ages: 5+.
Parent body:
English Heritage (South West Region)
Bristol, BS1 4ND, tel: 0117 975 0700, fax: 0117 975 0701

continued overleaf

Enquiries to: Custodian
Access:
Access to staff: By letter, by fax, by email
Access to building, collections or gallery: No prior appointment required
Hours: Apr to Oct: Mon to Fri, 1000 to 1600
Access for disabled people: Parking provided, ramped entry, toilet facilities

General description:
A former Cistercian Abbey that has yielded a vast quantity of archaeological material, including high quality mediaeval ceramic tiles and some very fine mediaeval roof bosses.
Information services:
Helpline available, tel no: 0870 333 1181.
Special visitor services: Tape recorded guides.
Education services: Group education facilities.
Services for disabled people: Displays and/or information at wheelchair height.
Catalogues:
Catalogue for all of the collections is only available in-house.

Internet home pages:
http://www.english-heritage.org.uk

595
CITY & COUNTY OF CARDIFF MUSEUM, THE
See - Council of Museums in Wales

596
CITY ART CENTRE
2 Market Street, Edinburgh, EH1 1DE

Tel: 0131 529 3993
Fax: 0131 529 3977
Email: enquiries@city-art-centre.demon.co.uk
Formed: 1980

Organisation type and purpose: Local government body, museum, art gallery, historic building, house or site, suitable for ages: all ages.
Parent body:
The City of Edinburgh Council's Department of Culture & Leisure
Museums and Galleries Service Division, tel: 0131 200 2000 (Main council) 0131 529 7844 (Culture & Leisure Department HQ))

Enquiries to: Curator
Direct tel: 0131 529 3955
Direct fax: 0131 529 3977
Other contacts: Marketing and Sponsorship Officer
Access:
Access to staff: By letter, by telephone, by fax, by email, in person, visitors by prior appointment
Hours: Mon to Sat, 1000 to 1700
Jul and Aug: Sun, 1200 to 1700
Access for disabled people: ramped entry, level entry, access to all public areas, toilet facilities

General description:
The City Art Centre stores and displays The City of Edinburgh Collection of fine art which includes more than 4000 paintings, drawings, prints, sculpture and textiles. All of the major movements and significant influences in the history of Scottish Art are represented.
The City Art Centre also stages major temporary exhibitions and information on past temporary exhibitions is available.
Collections:
Scottish Modern Arts Association. Scottish painting and sculpture. Late 19th century to 1960s c.374 items
Topography of Edinburgh. 18th-20th century
Miss Jean F Watson Bequest. Scottish paintings, drawings, sculpture, prints and textiles. 1965-present day c.1000 items
The Cavaye Collection of Thomas Begbie Prints
Victorian glass plate negatives 1857-1861 c. 451 items
Catalogues:
Catalogue for all of the collections is published.
Publications list:
is available in hard copy and online.
Printed publications:
The City of Edinburgh Museums and Galleries Service publishes a wide range of material, a list is available by telephoning 0131 529 3983, a selected list is available on our website

Address for ordering publications:
Printed publications:
Publishing Department, The City of Edinburgh Museums and Galleries Service
Tel: 0131 529 3983, email: Website: www.cac.org.uk

Internet home pages:
http://www.cac.org.uk
Website for The City of Edinburgh Museums and Galleries Service, it contains: information on each of the 11 venues and their permanent collections; details of current temporary exhibitions; information on past temporary exhibitions; details of selected publications.

597
CITY GALLERY
90 Granby Street, Leicester, LE1 1DJ

Tel: 0116 254 0595
Minicom no. 0116 254 0595
Fax: 0116 254 0593
Email: city.gallery@leicester.gov.uk

Organisation type and purpose: Local government body, art gallery, suitable for ages: 5+.
Managed by:
Leicester City Council

Enquiries to: Manager
Direct email: wrigs001@leicester.gov.uk
Access:
Access to staff: By email
Access to building, collections or gallery: No prior appointment required
Hours: Tue to Fri, 1100 to 1800; Sat, 1000 to 1700
Access for disabled people: level entry, access to all public areas, toilet facilities

General description:
The City Gallery is Leicester's leading contemporary art gallery, promoting the very best in contemporary art and craft. The gallery aims to provide an opportunity to the general public of all ages and abilities to become involved in the visual arts and crafts through a dynamic and accessible programme of changing exhibitions, artists' talks and education workshops. Gallery Main, Gallery Craft, Gallery Upstairs - available for hire. Gallery shop - stocked with new makers and famous names. Craft Council's list of Craft shops and galleries, active education programme.
The City Gallery - On Tour - taking contemporary art out of the gallery and into the community.
Information services:
Special visitor services: Materials and/or activities for children.
Education services: Group education facilities.
Services for disabled people: For the visually impaired; for the hearing impaired; displays and/or information at wheelchair height.

598
CITY OF LIVERPOOL MUSEUMS
See - Liverpool Museum

599
CITY OF SUNDERLAND EDUCATION AND COMMUNITY SERVICES DEPARTMENT
City Library and Arts Centre, Fawcett Street, Sunderland, Tyne and Wear, SR1 1RE

Tel: 0191 514 1235
Fax: 0191 514 8444
Email: enquiry.desk@sunderland.gov.uk
Formerly: Sunderland Leisure, Libraries and Arts

Organisation type and purpose: Local government body, art gallery, public library.
Part of:
NETWORK

Enquiries to: Principal Officer CLAC
Access:
Access to staff: By letter, by telephone, by fax, by email
Hours: Mon to Fri, 0900 to 1700
Access for disabled people: access to all public areas

General description:
General, local studies, commercial and technical fields, and art.
Collections:
Bob Mason Collection (maritime history)
Local collection on Sunderland and County Durham (8000 volumes, 12,000 illustrations, 2000 maps)
Standards API and BSI
Catalogues:
Catalogue for library is published. Catalogue for part of the collections is published.
Publications list:
is available in hard copy.
Printed publications:
Cyril Barton VC (£6.99)
Frances Fisher RIP (£6.99)
Out All Out (£3.00)
Sunderland Builds the Ships (£1.95)
Sunderland in the Blitz
The Likes of Us (£4.99)
Washington Then & Now (£3.99)
Electronic and video products:
The Barbary Coast (talking book, £6.50)

600
CLAN ARMSTRONG TRUST MUSEUM
Lodge Walk, Castleholm, Langholm, Dumfries & Galloway, DG13 0ND

Tel: 01387 381531
Fax: 01387 381243
Email: info@borderheritage.com
Formed: 1978
Formerly: Janet Armstrong Museum

Organisation type and purpose: Registered charity (charity number RO 1312), museum, suitable for ages: 5+.

Enquiries to: Chairman
Access:
Access to staff: By letter, by telephone, by fax, by email
Hours: Mon to Fri, 0900 to 1700
Access to building, collections or gallery: No prior appointment required
Hours: Sat, Sun, Tue, Wed, Fri, 1400 to 1700
Also Easter Bank Holiday Mon
Access for disabled people: Parking provided, ramped entry, access to all public areas

General description:
Armstrong history and archives, tells the story of this formidable Borders' Clan, armour and flags, coats of arms, photographs and paintings, a Model Reiver, archives on Armstrong history.
Collections:
Largest collection of Armstrong archives in the world
Memorabilia, pictures, documents, coats of arms, armour
Catalogues:
Catalogue for library is in-house only. Catalogue for all of the collections is only available in-house.
Printed publications:
Research material (available direct)

Internet home pages:
http://www.armstrongclan.org

601
CLAN CAMERON MUSEUM

Achnacarry, Spean Bridge, Inverness-shire, PH34 4EJ

Tel: 01397 712090
Email: museum@achnacarry.fsnet.co.uk
Formed: 1989

Organisation type and purpose: Independently owned, registered charity, museum.

Enquiries to: Curator
Access:
Access to staff: By letter, by email, in person
Access to building, collections or gallery: No prior appointment required
Hours: Apr to Mid Oct: daily, 1330 to 1700
Jul, Aug: daily, 1100 to 1700
Access for disabled people: Parking provided, level entry

General description:
The history of Clan Cameron; displays about the Queen's Own Cameron Highlanders and the Army Commandos.
Information services:
Library available for reference (for conditions see Access above)
Special visitor services: Materials and/or activities for children..
Catalogues:
Catalogue for library is in-house only. Catalogue for all of the collections is only available in-house.
Publications list:
is available on-line.
Printed publications:
The Camerons - A history of Clan Cameron (book, Stewart J of Ard Vorlich)

Internet home pages:
http://www.clan-cameron.org

602
CLAN DONALD CENTRE

See - Museum of the Isles

603
CLAN MACPHERSON MUSEUM

Main Street, Newtonmore, Inverness-shire, PH20 1DE

Tel: 01540 673332
Formed: 1952

Organisation type and purpose: Independently owned, registered charity (charity number CR 40246), museum, suitable for ages: all ages.

Enquiries to: Curator
Access:
Access to staff: By letter, by telephone, in person
Hours: Apr to Oct: Mon, Tue, Wed, Fri, 1000 to 1700; Thu, 1000 to 1200
Access to building, collections or gallery: No prior appointment required
Hours: Apr to Oct: Mon to Sat, 1000 to 1700; Sun, 1400 to 1700
Access for disabled people: Parking provided, ramped entry, access to all public areas, toilet facilities

General description:
History of the Clan Macpherson, its associated families and its place in the past and present.
Information services:
Library available for reference (for conditions see Access above)
Displays/information at wheelchair height where possible.
Special visitor services: Guided tours.
Services for disabled people: Displays and/or information at wheelchair height.
Catalogues:
Catalogue for library is in-house only. Catalogue for all of the collections is only available in-house.

604
CLAN MUNRO HERITAGE LIMITED

Storehouse of Foulis, Foulis Ferry, Evanton, Dingwall, Ross-shire, IV16 9UX

Tel: 01349 830000
Fax: 01349 830204
Email: clan@storehouseoffoulis.co.uk
Acronym or abbreviation: CMHL
Formed: 1997
Formed from: Clan Munro (Association)

Organisation type and purpose: International organisation, independently owned, registered charity (charity number SCO 23942), museum, historic building, house or site, suitable for ages: 8+.
Other addresses:
Honorary Secretary
Clan Munro (Association)
c/o Foulis Castle, Evanton, Ross-shire, IV16 9UA

Enquiries to: Company Secretary
Access:
Access to staff: By letter, by email
Access to building, collections or gallery: No prior appointment required
Hours: Summer: daily, 1000 to 1700
Winter: daily, 1100 to 1600
Other restrictions: Prior appointment required for library.
Access for disabled people: Parking provided, level entry, toilet facilities
Other restrictions: Access to exhibition but not to offices.

General description:
The fully restored 18th century Storehouse of Foulis, houses a series of entertaining and educational history and wildlife exhibitions about the Clan Munro, its peoples and its lands, stepping back in time with the sights, sounds and smells of the past. Outside there is an exhibition of local fishing boats, and the visitor can stroll on the shore to watch the seals. The licensed restaurant has stunning panoramic views of the Cromarty Firth, and serves a full range of excellent value home-made meals and snacks, specialising in local produce. The shop is well-stocked with unusual quality locally produced gifts and souvenirs.
Information services:
Library available for reference (for conditions see Access above)
Special visitor services: Guided tours, tape recorded guides.
Services for disabled people: Displays and/or information at wheelchair height.
Collections:
Library of Munro books and associated documents
Catalogues:
Catalogue for part of the collections is only available in-house.
Printed publications:
Clan Munro History (Fraser C I of Reelig)
Mapping The Clan Munro

Internet home pages:
http://www.clan-munro-assoc.co.uk
http://www.clanmunrousa.org
http://www.storehouseoffoulis.co.uk

605
CLANDON PARK

West Clandon, Guildford, Surrey, GU4 7RQ

Tel: 01483 222482
Fax: 01483 223176
Email: clandonpark@nationaltrust.org.uk
Formed: 1956

Organisation type and purpose: National organisation, registered charity (charity number 205846), museum, historic building, house or site, suitable for ages: all ages.
Parent body:
The National Trust (South and South East Region)
South East Regional Office, tel: 01372 453401
South East Regional Office:
Polesden Lacey
Great Bookham, Surrey, RH5 6BD, tel: 01372 453401, fax: 01372 452023, email/website: polesdenlacey@nationaltrust.org.uk

Enquiries to: Administration Assistant
Other contacts: Property Secretary for group bookings, thorough knowledge of property.
Access:
Access to staff: By telephone, by fax, by email, visitors by prior appointment
Access to building, collections or gallery: No prior appointment required
Hours: House: Tue, Wed, Thu, Sun, 1100 to 1700
Museum: Tue, Wed, Thu, Sun, 1200 to 1700
Open Bank Holiday Mondays, Good Friday and Easter Saturday
Access for disabled people: Parking provided, toilet facilities
Other restrictions: Drop-off point. 3 manual wheelchairs available. Steps to entrance. Stairclimber available. Ground floor fully accessible. No access to other floors. Level entrance to shop and to restaurant. Porcelain Collection is situated on first floor, not accessible to wheelchair users or people with walking difficulties.

General description:
A grand Palladian mansion, built c.1730 by the Venetian architect, Giacomo Leoni, and notable for its magnificent two-storeyed Marble Hall. The house is filled with the superb collection of 18th century furniture, porcelain, textiles and carpets acquired in the 1920s by the connoisseur Mrs David Gubbay, and also contains the Ivo Forde Meissen collection of Italian comedy figures and a series of Mortlake tapestries. The attractive gardens contain a parterre, grotto, sunken Dutch garden and a Maori meeting house with a fascinating history.
Object in Focus - one artefact specially displayed and described.
Information services:
Helpline available, tel no: Infoline 01483 225971.
Braille guide.
Front-carrying baby slings for loan. Hip-carrying infant seats for loan.
Children's quiz/trail.
Special visitor services: Materials and/or activities for children.
Services for disabled people: For the visually impaired; for the hearing impaired.
Collections:
The house is filled with the superb collection of 18th century furniture, porcelain, textiles and carpets acquired in the 1920s by the connoisseur Mrs David Gubbay
The Ivo Forde Meissen collection of Italian comedy figures
A series of Mortlake tapestries
Catalogues:
Catalogue for library is in-house only. Catalogue for all of the collections is only available in-house.
Printed publications:
Various guides and leaflets (direct)

Internet home pages:
http://www.nationaltrust.org.uk

606
CLAREMONT LANDSCAPE GARDEN

Portsmouth Road, Esher, Surrey, KT10 9JG

Tel: 01372 467806
Fax: 01372 464394
Email: claremont@nationaltrust.org.uk

Organisation type and purpose: (charity number 205846), suitable for ages: all ages.
Parent body:
National Trust (South and South East Region)
South East Regional Office, tel: 01372 453401, fax: 01372 45023

Enquiries to: Manager

continued overleaf

Access:
Access to staff: By letter, by telephone, by fax, by email
Access to building, collections or gallery: No prior appointment required
Hours: 1 Apr to 31 Oct, Mon to Fri, 1000 to 1800, Sat and Sun, 1000 to 1900;
Nov to end of Mar, Tue to Sun, 1000 to 1700, Bank Holiday Monday 1000 to 1900;
Belvedere Tower open first weekend each month April to Oct.
Other restrictions: Nov to end Mar closes at dusk. Closed 25 Dec; and closes on major event days in July.
Late night openings in May and June until 2100, please phone for dates.
Access for disabled people: Parking provided, level entry, toilet facilities
Other restrictions: Garden partly accessible, recommended route map.

General description:
Claremont's creation and development involved some of the great names in garden history, including Sir John Vanbrugh, Charles Bridgeman, William Kent and Capability Brown. The first gardens were begun c.1715 and later the delights of Claremont were famed throughout Europe. Since 1975 the Trust has been restoring this layout following years of neglect. The many features include a lake, island with pavilion, grotto, turf amphitheatre, viewpoints and vistas.
Information services:
Guided tours for booked groups (min. 15)
Unbooked tours 1st and 3rd Sat, 2nd Wed and last Sun of each month from Apr to Oct, at 1400 at entrance kiosk.
Plant Fair May. Open-air concerts July. For details of events send s.a.e.
Suitable for school groups. Children's quiz/trail
Special visitor services: Guided tours, materials and/or activities for children..

Internet home pages:
http://www.nationaltrust.org.uk

607
CLASSIC BOAT MUSEUM
Seaclose Wharf, Town Quay, Newport, Isle of Wight, PO30 4PF

Tel: 01983 533493
Fax: 01983 533505
Formed: 1996

Organisation type and purpose: Registered charity (charity number 1064643), museum, suitable for ages: all ages, research organisation. Research and restoration.

Enquiries to: Curator
Direct tel: 01983 291433
Direct email: kimlyall@supanet.com
Access:
Access to staff: By telephone
Access to building, collections or gallery: No prior appointment required
Hours: Apr to Oct: daily, 1030 to 1630
Access for disabled people: Parking provided, level entry, access to all public areas, toilet facilities

General description:
A collection of unique and historic boats, with associated maritime displays and artefacts. Restoration work on view and undertaken.
Information services:
Library available for reference (for conditions see Access above)
Special visitor services: Guided tours.
Services for disabled people: Displays and/or information at wheelchair height.
Collections:
Relevant books and magazines (all catalogued) available for research.
Catalogues:
Catalogue for library is in-house only. Catalogue for all of the collections is only available in-house.
Printed publications:
Museum Guide (£1.50)

608
CLASSIC CAR COLLECTION MOTOR MUSEUM LIMITED
See - Motoring Heritage Centre

609
CLASSIC KAWASAKI CLUB
PO Box 235, Nottingham, NG8 6DT

Tel: 0115 913 1333
Fax: 0115 913 4223
Email: classkawa@aol.com
Acronym or abbreviation: CKC
Formed: 1980
Formerly: Kawasaki Triples Club, date of change, 1996

Organisation type and purpose: International organisation, membership association (membership is by subscription), present number of members: 1100, museum.
Has connections with:
Various world wide clubs

Enquiries to: Membership Secretary
Access:
Access to staff: By letter, by telephone, by fax, by email, visitors by prior appointment, Internet web pages
Hours: Mon to Fri, 0900 to 1700
Access to building, collections or gallery: No prior appointment required
Other restrictions: Museum visits by appointment only.

General description:
Historical reference for Kawasaki motorcycles.
Collections:
Technical, historical and reference data held on computer and hard copy
Printed publications:
Magazine (6 times a year, members)
Electronic and video products:
Reference Guides (CD-ROM)

Internet home pages:
http://www.classickawasakiclub.com
Reference, photographs, adverts, message board.

610
CLAY TOBACCO PIPE MUSEUM
Duke Street, Broseley, Shropshire, TF12 5NA

Tel: 01952 882445

Organisation type and purpose: Museum, historic building, house or site.
Parent organisation:
Ironbridge Gorge Museum Trust
Ironbridge, Telford, Shropshire, TF8 7AW, tel: 01952 433522

General description:
Clay tobacco pipes.

611
CLAYDON HOUSE
Middle Claydon, Near Buckingham, Buckinghamshire, MK18 2EY

Tel: 01296 730349
Fax: 01296 738511
Email: claydon@nationaltrust.org.uk
Formed: 1771

Organisation type and purpose: Registered charity (charity number 205846), historic building, house or site, suitable for ages: 5+.
Parent body:
The National Trust (South and South East Region)
Thames and Solent Regional Office, tel: 01494 528051
Other addresses:
Hushenden Manor
High Wycombe, Buckinghamshire, tel: 01494 755500

Enquiries to: Manager
Other contacts: House Steward
Access:
Access to staff: By letter, by telephone, by fax
Access to building, collections or gallery: No prior appointment required
Hours: Gardens: end Mar to beg Nov, daily, 1200 to 1800
House: end Mar to beg Nov, daily, 1300 to 1700
Other restrictions: House closes at 1600 on events days.
Access for disabled people: Parking provided, ramped entry, toilet facilities
Other restrictions: Half-price admission for disabled visitors unable to climb stairs. Drop-off point. 2 manual wheelchairs available, booking essential. Steps to entrance. Accessible entrance different from main entrance. Ground floor accessible with assistance. No access to other floors.
Photograph album.

General description:
One of England's most extraordinary houses displaying some of the most remarkable 18th century rococco and chinoiserie decoration. Features of the house include the unique Chinese Room and parquetry Grand Stairs. In continuous occupation by the Verney family for over 380 years, the house has mementoes of their relation, Florence Nightingale, who was a regular visitor. 'Verney at War' exhibition about the English Civil War.
Information services:
Helpline available, tel no: Infoline 01494 755561.
Suitable for school groups. Family guide. Children's guide.
Leaflets available in French, German and Spanish.
Special visitor services: Guided tours, materials and/or activities for children.
Services for disabled people: Displays and/or information at wheelchair height.
Collections:
Pictures, furniture and superb wood carving of the Chinese Room to the breathtaking parquetry staircase
17th, 18th and 19th century portraits
Catalogues:
Catalogue for library is in-house only. Catalogue for all of the collections is only available in-house.
Printed publications:
IPL
Handbooks
Childrens' Guides
Event leaflets
Leaflets
Postcards
Writer Guides

Internet home pages:
http://www.nationaltrust.org.uk

612
CLAYMILLS PUMPING ENGINE TRUST
Meadow Lane, Stretton, Burton-on-Trent, Staffordshire, DE13 0DB

Tel: 01283 509929
Email: the@archivist.plus.com

Organisation type and purpose: Voluntary organisation, museum.
Restoration and operation of the site carried out by the Trust.
Member of:
North Staffordshire Museums Association
Access:
Access to staff: By letter, by telephone, by email

General description:
The pumping station at Claymills is a rare example of a complete Victorian working site, containing four enormous beam engines, one working, 13 other working steam engines, steam-powered workshop, blacksmith's shop and dynamo house, and the original working boiler house.

613
CLAYRACK DRAINAGE MILL

East bank of River Ant, O.S. TG 369 194, How Hill, Norfolk

Organisation type and purpose: Historic building, house or site.

General description:
Unique hollow post drainage mill with a full set of patent sails which drive a scoop wheel, operates occasionally.

614
CLEARWELL CAVES ANCIENT IRON MINES

Clearwell Caves, The Rocks, Clearwell, Coleford, Gloucestershire, GL16 8JR

Tel: 01594 832535
Fax: 01594 83362
Email: jw@clearwellcaves.com
Acronym or abbreviation: Clearwell Caves
Formed: 1968

Organisation type and purpose: Independently owned, museum, historic building, house or site, suitable for ages: all ages.
Mining museum, the only working ochre mines in the British Isles, set in a natural cave system tunnelled into by miners since the Iron Age, over 2000 years ago.
To research and provide centre for study of local iron mining in Forest of Dean.
Parent body:
Clearwell Mine Management Limited
Links with:
British Cave Research Association (BCRA)
Tel: 01298 873807
National Association of Mining History Organisations (NAMHO)
Tel: 01629 583834
National Caving Association (NCA)
Tel: 015396 22040
Royal Forest of Dean Free Miner's Association (RFDFMA)
Tel: 01594 832535

Enquiries to: Director
Access:
Access to staff: By letter, by telephone, by email, in person
Hours: Open from 1 March to 31 October, daily, 1000 to 1700. January and February weekends, 1000 to 1700
Access to building, collections or gallery: Prior appointment required
Hours: As arranged
Other restrictions: Guided tours and caving activities available for groups (pre-booking required).
Access for disabled people: Parking provided, ramped entry, toilet facilities
Other restrictions: Access to mine workings require prior arrangement for persons with walking difficulties.
Underground site not suitable for persons with walking difficulties.

General description:
Over the past 4000 years, ochre pigments have been mined in the Royal Forest of Dean.
Clearwell Caves now welcome visitors, and still produce ochre for artists' and traditional paints.
Exciting to visit, the caves which cover 600 acres, are a fascinating insight into a very ancient mining tradition.
A great underground experience, geological and mining displays, 9 impressive caverns open to visitors, guided tours and caving activities available for groups (pre-booking required).
A mining museum shows the history of iron mining in the Forest of Dean over 2500 years until 1945. Mining and geological displays.
Information services:
Library available for reference (for conditions see Access above)
Hands-on exhibits by arrangement.
Special visitor services: Guided tours, tape recorded guides, materials and/or activities for children.
Services for disabled people: For the visually impaired.
Collections:
Mining machinery and tools: Neolithic to 20th century, over 1000 items
Geological samples
Local mining history library
Printed publications:
Guide Book
Several facsimile reproductions of local 19th and 20th century publications

Internet home pages:
http://www.clearwellcaves.com
General history, event information and opening times, prices, etc.

615
CLEETHORPES COAST LIGHT RAILWAY

Lakeside Station, Kings Road, Cleethorpes, Lincolnshire, DN35 0AG

Tel: 01472 604657
Fax: 01472 291903
Email: genoff@cclrltd.freeserve.co.uk
Acronym or abbreviation: CCLR
Formed: 1948

Organisation type and purpose: Independently owned, suitable for ages: 5+.
Heritage tourist railway.
Supporters body:
Cleethorpes Coast Light Railway Supporters Association (CCLRSA)
at the same address

Enquiries to: Managing Director
Direct email: chris@cclrltd.freeserve.co.uk
Access:
Access to staff: By letter, by telephone, by email, visitors by prior appointment
Access for disabled people: access to all public areas, toilet facilities

General description:
Seaside miniature and pleasure railways of the UK, the Sutton Coldfield Miniature Railway.
Collections:
The complete Sutton Coldfield Miniature Railway (everything from locos to buildings) saved in 2002 and transported and re-erected at Cleethorpes

Internet home pages:
http://www.cleethorpescoastlightrailway.co.uk

616
CLEEVE ABBEY

Abbey Road, Washford, Watchet, Somerset, TA23 0PS

Tel: 01984 640377

Organisation type and purpose: National organisation, advisory body, historic building, house or site.
Parent body:
English Heritage (South West Region)
Tel: 0117 975 0700
Access:
Access to staff: By letter, by telephone
Access to building, collections or gallery: No prior appointment required
Hours: 29 Mar to 30 Sep: daily, 1000 to 1800,1 to 31 Oct: daily, 1000 to 1700,1 Nov to 31 Mar: daily, 1000 to 1300 and 1400 to 1600
Other restrictions: Closed 24 to 26 Dec and 1 Jan
Opening times are subject to change, for up-to-date information contact English Heritage by phone or visit the website.

General description:
One of the few 13th century monastic sites left where you can see such a complete set of cloister buildings. Also home to 15th century wall paintings of St Catherine and St Margaret. Following a major conservation programme, the Abbey can now be fully explored again.

Internet home pages:
http://www.english-heritage.org.uk

617
CLEVEDON COURT

Tickenham Road, Clevedon, North Somerset, BS21 6QU

Tel: 01275 872257
Fax: 01275 872257

Organisation type and purpose: National organisation, registered charity (charity number 205846), historic building, house or site, suitable for ages: all ages.
Parent body:
The National Trust (South West Region)
Wessex Regional Office, tel: 01985 843600
Other addresses:
The National Trust
Wessex Regional Office
Eastleigh Court, Bishopstrow, Warminster, BA12 9HW, tel: 0198584 3600

Enquiries to: Administrator
Access:
Access to staff: By letter, by telephone
Hours: Mon to Thu, 0900 to 1700
Access for disabled people: Parking provided
Other restrictions: Designated parking 15yds. Drop-off point. Steps to entrance. Ground floor largely accessible. No access to other floors. Photograph album.

General description:
An outstanding 14th century manor house, with much of the original building still evident, incorporating a massive 12th century tower and 13th century great hall. Altered and added to by the Elizabethans, it has been home to the Elton family since 1709. The house contains many striking Eltonware pots and vases and a fascinating collection of Nailsea glass. There is also a beautiful 18th century terraced garden.
Information services:
Guided tours for groups only.
Braille guide. Large-print guide.
Suitable for school groups. Children's guide. Children's quiz/trail.
Special visitor services: Materials and/or activities for children.
Education services: Group education facilities.
Services for disabled people: For the visually impaired.
Collections:
Collection of Eltonware art pottery
Collection of Nailsea glass
Printed publications:
Guide Book
Children's Guide Book

Internet home pages:
http://www.nationaltrust.org.uk/regions/wessex

618
CLEVEDON STORY HERITAGE CENTRE

Waterloo House, 4 The Beach, Clevedon, Somerset, BS21 7QU

Tel: 01275 341196
Formed: 1992

Organisation type and purpose: Registered charity (charity number 283629), museum.

Enquiries to: Manager
Access:
Access for disabled people: ramped entry, toilet facilities

General description:
Contains reproduction photographs and prints with texts illustrating the growth of Clevedon, supported with some original artefacts.

619
CLEVELAND IRONSTONE MINING MUSEUM
Skinningrove, Saltburn-by-the-Sea, Cleveland, TS13 4AP

Tel: 01287 642877
Fax: 01287 642970
Formed: 1983
Formerly: Tom Leonard Mining Museum, date of change, 1999

Organisation type and purpose: Independently owned, registered charity (charity number 1080246), museum, suitable for ages: 5+.

Enquiries to: Curator
Access:
Access to staff: By letter
Hours: Mon to Fri, 0900 to 1600

General description:
Located on the site of the old Loftus Ironstone Mine, the museum preserves and interprets the ironstone mining heritage of Cleveland, North-East England. It offers visitors an interesting and authentic underground experience. Discover the special skills, customs and domestic life of the miners who made Cleveland the most important ironstone mining area in Victorian and Edwardian Britain.
Information services:
Special visitor services: Guided tours, materials and/or activities for children.
Education services: Group education facilities, resources for Key Stages 1 and 2..
Collections:
A substantial collection of original tools, safety lamps and equipment, old photographs and social history objects.

620
CLIFFE CASTLE MUSEUM
Spring Gardens Lane, Keighley, West Yorkshire, BD20 6LH

Tel: 01535 618230
Fax: 01535 610536
Formed: 1959

Organisation type and purpose: Local government body, museum, art gallery, suitable for ages: all ages.
Administered by:
City of Bradford Metropolitan District Council

Enquiries to: Curator
Access:
Access to staff: By letter, by telephone, by fax, visitors by prior appointment
Other restrictions: Prior appointment to see staff.
Access to building, collections or gallery: No prior appointment required
Hours: Museum: Tue to Sat, 1000 to 1700; Sun, 1200 to 1700
Access for disabled people: Parking provided, ramped entry, toilet facilities

General description:
Local archaeology; history; geology and natural history.
Some fine and decorative art including stained glass (Morris and Co) and pottery.
Information services:
Education services: Group education facilities, resources for Key Stages 1 and 2, 3, 4 and Further or Higher Education.
Services for disabled people: Displays and/or information at wheelchair height.
Collections:
Displays and reference collection of rocks, minerals, fossils, flora and fauna; social history; art, fine and decorative, including Morris Stained Glass and pottery

621
CLIFFORD'S TOWER
York

Tel: 01904 646940

Organisation type and purpose: National organisation, advisory body, historic building, house or site.
Parent body:
English Heritage (Yorkshire Region)
Tel: 01904 601901

Enquiries to: Manager
Access:
Access to staff: By letter, by telephone
Access to building, collections or gallery: No prior appointment required
Hours: 29 Mar to 30 Sep: daily, 1000 to 1800 (17 Jul to 31 Aug: 0930 to 1900)
1 to 31 Oct: daily, 1000 to 1700,1 Nov to 31 Mar: daily, 1000 to 1600
Other restrictions: Closed 24 to 26 Dec and 1 Jan
Opening times are subject to change, for up-to-date information contact English Heritage by phone or visit the website.

General description:
Standing high on a mound, this 13th century tower includes one of two towers built to help William the Conqueror subdue the north. One hundred years later, in 1190, York's Jewish community took shelter in the castle when threatened by a violent mob. Many took their own lives rather than be murdered. The Tower's association with national events and royalty continued until the Civil War in the 17th century, when it was largely destroyed by a fire. Today, spectacular views from the Tower show why it played such a key role in the control of northern England.

Internet home pages:
http://www.english-heritage.org.uk

622
CLIFTON PARK MUSEUM
Clifton Park, Rotherham, South Yorkshire, S65 2AA

Tel: 01709 823635
Fax: 01709 823631
Email: steve.blackbourn@rotherham.gov.uk
Formed: 1893
Formerly: Rotherham Museum

Organisation type and purpose: Local government body, museum.

Enquiries to: Manager
Access:
Access to staff: By letter, by telephone, by fax, by email, visitors by prior appointment
Hours: Mon to Thu, Sat, 1000 to 1700; Sun, 1330 to 1630; (Sun, 1330 to 1700 in summer); Closed Fri
Access to building, collections or gallery: No prior appointment required
Hours: Mon to Thu, Sat, 1000 to 1700; Sun, 1330 to 1630; (Sun, 1330 to 1700 in summer); Closed Friv
Other restrictions: Prior appointment required for library and reserve collections.

General description:
South Yorkshire potteries, Swinton pottery, Rockingham porcelain; natural, social and industrial history of the Rotherham area, archaeology from antiquity (with special reference to the Roman fort at Templeborough) to the present day.
Collections:
Beatson Clarke and Spurley Hey Collection of glass
Rockingham Pottery Collection
Roman relics from Templeborough
Young Lepidoptera Collection (not on display)
Printed publications:
Books, booklets and information sheets

Internet home pages:
http://www.rmu.org

623
CLINK PRISON MUSEUM
1 Soho Wharf, Clink Street, London, SE1 9DG

Tel: 020 7378 1558 (museum enquiries)
Fax: 020 7403 5813
Email: jdh@clink.co.uk
Formed: 1989

Organisation type and purpose: Independently owned, museum, suitable for ages: 8+.
Other telephone numbers:
Admissions and Museum Enquiries
Tel: 020 7378 1558
Corporate Bookings
Tel: 020 7403 6515
General Management
Tel: 020 7403 0900

Enquiries to: Curator/General Manager
Access:
Access to staff: By telephone, by fax, by email, in person, visitors by prior appointment

General description:
The museum is on the site of the original prison known as The Clink from the 15th century and owned by successive Bishops of Winchester. This fascinating exhibition examines some of London's unsavoury past.
Information services:
Guided tours by arrangement only.
Educational services plans under development.
Special visitor services: Guided tours..

Internet home pages:
http://www.clink.co.uk

624
CLITHEROE CASTLE MUSEUM
Castle Hill, Clitheroe, Lancashire, BB7 1BA

Tel: 01200 424635
Email: museum@ribblevalley.gov.uk
Formed: 1938

Organisation type and purpose: Local government body, museum, suitable for ages: all ages.
Parent body:
Ribble Valley Borough Council (RVBC)
Church Walk, Clitheroe, BB7 2RA, tel: 01200 414496, email: tourism@ribblevalley.gov.uk
Links:
Lancashire County Museum Services
Stanley Street, Preston, Lancashire, PR1 4YP, tel: 01772 264061, fax: 01772 264079, email/website: museum@lancs.co.uk

Enquiries to: Custodian
Other contacts: Curator, Tel 01200 424568, 01772 264202; Fax 01200 424568; Email: hannah.chalk@mus.lancscc.gov.uk for enquiries regarding geology and educational projects.
Access:
Access to staff: By letter, by telephone, by email, in person
Hours: Low Season: Sat to Wed, 1100 to 1630
High Season: Mon to Sun, 1100 to 1630
Other restrictions: Open weekends only in winter (closed Jan); also open all Bank Holidays; open every day Easter to Oct; closed Thu, Fri, in spring.
Access to building, collections or gallery: No prior appointment required
Hours: Collections: Mon to Fri, 0930 to 1700
Other restrictions: Contact Curator only on telephone/fax 01200 424568.

General description:
Social history of Clitheroe, including agriculture; reconstructions of Edwardian kitchen, printers, cloggers' shop and 18th century lead mine (sound tracks in clogs and kitchen).
History of witchcraft; local industry; geology of the Ribble Valley, nationally famous for its fossils; minerals from around the world; earth sciences (Key Stage 2) for schools.
Information services:
Education services: Group education facilities, resources for Key Stage 2.

Services for disabled people: For the hearing impaired.
Collections:
Lancashire Geology Collection
Learoyd-Ranson, international geological collection, c. 20,000 specimens
Westhead Bequest
Ribble Valley Archaeology and Social History
Catalogues:
Catalogue for part of the collections is only available in-house.
Printed publications:
Clitheroe Castle (£1.50)
Lancashire Witch-Craze (£7)
Salthill Geology Trail (£2.99)
Walking Local Roman Roads (£5.95)

Internet home pages:
http://www.ribblevalley.gov.uk
Displays and opening times.

625
CLIVE HOUSE MUSEUM
See - Shrewsbury Museums Service

626
CLIVEDEN
Taplow, Maidenhead, Buckinghamshire, SL6 0JA

Tel: 01628 605069
Fax: 01628 669461
Email: cliveden@nationaltrust.org.uk

Organisation type and purpose: National organisation, registered charity (charity number 205846), historic building, house or site, suitable for ages: .
Parent Body:
The National Trust (South and South East Region)
Thames and Solent Regional Office, tel: 01494 528051

Enquiries to: Manager
Access:
Access to staff: By letter, by telephone, by fax, by email
Access to building, collections or gallery: No prior appointment required
Hours: House and Octagonal Temple: Apr to Oct, 1500 to 1730, Thu and Sun;
Estate and Garden: Mid Mar to Oct, Daily, 1100 to 1800; Nov and Dec, daily, 1100 to 1600
Other restrictions: Admission to house by timed ticket, obtainable from information kiosk only. Some areas of formal garden may be roped off when ground conditions bad.
Access for disabled people: Parking provided, toilet facilities
Other restrictions: Drop-off point. 3 manual wheelchairs available. Powered mobility vehicles: 2 single-seater, 2 two-seater, booking essential. Level entrance. Ground floor largely accessible, 2 steps on visitor route, can exit, use alternative entrance and rejoin tour. No access to other floors. Level entrance to shop and to restaurant. Grounds largely accessible. Recommended route map.

General description:
This spectacular estate overlooking the River Thames has a series of gardens, each with its own character, featuring topiary, statuary, water gardens, a formal parterre, informal vistas, woodland and riverside walks. The present house, the third on the site, was built by Charles Barry for the Duke of Sutherland in 1851. Once the home of Nancy, Lady Astor, it is now let as an hotel and is open only on certain days.
Information services:
Helpline available, tel no: Infoline: 01494 755562.
Braille guide. Large-print guide. Scented plants. Fountains and water garden.
All terrain buggies for hire . Children's guide.
Special visitor services: Materials and/or activities for children.
Services for disabled people: For the visually impaired.

Internet home pages:
http://www.nationaltrust.org.uk

627
CLOTWORTHY ARTS CENTRE
Antrim Castle Gardens, Randalstown Road, Antrim, BT41 4LH

Tel: 028 9442 8000
Fax: 028 9446 0360
Email: clotworthy@antrim.gov.uk
Formed: 1983

Organisation type and purpose: Local government body, art gallery, historic building, house or site, suitable for ages: 5+.
Parent body:
Antrim Borough Council
Steeple Offices, Antrim, BT41 1BJ, tel: 02894 463113, fax: 02894 464469

Enquiries to: Development Officer (Arts & Heritage)
Other contacts: Assistant Arts & Heritage Officer
Access:
Access to staff: By letter, by telephone, by fax, by email, visitors by prior appointment
Access to building, collections or gallery: No prior appointment required
Hours: Mon to Fri, 0930 to 2130; Sat, 1000 to 1700
Access for disabled people: Parking provided, ramped entry, toilet facilities
Other restrictions: Events Programme in large type and Braille, hearing loop in function rooms, Sennheiser System in theatre, textphone facility.

General description:
Three art galleries, theatre, Battle of Antrim interactive kiosk, historic 17th century water gardens, formal parterre, 12th century motte, gardens interpretative display.
Information services:
Special visitor services: Guided tours.
Services for disabled people: For the visually impaired; for the hearing impaired; displays and/or information at wheelchair height.
Printed publications:
Information leaflets (free)

Internet home pages:
http://www.antrim.gov.uk
General information on borough services.

628
CLOUDS HILL
Wareham, Dorset, BH20 7NQ

Tel: 01929 405616 (Custodian)

Organisation type and purpose: National organisation, registered charity (charity number 205846), museum, historic building, house or site, suitable for ages: 12+.
Parent Body:
The National Trust (South West Region)
Wessex Regional Office, tel: 01985 843600

Enquiries to: Custodian
Access:
Access to staff: By letter, by telephone
Access to building, collections or gallery: No prior appointment required
Hours: Apr to Oct, Thu to Sun, 1200 to 1700
Open Bank Holiday Mondays
Other restrictions: Closes at dusk if earlier than 1700. No electric light. Groups wishing to visit at other times must telephone in advance.

General description:
A tiny isolated brick and tile cottage, bought in 1925 by T E Lawrence ('Lawrence of Arabia') as a retreat. The austere rooms inside are much as he left them and reflect his complex personality and close links with the Middle East.. A new exhibition details Lawrence's extraordinary life.
Information services:
Services for disabled people: For the visually impaired.

Internet home pages:
http://www.nationaltrust.org.uk/regions/wessex

629
CLUMBER PARK
The Estate Office, Clumber Park, Worksop, Nottinghamshire, S80 3AZ

Tel: 01909 476592
Fax: 01909 500721
Email: clumberpark@nationaltrust.org.uk

Organisation type and purpose: National organisation, registered charity (charity number 205846), historic building, house or site, suitable for ages: 8+.
Parent body:
National Trust (East Midlands Region)
East Midlands Regional Office, tel: 01909 486411

Enquiries to: Estate Manager
Other contacts: Education Officer 01909 544918
Access:
Access to staff: By letter, by telephone, by fax, by email, in person, Internet web pages
Access for disabled people: Parking provided, toilet facilities
Other restrictions: 5 manual wheelchairs available. Powered mobility vehicles: 2 single-seater. Ramped entrance to shop. Ramped entrance to tea-room. Parts are accessible. Ramp access from conservatory to garden.

General description:
Over 1500ha (3800 acres) of parkland, peaceful woods, open heath and rolling farmland with a superb serpentine lake at its heart. Part of Nottinghamshire's famed 'Dukeries', Clumber was formerly home to the Dukes of Newcastle. The house was demolished in 1938, but many fascinating features of the estate remain, including an outstanding Gothic Revival Chapel, Hardwick village and walled kitchen garden.
Information services:
Helpline available, tel no: 01909 544917.
Suitable for school groups. Education room/centre. Hands-on activities. Children's guide. Children's quiz/trail. Family activity packs. Adult study days
Programme of concerts, Box Office 01909 51106
Special visitor services: Guided tours, materials and/or activities for children.
Education services: Group education facilities..

Internet home pages:
http://www.nationaltrust.org.uk

630
CLUN LOCAL HISTORY MUSEUM
Town Hall, The Square, Clun, Shropshire, SY7 8JA

Tel: 01588 640681
Fax: 01588 640681
Email: ktomey@fish.co.uk
Formed: 1924

Organisation type and purpose: Voluntary organisation, registered charity (charity number 208408), museum.
Governing body:
Clun Town Trust

Enquiries to: Curator
Access:
Access to staff: By letter, by telephone, by fax, by email

General description:
A comprehensive collection of domestic and agricultural items illustrating the local history of the area.
Collections:
Over 1000 prehistoric flints, tools and weapons, all brought to this flintless area by trade via the Clun-Clee Ridgeway. Includes a set of surgical instruments used in trepanning.
Agricultural and domestic bygones of various periods and photographs
Publications list:
is available in hard copy.
Printed publications:
Brief History of Clun (85p)

continued overleaf

Clun Castle (85p)
Clun Town Trail (85p)
The Recollections of Rev Henry Cresswell and His Family (50p)

631
CLWYD COUNTY MUSEUM SERVICE
See - Greenfield Valley Heritage Park

632
CLYDEBANK MUSEUM
Town Hall, Dumbarton Road, Clydebank, Strathclyde, G81 1UE

Tel: 01389 738 702
Fax: 0141 952 1243
Email: curator@clybankmuseum.sol.co.uk
Formed: 1980
Formerly: Clydebank District Museum, date of change, 1995

Organisation type and purpose: Local government body, museum.
Parent body:
West Dunbartonshire Council
Council Buildings, Garshake Road, Dumbarton, tel: 01389 730 000

Enquiries to: Curator
Access:
Access to staff: By letter, by telephone, by fax, in person
Hours: Mon, Wed, Thu, Fri, 1400 to 1630; Tue, Sat, 1000 to 1630; other times by prior arrangement
Access to building, collections or gallery: No prior appointment required

General description:
Clydebank shipbuilding, sewing machine industry, Clydebank local history, some World War II material - Clydebank Blitz.
Collections:
Collection of sewing machines, including photographic and technical archive
Publications list:
is available in hard copy.
Printed publications:
Antique Sewing Machines (£5.00)
Beardmore Built (hardback £14.95, paperback £9.95)
Down the Burma Road (£6.95)
History of Old Kilpatrick (£7.95)
Liners of the Clyde (£8.95)
Long Live Queen Mary (£14.95)
Memories of the Clyde (£4.95)
Old Clydebank in Pictures (£5.85)
Old Sewing Machines (£2.95)
OS Map of Clydebank 1896 (£1.25)
QE2 (£6.95)
RMS Queen Elizabeth (£8.95)
RMS Queen Mary (£4.95)
The Clydebank Blitz (£2.50)
To the Coast (£4.80)
Electronic and video products:
Canoes to Cunarders (VHS and NTSC)
Singer Clydebank Memories (VHS and NTSC)

Internet home pages:
http://www.west-dunbarton.gov.uk

633
CLYDEBUILT
See - Scottish Maritime Museum, Glasgow

634
COACH HOUSE MUSEUM (THE MUSEUM OF THE PURBECK STONE INDUSTRY)
See - Langton Matravers Museum

635
COALPORT CHINA MUSEUM
Ironbridge Gorge Museum Trust, Coach Road, Coalbrookdale, Telford, Shropshire, TF8 7DQ

Tel: 01952 580650
Fax: 01952 580650
Email: coalport@ironbridge.org.uk

Organisation type and purpose: Registered charity (charity number 503717-R), museum, historic building, house or site, suitable for ages: 5+.
Parent body:
The Ironbridge Gorge Museum Trust
Tel: 01952 433522
Access:
Access to staff: By letter, by telephone, by fax, by email, visitors by prior appointment
Access to building, collections or gallery: No prior appointment required
Hours: 1000 to 1700, daily
Other restrictions: Closed 24th and 25th Dec, 1st Jan.
Access for disabled people: Parking provided, ramped entry, toilet facilities
Other restrictions: Only one floor inaccessible. Access guide for disabled visitors available on request.

General description:
The National Collections of Caughley and Coalport china are displayed in the restored buildings of the old Coalport China works. Galleries show the beautiful china and explore the hardships of factory life.
Information services:
Demonstrations of ceramic techniques, workshops and a speciality china shop, activities vary from day to day. Please telephone for details.
Family trails. Children's activities, each school holiday, Mon to Fri.
Braille and large print guides.
Special visitor services: Materials and/or activities for children.
Education services: Group education facilities, resources for Key Stages 1 and 2, 3, 4 and Further or Higher Education.
Services for disabled people: For the visually impaired; displays and/or information at wheelchair height.
Collections:
National collections of Caughley and Coalport china

Internet home pages:
http://www.ironbridge.org.uk

636
COALVILLE LIBRARY
See - Coleorton Collection

637
COATS OBSERVATORY
49 Oakshaw Street West, Paisley, Renfrewshire, PA1 2DE

Tel: 0141 889 2013
Fax: 0141 889 9240
Formed: 1883

Organisation type and purpose: Local government body, museum, research organisation.
Observatory.
Parent body:
Renfrewshire Council

Enquiries to: Observatory Officer
Access:
Access to staff: By letter, by telephone, by fax, in person, visitors by prior appointment
Hours: Tue to Sat, 1000 to 1700; Sun, 1400 to 1700; closed Mon
Access to building, collections or gallery: No prior appointment required
Hours: Special Winter evening opening on Thu for astronomical observations by the Renfrewshire Astronomical Society

General description:
An astronomical observatory with seismic and meteorological functions dating from 1883. The building was designed by John Honeyman.
Collections:
Astronomical instruments
Seismometer with outstations connected to the British Geological Survey

Internet home pages:
http://homepage.ntlworld.com/mark.pollock/index.html
Renfrewshire Astronomical Society.

638
COBBATON COMBAT COLLECTION
Cobbaton, Chittlehampton, Umberleigh, Devon, EX37 9RZ

Tel: 01769 540740
Fax: 01769 540141
Email: info@cobbatoncombat.co.uk
Formed: 1981

Organisation type and purpose: Independently owned, museum, suitable for ages: 5+.

Enquiries to: Curator
Access:
Access to staff: By letter, by telephone, by fax, by email, in person, Internet web pages
Access for disabled people: Parking provided, ramped entry, access to all public areas, toilet facilities

General description:
Over 60 vehicles and equipment, mainly from WWII period.
Collections:
Over 60 vehicles, artillery pieces plus weapons and equipment
Home Front Section
Printed publications:
Guide Book (£1.50)
Leaflets (free)

Internet home pages:
http://cobbatoncombat.co.uk

639
COBHAM BUS MUSEUM
Redhill Road, Cobham, Surrey, KT11 1EF

Tel: 01932 868665 (weekends only)
Email: cobhambusmuseum@aol.com
Acronym or abbreviation: LBPT
Formed: 1972

Organisation type and purpose: Independently owned, registered charity (charity number 293319), museum, suitable for ages: 5+.
Parent body:
London Bus Preservation Trust (LBPT)

Enquiries to: Secretary
Access:
Access to staff: By letter, by email
Access to building, collections or gallery: Prior appointment required
Hours: Special event days only, telephone for details
Other restrictions: At other weekends, visitors are welcome by prior appointment only.
Access for disabled people: level entry
Other restrictions: Wheelchair user car spaces (currently no special toilet facilities).

General description:
History of the Omnibus in London.
Information services:
Special visitor services: Guided tours..
Collections:
30 Buses and Coaches, mostly of London origin, the widest selection under one roof of ex-London Transport motor vehicles in the world
Various items of street furniture and other transport artefacts
Photographic history of the London Motor-Bus
Video of the Museum's History and Bus preservation activities - housed on board a 1937 London Transport Double-Decker Bus

Internet home pages:
http://www.kevinmcgowan.org
Comprehensive information on the museum, the buses and event days.

640
CODY MUSEUM TRUST (1993)
8 Ash Green Lane West, Ash Green, Surrey, GU12 6HL

Tel: 01252 673872
Acronym or abbreviation: CMT
Formed: 1993

Organisation type and purpose: Independently owned, suitable for ages: 12+, consultancy, research organisation.
Education of young people etc.
Associated with:
Cody Society
Ash Green, Surrey
Farnborough Air Sciences Trust (FAST)
Farnborough, Hampshire

Enquiries to: Secretary
Access:
Access to staff: By letter only
Access to building, collections or gallery: Prior appointment required

General description:
Colonel Samuel Franklin Cody and the early pioneers of aviation in the UK.
Farnborough Aerospace Heritage.
Collections:
Extensive library of early aviation history photographs, documents etc
Catalogues:
Catalogue for all of the collections is only available in-house.
Publications list:
is available in hard copy.
Printed publications:
Various - aviation history
Monographs (for purchase)
Newsletter

Internet home pages:
http://www.hants.gov.uk/cousin/cousinweb/cody.html
Early history.

641
COGGES MANOR FARM MUSEUM
Church Lane, Witney, Oxfordshire, OX28 3LA

Tel: 01993 772602
Fax: 01993 703056
Formed: 1976

Organisation type and purpose: Local government body, museum, suitable for ages: all ages.
Connected with:
West Oxfordshire District Council
Woodgreen, Witney, Oxfordshire, OX28 1NB

Enquiries to: Manager
Access:
Access to staff: By letter, by telephone, by fax, visitors by prior appointment
Other restrictions: Front of house staff are accessible during open hours.
Access to building, collections or gallery: No prior appointment required
Hours: Tue to Fri, 1030 to 1730; Sat, Sun, 1200 to 1730
Access for disabled people: Parking provided, level entry, toilet facilities

General description:
Historic house, historic farm buildings, Victorian farm, Victorian room displays, rare animal breeds, agricultural collection.
Information services:
Helpline available
Special visitor services: Guided tours, materials and/or activities for children.
Education services: Group education facilities, resources for Key Stages 1 and 2..

642
COGGESHALL GRANGE BARN
Grange Hill, Coggeshall, Colchester, Essex, CO6 1RE

Tel: 01376 562226

Organisation type and purpose: National organisation, registered charity (charity number 205846), historic building, house or site, suitable for ages: 8+.
Parent body:
The National Trust

Enquiries to: Manager
Access:
Access to staff: By letter, by telephone
Access for disabled people: level entry, toilet facilities
Other restrictions: Ground floor fully accessible.

General description:
One of the oldest surviving timber-framed barns in Europe, dating from the 13th century and originally part of a Cistercian monastery. It was restored in the 1980s by The Coggeshall Grange Barn Trust, Braintree District Council and Essex County Council, and contains a small collection of farm carts and wagons. The Essex Way long-distance footpath passes the barn.

643
COLCHESTER AND DISTRICT VISUAL ARTS TRUST
See - Firstsite@The Minories

644
COLCHESTER CASTLE MUSEUM
Castle Park, Colchester, Essex, CO1 1TJ

Tel: 01206 282939 and 282931

Enquiries to: Curator
Access:
Access to staff: By letter, by telephone
Access to building, collections or gallery: No prior appointment required
Hours: Mon to Sat, 1000 to 1700; Sun, 1100 to 1700
Access for disabled people: toilet facilities
Other restrictions: Unstepped to the ground floor, a lift to the first floor. Tours include two sets of steep stairs.

General description:
Colchester Castle with the largest keep ever built by the Normans and material from the Bronze Age to the Civil War.
Information services:
Audio-visual dramas.
Special visitor services: Guided tours.
Services for disabled people: For the hearing impaired.

Internet home pages:
http://www.colchestermuseums.org.uk

645
COLCHESTER MUSEUMS
Museum Resource Centre, 14 Ryegate Road, Colchester, Essex, CO1 1YG

Tel: 01206 282931
Fax: 01206 282925
Email: marie.taylor@colchester.gov.uk
Formed: 1860
Formerly: Colchester & Essex Museum

Organisation type and purpose: Local government body, museum, suitable for ages: all ages.
Parent body:
Colchester Borough Council
Houses the library of:
Essex Archaeological Society in Hollytrees
Includes the:
Castle (archaeology)
Tel: 01206 282939, fax: 01206 282925, email/website: phillip.wise@colchester.gov.uk
Hollytrees (later antiquities, toys and costume)
Tel: 01206 282940, fax: 01206 282925, email/website: tom.hodgson@colchester.gov.uk
Natural History Museum in All Saints Church
Tel: 01206 282941, fax: 01206 282925, email/website: terry.bowdrey@colchester.gov.uk
Tymperleys Clock Museum
Tel: 01206 282943, fax: 01206 282925, email/website: tom.hodgson@colchester.gov.uk

Enquiries to: Information Officer
Direct tel: 01206 282937
Direct fax: 01206 282925
Access:
Access to staff: By telephone, by fax, by email, visitors by prior appointment, Internet web pages
Hours: Mon to Fri, 0900 to 1700
Access for disabled people: ramped entry, level entry, access to all public areas, toilet facilities
Other restrictions: No access to vaults tour

General description:
Archaeology, antiquities and natural history of Essex and Britain; social history of Colchester area; Colchester-made clocks; Roman Britain.
Information services:
Library available for reference (for conditions see Access above)
Special visitor services: Guided tours, materials and/or activities for children.
Education services: Group education facilities, resources for Key Stages 1 and 2.
Services for disabled people: For the visually impaired; for the hearing impaired; displays and/or information at wheelchair height.
Collections:
Major collections relating to the human and natural history of North East Essex
Catalogues:
Catalogue for part of the collections is on-line.
Printed publications:
Colchester Castle Guide
Colchester Town Guide
Museum leaflet
Town Hall Guide
Summer events leaflet

Internet home pages:
http://www.colchestermuseums.org.uk

646
COLDHARBOUR MILL, WORKING WOOL MUSEUM
Uffculme, Cullompton, Devon, EX15 3EE

Tel: 01884 840960
Fax: 01884 840858
Email: info@coldharbourmill.org.uk
Formed: 1982

Organisation type and purpose: Museum, suitable for ages: 5+.

Enquiries to: Curator
Other contacts: General Manager for advertising.
Access:
Access to staff: By letter, by telephone, by fax, by email, in person
Hours: Mon to Fri, 1030 to 1700
Access for disabled people: Parking provided, level entry, toilet facilities
Other restrictions: Access to most areas.
Due to historical nature of building, there are some access issues - telephone for details.

General description:
History of woollen and worsted industry through the story of The Fox Brothers' Company, from 1797-1981; textiles, late 19th and 20th century period spinning and weaving machinery.
Information services:
Special visitor services: Guided tours.
Education services: Group education facilities, resources for Key Stages 1 and 2, 3, 4 and Further or Higher Education.
Services for disabled people: For the visually impaired; for the hearing impaired.
Collections:
Worsted machinery, working gill box, draw box, spinning and twisting frames, 1898-1958. 20 items

continued overleaf

Woollen machinery, carding machine, spinning mule and dobby loom, 1903-1955, 6 items
Archive directly related to Fox Brothers Company
1867 Beam Engine
1910 Pollit & Wigzell cross-compound steam engine
1888 and 1910 Galloways Lancashire Boilers
New World tapestry, tells story of the colonisation of America, 1583-1642, 10 panels (100 ft.)

Catalogues:
Catalogue for all of the collections is only available in-house.

Internet home pages:
http://www.coldharbourmill.org.uk

647
COLDSTREAM MUSEUM

12 Market Square, Coldstream, Borders, TD12 4BD

Tel: 01890 882630
Fax: 01890 882631
Formed: 1994

Organisation type and purpose: Local government body, museum, suitable for ages: 5+.
Parent body:
Scottish Borders Council Museum and Gallery Service
Tel: 01750 20096

Enquiries to: Curator
Access:
Access to staff: By letter, by telephone, by fax
Other restrictions: Contact Scottish Borders Council Museum Service when closed.
Access to building, collections or gallery: No prior appointment required
Hours: Easter to end of Sep, Mon to Sat, 1000 to 1600, Sun 1400 to1600;
Oct, Mon to Sat, 1300 to 1600
Access for disabled people: Parking provided, access to all public areas, toilet facilities

General description:
The history of Coldstream and its people. The regiment of Coldstream Guards was named after the town following its stay in the area in 1659. Museum gallery with temporary exhibitions.

Internet home pages:
http://www.scotborders.gov.uk
http://www.scotborders.org.uk

648
COLEORTON COLLECTION

Leicestershire Libraries and Information Service, Coalville Library, High Street, Coalville, Leicestershire, LE67 3EA

Tel: 01530 835951
Fax: 01530 832019
Full name: Coleorton Parish Priests Collection
Formed: 1727

Organisation type and purpose: Local government body, public library.
Connections with:
Leicestershire Libraries and Information Service
County Hall, Glenfield, Leicester, LE3 8RA

Enquiries to: Librarian
Access:
Access to staff: By letter, by telephone, by fax, in person
Access for disabled people: Parking provided, ramped entry, access to all public areas, toilet facilities

General description:
Philosophy, religion, some history, especially strong in 19th century religious works.
Collections:
Contents of an 18th century Parish Priest's Library
Catalogues:
Catalogue for library is in-house only.

649
COLERIDGE COTTAGE

35 Lime Street, Nether Stowey, Bridgwater, Somerset, TA5 1NQ

Tel: 01278 732662

Parent body:
The National Trust (South West Region)
Wessex Regional Office, tel: 01985 843600

Enquiries to: Manager
Access:
Access to staff: By letter, by telephone
Access to building, collections or gallery: No prior appointment required
Hours: End Mar to end Sep, Tue to Sun, 1400 to 1700

General description:
The home of Samuel Taylor Coleridge for three years from 1797, with mementoes of the poet on display. It was here that he wrote 'The Rime of the Ancient Mariner', part of 'Christabel' and 'Frost at Midnight'.
Information services:
Services for disabled people: For the visually impaired.

Internet home pages:
http://www.nationaltrust.org.uk/regions/wessex

650
COLETON FISHACRE HOUSE AND GARDEN

Coleton, Brownstone Road, Kingswear, Dartmouth, Devon, TQ6 0EQ

Tel: 01803 752466
Fax: 01803 753017
Email: coletonfishacre@nationaltrust.org.uk
Formed: 1983

Organisation type and purpose: National organisation, registered charity (charity number 205846), historic building, house or site, suitable for ages: 8+.
Parent body:
The National Trust (South West Region)
Devon and Cornwall Regional Office, tel: 01392 881691

Enquiries to: Property Manager
Access:
Access to staff: By letter, by telephone, by fax
Access for disabled people: Parking provided, ramped entry, level entry, toilet facilities
Other restrictions: Designated parking 20yds. Drop-off point. 3 manual wheelchairs available, booking essential. Ramped entrance. Ground floor fully accessible. No access to other floors. Photograph album. Level entrance to shop and to tea-room. Garden: limited access, upper paths reasonably flat with some grass paths, but steep slopes (strong companion for wheelchair users essential). Recommended route map.

General description:
Spectacularly set in a stream-fed valley on a beautiful stretch of the NT South Devon coastline, the house was designed in 1925 for Rupert and Lady Dorothy D'Oyly Carte, who created the luxuriant garden around it. The house reflects the Arts & Crafts tradition, but also has refreshingly modern interiors; the garden has year-round interest with a gazebo, water features and fine collection of rare and exotic plants.
Information services:
Braille guide. Audio guide. Scented plants
Occasional guided walks by arrangement or as advertised under special events.
Hip-carrying infant seats for loan.
Children's quiz/trail.
Special visitor services: Guided tours, materials and/or activities for children.
Services for disabled people: For the visually impaired.

Collections:
No specific collections held but some original carpets, furniture and light fittings from the 1920s and 1930s
Publications list:
is available in hard copy.
Printed publications:
Guide Book (£2.50)
Short House Guide (20p)
Garden Guide (30p)

Internet home pages:
http://www.nationaltrust.org.uk/regions/southwest

651
COLLINS GALLERY

University of Strathclyde, 22 Richmond Street, Glasgow, G1 1XQ

Tel: 0141 548 2558
Fax: 0141 552 4053
Email: collinsgallery@strath.ac.uk
Formed: 1973
Formed from: University of Strathclyde

Organisation type and purpose: Art gallery, university department or institute, suitable for ages: 5+.
Parent body:
University of Strathclyde

Enquiries to: Curator
Direct tel: 0141 548 4145
Access:
Access to staff: By letter, by telephone, by fax, by email, visitors by prior appointment
Access for disabled people: Parking provided, level entry, access to all public areas, toilet facilities

General description:
Temporary exhibition programme of ten shows per annum covering fine and applied art, design and mixed media installation by contemporary artists from UK and abroad.
Information services:
Special visitor services: Guided tours, materials and/or activities for children.
Education services: Group education facilities, resources for Further or Higher Education.
Services for disabled people: Displays and/or information at wheelchair height.
Collections:
The following are to be viewed by appointment only:
Fine Art - mainly Scottish from 18th century to present day
Historic scientific instruments, including collection of Professor John Anderson, founder of the university, from 18th century to mid 20th century, c. 400 items
Catalogues:
Catalogue for all of the collections is only available in-house.
Publications list:
is available in hard copy and online.
Printed publications:
Annual Calendar of Exhibitions and Related Events (free of charge)

Internet home pages:
http://www.collinsgallery.strath.ac.uk

652
COLNE VALLEY MUSEUM

Cliffe Ash, Golcar, Huddersfield, West Yorkshire, HD7 4PY

Tel: 01484 659762
Formed: 1970

Organisation type and purpose: Independently owned, membership association (membership is by subscription), present number of members: 375, voluntary organisation, registered charity (charity number 529316), museum, suitable for ages: all ages.

Enquiries to: Executive Committee Member
Access:
Access to staff: By letter, charges to non-members

General description:
The museum recreates a hand weaver's home and working life, c. 1840-1850. Includes a Loom Chamber, with working hand looms and a Spinning Jenny; a Spinning Room, with Great Wheel and Saxony Wheels; and a Clogger's Shop, fully equipped with period tools and equipment from 1910.
Information services:
Education services: Group education facilities, resources for Key Stages 1 and 2, 3, 4 and Further or Higher Education..

653
COLNE VALLEY RAILWAY
The Station, Castle Hedingham, Halstead, Essex, CO9 3DZ

Tel: 01787 461174
Fax: 01787 462254
Formed: 1972

Organisation type and purpose: Membership association, voluntary organisation, museum, suitable for ages: all ages.
Tourist railway and education centre (primary only).
Connections with:
Colne Valley Railway Preservation Society at the same address

Enquiries to: Managing Director
Access:
Access to staff: By letter, by telephone, charges to non-members
Hours: Mon to Fri, 0900 to 1700

General description:
General railway history, science, energy and nature.
Collections:
Over 80 vintage carriages, wagons, steam and diesel locomotives
Victorian Buildings, stations and signal boxes
Railwayiana
Printed publications:
Guide and stock books
Nature folders
Topic books (for schools)
Various books on local railway lines

Internet home pages:
http://www.cvr.org.uk

654
COLOUR MUSEUM, THE
Perkin House, Providence Street, Bradford, West Yorkshire, BD1 2PW

Tel: 01274 390955
Fax: 01274 392888
Email: museum@sdc.org.uk
Formed: 1978

Organisation type and purpose: Learned society, professional body, registered charity, museum.

Enquiries to: Curator
Access:
Access to staff: By letter, by telephone, by fax, by email, visitors by prior appointment, Internet web pages
Hours: Tue to Fri, 1000 to 1600
Access to building, collections or gallery: No prior appointment required
Hours: Tue to Sat, 1000 to 1600
Access for disabled people: ramped entry, access to all public areas

General description:
Colour and coloration.
Information services:
Education services: Group education facilities, resources for Key Stages 1 and 2.
Services for disabled people: Displays and/or information at wheelchair height.
Catalogues:
Catalogue for part of the collections is only available in-house.

Internet home pages:
http://www.sdc.uk/museum/mus.htm

655
COMBE MARTIN MUSEUM
Flat 1, Atlantic House, Borough Road, Combe Martin, Devon, EX34 0AN

Tel: 01271 882920

Organisation type and purpose: Registered charity (charity number 1040191), museum, suitable for ages: 8+.

Enquiries to: Honorary Secretary
Access:
Access to staff: By letter, by telephone
Access to building, collections or gallery: Prior appointment required
Hours: Variable, contact museum in advance of visit
Other restrictions: Key held in Tourist Information Centre, Cross Street, Combe Martin during Spring, Summer and Autumn (end of Oct).
Access for disabled people: ramped entry

General description:
A small village museum which aims to illustrate through photographs, documents and artefacts the industrial and social history of the village and its immediate environs, from early times to the late 19th century. Silver and lead has been mined and smelted locally, and lime quarrying and burning was a major industry until early this century.
Catalogues:
Catalogue for part of the collections is only available in-house.

656
COMMANDERY, THE
Sidbury, Worcester, WR1 2HU

Tel: 01905 361821
Minicom no. 01905 772156
Fax: 01905 361822
Email: thecommandery@cityofworcester.gov.uk
Formed: 1977

Organisation type and purpose: Museum, historic building, house or site.
Parent body:
City of Worcester

Enquiries to: Manager
Direct tel: 01905 361829
Other contacts: Marketing and Events Assistant
Access:
Access to staff: By letter, by email
Hours: Mon to Sat, 1000 to 1700; Sun 1330 to 1700
Closed 25 Dec to 2 Jan
Access to building, collections or gallery: No access other than to staff
Hours: Mon to Sat, 1000 to 1700; Sun 1330 to 1700
Closed 25 Dec to 2 Jan

General description:
The story of England's Civil War and the battle of Worcester 1651. Worcester history Saxon/Roman to present day. Worcester archaeology. History of the building.
Printed publications:
Guide books
Electronic and video products:
Worcester History (CD-ROM products)

Internet home pages:
http://www.worcestercitymuseums.org.uk
http://www.cityofworcester.gov.uk

657
COMMERCIAL GALLERY, LONDON
See - Spitz Gallery - element 3

658
COMPTON CASTLE
Marldon, Paignton, Devon, TQ3 1TA

Tel: 01803 875740 (answerphone)
Fax: 01803 875740
Formed: 1350

Organisation type and purpose: Registered charity (charity number 205846), historic building, house or site, suitable for ages: 5+.
Parent body:
The National Trust (South West Region)
Devon and Cornwall Regional Office, tel: 01392 881691
Occupied and administered by:
Mr and Mrs G E Gilbert

Enquiries to: Administrator
Access:
Access to staff: By letter, by telephone, charges to non-members
Access to building, collections or gallery: No prior appointment required
Hours: Apr to Oct: Mon, Wed, Thu, 1000 to 1215 and 1400 to 1700
Access for disabled people: Parking provided
Other restrictions: Very limited access. Ground floor accessible with assistance. Rose garden and solar inaccessible for wheelchairs.

General description:
A magical fortified manor house, built between the 14th and 16th centuries and home to the Gilbert family for most of the last six hundred years. Sir Humphrey Gilbert (1539-1583) was coloniser of Newfoundland and half-brother to Sir Walter Raleigh. The dramatic towers and battlements shelter a stone courtyard and restored Great Hall with minstrels' gallery, solar, chapel and old kitchen. The rose garden is also open. Direct descendants of Sir Humphrey Gilbert still live at the castle.
Information services:
Guide cards for self-guided tour.
Suitable for school groups. Children's guide. Children's quiz/trail.
Front-carrying baby slings and toddlers' reins for loan.
Special visitor services: Materials and/or activities for children..
Printed publications:
Guide Book (£1.75)
Children's Guide Book (85p)
Children's Trail (5-8 years) (25p)
Postcards of Exterior, Great Hall, Old Kitchen and Sir Humphrey Gilbert (15p)

Internet home pages:
http://www.nationaltrust.org.uk/regions/devon

659
COMPTON VERNEY
Compton Verney House Trust, Compton Verney, Warwick, CV35 9HZ

Tel: 01926 645500
Fax: 01926 645501
Email: cvht@comptonverney.org.uk
Formed: 1993

Organisation type and purpose: Registered charity (charity number 1032478), art gallery, suitable for ages: 5+.

Enquiries to: Director of Communications & Visitor Services
Direct tel: 01926 645540
Direct email: katherine.gorbing@comptonverney.org.uk
Other contacts: (1) Director; (2) Director of Art; (3) Director of Finance and Administration; (4) Press Officer for (1) organisational matters; (2) collection & exhibitions; (3) recruitment, finance, admin matters (4) press, publicity, adverts.
Access:
Access to staff: By letter, by telephone, by fax, by email, visitors by prior appointment, Internet web pages
Access to building, collections or gallery: Prior appointment required
Hours: Gallery and parkland closed to visitors
Restoration opening 2003/2004
Access for disabled people: Parking provided, ramped entry, access to all public areas, toilet facilities

continued overleaf

General description:
Compton Verney's house and grounds are currently closed to visitors. Building and restoration work on the Grade I Robert Adam mansion house and 'Capability' Brown grounds is underway. Once completed, Compton Verney will open as an art gallery.
Besides the collection, the gallery will host exhibitions and run a programme of events and activities. In the meantime, a series of 'off-site' projects are being commissioned so that artists and audiences can engage with and learn about Compton Verney.
Information services:
Education services: Group education facilities.
Services for disabled people: For the visually impaired; for the hearing impaired.
Collections:
The collection includes:
South European painting, particularly Neapolitan (1450-1800)
Northern European painting (1450-1600)
A British Collection (1500-1800) including some items related to Compton Verney's history
The Asian Collection specialising in Chinese bronzes
Compton Verney will also house the British Folk Art Collection and the Enid Marx collection which was a bequest to the gallery
Catalogues:
Catalogue for library is in-house only. Catalogue for all of the collections is only available in-house.
Publications list:
is available in hard copy.
Printed publications:
Various publications available free, direct

Internet home pages:
http://www.comptonverney.org.uk/
Publications list

660
COMUNN EACHDRAIDH BHARRAIDH
See - Barra Heritage & Cultural Centre

661
CONFEDERATION OF BRITISH ROAD PASSENGER TRANSPORT

Acronym or abbreviation: CPT
See - National Tramway Museum

662
CONISBROUGH CASTLE
Castle Hill, Conisbrough, Doncaster, South Yorkshire, DN12 3BU

Tel: 01709 863329
Fax: 01709 866773
Email: info@conisbroughcastle.org.uk
Formed: 1988

Organisation type and purpose: Registered charity (charity number 519805), historic building, house or site, suitable for ages: 5+.
12th century castle tourist attraction.
Parent body:
English Heritage (Yorkshire Region)
Tel: 01904 601901
Managed by:
Ivanhoe Trust

Enquiries to: Director
Access:
Access to staff: By letter, by telephone, by fax, by email, in person, Internet web pages
Hours: Daily, 0900 to 1700
Access for disabled people: Parking provided, ramped entry, toilet facilities

General description:
Spectacular circular white keep of this 12th century castle, made of magnesian limestone, is the oldest of its kind in England. Recently restored, with two new floors and a roof, it is a fine example of medieval architecture, and was the inspiration for Walter Scott's classic novel 'Ivanhoe'.

Information services:
Guided evening and school party tours are available.
Special visitor services: Guided tours..

Internet home pages:
http://www.conisbroughcastle.org.uk

663
CONSERVATION CENTRE, THE
National Museums & Galleries on Merseyside, White Chapel, Liverpool, L1 6HZ

Tel: 0151 478 4999
Fax: 0151 478 4990
Acronym or abbreviation: NMGM
Formed: 1986

Organisation type and purpose: Suitable for ages: all ages.

Enquiries to: Director
Other contacts: Marketing Manager for advertising.
Access:
Access to staff: By letter only
Access for disabled people: Parking provided, ramped entry, level entry, access to all public areas, toilet facilities

General description:
The work of conservators in preserving and restoring everything from fine art and sculpture to space suits and ancient archaeological treasures.
Information services:
Helpline available, tel no: 0151 207 0001.
Expert opinion on looking after heirlooms.
Special visitor services: Tape recorded guides..
Catalogues:
Catalogue for library is on-line.
Publications list:
is available in hard copy.

Internet home pages:
http://www.nmgm.org.uk

664
CONTEMPORARY ART SOCIETY
17 Bloomsbury Square, London, WC1A 2LP

Tel: 020 7831 7311
Fax: 020 7831 7345
Email: cas@contempart.org.uk
Acronym or abbreviation: CAS
Formed: 1910

Organisation type and purpose: Learned society, consultancy.

Enquiries to: Director
Access:
Access to staff: Visitors by prior appointment
Hours: Mon to Fri, 1000 to 1800

General description:
Promotion of the understanding, enjoyment and collecting of contemporary art; acquisition of works of contemporary art for gifts to public museums and galleries; an extensive knowledge of British contemporary art.
Collections:
Extensive data on contemporary artists
Information is held on all CAS purchases since 1910

Internet home pages:
http://www.contempart.org.uk

665
CONWY SUSPENSION BRIDGE
Conwy, Gwynedd, LL32 8LD

Tel: 01492 573282

Organisation type and purpose: National organisation, registered charity (charity number 205846), historic building, house or site.
Parent body:
The National Trust Office for Wales
Trinity Square, Llandudno, LL30 2DE, tel: 01492 860123, fax: 01492 860233

Enquiries to: Manager

Access:
Access to staff: By letter, by telephone
Access to building, collections or gallery: No prior appointment required
Hours: Apr to Oct, daily, 1000 to 1700

General description:
Designed and built by Thomas Telford, this elegant suspension bridge was completed in 1826. It replaced the ferry, which was previously the only means of crossing the river. The tollkeeper's house has recently been restored and furnished as it would have been a century ago.

666
COOKWORTHY MUSEUM
The Old Grammar School, 108 Fore Street, Kingsbridge, Devon, TQ7 1AW

Tel: 01548 853235
Formed: 1971
Formerly: William Cookworthy Museum Society

Organisation type and purpose: Registered charity (charity number 20631 R), museum, historic building, house or site, suitable for ages: all ages.
Museum and Local Heritage Resource Centre in historic building.

Enquiries to: Chairman
Access:
Access to staff: By letter, by telephone, by email, in person
Access to building, collections or gallery: No prior appointment required
Hours: Museum, 31st March to 1st November, Mon to Sat, 1030 to 1700, October 1030 to 1600
Local Heritage Resource Centre, open throughout the year, Mon to Thu 1000 to 1200, Wed, 1400 to 1600, other times by appointment.
Other restrictions: Prior appointment is required for group visits to the museum throughout the year

General description:
A local museum housed in nine galleries of the old Kingsbridge Grammar School showing rural life in the South Hams, South Devon. Period displays include an Edwardian pharmacy; Victorian kitchen; and the original 17th century schoolroom, and a new display 'And so to Bed'. There is a farm gallery in the walled garden. Changing exhibitions are featured in the costume and photographic galleries.
Information services:
Local history data base
Devon Record Office Service Point
Newsplan - microfilm of local papers
Special visitor services: Materials and/or activities for children.
Education services: Group education facilities.
Services for disabled people: For the visually impaired; displays and/or information at wheelchair height.
Collections:
Social History Collections including costume, images, archives and ephemera.
Horse- and hand-powered tools and machinery necessary to run an average 200 acre farm in the South Hams pre 1939, displayed in the Farm Gallery
Cookworthy porcelain, examples of the first porcelain made in Britain, c. 1770
Good collection of women's dress to 1910 and from 1960-1975
A complete Edwardian Pharmacy. c. 1910
Catalogues:
Catalogue for library is in-house only. Catalogue for all of the collections is only available in-house.

667
COOPER GALLERY
Church Street, Barnsley, South Yorkshire, S70 2AH

Tel: 01226 242905
Fax: 01226 297213

Formed: 1913

Organisation type and purpose: Local government body, art gallery.
Connected to:
Barnsley Metropolitan Borough Council Culture, Sport and Tourism, Central Library, Shambles Street, Barnsley, South Yorkshire

Enquiries to: Keeper
Access:
Access to staff: By letter, by telephone, by fax
Access for disabled people: Parking provided, level entry, access to all public areas, toilet facilities

General description:
Paintings, drawings, statuary etc in Cooper Art Collection.
Collections:
Cooper Bequest: mainly Continental and British 19th century oils
Sadler Gift: English watercolours, drawings c.1750 to 1933
Sadler Gift: French watercolours, drawings, mainly 19th century

668
CORBRIDGE ROMAN SITE MUSEUM

The Roman Site, Corbridge, Northumberland, NE45 5NT

Tel: 01434 632349

Organisation type and purpose: National government body, historic building, house or site, suitable for ages: 5+.
Parent body:
English Heritage (North East Region) (EH) Tel: 0191 269 1227/8, fax: 0191 261 1130

Enquiries to: Custodian
Other contacts: Curator, tel: 01434 633168 for enquiries relating to collections.
Access:
Access to staff: By letter, by telephone, visitors by prior appointment
Access to building, collections or gallery: No prior appointment required
Hours: Apr to Sep: daily, 1000 to 1800; Oct: daily, 1000 to 1700
Nov to Mar: Wed to Sun, 1000 to 1600
Other restrictions: Closed 24 to 26 Dec, 1 Jan. Opening times are subject to change, for up-to-date information contact English Heritage by phone or visit the website.
Access for disabled people: Parking provided, level entry, toilet facilities

General description:
Roman archaeology (Hadrian's Wall).
Archaeological artefacts excavated from the garrison town of Corbridge provide an insight into life at Hadrian's Wall between 85 AD and 400 AD.
Information services:
Handling collection for educational use (pre-booking necessary).
Special visitor services: Tape recorded guides, materials and/or activities for children.
Education services: Resources for Key Stage 2..
Collections:
Corbridge hoard of weapons, armour, tools, etc. c. AD 122-138
Printed publications:
Various publications for sale, direct

Internet home pages:
http://www.english-heritage.org.uk

669
CORFE CASTLE MUSEUM

Town Hall, West Street, Corfe Castle, Dorset, BH20 5HA

Tel: 01929 480974
Fax: 01929 480181
Email: kenwollaston@tesco.net
Formed: 1889

Organisation type and purpose: Registered charity (charity number 214278), museum, historic building, house or site, suitable for ages: 16+.

Enquiries to: Chairman
Access:
Access to staff: By letter, by email
Access for disabled people: level entry
Other restrictions: Parking and toilets nearby.

General description:
A small collection of local memorabilia and artefacts from the past. The museum is unmanned and makes no charge for entry. Collections include a set of dinosaur footprints; local agriculture, clay and stone mason's tools; domestic implements; a copy of the 16th century town mace; and photographs of the local clay pits and quarries.
Collections:
An archive of pictures, postcards and documents relating to the village. Access is by appointment.
Catalogues:
Catalogue for all of the collections is only available in-house.

670
CORFE CASTLE

The Square, Corfe Castle, Wareham, Dorset, BH20 5EZ

Tel: 01929 481294
Fax: 01929 481294
Email: corfecastle@nationaltrust.org.uk

Organisation type and purpose: National organisation, registered charity (charity number 205846), historic building, house or site, suitable for ages: 5+.
Conservation and preservation.
Parent body:
The National Trust (South West Region) Wessex Regional Office, tel: 01985 843600

Enquiries to: Visitor Services Manager
Other contacts: Education Officer for education enquiries.
Access:
Access to staff: By letter, by telephone, by fax, by email, in person
Access to building, collections or gallery: No prior appointment required
Hours: Mar: daily, 1000 to 1700
Apr to Oct: daily, 1000 to 1800
Nov to Feb, daily, 1000 to 1600
Other restrictions: Last entry 30 minutes before closing.
Closed 25, 26 Dec and 1 day mid-March. Tea-room closed last two weeks in Jan 2004 for internal repair and decoration.
Access for disabled people: Parking provided, level entry, toilet facilities

General description:
One of Britain's most majestic ruins, the castle controlled the gateway through the Purbeck Hills and has been an important stronghold since the time of William the Conqueror. Its history as a fortification runs from the early medieval to the late 17th century. Defended during the Civil War by the redoubtable Lady Bankes, the castle fell to treachery from within, and was heavily slighted afterwards by the Parliamentarians. Many fine Norman and Early English features remain. Archaeology, architecture, lowland heaths, wildlife, flora/ fauna, English Civil War, rural settlement.
Information services:
Braille guide. Large-print guide. Handling collection. Many items and surfaces can be touched.
Castle View interactive exhibition centre in NT car park. Guided tours of castle often available during opening hours, April to Oct. Private groups by arrangement.
Suitable for school groups. Education room/ centre. Family guide. Children's guide.
Children's quiz/trail. Family activity packs .
Front-carrying baby slings for loan.
Special visitor services: Guided tours, materials and/or activities for children.
Education services: Group education facilities, resources for Key Stages 1 and 2, 3, 4 and Further or Higher Education.
Services for disabled people: For the visually impaired; displays and/or information at wheelchair height.
Collections:
Archaeological finds dating back to medieval period.
Printed publications:
Children's Guide (£1.80)
History Guide (£1.95)
Souvenir Guide (£1.75)
History leaflet (50p)
Welcome leaflet (free)
Plus many more available direct from the shop

Internet home pages:
http://www.nationaltrust.org.uk

671
CORINIUM MUSEUM

Park Street, Cirencester, Gloucestershire, GL7 2BX

Tel: 01285 655611
Fax: 01285 643286
Formed: 1938
Formerly: Cirencester Museum

Organisation type and purpose: Local government body, museum, suitable for ages: 5+.
Parent body:
Cotswold District Council
Member of:
Museums Association
South West Area Museums Council
South West Federation of Museums and Galleries

Enquiries to: Museums Service Manager
Direct email: john.paddock@cotswold.gov.uk
Access:
Access to staff: By letter, by telephone, by fax, by email, in person, visitors by prior appointment, Internet web pages
Other restrictions: Visitors to see staff - by prior appointment.
Access for disabled people: level entry, toilet facilities

General description:
Cotswold local history and archaeology, especially Romano-British archaeology.
Important Roman collections relating to Cirencester and the Cotswolds (on display). Also displays on medieval - English Civil War in the Cotswolds.
Important Anglo-Saxon Collection (currently not on display).
Small reference library.
Information services:
Education services: Group education facilities, resources for Key Stages 1 and 2 and 4.
Services for disabled people: For the hearing impaired; displays and/or information at wheelchair height.
Collections:
Bathhurst/Cripps Collections of Roman material related to Cirencester and surrounding connections
Butler's Field site, Lechlade archive and finds (Anglo-Saxon)
Stonework from Cirencester Abbey
Extensive collection of archaeological and historical material relating to Cirencester and Cotswold District area
Materials from Corinium, the second largest town in Roman Britain
Printed publications:
Corinium Museum Guide (75p)

continued overleaf

Acrostic Leaflet (free)
Cirencester Roman Amphitheatre Leaflet (£1)
Roman Food and Cooking (90p)
Roman Gardens (50p)

Internet home pages:
http://www.cotswold.gov.uk

672
CORNICE SCOTTISH MUSEUM OF ORNAMENTAL PLASTERWORK

Innerleithen Road, Peebles, Borders, EH45 8BA

Tel: 01721 720212
Fax: 01721 720212
Formed: 1987

Organisation type and purpose: Independently owned, museum.
Access:
Access to staff: By letter, by telephone, by fax, visitors by prior appointment
Access for disabled people: access to all public areas

General description:
The museum illustrates the various methods by which ornamental plasterwork is made.
Collections:
Probably Scotland's largest collection of plaster masters (termed originals in trade). Mainly Victorian times to present time, with some earlier pieces. 2000 plus items

673
CORNISH MINES AND ENGINES

Pool, Redruth, Cornwall, TR15 3NP

Tel: 01209 315027, 01209 210900 (Booking)
Fax: 01209 315027
Email: info@trevithicktrust.com

Organisation type and purpose: National organisation, registered charity (charity number 205846), museum, historic building, house or site, suitable for ages: 5+.
Parent body:
The National Trust (South West Region)
Devon and Cornwall Regional Office, tel: 01208 74281
Managed by:
Trevithick Trust
Tel: 01209 210900

Enquiries to: Manager
Access:
Access to staff: By letter, by telephone, by email
Access to building, collections or gallery: No prior appointment required
Hours: Museum: all year, Mon to Fri, 0900 to 1700
Centre: Apr to Jul, Mon to Fri and Sun, 1100 to 1700; Aug, daily, 1100 to 1700 ; Sep to beg Nov, Mon to Fri and Sun, 1100 to 1700
Trevithick Cottage: Apr to Oct, Wed, 1400 to 1700
Other restrictions: Nov to March 2004: by arrangement only; for details and group visits during this period and at other times tel./fax booking office.

General description:
Cornwall's engine houses are dramatic reminders of the time when the county was a powerhouse of tin, copper and china clay mining. These two great beam engines were used for pumping water (from a depth of over 550m) and for winding men and ore up and down. The engines were originally powered by high-pressure steam, introduced by the local engineer Richard Trevithick. Today one is rotated by electricity. The site also includes the Industrial Discovery Centre at East Pool, which provides an overview of Cornwall's industrial heritage and incorporates a fascinating audiovisual presentation. Nearby is the Geological Museum of the Camborne School of Mines, where the Trust's Norris collection of minerals can be seen. Trevithick Cottage, which is owned by the Trevithick Trust, is nearby at Penponds and is open to vistors free of charge (donations welcome).
Information services:
Services for disabled people: For the visually impaired.
Collections:
Taylor's 90 single cylinder pumping engine 1892
Michell's 1887 winding or whim engine

Internet home pages:
http://www.nationaltrust.org.uk/regions/cornwall

See also - ***Camborne School of Mines Geological Museum and Gallery***

674
CORNWALL HERITAGE TRUST

Registered Office, 9 Tregarne Terrace, St Austell, Cornwall, PL25 4DD

Tel: 01208 873039
Fax: 01208 873039
Email: cht@cornwallheritage.nildram.co.uk
Acronym or abbreviation: CHT
Formed: 1985

Organisation type and purpose: Registered charity (charity number 291607).
To take action swiftly and efficiently whenever possible to help safeguard Cornwall's heritage.
Address for Administration Office:
Cornwall Heritage Trust
16 Trewithan Park, Lostwithiel, Cornwall, PL22 0BD, tel: 01208 873039, fax: 01208 873039, email/website: cht@cornwallheritage.nildram.co.uk

Enquiries to: Administration Secretary
Access:
Access to staff: By letter, by telephone, by email
Hours: Mon to Fri, 0900 to 1300 and 1400 to 1600

General description:
An organisation which protects Cornwall's ancient landmarks. It owns and maintains places of interest such as Treffig Viaduct, Castle-an Dinas, Sancreed Beacon, The Paul Smales Legacy, Trevanion Culverhouse. Newer sites include Hurlers Stone, St Breoks Downs Monolith (known as Men Gurta)
Trethevy Quiot.

Internet home pages:
http://www.cornwallheritage.nildram.co.uk

675
CORNWALL MARITIME MUSEUM

See - ***National Maritime Museum Cornwall***

676
CORPORATION OF LONDON

See - ***Tower Bridge Experience***

677
CORRIGALL FARM MUSEUM

See - ***Orkney Museum***

678
CORRIGALL FARM MUSEUM

Harray, Orkney, KW17 2LQ

Tel: 01856 873191
Fax: 01856 871560
Formed: 1980

Organisation type and purpose: Local government body, museum, historic building, house or site, suitable for ages: 8+.

Enquiries to: Curator
Access:
Access to staff: By letter, by telephone, by fax
Access for disabled people: Parking provided, level entry, access to all public areas, toilet facilities

General description:
An Orkney farmstead of the late 19th century. House has a peat fire and box beds, there is a parish weaver's loom and a grain-drying kiln, traditional livestock.
Information services:
Special visitor services: Guided tours..
Collections:
Local straw and heather crafts
Horse-powered and hand-powered farm machinery

679
COSMESTON MEDIEVAL VILLAGE

Cosmeston Country Park, Penarth, South Glamorgan, CF64 5UY

Tel: 029 2070 1678
Fax: 029 2070 8686
Email: ncoles@valeofglamorgan.gov.uk

Organisation type and purpose: Local government body, museum, historic building, house or site, suitable for ages: 5+, research organisation.
Reconstructed medieval village.

Enquiries to: Manager
Access:
Access to staff: By letter, by email
Access to building, collections or gallery: No prior appointment required
Access for disabled people: Parking provided, ramped entry, access to all public areas, toilet facilities

General description:
A living history museum consisting of a partially reconstructed 14th century Welsh village on its original site, and a static museum with artefacts from the site.
Information services:
Special visitor services: Guided tours, tape recorded guides.
Education services: Group education facilities, resources for Key Stages 1 and 2, 3, 4 and Further or Higher Education.
Services for disabled people: For the visually impaired; for the hearing impaired; displays and/or information at wheelchair height.
Collections:
The village itself is unique, 14th century

Internet home pages:
http://www.valeofglamorgan.gov.uk

680
COSTUME AND TEXTILE ASSOCIATION FOR NORFOLK MUSEUMS

See - ***Costume and Textile Study Centre***

681
COSTUME AND TEXTILE STUDY CENTRE

Carrow House, 301 King Street, Norwich, Norfolk, NR1 2TS

Tel: 01603 223870
Email: museums@norfolk.gov.uk

Organisation type and purpose: Local government body, museum, historic building, house or site, suitable for ages: 8+.
To collect, preserve and provide access to our collection of British clothing, accessories, needlecrafts and home furnishings dating from the 18th century to the present day.
Parent body:
Norfolk Museum & Archaeological Service
Tel: 01603 493625
Based at the centre:
The Costume and Textile Association for Norfolk Museums
Tel: 01603 493625

Enquiries to: Assistant Keeper
Direct tel: 01603 223873 (answerphone)

Access:
Access to staff: By letter, by telephone, by email
Access to building, collections or gallery: Prior appointment required
Hours: The house is open on Tue and Thu
Other restrictions: Appointments can be made for groups or individuals.
At least three weeks' notice is required for group bookings or to view items, and one week's notice to use the library

General description:
Carrow House has an exceptional collection of period costume, textiles and related material on display. The collection reflects changing fashions, styles and technology in clothing and textiles, and the historic importance of Norwich in weaving and clothing production.
Information services:
Education services: Group education facilities..
Collections:
Male, female and children's 18th, 19th and 20th century costumes for all occasions
Shawl Collection: over 600 printed woven and embroidered shawls, and over 100 Norwich shawls, pattern books and designs
Domestic furnishings and linens
Knitting, crochet, netting and macrame
Patchwork, quilting and appliqué.
Lace and lace making equipment
Emboidery samplers (17th to 20th century)
Craft equipment and needlework tools
Specialist reference library, 2000 books plus journals, women's magazines, catalogues and patterns
Picture references, photographs and fashion plates
Catalogues:
Catalogue for all of the collections is only available in-house.

Internet home pages:
http://www.norfolk.gov.uk/tourism/museums

682
COTEHELE MILL
c/o Cotehele House, St. Dominick, Saltash, Cornwall, PL12 6TA

Tel: 01579 350606 (opening hours)
Email: cotehele@nationaltrust.org.uk

Organisation type and purpose: National organisation, registered charity (charity number 205846), museum, historic building, house or site, suitable for ages: all ages.
Parent body:
National Trust (South West)
Devon and Cornwall Regional Office, tel: 01208 74281

Enquiries to: Manager
Other contacts: 01579 351346 (Booking) 01579 351346 (Education)
Access:
Access to staff: By letter, by telephone, by fax, by email, in person, Internet web pages

General description:
Tucked away in dense woodland, this water mill, restored to working order, is a fine reminder of the recent past when corn was ground here for the local community. Nearby, a range of agricultural outbuildings containing a collection of blacksmiths', carpenters', wheelwrights' and saddlers' tools is presented as workshops, giving an insight into working life of local craftsmen.
Information services:
Suitable for school groups. Children's quiz/trail
Handling collection for the visually impaired
Special visitor services: Materials and/or activities for children.
Services for disabled people: For the visually impaired.

Internet home pages:
http://www.nationaltrust.org.uk/regions/cornwall

683
COTEHELE
St. Dominick, Saltash, Cornwall, PL12 6TA

Tel: 01579 351346
Fax: 01579 351222
Email: cotehele@nationaltrust.org.uk

Organisation type and purpose: National organisation, registered charity (charity number 205846), museum, art gallery, historic building, house or site, suitable for ages: 5+.
Parent body:
The National Trust (South West Region)
Devon and Cornwall Regional Office, tel: 01208 74281

Enquiries to: Property Manager
Access:
Access to staff: By letter only
Access to building, collections or gallery: Prior appointment required
Hours: House: 22 Mar to end Sep, Sat to Thu, 1100 to 1700; Oct to beg Nov, Sat to Thu, 1100 to 1630
Quay Gallery: 22 Mar to beg Nov, daily, 1200 to 1700
Garden: all year, 1030 to dusk
Other restrictions: Open Good Friday.
Shop, Restaurant and Quay Gallery: Nov & Dec, Christmas opening (tel. for details).
Edgcumbe Arms and Quay Gallery close at dusk if earlier than 5.
There is no electric light, so visitors should avoid dull days early and late in the season.
Access for disabled people: Parking provided, ramped entry, toilet facilities
Other restrictions: Designated parking. Drop-off point. 2 manual wheelchairs available. Steps to entrance. Ground floor largely accessible. No access to other floors. Photograph album. Hall, kitchen and Edgcumbe Room accessible. Steps to shop entrance. Level entrance to restaurant.

General description:
At the heart of this riverside estate, the house at Cotehele was mainly built between 1485 and 1627 and was a home of the Edgcumbe family for centuries. Its granite and slatestone walls contain intimate chambers adorned with tapestries, original furniture and armour. Outside, the formal gardens overlook the richly planted valley garden below, with medieval dovecote, stewpond and Victorian summerhouse, and 18th century tower above. At the Quay there are interesting old buildings housing an art and craft gallery and an outstation of the National Maritime Museum. The restored Tamar sailing barge, Shamrock, is moored alongside. A network of footpaths throughout the estate provides a variety of riverside and woodland walks with a high nature conservation and industrial archaeology interest.
Information services:
Helpline available, tel no: 01579 352739 (Infoline).
Suitable for school groups. Education room/centre. Children's guide. Children's quiz/trail. Adult study days.
Braille guide. Touch list. Scented plants
Tour of garden by prior appointment at an additional charge. Estate walk leaflets available.
Hip-carrying infant seats for loan.
Special visitor services: Materials and/or activities for children.
Education services: Group education facilities.
Services for disabled people: For the visually impaired.

Internet home pages:
http://www.nationaltrust.org.uk/regions/cornwall

684
COTSWOLD HERITAGE CENTRE
Fosseway, North Leach, Gloucestershire, GL54 3JH

Tel: 01451 860715
Fax: 01451 860091

Formed: 1981

Organisation type and purpose: Local government body, museum, historic building, house or site, suitable for ages: 5+.
Parent body:
Cotswold District Council
Other addresses:
Corinium Museum
Cirencester, tel: 01285 655611, fax: 01285 643286

Enquiries to: Museums Service Manager
Direct tel: 01285 655611
Direct fax: 01285 643286
Direct email: john.paddock@cotswold.gov.uk
Access:
Access to staff: By letter, by telephone, by fax, by email, in person, Internet web pages
Other restrictions: Visitors to see staff by prior appointment.
Curatorial Staff based at Corinium Museum.
Access for disabled people: Parking provided, level entry, toilet facilities

General description:
A museum of Cotswold rural life set in an 18th century House of Correction. The agricultural collections on display come from the Cotswolds, and there are displays showing a Victorian country kitchen and dairying. The waggons are of particular note. The building itself, was one of the few surviving prisons of the 18th century Prison Reform Movement, and the court room and one block of cells survive.
Information services:
Special visitor services: Guided tours, materials and/or activities for children.
Education services: Group education facilities, resources for Key Stages 1 and 2 and 4.
Services for disabled people: For the hearing impaired.
Collections:
Lloyd-Baker Collection of agricultural vehicles and implements
Farming in the Cotswolds pre-mechanisation
Publications list:
is available in hard copy.
Printed publications:
Museum Guide (75p)

Address for ordering publications:
Printed publications:
Cotswold Heritage Trust
at the same address, tel: 01451 860715; 01285 655611 (in winter), fax: 01451 860091, email: simone.clark@cotswold.gov.uk

Internet home pages:
http://www.cotswold.gov.uk

685
COTTAGE MUSEUM
15 Castle Hill, Lancaster, LA1 1YS

Organisation type and purpose: Museum, historic building, house or site, suitable for ages: 5+.
Other addresses:
Lancaster City Museums
Market Square, Lancaster, Lancashire, LA1 1HT, tel: 01524 64637, fax: 01524 841692, email/website: HMoore.LCM@ednet.lancs.ac.uk

Enquiries to: Head of Museums
Access:
Access to staff: By letter, by telephone, by email
Access to building, collections or gallery: No prior appointment required
Hours: Easter to Sep: daily, 1400 to 1700

General description:
Furniture and utensils appropriate to an artisan's house of the 1820s.

686
COTTAGE MUSEUM
Iddesleigh Road, Woodhall Spa, Lincolnshire, LN10 6SH

Tel: 01526 353775

continued overleaf

Formed: 1987

Organisation type and purpose: Independently owned, registered charity (charity number 700211), museum, suitable for ages: 16+.
Parent body:
Woodhall Spa Cottage Museum Trust

Enquiries to: Curator
Access:
Access to staff: By letter, by telephone, in person, charges made to all users
Access to building, collections or gallery: No prior appointment required
Hours: Easter to End Oct: Mon to Sat, 1000 to 1700; Sun, 1100 to 1700

General description:
Photographs from 1900-1930 of Woodhall Spa, history of Petwood Hotel, history of the Spa and Well, some history of 617 Squadron RAF (The Dambusters).

687
COUGHTON COURT

Alcester, Warwickshire, B49 5JA

Tel: 01789 400777
Fax: 01789 765544
Email: office@throckmortons.co.uk

Organisation type and purpose: National organisation, registered charity (charity number 205846), historic building, house or site, suitable for ages: 12+.
Parent body:
The National Trust (West Midlands)
West Midlands Regional Office, tel: 01743 708100

Enquiries to: Manager
Access:
Access to staff: By telephone, by fax, by email, by letter
Access for disabled people: Parking provided, ramped entry, toilet facilities
Other restrictions: Designated parking 120yds. Drop-off point. 3 manual wheelchairs available. Ground floor accessible with assistance. No access to other floors. Ramped entrance to shop. Level entrance to restaurant. Easy access to restaurant. Grounds largely accessible. There are gravel paths in the gardens and grounds. Recommended route map.

General description:
The Throckmorton family home since 1409 is one of England's finest Tudor houses, located within 47 acres of beautiful Warwickshire countryside. The house has a fine collection of furniture, porcelain and family portraits. Within the varied grounds is a 0.6ha walled garden containing stunning displays of roses and herbaceous plants. There are two churches to visit and a fascinating exhibition on the Gunpowder Plot of 1605, which has family connections.
Information services:
Helpline available, tel no: Infoline: 01789 762435.
Evening guided tours of the house and/or gardens by appointment. No group rate or membership concessions for out-of-hours visits.
A full events programme takes place throughout the year. In particular the Fine Living series demonstrates house and gardens skills used by the Throckmorton family staff. See website or send s.a.e. to Coughton Court for full details.
Frontcarrying baby slings for loan.
Suitable for school groups. Family guide. Children's quiz/trail. 'House and history' and 'Gunpowder plot' videos.
Special visitor services: Materials and/or activities for children.
Education services: Group education facilities, resources for Key Stages 2 and 3..

Internet home pages:
http://www.coughtoncourt.co.uk

688
COUNCIL FOR BRITISH ARCHAEOLOGY SCOTLAND

See - Council for Scottish Archaeology

689
COUNCIL FOR MUSEUMS AND GALLERIES IN SCOTLAND

See - Scottish Museums Council

690
COUNCIL FOR MUSEUMS, LIBRARIES AND ARCHIVES

16 Queen Anne's Gate, London, SW1H 9AA

Tel: 020 7273 1444
Fax: 020 7273 1404
Email: info@resource.gov.uk
Acronym or abbreviation: Resource
Formed: 1931
Formerly: Museums & Galleries Commission (MGC), date of change, 31 March 2000

Organisation type and purpose: Advisory body, registered charity (charity number 295943). Government advisory body. A strategic agency working with and on behalf of museums, archives and libraries. It has three main objectives, to provide strategy, advocacy and advice. The organisation undertakes work in all three of these areas to improve the context in which museums, archives and libraries operate and to improve services for users and potential users.
Non-departmental government body funded by the:
Department for Culture, Media and Sport
Work closely with:
Area Museum Council for the South West
Tel: 01823 259696
Council of Museums in Wales
Tel: 029 2022 5432
East Midlands Museum Service
Tel: 0115 985 4534
North of England Museum Service
Tel: 0191 222 1661
North West Museum Service
Tel: 01254 670211
Northern Ireland Museums Council
Tel: 028 9055 0215
Scottish Museums Council
Tel: 0131 229 7465
South Eastern Museum Service
Tel: 020 7600 0219
West Midlands Regional Museums Council
Tel: 01527 872258
Yorkshire & Humberside Museums Council
Tel: 0113 263 8909

Enquiries to: Media and Events Officer
Access:
Access to staff: Visitors by prior appointment
Hours: Mon to Fri, 0900 to 1700
Access for disabled people: ramped entry, toilet facilities

General description:
All aspects of museum, archive and library activity; museum, archive and library curatorship; conservation, education, security, safety, environmental concerns, funding, grants.
Collections:
Books and Periodicals on Conservation of Cultural Heritage
Publications list:
is available in hard copy and online.
Printed publications:
A number of publications are available free of charge on the following topics: education, disability and access, museum management, security, conservation and registration
Access and Management Publications
Annual Reports 1988 to 1995 each presenting a special topic
Conservation Publications
Disability Resource Directory for Museums
Environment Management: Guidelines for museums and galleries
Fundraising for Museums and the Arts (Taylor R W, £7.00)
Integrated Pest Management
Leaflets, booklets and guidelines
Museums Environment Energy (£15)
Museum Matters (newsletter, quarterly)
Museums Matter - An overview of museum provision and its contribution (cost £7.50)
Standards in the Museum Care of Collections Series
The Care of Photographic Materials & Related Material

Internet home pages:
http://www.resource.gov.uk

691
COUNCIL FOR SCOTTISH ARCHAEOLOGY, THE

c/o National Museums of Scotland, Chambers Street, Edinburgh, EH1 1JF

Tel: 0131 247 4119
Fax: 0131 247 4126
Email: csa@nms.ac.uk
Acronym or abbreviation: CSA
Formed: 1944
Formerly: The Council for British Archaeology Scotland (CBA Scotland)

Organisation type and purpose: National organisation, membership association (membership is by subscription), present number of members: c. 900, voluntary organisation, registered charity (charity number CR43304), suitable for ages: 8 to 16.
To promote informed opinion concerning the conservation of Scotland's archaeological heritage.
Sister body of the:
Council for British Archaeology

Enquiries to: Director
Other contacts: Assistant Director for co-ordinator of Young Archaeologists' Club Scottish network.
Access:
Access to staff: By letter, by telephone, by fax, visitors by prior appointment
Hours: Mon to Fri, 0900 to 1700

General description:
Archaeology, including education, careers, excavations, sources of information on sites, cultural resource management and integrated environmental approaches, who to contact in other bodies etc.
Collections:
Inventory of the Scottish Church Heritage - A database of all sites in Scotland and how to access further details
Publications list:
is available in hard copy.
Printed publications:
Discovery & Excavation in Scotland (annually, some out of print)
Scottish Archaeological News (3 times a year)

Internet home pages:
http://www.britarch.ac.uk/csa/
Details of activities of the organisation.

692
COUNCIL OF MUSEUMS IN WALES

The Courtyard, Letty Street, Cardiff, CF24 4EL

Tel: 029 2022 5432 or 228238
Fax: 029 2066 8516
Email: info@cmw.org.uk
Acronym or abbreviation: CMW
Formed: 1969

Organisation type and purpose: Professional body, registered charity (charity number 512031). Area Museum Council.
To support registered museums in Wales through the provision of professional advisory services, training and grant aid.
Also at:
Council of Museums in Wales

Unit 15 Gwerfno, Wrexham Technology Park, Wrexham, LL13 7YP, tel: 01978 314402, fax: 01978 314410, email/website: nwales@cmw.org.uk

Enquiries to: Director
Access:
Access to staff: By letter, by telephone, by fax, by email, visitors by prior appointment
Hours: Mon to Fri, 0900 to 1700
Access to building, collections or gallery: No prior appointment required
Hours: Mon to Fri, 0900 to 1700
Access for disabled people: Parking provided

General description:
Museum administration, curatorship, training, conservation, preventative conservation, display and exhibition techniques.
Collections:
Specialist training library including audiovisual material
Working library on museum management and conservation
Catalogues:
Catalogue for library is in-house only.
Printed publications:
Annual Report
Cysylltu (newsletter, monthly)

Internet home pages:
http://www.cmw.org.uk

693
COUNTY AND REGIMENTAL MUSEUMS
See - Lancashire County Museum Service

694
COUNTY BOROUGH MUSEUM
Regent Street, Wrexham, Clwyd, LL11 1RB

Tel: 01978 317970
Fax: 01978 317982
Email: museum@wrexham.gov.uk
Formed: 1996

Organisation type and purpose: Local government body, museum, suitable for ages: 8+.

Enquiries to: Manager
Access:
Access to staff: By letter, by telephone, by fax, by email, in person
Access to building, collections or gallery: Prior appointment required
Hours: Mon, Wed, Fri, 1000 to 1700; Tue, 1000 to 1900; Sat, 1030 to 1530
Access for disabled people: Parking provided, level entry, access to all public areas, toilet facilities

General description:
Local history and archaeology including Brynks Man. History and family history research facilities. Welsh football collection. Temporary exhibition gallery.
Information services:
Library available for reference (for conditions see Access above)
Special visitor services: Materials and/or activities for children..
Collections:
Local archaeology, social history including extensive bricks, tiles and terracotta collection
Football material from Welsh Football Collection
Catalogues:
Catalogue for part of the collections is only available in-house.

Internet home pages:
http://www.wrexham.gov.uk
General information plus details of Welsh Football Collection.

695
COUNTY HALL GALLERY LIMITED
Riverside Building, County Hall, Westminster Bridge Road, London, SE1 7PB

Tel: 020 7620 2720
Fax: 020 7620 3120
Email: info@daliuniverse.com
Formed: 2000
Trading as: Dali Universe

Organisation type and purpose: Independently owned, museum, suitable for ages: 5+.

Enquiries to: Business Manager
Direct tel: 020 7450 7603
Direct email: antonia@daliuniverse.com
Access:
Access to staff: By letter, by telephone, by fax, by email, in person, visitors by prior appointment, Internet web pages
Access to building, collections or gallery: No prior appointment required
Hours: Daily, 1000 to 1730
Access for disabled people: access to all public areas, toilet facilities
Other restrictions: Disabled access available in accordance with limitations of a Grade II listed building.

General description:
A large collection of bronze sculptures and illustrations, 50 bronze Dali Sculptures - one of the biggest collections in Europe. Lithographs and illustrations of classic themes including Romeo & Juliet, Casanova, The Tribes of Israel and more, gold jewellery, the Mac West Lips Sofa.
Catalogues:
Catalogue for all of the collections is published.
Printed publications:
Catalogue available for purchase by telephone, online or in the bookshop

Internet home pages:
http://www.daliuniverse.com
Overview of exhibition.

696
COURTAULD INSTITUTE GALLERY
Somerset House, Strand, London, WC2R 0RN

Tel: 020 7848 2526
Fax: 020 7848 2589
Email: galleryinfo@courtauld.ac.uk
Formed: 1932

Organisation type and purpose: Art gallery, university department or institute, suitable for ages: 5+.

Enquiries to: Public Relations Manager
Direct tel: 020 7848 2549
Other contacts: Public Affairs Department
Access:
Access to staff: By fax, by email
Hours: Mon to Fri, 1000 to 1800
Access to building, collections or gallery: No prior appointment required
Hours: Daily, 1000 to 1800
Access for disabled people: ramped entry, access to all public areas, toilet facilities

General description:
Somerset House is the masterpeice of Sir William Chambers (1723-1796), tutor and architect to George III, and one of the most important buildings of the Enlightenment in Britain. The Strand Block, where the Courtauld is situated, was built to house the newly formed Royal Academy of Arts, the Royal Society and the Society of Antiquaries. Commissioned in 1775, Somerset House was completed in 1801. In May 2000, Somerset House's courtyard, river terrace and south wing opened to the public, including a new museum for the magnificent Gilbert Collection of decorative arts.

The Gallery is an integral part of the Courtauld Institute of Art, founded in 1931 and the oldest teaching establishment for the History of Art in Britain. The Courtauld Institute moved to Somerset House in 1990, the teaching Institute from Home House in Portland Square, and the Gallery from Woburn Square where it has been housed since 1957 when the collection outgrew space in Home House.
Information services:
Library available for reference (for conditions see Access above)
Special visitor services: Materials and/or activities for children.
Education services: Group education facilities, resources for Key Stages 1 and 2, 3, 4 and Further or Higher Education.
Services for disabled people: For the visually impaired.
Collections:
The Courtauld Gallery has one of the finest collections of Impressionist paintings in the world, and is housed in one of the most beautiful 18th century buildings in London
It includes masterpieces by Manet, Renoir, Monet, Degas, Cézanne, van Gogh and Gaugin, and distinguished earlier collections from the Renaissance to the 18th century including paintings by Botticelli, Rubens, Tiepolo, Goya and Gainsborough
The Gallery reopened in October 1998 after a major lottery-funded refurbishment
Made up of private collections, the Gallery retains the atmosphere of a magnificent private collection in a grand Georgian interior
The most important bequest is Samuel Courtauld's founding collection of world-famous Impressionist and Post-Impressionist paintings, including:
Van Gogh's 'Self-Portrait with Bandaged Ear'
Manet's 'Bar at the Folies Bergère'
Cézanne's 'Montagne Sainte-Victoire
Renoir's 'La Loge'.
Other important collections include
The Princess Gate Collection, bequeathed in 1978 by Count Antoine Seilern, including paintings by Rubens, Tiepolo and Impressionist painters
The Lee Collection bequeathed by Lord Lee of Farnham, including paintings by Botticelli, Gainsborough and Goya
The Gallery holds an important collection of Old Master Prints and Drawings
Temporary exhibitions from the collection of 7000 drawings and 27,000 prints are held each year in a special exhibition space in Somerset House
Printed publications:
Courtauld Gallery Guide (publ Thames & Hudson, £8.95)

Internet home pages:
http://www.courtauld.ac.uk

697
COURTAULD INSTITUTE OF ART, BOOK LIBRARY
Somerset House, Strand, London, WC2R 0RN

Tel: 020 7848 2701
Fax: 020 7848 2887
Email: booklib@courtauld.ac.uk
Formed: 1933

Organisation type and purpose: University department or institute.
Library.
Specialised institute within:
London University

Enquiries to: Librarian
Access:
Access to staff: By letter, by fax, by email, visitors by prior appointment
Hours: Term time: 0930 to 1900
Vacations: 1030 to 1700
Other restrictions: A last resort reference library.

General description:
Fine arts (painting, sculpture, architecture) in post-classical Europe and post-Columbian America.

continued overleaf

Collections:
Extensive photographic collections administered separately from the Book Library
Catalogues:
Catalogue for library is in-house only.

Internet home pages:
http://www.courtauld.ac.uk

698
COVENTRY TOY MUSEUM

Whitefriars Gate, Much Park Street, Coventry, Warwickshire, CV1 2LT

Tel: 024 7622 7560

Organisation type and purpose: Independently owned, museum, historic building, house or site, suitable for ages: all ages.
Pleasure and education.

Enquiries to: Proprietor
Direct tel: 024 7622 7560
Access:
Access to building, collections or gallery: Prior appointment required
Other restrictions: Prior appointment required for school parties: 1000 to 1300

General description:
Toys.
Catalogues:
Catalogue for part of the collections is only available in-house.

699
COWBRIDGE AND DISTRICT MUSEUM

Town Hall Cells, Town Hall, High Street, Cowbridge, Vale of Glamorgan, CF71 7AD

Tel: 01446 775139
Formed: 1981

Organisation type and purpose: Registered charity (charity number 517702), museum.

Enquiries to: Curator
Access:
Access to staff: By letter, by telephone, in person
Access to building, collections or gallery: No prior appointment required
Hours: 1st Sat in month, 1100 to 1600

General description:
A museum of local history contained in the cells of an 1806 prison. The history is illustrated by a 180 million year-old ammonite, finds from the Bronze, Iron and Roman periods, documents and charters of the Roman and Mediaeval period, and artefacts and photographs of the 19th and 20th Centuries.
Information services:
Special visitor services: Guided tours..
Catalogues:
Catalogue for part of the collections is only available in-house.

700
COWES LIBRARY AND MARITIME MUSEUM

Beckford Road, Cowes, Isle of Wight, PO31 7SG

Tel: 01983 293341 or 293394
Fax: 01983 293341
Email: tony.butler@iow.gov.uk
Formed: 1975

Organisation type and purpose: Local government body, museum, public library, suitable for ages: 12+.
Part of:
Isle of Wight Council
Education and Community Development, tel: 01983 823847, fax: 01983 823841, email/ website: tony.butler@iow.gov.uk
Other address:
Museum of Island History
The Guildhall, Newport, Isle of Wight, tel: 01983 823433, fax: 01983 823841, email/ website: tonybutler@iow.gov.uk

Enquiries to: Curator
Direct tel: 01983 823433
Direct fax: 01983 823841
Access:
Access to staff: By letter, by telephone, in person, visitors by prior appointment
Hours: Mon, Tue, Wed and Fri, 0930 to 1800; Sat, 0930 to 1630

General description:
Isle of Wight maritime history, including J Samuel White and Co Ltd, Shipbuilders; Uffa Fox, naval architect and his craft; yachting, lifeboats.
Collections:
5 Uffa Fox dinghies and day boats
7000 maritime books and periodicals
Collection of yachting photographs by Kirk of Cowes
Photographs of construction, launches and trials of craft built by J Samuel White and Co Ltd, plus archives, plans and exhibits for the firm
Catalogues:
Catalogue for library is in-house only. Catalogue for part of the collections is only available in-house.

701
COWPER AND NEWTON MUSEUM

Orchard Side, Market Place, Olney, Buckinghamshire, MK46 4AJ

Tel: 01234 711516
Email: cnm@mkheritage.co.uk
Acronym or abbreviation: OLNCN
Formed: 1900
Formerly: Cowper Memorial Museum

Organisation type and purpose: Independently owned, voluntary organisation, registered charity (charity number 310521), museum, suitable for ages: 12+.
Registered museum No. RD1165.
Links with:
Milton Keynes Heritage Association (MKHA)
Tel: 01908 642540

Enquiries to: Custodian
Other contacts: Chairman of Trustees
Access:
Access to staff: By letter, by telephone, by fax, by email, in person, visitors by prior appointment

General description:
William Cowper, particularly his life at Olney, mementoes, books and manuscripts; Rev John Newton, life and work, to a lesser degree; lace and lacemaking; local history, local family history.
Information services:
Library available for reference (for conditions see Access above)
Special visitor services: Guided tours, tape recorded guides, materials and/or activities for children.
Services for disabled people: For the visually impaired.
Collections:
Books about William Cowper and the Reverend John Newton, their letters and writings and some original manuscripts
Most of ALS/MS owned by the museum are lodged with the County Record Office, Aylesbury, Buckinghamshire, HP20 1VA
Collection of lace and bobbins
Catalogues:
Catalogue for library is in-house only. Catalogue for all of the collections is only available in-house.
Publications list:
is available in hard copy and online.
Printed publications:
Books by or about John Newton and William Cowper including:
Letters of John Newton
John Newton and the English Evangelical Tradition
William Cowper Selected Poems
The Task and Selected Poems by William Cowper
Other books on contemporaries of Cowper and Newton
The Olney Hymns (facsimile of the 1779 First Edition)
How Sweet the Sound
Electronic and video products:
The Hymn Makers (CD or audio cassette)

Address for ordering publications:
Printed publications:
Mail Order Department
Email: museum@onley.co.uk

Internet home pages:
http://www.mkheritage.co.uk
Cowper and Newton Museum link.
http://www.cowperandnewtonmuseum.org
Opening times, location, history of house and garden, biography of Wm Cowper, virtual tour of rooms, books etc available, events, exhibitions.

702
CRAFTS STUDY CENTRE

See - Holburne Museum of Art

703
CRAGSIDE HOUSE, GARDENS AND ESTATE

Rothbury, Morpeth, Northumberland, NE65 7PX

Tel: 01669 620333/620150, Ext 4 (infoline), Ext 7 (Learning)
Fax: 01669 620066
Email: cragside@nationaltrust.org.uk

Organisation type and purpose: National organisation, registered charity (charity number 205846), museum, historic building, house or site, suitable for ages: 8+.
Parent body:
The National Trust (Yorkshire and North East)
North East Regional Office, tel: 01670 774691

Enquiries to: Manager
Access:
Access to staff: By letter, by telephone, by fax, by email
Access for disabled people: Parking provided, ramped entry, toilet facilities
Other restrictions: House: 1 space 20yds from entrance. Drop-off point on gravel forecourt. Visitor centre: 4 spaces 10yds from entrance. Drop-off point. 9 spaces 100yds from entrance in main car park. 5 manual wheelchairs available, booking essential. Ground floor largely accessible. No wheelchair access to scullery and plunge bath. Access to other floors via lift. Tel. for details. Level entrance to shop. Level entrance to restaurant. Only one terrace is accessible.

General description:
Built on a bare and rugged hillside above Rothbury by the 1st Lord Armstrong, Cragside was one of the most modern and surprising houses for its time in the country. In the 1880s the house had hot and cold running water, central heating, fire alarms, telephones, a Turkish bath suite and a passenger lift, but most remarkable of all it was the first house in the world to be lit by hydroelectricity. No wonder it was described as 'the Palace of a Modern Magician'. Around and below the house is one of Europe's largest rock gardens; across the valley lies the terraced garden. Here exotic fruits were nurtured throughout the year in glasshouses, and still are today in the Orchard House. Seven million trees and bushes were planted to cover the bare hillside and create the 404ha (1000 acre) forest garden you can explore today.
Information services:
Education services: Group education facilities.
Services for disabled people: For the visually impaired.

Internet home pages:
http://www.nationaltrust.org.uk

704
CRAIGIEVAR CASTLE
Alford, Aberdeenshire, AB33 8JF

Tel: 013398 83635
Fax: 013398 83280

Organisation type and purpose: Museum, historic building, house or site.
Parent body:
National Trust for Scotland (North-East Region)

Enquiries to: Property Manager
Access:
Access to staff: By letter, by telephone, by fax, in person
Access to building, collections or gallery: No prior appointment required
Hours: End Mar to end Oct, Thu to Mon, 1200 to 1700
Other restrictions: Guided tours only, no coaches, no groups

General description:
An example of the best of Scottish Baronial architecture. The Great Tower stands just as it was when it was completed in 1626.
Information services:
Explanatory text in French, German, Italian, Spanish.
Special visitor services: Guided tours..

Internet home pages:
http://www.nts.org.uk

705
CRAIL MUSEUM
62-64 Marketgate South, Crail, Fife, KY10 3TL

Tel: 01333 450869
Formed: 1979
Formerly: Crail Preservation Society, date of change, 1992

Organisation type and purpose: Voluntary organisation, registered charity (charity number SCO 23505), museum.

Enquiries to: Curator
Access:
Access to staff: By letter, by telephone, visitors by prior appointment
Hours: 1 Jun to 30 Sep: Mon to Sat, 1000 to 1300 and 1400 to 1700; Sun, 1400 to 1700
Apr and May, Weekends and Holidays: 1400 to 1700
Access for disabled people: Parking provided, ramped entry
Other restrictions: Free public parking.

General description:
History of ancient Royal Burgh of Crail, its Kirk, seafaring tradition, 13th century church and harbour, 200 year-old golf club and airfield (HMS Jackdaw - fleet air arm WWII station, HMS Bruce boys training school and JSSL).
Collections:
Local history
Crail Golfing Society, established 1786
Catalogues:
Catalogue for part of the collections is only available in-house.

706
CRAKEHALL WATER MILL
Little Crakehall, Bedale, North Yorkshire, DL8 1HU

Tel: 01677 423240
Formed: 1086

Organisation type and purpose: Independently owned, historic building, house or site, suitable for ages: 5+.
Water Mill.

Enquiries to: Owner
Access:
Access to staff: By letter, by telephone

General description:
Working water mill on the site of a Domesday mill AD 1086. Once owned by the Neville family of Middleham Castle, it became Crown property in the 15th century and was sold by James I in 1624. The present building dates from the 17th century, and its machinery from the 18th and 19th centuries, some made nearby at Leeming Bar. It was restored in 1977, and from 1980 has ground corn producing stoneground wholemeal flour.
Information services:
Special visitor services: Guided tours..
Collections:
Small collection of farm, rural and mill artefacts.

707
CRAMPTON TOWER MUSEUM
Rear of Post Office, High Street, Broadstairs, Kent, CT10 2AB

Tel: 01843 864446
Formed: 1978

Organisation type and purpose: Registered charity (charity number 276034), museum, suitable for ages: 5+ 16+.
To promote the life and works of T R Crampton (1816-1888), notable Victorian civil engineer, and to promote local transport displays.

Enquiries to: Curator
Access:
Access to staff: By letter only
Access to building, collections or gallery: No prior appointment required
Hours: Easter to end Oct: Mon, Tue, Thu, Fri, Sun, 1430 to 1700;
Wed, 1430 to 1700 during school holidays
Other restrictions: Admission charged.

General description:
Thomas Russell Crampton (1816-1888) was a Victorian civil engineer and designer of locomotives. He was the first to lay a Pentical Submarine Telegraph Cable to the continent. The collection contains his original patents and drawings of locomotives, and other items related to his inventions. Also features transport in general and local transport, including the Broadstairs to Canterbury Stage Coach. Also there are six working layouts, 'N', '00', '0' and gauge one. Some interactive exhibits.
Information services:
Special visitor services: Guided tours, materials and/or activities for children..
Collections:
Thomas Russell Crampton. Original drawings and patents. 1816-1888.
All of T R Crampton's drawings and patents now belong to the Museum
The collection is of original drawings and patents, and displays of railwaying, local transport, Thanet Tramways, Railways to Thanet, including Ramsgate Tunnel Railway
The Broadstair to Canterbury Stage Coach, apart from the Stage Coach which is owned by the local Town Council, the other displays have been loaned, on short or long term
Catalogues:
Catalogue for all of the collections is only available in-house.

Address for ordering publications:
Printed publications:
Curator, Crampton Tower Museum
c/o 42 Northdown Hill, St Peter's, Broadstairs, Kent, CT10 3HH

708
CRANBROOK MUSEUM
Carriers Road, Cranbrook, Kent, TN17 3JX

Formed: 1971

Organisation type and purpose: Independently owned, registered charity, museum, historic building, house or site.
Promotion of local history.

Enquiries to: Curator
Direct tel: 01580 715542
Access:
Access to staff: By letter only

General description:
Set in a large Grade II listed building, the collection reveals the broad spectrum of trades, domestic life and agriculture of a thriving Wealden Town in the 19th and early 20th Centuries. There is a wide range of exhibits from the immediate neighbourhood.
Artefacts - all aspects of Cranbrook local history.
Archives - Cranbrook and District local history, documents and books.
Oral History - tapes - transcripts of local interviews.
Collections:
Boyd Alexander Collection of Kent & Sussex Birds, 1900-1901
Cranbrook Colony of Painters, details of work, their history and background, 1850-1878, c. 35 illustrations
Artefacts Collection on computer database (catalist)
Publications list:
is available in hard copy.

Internet home pages:
http://www.localmuseum.freeserve.co.uk

709
CRANBROOK UNION MILL
Cranbrook, Kent

Tel: 01580 712256 or 712984

Organisation type and purpose: Historic building, house or site.
Member of:
Kent Windmills
Owned by:
Kent County Council

General description:
Built in 1814, the tallest smock mill in England.

710
CRATHES CASTLE, GARDEN & ESTATE
Banchory, Aberdeenshire, AB31 5QJ

Tel: 01330 844525
Fax: 01330 844797
Email: crathes@nts.org.uk

Organisation type and purpose: Museum, historic building, house or site.
Parent body:
National Trust for Scotland (North-East Region)

Enquiries to: Property Manager
Access:
Access to staff: By letter, by telephone, by fax, by email, in person
Access to building, collections or gallery: No prior appointment required
Hours: Castle and Visitor Centre: end Mar to end Sep, daily, 1000 to 1730: Oct, daily, 1000 to 1630;
Garden and grounds, all year, daily, 0900 to sunset
Access for disabled people: toilet facilities
Other restrictions: Access to ground floor of castle, garden and grounds, viewpoint trail, exhibitions, shop, restaurant, wheelchairs available

General description:
Superb example of a tower house built in second half of the 16th century. Some rooms retain their original painted ceilings, and collections of family portraits and furniture.
Information services:
Services for disabled people: For the visually impaired.

Internet home pages:
http://www.nts.org.uk

711
CRAVEN MUSEUM

Town Hall, High Street, Skipton, North Yorkshire, BD23 1AH

Tel: 01756 794079
Fax: 01756 706412
Email: museum@cravendc.gov.uk
Formed: 1929

Organisation type and purpose: Local government body, museum, suitable for ages: 5+.

Enquiries to: Curator
Access:
Access to staff: By letter, by telephone, by fax, by email, in person

General description:
A local museum with a few large graphic panels and many artefacts, curios and items of beauty. Particularly stong on archaeology and geology.
Information services:
Special visitor services: Materials and/or activities for children.
Education services: Group education facilities, resources for Key Stages 1 and 2 and Further or Higher Education.
Services for disabled people: Displays and/or information at wheelchair height.
Collections:
Craven Herbarium, plants largely from Craven, over 1000
Elbolton Cave, bones from cave site, *c.* 5000 BC to 200 AD; over 1000
Richardson Collection, prehistoric flints, over 1000
Tiddeman Collection, Reef Knoll fossils, over 1000
Catalogues:
Catalogue for part of the collections is only available in-house.

712
CRAWFORD ARTS CENTRE

93 North Street, St Andrews, Fife, KY16 9AD

Tel: 01334 474610
Fax: 01334 479880
Email: crawfordarts@crawfordarts.free-online.co.uk
Full name: Crawford Arts Centre (St Andrews) Limited
Formed: 1977

Organisation type and purpose: Independently owned, registered charity (charity number SCO 07748), art gallery, suitable for ages: all ages.
Supported by:
Friends of the Crawford Arts Centre at the same address

Enquiries to: Exhibitions Officer
Access:
Access to staff: By letter, by telephone, by fax, by email, in person, visitors by prior appointment
Hours: Mon to Fri, 1000 to 1700
Access to building, collections or gallery: No prior appointment required
Hours: Mon to Sat, 1000 to 1700; Sun, 1400 to 1700
Other restrictions: Closed Christmas and New Year.
Access for disabled people: Parking provided, level entry, toilet facilities
Other restrictions: Access to all areas within gallery.

General description:
Regularly changing exhibitions of mostly contemporary visual art and craft.
Information services:
Guided tours - occasionally.
Materials/activities for children - organised regularly.
Art classes for adults.
Friends' events.
Special visitor services: Guided tours, materials and/or activities for children..
Publications list:
is available in hard copy.
Printed publications:
A large number of publications on applied arts and design, architecture, contemporary artists, historical artists, and photography, available for purchase, direct

Internet home pages:
http://www.crawfordarts.free-online.co.uk
Listing of gallery exhibitions and related events, contact information, background to centre.

713
CREETOWN GEM ROCK MUSEUM

Chain Road, Newton Stewart, Dumfries & Galloway, DG8 7HJ

Tel: 01671 820357
Fax: 01671 820554
Email: gem.rock@btinternet.com
Formed: 1971

Organisation type and purpose: Museum. Privately owned.

Enquiries to: Managers
Direct fax: 01671 820557
Access:
Access to staff: By letter, by telephone, by fax, by email, in person, visitors by prior appointment, Internet web pages
Other restrictions: Closed from 23 Dec till end of Jan.
Access for disabled people: Parking provided, level entry, access to all public areas, toilet facilities

General description:
Gemmology; crystallography; mineralogy; geology; palaeontology.
Collections:
A spectacular collection of large gems, crystals, rocks and minerals
Many beautiful examples of the lapidary's work
World Class British specimens eg fluorite, calcite, hematite
Good local agate collection cut and uncut
Dinosaur's egg, jawbone and dung
Gold and Silver Collection
African and Australian Collections
Quartz-cut replicas of world's large diamonds
Printed publications:
Guide

Internet home pages:
http://www.gemrock.net

714
CREETOWN HERITAGE MUSEUM TRUST LIMITED

The Exhibition Centre, 91 St Johns Street, Creetown, Newton Stewart, Dumfries & Galloway, DG8 7JE

Tel: 01671 820343
Formed: 1991

Organisation type and purpose: Independently owned, registered charity (charity number SCO 022750), museum, suitable for ages: 5+.

Enquiries to: Committee Member
Direct tel: 01671 820471
Direct email: andoris@btopenworld.com
Access:
Access to staff: By letter, by telephone
Access to building, collections or gallery: No prior appointment required
Hours: Apr, May, Sep, Oct: Sun, Tue, Thu, 1100 to 1600
Jun to Aug: daily, 1100 to 1600
Access for disabled people: Parking provided, level entry, access to all public areas, toilet facilities

General description:
The exhibition is of Creetown both past and present. The village is portrayed from its eighteenth century beginnings as a fishing hamlet, through the growth and decline of its famous granite quarries, to the present day. Displays include a large collection of old photographs, war-time memorabilia, village shop, information on the Wigtown Bay Nature Reserve, and the work of local artists, wood-carvers, and sculptor. Presentation includes videos, audio commentaries, 'hands-on' exhibits and children's activities.
Information services:
Special visitor services: Materials and/or activities for children..
Catalogues:
Catalogue for all of the collections is only available in-house.
Printed publications:
Glimpses of Old Creetown (pub Dumfries and Galloway Libraries, £2.50)

Internet home pages:
http://www.scotland-creetown.com
http://www.dumfriesandgalloway.co.uk

715
CRESSING TEMPLE BARNS

Witham Road, Braintree, Essex, CM7 8PD

Tel: 01376 584903
Fax: 01376 584864
Email: cressingtemple@essexcc.gov.uk
Formed: 1987

Organisation type and purpose: Local government body, historic building, house or site.
Parent body:
Essex County Council

Enquiries to: Administrator
Access:
Access to staff: By letter, by telephone, by fax, by email, visitors by prior appointment
Access for disabled people: Parking provided, ramped entry, access to all public areas, toilet facilities

General description:
Built by the Knights Templar in the 13th century, Cressing Temple has the finest remaining pair of medieval barns in Europe. Also an Elizabethan granary, thatched cart lodge and Tudor walled garden featuring knot gardens, flowery mead, nosegay garden and physic plant area, and wheelwright's shop, old forge and bakehouse.
Information services:
Conference and meeting room facilities.
Special visitor services: Guided tours, materials and/or activities for children.
Education services: Group education facilities, resources for Key Stages 2 and 3..
Printed publications:
The Wheelwright's Shop from Kedington (10p)
Guide Book (£1.50)
Walled Garden Leaflet (20p)
Children's Worksheet (50p)

Internet home pages:
http://www.essexcc.gov.uk

716
CREWKERNE AND DISTRICT MUSEUM, THE

The Heritage Centre, Market Square, Crewkerne, Somerset, TA18 7JU

Tel: 01460 77079
Formed: 2000

Organisation type and purpose: Museum, suitable for ages: all ages.

Enquiries to: Chairman
Access:
Access to staff: By letter, by telephone
Access to building, collections or gallery: No prior appointment required
Hours: Easter to end Sep: Wed to Fri and Bank Holidays, 1030 to 1300 and 1400 to 1630; Sat, 1030 to 1300
Jun, Jul and Aug also: Sun, 1400 to 1630
Access for disabled people: level entry, toilet facilities
Other restrictions: Partial disabled access.

General description:
The objective of the Museum is to collect, document, preserve, interpret and exhibit, for the public benefit, material relating to the social and industrial history of Crewkerne and surrounding parishes.

717
CRICH TRAMWAY VILLAGE
See - National Tramway Museum

718
CRICKLADE MUSEUM
16 Calcutt Street, Cricklade, Wiltshire, SN6 6BB

Tel: 01793 750756
Formed: 1950

Organisation type and purpose: Learned society, registered charity (charity number 292887), museum, suitable for ages: 8+, research organisation.
Parent body:
Cricklade Historical Society

Enquiries to: Curator
Access:
Access to staff: By letter, by telephone

General description:
The social history of Cricklade and nearby villages from Roman to modern times. Over 2000 photographs.
Information services:
Special visitor services: Guided tours, tape recorded guides, materials and/or activities for children.
Education services: Group education facilities, resources for Key Stages 3, 4 and Further or Higher Education..
Collections:
Archaeological records of excavation of 9th century Saxon ramparts.
Records of parliamentary elections between 1780 and 1883
Artefacts, pictures, prints, photographs, books, documents, manuscripts
Catalogues:
Catalogue for library is in-house only. Catalogue for all of the collections is only available in-house.

719
CROFT CASTLE
Leominster, Herefordshire, HR6 9PW

Tel: 01568 780246
Fax: 01568 780462
Email: croftcastle@nationalrust.org.uk

Organisation type and purpose: National organisation, registered charity (charity number 205846), historic building, house or site, suitable for ages: 8+.
Parent body:
The National Trust (West Midlands)
West Midlands Regional Office, tel: 01743 708100

Enquiries to: Manager
Access:
Access to staff: By letter, by telephone, by fax, by email
Access for disabled people: Parking provided, ramped entry, toilet facilities
Other restrictions: Designated parking 20yds. Drop-off point. 2 manual wheelchairs available. Ground floor fully accessible, one step down to dining room. No access to other floors. Level entrance to shop and to tea-room. Grounds largely accessible.

General description:
Croft Castle re-opens in mid-April 2003 after a major refurbishment programme, with additional showrooms opening for visitors to enjoy, complementing the fine Georgian interior and period furnishings. The gardens and park offer pleasant walks and magnificent views.
Information services:
Outdoor theatre and concerts.
Braille guide. Large-print guide.
Family guide. Children's quiz/trail.
Special visitor services: Materials and/or activities for children.
Services for disabled people: For the visually impaired.

Internet home pages:
http://www.nationaltrust.org.uk

720
CROFTON ROMAN VILLA
Crofton Road, Orpington, Kent, BR6 8AD

Tel: 01689 873826 or 020 8462 4737 (no telephone on site)
Fax: 020 8462 4737
Email: bromley.museum@bromley.gov.uk
Formed: 1992

Organisation type and purpose: Local government body, museum, historic building, house or site, suitable for ages: 5+.
Parent body:
London Borough of Bromley Museum
The Priory, Church Hill, Orpington, BR6 0HH, tel: 01689 873826, email: bromley.museum@bromley.gov.uk
Address for Site Manager:
Kent Archaeological Rescue Unit (KARU)
5 Harvest Bank Road, West Wickham, BR4 9DL, tel: 020 8462 4737, fax: 020 8462 4737

Enquiries to: Manager
Direct tel: 020 8462 4737
Direct fax: 020 8462 4737
Other contacts: Curator
Access:
Access to staff: By letter, by telephone, by fax, by email
Other restrictions: Staff on site during opening hours.
Access to building, collections or gallery: No prior appointment required
Hours: 1 Apr to 31 Oct: Wed, Fri, Bank Holiday Mon, 1000 to 1300 and 1400 to 1700; Sun, 1400 to 1700
Access for disabled people: ramped entry, level entry, access to all public areas
Other restrictions: Parking in adjacent carpark, but no dedicated spaces.

General description:
Romano-British archaeology of the site in its local and regional context. The only Roman Villa open to the public in Greater London.
Information services:
Catalogue published in excavation report.
Special visitor services: Guided tours, tape recorded guides, materials and/or activities for children.
Education services: Group education facilities.
Services for disabled people: Displays and/or information at wheelchair height.
Collections:
Excavated material from the site is held in Bromley Museum
Catalogues:
Catalogue for part of the collections is published.
Printed publications:
A printed list of KARU publications is available but most do not refer to this site
The Roman Site at Orpington, Kent (Philp B, 1996, £12)
Crofton Roman Villa (Philp B, 80p)

Address for ordering publications:
Printed publications:
Publications, Kent Archaeological Rescue Unit
5 Harvest Bank Road, West Wickham, BR4 9DL, tel: 020 8462 4737, fax: 020 8462 4737

Internet home pages:
http://www.bromley.gov.uk/museums
General information.

721
CROMARTY COURTHOUSE TRUST
Church Street, Cromarty, Ross-shire, IV11 8XA

Tel: 01381 600418
Fax: 01381 600418
Email: courthouse@mail.cali.co.uk
Formed: 1988

Organisation type and purpose: Independently owned, registered charity, museum, suitable for ages: 5+.

Enquiries to: Curator
Access:
Access to staff: By letter, by telephone, by email, visitors by prior appointment
Access to building, collections or gallery: No prior appointment required
Hours: Apr to Oct: daily, 1000 to 1700
Nov, Dec, Mar: daily, 1200 to 1600
Access for disabled people: Parking provided

General description:
Covers the history of the immediate area.
Information services:
Special visitor services: Tape recorded guides, materials and/or activities for children.
Education services: Group education facilities, resources for Further or Higher Education.
Services for disabled people: For the hearing impaired.
Collections:
Coins, from Burgh fair site, 1200-1850, c. 700 items
Lead customs seals (Russian), from trade in hemp, 1760-1890, 70 items
Catalogues:
Catalogue for all of the collections is only available in-house.
Publications list:
is available in hard copy.
Printed publications:
Books on local history include:
Old Cromarty Castle (Gordon Slade H, £2.75)
The Resolis Riot (Alston D, £2.75)
Coin finds from Cromarty (Bateson J D, £2.75)
The Legend of Hugh Miller (Gostwick M, £2.75)
Cromarty's Emigrants and Emigrant Ships (Fyfe J, £2.75)
The Cromarty and Dingwall Light Railway (Malcolm E H, £2.75)
East Church, Cromarty - Gravestone Inscriptions (£3.50)
Electronic and video products:
Generations in Stone - Virtual Tour of Cromarty (CD-ROM, £16.99)

Internet home pages:
http://www.cali.co.uk/users/freeway/courthouse

722
CROMER LIFEBOAT MUSEUM
See - Henry Blogg Museum

723
CROMER MUSEUM
Tucker Street, Cromer, Norfolk, NR27 9HB

Tel: 01263 513543
Fax: 01263 511651
Email: alistair.murphy.mus@norfolk.gov.uk
Formed: 1978

Organisation type and purpose: Museum.
Parent body:
Norfolk Museums and Archaeological Service
Tel: 01603 493625, fax: 01603 493623

Enquiries to: Administrator
Access:
Access to staff: By letter, by telephone, by fax, by email, in person
Hours: Mon, 1000 to 1300 & 1400 to 1700; Tue to Sat, 1000 to 1700; Sun 1400 to 1700

continued overleaf

General description:
North Norfolk crab and fishing industry, including collection of fisherman's Ganseys. Quaternary geology - Cromer forest bed and West Runton Elephant. Development of North Norfolk tourism, particularly Victorian Cromer.
Collections:
Traditional fisherman's jumpers (ganseys)
Wallpapers from local houses and cottages
Fossils from the North Norfolk coast
Photographs of Cromer
Longshore fishing gear
Catalogues:
Catalogue for all of the collections is only available in-house.

Internet home pages:
http://www.norfolk.gov.uk/tourism/museums

724
CROMWELL MUSEUM

Grammar School Walk, Huntingdon, Cambridgeshire, PE29 3LF

Tel: 01480 375830
Fax: 01480 459563
Formed: 1962

Organisation type and purpose: Local government body, museum.
Parent body:
Cambridgeshire County Council
Tel: 01223 717111

Enquiries to: County Museum Officer
Direct tel: 01223 718136
Direct fax: 01223 362425
Direct email: john.goldsmith @cambridgeshire.gov.uk
Access:
Access to staff: By letter, by email
Access to building, collections or gallery: No prior appointment required
Hours: Vary throughout year, closed Mon
Other restrictions: Telephone to confirm opening hours.
Access for disabled people: level entry

General description:
Oliver Cromwell 1599-1658 and the Cromwellian period.
Information services:
Special visitor services: Guided tours, materials and/or activities for children.
Education services: Resources for Key Stages 2 and 3..
Catalogues:
Catalogue for all of the collections is only available in-house.
Publications list:
is available in hard copy.
Printed publications:
Cromwell Museum Guide

Address for ordering publications:
Printed publications:
Museum Assistant, Cromwell Museum
Grammar School Walk, Huntingdon, Cambridgeshire, PE29 3LF

Internet home pages:
http://edweb.camcnty.gov.uk/cromwell

725
CROOME PARK

NT Estate Office, The Builders' Yard, High Green, Severn Stoke, Worcestershire, WR8 9JS

Tel: 01905 371006
Fax: 01905 371090
Email: croomepark@nationaltrust.org.uk

Organisation type and purpose: National organisation, registered charity (charity number 205846), historic building, house or site, suitable for ages: all ages.
Parent body:
The National Trust (West Midlands)
West Midlands Regional Office, tel: 01743 708100

Enquiries to: Property Manager
Access:
Access to staff: By letter, by telephone, by fax, by email

General description:
Croome was 'Capability' Brown's first complete landscape, making his reputation and establishing a new style of parkland design which became universally adopted over the next fifty years. The elegant park buildings and other structures are mostly by Robert Adam and James Wyatt. The Trust acquired 270ha (670 acres) of the park in 1996 with substantial grant aid from the Heritage Lottery Fund.
The Trust has embarked on a 10-year restoration plan, including dredging the water features, clearance and replanting of the gardens and parkland.

Internet home pages:
http://www.nationaltrust.org.uk

726
CROSSNESS ENGINES MUSEUM

Thames Water, Belvedere Road, Abbey Wood, London, SE2 9AQ

Tel: 020 8303 6723
Fax: 020 8303 6723
Formed: 1985
Formerly: The Crossness Engines Trust

Organisation type and purpose: Independently owned, membership association (membership is by subscription), present number of members: 282, voluntary organisation, registered charity (charity number 297585), museum, historic building, house or site, suitable for ages: 8+.
The aim of the Trust is the restoration of the steam beamengines, pumps and buildings of the sewage pumping station at Crossness and to create a supporting museum related to the work of the site.
Connections with:
Association of London Pumping Heritage Attractions (ALPHA)
58 Palmiera Road, Bexley Heath, DA7 4UX, tel: 020 8301 5917
Other address:
The Crossness Engines Trust
8 Yorkland Avenue, Welling, DA16 2LF, tel: 020 8303 6723, fax: 020 8303 6723

Enquiries to: Executive Secretary
Other contacts: Museum Manager for museum display items.
Access:
Access to staff: By letter, by telephone, by fax, visitors by prior appointment
Hours: Tue and Sun, 0930 to 1600
Access to building, collections or gallery: Prior appointment required
Hours: 1 Sun and 1 Tue per month
Other restrictions: Visits start at 13.45 and must be booked. Tel: 020 8311 3711.
Access for disabled people: Parking provided, ramped entry

General description:
Crossness southern outfall works; London main drainage; sewerage and domestic sanitation; drainage and sanitation engineering; steam beamengines built by James Watt & Sons converted by Benjamin Goodfellows; sludge-disposal boats; engineering workshop practice; Sir Joseph Bazalgette (engineer); Charles H Driver (architect); William Webster Snr (contractor); William Webster Jnr.
Information services:
Library available for reference (for conditions see Access above). Helpline available, tel no: 020 8311 3711.
Special visitor services: Guided tours.
Education services: Group education facilities, resources for Further or Higher Education.
Services for disabled people: Displays and/or information at wheelchair height.
Collections:
Library of books, photographs, plans and archive material relating to subjects
The largest rotative beam engines in the world
Printed publications:
Leaflet (free)
Electronic and video products:
Video (£12)

Internet home pages:
http://www.crossness.org.uk
History and description of the site and main display.

727
CROWN LIQUOR SALOON, THE

46 Great Victoria Street, Belfast, BT2 7BA

Tel: 028 9027 9901

Organisation type and purpose: National organisation, registered charity (charity number 205846), historic building, house or site.
Parent body:
The National Trust

Enquiries to: Manager
Access:
Access to staff: By letter, by telephone

General description:
The most famous pub in Belfast and one of the finest examples of a High Victorian public house in existence, with rich ornamentation and snugs still intact.

Internet home pages:
http://www.belfasttelegraph.co.uk/crown

728
CROYDON NATURAL HISTORY AND SCIENTIFIC SOCIETY MUSEUM

Chipstead Valley Primary School, Chipstead Valley Road, Coulsdon, Surrey, CR5 3BW

Acronym or abbreviation: CNHSS
Formed: 1870
Formerly: Croydon Microscopical Club, date of change, 1877; Croydon Microscopical and Natural History Club, date of change, 1901

Organisation type and purpose: Learned society, registered charity (charity number 260739), suitable for ages: 16+.
Other addresses:
Croydon Natural History & Scientific Society Limited
96a Brighton Road, South Croydon, Surrey, CR2 6AD

Enquiries to: Curator
Direct tel: 020 8669 1501
Direct email: john@greig51.freeserve.co.uk
Other contacts: (1) Librarian; (2) General Secretary for (1) archives; (2) widespread contacts.
Access:
Access to staff: By letter, by telephone, by email, visitors by prior appointment, Internet web pages
Access to building, collections or gallery: Prior appointment required

General description:
Geology, archaeology, industrial studies, local history, natural history of the Croydon area.
Collections:
Geology, archaeology, social history, ethnography, natural history - mainly local area but some material in the Bennett Collection (geology, archaeology, ethnography) with worldwide sources
Catalogues:
Catalogue for library is in-house only. Catalogue for all of the collections is only available in-house.
Publications list:
is available in hard copy.
Printed publications:
Victorian Croydon Illustrated (2nd edn 1987, £3.25)

Edwardian Croydon Illustrated (2nd edn 1990, £4.25)
Croydon Between The Wars (2nd edn 1993, £4.75)
Croydon From Above (1999, £6.75)
Other illustrated local history books and miscellaneous publications

Address for ordering publications:
Printed publications:
Sales Officer, Croydon Natural History and Scientific Society
96a Brighton Road, South Croydon, Surrey, CR2 6AD

Internet home pages:
http://www.greig51.freeserve.co.uk/cnhss/

729
CRYSTAL PALACE MUSEUM

Anerley Hill, London, SE19 2BA

Tel: 020 8676 0700
Fax: 020 8676 0700
Formed: 1987

Organisation type and purpose: Voluntary organisation, registered charity (charity number 293693), museum, suitable for ages: 8+.

Enquiries to: Curator
Access:
Access to staff: By letter, by telephone, by fax
Hours: Sun and Bank Holiday Mon, 1100 to 1700, only

General description:
History of the Crystal Palace, Hyde Park and Sydenham; social, historical and technical.
World's leading authority on constructional details of the Sydenham Crystal Palace Building including I K Brunel's two unique water towers each designed to hold 1500 tons of water over 250 feet above ground level.
Information services:
Group tours by arrangement
Temporary exhibitions
Audio/video presentations
Research facilities available
Education packs
Special visitor services: Guided tours..
Collections:
Books, pictures, photographs, objects all relating to the Crystal Palace
Catalogues:
Catalogue for all of the collections is only available in-house.

730
CUCKFIELD MUSEUM

Queen's Hall, High Street, Cuckfield, West Sussex, RH17 5EL

Tel: 01444 400268 / 454276
Formed: 1980

Organisation type and purpose: Registered charity, museum, suitable for ages: 5+.

Enquiries to: Honorary Curator
Direct email: frances_stenlake@yahoo.com
Access:
Access to staff: By letter, by telephone, by fax, by email, in person, visitors by prior appointment
Access for disabled people: ramped entry, access to all public areas, toilet facilities

General description:
A small village enterprise organised and run entirely by volunteers. The museum illustrates all aspects of local history.
It presents 2 stories unique to Cuckfield:
1) the discovery in the 1820s by Dr Gideon Mantell of the Iguanadon.
2) the upbringing at Horsgate of Robert Bevan, the artist who became friendly with Gauguin in the 1890s and later a founder member of the Camden Town Group.
Information services:
Education services: Group education facilities, resources for Key Stages 1 and 2, 3, 4 and Further or Higher Education.
Services for disabled people: Displays and/or information at wheelchair height.
Collections:
Small library (reference only) of local history books
Locally donated collections, eg English pottery, birds' eggs, Sussex 'bygones'.
Pictures, photographs and postcards of Cuckfield and surrounding area
Local records
Artefacts and documents to do with WWI and WWII Home Front
Catalogues:
Catalogue for all of the collections is only available in-house.
Printed publications:
4 postcards of landscapes (50p each) by artist Robert Bevan painted in 1911 and 1914 while staying with his father at Horsgate, Cuckfield. 3 are in public collections: Cardiff, Reading and Stoke-on-Trent; 1 is in a private collection
A Chronicle of Cuckfield (Wright M, £5.95)
From Cuckfield to Camden Town - the story of artist Robert Bevan (Stenlake F, £6.99)
A Small Town at War (Miller A, £6.95)
A Record Reign (Smith N, £4.50)
Nurse Stoner's Diaries (£2.95)
Education in Cuckfield (Ward J, £1.50)

Internet home pages:
http://www.semuseums.org.uk/cuckfieldmuseum
General description, opening hours.

731
CUCKOOLAND

Old School House, Chester Road, Tabley, Knutsford, Cheshire, WA16 0HL

Tel: 01565 633039
Fax: 01565 750462
Email: post@cuckoolanduk.com
Formed: 1990
Formerly: Cuckoo Clock Museum, date of change, 2001

Organisation type and purpose: Independently owned, advisory body, professional body, service industry, museum, suitable for ages: 5+, consultancy, research organisation.

Enquiries to: Curator
Access:
Access to staff: By letter, by telephone, by fax, by email, in person, visitors by prior appointment
Access to building, collections or gallery: Prior appointment required
Access for disabled people: Parking provided, level entry, access to all public areas, toilet facilities

General description:
History of the Cuckoo Clock Industry in the Black Forest Germany, Black Forest Fair Ground Organs, tools and machines, collection of vintage and classic motor cycle combinations.
Catalogues:
Catalogue for library is in-house only. Catalogue for all of the collections is only available in-house.

Internet home pages:
http://www.cuckoolanduk.com

732
CULLODEN MOOR VISITORS CENTRE

Culloden Moor, Inverness, Highland, IV2 5EU

Tel: 01463 790607
Fax: 01463 794294
Email: rmackenzie@nts.org.uk
Formed: 1931

Organisation type and purpose: National organisation, registered charity, historic building, house or site.
Parent body:
National Trust for Scotland Highlands and Islands Office (North)

Enquiries to: Property Manager
Access:
Access to staff: By letter, by telephone, by fax, by email, in person, charges to non-members, Internet web pages
Access to building, collections or gallery: No prior appointment required
Hours: Apr 1 to Oct 31: Daily, 0900 to 1800
Jan 15 to Mar 31 and Nov 1 to Dec 31: Daily, 1000 to 1600
Access for disabled people: Parking provided, level entry, access to all public areas, toilet facilities
Other restrictions: Motorised wheelchair available

General description:
18th century battle site; visitor centre; weapons and artefact collection relating to Jacobite risings; Leanach cottage surviving 18th century farmhouse; military history; Highland history.
Information services:
Resources for Scottish Key Stages education facilities, Braille guidebook, raised maps, audio tour, induction loop, subtitled AV programme, special AV channel, guidebook in French and German, AV programme in French, Gaelic, German, Italian and Japanese.
Special visitor services: Guided tours, tape recorded guides.
Education services: Group education facilities.
Services for disabled people: For the visually impaired; for the hearing impaired; displays and/or information at wheelchair height.
Collections:
Collection of 18th century weapons (pistols and other guns), swords, farges, artefacts relating to battle and Jacobite risings
Jacobite and Hanoverian propaganda medals
Printed publications:
Range of postcards (35p each)
Guide Books (English, French, German, £3.50)

Internet home pages:
http://www.nts.org.uk

733
CULROSS PALACE

See - Royal Burgh of Culross

734
CULTURAL HERITAGE NATIONAL TRAINING ORGANISATION

Glyde House, Glydegate, Bradford, West Yorkshire, BD5 0UP

Tel: 01274 391056
Fax: 01274 394890
Email: mail@chnto.co.uk
Acronym or abbreviation: CHNTO
Formed: 1998
Formerly: Museum Training Institute (MTI), date of change, 1998

Organisation type and purpose: National government body, registered charity (charity number 1003074).
National training organisation.
To provide a focus for training activities and information in the museums and heritage field and to develop NVQ and SVQ standards for the sector.
To develop National occupational standards and vocational qualifications for those working in the museums, heritage and conservation sector.
To undertake research into the labour market, sector training needs and management development projects.

Enquiries to: Communications Officer
Direct tel: 01274 391087
Direct email: kathryn@chnto.co.uk
Access:
Access to staff: By letter, by telephone, by fax, by email
Hours: Mon to Fri, 0900 to 1700
Other restrictions: Working office - not open to the public.

continued overleaf

General description:
Careers in the museums, heritage and conservation sector, labour market information, courses information, skills development, modern apprenticeships, management development, equal opportunities, vocational qualifications and occupational standards.
Trade and statistical:
Data on the numbers and characteristics of the heritage workforce.
Data on training needs and skills shortages in this sector.
Publications list:
is available in hard copy.
Printed publications:
Careers booklet
NVQ and SVQ support materials
Standards of Occupational Competence
Electronic and video products:
Noticeboard (electronic bulletin)

Address for ordering publications:
Printed publications:
Information Assistant, Cultural Heritage National Training Organisation

Internet home pages:
http://www.chnto.co.uk/library
Access to information about the range of CHNTO's work, including toolkits, reports, latest news, press releases etc.

735
CULZEAN CASTLE AND COUNTRY PARK
Maybole, South Ayrshire, KA19 8LE

Tel: 01655 884455
Fax: 01655 884503
Email: culzean@nts.org.uk

Organisation type and purpose: Registered charity, historic building, house or site, suitable for ages: 5+.
Parent body:
National Trust for Scotland (West Region)
Email: dheron@nts.org.uk

Enquiries to: Manager
Other contacts: Castle Operations Manager
Access:
Access to staff: By letter, by telephone, by fax, by email, visitors by prior appointment, Internet web pages
Access for disabled people: Parking provided, level entry, access to all public areas, toilet facilities
Other restrictions: Access to Castle and Visitor Centre via lifts only
Wheelchairs and self-drive battery cars available bookable in advance

General description:
Robert Adams converted a fortified tower castle into a fine Georgian castle for the Earl of Cassillis between 1777 and 1792. The Circular Saloon and Oval Staircase are fine examples of Robert Adams work.
Information services:
Services for disabled people: For the visually impaired; for the hearing impaired.

Internet home pages:
http://www.culzeancastle.net

736
CUMBERLAND PENCIL MUSEUM
Southey Works, Main Street, Keswick, Cumbria, CA12 5NG

Tel: 017687 73626
Fax: 017687 74679
Email: museum@acco-uk.co.uk
Formed: 1981

Organisation type and purpose: Museum.

Enquiries to: Supervisor
Access:
Access to staff: By letter, by telephone, by fax, by email, charges made to all users
Hours: Mon to Fri, 0930 to 1600 (last admission)
Access for disabled people: access to all public areas

General description:
The history of pencil-making in Keswick from early beginnings to present day pencil manufacturing.
Collections:
The collection consists of items relating to the Cumberland Pencil Company - in the form of pencils, pencil manufacturing machinery, cedar products, old packaging, etc.
Printed publications:
History of Pencil Making (£1.99)
Making Pencils (£2.99)
Electronic and video products:
Three in One Video (pencil manufacture, watercolour pencil techniques and scenic Lake District talk, £11.99)

Internet home pages:
http://www.pencils.co.uk/
All about the museum and product history.

737
CUMBERLAND TOY & MODEL MUSEUM, THE
Banks Court, Market Place, Cockermouth, Cumbria, CA13 9NG

Tel: 01900 827606
Formed: 1989

Organisation type and purpose: Museum, suitable for ages: 4+.

Enquiries to: Curator
Access:
Access to staff: By letter, by telephone, in person
Hours: 1 Feb to 30 Nov: Mon to Sun, 1000 to 1700
Other restrictions: Telephone in Dec and Jan as times vary.

General description:
Housed in carefully restored late 18th century buildings, one a former hat factory and the other a joiner's workshop with its original tools. Toys and models in general, especially 1920 to 1980; specialised information on many manufacturers such as Hornby, Meccano, Dinky Toys, Micromodels, Lego, Tri-ang, Sutcliffe, Meccano, Minic, Airfix, etc.
Vistor operated displays and buttons to press including 0 and 00 tinplate trains, Scalextric cars, Meccano, Lego models and even a helicopter to fly.
Information services:
Special visitor services: Materials and/or activities for children.
Education services: Resources for Key Stages 1 and 2, 3, 4 and Further or Higher Education.
Services for disabled people: For the visually impaired.
Collections:
Micromodels; card model sets, individual sheets and built models from the firms of Modelcraft and Micromodels Ltd, 1941-1956, c. 200 items
Catalogues:
Catalogue for part of the collections is only available in-house.

Internet home pages:
http://www.toyandmodelmuseum.gbr.cc

738
CUMBERNAULD MUSEUM
Cumbernauld Library, Allander Walk, Town Centre, Cumbernauld, North Lanarkshire, G67 1EE

Tel: 01236 725664
Formed: 1998

Organisation type and purpose: Local government body, museum, suitable for ages: 8+.
Parent body:
North Lanarkshire Council
Museums Section

Enquiries to: Curator
Direct tel: 0141 304 1975
Direct fax: 0141 304 1902
Access:
Access to staff: By letter, by fax
Access to building, collections or gallery: No prior appointment required
Access for disabled people: Parking provided, ramped entry, access to all public areas, toilet facilities

General description:
Situated within the Cumbernauld town centre library, the Museum Room takes the visitor from the days of the Romans to the development of the new town in the 1950s and 60s. No curator on-site, but schools workshops and holiday activities are arranged throughout the year.
Information services:
Education services: Group education facilities, resources for Key Stages 2 and 3..
Collections:
Limited display of artefacts relating to area's Roman Heritage
19th century industries and agriculture
Growth of Cumbernauld new town in 1960s
Catalogues:
Catalogue for all of the collections is published.

739
CUMING MUSEUM
155-157 Walworth Road, London, SE17 1RS

Tel: 020 7703 1342
Fax: 020 7701 1342
Email: cuming.museum@southwark.gov.uk
Formed: 1906

Organisation type and purpose: Local government body, professional body, museum, suitable for ages: 5+.
Part of:
London Borough of Southwark
Education & Lifelong Learning
15 Spa Road, London, SE16 3QW, tel: 020 7525 1993

Enquiries to: Museum Manager
Direct email: janebird@southwark.gov.uk
Access:
Access to staff: By letter, by telephone, by fax, by email, visitors by prior appointment

General description:
Social history and archaeology of the Southwark area, London charms (superstitions), local history.
Collections:
Archaeology of Southwark
The Cuming Museum is the Museum of Southwark's history and the home of the rich and unusual Cuming Collection
Between 1780 and 1900, the Cuming Family collected over 100,000 objects from all over the world, this unique collection of everyday and extraordinary objects was left to the people of Southwark and the gallery was opened in 1906
Cuming Family Collection (antiquities and natural history)
Edward Lovett Collection (superstitions)
Publications list:
is available in hard copy.
Printed publications:
Local History Topics (available from Museum Shop)
Provisional Reports on excavations (available from Museum Shop)

740
CURTIS MUSEUM
3 High Street, Alton, Hampshire, GU34 1BA

Tel: 01420 82802
Fax: 01420 84227
Email: musmtc@hants.gov.uk
Formed: 1855
Formerly: Alton Museum

Organisation type and purpose: Local government body, museum, historic building, house or site.
The local museum for the Alton area,

Hampshire; displays of local history, archaeology, natural science including geology.
Parent body:
Hampshire County Council Museums Service
Tel: 01962 846304, fax: 01962 869836

Enquiries to: Curator
Access:
Access to staff: By letter, by telephone, by fax, by email, in person

General description:
Local history of the Alton area, archaeology, natural science, aquarium, recreation, toys, agriculture, hop growing, brewing; housed in the old mechanics' institute, library and museum, originally built in 1878.
Catalogues:
Catalogue for all of the collections is on-line.
Printed publications:
Publications list is available from the Librarian, Hampshire County Council Museums Service Headquarters, Chilcomb House, Winchester, SO23 8RD

Address for ordering publications:
Printed publications:
Registrar, Hampshire County Council Museums Service HQ

Internet home pages:
http://www.hants.gov.uk/museums/
HMCMS web catalogue, whole collection, 100,000 plus web pages.

741
CUSTARD FACTORY, THE
Gibb Street, Birmingham, B9 4AA

Tel: 0121 693 7777
Fax: 0121 693 4817
Email: info@custardfactory.com
Formed: 1995

Organisation type and purpose: Independently owned, historic building, house or site, suitable for ages: 16+.
Converted factory building.
Connections with:
The SPACE Foundation
(Society for the Promotion of Artistic and Creative Enterprise) (SPACE)
at the same address

Enquiries to: Manager
Access:
Access to staff: By letter, by fax, by email
Access to building, collections or gallery: Prior appointment required
Access for disabled people: Parking provided

General description:
Housed in an old factory used to make custard powder, there is: Dance Studio (for hire), gallery (available for hire), office and retail space to let, bar and café, food and entertainments, lake and sculpture yard.

Internet home pages:
http://www.custardfactory.com

742
CUSTOM HOUSE, THE
Purfleet Quay, King's Lynn, Norfolk, PE30 1HP

Tel: 01553 763044

Organisation type and purpose: Museum, historic building, house or site, suitable for ages: all ages.

Enquiries to: Curator

General description:
The restored Custom House has displays which tell the stories of King's Lynn's merchants and sailors.

743
CUSTOMS HOUSE GALLERY
Customs House Trust Limited, Mill Dam, South Shields, Tyne and Wear, NE33 1ES

Tel: 0191 454 1234
Fax: 0191 456 5979
Email: wendy@customshouse.co.uk
Formed: 1994

Organisation type and purpose: Registered charity, art gallery, suitable for ages: all ages.
Art centre, gallery, theatre, centre.

Enquiries to: Visual Arts Development Officer
Access:
Access to staff: By letter, by email
Access to building, collections or gallery: Prior appointment required
Access for disabled people: Parking provided, ramped entry, access to all public areas, toilet facilities

General description:
Arts centre with theatre, cinema, music and temporary exhibitions of visual arts.

Internet home pages:
http://www.customshouse.co.uk

744
CUSWORTH HALL MUSEUM
See - Museum of South Yorkshire Life

745
CUTTY SARK (CLIPPER SHIP MUSEUM)
King William Walk, Greenwich, London, SE10 9HT

Tel: 020 8858 3445
Fax: 020 8853 3589
Email: info@cuttysark.org.uk
Formed: 1869

Organisation type and purpose: Independently owned, registered charity (charity number 1080462), museum, historic building, house or site, suitable for ages: all ages.
Affiliated to:
Maritime Trust
2 Greenwich Church Street, Greenwich, London, SE10 9BG, tel: 020 8858 2698, fax: 020 8858 6976, email/website: info@cuttysark.org.uk
Other addresses:
Cutty Sark Trust
2 Greenwich Church Street, London, SE10 9BG, tel: 020 8858 2698, fax: 020 8858 6976, email/website: info@cuttysark.org.uk

Enquiries to: Chief Executive
Direct tel: 020 8858 2698
Direct fax: 020 8858 6976
Access:
Access to staff: By letter, by telephone, by email, Internet web pages
Access for disabled people: level entry
Other restrictions: Limited disabled access.

General description:
History of the Cutty Sark clipper ship, 1869 to present. The Main Deck houses the crew and officers' accommodation, restored to 1870s condition. The Galley, Carpenter's workshop and the masts can also be seen complete with their eleven miles of rigging.
Information services:
Children's hands-on activities.
Special visitor services: Guided tours, tape recorded guides, materials and/or activities for children.
Education services: Resources for Key Stages 2 and 3.
Services for disabled people: For the visually impaired; for the hearing impaired; displays and/or information at wheelchair height.
Collections:
Cumbers collection of merchant ships' figureheads
Publications list:
is available in hard copy.
Printed publications:
Copy of the Original Register of Cutty Sark (£14.95 plus £1.50 p&p)
Plans - general arrangement or rigging or sail (£2.50 each plus 50p p&p)
The Maritime Trust Silver Jubilee book (£1.50 plus £1 p&p)

Internet home pages:
http://www.cuttysark.org.uk
History of Cutty Sark and details of the ship.

746
CUTTY SARK TRUST
2 Greenwich Church Street, Greenwich, London, SE10 9BG

Tel: 020 8858 2698
Fax: 020 8858 6976
Email: info@cuttysark.org.uk
Formed: 1969

Organisation type and purpose: Registered charity.
Member of:
International Congress of Maritime Museums

Enquiries to: Development Manager
Access:
Access to staff: By letter, by telephone, by fax, by email, Internet web pages

General description:
Information on and restoration of the sole surviving tea clipper, Cutty Sark (1869).
Collections:
Cutty Sark restoration photographs 1991 to present
Long John Silver collection of ships' figureheads and nautical bric-à-brac (the Cumbers Bequest)

Internet home pages:
http://www.cuttysark.org.uk
History of the Cutty Sark.

747
CWMMAU FARMHOUSE
Brilley, Whitney-on-Wye, Herefordshire, HR3 6JP

Tel: 01885 483075 (Property Manager)

Organisation type and purpose: National organisation, registered charity (charity number 205846), museum, historic building, house or site, suitable for ages: 8+.
Parent body:
The National Trust (West Midlands Region)
West Midlands Regional Office, tel: 01743 708100

Enquiries to: Property Manager

General description:
Cwmmau is a superb example of an early 17th century timber-framed and stone-tiled farmhouse. Bequeathed to the National Trust in 1965, it had been restored from its derelict state by the donor from 1934 onwards.
The property includes a fine range of vernacular farm buildings, barns and a medieval building thought to have been built as a reconstruction in about 1700.

Internet home pages:
http://www.nationaltrust.org.uk

748
CYFARTHFA CASTLE MUSEUM & ART
Cyfarthfa Park, Brecon Road, Merthyr Tydfil, Mid Glamorgan, CF47 8RE

Tel: 01685 723112
Fax: 01685 723112
Email: museum@cyfarthfapark.freeserve.co.uk
Formed: 1910

Organisation type and purpose: Local government body, museum, art gallery, suitable for ages: 5+.
Parent body:
Merthyr Tydfil Borough Council

continued overleaf

Enquiries to: Curator
Other contacts: Education Officer for school groups.
Access:
Access to staff: By letter, by telephone, by fax, by email, visitors by prior appointment
Access for disabled people: ramped entry, access to all public areas, toilet facilities
Other restrictions: Ramped entry via rear entrance.

General description:
History of Merthyr Tydfil, iron industry, fine art, ceramics, Egypt.
Information services:
Education services: Group education facilities, resources for Key Stages 1 and 2, 3, 4 and Further or Higher Education..
Collections:
'City Status' Art Collection
Swansea & Nantgarw Ceramic Collection
Southey Bequest - Egyptian Collection
Crawshay Brass Band Instruments

749
CYFARTHFA CASTLE MUSEUM AND ART GALLERY

Brecon Road, Merthyr Tydfil, Mid Glamorgan, CF47 3NG

Tel: 01685 723112
Fax: 01685 723112
Email: museum@cyfarthfapark.freeserve.co.uk

Organisation type and purpose: Local government body, museum, art gallery, suitable for ages: 5+.

Enquiries to: Museum Officer
Access:
Access to staff: By letter, by telephone, by fax, by email, in person
Access for disabled people: access to all public areas, toilet facilities
Other restrictions: Ramped entry at rear.

General description:
Once the Regency home of the Crawshay ironmasters and now the regional museum for the Merthyr Valley. Contains fine art, especially 20th century; ceramics; ethnography - one of only a few such collections in Wales; items relating to the iron, steel and coal trades; and social history.
Information services:
Special visitor services: Guided tours, materials and/or activities for children.
Education services: Group education facilities, resources for Key Stages 1 and 2, 3, 4 and Further or Higher Education..
Collections:
Ceramics. European and some Chinese and Japanese, good Swansea and Nantgarw. Mainly 18th and 19th century. 600 items
Contemporary Art Society Wales (CASW). 20th century paintings - oil, watercolour and others. 20th century. 40 items
Crawshay. Photographs, silver, glass and printed and written material on the Crawshay family. 1800-1890s. 200 items
Southey. Egyptian and eastern. Wide. 200-300 items
Catalogues:
Catalogue for part of the collections is only available in-house.

750
CYNGOR CELFYDDYDAU CYMRU

See - Arts Council of Wales

751
CYWGER AMEUEDDFEYDD YNG NGHYMRU

See - Council of Museums in Wales

752
DACORUM HERITAGE TRUST LIMITED, THE

The Museum Store, Clarence Road, Berkhamsted, Hertfordshire, HP4 3YL

Tel: 01442 879525
Acronym or abbreviation: DHT
Formed: 1993

Organisation type and purpose: Museum.

Enquiries to: Curator
Access:
Access to staff: By letter, by telephone
Access to building, collections or gallery: Prior appointment required
Hours: Mon to Fri, 0900 to 1700
Access for disabled people: Parking provided

General description:
The trust operates from a museum store - there is no museum for the public to wander round.
Collections:
Wide variety of collections representing the history of the Borough of Dacorum

Internet home pages:
http://www.hertsmuseums.org.uk/dacorum

753
DALES COUNTRYSIDE MUSEUM

Station Yard, Hawes, North Yorkshire, DL8 3NT

Tel: 01969 667494
Fax: 01969 667165
Formed: 1979
Formerly: Upper Dales Folk Museum, date of change, 1990

Organisation type and purpose: Local government body, advisory body, museum.
Parent body:
Yorkshire Dales National Park Authority

Enquiries to: Manager
Access:
Access to staff: By letter, by telephone, by fax, visitors by prior appointment
Hours: Mon to Sun, 1000 to 1700
Other restrictions: Winter, daily, telephone for times.
Access for disabled people: Parking provided, ramped entry, level entry, access to all public areas, toilet facilities

General description:
The history of the Yorkshire Dales over 10,000 years. Including collections relating to people and the environment in the Yorkshire Dales, includes archaeology; agriculture; industry; crafts; social history; domestic life; childhood items; and tourism.
Information services:
Education services: Group education facilities..
Collections:
Doctor's surgery with his pharamacy
Dales' kitchen
Makers and menders tools
Farming life past and present
Agar collection of knitting sheaths, 1700-1900
Hartley/Ingilby collection of knitting sheaths, 1700-1900
Catalogues:
Catalogue for library is in-house only. Catalogue for all of the collections is only available in-house.

Internet home pages:
http://www.yorkshiredales.org.uk

754
DALGARVEN MILL TRUST

Dalry Road, Dalgarven, Kilwinning, Ayrshire, KA13 6PL

Tel: 01294 552448
Fax: 01294 552448
Email: admin@dalgarvenmill.org.uk
Full name: The Museum of Ayrshire Country Life and Costume
Formed: 1987

Organisation type and purpose: Registered charity (charity number SC 022937), museum, historic building, house or site, suitable for ages: all ages.
Museum and archive housed in group of listed grain mill buildings dated 12th, 16th, 17th, 19th century.

Enquiries to: Chairman
Other contacts: Administrator for bookings and opening hours.
Access:
Access to staff: By letter, by telephone, by fax, by email
Hours: Easter to end Oct: Tue to Sun, 1000 to 1700
Nov to Easter: Tue to Fri, 1000 to 1600; Sat, Sun, 1000 to 1700
Other restrictions: Ground floor and catering accessible for disabled.
Access for disabled people: Parking provided, ramped entry, toilet facilities
Other restrictions: Access to refreshments and ground floor displays.

General description:
The listed buildings themselves are important and show construction methods from the 16th century onwards.
The rural life collection houses, tools, artefacts, furniture, costume and records including photographs from 1850 to post World War II.
Over 1000 costumes from 1775 to 1975 are shown in rotating exhibitions.
Collections:
Collection covering Ayrshire's dairy industry, 1850-1950, 100 items
Ferguson collection, local costumes both aristocratic and working class, 1780-1980, 700 items
Catalogues:
Catalogue for all of the collections is only available in-house.
Printed publications:
Leaflet, brief history of the mill

755
DALI UNIVERSE

See - County Hall Gallery Limited

756
DALMENY HOUSE

South Queensferry, West Lothian, EH30 9TQ

Tel: 0131 331 1888
Fax: 0131 331 1788
Email: events@dalmeny.co.uk
Formed: 1814

Organisation type and purpose: Independently owned, historic building, house or site, suitable for ages: 16+.

Enquiries to: Administrator
Access:
Access to staff: By letter, by fax, by email, visitors by prior appointment
Hours: Mon to Fri, 0900 to 1645
Access for disabled people: toilet facilities

General description:
The Tudor Gothic house, built in 1815, contains the superb Rothschild Mentmore Collection of 18th century French furniture, porcelain and tapestries. Fine paintings include portraits by Gainsborough, Raeburn, Reynolds and Lawrence. The important Napoleonic collection was assembled by the fifth Earl of Rosebery - Prime Minister, historian and owner of three Derby winners.
Information services:
Special visitor services: Guided tours..
Collections:
Rothschild French 18th century furniture
Rosebery Napoleonic Collection, portraits and possessions of the Emperor
French 18th century Porcelain, Vincenie, Sèvres

Printed publications:
Guide Book (£3)

Internet home pages:
http://www.dalmeny.co.uk

757
DALTON CASTLE
Market Place, Dalton-in-Furness, Cumbria, LA15 8AX

Tel: 01524 701178
Email: daltoncastle@nationaltrust.org.uk

Organisation type and purpose: National government body, registered charity (charity number 205846), historic building, house or site.
Parent body:
The National Trust (North West)
North West Regional Office, tel: 0870 609 5391
Opened on behalf of the Trust by:
Friends of Dalton Castle

Enquiries to: Property Manager
Access:
Access to staff: By letter, by telephone, by email
Access for disabled people: Parking provided
Other restrictions: Designated parking 15yds. Steps to entrance. Ground floor accessible with assistance. No access to other floors.

General description:
A 14th century tower in the main street of the town, with a local exhibition by the Friends of Dalton Castle and a display about the painter George Romney, a native of Dalton.

Internet home pages:
http://www.nationaltrust.org.uk

758
DARBY HOUSES, THE
Ironbridge Gorge Museum Trust, Coach Road, Coalbrookdale, Telford, Shropshire, TF8 7DQ

Tel: 01952 433522
Email: visits@ironbridge.org.uk

Organisation type and purpose: Registered charity (charity number 503717-R), museum, historic building, house or site, suitable for ages: 5+.
Parent body:
Ironbridge Gorge Museum Trust
Tel: 01952 433522
Access:
Access to staff: By letter, by telephone, in person
Access to building, collections or gallery: No prior appointment required
Hours: 1000 to 1700, daily
Other restrictions: Closed 24 and 25 Dec, 1 Jan. Closed Nov to Mar, tel: 01952 432 166 to check winter opening times
Access for disabled people: Parking provided, level entry, toilet facilities
Other restrictions: Ground floor only. Access guide for disabled visitors available on request.

General description:
Restored Quaker ironmasters' homes overlooking the Darby furnace.
Information services:
Special visitor services: Guided tours, materials and/or activities for children.
Education services: Group education facilities, resources for Key Stages 1 and 2, 3, 4 and Further or Higher Education..
Collections:
The Darby Collection: collection of furniture and personal effects of the Darby family

Internet home pages:
http://www.ironbridge.org.uk

759
DARLINGTON RAILWAY CENTRE AND MUSEUM
North Road Station, Darlington, Co Durham, DL3 6ST

Tel: 01325 460532
Fax: 01325 287746
Email: museum@darlington.gov.uk
Formed: 1975

Organisation type and purpose: Local government body, museum.
Parent body:
Darlington Borough Council
Subsidiary:
Ken Hoole Study Centre for North-East Railway History
Tel: 01325 460532, email/website: ann@khoolearchive.demon.co.uk

Enquiries to: Curator
Other contacts: Documentation Officer (for Study Centre enquiries)
Access:
Access to staff: By letter, by telephone, in person
Hours: Mon to Fri, 1000 to 1700
Other restrictions: Appointment advisable for use of Study Centre. Study Centre is accessible by email.
Access for disabled people: Parking provided, level entry, access to all public areas, toilet facilities

General description:
History of the Stockton and Darlington Railway and the North Eastern Railway; history of the museum building, North Road Station, dating from 1842, part still in use for passenger trains; history of the railway industry in Darlington.
Information services:
Special visitor services: Materials and/or activities for children.
Education services: Group education facilities..
Collections:
Cleveland Bridge Company collection: Bridge Design and Construction
Ken Hoole collection: Railways of North-East England
North Eastern Railway Association Library
Some exhibits on loan from the National Railway Museum
Catalogues:
Catalogue for library is in-house only. Catalogue for part of the collections is only available in-house.
Printed publications:
Publicity leaflet
Study Centre leaflet

760
DART VALLEY LIGHT RAILWAY PLC (COMPANY NAME)
See - Paignton and Dartmouth Steam Railway

761
DARTMOUTH CASTLE
Castle Road, Dartmouth, Devon, TQ6 0JN

Tel: 01803 833588
Email: customers@english-heritage.org.uk

Organisation type and purpose: National organisation, historic building, house or site, suitable for ages: 8+.
Parent body:
English Heritage (South West Region)
Tel: 0117 975 0700, fax: 0117 975 0701

Enquiries to: Curator
Access:
Access to staff: By letter

General description:
This brilliantly positioned defensive castle juts out into the narrow entrance to the Dart Estuary, with the sea lapping at its foot. Begun late in the 14th century, when the merchants of Dartmouth felt the need to protect their homes and warehouses from invasion, it was one of the first castles constructed with artillery in mind. Since the 14th century, Dartmouth has seen 600 years of fortification and preparation for war.
Information services:
Education services: Group education facilities..

Address for ordering publications:
Printed publications:
English Heritage Postal Sales
c/o Gillards, Trident Works, Temple Cloud, Bristol, BS39 5AZ, tel: 01761 452966, fax: 01761 453408, email: ehsales@gillards.com

Internet home pages:
http://www.english-heritage.org.uk

762
DARTMOUTH MUSEUM
The Butterwalk, Duke Street, Dartmouth, Devon, TQ6 9PZ

Tel: 01803 832923
Formed: 1953

Organisation type and purpose: Membership association (membership is by subscription), registered charity (charity number 306635), museum, historic building, house or site, suitable for ages: all ages.

Enquiries to: Honorary Secretary
Other contacts: Honorary Curator
Access:
Access to staff: By letter, by telephone, in person
Access to building, collections or gallery: No prior appointment required
Hours: Summer: 1100 to 1630
Winter: 1200 to 1500

General description:
A small and interesting museum housed in an Old Merchant's House, dated 1640. Contains local and maritime information; many ship models; pictures; and artefacts of their ancient little town.
Collections:
Documents, manuscripts, pictures, photographs and other materials
Ship models and ships in bottles
Oil paintings of local views
Catalogues:
Catalogue for all of the collections is only available in-house.

763
DAVENTRY MUSEUM
The Moot Hall, Market Square, Daventry, Northamptonshire, NN11 4BH

Tel: 01327 302463
Fax: 01327 876684
Email: museum@daventrydc.gov.uk
Formed: 1989

Organisation type and purpose: Local government body, museum, suitable for ages: 5+.

Enquiries to: Curator
Other contacts: Education Officer for school or group visits.
Access:
Access to staff: By letter, by telephone, by fax, by email

General description:
Collection covering the social and local history of Daventry and the surrounding area.
Information services:
Education services: Group education facilities, resources for Key Stages 1 and 2..
Collections:
Social history, local history, some archaeology

764
DAVIDSON'S MILL
Mill Lane, Stelling Minnis, Canterbury, Kent

Tel: 01227 709238/709550

Organisation type and purpose: Historic building, house or site.

continued overleaf

General description:
Smock mill built 1866 and working until 1970. Works by wind or 1912 Ruston & Hornsby oil engine.
Catalogues:
Catalogue for library is in-house only. Catalogue for part of the collections is only available in-house.

765
DAVIES & TOOTH LIMITED
32 Dover Street, London, W1S 4NE

Tel: 020 7409 1516
Fax: 020 7409 1856
Email: art@davies-tooth.com
Formed: 1990

Organisation type and purpose: Art gallery, consultancy.
To advise corporate and private clients on the sale and purchase of contemporary art.

Enquiries to: Director
Access:
Access to staff: Visitors by prior appointment, by letter, by telephone, by fax, by email, Internet web pages
Hours: Mon to Fri, 1000 to 1800

General description:
Paintings, watercolours, limited edition prints, sculpture, tapestry, stained and etched glass, textiles by artists working from 1850 to the present day.
Collections:
Slide and photographic library containing examples of the works of over 2000 living artists
Publications list:
is available in hard copy.

Internet home pages:
http://www.davies-tooth.com
Outline of services available.

766
DAVY FARADAY RESEARCH LABORATORY
See - Royal Institution of Great Britain

767
DAWLISH MUSEUM SOCIETY
The Knowle, Barton Terrace, Dawlish, Devon, EX7 9QH

Tel: 01626 888557
Email: dawlish@devonmuseums.net
Formed: 1968

Organisation type and purpose: Voluntary organisation, registered charity (charity number 230246), museum, suitable for ages: all ages.
Eleven rooms.
Parent body:
Dawlish Local History Group (SWMC)

Enquiries to: Honorary Secretary
Direct tel: 01626 866124
Access:
Access to staff: By letter, by telephone
Access for disabled people: Parking provided, level entry
Other restrictions: Chairlift to first floor.

General description:
The collection, housed in a listed 19th century building, consists mainly of Victoriana of local interest. Displays include agriculture; local industries (mills, smithies, violet trade); militaria; railway; clothes; photographs; prints; china; toys; and a Victorian parlour, kitchen, shop and bedroom.
Information services:
Special visitor services: Materials and/or activities for children.
Education services: Resources for Key Stages 1 and 2.
Services for disabled people: For the visually impaired.
Collections:
Collection of Local Newspapers from 1897
Photographs (part of Chapman Collection, early 20th century)
Exceptional Victorian Collection
Copy of Parish Church list of baptisms, marriages and burials from the late 1600s to the early 1800s.
Catalogues:
Catalogue for library is in-house only.
Publications list:
is available in hard copy.
Printed publications:
Various publications available direct

Internet home pages:
http://www.devonmuseums.net/dawlish
Site, collections and diary of events.

768
D-DAY MUSEUM AND OVERLORD EMBROIDERY
Clarence Esplanade, Portsmouth, Hampshire, PO5 3NT

Tel: 023 9282 7261
Minicom no. 023 9287 6550
Fax: 023 9287 5276
Email: enquiries@ddaymuseum.co.uk
Formed: 1984

Organisation type and purpose: Local government body, museum, suitable for ages: 8+.

Enquiries to: Curator
Other contacts: Visitor Services Officer for group visits.
Access:
Access to staff: By letter, by telephone, by fax, by email
Access to building, collections or gallery: No prior appointment required
Hours: Apr to Sep: Daily, 1000 to 1730
Oct to Mar: Daily, 1000 to 1700
Access for disabled people: Parking provided, level entry, access to all public areas, toilet facilities

General description:
Portsmouth's D-Day Museum tells the dramatic story of the Allied landings in Normandy, 6th June 1944. Centrepiece is the magnificent 'Overlord Embroidery'. 83 metres long. Step back in time to scenes of wartime Britain. Military equipment, vehicles, landing craft and personal memories complete this special story.
Collections:
Overlord Embroidery
Cmdr Rupert Curtis bequest: Collection of documents and photographs on D-Day landing craft
Military History Collection
Objects, photographs, documents, maps and books relating to Operation Overlord
Catalogues:
Catalogue for part of the collections is on-line.

Internet home pages:
http://www.ddaymuseum.co.uk
Full website.

769
DE HAVILLAND AIRCRAFT HERITAGE CENTRE, THE
PO Box 107, Salisbury Hall, London Colney, St Albans, Hertfordshire, AL2 1EX

Tel: 01727 822051
Fax: 01727 826400
Formed: 1959
Formerly: Mosquito Aircraft Museum

Organisation type and purpose: Independently owned, registered charity (charity number 286794), museum, suitable for ages: 8+.
Preserve de Havilland aircraft and associated material.

Enquiries to: Director
Direct tel: 020 8954 5080
Direct fax: 020 8954 5080
Access:
Access to staff: By letter, by telephone, by fax
Access to building, collections or gallery: No prior appointment required
Hours: Tue, Thu, Sat, 1400 to 1730; Sun and Bank Holidays, 1030 to 1730
Access for disabled people: Parking provided, level entry, toilet facilities

General description:
Variety of de Havilland aircraft and sections from DH Moth to modern 1950-60 military and civil jets, included the prototype DH Mosquito.
Work in progress on certain aircraft projects.
Collection of de Havilland aircraft engines.
Storyboard history of de Havilland Aircraft Enterprise.
Information services:
Special visitor services: Guided tours.
Services for disabled people: Displays and/or information at wheelchair height.
Catalogues:
Catalogue for library is in-house only. Catalogue for all of the collections is only available in-house.
Printed publications:
Museum leaflets (free)
Museum Newsletter (£1.50)
Other inhouse publications (£2 to £5)

Internet home pages:
http://www.dehavillandmuseum.co.uk
http://www.hertsmuseums.org.uk
General information only.

770
DEAL CASTLE
Victoria Road, Deal, Kent, CT14 7BA

Tel: 01304 372762

Organisation type and purpose: Museum, historic building, house or site, suitable for ages: 5+.
Parent body:
English Heritage (South East Region)
Eastgate Court, 195-205 High Street, Guildford, Surrey, GU1 3EH, tel: 01483 252000, fax: 01483 252001, email: www.english-heritage.org.uk

Enquiries to: Manager
Access:
Access to staff: By letter, by telephone, in person
Access to building, collections or gallery: No prior appointment required
Hours: Apr to Sep: daily, 1000 to 1800
Oct: daily, 1000 to 1700
Nov to Mar: Wed to Sun, 1000 to 1600
Other restrictions: Closed Dec 24 to 26 and Jan 1
Opening times are subject to change, for up-to-date information contact English Heritage by phone or visit the website.
Access for disabled people: Parking provided
Other restrictions: Access to courtyards and ground floor only.

General description:
Largest of the three great forts of Sandown, Deal and Walmer built by Henry VIII, Deal Castle was built as an artillery fortress to counter the threat of invasion from the Catholic alliance of France and Spain during the mid-16th century. Its huge, rounded bastions, which were designed to deflect shots, once carried 66 guns. It is a fascinating castle to explore, with long, dark passages, battlements and a massive basement which houses an exciting exhibition. Tudor and Civil War interactive displays.
Information services:
Audio tours also available in French, German and Dutch.
Special visitor services: Tape recorded guides..

Internet home pages:
http://www.english-heritage.org.uk

771
DEAL MARITIME & LOCAL HISTORY MUSEUM, THE
22 St George's Road, Deal, Kent, CT14 6BA

Tel: 01304 381344
Email: dealmuseum@lineone.net
Formed: 1971
Formed from: Deal Walmer & District History Society (Nominates six of the Museum's Trustees)

Organisation type and purpose: Independently owned, registered charity, museum, suitable for ages: 5+.
Supported by:
Association of Friends of the Deal Museum & Local History Museum
at the same address

Enquiries to: Secretary
Other contacts: Chairman for curatorial enquiries.
Access:
Access to staff: By letter, by email, in person, visitors by prior appointment, charges to non-members
Access to building, collections or gallery: No prior appointment required
Hours: 1 Apr to 30 Sep: Mon to Sat, 1400 to 1700
Other restrictions: Prior appointment required for Reserve Collection.
Access for disabled people: ramped entry
Other restrictions: Pay parking nearby; access to all ground floor areas.

General description:
Surviving evidence on the history and development of the Port of Deal, its anchorage, The Downs, its boats and boatmen, its trade and its function as a naval base in the sailing ship era. The Tudor castles, the barracks and hospital and services to international shipping are illustrated in paintings, prints and drawings, ship and boat models, figureheads, carvings and relics. An actual Walmer galley, the 'Saxon King', is preserved, as are records of the three local lifeboats round the Goodwin Sands. In the courtyard is a 27ft naval whaler, ex-Royal Marines, also old tombstones, a battery of small saluting cannon and other objects of interest. In the detached stable building is a gallery devoted to the Armed Forces & Civil Defence in World War II. Upstairs, the 'Face of Deal' is illustrated by paintings, drawings, prints and photographs, as are various local worthies. There is a small library including parish records and works of reference, open to members of the Association of Friends of the Museum.
Collections:
W Honey Collections of photographs of local interest
Moses Collection - 20 pages of sepia pen and wash drawings from a sketch book of the summer of 1840 showing Deal beach, boats etc by Henry Moses (1782-1870), artist and engraver
Shelvey Bequest - Antiquarian and other books of local interest with a collection of topographical engravings from Mr & Mrs Shelvey, local collectors
Catalogues:
Catalogue for part of the collections is only available in-house.
Printed publications:
The Life & Times of a Small House in Deal - A contribution to the Celebration of the 300th Anniversary of the Granting of Deal's Charter (Sargent A, 1999, 4to. pp34, Illust, 6 maps, paperback, £5 plus p&p)

Internet home pages:
http://home.freeuk.com/deal-museum/

772
DEAN CASTLE
Dean Road, Kilmarnock, Ayrshire, KA3 1XB

Tel: 01563 554701
Fax: 01563 554720
Email: museums@east-ayrshire.gov.uk

Organisation type and purpose: Local government body, historic building, house or site, suitable for ages: all ages.

Enquiries to: Manager
Direct tel: 01563 554731 (Visitor services)
Access:
Access to staff: By letter, by telephone, by fax, by email, visitors by prior appointment
Access for disabled people: Parking provided, ramped entry, toilet facilities
Other restrictions: Limited access.

General description:
Dean Castle is a magnificent collection of restored buildings dating from the 1350s. Important collections of arms and armour, musical instruments and manuscripts by Robert Burns are on display in public rooms - guided tours only.
Information services:
Special visitor services: Guided tours..
Collections:
Van Raalte. Early European musical instruments, 1500-1900, 100 itmes
Howard de Walden. Arms and armour, 900-1800, 300 items

Internet home pages:
http://www.east-ayrshire.gov.uk
General information on museums in East Ayrshire.

773
DEAN FOREST RAILWAY MUSEUM
Norchard Railway Centre, Forest Road, New Mills, Lydney, Gloucestershire, GL15 4ET

Tel: 01594 845840
Fax: 01594 845840
Formed: 1971

Organisation type and purpose: Independently owned, voluntary organisation, registered charity (charity number 1041295), museum, suitable for ages: all ages.
Administrating body:
Dean Forest Railway Museum Trust
Tel: 01594 845840, fax: 01594 845840

Enquiries to: Curator
Direct tel: 01452 713642
Access:
Access to staff: By letter, by telephone, visitors by prior appointment
Access to building, collections or gallery: No prior appointment required
Hours: Easter to Christmas: Daily, 1100 to 1600 Weekends all year
Access for disabled people: Parking provided, ramped entry, access to all public areas, toilet facilities

General description:
Artefacts (plates, signs, station furniture, etc.) from the four main group railway companies and British Rail, with special priority given to items from the former Severn and Wye Joint Railway, the Forest of Dean tramways and railways. Illustrated panels tell the history of this railway from 1810 to date.
Collections:
8 illustrated information panels telling the history of the Severn and Wye Railway
Small railway artefacts, cast iron and enamel signs, pictures, photographs etc

774
DEAN FOREST RAILWAY SOCIETY
Forest Road, Lydney, Gloucestershire, GL15 4ET

Tel: 01594 843423 (information line, recorded times & dates of services)
Acronym or abbreviation: DFRS
Formed: 1970
Formed from: Dean Forest Railway Preservation Society

Organisation type and purpose: Membership association.
Members operate the Dean Forest Railway Co Ltd and Dean Forest Railfreight Ltd.
Holding company:
Forest of Dean Railway Ltd
95 Melville Road, Churchdown, Gloucester, GL3 2RF
Subsidiary companies:
Dean Forest Railfreight Ltd
95 Melville Road, Churchdown, Gloucester, GL3 2RF
Dean Forest Railway Co Ltd
95 Melville Road, Churchdown, Gloucester, GL3 2RF

Enquiries to: Commercial Director
Direct tel: 01594 845840 (shop)
Direct fax: 01594 845840
Other contacts: DFRS Membership Secretary for membership applications.
Access:
Access to staff: By letter only, visitors by prior appointment
Hours: Jan to Easter, Wed, Sat, Sun, 1000 to 1700: Easter to Oct, daily, 1000 to 1700; Nov to Jan 1st, daily, 1000 to 1500
Access to building, collections or gallery: No prior appointment required
Hours: Library and Gift shop: Jan to Easter, Wed, Sat, Sun, 1000 to 1700: Easter to Oct, daily, 1000 to 1700; Nov to Jan 1st, daily, 1000 to 1500
Access for disabled people: Parking provided, ramped entry, toilet facilities
Other restrictions: Access to shop, station etc only at Norchard.

General description:
Dean Forest Railway is a predominantly steam-powered standard gauge tourist railway operating between Norchard and Lydney Junction. It is adjacent, and connected, to Railtrack. The line north of Norchard to Parkend is undergoing restoration. The railway is the sole surviving remnant of the Severn and Wye railway. The headquarters at Norchard are on the site of the former West Gloucestershire Power Station and Norchard Colliery. Railway artefacts plus a working telephone system.
Printed publications:
Colour brochure/timetable (annual, free, please enclose stamped addressed envelope)
Forest Venturer (Society's magazine, £1.50 plus p&p, free to Society members)
Electronic and video products:
Norchard/Dean Forest Railway (video, £10.95 plus p&p, available from railway)

Address for ordering publications:
Printed publications:
Dean Forest Railway Co. Ltd
Norchard Railway Centre, at the same address, tel: 01594 845840

Internet home pages:
http://www.deanforestrailway.co.uk

775
DEAN GALLERY
Belford Road, Edinburgh, EH4 3DS

Tel: 0131 624 6200
Fax: 0131 623 7126
Email: enquiries@nationalgalleries.org
Formed: 1999

Organisation type and purpose: National organisation, art gallery, suitable for ages: 5+.

continued overleaf

Parent body:
The National Galleries of Scotland
Belford Road, Edinburgh, EH4 3DR, tel: 0131 624 6200, fax: 0131 343 3250, email: enquiries@natgalscot.ac.uk

Enquiries to: Curatorial Dept for academic enquiries
Other contacts: Press and Information Dept for general public enquiries.
Access:
Access to staff: By letter, by telephone, by fax, by email, Internet web pages
Access for disabled people: Parking provided, level entry, access to all public areas, toilet facilities

General description:
The Dean Gallery is a magnificent art centre situated in parkland opposite the Scottish National Gallery of Modern Art. Opened in 1999, it provides a home for the Eduardo Paolozzi gift of sculpture and graphic art, including a reconstruction of Paolozzi's studio, made possible by the artist's generous donation of the entire contents of his studio. It also houses the Gallery of Modern Art's renowned Dada and Surrealist collections, one of the best collections of Surrealist art in the world. The Dean Gallery also contains a superb library and archive, and a gallery fitted out as a library for the display of artists' books. The Gallery's large shop is well established as the place to buy presents with a Surrealist edge, whilst Café Newton is a modern take on the coffee-houses of Vienna. Temporary exhibitions change on a regular basis, details of which can be found on the website.
Information services:
Education services: Group education facilities..
Catalogues:
Catalogue for library is in-house only. Catalogue for all of the collections is published.
Publications list:
is available in hard copy and online.
Printed publications:
Variety of leaflets available on request

Address for ordering publications:
Printed publications:
Publications Department, National Galleries of Scotland
Dean Gallery, tel: 0131 624 6257/6259/6261, fax: 0131 315 2963, email: publications@nationalgalleries.org

Internet home pages:
http://www.nationalgalleries.org

776
DEAN HERITAGE MUSEUM
Camp Mill, Soudley, Cinderford, Gloucestershire, GL14 2UB

Tel: 01594 822170
Fax: 01594 823711
Email: deanmuse@btinternet.com
Formed: 1983

Organisation type and purpose: Independently owned, registered charity (charity number 298647), museum.
Educational charity.

Enquiries to: Director
Access:
Access to staff: By letter, by telephone, by fax, by email, in person
Access to building, collections or gallery: No prior appointment required
Hours: Apr to Sep: daily, 1000 to 1730
Oct to Mar: daily, 1100 to 1600
Other restrictions: Gage Library open by prior appointment, Mon, Wed, 1400 to 1700.
Access for disabled people: Parking provided, ramped entry, toilet facilities
Other restrictions: Wheelchair available.

General description:
Set in a 19th century Corn Mill, the Museum tells the story of the Forest of Dean, from prehistory until the modern day. Social and industrial history, archaeology, natural history, rural skills demonstrations on-site.
Information services:
Library available for reference (for conditions see Access above)
Special visitor services: Guided tours, materials and/or activities for children.
Education services: Group education facilities, resources for Key Stages 1 and 2, 3, 4 and Further or Higher Education.
Services for disabled people: For the visually impaired; displays and/or information at wheelchair height.
Collections:
Social and industrial history artefacts, including:
Working Beam Engine from Lightmoor Colliery
The Voyce Collection of 18th century Long Case Clocks
Archaeological and geological collections
Gage Library of books, documents, maps and images of the Forest of Dean and surrounding areas
Community archive database, including oral history collection
Forest of Dean tramways; archive and objects
Forest of Dean old postcards; a substantial collection, exceeding 1500.
Women's Timber Corps of the Women's Land Army; archives, recollections and uniforms
Catalogues:
Catalogue for library is in-house only. Catalogue for all of the collections is only available in-house.

Internet home pages:
http://www.fweb.org.uk/deanmuseum
http://www.deanmuse.co.uk

777
DENBIGH LIBRARY, MUSEUM & GALLERY
Hall Square, Denbigh, Clwyd, LL16 3NU

Tel: 01745 816313
Fax: 01745 816427
Formed: 3 April 1992

Organisation type and purpose: Local government body, professional body, museum, art gallery, public library, suitable for ages: all ages.

Enquiries to: Curator
Direct tel: 01824 708223
Direct fax: 01824 708258
Direct email: rose.mcmahon@hotmail.com
Access:
Access to staff: By letter, by email
Hours: Mon to Fri, 1000 to 1700
Access to building, collections or gallery: No prior appointment required
Hours: Mon to Fri, 1000 to 1700; Sat, 0930 to 1200
Access for disabled people: level entry, access to all public areas, toilet facilities

General description:
The museum collection relates to the foundation of the town and its development through to 1945, its social, industrial and economic growth and its cultural heritage.
Printed publications:
Teachers' Pack (£10 plus p&p)

778
DENBIGHSHIRE HERITAGE SERVICE
46 Clwyd Street, Ruthin, Denbighshire, LL15 1HP

Tel: 01824 708223
Fax: 01824 708258

Organisation type and purpose: Local government body.
Administrative body for the libraries, museums, art galleries and historical sites which are under the care of Denbighshire County Council.
Parent body:
Denbighshire County Council
Tel: 01824 708200, fax: 01824 708202

Enquiries to: Curator
Direct email: rose.mcmahon@denbighshire.gov.uk
Access:
Access to staff: By letter, by telephone, by fax, by email, Internet web pages

General description:
Administrative office for the museums and properties in the Denbighshire area which are under the control of the local authority. The conservation of Denbighshire heritage.

Internet home pages:
http://www.denbighshire.gov.uk

See also - Rhyl Library, Museum and Arts Centre; Ruthin Gaol

779
DENBY POTTERY VISITOR CENTRE
Derby Road, Denby, Derbyshire, DE5 8NX

Tel: 01773 740799
Fax: 01773 740749
Email: visitor.centre@denby.co.uk
Formed: 1809

Organisation type and purpose: Independently owned.
Pottery manufacturer.
Visitor centre for the pottery.

Enquiries to: Senior Tours Administrator
Access:
Access to staff: By letter, by telephone, by fax
Access for disabled people: Parking provided, level entry, toilet facilities
Other restrictions: No access to full factory tour. Access to Craftsman's workshop by lift and all other areas.

General description:
Enquiries about the history of Denby Pottery.
Tours of the working factory and Craftsman's Workshop.
The Visitor Centre is next to the pottery and welcomes tourists, organised groups (including schools). Includes factory shops, museum, restaurant, glass-blowing studio and tours of the factory.
Information services:
Special visitor services: Guided tours.
Services for disabled people: For the visually impaired; displays and/or information at wheelchair height.
Collections:
Small museum with examples of Denby Pottery from 1820s to present day
Printed publications:
Books on history of Denby Pottery (for purchase, direct)

Internet home pages:
http://www.denby.co.uk
Tableware and accessories, current history, visitor centre, factory tours.

780
DENNY ABBEY AND THE FARMLAND MUSEUM, THE
Ely Road, Waterbeach, Cambridge, CB5 9PQ

Tel: 01223 860988
Fax: 01223 860988
Email: f.m.denny@tesco.net
Formed: 1997

Organisation type and purpose: Independently owned, registered charity (charity number 289555), museum, historic building, house or site, suitable for ages: all ages.

Enquiries to: Curator
Access:
Access to staff: By letter, by telephone, by fax, by email, in person, visitors by prior appointment
Access for disabled people: Parking provided, ramped entry, level entry, toilet facilities
Other restrictions: Stairs to upper floor of Abbey.

General description:
Denny Abbey was founded in1159 by Benedictine monks as a dependent priory of the great cathedral monastery of Ely. At the heart of Denny stand the medieval Franciscan refectory and the church. Begun by the Benedictines and adapted under the Templars, the church underwent its most radical alterations when Denny was given to the Countess of Pembroke in 1327. At the Farmland Museum discover farming through time and learn about the rural history of Cambridgeshire. Visit a traditional farmworker's cottage and see a magnificent 17th century stone barn and workshops.
Information services:
Special visitor services: Guided tours, materials and/or activities for children.
Education services: Group education facilities, resources for Key Stages 1 and 2, 3 and Further or Higher Education..
Collections:
Agricultural machinery, tools, furniture and furnishing, objects, local history
Catalogues:
Catalogue for part of the collections is only available in-house.
Printed publications:
Leaflet (free, directly)

781
DENNY SHIP MODEL EXPERIMENTAL TANK

Castle Street, Dumbarton, West Dunbartonshire, G82 1QS

Tel: 01389 763444
Fax: 01389 743093

Organisation type and purpose: Museum.
Affiliated to:
Scottish Maritime Museum
Gottries Road, Irvine, Ayrshire, KA12 8QE

Enquiries to: Research Officer
Access:
Access to staff: By letter, by telephone, in person
Access to building, collections or gallery: Prior appointment required

General description:
Ship hydrodynamics, model testing.
Collections:
Completed records of ship model hydrodynamics experiments conducted by Denny Brothers (shipbuilders) between 1883 and 1963 in the world's first commercially built ship model test tank

782
DEPARTMENT OF EARTH SCIENCE

See - University College London, Department of Earth Science

783
DEPARTMENT OF GEOLOGICAL SCIENCES

See - University College London, Department of Earth Science

784
DEPARTMENT OF INDUSTRY

See - National Museums and Galleries of Wales

785
DEPARTMENT OF SOUND RECORDS

See - Imperial War Museum

786
DEPARTMENT OF THE ENVIRONMENT FOR NORTHERN IRELAND

Environment and Heritage Service, Monuments and Buildings Record, 5-33 Hill Street, Belfast, BT1 2LA

Tel: 028 9054 3004
Fax: 028 9054 3111
Email: mbr@doeni.gov.uk
Acronym or abbreviation: MBR
Formed: 1992
Formerly: Archaeological Survey

Organisation type and purpose: National government body.
Parent body:
Department of the Environment
Clarence Court, Belfast, BT2 8GB, tel: 028 9054 0540

Enquiries to: Secretary
Access:
Access to staff: By letter, by telephone, by fax, by email, in person
Hours: 0930 to 1300, 1400 to 1630
Access for disabled people: ramped entry, toilet facilities

General description:
Archaeological sites, listed buildings listings, photographic and drawings archive library, historic monuments and buildings, historic gardens, industrial archaeology, maritime archaeology.
Collections:
Clokey collection (stained glass)
J S Curl photographic collection (of historic buildings)
McCutcheon archive (industrial archaeology)
McKinstry and McGeagh architectural archives
Northern Ireland sites and monuments record
Catalogues:
Catalogue for library is in-house only. Catalogue for all of the collections is only available in-house.
Printed publications:
Carrickfergus Castle, Co Antrim
Historic Monuments of Northern Ireland

Internet home pages:
http://www.ehsni.gov.uk

See also - Department of Regional Development

787
DERBY INDUSTRIAL MUSEUM

Full Street, Derby, DE1 3AR

Tel: 01332 255308
Fax: 01332 716670
Formed: 1974

Organisation type and purpose: Local government body, museum.
Parent body:
Derby City Museums
The Strand, Derby, DE1 2BS, tel: 01332 716659, fax: 01332 716670

Enquiries to: Curator
Access:
Access to staff: By letter, by telephone, visitors by prior appointment
Access to building, collections or gallery: No prior appointment required
Hours: Mon, 1100 to 1700; Tue to Sat, 1000 to 1700; Sun and Bank Holidays, 1400 to 1700
Other restrictions: Phone in advance for Christmas Opening Times.
Access for disabled people: level entry, access to all public areas, toilet facilities
Other restrictions: Parking provided if reserved in advance.

General description:
Museum is housed on the site of Lombe Brothers' Silk Mill, first factory in England (1721). It introduces visitors to Derbyshire's industrial history; local history (Derby); technology; railways and aero-engines. There are galleries on Railway Engineering and Research. The Power for Industry Gallery contains a number of stationary engines and hands-on displays. Visitors can also see the world's largest collection of Rolls-Royce aero engines. The Museum also has temporary exhibitions, a shop, and admission is free.
Information services:
Library available for reference (for conditions see Access above). Helpline available, tel no: 01332 255308.
Special visitor services: Guided tours, materials and/or activities for children.
Education services: Group education facilities, resources for Key Stages 1 and 2.
Services for disabled people: For the hearing impaired.
Collections:
Rolls-Royce, over 30 Derby built Rolls-Royce aero engines from 1915 to the present, 1904-present, c. 1000 items
Collection of Derby railway material especially the Midland Railway, 1839 to the present, c. 60,000 items
Lawnmowers of Qualcast of Derby, 1920-1984, c. 100 items
Fletcher and Stewart, Engine, bike of George Fletcher-Serger, machinery models of Fletcher and Stewart, 1840-1980, c. 50 items
Catalogues:
Catalogue for part of the collections is only available in-house.

Internet home pages:
http://www.derby.gov.uk/museums

788
DERBY MUSEUMS AND ART GALLERY

The Strand, Derby, DE1 1BS

Tel: 01332 716659
Minicom no. 01332 256666
Fax: 01332 716670
Formed: 1869
Formerly: Derby City Council

Organisation type and purpose: Local government body, museum, art gallery, suitable for ages: 5+.
Links with:
Friends of Derby Museums and Art Gallery at the same address
Other addresses:
Derby Industrial Museum
Full Street, Derby, DE1 3AR, tel: 01332 255308, fax: 01332 716670
Pickfords House Museum
41 Friargate, Derby, DE1 1DA, tel: 01332 255363, fax: 01332 255277

Enquiries to: Curator
Other contacts: Assistant Director, Development & Cultural Services
Access:
Access to staff: By letter, by telephone, by fax, in person, visitors by prior appointment
Access to building, collections or gallery: No prior appointment required
Hours: Mon, 1100 to 1700; Tue to Sat, 1000 to 1700; Sun & Bank Holidays, 1400 to 1700
Other restrictions: Admission free.
Access for disabled people: ramped entry, access to all public areas, toilet facilities

General description:
Fine and decorative art (especially the work of Joseph Wright, ARA), applied art (especially Derby porcelain), local archaeology, social history and natural history, coins, costume and textiles, toy theatres, military history, industry, Rolls Royce aero engines.
Information services:
Identification service (no valuations).
Education service.
Special visitor services: Guided tours, materials and/or activities for children.
Education services: Group education facilities, resources for Key Stages 1 and 2 and Further or Higher Education..

continued overleaf

Collections:
Alfred Goodey Collection (old Derby pictures)
Archive of local photographs
Derby Porcelain
Frank Bradley Toy Theatre Collection
Joseph Wright (1734-1797) Collection (Derby paintings and drawings)
Catalogues:
Catalogue for part of the collections is available in-house and part is on-line.
Publications list:
is available in hard copy.
Printed publications:
Postcards (historical images 18th century)
Catalogues and books
Slides (Joseph Wright)
Information Sheets
Joseph Wright of Derby (Fraser D, £1.95)
Wright of Derby (Egerton J, £35)
Joseph Wright Bicentenary Catalogue (Wallis J, £12)

Internet home pages:
http://www.derby.gov.uk/museums
Principal works by painter Joseph Wright (1734-97) and associated information.

See also - Derby Industrial Museum; Pickford's House Museum

789
DERBYSHIRE CONSTABULARY POLICE MEMORABILIA MUSEUM
16 St Mary's Gate, Derby, DE1 3JN

Formed: 1970

Organisation type and purpose: Local government body, museum, suitable for ages: 8+.
Connections with:
Police History Society

Enquiries to: Curator
Access:
Access to staff: By letter, in person
Hours: Tue, 0930 to 1230; Thu, 1330 to 1630
Access to building, collections or gallery: No prior appointment required
Hours: Tue, 0930 to 1230; Thu, 1330 to 1630
Access for disabled people: ramped entry, access to all public areas, toilet facilities

General description:
Museum of police history and artefacts.
Information services:
Services for disabled people: Displays and/or information at wheelchair height.
Collections:
PC John Cork Collection - British police helmet plates
Records of the Local Force, history of the County and Borough Forces
Truncheons, handcuffs and police uniforms
International displays

790
DERRY CITY COUNCIL HERITAGE & MUSEUMS SERVICE
See - Harbour Museum; Tower Museum

791
DERRYMORE HOUSE
Bessbrook, Newry, Co Armagh, BT35 7EF

Tel: 028 3083 8361

Organisation type and purpose: National organisation, registered charity (charity number 205846), historic building, house or site.
Parent body:
National Trust Office for Northern Ireland
Rowallane House, Saintfield, Ballynahinch, Co Down, BT24 7LH, tel: 020 9751 0721, fax: 028 9751 1242

Enquiries to: Manager
Access:
Access to staff: By letter, by telephone, in person
Access to building, collections or gallery: No prior appointment required
Hours: House: May to Aug, Thu, Fri, Sat, 1400 to 1730
Grounds: May to Sep, 1000 to 2000; Oct to Apr, 1000 to 1600
Other restrictions: Access to house by guided tour only.
Access for disabled people: Parking provided
Other restrictions: Designated parking 30yds. Steps to entrance. Ground floor fully accessible. Main access route through property could be used by wheelchair users with strong companion. Grounds accessible.

General description:
An elegant late 18th century thatched cottage, built by Isaac Corry, who represented Newry in the Irish House of Commons for thirty years from 1776. Set amidst a picturesque estate, it is typical of the informal thatched retreats boasted by many estates in the 18th century.
Information services:
Special visitor services: Guided tours..

Internet home pages:
http://www.ntni.org.uk

792
DERWENT ISLAND HOUSE
In Derwentwater, Cumbria

Tel: 0870 609 5391(Regional Office)
Email: derwentislandhouse@nationaltrust.org.uk

Organisation type and purpose: National organisation, registered charity (charity number 205846), historic building, house or site.
Parent body:
The National Trust (North West)
North West Regional Office, tel: 0870 609 5391

Enquiries to: Manager
Access:
Access to staff: By letter, by telephone, by email
Access to building, collections or gallery: Prior appointment required
Other restrictions: Admission is by timed ticket. The house is privately let, but parts are open to the public by booked timed ticket on five days of the year. For information, contact regional office. For booking form send s.a.e. to: The National Trust (Derwent Island Bookings), The Hollens

Grasmere, Ambleside, Cumbria LA22 9QZ.

General description:
An intriguing Italianate house of the 1840s, set on an idyllic wooded island in Derwentwater, with a restrained classical interior and restored garden.

Internet home pages:
http://www.nationaltrust.org.uk

793
DERWENT VALLEY MILLS
See - Belper North Mill Trust

794
DERWENTCOTE STEEL FURNACE
Forge Lane, Hamsterley Colliery, Newcastle upon Tyne, NE39 1QA

Organisation type and purpose: Historic building, house or site.
Parent body:
English Heritage (North East Region)
Tel: 0191 269 1227/8, fax: 0191 261 1130

Enquiries to: Manager
Other contacts: English Heritage (North East Region), tel 0161 242 1400

General description:
Built in the 18th century, Derwentcote is the earliest and most complete steel-making furnace to have survived.

Internet home pages:
http://www.english-heritage.org.uk

795
DESIGN MUSEUM
Butlers Wharf, 28 Shad Thames, London, SE1 2YD

Tel: 020 7403 6933
Fax: 020 7378 6540
Formed: 1989

Organisation type and purpose: Registered charity, museum.

Enquiries to: Curator
Access:
Access to staff: By letter only
Access to building, collections or gallery: No prior appointment required
Access for disabled people: access to all public areas, toilet facilities

General description:
The Design Museum collection comprises industrial-designed, mass-produced consumer products and graphics, largely from the 20th and 21st Centuries. The collection covers furniture, domestic appliances, consumer electronic products, cameras, glass and ceramics, office equipment, road transport and architecture.
Information services:
Education services: Group education facilities, resources for Key Stages 1 and 2, 3, 4 and Further or Higher Education.
Services for disabled people: Displays and/or information at wheelchair height.
Collections:
A collection of industrial produced design from the 20th and 21st century including furniture, tableware, lighting, packaging, product design and transport
The Design Museum also manages the Heal's archive. Please note: the archive is not open for public access.
Catalogues:
Catalogue for library is in-house only. Catalogue for all of the collections is available in-house and part is on-line.

Internet home pages:
http://www.designmuseum.org

796
DEVON GUILD OF CRAFTSMEN
Riverside Mill, Bovey Tracey, Devon, TQ13 9AF

Tel: 01626 832223
Fax: 01626 834220
Email: devonguild@crafts.org.uk
Formed: 1955

Organisation type and purpose: Registered charity (charity number 296568), art gallery, suitable for ages: 5+.

Enquiries to: Assistant Director
Direct email: jenny@crafts.org.uk
Other contacts: Exhibitions Officer for forthcoming exhibitions and policy.
Access:
Access to staff: By letter, by telephone, by fax, by email, in person
Access for disabled people: Parking provided, level entry
Other restrictions: Access to downstairs facilities only, craft showrooms, exhibition areas, café.

General description:
The South West's leading gallery and craft shop selling and exhibiting craftwork from over 240 designer/makers specialising in contemporary art and craft work, including ceramics; wood; textiles; jewellery; furniture; metalwork; and original prints. Gallery café with outdoor seating, commissioning resource, wedding list, Artcred, Crafts Council Photostore.
Information services:
Education services: Group education facilities, resources for Key Stages 1 and 2, 3, 4 and Further or Higher Education.

Services for disabled people: Displays and/or information at wheelchair height.
Collections:
Crafts Council Photostore touch screen facility - access to over 40,000 craftworks
Commissioning Resource - folders of work and makers
Small Library
Craft Shop exhibiting work selected from around 240 makers
Changing themed and touring exhibitions in upstairs gallery space
Photographic portraits of members of the Devon Guild, taken by Alan Richards, FRSP, part of a continuing project, 1988- present, c. 200 items

Internet home pages:
http://www.crafts.org.uk
Online craft shop, education and information resource, over 200 makes and work represented with images.

797
DEVONSHIRE COLLECTION OF PERIOD COSTUME
See - Totnes Costume Museum

798
DEWA ROMAN EXPERIENCE
Pierpoint Lane, Off Bridge Street, Chester, Cheshire, CH1 2BJ

Tel: 01244 343407
Fax: 01244 347737
Formed: 1993

Organisation type and purpose: Independently owned, museum, suitable for ages: all ages but particularly Key Stage 2 History.
Education, hands-on.

Enquiries to: Manager
Access:
Access to staff: By letter, by telephone, by fax, in person
Access for disabled people: ramped entry
Other restrictions: 90% disabled access.

General description:
Reconstructions and a traditional museum section help explain Roman social and military history and its relation to Chester and the North West.
The subject of archaeology is introduced in the form of open excavations and artefact handling.
Guided tours of the centre, and external Roman Soldier Patrols, can be booked to give a deeper understanding and enjoyment of these subjects.
Information services:
Special visitor services: Guided tours, materials and/or activities for children.
Education services: Group education facilities, resources for Key Stages 1 and 2, 3, 4 and Further or Higher Education.
Services for disabled people: Displays and/or information at wheelchair height.
Collections:
Open excavations showing Roman, Saxon, medieval and post-medieval layers and archaeology
Roman finds displayed, from Chester and the Roman Empire
Printed publications:
Teachers Resource Pack (available for purchase)

799
DICK INSTITUTE ART GALLERY & MUSEUM
Dick Institute, Elmbank Avenue, Kilmarnock, Ayrshire, KA1 3BU

Tel: 01563 554343
Fax: 01563 554344
Email: museums@east-ayrshire.gov.uk
Formed: 1901

Organisation type and purpose: Local government body, museum, art gallery, suitable for ages: all ages.

Enquiries to: Manager
Access:
Access to staff: By letter, by telephone, by fax, by email, visitors by prior appointment
Access for disabled people: Parking provided, ramped entry, access to all public areas, toilet facilities

General description:
Temporary and permanent exhibitions over two floors of this grand Victorian building. Fine art, social and natural history collections are upstairs, whilst galleries downstairs house temporary exhibitions of visual art and craft. Free admission, craft shop sells locally made items.

Internet home pages:
http://www.eastayrshire.gov.uk
General information on museums in East Ayrshire.

800
DICKENS HOUSE MUSEUM AND LIBRARY
48 Doughty Street, London, WC1N 2LX

Tel: 020 7405 2127
Fax: 020 7831 5175
Email: dhmuseum@rmplc.co.uk
Formed: 1925

Organisation type and purpose: Registered charity (charity number 212172), museum, research organisation.
Houses, and is closely linked with, the:
Dickens Fellowship

Enquiries to: Curator
Access:
Access to staff: By letter, by telephone, by fax, by email, visitors by prior appointment, Internet web pages
Hours: Mon to Fri, 1000 to 1700

General description:
Charles Dickens and his works.
Collections:
Aylmer Papers
Carlton Papers
Matz Collection
Storey Papers
Suzannet Collection
Wright Papers

Internet home pages:
http://www.dickensmuseum.com
Information about museum and services.

801
DICKENS HOUSE MUSEUM
Victoria Parade, Broadstairs, Kent, CT10 1QS

Tel: 01843 861232
Fax: 01843 863453
Email: aleeault@aol.com
Formed: 1973

Organisation type and purpose: Local government body, learned society, museum, historic building, house or site, suitable for ages: all ages.
Celebrating Dickens association with Broadstairs where he spent holidays here from 1837 to 1851.

Enquiries to: Curator
Direct tel: 01843 863453
Access:
Access to staff: By letter, by telephone, by fax, by email
Access to building, collections or gallery: No prior appointment required

General description:
Dickens memorabilia; letters; prints; photographs Dickensian and local; costume and Victoriana.
Information services:
Library available for reference (for conditions see Access above). Helpline available, tel no: 01843 863453.
Special visitor services: Guided tours, materials and/or activities for children.
Education services: Group education facilities.
Services for disabled people: Displays and/or information at wheelchair height.
Catalogues:
Catalogue for library is in-house only. Catalogue for all of the collections is only available in-house.

Internet home pages:
http://www.dickenshouse.co.uk

802
DINEFWR
Llandeilo, Carmarthenshire, SA19 6RT

Tel: 01558 823902
Fax: 01558 825925
Email: dinefwr@nationaltrust.org.uk
Formed: 1996

Organisation type and purpose: National organisation, registered charity (charity number 205846), historic building, house or site, suitable for ages: all ages.
Parent body:
The National Trust Office for Wales
Tel: 01492 860123, fax: 01492 860233

Enquiries to: Manager
Access:
Access to staff: By letter, by telephone, by fax, visitors by prior appointment
Other restrictions: Limited staff presence Tue, Wed in open season.
Access to building, collections or gallery: No prior appointment required
Hours: Easter to November, Mon, Thu to Sun, 1100 to 1700
Other restrictions: Last admission 1615. On Tues and Wed the house is available for pre-arranged private events.
Access for disabled people: Parking provided, ramped entry, toilet facilities
Other restrictions: Drop-off point. 1 manual wheelchair available, booking essential. Ground floor fully accessible. No access to other floors. Ramped entrance to tea-room.

General description:
An 18th century landscape park, enclosing a medieval deer park, Dinefwr is home to more than one hundred fallow deer and a small herd of Dinefwr White Park Cattle. A number of scenic walks are available including access to Dinefwr Castle, with fine views across the Towy Valley. There is also a wooded boardwalk, particularly suitable for families and wheelchair users. Newton House, built in 1660, but now with a Victorian façade and a fountain garden, is at the heart of the site. It has two showrooms open to the public, a tea-room which looks out onto the deer park, and an exhibition on the history of Dinefwr in the basement.
Information services:
Guided tours by appointment. Badger watches can also be booked.
Events during season.
Braille guide.
Suitable for school groups. Education room/ centre. Children's quiz/trail.
Special visitor services: Guided tours, materials and/or activities for children.
Education services: Group education facilities, resources for Key Stages 1 and 2 and 3.
Services for disabled people: For the visually impaired.
Collections:
Collections are on loan from various sources

Internet home pages:
http://www.nationaltrust.org.uk

803
DINOSAUR ISLE
Culver Parade, Sandown, Isle of Wight, PO36 8QA

Tel: 01983 404344
Fax: 01983 407502
Email: dinosaur@iow.gov.uk
Formed: 1914

continued overleaf

Formed from: Isle of Wight Geological Museum, date of change, 2001

Organisation type and purpose: Local government body, museum, suitable for ages: 5+.

Enquiries to: Curator
Other contacts: Administration Officer for bookings.
Access:
Access to staff: By letter, by telephone, by fax, by email, in person
Access to building, collections or gallery: No prior appointment required
Hours: Oct to Mar: daily, 1000 to 1600
Apr to Sep: daily, 1000 to 1800
Access for disabled people: Parking provided, level entry, access to all public areas, toilet facilities

General description:
Displays of Isle of Wight geology and palaeontology, mostly relating to 125 million year old dinosaurs.
Information services:
Library available for reference (for conditions see Access above)
Special visitor services: Materials and/or activities for children.
Education services: Group education facilities, resources for Key Stages 1 and 2, 3, 4 and Further or Higher Education.
Services for disabled people: For the visually impaired; for the hearing impaired; displays and/or information at wheelchair height.
Collections:
Fossils, invertebrates, vertebrates and plants of cretaceous, palaeogene and quaternary ages

Internet home pages:
http://www.miwg.freeserve.co.uk/index.htm

804
DINOSAUR MUSEUM
Icen Way, Dorchester, Dorset, DT1 1EW

Tel: 01305 269880
Fax: 01305 268885
Email: info@dinosaur-museum.org.uk
Formed: 1984

Organisation type and purpose: Museum.
Parent body:
World Heritage
25 High West Street, Dorchester, Dorset, DT1 1UW, tel: 01305 269741, fax: 01305 268885

Enquiries to: Curator
Direct tel: 01305 269741
Access:
Access to staff: By letter, by telephone, by fax, by email, in person, Internet web pages
Hours: Mon to Fri, 0930 to 1730
Access to building, collections or gallery: No prior appointment required
Hours: All year, daily, 0930 to 1730

General description:
Dinosaurs; their evolution, development and extinction, fossilisation and palaeontology, the science of dinosaurs.
Information services:
Education services: Group education facilities, resources for Key Stage 1.
Services for disabled people: Displays and/or information at wheelchair height.
Collections:
Computer and hands-on displays
Fossils: both dinosaurian and contemporary
Life-size reconstructions of dinosaurs
Printed publications:
Wide range of books by other publishers on dinosaurs, and fossilization, available directly from the shop or by mail order
Electronic and video products:
Dinosaur videos and computer programs

Internet home pages:
http://www.dinosaur-museum.org.uk

805
DINOSAURLAND
Jurassic Attraction, Coombe Street, Lyme Regis, Dorset, DT7 3PY

Tel: 01297 443541
Email: steve@dinosaurland.co.uk
Formed: 1995

Organisation type and purpose: Museum.

Enquiries to: Curator
Access:
Access to staff: By letter, by email, visitors by prior appointment
Access to building, collections or gallery: No access other than to staff
Hours: Mon to Sun 1000 to 1700

General description:
Dinosaurs. Contains fossils collected along the Dorset coast. Includes ammonites; Ichthyosaur; Plesiosaur; and other marine fossils. A geological timescale puts the exhibits in perspective. There are also live fish, reptiles and birds. The History Room illustrates the history of Lyme Regis.

Internet home pages:
http://www.dinosaurland.co.uk

806
DISCOVER
383-387 High Street, Stratford, London, E15 4QZ

Tel: 020 8536 5540
Fax: 020 8522 1003
Formed: 1998
Formerly: Children's Discovery Centre, date of change, 2001

Organisation type and purpose: Membership association, registered charity (charity number 1070468), museum, suitable for ages: 2 to 7 years.
Hands-on learning centre for children aged 2 to 7 and their parents, carers and teachers, theme of stories.

Enquiries to: Assistant Director
Direct tel: 020 8536 5544
Direct email: anna.salaman@childrensdiscoverycentre.com
Access:
Access to staff: By letter, by telephone, by fax, by email
Access to building, collections or gallery: Prior appointment required
Hours: Daily, 1000 to 1700
Access for disabled people: Parking provided, ramped entry, level entry, access to all public areas, toilet facilities

General description:
Early years literacy, stories.
Information services:
Education services: Group education facilities, resources for Key Stage 1..
Collections:
Hands-on exhibitions on theme of stories to motivate visitors to use their imaginations
Publications list:
is available in hard copy.
Printed publications:
Off to a Flying Start - A creative partnership between Discover and Newham Sure Start
Playing to Learn? The Educational Role of Children's Museums Hands On! Europe Conference 2001

Internet home pages:
http://www.childrensdiscoverycentre.com
Describes organisation and its activities, showcases projects and provides a forum for children's creative work.

807
DISCOVERY CENTRE
See - Thinktank - Birmingham Museum of Science and Discovery

808
DISCOVERY MUSEUM
Blandford Square, Newcastle upon Tyne, NE1 4JA

Tel: 0191 232 6789
Fax: 0191 230 2614
Email: discovery@twmuseums.org.uk
Formed: 1934

Organisation type and purpose: Local government body, registered charity, museum, suitable for ages: 5+.
Parent body:
Tyne & Wear Museums (TWM)
Discovery Museum, at the same address

Enquiries to: Curator
Other contacts: Education Officer for school visits and activities.
Access:
Access to staff: By letter, by telephone, by fax
Other restrictions: By prior appointment only.
Access to building, collections or gallery: No prior appointment required
Hours: Mon to Sat, 1000 to 1700; Sun, 1400 to 1700
Access for disabled people: level entry, access to all public areas, toilet facilities

General description:
Interactive science gallery, Turbinia - the record-breaking ship, fashion gallery, history of Newcastle gallery from Romans to present, maritime gallery.
Information services:
Special visitor services: Materials and/or activities for children.
Education services: Group education facilities, resources for Key Stages 1 and 2, 3, 4 and Further or Higher Education.
Services for disabled people: For the visually impaired; for the hearing impaired; displays and/or information at wheelchair height.
Collections:
Science & industry - working engines, Turbinia
Maritime - ship models and full-size craft
Costume and textiles
Social history
Military
Examples of world 'Firsts' include
Charles Parson's Turbinia, the first vessel to be powered by steam turbine
Joseph Swan's historic lightbulbs

Internet home pages:
http://www.twmuseums.org
Facilities, galleries, collections, education activities.

809
DISCOVERY OUTPOST
See - Look Out Discovery Centre

810
DISCOVERY POINT
See - Royal Research Ship Discovery

811
DISCOVERY QUAY ENTERPRISES LIMITED

Acronym or abbreviation: DQE
See - National Maritime Museum Cornwall

812
DITCHLING MUSEUM
Church Lane, Ditchling, West Sussex, BN6 8TB

Tel: 01273 844744
Fax: 01273 844744
Email: info@ditchling-museum.com
Formed: 1985

Organisation type and purpose: Local government body, registered charity, museum, historic building, house or site, suitable for ages: all ages.
Links with:
Friends Association

Enquiries to: Director
Access:
Access to staff: By letter, by telephone, by email, visitors by prior appointment, Internet web pages
Hours: Mon to Fri, 1030 to 1700
Access to building, collections or gallery: No prior appointment required
Hours: Mid Feb to mid Dec: Tue to Sat and Bank Holidays, 1030 to 1700; Sun, 1400 to 1700
Access for disabled people: Parking provided, ramped entry, access to all public areas, toilet facilities

General description:
Local history of Ditchling and its arts and crafts heritage. Housed in a late Victorian village school the collection features the farmer and his wife in their Victorian kitchen; farm crafts and implements; local prehistory and history; period costumes in appropriate settings; Victorian-Edwardian toys and children's illustrated books; and numerous examples of embroidery and stitch work.
Information services:
Library available for reference (for conditions see Access above)
Special visitor services: Guided tours, materials and/or activities for children.
Education services: Group education facilities, resources for Key Stages 1 and 2, 3, 4 and Further or Higher Education..
Collections:
Information on 20th century artists and craftsmen
Work of the arts and crafts community established by Eric Gill and Hilary Pepler. Collections of work of Eric Gill, Edward Johnston, Ethel Mairet, Sir Frank Brangwyn, David Jones; examples include sculpture, printing, weaving, silversmithing
Permanent collection (in the new Hilary Bourne Gallery) of work by Eric Gill, Edward Johnston, the St Dominic's Press, David Jones, Joseph Cribb, Philip Hagreen, Valentine Kilbride, Dunstan Pruden and other members of the Guild of St George and St Dominic, with other famous artists of the 1920s.
Small collection of calligrapher Edward Johnston's work, painter Frank Brangwyn and Ethel Mairet, weaver
Catalogues:
Catalogue for library is in-house only. Catalogue for all of the collections is only available in-house but part is published.
Printed publications:
Font (£7.50)
Spring Lines (£9)
Exhibition Catalogues
Handwriting Everyones Art (£7.50)
Electronic and video products:
Hilary Bourne in Ditchling (video, £11.99)

Internet home pages:
http://www.ditchling-museum.com
Museum opening times, exhibitions programme, introduction to collection, general introduction to arts and crafts, educational material (in development).

813
DOBWALLS ADVENTURE PARK
See - John Southern Gallery

814
DOCK MUSEUM
North Road, Barrow-in-Furness, Cumbria, LA14 2PW

Tel: 01229 894444
Fax: 01229 811361
Email: dockmuseum@barrowbc.gov.uk
Formed: 1994

Organisation type and purpose: Local government body, museum, suitable for ages: all ages.

Enquiries to: Operations Manager
Other contacts: Collections Officer for curatorial matters.
Access:
Access to staff: By letter, by telephone, by fax, by email, visitors by prior appointment, Internet web pages
Other restrictions: Appointments required for access to Operations Manager and Collections Officer.
Access to building, collections or gallery: No prior appointment required
Hours: High Season: Tue to Sun
Low Season: Wed to Sun
Other restrictions: Prior appointments required for access to Reserve Collections.
Access for disabled people: Parking provided, ramped entry, access to all public areas, toilet facilities
Other restrictions: Passenger lift, hearing loop, information in Braille and large print, personal guide available for visualy impaired visitors.

General description:
Maritime, industrial and social history of Barrow-in-Furness, archaeology; fine art; geology; and natural history.
Information services:
Special visitor services: Guided tours, tape recorded guides, materials and/or activities for children.
Education services: Group education facilities, resources for Key Stages 1 and 2 and Further or Higher Education.
Services for disabled people: For the visually impaired; for the hearing impaired; displays and/or information at wheelchair height.
Collections:
VSEL Glass Negative Archive. Photographic collection covering the development of Barrow shipyard. 1870-1950, 11,000 negatives
VSEL Shipmodel Collection. Significant British ships originating from Barrow shipyard. 1881-1950, 11 items
Fine Art Collection
Publications list:
is available on-line.
Printed publications:
The Barrow Story (Apr 2000)
Electronic and video products:
Reflections in the Dock (video)

Internet home pages:
http://www.dockmuseum.co.uk
Time-line of museum, collection information, visitor service information, booking forms, education service, events, exhibitions.

815
DOCKLANDS FORUM
See - Museum in Docklands

816
DOLAUCOTHI GOLD MINES
Pumsaint, Llanwrda, Carmarthenshire, SA19 8RR

Tel: 01558 650177 (Admissions and booking), 01558 650707 (Estate Office)
Fax: 01588 01558 650707
Email: dolaucothi@nationaltrust.org.uk

Organisation type and purpose: National organisation, registered charity (charity number 205846), historic building, house or site, suitable for ages: 12+.
Parent body:
The National Trust Office for Wales
Trinity Square, Llandudno, LL30 2DE, tel: 01492 860123, fax: 01492 860233

Enquiries to: Manager
Access:
Access to staff: By telephone, by email
Access to building, collections or gallery: No prior appointment required
Hours: Apr to Oct: daily, 1000 to1700
Other restrictions: Last tour 1630
Access for disabled people: ramped entry
Other restrictions: Drop-off point. Ground floor largely accessible, Ramps into all but 2 buildings. Audio-visual/video. Ramped entrance to shop and to tearoom.

General description:
These unique gold mines are set amid wooded hillsides overlooking the beautiful Cothi Valley. The Romans who exploited the site almost 2000 years ago left behind a complex of pits, channels, adits and tanks. Mining resumed in the 19th century and continued through the 20th century, reaching a peak in 1938. Guided tours take visitors through the Roman and more recent underground workings. The main mine yard contains a collection of 1930's mining machinery and an exhibition explaining the history of the site, video and interpretation. Gold-panning gives visitors the opportunity to experience the frustrations of the search for gold. Other attractions include waymarked walks, cycle hire and Information Centre in Pumpsaint.
Information services:
Helpline available, tel no: Infoline 01558 650146.
Underground guided tours, tel for information.
Suitable for school groups. Education room/centre. Children's quiz/trail.
Special visitor services: Guided tours, materials and/or activities for children.
Education services: Group education facilities, resources for Key Stage 2..

Internet home pages:
http://www.nationaltrust.org.uk

817
DOLLAR MUSEUM
Castle Campbell Hall, High Street, Dollar, Clackmannanshire, FK14 7AY

Email: curator.dollarmuseum@btopenworld.com
Formerly: Dollar Museum Trust

Organisation type and purpose: Membership association (membership is by subscription), present number of members: 205 (friends), registered charity (charity number SC 022185), museum.

Enquiries to: Curator
Direct tel: 01259 742895
Access:
Access to staff: By letter, by telephone
Access to building, collections or gallery: No access other than to staff
Hours: Sat, 1100 to 1300 and 1400 to 1630; Sun, 1400 to 1630
Other restrictions: Other times by appointment with the Curator.
Access for disabled people: Parking provided, ramped entry, toilet facilities

General description:
Local history; Devon Valley railway.
Collections:
Peter Wilson collection of many photographs and memorabilia of the Devon Valley Railway (Alloa-Kinross), 1940s-1974
Catalogues:
Catalogue for all of the collections is only available in-house.

818
DOLLS MUSEUM
198 High Street, Musselburgh, Midlothian, EH21 7DX

Tel: 0131 665 5012
Fax: 0131 665 5012
Formed: 2002

Organisation type and purpose: Independently owned, museum, suitable for ages: 5+.

Enquiries to: Curator
Access:
Access to staff: By letter, by telephone, by fax
Access to building, collections or gallery: No prior appointment required
Access for disabled people: ramped entry, level entry, access to all public areas, toilet facilities

continued overleaf

General description:
Display of dolls and Royalty Collection, sale of goods displayed.
Information services:
Services for disabled people: Displays and/or information at wheelchair height.

819
DOLPHIN SAILING BARGE MUSEUM

Crown Quay Lane, Sittingbourne, Kent, ME10 3SN

Tel: 01795 424132
Formed: 1968

Organisation type and purpose: Registered charity (charity number 260519), museum. Independent museum staffed by volunteers.
Other address:
Dolphin Sailing Barge Museum
c/o 131 Milton High Street, Sittingbourne, Kent, ME10 2AR, tel: 01795 423215

Enquiries to: Honorary Secretary
Access:
Access to staff: By letter, by telephone, in person, visitors by prior appointment
Hours: Answerphone
Access to building, collections or gallery: No prior appointment required
Hours: Easter to End Oct: Sun and Bank Holidays, 1100 to 1700
Other restrictions: Museum can be opened at mutually convenient times; preferably for groups or parties.
Access for disabled people: Parking provided, level entry, toilet facilities

General description:
The museum specialises in the Thames Spritsail Barge (c. 1800-1950), displaying barge building tools, artefacts and pictures in an original shipwright's shop, sail-loft and forge. The Basin contains barges undergoing repair. The history and development of the Thames Sailing Barge and details of barges currently in full sailing condition.
Collections:
Small collection of books, booklets, leaflets on barges plus a collection of photographs, prints and drawings of barges
Barge builders' tools, 1800-1950, 100 items
Sail-makers' tools and materials, 1800-1950
Blacksmiths' forge and tools, 1800-1950
Brickmakers' tools and specimen bricks, 1800-1950
Models of barges, fully rigged, 1800-1950
Barge Yard operational and Steam Chest
Set of barge blocks with a barge using them
Catalogues:
Catalogue for library is in-house only.
Trade and statistical:
Access to details of all sailing barges built in Kent and Essex since 1800.
Publications list:
is available in hard copy.
Printed publications:
The Story of a Sailmaker (booklet)
Photographs of barges

Address for ordering publications:
Printed publications:
Dolphin Sailing Barge Museum
131 Milton High Street, Sittingbourne, Kent, ME10 2AR, tel: 01795 423215

820
DONCASTER AEROVENTURE

See - South Yorkshire Aviation Museum

821
DONINGTON GRAND PRIX COLLECTION, THE

Donington Park, Castle Donington, Derby, DE74 2RP

Tel: 01332 811027
Fax: 01332 812892
Email: enquiries@doningtoncollection.co.uk
Formed: 1973

Organisation type and purpose: Independently owned, museum, suitable for ages: 5+.

Enquiries to: Manager
Access:
Access to staff: By letter, by telephone, by fax, by email, in person, Internet web pages
Access for disabled people: Parking provided, ramped entry, access to all public areas

General description:
100 years of motorsport history.
Information services:
Special visitor services: Guided tours, materials and/or activities for children.
Services for disabled people: Displays and/or information at wheelchair height.
Collections:
Motorsport History:
From the turn of the 20th century to the New Millennium, its all here:
the largest collection of McLaren racing cars on public display
the world's only complete collection of the famous racing green Vanwalls
every Williams F1 car from 1983 to 1999
a superb BRM display
more rare four wheel drive racing cards than anywhere else
Ferraris driven by Ascari and Ichx
Senna's winning McLaren from the 1993 European Grand Prix at Donington
Stirling Moss's Lotus which defeated the might of the works Ferrari at Monaco in 1961
Jim Clark's beautiful Lotus 25
Ronnie Peterson's unique 6 wheel Tyrrell
several other examples of this marque including Jackie Stewart's Tyrrell 001
Plus many, many more
Printed publications:
Souvenir guide and inventory

Internet home pages:
http://www.doningtoncollection.com
Details of the collection, opening times, admission prices, directions.

822
DONINGTON-LE HEATH MANOR HOUSE, THE

Manor Road, Donington-le-Heath, Coalville, Leicestershire, LE67 2FW

Tel: 01530 831259
Fax: 01530 831259
Email: museums@leics.gov.uk
Formed: 1290

Organisation type and purpose: Local government body, museum, historic building, house or site, suitable for ages: all ages.
Parent body:
Leicestershire Museums Arts & Records Service
Leicestershire County Council (LMARS)
County Hall, Glenfield, Leicestershire, LE3 8TB

Enquiries to: Curator
Direct tel: 0116 2656791
Direct fax: 0116 2652788
Other contacts: Keeper of Archaeology for advice on archaeology of Leicestershire.
Access:
Access to staff: By telephone
Hours: Mon to Fri, 1100 to 1700
Other restrictions: Closed weekdays Dec to Feb.
Access to building, collections or gallery: No prior appointment required
Hours: Oct to Mar: daily, 1100 to 1500
Apr to Sep: daily, 1100 to 1700
Access for disabled people: Parking provided, ramped entry, toilet facilities
Other restrictions: Photograph album of inaccessible areas, touch and smell table for visually impaired. Gardens and tea-room.

General description:
Archaeology of Leicestershire, local history. Listed stone building dating from late 13th century with 17th century refurbishments. The site has a 17th century style garden with ornamental maze. The four-poster bed is reputed to have been slept in by Richard III.
Information services:
Helpline available, tel no: 0116 2656791.
Special visitor services: Guided tours, materials and/or activities for children.
Education services: Group education facilities, resources for Key Stages 2, 3 and 4.
Services for disabled people: For the visually impaired; for the hearing impaired; displays and/or information at wheelchair height.
Collections:
Museum of archaeology - local archaeology on display
Regular change of temporary exhibitions
Publications list:
is available in hard copy.

823
DORCHESTER ABBEY MUSEUM

Abbey Guest House, Dorchester-on-Thames, Oxfordshire, OX10 7HZ

Formed: 1959

Organisation type and purpose: Registered charity, museum.
Parent body:
Dorchester Abbey PCC

Enquiries to: Secretary
Direct tel: 01865 340751
Access:
Access to staff: By letter only
Hours: 1 May to 30 Sep only: Tue to Sat, 1100 to 1700; Sun, 1400 to 1700

General description:
The theme of the Museum shows evidence of continuity and change in Dorchester and its neighbourhood from 2500 BC with the Abbey as the centre of Christian and community life. The Museum building itself, dating from the 14th and 15th Centuries, is part of this history.

824
DORKING & DISTRICT MUSEUM

The Old Foundry, 62 West Street, Dorking, Surrey, RH4 1BS

Tel: 01306 876591
Formed: 1976
Formerly: Dorking and District Preservation Society

Organisation type and purpose: Independently owned, voluntary organisation, registered charity (charity number 246806), museum, suitable for ages: 8+.
Parent body:
The Dorking and District Preservation Society
Affiliated to the:
Surrey Museums Group

Enquiries to: Honorary Secretary
Direct tel: 01306 743821
Access:
Access to staff: By letter, by telephone
Hours: Wed and Thu, 1400 to 1700; Sat, 1000 to 1600
Access to building, collections or gallery: No access other than to staff
Hours: Wed and Thu, 1400 to 1700; Sat, 1000 to 1600
Access for disabled people: level entry

General description:
Collection of domestic bygones and agricultural implements illustrating the history of Dorking and surrounding villages. Contains Lord Ashcombe's collection of minerals and fossils. The library (in an adjoining building) contains books and records illustrative of Dorking's social history, including census returns, parish registers, and newspaper cuttings from late 19th century. There is also a very large collection of photographs, sales particulars of properties, and maps covering a wide historical spectrum, a fine collection of paintings by local artists (some of

which are now being restored) and a collection of costumes.
Information services:
Library available for reference (for conditions see Access above)
Special visitor services: Guided tours, materials and/or activities for children.
Education services: Group education facilities, resources for Key Stages 1 and 2.
Services for disabled people: Displays and/or information at wheelchair height.
Collections:
Lord Ashcombe's Collection of minerals and fossils
General information on Vaughan Williams, one-time resident in Dorking and the Leith Hill Music Festival, of which he was the founder
Catalogues:
Catalogue for library is in-house only.
Publications list:
is available on-line.
Printed publications:
Leaflet about the museum
A number of publications written by members of the sister organisation, the Dorking Local History Group

825
DORMAN MUSEUM
Linthorpe Road, Middlesbrough, North Yorkshire, TS5 6LA

Tel: 01642 813781
Formed: 1904

Organisation type and purpose: Museum, suitable for ages: all ages.
Archives and Library.

Enquiries to: Curator
Direct tel: 01642 358103
Direct fax: 01642 358100
Direct email: ken_sedman@middlesbrough.gov.uk
Access:
Access to staff: By letter, by telephone, by fax, in person, visitors by prior appointment
Hours: Tue to Sat, 1000 to 1730; Sun, 1430 to 1700
Access to building, collections or gallery: Prior appointment required
Hours: Mon to Fri, 0900 to 1600
Access for disabled people: Parking provided, ramped entry, access to all public areas, toilet facilities

General description:
The museum reflects the local and industrial history of Middlesbrough and its surrounding area, it includes: natural sciences, archaeology, local history, local pottery, Linthorpe Art Pottery, costume, library, photographs and archives.
Information services:
Library available for reference (for conditions see Access above)
Special visitor services: Guided tours, materials and/or activities for children.
Education services: Group education facilities, resources for Key Stages 1 and 2, 3 and 4.
Services for disabled people: For the visually impaired; for the hearing impaired; displays and/or information at wheelchair height.
Collections:
Frank Elgee Archaeology Collection
E Simpson. British fossils. Early 20th century. 500 items
L Greenbank. Northern England minerals. 1970-. 30 items
Linthorpe pottery.
Local art pottery (including Christopher Dresser Designs)
Herbarium. Margaret Stovin (traveller) collection of pressed plants and flowers
Rev J Hawell. Marske Quarry Jurassic plants. 1903. 150 items
R W Barstow. UK minerals. 1960-. 200 items
T H Nelson Collection of large stuffed birds, eggs. nests and library

Printed publications:
A Catalogue of the Herbarium of the British Flora - Collected by Margaret Stonian (1756-1846) (Simmons M)
James Cook Genealogical Study (Burnicle A)
Electronic and video products:
Transporter Bridge Interactive, includes history of St Hilda's area (CD-ROM)
Town in Time - Songs and Tunes of Middlesbrough by Richard Grainger (CD-ROM, audio tape)

826
DORNEYWOOD GARDEN
Dorneywood, Burnham, Buckinghamshire, SL1 8PY

Tel: 01494 528051 (Regional Office)
Email: dorneywood@nationaltrust.org.uk

Organisation type and purpose: National organisation, registered charity (charity number 205846), historic building, house or site.
Parent body:
National Trust (South and South East Region)
Thames & Solent Regional Office, tel: 01491 528051, fax: 01491 463310

Enquiries to: Manager
Access:
Access to staff: By letter only

General description:
The house was given to the National Trust as an official residence for either a Secretary of State or Minister of the Crown. Only the garden is open, with herbaceous borders, a rose garden, cottage and kitchen gardens maintained in the style of the 1930s.
Conservatory and lily pond.

Internet home pages:
http://www.nationaltrust.org.uk

827
DORSET COUNTY MUSEUM
High Street West, Dorchester, Dorset, DT1 1XA

Tel: 01305 262735
Fax: 01305 257180
Email: dorsetcountymuseum@dor-mus.demon.co.uk
Formed: 1846

Organisation type and purpose: Learned society (membership is by subscription), present number of members: 2100, voluntary organisation, museum, suitable for ages: 6 to 16, research organisation, publishing house.
Parent body:
Dorset Natural History and Archaeological Society (DNH&AS)

Enquiries to: Curator
Access:
Access to staff: By letter, by telephone, by fax, by email, visitors by prior appointment, charges to non-members
Hours: Mon to Fri, 1000 to 1700
Access to building, collections or gallery: No prior appointment required
Hours: Mon to Fri, 1000 to 1700
Other restrictions: No prior appointment required for members.

General description:
Archaeology; palaeontology; natural history; local history; maps; photographs; literary archives; prints and watercolours.
Catalogues:
Catalogue for library is in-house only. Catalogue for all of the collections is only available in-house.
Publications list:
is available in hard copy.
Printed publications:
Books, proceedings, monographs, newsletters, annual report

828
DORSET MILITARY MUSEUM
See - Military Museum of Devon and Dorset

829
DORSET REGIMENT MUSEUM
See - Military Museum of Devon and Dorset

830
DORSET TEDDY BEAR HOUSE
Antelope Walk, Dorchester, Dorset, DT1 1BE

Tel: 01305 263200
Fax: 01305 268885
Email: info@teddybearhouse.co.uk
Full name: The Dorset Teddy Bear Museum and Teddy Bear House
Formed: 1995
Formerly: Teddy Bear House

Organisation type and purpose: Museum.
Parent body:
World Heritage
25 High West Street, Dorchester, Dorset, tel: 01305 269741, fax: 01305 268885, email: info@world-heritage.org.uk

Enquiries to: Manager
Direct tel: 01305 269741
Direct fax: 01305 268885
Access:
Access to staff: By letter, by telephone, by fax, by email, in person, visitors by prior appointment, Internet web pages
Hours: Mon to Fri, 0930 to 1700
Access to building, collections or gallery: No prior appointment required
Hours: All year, daily, 0930 to 1700

General description:
Teddy Bears, their history.
Collections:
Hundreds of teddy bears from the very earliest bears of the 1900s to the modern day. Famous bears such as Winnie the Pooh, Paddington and Rupert, plus some special human-sized bears in an Edwardian home setting

Internet home pages:
http://www.teddybearhouse.co.uk

831
DOUGHTY MUSEUM
See - Welholme Galleries

832
SIR HENRY DOULTON GALLERY
See - Royal Doulton Visitor Centre & Sir Henry Doulton Gallery

833
DOVE COTTAGE AND THE WORDSWORTH MUSEUM
Grasmere, Ambleside, Cumbria, LA22 9SH

Tel: 015394 35544
Fax: 015394 35748
Email: enquiries@wordsworth.org.uk
Formed: 1891

Organisation type and purpose: Registered charity (charity number 1066184), museum, art gallery, historic building, house or site, suitable for ages: all ages, research organisation.
Centre for British Romanticism.
Links with:
Wordsworth Trust
at the same address

Enquiries to: Press Officer
Other contacts: Marketing Manager for residential courses.
Access:
Access to staff: By letter, by telephone, by fax, by email, in person, visitors by prior appointment
Other restrictions: Visitors to the library by prior appointment only.

continued overleaf

General description:
Wordsworth and his family, members of his circle including Coleridge, British and European Romanticism, Lake District life.
Information services:
Library available for reference (for conditions see Access above)
Special events including a programme of contemporary poetry readings, three annual residential courses incorporating lectures, seminars, walks and excursions.
Special visitor services: Guided tours.
Education services: Group education facilities, resources for Key Stages 2, 3 and 4..
Collections:
90% of Wordsworth papers
50,000 prints and paintings
Wordsworth memorabilia
Publications list:
is available in hard copy and online.
Printed publications:
William Wordsworth, An Illustrated Selection (ed Wordsworth J)
William and Dorothy Wordsworth: The Dove Cottage Years (ed Wordsworth J, £2.25)
Introducing Wordsworth: Classic Poems for Literacy Teaching at Key Stage 2 (N Martin, £16)
Dove Cottage: The Home of Wordsworth 1799-1808. A Pitkin Guide
Dorothy Wordsworth, Writer (Pamela Woof)
Exhibition catalogues: Romantic Icons, John Keats, Towards Tintern Abbey

Internet home pages:
http://www.wordsworth.org.uk

834
DOVER CASTLE
The Keep, Dover, Kent, CT16 1HH

Tel: 01304 201628

Organisation type and purpose: Museum, historic building, house or site, suitable for ages: 5+.
Parent body:
English Heritage (South East Region)
Eastgate Court, 195-205 High Street, Guildford, Surrey, GU1 3EH, tel: 01483 252000, fax: 01483 252001

Enquiries to: Curator
Access:
Access to staff: By letter, by telephone
Access to building, collections or gallery: No prior appointment required
Hours: 1st April to 30th September, daily, 1000 to 1800, 1st to 31st October, daily, 1000 to 1700, November to 31st March, daily 1000 to 1600.
Other restrictions: Closed December, 24th to 26 and January 1st.
Last tour one hour before castle closes.
Opening times are subject to change, for up-to-date information contact English Heritage by phone or visit the website.

General description:
No fortress in England can boast a longer history than Dover Castle. With its commanding position above the White Cliffs of Dover, it has been a strategic military site since Roman times. Today, visitors can discover 2000 years of history within its walls. An exhibition reveals the Tudor court on the move, and the latest sound, light, and film technology take you back to 1216 when Prince Louis of France besieged the castle. Wartime personnel were stationed here during WWII, and it was the nerve station for 'Operation Dynamo', where Sir Winston Churchill planned the evacuation of Dunkirk.
Information services:
Audio tours also available in French, German and Japanese.
Special visitor services: Tape recorded guides, materials and/or activities for children.
Education services: Group education facilities..
Collections:
Queen Elizabeth's pocket pistol
16th century ornamental bronze basilisk
World War II espionage devices
2 mortars, 2 anti-aircraft guns, and several cannon
A collection of 1940s/50s/60s civic defence telephone equipment is displayed in the underground works
Archaeological and architectural material from various excavations at English Heritage sites in the South East

Internet home pages:
http://www.english-heritage.org.uk

835
DOVER MUSEUM
Market Square, Dover, Kent, CT16 1PB

Tel: 01304 201066
Fax: 01304 241186
Formed: 1836

Organisation type and purpose: Local government body, museum, suitable for ages: all ages.
Parent body:
Dover District Council
White Cliffs Business Park, Whitfield, Dover, Kent, tel: 01304 821199, fax: 01304 872062

Enquiries to: Curator
Other contacts: Assistant Curator
Access:
Access to staff: By letter, by telephone, by fax, in person
Hours: Mon to Fri, 1000 to 1730
Other restrictions: Curatorial staff not available weekends.
Access for disabled people: ramped entry, access to all public areas, toilet facilities

General description:
Local history of Dover, Deal, Sandwich and local villages, archaeology of Dover, images of Dover, maritime and military history, Dunkirk evacuation, Roman history, Bronze Age boats, museum management, coins, ceramics and medals.
Information services:
Library available for reference (for conditions see Access above)
Object identification.
Digital image catalogue and museum collections database on free public access.
Special visitor services: Materials and/or activities for children.
Education services: Group education facilities, resources for Key Stages 1 and 2, 3, 4 and Further or Higher Education..
Collections:
Archives of the Cinque Port Pilots
Ray Warner collection (16mm film of Dover district 1949-1990)
Kent coal mining collections
Local History Archives (documents and manuscripts)
Prints, photographs and paintings
Social history collections
Channel Swimming photographs and documents, including the 'Sam Rockett' Collection
Electronic and video products:
Annual Review of Events in Dover District since 1990 (video)
The Dover Bronze Age Boat (video)

Internet home pages:
http://www.dovermuseum.co.uk
http://www.doveruk.com/museums/
Guide to museum.

836
DOVER ROMAN PAINTED HOUSE TRUST
See - Roman Painted House Trust

837
DOWN HOUSE
Luxted Road, Down, Biggin Hill, Kent, BR6 7JT

Tel: 01689 859119

Organisation type and purpose: Historic building, house or site, suitable for ages: 8+.
Parent body:
English Heritage (London Region)
23 Savile Row, London, W1X 1AB, tel: 020 7973 3000, email: www.english-heritage.org.uk

Enquiries to: Curator
Access:
Access to staff: By letter, by telephone, by fax, by email, charges to non-members

General description:
Down House was Charles Darwin's family home for over 40 years and is where he wrote his revolutionary book, 'On the Origin of Species'. Built during the late 18th century, the house remains much as it was when Darwin lived there. Visitors can explore the family rooms, where the paintings and pictures have been painstakingly restored, and see his writing desk and chair, along with parts of the collection of 5000 objects connected with his work.
Information services:
Audio tour in English, French, German and Japanese.
Special visitor services: Tape recorded guides.
Services for disabled people: For the visually impaired; for the hearing impaired.
Collections:
Collection of 5000 objects connected with Darwin's work

Internet home pages:
http://www.english-heritage.org.uk

838
DOWNHILL ESTATE
North Derry Office, Hezlett Farm, 107 Sea Road, Castlerock, Coleraine, Co Londonderry, BT51 4TW

Tel: 028 7084 8728
Fax: 028 7084 8728
Email: downhillcastle@nationaltrust.org.uk

Organisation type and purpose: National organisation, registered charity (charity number 205846), historic building, house or site, suitable for ages: 8+.
Parent body:
National Trust Office for Northern Ireland
Tel: 028 9751 0721

Enquiries to: Manager
Other contacts: Education Officer: 028 2073 1582
Access:
Access to staff: By letter, by telephone, by fax, by email
Access for disabled people: level entry, toilet facilities
Other restrictions: Recommended route map.

General description:
Set on a stunning and wild headland with fabulous clifftop walks and views over Ireland's north coast is the landscaped estate of Downhill, laid out in the late 18th century by the eccentric Earl and Bishop, Frederick Hervey. Estate includes ruins, mausoleum, beautiful gardens and the renowned Mussenden Temple perched on the cliff edge.

Internet home pages:
http://www.nationaltrust.org.uk

See also - Hezlett House

839
DOWNPATRICK RAILWAY MUSEUM
Downpatrick Station, Market Street, Downpatrick, Co Down, BT30 6LZ

Tel: 028 4461 5779
Email: drm@icom43.net
Acronym or abbreviation: DRM
Formed: 1987
Formed from: Downpatrick and Ardglass Railway Co Ltd, date of change, 1993; Downpatrick Steam Railway, date of change, 1995

Organisation type and purpose: Membership association (membership is by subscription), present number of members: 183, voluntary organisation, registered charity (charity number XO858), museum, historic building, house or site, suitable for ages: all ages.
A working railway museum of mainline 5ft 3in gauge, to show a typical market town station c1920-1950 period.
Has links with:
Downpatrick Railway Society
at same address, tel: 028 9145 1768, email/website: burkewalmae@cs.com

Enquiries to: Marketing Manager
Direct tel: 028 9145 1768
Other contacts: Director
Access:
Access to staff: By letter, by telephone, by email, in person, Internet web pages
Hours: Mon to Fri, 0900 to 1200; Sat, 1000 to 1600

General description:
Irish railway heritage, the restoration and preservation of many examples of this heritage.
Printed publications:
DRS News (periodically)
Downrail (annually)

Internet home pages:
http://www.downrail.com
The official online guide to the DRM. Contains detailed history, links and contact addresses.

840
DRAPERS MILL

College Road, Margate, Kent

Tel: 01843 291696

Member of:
Kent Windmills
Owned by:
Kent County Council
General description:
Smock corn mill built in 1845 by John Holman. Worked by wind until 1916, and by gas engine until 1933. Restored to working order 1965-75.

841
DRUM CASTLE, GARDEN & ESTATE

Drumoak, Banchory, Aberdeenshire, AB31 5EY

Tel: 01330 811204
Fax: 01330 811962
Email: drum-castle@nts.org.uk
Formed: c1286

Organisation type and purpose: National organisation, registered charity (charity number SCO 07410), museum, historic building, house or site, suitable for ages: 5+.
Parent body:
National Trust for Scotland (North-East Region)
Address for Head Office:
The National Trust for Scotland
28 Charlotte Square, Edinburgh, EH2 4ET, tel: 0131 243 9300, fax: 0131 243 9444, email/website: information@nts.org.uk

Enquiries to: Manager
Access:
Access to staff: By letter, by telephone, by fax, by email, visitors by prior appointment, charges to non-members, Internet web pages
Other restrictions: When property open to public there may be restrictions on access to staff.
Access to building, collections or gallery: No prior appointment required
Hours: Mar to May and Sep to Oct: daily, 1230 to 1730
Jun to Aug: daily, 1000 to 1730
Grounds: all year, daily, 0930 to sunset
Access for disabled people: Parking provided, toilet facilities
Other restrictions: Wheelchair available

General description:
The keep, built in the late 13th century, is one of the oldest tower houses surviving in Scotland. The original house was enlarged with the creation of a fine Jacobean mansion house in 1619 and a later addition during the reign of Queen Victoria. Houses an excellent collection of family portraits and good Georgian furniture.
Information services:
Guided tours by prior arrangement.
Special visitor services: Guided tours, materials and/or activities for children.
Education services: Group education facilities, resources for Key Stage 1 and Further or Higher Education..
Catalogues:
Catalogue for library is in-house only. Catalogue for all of the collections is only available in-house.
Publications list:
is available in hard copy and online.
Printed publications:
Guide Book (£3.50)

Internet home pages:
http://www.drum-castle.org.uk

842
DRUMCROON EDUCATION ART CENTRE

2 Parsons Walk, Wigan, Lancashire, WN1 1RS

Tel: 01942 321840
Fax: 01942 233303
Email: drumcroon@wiganmbc.gov.uk
Formed: 1981

Organisation type and purpose: Local government body, art gallery, suitable for ages: 5+.
Raising standards of art education for all, public art gallery.

Enquiries to: Manager
Other contacts: Administration Assistant for general information and exhibitions.
Access:
Access to staff: By letter, by telephone, by fax, by email, in person, Internet web pages
Access for disabled people: Parking provided, ramped entry
Other restrictions: Access to ground floor only.

General description:
Public gallery, 4 gallery spaces of which 3 on ground floor and 1 upstairs, resources in library, access to approximately 2000 art books and internet access.
Picture loan available to schools, colleges.
Education establishments can borrow original works of art from our collection of 3000 items on a termly basis at a very good price.
Daily visits of school children who work in the galleries with Gallery Staff in the mornings, and enjoy a practical workshop in the afternoon relating to current exhibitions.
Information services:
Education services: Group education facilities, resources for Key Stages 1 and 2, 3, 4 and Further or Higher Education..
Collections:
Approximately 3000 items including original, and reproductions in Picture Loan Collection
These are in all mediums, textiles, paintings, 3D, ceramics, sculpture, photographs, prints etc
Approximately 2000 books in library (all art books), back catalogues of magazines including Artist Network, Crafts, Artist Illustrators etc
Current and past exhibition catalogues, posters, teachers' notes etc
Vast number of slides, including Old Masters and past exhibitions at Drumcroon
Catalogues:
Catalogue for library is in-house only. Catalogue for all of the collections is only available in-house.
Printed publications:
Exhibition Catalogues, past and present (£1 to £1.50 each)
Posters (£1)
Exhibition Programme for Year (acadamic years, FOC)
Teachers Notes - aids for exhibitions (£4 each)
Electronic and video products:
Past exhibition catalogues, teachers' notes, artist-in-residence information, current exhibition images, and catalogues all on our Website

Internet home pages:
http://www.wiganmbc.gov.uk

843
DRUMLANRIGS TOWER VISITOR CENTRE

1 Tower Knowe, Hawick, Borders, TD9 9EN

Tel: 01450 377615
Fax: 01450 378506

Organisation type and purpose: National organisation, registered charity, art gallery, historic building, house or site.
Parent body:
Scottish Borders Council Museum and Gallery Service
Tel: 01750 20096

Enquiries to: Information Officer
Access:
Access to staff: By letter, by telephone, by fax
Access to building, collections or gallery: No prior appointment required
Hours: Apr, May, Jun, Sep, Mon to Sat, 1000 to 1700; Sun, 1300 to 1600;
Jul and Aug, Mon to Sat, 1000 to 1800, Sun, 1300 to 1700;
Oct, Mon to Sat, 1000 to 1800

General description:
The restored tower has period display rooms and costumed figures to tell the history of the tower.
Information services:
Interactive audiovisual programme available
Tourist information
Family history enquiry service (Wed to Fri)
Available for private functions
Venue for civil marriages
Special visitor services: Tape recorded guides.
Education services: Group education facilities..

Internet home pages:
http://www.scotborders.gov.uk
http://www.scotborders.org.uk

844
DAPHNE DU MAURIER'S SMUGGLERS AT JAMAICA INN

Jamaica Inn, Bolventor, Launceston, Cornwall, PL15 7TS

Tel: 01566 86025
Fax: 01566 86838
Formed: 1998

Organisation type and purpose: Independently owned, museum, suitable for ages: all ages.

Enquiries to: Manager
Direct tel: 01566 86838
Access:
Access to staff: By letter, by telephone, by fax
Access for disabled people: Parking provided, ramped entry, toilet facilities
Other restrictions: Partial access to museum - on 3 floors.

General description:
Smuggler's Museum contains tableaux in light and sound of scenes from Daphne du Maurier's book, Jamaica Inn.
Collections:
Some history of the Browning family, Daphne du Maurier's married name
Smuggling artefacts, ancient and modern
Printed publications:
Publications available on request for purchase, direct or mail order

845
DUALCHAS, SKYE AND LOCHALSH AREA MUSEUMS SERVICE

Park Lane, Portree, Isle of Skye, Inverness-shire, IV51 9GP

Tel: 01478 613857
Fax: 01478 613751

Organisation type and purpose: Local government body, museum.

Enquiries to: Heritage Officer
Other contacts: Museums Assistant (part-time) for photographic enquiries and general information.

Access:
Access to staff: By letter, by telephone, visitors by prior appointment
Access for disabled people: level entry, toilet facilities

General description:
Skye and Lochalsh area: local history and culture, landscape and archaeology, museum planning and interpretation.

Collections:
Paintings and prints, photographs and postcards
The Duncan Macpherson Collection of nearly 2000 photographic images from the late 19th to early 20th centuries
Maps, archaeological survey reports, archives, library of 3000 volumes, miscellaneous artefacts
The Dualchas Collections include an extensive range of over 10,000 photographs

Catalogues:
Catalogue for library is in-house only. Catalogue for part of the collections is only available in-house.

Printed publications:
Set of 8 postcards: Castles of Skye and Lochalsh (£2 plus p&p)

Electronic and video products:
'An Ceol Againn Fhin'local traditional music and Gaelic song (CD-ROM, £11 plus p&p, tape, £7 plus p&p)

Internet home pages:
http://www.highland.gov.uk/educ/publicservices/museumdetails/dualchas.htm

846
DUDLEY MUSEUM & ART GALLERY

3 St James's Road, Dudley, West Midlands, DY1 1HY

Tel: 01384 815575
Fax: 01384 815576
Email: Dudley.museum@mbc.dudley.gov.uk
Formed: 19th century

Organisation type and purpose: Local government body, museum, suitable for ages: 5+.

Enquiries to: Director
Direct fax: 01384 812746
Direct email: glass.pls@mbc.dudley.gov.uk
Other contacts: Exhibitions Officer, tel: 01384 815573

Access:
Access to staff: By letter, by telephone, by fax, by email, visitors by prior appointment
Access for disabled people: ramped entry
Other restrictions: Poor disabled access - telephone for details.

General description:
The museum is housed in a Victorian red brick building of two stories with a number of mezzanine floors. Changing programme of exhibitions and activities.
Currently limited geological collections on display because of gallery repairs. Phone for details.

Information services:
Education services: Group education facilities, resources for Key Stages 1 and 2, 3 and Further or Higher Education.
Services for disabled people: For the hearing impaired; displays and/or information at wheelchair height.

Collections:
The Fine Art Collection, started in the 1880s now numbers nearly 2000 works, including 250 oils, 750 drawings and watercolours, 450 engravings and 350 modern original prints. These include the view of Dudley Castle by J M W Turner, and works by David Cox, Frank Brangwyn and Percy Shakespeare
Geological Collection includes the collections of the former Dudley and Midland Geological Society and its successor, the Dudley and Midland Geological and Scientific Society. It now comprises some 12,000 fossil, rock and mineral specimens. The main strength is its definitive assemblage of marine invertebrate fossils from the local Silurian rocks.
Brooke Robinson Museum housed on the 2nd floor of the Museum, contains paintings, sculpture and decorative arts

Internet home pages:
http://www.dudley.gov.uk/tourism/dudleymuseum/index.asp

847
DUDMASTON HALL

Quatt, Bridgnorth, Shropshire, WV15 6QN

Tel: 01746 780866
Fax: 01746 780744
Email: dudmaston@nationaltrust.org.uk
Formed: 1980

Organisation type and purpose: National organisation, registered charity (charity number 205846), historic building, house or site, suitable for ages: 8+.

Parent body:
The National Trust (West Midlands)
West Midlands Regional Office, tel: 01743 708100

Enquiries to: House and Visitor Services Manager

Access:
Access to staff: By letter, by telephone, by email
Access to building, collections or gallery: Prior appointment required
Hours: House: Apr to Sep, Sun, Tue, Wed, 1400 to 1730
Garden: Apr to Sep, Sun to Wed, 1200 to 1800
Open Bank Holiday Mondays
Access for disabled people: Parking provided, ramped entry, toilet facilities
Other restrictions: Designated parking. Drop-off point. 3 manual wheelchairs available. 1 single-seater powered mobility vehicle. Ground floor fully accessible. No access to other floors. Ramped entrance to shop. Level entrance to tea-room. Grounds largely accessible. Recommended route map.

General description:
A late 17th century house with intimate family rooms containing fine furniture and Dutch flower paintings, as well as interesting contemporary paintings and sculpture. The delightful gardens are a mass of colour in spring and include a walk in the Dingle, a wooded valley. There are also estate walks starting from Hampton Loade.
Dudmaston is the home of Colonel and Mrs Hamilton-Russell.

Information services:
Braille guide. Large-print guide. Audio guide. Touch list.
Front-carrying baby slings for loan.
Children's quiz/trail.
Free tours with gardener Mondays 1200 to 1800.
Special visitor services: Materials and/or activities for children.
Services for disabled people: For the visually impaired; for the hearing impaired.

Collections:
17th century house with intimate family rooms
Fine furniture and Dutch flower paintings
Contemporary paintings and sculpture
Spanish modern art, abstract art, 1960-1966
Belgian modern art, abstract art, 1955-1960.
British modern art sculptures and paintings. Pieces by Henry Moore, Ben Nicholson, Barbara Hepworth, augmented by 'Paris School' of artists between 1950/1960s, Harting Dubuffet, Vasarely, Riojelle works, 1948/1963
Chinese porcelain and botanic prints

Printed publications:
Guide Book (£2.50)
Estate Walk Map (£1)
Dingle Walk (35p)
Botanic Prints (25p)
Events Leaflet (free)
Babbage Bus Leaflet (free)
Labouchere Collection Leaflet (free)

Internet home pages:
http://www.nationaltrust.org.uk/westmidlands

848
DUDSON MUSEUM

The Dudson Centre, Hope Street, Hanley, Stoke-on-Trent, Staffordshire, ST1 5DD

Tel: 01782 285286
Fax: 01782 824412
Email: info@dudson-group.co.uk
Formed: 1999

Organisation type and purpose: Independently owned, museum, historic building, house or site, suitable for ages: 12+.

Parent body:
Dudson Limited
Scotia Road, Tunstall, Stoke-on-Trent, tel: 01782 819337, fax: 01782 813230, email: info@dudson-group.co.uk

Enquiries to: Administrator

Access:
Access to staff: By letter, by telephone, by email, in person
Access for disabled people: Parking provided, ramped entry, toilet facilities
Other restrictions: Access to ground floor.

General description:
History of Dudson ceramics.

Information services:
Study area.
Special visitor services: Guided tours..

Collections:
Examples of Dudson ceramics from 1800 to present day, housed in listed bottle oven on original factory site

Catalogues:
Catalogue for part of the collections is only available in-house.

Publications list:
is available in hard copy.

Printed publications:
Dudson - A Family of Potters Since 1800 (Dudson A M, £24 plus £5 p&p)
A Pottery Panorama (Dudson A M, £10 plus £4 p&p)
Cheese Dishes (Dudson A M, £10 plus £3 p&p)

Internet home pages:
http://www.dudson.co.uk
Dudson products and services.

849
DUFF HOUSE COUNTRY GALLERY

Duff House, Banff, AB45 3SX

Tel: 01261 818181
Fax: 01261 818900
Email: enquiries@duffhouse.org.uk
Formed: 1995

Organisation type and purpose: National government body, local government body, art gallery, historic building, house or site, suitable for ages: 8+.

Parent body:
National Galleries of Scotland (NGS)
Belford Road, Edinburgh, EH4 3DR, tel: 0131 624 6200, fax: 0131 343 3250, email: enquiries@natgalscot.ac.uk

Connections with:
Historic Scotland (HS)
Longmore House, Salisbury Place, Edinburgh, tel: 0131 686 8600

Enquiries to: Chamberlain
Other contacts: Administrative Officer for booking or general enquiries.
Access:
Access to staff: By letter, by telephone, by fax, by email, in person, Internet web pages
Access for disabled people: Parking provided, level entry, access to all public areas, toilet facilities

General description:
An 18th century mansion designed by William Adam, restored interiors fitted with period furniture and hung with Scottish, English, Italian, Spanish, Dutch and German paintings.
Information services:
Programme of changing exhibitions, concerts, lectures and workshops.
Special visitor services: Guided tours, materials and/or activities for children.
Education services: Group education facilities.
Services for disabled people: For the hearing impaired; displays and/or information at wheelchair height.
Collections:
Information held on the Duff, Earl Fife family who commissioned the architect William Adam
Information held on William Adam
Information available to interested students and members of the general public
Catalogues:
Catalogue for part of the collections is published.
Printed publications:
Guide Book
Painting Catalogue
Footsteps on the Stairs: Tales of Duff House
The World from the Window: A Duff House Childrens' Story

Internet home pages:
http://www.duffhouse.com

850
DUFFTOWN MUSEUM
See - Whisky Museum

851
DUKE OF CORNWALL'S LIGHT INFANTRY REGIMENTAL MUSEUM
The Keep, The Barracks, Bodmin, Cornwall, PL31 1EG

Tel: 01208 72810
Fax: 01208 72810
Email: dclimus@talk21.com
Acronym or abbreviation: DCLI Museum
Formed: 1925
Also known as: Military Museum - Bodmin
Formed from: The Light Infantry, date of change, 1969

Organisation type and purpose: Registered charity (charity number 272359), museum, suitable for ages: 8+.
Military reference library.
To preserve the history of The County Regiment of Cornwall 1702 to 1959, and display for the learning and enjoyment of future generations.
Headquarters of:
The Light Infantry
RHQ The Light Infantry, Peninsula Barracks, Romsey Road, Winchester, Hampshire, SO23 8TS, tel: 01962 82827, fax: 01962 82834

Enquiries to: Curator
Direct email: dcli@talk21.com
Access:
Access to staff: By letter, by telephone, by fax, by email, in person
Access for disabled people: Parking provided, toilet facilities
Other restrictions: Museum on 2nd floor - no lift.

General description:
History of the Duke of Cornwall's Light Infantry and its ancestors from 1702. Archival information on members of the Regiment; general information on military history.
Information services:
Library available for reference (for conditions see Access above)
Special visitor services: Guided tours..
Collections:
Army lists 1761-1994
British infantry small arms 1790-1950
Medals and decorations: large collection of 32nd, 46th and DCL1 1815 to 1945
Regimental colours: 32nd
1844-1866, Roseland militia colours 1793-1816
Catalogues:
Catalogue for library is in-house only. Catalogue for all of the collections is only available in-house.
Printed publications:
The following publications plus p&p £2 in UK:
Costume of the 46th Regiment of Foot (£1)
More Than Twice a Hero - McCabe of Lucknow (£1.50)
History of The Duke of Cornwall's Light Infantry (Major E C Godfrey MC, £10)
Brasso Blanco & Bull - About National Service (£6.99)
Pictorial History of the DCLI - Images of England - Archive Photographs (£9.99)
Electronic and video products:
Several Audio CD-ROMs by The Band of The Light Division

Internet home pages:
http://www.armymuseums.org.uk

852
DUKE OF LANCASTERS OWN YEOMANRY MUSEUM
See - Museum of Lancashire

853
DULWICH PICTURE GALLERY
College Road, Dulwich, London, SE21 7AD

Tel: 020 8693 5254
Formed: 1811

Organisation type and purpose: Independently owned, registered charity (charity number 1040942), museum, art gallery, historic building, house or site, suitable for ages: all ages.
The Gallery's collection is 17th and 18th century Old Master paintings. Its purpose is to encourage the enjoyment of the visual arts.
Links with:
The Friends of Dulwich Picture Gallery
The Trustees of the Dulwich Picture Gallery
c/o Dulwich Picture Gallery, tel: 020 8693 5254, fax: 020 8299 8700, email/website: info@dulwichpicturegallery.org.uk

Enquiries to: Head of Press and Marketing
Other contacts: Curator for knowledge of the Collection.
Access:
Access to staff: By letter, by telephone, by fax, by email
Hours: Mon to Fri, 1000 to 1700
Access to building, collections or gallery: No prior appointment required
Hours: Gallery: Tue to Fri, 1000 to 1700; Sat, Sun & Bank Holiday Mon, 1100 to 1700
Other restrictions: Closed: Mon, Good Friday, Christmas Eve, Christmas Day and New Year's Day.
Access for disabled people: Parking provided, ramped entry, level entry, access to all public areas, toilet facilities
Other restrictions: Loop in lecture hall.

General description:
Houses an outstanding collection of 17th and 18th century Old Master paintings. The building, designed by Sir John Soane in 1811 is a seminal building for the display of pictures with its use of natural daylight.
Information services:
Library available for reference (for conditions see Access above)
Education Service, tel: 020 8693 6911.
Education for schools, outreach and general education of everyone.
Special visitor services: Guided tours, materials and/or activities for children.
Education services: Group education facilities.
Services for disabled people: For the visually impaired; for the hearing impaired.
Catalogues:
Catalogue for library is published. Catalogue for all of the collections is published.
Publications list:
is available in hard copy.
Printed publications:
Catalogues of the Collection (the complete catalogue)
Exhibition catalogues
Book about the building

Address for ordering publications:
Printed publications:
Commercial Manager, Dulwich Picture Gallery
Tel: 020 8299 8704, fax: 020 8299 8704, email: l.hutton@dulwichpicturegallery.org.uk

Internet home pages:
http://www.dulwichpicturegallery.org.uk
Information on collection, history, exhibitions, events.

854
DUMFRIES AND GALLOWAY AVIATION MUSEUM
Heathhall Industrial Estate, Heathhall, Dumfries, DG1 3PH

Tel: 01387 251623
Email: info@dgam.co.uk
Formed: 1977

Organisation type and purpose: Independently owned, registered charity, museum, historic building, house or site, suitable for ages: 5+.
Maintained by members of the:
Dumfries and Galloway Aviation Group
Member of:
British Aircraft Preservation Council (BAPC)

Enquiries to: Chairman
Direct tel: 01387 720487
Other contacts: Curator, tel: 01387 259546
Access:
Access to staff: By letter, by telephone, in person, Internet web pages
Access for disabled people: Parking provided, ramped entry, level entry
Other restrictions: Partial access to external and ground floor only.

General description:
Based around the original control tower of the former RAF Dumfries, the museum has a range of aircraft and aviation memorabilia from the earliest days of flight to the present day.
Unusual 3 storey control tower, with numerous displays.
Information services:
Special visitor services: Guided tours, materials and/or activities for children.
Education services: Group education facilities..
Collections:
Aircraft, including a Supermarine Spitfire MkII, F-100 Super Sabre, Lockheed T33, De Havilland Vampire T11, British Airways Trident 111 and the Gloster Meteor T7
Engines including a Rolls-Royce Merlin
Memorabilia, photographs, books, documents, log-books
Printed publications:
Leaflet

Internet home pages:
http://www.dgam.co.uk

855
DUMFRIES AND GALLOWAY MUSEUM SERVICE

Dumfries Museum & Camera Obscura, The Observatory, Church Street, Dumfries, DG2 7SW

Tel: 01387 253374
Fax: 01387 265081
Email: dumfriesmuseum@dumgal.gov.uk

Organisation type and purpose: Suitable for ages: all ages.
Parent body:
Dumfries and Galloway Council
Council Offices, English Street, Dumfries, DG1 2DD, tel: 01387 260000, fax: 01387 260034

Enquiries to: Museum Service Manager
Access:
Access to staff: By letter, by telephone, by fax, by email, Internet web pages

General description:
Administrative office for the museums, art galleries and historic properties in the care of Dumfries and Galloway Council.

Internet home pages:
http://www.dumgal.gov.uk/museum

See also - Camera Obscura at Dumfries Museum; Castle Douglas Art Gallery; Castle of St John; Dumfries Museum, The Observatory; Historic Resources Centre; Old Bridge House Museum; Robert Burns Centre; Robert Burns House; Sanquhar Tolbooth Museum; Stewartry Museum; Stranraer Museum; Tolbooth Art Centre

856
DUMFRIES MUSEUM

The Observatory, Church Street, Dumfries, DG2 7SW

Tel: 01387 253374
Fax: 01387 265081
Email: dumfriesmuseum@dumgal.gov.uk
Formed: 1936

Organisation type and purpose: Local government body, museum.
Parent body:
Galloway and Dumfries Museum Service
At same address, tel: 01387 253374
Administers the:
Dumfries Archive Centre
Other museums:
Castle Douglas Art Gallery
Market Street, Castle Douglas, DG7 1BE, tel: 01557 331643, fax: 01557 331643, email/website: davidd@dumgal.gov.uk
Castle of St John
Castle Street, Stranraer, DG9 7RT, tel: 01776 705088, fax: 01776 705544, email/website: johnpic@dumgal.gov.uk
Gracefield Arts Centre
28 Edinburgh Road, Dumfries, DG1 1JQ, tel: 01387 262084
Historic Resources Centre
Bank Street, Annan, tel: 01461 201384, fax: 01461 205876, email/website: anner@dumgal.gov.uk
Robert Burns House
Burns Street, Dumfries, DG1 2PS, tel: 01387 255297, fax: 01387 265081, email/website: elainek@dumgal.gov.uk
Sanquhar Tolbooth Museum
Hign Street, Sanquhar, DG4 6BN, tel: 01659 50186, fax: 01387 265081, email/website: elainek@dumgal.gov.uk
Stranraer Museum
55 George Street, Stranraer, DG9 7JP, tel: 01776 705088, fax: 01776 705544, email/website: johnpic@dumgal.gov.uk
The Observatory and Camera Obscura
Church Street, Dumfries, DG2 7SW, tel: 01387 253374, fax: 01387 265081, email/website: elainek@dumgal.gov.uk
The Old Bridge House
Mill Road, Dumfries, DG2 7BE, tel: 01387 256904, fax: 01387 265081, email/website: elainek@dumgal.gov.uk
The Robert Burns Centre
Mill Road, Dumfries, DG2 7BE, tel: 01387 264808, fax: 01387 264808, email/website: elainek@dumgal.gov.uk
The Stewartry Museum
St Mary Street, Kirkcudbright, DG6 4AQ, tel: 01557 331643, fax: 01557 331643, email/website: davidd@dumgal.gov.uk
Tolbooth Art Centre
High Street, Kirkcudbright, DG6 4JL, tel: 01557 331556, fax: 01557 331643, email/website: davidd@dumgal.gov.uk

Enquiries to: Manager
Direct email: elainek@dumgal.gov.uk
Other contacts: Museums Officer
Access:
Access to staff: Visitors by prior appointment, by letter, by telephone, by fax

General description:
Local studies relating to Dumfries and Galloway region, archaeology, civic and social history, numismatics, material culture, photographic records.
Catalogues:
Catalogue for part of the collections is only available in-house.
Publications list:
is available in hard copy.
Printed publications:
93 leaflets on the collections and local subjects
Museum information leaflets in several languages
Occasional publications

Internet home pages:
http://www.dumgal.gov.uk/museum

857
DUNASKIN OPEN AIR MUSEUM

Dalmellington Road, Waterside, Patna, Ayrshire, KA6 7JF

Tel: 01292 531144
Fax: 01292 532314
Email: dunaskin@btconnect.com
Formed: 1982

Organisation type and purpose: Independently owned, registered charity, museum.
Visitor attraction.
Operating company:
Dalmellington & District Conservation Trust (DDCT)

Enquiries to: Administrator
Other contacts: Visitor Services Manager
Access:
Access to staff: By letter, by telephone, by fax, by email
Access for disabled people: Parking provided, ramped entry, level entry, access to all public areas, toilet facilities

General description:
The Dalmellington Iron Company was founded in 1848. At its zenith, the company's eight furnaces provided employment for around 1400 people. The last furnace was blown out in 1921, but the company produced coal, and later bricks up to 1976. The site has been preserved as Europe's best remaining example of a Victorian ironworks. Ironworking, coal-mining, brickmaking, the story of the people and places of the Doon Valley through the Industrial Revolution up to modern times.
Information services:
Special visitor services: Guided tours, tape recorded guides, materials and/or activities for children.
Services for disabled people: For the hearing impaired; displays and/or information at wheelchair height.
Collections:
Artefacts, photographs, books, documents, oral history archive
Printed publications:
General Leaflet

Internet home pages:
http://home.btconnect.com/Dunaskin

858
DUNCAN SAVINGS BANK MUSEUM

See - Savings Banks Museum

859
DUNDEE ART GALLERIES AND MUSEUMS

See - Dundee City Council, Leisure and Arts Department

860
DUNDEE CITY COUNCIL

Leisure and Arts Department, Dundee Contemporary Arts, Floor 13, Tayside House, 152 Nethergate, Dundee

Tel: 01382 433827
Fax: 01382 432252
Email: arts.heritage@dundeecity.gov.uk
Formed: 2001
Formerly: Dundee Art Galleries and Museums, date of change, 1994; Arts and Heritage Department, date of change, 2001

Organisation type and purpose: Local government body, museum, art gallery.
Heritage facilities.

Enquiries to: Arts & Heritage Manager
Direct tel: 01382 432323
Direct fax: 01382 432252
Access:
Access to staff: By letter
Hours: Mon to Fri, 0900 to 1700

General description:
Tayside and North Fife region: archaeology, including sites research, history, natural sciences and environmental studies; museum education services; fine and applied art; Egyptology; astronomy; numismatics; field archaeology.
Collections:
Scottish Provincial Silver
Simpson Collection of Keyboard Instruments
Whaling records and collections
Printed publications:
Ale and A'thing: the Grocer and Licensed Trade in Dundee
Art Catalogue
Fishing for the Whale
Local history books
Studies in Archaeology

Internet home pages:
http://www.dca.org.uk
http://www.dundeecity.gov.uk

See also - Broughty Castle Museum; McManus Galleries; Mills Observatory

861
DUNDEE UNIVERSITY MUSEUM COLLECTIONS

University of Dundee, Dundee, DD1 4HN

Tel: 01382 344310
Email: museum@dundee.ac.uk
Formed: 1994

Organisation type and purpose: University department or institute.
Part of:
University of Dundee Archive, Records Management & Museum Services (ARMMS)

Enquiries to: Curator
Access:
Access to staff: By letter, by telephone, by email, visitors by prior appointment
Access to building, collections or gallery: No prior appointment required
Hours: Tower and Lamb Gallery: Mon to Fri, 0900 to 2030; Sat, 0930 to 1630
Other restrictions: Other displays and collections by prior appointment.

General description:
Tower Foyer and Lamb Gallery, changing exhibitions (mainly art), other displays and collections (by appointment) - art, design,

medical history, science, ethnography and natural history.
Information services:
Special visitor services: Guided tours..
Collections:
Fine Art - mainly Scottish Artists 19th and 20th century
Student Art - from Duncan of Jordanstone College
Scottish Arts Council Bequest - 20th century prints
Alan Woods Bequest - Contemporary Scottish Art
Textiles - Needlework Development Scheme
Furniture - 20th century design pieces
Ethnography - material from Tiberias, Palestine
Medical history
Scientific instruments and equipment
Natural History - Herbarium and D'Arcy Thompson Zoology Collection
Mathematical models, audiovisual equipment, aero engines, dental equipment, silver and ceramics
Catalogues:
Catalogue for all of the collections is available in-house and part is on-line.
Printed publications:
Museum Collections leaflet
Art Collection booklets
Electronic and video products:
Textile Collection (CD-ROM)

Internet home pages:
http://www.dundee.ac.uk/museum/
Site which links pages on art, science and exhibition pages.

862
DUNFERMLINE HERITAGE CENTRE
See - Abbot House Heritage Centre

863
DUNFERMLINE HERITAGE TRUST

864
DUNFERMLINE MUSEUM
Viewfield Terrace, Dunfermline, Fife, KY12 7HY

Tel: 01383 313838
Fax: 01383 313837
Email: lesley.botten@fife.gov.uk
Formed: 1963
Formerly: Dunfermline District Museum and Small Gallery

Organisation type and purpose: Local government body, museum, suitable for ages: all ages.
Parent body:
Fife Council Museums West
HQ at same address

Enquiries to: Curator
Access:
Access to staff: By letter, by telephone, by fax, by email, visitors by prior appointment
Access to building, collections or gallery: Prior appointment required
Hours: Open by appointment only, phone 01383 313838
Access for disabled people: Parking provided, ramped entry, toilet facilities

General description:
The history of Dunfermline and the 19th & 20th century luxury linen and silk weaving important to the town until around 1950.
Collections:
Collection of machinery, designes and products from the luxury damask linen and silk industry of 19th/20th century Dunfirmline
Printed publications:
Coalmining in West Fife, A bibliography of material held in Dunfermline Central Library
Dunfermline Linen, An Outline History, 1986
Everyday Life in Dunfermline in the late 18th century, 1978
Black Diamonds, Photographs of Longannet Mine Fife (Cavers C, 2001)
Local Maps, a revised guide, 1988
The Kingdom of Fife, selected list of books available, 1985

865
DUNHAM MASSEY
Altrincham, Greater Manchester, WA14 4SJ

Tel: 0161 941 1025
Fax: 0161 929 7508
Email: dunhammassey@nationaltrust.org.uk

Organisation type and purpose: National organisation, registered charity (charity number 205846), historic building, house or site, suitable for ages: 5+.
Parent body:
The National Trust (North West)
North West Regional Office, tel: 0870 609 5391

Enquiries to: Collections Manager
Other contacts: (1) House Steward; (2) Property Manager for (1) deputy to Collections Manager; (2) person in overall charge of property.
Access:
Access to staff: By letter, by telephone, by fax, visitors by prior appointment
Access for disabled people: Parking provided, toilet facilities
Other restrictions: Drop-off point. 4 manual wheelchairs available. 2 single-seater powered mobility vehicles available

booking essential. Steps to entrance. Stairclimber (please book) allows access to ground floor. Ground floor accessible with assistance. No access to other floors. Level entrance to shop. Lift to restaurant on first floor.

General description:
An early Georgian house, Dunham Massey was extensively reworked in the early years of the 20th century. The result is one of Britain's most sumptuous Edwardian interiors, housing exceptional collections of 18th century walnut furniture, paintings and Huguenot silver, as well as extensive servants' quarters. Here is one of the North West's great plantsman's gardens with richly planted borders and majestic trees, as well as an orangery, Victorian bark-house and well-house. The ancient deer park contains a series of beautiful avenues and ponds, and a working Elizabethan sawmill.
Information services:
Helpline available, tel no: Infoline: 0161 928 4351.
Catalogue for all the collections 95% in-house.
Education Service for visually impaired.
Braille guide.
Front-carrying baby slings for loan.
Suitable for school groups. Education room/centre. Live interpretation. Hands-on activities. Children's quiz/trail. Family tours.
Special visitor services: Guided tours, materials and/or activities for children.
Education services: Group education facilities, resources for Key Stages 1 and 2 and Further or Higher Education.
Services for disabled people: For the visually impaired.
Collections:
Collections held: silver, paintings, furniture, household textiles, costume, books, Country House technology, 19th and 20th century ceramics (native to the house)
Catalogues:
Catalogue for all of the collections is only available in-house.

Internet home pages:
http://www.nationaltrust.org.uk

866
DUNHAM MASSEY: WHITE COTTAGE
Little Bollington, Altringham, Greater Manchester, WA14 4TJ

Tel: 0870 609 5391 (Regional Office)

Organisation type and purpose: National organisation, registered charity (charity number 205846), historic building, house or site, suitable for ages: 8+.
Parent body:
National Trust (North West Area)
North West Regional Office, tel: 0870 609 5391

Enquiries to: Property Manager
Access:
Access to building, collections or gallery: Prior appointment required
Hours: Apr to Oct, Sun, 1400 to 1700; only open last Sun of each month
Other restrictions: All visits must be booked through the Stamford Estates Office, tel. 0161 928 0075
Mon to Fri 0900 to 1700

General description:
An important timber-framed cottage, built c.1500 as a cruck-trussed open hall and altered in the 17th century.
Recently restored by the Trust using traditional materials and techniques and now a private residence, it is open to visitors by kind permission of the tenants.

Internet home pages:
http://www.nationaltrust.org.uk

867
DUNKELD AND THE HERMITAGE
Dunkeld, Perthshire

Tel: 01350 728641 (Ranger Office)
Fax: tel/fax 01796 473233 (Killiecrankie Visitor Centre)

Parent body:
National Trust for Scotland

General description:
13 hectares of woodland and a picturesque folly, 'Ossian's Hall', built in 1758.

868
DUNKELD
Ell Shop, The Cross, Dunkeld, Perthshire, PH8 0AN

Tel: 01350 727460
Email: dunkeld@nts.org.uk

Organisation type and purpose: Historic building, house or site.
Parent body:
National Trust for Scotland
Access:
Access for disabled people: toilet facilities
Other restrictions: Access to the Ell shop, toilets 25 yards

General description:
Trust owns 20 restored houses dating from the rebuilding of the town after the Battle of Dunkeld in1689. Although these are not open to the public, visitors are welcome to the Trust's Ell Shop, which takes it name from the ell or weaver's measure fixed to the wall outside.
Information services:
Services for disabled people: For the hearing impaired.

Internet home pages:
http://www.nts.org.uk

869
DUNNOTTAR CASTLE
Stonehaven, Aberdeenshire, AB39

Tel: 01569 762173

continued overleaf

Organisation type and purpose: Independently owned, historic building, house or site, suitable for ages: all ages.

Enquiries to: Curator
Access:
Access to staff: By letter, by telephone, in person
Access to building, collections or gallery: No prior appointment required
Hours: Summer: Mon to Sat, 0900 to 1800; Sun, 1400 to 1700
Winter: Fri to Mon, 0930 to sunset
Last entry 30 mins before closing
Other restrictions: Closed 25, 26 Dec and 1 Jan.

General description:
Spectacular ruin, impregnable fortress of the Earls Marischal of Scotland. The site for the successful protection of the Scottish Crown Jewels against the might of Cromwell's Army. A castle dreams are made of, a must for anyone who takes Scottish history seriously.
Printed publications:
Guide Book (£3.50)
Set of 5 postcards (£1)

870
DUNS EXHIBITION ROOM
Library Building, 44 Newtown Street, Duns, Borders, TD11 3AU

Tel: 01361 884114

Organisation type and purpose: Local government body, museum, historic building, house or site.
Parent body:
Scottish Borders Council Museum and Gallery Service
Tel: 01750 20096, fax: 01750 23282

Enquiries to: Curator
Access:
Access to staff: By letter, by telephone
Other restrictions: All enquiries should be addressed to the Scottish Borders Council Museums Service.
Access for disabled people: access to all public areas

General description:
Changing exhibitions.

Internet home pages:
http://www.scotborders.gov.uk

871
DUNSTANBURGH CASTLE
c/o 14 Queen Street, Alnwick, Northumberland, NE66 1RD

Tel: 01665 576231

Organisation type and purpose: Historic building, house or site.
Parent body:
The National Trust
In the guardianship of:
English Heritage (North East Region)
Tel: 0191 269 1227/8, fax: 0191 261 1130

Enquiries to: Manager
Access:
Access to staff: By letter, by telephone
Access to building, collections or gallery: No prior appointment required
Hours: End Mar to end Sep, daily, 1000 to 1800; Oct, daily, 1000 to 1700; beg Nov to end Mar, Wed to Sun, 1000 to 1600
Other restrictions: Closed 24 to 26 Dec, 1 Jan. Opening times are subject to change, for up-to-date information contact English Heritage by phone or visit the website

General description:
Magnificent ruin of a 14th century castle. Now an eerie skeleton, the castle features a large gatehouse which later became the keep, and extensive curtain walls and towers.

Internet home pages:
http://www.english-heritage.org.uk

872
DUNSTER CASTLE
Dunster, Minehead, Somerset, TA24 6SL

Tel: 01643 821314
Fax: 01643 823000
Email: dunstercastle@nationaltrust.org.uk

Organisation type and purpose: Registered charity (charity number 205846), historic building, house or site, suitable for ages: 5+.
Parent body:
The National Trust (South West Region)
Wessex Regional Office, tel: 01985 843600

Enquiries to: Visitor Services Manager
Access:
Access to staff: By letter, by telephone, by fax, by email
Hours: Daily, 0900 to 1700
Access for disabled people: Parking provided, access to all public areas, toilet facilities
Other restrictions: Designated parking 300yds. Drop-off point. 2 manual wheelchairs available. 1 single-seater powered mobility vehicle. Steps to entrance. Ground floor accessible with assistance, steps into conservatory and billiard room. Access to other floors via stairclimber. Visitors should tel. in advance to check availability of stairclimber and mobility vehicles. Level entrance to shop. Some steep paths. Recommended route map.

General description:
Dramatically sited atop a wooded hill, there has been a castle here since at least Norman times. The 13th century gatehouse survives, but the present building was remodelled in 1868-72 by Antony Salvin for the Luttrell family, who lived here for 600 years. The fine oak staircase and plasterwork of the 17th century house he adapted can still be seen. There is a sheltered terrace to the south on which tender plants and shrubs grow, and beautiful parkland in which to walk. Home to the National Collection of Strawberry Trees and Britain's oldest lemon tree.
Information services:
Helpline available, tel no: 01643 823004 (Infoline).
Tape recording guides for the visually impaired. Braille guide. Large-print guide.
Touch list. Handling collection. Scented plants.
Suitable for school groups. Education room/centre. Live interpretation. Children's guide. Children's quiz/trail. Adult study days.
Tel. for details of out of hours guided tours of house and/or attics and basements.
Special visitor services: Tape recorded guides, materials and/or activities for children.
Education services: Group education facilities.
Services for disabled people: For the visually impaired.
Collections:
National Collection of Strawberry Trees

Internet home pages:
http://www.nationaltrust.org.uk/regions/wessex

873
DUNSTER WORKING WATERMILL
Mill Lane, Dunster, Minehead, Somerset, TA24 6SW

Tel: 01643 821759

Organisation type and purpose: National organisation, registered charity (charity number 205846), historic building, house or site, suitable for ages: 12+.
Parent Body:
The National Trust (South West Region)
Wessex Regional Office, tel: 01985 843600

Enquiries to: Manager
Access:
Access to staff: By letter
Access to building, collections or gallery: No prior appointment required
Hours: 22 Mar to 23 May, Mon, Tue, Wed, Thu, Sat, Sun, 1030 to 1700;
24 May to 26 Sep, daily, 1030 to 1700;
27 Sep to 2 Nov, Mon, Tue, Wed, Thu, Sat, Sun, 1030 to 1700
Open Good Friday
Other restrictions: The mill is a private business and all visitors, including National Trust members, pay the admission charge.
Access for disabled people: level entry
Other restrictions: Ground floor accessible with assistance. No access to other floors. Level entrance to shop. Steps to tea-room entrance.

General description:
Built on the site of a mill mentioned in the Domesday Survey of 1086, the present mill dates from the 18th century and was restored to working order in 1979.

Internet home pages:
http://www.nationaltrust.org.uk/regions/wessex

874
DUNWICH MUSEUM
St James Street, Dunwich, Saxmundham, Suffolk, IP17 3DT

Tel: 01728 648796
Formed: 1972

Organisation type and purpose: Independently owned, museum, suitable for ages: 8+.

Enquiries to: Manager
Access:
Access to staff: By letter, by telephone, visitors by prior appointment
Hours: 1st Apr to 31st Oct: 1130 to 1630

General description:
History of Dunwich from Roman times with model of the town in the 12th century; also local wildlife and social history; souvenir shop; books for sale.
Catalogues:
Catalogue for library is in-house only.

875
DURHAM ART GALLERY
See - Durham Light Infantry Museum & Durham Art Gallery

876
DURHAM CATHEDRAL, THE
Treasures of St Cuthbert Exhibition, Durham, DH1 3EH

Tel: 0191 386 4266
Fax: 0191 386 4267
Email: enquiries@durhamcathedral.co.uk
Formed: 1975

Organisation type and purpose: Independently owned, museum, suitable for ages: 8+.
Parent body:
The Chapter of Durham Cathedral
Address for Correspondence:
The Chapter of Durham Cathedral
The Chapter Office, The College, Durham, DH1 3EH

Enquiries to: The Chapter Steward
Access:
Access to staff: By letter, by fax, by email, Internet web pages
Access for disabled people: level entry, toilet facilities
Other restrictions: Access to all areas of exhibition.
Large print version of display information and some booklets available.

General description:
A museum of cathedral artefacts. It contains the coffin of St Cuthbert (7th century); opus anglicanum vestments (10th century); decorated manuscripts (8th-12th Centuries); episcopal rings (12th/13th Centuries); Church plate (17th-18th Centuries); a sanctuary knocker (12th century); and a 13th century conyers falchion tenure sword.

Information services:
Education services: Group education facilities, resources for Key Stages 1 and 2, 3 and 4.
Services for disabled people: For the visually impaired; displays and/or information at wheelchair height.
Collections:
St Cuthbert's Coffin and Pectoral Cross
Anglo-Saxon embroideries
Seals: 12-15th centuries
Manuscripts: 8-12th century
Plate and silverware: 17th and 18th century
Anglo-Saxon sculptured stones in the monks' dormitory, 8th-11th Centuries
Printed publications:
Guide Book (£5, direct from the Chapter Office)
Various leaflets (50p to £5, direct from the Chapter Office)

877
DURHAM COUNTY COUNCIL CULTURAL SERVICES

County Hall, Durham, DH1 5TY

Tel: 0191 383 3595
Fax: 0191 384 1336
Email: alm@durham.gov.uk
Formed: 1991
Formerly: Durham County Library, Durham Arts, Libraries and Museums Department

Organisation type and purpose: Local government body, museum, art gallery, public library.
Archives department.
Involved in Arts Development work in Co Durham.
Parent body:
Durham County Council
Tel: 0191 386 4411, email: help@durham.gov.uk
Responsible for:
Binchester Roman Fort
Binchester, Wear Valley, Co Durham, DL14 8DJ, tel: 01388 663089, fax: 0191 384 1336, email/website: archaeology@durham.gov.uk
Durham Archaeology Department
County Hall, Durham, DH1 5TY, tel: 0191 383 3000, fax: 0191 384 1336
Durham Light Infantry Museum & Durham Art Gallery
Aykley Heads, Durham, DH1 5TU, tel: 0191 384 2214, fax: 0191 386 1770, email/website: info@durham.gov.uk/dli
Killhope Lead Mining Museum
Lanehead, Upper Weardale, Bishop Auckland, Co Durham, DL13 1AR, tel: 01388 537505, fax: 01388 537617, email/website: killhope@durham.gov.uk
Public libraries

Enquiries to: Director
Direct tel: 0191 383 3600
Access:
Access to staff: By letter, by telephone, by fax, by email, visitors by prior appointment, Internet web pages
Hours: Mon to Fri, 0900 to 1700

General description:
General, social sciences, humanities, music, local studies resources at Durham City Library, history of the Durham Light Infantry in the DLI Museum. Archives in the County Record Office.
Collections:
Local Studies Collections (at Durham City)
Catalogues:
Catalogue for library is in-house only. Catalogue for all of the collections is only available in-house.
Publications list:
is available in hard copy.
Printed publications:
Community Information listings
Local History Publications Series
Local Society booklets
Prints
Sectional Catalogues (local studies)

Internet home pages:
http://www.durham.gov.uk
Small site describing County Council services.

878
DURHAM LIGHT INFANTRY MUSEUM & DURHAM ART GALLERY

Aykley Heads, Durham, DH1 5TU

Tel: 0191 384 2214
Fax: 0191 386 1770
Email: info@durham.gov.uk/dli
Formed: 1968
Formerly: Durham Light Infantry Museum

Organisation type and purpose: Local government body, museum, art gallery, suitable for ages: 5+.
Parent body:
Durham County Council Cultural Services
County Hall, Durham, DH1 5TY, tel: 0191 383 3595, fax: 0191 384 1336

Enquiries to: Manager
Access:
Access to staff: By letter, by telephone, by fax, by email, in person, Internet web pages
Access for disabled people: Parking provided, level entry, access to all public areas, toilet facilities

General description:
History of the Durham Light Infantry Regiment, 1758-1968, plus militia and volunteers of County Durham.
Durham Art Gallery features temporary exhibitions of arts/crafts, full details in events brochure or on website.
Information services:
Special visitor services: Materials and/or activities for children.
Education services: Group education facilities, resources for Key Stages 2, 3 and Further or Higher Education.
Services for disabled people: For the visually impaired; displays and/or information at wheelchair height.
Collections:
Uniforms, badges, documents, photographs, medals, letters, diaries, weapons and equipment relating to The Durham Light Infantry and its soldiers, including general issue items required to fill gaps in displays, 1758-1968
Archive of DLI records and photographs is now held at Durham County Record Office (website www.durham.gov.uk/cro). Catalogue will be published via web 2003
Books either referring directly to the DLI or to campaigns in which the regiment served
Catalogues:
Catalogue for library is in-house only. Catalogue for all of the collections is only available in-house.
Publications list:
is available on-line.

Internet home pages:
http://www.durham.ac.uk/dli

879
DURHAM UNIVERSITY

Museum of Archaeology, The Old Fulling Mill, The Banks, Durham, DH1 3EB

Tel: 0191 374 3623
Email: L.M.Brewster@durham.ac.uk

Organisation type and purpose: Registered charity (charity number Exempt), museum, university department or institute, suitable for ages: 8+.
Parent body:
University of Durham
Old Shire Hall, Old Elvet, Durham, DH1 3HP, tel: 0191 374 2000, fax: 0191 374 7250

Enquiries to: Curator
Direct tel: 0191 374 7911
Direct fax: 0191 374 7911
Other contacts: Shop Manager at the Fulling Mill for sales, opening times, events.
Access:
Access to staff: By telephone, by email
Access to building, collections or gallery: No prior appointment required
Hours: Apr to Oct: daily, 1100 to 1600
Nov to Mar: Fri, Sat, Sun, Mon, 1130 to 1530

General description:
A museum of local archaeology and also the repository for research material for Durham University. It is the fundamental archaeological resource for the world heritage site of Durham, and also includes significant collections of Roman pottery and epigraphy.
Information services:
Education services: Group education facilities, resources for Key Stages 1 and 2, 3, 4 and Further or Higher Education..
Collections:
Cathedral Library. Collection of altars and inscribed stones and sculpture from Hadrian's Wall and other northern sites. Roman. 52 items
Hoopell collection, Roman remains from Binchester, Co. Durham. Roman. Several hundred items
Oswald-Plicque collection of Samian pottery. Roman. Several 1000 sherds
Catalogues:
Catalogue for all of the collections is only available in-house.

Internet home pages:
http://www.dur.ac.uk/fulling.mill
General information.

880
DURHAM UNIVERSITY

Oriental Museum, Elvet Hill, Durham, DH1 3TH

Tel: 0191 374 7911
Fax: 0191 374 7911
Email: Oriental.Museum@durham.ac.uk
Formed: 1960
Formerly: Gulbenkian Museum of Oriental Art, date of change, 1983

Organisation type and purpose: Registered charity, museum, university department or institute, suitable for ages: all ages.
Parent body:
University of Durham
Old Shire Hall, Old Elvet, Durham, DH1 3HP, tel: 0191 374 2000, fax: 0191 374 7250

Enquiries to: Curator
Access:
Access to staff: By letter, by telephone, by fax, by email
Hours: Mon to Fri, 1000 to 1700; Sat, Sun, 1200 to 1700
Access for disabled people: Parking provided, ramped entry, access to all public areas, toilet facilities

General description:
Chinese arts and crafts, ancient Egyptian arts and crafts, general information on other oriental archaeology, arts and crafts.
Collections:
4th Duke of Northumberland Collection of Egyptian antiquities
H de Lazlo, Chinese antiquities
Marshall Collection of photographs of Indian archaeological monuments
Right Honourable Malcolm MacDonald Collection of Chinese ceramics
Sir Charles Hardinge Collection of Chinese jade and hardstone carvings
Printed publications:
Exhibition catalogues, postcards
Catalogue of the Egyptian Antiquities at Alnwick Castle (Birds S, London, 1880) the collection now at the Oriental Museum
Catalogue of the MacDonald Collection of Chinese Art

continued overleaf

Microform products:
Slides

Internet home pages:
http://www.dur.ac.uk/oriental.museum
Introduction to the Oriental Museum, virtual tours.

881
SIR HERBERT DUTHIE LIBRARY

Archives & Historical Section, University of Wales College of Medicine, Heath Park, Cardiff, CF14 4XN

Tel: 029 2074 2875
Fax: 029 2074 3651
Email: duthielib@cf.ac.uk

Organisation type and purpose: University department or institute, suitable for ages: 16+.
Other addresses:
Cochrane Archive
Llandough Library
Llandough Hospital
Penarth, Cardiff, tel: 029 2071 1711 ext 5497

Enquiries to: Reader Services, Librarian
Direct tel: 029 2074 4912
Other contacts: Archivist, Cochrane Library
Access:
Access to staff: By letter, by telephone, by email, visitors by prior appointment
Access to building, collections or gallery: Prior appointment required
Hours: Mon to Fri, 0900 to 1700
Access for disabled people: Parking provided, level entry

General description:
This collection consists of important textbooks on clinical medicine, including dermatology and paediatrics, surgery, obstetrics and gynaecology and public health of the 17th, 18th and 19th Centuries. There are a number of important pharmacopoeias and works on materia medica. The works are mainly British but there are a number of French texts. The range of material is comprehensive. It provides an important source of reference material for the practice of medicine and surgery from the 16th to the early 20th century. It is well housed with excellent facilities for reading and researching. No other such source exists in Wales.
Archive of material relating to medical education in Cardiff since 1900.
Material relating to work of Professor Archie Cochrane.
Collections:
Archive of documents relating to history of medical education in Cardiff
Archive of material relating to life and work of Professor Archie Cochrane
Collection of textbooks on clinical medicine of the 17th, 18th and 19th centuries
Catalogues:
Catalogue for part of the collections is only available in-house.

882
DUXFORD AIRFIELD

See - Imperial War Museum, Duxford

883
DYMCHURCH MARTELLO TOWER

Dymchurch, Kent

Tel: 01304 211067

Parent body:
English Heritage (South East Region)
Tel: 01483 252000, fax: 01483 252001

Enquiries to: Manager
Access:
Access to staff: By telephone
Access to building, collections or gallery: No prior appointment required
Hours: Tel: 01304 211067 for opening times

General description:
One of many artillery towers that formed part of a chain of strongholds to resist Napoleon.

Internet home pages:
http://www.english-heritage.org.uk

884
DYRHAM PARK

Dyrham, Chippenham, Gloucestershire, SN14 8ER

Tel: 01179 372501
Fax: 01179 371353
Email: dyrhampark@ntrust.org.uk
Formed: 1895

Organisation type and purpose: National organisation, advisory body, membership association (membership is by subscription), registered charity (charity number 205846), museum, historic building, house or site, suitable for ages: all ages.
Parent body:, The National Trust (South West Region)
Wessex Regional Office, tel: 01985 843600
Regional Offices:
The National Trust
Wessex Regional Office, Eastleigh Court, Warminster, Wiltshire, BA12 9HW, tel: 01985 843600, fax: 01985 893624

Enquiries to: Property Manager
Access:
Access to staff: By letter, by telephone, visitors by prior appointment, charges to non-members
Access for disabled people: level entry, toilet facilities
Other restrictions: Transfer available. Drop-off point. 2 manual wheelchairs available. Steps to entrance. Accessible entrance via East door. Ground floor fully accessible, domestic rooms accessible via separate entrance. No access to other floors. Only four upstairs rooms inaccessible, photograph album of these rooms available. Ramped entrance to shop and to restaurant. Grounds largely accessible.

General description:
Dyrham Park was built between 1691 and 1702 for William Blathwayt, William III's Secretary at War and Secretary of State. The rooms have changed little since they were furnished by Blathwayt and their contents are recorded in his housekeeper's inventory. There are many fine textiles and paintings, as well as items of blue-and-white Delftware, reflecting the contemporary taste for Dutch fashions. Restored Victorian domestic rooms which are open include kitchen, bells passage, bakehouse, larders, tenants' hall and Delft-tiled dairy. Please note that due to the fragile nature of their contents, some rooms have very low light levels.
Information services:
CD-ROM based services
Suitable for school groups. Education room/centre.
Braille guide. Large-print guide. Audio guide. Sympathetic Hearing Scheme. Hearing loop in reception buildings and some rooms in house
Family activity packs. CD-ROM available for purchase. Children's guidebook illustrated by member of the Blathwayt family.
Guide leaflets to the house in several languages.
Hip-carrying infant seats for loan.
Specialist guided tours some weekdays, tel. for details. Access for walkers and cyclists from Cotswold Way, and Avon and Wiltshire cycleways. 'Tracker Packs' in the house for families.
Special visitor services: Tape recorded guides, materials and/or activities for children.
Education services: Group education facilities.
Services for disabled people: For the visually impaired; for the hearing impaired.
Printed publications:
Guide Book
Electronic and video products:
CD-ROM

Internet home pages:
http://www.nationaltrust.org.uk/regions/wessex

885
DYSON PERRINS MUSEUM

See - Museum of Worcester Porcelain

886
EARLS BARTON MUSEUM OF LOCAL LIFE

27 The Square, Earls Barton, Northampton, NN6 0HD

Tel: 01604 811735 (private)
Formed: 1987

Organisation type and purpose: Registered charity (charity number 800531), museum, suitable for ages: all ages.

Enquiries to: Chairman
Access:
Access to staff: By letter, by telephone

General description:
The collections show aspects of village life, particularly shoe- making and lace making, which were important at the turn of the century. There is a reconstruction of the ground floor of a shoe worker's house (Victorian); a small corner shop; and other exhibitions which change quarterly, and which are collections belonging to local people.
Information services:
Special visitor services: Guided tours..
Collections:
Photographs, documents, census returns

887
EARTH CENTRE

Denaby Main, Doncaster, South Yorkshire, DN12 4EA

Tel: 01709 512000
Fax: 01709 512010
Email: info@earthcentre.org.uk
Formed: 1999
Still known as: Museum of the Earth, date of change, 1994

Organisation type and purpose: International organisation, registered charity, museum, suitable for ages: all ages, consultancy.
Visitor centre.
Visitor attraction on 400 acre site whose mission is to inspire understanding of sustainable development and to help people become involved in the process of achieving it in their own lives and for the world.
Wide range of funding partners from the private, public and independent sectors::
Numerous individual organisations

Enquiries to: Chief Executive
Direct tel: 01709 513915
Direct fax: 01709 512010
Direct email: info@earthcentre.org.uk
Access:
Access to staff: By letter, by fax, by email, in person, Internet web pages
Hours: Mon to Sun, 1000 to 1800
Access for disabled people: Parking provided, level entry, access to all public areas, toilet facilities

General description:
All areas relating to sustainable development: renewable energy; energy and resource - efficient building design; organic gardening and permaculture; non-polluting, resource efficient water treatment; environmentally-sensitive land management; fair trade and sustainable economics etc.
Catalogues:
Catalogue for part of the collections is only available in-house.
Printed publications:
Annual Report 2000
Education Resources
Information sheets

Internet home pages:
http://www.earthcentre.org.uk
Detailed information on Earth Centre.

888
EAST ANGLIA TRANSPORT MUSEUM

Chapel Road, Carlton Colville, Lowestoft, Suffolk, NR33 8BL

Tel: 01502 518459
Fax: 01502 584658
Email: enquiries@eatm.org.uk
Acronym or abbreviation: EATM
Formed: 1972

Organisation type and purpose: Museum, suitable for ages: 5+.
Affiliated to:
Association for Independent Museums
Association for Suffolk Museums
National Association for Road Transport Museums
Transport Trust

Enquiries to: Secretary
Direct tel: 01502 731459
Other contacts: Publicity Officer for all matters relating to publicity.
Access:
Access to staff: By letter, by telephone
Access for disabled people: Parking provided, level entry, toilet facilities

General description:
A working transport museum in a re-constructed street scene of the 1930s, featuring tram and trolleybus lines; a narrow-gauge railway; vehicles on exhibition include electric, petrol, diesel and steam examples of many types.
Information services:
Library available for reference (for conditions see Access above)
Special visitor services: Guided tours.
Education services: Group education facilities, resources for Key Stages 1 and 2 and 3..
Collections:
Transport vehicles, photographs, books, documents, badges, ticket machines, tickets etc
Various UK and Amsterdam trams 1900-1950
Various UK and Continental trolleybuses 1930-1960
Catalogues:
Catalogue for library is in-house only. Catalogue for all of the collections is only available in-house.
Printed publications:
Museum Guide Book (full colour, £1)

Internet home pages:
http://www.eatm.org.uk
Full details of museum and major exhibits.

889
EAST GRINSTEAD TOWN MUSEUM

East Court, College Lane, East Grinstead, West Sussex, RH19 3LT

Formed: 1976

Organisation type and purpose: Voluntary organisation, registered charity (charity number 1047505), museum.
Supporters group:
East Grinstead Museum Society
at the same address

Enquiries to: Curator
Direct tel: 01342 712087 (home)
Other contacts: Keeper of Photography
Access:
Access to staff: By letter, visitors by prior appointment
Hours: By arrangement, any reasonable time
Other restrictions: Difficult access for disabled (steep narrow steps).
Access to building, collections or gallery: No access other than to staff
Hours: Wed and Sat, 1400 to 1600
Other restrictions: Prior appointment for library and photographs.

General description:
Local history of East Grinstead and neighbouring parishes in Sussex, Surrey and Kent. Limited genealogical information within that area.
Collections:
5000 photographic images of the area, objects and pictures from East Grinstead's history
Reference collection of books on the area in formation
The Museum's archive collection is at West Sussex Record Office, Chichester
Local pottery
Catalogues:
Catalogue for all of the collections is only available in-house.
Printed publications:
East Grinstead Museum Compass (3 times a year, journal, £1 plus p&p))
Information leaflets, newsletter, bulletins (back numbers available)
Books, booklets and postcards of local interest

Internet home pages:
http://www.
Under construction.

890
EAST KENT RAILWAY

Station Road, Shepherdswell, Dover, Kent, CT15 7PD

Tel: 01304 832042
Formed: 1989
Formerly: White Cliffs Colliery Line

Organisation type and purpose: Independently owned, registered charity (charity number 297767), museum, suitable for ages: 12+.
Railway preservation.

Enquiries to: Treasurer
Access:
Access to staff: By letter, by telephone
Access to building, collections or gallery: No prior appointment required
Hours: Daily, 0900 to 1500 - no trains
Mar to Oct: Sun, 0900 to 1700 - train service
Access for disabled people: Parking provided

General description:
Originally constructed to carry coal from the local mines, the East Kent Railway now carries passengers from Shepherdswell to the village of Eythorne using steam and diesel locomotives.
Information services:
Special visitor services: Guided tours..
Collections:
Artefacts, photographs of East Kent Railway history
Rolling stock, locomotives, steam and diesel on site

Internet home pages:
http://www.eastkentrailway.com

891
EAST LANCASHIRE REGIMENT

See - Queen's Lancashire Regimental Museum

892
EAST LOTHIAN COUNCIL MUSEUMS SERVICE HEADQUARTERS

Library and Museums Headquarters, Dunbar Road, Haddington, East Lothian, EH41 3PJ

Tel: 01620 828203
Fax: 01620 828201
Email: elms@eastlothian.gov.uk
Acronym or abbreviation: ELMS
Formed: 1990

Organisation type and purpose: Local government body, museum.

Enquiries to: Museums Officer
Direct email: pgray@eastlothian.gov.uk
Access:
Access to staff: By letter, by telephone, by fax, by email, visitors by prior appointment, Internet web pages
Access to building, collections or gallery: Prior appointment required
Access for disabled people: Parking provided, level entry, access to all public areas, toilet facilities

General description:
Local history, natural history, archaeology, social and industrial history, fine art, numismatics.
Catalogues:
Catalogue for all of the collections is only available in-house.

Internet home pages:
http://www.elothian-museums.demon.co.uk/
http://www.historyshelf.org/
Digitisation projects.

893
EAST MIDLANDS MUSEUMS SERVICE

PO Box 7221, Wollaton Park, Nottingham, NG12 3WH

Tel: 01949 81734
Fax: 01949 81859
Email: emms@emms.org.uk
Acronym or abbreviation: EmmS
Formed: 1981
Formerly: East Midlands Area Museum Service, date of change, 1991

Organisation type and purpose: Advisory body, membership association (membership is by subscription), present number of members: 129, registered charity (charity number 1009683), training organisation, consultancy, research organisation.
Regional agency to enhance and improve standards in care and public use of museums collections in the East Midlands.

Enquiries to: Network Coordinator
Access:
Access to staff: By letter, by telephone, by fax, by email
Hours: Variable but consistent

General description:
Museum management, organisation and practice, museum collections in the East Midlands, collections care.
Trade and statistical:
Data on visitors and visits made to museums in the East Midlands.
Economic contribution of East Midlands Museums.
Employment data on East Midlands Museums.
Advice and information relating to museums in the East Midlands
Regional emergencies and disaster squad
Freelance education workers.
Publications list:
is available in hard copy.
Printed publications:
Annual Report
HOT NEWS (monthly, £24 a year)
Access Guide to Museums in the East Midlands (1996)
Facing Forward: A Museum Strategy for the East Midlands 1996-2001 (1996, £3)
Knowing Our Visitors
Museum and Record Office Emergency Disaster manual (for historic buildings and collections)
Good Practice Notes, Factsheets

Address for ordering publications:
Printed publications:
also available from the, Leicester University Bookshop

Internet home pages:
http://www.emms.org.uk

894
EAST RIDDLESDEN HALL
Bradford Road, Keighley, West Yorkshire, BD20 5EL

Tel: 01535 607075
Fax: 01535 691462
Email: eastriddlesden@nationaltrust.org.uk
Formed: 1895

Organisation type and purpose: National organisation, registered charity (charity number 205846), museum, historic building, house or site, suitable for ages: 8+.
The National Trust for places of historic interest and natural beauty.
Parent body:
The National Trust (Yorkshire and North East)
Yorkshire Regional Office, tel: 01904 702021

Enquiries to: Visitor Services Manager
Access:
Access to staff: By letter, by telephone, by fax, by email
Hours: Mon to Sun, 0830 to 1700
Access to building, collections or gallery: Prior appointment required
Hours: House: Apr to Jun, Tue, Wed, Sat, Sun, 1200 to 1700; Jul and Aug, Mon, Tue, Wed, Sat, Sun, 1200 to 1700; Sep to beg Nov, Tue, Wed, Sat, Sun, 1200 to 1700
Open Bank Holiday Mondays and Good Friday. Open additional days in school holidays.
Other restrictions: House opens at 1300 on Saturdays. Mornings - by prior appointment.
Access for disabled people: Parking provided, toilet facilities
Other restrictions: Designated parking 100yds. Drop-off point. 1 manual wheelchair available. Steps to entrance. Accessible entrance via 1 step. Ground floor fully accessible. No access to other floors. Photograph album. Steps to shop entrance. Steps to tea-room entrance. Grounds largely accessible.

General description:
A characterful 17th century manor house and buildings, originally belonging to the merchant James Murgatroyd of Halifax, with distinctive architectural details, set in mature grounds with beech trees, ducks and a pond. The house has a wonderful ambience and is furnished with delicate needlework pictures and embroideries, textiles, Yorkshire oak furniture and pewter. There is also a handling collection for you to discover. The ruined Starkie Wing façade, covered in clambering clematis, honeysuckle and roses, provides a dramatic backdrop to the garden. Wildflowers, bulbs, perennials, lavender and a fragrant herb border provide a changing carpet of colour throughout the year. A magnificent 17th century oak-framed barn also stands in the grounds.
Information services:
Braille guide. Large-print guide. Touch list. Handling collection.
Sympathetic Hearing Scheme.
Front-carrying baby slings for loan.
Suitable for school groups. Live interpretation. Children's guide. Children's quiz/trail. Adult study days.
Special visitor services: Guided tours, materials and/or activities for children.
Education services: Group education facilities, resources for Key Stage 2.
Services for disabled people: For the visually impaired; for the hearing impaired; displays and/or information at wheelchair height.
Collections:
Textiles, embroideries
Catalogues:
Catalogue for library is in-house only.
Printed publications:
Various products available

Internet home pages:
http://www.nationaltrust.org.uk

895
EAST SURREY MUSEUM
1 Stafford Road, Caterham, Surrey, CR3 6JG

Tel: 01883 340275
Email: es@emuseum.freeserve.co.uk
Formed: 1980

Organisation type and purpose: Independently owned, registered charity (charity number 283036), museum, suitable for ages: all ages.
Local history museum.

Enquiries to: Curator
Other contacts: Honorary Secretary for administrative queries.
Access:
Access to staff: By letter, by telephone, by email, in person
Access to building, collections or gallery: No prior appointment required
Hours: Wed to Sat, 1000 to 1700; Sun, 1400 to 1700
Access for disabled people: access to all public areas

General description:
Changing displays on local history, access to the collection for study and research, visits arranged to schools and community groups, school loan box available.
Information services:
Special visitor services: Materials and/or activities for children.
Education services: Group education facilities, resources for Key Stages 1 and 2 and 3..
Catalogues:
Catalogue for library is in-house only. Catalogue for all of the collections is only available in-house.
Printed publications:
Leaflet at the museum or on request (free)

896
EASTBOURNE LIFEBOAT MUSEUM
Grand Court, King Edwards Parade, Eastbourne, East Sussex, BN21 4BU

Tel: 01323 730717
Formed: 1937

Organisation type and purpose: Registered charity (charity number 209603), museum, suitable for ages: 8+.

Enquiries to: Curator
Access:
Access to staff: By letter, in person
Access to building, collections or gallery: No prior appointment required
Hours: Daily, 1000 to 1700
Other restrictions: Closed Christmas to Easter.
Access for disabled people: Parking provided, level entry

General description:
A history of Eastbourne Lifeboat. Accounts of rescues, models etc, plus shop.
Collections:
Objects, pictures and photographs of casualties over the years
Printed publications:
The History of Eastbourne Lifeboat (£3.50, available direct from curator, museum shop)

Address for ordering publications:
Printed publications:
Honorary Curator

897
EASTBURY MANOR HOUSE
Eastbury Square, Barking, London, IG11 9SN

Tel: 020 8507 0119
Fax: 020 8507 0118

Organisation type and purpose: National organisation, registered charity (charity number 205846), historic building, house or site.
Parent body:
The National Trust (South and South East Region)
Thames and Solent Regional Office, tel: 01494 528051
Managed by:
London Borough of Barking and Dagenham

Enquiries to: Manager
Access:
Access to staff: By letter, by telephone, by fax

General description:
An important example of a medium-sized brick built Elizabethan manor house. The house is architecturally distinguished and well-preserved. Recent restoration has revealed notable wall paintings. Described by Daniel Defoe in 'A Tour Through the Whole Island of Great Britain' as 'where tradition says the Gunpowder Treason Plot was first contrived'. The house is managed by the London Borough of Barking and Dagenham.

Internet home pages:
http://www.nationaltrust.org.uk

898
EASTLEIGH MUSEUM
25 High Street, Eastleigh, Hampshire, SO50 5LF

Tel: 023 8064 3026
Fax: 023 8065 3582
Email: musmst@hants.gov.uk
Formed: 1986

Organisation type and purpose: Professional body, museum, art gallery, historic building, house or site.
Parent body:
Hampshire County Council Museums Service (HCCMS)
Chilcomb House, Chilcomb Lane, Winchester, Hampshire, SO23 8RD, tel: 01962 846304, fax: 01962 869836

Enquiries to: Curator
Access:
Access to staff: By letter, by telephone, by fax, by email, in person, visitors by prior appointment, Internet web pages
Access to building, collections or gallery: No prior appointment required
Hours: Tue to Fri, 1000 to 1700; Sat 1000 to 1600
Access for disabled people: level entry, access to all public areas
Other restrictions: Level access to all display

General description:
Local and social history from 1850. The local museum for Eastleigh, Hampshire. Displays of local history including the brickmaking and LSWR Eastleigh Carriage and Wagon Works, and a temporary exhibition gallery.
Collections:
Eric Forge Collection, LSWR transport history
Local books, photographs, documents and maps about the Borough of Eastleigh and its history
Catalogues:
Catalogue for library is in-house only. Catalogue for all of the collections is available in-house and part is on-line.
Printed publications:
Publications list is available from the Librarian, Hampshire County Council Museums Service Headquarters, Chilcomb House, Winchester, SO23 8RD
Available from the Museum

Internet home pages:
http://www.hants.gov.uk/museum/eastlmus
Collections etc.

899
EASTTHORPE VISUAL ARTS
Huddersfield Road, Mirfield, West Yorkshire, WF14 8AN

Tel: 01924 497646
Fax: 01924 497646

Organisation type and purpose: Registered charity, art gallery, suitable for ages: 8+.
Community print workshop.

Enquiries to: Administrator
Direct email: eva@pop3.poptel.org.uk
Access:
Access to staff: By telephone, by email, visitors by prior appointment
Access to building, collections or gallery: No prior appointment required
Hours: Gallery: Tue to Sat, 1200 to 1600
Printmaking facilities: Mon, 1400 to 1600; Tue 1200 to 1600; Wed to Sat, 1200 to 1600
Access for disabled people: Parking provided, ramped entry, level entry, access to all public areas, toilet facilities

General description:
The EVA Centre houses the archetype@EVA retail space, exhibiting gallery, seven studios, a community photographic darkroom, professional etching and screen printing workshops.
Information services:
Special visitor services: Guided tours.
Education services: Group education facilities.
Services for disabled people: For the visually impaired.

Internet home pages:
http://homepages.poptel.org.uk/eva/index.html

900
ECOACTIVE EDUCATION CENTRE, THE
All Saints Hall, Haggerston Street, London, E8 4HT

Tel: 020 7923 7899
Fax: 020 7923 7966
Email: hcr-ecoactive@lineone.net
Formed: 1995
Formed from: Rubbish Dump Waste Not Recycling, date of change, 1999

Organisation type and purpose: Suitable for ages: 5+.
To develop environmental awareness through project work linked to National Curriculum for schools and to support environmental action/ activities for schools and youth community groups.
Parent body:
Hackney Community Transport (HCT)
1 Hertford Road, London, N1 5SH, tel: 020 7275 2450, fax: 020 7275 9779

Enquiries to: Manager
Access:
Access to staff: By telephone, by email, visitors by prior appointment
Hours: Mon to Thu, 0900 to 1700
Access to building, collections or gallery: Prior appointment required
Hours: Mon to Thu, 0900 to 1700
Access for disabled people: level entry, access to all public areas, toilet facilities

General description:
Environmental issues, mainly waste, energy, biodiversity and food.
Education focus, mainly science, geography, citizenship, education for sustainability, workshop.
Information services:
Special visitor services: Guided tours, materials and/or activities for children.
Education services: Group education facilities, resources for Key Stages 1 and 2, 3 and 4.
Services for disabled people: Displays and/or information at wheelchair height.
Collections:
Interactive exhibits, eg 2 bikes to cycle which light up the story comparing aluminium can-making from raw materials and by recycling cans
Large model magnetic can sorter to separate aluminium from steel, bins which open to compare rubbish of 1930 with present day
Large collection of useful and attractive objects made from re-used scrap materials
Magnetic world map with collection of models demonstrating issues of fair trade, organic foods, food miles, food chains etc.
Workshop area for activities such as paper-making, art from scrap, science experiments
Ecokitchen exhibits of energy/water conservation appliances; interactive greenhouse effect model; and lightbulb types comparison model
Large library of environmental information collected from:
Education organisations
Government departments
Environmental organisations
Catalogues:
Catalogue for library is in-house only.
Publications list:
is available in hard copy.
Printed publications:
Reduce, Reuse, Recycle, Throw Away
Too Good to Bin
Cool Clean & Green

901
EDINBURGH PRINTMAKERS STUDIO & GALLERY
23 Union Street, Edinburgh, EH1 3LR

Tel: 0131 557 2479
Fax: 0131 558 8418
Email: printmakers@ednet.co.uk
Formed: 1967

Organisation type and purpose: International organisation, registered charity (charity number SCO 09015), art gallery, suitable for ages: 8+.
Open access for artists and the public.

Enquiries to: Administrator
Access:
Access to staff: By letter, by fax, by email, visitors by prior appointment
Access to building, collections or gallery: No prior appointment required
Hours: Tue to Sat, 1000 to 1800

General description:
This is Edinburgh's main studio for practising artists who make limited edition prints - etchings, lithographs, screen prints and relief prints. Visitors may watch artists at work and purchase prints from the gallery.
Information services:
Special visitor services: Guided tours, materials and/or activities for children.
Education services: Group education facilities..
Collections:
Artists' prints shown include works by John Bellany, Hugh Buchanan, Sylvia von Hartmann, Elspeth Lamb, Robert Maclaurin, Barbara Rae
Catalogues:
Catalogue for part of the collections is on-line.
Publications list:
is available in hard copy and online.

Internet home pages:
http://www.edinburgh-printmakers.co.uk

902
EDINBURGH SCOUT MUSEUM
7 Valleyfield Street, Edinburgh, EH3 9LP

Tel: 0131 229 3756
Formed: 1973

Organisation type and purpose: Museum, suitable for ages: 8+.

Enquiries to: Administrator
Access:
Access to staff: By letter
Access to building, collections or gallery: Prior appointment required

General description:
Museum of the history and development of the Scout Movement, especially in the city of Edinburgh.
Collections:
Scouting ephemera, 1907-date, 9000 items

903
EDINBURGH UNIVERSITY COLLECTION OF HISTORIC MUSICAL INSTRUMENTS
Reid Concert Hall, Bristo Square, Edinburgh, EH8 9AG

Tel: +44 131 650 2422 (International) 0131 650 2423 (UK only)
Fax: 0131 650 2425
Email: euchmi@ed.ac.uk

Organisation type and purpose: Suitable for ages: all ages.
Governing body:
University of Edinburgh

Enquiries to: Director/Curator
Other contacts: (1) Assistant Curator; (2) Collection Secretary

General description:
Historic musical instruments; the history of the instruments of the orchestra, the wind band, theatre, dance, popular music, domestic music-making, brass bands etc.
The Sound Laboratory is a new hands-on approach showing how musical instruments work, with live sounds, physical models, computer displays and visual effects.
Collections:
The Collection contains over 2800 items including some 2000 instruments, about half of which are on display
Outstanding display of over 1000 musical instruments showing 400 years of history of folk and domestic music, bands and orchestras, plus interactive devices
Catalogues:
Catalogue for all of the collections is only available in-house.
Printed publications:
Catalogues (for purchase)
Guide to the Collection (for purchase)
Postcards (for purchase)

Internet home pages:
http://www.music.ed.ac.uk/euchmi/

904
EDWARD HAUGHEY AVIATION HERITAGE CENTRE
See - Solway Aviation Museum

905
EDZELL CASTLE
Edzell, Brechin, Angus, DD9 7UE

Tel: 01356 648631

Organisation type and purpose: Historic building, house or site.
Parent body:
Historic Scotland

Enquiries to: Curator
Access:
Access to staff: By letter
Access for disabled people: Parking provided, level entry, toilet facilities

General description:
16th century courtyard mansion with late medieval tower house and walled garden, early 17th century summer house.
Printed publications:
Guide Book (£1.75)

Internet home pages:
http://www.historic-scotland.gov.uk

906
EGYPT CENTRE
University of Wales, Swansea, Singleton Park, Swansea, West Glamorgan, SA2 8PP

Tel: 01792 295960
Email: c.a.graves-brown@swansea.ac.uk
Formed: September 1998
Formerly: Wellcome Museum, date of change, 1998

continued overleaf

Organisation type and purpose: Museum.

Enquiries to: Curator
Access:
Access to staff: By letter, by telephone, by email
Hours: Tue to Sat, 1000 to 1600
Access to building, collections or gallery: No access other than to staff
Hours: Tue to Sat, 1000 to 1600
Access for disabled people: access to all public areas

General description:
Most of the material was collected by Sir Henry Wellcome and largely comprises Egyptian artefacts, ranging from the Pre-Dynastic to the Coptic periods. There is a small collection of classical antiquities.
Catalogues:
Catalogue for all of the collections is only available in-house.

Internet home pages:
http://www.swansea.ac.uk/egypt

907
EILEAN DONAN CASTLE
Dornie, Kyle, Ross-shire, IV40 8DX

Tel: 01599 555 202
Fax: 01599 555 262
Email: info@eileandonancastle.com
Formed: 1955

Organisation type and purpose: Historic building, house or site, suitable for ages: 5+.

Enquiries to: Manager
Access:
Access to staff: By letter, by telephone, by fax, by email, in person, Internet web pages
Access to building, collections or gallery: No prior appointment required
Hours: Daily, 1000 to 1730
Other restrictions: Closed Dec, Jan, Feb.

General description:
The site has been fortified at least since the 13th century. However in 1719 the then castle was ruined and abandoned after bombardment by Government frigates. In 1911 it was bought by John McRae-Gilstrap who completed its reconstruction in 1932 with a bridge to the island. The rooms are now furnished and displayed as living history.
Information services:
Special visitor services: Guided tours, tape recorded guides, materials and/or activities for children..
Collections:
Furniture, arms, family possesions, displays relating the history of the castle

Internet home pages:
http://www.eileandonancastle.com

908
ELGIN LIBRARY LOCAL STUDIES SECTION
See - Moray Council

909
ELGIN MUSEUM
1 High Street, Elgin, Moray, IV30 1EQ

Tel: 01343 543675
Fax: 01343 543675
Email: curator@elginmuseum.org.uk
Formed: 1836

Organisation type and purpose: Independently owned, learned society, present number of members: c. 400, registered charity (charity number SC 01756), museum, suitable for ages: all ages.
Parent body:
The Moray Society
at the same address

Enquiries to: Curator
Access:
Access to staff: By letter, by telephone, by email, in person, visitors by prior appointment
Access for disabled people: ramped entry, toilet facilities

General description:
Fish and reptile fossils, geology, Pictish stones, archaeology, natural history, social history, art, science, ethnography, photographs.
Information services:
Library available for reference (for conditions see Access above)
Educational resources for 5-14 Environmental Studies.
Special visitor services: Guided tours, materials and/or activities for children.
Education services: Group education facilities, resources for Further or Higher Education.
Services for disabled people: For the visually impaired; displays and/or information at wheelchair height.
Collections:
Gordon Archive (Dr George Gordon of Birnie): Family papers and scientific correspondence
Grant Archive (Grant of Wester Elchies)
Catalogues:
Catalogue for library is in-house only. Catalogue for all of the collections is only available in-house but part is published.

Internet home pages:
http://www.elginmuseum.org.uk
General information about the museum.

910
ELIZABETHAN HOUSE MUSEUM
4 South Quay, Great Yarmouth, Norfolk, NR30 2QH

Tel: 01493 855746, 01493 745526 (out of season only)
Fax: 01493 745459

Organisation type and purpose: National organisation, registered charity (charity number 205846), museum, historic building, house or site, suitable for ages: 8+.
Parent body:
The National Trust (East of England)
East Anglia Regional Office, tel: 0870 609 5388
Managed by:
Norfolk Museums and Archaeology Service

Enquiries to: Manager
Access:
Access to staff: By letter, by telephone, by fax
Access for disabled people: level entry
Other restrictions: Ground floor accessible with assistance, one step into kitchen, one step to small back garden. No access to other floors. Photograph album. Level entrance to shop.

General description:
A 16th century building with rooms displayed to reflect the lives of the families who have lived here through history. Collection covering social history and domestic life; decorative and applied arts; furniture; ceramics and glass; toys and games; kitchen and cleaning equipment. Also some costume and accessories.
Of particular interest are a Tudor bedroom and dining-room, Victorian kitchen, scullery and parlour, and the Conspiracy Room, where the trial and execution of King Charles I were allegedly plotted. There is also a special children's room with replica toys, and there are hands-on activities throughout the house.
Information services:
Education services: Group education facilities, resources for Key Stage 2..
Collections:
The Absolon collection. Examples of the work of William Absolon of Great Yarmouth, a decorator of pottery and glassware, 1785-1815, 35 items
Catalogues:
Catalogue for part of the collections is only available in-house.

Internet home pages:
http://www.nationaltrust.org.uk
http://www.norfolk.gov.uk/tourism/museums
http://www.great-yarmouth.co.uk

911
ELLEN TERRY MEMORIAL MUSEUM
Smallhythe Place, Smallhythe, Tenterden, Kent, TN30 7NG

Tel: 01580 762334
Fax: 01580 762334
Email: smallhytheplace@nationaltrust.org.uk
Formed: 1929

Organisation type and purpose: National organisation, registered charity (charity number 205846), museum, historic building, house or site.
To secure the home of Dame Ellen Terry and its contents.
Parent body:
The National Trust

Enquiries to: Custodian
Access:
Access to staff: By letter, by telephone, by email, in person, visitors by prior appointment
Other restrictions: Research access Nov to Feb.

General description:
A 16th century half-timbered house, once the home of Ellen Terry. It contains stage costumes; personal and theatrical possessions; and mementoes of many great theatrical names. There is a large archive of letters, programmes, playbills and photographs, and many pictures and paintings. All largely mid- late 19th century and early 20th century.
Information services:
Special visitor services: Guided tours, materials and/or activities for children.
Services for disabled people: For the visually impaired.
Catalogues:
Catalogue for library is published. Catalogue for all of the collections is only available in-house.

Internet home pages:
http://www.nationaltrust.co.uk

912
ELLENROAD TRUST
Elizabethan Way, Milnrow, Rochdale, Lancashire, OL16 4LG

Tel: 01706 881952
Email: ellenroad@aol.com
Formed: 1985

Organisation type and purpose: Registered charity (charity number 700197), historic building, house or site, suitable for ages: 5+.
Parent body:
Friends of Ellenroad
Tel: 0870 131 7421

Enquiries to: Chairman
Access:
Access to staff: By letter, by telephone, by fax, by email
Hours: 24 hours, 7 days a week
Access to building, collections or gallery: No prior appointment required
Hours: Mon to Sat, 1200 to 1600; first Sun in month excluding Jan
Access for disabled people: Parking provided, ramped entry, access to all public areas

General description:
The largest working steam mill engine in the world, in steam. Also in steam, 1841 beam engine, coal-fired Lancashire boiler and associated steam plant, high speed steam electrical generator.
Information services:
Special visitor services: Guided tours, materials and/or activities for children..
Collections:
Largest steam mill engine in the world
1841 Whitelees Beam Engine
Steam Weir pump
Lancashire boiler, coal-fired
High speed steam generating set
Barring engine
Technical drawings of the Ellenroad Engine

Printed publications:
Ellenroad Guide Book (£1.50)
Electronic and video products:
Ellenroad (video, £12)

Internet home pages:
http://www.ellenroad.org.uk
Events list, details of Friends activities.

913
ELLISLAND TRUST
Holywood Road, Dumfries, DG2 0RP

Tel: 01387 740426
Formed: 1929

Organisation type and purpose: Registered charity (charity number SCO 27994), art gallery. Trust. Heritage Centre within cottage and farm buildings occupied by Robert Burns, Scotland's national bard.

Enquiries to: Curator
Access:
Access to staff: By letter, by telephone, in person
Access for disabled people: Parking provided, toilet facilities

General description:
Ellisland Farm, home of Robert Burns 1788-1791. Museum within Burns' Cottage, video of Burns' life in Granary, riverside walk, walk to Hermitage (in grounds of Friars Carse), horse-drawn implements displayed in orchard.
Information services:
Services for disabled people: Displays and/or information at wheelchair height.
Printed publications:
Postcards and miscellaneous gift items

Internet home pages:
http://www.ellislandfarm.co.uk

914
ELMBRIDGE MUSEUM
Church Street, Weybridge, Surrey, KT13 8DE

Tel: 01932 843573
Fax: 01932 846552
Email: info@elm-mus.datanet.co.uk
Formed: 1909
Formerly: Weybridge Museum, date of change, 1992

Organisation type and purpose: Local government body, museum, suitable for ages: under 5s upwards.
Member of:
Area Museums Service for South Eastern England
Museums Association
Surrey Museums Consultative Committee
Surrey Museums Group

Enquiries to: Manager
Other contacts: Assistant Manager for educational visits.
Access:
Access to staff: By letter, by telephone, by fax, by email, in person, visitors by prior appointment, Internet web pages
Hours: Mon, Tue, Wed and Fri, 1100 to 1700; Sat, 1000 to 1300 and 1400 to 1700
Other restrictions: Closed on Thu, Sun and Bank Holidays.

General description:
Local history, archaeology, costume, natural history, oral history, fine art, geology, film heritage archive, local studies room.
Information services:
Museums Loans Box Service for schools, colleges, community groups and societies.
Special visitor services: Materials and/or activities for children.
Education services: Group education facilities, resources for Key Stages 1 and 2 and 3.
Services for disabled people: For the visually impaired; displays and/or information at wheelchair height.
Collections:
Local photograph collection - Elmbridge
Rogers Family Collection
Surrey Costume Collection
Catalogues:
Catalogue for library is in-house only. Catalogue for all of the collections is only available in-house.
Printed publications:
Books on local history and related subjects

Internet home pages:
http://www.surrey-online.co.uk/elm-mus

915
ELSECAR HERITAGE CENTRE
Wath Road, Elsecar, Barnsley, South Yorkshire, S74 8HJ

Tel: 01226 740203
Fax: 01226 350239
Email: elsecarheritagecentre@barnsley.gov.uk
Formed: 1994
Formerly: Elsecar Workshops, date of change, 1994; Elsecar at Barnsley, date of change, 1995; Elsecar Discovery Centre, date of change, 1997

Organisation type and purpose: Local government body, museum, historic building, house or site, suitable for ages: all ages.
Links with:
Barnsley MBC, Environment & Development Programme Area
Central Offices, Kendray Street, Barnsley, South Yorkshire, S70 2TN

Enquiries to: Manager
Other contacts: Assistant Manager, Projects Manager for education, bookings.
Access:
Access to staff: By letter, by telephone, by fax, by email, visitors by prior appointment, charges made to all users
Hours: Mon to Sun, 1000 to 1700
Access to building, collections or gallery: No prior appointment required
Hours: Mon to Sun, 1000 to 1700
Access for disabled people: toilet facilities

General description:
Industrial heritage (South Yorkshire) 1850 to present day; Newcomen beam engine; science: forces, power and energy; Victorian inventions and engineers; bottles, pot lids and advertising; printing; candle making; paper making. Features hands-on exhibits on power and energy in the powerhouse. There is also a social and industrial history collection concerned with Elsecar village, the Fitzwilliam family, and surrounding local history, as featured in the Elsecar people exhibition.
Information services:
Wide variety of events, entertainments programme.
Special visitor services: Guided tours, materials and/or activities for children.
Education services: Group education facilities..
Collections:
Coddswallop: a museum of bottles and their manufacturers
Interactive science exhibits
Memorabilia:1850s to present day, industrial and social
Photographs: local interest
Catalogues:
Catalogue for all of the collections is only available in-house.
Publications list:
is available in hard copy.
Printed publications:
What's On (general leaflet)
Teacher's Pack

Internet home pages:
http://www.barnsley.gov.uk
General information

916
ELSTOW MOOT HALL MUSEUM
See - Moot Hall Museum

917
ELTHAM PALACE
Court Yard, Eltham, London, SE9 5QE

Tel: 020 8294 2548
Fax: 020 8294 2621

Organisation type and purpose: Historic building, house or site, suitable for ages: all ages.
Parent body:
English Heritage (London Region)
23 Savile Row, London, W1X 1AB, tel: 020 7973 3000, fax: 020 7937 3001

Enquiries to: Curator
Direct tel: 020 7973 3426
Other contacts: House Manager
Access:
Access to staff: By letter, by telephone, by fax
Access to building, collections or gallery: No prior appointment required
Hours: Apr to Sep: Wed to Fri, Sun and Bank Holidays, 1000 to 1800
Oct: Wed to Fri, Sun, 1000 to 1700
Nov to Mar: Wed to Fri, Sun 1000 to 1600
Other restrictions: Closed 22 Dec to 1 Feb
Opening times are subject to change, for up-to-date information contact English Heritage by phone or visit the website.

General description:
A magnificent example of the 1930s Art Deco style. Built by millionaire Stephen Courtauld as a lavish venue in which to host the fashionable parties of the era, it is home to many fascinating creative design ideas and painstakingly recreated interiors. Surrounded by stunning moated gardens it is also linked to the Great Hall of a medieval royal palace - built for Edward IV, and Henry VIII's home as a child.
Information services:
Available for private and corporate events
Audio tours also available in French and German.
Special visitor services: Tape recorded guides, materials and/or activities for children.
Education services: Group education facilities.
Services for disabled people: For the hearing impaired.

Internet home pages:
http://www.english-heritage.org.uk/

918
ELVASTON CASTLE WORKING ESTATE MUSEUM
Elvaston

Closed, date of change, 2001

919
ELY CATHEDRAL
Ely, Cambridgeshire, CB7 4DL

Tel: 01353 667735
Fax: 01353 665658
Email: receptionist@cathedral.ely.anglican.org
Formed: 673 AD

Organisation type and purpose: Voluntary organisation, registered charity, historic building, house or site, suitable for ages: all ages.
Place of worship.
Parent body:
Church of England

Enquiries to: Visits Manager
Other contacts: (1) The Bursar; (2) Education Officer for (1) marketing; (2) school visits.
Access:
Access to staff: By letter, by telephone, by fax, by email
Access for disabled people: ramped entry, toilet facilities
Other restrictions: Level entry - South Door.

General description:
Via website, information on architecture, history of building, current worship patterns etc of Ely Cathedral.
Information services:
On-line searching

continued overleaf

Special visitor services: Guided tours, materials and/or activities for children.
Education services: Group education facilities, resources for Key Stages 1 and 2 and 3.
Services for disabled people: For the visually impaired.
Printed publications:
Various guide books and publications associated with the Cathedral as a heritage site and place of worship

Address for ordering publications:
Printed publications:
Shop Manager, Ely Cathedral

Internet home pages:
http://www.cathedral.ely.anglican.org
Services, events, etc.

See also - Stained Glass Museum

920
ELY MUSEUM
The Old Gaol, Market Street, Ely, Cambridgeshire, CB7 4LS

Tel: 01353 666655
Fax: 01353 659259
Formed: 1972

Organisation type and purpose: Registered charity (charity number 274253), museum.

Enquiries to: Curator
Other contacts: (1) Chairman of Trustees (2) Chairman of Friends (3) Membership Secretary for (1) contacting trustees of Ely Museum (2) contacting friends of Ely Museum (3) joining friends of Ely Museum.
Access:
Access to staff: By letter, by telephone, by fax
Hours: Mon to Sun, 1030 to 1630 (Summer, 1030 to 1730)

General description:
Archaeology, social history, history of Isle of Ely and Fens, Cambridge Regiment.

921
EMBSAY & BOLTON ABBEY STEAM RAILWAY
Bolton Abbey Station, Bolton Abbey, Skipton, North Yorkshire, BD23 6AF

Tel: 01756 710614
Fax: 01756 710720
Email: embsay.steam@btinternet.com
Formed: 1968
Formerly: Embsay Steam Railway, Yorkshire Dales Railway

Organisation type and purpose: Learned society (membership is by subscription), present number of members: 1500, voluntary organisation, registered charity (charity number 517804), museum, publishing house.
Operating steam railway museum.
Parent body:
Yorkshire Dales Railway Museum Trust
at the same address
Member of:
Association of Independent Museums
Association of Independent Railways
Association of Railway Preservation Societies
Registered with the:
Museums and Galleries Commission
Other address:
Embsay & Bolton Abbey Steam Railway
Embsay Railway Station, East Lane, Embsay, Skipton, North Yorkshire, BD23 6QX, tel: 01756 794727, fax: 01756 795189, email/website: embsay.steam@btinternet.com

Enquiries to: Business Manager
Access:
Access to staff: By letter, by telephone, by fax, by email, visitors by prior appointment, Internet web pages
Hours: Mon to Fri, 1000 to 1500
Access to building, collections or gallery: No prior appointment required
Hours: Jan to Mar and Nov, Sundays only
Apr, May, Oct and Dec, Sat and Sun
Jun to mid Jul, Tue, Sat and Sun
Mid Jul and Aug, daily; open bank holidays and autumn half term.

General description:
History of Yorkshire Dales Railway, Midland Railway, industrial railways, Yorkshire built industrial locomotives, Skipton to Ilkley Railway. Operation of the Embsay and Bolton Abbey Steam Railway.
Collections:
Locomotives and rolling stock
Yorkshire Dales Railway and Midland Railway documents

Internet home pages:
http://www.embsayboltonabbeyrailway.org.uk
http://www.kidsnet.co.uk/yorkshire/embsay
http://www.daclnet.co.uk

922
EMMETTS GARDEN
Ide Hill, Sevenoaks, Kent, TN14 6AY

Tel: 01732 750367
Fax: 01732 750490
Email: emmetts@nationaltrust.org.uk

Organisation type and purpose: National organisation, registered charity (charity number 205846), historic building, house or site, suitable for ages: all ages.
Parent body:
The National Trust (South & South East Region)
South East Regional Office, tel: 01372 453401

Direct tel: 01732 868381(Enquiries Chartwell Office)
Access:
Access to staff: By letter, by telephone, by fax, by email
Access to building, collections or gallery: No prior appointment required
Hours: Mar to end of June, Wed to Sun, 1100 to 1700; Jul to 2 Nov, Wed, Sat and Sun, 1100 to 1700; open Bank Holiday Mondays
Other restrictions: Last admission 1615
Access for disabled people: Parking provided, toilet facilities
Other restrictions: Transfer available. Ramped entrance to shop and tea-room. Grounds largely accessible.
Steps, slopes and uneven paths in some areas. Caution: sheer drop at end of shrub garden.

General description:
Influenced by William Robinson, this charming and informal garden - with the highest treetop in Kent - was laid out in the late 19th century, with many exotic and rare trees and shrubs from across the world. While there are glorious shows of spring flowers and shrubs, a rose garden and rock garden, Emmetts is equally attractive for its spectacular views at all times and for its autumn colours.

Internet home pages:
http://www.nationaltrust.org.uk/regions/

923
EMSWORTH MUSEUM
10b North Street, Emsworth, Hampshire, PO10 7DD

Tel: 01243 378091
Acronym or abbreviation: EM&HT
Full name: Emsworth Maritime & Historical Trust
Formed: 1988

Organisation type and purpose: Independently owned, registered charity (charity number 294965), museum, suitable for ages: 5+.
Administered by:
Emsworth Maritime & Historical Trust
at the same address
Honorary Secretary:
Emsworth Maritime & Historical Trust
24 Hollybank Lane, Emsworth, Hampshire, PO10 7UE, tel: 01243 373780

Enquiries to: Honorary Secretary
Direct tel: 01243 373780
Access:
Access to staff: By letter, by telephone, visitors by prior appointment
Access to building, collections or gallery: No prior appointment required
Hours: Easter to end Oct: Sat, Bank Holidays and Fri in Aug, 1030 to 1630; Sun, 1430 to 1630

General description:
Emsworth Museum is packed with exhibits which reflect the history of the village and the people who lived and worked there. Many of the exhibits are maritime. In the 18th and 19th centuries Emsworth was the principal port of Chichester Harbour. By 1900 J D Foster (1858-1940) had a fleet of 13 large oyster smacks at sea - The Echo was the largest sailing fishing vessel ever to work out of any English Port.
Information services:
Special visitor services: Materials and/or activities for children..
Collections:
Photographs and documents reflecting Maritime and Local Community/Social History (also audio tapes and videos)
Books, photographs and documents relating to P G Wodehouse who lived in Emsworth 1904-1914
Printed publications:
Brochure

924
ENGINUITY
Ironbridge Gorge Museum Trust, Coach Road, Coalbrookdale, Telford, Shropshire, TF8 7DQ

Tel: 01952 435905

Organisation type and purpose: Registered charity (charity number 503717-R), museum, historic building, house or site, suitable for ages: 5+.
Interactive discovery centre.
Parent body:
Ironbridge Gorge Museum Trust
Tel: 01952 433522
Access:
Access to building, collections or gallery: No prior appointment required
Hours: 1000 to 1700, daily
Other restrictions: Closed 24 and 25 Dec, 1 Jan.
Access for disabled people: Parking provided, level entry, access to all public areas, toilet facilities
Other restrictions: Access guide for disabled visitors available on request.

General description:
Interactive Technology Centre. Become an apprentice engineer for the day, free to experiment with the gadgets and know-how involved in producing things we use every day. Find out how you can pull a real locomotive, control water to generate electricity, test your speed and accuracy against a robot, or work as a team to make the Crazy Boiler blow up.
Information services:
Conference and corporate catering.
Special visitor services: Materials and/or activities for children.
Education services: Group education facilities, resources for Key Stages 1 and 2, 3, 4 and Further or Higher Education.
Services for disabled people: Displays and/or information at wheelchair height.

Internet home pages:
http://www.ironbridge.org.uk

925
ENGLESEA BROOK CHAPEL AND MUSEUM OF PRIMITIVE METHODISM
Englesea Brook Lane, Englesea Brook, Crewe, Cheshire, CW2 5QW

Tel: 01270 820836
Email: engleseabrook-methodist-museum@supanet.com

Formed: 1987

Organisation type and purpose: Registered charity (charity number Exempt), museum, suitable for ages: 16+, research organisation.
Parent body:
The Methodist Church
Member of:
North Staffordshire Museums Association

Enquiries to: Development Officer
Access:
Access to staff: By letter, by telephone, in person, visitors by prior appointment
Hours: Answerphone always available
Access to building, collections or gallery: No prior appointment required
Hours: Apr to Nov: Thu, Fri, Sat and Bank Holiday Mon, 1030 to 1715; Sun, 1330 to 1715
During Aug: Tue to Sun, 1030 to 1715
Other restrictions: Prior appointment advised for access to library.

General description:
The Museum houses artefacts relating to Hugh Bourne and William Clowes and to The Primitive Methodist Church which they established in the early 19th century. There are various displays, including chapel life, P M Pottery, banners, home and overseas mission, political involvement and women preachers. There is an audiovisual introduction. The Museum has full registration with Resource, prime exhibits include the first pulpit, the first printing press (1830s) and the first organ (1828) used in the movement. Artefacts include a chest of drawers; pottery; books; and ephemera.
Information services:
Library available for reference (for conditions see Access above)
Special visitor services: Guided tours.
Education services: Group education facilities, resources for Key Stage 2.
Services for disabled people: Displays and/or information at wheelchair height.
Collections:
The collection is particularly strong in ceramic items, banners, books and printed ephemera
Part of the collection came from the former P M Ministerial Training College at Manchester
Catalogues:
Catalogue for library is in-house only. Catalogue for all of the collections is only available in-house.
Printed publications:
Several pamphlets on aspects of Primitive Methodism available
Related and general second-hand books (for purchase)
Hymn Singing (CD-ROM, for purchase)

Internet home pages:
http://www.engleseabrook-museum.org.uk
Brief description of museum, opening times.

926
ENGLISH HERITAGE (EAST MIDLANDS REGION)
44 Derngate, Northampton, NN1 1UH

Tel: 01604 735400
Fax: 01604 735401

Organisation type and purpose: National organisation, advisory body, membership association (membership is by subscription), suitable for ages: all ages.
Independent but government-sponsored body.
English Heritage site administration and information service, including dates, times of opening and special events.

Enquiries to: Marketing Manager
Access:
Access to staff: By letter, by telephone, by fax

General description:
English Heritage East Midlands Region, administers and cares for properties and sites in Derbyshire, Northamptonshire, Rutland, Lincolnshire and Leicestershire, the conservation and preservation of the historic environment.

See also - ***Ashby de la Zouch Castle; Bolsover Castle; Gainsborough Old Hall; Hardwick Old Hall; Kirby Hall; Kirby Muxloe Castle; Lincoln Medieval Bishops' Palace; Lyddington Bede House; Peveril Castle; Rushton Triangular Lodge; Sibsey Trader Windmill; Wingfield Manor***

927
ENGLISH HERITAGE (EAST OF ENGLAND REGION)
Brooklands, 24 Brooklands Avenue, Cambridge, CB2 2BU

Tel: 01223 582700
Fax: 01223 582701

Organisation type and purpose: National organisation, suitable for ages: all ages.
Independent but government-sponsored body.
English Heritage site information service, including dates, times of opening and special events.
Heritage sites:
Audley End House & Gardens
Saffron Walden, Essex, CB11 4JF, tel: 01799 541354
Berney Arms Windmill
8 Manor Road, Southtown, Norfolk, NR31 0QA, tel: 01493 700605
Castle Acre Priory and Castle
Stocks Green, Castle Acre, Kings Lynn, Norfolk, PE32 2XD, tel: 01760 755394
Castle Rising Castle
King's Lynn, Norfolk, tel: 01553 631330
Denny Abbey & The Farmland Museum
Near Waterbeach, Cambridge, tel: 01223 860489
Framlingham Castle
Framlingham, Suffolk, IP8 9BT, tel: 01728 724189
Grimes Graves
Lynford, Thetford, Norfolk, IP26 5DE, tel: 01842 810656
Hill Hall
Epping, Essex, tel: 01223 582700
Landguard Fort
Felixstowe, Suffolk
Longthorpe Tower
Thorpe Road, Longthorpe, Cambridgeshire, PE1 1HA, tel: 01733 268482
Orford Castle
Orford, Woodbridge, Suffolk, tel: 01394 450472
Row 111 House / Old Merchants House
South Quay, Great Yarmouth, Norfolk, IP13 2RQ, tel: 01493 745 526 (Norfolk Museums Service)
Saxtead Green Post Mill
The Mill House, Saxtead Green, Suffolk, IP13 9QQ, tel: 01728 685789
Tilbury Fort
No 2 Office Block, The Fort, Tilbury, Essex, RM18 7NR, tel: 01375 858489
West Park Gardens
Silsoe, Luton, Bedfordshire, MK45 4HS, tel: 01525 860152 (weekends only)

Enquiries to: Regional Marketing Manager
Access:
Access to staff: By letter, by telephone, by fax, by email
Hours: Mon to Fri, 0900 to 1700

General description:
The conservation and preservation of the historic environment of Eastern England.

Internet home pages:
http://www.english-heritage.org.uk

See also - ***Audley End House and Gardens; Berney Arms Windmill; Castle Acre Priory; Castle Rising Castle; Denny Abbey and the Farmland Museum; Framlingham Castle; Grime's Graves; Hill Hall; Landguard Fort; Lanman Museum; Longthorpe Tower; Orford Castle; Row III House / Old Merchant's House; Saxtead Green Post Mill; Tilbury Fort; Wrest Park Gardens***

928
ENGLISH HERITAGE (LONDON REGION)
23 Savile Row, London, W1X 1AB

Tel: 020 7973 3000
Fax: 020 7937 3001

Organisation type and purpose: National organisation, membership association (membership is by subscription), suitable for ages: all ages.
Independent but government-sponsored body.
English Heritage sites administration and information service, including dates, times of opening and special events.

Enquiries to: Marketing Officer
Access:
Access to staff: By letter, by telephone, by fax, visitors by prior appointment

General description:
English Heritage London Region, administers and cares for properties and sites in the London area, the conservation and preservation of the historic environment.

Internet home pages:
http://www.english-heritage.org.uk

See also - ***Chiswick House; Down House; Eltham Palace; Jewel Tower; Kenwood House; Marble Hill House; Wellington Arch; Wernher Collection at Ranger's House; Westminster Abbey, Chapter House***

929
ENGLISH HERITAGE (NORTH EAST REGION)
Bessie Surtees House, 41-44 Sandhill, Newcastle upon Tyne, NE1 3JF

Tel: 0191 261 1585

Organisation type and purpose: National organisation, advisory body, membership association (membership is by subscription), suitable for ages: all ages.
Independent but government-sponsored body.
English Heritage site administration and information service, including dates, times of opening and special events.

Enquiries to: Marketing Manager
Access:
Access to staff: By letter, by telephone, visitors by prior appointment

General description:
English Heritage North East Region administers and cares for properties and sites in Northumberland, Tyne & Wear, County Durham and Teesside, the conservation and preservation of the historic environment.

Internet home pages:
http://www.english-heritage.org.uk

See also - ***Aydon Castle; Barnard Castle; Belsay Hall, Castle and Gardens; Berwick-upon-Tweed Barracks; Brinkburn Priory; Chesters Roman Fort and Museum; Dunstanburgh Castle; Etal Castle; Finchale Priory; Hadrian's Wall and Housesteads Roman Fort; Hadrian's Wall Museums; Hadrian's Wall Tourism Partnership; Lindisfarne Priory; Norham Castle; Prudhoe Castle; Tynemouth Castle and Priory; Warkworth Castle and Hermitage***

930
ENGLISH HERITAGE (NORTH WEST REGION)
Canada House, 3 Chepstow Street, Manchester, M1 5FW

Tel: 0161 242 1400

Organisation type and purpose: National organisation, advisory body, membership association (membership is by subscription), suitable for ages: all ages.
Independent but government-sponsored body.
English Heritage site administration and

continued overleaf

information service, including dates, times of opening and special events.

Enquiries to: Marketing Manager

Access:

Access to staff: By letter, by telephone, visitors by prior appointment
Hours: Mon to Fri, 0900 to 1700

General description:

English Heritage North West Region administers and cares for properties and sites in Cheshire, Merseyside, Greater Manchester, Lancashire and Cumbria, the conservation and preservation of the historic environment.

Internet home pages:

http://www.english-heritage.org.uk

See also - ***Ambleside Roman Fort; Beeston Castle; Brough Castle; Brougham Castle; Carlisle Castle; Furness Abbey; Hadrian's Wall Museums; Hadrian's Wall Tourism Partnership; Lanercost Priory; Stott Park Bobbin Mill***

931 ENGLISH HERITAGE (SOUTH EAST REGION)

Eastgate Court, 195-205 High Street, Guildford, Surrey, GU1 3EH

Tel: 01483 252000
Fax: 01483 252001

Organisation type and purpose: National organisation, advisory body, suitable for ages: all ages.
Independent but government-sponsored body.
English Heritage site administration and information service, including dates, times of opening and special events.

Heritage sites:

Abingdon County Hall
Appuldurcombe House
Wroxall, Ventnor, Isle of Wight, PO38 3EW, tel: 01983 852484, fax: 01983 840188
Battle Abbey and Battlefield
High Street, Battle, East Sussex, TN33 0AD, tel: 01424 773792
Bayham Old Abbey
Bayham, Lamberhurst, Kent, TN8 8DE
Bishop's Waltham Palace
Bishop's Waltham, Hampshire, SO32 1DH
Calshot Castle
Camber Castle
Carisbrooke Castle and Museum
Carisbrooke, Newport, Isle of Wight, PO30 6JY, tel: 01983 523112, fax: 01983 532126, email/website: carismus@lineone.net
Deal Castle
Victoria Road, Deal, Kent, CT14 7BA, tel: 01304 372762
Dover Castle
The Keep, Dover, Kent, CT16 1HU, tel: 01304 201628
Down House
Luxted Road, Downe, Biggin Hill, Kent, BR6 7JT, tel: 01689 859119
Dymchurch Martello Tower
High Street, Dymchurch, Kent, CT16 1HU
Farnham Castle Keep
Castle Hill, Farnham, Surrey, GU6 0AG
Fort Brockhurst
Gunners Way, Elson, Hampshire, PO12 4DS
Hurst Castle
Lullingstone Roman Villa
Lullingstone Lane, Eynsford, Kent, DA4 0JA, tel: 01322 863467
Medieval Merchant's House
58 French Street, Southhampton, SO23 8NB
Osborne House
York Avenue, East Cowes, Isle of Wight, PO32 6JY, tel: 01983 200022, fax: 01983 281380
Pevensey Castle
Pevensey, East Sussex, BN24 5LE, tel: 01323 762604
Portchester Castle
Portchester, Hampshire, PO16 9QW, tel: 023 923 78291
Richborough Roman Fort
Sandwich, Kent, CT13 9JW
Rochester Castle
Boley Hill, Rochester, Kent, ME1 1SW, tel: 01634 402276
Rycote Chapel
St Augustine's Abbey and Museum
Longport, Canterbury, Kent, CT1 1TF, tel: 01227 767345, fax: 01227 767345
Temple Manor
Strood, Rochester, Kent, tel: 01634 827980
Upnor Castle
Wainscott, Rochester, Kent, tel: 01634 718742
Walmer Castle & Gardens
Kingsdown Road, Deal, Kent, CT14 7LJ, tel: 01304 364288, fax: 01304 364826
Wolvesey Castle (Old Bishop's Palace)
College Street, Winchester, SO23 8NB
Yarmouth Castle
Quay Street, Yarmouth, Isle of Wight, PO41 0PB, tel: 01983 760678

Enquiries to: Marketing Assistant

Access:

Access to staff: By letter, by telephone, by fax
Hours: Mon to Fri, 0900 to 1700

General description:

English Heritage South East Region administers and cares for properties and sites in Kent, Surrey, Sussex, Hampshire and the Isle of Wight; conservation and preservation of the historic environment.

Internet home pages:

http://www.english-heritage.org.uk

See also - ***Abingdon County Hall; Appuldurcombe House; Battle Abbey and Battlefield; Bayham Old Abbey; Bishop's Waltham Palace; Calshot Castle; Camber Castle; Carisbrooke Castle and Museum; Deal Castle; Dover Castle; Down House; Dymchurch Martello Tower; Farnham Castle Keep; Fort Brockhurst; Hurst Castle; Lullingstone Roman Villa; Medieval Merchant's House; Osborne House; Pevensey Castle; Portchester Castle; Richborough Roman Fort; Rochester Castle; Rycote Chapel; St Augustine's Abbey and Museum; Temple Manor; Upnor Castle; Walmer Castle & Gardens; Wolvesey Castle (Old Bishop's Palace); Yarmouth Castle***

932 ENGLISH HERITAGE (SOUTH WEST REGION)

29 Queen Square, Bristol, BS1 4ND

Tel: 0117 975 0700

Organisation type and purpose: National organisation, advisory body, membership association (membership is by subscription), suitable for ages: all ages, publishing house.
English Heritage South West Region administers and cares for properties and sites in Bristol, Cornwall, Devon, Dorset, Gloucestershire, Isles of Scilly, Somerset, and Wiltshire.

Heritage Site:

Berry Pomeroy Castle
Totnes, Devon, TQ9 6NJ
Chysauster Ancient Village
Newmill, Penzance, Cornwall, TR20 8XA
Cleeve Abbey
Washford, Warchet, Somerset, TA23 0PS
Dartmouth Castle
Castle Road, Dartmouth, Devon, TQ6 0JN
Farleigh Hungerford Castle
Farleigh Hungerford, Bath, Somerset, BA3 6RS
Hailes Abbey
Winchcombe, Cheltenham, Gloucester, GL54 5PB
Launceston Castle
Castle Lodge, Launceston, Cornwall, PL15 7DR
Muchelney Abbey
Muchelney, Langport, Somerset, TA10 0DQ
Okehampton Castle
Castle Lodge, Okehampton, Devon, EX20 1JB
Old Sarum
Castle Roads, Salisbury, Wiltshire, SP1 3SD
Old Wardour Castle
Tisbury, Salisbury, Wiltshire, SP3 6RR
Pendennis Castle
Falmouth, Cornwall, TR11 4LP
Portland Castle
Castleton, Portland, Dorset, DT5 1AZ
Restormel Castle
Lostwithiel, Cornwall, PL22 0BD
Sherborne Old Castle
Castleton, Dorset, 19 0SY
St Mawes Castle
St Mawes, Cornwall, TR2 3AA
Stonehenge
Stone Circle, Wiltshire, SP4 7DE
Tintagel Castle
Tintagel, Cornwall, DL34 0AA
Totnes Castle
Castle Street, Totnes, Devon, TQ9 5NU

Access:

Access to staff: By letter, by telephone, in person
Hours: Mon to Fri, 0900 to 1700

General description:

The conservation and preservation of the historic environment.

Internet home pages:

http://www.english-heritage.org.uk

See also - ***Berry Pomeroy Castle; Chysauster Ancient Village; Cistercian Museum; Cleeve Abbey; Dartmouth Castle; Farleigh Hungerford Castle; Hailes Abbey; Launceston Castle; Muchelney Abbey; Okehampton Castle; Old Sarum; Old Wardour Castle; Pendennis Castle; Portland Castle; Restormel Castle; Sherborne Old Castle; St Mawes Castle; Stonehenge; Tintagel Castle; Totnes Castle***

933 ENGLISH HERITAGE (WEST MIDLANDS REGION)

112 Colemore Row, Birmingham, B3 3AG

Tel: 0121 625 6820

Organisation type and purpose: National organisation, advisory body.
Independent but government-sponsored body.
English Heritage West Midlands Region administers and cares for properties and sites in Herefordshire, Shropshire, Staffordshire, Warwickshire, West Midlands and Worcestershire.

Heritage Site:

Boscobel House and the Royal Oak
Brewood, Bishops Wood, Shropshire, ST19 9AR
Buildwas Abbey
Ironbridge, Telford, TF8 7BW
Goodrich Castle
Goodrich, Ross on Wye, Worcestershire, HR9 6HY
Halesowen Abbey
Haughmond Abbey
Upton Magna, Uffington, Shropshire, SY4 4RW
Kenilworth Castle
Kenilworth, Warwickshire, CV8 1NE
Stokesay Castle
Craven Arms, Shropshire, SY7 9AH
Wall Roman Site (Letocetum)
Watling Street, Lichfield, Staffordshire, WS14 0AW
Wenlock Priory
Much Wenlock, Shropshire, TF13 6HS
Witley Court
Great Witley, Worcestershire, WR6 6JT
Wroxeter Roman City
Wroxeter, Shropshire, SY5 6PH

Access:

Access to staff: By letter, by telephone, in person
Hours: Mon to Fri, 0900 to 1700

General description:

The conservation and preservation of the historic environment.
English Heritage site administration and information service, including dates, times of opening and special events.

Internet home pages:
http://www.english-heritage.org.uk

See also - ***Boscobel House and the Royal Oak; Buildwas Abbey; Goodrich Castle; Halesowen Abbey; Haughmond Abbey; Jerwood Sculpture Park; Kenilworth Castle; Stokesay Castle; Wall Roman Site (Letocetum) Baths and Museum; Wenlock Priory; Witley Court; Wroxeter Roman City***

934
ENGLISH HERITAGE (YORKSHIRE REGION)

37 Tanner Row, York, YO1 6WP

Tel: 01904 601901

Organisation type and purpose: National organisation, advisory body.
Independent but government-sponsored body.
English Heritage Yorkshire Region administers and cares for properties and sites in East Riding of Yorkshire, North East Lincolnshire, North Lincolnshire, North Yorkshire, South Yorkshire and West Yorkshire.

Heritage Site:
Aldborough Roman Site
Main Street, Boroughbridge, Yorkshire, YO5 9EF
Brodsworth Hall and Gardens
Brodsworth, Doncaster, South Yorkshire
Byland Abbey
Coxwold, North Yorkshire, YO6 4BD
Clifford's Tower
Clifford Street, York, YO11 1HY
Conisbrough Castle
Helmsley Castle
Helmsley, North Yorkshire, YO6 5AB
Kirkham Priory
Whitwell-on-the-Hill, North Yorkshire, YO6 7JS
Middleham Castle
Middleham, Leyburn, North Yorkshire, DL8 4QG
Mount Grace Priory
Saddle Bridge, Northallerton, North Yorkshire, DL6 3JG
Pickering Castle
Pickering, North Yorkshire, YO18 7AX
Richmond Castle
Richmond, North Yorkshire, DL10 4QW
Rievaulx Abbey
Rievaulx, Helmsley, North Yorkshire, DL10 5LB
Roche Abbey
Maltby, Rotherham, South Yorkshire, S66 8NW
Scarborough Castle
Castle Road, Scarborough, North Yorkshire, YO11 1HY
Whitby Abbey
Whitby, North Yorkshire, YO22 4JT

Access:
Access to staff: By letter, by telephone, in person
Hours: Mon to Fri, 0900 to 1700

General description:
The conservation and preservation of the historic environment.
English Heritage site administration and information service, including dates, times of opening and special events.

Internet home pages:
http://www.english-heritage.org.uk

See also - ***Aldborough Roman Site; Brodsworth Hall and Gardens; Byland Abbey; Clifford's Tower; Conisbrough Castle; Helmsley Castle; Kirkham Priory; Middleham Castle; Mount Grace Priory; Pickering Castle; Richmond Castle; Rievaulx Abbey; Roche Abbey; Scarborough Castle; Whitby Abbey***

935
ENGLISH HERITAGE

Education, 23 Savile Row, London, W1S 2ET

Tel: 020 7973 3442
Fax: 020 7973 3443
Email: education@english-heritage.org.uk
Formed: 1984
Formerly: Historic Buildings and Monuments Commission for England, date of change, 1984

Organisation type and purpose: National government body, advisory body, statutory body, membership association (membership is by subscription), suitable for ages: 5 to 18 (formal) and informal.
To provide an advisory and support service for primary and secondary schools in the teaching of history and the use of the historic environment.

Other addresses:
English Heritage
Customer Services Department, National Monuments Record Centre, Kemble Drive, Swindon, Wiltshire, SN2 2GZ, tel: 01793 414926

Regional addresses:
English Heritage
Education Officer, North West Region, Canada House, 3 Chepstow Street, Manchester, M1 5FW, tel: 0161 242 1425, fax: 0161 242 1401
English Heritage
Education Officer, South East Region, Eastgate Court, 195-205 High Street, Guildford, GU1 3EH, tel: 01483 252000, fax: 01483 252001
English Heritage
Education Officer, West Midlands Region, 112 Colmore Row, Birmingham, B3 3AG, tel: 0121 625 6863, fax: 0121 625 6821
English Heritage
Education Officer, North East Region, Bessie Surtees House, 441 Sandhill, Newcastle upon Tyne, NE1 8JF, tel: 0191 269 1585, fax: 0191 261 1130
English Heritage
Education Officer, Yorkshire Region, G10, 37 Tanner Row, York, YO1 6WP, tel: 01904 601962, fax: 01904 601999
English Heritage
Education Officer, East of England Region, 62-74 Burleigh Street, Cambridge, CB1 1DJ, tel: 01223 582715, fax: 01223 582701
English Heritage
Education Officer, East Midlands Region, 44 Derngate, Northampton, NN1 1UH, tel: 01604 735400, fax: 01604 735401
English Heritage
Education Officer, London Region, Savile Row, London, W1S 2ET, tel: 020 7973 3485, fax: 020 7973 3470
English Heritage
Education Officer, South West Region, 29/30 Queen Square, Bristol, BS1 4ND, tel: 0117 975 0729, fax: 0117 975 0701

Enquiries to: Head of Education

Access:
Access to staff: By letter, by telephone, by fax, by email
Hours: Mon to Fri, 0900 to 1700
Other restrictions: Access for visitors with disabilities should be checked with the regional office before booking a visit.

General description:
The historic environment of Britain, its preservation and use. Archaeology, architecture, ancient monuments, conservation and listed buildings.

Publications list:
is available in hard copy and online.

Printed publications:
English Heritage advise that you contact them and ask for a free Resources Catalogue, or visit their website for the complete range of publications
Large selection of resources: books, posters, computer software and videos for Key Stages 1, 2, 3, GCSE and Adult Education. Published topics include: Local Studies, Romans, Anglo-Saxons and Vikings, Victorian Britain, Medieval World and Prehistory
Art and the Historic Environment (Lockey M, £6.99)
Design and Technology and the Historic Environment (Barnes J, £6.99)
Heritage Learning Magazine (aimed at teachers, free)
Primary History - Guide to using historic sites for all aspects of primary school history ((£7.99)
Teacher's Guide - History through role play (Fairclough J, £6.99)
Free Educational Visits (how to book free educational visits to sites, free)

Electronic and video products:
The Resources Catalogue lists all videos, CD-ROMs, etc. Most videos are available on free loan
Teaching Primary History (video, £12.99)
Real Victorians (CD-ROM, £14.99)
The Key Stage 1 Curriculum (video, £12.99)
Video Role Up - role play with mixed ability class (video, £12.99)

Address for ordering publications:
Printed publications:
English Heritage
c/o Gillards, Trident Works, Temple Cloud, Bristol, BS39 5AZ, tel: 01761 452966, fax: 01761 453408

Internet home pages:
http://www.english-heritage.org.uk
Full details of all resources and up-to-date information about the education service and the work of the English Heritage.
http://www.heritageeducation.org.uk

936
ENGLISH TOURIST COUNCIL/ BRITISH TOURIST AUTHORITY

Library, Thames Tower, Black's Road, Hammersmith, London, W6 9EL

Tel: 020 8563 3000
Fax: 020 8563 3391
Acronym or abbreviation: ETC/BTA
Formed: 1969
Formerly: English Tourist Board, date of change, 1969; British Tourist Authority/English Tourist Board (BTA/ETB), date of change, 1969 -1999

Organisation type and purpose: National government body.
National government body for tourism.

Enquiries to: Information Resources Manager
Direct tel: 020 8563 3011
Direct email: gevans@englishtourism.org.uk

Access:
Access to staff: By letter, by email, visitors by prior appointment
Hours: Mon to Fri, 0900 to 1700
Access to building, collections or gallery: No access other than to staff
Hours: Access to the library is available to ETC/BTA Staff and partners only.
Access for disabled people: ramped entry, access to all public areas

General description:
Tourism statistics and all other aspects of tourism; Britain as a tourist destination.

Collections:
Books
Information files
Journals
Press cuttings
Research reports

Catalogues:
Catalogue for library is in-house only.

Trade and statistical:
Data on the volume and value of tourism in and to the UK.

Publications list:
is available in hard copy and online.

Printed publications:
Digest of Tourist Statistics No.24
English Heritage Monitor 2001
Tourism Research and Strategic Intelligence

continued overleaf

People with Disabilities and Holiday Taking (free)
Measuring the Local Impact of Tourism (free)
The Heritage Monitor (2000, £20)
Making the Connections - A practical guide to tourism management in historic towns (£25)
Providing Service for All in Education (£5)
Providing Accessible Visitor Attractions (£5)
Somewhere Special 2001 (£7.99)

Address for ordering publications:
Printed publications:
English Tourism Council
at the same address, tel: 0870 606 7204, fax: 020 8563 3048

Internet home pages:
http://www.britishtouristauthority.org
Corporate website.
http://www.staruk.org.uk
Statistics and research on UK tourism, domestic and inbound data, who's who in UK tourism, details of joint national tourist board surveys.
http://www.englishtourism.org.uk
Corporate website.

937
ENGLISH WINE CENTRE

Drusillas Roundabout, Polegate, Alfriston, East Sussex, BN26 5QS

Tel: 01323 870164
Fax: 01323 870005
Email: bottles@englishwine.co.uk
Formed: 1972

Organisation type and purpose: Museum. Corporate functions, wedding receptions, wine shop.

Enquiries to: Proprietor
Access:
Access to staff: By letter, by telephone, by fax, by email, in person, visitors by prior appointment
Hours: Sun to Sat, 1000 to 1700
Access for disabled people: Parking provided, level entry, access to all public areas, toilet facilities

General description:
The production of wine in England from Roman times to the present day and including the dissolution of the monasteries.
Collections:
Artefacts for the production of wine
Corkscrews
Drinking vessels

Internet home pages:
http://www.englishwine.co.uk

938
ENNISCORTHY CASTLE

See - Wexford County Museum

939
ENNISKILLEN CASTLE

See - Fermanagh County Museum

940
EPPING FOREST MUSEUM

See - Queen Elizabeth's Hunting Lodge

941
EPWORTH OLD RECTORY

1 Rectory Street, Epworth, Doncaster, South Yorkshire, DN9 1HX

Tel: 01427 872268
Email: curator@epwortholdrectory.org.uk
Formed: 1957

Organisation type and purpose: International organisation, independently owned, museum, historic building, house or site, suitable for ages: 8+.

Enquiries to: Curator
Access:
Access to staff: By letter, by telephone, by email
Access to building, collections or gallery: Prior appointment required
Hours: Mar, Apr, Oct: Mon to Sat, 1000 to 1200 and 1400 to 1600; Sun, 1400 to 1600
May to Sep: Mon to Sat, 1000 to 1630; Sun, 1400 to 1630
Other restrictions: At other times by prior appointment only.
Access for disabled people: Parking provided, level entry, toilet facilities
Other restrictions: Access to ground floor only - Grade I listed building.

General description:
Story of Methodism and the Wesley family.
Information services:
Library available for reference (for conditions see Access above)
Audio/Visual presentation.
Special visitor services: Guided tours, materials and/or activities for children..
Collections:
Pictures, prints, documents, furniture, library
Catalogues:
Catalogue for library is in-house only. Catalogue for all of the collections is only available in-house.
Electronic and video products:
Videos

Internet home pages:
http://www.epwortholdrectory.org.uk/

942
ERASMUS DARWIN CENTRE, THE

Darwin House, Beacon Street, Lichfield, Staffordshire, WS13 7AD

Tel: 01543 306260
Email: erasmus.d@virgin.net

Member of:
North Staffordshire Museums Association
Access:
Access for disabled people: Parking provided, toilet facilities
Other restrictions: Lift

General description:
The home of Erasmus Darwin, founder of the Lunar Society, a driving force behind the Industrial Revolution and grandfather of Charles Darwin. Other members of the Society included Matthew Boulton, James Watt, Josiah Wedgwood and later Joseph Priestley. Interactives and computer technology tell the story of this remarkable man.
Collections:
Period furnishings
Herb garden

Internet home pages:
http://www.erasmus-darwin.org/

943
ERDDIG HALL

Wrexham, Clwyd, LL13 0YT

Tel: 01978 355314
Fax: 01978 313333
Email: erddig@nationaltrust.org.uk
Formed: 1895

Organisation type and purpose: National organisation, registered charity (charity number 205846), historic building, house or site, suitable for ages: 8+.
Parent body:
The National Trust Office for Wales
Trinity Square, Llandudno, LL30 2DE, tel: 01492 860123, fax: 01492 860233

Enquiries to: Visitor Services Supervisor
Direct tel: 01978 315170
Direct email: geruss@smtp.ntrust.co.uk
Other contacts: House Manager for knowledge of collections.
Access:
Access to staff: By letter, by fax
Hours: Contact General Office
Access for disabled people: Parking provided, level entry, toilet facilities
Other restrictions: Designated parking 75yds. Drop-off point. 3 manual wheelchairs available. Access across rough gravel, tel. in advance to discuss visit. Ground floor fully accessible. No access to other floors. Audiovisual/video. Induction loop in AV room. Model of house on ground floor. Level entrance to shop. Steps to restaurant entrance. Lift available. Access restricted to 3 wheelchair users at any one time. Parlour accessible to all visitors.

General description:
Erddig is one of the most fascinating houses in Britain, not least because of the unusually close relationship that existed between the family of the house and their servants. The beautiful and evocative range of outbuildings includes kitchen, laundry, bakehouse, stables, sawmill, smithy and joiner's shop, while the stunning state rooms display most of their original 18th and 19th century furniture and furnishings, including some exquisite Chinese wallpaper. The large walled garden has been restored to its 18th century formal design and has a Victorian parterre and yew walk. It also contains the National Collection of Ivies. There is an extensive park with woodland walks.
Information services:
Helpline available, tel no: Infoline: 01978 315151.
Garden tours (groups 20+) by arrangement with Head Gardener. House tours (20+) by arrangement with House Manager.
Braille guide.
Front-carrying baby slings for loan.
Suitable for school groups. Education room/ centre. Children's guide.
Most rooms have no electric light; visitors wishing to make a close study of pictures and textiles should avoid dull days.
Special visitor services: Guided tours.
Education services: Group education facilities, resources for Key Stages 1 and 2, 3, 4 and Further or Higher Education.
Services for disabled people: For the visually impaired; for the hearing impaired.
Collections:
Paintings, photographs of servants
Doggerel verse on subject of servants
Early 18th century furniture and textiles
Complete 'Country House' Collection to 1920s
18th century Gentry Library
Wallpapers 1714 to 1960s
Metal Ceiling c1907
Printed publications:
Guide Books
Children's Guide
Property Leaflet (free)
Events (free)
Servants' Poems
Facts & Fancies (1924 guide to house)

Internet home pages:
http://www.nationaltrust.org.uk

944
ERITH MUSEUM

Walnut Tree Road, Erith, Kent, DA8 1RS

Tel: 01322 336582
Email: contact@erithmuseum.org.uk
Formed: 1934

Organisation type and purpose: Local government body, museum.
Other office:
Bexley Museum Service
Hall Place, Bourne Road, Bexley, Kent, DA5 1PQ, tel: 01322 526574, fax: 01322 522921, email/website: janice@bexleymuseum.freeserve.co.uk

Enquiries to: Curator
Direct tel: 01322 526574
Access:
Access to staff: By letter, by telephone
Access to building, collections or gallery: No prior appointment required
Hours: Mon, Wed, 1415 to 1715; Sat, 1415 to 1645
Other restrictions: Closed Bank Holidays, open

at other times by appointment for group visits.

General description:
Local history, geology and archaeology, social history and especially maritime and industrial history.

Internet home pages:
http://www.erithmuseum.org.uk
http://www.bexley.gov.uk
Location, opening hours.

945
ESSEX COUNTY COUNCIL

See - Cressing Temple Barns

946
ESSEX REGIMENT MUSEUM

Oaklands Park, Moulsham Street, Chelmsford, Essex, CM2 9AQ

Tel: 01245 615101
Fax: 01245 611250
Email: pompadour@chelmsfordbc.gov.uk
Formed: 1973

Organisation type and purpose: Local government body, registered charity (charity number 246632), museum, suitable for ages: 5+.

Enquiries to: Keeper of the Essex Regiment Museum

Access:
Access to staff: By letter, by telephone, by fax, by email, in person, visitors by prior appointment
Access for disabled people: Parking provided, ramped entry, toilet facilities
Other restrictions: Access currently to ground floor only.

General description:
Military and social history of the Essex Regiment and its antecedents, 44th and 56th Foot, and of Essex military subjects. Collections of the Essex Yeomanry and other Auxiliary units.

Information services:
Education services: Resources for Key Stages 1 and 2 and Further or Higher Education..

Collections:
Uniform, badges, flags, colours, silver, ceramics, weapons, archive, photographs, personal relics of the Essex Regiment and Essex Yeomanry
Includes the Eagle Standard of the French 62nd Regiment captured at the Battle of Salamanca, July 1812

Catalogues:
Catalogue for all of the collections is only available in-house.

Internet home pages:
http://www.chelmsfordbc.gov.uk/museums/regi.shtml

947
ESTORICK COLLECTION OF MODERN ITALIAN ART, THE

39a Canonbury Square, London, N1 2AN

Tel: 020 7704 9522
Fax: 020 7704 9531
Email: curator@estorickcollection.com
Formed: 1998
Formerly: Estorick Foundation

Organisation type and purpose: Registered charity (charity number 1046374), art gallery, suitable for ages: 16+.

Enquiries to: Director

Access:
Access to staff: By telephone, by email, Internet web pages
Access for disabled people: Parking provided, ramped entry
Other restrictions: Galleries 1-2 by ground floor access. Galleries 3-4, by 1st floor ramp.

General description:
Futurist art and figurative art from 1895-1950s in modern Italian Art permanent collection. Plus regular temporary exhibitions.

Information services:
Education services: Group education facilities, resources for Key Stage 4.
Services for disabled people: For the hearing impaired.

Collections:
Italian aviation posters 1910-1943
Art library of over 2000 books, periodicals and catalogues specialising in 20th century Italian art
The collection of Eric Estorick (1913-1993)
Futurist paintings
Figurative art from 1890 to the 1950s

Catalogues:
Catalogue for library is published. Catalogue for all of the collections is published.

Printed publications:
Estorick Collection Catalogue (£15)

Internet home pages:
http://www.estorickcollection.com

948
ETAL CASTLE

Etal, Cornhill on Tweed, Northumberland, TD12 4TN

Tel: 01890 820332

Organisation type and purpose: Historic building, house or site.

Parent body:
English Heritage (North East Region)
Tel: 0191 269 1227/8, fax: 0191 261 1130

Enquiries to: Manager

Access:
Access to staff: By letter, by telephone, in person
Access to building, collections or gallery: No prior appointment required
Hours: End Mar to end Sep: daily, 1000 to 1800
Oct: daily, 1000 to 1700
Other restrictions: Opening times are subject to change, for up-to-date information contact English Heritage by phone or visit the website.
Access for disabled people: access to all public areas

General description:
14th century border castle including a gatehouse and three-storey keep. Exhibition tells the story of the Battle of Flodden and of border warfare which existed here before the union of the English and Scottish crowns in 1603.

Information services:
Audio tour guides around castle and exhibition, audio tapes also for visitors with hearing difficulties and learning disabilities.
Special visitor services: Tape recorded guides.
Services for disabled people: For the hearing impaired.

Internet home pages:
http://www.english-heritage.org.uk

949
ETRURIA INDUSTRIAL MUSEUM

Lower Bedford Street, Shelton, Stoke-on-Trent, Staffordshire, ST4 7AF

Tel: 01782 233144
Fax: 01782 233145
Email: etruria@stoke.gov.uk
Formed: 1990
Formerly: Shirley's Bone and Flint Mill

Organisation type and purpose: Historic building, house or site, suitable for ages: 5+.

Parent body:
Stoke-on-Trent City Council

Enquiries to: Manager

Access:
Access to staff: By letter, by telephone, by email
Hours: Sat to Wed, 1200 to 1630
Access to building, collections or gallery: Prior appointment required
Hours: Sat to Wed, 1200 to 1630
Closed weekends Jan to Mar
Access for disabled people: Parking provided, ramped entry, toilet facilities
Other restrictions: Next to museum, please ring for directions

General description:
This is a steam-powered potters' mill. Built in 1856, it contains the original bone-grinding machinery and steam engine. Monthly steaming demonstrations are given April to December. There is also a working blacksmith's forge on the site. The mill is Britain's sole surviving steam-powered potters' mill. 1856-1972 (in use).

Information services:
Education services: Group education facilities, resources for Key Stages 2, 3 and Further or Higher Education..

Collections:
1820s beam engine 'Princess' believed to be oldest of its type still in use in the UK

Internet home pages:
http://www.stoke.gov.uk/museums

950
EUREKA! THE MUSEUM FOR CHILDREN

Discovery Road, Halifax, West Yorkshire, HX1 2NE

Tel: 01422 330069
Fax: 01422 330275
Email: info@eureka.org.uk
Formed: July 1992

Organisation type and purpose: Registered charity (charity number 292758), museum, suitable for ages: 5+.
Interactive discovery centre.

Enquiries to: Director

Access:
Access to staff: By letter, by telephone, by fax, by email, visitors by prior appointment
Hours: Mon to Fri, 0900 to 1700
Access for disabled people: Parking provided, level entry, access to all public areas, toilet facilities

General description:
Key Stages 1 and 2, interactive learning.

Internet home pages:
http://www.eureka.org.uk
General museum services and products.

951
EUSTON WATERMILL

Euston, Suffolk

Tel: 01842 766366

Organisation type and purpose: Historic building, house or site.

Access:
Access to staff: By telephone
Access for disabled people: toilet facilities
Other restrictions: Access for wheelchairs.

General description:
1670's mill, rebuilt in 1731 as a gothic church. Iron waterwheel added in 1859.

952
EVESHAM TOURIST INFORMATION AND HERITAGE CENTRE

See - Almonry Heritage Centre

953
EXPLOSION! - MUSEUM OF NAVAL FIREPOWER

Priddy's Hard, Gosport, Hampshire, PO12 4LE

Tel: 023 9250 5600
Fax: 023 9250 5605
Email: info@explosion.org.uk
Formed: March 2001
Formerly: Museum of Naval Armaments

Organisation type and purpose: Registered charity (charity number 1084982), museum, suitable for ages: 5+.

Enquiries to: Director

continued overleaf

Other contacts: Curator for technical/collections information.
Access:
Access to staff: By letter, by fax, by email, visitors by prior appointment
Access for disabled people: level entry, access to all public areas, toilet facilities
General description:
A new museum tracing the technological development of naval firepower and its associated naval and social history. Extensive collections of naval armaments housed in 18th century former naval ordnance depot at Priddy's Hard. Cafe, shop, Portsmouth Harbour Waterbus.
Information services:
Library available for reference (for conditions see Access above)
Special visitor services: Materials and/or activities for children.
Education services: Group education facilities, resources for Key Stages 1 and 2 and 3..
Collections:
Naval armaments, including cannon, shell, small arms, large guns, mines, torpedoes and missiles; naval memorabilia and artefacts, photographs and documents
Catalogues:
Catalogue for part of the collections is only available in-house.

954
EYAM HALL

Eyam, Hope Valley, Derbyshire, S32 5QW

Tel: 01433 631976
Fax: 01433 631603
Email: nicwri@eyamhall.co.uk

Organisation type and purpose: Independently owned, historic building, house or site, suitable for ages: all ages.
Member of:
Historic Houses Association
2 Chester Street, London, SW1X 7BB

Enquiries to: Administrator
Access:
Access to staff: By letter, by telephone, by fax, by email
Access to building, collections or gallery: No prior appointment required
Hours: Jun to Aug: Wed, Thu, Sun, Bank Holiday Mon, 1100 to 1600
Other restrictions: Craft Centre, Restaurant and Shop open all year, Tue to Sun.
Access for disabled people: Parking provided, level entry, toilet facilities
Other restrictions: Access to ground floor only.

General description:
17th century manor house, home of the Wright family for over 300 years. 17th to 20th century family life. Farm buildings now house a range of craft units.
Information services:
Special visitor services: Guided tours, materials and/or activities for children.
Education services: Group education facilities.
Services for disabled people: Displays and/or information at wheelchair height.
Collections:
Portraits, photographs, documents, textiles, artefacts, glass and china, special exhibitions
Catalogues:
Catalogue for library is in-house only.
Printed publications:
Guide Book (direct)
Village Guide (direct)
Post Cards (direct)

Internet home pages:
http://www.eyamhall.co.uk
All activities on site including weddings, events, catering, house opening details.
http://www.eyamhall.com

955
EYAM MUSEUM

Hawkhill Road, Eyam, Hope Valley, Derbyshire, S32 5QP

Tel: 01433 631371
Fax: 01433 630777
Formed: 1994

Organisation type and purpose: Museum, suitable for ages: 5+.

Enquiries to: Secretary
Access:
Access to staff: By letter, by telephone, by fax
Access to building, collections or gallery: No prior appointment required
Hours: Apr to 3 Nov: Tue to Sun, Bank Holidays, 1000 to 1630 (last admission 1600)
Access for disabled people: ramped entry
Other restrictions: Toilet facilities and parking nearby, stairlift to upper floor.

General description:
The Museum tells of the 1665/6 outbreak of Bubonic Plague in Eyam, when the villagers quarantined themselves to prevent the spread of the disease. Stories of families affected by the Plague are told. Recent research has revealed new information about the effect on the village during its period of quarantine. Vivid paintings and a mural add to this unique story.The recovery follows, with growth of local industries, and the display ends with the local geology.
Information services:
Special visitor services: Materials and/or activities for children.
Education services: Group education facilities..
Collections:
Local documents and photographs
Clarence Daniel collection.
Archaeological material
Local fossils and minerals
Catalogues:
Catalogue for all of the collections is only available in-house.
Publications list:
is available in hard copy and online.
Printed publications:
Teachers Pack (£4.95 plus £1.30 p&p)

Internet home pages:
http://www.eyammuseum.demon.co.uk
General information, educational material and book list.
http://www.cressbrook.co.uk/eyam/museum
General information page on tourist site

956
EYEMOUTH MUSEUM

Auld Kirk, Manse Road, Eyemouth, Berwickshire, TD14 5JE

Tel: 01890 750678
Full name: Eyemouth Museum Trust Limited
Formed: 1981

Organisation type and purpose: Independently owned, registered charity (charity number ED.CR42587), museum, suitable for ages: 5+.
Parent body:
Eyemouth Museum Trust Limited
Same address
Managed and administered by:
Scottish Borders Council Museum Service
Tel: 01750 20096, fax: 017502382

Enquiries to: Curator
Other contacts: Chairman for appointments.
Access:
Access to staff: By letter, by telephone, visitors by prior appointment
Hours: Apr to Oct: Mon to Sat, 1000 to 1700
Nov to Mar: Tue and Fri, 1000 to 1300 only
Access to building, collections or gallery: No prior appointment required
Hours: Easter to end of Oct,
Apr, May, Jun, Sep, Mon to Sat, 1000 to 1700,
Sun, 1300 1500;
Jul, Aug, 1000 to 1800
Sun, 1130 to 1630
Oct, Mon to Sat, 1000 to 1600, closed Sun
Access for disabled people: Parking provided, ramped entry
General description:
Local history with particular reference to the fishing industry and the Great Disaster of 1881. Displayed is the Eyemouth Tapestry commemorating the disaster of 1881 when 189 local fishermen were drowned during a great storm.
Catalogues:
Catalogue for all of the collections is only available in-house.
Printed publications:
Museum Booklet (£1)
An Old Eyemouth Album (photographic collection, £2 plus p&p)
The Berwickshire News, October 18th 1881 (95p plus p&p)
Walks in and around Eyemouth (50p)

Internet home pages:
http://www.scotborders.gov.uk
http://www.scotborders.org.uk

957
FAIRBOURNE AND BARMOUTH RAILWAY

Beach Road, Fairbourne, Dolgellau, Gwynedd, LL38 2PZ

Tel: 01341 250362
Fax: 01341 250240
Email: enquiries@fairbourne-railway.co.uk
Acronym or abbreviation: FBSR
Formed: 1995
Formerly: North Wales Narrow Gauge Railway Ltd

Organisation type and purpose: Membership association, service industry, museum.
Narrow gauge railway.
Affiliated to:
North Wales Coast Light Railway Ltd
Unit 8, Centre One, Lysander Way, Old Sarum, Salisbury, Wiltshire

Enquiries to: Manager
Other contacts: Managing Director, Engineering Manager
Access:
Access to staff: By letter, by telephone, by fax
Hours: Mon to Fri, 0900 to 1700

General description:
Narrow gauge railway operation on a $2\frac{1}{2}$ mile track originally laid out in 1895 by Mr Arthur McDougall (of flour fame) to transport building materials for the construction of Fairbourne village. It runs between Fairbourne station and Penrhyn Point.
The Station Museum contains photographs and documents connected with over 100 years of Fairbourne's history, also railway memorabilia.
Information services:
Special visitor services: Materials and/or activities for children..

Internet home pages:
http://www.fairbourne-railway.co.uk
http://www.fairbourne-wales.com

958
FAIRLYNCH MUSEUM AND ARTS CENTRE

27 Fore Street, Budleigh Salterton, Devon, EX9 6NP

Tel: 01395 442666
Email: fairlynch@devonmuseums.net
Formed: 1967

Organisation type and purpose: Voluntary organisation, registered charity (charity number 306636), museum, suitable for ages: all ages.
Independent organisation:
Friends of Fairlynch
Tel: 01395 442666
Member of:
Museums Association
Resource

Enquiries to: Administrator
Other contacts: Publicity Office
Access:
Access to staff: By letter, by telephone, visitors by prior appointment, charges made to all users
Access for disabled people: ramped entry, toilet facilities

General description:
Archaeology; geology, including the pebble beds and radioactive nodules; period costumes, especially Victorian; dolls, toys, lace and lacemaking; development and growth of Budleigh Salterton; local history, local archaeology, geology, natural history, local authors, local plans, maps, history of the area.
Printed publications:
Fairlynch - a History
Leaflet on local geology
Notes on Local Archaeology and History
Postcards, greetings cards (local artists and interest)
Radioactive Nodules from Devonshire
The Budleigh Salterton Railway

Internet home pages:
http://www.devonmuseums.net

959
FAKENHAM MUSEUM OF GAS AND LOCAL HISTORY
Hempton Road, Fakenham, Norfolk, NR21 7LA

Formed: 1987

Organisation type and purpose: Independently owned, registered charity (charity number 294371), museum, historic building, house or site, suitable for ages: 12+.

Enquiries to: Chairman
Direct tel: 01328 863150 (general enquiries); 01328 863507 (enquiries for group visits)
Access:
Access to staff: By letter, in person, visitors by prior appointment
Access to building, collections or gallery: No prior appointment required
Hours: Thu, 1030 to 1300
Summer: Thu, 1030 to 1530
Other restrictions: Other times by prior appointment.
Access for disabled people: level entry
Other restrictions: Two upstairs rooms (local history) not accessible for disabled.

General description:
The only complete (non-working) gasworks left in England or Wales. It was in use from 1846 to 1965 (when North Sea gas was introduced).
The exhausters and all other equipment have been left in exactly the state they were in when the gasworks closed in 1965. Some items may be seen in action on Thursdays.
Ancillary displays of domestic gas-powered equipment.
Local history museum in two rooms, giving additional insight into the history of Fakenham Town.
Information services:
Guided tours by prior appointment.
Special visitor services: Guided tours.
Services for disabled people: Displays and/or information at wheelchair height.
Collections:
Collections of:
Gas meters
Gas domestic equipment: cookers, lights, fires, geysers etc
Gas equipment for maintenance
Library of gas publications
Local history of Fakenham area
Catalogues:
Catalogue for library is in-house only. Catalogue for all of the collections is only available in-house.

960
FALCONER MUSEUM
Tolbooth Street, Forres, Moray, IV36 1PH

Tel: 01309 673701
Fax: 01309 675863
Email: alasdair.joyce@techleis.moray.gov.uk
Formed: 1871

Organisation type and purpose: Museum.

Enquiries to: Senior Museums Officer
Direct tel: 01309 676688
Access:
Access to staff: By letter, by telephone, by fax, by email, in person
Hours: Apr to Oct: Mon to Sat, 1000 to 1700
Nov to Mar: Mon to Thu, 1100 to 1230 and 1300 to 1530
Other restrictions: No wheelchair access to gallery.
Access to building, collections or gallery: No access other than to staff

General description:
The Moray collection of social history; archaeology; and geology. Includes the bequests of Alexander and Hugh Falconer, including Indian palaeontology.
Collections:
The Corries folk group, c. 1960-1990
Catalogues:
Catalogue for all of the collections is on-line.

Internet home pages:
http://www.moray.gov.uk
http://www.moray.org/museums/homepage.htm

961
FALKIRK COUNCIL

Libraries:
Bo'ness Library
Scotland's Close, Bo'ness, EH51 0AH, tel: 01506 778520
Bonnybridge Library
Bridge Street, Bonnybridge, FK4 1AD, tel: 01324 503295
Denny Library
49 Church Walk, Denny, FK6 6DF, tel: 01324 504242
Falkirk Library
Hope Street, Falkirk, FK1 5AU, tel: 01324 503605
Grangemouth Library
Bo'ness Road, Grangemouth, FK3 8AG, tel: 01324 504690
Larbert Library
Main Street, Stenhousemuir, Larbert, FK5 3JX, tel: 01324 503590
Slamannan Library
The Cross, Slamannan, tel: 01324 851373
The Information Centre
The Steeple, High Street, Falkirk, tel: 01324 628038
Museums:
Falkirk Museum
Callendar House, Callendar Park, Falkirk, tel: 01324 612134
Grangemouth Museum
Victoria Library, Bo'ness Road, Grangemouth, tel: 01324 483291
Kinneil Museum
Duchess Anne Cottages, Kinneil Estate, Bo'ness, tel: 01506 824318

962
FALKIRK COUNCIL ARCHIVES
Falkirk Museums, Callendar House, Callendar Park, Falkirk, Strathclyde, FK1 1YR

Tel: 01324 503779
Fax: 01324 503771
Email: callendar.house@falkirk.gov.uk
Full name: Falkirk Museums History Research Centre
Formed: 1924

Organisation type and purpose: Local government body.
Archives.
Local authority archive service run by Falkirk Museums for Falkirk Council.
Parent body:
Falkirk Council

Enquiries to: Archivist
Other contacts: Museums Assistant for search room enquiries.
Access:
Access to staff: By letter, by telephone, by fax, by email, in person
Hours: Mon to Fri, 1000 to 1230 and 1330 to 1700
Other restrictions: Closed on local public holidays.
Access to building, collections or gallery: No prior appointment required
Hours: Mon to Sat, 1000 to 1700
Access for disabled people: Parking provided, level entry, access to all public areas, toilet facilities

General description:
Archaeology (Roman and industrial), brickmaking, ceramics, engineering, ironfounding, mining, shipbuilding, shipbreaking, timber, transport, social history, industrial history, local history, local photography.
Collections:
Funds Level Finding Aid will be available via the Scottish Archives Network
Business records including: Grangemouth Dockyard, Cruikshank & Co, P&M Hurll, J Baird & Co, Grahamston Iron Co, James Ross & Co, Scottish Tar Distillers
Falkirk Herald 1845-1900 (microfilm)
Family and personal papers including: Forbes of Callendar Papers, Dewar family, Louden family, Burns family, Love Collection
Local authority records (Falkirk Burgh 1803-1975, Grangemouth Burgh 1872-1975, Bo'ness Burgh, Denny & Dunipace Burgh 1833-1975, Falkirk District 1975-1995, Stirling County District Councils 1930-1975, West Lothian County District Councils 1930-1975, Parish Councils and Parochial Boards
Photograph collection, over 30,000 images
Records of local organisations, trade unions, professional associations
Small reference library
Catalogues:
Catalogue for library is in-house only. Catalogue for all of the collections is only available in-house.

Internet home pages:
http://www.falkirk.gov.uk

963
FALKIRK MUSEUM WORKSHOPS
Abbotsinch Road, Grangemouth, Stirlingshire, FK3 9UX

Tel: 01324 504689

Organisation type and purpose: Local government body, museum.
Parent body:
Falkirk Council
Connections with:
Falkirk Museums
Other address:
Falkirk Museums
Callendar House, Callendar Park, Falkirk, FK1 1YR, tel: 01324 503770, fax: 01324 503771, email/website: callendar.house@falkirk.gov.uk

Enquiries to: Collections Manager
Access:
Access to staff: Visitors by prior appointment
Access to building, collections or gallery: No prior appointment required

General description:
Local history; Romans; archaeology; industry; social history; local ceramics; Dunmore pottery; Bo'ness pottery; Carron Company; ironfounding; local communion tokens; natural science

continued overleaf

specimens; transport; agriculture; bookbinding; brickmaking; aerated water manufacture; domestic items.

964
FALKIRK MUSEUMS

Callendar House, Callendar Park, Falkirk, Strathclyde, FK1 1YR

Tel: 01324 503770
Fax: 01324 503771
Email: callendar.house@falkirk.gov.uk
Formed: 1926
Formerly: Falkirk District Museums

Organisation type and purpose: Local government body, museum, art gallery, historic building, house or site.
Parent body:
Falkirk Council
Also at:
Grangemouth Museum
Bo'ness Road, Grangemouth, tel: 01324 504699
History Research Centre
Callendar House, Callendar Park, Falkirk, tel: 01324 503779
Kinneil Museum
Kinneil Estate, Bo'ness, tel: 01506 778530
Museum Stores and Workshop
7-11 Abbotsinch Road, Grangemouth, tel: 01324 504689
The Park Gallery
Callendar Park, Falkirk, tel: 01324 503789

Enquiries to: Assistant Museums Manager
Direct tel: 01324 503777
Other contacts: (1) Archivist (2) Collections Manager (3) Archaeologist for access to collections or specialist information.
Access:
Access to staff: By letter, by telephone, by fax, by email, in person
Hours: Callendar House: all year; Mon to Sat, 1000 to 1700, Apr to Sep; Sun, 1400 to 1700, Kinneil Museum: Mon to Sat, 1230 to 1600 Grangemouth Museum: Mon to Sat, 1230 to 1700
The Park Gallery, Oct to Apr, Mon to Sat, 1000 to 1600, Apr to Sep, Mon to S
Access to building, collections or gallery: No prior appointment required
Other restrictions: Access to collections by prior appointment.
Museum Stores and Workshop, Grangemouth, access by prior appointment
Access for disabled people: Parking provided, level entry, access to all public areas, toilet facilities

General description:
Local history; industrial and social history; Romans (especially Antonine Wall); ceramics; Georgian period; visual arts and crafts; archaeology; archives; clocks and clockmaking; printing; photograph collection; industry; brickmaking; ironfounding; bookbinding; agriculture; transport; public health; environmental studies; domestic life.
Information services:
Library available for reference (for conditions see Access above)
Special visitor services: Materials and/or activities for children.
Education services: Group education facilities.
Services for disabled people: Displays and/or information at wheelchair height.
Catalogues:
Catalogue for library is in-house only. Catalogue for all of the collections is only available in-house.
Publications list:
is available on-line.
Printed publications:
Casson, Crucible of Scotland (Whittaker C, 1999)
Callendar House: The Restoration 1990-1998 (Whittaker C)
A select bibliography and source guide to the Romans in Falkirk District (1982)
Dear Auld Home (Sneddon C, 1997)
Locks Stocks and Bodies in Barrels (Bailey G)
Falkirk 400 (Bailey G, 2000)
The Edinburgh and Glasgow Union Canal (Massey A, 1983)

965
FALKIRK MUSEUMS HISTORY RESEARCH CENTRE

Callendar House, Callendar Park, Falkirk, Strathclyde, FK1 1YR

Tel: 01324 503779
Email: callendar.house@falkirk.gov.uk
Formed: 1994
Also known as: Falkirk Council Archive

Organisation type and purpose: Local government body.
Archives.
Local authority archive service run by Falkirk Museums for Falkirk Council.
Parent body:
Falkirk Council

Enquiries to: Archivist
Other contacts: Museums Assistant for search room enquiries.
Access:
Access to staff: By letter, by telephone, by fax, by email, in person
Hours: Mon to Fri, 1000 to 1230 and 1330 to 1700
Other restrictions: Closed public holidays.
Access to building, collections or gallery: No prior appointment required
Hours: Mon to Fri, 1000 to 1230 and 1330 to 1700
Other restrictions: Access is free to HRC although there is an admission charge for Callendar House.
Access for disabled people: Parking provided, level entry, access to all public areas, toilet facilities

General description:
Local history, industry, social history, local photography, archaeology, (Roman and industrial); brickmaking, ceramics, engineering, ironfoundry, mining, shipbuilding, shipbreaking, timber, transport.
Information services:
Education services: Group education facilities..
Collections:
Fonds Level Finding Aid will be available via Scottish Archives Network
Photographic collection over 30,000 images
Business records
Family and personal papers
Local Authority records (Falkirk Burgh 1803-1975, Grangemouth Burgh 1872-1975, Bo'ness Burgh 1744-1975, Denay & Denepace Burgh 1833-1975, Falkirk District 1975-1995, Stirling County District Councils 1930-1975, Parish Councils, West Lothian County District Councils 1930-1975)
Records of local organisations, trade unions, professional associations
Catalogues:
Catalogue for library is in-house only. Catalogue for all of the collections is only available in-house.

966
FALKLAND PALACE

Falkland, Cupar, Fife, KY15 7BU

Tel: 01337 857397
Fax: 01337 857980
Email: falklandpalace@nts.org.uk

Organisation type and purpose: National organisation, registered charity (charity number SCO 07410), historic building, house or site, suitable for ages: all ages.
Parent body:
National Trust for Scotland (South Region)
Northgate House, 32 Northgate, Peebles, EH45 8RS, tel: 01721 722502, fax: 01721 726000, email: jgreig@nts.org.uk

Enquiries to: Property Manager
Other contacts: Marketing Manager
Access:
Access to staff: By letter, by telephone, by fax, by email
Access to building, collections or gallery: No prior appointment required
Hours: Beginning of March to end of October, Mon to Sat, 1000 to 1800, Sun, 1300 to 1700

General description:
Royal palace; information on Stuart kings and queens, including Mary, Queen of Scots.
Information services:
Scented garden, basic language tape tour for visitors with learning difficulties, guidebook in French and German, explanatory text in Dutch, French, German, Italian, Japanese, Spanish, Swedish
Special visitor services: Guided tours, tape recorded guides, materials and/or activities for children..
Collections:
Original Royal Tennis Court built 1539, still in use.
Portraits of Stuart monarchs
Small herb garden featuring quotations from John Gerard's book'Herball'(1597)
Tapestry hangings

967
FALMOUTH ART GALLERY

Municipal Buildings, The Moor, Falmouth, Cornwall, TR11 2RT

Tel: 01326 313863
Email: info@falmouthartgallery.com
Formed: 1978

Organisation type and purpose: Local government body, art gallery, suitable for ages: all ages, consultancy, research organisation, publishing house.
Local authority art gallery.
Parent body:
Falmouth Town Council

Enquiries to: Director
Other contacts: Gallery Manager
Access:
Access to staff: By letter, by telephone, by email, in person, Internet web pages
Hours: Mon to Sat, 1000 to 1700
Access to building, collections or gallery: No prior appointment required
Hours: Mon to Sat, 1000 to 1700
Other restrictions: Groups advised to book to avoid double bookings.
Access for disabled people: access to all public areas, toilet facilities
Other restrictions: Lift via Webber Street entrance.

General description:
The Town's art collection is one of the most important in Cornwall and features major works by British artists including Sir Edward Coley Burne-Jones, Dame Laura Knight, Sir Alfred Munnings, Henry Scott Tuke, John William Waterhouse RA.
Information services:
Education services: Group education facilities, resources for Key Stages 1 and 2, 3, 4 and Further or Higher Education.
Services for disabled people: For the visually impaired; displays and/or information at wheelchair height.
Collections:
De Paas Collection, prints include works by Claude, Durer, Piranesi and Rembrandt - see www.chain.org.uk
Topographical collection
Publications list:
is available in hard copy.
Printed publications:
Publications available through Gallery Shop
Electronic and video products:
Video available through Gallery Shop

Internet home pages:
http://www.falmouthartgallery.com

968
FALMOUTH MARITIME MUSEUM AND TRUST
See - National Maritime Museum Cornwall

969
FALMOUTH PACKET SHIP SERVICE
See - National Maritime Museum Cornwall

970
FAN MUSEUM, THE
12 Crooms Hill, Greenwich, London, SE10 8ER

Tel: 020 8305 1441
Fax: 020 7293 1889
Email: admin@fan-museum.org
Formed: 1991

Organisation type and purpose: Voluntary organisation, registered charity (charity number 295303), museum, suitable for ages: 16+.
Specialised museum with many international links.
Links with:
Fan Museum Trust
at the same address
Friends of the Fan Museum
at the same address

Enquiries to: Director
Other contacts: Marketing Manager
Access:
Access to staff: By letter, by telephone, by fax, by email, visitors by prior appointment, charges to non-members, Internet web pages
Hours: Mon closed except by appointment; Tue to Sat, 1100 to 1700; Sun 1200 to 1700
Other restrictions: Disabled access and facilities available.
Access to building, collections or gallery: No prior appointment required
Hours: Tue to Fri, 1100 to 1700
Other restrictions: Donation welcome.
Not open at weekends, no flash photography, no ink.
Access for disabled people: ramped entry, access to all public areas, toilet facilities

General description:
This is a specialised fan museum. Books on fans in several languages available in the library, many periodicals and articles (good index), visual archive, catalogues of exhibitions in this museum and elsewhere.
There is a small permanent display (audio explanation); thematic exhibitions changing every 4 months for conservation reasons.
Collections:
Alexander collection, fans and fan leaves, 17th century to 20th century, c. 2000 items
Josy Wall collection, fans, mainly ethnographic, 19th-20th century, c. 130 items
Fonds Duvelleroy. Duvelleroy archive (Duvelleroy was the oldest established fan maker), 19th-20th century, c. 100 items
Publications list:
is available in hard copy and online.

Internet home pages:
http://www.fan-museum.org
All levels of information regarding the museum, workshops, shop, books, functions.

971
FAREHAM MUSEUM
See - Westbury Manor Museum

972
FARINGDON COLLECTION TRUST, THE
Buscot Park, Faringdon, Oxfordshire, SN7 8BU

Tel: 01367 240786
Fax: 01367 241794
Email: estbuscot@aol.com
Acronym or abbreviation: FCT
Formed: 1956

Organisation type and purpose: Registered charity (charity number 203770), historic building, house or site, suitable for ages: 16+.
Historic house and park.
Parent body:
The National Trust
Administered by:
Faringdon Collection Trust
Contents, Art & Furniture Collection owned by:
Faringdon Collection Trust

Enquiries to: Secretary
Access:
Access to staff: By letter, by telephone, by fax, by email, Internet web pages
Access to building, collections or gallery: No prior appointment required
Hours: Most but not all, Wed to Sun: Apr to Sep, 1400 to 1800
Call Information Line fro details: 0845 345 3387
Access for disabled people: Parking provided, toilet facilities
Other restrictions: Not ideal due to gravel paths, incline and steep steps to house.

General description:
Buscot Park was built by Edward Loveden Townsend in the 1770s. The 18th century house is a dignified example of the Italianate country house inspired by Palladio. It contains the Faringdon Collection of fine paintings and furniture, set in attractive parkland featuring two lakes, water gardens and a walled garden.
Collections:
The Faringdon Collection of fine paintings and furniture
Paintings include works by
Rembrandt
Murillo
Reynolds
Burne-Jones
Catalogues:
Catalogue for part of the collections is published and part is on-line.
Printed publications:
Guide Book (£3)

Internet home pages:
http://www.buscot-park.com
Tour of house and gardens, history, picture collection.

973
FARLEIGH HUNGERFORD CASTLE
Farleigh Hungerford, Bath, BA3 6RS

Tel: 01225 754026
Fax: 01225 754026
Email: customers@english-heritage.org.uk
Formed: 1984

Organisation type and purpose: National organisation, historic building, house or site.
Parent body:
English Heritage (South West Region)
Tel: 0117 975 0700, fax: 0117 975 0701

Enquiries to: Head Custodian
Access:
Access to staff: By letter, by fax
Hours: Apr to Sep, daily, 1000 to 1800; Sep, daily, 1000 to 1700; Nov to Mar, Wed to Sun, 1000 to 1600
Access to building, collections or gallery: No prior appointment required
Hours: Apr to Sep, daily, 1000 to 1800; Sep, daily, 1000 to 1700; Nov to Mar, Wed to Sun, 1000 to 1600
Other restrictions: Closed 24-26 Dec and 1 Jan 2003
To make an appointment for educational parties ring 0117 9750720

General description:
Sir Thomas Hungerford acquired and fortified Farleigh Manor in 1370 and over time it became Farleigh Hungerford Castle. Of the original castle, there remain the two south towers and parts of the curtain wall. The 14th century chapel with wall paintings and the crypt are also preserved.
Information services:
Special visitor services: Tape recorded guides.
Education services: Group education facilities..

974
FARNBOROUGH HALL
Banbury, Warwickshire, OX17 1DU

Tel: 01295 690002
Email: farnboroughhall@nationaltrust.org.uk

Organisation type and purpose: National organisation, registered charity (charity number 205846), historic building, house or site, suitable for ages: 12+.
Parent body:
The National Trust (West Midlands)
West Midlands Regional Office, tel: 01743 708100
Occupied and administered by the:
Holbech Family

Enquiries to: Manager
Access:
Access to staff: By letter, by telephone, by email
Access for disabled people: Parking provided
Other restrictions: Designated parking 10yds. Ground floor fully accessible. No access to other floors.

General description:
A beautiful honey-coloured stone house, richly decorated in the mid-18th century and the home of the Holbech family for over 300 years. The interior plasterwork is quite outstanding and the charming grounds contain 18th century temples, a terrace walk and an obelisk.
Information services:
Children's quiz/trail.
Special visitor services: Materials and/or activities for children..

Internet home pages:
http://www.nationaltrust.org.uk

975
FARNE ISLANDS
Northumberland

Tel: 01665 720651

Organisation type and purpose: National organisation, registered charity (charity number 205846), historic building, house or site, suitable for ages: 8+.
Parent body:
The National Trust (Yorkshire and North East)
North East Regional Office, tel: 01670 774691

Enquiries to: Manager
Access:
Access to staff: By letter, by telephone

General description:
One of Britain's most important seabird sanctuaries, home to more than 20 different species, including puffins, eider ducks and four species of tern. Many of the birds are extremely confiding and visitors can enjoy close views. There is also a large colony of seals. St Cuthbert died on Inner Farne in 687 and the chapel built in his memory can be visited.

Internet home pages:
http://www.nationaltrust.org.uk

976
FARNHAM CASTLE KEEP
Farnham, Surrey

Tel: 01252 713393
Formed: 1138

Organisation type and purpose: Historic building, house or site, suitable for ages: 5+.
Parent body:
English Heritage (South East Region)
Eastgate Court, 195-205 High Street, Guildford, Surrey, GU1 3EH, tel: 01483 252000, fax: 01483 252001

continued overleaf

Enquiries to: Curator
Access:
Access to building, collections or gallery: No prior appointment required
Hours: Apr to Sep: daily, 1000 to 1800
Oct: daily, 1000 to 1700
Other restrictions: Opening times are subject to change, for up-to-date information contact English Heritage by phone or visit the website.

General description:
This motte and bailey castle has been in continuous occupation since the 12th century.
Information services:
Special visitor services: Tape recorded guides..

Internet home pages:
http://www.english-heritage.org.uk

977
FEDERATION OF BRITISH CRAFTS SOCIETIES
See - Lace Guild

978
FELBRIGG HALL, GARDEN AND PARK
Felbrigg, Norwich, Norfolk, NR11 8PR

Tel: 01263 837444
Fax: 01263 837032
Email: felbrigg@nationaltrust.org.uk
Formed: 1895

Organisation type and purpose: National organisation, registered charity (charity number 205846), historic building, house or site, suitable for ages: 8+.
Parent body:
The National Trust (East of England)
East Anglia Regional Office, tel: 0870 609 5388

Enquiries to: Property Manager
Other contacts: Property Secretary
Access:
Access to staff: By letter, by fax, by email
Other restrictions: Appointments required.
Access to building, collections or gallery: Prior appointment required
Hours: House: End Mar to end Oct, Sat to Wed, 1300 to 1700; End Oct to beg Nov, Sat to Wed, 1300 to 1600
Gardens: End Mar to Nov, Sat to Wed, 1100 to 1730
Walled Garden: End Mar to mid Jul, Sat to Wed, 1200 to 1600; Mid Jul to end Aug, daily, 1200 to 1600
Other restrictions: Open Bank Holiday Mondays, 1100 to 1700
Access for disabled people: Parking provided, level entry, toilet facilities
Other restrictions: Designated parking 100yds. Drop-off point. 1 single-seater powered mobility vehicle. Level entrance. Ground floor accessible with assistance, Small step from Bird corridor to kitchen corridor. No access to other floors. Photograph album. Level entrance to shop and to restaurant. Grounds largely accessible. Gravel pathways around garden accessible to wheelchairs. Recommended route map.

General description:
One of the finest 17th century country houses in East Anglia. The Hall contains its original 18th century furniture and one of the largest collections of Grand Tour paintings by a single artist. The library is outstanding. The Walled Garden has been restored and features a series of potager gardens, a working dovecote and National Collection of Colchicums.
Information services:
Braille guide.
Front-carrying baby slings for loan.
Suitable for school groups. Children's guide. Children's quiz/trail
Introductory tour of house at 12 noon on open days except Bank Holidays. Numbers limited. (Charge inc. NT members). Special guided group tours of Hall outside normal opening times; guided group tours of gardens; guided group walks of estate.
Special themed suppers monthly and events throughout year. Send s.a.e. to Property Manager for details.
Special visitor services: Guided tours.
Education services: Group education facilities, resources for Key Stage 2.
Services for disabled people: For the visually impaired.
Collections:
Grand Tour Paintings
Books
Catalogues:
Catalogue for library is in-house only. Catalogue for all of the collections is only available in-house.
Printed publications:
Guide Book
Children's Guide
Short Guide

Internet home pages:
http://www.nationaltrust.org.uk

979
FELIXSTOWE MUSEUM, THE
Viewpoint Road, Landguard Point, PO Box 50, Felixstowe, Suffolk, IP11 7JG

Tel: 01394 674355
Acronym or abbreviation: FHMS
Full name: Felixstowe History and Museum Society
Formed: 1982

Organisation type and purpose: Membership association, voluntary organisation, registered charity (charity number 278342/R), museum, historic building, house or site, suitable for ages: all ages, research organisation.

Enquiries to: Archivist
Direct tel: 01394 285506
Other contacts: Secretary fax: 01394 672284 email ronman16@tiscali.co.uk
Access:
Access to staff: By letter, by telephone, by fax, by email, in person, visitors by prior appointment
Access to building, collections or gallery: No prior appointment required
Hours: Easter to end Sep; Wed, 1300 to 1730
Easter to end Oct; Sun 1300 to 1730
Bank Holidays, 1300 to 1730
Other restrictions: Other times by appointment. Entry charge, half price to English Heritage members
Access for disabled people: ramped entry, access to all public areas

General description:
Primarily local history, military and civil.
Information and artefacts relating to the Ravelin Block, next door to the Fort, which houses the museum - dates from 1878 - a submarine mining establishment.
Naval room with coastal forces, including HMS Beehive memorabilia.
Many models of aircraft, ships etc, Port of Felixstowe.
Archaeology, geology, Roman collection relating to the Roman fort at Felixstowe.
Paddle steamer room.
Local shop reconstructed.
Information services:
Library available for reference (for conditions see Access above)
Some displays and information at wheelchair height.
Special visitor services: Materials and/or activities for children.
Education services: Group education facilities, resources for Key Stages 1 and 2, 3, 4 and Further or Higher Education..
Collections:
Reference Library
Roman artefacts
Military history of Landguard Fort
Social history of Felixstowe - Victorian/ Edwardian and other WWII history
History of flying from 1912, including the Marine Aircraft Experimental Establishment
Artefacts from St Audry's Hospital, Melton - mental hospital with roots from 1700s
Comprehensive collection of maps
Models of planes, ships, tanks etc
Photographs including the collection of G F Cordy - local photographer
Catalogues:
Catalogue for library is in-house only. Catalogue for part of the collections is only available in-house.
Printed publications:
Publicity leaflet (free, direct)

See also - Landguard Fort

980
FENDERESKY GALLERY
2-4 Crescent Arts Centre, University Road, Belfast, BT7 1NH

Tel: 028 9023 5245
Formed: 1984

Organisation type and purpose: National organisation, art gallery, suitable for ages: 12+.

Enquiries to: Curator
Access:
Access to staff: By letter only
Access to building, collections or gallery: No prior appointment required
Access for disabled people: level entry, toilet facilities

981
FENTON HOUSE
Windmill Hill, Hampstead, London, NW3 6RT

Tel: 020 7435 3471
Fax: 020 7435 3471
Email: fentonhouse@nationaltrust.org.uk
Formed: 1952

Organisation type and purpose: National organisation, registered charity (charity number 205846), museum, historic building, house or site, suitable for ages: 5+.
Parent body:
The National Trust (London Region)
London Central Office, tel: 0870 609 5380

Enquiries to: Custodian
Access:
Access to staff: By letter, by telephone, by fax, by email, visitors by prior appointment
Hours: Wed to Sun, 0900 to 1800
Access for disabled people: ramped entry
Other restrictions: Tel. for parking arrangements. Steps to entrance. Portable ramp available. Ground floor fully accessible. No access to other floors. Photograph album. WCs on first floor, only accessible via staircase. Upper walk and south garden accessible to wheelchair users.

General description:
A late 17th century house with an outstanding collection of porcelain, 17th century needlework pictures, Georgian furniture and early keyboard instruments, most of which are in working order. The delightful walled garden includes fine displays of roses, an orchard and a vegetable garden.
Information services:
Helpline available, tel no: Infoline: 01494 755563.
Demonstration tours (max. 20) of instruments by the Keeper on certain dates, 1-2hrs, apply to Custodian for details.
Braille guide. Large-print guide.
Suitable for school groups. Children's quiz/trail.
Special visitor services: Materials and/or activities for children.
Services for disabled people: For the visually impaired.
Collections:
Benton Fletcher Collection of early keyboard instruments
Binning Collections of 18th century porcelain and pottery, furniture and Stuart embroidered pictures

Catalogues:
Catalogue for library is in-house only. Catalogue for all of the collections is only available in-house.
Printed publications:
Guide Book
Short Guide
Guide to the Keyboard Instruments

Internet home pages:
http://www.nationaltrust.org.uk

982
FERENS ART GALLERY
Queen Victoria Square, Hull, East Yorkshire, HU1 3RA

Tel: 01482 613902
Formed: 1927

Organisation type and purpose: Local government body, art gallery, suitable for ages: 5+.
Parent body:
Kingston upon Hull City Council
Tel: 01482 300300

Enquiries to: Curator
Access:
Access to staff: By letter, by telephone
Access to building, collections or gallery: No prior appointment required
Hours: Mon to Sat 1000 to 1700, Sun 1330 to 1630

General description:
The Gallery has an internationally renowned permanent collection of displays of paintings and sculpture from the medieval period to the present day, as well as temporary exhibitions and live art.
Information services:
Education and events programme, including tours, talks and art workshops
Children's gallery
Special visitor services: Materials and/or activities for children.
Education services: Group education facilities..
Collections:
European Old Masters, particularly Dutch and Flemish
Modern and contemporary British art
Masterpieces by Frans Hals, Antonio Canaletto, Stanley Spencer, David Hockney, Helen Chadwick and Peter Howson

Internet home pages:
http://www.hullcc.gov.uk./museums

983
FERGUSSON GALLERY, THE
Marshall Place, Perth, Tayside, PH2 8NU

Tel: 01738 441944
Fax: 01738 621152
Email: museum@pkc.gov.uk
Formed: 1992
Formed by: The J D Fergusson Art Foundation

Organisation type and purpose: Art gallery.
Parent body:
Perth and Kinross Council, Education and Children's Services, Arts and Heritage Division
2-5 High Street, Perth, tel: 01738 475000

Enquiries to: Curator
Access:
Access to staff: By letter, by telephone, by fax, by email, in person, visitors by prior appointment
Hours: Mon to Fri, 1000 to 1700
Access to building, collections or gallery: No prior appointment required
Hours: Mon to Sat, 1000 to 1700
Access for disabled people: ramped entry, toilet facilities
Other restrictions: Access to galleries 1 and 2.

General description:
The gallery is devoted to the promotion of the life and work of Scottish colourist artist, J D Fergusson (1874 to 1961). Large permanent collection includes; oil paintings, watercolours, drawings, sculpture and extensive archive of photographs, letters, press-cuttings etc.
Permanent collection also contains works by related artists, including members of the New Scottish Group.
Information services:
Library available for reference (for conditions see Access above)
J D Fergusson Arts Award Trust (annual award available to Scottish Artists).
Special visitor services: Materials and/or activities for children.
Services for disabled people: For the visually impaired.
Collections:
The Fergusson Collection, a series of sketchbooks made by the artist whilst living in Paris between 1907-1914, 40 sketchbooks
Catalogues:
Catalogue for part of the collections is published.
Printed publications:
Gallery booklet, postcards, prints, available for purchase
Living Paint, J D Ferguson 1874-1961 a biography of the artist and catalogue of the collection

Internet home pages:
http://www.pkc.gov.uk/ah/fergussongallery.htm
Exhibitions, events and descriptions of the collections including images.

984
FERMANAGH COUNTY MUSEUM
Enniskillen Castle, Castle Barracks, Enniskillen, Co Fermanagh, BT74 7HL

Tel: 028 6632 5000
Fax: 028 6632 7342
Formed: 1976

Organisation type and purpose: Local government body, museum.
Parent body:
Fermanagh District Council
Member of:
Irish Museums Association
Northern Ireland Museums Council
Visitor Attractions Association of Northern Ireland

Enquiries to: Curator
Other contacts: Education Officer, Development Officer for educational visits.
Access:
Access to staff: By letter, by telephone, by fax, by email, in person
Access to building, collections or gallery: No prior appointment required
Hours: May, Jun, Sep: Mon, Sat, 1400 to 1700; Tue to Fri, 1000 to 1700
Jul, Aug: Mon, Sat, Sun, 1400 to 1700; Tue to Fri, 1000 to 1700
Oct to Apr: Mon, 1400 to 1700; Tue to Fri, 1000 to 1700
Open Bank Holidays, 1000 to 1700
Access for disabled people: Parking provided, toilet facilities
Other restrictions: Partial access to Castle Keep.

General description:
The castle was built in the early 15th century by Hugh the Hospitable under Macguire patronage. There are now the 19th century barracks buildings surrounding the medieval Castle Keep, the 17th century Watergate and the more recent heritage centre.
The Keep houses the Royal Inniskilling Fusiers Museum and dsiplays the history of the regiment from its formation in 1689.
The Keep also displays the history of the Castle and the development of the town.
The Barracks contains displays relating to the archaeology, history and environment of Fermanagh.
Information services:
Helpline available, tel no: 028 6632 5000.
Curriculum-linked tours and education programmes.
Guided tours, groups only.
Special visitor services: Guided tours, materials and/or activities for children.
Education services: Group education facilities, resources for Key Stages 1 and 2, 3, 4 and Further or Higher Education.
Services for disabled people: For the hearing impaired.
Collections:
Items of local historic interest, Belleek china, lace, local photographs and paintings
Printed publications:
Enniskillen Castle Newsletter (available to Friends of the Museum Association, teachers)
Electronic and video products:
Maguires of Fermanagh (video, available to purchase from Museum)
Enniskillen Today and Yesterday (video, available to purchase from museum)

985
FERRERS GALLERY
Staunton Harold, Ashby-de-la-Zouch, Leicestershire, LE65 1RU

Tel: 01332 863337
Fax: 01332 865408
Email: jayne@ferrersgallery.co.uk
Full name: Ferrers Centre for Arts & Crafts
Formed: 1974

Organisation type and purpose: Independently owned, art gallery, suitable for ages: 16+.
Contemporary arts selling British-made works.

Enquiries to: Manager
Access:
Access to staff: By letter, by telephone, by fax, by email
Hours: Tue to Sun, 1100 to 1700
Access to building, collections or gallery: No prior appointment required
Hours: Tue to Sun, 1100 to 1700
Access for disabled people: Parking provided, toilet facilities
Other restrictions: Access to ground floor.

General description:
The Centre occupies the fine Georgian stable block of nearby Staunton Hall. The main purpose and use of the Ferrers Centre is to provide workspace for artists and craftspeople. 17 different workshops and studios operate here, with skilled craftspeople making individual items. A wide variety of disciplines are represented, furniture, ceramics, textiles and gallery.
Printed publications:
Centre leaflet
Walks Around Staunton Harold Estate (leaflet, 60p)

Address for ordering publications:
Printed publications:
Manager, Ferrers Centre for Arts & Crafts

Internet home pages:
http://www.ferrerscentre.co.uk
http://www.ferrersgallery.co.uk

986
FIFE COUNCIL MUSEUMS - EAST
County Buildings, St Catherine Street, Cupar, Fife, KY15 4TA

Tel: 01334 412933/4
Fax: 01334 413214
Email: museums.east@fife.gov.uk
Formed: 1983
Formerly: North East Fife District Museums Service, date of change, 1996

Organisation type and purpose: Museum.
Branch museum:
Newburgh
St Andrews

Enquiries to: Curator

continued overleaf

Access:
Access to staff: By letter, by telephone, by fax, by email, visitors by prior appointment
Hours: Mon to Fri, 0930 to 1630

General description:
Collections of prehistoric and mediaeval archaeology; 19th century ethnography; fine and decorative art; geology and natural history; militaria; phrenology; and social history, relating to North East Fife.
Collections:
St Andrews University Archaeology Collection, prehistoric and historic artefacts, 6000 BC to 1900 AD, very extensive collection
Cynicus Collection, relating to Martin Anderson (1854-1932) Tayport-based Edwardian cartoonist, c. 1870-1932, large collection, still being added to
Robert Young (1866-1932) collection, Tabura items from NE Zambia, c. 1800-1917
John Anderson (1796-1864) collection, fossil fish
James Bonnar (1849-1930) collection, ethnography, militaria, etc c. 1800-1930
Alexander Laing (1808-1892) collection, ethnography, Victorian collections, 19th century
Cupar Phrenological Society collection, part of the society's collections, 19th century, 17 heads and deathmasks

See also - St Andrews University Museum Collections

987
FIFE COUNCIL MUSEUMS WEST
Museum HQ, Dunfermline Museum, Viewfield Terrace, Dunfermline, Fife, KY12 7HY

Tel: 01383 313838
Fax: 01383 313837
Email: lesley.botten@ fife.gov.uk
Acronym or abbreviation: FCMW
Formed: 1996
Formerly: Dunfermline District Museum and Small Gallery, date of change, 1997

Organisation type and purpose: Local government body, museum, suitable for ages: all ages.
Headquarters of Fife Council Museums West.
Parent body:
Fife Council
Access:
Access to staff: By telephone, by fax, by email, visitors by prior appointment, by letter
Access to building, collections or gallery: Prior appointment required
Access for disabled people: ramped entry, level entry

General description:
Local history and archaeology; 19th and 20th century luxury linen damask weaving industry history; costume; coal mining; west Fife area.
Collections:
Comprehensive collection of machinery, designs and products from the luxury damask linen and silk industry of 19/20th century Dunfermline

See also - Dunfermline Museum; Inverkeithing Museum; Pittencrieff House Museum; St Margaret's Cave

988
FIFE FOLK MUSEUM
High Street, Ceres, Cupar, Fife, KY15 5NF

Tel: 01334 828180
Formed: 1968

Organisation type and purpose: Museum.

Enquiries to: Curator
Access:
Access to staff: By letter, by telephone, visitors by prior appointment
Access for disabled people: Parking provided
Other restrictions: Limited disabled access.

General description:
A category A listed building housing the museum of local history; agricultural history; local architecture; antiquities.
Collections:
Bars of soap, box beds, bicycle, dolls' prams, farm carts, mouse traps and steam engines
Burgh tolbooth dating from the 1600s
Cottage of a hand-loom weaver
Homes, farms and workshops
a dresser displaying the pottery and china from home
Large collection of lace, patchwork, samplers, clothes and accessories
Boot of David Hackston of Rathillet (murderer of Archbishop Sharp), 17th century
Catalogues:
Catalogue for all of the collections is only available in-house.

989
FILCHING MANOR MOTOR MUSEUM, THE
Filching Manor, Wannock, Polegate, East Sussex, BN26 5QA

Tel: 01323 487933; 487838; 487124
Fax: 01323 486331
Email: campbellcircut@aol.com
Formed: 1947

Organisation type and purpose: International organisation, independently owned, museum, art gallery, historic building, house or site, consultancy, research organisation, publishing house.
Conservation, restoration, preservation.

Enquiries to: Lord of the Manor of Filching Wannock
Access:
Access to staff: By letter, by telephone, by fax, by email, visitors by prior appointment
Access to building, collections or gallery: Prior appointment required
Hours: Easter to Oct and Bank Holidays: Conducted tours by appointment only
Other restrictions: Owing to security, admission is by appointment by phone, fax or letter only.
Access for disabled people: Parking provided, ramped entry, level entry, access to all public areas, toilet facilities

General description:
Visit the ancient Saxon site of the ffulchings, set in 28 acres of beautiful Sussex Downland and formal gardens. The building is a 15th century Wealden House, rebuilt in 1450 from the then existing building. The Great Hall features a minstrel's gallery and early oak panelling.
There you can see the unique and exclusive collection of some of the rarest sports and racing cars in the world. Filching is the home of many well known London to Brighton run cars, and the Bluebird K3 speedboat with its Rolls Royce racing 'R' type engine, which broke the world water speed record in 1937 with Sir Malcolm Campbell at the helm. Also the Bluebird K7 Hydroplane built for the successful BBC film 'Across the Lake'. The story of Donald Campbell.
There are three amazing Bugatti cars together with original Bugatti furniture. Also on display are antiquities, arms and armour, not forgetting the original Wealden Hall House of the Manor itself with its hall, minstrel's gallery and early oak panelling. The front door is reputed to be the oldest in domestic use in Britain.
Collections:
7500 books on motor cars, no public access to books or archive, help given at times with photostats etc and research
24,000 catalogues on cars, motorcycles and cycles
Collection of art, antiques, paintings and sculpture, ethnographic art
Collection of model cars
Collection of Aronortica, R37 Rolls-Royce Schnider Trophy engine, Metrovic engine from Bluebird K7, 1909 Anzani engine, 1915 ABC engine, 1914 Isotta-Fraschini engine, 1895 Mellor Rotary engine
Malcolm and Donald Campbell archive/collection
2 Campbell Bluebirds
2 Campbell cars
1 Campbell Airoplane wreck
Collection of motoring art and trophies
Bugatti Furniture

Internet home pages:
http://www.filchingmanor.co.uk

990
FILEY MUSEUM
8-10 Queen Street, Filey, North Yorkshire, YO14 9HB

Tel: 01723 515013
Formed: 1971

Organisation type and purpose: Independently owned, registered charity (charity number 1081130), museum, historic building, house or site, suitable for ages: 8+.
Registered museum.

Enquiries to: Honorary Curator
Direct tel: 01723 515945
Other contacts: Secretary to Trustees, tel: 01723 513468
Access:
Access to staff: By letter, by telephone, in person
Access for disabled people: level entry, toilet facilities
Other restrictions: Ramped entry to garden area, talking labels in each room, crystal aids for hearing impaired, video of upper floor viewed on TV from ground floor.

General description:
The museum is housed in a Grade II listed building dating from 1696. Displays relating to the sea-shore, the lifeboat service, fishing, Filey as a community, Victorian life, rural and domestic crafts, photographs, and costume, replica baiting shed.
Information services:
Special visitor services: Guided tours.
Services for disabled people: For the visually impaired; for the hearing impaired; displays and/or information at wheelchair height.
Collections:
Old Local Newspapers from 1876 and 1943
Photographic Collection from late 1800 and 1900
Catalogues:
Catalogue for library is in-house only. Catalogue for all of the collections is only available in-house.

991
FINAVON DOOCOT
Finavon, Angus

Organisation type and purpose: Historic building, house or site.
Parent body:
National Trust for Scotland (North-East Region)
Access:
Access to building, collections or gallery: No prior appointment required
Hours: End Mar to end Oct, daily
Other restrictions: Keys from Finavon Hotel

General description:
Largest doocot in Scotland, believed to have been built in the 16th century.

992
FINCH FOUNDRY
Sticklepath, Okehampton, Devon, EX20 2NW

Tel: 01837 840046
Full name: Finch Foundry Museum of Rural Industry
Formed: 1994

Organisation type and purpose: National organisation, registered charity (charity number 205846), museum, suitable for ages: all ages.

Parent body:
The National Trust (South West Region)
Regional Office for Devon and Cornwall, tel: 01392 881691

Enquiries to: Custodian
Access:
Access to staff: By letter only
Hours: Mon, Wed, Thu, Fri, 0900 to 1700
Access to building, collections or gallery: No access other than to staff
Hours: Apr to Oct: Mon, Wed to Sun, 1100 to 1730
Other restrictions: Not suitable for coaches.

General description:
Finch Foundry is a museum of agriculture housed in a 19th century forge used for making edge tools such as sickles, scythes, axes and shovels for both agriculture and mining. There are three large working waterwheels which power a fan for the forges, drop hammers, shears, grinding wheel, bandsaw, and a tilt hammer.
Information services:
Braille guide. Handling collection. Volunteers explain the history of the foundry.
Suitable fo school groups. Children's quiz-trail.
Special visitor services: Materials and/or activities for children..
Collections:
Collection of edge tools made by the Finch family during the 19th century.
Catalogues:
Catalogue for all of the collections is only available in-house.
Printed publications:
Guide Book (£2.25)

Internet home pages:
http://www.nationaltrust.org.uk/regions/devon

993
FINCHALE PRIORY
Brasside, Newton Hall, Co Durham, DH1 5SH

Tel: 0191 386 3828

Organisation type and purpose: Historic building, house or site.
Parent body:
English Heritage (North East Region)
Tel: 0191 269 1227/8, fax: 0191 261 1130

Enquiries to: Manager
Access:
Access to staff: By letter, by telephone, in person
Access to building, collections or gallery: No prior appointment required
Hours: End Mar to end Sep: daily, 1000 to 1800
Other restrictions: Opening times are subject to change, for up-to-date information contact English Heritage by phone or visit the website.

General description:
13th century priory ruins.

Internet home pages:
http://www.english-heritage.org.uk

994
FIREPOWER
The Royal Artillery Museum, Royal Arsenal, Woolwich, London, SE18 6ST

Tel: 020 8855 7755
Fax: 020 8855 7100
Email: info@firepower.org.uk
Formed: 2001
Formerly: Royal Artillery Experience; Royal Artillery Library (moved to new site and opened), Museum of Artillery in the Rotunda (moved to new site and opened), date of change, 2001

Organisation type and purpose: Independently owned, museum, suitable for ages: all ages.
Parent body:
Royal Artillery Historical Trust
c/o Firepower, Royal Artillery Museum, tel: 020 8855 7755

Other addresses:
Museum of Artillery in the Rotunda
Repository Road, London, SE18 4BQ, tel: 020 8782 3127, email/website: less@firepower.org.uk
Royal Artillery Institution Library, James Clavell Library
Firepower Royal Artillery Museum, Royal Arsenal (West), Warren Lane, Woolwich, London, SE18 6ST, tel: 020 8312 7125

Enquiries to: Chief Executive
Other contacts: Historical Secretary for research enquiries.
Access:
Access to staff: By letter, Internet web pages
Hours: Telephone or check website
Access to building, collections or gallery: No prior appointment required
Hours: Telephone or check website
Access for disabled people: Parking provided, level entry, access to all public areas, toilet facilities
Other restrictions: Wheelchairs supplied, induction loop, braille captions and outlies of objects.

General description:
History of artillery, historic collection of the Royal Regiment up to present day, missile systems and self-propelled guns. Medals, artefacts, hands-on displays and interactives, library and archive, history of artillery and of the regiment.
Information services:
Library available for reference (for conditions see Access above)
Corporate hire facilities, children's parties.
Special visitor services: Materials and/or activities for children.
Education services: Group education facilities, resources for Key Stages 2, 3 and Further or Higher Education.
Services for disabled people: For the visually impaired; for the hearing impaired; displays and/or information at wheelchair height.
Collections:
Collections:
Royal Artillery Institution Library
James Clavell Library
Subject Coverage includes:
Royal Artillery Regimental history, artillery equipments, armed forces, warfare, tactics, training, fortification, military history, military geography and biography
Stock includes:
books, journals, pamphlets, manuscripts, diaries, maps, plans, drawings, photographs, film and microfiche
Publications list:
is available on-line.
Printed publications:
History of the Royal Regiment of Artillery (vols I-VI, vol VII in production)

Address for ordering publications:
Printed publications:
Royal Artillery Shop
Tel: 020 8312 7134, email: shop@firepower.org.uk

Internet home pages:
http://www.firepower.org.uk
General information.

See also - Museum of Artillery in the Rotunda; Royal Artillery Institution library

995
FIRST GARDEN CITY HERITAGE MUSEUM
296 Norton Way South, Letchworth Garden City, Hertfordshire, SG6 1SU

Tel: 01462 482710
Fax: 01462 486056
Email: fgchm@letchworth.com
Acronym or abbreviation: FGCHM
Formed: 1977

Organisation type and purpose: Museum.
Parent body:
Letchworth Garden City Heritage Foundation
Suite 401, Spirella Building, Bridge Road, Letchworth, Hertfordshire, SG6 4ET, tel: 01462 476000, fax: 01462 476050, email: info@letchworth.com

Enquiries to: Curator
Other contacts: Documentation Officer for enquiries.
Access:
Access to staff: By letter, by telephone, by fax, by email, in person, visitors by prior appointment
Hours: Mon to Sat, 1000 to 1700
Access to building, collections or gallery: No prior appointment required
Hours: Mon to Sat, 1000 to 1700

General description:
History of the garden city movement, its structure, personalities; history of Letchworth Garden City from its formation in 1903 up to the present; many aspects are covered including industrial, political, social etc.
Information services:
Library available for reference (for conditions see Access above)
Special visitor services: Guided tours, materials and/or activities for children.
Education services: Group education facilities, resources for Key Stages 1 and 2, 3, 4 and Further or Higher Education..
Collections:
Documents relating to First Garden City Ltd
Minute Books plus other sources for other organisations within Letchworth
Primary source of information through a series of cuttings and books from 1902-1917
Small but important library on garden city movement, Co-operative movement, Letchworth history
Printed publications:
Leaflets, books, postcards (available, museum shop)

Internet home pages:
http://www.letchworth.com

996
FIRSTSITE@THE MINORIES
74 High Street, Colchester, Essex, CO1 1UE

Tel: 01206 577067
Fax: 01206 577161
Email: info@firstsite-online.org.uk
Formed: 1993
Formerly: Colchester and District Visual Arts Trust (CADVAT), date of change, 1995

Organisation type and purpose: Registered charity (charity number 1031800), art gallery, suitable for ages: 3+, consultancy, publishing house.
Visual Arts (Contemporary).
To promote contemporary visual arts in Essex and on tour in the UK and abroad.
HQ:
Minories Art Gallery

Enquiries to: Administrator
Access:
Access to staff: By letter, by telephone, by fax, by email, in person
Other restrictions: Director by prior appointment only.
Access to building, collections or gallery: No prior appointment required
Hours: Mon to Sat, 1000 to 1700
Access for disabled people: ramped entry, toilet facilities

General description:
Contemporary visual arts.
Information services:
Library available for reference (for conditions see Access above)
Special visitor services: Materials and/or activities for children.
Education services: Group education facilities, resources for Key Stages 1 and 2, 3, 4 and Further or Higher Education.
Services for disabled people: For the hearing impaired.

continued overleaf

Collections:
The Victor Batte-Lay Trust Collection
Catalogues:
Catalogue for all of the collections is only available in-house.
Publications list:
is available in hard copy and online.
Printed publications:
Exhibition Catalogues
Artists' Books

Internet home pages:
http://www.firstsite.uk.net

997
FISHBOURNE ROMAN PALACE MUSEUM

Salthill Road, Fishbourne, Chichester, West Sussex, PO19 3QR

Tel: 01243 785859
Fax: 01243 539266
Email: adminfish@sussexpast.co.uk
Formed: 1968

Organisation type and purpose: Museum.
Parent body:
Sussex Past
Bull House, 92 High Street, Lewes, East Sussex, BN7 1XH, tel: 01273 486260, fax: 01273 486990, email: admin@sussexpast.co.uk

Enquiries to: Director
Other contacts: Secretary for visit bookings.
Access:
Access to staff: By letter, by email
Access to building, collections or gallery: No access other than to staff
Hours: Mar to July and Sep, Oct, daily, 1000 to 1700
Aug, daily, 1000 to 1800
Nov to mid Dec, daily 1000 to 1600
Mid Dec to 31 Jan, daily Sat, Sun, 1000 to 1600
Feb, daily, 1000 to 1600
Access for disabled people: Parking provided, level entry, access to all public areas, toilet facilities

General description:
Romano-British mosaics; Fishbourne Roman Palace; Roman gardens. The remains of part of a 1st century AD palatial building, containing many 1st-3rd century insitu mosaics, and two 4th century mosaics from the area.
Information services:
Special visitor services: Guided tours, tape recorded guides, materials and/or activities for children.
Education services: Group education facilities, resources for Key Stages 2, 3, 4 and Further or Higher Education.
Services for disabled people: For the visually impaired.
Collections:
Excavated material from 1960 onwards, including Britain's largest collection of insitu mosaics
50% recorded on computer database, 25% in other publications
Catalogues:
Catalogue for part of the collections is only available in-house.
Printed publications:
Promotional leaflet

Internet home pages:
http://www.sussexpast.co.uk

998
FITZWILLIAM MUSEUM

Library, Trumpington Street, Cambridge, CB2 1RB

Tel: 01223 332900
Fax: 01223 332923

Organisation type and purpose: Museum, university department or institute.
Parent body:
University of Cambridge

Enquiries to: Librarian
Other contacts: Keeper of Manuscripts and Printed Books for materials relating specifically to the curatorial collections.
Access:
Access to staff: By letter, by telephone, by email, in person, visitors by prior appointment, letter of introduction required
Hours: CLOSED 2002 TO 2003 owing to building work
(Tue to Fri, 1000 to 1200 and 1330 to 1630)
Other restrictions: Access restrictions apply only to the users of curatorial materials (ie manuscripts and rare books).
Access to building, collections or gallery: No access other than to staff
Hours: CLOSED 2002 TO 2003 owing to building work
(Tue to Fri, 1000 to 1200 and 1330 to 1630)

General description:
The collection is valuable for its form rather than subject coverage: illuminated manuscripts, music manuscripts and printed music, autograph letters, rare books of all periods, art reference works, literary manuscripts, fine arts and antiquities.
Collections:
Collections include:
Most of music and some of the other manuscript material on microfilm
Music by Patrick Hadley, MacFarren, Handel
William Hayley papers
W S Blunt papers
Catalogues:
Catalogue for library is on-line. Catalogue for part of the collections is published and part is on-line.
Printed publications:
Annual Report
Catalogues of the collections
Newsletter (3 times a year)
Microform products:
Microfilm, photographs available for purchase via Photographic Sales Officer

Internet home pages:
http://www.fitzmuseum.cam.ac.uk
Museum web pages.

999
FITZWILLIAM MUSEUM

Trumpington Street, Cambridge, CB2 1RB

Tel: 01223 332900
Fax: 01223 332923
Email: fitzmuseum-enquiries@lists.cam.ac.uk
Formed: 1816

Organisation type and purpose: Museum, art gallery, historic building, house or site, university department or institute, suitable for ages: all ages.
Museum opened to public 1848.
Parent body:
University of Cambridge

Enquiries to: Administrator
Access:
Access to staff: By letter, by telephone, by fax, by email

General description:
Fine arts: including paintings, drawings and prints, antiquities, sculpture, arms and armour, furniture, porcelain, ceramics, pottery, glass and enamels, silver, coins and medals, jewellery, gems and cameos, textiles and fans.
Information services:
Special visitor services: Guided tours, materials and/or activities for children.
Education services: Group education facilities, resources for Key Stages 1 and 2, 3, 4 and Further or Higher Education..
Collections:
Important international collections in the subject categories including:
Paintings (masterpieces of the Italian, Dutch, Flemish, French and English Schools)
English Watercolours and drawings (a large collection of William Blake) and portrait miniatures
One of the finest collections of Rembrandt prints in the world
Antiquities, including Egyptian (the Gayer-Anderson Collection), West Asiatic, Greek and Roman
English furniture and clocks, and sculpture in ivory, bronze, terracotta and marble
Islamic pottery and glass
Chinese porcelain, bronzes and jade
Japanese porcelain and lacquer and the Gompertz Collection of Korean ceramics
Manuscripts (notably mediaeval illuminated manuscripts and important music manuscripts, including the Fitzwilliam Virginal Book) and printed books
Coins including:
The McClean Collection of Greek coins
The Grierson Collection of Mediaeval coins
The Blunt Collection of Anglo-Saxon coins
Fine Italian and English Medals
Catalogues:
Catalogue for library is on-line. Catalogue for part of the collections is published and part is on-line.
Publications list:
is available on-line.
Printed publications:
Catalogues of temporary exhibitions
Publications on the permanent collections

Internet home pages:
http://www.fitzmuseum.cam.ac.uk

1000
FLAG FEN BRONZE AGE CENTRE

The Croveway, Northey Road, Peterborough, Cambridgeshire, PE6 7QJ

Tel: 01733 313414
Fax: 01733 349957
Email: info@flagfen.com
Formed: 1986

Organisation type and purpose: Independently owned, registered charity (charity number 295116), historic building, house or site, suitable for ages: 5+.
Parent body:
Fenland Archaeological Trust

Enquiries to: Manager
Access:
Access to staff: By letter, by telephone, by fax, by email
Hours: All week, 1000 to 1700
Access for disabled people: Parking provided, access to all public areas, toilet facilities

General description:
Flag Fen is a Bronze Age site that covers a 20 acre park. The excavations and the Museum of the Bronze Age can be viewed all year round, as can the reconstructed roundhouses and natural wildlife. Interpretation is provided throughout the site to help guide visitors around the park.
Information services:
Guided tours must be pre-booked.
Special visitor services: Guided tours.
Education services: Group education facilities, resources for Key Stages 1 and 2, 3 and Further or Higher Education.
Services for disabled people: For the visually impaired; displays and/or information at wheelchair height.
Collections:
Over 300 pieces of bronze metalwork ranging from jewellery to swords and daggers
Unique range of Bronze Age finds
Prehistoric wood, earliest wheel in England, 'shoe' box housing shears, willow scoop, axle, etc. 1350-100 BC
Printed publications:
The Flag Fen Basin
Guide Book
Postcards

Internet home pages:
http://www.flagfen.com
History of the site including what is on offer to visitors.

1001
FLAGSHIP PORTSMOUTH TRUST
See - Portsmouth Historic Dockyard

1002
FLAMBARDS VILLAGE THEME PARK
Culdrose Manor, Helston, Cornwall, TR13 0QA

Tel: 01326 573404
Fax: 01326 573344
Email: info@flambards.co.uk
Formed: 1976
Formerly: The Cornwall Aircraft Park (Helston) Limited

Organisation type and purpose: Suitable for ages: all ages.
Private family owned business.
Family leisure park.

Enquiries to: Managing Director
Other contacts: Director of Marketing for point of contact.
Access:
Access to staff: By fax, visitors by prior appointment
Access to building, collections or gallery: No prior appointment required
Hours: Easter to end Oct: 1030 to 1700
Aug: 1030 to 1800
Other restrictions: Closed some Mon and Fri in low season.
Access for disabled people: Parking provided, ramped entry, level entry, toilet facilities
Other restrictions: Free wheelchair loan, free route guide.

General description:
A Victorian village containing over 50 fully equipped homes, shops and trade premises. Includes galleries containing items of interest concerning Cornwall and World War II, Britain in the Blitz and the Home Front. Other collections include advertising ephemera; helicopters; and aircraft.
Information services:
Special visitor services: Tape recorded guides..
Collections:
Victorian village, recreated village, 1860-1910
War galleries, showcases of events, 1938-1947
Bovril advertising, company advertising thresholds, up to 1970
Aero Park, aircraft/helicopters, up to 1980
Items made from World War I aircraft propellers, 1914-1919
Catalogues:
Catalogue for all of the collections is only available in-house.
Printed publications:
Information leaflet (annually, available Spring)

Internet home pages:
http://www.flambards.co.uk

1003
FLATFORD: BRIDGE COTTAGE
Flatford, East Bergholt, Colchester, Essex, CO7 6OL

Tel: 01206 298260
Fax: 01206 299193
Email: flatfordbridgecottage @nationaltrust.org.uk

Organisation type and purpose: National organisation, registered charity (charity number 205846), historic building, house or site, suitable for ages: 8+.
Parent body:
The National Trust (East of England)
East Anglia Regional Office, tel: 0870 609 5388
National Trust sites:
Bridge Cottage
Flatford, East Bergholt, Colchester, Suffolk, CO7 6OL, tel: 01206 299193

Enquiries to: Manager
Access:
Access to staff: By letter, by telephone, by fax, by email
Access for disabled people: Parking provided, level entry, toilet facilities
Other restrictions: 1 manual wheelchair available. Ground floor accessible with assistance, floor in Bridge Cottage very uneven. Level entrance to shop and to tea-room.

General description:
A 16th century thatched cottage, just upstream from Flatford Mill and housing an exhibition on John Constable, several of whose paintings famously depict this property.
Information services:
Audio guide.
Front-carrying baby slings for loan.
Suitable for school groups. Audio guide. Children's quiz/trail.
Flatford Mill, Valley Farm and Willy Lott's House are leased to the Field Studies Council which runs arts-based courses for all age groups. For information on courses tel: 01206 298283. There is no general public access to these buildings, but the Field Studies Council will arrange tours for groups.
Special visitor services: Tape recorded guides, materials and/or activities for children.
Education services: Resources for Key Stage 2.
Services for disabled people: For the visually impaired.

Internet home pages:
http://www.nationaltrust.org.uk

1004
FLEECE INN, THE
Bretforton, Nr Evesham, Worcestershire, WR11 5JE

Tel: 01386 831173
Email: fleeceinn@nationaltrust.org.uk

Organisation type and purpose: National organisation, registered charity (charity number 205846), historic building, house or site, suitable for ages: 16+.
Parent body:
The National Trust (West Midlands Region)
West Midlands Regional Office, tel: 01743 708100

Enquiries to: Property Manager

General description:
A black-and-white half-timbered medieval farmhouse, largely unaltered since first becoming a licensed house in 1848.

Internet home pages:
http://www.nationaltrust.org.uk

1005
FLEET AIR ARM MUSEUM
Box D6, Royal Naval Air Station, Yeovilton, Ilchester, Somerset, BA22 8HT

Tel: 01935 840565
Fax: 01935 840181
Acronym or abbreviation: FAAM
Formed: 1964

Organisation type and purpose: National organisation, independently owned, museum, suitable for ages: 5+.
Member of:
British Aircraft Preservation Council
Museums Association

Enquiries to: Curator
Access:
Access to staff: By letter, by telephone, by fax, in person, visitors by prior appointment
Hours: Mon to Fri, 0900 to 1700
Access for disabled people: Parking provided, level entry, toilet facilities
Other restrictions: Access to almost all areas.

General description:
History of the Fleet Air Arm and the Royal Naval Air Service, aircraft carriers, naval aircraft, shore stations and associated equipment and topics.
Information services:
Education services: Group education facilities, resources for Key Stages 1 and 2, 3, 4 and Further or Higher Education.
Services for disabled people: Displays and/or information at wheelchair height.
Collections:
Information on most aspects of Naval Aviation: Collections include
Aircraft and Aeronautical hardware, clothing
Papers of a wide variety of naval aviators
Photograph library
Record books
Squadron line books
Technical publications and aircraft records
Catalogues:
Catalogue for library is in-house only. Catalogue for all of the collections is only available in-house.

1006
FLEETWOOD MUSEUM
Queens Terrace, Fleetwood, Lancashire, FY7 6BT

Tel: 01253 876621
Fax: 01253 878088
Email: fleetwoodmuseum @museumoflancs.org.uk
Formed: 1974

Organisation type and purpose: Local government body, museum, historic building, house or site, suitable for ages: 5+.
Parent body:
Lancashire County Museum Service (LCMS)
Stanley Street, Preston, PR1 4YP, tel: 01772 264061, fax: 01772 264079

Enquiries to: Curator
Access:
Access to staff: By letter, by telephone, by fax, visitors by prior appointment
Access to building, collections or gallery: No prior appointment required

General description:
Local history; maritime history (especially deep sea and inshore fishing); natural history.
Information services:
Library available for reference (for conditions see Access above). Helpline available
Special visitor services: Guided tours, tape recorded guides, materials and/or activities for children.
Education services: Group education facilities, resources for Key Stages 1 and 2, 3, 4 and Further or Higher Education.
Services for disabled people: For the visually impaired; for the hearing impaired.
Collections:
Maritime history
Local history
Natural history
Catalogues:
Catalogue for library is in-house only. Catalogue for part of the collections is only available in-house.

Internet home pages:
http://www.nettingthebay.org.uk

1007
FLEUR DE LIS HERITAGE CENTRE
10-13 Preston Street, Faversham, Kent, ME13 8NS

Tel: 01795 534542
Fax: 01795 533261
Email: museum@favershamsociety.co.uk
Formed: 1977

Organisation type and purpose: Registered charity (charity number 250945), museum, art gallery, historic building, house or site, suitable for ages: all ages, publishing house.

continued overleaf

Parent body:
The Faversham Society
at the same address
Member of:
South East England Tourist Board Association
Other location:
Chart Gunpowder Mills
Chart Close, off Stonebridge Way, Faversham, Kent, ME13 7SE, tel: 01795 534542, fax: 01795 533261, email/website: faversham@btinternet.com
Maison Dieu
Ospringe Street, Faversham, Kent, ME13 8TW, tel: 01795 534542, fax: 01795 533261, email/website: faversham@btinternet.com

Enquiries to: Honorary
Access:
Access to building, collections or gallery: No prior appointment required
Hours: Mon to Sat, 1000-1600, Sun 1000-1300 (except January and February)
Access for disabled people: level entry, toilet facilities
Other restrictions: Access to all ground floor areas

General description:
History of the Faversham area, including the port, Faversham and industries.
Family history In the Faversham area, and the history of the explosives industry.
Information services:
Education services: Group education facilities.
Services for disabled people: Displays and/or information at wheelchair height.
Collections:
Artefacts, photographs, books and documents relating to the history of the area
Explosives manufacture, 1760-1934, 40 small items
Also house (but do not own) at Doddington Parochial Library, a collection of about 400 books from 1501 to c. 1750
Working Strowger telephone exchange, c. 1945, all equipment plus 10 phones (handsets)
Publications list:
is available in hard copy.
Printed publications:
Large selection of monographs and historical publications
Electronic and video products:
Videos

Address for ordering publications:
Printed publications:
The Faversham Society Publications
at same address

Internet home pages:
http://www.faversham.org
Full details of the centre and the society.

1008
FLINTSHIRE MUSEUM SERVICE
County Hall, Mold, Flintshire, CH7 6NW

Tel: 01352 704400
Email: communication@flintshire.gov.uk
Formed: 1996
Formerly: Clwyd County Museum Service, date of change, 1974-1996

Organisation type and purpose: Local government body.
Local authority museum service.
Administers the:
Basingwerk Abbey
Flint Castle
Museum addresses:
Buckley Library and Heritage Centre
The Precinct, Buckley, Flintshire, CH7 2EF, tel: 01244 549210
Mold Library Museum and Gallery
Earl Road, Mold, Flintshire, CH7 1AP, tel: 01352 754791

Enquiries to: Head of Libraries, Culture and Hertiage
Access:
Access to staff: By letter, by telephone, Internet web pages
Hours: Mon to Fri, 0900 to 1700
Access to building, collections or gallery: No prior appointment required

General description:
The support of local culture and history.
Catalogues:
Catalogue for part of the collections is only available in-house.

Internet home pages:
http://www.flintshire.gov.uk

1009
FLORA TWORT GALLERY
Church Path, 21 The Square, Petersfield, Hampshire, GU32 3HS

Tel: 01730 260756
Email: musmtc@hants.gov.uk
Formed: 1991

Organisation type and purpose: Local government body, museum.
Parent body:
Hampshire County Council Museums Service
Chilcomb House, Winchester, SO23 8RD, tel: 01962 846304, fax: 01962 869836

Enquiries to: Curator
Access:
Access to staff: By letter, by telephone, by fax, by email, in person
Access to building, collections or gallery: No prior appointment required
Hours: Tue to Sat, 0930 to 1700

General description:
Paintings by Flora Twort, 1893 to 1985; and temporary exhibitions; fine art, local history, object painting in the Petersfield area, Hampshire from 1920 to 1985.
Collections:
Paintings by Flora Twort (1893-1985)
Catalogues:
Catalogue for all of the collections is on-line.
Printed publications:
Publications list is available from the Librarian, Hampshire County Council Museums Service Headquarters, Chilcomb House, Winchester, SO23 8RD

Address for ordering publications:
Printed publications:
Registrar, Hampshire County Council Museums Service HQ

Internet home pages:
http://www.hants.gov.uk/museums/
HMCMS web catalogue, whole collection, 100,000 plus web pages.

1010
FLORENCE COURT
Enniskillen, Co Fermanagh, BT92 1DB

Tel: 028 6634 8249
Fax: 028 6634 8873
Email: florencecourt@nationaltrust.org.uk
Formed: 1895

Organisation type and purpose: National organisation, registered charity (charity number 205846), museum, historic building, house or site, suitable for ages: 5+.
Parent body:
The National Trust Office for Northern Ireland
Rowallane House, Saintfield, Ballynahinch, Co Down, BT24 7LH, tel: 028 9751 0721, fax: 028 9751 1242

Enquiries to: Property Manager
Other contacts: House Steward
Access:
Access to staff: By letter, by telephone, by fax, by email
Hours: Mon to Fri, 1000 to 1700
Access for disabled people: Parking provided, ramped entry, toilet facilities
Other restrictions: Designated parking. Drop-off point. 2 manual and 1 single-seater powered mobility vehicles available. Ground floor fully accessible. Photograph album. Level entrance to shop and to restaurant. Grounds largely accessible. Recommended route map.
Large print guide available and Braille guide, 2 wheelchairs and a self-drive Batricar may be borrowed. Please enquire at the ticket office.

General description:
One of the most important houses in Ulster, built by the 1st Lord Mount Florence between c. 1756 and 1764 of rendered brick in a lively classical style and embellished with superb rococo plasterwork. It was the home of the Earls of Enniskillen until 1954. The house tour includes the exquisite rococo decoration, fine Irish furniture and service quarters. The pleasure grounds have an ice house and water-powered sawmill.
Information services:
Braille guide. Large-print guide. Sympathetic Hearing Scheme.
Front-carrying baby slings for loan.
Suitable for school groups. Education room/centre. Live interpretation. Hands-on activities. Children's quiz/trail.
Programme of concerts, family days, guided walks and country fairs.
Special visitor services: Guided tours, materials and/or activities for children.
Education services: Group education facilities, resources for Key Stages 1 and 2.
Services for disabled people: For the visually impaired; for the hearing impaired.
Collections:
The Enniskillen family's dining room furniture
A representative sample of the family's famous 18th century collections of Irish silver and porcelain
The library
Family pictures and historic items

Internet home pages:
http://www.nationaltrust.org.uk

1011
FLORENCE NIGHTINGALE MUSEUM
2 Lambeth Palace Road, London, SE1 7EW

Tel: 020 7620 0374
Fax: 020 7928 1760
Email: curator@florence-nightingale.co.uk
Acronym or abbreviation: FNM
Formed: 1989

Organisation type and purpose: Registered charity (charity number 299576), museum, suitable for ages: all ages.

Enquiries to: Assistant Curator
Other contacts: Schools Officer for group bookings.
Access:
Access to staff: By letter, by telephone, by fax, by email, in person, visitors by prior appointment
Hours: Mon to Fri, 1000 to 1700; Sat, Sun, 1130 to 1630
Access for disabled people: access to all public areas

General description:
Life and work of Florence Nightingale; establishment of the nursing profession; health condition of the British Army; public health; district nursing.
Information services:
Special visitor services: Guided tours.
Education services: Group education facilities, resources for Key Stages 1 and 3..
Collections:
Military history and medical history
Florence Nightingale personalia and memorabilia
Catalogues:
Catalogue for all of the collections is only available in-house.

Internet home pages:
http://www.florence-nightingale.co.uk
Information about Florence Nightingale and the museum.

1012
FOLKESTONE MUSEUM
2 Grace Hill, Folkestone, Kent, CT20 1HD

Tel: 01303 850123
Minicom no. 01303 240258
Fax: 01303 256710 (phone/fax)
Email: janet.adamson@kent.gov.uk
Formed: 1888

Organisation type and purpose: Local government body, museum, art gallery, suitable for ages: 5+.

Enquiries to: Curator
Access:
Access to staff: By letter, by telephone, by fax, by email, in person
Other restrictions: Appointment advised.
Access to building, collections or gallery: No prior appointment required
Hours: Mon, Tue, Thu, 0930 to 1800; Wed, Sat, 0930 to 1700; Fri, 0930 to 1900
Other restrictions: Prior appointment required for items in store.
Access for disabled people: level entry, toilet facilities
Other restrictions: Lift access to first floor of building.

General description:
Local history, family history, paintings and prints, social history. The development of the town from its Anglo-Saxon origins; through its growth as a busy medieval port, a smuggler's haven, fashionable holiday resort right up to the present day.
Information services:
Library available for reference (for conditions see Access above)
Folkestone on film, hands-on activities for children.
Special visitor services: Materials and/or activities for children.
Services for disabled people: For the hearing impaired; displays and/or information at wheelchair height.
Collections:
Sassoon Gallery, contemporary fine art and craft
Fossils, coins, natural history specimens and social history artefacts
Photographic collection
Map collection
Catalogues:
Catalogue for library is in-house only. Catalogue for all of the collections is only available in-house.
Printed publications:
Local studies leaflets
Microform products:
Creed's, Sinnock's, Pike's, Parson's and Kelly's Directories 1871-1938 (microfiche)
Electronic and video products:
Living in Kent (CD-ROM, £14.99)

Internet home pages:
http://www.kent.gov/e&l/artslib/museums/folkstone.html

1013
FORD GREEN HALL
Ford Green Road, Smallthorne, Stoke-on-Trent, Staffordshire, ST6 1NG

Tel: 01782 233195
Fax: 01782 233194
Email: ford.green.hall@stoke.gov.uk
Formed: 1952

Organisation type and purpose: Local government body, museum, historic building, house or site, suitable for ages: 5+.

Enquiries to: Manager
Access:
Access to staff: By letter, by telephone, by email, in person
Hours: Sun to Thu, 1300 to 1700
Access to building, collections or gallery: No prior appointment required
Hours: Mon to Thu, 1300 to 1700
Access for disabled people: Parking provided, toilet facilities
Other restrictions: Access to ground floor.

General description:
17th century timber-framed house with 18th century additions, complete with period garden. A designated collection of furniture, ceramics and textiles.
Information services:
Guided tours for groups.
Special visitor services: Guided tours, materials and/or activities for children.
Education services: Group education facilities, resources for Key Stages 1 and 2, 3 and Further or Higher Education..
Collections:
17th and 18th century textiles (reproduction) and ceramics
A collection of oak country furniture ranging in date from the 15th to the 19th century, but with particular emphasis upon the 17th century.

Internet home pages:
http://www.stoke.gov.uk/fordgreenhall

1014
FORDE ABBEY
Chard, Somerset, TA20 4LU

Tel: 01460 221290
Email: forde.abbey@virgin.net
Formed: 1140

Organisation type and purpose: Independently owned, historic building, house or site, suitable for ages: 16+.

Enquiries to: Owner
Direct tel: 01460 220231
Access:
Access to staff: By letter, by telephone, by email, in person, charges made to all users
Access to building, collections or gallery: No access other than to staff
Hours: 1 Apr to 31 Oct, Tue to Fri, Sun, Bank holiday Mons, 1300 to 1630
Other restrictions: Gardens open daily throughout the year from 1000
Access for disabled people: Parking provided, toilet facilities

General description:
Former Cistercian monastery, private home since 1539, 30 acres of world-famous gardens.
Collections:
Magnificent Mortlake tapestries
Moulded plaster ceilings c. 1658
Publications list:
is available in hard copy.
Printed publications:
Guide Book (£3.50)

Internet home pages:
http://www.fordeabbey.co.uk

1015
FORDINGBRIDGE MUSEUM TRUST
King's Yard, Salisbury Street, Fordingbridge, Hampshire, SP6 1AB

Tel: 01425 655222
Email: fordingbridge@storytelling.freeserve.co.uk
Formed: 1998

Organisation type and purpose: Registered charity (charity number 1072427), art gallery.

Enquiries to: Secretary General
Access:
Access to staff: By letter
Hours: Mon to Fri, 1100 to 1600
Access to building, collections or gallery: No prior appointment required
Hours: Daily, 1100 to 1600

General description:
Collection of artefacts from the town generally, from the last 100 years. Exhibition shops with cycle, footwear and hardware themes. Local handmade bricks, washing machines and blacksmith's tools. Photographs of local villages and regatta.
Collections:
1000 Photographs
Oldest washing machine in the country
Printed publications:
Museum Leaflet

Internet home pages:
http://www.fordingbridgemuseum.co.uk

1016
FORDYCE JOINER'S WORKSHOP VISITOR CENTRE
Church Street, Fordyce, Portsoy, AB45 2SL

Tel: 01771 622906
Fax: 01771 622884
Formed: 1993

Organisation type and purpose: Local government body, museum, historic building, house or site, suitable for ages: 5+.
Parent body:
Aberdeenshire Heritage
Tel: 01771 622906, fax: 01771 622884

Enquiries to: Curator
Access:
Access to staff: By letter, by telephone, by fax

General description:
Late 19th century and early 20th century rural joiner's workshop, with machinery and tools, craftsman's workshop attached.
Collections:
Joiner's tools and machinery
Catalogues:
Catalogue for part of the collections is only available in-house.

1017
FORFAR MUSEUM AND ART GALLERY
See - Meffan Museum & Gallery

1018
FORGE MILL MUSEUM & BORDESLEY ABBEY VISITOR CENTRE
Needle Mill Lane, Riverside, Redditch, Worcestershire, B98 8HY

Tel: 01527 62509
Email: museum@redditchbc.gov.uk
Formed: 1983

Organisation type and purpose: Local government body, museum, suitable for ages: 5+.

Enquiries to: Manager
Access:
Access to staff: By letter, by telephone, by email, visitors by prior appointment
Access to building, collections or gallery: No access other than to staff
Hours: Easter to Sep: Mon to Fri, 1100 to 1630; Sat & Sun, 1400 to 1700
Feb to Easter and Oct to Nov: Mon to Thu 1100 to 1600; Sun 1400 to 1700
Other restrictions: Closed Dec to Jan.
Access for disabled people: Parking provided, toilet facilities
Other restrictions: Access to ground floor galleries.

General description:
Forge Mill Museum is a working 18th century water-powered needle scouring (polishing) mill. The material held relates to the local fishing tackle and needle industries. The collection is comprised of a vast range of needles (many unique), needle cases and needlework accessories, needle packets and needle making machinery, plus documents and ephemera.
The Bordesley Abbey Visitor Centre exhibits artefacts excavated from the adjacent mediaeval Cistercian Abbey, which includes metal work; carved stone; floor tiles; and objects from daily

continued overleaf

life; plus timbers from an early 12th-14th century water- powered metal working mill.
Information services:
Helpline available, tel no: 01527 62509.
Special visitor services: Guided tours, tape recorded guides.
Education services: Group education facilities, resources for Key Stages 1 and 2 and 3..
Collections:
Archaeological finds from excavation of Cistercian abbey church, gateway chapel and watermill
Fishing tackle catalogues, (some photocopied), 1866-1970s, 70-80 items
Needles, needle machinery and needle industry archives
Needle and smallware catalogues (also surgical), 1888-1994, 200 items
Catalogues:
Catalogue for all of the collections is only available in-house.

Internet home pages:
http://www.redditchbc.gov.uk
General information, current exhibitions and events.

1019
FORT BROCKHURST

Gunners Way, Elson, Gosport, Hampshire, PO12 4DS

Tel: 02392 581059
Fax: 02392 522659

Organisation type and purpose: National government body, historic building, house or site.
Parent body:
English Heritage (South East Region)
Tel: 01483 252000, fax: 01483 252001

Enquiries to: Administrator
Direct email: plbraddo@english-heritage.org.uk
Access:
Access to staff: By letter, by telephone, by fax
Access to building, collections or gallery: No prior appointment required
Hours: Apr to 30 Sep: Sat, Sun and Bank Holidays, 1000 to 1800
Oct: Sat, Sun, 1000 to 1700
Other restrictions: Prior appointment is required Mon to Fri.
Opening times are subject to change, for up-to-date information contact English Heritage by phone or visit the website.
Access for disabled people: Parking provided, level entry, toilet facilities

General description:
When it was built in the 19th century, this was the latest in defence design and the fort was able to protect Portsmouth with its formidable fire power. Largely unaltered, the parade ground, gun ramps and moated keep can all be viewed.

Internet home pages:
http://www.english-heritage.org.uk

1020
FOSSIL GROVE

Victoria Park, Glasgow, G14 1BN

Tel: 0141 287 2000
Fax: 0141 950 1148

Organisation type and purpose: Local government body, museum, suitable for ages: 5+.
Parent body:
Glasgow Museums

Enquiries to: Administrator
Access:
Access to staff: By letter, by telephone, in person
Access to building, collections or gallery: No prior appointment required
Hours: Apr to Sep, Daily, 1200 to 1700
Other restrictions: Closed 25, 26 Dec and 1, 2 Jan

General description:
Fossil tree stumps, discovered following excavation in 1887, depict the extinct plant clubmoss. They grew in swampy tropical forests 330 million years ago.

Internet home pages:
http://www.glasgow.gov.uk

1021
FOUNTAINS ABBEY & STUDLEY ROYAL

Fountains, Ripon, North Yorkshire, HG4 3DY

Tel: 01765 608888
Fax: 01765 601002

Organisation type and purpose: National organisation, registered charity (charity number 205846), historic building, house or site, suitable for ages: all ages.
Parent body:
The National Trust (Yorkshire and North East)
Yorkshire Regional Office, tel: 01904 702021
In partnership with:
English Heritage (Yorkshire Region)
Tel: 01904 601901

Enquiries to: Administrator
Other contacts: Box office: tel: 01909 511061
Access:
Access to staff: By letter, by telephone, by email
Access for disabled people: Parking provided, level entry, access to all public areas, toilet facilities
Other restrictions: Designated parking. Drop-off point. 6 manual wheelchairs and 2 single-seater Batricars for hire, booking essential, free of charge. 3-wheel battery cars not permitted due to uneven terrain. Level access into Abbey and Mill. Limited access to Fountains Hall, approx. 20 steps with handrails. Ramp into St Mary's Church. All outside major events wheelchair accessible. Ramped entrance to shop and to restaurant. Grounds largely accessible. Recommended route map.

General description:
Over 800 years of history and a World Heritage Site, comprising the most complete ruins of a Cistercian monastery in Britain, abbey and monastic watermill, an Elizabethan mansion (two rooms open to visitors) and one of the best surviving examples of a Georgian water garden. Elegant ornamental lakes, canals, temples and cascades provide a succession of dramatic eye-catching vistas. St Mary's Church gives a majestic focus to the medieval deer park, home to 500 deer and a wealth of flora and fauna.
Information services:
Free volunteer-led guided tours of the Abbey and water garden April to Oct plus extended tours of the complete estate, available throughout the year. Floodlit tours of the Abbey: late Aug to mid Oct every Fri 1945 and 2015. Specialist guides for booked groups.
Extensive programme of events throughout year: open-air Shakespeare, concerts, fireworks and Christmas entertainment; details from Box Office. Extensive programme of wildlife and historical tours, music events and family activities.
Braille guide. Sympathetic Hearing Scheme. Audio loop in Fountains Abbey Mill.
Programme of children's activities in school holidays. Suitable for school groups. Education room/centre. Hands-on activities. Children's guide. Children's quiz/trail. Adult study days.
Special visitor services: Guided tours, tape recorded guides, materials and/or activities for children.
Education services: Group education facilities, resources for Key Stages 1 and 2 and 3.
Services for disabled people: For the visually impaired; for the hearing impaired; displays and/or information at wheelchair height.
Printed publications:
Property leaflet (available direct, on request)

Internet home pages:
http://www.fountainabbey.org.uk
All visitor information.

1022
FOX TALBOT MUSEUM

Lacock, Chippenham, Wiltshire, SN15 2LG

Tel: 01249 730459
Fax: 01249 730501
Formed: 1975

Organisation type and purpose: National organisation, registered charity (charity number 205846), museum, suitable for ages: 16+.
Photographic museum, dedicated to showing the life works of William Henry Fox Talbot (1800-1877).
Parent body:
The National Trust
Eastleigh Court, Bishopston, Warminster, Wiltshire, BA11 12LA

Enquiries to: Curator
Access:
Access to staff: By letter only
Other restrictions: Curator available only by prior appointment.
Access to building, collections or gallery: No prior appointment required
Hours: Daily, 1100 to 1700
Access for disabled people: Parking provided, ramped entry

General description:
History of photography, botany, chemistry, physics.
Collections:
Photographs, papers, correspondence of William Henry Fox Talbot
Catalogues:
Catalogue for library is in-house only. Catalogue for all of the collections is available in-house and part is on-line.

Internet home pages:
http://www.ikons-centre.org

See also - Lacock Abbey and Fox Talbot Museum and Village

1023
FOXFIELD RAILWAY

Caverswall Road Station, Blythe Bridge, Stoke-on-Trent, Staffordshire, ST11 9BG

Tel: 01782 396210

Secretary:
Foxfield Railway
PO Box 1967, Stoke-on-Trent, Staffordshire, ST4 8YT
Access:
Access for disabled people: Parking provided

General description:
Covers industrial railways and the railways of North Staffordshire. The museum is based on a preserved colliery railway. Steam railway running on a line with a five-minute journey time.
Collections:
Large collection of locomotives, rolling stock and artefacts
Unique collection of ten North Staffordshire built industrial locomotives, 1880-1950
Collection covering the development of industrial diesel traction, 1920-1970

Internet home pages:
http://www.foxfieldrailway.co.uk

1024
FOXTON INCLINED PLANE TRUST

Foxton Canal Museum, Middle Loch, Gumley Road, Foxton, Leicestershire, LE16 7RA

Tel: 0116 279 2657
Email: mike@foxcm.freeserve.co.uk
Acronym or abbreviation: FIPT
Formed: 1980

Formerly: Foxton Canal Museum
Trust formed 1980

Organisation type and purpose: Membership association (membership is by subscription), voluntary organisation, registered charity (charity number 513241), museum, suitable for ages: all ages.
Independent trust.
The FIPT is dedicated to the restoration of the Victoria Boat Lift constructed by Gordon Thomas for the Grand Junction Canal Company in 1900.

Enquiries to: Keeper
Access:
Access to staff: By letter, by telephone, by email, in person, visitors by prior appointment, Internet web pages
Access for disabled people: Parking provided, level entry, access to all public areas, toilet facilities
Other restrictions: Parking and toilet facilities are in County Council Car Park, the site has some steep slopes and can be difficult, please telephone for advice.

General description:
The ten locks at Foxton were opened in 1814, connecting the Leicestershire & Northants Union Canal with the Grand Union Canal, they raise the canal by 75 ft and use 25,000 gallons of water for each boat passing through. These were replaced by the Lift in 1900. This lift is being restored whilst the locks are still in use. Canals and boat lifts, canal people, canal boats, industrial archaeology, steam boats, Measham pottery.
Information services:
Library available for reference (for conditions see Access above)
Educational and guided tours for all ages.
Special visitor services: Guided tours, materials and/or activities for children.
Education services: Group education facilities, resources for Key Stages 1 and 2, 3, 4 and Further or Higher Education.
Services for disabled people: Displays and/or information at wheelchair height.
Collections:
Waterway objects relating to the local waterway
Archives including information and photographs of local and international canals, and boat lifts
Canal items including rare Legging Boards, painted ware, parts from boats and locks, costume, lift parts, models
Catalogues:
Catalogue for library is in-house only. Catalogue for all of the collections is only available in-house.
Publications list:
is available in hard copy and online.
Printed publications:
Plane Informer (free to members, includes the latest research)
Foxton Locks and Inclined Plane (a detailed history, £2 plus p&p)
Foxton Photo Guide (in several languages, £1.25 plus p&p)
Other waterway books in stock - ring for details
Electronic and video products:
Canal videos in stock - ring for details

Internet home pages:
http://www.foxcanal.fsnet.co.uk
Foxton Locks, Lift and Local Waterways - with pictures, information on organisation.

1025
FRAMEWORK KNITTERS MUSEUM
See - Ruddington Framework Knitters' Museum

1026
FRAMLINGHAM CASTLE
Framlingham, Woodbridge, Suffolk, IP13 9BP

Tel: 01728 724189

Organisation type and purpose: Museum, historic building, house or site, suitable for ages: all ages.
Parent body:
English Heritage (East of England Region)
Brooklands, 24 Brooklands Avenue, Cambridge, CB2 2BU, tel: 01223 582700, fax: 01223 582701
Access:
Access to staff: By letter, by telephone
Other restrictions: Closed Christmas and New Year's Day.
Access to building, collections or gallery: No prior appointment required
Hours: Apr to Sep: daily, 1000 to 1800
Oct: daily, 1000 to 1700
Nov to Mar: daily, 1000 to 1600
Closed 24 to 26 Dec and 1 Jan
Other restrictions: Opening times are subject to change, for up-to-date information contact English Heritage by phone or visit the website.

General description:
Built in the 12th century, Framlingham Castle, hidden behind curtain walls linking 13 towers, includes castle gatehouse and battlements encircling the castle site. It has had an enormously varied history, its roles ranging from its time as a fortress to a temporary home for Mary Tudor in 1553 prior to her accession to the throne, from an Elizabethan prison to a 17th century poor house, and even a school.
Information services:
Special visitor services: Tape recorded guides, materials and/or activities for children..

See also - Lanman Museum

1027
FRAMSDEN WINDMILL
On B 1077, Framsden, Suffolk

Tel: 01473 890328

Organisation type and purpose: Historic building, house or site.
Access:
Access to staff: By telephone
Access to building, collections or gallery: Prior appointment required
Hours: All year, Sat, Sun

General description:
Tall post mill dating from 1760 with intact machinery; restored in the 1960s.
Collections:
Country bygones

1028
FRANK HAYNES GALLERY, THE
50 Station Road, Great Bowden, Market Harborough, Leicestershire, LE16 7HN

Tel: 01858 464862
Formed: 1987

Organisation type and purpose: Independently owned, art gallery, suitable for ages: 20+.
Sells paintings and ceramics.

Enquiries to: Proprietor
Access:
Access to staff: By letter, by telephone, in person
Access for disabled people: Parking provided, level entry, access to all public areas

General description:
Artists/painters in Leicestershire, Northamptonshire and Rutland. Makers of ceramics in the Midlands.
Collections:
Regular exhibitions of paintings from Leicestershire, Northamptonshire, Rutland
Regular exhibitions of ceramics from the Midlands etc

Internet home pages:
http://www.marketharborough.com/gallery
Current exhibition (10 per year)

1029
FREUD MUSEUM
20 Maresfield Gardens, London, NW3 5SX

Tel: 020 7435 2002
Fax: 020 7431 5452
Email: freud@gn.apc.org
Formed: 1986

Organisation type and purpose: Registered charity (charity number 281124), museum, suitable for ages: 16+.

Enquiries to: Director
Access:
Access to staff: By letter, by email, visitors by prior appointment
Hours: Mon to Fri, 1030 to 1700
Access to building, collections or gallery: Prior appointment required

General description:
The life and works of Sigmund Freud (1856-1939).
Information services:
Education services: Group education facilities, resources for Further or Higher Education..
Collections:
Artefacts - Freud's Antiquities Collection
Library - Freud's Personal Library
Reference Library - Psychoanalysis etc
Archive
Catalogues:
Catalogue for library is in-house only. Catalogue for all of the collections is only available in-house.

Internet home pages:
http://www.freud.org.uk

1030
FRIENDS OF BRECKNOCK MUSEUM
See - Brecknock Society and Museum Friends

1031
FRIENDS OF THE ULSTER MUSEUM
12 Malone Road, Belfast, BT9 5BN

Tel: 028 9068 1606
Formed: 1970

Organisation type and purpose: Voluntary organisation.

Enquiries to: Administrator
Access:
Access to staff: By letter, visitors by prior appointment
Hours: Part-time availability days, hours vary.
Access to building, collections or gallery: Prior appointment required

General description:
Support body for the Ulster Museums, gives members of the public an opportunity to participate in the Museum's work through social activities and to assist in efforts to add to the collections through fundraising and donation.

Internet home pages:
http://www.ulstermuseum.org.uk/friends

1032
FRINTON AND WALTON HERITAGE CENTRE MUSEUM
See - Walton Maritime Museum

1033
FRITH STREET GALLERY
59-60 Frith Street, London, W1D 3JJ

Tel: 020 7494 1550
Fax: 020 7287 3733
Email: info@frithstreetgallery.com
Formed: 1989
Formerly: Jane Frith

Organisation type and purpose: Independently owned, art gallery, suitable for ages: 5+.

continued overleaf

Enquiries to: Director
Direct email: david@frithstreetgallery.com
Access:
Access to staff: By letter, by telephone, by fax, by email, in person, Internet web pages
Access to building, collections or gallery: No prior appointment required
Hours: Mon to Fri, 1000 to 1800; Sat, 1100 to 1600
Access for disabled people: level entry
Other restrictions: Stairs to basement galleries, no lift.

General description:
Since opening in 1989, Frith Street Gallery has developed a programme of exhibitions by international artists working in painting, photography, sculptures, film and video. We currently represent 16 artists both from Britain and abroad, as well as collaborating with other artists on specific projects. A full list of represented artists can be seen via the website.
Publications list:
is available in hard copy and online.
Printed publications:
Some publications available direct, others through distributors
Microform products:
Visual material sometimes available for loan
Electronic and video products:
Visual material sometimes available for loan

Internet home pages:
http://www.frithstreetgallery.com
List of artists, information, visuals, biographies, list of publications, current exhibition, upcoming exhibition information, list of staff and contact details.

1034
FRY ART GALLERY
Bridge End Gardens, Castle Street, Saffron Walden, Essex, CB10 1BD

Tel: 01799 513779
Formed: 1985

Organisation type and purpose: Membership association (membership is by subscription), registered charity (charity number 295904), art gallery, suitable for ages: 16+.
Supported by:
Fry Art Gallery Society
at the same address

Enquiries to: Honorary Secretary
Access:
Access to staff: By letter, by telephone
Access to building, collections or gallery: No prior appointment required
Hours: Sat, Sun & Bank Holidays 1430 to 1730 from Easter Sunday to end of Oct
Other restrictions: Out of hours appointments possible for group visits.
Access for disabled people: ramped entry

General description:
The Gallery contains the North West Essex collection of work by eminent 20th century artists, including Sir George Clausen, Edward Bawden, Erik Ravilious, Michael Rothenstein, Marianne Straub, Isabel Lambert, John Norris Wood, Audrey Cruddas, John Aldridge, Kenneth Rowntree, Duffy Ayers, Richard Bawden, Sheila Robinson, Chloë Cheese, Walter Hoyle, Bernard Cheese and others who have lived or worked in North West Essex, particularly Great Barfield and Saffron Walden, and made significant contribution to their field.
The gallery was designed to house the collection of Francis Gibson, a local businessman who died in 1859, and the building passed by descent to the Fry family.
Information services:
Special exhibitions as well as the permanent collection.
Special visitor services: Guided tours.
Education services: Group education facilities, resources for Further or Higher Education..
Collections:
North West Essex Collection - watercolours, prints, oils, illustrated papers and books
Watercolours and oils by Lewis George Fry, RBA, RWA 1860-1933
Works by Roger Fry, 1866-1934 and Anthony Fry
Catalogues:
Catalogue for part of the collections is published.
Publications list:
is available in hard copy.
Printed publications:
30 postcards of works on display, including Bawden (5), Ravilious (5), Rowntree (4) and Rothenstein (2) for sale by post, sample pack of each unique card £7.50, order form/list free
Newsletters (members)

Internet home pages:
http://www.fryartgallery.org

1035
FULNECK MORAVIAN SETTLEMENT AND MORAVIAN MUSEUM
55-57 Fulneck, Pudsey, West Yorkshire, LS28 8NT

Tel: 0113 256 4147
Formed: 1969

Organisation type and purpose: Registered charity (charity number 251211), museum, historic building, house or site, suitable for ages: 16+.
Moravian Church & Settlement built mid-1700s.
The only Moravian Museum in England.
To provide information on The Moravians in England and Overseas.

Enquiries to: Information Officer
Other contacts: Resident Minister
Access:
Access to staff: By letter, by telephone, visitors by prior appointment
Access to building, collections or gallery: Prior appointment required
Hours: Mar to Oct: Wed to Sat, 1400 to 1630
Other restrictions: Groups any other time by prior appointment.

General description:
Moravian memorabilia, only working fire engine (built 1700s), Victorian doll collection, weaving loom, cottage living room and kitchen, Moravian lace.
Information services:
Special visitor services: Tape recorded guides..
Collections:
Moravian artefacts, pictures, photographs, samplers

1036
FURNESS ABBEY
Barrow-in-Furness, Cumbria, LA13 0TJ

Tel: 01229 823420
Formed: 1123

Organisation type and purpose: National government body, museum, historic building, house or site, suitable for ages: all ages.
Parent body:
English Heritage (North West Region)
Canada House, 3 Chepstow Street, Manchester, M1 5FW, tel: 0161 242 1400

Enquiries to: Custodian
Access:
Access to staff: By letter, by telephone
Access to building, collections or gallery: No prior appointment required
Hours: Apr to Sep, daily, 1000 to 1800
Oct, daily, 1000 to 1700
Nov to Mar, Wed to Sun, 1000 to 1300 and 1400 to 1600
Other restrictions: Closed 24, 25, 26 Dec and 1 Jan
Opening times are subject to change, for up-to-date information contact English Heritage by phone or visit the website.
Access for disabled people: toilet facilities

General description:
St Mary of Furness was founded in 1123 by Stephen, later King of England. It originally belonged to the small Order of Savigny and then, in 1147, to the Cistercians. The small, ornate church built by the Savigniac order was gradually rebuilt and enlarged by the Cistercians. This second church was itself remodelled in the 15th century.
Information services:
Exhibition about the history of Furness Abbey.
Audio tours also available for the visually impaired and those with learning difficulties
Special visitor services: Tape recorded guides..

Internet home pages:
http://www.english-heritage.org.uk/

1037
FURSDON HOUSE
Cadbury, Thorverton, Exeter, Devon, EX5 5JS

Tel: 01392 860860
Fax: 01392 860126
Email: admin@fursdon.co.uk

Organisation type and purpose: Suitable for ages: 18+.
Historic house.

Enquiries to: Owner
Access:
Access to staff: Visitors by prior appointment, by letter, by telephone, by fax, by email, Internet web pages

General description:
Fursdon is an historic house with the museum showing family mementos, possessions and costumes which have been used at Fursdon, illustrating their involvement in local landowning from the 13th century to the present day.
No specialised knowledge offered.
Collections:
Fursdon costumes (including a mantilla or court dress) and other women's items 17th, 18th and 19th Centuries
Printed publications:
Guide Book (£2)

Internet home pages:
http://www.fursdon.co.uk

1038
FYLINGDALES MUSEUM
See - Robin Hood's Bay and Fylingdales Museum

1039
FYNE COURT
Broomfield, Bridgewater, Somerset, TA5 2EQ

Tel: 0183 45157

Organisation type and purpose: National organisation, registered charity (charity number 205846), historic building, house or site, suitable for ages: 5+.
Parent body:
National Trust (South West)
Wessex Regional Office, tel: 01985 843600

Enquiries to: Warden
Access:
Access to staff: By letter, by telephone
Access for disabled people: toilet facilities
Other restrictions: Grounds largely accessible. Recommended route map.

General description:
Formerly the pleasure grounds of the now demolished home of the pioneer electrician, Andrew Crosse (1784-1855), this nature reserve is now the headquarters of the Somerset Wildlife Trust and a visitor centre for the Quantocks.

Internet home pages:
http://www.nationaltrust.org.uk/regions/wessex

1040
FYVIE CASTLE
Fyvie, Turriff, Aberdeenshire, AB53 8JS

Tel: 01651 891266
Fax: 01651 891107

Organisation type and purpose: Museum, art gallery, historic building, house or site.
Parent body:
National Trust for Scotland (North-East Region)

Enquiries to: Property Manager
Access:
Access to staff: By letter, by telephone, by fax, in person
Access to building, collections or gallery: No prior appointment required
Hours: End Mar to end Jun and beg Sep to end Oct, Sat to Wed, 1200 to 1700; end June to beg Sep, daily, 1000 to 1700
Grounds, all year, daily, 0930 to sunset
Access for disabled people: toilet facilities
Other restrictions: Wheelchair available

General description:
Fyvie was once a royal stronghold, one of a chain of fortresses throughout medieval Scotland. It is probably the finest example of Scottish baronial architecture. Oldest part dates from 13th century, and within its ancient walls houses a great wheel-stair, the finest in Scotland. Contemporary panelling and plaster ceilings of the 17th century survive. Opulence of the Edwardian era is reflected in its interiors. There is a fine collection of arms and armour, 17th century tapestries and a rich portrait collection.
Information services:
Services for disabled people: For the visually impaired.

Internet home pages:
http://www.nts.org.uk

1041
GAINSBOROUGH OLD HALL
Parnell Street, Gainsborough, Lincolnshire, DN21 2NB

Tel: 01427 612669
Fax: 01427 612779
Email: gainsborougholdhall @lincolnshire.gov.uk

Organisation type and purpose: Local government body, historic building, house or site.
Parent body:
English Heritage (East Midlands Region)
44 Derngate, Northampton, NN1 1UH, tel: 01604 735400, fax: 01604 735401
Managed by:
Lincolnshire County Council

Enquiries to: Principal Keeper
Access:
Access to staff: By letter, by telephone, by fax, by email
Access to building, collections or gallery: No prior appointment required
Hours: Easter to 31 Oct: Mon to Sat, 1000 to 1700, Sun 1400 to 1730;
1 Nov to Easter: Sat, Mon to Sat, 1000 to 1700;
Other restrictions: Closed Good Friday, 24-26 Dec and 1 Jan
Opening times are subject to change, for up-to-date information contact English Heritage by phone or visit the website.

General description:
A late medieval manor with timber framing and brick construction. The house is a good example of medieval building techniques. It has a Great Hall and suites of rooms. It has a fine recreated medieval kitchen display. The collections are displayed principally as room settings.
Information services:
Special event days.
Special visitor services: Guided tours, tape recorded guides, materials and/or activities for children.
Education services: Group education facilities, resources for Key Stages 1 and 2, 3 and 4..
Collections:
Historic furniture and artefacts
Oak furniture, 17th-18th century

Internet home pages:
http://www.english-heritage.org.uk

1042
GAINSBOROUGH'S HOUSE
46 Gainsborough Street, Sudbury, Suffolk, CO10 2EU

Tel: 01787 372958
Fax: 01787 376991
Email: mail@gainsborough.org
Full name: Gainsborough's House Society
Formed: 1961

Organisation type and purpose: Registered charity (charity number 214046), art gallery, suitable for ages: 5+.

Enquiries to: Curator
Access:
Access to staff: By letter, by telephone, by fax, by email, visitors by prior appointment, Internet web pages
Access for disabled people: ramped entry, toilet facilities

General description:
The birthplace of the 18th century landscape and portrait painter, Thomas Gainsborough. Includes paintings, drawings, etchings and letters by him, plus other works by artists influenced by or influencing him. Also some East Anglia work.
Catalogues:
Catalogue for library is in-house only. Catalogue for all of the collections is published.
Publications list:
is available in hard copy and online.
Printed publications:
Gainsborough's House Review (annually, Sep)
Constable's Country (1976)
The Painter's Eye (1977)
The Muses' Bower: Vauxhall Gardens 1728-86 (1978)
John Sell Cotman (1782-1842) (1978)
John Crome (1768-1821) (1980)

Internet home pages:
http://www.gainsborough.org
Information about facilities and Gainsborough.

1043
GAIRLOCH HERITAGE MUSEUM
Achtercairn, Gairloch, Ross-shire, IV21 2BP

Tel: 01445 712287
Email: info@gairlochheritagemuseum.org.uk
Formed: 1977

Organisation type and purpose: Registered charity (charity number SCO 10249), museum, suitable for ages: all ages.
Local heritage.

Enquiries to: Curator
Access:
Access to staff: By letter, by email, visitors by prior appointment
Hours: Apr to Sep: Mon to Sat, 1000 to 1700; Oct: Mon to Fri, 1000 to 1330
Other restrictions: Winter months, Nov to Mar by prior arrangement.
Access to building, collections or gallery: No prior appointment required
Hours: Mon to Fri, 1000 to 1700
Access for disabled people: Parking provided

General description:
A local history collection. The displays are arranged in sections. These include prehistory; religion; fishing; a school room; agriculture; dairy; a shop; a croft house room; mills and milling; and natural history. All are situated in a complex of former farm buildings.
Information services:
Library available for reference (for conditions see Access above)
Family history material.
Special visitor services: Materials and/or activities for children..
Collections:
Social history, photographs, maps, books
Oral history, aspects of local history, 90% recorded in Gaelic, 1900 onwards
Catalogues:
Catalogue for library is in-house only. Catalogue for all of the collections is only available in-house.
Publications list:
is available in hard copy and online.
Printed publications:
A variety of publications relating to the Area (from between 25p to £20)
Dixon's Gairloch and Guide to Loch Maree (museum is only stockist)

Internet home pages:
http://www.ghmr.freeserve.co.uk
Information on the museum.

1044
GALLERIES OF JUSTICE
Shire Hall, High Pavement, Lace Market, Nottingham, NG1 1HN

Tel: 0115 952 0555
Fax: 0115 993 9828
Email: info@galleriesofjustice.org.uk
Full name: Museum of Law Trust
Formed: 1993

Organisation type and purpose: Independently owned, registered charity (charity number 1030554), museum, suitable for ages: 7+.
Parent body:
Nottingham Trent University (NTU)
Burton Street, Nottingham, NG1 4BU, tel: 0115 941 8418, email: ntu@nottingham.ac.uk
Connections with:
Museum of Law Trust Company
at the same address

Enquiries to: Curator
Direct email: louise.connell @galleriesofjustice.org.uk
Other contacts: Librarian or Archivist
Access:
Access to staff: By letter, by telephone, by fax, visitors by prior appointment
Hours: Library: Mon to Fri, 0900 to 1700
Access to building, collections or gallery: No access other than to staff
Hours: Museum: Tue to Sun and Bank Holidays, 1000 to 1600
Other restrictions: Closed 24 to 26 Dec and 1 Jan. Last admission to museum 1 hour prior to close.
Access for disabled people: toilet facilities
Other restrictions: Restricted access - lifts access.

General description:
The Galleries of Justice Building occupies Nottingham's Shire Hall comprising an 1800 prison, 1905 police station, 1838 prison bath house and laundry, and criminal and civil courts dated 1878.
Collections of local and national importance covering all aspects of the law and its history. Legal costumes, legal personalities, police and penology, crime and criminal evidence, legal cases. Changing temporary exhibitions.
The library houses a collection of books dating from 1655 to 1998, includes historical texts such as the first edition of 'A History of the Police of Metropolis', as well as contemporary books such as popular books, academic and reference books.
The Museum of Law is one of three elements within the Galleries of Justice. Complementing the museum are a Law Education Centre and a lively interpretation of the galleries' main asset; the Shire Hall - a 19th century courthouse and 17th century gaol.
An interactive and atmospheric tour of over 300 years of crime and punishment. Based on unique historic site, comprising Victorian courtrooms, 19th century County Gaol and medieval cave systems, as well as Edwardian police station.
The collections include material relating to

continued overleaf

criminal law, civil law and law enforcement. an extensive library and archives, as well as a resource centre, and includes an enquiry service.
Information services:
Library available for reference (for conditions see Access above)
Special visitor services: Guided tours, materials and/or activities for children.
Education services: Group education facilities, resources for Key Stages 1 and 2, 3, 4 and Further or Higher Education.
Services for disabled people: For the visually impaired; for the hearing impaired.
Collections:
Archive dating from 1700 to 1998 relating to famous trials, legal personalities, criminal evidence, examples of legal papers through time, object and library collections related to the history of law, and crime and punishment
Large collection of legal and police costumes
Largest collection of restraints in Europe
Collection relating to the history and development of the police, includes equipment
Ross Simms Collection of police uniforms, etc. 1750-1994, c. 1000 items
Bramshill Collection, police truncheons, tipstaffs, maces, 1430-1976, c. 600 items
Archival Material includes:
Personal scrapbooks of Lord Justice Lawrence of the Nuremberg War Criminal Trials (copy held on microfiche)
Forensic evidence relating to cases handled by Marshall Hall as well as Great Train Robbery evidence
Marshall Hall, Black collection and personal papers, 1920s, c. 20 items
Rainer Foundation Archive consists of minute books, annual reports, letters, photographs relating to several Reformatory Institutions, London Police Court Mission
Loup, Musical covers (sheet) legal themes, 1890s-1920s, 54 items
The Foundation of the Probation Service includes material related to Elizabeth Fry
Oaksey, papers from Nuremburg War Trials, 1946-1947, 4 scrapbooks
Archive Material from Nottingham City Police / Nottinghamshire Police including photographs
Library consisting of approximately 4000 books both historic and contemporary texts on all aspects of the history of law, and crime and punishment
Catalogues:
Catalogue for part of the collections is only available in-house.

Internet home pages:
http://www.galleriesofjustice.org.uk

1045
GALLERY OF COSTUME
Platt Hall, Rusholme, Manchester, M14 5LL

Tel: 0161 224 5217
Fax: 0161 256 3278
Formed: 1947
Formerly: Manchester City Art Galleries (Manchester City Council)

Organisation type and purpose: Local government body, museum, suitable for ages: all ages.
Parent body:
Manchester City Art Galleries
Tel: 0161 235 8888, fax: 0161 235 8899, email: cityart@mcrl.poptel.org.uk

Enquiries to: Curator
Access:
Access to staff: By letter, by telephone, by fax, visitors by prior appointment
Access to building, collections or gallery: No prior appointment required
Hours: Museum displays: Tue to Sun, 1000 to 1730
Research facilities: Mon to Fri, 1000 to 1630
Nov to Feb close at 1600
Other restrictions: Prior appointment required for reserve collections.
Access for disabled people: Parking provided, ramped entry
Other restrictions: Ground floor access only. Guide dogs and hearing dogs welcome

General description:
One of the largest collections of clothing and accessories in Britain. The collection is housed in Platt Hall, an elegant Georgian mansion. It has displays on two floors, exhibiting the history of English costume from *c.* 1600 to the present day. New displays and exhibitions are mounted each year.
Information services:
Education services: Group education facilities, resources for Further or Higher Education..
Collections:
Archives of fashion magazines, trade catalogues, photographs, tailoring books and paper patterns from 1800 to the present
Over 23,000 items of clothing
Publications list:
is available in hard copy.
Printed publications:
Books
Catalogue picture books (£1 plus p&p)
Information Pack (£2 plus p&p)
Postcards (25p each)

1046
GALLERY OF ENGLISH COSTUME
See - Gallery of Costume

1047
GALLERY OF MODERN ART
Royal Exchange Square, Glasgow, G1 3AH

Tel: 0141 229 1996
Fax: 0141 204 5316
Acronym or abbreviation: GoMA

Organisation type and purpose: Art gallery, suitable for ages: 5+.
Parent body:
Glasgow Museums

Enquiries to: Curator
Access:
Access to staff: By letter, by telephone, by fax
Access to building, collections or gallery: No prior appointment required
Hours: Mon to Thu, Sat 1000 to 1700; Fri and Sun, 1100 to 1700
Other restrictions: Closed 25, 26 Dec and 1, 2 Jan
Access for disabled people: access to all public areas, toilet facilities

General description:
Works on display include the latest works of Scottish and worldwide artists.
Information services:
Education services: Group education facilities, resources for Further or Higher Education..

Internet home pages:
http://www.goma.glasgow.gov.uk

1048
GALLERY OLDHAM
Greaves Street, Oldham, Lancashire, OL1 1AL

Tel: 0161 911 4657
Fax: 0161 911 4669
Email: ecs.galleryoldham@oldham.gov.uk
Formed from: Oldham Museum
Formerly: Oldham Gallery

Organisation type and purpose: Local government body, museum, art gallery.
Parent body:
Oldham Metropolitan Borough, Education & Cultural Services (OMBC)
Civic Centre, Level 5, West Street

Enquiries to: Programme & Exhibitions Manager
Direct tel: 0161 911 4650
Access:
Access to staff: By letter, by telephone, by fax, by email
Hours: Mon to Fri, 1000 to 1700
Access to building, collections or gallery: No prior appointment required
Hours: Mon to Sat, 1000 to 1700
Access for disabled people: Parking provided, level entry, access to all public areas, toilet facilities
Other restrictions: Audio guides, hearing loop.

General description:
A local museum with collections relating to Oldham's human and natural history, including geological and archaeological collections. The museum also houses a large collection of photographs and paper ephemera.
Information services:
Special visitor services: Guided tours, tape recorded guides.
Education services: Group education facilities.
Services for disabled people: For the visually impaired; for the hearing impaired.
Collections:
Traditional gallery and museum collections
Specific collections of library and research interest
Large collection of printed ephemera local and national interest including first election posters relating to Winston Churchill
Costume, accessories and clothing, 18th-20th century, 5000 items
Photographs, local collection, 19th-20th century, 20,000 items
Catalogues:
Catalogue for library is in-house only.
Publications list:
is available in hard copy.
Printed publications:
Charles Lees Watercolour Collection
Various exhibition catalogues
Electronic and video products:
Building Stones of Oldham Walk - audio tour to geological items in the town (tape)
Sussed - interactive game looking at issues relating to sustainable development (CD-ROM)
Billy Small - cartoon storyline, information and interactive on issues of sustainability (CD-ROM)

Internet home pages:
http://www.galleryoldham.org.uk

1049
GARDNER ARTS CENTRE LIMITED
University of Sussex, Falmer, Brighton, East Sussex, BN1 9RA

Tel: 01273 685447 (Admin) / 01273 685861 (Box Office)
Fax: 01273 678551
Email: info@gardnerarts.co.uk
Formed: 1969

Organisation type and purpose: Independently owned, registered charity (charity number 292586), historic building, house or site, suitable for ages: all ages.
Access to the arts through participation. We run three seasons providing a mixed programme of contemporary performing and visual arts and a healthy education programme.

Enquiries to: Administrator
Access:
Access to staff: By letter, by telephone, by email
Hours: Mon to Fri, 1000 to 1800
Box Office: Mon to Fri, 1000 to 1900
Access to building, collections or gallery: No prior appointment required
Hours: Gallery: daily, 1000 to 1800 and when performances are on
Access for disabled people: Parking provided, toilet facilities
Other restrictions: Access currently limited with stairs to auditorium and gallery - phone to discuss needs.

General description:
Arts centre, theatre and gallery, housed in a Grade II listed building.

Internet home pages:
http://www.gardnerarts.co.uk

1050
GARLOGIE MILL POWER HOUSE MUSEUM

Garlogie, Skene, Westhill, Aberdeenshire, AB32 6RX

Tel: 01771 622906
Fax: 01771 622884
Formed: 1995

Organisation type and purpose: Local government body, museum, suitable for ages: 5+.
Parent body:
Aberdeenshire Heritage
Tel: 01771 622906, fax: 01771 622884

Enquiries to: Curator
Access:
Access to staff: By letter, by telephone, by fax
Access to building, collections or gallery: No prior appointment required
Other restrictions: May to Sep, Sat, Sun, 1400 to 1630
Access for disabled people: toilet facilities
Other restrictions: No disabled access to the beam engine itself

General description:
Early 19th century beam engine, early 20th century turbine.
Collections:
Only the beam engine and turbine
Catalogues:
Catalogue for part of the collections is only available in-house.

1051
GARSTANG & DISTRICT ART SOCIETY, THE

The Old Grammar School Arts Centre, Croston Road, Garstang, Preston, Lancashire, PR3 1EB

Tel: 01995 606648
Formed: 1969

Organisation type and purpose: Registered charity (charity number 259715).
Arts society embracing visual and performing arts.

Enquiries to: Chairman
Direct tel: 01995 603288
Access:
Access to staff: By letter, by telephone, in person
Access to building, collections or gallery: No prior appointment required
Hours: Tue, 1000 to 1230 and 1400 to 1600; Thu, 1000 to 1600; Sat, 1000 to 1230
Access for disabled people: level entry, access to all public areas, toilet facilities

General description:
Exhibition of paintings, photographs or other materials together with concerts and demonstrations.
Collections:
Memorabilia connected with previous Garstang Town Council including:
Halberds
Town Crier's Bell
Weights, Measures
Branding iron and handcuffs

1052
GARU NANAK SIKH MUSEUM

9 Holy Bones, Leicester, LE1 4LJ

Tel: 0116 262 8606
Fax: 0116 262 8606
Email: info@thesikhmuseum.com
Acronym or abbreviation: GN Sikh Museum
Formed: 1992

Organisation type and purpose: Registered charity (charity number 1076280), museum, suitable for ages: 5+.
Registered as museum by the Council for Museums, Archives and Libraries.
The museum seeks to promote the understanding and appreciation of Sikh religion, history and culture by maintaining a collection of artefacts and manuscripts as evidence of the Sikh Heritage. The collection will be recorded, researched, conserved and displayed for the public benefit.
Member of:
Council for Museums, Archives and Libraries

Enquiries to: Project Co-ordinator
Access:
Access to staff: By letter, by telephone, by fax, by email, visitors by prior appointment
Access for disabled people: Parking provided, access to all public areas, toilet facilities
Other restrictions: Arrangements in advance for lift which operates from Car Park Level.

General description:
The first registered Sikh Museum opened in 1992, depicting the history of the Sikh Nation, in the form of dramatic paintings, coins, hand craft, manuscripts and spectacular models of shrines including the Golden Temple at Amritsar.
Photographic displays include the role played by Sikh soldiers in both World Wars.
Information services:
Special visitor services: Guided tours, materials and/or activities for children.
Education services: Group education facilities, resources for Key Stages 1 and 2, 3, 4 and Further or Higher Education..
Collections:
The Museum holds special exhibitions in the months of April and November
The exhibition in November includes workshops on different aspects of the Sikh way of life, Sikh costumes, turban trying by visitors, Panjabi foods, language, Sikh music
A large collection of fine art paintings and photographs on permanent display
Catalogues:
Catalogue for all of the collections is only available in-house.
Printed publications:
All leaflets (free)
A Visit to Gurdwara - Sikh Temple (free to educational institutions)
The Formation of 'Khalsa' (poster, £5)
Other posters (for purchase)
Electronic and video products:
Videos (for purchase)

Internet home pages:
http://www.thesikhmuseum.com
More details on website
http://www.panjab2000.co.uk
http://www.kidsnet.co.uk

1053
GAWTHORPE HALL

Padiham, Burnley, Lancashire, BB12 8UA

Tel: 01282 771004
Fax: 01282 770178/770353
Email: gawthorpehall@nationaltrust.org.uk

Organisation type and purpose: Local government body, registered charity (charity number 205846), museum, art gallery, historic building, house or site, suitable for ages: 8+.
Parent body:
The National Trust (North West)
North West Regional Office, tel: 0870 609 5391
Leased to:
Lancashire County Museum Service (LCMS)
Stanley Street, Preston, PR1 4YP, tel: 01772 264061

Enquiries to: Manager
Access:
Access to staff: By letter, by telephone, by fax, in person
Access to building, collections or gallery: No prior appointment required
Hours: Apr to beg Nov, Tue to Thu, Sat and Sun, 1300 to 1700
Open Bank Holiday Mondays and Good Friday
Access for disabled people: toilet facilities
Other restrictions: Drop-off point. Steps to entrance. Ground floor accessible with assistance. No access to other floors. Photograph album. Four steps from outside to entrance hall. Steps from dining-room difficult. Urdu interpretation of RBKS textile collection. Steps to tea-room entrance. External seating just up 2 steps. Route from car park to lawn level. Gradient route through trees.

General description:
17th century architecture, panelling, plaster ceilings and furniture; mid 19th century work of Sir Charles Barry and A W N Pugin;
Shuttleworth family history.
Information services:
Special events and exhibitions all season.
Education facilities include role-play for Key Stage Two pupils.
Group evening guided tours and special activities available.
Suitable for school groups. Live interpretation. Hands-on activities. Children's quiz/trail. Adult study days.
Special visitor services: Materials and/or activities for children.
Education services: Group education facilities, resources for Key Stage 2..
Collections:
Collection of textiles, embroidery, needlework, lace, treen, and ceramics.
17th century portraits on permanent loan from the National Portrait Gallery
Ryder Bequest: 17th century furniture and domestic artefacts
The Rachel B Kay-Shuttleworth Collections of Textiles
Printed publications:
Gawthorpe Hall - National Trust Guide Book (£2)
Backcloth to Gawthorpe (Conroy M P, £5.95)

Internet home pages:
http://www.nationaltrust.org.uk

1054
GEEVOR TIN MINE HERITAGE CENTRE

Boscaswell, Pendeen, Penzance, Cornwall, TR19 7EW

Tel: 01736 788662
Fax: 01736 786059
Email: pch@geevor.com
Formed: 2001
Organisations still looked for as: Pendeen Community Heritage won the Management Contract from The Trevithick Trust, date of change, October 2001
Site owned by: Cornwall County Council

Organisation type and purpose: Registered charity (charity number 1087755), museum, suitable for ages: 5+.
Education and heritage centre.
Conservation and interpretation of local mining heritage, management and conservation of Geevor site, education, creation of employment.
Parent body:
Cornwall County Council
Managed by:
Pendeen Community Heritage (PCH)
Tel: 01736 788662, fax: 01736 786095, email/website: pch@geevor.com

Enquiries to: Chairman
Other contacts: Mine Manager for bookings, silt operation.
Access:
Access to staff: By letter, by telephone, by fax, by email, Internet web pages
Access to building, collections or gallery: Prior appointment required
Hours: Nov to Easter: Mon to Fri, 1000 to 1600
Easter to end Oct: Sun to Fri, 1000 to 1700
plus Bank Holiday Sat

continued overleaf

Access for disabled people: Parking provided, toilet facilities
Other restrictions: Ramped entry to some buildings.

General description:
Geevor Tin Mine was the last mine to work in the far west of Cornwall, finally closing in 1990. Until then tin was won for centuries in workings which eventually stretched far out under the sea. Geevor is now the largest complete mining history site in Britain, where visitors can follow the story of the mining and processing of tin.
In the museum building are mining artefacts, memorabilia, photographs, mineral displays, 3D model of coastal mine workings, the history of tin and allied mining in the local area and local history.
Surface buildings including compressor and winder houses; mill processing plant where the ore was crushed, ground, separated and the tin concentrate was produced. Underground mine tour in 18th century Wheal Mexico Adit Mine set in magnificent coastal scenery with wealth of wildlife. Nearby along coastal footpath are famous Levant and Botallack Mines, inland prehistoric archaeological sites and structures in unspoilt countryside. Archives available by appointment.

Information services:
Library available for reference (for conditions see Access above)
Educational facilities.
Special visitor services: Guided tours, materials and/or activities for children.
Education services: Group education facilities, resources for Key Stages 1 and 2, 3, 4 and Further or Higher Education.
Services for disabled people: For the visually impaired.

Collections:
Compressors (not working) in Compressor House
Electric Winder (not working) in Winder House
Original Steam Winder (not working) in Winder House
Processing Machinery (not working) in Mill Processing Plant
Other surface buildings, photographs of mines and miners, mining memorabilia, mineral collection
Archives available on request
Collection of Geevor minerals and artefacts
Trevithick Society collection (Richard Trevithick)
Geevor Archive - historical material re Geevor Tin Mines plc and some associated operations

Catalogues:
Catalogue for library is in-house only. Catalogue for all of the collections is only available in-house.

Publications list:
is available in hard copy.

Printed publications:
Guides

Electronic and video products:
Educational CD-ROM (2002)

Internet home pages:
http://www.geevor.com
Description of Geevor Tin Mine and history, links to education, surrounding area.

1055
GEFFRYE MUSEUM
Kingsland Road, London, E2 8EA

Tel: 020 7739 9893
Fax: 020 7729 5647
Formed: 1914

Organisation type and purpose: Independent trust museum.
Parent body:
Geffrye Museum Trust
Member of:
Furniture History Society
Group for Educational Services in Museums
London Museums Agency
Regional Furniture Society
Supported by:
Friends of the Geffrye

Enquiries to: Director
Access:
Access to staff: Visitors by prior appointment
Hours: Mon to Fri, 0900 to 1700

General description:
English furniture, English domestic life, decorative arts, paintings and domestic interiors 1600-1950, East End furniture industry, education in museums, herb gardens.
Collections:
Archive related to the East London furniture trade
Collections of English furniture, paintings and decorative arts, from 1600 to present day
Publications list:
is available in hard copy.
Printed publications:
Events Bulletin (quarterly)
Microform products:
Slides

1056
GEOLOGICAL MUSEUM
London
See - Natural History Museum

1057
GEOLOGICAL MUSEUM, SANDOWN
See - Dinosaur Isle

1058
GEOLOGY AND ENVIRONMENTAL RESOURCES
Cleveland County Council

1059
GEOLOGY DEPARTMENT MUSEUM
See - Aberdeen University, Geology Department Museum

1060
GEORGE INN, THE
The George Inn Yard, 77 Borough High Street, Southwark, London, SE1 1NH

Tel: 020 7407 2056

Organisation type and purpose: National organisation, registered charity (charity number 205846), historic building, house or site.
Parent body:
The National Trust (South and South East Region)
Thames and Solent Regional Office, tel: 01494 528051

Enquiries to: Manager
Access:
Access to staff: By letter, by telephone

General description:
The last remaining galleried inn in London, famous as a coaching inn during the 17th century and mentioned by Dickens in Little Dorrit. Leased to a private company and still in use as a public house.

Internet home pages:
http://www.nationaltrust.org.uk

1061
GEORGE STEPHENSON'S BIRTHPLACE
Street House, Wylam, Newcastle upon Tyne, NE41 8BP

Tel: 01661 853457
Fax: 01670 774317

Organisation type and purpose: National organisation, registered charity (charity number 205846), museum, historic building, house or site.
Parent body:
The National Trust (Yorkshire and North East)
North East Regional Office, tel: 01670 774691

Enquiries to: Manager
Access:
Access to staff: By letter, by telephone, by fax

General description:
A small stone tenement, built c.1760 to accommodate mining families. The furnishings reflect the year of Stephenson's birth here (1781), his whole family living in the one room.

Internet home pages:
http://www.nationaltrust.org.uk

1062
GEORGIAN HOUSE, THE
7 Charlotte Square, Edinburgh, EH2 4DR

Tel: 0131 226 3318
Fax: 0131 226 3318
Email: thegeorgianhouse@nts.org.uk

Organisation type and purpose: National organisation, registered charity (charity number SCO 07410), historic building, house or site, suitable for ages: all ages.
Parent body:
National Trust for Scotland
Tel: 01721 722502, fax: 01721 726000, email: jgreig@nts.org.uk

Enquiries to: Property Manager
Other contacts: Marketing Manager
Access:
Access to staff: By letter, by telephone, by fax, by email
Access to building, collections or gallery: No prior appointment required
Hours: End Jan to end Mar and end Oct to 24 Dec: daily, 1100 to 1600
End Mar to end Oct, daily, 1000 to 1800
Closed for Christmas and for most of January
Other restrictions: Opening dates vary slightly each year

General description:
Georgian architecture.
Information services:
Video programme, interactive CD-ROM for use at the house, Braille guidebook, induction loop, sub-titled video, explanatory text in Chinese, Danish, Dutch, French, German, Italian, Japanese, Portuguese, Russian, Spanish, Swedish
Special visitor services: Guided tours, materials and/or activities for children.
Services for disabled people: For the visually impaired; for the hearing impaired.
Collections:
China, silver, paintings and furniture of the period

Internet home pages:
http://www.nts.org.uk

1063
GEORGIAN HOUSE MUSEUM, THE
7 Great George Street, Bristol, BS1 5RR

Tel: 0117 921 1362
Formed: 1939

Organisation type and purpose: Local government body, registered charity (charity number 311502), historic building, house or site.
Branch of:
City Museum & Art Gallery
Queen's Road, Bristol, BS8 1RL

Enquiries to: Curator
Direct tel: 0117 922 3588
Direct fax: 0117 922 2047
Direct email: karin_walton@bristol-city.gov.uk
Access:
Access to staff: By letter, by email, visitors by prior appointment

Information services:
Education services: Group education facilities..
Collections:
Furniture, paintings
Printed publications:
Postcards

1064
GIANT'S CAUSEWAY
44a Causeway Road, Bushmills, Co Antrim, BT57 8SU, Northern Ireland

Tel: 028 2073 1159/1582

Parent body:
The National Trust
Access:
Access to building, collections or gallery: No prior appointment required
Hours: Stones and North Antrim Coastal Path, all year
Access for disabled people: Parking provided
Other restrictions: Close parking, minibus with hoist for transport to Causeway during season. Shop, tearoom and Visitor Centre, ramped access. Wheelchair accessible paths.

General description:
World Heritage site and National Nature Reserve. Famous for its renowned geological phenomenon of polygonal columns of basalt, resulting from a volcanic eruption 60 million years ago. Coast and cliff paths and wreck site of a Spanish Armada treasure ship can be seen. Visitors' Centre with interpretative displays and audiovisual theatre.
Information services:
Education services: Group education facilities, resources for Key Stages 1 and 2, 3 and 4.
Services for disabled people: For the visually impaired; for the hearing impaired.

1065
GIBSIDE
nr Rowlands Gill, Burnopfield, Newcastle upon Tyne, NE16 6BG

Tel: 01207 542255 (Estate Office)
Fax: 01207 542255
Email: gibside@nationaltrust.org.uk

Parent body:
The National Trust (Yorkshire and North East)
North East Regional Office, tel: 01670 774691

Enquiries to: Property Manager
Direct tel: 01207 542741
Access:
Access to staff: By letter, by telephone, by fax, by email
Access for disabled people: Parking provided, toilet facilities
Other restrictions: Designated parking 100yds. 2 manual wheelchairs available, booking essential. 1 single-seater
powered mobility vehicle, booking essential. Steps to entrance. Photos in information centre. Chapel: steps to entrance. Ramped entrance to shop and to tea-room. Grounds largely accessible. Recommended route map.

General description:
One of the North's finest landscapes, much of which is a Site of Special Scientific Interest (SSSI), a 'forest garden' currently under restoration and embracing many miles of riverside and forest walks. There are several outstanding buildings, including a Palladian chapel, Column of Liberty, and others awaiting or undergoing restoration. The estate is the former home of the Queen Mother's family, the Bowes-Lyons.
Information services:
Braille guide.
Suitable for school groups. Children's quiz/trail. Family activity packs.
Concerts and children's events. Send s.a.e. for details.
Special visitor services: Materials and/or activities for children.
Services for disabled people: For the visually impaired.

Internet home pages:
http://www.nationaltrust.org.uk

1066
GILBERT WHITE'S HOUSE & THE OATES MUSEUM
The Wakes, Selborne, Alton, Hampshire, GU34 3JH

Tel: 01420 511275
Fax: 01420511040
Email: gilbertwhite@btinternet.com

Organisation type and purpose: Museum, historic building, house or site.
Access:
Access for disabled people: Parking provided, ramped entry, toilet facilities
Other restrictions: Access to ground floor and garden.

General description:
The Rv Gilbert White (1720-1793), author of the famous Natural History of Selborne, lived here in the 18th century. The rooms have been restored following descriptions in White's correspondence and include items of his furniture, beautifully embroidered bedhangings and family portraits.
The garden is well documented by White and has been largely restored to its 18th century form.
Due to major building works there is at present a temporary exhibition on the Oates family, featuring new acquisitions relating to Captain Lawrence Oates, hero of the ill-fated expedition to the South Pole.
Information services:
Education services: Group education facilities..
Collections:
House, gardens, furniture and effects, books and papers of, and relating to, Gilbert White, the 18th century naturalist, gardener and author
Papers, effects and artefacts relating to Laurence Oates the Antarctic explorer, and his family
Garden with plants of the time displayed in 'Six Quarters', ornamental 'basons', a wild flower garden and vegetable plot. A revolving 'Wine Pipe' overlooks the miniature landscape garden and a magnificent beech clad 'Hanger'.

1067
GILLINGHAM MUSEUM
Chantry Fields, Gillingham, Dorset, SP8 4UA

Tel: 01747 821119
Email: gillinghammuseum@waitrose.com
Formed: 1958

Organisation type and purpose: Registered charity (charity number 1014970), museum, suitable for ages: all ages.

Enquiries to: Honorary Secretary
Access:
Access to staff: By letter, by email
Access to building, collections or gallery: No prior appointment required
Hours: Mon, Tue, Thu, Fri, 1000 to 1700; Sat, 0930 to 1230
Other restrictions: Closed Wed, Sun, Bank Holidays.
Access for disabled people: level entry, access to all public areas

General description:
The museum shows Gillingham's geology and archaeology - including locally found fossils; evidence of Roman, Saxon and Mediaeval occupation; Gillingham forest; the story of the artist John Constable's association with the town, including full size colour reproductions of all his local works; the 1790 fire engine, and the history of the fire brigade; the coming of the railway to Gillingham and its influence on the town's industrial development; Victorian Gillingham; the Dorset Volunteers and Dorset Yeomanry, and the first and second World Wars.
Information services:
Services for disabled people: Displays and/or information at wheelchair height.
Collections:
All collections refer to Gillingham and local villages
All photographs on modes
All items in process of being put on modes
Catalogues:
Catalogue for library is in-house only. Catalogue for all of the collections is only available in-house.
Printed publications:
Gylla's Home Town (Howe C, £4.50)
Around Gillingham in Photographs (Crocker P, £7.99 plus p&p)
Around Gillingham in Photographs (Lloyd D, £9.99 plus p&p)
Miscellaneous smaller documented items

Address for ordering publications:
Printed publications:
Mr C Burfoot, Gillingham Museum

Internet home pages:
http://www.brwebsites.com/gillingham.museum

1068
GLADSTONE COURT MUSEUM
Biggar, Lanarkshire, ML12 6DT

Tel: 01899 221573
Fax: 01899 221050
Email: margaret@bmtrust.freeserve.co.uk
Formed: 1968
Formed from: Biggar Museum Trust

Organisation type and purpose: Independently owned, museum, suitable for ages: 5+.
Parent body:
Biggar Museum Trust
Moat Park Heritage Centre, Biggar, ML12 6DT, tel: 01899 221050, fax: 01899 221050, email: margaret@bmtrust.freeserve.co.uk

Enquiries to: Administrator
Access:
Access to staff: By letter, by telephone, by fax, by email
Access for disabled people: ramped entry

General description:
Children of all ages can stroll along the 'Real' Victorian Street and visit the small shops - or perhaps sit in the schoolroom to recall the not-so-good old days. This is a museum which gives children a living experience of Victorian social history.
Information services:
Library available for reference (for conditions see Access above). Helpline available, tel no: 01899 221050.
Special visitor services: Materials and/or activities for children.
Education services: Group education facilities.
Services for disabled people: Displays and/or information at wheelchair height.
Collections:
Furniture and fixtures of the Victorian era
Catalogues:
Catalogue for library is in-house only.
Printed publications:
Brochure

Internet home pages:
http://www.biggar.net.co.uk

1069
GLADSTONE POTTERY MUSEUM
Uttoxeter Road, Longton, Stoke-on-Trent, Staffordshire, ST3 1PQ

Tel: 01782 319232
Fax: 01782 598640
Email: gladstone@stoke.gov.uk

continued overleaf

Formed: 1975

Organisation type and purpose: Local government body, museum, suitable for ages: 5+.

Enquiries to: Administration Officer
Direct tel: 01782 311378
Other contacts: Curator for historical information.
Access:
Access to staff: By letter, by telephone, by fax, by email, visitors by prior appointment
Hours: Daily 1000 to 1700
Closed Dec 25 to Jan 2
Access for disabled people: Parking provided, ramped entry, level entry, access to all public areas, toilet facilities

General description:
The Gladstone Pottery Museum is housed in a Victorian pottery factory, complete with bottle ovens. There are collections of machinery and tools relating to pottery-making. Also features ceramic sanitaryware; tiles; and the colouring and decoration of pottery. Pottery-making processes, life and work of the North Staffs pottery world.
Information services:
Library available for reference (for conditions see Access above). Helpline available, tel no: 01782 311378.
Guided tours for groups with prior booking.
Special visitor services: Guided tours, materials and/or activities for children.
Education services: Group education facilities, resources for Key Stages 1 and 2, 3, 4 and Further or Higher Education.
Services for disabled people: For the hearing impaired.
Collections:
Photographs
Books
Transcripts and video interviews of pottery workers
Machinery and tools
Ceramic tiles - Over 1000 tiles in new gallery
Victorian WC's
Architectural ceramics
Catalogues:
Catalogue for library is in-house only. Catalogue for all of the collections is available in-house, part is published and part is on-line.

Internet home pages:
http://www.stoke.gov.uk/gladstone

1070
GLADSTONE'S LAND
477B Lawnmarket, Edinburgh, EH1 2NT

Tel: 0131 226 5856
Fax: 0131 226 4851

Organisation type and purpose: Historic building, house or site.
Parent body:
National Trust for Scotland (South Region)

Enquiries to: Property Manager
Access:
Access to staff: By letter, by telephone, by fax, in person, charges to non-members
Access to building, collections or gallery: No prior appointment required
Hours: End Mar to end Oct, Mon to Sat, 1000 to 1700, Sun, 1300 to 1700
Other restrictions: Sun, 1-2 guided tours only, maximum ten people

General description:
17th century tenement building.
Information services:
Explanatory text in Dutch, French, German, Italian, Japanese, Norwegian, Spanish.
Special visitor services: Guided tours.
Services for disabled people: For the visually impaired.

Internet home pages:
http://www.nts.org.uk

1071
GLAMIS CASTLE
Glamis, Angus, DD8 1RJ

Tel: 01307 840393
Fax: 01307 840733
Email: admin@glamis-castle.co.uk

Organisation type and purpose: Historic building, house or site, suitable for ages: 5+.

Enquiries to: Administrator
Access:
Access to staff: By telephone, by email
Access for disabled people: Parking provided, ramped entry
Other restrictions: Access to ground floor only.

General description:
Family home of the Earls of Strathmore and Kinghorne. A Royal residence since 1372. Childhood home of the late Queen Elizabeth, the Queen Mother.
Collections:
Furniture, portraits and porcelain collections
Publications list:
is available in hard copy and online.

Internet home pages:
http://www.glamis-castle.co.uk

1072
GLANDFORD SHELL MUSEUM
Glandford, Holt, Norfolk, NR25 7JR

Tel: 01263 740081
Fax: 01263 740081
Email: sushell@dircon.co.uk
Formed: 1915

Organisation type and purpose: Registered charity (charity number 311106), museum, suitable for ages: all ages.
Collection of worldwide seashells, artefacts, minerals and tapestry depicting the North Norfolk coast.

Enquiries to: Curator
Access:
Access to staff: By letter, by fax, by email
Access for disabled people: Parking provided, level entry, access to all public areas

General description:
Worldwide seashell collections, artefacts, minerals and $14\frac{1}{2}$ ft by 16 in wide tapestry depicting the North Norfolk coast.
Printed publications:
Museum brochure and postcards

1073
GLASGOW MUSEUM OF TRANSPORT
Kelvin Hall, 1 Bunhouse Road, Glasgow, G3 8DP

Tel: 0141 287 2723
Fax: 0141 287 2692
Formed: 1964

Organisation type and purpose: Local government body, museum, suitable for ages: all ages.
Parent body:
Glasgow Museums

Enquiries to: Curator
Other contacts: Administration Officer for messages and will pass information on.
Access:
Access to staff: By letter, by telephone, by fax, visitors by prior appointment
Access to building, collections or gallery: Prior appointment required
Hours: Mon to Thu, Sat, 1000 to 1700; Fri, Sun, 1100 to 1700
Other restrictions: Closed 25, 26 Dec and 1, 2 Jan.
Access for disabled people: Parking provided, access to all public areas, toilet facilities
Other restrictions: Lift.

General description:
Transport, especially Glasgow and the West of Scotland.
The Museum of Transport houses many exhibits of national and international importance.
Displays tell the story of transport by land and sea with particular reference to Glasgow. Kelvin Street has been recreated as in 1938.
Information services:
Records of collections are mostly held on computer for internal use. Some hand lists of archives, photographic collections etc.
Special visitor services: Guided tours, materials and/or activities for children.
Education services: Group education facilities..
Collections:
Famous locomotives include Caledonian Railway No 123 'The Caley Single', Highland Railway No 103 'The Jones Goods', and Great North of Scotland Railway No 49 'Gordon Highlander'.
Glasgow Trams
Horse-drawn vehicles, fire engines and other emergency service vehicles, motor cycles and caravans, also toy cars and prams
In the Clyde Room are some 250 ship models (representing the gigantic contribution of the River Clyde and its shipbuilders and engineers to the world of maritime trade) from the Comet of 1812 to fabulous builders models of the 'Hood', 'Howe', 'Queen Mary', 'Queen Elizabeth' and 'Queen Elizabeth 2'.
The finest collection in the world of Scottish-built cars including such world famous marques as Argyll, Arrol Johnston and Albion
The World's oldest surviving pedal cycle
Printed publications:
A Guide to the Museum of Transport (£2.95)
Friends Preview (magazine, quarterly, free, ISSN 0962-2470)
Museum of Transport Ship Models (£3.50)

Address for ordering publications:
Printed publications:
Marketing Department, Culture and Leisure Services
32 Albion Street, Glasgow

Internet home pages:
http://www.glasgow.gov.uk

1074
GLASGOW MUSEUMS
Art Gallery and Museum, Kelvingrove, Glasgow, G3 8AG

Tel: 0141 287 2699
Fax: 0141 287 2690
Formed: 1901
Formerly: Glasgow Museums and Art Galleries

Organisation type and purpose: Local government body, museum, art gallery, suitable for ages: all ages.
Glasgow Museums is the corporate title for Glasgow City Council, Culture & Leisure Services', Museums Service, and administers Glasgow's ten municipal museums and art galleries.
Parent body:
Glasgow City Council, Culture and Leisure Services
20 Trongate, Glasgow, G1 5ES, tel: 0141 287 4350, fax: 0141 287 5558

Enquiries to: Director
Direct tel: 0141 287 2600
Direct fax: 0141 287 2690
Other contacts: Marketing Officer
Access:
Access to staff: By letter, by telephone, by fax, visitors by prior appointment
Hours: Mon to Thu, Sat, 1000 to 1700; Fri, Sun, 1100 to 1700
Access for disabled people: Parking provided, level entry, access to all public areas, toilet facilities

General description:
The subjects covered by the ten museums of Glasgow include art, history, British history, worldwide ethnography, sociology, natural history, history of science, history of transport,

religious history, and content and conservation science.
Information services:
The Open Museum Department lends objects and displays to community groups in Glasgow and Strathclyde.
Glasgow Museums offers touring exhibitions to venues in UK and elsewhere. For Museum Education Department tel: 0141 287 2748.
Special visitor services: Guided tours, materials and/or activities for children.
Education services: Group education facilities..
Trade and statistical:
Glasgow's municipal art and design collections of over 1 million objects, a substantial proportion of which relate to the City's artistic, cultural, political and social history.
Printed publications:
Variety of publications including:
1745: Charles Edward and the Jacobites (£11.95)
Burrell: Portrait of a Collector (R Marks, £6.99)
European Arms and Armour at Kelvingrove (J G Scott, £1.75)
Friends Preview Magazine (free of charge)
Glasgow Art Gallery and Museum: The Buildings and the Collections (£6.95)
Guide to the Museum of Transport (£2.95)
The Burrell Collection: a guide (£6.95)
The People's Palace and Glasgow Green (E King, £3.99)
The St Mungo Museum of Religious Life and Art (M O'Neill, £4.99)
The Strike of the Glasgow Weavers (E King, £1.65)

Address for ordering publications:
Printed publications:
Marketing Department, Culture and Leisure Services
32 Albion Street, Glasgow

Internet home pages:
http://www.glasgow.gov.uk/cls

*See also - **Burrell Collection; Fossil Grove; Gallery of Modern Art; Glasgow Museum of Transport; Kelvingrove Art Gallery & Museum; Martyrs' School; McLellan Galleries; Open Museum; People's Palace; Pollok House; Provand's Lordship; Scotland Street School Museum; St Mungo Museum of Religious Life and Art***

1075
GLASGOW SCIENCE CENTRE, THE

50 Pacific Quay, Glasgow, G51 1EA

Tel: 0141 420 5000
Fax: 0141 420 5011
Acronym or abbreviation: GSC
Formed: 2000 (IMAX)

Organisation type and purpose: Registered charity (charity number SCO 030809), suitable for ages: all ages.
Science centre, science mall and tower formed 2001.
To promote science and technology in Scotland, and to provide a world class visitor attraction.
Key Funders:
Glasgow City Council
Scottish Enterprise Glasgow
Strathclyde European Partnership ERDF Objective 2 Programme
The Millennium Commission
The Wellcome Trust

Enquiries to: Media Manager
Direct tel: 0141 420 5010
Direct email: david.grimmer@gsc.org.uk
Access:
Access to staff: By letter, by telephone, by email, in person, visitors by prior appointment, Internet web pages
Access to building, collections or gallery: No prior appointment required
Hours: 23 Mar to 31 Oct: Daily, 1000 to 1800; also Tower and IMAX, Thu, Fri and Sat, to 2000,1 Nov to 31 Mar: Daily, 1000 to 1700; also Tower and IMAX, Fri, Sat, to 1900
Other restrictions: Closed 24, 25 Dec and 1 Jan.
Access for disabled people: Parking provided, level entry, access to all public areas, toilet facilities
Other restrictions: 2 manual wheelchairs available for loan, dependent on demand on day of visit.

General description:
Glasgow Science Centre is a collection of three buildings at Pacific Quay on the Clyde. The project has three aims - to boost Glasgow's stock of tourism attractions, to provide new educational resources, and to spark further development on the former Garden Festival site. GSC's unique buildings include a large-format IMAX cinema, which shows factual films on Scotland's biggest cinema system with a 80 x 60ft screen and 12,000 watt sound. The Glasgow Tower, a unique structure which is the only ground-up 360 degree rotating tower in the world, offers a new window on the past, present and future of the city. And finally, the Science Mall is the centrepiece of GSC - a shimmering crescent with four floors packed with exhibits, new theatres including Scotland's best planetarium, and the latest visitor facilities.
The GSC's educational programme works both on-site and through outreach programmes visiting schools, colleges and local venues throughout the country.
Information services:
Education services: Group education facilities.
Services for disabled people: For the hearing impaired; displays and/or information at wheelchair height.
Collections:
Over 300 hands-on interactive exhibits held within the four floor Science Mall at GSC
A full listing of these world class exhibits is available to teachers and educationalists upon request
Printed publications:
Spark (quarterly newsletter, free)
Information leaflets for Tower, IMAX, Science Mall (free)
GSC Official Guide
Electronic and video products:
Audiovisual (CD-ROM)

Internet home pages:
http://www.gsc.org.uk

1076
GLASGOW UNIVERSITY

Hunterian Art Gallery, 82 Hillhead Street, Glasgow, G12 8QQ

Tel: 0141 330 5431
Fax: 0141 330 3618
Email: hunter@museum.gla.ac.uk
Acronym or abbreviation: HAG
Formed: 1807

Organisation type and purpose: Registered charity (charity number CR 43991), art gallery, university department or institute, research organisation.

Enquiries to: Administrator
Other contacts: Curator for queries regarding works of art.
Access:
Access to staff: By letter, by telephone, by email, in person, Internet web pages
Hours: Mon to Sat, 0930 to 1700
Access for disabled people: ramped entry

General description:
The Hunterian Art Gallery holds a remarkable collection of European art. C R Mackintosh, Whistler, Scottish Art, Old Masters, prints and sculpture.
Works on paper feature in our exhibition programme and can also be viewed by prior appointment in the Print Room. The reconstruction of the interiors of The Mackintosh House forms part of the Mackintosh collection.
Information services:
Special visitor services: Materials and/or activities for children.
Education services: Group education facilities..
Collections:
Graphics Collection, one of the most important in Scotland, holds 30,000 prints
Major displays of paintings by the Scottish Colourists, Fergusson, Peploe, Cadell and Hunter
16th-17th century Paintings
18th-early 19th century Paintings
19th century French and Scottish Paintings
19th-20th century Art
The Print Gallery
The Sculpture Courtyard
A popular feature of the Charles Rennie Mackintosh collection is the reconstruction of the interiors of The Mackintosh House.
The founding collection of Dr William Hunter includes outstanding paintings by Rembrandt, Koninck, Chardin and Stubbs.
The Whistler Collection - unrivalled holdings of work by James McNeill Whistler include paintings, pastels and prints
Catalogues:
Catalogue for part of the collections is only available in-house.
Publications list:
is available on-line.
Printed publications:
Books, catalogues, postcard packs, postcards, greeting cards, mounted artboards, posters, exhibition posters - Mackintosh related
A Guidebook to the Hunterian Art Gallery
Beatrice Whistler: Artist and Designer
James McNeill Whistler at the Hunterian Art Gallery
Mackintosh at The Hunterian: Teacher Pack
Mackintosh Flower Drawings
Prints and Printmaking
The Mackintosh House
C R Mackintosh: Architectural Sketches
C R Mackintosh: The Architectural Papers
C R Mackintosh at the Hunterian Art Gallery
Charles Rennie Mackintosh: Textile Designs
Charles Rennie Mackintosh: The Chelsea Years
A Thoroughly Modern Afternoon: Margaret Macdonald Mackintosh and the Salon Waerndorfer in Vienna: 4 Essays
Mackintosh and Others: Aspects of the George Smith Collection
The Chronycle - The Letters of Charles Rennie Mackintosh to Margaret Macdonald Mackintosh. 1927
Microform products:
Slides - General
Slides - Mackintosh
Slides - Whistler

Address for ordering publications:
Printed publications:
Publications Officer, Hunterian Art Gallery
Tel: 0141 330 2767, fax: 0141 330 3618, email: lclark@museum.gla.ac.uk

Internet home pages:
http://www.hunterian.gla.ac.uk
Full description of events, history, collections of Hunterian Museum and Art Gallery.

1077
GLASGOW UNIVERSITY

Hunterian Museum, University Avenue, Glasgow, G12 8QQ

Tel: 0141 330 4221
Fax: 0141 330 3617
Email: hunter@museum.gla.ac.uk
Acronym or abbreviation: GLAHM
Formed: 1807

Organisation type and purpose: Learned society, museum, university department or institute, suitable for ages: all ages.

Enquiries to: Curator
Direct tel: 0141 330 3599
Direct email: nclark@museum.gla.ac.uk
Access:
Access to staff: By letter, by telephone, by fax, by email, visitors by prior appointment, Internet web pages

continued overleaf

Hours: Mon to Sat, 0930 to 1700
Other restrictions: Closed on public holidays.
Access to building, collections or gallery: No prior appointment required
Hours: Mon to Sat, 0930 to 1700
Other restrictions: Collections closed on Sat.
Access for disabled people: toilet facilities
Other restrictions: Lift to most levels.

General description:
Zoology, palaeontology, dinosaurs, mineralogy, petrology, geology, archaeology, Romans in Scotland, numismatics, scientific instruments.
Information services:
Education services: Group education facilities, resources for Key Stages 1 and 2, 3, 4 and Further or Higher Education..
Collections:
Archaeological and ethnographical artefacts, palaeontological, geological and biological specimens, some computer catalogued
Items collected on Captain Cook's voyages in the Pacific, late 18th century, 210 items
Catalogues:
Catalogue for part of the collections is available in-house, part is published and part is on-line.
Trade and statistical:
Conservation of geological sites.
Publications list:
is available on-line.

Internet home pages:
http://www.hunterian.gla.ac.uk
All aspects of museum on many pages, virtual museum visits.

1078
GLASTONBURY ABBEY
The Abbey Gatehouse, Magdalene Street, Glastonbury, Somerset, BA6 9EL

Tel: 01458 832267
Fax: 01458 832267
Email: glastonbury.abbey@dial.pipex.com
Full name: Glastonbury Abbey Estate
Formed: 940 Museum 1994

Organisation type and purpose: Registered charity (charity number 222448), museum, historic building, house or site, suitable for ages: all ages.
Historic monument and visitor attraction.

Enquiries to: Custodian
Other contacts: (1) Deputy Custodian; (2)Education Officer for (1) Group Travel, Marketing, Accounts; (2) Education for school groups.
Access:
Access to staff: By letter, by telephone, by fax, by email, in person, visitors by prior appointment
Hours: Office Hours: Mon to Fri, 0900 to 1530
Access to building, collections or gallery: Prior appointment required
Hours: Mon to Fri, 0900 to 1500
Other restrictions: May apply, depending on the request made.
Access for disabled people: ramped entry, toilet facilities
Other restrictions: Parking nearby.

General description:
Glastonbury Abbey, by tradition founded on the site chosen by St Joseph of Arimathea, and now a ruin; St Mary's Chapel dating from 1186 is elaborately carved in the transitional Norman style; the Abbot's Kitchen dating from the 1340s is the only complete building; St Patrick's Chapel dating from the 16th century is still in use. The museum illustrates the history and the life of the abbey and contains a model of the pre-Reformation Abbey. Surrounding the ruins are 36 acres of park with fish pond, duck pond and cider orchard. Adjacent is the Abbot House now a retreat house.
Information services:
Helpline available, tel no: 01458 832267.
Available periodically by appointment with museum consultant.
Special visitor services: Guided tours, tape recorded guides, materials and/or activities for children.
Education services: Group education facilities, resources for Key Stages 1 and 2, 3, 4 and Further or Higher Education.
Services for disabled people: For the visually impaired; for the hearing impaired.
Collections:
General collections of stone, tiles, pottery, archives, textiles, decorative and applied arts, fine art, numismatics
Anglo-Saxon glass, fragments of a Saxon glass-making kiln and window and vessel glass, 950-1050
Painted coloured window glass, 1170-1184, about 30 items
Catalogues:
Catalogue for part of the collections is only available in-house.
Printed publications:
Leaflets (available, free singularly, postage required if in bulk)

1079
GLASTONBURY LAKE VILLAGE MUSEUM
The Tribunal, 9 High Street, Glastonbury, Somerset, BA6 8DB

Tel: 01458 832954
Fax: 01458 832949
Email: glastonbury.tic@ukonline.co.uk

Organisation type and purpose: Local government body, museum, historic building, house or site, suitable for ages: all ages.
Parent body:
Somerset County Museums Service
Tel: 01823 320200, email: county-museums@somerset.gov.uk

Enquiries to: Manager
Access:
Access to staff: By letter, by telephone, by fax, by email, Internet web pages
Access to building, collections or gallery: No prior appointment required
Hours: Apr to Sep, Sun to Thu, 1000 to 1700, Fri and Sat, 1000 to 1730;
Oct to Mar, daily 1000 to 1600

General description:
The Lake Village Museum, housed in a medieval building, presents an interesting insight into everyday life in an Iron Age settlement, dating from around 2000 years ago. An interesting collection of artefacts is held, and the whole history and background has been brought to life through imaginative displays and artists' reconstructions.
Collections:
Archaeological artefacts from the Somerset Levels.
Catalogues:
Catalogue for all of the collections is only available in-house.

Internet home pages:
http://www.glastonburytic.co.uk

1080
GLASTONBURY TOR
Near Glastonbury, Somerset

Tel: 01985 843600 (Regional Office)

Organisation type and purpose: National organisation, registered charity (charity number 205846), historic building, house or site, suitable for ages: 8+.
Parent body:
National Trust (South West)
Regional Office for Wessex, tel: 01985 843600

Enquiries to: Manager

General description:
The dramatic and evocative Tor dominates the Somerset Levels and offers spectacular views over Somerset, Dorset and Wiltshire. At the summit of this very steep hill an excavation has revealed the plans of two superimposed churches of St Michael, of which only the 15th century tower remains.
Printed publications:
Information leaflet 50p plus p&p (available from Regional box office, 01985 843601)

Internet home pages:
http://www.nationaltrust.org.uk/regions/wessex

1081
GLEASTON WATER MILL
Gleaston, Near Ulverston, Cumbria, LA12 0QH

Tel: 01229 869244
Fax: 01229 869764
Email: info@watermill.co.uk
Formed: 1990

Organisation type and purpose: Independently owned, historic building, house or site, suitable for ages: all ages.
Member of:
North West Mills Group
Working in association with:
Furness Bee Keepers

Enquiries to: Managing Partner
Access:
Access to staff: By letter, by telephone, by fax, by email, in person, visitors by prior appointment, Internet web pages
Hours: Tue to Sun, 0900 to 1700
Other restrictions: Small organisation - prior notice is preferred.
Access for disabled people: Parking provided, ramped entry, toilet facilities
Other restrictions: Ground floor access only. Full access to restaurant facilities and retail outlet.

General description:
Water corn milling process and corn milling machinery, pig-keeping, bee-keeping, local archaeology, local dialect and folklore.
Information services:
Special visitor services: Guided tours, materials and/or activities for children.
Education services: Group education facilities, resources for Key Stages 1 and 2, 3, 4 and Further or Higher Education.
Services for disabled people: For the visually impaired; for the hearing impaired; displays and/or information at wheelchair height.
Collections:
Comprehensive selection of milling hand tools and water powered equipment to back up complete working (but not producing) 18th century corn milling machinery
Local pig-keeping, killing and preserving equipment
Bee-keeping equipment and observation hive (spring and summer only)
On-site training apiary - opportunities for 'one-off' visits
Chris Salisbury's Mesolithic and 11th century archaeological finds from excavations 1993-2000 in mill meadows
Hand farm tool collection and local stuffed animals on display in Dusty Miller's café/ restaurant adjoining watermill
Catalogues:
Catalogue for part of the collections is only available in-house.
Printed publications:
In preparation
Electronic and video products:
In preparation

Internet home pages:
http://www.watermill.co.uk
http://www.pigswhisper.com
http://www.lilecottage.com
http://www.dustymillers.com

1082
GLENCOE AND DALNESS
The National Trust for Scotland Visitor Centre, Glencoe, Argyll, PH49 4LA

Tel: 01855 811729
Fax: 01855 811772
Email: glencoe@nts.org.uk

Organisation type and purpose: Historic building, house or site.
Parent body:
National Trust for Scotland

Enquiries to: Property Manager
Other contacts: 01855 811307 (summer only)
Access:
Access to staff: By telephone, by fax, by email, in person
Access to building, collections or gallery: No prior appointment required
Hours: Site, all year, daily
Visitor Centre, shop and café, beg May to end Oct, daily 1000 to 1800
Access for disabled people: toilet facilities

General description:
Site of the infamous massacre of 1692.

1083
GLENCOE AND NORTH LORN FOLK MUSEUM
Glencoe, Ballachulish, Argyll, PA49 4HS

Tel: 01855 811664
Formed: 1967

Organisation type and purpose: Registered charity, museum.

Enquiries to: Trustees
Access:
Access to staff: By letter, in person
Hours: Easter Week & mid-May to end Sep: Mon to Sat, 1000 to 1730; other times by arrangement
Access for disabled people: level entry

General description:
Local history, social history, costumes and textiles, Royal Family Commemorative china, military, clans, agricultural and work history, Jacobites.
Catalogues:
Catalogue for all of the collections is only available in-house.
Publications list:
is available in hard copy and online.

1084
GLENESK FOLK MUSEUM
The Retreat, Glenesk, Brechin, Angus, DD9 7YT

Tel: 01356 670254
Email: retreat@angusglens.co.uk
Formed: 1955

Organisation type and purpose: Independently owned, registered charity (charity number SCO 15078), museum, suitable for ages: 8+.

Enquiries to: Curator
Access:
Access to staff: By letter, by telephone, by email, visitors by prior appointment, Internet web pages
Access for disabled people: Parking provided, ramped entry, toilet facilities

General description:
The museum, housed in a former shooting lodge and run by the people of Glenesk, houses a fascinating and unique collection of antiques, documents and artefacts, reflecting the history of the folk in the Glen and surrounding area. The object is to show life as it was lived, how they did their work. Kitchen utensils, costume exhibits, farm implements, horse harness, cheese presses, fiddles, pianos, a large relief map of the Glen and panels telling of the flora and fauna of the area.
Collections:
Books, documents, crockery, farming equipment, costumes, sewing equipment, pictures, photographs
Everything significant to the area depicting life in a small glen rural community

Internet home pages:
http://www.angusglens.co.uk

1085
GLENFINNAN MONUMENT
National Trust for Scotland Information Centre, Glenfinnan, Highland, PH37 4LT

Tel: 01397 722250
Fax: 01397 722250
Email: glenfinnan@nts.org.uk

Organisation type and purpose: Historic building, house or site.
Parent body:
National Trust for Scotland Highlands and Islands Office (South)

Enquiries to: Property Manager
Access:
Access to staff: By letter, by telephone, by fax, by email, in person
Access to building, collections or gallery: No prior appointment required
Hours: Site, all year, daily
Visitor Centre, shop and snack-bar, end Mar to middle May and beg Sep to end Oct, daily 1000 to 1700; middle May to beg Sep, daily, 0930 to 1800
Access for disabled people: toilet facilities
Other restrictions: Exhibition, shop and snack-bar accessible, wheelchair available

General description:
The monument erected in 1815 by Alexander Macdonald of Glenaladale pays tribute to the clansmen who fought and died in the cause of Bonnie Prince Charlie.
The Visitor Centre exhibition portrays the campaign from Glenfinnan to Derby and back to the final defeat at Culloden.

Internet home pages:
http://www.nts.org.uk

1086
GLENLUCE ABBEY AND GLEBE
Glenluce, Newton Stewart, Dumfries & Galloway, DG8

Tel: 01581 300541

Owned by:
National Trust for Scotland
Under guardianship of:
Historic Scotland
Access:
Access to staff: By telephone

General description:
Ruined Cistercian Abbey founded by Rolland, Lord of Galloway in 1192.

Internet home pages:
http://www.historic-scotland.gov.uk

1087
GLOSSOP HERITAGE CENTRE
Bank House, Henry Street, Glossop, Derbyshire, SK13 8BW

Tel: 01457 869176
Formed: 1986

Organisation type and purpose: Independently owned, registered charity, museum, art gallery, suitable for ages: all ages, consultancy, research organisation.
Parent body:
Glossop Heritage Trust
at the same address

Enquiries to: Executive Secretary
Other contacts: Archivist
Access:
Access to staff: By letter, by telephone, in person, visitors by prior appointment
Access to building, collections or gallery: No prior appointment required
Hours: Mon to Sat, 1030 to 1630
Other restrictions: Closed 25, 26 Dec and 1 Jan.
Access for disabled people: ramped entry

General description:
Two exhibition rooms: one for a permanent exhibition on local history, the other for changing exhibitions of local interest.
Art Gallery with changing exhibitions. Victorian kitchen, family history research with microfiche facilities, history of Glossop and district. Roman, medieval, Victorian, Industrial Revolution and cotton industry, war-time (1939-45), present day, collection of local newspapers from 1896 to present day.
Information services:
Special visitor services: Guided tours, materials and/or activities for children.
Education services: Group education facilities, resources for Key Stages 1 and 2, 3, 4 and Further or Higher Education..
Collections:
Pictures, postcards, books, research files, catalogued newspapers 1896 to present day
Victorian memorabilia
Roman artefacts
Farming equipment
General local photographs
War-time memorabilia
Costumes
Printed publications:
Glossopdale, Manor & Borough (£3.50)
Annals of Glossop (£2.50)
Glossop Tramways (£4.50)
Glossop Heritage (£2.50)
Glossop / Longdendale - Archive Series
Glossop (Archive Photograph) (£9.99)
Relfections of Glossop
More Reflections of Glossop
History of Parish Church
I Remember (personal reminiscences)
Woodhead Railway Books 2 & 3
History in a Pint Pot (all the pubs)
And various other publications including Guide, Postcards
Microform products:
List of Microfiche (75p)

Internet home pages:
http://www.glossopheritage.co.uk

1088
GLOUCESTER CITY COUNCIL
Culture, Learning & Leisure, Herbert Warehouse, The Docks, Gloucester, GL1 2EZ

Tel: 01452 396620
Fax: 01452 296622
Email: culture@gloucester.gov.uk

Organisation type and purpose: Local government body, museum, art gallery, historic building, house or site, suitable for ages: 5+.
Oversight of cultural services, including museums, art gallery, archaeology, arts centre, arts development, festivals.
Parent body:
Gloucester City Council
North Warehouse, The Docks, Gloucester
Other addresses:
Gloucester City Museum and Art Gallery
Gloucester Folk Museum

Enquiries to: Strategic Cultural Manager
Other contacts: Museum Manager for museum-specific information.
Access:
Access to staff: By letter, by telephone, by fax, by email, in person, visitors by prior appointment, Internet web pages
Access for disabled people: Parking provided, ramped entry, access to all public areas, toilet facilities
Other restrictions: Access to museums varies, please check.

continued overleaf

General description:
Archaeology of Gloucester and Gloucestershire, natural history, fine arts, decorative arts (limited), social history (mainly of Gloucestershire).
Collections:
Marling Bequest of furniture, paintings, ceramics, silver, clocks, barometers etc

Internet home pages:
http://www.gloucester.gov.uk/libraries/templates/page.asp?FolderID=29

1089
GLOUCESTER CITY MUSEUM & ART GALLERY
Brunswick Road, Gloucester, GL1 1HP

Tel: 01452 396131
Email: citymuseum@gloucester.gov.uk
Formed: 1860

Organisation type and purpose: Local government body, museum, art gallery, historic building, house or site, suitable for ages: 5+.
Parent body:
Gloucester City Council
Culture, Learning & Leisure, Herbert Warehouse, The Docks, Gloucester, GL1 2EZ, tel: 01452 396620, fax: 01452 396622, email: culture@gloucester.gov.uk

Enquiries to: Manager
Access:
Access to staff: By letter, by telephone, by fax, by email, in person, visitors by prior appointment, Internet web pages
Access to building, collections or gallery: No prior appointment required
Hours: 1000 to 1700, Tue to Sat
Access for disabled people: Parking provided, access to all public areas
Other restrictions: Some displays/information at wheelchair height.

General description:
Covers the geology and natural history relating to Gloucester and Gloucestershire, with wider collections of minerals and marine shells. Also covers the archaeology of Gloucester, including finds from Roman and mediaeval Gloucester. There are collections of coins and tokens; sculpture; paintings; watercolours; drawings and prints, including works of Gloucestershire topography or by Gloucestershire artists; silver; glass; ceramics; clocks; watches; and furniture. Fine and applied art, mainly British but some European.
Information services:
Special visitor services: Guided tours, materials and/or activities for children.
Education services: Group education facilities, resources for Key Stages 1 and 2, 3 and 4.
Services for disabled people: For the hearing impaired; displays and/or information at wheelchair height.
Collections:
Jourdain collection, palaearctic birds eggs, 50,000 items
Saxo-Norman pennies of Gloucester mints, 10th-13th century, 180 items
Work of William Corsley, Gloucester silversmith, 1660-1680, 12 items
Marling bequest, domestic barometers, 17th-18th century, 18 items
Printed publications:
Apply for information

Internet home pages:
http://www.mylife.gloucester.gov.uk/City%20Museum/city.htm
http://www.livinggloucester.co.uk
http://www.gloucester.gov.uk/libraries/templates/page.asp?URN=919

1090
GLOUCESTER FOLK MUSEUM
99-103 Westgate Street, Gloucester, GL1 2PG

Tel: 01452 396467
Fax: 01452 330495
Email: folk.museum@glos-city.gov.uk
Formed: 1935
Formerly: City Museum and Art Gallery, Gloucester

Organisation type and purpose: Local government body, museum, historic building, house or site, suitable for ages: all ages.
Gloucester Folk Museum exists to collect, preserve, document, display, interpret and care for material evidence of social history, crafts, trades and industries showing how people lived and worked in and around Gloucester from 1500 to the present, so that visitors of all ages, backgrounds and abilities may better understand their heritage and themselves.
Parent body:
Gloucester City Council
Culture, Learning & Leisure, Herbert Warehouse, The Docks, Gloucester GL1 2EZ, tel: 01452 396620, fax: 01452 396622, email: culture@gloucester.gov.uk
Other branch:
Transport Museum
The Old Fire Station, Longsmith Street, Gloucester, GL1 2JF, tel: 01452 396467, fax: 01452 330495, email/website: folk.museum@gloucester.gov.uk

Enquiries to: Manager
Direct email: christopherm@glos-city.gov.uk
Other contacts: Curator of Social History for appointments to view collections for research etc.
Access:
Access to staff: By letter, by telephone, by fax, by email, visitors by prior appointment, Internet web pages
Hours: Mon to Fri, 0900 to 1700
Other restrictions: Researchers by prior appointment.
Access to building, collections or gallery: No prior appointment required
Hours: Tue to Sat, 1000 to 1700
Other restrictions: free to local residents and under 18's, others £2 admission (£1 concessions).
Prior appointments required for access to reserve collection and to library and collections for research.
Access for disabled people: ramped entry
Other restrictions: Ground floor access only (c.40% of total display area). Some displays and information at wheelchair height.

General description:
Museum is housed in a complex of timber-framed houses which have associations with the protestant martyr, Bishop Hooper. It chronicles the lives of ordinary people. Trades and occupations are demonstrated through tools and reconstructed workshops and rooms. Collections cover the social history, crafts, trades and industries of the City and County of Gloucester from c.1500 to the present. Enquiries are welcome on any aspect of the collections or buildings, the latter including Grade II* Tudor and Jacobean timber-framed buildings. Subjects on display include Victorian classroom; pin-making; agriculture; dairy farming; siege of Gloucester; childhood and toys' gallery; glass, pewter and ceramics; treen; Gloucestershire folklore; domestic life - cooking, washing and ironing; horn industry; ironmonger's shop; wheelwright and carpenter workshops. Regular temporary special exhibitions display special collections using themes such as Severn Fisheries, Bishop Hooper, the 1643 Siege of Gloucester and pin-making (the building houses an 18th century pin factory). New 'Portal' gallery with interactive computer quizzes and information.
Information services:
Library available for reference (for conditions see Access above)
Help given to any local history enquiries, school projects, loans or other educational services required.
Special activities for schools includes a session in the Victorian schoolroom, to give a taste of Victorian education.
Special visitor services: Guided tours, tape recorded guides, materials and/or activities for children.
Education services: Group education facilities, resources for Key Stages 1 and 2, 3, 4 and Further or Higher Education.
Services for disabled people: Displays and/or information at wheelchair height.
Catalogues:
Catalogue for all of the collections is available in-house and part is on-line.
Publications list:
is available on-line.
Printed publications:
Various exhibition catalogues, information sheets, pamphlets, quiz sheets, bibliographies, colouring book, postcards (to purchase)
Many titles from the range of Shire Albums: Gloucester in Old Photographs (Voyce Jill, £5.95)
Many local history and museum-related books available from the shop

Internet home pages:
http://www.mylife.gloucester.gov.uk/Folk%20Museum/folk.htm
Folk Museum website, objects, images and information about the collections via onsite computers.
http://www.livinggloucester.co.uk
Dedicated Museum website as part of the 'Living Gloucester' project.
http://www.gloucester.gov.uk/libraries/templates/page.asp?URN=929

1091
GLOUCESTERSHIRE COUNTY LIBRARY, ARTS AND MUSEUMS SERVICE
Quayside House, Shire Hall, Gloucester, GL1 2HY

Tel: 01452 425020
Minicom no. 01452 426973
Fax: 01452 452042
Email: clams@gloscc.gov.uk

Organisation type and purpose: Local government body, public library.
Library headquarters, there are 39 libraries in the County.
Parent body:
Gloucestershire County Council
Other sites:
39 libraries
Strategic libraries at:
Cheltenham, Cinderford, Cirencester, Gloucester, Stroud and Tewkesbury

Enquiries to: Information Officer
Direct tel: 01452 425027
Direct email: pgaw@gloscc.gov.uk
Other contacts: Senior Librarian Information Services for Assistant.
Access:
Access to staff: By letter, by telephone, by fax, by email, Internet web pages
Hours: Mon to Fri, 0900 to 1700

General description:
General reference, business information, Gloucestershire local studies, Gloucestershire arts and crafts.
Information services:
Library available for reference (for conditions see Access above), on-line searching, CD-ROM based services
Can direct public to most appropriate library within County. Nearest is Gloucester library which holds a European and official publications collection.

Special visitor services: Materials and/or activities for children.
Services for disabled people: For the visually impaired; for the hearing impaired.
Collections:
Art Collection
Arts - Cheltenham
Burchall English Civil War Collection
Business Information - Cheltenham
European Public Information Centre - Gloucester
Gloucester Collection (Historical)
Hitchings Collection of Bibles
Local Studies - Gloucester
Official Publications - Gloucester
Catalogues:
Catalogue for all of the collections is on-line.

Internet home pages:
http://www.gloscc.gov.uk
GlosNet: community information, local government, public services, tourism, business etc.
http://www.gloscc.gov.uk/locate
http://www.findabook.gloscc.gov.uk
http://www.gloscc.gov.uk/pubserv/gcc/clamx/index.htm

1092
GLOUCESTERSHIRE WARWICKSHIRE STEAM RAILWAY

The Railway Station, Toddington, Gloucestershire, GL54 5DT

Tel: 01242 621405
Acronym or abbreviation: GWSRPLC
Formed: 1981

Organisation type and purpose: Voluntary organisation.
Heritage steam railway.
Associated membership body:
Gloucestershire Warwickshire Railway Limited by guarantee (GWRL)

Enquiries to: Company Secretary
Access:
Access to staff: By letter
Hours: Summer only: Mon to Fri, 0900 to 1700; All year: Sat and Sun, 1045 to 1730

General description:
Heritage railway operation; heritage railway construction; heritage steam locomotive maintenance and operation; heritage diesel locomotive restoration, maintenance and operation.
Publications list:
is available in hard copy and online.
Printed publications:
Guide books, local walking books etc (at varying prices)
Timetable (free)
Electronic and video products:
Videos of operations through the tracks (price on application)

Address for ordering publications:
Printed publications:
Shop Manager

Internet home pages:
http://www.gwsr.plc.uk

1093
GLYNN VIVIAN ART GALLERY

Alexandra Road, Swansea, West Glamorgan, SA1 5DZ

Tel: 01792 655006 or 651738
Fax: 01792 651738
Email: glynn.vivian.gallery@swansea.gov.uk

Organisation type and purpose: Local government body, art gallery.

Enquiries to: Curator
Access:
Access to staff: By letter, by telephone, by email
Access for disabled people: ramped entry

General description:
Based on original Richard Glynn Vivian art collection, the Gallery features 20th century works by Welsh artists including Augustus and Gwen John, Ceri Richards, etc.; Swansea pottery and porcelain; Oriental and European ceramics; glass; and clocks. The Vivian Collection includes French and Italian art, e.g. by Gustave Doré; fine arts - paintings, sculpture, prints, drawings; decorative arts - ceramics; glass (including paperweights); clocks; and Toby Jugs.
Collections:
Swansea and Nantgarw pottery and porcelain
Glass paperweights
Toby Jugs
Deffett Francis works
Fine art by Gustave Doré.

1094
GNOME RESERVE, WILD FLOWER GARDEN & PIXIE KILN

West Putford, Nr Bradworthy, Holsworthy, Devon, EX22 7XE

Tel: 01409 241435
Fax: 01409 241435
Email: info@gnomereserve.co.uk
Formed: 1979

Organisation type and purpose: Independently owned.

Enquiries to: Manager
Access:
Access to staff: By letter, by telephone, by email, in person, Internet web pages
Access for disabled people: Parking provided, toilet facilities

General description:
Contains c. 1000 gnomes living in an idyllic $1\frac{1}{2}$ acre beechwood with a stream, and a 2 acre wild flower garden. There are also c. 250 labelled species of wild flowers, herbs, grasses and ferns. Concrete/hand-painted garden gnomes made on site and kiln-fired, individually modelled indoor pottery pixies.
Collections:
Indoor collection of rare gnomes surviving from Victorian times to the 1940s period, made in pottery and metal. 60 plus.

Internet home pages:
http://www.gnomereserve.co.uk

1095
GODALMING MUSEUM

109A High Street, Godalming, Surrey, GU7 1AQ

Tel: 01483 426510
Fax: 01483 523495
Email: museum@godalming.ndo.co.uk
Formed: 1923

Organisation type and purpose: Independently owned, registered charity (charity number 292155), museum, historic building, house or site, suitable for ages: all ages.
Local studies library.
To promote the enjoyment and understanding of the heritage of the town and its surrounding villages, and to encourage and support life-long learning, by collecting, safeguarding and making accessible, local artefacts and knowledge within a welcoming, stimulating and inclusive environment.

Enquiries to: Curator
Access:
Access to staff: By letter, by telephone, by fax, by email, in person
Access for disabled people: ramped entry
Other restrictions: Wheelchair access to ground floor, headphones, portable induction loop and transcript available for interactive computers, parking for orange badge holders on High Street.

General description:
The geology, archaeology and history of Godalming and the surround villages, including the life and work of local characters such as Gertrude Jekyll, Sir Edwin Lutyens, Jack Phillips (wireless operator on the Titanic) and General Oglethorpe (founder of Georgia).
Information services:
Library available for reference (for conditions see Access above)
Interactive touch screens for history of Godalming and Gertrude Jekyll.
Special visitor services: Materials and/or activities for children.
Education services: Group education facilities, resources for Key Stages 1 and 2, 3, 4 and Further or Higher Education.
Services for disabled people: For the hearing impaired; displays and/or information at wheelchair height.
Collections:
Geology, archaeology and local history items relating to Godalming and the surrounding villages
The archaeology collections include mesolithic flints from field walking in the local area, material from Binscombe Roman villa, and site archives from recent excavations in Godalming (finds from Anglo-Saxon to modern periods)
Local history material includes local studies library and archive collections including:
Items relating to Gertrude Jekyll include sketches and watercolour and oil paintings by her, her planting notebooks, personal memorabilia and the Godalming women's suffrage banner designed by her, also Helen Allingham's painting of the South Border at Munstead Wood
Items relating to local industries and trades, especially the wool trade and framework knitting in the 18th to 20th centuries, also clocks by Stedman, Stephens and Edwards, items representing the rural economy include locally made tools and a black 19th century smock, brackets and wiring from the world's first public electricity suply (Godalming 1881)
Items relating to childhood include an 18th century child's shoe, found in the rafters of a house in Hascombe and a plate commemorating a baptism and dated 1807 (the latest date recorded on a piece of English delftware)
The Percy Woods Collection - a massive collection of transcripts and original research relating to the Godalming Hundred, compiled by Percy Woods (1842-1922) indexed by person and place name - an excellent resource for family historians
Wartime memorabilia includes a loin cloth worn by a prisoner in a Japanese camp in WWII, it is signed by the other POWs and by some of the Japanese guards
Catalogues:
Catalogue for library is in-house only. Catalogue for all of the collections is only available in-house.
Publications list:
is available in hard copy.
Printed publications:
Gertrude Jekyll and Sir Edwin Lutyens - a local introduction to their lives and work (Coombs D, 1999, £1.50)
Westbrook and the Oglethorpes (Dedman S C, 1990, revised ed. 75p)
Planting Design for the Museum Garden (Edwards M and F, 1990, 75p)

Internet home pages:
http://www.godalming-museum.org.uk
General information about the museum, information about Gertrude Jekyll, Edwin Lutyens and Jack Phillips (Titanic).

1096
GODOLPHIN ESTATE, THE

Lizard Countryside Office, Helston, Cornwall

Tel: 01326 561407 (Lizard Countryside Office)
Fax: 01326 562882
Email: godolphin@nationaltrust.org.uk

continued overleaf

Organisation type and purpose: Independently owned, historic building, house or site, suitable for ages: .
Parent body:
The National Trust (South West Region)
Devon and Cornwall Regional Office, tel: 01392 881691

Enquiries to: Manager
Access:
Access to staff: By letter, by telephone, by fax, by email

General description:
The National Trust acquired this ancient estate of 222ha (555 acres) in 2000; improvements to public access have been, and continue to be, made. The historic landscape includes Godolphin Hill, from which there are wonderful views over west Cornwall, and more than 400 recorded archaeological features ranging from Bronze Age enclosures to dramatic 19th century mine buildings.

Internet home pages:
http://www.nationaltrust.org.uk/regions/cornwall

1097
GOLDEN HIND MUSEUM SHIP
Inner Harbour, Brixham, Devon, TQ5 8AW

Tel: 01803 856223
Email: postmaster@goldenhind.co.uk
Formed: 1965

Organisation type and purpose: Museum.

Enquiries to: Curator
Access:
Access to staff: By letter, by telephone, in person
Hours: Mar to Oct; daily, 0900 to 1700
Jul and Aug; 0900 to 2200

General description:
The Golden Hind ship, life at sea in the 16th century. A full-size seagoing replica of Sir Francis Drake's famous ship in which he circumnavigated the world, 1577-1580, and on which he was knighted on board by Queen Elizabeth I. There are historical displays throughout the ship.
Publications list:
is available on-line.

Internet home pages:
http://www.goldenhind.co.uk

1098
GOLDEN HINDE, THE
St Mary Overie Dock, Cathedral Street, London, SE1 9DE

Tel: 08700 11 8700
Fax: 020 7407 5908
Email: info@goldenhinde.co.uk
Formed: 1984

Organisation type and purpose: Independently owned, museum, historic building, house or site, suitable for ages: 5+.
Travelling educational museum/memorial to Drake, 1973 to 1996.
The Golden Hinde is not a collection-based museum. It is a working replica of the original 16th century Galleon. It is now a stationary educational and activity museum.
To provide a range of educational and enjoyable activities and events for adults and children.

Enquiries to: Manager
Direct tel: 020 7403 0123
Direct email: catherine@goldenhinde.co.uk
Other contacts: Director/Owner
Access:
Access to staff: By letter, by telephone, by fax, by email, Internet web pages
Hours: Mon to Fri, 0930 to 1730
Access to building, collections or gallery: No prior appointment required
Hours: Winter: daily 0930 to 1700
Summer: Occasionally hired out for private functions - advisable to ring before visiting.
Other restrictions: Telephone for opening hours to library.

General description:
The reconstruction of Sir Francis Drake's 16th century galleon. This ship has a colourful history of her own, with a circumnavigation and over 200,000 kilometres under sail. Visitors can explore 5 levels of decks, including the 14 cannon gun deck, giving them the opportunity to experience life aboard an Elizabethan ship.
Information services:
Special visitor services: Guided tours, materials and/or activities for children.
Education services: Group education facilities, resources for Key Stages 1 and 2 and 3..
Printed publications:
Brochures of ship
Children's colouring book and story
Guide Book

Internet home pages:
http://www.goldenhinde.co.uk
All museum programmes and activities.

1099
GOODRICH CASTLE
Goodrich, Ross-on-Wye, Herefordshire, HR9 6HY

Tel: 01600 890538

Organisation type and purpose: National organisation, historic building, house or site.
Parent body:
English Heritage (West Midlands Region)
Tel: 0121 625 6820

Enquiries to: Manager
Access:
Access to staff: By letter, by telephone
Access to building, collections or gallery: No prior appointment required
Hours: 29 Mar to 30 Sep: daily, 1000 to 1800,1 to 31 Oct: daily, 1000 to 1700,1 Nov to 28 Mar: Wed to Sun, 1000 to 1300 and 1400 to 1600
Other restrictions: Closed 24 to 26 Dec and 1 Jan.
Opening times are subject to change, for up-to-date information contact English Heritage by phone or visit the website.

General description:
One of the most complete medieval castles in Britain, this fortress stands majestically on a sandstone crag with exhilarating views over the River Wye. Visitors can explore its 12th century keep, chapel and a maze of small rooms and passageways, and peer through its defensive 'murder-holes'. The castle was besieged during the Civil War, and was a tourist attraction as long ago as the 17th century, after its ruination by Parliamentarian forces.
Information services:
Special visitor services: Tape recorded guides..

Internet home pages:
http://www.english-heritage.org.uk

1100
GOODWOOD HOUSE
Goodwood, Chichester, West Sussex, PO18 0PX

Tel: 01243 755000
Fax: 01243 755005
Email: curator@goodwood.co.uk

Organisation type and purpose: Historic building, house or site, suitable for ages: 5+.

Enquiries to: Curatorial Assistant
Other contacts: House Sales Manager for bookings, arranging corporate events and weddings in the house.
Access:
Access to staff: By letter, by telephone, by fax, by email, Internet web pages
Hours: Mon to Thu, 0900 to 1730
Access to building, collections or gallery: Prior appointment required
Hours: 1 April to 30 September, most Sunday and Monday afternoons
August, Sun to Thu
Access for disabled people: Parking provided, ramped entry, access to all public areas, toilet facilities

General description:
History of Goodwood House, history of the Dukes of Richmond who first came to Goodwood House in 1697; Regency architecture.
Information services:
Special visitor services: Guided tours.
Education services: Group education facilities, resources for Key Stages 1 and 2, 3, 4 and Further or Higher Education..
Collections:
Goodwood Collection amassed by the Dukes of Richmond from early 18th century to the present day. Consists of 18th century French porcelain, tapestries and furniture
Paintings, including works by Canaletto, Stubbs, Van Dyke and Reynolds
18th century British sporting art
17th and 18th century British portraiture
Printed publications:
Goodwood House Guidebook

Internet home pages:
http://www.goodwood.co.uk

1101
GOOLE MUSEUM
Carlisle Street, Goole, East Yorkshire, DN14 5DB

Tel: 01405 768963
Fax: 01482 392782
Email: janet.tierney@eastriding.gov.uk
Formed: 1968

Organisation type and purpose: Museum, art gallery.
Parent body:
East Riding of Yorkshire Museum Service
The Chapel, 10 Lord Roberts Road, Beverley, HU17 9BG, tel: 01482 329770, fax: 01482 392779
Correspondence address:
Goole Museum
ERYC Offices, Church Street, Goole, Yorkshire, DN14 5BG, tel: 01482 392777, fax: 01483 392782, email/website: janet.tierney@eastriding.gov.uk

Enquiries to: Curator
Access:
Access to staff: By letter, by telephone, by fax, by email, in person, visitors by prior appointment
Hours: Mon to Fri, 0900 to 1730
Access to building, collections or gallery: No prior appointment required
Hours: Mon, 1400 to 1700; Tue to Fri, 1000 to 1700; Sat, 0900 to 1300
Other restrictions: Closed all public holidays and 25 Dec to 1 Jan.
Access for disabled people: level entry, toilet facilities
Other restrictions: Lift to 1st Floor.

General description:
Maritime paintings, social history, photography, maritime history, local history, illustrating the formation and development of Goole as a town and as an inland port.
Information services:
Special visitor services: Materials and/or activities for children.
Education services: Group education facilities, resources for Key Stages 1 and 2 and 3.
Services for disabled people: Displays and/or information at wheelchair height.
Collections:
Maritime paintings by the Goole-born artist Reuben Chappell, (1870-1940)
Garside Collection (photographs, documents, general local history)
Shand Collection (social history)
Catalogues:
Catalogue for all of the collections is only available in-house.
Printed publications:
Information sheets (general social history topics, free)

Photographs from extensive local maritime collection (copy for private study, if for commercial use by arrangement only)

Address for ordering publications:
Printed publications:
Curator, Goole Museum
ERYC Offices, Church Street, Goole, DN14 5BG, tel: 01482 392777, fax: 01482 392782, email: janet.tierney@eastriding.gov.uk

1102
GORDON HIGHLANDERS MUSEUM, THE

St Luke's, Viewfield Road, Aberdeen, AB15 7XH

Tel: 01224 311200
Fax: 01224 319323
Email: museum@gordonhighlanders.com
Formed: 1997

Organisation type and purpose: Independently owned, registered charity (charity number SCO 22039), museum, suitable for ages: 5+.

Enquiries to: Curator
Direct email: curator@gordonhighlanders.com
Access:
Access to staff: By letter, by telephone, by fax, by email, visitors by prior appointment, Internet web pages
Other restrictions: Charge made for research.
Access to building, collections or gallery: No prior appointment required
Hours: Apr to Oct, Tue to Sat, 1030 to 1630; Sun, 1330 to 1630
Other restrictions: By appointment only from Nov to Mar.
Access for disabled people: Parking provided, ramped entry, toilet facilities

General description:
Gordon Highlanders' history and records.
Information services:
Library available for reference (for conditions see Access above)
Special visitor services: Materials and/or activities for children.
Education services: Group education facilities, resources for Key Stages 1 and 2, 3 and 4.
Services for disabled people: For the visually impaired; for the hearing impaired; displays and/or information at wheelchair height.
Catalogues:
Catalogue for all of the collections is only available in-house.

Internet home pages:
http://www.gordonhighlanders.com

1103
GOSPORT MUSEUM

Walpole Road, Gosport, Hampshire, PO12 1NS

Tel: 023 9258 8035
Fax: 023 9250 1951
Email: musmie@hants.gov.uk
Formed: 1975

Organisation type and purpose: Local government body, museum.
Parent body:
Hampshire County Council Museums Service
Chilcomb House, Winchester, SO23 8RD, tel: 01962 846304, fax: 01962 869836

Enquiries to: Curator
Access:
Access to staff: By letter, by telephone, by fax, by email, in person, visitors by prior appointment, Internet web pages
Access to building, collections or gallery: No prior appointment required
Hours: Tue to Sat, 1000 to 1700
Access for disabled people: ramped entry, level entry, access to all public areas
Other restrictions: Audio guide for visually impaired

General description:
The story of Gosport from prehistoric times to the present day, local history, archaeology, natural science and geology.
Information services:
Services for disabled people: For the visually impaired.
Catalogues:
Catalogue for all of the collections is on-line.
Publications list:
is available in hard copy.
Printed publications:
Publications list available from the Librarian at Hampshire County Council Museums Service Headquarters, Chilcomb House, Winchester, SO23 8RD

Address for ordering publications:
Printed publications:
Registrar, Hampshire County Council Museums Service HQ

Internet home pages:
http://www.hants.gov.uk/museums/
HMCMS web catalogue, whole collection, 100,000 plus web pages.
http://www.hants.gov.uk/museum/gosport
Museum website

1104
GOVERNMENT ART COLLECTION

Information Centre, Department for Culture, Media and Sport, 2-4 Cockspur Street, London, SW1Y 5DH

Tel: 020 7211 6200
Fax: 020 7211 6032
Email: enquiries@culture.gov.uk
Acronym or abbreviation: GAC
Formed: 1898

Organisation type and purpose: National government body.
Working collection.
Display of works of art in major government buildings in the UK and abroad.
Division of the:
Department for Culture, Media and Sport (DCMS)

Enquiries to: Administrator
Access:
Access to staff: By letter
Access to building, collections or gallery: No prior appointment required

General description:
Works of art owned or administered by the Government Art Collection. Various paintings, prints and drawings, sculpture and tapestries, by British artists from the 16th century to the present day.
Collections:
Works of British Art dating from 16th century to present day
Works by WWII artists, 1939-1945
Works commissioned to commemorate the Coronation of Elizabeth II, 1953
Catalogues:
Catalogue for all of the collections is only available in-house but part is published.
Printed publications:
Published material on the Government Art Collection
Catalogues of works of art on loan to Embassies:
The British Embassy, Bonn (1991)
The British Embassy, Paris (1993)
Works of Art in the British Embassy, Tel Aviv (1998)
General:
The Twentieth Century, A Summary Catalogue (1997)
Report on Acquisitions (published every year since 1976-77)

1105
GOWER HERITAGE CENTRE

Y Felin Ddwr, Parkmill, Gower, Swansea, West Glamorgan, SA3 2Eh

Tel: 01792 371206
Fax: 01792 371206
Email: info@gowerheritagecentre.sagehost.co.uk
Formed: 1990

Organisation type and purpose: Registered charity (charity number 1054567), historic building, house or site, suitable for ages: 5+.

Enquiries to: Manager
Direct fax: 01792 371471
Access:
Access to staff: By letter, by telephone, by fax, by email, in person, Internet web pages
Hours: Nov to Mar: daily, 1000 to 1600
Apr to Oct: daily, 1000 to 1730
Access to building, collections or gallery: No prior appointment required
Hours: Nov to Mar: daily, 1000 to 1600
Apr to Oct: daily, 1000 to 1730
Access for disabled people: Parking provided, level entry, access to all public areas, toilet facilities

General description:
The Gower Heritage Centre is situated in the village of Parkmill, set in the beautiful Gower Peninsula, 8 miles West of Swansea in South Wales. In 1956 the Gower Peninsula was designated the UK's first area of outstanding natural beauty. The Heritage Centre is based around a 12th century Water-Powered Cornmill. The Centre also has a number of craft workshops, large tea-rooms and all facilities for an enjoyable family day out, and we provide a specialised guided tour service for all types of groups. The average tour takes about 2 hours, and visitors can see the cornmill working, together with workshops in action, and enjoy a walk along the river which supplies water to the Mill. There is a farming museum.
Crafts people working at the centre include artisans, a potter, blacksmith, jeweller, wheelright, mason, fret sawyer and traditional carpenter. There is also a puppet workshop and theatre.
Information services:
Special visitor services: Guided tours, materials and/or activities for children.
Education services: Group education facilities..
Collections:
Millstones, 1600-1700

Internet home pages:
http://www.gowerheritagecentre.co.uk

1106
GRACE DARLING MEMORIAL MUSEUM

1 Radcliffe Road, Bamburgh, Northumberland, NE69 7AE

Tel: 01668 214465
Fax: 01668 214465
Formed: 1938

Organisation type and purpose: Voluntary organisation, registered charity, museum, suitable for ages: 8+.
Administered by:
Royal National Lifeboat Institution

Enquiries to: Honorary Curator
Access:
Access to staff: By fax
Hours: Mon to Sat, 1000 to 1700; Sun, 1200 to 1700

General description:
The museum commemorates the rescue by Grace Darling and her father of 9 survivors of the S. S. Forfarshire which was wrecked off the Faroe Islands on 7.9.1838 - a rescue which made her a national heroine.
Information services:
Education services: Resources for Key Stages 2 and 3..

continued overleaf

Collections:
Papers and relics relating to her life
Several personal letters to and from Grace and her father
Original coble on which the rescue was made
Original oils, watercolours, etc. by distinguished artists of the wreck and the rescue
Artefacts from SS Forfarshire, flag, china, cutlery, etc
William Darling's manuscript report and log book recording the rescue
Replicas of medals presented to Grace
Printed publications:
Grace Darling and the Story of the Rescue
Leaflet on the museum (free)
Grace Darling - A colouring book to keep (for young children and National Curriculum Key Stage 1 and 2)
Electronic and video products:
Tape for purchase direct from Museum

1107
GRACEFIELD ARTS CENTRE
28 Edinburgh Road, Dumfries, DG1 1JQ

Tel: 01387 262084
Fax: 01387 255173
Formed: 1951

Organisation type and purpose: Local government body, art gallery.
Parent body:
Dumfries & Galloway Council
Community Resources (DGC)
118 English Street, Dumfries, tel: 01387 260070

Enquiries to: Curator
Access:
Access to staff: By letter, by telephone, by fax
Access for disabled people: Parking provided, ramped entry, level entry, toilet facilities
Other restrictions: First floor of one building inaccessible.

General description:
Art and craft exhibitions, events and activities. Work from local, national and international artists and makers exhibited in the galleries and studios, exhibition spaces throughout the year.
Information services:
Helpline available, tel no: 01387 262084.
Special visitor services: Materials and/or activities for children..
Collections:
Collection of mainly Scottish fine art dating from the 1840s to the present day, shown in selected exhibitions 3 to 4 times throughout the year
Work by the 'Glasgow Boys', the Scottish Colourists and contemporary Glasgow artists, 1890 to present

Internet home pages:
http://www.artsandcraftssouthwestscotland.com
http://www.dumgal.gov.uk

1108
GRAMPIAN TRANSPORT MUSEUM
Main Street, Alford, Aberdeenshire, AB33 8AE

Tel: 019755 62292
Fax: 019755 62180
Email: info@gtm.org.uk
Acronym or abbreviation: GTM
Formed: 1983

Organisation type and purpose: Membership association (membership is by subscription), present number of members: 350, registered charity (charity number SCO 17625), museum, suitable for ages: 3+.

Enquiries to: Curator
Access:
Access to staff: By letter, by telephone, by fax, by email, charges to non-members, Internet web pages
Hours: Museum Office: 31 Mar to 31 Oct: daily, 1000 to 1700,1 Nov to 30 Mar: Mon to Fri, 0900 to 1700 visitors by prior appointment
Access to building, collections or gallery: No prior appointment required
Hours: 31 Mar to 31 Oct: daily, 1000 to 1700
Museum closed Nov to Mar inclusive
Other restrictions: Prior appointment required for access to reference library.
Access for disabled people: Parking provided, level entry, access to all public areas, toilet facilities
Other restrictions: No access to small balcony area.

General description:
The Grampian Transport Museum houses an extensive collection of vintage, classic and modern vehicles which include cycles, cars, motorcycles, horse-drawn, steam, commercial and military. Many have strong local associations. Constantly changing displays and climb aboard and working exhibits. Railway exhibition in Alford's reconstructed railway station.
Information services:
Library available for reference (for conditions see Access above)
Guided tours for school groups.
Special visitor services: Guided tours, materials and/or activities for children.
Education services: Group education facilities, resources for Key Stages 1 and 2, 3 and 4.
Services for disabled people: Displays and/or information at wheelchair height.
Collections:
Collection of approximately 100 road vehicles and transport-related items and exhibits, many with a North East of Scotland connection
Small railway items displayed in the Railway Museum Station
Craigievar Express, 1895 steam tricyclecar built by local postman, vehicle and supporting material
Cruden Bay Tram, one of only two trams built to service Cruden Bay Hotel, 1899, vehicle and supporting material.
Catalogues:
Catalogue for library is in-house only. Catalogue for all of the collections is only available in-house but part is published.

Internet home pages:
http://www.gtm.org.uk

1109
GRANGE MUSEUM OF COMMUNITY HISTORY
Neasden Lane, London, NW10 1QB

Tel: 020 8452 8311
Fax: 020 8208 4233
Email: grangemuseum@brent.gov.uk
Formed: 1977

Organisation type and purpose: Local government body, museum, suitable for ages: all ages.

Enquiries to: Curator
Other contacts: Education and Lifelong Learning Officer for school service, adult learners, holiday activities.
Access:
Access for disabled people: level entry
Other restrictions: Parking available, no lift to first floor.

General description:
Fascinating local community history museum - an oasis on the busy Neasden roundabout.
Brent People Gallery: Brent's diverse history is brought to life through photographs, objects and spoken memories from the 1920s to the present day.
Permanent Displays: Include a Victorian parlour room, an Edwardian draper's shop from Willesden High Road, and furniture, paintings, ceramics and household objects from 1700 to the 1950s.
Collections:
Social history collections 1700 to 1990s
British Empire Exhibition material (1924-25)
Edwardian Draper's Shop
Victorian Parlour Room
Paintings, ceramics, furniture, household objects
Catalogues:
Catalogue for part of the collections is only available in-house.

Internet home pages:
http://www.brent.gov.uk/grangemuseum
Access details, collection and exhibition details.

1110
GRANGEMOUTH MUSEUM
Bo'ness Road, Grangemouth, Stirlingshire

Tel: 01324 504699
Formerly: Falkirk District Museums, date of change, 1996

Organisation type and purpose: Local government body, museum.
Parent body:
Falkirk Council
Falkirk Museums
Address for all correspondence:
Falkirk Museums
Callendar House, Callendar Park, Falkirk, FK1 1YR

Enquiries to: Assistant Museums Manager
Direct tel: 01324 503770
Direct fax: 01324 503771
Direct email: callendar.house@falkirk.gov.uk
Other contacts: Museum Attendant for staff on site.
Access:
Access to staff: By letter, by telephone, by fax, by email, in person
Hours: Mon to Sat, 1230 to 1700
Access to building, collections or gallery: No prior appointment required
Hours: Mon to Sat, 1230 to 1700
Closed public holidays
Other restrictions: No appointment required for access to library.

General description:
Displays relating to formation of Grangemouth as Victorian town to present day as petrochemical centre and port.

1111
GRANGEMOUTH MUSEUM STORES AND WORKSHOP (FALKIRK DISTRICT MUSEUMS)
7-11 Abbotsinch Road, Abbotsinch Industrial Estate, Grangemouth, Stirlingshire, FK3 9UX

Tel: 01324 471853
Access:
Access to building, collections or gallery: Prior appointment required
Other restrictions: Appointments should be made through Falkirk Museums, Callendar House, tel: 01324 503770

General description:
Contains material relating primarily to local social and industrial history, especially ironfounding and engineering. Also significant natural history; local pottery; costume; and hand tool collections. The museum also runs Callendar House (working 19th century kitchen and exhibitions); Grangemouth Museum (local history); and Kinneil Museum (natural and local history).
Collections:
Carron Collection, foundry patterns and products, 19/20th century, c. 1000 items
Hand tools, wide variety of trades eg. decorating, moulding, carpentry, musical instrument making, coopering, etc, 19/20th century, c. 10,000 items

1112
GRANT MUSEUM OF ZOOLOGY AND COMPARATIVE ANATOMY

Biology Department, Darwin Building, University College London, Gower Street, London, WC1E 6BT

Tel: 020 7679 2647
Fax: 020 7679 7096
Email: zoology.museum@ucl.ac.uk
Acronym or abbreviation: GMZ, UCL
Formed: 1828
Formerly: Museum of Zoology and Comparative Anatomy, date of change, 1996

Organisation type and purpose: Museum, university department or institute.

Enquiries to: Curator
Access:
Access to staff: By letter, by telephone, by fax, by email, in person, visitors by prior appointment, Internet web pages
Access for disabled people: ramped entry, toilet facilities

General description:
An historic natural history collection dating to the 1820s. The collection covers the whole of the animal kingdom, and includes examples of rare and extinct animals such as the Quagga (an extinct species of Zebra), Marsupial Wolf or Thylacine, and Dodo remains. The collection retains an air of the avid Victorian Collectors and can be enjoyed and used by all (researchers, students of all ages and the general public).
Information services:
Catalogue for the collections in-house only, and online via web planned for the future.
Service of tape recorded guides for the visually impaired planned for the future.
Special visitor services: Guided tours, tape recorded guides, materials and/or activities for children.
Education services: Group education facilities, resources for Key Stages 2, 3, 4 and Further or Higher Education.
Services for disabled people: For the visually impaired.
Collections:
Biological material - animal skeletons, specimens preserved in fluid, taxidermy specimens, dried material
Microscope slide collection
Archive: books, documents, photographs relating to the history of the collection
Robert E Grant. Sponges, fossils, etc. 1820-1874
E Ray Lankester. Arthropods, etc.1880-1890
Chalmers Mitchell. Birds, 1920-1930
J P Hill. Marsupials, 1906-1921
D M S Watson. Fossil and coal bark slides, 1918-1954
T H Huxley. Vertebrate dissections, 1830-1850
Catalogues:
Catalogue for library is in-house only. Catalogue for all of the collections is only available in-house.

Internet home pages:
http://collections.ucl.ac.uk/zoology

1113
GRANTHAM HOUSE

Castlegate, Grantham, Lincolnshire, NG31 6SS

Tel: 01909 486411 (Regional Office)

Organisation type and purpose: National organisation, registered charity (charity number 205846), historic building, house or site, suitable for ages: 8+.
Parent body:
National Trust (East Midlands Region)
East Midlands Regional Office, tel: 01909 486411

Enquiries to: Tenant
Access:
Access to staff: By letter only
Access to building, collections or gallery: Prior appointment required
Hours: April to Sep, Wed, 1400 to 1700, Gound floor only
Other restrictions: Admission by written appointment only with the tenant, Major-General Sir Brian Wyldbore-Smith
Not suitable for large groups.(max of seven in group)

General description:
Dating from 1380, the house has been extensively altered since then and presents an attractive mixture of styles. There are delightful walled gardens running down to the river.

Internet home pages:
http://www.nationaltrust.org.uk

1114
GRANTHAM MUSEUM

St Peter's Hill, Grantham, Lincolnshire, NG31 6PY

Tel: 01476 568783
Fax: 01476 592547
Email: grantham.museum@lincolnshire.gov.uk
Formed: 1926

Organisation type and purpose: Local government body, museum, suitable for ages: 5+.
Parent body:
Lincolnshire County Council

Enquiries to: Principal Keeper
Access:
Access to staff: By letter, by email
Hours: Mon to Sat, 1000 to 1700
Access to building, collections or gallery: No prior appointment required
Access for disabled people: ramped entry, access to all public areas
Other restrictions: Induction loop.

General description:
Collection covering the local history of the area from pre- historic times to the present day; ethnographical collections from Egypt, Africa and Oceania.
Collections:
Agriculture and industry
Grantham's Friendly Invasion (US IXth Troop Carrier Command); primarily photographs, oral histories, letters 1943-45, and interviews with local and US individuals
Archaeology
Dambusters
Isaac Newton
Margaret Thatcher, Lady Thatcher, Prime Minister 1979-1990.

1115
GRANTOWN MUSEUM & HERITAGE TRUST

Burnfield House, Burnfield Avenue, Grantown on Spey, Moray, PH26 3HH

Tel: 01479 872478
Fax: 01479 872478
Email: molly.duckett@btinternet.com
Formed: 1999

Organisation type and purpose: Museum.

Enquiries to: Curator
Access:
Access to staff: By letter, by telephone, by fax, by email, in person, visitors by prior appointment, Internet web pages
Hours: Mon to Fri, 0900 to 1700
Access to building, collections or gallery: No prior appointment required
Hours: Mar to Dec: Mon to Fri, 1000 to 1600
Access for disabled people: Parking provided, ramped entry, access to all public areas, toilet facilities

General description:
Local history, research facility, internet access. Material relevant to Strathspey and the history of the planned town of Grantown on Spey with emphasis on the River Spey, its wildlife and associated sports and industries such as fishing, golf and distilling.
Catalogues:
Catalogue for part of the collections is only available in-house.

Internet home pages:
http://www.grantown-on-spey.co.uk/museum.htm

1116
GRASSIC GIBBON CENTRE, THE

Arbuthnott, Laurencekirk, Kincardineshire, AB30 1PB

Tel: 01561 361668
Fax: 01561 361742
Email: lgginfo@grassicgibbon.com
Formed: 1992

Organisation type and purpose: Independently owned, registered charity (charity number ED 935/89/MEB), suitable for ages: 16+.
Community business, visitor centre.

Enquiries to: Manager
Access:
Access to staff: By letter, by telephone, by fax, by email
Access for disabled people: Parking provided, ramped entry, access to all public areas, toilet facilities

General description:
Scottish literature, heritage.
Information services:
Helpline available, tel no: 01561 361668.
Special visitor services: Guided tours.
Education services: Group education facilities.
Services for disabled people: For the visually impaired; displays and/or information at wheelchair height.
Collections:
Lewis Grassic Gibbon related collection
Arbuthnott Parish Church records
Catalogues:
Catalogue for library is in-house only. Catalogue for all of the collections is only available in-house.

Internet home pages:
http://www.grassicgibbon.com

1117
GRAVES ART GALLERY

Surrey Street, Sheffield, South Yorkshire, S1 1XZ

Tel: 0114 278 2600
Fax: 0114 278 2604
Email: info@sheffieldgalleries.org.uk
Formed: 1934

Organisation type and purpose: Local government body, registered charity (charity number 1068850), art gallery, suitable for ages: 5+.
Parent body:
Sheffield Galleries & Museums Trust

Enquiries to: Curator
Access:
Access to staff: By telephone, by fax
Hours: Tue to Sat, 1000 to 1700
Other restrictions: Limited disabled access.
Access for disabled people: toilet facilities
Other restrictions: Parking on Surrey Street, access by rear entrance.

General description:
Visual arts, especially British art.
Information services:
Programme of family activities
Adult workshops
Education programme
Special visitor services: Materials and/or activities for children.
Education services: Group education facilities..
Printed publications:
Exhibition Catalogues
Postcards and Greetings Cards

1118
GRAY'S PRINTING PRESS

49 Main Street, Strabane, Co Tyrone, BT82 8AU

Tel: 028 7188 4094

Organisation type and purpose: National organisation, registered charity (charity number 205846), museum, historic building, house or site, suitable for ages: 8+.

Parent body:

National Trust Office for Northern Ireland
Rowallane House, Saintfield, Ballynahinch, Co Down, BT24 7LH, tel: 020 9751 0721, fax: 028 9751 1242

Enquiries to: Manager

Access:

Access to staff: By letter, by telephone, by email, in person

Access to building, collections or gallery: No prior appointment required

Hours: Apr to Sep, Tue to Sat, 1400 to 1700

Other restrictions: Admission by guided tour. Closed Bank Holidays. Other times by arrangement

Access for disabled people: toilet facilities

Other restrictions: Ground floor fully accessible. Audiovisual display accessible.

General description:

Eighteenth century printing press and collection of 19th century hand printing machines; reputedly where John Dunlap, who printed the American Declaration of Independence, learned his trade.

Information services:

Audio guide.
Booked school visits welcome.

Special visitor services: Guided tours, tape recorded guides.

Services for disabled people: For the visually impaired.

Internet home pages:

http://www.nationaltrust.org.uk

1119
GREAT BARN MUSEUM

See - Barn Gallery

1120
GREAT CENTRAL RAILWAY (NOTTINGHAM) LTD

Nottingham Transport Heritage Centre, Mere Way, Ruddington, Nottingham, NG11 6NX

Tel: 0115 940 5705
Fax: 0115 940 5905

Acronym or abbreviation: GCR

Formed: 1990

Organisation type and purpose: Voluntary organisation.
The organisation runs the only steam railway in Nottinghamshire and also a transport heritage centre.

Home to:

Nottingham Society of Model Engineers (NSMEE)

Enquiries to: Information Officer

Access:

Access to staff: By letter, by telephone, by fax

Hours: Mon to Fri, 0900 to 1700

General description:

Steam and diesel locomotives, and GCR rolling stock, miniature railways run by the Nottingham Society of Model Engineers, public transport (buses) preservation and restoration. Six miles of track from Ruddington to Gotham Moor on the old GCR line with plans to extend by a further ten miles to Loughborough.

Printed publications:

Newsletter (quarterly, available on application £1 including postage)

1121
GREAT CHALFIELD MANOR

Melksham, Wiltshire, SN12 8NJ

Tel: 01225 782239
Fax: 01225 783379

Organisation type and purpose: National organisation, registered charity (charity number 205846), historic building, house or site.

Parent body:

The National Trust (South West Region)
Wessex Regional Office, tel: 01985 843600

National Trust sites:

Great Chalfield Manor
Melksham, Wiltshire, SN12 8NJ, tel: 01225 782239, fax: 01225 783379

Enquiries to: Manager

Access:

Access to staff: By letter, by telephone, by fax

Access for disabled people: toilet facilities

Other restrictions: Steps to entrance. Ground floor accessible with assistance. No access to other floors. There is limited access to the garden.

General description:

A charming manor house, enhanced by a moat and gatehouse and with beautiful oriel windows and a great hall. Completed in 1480, the manor and gardens were restored c.1905-11 by Major R. Fuller, whose family live here and manage the property. The garden, designed by Alfred Parsons to complement the manor, has been replanted.

Information services:

Special visitor services: Guided tours..

Internet home pages:

http://www.nationaltrust.org.uk/regions/wessex

1122
GREAT COXWELL BARN

Great Coxwell, Faringdon, Oxfordshire

Tel: 01793 762209 (Coleshill Estate Office)
Email: greatcoxwellbarn@nationaltrust.org.uk

Organisation type and purpose: National organisation, registered charity (charity number 205846), historic building, house or site, suitable for ages: all ages.

Parent body:

The National Trust (South & South East Region)
Thames & Solent Regional Office, tel: 01491 528051

Enquiries to: Property Manager
Direct tel: 01491 528051

Access:

Access to staff: By letter, by telephone, by email

Access to building, collections or gallery: No prior appointment required

Hours: Daily throughout the year, early to dusk

General description:

A 13th century monastic barn, stone-built with a stone-tiled roof and interesting timber structure.

Internet home pages:

http://www.nationaltrust.org.uk/regions/

1123
GREAT DUNMOW MALTINGS PRESERVATION TRUST LIMITED, THE

The Maltings, Mill Lane, Great Dunmow, Essex, CM6 1BG

Tel: 01371 878979

Acronym or abbreviation: The Great Dunmow Maltings

Formed: 1996

Organisation type and purpose: National organisation, registered charity (charity number 1057124), museum, historic building, house or site, suitable for ages: 16+.

Registered office:

Great Dunmow Maltings Preservation Trust Limited
46 Barnston Green, Barnston, Great Dunmow, CM6 1PH, tel: 01371 873958, fax: 01371 873958

Enquiries to: Chairman
Direct tel: 01371 873958
Direct fax: 01371 873958

Access:

Access to staff: By telephone, by fax

Access for disabled people: ramped entry, access to all public areas, toilet facilities

General description:

A rare example of a small, timber-framed maltings, the building is an authentic restoration from the early brewery trade. It has been dated as far back as 1565, but was known to be operational until 1948 when it was last used for traditional malt production by the local brewers, Randall, Gibbons, Ingold and Company. Now listed Grade II*.
The ground floor houses the town museum.

1124
GREAT HALL MUSEUM

Castle Avenue, Winchester, Hampshire, SO23 8US

Tel: 01962 846476
Fax: 01962 841326

Formed: 1984

Organisation type and purpose: Local government body, historic building, house or site, suitable for ages: 5+.

Enquiries to: Manager
Direct tel: 01962 846663
Other contacts: Senior Custodian for Manager who is in a distant office.

Access:

Access to staff: By letter, by telephone, by fax, in person, visitors by prior appointment

Access for disabled people: access to all public areas, toilet facilities, ramped entry, level entry

General description:

13th century medieval Great Hall, home to King Arthur's Round Table, gallery exhibition of castle history, replica herbarium - Queen Eleanor's Garden.

Information services:

Guided tours by pre-booking.

Special visitor services: Guided tours..

Collections:

Gallery of pictures and photographs
King Arthur's Round Table
Models of castle

Internet home pages:

http://www.hants.gov.uk/leisure/greathall

1125
GREAT ORME BRONZE AGE COPPER MINES

Great Orme, Llandudno, Gwynedd

Tel: 01492 870447
Fax: 01492 870447
Email: gomines@greatorme.freeserve.co.uk

Organisation type and purpose: Historic building, house or site, suitable for ages: 8+.

Enquiries to: Manager

Access:

Access to staff: By letter, by telephone, by fax, by email, Internet web pages

General description:

This is the oldest copper mine open to the public. In this mine, worked 4000 years ago, view the ancient passages, the prehistoric cavern and areas exposed by archaeological exploration during the past ten years.
The Visitor Centre, open to non-mine visitors, has displays of life during the Bronze Age.

Internet home pages:

http://www.greatorme.freeserve.co.uk

1126
GREAT ORME TRAMWAY, THE
Victoria Station, Church Walks, Llandudno, Gwynedd, LL30 1AZ

Tel: 01492 575275
Email: enq@greatormetramway.com

Organisation type and purpose: Suitable for ages: all ages.

Enquiries to: Manager
Access:
Access to staff: By letter, by telephone, by email, Internet web pages

General description:
The one hundred year old trammway is the only cable-hauled street tramway in Britain. It still uses the original Victorian carriages.
An historic Tramway exhibition is situated at the Halfway Station.

Internet home pages:
http://www.greatormetramway.com

1127
GREAT WESTERN RAILWAY MUSEUM
The Old Railway Station, Railway Drive, Coleford, Gloucestershire, GL16 8AZ

Tel: 01594 833569
Fax: 01594 832032 (office hours only)
Formed: 1988

Organisation type and purpose: Museum, suitable for ages: 8+, consultancy.
To preserve ex-GWR Goods Station of c. 1883 and signal box of 1906.
Other address:
Great Western Railway Museum
Curator, c/o 6 Grove Crescent, Coleford, Gloucestershire, GL16 8AZ, tel: 01594 832032, fax: 01594 832032

Enquiries to: Curator
Access:
Access to staff: By letter, by telephone, visitors by prior appointment
Access to building, collections or gallery: Prior appointment required
Hours: Sat, 1430 to 1700
Other restrictions: Groups by prior arrangement.

General description:
Severn & Wye Railway and GWR, local railways in the Royal Forest of Dean, Gloucestershire.
Information services:
Special visitor services: Guided tours..
Collections:
Severn & Wye Railway Company Limited
GWR local railways in the Forest of Dean, Gloucestershire
Printed publications:
Museum Guide and Map of FOD Railways 1917 (£1 plus p&p)

See also - Steam: Museum of the Great Western Railway

1128
GREAT WESTERN SOCIETY LIMITED
Didcot Railway Centre, Didcot, Oxfordshire, OX11 7NJ

Tel: 01235 817200
Fax: 01235 510621
Email: didrlyc@globalnet.co.uk
Acronym or abbreviation: GWS
Formed: 1961

Organisation type and purpose: Membership association (membership is by subscription), voluntary organisation, registered charity (charity number 272616), museum.
Affiliated to:
Heritage Railway Association
Transport Trust

Enquiries to: Secretary
Access:
Access to staff: By letter, by telephone, by email, Internet web pages
Hours: Mon to Fri, 0900 to 1700

General description:
Great Western Railway.
Catalogues:
Catalogue for part of the collections is published and part is on-line.
Printed publications:
Didcot Railway Centre Guidebook (irregular)
Great Western Echo (quarterly, to members)

Internet home pages:
http://www.didcotrailwaycentre.org.uk

1129
GREAT YARMOUTH MARITIME MUSEUM
See - Tower Curing Works Museum

1130
GREAT YARMOUTH MUSEUMS
Museum Office, Central Library, Tolhouse Street, Great Yarmouth, Norfolk, NR30 2SH

Tel: 01493 745526
Fax: 01493 745459
Email: yarmouth.museums@norfolk.gov.uk

Organisation type and purpose: Local government body, suitable for ages: all ages.
Great Yarmouth museums, site administration and information service, including dates, times of opening and special events.
Parent body:
Norfolk Museums & Archaeology Service

Enquiries to: Administrator
Other contacts: Chief Custodian
Access:
Access to staff: By letter, by telephone, by fax, by email, in person, visitors by prior appointment, Internet web pages

General description:
Administrative office for the museums and properties in the Great Yarmouth area which are under the control of Norfolk County Council.
Collections:
Collections are almost exclusively paintings and drawings. There are c. 200 oils; 400 watercolours/drawings; and 500 prints, mostly local interest
Broadland watercolours, C H Harrison, S J Batchelder, late 19th/early 20th century
Watercolours and oils by J C and W Joy, early 19th century
Oils by Norwich School artists, A Stanndard, G Vincent, R Ladbrooke
Oils and watercolours by Rowland Fisher RSMA

Internet home pages:
http://www.great-yarmouth.co.uk
http://www.norfolk.gov.uk/tourism/museums

See also - Elizabethan House Museum; Tolhouse Museum; Tower Curing Works Museum

1131
GREAT YARMOUTH POTTERIES AND HERRING SMOKING MUSEUM
Trinity Place/Blackfriar's Road, Great Yarmouth, Norfolk

Organisation type and purpose: Museum, art gallery, historic building, house or site, suitable for ages: all ages.

Enquiries to: Manager
Access:
Access to staff: By letter
Access to building, collections or gallery: No prior appointment required
Hours: Open throughout the year, Mon to Fri, 0915 to 1215 and 1315 to 1700; open all day in Summer
Other restrictions: Last admission 1615

General description:
Former Herring Curing Works and working pottery.

1132
GREAT YARMOUTH TOWN HALL
Town Hall, Great Yarmouth, Norfolk, NR30 2QF

Tel: 01493 856100
Fax: 01493 846332

Organisation type and purpose: Local government body, historic building, house or site, suitable for ages: all ages.
Access:
Access to staff: By letter, by telephone, by fax
Access to building, collections or gallery: Prior appointment required
Other restrictions: Group guided tours must be booked at the Town Hall Reception

General description:
A magnificent building opened by the Prince of Wales in 1882, epitomising the town's former wealth, and illustrating the status created by maritime industries.
Collections:
Borough civic plate

1133
GREATER MANCHESTER MUSEUM OF SCIENCE & INDUSTRY
See - Museum of Science and Industry

1134
GREEN HOWARDS MUSEUM
Trinity Church Square, Richmond, North Yorkshire, DL10 4QN

Tel: 01748 822133
Fax: 01748 826561
Formed: 1935

Organisation type and purpose: Registered charity, museum.
Regimental museum.
Member of:
Army Museum's Ogilby Trust
Association of Independent Museums
Museums Association
Yorkshire Tourist Board
Yorkshire, Humberside Museums Association

Enquiries to: Curator
Access:
Access to staff: By letter, by telephone, by fax, by email, visitors by prior appointment, charges to non-members
Hours: Mon to Fri, 0900 to 1700
Access to building, collections or gallery: No prior appointment required

General description:
Regimental history of the Green Howards (Alexandra Princess of Wales's Own Yorkshire Regiment) from its formation in 1688, told in three galleries and a separate medal room; uniforms, medals and militaria generally.
Collections:
4 items of regimental equipment from 1688
Archives from the early 18th century
VCs in special display
Catalogues:
Catalogue for library is in-house only. Catalogue for all of the collections is only available in-house.
Printed publications:
Museum Handbook
Museum leaflet
The History of the Green Howards (G S Powell, 1992, revised 2001)
Electronic and video products:
Video, CD-ROM and audio guides

1135
GREEN QUAY, THE
South Quay, King's Lynn, Norfolk, PE30 5DT

Tel: 01553 818500

Organisation type and purpose: Museum, historic building, house or site, suitable for ages: all ages.

Enquiries to: Curator
Access:
Access to building, collections or gallery: No prior appointment required
Hours: Apr to Sep, daily, 1000 to 1700; Oct to Mar, daily, 1000 to 1600

General description:
Housed in a 16th century warehouse, an interactive discovery centre about the Wash.

Internet home pages:
http://www.thegreenquay.co.uk

1136
GREENFIELD VALLEY HERITAGE PARK
Admin Centre, Basingwerk House, Greenfield, Holywell, Flintshire, CH8 7GH

Tel: 01352 714172
Email: info@greenfieldvalley.com

Organisation type and purpose: Independently owned, registered charity (charity number 518532), museum, historic building, house or site, suitable for ages: 5+.
Trust.
Parent body:
Clwyd County Museum Service
Member of:
Association of Independent Museums (AIM)
Council for Museums in Wales
Joint Area Museums Education Service (JAMES)

Enquiries to: Operations Manager
Other contacts: Company Secretary; Chair of Trustees
Access:
Access to staff: By letter, by telephone, by email, visitors by prior appointment
Access to building, collections or gallery: No prior appointment required
Hours: 23 Mar to 31 Oct: daily, 1000 to 1630
Other restrictions: Other times by prior appointment.
Access for disabled people: Parking provided

General description:
A collection of original and reconstructed local buildings, complementary display of agricultural equipment and implements. Victorian school with authentic furnishings. Seventy acre country park with woodlands, reservoirs and remains of industrial era in the Valley, including copper, brass, lead, tinplate, wire, textiles and paper industries. Fishing and bird-watching, woodland walks, farm animals and adventure playground.
Information services:
Special visitor services: Materials and/or activities for children.
Education services: Group education facilities, resources for Key Stages 1 and 2..
Collections:
17th and 19th century farmhouses reconstructed on site complete with period furnishings, utensils
Victorian schoolroom reconstructed on site complete with authentic furnishing, farming history exhibits
Working blacksmith's forge and steam driven bottling plant - contact Admin Centre for operating times
Adjacent to: remains of Basingwerk Abbey, Cistercian foundation in the care of CADW
Catalogues:
Catalogue for part of the collections is only available in-house.
Printed publications:
Greenfield Valley Heritage Park: Resources for schools bi-lingual (English/Welsh) pack (£10, direct)
Internet home pages:
http://www.greenfieldvalley.com

1137
GREENHILL COVENANTERS' HOUSE MUSEUM
Burn Braes, Biggar, Lanarkshire, ML12 6DT

Tel: 01899 221572
Fax: 01899 221050
Email: margaret@bmtrust.freeserve.co.uk
Acronym or abbreviation: BMT
Full name: Biggar Museum Trust
Formed: 1975
Formed from: Biggar Museum Trust

Organisation type and purpose: Independently owned, registered charity, museum, historic building, house or site, suitable for ages: 5+.
Parent body:
Biggar Museum Trust
Moat Park Heritiage Centre, Biggar, ML12 6DT, tel: 01889 221572, fax: 01899 221050, email: margaret@bmtrust.freeserve.co.uk

Enquiries to: Administrator
Access:
Access to staff: By letter, by telephone, by fax, by email
Access for disabled people: level entry

General description:
Biggar Museum Trust rescued this 17th century farmhouse from its original site at Wiston about 13km away. They rebuilt and refurbished it in the Burn Braes in 1975. Here you return to the troubled century of the signing of the national covenant and the 'Killing Times' when people were hunted down for worshipping in the open fields rather than attending state-controlled churches.
Information services:
Helpline available, tel no: 01899 221050.
Special visitor services: Tape recorded guides, materials and/or activities for children.
Education services: Group education facilities..
Collections:
All collections relate to Covenanters Period
Books
Furniture
Catalogues:
Catalogue for library is in-house only. Catalogue for part of the collections is only available in-house.

Internet home pages:
http://www.biggar-net.co.uk

1138
GREEN'S MILL & SCIENCE MUSEUM
Windmill Lane, Sneinton, Nottingham, NG2 4QB

Tel: 0115 915 6878
Fax: 0115 915 6875
Email: enquiries@greensmill.org.uk
Acronym or abbreviation: Green's Mill
Formed: 1985
Formed from: Nottingham City Museums & Galleries

Organisation type and purpose: Local government body, museum, suitable for ages: 5+.
Museum and science centre.
Parent body:
Nottingham City Museums & Galleries
Links with:
George Green Memorial Fund
At the same address

Enquiries to: Manager
Direct tel: 0115 915 3691
Direct fax: 0115 915 3653
Direct email: access@ncmg.demon.co.uk
Other contacts: (1) Senior Museum Assistant; (2) Education/Interpretation Officer for (1) queries/bookings related to site; (2) further information about George Green and the Mill.
Access:
Access to staff: By letter, by telephone, by fax, by email, visitors by prior appointment
Hours: Wed to Sun, 0900 to 1700
Access to building, collections or gallery: No prior appointment required
Hours: Wed to Sun, 1000 to 1600
Access for disabled people: Parking provided, toilet facilities
Other restrictions: Cobbled and uneven mill yard, but parking provided in the mill yard very close to mill and centre.
Access inside mill not possible for people with limited mobility.

General description:
A restored working 19th century tower windmill once owned by mathematical physicist George Green (1793-1841). The centre tells the story of mills and milling, and of Green's remarkable contribution to science, through exhibits and hands-on interactive displays.
Science - in particular light, magnetism and electricity.
Organic flour and milling.
Information services:
Guided tours by prior appointment.
The Hand's On interactive science exhibits are suitable for people who are visually or hearing impaired, and for those with special educational needs.
Special visitor services: Guided tours, materials and/or activities for children.
Education services: Group education facilities, resources for Key Stages 1 and 2.
Services for disabled people: Displays and/or information at wheelchair height.
Collections:
Information and documentation relating to George Green's life and the history of Green's Mill
Information on mills and milling in general

Internet home pages:
http://www.greensmill.org.uk
Information on the mill and science centre, public and education events and sessions, George Green and the Mill.

1139
GREENWAY
Greenway Road, Galmpton, Brixham, Devon, TQ5 0ES

Tel: 01803 842382 (Infoline)
Fax: 01803 661900
Email: greenway@nationaltrust.org.uk

Organisation type and purpose: National organisation, registered charity (charity number 205846), historic building, house or site, suitable for ages: all ages.
Parent body:
National Trust (South West)
Regional Office for Devon and Cornwall, tel: 01392 881691

Enquiries to: Warden
Access:
Access to staff: By letter, by telephone, by fax, by email, in person, Internet web pages
Access for disabled people: toilet facilities
Other restrictions: Designated parking must be booked, drop-off point, Level entrance to shop. Ramped entrance to restaurant. Barn gallery upstairs accessed by ramp for functions/lectures/workshops. Greenway is not easily accessible having some steep and slippery paths. Please see visitor reception for routes.
No mobility vehicles allowed in gardens, as paths are narrow.

General description:
Greenway is a glorious woodland garden on the banks of the River Dart that time seems to have passed by. Renowned for rare half-hardy plants underplanted by native wild flowers, a true 'secret' garden of peace and tranquillity. A unique and important estate on the Dart estuary. Bathing room, saloon room, balcony and

Greenway's famous 'boathouse' are open.
Barn Gallery exhibits contemporary art by local artists.
Information services:
Lectures and workshops in the Barn Gallery.
Garden days.
Special visitor services: Guided tours..

Internet home pages:
http://www.nationaltrust.org.uk/regions/devon

1140
GREENWICH BOROUGH MUSEUM
232 Plumstead High Street, London, SE18 1JT

Tel: 020 8855 3240
Fax: 020 8316 5754
Email: beverley.burford@greenwich.gov.uk
Formed: 1919
Formerly: Plumstead Museum

Organisation type and purpose: Local government body, museum, suitable for ages: 5+.
Connections with:
Greenwich Council

Enquiries to: Curator
Access:
Access to staff: By letter, by telephone, by fax, by email, in person

General description:
Local history museum with displays and collections of social history, archaeology, natural history and ethnography.
Information services:
Programme of temporary exhibitions
Lectures and workshops for adults and childrens
Special visitor services: Materials and/or activities for children.
Education services: Group education facilities..
Collections:
Social History: objects, pictures, photographs, documents and material on local industries
Archaeology: objects, photographs, reports; collection includes Neolithic, Roman, Medieval and Post-Medieval material
Natural History: Lepidoptera including Dawson & L T Ford Collections
Invertebrates
Marriott Herbarium
Mammals, Birds, Insects, local Mollusca
Fossils inlcuding Busbridge Collection
Catalogues:
Catalogue for part of the collections is only available in-house.
Printed publications:
Aspects of the Arsenal: The Royal Arsenal, Woolwich (£11.99)
Romans in Greenwich (25p)
The Thames on our Doorstep (45p)

1141
GREENWICH LOCAL HISTORY LIBRARY
Woodlands, 90 Mycenae Road, Blackheath, London, SE3 7SE

Tel: 020 8858 4631
Fax: 020 8293 4721
Email: local.history@greenwich.gov.uk
Formed: 1972

Organisation type and purpose: Local government body, public library, suitable for ages: all ages.
Parent body:
Greenwich Council
Tel: 020 8854 8888

Enquiries to: Librarian
Access:
Access to staff: By letter, by telephone, by fax, by email, in person
Hours: Mon, Tue, 0900 to 1730; Thu, 0900 to 2000; Sat, 0900 to 1700; Wed and Fri, closed
Other restrictions: No disabled access.

General description:
History of the London Borough of Greenwich.
Collections:
Books, pamphlets, maps, illustrations, local authority archives, manuscripts, microfilms and fiche, audiotapes, and videotapes
Documents relating to the history, topography and people of Deptford, Blackheath, Greenwich, Kidbrooke, Charlton, Woolwich, Plumstead, Shooters Hill and Eltham
Martin Collection, 10,000 items relating to the history of Blackheath, Greenwich, Kidbrooke, Charlton and Lewisham
Official repository of the records of the London Borough of Greenwich and its predecessors
Catalogues:
Catalogue for library is in-house only. Catalogue for part of the collections is only available in-house.
Publications list:
is available on-line.
Printed publications:
Sugar, Spices and Human Cargo: an early Black History of Greenwich (Anim-Addo J, 1996)
Family History in Greenwich: a Guide to Sources (Reilly L, 1991, £1)
Free for All (Watson J and Gregory W, 1993)
In the Meantime: a Book on Greenwich (Watson J and Gregory K, 1988)
Woolwich Reviewed (Watson J, 1986)

Internet home pages:
http://www.greenwich.gov.uk/council/publicservices/lhistory.htm
Guide to the library and its sources; detailed guide to family history sources.

1142
GREG'S MILL
See - Quarry Bank Mill and Styal Estate

1143
GREYFRIARS, THE
Friar Street, Worcester, WR1 2LZ

Tel: 01905 23571
Email: greyfriars@nationaltrust.org.uk

Organisation type and purpose: Registered charity (charity number 205846), historic building, house or site, suitable for ages: 16+.
Parent body:
The National Trust (West Midlands)
West Midlands Regional Office, tel: 01743 708100

Enquiries to: Administrator
Access:
Access to staff: By letter, by telephone

General description:
A fine timber-framed merchant's house, built in 1480 next to the Franciscan friary. Rescued from demolition and carefully restored, the panelled interior contains interesting textiles and furnishings. An archway leads through to the delightful walled garden.
Information services:
Guided tours for booked groups available.
Braille guide.
Children's guide.
Special visitor services: Guided tours, materials and/or activities for children.
Services for disabled people: For the visually impaired.

Internet home pages:
http://www.nationaltrust.org.uk

1144
GREYS COURT
Rotherfield Greys, Henley-on-Thames, Oxfordshire, RG9 4PG

Tel: 01491 628529
Fax: greyscourt@nationaltrust.co.uk
Telex: 01491 628935

Organisation type and purpose: National organisation, registered charity (charity number 205846), historic building, house or site, suitable for ages: 8+.
Parent body:
The National Trust (South and South East Region)
Thames and Solent Regional Office, tel: 01494 528051

Enquiries to: Manager
Access:
Access to staff: By letter, by telephone, by fax, by email
Access to building, collections or gallery: No prior appointment required
Hours: Apr to Sep, Wed, Thu, Fri, 1400 to 1800
Open Bank Holiday Mondays
Other restrictions: Closed Good Friday.
Access for disabled people: Parking provided, ramped entry, toilet facilities
Other restrictions: Drop-off point. 1 manual wheelchair available, booking essential. Ground floor largely accessible, half the rooms are accessible, photo album for other areas available. No access to other floors. Photograph album. Steps to shop entrance. Ramped entrance to tea-room. Garden partially accessible for wheelchairs.

General description:
A picturesque and intriguing house, originally 14th century but much added to later, with a beautiful courtyard and one surviving tower dating from 1347. The house has an interesting history and was involved in Jacobean court intrigue. Inside, the intimate rooms contain some outstanding 18th century plasterwork. The outbuildings include a Tudor wheelhouse, beautiful walled gardens full of old-fashioned roses and wisteria, and an ornamental vegetable garden.
Information services:
Helpline available, tel no: Infoline 01494 755564.
Guided tours of gardens only.
Children's quiz/trail.
Special visitor services: Materials and/or activities for children..

Internet home pages:
http://www.nationaltrust.org.uk

1145
GRIME'S GRAVES
nr Stanton Downham, Thetford, Norfolk

Tel: 01842 810656

Organisation type and purpose: Historic building, house or site.
Parent body:
English Heritage (East of England Region)
Brooklands, 24 Brooklands Avenue, Cambridge, CB2 2BU, tel: 01223 582700, fax: 01223 582701
Access:
Access to staff: By telephone
Access to building, collections or gallery: No prior appointment required
Hours: Apr to Sep: daily, 1000 to 1800
Oct: daily, 100 to 1700
Nov to Mar: Wed to Sun, 1000 to 1600
Last visit to the site is 30 mins before closing
Other restrictions: Closed 1300 to 1400 through the year, and 24 to 26 Dec and 1 Jan
Entry to the mines for children under 5 years will be at discretion of custodian.

General description:
Named Grim's Graves by the Anglo-Saxons after the pagan god Grim, it was not until some of them were first excavated in 1870 that they were found to be flint mines dug some 4000 years ago. The mines provided the materials needed to make tools and weapons. Today visitors can descend 10 metres (30 feet) by ladder into one excavated shaft.

1146
GRIMSBY MUSEUMS AND HERITAGE SERVICE
See - Welholme Galleries

1147
GRIMSTHORPE CASTLE
Grimsthorpe Estate Office, Bourne, Lincolnshire, PE10 0LY

Tel: 01778 591205
Fax: 01778 591259
Email: ray@grimsthorpe.co.uk
Full name: Grimsthorpe and Drummond Castle Trust
Formed: 1978

Organisation type and purpose: Registered charity (charity number 507478), historic building, house or site, suitable for ages: 8+.

Enquiries to: Manager
Access:
Access to staff: By letter
Access to building, collections or gallery: Prior appointment required
Access for disabled people: Parking provided, ramped entry, toilet facilities

General description:
Willoughby De Eresby family history, 18th century architecture.
Information services:
Special visitor services: Guided tours.
Education services: Group education facilities..
Collections:
Family furniture, paintings, tapestries
Publications list:
is available in hard copy.
Printed publications:
Guide Book (for purchase, direct)

Internet home pages:
http://www.grimsthorpe.co.uk
Opening times, admission charges, general background information.

1148
GROAM HOUSE MUSEUM
High Street, Rosemarkie, Ross-shire, IV10 8UF

Tel: 01381 620961
Fax: 01381 621730
Email: groamhouse@ecosse.net
Formed: 1989

Organisation type and purpose: Independently owned, registered charity (charity number SCO 04435), museum, suitable for ages: 5+, consultancy, research organisation, publishing house.
Pictish Interpretation Centre.

Enquiries to: Curator
Access:
Access to staff: By letter, by telephone, by fax, by email, visitors by prior appointment
Access for disabled people: level entry
Other restrictions: Partial access - ground floor only.

General description:
Nine Pictish Class 2 and Class 3 sculpted stones (8th-9th century), and four stones on loan, in an interpretive exhibition. The centre-piece is a magnificent Class 2 cross-slab. The museum also holds the National collection of the work of George Bain, Master of Celtic Art. The Museum exists to safeguard the history of the inhabitants of Ross & Cromarty with particular reference to the Picts. Annually a series of lectures are held and each year an academic lecture is presented with publication. For research purposes we have a comprehensive collection of photographs of Pictish stones and also a local archive for comparing the old villages with those of today. Original photographic prints (research copies displayed) relating to the social history of Rosemarkie, Fortrose and Avoch, c. 1890 onwards.
Information services:
Library available for reference (for conditions see Access above)
Special visitor services: Guided tours, materials and/or activities for children..
Collections:
Collection of Pictish sculptured stones
The George Bain Collection of his original Celtic art
14th century Church Seals
Modern black and white record photograph by T E Gray of Scottish Pictish Stones, available for research.
Local social history information and photographs
Catalogues:
Catalogue for library is in-house only. Catalogue for all of the collections is available in-house and part is on-line.
Publications list:
is available in hard copy.
Printed publications:
Earl & Mormaer, Norse-Pictish relationships in Northern Scotland (Crawford B, (£3.95)
Perceptions of the Picts: from Eumenius to John Buchan (Ritchie A, £3.95)
A persona for the Northern Picts (Hunter J, £3.95)
The Picts and their Place Names (Nicolaisen W F H, £3.95)
Recording Early Christian Monuments in Scotland (Ritchie J N G, £3.95)
Place, Space and Odyssey - Exploring the future of early medieval sculpture (Foster S M, £3.95)
George Bain: Master of Celtic Art (Seright S E, £3.95)

Internet home pages:
http://www.scran.ac.uk
Detailed examination of Pictish stones based on new research (Rosemarkie's Pictish Stones).
http://www.cali.co.uk/highexp/Fortrose/GROAM.htm

1149
GROSVENOR MUSEUM
See - Chester Museums

1150
GROUDLE GLEN RAILWAY
29 Hawarden Avenue, Douglas, Isle of Man, IM1 4BP, Isle of Man

Tel: 01624 622138 (evenings only) 01624 670453 (weekends only)
Formed: 1982

Organisation type and purpose: Membership association (membership is by subscription), present number of members: 700, voluntary organisation, registered charity (charity number Isle of Man No 406).
Restoration and operation of a narrow gauge railway.
Affiliated to:
Isle of Man Steam Railway Supporters Association
at the same address

Enquiries to: Honorary Secretary
Access:
Access to staff: By letter only, visitors by prior appointment
Hours: Mon to Fri, 0900 to 1700

General description:
Railway restoration and operation of a 2ft gauge line with steam and diesel locomotives over 3/4 mile track.
Printed publications:
Magazine (quarterly, to members)

1151
GRUNDY ART GALLERY
Queen Street, Blackpool, Lancashire, FY1 1PX

Tel: 01253 478170
Fax: 01253 478172
Email: grundyartgallery@blackpool.gov.uk
Formed: 1911

Organisation type and purpose: Local government body, art gallery, suitable for ages: 5+.

Enquiries to: Curator
Access:
Access to staff: By letter, by telephone, by fax, by email, in person
Access to building, collections or gallery: No prior appointment required
Hours: Mon to Sat, 1000 to 1700
Access for disabled people: ramped entry, level entry
Other restrictions: Access to all downstairs galleries.

General description:
Fine art, decorative art, local history, contemporary craft.
Information services:
Special visitor services: Materials and/or activities for children.
Education services: Group education facilities, resources for Key Stages 1 and 2, 3, 4 and Further or Higher Education.
Services for disabled people: Displays and/or information at wheelchair height.
Collections:
British paintings, particularly 19th and 20th century
Prints
Sculpture
Local historical paintings, photographs and objects
Oriental decorative art, including ivories
Contemporary craft jewellery
Catalogues:
Catalogue for all of the collections is only available in-house.

Internet home pages:
http://www.blackpool.gov.uk
Brief gallery details (click on services link).

1152
GUARDS MUSEUM
Wellington Barracks, Birdcage Walk, London, SW1E 6HQ

Tel: 020 7414 3428
Fax: 020 7414 3429
Formed: 1988

Organisation type and purpose: Registered charity, museum, art gallery.

Enquiries to: Secretary
Other contacts: Curator for research.
Access:
Access to staff: By letter only, visitors by prior appointment
Access to building, collections or gallery: No prior appointment required
Hours: Daily, 1000 to 1600
Other restrictions: Closed on Ceremonial Days.
Access for disabled people: level entry

General description:
A collection of colours, weapons, uniforms and much personal military memorabilia covering the Grenadier, Coldstream, Scots, Irish and Welsh Guards.
No personal documents or records.
Information services:
Guided tours by prior appointment.
Special visitor services: Guided tours, tape recorded guides.
Services for disabled people: Displays and/or information at wheelchair height.

1153
GUILD OF CAMPANOLOGISTS
See - Wiltshire Education & Libraries

1154
GUILD OF HANDICRAFT TRUST
Silk Mill, Sheep Street, Chipping Campden, Gloucestershire, GL55 6DS

Tel: 01386 859135/858180
Email: gofhtrust@ukonline.co.uk
Acronym or abbreviation: GofHT
Formed: 1990

Organisation type and purpose: Registered charity (charity number 1007696), museum, suitable for ages: 5+.
Collections of material relating to art, craft and design in Chipping Campden and the North

Cotswolds.
To preserve, promote and encourage an understanding of the work of artists, craftsmen and women, and designers of Chipping Campden and the North Cotswolds.

Enquiries to: Secretary
Access:
Access to staff: By letter, by telephone, by email, visitors by prior appointment
Hours: Any reasonable time.

General description:
Information and material relating: to C R Ashbee's Guild of Handicraft in Chipping Campden 1902-1919; R Welch (silversmith and product designer); and others associated with the area eg Alec Miller (woodcarver/sculptor), George Hart (silversmith) and Paul Woodroffe (stained glass/book illustrator). Information relating to F L Griggs, RA (etcher/engraver) and Gordon Russell (furniture designer and maker).
Catalogues:
Catalogue for part of the collections is only available in-house.
Publications list:
is available in hard copy.
Printed publications:
A range of publications on sale at the Guild or by post (plus p&p):
A Child in Arcadia. The Chipping Campden boyhood of H T Osborn 1902-07 (£5)
Alec Miller: Guildsman & Sculptor in Chipping Campden (Wilgress J, £5)
Arts & Crafts at Campden: Guild of Handicraft catalogue reprint (£3)
F Griggs, RA and Chipping Campden (Powell G, reprint from Gloucestershire History, 1989, 50p)
Robert Welch: Designer-Silversmith. Catalogue of the Retrospective Exhibition 1955-1995 (£2)
Ruskin re-considered: an essay by Alec Miller (£2)
Electronic and video products:
Material in process of preparation
Biography of Janet Ashbee (wife of C R Ashbee) (Ashbee F)
Guide to the Arts and Crafts of Chipping Campden and Broadway (Crawford A)

1155
GUILDFORD HOUSE GALLERY
155 High Street, Guildford, Surrey, GU1 3AJ

Tel: 01483 444740
Fax: 01483 444742
Email: guildfordhouse @remote.guildford.gov.uk
Formed: 1959

Organisation type and purpose: Local government body, museum, art gallery, historic building, house or site, suitable for ages: 12+.
Parent body:
Guildford Borough Council
Millmead, Guildford, Surrey, GU2 5BB, tel: 01483 505050

Enquiries to: Collections & Exhibitions Officer
Direct tel: 01483 444741
Other contacts: Curator for policy, collections management, personnel etc.
Access:
Access to staff: By letter, by telephone, by fax, by email, in person, visitors by prior appointment
Hours: Tue to Sat, 1000 to 1645
Access to building, collections or gallery: No prior appointment required
Hours: Mon to Fri, 0900 to 1630
Other restrictions: Letter of application and at least 2 weeks' notice.

General description:
1660 house with many original features, including plaster ceilings, carved staircase, wrought iron work on windows.
Local collection of local artists including John Russell RA (1745 to 1806) and local scenes, shown periodically.
Changing programme of exhibitions.
Information services:
On-line searching. Helpline available, tel no: 01483 444740.
Special visitor services: Guided tours.
Education services: Group education facilities..
Collections:
Large public collection of work by John Russell RA (1745-1806)
William Hyde (1859-1925), mezzotints/ engravings
Henry J Sage (1868-1953), watercolours of local scenes in and around Guildford 1853-1920
Printed publications:
Various postcards and greeting cards featuring the Borough Collection

Internet home pages:
http://www.guildfordborough.co.uk/pages/ leisure/culture/housegt.htm
Exhibition details, events, information on House.

1156
GUILDFORD MUSEUM
Castle Arch, Guildford, Surrey, GU1 3SX

Tel: 01483 444751
Fax: 01483 532391
Email: museum@remote.guildford.gov.uk
Formed: 1878

Organisation type and purpose: Local government body, museum.
Administered by:
Guildford Borough Council
Tel: 01483 505050, fax: 01483 444444
Links with:
Guildford Muniment Room
at the same address
Surrey Archaeological Society
at the same address, tel: 01483 532454

Enquiries to: Curator
Access:
Access to staff: By letter, by telephone, by fax, by email, visitors by prior appointment
Hours: Mon to Sat, 0900 to 1700
Other restrictions: Limited disabled access.

General description:
Archaeology and local history of Surrey; needlework (especially British embroidery and smocks).
Collections:
Jekyll Collection of rural byegones
Lewis Carroll Collection
Needlework collection
Pottery and glass collection of international importance
Victorian Childhood Collection
Wetton token collection
Catalogues:
Catalogue for all of the collections is only available in-house.
Publications list:
is available in hard copy.
Printed publications:
Guildford History: an outline
Surrey from the Stone Age to the Saxons

Internet home pages:
http://www.guildfordborough.co.uk
Description of services offered by Guildford Museum and collections, also information on forthcoming events.

1157
GUILDHALL ART GALLERY, CORPORATION OF LONDON
No 2 Guildhall Yard, London, EC2P 2EJ

Tel: 020 7606 3030 ext 1632/1856
Fax: 020 332 3342
Telex: 265608 LONDON G
Email: guildhall.artgallery @corpoflondon.gov.uk
Formed: 1886

Organisation type and purpose: Local government body, art gallery, suitable for ages: all ages.
Parent body:
Corporation of London

Enquiries to: Curator
Direct tel: 020 7332 1632 or 1856
Direct fax: 020 7332 3342
Access:
Access to staff: By letter, by telephone, by fax, by email, in person, visitors by prior appointment, Internet web pages
Access for disabled people: level entry, access to all public areas, toilet facilities

General description:
Specialist information regarding Corporation's Permanent Collection, history of Guildhall Art Gallery, general information on fine art.
Information services:
Recorded information, tel no 020 7332 3700
Special visitor services: Materials and/or activities for children.
Education services: Resources for Key Stages 1 and 2 and Further or Higher Education.
Services for disabled people: Displays and/or information at wheelchair height.
Collections:
Charles Gassiot Bequest
Greater London Council Heritage Collection
Harold Samuel Collection of Dutch and Flemish 17th century paintings
Sir John Gilbert Gift
Sir Matthew Smith Collection
Wakefield Bequest
Catalogues:
Catalogue for all of the collections is on-line.
Printed publications:
Children in Painting, Guildhall Art Gallery (1999, Supreme Publishing Services)
Dutch and Flemish 17th Century Painting: The Harold Samuel Collection (1992, pub. CUP, reprinted 1997, Corporation of London)
Guildhall Art Gallery Handbooks (5 titles)
Landscapes and Sea Views, Guildhall Art Gallery (1999, Supreme Publishing Services)
London in Paintings, Guildhall Art Gallery (1999, Supreme Publishing Services)
Modern Pictures, Guildhall Art Gallery (1999, Supreme Publishing Services)
Portraits, Guildhall Art Gallery (1999, Supreme Publishing Services)
The History of Guildhall Art Gallery (1999, Supreme Publishing Services)
The Two Mr Smiths: The Life and Work of Matthew Smith (Lund Humphries in association with the Corporation of London, 1995)
Victorian Pictures, Guildhall Art Gallery (1999, Supreme Publishing Services)
Works of Art of the Corporation of London (Woodhead-Faulkner, 1986)

Internet home pages:
http://www.guildhall-art-gallery.org.uk

1158
GUILDHALL EXHIBITION
See - Royal Borough Museum Collection

1159
GUILDHALL GALLERY, THE
The Broadway, Winchester, Hampshire, SO23 9BE

Tel: 01962 848289 or 848269
Email: cbradbury@winchester.gov.uk

Organisation type and purpose: Local government body, art gallery, historic building, house or site.
Linked to:
Winchester Museums Service
Tel: 01962 848269, fax: 01962841365, email/ website: museums@winchester.gov.uk
Address for correspondence:
Historic Resources Centre
75 Hyde Street, Winchester, SO23 7DW, tel: 01962 848269
Access:
Access to building, collections or gallery: No prior appointment required

continued overleaf

Hours: 1000 to 1600, Tue to Sat, 1400 to1600, Sun
Access for disabled people: access to all public areas

General description:
The Gallery provides a professional exhibition space accommodating practising artists and talented local amateur groups. The work encompasses nearly all artistic disiplines: contemporary paintings, sculpture, ceramics, photography, crafts and an annual selection of the City's topographical collection of oil paintings, prints and drawings. Exhibitions change every three weeks.

Internet home pages:
http://www.winchester.gov.uk/heritage

1160
GUILDHALL, THE
Guildhall Lane, Leicester, LE1 5FQ

Tel: 0116 253 2569
Fax: 0116 253 9626

Organisation type and purpose: Local government body, museum.
Parent body:
Leicester City Museum Service
Block A, New Walk Centre, Welford Place, Leicester, LE1 6ZG

Enquiries to: Head of Museums & Heritage Services
Direct tel: 0116 252 8912
Direct fax: 0116 225 6048
Direct email: levis001@leicester.gov.uk
Access:
Access to staff: By email

General description:
One of the best preserved timber-framed halls in the country, dating back 600 years. Best known today as an excellent performance venue.

1161
GUILDHALL MUSEUM
High Street, Rochester, Kent, ME1 1PY

Tel: 01634 848717
Fax: 01634 832919
Email: guildhall.museum@medway.gov.uk
Formed: 1897

Organisation type and purpose: Museum.

Enquiries to: Curator
Access:
Access to staff: By letter, by telephone, by fax, by email
Hours: Daily, 1000 to 1630
Access to building, collections or gallery: No prior appointment required
Hours: Daily, 1000 to 1630

General description:
Social history of the Medway Towns. Local geology, archaeology and social history, special features include 'The Hulks Experience' portraying life and conditions experienced by Napoleonic prisoners of war on the Medway prison hulks, and life in Edwardian and Victorian times.
Information services:
Special visitor services: Materials and/or activities for children.
Education services: Group education facilities, resources for Key Stages 1 and 2, 3 and 4..
Collections:
Fitzgerald Collection of Dickensiana (objects and printed material)
The Horton Collection of Victoriana
The Norris Collection - lamps and lighting
The Prentice Natural History Collection
Charles Spencelagh Art Collection
Medway Archaeology Collection
Ephemera (Medway Social History Collection)
Glass plate negatives
Catalogues:
Catalogue for part of the collections is only available in-house.

Internet home pages:
http://www.medway.gov.uk
Details of forthcoming events and exhibitions.

1162
GUILDHALL MUSEUM, CHICHESTER
See - Chichester District Museum

1163
GUILDHALL MUSEUM, LONDON
See - Museum of London

1164
GUILDHALL MUSEUM, NEWPORT
See - Museum of Island History

1165
GUILDHALL OF CORPUS CHRISTI, THE
Market Place, Lavenham, Sudbury, Suffolk, CO10 9QZ

Tel: 01787 247646
Email: lavenhamguildhall@nationaltrust.org.uk

Organisation type and purpose: National organisation, independently owned, registered charity (charity number 205846), museum, historic building, house or site, suitable for ages: 8+.
Parent body:
The National Trust (East of England Region)
East Anglia Regional Office, tel: 0870 609 5388

Enquiries to: Administrator
Access:
Access to staff: By letter, by telephone, by email, visitors by prior appointment, charges to non-members
Access for disabled people: level entry, toilet facilities
Other restrictions: Ground floor accessible with assistance. No access to other floors. Photograph album. Level entrance to shop. Ramped entrance to tea-room.

General description:
Spectacular timber-framed building dominating the Market Place of historic Lavenham, once the 14th richest town in England. Houses local history museum with displays on the medieval cloth trade, farming and medieval guilds. Tranquil courtyard garden with unique dye plants used in the medieval cloth industry. Restored 19th century lock-up and mortuary.
Information services:
Introductory talks by arrangement.
Blue-badge guided walks around Lavenham village, (groups of 15+)
Suitable for school groups.
Children's guide
Special visitor services: Materials and/or activities for children.
Education services: Group education facilities.
Services for disabled people: For the visually impaired; displays and/or information at wheelchair height.
Collections:
Private collections of objects, photographs, working models etc relevant to local history museum
Catalogues:
Catalogue for all of the collections is only available in-house.
Publications list:
is available in hard copy.
Printed publications:
Short Guide
Full colour guide
Cloth Trade information
French and German translations
Children's Guide

Internet home pages:
http://www.nationaltrust.org.uk/regions

1166
GUILDHALL, THE
Ramparts Walk, Totnes, Devon, TQ9 5QH

Tel: 01803 862147
Fax: 01803 864275
Email: totnestowncouncil@btinternet.com
Formed: 1086

Organisation type and purpose: Historic building, house or site, suitable for ages: 5+.
Parent body:
Totnes Town Council (TTC)

Enquiries to: Administrator
Access:
Access to staff: By letter, by telephone, by fax, by email, in person
Access to building, collections or gallery: No prior appointment required
Hours: 1 Apr to 31 Oct: daily, 1030 to 1300 and 1400 to 1630

General description:
Range of exhibits relating to history of Totnes.
Publications list:
is available in hard copy.
Printed publications:
Information leaflet

1167
GUINNESS ARCHIVES
Park Royal Brewery, London

Closed: Records moved to Visitor Centre in Dublin

1168
GUISBOROUGH MUSEUM
Sunnyfield House, 36 Westgate, Guisborough, Cleveland, TS14 6AY

Tel: 01287 203617
Email: guisboro.museum@care4free.co.uk
Formed: 1989

Organisation type and purpose: Independently owned, registered charity (charity number 1009236), museum, suitable for ages: all ages.

Enquiries to: Information Officer
Direct tel: 01287 646834
Direct email: jacky.quarmby@virgin.net
Access:
Access to staff: By letter, by telephone, by email
Hours: Thu, 0900 to 1200
Access to building, collections or gallery: No prior appointment required
Hours: Apr to Oct: Thu to Sat, 1000 to 1600
Access for disabled people: Parking provided, ramped entry

General description:
A museum of social history telling the story of a typical market town through the history of Guisborough.
Collections:
General Archive. c. 3000 photographs and items of printed ephemera, 1800 to 1994
Catalogues:
Catalogue for part of the collections is only available in-house.

1169
GULBENKIAN MUSEUM OF ORIENTAL ART
See - Durham University

1170
GUN BARREL PROOF HOUSE MUSEUM AND LIBRARY
Banbury Street, Birmingham, B5 5RH

Tel: 0121 643 3860
Fax: 0121 643 7872
Email: info@gunproof.com
Formed: 1813

Organisation type and purpose: Museum, historic building, house or site, suitable for ages: 16+.

Enquiries to: Librarian/Curator
Access:
Access to staff: By letter, by telephone, by email, Internet web pages
Access to building, collections or gallery: Prior appointment required
Hours: Mon to Thu, 0900 to 1645
Other restrictions: Charges made
Access for disabled people: level entry

General description:
There are two museums, one on arms, the other on ammunition and blown up weapons.
Information services:
Library available for reference (for conditions see Access above)
Conducted tours start at 1000 and last 3 hours, groups only, parties to be made up by visitors not by Proof House
Special visitor services: Guided tours..
Collections:
Library on weapons and ammunition
Publications list:
is available on-line.

Internet home pages:
http://www.gunproof.com

1171
GUNBY HALL ESTATE: MONKSTHORPE CHAPEL

Monksthorpe, Nr Spilsby, Lincolnshire

Tel: 01909 486411 (Regional Office)

Organisation type and purpose: National organisation, registered charity (charity number 205846), historic building, house or site, suitable for ages: 8+.
Parent body:
The National Trust (East Midlands Region)
East Midlands Regional Office, tel: 01909 486411

Enquiries to: Property Manager
Access:
Access to staff: By letter, by telephone, by fax
Other restrictions: All enquiries should be directed to Regional Office.
Access for disabled people: level entry
Other restrictions: Drop-off point, ground floor largely accessible. Grounds largely accessible

General description:
One of the two best surviving English examples of a Baptist Chapel from the late 17th century. This remote Chapel, originally a brick barn, with outdoor baptistry was used by local Baptists as a secluded place of worship. The Chapel was substantially altered to its present appearance in the early 19th century.

Internet home pages:
http://www.nationaltrust.org.uk

1172
GUNBY HALL ESTATE: WHITEGATES COTTAGE

Mill Lane, Bratoft, Nr Spilsby, Lincolnshire

Tel: 01909 486411 (Regional Office)

Organisation type and purpose: National organisation, registered charity (charity number 205846), historic building, house or site, suitable for ages: 8+.
Parent body:
The National Trust (East Midlands Region)
East Midland Regional Office, tel: 01909 486411

Enquiries to: Property Manager
Access:
Access to staff: By letter, by telephone, by fax, in person
Other restrictions: All enquiries should be directed to Regional Office.
Access to building, collections or gallery: Prior appointment required
Hours: Apr to Sep, Wed, 1400 to 1800
Other restrictions: Written appiontment only with regional office
Access for disabled people: level entry
Other restrictions: Ground floor largely inaccessible, small rooms with narrow doorways; inadequate turning space. No access to other floors

General description:
A small thatched cottage, built c.1770 to provide accommodation for estate workers. Notable for its mud and stud walling, it has been restored using traditional methods and materials.

Internet home pages:
http://www.nationaltrust.org.uk

1173
GUNBY HALL

Gunby, Spilsby, Lincolnshire, PE23 5SS

Tel: 01909 486411 (Regional Office)
Email: gunbyhall@ic24.net

Organisation type and purpose: National organisation, registered charity (charity number 205846), historic building, house or site, suitable for ages: 5+.
Parent body:
National Trust (East Midlands Region)
East Midlands Regional Office, tel: 01909 486411

Enquiries to: Head Gardener
Direct tel: 07790 810039
Access:
Access to staff: By letter, by email, in person, visitors by prior appointment, charges to non-members, Internet web pages
Access for disabled people: Parking provided
Other restrictions: Drop-off point; 1 manual wheelchair available, booking essential; Steps to entrance, ground floor
largely inaccessible. No access to other floors. Grounds largely accessible

General description:
A fine red-brick house, dating from 1700 (with later extensions) and located in one of England's most remote corners. Many of the rooms are panelled and there is a beautiful oak staircase, as well as many fine paintings and items of furniture and china. The exquisite walled garden is planted with traditional English vegetables, fruit and flowers.

Internet home pages:
http://www.gunbyhall.ic24.net
Regularly updated information re special events etc.
http://www.nationaltrust.org.uk

1174
GUNNERSBURY PARK MUSEUM

Gunnersbury Park, London, W3 8LQ

Tel: 020 8992 1612
Fax: 020 8752 0686
Acronym or abbreviation: GPM
Formed: 1929

Organisation type and purpose: Local government body, museum, historic building, house or site, suitable for ages: all ages.
Gunnersbury Park joint committee, has links with:
London Borough of Hounslow & London Borough of Ealing

Enquiries to: Curator
Other contacts: Deputy Curator
Access:
Access to staff: By letter, by telephone, by fax, visitors by prior appointment
Hours: Nov to Apr: 1300 to 1600; May to Oct; 1300 to 1700
Weekends and bank holidays, 1300 to 1800
Access for disabled people: Parking provided, ramped entry, toilet facilities
Other restrictions: Visually impaired by special arrangement.

General description:
Local history of the area of the above two boroughs; carriages, Victorian kitchens, the Rothschilds at Gunnersbury, costume history.
Information services:
Guided tours by prior arrangement.
Visually impaired by special arrangement.
Special visitor services: Guided tours, materials and/or activities for children.
Education services: Group education facilities, resources for Key Stage 2.
Services for disabled people: For the visually impaired.
Collections:
Gunnersbury Park archive
Local photographic and picture archive
Local trades archive and industries eg Great West Road firms
Sadler Collection (literature by famous local writers eg Bulwer Lytton)
Catalogues:
Catalogue for all of the collections is only available in-house.
Publications list:
is available in hard copy.
Printed publications:
Free leaflets

1175
GUNTON PARK SAWMILL

O.S. TG 224 335, Gunton Hall, Norfolk

Organisation type and purpose: Historic building, house or site.
Links with:
Norfolk Industrial Archaeology Society

General description:
Extremely rare water-powered sawmill, waterwheels and timber sawing on open days.

1176
GURKHA MUSEUM

Peninsula Barracks, Winchester, Hampshire, SO23 8TS

Tel: 01962 842832
Fax: 01962 877597
Email: curator@thegurkhamuseum.co.uk
Formed: 1990

Organisation type and purpose: Museum, suitable for ages: 5+, research organisation.

Enquiries to: Curator
Other contacts: Assistant Curator
Access:
Access to staff: By letter, by telephone, by fax, by email, Internet web pages
Hours: Sat, 1000 to 1630; Sun, 1200 to 1600
Access to building, collections or gallery: No prior appointment required
Hours: Sat, 1000 to 1700; Sun, 1200 to 1600
Access for disabled people: Parking provided, ramped entry, access to all public areas, toilet facilities
Other restrictions: Chairlift, lift.

General description:
Gurkha service to British Crown and people.
Information services:
Library available for reference (for conditions see Access above)
Special visitor services: Guided tours, materials and/or activities for children.
Education services: Group education facilities, resources for Key Stages 1 and 2, 3, 4 and Further or Higher Education.
Services for disabled people: Displays and/or information at wheelchair height.
Collections:
Dioramas, medals, uniforms, weapons, pictures, badges, jewellery, silver, gold
Catalogues:
Catalogue for library is published. Catalogue for all of the collections is published.
Publications list:
is available in hard copy and online.
Printed publications:
Various available

continued overleaf

Microform products:
Various available
Electronic and video products:
Various publications available

Internet home pages:
http://www.thegurkhamuseum.co.uk

1177
GWENT RURAL LIFE MUSEUM
See - Usk Rural Life Museum

1178
GWILI RAILWAY COMPANY LIMITED
Bronwydd Arms Station, Bronwydd, Carmarthen, SA33 6HT

Tel: 01267 230666
Email: company@gwili-railway.co.uk
Formed: 1975

Organisation type and purpose: Membership association (membership is by subscription), present number of members: over 1000, voluntary organisation, museum.
A limited company and preservation society operating a heritage steam railway, staffed entirely by volunteers.
Operating a tourist steam railway.
Associated with:
Caerphilly Railway Society
Gwili Railway Preservation Society
Railway Clubs of Wales
Vale of Neath Railway Society

Enquiries to: Publicity Officer
Direct tel: 01267 236291
Direct fax: 01267 236291
Access:
Access to staff: By letter, by telephone, by email
Hours: Daily during School Spring, Summer and half-term holidays, weekends at other times.

General description:
History of railways in South Wales.
Collections:
Photographs and documents

Internet home pages:
http://www.gwili-railway.co.uk
History of railway, current timetable and fares, stock list

1179
GWYNEDD AND ANGLESEY FEDERATION OF MARITIME MUSEUMS
See - Holyhead Maritime Museum; Lleyn Historical & Maritime Museum; Porthmadog Maritime Museum; Seiont II Maritime Trust (Caernarfon Maritime Museum)

1180
GWYNEDD ARCHAEOLOGICAL TRUST LIMITED
Craig Beuno, Garth Road, Bangor, Gwynedd, LL57 2RT

Tel: 01248 352535
Fax: 01248 370925
Email: gat@heneb.co.uk
Acronym or abbreviation: GAT
Formed: 1974

Organisation type and purpose: Professional body, registered charity, suitable for ages: 8+, consultancy.
Archaeological Trust.
The principal objective of the Trust is to advance the education of the public in archaeology.

Enquiries to: Director
Other contacts: Deputy Director
Access:
Access to staff: By letter, by telephone, by fax, by email
Other restrictions: By prior appointment only.
Access for disabled people: ramped entry

General description:
The archaeology of North-West Wales.
Printed publications:
Publish in journals and general publications
Leaflets

Internet home pages:
http://www.hneb.co.uk

1181
GWYNEDD ARCHIVES & MUSEUMS SERVICE
Victoria Dock, Caernarfon, Gwynedd

Tel: 01286 679095
Fax: 01286 679637
Email: archives.caernarfon@gwynedd.gov.uk

Organisation type and purpose: County Record Office.
Other address:
Gwynedd Archives
Dolgellau Area Record Office

Enquiries to: Archivist
Access:
Access to staff: By telephone, by fax, by email, in person
Hours: Closed Mon; Tue, Thu, Fri, 0930 to 1230 and 1330 to 1700; Wed, 0930 to 1230 and 1330 to 1900
Access to building, collections or gallery: No prior appointment required
Hours: Closed Mon; open Tue, Thu, Fri, 0930 to 1230 and 1330 to 1700; Wed, 0930 to 1230 and 1330 to 1900
Other restrictions: CARN readers ticket required.
Appointment advised for microfiche and microfilm readers
Access for disabled people: level entry, access to all public areas, toilet facilities

General description:
Usual county archive collection with particular strengths in the industrial (quarrying), maritime and estate records.
Information services:
Education services: Group education facilities, resources for Key Stages 1 and 2 and 3..
Catalogues:
Catalogue for all of the collections is available in-house and part is on-line.
Publications list:
is available on-line.

Internet home pages:
http://www.gwynedd.gov.uk/archives

See also - Beaumaris Gaol and Court

1182
GWYNEDD MUSEUM AND ART GALLERY, BANGOR
Ffordd Gwynedd, Bangor, Gwynedd, LL57 1DT

Tel: 01248 353368
Fax: 01248 370149
Email: patwest@gwynedd.gov.uk
Formed: 1884
Formerly: Museum of Welsh Antiquities, date of change, 1993

Organisation type and purpose: Local government body, museum.
Parent body:
Gwynedd Council, Education, Culture and Leisure Department

Enquiries to: Curator
Access:
Access to staff: By letter, by telephone, by fax, by email, Internet web pages
Hours: Mon to Fri, 0900 to 1700

General description:
Bangor and North Wales antiquities, archaeology, costume, furniture, local history, photographs and prints.
Information services:
Education services: Group education facilities..

Collections:
Archaeology eg special collections from the Bronze Age and Roman periods
Florence Leach collections of fans (18th to 20th centuries)
John Griffiths archaeology collection including Viking and Saxon hoard
Lieut Col T W L Hughes' costumes collection
Mrs Drage's lace collections
Welsh kitchen, Elizabeth Williams collection
Ynysgain Collection (Dorothea Pugh-Jones) furniture from the farming household (upper class) (17th to 19th centuries)

Internet home pages:
http://www.gwynedd.gov.uk/museums
General information: location, opening hours, collections, policies, education services, what's on.

1183
GWYNEDD MUSEUMS SERVICE
Gwynedd Council, Caernarfon, Gwynedd, LL55 1SH

Tel: 01286 679098
Fax: 01286 679637
Email: amgueddfeydd-museums@gwynedd.gov.uk
Formed: 1985

Organisation type and purpose: Local government body, museum, art gallery, historic building, house or site, suitable for ages: 5+.
To collect, care for and provide access to the material that reflects the culture, people and life in Gwynedd.
Museums are:
Barmouth Sailor's Institute
Barmouth, Gwynedd, tel: 01341 241333
Gwynedd Museum & Art Gallery, Bangor
Ffordd, Bangor, Gwynedd, tel: 01248 353368
Lloyd George Museum
Llanystumdwy, Criccieth, Gwynedd, LL52 0SH, tel: 01766 522071, fax: 01766 522071
Oriel Pendeitsh Gallery
Castle Ditch, Caernarfon, Gwynedd, LL55 2AY, tel: 01286 679 564, fax: 01286 677 647
Quaker Heritage Centre
Ty Meirion, Sgwar Eldon Square, Dolgellau, Gwynedd, tel: 01341 424442

Enquiries to: Museums and Galleries Officer
Other contacts: (1) Principal Archivist and Heritage Officer (2) Assistant Director of Culture (3) Collections Management Officer (4) Education Officer for (1) and (2) strategic (3) collections (4) education.
Access:
Access to staff: By letter, by telephone, by fax, by email, visitors by prior appointment, Internet web pages
Access to building, collections or gallery: No prior appointment required
Hours: Each site has different hours of opening.

General description:
The history of Gwynedd including archaeology; furniture; general social history; David Lloyd George; The Quakers; costume; traditions; Victorian times.
Information services:
Education services: Group education facilities, resources for Key Stages 1 and 2, 3, 4 and Further or Higher Education..

Internet home pages:
http://www.gwynedd.gov.uk/museums
Information on our museums and interpretations site.

1184
HACK GREEN SECRET NUCLEAR BUNKER
PO Box 127, Nantwich, Cheshire, CW5 8AQ

Tel: 01270 629219
Email: coldwar@hackgreen.co.uk
Formed: 1997

Organisation type and purpose: Museum, historic building, house or site.

Enquiries to: Curator
Access:
Access to staff: By letter only
Access to building, collections or gallery: No prior appointment required
Hours: Daily, 1000 to 1730
Access for disabled people: ramped entry, toilet facilities

General description:
Former regional government nuclear war headquarters. 35,000 sq ft blastproof bunker. Operations and communication rooms etc, Cold War collection and nuclear weapon collection, also former WWII radar station.
Information services:
Library available for reference (for conditions see Access above)
Special visitor services: Guided tours, materials and/or activities for children.
Education services: Group education facilities, resources for Key Stages 3 and 4.
Services for disabled people: For the visually impaired; for the hearing impaired.
Collections:
Working Marconi 264 Radar
Nuclear Weapons Collection
Cold War & Radar Museum
Military Vehicles
Catalogues:
Catalogue for library is in-house only. Catalogue for all of the collections is only available in-house.
Publications list:
is available in hard copy.

Internet home pages:
http://www.hackgreen.co.uk

1185
HACKNEY MUSEUM
Hackney Technology & Learning Centre, 1 Reading Lane, London, E8 1GQ

Tel: 020 8356 3500
Fax: 020 8356 2563
Email: hmuseum@hackney.gov.uk
Formed: 1987

Organisation type and purpose: Museum, suitable for ages: all ages.

Enquiries to: Curator
Other contacts: Education Officer for education.
Access:
Access to staff: By letter, by telephone, by fax, by email, in person, Internet web pages
Hours: Mon, Tue, Thu, Fri, 0930 to 1730
Other restrictions: Closed Wed.
Access to building, collections or gallery: No prior appointment required
Hours: Mon, Tue, Thu, Fri, 0930 to 1730; Sat, 1000 to 1700
Other restrictions: Closed Wed
Access for disabled people: level entry, access to all public areas, toilet facilities

General description:
The local history museum for Hackney, telling the story of Hackney and its people and immigration, with a diverse collection of multicultural material.
Information services:
Special visitor services: Materials and/or activities for children.
Education services: Group education facilities, resources for Key Stages 1 and 2.
Services for disabled people: Displays and/or information at wheelchair height.
Collections:
Social history, artefacts, prints, photographs
Chalmer Bequest Collection of mainly 19th century art works
Catalogues:
Catalogue for all of the collections is only available in-house.

Internet home pages:
http://www.hackney.gov.uk/hackneymuseum

1186
HADDO HOUSE ARTS TRUST
Haddo House, Ellon, Aberdeenshire, AB41 7ER

Tel: 01651 851770

General description:
Watercolour views of Aberdeenshire castles which were painted between 1838 and 1855 by local artist James Giles, RSA: 1801-1870.
Collections:
Canadian State Dinner Service; hand painted by the women artists of Canada

1187
HADDO HOUSE
Ellon, Aberdeenshire, AB41 7EQ

Tel: 01651 851440
Fax: 01651 851888
Email: haddo@nts.org.uk

Organisation type and purpose: Museum, art gallery, historic building, house or site.
Parent body:
National Trust for Scotland (North-East Region)

Enquiries to: Property Manager
Access:
Access to staff: By letter, by telephone, by fax, by email, in person
Access to building, collections or gallery: No prior appointment required
Hours: House and garden, end Jun to beg Sep, daily, 1000 to 1700
Aberdeenshire Council Country Park, open all year, daily, 0930 to sunset
Access for disabled people: toilet facilities
Other restrictions: Access to house (lift for wheelchairs), garden and Country Park, shop, restaurant, wheelchairs available

General description:
Designed by William Adam in 1732 and refurbished in the 1880s, the house blends crisp Georgian architecture with sumptuous late Victorian interiors. It is noted for its fine furniture, paintings and objets d'art. Throughout the house and grounds, personal portraits, monuments, plaques and memorabilia build up a fascinating account of the Gordon family who have lived at Haddo continuously for over 400 years.

Internet home pages:
http://www.nts.org.uk

1188
HADEN HILL HOUSE MUSEUM
Halesowen Road, Cradley Heath, West Midlands, B64 7JU

Tel: 01384 569444
Fax: 01384 412623
Formed: 1875

Organisation type and purpose: Local government body, museum, historic building, house or site, suitable for ages: 5+.
Parent body:
Sandwell MBC (SMBC)
Council House, Oldbury, tel: 0121 569 2200
Other addresses:
Oak House Museum
Oak Lane, West Bromwich, tel: 0121 553 0759
Wednesbury Museum & Art Gallery
Holyhead Road, Wednesbury, WS10 7DF, tel: 0121 556 0683

Enquiries to: Curator
Other contacts: Visitor Services Manager for daily management issues of site.
Access:
Access to staff: By letter, by telephone, by fax, in person, visitors by prior appointment
Other restrictions: Curator, Visitor Services Manager not always on site.
Access to building, collections or gallery: No prior appointment required
Hours: Mon to Thu, 1000 to 1700; Fri, 1000 to 1630; Sat, Sun, 1300 to 1700
Last admission 30 mins prior to closing
Access for disabled people: Parking provided, ramped entry, level entry, toilet facilities
Other restrictions: Access to ground floor only.

General description:
History of Cradley Heath and surrounding area, social history is a specialised area.
Information services:
Special visitor services: Guided tours, materials and/or activities for children.
Education services: Group education facilities..
Collections:
Period displays from late Victorian/early Edwardian period
Archive concerning occupation of house by Best Family from building 1878 and subsequent history of building
Collection of social history objects from Victorian period to present day

Internet home pages:
http://www.sandwellmbc.gov.uk
General information about Sandwell Museum Service.

1189
HADRIAN'S WALL AND HOUSESTEADS ROMAN FORT, THE
Haydon Bridge, Hexham, Northumberland, NE47 6NN

Tel: 01434 344363 (English Heritage Custodian)

Organisation type and purpose: National organisation, registered charity (charity number 205846), museum, historic building, house or site, suitable for ages: 12+.
Maintained and managed by:
English Heritage (North East Region)
Tel: 0191 269 1227/8, fax: 0191 261 1130
Owned by:
The National Trust (Yorkshire and North East)
North East Regional Office, tel: 01670 774691, fax: 01670 774317

Enquiries to: Custodian
Access:
Access to staff: By letter, by telephone
Access to building, collections or gallery: No prior appointment required
Hours: Apr to Sep, daily, 1000 to 1800; Oct, daily, 1000 to 1700; Nov to Mar, daily, 1000 to 1600
Other restrictions: Closed 24-26 Dec, 1 Jan
Opening times are subject to change, for up-to-date information contact English Heritage by phone or visit the website.
Access for disabled people: Parking provided, ramped entry, toilet facilities
Other restrictions: Ramped entrance. Ask at information centre for details. On request at National Trust visitor centre, cars can be taken up to English Heritage Museum 100yds from Fort. Ramped access to Wall at Steel Rigg. Ramped entrance to shop.

General description:
One of Rome's most northerly outposts, the Wall was built when the Roman Empire was at its height. Snaking across dramatic countryside, it remains one of Britain's most impressive ruins. Housesteads Fort, one of thirteen permanent bases along the Wall, is one of the best-preserved, and conjures an evocative picture of Roman military life. It is the most complete example of a Roman fort in Britain and was a permanent fort built in AD 124. The remains include gates, commandant's house, barracks, granaries, hospital and latrines.
Information services:
A volunteer guide may be available if booked in advance.
Braille guide.

continued overleaf

Suitable for school groups. Education room/ centre. Children's guide.
Special visitor services: Materials and/or activities for children.
Education services: Group education facilities.
Services for disabled people: For the visually impaired.
Collections:
250 items excavated from the Roman Fort and civil settlement at Housesteads (dating ca. 120 AD-AD 400), and a range of models.
20 items of religious sculpture/epigraphy; probably the most important part of the collection.

Internet home pages:
http://www.english-heritage.org.uk

1190
HADRIAN'S WALL MUSEUMS

The Roman Site, Corbridge, Northumberland, NE45 5NT

Tel: 01434 632239

Organisation type and purpose: National government body, museum, historic building, house or site, suitable for ages: all ages.
Parent body:
English Heritage (North West Region)
Canada House, 3 Chepstow Street, Manchester, M1 5FW, tel: 0161 242 1400

Enquiries to: Custodian
Other contacts: Curator 01434 633168 for enquiries relating to collections.
Access:
Access to staff: By letter, by telephone, visitors by prior appointment
Access to building, collections or gallery: No prior appointment required
Hours: Apr to Sep: daily, 1000 to 1800
Oct: daily, 1000 to 1700
Nov to Mar: Wed to Sun, 1000 to 1600
Other restrictions: Closed 24 to 26 Dec, 1 Jan.
Access for disabled people: Parking provided, level entry, toilet facilities

General description:
Roman Archaeology relating to Hadrian's Wall. Roman inscriptions, sculpture, small finds and pottery excavated from the Roman sites of Corbridge, Chesters and Homesteads, illustrating both the history of Hadrian's Wall and its military and civilian use.
Information services:
Handling collection available for educational use. Must be pre-booked.
Special visitor services: Tape recorded guides, materials and/or activities for children.
Education services: Group education facilities, resources for Key Stage 2..
Collections:
Corbridge hoard of weapons, armour, tools, etc. ca. AD 122-138. ca. 360 items
Printed publications:
Various publications available at the sites.

Internet home pages:
http://www.english-heritage.org.uk

See also - Chesters Roman Fort and Museum; Corbridge Roman Site Museum; Hadrian's Wall and Housesteads Roman Fort

1191
HADRIAN'S WALL TOURISM PARTNERSHIP

Tel: 01434 602505
Email: info@hadrians-wall.org

Organisation type and purpose: Public/private partnership.
To develop sustainable tourism and linked community and environmental initiatives throughout the whole of the Hadrian's Wall World Heritage Site.
Partner is:
Countryside Agency
Cumbria Tourist Board
English Heritage
National Trust
Newcastle University
Northumbria Tourist Board
Vindolanda Trust
Access:
Access to staff: By telephone, by email, Internet web pages

General description:
Hadrian's Wall.

Internet home pages:
http://www.hadrians-wall.org
Information on any of the Partnership's projects.

1192
HAIG COLLIERY MINING MUSEUM

Solway Road, Kells, Whitehaven, Cumbria, CA28 9BG

Tel: 01946 599949
Fax: 01946 599949
Email: museum@haigpit.com
Formed: 1993
Formerly: Haig Pit Restoration Group

Organisation type and purpose: Membership association (membership is by subscription), voluntary organisation, registered charity (charity number 1050534), museum, suitable for ages: all ages, training organisation, research organisation.

Enquiries to: Manager
Other contacts: Heritage Officer for information relating to archives and collection.
Access:
Access to staff: By letter, by telephone, by fax, by email, in person, Internet web pages
Hours: Daily, 1100 to 1700; closed Wed
Access to building, collections or gallery: No prior appointment required
Hours: Daily, 1100 to 1700; closed Wed
Access for disabled people: Parking provided, ramped entry, toilet facilities

General description:
Coalmining.
Catalogues:
Catalogue for library is on-line. Catalogue for all of the collections is on-line.
Publications list:
is available on-line.
Printed publications:
Employment Commission Evidence for Cumberland 1842
Museum Guide
Electronic and video products:
Oral archive (CD-ROM)

Internet home pages:
http://www.haigpit.com

1193
HAILES ABBEY

Near Winchcombe, Cheltenham, Gloucestershire, GL54 5PB

Tel: 01242 602398
Email: customers@english-heritage.org.uk
Formed: 1246

Organisation type and purpose: National government body, registered charity (charity number 205846), historic building, house or site, suitable for ages: 16+.
Maintained and managed by:
English Heritage (South West Region)
Tel: 0117 975 0700, fax: 0117 975 0701
Owned by:
The National Trust (South West Region)
Tel: 01985 843600
Other branches:
English Heritage
South West Region
29 Queen Square, Bristol, BS1 4ND, tel: 0117 9750700, fax: 0117 9750701

Enquiries to: Custodian
Access:
Access to staff: By letter only
Access to building, collections or gallery: No prior appointment required
Hours: Apr to Sep, daily, 1000 to 1800; Oct, daily, 1000 to 1700
Other restrictions: Opening times are subject to change, for up-to-date information contact English Heritage by phone or visit the website.
Access for disabled people: ramped entry, toilet facilities
Other restrictions: General access, 1 step to museum.

General description:
Hailes Abbey, built in the 13th century, became famous when presented with a phial said to contain the Holy Blood of Christ. Pilgrims from far and wide were attracted to the magnificent Cistercian Abbey until the 16th century. Today, the museum displays fine sculpture and other exciting finds from the Abbey, and the site retains an atmosphere of deep serenity.
Information services:
Braille guide. Audio tour also for visually impaired visitors, those with learning difficulties and for wheelchair users.
Suitable for school groups.
Special visitor services: Tape recorded guides.
Education services: Group education facilities.
Services for disabled people: For the visually impaired; for the hearing impaired.
Printed publications:
Site Guide Book

Address for ordering publications:
Printed publications:
Gillards, Trident Works
Temple Works, Bristol, tel: 01761 452966, fax: 01761 453408

Internet home pages:
http://www.english-heritage.org.uk
http://www.nationaltrust.org.uk/regions/wessex

1194
HALESOWEN ABBEY

Halesowen, West Midlands

Organisation type and purpose: National organisation, historic building, house or site.

Enquiries to: Manager
Access:
Access to staff: By letter

General description:
Remains of an abbey founded by King John in the 13th century.

1195
HALESWORTH AND DISTRICT MUSEUM

The Railway Station, Station Road, Halesworth, Suffolk, IP19 8BZ

Formed: 1984

Organisation type and purpose: Independently owned, registered charity (charity number 1002545), museum, suitable for ages: all ages. Registered museum in refurbished railway station.
To preserve and record the history of the area.

Enquiries to: Curator
Direct tel: 01986 873030 (Curator's Home Number)
Access:
Access to staff: By letter, by telephone, in person
Access to building, collections or gallery: No prior appointment required
Hours: May to Sep: Tue & Wed, 1000 to 1230 & 1400 to 1600; Thu & Sat, 1000 to 1230; Bank Holidays, 1400 to 1600
Oct to Apr: most Tue and Thu, 1000 to 1230
Other times by appointment
Access for disabled people: Parking provided, ramped entry, access to all public areas, toilet facilities

General description:
Archaeology, geology and local history: Hooker (father and son) first two Directors of Kew Gardens; brewing and maltings; LNER and Southwold Railways, photographs, paper archives, books and ephemera.
Information services:
Library available for reference (for conditions see Access above)
The Museum is able to provide activities and resources to support education work of schools and groups of all ages and abilities. Visits can be arranged to suit the requirements of groups and individuals. There are study loan boxes and Halesworth's restored signal box is nearby.
Special visitor services: Guided tours, materials and/or activities for children.
Education services: Group education facilities, resources for Key Stages 1 and 2 and Further or Higher Education.
Services for disabled people: For the visually impaired; displays and/or information at wheelchair height.
Catalogues:
Catalogue for library is in-house only. Catalogue for all of the collections is only available in-house.
Publications list:
is available in hard copy.
Printed publications:
Archaeological reports on local sites and excavations
Local history books:
Constables of Suffolk: a Brief History (£6.50 plus £1 p&p)
Emmanuel Bowyer's 1759 Suffolk Map (£2.50 plus 50p p&p)
Ghosts and Witchcraft (20p plus 20p p&p)
Halesworth Through the Ages (7 vols, Pre-history to 20th century, £3.99 plus 50 p&p)
The Agricultural Labourer (£1 plus 50p p&p)
The Halesworth Area in the 11th Century (£1 plus 50p p&p)
The History of a Gothic House (£4.99 plus 50p p&p)
The People of a Suffolk Town (£9.50 plus £1 p&p)
Suffolk Map & Guidebook in One (Goldeneye, £4.99 plus 50p p&p)

Address for ordering publications:
Printed publications:
Publicity Officer, Halesworth and District Museum
at the address above

1196
HALL I'TH' WOOD MUSEUM
See - Bolton Museums, Art Gallery and Aquarium

1197
HALL PLACE & GARDENS
See - Bexley Heritage Trust

1198
HALLIWELL'S HOUSE MUSEUM & ROBSON GALLERY
Market Place, Selkirk, Borders, TD7 4BL

Tel: 01750 20096
Fax: 01750 23282
Email: museums@scotborders.gov.uk
Formed: 1984

Organisation type and purpose: Local government body, museum, art gallery, suitable for ages: 5+.
Parent body:
Scottish Borders Council Museum and Gallery Service
Municipal Buildings, High Street, Selkirk, TD7 4JX, tel: 01750 20096, fax: 01750 23282, email: museums@scotborders.gov.uk

Enquiries to: Curator
Access:
Access to staff: By letter, by telephone, by fax, by email, in person
Access to building, collections or gallery: No prior appointment required
Hours: Apr to Oct: Mon to Sat, 1000 to 1700; Sun, 1400 to 1700
Access for disabled people: Parking provided, ramped entry, access to all public areas, toilet facilities
Other restrictions: Lift to first floor.

General description:
Recreating the building's former use as a home and ironmonger's shop, the displays tell the story of the Royal Burgh of Selkirk, Ettick and Yarrow Valleys.
Ironmongery and domestic collections.
Information services:
Temporary exhibitions in the Robson Gallery
Special visitor services: Guided tours, tape recorded guides, materials and/or activities for children.
Education services: Group education facilities..
Collections:
Artefacts relating to the woolen trade
Ironmongery and domestic collections.
Robson; domestic ironmongery as sold from ironmonger's shop, some material predates main collection, c.1850 - c.1950, 2500 items
Flodden Flag, reputed to have been brought back to Selkirk from Battle of Flodden, 1513
Catalogues:
Catalogue for all of the collections is only available in-house.
Publications list:
is available in hard copy.

Internet home pages:
http://www.scotborders.gov.uk
http://www.scotborders.org.uk

1199
HALTON CHEMICAL INDUSTRY MUSEUM TRUST
See - Catalyst

1200
HAM HOUSE
Richmond-upon-Thames, Surrey, TW10 7RS

Tel: 020 8940 1950
Fax: 020 8332 6903
Email: hamhouse@nationaltrust.org.uk

Organisation type and purpose: Local government body (charity number 205846), museum, art gallery, public library.
Parent body:
The National Trust (South and South East Region)
Thames and Solent Regional Office, tel: 01494 528051
National Trust sites:
Ham House
Richmond-upon-Thames, Surrey, TW10 7RS, tel: 020 8940 1950, fax: 020 8332 6903, email/website: hamhouse@ntrust.org.uk

Enquiries to: Manager
Access:
Access to staff: By letter, by telephone, by fax, by email
Access for disabled people: Parking provided, access to all public areas, toilet facilities
Other restrictions: 2 manual wheelchairs and 1 single-seater powered mobility vehicle available, booking essential. Steps to entrance. Stairclimber available for most types of wheelchair. Please tel. in advance. Ground floor fully accessible, small lift to all floors on request. Level entrance to shop. Ramped entrance to tea-room. Grounds largely accessible. Recommended route map.

General description:
Ham House is unique in Europe as the most complete survival of 17th century fashion and power. It was built in 1610 and then enlarged in the 1670s when it was at the heart of Restoration court life and intrigue. The Earl's 18th century drawing room in the private apartments and the 17th century statues in the wilderness garden have now been restored. The garden is significant as one of the few formal gardens to survive the English Landscape Movement in the 18th century. The garden restoration, begun in 1973, has influenced recent restorations of some of the great gardens in Europe. An exhibition about the history and development of the garden, accompanied by a video of the history of the house, is on show in the 18th century dairy buildings, and the interior of the earliest identifed still house in England can be seen.
Information services:
Guided tours of house available by arrangement on Wed mornings only during the open season. Guided tours of gardens 1400 and 1500 on Weds (dates as house). Ghost tours in Nov (booking essential).
Open-air concerts during the summer. House and ghost tours; school holiday family events; 'Putting the House to Bed'; lecture lunches; Christmas carols (tel. for details). Braille guide. Large-print guide. Touch list. Handling collection. Scented plants.
Sympathetic Hearing Scheme.
Front-carrying baby slings for loan.
Suitable for school groups. Education room/centre. Hands-on activities. Children's guide. Children's quiz/trail.
Special visitor services: Guided tours, materials and/or activities for children.
Education services: Group education facilities.
Services for disabled people: For the visually impaired; for the hearing impaired.
Collections:
Collection of 17th century furniture, textiles and pictures, including miniatures, original to the house

Internet home pages:
http://www.nationaltrust.org.uk

1201
HAMILTON DISTRICT MUSEUM
See - Low Parks Museum

1202
HAMPSHIRE COUNTY COUNCIL MUSEUMS SERVICE HEADQUARTERS
Chilcomb House, Chilcomb Lane, Winchester, Hampshire, SO23 8RD

Tel: 01962 846304
Fax: 01962 869836
Email: musmrg@hants.gov.uk
Formed: 1944

Organisation type and purpose: Local government body.
The headquarters service, including administration, documentation, museum library, stores, conservation workshops, photographic studio, design studio, etc.
Parent body:
Hampshire County Council

Enquiries to: Director
Access:
Access to staff: By letter, by telephone, by fax, by email, in person, visitors by prior appointment
Hours: Mon to Fri, 0900 to 1700

General description:
The main subject areas are Hampshire history, archaeology, local history, social history, decorative art, ceramics, textiles, costume, toys, horology, firearms, natural science, botany, zoology, geology, conservation (museum), museology.
Collections:
Archaeological site archives
Blair Collection (entomologist's notes)
Tasker Collection (steam machinery, engineering drawings, archives and plans)
Printed publications:
List available from the Librarian at this address

continued overleaf

Internet home pages:
http://www.hants.gov.uk/museums/
Catalogue, whole collection, over 100,000 pages.

See also - Aldershot Military Museum; Allen Gallery; Andover Museum; Basing House Historic Ruin; Bursledon Windmill; Curtis Museum; Eastleigh Museum; Flora Twort Gallery; Gosport Museum; Havant Museum; Milestones; Monitor 33; Museum of the Iron Age; Red House Museum and Gardens; Rockbourne Roman Villa; Rushmoor Local History Gallery; SEARCH; St Barbe Museum & Art Gallery; Treadgold Industrial Heritage Museum; Westbury Manor Museum; Willis Museum of Basingstoke Town and Country Life

1203
HAMPSHIRE FARM MUSEUM
See - Manor Farm Country Park

1204
HAMPSHIRE MUSEUM EDUCATION SERVICE
See - SEARCH

1205
HAMPSHIRE TRANSPORT AND TECHNOLOGY MUSEUM
See - Milestones

1206
HAMPSTEAD MUSEUM
Burgh House, New End Square, London, NW3 1LT

Tel: 020 7431 0144
Fax: 020 7435 8817
Email: hampsteadmuseum@talk21.com
Full name: Hampstead Museum, Burgh House
Formed: 1979

Organisation type and purpose: Independently owned, museum, suitable for ages: 8+, research organisation.
Connections with:
Association of Independent Museums (AIM)
Weald and Downland Museum, Singleton, Chichester, West Sussex, PO18 0EU
Camden History Society
London Museums Agency (LMA)
Cloister Court, 22-26 Farringdon Lane, London, EC1R 3 AJ, tel: 020 7600 0219
Museums Association (MA)
24 Calvin Street, London, E1 6NW, tel: 020 7608 2933, fax: 020 7250 1929
Other address:
Burgh House Trust
at the same address

Enquiries to: Curator
Access:
Access to staff: By letter, by telephone, by fax, visitors by prior appointment
Hours: Wed to Sun, 1200 to 1700 (Sat by appointment)
Closed Mon, Tue, Christmas to New Year, Good Friday and Easter Monday
Access for disabled people: ramped entry, toilet facilities
Other restrictions: Ramped entry at back of house, ground floor only.

General description:
Helen Allingham Collection.
Local artists, theatrical associations and musical associations; local architecture; famous people who have lived in Hampstead; 18th century Hampstead and the history of The Wells; local industry; Hampstead Heath; Isokon chair, furniture, flats.
Collections:
Local history archive of photographs, documents, prints etc
Helen Allingham Bequest of paintings, books, memorabilia
Constable Display
Isokon Chair from Wells Coates Lawn Road flats
Scouts Collection
Catalogues:
Catalogue for library is in-house only. Catalogue for all of the collections is only available in-house.
Printed publications:
Various printed publications such as:
Constable's Hampstead
Hampstead at War
Who Lived Where in Hampstead
Theatrical Hampstead
Historic Taverns

See also - Burgh House Trust

1207
HAMPTON COURT PALACE
East Molesey, Surrey, KT8 9AU

Tel: 020 8781 9500
Fax: 020 8781 9509
Email: curators@hrp.org.uk
Acronym or abbreviation: HRP
Formed: 1990
Formerly: Historic Royal Palaces Agency, date of change, 1998

Organisation type and purpose: National government body, suitable for ages: all ages.

Enquiries to: Curator
Direct tel: 020 8781 9781
Direct fax: 020 8781 9782
Access:
Access to staff: By letter, by telephone, by fax, by email, visitors by prior appointment
Access to building, collections or gallery: No prior appointment required

General description:
Collection of paintings, tapestry and furniture housed in the impressive State Apartments, the Lower Orangery Gallery and the Renaissance Picture Gallery.
Information services:
Special visitor services: Guided tours, tape recorded guides, materials and/or activities for children.
Education services: Group education facilities, resources for Further or Higher Education..

1208
HANBURY HALL
School Road, Hanbury, Droitwich, Worcestershire, WR9 7EA

Tel: 01527 821214
Fax: 01527 821251
Email: hanburyhall@ntrust.org.uk
Formed: 1895

Organisation type and purpose: Registered charity (charity number 205846).
Historic house.
Parent body:
The National Trust

Enquiries to: Property Manager
Access:
Access to staff: By letter, by telephone, by fax, by email
Access for disabled people: Parking provided, ramped entry, toilet facilities

General description:
Thornhill painted staircase; Dutch flower paintings; Watney porcelain collection; restored 18th century gardens. An historic country house - red brick in the style of Wren, built c. 1700 and little altered; fine painted ceilings and a staircase by Sir James Thornhill (artist of Great Hall at Greenwich) c. 1710; 18th century collection of porcelain and Dutch flower paintings; 18th century marquetry furniture; angle bed with original fabrics c. 1720; handsome Orangery and excellent example of ice house, both c. mid 18th century.
Collections:
Porcelain. 18th century figures. Collection of armorial dinner plates and two armorial dinner services
Dutch flower paintings, mid 17th century-18th century
Angle bed c. 1720 with original blue wool damask fabrics
Printed publications:
Braille Guide
Guide Books

1209
HANCOCK MUSEUM
Barras Bridge, Newcastle upon Tyne, NE2 4PT

Tel: 0191 222 6765
Minicom no. 0191 222 6805
Fax: 0191 222 6753
Email: hancock.museum@ncl.ac.uk
Formed: 1829
Formed from: Natural History Society of Northumberland, Durham and Newcastle upon Tyne, Lit & Phil (Newcastle), Natural History Society of Northumbria
Formerly: The Newcastle Museum

Organisation type and purpose: Local government body, independently owned, learned society, registered charity, museum, university department or institute, suitable for ages: 5+, research organisation.
Natural history museum (with Egyptology and ethnography).
Parent body:
The Natural History Society of Northumbria
Administered by:
Tyne & Wear Museums (TWM)
Discovery Museum, Blandford Square, Newcastle, tel: 0191 232 6789, fax: 0191 230 2614
Funded by:
University of Newcastle

Enquiries to: Curator
Direct tel: 0191 222 7868
Direct email: s.g.mclean@ncl.ac.uk
Other contacts: Education Officer for school groups, activities.
Access:
Access to staff: By letter, by telephone, by fax, by email, visitors by prior appointment, Internet web pages
Hours: Mon to Fri, 0900 to 1700
Access to building, collections or gallery: No prior appointment required
Hours: Mon to Sat, 1000 to 1700; Sun, 1400 to 1700
Other restrictions: Prior appointment required to view collections not on public display.
Access for disabled people: Parking provided, ramped entry, toilet facilities
Other restrictions: 95% access to all areas.

General description:
The North East's premier Natural History Museum unravels the secrets of the natural world through sensational galleries and close encounters with reptiles and insects. From the dinosaurs to live animals. It contains permanent galleries of environment, ecology, geology, mineralogy, insects, birds, mammals, Egyptology and ethnography. An important collection designated as of outstanding national importance and containing approximately 750,000 items.
The Hancock is home to creatures past and present, and even the odd Egyptian Mummy or two.
Information services:
Library available for reference (for conditions see Access above)
Special visitor services: Tape recorded guides, materials and/or activities for children.
Education services: Group education facilities, resources for Key Stages 1 and 2, 3, 4 and Further or Higher Education.
Services for disabled people: For the hearing impaired; displays and/or information at wheelchair height.

Collections:
The museum has an extensive paper archive collection and in fact devotes a complete store to this purpose. The collection is too extensive to list here and only some of the more important collections are named - dates refer to actual periods covered, or estimates
Predominantly Natural History including: entomology, osteology, vertebrate and invertebrate palaeontology, palaeobotany, mineralogy, petrology, botany, vertebratre and invertebrate zoology, spirit collections, but also including significant collections of ethnography and archaeology
Material originating in 18th century collection including those of numerous important Victorian collectors
Nathaniel John Winch Collection
Vascular plants, author of the first flora of Northumberland, lower plants 1768-1838, 4000+ artefacts
Frederic Raine Collection
Vascular plants mainly from Southern Europe 1851-1919, 8000+ artefacts
Birds nests and eggs, 3000 artefacts
Butterflies, mainly European, 11000 artefacts
George Ralph Tate Collection
Vascular plants, co-author of A new flora of Northumberland and Durham 1835-1874
Sir Walter Calverley Trevelyan of Wallington Hall Collection
Vascular plants, lower plants 1797-1879, 1300 artefacts
Robert Benson Bowman Collection
Vascular plants, 1808-1882, 1400 artefacts
One of the largest collections in the world of the watercolours and engravings of Newcastle-born 18th century artist and engraver, Thomas Bewick
Professor George Brady Collection
Micro-crustacea (spirit and slide collections), much Type material, includes material from the HMS Challenger voyage, 1832-1921, 4000+ artefacts
Hancock Letters
John Hancock correspondence c. 1830-1890
Catalogues:
Catalogue for library is in-house only. Catalogue for all of the collections is published and is also on-line.
Publications list:
is available in hard copy.
Printed publications:
Contact Museum for details

Internet home pages:
http://www.ncl.ac.uk/hancock
Facilities, galleries, collections, education
http://www.ncl.ac.uk/publications/

1210
HANLEY MUSEUM
See - Potteries Museum & Art Gallery

1211
HARBOROUGH MUSEUM
Council Offices, Adam and Eve Street, Market Harborough, Leicestershire, LE16 7AG

Tel: 01858 821085
Fax: 01858 821086
Email: museum@leics.gov.uk
Formed: 1983

Organisation type and purpose: Local government body, museum, suitable for ages: all ages.
Parent body:
Leicester Museums, Arts & Records Service (LMARS)
Room 700, County Hall, Glenfield, Leicester, LE3 8TB, tel: 0116 265 6783, fax: 0116 265 6788, email: museums@leics.gov.uk

Enquiries to: Curator
Direct tel: 01858 821087
Access:
Access to staff: By letter, by telephone, by fax, by email, in person

General description:
Harborough Museum is a small, local history museum looking at the history of the town, its people and its industries from Roman times to present day.
Displays and specialist knowledge include: the Symington Corset Collection, a collection of Tudor street toys, a reconstructed shoe-maker's shop, a Roman mosaic, and extensive archives on W Symington dried food manufacturers.
Information services:
Special visitor services: Materials and/or activities for children.
Education services: Resources for Key Stages 1 and 2.
Services for disabled people: For the hearing impaired.
Collections:
Extensive local photographs collection dating from 1850 to present day
Tudor Street Toys
R & W H Symington Corset Collection
W Symington Collection of packaging and archive material
Local oral history archive, taped interviews with local residents on a wide variety of topics, 1900s-date, c. 300 hours (ongoing)
Harold Jones Collection, rubbings of local Swithland slate gravestones, 1690-1900, c. 750 items
St Dionysius Toy Hoard. Children's toys found walled up in Parish Church, c. 1650, c. 300 items
Contemporary Christmas cards. Well-provenanced collections of contemporary Christmas cards, 1988-date, c. 2000 (ongoing)
William Law Collection, calotype photographs of Welland Valley area, 1850s c. 70 items
Ernest Elliott Collection, artefacts relating to the work of Elliott as a popular entertainer, 1920s-1950s, c. 50 items
Catalogues:
Catalogue for all of the collections is available in-house and part is on-line.

1212
HARBOUR COTTAGE GALLERY, THE
Castlebank, Kirkcudbright, Dumfries & Galloway, DG6 4LB

Tel: 01557 330073
Formed: 1957

Organisation type and purpose: Art gallery, suitable for ages: 12+.
Trust.
Parent body:
Kirkcudbright Harbour Cottage Gallery Trust
12 Castle Street, Kirkcudbright, DG6 4JA

Enquiries to: Honorary Secretary
Access:
Access to staff: By letter, by telephone

General description:
Exhibitions of original paintings by artists in Galloway, local crafts exhibitions, open exhibition - open to artists outwith Galloway, and Gallery's paintings of old Kircudbright artists.

Internet home pages:
http://www.kirkcudbright.co.uk
Kirkcudbright website information on Gallery programme and artists

1213
HARBOUR MUSEUM
Harbour Square, Londonderry, BT48 6AF

Tel: 028 7137 7331
Fax: 028 7137 7633
Email: museums@derrycity.gov.uk
Formed: 1995
Formed from: Derry City Council Heritage & Museums Service
Formerly: Tower Museum

Organisation type and purpose: Local government body, museum, suitable for ages: 8+.
Parent body:
Derry City Council (DCC)
98 Strand Road, Derry, tel: 028 7136 5151

Enquiries to: Curator
Access:
Access to staff: By letter, by telephone, by fax, by email, in person, visitors by prior appointment
Hours: Mon to Fri, 0900 to 1300 and 1400 to 1700
Access to building, collections or gallery: No prior appointment required
Hours: Daily, 1000 to 1300 and 1400 to 1630
Access for disabled people: toilet facilities
Other restrictions: Ground floor access.

General description:
A small collection of maritime and river-related objects of local interest.
Catalogues:
Catalogue for part of the collections is only available in-house.

See also - Tower Museum

1214
HARDKNOTT ROMAN FORT
See - Wasdale, Eskdale and Duddon

1215
HARDLEY MILL
O.S. TG 387 024, Hardley Street, Norfolk

Organisation type and purpose: Historic building, house or site.

General description:
Undergoing extensive restoration.

1216
HARDWICK HALL
Doe Lea, Chesterfield, Derbyshire, S44 5QJ

Tel: 01246 850430
Fax: 01246 854200
Email: hardwickhall@nationaltrust.org.uk

Organisation type and purpose: National organisation, registered charity (charity number 205846), historic building, house or site, suitable for ages: 8+.
Parent body:
The National Trust (East Midlands Region)
East Midlands Regional Office, tel: 01909 486411

Enquiries to: Property Manager
Other contacts: Education Officer (01246 850430) for education facilities.
Access:
Access to staff: By letter, by telephone, by fax, by email, in person, Internet web pages
Access to building, collections or gallery: No prior appointment required
Hours: Hall: end of Mar to June, and Sep, Wed, Thu, Sat and Sun, 1230 to 1700: Jul to Aug, Wed, Thu, Sat, Sun and Mon 1230 to 1700; Oct, Wed, Thu, Sat and Sun, 1230 to1600
Garden: end of Mar to end of Oct, 1100 to 1730
Other restrictions: Extensive building work throughout 2003 may lessen visitors' enjoyment. Due to limited lighting, visitors wishing to make a close study of tapestries and textiles should avoid dull days early and late in the season.
To avoid congestion, access to the house may be limited at peak periods. Visitors are advised to allow one hour to tour the house. The remains of Hardwick Old Hall in the grounds are in the guardianship of English Heritage (01246 850431)
Access for disabled people: Parking provided, ramped entry, toilet facilities
Other restrictions: Drop-off point. 3 manual wheelchairs available, booking essential. Ground floor largely accessible, no battery-powered wheelchairs allowed (except

continued overleaf

children). No access to other floors.
Photograph album. Many narrow steep stairs.
Staff trained to assist hard of hearing and sight-impaired visitors - please pre-book.
Ramped entrance to shop. Ramped entrance to restaurant. Wheelchair-adapted table - booking essential. Grounds largely accessible.
Recommended route map.

General description:
One of Britain's foremost Elizabethan houses and a magnificent statement of the wealth and authority of its builder, Bess of Hardwick. Like a huge glass lantern, the house dominates the surrounding area and contains outstanding collections of 16th century furniture, tapestries and needlework. All are owned by the Devonshire family. Some were acquired specifically for Hardwick, while others were brought in at various stages in the hall's history. Walled courtyards enclose fine gardens, orchards and a herb garden, and the surrounding country park contains rare breeds of cattle and sheep.
Information services:
Braille guide, large-print guide, touch list, handling collection, tactile map of garden and park.
Suitable for school groups. Education room/centre; live interpretation.
Education visits Wed & Thur plus Mon in July.
Children's guide. Children's quiz/trail.
Adult study days.
Tours of stonemasons' yard Wed/Thu pm
Hall and roof guided tours Mon in July & Aug (not BH Mon)
Roof tours Wed & Thur 30 July - 28 Aug (weather permitting); no children under 12 or unaccompanied children under 17.
Special events programme.
Special visitor services: Materials and/or activities for children.
Education services: Group education facilities, resources for Key Stage 2 and Further or Higher Education.
Services for disabled people: For the visually impaired; for the hearing impaired.
Collections:
Needlework, including many embroideries worked by Bess of Hardwick and rare appliqué wall hangings, late 16th/early 17th Centuries, c. 500 items or groups of items in general category of textiles
Furniture, various items of which appear in the 1601 inventory of the contents of Hardwick including the famous Sea Dog and Eglantine Tables c. 50 items

Internet home pages:
http://www.nationaltrust.org.uk

See also - Stainsby Mill: Hardwick Estate

1217
HARDWICK OLD HALL
Doe Lea, Chesterfield, Derbyshire, S44 5QJ

Tel: 01246 850431

Organisation type and purpose: Historic building, house or site.
Parent body:
National Trust (East Midlands Regional Office)
Tel: 01909 486411, fax: 01909 486377
Maintained and managed by:
English Heritage (East Midlands Region)
44 Derngate, Northampton, NN1 1UH, tel: 01604 735400, fax: 01604 735401

Enquiries to: House Manager
Access:
Access to staff: By letter, by telephone
Other restrictions: Contact Regional Office when property closed, 01604 735400.
Access to building, collections or gallery: No prior appointment required
Hours: 1 Apr to 30 Sep, Mon, Wed, Thu, Sat and Sun, 1100 to 1800; Oct, Mon, Wed, Thu, Sat and Sun, 1100 to 1700;
Other restrictions: Opening times are subject to change, for up-to-date information contact English Heritage by phone or visit the website.
Access for disabled people: Parking provided, toilet facilities

General description:
The family home of Bess of Hardwick, one of the most remarkable women of the Elizabethan Age who embarked on several grand building projects to display her immense wealth and authority. This large, ruined house, finished in 1591, lies on the crest of the hill next to the stupendous 'New' Hall she built in the 1590s. The Old Hall displays Bess of Hardwick's innovative planning and decorative plasterwork. The views from the top floor are spectacular.
Information services:
Special visitor services: Tape recorded guides..

Internet home pages:
http://www.english-heritage.org.uk

1218
HARDY MONUMENT
Black Down, Portesham, Dorset

Tel: 01297 561900 (West Dorset Office)
Fax: 01297 561901

Organisation type and purpose: National organisation, registered charity (charity number 205846), historic building, house or site.
Parent body:
National Trust (South West)
Regional Office for Wessex, tel: 01985 843600

Enquiries to: Manager
Access:
Access to staff: By letter, by telephone, by fax

General description:
A monument erected in 1844 in memory of Vice-Admiral Sir Thomas Masterman Hardy, Flag-Captain of HMS Victory at the Battle of Trafalgar. It has been recently restored by the NT.

Internet home pages:
http://www.nationaltrust.org.uk/regions/wessex

1219
HARDY'S COTTAGE
Higher Bockhampton, Dorchester, Dorset, DT2 8QJ

Tel: 01305 262366 (Custodian)

Organisation type and purpose: National organisation, registered charity (charity number 205846), museum, historic building, house or site, suitable for ages: 5+.
Parent body:
The National Trust (South West Region)
Wessex Regional Office, tel: 01985 843600

Enquiries to: Custodian
Access:
Access to staff: By letter, by telephone
Access to building, collections or gallery: No prior appointment required
Hours: Beg Apr to beg Nov, Mon, Thu, Fri, Sat, Sun, 1100 to 1700
Other restrictions: Closes dusk if earlier than 1700.
No coach parking.

General description:
The small cob and thatch cottage where novelist and poet Thomas Hardy was born in 1840 and from where he would walk to school every day in Dorchester, six miles away. It was built by his great-grandfather and is little altered since. The interior has been furnished by the National Trust (see also Max Gate). His early novels 'Under the Greenwood Tree' and 'Far from the Madding Crowd' were written here. Charming cottage garden.
Information services:
Services for disabled people: For the visually impaired.

Internet home pages:
http://www.nationaltrust.org.uk/regions/wessex

See also - Max Gate

1220
HARESTONES COUNTRYSIDE VISITOR CENTRE
by Ancrum, Jedburgh, Borders, TD8 6UQ

Tel: 01835 830306
Fax: 01835 830734

Organisation type and purpose: Local government body, suitable for ages: 5+.
Visual Arts and historical exhibition centre.
Parent body:
Scottish Borders Council Museum and Gallery Service
Tel: 01750 23282
Grant-aided by, the European Union Regional Development Fund:
Scotish National Heritage
Grant-aided by the, the European Union Regional Development Fund:
European Union Regional Development Fund

Enquiries to: Manager
Access:
Access to staff: By letter, by telephone, by fax
Access for disabled people: Parking provided, access to all public areas

General description:
Scottish Borders countryside, parkland.

Internet home pages:
http://www.scotborders.org.uk
http://www.scotborders.gov.uk

1221
HAREWOOD HOUSE TRUST
Moor House, Harewood, Leeds, West Yorkshire, LS17 9LQ

Tel: 0113 218 1010
Fax: 0113 218 1002
Email: business@harewood.org
Formed: 1950

Organisation type and purpose: Registered charity (charity number 517753), museum, historic building, house or site, suitable for ages: all ages, research organisation.

Enquiries to: Director
Direct tel: 0113 218 1006
Direct email: director@harewood.org
Access:
Access to staff: By letter, by email, Internet web pages
Access to building, collections or gallery: No prior appointment required
Hours: Daily, 1000 to 1800
Access for disabled people: Parking provided, ramped entry, toilet facilities

General description:
History of house and related subjects, Princess Mary and related collections.
Information services:
Special visitor services: Guided tours, tape recorded guides, materials and/or activities for children.
Education services: Group education facilities, resources for Key Stages 2, 3, 4 and Further or Higher Education..
Collections:
Chippendale furniture and other 18th century decorative art
Adam interiors
18th century paintings eg Reynolds, Gainsborough, Turner watercolours
Italian Renaissance paintings
Sèvres Porcelain
Chinese Celadon Porcelain
20th century art including Sickert, Bacon, Munnings and Picasso
Publications list:
is available in hard copy.

Printed publications:
The Art of Thomas Chippendale (exhibition catalogue, hardback £9.95, softback £5.95)
Thomas Girtin: Genius in the North (Hill D, £3)
Thomas Hartley Cromek: A Classical Vision (Zack S, £2.95)
Watercolours by Charlotte, Viscountess Canning (Millar D, £4.95)
Harewood Masterpieces, English Watercolours and Drawings (Hill D, hardback £9.95, softback £5.95)
Harewood Souvenir Brochure (£3)
Harewood House (Mauchline M, £9.95)

Internet home pages:
http://www.harewood.org

1222
HARINGEY ARCHIVE SERVICE

Bruce Castle Museum, Lordship Lane, London, N17 8NU

Tel: 020 8808 8772
Fax: 020 8808 4118
Email: museum.services@haringey.gov.uk

Organisation type and purpose: Local government body, museum.

Enquiries to: Local History Officer
Access:
Access to staff: By letter, by telephone, visitors by prior appointment
Hours: Wed to Fri, 1300 to 1645; alternate Sat, 1300 to 1645
Other restrictions: Appointment required.

General description:
Archives and local history of the present local authority (Borough of Haringey) and its predecessors (Tottenham, Wood Green and Hornsey).
Collections of maps, photographs, postcards, 1841 to 1891 census returns on 35mm microfilm for Tottenham, Wood Green and Hornsey, newspapers, directories.
Catalogues:
Catalogue for part of the collections is only available in-house.

1223
HARINGEY LIBRARIES, MUSEUM AND ARCHIVES SERVICE

Haringey Central Library, High Road, Wood Green, London, N22 6XD

Tel: 020 8489 0000
Fax: 020 8889 0110
Formerly: Haringey Library Services

Organisation type and purpose: Local government body, public library.
Parent body:
London Borough of Haringey Education Service
Branch libraries:
Alexandra Park
Tel: 020 8883 8553
Coomes Croft
Tel: 020 8808 0022
Highgate
Tel: 020 8348 3443
Hornsey
Tel: 020 8489 1429
Marcus Garvey
Tel: 020 8489 5350
Muswell Hill
Tel: 020 8883 6734
St Anns
Tel: 020 8800 4390
Stroud Green
Tel: 020 8348 4363

Enquiries to: Head of Library Services
Other contacts: Principal Librarian Systems and Support Services for Head of Bibliographic and Computer Services.
Access:
Access to staff: By letter, by telephone, by fax, in person
Hours: Central Library: Mon to Thu, 0900 to 1900; Fri closed; Sat, 0900 to 1700
Other restrictions: Contact other branch libraries for information regarding opening times and disabled access facilities.
Access to building, collections or gallery: No access other than to staff
Access for disabled people: level entry, access to all public areas, toilet facilities

General description:
General; instrumental recitals and the works of Telemann (under the Greater London Audio Subject Specialisation scheme GLASS).
Collections:
Public health engineering under the LASCRA specialisation
Heath Robinson Collection (at Hornsey Library tel: 020 8489 0000)
Printed publications:
Connections by Sylvia Caldecott
How Things Were
Lost Houses of Haringey

Internet home pages:
http://www.haringey.gov.uk
Library news, opening hours, what's on, links, contact us.

1224
HARLEY GALLERY

Welbeck, Worksop, Nottinghamshire, S80 3LW

Tel: 01909 501700
Formed: 1994
Formerly: The Harley Foundation

Organisation type and purpose: Registered charity (charity number 276611), museum, art gallery, suitable for ages: all ages.

Enquiries to: Director
Other contacts: Education Officer for education facilities.
Access:
Access to staff: By letter, by telephone
Access for disabled people: Parking provided, level entry, access to all public areas, toilet facilities

General description:
An architecturally acclaimed adaptation of the ruins of the 5th Duke of Portland's Welbeck Estate gasworks of c. 1865. The new Gallery, designed by Leo Godlewski, was built by local craftsmen, demonstrating that very high standards of craftsmanship are still available in the building industry today. There are changing exhibitions of contemporary crafts and fine arts with early work of art, many of national importance, shown in the secure Treasury.
Information services:
Art and craft workshops for schools and holiday workshops.
Art and craft shop, and exhibitions of contemporary art and craft held annually.
Special visitor services: Guided tours, materials and/or activities for children.
Education services: Group education facilities, resources for Key Stages 1 and 2, 3 and 4..
Collections:
Duke of Portland's Art Collection

1225
HARMER CLASSICS

See - Norfolk Motorcycle Museum

1226
HARRIS MUSEUM & ART GALLERY

Market Square, Preston, Lancashire, PR1 2PP

Tel: 01772 258248
Fax: 01772 886764
Email: harris.museum@preston.gov.uk
Formed: 1893

Organisation type and purpose: Local government body, museum, art gallery, historic building, house or site, suitable for ages: all ages.
Parent body:
Preston Borough Council, Leisure Services Department

Enquiries to: Development Officer
Access:
Access to staff: By letter, by email, visitors by prior appointment
Hours: Mon to Fri, 1000 to 1700
Access to building, collections or gallery: No access other than to staff
Hours: Mon to Sat, 1000 to 1700
Other restrictions: Prior appointment required to see items not on public display.
Closed Sun and Bank Holidays.
Access for disabled people: Parking provided, ramped entry, access to all public areas, toilet facilities

General description:
Fine art; contemporary art; decorative art; local history, all housed in a Grade I listed building.
Information services:
Special visitor services: Guided tours.
Education services: Group education facilities, resources for Key Stages 1 and 2, 3, 4 and Further or Higher Education.
Services for disabled people: For the visually impaired; displays and/or information at wheelchair height.
Collections:
Collections of local and social history
Other collections of fine and decorative art; mainly 18th to 20th century
Contemporary photography collection
Mrs French collection of perfume bottles, 1750-1990, 3000 items
Mrs French collection of visiting card cases, 1750-1990, 1000 items
Items relating to the Preston Guild, 1780-1990, 2000 items
Paintings by Arthur and Anthony Devis, 1750-1816, 150 items
Greetings cards, 1790-1990, 4700 items
Cigarette and tea cards, 1890-1970, 10,000 items
Polished eggs, 800 items
Dolls, 1830-1920, 210 items
Music covers, 1800-1930, 1500 items

Internet home pages:
http://www.preston.gov.uk
http://www.visitpreston.com
General guide to exhibitions, events, collections and other services.

1227
HARROW MUSEUM & HERITAGE CENTRE

Headstone Manor, Pinner View, Harrow, Middlesex, HA2 6PX

Tel: 020 8861 2626
Fax: 020 8863 6407
Email: jan@hacserve.tcom.uk
Formed: 1985/86
Formerly: Harrow Arts Council

Organisation type and purpose: Voluntary organisation, registered charity (charity number 1035534), museum, suitable for ages: all ages.
Parent body:
Harrow Arts Council (HAC)
Harrow Arts Centre, Uxbridge Road, Hatch End, HA5 4EA, tel: 020 8428 0123

Enquiries to: Curator
Other contacts: General Manager
Access:
Access to staff: By letter, by telephone, by fax, by email, in person, Internet web pages
Hours: Thu to Sat, 1230 to 1700 or dusk in winter
Sun and Bank Holidays 1030 to 1700

General description:
Illustrates the local history of Harrow - with 4 listed buildings on a moated site which is an ancient monument. The collection covers archaeology; industry; social and agricultural history.
Collections:
Whitefriars Glass. Collection of glass-makers' tools, patterns, catalogues, products, photographs. 1923 to 1980. ca. 1000,1930s Collection. Domestic and trade items,

continued overleaf

photographs and documents of housing. 1920-1939. ca. 2000 items
Hamiltons. Hand-made decorators' and artists' brushes, tools, etc. and an archive. 1899 to 1982. ca. 1000 items
Local history
Catalogues:
Catalogue for all of the collections is only available in-house.

Internet home pages:
http://www.harrowarts.org.uk/

1228
HARTLEBURY CASTLE

Kidderminster, Worcestershire, DY11 7XZ

Tel: 01299 250416
Fax: 01299 251890
Email: museum@worcestershire.gov.uk
Formed: 1966
Formerly: Hereford & Worcester County Museum, date of change, 1998

Organisation type and purpose: Local government body, museum, historic building, house or site, suitable for ages: all ages.
Parent body:
Worcestershire County Museum

Enquiries to: County Museums Officer
Access:
Access to staff: By letter, by telephone, by fax, by email, visitors by prior appointment
Hours: Mon to Thu, 1000 to 1700; Fri, 1400 to 1700
Access to building, collections or gallery: No prior appointment required
Hours: Mon to Thu, 1000 to 1700; Fri and Sun, 1400 to 1700; Bank Holidays, 1100 to 1700
Access for disabled people: Parking provided, toilet facilities
Other restrictions: Level entry to ground floor and external exhibits.

General description:
The County Museum of Worcestershire is housed in the North Wing of Hartlebury Castle, the sandstone home of the Bishops of Worcester for over a thousand years. The museum depicts life in the county from earliest times until the twentieth century, but is particularly strong on the last two centuries. Galleries in the main museum building show life in the castle in the Victorian period, as well as significant themes from the wider county. In addition there are exterior displays that include a reconstructed Cider Mill and a Transport Gallery. Access to the State Rooms of the castle forms part of the museum package on Tue to Thu inclusive.
Information services:
Library available for reference (for conditions see Access above)
Special visitor services: Guided tours, materials and/or activities for children.
Education services: Group education facilities, resources for Key Stages 1 and 2 and 3..
Collections:
All collections relate to the historic county of Worcestershire and include archaeology, transport, social/domestic life, applied arts, crafts/industries and costume/textiles
Particularly notable are current displays of horse-drawn vehicles, including six gypsy caravans, the county's Roman past, ladies' fashions from the late 18th and 19th centuries, decorative art and craft work from the Bromsgrove Guild, and a wide range of Georgian/Victorian domestic/personal items
Incorporated into the museum collection is the former museum from Tickenhill Manor, which was established by the Parker Family during the inter-war years and passed to the care of the County Council in the 1960s
Catalogues:
Catalogue for library is in-house only. Catalogue for all of the collections is available in-house and part is on-line.

1229
HASLEMERE EDUCATIONAL MUSEUM

78 High Street, Haslemere, Surrey, GU27 2LA

Tel: 01428 642112
Fax: 01428 645234
Acronym or abbreviation: HEM
Formed: 1888

Organisation type and purpose: Independently owned, registered charity (charity number 1071244), museum, suitable for ages: all ages.

Enquiries to: Curator
Access:
Access to staff: By letter, by telephone, by fax
Hours: Mon to Fri, 1000 to 1700
Access to building, collections or gallery: No prior appointment required
Hours: Tue to Sat, 1000 to 1700
Access for disabled people: access to all public areas, toilet facilities

General description:
Permanent galleries: geology, natural history, archaeology, history and an unusual collection of European Folk art, full programme of events.
Information services:
Library available for reference (for conditions see Access above)
Special visitor services: Materials and/or activities for children.
Education services: Group education facilities, resources for Key Stages 1 and 2, 3, 4 and Further or Higher Education.
Services for disabled people: Displays and/or information at wheelchair height.
Collections:
Human History:
Prehistoric British flints, Romano-British pottery, Egyptian mummy, social history, Peasant art, local archives
Natural History:
Botany, British mammals, Mozers shell collection, insect collection, British caged birds, game heads, bones, reptiles
Geology:
Geikie archive, fossils (Icthyosaur), Burgess shale, minerals, meteorite, moa skeleton, Irish elk antlers
Catalogues:
Catalogue for library is in-house only. Catalogue for all of the collections is only available in-house.

1230
HASTINGS FISHERMEN'S MUSEUM

Rock-a-Nore Road, Hastings, East Sussex, TN34 3DW

Tel: 01424 461446
Formed: 1956

Organisation type and purpose: Registered charity, museum, research organisation.
Parent body:
Old Hastings Preservation Society

Enquiries to: Curator/Shipkeeper
Access:
Access to staff: By letter, by telephone
Access for disabled people: level entry

General description:
Maritime past and present of Hastings, especially the ancient fishing industry, fishing industry in East Sussex, Hastings as a seaport.
Information services:
Special visitor services: Guided tours..
Collections:
Actual 28 foot sailing lugger on display plus many models, photos, paintings and items of fishing gear
Three wooden fishing boats on display outside museum

1231
HASTINGS MUSEUM AND ART GALLERY

Johns Place, Cambridge Road, Hastings, East Sussex, TN34 1ET

Tel: 01424 781155
Fax: 01424 781165
Email: museum@hastings.gov.uk
Formed: 1890

Organisation type and purpose: Local government body, museum, art gallery, suitable for ages: 5+.
Exhibition Gallery.
Parent body:
Hastings Borough Council
Town Hall, Queens Road, Hastings, East Sussex, tel: 01424 781066
Other address:
Old Town Hall Museum
High Street, Hastings, tel: 01424 781155, email/website: oldtownmuseum@hastings.gov.uk

Enquiries to: Curator
Direct tel: 01424 781150
Direct email: vwilliams@hastings.gov.uk
Access:
Access to staff: By letter, by telephone, by fax, visitors by prior appointment
Access to building, collections or gallery: No prior appointment required
Hours: Mon to Sat, 1000 to 1700; Sun, 1400 to 1700
Access for disabled people: Parking provided, ramped entry, toilet facilities

General description:
Local studies in geology, zoology, archaeology, topography, art, ceramics, ironwork, history, folklife, biography, architecture, archives; British, European and oriental art, especially ceramics; ethnography, particularly of Oceania and native American collections.
Collections:
Brassey collection of Ethnography and Oriental Art
Edward Blackmore collection of Native American Art
Markwick Library
Catalogues:
Catalogue for part of the collections is only available in-house.
Printed publications:
Outline of Hastings History
Other local history publications eg the Cinque Ports, the Wealden Iron Industry, Painters of Hastings
Schools' worksheets

1232
HATCHLANDS PARK

East Clandon, Guildford, Surrey, GU4 7RT

Tel: 01483 222482
Fax: 01483 223176
Email: hatchlands@nationaltrust.org.uk

Organisation type and purpose: National organisation, registered charity (charity number 205846), historic building, house or site, suitable for ages: 5+.
Parent body:
The National Trust (South and South East Region)
South East Regional Office, tel: 01372 453401

Enquiries to: Manager
Access:
Access to staff: By letter, by telephone, by fax, by email
Access to building, collections or gallery: No prior appointment required
Hours: Apr to Jul, Tue, Wed, Thu, Sun, 1400 to 1730;
Aug, Tue, Wed, Thu, Fri, Sun, 1400 to 1730;
Sep and Oct, Tue, Wed, Thu, Sun, 1400 to 1730
Open Bank Holiday Mondays

Access for disabled people: Parking provided, ramped entry, toilet facilities
Other restrictions: Designated parking 100yds. Transfer available. 3 manual wheelchairs available. Ground floor fully accessible. Level entrance to shop and to restaurant.

General description:
Built in the 1750s for Admiral Boscawen, hero of the Battle of Louisburg, and set in a beautiful 170ha (430 acre) Repton park offering a variety of park and woodland walks, Hatchlands contains splendid interiors by Robert Adam, decorated in appropriately nautical style. It houses the Cobbe Collection, the world's largest group of keyboard instruments associated with famous composers such as Purcell, J. C. Bach, Chopin, Mahler and Elgar. There is also a small garden by Gertrude Jekyll, flowering from late May to early July and a stunning bluebell wood in May.
Information services:
Helpline available, tel no: Infoline 01483 225971.
Braille guide. Audio guide.
Children's audio guide. Children's quiz/trail.
Special visitor services: Materials and/or activities for children.
Services for disabled people: For the visually impaired.

Internet home pages:
http://www.nationaltrust.org.uk

1233
HATFIELD HOUSE
Hatfield, Hertfordshire, AL9 5NQ

Tel: 01707 287010
Fax: 01707 287033
Email: curator@hatfield-house.co.uk
Formed: 1948

Organisation type and purpose: Independently owned, historic building, house or site, suitable for ages: 7+.

Enquiries to: Curator's Office
Other contacts: Archivist for library and family papers.
Access:
Access to staff: By letter, by telephone, by fax, visitors by prior appointment
Hours: Mon to Fri 0930 to 1730
Access to building, collections or gallery: No prior appointment required
Hours: Easter Saturday to 30 Sep daily:
House, 1200 to 1600
Gardens, Park, Shops and Restaurant, 1100 to 1730
Other restrictions: Access to political and family papers - specialist appointments only
Access for disabled people: Parking provided, ramped entry, access to all public areas, toilet facilities
Other restrictions: All disabled people welcomed

General description:
Jacobean house, formal organic gardens, Great Park, early life of Elizabeth I, Elizabethan and Victorian political history.
Information services:
Library available for reference (for conditions see Access above)
Living history days throughout the year for all ages from 7 upwards.
Special visitor services: Guided tours, materials and/or activities for children.
Education services: Group education facilities, resources for Key Stage 2..
Collections:
'Ermine' and 'Rainbow' protraits of Elizabeth I
Cecil family portraits from 16 century
Appropriate furniture and artefacts
Catalogues:
Catalogue for part of the collections is published.
Printed publications:
Standard, young persons', and garden guides
Catalogue of sculpture and paintings
Nature trails leaflet
Historic trail for schools

Internet home pages:
http://www.hatfield-house.co.uk
General, opening arrangements, events programme, commercial and residential property, forestry and farm produce

1234
HATTON GALLERY
University of Newcastle upon Tyne, Newcastle upon Tyne, NE1 7RU

Tel: 0191 222 6059
Fax: 0191 222 6059
Email: hatton-gallery@ncl.ac.uk
Acronym or abbreviation: HG
Full name: The Hatton Gallery
Formed: 1926

Organisation type and purpose: Museum, art gallery, university department or institute, suitable for ages: all ages.
Part of:
Newcastle University
Newcastle upon Tyne, tel: 0191 222 6000

Enquiries to: Curator
Direct tel: 0191 222 6057
Direct email: lucy.whetstone.ncl.ac.uk
Access:
Access to staff: By letter, by telephone, by fax, by email, in person, Internet web pages
Hours: Mon to Fri, 1000 to 1730; Sat, 1000 to 1630
Access to building, collections or gallery: No prior appointment required

General description:
African art collection; 20th century art; 20th century painting; Renaissance art; drawings, prints, paintings and watercolours. On permanent display is the 'Elterwater Merzbarn', a unique installation by German Dada artist Kurt Schwitters.
Information services:
Education services: Group education facilities, resources for Key Stages 1 and 2, 3, 4 and Further or Higher Education..
Collections:
Fred & Diana Uhlman Collection of African sculpture
20th century paintings
Arts Council
Renaissance Art
3500 works on paper or canvas including Bosanquet. Textile samples. 19th century, 144 items
John Charlton drawings (local), mid-19th century, 40 items
William Henry Charlton, watercolours, early 20th century, 1500 items
Crawhall, drawings, 19th century, 24 items
Hair, watercolours (local), 19th century, 43 items
Hall, Baxter prints, 19th century, 500 items
Publications list:
is available in hard copy and online.
Printed publications:
Derek Jarman - a portrait
Impressionist and Modern - art collection
Whistler, Haden and the Rise of the Painter-Etcher (exhibition catalogue)

Internet home pages:
http://www.ncl.ac.uk/hatton

1235
HAUGHMOND ABBEY
Shrewsbury, Shropshire

Tel: 01743 709661

Organisation type and purpose: National organisation, historic building, house or site.
Parent body:
English Heritage (West Midlands Region)
Tel: 0121 625 6820

Enquiries to: Manager
Access:
Access to staff: By telephone
Access to building, collections or gallery: No prior appointment required
Hours: 29 Mar to 30 Sep: daily, 1100 to 1700
Other restrictions: Opening times are subject to change, for up-to-date information contact English Heritage by phone or visit the website.

General description:
The extensive remains of this 12th century Augustinian abbey include some fine medieval sculpture.

Internet home pages:
http://www.english-heritage.org.uk

1236
HAVANT MUSEUM
Old Town Hall, 56 East Street, Havant, Hampshire, PO9 1BS

Tel: 023 9245 1155
Fax: 023 9249 8707
Email: musmcp@hants.gov.uk
Formed: 1977

Organisation type and purpose: Local government body, museum, historic building, house or site.
Local museum for Havant and district, and aquarium.
Parent body:
Hampshire County Council Museums Service
Chilcomb House, Chilcomb Lane, Winchester, Hampshire, SO23 8RD, tel: 01962 846304, fax: 01962 869836

Enquiries to: Curator
Access:
Access to staff: By letter, by telephone, by fax, by email, in person
Hours: Tue to Sat, 1000 to 1700
Access to building, collections or gallery: No prior appointment required
Hours: Tue to Sat, 1000 to 1700

General description:
Local history of Havant and district, local studies collection, trade in the area 1850 to date, photographers and glovemakers, transport, railways, natural science, zoology, agriculture, hunting, firearms.
Collections:
Aquarium
Display of local history
Guns, puntguns, rifles
Hayling Billy locomotive
Vokes Collection of firearms
Catalogues:
Catalogue for all of the collections is on-line.
Printed publications:
Publications list is available from the Librarian, Hampshire County Council Museums Service, Chilcomb House, Winchester, SO23 8RD

Internet home pages:
http://www.hants.gov.uk/museums/
Whole collection, 100,000 plus web pages

1237
HAVERFORDWEST TOWN MUSEUM
Castle House, Haverfordwest, Pembrokeshire, SA61 2EF

Tel: 01437 763087
Formed: 1996
Formerly: Castle Museum

Organisation type and purpose: Registered charity (charity number 1072596), museum, suitable for ages: 8+.

Enquiries to: Manager
Access:
Access to staff: By letter, by telephone, in person
Access for disabled people: Parking provided, level entry
Other restrictions: Access computer allows upstairs rooms and artefacts to be viewed from reception room downstairs.

continued overleaf

General description:
The Haverfordwest Town Museum is located within the grounds of the castle and reflects the history of the town from Norman times to the present day. It covers many aspects of the history of Haverfordwest. Displays on civic regalia, local archaeological finds, finds from excavations at the Augustinian Priory. Each room has a different theme.
Information services:
Guided tours by prior arrangement.
Children's quiz sheet.
Special visitor services: Guided tours, materials and/or activities for children..
Collections:
There is a display on the 1652 Plague outbreak at Haverfordwest, together with uniforms of the local yeomanry
The Museum has a display of local coinage, billheads, a famous Llewellin Butter Churn
Many artefacts, photographs, paintings and a touch-screen computer display
Catalogues:
Catalogue for part of the collections is only available in-house.

Internet home pages:
http://www.haverfordwest-town-museum.org.uk

1238
HAVERHILL LOCAL HISTORY CENTRE
Town Hall Arts Centre, High Street, Haverhill, Suffolk, CB9 8AR

Tel: 01440 714962
Formed: 1985

Organisation type and purpose: Registered charity (charity number 26457), museum.
Parent body:
Haverhill & District Local History Group at the same address

Enquiries to: Honorary Secretary
Direct tel: 01440 762570
Access:
Access to staff: By letter, by telephone, in person, visitors by prior appointment
Hours: Tue, 1900 to 2100; Wed to Fri, 1400 to 1600; Sat, 1030 to 1530
Access to building, collections or gallery: No prior appointment required
Hours: Tue, 1900 to 2100; Wed to Fri, 1400 to 1600; Sat, 1030 to 1530
Access for disabled people: Parking provided, ramped entry, access to all public areas, toilet facilities

General description:
Over 4000 photographs and 2000 publications and research papers relating to Haverhill and surrounding district.
Information services:
Library available for reference (for conditions see Access above)
Special visitor services: Guided tours, materials and/or activities for children.
Services for disabled people: Displays and/or information at wheelchair height.
Collections:
Grace Gulteen. Photographic collection of the Gulteens, the most important family in the town, especially during the 2nd half of the 19th century. 1860s to 1930s
Chris Davey. A professional photographer in the town, now retired, he donated some 300 large format negatives of Haverhill, its surrounding parishes, and its people. Mainly 1950s to 1960s.
There are file copies of the Haverhill 'Echo' and its predecessor the 'South West Suffolk Echo'.
Catalogues:
Catalogue for all of the collections is only available in-house.
Printed publications:
Haverhill Historian (2 times a year, 99p each)
Pictorial histories of different eras

1239
HAWFORD DOVECOTE
Hawford, Worcester

Tel: 01743 708100 (Regional Office)
Email: hawforddovecote@nationaltrust.org.uk

Organisation type and purpose: National organisation, registered charity (charity number 205846), historic building, house or site.
Parent body:
The National Trust (West Midlands)
West Midlands Regional Office, tel: 01743 708100

Enquiries to: Manager
Access:
Access for disabled people: level entry
Other restrictions: Ground floor largely accessible. No WC

General description:
A 16th century half-timbered dovecote, the remnant of a former monastic grange.

Internet home pages:
http://www.nationaltrust.org.uk

1240
HAWICK MUSEUM & SCOTT GALLERY
Wilton Lodge Park, Hawick, Borders, TD9 7JL

Tel: 01450 373457
Fax: 01450 378506

Organisation type and purpose: Local government body, museum, art gallery, suitable for ages: 5+.
Parent body:
Scottish Borders Council Museum and Gallery Service
Tel: 01750 20096

Enquiries to: Curator
Access:
Access to staff: By letter, by telephone, by fax
Access to building, collections or gallery: No prior appointment required
Hours: Apr to Sep, Mon to Fri, 1000 to 1200, 1300 to 1700, Sat and Sun, 1400 to 1700;
Oct to Mar, Mon to fri, 1300 to 1600, (closed Sat), Sun, 1400 to 1600

General description:
Local history of Hawick, changing exhibitions of archaeology, ethnography, fine art, knitware and sporting heritage.
The Scott Gallery houses temporary exhibitions of fine art and selections from the permanent art collection.
Information services:
Interpretation leaflets in French, German, Italian, Dutch and Japanese.
Wide range of workshops
Special visitor services: Materials and/or activities for children.
Education services: Group education facilities..

Internet home pages:
http://www.scotborders.gov.uk
http://www.scotborders.org.uk

1241
HAWKSHEAD AND CLAIFE
Unit 9, Scutcheon Buildings, Far Sawrey, Cumbria, LA22 0LQ

Tel: 015394 47997
Fax: 015394 47997
Email: hawkshead@nationaltrust.org.uk

Organisation type and purpose: National organisation, registered charity (charity number 205846), historic building, house or site, suitable for ages: 8+.
Parent body:
National Trust (North West Area)
North West Regional Office, tel: 0870 609 5391

Enquiries to: Warden
Direct tel: 015394 44746/46534
Access:
Access to staff: By letter, by telephone, by fax, by email, in person, Internet web pages

General description:
Hawkshead is a classic Lakeland village, surrounded by beautiful scenery, much of which is owned by the National Trust. Claife Woodlands and the low-lying small farms between the village and Lake Windermere are typical of the area.
Just north of Hawkshead itself is the Courthouse, which dates from the 15th century and is all that remains of the village manorial buildings (once held by Furness Abbey).
Claife Station, on the west bank of Windermere, is a former Victorian viewing station with glimpses of the lake.
Wray Castle is currently let as a college, with limited access to the grounds and occasional access to the castle, tel. property office for details.
Information services:
Guided walks available
Suitable for school groups
There is a NT campsite in a superb location on the lake shore at Low Wray open Easter to end Oct; tel. for details
Special visitor services: Guided tours..

Internet home pages:
http://www.nationaltrust.org.uk

1242
HAXTED WATER MILL
Haxted Road, Edenbridge, Kent, TN8 6PU

Tel: 01732 862914
Email: david@haxtedmill.co.uk

Organisation type and purpose: Historic building, house or site, suitable for ages: 5+.

Enquiries to: Owner
Access:
Access to staff: By email, Internet web pages
Access for disabled people: Parking provided

General description:
A unique combination of a working watermill alongside a museum of functional mill machinery with an emphasis on the history, development and multiple uses of water power and the processes of grinding flour, past and present.
Information services:
Education services: Group education facilities, resources for Further or Higher Education..
Collections:
Artefacts, photographs, books, documents
Picture Gallery, with watercolours, old postcards, photographs and drawings, and site maps; some of the items are the only relics of mills long disappeared. Probably the oldest surviving wooden waterwheel, a mysterious grindstone dug up under the new Tesco in Croydon, and a unique hydraulic water level control.

Internet home pages:
http://www.haxtedmill.co.uk

1243
HAYNES MOTOR MUSEUM
Sparkford, Yeovil, Somerset, BA22 7LH

Tel: 01963 440804
Fax: 01963 441004
Email: mike@haynesmotormuseum.co.uk
Formed: 1985
Formerly: Sparkford Motor Museum, Haynes Sparkford Motor Museum

Organisation type and purpose: Membership association (membership is by subscription), present number of members: 320, registered charity (charity number 292048), museum, suitable for ages: 5+, consultancy, research organisation.
To preserve and restore items of motoring and motorcycling interest in the UK. To promote safe and enjoyable driving. To educate and entertain.

Enquiries to: Curatorial Director
Access:
Access to staff: By letter, by telephone, by fax, by email, in person, charges to non-members, Internet web pages
Hours: Daily, 0930 to 1730
Access to building, collections or gallery: No prior appointment required
Hours: Prior appointment required for the library, Mon to Fri, 1000 to 1600
Access for disabled people: Parking provided, ramped entry, level entry, access to all public areas, toilet facilities

General description:
Motoring history generally. Leaning towards British and American cars as preference, but have a truly international collection of over 200 motor vehicles from the turn of the century to the present day. Covers all aspects of motoring on four and two wheels. There are American, British and European vehicles, including some oddities from Third World countries.
Collections:
Red collection, red sports cars, 1922-1984, 40 plus
Racing cars and motorcycles, 1920s-1970s, 30 plus
William Morris collection, vehicles with William Morris connection, 1920s-1970s, 40 plus
American cars, 1920s-1985, 30 plus
Catalogues:
Catalogue for library is in-house only. Catalogue for all of the collections is published.
Publications list:
is available in hard copy and online.
Printed publications:
All Haynes Workshop Manuals and books

Internet home pages:
http://www.haynesmotormuseum.co.uk

1244
HEATHERBANK MUSEUM
Glasgow Caledonian University, Cowcaddens Road, Glasgow, G4 0BA

Tel: 0141 331 8637
Fax: 0141 331 3005
Email: a.ramage@gcal.ac.uk
Acronym or abbreviation: HMSW
Full name: Heatherbank Museum of Social Work
Formed: 1975

Organisation type and purpose: Registered charity (charity number SCO 05882), museum, university department or institute, suitable for ages: 16+.
Connections with:
University Museums in Scotland (UMIS)
c/o Marischal Museum, University of Aberdeen, email/website: n.curtis@abdn.ac.uk

Enquiries to: Curator
Other contacts: Museum Manager for overall planning, financial control.
Access:
Access to staff: By letter, by telephone, by fax, by email, in person, Internet web pages
Access for disabled people: ramped entry, access to all public areas, toilet facilities

General description:
A museum of social work, social care, social welfare, social policy and administration, healthcare, childcare, penology and homelessness, with a library of 2000 books and a picture library of 5000 prints, slides, etc.
Contains archives; artefacts; and public exhibitions; and offers research and educational facilities.
Information services:
Library available for reference (for conditions see Access above)
Book library, picture library, resources library, ephemera library, audiovisual library, artefact collections.
Special visitor services: Guided tours, materials and/or activities for children.
Education services: Resources for Further or Higher Education..
Collections:
Rare Books, books from the 18th century onwards, some unique
Reports of Government Committees
Archives, Social Work Institutions now closed, 1900-.
Ephemera Collection, materials relating to social work - press cuttings, etc. pamphlets and journals, 1860-1985
Catalogues:
Catalogue for library is on-line. Catalogue for all of the collections is on-line.
Publications list:
is available on-line.
Printed publications:
All publications now out of print - file copies held
12 Fact sheets (free of charge)
Electronic and video products:
Videos available, see website

Internet home pages:
http://www.lib.gcal.ac.uk/heatherbank/
Full details of Museum, catalogues, fact sheets.

1245
HEATHERSLAW CORNMILL
Cornhill on Tweed, Northumberland, TD12 4TJ

Tel: 01890 820338

Organisation type and purpose: Historic building, house or site, suitable for ages: 8+.

Enquiries to: Manager
Access:
Access to staff: By letter, by telephone
Access to building, collections or gallery: No prior appointment required
Hours: Easter to Oct, daily, 1000 to 1800
Other restrictions: Winter by arrangement

General description:
A restored and working 19th century watermill. Everything is visible, from the huge water wheel to the finished flour.
Information services:
Demonstrations and a children's trail.
Special visitor services: Materials and/or activities for children..

1246
HEATON COOPER STUDIO, THE
Grasmere, Near Ambleside, Cumbria, LA22 9SX

Tel: 015394 35280
Fax: 015394 35797
Email: info@heatoncooper.co.uk
Formed: 1939

Organisation type and purpose: Independently owned, art gallery, suitable for ages: all ages.

Enquiries to: Managing Director
Direct email: john@heatoncooper.co.uk
Access:
Access to staff: By letter
Access to building, collections or gallery: No prior appointment required
Hours: Mon to Sat, 0900 to 1700; Sun, 1200 to 1700
Access for disabled people: Parking provided, ramped entry, access to all public areas

General description:
The landscape of Lakeland in paintings from 1900 to present day.
Collections:
Original paintings and prints
Catalogues:
Catalogue for library is on-line. Catalogue for all of the collections is on-line.
Publications list:
is available in hard copy and online.

Internet home pages:
http://www.heatoncooper.co.uk
History and products, paintings etc.

1247
HEATON HALL
Heaton Park, Prestwich, Manchester, M25 5SW

Tel: 0161 773 1231
Minicom no. 0161 235 8893
Fax: 0161 798 9564

Organisation type and purpose: Local government body, museum, historic building, house or site, suitable for ages: all ages.
Parent body:
Manchester City Galleries
Mosley Street, Manchester, M2 3JL, tel: 0161 235 8888, fax: 0161 235 8893

Enquiries to: Development Officer
Other contacts: Education Assistant for educational visits.
Access:
Access to staff: By letter, by telephone, by fax
Access to building, collections or gallery: No prior appointment required
Hours: Apr to end of Sep, Sunday and Bank Holidays, 1000 to 1700
Access for disabled people: ramped entry
Other restrictions: Wheelchair access only available to ground floor, guide dogs and hearing dogs welcome, information booklet available in Braille, on tape and in large print.

General description:
Late 18th and early 19th century fine and decorative arts are displayed in a neo-classical historic country house, formerly the home of the Egertons (later Earls of Wilton). The house remains much as it was in the late 18th century, with some rooms restored to provide an impression of the period.
The park is being restored to the way it was at the beginnig of the 20th century. Also within the park is the Farm Centre, the Boating Lake, The Horticultural Centre and the Tram Museum.
Collections:
Drawings and furniture relating to James Wyatt and Heveningham Hall, 1780s to 1840s, 36 items
Musical instruments, Samuel Green organ in working order, and other period musical instruments, 1770-1825, 6 items

Internet home pages:
http://www.manchestergalleries.org

1248
HEATON PARK TRAMWAY, THE
Tram Depot, Middleton Road, Prestwich, Manchester, M25 5SW

Tel: 0161 740 1919
Full name: Manchester Transport Museum Society Limited
Formed: 1980

Organisation type and purpose: Registered charity (charity number 505601), museum, suitable for ages: 8+.
Affiliated to:
Manchester Tramway Company Limited
Heaton Park, Manchester, M25 5SN, tel: 0161 773 1085

Enquiries to: Curator
Direct tel: 0161 330 5531
Other contacts: Membership Secretary, tel: 0161 442 7682
Access:
Access to staff: By letter, by telephone, visitors by prior appointment
Hours: Sun, 1300 to 1700
Access to building, collections or gallery: No prior appointment required
Hours: Sun and Bank Holidays, 1300 to 1700
Jun and Jul: Wed, 1100 to 1400

General description:
Operating $\frac{1}{2}$ mile electric tramway to municipal parks - restoration and maintenance of historic Manchester Tramway. Books and manuscripts relating to tramways in the Greater Manchester area between 1870 and present day.

continued overleaf

Collections:
Working Tramway:
c. 1880 - double-deck horse tramcar ex Manchesters tramways
1901 - single-deck converted electric tramcar ex Hull tramways
1914 - single-deck 8 wheel electric tramcar ex Manchester's tramways
1902 - double-deck 4 wheel electric tramcar ex Manchester's tramways (one of Manchester's first electric trams)
Single-deck Rawtenstall electric tramcar - in store pending restoration
Drawings and blue-prints, historic documents and tickets, 2500 photographs depicting Greater Manchesters streets and tramways
Catalogues:
Catalogue for library is in-house only. Catalogue for part of the collections is only available in-house.
Publications list:
is available in hard copy.

Address for ordering publications:
Printed publications:
Sales Manager, Heaton Park Tramway Museum
25 Branch Road, Darwen, Lancashire, BE3 0PQ, tel: 01254 665119

Internet home pages:
http://www.mtms.org.uk
Museum details and tramway history.

1249
HEDINGHAM CASTLE
Castle Hedingham, Halstead, Essex, CO9 3DJ

Tel: 01787 460261
Fax: 01787 461473
Email: mail@hedinghamcastle.co.uk
Formed: 1140

Organisation type and purpose: Independently owned, historic building, house or site, suitable for ages: 5+.
Tourist attraction/venue.

Enquiries to: Administrator
Access:
Access to staff: By telephone, by email, visitors by prior appointment, Internet web pages
Access to building, collections or gallery: No prior appointment required
Hours: Easter to end Oct: daily, 1000 to 1700
Other restrictions: Closed end Oct to Easter. Guided tours by prior arrangement.
Access for disabled people: Parking provided
Other restrictions: Castle not suitable for wheelchair users.
Partial access to grounds.

General description:
Family and estate history.
Information services:
Guided tours by prior arrangement.
Special visitor services: Guided tours.
Education services: Group education facilities, resources for Key Stages 1 and 2, 3 and 4..
Printed publications:
Guide Book (£4)
Numerous related books (direct in Gift Shop)

Internet home pages:
http://www.hedinghamcastle.co.uk
Full information on all aspects of Castle and Mansion House.

1250
HEDON MUSEUM
Town Hall Complex, St Augustine's Gate, Hedon, East Yorkshire, HU12 8EX

Tel: 01482 890908
Email: hedon.museum@widehorizon.net
Formed: 1988

Organisation type and purpose: Membership association, voluntary organisation, museum. Archive.
Parent body:
Hedon Museum Society

Enquiries to: Honorary Secretary

General description:
Heritage museum covering South Holderness in the East Riding of Yorkshire.
Collections:
Archaeological finds
Archive of documents
Local artefacts
Photographs

Internet home pages:
http://www.museum.hedon-uk.com

1251
HEINZ ARCHIVE AND LIBRARY
See - National Portrait Gallery

1252
HELICOPTER MUSEUM, THE
Western Heliport, Locking Moor Road, Weston-Super-Mare, Somerset, BS24 8PP

Tel: 01934 635227
Fax: 01934 645230
Email: office@helimuseum.fsnet.co.uk
Full name: The British Rotorcraft Museum and Avon Air Collection
Formed: 1988
Formerly: British Rotorcraft Museum (BRM), date of change, 1986; The International Helicopter Museum (IHM), date of change, 1998

Organisation type and purpose: Membership association (membership is by subscription), present number of members: 150/200, voluntary organisation, registered charity (charity number 281053), museum, suitable for ages: 5+.
Helicopter presentation, restoration, preservation and information.

Enquiries to: Manager
Other contacts: (1) Aircraft Restoration Manager (2) Chairman of Trustees for (1) information on restoration (2) archival information.
Access:
Access to staff: By letter, by telephone, by fax, by email, in person, Internet web pages
Access to building, collections or gallery: No prior appointment required
Hours: Open April to October: Wed to Sun, 1000 to 1800
November to March Wed to Sun 1000 to 1600
Open Daily during Easter and Summer School Holidays
Other restrictions: Closed Christmas Eve, Christmas Day, Boxing Day and New Year's Day.
Access for disabled people: Parking provided, ramped entry, access to all public areas, toilet facilities

General description:
Helicopter/aircraft restoration.
Catalogues:
Catalogue for library is in-house only. Catalogue for part of the collections is on-line.
Publications list:
is available on-line.
Printed publications:
Visitor Guide incorporating fleet list

Internet home pages:
http://www.helicoptermuseum.co.uk
History of the museum, travel information, list of main exhibits, links to other heli-sites.

1253
HELMSDALE HERITAGE SOCIETY
See - Timespan Heritage Centre & Art Gallery

1254
HELMSHORE TEXTILE MUSEUMS
Holcombe Road, Helmshore, Rossendale, Lancashire, BB4 4NP

Tel: 01706 226459
Fax: 01706 218554
Email: helmshore.museum@mus.lancscc.gov.uk
Full name: Museum of the Lancashire Textile Industry
Formed: 1983
Formerly: Higher Mill Museum

Organisation type and purpose: Local government body, registered charity (charity number 254660), museum, suitable for ages: 5+.
Higher Mill Museum Trust owns the freehold of Higher Mill which it leases to Lancashire County Council.
The trust seeks to promote the history of Lancashire's wool textile industry.
Parent body:
Lancashire County Museum Service (LCMS)
Stanley Street, Preston, PR1 4YP, tel: 01772 264062, fax: 01772 264079

Enquiries to: Keeper
Direct email: catriona.west@mus.lancscc.gov.uk
Other contacts: Visitor Services Officer for bookings and information/assistance other than curatorial enquiries.
Access:
Access to staff: By letter, by telephone, by fax, by email, in person, visitors by prior appointment
Access to building, collections or gallery: No prior appointment required
Hours: 1 Apr to 3 Nov: Mon to Fri, 1200 to 1600; Sat, Sun, 1200 to 1700
Other restrictions: Closed Nov to Mar, except by prior arrangement.
Collections - prior appointment required for research purposes only.
Access for disabled people: Parking provided, level entry, toilet facilities
Other restrictions: Level entry and full access to one building.
Ramped entry and ground floor acccess only to second building.

General description:
Lancashire's wool textile industry. 18th century woollen fulling mill, with original machinery and working waterwheel. Adjacent 19th century condenser cotton spinning mill, also with original machinery in working order. Collections include related books, small instruments and weaving machinery, not currently available to casual visitors but may be seen by arrangement (for research purposes only).
Information services:
Special visitor services: Guided tours, materials and/or activities for children.
Education services: Group education facilities, resources for Key Stages 1 and 2, 3, 4 and Further or Higher Education.
Services for disabled people: For the visually impaired; for the hearing impaired; displays and/or information at wheelchair height.
Collections:
Spinning floor with working carding and spinning machinery (mules)
Carding, spinning, weaving and other machines for cotton working in their original mill environments
Wool cloth finishing plant (fulling mill) preserved, working, insitu with waterwheel drive
An original Arkwright's water frame
Early Spinning Jenny
Arkwright preparation and carding machinery
Other wool cloth finishing machines, artefacts and documents
Books, manufacturers' catalogues, photographs
Catalogues:
Catalogue for library is in-house only. Catalogue for all of the collections is only available in-house.
Printed publications:
Guide to the Fulling Mill (available from the Mill at a nominal charge)
Guide to Londener Cotton Spinning (available from the Mill at a nominal charge)

Internet home pages:
http://www.bringinghistoryalive.co.uk
Full information on costumed role-play sessions.

1255
HELMSLEY CASTLE

Helmsley, North Yorkshire, YO6 5AB

Tel: 01439 770442

Organisation type and purpose: National organisation, advisory body, historic building, house or site.
Parent body:
English Heritage (Yorkshire Region)
Tel: 01904 601901

Enquiries to: Manager
Access:
Access to staff: By letter, by telephone
Access to building, collections or gallery: No prior appointment required
Hours: 29 Mar to 30 Sep: daily, 1000 to 1800,1 to 31 Oct: daily, 1000 to 1700,1 Nov to 31 Mar: Wed to Sun, 1000 to 1600
Other restrictions: Closed 1300 to 1400 through the year (except 29 Mar to 30 Sep).
Closed 24 to 26 Dec and 1 Jan.
Opening times are subject to change, for up-to-date information contact English Heritage by phone or visit the website.

General description:
Spectacular earthworks surround the great keep of this 12th century castle, ruined during the Civil War by the Parliamentary army following a torturous three-month siege.

Internet home pages:
http://www.english-heritage.org.uk

1256
HELSTON FOLK MUSEUM

Market Place, Helston, Cornwall, TR13 8TH

Tel: 01326 564027
Fax: 01326 569714
Email: enquiries@helstonmuseum.org.uk
Formed: 1949

Organisation type and purpose: Local government body, museum, art gallery, suitable for ages: all ages.
Parent body:
Kerrier District Council
Dolcoath Avenue, Cambourne, Cornwall, TR14 8RY, tel: 01209 614000

Enquiries to: Assistant Curator
Other contacts: Heritage Development Officer
Access:
Access to staff: By letter, by fax, by email
Access to building, collections or gallery: No prior appointment required
Hours: Mon to Sat, 1000 to 1700
Access for disabled people: ramped entry, toilet facilities
Other restrictions: No upstairs access at present.

General description:
Displays relating to Henry Trengrouse (inventor of the rocket lifesaving apparatus) and Robert Fitzsimmons (holder of the heavyweight boxing championship and other titles in three weights); mining; fishing; trades and professions relating to life on the Lizard Peninsula.
Information services:
Guided tours for visually and hearing impaired.
Education Services, hope to include Key Stage 3 shortly.
Special visitor services: Materials and/or activities for children.
Education services: Group education facilities, resources for Key Stages 1 and 2..
Collections:
Collection relates to former crafts and industries locally in the 19th and 20th centuries
Transport and trades, domestic, home life, fishing and mining, gardening, civic, fire engines, farm wagons and machinery
Bob Fitzsimmons, World Heavyweight Boxing Champion, born in Helston
Costume collection
Henry Trengrouse (1772-1854) Lifesaving Apparatus Section, born in Helston
Catalogues:
Catalogue for all of the collections is only available in-house.
Printed publications:
Leaflet (free)

Internet home pages:
http://www.helstonmuseum.org.uk
Shop, home, events, local personalities.

1257
HENFIELD MUSEUM

Henfield Hall, Cooper's Way, Henfield, West Sussex, BN5 9DB

Tel: 01273 492546
Formed: 1948

Organisation type and purpose: Local government body, museum, suitable for ages: all ages.

Enquiries to: Curator
Access:
Access to staff: By telephone
Access for disabled people: Parking provided, ramped entry, access to all public areas, toilet facilities

General description:
Collection of local history and domestic bygones; farm tools; Victorian and Edwardian costume; local geology and archaeology; local paintings and photographs; and Sussex rifle volunteer uniforms.
Information services:
Services for disabled people: Displays and/or information at wheelchair height.
Collections:
Paintings of Old Henfield. 1830-1950. 30 items
Photographs of Old Henfield. 1890-1950. 2000 items
Catalogues:
Catalogue for all of the collections is only available in-house.

1258
HENRY BLOGG MUSEUM

RNLI Cromer, The Gangway, Cromer, Norfolk, NR27 9HE

Tel: 01263 511294
Email: rnlicromermuseum@rnli.org.uk
Formed: 1967
Formerly: Cromer Lifeboat Museum

Organisation type and purpose: National organisation, registered charity (charity number 209603), museum, suitable for ages: all ages, research organisation.
Local lifeboat history.
To promote the history of Cromer lifeboats and their 200 years of service to mariners, and the exploits of Henry Blogg and other crews of the lifeboats.
Parent body:
Royal National Lifeboat Institution (RNLI)
West Quay Road, Poole, Dorset, BH15 1HZ, tel: 01202 663000, fax: 01202 663167

Enquiries to: Curator
Direct tel: 01263 513018
Direct email: rfmuirhead@csma-netlink.co.uk
Access:
Access to staff: By letter, by telephone, by email
Access for disabled people: ramped entry, access to all public areas

General description:
Contains the RNLI Lifeboat H F Bailey, coxed by Henry Blogg from 1935 to 1945, and which saved 502 lives. Photographs and models of the Cromer Lifeboat history from 1804.
Collections:
The complete set of medals of Coxswain Henry Blogg. Includes 3 gold medals, 4 silver medals, George Cross, BEM and other foreign awards (replicas)
Catalogues:
Catalogue for part of the collections is only available in-house.

1259
HENRY MOORE INSTITUTE

74 The Headrow, Leeds, West Yorkshire, LS1 3AH

Tel: 0113 246 7467
Fax: 0113 246 1481
Email: hmi@henry-moore.ac.uk
Formed: 1993

Organisation type and purpose: Registered charity (charity number 271370), art gallery, suitable for ages: 16+ and graduate or postgraduate.
Sculpture institute, library, archives and galleries.
To promote sculpture.

Enquiries to: Administrator
Access:
Access to staff: By letter, by fax, by email, Internet web pages
Hours: Mon, Tue, Thu, Fri, 1000 to 1730; Wed, 1000 to 2100
Access for disabled people: access to all public areas, toilet facilities
Other restrictions: Lift, Braille and large print literature

General description:
A collection devoted to sculpture of all periods, but principally the 20th century. Contains a cross-section of study resources from sculpture; magnettes; drawings; documents; photographs; books; slides; and videos.
Information services:
Library available for reference (for conditions see Access above)
Special visitor services: Guided tours.
Services for disabled people: For the visually impaired.
Collections:
Sculpture, 18th-20th century, c. 250 items
Archive, Sculptors' papers, 18th-20th century, c. 5000 items
Library, c.14,000 books on sculpture, 15th-20th century
Some 5000 slides on sculpture of the 18th-20th century
Catalogues:
Catalogue for library is in-house only.
Publications list:
is available in hard copy.
Printed publications:
Catalogues (for sale)
Exhibition information (free)
Over 30 books on the archives and the collections

Internet home pages:
http://www.henry-moore-fdn.co.uk

1260
HERBERT ART GALLERY AND MUSEUM

Jordan Well, Coventry, Warwickshire, CV1 5QP

Tel: 024 7683 2565
Minicom no. 024 7683 2340
Fax: 024 7683 2410
Email: artsandheritage@coventry.gov.uk
Acronym or abbreviation: HAGM
Formed: 1960
Also known as: The Herbert

Organisation type and purpose: Local government body, independently owned, museum, art gallery, suitable for ages: all ages.
Parent body:
Coventry Arts & Heritage
Coventry City Council

continued overleaf

Enquiries to: Manager
Direct tel: 024 7683 2385
Direct fax: 024 7683 2410
Access:
Access to staff: By letter, by telephone, by fax, by email, in person
Hours: Mon to Fri, 0900 to 1700 or by appointment
Access for disabled people: Parking provided, level entry, access to all public areas, toilet facilities

General description:
History of Coventry, including archaeology, social history and industrial history.
Visual arts and natural history.
Information services:
Helpline available, tel no: 024 7683 2381.
Temporary exhibitions programme.
Special visitor services: Tape recorded guides, materials and/or activities for children.
Education services: Group education facilities, resources for Key Stages 1 and 2, 3 and 4.
Services for disabled people: Displays and/or information at wheelchair height.
Collections:
Archaeological finds
Industrial history artefacts including:
Clocks
Textiles
Ribbons
Watches
Social History
Natural History
Visual Arts including: Godiva paintings, Sutherland drawings.
Silk Ribbon collection
Topographical prints
Catalogues:
Catalogue for all of the collections is available in-house and part is on-line.
Publications list:
is available on-line.
Printed publications:
Various products available via Coventry Archives, available free or for purchase, direct

Address for ordering publications:
Printed publications:
Coventry Archives
Tel: 024 7683 2418

Internet home pages:
http://www.coventrymuseum.org.uk
http://www.virtualgallery.org.uk

1261
HEREFORD AND WORCESTER COUNTY MUSEUM
See - Worcestershire County Museum

1262
HEREFORD CIDER MUSEUM TRUST
See - Cider Museum & King Offa Distillery

1263
HERIOT-WATT UNIVERSITY
Archive, Records Management and Museum Service, Riccarton, Edinburgh, EH14 4AS

Tel: 0131 541 3219

Organisation type and purpose: Museum, university department or institute, suitable for ages: 16+.

Enquiries to: Archivist
Access:
Access to staff: By letter, by telephone
Hours: Mon to Fri, 0900 to 1700
Access to building, collections or gallery: No prior appointment required

General description:
The history of the University and its predecessor bodies.
Collections:
Archives, objects and works of art recording the history of the University, its predecessor bodies and people associated with it
Also responsible for a textile archive at the Galashiels Campus

Internet home pages:
http://www.hw.ac.uk/archive
A brief history of the University and overview of the collections.

1264
HERITAGE CENTRE, THE
Hexham, Northumberland, NE48 2AU

Tel: 01434 220050
Formed: 1994

Organisation type and purpose: Registered charity (charity number 1041300), museum.

Enquiries to: The Committee
Direct tel: 01434 220316
Access:
Access to staff: By letter
Access to building, collections or gallery: No prior appointment required
Hours: Fri to Mon, 1030 to 1630
Access for disabled people: Parking provided, level entry, access to all public areas, toilet facilities

General description:
Folk museum - life in past centuries in North Tynedale and Redesdale.
Information services:
Special visitor services: Guided tours, materials and/or activities for children.
Services for disabled people: Displays and/or information at wheelchair height.
Collections:
Unique collection of photographs and artefacts relating to the North British Railway
The photographs of W P Collier (shop in village 1911-1932)
The Border Reivers
Other exhibitions change according to which local organisations we involve

1265
HERITAGE CENTRE, THE
Main Street, West Lulworth, Wareham, Dorset, BH20 5RQ

Tel: 01929 400587
Formed: 1994

Organisation type and purpose: Heritage centre.

Enquiries to: Countryside Rangers
Other contacts: Retail Manager for building, reception and retail areas.
Access:
Access to staff: By letter, by telephone, in person
Hours: Winter: Mon to Fri, 1000 to 1600
Summer: daily, 1000 to 1800
Other restrictions: Rota worked - not all staff present every day.
Access to building, collections or gallery: No prior appointment required
Hours: Winter: Mon to Fri, 1000 to 1600
Summer: daily, 1000 to 1800
Other restrictions: Free admission
Access for disabled people: Parking provided, ramped entry, level entry, toilet facilities

General description:
Displays on geology, local history, wildlife of the Lulworth area.
Information services:
Education services: Group education facilities, resources for Key Stages 2, 3, 4 and Further or Higher Education.
Services for disabled people: Displays and/or information at wheelchair height.
Printed publications:
Lulworth Rocks (booklet, 24 page full colour, for purchase)
Postcards
Electronic and video products:
The Power of the Sea etc (video)

Internet home pages:
http://www.lulworth.com

1266
HERITAGE CENTRE, BELLINGHAM, THE
Old Station Yard, Woodburn Road, Bellingham, Hexham, Northumberland, NE48 2DF

Tel: 01434 220050
Formed: 1994

Organisation type and purpose: Registered charity (charity number 1041300), museum, suitable for ages: 5+.
Quote from constitution: To promote, encourage, preserve and interpret the heritage of North Tynedale and Redesdale.

Enquiries to: Honorary Treasurer
Direct tel: 01434 220361
Access:
Access to staff: By letter, by telephone
Access to building, collections or gallery: No prior appointment required
Hours: May to end Sep: Fri, Sat, Sun, Mon, 1030 to 1630
Access for disabled people: Parking provided, level entry, access to all public areas, toilet facilities

General description:
The Border Counties Railway - modern and early photographs, artefacts, notices, etc. A unique collection.
The photographs of W P Collier, local photographs, monochrome postcards illustrating life in the area in the early 20th century.
The Border Reisers - information, illustration, artefacts relating to the activities of the reisers of North Tynedale and Redesdale, The notorious Charlton grayne.
Children's activities - 'Life in the early 20th century village' by local Women's Institutes.
Collections:
Border Counties Railway
W P Collier's shop - pictures, cameras, developing, printing, enlarging materials and artefacts dating from early 20th century
19th century and early 20th century artefacts and recorded accounts to bring alive life in a village or farmhouse at that period
Farming and small-scale mining are included
Photographs, artefacts, accounts of Border Life from 13th to 17th centuries, the time of the Border Reisers

1267
HERITAGE CENTRE, CREWKERNE
See - Crewkerne and District Museum

1268
HERITAGE CENTRE, LYTHAM
See - Lytham Hall

1269
HERITAGE MOTOR CENTRE
See - British Motor Industry Heritage Trust

1270
HERITAGE RAILWAY ASSOCIATION
7 Robert Close, Potters Bar, Hertfordshire, EN6 2DH

Tel: 01707 643568
Fax: 01707 643568
Acronym or abbreviation: HRA
Formed: 1996
Formed by the merger of: Association of Independent Railways (AIR), date of change, 1959; Association of Railway Preservation Societies Limited (ARPS), date of change, 1996

Organisation type and purpose: Advisory body, trade association (membership is by subscription), present number of members: 800, service industry, voluntary organisation, training organisation, consultancy, research organisation.
National coordination of preserved railways and museums.

Affiliated to:
International Association of Transport Museums
Members of:
British Incoming Tour Operators Association (BITOA)
European Federation of Museum and Tourist Railways (FEDECRAIL)
International Association of Transport and Communication Museums (IATM)
Railway Industry Training Council (RITC)
The Railway Forum
Managing Director:
Heritage Railway Association (HRA)
8 Ffordd Dyfrig, Tywyn, Gwynedd, LL36 9EH, tel: 01654 710344

Enquiries to: Press Officer
Other contacts: Managing Director
Access:
Access to staff: By letter, by telephone, by fax
Hours: Mon to Fri, 0900 to 1700
Other restrictions: Not by overnight fax.

General description:
Preserved railways, details of locomotives, rolling stock, operating and maintenance equipment, setting up and operating railway preservation organisations.
Publications list:
is available in hard copy.
Printed publications:
Guide to Steam Trains in the British Isles (annually, send sae)
Information Papers (on request)
Journal (quarterly)
Railways Restored (annually)

Internet home pages:
http://www.ukhrail.uel.ac.uk/hra.html
Details of organisation and of many members who operate heritage railways or railway centres.

1271
HERNE WINDMILL
Off Mill Lane, Herne, Kent

Tel: 01227 361326/374539

Organisation type and purpose: Historic building, house or site.
Member of:
Kent Windmills
Owned by:
Kent County Council

General description:
Black smock-mill containing original machinery. Restored to working order 1998-9.

1272
HERON CORN MILL AND MUSEUM OF PAPERMAKING
By Waterhouse Mills, Beetham, Milnthorpe, Cumbria, LA7 7AR

Tel: 015395 65027
Fax: 015395 65033
Email: nt.stobbs@virgin.net
Formed: 1975

Organisation type and purpose: Registered charity (charity number 503387), museum, historic building, house or site, suitable for ages: all ages.
Museum formed in 1988.
Educational resource.

Enquiries to: Administrator
Access:
Access to staff: By letter, by telephone, by fax, by email, in person, charges made to all users

General description:
A working watermill housed in a restored 18th century building. This is a good example of a Lowdertype Mill. All machinery is driven by a 14 ft. high breast shot wheel. Also contains a museum of papermaking, housed in a restored 18th century carter's barn, which shows the craft of papermaking (modern and historic) with demonstrations of the handmaking of paper.
Information services:
Special visitor services: Guided tours, tape recorded guides.
Education services: Group education facilities, resources for Key Stages 1 and 2 and 3.
Services for disabled people: For the hearing impaired.
Collections:
Parts of the machinery appear to be contemporary with the 18th century building. Shows the development of mill technology up to the mid-20th century.
Museum has various artefacts connected to the paper industry
Displays explain modern industry and previous methods
Catalogues:
Catalogue for library is in-house only. Catalogue for all of the collections is only available in-house.

1273
HERRINGFLEET DRAINAGE WINDMILL
Herringfleet, Suffolk

Organisation type and purpose: Historic building, house or site.

General description:
19th century smock mill in working order. The mill can be seen pumping on open days.

1274
HERTFORD MUSEUM
18 Bull Plain, Hertford, SG14 1DT

Tel: 01992 582686
Fax: 01992 534797
Formed: 1903

Organisation type and purpose: Registered charity (charity number 312142), museum, suitable for ages: 5+.

Enquiries to: Curator
Access:
Access to staff: By letter, by telephone, in person
Access to building, collections or gallery: No prior appointment required
Hours: Tue to Sat, 1000 to 1700
Access for disabled people: level entry, toilet facilities
Other restrictions: Access to ground floor only.

General description:
A local history museum housed in an early 17th century town house with a recreated Jacobean knot garden, it covers local social history, archaeology, geology, photographs, prints, paintings, foreign ethnography and the Hertfordshire Regiment Collection.
Information services:
Education services: Group education facilities, resources for Key Stages 1 and 2..
Collections:
Objects, photographs, books, documents
Hertfordshire trade tokens, 17th century
Hertfordshire maps
Hertfordshire Regiment collection
Catalogues:
Catalogue for library is in-house only. Catalogue for all of the collections is only available in-house.
Printed publications:
General leaflet
Newsletter (3 times a year)

Internet home pages:
http://www.hertford.net/museum

1275
HERTFORDSHIRE ARCHAEOLOGICAL TRUST
Maidenhead Yard, The Wash, Hertford, SG14 1PX

Tel: 01992 558170
Fax: 01992 553359
Email: info@hertfordshire-archaeological-trust.co.uk

Acronym or abbreviation: HAT
Formed: 1987

Organisation type and purpose: National organisation, registered charity (charity number 281819), suitable for ages: 8+.
Independent archaeological company.

Enquiries to: Community Archaeology Officer
Access:
Access to staff: By letter, by telephone, by fax, by email, visitors by prior appointment, Internet web pages
Hours: Mon to Fri, 0800 to 1630
Access to building, collections or gallery: Prior appointment required

General description:
Archaeology, archaeological finds, research, professional archaeological services provided, membership open to the public, occasional community events, and educational services also provided.
Information services:
Education services: Group education facilities, resources for Key Stages 1 and 2, 3 and 4..
Publications list:
is available on-line.

Internet home pages:
http://www.hertfordshire-archaeological-trust.co.uk

1276
HEVER CASTLE
Edenbridge, Kent, TN8 7NG

Tel: 01732 865224
Fax: 01732 866796
Email: mail@hevercastle.co.uk
Full name: Hever Castle Limited
Formed: 1983

Organisation type and purpose: Independently owned, historic building, house or site, suitable for ages: 5+.

Enquiries to: Managing Director
Access:
Access to staff: By letter, by email
Access for disabled people: Parking provided, ramped entry, toilet facilities
Other restrictions: Castle - ground floor only.

General description:
13th century moated castle, the former home of Anne Boleyn and in 1903, William Waldorf Astor.
Information services:
Special visitor services: Guided tours, materials and/or activities for children..
Publications list:
is available in hard copy.
Printed publications:
Castle Guide Book
Gardens Guide Book

Internet home pages:
http://www.hevercastle.co.uk

1277
HEXHAM ABBEY
Beaumont Street, Hexham, Northumberland, NE46 3NB

Tel: 01434 602031
Fax: 01434 606116
Email: hexamabbey@ukonline.co.uk
Formed: c. 674

Organisation type and purpose: Historic building and place of worship.

Enquiries to: Administrator
Access:
Access to staff: By letter, by fax, in person
Hours: Mon to Fri, 0930 to 1300; Sat, 1000 to 1230
Access for disabled people: level entry

General description:
The original Benedictine abbey was founded by Wifred, Bishop of York in 674 and replaced by an Augustinian priory in the 12th century. The

continued overleaf

present church was built between 1170 and 1250 and continued as the parish church of Hexham following the dissolution of the monasteries in1537.
Information services:
Special visitor services: Guided tours..
Printed publications:
Guide Book (available for purchase from Abbey Shop)
Information sheets on points of historical interest in the Abbey (available, 20p each)

Internet home pages:
http://www.hexhamabbey.org.uk
Information on services, weekly newsletter, music events, history.

1278
HEYSHAM HERITAGE CENTRE

Main Street, Heysham, Lancashire, LA3 2RX

Tel: 01524 853465
Formed: 2000

Organisation type and purpose: Museum, suitable for ages: 8+.
Centre run by:
Heysham Heritage Association
(voluntary organisation) (HHA)
80 Twemlow Parade, Heysham, LA3 2AL
Owners of the building:
Heritage Trust for the North West
(also mount exhibitions) (HTNW)
Pendle Heritage Centre, Barrowfield, Nelson, BB9 6JQ

Enquiries to: Honorary Secretary
Direct tel: 01524 859517
Access:
Access to staff: By letter
Access to building, collections or gallery: No prior appointment required
Hours: Apr to Sep, 1100 to 1600
Access for disabled people: level entry

General description:
Permanent exhibition (maily display panels) of the history of Heysham; maps.
Information services:
Special visitor services: Materials and/or activities for children..
Publications list:
is available in hard copy.
Printed publications:
Heysham - a History (Dent E J, 1997, £2 plus p&p)
Voices of Heysham (Dent E J, 2000, £2 plus p&p)
St Patrick's Chapel (Procter J C, 1997, £2 plus p&p)
The Heysham Peninsula (ed Dent E J, 2000, £4.95 plus p&p)
The History of Heysham (Flaxington D, 2001 £4.95 plus p&p)

Internet home pages:
http://www.htnw.co.uk/HHA.html

1279
HEZLETT HOUSE

107 Sea Road, Castlerock, Coleraine, Co Londonderry, BT51 4TW

Tel: 028 7084 8728
Fax: 028 7084 8728
Email: hezletthouse@nationaltrust.org.uk

Organisation type and purpose: National organisation, registered charity (charity number 205846), museum, historic building, house or site, suitable for ages: 8+.
Parent body:
National Trust Office for Northern Ireland
Rowallane House, Saintfield, Ballynahinch, Co Down, BT24 7LH, tel: 028 9751 0721, fax: 028 9751 1242

Enquiries to: Manager
Access:
Access to staff: By letter, by telephone, by fax, by email
Access to building, collections or gallery: No prior appointment required
Hours: House: Mid Mar to end May and Sep, Sat and Sun, 1200 to 1700; Jun to Aug, Wed to Mon, 1200 to 1800
Open Bank Holiday Mondays and Good Friday; also open Bank Holidays in Northern Ireland
Other restrictions: Admission by guided tour, parties must book in advance (max 15 in house at any one time)
Access for disabled people: Parking provided, level entry, toilet facilities
Other restrictions: Designated parking 10yds. Ground floor accessible with assistance, 2 rooms & outbuildings only. No access to other floors.

General description:
One of the few buildings in Northern Ireland surviving from before the 18th century, this 17th century thatched house has an interesting cruck-truss roof construction and is simply furnished in late Victorian style. There is a small museum of farm implements.
Information services:
Booked school groups welcome.
Special visitor services: Guided tours..

Internet home pages:
http://www.ntni.org.uk

See also - Downhill Estate

1280
HIDCOTE MANOR GARDEN

Hidcote Bartrim, Nr Chipping Campden, Gloucestershire, GL55 6LR

Tel: 01386 438333
Fax: 01386 438817
Email: hidcote@nationaltrust.org.uk

Organisation type and purpose: National organisation, registered charity (charity number 205846), historic building, house or site, suitable for ages: 8+.
Parent body:
National Trust (South West)
Regional Office for Wessex, tel: 01985 843600

Enquiries to: Warden
Access:
Access to staff: By letter, by telephone, by fax, by email, Internet web pages
Access for disabled people: ramped entry, toilet facilities
Other restrictions: Drop-off point, powered mobility vehicles available for hire, recommended route map.

General description:
One of England's great gardens, an 'Arts & Crafts' masterpiece created by the horticulturist Major Lawrence Johnston. A series of outdoor rooms, each with a different character and separated by walls and hedges of many different species, the garden is famous for its rare shrubs and trees, outstanding herbaceous borders and unusual plant species from all over the world. The varied styles of the outdoor rooms peak at different times of year, making for an interesting visit at any time.
Information services:
Scented plants, braille guide and audio guide for the visually impaired.
Special visitor services: Tape recorded guides, materials and/or activities for children.
Services for disabled people: For the visually impaired.

Internet home pages:
http://www.nationaltrust.org.uk/regions/wessex

1281
CECIL HIGGINS ART GALLERY, THE

Castle Lane, Bedford, MK40 3RP

Tel: 01234 211222
Fax: 01234 327149
Email: chag@bedford.gov.uk
Formed: 1949

Organisation type and purpose: Local government body, registered charity (charity number 290703), museum, art gallery, suitable for ages: 5+.

Enquiries to: Curator
Access:
Access to staff: By letter, by telephone, by fax, by email, in person, visitors by prior appointment, Internet web pages
Access to building, collections or gallery: No prior appointment required
Hours: Tue to Sat, 1100 to 1700; Sun, Bank Holiday Mon, 1400 to 1700
Other restrictions: Closed Mon, Good Friday, 25, 26 Dec, 1 Jan.
Access for disabled people: ramped entry, access to all public areas, toilet facilities

General description:
Founded in 1949, the Cecil Higgins Art Gallery houses one of the best collections of fine and decorative arts from the 18th to the 20th centuries, principally watercolours; prints; ceramics; glass; furniture; textiles; lace; and costume. Also includes smaller collections of Valentines; toys; silver; jewellery; oils; miniatures; and sculpture.
Information services:
Exhibitions throughout the year.
Special visitor services: Guided tours, materials and/or activities for children.
Education services: Group education facilities, resources for Key Stages 1 and 2, 3, 4 and Further or Higher Education.
Services for disabled people: Displays and/or information at wheelchair height.
Collections:
Recreated Victorian mansion housing fine and decorative arts collection from the 18th to 20th centuries
Special Collections include:
Bedford Corporation. Paintings of Bedford. 16th-20th century, about 100 items
Edward Bawden Archive
Handley-Read. Fine and decorative arts. 19th/20th century, about 200 items
Thomas Lester. Lace. 19th century.
William Burges. Furniture and decorative arts. 19th century
European ceramics and glass from Renaissance to 20th century
Watercolours, drawings, oils, prints, books, furniture (including clocks), silver, pewter, photographs, costume, textiles, lace, Valentines, jewellery, toys
Printed publications:
Guide Book
Bedford Portrayed
Lace Publications (Bedfordshire)
Watercolours and Drawings Catalogue
Free leaflets: introduction in various languages etc

Internet home pages:
http://www.cecilhigginsartgallery.org
Collections, exhibitions and events, educational, friends organisation.

1282
HIGH PEAK ESTATE

High Peak Estate Office, Edale End, Hope Valley, Derbyshire, S33 6RF

Tel: 01433 670368
Fax: 01433 670397
Email: highpeakestate@nationaltrust.org.uk

Organisation type and purpose: National organisation, registered charity (charity number 205846), historic building, house or site, suitable for ages: 12+.
Parent body:
The National Trust (East Midlands Region)
East Midlands Regional Office, tel: 01909 486411

Enquiries to: Estate Manager
Access:
Access to staff: By letter, by telephone, by fax, by email, in person, Internet web pages

Access to building, collections or gallery: No prior appointment required
Hours: Open and unrestricted access for walkers all year to moorland, subject to occasional management closures (which are advertised locally). Access to farmland is via public rights of way and permitted paths.
Other restrictions: Five information shelters are open all year: Lee Barn (110:SK096855) on Pennine Way near Jacob's Ladder; Dalehead (110: SK101843) in Edale; South Head Farm (SK060854) at Kinder; Edale End (SK161864) between Edale and Hope; Grindle Barns above Ladybower Reservoir
(SK189895)

General description:
The High Peak is outstanding walking country, stretching from the heather-clad moors of Park Hall to the gritstone of Derwent Edge, and from the peat bogs of Bleaklow to the limestone crags of Winnats Pass. The wild and dramatic Pennine moorlands are of international importance for their populations of breeding birds, including golden plover, merlin and red grouse.
Sites of particular interest include:-
Mam Tor, with its spectacular views, landslip and prehistoric settlement;
Odin Mine, one of the oldest lead mines in Derbyshire;
Kinder Scout, the highest point for fifty miles around and where the Mass Trespass of 1932 took place;
and the unspoilt valley of Snake Pass.
The Trust also owns several farms in the beautiful Edale valley. A major woodland restoration project (in partnership with the Forestry Commission) is now underway in the recently acquired Alport Valley.
Information services:
Suitable for school groups. Live interpretation. Hands-on activities. Children's guide
Special events programme, send s.a.e or email for details of events and wide range of leaflets
Special visitor services: Materials and/or activities for children.
Education services: Group education facilities..

Internet home pages:
http://www.nationaltrust.org.uk

1283
HIGH WYCOMBE ART GALLERY AND MUSEUM
See - Wycombe Museum

1284
HIGHAM PARK HOUSE AND GARDENS
Higher Park Bridge, Canterbury, Kent, CT4 5BE

Tel: 01227 830830
Fax: 01227 830830
Email: highampark@aol.com
Formed: 1998

Organisation type and purpose: Independently owned, historic building, house or site, suitable for ages: 5+.
Restoration of the house and gardens.

Enquiries to: Director
Access:
Access to staff: By letter, by telephone, by fax, by email, Internet web pages
Hours: Sun to Thu, 1100 to 1700
Access to building, collections or gallery: No prior appointment required
Hours: Gardens: Apr to Sep, Sun to Thu, 1100 to 1700
House tours: Apr to Sep, Sun to Thu, 1230 to 1430
Access for disabled people: Parking provided, ramped entry, toilet facilities
Other restrictions: Access to most of the gardens

General description:
History of the house and its occupants, 25 acres of gardens. The house's past can be traced back to Edward II (1320), it was home to James Hallet. Owners include Thomas Culpepper of Bedgebury 1534, the Countess Margaret Zborowski (Née Astor) and her son Count Louis Zborowski the creator of the series of Chitty Bang Bang racing cars, followed by Walter Whigham of the Bank of England who chose to rename Higham, Highland Court.
Information services:
Special visitor services: Guided tours..

Internet home pages:
http://www.higham-park.co.uk

1285
HIGHCLERE CASTLE
Newbury, Berkshire, RG20 9RN

Tel: 01635 253210
Fax: 01635 255315
Formed: 1988

Organisation type and purpose: Historic building, house or site.

Enquiries to: General Manager
Direct email: theoffice@highclerecastle.co.uk
Access:
Access to staff: By letter, by telephone, by fax, by email, visitors by prior appointment
Access for disabled people: Parking provided, ramped entry, toilet facilities

General description:
5th Earl of Carnarvon, Howard Carter, discovery of the tomb of Tutankhamun, now the home of the 8th Earl. Victorian house created by Sir Charles Barry the grounds influenced by Capability Brown a tour of which may take $1\frac{1}{2}$ to $2\frac{1}{2}$ hours.
Information services:
Helpline available, tel no: 01635 253204.
Education service for schools and colleges.
Registered for civil weddings.
Special visitor services: Guided tours.
Education services: Group education facilities, resources for Key Stages 1 and 2..
Collections:
Egyptian artefacts discovered by 5th Earl of Carnarvon and Howard Carter
Horseracing Exhibition
Printed publications:
Guide Book

Internet home pages:
http://www.highclerecastle.co.uk

1286
HIGHER MILL MUSEUM
See - Helmshore Textile Museums

1287
HIGHLAND COUNCIL, THE
See - Highland Folk Museum

1288
HIGHLAND FOLK MUSEUM, THE
Duke Street, Kingussie, Inverness-shire, PH21 1JG

Tel: 01540 661307
Fax: 01540 661631
Email: highland.folk@highland.gov.uk
Formed: 1944

Organisation type and purpose: Local government body, museum, suitable for ages: 5+.
Parent body:
The Highland Council
Council Offices, Ruthven Road, Kingussie, PH21 1EJ, tel: 01540 664530, fax: 01540 661004, email: cls_badenoch&strathspey@highland.gov.uk
Other site:
Highland Folk Museum
Aultlarie, Newtonmore, tel: 01540 661307

Enquiries to: Curator
Direct email: ross.noble@highland.gov.uk
Access:
Access to staff: By letter, by telephone, by fax, by email, visitors by prior appointment
Other restrictions: Closed Christmas and New Year.
Access to building, collections or gallery: No prior appointment required
Hours: Easter to Oct: telephone for details
Nov to Easter: Mon to Fri, 1100 to 1300
Access for disabled people: Parking provided, ramped entry, level entry, toilet facilities
Other restrictions: Access to all areas at Kingussie site.
Some restrictions at Newtonmore site.

General description:
Social history of the Scottish Highlands from c. 1700. Agriculture, domestic life, costume, furniture, handcrafts. Open-air museum with reconstructed buildings.
Information services:
Library available for reference (for conditions see Access above)
Special visitor services: Guided tours.
Education services: Group education facilities..
Collections:
Agriculture, domestic life, costume, furniture, handcrafts
Catalogues:
Catalogue for library is in-house only. Catalogue for all of the collections is only available in-house.
Publications list:
is available in hard copy.
Printed publications:
Leaflets
Educational Packs for teachers and further education groups

Internet home pages:
http://www.highlandfolk.com
Information on Kingussie and Newtonmore sites.
View of Highland history by Jim Hunter.

1289
HIGHLAND FOLK MUSEUM
Kingussie Road, Aultlarie, Newtonmore, Inverness-shire, PH20 1AY

Tel: 01540 661307
Fax: 01540 661631
Email: highland.folk@highland.gov.uk
Full name: Highland Folk Museum Newtonmore
Formed: 1935

Organisation type and purpose: Local government body, museum, suitable for ages: all ages.
Other addresses:
Highland Folk Museum
Duke Street, Kingussie, Inverness-shire, tel: 01540 661307, fax: 01540 661631

Enquiries to: Curator
Direct email: ross.noble@highland.gov.uk
Access:
Access to staff: By letter, by telephone, by fax, by email, in person, visitors by prior appointment
Hours: Kingussie Site: Mon to Fri, 0900 to 1700
Other restrictions: Curatorial Staff based at Kingussie Site.
Access for disabled people: Parking provided, level entry, toilet facilities
Other restrictions: Access to most areas.

General description:
Farming and social history from 1700-1936.
Information services:
Special visitor services: Materials and/or activities for children.
Education services: Group education facilities, resources for Further or Higher Education..
Collections:
Re-constructed buildings and other major artefacts
Major handling collections

continued overleaf

Catalogues:
Catalogue for part of the collections is only available in-house.
Printed publications:
Leaflets
Educational Packs for Teachers and Further Education Groups
Electronic and video products:
The Highland Folk Museum - Through Windows of Time (video, for purchase)

Internet home pages:
http://www.highlandfolk.com

1290
HIGHLAND MUSEUM OF CHILDHOOD

The Old Station, Strathpeffer, Ross-shire, IV14 9DH

Tel: 01997 421031
Fax: 01997 412031
Email: info@hmoc.freeserve.co.uk
Formed: 1992

Organisation type and purpose: Museum, suitable for ages: all ages.
An independent museum run by a charitable trust.

Enquiries to: Manager
Other contacts: Curator for collections information.
Access:
Access to staff: By letter, by telephone, by fax, by email, in person
Access to building, collections or gallery: No prior appointment required
Hours: Apr to Oct: Mon to Sat, 1000 to 1700; Sun, 1400 to 1700
July and Aug: Mon to Fri, 1000 to 1900; Sat, 1000 to 1700; Sun, 1400 to 1700
Other restrictions: Closed 1 Nov to 31 Mar, open before 1 Apr if Easter is early.
Access for disabled people: Parking provided, level entry, access to all public areas

General description:
A comprehensive collection of dolls, toys and other childhood artefacts.
Interpretative panels with the history of childhood in the Highlands of Scotland.
Evocative photographs of childhood. Award winning history video, small costume collection.
Information services:
Guided tours by appointment only.
Some displays/information at wheelchair height.
Special visitor services: Guided tours, tape recorded guides, materials and/or activities for children.
Education services: Group education facilities, resources for Key Stages 1 and 2, 3 and 4.
Services for disabled people: For the visually impaired; displays and/or information at wheelchair height.
Collections:
Angela Kellie doll and toy collection
Small collection of children's books, cradles, prams, dolls' house furniture
Small collection of baby and children's costume
Catalogues:
Catalogue for all of the collections is only available in-house.
Printed publications:
Children's Activity Sheets
Information sheets on Local Landmarks
Short History Guide to Village
Museum leaflet

Internet home pages:
http://www.hmoc.freeserve.co.uk
Introduction to the museum, collections, history, location, outreach, education, access etc.

1291
HILL HALL

c/o English Heritage (East of England Region), Brooklands, 24 Brooklands Avenue, Cambridge, CB2 2BU

Tel: 01223 582700
Fax: 01223 582701

Organisation type and purpose: Historic building, house or site.
Parent body:
English Heritage (East of England Region)

General description:
Elizabethan architecture and art.

Internet home pages:
http://www.english-heritage.org.uk

1292
HILL HOUSE, THE

8 Upper Colquhoun Street, Helensburgh, G84 9AJ

Tel: 01436 673900
Fax: 01436 674685
Email: thehillhouse@nts.org.uk
Formed: 1902

Organisation type and purpose: Registered charity, historic building, house or site.
Parent body:
National Trust for Scotland (West Region)
Other addresses:
National Trust for Scotland (NTS)
28 Charlotte Square, Edinburgh, EH2 4ET, tel: 0131 243 9300, fax: 0131 243 9301

Enquiries to: Property Manager
Access:
Access to staff: By letter, by telephone, by email, visitors by prior appointment
Access to building, collections or gallery: No prior appointment required
Hours: End Mar to end Oct: daily, 1330 to 1730
Other restrictions: Groups must pre-book
Access for disabled people: ramped entry, toilet facilities

General description:
The house, its furniture and fittings were designed by Charles Rennie Mackintosh, 1902/1903. It contains Mackintosh drawings; sketches; plans; and watercolours. Also contains oil paintings by Raeburn and J D Fergusson; watercolours by Pringle; a Gesso Panel by M M Mackintosh; and book covers and wall sconce by Talwin Morris. There is also an annual exhibition of modern domestic design.
Information services:
Services for disabled people: For the visually impaired; displays and/or information at wheelchair height.
Collections:
Furniture, Interior Decoration, Drawings and Plans
C R Mackintosh - water colour painting
Pringle - water colour paintings
J D Ferguson - oil painting
Raeburn - oil painting
Several other minor artists
Catalogues:
Catalogue for library is in-house only. Catalogue for all of the collections is only available in-house.

Internet home pages:
http://www.nts.org.uk

1293
HILL OF TARVIT MANSION HOUSE & GARDENS

Cupar, Fife, KY15 5PB

Tel: 01334 653127
Fax: 01334 653127
Formed: 1906

Organisation type and purpose: National organisation, membership association, voluntary organisation, registered charity, historic building, house or site, suitable for ages: 8+.
Parent body:
National Trust for Scotland
28 Charlotte Square, Edinburgh, EH2 4ET, tel: 0131 243 9300

Enquiries to: Manager
Access:
Access to staff: By letter, by telephone, by fax
Access for disabled people: Parking provided, ramped entry, toilet facilities
Other restrictions: Wheelchair access to ground floor of mansion house, tearoom and shop, wheelchair available

General description:
Mansion house rebuilt in 1906 by Sir Robert Lorimer. Fine example of early 20th century architecture. Collection of furniture, paintings, porcelain remain in the house. Large estate including formal gardens, woodland walks, Edwardian laundry, hilltop viewpoint.
Scotstarvit Tower, known to have existed in 1579 close to mansion house. Keys available during mansion house opening hours.
Information services:
Explanatory text in French, German, Italian, Spanish.
Special visitor services: Guided tours.
Education services: Group education facilities, resources for Key Stages 1 and 2, 3 and Further or Higher Education..
Collections:
Furniture including French, Chippendale-style and vernacular
Dutch paintings and pictures by Raeburn and Ramsay
Flemish tapestries
Chinese porcelain and bronzes
Interior of mansion house very much in the Edwardian Style
Edwardian laundry contains original fittings and equipment
Printed publications:
Guide Book (£1.95)
Range of postcards (available for purchase)

Address for ordering publications:
Printed publications:
Merchandise Department, The National Trust for Scotland
28 Charlotte Square, Edinburgh, EH2 4ET, tel: 0131 243 9300

Internet home pages:
http://www.nts.org.uk

1294
HILL TOP

Near Sawrey, Ambleside, Cumbria, LA22 0LF

Tel: 015394 36269
Fax: 015394 36811
Email: hilltop@nationaltrust.org.uk

Organisation type and purpose: National organisation, registered charity (charity number 205846), museum, historic building, house or site, suitable for ages: 5+.
Parent body:
The National Trust (North West)
North West Regional Office, tel: 0870 609 5391

Enquiries to: Manager
Access:
Access to staff: By letter, by telephone, by fax, by email

General description:
Beatrix Potter wrote many of her famous children's stories in this little 17th century house and it has been kept exactly as she left it, complete with her furniture and china. There is a traditional cottage garden attached. A selection of her original illustrations may be seen at the Beatrix Potter Gallery.
Information services:
Children's guidebook about Beatrix Potter.
Special visitor services: Materials and/or activities for children..

Collections:
Beatrix Potter's furniture and china

Internet home pages:
http://www.nationaltrust.org.uk

See also - Beatrix Potter Gallery

1295
HINCKLEY & DISTRICT MUSEUM

Framework Knitters' Cottages, Lower Bond Street, Hinckley, Leicestershire, LE10 1QU

Tel: 01455 251218
Formed: 1992

Organisation type and purpose: Registered charity (charity number 1015922), museum, suitable for ages: 8+.

Enquiries to: Secretary
Direct email: plindhinckley@hotmail.com
Access:
Access to staff: By letter
Hours: Museum Easter Mon to end Oct: Sat & bank holiday Mon, 1000 to 1600; Sun 1400 to 1700; other times by appointment

General description:
Hinckley and District from prehistory to modern times. Hosiery industry in the Hinckley area.
Information services:
Special visitor services: Guided tours, materials and/or activities for children..
Catalogues:
Catalogue for all of the collections is only available in-house.
Publications list:
is available in hard copy.
Printed publications:
The Accounts of the Great Foeffment Charity of Hinckley 1623-1759 (ed David J Knight, 1998, £12)
Old Hinckley and Other Writings (Thomas Harrold, ed David J Knight, 1996, £3.50)
Lady Byron and Earl Shilton (David Herbert, 1997, £7.50)
Hinckley from the Stone Age to Medieval Times: an Illustrated picture book and education pack (1996, 50p)
The Museum Cottages: an illustrated guide (David J Knight, 1996, £1)
The History and Antiquities of Hinckley. An abridged reproduction of the 1782 edition (ed David J Knight, 1993)
Hinckley and District Hospital: a centenary history (Beavin H A, 2000, £2.50)
Pamphlets to accompany permanent exhibitions (David J Knight, 1998, 30p each):
Anglo-Saxon Hinckley
Hinckley Castle
Medieval Hinckley
Prehistoric Hinckley
Roman Hinckley

1296
HINTON AMPNER

Bramdean, Alresford, Hampshire, SO24 0LA

Tel: 01927 771305
Fax: 01962 793101
Email: hintonampner@nationaltrust.org.uk

Organisation type and purpose: National organisation, registered charity (charity number 205846), historic building, house or site, suitable for ages: 8+.
Parent body:
The National Trust (South and South East Region)
Thames and Solent Regional Office, tel: 01494 528051

Enquiries to: Manager
Access:
Access to staff: By letter, by telephone, by fax, by email
Access to building, collections or gallery: No prior appointment required
Hours: Garden: End Mar to Sep, Sat to Wed, 1200 to 1700
House: Apr to Jul, Tue, Wed, 1330 to 1700; Aug, Tue, Wed, Sat, Sun, 1330 to 1700; Sep, Tue, Wed, 1330 to 1700
Access for disabled people: Parking provided, ramped entry, access to all public areas, toilet facilities
Other restrictions: 4 manual wheelchairs available. House fully accessible. Ramped entrance to tea-room.
Grounds largely accessible. Recommended route map.

General description:
One of the great gardens of the 20th century. A masterpiece of design by Ralph Dutton, 8th and last Lord Sherborne, uniting a formal layout with varied and informal plantings in pastel shades. A garden of all-year-round interest with scented plants and magnificent vistas over parkland and rolling Hampshire countryside. The house, which is tenanted, contains Ralph Dutton's fine collection of English furniture, Italian paintings and hardstones.
Information services:
Braille guide. Large-print guide. Touch list. Scented plants.
Children's quiz/trail.
Special visitor services: Materials and/or activities for children.
Services for disabled people: For the visually impaired.

Internet home pages:
http://www.nationaltrust.org.uk

1297
HIRSEL HOMESTEAD MUSEUM

The Hirsel, Coldstream, Borders, TD12 4LP

Tel: 01890 882834

Organisation type and purpose: Museum, historic building, house or site, suitable for ages: 5+.
Access:
Access to staff: By letter, by telephone
Access for disabled people: toilet facilities
Other restrictions: Disabled access

General description:
Collection of artefacts pertaining to the history of the Hirsel Estate - covers archaeology; agriculture; blacksmiths; botany; fishing; forestry; farming; horticulture; joinery; laundry; and ornithology.
Catalogues:
Catalogue for part of the collections is only available in-house.

1298
HISTORIC DOCKYARD

See - Museum of the Royal Dockyard

1299
HISTORIC FARM BUILDINGS GROUP

c/o Museum of English Rural Life, University of Reading, PO Box 229, Whiteknights, Reading, Berkshire, RG6 6AG

Tel: 0118 931 8663
Fax: 0118 975 1264
Email: r.d.brigden@reading.ac.uk
Acronym or abbreviation: HFBG
Formed: 1985

Organisation type and purpose: Learned society.

Enquiries to: Secretary
Access:
Access to staff: By email, by letter
Hours: Mon to Fri, 0900 to 1700

General description:
History of old farm buildings.
Printed publications:
Annual Journal

Internet home pages:
http://www.chelt.ac.uk/ccru/hfbg
Information about the group, contacts and newsletter

1300
HISTORIC HEXHAM TRUST, THE

Priestpopple House, Priestpopple, Hexham, Northumberland, NE46 1PL

Tel: 01434 602031
Fax: 01434 606116
Email: museum@tynedale.gov.uk
Formed: 1996

Organisation type and purpose: Registered charity (charity number 1069497), museum, historic building, house or site, suitable for ages: 8+.
Other addresses:
Hexham Abbey Parish Centre
Beaumont Street, Hexham, NE46 3NB
Tynedale Museums
Moot Hall, Hexham

Enquiries to: Secretary
Direct tel: 01434 603562
Direct email: tom.corfe@ukonline.co.uk
Access:
Access to staff: By letter, by telephone, by fax, by email
Access to building, collections or gallery: No prior appointment required

General description:
Local history and archaeology of Hexham and Tynedale.
Information services:
Special visitor services: Guided tours.
Education services: Group education facilities, resources for Key Stages 2 and 3..
Collections:
Anglo-Saxon sculpture at present in Hexham Abbey
Local artefacts, pictures and records
Printed publications:
Newsletter (occasional)

Internet home pages:
http://www.tynedale-online.co.uk/hexhamhistory
Information on the town, historic buildings, and the Trust.

1301
HISTORIC RESOURCES CENTRE

6 Bank Street, Annan, Dumfries & Galloway, DG12 6AA

Tel: 01461 201384
Fax: 01461 205876
Email: AnneR@dumgal.gov.uk

Parent body:
Dumfries and Galloway Museum Service
Tel: 01387 253374

General description:
Exhibition centre.

1302
HISTORIC WARSHIPS AT BIRKENHEAD

Corn Warehouse Quay, East Float Dock, Dock Road, Birkenhead, Merseyside, CH41 1DJ

Tel: 0151 650 1573
Fax: 0151 650 1473
Email: manager@warships.freeserve.co.uk

Organisation type and purpose: Independently owned, registered charity, museum, historic building, house or site.

Enquiries to: Project Director
Direct email: wbennett@historicwarships.freeserve.co.uk
Access:
Access to staff: By letter, by email
Access for disabled people: Parking provided, ramped entry

continued overleaf

General description:
Corn Warehouse Quay with preserved warships and submarines, visitor centre with displays of artefacts, scale models and static display boards.
Information services:
Guided tours for U534 only.
Special visitor services: Guided tours.
Services for disabled people: Displays and/or information at wheelchair height.
Collections:
HMS Plymouth, last action the Falklands campaign
HMS Onyx, a non-nuclear submarine, also in the Falklands campaign
U534, the only German submarine to be raised from the seabed after having been sunk
Printed publications:
Information Leaflet (free)
HMS Plymouth and HMS Onyx Brochure (£2)
U534 Brochure (£2.50)
A wide range of books on naval heritage (available for purchase)
Electronic and video products:
A wide range of related videos available for purchase

Internet home pages:
http://www.warships.freeserve.co.uk
Comprehensive information on vessels in preservation.

1303
HISTORICAL MANUSCRIPTS COMMISSION
See - National Archives

1304
HISTORY SHOP, THE
Library Street, Wigan, Lancashire, WN1 1NU

Tel: 01942 828128
Email: heritage@wiganmbc.gov.uk
Full name: Wigan Council Wigan Heritage Service
Formed: 1992
Formed from: Wigan Museum Service, Wigan Record Office, date of change, 1989

Organisation type and purpose: Local government body, museum, art gallery, historic building, house or site, suitable for ages: 16+.
Parent body:
Wigan Heritage Service
At the same address

Enquiries to: Manager
Other contacts: (1) Collections Development Manager; (2) Local/Family History Officer for (1) questions on the collection or possible donations; (2) local history/genealogy.
Access:
Access to staff: By letter, by telephone, by email, in person, Internet web pages
Access to building, collections or gallery: No prior appointment required
Hours: Mon, 1000 to 1900; Tue to Fr, 1000 to 1700; Sat, 1000 to 1300
Access for disabled people: ramped entry, toilet facilities

General description:
Local history museum and art gallery in an historic 1878 library setting. Local and family history study facilities, museum galleries, art gallery, shop, meeting room (for hire).
Collections - local to the area of all types plus newspaper and photograph archive, maps, parish records etc.
Information services:
Library available for reference (for conditions see Access above)
Special visitor services: Guided tours.
Education services: Group education facilities..
Collections:
Collections all relating to the local area: objects, machinery, pictures, photographs, books, documents, manuscripts, parish records, maps, census returns, family and business records
Catalogues:
Catalogue for library is in-house only. Catalogue for part of the collections is only available in-house.
Printed publications:
Many local history titles, some Wigan Heritage Service publications (telephone for details)
Past Forward (magazine, 3 times a year, by subscription, £5 per annum)

Address for ordering publications:
Printed publications:
The History Shop Shop

Internet home pages:
http://www.wiganmbc.gov.uk
Information on the Heritage Service and its venues.

1305
HITCHIN MUSEUM & ART GALLERY
Payne's Park, Hitchin, Hertfordshire, SG5 1EQ

Tel: 01462 434476
Fax: 01462 431316
Email: caroline.frith@nhdc.gov.uk
Formed: 1941

Organisation type and purpose: Local government body, museum, art gallery, historic building, house or site, suitable for ages: 5+.
Parent body:
North Hertfordshire District Council (NHDC)

Enquiries to: Curator
Direct email: gillian.riding@nhdc.gov.uk
Other contacts: Assistant Curator
Access:
Access to staff: By letter, by telephone, by fax, by email, visitors by prior appointment
Hours: Mon to Fri, 0900 to 1730
Access for disabled people: Parking provided
Other restrictions: Limited disabled access to ground floor. 1st floor only accessible by stairs, no public toilets on site.

General description:
Housed in a Georgian Townhouse:
Herts Yeomanry. World War I and World War II.
Displays on local industries and domestic life.
Collections of historical costume.
Victorian Chemist Shop and Physic Garden.
Information services:
Guided tours by arrangement.
Education service for schools and local groups via education officer 01462 422946.
Study room for local history research, museum gift shop, temporary exhibition programmes and events.
Special visitor services: Guided tours, materials and/or activities for children.
Education services: Group education facilities, resources for Key Stages 1 and 2, 3, 4 and Further or Higher Education..
Collections:
Collections relating to the history of Hitchin and the surrounding area (North Hertfordshire)
Photographs and negative archive
Local artists (Margaret Thompson), oil paintings, watercolours, sketchbooks, prints
Watercolours and drawings by Sammuel Lucas senior and Sammuel Lucas junior, 1825-1919, 1200 items
Etchings and drypoints by Frederick Landseer, Maur Griggs, 1878-1939, 50 items
Newspapers (originals):
Herts Express 1865-1934, 1966-1970
Herts & Beds Express 1940-1966
Hitchin Gazette 1970-1978
The Citizen 1908-1970
Letchworth & Baldock Gazette 1973-1979
The Pictorial 1928-1959
Costume Collection, 1800-1995, 4000 items
Herts Yeomanry Collection costume and medals, 1800-1945, 500 items
Lewis Victorian pharmacy, reconstructed, 1780-1950, 5000 items
Social history objects of 18th to 19th century
Catalogues:
Catalogue for library is in-house only. Catalogue for all of the collections is available in-house and part is on-line.

Internet home pages:
http://www.nhdc.gov.uk
Hitchin Museum has a link from the NHDC website with information about events and the collections.

1306
HM CUSTOMS & EXCISE NATIONAL MUSEUM
National Museums & Galleries on Merseyside, Albert Dock, Liverpool, L3 4AQ

Tel: 0151 478 4499
Fax: 0151 478 4590
Acronym or abbreviation: NMGM
Formed: 1986

Organisation type and purpose: Suitable for ages: all ages.
Parent body:
National Museums & Galleries on Merseyside (NMGM)

Enquiries to: Director
Other contacts: Marketing Manager for advertising.
Access:
Access to staff: By letter only
Access to building, collections or gallery: No prior appointment required
Hours: Daily, 1000 to 1700

General description:
The story of smuggling and contraband from the 1700s to the present day.
Collections:
National collection of the Department of Customs & Excise: tools, prints, paintings and photographs
Publications list:
is available in hard copy.

Internet home pages:
http://www.nmgm.org.uk

1307
HM FRIGATE UNICORN
Victoria Dock, Dundee, DD1 3JA

Tel: 01382 200900
Fax: 01382 200923
Email: mail@frigateunicorn.org
Formed: 1974

Organisation type and purpose: Independently owned, registered charity, suitable for ages: pre-school+.
Historic ship. Preservation society formed 1968.
Maintained by:
The Unicorn Preservation Society
Member of:
Scottish Museums Council (SMC)
County House, 20/22 Turphichen Street, Edinburgh, EH3 8JB, tel: 0131 229 7465, fax: 0131 229 2728

Enquiries to: Manager
Other contacts: Chairman for information required, any necessary action can only be taken at Board Level.
Access:
Access to staff: By letter, by telephone, by fax, in person, charges made to all users
Access to building, collections or gallery: No prior appointment required
Hours: Apr to Oct: daily, 1000 to 1700
Nov to Mar: Wed to Sun variable, 1000 to 1600

General description:
The Frigate Unicorn is the oldest British-built ship afloat and Scotland's only example of a wooden hulled warship. It was built in the Royal Dockyard at Chatham and named after the Scottish Royal Beast.
The ship is the most important artefact in the collection.
The other items in the collection cover a wide variety of naval memorabilia, ship models, paintings, tools and equipment used by shipwrights and sailmakers and a variety of replica and original ordnance.
There is an extensive archive of relevant books, plans and charts. However, these are not readily accessible at present, and an appointment would be required for access.
Information services:
Library available for reference (for conditions see Access above). Helpline available, tel no: 01382 200900/200893.
School groups welcome, education pack available.
No specific aids for people with disabilities. However, because of the nature of the ship and layout of the main entrance deck, all displays and information here are at wheelchair height.
Special visitor services: Guided tours.
Education services: Group education facilities.
Services for disabled people: Displays and/or information at wheelchair height.
Collections:
The Collections include: books, photographs and documents relating to the formation of the Preservation Society
Paintings and prints, plaques including the Naval War Memorial, musical instruments, uniforms, ship models, items of furniture from the Georgian period, replica 18 pounder long guns, 32 pounder carronades, 3 sets of small guns (Menzies, Duncan & Mountbatten)
Assorted shipwrights, riggers and sailmakers tools
Ships bells, and items from the Tay Division RNVRA Collection
Memorabilia from the RN Voluntary Aid Detatchment
Printed publications:
Visitor information leaflet (free of charge)
Guide Book (available direct or mail order)
Guns of the Frigate Unicorn (booklet, £2, direct)
Other printed products include: postcards, greeting cards and posters (prices from 25p)

Internet home pages:
http://www.frigateunicorn.org
General information about the ship, life in the navy of the period and a wide range of photographic images.

1308
HM PRISON SERVICE MUSEUM

Newbold Revel, Rugby, Warwickshire, CV23 0TH

Tel: 01788 834168
Fax: 01788 834186
Email: museum@breathemail.net
Acronym or abbreviation: HMPSM
Formed: 1982

Organisation type and purpose: National government body, national organisation, museum, suitable for ages: 8+.
Parent body:
HM Prison Service (HMPS T&DG)
Training & Development Group, at the same address, tel: 01788 834104

Enquiries to: Curator
Access:
Access to staff: By letter, by telephone, by fax, by email, in person, Internet web pages
Access to building, collections or gallery: No prior appointment required
Hours: Mon to Fri, 0900 to 2000
Other restrictions: Open at other times by appointment on request.
Access for disabled people: Parking provided, level entry, toilet facilities
Other restrictions: Access to ground floor displays only.

General description:
Contains the national collection of the HM Prison Service.
The museum provides a history of punishment and imprisonment from the Middle Ages to the modern prison service.
Collections include objects, uniforms, photographs, archives, paintings and architectural plans relating to HM Prison Service.
Information services:
Library available for reference (for conditions see Access above)
Special visitor services: Guided tours, materials and/or activities for children.
Education services: Group education facilities, resources for Key Stages 1 and 2 and Further or Higher Education..
Collections:
Prison uniforms: staff/prisoners
Prison furniture, fitments
Newgate flogging block
Stocks, gibbet irons, fetters, shackles etc
Oscar Wilde's cell door
Photographs: individual and albums
Objects made by prisoners
Prisoner art work
Archival material, eg rules and regulations
Medical equipment
Arms, guns, swords
Cameras - Gandoffi
Executioner's equipment
Gallows
Catalogues:
Catalogue for all of the collections is only available in-house.
Publications list:
is available on-line.
Printed publications:
Museum information sheet, leaflet, education leaflet, posters, trail sheets
Information sheets on history of punishment and imprisonment
Education Book and Education Activities - aimed at KS2 and KS3, emphasis on citizenship

Internet home pages:
http://www.hmprisonservice.gov.uk
Under Prison Life
http://www.pmnw.co.uk
Under contacts.

1309
HMS BELFAST

Morgan's Lane, Tooley Street, London, SE1 2JH

Tel: 020 7940 6300
Fax: 020 7403 0719
Email: hmsbelfast@iwm.org.uk
Formed: 1971

Organisation type and purpose: Museum. Historic warship.
Parent body:
Imperial War Museum
Lambeth Road, London, SE1 6HZ, tel: 020 7416 5000, fax: 020 7416 5374, email: info@iwm.org.uk

Enquiries to: Director
Direct tel: 020 7940 6332
Other contacts: Marketing Officer for marketing and advertising matters.
Access:
Access to staff: By letter, by telephone, by fax, by email, visitors by prior appointment, Internet web pages
Hours: 1000 to 1800, Mar 1 to Oct 31, Mon to Fri; 1000 to 1700, Nov 1 to Feb 28, Mon to Fri
Other restrictions: Closed 24, 25, 26 Dec.
Access for disabled people: ramped entry, toilet facilities
Other restrictions: Access inevitably somewhat restricted but main decks are fully accessible.

General description:
World War II naval history.
Collections:
Europe's last big gun armoured warship from World War II, a cruiser: operations room, decks, bridges, engine room, gun turrets, displays which recreate the conditions of life on-board for officers and men
Publications list:
is available in hard copy.
Printed publications:
HMS Belfast (illustrated history)
HMS Belfast education pack, quiz trails, project sheets
HMS Belfast ticket/guide leaflet
Microform products:
See IWM entries
Electronic and video products:
See IWM entries

Internet home pages:
http://www.iwm.org.uk
Ship's history.
http://www.livesights.com
Thames live cam.

1310
HMS WARRIOR (1860) MUSEUM

Victory Gate, HM Naval Base, Portsmouth, Hampshire, PO1 3QX

Tel: 023 9277 8600
Fax: 023 9277 8601
Email: info@hmswarrior.org
Acronym or abbreviation: WPT
Full name: Warrior Preservation Trust
Formed: 1985
Formerly: Maritime Trust, date of change, 1983; Ship's Preservation Trust, date of change, 1985

Organisation type and purpose: Registered charity (charity number 256756), museum, historic building, house or site, suitable for ages: 5+.
Historic ship.
Parent body:
The Warrior Preservation Trust

Enquiries to: Chief Executive
Access:
Access to staff: By letter, by telephone, by fax, by email, in person, visitors by prior appointment, Internet web pages
Access for disabled people: Parking provided, ramped entry, toilet facilities
Other restrictions: Lift to lower deck.

General description:
Access to all 4 decks of a Victorian warship which is presented as the ship would have been in 1860.
Subjects covered are life at sea in the Victorian Navy, life in Victorian times, warship design, machinery, armament and seamanship.
Information services:
Library available for reference (for conditions see Access above)
Special visitor services: Guided tours, tape recorded guides, materials and/or activities for children.
Education services: Group education facilities, resources for Key Stages 1 and 2, 3, 4 and Further or Higher Education.
Services for disabled people: For the visually impaired; for the hearing impaired; displays and/or information at wheelchair height.
Collections:
The ship is fully fitted out with a range of furniture, guns, machinery, equipment, nautical artefacts and a library containing books related to the ship and the Victorian Navy
Catalogues:
Catalogue for library is in-house only.
Printed publications:
Guide Book (£2.50)
The Immortal Warrior (Captain John Wells RN, £16.50)
Building a Working Model Warship (Mowth W, £10)

continued overleaf

Internet home pages:
http://www.hmswarrior.org
Information on the ship including visual images and details of our corporate services eg weddings, dinners etc.

1311
HOGARTH'S HOUSE

Hogarth Lane, Great West Road, Chiswick, London, W4 2QN

Tel: 020 8994 6757
Formed: 1904

Organisation type and purpose: Local government body, historic building, house or site.

Enquiries to: Heritage and Tourism Manager
Direct tel: 020 8583 4545
Direct fax: 020 8583 4595
Access:
Access to staff: By letter, by telephone
Access for disabled people: toilet facilities
Other restrictions: Access to ground floor only.

General description:
Country home of the great artist and satirist William Hogarth from 1749 until his death in 1764. Contains an excellent display of Hogarth's prints and interpretive material telling the story of Hogarth and his life and work; also a small gallery with temporary exhibitions. There is a small shop selling publications and other items connected with Hogarth.
Collections:
One of the largest public exhibitions of Hogarth's prints in existence, including:
'A Harlot's Progress'
'A Rake's Progress'
'Marriage-à-la-Mode'
'Gin Lane' and 'Beer Street', etc
Catalogues:
Catalogue for part of the collections is only available in-house.
Printed publications:
Guide to Hogarth's House (£3)
Range of postcards and books about Hogarth

Address for ordering publications:
Printed publications:
Heritage & Tourism Manager, Hounslow Library Centre Space, Treaty Centre, High Street, Hounslow, TW3 1ES, tel: 020 8583 4545, fax: 020 8583 4595

1312
HOGHTON TOWER

Hoghton, Preston, Lancashire, PR5 0SH

Tel: 01254 852986
Fax: 01254 852109
Email: mail@hoghtontower.co.uk

Organisation type and purpose: Historic building, house or site, suitable for ages: all ages.

Enquiries to: Administrator
Access:
Access to staff: By letter, by telephone, by fax, by email
Access for disabled people: Parking provided

General description:
16th century fortified hilltop manor house, ancestral home of the de Hoghton family since William the Conqueror. King's Ante-Chamber, Ballroom, King's Bedchamber and other staterooms.
Information services:
School visits.
Special visitor services: Guided tours.
Education services: Group education facilities..
Collections:
Tudor Well House with horse-drawn pump and oaken windlass
Dungeons
Publications list:
is available in hard copy and online.

Internet home pages:
http://www.hoghtontower.co.uk

1313
HOLBURNE MUSEUM OF ART, THE

Great Pulteney Street, Bathwick, Bath, BA2 4DB

Tel: 01225 466669
Fax: 01225 333121
Email: holburne@bath.ac.uk
Formed: 1893
Formerly: Holburne of Menstrie Museum; Holburne Museum & Crafts Study Centre, date of change, 2000

Organisation type and purpose: Independently owned, registered charity (charity number 310288), museum, art gallery, historic building, house or site, suitable for ages: 5+.
Affiliated to:
University of Bath
Tel: 01225 826826

Enquiries to: Director
Other contacts: (1) Marketing & Publicity Officer (2) Curator 3) Education Officer for (1) information (2) enquiries relating to collections (3) events relating to schools and coures.
Access:
Access to staff: By letter, by telephone, by fax, by email, visitors by prior appointment
Access to building, collections or gallery: No prior appointment required
Hours: Tue to Sat, 1000 to 1700, Sun1430 to 1730
Other restrictions: Closed Mon except for Bank Holiday or for pre-arranged group bookings
Access for disabled people: Parking provided, level entry, toilet facilities
Other restrictions: Lift to all foors

General description:
The museum began life in 1796 as the Sydney Hotel, entertaining visitors to the Sydney Pleasure Gardens with balls, fireworks and public breakfasts. It houses the art collection of Sir William Holburne, a great collector of 19th century Bath.
17th and 218th century fine and decorative art, paintings, portrait miniatures, silver, porcelain, glass, furniture, majolica, bronzes, Old Masters, lovely grounds, licenced tea house, travelling exhibitions, talks, events, book and gift shop.
Information services:
Events programme for families, with regular events for under fives
Special visitor services: Guided tours, materials and/or activities for children.
Education services: Group education facilities, resources for Key Stages 1 and 2, 3, 4 and Further or Higher Education..
Collections:
Collections of fine and decorative art including:
Paintings, drawings, portrait miniatures, prints, silver, glass, ceramics, textiles, furniture
Landscapes by Guardi and Turner and portraits by Stubbs, Ramsay, Zoffany and Thomas Gainsborough
Sir William Holburne (1793-1874): His collections of fine art and paintings form the nucleus of the works of art
Minerals and books
Printed publications:
A Gift to the Nation
Ernest Cook centenary publication: Miniatures catalogue (Bayne-Powell)
The History and the Collections: A Fine Line (Hammond, H)
Programme of Events
Numerous publications on the contents of the museum covering:
Decorative Art and Mixed Exhibitions
Secret Passion to Noble Fashion - Portrait Miniatures (Sumner)
Holburne Museum of Art Guide Book 1999
Fine Art Catalogues
Catalogue of Miniatures
Catalogue of Silver
Exhibition catalogues
Souvenir Guide Book

Internet home pages:
http://www.bath.ac.uk/holburne
General information, opening hours, forthcoming exhibitions, events and courses.

1314
HOLKER HALL AND GARDENS

See - Lakeland Motor Museum

1315
HOLLYCOMBE STEAM AND WOODLAND GARDEN SOCIETY

Iron Hill, Midhurst Road, Liphook, Hampshire, GU30 7LP

Tel: 01428 724900
Fax: 01428 723682
Email: hollycombe@talk21.com
Formed: 1971

Organisation type and purpose: Membership association (membership is by subscription), present number of members: 150, voluntary organisation, registered charity, museum, suitable for ages: all ages.
Operates Hollycombe Steam Collection, a working steam power museum of national importance in the UK. Open to the public as advertised.

Enquiries to: Information Officer
Access:
Access to staff: By letter, by telephone, by fax, by email, in person, Internet web pages
Hours: Office: Mon to Fri, 0900 to 1700
Access to building, collections or gallery: No prior appointment required
Hours: Collection open to public: Sun and Public holidays; Easter to mid Oct; daily late Jul to late Aug, 1200 to 1700
Other restrictions: Admission charge published. Prior appointment is required when closed to the public.
Access for disabled people: Parking provided, level entry, toilet facilities
Other restrictions: Access to most areas.

General description:
History and application of steam power to transport, agriculture, fairground, marine, industry. Shown working when open.
Printed publications:
Museum Guide Book
Publicity leaflet
Electronic and video products:
Fairground Organ Tapes (available for purchase)

Internet home pages:
http://www.hollycombe.co.uk
Details of museum, Description of artefacts. Open days, exhibits.Up-to-date news.

1316
HOLLYTREES MUSEUM

Castle Park, High Street, Colchester, Essex, CO1 1UG

Tel: 01206 282940
Minicom no. 01206 500145
Fax: 01206 282925
Email: tom.hodgson@colchester.gov.uk

Organisation type and purpose: Museum, historic building, house or site, suitable for ages: all ages.
Parent body:
Museum Resource Centre
14 Rygate Road, Colchester, Essex, tel: 01206 282931, fax: 01206 282932

Enquiries to: Curator
Access:
Access to staff: By letter, by telephone, by fax, by email, visitors by prior appointment, Internet web pages

Access to building, collections or gallery: No prior appointment required
Hours: Mon to Sat, 1000 to 1700; Sun, 1100 to 1700
Access for disabled people: level entry, toilet facilities
Other restrictions: A lift to all public spaces, access may be limited for users of larger wheelchairs, a manual wheelchair is available.

General description:
Georgian town house built 1718 for Elizabeth Cornelisen and since owned by some of the wealthiest families in Colchester. Home life in Colchester over the last 300 years.
Collections:
17th and 18th century books (history and religion)
Archaeological Journals
Brass rubbing collection (A H Brown)
Definitive collection of rubbings of Essex brasses (Christy, Porteous and Smith)
Essex Parish Histories
Transcripts of Essex Parish Registers
Toys
Domestic life objects
Catalogues:
Catalogue for library is in-house only. Catalogue for part of the collections is published and part is on-line.
Printed publications:
Holytrees Guide Book

Internet home pages:
http://www.colchestermuseums.org.uk
Collections on-line, general information on all four museums, education visits, feedback, street finder

1317
HOLMFIRTH POSTCARD EXHIBITION
See - Bamforth & Co Postcard Museum

1318
HOLMWOOD HOUSE
61-63 Netherlee Road, Cathcart, Glasgow, G44 3YG

Tel: 0141 637 2129
Fax: 0141 637 2129
Email: holmwood@nts.org.uk

Organisation type and purpose: Historic building, house or site.
Parent body:
National Trust for Scotland (West Region)

Enquiries to: Property Manager
Access:
Access to staff: By letter, by telephone, by fax, by email
Access for disabled people: access to all public areas, toilet facilities
Other restrictions: Access to house and grounds, wheelchair lift to first floor

General description:
Nineteenth century house, interior designed by Alexander 'Greek' Thomson in 1857-58.
Information services:
CD-ROM, audio tour in French and German, basic language tape tour for visitors with learning difficulties.
Special visitor services: Tape recorded guides..
Printed publications:
Selection of 'Greek' Thomson-related books and books of architectural interest

Internet home pages:
http://www.nts.org.uk

1319
HOLNICOTE ESTATE
Selworthy, Minehead, Somerset, TA24 8TJ

Tel: 01643 862452
Fax: 01643 863011
Email: holnicote@nationaltrust.org.uk

Organisation type and purpose: National organisation, registered charity (charity number 205846), historic building, house or site, suitable for ages: 8+.
Parent body:
National Trust (South West)
Regional Office for Wessex, tel: 01985 843600

Enquiries to: Warden
Access:
Access to staff: By letter, by telephone, by fax, by email, in person, Internet web pages
Access to building, collections or gallery: No prior appointment required
Hours: Estate: open access throughout the year Information Centre: daily, 15 Mar to 30 April, 1100 to 1600; May to Sep, 1100 to 1700; Oct, 1100 to 1600
Access for disabled people: toilet facilities
Other restrictions: Easy access trail at North Hill and Webbers Post, adapted bird hide, telephone for further details of these and other trails. Adapted WC at Bossington and Horner car parks.

General description:
The Holnicote Estate covers 5042ha (12,500 acres) of Exmoor National Park and includes the high tors of Dunkery and Selworthy Beacons. Its traditional cottages and farms are grouped in and around the villages and hamlets, which include Selworthy, Allerford, Bossington, Horner and Luccombe.
'Hands on' interpretation at Selworthy information centre, offering insights into the abundance of wildlife and ancient buildings. Jubilee wind and weather hut at Webbers Post.

Internet home pages:
http://www.nationaltrust.org.uk/regions/wessex

1320
HOLST BIRTHPLACE MUSEUM
4 Clarence Road, Cheltenham, Gloucestershire, GL52 2AY

Tel: 01242 524846
Fax: 01242 580182
Email: holstmuseum@btconnect.com
Formed: 1975

Organisation type and purpose: Independently owned, registered charity (charity number 1078599), museum, suitable for ages: 5+. Independent trust.

Enquiries to: Curator
Direct tel: 01242 580182
Other contacts: Chairman of Trustees
Access:
Access to staff: By letter, by telephone, by fax, by email, visitors by prior appointment, Internet web pages
Other restrictions: Appointment necessary to see Curator.

General description:
Life and music of Gustav Holst; Regency and Victorian lifestyles.
Information services:
Library available for reference (for conditions see Access above)
Special visitor services: Guided tours, materials and/or activities for children.
Education services: Resources for Key Stages 1 and 2 and Further or Higher Education..
Collections:
Complete published works of Gustav Holst
Concert programmes and press cuttings (20 volumes, assembled by Holst)
Photographs
Catalogues:
Catalogue for all of the collections is only available in-house.
Printed publications:
Guide book to the Holst Birthplace Museum
Pictorial Scrapbook for the Holst Birthplace Museum
Holst's Country (leaflet)
Pittville Guided Walk (leaflet)

Internet home pages:
http://www.accessarts.org.uk
http://www.holstmuseum.org.uk

1321
HOLTON WINDMILL
Mill House, Holton, Halesworth, Suffolk

Tel: 01986 872367

Organisation type and purpose: Historic building, house or site.
Access:
Access to staff: By letter, by telephone

General description:
18th century post mill on roundhouse, the exterior now fully restored.

1322
HOLYHEAD MARITIME MUSEUM
Newry Beach, Beach Road, Holyhead, Gwynedd, LL65 1YD

Tel: 01407 769745

Organisation type and purpose: Registered charity (charity number 514840), museum, historic building, house or site, suitable for ages: 8+.
Member of the:
Gwynedd and Anglesey Federation of Maritime Museums

Enquiries to: Curator
Access:
Access to staff: By letter, by telephone

General description:
The museum is housed in the old lifeboat house (c. 1858). It contains a display of models, photographs and artefacts relating to local maritime history from the Roman period.
Collections:
Local historical photographs

1323
HOME FRONT EXPERIENCE, THE
New Street, Llandudno, Gwynedd, LL30 2YF

Tel: 01492 871032

Enquiries to: Curator
Access:
Access to staff: By letter, by telephone

General description:
Civilian life during the Second World War, its sights, sounds and smell. Interactive displays include experience in an Anderson shelter during an air raid, the blackout, the air raid siren, gas masks and food rationing.

1324
HOME OF THE TROLLEYBUS
See - Trolleybus Museum at Sandtoft

1325
HONEYWOOD HERITAGE CENTRE
Honeywood Walk, Carshalton, Surrey, SM5 3NX

Tel: 020 8770 4297
Fax: 020 8770 4297
Email: lbshoneywood@ukonline.co.uk
Formed: 1990
Formerly: Sutton Heritage Centre, date of change, 1998

Organisation type and purpose: Local government body, museum, suitable for ages: 5+.
Parent body:
London Borough of Sutton Heritage Service
Central Library, St Nicholas Way, Sutton, SM1 1EA, tel: 020 8770 4781/2, fax: 020 8770 4777

Enquiries to: Curator
Access:
Access to staff: By letter, by telephone, by fax, by email, in person, Internet web pages

continued overleaf

Access for disabled people: Parking provided, level entry, toilet facilities
Other restrictions: Disabled parking - 1 bay only.

General description:
Local history of the area (Beddington, Wallington, Carshalton, Sutton, Cheam) including industrial and social history associated with River Wandle.
Information services:
Guided tours by prior arrangement.
Special visitor services: Guided tours, materials and/or activities for children.
Education services: Group education facilities, resources for Key Stages 1 and 2..
Collections:
Local Art Collection
Artefacts from Beddington Roman Villa, 1st-4th century AD
Photographs of the local area
Catalogues:
Catalogue for part of the collections is only available in-house.
Publications list:
is available in hard copy.
Printed publications:
A number of publications on various local history subjects including:
Croissants at Croydon: The Memoirs of Jack Bamford (Bamford J, ISBN 0 907335 15 2, £1.50
Five Centuries of Artists in Sutton: A Biographical Dictionary of Artists associated with Sutton, London (Beasley M, ISBN 0 907335 19 5, £4.95)
Croydon Airport and the Battle for Britain, 1939-1940 (Bogle J, Cluett D, Learmonth B, ISBN 0 907335 11 X, £2.95)
The Past in Pictures: A further collection of photographs of the London Borough of Sutton over the last century (ed Broughton J, 2nd rev.ed, ISBN 0 907335 24 1, £2.95)

Address for ordering publications:
Printed publications:
Leisurestop, London Borough of Sutton
Central Library, St Nicholas Way, Sutton, SM1 1EA, tel: 020 8770 4444

Internet home pages:
http://www.sutton.gov.uk/lfl/heritage/honeywood
General information on house and events/exhibitions programme.

1326
HORNEL ART GALLERY, THE
Broughton House, High Street, Kirkcudbright, Dumfries & Galloway, DG6 4JX

Tel: 01557 330437
Formed: 1901

Organisation type and purpose: Art gallery, historic building, house or site.
Parent body:
The National Trust for Scotland

Enquiries to: Curator

General description:
The paintings of A E Hornel, his house and artefacts.
Collections:
Fine antique furniture and oriental curios
Library of over 20,000 books and manuscripts
Paintings by Hornel

1327
E A HORNEL GALLERY
See - Broughton House

1328
HORNIMAN MUSEUM AND GARDENS
100 London Road, Forest Hill, London, SE23 3PQ

Tel: 020 8699 1872
Fax: 020 8291 5506
Email: enquiry@horniman.ac.uk

Formed: 1901

Organisation type and purpose: Registered charity (charity number 2456393), museum.
Administered by an independent charitable trust funded by the:
Department of Culture, Media and Sport

Enquiries to: Librarian
Direct tel: 020 8291 8681
Direct fax: 020 8291 5506
Direct email: dallen@horniman.ac.uk
Access:
Access to staff: By letter, by telephone, by fax, by email, in person, Internet web pages
Hours: Access to Library Tue to Sat, 1030 to 1730; Sun, 1400 to 1730, closed Mon and Bank Holidays
No appointment needed
Access to building, collections or gallery: No prior appointment required
Hours: Mon to Sat, 1030 to 1730; Sun, 1400 to 1730

General description:
Anthropology and ethnography (especially material culture), musical instruments (especially organology), natural history.
Information services:
Education services: Group education facilities, resources for Key Stages 1 and 2, 3, 4 and Further or Higher Education.
Services for disabled people: For the visually impaired; for the hearing impaired; displays and/or information at wheelchair height.
Collections:
18th century works on botany and zoology
250,000 natural history specimens
50,000 ethnographic specimens
6000 musical instruments from Africa, The Americas, Antarctica, Asia, Europe and Oceania
Adam Carse Collection of wind instruments and archives
Early Africana
Ridley Collection of books on organs
Catalogues:
Catalogue for library is in-house only.
Publications list:
is available in hard copy.
Printed publications:
Collectors: Individuals and Institutions (Shelton A, 2001)
Oriental Visions: Exhibitions, Travel and Collecting in the Victorian Age (Levell N, 2001)
Re-Visions: New perspectives on the African Collections of the Horniman Museum (Arnaut K, 2001)
Collectors: Expressions of Self and Other (Shelton A, 2001)
Nomads: Nomadic Material Culture in the Collections of the Horniman (Teague K, 2000)
Ekpu (Nicklin K, 1999)

Address for ordering publications:
Printed publications:
Global Book Marketing
38 King Street, London, WC2E 8JJ, tel: 020 7836 3020

Internet home pages:
http://www.horniman.ac.uk
Basic access information, plus email contact and research guide to the collections and musical instruments.

1329
HORNSEA MUSEUM
Burns Farm, Newbegin, Hornsea, East Yorkshire, HU18 1AB

Tel: 01964 533443
Formed: 1978

Organisation type and purpose: Registered charity (charity number 509615), museum, suitable for ages: 5+.

Enquiries to: Administrator
Access:
Access to staff: By letter, by telephone
Access for disabled people: ramped entry, toilet facilities

General description:
East Riding rural life, 16th century farmhouse and grounds containing displays on farming, domestic life, local trades, crafts, history and personalities; Hornsea Pottery display.
Information services:
Special visitor services: Guided tours, materials and/or activities for children.
Education services: Group education facilities, resources for Key Stages 1 and 2..
Collections:
Farm machinery and tools, domestic tools and furniture, costume, photographs, toys, trade tools, dairy equipment
Hornsea Pottery

Internet home pages:
http://www.hornseamuseum.com

1330
HORSEY WINDPUMP
Horsey, Great Yarmouth, Norfolk, NR29 4EF

Tel: 0870 609 5388 (Regional Office); 01493 393904 (open days only)
Email: horseywindpump@nationaltrust.org.uk

Organisation type and purpose: National organisation, registered charity (charity number 205846), historic building, house or site.
Parent body:
The National Trust (East of England)
East Anglia Regional Office, tel: 0870 609 5388

Enquiries to: Manager
Access:
Access to staff: By letter, by telephone, by email
Access for disabled people: ramped entry, toilet facilities
Other restrictions: Ground floor accessible with assistance. Level entrance to shop and to tea-room. WC not always available.

General description:
A restored drainage windpump that affords striking views across Horsey Mere, one of the Norfolk Broads. The mere is particularly well known for wintering wildfowl.

Internet home pages:
http://www.nationaltrust.org.uk

1331
HORSFORTH VILLAGE MUSEUM
5 The Green, Horsforth, Leeds, West Yorkshire, LS18 5JB

Tel: 0113 2819877
Acronym or abbreviation: HVM
Formed: 1988

Organisation type and purpose: Registered charity, museum.

Enquiries to: Manager
Access:
Access to staff: By letter
Access for disabled people: ramped entry

General description:
Local history. A collection of photographs, documents, maps and artefacts relating to the history of Horsforth (which was listed in Domesday in 1085). Items are on display as well as in storage for retrieval for study purposes.
Information services:
Special visitor services: Guided tours.
Education services: Group education facilities..
Collections:
How we lived, including Home Front, 1920-1950, 100 items plus documents
Printed publications:
Horsforth History Guides 1-6
Photograph Books
Guided Walks 1 and 2

Internet home pages:
http://www.yourhorsforth.co.uk/history.htm

1332
HORSHAM MUSEUM
9 The Causeway, Horsham, West Sussex, RH12 1HE

Tel: 01403 254959
Email: museum@horsham.gov.uk
Formed: 1893
Formerly: Horsham Museum Society

Organisation type and purpose: Museum.

Enquiries to: Curator
Access:
Access to staff: By letter, by telephone, by email, in person, visitors by prior appointment
Hours: Mon to Sat, 0900 to 1700
Other restrictions: Closed public holidays.
Access to building, collections or gallery: No prior appointment required
Hours: Daily, 1000 to 1700
Other restrictions: Appointment to view documents requires 3 days' notice. Appointment required to view museum society library.
Access for disabled people: ramped entry, toilet facilities

General description:
Horsham history; Shelley; Thomas Medwin; ephemera; photographs.
Information services:
Education services: Group education facilities, resources for Key Stages 1 and 3.
Services for disabled people: Displays and/or information at wheelchair height.
Collections:
Geology, 3 types of specimens, 2 Wealden fossil dragonflies, 1 Polacanthus
Albery Collection, an extensive collection of saddlery and bridle bits, 18th-19th century, 890 bridle bits, c. 400 saddlery items including tools
Early bicycles from the 'bone shaker' to 1930s tradesman, 1880s-1930s, over 20 items
Catalogues:
Catalogue for part of the collections is published.
Publications list:
is available in hard copy.
Printed publications:
Publications include:
Shelley A Life Told Through Books - A catalogue of Shelley Collection
Shelleys of Field Place
Shelleys P B and Thomas - Letters
Horsham Companion
Horsham and its History
Horsham of Medwin
Horsham Post
Victorian Horsham

1333
HORTON COURT
Horton, Chipping Sodbury, Gloucestershire, BS37 6QR

Tel: 01249 730141
Fax: 01249 730501

Organisation type and purpose: National organisation, registered charity (charity number 205846), historic building, house or site.
Parent body:
http://www.nationaltrust.org.uk/regions/wessex
Wessex Regional Office, tel: 01985 843600

Enquiries to: Tenant
Access:
Access to staff: By letter, by telephone, by fax
Access to building, collections or gallery: No prior appointment required
Hours: Beg Apr to beg Nov, Wed and Sat, 1400 to 1800
Other restrictions: Closes dusk if earlier. Other times by written appointment with tenant.
Access for disabled people: Parking provided
Other restrictions: Designated parking on application to tenant. Steps to entrance. Accessible entrance different from main entrance. Ambulatory is accessible

General description:
A Norman hall and an exceptionally fine detached ambulatory are all that remain of what is probably the oldest rectory in England. There are interesting early renaissance features, including stucco caricatures of classical figures. House not open to the public. Horton Camp, an Iron Age hill-fort with open access, is situated 500m south of Horton Court.

Internet home pages:
http://www.nationaltrust.org.uk/regions/wessex

1334
HOUGHTON MILL
Houghton, Huntingdon, Cambridgeshire, PE28 2AZ

Tel: 01480 301494 (Custodian)
Fax: 01480 469641

Organisation type and purpose: National organisation, registered charity (charity number 205846), museum, art gallery, historic building, house or site.
Parent body:
The National Trust (East of England)
East Anglia Regional Office, tel: 0870 609 5388

Enquiries to: Manager
Access:
Access to staff: By letter, by telephone, by fax
Access for disabled people: level entry, toilet facilities
Other restrictions: Ground floor fully accessible. No access to other floors. Ramped entrance to tea-room.

General description:
A large timber-built watermill on an island in the Great Ouse, with intact machinery which is still operational. Milling takes place on Sundays and Bank Holiday Mondays, and the flour is for sale. An art gallery exhibits work by local artists and photographers.
Information services:
Guided tours by arrangement.
Braille guide. Handling collection.
Suitable for school groups. Hands-on activities. Family guide. Children's guide. Children's quiz/trail.
Special visitor services: Materials and/or activities for children.
Education services: Group education facilities, resources for Key Stages 2 and 3.
Services for disabled people: For the visually impaired.

Internet home pages:
http://www.nationaltrust.org.uk

1335
HOUSE OF DUN
Montrose, Angus, DD10 9LQ

Tel: 01674 810264
Fax: 01674 810722
Email: houseofdun@nts.org.uk

Organisation type and purpose: Museum, historic building, house or site.
Parent body:
National Trust for Scotland

Enquiries to: Property Manager
Access:
Access to staff: By letter, by telephone, by fax, by email, in person
Access to building, collections or gallery: No prior appointment required
Hours: House and shop, end Mar to end Oct, Fri to Tue, 1200 to 1700; end Jun to beg Sep, Fri to Tue, 1100 to 1800
Garden and grounds, all year, daily, 0930 to sunset
Other restrictions: Guided tours of house only
Access for disabled people: toilet facilities
Other restrictions: Stairlift, wheelchair available

General description:
Georgian house built by William Adam in 1730. Contains superb contemporary plasterwork, royal mementos, woolwork and embroidery, family collection of portraits, furniture, and porcelain.
Courtyard buildings include a handloom weaving workshop.
Information services:
Miniature theatre display, video, Braille information sheets, subtitled video, explanatory text in French and German.
Special visitor services: Guided tours.
Services for disabled people: For the visually impaired; for the hearing impaired.

Internet home pages:
http://www.nts.org.uk

1336
HOUSE OF THE BINNS
Linlithgow, West Lothian, EH49 7NA

Tel: 01506 834255
Email: houseofthebinns@nts.org.uk

Organisation type and purpose: Historic building, house or site.
Parent body:
National Trust for Scotland

Enquiries to: Property Manager
Access:
Access to staff: By letter, by telephone, by email, in person, charges to non-members
Access to building, collections or gallery: No prior appointment required
Hours: May to Sep, daily except Fri, 1300 to 1700

General description:
Seventeenth century house showing transition in Scottish architecture from fortified stronghold to more spacious mansion. The family home of the Dalyells since 1612 containing a fine collection of furniture; paintings; clocks; and porcelain, collected over 400 years. Of particular interest are the plaster ceilings of 1630 and the family's involvement in historical events.
Information services:
Services for disabled people: For the visually impaired.
Collections:
General Tam Dalyell (1615-1685), a Royalist General, signed the National Covenant but fought for King in the Civil War. Captured at Worcester in 1651; imprisoned in Tower; escaped to Russia, where he reformed the Tsar's Army until recalled after the Restoration to become Commander-in-Chief of the King's Forces in Scotland. He became the scourge of the Covenanters and so became known as 'The Bloody Muscovite'.

Internet home pages:
http://www.nts.org.uk

1337
HOUSE ON THE HILL TOY MUSEUM
Grove Hill, Stansted, Essex, CM24 8SP

Tel: 01279 813237 (Admin) 01279 813567 (Collector Shop)
Fax: 01279 816391
Email: gold@enta.net
Formed: 1991

Organisation type and purpose: Museum, suitable for ages: all ages.

Enquiries to: Curator
Access:
Access to staff: By letter, by telephone, by fax, by email, Internet web pages
Hours: Mon to Fri, 1000 to 1600

General description:
Toy Museum displays include: train layout, Star Wars, dolls and soft toys, Meccano, games, annuals, Action Man, Rock 'n Roll memorabilia and End-of-the-Pier slot machines.

continued overleaf

Internet home pages:
http://www.gold.enta.net
Detailed information on what the museum has on offer for visitors; opening times; prices etc.

1338
HOUSEHOLD CAVALRY MUSEUM

Combermere Barracks, St Leonards Road, Windsor, Berkshire, SL4 3DN

Tel: 01753 755112
Fax: 01753 755161
Email: homehq@householdcavalry.co.uk
Formed: 1964

Organisation type and purpose: Registered charity (charity number 274185), museum, suitable for ages: 8+, research organisation.
Affiliated to:
National Army Museum
Ogilby Trust, Area Museum South East England

Enquiries to: Curator
Access:
Access to staff: By letter only, charges made to all users
Hours: Mon to Fri, 0900 to 1700
Access to building, collections or gallery: No prior appointment required
Access for disabled people: toilet facilities

General description:
Personal records, uniform, arms and armour, traditions; marriage details, births and historical records etc of officers and soldiers of the Life Guards (early 19th century to date), Horse Grenadiers, Royal Horse Guards (The Blues, 1780 to date), and the 1st Royal Dragoons (1661-1969); the library contains reference works on military history, especially cavalry and Household Cavalry, equitation, personal records and orders in manuscript.
Collections:
Court martial books
Historical record books
Officers' service details
Private letters
Records of state occasions
Soldier service details
Standing orders
Regimental magazines 1862-1993
War diaries
Printed publications:
Regimental Histories
The Blues and Royals
The Life Guards

1339
HOVE MUSEUM & ART GALLERY

19 New Church Road, Hove, East Sussex, BN3 4AB

Tel: 01273 290200
Fax: 01273 202827
Formed: 1927

Organisation type and purpose: Local government body, museum, art gallery, suitable for ages: 5+.
Parent body:
Brighton & Hove District Council

Enquiries to: Keeper
Access:
Access to staff: By letter, by telephone, by fax, visitors by prior appointment
Access for disabled people: Parking provided, ramped entry, access to all public areas, toilet facilities

General description:
The museum is housed in a Victorian villa designed in the 1870s by the architect Thomas Vallance in an Italianate style for John Oliver Vallance who died in 1893. The museum has a Childhood Room; Toy Gallery; interactive Film Library; Local History Gallery with displays of the Roman settlement at West Blatchington, Norman manors and churches, Hangleton' early medieval village, the Regency development of Brunswick and the growth of Victorian and 20th century Hove; Paintings Gallery with fine art collections and a Research Room.
Information services:
Special visitor services: Guided tours, tape recorded guides, materials and/or activities for children.
Education services: Group education facilities, resources for Key Stages 1 and 2, 3, 4 and Further or Higher Education.
Services for disabled people: For the visually impaired; displays and/or information at wheelchair height.
Collections:
Collection of over 20,000 toys
Working train set
Working optical toys, magic lanterns, cameras and rare apparatus
Prehistoric Amber Cup
Pocock Collection of British ceramics, 17th-20th century, c. 500 items
Printed publications:
Publications for purchase from Museum Shop
Electronic and video products:
For purchase from Museum Shop

Internet home pages:
http://www.hove.virtualmuseum.info

1340
HOVERCRAFT MUSEUM TRUST & SOCIETY

Argus Gate, HMS Daedalus, Chark Lane, off Broom Way, Lee-on-Solent, Gosport, Hampshire, PO13 9NY

Tel: 023 9255 2090
Fax: 023 9255 2090
Email: enquiries@hovercraft-museum.org
Acronym or abbreviation: THS or Hovercraft Museum
Formed: 1971
Formerly: United Kingdom Hovercraft Society, date of change, 1971

Organisation type and purpose: Learned society (membership is by subscription), registered charity, museum, suitable for ages: all ages, consultancy.
Other addresses:
Hovercraft Museum Trust
15 St Marks Road, Gosport, Hampshire, PO12 2DA, tel: 02392 601310

Enquiries to: Secretary
Other contacts: TV and Film c/o 02392 601310
Access:
Access to staff: By letter, by telephone, by fax
Hours: Mon to Fri, 0900 to 1700
Other restrictions: To library, by appointment.
Access to building, collections or gallery: Prior appointment required
Hours: By appointment only
Access for disabled people: Parking provided, level entry, toilet facilities

General description:
Application of the air cushion principle; hovercraft applications in materials handling, civil engineering and medicine; ferries, transport, leisure, military.
Collections:
Early papers and books on the hovercraft principle, papers and proceedings, videos, photographs, films and slides
SRNI log book
3 Cross-Channel Hovercraft
Many early historic craft - last of types
Last SRNS and many pioneer vehicles
A collection of 40 hovercraft, and 5000 plus books, pictures, etc.
Publications list:
is available in hard copy and online.
Printed publications:
Hovercraft Bulletin (monthly)
Proceedings
Electronic and video products:
Set of 5 videos (£15 each)

Internet home pages:
http://www.hovercraft-museum.org
2000 pages and pictures

1341
HOW WE LIVED THEN - MUSEUM OF SHOPS

20 Cornfield Terrace, Eastbourne, East Sussex, BN21 4NS

Tel: 01323 737143
Formed: 1988

Organisation type and purpose: Independently owned, museum, suitable for ages: all ages.
Museum of shops and social history.

Enquiries to: Owner
Access:
Access to staff: By letter, by telephone, in person

General description:
Mr Barton the Grocer; The Admiral Lord Nelson Inn; Chemist, Ironmonger, Office and Boot Repairer's; Draper's and Tailor's; Photographer's; Music Shop; Toy Shop; Village Post Office; Jeweller's; WWII kitchen/living room complete with under-the-stairs air-raid shelter; Edwardian kitchen.
Collections:
Over 100,000 exhibits
Printed publications:
Information leaflets and worksheets available upon request

1342
HOWELL HARRIS MUSEUM

Coleg Trefeca, Brecon, Powys, LD3 0PP

Tel: 01874 711423
Fax: 01874 712212
Email: post@trefeca.org.uk
Formed: 1752
Formerly: Trefecca College, Trevecka College, date of change, 1972

Organisation type and purpose: Registered charity (charity number 258456), museum, historic building, house or site, suitable for ages: 8+.
Christian training, retreat and conference centre and museum.
Parent body:
Presbyterian Church of Wales (PCW EBC)
53 Richmond Road, Cardiff, CF24 3WJ, tel: 029 2049 4913, fax: 029 2046 4293, email: ebcpcw@aol.com

Enquiries to: Warden
Access:
Access to staff: By letter, by telephone, by fax, by email, visitors by prior appointment
Hours: Daily, 0900 to 1600
Access to building, collections or gallery: Prior appointment required
Hours: Daily, 0900 to 1600
Other restrictions: Other times strictly by appointment only.
Dec to Feb: closed Sat, Sun.
Closed Good Friday to Easter Tuesday and Christmas.
Access for disabled people: Parking provided, ramped entry, toilet facilities
Other restrictions: Access to museum area by chair lift.
Access to historic house involves one step.

General description:
The Welsh Methodist revival by means of an audiovisual presentation. Artefacts include the Trefeca 'Family' period. Also features contacts with English Methodists such as Wesley, Whitefield and the Countess of Huntingdon. Library on Welsh Methodist history and related subjects, in English and Welsh, historic Grade II listed building (1752 onwards), extensive training, retreat and conference programme.
Information services:
Library available for reference (for conditions see Access above)

Special visitor services: Guided tours, materials and/or activities for children.
Education services: Resources for Key Stages 1 and 2, 3, 4 and Further or Higher Education.
Services for disabled people: For the hearing impaired; displays and/or information at wheelchair height.
Collections:
Electrifying Machine. 1763
Howell Harris Preaching Chair/Pulpit. Field Pulpit. ca. 1741
Joseph Harris' Telescope (recorded the transit of Venus over sun - experiment presented to Royal Society) 1761
Pulpit from the Countess of Huntingdon's College, Trefeca
Turrett clock and bell. Rose drums of Yew. 1754 added to house, restored by Barometer Shop, Leominster, 1999
Swords and guns. Brecknock Militia ('Seven Year's War', 1756)
Books published by Treveka Press 1756-1800
Catalogues:
Catalogue for library is in-house only. Catalogue for all of the collections is only available in-house.
Printed publications:
There was a man sent . . . A short history of Howell Harris and the Methodist revival (£1.25)
Treveka 1714-1964 (Davies G, £1.75)
Internet home pages:
http://www.trefeca.org.uk/
Historical and general outline of work of the college.
http://www.ebcpcw.org.uk
General information regarding Presbytarian Church of Wales including Coleg Trefeca.

1343
HUDDERSFIELD LIBRARY & ART GALLERY
Princess Alexandra Walk, Huddersfield, West Yorkshire, HD1 2SU

Tel: 01484 221962
Fax: 01484 221952
Formed: 1898

Organisation type and purpose: Local government body, art gallery, suitable for ages: 5+.
Parent body:
Kirklees Cultural Services
Headquarters, Red Doles Lane, Huddersfield, HD2 1YF, tel: 01484 226300

Enquiries to: Principal Visual Arts Officer
Direct tel: 01484 221964
Direct email: robert.hall@kirkleesmc.gov.uk
Access:
Access to staff: By letter, by telephone, by fax, by email, visitors by prior appointment
Hours: Mon to Fri, 1000 to 1700; Sat, 1000 to 1600
Access to building, collections or gallery: No prior appointment required
Hours: Mon to Fri, 1000 to 1700; Sat, 1000 to 1600
Access for disabled people: ramped entry, access to all public areas, toilet facilities

General description:
Chiefly British art of past two centuries - paintings, drawings, prints, sculpture and some decorative art/craft.
Temporary exhibitions and events programme - local and regional artists and societies, touring shows, contemporary art.
Information services:
Special visitor services: Materials and/or activities for children.
Education services: Resources for Key Stages 2, 3 and Further or Higher Education..
Collections:
British Art from c. 1800 and small collections of European paintings, Japanese prints, contemporary crafts, 18th century watercolours, local and Yorkshire artists
19th century artists include: G F Watts, Atkinson Grimshaw, B W Leader, William Holman Hunt
20th century artists include: Camden Town (Gilman, Ginner, Bevan, Drummond, Pissarro, John, Sickert, Spencer Gore, Lowry, Bacon, Hockney, Bomberg, Colquhoun, Moore, Dobson, Epstein, Spencer, Irvin, Burra, Eurich, Eardley, Auerbach and Wadsworth)
Catalogues:
Catalogue for all of the collections is only available in-house but part is published.
Printed publications:
Exhibition Catalogues Recent:
Time Was . . . Recent Work by Shirley Diamond (£3.50)
Arturo Di Stefano Paintings, Counterproofs and Woodcuts (£6)

Internet home pages:
http://www.kirkleesmc.gov.uk

1344
HUDDERSFIELD NARROW CANAL
See - Marsden Moor Estate

1345
HUGH MILLER'S COTTAGE
Church Street, Cromarty, Ross-shire, IV11 8XA

Tel: 01381 600245

Organisation type and purpose: Museum, historic building, house or site.
Parent body:
National Trust for Scotland Highlands and Islands Office (North)

Enquiries to: Property Manager
Access:
Access to staff: By letter, by telephone, in person
Access to building, collections or gallery: No prior appointment required
Hours: Beg May to end Sep, daily, 1200 to1700

General description:
Hugh Miller's birthplace, built by his great-grandfather c1698. Furnished cottage containing an exhibition and video of his life and work.
Information services:
Services for disabled people: For the visually impaired.
Collections:
Fossils from old red sandstone of special local and regional importance, 1820-1854, 8 cases of unique and rare exhibits

Internet home pages:
http://www.nts.org.uk

1346
HUGHENDEN MANOR ESTATE
Hughenden Valley, High Wycombe, Buckinghamshire, HP14 4LA

Tel: 01494 755573
Fax: 01494 474284
Formed: 1895

Organisation type and purpose: Registered charity (charity number 205846), museum, suitable for ages: 7+.
Parent body:
National Trust (South and South East Region)
Thames and Solent Regional Office, tel: 01494 528051, fax: 01494 463310

Enquiries to: Visitor Services Manager
Access:
Access to staff: By letter, by fax
Access to building, collections or gallery: No prior appointment required
Hours: Manor, Mar, weekends only; Apr to Oct inc, Wed to Sun and Bank holidays 1300 to 1700, last admissions 1630
Garden, Mar also Sat and Sun, 1200 to 1700
Open Good Friday
Other restrictions: Contact Estate office on 01494 755573.
Access for disabled people: Parking provided, level entry, toilet facilities
Other restrictions: 3 manual wheelchairs available. Ground floor fully accessible. No access to other floors. Level entrance to shop and restaurant. Gravel paths difficult for wheelchairs. Access to terrace for view of garden.

General description:
The home of Benjamin Disraeli, Victorian prime minister and statesman, from 1848 until his death in 1881. Most of his furniture, books and pictures remain in this, his private retreat from the rigours of parliamentary life in London. There are beautiful walks through the surrounding park and woodland, and the garden is a recreation of the colourful design of his wife, Mary Anne.
Information services:
Photograph album. Braille guide, large print guide, sympathetic hearing scheme.
Loan of all-terrain buggy for outdoors.
Suitable for school groups, education room/centre, live interpretation, hands-on activities, children's guide.
Special visitor services: Materials and/or activities for children.
Education services: Group education facilities.
Services for disabled people: For the visually impaired; for the hearing impaired.
Collections:
Hughenden Papers, kept at the Bodleian Library, Oxford
Catalogues:
Catalogue for part of the collections is only available in-house.
Publications list:
is available in hard copy.
Printed publications:
Guide Book
Short Guide
Estate leaflet
Children's guide
Property leaflet (free)
Group bookings (free)
Events (free)

Internet home pages:
http://www.nationaltrust.org.uk
Information about the National Trust and its work, including places to visit

1347
HULL CITY MUSEUMS, ART GALLERIES AND ARCHIVES
Monument Building, Ferens Art Gallery, Queen Victoria Square, Kingston upon Hull, East Yorkshire, HU1 3RA

Tel: 01482 613902
Fax: 01482 613710
Email: museums@hullcc.gov.uk
Formed: 1822
Formerly: Kingston upon Hull City Museums

Organisation type and purpose: Local government body, museum, art gallery, suitable for ages: all.
Administrative office for the museums and art galleries of Hull.
Parent body:
Hull City Council
Guildhall, Hull, HU1 2AA, tel: 01482 610610
Other addresses:
Arctic Corsair
Ferens Art Gallery
Hands on History
Hull & East Riding Museum
Hull Maritime Museum
Queen Victoria Square, Hull, HU1 3RA
Spurn Lightship
Streetlife
The Deep
Wilberforce House

Enquiries to: Head of Museums
Direct tel: 01482 613904
Direct fax: 01482 613710
Other contacts: Customer Services Manager for Deputy to Head of Service.

continued overleaf

Access:
Access to staff: By letter, by telephone, by fax, by email, visitors by prior appointment
Hours: Mon to Fri, 1000 to 1700
Access to building, collections or gallery: No access other than to staff
Hours: Museum open Mon to Sat, 1000 to 1700; Sun, 1330 to 1630
Other restrictions: Prior appointment required for library.

General description:
Marine painting 18th to 20th century; British painting of 19th to 20th century; port of Hull; shipbuilding, Hull and East Yorkshire; Humber merchant shipping; whaling and deep water fishing 18th to 20th centuries; maritime transport and social history of Hull; Hull silver; William Wilberforce and abolition of the Slave Trade; whaling, fishing and shipping of Hull; archaeology of Hull and the East Riding; local natural history, geology; marine painters, other local artists, Dutch art, modern art, live art.
Collections:
Archives relating to the City of Hull
Arctic Whaling: artefacts, documents (log books, journals), specialist library, photographs
Deep Water Fishing: photos, models, artefacts
Library of William Wilberforce
Marine Painting extensive collection especially Hull School
Marcus Barnard, ship photographer (1900-1925)
Photographic collection of Harry Cartidge (1910-1970)
Ship plans - Beverley and Selby shipyards
The Hull Arctic Whaling Trade (1750-1869)
Wilson Line: models, artefacts, photographs
Publications list:
is available on-line.

Internet home pages:
http://www.hullcc.gov.uk/museums

1348
HULL MARITIME MUSEUM
Victoria Square, Hull, East Yorkshire, HU1 3DX

Tel: 01482 613902
Fax: 01482 613710
Formed: 1975
Formed from: Hull City Museums
Formerly: Kingston upon Hull Town Docks Museum; Town Docks Museum, date of change, 1999

Organisation type and purpose: Local government body, museum, historic building, house or site, suitable for ages: 5+.

Enquiries to: Curator
Access:
Access to staff: By letter, by telephone, by fax, visitors by prior appointment
Access to building, collections or gallery: No prior appointment required
Hours: Mon to Sat, 1000 to 1700; Sun, 1230 to 1630
Access for disabled people: ramped entry, access to all public areas, toilet facilities
Other restrictions: Wheelchair available.

General description:
Whaling: Arctic whaling of 19th century and 20th century, 'factory' whaling. Paintings, personalia, weapons, tools and decorative arts - Scrimshaw, the art of the whaler, skeletons of whales.
Fishing: East Coast fishing, deep sea trawling, models from coastal craft to steam trawlers, photographs, equipment.
Merchant Trade: decorative arts, marine paintings, models relating to Hull Docks and trade, local steamship companies, figureheads, life-saving, navigation.
Information services:
Library available for reference (for conditions see Access above)
Guided tours by arrangement.
Special visitor services: Guided tours, materials and/or activities for children.
Education services: Group education facilities, resources for Key Stages 1 and 2, 3 and 4.
Services for disabled people: Displays and/or information at wheelchair height.
Collections:
Outstanding collection of marine paintings by local artists 19-20th centuries
Largest collection of 'Scrimshaw' - decorative whale kett, whalebone etc, this side of the Atlantic
Catalogues:
Catalogue for library is in-house only. Catalogue for part of the collections is only available in-house.
Printed publications:
Inhouse gallery guide and local publications, exhibition catalogues (available direct)

Internet home pages:
http://www.hullcc.gov.uk/museums
General information regarding access.

1349
HULL UNIVERSITY ART COLLECTION
The Middleton Hall, University of Hull, Cottingham Road, Hull, East Yorkshire, HU6 7RX

Tel: 01482 346311
Fax: 01482 465192
Email: j.g.bernasconi@hist.hull.ac.uk
Formed: 1963

Organisation type and purpose: Art gallery.
Parent body:
University of Hull

Enquiries to: Director
Direct tel: 01482 465035
Access:
Access to staff: By letter, by telephone, by fax, by email, visitors by prior appointment
Access to building, collections or gallery: No prior appointment required
Hours: Mon, Tue, Thu, Fri, 1400 to 1600; Wed, 1230 to 1600

General description:
An internationally known art collection specialising in art in Britain 1890-1940. It features paintings, sculpture, drawings and prints, including works by Beardsley, Sickert, Steer, Lucien Pissarro, Augustus John, Stanley Spencer, Wyndham Lewis and Ben Nicholson as well as sculpture by Epstein, Gill, Gaudier- Brzeska and Henry Moore. The Camden Town Group and Bloomsbury artists are particularly well represented.
Collections:
Paintings, drawings, sculpture, prints
Thompson Collections of Chinese ceramics (on long loan)
Catalogues:
Catalogue for all of the collections is only available in-house.
Publications list:
is available in hard copy.
Printed publications:
Exhibition catalogues

Address for ordering publications:
Printed publications:
The Director, University Art Collection University of Hull

Internet home pages:
http://www.hull.ac.uk/history/art/

1350
HUNTER HOUSE MUSEUM
Calderwood Cottages, Maxwellton Road, Glasgow, G74 3LW

Tel: 01355 261261
Formed: 1996

Organisation type and purpose: Local government body, museum, suitable for ages: 5+.

Enquiries to: Visitor Services Officer
Direct tel: 01355 236644
Other contacts: Curator
Access:
Access to staff: By letter, by telephone
Hours: Mon to Fri, 0900 to 1600
Access to building, collections or gallery: Prior appointment required
Hours: Mon to Fri, 1230 to 1630; Sat, Sun, 1200 to 1700
Access for disabled people: Parking provided, level entry, access to all public areas, toilet facilities

General description:
Was home to John and William Hunter, famous medical brothers, born and raised here in 18th century.
Hunter House makes learning about medicine a fine experience. The museum is a combination of traditional and modern methods to describe anatomy and surgery in a way which especially interests children. A recreated kitchen scene reinacts the brother's early days. 'Bodyvents' explains 18th century surgical practice.
Information services:
Special visitor services: Materials and/or activities for children.
Education services: Group education facilities.
Services for disabled people: Displays and/or information at wheelchair height.
Printed publications:
CD-ROM allows an exciting insight into the origins of modern medicine

1351
HUNTERIAN ART GALLERY
See - Glasgow University, Hunterian Art Gallery

1352
HUNTERIAN COLLECTION
See - Museums of the Royal College of Surgeons

1353
HUNTERIAN MUSEUM
See - Glasgow University, Hunterian Museum

1354
HUNTLY HOUSE MUSEUM
See - Museum of Edinburgh

1355
HUNTLY MUSEUM
See - Brander Museum, Huntly

1356
HURST CASTLE
Milford-on-Sea, Keyhaven, Limington, Hampshire, SO41 0QU

Tel: 01590 642344

Organisation type and purpose: Historic building, house or site, suitable for ages: 5+.
Parent body:
English Heritage (South East Region)
Eastgate Court, 195-205 High Street, Guildford, Surrey, GU1 3EH, tel: 01483 252000, fax: 01483 252001

Enquiries to: Curator
Access:
Access to staff: By letter, by telephone
Access to building, collections or gallery: No prior appointment required
Hours: April to 31st October, daily, 1030 to 1730 or dusk

General description:
Fortress built by Henry VIII and strengthened in the 19th and 20th centuries, it controls the entrance to the Solent.

1357
HUTCHESONS' HALL

158 Ingram Street, Glasgow, G1 1EJ

Tel: 0141 552 8391
Fax: 0141 552 7031
Email: hutchesonshall@nts.org.uk

Organisation type and purpose: Museum, art gallery, historic building, house or site.
Parent body:
National Trust for Scotland (West Region)

Enquiries to: Property Manager
Access:
Access to staff: By letter, by telephone, by fax, by email
Access for disabled people: toilet facilities
Other restrictions: Access to gallery

General description:
Built in 1802-5 to a design by David Hamilton, interior hung with portraits of Glasgow worthies, permanent multimedia exhibition, 'Glasgow Style', includes film and a gallery selling work by young Glasgow designers.

Internet home pages:
http://www.nts.org.uk

1358
HYTHE LOCAL HISTORY ROOM

Oaklands, Stade Street, Hythe, Kent, CT21 6BG

Tel: 01303 266152
Formed: 1933

Organisation type and purpose: Museum, art gallery, suitable for ages: 8+.
Parent body:
Hythe Town Council

Enquiries to: Curator
Direct tel: 01303 850123
Direct fax: 01303 256710
Direct email: janet.adamson@kent.gov.uk
Access:
Access to staff: By letter, by telephone, visitors by prior appointment
Hours: Mon, 0930 to 1800; Tue, Wed, Thu, 0930 to 1700; Fri, 0930 to 1900; Sat, 0930 to 1600
Access to building, collections or gallery: No prior appointment required
Access for disabled people: Parking provided, level entry, access to all public areas, toilet facilities

General description:
Cinque Ports. History of Hythe.
Catalogues:
Catalogue for all of the collections is only available in-house.

1359
ICKWORTH HOUSE, PARK & GARDENS

Ickworth, The Rotunda, Horringer, Bury St Edmunds, Suffolk, IP29 5QE

Tel: 01284 735270
Fax: 01284 735175
Email: ickworth@nationaltrust.org.uk
Formed: 1956

Organisation type and purpose: National organisation, registered charity (charity number 205846), historic building, house or site, suitable for ages: all ages.
Parent body:
The National Trust (East of England)
East Anglia Regional Office, tel: 0870 609 5388

Enquiries to: Events & Marketing Co-ordinator
Direct tel: 01284 735961
Direct email: aihkee@nationaltrust.org.uk
Access:
Access to staff: By letter, by telephone, by fax, by email, in person
Access for disabled people: Parking provided, ramped entry, access to all public areas, toilet facilities
Other restrictions: Designated parking 10yds. Drop-off point. 2 single-seater powered mobility vehicles available. Steps to entrance. Ramp available to front door. Ground floor fully accessible, all ground floor rooms on one level. Photograph album. Lift to first floor, takes small wheelchairs only. Restricted access in house for large, powered vehicles. Wheelchair on each floor, for use in house only. Fire and evacuation regulations only allow one wheelchair on first floor at any one time. Steps to shop and to restaurant entrances. Stairlift to shop and restaurant available for wheelchair users able to transfer. Garden largely accessible, some changes of level; gravel drive and paths. Lady Geraldine's Walk, a circular, edge-marked walk with level gravel surface. Recommended route map.

General description:
The eccentric 4th Earl of Bristol created this equally eccentric house, with its central rotunda and curved corridors, in 1795 to display his collections. Paintings by Titian, Gainsborough and Velázquez and a magnificent Georgian silver collection are on display. An Italianate garden lies to the south of the house, which is set in a 'Capability' Brown park with woodland walks, deer enclosure, vineyard, Georgian summer house, church, canal and lake.
Information services:
Taster tours each day except Wed and Thur during open season at 1215.
Booked guided tours and special openings of house for groups with particular interests. Also booked tours for groups of Italianate garden, woods, parkland and vineyard. Details from property. Many events throughout the season including Christmas. Programme of themed restaurant events/ meals. Family woodland rambles. School holiday activities.
Braille guide. Large-print guide. Touch list. Handling collection. Scented plants. Frontcarrying baby slings for loan. Hip-carrying infant seats for loan. All-terrain pushchair available for outdoor use.
Suitable for school groups. Hands-on activities. Children's guide. Children's quiz/trail. Adult study days.
Special visitor services: Guided tours, materials and/or activities for children.
Education services: Group education facilities.
Services for disabled people: For the visually impaired.
Catalogues:
Catalogue for library is in-house only. Catalogue for all of the collections is only available in-house.
Printed publications:
Children's Guide (£1.70)
Guide Book (£2.95)
Short Guide (25p)
Walks Map (£1)

Internet home pages:
http://www.nationaltrust.org.uk/regions/eastanglia
General.

1360
IGHTHAM MOTE

Ivy Hatch, Sevenoaks, Kent, TN15 0NT

Tel: 01732 810378
Fax: 01732 811029
Email: igthammote@nationaltrust.org.uk
Formed: 1330

Organisation type and purpose: Registered charity (charity number 205846), historic building, house or site, suitable for ages: 5+.
Parent body:
The National Trust (South and South East Region)
South East Regional Office, tel: 01372 453401

Enquiries to: Visitor Services Manager
Other contacts: Property Manager
Access:
Access to staff: By letter, by telephone, by email
Access for disabled people: Parking provided, level entry, toilet facilities
Other restrictions: Drop-off point. 3 manual wheelchairs available. Accessible entrance, contact property office in advance or ask at ticket office on arrival. Ground floor accessible with assistance, some changes in level. No access to other floors. Photograph album. Virtual tour of upstairs rooms. Conservation exhibition at ticket office accessible. Cobbled courtyard. Level entrance to shop and to restaurant.

General description:
A superb moated manor house, nestling in a sunken valley and dating from 1330. The main features of the house span many centuries and include the Great Hall, Old Chapel, crypt, Tudor chapel with painted ceiling, drawing room with Jacobean fireplace, frieze and 18th century wallpaper, and billiards room. There is an extensive garden and interesting walks in the surrounding woodland. A comprehensive ongoing programme of repair was begun in 1988 and is the subject of a 'Conservation in Action' exhibition in the ticket office.
Information services:
Helpline available, tel no: Infoline 01732 811145.
Braille guide. Large-print guide. Touch list. Sympathetic Hearing Scheme.
Front-carrying baby slings for loan.
Suitable for school groups. Children's guide.
Free introductory talks. Regular garden tours. Booked special guided tours for groups of 15+ on open weekday mornings only. Occasional guided walks.
Special visitor services: Guided tours, materials and/or activities for children.
Education services: Resources for Key Stages 1 and 2 and 3.
Services for disabled people: For the visually impaired; for the hearing impaired.
Printed publications:
Guide Book
Estate Leaflet
Garden Leaflet
Children's Quiz and Guide
Foreign Guides
Teachers Resource Book
Property leaflet, events leaflet, group bookings leaflet (free)

Internet home pages:
http://www.nationaltrust.org.uk

1361
IKON GALLERY

1 Oozells Square, Brindleyplace, Birmingham, B1 2HS

Tel: 0121 248 0708
Fax: 0121 248 0709
Email: art@ikon-gallery.co.uk
Formed: 1966

Organisation type and purpose: International organisation, registered charity (charity number 528892), art gallery, suitable for ages: 5+.

Enquiries to: Marketing Assistant
Access:
Access to staff: By letter, by telephone, by fax, by email, in person, visitors by prior appointment, Internet web pages
Access for disabled people: level entry, access to all public areas, toilet facilities

General description:
Ikon Gallery is an internationally acclaimed contemporary art venue situated in the refurbished neo-gothic Oozells Street School building in Brindleyplace, central Birmingham. Ikon shows a continuous programme of changing exhibitions on two floors, with 440 square metres of exhibition space. A variety of media are represented including sound, video, mixed media, photography, painting, sculpture and installation. In addition to the galleries, exhibitions and projects also take place in Ikon's Foyer, Events Room and Tower. Ikon Offsite Projects develop the relationship between art,

continued overleaf

artists and audiences in projects outside the gallery. Ikon runs an extensive education programme, with events relating to each exhibition including talks, workshops, seminars and guided tours.
Information services:
Special visitor services: Materials and/or activities for children.
Education services: Group education facilities.
Services for disabled people: For the hearing impaired.
Publications list:
is available in hard copy.

Internet home pages:
http://www.ikon-gallery.co.uk

1362
ILCHESTER MUSEUM

The Town Hall and Community Centre, The High Street, Ilchester, Somerset, BA22 8NQ

Tel: 01935 841247
Full name: The Ilchester Community Museum
Formed: 1989

Organisation type and purpose: Registered charity, museum, suitable for ages: 8+.
Trust.
To show the history of Ilchester by artefacts, photographs, text etc, for locals and visitors. To research into history and to hold artefacts that would otherwise be lost to the community for the future.
Parent body:
Ilchester Town Trust

Enquiries to: Honorary Administrator
Direct tel: 01935 841648
Access:
Access to staff: By letter, by telephone, in person, visitors by prior appointment
Access for disabled people: access to all public areas, toilet facilities
Other restrictions: Level entry - Front Door of Town Hall for museum by prior arrangement with Caretaker 01935 841247.

General description:
A locally focused narrative supporting mainly small finds, illustrating the 2000 plus year history of the area's settlements.
The history and evidence of Ilchester from prehistory to the present day using narrative, plans, maps, photographs and artefacts.
Information services:
Guided tours of museum and village.
Visually impaired facilities under development.
Displays/information - mostly at wheelchair height.
Special visitor services: Guided tours.
Education services: Resources for Key Stage 3.
Services for disabled people: For the visually impaired; displays and/or information at wheelchair height.
Collections:
Small Finds donated or loaned by local people to the Ilchester Community Museum and the Somerset County Council Museum Taunton, or owned by the Ilchester Town Trust
Photographs, documents - original and copies
Catalogues:
Catalogue for library is in-house only. Catalogue for all of the collections is only available in-house.

1363
ILFRACOMBE MUSEUM

Wilder Road, Ilfracombe, Devon, EX34 8AF

Tel: 01271 863541
Email: ilfracombe@devonmuseums.net
Formed: 1932

Organisation type and purpose: Registered charity (charity number 269379), museum.

Enquiries to: Information Officer
Access:
Access to staff: By letter, by telephone
Other restrictions: By appointment.

General description:
Natural history, Victoriana, maritime, minerals, archaeology, maps, paintings, photos, militaria, costume, and local history.

Internet home pages:
http://www.devonmuseums.net

1364
ILKLEY TOY MUSEUM

Whitton Croft Road, Ilkley, West Yorkshire, LS29 9HR

Tel: 01943 603855
Fax: 01943 602043
Email: ilkleytoymuseum@supanet.com
Formed: 1997

Organisation type and purpose: Independently owned, museum, suitable for ages: all ages.

Enquiries to: Director
Direct tel: 01943 602043
Access:
Access to staff: By letter, by telephone, by fax, by email
Access to building, collections or gallery: No prior appointment required
Hours: Sat, 1000 to 1600; Sun and Bank Holidays, 1200 to 1600
Other restrictions: Open to groups on weekdays by prior appointment.
Open some weekdays in School Holidays (ring for details).
Access for disabled people: ramped entry, toilet facilities
Other restrictions: Access to ground floor only for wheelchair users.

General description:
One of the finest private collections of toys in the North of England.
Information services:
Some displays/information at wheelchair height.
Special visitor services: Materials and/or activities for children.
Education services: Resources for Key Stages 1 and 2..
Collections:
Dolls including a fine display of early English wooden dolls
Teddy bears
Dolls-houses and miniature shops
Tin-plate toys
Lead figures
Games
1940s working model fairground
Printed publications:
General Information Leaflet (free)
Various Children's Quizzes (free)

Internet home pages:
http://www.ilkleytoymuseum.co.uk
Opening hours, location, collection details, information for school visits.

1365
IMPERIAL DEFENCE COLLEGE

See - Royal College of Defence Studies

1366
IMPERIAL WAR MUSEUM

Duxford, Cambridgeshire, CB2 4QR

Tel: 01223 835000
Fax: 01223 837267
Email: duxford@iwm.org.uk
Formed: September 1971

Organisation type and purpose: Museum.
Administered in conjunction with the:
Cambridgeshire County Council
Tel: 01223 717111
Duxford Aviation Society
Tel: 01223 836593
Other branches at:
Cabinet War Rooms
Tel: 020 7930 6961
HMS Belfast
Tel: 020 7407 6434
Imperial War Museum
London, tel: 020 7820 1683

Enquiries to: Marketing Manager
Other contacts: Head of Marketing
Access:
Access to staff: By letter, by telephone, by fax, by email, visitors by prior appointment
Hours: 14 Mar to 23 Oct, 1000 to 1800; 24 Oct to 13 Mar, 1000 to 1600

General description:
Duxford Airfield was one of the RAF's first stations and in 1940 played a vital role in the Battle of Britain. Now part of the Imperial War Museum, Duxford is one of Europe's most popular aviation museums, with over 140 aircraft on display. Aircraft from the First World War through to Concorde are on show all year round. 20th century military aircraft, tanks, artillery pieces; naval exhibits; British civil airliners.
Information services:
Special visitor services: Materials and/or activities for children.
Education services: Group education facilities, resources for Key Stages 1 and 2, 3 and 4..
Collections:
Rare and historic aircraft, 1914 to present day, over 90 aeroplanes
Military vehicles
Fighter collection, old flying machine company, 1914 onwards, over 30 aeroplanes
Restored original Second World War Battle of Britain ops room
Printed publications:
Duxford Handbook (annually, £2.70)

Internet home pages:
http://www.iwm.org.uk
Basic information.

1367
IMPERIAL WAR MUSEUM

Sound Archive, Lambeth Road, London, SE1 6HZ

Tel: 020 7416 5363
Fax: 020 7416 5379
Email: sound@iwm.org.uk
Formed: 1972
Formerly: Department of Sound Records, date of change, 1995

Organisation type and purpose: National government body, museum.
Archive within museum.
Member of:
British Association of Sound Collections
International Association of Sound Archives
Oral History Society
Women Heritage and Museums

Enquiries to: Office Manager
Access:
Access to staff: By letter, by telephone, by fax, by email, visitors by prior appointment, Internet web pages
Hours: Mon to Fri, 0900 to 1700

General description:
History including military history, social history and peace studies, women's studies, oral history methodology: over 36,000 hours, including interviews, speeches, lectures, sound effects etc relating to conflict in the Twentieth and Twenty-first Centuries.
Main oral history projects to date:
Boer War 1898-1901
Military and Naval Aviation 1914-1918
Western Front: Life and Operations
Gallipoli 1915
Royal Navy: Lower Deck 1910-1922
The Anti-War Movement 1914-1918
War Work 1914-1918
British Army in India 1919-1939
Mechanisation of the British Army 1919-1939
The RAF and the development of Air Power 1919-1939
Invergordon Mutiny 1931
British Army in Africa 1919-1939
Middle East: British Military Personnel 1919-1939
British Servicemen in the Far East 1919-1939

British Involvement in the Spanish Civil War 1936-1939
Britain and the Refugee Crisis 1933-1947
The Anti-War Movement 1939-1945
British Service Cameramen 1939-1945
British POWs in Europe and the Far East 1939-1945
Enemy Internment of British civilians 1939-1945
Civilian Evacuation in Britain 1939-1945
Gort's Army: The BEF of 1939-1940
Norway Campaign 1940
East Africa Campaign 1940-1941
North Africa Campaign 1940-1943
Sinking of HMS Prince of Wales and HMS Repulse 1941
Life in Nazi Europe 1933-45 and the Holocaust
Air Offensive against Europe 1939-1945
Commandos and Special Forces 1939-1945
Philippines Campaign 1941-1942
Burma 1942-1945
Women's Land Army
Italian Campaign 1943-1945
D Day and NW Europe Campaign 1944-1945
The Blitz in Britain 1940-1945
War Work 1939-1945
War Brides
Submarines 1939-1945
Captain Class Frigates
Wartime Reporting and Filming
Wartime Medicine and Science
Wartime Politics
The Secret War 1939-1945 including Special Operations Executive
Military Training
Post-Colonial Conflicts eg Malay Emergency, Mau Mau etc
Nuclear Testing and Warfare
VE and VJ Day 1945
Palestine before 1948
The Peace Movement since 1945
The Middle East since 1948 including Suez
Korean War 1950-1952
Artists in an age of conflict
Falkland Islands 1982
The Gulf War 1991
Conflict in the former Yugoslavia.

Collections:
In addition to the eyewitness accounts, thousands of hours of speeches, poetry, sound effects etc plus
The Nuremberg War Crimes Trials
BBC Second World War Broadcasts

Catalogues:
Catalogue for all of the collections is on-line.

Publications list:
is available in hard copy.

Printed publications:
Printed catalogues, or duplicated lists are available for most of the oral history projects and special collections. They may be consulted at the Museum or ordered by post

Electronic and video products:
Over 36,000 hours of recordings, copies of most are available on tape or CD-ROM, for purchase

Internet home pages:
http://www.iwm.org.uk/collections/sound.htm
General information, contacts, examples from collection etc.

1368
IMPERIAL WAR MUSEUM

Department of Art, Lambeth Road, London, SE1 6HZ

Tel: 020 7416 5211
Fax: 020 7416 5409
Email: art@iwm.org.uk
Acronym or abbreviation: IWM
Formed: 1917

Organisation type and purpose: Museum.

Enquiries to: Keeper of the Department of Art
Direct tel: 020 7416 5210
Direct fax: 020 7416 5409
Direct email: aweight@iwm.org.uk
Other contacts: Research & Information Officer for Print Room visitor services.

Access:
Access to staff: By letter, by telephone, by fax, by email, visitors by prior appointment
Hours: Mon to Fri, 1000 to 1700 (Print Room)
Access to building, collections or gallery: No access other than to staff
Hours: Public Galleries: Mon to Sun, 1000 to 1800
Access for disabled people: access to all public areas, toilet facilities
Other restrictions: Level entry by the side door

General description:
Works of art executed under official war artist schemes, 1914-1918 and 1939-1945; contemporary art, paintings, sculpture, war posters, art medals, printed ephemera, war artists' correspondence - official archive.

Information services:
Library available for reference (for conditions see Access above)
Special visitor services: Guided tours, materials and/or activities for children.
Education services: Group education facilities.
Services for disabled people: For the hearing impaired; displays and/or information at wheelchair height.

Collections:
Archive of correspondence between artists and the War Artist Committees

Catalogues:
Catalogue for library is in-house only. Catalogue for all of the collections is only available in-house.

Printed publications:
War Art exhibition catalogues, list on request

Microform products:
Colour transparencies (war art and war posters), hire service

Electronic and video products:
Mediastore, electronic image database available in the Print Room, colour printouts may be ordered

Internet home pages:
http://www.iwm.org.uk
Introduction to the collections, contact and exhibition information

1369
IMPERIAL WAR MUSEUM

Department of Documents, Lambeth Road, London, SE1 6HZ

Tel: 020 7416 5221/2/3
Fax: 020 7416 5374
Email: docs@iwm.org.uk
Acronym or abbreviation: IWM

Organisation type and purpose: Department of a national museum.

Enquiries to: Keeper, Department of Documents

Access:
Access to staff: By letter, by telephone, by fax, by email, in person, visitors by prior appointment
Hours: Mon to Sat, 1000 to 1700

General description:
German documents from the period of the Third Reich; records of the major War Crimes Trials; private papers of 20th century British and some Commonwealth servicemen and women and civilians in wartime; information on the holdings of other British, European and American archives in the field of contemporary history.

Collections:
Detailed information about the individual collections may be obtained from the Department; sources of reference are also given in the Department's information leaflet; new acquisitions are listed in the Annual List of Accessions to Repositories published by the Royal Commission on Historical Manuscripts
Major collections of papers of:
FM Sir Henry Wilson (1864-1922)
FM Sir John French (1852-1925)
FM Viscount Montgomery (1887-1976)
German Ministry of Armaments and War Production and Reich Air Ministry records
Isaac Rosenberg (1890-1918)
Siegfried Sassoon (1886-1967)
Biographical files on holders of the VC and GC
Copies of Second World War Wehrmacht operational records
Transcripts of proceedings of major War Crimes Trials at Nuremberg and Tokyo

Catalogues:
Catalogue for part of the collections is only available in-house.

Publications list:
is available in hard copy.

Internet home pages:
http://www.iwm.org.uk/collections/docs.htm
Main home page for the Department, including a broad description of its holdings and contact information.

1370
IMPERIAL WAR MUSEUM

Film and Video Archive, Lambeth Road, London, SE1 6HZ

Tel: 020 7416 5000
Fax: 020 7416 5299
Email: film@iwm.org.uk
Acronym or abbreviation: IWMFVA
Formed: 1920
Alternately: IWM Film Department, date of change, 1995
Formerly: IWM Department of Film, date of change, 1995

Organisation type and purpose: Museum, public library.
Film archive; national museum department.

Enquiries to: Keeper of Archive
Direct tel: 020 7416 5290
Direct email: Rsmither@iwm.org.uk
Other contacts: Production Office, tel no: 020 7416 5291/2 for preferred point of contact for general enquiries.

Access:
Access to staff: By letter, by telephone, by fax, by email, visitors by prior appointment, Internet web pages
Hours: Mon to Fri, 0900 to 1700

General description:
The two World Wars and other military operations involving Britain or the Commonwealth since 1914, including post-1945 conflicts (military, social, diplomatic and political aspects).

Collections:
About 35,000 items of film and videotape with supporting documentation
British Ministry of Information Collection (both World Wars)
British, German and Russian newsreels
Record film and supporting 'dopesheets' (cameraman's daily reports shot by Army and RAF film units during the Second World War)

Publications list:
is available in hard copy.

Printed publications:
Film and Video Archive Handbook, 1997
Departmental leaflet
IWM Film Catalogue volume I: The First World War Archive (1994)

Electronic and video products:
Large selection of videos from film archive (list available)

Internet home pages:
http://www.iwm.org.uk
General information on the Imperial War Museum and its activities.

1371
IMPERIAL WAR MUSEUM

Lambeth Road, London, SE1 6HZ

Tel: 020 7416 5000
Fax: 020 7416 5374
Email: mail@iwm.org uk
Acronym or abbreviation: IWM
Formed: 1917

Organisation type and purpose: National organisation, museum, suitable for ages: all ages.

continued overleaf

Links with:
Friends of the Imperial War Museum
Tel: 020 7416 5255
Other locations:
Cabinet War Rooms
Clive Steps, King Charles Street, London, SW1A 2AQ, tel: 020 7930 6961, fax: 020 7839 5897
HMS Belfast
Morgans Lane, Tooley Street, London, SE1 2JH, tel: 020 7940 6300, fax: 020 7430 0719, email/website: hmsbelfast@iwm.org.uk
Imperial War Museum Duxford
Duxford, Nr Cambridge, CR2 4QR, tel: 01223 835000, fax: 01223 837267
Imperial War Museum North
Trafford Wharf Road, Trafford Park, Manchester, M17 1TZ, tel: 0161 836 4000, fax: 0161 836 4003

Enquiries to: Enquiries
Direct tel: 020 7416 5320
Other contacts: Collections Division for collections related enquiries 020 7416 5337.
Access:
Access to staff: By letter, by telephone, by fax, by email, in person, Internet web pages

General description:
The story of 20th century conflict on the home front and in the front line through a series of exhibitions and displays arranged over six floors. Exhibits range from a Battle of Britiain Spitfire to Hitler's last will and testament. Highlights include the Holocaust Exhibition, the Blitz Experience complete with sounds, smells and other special effects, the Secret War exhibition, and the Victoria Cross and George Cross Gallery.
Information services:
Library available for reference (for conditions see Access above)
Recorded information 0900 1600140, 24 hours
Imperial War Museum Battlefield Tours with Experts; tours organised in association with Tours With Experts Limited tel 0151 520 1290, fax 0151 531 0052.
Introductory tours by friends of the IWM
Special visitor services: Materials and/or activities for children.
Education services: Group education facilities, resources for Key Stages 1 and 2, 3, 4 and Further or Higher Education.
Services for disabled people: For the visually impaired; for the hearing impaired; displays and/or information at wheelchair height.
Collections:
Art, exhibits, documents, photographs, film and videos, books and oral history/sound recordings
Catalogues:
Catalogue for library is in-house only. Catalogue for all of the collections is only available in-house but part is published.
Publications list:
is available in hard copy.

Address for ordering publications:
Printed publications:
Imperial War Museum Mail Order, Duxford Airfield
Cambridge, CB2 4QR, tel: 01223 499348

Internet home pages:
http://www.iwm.org.uk
Collections, publications and shopping
http://www.iwm.org.uk/tours/
Battlefield Tours with Experts

See also - HMS Belfast

1372
IMPERIAL WAR MUSEUM
Department of Printed Books, Lambeth Road, London, SE1 6HZ

Tel: 020 7416 5342
Fax: 020 7416 5246
Email: books@iwm.org.uk
Acronym or abbreviation: IWM
Formed: 1917

Organisation type and purpose: Museum, suitable for ages: 16+.
The Department of Printed Books forms part of the Museum's Collections Division consisting of::
Department of Art
Tel: 020 7416 5211, email/website: art@iwm.org.uk
Department of Documents
Tel: 020 7416 5221, email/website: docs@iwm.org.uk
Department of Exhibits & Fire Arms
Tel: 020 7416 5272, email/website: exfire@iwm.org.uk
Photograph Archive
Tel: 020 7416 5333, email/website: photos@iwm.org.uk
Sound Archive
Tel: 020 7416 5363, email/website: sound@iwm.org.uk
United Kingdom National Inventory of War Memorials
Tel: 020 7416 5353, email/website: memorials@iwm.org.uk

Enquiries to: Keeper, Department of Printed Books
Access:
Access to staff: By letter, by telephone, by fax, by email, visitors by prior appointment
Hours: Telephone access hours: Mon to Fri, 0900 to 1700
Access for disabled people: Parking provided, ramped entry, toilet facilities
Other restrictions: Wheelchair accessible study area available during above opening hours, by appointment.

General description:
Study of conflicts in which British and Commonwealth forces have been engaged in the 20th century, particularly the two World Wars; naval, military and air operations; unit records; social, political, economic and literary aspects of modern warfare.
Collections:
Over 100,000 books, 25,000 pamphlets and 15,000 maps, ephemera collections, etc
British, French, German and American unit histories
Pamphlet Collection (wartime propaganda, ration books, and other ephemera)
United States Strategic Bombing Survey Reports
Women's Activities in the First World War
Catalogues:
Catalogue for library is in-house only.
Publications list:
is available in hard copy and online.
Printed publications:
Bibliographies and book lists (on some 500 topics)
Catalogue of library reprint publications (pub by the Department of Printed Books)
List of current journals (held by the Department of Printed Books)
Tracing Your Family History - series of guides on Army, Navy, RAF and Merchant Navy
Electronic and video products:
Official History of the Great War - Military Operations France & Belgium 1914-1918 MAPS (CD-ROM, from Naval & Military Press)
Imperial War Museum Trench Map (Great War) Archive (CD-ROM, from Naval & Military Press)

Address for ordering publications:
Electronic publications:
Naval & Military Press
Tel: 01825 749494, email: order.dept@naval-military-press.co.uk
Printed publications:
Mail Order, Imperial War Museum
Duxford Air Field, Cambridge, CB2 4QR, tel: 01223 499348, fax: 01223 839688, email: mailorder@iwm.org.uk

Internet home pages:
http://www.iwm.org.uk
Includes catalogue of the Department's own publications and advice pages on family history research.

1373
IMPERIAL WAR MUSEUM
UK National Inventory of War Memorials, Lambeth Road, London, SE1 6HZ

Tel: 020 7416 5353/5281/5445
Fax: 020 7416 5379
Email: memorials@iwm.org.uk
Acronym or abbreviation: UKNIWM
Formed: 1989

Organisation type and purpose: Museum, university department or institute.

Enquiries to: Project Officer
Access:
Access to staff: By letter, by telephone, by fax, by email, visitors by prior appointment, Internet web pages
Hours: Mon to Fri, 1000 to 1630

General description:
Inventory of war memorials throughout the United Kingdom commemorating all conflicts not just the First and Second World Wars. They include those erected to the fallen from communities and regiments as well as those to individuals. All types of memorial are recorded including crosses, obelisks, village halls, plaques and tablets, church fabrics and fittings, avenues of trees etc. The database contains information on location, inscription transcripts and name lists in the files, design, details on the histroical background of the memorials and who built them. To date 47,000 memorials have been input into the database with a further 4000 awaiting inputting.
Collections:
Collection of contemporary postcards of war memorials
Catalogues:
Catalogue for all of the collections is only available in-house.
Publications list:
is available on-line.
Printed publications:
The War Memorials Handbook (gives information on the care and conservation of war memorials as well as details about the inventory, £4.99)

Address for ordering publications:
Printed publications:
Mail Order, Imperial War Museum
Duxford, Cambridge, CB2 4QR, tel: 01223 499345, fax: 01223 839688, email: mailorder@iwn.org.uk

Internet home pages:
http://www.iwm.org.uk/collections/niwm/index.htm

1374
IMPERIAL WAR MUSEUM
Photograph Archive, All Saints Annexe, Austral Street, London, SE11 4SL

Tel: 020 7416 5333 or 5338
Fax: 020 7416 5355
Email: photos@iwm.org.uk
Acronym or abbreviation: IWM

Organisation type and purpose: National government body, museum.
Photographic archive.
Other addresses:
Imperial War Museum
Lambeth Road, London, SE1 6HZ, tel: 020 7416 5000, fax: 020 7416 5374

Enquiries to: Head of Department
Direct tel: 020 7416 5287
Direct fax: 020 7416 5355
Direct email: bking@iwm.org.uk

Access:
Access to staff: By letter, by telephone, by fax, by email, visitors by prior appointment, Internet web pages
Hours: Mon to Fri, 0900 to 1700

General description:
Every theatre of operations in the two World Wars, including the home front; subsequent conflicts involving Britain and the Commonwealth; ships, military equipment and aircraft of many countries (some five million photographs from official, private and agency sources).
Printed publications:
Information leaflet (free)
Lists of photographs on popular subjects

Internet home pages:
http://www.iwm.org.uk

1375
IMPERIAL WAR MUSEUM NORTH

Trafford Wharf Road, Trafford Park, Manchester, M17 1TZ

Tel: 0161 836 4000
Fax: 0161 836 4003
Email: info@iwmnorth.org.uk
Formed: July 2002

Organisation type and purpose: National government body, museum.
Parent body:
Imperial War Museum
Lambeth Road, London, SE1 6HZ, tel: 020 7416 5320, fax: 020 7416 5374
Access:
Access to staff: By letter, by telephone, by email, Internet web pages
Access for disabled people: level entry, access to all public areas, toilet facilities
Other restrictions: Reserved parking provided

General description:
All aspects of conflict, military, civilian, social, economic etc, in which British or Commonwealth forces have been involved, from 1914 to present day.
Information services:
Education services: Group education facilities, resources for Key Stages 1 and 2, 3, 4 and Further or Higher Education.
Services for disabled people: For the visually impaired; for the hearing impaired; displays and/or information at wheelchair height.
Electronic and video products:
Learning CD-ROM (via Learning & Access Department tel 0161 836 4064)

Internet home pages:
http://www.iwm.org.uk

1376
IMPRESSIONS GALLERY OF PHOTOGRAPHY LIMITED

29 Castlegate, York, YO1 9RN

Tel: 01904 654724
Fax: 01904 651509
Email: enquiries@impressions-gallery.com
Formed: 1972

Organisation type and purpose: Suitable for ages: 5+.
Contemporary photography gallery.

Enquiries to: Office Manager
Other contacts: Education/Events Bookings Officer for general public, schools and colleges.
Access:
Access to staff: By letter, by telephone, by email, Internet web pages
Hours: Mon to Fri, 1000 to 1700
Access to building, collections or gallery: No prior appointment required
Hours: Winter: Mon to Sat, 1000 to 1730
Summer: Mon to Sat, 1000 to 1800
Access for disabled people: Parking provided, ramped entry
Other restrictions: Access to ground floor galleries and café bar.

General description:
Contemporary photography, new media, installation.
Information services:
Special visitor services: Guided tours.
Education services: Group education facilities, resources for Key Stages 1 and 2, 3, 4 and Further or Higher Education..

Internet home pages:
http://www.impressions-gallery.com
Programme both exhibition past and future, events, policies.

1377
INDUSTRIAL DISCOVERY CENTRE

Trevithick Road, East Pool, Redruth, Cornwall, TR15 3NP

Tel: 01209 315027
Fax: 01209 315027

Organisation type and purpose: Independently owned, suitable for ages: all ages.
Parent body:
The Trevithick Trust
Tel: 01209 210900

Enquiries to: Manager
Access:
Access to staff: By letter, by telephone, by fax
Access for disabled people: toilet facilities

General description:
The centre provides an overview of Cornwall's industrial heritage and incorporates a stunning audiovisual presentation.
Information services:
Special visitor services: Guided tours.
Education services: Group education facilities..

Internet home pages:
http://www.trevithicktrust.com

1378
INDUSTRIAL MUSEUM

Moorside Road, Bradford, West Yorkshire, BD2 3HP

Tel: 01274 435900
Fax: 01274 636362
Formed: 1974

Organisation type and purpose: Museum, suitable for ages: 5+.

Enquiries to: Senior Keeper Technology
Access:
Access to staff: By letter, by telephone, by fax, by email, in person
Access for disabled people: Parking provided, level entry, toilet facilities

General description:
Original worsted spinning mill with mill manager's house, back-to-back houses, mill stables (with working horses), transport gallery, motive power gallery and Cinton engine shed, printing, tram and trolley bus shed.
Steam/gas/oil engines, spinning, carding, combing, warping, winding, weaving machines, printing and furniture, reference library.
Information services:
Special visitor services: Tape recorded guides, materials and/or activities for children.
Education services: Resources for Key Stages 2 and 3.
Services for disabled people: For the hearing impaired.
Printed publications:
Victorian School Room Booklets - writing, drawing, reading
Literary packs
Power House Book
Guide Book
Guide Leaflet (free)

1379
INSCH CONNECTION MUSEUM

North Road, Insch, Aberdeenshire, AB52 6XP

Tel: 01464 821354
Formed: 1997

Organisation type and purpose: Registered charity (charity number SCO 28432), museum. Run by volunteers.

Enquiries to: Secretary
Access:
Access to staff: In person, visitors by prior appointment
Access to building, collections or gallery: Prior appointment required
Hours: Apr to Oct: Wed and Sun, 1330 to 1700
Other restrictions: Or by prior appointment.
Access for disabled people: Parking provided, ramped entry, access to all public areas, toilet facilities

General description:
Displays which change annually, encompass both railway and local history with an Insch connection.
Collections:
Scale model of Insch Station, photographs, artefacts and every day stories of how life used to be in Insch
Archive material about Insch and District is available for research

1380
INSPIRE HANDS-ON SCIENCE CENTRE

St Michaels Church, Coslany Street, Norwich, Norfolk, NR3 3DT

Tel: 01603 612612
Email: inspire@science-project.org
Formed: 1995

Organisation type and purpose: Registered charity (charity number 298542), suitable for ages: 5+.
Science centre.
Science communication.
Parent charity:
Science Projects
20 St James' Street, Hammersmith, London, W8 9RW
Other addresses:
The Observatory
Herstmonceux, Hailsham, Sussex

Enquiries to: Director
Access:
Access to staff: By letter, by telephone, by email
Access to building, collections or gallery: No prior appointment required
Hours: Daily, 1000 to 1730
Access for disabled people: ramped entry, access to all public areas

General description:
Hands-on science exhibition with regular science shows and special events.
Information services:
Special visitor services: Materials and/or activities for children.
Education services: Group education facilities, resources for Key Stages 1 and 2, 3, 4 and Further or Higher Education..
Collections:
Hands-on science exhibits

Internet home pages:
http://www.science-project.org
Information on centre and services.

1381
INSTITUTE OF CONTEMPORARY ARTS

12 Carlton House Terrace, London, SW1Y 5AH

Tel: 020 7930 0493
Fax: 020 7873 0051
Email: info@ica.org.uk
Acronym or abbreviation: ICA
Formed: 1947

continued overleaf

Organisation type and purpose: Membership association, registered charity (charity number 236848), art gallery, suitable for ages: 16+.
Arts Centre.
Subsidiary body:
ICA Projects Ltd

Enquiries to: Administrative Assistant
Other contacts: Education Officer for tel no: 020 7766 1423.
Access:
Access to staff: By letter, by telephone, by fax, by email, visitors by prior appointment, charges to non-members, Internet web pages
Hours: Mon to Fri, 1200 to 1930
Access to building, collections or gallery: No prior appointment required
Hours: Mon to Fri, 1200 to 1930

General description:
Contemporary cultural activities, including film, theatre, dance and music; events and exhibitions.
Collections:
Pre-1990 collection at the Tate
Publications list:
is available in hard copy.
Electronic and video products:
1500 audio recordings of lectures
Over 200 videos of art events

Internet home pages:
http://www.ica.org.uk
Events, listings, archive etc.

1382
INVERARAY MARITIME MUSEUM
Inveraray Pier, Inveraray, Argyll, PA33 8UY

Tel: 01499 302213
Formed: 1992
Formerly: Arctic Penguin Maritime Heritage Centre, date of change, 1996

Organisation type and purpose: Independently owned, museum, suitable for ages: all ages.

Enquiries to: Manager
Access:
Access to staff: By letter, by telephone
Access to building, collections or gallery: No prior appointment required
Hours: Oct to Mar: daily, 1000 to 1700
Apr to Sep: daily, 1000 to 1800

General description:
West of Scotland and Clyde maritime history through displays, memorabilia, archive film and hands-on activities, aboard three-masted schooner built in 1911. In Summer, trips aboard the Museum's Clyde Puffer 'Eilean Eisdell'.
Information services:
Special visitor services: Guided tours, tape recorded guides.
Education services: Group education facilities..
Collections:
Clyde artefacts and memorabilia, and photographic prints of many Clyde-built 19th century sailing ships
Publications list:
is available in hard copy.

1383
INVERKEITHING MUSEUM
The Friary, Queen Street, Inverkeithing, Fife, KY11 1LS

Tel: 01383 410495

Organisation type and purpose: Local government body, museum, historic building, house or site.
Parent body:
Fife Council
Museum headquarters:
Fife Council Museums West
Dunfermline Museum, Viewfield Terrace, Dunfermline, KY12 7HY, tel: 01383 313838, fax: 01383 313837, email/website: lesley.botten@fife.gov.uk
Other branch museum:
Pittencrieff House Museum
Pittencrieff Park, Dunfermline, tel: 01383 313838, fax: 01383 313837, email/website: lesley.botten@fife.gov.uk
St Margaret's Cave
Tel: 01383 313838, fax: 01383 313837, email/website: lesley.botten@fife.gov.uk
Access:
Access to staff: By email, visitors by prior appointment, by letter, by telephone, by fax
Other restrictions: All communication to staff should be made through Dunfermline Museum only.
Access to building, collections or gallery: No prior appointment required
Hours: Thur to Sun, 1000 to 1230, 1300 to 1600, Closed Mon to Wed, and Dec, 25th and 26th, Jan 1st and 2nd

General description:
A local history museum with material about Inverkeithing and Rosyth. Covers social history; industrial history; archaeology; and fine art. Also contains material on Admiral Greig - born in Inverkeithing - who was the Father of the Russian Navy.

1384
INVERNESS MUSEUM AND ART GALLERY
Castle Wynd, Inverness, IV2 3EB

Tel: 01463 237114
Fax: 01463 225293
Email: inverness.museum@highland.gov.uk
Formed: 1882

Organisation type and purpose: Local government body, museum, art gallery, suitable for ages: 5+.
Parent body:
The Highland Council

Enquiries to: Curator
Access:
Access to staff: By letter, by telephone, by fax, by email, in person, visitors by prior appointment, Internet web pages
Access to building, collections or gallery: No prior appointment required
Hours: Mon to Sat, 0900 to 1700
Access for disabled people: Parking provided, ramped entry, access to all public areas

General description:
Silver - Highland Provincial; Jacobite memorabilia; Highland art; Inverness history; Highland botany, zoology and geology; archaeology of Highlands; Class 1 Pictish stones; limited map and numismatic collection.
Information services:
New discovery centre, Hands on the Highlands.
Full programme, temporary exhibitions and events.
Special visitor services: Materials and/or activities for children.
Education services: Group education facilities..
Collections:
The archaeology, natural history and local history of Inverness and the Highlands
Silver - Highland Provincial
Class 1 Pictish stones, excavation archives and small finds from across Highlands
Highland coin and medal collection
Highland weapons
Photographs - Highland - Joseph Cook, Mem Donaldson and Photographic Archive (David Whyte)
Small art collection - Highland artists or Highland subject matter, ephemera, manuscript collections including Town Charters
Small collection of early maps for Inverness and Highlands
Social history 1946 to present
Printed publications:
A Catalogue of the Class 1 Pictish Carved Stones in Inverness Museum & Art Gallery (Hanley R, 1994, direct)

Internet home pages:
http://www.highland.gov.uk/educ/publicservices/museumdetails/imag.htm
Basic information on services provided and opening hours.

1385
INVERURIE MUSEUM
See - Carnegie Museum

1386
IPSWICH MUSEUMS SERVICE
High Street, Ipswich, Suffolk, IP1 3QH

Tel: 01473 433550
Fax: 01473 433558
Email: museums.service@ipswich.gov.uk
Formed: 1849
Formerly: Ipswich Museums and Art Gallery

Organisation type and purpose: Local government body, museum, art gallery, suitable for ages: all ages.
Other address:
Christchurch Mansion
Soane Street, Ipswich, tel: 01473 433554, fax: 01473 433564

Enquiries to: Head of Service
Access:
Access to staff: By letter, by telephone, by fax, by email, visitors by prior appointment
Access for disabled people: ramped entry, toilet facilities
Other restrictions: Ipswich Museum - Lift to 1st floor.

General description:
Natural sciences, botany, zoology and geology; archaeology and ethnography, local and social history, fine and applied arts, costume, furniture, glass and ceramics; regional art collection including notable collections of Gainsborough and Constable.
Information services:
Special visitor services: Guided tours, materials and/or activities for children.
Education services: Group education facilities, resources for Key Stages 1 and 2.
Services for disabled people: For the hearing impaired.
Collections:
Basil Brown diaries (excavation of Sutton Hoo 1938-1939)
Christopher Dresser Sketchbook

1387
IPSWICH TRANSPORT MUSEUM
Old Trolley Bus Depot, Cobham Road, Ipswich, Suffolk, IP3 9JD

Tel: 01473 715666
Full name: Ipswich Transport Museum Limited
Formed: 1966
Formerly: Ipswich Transport Preservation Group, date of change, 1970; Ipswich Transport Society, date of change, 1977

Organisation type and purpose: Independently owned, registered charity (charity number 276626), museum, suitable for ages: 5+.
Collects material relating to transport and engineering history of Ipswich area.
Links with:
Friends of Ipswich Transport Museum
at the same address, tel: 01473 715666
Trading subsidiary:
Ipswich Transport Museums Services Limited
at the same address, tel: 01473 715666

Enquiries to: Chairman
Direct tel: 01473 832260
Direct email: brian.dyer@btclick.com
Access:
Access to staff: By letter, by telephone, in person, Internet web pages
Hours: Open: Sun and Bank Holiday Mon, Apr to Nov, 1100 to 1630
School Holidays: Mon to Fri, May to Oct, 1300 to 1600

Other restrictions: Hours - At other times by appointment.
Access for disabled people: Parking provided, ramped entry, access to all public areas, toilet facilities

General description:
Transport and engineering history relating to Ipswich Area, especially Ipswich Corporation Transport, Eastern Counties Roadcar Company, Eastern Counties Omnibus Company, Ipswich Fire Brigade. Collections include: cycles; horse drawn carriages; baby carriages; public transport; heavy haulage; lifting and handling; fire fighting; service vehicles and local deliveries. Displays also cover air, rail and water transport.
Information services:
Library available for reference (for conditions see Access above)
Special visitor services: Guided tours.
Education services: Group education facilities, resources for Key Stages 1 and 2.
Services for disabled people: Displays and/or information at wheelchair height.
Collections:
Vehicles, costumes, archives, library, photographs
Catalogues:
Catalogue for library is in-house only. Catalogue for all of the collections is available in-house and part is on-line.

Internet home pages:
http://www.ipswichtransportmuseum.co.uk
Short description (including picture) of major objects in collection; short histories of transport-related subjects; details of museum.

1388
IRIS IMAGING
7 Magpie Close, High Wycombe, Buckinghamshire, HP10 9DZ

Tel: 01628 533228
Fax: 01628 533228
Email: joycepeck@lineone.net
Formed: 1994

Organisation type and purpose: Independently owned.
Producing art works.

Enquiries to: Managing Director
Access:
Access to staff: By email
Access to building, collections or gallery: Prior appointment required
Access for disabled people: ramped entry, toilet facilities

General description:
Art works, photography, holograms, digital printing.
Collections:
Pictures, prints, photographs, holograms

Internet home pages:
http://www.art-science.com/Joyce_Peck/index.html
http://ourworld.compuserve.com/homepages/Joyce_Peck_2/

1389
IRISH LINEN CENTRE AND LISBURN MUSEUM
Market Square, Lisburn, Co Antrim, BT28 1AG

Tel: 028 9266 3377
Fax: 028 9267 2624
Email: irishlinencentre@lisburn.gov.uk
Formed: 1981

Organisation type and purpose: Local government body, museum.
Parent body:
Lisburn Borough Council
The Island Civic Centre, Lisburn, BT27 4RL, tel: 028 9250 9509

Enquiries to: Curator
Other contacts: Research Officer
Access:
Access to staff: By letter, by telephone, by fax, by email, in person
Hours: Mon to Fri, 0930 to 1700
Access for disabled people: Parking provided, level entry, toilet facilities

General description:
History of the Irish linen industry, technical aspects of linen production, textiles in general, costume, with special reference to linen, Irish history, local history of Lisburn and the Lagan Valley.
Information services:
Library available for reference (for conditions see Access above)
Sign language interpretation.
Special visitor services: Guided tours, materials and/or activities for children.
Services for disabled people: For the visually impaired; for the hearing impaired.
Collections:
Local newspapers
Maps
Photographic collection
Research library covering the subject areas of the collections
Special collection of library of the former Linen Research Institute (Lambeg Industrial Research Association)
Catalogues:
Catalogue for library is in-house only. Catalogue for all of the collections is only available in-house.
Printed publications:
Flax to Fabric - The Story of Irish Linen (1994)
The Huguenots in Ulster (1985, temporarily out of print)

1390
IRON BRIDGE AND TOLLHOUSE, THE
Ironbridge Gorge Museum Trust, Coach Road, Coalbrookdale, Telford, Shropshire, TF8 7DQ

Tel: 01952 433522

Organisation type and purpose: Registered charity (charity number 503717-R), historic building, house or site, suitable for ages: 5+.
Parent body:
Ironbridge Gorge Museum Trust
Tel: 01952 433522
Access:
Access for disabled people: Parking provided, access to all public areas
Other restrictions: Access guide for disabled visitors available on request.

General description:
The great symbol of success of the iron industry was the Iron Bridge. Cast in 1779 by Abraham Darby III, its great arch enthralled visitors of the time, just as it does today. An exhibition about its history is in the original Tollhouse on the south side of the bridge.

Internet home pages:
http://www.ironbridge.org.uk

1391
IRONBRIDGE GORGE MUSEUM TRUST, THE
Museum Library, Coach Road, Coalbrookdale, Telford, Shropshire, TF8 7DQ

Tel: 01952 432141
Fax: 01952 432237
Email: library@ironbridge.org.uk
Formed: 1968

Organisation type and purpose: Registered charity, suitable for ages: 16+.
Private library. Courses at the Library run from Birmingham University.
Links with:
Birmingham University

Enquiries to: Librarian and Information Officer
Access:
Access to staff: By letter, by telephone, by fax, by email, visitors by prior appointment
Hours: Mon to Fri, 0900 to 1700
Access to building, collections or gallery: Prior appointment required
Hours: 0930 to 1700, Mon to Fri
Access for disabled people: toilet facilities
Other restrictions: Many stairs, access to ground floor only and not to library itself. Staff happy to assist disabled users, please telephone for information.

General description:
Industrial history, particularly East Shropshire Coalfield; history of technology; museology.
Information services:
Education services: Group education facilities, resources for Further or Higher Education..
Catalogues:
Catalogue for library is in-house only. Catalogue for all of the collections is only available in-house.

Internet home pages:
http://www.ironbridge.org.uk

1392
IRONBRIDGE GORGE MUSEUM TRUST, THE
Coach Road, Coalbrookdale, Telford, Shropshire, TF8 7DQ

Tel: 01952 433522
Fax: 01952 433204
Email: info@ironbridge.org.uk
Acronym or abbreviation: Ironbridge Gorge Museums
Formed: 1967

Organisation type and purpose: Registered charity (charity number 503717-R), museum, suitable for ages: 5+.
Maintains the:
Blists Hill Open Air Museum
Broseley Pipeworks Museum
Coalbrookdale Museum of Iron and Furnace
Coalport China Museum
Jackfield Tile Museum
Long Warehouse which houses the Ironbridge Institute and the Museum library and archives
Museum of the Gorge
Secretariat of the:
Association for Industrial Archaeology (AIA)
Historic Site:
Blists Hill Victorian Town
Broseley Pipeworks
Coalport China Museum
Enginuity
Ironbridge Gorge Museum Trust
Jackfield Tile Museum
Museum of Iron
Museum of the Gorge
Tar Tunnel
The Darby Houses
The Iron Bridge and Tollhouse
The Merrythought Teddy Bear Shop and Museum
Links with:
Association for Industrial Archaeology
Manages:
Ironbridge Institute

Enquiries to: Head of Marketing
Direct email: marketing@ironbridge.org.uk
Access:
Access to staff: By letter, by fax, by email
Hours: Mon to Fri, 0900 to 1700
Access for disabled people: Parking provided, ramped entry, toilet facilities
Other restrictions: Sites vary, access guides available on request.

General description:
A series of museums and monuments which capture the stories of Britain's Industrial Revolution. Ten museums covering six square miles of East Shropshire coalfields.
Information services:
Library available for reference (for conditions see Access above)

continued overleaf

Educational and school visits, Tel: 01952 433970 or e-mail: education@ironbridge.org.uk.
Group visits: telephone, or e-mail: visits@ironbridge.org.uk.
Special visitor services: Guided tours, materials and/or activities for children.
Education services: Group education facilities, resources for Key Stages 1 and 2, 3, 4 and Further or Higher Education.
Services for disabled people: For the visually impaired; for the hearing impaired; displays and/or information at wheelchair height.
Collections:
Collection on the life and works of Thomas Telford
Elton Collection (paintings, prints, book, pamphlets and memorabilia relating to the history of the Industrial Revolution)
Catalogues:
Catalogue for library is on-line. Catalogue for all of the collections is available in-house, part is published and part is on-line.
Printed publications:
Educational publications
Site specific guidebooks available to purchase
Souvenir Guide which covers all main sites
Various books which cover site subject matter, available on request
Electronic and video products:
Souvenir Video

Address for ordering publications:
Printed publications:
Mail Order Departement

Internet home pages:
http://www.ironbridge.org.uk

See also - ***Association for Industrial Archaeology; Blists Hill Victorian Town; Broseley Pipeworks; Coalport China Museum; Darby Houses; Enginuity; Iron Bridge and Tollhouse; Jackfield Tile Museum; Merrythought Teddy Bear Shop and Museum; Museum of Iron; Museum of the Gorge; Tar Tunnel***

1393
IRONBRIDGE OPEN AIR MUSEUM OF STEEL SCULPTURE
Moss House, Cherry Tree Hill, Coalbrookdale, Telford, Shropshire, TF8 7EF

Tel: 01952 433152
Email: pam.brown@virgin.net
Acronym or abbreviation: MOSS
Full name: Museum of Steel Sculpture
Formed: 1989

Organisation type and purpose: National organisation, membership association (membership is by election or invitation), present number of members: 4, voluntary organisation, registered charity (charity number 701102), museum, art gallery, suitable for ages: all ages, research organisation.

Enquiries to: Director
Access:
Access to staff: By letter, by telephone, by email, visitors by prior appointment
Access for disabled people: Parking provided, toilet facilities
Other restrictions: Much of the site is accessible to wheelchair users and an electrically powered wheelchair is available though prior booking. Guide dogs are welcome, but no other dogs are allowed.

General description:
20th/21st century British steel sculpture.
Collections:
Outdoor collection of iron and steel sculptures, including a substantial body of works by the Museum's Founder, Roy Kitchen
Catalogues:
Catalogue for all of the collections is only available in-house.
Printed publications:
Information leaflet - free

Internet home pages:
http://www.go2.co.uk/steelsculpture
General information, further information, admission and opening times and location map

1394
IRONBRIDGE TOY MUSEUM
Telford

Closed

1395
IRVINE BURNS CLUB & BURGH MUSEUM
28 Eglinton Street, Irvine, Ayrshire, KA12 8AS

Tel: 01294 274511
Email: sylvander@irvineburns.ndirect.co.uk
Formed: 1826

Organisation type and purpose: Independently owned, registered charity, museum, suitable for ages: 8+.
Burns Club and Burgh museum.

Enquiries to: Secretary
Direct tel: 01294 279646
Access:
Access to staff: By letter, by telephone, by email, in person, visitors by prior appointment

General description:
R Burns; the local history of Irvine.
Information services:
Special visitor services: Guided tours, tape recorded guides..
Collections:
Artefacts, pictures, prints, photographs, books, documents, manuscripts

Internet home pages:
http://www.irvineburns.ndirect.co.uk

1396
ISLAND HISTORY TRUST
197 East Ferry Road, London, E14 3BA

Tel: 020 7987 6041
Email: eve@islandhistory.org.uk
Formed: 1980

Organisation type and purpose: Registered charity (charity number 292530), museum.

Enquiries to: Curator
Access:
Access to staff: By letter, by telephone, by email, in person, Internet web pages

General description:
Contains 4000 photographs with detailed captions including thousands of named individuals, covering the period 1880-1980 with a concentration on the 1920s and 1930s, depicting all aspects of social, cultural, family, and economic life on the Isle of Dogs in London's Docklands.
Catalogues:
Catalogue for all of the collections is only available in-house.
Printed publications:
A Brief History of the Isle of Dogs Vols I and II (available for purchase, direct)

Internet home pages:
http://www.islandhistory.org.uk

1397
ISLE OF WIGHT BUS MUSEUM
The Quay, Newport, Isle of Wight, PO30 2EH

Tel: 01983 533352
Formed: 1997

Organisation type and purpose: Membership association (membership is by subscription), present number of members: 350, voluntary organisation, museum.
Membership Secretary:
Isle of Wight Bus Museum
9 St John Wood Road, Ryde, Isle of Wight

Enquiries to: Administration Manager
Access:
Access to staff: By letter, by telephone, in person
Hours: May to Sep, Mon to Sun, 1100 to 1600

General description:
Buses.

1398
ISLE OF WIGHT GEOLOGICAL MUSEUM
See - Dinosaur Isle

1399
ISLE OF WIGHT MUSEUM SERVICE
The Guildhall, High Street, Newport, Isle of Wight, PO30 1TY

Tel: 01983 821000
Fax: 01983 823841
Email: mbishop@iwight.gov.uk
Formed: 1975
Formerly: Isle of Wight County Museum and Heritage Service, date of change, 1997

Organisation type and purpose: Local government body, museum.
Section of:
Isle of Wight Council
County Hall, Newport, Isle of Wight, PO30 1UD, tel: 01983 821000, fax: 01983 823333
Branches:
Cowes Maritime Museum
Cowes Library, Beckford Road, Cowes, PO31 7SG, tel: 01983 293394
Museum of Island History
at the same address, tel: 01983 823366
Museum of Isle of Wight Geology
Sandown Library, High Street, Sandown, tel: 01983 404344
Newport Roman Villa
Cypress Road, Newport, PO30 1HE, tel: 01983 529720

Enquiries to: Museums Officer
Direct email: mbishop@iwight.gov.uk
Access:
Access to staff: By letter, by telephone, by fax, by email

General description:
The collections comprise archaeology; geology and palaeontology; maritime history; social history; fine art; and natural history. They are housed in several museums on the Island at Sandown, Newport, Ryde and Cowes.
Collections:
Geological collections, especially rich in Cretaceous dinosaurs and Neogene fossils
Archaeology collections, rich in local prehistoric and Romano-British material
Local social history collections, including the Brigstoke Collection of porcelain
Catalogues:
Catalogue for part of the collections is only available in-house.

Internet home pages:
http://www.iwight.gov.uk

1400
ISLE OF WIGHT RAILWAY COMPANY LIMITED, THE
The Railway Station, Havenstreet, Ryde, Isle of Wight, PO33 4DS

Tel: 01983 882204
Fax: 01983 884515
Email: info@iwsteamrailway.co.uk
Formed: 1972

Enquiries to: Secretary
Access:
Access to staff: By letter, by fax, by email, Internet web pages
Hours: Mon tot Fri, 0900 to 1700
Access for disabled people: ramped entry, toilet facilities

General description:
History of the railways of the Isle of Wight.

Collections:
Books, selected archival material, photographs, tickets, ephemera, railway artefacts
Printed publications:
Island Rail News (magazine, quarterly, free to members, or by purchase)

Internet home pages:
http://www.iwsteamrailway.co.uk
Gives information on the railway, operating dates, current events, survey of locomotives and rolling stock

1401
ISLES OF SCILLY MUSEUM
Church Street, St Mary's, Isles of Scilly, TR21 0JT

Tel: 01720 422337
Fax: 01720 422337
Email: info@iosmuseum.org
Formed: 1967

Organisation type and purpose: Registered charity (charity number 270055), museum, suitable for ages: 12+.
To preserve, for the benefit of the public, matters relating to the archaeology and history (natural and social) of the Isles of Scilly.

Enquiries to: Honorary Secretary
Direct tel: 01720 422224
Other contacts: Curator for specific enquires about museum accessions.
Access:
Access to staff: By letter, by telephone, by fax, by email
Access to building, collections or gallery: No prior appointment required
Hours: Apr to Oct: daily, 1000 to 1200 and 1330 to 1630
Jun, Jul, Aug: daily, 1930 to 2100
Winter: Wed, 1400 to 1600
Access for disabled people: ramped entry

Collections:
Collections contain items dealing with the geology, archaeology, history and natural history of the Isles of Scilly; shipwreck material;
Library relating to Scilly
Our most significant collection and artefacts have been assessed as:
Archaeology Knackyboy Collection (Bronze Age)
Nornour Collection (Romano-British) broaches, coins and artefacts, 1st and 4th century, 1500 items
Wrecks: 'Association' and 'Hollandia' Collections
Klondyke, Gig (7-oared vessel), 1872
Natural History: shell collection; Dorrien-Smith bird collection from Tresco
Catalogues:
Catalogue for part of the collections is only available in-house.

Internet home pages:
http://www.aboutbritain.com/islesofScillyMuseum.htm
General information, links with www.scillynews.co.uk
http://www.iosmuseum.org
The Museum's own specific website is under construction.

1402
ISLINGTON MUSEUM
Foyer Gallery, Town Hall, Islington, London, N1 2UD

Tel: 020 7527 3235/2837
Fax: 020 7527 3049
Email: alison.lister@islington.gov.uk
Formed: 1993

Organisation type and purpose: Local government body, museum, art gallery, suitable for ages: 5+.
To interpret the history of Islington, its people and cultures.

Enquiries to: Manager
Direct email: as above or valerie.munday@islington.gov.uk
Access:
Access to staff: By letter, by telephone, by fax, by email, visitors by prior appointment
Hours: Mon to Fri, 1000 to 1400
Access to building, collections or gallery: No prior appointment required
Hours: Wed to Sat, 1100 to 1700; Sun, 1400 to 1600
Access for disabled people: Parking provided, level entry
Other restrictions: Toilet facilities adjacent.

General description:
Story of Islington display, programme of temporary exhibitions, costume.
Information services:
Small local history shop.
Special visitor services: Guided tours.
Education services: Group education facilities, resources for Key Stages 1 and 2, 3, 4 and Further or Higher Education..
Collections:
Local and social history of Islington - photographs, paintings, costume, objects
Publications list:
is available in hard copy.
Printed publications:
Local history books and leaflets

Internet home pages:
http://www.islington.gov.uk

1403
IZAAK WALTON'S COTTAGE
Worston Lane, Shallowford, Stafford, ST15 0PA

Tel: 01785 760278 Apr to Oct / 01785 619619 Nov to Mar
Fax: 01785 760278 Apr to Oct
Formed: 1924

Organisation type and purpose: Local government body, museum, historic building, house or site, suitable for ages: 8+.
Parent body:
Stafford Borough Council
Civic Centre, Riverside, Stafford, ST16 3AQ, tel: 01785 619000

Enquiries to: Manager
Access:
Access to staff: By letter, by telephone
Access for disabled people: Parking provided, toilet facilities
Other restrictions: Ramped entry to ground floor only.

General description:
Izaak Walton - his life and his famous book 'The Compleat Angler'.
Information services:
Special visitor services: Guided tours..
Collections:
Angling Museum - fishing tackle c. 1800-1950

Internet home pages:
http://www.staffordbc.gov.uk

1404
JACKFIELD TILE MUSEUM
Ironbridge Gorge Museum Trust, Coach Road, Coalbrookdale, Telford, Shropshire, TF8 7DQ

Tel: 01952 882030

Organisation type and purpose: Registered charity (charity number 503717-R), museum, historic building, house or site, suitable for ages: 8+.
Parent body:
Ironbridge Gorge Museum Trust
Coach Road, Coalbrookdale, Telford, Shropshire, TF8 7DQ, tel: 01952 433522

Enquiries to: Curator

General description:
Discover why tiles from Jackfield could be found everywhere from palaces to public toilets. Displays of magnificent decorative tiles and ceramics can be seen in the gas-lit galleries and showrooms. Drop-in workshops and fascinating hands-on exhibits. The Great Rock Sandwich Exhibition explains the geology under our feet.

Internet home pages:
http://www.ironbridge.org.uk

1405
JAGUAR DAIMLER HERITAGE TRUST
c/o Jaguar Cars, Browns Lane, Allesley, Coventry, West Midlands, CV5 9DR

Tel: 024 7640 2121
Fax: 024 7620 2777
Email: jagtrust@jaguar.com
Acronym or abbreviation: JDHT
Formed: 1983

Organisation type and purpose: Independently owned, registered charity (charity number 286863), museum, suitable for ages: 12+.

Enquiries to: Administrator
Direct tel: 024 7620 3322
Direct email: jbingha1@jaguar.com
Other contacts: Archivist for archive enquiries.
Access:
Access to staff: By letter, by telephone, by fax, by email, in person, visitors by prior appointment, Internet web pages
Access for disabled people: Parking provided, ramped entry, level entry, access to all public areas, toilet facilities

General description:
Vehicle collection of Jaguars, Daimlers, Lanchesters and SS cars, plus an Art Gallery.
Information services:
Services for disabled people: Displays and/or information at wheelchair height.
Collections:
Some on show, otherwise an appointment with the Archivist is required
Catalogues:
Catalogue for library is in-house only. Catalogue for all of the collections is only available in-house.

Internet home pages:
http://www.jaguarcars.com/uk/jdht/services.html

1406
JAMES DUN'S HOUSE
Aberdeen

Closed, date of change, 1997

1407
JANE AUSTEN'S HOUSE
Chawton, Alton, Hampshire, GU34 1SD

Tel: 01420 83262
Fax: 01420 83262
Acronym or abbreviation: JAMT
Full name: Jane Austen Memorial Trust
Formed: 1949

Organisation type and purpose: Registered charity (charity number 307252), museum.
Running and maintenance of the author's house.
Parent body:
Jane Austen Memorial Trust

Enquiries to: Curator
Other contacts: Trustee
Access:
Access to staff: By letter, by telephone, by fax, in person, visitors by prior appointment
Other restrictions: Appointment required for detailed enquiries.
Access to building, collections or gallery: No access other than to staff
Hours: Mon to Sun, 1100 to 1630;
Closed 25-26 Dec and weekdays Jan and Feb

General description:
Life and times of Jane Austen, literary and historical 18th century writings, memorabilia etc.
Collections:
Books, manuscripts, memorabilia etc

continued overleaf

Printed publications:
Brochure Guide leaflet

Address for ordering publications:
Printed publications:
Mail Order Secretary, Jane Austen Memorial Trust
Jane Austen's House

Internet home pages:
http://www.janeaustenmuseum.org.uk

1408
JANET ARMSTRONG MUSEUM
See - Clan Armstrong Trust Museum

1409
JARROW 700 AD LIMITED
See - Bede's World

1410
JEDBURGH CASTLE JAIL & MUSEUM
Castlegate, Jedburgh, Borders, TD8 6QD

Tel: 01835 864750
Fax: 01835 864750

Organisation type and purpose: Local government body, museum, historic building, house or site, suitable for ages: 5+.
Parent body:
Scottish Borders Council Museum and Gallery Service
Tel: 01750 20096

Enquiries to: Curator
Access:
Access to staff: By letter, by telephone, by fax
Other restrictions: When closed contact Scottish Borders Council Museum and Gallery Service.
Access to building, collections or gallery: No prior appointment required
Hours: Easter to end Oct, Mon to Sat, 1000 to 1630, Sun 1300 to 1600

General description:
A 19th century jail on the site of Jedburgh castle. Costumed figures and period rooms tell the story of the Howard Reform Prison. In the jailer's house are exhibitions of the history of Jedburgh.
Information services:
Interactive audiovisual programme and audio tour
Interpretation leaflets available in French, German, Italian, Dutch and Japanese
Temporary exhibitions
Special visitor services: Tape recorded guides..

Internet home pages:
http://www.scotborders.gov.uk
http://www.scotborders.org.uk

1411
JENNER MUSEUM, THE
Church Lane, Berkeley, Gloucestershire, GL13 9BN

Tel: 01453 810631
Fax: 01453 811690
Email: manager@jennermuseum.com
Full name: The Edward Jenner Museum
Formed: 1985

Organisation type and purpose: Registered charity (charity number 284085), museum, historic building, house or site, suitable for ages: 5+.
To preserve and promote the memory of Dr Edward Jenner, discoverer of vaccination against smallpox.

Enquiries to: Director
Access:
Access to staff: By letter, by telephone, by fax, by email, in person, Internet web pages
Access to building, collections or gallery: No prior appointment required
Hours: Apr to end Sep: Tue to Sat, 1230 to 1730; Sun, 1300 to 1730
Oct: Sun only, 1300 to 1730
Other restrictions: Closed Mon, except Bank Holidays.
Access for disabled people: Parking provided, level entry, toilet facilities

General description:
Dr Edward Jenner (1749 to 1823). The museum is housed in Edward Jenner's Georgian House. It contains collections relating to Jenner's early life and studies into the natural history of cuckoos and hedgehogs; Jenner's discovery of vaccination against smallpox; the eradication of smallpox from the world. There is a reconstruction of Jenner's study.
Collections:
Archive of material relevant to Edward Jenner and smallpox
Catalogues:
Catalogue for all of the collections is only available in-house.
Publications list:
is available in hard copy and online.
Printed publications:
Books, booklets, prints, postcards, 35mm transparencies relating to Jenner to purchase by mail order
The Eradication of Smallpox (Bazin H, £26.95 plus p&p)
Jenner (Perry B, £2.50 plus p&p)
Jenner, the Man and His Work (Gethyn-Jones et al, 50p plus p&p)
Smallpox is Dead (for children, Sanderson, £5 plus p&p)
The Chantry (Gethyn-Jones, 50p plus p&p)
The Origin of the Vaccine (facsimile of paper, Jenner E, £3 plus p&p)
Vaccination - Jenner's Legacy (Baxby D, £3 plus p&p)
Electronic and video products:
Edward Jenner (video, £12.95 plus p&p)

Internet home pages:
http://www.jennermuseum.com
Information about Edward Jenner and smallpox vaccination, and about the Jenner Museum.

1412
JERSEY BATTLE OF FLOWERS MUSEUM
La Robeline, Mont des Corvees, St Ouen, Jersey, JE3 2ES, Channel Islands

Tel: 01534 482408
Formed: 1971

Organisation type and purpose: Independently owned, museum, suitable for ages: all ages.

Enquiries to: Curator
Access:
Access to staff: By letter, by telephone
Hours: Mon to Fri, 1000 to 1700
Access for disabled people: Parking provided, ramped entry, access to all public areas, toilet facilities

General description:
This museum houses wild flower exhibits which have taken part in the famous Jersey Battle of Flowers parade, and all are major award-winners.
Information services:
Special visitor services: Tape recorded guides..
Collections:
This collection is unique and houses life-size animals and birds, etc. Included are 101 dalmatians, ostriches, pink flamingoes, horses, emus, reindeer, elephants, jaguars, and many more. All exhibits are covered in dried Harestails and Marram Grass.
Catalogues:
Catalogue for all of the collections is only available in-house.

1413
JERSEY HERITAGE TRUST
Jersey Museum, The Weighbridge, St Helier, Jersey, JE2 3NF, Channel Islands

Tel: 01534 633300
Fax: 01534 633301
Email: museum@jerseyheritagetrust.org
Formerly: Jersey Museums Service

Organisation type and purpose: Professional body, registered charity, museum, art gallery, suitable for ages: 5+, primary and secondary.

Enquiries to: Registrar
Access:
Access to staff: By letter, by telephone, by fax, by email, visitors by prior appointment, Internet web pages
Hours: Mon to Fri, 0900 to 1700
Access to building, collections or gallery: No prior appointment required
Hours: Every day, Summer, 1000 to 1700. Winter, 1000 to 1600
Access for disabled people: Parking provided, level entry, access to all public areas, toilet facilities

General description:
Collection relates to local history, art and archaeology.
Information services:
Special visitor services: Guided tours.
Education services: Group education facilities, resources for Key Stages 1 and 2, 3 and 4.
Services for disabled people: Displays and/or information at wheelchair height.
Collections:
The collections on display explore thematically the island's natural, social, political and maritime history.
4000 works of art, the majority by local artists or of local subjects and including Millais.
Archaeological collection - prehistoric, Gallo-Roman and mediaeval finds from Jersey including material from neolithic tombs
Collection relating to the German occupation, military and civilian 1940-1945
Early photographs
Extensive collection of material relating to Surrealist artist Claude Cahun
Rural collection
Local geological collection
Local natural history collection
Social history collection - mainly late Victorian
Special Collections:
La Cotte Collection of palaeolithic flint tools and associated fossils of mammoth, woolly rhino and other animals
Photographic. Extensive collection. 1860-. 30,000 images
Maritime Art. Ship portraits, etc c.300
Lillie Langtry. Memorabilia
Jersey Silver. Local silverware c.100 items
Catalogues:
Catalogue for all of the collections is available in-house and part is on-line.

Internet home pages:
http://www.jerseyheritagetrust.org
Information/opening hours for the seven sites run by the Heritage Trust.
Online catalogue for Art & Archive collections.
Virtual exhibitions highlighting parts of the collection.

1414
JERSEY MOTOR MUSEUM
Closed

1415
JERWOOD SCULPTURE PARK
Witley Court, Great Witley, Worcestershire, WR6 6JT

Tel: 01782 816430
Fax: 01782 816430
Formed: 2000

Organisation type and purpose: Sculpure Park.

Parent body:
English Heritage (West Midlands Region)
Tel: 0121 625 6820
Access:
Access to staff: By letter only
Access to building, collections or gallery: Prior appointment required
Hours: Apr to Sep: Mon to Sun, 1000 to 1800
Oct: 1000 to 1700
Nov: Wed to Sun, 1000 to 1600
Access for disabled people: Parking provided, ramped entry

General description:
Sculpture.
Information services:
Special visitor services: Guided tours..

See also - Witley Court

1416
JERWOOD SPACE
171 Union Street, London, SE1 0LN

Tel: 020 7654 0171
Fax: 020 7654 0172
Email: space@jerwoodspace.co.uk
Formed: 1997
Formerly: Jerwood Gallery

Organisation type and purpose: Independently owned, art gallery, historic building, house or site.
Rehearsal and event space, support organisation. Provision of rehearsal space to young and emerging artists, with a free, public art gallery and café. The Jerwood Space is a beautifully refurbished Victorian school on London's thriving Bankside.

Enquiries to: Director
Direct email: richard.lee@jerwoodspace.co.uk
Access:
Access to staff: By letter, by email, Internet web pages
Access for disabled people: Parking provided, ramped entry, access to all public areas, toilet facilities

General description:
Varying exhibitions in the gallery throughout the year, including the Jerwood painting, drawing and sculpture prizes.

Internet home pages:
http://www.jerwoodspace.co.uk

1417
JEWEL TOWER
Abingdon Street, Westminster, London, SW1P 3JY

Tel: 020 7222 2219
Fax: 020 7222 2219
Formed: 1365

Organisation type and purpose: Historic building, house or site.
Parent body:
English Heritage (London Region)
23 Savile Row, London, W1X 1AB, tel: 020 7973 3000, fax: 020 7937 3001

Enquiries to: House Manager
Access:
Access to staff: By letter, by telephone, by fax
Access to building, collections or gallery: No prior appointment required
Hours: 1 Apr to 30 Sep, Daily, 1000 to 1800; Oct, Daily, 1000 to 1700; 1 Nov to 31 Mar, Daily, 1000 to 1600.
Other restrictions: Closed 24, 25, 26, Dec and 1 Jan.
Opening times are subject to change, for up-to-date information contact English Heritage by phone or visit the website.

General description:
One of only two surviving buildings of the original Palace of Westminster, The Jewel Tower was built around 1365 to house Edward III's personal treasure and wardrobe. Today it is home to the 'Parliament: Past and Present' exhibition detailing a fascinating account of the House of Commons and the House of Lords.
Catalogues:
Catalogue for all of the collections is only available in-house.

Internet home pages:
http://www..english-heritage.org.uk

1418
JEWELLERY QUARTER DISCOVERY CENTRE
See - Museum of the Jewellery Quarter

1419
JEWISH MUSEUM FINCHLEY, THE
The Sternberg Centre, 80 East End Road, London, N3 2SY

Tel: 020 8349 1143
Fax: 020 8343 2162
Email: enquiries@jewishmuseum.org.uk
Formed: 1983
Still known as: London Museum of Jewish Life, Museum of the Jewish East End, date of change, 1996

Organisation type and purpose: Independently owned, registered charity (charity number 1009819), museum, suitable for ages: 8+.
Other addresses:
Jewish Museum, Camden
129-131 Albert Street, London, NW1 7NB, tel: 020 7284 1997, fax: 020 7267 9008, email/website: admin@jmus.org.uk

Enquiries to: Administrator
Other contacts: (1) Director; (2) Curator
Access:
Access to staff: By letter, by telephone, by email, visitors by prior appointment
Hours: Mon to Thu, 1030 to 1700
Other restrictions: Access to collections in store as for access to staff.
Access to building, collections or gallery: No prior appointment required
Hours: Mon to Thu, 1030 to 1700; Sun, 1030 to 1630
Other restrictions: Closed all public and Jewish holidays.
Access for disabled people: level entry, toilet facilities
Other restrictions: Access to ground floor gallery only.

General description:
History of Jews in Britain, with particular interest in the Jewish East End, refugees from Nazism, Holocaust education.
Information services:
Library available for reference (for conditions see Access above)
Special visitor services: Materials and/or activities for children.
Education services: Group education facilities, resources for Key Stages 2, 3, 4 and Further or Higher Education.
Services for disabled people: For the visually impaired.
Collections:
Objects, documents, photographic archive and oral history archive relating to late 19th and 20th century Jewish social history
Catalogues:
Catalogue for library is in-house only. Catalogue for all of the collections is only available in-house.
Publications list:
is available in hard copy and online.
Printed publications:
Guide Book (available direct, for purchase)
Exhibition Catalogues (available direct, for purchase)

1420
JEWISH MUSEUM
Raymond Burton House, 129-131 Albert Street, Camden Town, London, NW1 7NB

Tel: 020 7284 1997
Fax: 020 7267 9008
Email: admin@jmus.org.uk
Full name: Jewish Museum, London
Formed: 1932
Formerly: Museum of the Jewish East End
Incorporates the former: London Museum of Jewish Life

Organisation type and purpose: Independently owned, registered charity (charity number 1009819), museum, suitable for ages: 5+.
Operates on two sites with the:
Jewish Museum, Finchley (formerly the London Museum of Jewish Life)
80 East End Road, Finchley, London, N3 2SY, tel: 020 8349 1143, fax: 020 8343 2162, email/website: jml.finchley@lineone.net

Enquiries to: Curator
Access:
Access to staff: By letter, by telephone, by fax, by email, visitors by prior appointment, Internet web pages
Hours: Mon to Thu, 1000 to 1600
Other restrictions: No access to staff Fri to Sun, Jewish Festivals & Public Holidays.
Access to building, collections or gallery: No prior appointment required
Hours: Mon to Thu, 1000 to 1600; Sun, 1000 to 1700
Other restrictions: Closed Fri, Sat, Jewish Festivals & Public Holidays
Access for disabled people: access to all public areas, toilet facilities
Other restrictions: Pay and display parking outside museum.

General description:
Jewish ceremonial art; modern Jewish history, with special reference to Britain; Jewish life, religion and customs; related topics in temporary exhibitions.
Information services:
Special visitor services: Materials and/or activities for children.
Education services: Group education facilities, resources for Key Stages 1 and 2, 3, 4 and Further or Higher Education.
Services for disabled people: For the hearing impaired.
Collections:
Alfred Rubens Collection of prints and drawings
Handlist of the manuscript collection available at the National Register of Archives and at the Parkes Library, Southampton University
Judaica Collection (awarded designated status)
Publications list:
is available in hard copy and online.
Printed publications:
150 Years of Progressive Judaism in Britain 1840-1900
Boris - The Studio Photographer
Child's Play - Jewish Children's Books and Games from the Past
Leon Greenman - Auschwitz Survivor 98288
Diaries of Sir Moses and Lady Montefiore (a facsimile of the 1890 edn, £15)
Immigrant Furniture Workers in London 1881-1939 - and the Jewish contribution to the Furniture Trade
Living Up West - Jewish Life in London's West End
Map of the Jewish East End
The Jewish Museum (guide)
The Jews of Aden
The Last Goodbye - The Rescue of Children from Nazi Europe
The Permanent and Loan Collections of the Jewish Museum, London (out of print)
The Portuguese Jewish Community in London (1656-1830)

continued overleaf

What About the Children? 200 years of Norwood Child Care 1795-1995
Yiddish Theatre in London 1880-1987
There are also publications by the Museum of the Jewish East End and the former London Museum of Jewish Life
Research Papers
Electronic and video products:
From the Cradle to the Grave
Sabbaths & Festivals
Wandering Stars (Yiddish theatre in London)
Video tapes (£15 each)

Internet home pages:
http://www.jewishmuseum.org.uk
General information, publications list.

1421
JEWRY WALL MUSEUM
St Nicholas Circle, Leicester, LE1 4LB

Tel: 0116 225 4971
Fax: 0116 225 4966
Formed: 1849

Organisation type and purpose: Local government body, museum, historic building, house or site, suitable for ages: 5+.
Parent body:
Leicester City Museum Service
New Walk Centre, Welford Place, Leicester

Enquiries to: Curator
Direct tel: 0116 225 4970
Access:
Access to staff: By letter, by telephone
Access for disabled people: level entry, access to all public areas, toilet facilities

General description:
Covers the archaeology of Leicestershire from earliest times to the 16th century.
Information services:
Library available for reference (for conditions see Access above)
Special visitor services: Guided tours, materials and/or activities for children.
Education services: Group education facilities..
Collections:
Archaeology
Catalogues:
Catalogue for library is in-house only. Catalogue for all of the collections is only available in-house.

Internet home pages:
http://www.leicestermuseums.ac.uk
Information on Leicester Museums, events and activities.

1422
JIM CLARK ROOM, THE
44 Newton Street, Duns, Borders, TD11 3AU

Tel: 01361 883960

Organisation type and purpose: Local government body, museum, suitable for ages: 12+.
Paerent body:
Scottish Borders Council Museum and Gallery Service
Tel: 01750 20096

Enquiries to: Manager
Access:
Access to staff: By letter, by telephone
Other restrictions: Contact Scottish Borders Council Museum and Gallery Service when closed.

General description:
A celebration of the career of Jim Clark, Berwickshire farmer and winner of the World Motor Racing Championships on two occasions during the 1960s.
Collections:
Trophies, photographs and memorabilia

Internet home pages:
http://www.scotborders.gov.uk
http://www.scotborders.org.uk

1423
JOHN BUCHAN CENTRE, THE
Broughton, Peebles, Borders, ML12 6HQ

Tel: 01899 830223
Formed: 1982
Formed from: Biggar Museum Trust (Moat Park)

Organisation type and purpose: Museum, suitable for ages: 16+, consultancy.
To tell the life story of John Buchan, author, politician.

Enquiries to: Chairman
Access:
Access to staff: By letter only
Hours: May to Sep: daily, 1400 to 1700
Access to building, collections or gallery: No prior appointment required
Hours: May to Sep: daily, 1400 to 1700
Access for disabled people: Parking provided, ramped entry

General description:
Pictures, story, memorabilia of John Buchan as country lover, author, politician, South African and Canadian careers.
Catalogues:
Catalogue for library is in-house only. Catalogue for all of the collections is only available in-house.
Printed publications:
Brochure (leaflet)

1424
JOHN BUNYAN MUSEUM
Bunyan Meeting Free Church, Mill Street, Bedford, MK40 3EU

Tel: 01234 213722 (church office)
Fax: 01234 213722
Email: bmeeting@dialstart.net
Formed: 1998

Organisation type and purpose: Registered charity (charity number 248195), museum, historic building, house or site, suitable for ages: all ages.
Bunyan Meeting Free Church and John Bunyan Museum (place of worship); John Bunyan was minister of this church 1671-1688.

Enquiries to: Trustee
Access:
Access to staff: By letter, by fax, by email
Access for disabled people: ramped entry, access to all public areas, toilet facilities

General description:
John Bunyan (1628-88), his life and work. The John Bunyan Museum is housed in a new building (opened 1998), in the grounds of the church where John Bunyan was the Minister from 1671-1688. Visitors can experience the life and times of John Bunyan, author of 'The Pilgrim's Progress'. Follow in his footsteps through Bedford's cobbled streets, stand in a pulpit where he preached and visit him in his prison cell.
There is a trail around the town of Bedford and the countryside of Bedfordshire, relating to sites he would have known or wrote about.
Information services:
Library available for reference (for conditions see Access above)
Teachers' Resource Pack.
Special visitor services: Guided tours.
Education services: Resources for Key Stages 1 and 2.
Services for disabled people: Displays and/or information at wheelchair height.
Collections:
The Pilgrim's Progress in over 170 languages
Items belonging to Bunyan including his anvil and violin. Items relating to his imprisonment such as his cell door, and the jug used to take him his soup.
17th century vestry chair, pulpit, church doors
The Church:
Scenes from 'The Pilgrim's Progress' are depicted on the magnificent bronze entrance doors, and in some of the finest examples of 20th and 21st century stained glass windows
Catalogues:
Catalogue for library is published.
Publications list:
is available in hard copy.
Printed publications:
Publicity leaflets
Teachers' Resource Pack - Ideal for KS 1 & 2 (£8 incl p&p, Account: Trustees of Bunyan Meeting (Museum Account))
Bunyan Museum Library Catalogue (£10, £13 incl p&p, Account: Trustees of Bunyan Meeting (Museum Account))

Internet home pages:
http://www.museums.bedfordshire.gov.uk/sites/bunyan/index.htm

1425
JOHN CREASEY MUSEUM
Salisbury Library, Market Place, Salisbury, Wiltshire, SP1 1BL

Tel: 01722 410614
Fax: 01722 413214

Organisation type and purpose: Registered charity (charity number 309535), museum, art gallery, suitable for ages: 8+.

Enquiries to: Curator
Other contacts: District Librarian
Access:
Access to staff: By letter, by telephone, by fax, by email, visitors by prior appointment
Access to building, collections or gallery: No prior appointment required
Hours: Mon, 1000 to 1900, Tue, Wed and Fri, 0900 to 1900, Thu and Sat, 0900 to 1700
Access for disabled people: level entry, access to all public areas, toilet facilities

General description:
A literary and contemporary art museum celebrating the life and work of John Creasey MBE, 1908-1973.
Collections:
The Literary Museum, artefacts and books relating to the life and literary work of John Creasey, 2600 items
125 works of contemporary art by distinguished artists with a Wiltshire connection; John Hoyland, Cecil Beaton, Howard Hodgkin, Fay Godwin, etc
Catalogues:
Catalogue for library is in-house only. Catalogue for all of the collections is only available in-house.

1426
JOHN DORAN GAS MUSEUM
See - National Gas Museum Trust

1427
JOHN GOODCHILD'S LOCAL HISTORY STUDY CENTRE
Central Library, Drury Lane, Wakefield, West Yorkshire, WF1 2DT

Tel: 01924 298929
Formed: 1950

Organisation type and purpose: Independently owned, suitable for ages: 16+, consultancy, research organisation.
Independent local history study centre, no charges made, financed from own pension.

Enquiries to: Archivist
Access:
Access to staff: By letter, by telephone, in person, visitors by prior appointment

General description:
Collections relate to central part of West Riding. Virtually every subject has material relating to it; material from c1200.
Specialised information on coalmining, local industries, textiles, waterways, railways, turnpikes, town development, administration local and regional, country estates, banking, charities, friendly societies etc.
All services are free of charge.
Information services:
Library available for reference (for conditions see Access above)
Lecture service (gratuitous).
Special visitor services: Guided tours.
Education services: Resources for Further or Higher Education..
Collections:
MSS, books, plans, illustrations, a small collection of 3D items which relate to the MSS
Catalogues:
Catalogue for library is in-house only. Catalogue for all of the collections is only available in-house.
Printed publications:
Some 150 and more publications of proprietor's print (not direct)

1428
JOHN HASTIE MUSEUM
8 Threestanes Road, Strathaven, Lanarkshire, ML10 6DX

Tel: 01357 521257

Organisation type and purpose: Local government body, museum, suitable for ages: all ages.
Parent body:
East Kilbride District Council

Enquiries to: Curator

General description:
Covers the local history of Strathaven and surrounding landward area, including Strathaven Castle; weaving; old photographs; the Covenanters and the Battle of Drumclog; Friendly Societies; Strathaven toffee; James Wilson and the 1820 Radical Rising; and ceramics. Temporary exhibitions.
Collections:
John Hastie Collection of trophies and artefacts
Guns not on exhibition
Burnbrae bequest of ceramics (late 19th and early 20th Centuries), donated by Joseph Turner. (Related collection held by Renfrew District Council at Paisley Museum). Ceramics include J and M P Bell, Wedgwood, Royal Doulton, Minton, Ainsley, Royal Worcester, Cauldon, Kinkozan, Noritake, and Royal Dux.

1429
JOHN INNES FOUNDATION HISTORICAL COLLECTIONS
John Innes Centre, Norwich Research Park, Colney, Norwich, Norfolk, NR4 7UH

Tel: 01603 450674
Email: elizabeth.stratton@bbsrc.ac.uk
Formed: 1910
Formerly: John Innes Institute (JII), date of change, 1994

Organisation type and purpose: International organisation, registered charity, suitable for ages: adults.
Archives and rare books, research institution. Plant research.
Connections with:
John Innes Centre

Enquiries to: Archivist
Access:
Access to staff: By email
Access to building, collections or gallery: Prior appointment required
Access for disabled people: Parking provided

General description:
Plant development.

Collections:
Archives and a special collection of rare botanical books embracing over four centuries of botanical art and literature.
Catalogues:
Catalogue for library is in-house only.

Internet home pages:
http://www.jic.bbsrc.ac.uk/corporate/Library/index.htm

1430
JOHN JARROLD PRINTING MUSEUM
Whitefriars, Norwich, Norfolk, NR3 1SH

Tel: 01603 660211
Formed: 1982

Organisation type and purpose: Independently owned, museum, suitable for ages: 12+.
Set up to preserve the historic printing equipment and crafts of the printing and bookbinding industry prior to the 1960s.

Enquiries to: Secretary
Access:
Access to staff: By letter
Access for disabled people: level entry, toilet facilities

General description:
The museum houses a collection of letterpress, lithographic and bookbinding tools and equipment reflecting the art and craft of printing and bookbinding up to the mid-20th century, the history and practice of printing in all its aspects.
Information services:
Library available for reference (for conditions see Access above)
Special visitor services: Guided tours..
Collections:
Collection of equipment, machines, artefacts held on database

1431
JOHN KNOX HOUSE
See - Netherbow Arts Centre/John Knox House

1432
JOHN MUIR BIRTHPLACE
126 High Street, Dunbar, East Lothian, EH42 1JJ

Tel: 01368 862585
Email: trust@jmbt.org.uk
Acronym or abbreviation: JMBT
Formed: 1998

Organisation type and purpose: Registered charity (charity number SCO 28244), historic building, house or site, suitable for ages: 5+.
Site operated by:
East Lothian Council Museums Service
Library & Museums Headquarters, Dunbar Road, Haddington, EH41 3PJ, tel: 01620 828203, fax: 01620 828201, email/website: elms@eastlothian.gov.uk

Enquiries to: Manager
Direct tel: 01620 828203
Direct fax: 01620 828201
Direct email: pgray@eastlothian.gov.uk
Access:
Access to staff: By letter, by telephone, by fax, by email

General description:
An interpretation of the life and work of John Muir (1838-1914) who emigrated to Canada and moved to Wisconsin and then California. Founding father of the environmental movement, the Sierra Club and National Parks in the USA, particularly Yosemite.

Internet home pages:
http://www.jmbt.org.uk
http://www.elothian-museums.demon.co.uk/jmb/

1433
JOHN SOUTHERN GALLERY
Adjacent to and part of, Dobwalls Adventure Park, Havett Road, Dobwalls, Liskeard, Cornwall, PL14 6HB

Tel: 01579 320325
Fax: 01579 321345
Formed: 1972
Formerly: Thorburn Museum & Gallery, date of change, 1995

Organisation type and purpose: Independently owned, art gallery, suitable for ages: all ages.
Part of:
Dobwalls Adventure Park

Enquiries to: Chairman
Access:
Access to staff: By letter, by telephone, by fax
Access for disabled people: Parking provided, level entry, access to all public areas, toilet facilities

General description:
A large permanent display of signed limited edition prints by Steven Townsend, born 1955, Lancashire Artist of the Year 1999. Examples of each for sale, also original watercolours.
The largest permanent display in the world of signed limited edition prints by Carl Brenders, born 1937 Belgium.
Some 100 images on show, examples of each can be obtained.
Information services:
Guided tours by prior arrangement.
Special visitor services: Guided tours.
Services for disabled people: Displays and/or information at wheelchair height.

1434
JOHN WESLEY'S HOUSE
See - Wesley's Chapel, Museum of Methodism and Wesley's House

1435
DR JOHNSON'S HOUSE
17 Gough Square, London, EC4A 3DE

Tel: 020 7353 3745
Fax: 020 7353 3745
Email: curator@drjh.dircon.co.uk
Formed: 1912

Organisation type and purpose: Museum, historic building, house or site, suitable for ages: 8+.

Enquiries to: Curator
Access:
Access to staff: By letter, by telephone, by email, visitors by prior appointment
Hours: Oct to Apr: Mon to Sat, 1100 to 1700; May to Sep: Mon to Sat, 1100 to 17.30
Other restrictions: Closed Sun and Bank Holidays.
Access to building, collections or gallery: No prior appointment required
Other restrictions: Prior appointment required for the library.

General description:
Dr Johnson, his life and times. This was the home of Dr Samuel Johnson where he compiled the first comprehensive English dictionary. The collection comprises 18th century period furniture; paintings; engravings; books; and relics related to Dr Johnson and his friends.
Information services:
Library available for reference (for conditions see Access above)
Special visitor services: Guided tours..
Collections:
First editions of many of Johnson's works
China, once the property of Sir Joshua Reynolds, cup, saucer and tea caddy
China, once the property of James Boswell, beer mug and coffee cup
China, once the property of Mrs Thrale, tea equipage

1436
JOSEPH PARRY'S COTTAGE

4 Chapel Row, Georgetown, Merthyr Tydfil, Mid Glamorgan, CF48 1AG

Tel: 01685 723112
Fax: 01685 723112
Email: museum@cyfarthfapark.freeserve.co.uk
Formed: 1986

Organisation type and purpose: Museum, suitable for ages: 5+.

Enquiries to: Museums Officer
Access:
Access to staff: By letter, by telephone, by fax, by email, visitors by prior appointment
Hours: 1 Apr to 30 Sep: daily, 1000 to 1800,1 Oct to 31 Mar: Tue to Fri, 1000 to 1600; Sat, Sun, 1200 to 1600
Access for disabled people: level entry

General description:
An iron worker's cottage built in 1825, which was the birthplace of Joseph Parry, composer of works such as 'My Family'. It now contains a museum, set in the 1840s period, with collections of documents and ephemera related to Parry's life and work.
Information services:
Education services: Group education facilities, resources for Key Stages 1 and 2, 3, 4 and Further or Higher Education..

1437
JOSIAH WEDGWOOD & SONS LIMITED

Barlaston, Stoke-on-Trent, Staffordshire, ST12 9ES

Tel: 01782 204141
Fax: 01782 204666
Formed: 1759

Organisation type and purpose: Manufacturing industry, museum.

Enquiries to: Public Relations Manager
Direct tel: 01782 282516
Direct fax: 01782 204433
Direct email: andrew.stanistreet@wedgwood.com
Access:
Access to staff: By letter, by fax, by email
Hours: Mon to Fri, 0900 to 1700

General description:
Manufacturing processes of fine bone china and earthenware, company history from 1759.
Collections:
Museum of ceramics and manuscripts

Internet home pages:
http://www.wedgwood.co.uk
Company history, product information, visitor centre, events, company magazine, gift ideas.

1438
JUDGE'S LODGING, THE

Broad Street, Presteigne, Powys, LD8 2AD

Tel: 01544 260650
Fax: 01544 260652
Email: info@judgeslodging.org.uk
Formed: 1997
Formerly: Presteigne & District Museum, date of change, 1997

Organisation type and purpose: Registered charity (charity number 1062215), museum, historic building, house or site, suitable for ages: 5+.
Parent body:
Powys County Council
County Hall, Llandrindod Wells, Powys, LD1 5LG
Administrated by:
Presteigne Shire Hall Museum Trust

Enquiries to: Manager
Other contacts: Museum Assistant for collection details and education.

Access:
Access to staff: By letter, by telephone, by fax, by email, visitors by prior appointment, Internet web pages
Access to building, collections or gallery: No prior appointment required
Hours: 1 Mar to 31 Oct: daily, 1000 to 1800 Nov, Dec: Wed to Sun, 1000 to 1600
Other restrictions: At other times by prior appointment.
Access for disabled people: ramped entry
Other restrictions: Photopack of inaccessible rooms for wheelchair users. Ground floor access only, lift to this level.

General description:
The faithful restoration of an 1870s gas-lit courthouse and Victorian Judge's grand residence, with original furniture and fittings. Once occupied by Lord Chief Justice Campbell, 1855. Local history exhibitions and legal memorabilia, Presteigne and Radnorshire social history, Radnorshire law and order, Victorian domestic furnishings.
Information services:
Transcripts in French, German and Welsh.
Has ambient sound guides.
Houses the town's collections and tourist information centre.
Special visitor services: Guided tours, tape recorded guides, materials and/or activities for children.
Education services: Group education facilities, resources for Key Stages 1 and 2, 3, 4 and Further or Higher Education.
Services for disabled people: For the visually impaired; for the hearing impaired; displays and/or information at wheelchair height.
Collections:
Artefacts, photographs, paintings, furnishings and books relating to history of the building and Presteigne
Presteigne Town local history collection
Radnorshire legal collections and constabulary memorabilia
Victorian domestic furnishings
Catalogues:
Catalogue for all of the collections is only available in-house.
Printed publications:
Guide Books, Booklets on local history and Victorian subjects (contact direct for details)
Pamphlets on Victorian Crime and Punishment and Local History (produced regularly, list available on request)
Electronic and video products:
Tour of Building (audio tape)

Internet home pages:
http://www.judgeslodging.org.uk
Details of period rooms, events and facilities, educational resources.

1439
JUDGES' LODGINGS MUSEUM

Church Street, Lancaster, LA1 1YS

Tel: 01524 32808
Fax: 01524 846315
Email: judges.lodgings@mus.lancscc.gov.uk

Organisation type and purpose: Local government body, museum, historic building, house or site, suitable for ages: 5+.
Parent body:
Lancashire County Museum Service (LCMS)
Stanley Street, Preston, PR1 4YP, tel: 01772 264061

Enquiries to: Manager
Access:
Access to staff: By letter, by telephone, by fax, by email
Access to building, collections or gallery: No prior appointment required
Hours: Good Friday to end of Oct;
Good Fri to end of Jun and Oct, Mon to Fri, 1300 to 1600; Sat and Sun, 1200 to 1600;
Jul to Sep, Mon to Fri 1000 to 1600; Sat and Sun, 1200 to 1600;
Other restrictions: Schools and group bookings all year round by prior appointment.

General description:
Built at the beginning of the 17th century, this town house was, in 1612, the home of the keeper of the castle, Thomas Covell. It was later used by judges visiting Lancaster to attend the Assize Courts.
Period room displays feature the work of the 18th/19th century local furniture makers, Gillows of Lancaster. A special gallery is dedicated to the history of the family.
Fine portrait collection, and childhood collection.
Collections:
Children's collection: toys, dolls and games from 18th century to the present day
Furniture by Gillows of Lancaster

Internet home pages:
http://www.bringinghistoryalive.co.uk

1440
JULIA MARGARET CAMERON TRUST

Dimbola Lodge, Terrace Lane, Freshwater Bay, Freshwater, Isle of Wight, PO40 9QE

Tel: 01983 756814
Fax: 01983 755578
Email: administrator@dimbola.co.uk
Acronym or abbreviation: JMC Trust
Formed: 1993
Formerly: Dimbola Lodge

Organisation type and purpose: Independently owned, membership association (membership is by subscription), present number of members: 450, registered charity (charity number 1026339), museum, art gallery, historic building, house or site, suitable for ages: 12+.
Friends organisation. To advance knowledge of Julia Margaret Cameron, and display her work and contemporary photographic work as well.
Connected with:
Friends of JMC Trust
Dimbola Lodge

Enquiries to: Executive Secretary
Other contacts: (1) Chairman (2) Curator for (1) overall charge of project (2) museum/historical.
Access:
Access to staff: By letter, by telephone, by fax, by email, in person, visitors by prior appointment
Hours: Tue to Sun, 1000 to 1700 including Bank Holiday Mon; closed for 5 days at Christmas
Access to building, collections or gallery: Prior appointment required
Hours: Mon to Sun, 0900 to 1700 for research; public opening times: Tue to Sun, 1000 to 1700 including Bank Holiday Mon; closed for 5 days at Christmas
Access for disabled people: Parking provided, ramped entry, access to all public areas, toilet facilities

General description:
Julia Margaret Cameron 1815-1879 and her work, associates etc in Victorian times; historical photographic processes and photography in general.
Information services:
Library available for reference (for conditions see Access above)
Special visitor services: Guided tours.
Education services: Group education facilities..
Catalogues:
Catalogue for library is published and is on-line.
Catalogue for all of the collections is published and is also on-line.
Publications list:
is available in hard copy and online.
Printed publications:
Books, cards
Electronic and video products:
Video of specialised talk on early photographers

Internet home pages:
http://www.dimbola.co.uk

1441
JURASSIC ATTRACTION
See - Dinosaurland

1442
K VILLAGE HERITAGE CENTRE
K Village, Kendal, Cumbria, LA9 7DA

Tel: 01539 732363
Access:
Access to staff: By letter, by telephone, by fax
Access to building, collections or gallery: No prior appointment required
Hours: Sat, 0900 to 1800; Sun, 1100 to 1700
Access for disabled people: Parking provided, ramped entry, access to all public areas, toilet facilities

General description:
The history of shoe production and development in Kendal from the 1890s forward.

1443
KAWASAKI TRIPLES CLUB
See - Classic Kawasaki Club

1444
KEATS HOUSE
Wentworth Place, Keats Grove, Hampstead, London, NW3 2RR

Tel: 020 7794 6829
Fax: 020 7431 9293
Email: lma@corpoflondon.gov.uk
Formed: 1925
Formerly: Keats Memorial Library

Organisation type and purpose: Local government body, museum, suitable for ages: 12+.
Parent body:
Corporation of London
Department of:
London Metropolitan Archives
40 Northampton Road, London, EC1R 0HB, tel: 020 7332 3820, fax: 020 7833 9136, email/website: lma@corpoflondon.gov.uk

Enquiries to: Manager
Access:
Access to staff: By letter, by telephone, by fax, by email, visitors by prior appointment, letter of introduction required
Access to building, collections or gallery: No prior appointment required
Hours: Mon, closed; Tue to Sat, 1200 to 1700 general opening; 1000 to 1200, tours by appointment; 1 weekday, 6-8 guided tours and events; Sun, 1200 to 1700, general opening

General description:
John Keats and his contemporaries.
Information services:
Library available for reference (for conditions see Access above)
Special visitor services: Guided tours, materials and/or activities for children.
Education services: Group education facilities, resources for Key Stages 2, 3, 4 and Further or Higher Education.
Services for disabled people: For the visually impaired; displays and/or information at wheelchair height.
Collections:
John Keats and his contemporaries
Catalogues:
Catalogue for library is in-house only. Catalogue for all of the collections is only available in-house.
Publications list:
is available on-line.
Printed publications:
Guide to Keats House
Microform products:
Catalogue of manuscripts at Keats house - University Microfilms

Internet home pages:
http://www.keatshouse.org.uk
http://www.cityoflondon.gov.uk

1445
KEDLESTON HALL
Kedleston, Derby, DE22 5JH

Tel: 01332 842191
Fax: 01332 841972
Email: kedlestonhall@nationaltrust.org.uk
Formed: 1895

Organisation type and purpose: Registered charity (charity number 205846), historic building, house or site, suitable for ages: 5+. Registered museum.
Parent body:
The National Trust (East Midlands Region)
East Midlands Regional Office, tel: 01909 486411

Enquiries to: Property Secretary
Access:
Access to staff: By letter, by telephone, by fax, by email, in person, visitors by prior appointment, charges to non-members
Other restrictions: Times and dates vary year to year.
Access for disabled people: Parking provided, access to all public areas, toilet facilities
Other restrictions: House: access via stairclimber (last entry 1530); Garden, Restaurant and Shop: accessible.
Wheelchairs and self-drive vehicle for garden, and limited use in park subject to availability.

General description:
A classical Palladian mansion built 1759-65 for the Curzon family who have lived in the area since the 12th century. The house boasts the most complete and least-altered sequence of Robert Adam interiors in England, with the magnificent state rooms retaining their great collections of paintings and original furniture. The Eastern Museum houses a remarkable range of objects collected by Lord Curzon when Viceroy of India (1899-1905). The gardens have been restored in part to an 18th century 'pleasure ground' and the surrounding park, also designed by Adam, includes a fine bridge, fishing pavilion and a beautiful series of lakes and cascades. All Saints' Church is the only survivor of the medieval village of Kedleston and contains a fascinating collection of monuments and memorials to the Curzon family.
Recently opened, 'The Wilderness Walk': 2 or 3 mile easy-going unsurfaced walk on north side of Park.
Information services:
Braille guide; sympathetic hearing scheme
Suitable for school groups. Live interpretation.
Children's guide. Children's quiz/trail
Introductory talks from 18th century housekeeper. Guided walks around park, stables, fishing room and gardens, tel. for dates and times
Programme of major events including open-air concert, antiques fair, working craft fair and garden fete.
Special visitor services: Guided tours, materials and/or activities for children.
Education services: Group education facilities.
Services for disabled people: For the visually impaired; for the hearing impaired.
Collections:
18th century furniture
17th and 18th century paintings
Robert Adam Interior - plaster work etc
18th century silverware
18th and 19th century ceramics
Substantial collection of Indian and other Asian material - Eastern Museum
18th and 19th century book collection
Sculpture
Archives: by appointment, recommendation; also a facility fee charged
Catalogues:
Catalogue for part of the collections is only available in-house.
Publications list:
is available in hard copy.
Printed publications:
Guide Book, for purchase, direct
Short Guide, for purchase, direct
Children's Guide, for purchase, direct

Internet home pages:
http://www.nationaltrust.org.uk

1446
KEELE UNIVERSITY ART COLLECTION
The Art Gallery, Chancellors Building, Keele University, Keele, Staffordshire, ST5 5BG

Tel: 01782 583376
Fax: 01782 584165
Email: m.gidman@uso.keele.ac.uk
Formed: 1950

Organisation type and purpose: Art gallery, university department or institute, suitable for ages: 16+.

Enquiries to: Curator
Direct email: m.gidman@keele.ac.uk
Access:
Access to staff: By letter, by telephone, by fax, by email, visitors by prior appointment
Access for disabled people: Parking provided, ramped entry, access to all public areas, toilet facilities

General description:
Contains decorative/applied arts; fine art; and photography. A diverse collection including work donated in 1957 by Sir Barnett and Lady Stross. Also contains drawings and paintings by Jacob Kramer and Rowley Smart.
Collections:
Barnett-Stross Bequest of 20th century British art.

1447
KEEP MILITARY MUSEUM
See - Military Museum of Devon and Dorset

1448
KEGWORTH MUSEUM
52 High Street, Kegworth, Derbyshire, DE74 2DA

Tel: 01509 672886
Formed: 1992

Organisation type and purpose: Independently owned, voluntary organisation, registered charity (charity number 501573), museum, suitable for ages: 8+.

Enquiries to: Secretary
Access:
Access to staff: By letter, by telephone
Access for disabled people: ramped entry, toilet facilities
Other restrictions: Access to ground floor only.

General description:
Collection covering local history related to Kegworth. Includes domestic artefacts; saddlery tools; hand knitting machine; industry; the local school; war memorabilia, etc. There is also a photographic collection of local people and places.
Collections:
Local industry, school, photographs
Royal British Legion

1449
KEIGHLEY AND WORTH VALLEY RAILWAY PRESERVATION SOCIETY
The Railway Station, Haworth, Keighley, West Yorkshire, BD22 8NJ

Tel: 01535 645214
Fax: 01535 647317
Acronym or abbreviation: KWVR

Organisation type and purpose: Voluntary organisation, historic building, house or site. Independent standard gauge steam-operated branch line railway.

continued overleaf

Enquiries to: Publicity Secretary
Other contacts: Society Chairman
Access:
Access to staff: By letter, by telephone, by fax, in person
Hours: Mon to Fri, 0900 to 1700

General description:
Vintage steam trains, operated on a preserved complete branch line.
Collections:
Archive documents
Award Winning Stations
Historic Signs
Independent Railway of the Year
Printed publications:
Annual Timetable (500,000 copies for free distribution)
Push & Pull (magazine, quarterly)
Guide, Stockbook, and other publications

Internet home pages:
http://www.kwvr.co.uk

See also - Vintage Carriages Trust

1450
KEIGHLEY BUS MUSEUM TRUST LIMITED

Halifax Road, Bradford, West Yorkshire, BD13 4EN

Tel: 01282 413179
Fax: 01282 413179
Email: info@kbmt.org.uk
Acronym or abbreviation: KBMT
Formed: 1991

Organisation type and purpose: Independently owned, registered charity (charity number 1060457), museum, suitable for ages: 12+.
Establishment of a permanent museum of road passenger transport in Keighley area.
Address for correspondence:
Keighley Bus Museum Trust Limited
47 Brantfell Drive, Burnley, Lancashire, BB12 8AW
Museum premises are located at:
Keighley Bus Museum
Denholme House Farm, Halifax Road, Denholme
Other Site:
Keighley Bus Museum Trust Limited
Old Dalton Lane, Keighley

Enquiries to: Secretary
Other contacts: Press Officer, tel: 01535 645454 for all media contacts.
Access:
Access to staff: By letter, by telephone, by fax, by email, Internet web pages
Hours: Any reasonable time (answerphone facility)
Access for disabled people: Parking provided, level entry
Other restrictions: Some narrow gangways, unsuitable for wheelchairs.

General description:
A collection of 60 buses, coaches, trolleybuses and anciliary vehicles from 1924 to 1980, some restored, some awaiting or under restoration. Visitors can ride on historic vehicles, some of which are available for hire. We also have spares, manuals and can help with technical knowledge on repair, history and operation of buses and coaches.
Collections:
Buses, coaches, trolleybuses, lorries, bus shelters, stop poles and flags, workshop manuals and spare parts, including:
Oldest known double deck trolleybus (1924)
Britain's last operational trolleybus
Collection of ex Leeds and Bradford motor buses
Catalogues:
Catalogue for library is published. Catalogue for part of the collections is published and part is on-line.
Printed publications:
Guide Book (£3)
Events Leaflet (annually)
Members Magazine (quarterly)

Internet home pages:
http://www.kbmt.org.uk

1451
KEITH HARDING'S WORLD OF MECHANICAL MUSIC

Oak House, High Street, Northleach, Cheltenham, Gloucestershire, GL54 3ET

Tel: 01451 860181
Fax: 01451 861133
Email: keith@mechanicalmusic.co.uk

Organisation type and purpose: Museum.

Enquiries to: Owner
Access:
Access to staff: By letter, by telephone, by fax, by email
Hours: Mon to Sun, 1000 to 1700
Access to building, collections or gallery: No prior appointment required
Hours: Mon to Sun, 1000 to 1700

General description:
Three centuries of self-playing musical instruments, workshops for the repair and restoration of clocks, musical boxes and automata.
These items were an important feature of domestic life before regular broadcasting started in 1924, and all are maintained in perfect order, and introduced and played by museum guides in the form of a live entertainment.
Catalogues:
Catalogue for all of the collections is only available in-house.

Internet home pages:
http://www.mechanicalmusic.co.uk

1452
KELHAM ISLAND MUSEUM

Kelham Island, Alma Street, Sheffield, South Yorkshire, S3 8RY

Tel: 0114 272 2106
Fax: 0114 275 7847
Email: simt@argonet.co.uk
Formed: 1982

Organisation type and purpose: Registered charity (charity number 1042287), museum, suitable for ages: 5+.
Parent body:
Sheffield Industrial Museums Trust
Tel: 0114 272 2106
Sister Museum:
Abbeydale Industrial Hamlet
Abbeydale Road, South Sheffield, tel: 0114 272 2106
Shepherd Wheel
Tel: 0114 272 2106

Enquiries to: Executive Director
Access:
Access to staff: By letter, by telephone, by fax, visitors by prior appointment
Access for disabled people: level entry, access to all public areas, toilet facilities

General description:
Industrial history, local history, steel manufacture.
Collections:
Documents, film, objects, pictures, photographs: all in the process of being catalogued on computer
Catalogues:
Catalogue for library is in-house only. Catalogue for part of the collections is only available in-house.
Printed publications:
Guide Book (£1.50 direct)

Internet home pages:
http://www.simt.co.uk
Introduction to the Museum.

1453
KELLIE CASTLE AND GARDEN

Pittenweem, Anstruther, Fife, KY10 2RF

Tel: 01333 720271
Fax: 01333 720326

Organisation type and purpose: International organisation, membership association (membership is by subscription), voluntary organisation, registered charity, museum, historic building, house or site.
Parent body:
National Trust for Scotland
28 Charlotte Square, Edinburgh, EH2 4ET

Enquiries to: Property Manager
Other contacts: Head Gardener for advice for organic garden.
Access:
Access to staff: By letter, by telephone, by fax, in person
Access to building, collections or gallery: No prior appointment required
Hours: End Mar to end Sep, Thu to Mon, 1200 to 1700
Access for disabled people: Parking provided, level entry, toilet facilities
Other restrictions: Ground floor only and gardens, wheelchair available

General description:
A fine example of lowland Scotland domestic architecture, dating from the 14th century. Sympathetically restored by the Lorimer family in the late 19th century. There are magnificent plaster ceilings; painted panelling; and fine furniture designed by Sir Robert Lorimer. The Victorian nursery and 1930s kitchenware are of particular interest.
Information services:
Services for disabled people: For the hearing impaired.

1454
KELVINGROVE ART GALLERY & MUSEUM

Kelvingrove, Glasgow, G3 8AG

Tel: 0141 287 2699
Telex: 0141 287 2690
Formed: 1901

Organisation type and purpose: Local government body, museum, art gallery, suitable for ages: all ages.
Parent body:
Glasgow Museums
Glasgow City Council
20 Trongate, Glasgow
Access:
Access to staff: By letter, by telephone, by fax
Access to building, collections or gallery: No prior appointment required
Hours: Tue, Wed, Thu, Sat, 1000 to 1700; Fri, Sun, 1100 to 1700
Other restrictions: The Gallery will close for two years in 2003, for refurbishment.The art treasures will be stored at the McLellan Galleries where some will be displayed from June 2003.
Access for disabled people: Parking provided, level entry, access to all public areas, toilet facilities

General description:
This fine national art collection contains superb paintings and sculptures, silver and ceramics, European armour, weapons and firearms, clothing and furniture. The natural history of Scotland is treated in depth, and there are displays of relics from Scotland's history and prehistory.
Information services:
Activities for children
Temporary exhibitions
Special visitor services: Guided tours, tape recorded guides, materials and/or activities for children.
Education services: Group education facilities.
Services for disabled people: Displays and/or information at wheelchair height.

Printed publications:
Preview Magazine (free)

1455
KENDAL MUSEUM
Station Road, Kendal, Cumbria, LA9 6BT

Tel: 01539 721374
Fax: 01539 737976
Email: info@kendalmuseum.org.uk
Full name: Kendal Museum of Natural History and Archaeology
Formed: 1796

Organisation type and purpose: Local government body, museum, suitable for ages: 5+.
Parent body and Administrators:
Lakeland Arts Trust
Abbot Hall, Kendal, Cumbria, tel: 01539 722464
Owned by:
South Lakeland District Council

Enquiries to: Curator
Access:
Access to staff: By letter, by telephone, by email, visitors by prior appointment, Internet web pages
Hours: Mon to Fri, 1030 to 1600
Access to building, collections or gallery: No prior appointment required
Hours: Mon to Sat, 1030 to 1700
Nov, Dec, Feb, Mar: Mon to Sat, 1030 to 1600
Access for disabled people: ramped entry, toilet facilities

General description:
Archaeology, natural history and geology of South Lakeland.
Information services:
Special visitor services: Materials and/or activities for children.
Education services: Group education facilities, resources for Key Stages 1 and 2, 3 and 4..
Collections:
Artefacts: natural history, archaeology, geology, social history, Alfred Wainwright material
Catalogues:
Catalogue for all of the collections is only available in-house.

Internet home pages:
http://www.kendalmuseum.org.uk
Introduction to the museum; description of collections; facilities; education facilities; events and children's activities; research access form.

1456
KENILWORTH CASTLE
Castle Green, Kenilworth, Warwickshire, CV8 1NE

Tel: 01926 852078

Organisation type and purpose: National government body, registered charity, suitable for ages: 5+.
Parent body:
English Heritage (West Midlands Region)
English Heritage
Tel: 0121 625 6820
Other addresses:
English Heritage
112 Comore Row, Birmingham, B3 3AG, tel: 0121 625 6820, fax: 0121 625 6821

Enquiries to: Manager
Access:
Access to staff: By letter, by telephone, in person
Access to building, collections or gallery: No prior appointment required
Hours: 29 Mar to 30 Sep, daily, 1000 to 1800,1 to 31 Oct, daily, 1000 to 1700,1 Nov to 28 Mar, daily 1000 to 1600
Other restrictions: Closed 24 to 26 Dec and 1 Jan
Opening times are subject to change, for up-to-date information contact English Heritage by phone or visit the website.
Access for disabled people: Parking provided
Other restrictions: Disabled visitors advised to use north entrance when open.

General description:
Tudor gardens, impressive Norman Keep and John of Gaunt's Great Hall. The largest castle ruin in England, first castle built 50 years after Norman Conquest, radically extended by King John. Kenilworth stayed in royal hands until 1253 when it was given to Simon de Montfort. The castle was besieged in the Barons' War in 1266. Edward II was imprisoned here. Henry V retired here after Battle of Agincourt in 1415. Acquired by John Dudley, Duke of Northumberland, who was executed for trying to put Lady Jane Grey on the throne in 1553. Partially demolished by Parliamentarian Troops after Civil War. Over the years it was allowed to fall further into ruin, and its great lake drained away.
Information services:
Free planned educational visits, interactive display, tape tours, guided tours by arrangement, educational acitivities, events.
Special visitor services: Tape recorded guides, materials and/or activities for children..
Printed publications:
Kenilworth Castle Guide Book

Internet home pages:
http://www.english-heritage.org.uk

1457
KENSINGTON AND CHELSEA (ROYAL BOROUGH) LIBRARIES AND ARTS SERVICES
Central Library, Phillimore Walk, London, W8 7RX

Tel: 020 7937 2542
Fax: 020 7361 2976
Email: information.services@rbkc.gov.uk
Acronym or abbreviation: RBKC
Full name: Royal Borough of Kensington and Chelsea
Formed: 1965

Organisation type and purpose: Local government body, museum, art gallery, public library.

Enquiries to: Head of Libraries and Arts
Other contacts: Head of Service
Access:
Access to staff: By letter, by telephone, by fax, by email, in person, Internet web pages
Hours: Mon, Tue, Thu, Fri, 0930 to 2000; Wed, Sat, 0930 to 1700

General description:
General, biography and genealogy, customs and folklore, language and languages.
Collections:
Samborne Family Archive
Correspondence of Frederick, Lord Leighton (1830-1896)
Historical collection of children's books
Illustrated books of the 1860s
Illustrations, portraits and heraldry
Kensington and Chelsea local history and current information
Music and sound recordings library
Records of the Chelsea Arts Club 1890-1974
Catalogues:
Catalogue for library is in-house only. Catalogue for all of the collections is only available in-house.
Publications list:
is available in hard copy.
Printed publications:
Historic Chelsea in Maps
Historic Kensington in Maps
Kensington and Chelsea Street Names
Lord Leighton: a catalogue of letters
St Mary Abbots Church Registers; marriage entries 1676-1775
Kensington & Chelsea in old Photographs (Barbara Denny & Carolyn Starren, £7.99)

Internet home pages:
http://www.rbkc.gov.uk/general/default.asp?/libraries/zone=service

1458
KENSINGTON PALACE STATE APARTMENTS AND ROYAL CEREMONIAL DRESS COLLECTION
London, W8 4PX

Tel: 020 7937 9561
Fax: 020 7376 0198

Organisation type and purpose: Registered charity (charity number NDPB), museum, art gallery, historic building, house or site.
Connections with:
Historic Royal Palaces
Hampton Court Palace, Surrey, KT8 9AU

Enquiries to: Director
Access:
Access to staff: By letter, by telephone, by fax
Hours: Mon to Fri, 1000 to 1700
Access for disabled people: toilet facilities
Other restrictions: Limited disabled access; no parking.

General description:
Royal and ceremonial dress; history of Kensington Palace.

Internet home pages:
http://www.hrp.org.uk

1459
KENT AND SHARPSHOOTERS YEOMANRY MUSEUM
Hever Castle, Edenbridge, Kent, TN8 7NG

Tel: 01732 865224
Acronym or abbreviation: KSY Museum
Formed: 1970

Organisation type and purpose: Museum.

Enquiries to: Curator
Access:
Access to staff: By letter only
Access to building, collections or gallery: No prior appointment required
Hours: 1 Mar to 30 Nov: Mon to Sun, 1200 to 1700
Access for disabled people: Parking provided, toilet facilities

General description:
Regimental history.
Collections:
Collections of pictures, uniforms, badges and medals; artefacts and records of the East Kent Yeomanry; the West Kent Yeomanry; and the 3rd/4th County of London Yeomanry (Sharpshooters)

1460
KENWOOD HOUSE
The Iveagh Bequest, Hampstead Lane, London, NW3 7JR

Tel: 020 8348 1286
Fax: 020 8793 3891

Parent body:
English Heritage (London Region)
23 Savile Row, London, W1X 1AB, tel: 020 7973 3000, fax: 020 7937 3001

Enquiries to: Curator
Access:
Access to staff: By letter, by telephone, by fax

continued overleaf

General description:
Beautiful neoclassical architecture, landscaped grounds and stunning art collection, Kenwood House has something for everyone. The grounds have meandering pathways, through 112 acres of woodland and lakes and some famous sculptures.
Collections:
Iveagh Bequest Art Collection, famous works by Rembrant, Vermeer, Turner, Reynolds, Gainsborough and Van Dyke, amongst others
The Suffolk Collection
Sculptures by Henry Moore and Barbara Hepworth
Printed publications:
Guide Books

Internet home pages:
http://www.english-heritage.org.uk

1461
KESWICK MUSEUM & ART GALLERY
Station Road, Keswick, Cumbria, CA12 4NF

Tel: 017687 73263
Fax: 017687 80390
Email: keswick.museum@allerdale.gov.uk
Formed: 1873
Formed from: Fitz Park Trust
Formerly: Fitz Park Museum, date of change, c.1989

Organisation type and purpose: Local government body, registered charity (charity number 1088956), museum, art gallery, suitable for ages: 5+.
Parent body:
Allerdale Borough Council
Heritage & Arts Unit

Enquiries to: Curator
Access:
Access to staff: By letter, by telephone, by fax, by email
Access for disabled people: ramped entry, access to all public areas

General description:
The museum is set in Fitz Park. It covers local history, natural history, geology, social history, fine and decorative art, literary manuscripts of Lake Poets, especially Robert Southey and Hugh Walpole.
Information services:
Library available for reference (for conditions see Access above)
Catalogue for some of the collections can be sent via e-mail.
Special visitor services: Materials and/or activities for children.
Services for disabled people: Displays and/or information at wheelchair height.
Collections:
Large collection of literary manuscripts of Lake Poets: Robert Southey and Hugh Walpole
Geology collection of national and international importance, covering the Lake District. The mineral collection is especially fine. Also many type specimens in the fossil collection, c. 2000 items
Catalogues:
Catalogue for part of the collections is only available in-house.

Internet home pages:
http://www.allerdale.gov.uk
General information for museum and art gallery.

1462
KETTLE'S YARD
Castle Street, Cambridge, CB3 0AQ

Tel: 01223 352124
Fax: 01223 324377
Email: mail@kettlesyard.cam.ac.uk
Formed: 1957

Organisation type and purpose: Museum, art gallery, university department or institute.
Parent body:
University of Cambridge
The Old Schools, Trinity Lane, Cambridge, CB2 1TN, tel: 01223 332200, fax: 01223 332277

Enquiries to: Curator
Other contacts: Public Relations Officer for hire of gallery for corporate events and information regarding Kettle's Yard music programme.
Access:
Access to staff: By letter, by telephone, by email, visitors by prior appointment
Hours: Tue to Sun, 1400 to 1600
Other restrictions: Closed Mon.
Access to building, collections or gallery: No access other than to staff
Hours: Tue to Sun, 1400 to 1600
Access for disabled people: level entry, toilet facilities

General description:
20th century painting and sculpture, particularly British and European, furniture, applied arts and crafts, a specialist art library is available for consultation and the archive includes the correspondence between the founder, H S Ede (1895 to 1990), and Ben Nicholson (1894 to 1982), Winifred Nicholson (1893 to 1981), David Jones (1895 to 1974), and William Congdon (1912 to 1998). We have substantial archival material on Henri Gaudier-Brzeska (1891 to 1915).
Collections:
A computerised collection catalogue is maintained, a catalogue of archival material is in preparation
Gaudier-Brzeska sculptures and drawings
St Ives School, 1920s-1960s, works by Ben and Winifred Nicholson, Wallis, Wood and Hepworth
Catalogues:
Catalogue for library is in-house only. Catalogue for all of the collections is only available in-house.
Printed publications:
A Way of Life (Cambridge, 1995, £45)
Kettle's Yard and Its Artists (Kettle's Yard, Cambridge, 1995, £6.95)
A range of temporary exhibition catalogues, posters and postcards

Address for ordering publications:
Printed publications:
Bookshop Manager

Internet home pages:
http://www.kettlesyard.co.uk

1463
KEW BRIDGE STEAM MUSEUM
Green Dragon Lane, Brentford, Middlesex, TW8 0EN

Tel: 020 8568 4757
Fax: 020 8569 9978
Email: info@kbsm.org
Formed: 1975

Organisation type and purpose: Independently owned, registered charity (charity number 269285), museum, historic building, house or site, suitable for ages: all ages.
Membership scheme open to supporters of the museum's work.
Associate of:
Independent Museums & Museums Association
Member of:
Association of London Pumping Heritage Attractions (ALPHA)

Enquiries to: Manager
Direct email: lesley@kbsm.org
Other contacts: Education Officer
Access:
Access to staff: By letter, by telephone, by fax, by email, Internet web pages
Hours: Mon to Sun, 1100 to 1700
Access to building, collections or gallery: No access other than to staff
Hours: Mon to Sun, 1100 to 1700
Other restrictions: Closed week prior to Christmas and on Good Friday.
Prior appointment for access to reserve collections.
Access for disabled people: Parking provided, level entry, toilet facilities
Other restrictions: Advance booking of parking needed to ensure space.

General description:
A 19th century pumping station with a 90 inch working beam engine. The collection of water pumping engines powered by steam, diesel and water. The station was originally built to supply water to London and the museum displays the history of London's water from Roman times to the Thames Water Ring Main. The waterworks railway is demonstrated by a short line with 'Cloister' and 'Wendy' steam locomotives operated by the Hampshire Narrow Gauge Railway Society.
Information services:
Special events include the Live Steam Model Railway Show and the Festival of Steam.
Restoration of all types of steam and other industrial artefacts.
Special weekday visits can be arranged for schools and colleges, for information contact the Education Officer. Also touch tours for partially sighted people.
Special visitor services: Guided tours, materials and/or activities for children.
Education services: Group education facilities, resources for Key Stages 1 and 2 and Further or Higher Education.
Services for disabled people: Displays and/or information at wheelchair height.
Collections:
Most collections relate to water supply, visitors can view CD-ROM with collections information on a terminal at museum
Cornish beam engines, including the largest surviving working example - Grand Junction 90 inch engine, 1820-1871
Catalogues:
Catalogue for part of the collections is only available in-house.
Printed publications:
Guide Book
Museum shop stocks wide range of industrial archaeology titles
Electronic and video products:
CD-ROM produced to support recent exhibition on Henry Maudslay (£7 inc p&p)

Internet home pages:
http://www.kbsm.org
General information on museum and services it offers; special events etc.

1464
KIDWELLY CASTLE
Castle Road, Kidwelly, Carmarthenshire, SA17 5BQ

Tel: 01554 890104
Fax: 01554 890104

Organisation type and purpose: National government body, historic building, house or site, suitable for ages: 5+.
Parent body:
Welsh Historic Monuments (CADW)
Parent body:
National Assembly for Wales (NAFW / CADW)
Crown Buildings, Cathays Park, Cardiff

Enquiries to: Head Custodian
Access:
Access to staff: By letter, by telephone, by fax
Hours: Daily, 1000 to 1600
Access to building, collections or gallery: No prior appointment required
Hours: Apr to May, Oct: daily, 0930 to 1700
End May to end Sep: daily, 0930 to 1800
Nov to end Mar: Mon to Sat, 0930 to 1600; Sun, 1100 to 1600
Access for disabled people: ramped entry, toilet facilities
Other restrictions: Ground level access only inside Castle.

General description:
The castle was founded by the Normans as an earth and timber stronghold in 1106. It was rebuilt in stone in the 13th century with the great gatehouse being added in 1422 and other improvements being added over the centuries.
Information services:
Free entry for full-time education groups, Mon to Fri during school terms - pre-booking essential.
Special visitor services: Tape recorded guides.
Services for disabled people: For the hearing impaired.
Publications list:
is available in hard copy.
Printed publications:
Publications List available from HQ Cardiff
Kidwelly Castle Guide Book (available direct, £3.25, and mail order from HQ)

Address for ordering publications:
Printed publications:
Sales Officer, CADW
Crown Buildings, Cathays Park, Cardiff, tel: 02920 826175

Internet home pages:
http://www.cadw.wales.gov.uk
Information on all sites in care of CADW.

1465
KIDWELLY INDUSTRIAL MUSEUM
Broadford, Kidwelly, Carmarthenshire, SA17 4LW

Tel: 01554 891078

Organisation type and purpose: Registered charity (charity number 513188), museum, suitable for ages: 8+.

Enquiries to: Secretary (Volunteer)
Direct tel: 01554 891084
Access:
Access to staff: By letter, by telephone
Access for disabled people: Parking provided, ramped entry, toilet facilities

General description:
Specialist machinery used in the tinplate industry - pack mill process. Museum interprets the tinplate industry, small coal-mining museum and local history exhibition.
Information services:
Guided tours by prior appointment only.
Special visitor services: Guided tours.
Services for disabled people: Displays and/or information at wheelchair height.
Collections:
Heavy industrial machinery:
Hot rolling mill and cold rolling mill for tinplate industry
Winding engine and head frame for coal industry
Machinery static at present, hoping to mechanise some

1466
KILLERTON HOUSE
Broadclyst, Exeter, Devon, EX5 3LE

Tel: 01392 881345
Fax: 01392 883112
Email: killerton@nationaltrust.org.uk
Given to: The National Trust, date of change, 1944
Opened, date of change, 1978

Organisation type and purpose: Registered charity (charity number 205846), historic building, house or site.
Parent body:
The National Trust (South West Region)
Devon and Cornwall Regional Office, tel: 01392 881691

Enquiries to: Property Manager
Other contacts: Costume Curator for costume collection.

Access:
Access to staff: By letter
Hours: Costume Staff: Mon, Tue, Wed, 0900 to 1700
Access to building, collections or gallery: No prior appointment required
Hours: Mid Apr to beg Nov, daily, 1100 to 1730; Mid Dec to Christmas, daily, 1400 to 1600
Other restrictions: Closed Tue except in August. Please telephone if visiting in April to check house reopening date. In winter, the shop may not open in bad weather.
Access for disabled people: Parking provided, ramped entry, toilet facilities
Other restrictions: Designated parking. Transfer available. Drop-off point. 4 manual wheelchairs available. Steps to entrance. Ramp available. Ground floor fully accessible. Photograph album. No access to costume exhibition. Stable block: cobbled access to tea-room (steps between servery and seat in garden), wheelchair lift to shop. Garden: steep gradients in garden so access restricted unless companion strong. Gravel paths. Golf buggy in garden driven by volunteers, carries 3 passengers. Buggy not suitable for wheelchairs. Recommended route map.

General description:
An 18th century house with period rooms furnished with mainly 19th century furniture, family portraits, silver and ceramics. The house contains displays from the Killerton costume collection and a Victorian laundry. There is an introductory exhibition in the stable courtyard and an interesting 19th century chapel. The delightful hillside garden features rhododendrons, magnolias, herbaceous borders and rare trees, as well as an ice-house and early 19th century rustic-style summerhouse known as The Bear's Hut. The surrounding parkland and woods offer a number of beautiful circular walks giving access to the 2500ha (6100 acre) estate, and there is also a discovery centre offering varied activities.
Information services:
Braille guide. Audio guide. Scented plants.
Musicians may play grand piano and organ.
Introductory talks on house and garden by arrangement.
Children's play area. Family activities and discovery centre open in school holidays. Suitable for school groups. Education room/centre. Children's guide. Children's quiz/trail.
Special visitor services: Tape recorded guides, materials and/or activities for children.
Education services: Group education facilities, resources for Key Stages 1 and 2.
Services for disabled people: For the visually impaired; for the hearing impaired.
Collections:
Killerton Costume Collection 18th-20th century, started with Paulise de Bush Collection given to Trust in 1978 - since increased to 9000 items
Portraits of Acland family including Reynolds, Lawrence
Collection of portraits of Grillian Club - 19th century dining club in London, sketches of members includes Gladstone, Lord Shaftesbury and other eminent Victorians. 90 portraits.
Publications list:
is available in hard copy.
Printed publications:
House and Garden (colour guide, £2.95)

Internet home pages:
http://www.nationaltrust.org.uk/regions/devon

1467
KILLERTON: BUDLAKE OLD POST OFFICE ROOM
Broadclyst, Exeter, Devon, EX5 3LW

Tel: 01392 881690 (Tenant)

Organisation type and purpose: National organisation, registered charity (charity number 205846), historic building, house or site, suitable for ages: 5+.
Parent body:
National Trust (South West)
Regional Office for Devon and Cornwall, tel: 01392 881691
Access:
Access to staff: By letter, by telephone, in person
Access to building, collections or gallery: No prior appointment required
Hours: 30 Mar to 2 Nov, Mon, Tue and Sun, 1400 to 1700

General description:
A charming example of a 1950s Post Office Room with cottage garden.

Internet home pages:
http://www.nationaltrust.org.uk/regions/devon

1468
KILLERTON: CLYSTON MILL
Broadclyst, Exeter, Devon, EX5 3EW

Tel: 01392 462425, 01392 881345 (Killerton House)

Organisation type and purpose: National organisation, registered charity (charity number 205846), museum, historic building, house or site, suitable for ages: 5+.
Access:
Access to staff: By letter, by telephone
Access to building, collections or gallery: No prior appointment required
Hours: End Mar to beg Nov, Mon, Tue, Sun, 1400 to 1700
Other restrictions: Children need to be supervised as mill is on three floors.
Access for disabled people: level entry
Other restrictions: Ground floor fully accessible. No access to other floors.

General description:
A water-powered grain mill in working order, believed to date from the early 19th century.
Information services:
Suitable for school groups. Children's quiz/trail.
Small groups welcome by arrangement.
Special visitor services: Materials and/or activities for children.
Education services: Group education facilities..

1469
KILLERTON: MARKER'S COTTAGE
Broadclyst, Exeter, Devon, EX5 3HR

Tel: 01392 461546, 01392 881345 (Killerton House)

Organisation type and purpose: National organisation, registered charity (charity number 205846), museum, historic building, house or site.
Parent Body:
The National Trust (South West Region)
Devon and Cornwall Regional Office, tel: 01392 881691

Enquiries to: Manager
Access:
Access to staff: By letter, by telephone
Access to building, collections or gallery: No prior appointment required
Hours: End Mar to beg Nov, Mon, Tue, Sun, 1400 to 1700

General description:
A fascinating medieval cob house containing a cross-passage screen decorated with a painting of St Andrew and his attributes. Cob summer house.

Internet home pages:
http://www.nationaltrust.org.uk/regions/devon

1470
KILLERTON: NEWHALL EQUESTRIAN CENTRE

Broadclyst, Exeter, Devon, EX5 3LW

Tel: 01392 462453 (Leaseholders)
Full name: Newhall Equestrian & Visitors Centre (National Trust Killerton)
Formed: 1933
Formerly: Newhall Farm

Organisation type and purpose: National organisation, registered charity (charity number 205846), museum, art gallery, historic building, house or site.
Parent body:
The National Trust (South West Region)
Devon and Cornwall Regional Office, tel: 01392 881691
Leased and managed by:
Mr and Mrs D Llewellin

Enquiries to: Curator
Access:
Access to staff: By letter, by telephone, visitors by prior appointment
Access for disabled people: Parking provided, level entry, access to all public areas, toilet facilities
Other restrictions: Interesting guided tours for disabled visitors by prior appointment. Ground floor fully accessible. No access to other floors. Photograph album. Level entrance to shop and tea-room.

General description:
The finest range of vernacular farm-buildings on the Killerton Estate. Listed Grade II*, the buildings are arranged around two courtyards and retain many original features. They are now used as a livery yard, equestrian centre and thoroughbred National Hunt stud, with exhibitions of equestrian art, a small carriage museum, pets' corner and aviary.
Information services:
Services for disabled people: For the visually impaired; for the hearing impaired.
Collections:
Horse-drawn vehicles
Equestrian paintings and sculpture

Internet home pages:
http://www.nationaltrust.org.uk/regions/devon

1471
KILLHOPE, THE NORTH OF ENGLAND LEAD MINING MUSEUM

Killhope, Lanehead, Weardale, Bishop Auckland, Co Durham, DL13 1AR

Tel: 01388 537505
Fax: 01388 537617
Email: killhope@durham.gov.uk
Acronym or abbreviation: Killhope
Formed: 1984

Organisation type and purpose: Local government body, museum, historic building, house or site, suitable for ages: all ages.
Parent body:
Durham County Council Cultural Services
County Hall, Durham, DH1 5TY, tel: 0191 383 3595, fax: 0191 384 1336

Enquiries to: Manager
Other contacts: Deputy Manager for educational visits.
Access:
Access to staff: By letter, by fax, by email, visitors by prior appointment, Internet web pages
Hours: Mon to Fri, 0930 to 1700
Access to building, collections or gallery: No prior appointment required
Hours: Sun to Sat, 0930 to 1700
Other restrictions: Closed Nov to Mar.
Access for disabled people: Parking provided, level entry, toilet facilities

General description:
Lead mining in the Northern Pennines. The original buildings and machinery have been restored on site.
Collections:
Great Wheel, 33ft 6ins high which powered the crushing mill

Internet home pages:
http://www.durham.gov.uk/killhope
Basic information on museum.

1472
KILLIECRANKIE VISITOR CENTRE

Pitlochry, Perthshire, PH16 5LG

Tel: 01796 473233
Fax: 01796 473233
Email: killiecrankie@nts.org.uk

Organisation type and purpose: Registered charity (charity number SCO 07410), museum, suitable for ages: 5+.
Parent body:
National Trust for Scotland (North-East Region)

Enquiries to: Property Manager and Senior Ranger
Access:
Access to staff: By letter, by telephone, by fax, by email, in person
Access to building, collections or gallery: No prior appointment required
Hours: Apr to Jun and Sep to end Oct, daily 1000 to 1730; Jul to Sep, daily, 0930 to 1900
Access for disabled people: Parking provided, access to all public areas, toilet facilities

General description:
A Jacobite army, led by Bonnie Dundee, defeated the English in 1689. An exhibition features the battle and natural history of the area which has been designated a Site of Special Scientific Interest.

Internet home pages:
http://www.nts.org.uk

1473
KILMARTIN HOUSE MUSEUM OF ANCIENT CULTURE

Kilmartin House, Kilmartin, Argyll, PA31 8RQ

Tel: 01546 510278
Fax: 01546 510330
Email: museum@kilmartin.org
Formed: 1997

Organisation type and purpose: Registered charity (charity number SCO 22744), museum, suitable for ages: all ages, research organisation, publishing house.

Enquiries to: Marketing Officer
Access:
Access to staff: By letter, by telephone, by fax, by email, Internet web pages
Access for disabled people: Parking provided, level entry, access to all public areas, toilet facilities

General description:
Archaeology and landscape of the Kilmartin Valley.
Information services:
Library available for reference (for conditions see Access above)
Special visitor services: Guided tours, materials and/or activities for children.
Education services: Group education facilities, resources for Key Stages 1 and 2, 3, 4 and Further or Higher Education.
Services for disabled people: For the visually impaired; for the hearing impaired; displays and/or information at wheelchair height.
Collections:
Local archaeological artefacts on display in Museum
Library holding
Kilmartin House
Marion Campbell Collection
Natural History & Antiquarian Society of Mid Argyll
Catalogues:
Catalogue for library is in-house only. Catalogue for all of the collections is only available in-house.
Publications list:
is available on-line.
Printed publications:
The following publications available direct (shop) or via website
Kilmartin An Introduction and Guide to Scotland's Richest Prehistoric Landscape (Butter, R)
Kilmartin Prehistoric & Early Historic Monuments - Royal Commission for Ancient & Historic Monuments of Scotland
Electronic and video products:
The Kilmartin Sessions - The Sounds of Ancient Scotland (CD-ROM, available direct (shop) or via website)

Address for ordering publications:
Printed publications:
Kilmartin House Trust

Internet home pages:
http://www.kilmartin.org
Full information on Museum and all aspects of the Trust's work with full visitor information on local area, publications.

1474
KILVERT GALLERY OF CONTEMPORARY ART

Ashbrook House, Clyro, Herefordshire, HR3 5RZ

Tel: 01497 820831
Fax: 01497 820831
Email: art@clyro.co.uk
Formed: 1987

Organisation type and purpose: Independently owned, art gallery, historic building, house or site, suitable for ages: 5+, consultancy, research organisation.

Enquiries to: Owner/Administrator
Access:
Access to staff: By letter, by telephone, by fax, by email, Internet web pages

General description:
Work by up-and-coming artists - paintings, sculpture, ceramics, jewellery, textiles, items of clothing, all original articles by gallery artists.
A showcase of Kilvert memorabilia.
Collections:
Kilvert Memorabilia
Collection of artefacts connected with the Reverend Francis Kilvert, Victorian Diarist, 1840-1879
He lived in the house from 1865-1872 and wrote the major part of his diaries here

Internet home pages:
http://www.clyro.co.uk/

1475
KING CHARLES TOWER

City Walls, Chester, Cheshire

Tel: 01244 321616

Parent body:
Chester City Council, Chester Museums

General description:
Displays relating the story of Chester during the English Civil War, housed in a Mediaeval Tower on the city wall - the former meeting place of Painters' and Stationers' Company.

1476
KING EDWARD MINE

Troon, Camborne, Cornwall

Tel: 01209 614681
Email: info@ trevithicktrust.com

Organisation type and purpose: Independently owned, historic building, house or site, suitable for ages: 8+.
Parent body:
The Trevithick Trust
Tel: 01209 210900

Enquiries to: Manager
Access:
Access to staff: By letter, by telephone
Access to building, collections or gallery: No prior appointment required
Hours: End of May to Sep, Sun to Fri, 1030 to 1700; for one week during Easter period and May Bank Holiday 1030 to 1700

General description:
The mill of this training mine has been restored by volunteers and contains the last working Californian stamps in Britain, and working examples of round frames, rag frames and a Cornish buddle.

Internet home pages:
http://www.trevithicktrust.com

1477
KING JOHN'S HUNTING LODGE

The Square, Axbridge, Somerset, BS26 2AP

Tel: 01934 732012

Organisation type and purpose: National organisation, registered charity (charity number 205846), museum, historic building, house or site.
Parent body:
The National Trust (South West Region)
Wessex Regional Office, tel: 01985 843600
In cooperation with:
Axbridge Archaeological and Local History Society
Sedgemoor District Council
Somerset County Museums Service
Run by:
Axbridge and District Museum Trust

Enquiries to: Manager
Access:
Access to staff: By letter, by telephone
Access to building, collections or gallery: No prior appointment required
Hours: Apr to Sep, daily, 1300 to 1600

General description:
An early Tudor merchant's house, extensively restored in 1971 and now a local history museum.
Information services:
Services for disabled people: For the hearing impaired.

Internet home pages:
http://www.nationaltrust.org.uk/regions/wessex

1478
KING'S COLLEGE

King's Parade, Cambridge, CB2 1ST

Tel: 01223 331212
Fax: 01223 331212/331315
Email: derek.buxton@kings.cam.ac.uk
Formed: 1441

Organisation type and purpose: Independently owned, historic building, house or site.

Enquiries to: Information Officer
Access:
Access to staff: By telephone, by fax, by email, visitors by prior appointment, Internet web pages
Access for disabled people: ramped entry, access to all public areas

General description:
Information about Cambridge, the chapel and choir.
Printed publications:
Book about King's College available in several languages
Electronic and video products:
CDs of King's College choir and organ music

Address for ordering publications:
Printed publications:
The Manager, Chapel Shop
King's College

Internet home pages:
http://www.kings.cam.ac.uk

1479
KING'S HEAD, THE

King's Head Passage, Market Square, Aylesbury, Buckinghamshire, HP20 2RW

Tel: 01296 381501
Fax: 01296 381502
Email: kingshead@nationaltrust.org.uk

Organisation type and purpose: National organisation, registered charity (charity number 205846), historic building, house or site, suitable for ages: 16+.
Parent body:
The National Trust (South and South East Region)
Thames and Solent Regional Office, tel: 01494 528051
Other addresses:
Hughendon Manor
High Wycombe, Buckinghamshire, tel: 01494 756600

Enquiries to: Manager
Other contacts: Custodian
Access:
Access to staff: By letter, by telephone, by fax, in person, visitors by prior appointment
Access to building, collections or gallery: Prior appointment required
Hours: All year, daily, licensing hours
Other restrictions: Groups, (maximum 4 visitors per tour) must be booked in advance.
Access for disabled people: Parking provided, toilet facilities
Other restrictions: Steps to entrance. Ground floor accessible with assistance. No access to other floors.

General description:
A restored and operating former coaching inn dating from 1455 and of particular interest for its large mullioned window, spacious public courtyard and extensive timber framing.
Information services:
Special visitor services: Guided tours..
Collections:
Many historic items of interest belonging to the property on display: paintings, furniture and artefacts, good example of a traditional, unchanged coaching inn with links to the Civil War and close links with Oliver Cromwell
Catalogues:
Catalogue for library is in-house only. Catalogue for all of the collections is only available in-house.
Printed publications:
IPL - T&S leaflet

Internet home pages:
http://www.nationaltrust.org.uk

1480
KING'S LYNN FESTIVAL AND ARTS CENTRE

See - St George's Guildhall

1481
KING'S LYNN MUSEUMS

See - Lynn Museum

1482
KING'S OWN REGIMENT MUSEUM

See - Lancaster City Museums

1483
KING'S OWN ROYAL BORDER REGIMENT MUSEUM

See - Border Regiment and King's Own Royal Border Regiment Museum

1484
KING'S OWN SCOTTISH BORDERERS REGIMENTAL MUSEUM

The Barracks, Berwick-upon-Tweed, Northumberland, TD15 1DG

Tel: 01289 307426
Fax: 01289 331928
Email: rhqkosb@kosb.co.uk
Acronym or abbreviation: KOSB
Formed: 1689
Formerly: 25th Regiment of Foot

Organisation type and purpose: Museum, historic building, house or site, suitable for ages: 5+.
Regimental museum.
Building under the custodionship of:
English Heritage
Tel: 0191 261 1585

Enquiries to: Regimental Secretary
Access:
Access to staff: By letter, by telephone, by fax, by email
Access to building, collections or gallery: No prior appointment required
Hours: Winter: Mon to Sat, 1000 to 1600
Summer: Mon to Sat, 1000 to 1800
Other restrictions: Closed Sun and some Bank Holidays.
Prior appointment required for Archives. Please phone if wishing to see a specific item to check that the museum is open.
Access for disabled people: toilet facilities

General description:
History and records of the King's Own Scottish Borderers Regiment from 1689 until the present day, with artefacts and pictorial material.
Information services:
Education services: Group education facilities..
Collections:
A wide collection of material (written, pictorial and objects) depicting the Regiment's history since 1689 both at home and abroad
Extensive collections of medals, badges and uniforms
Regimental archives and photographic library
Catalogues:
Catalogue for all of the collections is only available in-house.
Printed publications:
A Short Regimental History
Off At Last - War History of 7 KOSB 1939-45 (Sigmond R)

Internet home pages:
http://www.kosb.co.uk
Regimental history, details of museum and archives, contacts, information about Regiment today, guest page/bulletin board.

See also - Berwick-upon-Tweed Barracks

1485
KING'S ROYAL HUSSARS MUSEUM IN WINCHESTER, THE

Peninsula Barracks, Romsey Road, Winchester, Hampshire, SO23 8TS

Tel: 01962 828539
Fax: 01962 828538
Email: beresford@krhmuseum.freeserve.co.uk
Formed: 1980
Formerly: Royal Hussars Museum, date of change, 1999

Organisation type and purpose: Museum.

Enquiries to: Curator
Access:
Access to staff: By letter, by telephone, by fax, by email

continued overleaf

Access to building, collections or gallery: No prior appointment required
Hours: Tue to Fri, 1000 to 1245 and 1315 to 1600
Sat, Sun, Bank Holidays and Half-Term Mon, 1200 to 1600
Access for disabled people: Parking provided, ramped entry, access to all public areas, toilet facilities

General description:
Covers the history of the 10th Royal Hussars (PWO) and the 11th Hussars (PAO) from 1715 to 1969, and of The Royal Hussars (PWO) from 1969-1992.

1486
KING'S WESTON ROMAN VILLA

Long Cross, Lawrence Weston, Bristol, BS11 0LP

Organisation type and purpose: Local government body, historic building, house or site, suitable for ages: 5+.

Enquiries to: Curator

General description:
The remains of a Roman Villa.

Internet home pages:
http://www.bristol-city.gov.uk/museums

1487
KINGSBURY WATERMILL MUSEUM LIMITED

St Michael's Street, St Albans, Hertfordshire, AL3 4SJ

Tel: 01727 853502
Fax: 01727 832662
Formed: 1982

Organisation type and purpose: Museum.

Enquiries to: Director
Access:
Access to staff: By letter only

General description:
Watermills.

1488
KINGSMILL VISITOR CENTRE

Wrexham

Closed to the public

1489
KINGSTON LACY

Wimbourne Minster, Dorset, BH21 4EA

Tel: 01202 883402, 01202 842913 (Sat and Sun 1100 to 1700)
Fax: 01202 882402
Email: kingstonlacy@nationaltrust.org.uk

Organisation type and purpose: National organisation, registered charity (charity number 205846), historic building, house or site, suitable for ages: 5+.
Parent body:
The National Trust (South West Region)
Wessex Regional Office, tel: 01985 843600

Enquiries to: Manager
Access:
Access to staff: By letter, by telephone
Access to building, collections or gallery: No prior appointment required
Hours: House: 22 Mar to beg Nov, Wed to Sun, 1100 to 1700;
Open Bank Holiday Mondays.
Other restrictions: Last admission one hour before closing.
Access for disabled people: Parking provided, toilet facilities
Other restrictions: 4 manual wheelchairs available.One single-seater powered mobility vehicle, booking essential. Steps to entrance. Ground floor largely inaccessible. No access to other floors. Chairs available in each room. Two access days for less able visitors, tel. property manager for details. Steps to shop entrance. Level entrance to restaurant. Loose gravel on garden paths.

General description:
Home of the Bankes family for over 300 years, having replaced the ruined family seat at Corfe Castle, this 17th century house was radically altered in the 19th century by Sir Charles Barry. The house contains the outstanding collection of paintings and other works of art accumulated by William Bankes. It is famous for its dramatic Spanish Room, with walls hung in magnificent gilded leather. The house and garden are set in a wooded park with attractive waymarked walks and a fine herd of North Devon cattle. The surrounding estate is crossed by many paths (leaflet available from shop) and dominated by the Iron Age hill-fort of Badbury Rings. The botanically rich Rings are managed by grazing, and dogs are not permitted.
Information services:
Helpline available, tel no: 01202 880413 (Infoline).
Special snowdrop days in Jan and Feb, for details tel Infoline.
Pre-booked guided tours for groups of more than 15 visitors.
Large print guide. One-to-one touch tours available free.
Suitable for school groups. Education room/centre. Hands-on activities. Children's guide. Children's quiz/trail. Adult study days.
Front-carrying baby slings for loan.
Special visitor services: Guided tours, materials and/or activities for children.
Education services: Group education facilities, resources for Key Stages 1 and 2.
Services for disabled people: For the visually impaired.

Internet home pages:
http://www.nationaltrust.org.uk/regions/wessex

1490
KINGSTON MUSEUM & HERITAGE SERVICE

Local History Room, North Kingston Centre, Richmond Road, Kingston upon Thames, Surrey, KT2 5PE

Tel: 020 8547 6738
Fax: 020 8547 6747
Email: local.history@rbk.kingston.gov.uk
Formed: 1904
Formerly: Kingston Heritage Centre, date of change, 1992

Organisation type and purpose: Local government body, museum, art gallery, suitable for ages: all ages.
Archive service, local history room.
Associated with:
Kingston upon Thames Archaeological Society
Surrey Archaeological Society
Surrey History Centre
Tel: 01483 594594, fax: 01483 594595, email/website: shs@surreycc.gov.uk
Part of:
Kingston upon Thames Corporation's Education and Leisure Department
Museum address:
Kingston Museum
Wheatfield Way, Kingston upon Thames, Surrey, KT1 2PS, tel: 020 8547 6755, fax: 020 8547 6747

Enquiries to: Local Studies Officer
Other contacts: (1) Archivist (2) Heritage Officer, tel: 020 8547 6756 for archives for Royal Borough accessible at local history room.
Access:
Access to staff: By letter, by telephone, by fax, by email, in person, Internet web pages

General description:
Local history, topography, archaeology and environmental studies relevant to the Royal Borough of Kingston upon Thames and also of the County of Surrey, Thames Valley, and including Kingston Town, Norbiton, Surbiton, Hook, Tolworth, New Malden and Chessington.
Collections:
Archives, archaeology and local history collection have been transferred to the Heritage Centre from the Kingston Library
Eadweard Muybridge Collection (local pioneer of cinematography)
Local History Collection
Martinware (pottery) Collection
Thomas Rowlandson Collection (18th century, watercolours, etc.)
Catalogues:
Catalogue for library is in-house only. Catalogue for all of the collections is only available in-house.
Printed publications:
Information sheets
Reproductions of local photographs (portfolios of special areas or subjects, with booklet)
Reproductions of local postcards, graphic work and broadsides etc
Microform products:
Microfilm service: Surrey Comet, and Census Returns 1841-1891
Electronic and video products:
Some local history videos

Internet home pages:
http://www.kingston.gov.uk/enjoying/museum/local+history+and+archives.htm
http://www.kingston.ac.uk/Muybridge
Eadweard Muybridge Collection only.

1491
KINGSTON MUSEUM

Wheatfield Way, Kingston upon Thames, Surrey, KT1 2PS

Tel: 020 8546 5386
Email: museum@rbk.kingston.gov.uk
Formed: 1904

Organisation type and purpose: Local government body, museum, suitable for ages: 5+.

Enquiries to: Curator
Access:
Access to staff: By letter, by telephone, by email, in person, Internet web pages
Access to building, collections or gallery: No prior appointment required
Hours: Mon, Tue, Thu, Fri, Sat, 1000 to 1700
Access for disabled people: level entry, access to all public areas, toilet facilities

General description:
Archaeology, social and economic history of Kingston upon Thames. Also holds the archive of Eadweard Muybridge, a famous early photographer.
Information services:
Special visitor services: Materials and/or activities for children.
Education services: Group education facilities, resources for Key Stages 1 and 2.
Services for disabled people: Displays and/or information at wheelchair height.
Collections:
Photographs and objects connected to Eadweard Muybridge
Pottery Collection bequeathed by Ernest Marsh
Objects connected to the history of Kingston upon Thames
Publications list:
is available on-line.

Internet home pages:
http://www.kingston.gov.uk/museum

1492
KINGSTON UPON HULL TOWN DOCKS MUSEUM

See - Hull Maritime Museum

1493
KINNEIL MUSEUM
Duchess Anne Cottages, Kinneil Estate, Bo'ness, West Lothian, EH51 0PR

Tel: 01506 778530
Formed: 1976
Formerly: Falkirk District Museums, date of change, 1996

Organisation type and purpose: Local government body, museum, historic building, house or site.
Parent body:
Falkirk Council
Falkirk Museums
Address for all correspondence:
Falkirk Museums
Callendar House, Callendar Park, Falkirk, FK1 1YR, tel: 01324 503770

Enquiries to: Assistant Museums Manager
Direct tel: 01324 503770
Direct fax: 01324 503771
Direct email: callendar.house@falkirk.gov.uk
Other contacts: Museum Attendant for direct contact for Kinneil Museum.
Access:
Access to staff: In person
Access to building, collections or gallery: No prior appointment required
Hours: Mon to Sat, 1230 to 1600
Closed public holidays
Other restrictions: For all specialised information contact Falkirk Museums.
Access for disabled people: Parking provided

General description:
Local history; displays relating to Kinneil Estate; medieval village and church; James Watt's cottage; 16th century Kinneil House; Roman wall and fortlet.
Information services:
Education services: Group education facilities..

Address for ordering publications:
Printed publications:
Falkirk Museums
Callendar House, Callendar Park, Falkirk, FK1 1YR

1494
KINVER EDGE AND HOLY AUSTIN ROCK HOUSES
The Warden's Lodge, The Compa, Kinver, Stourbridge, Staffordshire, DY7 6HU

Tel: 01384 872418, 01384 872553 (Custodian)
Email: kinveredge@nationaltrust.org.uk

Organisation type and purpose: National organisation, registered charity (charity number 205846), historic building, house or site.
Parent body:
The National Trust (West Midlands)
West Midlands Regional Office, tel: 01743 708100

Enquiries to: Custodian
Access:
Access to staff: By letter, by telephone, by email

General description:
A sandstone ridge, covered in woodland and heath and from which there are dramatic views across surrounding counties. The famous Holy Austin rock houses, which were inhabited until the 1950s, have now been restored and parts are open to visitors at selected times.

Internet home pages:
http://www.nationaltrust.org.uk

1495
KINWARTON DOVECOTE
Kinwarton, Alcester, Warwickshire

Tel: 01743 708100 (Regional Office)
Email: kinwartondovecote@nationaltrust.org.uk

Organisation type and purpose: National organisation, registered charity (charity number 205846), historic building, house or site.
Parent body:
The National Trust (West Midlands)
West Midlands Regional Office, tel: 01743 708100

Enquiries to: Manager
Access:
Access to staff: By letter, by telephone, by email

General description:
A circular 14th century dovecote, still housing doves and retaining its potence, an unusual pivoted ladder from which access is possible to the nesting boxes.

Internet home pages:
http://www.nationaltrust.org.uk

1496
KIPPERS CAT MEOWSEUM
Bury

Closed

1497
KIRBY HALL
Corby, Northamptonshire

Tel: 01536 203230
Formed: 1570

Organisation type and purpose: Historic building, house or site.
Parent body:
English Heritage (East Midlands Region)
44 Derngate, Northampton, NN1 1UH, tel: 01604 735400, fax: 01604 735401

Enquiries to: House Manager
Access:
Access to staff: By letter, by telephone
Access to building, collections or gallery: No prior appointment required
Hours: Apr to Sep: daily, 10oo to 1800
Oct: daily, 1000 to 1700
Nov to Mar: Sat, Sun, 1000 to 1600
Other restrictions: Closed 24 to 26 Dec and 1 Jan.
Opening times are subject to change, for up-to-date information contact English Heritage by phone or visit the website.

General description:
With formal gardens that gained the reputation in the 17th century as being the finest in all England, and amazing Renaissance architectural detail, Kirby Hall is one of the most outstanding Elizabethan mansions in the country. Built in Weldon stone. Although now empty, the state rooms contain reconstruction drawings of how it appeared in 1619 when James I visited the hall. Most of the year one of the most relaxing and peaceful places imaginable, in August Kirby Hall is transformed by the annual History in Action event, a truly spectacular historical re-enactment.
Information services:
Gardens exhibition.
Special visitor services: Tape recorded guides..

Internet home pages:
http://www.english-heritage.org.uk

1498
KIRBY MUXLOE CASTLE
Kirby Muxloe, Leicester

Tel: 01162 386886

Organisation type and purpose: Historic building, house or site.
Parent body:
English Heritage (East Midlands Region)
44 Derngate, Northampton, NN1 1UH, tel: 01604 735400, fax: 01604 735401

Enquiries to: Manager
Access:
Access to staff: By telephone
Hours: Apr to Oct, Sat, Sun and Bank Holidays only, 1200 to 1700.
Other restrictions: Contact regional office when property closed, tel: 01604 735400.
Access to building, collections or gallery: No prior appointment required
Hours: Apr to Oct: Sat, Sun and Bank Holidays, 1200 to 1700
Other restrictions: Opening times are subject to change, for up-to-date information contact English Heritage by phone or visit the website.

General description:
Moated, brick castle, started in 1480 and unfinished at the time of owner's (William, Lord Hastings), execution in 1483. Remains much as Lord Hastings left it.

Internet home pages:
http://www.english-heritage.org.uk

1499
KIRKALDY TESTING MUSEUM
99 Southwark Street, Southwark, London, SE1 0JF

Tel: 01322 332195
Formed: 1983

Organisation type and purpose: Voluntary organisation, registered charity (charity number 297557), museum, suitable for ages: 16+.

Enquiries to: Manager
Access:
Access to staff: By letter, by telephone, visitors by prior appointment

General description:
The aim of the museum is to promote the history of materials testing with special reference to the work of David Kirkaldy and his family, and to demonstrate the standardisation of materials testing developed by this independent works.
Catalogues:
Catalogue for library is in-house only.

1500
KIRKCALDY MUSEUM & ART GALLERY
War Memorial Gardens, Kirkcaldy, Fife, KY1 1YG

Tel: 01592 412860
Fax: 01592 412870
Formed: 1925

Organisation type and purpose: Local government body, museum, art gallery, suitable for ages: all ages.

Enquiries to: Curator
Other contacts: Exhibitions Officer for publicity.
Access:
Access to staff: By letter, by telephone, by fax, in person
Hours: Mon to Sat, 1030 to 1700; Sun, 1400 to 1700
Access for disabled people: Parking provided, ramped entry, access to all public areas, toilet facilities

General description:
Fine art collection specialising in 18th to 21st century Scottish paintings.
Largest public collection of works by William McTaggart and S J Peploe outside the National Galleries of Scotland.
Wemyss Ware pottery displays.
Collections:
J W Blyth Collection, paintings - including large number of works of S J Peploe and Wm McTaggart, 18th-20th century
Linoleum, samples, archives, tools, printing blocks, etc 1870s-1990s
Kirkcaldy made pottery - including Wemyss Ware, c. 1800-1930
Catalogues:
Catalogue for part of the collections is published.
Publications list:
is available in hard copy.
Printed publications:
Catalogue of the Fine Art Collection and others

1501
KIRKHAM PRIORY
Whitwell on the Hill, North Yorkshire, YO60 7JS

Tel: 01653 618768

Organisation type and purpose: National organisation, advisory body, historic building, house or site.
Parent body:
English Heritage (Yorkshire Region)
Tel: 01904 601901

Enquiries to: Manager
Access:
Access to staff: By letter, by telephone
Access to building, collections or gallery: No prior appointment required
Hours: 29 Mar to 30 Sep: daily, 1000 to 1300 and 1400 to 1800,1 to 31 Oct: daily, 1000 to 1300 and 1400 to 1700
Other restrictions: Opening times are subject to change, for up-to-date information contact English Heritage by phone or visit the website.

General description:
The ruins of an Augustinian priory, set in a peaceful valley by the River Derwent.

Internet home pages:
http://www.english-heritage.org.uk

1502
KIRKLEATHAM MUSEUM
Kirkleatham, Redcar, Cleveland, TS10 5NW

Tel: 01642 479500
Fax: 01642 474199
Email: museum_services@redcar-cleveland.gov.uk
Acronym or abbreviation: RCMS/KM
Formed: 1981
Formerly: Kirkleatham Old Hall Museum

Organisation type and purpose: Local government body, museum, art gallery, historic building, house or site, suitable for ages: 5+.
Local history museum for the Redcar and Cleveland Borough areas.
Parent body:
Redcar & Cleveland Borough Council
Redcar & Cleveland Museums Service, tel: 01642 444000
Other address:
Margrove Heritage Centre (MHC)
Margrove Park, Boosbeck, Saltburn-by-Sea, TS12 3BZ, tel: 01287 610368, fax: 01287 610368, email/website: museum_services@redcar-cleveland.gov.uk

Enquiries to: Museums Curator
Access:
Access to staff: By letter, by telephone, by fax, by email, in person, visitors by prior appointment
Access to building, collections or gallery: Prior appointment required
Hours: Apr to Sept: Tue to Sun, 1000 to 1700
Oct to Mar: Tue to Sun, 1000 to 1600
Other restrictions: Closed Mon, except Bank Holidays.
Access for disabled people: Parking provided, level entry, access to all public areas, toilet facilities

General description:
A local history museum for Langbaurgh-on-Tees Borough. Covers working life; maritime history; domestic life; toys, dolls and games; natural history; archaeology; geology; photographs; paintings; prints and drawings.
Collections:
Kirkleatham the story of the village to the present day
Sea rescue, the Zetland and Sir James Knott Life Boats, 1802-1985
Fishing, 'Sea Mew' and 'Volente' fishing boats, 1900-1993
Staithes Group, paintings and Laura Knight sketches, c. 1890-1950, 20 plus
Photographs of local topography and various topics, c. 1870 onwards, 10,000 items
Ironstone mining, tools, equipment, photographs, etc c. 1850-1960, 100 items
Iron making, blast furnace tools and equipment, c. 1993, 100 items
Rock Candy, lettered rock manufacture, c. 1940-1990, 200 items
Printed ephemera, posters, adverts, packaging, etc c. 1850, 2000 items
Ship building, Smiths Dock models and photographs, c. 1900-1985, 5000 items
TRTB Trolleybus and artefacts, c. 1950s-1971
Publications list:
is available in hard copy.

1503
KIRKLEES LIGHT RAILWAY
The Railway Station, Park Mill Way (off A636), Clayton West, Near Huddersfield, West Yorkshire, HD8 9XJ

Tel: 01484 865727
Full name: Yorkshire's Great Little Steam Train
Formed: 1991

Organisation type and purpose: Independently owned, suitable for ages: 5+.
Tourist attraction, narrow gauge steam railway.
Purpose-built narrow gauge steam railway, built on trackbed of old BR Clayton West Branch Line. Provides a 50 minute scenic return trip.
Member of:
English Tourist Board
Heritage Railways
Penistone Line Partnership
Pennine Yorkshire Tourism Association
Yorkshire Tourist Board

Enquiries to: Information Officer
Access:
Access to staff: By telephone
Hours: Daily, 0900 to 1700
Access to building, collections or gallery: No prior appointment required
Hours: Spring Bank Holiday to End Aug: Daily, 1100 to 1600; 1100 to 1500 in Winter
Other restrictions: Open all weekends, most school holidays.
Access for disabled people: Parking provided, ramped entry, toilet facilities
Other restrictions: Access to most areas.

General description:
The 15 inch gauge line was laid along the old Lancashire & Yorkshire Clayton West Branch Line which used to connect Clayton West and Skelmanthorpe with the main Sheffield to Huddersfield line.
Printed publications:
Leaflet (annually)

1504
KIRRIEMUIR GATEWAY TO THE GLENS MUSEUM
The Town House, 32 High Street, Kirriemuir, Angus, DD8 4BB

Tel: 01575 575479
Email: kirriegateway@angus.gov.uk
Formed: 2001

Organisation type and purpose: Local government body, museum, historic building, house or site, suitable for ages: all ages.
Connections with:
Friends of Kirriemuir Gateway to the Glens Museum
Bank House, Bank Street, Kirriemuir, Angus, tel: 01575 572355

Enquiries to: Curator
Other contacts: Museums Manager for Curator who is part-time.
Access:
Access to staff: By letter, by telephone, by email, in person
Access to building, collections or gallery: No prior appointment required
Hours: Mon, Tue, Wed, Fri, Sat, 1000 to 1700; Thu, 1300 to 1700
Access for disabled people: level entry, toilet facilities

General description:
The Town House was originally built in 1604 and was once the town's jail and courthouse. A detailed model of the town square in 1604 shows vividly what market day was like hundreds of years ago.
The Museum explores the fascinating history of 'The Wee Red Toon's' development from its foundation as an ecclesiastical site in Pictish Times through its handloom weaving times to its place today as Gateway to the Western Angus Glens. The geology and wildlife are captured in a stunning diorama and an encyclopaedic multimedia programme.
Information services:
Special visitor services: Guided tours, tape recorded guides, materials and/or activities for children.
Services for disabled people: Displays and/or information at wheelchair height.
Collections:
Objects relating to the history of Kirriemuir and the Glens:
Pictish carved stones, civic and ecclesiastical material, literary and cultural artefacts, photographs
Publications list:
is available in hard copy.
Printed publications:
Leaflet
Poster
Bookmark

1505
KNARESBOROUGH CASTLE & MUSEUM
Castle Yard, Knaresborough, North Yorkshire, HG5 8AS

Tel: 01423 556188
Fax: 01423 556130
Email: lg12@harrogate.gov.uk
Formed: 1977

Organisation type and purpose: Local government body, historic building, house or site, suitable for ages: all ages.
Parent body:
Harrogate Borough Council

Enquiries to: Administrator
Access:
Access to staff: By letter, by telephone, by email, visitors by prior appointment
Access to building, collections or gallery: No prior appointment required
Hours: Good Fri to end Sep: daily, 1030 to 1700

General description:
Knaresborough's Royal Castle stands towering over the River Nidd. Attractions include The Keep, the mysterious underground Sallyport and an original Tudor Courtroom in the Castle's Old Courthouse Museum.
Information services:
Special visitor services: Guided tours, materials and/or activities for children.
Education services: Group education facilities, resources for Key Stages 1 and 2..
Collections:
Archaeology and local history
Catalogues:
Catalogue for part of the collections is only available in-house.
Printed publications:
Guidebook

Address for ordering publications:
Printed publications:
Harrogate Museum & Arts, Royal Pump Room Museum
Crown Place, Harrogate, HG1 2RY

Internet home pages:
http://www.harrogate.gov.uk/museums

1506
KNEBWORTH HOUSE

The Estate Office, Knebworth House, Knebworth, Hertfordshire, SG3 6PY

Tel: 01438 812661
Fax: 01438 811908
Email: info@knebworthhouse.com
Formed: 1490

Organisation type and purpose: Registered charity, historic building, house or site, suitable for ages: 5+.

Enquiries to: Administrator
Direct tel: 01438 810934
Direct email: j.birch@knebworthhouse.com
Other contacts: (1) Archivist (2) Group Bookings Organiser for (1) archive enquiries (2) group bookings..

Access:
Access to staff: By letter, by fax, by email, Internet web pages
Hours: Estate Office only Mon to Fri, 0900 to 1700
Access for disabled people: Parking provided, ramped entry, toilet facilities
Other restrictions: Ground floor access only for wheelchair users

General description:
Lytton Family home for 500 years.
Architecture - Tudor, Victorian Gothic, Sir Edward Lutyens.
Political links - Queen Elizabeth I, Cromwell, Victoria, Disraeli, Churchill.
Literary links - Owen Meredith (pseud Edward Bulwer Lytton), Dickens.
Other interest - British Raj, women's rights, rock concerts and filming.

Information services:
Library available for reference (for conditions see Access above)
Special visitor services: Guided tours, materials and/or activities for children.
Education services: Group education facilities, resources for Key Stages 1 and 2 and Further or Higher Education..

Collections:
Artefacts relating to all the subjects.

Internet home pages:
http://www.knebworthhousegiftshop.com
Gifts and publication ordering
http://www.knebworthhouse.com
Opening times, events, press page, film location info, special tours

1507
KNIGHTSHAYES COURT

Bolham, Tiverton, Devon, EX16 7RQ

Tel: 01884 254665, 01884 257381 (Visitor reception)
Fax: 01884 243050
Email: knightshayes@nationaltrust.org.uk

Organisation type and purpose: National organisation, registered charity (charity number 205846), historic building, house or site, suitable for ages: 5+.

Parent body:
The National Trust (South West Region)
Devon and Cornwall Regional Office, tel: 01985 843600

Enquiries to: Manager

Access:
Access to staff: By letter, by telephone, by fax, by email, Internet web pages
Access to building, collections or gallery: No prior appointment required
Hours: 22 Mar to end Sep, Mon, Tue, Wed, Thu, Sat, Sun, 1100 to 1730
Oct to beg Nov, Mon, Tue, Wed, Thu, Sat, Sun, 1100 to 1600
Open Good Friday
Access for disabled people: Parking provided, ramped entry, toilet facilities
Other restrictions: Designated parking. Drop-off point. 3 manual wheelchairs available. Ramped entrance. Ground floor fully accessible. Lift to 1st floor if visitors are able to stand. Level entrance to shop. Level entrance to restaurant. Grounds largely accessible. Garden on an incline but well routed for less able visitors. Recommended route map.

General description:
Designed by William Burges and begun in 1869, Knightshayes is a rare survival of his work. The rich interiors combine medieval romanticism with lavish Victorian decoration, and the smoking and billiard rooms, elegant boudoir and drawing room all give an atmospheric insight into grand country house life. A new room is open with original Burges interior designs, featuring Burges furniture and wall-paintings of eighty-three birds. The celebrated garden features a water lily pool and topiary, fine specimen trees, rare shrubs and delightful seasonal colours. Attractive woodland walks lead through the grounds.

Information services:
Braille guide. Audio guide. Handling collection. Scented plants.
Guided tours of house and garden for groups by arrangement during season and also on Sun during Nov and Dec.
Front-carrying baby slings for loan.
Suitable for school groups. Education room/centre. Hands-on activities. Children's guide. Children's quiz/trail. Adult study days.
Special visitor services: Materials and/or activities for children.
Education services: Group education facilities, resources for Key Stages 1 and 2 and 3.
Services for disabled people: For the visually impaired.

Internet home pages:
http://www.nationaltrust.org.uk/regions/devon

1508
KNOLE

Sevenoaks, Kent, TN15 0RP

Tel: 01732 462100
Fax: 01732 465528
Email: knole@nationaltrust.org.uk

Organisation type and purpose: National organisation, registered charity (charity number 205846), historic building, house or site, suitable for ages: 5+.

Parent body:
The National Trust (South and South East Region)
South East Regional Office, tel: 01372 453401

Enquiries to: Manager

Access:
Access to staff: By letter, by telephone, by fax, by email
Access to building, collections or gallery: No prior appointment required
Hours: House: End Mar to beg Nov, Wed to Sun, 1100 to 1600; open Bank Holiday Mondays
Park: daily for pedestrians only
Garden: May to Sept, first Wed in each month only, 1100 to 1600 (last admission 1500), by courtesy of Lord Sackville
Access for disabled people: Parking provided, ramped entry, toilet facilities
Other restrictions: Designated parking 30yds. Drop-off point. 2 manual wheelchairs available. Ground floor accessible with assistance, 1 step in Great Hall. No access to other floors. Photograph album. Virtual reality tour. All showrooms (other than the Great Hall) are on the first floor, accessible by stairs. Ramped entrance to shop. Level entrance to tea-room. Surrounding area is very hilly and unsuitable for some types of wheelchair.

General description:
One of the great treasure houses of England, set in a magnificent deer park. The original 15th century house was enlarged and embellished in 1603 by the 1st Earl of Dorset, one of Queen Elizabeth's favourites, and has remained unaltered ever since - a rare survival. The thirteen state rooms open to the public contain magnificent collections: 17th century royal Stuart furniture, including three state beds, silver furniture and the prototype of the famous Knole Settee, outstanding tapestries and textiles, and important portraits by Van Dyck, Gainsborough, Lely, Kneller and Reynolds.

Information services:
Helpline available, tel no: Infoline 01732 450608.
Guided tours for groups (15+ by arrangement).
Virtual reality tour of showrooms. Children's period costume events and family activities (tel. for details). Concerts in the Great Hall and courtyard. Easter egg trails.
Braille guide. Large-print guide. Touch list. Sympathetic Hearing Scheme.
Front-carrying baby slings for loan.
Suitable for school groups. Education room/centre. Hands-on activities. Children's quiz/trail. Family activity packs.
Special visitor services: Materials and/or activities for children.
Education services: Group education facilities, resources for Key Stages 1 and 2, 3 and 4.
Services for disabled people: For the visually impaired; for the hearing impaired.

Internet home pages:
http://www.nationaltrust.org.uk

1509
KNOWSLEY MUSEUM SERVICE

Prescot Museum, 34 Church Street, Prescot, Knowsley, Merseyside, L34 3LA

Tel: 0151 430 7787
Fax: 0151 430 7219
Email: prescot.museum.dlcs@knowsley.gov.uk
Formed: 1982

Organisation type and purpose: Local government body, museum, suitable for ages: 5+.

Enquiries to: Manager
Other contacts: Curator (Horology) for specialist enquiries.

Access:
Access to staff: By letter, by telephone, by fax, by email, in person, visitors by prior appointment, Internet web pages
Access to building, collections or gallery: No prior appointment required
Hours: Tue to Sat, 1000 to 1300 and 1400 to 1700; Sun, 1400 to 1700
Access for disabled people: ramped entry

General description:
Local history, horology.

Information services:
Library available for reference (for conditions see Access above)
Outreach services.
Special visitor services: Guided tours, materials and/or activities for children.
Education services: Group education facilities, resources for Key Stages 1 and 2, 3, 4 and Further or Higher Education.
Services for disabled people: For the visually impaired; displays and/or information at wheelchair height.

Collections:
National collection of clocks and watches

Catalogues:
Catalogue for library is in-house only. Catalogue for all of the collections is only available in-house.

Internet home pages:
http://www.knowsley.gov.uk/leisure/museum

1510
KYMIN, THE

Naval Temple and Round House, Monmouth, Gwent, NP25 3SE

Tel: 01600 719241(Custodian)
Fax: 01600 719241

continued overleaf

Organisation type and purpose: Registered charity, historic building, house or site, suitable for ages: all ages.
Parent body:
The National Trust Office for Wales
Tel: 01492 860123

Enquiries to: Custodian
Access:
Access to staff: By letter, by telephone, by fax, by email
Access to building, collections or gallery: No prior appointment required
Hours: Apr to Oct, Sun and Mon, 1100 to 1600
Other restrictions: Round House: last entry 1545
Access for disabled people: ramped entry
Other restrictions: Transfer available. Ramped entrance. Accessible entrance via kitchen. Ground floor fully accessible. No access to other floors. Pleasure grounds are mostly lawns.

General description:
Once visited by Nelson and set in 4ha (9 acres) of woods and pleasure grounds, this property encompasses a small two-storey circular Georgian banqueting house and naval temple, a monument dedicated to the glories of the British Navy. The hilltop grounds near Monmouth in the Wye valley afford spectacular views of the surrounding countryside. After substantial renovations in 2001, the banqueting house was opened to the public for the first time in spring 2002.

Internet home pages:
http://www.nationaltrust.org.uk

1511
LACE GUILD

The Hollies, 53 Audnam, Stourbridge, West Midlands, DY8 4AE

Tel: 01384 390739
Fax: 01384 444415
Email: hollies@laceguild.org
Full name: The Lace Guild
Formed: 1976

Organisation type and purpose: International organisation, national organisation, membership association (membership is by subscription), present number of members: 5000 approx, registered charity (charity number 274397), museum, suitable for ages: all ages.
Registered museum no RD 1950.
The role of The Lace Guild is to promote understanding and appreciation of all aspects of lace and lacemaking.

Enquiries to: Secretary
Other contacts: Headquarters staff for available on a daily basis.
Access:
Access to staff: By letter, by telephone, by fax, by email, visitors by prior appointment, Internet web pages
Hours: Mon to Fri, 0900 to 1600
Access to building, collections or gallery: Prior appointment required

General description:
All aspects of lace including: history (social and technical); making of all English and most European bobbin, needle and craft laces; equipment and materials; publications; exhibitions; courses.
Collections:
Collections of lace and lace-related artefacts, including patterns, tools, materials, sample books
Comprehensive library of books, magazines (from around the world), photographs, documents and study folios covering every aspect of lace
Catalogues:
Catalogue for library is published. Catalogue for part of the collections is only available in-house.
Printed publications:
Information leaflets
Instruction books
Magazine and Newsletter (quarterly, members)
Patterns and Pattern books
Young Lacemakers Magazine

Internet home pages:
http://www.laceguild.demon.co.uk
Home page with links to: About the Guild; Craft of Lace; Lace magazine; events; publications; suppliers.

1512
LACE MARKET CENTRE

See - Museum of Nottingham Lace

1513
LACKHAM MUSEUM OF AGRICULTURE AND RURAL LIFE

Wiltshire College Lackham, Lacock, Chippenham, Wiltshire, SN15 2NY

Tel: 01249 466847
Fax: 01249 444474
Email: daviaj@wiltscoll.ac.uk
Formed: 1946
Formerly: Lackham Museum, date of change, 2001

Organisation type and purpose: Independently owned, registered charity (charity number 1085573), museum, suitable for ages: 5+.
Parent body:
Lackham Museum of Agriculture and Rural Life Trust

Enquiries to: Curator
Access:
Access to staff: By letter, by telephone, by fax, by email, visitors by prior appointment
Access to building, collections or gallery: Prior appointment required
Hours: Seasonal openings - please telephone for details
Access for disabled people: Parking provided, level entry, toilet facilities
Other restrictions: Partial ramped entry.

General description:
A collection housed in a reconstructed threshing barn and granaries, with an exhibition area concentrating on rural crafts; engines and machinery; farming; and butter and cheese making. Artefacts, books and papers relating to Wiltshire agriculture and rural life.
Information services:
Special visitor services: Guided tours, materials and/or activities for children.
Education services: Group education facilities, resources for Key Stages 1 and 2, 3 and Further or Higher Education.
Services for disabled people: Displays and/or information at wheelchair height.
Collections:
Brown & May portable steam engine
Wiltshire wagons and carts
Historic agricultural buildings - barns and granaries
Shepherd's lambing hut
Fixed barn threshing machine, ploughs, seed drills
'Waterloo Boy' John Deere Overtime Tractor
Catalogues:
Catalogue for all of the collections is only available in-house.

1514
LACOCK ABBEY AND FOX TALBOT MUSEUM AND VILLAGE

Lacock, Chippenham, Wiltshire, SN15 2LG

Tel: 01249 730227 (Abbey), 01249 730459 (Museum)
Fax: 01249 730227 (Abbey), 01249 730501 (Museum/Estate Office)
Formed: 1232

Organisation type and purpose: Registered charity (charity number 205846), museum, historic building, house or site, suitable for ages: 8+.
Parent body:
The National Trust (South West Region)
Wessex Regional Office, tel: 01985 843600
Other addresses:
The National Trust
36 Queen Anne's Gate, London, SW1H 9AS, tel: 0870 609 5380, fax: 020 7222 5097

Enquiries to: Custodian
Other contacts: Property Manager
Access:
Access to staff: By letter, by telephone, by fax, visitors by prior appointment
Access to building, collections or gallery: No prior appointment required
Hours: Museum, Cloisters and Garden: Mar to beg Nov, daily, 1100 to 1730;
Abbey: end Mar to beg Nov, Mon, Wed to Sun, 1300 to 1730
Other restrictions: Abbey closed Tuesdays. Closed Good Friday.
Museum (only) open winter weekends, but closed 20 Dec to 28 Dec.
Prior appointment required for guided tours.
Access for disabled people: Parking provided, ramped entry, toilet facilities
Other restrictions: Drop-off point. 2 manual wheelchairs available. 1 single-seater powered mobility vehicle. Steps to entrance. Ground floor largely accessible, access inside Abbey is difficult with 3 sets of steps. Ramped access into Abbey cloisters. No access to other floors. Photograph album. Ramped entrance to shop. Grounds largely accessible. Recommended route map. Grounds - level.

General description:
Founded in 1232 and converted into a country house c.1540, the fine medieval cloisters, sacristy, chapter house and monastic rooms of the Abbey have survived largely intact. The handsome 16th century stable courtyard has half-timbered gables, a clockhouse, brewery and bakehouse. The Victorian woodland garden boasts a fine display of spring flowers, magnificent trees, an 18th century summer house, Victorian rose garden, newly restored botanic garden and ha-ha. The Museum of Photography commemorates the achievements of a former resident of the Abbey, William Henry Fox Talbot (1800-77), inventor of the negative/positive photographic process and whose descendants gave the Abbey and village to the Trust in 1944. The village dates from the 13th century and has many limewashed half-timbered and stone houses.
Information services:
Suitable for school groups. Education room/centre (telephone 01294 730141). Children's guide. Children's quiz/trail.
Guided tours by arrangement.
Braille guide. Large-print guide. Audio guide.
Front-carrying baby slings for loan.
Special visitor services: Guided tours, materials and/or activities for children.
Education services: Group education facilities.
Services for disabled people: For the visually impaired.
Collections:
General country house contents eg furniture and paintings
Fox Talbot Collection - early history of photography and William Henry Fox Talbot held in museum gates of Abbey
Catalogues:
Catalogue for library is in-house only. Catalogue for part of the collections is only available in-house.
Printed publications:
Guide Book (£2)
Colour Souvenir (£2.50)
Children's Guide (50p)
Short Guide (50p)

Internet home pages:
http://www.nationaltrust.org.uk/regions/wessex

See also - Fox Talbot Museum

1515
LADY LEVER ART GALLERY

National Museums & Galleries on Merseyside, Port Sunlight Village, Bebbington, Liverpool, L62 5EQ

Tel: 0151 478 4136

Organisation type and purpose: Art gallery, suitable for ages: all ages.
Parent body:
National Museums & Galleries on Merseyside (NMGM)

Enquiries to: Curator
Other contacts: Marketing Manager for advertising.
Access:
Access to building, collections or gallery: No prior appointment required
Hours: Mon to Sat, 1000 to 1700; Sun, 1200 to 1700

General description:
A collection of British paintings and sculpture 1750-1930, especially 18th century portraits and Pre-Raphaelite paintings. There is also British and European furniture 1500-1830, Chinese porcelain (17th and 18th century), Wedgwood pottery, and examples of 17th and 18th century English embroidery.
Collections:
The 'New Sculpture' 1880-1920
Collections related to the history of Freemasonry
Old Master drawings
English commodes 1750-1800
Greek vases
Chinese porcelain, enamels and hardstones
European straw-work
Publications list:
is available in hard copy.

Internet home pages:
http://www.nmgm.org.uk

1516
LADY WATERFORD HALL

Cornhill-on-Tweed, Northumberland

Tel: 01890 820338

Organisation type and purpose: Historic building, house or site, suitable for ages: 8+.

Enquiries to: Curator
Access:
Access to staff: By letter, by telephone
Access to building, collections or gallery: No prior appointment required
Hours: Easter to Oct, daily, 1030 to 1230, 1330 to 1730
Other restrictions: Out of season by appointment

General description:
The village school built by Lady Waterford in 1860 which she decorated with murals, illustrating people living in the village at the time.

1517
LAIDHAY CROFT MUSEUM

Dunbeath, Caithness, KW6 6EH

Tel: 01593 731244
Formed: 1974

Organisation type and purpose: Independently owned, registered charity, museum, suitable for ages: 5+.
Agricultural museum and household artefacts.
Parent body:
Laidhay Preservation Trust

Enquiries to: Secretary
Access:
Access to staff: By letter, by telephone, in person, charges made to all users
Access for disabled people: access to all public areas, toilet facilities

General description:
A typical north of Scotland thatched croft long-house and a cruck constructed barn. Agricultural history, life in a croft-building which was derived from a long-house or byre-building, common prior to the 18th and 19th centuries. Displays include croft machinery; implements; and household artefacts. Some items were in common use until World War II.
Information services:
Special visitor services: Guided tours.
Education services: Group education facilities..
Catalogues:
Catalogue for all of the collections is only available in-house.
Printed publications:
The Caithness Croft (1976)

1518
LAING ART GALLERY

New Bridge Street, Newcastle, Newcastle upon Tyne, NE1 8AG

Tel: 0191 232 7734
Minicom no. 0191 211 2129/2127
Fax: 0191 222 0952
Email: laing@twmuseums.org.uk
Formed: 1901
Formed from: Tyne & Wear Museums (TWM)
Formerly: Tyne & Wear Museums (TWM)

Organisation type and purpose: Local government body, registered charity, art gallery, suitable for ages: 5+.
Parent body:
Tyne and Wear Museums (TWM)
Discovery Museum, Blandford Square, Newcastle upon Tyne, NE1 4JA, tel: 0191 232 6789, fax: 0191 230 2614, email: sharon.granville@tyne-wear-museums.org.uk

Enquiries to: Curator
Other contacts: Education Officer for school Visits and Activities.
Access:
Access to staff: By letter, by telephone, by fax, by email, visitors by prior appointment
Other restrictions: By appointment only.
Access to building, collections or gallery: No prior appointment required
Hours: Mon to Sat, 1000 to 1700, Sun, 1400 to 1700
Other restrictions: Public displays and exhibitions only.
Access for disabled people: access to all public areas, toilet facilities

General description:
The Laing Art Gallery combines a permanent display of works with a wide-ranging exhibition programme that caters for all tastes and ages. The Baroque style building is home to a collection with a designated status of national and international significance. Works from the collection can be seen along with a popular and high profile temporary exhibition programme of both historical and contemporary art.
Information services:
Special visitor services: Guided tours, materials and/or activities for children.
Education services: Group education facilities, resources for Key Stages 1 and 2, 3, 4 and Further or Higher Education.
Services for disabled people: For the visually impaired; for the hearing impaired; displays and/or information at wheelchair height.
Collections:
The Laing houses an extensive collection of British oil paintings, watercolours, ceramics, silver and glassware
The collections are of national and international significance and are of designated status
Key works include:
Isabella and the Pot of Basil by William Holman Hunt
Laus Veneris by Edward Coley Burne-Jones
An important group of works by John Martin
Catalogues:
Catalogue for all of the collections is only available in-house.
Publications list:
is available in hard copy.

Address for ordering publications:
Printed publications:
Commercial Department, Tyne and Wear Museums
Newcastle Discovery, Blandford Square, Newcastle upon Tyne, NE1 4JA, tel: 0191 2326789, fax: 0191 2302614, email: vera.faulkner@tyne-wear-museums.org.uk

Internet home pages:
http://www.twmuseums.org.uk
Facilities, galleries, collections, education activities.

1519
LAING MUSEUM

High Street, Newburgh, Fife, KY15 0LA

Tel: 01337 883016 / 01334 412933
Fax: 01334 413214
Email: museums.east@fife.gov.uk

Organisation type and purpose: Local government body, museum, suitable for ages: 5+.
Parent body:
Fife Council Museums East
County Buildings, St Catherine Street, Cupar, KY15 4TA, tel: 01334 412933, fax: 01334 413214, email/website: museums.east@fife.gov.uk

Enquiries to: Museum Access Co-ordinator
Access:
Access to staff: By letter, by telephone, by fax, by email
Access to building, collections or gallery: No prior appointment required
Hours: Apr to Sep: daily, 1200 to 1700
Other restrictions: Prior appointment for research etc.

General description:
Displays tell of Alexander Laing who collected artefacts and books - the foundation of the museum and library.
Temporary exhibitions on local themes.
Information services:
Special visitor services: Materials and/or activities for children..
Collections:
Collections are part of Fife Council Museums East - local history, material associated with Alexander Laing, archaeology

1520
LAKE DISTRICT VISITOR CENTRE AT BROCKHOLE

Windermere, Cumbria, LA23 1LJ

Tel: 01539 446601
Minicom no. 01539 731263
Fax: 01539 445555
Formed: 1950

Organisation type and purpose: Historic building, house or site, suitable for ages: 5+.
Visitor Centre for the Lake District National Park.
Parent body:
Lake District National Park Authority (LDNPA)

Enquiries to: Manager
Direct email: helenlister@lake-district.gov.uk
Access:
Access to staff: In person
Access for disabled people: Parking provided, level entry, toilet facilities

General description:
The Lake District National Park.
Information services:
Special visitor services: Guided tours, tape recorded guides.
Education services: Group education facilities, resources for Key Stages 1 and 2, 3, 4 and Further or Higher Education.

continued overleaf

Services for disabled people: For the visually impaired; for the hearing impaired; displays and/or information at wheelchair height.
Publications list:
is available on-line.
Printed publications:
Many publications concerning: walking routes both easy and more demanding, town trails, lake user guides, safety and codes of conduct, LDNPA Properties, education, planning and conservation advice, LDNP management, byelaws (very many free of charge)
Lime Kilns in the Lake District
Honister Slate Mines & Quarries
National Park News (residents newsletter)
Lake Windermere Newsletter
Members Information Bulletin
Welcome to the Lake District National Park
Local Information Points
Events for Children and Families
Grasmere: A Contrasting Locality in a Mountain Environment (education pack, £18 inc p&p)
Electronic and video products:
Victorian Tourism and Change (CD-ROM, £15)

Internet home pages:
http://www.lake-district.gov.uk
Information on the 880 square miles the Lake District National Park covers

1521
LAKELAND ARTS TRUST
See - Abbot Hall Art Gallery; Kendal Museum

1522
LAKELAND MOTOR MUSEUM
Holker Hall and Gardens, Cark-in-Cartmel, Grange-over-Sands, South Lakeland, Cumbria, LA11 7PL

Tel: 015395 58509
Fax: 015395 58509
Formed: 1978

Organisation type and purpose: Museum, suitable for ages: 5+.
Preservation of motoring heritage.

Enquiries to: Manager
Access:
Access to staff: By letter, by telephone, by fax
Access for disabled people: Parking provided, ramped entry, toilet facilities
Other restrictions: Access to all areas except for small first floor exhibition area.

General description:
A nostalgic reminder of transport bygones offering a truly astonishing insight into our forefathers' inventiveness and dexterity. Classic and vintage cars, motor cycles, bicycles, scooters, tractors, engines and automobilia. Over 20,000 items tastefully presented in a quaint former shire horse stables setting. 1920s garage re-creation. Campbell Legend Bluebird Exhibition.
Information services:
Services for disabled people: For the visually impaired; for the hearing impaired.

1523
LAKESIDE AND HAVERTHWAITE RAILWAY
Haverthwaite Station, Ulverston, Cumbria, LA12 8AL

Tel: 01539 531594
Fax: 01539 531594
Formed: 1973

Organisation type and purpose: Voluntary organisation.
Steam Railway.

Enquiries to: Information Officer
Access:
Access to staff: By letter, by telephone, by fax, in person
Hours: Mon to Fri, 0900 to 1700

General description:
Steam railway operation.

Printed publications:
Timetable Brochure

1524
LAMB HOUSE
West Street, Rye, East Sussex, TN31 7ES

Tel: 01372 453401 (Regional Office)

Organisation type and purpose: National organisation, registered charity (charity number 205846), historic building, house or site.
Parent body:
The National Trust (South and South East Region)
South East Regional Office, tel: 01372 453401
Administered and largely maintained by:
a tenant

Enquiries to: Manager
Access:
Access to staff: By letter, by telephone

General description:
A delightful brick-fronted house dating from the early 18th century and typical of the attractive town of Rye. This was the home of writer Henry James from 1898 to 1916, and later of author E. F. Benson. Some of James's personal possessions can be seen and there is a charming walled garden.

Internet home pages:
http://www.nationaltrust.org.uk

1525
LAMB SCULPTURE STUDIO
24 Market Street, Montrose, Angus, DD10 8NB

Tel: 01674 673232
Formed: 1978
Formerly: William Lamb Memorial Studio, date of change, 2000

Organisation type and purpose: Local government body, museum, art gallery.
Parent body:
Montrose Museum & Art Gallery
Panmure Place, Montrose, DD10 8HE, tel: 01674 673232, email: montrose.museum@angus.gov.uk

Enquiries to: Curator
Access:
Access to staff: By letter, by telephone, by email, in person, visitors by prior appointment
Access for disabled people: level entry

General description:
The studio of William Lamb RSA (1893-1951), a native of Montrose and an artist of exceptional talent. The building houses many of his works, including busts of the Duchess of York, Princess Elizabeth and Princess Margaret Rose, Hugh Macdiarmid as well as native Montrosians. Bronze casts and plaster sculptures, woodcarvings, watercolours and books of his etchings.
Information services:
Organised activities - occasionally.
Annual clay-modelling competition.
Special visitor services: Guided tours, materials and/or activities for children..
Collections:
Sculptures in various mediums
Paintings - watercolours
Pen & ink drawings
Etchings
Work tools
Printed publications:
William Lamb Catalogue (£3)
William Lamb Cards (11p and 25p), Notepads (£1), Notelets (£1.50)

Address for ordering publications:
Printed publications:
Curator, Montrose Museum & Art Gallery
Panmure Place, Montrose, Angus, DD10 8HE, tel: 01674 673232

1526
LAMBEG INDUSTRIAL RESEARCH ASSOCIATION
Acronym or abbreviation: LIRA
See - Irish Linen Centre and Lisburn Museum

1527
LAMBRETTA SCOOTER MUSEUM
77 Alfred Street, Weston-Super-Mare, Somerset, BS23 1PP

Tel: 01934 614614
Fax: 01934 620120
Email: enquiries@westonscooterparts.co.uk
Formed: Aug 1986

Organisation type and purpose: Independently owned, museum, suitable for ages: 12+.
Private Collection.
Also:
Weston Scooter Parts
at the same address

Enquiries to: Manager
Direct tel: 01934 822075
Other contacts: Owner
Access:
Access to staff: By telephone, by fax, in person, visitors by prior appointment
Access to building, collections or gallery: No prior appointment required
Hours: Mon, Tue, 1000 to 1730; Thu, Fri, Sat, 1000 to 1730

General description:
Every model of Lambretta Scooters ever made from Oct 1947 to May 1971 and world's largest collection of memorabilia and accessories for Lammy's.
Printed publications:
Lambretta - An illustrated history (Cox N, publ Haynes Publishing of Yeovil, ISBN 1 85960 852 3 £14.99, can be signed by author if purchased)
Electronic and video products:
Brussels Rally 1960 (Video, £6)

Internet home pages:
http://www.westonscooterparts.co.uk

1528
LANARK GALLERY
116 North Vennel, Lanark, ML11 7PT

Tel: 01555 662565
Full name: Lanark Gallery Picture Framers
Formed: 2000

Organisation type and purpose: Independently owned, art gallery, suitable for ages: 16+.
Sales.

Enquiries to: Manager
Access:
Access to staff: By letter only
Access for disabled people: level entry, access to all public areas

General description:
Paintings by local artists; antique prints.
Collections:
Original paintings by local artists and leading Scottish artists
Comprehensive collection of antique prints

1529
LANARK MUSEUM
8 Westport, Lanark, ML11 9HD

Tel: 01555 666680
Email: user@lanark-museum.1n2home.co.uk
Full name: The Royal Burgh of Lanark Museum
Formed: 1988

Organisation type and purpose: Voluntary organisation, registered charity (charity number SCO 11883), museum, suitable for ages: 5+.
Member of:
South Lanarkshire Museums Forum

The Scottish Museums Council (SMC)
Registered museum with:
Resource

Enquiries to: Honorary Secretary
Other contacts: Keeper of Collections for enquiries on collections.
Access:
Access to staff: By letter, by telephone, by email, visitors by prior appointment, Internet web pages
Access to building, collections or gallery: No prior appointment required
Hours: Apr to Sep: Fri and Sat, 1030 to 1630
Library occasional evening and weekend access by appointment
Other restrictions: Visitors requiring access or information on collections or local history should arrange an appointment.

General description:
History of the Royal Burgh of Lanark, a collection of objects, documents and photography, tools (saddlers and stonemasons), early aviation meeting (1910), illustrating the social, commercial and industrial history of the town and surrounding area, particularly since the mid-12th century; weights and measures (Scottish); early aviation meeting (1910).
Information services:
CD-ROM based services
CD-ROM data and other databases accessible through terminal in museum display area, access by appointment or during museum opening hours.
Special visitor services: Guided tours, materials and/or activities for children.
Education services: Group education facilities..
Collections:
General collection of books, photographs, ephemera and artefacts connected with Lanark
Morrison & Marr Collections: mainly early 19th century, maps and plans, primarily Lanarkshire roads and railways
Lanark - Industry and Trade
Papers of the Caledonian Mineral Oil Co (1891-1906)
Papers of Lanark Gas Consumers Co (1906-1914)
Lanimer Collection:
Brochures, photographs and ephemera
Lawrie & Symington (Agricultural Auctioneers) Business Records: on deposit at South Lanarkshire railway archives
Morrison and Marr Collection:
Plans, maps, etc of roads, railways and buildings (c1813-1850)
Minute Books including:
Lanark Boat Club (1882-1900)
Lanark Female Society (1948-1992)
Lanark Toastmasters Club (1951-1986)
Photographic Collection:
3000+ 19th, 20th and 21 century, including collections of Lanimers, press photographs and Archibald Brown and Co
Printed publications:
Fancy Woodworkers (Archibald Brown and Co, Lanark, £2.50 inc p&p)
Price on application for the following publications:
Cleghorn Terra Cotta Company Limited 1895-1900
Handloom Weaving: A Cottage Industry of The Royal Burgh of Lanark
Paraffin Oil: The Oil Processing Industry in The Royal Burgh of Lanark
William Smellie MD

Internet home pages:
http://www.biggar-net.co.uk/lanarkmuseum
Basic information about museum and history of Lanark with details of current exhibition; related sites.

1530
LANCASHIRE COUNTY MUSEUM SERVICE
Stanley Street, Preston, Lancashire, PR1 4YP

Tel: 01772 264075
Fax: 01772 264079
Email: museum.enquiries@mus.lancscc.gov.uk
Formed: 1983
Formerly: County and Regimental Museums, date of change, 1997

Organisation type and purpose: Local government body, suitable for ages: all ages. Administrative body for the local government museums.
Parent body:
Lancashire County Council
County Hall, Preston, Lancashire
Museums, Galleries or Historic Sites:
Fleetwood Museum
Queens Terrace, Fleetwood, Lancashire, FY7 6BT, tel: 01253 876621, fax: 01253 878088, email/website: fleetwoodmuseum@museumoflancs.org.uk
Gawthorpe Hall
Padiham, Nr Burnley, BB12 8UA, tel: 01282 771004, fax: 01282 770178, email/website: gawthorpehall@museumoflancs.org.uk
Helmshore Textile Museums
Holcombe Road, Helmshore, Rosendale, Lancashire, BB4 4NP, tel: 01706 226459, fax: 01706 218554, email/website: helmshoremuseum@museumoflancs.org.uk
Judges' Lodgings
Church Street, Lancaster, LA1 1YS, tel: 01524 32808, email/website: judgeslodgings.lcc@btinternet.com
Museum of Lancashire
Stanley Street, Preston, PR1 4YP, tel: 01772 264075, fax: 01772 264079
Queen Street Mill
Harle Skye, Burnley, Lancashire, BB10 2HX, tel: 01282 412555, fax: 01282 430220
Turton Tower
Chapeltown Road, Turton, Nr Bolton, Lancashire, BL7 0HG, tel: 01204 852203, fax: 01204 853759, email/website: turtontower.lcc@btinternet.com

Enquiries to: Marketing Assistant
Access:
Access to staff: By letter, by telephone, by email, Internet web pages
Hours: Mon to Fri, 0900 to 1700
Access for disabled people: ramped entry, access to all public areas, toilet facilities

General description:
The subjects covered by the museums of Lancashire include: military history, local history, social history, maritime history, textile machinery, art, fine art, childhood collections, geology, natural science and conservation.

Internet home pages:
http://www.bringinghistoryalive.co.uk

See also - Fleetwood Museum; Gawthorpe Hall; Helmshore Textile Museums; Judges' Lodgings Museum; Museum of Lancashire; Queen Street Mill; Turton Tower

1531
LANCASHIRE MINING MUSEUM
closed to the public
See - Salford Museums Heritage Service

1532
LANCASHIRE REGIMENT AND RELATED MILITIA, VOLUNTEER, TERRITORIAL ARMY, HOME GUARD AND CADET UNITS
See - Queen's Lancashire Regimental Museum

1533
LANCASHIRE REGIMENT MUSEUM
See - Queen's Lancashire Regimental Museum

1534
LANCASTER CASTLE
Shire Hall, Castle Parade, Lancaster, LA1 1YJ

Tel: 01524 64998
Fax: 01524 847914
Email: christine.goodier@property.lancscc.gov.uk
Formed: 1954

Organisation type and purpose: Local government body, historic building, house or site, suitable for ages: 5+.

Enquiries to: Manager
Direct tel: 01772 263315
Direct fax: 01772 262825
Direct email: lynette.morrissey@property.lancscc.gov.uk
Access:
Access to staff: By letter, by telephone, by fax, by email, in person, visitors by prior appointment, Internet web pages
Access to building, collections or gallery: No prior appointment required
Hours: Daily, 1000 to 1700

General description:
Crime and punishment, monarchy, religious persecution, heraldry, witchcraft.
Information services:
Helpline available, tel no: 01524 64998.
Special visitor services: Guided tours.
Education services: Resources for Key Stages 2 and 3..
Printed publications:
Guide Book
Information leaflets

Internet home pages:
http://www.lancastercastle.com

1535
LANCASTER CITY MUSEUMS
Market Square, Lancaster, LA1 1HT

Tel: 01524 64637
Fax: 01524 841692
Email: awhite@lancaster.gov.uk
Formed: 1923

Organisation type and purpose: Local government body, museum, suitable for ages: 5+.
Parent body:
Lancaster City Council
at the same address
Comprises 3 local Government Museums and a trustee museum:
King's Own Regimental Museum
Supported by:
Friends of Lancaster City Museum
at the same address
Museum sites:
City Museum
same address
Cottage Museum
15 Castle Hill, Lancaster
Lancaster Maritime Museum
St George's Quay, Lancaster, LA1 1RB, tel: 01524 64637, fax: 01524 841692, email/website: awhite@lancaster.gov.uk

Enquiries to: Head of Museums Service
Access:
Access to staff: By letter, by telephone, by fax, by email, in person, visitors by prior appointment, Internet web pages
Hours: Mon to Sat, 1000 to 1700
Other restrictions: Prior appointment preferred.
Access to building, collections or gallery: No prior appointment required
Hours: Mon to Sat, 1000 to 1700
Other restrictions: Closed Christmas and New Year.
Access for disabled people: ramped entry, access to all public areas

continued overleaf

General description:
King's Own Royal Regiment, maritime history, archaeology, local history, social history, costume, numismatics, fine art, decorative art, transport, military history.
Information services:
Catalogue for all the collections also online via web (basic level).
Guided tours on request.
Special visitor services: Guided tours, materials and/or activities for children.
Education services: Group education facilities, resources for Key Stages 1 and 2, 3, 4 and Further or Higher Education.
Services for disabled people: For the visually impaired; displays and/or information at wheelchair height.
Collections:
Archive and library relating to the King's Own Royal Regiment (Lancaster) (inc important MSS)
Catalogues:
Catalogue for all of the collections is on-line.
Printed publications:
Exhibition leaflets (*c.* 2 times a year)
Exhibition lists (annually)
Local history publications (21 titles), irregular additions, for sale
Museum guidebooks (2) for sale
Subject leaflets (12, irregular additions, for sale)

Internet home pages:
http://www.lancaster.gov.uk/
Brief history, opening hours, brief details of collections.

See also - Cottage Museum; Lancaster Maritime Museum

1536
LANCASTER MARITIME MUSEUM

Custom House, St. George's Quay, Lancaster, LA1 1RB

Tel: 01524 64637
Fax: 01524 841692
Formed: 1985

Organisation type and purpose: Local government body, museum, art gallery.
Supported by:
Friends of Lancaster Maritime Museum
Outstation of:
Lancaster City Museums
Old Town Hall, Lancaster, LA1 1HT, tel: 01524 64637, fax: 01524 841692

Enquiries to: Head of Museums
Direct tel: 01524 64637 ext 28
Direct email: awhite@lancaster.gov.uk
Access:
Access to staff: By letter, by telephone, by email, in person, visitors by prior appointment
Access to building, collections or gallery: No prior appointment required
Hours: Easter to Oct: Mon to Sun, 1100 to 1700
Nov to Easter: Mon to Sun, 1230 to 1600
Other restrictions: Closed Christmas and New Year.
Access for disabled people: level entry, access to all public areas, toilet facilities
Other restrictions: Audio loops.

General description:
Maritime history of Lancaster, Morecambe and the coast of Morecambe Bay including Heysham, Glasson Dock and Sunderland Point.
Lancaster Canal; River Lune; Lancaster Port Commission; Shipbreaking at Morecambe 1905 to 1933; Irish Sea Shipping services to Ireland and the Isle of Man; local shipbuilding. Deals with local inshore fishing, Lancaster's 18th century Atlantic trade (including slavery).
Collections:
U B Shaw Collection of Lancaster Port Commission material
John Walker photograph collection of local shipping and coastal activity, c.1890-1914, c. 1500 images
Willmott Collection of Heysham Harbour and Irish Sea Shipping ephemera and photographs, 1950s-1960s, c. 300 images
Catalogues:
Catalogue for part of the collections is only available in-house.
Printed publications:
Series of local studies booklets

1537
LANDGUARD FORT

Viewpoint Road, Landguard Point, Felixstowe, Suffolk, IP11 7JG

Parent body:
English Heritage (East of England Region)
Brooklands, 24 Brooklands Avenue, Cambridge, CB2 2BU, tel: 01223 582700, fax: 01223 582701
Managed by:
Landguard Fort Trust
Access:
Access to staff: By letter, by telephone

General description:
18th century fort.

See also - Felixstowe Museum

1538
LANDMARK HERITAGE PARK

Carrbridge, Inverness-shire, PH23 3AJ

Tel: 01479 841613
Fax: 01479 841384
Formed: 1970

Organisation type and purpose: Independently owned, suitable for ages: all ages.
Heritage and adventure park.
Member of:
Association of Scottish Visitor Attractions (ASVA)
Stirling

Enquiries to: Manager
Other contacts: (1) Shop Manager; (2) Operations Manager
Access:
Access to staff: By letter, by telephone, by fax, by email, in person, charges made to all users
Access to building, collections or gallery: No prior appointment required
Hours: Daily, 1000 to 1700
Summer: daily, 1000 to 1800
Access for disabled people: Parking provided, ramped entry, toilet facilities
Other restrictions: Access to most areas.

General description:
Covers Scottish forestry tools and equipment. Also features a general exhibition and multivision show on Highland life, and the natural history of Scots pine.

1539
LANDMARK TRUST, THE

Shottesbrooke, Maidenhead, Berkshire, SL6 3SW

Tel: 01628 825920
Fax: 01628 825417
Formed: 1965

Organisation type and purpose: Registered charity (charity number 243312).
Building preservation charity.

Enquiries to: Public Relations Manager
Access:
Access to staff: By letter
Hours: Mon to Fri, 0900 to 1700

General description:
Restoration of historic buildings for self-catering holidays all year round.
Collections:
A photo slide library of all the Trust buildings, black and white prints of a survey before restoration but concentrating on the buildings after restoration
Printed publications:
Handbook (approximately once a year)
Legacy leaflets and brochures (occasional)
Newsletter (2 times a year)
Price List (annually)

Internet home pages:
http://www.landmarktrust.co.uk

1540
LANERCOST PRIORY

Lanercost, Brampton, Cumbria

Tel: 01697 73030

Organisation type and purpose: National organisation, historic building, house or site, suitable for ages: all ages.
Parent body:
English Heritage (North West Region)
Canada House, 3 Chepstow Street, Manchester, M1 5FW, tel: 0161 242 1400

Enquiries to: Custodian
Access:
Access to staff: By letter, by telephone
Access to building, collections or gallery: No prior appointment required
Hours: Apr to Sep: daily, 1000 to 1800
Oct: daily, 1000 to 1700
Other restrictions: Opening times are subject to change, for up-to-date information contact English Heritage by phone or visit the website.

General description:
12th century Augustinian Priory ruins. Situated near the Scottish border in Cumbria are the impressive remains of this 12th century Augustinian priory. From the relative tranquillity of Lanercost's life as a monastic house, to its involvement in the turbulent Anglo-Scottish wars of the 14th century and eventual dissolution under Henry VIII, the history of the priory is a rich and diverse one.
Information services:
Special visitor services: Tape recorded guides..

Internet home pages:
http://www.english-heritage.org.uk

1541
LANGTON MATRAVERS MUSEUM

Barton, The Hyde, Langton Matravers, Swanage, Dorset, BH19 3HE

Tel: 01929 423168
Email: localhistory@langtonia.org.uk
Formed: 1972
Incorporates: The Coach House Museum, The Museum of the Purbeck Stone Industry

Organisation type and purpose: Independently owned, registered charity (charity number 272407), museum, suitable for ages: 5+, research organisation.
To research, collect, publish and display information on the history of the Parish of Langton Matravers.
Parent body:
Langton Matravers Local History and Preservation Society
at the same address

Enquiries to: Honorary Curator
Access:
Access to staff: By letter, by telephone, by email, visitors by prior appointment, Internet web pages
Access for disabled people: Parking provided, level entry, access to all public areas

General description:
Local history, family history, local industries including Purbeck stone.
Information services:
Education services: Group education facilities, resources for Key Stages 1 and 2, 3, 4 and Further or Higher Education.
Services for disabled people: For the visually impaired; for the hearing impaired.

Catalogues:
Catalogue for library is in-house only. Catalogue for all of the collections is only available in-house.
Publications list:
is available in hard copy and online.
Printed publications:
A selection of publications in print include:
A Langton Quarrier's Apprentice (£1.60)
A Langton Smuggler - The story of smuggled brandy in the roof of St Georges Parish Church (£0.80)
Langton's Stone Quarries - History of the local stone and 'Marble' and the men who worked them (£0.80)
The Ancient Order of Purbeck Marblers and Stone Cutters - A mediaeval guild (£1.50)
A further 34 publications are planned of which 4 will be published in the year 2000

Internet home pages:
http://www.langton.ia.org.uk

1542
LANHYDROCK
Bodmin, Cornwall, PL30 5AD

Tel: 01208 73320
Fax: 01208 74084
Email: lanhydrock@nationaltrust.org.uk
Formed: 1953

Organisation type and purpose: Registered charity (charity number 205846), historic building, house or site, suitable for ages: all ages.
Parent body:
The National Trust (South West Region)
Devon and Cornwall Regional Office, tel: 01208 74281

Enquiries to: Property Manager
Access:
Access to staff: By letter, by telephone, by email
Hours: Phone property for details
Access to building, collections or gallery: No prior appointment required
Hours: Mar to Sep: Tue to Sun, 1100 to 1730
Oct and Nov: Tue to Sun, 1100 to 1700
Open Bank Holiday Mondays
Access for disabled people: Parking provided, ramped entry, toilet facilities
Other restrictions: Access to most areas. Designated parking. Drop-off point. 4 manual wheelchairs available. 1 single-seater powered mobility vehicle, booking essential. Accessible entrance different from main entrance. Ground floor largely accessible, 3 steps down to Billiard Room. Lift to first floor. Photograph album. Steps to shop entrance. Ramped entrance to restaurant. Grounds partly accessible. Recommended route map.

General description:
One of the most fascinating late 19th century houses in England, full of period atmosphere and the trappings of a high Victorian country house. Although the gatehouse and north wing (with magnificent 32yd-long gallery with plaster ceiling) survive from the 17th century, the rest of the house was rebuilt following a disastrous fire in 1881 with the latest in contemporary living, including central heating. The garden features a stunning collection of magnolias, rhododendrons and camellias, and offers fine colours right through into autumn. All this is set in a glorious estate of 364ha (900 acres) of woods and parkland running down to the River Fowey. There is an extensive network of footpaths.
Information services:
Braille guide. Touch list.
Suitable for school groups. Education room. Hands-on activities. Children's guide. Children's quiz/trail. Children's play area. Organised activities in school holidays.
Front carrying baby slings for loan.
Special visitor services: Materials and/or activities for children.
Education services: Group education facilities, resources for Key Stages 1 and 2, 3 and 4.
Services for disabled people: For the visually impaired.

Collections:
Pictures by Lely, Kneller, Gainsborough, Reynolds and Richmond
Fine Collections of ceramics and furniture dating from the 17th century
Unique library formed by the 1st Earl Radnor (d.1685) consisting of many theological works
Good examples of Victorian domestic services
Catalogues:
Catalogue for library is in-house only. Catalogue for all of the collections is only available in-house.
Printed publications:
Full House Guide (£2.95)
Short House Guide (50p)
Childrens Guide (£1.60)
Park Guide (£1)
Electronic and video products:
Lanhydrock: A Tale of Two Eras (vidoe, £9)

Address for ordering publications:
Printed publications:
Shop Manager, National Trust Enterprises Ltd

Internet home pages:
http://www.nationaltrust.org.uk/regions/cornwall

1543
LANMAN MUSEUM
The Castle, Framlingham, Woodbridge, Suffolk, IP13 9BP

Tel: 01728 724189

Organisation type and purpose: Museum, suitable for ages: all ages.
Parent body:
English Heritage (East of England Region)
Brooklands, 24 Brooklands Avenue, Cambridge, CB2 2BU, tel: 01223 582700, fax: 01223 582701
Access:
Access to staff: By letter, by telephone
Other restrictions: Closed 24 to 26 Dec and 1 Jan.

General description:
A local museum devoted to items collected from Framlingham and the surrounding villages. Its strengths include a good collection of prints, drawings and paintings of Framlingham and the Castle. The museum also has a collection of agricultural tools and a fine collection of local newspapers stretching back to 1859. A display of moated sites.
Collections:
Newspapers. Framlingham Weekly News. 1859-1938. Copy of all editions printed
Pictures. Drawings, prints, etc. 19th century. 50 plus.
Catalogues:
Catalogue for part of the collections is only available in-house.

See also - Framlingham Castle

1544
LANREATH FARM & FOLK MUSEUM
Lanreath, Looe, Cornwall, PL13 2NX

Tel: 01503 220321
Formed: 1973

Organisation type and purpose: Independently owned, professional body, museum, suitable for ages: all ages.

Enquiries to: Curator
Access:
Access to building, collections or gallery: No prior appointment required
Hours: Easter to 31 Oct: Mon to Sun, 1000 to 1800
Access for disabled people: Parking provided, level entry, access to all public areas

General description:
Farm machinery, plus much more. Many exhibits are of particular local interest, reflecting the Cornish countryside of yesteryear. Includes kitchen utensils; barn machinery; oil engines; a Marshall road roller; a Rack bench; an Allen excavator; radios from the 1920s onwards; telephones; and typewriters.
Printed publications:
Catalogues of exhibits

1545
LANTERN GALLERY OF FINE ART
18 South Guildry Sreet, Elgin, Moray, IV30 1QN

Tel: 01343 546864
Fax: roynmunn@aol.com
Formed: 1997

Organisation type and purpose: Independently owned, art gallery, suitable for ages: 16+.

Enquiries to: Owner
Access:
Access to staff: By letter, by telephone, by fax, in person
Hours: Tue to Sat, 1000 to 1700
Access to building, collections or gallery: No prior appointment required

General description:
Artistic impressions of landscapes, boats, birds, flowers and still life.

1546
LAPWORTH MUSEUM
School of Earth Sciences, University of Birmingham, Edgbaston, Birmingham, B15 2TT

Tel: 0121 414 7294
Fax: 0121 414 4942
Email: lapmus@bham.ac.uk
Full name: The Lapworth Museum of Geology
Formed: 1880

Organisation type and purpose: Museum, suitable for ages: 8+.

Enquiries to: Curator
Direct email: j.c.clatworthy@bham.ac.uk
Other contacts: Director
Access:
Access to staff: By letter, by telephone, by fax, by email, in person
Hours: Mon to Fri, 0900 to 1700
Access to building, collections or gallery: No prior appointment required
Hours: Mon to Fri, 0900 to 1700; Sat, Sun, 1400 to 1700
Access for disabled people: Parking provided, level entry

General description:
Rocks, minerals and fossils from the United Kingdom and around the world. There are particularly strong collections of West Midlands, Welsh Borders and Welsh fossil invertebrates, and also of fossil fish.
Information services:
Guided tours by arrangement.
Schools/Education: Loan Sets, evening lecture series and occasional weekend day schools
Special visitor services: Guided tours.
Education services: Group education facilities, resources for Key Stages 1 and 2, 3, 4 and Further or Higher Education..
Collections:
Dewey. Stone implements. 500 items
General Palaeontology Collections - 100,000 items (fossils from the UK and many important localities around the world)
Holcroft. Wenlock invertebrates 4000 items
Holcroft. Recent shells 1500 items
Ketley. Wenlock invertebrates 1650 items
Lapworth. Graptolites and other invertebrates 6000 items
Minerals. United Kingdom and international minerals 12,000 items
Type and figured. Illustrated fossil specimens 3500 items

continued overleaf

Humphreys Recent and fossil skulls and teeth 2000 items
Vertebrate. Fossil fish, reptiles and mammals 3000 items - All on a computer database
Archives: Letters, early maps and manuscripts etc, all of a geological nature - many thousands of items
Photographs: Photographs of a geological nature, 19th and early 20th century, includes approximately 6000 magic lantern slides

Catalogues:
Catalogue for part of the collections is only available in-house.

Internet home pages:
http://www.bham.ac.uk/EarthSciences/lapworth
Information regarding the museum and collections.

1547
LARGS AND DISTRICT HISTORICAL SOCIETY

Kirkgate House, 2 Manse Court, Largs, Ayrshire, KA30 8AW

Tel: 01475 687081
Formed: 1967

Organisation type and purpose: Museum.

Enquiries to: Curator
Access:
Access to staff: By letter only
Access to building, collections or gallery: No prior appointment required
Hours: Mid May to Mid Sep, Mon to Fri, 1400 to 1700

General description:
A local collection of books, papers, photographs, ephemera and artefacts illustrating the past of the burgh and parish of Largs.
Catalogues:
Catalogue for library is in-house only.

1548
LARGS MUSEUM

Kirkgate House, Manse Court, Largs, Ayrshire, KA30 8AW

Tel: 01475 687081
Formed: 1967

Organisation type and purpose: Museum.

Enquiries to: Curator
Access:
Access to staff: By letter only
Other restrictions: Staff - all volunteers - no fixed hours.
Access to building, collections or gallery: No prior appointment required
Hours: Mid May to Mid Sep: daily, 1400 to 1700
Other restrictions: Other times by prior appointment.
Access for disabled people: ramped entry

General description:
Local history.
Catalogues:
Catalogue for library is in-house only.
Publications list:
is available in hard copy.

1549
LASHENDEN AIR WARFARE MUSEUM

Headcorn Aerodrome, Ashford, Kent, TN27 9HX

Tel: 01622 890226 or 206783
Fax: 01622 206783
Telex: 966127
Email: lashairwar@aol.com
Formed: 1970

Organisation type and purpose: Membership association (membership is by election or invitation), present number of members: 25, voluntary organisation, registered charity (charity number 279883), museum, research organisation.

Enquiries to: Secretary
Direct tel: 01622 206783
Access:
Access to staff: By letter, by telephone, by fax, by email, in person
Hours: Mon to Sat, 0900 to 1700; Sun and Bank Holidays, 1030 to 1800
Access to building, collections or gallery: No access other than to staff
Access for disabled people: Parking provided, ramped entry, access to all public areas, toilet facilities

General description:
Contains relics showing aviation history from 1911 to date, including civilians at war and prisoners of war. Features a piloted prototype Fieseler F1 103 R4 (V1) flying bomb, and an FA 330 gyro kite.
Catalogues:
Catalogue for part of the collections is only available in-house.

1550
LAUDERDALE HOUSE ARTS & EDUCATION CENTRE

Lauderdale House, Waterlow Park, Highgate Hill, London, N6 5HG

Tel: 020 8348 8716
Minicom no. 020 8442 9189
Fax: 020 8442 9099
Email: admin@lauderdale.org.uk
Formed: 1978
Formerly: Lauderdale Community Art Centre

Organisation type and purpose: Registered charity (charity number 275502), art gallery, historic building, house or site, suitable for ages: all ages.
Arts and education centre.

Enquiries to: Director
Other contacts: General Manager
Access:
Access to staff: By telephone, by email, in person, visitors by prior appointment
Hours: By telephone: Mon to Fri, 1000 to 1800
Other restrictions: In person to reception only during access hours, visitors by prior appointment outside access hours.
All meetings by prior appointment.
Access to building, collections or gallery: No prior appointment required
Hours: Tue to Fri, 1100 to 1600; Sun, 1200 to 1700
Access for disabled people: Parking provided, toilet facilities
Other restrictions: Small ledge to level entry, access to all areas downstairs only.

General description:
Lauderdale House was built in 1582 as a merchant's house and has a number of architectural features demonstrating how it has evolved over the centuries. It has no permanent collection but currently runs as an arts and education centre featuring two art exhibitions (changes every two weeks) and a regular programme of jazz, cabaret, classical concerts, poetry readings, family days, children's shows, children's and adult classes.
Information services:
Special visitor services: Materials and/or activities for children..

Internet home pages:
http://www.lauderdale.org.uk

1551
LAUNCESTON CASTLE

Castle Lodge, Guildhall Square, Launceston, Cornwall, PL15 7DR

Tel: 01566 77365

Organisation type and purpose: National organisation, advisory body, historic building, house or site.

Parent body:
English Heritage (South West Region)
Tel: 0117 975 0700, fax: 0117 975 0701

Enquiries to: Manager
Access:
Access to staff: By letter, by telephone
Access to building, collections or gallery: No prior appointment required
Hours: 29 Mar to 30 Sep: daily, 1000 to 1800,1 to 31 Oct: daily, 1000 to 1700,1 Nov to 28 Mar: Fri to Sun, 1000 to 1300 and 1400 to 1600
Other restrictions: Closed 24 to 26 Dec and 1 Jan.
Opening times are subject to change, for up-to-date information contact English Heritage by phone or visit the website.

General description:
Launceston Castle is set on the high motte of a stronghold built soon after the Norman Conquest. It is not only an imposing fortress dominating the main routes to Cornwall, but was famously used as a jail for George Fox during the reign of Charles II. As the venue for the County Assizes and Jail, the castle witnessed the trials and hangings of numerous criminals, with the last execution recorded in 1821.

Internet home pages:
http://www.english-heritage.org.uk

1552
LAUREL AND HARDY MUSEUM

4C Upper Brook Street, Ulverston, Cumbria, LA12 7BH

Tel: 01229 582292
Fax: 01229 582292
Formed: 1976

Organisation type and purpose: Museum.

Enquiries to: Curator
Direct tel: 01229 861614
Access:
Access to staff: By letter, by telephone, by fax, in person, charges made to all users
Hours: Daily, 1000 to 1630; closed January
Access for disabled people: access to all public areas, toilet facilities

General description:
The lives and times of Stan Laurel and Oliver Hardy and their films.

1553
LAURENCE STERNE TRUST, THE

Shandy Hall, Coxwold, York, YO61 4AD

Tel: 01347 868465
Formed: 1967

Organisation type and purpose: Registered charity (charity number 529593), historic building, house or site.

Enquiries to: Curator
Access:
Access to staff: By letter, by telephone

General description:
Early 15th century house added to by Sterne contains an extensive collection of editions of Sterne's novels. Prints and paintings illustrating his work, ie 'Tristram Shandy' and 'A Sentimental Journey'.
Information services:
Special visitor services: Guided tours..
Collections:
Monkman collection of early editions of works of Laurence Sterne and related works, 1760-1990
Printed publications:
Laurence Sterne and Shandy Hall (Cash A M, £1)
The Shandean - an annual volume devoted to L Sterne and his works (£19)
Postcards (25p)

Internet home pages:
http://www.let.uu.nl/peter.devoogd/shandean/trust/html

1554
LAURISTON CASTLE

Cramond Road South, Davidson's Mains, Edinburgh, EH4 5QD

Tel: 0131 336 2060
Fax: 0131 312 7165
Formed: 1927

Organisation type and purpose: Local government body, museum, historic building, house or site, suitable for ages: 16+.
Part of:
The City of Edinburgh Museums and Galleries Service
Which is a division of:
The City of Edinburgh Council's Culture & Leisure Department
Tel: 0131 200 2000 (main Council) 0131 529 7844 (Culture & Leisure Department HQ)

Enquiries to: Custodian
Direct tel: 0131 529 4052
Access:
Access to staff: By letter, by telephone, by fax, by email, in person, visitors by prior appointment
Hours: Apr to Oct: Sat to Thu, 1100 to 1300 and 1400 to 1700
Nov to Mar: Sat, Sun, 1400 to 1600
Access for disabled people: Parking provided, toilet facilities

General description:
16th century tower house, with 18th and 19th century additions, standing in tranquil grounds overlooking the Firth of Forth at Cramond. The last private owners, the Reids, makers and collectors of fine furniture and objets d'art, left the property to the nation with the proviso that the interior should remain unchanged, a wealthy home of the Edwardian Era with rich collections. Lauriston contains strong collections of prints, paintings, tapestries, textiles, porcelain, Sheffield-Plate, Blue John and continental furniture.
Information services:
Special visitor services: Guided tours, tape recorded guides.
Education services: Group education facilities..
Catalogues:
Catalogue for all of the collections is published.
Publications list:
is available on-line.

Internet home pages:
http://www.cac.org.uk

1555
LAWNMOWER MUSEUM

See - British Lawnmower Museum

1556
LAWRENCE HOUSE MUSEUM

9 Castle Street, Launceston, Cornwall, PL15 8BA

Tel: 01566 773277

Parent body:
The National Trust

General description:
A collection primarily of local history from the Bronze Age to the present day, including Victorian/Edwardian collections. Includes feudal dues; agricultural implements; and a domestic room; and a feature on the Australian Connection (Launceston, Tasmania); local early settlers: Philip Gidley King, 3rd Governor New South Wales, William Bryant, James Ruse.

Internet home pages:
http://www.nationaltrust.org.uk

1557
LAXFIELD AND DISTRICT MUSEUM

The Guildhall, Laxfield, Woodbridge, Suffolk, IP13 8DU

Tel: 01986 798026
Formed: 1970

Organisation type and purpose: Museum, suitable for ages: 5+.

Enquiries to: Secretary
Other contacts: Chairman, tel: 01986 798460
Access:
Access to staff: By letter, by telephone

General description:
Contains exhibits of local relevance and interest, including local and family history; natural history; and geology. Permanent exhibits include an early 20th century shop scene; a rural domestic scene; rural tradesmen's tools and agricultural tools; toys; and geology. Also includes costumes and photographs. The material is mostly late 19th and early 20th century.
Catalogues:
Catalogue for part of the collections is only available in-house.

1558
LAYER MARNEY TOWER

Layer Marney, Colchester, Essex, CO5 9US

Tel: 01206 330784
Fax: 01206 330884
Formed: 1990

Organisation type and purpose: Historic building, house or site, suitable for ages: all ages.

Enquiries to: Administrator
Access:
Access to staff: By letter only
Access to building, collections or gallery: Prior appointment required
Hours: Apr to Oct, Sun to Fri, 1200 to 1700
Access for disabled people: Parking provided, ramped entry, toilet facilities
Other restrictions: Access to the tower is not possible, otherwise reasonable access

General description:
Fine pieces of Italianate terracotta on the beautiful Tudor Gatehouse with gardens, church, medieval barn, farm and long gallery.
Information services:
Tea room, shop and holiday cottage.
Special visitor services: Guided tours, materials and/or activities for children.
Education services: Group education facilities, resources for Key Stages 1 and 2 and 3..
Printed publications:
Guide books

1559
LEADHILLS AND WANLOCKHEAD RAILWAY

The Station, Leadhills, Lanarkshire, ML12 6XP

Tel: 01555 820778
Formed: 1983
Formerly: Lowthers Railway Society

Organisation type and purpose: Membership association (membership is by subscription), voluntary organisation.

Enquiries to: Secretary
Direct tel: 01506 464666
Direct fax: 01506 463030
Direct email: secretary@leadhillsrailway.co.uk
Access:
Access to staff: By email
Hours: Mon to Fri, 0900 to 1700

General description:
Railway preservation.
Printed publications:
The Leadhills and Wanlockhead Light Railway (the original branch line, 1901-38, 64pp illustrated, £5)

Internet home pages:
http://www.leadhillsrailway.co.uk
History, rolling stock, operating times.

1560
LEAMINGTON SPA ART GALLERY AND MUSEUM

The Royal Pump Rooms, The Parade, Leamington Spa, Warwickshire, CV32 4AA

Tel: 01926 742700
Fax: 01926 742705
Email: prooms@warwickdc.gov.uk
Formed: 1914
Formerly: Royal Pump Rooms Art Gallery and Museum; Warwick District Council Art Gallery and Museum, date of change, 1999

Organisation type and purpose: Local government body, museum, art gallery, historic building, house or site, suitable for ages: 5+.
To provide opportunities for everyone to benefit from, enjoy and participate in the creation, interpretation and preservation of the Arts and Heritage.
Parent body:
Warwick District Council (WDC)
Leisure and Amenities, Marlborough House, Holly Walk, Royal Leamington Spa, CV32 4UJ, tel: 01926 450000, fax: 01926 317867

Enquiries to: Heritage & Arts Manager
Direct tel: 01926 742708
Direct email: jwatkin@warwickdc.gov.uk
Other contacts: (1) Bookings Officer (2) Events and Exhibitions Officer for (1) booking rooms for private hire (2) events and exhibitions queries.
Access:
Access to staff: By letter, by telephone, by email, visitors by prior appointment
Access to building, collections or gallery: No prior appointment required
Hours: Tue, Wed, Fri, Sat, 1030 to 1700; Thu, 1330 to 2000; Sun, 1100 to 1600
Other restrictions: Closed Mon.
Admission free.
Access for disabled people: Parking provided, ramped entry, access to all public areas, toilet facilities

General description:
Art collections of local and national significance. 17th and 19th to 21st century. Craft by major British artists and makers; watercolours, prints, photographs, sculpture, ceramics and glass.
Social history: costume, numismatics, ethnography and archaeology. Local history displays in former Turkish Bath area.
Information services:
Changing temporary exhibitions.
Special visitor services: Materials and/or activities for children.
Education services: Group education facilities, resources for Key Stages 1 and 2, 3, 4 and Further or Higher Education.
Services for disabled people: For the visually impaired; for the hearing impaired; displays and/or information at wheelchair height.
Collections:
Paintings, drawings and sculpture, 1235+ items (includes Alderman Alfred Holt collection of 20th century British and continental paintings, 108 items)
Ceramics and glass, 660 items (includes F H Jahn collection of late 17th to early 19th century drinking glasses, 168 items)
Social History, 2623 items
Prints and photographs, 2987 items
Ethnography (Northern Europe, Asia, Africa, Oceania)
Printed publications:
Various postcards (45p and 50p)
Guide Book: The Royal Pump Rooms and the growth of Leamington Spa

Internet home pages:
http://www.royal-pump-rooms.co.uk/main.htm.
Access, history, sponsorship, opening times, services.
http://www.royal-pump-rooms.co.uk/tic.htm
http://www.royal-pump-rooms.co.uk/gallery
http://www.royal-pump-rooms.co.uk/library
http://www.royal-pump-rooms.co.uk/assembly
http://www.royal-pump-rooms.co.uk/café

1561
LEATHERHEAD & DISTRICT LOCAL HISTORY SOCIETY

Leatherhead Museum, Hampton Cottage, 64 Church Street, Leatherhead, Surrey, KT22 8DP

Tel: 01372 386348
Email: leatherheadmuseum@localhistory.free-online.co.uk
Full name: Leatherhead Museum of Local History
Formed: 1980

Organisation type and purpose: Independently owned, registered charity, museum, suitable for ages: 5+.
Owned and operated by:
Leatherhead & District Local History Society (LDLHS)
at the same address

Enquiries to: Curator
Access:
Access to staff: By letter, by telephone, by email, in person
Hours: Mon to Fri, 0900 to 1700

General description:
Covers local history relating to Leatherhead, Ashtead, Bookham and Fetcham, and the surrounding area, housed in a 17th century timber-framed cottage.
Collections:
Ashtead pottery. Art deco pottery. 1923-1935. ca. 100 items
Ronson and Goblin products
Victorian and Edwardian memorabilia
Artefacts and photographs of local interest
Catalogues:
Catalogue for library is in-house only. Catalogue for all of the collections is only available in-house.
Publications list:
is available on-line.

Internet home pages:
http://www.leatherheadlocalhistory.org.uk
Information regarding Society activities, publications and the Museum.

1562
LEBRECHT MUSIC COLLECTION

58b Carlton Hill, London, NW8 0ES

Tel: 020 7625 5341
Fax: 020 7625 5341
Email: pictures@lebrecht.co.uk or lebrecht @btopenworld.com
Formed: 1992

Organisation type and purpose: Consultancy, research organisation.
Picture library.
To supply classical music images for commercial clients ie specialist music magazines, publishers, newspapers, TV etc.

Enquiries to: Director
Access:
Access to staff: By letter, by telephone, by fax, by email, visitors by prior appointment
Hours: Mon to Fri, 0900 to 1700

General description:
Opera, choirs, music scores, concert halls, composers, instruments, musicians, singers, monuments of famous composers.
Collections:
Alan Bush Foundation
Kurt Weill Foundation
Martinu Archives
Royal Academy of Music Collection of Images
Publications list:
is available on-line.

Internet home pages:
http://www.lebrecht.co.uk

1563
LEEDS CASTLE

Maidstone, Kent, ME17 1PL

Tel: 01622 765400
Fax: 01622 767855
Email: info@leeds-castle.com
Formed: 1975

Organisation type and purpose: Registered charity (charity number 1413563), historic building, house or site.

Enquiries to: Public Relations Manager
Access:
Access to staff: By letter, by telephone, by email
Hours: Mon to Fri, 0900 to 1730
Access to building, collections or gallery: No prior appointment required
Hours: Mar to Oct: daily, 1000 to 1700
Nov to Feb: daily, 1000 to 1500
Access for disabled people: Parking provided, ramped entry, toilet facilities

General description:
Over the centuries, Leeds Castle has been a Norman Fortress, a royal residence to six of England's Medieval Queens, a palace to Henry VIII and subsequently, a private home until as recently as 1974. Today Leeds Castle has become a national treasure - faithfully restored and preserved by the Leeds Castle Foundation.
Information services:
Helpline available, tel no: 0870 600 8880.
Special visitor services: Guided tours, materials and/or activities for children.
Education services: Group education facilities, resources for Key Stages 1 and 2.
Services for disabled people: For the visually impaired; displays and/or information at wheelchair height.
Collections:
One of the finest collections of medieval furnishing, paintings and tapestries - a place where literally hundreds of years of history come to life
The Aviary is home to over 100 species of rare and tropical birds
The Dog Collar Museum houses the world's finest public collection of collars with exhibits dating back to the 16th century
Publications list:
is available in hard copy.
Printed publications:
Guide Book
The Birds of Leeds Castle
Four Centuries of Dog Collars at Leeds Castle
Lady Baillie at Leeds Castle

Internet home pages:
http://www.leeds-castle.com

1564
LEEDS CITY ART GALLERY

The Headrow, Leeds, West Yorkshire, LS1 3AA

Tel: 0113 247 8248
Fax: 0113 244 9689
Email: leedscityart.gallery@virgin.net
Formed: 1888

Organisation type and purpose: Local government body, art gallery, suitable for ages: all ages.
Parent body:
Leeds Museums and Galleries
Friends organisation:
Leeds Art Collections Fund (LACF)

Enquiries to: Curator
Other contacts: (1) Education Officer tel: 0113 247 8248; (2) Visitor Services Manager tel: 0113 249 6453 for (1) education (2) exhibitions.
Access:
Access to staff: By letter, by telephone, by fax, by email, visitors by prior appointment
Access to building, collections or gallery: No prior appointment required
Hours: Mon to Sat, 1000 to 1700; Wed, 1000 to 2000; Sun, 1300 to 1700
Other restrictions: Closed Bank Holidays.
Access for disabled people: ramped entry, toilet facilities
Other restrictions: Access to upper floor by lift is possible with assistance.

General description:
Sculpture, primarily British 20th century. 20th century British painting as well as watercolours and prints late 18th to 20th century. Contemporary British Art. Museum studies.
Information services:
Large print format exhibit labels available.
Special visitor services: Materials and/or activities for children.
Education services: Group education facilities, resources for Key Stages 1 and 2, 3, 4 and Further or Higher Education..
Collections:
Post-1800 British art, especially strong in the field of sculpture, designated by HM Government as a collection of national importance
English watercolours
Fine Victorian academic and Pre-Raphaelite painting
Late 19th century British Art painting
Modern sculpture
Contemporary British art
Catalogues:
Catalogue for all of the collections is only available in-house but part is published.
Publications list:
is available on-line.
Printed publications:
Concise catalogue available on the website
Catalogues
Postcards

Address for ordering publications:
Printed publications:
Commercial Office, Leeds Museum Resource Centre
Moorfield Road, Moorfield Industrial Estate, Yeadon, Leeds, LS19 7BN, tel: 0113 214 6534, fax: 0113 214 6536

Internet home pages:
http://www.leeds.gov.uk/artgallery

1565
LEEDS INDUSTRIAL MUSEUM

Armley Mills, Canal Road, Armley, Leeds, West Yorkshire, LS12 2QF

Tel: 0113 263 7861
Fax: 0113 263 7861
Email: armleymills.indmuseum@virgin.net
Formed: 1982
Formerly: Armley Mills Museum

Organisation type and purpose: Local government body, professional body, museum.
Museum holding information on Leeds' industrial history.
Owned by:
Director of Museums and Galleries
Leeds City Council, Leisure Services Department, Museums & Galleries Division, Leeds Town Hall, Leeds, West Yorkshire

Enquiries to: Curator
Access:
Access to staff: By letter, by telephone, by fax, by email, in person, visitors by prior appointment, Internet web pages
Hours: Mon, by appointment only, 0900 to 1700; Tue to Fri, 0900 to 1700
Access for disabled people: Parking provided, ramped entry, toilet facilities
Other restrictions: Access to most areas; touch trail; lift to all floors.

General description:
Leeds industrial history, printing, photography, cinematography, engineering, textiles, ready made clothing, locomotive building, cranes, transport (road rollers etc).
Information services:
Library available for reference (for conditions see Access above)
Library available for reference by appointment.

Special visitor services: Materials and/or activities for children..
Collections:
Working exhibits include:
1904 Spinning Mule
Ploughing engine, mill engine, steam locomotive
1920s cinema
Archives of photographs/documents relating to Leeds Industries
Printed publications:
Guide Book
Building Sights (Beesley I, commissioned by Museum)

Internet home pages:
http://www.leeds.gov.uk
Web page covering areas of collections.
http://www.leeds.gov.uk/tourinfo/attract/museums/armley/index.html
Armley Mills homepage.
http://www.leeds.gov.uk/tourinfo/events/lmg_arm.html
Events listings.

1566
LEEDS MUSEUM RESOURCE CENTRE
1 Moorfield Road, Yeadon, Leeds, West Yorkshire, LS19 7BN

Tel: 0113 214 6526
Fax: 0113 214 6539
Formed: 1819

Organisation type and purpose: Local government body, museum.
Open access store and activity centre.
Parent body:
Leeds Museums and Galleries
Department of Leisure Services, Leeds Town Hall, Leeds, LS1

Enquiries to: Senior Curator
Other contacts: Education Officer, tel: 0113 214 6526
Access:
Access to staff: By letter, by telephone, visitors by prior appointment, Internet web pages
Hours: Mon to Thu, 0900 to 1700; Fri, 0900 to 1600
Access to building, collections or gallery: Prior appointment required

General description:
A multi-disciplinary traditional museum collection, founded in 1819. Its main strengths lie in international natural history, archaeology, anthropology, geology, ethnography, archaeology and numismatics.
Collections:
The Gott and Lord Saville collections of classical antiquities
Egyptian collection, including the Mummy of Natsef
Very large natural history collections

Internet home pages:
http://www.leeds.gov.uk

1567
LEEDS MUSEUM RESOURCE CENTRE, THE
Moorfield Road, Yeadon, Leeds, West Yorkshire, LS21 1AN

Tel: 0113 214 6526
Fax: 0113 214 6539
Email: adrian.norris@leeds.gov.uk
Acronym or abbreviation: LMRC
Formed: 1819-20
Formerly: Leeds City Museum, date of change, 1999

Organisation type and purpose: Local government body, museum, suitable for ages: 5+.
Exhibitions and outreach elsewhere in Leeds eg Leeds Central Library.
Parent body:
Literary and Philosophical Society, Leeds
c/o LMRC

Part of:
Leeds Museum and Galleries

Enquiries to: Senior Curator
Other contacts: (1) Curator of Anthropology; (2) Assistant Curator (Geology); (3) Assistant Curator (Archaeology) for general enquiries on these subject areas.
Access:
Access to staff: By letter, by telephone, by fax, by email, visitors by prior appointment
Access to building, collections or gallery: Prior appointment required
Hours: Mon to Thu, 1000 to 1600; Fri, 1000 to 1500
Other restrictions: Booking essential.
Access for disabled people: Parking provided
Other restrictions: Ramped area through loading bay; one step to normal entrance.

General description:
Large natural history store. Egyptian mummy, small displays of world cultures and geology.
Activity area for schools and public workshops.
Information services:
Library available for reference (for conditions see Access above)
Special visitor services: Guided tours, materials and/or activities for children.
Education services: Group education facilities, resources for Key Stages 2, 3, 4 and Further or Higher Education..
Collections:
Over 1 million items
Small reference library
Slime - the world of molluscs from giant squid and clams, to snails and slugs, and fossil ammonites
Catalogues:
Catalogue for library is in-house only. Catalogue for all of the collections is only available in-house.
Publications list:
is available on-line.
Printed publications:
Tales From Japan (information pack, 99p)
Electronic and video products:
Senior Curator has completed a web publication on the Molluscan Collections (see website)

Internet home pages:
http://www.leeds.gov.uk/

1568
LEEDS MUSEUMS AND GALLERIES
The Town Hall, The Headrow, Leeds, West Yorkshire, LS1 3AD

Tel: 0113 247 7241
Fax: 0113 247 7747
Formed: 1995

Organisation type and purpose: Local government body, museum, suitable for ages: all ages.
Administrative service for museums and historical sites under the care of Leeds City Council.
Parent body:
Leeds City Council

Enquiries to: Head of Support Services
Direct tel: 0113 247 7242
Direct fax: 0113 247 7747
Other contacts: Head of Collections for details of museum collections.
Access:
Access to staff: By letter, by telephone, visitors by prior appointment
Access for disabled people: toilet facilities
Other restrictions: Access is limited on some sites, please ring for details.

General description:
Archaeology, numismatics, ethnography and natural history, fine and decorative arts, industrial and social history.
Collections:
Designated collection of fine and decorative art
Major collections of specimens of international archaeology, ethnography, natural history

Address for ordering publications:
Printed publications:
Commercial Office, The Leeds Museum Resource Centre
1 Moorfield Road, Yeadon, LS19 7SN, tel: 0113 391 0649, fax: 0113 391 0446

Internet home pages:
http://www.leeds.gov.uk

See also - Leeds City Art Gallery; Leeds Industrial Museum; Leeds Museum Resource Centre; Lotherton Hall; Temple Newsam House; Thwaite Mills Watermill

1569
LEEDS PHILOSOPHICAL & LITERARY SOCIETY
City Museum, c/o The Town Hall, Leeds, West Yorkshire, LS1 3AD

Acronym or abbreviation: LPLS
Formed: 1819

Organisation type and purpose: Learned society, suitable for ages: 16+.

Enquiries to: Honorary Secretary
Access:
Access to staff: By letter only

General description:
The purpose of the Society is 'to promote the advancement of science, literature and the arts in the City of Leeds and elsewhere, and to hold, give or provide for meetings, lectures, classes and entertainments of a scientific, literary or artistic nature'.
Collections:
The Society's Library was donated to the University of Leeds Library in 1936, and is available to users of that library
Publications list:
is available in hard copy.
Printed publications:
Publications available for purchase, direct from the Society

Address for ordering publications:
Printed publications:
Honorary Secretary

Internet home pages:
http://www.leedsphilandlit.org.uk
Information on aims, history, constitution, annual reports, grants, events.

1570
LEEDS PHILOSOPHICAL AND LITERARY SOCIETY
See - Leeds Museums and Galleries

1571
LEEDS UNIVERSITY
See - Museum of the History of Education

1572
LEICESTER CITY MUSEUMS
New Walk Museum, 53 New Walk, Leicester, LE1 7EA

Tel: 0116 255 4100
Fax: 0116 247 3057
Formed: 1849

Organisation type and purpose: Local government body, museum.
To tell the story of Leicester, all its people and the world in which they live, through buildings and the objects we care for, record and collect, for everyone to learn from and enjoy.
Parent body:
Leicester City Council
New Walk Centre, Welford Place, Leicester, LE1 6ZG, tel: 0116 254 9922, fax: 0116 255 7870
Other museums and sites:
Abbey Pumping Station
Corporation Road, Abbey Lane, Leicester, LE4 5PX, tel: 0116 299 5111, fax: 0116 299 5125
Belgrave Hall and Gardens

continued overleaf

Church Road, Belgrave, Leicester, LE4 5PE, tel: 0116 266 6590, fax: 0116 261 3063
Jewry Wall Museum
St Nicholas Circle, Leicester, LE1 4LB, tel: 0116 247 3021, fax: 0116 251 2257
Newarke Houses Museum
The Newarke, Leicester, LE2 7BY, tel: 0116 247 3222, fax: 0116 247 0403
Raw Dykes Ancient Monument
Aylestone Road, (opposite Freeman's Common), tel: 0116 247 3021, fax: 0116 251 2257
The Guildhall
Guildhall Lane, Leicester, LE1 5FQ, tel: 0116 253 2569, fax: 0116 253 9626
Wygston's House
c/o The Guildhall, Guildhall Lane, Leicester, LE1 5FQ, tel: 0116 253 2569, fax: 0116 253 9626

Enquiries to: Head of Museums
Direct tel: 0116 252 8913
Direct fax: 0116 255 6048
Direct email: levis001@leicester.gov.uk
Other contacts: Quality and Development Manager; Marketing Officer; Exhibitions Officer; Officer Curators; Collections and Audience Development Manager for specific professional areas.
Access:
Access to staff: By letter, by telephone, by fax, by email, in person, Internet web pages

General description:
Archaeology, biology, costume, decorative and fine arts, ethnography, numismatics, performing arts, geology, history, ecology, technology, archives, photography, education; information and specimens relate primarily to Leicester and Leicestershire.
Information services:
On-line searching
Special visitor services: Guided tours, materials and/or activities for children.
Education services: Group education facilities, resources for Key Stages 1 and 2.
Services for disabled people: For the visually impaired; for the hearing impaired; displays and/or information at wheelchair height.
Collections:
Fine art, including German Expressionist art
Science and industry
Coins and medals
Collections on: archaeology, botany, costume, Egyptology, entomology, mineralogy, palaeontology (including the Rutland Dinosaur), social history and zoology
Decorative arts, including Gimson furniture
Photographic collections
Catalogues:
Catalogue for part of the collections is only available in-house.
Printed publications:
Contact New Walk Museum

Internet home pages:
http://www.leicestermuseums.ac.uk
Information on all museum sites; events and special topics.

1573
LEICESTER GAS MUSEUM
See - National Gas Museum Trust

1574
LEICESTER MUSEUM OF TECHNOLOGY
See - Abbey Pumping Station Museum of Science and Technology

1575
LEICESTERSHIRE LIBRARIES AND INFORMATION SERVICE
See - Coleorton Collection

1576
LEICESTERSHIRE MUSEUMS SERVICE
Suite 4 Bridge Park Plaza, Bridge Park Road, Thurmasten, Leicester, LE4 8BL

Tel: 0116 264 5800
Fax: 0116 264 5820
Email: museums@leics.gov.uk

Organisation type and purpose: Local government body, museum.

Enquiries to: Director
Access:
Access to staff: By letter, by telephone, by fax, by email, in person, visitors by prior appointment, Internet web pages
Hours: Mon to Fri, 0900 to 1630
Access to building, collections or gallery: Prior appointment required
Access for disabled people: Parking provided, toilet facilities

General description:
Headquarters of Leicestershire Museums.
Catalogues:
Catalogue for all of the collections is only available in-house.

Internet home pages:
http://www.leics.gov.uk/museums

1577
LEICESTERSHIRE MUSEUMS, ARTS AND RECORDS SERVICE
County Hall, Glenfield, Leicester, LE3 8TB

Tel: 0116 265 6782
Acronym or abbreviation: LMARS
Formed: 1849

Organisation type and purpose: Local government body, museum, art gallery.
Administrative office for Leicestershire galleries and museums.
Provides an art gallery, a wide ranging museums service and county records (archive) service.
Department of the:
Leicestershire County Council
Museums and Sites:
Charnwood Museum
Queen's Hall, Granby Street, Loughborough, Leicestershire, LE11 3QW, tel: 01509 233754, fax: 01509 268140
Harborough Museum
Council Offices, Adam and Eve Street, Market Harborough, Leicestershire, LE16 7AG, tel: 01858 821087, fax: 01858 821000
Holly Hayes Environmental Resources Centre
Holly Hayes, 216 Birstall Road, Birstall, Leicester, LE4 4DG, tel: 0116 267 1950, fax: 0116 267 7112
Leicestershire Record Office
Long Street, Wigston Magna, Leicester, LE18 2AH, tel: 0116 257 1080, fax: 0116 257 1120
Manor House
Manor Road, Donington-le-Heath, Coalville, Leicestershire, LE67 2FW, tel: 01530 831259, fax: 01530 831259
Melton Carnegie Museum
Thorpe End, Melton Mowbray, Leicestershire, LE13 1RB, tel: 01664 569946, fax: 01664 569946
Sherrier Resources Centre
Church Street, Lutterworth, Leicestershire, LE17 4AG, tel: 01455 552834, fax: 01455 552845
Snibston Discovery Park
Ashby Road, Coalville, Leicestershire, LE67 2LN, tel: 01530 510851, fax: 01530 813301

Enquiries to: Director
Other contacts: Assistant Director for general enquiries and information.
Access:
Access to staff: By letter, by telephone, by fax, in person
Hours: Mon to Sat, 1000 to 1730; Sun, 1400 to 1730
Other restrictions: Holly Hayes Environmental Resources Centre and Sherrier Record Office not open Sunday.
Access to building, collections or gallery: No prior appointment required
Other restrictions: For Holly Hayes and Sherrier Record Office.

General description:
Archaeology, biology, costume, decorative and fine arts, performing arts, geology, history, ecology, technology, archives, photography, education; information and specimens relate primarily to Leicestershire.
Collections:
Archaeology, botany, costume, entomology, mineralogy, palaeontology (including the Rutland Dinosaur), social history and zoology
County Record Office (several million documents) includes Exton collection
Decorative arts, including Gimson furniture
Ecological and archaeological records
Fine art, including German Expressionist art
Photographic collections, including Newton (Great Central Railway) and Henton (topographical)
Science and industry, including transport and typewriters
Symington corsetry
Catalogues:
Catalogue for library is in-house only. Catalogue for part of the collections is only available in-house.
Publications list:
is available in hard copy.

Internet home pages:
http://www.leics.gov.uk
Services provided and opening times.

1578
LEIGH LIBRARY
See - Turnpike Gallery

1579
LEIGHTON BUZZARD RAILWAY LIMITED
Page's Park Station, Billington Road, Leighton Buzzard, Bedfordshire, LU7 4TN

Tel: 01525 373888
Fax: 01525 377814
Email: inf@buzzrail.co.uk
Acronym or abbreviation: LBNGRS Ltd
Full name: Leighton Buzzard Narrow Gauge Railway Society Ltd
Formed: 1967
Formed from: Iron Horse Preservation Society (IHPS), date of change, 1969

Organisation type and purpose: Membership association (membership is by subscription), present number of members: 350, voluntary organisation, registered charity (charity number 20830R), museum.
The preservation and operation of former line of Leighton Buzzard Light Railway.
Subsidiary of:
Leighton Buzzard Narrow Gauge Railway Society Ltd

Enquiries to: Public Relations Manager
Access:
Access to staff: By letter, by telephone, by fax, by email, in person, Internet web pages
Hours: Mon to Fri, 1000 to 1100 plus times when train service is operating
Other restrictions: Answerphone available when closed.
Access for disabled people: Parking provided, ramped entry, toilet facilities

General description:
Narrow gauge industrial railways, Bedfordshire sand industry, steam railway preservation and the restoration of locomotives and rolling stock.
Collections:
Locomotives, over 50 from range of manufacturers
Over 100 wagons and 8 coaches
Various associated archive materials

Printed publications:
Two books detailing the history of the railway (£18.95 and £10.95 plus p&p)
Chaloner (magazine, quarterly, members, £2 non-members plus p&p)
Railway Guide Book (£1.95 plus p&p)
Railway Stock Book (£4.95 plus p&p)
Electronic and video products:
Railway video

Internet home pages:
http://www.buzzrail.co.uk
Description of line and principal locomotives, timetable and fares, special events diary, how to find, latest news.

1580
LEIGHTON HOUSE MUSEUM
12 Holland Park Road, London, W14 8LZ

Tel: 020 7602 3316
Fax: 020 7371 2467
Email: leightonhousemuseum@rbkc.gov.uk
Formed: 1927

Organisation type and purpose: Local government body, historic building, house or site, suitable for ages: 8+.
Parent body:
Royal Borough of Kensington & Chelsea (RBKC) Libraries & Arts Service, Central Library, Phillimore Walk, tel: 020 7361 3000

Enquiries to: Curator
Direct tel: 020 7602 3316 ext 301
Direct email: daniel.robbins@rbkc.gov.uk
Other contacts: Local Studies Librarian for issues relating to Leighton's correspondence, archive (see collections).
Access:
Access to staff: By letter, by telephone, by fax, by email, visitors by prior appointment, Internet web pages
Access to building, collections or gallery: No prior appointment required
Hours: Sun, Mon, Wed, Thu, Fri, Sat, 1100 to 1730
Other restrictions: Closed Winter Bank Holidays, 25 and 26 Dec.

General description:
Leighton House Museum is the former home of the eminent Victorian artist, Frederic, Lord Leighton. Built by Leighton as a studio-house, the original building was extended with the construction of the 'Arab Hall' designed to display Leighton's exceptional collection of Islamic tiles. The rooms are largely unfurnished but hung with works by Leighton and his contemporaries, including Millais and Burne-Jones. The museum also has an extensive collection of some 608 of Leighton's studies and sketches.
Collections:
Collection of Leighton's correspondence is held at the Kensington Central Library, Local Studies Department
Collection of archive material relating to the history of the house (especially 20th century) is also housed at Local Studies Department
Printed publications:
Guide Book (£3)

Internet home pages:
http://www.rbkc.gov.uk/leightonhousemuseum/general/

1581
LEITH HALL, GARDEN & ESTATE
Huntly, Aberdeenshire, AB54 4NQ

Tel: 01464 831216
Fax: 01464 831594
Email: leithhall@nts.org.uk

Organisation type and purpose: Museum, art gallery, historic building, house or site.
Parent body:
National Trust for Scotland

Enquiries to: Property Manager
Access:
Access to staff: By letter, by telephone, by fax, by email, in person
Access to building, collections or gallery: No prior appointment required
Hours: House and tearoom, end Mar to end Oct, Wed to Sun, 1200 to 1700
Garden and grounds, all year, daily, 0930 to sunset
Access for disabled people: toilet facilities
Other restrictions: Access to ground floor of house, pond walk and tearoom, wheelchair available

General description:
A charming and intimate Scottish family home, it includes an interesting variety of family furniture, artwork, tapestry and military memorabilia. The house offers a unique insight into the life of the family who has lived there over the last four centuries.

Internet home pages:
http://www.nts.org.uk

1582
LEITH HILL
Coldharbour, Dorking, Surrey

Tel: 01306 711777

Organisation type and purpose: National organisation, registered charity (charity number 205846), historic building, house or site, suitable for ages: all ages.
Parent body:
The National Trust (South & South East Region) South East Regional Office, tel: 01372 453401

Enquiries to: Warden
Other contacts: Education Officer (01306 742809)
Access:
Access to staff: By telephone, by fax

General description:
The highest point in south-east England, crowned by an 18th century Gothic tower with telescope on top. The surrounding woodland contains ancient stands of hazel and oak and there is a colourful display of rhododendrons in May and June.

Internet home pages:
http://www.nationaltrust.org.uk/regions/

1583
LEOMINSTER MUSEUM
Etnam Street, Leominster, Herefordshire, HR6 8AN

Tel: 01568 615186
Full name: Leominster Folk Museum
Formed: 1972

Organisation type and purpose: Independently owned, registered charity, museum.

Enquiries to: Curator
Direct tel: 01544 318263
Access:
Access to staff: By letter, by telephone, in person
Hours: Mon to Fri, 1030 to 1600; Sat, 1030 to 1300
Access for disabled people: level entry
Other restrictions: Access to ground floor only.

General description:
History of Leominster: agriculture; domestic items; costume; railways; police; cider making; dairying.
Small industries: hatting; glove making; shoemakers.
Information services:
Special visitor services: Materials and/or activities for children.
Services for disabled people: Displays and/or information at wheelchair height.
Catalogues:
Catalogue for all of the collections is only available in-house.

1584
LETCHWORTH MUSEUM
The Broadway, Letchworth, Hertfordshire, SG6 3PD

Tel: 01462 685647
Fax: 01462 481879
Email: letchworth.museum@north-herts.gov.uk
Formed: 1914

Organisation type and purpose: Local government body, museum, art gallery, suitable for ages: 5+.
Parent body:
North Hertfordshire District Council (NHDC) Gernon Road, Letchworth, Hertfordshire

Enquiries to: Curator
Access:
Access to staff: By letter, by telephone, by email
Access to building, collections or gallery: No prior appointment required
Hours: Mon, Tue, Thu, Fri, Sat, 1000 to 1700
Other restrictions: Closed Wed, Sun and Bank Holidays.

General description:
North Herts archaeology, Letchworth Garden City, William Ratcliffe, Francis King, North Herts wildlife and natural history.
Information services:
Displays/information at wheelchair height on ground floor only.
Special visitor services: Guided tours, materials and/or activities for children.
Education services: Group education facilities, resources for Key Stages 1 and 2.
Services for disabled people: Displays and/or information at wheelchair height.
Collections:
William Ratcliffe, sometime resident of Letchworth, and member of Camden Town group of artists, 200 paintings and sketches
North Herts archaeology
Art Collection
Ceramics, costume
North Herts wildlife, natural history
Romano-British Baldock, 1925-present, of national importance, 100,000 plus items
Catalogues:
Catalogue for all of the collections is available in-house and part is on-line.

Internet home pages:
http://www.north-herts.gov.uk
Go to 'leisure' and 'letchworth museum'.
Information on our collections and services, contact details.

1585
LETHERINGSETT WATERMILL
Riverside Road, Letheringsett, Holt, Norfolk, NR25 7YD

Tel: 01263 713153
Email: watermill@ic24.net
Formed: 1987

Organisation type and purpose: Historic building, house or site.
Working watermill.

Enquiries to: Proprietor
Access:
Access to staff: By letter, by telephone, by email, in person
Access to building, collections or gallery: No prior appointment required

General description:
Milling in the traditional way on grindstones.
Information services:
Special visitor services: Guided tours, tape recorded guides..
Printed publications:
Mill History

Internet home pages:
http://www.letheringsettwatermill.co.uk
For general information.

1586
LEVANT STEAM ENGINE, THE

Trewellard, Pendeen, St Just, Cornwall

Tel: 01736 786156 (opening hours only), 01736 796993 (Penwith Countryside Office)

Organisation type and purpose: National organisation, registered charity (charity number 205846), museum, historic building, house or site.

Parent body:
The National Trust (South West Region)
Devon and Cornwall Regional Office, tel: 01208 74281

Enquiries to: Manager

Access:
Access to staff: By letter, by telephone
Access to building, collections or gallery: No prior appointment required
Hours: Steaming: 1100 to 1700, 1 Mar to 21 Apr, Fri; 22 Apr to 30 May, Tue, Fri; Jun, Wed, Thu, Fri, Sun; Jul, Aug, Sep, Mon, Tue, Wed, Thu, Fri, Sun; Oct, Tue, Fri;
Not steaming: Nov to end Feb, 1100 to 1600
Other restrictions: Open Bank Holiday Sundays and Mondays .
Access for disabled people: Parking provided, ramped entry
Other restrictions: Accessible entrance different from main entrance. Ground floor largely inaccessible. No acess to other floors.

General description:
Tiny engine house, perched on the cliff edge, houses the famous Levant beam engine which is steaming again after sixty idle years. The sight, sounds and smells of this 160-year-old engine conjure up the feel of Cornwall's industrial past. Half a mile along the cliff is Geevor Mine (not National Trust) and a mining museum. A short underground tour takes the visitor from the miners' dry to the main engine shaft via a spiral staircase.

Internet home pages:
http://www.nationaltrust.org.uk/regions/cornwall

1587
LEWES CASTLE & MUSEUMS

169 High Street, Lewes, East Sussex, BN7 1YE

Tel: 01273 486290
Email: castle@sussexpast.co.uk
Formed: 1856
Formerly: Barbican House Museum, Sussex Archaeological Society

Organisation type and purpose: Independently owned, learned society, registered charity (charity number 207037), museum, historic building, house or site, suitable for ages: all ages.

Enquiries to: Curator
Other contacts: Honorary Librarian for specific library requests.

Access:
Access to staff: By letter, by email
Hours: Mon to Fri, 1000 to 1700
Access to building, collections or gallery: Prior appointment required
Hours: Mon to Fri, 1000 to 1700

General description:
Sussex history and archaeology. The site includes Lewes Castle and the Museum of Sussex Archaeology, plus an audio-visual presentation on Lewes. It contains important archaeological material from Sussex sites. Sussex archaeology from Palaeolithic to mediaeval periods (and later). Sussex topographical pictures, prints and photographs.

Information services:
Library available for reference (for conditions see Access above)
Special visitor services: Guided tours, tape recorded guides.
Education services: Group education facilities, resources for Key Stages 1 and 2..

Collections:
Artefacts, photographs, prints, books
Reeves collection of historic negatives.

Catalogues:
Catalogue for library is in-house only. Catalogue for all of the collections is only available in-house.

Internet home pages:
http://www.sussexpast.co.uk

1588
LEWIS TEXTILE MUSEUM

See - Blackburn Museum and Art Gallery

1589
LEYLAND HISTORIC VEHICLES

See - British Motor Industry Heritage Trust

1590
LIBRARY AND MUSEUM OF FREEMASONRY, THE

Freemasons' Hall, Great Queen Street, London, WC2B 5AZ

Tel: 020 7395 9251
Fax: 020 7404 7418
Full name: Library and Museum Charitable Trust of the United Grand Lodge
Formed: 1996
Formerly: United Grand Lodge of England, date of change, 1999

Organisation type and purpose: Professional body, registered charity (charity number 1058497), museum.
Research library.

Enquiries to: Director
Other contacts: Librarian for research queries.

Access:
Access to staff: By letter, by telephone, by fax, in person, charges made to all users
Hours: Mon to Fri, 1000 to 1700

General description:
Freemasonry, historical record and information, extensive library and artefact collection.

Catalogues:
Catalogue for library is in-house only. Catalogue for part of the collections is only available in-house.

1591
LIDDESDALE HERITAGE CENTRE

South Hermitage Street, Newcastleton, Roxburghshire, TD9 0QE

Tel: 013873 75283/75259

Organisation type and purpose: Local government body, suitable for ages: 5+.

Enquiries to: Curator

Access:
Access to staff: By letter, by telephone
Access to building, collections or gallery: No prior appointment required
Hours: Easter to Sep, Daily 1330 to 1630
Other restrictions: Closed Tue

General description:
The local history of Liddesdale and its people.

1592
LIFE BOAT MUSEUM

See - Royal National Lifeboat Institution

1593
LIGHT INFANTRY MUSEUM

Peninsula Barracks, Romsey Road, Winchester, Hampshire, SO23 8TS

Tel: 01962 828550
Fax: 01962 828534
Acronym or abbreviation: LI Museum
Formed: 1985

Organisation type and purpose: Museum.

Regimental Headquarters:
The Light Infantry
at the same address, tel: 01962 828530, fax: 01962 828534

Enquiries to: Curator
Direct tel: 01962 828530
Direct fax: 01962 828500
Other contacts: Chairman of Trustees for the Trustees.

Access:
Access to staff: By letter, by telephone, by fax, visitors by prior appointment
Hours: Mon to Fri, 0900 to 1600
Access to building, collections or gallery: No access other than to staff
Hours: Tue to Sat and Bank Holiday Mon, 1000 to 1600; (closed for lunch); Sun, 1200 to 1600
Access for disabled people: Parking provided, level entry, access to all public areas, toilet facilities

General description:
A Regimental Museum which shows some aspects of the distant past, but which concentrates on a modern Regiment, and more recent events around the world.

Collections:
Field Marshal Lord Harding of Petherton, uniforms, medals, banners, crests, etc.
Berlin Wall, large piece of wall with supporting uniform of Allies and Russian/German soldiers
Gulf War, items from the battlefield
Lt Gen Sir Peter de la Billière, uniform, medals and presentation submachine gun with gold trigger, etc.

Publications list:
is available in hard copy.

1594
LIGHT INFANTRY REGIMENTAL MUSEUM

See - Duke of Cornwall's Light Infantry Regimental Museum

1595
LILLIE ART GALLERY

71 Station Road, Milngavie, Glasgow, G62 8BZ

Tel: 0141 578 8847
Fax: 0141 570 0244
Email: hildegarde.berwick@eastdunbarton.gov.uk
Formed: 1962

Parent body:
East Dunbartonshire Council

Enquiries to: Curator

Access:
Access for disabled people: Parking provided, access to all public areas

General description:
Purpose-built art gallery opened in 1962. Temporary exhibition programme of fine and applied art including paintings, prints, textiles and ceramics. Temporary exhibitions also from the permanent collection.

Information services:
Materials/activities for children linked to certain exhibitions.
Special visitor services: Materials and/or activities for children..

Collections:
Collection of 20th century Scottish paintings, prints, sculptures and ceramics, including the Glasgow Boys, the Scottish Colourists, local artists William and Mary Armour
A collection of Jean Eardley drawings and works by contemporary artists including June Redfern, Barbara Rae, Lesley Banks and Adrian Wiszniewski

Catalogues:
Catalogue for all of the collections is only available in-house but part is published.

Printed publications:
Exhibitions Booklet (2 times a year)
Lille Art Gallery

List of Paintings, Prints, Drawings and Sculpture (1987)

Internet home pages:
http://www.eastdunbarton.gov.uk
Exhibitions listing.

1596
LILLIPUT DOLL & TOY MUSEUM

High Street, Brading, Sandown, Isle of Wight, PO36 0DJ

Tel: 01983 407231
Email: lilliput.museum@btconnect.com
Full name: The Lilliput Antique Doll and Toy Museum
Formed: 1974

Organisation type and purpose: Independently owned, museum, suitable for ages: all ages.

Enquiries to: Proprietor
Access:
Access to staff: By letter, by telephone, by email, Internet web pages
Hours: Mon to Sun, 1000 to 1700
Other restrictions: Closed Christmas Day.
Access for disabled people: ramped entry

General description:
A comprehensive collection of antique dolls from c. 2000 BC to c. 1945, including dolls made of Bisque China, wax, wax over composition, wood, rubber, metal, celluloid and cloth. The collection also includes teddy bears dating from c. 1905; doll's houses, Victorian and Edwardian rocking horses, and other pre-World War II toys and games.
Collections:
Over 2000 antique dolls and toys pre-1945

Internet home pages:
http://www.lilliputmuseum.com
Brief history of museum and some examples of exhibits on display.

1597
LINCOLN CASTLE

Castle Hill, Lincoln, LN1 3AA

Tel: 01522 511068
Fax: 01522 512150
Formed: 1068

Organisation type and purpose: Local government body, historic building, house or site, suitable for ages: 5+.
Castle, historic monument.
Visitor attraction.
Parent body:
Lincolnshire County Council (LCC)
County Hall, Lincoln

Enquiries to: Principal Keeper
Access:
Access to staff: By letter, by telephone, by fax, in person

General description:
An ancient monument built by William the Conqueror in 1068. Lincoln Castle contains the Observatory Tower, Lucy Tower and Cobb Hall, plus the Old Prison Chapel (audio and visual experience available). Original Lincoln Magna Carta - 1215, plus exhibition Victorian Prison and only remaining 'Pentonville Chapel'; wall walks; gardens; café, restaurant.
Collections:
Various items of furniture relating to the Prison, includes the Georgian Debtors' Prison Building 1787, and the Victorian Felons' Prison 1845

1598
LINCOLN CATHEDRAL

Minster Yard, Lincoln, LN2 1PX

Tel: 01522 544544
Fax: 01522 511307
Email: visitors@lincolncathedral.com
Full name: The Cathedral Church of the Blessed Virgin Mary of Lincoln
Formed: 1072

Organisation type and purpose: Registered charity (charity number X7802), historic building, house or site, suitable for ages: all ages.
Church of England Cathedral Church.
Other addresses:
Chapter Office
4 Priorygate, Lincoln, LN2 1PL, tel: 01522 530320, fax: 01522 511794, email/website: chiefexecutive@lincolncathedral.com

Enquiries to: Visitor Officer
Direct tel: 01522 530320
Direct fax: 01522 511794
Direct email: chiefexecutive @lincolncathedral.com
Access:
Access to staff: By letter, by telephone, by fax, by email, visitors by prior appointment
Access to building, collections or gallery: No prior appointment required
Hours: Summer: daily, 0715 to 2000
Winter: daily, 0715 to 1800
Other restrictions: Some areas may be roped off for services.
Library available for reference by prior appointment only.
Access for disabled people: ramped entry, toilet facilities
Other restrictions: Touch exhibition and 3D model for visually impaired.
Staff in attendance with wheelchair access where necessary, most of the Cathedral is readily accessible.

General description:
By prior notification, guides specialising in architecture, glazing, monuments etc of Lincoln Cathedral can be provided. Dedicated study day progammes with leading national speakers are arranged by volunteer guides - telephone for details.
New for 2002 was a Jubilee Tour, exploring the Monarchy's links with the Cathedral from 1066 to present day.
Information services:
Lincoln Cathedral Library may be accessed by contacting the Librarian by letter or telephone: 01522 544544 by prior appointment only.
Special visitor services: Guided tours, materials and/or activities for children.
Education services: Group education facilities, resources for Key Stages 1 and 2, 3, 4 and Further or Higher Education.
Services for disabled people: For the visually impaired; for the hearing impaired; displays and/or information at wheelchair height.
Collections:
Lincoln Cathedral Library
Library has 3 areas:
Medieval Library (dating from 1420s)
Wren Library (1675, housing collection of early printed books)
Reading Room (containing reference collection for students)
A chantry chapel, painted by the artist Duncan Grant, open during normal hours
Catalogues:
Catalogue for part of the collections is only available in-house.
Publications list:
is available on-line.
Printed publications:
Various books on the Cathedral (available direct from the Minster Shop, or website)

Internet home pages:
http://www.lincolncathedral.com

1599
LINCOLN MEDIEVAL BISHOPS' PALACE

Minster Yard, Lincoln, LN2 1PU

Tel: 01522 527468

Organisation type and purpose: National government body, historic building, house or site, suitable for ages: 5+.
Parent body:
English Heritage (East Midlands Region) (EH)
44 Derngate, Northampton, NN1 1UH, tel: 01604 735400, fax: 01604 735401

Enquiries to: Manager
Access:
Access to staff: By letter, by telephone, in person

General description:
Standing in the shadow of Lincoln Cathedral is the Medieval Bishops' Palace, once the hub of the largest diocese in medieval England. Built on terraces on the Lincoln hillside, this impressive palace provides a wonderful panorama of the Roman, medieval and modern city. Enjoy the walled terrace garden, part of our Contemporary Heritage Gardens scheme. Its design maximises space and enhances the views over Lincolnshire.
Information services:
Special visitor services: Tape recorded guides.
Education services: Group education facilities.
Services for disabled people: For the hearing impaired; displays and/or information at wheelchair height.

Internet home pages:
http://www.english-heritage.org.uk

1600
LINDISFARNE CASTLE

Holy Island, Berwick-upon-Tweed, Northumberland, TD15 2SH

Tel: 01289 389244
Fax: 01289 389349

Organisation type and purpose: National organisation, registered charity (charity number 205846), museum, historic building, house or site.
Parent body:
The National Trust (Yorkshire and North East)
North East Regional Office, tel: 01670 774691

Enquiries to: Manager
Access:
Access to staff: By letter, by telephone, by fax

General description:
Perched atop a rocky crag and accessible over a causeway at low tide only, the castle presents an exciting and alluring aspect. Originally a Tudor fort, it was converted into a private house in 1903 by the young Edwin Lutyens. The small rooms are full of intimate decoration and design, the windows looking down upon the charming walled garden planned by Gertrude Jekyll.
Information services:
Services for disabled people: For the visually impaired.

Internet home pages:
http://www.nationaltrust.org.uk

1601
LINDISFARNE PRIORY

Holy Island, Berwick-upon-Tweed, Northumberland, TD15 2RX

Tel: 01289 389200

Organisation type and purpose: Museum, historic building, house or site.
Parent body:
English Heritage (North East Region)
Tel: 0191 269 1227/8, fax: 0191 261 1130

Enquiries to: Manager
Access:
Access to staff: By letter, by telephone, in person
Access to building, collections or gallery: No prior appointment required
Hours: End Mar to end Sep, daily, 1000 to 1800; Oct, daily, 1000 to 1700; beg Nov to end Mar, daily, 1000 to 1600
Other restrictions: Closed 24-26 Dec, 1 Jan
Only reached via causeway at low tide.
Opening times are subject to change, for up-to-date information contact English Heritage by phone or visit the website

continued overleaf

General description:
Site of one of most important early centres of Christianity in Anglo-Saxon England, founded in AD635. For 1300 years it had been a place of pilgrimage and remains so today. A lively exhibition tells the story of Viking plunderers, and displays precious Anglo-Saxon carvings.
Information services:
Special visitor services: Materials and/or activities for children..

Internet home pages:
http://www.english-heritage.org.uk

1602
LINDSEY HOUSE
100 Cheyne Walk, Chelsea, London, SW10 0DQ

Tel: 01494 528051 (Regional Office)

Organisation type and purpose: National organisation, registered charity (charity number 205846), historic building, house or site.
Parent body:
The National Trust (South East Region)
Thames and Solent Regional Office, tel: 01494 528051

Enquiries to: Manager

General description:
Built on the former site of Sir Thomas More's garden and now part of Cheyne Walk. The house claims one of the finest 17th century exteriors in London.

Internet home pages:
http://www.nationaltrust.org.uk

1603
LINEN RESEARCH INSTITUTE
See - Irish Linen Centre and Lisburn Museum

1604
LINLEY SAMBOURNE HOUSE
18 Stafford Terrace, Kensington, London, W8 7BH

Tel: 020 7602 3316 ext 302
Fax: 020 7371 2467
Formed: 1981
Formerly: The Royal Borough of Kensington & Chelsea (RBK&C), date of change, 1986

Organisation type and purpose: Local government body, museum, historic building, house or site, suitable for ages: all ages.
Parent body:
The Royal Borough of Kensington and Chelsea (RBK&C)
Central Library, Phillimore Walk, London, W8 7RX
Other address:
Leighton House Museum
12 Holland Park Road, London, tel: 020 7602 3316, fax: 020 7371 2467, email/website: www.rbkc.gov.uk/leightonhousemuseum

Enquiries to: Curator
Other contacts: Curator of Collections and Research for special responsibility for house and collections.
Access:
Access to staff: By letter, by telephone, by fax
Access to building, collections or gallery: Prior appointment required

General description:
Linley Sambourne house was the home of Edward Linley Sambourne, a leading Punch cartoonist of the late Victorian and Edwardian period. The magnificent 'artistic' interior has survived largely unchanged. Its original wall decoration, fixtures and furniture have been preserved together with Sambourne's own pictures. The result is a unique and fascinating survival of a late Victorian town house.
Information services:
Library available for reference (for conditions see Access above). Helpline available
Special visitor services: Guided tours, materials and/or activities for children.
Education services: Resources for Key Stages 1 and 2 and Further or Higher Education..
Collections:
Collection of Sambourne family diaries from 1881-1920s (have been microfilmed)
Bills and letters from 1880-1960 (catalogued and computerised, available for consultation)
Collection of household decorative objects (catalogued and computerised)
Cyanotype photographs, 1860s-1910, 24,000. Total photographs/cyanotype, 11,000. Total copies, 13,000.
Catalogues:
Catalogue for part of the collections is only available in-house.
Printed publications:
Roy Sambourne, An Edwardian Bachelor (Nicholson S, for purchase)
A Victorian Household (Nicholson S, for purchase)
Public Artist, Private Passions: The World of Edward Linley Sambourne (exhibition catalogue, for purchase)
Other related material connected with the period
Microform products:
Microform products: Available for consultation at local studies library, Kensington

Internet home pages:
http://www.rbkc.gov.uk/linleysambournehouse

1605
LINLITHGOW HERITAGE TRUST
Annet House, 143 High Street, Linlithgow, West Lothian, EH49 7EJ

Tel: 01506 670677
Email: enquiries@linlithgowhistory.org.uk
Formed: 1991

Organisation type and purpose: Independently owned, registered charity (charity number SCO 17593), museum.

Enquiries to: Honorary Secretary
Access:
Access to staff: By letter, by telephone, by email, charges to non-members
Other restrictions: Outside period Easter to end Oct, contact by letter only.
Access to building, collections or gallery: No prior appointment required
Hours: Easter to end Oct: Mon to Sat, 1000 to 1700; Sun, 1300 to 1600

General description:
Displays relating to the history of the ancient and Royal Burgh of Linlithgow. These displays depict something of the history of Linlithgow Palace, and tell of the development of the town and its trades.
The garden contains examples of fruits and herbs of yesteryear, and offers fine views over the town towards the church and palace.
Information services:
Special visitor services: Guided tours.
Education services: Group education facilities..

Internet home pages:
http://www.linlithgowhistory.org.uk
General information about museum and activities, membership information.

1606
LINLITHGOW UNION CANAL SOCIETY
Canal Basin, Manse Road, Linlithgow, West Lothian, EH49 6AJ

Tel: 01506 671215
Email: info@lucs.org.uk
Acronym or abbreviation: LUCS
Full name: Linlithgow Canal Centre
Formed: 1975

Organisation type and purpose: Membership association (membership is by subscription), present number of members: 300, voluntary organisation, registered charity (charity number CR 45028), museum, suitable for ages: 5+.
Visitor attraction, 3 star grading includes boat trips.

Enquiries to: Publications and Marketing
Other contacts: (1) Membership (2) Booking Secretary (3) Tourism and Publications for (1) members (2) charters etc bookings (3) publications, webmaster.
Access:
Access to staff: By letter, by email, Internet web pages
Hours: Easter to mid Oct: Sat, Sun, 1400 to 1700
and Mon to Fri, during Jul and Aug
Other restrictions: Charters of boats, access to museum by arrangement.
Access for disabled people: ramped entry, access to all public areas, toilet facilities
Other restrictions: No access to boats.

General description:
Canals, particularly Edinburgh/Glasgow Union Canal and Millennium Link.
Collections:
Audiovisual Display
Museum with display, canal artefacts
Catalogues:
Catalogue for library is in-house only. Catalogue for all of the collections is only available in-house.
Publications list:
is available on-line.
Printed publications:
The Union Canal (a short history, Skinner B C)
Copy of Companion (1823)

Internet home pages:
http://www.lucs.org.uk
About the museum, tea room, boats, society (membership etc), events (past and forthcoming), links to other pages.

1607
LION SALT WORKS TRUST
Ollershaw Lane, Marston, Northwich, Cheshire, CW9 6ES

Tel: 01606 41823
Fax: 01606 41823
Email: afielding@lionsalt.demon.co.uk
Formed: 1993

Organisation type and purpose: Registered charity (charity number 1020258), museum, historic building, house or site, suitable for ages: 8+.
Museum of the salt industry.

Enquiries to: Director
Access:
Access to staff: By letter, by telephone, by email
Access to building, collections or gallery: No prior appointment required
Hours: Daily, 1330 to 1630
Access for disabled people: Parking provided, ramped entry

General description:
The last traditional salt works to evaporate 'wild brine', to make block salt by the open pan process, 5 pan houses, brine pump, engine house, pump house, brine tank, smithy, manager's office, railway siding.
To be restored as a working museum.
Collections:
All objects and documents relating to the site, its operation and items related to the Thompson Family (former owners, builders and operators of Henry Ingram Thompson's Red Lion Salt Works)
Also interests in Jabez Thompson Brickworks, Northwich
Printed publications:
Guide to the Lion Salt Works Marston (ISBN 0-9538502-0-X, £3.95)
Open Salt Making in Cheshire (ISBN 0-9538502-1-8, £9.50)
The Mundling Stick (newsletter, quarterly, free by post)

Internet home pages:
http://www.lionsaltworkstrust.co.uk/

1608
LISBURN MUSEUM
See - Irish Linen Centre and Lisburn Museum

1609
LITCHAM VILLAGE MUSEUM
Fourways, Mileham Road, Litcham, King's Lynn, Norfolk, PE32 2NZ

Tel: 01328 701383
Formed: 1991
Formed from: Litcham Historical & Amenity Society

Organisation type and purpose: Independently owned, museum, historic building, house or site, suitable for ages: all ages.
Parent body:
Litcham Historical & Amenity Society

Enquiries to: Director General
Other contacts: Curator
Access:
Access to staff: By letter, by telephone, visitors by prior appointment
Access for disabled people: Parking provided

General description:
All items are of local interest and are housed in a Grade II listed building. Contains agricultural, domestic and general items. Fine collection of over 1000 local photographs dating from 1860. Wide variety of local artefacts including Roman items. Underground lime kiln open on request. Local 'history walk' sheets available free from museum.
Information services:
Library available for reference (for conditions see Access above)
Special visitor services: Tape recorded guides..
Collections:
Photography. Black and white. Local interest. 1865-1990, 1400 items
Catalogues:
Catalogue for library is in-house only. Catalogue for all of the collections is only available in-house.
Printed publications:
Heritage Book
History of Litcham Book and Leaflets
History Walks through Litcham

1610
LITTLE CLARENDON HOUSE
Dinton, Salisbury, Wiltshire, SP3 5DZ

Tel: 01985 843600 (Regional Office)

Organisation type and purpose: National organisation, registered charity (charity number 205846), historic building, house or site.
Parent body:
The National Trust (South West Region)
Wessex regional Office, tel: 01895 843600
National Trust sites:
Little Clarendon House
Dinton, Salisbury, Wiltshire, SP3 5DZ, tel: 01985 843600 (Regional Office)

Enquiries to: Manager
Access:
Access to staff: By letter, by telephone
Access to building, collections or gallery: No prior appointment required
Hours: April to Oct, Mon, 1300 to 1700 and Fri, 1000 to 1300
Other restrictions: No parking, not suitable for coaches.

General description:
Tudor house, altered in the 17th century and with a 20th century Catholic chapel. The three principal rooms on the first floor are open to visitors and furnished with vernacular oak furniture.

Internet home pages:
http://www.nationaltrust.org.uk/regions/wessex

1611
LITTLE CRESSINGHAM WATERMILL
O.S. TG 870 003, Little Cressingham, Norfolk

Organisation type and purpose: Historic building, house or site.
General description:
A unique combined wind and water mill.

1612
LITTLE FLEECE BOOKSHOP
Bisley Street, Painswick, Gloucestershire, GL6 6QQ

Tel: 01452 802103

Organisation type and purpose: National organisation, registered charity (charity number 205846), historic building, house or site.
Parent body:
The National Trust (South West Region)
Wessex Regional Office, tel: 01985 843600

Enquiries to: Manager
Access:
Access to staff: By letter, by telephone
Access to building, collections or gallery: No prior appointment required
Hours: Beg Apr to end Oct, Tue, Wed, Thu, Fri, Sat, 1030 to1700; Nov to mid Dec, Sat, 1030 to 1700
Other restrictions: Closed Good Friday. Also closed between 1300 and 1400.
Access for disabled people: level entry
Other restrictions: Ground floor largely inaccessible.

General description:
A 17th century building, originally part of a former inn and restored in an exemplary 'Arts and Crafts' style in 1935. Now open as a bookshop with ground floor only on view.

Internet home pages:
http://www.nationaltrust.org.uk/regions/wessex

1613
LITTLE GIDDING TRUST, THE
Ferrar House, Little Gidding, Huntingdon, Cambridgeshire, PE28 5RJ

Tel: 01832 293383
Formed: 1998

Organisation type and purpose: Historic building, house or site, suitable for ages: 16+.

Enquiries to: Chairman
Access:
Access to staff: By letter, by telephone
Access to building, collections or gallery: No prior appointment required
Hours: Daily, 1000 to 1700
Access for disabled people: Parking provided, level entry, access to all public areas, toilet facilities

General description:
Artefacts and relics of the original 17th century Ferrar Christian community/family at Little Gidding, with subsequent references and reproduced material referring to same. Copies of reports of subsequent pilgrimages to Little Gidding displayed in a parlour museum and a former mediaeval church restored between the 17th and 19th centuries.
Collections:
15th century Flemish lectern and 17th century reredos, brass tablets and wood panelling and 18th century brass chandelier in a former mediaeval church
Copies of Ferrar crest/seal authentification, and books and papers used and signed by the Ferrar family.
Full set of 17th century communion silver and crucifix (inscribed)
Original unique 17th century brass font with brass crown cover
Original wool tapestry on canvaswork, reputedly woven by 17th century Ferrar household women
Publications list:
is available in hard copy.

1614
LITTLE HALL
Market Place, Lavenham, Sudbury, Suffolk, CO10 9QZ

Tel: 01787 247179
Fax: 01787 248341
Formed: 1974

Organisation type and purpose: Independently owned, historic building, house or site, suitable for ages: 16+.
Parent body:
Suffolk Building Preservation Trust Limited (SBPT)
Little Hall, at the same address

Enquiries to: Chairman
Access:
Access to staff: By letter, by telephone
Hours: Mon to Thu, 0900 to 1700; Fri, 0900 to 1230

General description:
A late 14th century, heavily timbered building with 16th and 17th century modifications, providing an opportunity to examine medieval construction methods and later developments. Furnished with antiques and paintings collected by the Gayer-Anderson brothers who purchased and renovated the house in the 1920s and 30s and bearing evidence of 2nd World War evacuee accommodation. The house also has a beautiful, well-kept, walled garden.
Information services:
Special visitor services: Guided tours, materials and/or activities for children..
Collections:
Paintings, furniture and objects.17-20th century, the furnishings of the modestly-sized house that the Gayer-Anderson brothers lived in from the 1920s until 1960
Printed publications:
Guide leaflet (available for purchase at reception desk, 50p)

1615
LITTLE HOLLAND HOUSE
40 Beeches Avenue, Carshalton, Surrey, SM5 3LW

Tel: 020 8770 4781
Fax: 020 8770 4777
Email: valary.murphy@sutton.gov.uk or sutton.museum@ukonline.co.uk
Formed: 1974

Organisation type and purpose: Local government body, museum, historic building, house or site, suitable for ages: 12+.
Parent body:
London Borough of Sutton
Heritage Service, Central Library, St Nicholas Way, Sutton, SM1 1EA
Other addresses:
Sutton Heritage Service
Central Library, St Nicholas Way, Sutton, SM1 1EA, tel: 020 8770 4781, fax: 020 8770 4777, email/website: valary.murphy@sutton.gov.uk

Enquiries to: Museum & Historic Houses Officer
Other contacts: Warden for access in an emergency when the Museum and Historic Houses Officer is not available.
Access:
Access to staff: By letter, by telephone, by fax, by email, in person, visitors by prior appointment

continued overleaf

Hours: By phone, fax, email: Tue to Fri, 0900 to 1730

General description:
The former home of artist, designer and craftsman Frank Dickinson (1874-1961). The Grade II listed interior features paintings; handmade furniture; metalwork carvings; and other craft objects created by Dickinson in the original setting of the house and garden he designed and built himself, inspired by the teachings of Ruskin and Morris.

Information services:
Special visitor services: Guided tours..

Collections:
Frank Dickinson Collection: paintings, photographs and manuscripts
Furniture and metalwork in the Arts & Crafts style

Catalogues:
Catalogue for part of the collections is only available in-house.

Printed publications:
A Novice Builds His Own Ideal House: An account by Frank Dickinson and the construction of Little Holland House (16pp, £1 plus p&p, direct)

Address for ordering publications:
Printed publications:
Sutton Heritage Service, Central Library
St Nicholas Way, Sutton, SM1 1EA, tel: 020 8770 4781, fax: 020 8770 4777, email: valary.murphy@sutton.gov.uk

Internet home pages:
http://www.sutton.gov.uk/lfl/heritage/lhh

1616
LITTLE MORETON HALL

Congleton, Cheshire, CW12 4SD

Tel: 01260 272018
Email: littlemoretonhall@nationaltrust.org.uk

Organisation type and purpose: National organisation, registered charity (charity number 205846), museum, historic building, house or site, suitable for ages: 8+.

Parent body:
The National Trust (North West)
North West Regional Office, tel: 0870 609 5391

Enquiries to: Manager

Access:
Access to staff: By letter, by telephone, by email
Access for disabled people: Parking provided, level entry, toilet facilities
Other restrictions: 3 manual wheelchairs available, booking essential. Ground floor fully accessible. No access to other floors. Photograph album. Cobbled courtyard. Level entrance to shop. Level entrance to restaurant. Grounds largely accessible. Recommended route map.

General description:
Britain's most famous, and arguably finest timber-framed moated manor house. The drunkenly reeling south front, topped by a spectacular long gallery, opens onto a cobbled courtyard and the main body of the Hall. Magnificent wall paintings and a notable knot garden are of special interest.

Information services:
Open-air theatre in July, plus regular events during normal opening hours.
Braille guide. Large-print guide. Touch list. Handling collection.
Suitable for school groups. Education room/centre. Live interpretation. Hands-on activities. Children's guide. Children's quiz/trail.
Special visitor services: Guided tours, materials and/or activities for children.
Education services: Group education facilities.
Services for disabled people: For the visually impaired.

Internet home pages:
http://www.nationaltrust.org.uk

1617
LITTLEHAMPTON MUSEUM

Manor House, Church Street, Littlehampton, West Sussex, BN17 5EW

Tel: 01903 738100
Fax: 01903 731690
Email: rebecca.fardell@arun.gov.uk
Formed: 1928

Organisation type and purpose: Local government body, museum, suitable for ages: all ages.

Enquiries to: Museum & Community Arts Officer

Access:
Access to staff: By letter, by telephone, by fax, by email, in person
Access to building, collections or gallery: No prior appointment required
Hours: Tue to Sat, 1030 to 1630
Access for disabled people: ramped entry, access to all public areas, toilet facilities

General description:
Contains prehistoric, Roman and mediaeval archaeological finds; local and social history - related artefacts; paintings, prints and photographs; maps and documentary information; anchors; cannon; ship models and other items related to maritime history; geological and natural history collections. Much of the above relates directly to Littlehampton and district.

Information services:
Library available for reference (for conditions see Access above)
Special visitor services: Materials and/or activities for children.
Education services: Group education facilities, resources for Key Stages 1 and 2, 3, 4 and Further or Higher Education.
Services for disabled people: Displays and/or information at wheelchair height.

Collections:
Local history
Maritime history
Cameras and photography
Archaeology
Paintings
Photographs

Catalogues:
Catalogue for all of the collections is only available in-house.

1618
LIVERPOOL METROPOLITAN CATHEDRAL OF CHRIST THE KING

Cathedral House, Mount Pleasant, Liverpool, L3 5TQ

Tel: 0151 709 9222
Fax: 0151 708 7274
Email: met.cathedral@cwcom.net
Formed: 1967

Organisation type and purpose: Registered charity (charity number 232709), historic building, house or site.
Roman Catholic Cathedral.

Cathedral Church of:
Archdiocese of Liverpool
Tel: 0151 522 1000, fax: 0151 522 1014

Enquiries to: Dean
Other contacts: (1) Dean's Assistant (2) Director of Music (3) Artistic Director (4) Archivist for (1) bookings for services, functions or tours (2) musical matters (3) artistic matters (4) historical matters.

Access:
Access to staff: By letter, by telephone, by fax, by email, visitors by prior appointment
Access to building, collections or gallery: No prior appointment required
Hours: Daily, 0800 to 1800
Access for disabled people: Parking provided, ramped entry, toilet facilities
Other restrictions: Access to all areas except the crypt.

Information services:
Special visitor services: Guided tours, materials and/or activities for children.
Education services: Group education facilities, resources for Key Stages 1 and 2, 3, 4 and Further or Higher Education.
Services for disabled people: For the hearing impaired.

Collections:
Diocesan and Cathedral Archives
Modern Christian Art - sculpture, mosaic, paintings and fabric
Photoghraphic archive and display of construction of Crypt and Cathedral

Catalogues:
Catalogue for all of the collections is only available in-house.

Printed publications:
Guide Books
Educational Material
Postcards

Address for ordering publications:
Printed publications:
The Manager, The Bookshop
Liverpool Metropolitan Cathedral of Christ The King, tel: 0151 707 2109, fax: 0151 708 7274, email: met.cathedral@cwcom.net

Internet home pages:
http://www.liverpoolmetrocathedral.org.uk
History, description, virtual tour, current events and sevices

1619
LIVERPOOL MUSEUM

National Museums & Galleries on Merseyside, William Brown Street, Liverpool, L3 8EN

Tel: 0151 207 0001
Fax: 0151 478 4390
Email: kate.johnson@nmgm.org
Acronym or abbreviation: NMGM
Formed: 1851
Formerly: City of Liverpool Museums from 1851 to 1974; Merseyside County Museums from 1974 to 1986

Organisation type and purpose: National government body, registered charity (charity number XN 74812), museum, suitable for ages: all ages.

Enquiries to: Curator

Access:
Access to staff: By letter, by telephone, by fax, by email, visitors by prior appointment, Internet web pages
Access to building, collections or gallery: No prior appointment required
Hours: Mon to Sat, 1000 to 1700; Sun, 1200 to 1700
Closed Dec 23 to 26 and Jan 1
Access for disabled people: Parking provided, ramped entry, level entry, access to all public areas, toilet facilities

General description:
Archaeology, botany, ethnology, geology, physical science, zoology.

Information services:
Library available for reference (for conditions see Access above)
Enquiry service available by personal application.
Objects can be brought for a curator's opinion each Thursday afternoon, 1400 to 1600hrs.
Special visitor services: Materials and/or activities for children.
Education services: Group education facilities, resources for Key Stages 1 and 2, 3, 4 and Further or Higher Education..

Collections:
Merseyside (Archaeological) Sites and Monuments Record

Catalogues:
Catalogue for library is in-house only. Catalogue for part of the collections is only available in-house.

Publications list:
is available in hard copy and online.
Printed publications:
Liverpool Museum (full colour guide)
Books on the permanent collections and loan exhibitions, monographs and guides including:
Precious Vessels: 200 Years of Chinese Pottery
The Lever and Hope Sculptures (Roman marble sculptures)
Tavern Checks from Liverpool and Vicinity
Historic Glass from Collections in North West England
Man and the Changing Landscape (an integrated landscape study of the Central Pennines)
The Archaeology of Merseyside
The Art of the Samurai
The Wetlands of Merseyside
Herbs in Medicine and in the Kitchen
Sand Dunes of the Sefton Coast
James Bolton of Halifax (botanical artist and naturalist 1735-1799)
The Dragonflies and Damselflies of Cheshire
The Butterflies of Cheshire

Address for ordering publications:
Printed publications:
NMGM Enterprises Ltd, National Museums and Galleries on Merseyside
127 Dale Street, Liverpool, L69 3LA, tel: 0151 478 4685, fax: 0151 478 4790, email: publications@nmgm.org

Internet home pages:
http://www.nmgm.org.uk
http://www.nmgm.org.uk/publications
Publications list.

1620
LIVERPOOL UNIVERSITY ART GALLERY
3 Abercromby Square, Liverpool, L69 7WY

Tel: 0151 794 2347/8
Fax: 0151 794 2343
Email: artgall@liverpool.ac.uk
Full name: University of Liverpool Art Gallery
Formed: 1979

Organisation type and purpose: Art gallery, university department or institute.
Other address:
Liverpool University Art Gallery
6 Abercromby Square, Liverpool, L69 7WY

Enquiries to: Curator
Direct email: acompton@liverpool.ac.uk
Access:
Access to staff: By letter, by telephone, by fax, by email
Hours: Mon to Fri, 0900 to 1700
Access to building, collections or gallery: No access other than to staff
Hours: Gallery: Mon, Tue, Thu, 1200 to 1400; Wed, Fri, 1200 to 1600

General description:
The collections of British art 1700 to present of the University of Liverpool have been accruing since 1881, mostly as gifts and bequests, but also with purchases since the late 1950s. They include works of fine and applied art, including paintings by Audubon, Wright of Derby and Turner; a representative collection of early English watercolours; another of early English porcelain; and sculpture by Epstein, Hepworth and Frink. Also contains prints, silver and glass 1700 to 1900; icons 1600 to 1900. The focus of the collections is the Art Gallery located in an early 19th century terraced house.
Collections:
Original works by John James Audubon, considered to be the largest outside the USA, early 19th century
Sir Sydney Jones. Early English watercolours, c. 60 items
Sir Sydney Jones. Early English porcelain, c. 300 items
Catalogues:
Catalogue for all of the collections is only available in-house.
Publications list:
is available in hard copy and online.
Printed publications:
Charles Reilly & Liverpool School of Architecture (Sharples etc, £15)
Public Sculpture of Liverpool (Cavanagh T, £15.95)
From Hogarth to Rowlandson: Medecine in Art (Haslam F, £18.99)
Barbara Hepworth Reconsidered (Thistlewood D ed, £22.50)
Publications and exhibition catalogues include:
Medieval Manuscripts on Merseyside (1993 exhibition catalogue, £6)

1621
LIVERPOOL UNIVERSITY
Museum of Dentistry, Edwards Building, Pembroke Place, Liverpool, L3 5PS

Formed: 1880

Organisation type and purpose: Museum, university department or institute.
Affiliated to:
North West Museums Association

Enquiries to: Curator
Direct tel: ext 5279
Access:
Access to staff: By letter only
Access to building, collections or gallery: Prior appointment required
Other restrictions: Write to make an appointment to view the collections.

General description:
History of dentistry and dental instruments; artefacts and archives.
Collections:
Early dental books and a collection of ivory dentures

1622
LIVERPOOL UNIVERSITY
Archaeology Museum, School of Archaeology, Classics and Oriental Studies, 14 Abercromby Square, Liverpool, L69 7WZ

Tel: 0151 794 2467
Fax: 0151 794 2220
Email: winkerpa@liv.ac.uk
Formed: 1904

Organisation type and purpose: Museum, university department or institute.

Enquiries to: Curator
Access:
Access to staff: By letter, by email

General description:
Egyptology, classical archaeology and Near Eastern archaeology.
Collections:
Artefacts and photographs
Mainly objects from the excavations of Professor John Garstang in Egypt and the Near East
Collections of classical Aegean and prehistoric antiquities, and a selection of coins from the Barnard and Chevasse collections

Internet home pages:
http://www.liv.ac.uk/sacos/facilities/museum.html

1623
LIVESEY MUSEUM FOR CHILDREN
682 Old Kent Road, London, SE15 1JF

Tel: 020 7639 5604
Fax: 020 7277 5384
Email: livesey.museum@southwark.gov.uk
Formed: 1974

Organisation type and purpose: Local government body, museum.
Interactive and educational children's museum for up to 12 year olds, their schools, families and carers.
Parent body:
Southwark Culture & Heritage Service

Enquiries to: Manager
Access:
Access to staff: By letter, by telephone, by fax, by email
Hours: Tue to Sat, 1000 to 1700

General description:
Interactive and educational exhibitions including, the Great Rubbish Show, Mind Your Language, Number Crunching, Transformations.
Information services:
Special visitor services: Materials and/or activities for children.
Education services: Group education facilities, resources for Key Stages 1 and 2..
Printed publications:
Information Packs provided for each exhibition (charge made)

1624
DAVID LIVINGSTONE CENTRE
165 Station Road, Blantyre, Glasgow, G72 9BT

Tel: 01698 823140
Fax: 01698 821424
Formed: 1929

Organisation type and purpose: Museum.
Parent body:
National Trust for Scotland (West Region)

Enquiries to: Education Officer
Access:
Access to staff: By letter, by telephone, by fax
Hours: Mon to Sat, 1000 to 1700; Sun, 1230 to 1700 (last admission 1630)

General description:
Housed in the birthplace of David Livingstone (1813 to 1873), this is a collection of artefacts is related to his life from his childhood, working in 19th century cotton mills to his explorations in Africa. There is also a social history collection pertaining to Blantyre and the local area, and some cotton and coal industry artefacts.
Information services:
Special visitor services: Guided tours.
Education services: Group education facilities..

1625
LIZARD COUNTRYSIDE OFFICE
See - Lizard Wireless Station; Marconi Centre

1626
LIZARD LIGHTHOUSE
The Lizard, Helston, Cornwall, TR12 7NT

Tel: 01326 290065
Fax: 01326 290065

Organisation type and purpose: Historic building, house or site, suitable for ages: 8+.
Managed by:
The Trevithick Trust
Tel: 01209 210900
Owned by:
Trinity House

Enquiries to: Manager
Access:
Access to staff: By letter, by telephone, by fax

General description:
Most Southerly Lighthouse on mainland Britain, first built 1751. Fog Signal survives; visitors can see the engine room and the top of the lighthouse tower.
Information services:
Special visitor services: Guided tours..

Internet home pages:
http://www.trevithicktrust.com

1627
LIZARD WIRELESS STATION
Bass Point, The Lizard, Nr Heston, Cornwall

Tel: 01326 290384

Organisation type and purpose: National organisation, registered charity (charity number

continued overleaf

205846), historic building, house or site, suitable for ages: 5+.
Parent body:
National Trust (South West)
Regional Office for Devon and Cornwall, tel: 01208 74281

Enquiries to: Warden
Direct tel: 01326 561407 (Lizard Countryside Office)
Direct fax: 01326 562882
Direct email: lizard@nationaltrust.org.uk
Access:
Access to staff: By letter, by telephone, by fax, by email
Access to building, collections or gallery: No prior appointment required
Hours: Please telephone for opening times
Access for disabled people: toilet facilities

General description:
This area has played a key role in the history of modern communications. Marconi's historic wireless experiments on the Lizard in 1901 are celebrated at the restored Lizard Wireless Station.

Internet home pages:
http://www.nationaltrust.org.uk/regions/cornwall

See also - Marconi Centre

1628
LLANCAIACH FAWR MANOR LIVING HISTORY MUSEUM
Nelson, Treharris, Mid Glamorgan, CF46 6ER

Tel: 01443 412248
Fax: 01443 412688
Formed: 1991

Organisation type and purpose: Local government body, museum, historic building, house or site, suitable for ages: all ages.
Parent body:
Caerphilly County Borough Council

Enquiries to: Manager
Access:
Access to staff: By letter, by telephone, by fax, by email
Access for disabled people: toilet facilities

General description:
Tudor semi-fortified manor refurbished to mid-17th century state, costumed interpreters, specialising in the Civil War years.
Information services:
Visitor centre, exhibition, gift shop and restaurant.
Special visitor services: Materials and/or activities for children.
Education services: Group education facilities, resources for Key Stages 1 and 2, 3 and 4..
Collections:
Llancaiach Fawr features an exhibition which includes an in-depth history of the site, its archaeological finds, and a selection of reproduction costumes and artefacts.

Internet home pages:
http://www.caerphilly.gov.uk

1629
LLANDUDNO MUSEUM
17-19 Gloddaeth Street, Llandudno, Gwynedd, LL30 2DD

Tel: 01492 876517
Fax: 01492 876517
Email: llandudno.museum@lineone.net
Formed: 1927
Formerly: The Chardon Trust

Organisation type and purpose: Independently owned, registered charity (charity number 217013), museum, historic building, house or site, suitable for ages: all ages.
Links with:
ChardonTrust
Tel: 01492 876517, fax: 01492 876517

Enquiries to: Curator
Other contacts: Honorary Secretary for any complaints.
Access:
Access to staff: By letter, by telephone, by fax, by email, visitors by prior appointment
Access to building, collections or gallery: Prior appointment required
Access for disabled people: ramped entry, toilet facilities
Other restrictions: No access to 1st floor.

General description:
Paintings, sculpture, objets d'art, archaeology, prehistoric, Roman and industrial, Welsh kitchen reconstruction, social history of Llandudno town resort from Victorian to 20th century, WWI and WWII memorabilia, artefacts from the Bronze Age Great Orme copper mines, and various temporary exhibitions.
Information services:
Available to assist research enquiries from public.
Special visitor services: Guided tours.
Education services: Resources for Key Stages 1 and 2..
Collections:
The Chardon Bequest of paintings, sculptures and objets d'art
Roman objects from Kanovium Port
Llandudno Field Club Collection (natural history & geology, not on display)
Llandudno Royal Artillery Association Collection

1630
LLANERCHAERON
Ciliau Aeron, Aberaeron, Ceredigion, SA48 8DG

Tel: 01545 570200
Fax: 01545 571759
Email: llanerchaeron@nationaltrust.org.uk

Organisation type and purpose: National organisation, registered charity (charity number 205846), historic building, house or site, suitable for ages: 8+.
Parent body:
The National Trust Office for Wales
Trinity Square, Llandudno, LL30 2DE, tel: 01492 860123, fax: 01492 860233

Enquiries to: Manager
Access:
Access to staff: By letter, by telephone, by email
Access to building, collections or gallery: No prior appointment required
Hours: Easter to November, Wed to Sun, 1130 1630,
Open Bank Holidays Mondays
Access for disabled people: ramped entry, toilet facilities
Other restrictions: Drop-off point. Ground floor fully accessible, Alternative entrance to service courtyard. No access to other floors. Grounds largely accessible.

General description:
Llanerchaeron is a small 18th century Welsh gentry estate, set in the beautiful Dyffryn Aeron. The estate survived virtually unaltered into the 20th century and was bequeathed to the National Trust by J. P. Ponsonby Lewes in 1989. The house was designed and built by John Nash in 1794-96 and is the most complete example of his early work. Llanerchaeron was a self-sufficient estate - evident in the dairy, laundry, brewery and salting house of the service courtyard, as well as the Home Farm buildings from the stables to the threshing barns. Llanerchaeron today is a working organic farm, and the two restored walled gardens also produce home-grown fruit and herbs. There are extensive walks around the estate and parkland.
Information services:
Helpline available, tel no: Infoline 01558 825147.
Guided tours of the garden and Home Farm start 1330 every Thur, Jun to Sep.
Hip-carrying infant seats for loan.
Suitable for school groups. Education room/centre. Children's quiz/trail.
Special visitor services: Guided tours, materials and/or activities for children.
Education services: Group education facilities..

Internet home pages:
http://www.nationaltrust.org.uk

1631
LLANGOLLEN CANAL MUSEUM
The Wharf, Wharf Hill, Llangollen, Denbighshire, LL20 8TA

Tel: 01978 860702
Fax: 01978 860702
Email: sue@horsedrawnboats.co.uk
Acronym or abbreviation: WCHC Ltd
Formed: 1884

Organisation type and purpose: Independently owned, suitable for ages: all ages.
Visitor attraction.

Enquiries to: Director
Access:
Access to staff: By letter, by telephone, by fax, by email, in person
Access to building, collections or gallery: No prior appointment required
Hours: Daily, 1000 to 1700
Access for disabled people: level entry, access to all public areas, toilet facilities
Other restrictions: Pick-up/drop-off point only.

General description:
The rise and decline of Britain's canal system.
Information services:
Special visitor services: Guided tours, materials and/or activities for children.
Education services: Group education facilities, resources for Key Stages 1 and 2 and 3..
Collections:
Working models of Anderton boat lift and a swing bridge
Boat engine, mock-up of boatman's cabin from working boat
Model showing various stages of canal-building etc

Internet home pages:
http://www.horsedrawnboats.co.uk
Trip and facilities information.

1632
LLANGOLLEN MOTOR MUSEUM
Pentre Felin, Llangollen, Denbighshire, LL20 8EE

Tel: 01978 860324
Email: llangollenmotormuseum@hotmail.com
Formed: 1986

Organisation type and purpose: Museum, suitable for ages: all ages.
Reference library of motoring books.

Enquiries to: Curator
Access:
Access to staff: By letter, by telephone
Access to building, collections or gallery: No prior appointment required
Hours: Feb to Nov: Tue to Sun, 1000 to 1700
Other restrictions: Closed Dec and Jan
Access for disabled people: Parking provided, level entry, access to all public areas

General description:
Motor vehicles, garage equipment, models, memorabilia, representations of garage life in the 1950s, 'Hands-on' examples of how things work, the oldest motor-drawn caravan in the UK, cutaway models for demonstration.
A small exhibition showing the development of our canal network, Owners are always ready to explain and demonstrate.
Information services:
Library available for reference (for conditions see Access above)
Special visitor services: Materials and/or activities for children.
Services for disabled people: Displays and/or information at wheelchair height.

Internet home pages:
http://www.llangollenmotormuseum.co.uk
General pictures and information about the museum.

1633
LLEYN HISTORICAL & MARITIME MUSEUM

Old St Mary's Church, Church Street, Nefyn, Gwynedd

Tel: 01758 720270

Organisation type and purpose: Registered charity (charity number 514365), museum, historic building, house or site, suitable for ages: 8+.
Member of the:
Gwynedd and Anglesey Federation of Maritime Museums
Access:
Access to staff: By letter, by telephone

General description:
The museum is housed in the Old Church on the site of a 6th century Celtic church. Paintings, photographs and artefacts relate the local maritime history including ship building, coasting vessels, the herring industry and also everyday life at the turn of the 19th century.

1634
LLOYD GEORGE MUSEUM AND HIGHGATE COTTAGE

Llanystumdwy, Criccieth, Gwynedd, LL52 0SH

Tel: 01766 522071
Fax: 01766 522071
Email: nestthomas@gwynedd.gov.uk
Formed: 1948

Organisation type and purpose: Local government body, registered charity, museum, historic building, house or site, suitable for ages: all ages, research organisation.
Parent body:
Gwynedd Council
Gwynedd Education and Culture, Museums Service, tel: 01286 679698, fax: 01286 679637, email: amgueddfeydd-museums@gwynedd.gov.uk
Close liaison with:
Council of Museums in Wales
National Museum of Wales
Other addresses:
Caernarfon Record Office
Caernarfon, Gwynned, LL55 1SH, tel: 01286 679098, email/website: nestthomas@gwynedd.gov.uk

Enquiries to: Museums and Gallery Officer
Direct tel: 01286 679698
Direct fax: 01286 679637
Other contacts: Archivist and Heritage Officer, Senior Custodian
Access:
Access to staff: By letter, by telephone, by fax, by email, visitors by prior appointment
Hours: Mon to Fri, 0900 to 1700
Access to building, collections or gallery: No prior appointment required
Hours: Easter, daily, 1030 to 1700
May, Mon to Fri, 1030 to 1700
June, Mon to Sat, 1030 to 1700
July to Sep, daily, 1030 to 1700
Oct, Mon to Fri, 1100 to 1600
Open bank holidays
Access for disabled people: toilet facilities
Other restrictions: Access to museum, the ground floor of the cottage and the shoemaker's house.

General description:
History, social, political and economic; geography; decorative art; Lloyd George, First World War.
Collections:
Collection of original Punch cartoons
Costumes, memorabilia
Lloyd George Library
Original Archives eg Versailles Peace Treaty
Social history artefacts at Highgate
The Lloyd George Museum Trust Collection
Catalogues:
Catalogue for library is in-house only. Catalogue for part of the collections is only available in-house.
Publications list:
is available in hard copy.
Printed publications:
Megan Lloyd George (£2.50)
Lloyd George Museum Souvenir Booklet (£3)
David Lloyd George (£3.95)

1635
LOCAL HISTORY AND ARCHAEOLOGICAL RESOURCE CENTRE

31 Stock Street, London, E13 0BX

Tel: 020 8472 4785
Email: susan.gosling@newham.gov.uk
Formed from: Newham Museum Service, Passmore Edwards Museum

Organisation type and purpose: Local government body, museum, suitable for ages: 16+.
Parent body:
London Borough of Newham
Newham Heritage Service
Leisure Services, tel: 020 8430 2457, email: leisure.heritage@newham.gov.uk
Other addresses:
Newham Heritage Service
The Old Dispensary, 30 Romford Road, Stratford, London, E15 4BX, tel: 020 8430 6393

Enquiries to: Collections Officer
Access:
Access to staff: By letter, by telephone, by email, visitors by prior appointment
Hours: Tue, Wed, Thu, 1000 to 1600
Access to building, collections or gallery: Prior appointment required
Access for disabled people: level entry

General description:
Archaeology relating to Newham area and some Essex sites.
Local history of Newham.
Information services:
Education services: Group education facilities, resources for Key Stage 2..
Collections:
Madge Gill (outsider artist)
Bow porcelain
Catalogues:
Catalogue for part of the collections is only available in-house.

Address for ordering publications:
Printed publications:
Local History and Archaeology Resource Centre, Newham Heritage Service
The Old Dispensary, 30 Romford Road, London, E15 4BZ

Internet home pages:
http://www.newham.gov.uk

1636
LOCAL STUDIES CENTRE

Central Library, Northumberland Square, North Shields, Tyne and Wear, NE30 1QA

Tel: 0191 200 5424
Fax: 0191 200 6118
Email: eric.hollerton@northtyneside.gov.uk
Formed: 1974

Organisation type and purpose: Local government body.
Archive.
Parent body:
North Tyneside Council

Enquiries to: Librarian
Access:
Access to staff: By letter, by telephone, by fax, by email, in person
Access for disabled people: level entry, access to all public areas, toilet facilities
Other restrictions: Wheelchair available.

General description:
Contains printed sources dealing with people and organisations in or from the present North Tyneside Borough, past, present and future.
There is also a collection of local photographs.
Collections:
Theatre Royal, North Shields, playbills. 1820s. Numerous
Shields Daily News. 1864-.
Catalogues:
Catalogue for library is in-house only.

Internet home pages:
http://www.northtyneside.gov.uk/libraries/index.htm
Access to libraries, current events.

1637
LODGE PARK AND SHERBORNE ESTATE

Aldsworth, Cheltenham, Gloucestershire, GL54 3PP

Tel: 01451 844130, 01451844257 (Estate Office)
Fax: 01451 844131
Email: lodgepark@ntrust.org.uk

Organisation type and purpose: National organisation, registered charity, historic building, house or site, suitable for ages: 5+.
Parent body:
The National Trust (South West Region)
Wessex Regional Office, tel: 01985 843600

Enquiries to: Manager
Access:
Access to staff: By letter, by telephone, by fax
Access to building, collections or gallery: No prior appointment required
Hours: Grandstand: end Mar to end Oct, 1100 to1600, Mon, Fri, Sun; Nov to end Mar, Sat, 1100 to 1500
Estate: all year, daily
Access for disabled people: Parking provided, toilet facilities
Other restrictions: Designated parking 50yards. Drop-off point. 1 manual wheelchair available, booking
essential. Steps to entrance. Ramp available. Ground floor accessible with assistance. No access to other floors. Audio-visual/video. Photograph album. Recommended route map.

General description:
Situated on the picturesque Sherborne Estate in the Cotswolds, Lodge Park was created in 1634 by John 'Crump' Dutton. Inspired by his passion for gambling and banqueting it is a unique survival of what would have been called a grandstand, with its deer course and park. It was the home of Charles Dutton, 7th Lord Sherborne, until 1982 when he bequeathed his family's estate to the National Trust. The grandstand has been reconstructed to its original form and is the first project of its kind undertaken by the Trust that relies totally on archaeological evidence. The park behind was designed by Charles Bridgeman in 1725. The Sherborne Estate is 1650ha (4000 acres) of rolling Cotswold countryside with sweeping views down to the River Windrush. Much of the village of Sherborne is owned by the Trust, including the post office and shop, school and social club. There are walks for all ages around the estate, which include the restored and working water meadows.
Information services:
Helpline available, tel no: Infoline 01684 855369.
Suitable for school groups. Education room/centre. Children's quiz/trail.
Introductory slide talks given at regular intervals throughout the day.
Out of hours guided tours and walks can be arranged.

continued overleaf

Braille guide.
Special visitor services: Materials and/or activities for children.
Education services: Group education facilities, resources for Key Stages 1 and 2, 3 and 4.
Services for disabled people: For the visually impaired.

Internet home pages:
http://www.nationaltrust.org.uk/regions/wessex

1638
LOGIE STEADING ART GALLERY

Logie, Forres, Moray, IV36 2QN

Tel: 01309 611378
Fax: 01309 611300
Email: panny@logie.co.uk
Formed: 1992

Organisation type and purpose: Independently owned, art gallery, suitable for ages: 16+.

Enquiries to: Manager
Direct tel: 01309 611278
Access:
Access to staff: By letter, by email
Access for disabled people: Parking provided, ramped entry, toilet facilities

General description:
Ever-changing exhibition of contemporary, predominantly Scottish, art. Oils, watercolours, original prints, drawings, wood, ceramics, bronzes, glass, cards.

Internet home pages:
http://www.logie.co.uk/steading/artgallery.htm

1639
LONDON AND GUILDHALL MUSEUMS

See - Museum of London

1640
LONDON BRASS RUBBING CENTRE

The Crypt, St Martin-in-the-Fields Church, Trafalgar Square, London, WC2N 4JJ

Tel: 020 7930 9306
Fax: 020 7930 9306
Acronym or abbreviation: LBRC
Formed: 1975

Organisation type and purpose: Independently owned.
Brass rubbing centre.
To bring the traditional hobby of brass rubbing to the widest possible public by providing an excellent cross-section of brasses - geographically, historically and in their social mix - and specialist materials.
Member of:
London Tourist Board
Glen House, Stag Place, London, SW1E 5LT
Monumental Brass Society
Society of Antiquaries, Piccadilly, London

Enquiries to: Director
Other contacts: Manager for operating details, group bookings, etc.
Access:
Access to staff: By letter, by fax
Hours: 1000 to 1800

General description:
Brasses in replica from 1297 to Victorian era form the collection with additions of some medieval woodcuts and images from Celtic illuminations. Social customs, development of costume and armour can all be traced. Making rubbings from these brasses is open to visitors with guidance from staff and provision of specialist materials. Suitable activity for everyone aged 7 and beyond. Inclusive prices for rubbing from £2.50.
Collections:
Studio display of brass rubbings covering the period 1311 to 1640, with three Victorian designs

1641
LONDON CANAL MUSEUM

12-13 New Wharf Road, London, N1 9RT

Tel: 020 7713 0836
Fax: 020 7689 6679
Email: info@canalmuseum.org.uk
Formed: 1992

Organisation type and purpose: Independently owned, voluntary organisation, registered charity (charity number 277484), museum, historic building, house or site.
Member of:
Association of Independent Museums (AIM)
Inland Waterways Association
Islington Voluntary Service Council
Transport Trust
Run by:
Canal Museum Trust

Enquiries to: Secretary
Access:
Access to staff: By letter, by fax, by email, in person, visitors by prior appointment, Internet web pages
Hours: Staff access by appointment only
Access to building, collections or gallery: No prior appointment required
Hours: Tue to Sun, 1000 to 1630
Other restrictions: Closed Mon.
Access for disabled people: level entry

General description:
United Kingdom canals, canal life and development, the ice trade.
Information services:
Library available for reference (for conditions see Access above)
Special visitor services: Materials and/or activities for children.
Education services: Group education facilities, resources for Key Stage 2.
Services for disabled people: For the hearing impaired; displays and/or information at wheelchair height.
Catalogues:
Catalogue for library is in-house only. Catalogue for all of the collections is available in-house and part is on-line.

Internet home pages:
http://www.canalmuseum.org.uk/wap/index.wml
WAP site.
http://www.canalmuseum.org.uk
Information about the museum, London's canals and their history, the ice trade, conference hire of building and related pages.

1642
LONDON FIRE BRIGADE MUSEUM

Winchester House, 94 Southwark Bridge Road, London, SE1 0EG

Tel: 020 7587 2894
Fax: 020 7587 2878
Email: museum@london-fire.gov.uk
Acronym or abbreviation: LFB Museum
Formed: c1960s

Organisation type and purpose: Museum, suitable for ages: 5+.

Enquiries to: Curator
Access:
Access to staff: By letter, by telephone, by fax, by email, visitors by prior appointment
Access to building, collections or gallery: Prior appointment required
Access for disabled people: toilet facilities

General description:
A collection of firefighting equipment and memorabilia. Illustrates the history of firefighting in London from the Great Fire of 1666 to modern times. Includes models; photographs; buttons and badges; uniforms; medals; World War II items.

Information services:
Special visitor services: Guided tours, materials and/or activities for children..
Collections:
Objects, fire applicances, paintings, photographs, uniforms, equipment, all relating to the fire service
London insurance firemarks, late 17th century, 60 plus items
Section of early London water main, 1650s
Publications list:
is available in hard copy.

1643
LONDON HOSPITAL MEDICAL COLLEGE

See - Royal London Hospital Archives and Museum

1644
LONDON MUSEUM OF JEWISH LIFE

Closed
See - Jewish Museum; Jewish Museum Finchley

1645
LONDON TOURIST BOARD LIMITED

5th Floor, 1 Warwick Row, London, SW1E 5ER

Tel: 020 7932 2044
Fax: 020 7932 2067
Acronym or abbreviation: LTB

Organisation type and purpose: Tourist Board.

Enquiries to: Information Officer
Direct tel: 020 7932 2000
Direct fax: 020 7932 0222
Direct email: enquiries@londontouristboard.co.uk
Access:
Access to staff: By letter, by telephone, by fax, by email, Internet web pages

General description:
What to see, and where to go and stay in London.
Publications list:
is available in hard copy and online.
Printed publications:
London Capital Breaks
Annual Events
London for the Travel Trade
Where to stay and what to do
Where to stay on a Budget
Events in London
Children's London

Address for ordering publications:
Printed publications:
Information Department, London Tourist Board

Internet home pages:
http://www.londontouristboard.co.uk
http://www.londontown.com/

1646
LONDON TOY AND MODEL MUSEUM

21-23 Craven Hill, Bayswater, London, W2 3EN

Tel: 020 7706 8000
Fax: 020 7706 8823
Formed: 1982

Organisation type and purpose: Museum.

Enquiries to: Curator
Access:
Access to staff: By letter, by telephone, by fax, visitors by prior appointment

General description:
History of toys and models from the 1850s to the present day, toy manufacturers.
Collections:
1899-1924 Model Engineer magazine
Bassett-Lowke and Meccano Collections

Doll Collection from 1 AD to 1930s
General Reference Toy and Model magazines
Open Air 2'and 7'gauge working model railways
Peter Bull Teddy Bear Collection
Printed publications:
Teachers' Pack: Victorian Playthings (1995, free)
Teachers' Pack: Steam to Battery - Toy Technology (1995, free)
London Toy and Model Museum Brochure/ Guide (1995, £2.50)

1647
LONDON UNIVERSITY
See - Courtauld Institute of Art, Book Library; Robertson Museum and Aquarium

1648
LONDON'S TRANSPORT MUSEUM
39 Wellington Street, Covent Garden, London, WC2E 7BB

Tel: 020 7379 6344
Fax: 020 7497 3527
Email: resource@ltmuseum.co.uk

Organisation type and purpose: (charity number 211091), museum.
The Museum manages Transport for London's historical collections and displays them on its behalf.
Links with:
The Friends of London's Transport Museum at the same address

Enquiries to: Librarian
Access:
Access to staff: By letter, by telephone, by fax, by email, visitors by prior appointment, charges made to all users, Internet web pages
Hours: Mon to Wed, 1000 to 1230 and 1400 to 1700; Fri, 1100 to 1230 and 1400 to 1700
Other restrictions: Libraries by appointment only.
Learning Centre is open on a drop-in basis, daily, 1000 to 1730.
Access to building, collections or gallery: No prior appointment required
Other restrictions: No prior appointment required for main gallery
Access for disabled people: ramped entry, toilet facilities
Other restrictions: Above facilities for the Main gallery.

General description:
Development of public transport in London (buses, trams, trolleybuses and underground railways architecture and design) since the beginning of the 19th century, particularly the history of London Transport, the organisation and its predecessor companies, subject from poster design to station architecture.
Information services:
Library available for reference (for conditions see Access above)
The Learning Centre is primarily intended as an adult learning area. Families are welcome, but unaccompanied children under 10 are admitted at the discretion of staff. The Museum offers a wide range of resources specifically designed for school groups; contact the School Visits Service, tel 020 7565 7298.
Special visitor services: Guided tours, materials and/or activities for children.
Education services: Group education facilities, resources for Key Stages 1 and 2, 3, 4 and Further or Higher Education.
Services for disabled people: For the visually impaired; for the hearing impaired; displays and/or information at wheelchair height.
Collections:
London Transport photograph archive, *c.* 1810 to present
London Transport poster archive, 1908 to present
Frank Pick Collection (documents and writings of Frank Pick)
Reinohl collection of tickets and transport ephemera
Video collection *c.* 1920s to present
Catalogues:
Catalogue for all of the collections is only available in-house.
Printed publications:
Exhibition Leaflets
London's Transport Museum Guide
Education Packs includes:
Nursery and KS1 pack
Numeracy pack
Literacy pack
Science pack
Victorian London pack

Internet home pages:
http://www.ltmuseum.co.uk
Introduction to the museum and its many collections
http://www.ltmuseum.co.uk/education
Information regarding school visits

1649
LONG CRENDON COURTHOUSE
Long Crendon, Aylesbury, Buckinghamshire, HP18 9AN

Tel: 01494 528051(Regional Office)

Organisation type and purpose: National organisation, registered charity (charity number 205846), historic building, house or site, suitable for ages: 12+.
Parent body:
The National Trust (South and South East Region)
Thames and Solent Regional Office, tel: 01494 528051
Other addresses:
Claydon House
Middle Claydon, MK18 2EY, tel: 01296 730349, email/website: claydon@nationaltrust.org.uk

Enquiries to: Manager
Direct tel: 01296 730344
Direct email: claydon@nationaltrust.org.uk
Access:
Access to staff: By letter, by telephone, by email
Access to building, collections or gallery: No prior appointment required
Hours: End Mar to Sep, Sat, Sun, Bank Holidays, 1100 to 1800; Wed, 1400 to 1800
Other restrictions: Upper floor only

General description:
A 15th century two-storeyed building, partly timbered and probably first used as a wool store. A fine example of early timber-frame construction. The manorial courts were held here from the reign of Henry V until Victorian times.

Internet home pages:
http://www.nationaltrust.org.uk

1650
LONG SHOP STEAM MUSEUM
Main Street, Leiston, Suffolk, IP16 4ES

Tel: 01728 832189
Fax: 01728 832189
Email: longshop@care4free.net
Formed: 1984
Formerly: Long Shop Museum, date of change, 1997

Organisation type and purpose: Registered charity (charity number 283444), museum, historic building, house or site, suitable for ages: 5+.
Parent body:
Long Shop Project Trust
Tel: 01728 832189, fax: 01728 832189, email: longshop@care4free.net
Federated with the:
Museum of East Anglian Life

Enquiries to: Manager
Access:
Access to staff: By letter, by telephone, by fax
Access to building, collections or gallery: No prior appointment required
Access for disabled people: access to all public areas, toilet facilities

General description:
Local, social and industrial history. The Long Shop built in 1852 by Richard Garrett was one of the first production lines for steam engines; the first Loman Doctor. Home of the Garrett Collection.
Catalogues:
Catalogue for library is in-house only. Catalogue for all of the collections is only available in-house.

Internet home pages:
http://www.longshop.care4free.net
Education website.
http://www.suffolkcc.gov.uk/libraries_and_heritage/sro/garrett/index.html
Libraries and heritage website. Garrett archives.

1651
LONGDALE CRAFT CENTRE AND MUSEUM
Longdale Lane, Ravenshead, Nottinghamshire, NG15 9AH

Tel: 01623 794888
Fax: 01623 794858
Email: longdale@longdale.co.uk
Formed: 1972
Access:
Access for disabled people: Parking provided, ramped entry, level entry, access to all public areas

General description:
Museum of Victorian goods. Craft workshops and courses.
Collections:
Victorian kitchen equipment, 1780-.
Farm equipment, 1700s
Stocking and knitting machines, 1780s
Clockmaker's equipment, 1800s
Lary collection of woodworking tools, 1746-.
Stained glass original windows, 1850
Stained glass original cartoons, 1850

1652
LONGSANDS MUSEUM
St Neots

Closed

1653
LONGTHORPE TOWER
Peterborough, Cambridgeshire

Tel: 01733 268482 (weekends only)

Organisation type and purpose: Historic building, house or site.
Parent body:
English Heritage (East of England Region)
Brooklands, 24 Brooklands Avenue, Cambridge, CB2 2BU, tel: 01223 582700, fax: 01223 582701
Access:
Access to building, collections or gallery: No prior appointment required
Hours: Apr to Oct: Sat-Sun and Bank Holidays only, 1200 to 17000
Other restrictions: Opening times are subject to change, for up-to-date information contact English Heritage by phone or visit the website.

General description:
Tower has the finest 14th century domestic wall paintings in northern Europe, showing many secular and spiritual subjects.

Internet home pages:
http://www.english-heritage.org.uk

1654
LOOK OUT DISCOVERY CENTRE, THE

Nine Mile Ride, Bracknell, Berkshire, RG12 7QW

Tel: 01344 354400
Fax: 01344 354422
Email: thelookout@bracknell-forest.gov.uk
Formed: 1991
Formerly: Discovery Outpost; The Look Out Discovery Park, date of change, 2000

Organisation type and purpose: Local government body, museum, suitable for ages: 5+.
Hands-on interactive science and nature exhibition.
Connections with:
Techniquest
Stuart Street, Cardiff, CF10 5BW, tel: 02920 475475

Enquiries to: Information Officer
Access:
Access to staff: By letter, by telephone, by fax, by email, in person, Internet web pages
Hours: Mon to Sun, 0930 to 1730
Access to building, collections or gallery: No prior appointment required
Hours: Daily, 1000 to 1700
Access for disabled people: Parking provided, ramped entry, access to all public areas, toilet facilities

General description:
Hands-on science and nature exhibition.
Information services:
Education services: Group education facilities, resources for Key Stages 1 and 2 and 3.
Services for disabled people: Displays and/or information at wheelchair height.
Publications list:
is available on-line.

Internet home pages:
http://www.bracknell-forest.gov.uk

1655
LOSTWITHIEL MUSEUM

Fore Street, Lostwithiel, Cornwall

Tel: 01208 872079

Organisation type and purpose: Registered charity, museum, historic building, house or site.

Enquiries to: Chairman
Access:
Access to staff: By letter
Access for disabled people: level entry

General description:
The museum is situated on the ground floor of the Guidhall, which was built in 1740 and originally housed the old Corn Exchange and town lock-up. A local history collection covering Lostwithiel and surroundings, with a wide range of domestic, trade and agricultural objects. Other items of interest include the town's 18th century fire engine, wooden stocks, and the cloak worn by the town serjeant when he was murdered in 1814. There is also a growing collection of local photographs.
Catalogues:
Catalogue for part of the collections is only available in-house.
Printed publications:
Civil War Diary
Lostwithiel Past & Present
Museum Matters

1656
LOTHERTON HALL

Lotherton Lane, Aberford, Leeds, West Yorkshire, LS25 3EB

Tel: 0113 281 3259
Fax: 0113 281 2100
Formed: 1969

Organisation type and purpose: Art gallery, historic building, house or site.

Enquiries to: Curator
Other contacts: (1) Supervisor (2) Director, Leeds Museums and Galleries for (1) group visits (2) strategic and policy issues.
Access:
Access to staff: By letter, by telephone, by fax
Hours: No access on Mon
Access to building, collections or gallery: No access other than to staff
Hours: Apr to Oct: Tue to Sat, 1000 to 1700; Sun 1300 to 1700
Nov to Mar: Tue to Sat, 1000 to 1600; Sun, 1300 to 1600
Other restrictions: Closed Mon (except Bank Holidays), Christmas Day, Boxing Day and New Year's Day.

General description:
Fine and decorative arts from the 18th century to the present day. Holdings include silver; ceramics; jewellery; furniture; paintings; sculpture; and costume - all within the setting of an Edwardian country house. Special emphasis on Victorian furniture and design, alongside objects from the Gascoigne family collections.
Information services:
Special visitor services: Guided tours.
Education services: Group education facilities, resources for Key Stages 2 and 3..
Collections:
Gascoigne Bequest: works of art, paintings, furniture, silver, ceramics, jewellery
The Frank Savery Bequest of early Chinese ceramics
Ranging from 18th century costumes and accessories to the work of contemporary British designers
Contemporary ceramics including work by leading makers such as Liz Fritsh, Hans Coper, Wally Keeler and Sutton Taylor.
Catalogues:
Catalogue for part of the collections is only available in-house.
Publications list:
is available in hard copy.

Address for ordering publications:
Electronic publications:
Commercial Office, Leeds Museum Resource Centre
Tel: 0113 391 0648
Printed publications:
Commercial Office, Leeds Museum Resource Centre
1 Moorfield Road, Moorfield Industrial Estate, Leeds, LS19 7BN, tel: 0113 391 0648

Internet home pages:
http://www.leeds.gov.uk

1657
LOUGHBOROUGH ARCHAEOLOGICAL AND HISTORICAL SOCIETY

See - Old Rectory Museum

1658
LOUGHWOOD MEETING HOUSE

Dalwood, Axminster, Devon, EX13 7DU

Tel: 01392 881691(Regional Office)
Fax: 01392 881954

Organisation type and purpose: National organisation, registered charity (charity number 205846), historic building, house or site.
Parent body:
The National Trust (South West Region)
Regional Office for Devon and Cornwall, tel: 01392 881691

Enquiries to: Manager
Access:
Access to staff: By letter, by telephone
Access to building, collections or gallery: No prior appointment required
Hours: All year, daily
Access for disabled people: level entry
Other restrictions: Steep slope from the car park. Ground floor fully accessible. No access to other floors.

General description:
Built c.1653 by the Baptist congregation of Kilmington, who attended services here at the risk of imprisonment or transportation. A simple but interesting building, with an interior fitted in the early 18th century.

Internet home pages:
http://www.nationaltrust.org.uk/regions/devon

1659
LOUTH MUSEUM

4 Broadbank, Louth, Lincolnshire, LN11 6EQ

Tel: 01507 601211
Acronym or abbreviation: LNALS
Full name: Louth Naturalists Antiquarian & Literary Society
Formed: 1910

Organisation type and purpose: Learned society, registered charity, museum, suitable for ages: all ages, publishing house.

Enquiries to: Honorary Curator
Access:
Access to staff: By letter, by telephone

General description:
A general museum of local history based on collections of natural history specimens; geology and fossils; and archaeology. Also houses a library based on similar subjects.
Information services:
Special visitor services: Guided tours..
Collections:
Bennett Hubbard. Sketches. 1806-1870. ca. 100 items
Louth-made carpets. 19th century. 8 items
Thomas Wilkinson Wallis. Carvings and plaster models. 1821-1903. 6 items
Catalogues:
Catalogue for part of the collections is only available in-house.
Publications list:
is available in hard copy.
Printed publications:
Publications list in preparation

1660
LOW PARKS MUSEUM

129 Muir Street, Hamilton, South Lanarkshire, ML3 6BJ

Tel: 01698 328232
Fax: 01698 328412
Formed: 1967
Formerly: Hamilton District Museum, Cameronians (Scottish Rifles) Regimental Museum, date of change, 1996

Organisation type and purpose: Local government body, museum.
Parent body:
South Lanarkshire Council
Council Offices, Almada Street, Hamilton, tel: 01698 45444

Enquiries to: Manager
Other contacts: Commercial Officer for functions hire, tel no: 01698 426213.
Access:
Access to staff: By letter
Access for disabled people: Parking provided, level entry, toilet facilities

General description:
A general local history museum for South Lanarkshire, with art; costume; textiles; social history; agriculture; coal mining; Hamilton Estate; transport; paintings; photography; archives; natural history; ceramics; and archaeology. Also contains the regimental museum of the Cameronians (Scottish Rifles) Regiment, disbanded 1968.
Collections:
Displays relating to Burgh histories, textiles, agriculture, mining and covenanting

Information relating to historic buildings in Hamilton
Military. Mixed campaigns of 26th and 90th regiments serving since 1689 and 1790

1661
LOWESTOFT MUSEUM

Nicholas Everitt Park, Lowestoft, Suffolk, NR33 9JR

Tel: 01502 511457
Formed: 1985

Organisation type and purpose: Membership association (membership is by election or invitation), present number of members: 61, registered charity (charity number 268011), museum.
Connected with:
Lowestoft Archaeological and Local History Society (LALHS)
The Secretary, 95 Carlton Road, Lowestoft, Suffolk, NR33 0LZ
Liaison Officer:
Lowestoft Museum
10 Constable Close, Lowestoft, NR32 2QU, tel: 01502 513795, fax: 01502 513795

Enquiries to: Information Officer
Direct tel: 01502 513795
Direct fax: 01502 513795
Other contacts: Schools Officer, tel no: 01502 530663 for school visits and study unit loans.
Access:
Access to staff: By letter, by telephone
Access to building, collections or gallery: No prior appointment required
Hours: End Mar to End Oct, Mon to Fri, 1030 to 1700; Sat, Sun, 1400 to 1700
Access for disabled people: level entry
Other restrictions: Access to ground floor only.

General description:
A local history museum covering all aspects of local history from pre-Stone Age up to the 1980s. Includes a nationally important collection of Lowestoft porcelain. Also covers domestic history. Lowestoft history and archaeology.
Information services:
Selective dissemination services. Helpline available, tel no: 01502 568560.
Special visitor services: Guided tours, materials and/or activities for children.
Education services: Group education facilities.
Services for disabled people: For the visually impaired.
Collections:
Historic photographs of Lowestoft and surrounding area
Lowestoft porcelain, fine examples of the various products from the Lowestoft factory, 1757 to 1799
Catalogues:
Catalogue for library is in-house only. Catalogue for all of the collections is only available in-house.
Printed publications:
The following booklets for purchase, 75p rrp, 50p for resale
Broad House
Lowestoft: A Brief History
Oulton Broad from Ancient Times
Roman Legacy in the Lowestoft Landscape
Round Tower Churches
Sir Samuel Marton Peto
The Church in Lothingland
Pakefield - A History

Internet home pages:
http://www.
Under construction.

1662
LOWFIELD HEATH WINDMILL TRUST, THE

141 Downland Drive, Southgate West, Crawley, West Sussex, RH11 8SL

Tel: 01293 409845
Email: peterjames@exanimo.freeserve.co.uk

Formed: 1987

Organisation type and purpose: Independently owned, registered charity (charity number 1066964), historic building, house or site.
The restoration, preservation and running of the Lowfield Heath Windmill, together with a small display of artefacts.

Enquiries to: Chairman
Access:
Access to staff: By letter, by telephone, by email, visitors by prior appointment
Other restrictions: Anytime by prior appointment.
Access for disabled people: Parking provided, ramped entry

General description:
A complete early 18th century Post Windmill restored to full working order. There is a detailed photographic exhibition showing the history and restoration. Also an audiovisual presentation of various Windmill Films. There is also a collection of artefacts from this and local mills.
Information services:
Special visitor services: Guided tours..
Collections:
Detailed exhibition of photographs on display
Printed publications:
Postcards (30p each)

1663
LOWRY, THE

Pier 8, Salford Quays, Manchester, M50 3AZ

Tel: 0161 876 2020
Minicom no. 0161 876 2002
Fax: 0161 876 2021
Email: info@thelowry.com
Formed: 2000
Formerly: The Lowry Centre, date of change, 1999

Organisation type and purpose: Art gallery, suitable for ages: all ages.
Arts centre (galleries and theatres).

Enquiries to: Office Administrator
Access:
Access to staff: By letter, by telephone, by fax, by email
Access to building, collections or gallery: No prior appointment required
Hours: Galleries open 7 days a week, 1100 to 1700 (late evenings occasionally)
Access for disabled people: Parking provided, access to all public areas, toilet facilities

General description:
A gallery dedicated to the life and work of L S Lowry, and the work of contemporary artists from the North West of England, Artworks, an ineractive gallery for children and adults provides the creative experience of exploring works of art.
Collections:
Collection of over 300 paintings and drawings by L S Lowry
Archive of photographs, letters, tape recordings and documents related to L S Lowry's life and work
Catalogues:
Catalogue for library is in-house only. Catalogue for part of the collections is published.
Publications list:
is available in hard copy.
Printed publications:
Lowry's City (Sandling J and Leber M, 2001, £14.95)
The Lowry Lexicon: An A-Z of L S Lowry (Rohde S, 2001, £15.95)
Lowry's Places (exhibition catalogue, 2000, £5.95)
Lowry's People (exhibition catalogue, 2000, £5.95)
A Visionary Artist (Howard M, 1999, £40)
L S Lowry Biography (Rohde S, 1999, £14.95)

Address for ordering publications:
Printed publications:
Galleries Co-ordinator, The Lowry
Tel: 0161 876 2054

Internet home pages:
http://www.thelowry.com
Publications list.

1664
LOYAL REGIMENT (NORTH LANCASHIRE)

*See - **Queen's Lancashire Regimental Museum***

1665
LUDLOW MUSEUM

Castle Street, Ludlow, Shropshire, SY8 1AS

Tel: 01584 875384
Fax: 01584 872019
Email: ludlow.museum@shropshire-cc.gov.uk
Acronym or abbreviation: SHRCM
Full name: Shropshire County Museum Service
Formed: 1833
Formerly: Buttercross Museum, date of change, 1993

Organisation type and purpose: Local government body, museum, suitable for ages: all ages.
Parent body:
Shropshire County Council, Community and Environment
Other addresses:
Acton Scott Historic Working Farm
Wenlock Lodge, Acton Scott, Church Stretton, Shropshire, SY6 6QN, tel: 01694 781 306/307, fax: 01694 781 569, email/website: acton.scott@shropshire-cc.gov.uk
Ludlow Museum Office
47 Old Street, Ludlow, Shropshire, SY8 1NQ, tel: 01584 873 857, fax: 01584 872019, email/website: ludlow.museum@shropshire-cc.gov.uk

Enquiries to: Curator
Direct tel: 01584 873857
Other contacts: Museum Assistant for general enquiries, school bookings etc.
Access:
Access to staff: By letter, by telephone, by email, in person, visitors by prior appointment
Hours: Mon to Fri, 0900 to 1300 and 1400 to 1700
Other restrictions: Office open all year.
Access to building, collections or gallery: No access other than to staff
Hours: Mon to Sat, 1030 to 1300 and 1400 to 1700
Other restrictions: Apr to Oct, Mon to Sat, Bank Holiday Sun; Sun in Jun, Jul and Aug.
Access for disabled people: level entry, access to all public areas, toilet facilities
Other restrictions: Access for disabled at museum displays, Castle Street.

General description:
Local history; geology; palaeontology; archaeology.
Information services:
Special visitor services: Materials and/or activities for children.
Education services: Group education facilities, resources for Key Stages 1 and 2.
Services for disabled people: Displays and/or information at wheelchair height.
Collections:
Biological specimens and records data for Shropshire
Geological specimens and site data for Shropshire
Local history, photographs, costumes and objects
Printed publications:
2 Geological Cards
3 prints of Ludlow

continued overleaf

Internet home pages:
http://www.shropshire-cc.gov.uk/museums.nsf

See also - Biological Records Centre & Ludlow Museum

1666
LULLINGSTONE ROMAN VILLA

Lullingstone Lane, Eynsford, Dartford, Kent, DA4 0JA

Tel: 01322 863467
Fax: 01322 863467
Formed: 1967

Organisation type and purpose: National government body, historic building, house or site, suitable for ages: 5+.
Parent body:
English Heritage (South East Region)
Tel: 01483 252000, fax: 01483 252001

Enquiries to: Head Custodian
Access:
Access to staff: By letter, by telephone, by fax
Access to building, collections or gallery: No prior appointment required
Hours: 29 Mar-30 Sep: 10am-6pm, daily. 1-31 Oct: 10am-5pm, daily. 1 Nov-31 Mar: 10am-4pm, daily
Other restrictions: Closed 24-26 Dec and 1 Jan 2003.
Closed 3pm during Jun and Jul due to opera evenings.
Access for disabled people: toilet facilities
Other restrictions: Can access all ground floor

General description:
Lullingstone is renowned not only for its stunning mosaics, but also for being the site of one of the first surviving Christian chapels in England. Possibly built as a luxury summer-house for a wealthy Roman official, the villa also features wall paintings and a display of skeletal remains uncovered on site.
Information services:
Audio tours also available in French and German, for the visually impaired and for those with learning difficulties.
Special visitor services: Guided tours, tape recorded guides, materials and/or activities for children.
Education services: Resources for Key Stage 3.
Services for disabled people: For the visually impaired; for the hearing impaired.

1667
LUNDY

Bristol Channel, Devon, EX39 2LY

Tel: 01237 431831
Fax: 01237 431832
Email: info@lundyisland.co.uk

Organisation type and purpose: National organisation, registered charity (charity number 205846), historic building, house or site, suitable for ages: all ages.
Parent body:
The National Trust (South West Region)
Regional Office for Devon, tel: 01208 74281
Financed, adninistered and maintained by:
The Landmark Trust
Access:
Access to staff: By letter, by telephone, by fax, by email

General description:
A unique and unspoilt island, undisturbed by cars, and home to a fascinating array of wildlife amidst dramatic scenery.
There is a small village with an inn and Victorian church, and nearby the 13th century Marisco Castle, and archaeological sites.

Internet home pages:
http://www..nationaltrust.org.uk/regions/devon

1668
LUNT ROMAN FORT MUSEUM

Coventry Road, Baginton Village, Coventry, Warwickshire, CV8 3AZ

Tel: 024 7683 2381
Email: artsandheritage@coventry.gov.uk
Formed: 1967

Organisation type and purpose: Local government body, museum, historic building, house or site, suitable for ages: 8+.
Parent body:
Coventry Arts & Heritage
Coventry City Council

Enquiries to: Manager
Access:
Access to staff: By letter, by email
Access for disabled people: Parking provided, ramped entry
Other restrictions: Telephone to arrange parking.

General description:
1st century AD Roman reconstruction; small Roman Museum.
Information services:
Special visitor services: Guided tours.
Education services: Resources for Key Stages 2, 3 and Further or Higher Education..
Collections:
Roman objects

1669
LUTON MUSEUM AND GALLERY

Wardown Park, Old Bedford Road, Luton, Bedfordshire, LU2 7HA

Tel: 01582 546723
Fax: 01582 546763
Formed: 1927

Organisation type and purpose: Local government body, museum.
Also at the same address:
Bedfordshire and Hertfordshire Regiment Museum
Tel: 01582 546723, fax: 01582 546763
Subsidiary body:
John Dony Field Centre
Hancock Drive, Bushmead, Luton, LU2 7SF, tel: 01582 486983, fax: 01582 546763
Stockwood Craft Museum and Gardens
Farley Hill, Luton, LU1 4BH, tel: 01582 546723, fax: 01582 546763

Enquiries to: Curator
Direct tel: 01582 746719
Other contacts: Visitor Services Officer, 01582 546739
Access:
Access to staff: By letter, by telephone, by fax, visitors by prior appointment
Hours: Tue to Fri, 1000 to 1700
Access for disabled people: Parking provided, level entry, access to all public areas, toilet facilities

General description:
Archaeology, social, local and natural history of Bedfordshire, lace-making, straw plait industry, hats and hat industry, childhood, including toys.
Collections:
Bagshawe Collection of Bedfordshire crafts and rural trades
Bagshawe library
Bedfordshire and Hertfordshire Regimental Collection
Mossman collection of horse-drawn vehicles
Publications list:
is available in hard copy.
Printed publications:
Bedfordshire Plant Atlas
Early Trades and Industries - Microcosm of Pyne (2 parts)
Hat Fashions 1787-1937
Luton and the Hat Industry
Old County Maps of Bedfordshire
Pillow Lace in the East Midlands
Railway Age
Turnpike Age
Waterways Heritage

Internet home pages:
http://www.luton.gov.uk/museums

1670
LYDD TOWN MUSEUM

The Old Fire Station, Queens Road, Lydd, Kent, TN29

Formed: 1978

Organisation type and purpose: Registered charity (charity number 274692), museum, suitable for ages: 8+.
Affiliated to:
Civic Trust
Commons Open Spaces
CPRE (Kent)
Romney Marsh Footpaths Preservation Society
Address for correspondence:
Friends of Lydd
The Chairman (FOL)
11 Seaview Road, Greatstone, TN28 8RH, tel: 01787 366566
Other addresses:
Friends of Lydd
Honorary Secretary (FOL)
Park Street House, Park Street, Lydd, TN29 7AZ

Enquiries to: Chairman
Direct tel: 01797 366566
Other contacts: Honorary Secretary
Access:
Access to staff: By letter, by telephone
Other restrictions: Letters to Chairman not to the Museum.
Access for disabled people: Parking provided, level entry, access to all public areas, toilet facilities

General description:
The museum occupies the old Fire Station, and shows artefacts of local history including the Lydd horse-drawn fire engine and bus, a Landour and a unique beach cart.
Farming, fishing, shoemaking tools and equipment used by local people.
Costumes from 1890 on view.
Information services:
Helpline available, tel no: 01797 366566.
Special visitor services: Guided tours, materials and/or activities for children.
Services for disabled people: Displays and/or information at wheelchair height.
Catalogues:
Catalogue for part of the collections is only available in-house.

1671
LYDDINGTON BEDE HOUSE

Blue Coat Lane, Lyddington, Near Uppingham, Rutland, LE15 9LZ

Tel: 01572 822438
Fax: 01572 822750
Formed: 1983

Organisation type and purpose: Historic building, house or site, suitable for ages: 5+.
Parent body:
English Heritage (East Midlands Region)
44 Derngate, Northampton, NN1 1UH, tel: 01604 735400, fax: 01604 735401
Other addresses:
English Heritage
East Midlands Regional Office
44 Derngate, Northampton, NN1 1UH, tel: 01604 735400, fax: 01604 735401

Enquiries to: Custodian
Direct fax: 01572 822570
Access:
Access to staff: By letter, by telephone, by fax
Access to building, collections or gallery: No prior appointment required
Hours: 29 Mar to 30 Sep: daily, 1000 to 1800,1 to 31 Oct: daily, 100 to 1700
Other restrictions: Opening times are subject to

change, for up-to-date information contact English Heritage by phone or visit the web site.

General description:
Medieval Bishops Palace, Tudor Alms House (used until 1930). Lyddington Bede House was originally a wing of a medieval rural palace of the Bishops of Lincoln. In 1600 the building was converted into an almshouse, and remained a home for pensioners until the 1930s. It contains fine 16th century rooms with decorated timber ceilings. Among the things to see on its three floors are the bedesmen's rooms with tiny windows and fireplaces, and the Great Chamber which features an exceptionally beautiful ceiling cornice.
Information services:
Helpline available, tel no: 0870 333 1181.
Special visitor services: Tape recorded guides..

Internet home pages:
http://www.english-heritage.org.uk

1672
LYDIARD PARK

Lydiard Tregoze, Swindon, Wiltshire, SN5 3PA

Tel: 01793 770401
Fax: 01793 877909
Formed: 1955

Organisation type and purpose: Local government body, historic building, house or site, suitable for ages: 5+.

Enquiries to: The Keeper
Access:
Access to staff: By letter, by telephone, by fax, visitors by prior appointment
Access to building, collections or gallery: No prior appointment required
Hours: Mon to Fri, 1000 to 1300 and 1400 to 1700; Sat, 1000 to 1700; Sun 1400 to 1700
Nov to Feb: early closing 1600
Other restrictions: Prior appointment required for groups.
Access for disabled people: Parking provided, level entry
Other restrictions: For access to house, telephone or write to request information sheet.

General description:
Ancestral home of the Bolingbrokes, set in rolling lawns and woodland. Palladian mansion contains fine family furnishings and portraits, exceptional plasterwork, rare 17th century window and room devoted to 18th society artist, Lady Diana Spencer. Exceptional monuments such as the 'Golden Cavalier' in adjacent church.
Information services:
Helpline available, tel no: 01793 770401.
Group education services for pre-school groups too.
Special visitor services: Guided tours, tape recorded guides, materials and/or activities for children.
Education services: Group education facilities, resources for Key Stages 1 and 2, 3 and Further or Higher Education.
Services for disabled people: For the visually impaired; displays and/or information at wheelchair height.
Collections:
St John family portraits and miniatures (16th-19th century)
Fine furniture (18th-19th century)
Library 18th to early 20th century
Decorative arts, family memorabilia and manuscripts
Catalogues:
Catalogue for all of the collections is only available in-house.
Printed publications:
Guide Book (£1.50)
Postcards (25p)
Series of historical booklets on Lydiard Park and aspects of the collection

Internet home pages:
http://www.swindon.gov.uk

1673
LYME PARK

Disley, Stockport, Cheshire, SK12 2NX

Tel: 01663 762023
Fax: 01663 765035
Email: lymepark@nationaltrust.org.uk

Organisation type and purpose: National organisation, registered charity (charity number 205846), museum, historic building, house or site, suitable for ages: 5+.
Parent body:
The National Trust (North West)
North West Regional Office, tel: 0870 609 5391
Partly financed by:
Stockport Metropolitan Borough Council

Enquiries to: House & Collections Manager
Other contacts: Education: 01663 761406
Access:
Access to staff: By letter, by telephone, by fax, by email, Internet web pages
Access for disabled people: Parking provided, toilet facilities
Other restrictions: Designated parking. Drop-off point. 4 manual wheelchairs available. Steps to entrance. Accessible entrance different from main entrance. Ground floor accessible with assistance. No access to other floors. Photograph album. Level entrance to shop. Ramped entrance to restaurant.

General description:
Originally a Tudor house, Lyme was transformed by the Venetian architect Leoni into an Italianate palace. Some of the Elizabethan interiors survive and contrast dramatically with later rooms. The state rooms are adorned with Mortlake tapestries, Grinling Gibbons wood-carvings and an important collection of English clocks. The 6.8ha (17 acre) Victorian garden boasts impressive bedding schemes, a sunken parterre, an Edwardian rose garden, Jekyll-style herbaceous borders, reflection lake, a ravine garden and Wyatt conservatory. The garden is surrounded by a medieval deer park of almost 566ha (1400 acres) of moorland, woodland and parkland, containing an early 18th century hunting tower. Lyme appeared as 'Pemberley' in the BBC's adaptation of Jane Austen's novel Pride and Prejudice, and also featured in the recent Granada production of The Forsyte Saga.
Information services:
Helpline available, tel no: Infoline: 01663 766492.
Taster tours of house at noon on open days.
Guided tours of house, garden & park available on some days, limited places.
Enquire at information centre on arrival.
House & garden tours by arrangement outside normal opening hours.
Braille guide.
Frontcarrying baby slings for loan.
Suitable for school groups. Education room/centre. Live interpretation. Children's guide.
Children's quiz/trail.
Special visitor services: Guided tours, materials and/or activities for children.
Education services: Group education facilities, resources for Key Stages 1 and 2, 3, 4 and Further or Higher Education.
Services for disabled people: For the visually impaired.
Collections:
Fine 18th century furniture
Mortlake tapestries
Wood carvings, some reputedly by Grinling Gibbons
Superb collection of English domestic clocks
Printed publications:
Guide Book (32.95)
Introductory Guide (70p)
Childrens Guide (£1.50)

Internet home pages:
http://www.nationaltrust.org.uk

1674
LYME REGIS PHILPOT MUSEUM

Bridge Street, Lyme Regis, Dorset, DT7 3QA

Tel: 01297 443370
Email: info@lymeregismuseum.co.uk
Acronym or abbreviation: LYMPH
Formed: 1921

Organisation type and purpose: Registered charity, museum, suitable for ages: all ages.

Enquiries to: Curator
Other contacts: Manager
Access:
Access to staff: By letter, by telephone, by email, visitors by prior appointment
Other restrictions: Some closure weekdays during winter.

General description:
The museum is housed in a charmingly idiosyncratic building, purpose-built in 1900 on the site of Mary Anning's birthplace. Lyme Regis area geology, history, topography, buildings etc.
The story of Lyme Regis in its landscape - part of the Jurassic Coast World Heritage Site.
The significance of Lyme to the scientific study of fossils from the early 1800s. The important part Mary Anning played in the early development of geology.
Literary connections from Jane Austen to John Fowles.
Lyme's fascinating history from the granting of its Royal Charter by Edward I, through the Civil War to modern times.
Its connection with the sea and shipping.
Information services:
Special visitor services: Materials and/or activities for children.
Education services: Resources for Key Stages 1 and 2.
Services for disabled people: For the visually impaired.
Collections:
Small local archaeological collection
700 paintings
4500 photographs
2000 postcards
General social history collection
Fossil Collection
John Fowles material
Maritime material etc
History of the Lyme-Axminster railway
Publications list:
is available on-line.
Printed publications:
Mary Anning a Souvenir (Charlesworth K, 1999, 16pp cartoons, £1.95, direct)
Mary Anning of Lyme Regis (Tickell C, 1996, 32pp, £2.99, direct)
Picture of Lyme Regis & Environs (Fowles J, 1985, reprint of 1817 guide with information, 27pp, 75p, direct)
Lyme Voices 1 & 2 (oral history, for purchase, direct)
Annual Reports (2001, direct)

Internet home pages:
http://www.lymeregismuseum.co.uk

1675
LYMINGTON MUSEUM TRUST

See - St Barbe Museum & Art Gallery

1676
LYNN MUSEUM, THE

Old Market Street, King's Lynn, Norfolk, PE30 1NL

Tel: 01553 775001
Fax: 01553 775001
Email: lynn.museum@norfolk.gov.uk
Formed: 1904
Formerly: King's Lynn Museums

Organisation type and purpose: Local government body, museum, art gallery, historic building, house or site, suitable for ages: all ages.
Parent body:
Norfolk Museums & Archaeology Service

continued overleaf

Shirehall, Market Avenue, Norwich, NR1 3JQ, tel: 01603 493669, fax: 01603 493651

Other branches:

Town House Museum
46 Queen Street, King's Lynn, PE30 5DQ, tel: 01553 773450, email/website: townhouse.museum@norfolk.gov.uk

Enquiries to: Area Museums Officer
Other contacts: Education Officer tel: 01553 773450

Access:

Access to staff: By letter, by telephone, by fax, by email, visitors by prior appointment
Hours: Mon to Fri, 1000 to 1700
Access to building, collections or gallery: No prior appointment required
Hours: Tue to Sat, 1000 to 1700
Access for disabled people: ramped entry, level entry, access to all public areas

General description:

The history, archaeology, natural history and geology of King's Lynn and West Norfolk; local art collections. Town House Museum: furniture and domestic life; social history; costume and toys from the mediaeval period to the 20th century.

Information services:

Education services: Group education facilities, resources for Key Stages 1 and 2, 3, 4 and Further or Higher Education..

Collections:

Collections relating to the social history, archaeology, natural history and geology of King's Lynn and West Norfok
Also local art collections and material from the engineering firm of Savages, makers of fairground rides; F Savage's engineering drawings, patterns and horses from fairground 1880-7
Lynn Glass, 18th/19th century
Mediaeval archaeology, leather, pottery
Mediaeval pilgrim badges, 1300s-1400s, 100 items
Nelson memorabilia, 20 items

Internet home pages:

http://www.visitwestnorfolk.com
http://www.norfolk.gov.uk/tourism/museums

1677
LYTES CARY MANOR

Charlton Mackrell, Somerton, Somerset, TA11 7HU

Tel: 01985 843600 (Regional Office)
Email: lytescarymanor@nationaltrust.org.uk

Organisation type and purpose: National organisation, registered charity (charity number 205846), historic building, house or site.

Parent body:

The National Trust (South West Region)
Wessex Regional Office, tel: 01985 843600

Enquiries to: Manager

Access:

Access to staff: By letter, by email, Internet web pages
Access to building, collections or gallery: No prior appointment required
Hours: Mid Apr to end Oct, Mon, Wed, Fri, Sun, 1100 to 1700
Other restrictions: Closes dusk if earlier.
Access for disabled people: toilet facilities
Other restrictions: Grounds largely accessible.

General description:

Manor house with a 14th century chapel and 15th century Great Hall, much added to in the 16th century and rescued from dereliction in the 20th century by Sir Walter Jenner. The interiors were refurnished in period style.

Information services:

Guided tours by arrangement. Guided walks, details from property.
Children's quiz/trail.
Braille guide and scented flowers.
Special visitor services: Materials and/or activities for children.
Services for disabled people: For the visually impaired.

Internet home pages:

http://www.nationaltrust.org.uk/regions/wessex

1678
LYTHAM HALL

Ballam Road, Lytham St Annes, Lancashire

Tel: 01282 661704
Formed: 1997
Formerly: Heritage Centre

Organisation type and purpose: Registered charity (charity number 508300), museum, historic building, house or site.

Enquiries to: Chief Executive
Direct fax: 01282 611718
Direct email: john.miller@htnw.co.uk

Access:

Access to staff: By letter, by telephone, by fax, by email, letter of introduction required, charges made to all users
Access to building, collections or gallery: Prior appointment required
Access for disabled people: Parking provided

General description:

Historic house.

Information services:

Special visitor services: Guided tours..

Collections:

Pictures and furniture

1679
LYTHAM HERITAGE GROUP

Lytham Heritage Centre, 2 Henry Street, Lytham St Annes, Lancashire, FY8 5LE

Tel: 01253 730767
Fax: 01253 730767
Email: thecentre@lythamheritage.fsnet.co.uk
Acronym or abbreviation: LHG
Formed: 1987

Organisation type and purpose: Independently owned, registered charity (charity number 701152), historic building, house or site, suitable for ages: 12+.
Exhibition centre and heritage display.
The Lytham Heritage Centre is owned and run by the Lytham Heritage Group.

Other addresses:

Lytham Windmill

Enquiries to: Public Relations Manager
Direct tel: 01253 730787; 07949 611472
Other contacts: The Secretary

Access:

Access to staff: By letter, by fax, by email, Internet web pages
Other restrictions: Volunteer staff - no regular working hours.
Access for disabled people: ramped entry, access to all public areas, toilet facilities

General description:

Lytham Heritage Centre: a restored Grade II listed building - built as a bank in 1899. Exhibitions on the history and heritage of Lytham. Changing exhibitions generally featuring local artists, arts and crafts and community groups.

Information services:

Special visitor services: Guided tours.
Education services: Group education facilities..

Collections:

Artefacts, memorabilia, pictures, postcards, photographs, documents related to the history and heritage of Lytham.

Catalogues:

Catalogue for part of the collections is only available in-house.

Printed publications:

Lytham - Our Town - An illustrated history of Lytham
The Lytham Heritage Centre - A description of the Centre: a Grade II listed building
The Lytham Heritage Group - The story of the founding and growth of the Group 1987-2000

Internet home pages:

http://www.lythamheritage.fsnet.co.uk
History and purpose of Lytham Heritage Group, details of exhibitions at Heritage Centre.

1680
LYTHAM WINDMILL

Lytham Heritage Group, 2 Henry Street, Lytham St Annes, Lancashire, FY8 5LE

Tel: 01253 730767
Fax: 01253 730767
Email: thecentre@lythamheritage.fsnet.co.uk
Formed: 1987

Organisation type and purpose: Independently owned, registered charity (charity number 701152), museum, historic building, house or site, suitable for ages: 12+.

Owned by:

Fylde Borough Council

The Museum in the Windmill is owned and run by:

Lytham Heritage Group

Enquiries to: Public Relations Manager
Direct tel: 01253 730787; 07949 611472
Other contacts: The Secretary

Access:

Access to staff: By letter, by fax, by email, Internet web pages
Other restrictions: Volunteer Staff only - no regular working hours.

General description:

Lytham Windmill - Built 1805 and used as a working mill until 1919 and now stages exhibitions on milling, North West Mills and the history of the mill. Tableaux of life in Victorian Lytham. A local landmark on Lytham Green, completely restored and renovated.

Information services:

Helpline available, tel no: 01253 730767.
Special visitor services: Guided tours.
Education services: Group education facilities..

Catalogues:

Catalogue for part of the collections is only available in-house.

Printed publications:

Lytham - Our Town, An Illustrated history of Lytham
The Lytham Heritage Group - The story of the founding and growth of the Group 1987-2000

Internet home pages:

http://www.lythamheritage.fsnet.co.uk
History and purpose of Lytham Heritage Group, details of exhibitions at Lytham Windmill Museum.

1681
LYVEDEN NEW BIELD

Oundle, Peterborough, Cambridgeshire, PE8 5AT

Tel: 01832 205358
Email: lyvedennewbield@nationaltrust.org.uk
Formed: 1895

Organisation type and purpose: National organisation, registered charity (charity number 205846), historic building, house or site, suitable for ages: 12+.

Parent body:

The National Trust (East Midlands Region)
East Midlands Regional Office, tel: 01909 486411

Enquiries to: Manager

Access:

Access to staff: By letter, by telephone, by email
Access to building, collections or gallery: No prior appointment required
Hours: Apr to Jul, Sep and Oct: Wed to Sun, 1030 to 1700

Aug: daily, 1030 to 1700
Nov to Mar: Sat and Sun, 1030 to 1600
Open Bank Holiday Mondays
Access for disabled people: Parking provided
Other restrictions: Steps to entrance. Ground floor largely accessible, low entrance to the building

General description:
An incomplete Elizabethan garden house and moated garden. Begun in 1595 by Sir Thomas Tresham to symbolise his Catholic faith, Lyveden remains virtually unaltered since work stopped when Tresham died in 1605. Lyveden has fascinating Elizabethan architectural detail, remains of one of the oldest garden layouts in Britain and is set amidst beautiful open countryside. Archaeology, garden history, heritage, architecture.
Information services:
Library available for reference (for conditions see Access above). Helpline available
Children's quiz/trail; family guide.
Tours for groups by arrangement
Special visitor services: Guided tours.
Education services: Group education facilities, resources for Key Stages 1 and 2, 3, 4 and Further or Higher Education..

Internet home pages:
http://www.nationaltrust.org.uk

1682
MACCLESFIELD MUSEUMS AND HERITAGE CENTRE, THE

Roe Street, Macclesfield, Cheshire, SK11 6UT

Tel: 01625 613210
Fax: 01625 617880
Email: silkmuseum@tiscali.co.uk
Formed: 1984

Organisation type and purpose: Independently owned, registered charity (charity number 519521), museum, historic building, house or site, suitable for ages: 5+.
Parent body:
Macclesfield Museums Trust
at the same address
Heritage and museum sites:
Paradise Mill
Park Lane, Macclesfield, Cheshire, SK11 6JY, tel: 01625 618228
The Macclesfield Silk Museum
The Heritage Centre, Roe Street, Macclesfield, tel: 01625 613210, fax: 01625 617880
The Silk Museum
Macclesfield School of Art, Park Lane, Macclesfield, Cheshire, SK11 6JY, tel: 01625 612045, fax: 01625 612048
West Park Museum
Prestbury Road, Macclesfield, Cheshire, SK10 3BJ, tel: 01625 619831

Enquiries to: Director
Other contacts: Education Officer
Access:
Access to staff: By letter, by telephone, by fax, by email, visitors by prior appointment
Hours: Bookings and general enquiries, Mon to Fri, 0900 to 1700
Other restrictions: Closed Bank Holidays, Christmas Day, Boxing Day, New Year's Day and Good Friday.
Access for disabled people: ramped entry, access to all public areas, toilet facilities
Other restrictions: Lift to upper floors

General description:
The Grade II* listed building, which is now The Heritage Centre, was built in 1813 as a Sunday School for the children of Macclesfield who worked in the silk mills. It was refurbished in the 1980s, and now provides conference, concert and function facilities, as well as housing one of the silk museums and the administrative offices of the Macclesfield Museums Trust. The Trust is responsible for the administration and management of the four museums in Macclesfield.
Information services:
Library available for reference (for conditions see Access above)
Conference and concert centre
Special visitor services: Guided tours, tape recorded guides, materials and/or activities for children..
Collections:
Silk Manufacturers Pattern Archive
Jacquard Silk handlooms, 1860
Publications list:
is available in hard copy and online.
Printed publications:
Child Labour
Factory Community
Family in Silk Street
Macclesfield -The Silk Industry (Collins, L and Stevenson, M)
Origins of the Silk Industry
Selection of Document Packs containing about 50 documents, illustrations, maps etc including:
Canals in Cheshire
Cheshire in the Great War
Macclesfield at War 1939-1945
Poor Law in Cheshire
Electronic and video products:
Macclesfield Memories for the Millennium (CD)
The Story of Silk in Macclesfield (video)

Internet home pages:
http://www.silk-macclesfield.org
Information, access to museums, calender of events, education, publications, and Friends of Macclesfield Silk Heritage.

See also - Macclesfield Silk Museum; Paradise Mill; Silk Museum; West Park Museum

1683
MACCLESFIELD SILK MUSEUM

The Heritage Centre, Roe Street, Macclesfield, Cheshire, SK11 6UT

Tel: 01625 613210
Fax: 01625 617880
Email: silkmuseum@tiscali.co.uk
Full name: Macclesfield Museums
Formed: 1987
Formerly: Silk Museum; Macclesfield Silk Heritage, date of change, 1982

Organisation type and purpose: Independently owned, registered charity (charity number 519521), museum, historic building, house or site, suitable for ages: all ages.
To collect the pictorial documentary and pictorial evidence of the silk industry.
Parent body:
Macclesfield Museums Trust
Reference Library:
The Silk Museum on Park Lane
Park Lane, Macclesfield, SK11 6TJ, tel: 01625 612045

Enquiries to: Director
Other contacts: Documentation Assistant
Access:
Access to staff: By letter, by telephone, by fax, by email, visitors by prior appointment
Access to building, collections or gallery: No prior appointment required
Hours: Daily, 1100 to 1700
Other restrictions: Closed Christmas Day, Boxing Day, New years Day
Access for disabled people: ramped entry, access to all public areas, toilet facilities
Other restrictions: Stair lift

General description:
The museum is housed within a Sunday School built in 1813 and describes, by means of an AV programme, models, exhibits and costumes, the history and development of silk, the industry and fashion, worldwide, nationally and with particular reference to Macclesfield, industrial archaeology and weaving processes.
Information services:
Services for disabled people: For the hearing impaired.
Collections:
Silk manufacturers and designers' pattern books, 1830-1970
Catalogues:
Catalogue for library is published. Catalogue for part of the collections is only available in-house.
Publications list:
is available in hard copy.
Printed publications:
Document packs on a variety of local history subjects
Source books with primary sources on subjects related to the local silk industry and Macclesfield
Information leaflets, postcards and other items suitable for schools relating to the needs of the National Curriculum

Internet home pages:
http://www.silk-macclesfield.org
General information.

1684
MCEWAN GALLERY

Ballater, Aberdeenshire, AB35 5UB

Tel: 013397 55429
Fax: 013397 55995
Email: art@mcewangallery.com
Formed: 1970

Organisation type and purpose: Art gallery, publishing house.

Enquiries to: Partner
Access:
Access to staff: By letter, by telephone, by fax, by email, in person, Internet web pages
Access to building, collections or gallery: No prior appointment required
Hours: Mon to Sat, 1000 to 1730; Sun, 1400 to 1730
Access for disabled people: Parking provided, level entry

Collections:
Pictures, prints, books, pottery, glass
Printed publications:
Dictionary of Scottish Artists (McEwan, P J M)

Internet home pages:
http://www.mcewangallery.com

1685
MCLEAN MUSEUM & ART GALLERY

15 Kelly Street, Greenock, Renfrewshire, PA16 8JX

Tel: 01475 715624
Fax: 01475 715626
Email: val.boa@inverclyde.gov.uk
Formed: 1876

Organisation type and purpose: Local government body, museum, art gallery, suitable for ages: all ages.
Connected to:
Innerclyde Council
Municipal Buildings, Clyde Square, Greenock, PA15 1LY, tel: 01475 717171

Enquiries to: Curator
Other contacts: Assistant Curators for enquiries.
Access:
Access to staff: By letter, by telephone, by fax, by email, visitors by prior appointment
Hours: Mon to Sat, 1000 to 1700
Other restrictions: Closed local and national public holidays.
Access to building, collections or gallery: No prior appointment required
Hours: Mon to Sat, 1000 to 1700
Access for disabled people: Parking provided, ramped entry, toilet facilities

General description:
Local and social history; James Watt, the engineer; maritime subjects; ethnography; natural history; geology; Egyptology and fine art

continued overleaf

(includes Caird Art Collection); programme of temporary exhibitions.
Information services:
Special visitor services: Guided tours, materials and/or activities for children.
Education services: Group education facilities.
Services for disabled people: For the hearing impaired.
Collections:
Caird art collection, paintings and prints, mainly Scottish School, 19th and 20th century
Paterson Photograph Collection of Clyde River Steamers, late 19th-early 20th century
Ethnographic collection, worldwide, particularly Japan, 19th and 20th century
R L Scott, big game, early 20th century
Catalogues:
Catalogue for part of the collections is only available in-house.
Printed publications:
Best of the McLean, highlights of the collections of the McLean Museum and Art Gallery (Oliver C and G, 1987, £1.99, plus £1 p&p)
The Clyde Pottery 1816 to 1905 (Boa V, Quail G, and Denhom P C, 1987, 99p, plus 50p p&p)
Greenock Morton 1874 to 1999 (Gillen V P, 1999, £5.95, plus £1 p&p)

Internet home pages:
http://www.inverclyde.gov.uk/museum/index.htm

1686
MCLELLAN GALLERIES
270 Sauchiehall Street, Glasgow, G2 3EH

Tel: 0141 565 4100
Fax: 0141 565 4111

Organisation type and purpose: Local government body, art gallery, suitable for ages: all ages.
Parent body:
Glasgow Museums
Access:
Access to staff: By letter, by telephone, by fax

General description:
Purpose-built exhibition galleries, refurnished in 1990 to house a series of high-quality temporary exhibitions from around the globe.

Internet home pages:
http://www.glasgow.gov.uk

1687
MCMANUS GALLERIES
Albert Square, Dundee, DD1 1DA

Tel: 01382 432084
Fax: 01382 432052
Email: mcmanus.galleries@dundeecity.gov.uk
Formed: 1873
Formerly: Dundee Art Galleries & Museums, date of change, 1996

Organisation type and purpose: Local government body, museum, art gallery, suitable for ages: all ages.
Parent body:
Dundee City Council
Leisure and Arts Department, tel: 01382 433827, fax: 01382 432252, email: arts.heritage@dundeecity.gov.uk
Other addresses:
Broughty Castle Museum
Mills Observatory

Enquiries to: Curator
Direct tel: 01382 432073
Direct fax: 01382 432052
Direct email: richard.brinklaw@dundeecity.gov.uk
Other contacts: Heritage Officers: Art, Natural Sciences, Human History for curatorial specialisms.
Access:
Access to staff: By letter, by telephone, by fax, by email, visitors by prior appointment
Access to building, collections or gallery: No prior appointment required
Hours: Fri to Wed, 1030 to 1700; Thu, 1030 to 1900; Sun, 1230 to 1600
Access for disabled people: Parking provided, level entry, access to all public areas, toilet facilities

General description:
Fine and decorative art, archaeology and human history, natural history.
Collections:
The collections of the former Barrack Street Museum
* Denotes computerised databases
*British (mainly Scottish) oils, watercolours and prints
*Orchar Collection (art) on 'www.scran.ac.uk'.
Local and social history, archaeology and *ethnography, numismatics, costume and textiles
*Geology, *zoology and *botany

Internet home pages:
http://www.dundeecity.gov.uk/mcmanus

1688
MAELDUNE HERITAGE CENTRE
St Peter's Church, Market Hill, Maldon, Essex

Tel: 01621 851628

Organisation type and purpose: Museum, art gallery.
Exhibitions of local artists' work, changed monthly.

General description:
History of Maldon.
Collections:
42ft long Maldon Embroidery celebrating the battle of Maldon AD991and depicting the history of Maldon AD991-1991
Photographic archive compiled by the Maldon Society

1689
MAGNA
Sheffield Road, Templeborough, Rotherham, South Yorkshire, S60 1DX

Tel: 01709 720002
Fax: 01709 820092
Email: info@magnatrust.co.uk
Full name: Magna Science Adventure Centre
Formed: 2001

Organisation type and purpose: Registered charity (charity number 1074578), suitable for ages: 5+.
Visitor attraction.
Parent body:
Rotherham Metropolitan Borough Council (RMBC)
Town Hall, The Cotts, Rotherham, tel: 01709 382121

Enquiries to: Marketing Executive
Direct tel: 01709 723108
Direct email: jeyre@magnatrust.co.uk
Other contacts: Deputy Chief Executive
Access:
Access to staff: By letter, by email, Internet web pages
Hours: Mon to Fri, 1000 to 1700
Access for disabled people: Parking provided, ramped entry, access to all public areas, toilet facilities
Other restrictions: Braille in the lifts, wheelchair hire.
Script of the Big Melt for the hard of hearing.

General description:
There are four pavillions based around the four elements, earth, air, fire and water. Once inside you can play on giant interactives such as real JCBs and water cannons. There are also three shows, the first being a sound and light show called Big Melt, which is a staged show re-enacting the melting of steel; there's the face of steel, a multimedia oral history of the workers at Templeborough 30 ft in the air; and the Living Robots Show in a specially built arena.
Information services:
Special visitor services: Guided tours, materials and/or activities for children.
Education services: Group education facilities, resources for Key Stages 1 and 2, 3, 4 and Further or Higher Education.
Services for disabled people: Displays and/or information at wheelchair height.
Collections:
Over 120 exhibits based around the four elements
25 pieces of specialised artwork specifically created for Magna
Catalogues:
Catalogue for library is on-line. Catalogue for all of the collections is on-line.
Printed publications:
Guide (£4)
Educational Pack (£3.50)
Other literature free
Electronic and video products:
High resolution images can be obtained, cost varies

Internet home pages:
http://www.magnatrust.org.uk

1690
MAIDENHEAD MUSEUM
See - Royal Borough Museum Collection

1691
MAIDSTONE MUSEUM & BENTLIF ART GALLERY
St Faith's Street, Maidstone, Kent, ME14 1LH

Tel: 01622 754497
Fax: 01622 685022
Acronym or abbreviation: Maidstone Museum
Formed: 1858

Organisation type and purpose: Local government body, museum.
Parent body:
Maidstone Borough Council
Also at the same address:
Bentlif Art Gallery
Links with:
Carriage Museum
Archbishops Stables, Mill Street, Maidstone, Kent

Enquiries to: Tourism & Marketing Manager
Direct tel: 01622 602462
Direct fax: 01622 602424
Other contacts: Collection Manager for details of collections.
Access:
Access to staff: By letter, by telephone, by fax, in person
Hours: Mon to Fri, 0900 to 1700
Access to building, collections or gallery: No prior appointment required
Other restrictions: Prior appointment is required for certain areas (ie library).
Access for disabled people: Parking provided, ramped entry

General description:
Local history, ceramics; natural history; archaeology; fine arts; costume; paintings; local industry; horse-drawn carriages; ethnography; Japanese fine and applied art.
Information services:
Library available for reference (for conditions see Access above)
Special visitor services: Materials and/or activities for children.
Education services: Group education facilities..
Collections:
Kent biological records centre
Catalogues:
Catalogue for all of the collections is only available in-house but part is published.

Internet home pages:
http://www.museum.maidstone.gov.uk

See also - Tyrwhitt-Drake Museum of Carriages

1692
MAISON DIEU
Ospringe Street, Faversham, Kent, ME13 8TW

Tel: 01795 534542
Fax: 01795 533261
Email: faversham@btinternet.com

Organisation type and purpose: Historic building, house or site, suitable for ages: all ages.
Medieval building, once part of a complex which served as a Royal Lodge, pilgrims' hostel, hospital and almshouse for retired royal retainers.
Parent body:
Faversham Society
Fleur de Lis Heritage Centre, Preston Street, Faversham, Kent, ME13 8NS, tel: 01795 534542, fax: 01795 533261, email: faversham@btinternet.com
Other location:
Chart Gunpowder Mills
Chart Close, off Stonebridge Way, Faversham, Kent, ME13 7SE, tel: 01795 534542, fax: 01795 533261, email/website: faversham@btinternet.com
Fleur de Lis Heritage Centre
10-13 Preston Street, Faversham, Kent, ME13 8NS, tel: 01795 534542, fax: 01795 533261, email/website: museum@favershamsociety.co.uk

Enquiries to: Honorary Director
Access:
Access to staff: By letter, by telephone, by fax, by email
Hours: Mon to Sat, 1000-1600
Other restrictions: Help and information available from the Fleur de Lis Heritage Centre and Museum in Preston Street Faversham.
Access to building, collections or gallery: No prior appointment required
Hours: Easter to October, Sat, Sun and Bank Holidays, 1400-1700
Other restrictions: English Heritage members free

General description:
Displays illustrating Ospringe's eventful history and Roman finds.

Internet home pages:
http://www.faversham.org
Details of historic Faversham.

1693
MAISTER HOUSE
160 High Street, Hull, East Yorkshire, HU1 1NL

Tel: 01482 324114
Fax: 01482 227003

Organisation type and purpose: National organisation, registered charity (charity number 205846), historic building, house or site.
Parent body:
The National Trust (Yorkshire and North East Region)
Yorkshire Regional Office, tel: 01904 702021

Enquiries to: Manager
Access:
Access to staff: By letter, by telephone, by fax

General description:
Rebuilt in 1743 during Hull's heyday as an affluent trading centre, this house is a typical but rare survivor of a contemporary merchant's residence. The restrained exterior belies the spectacular plasterwork staircase inside. The house is now let as offices.

Internet home pages:
http://www.nationaltrust.org.uk

1694
MAKING IT DISCOVERY CENTRE
Littleworth, Mansfield, Nottinghamshire, NG18 1AH

Tel: 01623 473273
Fax: 01623 473201
Email: info@makingit.org.uk
Acronym or abbreviation: Making It!
Full name: The Making It Industrial Heritage Trust Limited
Formed: 1996

Organisation type and purpose: Registered charity (charity number 1064919), suitable for ages: 5+.
Discovery Centre.
To promote education.

Enquiries to: Chief Executive
Direct tel: 01623 473200
Direct fax: 01623 473201
Direct email: susanwalters@makingit.org.uk
Other contacts: Education Manager for educational matters.
Access:
Access to staff: By letter, by fax, by email
Hours: Mon to Sun, 0930 to 1730
Access for disabled people: Parking provided, ramped entry, level entry, access to all public areas, toilet facilities
Other restrictions: Working towards Braille

General description:
Design Technology for Key Stages 1 to 5, business studies, art, science.
Information services:
Special visitor services: Materials and/or activities for children.
Education services: Group education facilities, resources for Key Stages 1 and 2, 3, 4 and Further or Higher Education.
Services for disabled people: For the visually impaired; for the hearing impaired; displays and/or information at wheelchair height.
Collections:
Local history oral archive of working lives

Internet home pages:
http://www.makingit.org.uk
Information about visits, education pack, games

1695
MAKING PLACE, THE
3 Exmoor Street, London, SW17 9NE

Tel: 020 8964 2684
Fax: 020 8964 2698
Email: info@the-making-place.co.uk
Formed: 1996

Organisation type and purpose: Suitable for ages: 5+.
Hands-on science centre.
Hands-on science workshops.

Enquiries to: Director
Access:
Access to staff: By telephone, by fax, by email, Internet web pages
Access to building, collections or gallery: Prior appointment required
Access for disabled people: Parking provided, ramped entry, access to all public areas, toilet facilities

General description:
Hands-on science activities and workshops for schools and family groups aimed at children age 5-12, inset training for teachers.
Information services:
Special visitor services: Materials and/or activities for children.
Education services: Group education facilities, resources for Key Stages 1 and 2..
Collections:
Examples of activities to make
Printed publications:
Publicity leaflets and flyers
Kits for making activities

Internet home pages:
http://www.the-making-place.co.uk

1696
MALDON AND DISTRICT AGRICULTURAL & DOMESTIC MUSEUM
Church Street, Goldhanger, Maldon, Essex

Tel: 01621 788647
Formed: 1985

Organisation type and purpose: Independently owned, museum.

General description:
Agricultural and domestic artefacts.
Collections:
Large collection of tractors, rotovators and static engines, pedal power saws and drills; garage equipment including petrol pumps; also domestic household equipment.

1697
MALDON DISTRICT MUSEUM
47 Mill Road, Maldon, Essex, CM9 5HX

Tel: 01621 842688
Email: bygones@maldonmuseum.fsnet.co.uk
Acronym or abbreviation: MDMA
Full name: Maldon District Museum Association
Formed: 1921
Formerly: Maldon Museum, date of change, 1997

Organisation type and purpose: Independently owned, registered charity (charity number 301362), museum.

Enquiries to: Chairman
Direct tel: 01621 828001
Direct email: laceysx@lineone.net
Other contacts: Membership Secretary for the Association.
Access:
Access to staff: By letter, by telephone, visitors by prior appointment, charges to non-members
Access to building, collections or gallery: Prior appointment required
Hours: Wed, Thu, Fri, 1400 to 1600; Sat, Sun, 1400 to 1700
Access for disabled people: ramped entry, toilet facilities

General description:
Social history of Maldon since 1750. Recreation of cobbler's shop, bakery, general store, pub, railway station, 1940s room.
Information services:
Helpline available
Guided tours by prior arrangement.
Special visitor services: Guided tours, materials and/or activities for children.
Services for disabled people: Displays and/or information at wheelchair height.
Collections:
Artefacts relating to social history of Maldon since 1750
Display of clay pipes, boatbuilding, sail-making equipment
Many artefacts from local industrial concerns now defunct especially John Sadd & Sons Ltd, Bentall's of Heybridge
Displays relating to local schools, cinemas, hospitals
Fire engine from 1877, hand pumper
Margery Allingham Society, devoted to the works of the author who lived locally, has a display space within the Museum; particularly her detective stories with the hero, Albert Campion
Catalogues:
Catalogue for all of the collections is only available in-house.
Publications list:
is available in hard copy.

Internet home pages:
http://www.maldonmuseum.fsnet.co.uk

1698
MALLAIG HERITAGE CENTRE
Station Road, Mallaig, Inverness-shire, PH41 4PY

Tel: 01687 462085
Email: curator@mallaigheritage.org.uk
Formed: 1994
Formerly: Mallaig Heritage Trust

Organisation type and purpose: Independently owned, registered charity (charity number ED661/84/PLB), museum, suitable for ages: 8+. Museum dedicated to the history of West Lochaber, Inverness-shire.

Enquiries to: Curator
Access:
Access to staff: By letter, by email, in person, Internet web pages
Access for disabled people: Parking provided, level entry, access to all public areas, toilet facilities

General description:
Material relevant to all aspects of the history of West Lochaber. At present the collection is largely photographic, drawn from other archives. Now housed in a new centre (opened March 1994), the collection is growing fast.
Information services:
Special visitor services: Guided tours..
Collections:
1841-1891 Censuses for Glenelg Parish, Ordnamurchan Parish
Wide range of photographs relevant to the local area, especially local people and the landscape, 800 items
Catalogues:
Catalogue for part of the collections is only available in-house.
Printed publications:
Jon Schueler 1916-1992 (ed. Salvesen M)
North Morar 1750-1900 (Rixson D)
Knoydart 1750-1894 (Rixson D)
Arisaig & S Morar (Rixson D)

Internet home pages:
http://www.mallaigheritage.org.uk/index.htm
Introduction, index to subjects covered.

1699
MALTON MUSEUM
Old Town Hall, Market Place, Malton, North Yorkshire, YO17 7LP

Tel: 01653 695136
Formed: 1982

Organisation type and purpose: Registered charity (charity number 508224), museum, suitable for ages: all ages.

Enquiries to: Chairman
Direct tel: 01653 692610
Access:
Access to staff: By letter, by telephone
Hours: Easter Sat to 31 Oct: Mon to Sat, 1000 to 1600
Access for disabled people: level entry
Other restrictions: Access to ground floor only.

General description:
Archaeology of the Roman Fort of Malton (Derventio), the Vicus and nearby villas, evidence and objects gathered from a long history of local excavation, potteries and coin hoards. Pre-historic artefacts from local sites. Later social history of town including local trades, such as brewing and racing, as well as items made in Malton.
Information services:
Special visitor services: Materials and/or activities for children..

1700
MALVERN MUSEUM
The Abbey Gateway, Abbey Road, Malvern, Worcestershire, WR14 3ES

Tel: 01684 567811
Formed: 1979

Organisation type and purpose: Independently owned, membership association (membership is by subscription), present number of members: 200, voluntary organisation, registered charity (charity number 508766), museum, historic building, house or site, suitable for ages: all ages, publishing house.
Museum and listed building owned by Malvern Museum Society.
Malvern Museum Association (eg Friends of the Museum), membership by subscription, provides the daily running and maintenance, organises lectures, meetings and other events for the membership and the public.

Enquiries to: Curator
Access:
Access to staff: By letter, by telephone, in person
Access for disabled people: level entry
Other restrictions: Level entry to sales and reception area only.
Audio system available to describe the other museum rooms on lower and upper floor.

General description:
Local history of the area from earliest times: geology of Malvern Hills; Malvern Chase, foundation of 11th century Priories; Malvern water, the 19th century Water Cure; Victorian Malvern - growth of town, architecture, schools, railways, motor cars, Santler and Morgan; Malvern Festival 1929 to present including Elgar's work; development of radar; Malvern during World Wars I and II.
Information services:
Guided tours by appointment.
School visits by appointment.
Special visitor services: Guided tours, tape recorded guides.
Education services: Resources for Key Stages 2 and 3..
Collections:
Medieval Timbers (late 14th century) from Guesten Hall windows
19th century bottles (commercial) linked to Water Cure
Late Victorian carpenter tools
Programmes and photographs of early Malvern Festival (theatrical) productions, 1929-.
Catalogues:
Catalogue for all of the collections is only available in-house.
Printed publications:
Ancient Hills (£1.20)
Aquae Malvernensis (£9.99)
Dr Wilson and his Malvern Hydro (£5.95)
Malvern Chase (£1)
The Malvern Hillforts (£1)
Malvern Voices: Childhood (first of a series of oral histories of the 20th century, £1.99)
Temperance, therapy and trilobytes: Dr Ralph Grindrod, Victorian Pioneer (£5.95)
Henry Ward, VC, 1823-1867 (£3.50)
Various booklets, maps, cards, postcards etc (list sent on request)

1701
MANCHESTER AIR AND SPACE MUSEUM
See - Museum of Science and Industry, Manchester

1702
MANCHESTER ART GALLERY
Mosley Street, Manchester, M2 3JL

Tel: 0161 235 8888
Minicom no. 0161 235 8893
Fax: 0161 235 8899
Formerly: Manchester City Art Gallery, date of change, 2001

Organisation type and purpose: Local government body, art gallery, historic building, house or site, suitable for ages: all ages.
Parent body:
Manchester City Galleries

Enquiries to: Information Officer
Access:
Access to staff: By letter, by telephone, by fax, visitors by prior appointment
Hours: Tue to Fri, 1000 to 1700
Other restrictions: Prior appointment preferred.
Access to building, collections or gallery: No prior appointment required
Hours: Tue to Sun and Bank Holiday Mon, 1000 to 1700
Other restrictions: Closed Dec 24 to 26, 31, Jan 1 and Good Friday
Access for disabled people: ramped entry, access to all public areas, toilet facilities

General description:
The Gallery houses one of the country's finest art collections; 19th century Pre-Raphaelite paintings, works of 18th century artists including Gainsborough, Reynolds and Stubbs. There are a number of specialist galleries. Each floor has a special interest gallery, which introduces particular aspects of the collection. The Manchester Gallery displays some of the city's creative achievements, works by Lowry and Valette and contemporary artists and designers. The Gallery of Craft and Design includes ceramics, glass, metalwork, furniture, textiles, toys and armour. The Clore Interactive Gallery for children aged 5 to 12 years, provides the experience of real works of art together with hands-on activities. Two new galleries provide space for a programme of changing national and international special exhibitions.
Information services:
Provides a programme of events, talks and workshops for visitors of all ages.
Programmes for schools and collages, contact education department.
Audio guide also available for families, and in Cantonese and Urdu .
Copies of the introductory panels for each room available, on loan, in a range of Asian and European languages.
Floor plans available.
Facilities available for corporate entertaining, receptions and meetings, contact 0161 235 8851.
Special visitor services: Guided tours, tape recorded guides, materials and/or activities for children.
Education services: Group education facilities, resources for Key Stages 1 and 2, 3 and 4.
Services for disabled people: For the visually impaired; for the hearing impaired.

Internet home pages:
http://www.manchestergalleries.org

1703
MANCHESTER CITY GALLERIES
Mosley Street, Manchester, M2 3JL

Tel: 0161 235 8888
Minicom no. 0161 235 8893
Fax: 0161 235 8899
Email: cityart@mcrl.poptel.org.uk
Formed: 1882
Formerly: Manchester City Art Galleries, date of change, 2001

Organisation type and purpose: Local government body, art gallery, historic building, house or site, suitable for ages: all ages.
Administrative body for the Manchester City Art Galleries and Museums.
Parent body:
Manchester City Council
Email: www.manchester.gov.uk
Galleries and historic houses:
Gallery of Costume
Platt Hall, Wilmslow Road, Rusholme, Manchester, M14 5LL, tel: 0161 224 5217, fax: 0161 256 3278
Heaton Hall
Heaton Park, Preswich, Manchester, M25 5SW, tel: 0161 773 1231
Manchester Art Gallery
Mosley Street, Manchester, M2 3JL, tel: 0161 235 8888, fax: 0161 235 8899

Queen's Park Conservation Studio
Queen's Park, Rochdale Road, Harpurhey, Manchester, M9 5SH, tel: 0161 205 2645, fax: 0161 205 6164
Wythenshawe Hall
Wythenshaw Park, Northenden, Manchester, M23 0AB, tel: 0161 998 2331

Enquiries to: Administration
Access:
Access to staff: By letter, by telephone, visitors by prior appointment, Internet web pages
Hours: Mon to Fri, 0900 to 1700

General description:
Fine and decorative art from antiquity to present day; costume, picture, decorative art, and costume restoration.
Information services:
Special visitor services: Guided tours, tape recorded guides, materials and/or activities for children.
Education services: Group education facilities, resources for Key Stages 1 and 2, 3, 4 and Further or Higher Education..
Collections:
20th century British Paintings
Assheton-Bennett Collection of English silver and 17th century Dutch painting
Old Masters
Pre-Raphaelites
Thomas Greg Collection of English pottery
Catalogues:
Catalogue for all of the collections is available in-house, part is published and part is on-line.
Printed publications:
Concise Catalogue of British Paintings (2 vols)
Foreign Paintings
Large selection of printed items eg posters, prints, postcards, greetings cards etc
Other catalogues of temporary exhibitions
Pre-Raphaelite Paintings

Internet home pages:
http://www.cityartgalleries.org.uk

See also - Gallery of Costume; Heaton Hall; Manchester Art Gallery; Queen's Park Art Studio; Wythenshawe Hall

1704
MANCHESTER JEWISH MUSEUM
190 Cheetham Hill Road, Manchester, M8 8LW

Tel: 0161 834 9879
Fax: 0161 834 9801
Email: info@manchesterjewishmuseum.com
Acronym or abbreviation: MJM
Formed: 1984

Organisation type and purpose: Independently owned, registered charity (charity number 508278), museum, historic building, house or site, suitable for ages: 5+.
Former Spanish and Portuguese Synagogue, now Grade II* listed building, beautifully restored, stained glass windows.

Enquiries to: Administrator
Access:
Access to staff: By letter, by telephone, by fax, by email, visitors by prior appointment
Access to building, collections or gallery: No prior appointment required
Hours: Mon to Thu, 1030 to 1600; Sun, 1030 to 1700
Other restrictions: Fri by prior appointment. Closed Sat and Jewish Holidays (phone in advance).

General description:
Social history of the Jewish Community in Manchester and Salford over the past 250 years.
Synagogue, torah, Jewish belief and associated subjects.
Information services:
Special visitor services: Guided tours, materials and/or activities for children.
Education services: Group education facilities, resources for Key Stages 1 and 2, 3, 4 and Further or Higher Education.
Services for disabled people: For the visually impaired.
Collections:
Photographs (c. 18,000) held as contact prints/negatives
Artefacts (social, religious, homelife, work, school etc)
Oral history (c. 700 hours of testimony on cassette tape)
Small number of books, pamphlets and paintings (not all held in this building)
Publications list:
is available in hard copy.
Printed publications:
A Visitor's Guide (direct, £3 incl p&p - UK)
Fact & Activity Packs (at both KS 1 and 2 and KS 3 and 4, direct)
A4 sheets in plastic folders on all main Jewish Festivals, Sabbath, Weddings and Bar & Bat Mitzvah (contains cross-curricular activities, photocopiable, direct)

Internet home pages:
http://www.manchesterjewishmuseum.com

See also - North West Sound Archive

1705
MANCHESTER TRANSPORT MUSEUM SOCIETY
See - Heaton Park Tramway

1706
MANCHESTER UNITED MUSEUM
Sir Matt Busby Way, Old Trafford, Manchester, M16 0RA

Tel: 0161 868 8631
Fax: 0161 868 8861
Email: tours@manutd.co.uk
Formed: 1986

Organisation type and purpose: Independently owned, museum.

Enquiries to: Manager
Direct tel: 0161 868 8626
Access:
Access to staff: By telephone
Access for disabled people: level entry, access to all public areas, toilet facilities
Other restrictions: Some parts of the stadium not available to wheelchair users.

General description:
The museum provides a background to the history of the World's Most Famous Football Club through displays, audio-visuals and a wide variety of interactives from its foundation as Newton Heath, Lancashire and Yorkshire Railway, Cricket and Football Club to the present day. It includes personal items from players past and present.
The tour takes visitors behind the scenes, and includes the Dressing Room so you can sit where your favourite player changes on match day.
Information services:
Special visitor services: Guided tours.
Education services: Group education facilities, resources for Key Stages 1 and 2, 3, 4 and Further or Higher Education.
Services for disabled people: For the visually impaired; displays and/or information at wheelchair height.
Collections:
Several thousand items running from trophies, medals, photographs, programmes, shirts, books etc
Catalogues:
Catalogue for library is in-house only. Catalogue for all of the collections is only available in-house.
Printed publications:
Information leaflet available free of charge direct

1707
MANDER & MITCHENSON THEATRE COLLECTION
Trinity College of Music, Jerwood Library of the Performing Arts, King Charles Court, Old Royal Naval College, Greenwich, SE10 9JF

Tel: 020 8305 3888
Fax: 020 8305 3999
Email: library@tcm.ac.uk
Full name: The Raymond Mander and Joe Mitchenson Theatre Collection
Formed: 1938

Organisation type and purpose: Registered charity (charity number 273339), museum, research organisation.

Enquiries to: Administrator
Access:
Access to staff: By letter, by telephone, by fax, by email, visitors by prior appointment
Hours: Mon to Fri, 1000 to 1600
Other restrictions: No disabled access.

General description:
Programmes, photographs, engravings, cuttings, books, all theatre and performing arts related (UK only).
Catalogues:
Catalogue for library is in-house only. Catalogue for part of the collections is only available in-house.

1708
MANGAPPS RAILWAY MUSEUM
Southminster Road, Burnham-on-Crouch, Essex, CM0 8QQ

Tel: 01621 784898

Enquiries to: Information Officer

General description:
East Anglian railway history, signalling equipment, steam and diesel locomotives, carriages and wagons.

Internet home pages:
http://www.mangapps.co.uk

1709
MANOR FARM COUNTRY PARK
Pylands Lane, Burseldon, Southampton, SO31 1XX

Tel: 01489 787055

Organisation type and purpose: Local government body, museum.
Parent body:
Hampshire County Council

Enquiries to: Curator

General description:
Working farm, farmhouse and garden of a bygone age, traditional farm buildings, machinery and equipment, rare breeds of farm animals.

1710
MANOR HOUSE MUSEUM, THE
5 Honey Hill, Bury St Edmunds, Suffolk, IP33 1HF

Tel: 01284 757076
Formed: 1933

Organisation type and purpose: Local government body, museum, historic building, house or site, suitable for ages: 5+.
Parent body:
St Edmundsbury Borough Council (St Eds BC)
Shire Hall, Honey Hill Mews, Bury St Edmunds, Suffolk, IP33 1HF

Enquiries to: Assistant Manager
Direct tel: 01284 757074
Direct fax: 01284 747231
Direct email: saskia.stent@stedsbc.gov.uk
Other contacts: Overall Museums Manager for Manor and Moyses.

continued overleaf

Access:
Access to staff: By letter, by telephone, by fax, by email
Other restrictions: Prior appointment preferred.
Access to building, collections or gallery: No prior appointment required
Hours: Wed to Sun, 1100 to 1600
Other restrictions: Large groups requiring guided tour by prior appointment.
Access for disabled people: Parking provided, ramped entry, access to all public areas, toilet facilities

General description:
The Manor House Museum is a beautifully restored 18th century Georgian mansion which overlooks the timeless tranquility of the Great Churchyard. Specialising in clocks, watches, paintings and costume.
Information services:
Special visitor services: Guided tours, materials and/or activities for children.
Education services: Group education facilities, resources for Key Stages 1 and 2 and 3.
Services for disabled people: For the visually impaired; displays and/or information at wheelchair height.
Catalogues:
Catalogue for library is on-line. Catalogue for part of the collections is only available in-house.
Printed publications:
Guide Book (£1)
Working Time (£1)
Rose Mead (£1.50)
Mary Beale (£1)
Wedding Dresses 1800s

Internet home pages:
http://www.stedmundsbury.gov.uk/manorhse.htm
General information with images.
Catalogue of the library.

1711
MANOR HOUSE MUSEUM, THE
Donington-le-Heath, Manor Road, Coalville, Leicestershire, LE67 2FE

Tel: 01530 831259
Formed: 1972

Organisation type and purpose: Local government body, museum, historic building, house or site, suitable for ages: 5+.
Parent body:
Leicestershire County Council
County Hall, Glenfield, Leicester, LE3 8TB, tel: 0116 265 6791
Other addresses:
Leicestershire County Council
County Hall, Glenfield, Leicester, LE3 8TB, tel: 0116 265 6791

Enquiries to: Curator
Direct email: museums@leics.gov.uk
Other contacts: Keeper for events.
Access:
Access to staff: By letter, by telephone, by fax, visitors by prior appointment
Hours: Mon to Fri, 1100 to 1700
Access for disabled people: Parking provided, ramped entry, level entry, toilet facilities
Other restrictions: Wheelchair available; photograph album of inaccessible parts of the house; touch/feel/smell table for visually impaired visitors.

General description:
Archaeology.
Information services:
Helpline available, tel no: 01530 831259.
Special visitor services: Guided tours, materials and/or activities for children.
Education services: Group education facilities, resources for Key Stages 2 and 3.
Services for disabled people: For the visually impaired; displays and/or information at wheelchair height.
Collections:
Archaeological information and artefacts can be viewed by arrangement
13th century stone built house with 17th century modifications
Collection of original 17th century furniture
17th century style gardens
Publications list:
is available in hard copy.

Internet home pages:
http://www.leics.gov.uk
Museum sites and opening times.

1712
MANOR HOUSE MUSEUM
c/o The Coach House, Sheep Street, Kettering, Northamptonshire, NN16 0AN

Tel: 01536 534381
Fax: 01536 534370
Formed: 1989
Part of: Kettering's Heritage Quarter

Organisation type and purpose: Local government body, museum, suitable for ages: 8+.
Parent body:
Kettering Borough Council (KBC)
Bowling Green Road, Kettering, tel: 01536 534394, fax: 01536 534370

Enquiries to: Curator
Direct tel: 01536 534394
Direct fax: 01536 534370
Access:
Access to staff: By letter, by telephone, by fax
Hours: Mon, Tue, Thu to Sat, 0930 to 1700; Wed, 1000 to 1700
Other restrictions: Closed Bank Holidays.
Access for disabled people: level entry, access to all public areas, toilet facilities

General description:
History of Kettering Borough: archaeology (especially Roman); geology; social history; industrial history (especially boot and shoe). Changing temporary exhibitions, permanent display, monthly events days and school holiday children's activities.
Information services:
Special visitor services: Materials and/or activities for children.
Education services: Resources for Key Stages 2 and 3..
Collections:
Works by Sir Alfred East, 1850s-1913 and T C Gotch, c. 1850-1900 (both artists born in Kettering)
Catalogues:
Catalogue for all of the collections is only available in-house but part is published.
Printed publications:
Publicity leaflets and local history leaflets only (free)

Internet home pages:
http://www.kettering.gov.uk

1713
MANSFIELD MUSEUM AND ART GALLERY
Leeming Street, Mansfield, Nottinghamshire, NG18 1NG

Tel: 01623 463088
Fax: 01623 412922
Formed: 1904

Organisation type and purpose: Local government body, museum, art gallery, historic building, house or site, suitable for ages: all ages.
Parent body:
Mansfield District Council
Chesterfield Road South, Mansfield, Nottinghamshire, NG19 7BH

Enquiries to: Curator
Access:
Access to staff: By letter, by telephone, in person
Hours: Mon to Sat, 1000 to 1700
Access for disabled people: level entry, access to all public areas, toilet facilities

General description:
History of Mansfield.
Collections:
Archives related to Mansfield
Natural history specimens and social history objects
Photographs related to Mansfield
Watercolours (130) by Albert Sorby Buxton, a record of the town at the turn of the century

1714
MAPPIN ART GALLERY
See - Sheffield City Museum and Mappin Art Gallery

1715
MARBLE HILL HOUSE
Richmond Road, Twickenham, Middlesex, TW1 2NL

Tel: 020 8892 5115
Fax: 020 8607 9976

Organisation type and purpose: Historic building, house or site, suitable for ages: all ages.
Parent body:
English Heritage (London Region)
23 Savile Row, London, W1X 1AB, tel: 020 7973 3000, fax: 020 7937 3001

Enquiries to: House Manager
Access:
Access to staff: By letter, by telephone, by fax
Access for disabled people: toilet facilities
Other restrictions: Access to ground floor only

General description:
A magnificent Thames-side Palladian villa, Marble Hill House built in the 1720s for Henrietta Howard, Countess of Suffolk and mistress of King George II. There are extravagant gilded rooms in which she entertained famous poets and wits of the age including Pope, Gay and Swift. The house is set in 66 acres of beautiful riverside grounds.
Information services:
Pre-booked tours available.
Exhibition
Special visitor services: Guided tours, tape recorded guides, materials and/or activities for children.
Education services: Group education facilities..
Collections:
Early 18th century paintings (Hogarth, Reynolds, Wilson, etc.) and furniture, including original overmantel and overdoors by Panini

Internet home pages:
http://www.english-heritage.org.uk

1716
MARCH & DISTRICT MUSEUM
High Street, March, Cambridgeshire, PE15 9JJ

Tel: 01354 655300 (answerphone)
Fax: 01354 653714
Formed: 1977

Organisation type and purpose: (charity number 286115), suitable for ages: all ages.

Enquiries to: Vice-Chairman
Access:
Access to staff: By letter, by fax
Access to building, collections or gallery: No prior appointment required
Hours: Wed, 1000 to 1200; Sat, 1030 to 1530; 1st Sun, Jun, Jul, Aug, Sep: 1400 to 1700
Other restrictions: Parties at other times by prior appointment (14 days' notice).
Access for disabled people: ramped entry, access to all public areas

General description:
Rural life museum reflecting life in the area - predominantly exhibits from 19th and 20th centuries.
Collections:
Local Government Rate Books, 1852 onwards

Local Council Minute Books
Medals awarded to Benjamin Gimbert (Soham Explosion 1944) - George Cross et al
Locomotive name plate 'Benjamin Gimbert GC'.
Church Plate given to 'Parishioners of March' by James Collier 1752
Doddington & Hamlets Cavalry Guidon (1798-1828)
Wide selection of photographs of March and District
Printed publications:
Small selection of books/booklets relevant to local history
Internet home pages:
http://www.marchtown.com
Brief description of current events.

1717
MARCONI CENTRE
Poldhu, The Lizard, Nr Helston, Cornwall

Tel: 01362 241656

Organisation type and purpose: National organisation, registered charity (charity number 205846), museum, suitable for ages: 5+.
Parent body:
National Trust (South West)
Regional Office for Devon and Cornwall, tel: 01208 74281

Enquiries to: Warden
Direct tel: 01326 561407 (Lizard Countryside Office)
Direct fax: 01326 562882
Direct email: lizard@nationaltrust.org.uk
Access:
Access to staff: By letter, by telephone, by fax, by email, in person, Internet web pages
Access to building, collections or gallery: No prior appointment required
Hours: Please telephone for opening times

General description:
The Lizard played a key role in the history of modern communications. Marconi's historic wireless experiments on the Lizard in 1901 are celebrated at this new centre.

Internet home pages:
http://www.nationaltrust.org.uk/regions/cornwall

See also - Lizard Wireless Station

1718
MARGATE MUSEUM
Old Town Hall, Market Street, Margate, Kent, CT9 1ER

Tel: 01843 231213
Fax: 01843 587765
Email: museum@ekmt.fsnet
Formed: 1987
Formerly: East Kent Maritime Trust, Margate Old Town Hall Local History Museum

Organisation type and purpose: Registered charity, museum.
Parent body:
East Kent Maritime Trust
The Clock House, Pier Yard, Royal Harbour, Ramsgate, Kent, CT11 8LS, tel: 01843 587765

Enquiries to: Curator
Direct tel: 01843 292831
Other contacts: Education Officer for group visits and facilities.
Access:
Access to staff: By letter, by telephone, by fax, by email, in person
Access to building, collections or gallery: No prior appointment required
Hours: Tue to Sun 1000 to 1700

General description:
The Town Hall forms the focal point of the old town of Margate. Within the complex can be found the local museum, the main theme of which is the local history of Margate from the 18th Century. The display material charts Margate's development as a premier resort, and Margate during World War II.
Collections:
Paddle Steamer. Models - prints, pictures. Early 19th Century
Pictures, photographs and postcards of Margate
Prints/Pictures. Rowlandson collections. Late 18th Century
Police items. Borough police items. Mid-19th Century
Rowe bequest. Romano-British items. 1st Century
WW1 and WW2. Items relating to the two wars. Mid-20th Century
Catalogues:
Catalogue for library is in-house only. Catalogue for all of the collections is only available in-house.

Internet home pages:
http://www.ekmt.fsnet.co.uk

1719
MARGERY ALLINGHAM SOCIETY
See - Maldon District Museum

1720
MARGROVE HERITAGE CENTRE
See - Kirkleatham Museum

1721
MARGROVE PARK HERITAGE CENTRE
Margrove Park, Boosbeck, Guisborough, Cleveland, TS12 3BZ

Tel: 01287 610368 or 01642 479500
Fax: 01642 474199
Email: museum_services@redcar-cleveland.gov.uk
Formed: 1990

Organisation type and purpose: Local government body, museum, suitable for ages: 5+.
Parent body:
Redcar & Cleveland Museums Service
Other addresses:
Kirkleatham Museum
Kirkleatham, Redcar, TS10 5NW, tel: 01642 479500, fax: 01642 474199

Enquiries to: Curator
Access:
Access to staff: By letter, by telephone, by fax, by email
Access for disabled people: Parking provided, ramped entry, access to all public areas, toilet facilities

General description:
Information on history, archaeology etc of Redcar & Cleveland Borough area.
Information services:
Special visitor services: Materials and/or activities for children.
Education services: Group education facilities, resources for Key Stages 1 and 2, 3, 4 and Further or Higher Education.
Services for disabled people: For the visually impaired; for the hearing impaired.
Collections:
Local and social history and other collections
Collection of historic maps
Publications list:
is available in hard copy.

1722
MARINE BIOLOGICAL ASSOCIATION
See - Robertson Museum and Aquarium

1723
MARISCHAL MUSEUM
See - Aberdeen University, Marischal Museum

1724
MARITIME MUSEUM
Sparrows Nest Gardens, Whapload Road, Lowestoft, Suffolk, NR32 1XG

Tel: 01502 561963
Full name: Lowestoft and East Suffolk Maritime Society
Formed: 1968

Organisation type and purpose: Registered charity, museum.

Enquiries to: Chairman
Other contacts: (1) Honorary Secretary (2) Curator
Access:
Access to staff: By letter, by telephone
Hours: May to Oct: Mon to Sun, 1000 to 1700

General description:
History of the Lowestoft fishing industry, from sail to steam, and modern vessels, models, paintings etc. The methods of fishing are also recorded, and the collection includes all gear associated with fishing.
Local wartime association with the Royal Navy, photographs and medals.
Evolution of RNLI Lifeboats, models, photographs and artefacts.
Local boat and shipbuilding, display of shipwrights' tools; picture gallery.
Collections:
Cox Memorial, evolution of East Coast lifeboats, 1900-1990, 250 items
Picture gallery of fishing vessels, 1800-1985, 300 items and the Battle of Lowestoft, 1665, with summary of event
Prunier Trophy sculptured in Purbeck marble, for the largest single catch of herring in one night's fishing, 1936-1966

1725
MARKET LAVINGTON VILLAGE MUSEUM
Church Street, Market Lavington, Wiltshire, SN10 4DT

Tel: 01380 818736
Formed: 1985

Organisation type and purpose: Registered charity, museum.
Other Addresses:
Honorary Secretary
Parsonage Mead, The Spring, Market Lavington, Wiltshire, SN10 4EB, tel: 01380 816222

Enquiries to: Honorary Curator
Other contacts: Honorary Secretary
Access:
Access to staff: By letter, by telephone, in person, visitors by prior appointment

General description:
A small cottage museum concentrating on all aspects of life in the village. A history of the village from all aspects past and present.
Information services:
Disabled aids being expanded.
Special visitor services: Materials and/or activities for children.
Education services: Group education facilities..
Collections:
19th century kitchen display.
Clothes.19th and 20th century
Photographs
Press cuttings.1950s to present day
Printed publications:
Village Under the Plain - The Story of Market Lavington (McGill B, available from Honorary Curator, £10)

1726
MARKET OVERTON INDUSTRIAL RAILWAY ASSOCIATION
See - Rutland Railway Museum

1727
MARKFIELD BEAM ENGINE & MUSEUM
Markfield Road, South Tottenham, London, N15 4RB

Tel: 020 8800 7061
Email: alan@mbeam.org
Acronym or abbreviation: MBEAM
Formed: 1984
Formed from: River Lea Industrial Archaeological Society (RLIAS)

Organisation type and purpose: Independently owned, registered charity (charity number 290486), museum, historic building, house or site, research organisation.
Connections with:
River Lea Industrial Archaeological Society (RLIAS)
Founding Member:
Association of London Pumping Houses Attractions (ALPHA)
Other members:
Kew Bridge, Kempton, Crossness, Old Hall
Office Address:
Markfield Beam Engine & Museum
c/o Nine Elms, Therfield, Royston, CG8 9QE, tel: 01763 287331, email/website: alan@mbeam.org

Enquiries to: Director
Direct tel: 0176 3287 331
Access:
Access to staff: By letter, by telephone
Access for disabled people: Parking provided
Other restrictions: Entry - normally 2 steps.

General description:
1886 Beam Pumping Engine - 2 cylinder. Wolf Compound, 100 hp, 4 million gallons per day of sewage, built by Wood Bros, Sowerby Bridge. Restored to full working order, using clean water.
Open steam days. Videos of it working shown, when not in steam.
Small associated museum display and presentation. Guided walk to view outdoor items of former small sewage treatment works - 6 acres - 2 1/2 hectares.

Internet home pages:
http://www.mbeam.org

See also - River Lea Industrial Archaeological Society

1728
MARLIPINS MUSEUM
36 High Street, Shoreham-by-Sea, West Sussex, BN43 5NN

Tel: 01273 462994
Email: smomich@sussexpast.co.uk
Formed: 1926

Organisation type and purpose: Independently owned, registered charity (charity number 207037), museum, historic building, house or site, suitable for ages: all ages.
Parent body:
Sussex Past
Bull House, 92 High Street, Lewes, East Sussex, BN7 1XH, tel: 01273 486260, fax: 01273 486990, email: admin@sussexpast.co.uk
Parent body:
Sussex Archaeological Society
Bull House, 92 High Street, Lewes, BN7 1XH, tel: 01273 486260, fax: 01273 486990, email/ website: admin@sussexpast.co.uk

Enquiries to: Curator
Direct tel: 01323 441279/01273 462994
Direct fax: 01323 844030
Access:
Access to staff: By letter, by email

General description:
A museum housed in a Norman and later building, containing collections of geology; archaeology; local history; and maritime history, relating to Shoreham and its immediate environs. Also contains an interesting collection of topographical paintings and maps.
Information services:
Special visitor services: Guided tours, materials and/or activities for children.
Education services: Group education facilities.
Services for disabled people: Displays and/or information at wheelchair height.
Collections:
Artefacts and images of Shoreham area
Maritime history through ship models, artefacts and pictures
Paintings of local buildings, etc. 19th-20th century
Portraits of Shoreham ships, 19th-20th century
Various ship models of varying quality, 19th-20th century
Catalogues:
Catalogue for part of the collections is only available in-house.
Printed publications:
Museum Guide Book
Books on social and local history of Shoreham area, including:
Bungalow Town - early film industry (Wouters N)

Internet home pages:
http://www.sussexpast.co.uk
Archaeology and historical research in Sussex, properties, and membership.

1729
MARSDEN MOOR ESTATE
Estate Office, The Old Goods Yard, Station Road, Marsden, Huddersfield, West Yorkshire, HD7 6DH

Tel: 01484 847016
Fax: 01484 847071
Email: marsdenmoor@nationaltrust.org.uk

Organisation type and purpose: National government body, registered charity (charity number 205846), historic building, house or site.
Parent body:
National Trust (Yorkshire and North East Region)
Yorkshire Regional Office, tel: 01904 702021

Enquiries to: Manager
Access:
Access to staff: By letter, by telephone, by fax

General description:
The estate, covering nearly 2429ha (5685 acres) of unenclosed common moorland and almost surrounding the village of Marsden, takes in the northern part of the Peak District National Park, with valleys, reservoirs, peaks and crags, as well as archaeological remains dating from pre-Roman times to the great engineering structures of the canal and railway ages. The landscape supports large numbers of
classic moorland birds such as the golden plover, red grouse, curlew and diminutive twite. The estate is a designated SSSI and forms part of an international Special Area of Conservation. The Huddersfield Narrow Canal has been restored and a Visitor Centre (not NT) is open at Tunnel End, Marsden, with car parking adjacent to the Estate Office. The 'Welcome to Marsden' exhibition traces the development of the village and its surroundings from Mesolithic times to the present. A new Heritage Trail enables visitors to explore Marsden and its sites of interest.

1730
MARTIN FOWLER MUSEUM
See - National Coracle Centre

1731
MARTYRS' SCHOOL
Parson Street, Glasgow, G4 0PX

Tel: 0141 552 2356
Fax: 0141 552 2356

Organisation type and purpose: Museum, historic building, house or site.
Parent body:
Glasgow Museums

General description:
One of the earliest buildings designed by Charles Rennie Mackintosh 1868-1928. It was opened in 1897 as a public primary school. It was restored in 1999.

Internet home pages:
http://www.glasgow.gov.uk

1732
MARY ARDEN'S HOUSE
Shakespeare Countryside Museum, Wimcote, Stratford-upon-Avon, Warwickshire, CV37 9UN

Tel: 01789 293455
Email: info@shakespeare.org.uk

Organisation type and purpose: Registered charity (charity number 209302), historic building, house or site, suitable for ages: all ages.
Parent body:
Shakespeare Birthplace Trust
Tel: 01789 204016, fax: 01789 296083, email: info@shakespeare.org.uk

Enquiries to: Public Relations Manager
Direct tel: 01789 201807
Direct fax: 01789 263138
Direct email: sarah.jervis@shakespeare.org.uk
Access:
Access to staff: By letter, by telephone, by fax, by email, in person, Internet web pages
Access for disabled people: Parking provided, ramped entry, level entry, toilet facilities

General description:
An early Tudor Farmhouse which belonged to Robert Arden, Shakespeare's grandfather. The site also includes Palmers Farmhouse and many farm buildings. This brings to life the work and traditions of the countryside around Stratford upon Avon from Shakespeare's time to the early 20th century.

Internet home pages:
http://www.shakespeare.org.uk

1733
MARY QUEEN OF SCOT'S HOUSE & VISITOR CENTRE
1 Queen Marys Gardens, Queen Street, Jedburgh, Borders, TD8 6EN

Tel: 01835 863331
Fax: 01450 378506

Organisation type and purpose: Local government body, historic building, house or site, suitable for ages: 8+.
Parent body:
Scottish Borders Council Museum and Gallery Service
Tel: 01750 20096

Enquiries to: Curator
Access:
Access to staff: By letter, by telephone, by fax
Other restrictions: When closed contact Scottish Borders Council Museum and Gallery Service.
Access to building, collections or gallery: No prior appointment required
Hours: Early Mar to end Nov, Mon to Sat, 1000 to 1700, Sun, 1200 to 1630;
Jun to Sep Sun 1000 to 1630

General description:
Late 16th century fortified 'Bastel' house set in formal gardens. Period room displays give insight into the life of Mary Queen of Scots who visited Jedburgh in 1566.
Information services:
Interactive audiovisual programme available
Interpretation leaflets in French, German, Italian, Dutch and Japanese
Temporary exhibitions
Special visitor services: Tape recorded guides..

Internet home pages:
http://www.scotborders.gov.uk
http://www.scotborders.org.uk

1734
MARY ROSE TRUST

College Road, HM Naval Base, Portsmouth, Hampshire, PO1 3LX

Tel: 023 9275 0521
Fax: 023 9287 0588
Email: gill-armstrong@maryrose-admin.freeserve.co.uk
Formed: 1979

Organisation type and purpose: Registered charity (charity number 277503), museum, suitable for ages: 7 to 11, research organisation. Tourist attraction.
To conserve and display the Mary Rose hull and artefacts (in Portsmouth's historic dockyard).
Project's friends organisation:
Mary Rose Society
PO Box 1545, Winchester, Hampshire, SO23 8YT

Enquiries to: Public Relations Manager
Access:
Access to staff: By letter, by telephone, by email, visitors by prior appointment
Hours: Mon to Fri, 1000 to 1700

General description:
Henry VIII's warship Mary Rose, 1510-1545, maritime history of the Tudor period, underwater technology, evolution of the wooden ship in the late medieval period, conservation and care of material excavated from wet sites.
Collections:
Excavation Archive, which is being computerised, covers the hull structure, the excavated artefacts and a large collection of skeletal material
Photographic library for hire
Printed publications:
Annual Reports
Leaflet and fact sheet
Firstwatch
Video for hire

Internet home pages:
http://www.maryrose.org
The Mary Rose.

1735
MARYLEBONE CRICKET CLUB LIBRARY

See - MCC

1736
MASHAMS TRUST, THE

Mashams, Ongar, Essex, CM5 0DZ

Tel: 01277 890242
Email: kingking@mashams.freeserve.co.uk
Formed: 1980

Organisation type and purpose: Registered charity (charity number 1015099), historic building, house or site, suitable for ages: 5+.

Enquiries to: Curator
Access:
Access to staff: By letter, by telephone, by email, visitors by prior appointment
Access for disabled people: Parking provided

General description:
A Grade II listed building, heavily timbered with a thatched roof and set in a large garden. Built around 1400.
Information services:
Special visitor services: Guided tours, materials and/or activities for children.
Education services: Group education facilities..

1737
MASSON MILLS

See - Sir Richard Arkwright's Masson Mills

1738
MAUD FOSTER WINDMILL

Willoughby Road, Boston, Lincolnshire, PE21 9EG

Tel: 01205 352188
Formed: 1819

Organisation type and purpose: Independently owned, historic building, house or site, suitable for ages: 5+.

Enquiries to: Managing Director
Access:
Access to staff: By letter, by telephone

1739
MAUD RAILWAY MUSEUM

Maud Railway Station, Peterhead, Aberdeenshire, AB42 5LY

Tel: 01771 622906
Fax: 01771 622884
Formed: 1995

Organisation type and purpose: Local government body, museum, suitable for ages: 5+.
Parent body:
Aberdeenshire Heritage
Tel: 01771 622906, fax: 01771 622884

Enquiries to: Curator
Access:
Access to staff: By letter, by telephone, by fax
Access for disabled people: access to all public areas

General description:
Northeast Scotland railway material - GNSR, LNER, BR.
Catalogues:
Catalogue for part of the collections is only available in-house.

1740
MAX GATE

Alington Avenue, Dorchester, Dorset, DT1 2AA

Tel: 01305 262538
Fax: 01305 250978

Organisation type and purpose: National organisation, registered charity (charity number 205846), historic building, house or site.
Parent Body:
The National Trust (South West Region)
Wessex Regional Office, tel: 01985 843600
Access:
Access to staff: By letter
Access to building, collections or gallery: No prior appointment required
Hours: Beg Apr to end Sep, Mon, Wed and Sun, 1400 to 1700
Other restrictions: Only hall, dining and drawing rooms and garden open. Private visits, tours and seminars by schools, colleges and literary societies, at other times, by appointment with the tenants, Mr and Mrs Andrew Leah.

General description:
Novelist and poet Thomas Hardy designed and lived in this house from 1885 until his death in 1928. Here he wrote 'Tess of the D'Urbervilles', 'Jude the Obscure' and 'The Mayor of Casterbridge', as well as much of his poetry. The house contains several pieces of his furniture.
Information services:
Services for disabled people: For the visually impaired.

Internet home pages:
http://www.nationaltrust.org.uk/regions/wessex

See also - Hardy's Cottage

1741
MCC

Library, Lord's Cricket Ground, St John's Wood, London, NW8 8QN

Tel: 020 7289 1611
Fax: 020 7432 1062
Telex: 297329 MCC G
Acronym or abbreviation: MCC
Full name: Marylebone Cricket Club
Formed: 1787

Organisation type and purpose: Membership association (membership is by election or invitation), historic building, house or site. Private Cricket Club.

Enquiries to: Curator
Direct email: glenys.williams@mcc.org.uk
Access:
Access to staff: Visitors by prior appointment
Hours: Mon to Thu, 1000 to 1700; Fri, 1000 to 1600
Other restrictions: Open Sat and Sun by arrangement on cricket days.
Access to building, collections or gallery: Prior appointment required

General description:
History of cricket, modern cricket, scores and statistics, real tennis, some other sports, history of Lord's and the MCC.
Collections:
Early cricket books and bats
Sir George Allen scrapbooks
Catalogues:
Catalogue for library is in-house only. Catalogue for part of the collections is only available in-house.

1742
MCC MUSEUM

Lord's Ground, London, NW8 8QN

Tel: 020 7289 1611
Fax: 020 7432 1062
Acronym or abbreviation: MCC Museum
Full name: Marylebone Cricket Club Museum
Formed: 1787

Organisation type and purpose: Independently owned, membership association (membership is by election or invitation), museum, art gallery, public library, suitable for ages: 8+.
Private cricket club.
Parent body:
Marylebone Cricket Club
Lord's Ground, London, NW8 8QN

Enquiries to: Curator
Direct tel: 010 7432 1036
Access:
Access to staff: By letter, by telephone, by fax, visitors by prior appointment
Hours: Mon to Fri, 1000 to 1700
Access to building, collections or gallery: No prior appointment required
Hours: Open match days in summer on Sat and Sun.
Other times access is via the Tours Manager, telephone 020 7432 1033.
Access for disabled people: Parking provided

General description:
Collection covering the history of cricket. There is also a section on real tennis.
Information services:
Library available for reference (for conditions see Access above), bibliography compilation
Special visitor services: Guided tours..
Collections:
A large collection of cricket paintings
Catalogues:
Catalogue for library is in-house only. Catalogue for part of the collections is only available in-house.

Internet home pages:
http://www.lords.org

1743
MDA (EUROPE)

Jupiter House, Station Road, Cambridge, CB1 2JZ

Tel: 01223 315760
Email: mda@mda.org.uk
Formed: 1977
Formerly: Museum Documentation Association (Mda)

Organisation type and purpose: International organisation, national government body, national organisation, registered charity.
To support the management and use of collections.
Funded by:
Resource, the Council for Museums Archives & Libraries

Enquiries to: Communications Manager
Other contacts: Information Officer for Assistant to Communications Manager.
Access:
Access to staff: By letter, by telephone, by fax, by email
Hours: Mon to Fri, 0900 to 1700
Access to building, collections or gallery: Prior appointment required

General description:
Support for the cultural sector, cultural initiatives, documentation and standards work.
Publications list:
is available in hard copy and online.
Printed publications:
Key texts, factsheets and pre-printed forms and registers for documenting collections.

Internet home pages:
http://www.mda.org.uk
Information and resources for cultural sector professionals.

1744
MEAD GALLERY

University of Warwick, Gibbet Hill Road, Coventry, Warwickshire, CV4 7AL

Tel: 024 7652 4524
Fax: 024 7657 2664
Email: meadgallery@warwick.ac.uk
Formed: 1986

Organisation type and purpose: Art gallery, university department or institute.

Enquiries to: Curator
Direct tel: 024 7652 4731
Other contacts: Assistant Curator for education matters.
Access:
Access to staff: By letter, by telephone, by fax, by email, visitors by prior appointment
Other restrictions: The University closes for some days during Christmas and Easter.
Access to building, collections or gallery: No prior appointment required
Hours: Term time only: Mon to Sat, 1200 to 2100; Closed Sun
Access for disabled people: Parking provided, ramped entry, access to all public areas, toilet facilities

General description:
The Mead Gallery staff curate the University of Warwick's 20th century art collection. The collection consists of paintings; prints; drawings; sculpture; and studio ceramics, dating from post-1945. The work is displayed throughout the university campus, including sculpture outdoors.
Information services:
Special visitor services: Guided tours.
Education services: Group education facilities..
Collections:
British abstract art, Terry Frost, Patrick Herun, John Hoyland, Paul Falen
1950s to the present day
British sculpture, Richard Deacon, Peter Randall Page, William Pye, Liliane Lijn
Catalogues:
Catalogue for part of the collections is published.
Publications list:
is available in hard copy.

1745
MEASHAM MUSEUM

High Street, Measham, Swadlincote, Leicestershire, DE12 7HZ

Tel: 01530 273596
Formed: 1992

Organisation type and purpose: Registered charity (charity number 1062716), museum, suitable for ages: all ages.

Enquiries to: Chairman
Direct tel: 01530 272761
Direct fax: 01530 272761
Access:
Access to staff: By letter, by telephone, in person
Access for disabled people: ramped entry
Other restrictions: Access difficult.

General description:
Local history of Measham and district.
Information services:
Special visitor services: Guided tours, materials and/or activities for children.
Education services: Group education facilities..
Printed publications:
Measham in Focus (book, £5.99)

1746
MECHANICAL MEMORIES AMUSEMENT MUSEUM

138 Edward Street, Brighton, East Sussex, BN2 2JL

Tel: 01273 608620
Acronym or abbreviation: MM
Formed: 1994
Formerly: National Museum of Penny Slot Machines

Organisation type and purpose: Trade association, voluntary organisation, museum, consultancy.
Preservation.
Connected with:
Sussex Museums Group (SMG)
Other address:
Mechanical Memories Amusement Museum
250C Kings Road Arches, Brighton

Enquiries to: Administrator
Other contacts: Daily Manager for on-site volunteer of the day.
Access:
Access to staff: By letter, by telephone, visitors by prior appointment, charges to non-members
Hours: Easter to Oct, weekends and school holidays
Jul to Sep: daily, 1200 to 1800
Other restrictions: Sea conditions, mainly winter high tides and winds as the public exhibition is on beach level.
Access to building, collections or gallery: Prior appointment required

General description:
History and technical information on coin-feed devices; amusements, mechanisms, money boxes; technical toys, mechanical music, fairground and advertising history.
Main collection: (as working museum) about 150 working/restored 'penny-slot' amusement games. Themes covered as well as above, early cinema viewers and working models.
Reserve collection, many unrestored; reproduction parts provided for collectors and other museums.
Information services:
Helpline available
Special visitor services: Guided tours.
Services for disabled people: For the visually impaired.
Collections:
Books, documents, various photographs
Printed publications:
Reproduction early trade catalogues
Internet home pages:
http://www.sussexmuseums.co.uk/index.html
Only via Sussex Museums Group.

1747
MECHANICAL MUSIC AND DOLL COLLECTION

Church Road, Portfield, Chichester, West Sussex, PO19 4HN

Tel: 01243 372646
Fax: 01243 370299
Email: harvej@cix.compulink.co.uk
Formed: 1983

Organisation type and purpose: Museum, suitable for ages: all ages.
Private museum.

Enquiries to: Managing Director
Access:
Access to staff: By letter, by telephone, by fax, visitors by prior appointment, charges made to all users
Access to building, collections or gallery: No prior appointment required
Hours: Jun, Jul, Aug, Sep; Wed, 1300 to 1600
Other restrictions: Prior appointment required for groups.
Access for disabled people: Parking provided, access to all public areas

General description:
Mechanical musical instruments: specialists in discs for disc-playing musical boxes of all types; early phonographs and gramophones, barrel pianos, barrel organs, orchestrions, Victorian and Edwardian dolls.
Information services:
Special visitor services: Guided tours..
Collections:
Lists of music-box discs now available from this museum
Original discs have been copied and listed to preserve this music and to enhance the original music-boxes on which they play and are available to museums and private collectors worldwide
Catalogues:
Catalogue for part of the collections is only available in-house.
Printed publications:
Lists of musical box metal discs available

1748
MECHANICAL MUSIC MUSEUM & BYGONES (TRUST), THE

Blacksmith Road, Cotton, Stowmarket, Suffolk, IP14 4QN

Tel: 01449 613876
Formed: 1982

Organisation type and purpose: Registered charity (charity number 801863), museum.
Working museum to educate and entertain all ages of the general public.
Mailing address:
The Secretary, Mechanical Music Museum & Bygones (Trust)
27 St Peter's Close, Stowmarket, Suffolk, IP14 1LF, tel: 01449 613876

Enquiries to: Secretary
Access:
Access to staff: By letter, by telephone
Hours: Mon to Fri, 0900 to 1700
Access to building, collections or gallery: No prior appointment required
Hours: Jun to end Sep; Sun, 1430 to 1730
Private parties minimum 20 by arrangement Jun to end Sep

General description:
A large varied collection of mechanical musical items including small music boxes; polyphons; organettes; and many unusual items including the larger street pianos; player organs, reed organs, the fair organs, the Wurlitzer Theatre pipe organ and the gigantic café organ.

Information services:
Special visitor services: Guided tours.
Services for disabled people: Displays and/or information at wheelchair height.
Printed publications:
Advertising leaflets (free, available from the Secretary)

1749
MEDICAL MUSEUM
See - Thackray Medical Museum

1750
MEDIEVAL MERCHANT'S HOUSE
58 French Street, Southampton

Tel: 02380 221503
Formed: 1290

Organisation type and purpose: National organisation, historic building, house or site, suitable for ages: 5+.
Parent body:
English Heritage (South East Region)
Tel: 01483 252000, fax: 01483 252001

Enquiries to: Curator
Access:
Access to staff: By letter, by telephone
Access to building, collections or gallery: No prior appointment required
Hours: Apr to Sep: daily, 1000 to 1800
Oct: daily, 1000 to 1700
Other restrictions: Opening times are subject to change, for up-to-date information contact English Heritage by phone or visit the website.

General description:
This house was built in about 1290 by John Fortin, a wealthy merchant who traded with merchants from Bordeaux. It was both a residence and a place of business located on one of the busiest streets in medieval Southampton. The house has been returned to its mid-14th century appearance by the removal of later floors, partitions and fireplaces.
Information services:
Audio guides also available for the visually impaired and those with learning difficulties.
Special visitor services: Tape recorded guides, materials and/or activities for children..

Internet home pages:
http://www.english-heritage.org.uk

1751
MEDWAY LIBRARY, INFORMATION & MUSEUM SERVICE
Civic Centre, Strood, Rochester, Kent, ME2 4AU

Tel: 01634 306000
Formed: 1998
Formerly: Kent County Council

Organisation type and purpose: Local government body, public library.
Other address:
Chatham Library
Riverside, Chatham, Kent, ME4 4SN, tel: 01634 843589, fax: 01634 827976, email/website: chatham.library@medway.gov.uk
Medway Archives and Local Studies Centre
Clocktower Building, Civic Centre, Strood, ME2 4AU, tel: 01634 332714
Medway Library Information and Museum Service, Education and Leisure
Civic Centre, Strood, Kent, ME2 4AU, tel: 01634 306000, fax: 01634 332756

Enquiries to: Librarian
Direct tel: 01634 843589
Direct fax: 01634 827976
Direct email: gill.butler@medway.gov.uk
Other contacts: Reference, Archives, Local Studies Manager for reference, local studies and archives.

Access:
Access to staff: By letter, by telephone, by fax, by email, in person, Internet web pages
Hours: Various

General description:
Local studies and archives, business information.
Collections:
See Leaflets
Catalogues:
Catalogue for library is on-line. Catalogue for part of the collections is on-line.

Address for ordering publications:
Printed publications:
Chatham Reference Library
Riverside, Chatham, Kent, ME4 4SN, email: chatham.library@medway.gov.uk

Internet home pages:
http://cityark.medway.gov.uk
Archives database.
http://libcat.medway.gov.uk
Library catalogue.

1752
MEFFAN MUSEUM & GALLERY, THE
20 West High Street, Forfar, Angus, DD8 1BB

Tel: 01307 464123/467017
Fax: 01307 468451
Email: the.meffan@angus.gov.uk
Formed: 1897
Formerly: The Meffan Institute, date of change, 2000

Organisation type and purpose: Local government body, museum, art gallery, suitable for ages: 5+.
Parent body:
Angus Council
Cultural Services, County Building, Market Street, Forfar, DD8 3WF, tel: 01307 473256, fax: 01307 462590, email: culture@angus.gov.uk

Enquiries to: Museums Manager
Direct email: kingm@angus.gov.uk
Other contacts: (1) Museum Assistant (2) Exhibitions Officer for (1) hire of Upper Gallery for meetings; (2) enquiries about temporary art exhibitions/gallery space.
Access:
Access to staff: By letter, by telephone, by email, in person, Internet web pages
Hours: Mon to Sat, 1000 to 1700
Access to building, collections or gallery: No prior appointment required
Hours: Mon to Sat, 1000 to 1700
Access for disabled people: toilet facilities
Other restrictions: Ramped entry with prior notice as 2 members of staff required for lifting ramp.

General description:
The Meffan hosts monthly contemporary art exhibitions in 2 galleries. The museum concentrates on a stunning display of the enigmatic Pictish carved stones and includes an interactive encyclopaedic programme covering all Angus Pictish Stories. An interactive computer allows the visitor to access a gazeteer of all Pictish Stones in Angus. Visitors then wander down a dark vennel full of typical Forfar trades: a handloom weaver, a clockmaker, a shoe maker, a sweetie shop and a baker with his bridies. Suddenly the visitor is confronted by an aspect of Forfar's darker history: a 'witch' is being condemned to be burnt.
Information services:
Special visitor services: Guided tours, materials and/or activities for children..
Collections:
Archaeology of Forfar and district including 11th century log boat
11th century dug-out oak canoe
Cardean Roman excavation material
Church history and ecclesiastical artefacts
Civic Regalia
Extensive Photographic Collection of Forfar & District
James Waterston Herald collection of paintings
Lord Ritchie Calder of Balmashanner Collection
Pictish stones
Social history collections
Witches Branks
Catalogues:
Catalogue for all of the collections is only available in-house.

Internet home pages:
http://www.angus.gov.uk

1753
MELBOURNE HALL
Church Square, Melbourne, Derbyshire, DE73 1EN

Tel: 01332 862502
Fax: 01332 862263
Formed: 1953

Organisation type and purpose: Independently owned, historic building, house or site, suitable for ages: 16+.
Connections with:
Historical Houses Association

Enquiries to: Curator
Access:
Access to staff: By letter, by telephone, by fax
Access for disabled people: ramped entry

General description:
A small privately owned historic house. The rooms on view are used by the family, and contain many treasures and works of art. This is the former home of Viscount Melbourne.
Information services:
Special visitor services: Guided tours..
Collections:
Historic house with paintings, antique furniture
Catalogues:
Catalogue for part of the collections is published.

1754
MELFORD HALL
Long Melford, Sudbury, Suffolk, CO10 9AA

Tel: 01787 880286
Email: melford@nationaltrust.org.uk
Formed: 1960

Organisation type and purpose: National organisation, registered charity (charity number 205846), historic building, house or site, suitable for ages: 5+.
Parent body:
The National Trust (East of England)
East Anglia Regional Office, tel: 0870 609 5388

Enquiries to: Manager
Access:
Access to staff: By letter, by telephone, by email
Access for disabled people: Parking provided, ramped entry, toilet facilities
Other restrictions: Drop-off point. 3 manual wheelchairs available. Ramped entrance. Ground floor fully accessible. Stairlift to first floor. Access to garden difficult.

General description:
One of East Anglia's most celebrated Elizabethan houses, little changed externally since 1578 and with an original panelled banqueting hall. The home of the Hyde Parker family since 1786. There is a Regency library, as well as Victorian bedrooms and good collections of furniture and porcelain. Small collection of Beatrix Potter memorabilia.The garden contains some spectacular specimen trees and a charming banqueting house, and there is an attractive walk through the park.
Information services:
Hip-carrying infant seats for loan.
Children's guide. Children's quiz/trail.
Braille guide. Large-print guide. Sympathetic Hearing Scheme.
Special visitor services: Guided tours, materials and/or activities for children.
Services for disabled people: For the visually impaired; for the hearing impaired.
Collections:
Chinese porcelain

continued overleaf

Beatrix Potter memorabilia
Dutch 17th century paintings, and others
Printed publications:
Guide (£1.50)
Leaflet (30p)

Internet home pages:
http://www.nationaltrust.org.uk/eastanglia/melfordhall

1755
MELLERSTAIN HOUSE

Gordon, Berwickshire, TD3 6LG

Tel: 01573 410225

Organisation type and purpose: Independently owned, historic building, house or site, suitable for ages: 5+.
Access:
Access to staff: By letter, by telephone
Access to building, collections or gallery: No prior appointment required
Hours: Easter: May to early Oct, Mon to Sat, 1230 to 1700

General description:
An Adam Mansion, with decorated ceilings in all main rooms. Fine examples of period furniture and art collection.
Exhibition of dolls' houses.

1756
MELTON CARNEGIE MUSEUM

Thorpe End, Melton Mowbray, Leicestershire, LE13 1RB

Tel: 01664 569946
Fax: 01664 564060
Email: museums@leics.gov.uk
Formed: 1977

Organisation type and purpose: Local government body, museum, historic building, house or site, suitable for ages: 8+.
Parent body:
Leicestershire Museums Arts & Records Service

Enquiries to: Curator
Access:
Access to staff: By letter, by telephone, by fax, by email, in person, Internet web pages
Access for disabled people: access to all public areas, toilet facilities

General description:
Recently undergone a complete refurbishment featuring permanent displays on the social, artistic and economic development of the borough and has a programme of events. A multi-disciplinary museum covering the natural and local history of Melton and the Vale of Belvoir.
Information services:
Special visitor services: Materials and/or activities for children.
Education services: Resources for Key Stages 1 and 2 and 3.
Services for disabled people: Displays and/or information at wheelchair height.
Catalogues:
Catalogue for part of the collections is only available in-house.

Internet home pages:
http://www.leics.gov.uk/museums

1757
MELTON LIBRARY ART GALLERY

Wilton Road, Melton Mowbray, Leicestershire, LE13 0UJ

Tel: 01664 560161
Fax: 01664 410199
Email: meltonmowbraylibrary@leics.gov.uk

Organisation type and purpose: Local government body, art gallery, suitable for ages: 5+.

Enquiries to: Administrator
Direct email: rpointer@leics.gov.uk
Access:
Access to staff: By letter, by telephone, by fax, by email, in person, visitors by prior appointment
Access to building, collections or gallery: No prior appointment required
Hours: Mon, Tue, Thu, 0900 to 1900; Wed, Fri, 0900 to 1700; Sat, 0930 to 1600
Access for disabled people: level entry, access to all public areas

General description:
Programme of temporary exhibitions - 6 to 10 per year, including solo exhibitions, community exhibitions (max 2 per year) and occasional touring exhibitions. Two- and three-dimensional work, which may be for sale. Occasional artists' workshops. Emphasis is on contemporary artists from the county and the region, working in a wide range of media.
Printed publications:
Programme (3 or 4 times a year, distributed to mailing list and via website)

Internet home pages:
http://www.leics.gov.uk/
Brief introduction to the gallery, programme of exhibitions, publicity for individual exhibitions.

1758
MENSTRIE CASTLE

Castle Street, Menstrie, Clackmannanshire

Organisation type and purpose: Museum, historic building, house or site, suitable for ages: 5+.

Enquiries to: Property Manager (Alloa Tower)
Direct tel: 01259 211701

General description:
Birthplace of Sir William Alexander, James VI's Lieutenant for the Plantation of Nova Scotia. Exhibition in the Scotia Commemoration Room tells story of this ill-fated scheme. Castle is not NTS property but the Trust, in co-operation with the then Clackmannanshire County Council, played a large part in saving it from demolition.

1759
MENZIES CAMPBELL DENTAL MUSEUM

See - Museums of the Royal College of Surgeons of Edinburgh

1760
MEOPHAM WINDMILL TRUST

Meopham Green, Kent, DA13 0QA

Tel: 01474 813518/812465
Formed: Mar 1969

Organisation type and purpose: Registered charity (charity number 258472), historic building, house or site, suitable for ages: 8+. Visitor attraction - working windmill.
Member of:
Kent Windmills
Owned by:
Kent County Council
Address for Honorary Secretary:
A Kubias
2 Podlar Walk, Meopham, Gravesend, Kent, DA13 0EB, tel: 01474 812465

Enquiries to: Honorary Secretary
Direct tel: 01474 812465
Access:
Access to staff: By letter, by telephone
Access to building, collections or gallery: Prior appointment required
Hours: May to Sep: Sun, 1430 to 1630
Other restrictions: Or by special arrangement via 01474 813518.

General description:
A black 19th century smock mill built in 1821, worked by hand until c. 1912, later powered by gas engine and now largely restored. Unusual in being six-sided.
Information services:
Helpline available, tel no: 01474 812465.
School and groups welcome by appointment.
Special visitor services: Guided tours.
Education services: Group education facilities..

1761
MERCER GALLERY

31 Swan Road, Harrogate, North Yorkshire, HG1 2SA

Tel: 01423 556188
Fax: 01423 556130
Email: lg12@harrogate.gov.uk
Formed: 1991

Organisation type and purpose: Local government body, art gallery, suitable for ages: all ages.
Parent body:
Harrogate Borough Council
Links with:
Friends of the Mercer Art Gallery
Tel: 01423 556188, fax: 01423 556130

Enquiries to: Administrator
Other contacts: Curator of Art for specific enquiries.
Access:
Access to staff: By letter, by telephone, by fax, by email, visitors by prior appointment
Access to building, collections or gallery: No prior appointment required
Hours: Gallery: Tue to Sat, 1000 to 1700; Sun 1400 to 1700 and Bank Holiday Mon
Closed 24, 25, 26 Dec and 1 Jan
Other restrictions: Appointment required for collections not on display.
Access for disabled people: Parking provided, ramped entry, access to all public areas, toilet facilities
Other restrictions: Parking - 1 space only.

General description:
Access to Harrogate's Fine Art Collection, changing exhibitions throughout the year, encompassing seven centuries of art, the catalogue reflects a variety of treasured objects. From the Victorian splendour of Frith's, The Birthday Party, 1856, and Burne-Jones' enchanting, The Choristers, c.1870, to the stunning modern works of David Mach and Andy Goldsworthy.
Information services:
Library available for reference (for conditions see Access above)
Object indentification. Guided tours on request.
Special visitor services: Guided tours, materials and/or activities for children.
Education services: Group education facilities.
Services for disabled people: Displays and/or information at wheelchair height.
Collections:
Mainly 19th and 20th century British painting. Contains 2500 items in the Fine Art Collection, including paintings, drawings, prints and photographs. Paintings by Turner, Burne-Jones, W P Frith, Atkinson Grimshaw, Sickert, Paul Nash, Wadsworth, Ravillions, Bomberg, Hitchens, Goldsworthy, Mach
Kent Collection of Egyptian, Roman, Greek and South American artefacts
Catalogues:
Catalogue for library is in-house only. Catalogue for part of the collections is published.
Publications list:
is available on-line.
Printed publications:
Harrogate's Fine Art Catalogue (£25 plus £5.50 p&p)
Guide to the Royal Pump Room Museum (£1.50 plus 39p p&p)
Guide to Knaresborough Castle and Museum (£1.50 plus 39p p&p)
Selection of postcards, posters and prints

Internet home pages:
http://www.harrogate.gov.uk/museums

1762
MERCHANT ADVENTURERS' HALL

Fossgate, York, YO1 9XD

Tel: 01904 654818
Fax: 01904 654818
Email: the.clerk@mahall-york.demon.co.uk
Full name: The Company of Merchant Adventurers' of The City of York
Formed: 1357

Organisation type and purpose: Membership association (membership is by election or invitation), registered charity (charity number 235256 co 700792), museum.
Historic building.

Enquiries to: The Clerk of the Company
Access:
Access to staff: By letter, by telephone, by fax, by email, visitors by prior appointment
Access to building, collections or gallery: No prior appointment required
Hours: Winter: Mon to Thu, 0900 to 1530; Fri, Sat, 0900 to 1500; closed Sun
Summer: Mon to Fri, 0900 to 1700; Sat, Sun, 1200 to 1600
Access for disabled people: ramped entry, toilet facilities
Other restrictions: Ramped entry to undercroft, toilet facilities in undercroft.

General description:
Archive of The Company of Merchant Adventurers of The City of York and the Merchant Adventurers' Hall. The Story of the Merchants since 1357.
Collections of paintings, furniture and silver.
Collections:
Archives, paintings, furniture, silver
Catalogues:
Catalogue for library is in-house only. Catalogue for all of the collections is only available in-house.
Printed publications:
Guide Books
History of the Company
Postcards

Internet home pages:
http://www.theyorkcompany.sagenet.co.uk

1763
MERLEY HOUSE MODEL MUSEUM

Wimborne

Closed

1764
MERRYTHOUGHT TEDDY BEAR SHOP AND MUSEUM, THE

Ironbridge Gorge Museum Trust, Coach Road, Coalbrookdale, Telford, Shropshire, TF8 7DQ

Tel: 01952 433116

Organisation type and purpose: Museum.
Access:
Access to staff: By letter, in person
Access to building, collections or gallery: No prior appointment required
Access for disabled people: level entry
Other restrictions: Access guide for disabled visitors available on request.

General description:
Collection of teddy bears.

Internet home pages:
http://www.ironbridge.org.uk

1765
MERSEYSIDE COUNTY MUSEUMS

See - National Museums & Galleries on Merseyside

1766
MERSEYSIDE MARITIME MUSEUM

Albert Dock, Liverpool, L3 4AQ

Tel: 0151 478 4499
Fax: 0151 478 4590
Acronym or abbreviation: NMGM
Formed: 1980

Organisation type and purpose: Museum, suitable for ages: all ages.
Parent body:
National Museums & Galleries on Merseyside

Enquiries to: Director
Other contacts: Marketing Manager for advertising.
Access:
Access to staff: By letter only
Access to building, collections or gallery: No prior appointment required
Hours: Daily, 1000 to 1700
Access for disabled people: Parking provided, ramped entry, level entry, access to all public areas, toilet facilities

General description:
Contains comprehensive collections related to British merchant navy history and trade, including historic ships and boats, marine paintings, ship models, navigational and technical equipment and archives, plus artefacts associated with maritime social and commercial activities. Includes historic buildings and quaysides.
Collections:
Marine paintings, watercolours and prints. Work by Liverpool and North-West artists, depictions of vessels and port, late 18th-20th century, 1000 items
Ship Models. Comprehensive collection of ship models, 18th-20th century, 2000 items
Wynn Collections. Maritime artefacts, including boats, associated with Wynn family of Fort Byan, North Wales, 18th-19th century, 500 items
Catalogues:
Catalogue for library is on-line.
Publications list:
is available in hard copy.

Internet home pages:
http://www.nmgm.org.uk

1767
MERTHYR TYDFIL BOROUGH COUNCIL MUSEUM

See - Cyfarthfa Castle Museum & Art

1768
MERTON ANTIQUES

See - Barometer World & Museum

1769
METROPOLITAN POLICE MOUNTED BRANCH MUSEUM

Mounted Branch Training Establishment, Imber Court, Ember Lane, East Molesey, Surrey, KT8 0BT

Tel: 020 8247 5480
Formed: 1986

Organisation type and purpose: National government body.
Connected with:
Mounted Police Association (MPA)
at the same address

Enquiries to: Curator
Access:
Access to staff: By letter only, visitors by prior appointment
Access to building, collections or gallery: Prior appointment required

General description:
History of mounted police; history and development of public order. The museum details the formation and development of the Metropolitan Mounted Police from the 1805 'Robin Redbreasts' to the present day.
Collections:
Items relating to Billie, 'The White Horse of Wembley', and his rider George Scorey, 1923

1770
METROPOLITAN TRAFFIC POLICE MUSEUM

68 Station Road, Hampton, Middlesex, TW12 2AX

Tel: 020 8247 6925
Fax: 020 8247 6990

Organisation type and purpose: Professional body, registered charity, museum, suitable for ages: 16+.
To preserve police vehicles and history used by the Metropolitan Police.

Enquiries to: Information Officer
Access:
Access to staff: By letter only
Access to building, collections or gallery: Prior appointment required
Other restrictions: Operational Police Traffic Patrol Garage.
Access for disabled people: ramped entry

General description:
Collection of police motor cars/motor cycles dating from the 1930s. Police uniforms and equipment in display cabinets. Police photographs and traffic memorabilia dating from generally the 1930s to the present day.
Collections:
Metropolitan Police motor vehicles including motorcycles

1771
MICHAEL BRUCE COTTAGE MUSEUM

The Cobbles, Kinnesswood, Kinross, Fife, KY13 9HL

Formed: 1906

Organisation type and purpose: Independently owned, registered charity, museum, historic building, house or site, suitable for ages: 12+.
To keep alive the memory of the life and poetical works of Michael Bruce (1746-1767).

Enquiries to: Chairman
Direct tel: 01592 840 203
Access:
Access to staff: By letter

General description:
Contains material relating to the life and works of the 18th century Scottish poet Michael Bruce who lived in the cottage. Also contains additional items reflecting the social history of Kinross-shire during the past 2 centuries.
Collections:
Artefacts relating to the parchment and vellum industry, 18th and 19th century, 20 items
Printed publications:
Range of postcards and books

1772
MICHAEL FARADAY MUSEUM

See - Royal Institution of Great Britain

1773
MICHELHAM PRIORY

Upper Dicker, Hailsham, East Sussex, BN27 3QS

Tel: 01323 844224

Organisation type and purpose: Registered charity (charity number 207037), historic building, house or site, suitable for ages: all ages.
Parent body:
Sussex Past
Bull House, 92 High Street, Lewes, East Sussex, BN7 1XH, tel: 01273 486260, fax: 01273 486990, email: admin@sussexpast.co.uk

Enquiries to: Manager

continued overleaf

Access:
Access to staff: By letter, by telephone
Access to building, collections or gallery: No prior appointment required
Hours: Mar to Apr: Tue to Sun, 1030 to 1600
Apr to Jul: Tue to Sun, 1030 to 1700
Aug: daily, 1030 to 1730
Sep: Tue to Sun, 1030 to 1700
Oct: Tue to Sun, 1030 to 1600
Open Bank Holidays Mondays
Access for disabled people: ramped entry, toilet facilities
Other restrictions: Wheelchair access to house limited to ground floor

General description:
Ancient moated priory.
Information services:
For Braille guides and tactile tours prior notice is reqested.
Special visitor services: Materials and/or activities for children.
Education services: Group education facilities.
Services for disabled people: For the visually impaired.

Internet home pages:
http://www.sussexpast.co.uk

1774
MIDDLE LITTLETON TITHE BARN
Middle Littleton, Evesham, Worcestershire

Tel: 01743 708100 (RegionalOffice)
Email: middlelittleton@nationaltrust.org.uk

Organisation type and purpose: National organisation, registered charity (charity number 205846), historic building, house or site.
Parent body:
The National Trust (West Midlands)
West Midlands Regional Office, tel: 01743 708100

Enquiries to: Manager
Access:
Access to staff: By letter, by telephone, by email

General description:
One of the largest and finest tithe barns in the country, dating from the 13th century.

Internet home pages:
http://www.nationaltrust.org.uk

1775
MIDDLEHAM CASTLE
Middleham, Leyburn, North Yorkshire

Tel: 01969 623899

Organisation type and purpose: National organisation, advisory body, museum, historic building, house or site.
Parent body:
English Heritage (Yorkshire Region)
Tel: 01904 601901

Enquiries to: Manager
Access:
Access to staff: By letter, by telephone
Access to building, collections or gallery: No prior appointment required
Hours: 29 Mar to 30 Sep: daily, 1000 to 1800,1 to 31 Oct: daily, 1000 to 1700,1 Nov to 31 Dec: daily, 1000 to 1300 and 1400 to 1600,2 Jan to 31 Mar: Wed to Sun, 1000 to 1300 and 1400 to 1600
Other restrictions: Closed 24 to 26 Dec and 1 Jan.
Opening times are subject to change, for up-to-date information contact English Heritage by phone or visit the website.

General description:
This impressive fortress, built in the 12th century, was the childhood home of Richard III who made it his main castle in the North of England. Before the present castle, a Norman motte and bailey fortification existed at Middleham. The principal building on the new site was a formidable stone keep, one of the largest in England, which today commands stunning views of the surrounding countryside.

Internet home pages:
http://www.english-heritage.org.uk

1776
MIDDLESBROUGH ART GALLERY
320 Linthorpe Road, Middlesbrough, Cleveland, TS1 3QY

Tel: 01642 247445

General description:
20th century British paintings, drawings and sculpture; 16th-19th century European paintings.
Collections:
Special collection of Scottish 20th century paintings

1777
MIDDLETON RAILWAY TRUST
The Station, Moor Road, Hunslet, Leeds, West Yorkshire, LS10 2JQ

Tel: 0113 271 0320
Email: info@middletonrailway.org.uk
Acronym or abbreviation: MRT
Formed: 1960

Organisation type and purpose: (membership is by subscription), voluntary organisation, registered charity (charity number 230387), museum.
Preservation of Middleton Railway.

Enquiries to: Public Relations Manager
Direct tel: 0113 272 4115
Access:
Access to staff: By letter, by telephone, by email, Internet web pages
Hours: Mon to Fri, 0900 to 1700
Access to building, collections or gallery: No prior appointment required
Hours: Sun to Sat, 1030 to 1630
Other restrictions: Weekends only from Easter to Christmas
Access for disabled people: Parking provided, level entry, access to all public areas, toilet facilities

General description:
A heritage railway, preserving the Middleton Railway (founded by the first railway Act of Parliament in 1758) and employing the first commercially successful steam locomotives in 1812. A museum is in course of construction. Archives and industrial railway artefacts. Educational for all age groups. A working railway with steam and diesel locomotives, many built locally in Hunslet, Leeds.
Collections:
Transport and historical journals and various local archives relating to all railways in the area
Publications list:
is available in hard copy and online.
Printed publications:
Guide to the Railway
History of Middleton Railway
Members Journal
Stock Book
Electronic and video products:
Middleton Railway (VHS (PAL) video)

Internet home pages:
http://www.middletonrailway.org.uk
Details of history, rolling stock, timetables and special events.

1778
MID-HANTS RAILWAY (WATERCRESS LINE)
Alresford Station, Alresford, Hampshire, SO24 9JG

Tel: 01962 733810
Fax: 01962 735448
Email: info@watercressline.co.uk
Acronym or abbreviation: Watercress Line
Formed: 1973
Still known as: Watercress Line

Organisation type and purpose: Voluntary organisation.
Preserved steam railway. Tourist attraction.

Enquiries to: Sales Administrator
Other contacts: Marketing Officer for publicity.
Access:
Access to staff: By letter, by telephone, by fax, by email, in person, Internet web pages
Hours: Mon to Fri; 0930 to 1630
Access for disabled people: Parking provided, toilet facilities

General description:
Standard gauge (steam) railways - especially Southern Railway/British Rail Southern Region and the Watercress Line from Alton to Alresford in particular.
Printed publications:
Guidebook
Journal (quarterly, members)

Internet home pages:
http://www.watercressline.co.uk
Regularly updated information on all services offered including booking forms for certain special events.

1779
MIDLAND RAILWAY CENTRE
Butterley Station, Ripley, Derbyshire, DE5 3QZ

Tel: 01773 747674
Fax: 01773 570721
Email: information@midlandrailwaycentre.co.uk
Formed: 1969

Organisation type and purpose: Membership association (membership is by subscription), present number of members: 1200, voluntary organisation, registered charity (charity number 502278), museum, training organisation.
Affiliated to:
Midland Railway Enterprises plc
Midland Railway Trust

Enquiries to: Manager
Access:
Access to staff: By letter, by telephone, by fax, visitors by prior appointment
Hours: Mon to Fri, 0900 to 1700
Access to building, collections or gallery: Prior appointment required
Hours: Static display: daily, 1000 to 1615
Closed Christmas Day
Access for disabled people: Parking provided, toilet facilities

General description:
Railway history, demonstration signal box, Victorian railwayman's church. 3.5 mile heritage railway, Golden Valley Light Railway (2ft gauge), Butterly Park Miniature Railway (3.5 and 5 in gauges), model railways.
Collections:
Archive of railway books, records and photography
Collection of railway equipment, mainly Midland Railway, its predecessors and successors
Princess Royal Class Locomotive Trust Depot
Midland Diesel Group collection of main line diesel power
Stationary Power Gallery
Printed publications:
The Wyvern (quarterly magazine)
Guide
Stockbook

1780
MID-SUFFOLK LIGHT RAILWAY COMPANY
62 Orford Street, Ipswich, Suffolk, IP1 3PE

Formed: 1990
Formerly: Mid-Suffolk Light Railway Society, date of change, 1996

Organisation type and purpose: Independently owned, registered charity (charity number 1063635), museum, suitable for ages: 8+, research organisation.
Member of:
Association of Suffolk Museums
Heritage Railway Association
South Eastern Museum Services
Address for Museum:
The Mid-Suffolk Light Railway Museum Brockford Station, Wetheringsett, Stowmarket, Suffolk, IP14 5PW, tel: 01449 766899

Enquiries to: Honorary Secretary
Direct tel: 01473 286907
Direct email: rob@murray36e.freeserve.co.uk
Access:
Access to staff: By letter, by telephone, by email
Hours: By prior arrangement.
Access for disabled people: Parking provided, toilet facilities
Other restrictions: Surfaces at site vary; some areas are difficult for disabled access.

General description:
The company maintains and operates a museum dedicated to interpreting the history of the Mid-Suffolk Light Railway. The Mid-Suffolk Light Railway was a branch line railway which operated in rural mid-Suffolk from 1902 until 1952.
Collections:
Buildings of original company re-erected and restored
Railway rolling stock typical of the original Mid-Suffolk Light Railway 1902-1924
Small artefacts, documents, and a large collection of photographs
Audio material and a small amount of film footage which is not stored electronically
Electronic and video products:
Recollections of Railway Staff (CD-ROM)

Internet home pages:
http://www.mslr.org.uk
Simple description of museum site and facilities, some photographs.

1781
MILDENHALL MUSEUM
6 King Street, Mildenhall, Bury St Edmunds, Suffolk, IP28 7EX

Tel: 01638 716970
Full name: Mildenhall and District Museum
Formed: 1954

Organisation type and purpose: Membership association (membership is by subscription), registered charity (charity number 281511), museum.
To display and interpret the history of Mildenhall and the surrounding area.

Enquiries to: Curator
Access:
Access to staff: By letter, by telephone, in person, visitors by prior appointment
Hours: Mar 1 to May 6; Sep 8 to Christmas: Wed, Thu, Sat, 1430 to 1630; Fri, 1100 to 1630
May 7 to Sep 7: Tue to Sat, 1100 to 1630
Other restrictions: Closed between Christmas and 1 March.
Access to building, collections or gallery: No prior appointment required
Other restrictions: Access to photograph collection by appointment.

General description:
Local history, natural history and archaeology. Displays include the story of RAF Mildenhall and the 1934 MacRobertson Mildenhall to Melbourne Air Race.
Collections:
Local history and archaeology
Collection of photographs of Mildenhall
RAF Mildenhall and surrounding villages

Internet home pages:
http://www.mildenhallmuseum.co.uk
Information relating to the museum, its displays, and to the history of Mildenhall.

1782
MILESTONES
Leisure Park, Basingstoke, Hampshire, RG21 6YR

Tel: 01256 477766
Fax: 01256 477784
Full name: Milestones - Hampshire's Living History Museum
Formed: 2000
Formerly: Hampshire Transport and Technology Museum

Organisation type and purpose: Local government body, museum, suitable for ages: 5+.

Enquiries to: Curator
Access:
Access to staff: By letter, by telephone, by fax, by email, in person
Access to building, collections or gallery: No prior appointment required
Hours: Tue to Fri, 1000 to 1700; Sat, Sun, 1000 to 1800; Bank Holidays, 1000 to 1700
Other restrictions: Closed Christmas Day, Boxing Day and New Year's Day.
Access for disabled people: Parking provided, level entry, access to all public areas, toilet facilities
Other restrictions: Lifts from Reception to displays, some streets are cobbled, but there are no steps

General description:
Hampshire's living history museum to display the transport and technology, trade and social life of the county.
Information services:
Audio recorded guides, some visually impaired and some displays/information at wheelchair height.
Special visitor services: Materials and/or activities for children.
Education services: Group education facilities, resources for Key Stages 1 and 2.
Services for disabled people: For the visually impaired; for the hearing impaired; displays and/or information at wheelchair height.
Catalogues:
Catalogue for library is in-house only. Catalogue for all of the collections is on-line.
Printed publications:
Publications list is available from the Librarian, Hampshire County Council Museums Service Headquarters, Chilcomb House, Winchester, SO23 8RD

Internet home pages:
http://www.hants.gov.uk/museums/
HMCMS web catalogue, whole collection, 100,000 plus web pages
http://milestones-museum.com/index.html

1783
MILFORD HAVEN HERITAGE & MARITIME MUSEUM
The Old Custom House, The Docks, Milford Haven, Dyfed, SA73 3AF

Tel: 01646 694496
Fax: 01646 699454
Formed: 1980

Organisation type and purpose: Registered charity (charity number 1036633), museum.
To relate the history and development of the town and waterway of Milford Haven.

Enquiries to: Curator
Access:
Access to staff: By letter, by telephone, by fax, in person
Access for disabled people: level entry, toilet facilities

General description:
Material covering the founding and history of the town; Quakers; whaling; the fishing industry; the oil era; and social history.
Information services:
Special visitor services: Guided tours.
Education services: Group education facilities..
Catalogues:
Catalogue for all of the collections is only available in-house.
Printed publications:
A Remarkable Relationship (£5.50)
Milford Haven - Waterway and Town (£9.99)
Museum Guide (50p) (Welsh edition 50p)
The Rotches of Castle Hall (£3.50)
The Story of Milford Haven (£3.50)
A Vision of Greatness (£10.50)
Electronic and video products:
A Vision of Greatness (video, £10)

1784
MILITARY & AEROSPACE MUSEUMS (ALDERSHOT), THE
Closed

1785
MILITARY MUSEUM OF DEVON AND DORSET
The Keep, Bridport Road, Dorchester, Dorset, DT1 1RN

Tel: 01305 264066
Fax: 01305 250373
Email: keep.museum@talk21.com
Formed: 1927
Formerly: Dorset Military Museum

Organisation type and purpose: Registered charity (charity number 1054956), museum, suitable for ages: 12+, research organisation.
Museum, collections owned by charitable trust in Ministry of Defence building.
Connections with:
The Devonshire & Dorset Regiment
The Devonshire Regiment
The Dorset Regiment
The Queen's Own Dorset Yeomanry
The Royal Devon Yeomanry
Trustees the:
Devonshire and Dorset Regimental Charity Devonshire and Dorset Regiment, RHQ, Wyvern Barracks, Exeter, EX2 6AE

Enquiries to: Curator
Access:
Access to staff: By letter, by telephone, by fax, visitors by prior appointment, charges made to all users
Hours: Apr to Sep: Mon to Sat, 0900 to 1700; July and August: Sun, 1030 to 1600; Oct to Mar: Tue to Sat, 0900 to 1700
Access to building, collections or gallery: No prior appointment required
Access for disabled people: Parking provided, ramped entry, toilet facilities

General description:
History of the units raised in the two Counties being The Devonshire and Dorset Regiment with its antecedents The Devonshire Regiment and The Dorset Regiment including militia and volunteers and The Queen's Own Dorset Yeomanry, the Royal Devon Yeomanry.
Collections:
Archives of the units and photographs, small reference library
Publications list:
is available in hard copy.
Printed publications:
March On, 2nd Battalion Dorset Regiment, Burma 1943 to 1945
Memorable Days, Normandy 1944 and 1994
The Dorsetshire Regiment (photographic images)
The Bloody 11th, Volume II and III
Electronic and video products:
Military Band Music (CD-ROM's)

1786
MILITARY MUSEUM, BODMIN
Information services:
Education services: Resources for Key Stage 4..
See - Duke of Cornwall's Light Infantry Regimental Museum

1787
MILITARY VEHICLE MUSEUM
Exhibition Park, 2 Great North Road, Jesmond, Newcastle upon Tyne, NE2 4PZ

Tel: 0191 281 7222
Email: miltmuseum@aol.com
Full name: Military Vehicle Museum
Formed: 1983

Organisation type and purpose: Registered charity (charity number 516848), museum.

Enquiries to: Chairman
Access:
Access to staff: By letter, by telephone, by email, in person
Hours: Mon to Fri, 1000 to 1600,1Nov to 1 Mar: Sat and Sun, 1000 to 1600
Access for disabled people: ramped entry, access to all public areas

General description:
History of World War I and World War II, pertaining to vehicles and other memorabilia.
Information services:
Education services: Group education facilities.
Services for disabled people: Displays and/or information at wheelchair height.
Collections:
World War I mock-up trench
World War ll vehicles, guns, search lights, radio equipment
70 cabinets, mostly World War ll artefacts
Medals, uniforms, documents, firearms etc
Printed publications:
Schools Teaching Pack

Internet home pages:
http://www.military-museum.org.uk

1788
MILL MEECE PUMPING STATION, THE
The Mill Meece Pumping Station Preservation Trust, Cotes Heath, Eccleshall, Staffordshire, ST21 6QH

Tel: 01270 873863 (Hon Secretary)

Organisation type and purpose: Museum, historic building, house or site.
Member of:
North Staffordshire Museums Association

Enquiries to: Honorary Secretary
Access:
Access for disabled people: Parking provided, access to all public areas

General description:
Built in 1914, the Grade II listed buildings, in their rural setting, are home to two giant horizontal tandem steam engines and pumping sets which once pumped 3.5 million gallons of water daily to the Potteries.

1789
MILLENNIUM GALLERIES
Arundel Gate, Sheffield, South Yorkshire, S1 2PP

Tel: 0114 278 2600
Fax: 0114 278 2604
Email: info@sheffieldgalleries.org.uk
Formed: 2001
Formerly: Ruskin Gallery & Ruskin Craft Gallery, date of change, 2000

Organisation type and purpose: Independently owned, registered charity (charity number 1068850), art gallery, suitable for ages: all ages.
Parent body:
Sheffield Galleries & Museums Trust
Tel: 0114 278 2600, fax: 0114 278 2604, email: info@sheffieldgalleries.org.uk

Enquiries to: Press & Publicity Officer
Direct tel: 0114 278 2612
Direct email: stephanie.potts @sheffield.galleries.org.uk
Access:
Access to staff: By letter
Access for disabled people: access to all public areas

General description:
The Ruskin Gallery houses the collection of the Guild of St George, which was founded by John Ruskin (1819-1900) in 1875, and comprises minerals; watercolours; mediaeval illustrated manuscripts; photographs; plastercasts; coins; ornithological prints; and a fine library.
Adjoining the Ruskin Gallery is the Ruskin Craft Gallery which has a wide-ranging exhibition programme, drawn from the work of professional craftspeople nationwide.
Metalwork Gallery.
Information services:
Programme of family activities
Adult workshops
Education programme
Special visitor services: Materials and/or activities for children.
Education services: Group education facilities, resources for Key Stages 1 and 2, 3, 4 and Further or Higher Education.
Services for disabled people: Displays and/or information at wheelchair height.
Collections:
Visual Arts
Metalwork Collection
Ruskin Collection

Internet home pages:
http://www.sheffieldgalleries.org.uk
Home page, information on all galleries, opening times, collections etc.

1790
MILLS OBSERVATORY
Glamis Road, Balgay Park, Dundee, DD2 2UB

Tel: 01382 435846
Fax: 01382 435962
Email: mills.observatory@dundeecity.gov.uk
Formed: 1935

Organisation type and purpose: Museum. Public observatory and planetarium.
Parent body:
Dundee City Council
Leisure and Arts Department
Arts and Heritage, 152 Nethergate, Dundee, DD1 4DY, tel: 01382 432321, fax: 01382 432252, email: arts.heritage@dundeecity.gov.uk http://www.dundeecity.gov.uk

Enquiries to: Curator
Access:
Access to staff: By letter, by telephone, by fax, by email, in person
Access for disabled people: Parking provided
Other restrictions: Access is difficult for people with limited mobility, 4 steps to enter the main area and no lift available to access the upper levels.

General description:
Britain's only full-time public observatory.
Astronomy, space exploration.
Collections:
Astronomy Library
Telescopes - Historic and Modern
Catalogues:
Catalogue for library is in-house only. Catalogue for all of the collections is only available in-house.
Printed publications:
Night Sky Leaflets (monthly, free)

Internet home pages:
http://www.dundeecity.gov.uk/mills/main.htm

1791
MILTON KEYNES GALLERY
900 Midsummer Boulevard, Central Milton Keynes, Buckinghamshire, MK9 3QA

Tel: 01908 676900
Fax: 01908 558308
Email: mkgallery@mktgc.co.uk
Acronym or abbreviation: Mk G
Formed: 1999
Formerly: Milton Keynes Theatre & Gallery Company (MKTGC)

Organisation type and purpose: National organisation, registered charity, art gallery.
To present a changing programme of modern and contemporary art - bringing new art to new audiences.
Subsidiary:
Milton Keynes Theatre & Gallery Company (MKTGC)
3 Theatre Walk, Central Milton Keynes, MK9 3PX

Enquiries to: Head of Press & Marketing
Direct tel: 01908 558302
Direct email: k.sorensen@mktgc.co.uk
Other contacts: (1) Director (2) Education Co-ordinator for (1) exhibition proposals (2) educational events tel 01908 558 305.
Access:
Access to staff: By letter, by telephone, by fax, by email
Access to building, collections or gallery: No prior appointment required
Hours: Tue to Sat, 1000 to 1700; Sun, 1100 to 1700
Access for disabled people: level entry, access to all public areas, toilet facilities
Other restrictions: Disabled parking spaces in the vicinity.

General description:
Modern and contemporary art gallery, showing about ten exhibitions per year featuring contemporary art and crafts, and social history.
Information services:
Special visitor services: Materials and/or activities for children.
Education services: Group education facilities, resources for Key Stages 1 and 2 and 3..
Collections:
Resources area library - a small art catalogue and magazine resource principally for staff research purposes
Publications list:
is available in hard copy.
Printed publications:
MKG Catalogues and Postcards (direct or via Cornerhouse Pubs, Manchester)

Address for ordering publications:
Printed publications:
Cornerhouse Publications
Manchester

Internet home pages:
http://www.mkweb.co.uk/mkg
Exhibition background, contacts, events, education, friends.

1792
MILTON KEYNES THEATRE AND GALLERY COMPANY LIMITED
See - Milton Keynes Gallery

1793
MILTON'S COTTAGE
Deanway, Chalfont St Giles, Buckinghamshire, HP8 4JH

Tel: 01494 872313
Email: info@miltonscottage.org
Full name: John Milton's Cottage
Formed: 1887
Formerly: Milton's Cottage Trust

Organisation type and purpose: Registered charity (charity number 204997), museum, art gallery, public library, historic building, house or site, suitable for ages: 15+.

Enquiries to: Curator
Other contacts: Chairman of Trust
Access:
Access to staff: By letter, by telephone, by email, in person, Internet web pages
Hours: 1 Mar to 31 Oct: Tue to Sun, 1000 to 1300 and 1400 to 1800
Other restrictions: Closed Mondays, except Bank Holidays.
Access to building, collections or gallery: No prior appointment required

Hours: 1 Mar to 31 Oct: Tue to Sun, 1000 to 1300 and 1400 to 1800

General description:
John Milton, poet, parliamentarian, religious and political thinker, and ideologist.
Collections:
1st editions onwards of all his works
Early editions of Paradise Lost, in every language worldwide
Catalogues:
Catalogue for library is in-house only.
Trade and statistical:
World data on John Milton.
Printed publications:
Catalogue (library) (£20 direct purchase)
Cottage History (70p, direct purchase)
John Milton Chronology (£1, direct purchase)
Electronic and video products:
Paradise Lost (CD-ROM, £22.50, direct purchase)

Internet home pages:
http://www.miltonscottage.org

1794
MINORIES ART GALLERY
See - Firstsite@The Minories

1795
MINSTER ABBEY GATEHOUSE MUSEUM
Union Road, Minster, Sheerness, Kent, ME12 2HW

Tel: 01795 872303
Formed: 1981

Organisation type and purpose: Museum, historic building, house or site, suitable for ages: all ages.
Voluntary local history museum in leased council property.
Parent body:
Sheppey Local History Society

Enquiries to: Secretary
Direct tel: 01795 661119 (out of hours)
Access:
Access to staff: By letter, by telephone, visitors by prior appointment
Hours: Any reasonable time.
Access to building, collections or gallery: Prior appointment required
Hours: Easter, May, Spring Bank Holiday: Sat, Sun, 1400 to 1700
Jun to mid-Jul: Sat, Sun, 1400 to 1700
Mid-Jul to mid-Sep: Fri to Wed, 1400 to 1700
Access for disabled people: Parking provided, ramped entry
Other restrictions: Very restricted access - listed medieval building, newel stair, 4 levels.

General description:
History of Isle of Sheppey.
Information services:
Library available for reference (for conditions see Access above). Helpline available, tel no: 01795 661119.
Special visitor services: Guided tours.
Education services: Resources for Key Stages 1 and 2, 3, 4 and Further or Higher Education..
Collections:
Local artefacts (Iron Age to WWII), fossils, costumes
Toys, school room, childhood collections
Local newspapers (bound annual volumes - not complete list, several missing, late 19th century onwards)
Catalogues:
Catalogue for library is in-house only. Catalogue for all of the collections is only available in-house.
Printed publications:
Sheerness and the Mutiny at the Nore (ISBN 09530665 0 9)
Sheerness Dockyard and Fort the Early Years (ISBN 09530665 1 7)
Gatehouse Visitors' Guide

1796
MIREHOUSE HISTORIC HOUSE
Underskiddaw, Keswick, Cumbria, CA12 4QE

Tel: 017687 72287
Email: info@mirehouse.com
Formed: 1981

Organisation type and purpose: Independently owned, historic building, house or site, suitable for ages: all ages.

Enquiries to: Administrator
Access:
Access to staff: By letter, by telephone, by fax, by email, visitors by prior appointment
Access to building, collections or gallery: No prior appointment required
Hours: Apr to Oct: Sun, Wed, also Fri in Aug, 1400 to 1700
Other restrictions: Last entry 1630.
Access for disabled people: level entry, access to all public areas, toilet facilities

General description:
Mirehouse is a family house, built in 1666 and only sold once, in 1688. Connections with Tennyson, Wordsworth, Southey, Coleridge, Francis Bacon, Thomas Carlyle, Constable are all supported with manuscripts. The Spedding collection of letters is kept at Dove Cottage with the exception of those displayed at Mirehouse. Pictures by Romney, Turner, Gastimeau, Hearne, Girtin, Sutton. Poetry exhibition in the gardens changes three times a year. Won NPI Heritage Award 1999 'Best Property for Families in the UK'.
Information services:
Gardens and lakeside walk. Children's history trail.
Special visitor services: Guided tours, materials and/or activities for children.
Education services: Group education facilities, resources for Key Stages 1 and 2 and 3.
Services for disabled people: For the visually impaired; displays and/or information at wheelchair height.
Collections:
Library collected by John and Tom Spedding, 1800-1850, 3000-4000 books

Internet home pages:
http://www.mirehouse.com

1797
MOAT PARK HERITAGE CENTRE
Moat Park, Biggar, Lanarkshire, ML12 6DT

Tel: 01899 221050
Fax: 01899 221050
Email: margaret@bmtrust.freeserve.co.uk
Acronym or abbreviation: BMT
Full name: Biggar Museum Trust
Formed: 1987

Organisation type and purpose: Independently owned, museum, suitable for ages: 5+, research organisation.
Parent body:
Biggar Museum Trust
Tel: As before

Enquiries to: Administrator
Access:
Access to staff: By letter, by telephone, by fax, by email, in person, Internet web pages
Access to building, collections or gallery: Prior appointment required
Hours: Mon to Sat, 1030 to 1700; Sun, 1400 to 1700
Access for disabled people: Parking provided, ramped entry, toilet facilities

General description:
Here you will find models of Clydesdale's past from geological times to the 18th century. Meet an Iron Age family or one of the Roman soldiers who were the scourge of the 'locals' whose fortified houses of many ages can be seen on display. Observe our live bees (in season), appreciate the fascinating finds of our archaeology team, admire the many genuine costumes on display and the unique Menzies Moffat Tapestry.
Information services:
Library available for reference (for conditions see Access above)
Special visitor services: Guided tours, materials and/or activities for children.
Education services: Group education facilities.
Services for disabled people: For the visually impaired.
Collections:
Archaeology
Photographs
Costume
Books
Catalogues:
Catalogue for library is in-house only. Catalogue for part of the collections is only available in-house.
Printed publications:
Brochure

Internet home pages:
http://www.biggar-net.co.uk

See also - Biggar Museum Trust

1798
MODEL RAILWAY HERITAGE TRUST LIMITED, THE
Smethwick

Closed

1799
MODERN ART OXFORD
30 Pembroke Street, Oxford, OX1 1BP

Tel: 01865 722733 / 01865 813830 (recorded information)
Fax: 01865 722573
Email: info@moma.org.uk
Formed: 1965
Formerly: The Museum of Modern Art, Oxford (MOMA), date of change, 2002

Organisation type and purpose: Registered charity (charity number 868757), art gallery, suitable for ages: 5+, publishing house.

Enquiries to: Press Officer
Direct tel: 01865 813813
Direct email: rachel.tomkins@moma.org.uk
Other contacts: Exhibition Programme Administrator for exhibition archivist.
Access:
Access to staff: By letter, by telephone, by fax, by email
Hours: Mon to Fri, 0930 to 1730
Access to building, collections or gallery: No prior appointment required
Hours: Tue to Sat, 1100 to 1730; Thu, 1100 to 2000; Sun, 1200 to 1730
Other restrictions: Prior appointment required for group bookings.
Access for disabled people: Parking provided, ramped entry, access to all public areas, toilet facilities

General description:
MOMA's key aim is to widen the understanding, appreciation and enjoyment of modern and contemporary visual art and culture and to build new audiences.
Its pioneering exhibition programme covers 20th century painting, sculpture, photography, film, video, architecture, design and performance from all over the world. Contemporary and modern arts - national and international temporary exhibitions.
Information services:
Helpline available, tel no: 01865 813830.
Signed talks available on request.
Special visitor services: Guided tours, materials and/or activities for children.
Education services: Group education facilities, resources for Key Stages 1 and 2, 3, 4 and Further or Higher Education.
Services for disabled people: For the hearing impaired.

continued overleaf

Collections:
No permanent collections
Publications list:
is available in hard copy and online.
Printed publications:
Exhibition Catalogues
Exhibition News Sheets
Exhibition Guides
Postcards

Address for ordering publications:
Printed publications:
Cornerhouse Publications
70 Oxford Street, Manchester, M1 5NH, tel: 0161 200 1503, fax: 0161 200 1504

Internet home pages:
http://www.moma.org.uk
Exhibitions, events, about MOMA, education, press, friends, publications, MOMA links.
http://www.moma.org.uk/publications.

1800
MOIRA FURNACE MUSEUM
Moira Workshops, Furnace Lane, Moira, Swadlincote, Derbyshire, DE12 6AT

Tel: 01283 224667
Fax: 01283 224667

Organisation type and purpose: Registered charity (charity number 702783), museum, suitable for ages: all ages.

Enquiries to: Manager
Direct tel: 07976 637858
Access:
Access to staff: By letter, by telephone, by fax, in person
Access to building, collections or gallery: No prior appointment required
Hours: Summer: Tue to Sun, 1130 to 1700
Winter: Wed to Sun, 1230 to 1600
Open all Bank Holidays: 1100 to 1600
Access for disabled people: Parking provided, ramped entry, level entry, access to all public areas, toilet facilities

General description:
An early 19th century iron-making furnace with lime kilns recently restored and reopened with new interactive and educational displays relating to the iron-making process and the story of the buildings' inhabitants. Transport, economic history and natural history can also be studied. Canal boat rides, pond-dipping, adventure playground, the newly opened Moira lock, furnace, woodland, tramways and tow paths and adjoining Danisthorpe Country Park are all open to visitors. The site also has a tea-room and craft workshops, picnic areas and gift shop.
Information services:
Helpline available, tel no: 07976 637858 / 01283 224667.
Special visitor services: Guided tours, materials and/or activities for children.
Education services: Group education facilities, resources for Key Stages 1 and 2, 3, 4 and Further or Higher Education.
Services for disabled people: Displays and/or information at wheelchair height.

Internet home pages:
http://www.moirafurnace.com

1801
MOIRLANICH LONGHOUSE
Near Killin, Stirling

Organisation type and purpose: Museum, historic building, house or site.
Parent body:
National Trust for Scotland (West Region)
Enquiries to:
NTS Office
Lynedoch, Main Street, Killin, FK21 8UW, tel: 01567 820988, fax: 01567 820988

Enquiries to: Groundsman
Access:
Access to building, collections or gallery: No prior appointment required
Hours: End Mar to end Oct, Wed and Sun, 1400 to 1700
Other restrictions: Limited car parking access, unsuitable for coaches
Access for disabled people: toilet facilities
Other restrictions: Access to Reception building

General description:
Traditional cruck-framed cottage and byre dating from the mid-19th century. Building has been little altered and retains many of its original features, such as the 'hingin lum' and box beds. A small adjacent building displays a rare collection of working and 'Sunday best' clothes found in the Longhouse, and an exhibition interprets the history and restoration of the building.

Internet home pages:
http://www.nts.org.uk

1802
MOLD LIBRARY MUSEUM AND GALLERY
Earl Road, Mold, Flintshire, CH7 1AP

Tel: 01352 754791

Parent body:
Flinshire Museums Service
County Museums Officer

General description:
Collections relating to the life and works of the Welsh novelist Daniel Owen, together with collections of local, social and industrial history relating to the town of Mold.
Information services:
Education services: Group education facilities, resources for Key Stages 1 and 2..

1803
MOMPESSON HOUSE
The Close, Salisbury, Wiltshire, SP1 2EL

Tel: 01722 335659, 01722 420980 (Infoline)
Fax: 01722 321559
Email: mompessonhouse@ntrust.org.uk

Organisation type and purpose: National organisation, registered charity (charity number 205846), museum, historic building, house or site.
Parent body:
The National Trust (South West Region)
Wessex Regional Office, tel: 01985 843600
National Trust sites:
Mompesson House
The Close, Salisbury, Wiltshire, SP1 2EL, tel: 01722 335659, fax: 01722 321559, email/website: mompessonhouse@ntrust.org.uk

Enquiries to: Manager
Access:
Access to staff: By letter, by email, Internet web pages
Access to building, collections or gallery: No prior appointment required
Hours: End Mar to end Sep, Mon, Tue, Wed, Sat, Sun, 1100 to 1700
Other restrictions: Open Good Friday.
Access for disabled people: toilet facilities
Other restrictions: Drop-off point. Steps to main entrance. Alternative accessible entrance. Ground floor accessible with assistance. Ramps for single steps. No access to other floors. Steps to shop and tea-room entrances.

General description:
Elegant and spacious 18th century house in Cathedral Close with magnificent plasterwork and fine oak staircase. Contains pieces of very good-quality furniture.
Information services:
Out-of-hours tours of house and/or garden by arrangement.
Braille guide, large-print guide, scented plants.
Children's guide.
Front-carrying baby sling for loan.
Special visitor services: Materials and/or activities for children.
Services for disabled people: For the visually impaired.
Collections:
Turnbull collection of 18th century drinking glasses

Internet home pages:
http://www.nationaltrust.org.uk/regions/wessex

1804
MONITOR 33
Treadgolds Museum, 1 Bishop Street, Portsmouth, Hampshire, PO1 3DA

Tel: 023 9287 6253

Organisation type and purpose: Local government body, historic building, house or site.
Naval ship.
Parent body:
Hampshire County Council Museums Service
Chilcomb House, Chilcomb Lane, Winchester, SO23 8RD, tel: 01962 846304, fax: 01962 869836
Other location:
Treadgolds of Portsea Museum
1 Bishop Street, Portsmouth, PO1 3DA, tel: 023 9282 4745, fax: 023 9283 7310

Enquiries to: Curator
Access:
Access to building, collections or gallery: No access other than to staff
Other restrictions: Closed for refurbishment, contact Treadgolds for up-to-date information.

General description:
Monitor 33, later known as HMS Minerva, one of five 6 inch monitors for inshore bombardment, built by Workman Clark under contract to Harland and Wolff, Belfast, 15; served in the Gallipoli Campaign, World War I; converted to a coastal mine sweeper 1924; used for instructional purposes 1939 onwards.
Publications list:
is available in hard copy.
Printed publications:
Publications list is available from the Librarian, Hampshire County Council Museums Service Headquarters, Chilcomb House, Winchester, SO23 8RD

Internet home pages:
http://www.hants.gov.uk/museums/
HMCMS web catalogue, whole collection, 100,000 plus web pages

1805
MONKBAR MUSEUM
See - Richard III Museum

1806
MONK'S HOUSE
Rodmell, Lewes, East Sussex, BN7 3HF

Tel: 01372 453401 (Regional Office)

Organisation type and purpose: National organisation, registered charity (charity number 205846), historic building, house or site.
Parent body:
The National Trust (South and South East Region)
South East Regional Office, tel: 01372 453401

Enquiries to: Manager
Access:
Access to staff: By letter, by telephone

General description:
A small weather-boarded house, the home of Leonard and Virginia Woolf until Leonard's death in 1969. The rooms reflect the life and times of the literary circle in which they moved.

Internet home pages:
http://www.nationaltrust.org.uk

1807
MONKSTHORPE CHAPEL
See - Gunby Hall Estate: Monksthorpe Chapel

1808
MONKWEARMOUTH STATION MUSEUM
North Bridge Street, Sunderland, Tyne and Wear, SR5 1AP

Tel: 0191 567 7075
Fax: 0191 553 7828
Formed: 1973

Organisation type and purpose: Local government body, registered charity, museum, suitable for ages: all ages.
Parent body:
Tyne and Wear Museums (TWM)
Discovery Museum, Blandford Square, Newcastle, tel: 0191 232 6789, fax: 0191 230 2614
Other addresses:
Sunderland Museum and Winter Gardens
Burdon Road, Sunderland, SR1 1PP, tel: 0191 553 2323, fax: 0191 553 9828, email/website: sunderland.museum@tyne-wear-museums.org.uk

Enquiries to: Curator
Direct tel: 0191 553 2323
Direct fax: 0191 553 7820
Direct email: sunderland.museum@tyne-wear-museums.org.uk
Other contacts: Education Officer for school bookings.
Access:
Access to staff: By letter, by telephone, by fax
Other restrictions: By appointment only.
Access to building, collections or gallery: No prior appointment required
Access for disabled people: Parking provided, ramped entry, access to all public areas, toilet facilities

General description:
The splendid Victorian classical railway station of 1848 with restored booking office recreates a sense of train travel in times past. Explore the ticket office as it would have looked in Victorian times, see the guards van and goods wagon in the railway sidings, and watch today's trains zoom past. Displays on history of local railways. The Children's Gallery has a range of toys and dressing-up clothes. Special temporary exhibitions.
Information services:
Education services: Group education facilities, resources for Key Stages 1 and 2, 3, 4 and Further or Higher Education.
Services for disabled people: For the visually impaired; for the hearing impaired; displays and/or information at wheelchair height.
Collections:
The collections at Monkwearmouth all relate to transport, they include the contents of the 1866 booking office, and rolling stock such as guard's and goods wagon, in the sidings
There is a collection of printed material, photographs and models relating to railways, particularly those in Tyne and Wear
Sunderland Corporation Transport is also represented and there is a significant collection of bicycles

Internet home pages:
http://www.twmuseums.org.uk

1809
MONMOUTH MUSEUM
See - Nelson Museum and Local History Centre, Monmouth

1810
MONTACUTE HOUSE
Montacute, Somerset, TA15 6XP

Tel: 01935 823289
Fax: 01935 826921
Email: montacute@nationaltrust.org.uk

Organisation type and purpose: National government body, registered charity (charity number 205846), museum, art gallery, historic building, house or site.
Parent body:
The National Trust (South West Region)
Wessex Regional Office, tel: 01985 843600

Enquiries to: Manager
Other contacts: Box office, Tel: 01985 843601
Access:
Access to staff: By letter, by email, Internet web pages
Access to building, collections or gallery: No prior appointment required
Hours: End Mar to beg Nov, Mon, Wed to Sun, 1100 to 1700
Other restrictions: Closed Tuesdays. Park and Estate unlimited opening.
Access for disabled people: Parking provided, toilet facilities
Other restrictions: 3 manual wheelchairs available. Ground floor accessible with assistance. No access to other floors. Level entrance to shop and restaurant. Grounds largely accessible.

General description:
Elizabethan house, adorned with elegant chimneys, carved parapets and other Renaissance features, including contemporary plasterwork, chimneypieces and heraldic glass. Magnificent state rooms, including a long gallery which is the largest of its type in England, are full of fine 17th and 18th century furniture, and Elizabethan and Jacobean portraits from the National Portrait gallery. There are also good-quality textiles, including an exhibition of 17th century samplers.
Information services:
Guided tours for groups by arrangement with the House manager. Out-of-hours tours and activities also available by arrangement.
Braille guide, large-print guide, touch list, scented plants. Sympathetic Hearing Scheme.
Children's guide, children's quiz/trail.
For details of events, telephone Wessex regional box office.
Special visitor services: Guided tours, materials and/or activities for children.
Education services: Group education facilities.
Services for disabled people: For the visually impaired; for the hearing impaired.

Internet home pages:
http://www.nationaltrust.org.uk/regions/wessex

1811
MONTACUTE TV & RADIO MEMORABILIA MUSEUM
1 South Street, Montacute, Somerset, TA15 6XD

Tel: 01935 823024
Email: montacutemuseum@aol.com
Formed: 1994

Organisation type and purpose: Independently owned, museum, suitable for ages: 5+.
Private museum.

Enquiries to: Curator
Other contacts: Marketing Officer
Access:
Access to staff: By letter, by telephone, by email, visitors by prior appointment, charges made to all users

General description:
A nostalgic trip through the world of radio and TV particularly memorabilia, books, toys and games related to radio and TV programmes.
Mad Hatter's tea-rooms.
Collections:
Over 500 radios and radiograms from vintage wireless (particularly 1930s) through to novelty transistors
Some 1950s TVs
Extensive collection of radio and TV programme related memorabilia, books, toys and games
Alice in Wonderland Collection

1812
MONTAGU COLLECTION OF WORLD MUSICAL INSTRUMENTS
171 Iffley Road, Oxford, OX4 1EL

Tel: 01865 726037
Email: jeremy.montagu@music.oxford.ac.uk
Formed: 1960

Organisation type and purpose: Museum.

Enquiries to: Curator
Access:
Access to staff: By letter, by email, visitors by prior appointment
Hours: Any mutually convenient times
Other restrictions: Charges may be made to users.

General description:
History, development, identification, classification of musical instruments of all types, advice on maintenance and display of instruments.
Collections:
Books and illustrations of musical instruments, all types, all periods
Small collection of recordings on disk, CD-ROM, cassette
Catalogues:
Catalogue for part of the collections is published.
Printed publications:
The Magpie in Ethnomusicology (0-9527606-1-4 £2.50 plus 50p p&p)
A number of relevant books by the curator commercially published and available in libraries as well as numerous periodical articles eg
Reed Instruments (partial catalogue of the collection, Scarecrow Press, Lanlan MD 0-8108-3938-5)
Timpani and Percussion (Yale, UP New Haven and London, 0-300-09337-3 and 0-300-09500-7)
Making Early Percussion Instruments (available direct only)

1813
MONTAGU MOTOR MUSEUM
See - National Motor Museum

1814
MONTGOMERY CIVIC SOCIETY
See - Old Bell Museum

1815
MONTROSE AIR STATION MUSEUM
Waldron Road, Broomfield, Montrose, Angus, DD10 9BB

Tel: 01674 674210
Fax: 01674 674210
Email: pd.mams@btopenworld.com
Acronym or abbreviation: MAMS
Formed: 1983

Organisation type and purpose: Registered charity, museum.

Enquiries to: Administrator
Access:
Access to staff: By letter only
Hours: Sun, 1200 to 1700
Access to building, collections or gallery: Prior appointment required
Hours: Sun, 1200 to 1700
Access for disabled people: Parking provided, ramped entry

continued overleaf

General description:
The collection relates to Montrose Air Station, Britain's first operational aerodrome, which opened on 26 February 1913, in all its aspects. Includes aircraft and vehicles to supplement collections of smaller artefacts and aviation-related memorabilia.
Information services:
Library available for reference (for conditions see Access above)
Special visitor services: Guided tours, materials and/or activities for children.
Education services: Group education facilities..
Collections:
History of Site, 1913-1950
Catalogues:
Catalogue for library is in-house only. Catalogue for all of the collections is only available in-house.
Publications list:
is available on-line.
Printed publications:
RAF Montrose History (£12.99 inc p&p)

Internet home pages:
http://ourworld.compuserve.com/homepages/AirspeedNews

1816
MONTROSE MUSEUM AND ART GALLERY
Panmure Place, Montrose, Angus, DD10 8HE

Tel: 01674 673232
Fax: 01307 462590
Email: montrose.museum@angus.gov.uk
Formed: 1842

Organisation type and purpose: Local government body, museum, art gallery.

Enquiries to: Curator
Access:
Access to staff: By email, in person, by letter, by telephone, by fax, Internet web pages
Hours: Mon to Sat, 1000 to 1700
Other restrictions: Limited disabled access, no permanent ramp at front door. Wheelchair access restricted to ground floor. No disabled toilet provision.
Access to building, collections or gallery: No access other than to staff

General description:
Local archaeology, history and geology.
Information services:
Guided tours by appointment.
Special visitor services: Guided tours, materials and/or activities for children..
Collections:
Extensive collections cover the history of Montrose from pre-historic times to local government reorganisation, the maritime history of the port, the natural history of Angus, and local art exhibits include Pictish stones, Montrose silver and pottery, whaling, artefacts and Napoleonic items
Collections of the former Sunnyside Museum dealing with the two hundred years of the story of the Sunnyside asylum and including the Sunnyside Chronicle containing articles by the patients, and art works produced by the patients
Catalogues:
Catalogue for all of the collections is only available in-house.
Printed publications:
Auchmithie Album (£1.95)
Auchmithie - Home of the Smokie (£4.95)
Burn the Witch (£5.95)
Caa Dune the Mune (£1)
Doors Open Day (£2)
Dorward House (£4.50)
The Early History of Montrose (£3.50)
The Mid Links (£3.50)
Reading a Burgh Archive (£5)
Tombstones of Angus C Mearns (£10)
Walks into History (£2)
Wm Lamb Catalogue (£3)

Internet home pages:
http://www.angus.gov.uk

1817
MOORCROFT MUSEUM & FACTORY SHOP
Sandbach Road, Burslem, Stoke-on-Trent, Staffordshire, ST6 2DQ

Tel: 01782 207943
Email: shop@moorcroft.com

Organisation type and purpose: Museum.

Enquiries to: Manager
Access:
Access for disabled people: ramped entry, access to all public areas, toilet facilities
Other restrictions: Car park adjacent.

General description:
In cabinets made by Liberty of London in 1924 are displayed examples of the very first pieces designed by William Moorcroft at the end of the 19th century, through the great renaissance of Moorcroft's art ten years ago its centenary year in 1997.

Internet home pages:
http://www.moorcroft.com

1818
MOOT HALL, THE
High Street, Maldon, Essex, CM9 5PN

Tel: 01621 857373

Organisation type and purpose: Local government body, historic building, house or site, suitable for ages: all ages.
Access:
Access to building, collections or gallery: No prior appointment required
Hours: March to October, Sat tours 1400 and 1530
Other restrictions: Tours at other times can be arranged with Maldon Town Council, tel: 01621 857373

General description:
The Hall has been the centre of local government since 1576. It has a medieval spiral staircase, a Dickensian Court House, a Georgian Council Chamber and the remains of an old borough Gaol with prisoners' exercise yard.
Information services:
Special visitor services: Guided tours..

Internet home pages:
http://www.maldon.cwc.net/moothall

1819
MOOT HALL MUSEUM
Church End, Elstow, Bedford, MK42 9XT

Tel: 01234 266889

Organisation type and purpose: Museum, historic building, house or site, suitable for ages: 8+.
Parent body:
Bedfordshire County Council
Department of the Environment and Economic Development (DEED)

Enquiries to: Curator
Other contacts: Caretaker for bookings for groups, 01234 304640.
Access:
Access to staff: By letter, by telephone
Hours: Apr to Sep: Tue, Wed, Thu, Sun, Bank Holidays, 1300 to 1600
Access to building, collections or gallery: Prior appointment required
Hours: Apr to Sep: Tue, Wed, Thu, Sun, Bank Holidays, 1300 to 1700

General description:
A collection of 17th century domestic artefacts and furniture, and illustrations of traditional crafts. Also includes illustrations and translations of John Bunyan's many works, including panels by William Blake.
Collections:
Illustrations, translations and rare copies of John Bunyan's works, 17th century to present
17th century furniture
Artefacts relating to John Bunyan: pulpit, jail doors, etc. 17th century

1820
MORAVIAN MUSEUM
See - Fulneck Moravian Settlement and Moravian Museum

1821
MORAY COUNCIL
Local Heritage Centre, Grant Lodge, Elgin, Moray, IV30 1HS

Tel: 01343 562644
Fax: 01343 549050
Email: graeme.wilson@moray.gov.uk
Formed: 1996
Formed from: Elgin Library Local Studies Section, Moray District Record Office, date of change, 1996

Organisation type and purpose: Local government body, research organisation.

Enquiries to: Local Heritage Officer
Access:
Access to staff: By letter, by telephone, by fax, by email, in person, Internet web pages
Access to building, collections or gallery: No prior appointment required
Hours: Oct to Apr: Mon, Thu, Fri, 1000 to 1700; Tue, 1000 to 2000; Sat, 1000 to 1200
May to Sep: also Wed, 1000 to 1700
Access for disabled people: ramped entry, access to all public areas

General description:
Sources relating to Moray including archives, books, maps, newspapers and genealogical records.
Information services:
Education services: Resources for Further or Higher Education..
Catalogues:
Catalogue for library is in-house only. Catalogue for all of the collections is only available in-house.

Internet home pages:
http://www.moray.org/heritage/roots.html
http://www.moray.org/heritage/index.html

1822
MORDEN HALL PARK
Morden Hall Road, Morden, Surrey, SM4 5JD

Tel: 020 8648 1845
Fax: 020 8687 0094
Email: mordenhallpark@nationaltrust.org.uk

Organisation type and purpose: Registered charity (charity number 205846), historic building, house or site, suitable for ages: 5+.
Parent body:
The National Trust (South and South East Region)
Thames and Solent Regional Office, tel: 01494 528051

Enquiries to: Manager
Access:
Access to staff: By letter, by telephone, by fax, by email
Access to building, collections or gallery: No prior appointment required
Hours: Park open dailyduring daylight hours
Other restrictions: Car park closes at 1800
Access for disabled people: Parking provided
Other restrictions: Wheelchair path through rose garnen and beside river, cafeshop and garden centre accessible

General description:
This oasis in the heart of suburbia covers over 50ha (125 acres) of parkland with the River Wandle meandering through. The river plays an important role in the park with an old Snuff Mill, now used as an Environmental Centre, and a variety of bridges traversing the river. The park has hay meadows and a collection of old estate buildings, as well as an impressive rose garden with over 2000 roses. The workshops now house local craftworkers. There is an independently run garden centre and a city farm.
Information services:
Full programme of year round events
May, Craft Fair; details from Four Seasons Events (tel. 01276 679419)
Programme of walks
Braille guide. Large-print guide
Craft workshops closed on Tues
Suitable for school groups. Snuff Mill Environmental Centre for community and family holiday activities
Special visitor services: Guided tours, materials and/or activities for children.
Education services: Group education facilities..

Internet home pages:
http://www.nationaltrust.org.uk

1823
MORLEY HEWITT MEMORIAL MUSEUM
See - Rockbourne Roman Villa

1824
MORPETH CHANTRY BAGPIPE MUSEUM
Bridge Street, Morpeth, Northumberland, NE61 1PJ

Tel: 01670 519466
Fax: 01670 511326
Email: amoore@castlemorpeth.gov.uk
Formed: 1987

Organisation type and purpose: Museum.
Parent body:
Society of Antiquaries of Newcastle though
Links with:
Northumbrian Pipers' Society
Museum is run by the:
Castle Morpeth Borough Council

Enquiries to: Curator
Access:
Access to staff: By letter, by telephone, by fax, by email, in person
Hours: Mon to Sat, 1000 to 1700
Access to building, collections or gallery: Prior appointment required
Hours: Displays, 1000 to 1700
Other restrictions: Library and reserve collections by prior appointment.

General description:
Music, specifically bagpipes, emphasis on Northumbrian and Irish pipes.
Collections:
W A Cocks collection of bagpipes and related material (library of manuscripts, tunebooks, music etc)

1825
MORVILLE HALL
Morville, Bridgnorth, Shropshire, WV16 5NB

Tel: 01743 708100 (Regional Office)
Email: morvillehall@nationaltrust.org.uk

Organisation type and purpose: National organisation, registered charity (charity number 205846), historic building, house or site.
Parent body:
The National Trust (West Midlands)
West Midlands Regional Office, tel: 01743 708100

Enquiries to: Manager
Access:
Access to staff: By letter, by telephone, by email
Access to building, collections or gallery: Prior appointment required
Other restrictions: Access is by guided tour only, by written appointment with the tenants, Dr and Mrs C Douglas.

General description:
An Elizabethan house of mellow stone, converted in the 18th century and set in attractive gardens.

Internet home pages:
http://www.nationaltrust.org.uk

1826
MOSELEY OLD HALL
Moseley Old Hall Lane, Fordhouses, Wolverhampton, Staffordshire, WV10 7HY

Tel: 01902 782808
Fax: 01902 782808
Email: moseleyoldhall@nationaltrust.org.uk
Formed: 1895

Organisation type and purpose: National organisation, registered charity (charity number 205846), historic building, house or site, suitable for ages: 8+.
Parent body:
The National Trust (West Midlands)
West Midlands Regional Office, tel: 01743 708100
Headquarters:
National Trust
36 Queen Anne's Gate, London, SW1H 9AS, tel: 0870 609 5380, fax: 020 7222 5097

Enquiries to: Property Manager
Access:
Access to staff: By letter, by telephone
Access to building, collections or gallery: No prior appointment required
Hours: Late Mar to beg Nov: Sat, Sun, Wed, 1300 to 1700
Early Nov to mid Dec: Sun, 1300 to 1600
Open Bank Holiday Mons, 1100 to 1700 and following Tue, 1300 to 1700
Other restrictions: Tea-room and Garden open from 1200.
Access for disabled people: Parking provided, level entry, toilet facilities
Other restrictions: Designated parking 10 yds. 1 manual wheelchair available. Accessible entrance by route from reception avoiding steps. Ground floor fully accessible. No access to other floors. Level entrance to shop. Level entrance to tea-room. Grounds largely accessible.

General description:
An Elizabethan House, altered in the 19th century and famous for its association with Charles II who hid here after the battle of Worcester (1651). The story of his escape is reconstructed in an exhibition in the barn, and there is an interesting garden full of 17th century plants.
Information services:
Optional free guided tours; last guided tour 1545. Contact property for details of out-of-hours tours, inc. evening tours.
Braille guide. Large-print guide. Touch list.
Front-carrying baby slings for loan.
Suitable for school groups. Live interpretation. Hands-on activities. Children's guide.
Children's quiz/trail.
Special visitor services: Guided tours, materials and/or activities for children.
Education services: Group education facilities, resources for Key Stages 1 and 2 and 3.
Services for disabled people: For the visually impaired; for the hearing impaired; displays and/or information at wheelchair height.
Collections:
Mainly 17th century oak furniture
Paintings
Printed 17th century proclamations and posters
Catalogues:
Catalogue for all of the collections is only available in-house.
Printed publications:
Colour Guide (£2.50)
Children's Guide (85p)
Garden Leaflet (10p)

Internet home pages:
http://www.nationaltrust.org.uk

1827
MOSQUITO AIRCRAFT MUSEUM
See - de Havilland Aircraft Heritage Centre

1828
MOSSMAN COLLECTION
See - Stockwood Craft Museum and Mossman Collection

1829
MOTHERWELL HERITAGE CENTRE
1 High Road, Motherwell, North Lanarkshire, ML1 3HQ

Tel: 01698 251000
Fax: 01698 268867
Formed: 1996

Organisation type and purpose: Local government body, museum, suitable for ages: 8+.
Parent body:
Museums Section
North Lanarkshire Council, Buchan Business Park, Stepps, Glasgow, G33 6HR, tel: 0141 304 1975, fax: 0141 304 1902

Enquiries to: Manager
Access:
Access to staff: By letter, by telephone, by fax
Access for disabled people: Parking provided, level entry, access to all public areas, toilet facilities

General description:
Main feature is the interactive audiovisual display, 'Technopolis', which takes the visitor from Roman Times, through the rise and fall of the area's heavy industries, to post-industrial Motherwell. Also specially equipped local studies room, exhibition gallery and shop.
Information services:
Education services: Group education facilities, resources for Key Stages 2, 3 and 4..
Collections:
Collections relate to local industries eg Hurst-Nelson Archive of Locomotives
The family papers of the Hamiltons of Dalzell
Extensive collection of general artefacts relating to the life and work of 19th century Motherwell Area
Catalogues:
Catalogue for library is published. Catalogue for all of the collections is published.

Internet home pages:
http://motherwell.museum.com

1830
MOTOR HOUSE COLLECTION
See - War Room and Motor House Collection

1831
MOTORBOAT MUSEUM, THE
Wat Tyler Country Park, Pitsea Hall Lane, Basildon, Essex, SS16 4UH

Tel: 01268 550077
Fax: 01268 584207
Formed: 1986
Formerly: National Motorboat Museum

Organisation type and purpose: Local government body, museum.
To promote knowledge of the history of power boating in the sports and leisure field. Over 35 exhibits on display, fine collection of inboard and outboard motors.
Parent body:
Basildon District Council (BDC)
The Basildon Centre, Pagel Mead, Basildon, Essex, SS14 1DL, tel: 01268 533333

continued overleaf

Enquiries to: Museum Officer
Other contacts: Manager, tel no 01268 550088
Access:
Access to staff: By letter, by telephone, by fax, in person
Access for disabled people: Parking provided, ramped entry, toilet facilities

General description:
Sporting and leisure motor craft, outboard engines, racing archives.
Information services:
Library available for reference (for conditions see Access above)
Library searches and permission to reproduce documents by arrangement.
Special visitor services: Guided tours..
Collections:
Bert Savidge Collection (Outboard Engines)
Carstairs Collection - Over 30 Silver Racing Trophies in display case belonging to the late Marion Barbara Carstairs who was born in 1900, successful racer in her time
The Charlie Sheppherd Archives (Inshore Circuit Racing Archives)
Ray Bulman Photographic Archive - over 3000 negatives for the racing years, spanning 30 years
UKOBA Archive (Racing Archive Offshore)
Catalogues:
Catalogue for part of the collections is only available in-house.

1832
MOTORING HERITAGE CENTRE
Loch Lomond Outlets, Main Street, Alexandria, Dumbartonshire, G83 0UG

Tel: 01389 607 862
Fax: 01389 607 862
Email: info@motoringheritage.co.uk
Formed: 1995
Formerly: Argyll Motor Museum Limited

Organisation type and purpose: Voluntary organisation, registered charity (charity number SCO 28515), museum, suitable for ages: 5+.
Parent body:
Scottish Motor Museum Trust
at same address

Enquiries to: Administrator
Access:
Access to staff: By letter, by telephone, by fax, by email, in person, Internet web pages
Access to building, collections or gallery: No prior appointment required
Hours: Daily, 0930 to 1730
Access for disabled people: Parking provided, ramped entry, level entry, access to all public areas, toilet facilities

General description:
Situated in the largest and most palatial motor works of its day. Built in 1906, the Motor Heritage Centre tells the story of Scotland's motoring history, exhibiting Scottish built cars.
Information services:
Library available for reference (for conditions see Access above)
Special visitor services: Guided tours, materials and/or activities for children.
Education services: Group education facilities, resources for Key Stage 3.
Services for disabled people: Displays and/or information at wheelchair height.
Collections:
Film archive of Scottish motoring
Library of photographic images of Scottish motoring and moving images
Motor vehicles of Scottish origin
Catalogues:
Catalogue for part of the collections is only available in-house.
Microform products:
Collection Cine Film of Scottish Motoring
Electronic and video products:
Videos of Scottish motoring

Internet home pages:
http://www.motoringheritage.co.uk
http://www.visitlochlomond.com

1833
MOTTISFONT ABBEY, GARDEN, HOUSE AND ESTATE
Mottisfont, Romsey, Isle of Wight, SO51 0LP

Tel: 01794 340757
Fax: 01794 341492
Email: mottisfontabbey@nationaltrust.org.uk

Organisation type and purpose: National organisation, registered charity (charity number 205846), historic building, house or site.
Parent body:
The National Trust (South and South East Region)
Thames and Solent Regional Office, tel: 01494 528051

Enquiries to: Manager
Access:
Access to staff: By letter, by telephone, by fax, by email
Access to building, collections or gallery: No prior appointment required
Hours: Garden only: 1 Mar to 16 Mar, Sat and Sun
1100 to 1600; Jun, Daily, 1100 to 2030
House only: Jun, daily, 1100 to 1800
House and garden: End Mar to beg Jun, 1100 to 18oo, Sat to Wed; Jul and Aug, Sat to Thu, 1100 to 1800; Sep to beg Nov, Sat to Wed
Other restrictions: Open Good Friday, 1100 to 1800. Last admission to house 1 hour before closing.
Access for disabled people: Parking provided, ramped entry, toilet facilities
Other restrictions: Designated parking 200yds. 6 manual wheelchairs available. Ground floor fully accessible. Audiovisual/video. Photograph album. 1 five-seater powered mobility vehicle. Ramped entrance to shop. Level entrance to restaurant. Grounds largely accessible.

General description:
Set amidst glorious countryside along the River Test, this 12th century Augustinian priory was converted into a private house after the Dissolution, and still retains the spring or 'font' from which its name is derived. The abbey contains a drawing room decorated by Rex Whistler and Derek Hill's 20th century picture collection, but the key attraction is the grounds with magnificent trees, walled gardens and National Collection of Old-fashioned Roses. The estate includes Mottisfont village and surrounding farmland and woods.
Information services:
Helpline available, tel no: Infoline 01794 341220.
Braille guide. Scented plants.
Children's quiz/trail.
Special visitor services: Materials and/or activities for children.
Services for disabled people: For the visually impaired.

Internet home pages:
http://www.nationaltrust.org.uk

1834
MOTTISTONE MANOR
The Gardener, Manor Cottage, Hoxall Lane, Mottistone, Isle of Wight, PO30 4ED

Tel: 01983 741302

Organisation type and purpose: National organisation, registered charity (charity number 205846), historic building, house or site, suitable for ages: all ages.
Parent body:
The National Trust (South & South East Region)
Thames & Solent Regional Office, tel: 01491 528051

Enquiries to: Head Gardener

Access:
Access to staff: By letter, by telephone
Access for disabled people: toilet facilities
Other restrictions: Level entrance to shop. Level entrance to tearoom. Limited access for wheelchair users because of steep slopes.

General description:
A garden noted for its colourful herbaceous borders, grassy terraces planted with fruit trees and its sea views. The 16th- and 17th century manor house, which is tenanted, lies at the heart of the Mottistone Estate, which offers delightful walks between the Downs and the coast.
Information services:
Summer open-air concerts; children's quiz/trail
Special visitor services: Materials and/or activities for children..

Internet home pages:
http://www.nationaltrust.org.uk/regions/

1835
MOULTON HALL
Moulton, Richmond, North Yorkshire, DL10 6QH

Tel: 01325 377227

Organisation type and purpose: National organisation, registered charity (charity number 205846), historic building, house or site.
Parent body:
The National Trust (Yorkshire and North East)
Yorkshire Regional Office, tel: 01904 70202

Enquiries to: Manager
Access:
Access to staff: By letter, by telephone
Access to building, collections or gallery: Prior appointment required
Other restrictions: By arrangement with the tenant, Viscount Eccles.

General description:
A compact stone manor house, dating from 1650 and with a very fine carved wood staircase.

Internet home pages:
http://www.nationaltrust.org.uk

1836
MOULTON PACKHORSE BRIDGE
Moulton, Newmarket, Suffolk, CB

Organisation type and purpose: Historic building, house or site.
Parent body:
English Heritage (East of England Region)
Brooklands, 24 Brooklands Avenue, Cambridge, CB2 2BU, tel: 01223 582700, fax: 01223 582701
Access:
Access to building, collections or gallery: No prior appointment required
Hours: Any reasonable time
Access for disabled people: access to all public areas

General description:
Medieval four-arched bridge spanning the River Kennett.

Internet home pages:
http://www.english-heritage.org.uk

1837
MOULTON WINDMILL PROJECT LIMITED
c/o 4 Hawthorn Chase, Moulton, Spalding, Lincolnshire, PE12 6GA

Tel: 01406 373368
Formed: 1998

Organisation type and purpose: Registered charity (charity number 1078747), historic building, house or site, suitable for ages: 5+.
Other addresses:
Secretary
Moulton Windmill Project Limited
571 Broadgate, Weston Hills, Spalding, PE12 6DB, tel: 01775 724929

Enquiries to: Chairman
Access:
Access to staff: Visitors by prior appointment
Access to building, collections or gallery: Prior appointment required
Hours: Daily, 1000 to 1600

General description:
The windmill is currently undergoing renovation but is open to the public with limited access. All original machinery intact, and when restored will be the newest mill in the country.
Collections:
Milling artefacts, photographic displays, grind your own corn with our hand-operated quern
Printed publications:
Publications available direct

1838
MOUNT EDGCUMBE HOUSE & COUNTRY PARK

Cremyll, Torpoint, Cornwall, PL10 1HZ

Tel: 01752 822236
Fax: 01752 822199
Formed: 1971
Formerly: Plymouth City Council, Cornwall County Council

Organisation type and purpose: Local government body, museum, art gallery, suitable for ages: all ages.
Access to historic house and gardens.
Jointly owned by:
Cornwall County Council and Plymouth City Council
Tel: 01752 822236

Enquiries to: Manager
Other contacts: Museum Officer for collections; garden history.
Access:
Access to staff: By letter, by telephone, by fax, visitors by prior appointment
Hours: Mon to Fri, 0900 to 1650
Other restrictions: 29 Mar to 29 Sep: Wed to Sun, 1100 to 1630; Bank Holidays.
Access for disabled people: ramped entry, toilet facilities
Other restrictions: Lift in house.

General description:
Former home of the Earls of Mount Edgcumbe. Tudor home built 1547, red stone, suffered damage in WWII, restored 1958. Grounds used by US Force pre D-Day. Damaged in Civil War of 1644. Early design took advantage of stunning site overlooking Plymouth Sound.
History of Earls of Mount Edgcumbe; their houses and historic gardens; family portraits; furniture; national camellia collection; archaeology; geology; wildlife; forestry; fortifications; follies; 18th century garden buildings within the country park.
Collections:
Family possessions including paintings by Sir Joshua Reynolds, Gerard Edema and Willem van der Velde
Irish bronze age horns
16th century tapestries
18th century Chinese and Plymouth porcelain
Special exhibition during season
Catalogues:
Catalogue for library is in-house only. Catalogue for all of the collections is only available in-house.
Printed publications:
Mount Edgcumbe House: The Historic Gardens
Leaflets on the house; the Earl's garden; the historic gardens; geology (for purchase, directly)
Guide Book
Geology in Mount Edgcumbe Park
Mount Edgcumbe House and Country Park - A Guide (£2.95, £3.60 incl p&p)
Camellias

Internet home pages:
http://www..gardensincornwall.co.uk
Information on House and Country Park

1839
MOUNT GRACE PRIORY

Osmotherley, Northallerton, North Yorkshire, DL6 3JG

Tel: 01609 883494

Organisation type and purpose: National organisation, advisory body, historic building, house or site.
Maintained and managed by:
English Heritage (Yorkshire Region)
Tel: 01904 601901
Owned by:
The National Trust (Yorkshire and North East)
Yorkshire Regional Office, tel: 01904 70202

Enquiries to: Manager
Access:
Access to staff: By letter, by telephone
Access to building, collections or gallery: No prior appointment required
Hours: Apr to Sep, daily, 1000 to 1800; Oct, daily, 1000 to 1700; Nov to Mar, Wed to Sun, 1000 to 1600
Other restrictions: Closed 24 to 26 Dec and 1 Jan.
Closed for lunch Nov to Mar, 1300 to1400.
Opening times are subject to change, for up-to-date information contact English Heritage or the National Trust by phone or visit the website.

General description:
Mount Grace Priory is the best preserved of the medieval Carthusian monasteries or 'charterhouses' in Britain. Founded in 1398, its site, among attractive woodland below the escarpment of the North York Moors, was chosen for the peace and tranquillity that still survives today. One cell and its enclosed garden has been reconstructed and furnished as it would have been in the early 16th century, and the great cloister and the church survive well today.
Information services:
Education services: Group education facilities..

Internet home pages:
http://www.nationaltrust.org.uk

1840
MOUNT STEWART HOUSE, GARDEN AND TEMPLE OF THE WINDS

Portaferry Road, Newtownards, Co Down, BT22 2AD

Tel: 028 4278 8387
Fax: 028 4278 8569
Email: mountstewart@nationaltrust.org.uk

Organisation type and purpose: National organisation, registered charity (charity number 205846), historic building, house or site, suitable for ages: 5+.
Parent body:
National Trust Office for Northern Ireland
Rowallane House, Saintfield, Ballynahinch, Co Down, BT24 7LH, tel: 028 9751 0721, fax: 028 9751 1242

Enquiries to: Manager
Other contacts: Education Officer: 028 4278 8830
Access:
Access to staff: By letter, by telephone, by fax, by email
Access for disabled people: Parking provided, level entry, toilet facilities
Other restrictions: Designated parking 100yds. 2 single-seater powered mobility vehicles, booking essential. Ground floor fully accessible. Photograph album. Level entrance to shop and to restaurant. Grounds largely accessible. Recommended route map.

General description:
Fascinating 18th century house, with 19th century additions, home of Lord Castlereagh. Boasts one of the greatest gardens in the British Isles, planted in the 1920s and now designated a World Heritage Site. Magnificent series of 'outdoor rooms' and vibrant parterres contain many rare plants that thrive in the mild climate of the Ards. House tour includes world famous paintings and stories about the prominent political figures to whom the Londonderry family played host.
Information services:
Scented plants. Sympathetic Hearing Scheme.
Suitable for school groups. Education room/centre. Live interpretation. Hands-on activities. Children's quiz/trail.
Drama, music and craft events.
Special visitor services: Guided tours, materials and/or activities for children.
Education services: Group education facilities, resources for Key Stages 1 and 2.
Services for disabled people: For the visually impaired; for the hearing impaired.

Internet home pages:
http://www.ntni.org.uk

1841
MOYSE'S HALL MUSEUM

Cornhill, Bury St Edmunds, Suffolk, IP33 3YU

Tel: 01284 706183
Fax: 01284 765373
Email: moyses-hall@stedsbc.gov.uk
Formed: 1899

Organisation type and purpose: Local government body, museum, suitable for ages: 5+.

Enquiries to: Assistant Manager
Direct tel: 01284 725986
Direct email: gill.hawkins@stedsbc.gov.uk
Access:
Access to staff: By letter, by telephone, by fax, by email, in person, visitors by prior appointment
Access for disabled people: level entry, access to all public areas, toilet facilities
Other restrictions: Disabled parking outside except Wed and Sat.

General description:
The collections of local history, natural history and archaeology are housed in one of England's rare surviving Norman houses where the original features are still clearly visible. In its long history, Moyse's Hall has been used as a gaol, fire station and railway parcels office before opening as a museum in 1899.
Local history - William Corder/Red Barn Murder, archaeological collections, Suffolk Regiment gallery, children's activities.
Information services:
Special visitor services: Guided tours, tape recorded guides, materials and/or activities for children.
Education services: Group education facilities, resources for Key Stages 1 and 2, 3, 4 and Further or Higher Education.
Services for disabled people: For the visually impaired; for the hearing impaired; displays and/or information at wheelchair height.
Collections:
Isleham Hoard, the largest Bronze Age hoard in Europe, 9th/10th century BC
Red Barn Murder, collection of items from this famous murder, 1827 c 30 items
Printed publications:
General leaflet and events

Internet home pages:
http://www.stedmundsbury.gov.uk/moyses.htm

1842
MUCHELNEY ABBEY

Muchelney, Somerset

Tel: 01458 250664

Organisation type and purpose: National organisation, advisory body, historic building, house or site.
Parent body:
English Heritage (South West Region)
Tel: 0117 975 0700, fax: 0117 975 0701

Enquiries to: Manager

continued overleaf

Access:
Access to staff: By letter, by telephone
Access to building, collections or gallery: No prior appointment required
Hours: 29 Mar to 30 Sep: daily, 1000 to 1800,1 to 31 Oct: daily, 1000 to 1700
Other restrictions: Opening times are subject to change, for up-to-date information contact English Heritage by phone or visit the website.

General description:
The monastery was first established at Muchelney by Ine, a 7th century King of Wessex. It did not survive the Viking invasions, but the abbey was refounded about AD950 and lasted for nearly six centuries. The present remains date largely from the 12th century. The best-preserved feature of the site today is the Abbot's Lodging which had only just been completed when the abbey was surrendered to Henry VIII in 1539.

Internet home pages:
http://www.english-heritage.org.uk

1843
MUIR STREET MUSEUMS
See - Low Parks Museum

1844
MULL AND WEST HIGHLAND NARROW GAUGE RAILWAY
Old Pier Station, Craignure, Isle of Mull, Argyll, PA65 6AY

Tel: 01680 812494 or 812567
Fax: 01680 300595
Email: torosay@aol.com
Acronym or abbreviation: Mull Rail
Formed: 1980

Organisation type and purpose: Service industry.
Tourist railway.

Enquiries to: Chairman
Direct tel: 01680 812421
Other contacts: (1) Operations Manger (2) Marketing/Sales Director for (1) Operation of the railway (2) Services available.
Access:
Access to staff: By letter, by telephone, by fax, by email, in person, Internet web pages
Hours: Mon to Fri, 0900 to 1700
Other restrictions: Railway closed mid-Oct to Easter; contact should be made by fax or 01680 812494 or 812421.
Access for disabled people: ramped entry

General description:
Running the narrow guage steam and diesel railway from Craignure Station, linking the ferry to Torosay Castle. Expertise on the building of 260mm gauge railways and sourcing of materials.
Publications list:
is available in hard copy.
Printed publications:
Guide books, postcards etc
Timetable (free)

Internet home pages:
http://www.mullrail.co.uk

1845
MULL MUSEUM
Columba Buildings, Main Street, Tobermory, Isle of Mull, Argyll, PA75 6NU

Tel: 01688 302493
Full name: Isle of Mull Museum Trust
Formed: 1972

Organisation type and purpose: Independently owned, registered charity (charity number SCO 000223), museum, suitable for ages: 8+.
The Isle of Mull Life from first man to present day.

Enquiries to: Curator
Other contacts: Archivist for archive type queries.
Access:
Access to staff: By letter, by telephone
Access to building, collections or gallery: No prior appointment required
Hours: Mon to Fri, 1000 to 1600
Access for disabled people: level entry, access to all public areas
Other restrictions: Access to all areas except for archive and library.

General description:
Life on the Isle of Mull, some family history.
Information services:
Catalogue of archives - Published.
Special visitor services: Materials and/or activities for children..
Collections:
Collection of 3000+ photographs (database and card index) almost entirely Mull subjects
Catalogues:
Catalogue for part of the collections is only available in-house.
Printed publications:
Isle of Mull Museum Archive List (1999)

1846
MULLACH BAN FOLK MUSEUM
Tullymacrieve, Mullach Ban, Co Armagh, BT35 9XA

Tel: 028 3088 8278
Fax: 028 3088 8100
Email: michealmccoy@ireland.com
Formed: 1965
Formerly: Mullach Ban Folklore and Historical Society

Organisation type and purpose: Membership association (membership is by election or invitation), present number of members: 25, museum.

Enquiries to: Director
Access:
Access to staff: By email
Access to building, collections or gallery: Prior appointment required
Access for disabled people: toilet facilities

General description:
Roadside cottage (thatched) contains artefacts pertaining to turn of the century (19th) agricultural society.
Printed publications:
A series of volumes on local society in the region (for purchase only)

1847
MULTIMEDIA TEAM LIMITED, THE
National Museums of Scotland, 11a High Street, Dingwall, Ross-shire, IV15 9RU

Tel: 01349 866370
Fax: 01349 866351
Email: info@theteam.demon.co.uk
Acronym or abbreviation: TMT Limited
Formed: 1993
Formed from: National Museums of Scotland

Organisation type and purpose: International organisation, service industry, museum, suitable for ages: all ages, consultancy.
Production of interactive multimedia programmes for cultural and educational organisations for use in galleries, schools, museums etc. Project management consultancy.
Enterprise company of:
National Museums of Scotland
Chambers Street, Edinburgh, EH1 1JF, tel: 0131 225 7534
Other main office:
The Multimedia Team Limited, National Museums of Scotland
Chambers Street, Edinburgh, EH1 1JF, tel: 0131 247 4437, fax: 0131 247 4304, email/website: info@theteam.demon.co.uk

Enquiries to: Managing Director
Direct tel: 0131 247 4433
Direct fax: 0131 247 4304
Direct email: mike@theteam.demon.co.uk
Other contacts: Project Manager for general enquiries.
Access:
Access to staff: By letter, by telephone, by fax, by email, visitors by prior appointment, Internet web pages
Access to building, collections or gallery: Prior appointment required
Hours: Mon to Fri, 0900 to 1730

General description:
Scottish history and culture, e-learning, web development, digital interpretation of collections.
Collections:
Access to database of National Museums of Scotland
Publications list:
is available on-line.
Electronic and video products:
Investigating The Lewis Chess Pieces (CD-ROM)
Looking for Vikings (CD-ROM)
Scottish Currency (CD-ROM)

Address for ordering publications:
Printed publications:
Dingwall Office

Internet home pages:
http://team.nms.ac.uk
The Multimedia Team website.

1848
MUNCASTER CASTLE
Ravenglass, Cumbria, CA18 1RQ

Tel: 01229 717614
Fax: 01229 717010
Email: info@muncaster.co.uk

Organisation type and purpose: Independently owned, historic building, house or site.

Enquiries to: Administrator
Other contacts: Marketing Director for event and exhibition information.
Access:
Access to staff: By letter, by telephone, by fax, by email, in person
Access for disabled people: Parking provided, ramped entry, toilet facilities
Other restrictions: Access to ground floor of the castle only

Information services:
Library available for reference (for conditions see Access above)
Special visitor services: Tape recorded guides.
Education services: Group education facilities, resources for Key Stages 1 and 2.
Services for disabled people: For the hearing impaired; displays and/or information at wheelchair height.
Collections:
Pictures, books, documents, embroideries (Oriental and English), tapestries
Persian rugs and lace
Toy soldiers (on loan from Abbott Hall, Kendal)
17th century furniture
European works of art
Catalogues:
Catalogue for part of the collections is only available in-house.
Printed publications:
Guide Book (£2)
Postcards
Accommodation, wedding and corporate information

Internet home pages:
http://www.muncaster.com

1849
MUNICIPAL ART GALLERY & MUSEUM, WOLVERHAMPTON
See - Wolverhampton Art Gallery

1850
MUNICIPAL TRAMWAYS ASSOCIATION

Acronym or abbreviation: MTA
See - National Tramway Museum

1851
SIR ALFRED MUNNINGS ART MUSEUM

Castle House, Dedham, Colchester, Essex, CO7 6AZ

Tel: 01206 322127
Fax: 01206 322127 (office hours only)
Formed: 1961
Formerly: Castle House Trust

Organisation type and purpose: Registered charity (charity number 310671), museum, art gallery.

Enquiries to: Administrator
Access:
Access to staff: By letter, by telephone
Hours: Mon to Fri, 0930 to 1230
Other restrictions: Museum open from Easter Sun to 1st Sun in Oct.
Access to building, collections or gallery: No prior appointment required
Hours: Sun, Wed and Bank Holiday Mon, 1400 to 1700; additionally Thu and Sat in Aug, 1400 to 1700

General description:
The life and works of Sir Alfred Munnings, KCVO, PRA. President of the Royal Academy 1944-1949.
Castle House is the home, studios and grounds where Sir Alfred Munnings lived and worked from 1919 until his death in 1959. Along with his original furniture in the part-Tudor, part-Georgian house is a large permanent collection of his work, including many examples of the racing theme, together with paintings demonstrating his great versatility.
Each year there is a special exhibition.
Catalogues:
Catalogue for part of the collections is only available in-house.
Publications list:
is available in hard copy and online.
Printed publications:
Prints, greeting cards, postcards, notelets, tea towel
Sir Alfred Munnings 1878 to 1959 an appreciation (Booth S, book, £7 plus p&p UK £2.50)
Catalogue, list of paintings on exhibition for season (50p)
The following publications available free or for purchase, direct:
Guide to House (brochure, £1.50, plus p&p UK £2.50)

1852
MURTON PARK

See - Yorkshire Museum of Farming

1853
MUSEUM AND LIBRARY OF ORDER OF ST JOHN

St John's Gate, St John's Lane, Clerkenwell, London, EC1M 4DA

Tel: 020 7324 4070
Fax: 020 7336 0587
Email: museum@nhq.sja.org.uk
Acronym or abbreviation: The Order of St John
Full name: The Priory of England and the Islands of the Most Venerable Order of the Hospital of St John of Jerusalem
Formed: 1888
Formerly: The Grand Priory of the Most Venerable Order of the Hospital of St John of Jerusalem, date of change, 1997

Organisation type and purpose: Registered charity (charity number 1077265), museum, historic building, house or site.
Order of Chivalry.
The museum and library aims to make the history of the Order and its foundation available to members of St John in particular and the widest possible public in general. The museum and library collects, conserves, researches, interprets and displays material evidence of the Order of St John in the widest sense.
The Order of St John founded:
St John Ambulance
National Headquarters, 1 Grosvenor Crescent, London, SW1X 7EF, tel: 020 7324 4000, fax: 020 7324 4001, email/website: info@nhq.sja.org.uk

Enquiries to: Curator
Other contacts: Deputy Curator
Access:
Access to staff: By letter, by email, Internet web pages

General description:
Clerkenwell, heraldry, Order of St John of Jerusalem, Crusades, first aid and first aid training, hygiene, nursing in general, Islington, Cyprus, Malta, Rhodes, Middle and Near East, St John Ambulance in the Boer War, WWI, WWII, family history of St John members, military religious orders.
Collections:
Museum and library
History of the Order of St John of Jerusalem, of Rhodes and of Malta (the Knights Hospitallers); Cyprus; Holy Land; Rhodes; Malta; heraldry; genealogy; history of the Crusades and military religious Orders; medieval Order properties in Britain and Europe
History of St John Ambulance Association and Brigade
Local history of Clerkenwell and Islington
Catalogues:
Catalogue for library is in-house only. Catalogue for part of the collections is available in-house and part is published.
Publications list:
is available in hard copy.
Printed publications:
St John Historical Society Proceedings (annually)
First Aid Manuals, and other books on first aid
Information packs (free)
Books and pamphlets on the work and history of the order including:
Hospitallers - The History of the Order of St John (Riley-Smith J)
The Crusades: Cultures in Conflict (Kernaghan P)
The First Crusaders 1095-1131 (Riley-Smith J)
The Military Orders - Fighting for the Faith and Caring for the Sick (Barber M ed)
Microform products:
Slide pack
Electronic and video products:
The Story of the Eight-Pointed Cross (Video, £15)
Multimedia exhibits on site

Internet home pages:
http://www.sja.org.uk/history
Site includes information on the history of the Order of St John and visiting the museum and library, and/or using its services.

1854
MUSEUM BHARRAIGH AGUS BHATARSAIDH

See - Barra Heritage & Cultural Centre

1855
MUSEUM BOOKSHOP, THE

36 Great Russell Street, London, WC1B 3QB

Tel: 020 7580 4086
Fax: 020 7436 4364
Email: mbooks@btconnect.com
Formed: 1979

Organisation type and purpose: Retail bookshop, specialities: ancient history; conservation, museum studies.

Enquiries to: Managing Director
Access:
Access to staff: By letter, by telephone, by fax, by email
Access to building, collections or gallery: No prior appointment required
Hours: Mon to Sun, 1000 to 1730

General description:
Egyptology; Middle East; Classical Archaeology; Roman and Prehistoric Britain; museum studies and conservation.
Publications list:
is available in hard copy and online.

Internet home pages:
http://www.themuseumbookshop.com

1856
MUSEUM ETHNOGRAPHERS GROUP

National Museums of Scotland, Chambers Street, Edinburgh, EH1 1JF

Tel: 0131 247 4065
Fax: 0131 247 4070
Acronym or abbreviation: MEG
Formed: 1976

Organisation type and purpose: Membership association (membership is by subscription), voluntary organisation, registered charity (charity number 1023150).
To promote the understanding of Museum Ethnography and encourage the exchange of information.

Enquiries to: Secretary
Access:
Access to staff: By letter, by fax

General description:
Ethnographic collections in the UK via membership; curatorial, conservation specialists.
Publications list:
is available in hard copy.
Printed publications:
Journal of Museum Ethnography (yearly)
MEG News (quarterly)
Occasional Papers

1857
MUSEUM IN DOCKLANDS

Docklands Library and Archives, No 1 Warehouse, West India Quay, Hertsmere Road, London, E14 4AL

Tel: 020 7001 9800
Fax: 020 7001 9801
Email: info@museumsindocklands.org.uk
Formed: 1984

Organisation type and purpose: Museum, historic building, house or site, suitable for ages: 5+.
Parent body:
Museum of London
150 London Wall, tel: 020 7600 3699
Funded jointly by:
Corporation of London (COL)
Department for Culture, Media and Sport (DCMS)
Museum:
Museum in Docklands
At same address

Enquiries to: Librarian & Archivist
Direct tel: 020 7001 9825
Direct email: bobaspinall@museumsindocklands.org.uk
Access:
Access to staff: By letter, by telephone, by fax, by email, visitors by prior appointment
Hours: Mon to Fri, 0900 to 1700
Access for disabled people: Parking provided, ramped entry, access to all public areas, toilet facilities

continued overleaf

Other restrictions: Dedicated disabled persons lift

General description:
The history and development of the Port of London from 1770 to date, including the current regeneration of London's Docklands, the enclosed docks and riverside wharves, the docks and river, cargo handling, dock trades, dock police, dock equipment, labour history of the docks, tools and equipment used in the docks.

Collections:
20,000 photographs of docks and river
British Ports Authority archive covering the port transport industry nationally from 1911-1975
Coal Meter's Society archive *c.* 1750 to *c.* 1980
Data on the registered dock labour force in London (1950-1988)
Data on the trade of the port of London (1800 to the present)
Docklands Forum archive 1975-1995
Historic films of docks 1921-1970
Port of London Authority records 1909 to date (historic records only ie non-operational)
Records of the Corporation of London River Thames Committee (1770-1857) and the Thames Conservators (1857-1909)
The surviving business records of the private dock companies operating on the Thames (1799-1909)

Catalogues:
Catalogue for library is in-house only. Catalogue for all of the collections is only available in-house.

Trade and statistical:
Data on the trade of the Port of London (1800 to the present).
Data on the registered dock labour force in London 1950-1988.

Printed publications:
Dockland Life: historic and social history 1860-1970 (for sale)
Gateway to the East (for sale)
Liquid History: the first 50 years of the PLA (for sale)

Electronic and video products:
City of Ships (1938) video (for sale)
Waters of Time (1951) video (for sale)

1858
MUSEUM IN DOCKLANDS

No 1 Warehouse, West India Quay, Hertsmere Road, London, E14 4AL

Tel: 020 7001 9800
Fax: 020 7001 9801
Email: info@museumindocklands.org.uk
Formed: 2003

Organisation type and purpose: Museum, historic building, house or site, suitable for ages: 5+.

Parent body:
Museum of London

Funded jointly by:
Corporation of London (COL)
Department for Culture, Media and Sport (DCMS)

Museum in Docklands:
Docklands Library and Archives
At same address

Enquiries to: Strategic Development Officer
Direct tel: 020 7001 9821

Access:
Access to staff: By letter, by telephone, by fax, by email
Access to building, collections or gallery: No prior appointment required
Hours: Mon to Sat, 1000 to 1800; Sun, 1200 to 1800
Other restrictions: Opening Easter 2003
Access for disabled people: Parking provided, ramped entry, access to all public areas, toilet facilities
Other restrictions: Dedicated disabled person's lift

General description:
Displays about the river, port and people of London from Roman times to the present day.

Information services:
Guided tours may be booked
Educational interpretation department
Dedicated children's gallery
Auditorium for corporate hire, lectures etc
Video displays throughout the museum
Information available in French, German, Spanish, Italian, Japanese, Urdu and Cantonese.
Special visitor services: Guided tours, materials and/or activities for children.
Education services: Group education facilities.
Services for disabled people: For the hearing impaired; displays and/or information at wheelchair height.

Catalogues:
Catalogue for all of the collections is only available in-house.

Internet home pages:
http://www.museumindocklands.org.uk

1859
MUSEUM IN THE PARK

Stroud District Museum Service, Stratford Park, Stroud, Gloucestershire, GL5 4AF

Tel: 01453 763394
Fax: 01453 752400
Email: museum@stroud.gov.uk
Formed: 1899
Formed from: Cowle Trust
Formerly: Stroud District Museum, date of change, 2001

Organisation type and purpose: Local government body, registered charity (charity number 311486), museum, art gallery, historic building, house or site, suitable for ages: all ages.

Parent body:
Stroud District Council
Ebley Mill, Stroud, Gloucestershire

Enquiries to: Curator

Access:
Access to staff: By letter, by telephone, by email, visitors by prior appointment
Access to building, collections or gallery: No prior appointment required
Hours: Tue to Fri, 1300 to 1700; Sat, Sun, 1100 to 1600
Other restrictions: Appointment necessary to view reserve collections.
Access for disabled people: Parking provided, level entry, access to all public areas, toilet facilities

General description:
Archaeology, geology, social history, industrial history, decorative arts.

Information services:
Special visitor services: Materials and/or activities for children.
Education services: Group education facilities.
Services for disabled people: For the hearing impaired; displays and/or information at wheelchair height.

Collections:
Fisher Collection of lace
Local dinosaur bones and other fossils
Roman altars

Catalogues:
Catalogue for all of the collections is only available in-house.

1860
MUSEUM NAN EILEAN

Sgoil Lionacleit, Lionacleit, Benbecula, Western Isles, HS7 5PJ

Tel: 01870 602864
Fax: 01870 602053
Email: danamacphee@cne-siar.gov.uk
Formed: 1988

Organisation type and purpose: Local government body, museum, suitable for ages: 5+.

Parent body:
Comhairle Nan Eilean Siar
Sandwick Road, Stornoway, Isle of Lewis, Western Isles, tel: 01851 703773

Other addresses:
Museum Nan Eilean
Francis Street, Stornoway, Isle of Lewis, Western Isles, tel: 01851 703773, fax: 01851 706318

Enquiries to: Museums Officer

Access:
Access to staff: By letter, by telephone, by fax, by email, in person, visitors by prior appointment, Internet web pages
Access to building, collections or gallery: No prior appointment required
Hours: Mon, Wed, Thu, 0900 to 1600; Tue, Fri, 0900 to 1900; Sat, 1100 to 1600
Access for disabled people: Parking provided, level entry, access to all public areas, toilet facilities

General description:
Changing exhibition programme covering aspects of Island life, including crofting and other social history topics.

Collections:
Collections cover aspects of Island lifestyle, language and culture, these include agricultural artefacts, oral readings and photographs

Catalogues:
Catalogue for all of the collections is only available in-house.

Internet home pages:
http://www.cne-siar.gov.uk
Exhibition programme and contact details.

1861
MUSEUM OF ADVERTISING

See - Advertising Archives

1862
MUSEUM OF ADVERTISING & PACKAGING

Albert Warehouse, The Docks, Gloucester, GL1 2EH

Tel: 01452 302309
Formed: 1984

Organisation type and purpose: Museum.

Enquiries to: Curator

General description:
Advertising, packaging and social history 1850 to present.

Collections:
Television commercial programmes
The Robert Opie Collection (300,000 items relating to the history of the consumer society)

Internet home pages:
http://www.themuseum.co.uk

1863
MUSEUM OF ANTIQUITIES

See - National Museums of Scotland

1864
MUSEUM OF ANTIQUITIES

University of Newcastle upon Tyne, Newcastle upon Tyne, NE1 7RU

Tel: 0191 222 7849
Fax: 0191 222 8561
Email: m.o.antiquities@ncl.ac.uk
Full name: Museum of Antiquities of the University and Society of Antiquaries of Newcastle upon Tyne
Formed: 1960
Formerly: Society of Antiquaries of Newcastle upon Tyne

Organisation type and purpose: Museum.
The mission of the Museum of Antiquities is to curate, display and enhance the collections in its care, and disseminate archaeological information by publication and educational services.

Connected with:
University of Newcastle upon Tyne
Kensington Terrace, Newcastle upon Tyne

Enquiries to: Director

Direct email: l.allason-jones@ncl.ac.uk
Access:
Access to staff: By letter, by telephone, by fax, by email, visitors by prior appointment
Hours: Mon to Sat, 0900 to 1700
Access for disabled people: ramped entry, access to all public areas

General description:
Archaeology of the North of England, particularly the Romans and Hadrian's Wall; Prehistoric, Roman, Anglo-Saxon and medieval collections chiefly from Northumberland; models of Hadrian's Wall and Mithraeum.
Information services:
Selective dissemination services
Special visitor services: Guided tours.
Education services: Group education facilities, resources for Key Stages 2, 3, 4 and Further or Higher Education.
Services for disabled people: For the visually impaired.
Collections:
The following are all slides or photographs:
Aerial photographic collection
Hadrian's Wall archive, photographs of Hadrian's Wall, 19th-20th century, 3000 plus items
Pearce Collection
Sellars Collection
Gertrude Bell archive. Photographs of Middle East, 1890-1926, 6000 items
Libyan Society archive. Plans, photographs, etc of Libya, 19th-20th century
Catalogues:
Catalogue for library is in-house only. Catalogue for all of the collections is available in-house and part is on-line.
Publications list:
is available in hard copy and online.
Printed publications:
A Guide to the Inscribed and Sculptured Stones in the Museum of Antiquities (Allason-Jones L, 1989)
Beakers from Northumberland (Tait J, 1965, out of print)
Bronze Age Metalwork in Northern England, 100-700 (Burgess, C B, 1968, out of print)
Catalogue of the Anglo-Saxon and Viking Antiquities in the Museum of Antiquities, Newcastle upon Tyne (Cramp R J and Miket R, 1982)
Catalogue of the Early Northumbrian Coins in the Museum of Antiquities, Newcastle upon Tyne (Pirie E E, 1982)
Catalogue of the Romano-British Ironwork in the Museum of Antiquities, Newcastle upon Tyne (Manning W H, 1976)
Hadrian's Wall in Models (Smith, D J, 2nd ed, rev 1969 out of print; reprint being considered)
Illustrated Introduction to the Museum of Antiquities (Smith D J, 1974)
Mithras and his Temples on the Wall (Daniels C M, 3rd ed, rev 1989)

Address for ordering publications:
Printed publications:
SOP Manager, Museum of Antiquities
University of Newcastle upon Tyne, tel: 0191 222 8560, fax: 0191 222 8561, email: c.e.riley@ncl.ac.uk

Internet home pages:
http://www.ncl.ac.uk/antiquities
Includes exhibitions; object of the month; catalogue of the aerial photographic collection and an archive of Roman military equipment (Armamentarium).

1865
MUSEUM OF ARCHAEOLOGY
Durham University
See - Durham University

1866
MUSEUM OF ARCHAEOLOGY
God's House Tower, Winkle Street, Southampton, SO14 2NY

Tel: 023 8063 5904
Fax: 023 8033 9601
Email: historic.sites@southampton.gov.uk
Formed: 1960

Organisation type and purpose: Local government body, museum, historic building, house or site, suitable for ages: 5+.
Parent body:
Southampton City Council
Civic Centre, Southampton, SO14 7LP, tel: 023 8083 3333, fax: 023 8083 3381
Branch of:
Cultural Services
Civic Centre, Southampton, SO14 7LP, tel: 023 8063 5904, fax: 023 8033 9601, email/website: historic.sites@southampton.gov.uk

Enquiries to: Curator of Archaeological Collections
Other contacts: Cultural Services Manager for head of service covering museums.
Access:
Access to staff: By letter, by telephone, by fax, by email, in person

General description:
Artefacts from the Palaeolithic period through to the post-medieval from Southampton and the hinterland. The section relating to Saxon and medieval urban development is of international importance.
Designated status awarded 1997.
Information services:
Educational services and guided tours, by arrangement.
Special visitor services: Materials and/or activities for children.
Education services: Group education facilities, resources for Key Stages 1 and 2 and 3..
Catalogues:
Catalogue for all of the collections is on-line.

Internet home pages:
http://www.southampton.gov.uk/leisure/heritage/mus_arch.htm
Information about archaeological collections.
http://www.southampton.gov.uk/leisure/heritage
Information about the building and permanent exhibitions.

1867
MUSEUM OF ARMY FLYING
Middle Wallop, Stockbridge, Andover, Hampshire, SO20 8DY

Tel: 01980 674421
Fax: 01264 781694
Email: enquiries@flying-museum.org.uk
Formed: 1984

Organisation type and purpose: Professional body, registered charity (charity number 297897), museum, suitable for ages: 5+.

Enquiries to: Chief Executive
Direct fax: 01264 781086
Other contacts: Marketing Manager
Access:
Access to staff: By letter, by telephone, by fax, by email, visitors by prior appointment, Internet web pages
Hours: Mon to Fri, 1000 to 1630
Other restrictions: Archives by appointment only.
Access to building, collections or gallery: No prior appointment required
Hours: Mon to Fri, 1000 to 1630
Access for disabled people: Parking provided, ramped entry, level entry
Other restrictions: Lift, wheelchair.

General description:
A celebration of over 100 years of army aviation.
Information services:
Library available for reference (for conditions see Access above)
Special visitor services: Guided tours, materials and/or activities for children.
Education services: Group education facilities.
Services for disabled people: Displays and/or information at wheelchair height.
Collections:
Home to one of the country's finest historical collections of military kites, gliders, aeroplanes and helicopters
Dioramas and static displays trave the development of army flying from pre World War I to today's Army Air Corps
Catalogues:
Catalogue for library is in-house only. Catalogue for all of the collections is only available in-house.
Printed publications:
Various aviation books
Microform products:
Archival CD-ROM available late 2000
Electronic and video products:
Aviation videos

Address for ordering publications:
Printed publications:
Shop Manager
Tel: 01980 674421 ext 4421

Internet home pages:
http://www.flying-museum.org.uk

1868
MUSEUM OF ARMY TRANSPORT
Flemingate, Beverley, East Yorkshire, HU17 0NG

Tel: 01482 860445
Fax: 01482 872767
Formed: 1984

Organisation type and purpose: Registered charity (charity number 513683), museum, suitable for ages: 5+.

Enquiries to: Curator
Other contacts: Manager for group and school visits.
Access:
Access to staff: By letter, by telephone, by fax, visitors by prior appointment
Access to building, collections or gallery: No prior appointment required
Hours: Daily, 1000 to 1700
Other restrictions: Closed 24 Dec to 2 Jan. Entry fee.
Access for disabled people: Parking provided, level entry, toilet facilities
Other restrictions: Access to 95% of areas.

General description:
Army transport, vehicles and aircraft.
Information services:
Services for disabled people: Displays and/or information at wheelchair height.
Collections:
Over 110 vehicles on display showing methods of Army transport from Crimean War to present day
Last remaining Blackburn Beverley Aircraft
Archive Department - charge made for research

Internet home pages:
http://www.museum-of-army-transport.co.uk

1869
MUSEUM OF ARTILLERY IN THE ROTUNDA
Repository Road, Woolwich, London, SE18 4BQ

Formed: 1778

Organisation type and purpose: Museum. Managed by the Royal Artillery Historical Trust and staffed by the Royal Artillery Institution.
Parent body:
Royal Artillery Historical Trust
c/o Firepower, The Royal Artillery Museum
Museum:
Firepower

continued overleaf

Royal Artillery Museum, Royal Arsenal (West), Warren Lane, Woolwich, London, SE18 6ST, tel: 020 8855 7755, fax: 020 8855 7100, email/website:
research@firepower.org.uk
www.firepower.org.uk

Enquiries to: Curator

General description:
Land service (army) ordnance artefacts.
Collections:
Reserve collection for Firepower, The Royal Artillery Museum
British ordnance and artillery, 15th century to the present day; rockets from the 18th century; artillery ammunition; sidearms connected with artillery service
Printed publications:
Catalogues

1870
MUSEUM OF BADGES AND BATTLEDRESS
Bedale

Closed, date of change, 1999

1871
MUSEUM OF BARNSTAPLE & NORTH DEVON
The Square, Barnstaple, Devon, EX32 9BG

Tel: 01271 346747
Email: museum@northdevon.gov.uk
Formerly: Museum of North Devon

General description:
Housed in a Victorian house, the museum tells the story of North Devon and its historic centre, Barnstaple, from its formation to the present day.
Information services:
Identification and dating of artefacts (not valuations).
Special visitor services: Guided tours, materials and/or activities for children..
Collections:
Geology, natural history and archaeology of North Devon
North Devon pottery
North Devon at war
Catalogues:
Catalogue for part of the collections is only available in-house.

Internet home pages:
http://www.devonmuseums.net/barnstaple

1872
MUSEUM OF BERKSHIRE AVIATION
Mohawk Way, Woodley, Reading, Berkshire, RG5 4UE

Tel: 0118 944 8089 or 0118 934 0712
Email: Museumof BerkshireAviaition@fly.to
Formed: 1991

Organisation type and purpose: Registered charity (charity number 1008856), museum, suitable for ages: 5+, research organisation.

Enquiries to: Archivist
Access:
Access to staff: By letter only
Access to building, collections or gallery: Prior appointment required
Hours: Wed, Sat, Sun, 1030 to 1700
Winter: Wed, Sun, 1200 to 1600
Access for disabled people: Parking provided, ramped entry, toilet facilities
Other restrictions: Access to all areas except for Mezzanine.

General description:
History of aviation in Berkshire.
Information services:
Special visitor services: Guided tours..
Catalogues:
Catalogue for library is in-house only. Catalogue for all of the collections is only available in-house.
Electronic and video products:
Video

Internet home pages:
http://fly.to/MuseumofBerkshireAviation

1873
MUSEUM OF BRITISH PEWTER
Harvard House, High Street, Stratford-upon-Avon, Warwickshire, CV37 6HB

Tel: 01789 204507

Organisation type and purpose: Registered charity (charity number 209302), museum, historic building, house or site.
Parent body:
Shakespeare Trust
Tel: 01789 204016

Enquiries to: Marketing Manager
Direct tel: 01789 201807
Direct fax: 01789 263138
Direct email: info@shakespeare.org.uk
Access:
Access to staff: By letter, by telephone, by fax, by email

General description:
British pewter.
Collections:
Neish Collection of Pewter

1874
MUSEUM OF BRITISH ROAD TRANSPORT
St Agnes Lane, Hales Street, Coventry, Warwickshire, CV1 1PN

Tel: 024 7683 2425
Fax: 024 7683 2465
Email: museum@mbrt.co.uk
Acronym or abbreviation: MBRT
Formed: 1980

Organisation type and purpose: Local government body, museum, suitable for ages: 5+.

Enquiries to: Development Officer
Direct email: lucy.rumble@coventry.gov.uk
Other contacts: (1) Curator (2) Archive Assistant for enquiries relating specifically to the collection.
Access:
Access to staff: By letter, by telephone, by fax, by email, in person, visitors by prior appointment, Internet web pages
Hours: Mon to Sun, 1000 to 1700
Access to building, collections or gallery: No prior appointment required
Hours: Museum only: daily, 1000 to 1700
Other restrictions: Archive open Mon to Fri, 1000 to 1630, by appointment only.
Access for disabled people: level entry, access to all public areas, toilet facilities

General description:
Road transport in general to date; history of vehicle manufacture in Coventry; history of the manufacture of cycles specific in Coventry; general history of motor vehicle and cycle technology; social history of motor manufacture in Coventry.
Collections:
Books: a small specialist library is available for consultation
Computer: all major objects catalogued on Calm 2000 Laser disk/database of Daimler photographs
Documents: assorted documents, correspondence, sales material relating to a number of Coventry companies, especially the Rootes Group; specific company vehicle chassis registers
Objects: 200 cars and commercial vehicles 1896 to date; 200 cycles 1818 to date; 90 motorcycles 1920 to date; 'Thrust 2' and the land speed record story; Tiatsa Model Collection
Photographic Collection: 170,000 negatives relating to the Rootes Group (Humber, Hillman, Sunbeam, Talbot, Singer, Commer Karrier and others); 4000 Glass Plate Negatives relating to the Daimler Company (mostly pre 1st World War); 100 negatives relating to the Alvis Company; large photographic archive relating to vehicle factories of Coventry companies
Catalogues:
Catalogue for part of the collections is published.
Printed publications:
Assorted educational publications relating to the collection available direct from the museum

Internet home pages:
http://www.mbrt.co.uk
General information on museum.

1875
MUSEUM OF CANNOCK CHASE
Valley Road, Hednesford, Cannock, Staffordshire, WS12 5TD

Tel: 01543 877666
Fax: 01543 428272
Email: museum@cannockchasedc.gov.uk
Formed: 1998
Formerly: Valley Heritage Centre, date of change, 1998

Organisation type and purpose: Local government body, museum, suitable for ages: all ages.
Member of:
North Staffordshire Museums Association

Enquiries to: Principal Leisure Strategy & Development Officer
Other contacts: (1) Visitor Services Officer; (2) Museum Services Officer for (2) education.
Access:
Access to staff: By letter, by telephone, by fax, by email, in person, Internet web pages
Hours: Mon to Fri, 1100 to 1600
Other restrictions: Library for reference only by appointment.
Access to building, collections or gallery: No prior appointment required
Hours: Oct to Easter: Mon to Fri, 1100 to 1600
Easter to Sep: daily, 1100 to 1700
Other restrictions: Last admissions, 30 minutes before closing.
Closed for 2 weeks at Christmas.
Visitors by prior appointment outside normal opening hours.
Access for disabled people: Parking provided, ramped entry, level entry, access to all public areas, toilet facilities
Other restrictions: Lift, stairlift.

General description:
Local history, coal-mining, social history from the Cannock Chase District, mainly 19th and 20th century.
Information services:
Library available for reference (for conditions see Access above)
Tourist information point.
Special visitor services: Materials and/or activities for children.
Education services: Group education facilities, resources for Key Stages 1 and 2.
Services for disabled people: For the hearing impaired.

Collections:
Artefacts, photographs (database), books, documents relating to local history, and social history
Coal-mining, small artefacts used in coal-mining and mines on Cannock Chase coalfield
Books, union records, etc. 19th century to the present, c. 400
Catalogues:
Catalogue for library is in-house only. Catalogue for all of the collections is only available in-house.
Publications list:
is available in hard copy.
Printed publications:
Childhood Memories of a Miners Son (£2.50)
Dark & Dirty (the story of mining, for teachers, £3.95)
Toys and Games Teacher's Pack (£4.50)
Wizard of the Turf (£2)

Internet home pages:
http://www.museumofcannockchase.co.uk
Guide to the museum and its services.

1876
MUSEUM OF CHILDHOOD AT BETHNAL GREEN
Cambridge Heath Road, Bethnal Green, London, E2 9PA

Tel: 020 8980 2415
Fax: 020 8983 5225
Email: bgmc@vam.ac.uk
Formed: 1872
Formerly: Bethnal Green Museum of Childhood

Organisation type and purpose: National organisation, museum, suitable for ages: 5+.
Branch of:
The Victoria and Albert Museum (V&A)
Tel: 020 7942 5000

Enquiries to: Marketing Manager
Direct tel: 020 8980 5227
Direct fax: 020 8980 5225
Direct email: k.bines@vam.ac.uk
Access:
Access to staff: By letter, by telephone, by fax, by email, in person, visitors by prior appointment, Internet web pages
Access to building, collections or gallery: Prior appointment required
Hours: Daily, 1000 to 1750; closed Fri
Access for disabled people: Parking provided, ramped entry, level entry, access to all public areas, toilet facilities

General description:
A museum devoted to the material culture of childhood. There are major gallery displays and a research collection of toys (including dolls, dolls' houses, games and puppets). There is a children's book library (no public access at present). Also other displays and collections relating to childhood (e.g. children's dress, nursery antiques).
Information services:
Special visitor services: Materials and/or activities for children.
Education services: Group education facilities, resources for Key Stages 1 and 2..
Collections:
Renier Collection, historic and contemporary publications for children, 1585-present, 80,000 items

Internet home pages:
http://www.museumofchildhood.org.uk

1877
MUSEUM OF CHILDHOOD
42 High Street, Edinburgh, EH11 1TG

Tel: 0131 529 4142
Fax: 0131 558 3103
Email: admin@museumofchildhoo.fsnet.co.uk
Formed: 1955

Organisation type and purpose: Local government body, museum, suitable for ages: all ages.
Affiliated to:
City of Edinburgh Council

Enquiries to: Curator
Direct tel: 0131 529 4119
Other contacts: Marketing and Sponsorship Officer
Access:
Access to staff: By letter, by telephone, by fax, by email, in person, visitors by prior appointment
Hours: Curator, Mon to Fri, 0900 to 1700
Access to building, collections or gallery: No prior appointment required
Hours: Mon to Sat, 1000 to 1700; Sun during Jul and Aug, 1200 to 1700
Access for disabled people: level entry, toilet facilities

General description:
First museum in the world devoted to the experience of childhood.
Childhood-related subjects: toys, indoor and outdoor games, dolls, skills and hobbies, puppets, education, health and welfare, literature, costume, entertainments, ethnographic dolls.
Information services:
Library available for reference (for conditions see Access above)
Brass Rubbing Centre.
6 boxes of objects for handling (Reminiscence) loaned within Edinburgh.
Special visitor services: Materials and/or activities for children..
Collections:
The Lovett collection of ethnographic dolls, puppets
Toys, indoor and outdoor games, dolls, skill and hobby items, education material, child health artefacts, children's books, children's clothes, photographs of children
Catalogues:
Catalogue for all of the collections is only available in-house but part is published.
Publications list:
is available in hard copy.
Printed publications:
Colouring Books
Guides, catalogues, books and leaflets
In For a Penny - illustrated catalogue of money boxes, and savings items
Museum Children's Activity Guide Book
Resource Packs: Victorian Children; Schooldays; Health and Hygiene
The Lovett Collection of Ethnic and Unusual Dolls
Electronic and video products:
Films from the Golden City including:
The Singing Street - street games and songs in Edinburgh, 1951 (video, Norton Park Group)

Internet home pages:
http://www.cac.org.uk
General information, brief description.

1878
MUSEUM OF CHILDHOOD MEMORIES
1 Castle Street, Beaumaris, Anglesey, LL58 8AP

Tel: 01248 712498
Fax: 01248 716869
Email: bryn.brown@amserv.net
Formed: 1973
Formerly: Museum of Childhood

Organisation type and purpose: Independently owned, museum, suitable for ages: all ages. Extension of hobby.

Enquiries to: Owner
Access:
Access for disabled people: level entry
Other restrictions: Ground Floor only; wheelchair users free.

General description:
Children's toys, especially money boxes or savo's.
Collections:
Many tin toys - a collection of 250 children's toy saving boxes

Internet home pages:
http://www.aboutbritain.com/museumofchildhoodmemories.htm

1879
MUSEUM OF COSTUME & TEXTILES
51 Castle Gate, Nottingham, NG1 6AF

Tel: 0115 915 3500

Organisation type and purpose: Museum.
Part of:
Nottingham City Museums and Galleries

Enquiries to: Curator
Direct tel: 0115 915 3540
Access:
Access to staff: By letter, by telephone, visitors by prior appointment
Hours: Wed to Sun, 1000 to 1600 (general enquiries)
Mon to Fri, 1000 to 1800 (specific enquiries)

General description:
Costume: including accessories; textiles: embroidery, woven, printed, knitted; lace: hand-made, machine-made, especially Nottingham-made; fashion.
Collections:
Sample books, fashion magazines, fashion plates
Large collections of costume, some non-European, hand and machine-made lace
Smaller collections of embroideries, textiles (woven, printed, knitted), dolls
Catalogues:
Catalogue for all of the collections is only available in-house.

1880
MUSEUM OF COSTUME
Bath and North East Somerset Council, Heritage Services, Pump Room, Stall Street, Bath, BA1 1LZ

Tel: 01225 477750
Fax: 01225 477271
Email: stephen_bird@bathnes.gov.uk
Formed: 1979
Formerly: Bath Museums Service

Organisation type and purpose: Local government body, museum.
Parent body:
Bath & North East Somerset Council
Includes the:
18th Century Guildhall
Tel: 01225 477724
Fashion Research Centre
4 Circus, Bath, BA1 2EW, tel: 01225 477752, fax: 01225 444793, email/website: costume_enquiries@bathnes.gov.uk
Georgian Garden
Gravel Walk, Bath, tel: 01225 477752, fax: 01225 444793, email/website: costume_enquiries@bathnes.gov.uk
Museum of Costume & Assembly Rooms
Bennett Street, Bath, tel: 01225 477789, fax: 01225 444793, email/website: costume_enquiries@bathnes.gov.uk
Roman Bath Museum & Pump Room
Stall Street, Bath, BA1 1LZ, tel: 01225 477774, fax: 01225 477243
Victoria Art Gallery
Bridge Street, Bath, BA2 4AT, tel: 01225 477772, fax: 01225 477231, email/website: victoria_enquiries@bathnes.gov.uk

Enquiries to: Head of Service
Other contacts: Assistant Keeper Costume for fashion research centre.
Access:
Access to staff: By letter, by telephone, by fax, by email, Internet web pages
Hours: Mon to Fri, 0900 to 1700

continued overleaf

General description:
History and topography of Bath, archaeology of Bath, history of costume and fashion, fine and decorative arts.
Collections:
Collections of Museum objects: archaeology, local history, numismatics, silver, fine and decorative art, costume and textiles, furniture
Doris Langley Moore Costume Collection
Horstmann Collection of Antique Watches
Kimball Collection of Prints
Sunday Times Fashion Archive
Worth and Paquin Fashion Archive
Printed publications:
Victoria Art Gallery programme (twice a year)

Internet home pages:
http://www.romanbaths.co.uk
Virtual tour, 3D video computer reconstruction. On all three sites: museum shops, education, historic buildings venue hire, group bookings, contact, feedback.
http://www.museumofcostume.co.uk
Virtual tour, special exhibitions.
http://www.victoriagal.org.uk
Virtual tour, gallery, what's on.

1881
MUSEUM OF DOLLS AND BYGONE CHILDHOOD

See - Vina Cooke Museum of Dolls and Bygone Childhood

1882
MUSEUM OF DOMESTIC DESIGN & ARCHITECTURE

Middlesex University, Cat Hill, Barnet, Hertfordshire, EN4 8HT

Tel: 020 8411 5244
Fax: 020 8411 6639
Email: moda@mdx.ac.uk
Acronym or abbreviation: MoDA
Formed: 2000
Formerly: Silver Studio Collection

Organisation type and purpose: Museum, university department or institute, suitable for ages: 5+.
Part of:
Middlesex University

Enquiries to: Director
Direct tel: 020 8411 6614
Direct fax: 020 8411 5271
Direct email: k.mannering@mdx.ac.uk
Other contacts: Curator
Access:
Access to staff: By letter, by telephone, by fax, by email, visitors by prior appointment
Hours: Tue to Sat, 1000 to 1700; Sun, 1400 to 1700
Access to building, collections or gallery: No prior appointment required
Hours: Tue to Sat, 1000 to 1700; Sun, 1400 to 1700
Access for disabled people: Parking provided, access to all public areas, toilet facilities

General description:
The Museum of Domestic Design & Architecture, MoDA, houses one of the most important and comprehensive collections of late 19th and 20th century decorative design for the home. Its collections are recognised to be of outstanding national academic importance, and are a unique resource for scholars and design professionals.
Information services:
Library available for reference (for conditions see Access above)
Special visitor services: Guided tours, materials and/or activities for children.
Education services: Group education facilities, resources for Key Stages 1 and 2.
Services for disabled people: Displays and/or information at wheelchair height.
Collections:
MoDA has six collections in its care
Silver Studio Collection is the archive of a commercial studio, which produced designs, mostly for domestic textiles and wallcoverings, between 1880 and 1963
The collection contains over 40,000 designs, 5000 wallpaper samples, 5000 textile samples and the Studio's working records
It is recognised to be of outstanding national academic importance
Domestic Design Collection (1850-1960) contains more than 4000 books, magazines and trade catalogues relating to design for the home and household management
Crown Wallpaper Collection consists of wallpaper pattern books mainly from the 1950s
Sir J M Richards Library is a collection of architectural books and journals collected by Sir J M Richards (1907-1992), a leading spokesman and theorist of the Modern Movement in architecture in Britain
Peggy Angus Archive comprises the contents of the London studio of Peggy Angus (1904-1993), an artist, designer and teacher
Charles Hasler Collection is an archive relating to the work of Charles Hasler (1908-1992), a typographer and designer
Catalogues:
Catalogue for part of the collections is on-line.
Publications list:
is available on-line.
Printed publications:
Publications available direct from Museum Shop
Electronic and video products:
Direct from Museum Shop

Internet home pages:
http://www.moda.mdx.ac.uk

1883
MUSEUM OF EAST ASIAN ART, THE

12 Bennett Street, Bath, BA1 2QL

Tel: 01225 464640
Fax: 01225 461718
Email: museum@east-asian-art.freeserve.co.uk
Formed: 1992

Organisation type and purpose: Registered charity (charity number 328725), museum, suitable for ages: .

Enquiries to: Administrator
Other contacts: Curator for research.
Access:
Access to staff: By letter, by telephone, by fax, by email, visitors by prior appointment, Internet web pages
Hours: Mon to Fri, 1000 to 1700
Access to building, collections or gallery: No prior appointment required
Hours: Tue to Sat, 1000 to 1700; Sun, 1200 to 1700
Access for disabled people: access to all public areas, toilet facilities

General description:
East Asian art and culture, jade, ceramics, metalware.
Information services:
Library available for reference (for conditions see Access above)
Festival Promenade (interactive computer programme).
Special visitor services: Materials and/or activities for children.
Education services: Group education facilities, resources for Key Stages 1 and 2, 3, 4 and Further or Higher Education.
Services for disabled people: For the visually impaired; for the hearing impaired.
Catalogues:
Catalogue for library is in-house only. Catalogue for all of the collections is only available in-house.
Publications list:
is available in hard copy.
Printed publications:
Contact the Museum for details on prices etc for the following publications:
Between Bath & China, Trade and Culture in the West Country 1680 to 1840
Volumes 1-6 of the Museum Journal
Inaugural Exhibition Catalogue, Vol 1 Chinese Ceramics
Inaugural Exhibition Catalogue, Vol 2 Chinese Metalware and Decorative Art
Jades from China
One Hundred Treasures

Address for ordering publications:
Printed publications:
Retail Manager, Museum of East Asian Art at same address

Internet home pages:
http://www.east-asian-art.co.uk
Museum website.

1884
MUSEUM OF EAST YORKSHIRE

See - Sewerby Hall

1885
MUSEUM OF EDINBURGH, THE

142 Canongate, Royal Mile, Edinburgh, EH8 8DD

Tel: 0131 529 4143
Fax: 0131 557 3346
Formed: 1930s
Formerly: Huntly House Museum, date of change, 2000

Organisation type and purpose: Local government body, museum, historic building, house or site.
Part of:
The City of Edinburgh Museums and Galleries Service
Which is a division of:
The City of Edinburgh Council's Culture & Leisure Department
Tel: 0131 200 2000 (Main council) 0131 529 7844 (Culture & Leisure Department HQ)

Enquiries to: Curator
Direct tel: 0131 529 4052
Other contacts: Marketing and Sponsorship Officer
Access:
Access to staff: By telephone, by fax, visitors by prior appointment
Hours: Mon to Sat, 1000 to 1700
During Edinburgh Festival: Sun, 1400 to 1700

General description:
The Museum of Edinburgh is the city's local history museum. It contains extensive collections of Edinburgh silver, glass, pottery and ceramics. Also includes the 1638 National Covenant, and artefacts related to the famous Edinburgh canine character, Greyfriars Bobby.
Collections:
Scottish Pottery, mainly east coast, but other areas represented, 18th-20th century
Edinburgh and Canongate silver, 16th-20th century, 200 items
Life and work of Field Marshal Earl Haig, 19th-20th century, 500 items
Shop signs, mainly from Edinburgh, mainly 3-D figures, 18th-20th century
Ford-Rankin, glass from Edinburgh and Leith, 18th-20th century
Publications list:
is available in hard copy and online.
Printed publications:
The City of Edinburgh Museums and Galleries Service publishes a wide range of material, a list is available by telephoning 0131 529 3983, a selected list is available on our website

Address for ordering publications:
Printed publications:
Publishing Department, The City of Edinburgh Museums and Galleries Service
Tel: 0131 529 3983, email: website: www.cac.org.uk

Internet home pages:
http://www.cac.org.uk
Website for The City of Edinburgh Museums and Galleries Service, it contains: information on each of our 11 venues and their permanent collections; details of current temporary exhibitions; information on past temporary exhibitions; details of selected publications.

1886 MUSEUM OF EDUCATION

See - Scotland Street School Museum

1887 MUSEUM OF ETON LIFE

Eton College, Windsor, Berkshire, SL4 6DB

Tel: 01753 671177
Fax: 01753 671265
Formed: 1985

Organisation type and purpose: Museum.
Parent body:
Provost and Fellows of Eton College

Enquiries to: Visits Manager
Other contacts: Curator and College Archivist for queries on college history; family history.
Access:
Access to staff: By letter, by telephone, by fax, by email
Access to building, collections or gallery: No access other than to staff
Hours: Mar to Oct: Holiday, 1030 to 1630; Term, 1400 to 1630 (exact dates vary each year).
Other restrictions: Prior appointment required for groups.
Occasional closures for school functions.
Access for disabled people: toilet facilities

General description:
History of Eton College and of Etonians. Contains material relating to the daily life and studies of the boys.
Collections:
Objects used at the school. (There are separately administered archives, photographic collections and prints and drawings also relating to the history of Eton College, open by prior appointment.)
Catalogues:
Catalogue for all of the collections is only available in-house.

1888 MUSEUM OF FARMING LIFE

Pitmedden Garden, Ellon, Aberdeenshire, AB41 0PD

Tel: 01651 842352
Fax: 01651 843188
Email: sburgess@nts.org.uk
Formed: 1977

Organisation type and purpose: National organisation, registered charity (charity number SCO 07410), museum, historic building, house or site, suitable for ages: all ages.
Parent body:
National Trust for Scotland
28 Charlotte Square, Edinburgh, tel: 0131 243 9300, fax: 0131 243 9301, email/website: info@nts.org.uk

Enquiries to: Manager
Access:
Access to staff: By letter
Access for disabled people: Parking provided, level entry, toilet facilities
Other restrictions: Access to most areas.

General description:
A turn of the century display of farm buildings including a house, bothy, stable and byre housing extensive collections of implements, tractors, binders, ploughs and domestic furniture.
Information services:
Special visitor services: Guided tours.
Education services: Group education facilities, resources for Key Stages 1 and 2.
Services for disabled people: Displays and/or information at wheelchair height.
Catalogues:
Catalogue for all of the collections is only available in-house.

1889 MUSEUM OF FARNHAM

Wilmer House, 38 West Street, Farnham, Surrey, GU9 7DX

Tel: 01252 715094
Fax: 01252 715094
Email: fmuseum@waverley.gov.uk
Formed: 1961
Formerly: Willmer House Museum; Farnham Museum, date of change, 1992

Organisation type and purpose: Local government body, museum.
Parent body:
Waverley Borough Council; the William Cobbett Society is based at the museum

Enquiries to: Curator
Other contacts: Education Officer for education visits and enquiries.
Access:
Access to staff: By letter, by telephone, by fax, by email, in person, visitors by prior appointment
Hours: Tue to Sat, 1000 to 1700
Other restrictions: Disabled access to ground floor and garden only.

General description:
Farnham and environs local history and archaeology; fine and decorative arts; museum studies; hops and brewing.
Collections:
Books, documents, artefacts, photographs on Farnham history
George Sturt Collection (manuscripts, artefacts)
Harold Falkner Collection (architectural drawings and English street scenes)
John Henry Knight Collection (photographs, 1880-1990)
William Cobbett Collection of books, documents, prints and artefacts
Catalogues:
Catalogue for library is in-house only. Catalogue for all of the collections is only available in-house.
Printed publications:
Farnham and District Museum Society Newsletter (includes articles on local history topics (quarterly)
Variety of local history publications on Waverley Abbey, Farnham Castle, local artists etc

Internet home pages:
http://www.waverley.gov.uk/museumoffarnham

1890 MUSEUM OF FIRE

Brigade HQ, Lothian and Borders Fire Brigade, Lauriston Place, Edinburgh, EH3 9DE

Tel: 0131 228 2401 ext 267
Fax: 0131 229 8359
Formed: 1966

Organisation type and purpose: Local government body, professional body, museum, historic building, house or site, suitable for ages: 5+.
Professional body - registered office of The Institute of Fire Engineers (world-wide body).
Registered office of:
The Institution of Fire Engineers
at the same address

Enquiries to: Community Safety Officer
Direct tel: 0131 659 7267
Direct email: csg@lothian.fire-uk.org
Access:
Access to staff: By letter, by telephone
Access for disabled people: level entry, access to all public areas, toilet facilities

General description:
Fire Brigades, general and historical, specifically that of the Lothian and Borders Fire Brigade, the oldest municipal Fire Brigade in the UK; fire fighting and extinguishing.
Collections:
Books and manuscripts on Edinburgh Fire Brigade
A range of engines including manual, horse-drawn, steam, and motorised pumps from 1806
Fire related items from 1426
Printed publications:
Fire Safety Advice (seasonal)
Museum Leaflet

Internet home pages:
http://www.lothian.fire-uk.org

1891 MUSEUM OF FLIGHT

East Fortune Airfield, North Berwick, East Lothian, EH39 5LF

Tel: 01620 880308
Fax: 01620 880355
Email: museum_of_flight@sol.co.uk
Formed: 1975
Formed from: Royal Museum

Organisation type and purpose: National organisation, museum, suitable for ages: 5+.
Part of:
National Museums of Scotland (NMS)
Chambers Street, Edinburgh, tel: 0131 225 7534

Enquiries to: Curator
Other contacts: Administrator for marketing and updating information etc.
Access:
Access to staff: By letter, by telephone, by fax, by email, in person, Internet web pages
Access to building, collections or gallery: No prior appointment required
Hours: Summer: daily, 1030 to 1700 (Jul and Aug, 1800)
Winter: daily, 1030 to 1600
Other restrictions: Limited access in winter unless by prior arrangement.
Access for disabled people: Parking provided, ramped entry, level entry, toilet facilities
Other restrictions: Access to most areas.

General description:
Aviation in Scotland. Scottish or Scottish-based pioneers of aviation. The Museum occupies the site of an historic World War II airfield, and has an extensive collection of aeroplanes, rockets, aero engines, models and memorabilia.
Information services:
Library available for reference (for conditions see Access above)
Special visitor services: Guided tours, materials and/or activities for children.
Education services: Group education facilities.
Services for disabled people: Displays and/or information at wheelchair height.
Collections:
Scotland's National Aviation Collection, there are some fifty aircraft on site, rockets, hang-gliders, and microlights
The UK's oldest aircraft Pilcher's Hawk glider 1896
A de Havilland Puss Moth in which Glaswegian, Jim Mollison made the first ever east to west solo crossing of the Atlantic in 1932
Around 100 aircraft engines including an original 1910 Wright Brother's engine
Over 10,000 items of aircraft-related equipment, radar and radio units, weaponry, support equipment etc
Extensive collection of British rocketry including a Blue Streak
An extensive library of aviation books and leaflets with a comprehensive archive
Catalogues:
Catalogue for library is in-house only. Catalogue for part of the collections is on-line.
Publications list:
is available in hard copy and online.

continued overleaf

Printed publications:
Information leaflet
Short History of East Fortune Airfield (Newman G)
Percy Pilcher Booklet (Jarrett P)
Electronic and video products:
Official video of 2000 Air Show at East Fortune

Address for ordering publications:
Printed publications:
NMS Publishing, Royal Museum
Chambers Street, Edinburgh, EH1 1JF, tel: 0131 247 4026, fax: 0131 247 4012, email: fhk@nms.ac.uk

Internet home pages:
http://www.scotwings.com
http://www.nms.ac.uk/flight
Information on Museum, history, collections, events.

1892
MUSEUM OF FULHAM PALACE

Bishops Avenue, London, SW6 6EA

Tel: 020 7736 3233
Fax: 020 7736 3233
Formed: 1990

Organisation type and purpose: Registered charity, museum.
Parent body:
Fulham Palace Trust
Associate of the:
Museum of Fulham Palace
Member of:
Association of Independent Museums
Garden History Society
Group for Education in Museums
Museums Association
South Eastern Museums Service
Registered with the:
Museums and Galleries Commission

Enquiries to: Curator
Other contacts: Education Officer
Access:
Access to staff: By letter, by telephone, in person
Hours: Office: weekdays, 0930 to 1730
Other restrictions: Study room by prior appointment.

General description:
History of Fulham Palace the former residence of the Bishops of London, garden history, architecture, Tudor history, archaeology, history of the Church of England.
Collections:
Primary and secondary sources relating to history of the site, Bishops of London
Periodicals: Museums Journal, Garden History, AIM Bulletin, Gems Bulletin, Herb Society
Subsidiary sources on garden history, architecture, church history
Publications list:
is available in hard copy.
Printed publications:
Guidebooks
Information sheets

1893
MUSEUM OF GARDEN HISTORY

Lambeth Palace Road, London, SE1 7LB

Tel: 020 7401 8865
Fax: 020 7401 8869
Email: info@museumgardenhistory.org
Formed: 1977

Organisation type and purpose: International organisation, membership association (membership is by subscription), present number of members: 2000, registered charity (charity number 1088221), museum, suitable for ages: all ages.
The Museum of Garden History, aims to be the first stop for garden enthusiasts who wish to find out more on: plants and shrubs, their history, who introduced them, where they can be obtained etc.
Affiliated to:
Royal Horticultural Society
Owned by:
The Tradescant Trust

Enquiries to: Chief Executive
Other contacts: (1) Assistant Curator; (2) Shop Supervisor, (3) Venue Hire Co-ordinator for (1) information on exhibits/historical; (2) information on gift shop; (3) on hire facilities.
Access:
Access to staff: By letter, visitors by prior appointment, Internet web pages
Hours: Mon to Fri, 1000 to 1700
Access to building, collections or gallery: No prior appointment required
Hours: Museum: Daily, 1030 to 1700
Other restrictions: Library access for Friends of the Museum by appointment.
Access for disabled people: level entry

General description:
History of garden tools; John Tradescant; The Church of St Mary at Lambeth; Gardens in Britain; biographical information about gardeners; general plant history. Limited information is available on every aspect of the history of gardening.
Collections:
The collection consists of approximately 350 gardening tools and associated equipment, 50 horticultural coins and medals, 150 artworks, 500 documents and associated ephemera, 1000 booklets, leaflets and horticultural catalogues, 1000 photographs, 1000 living plant specimens, 100 monuments, tombs and commemorative windows plus a small and selective library
Printed publications:
Newsletter (3 times a year, members)
Buildings History (80p)
Museum History (£1.20)

Address for ordering publications:
Printed publications:
Mr Bill Knights
at the same address

Internet home pages:
http://www.museumgardenhistory.org
Museum history; garden history; activities, lectures and exhibitions.

1894
MUSEUM OF HAIRDRESSING, THE

Broken up into at least four parts and no longer exists

1895
MUSEUM OF INSTALLATION

175 Deptford High Street, London, SE8 3NU

Tel: 020 8692 8778
Fax: 020 8692 8122
Email: moi@dircon.co.uk
Acronym or abbreviation: MOI
Formed: 1990

Organisation type and purpose: Registered charity, museum, art gallery, suitable for ages: all ages.

Enquiries to: Administrator
Access:
Access to staff: By letter, by telephone, by fax, by email, in person, visitors by prior appointment, Internet web pages
Access to building, collections or gallery: No prior appointment required
Hours: Wed to Sat, 1200 to 1700
Other restrictions: Archive and reading room by appointment.

General description:
The Museum of Installation has 5 site-specific installations per year by UK and foreign artists who build their works in situ. Installation art: research production and dissemination.
Collections:
Slide/photo and video record of the works is available
Slide library of installation projects worldwide
Catalogues:
Catalogue for library is in-house only. Catalogue for all of the collections is available in-house and part is on-line.
Publications list:
is available in hard copy.
Printed publications:
Various printed materials, catalogues and books (direct)
Electronic and video products:
CD-ROM (direct, purchase)

Internet home pages:
http://www.moi.dircon.co.uk

1896
MUSEUM OF IRON

Ironbridge Gorge Museum Trust, Coach Road, Coalbrookdale, Telford, Shropshire, TF8 7DQ

Tel: 01952 433418

Organisation type and purpose: Registered charity (charity number 503717-R), museum, historic building, house or site, suitable for ages: 5+.
Parent body:
Ironbridge Gorge Museum Trust
Tel: 01952 433522
Access:
Access to staff: By letter, by telephone, in person
Access to building, collections or gallery: No prior appointment required
Hours: 1000 to 1700, daily
Other restrictions: Closed 24th and 25th Dec, 1st Jan.
Access for disabled people: level entry, access to all public areas, toilet facilities
Other restrictions: Lift, wheelchairs available. Access guide for disabled visitors available on request.

General description:
The name of Coalbrookdale became famous around the world for superb art castings, fountains, gates, garden furniture. It is now home to a museum that interprets the beginnings of industry and the lives of the people who lived and worked here. View the original iron smelting furnace of Abraham Darby I.
Information services:
Braille Guide.
Special visitor services: Materials and/or activities for children.
Education services: Group education facilities, resources for Key Stages 1 and 2, 3, 4 and Further or Higher Education.
Services for disabled people: For the visually impaired; displays and/or information at wheelchair height.

Internet home pages:
http://www.ironbridge.org.uk

1897
MUSEUM OF ISLAND HISTORY

High Street, Newport, Isle of Wight, PO30 2EE

Tel: 01983 823366
Fax: 01983 823841
Email: tony.butler@iow.gov.uk
Formed: 1996
Formerly: Guildhall Museum, date of change, 2001

Organisation type and purpose: Local government body, museum, suitable for ages: all ages.
Parent body:
Isle of Wight Council (IWC)
Directorate of Community Development, The Guildhall, High Street, Newport, Isle of Wight, tel: 01983 823822

Enquiries to: Curator
Direct tel: 01983 823433
Access:
Access to staff: By letter, by telephone, by fax, by email
Hours: Mon to Fri, 1000 to 1630
Access for disabled people: level entry

General description:
The Museum tells the story of the Isle of Wight from the dinosaurs to the present.
It emphasises the unique archaeology, geology, human history and biodiversity of the Island.
Collections:
Archaeology of Isle of Wight, especially Roman Wight
Brigstock Collection of export porcelain 16th to 19th centuries
Catalogues:
Catalogue for all of the collections is only available in-house.
Publications list:
is available in hard copy.

Address for ordering publications:
Printed publications:
The Curator of Human History

1898
MUSEUM OF ISLE OF WIGHT GEOLOGY
See - Dinosaur Isle

1899
MUSEUM OF KENT LIFE
Cobtree, Lock Lane, Sandling, Maidstone, Kent, ME14 3AU

Tel: 01622 763936
Fax: 01622 662024
Email: enquiries@museum-kentlife.co.uk
Full name: Museum of Kent Life - Cobtree
Formed: 1985

Organisation type and purpose: Registered charity (charity number 1028507), museum, suitable for ages: all ages.

Enquiries to: Director
Access:
Access to staff: By letter, by telephone, by fax, by email, in person
Access for disabled people: Parking provided, toilet facilities

General description:
Kentish rural life; hops; agricultural machinery; livestock; gardens.
Collections:
Kent rural life photographs
Catalogues:
Catalogue for all of the collections is only available in-house.
Printed publications:
Guide Book
Promotional leaflets

Internet home pages:
http://www.museum-kentlife.co.uk
General information about the museum and its services.

1900
MUSEUM OF LAKELAND LIFE
Abbot Hall, Kendal, Cumbria, LA9 5AL

Tel: 01539 722464
Fax: 01539 722494
Email: info@abbothall.org.uk
Formed: 1972
Formerly: Museum of Lakeland Life & Industry

Organisation type and purpose: Registered charity (charity number 526980), museum, suitable for ages: all ages.
Parent body:
Lakeland Arts Trust

Enquiries to: Director
Direct email: ek@abbothall.org.uk
Other contacts: Assistant Curator
Access:
Access to staff: By letter, by telephone, by fax, by email, visitors by prior appointment, charges made to all users, Internet web pages
Access to building, collections or gallery: No prior appointment required
Hours: Mon to Sat, 1030 to 1700; closing 1600 in Winter
Other restrictions: Closed 24 Dec to 14 Feb.
Access for disabled people: Parking provided, toilet facilities
Other restrictions: Partial access to lower levels.

General description:
Everyday life in the Lake District from *c.*1600 to the present day; social and economic history of the Lake District; identification of objects (but not valuations); arts and crafts movement such as Westmorland oak furniture, costume, farriery, farm tools, bobbin turning, wheelwrighting, shoemaking and clogging, patchwork, toys and dolls; weaver and wool trade.
Information services:
Special visitor services: Materials and/or activities for children.
Education services: Group education facilities, resources for Key Stages 1 and 2, 3, 4 and Further or Higher Education.
Services for disabled people: For the visually impaired; for the hearing impaired; displays and/or information at wheelchair height.
Collections:
17th and 18th century local vernacular oak furniture
Annie Garnett: fabric swatches, designs, colour notes
Arthur Ransome: furniture, personalia, books, typescripts
Arts and Crafts: movement furniture including Arthur Simpson and Stanley Davies
Lakeland photographic collection: some 30,000 glass negatives - not on open display
Publications list:
is available in hard copy.
Printed publications:
Information sheets, prints and maps, books, etc

Internet home pages:
http://www.lakelandlifemuseum.org.uk
http://www.lakelandartstrust.org.uk

1901
MUSEUM OF LANCASHIRE, THE
Stanley Street, Preston, Lancashire, PR1 4YP

Tel: 01772 264075
Fax: 01772 264079
Email: museums.enquiries@mus.lancscc.gov.uk
Formed: 1984
Formed from: County and Regimental Museum (C&R), date of change, 1996
Formerly: DLOY Museum; Duke of Lancasters Own Yeomanry Museum (DLOY), date of change, 1987

Organisation type and purpose: Local government body, museum, historic building, house or site, suitable for ages: 5+.
Education and life-long learning.
Parent body:
Lancashire County Museum Service (LCMS) Stanley Street, Preston, PR1 4YP, tel: 01772 264061

Enquiries to: Curator
Other contacts: (1) Military Curator; (2) Social History Curator; (3) Assistant Keeper
Access:
Access to staff: By letter, by telephone, by fax, by email, in person, visitors by prior appointment, Internet web pages
Access for disabled people: Parking provided, ramped entry, access to all public areas, toilet facilities

General description:
Social history, military history with emphasis on Lancashire. DLOY and 14th/20th Hussars. Fine art and Gillow furniture, local archaeology, conservation, toys, dolls and childhood items.
Information services:
Special visitor services: Guided tours, materials and/or activities for children.
Education services: Group education facilities, resources for Key Stages 1 and 2 and 3.
Services for disabled people: For the hearing impaired.
Collections:
Domestic, personal, community and social history collection
Lancashire Constabulary Collection
Collections relating to health and mental health
14/20th Kings Hussars, DLOY (Duke of Lancasters Own Yeomanry) - complete collections of both
Part of Queens Lancashire Regiment Collection
Catalogues:
Catalogue for all of the collections is only available in-house.

Internet home pages:
http://www.lancscc.gov.uk/education/lifelong/museums/lcc/mol.htm

1902
MUSEUM OF LAW TRUST
See - Galleries of Justice

1903
MUSEUM OF LEAD MINING, THE
Wanlockhead, By Biggar, Dumfries & Galloway, ML12 6UT

Tel: 01659 74387
Fax: 01659 74481
Email: ggodfrey@goldpan.co.uk
Formed: 1974

Organisation type and purpose: Independently owned, registered charity, museum, historic building, house or site, suitable for ages: all ages.

Enquiries to: Curator
Other contacts: Tourism Officer
Access:
Access to staff: By telephone, by fax, by email, in person, visitors by prior appointment, Internet web pages
Hours: 1 Apr to 31 Oct: Mon to Sun, 1100 to 1630
Other restrictions: Nov to Mar by appointment.
Access to building, collections or gallery: No access other than to staff
Hours: 1 Apr to 31 Oct: Mon to Sun, 1100 to 1630
Other restrictions: No direct handling of books for research unless by prior arrangement.
Access for disabled people: Parking provided, ramped entry, access to all public areas, toilet facilities

General description:
Mining, ore preparation, smelting of lead, geology, social history.
Information services:
Special visitor services: Guided tours.
Education services: Group education facilities, resources for Key Stages 1 and 2, 3, 4 and Further or Higher Education..
Collections:
The museum has a collection of 19th century tools relating to all aspects of the mining, smelting and ore preparation of lead
19th century examples of working clothing, two hats, and waterproof capes
There is a small textile collection; a geological and minerals collection; and a miners' library of 2800 books
Social history collection and archives of c. 1260 items
Minute books from local societies, ie curling, bowls, quoits and library
Catalogues:
Catalogue for library is in-house only.

Internet home pages:
http://www.leadminingmuseum.co.uk

1904
MUSEUM OF LEATHERCRAFT
See - Northampton Museums and Art Gallery

1905
MUSEUM OF LINCOLNSHIRE LIFE
See - Royal Lincolnshire Regimental Museum

1906
MUSEUM OF LIVERPOOL LIFE
National Museums & Galleries on Merseyside, Liverpool, L3 1PZ

Tel: 0151 478 4080
Fax: 0151 478 4090
Email: liverpoollife@nmgm.org
Acronym or abbreviation: NMGM
Formed: 1986

Organisation type and purpose: Local government body, museum, historic building, house or site, suitable for ages: all ages.

Enquiries to: Director
Other contacts: Marketing Manager for advertising.
Access:
Access to staff: By letter only
Hours: Mon to Fri, 100 to 1700
Access to building, collections or gallery: No prior appointment required
Hours: Mon to Sat, 1000 to 1700; Sun, 1200 to 1700
Access for disabled people: Parking provided, level entry, access to all public areas, toilet facilities

General description:
Housed in a former boat hall and building used by pilots controlling traffic along the river, the Museum celebrates the contribution of the people of Liverpool to national life. Recently expanded to include three new galleries, City Lives exploring the richness of Liverpool's cultural diversity, The River Room featuring life around the River Mersey, and City Soldiers about the Kings Regiment. Other galleries include Mersey Culture, from Brookside to the Grand National, Making a Living, and Demanding a Voice.
Information services:
Helpline available, tel no: 0151 207 0001.
Special visitor services: Materials and/or activities for children.
Education services: Group education facilities..
Collections:
Regional and national materials relating to housing, public health, transport, employment, trade unionism and recreation
Publications list:
is available in hard copy.

Internet home pages:
http://www.museumofliverpoollife.org.uk
http://www.nmgm.org.uk

1907
MUSEUM OF LOCAL CRAFTS AND INDUSTRIES
Towneley Hall Art Gallery & Museums, Off Todmorden Road, Burnley, Lancashire, BB11 3RQ

Tel: 01282 424213
Formed: 1971

Organisation type and purpose: Local government body, museum, suitable for ages: 5+.
Parent body:
Burnley Borough Council
Email: www.burnley.gov.uk

Enquiries to: Secretary
Access:
Access to staff: By letter, by telephone, by email, in person, visitors by prior appointment
Access for disabled people: Parking provided, ramped entry

General description:
Burnley's social and industrial history 1860-1950.
Collections:
A street scene with street furniture, trades, domestic equipment, brewing, coal-mining and textiles
Catalogues:
Catalogue for part of the collections is on-line.

Internet home pages:
http://www.www.burnley.gov.uk

1908
MUSEUM OF LOCAL LIFE
38-42 Tudor House, Friar Street, Worcester, WR1 2NA

Tel: 01905 722349
Formed: 1971
Formed from: Tudor House Museum, date of change, 1996

Organisation type and purpose: Local government body, museum, historic building, house or site, suitable for ages: all ages.
Parent body:
Worcester City Council
Part of:
Worcester City Museums Service

Enquiries to: Social History Officer
Direct email: nburnett@cityofworcester.gov.uk
Other contacts: Education Officer for education enquiries.
Access:
Access to staff: By letter, by telephone, in person
Access to building, collections or gallery: Prior appointment required
Hours: Mon, Tue, Wed, Fri, Sat, 1030 to 1700
Other restrictions: 14 days' notice for access to collections.
Access for disabled people: toilet facilities

General description:
History of Worcester and its people over past two hundred years. Including displays on Worcester at War, Victorian Kitchen, Edwardian School Room.
Information services:
Special visitor services: Guided tours, materials and/or activities for children.
Education services: Group education facilities, resources for Key Stages 1 and 2..
Collections:
Domestic history, toys and games, World War II memorabilia, social history, transport and agriculture
Printed publications:
Museum Guide (50p)

Internet home pages:
http://www.worcestercitymuseum.org.uk

1909
MUSEUM OF LONDON
150 London Wall, London, EC2Y 5HN

Tel: 020 7600 3699
Fax: 020 7600 1058
Email: info@museumoflondon.org.uk
Acronym or abbreviation: MOL
Formed: 1976
Collections of the former: London and Guildhall Museums

Organisation type and purpose: National organisation, museum, suitable for ages: all ages.
Affiliated to:
Museum of London Archaeological Service
Walker House, 87 Queen Victoria Street, London, EC4V 4AB, tel: 020 7410 2200

Enquiries to: Marketing Administrator
Direct tel: 020 7814 5502
Direct fax: 020 7814 5506
Direct email: jholmes@museumoflondon.org.uk
Access:
Access to staff: By letter, by telephone, by email
Hours: Mon to Fri, 0930 to 1730
Access for disabled people: Parking provided, level entry, access to all public areas, toilet facilities
Other restrictions: Telephone in advance to book the limited amount of parking

General description:
Archaeology, topography and social history of London and the London region from prehistoric times to the present, including costume; paintings, prints and drawings; current excavations; conservation.
Information services:
Recorded information on tel no: 020 7600 0807
Special visitor services: Tape recorded guides, materials and/or activities for children.
Education services: Group education facilities.
Services for disabled people: For the visually impaired; for the hearing impaired; displays and/or information at wheelchair height.
Collections:
King collection: of theatre and related material
Layton Collection: antiquarian collections of local archaeology, ethnography etc
London History Workshop collection: relates to oral and video record of London life
Port of London Authority collection: relates to the Port of London (all types of material)
Suffragette Fellowship collection: contains photographs, objects and archive
Tangye Collection of Civil War and Commonwealth period includes books, manuscripts, oil paintings and engravings
The Honeybourne collection: of prints and drawings of London and surrounding area
The Phillips collection: 19th century watercolours of London
The Power collection: prints, drawings and watercolours of London by a wide range of artists from Rowlandson and Pugin to Joseph Pennell and Stanley Anderson, also a range of cuttings and other material on London arranged topographically
Whitefriars Glass collection: relates to a London glasshouse (archive, tools and glass)
Young MSS: papers of Mrs G F Young, wife of Thames ship builder
Publications list:
is available in hard copy.
Printed publications:
Catalogues of some parts of the collections, maps, books etc
Events leaflets (3 times a year, free)
Gazetteer (3 volumes, 1998)
James Powell & Sons: Glassmakers of Whitefriars 1834-1980 (out of print)
London Alive! An Activity Book for Children (out of print)
London Bodies (1998)
London Eats Out 500 Years of Capital Dining (1999)
London in Paint
London on Film
London Wall Walk
Photographers' London: 1839-1990 (out of print)
The Rose Theatre, Past, Present & Future
The Spitalfields Roman (1999)
Vivienne Westwood (2000)
Roman London (2001)
Creative Quarters (2001)

Internet home pages:
http://www.museumoflondon.org.uk/

See also - Museum in Docklands

1910
MUSEUM OF MANKIND
See - British Museum

1911
MUSEUM OF METHODISM
See - Wesley's Chapel, Museum of Methodism and Wesley's House

1912
MUSEUM OF MODERN ART
See - Modern Art Oxford

1913
MUSEUM OF MODERN ART, WALES
See - Tabernacle Cultural Centre

1914
MUSEUM OF NATURAL HISTORY
See - Oxford University, Museum of Natural History

1915
MUSEUM OF NAVAL ARMAMENTS
See - EXPLOSION! - Museum of Naval Firepower

1916
MUSEUM OF NORTH DEVON
See - Museum of Barnstaple & North Devon

1917
MUSEUM OF NOTTINGHAM LACE
3-5 High Pavement, Nottingham, NG1 1HF

Tel: 0115 989 7365
Fax: 0115 989 7301
Email: info@nottinghamlace.org

Organisation type and purpose: Museum, historic building, house or site.

Enquiries to: Curator
Access:
Access to staff: By letter, by telephone, by fax, by email, Internet web pages
Access to building, collections or gallery: No prior appointment required
Hours: Daily, 1000 to 1700; closed Christmas and Boxing Day

General description:
The Lace Market built to house the industry 1550 years ago, and the history of lacemaking and the techniques used to produce it.
Information services:
Modern lace made at the Centre available for purchase.
Special visitor services: Tape recorded guides..
Printed publications:
Catalogue of items for sale

Internet home pages:
http://www.nottinghamlace.org

1918
MUSEUM OF NOTTINGHAM LIFE
See - Brewhouse Yard Museum

1919
MUSEUM OF PAPERMAKING
See - Heron Corn Mill and Museum of Papermaking

1920
MUSEUM OF PATHOLOGY/ ANATOMY
See - Museums of the Royal College of Surgeons of Edinburgh

1921
MUSEUM OF POWER
Steam Pumping Station, Hatfield Road, Langford, Malden, Essex

Tel: 01621 843183

Organisation type and purpose: Museum. The Museum site covers 7 acres.

General description:
Power sources of all types and the major roles which they have played in history.
Collections:
Triple expansion steam engine and pumps built by the Lillishall Company
2 ex. Dagenham, Simpson triple expansion engines of 1909 and 1916

1922
MUSEUM OF PRIMITIVE METHODISM
See - Englesea Brook Chapel and Museum of Primitive Methodism

1923
MUSEUM OF READING
Blagrave Street, Reading, Berkshire, RG1 1QH

Tel: 0118 939 9800
Fax: 0118 939 9881
Email: info@readingmuseum.org.uk
Formed: 1883
Formerly: Reading Museum and Art Gallery, date of change, 1993

Organisation type and purpose: Local government body, museum, art gallery, suitable for ages: all ages.
Parent body:
Reading Borough Council

Enquiries to: Director
Access:
Access to staff: By letter, by telephone, by fax, by email
Hours: Mon to Fri, 0900 to 1700
Access for disabled people: level entry, access to all public areas, toilet facilities

General description:
Archaeology, social history, natural history, art, mainly relating to the Reading and Berkshire region. Full-size replica of the Bayeux Tapestry.
Information services:
Identification of interesting objects, Thursdays 1400 to 1900, no valuations given.
Lunch-time talks focussing on different galleries and the interesting objects from the collection.
Special visitor services: Materials and/or activities for children.
Education services: Group education facilities, resources for Key Stages 1 and 2, 3, 4 and Further or Higher Education.
Services for disabled people: For the visually impaired; displays and/or information at wheelchair height.
Collections:
Excavations at Mesolithic Thatcham
Excavations at Roman Silchester
Huntley and Palmer Biscuits Archive
Reading Abbey sculpture

Internet home pages:
http://www.readingmuseum.org.uk
http://www.bayeuxtapestry.org.uk
Explore the Bayeux Tapestry online

1924
MUSEUM OF RICHMOND
Whittaker Avenue, Richmond-upon-Thames, Surrey, TW9 1TP

Tel: 020 8332 1141
Fax: 020 8948 7570
Email: musrich@globalnet.co.uk
Formed: 1988

Organisation type and purpose: Registered charity, museum.

Enquiries to: Curator
Access:
Access to staff: By letter, by telephone, by fax, by email, visitors by prior appointment
Hours: Tue to Sat, 1100 to 1700

General description:
History of Richmond.
Collections:
Computer databases

Internet home pages:
http://www.museumofrichmond.com

1925
MUSEUM OF RUGBY, THE
Twickenham Stadium, Rugby Road, Twickenham, Middlesex, TW1 1DZ

Tel: 020 8892 8877
Fax: 020 8892 2817
Formed: 1996

Organisation type and purpose: Independently owned, museum, suitable for ages: all ages, consultancy.
Parent body:
RFU
Rugby House, Rugby Road, TW1 1DS

Enquiries to: Librarian
Direct tel: 020 8831 6617
Direct fax: paulrudge@rfu.com
Other contacts: (1) Library Officer; (2) Brand Manager for (1) Reserve contact.
Access:
Access to staff: By letter, by email
Access to building, collections or gallery: No prior appointment required
Hours: Tue to Sat, 1000 to 1700; Sun, 1100 to 1700; last entry 1630
Access for disabled people: Parking provided, level entry, access to all public areas, toilet facilities

General description:
History of Rugby Football worldwide.
Information services:
Library available for reference (for conditions see Access above)
Special visitor services: Guided tours.
Education services: Group education facilities, resources for Key Stages 2 and 3.
Services for disabled people: Displays and/or information at wheelchair height.
Collections:
Rugby Memorabilia
Reference Library
Photographs
Printed publications:
Schools Packs - Key Stages 2 and 3
Museum Brochure (£4.99)

Internet home pages:
http://www.rfu.com

1926
MUSEUM OF SCIENCE AND ENGINEERING
See - Discovery Museum, Newcastle upon Tyne

1927
MUSEUM OF SCIENCE AND INDUSTRY, THE
Liverpool Road, Castlefield, Manchester, M3 4FP

Tel: 0161 606 0127
Fax: 0161 606 0184
Email: collections@msim.org.uk
Acronym or abbreviation: MSIM
Full name: Museum of Science and Industry in Manchester
Formed: 1983
Formerly: Greater Manchester Museum of Science & Industry

Organisation type and purpose: Registered charity, museum, suitable for ages: 5+.
Archives.
Material relating to science and industry in Manchester area.

Enquiries to: Archivist
Direct tel: 0161 606 0113
Direct fax: 0161 606 0115
Direct email: archive@msim.org.uk
Access:
Access to staff: By letter, by telephone, by fax, by email, in person, Internet web pages
Access to building, collections or gallery: No prior appointment required
Hours: Daily, 1000 to 1700
Other restrictions: No prior appointment required but recommended.
Access to archives Tue, Thu, 1000 to 1630
Closed 24 and 25 Dec.

continued overleaf

Access for disabled people: Parking provided, ramped entry, access to all public areas, toilet facilities
Other restrictions: Advance notification useful. Access to most areas.
Visually impaired by arrangement.

General description:
Objects and archives relating to science and industry in Manchester on the site of the world's oldest passenger railway station.
Subject areas include:
Air and Space: aviation, solar power, space

Transport: rail transport and travel, water transport and travel
Energy: electricity, wind and water power
Social History: business archives, water supply, sanitation and drainage
Textiles: textile industry and products
Printing: photographic equipment, papermaking
Science: computing, calculating, scientific instruments, scientific research, chemical industry
Communications: telecommunications, television, radio and the popular music industry.

Information services:
Library available for reference (for conditions see Access above)
Enquiry answering service.
Activities for the visually impaired by arrangement.
Collections Centre.
Special visitor services: Guided tours.
Education services: Group education facilities, resources for Key Stages 1 and 2, 3, 4 and Further or Higher Education.
Services for disabled people: For the hearing impaired; displays and/or information at wheelchair height.

Collections:
Archive of companies and people involved in science, industry and business in the Manchester area
Collections include working machinery
Pictures, photographs and moving images relating to:
Ferranti International
Beyer Peacock
Mathew & Platt
William Perkin
L & M
The Baby Computer
Metropolitan Vickers
Electricity Council
National archive of the electricity industry

Catalogues:
Catalogue for library is in-house only. Catalogue for all of the collections is only available in-house.

Printed publications:
Museum guide (£1.50 plus 50p p&p)

Internet home pages:
http://www.msim.org.uk
Description of museum site; galleries; services; special exhibitions; events and programmes.

1928
MUSEUM OF SCIENCE AND TECHNOLOGY, LEICESTER

See - Abbey Pumping Station Museum of Science and Technology

1929
MUSEUM OF SCOTTISH COUNTRY LIFE

Wester Kittochside, East Kilbride, G76 9HR

Tel: 01355 224181
Fax: 01355 571290
Formed: 2001
Formed from: Scottish Agriculture Museum, date of change, Closed 1998

Organisation type and purpose: Museum.
This new museum, the result of a partnership between the National Museums of Scotland and the National Trust for Scotland, shows how country people lived and worked in Scotland in the past and how this has shaped the countryside of today.

Parent body partnership between:
National Museums of Scotland (NMS)
Chambers Street, Edinburgh, EH1 1JF, tel: 0131 225 7534, fax: 0131 220 4819, email: info@nms.ac.uk
National Trust for Scotland (West Region)

Enquiries to: General Manager
Direct email: d.dornan@nms.ac.uk
Other contacts: (1) Head of Visitor Services; (2) Curator of Scottish Life Archive for general information on museum; (2) information on SLA.

Access:
Access to staff: By letter, by telephone, by fax, by email, in person, visitors by prior appointment, Internet web pages
Access to building, collections or gallery: No prior appointment required
Hours: Daily, 1000 to 1700
Access for disabled people: Parking provided, ramped entry, level entry, toilet facilities

General description:
Working life in Scotland 18th century to present day; agriculture and forestry; trades and crafts; fisheries; building; domestic work; social life/history.

Information services:
Library available for reference (for conditions see Access above)
Special visitor services: Guided tours, materials and/or activities for children.
Education services: Group education facilities, resources for Key Stages 1 and 2, 3, 4 and Further or Higher Education..

Collections:
Scottish Life archive c1700 to present - established in 1959 to record and preserve documentary and illustrative evidence as context to the country life collections of the National Museum of Antiquities of Scotland - has been extended to include maritime, urban and industrial society
Special Collections include:
National Countrylife Collections
Working Life Collections
Royal Highland Society Model Collection (c1800)
Peat Working Tools
Comprehensive contents of joiners' shops, smithies and shoemakers' premises
Angling equipment and contents of a sailmaker's workshop (1964)

Catalogues:
Catalogue for library is in-house only. Catalogue for all of the collections is only available in-house.

Printed publications:
Contact NMS Publishing Limited

Electronic and video products:
Contact The Multimedia Team Limited

Address for ordering publications:
Printed publications:
NMS Publishing Limited
Chambers Street, Edinburgh, EH1 1JF, tel: 0131 247 4026, email: c.shanley@nms.ac.uk

Internet home pages:
http://www.nms.ac.uk/countrylife

1930
MUSEUM OF SMUGGLING HISTORY

Botanic Garden, Undercliff Drive, Ventnor, Isle of Wight, PO38 1UL

Tel: 01983 853677
Formed: 1973

Organisation type and purpose: Independently owned, museum, suitable for ages: 8+.

Enquiries to: Curator

Access:
Access to staff: By letter, by telephone, in person

General description:
The artefacts illustrate methods of smuggling in England over a 700 year period to the present day.

Collections:
300 artefacts and tableaux showing what has been smuggled and how it was done

1931
MUSEUM OF SOUTH SOMERSET

Hendford, Yeovil, Somerset, BA20 1UN

Tel: 01935 424774
Email: marion.barnes@southsomerset.gov.uk
Formed: 1926
Formerly: Wyndham Museum of South Somerset

Organisation type and purpose: Local government body, museum, suitable for ages: 5+.

Enquiries to: Curator

Access:
Access to staff: By letter, by telephone, by email, in person, Internet web pages

General description:
Primarily social history and archaeology collections, with other collections of photographs, geology and costume.
Displays of social history related to the local area, particularly gloving manufacture, flax and hops production and engineering.
Archaeology displays founded on reproduction of Roman dining room and kitchen. All reserve collections available for study by appointment.
Particularly strong are collections of gloving material and Roman collections.

Information services:
Special visitor services: Guided tours, materials and/or activities for children.
Education services: Group education facilities, resources for Key Stages 1 and 2, 3 and Further or Higher Education..

Collections:
Collection of gloving material
Archives from excavations of Westland, Lufton and Ilchester Roman villas

Printed publications:
Series of local booklets

Internet home pages:
http://www.southsomerset.gov.uk/
Details of all museums in the South Somerset Service.

1932
MUSEUM OF SOUTH YORKSHIRE LIFE

Cusworth Hall Museum, Cusworth Hall, Cusworth Lane, Doncaster, South Yorkshire, DN5 7TU

Tel: 01302 782342
Fax: 01302 782342
Email: museum@doncaster.gov.uk
Formed: 1967

Organisation type and purpose: Local government body, museum, historic building, house or site.

Parent body:
Doncaster Metropolitan Borough Council

Enquiries to: Curator

Access:
Access to staff: By letter, by telephone, by fax, in person, visitors by prior appointment
Hours: Mon to Fri, 1000 to 1700; Sat, 1100 to 1700; Sun, 1300 to 1700 (closes 1600 Dec and Jan)
Access to building, collections or gallery: No prior appointment required
Hours: Mon to Fri, 1000 to 1700; Sat, 1100 to 1700; Sun, 1300 to 1700 (closes 1600 Dec and Jan)
Access for disabled people: Parking provided, toilet facilities
Other restrictions: Chairlift to ground floor, tearoom and shop accessible.

General description:
Social history of Doncaster and South Yorkshire area over the last 200 years including childhood, education, domestic life, transport, mining (coal), railway engineering, agriculture, community life, leisure, costume, crafts, pastimes. Three dimensional objects, printed ephemera and photographs relating to above are on display to the public; limited research files.
Information services:
Education services: Group education facilities, resources for Key Stages 1 and 2 and 3.
Services for disabled people: Displays and/or information at wheelchair height.
Collections:
Former industrial archive material now housed in Wakefield and Doncaster Borough archives services
Catalogues:
Catalogue for part of the collections is only available in-house.
Printed publications:
Caring for Cusworth (Morrish A V)
Cusworth Hall and the Battie-Wrightson family (Smith G)
Leaflet on History of Cusworth Hall and description of Museum

1933
MUSEUM OF SPEED
Old Caravan Site, Pendine, Carmarthen, SA33 4NY

Tel: 01994 453488
Formed: 1996

Organisation type and purpose: Local government body, museum, suitable for ages: 5+.
Displays material related to Pendine and land speed record attempts there.
Parent body:
Carmarthenshire County Museum
Abergwili, Carmarthen, Carmarthenshire, SA31 2SG, tel: 01267 231691, fax: 01267 223830, email/website: cdelaney@carmarthenshire.gov.uk

Enquiries to: Manager
Direct tel: 01267 231691
Direct fax: 01267 223830
Direct email: cdelaney@carmarthenshire.gov.uk
Access:
Access to staff: By letter, by telephone, by fax, by email, in person, visitors by prior appointment
Access to building, collections or gallery: No prior appointment required
Hours: May to Sep: Mon to Sun, 1000 to 1700
Apr and Oct: Fri to Mon, 1000 to 1700
Other restrictions: Closed for lunch.
Access for disabled people: Parking provided, level entry, access to all public areas, toilet facilities

General description:
Land speed attempts, particularly in 1920s; Campbell and Parry Thomas.
Collections:
Trophies, cups, medals, photographs
Catalogues:
Catalogue for all of the collections is only available in-house.

1934
MUSEUM OF ST ALBANS
Hatfield Road, St Albans, Hertfordshire, AL1 3RR

Tel: 01727 819340
Fax: 01727 837472
Email: a.wheeler@stalbans.gov.uk
Acronym or abbreviation: MOSTA
Formed: 1898

Organisation type and purpose: Local government body, museum, suitable for ages: all ages.
Parent body:
St Albans District Council
Tel: 01727 866100

Connections with:
Friends of St Albans Museums
Verulamium
St Michael's, St Albans, Hertfordshire, AL3 4SW, tel: 01727 751810, fax: 01727 859919, email/website: museum@stalbans.gov.uk

Enquiries to: Curator
Access:
Access to staff: By letter, by telephone, by fax, by email, in person, visitors by prior appointment, Internet web pages
Hours: Mon to Sat, 1000 to 1700
Access to building, collections or gallery: No prior appointment required
Hours: Mon to Sat, 1000 to 1700
Access for disabled people: Parking provided, ramped entry, toilet facilities

General description:
Local and social history of the historic cathedral city of St Albans, craft tools and history of craft industries of many kinds, biological and geological data, and wildlife garden.
Information services:
Education services: Group education facilities, resources for Key Stages 1 and 2, 3 and 4..
Collections:
Biological and geological data banks for Hertfordshire and Middlesex
Local and social history collection
Natural history collection
Salaman Collection of tools
Catalogues:
Catalogue for part of the collections is only available in-house.
Publications list:
is available in hard copy.
Printed publications:
Museum News (free to Friends)
St Albans: The Home Front (£3.99)

Internet home pages:
http://www.stalbansmuseums.org.uk

1935
MUSEUM OF STEAM POWER AND LAND DRAINAGE
See - Westonzoyland Pumping Station

1936
MUSEUM OF SUSSEX ARCHAEOLOGY
See - Lewes Castle & Museums

1937
MUSEUM OF THE BRITISH RESISTANCE ORGANISATION
See - 390th Bomb Group Memorial Air Museum

1938
MUSEUM OF THE BROADS, THE
Poor's Staithe, Stalham, Norfolk, NR12 9DA

Tel: 01692 581681
Email: motbroads@stalhamnfk.fsnet.co.uk
Formed: 1994

Organisation type and purpose: Museum, suitable for ages: all ages.

Enquiries to: Secretary
Access:
Access to staff: By letter, by telephone, by email, in person, visitors by prior appointment, Internet web pages
Hours: Mon, Wed, 1000 to 1300
Access for disabled people: Parking provided, ramped entry, level entry, access to all public areas, toilet facilities

General description:
Artefacts and models relating to the history of Norfolk and Suffolk Broadland. Videos of historical film and traditional Broads life of the people who lived and worked in it's traditional industries. The museum is situated at the head of Stalham dyke in a delightfully tranquil setting. It is the only museum in the UK to chronicle man's effect upon the Broadland environment.
Information services:
Guided tours by prior appointment.
Special visitor services: Guided tours, materials and/or activities for children.
Education services: Group education facilities, resources for Key Stages 1 and 2, 3, 4 and Further or Higher Education.
Services for disabled people: Displays and/or information at wheelchair height.
Collections:
Boats, wherry fittings, tools, models
Pictures, photographs, books, documents, manuscripts
Catalogues:
Catalogue for part of the collections is only available in-house.

Internet home pages:
http://www.norfolkbroads.com/broadsmuseum

1939
MUSEUM OF THE EARTH
See - Earth Centre

1940
MUSEUM OF THE GORGE
Ironbridge Gorge Museum Trust, Coach Road, Coalbrookdale, Telford, Shropshire, TF8 7DQ

Tel: 01952 432405
Email: visits@ironbridge.org.uk
Formerly: Museum of the River Visitor

Organisation type and purpose: Registered charity (charity number 503717-R), museum, historic building, house or site, suitable for ages: 5+.
Parent body:
Ironbridge Gorge Museum Trust
Tel: 01952 433522
Access:
Access to staff: By letter, by telephone, by email, in person, Internet web pages
Access to building, collections or gallery: No prior appointment required
Hours: 1000 to 1700, daily
Other restrictions: Closed 24th and 25th Dec, 1st Jan.
Access for disabled people: Parking provided, level entry, access to all public areas, toilet facilities
Other restrictions: Access guide for disabled visitors available on request.

General description:
The old Severn Warehouse is a short walk alongside the river from the Iron Bridge. Built in the 1830s, this gothic building was used by the Coalbrookdale Company as a riverside warehouse for their goods. Inside is an exhibition covering the whole history of the Gorge including a 40ft scale model of the river valley as it was in 1796.
Information services:
Special visitor services: Materials and/or activities for children.
Education services: Group education facilities, resources for Key Stages 1 and 2, 3, 4 and Further or Higher Education..

Internet home pages:
http://www.ironbridge.org.uk

1941
MUSEUM OF THE HISTORY OF EDUCATION
Leeds University, Parkinson Court, Leeds, West Yorkshire, LS2 9JT

Tel: 0113 233 4665/4545
Fax: 0113 233 4529
Formed: 1951

Organisation type and purpose: Museum. University collection and centre for research and publication.

Enquiries to: Curator

continued overleaf

Access:
Access to staff: By letter, by telephone, visitors by prior appointment
Hours: Mon, Wed, Fri, 1330 to 1630; Thu, 1330 to 1630; Tue closed
Access to building, collections or gallery: Prior appointment required
Other restrictions: The museum is closed for staff and public holidays and when in use by students.
Prior booking of visits advised.
Access for disabled people: ramped entry

General description:
History of education and educational administration.
Collections:
Board of Education files 1939-1945
Educational artefacts
Library of the history of education
Pupil exercise books
West Riding County Council Education Committee Minutes 1904-1974 and other documents
Printed publications:
Catalogue 1980
Educational Administration and History Monographs (list available from the Museum)
Journal of Educational Administration and History (2 times a year)

Internet home pages:
http://education.leeds.ac.uk/edu/inted/museum.htm

1942
MUSEUM OF THE HISTORY OF SCIENCE
Broad Street, Oxford, OX1 3AZ

Tel: 01865 277280
Fax: 01865 277288
Email: museum@mhs.ox.ac.uk
Formed: 1924

Organisation type and purpose: Museum.
Affiliated to:
Oxford University

Enquiries to: Director
Direct tel: 01865 277281
Direct email: jim.bennett@mhs.ox.ac.uk
Access:
Access to staff: By letter, by telephone, by fax, by email, in person
Hours: Tue to Sat, 1200 to 1600

General description:
History of science, scientific instruments.
Collections:
Books and manuscripts related to the history of science
Early scientific instruments
Catalogues:
Catalogue for library is on-line. Catalogue for all of the collections is on-line.
Publications list:
is available on-line.
Printed publications:
Exhibition catalogues
Sphaera (newsletter, 2 times a year)

Internet home pages:
http://www.mhs.ox.ac.uk/
Information on the museum, its contents and courses for students. Online exhibitions, online catalogues of collections and library.

1943
MUSEUM OF THE HOME
7 Westgate Hill, Pembroke, Dyfed, SA71 4LB

Tel: 01646 681200
Formed: 1986

Organisation type and purpose: Independently owned, museum, suitable for ages: 8+.

Enquiries to: Owner
Access:
Access to staff: By letter, by telephone, in person
Hours: May to Sep: Mon to Thu, 1100 to 1700
Access to building, collections or gallery: No prior appointment required
Hours: May to Sep: Mon to Thu, 1100 to 1700
Other restrictions: Children under 5 NOT admitted.

General description:
A unique private collection covering virtually every item of equipment used in the home. Items are grouped by function in a domestic setting. The main groups are: dairy; garden; small holding; toilet; baby care; medicine; cleaning; food storage; cooking; eating; drinking; tobacco; writing; dress accessories; needlework; toys and games. Domestic arts and crafts, Welsh folk art and costume, local historic maps, prints, photographs.
Collections:
Comprehensive collection of domestic artefacts 1650-1950
Traditional games, 100-1960, c. 300 items
Welsh costume and love tokens, 1730-1900, c. 20 items
Prints and photographs of Pembroke, 1740-1950, c. 150 items
Maps of Pembrokeshire, 1550-1940, c. 100 items
Catalogues:
Catalogue for all of the collections is only available in-house.

1944
MUSEUM OF THE IRON AGE
6 Church Close, Andover, Hampshire, SP10 1DP

Tel: 01264 366283
Fax: 01264 339152
Email: musmda@hants.gov.uk
Formed: 1986

Organisation type and purpose: Local government body, museum, public library.
Parent body:
Hampshire County Council Museums Service
Tel: 01962 846304, fax: 01962 869836

Enquiries to: Curator
Access:
Access to staff: By letter, by telephone, by fax, by email, in person

General description:
An interpretive exhibition of the archaeological finds and discoveries at the Danebury Ring Iron Age hillfort, Nether Wallop, Hampshire, 600BC.
Collections:
Iron Age artefacts from the Danebury Ring hillfort
Catalogues:
Catalogue for all of the collections is on-line.
Printed publications:
Publications list is available from the Librarian, Hampshire County Council Museums Service Headquarters, Chilcomb House, Winchester, SO23 8RD

Address for ordering publications:
Printed publications:
Registrar, Hampshire County Council Museums Service HQ

Internet home pages:
http://www.hants.gov.uk/museum/ironagem/
Iron Age Museum website.

1945
MUSEUM OF THE ISLES
Clan Donald Visitor Centre, Armadale, Sleat, Isle of Skye, IV45 8RS

Tel: 01599 534454
Fax: 01471 844275
Email: library@cland.demon.co.uk
Full name: Armadale Castle, Gardens & Museum of the Isles
Formed: 1976

Organisation type and purpose: Independently owned, registered charity (charity number SCO 07862), museum, suitable for ages: 16+.
Parent body:
Clan Donald Lands Trust
Armadale, Sleat, Isle of Skye, IV45 8RS, tel: 01471 844305, fax: 01471 844275, email: office@cland.demon.co.uk

Enquiries to: Curator
Other contacts: Archivist
Access:
Access to staff: By letter, by telephone, by fax, by email, charges to non-members
Access for disabled people: Parking provided, ramped entry, access to all public areas, toilet facilities

General description:
Scottish Highland history and in particular the history of Clan Donald.
West Highland genealogy research.
Collections:
Jacobite Collection of antiquarian books and pamphlets
Cunningham Collection of 18th century arms, paintings and Macdonnell of Glengarry artefacts
Harry Mathen's Collection: maps, prints and weapons
Archive and manuscript material including Macdonald estate papers for Skye & North Ulst
Photograph and Slide Collection
Reference books
Also, textiles, costume, decorative arts and social history collection

Internet home pages:
http://www.highlandconnection.org/clandonaldcentre.htm

1946
MUSEUM OF THE JEWELLERY QUARTER
75/79 Vyse Street, Hockley, Birmingham, B18 6HA

Tel: 0121 554 3598
Fax: 0121 554 9700
Formed: 1992
Formerly: Jewellery Quarter Discovery Centre

Organisation type and purpose: Local government body, museum, suitable for ages: 5+.
Parent body:
Birmingham Museum & Art Gallery (BM&AG)
Chamberlain Square, Birmingham, B3 3DH

Enquiries to: Curator
Other contacts: Education and Outreach Officer for education programme.
Access:
Access to staff: By letter, by telephone, by fax, visitors by prior appointment
Hours: Mon to Fri, 1000 to 1600
Access for disabled people: ramped entry, access to all public areas, toilet facilities

General description:
A perfectly preserved jewellery workshop little changed since 1900 gives a unique glimpse of working life in Birmingham's Jewellery Quarter. Guided tours of the original office and workshop, plus daily demonstrations of the skills of the jeweller at the workbench. Video, displays and exhibitions about jewellery, hallmarking and the Jewellery Quarter.
Information services:
Special visitor services: Guided tours, materials and/or activities for children.
Education services: Group education facilities, resources for Key Stages 1 and 2.
Services for disabled people: For the visually impaired.
Collections:
The contents of the Smith & Pepper jewellery factory (1899-1981), includes office paperwork, benches, chairs, working machinery, tools, workbenches, stools, jewellery, some 10,000 items
Catalogues:
Catalogue for part of the collections is only available in-house.

Internet home pages:
http://www.bmag.org.uk
Information about Birmingham Museums and Art Gallery, including the Museum of the Jewellery Quarter.

1947
MUSEUM OF THE JEWISH EAST END
See - Jewish Museum; Jewish Museum Finchley

1948
MUSEUM OF THE LANCASHIRE TEXTILE INDUSTRY
See - Helmshore Textile Museums; Queen Street Mill

1949
MUSEUM OF THE MOVING IMAGE
South Bank, London

Acronym or abbreviation: MOMI

Organisation type and purpose: Museum.
Parent body:
British Film Institute
21 Stephen Street, London, W1P 1PL

General description:
Film and television.
Collections:
Film and television memorabilia and artefacts

1950
MUSEUM OF THE PURBECK STONE INDUSTRY
See - Langton Matravers Museum

1951
MUSEUM OF THE ROYAL DOCKYARD, THE
The Historic Dockyard, Chatham, Kent, ME4 4TZ

Tel: 01634 832028
Formed: 1980

Organisation type and purpose: Learned society, registered charity (charity number 287263), museum, suitable for ages: 8+, research organisation.
To spread the knowledge of the dockyard and promote the museum.
Parent body:
Chatham Dockyard Historical Society (CDHS)

Enquiries to: Honorary Secretary
Direct tel: 01634 250647
Access:
Access to staff: By letter, by telephone, in person, members only
Hours: Mon to Fri, 1030 to 1700
Access to building, collections or gallery: No prior appointment required
Hours: Apr to end Oct: daily, 1030 to 1800
Nov, Feb, Mar: Wed, Sat, Sun, 1030 to 1800
Other restrictions: Closed to the public Dec and Jan.
Access for disabled people: Parking provided, level entry, toilet facilities

General description:
The history of the Navy and its men, ships etc.
Workers and trades in the Dockyard.
Information services:
Catalogue in preparation.
Special visitor services: Guided tours, materials and/or activities for children.
Services for disabled people: Displays and/or information at wheelchair height.
Collections:
Extensive reference library
Reserve collection of artefacts in addition to those on show
Publications list:
is available in hard copy.
Printed publications:
Research papers (direct)

1952
MUSEUM OF THE ROYAL DRAGOON GUARDS
3 Tower Street, York, YO1 9SB

Tel: 01904 642036
Fax: 01904 642036
Email: rdgmuseum@onetel.net.uk
Formed: 1992
Formerly: 7th Princess Royal's Dragoon Guards, 4th Royal Irish Dragoon Guards, 6th Inniskilling Dragoons, 5th (Princess Charlotte of Wales) Dragoon Guards; 4/7th Royal Dragoon Guards, 5th Royal Inniskilling Dragoon Guards, date of change, 1992

Organisation type and purpose: Registered charity, museum.

Enquiries to: Curator
Access:
Access to staff: By letter, by telephone, by fax, by email, in person
Hours: Mon to Sat, 0930 to 1630
Access for disabled people: level entry, toilet facilities
Other restrictions: Chairlift to lower floor.

General description:
Regimental history of all former Regiments listed from 1685.
Information services:
Services for disabled people: Displays and/or information at wheelchair height.
Catalogues:
Catalogue for library is in-house only. Catalogue for all of the collections is only available in-house.
Printed publications:
Journal
Postcards
Prints
History Books
Electronic and video products:
Videos, tapes and CD-ROMs

Internet home pages:
http://www.armymuseums.org.uk

1953
MUSEUM OF THE ROYAL LEICESTERSHIRE REGIMENT
c/o Newarke Houses Museum, The Newarke, Leicester, LE2 7BY

Tel: 0116 247 3222

Organisation type and purpose: Local government body, museum, historic building, house or site, suitable for ages: 5+.

Enquiries to: Curator
Access:
Access to staff: By letter only

General description:
No objects on display. Building is available to view internally.
Information services:
Special visitor services: Guided tours..
Collections:
Military collections from 1688-1950s relating to the Royal Leicestershire Regiment

1954
MUSEUM OF THE ROYAL PHARMACEUTICAL SOCIETY OF GREAT BRITAIN
1 Lambeth High Street, London, SE1 7JN

Tel: 020 7572 2210
Fax: 020 7572 2499
Email: museum@rpsgb.org.uk
Acronym or abbreviation: RPSGB
Formed: 1842
Formed from: Pharmaceutical Society of Great Britain (PSGB), date of change, 1988

Organisation type and purpose: Professional body, museum.
Parent body:
Royal Pharmaceutical Society of Great Britain

Enquiries to: Curator
Other contacts: Head of Information for information centre which includes Museum.
Access:
Access to staff: By letter, by telephone, by fax, by email, members only, Internet web pages
Other restrictions: No non-member visitor access.
Historical research and information enquiries via the library staff.
Library is free to members, non-members pay an access fee.

General description:
The museum focuses on the development of the profession of pharmacy in Britain. The emphasis is on retail and dispensing equipment. It holds important collections of English tin glazed drug jars; bell metal mortars; proprietary medicines; and associated promotional material. There are good collections of prints and photographs. The linked archive and library includes early pharmacopoeias and herbals.
Collections:
History of British Pharmacy: objects, pictures, photographs, books, manuscripts, ephemera
Catalogues:
Catalogue for library is in-house only. Catalogue for all of the collections is only available in-house.
Publications list:
is available on-line.
Printed publications:
Range of museum postcards, greetings cards and other items available to visitors from the library or by mail order
Electronic and video products:
Pharmacy History Database (published as part of RPS e-PIC by HCN)

Internet home pages:
http://www.rpsgb.org.uk/museum/index.html

1955
MUSEUM OF THE STAFFORDSHIRE YEOMANRY
The Ancient High House, Greengate Street, Stafford, ST16 2JA

Tel: 01785 619130

Member of:
North Staffordshire Museums Association

Enquiries to: Curator

General description:
Housed in the Ancient High House, an historic Elizabethan building, the museum celebrates the County's own volunteer cavalry regiment from 1794 to the present day.
Collections:
Uniforms, pictures, medals and weapons
Detailed models and an audiovisual display
Collection of photographs dating back to the invention of the camera

1956
MUSEUM OF THE WELSH WOOLLEN INDUSTRY
Dre-fach Felindre, Nr Newcastle Emlyn, Llandysul, Carmarthenshire, SA44 5UP

Tel: 01559 370929
Fax: 01559 371592
Acronym or abbreviation: MWWI
Formed: 1976

Organisation type and purpose: National government body, manufacturing industry, registered charity, museum, historic building, house or site, suitable for ages: 16+.
National museum.
To tell Wales about the world and the world about Wales.
Parent body:
National Museums & Galleries of Wales (NMGW)
Tel: 02920 397951
Other address:
NMGW

continued overleaf

Cathays Park, Cardiff, CF1 3NP, tel: 02920 397951, fax: 02920 373219

Enquiries to: Museum Manager
Direct tel: 01559 370929
Direct fax: 01559 371592
Other contacts: Marketing Officer for press/publicity/adverts.
Access:
Access to staff: By letter, by telephone, by fax, in person, visitors by prior appointment, letter of introduction required
Access for disabled people: toilet facilities

General description:
Welsh woollen textiles, textile machinery, processes of spinning, weaving and finishing.
Information services:
Most services supplied through the NMGW Library/Website.
Special visitor services: Guided tours.
Education services: Group education facilities, resources for Key Stages 1 and 2, 3, 4 and Further or Higher Education..
Catalogues:
Catalogue for library is in-house only. Catalogue for all of the collections is available in-house and part is on-line.
Publications list:
is available in hard copy.

Address for ordering publications:
Printed publications:
Commercial Manager or Marketing Officer, National Museums and Galleries of Wales
Cathays Park, Cardiff, tel: 029 2039 7951

Internet home pages:
http://www.nmgw.ac.uk
Pages on all NMGW sites.

1957
MUSEUM OF TRANSPORT

Boyle Street, Cheetham, Manchester, M8 8UW

Tel: 0161 205 2122
Fax: 0161 205 2122
Email: gmts.enquire@btinternet.com
Acronym or abbreviation: GMTS
Full name: Museum of Transport - Greater Manchester
Formed: 1977
Formed from: Selnec Transport Society, date of change, 1977

Organisation type and purpose: Registered charity (charity number 509772), museum, suitable for ages: all ages.
The Museum of Transport is owned by the Greater Manchester Passenger Transport Executive, a statutory body, but managed on its behalf by the volunteers of the Greater Manchester Transport Society.
Links with:
Greater Manchester Transport Society

Enquiries to: Honorary Secretary
Other contacts: Head of Collections Management for appointments for access to archives, reserve collections etc.
Access:
Access to staff: By letter, by telephone, by fax, by email, in person, visitors by prior appointment, charges to non-members, Internet web pages
Access to building, collections or gallery: No prior appointment required
Hours: Wed, Sat, Sun, Bank Holidays, 1000 to 1700
Access for disabled people: Parking provided, level entry
Other restrictions: Access to all areas, except store rooms.

General description:
A collection of over 80 vehicles, mainly buses and coaches, representing 170 years of transport in Greater Manchester, 'From Horse Bus to Metrolink'.
Information services:
Library available for reference (for conditions see Access above)
Talks service.
Vehicles and objects available for hire for filming etc.
Special visitor services: Guided tours, materials and/or activities for children.
Education services: Group education facilities, resources for Key Stages 1 and 2, 3, 4 and Further or Higher Education.
Services for disabled people: For the visually impaired; displays and/or information at wheelchair height.
Collections:
Collection of uniforms, ticket equipment, bus stops, road signs and similar ancillary items
Library/archives of photographs, film and video, printed and ms. resources - posters, magazines, books, tickets, annual reports, maps and plans, time and fare tables etc.
The P T E Core Display, a collection of c. 30 buses which have been restored. There is at least 1 bus from each of the municipal undertakings prior to the 1969 amalgamation of the Manchester area bus operators, 1925-1990 (total collection 80 vehicles)
Catalogues:
Catalogue for library is in-house only. Catalogue for all of the collections is only available in-house.
Printed publications:
Service Since 1824 (out of print)
Electronic and video products:
Travel By Coach - North Western Publicity Films (video, £13)
Mind How You Go - Manchester & Salford Road Safety Films of 1950s-1960s (video, £11.95)
Sights of the Seventies - Promotional Bus Videos (£12.95)

Internet home pages:
http://www.gmts.co.uk
Description of collections and services, directions, sales lists, vehicles list, latest news, coming events, booking forms, visitor comments, contact lists, links.

1958
MUSEUM OF WELSH ANTIQUITIES

See - Gwynedd Museum and Art Gallery, Bangor

1959
MUSEUM OF WELSH LIFE

St Fagans, Cardiff, CF5 6XB

Tel: 029 2057 3500
Fax: 029 2057 3490
Email: mwl@nmgw.ac.uk
Acronym or abbreviation: MWL
Formed: 1948
Formed from: National Museum of Wales/Amgueddfa Genedlaethol Cymru, date of change, 1948
Formerly: Welsh Folk Museum, date of change, 1995

Organisation type and purpose: National government body, registered charity (charity number 525774), museum, historic building, house or site, suitable for ages: all ages, research organisation.
Re-erected vernacular and historic buildings, gardens, museum specimens, library and archives.
Parent body:
National Museums & Galleries of Wales

Enquiries to: Director
Other contacts: (1) Archivist (2) librarian for (1) manuscripts, documents and photographs, audiovisual archive (2) Library.
Access:
Access to staff: By letter, by telephone, by fax, by email, visitors by prior appointment, Internet web pages
Access for disabled people: Parking provided
Other restrictions: Ramped entry where possible.

General description:
The life and culture of Wales, ethnography (ie folklife) of Wales, comprising vernacular architecture, furniture, horology, domestic life, costume, farming, rural life, folk customs, folklore, folk music, local history, corporate and cultural life, Welsh dialectology.
Information services:
Library available for reference (for conditions see Access above), bibliography compilation.
Helpline available, tel no: 029 2057 3446.
Information service, copies supplied from photographic archives.
Special visitor services: Materials and/or activities for children.
Education services: Group education facilities, resources for Key Stages 1 and 2, 3 and 4.
Services for disabled people: For the visually impaired; for the hearing impaired; displays and/or information at wheelchair height.
Collections:
Library
Archive of manuscripts and primary sources
Audiovisual archive
Oral history archive of interviews on tape, mainly in Welsh
Photographic collection
Museum specimens, including many historic buildings
Catalogues:
Catalogue for library is in-house only. Catalogue for all of the collections is only available in-house but part is published.
Publications list:
is available on-line.
Printed publications:
Amgueddfa (yearbook)
Annual Report
Premier (corporate newsletter)
Microform products:
Schedule of archives (manuscripts and documents, microfiche, Chadwyck-Healey)
Electronic and video products:
Audio cassettes selected from our extensive Audiovisual Archive and a video presenting the Museum can be purchased from the Museum shop
House and households = Tai a chartrefi - CD-ROM based on the Museum's collections and aimed at National Curriculum for history, Key Stage 2 (Pub Anglia Multimedia)

Address for ordering publications:
Printed publications:
Commercial Operations, National Museums and Galleries of Wales
Cathys Park, Cardiff, CF10 3NP, tel: 029 2057 3477

Internet home pages:
http://www.nmgw.ac.uk/mwl
Enquiries, access, education, general information, collections and what's on

1960
MUSEUM OF WITCHCRAFT

The Harbour, Boscastle, Cornwall, PL35 0HD

Tel: 01840 250111
Email: museumofwitchcraft@compuserve.com
Formed: 1951
Formerly: Witchcraft Museum

Organisation type and purpose: Independently owned, museum, suitable for ages: 5+, research organisation.

Enquiries to: Director
Access:
Access to staff: By letter, by email, visitors by prior appointment
Access to building, collections or gallery: No prior appointment required

General description:
Witchcraft, magic, occult, folklore.
Collections:
Museum of Witchcraft Collection and Library
Cecil Williamson Collection and Library

Catalogues:
Catalogue for library is in-house only. Catalogue for part of the collections is on-line.
Printed publications:
Museum Guide Books in English, French and German
Electronic and video products:
Chanting (CD-ROM)
Chanting (cassette)

Internet home pages:
http://www.museumofwitchcraft.com
Tour of museum, search.

1961
MUSEUM OF WORCESTER PORCELAIN
Royal Worcester Porcelain, Severn Street, Worcester, WR1 2NE

Tel: 01905 23221
Fax: 01905 617807
Email: museum@royal-worcester.co.uk
Formed: 1879
Formerly: Dyson Perrins Museum, date of change, 1995
Still looked for: Dyson Perrins Museum Trust

Organisation type and purpose: Registered charity (charity number 223753), museum, suitable for ages: all ages.
Archive.
Links with:
Friends of the Museum of Worcester Porcelain

Enquiries to: Curator
Other contacts: (1) Tours Organiser (2) Museum Manager for (1) group visits (2) business queries.
Access:
Access to staff: By letter, by telephone, by fax, by email, visitors by prior appointment, charges made to all users
Hours: Mon to Fri, 0900 to 1730
Access to building, collections or gallery: No prior appointment required
Hours: Mon to Sat, 0900 to 1730; Sun, 1100 to 1700
Other restrictions: Prior appointment required for archive, access to Curator Mon to Fri only. China enquiries Mon to Fri, by appointment only.
Access for disabled people: Parking provided, level entry, access to all public areas, toilet facilities

General description:
A large and comprehensive collection of Worcester Porcelain, including items from the earliest piece, the Wigornia Creamboat of 1751, through the glamour of the Regency, novelty of the Victorian age, to current products and technical innovations of Royal Worcester Ltd in the 20th century. The Worcester factories of Grainger and Hadley are also represented.
Information services:
Library available for reference (for conditions see Access above)
Special visitor services: Guided tours.
Services for disabled people: Displays and/or information at wheelchair height.
Collections:
Ceramics manufactured in the City of Worcester from 1751 to the present day, including Dr Wall, Giles, Flight, Chamberlain, Grainger, Hadley and Royal Worcester factories
Factory Archives including design library and personnel records
Worcester Porcelain 1751 to the present day, some oil paintings, archives and books
Catalogues:
Catalogue for library is in-house only. Catalogue for all of the collections is only available in-house.
Printed publications:
Guide Book and postcards (available, £2.99)
Electronic and video products:
Henry Sandon's Guide to Royal Worcester Porcelain (video)

1962
MUSEUM OF WORLD RAILWAYS
See - Railworld

1963
MUSEUM OF YORKSHIRE DALES LEAD MINING
Old Grammar School, School Lane, Earby, Lancashire, BB18 6QF

Tel: 01282 841422
Fax: 01282 841422
Full name: Earby Mines Research Group Museum Trust
Formed: 1972

Organisation type and purpose: Independently owned, registered charity (charity number 1068481), museum, suitable for ages: 5+.
Museum of the Yorkshire Dales lead mining.

Enquiries to: Honorary Secretary
Direct tel: 01282 841887
Other contacts: (1) Curator; (2) Secretary
Access:
Access to staff: By letter, by telephone, by fax, in person
Access for disabled people: ramped entry, toilet facilities

General description:
800 items on show featuring lead miners; tools and equipment; personal items; a large water wheel and lead crushing mill (in the grounds); photographs; minerals; and working models all housed in a 400 year old Grammar School.
Collections:
John McNeill Collection
Frank Woodall Collection of Models and Minerals
Dr A Raistrict small collection
Alan Butterfield Collection (various)

1964
MUSEUM OF ZOOLOGY AND COMPARATIVE ANATOMY
See - Grant Museum of Zoology and Comparative Anatomy

1965
MUSEUMS AND GALLERIES OF NORTHERN IRELAND
Botanic Gardens, Belfast, BT9 5AB

Tel: 028 9038 3000
Minicom no. 028 9038 3008
Fax: 028 9038 3006/ 3103
Email: director.um@nics.gov.uk

Organisation type and purpose: National government body, museum.
Parent body of:
Ulster American Folk Park, Omagh
Ulster Folk and Transport Museum, Holywood
Ulster Museum, Belfast including Armagh County Museum, Armagh
W5 Science Centre, Belfast
Subsidiary body:
Centre for Environmental Data and Recording (CEDaR)
Tel: 028 9038 3154, fax: 028 9038 3003, email/ website: damien.mcferran.um@nics.gov.uk

Enquiries to: Chief Executive
Access:
Access to staff: By letter, by telephone, by fax, in person, visitors by prior appointment, Internet web pages
Hours: Mon to Fri, 1000 to 1700
Access for disabled people: ramped entry, access to all public areas, toilet facilities

General description:
Administrative body responsible for mangement and development of the Ulster museums and galleries within its care.

Internet home pages:
http://www.magni.org.uk

See also - Ulster Folk and Transport Museum

1966
MUSEUMS ASSOCIATION
24 Calvin Street, London, E1 6NW

Tel: 020 7426 6970
Fax: 020 7426 6961
Email: info@museumsassociation.org
Acronym or abbreviation: MA
Formed: 1889

Organisation type and purpose: Professional body, registered charity (charity number 313024).

Enquiries to: Information Officer
Access:
Access to staff: By letter, by telephone, by fax, by email, Internet web pages
Hours: Mon to Fri, 0900 to 1700

General description:
Museums, particularly professional matters and training.
Publications list:
is available in hard copy.
Printed publications:
Museum Practice (3 times a year)
Museums Journal (monthly)
Museums Yearbook

Internet home pages:
http://www.museumsassociation.org

1967
MUSEUMS OF THE ROYAL COLLEGE OF SURGEONS
Royal College of Surgeons of England, 35-43 Lincoln's Inn Fields, London, WC2A 3PE

Tel: 020 7869 6560
Fax: 020 7869 6564
Email: museums@rcseng.ac.uk
Acronym or abbreviation: RCS
Formed: 1800

Organisation type and purpose: Professional body, service industry, registered charity (charity number 212808), museum.
Subsidiary bodies:
Hunterian Museum
(closed from July 2002 for approximately 18 months)
Tel: 020 7869 6560, fax: 020 7869 6564
Odontological Museum
(closed from July 2002 for approximately 18 months)
Wellcome Museum of Anatomy & Pathology

Enquiries to: Curator
Access:
Access to staff: By email
Hours: Mon to Fri, 1000 to 1700
Access to building, collections or gallery: No access other than to staff

General description:
Surgery; history of medicine; odontology; anatomy; pathology; natural history; museum conservation techniques; microscopy; historic surgical instruments.
Information services:
The Huntarian and Odontological Museums are due to close for refurbishment July 2002 for approximately 18 months. Wellcome Museum to stay open.
Special visitor services: Guided tours..
Collections:
Hunterian Collection: Comparative and Human Anatomy and Pathology, 1760-1793 some 3600 items
Hunterian collection of paintings (Stubbs, Hodges, etc.), 1760-1793, 24 items
Agasse Collection, animal paintings, early 19th century, 14 items
Cheselden Collection, skull paintings, ca. 1733, 7 items
Flower Collection, comparative osteology
Odontological Collection: Comparative and Human Dental Anatomy and Pathology
Catalogues:
Catalogue for part of the collections is published.

continued overleaf

Printed publications:
Historic Surgical Instruments (£1, purchase direct)
John Hunter's Casebooks (Royal Society of Medicine, £80)
The Hunter Story - William & John Hunter (£4)

Internet home pages:
http://www.rcseng.ac.uk/services/museums/
General introduction.
http://www.rcseng.ac.uk/services/museums/john_hunter_html
Biography of John Hunter.
http://www.rcseng.ac.uk/services/museums/collections
Description of collections.
http://www.rcseng.ac.uk/services/museums/history
History of museum.

1968
MUSEUMS OF THE ROYAL COLLEGE OF SURGEONS OF EDINBURGH
18 Nicolson Street, Edinburgh, EH8 9DW

Tel: 0131 527 1649
Fax: 0131 557 6406
Email: museum@rcsed.ac.uk
Formed: 1699

Organisation type and purpose: Independently owned, professional body, registered charity (charity number SC 5317), museum, suitable for ages: 16+, training organisation.
The College exists to maintain standards in surgery, arranges examinations for the Fellowship and training courses for surgeons from all over the world.

Enquiries to: Administrator
Access:
Access to staff: By letter, by telephone, by fax, by email, letter of introduction required
Other restrictions: Services are provided for Fellows and others connected with surgery, medicine, art.
Access to building, collections or gallery: Prior appointment required
Hours: Public Area: Mon to Fri, 1400 to 1600
Other restrictions: Pathology Museum: by special arrangement.

General description:
History of surgery and history of dental surgery, especially relating to Edinburgh. Includes the Museum of Pathology/Anatomy, Sir Jules Thorn exhibition of the history of surgery and the Menzies Campbell Dental Museum.
Catalogues:
Catalogue for library is in-house only.

Internet home pages:
http://www.rcsed.ac.uk

1969
MUSEUMS WEEK
See - Campaign for Museums

1970
MUSICAL MUSEUM
368 High Street, Brentford, Middlesex, TW8 0BD

Tel: 020 8560 8108
Formed: 1963
Formerly: British Piano Museum

Organisation type and purpose: Membership association (membership is by election or invitation), voluntary organisation, registered charity (charity number 2401088), museum.

Enquiries to: Curator
Access:
Access to staff: By letter, by telephone
Hours: Apr to Oct: Sat to Sun, 1400 to 1700
Jul and Aug: Wed, 1400 to 1600

General description:
Reproducing pianos, reproducing pipe organs, street barrel pianos and organs, automatic playing violins with piano accompaniment, orchestrions, the Aeolian residence pipe organ, Wurlitzer theatre organ and other related items.
Collections:
30,000 music rolls
Catalogues:
Catalogue for part of the collections is on-line.
Publications list:
is available in hard copy.
Printed publications:
Coloured brochures
List of Concerts (each Spring)
Newsletters (2 times a year; published by The Friends of the Museum)
Electronic and video products:
Tapes and CD-ROMs

Internet home pages:
http://www.musicalmuseum.co.uk

1971
MYRETON MOTOR MUSEUM
Aberlady, Longniddry, East Lothian, EH32 0PZ

Tel: 01875 870288
Formed: 1966

Organisation type and purpose: Independently owned, museum, suitable for ages: 5+.

Enquiries to: Owner Curator
Direct tel: 07947 066666
Access:
Access to staff: By letter, by telephone
Access for disabled people: Parking provided, level entry, access to all public areas, toilet facilities

General description:
A highly varied collection of motor cars from 1896; motor cycles from 1902; commercial vehicles from 1919; cycles from 1896; World War II British military vehicles; aircraft and car engines; a large collection of advertising posters; enamel signs; and ephemera.
Printed publications:
Photograph Album

1972
NAIRN FISHERTOWN MUSEUM
See - Nairn Museum

1973
NAIRN MUSEUM
Viewfield House, King Street, Nairn, Highland, IV12 4EE

Tel: 01667 456791
Fax: 01667 455399
Email: manager@nairnmuseum.freeserve.co.uk
Formed: 1860
Incorporates the former: Nairn Fishertown Museum

Organisation type and purpose: Independently owned, registered charity (charity number SCO 19425), museum, suitable for ages: 5+, research organisation.

Enquiries to: Manager
Access:
Access to staff: By letter, by telephone, by fax, by email, in person, Internet web pages
Hours: Mon to Sat, 1000 to 1630
Access to building, collections or gallery: No access other than to staff
Hours: Mon to Sat, 1000 to 1630
Access for disabled people: Parking provided, ramped entry, access to all public areas

General description:
The museum illustrates the history of the Burgh and County of Nairn through photographs and objects of interest. It is housed on the first floor of a Georgian House with an exhibition room and library on the ground floor.
The material from the former Nairn Fishertown Museum tells the story of fishing, and the fisherfolk of Nairn, with collections of models, photographs and memorabilia of line and herring fishing, mainly late 19th to early 20th century.

Information services:
Library available for reference (for conditions see Access above)
Help for disabled people available from guides.
Family and local history service.
Special visitor services: Guided tours, materials and/or activities for children..
Collections:
Brodie of Brodie Cabinet. Geology made up of minerals and rocks, about 2000 specimens
Fish fossils. Cawdor collection. Photographic. Old red sandstone fish fossils, local photographs of the town and people, about 400 specimens
Ethnographic collection. Included are items from Africa, America and the Far East
MacBean collection. Local Scottish history reference books. 16th-20th century about 1000 books.
Catalogues:
Catalogue for library is in-house only. Catalogue for all of the collections is only available in-house.
Publications list:
is available on-line.
Printed publications:
Information sheets available from the museum
Electronic and video products:
Currently being processed

Internet home pages:
http://www.nairnmuseum.co.uk
General information on museum opening times and services

1974
NARROW GAUGE RAILWAY MUSEUM
Wharf Station, Tywyn, Gwynedd, LL36 9EY

Tel: 01654 710472
Email: enquiries@ngrm.net
Formed: 1956

Organisation type and purpose: Registered charity (charity number 1040128), museum, suitable for ages: 8+.
Shared site with:
Talyllyn Railway
Wharf Station, Tywyn, LL36 9EY, tel: 01654 710472

Enquiries to: Honorary Secretary
Access:
Access to staff: By letter, by email, visitors by prior appointment
Access to building, collections or gallery: No access other than to staff
Hours: Easter to end Oct: daily, 0930 to 1730
Other restrictions: Other times by arrangement.
Access for disabled people: Parking provided, ramped entry, toilet facilities
Other restrictions: Access to most areas.

General description:
Collection of locomotives, wagons, signalling, track work, signs, tickets, posters and other items used on narrow gauge railways in the British Isles, especially relating to the slate industry of North Wales and the Talyllyn Railway in particular.
Collections:
Slate Industry transport, 1840-1980
Talyllyn Railway collection, 1865-2000
Collection of signalling equipment, 1870-1960
Track materials, 1790-1990
Catalogues:
Catalogue for all of the collections is available in-house and part is on-line.

Internet home pages:
http://www.talyllyn.co.uk/ngrm
Background information in five languages, details of collection etc.

1975
NATIONAL ARCHIVES

Quality House, Quality Court, Chancery Lane, London, WC2A 1HP

Tel: 020 7242 1198
Fax: 020 7831 3550
Email: nra@hmc.gov.uk
Acronym or abbreviation: NA
Formed: 1869
Formerly: National Register of Archives (NRA); Historical Manuscripts Commission (HMC), date of change, 1 April 2003; Royal Commission on Historical Manuscripts (RCHM), date of change, 2000

Organisation type and purpose: National government body, advisory body.
To provide information and advice about the location, nature and care of manuscript sources for British history.
Moving towards the end of 2003 to:
National Archives
Ruskin Avenue, Kew, Richmond-upon-Thames, Surrey, TW9 4DU

Enquiries to: Secretary
Access:
Access to staff: By letter, by fax, by email, in person, Internet web pages
Hours: Mon to Fri, 0930 to 1700
Access to building, collections or gallery: No prior appointment required
Hours: Mon to Fri, 0930 to 1700

General description:
Nature and whereabouts in the United Kingdom of papers, manuscript collections and archives of value for the study of British history, outside the public records; care and disposal of such records, advice on conservation and storage, associated published finding aids to historical manuscripts throughout the world.
Collections:
The National Register of Archives (NRA) includes over 43,000 lists of archives held by record offices, libraries, museums, universities, businesses, other public and private organisations and individuals.
Manorial Documents Register and other finding aids
Published finding aids to historical manuscripts throughout the world which are of importance to British history
The Commission does not hold collections of manuscripts
Publications list:
is available in hard copy and online.
Printed publications:
Annual Review 2000-2001 (2001, pub HMSO, £6)
Archive Buildings in the United Kingdom 1977-1992 (pub. HMSO, £17.95)
Guides to Sources for British History
Archives at the Millennium: the Twenty-eighth Report (1999, £9.50)
Prime Ministers' Papers (papers of nineteenth century statesmen)
Record Repositories in Great Britain (11th edn, 1999, £4.99)
Other titles listed in publications leaflet and on website

Internet home pages:
http://www.hmc.gov.uk/
General information on the HMC and its activities; HMC information sheets for researchers; the Indexes to the National Register of Archives, part of the Manorial Documents Register; the thematic digests of Accessions to Repositories, ARCHON - Archival Resources Online information gateway; Archives in Focus site providing introductory guide to archives and their use for lifelong learning.

1976
NATIONAL ARCHIVES

Ruskin Avenue, Kew, Richmond-upon-Thames, Surrey, TW9 4DU

Tel: 020 8876 3444
Minicom no. 020 8392 9198
Fax: 020 8878 8905
Email: enquiry@pro.gov.uk
Acronym or abbreviation: PRO
Formed: 1838
Formerly: Public Record Office (PRO), date of change, 1 April 2003

Organisation type and purpose: National government body.
National Archive Office.
Executive agency responsible to the:
Lord Chancellor
Other addresses:
The Family Records Centre
1 Myddleton Street, Islington, London, EC1R 1UW, tel: 020 8392 5300, fax: 020 8392 5307, email/website: enquiry@pro.gov.uk

Enquiries to: Contact Centre
Direct tel: 020 8392 5200
Access:
Access to staff: By letter, by telephone, by fax, by email, in person, Internet web pages
Hours: Mon, Wed, Fri, Sat, 0900 to 1700; Tue, 1000 to 1900; Thu, 0900 to 1900; Sat, 0930 to 1700
Other restrictions: Enquiries, as to contents of the Public Records and to methods of research in them, may be addressed to the Contact Centre. A reader's ticket is necessary in order to consult the records; the ticket may be obtained free of charge, upon proof of identity.
Access to building, collections or gallery: No prior appointment required
Hours: Mon, Wed, Fri, Sat, 0900 to 1700; Tue, 1000 to 1900; Thu, 0900 to 1900; Sat, 0930 to 1700
Access for disabled people: Parking provided, level entry, access to all public areas, toilet facilities

General description:
National Archives of England, Wales and the United Kingdom.
History of the British Isles and of all those parts of the world with which Great Britain has been involved since the 11th century; any central government activity (up to 30 years ago), including scientific research and exploration, medical and artistic administration etc, in addition to political, social, military, economic and administrative history; maps; archive science; records of Royal Courts of Law; genealogical material.
Collections:
The collections are too numerous to specify (documents number many millions, and currently cover 100 miles of shelving)
Famous documents include the Domesday Book, Shakespeare's will, the Log of HMS Victory, World Wars documents
Catalogues:
Catalogue for all of the collections is on-line.
Publications list:
is available in hard copy and online.
Printed publications:
Many titles include:
Information for Readers (free)
Army Records for Family Historians (£7.99)
Making Use of the Census (Lumas, 4th ed, £8.99)
Naval Records for Genealogists (Rodger, £10)
New to Kew? (Cox, £6.99)
Tracing Your Ancestors in the PRO (6th ed, Bevan, £14.99)
Using Manorial Records (Ellis, £7.99)
Using Navy Records (£3.99)
Using Poor Law Records (Fowler, £3.99)
Using Wills (£3.99)

Internet home pages:
http://catalogue.pro.gov.uk
There are descriptions of over 8.4 million documents in the Record Classes of the PRO. The scope and content of the Record Classes are described along with a link to Class List and further links to descriptions of the individual Class Listings. The visitor may either search or browse through the descriptions.
http://www.pro.gov.uk
General information about PRO.

1977
NATIONAL ARMY MUSEUM

Library, Royal Hospital Road, Chelsea, London, SW3 4HT

Tel: 020 7730 0717
Fax: 020 7823 6573
Email: info@national-army-museum.ac.uk

Organisation type and purpose: Registered charity (charity number 237902), museum, suitable for ages: all ages.

Enquiries to: Head of The Department of Printed Books
Access:
Access to staff: By letter, by telephone, by fax, by email, members only, Internet web pages
Hours: Library: Tue to Sat, 1000 to 1630
Museum: Sun to Sat, 1000 to 1730
Other restrictions: Personal access to Library for those over 18 who are holders of Readers' Tickets only.

General description:
The history of British, Indian and Commonwealth land forces.
Collections:
c. 45,000 books, c. 1500 feet of archives, c. 100,000 photographs, c. 30,000 prints and drawings
Papers of FM Lord Roberts; FM Viscount Gough; FM Lord Raglan; Gen. Lord 1st Marquess of Anglesey; Gen. Lord Chelmsford; Gen. Sir Frederick Haines; Gen Lord Rawlinson
Catalogues:
Catalogue for library is in-house only. Catalogue for part of the collections is only available in-house.
Publications list:
is available in hard copy.
Printed publications:
Sales list available upon application to the Museum shop

Internet home pages:
http://www.national-army-museum.ac.uk
Summary of museum and library services, suggestions for contacts for further research.

1978
NATIONAL COAL MINING MUSEUM FOR ENGLAND

Caphouse Colliery, New Road, Overton, Wakefield, West Yorkshire, WF4 4RH

Tel: 01924 848806
Fax: 01924 840694
Acronym or abbreviation: NCMME
Formed: 1988
Formerly: Yorkshire Mining Museum, date of change, 1995

Organisation type and purpose: National organisation, registered charity (charity number 517325), museum, suitable for ages: all ages.
Parent body:
National Coal Mining Museum for England Trust Limited

Enquiries to: Librarian
Access:
Access to staff: By letter, by telephone, by email, visitors by prior appointment
Access for disabled people: Parking provided, ramped entry, access to all public areas, toilet facilities

General description:
All aspects of coal mining in England: includes coal mining technology, literature and coal mining communities.
Collections:
Coal mining library of technology, social history and literature; includes periodicals, printed

continued overleaf

ephemera, photographs and art relating to coal mining primarily within England
Catalogues:
Catalogue for library is in-house only. Catalogue for all of the collections is only available in-house but part is published.
Publications list:
is available in hard copy.
Printed publications:
The British Coal Collection (£14.50, catalogue)
Danger in the Dark (children's Victorian story, £1.60)
Voices from the dark: women and children in Yorkshire coal mines (£1.80)
National Coal Mining Museum for England, Caphouse Colliery: souvenir guidebook (£1.99)
Coal mining and the camera: images of coal mining in England from the collections of the National Coal Mining Museum for England (£1.99)
Variety of education packs and books
Electronic and video products:
A Proud Tradition: Coalmining in Yorkshire (video, £9.99)

Internet home pages:
http://www.ncm.org.uk

1979
NATIONAL CORACLE CENTRE, THE
Bwythyn Tyr Felin, Cenarth, Newcastle Emlyn, Dyfed, SA38 9JL

Tel: 01239 710980
Fax: 01239 710980
Formed: 1991

Organisation type and purpose: Independently owned, museum, historic building, house or site, suitable for ages: 8+.

Enquiries to: Director
Access:
Access to staff: By letter, by telephone, by fax, by email, in person
Access for disabled people: Parking provided, ramped entry, access to all public areas

General description:
A unique collection of coracles from Wales and around the world. Set in the grounds of the 17th century flour mill beside the salmon river and falls.
Information services:
Special visitor services: Tape recorded guides.
Education services: Group education facilities..
Collections:
The Quffa, Iraq
The Indian Parisal
Vietnam coracle
Information on Tibet
2 Irish Currachs
9 Welsh coracles
Scottish and English examples.

Internet home pages:
http://www.coraclecentre.co.uk

1980
NATIONAL CYCLE COLLECTION
The Automobile Palace, Temple Street, Llandrindod Wells, Powys, LD1 5DL

Tel: 01597 825531
Fax: 01597 825531
Email: cycle.museum@care4free.net
Formed: 1984
Formerly: National Cycle Museum

Organisation type and purpose: Independently owned, registered charity (charity number 511257), museum, historic building, house or site, suitable for ages: 5+.
Museum, reference, archive.
Parent and administrative body:
National Cycle Museum Trust
at same address
Museum Paper Archive held at:
Warwick University
Modern Records Office, University of Warwick, Coventry, CV4 7AL

Enquiries to: Curator
Other contacts: Secretary and Treasurer of National Cycle Museum Trust
Access:
Access to staff: By letter, by telephone, by fax, by email, in person, Internet web pages
Access to building, collections or gallery: No prior appointment required
Hours: 1 Mar to end Oct: daily, 1000 to 1600
Other restrictions: Winter: restricted opening telephone or check website for details
Access for disabled people: Parking provided, level entry, access to all public areas, toilet facilities

General description:
Housed in a building constructed in 1907 in the art nouveau style. Bicycle history 1819-1990s and DEL records.
Information services:
Guide Dogs welcome, also pets.
Special visitor services: Guided tours.
Education services: Group education facilities, resources for Key Stages 1 and 2, 3, 4 and Further or Higher Education.
Services for disabled people: Displays and/or information at wheelchair height.
Collections:
The following are all on display at the museum:
Approximately 240 cycles on display from 1818 until today.
Artefacts and accessories, and display and advertising material.
David Higman Collection
Dunlop Archive (3000 papers)
Frank Patterson Prints
Special collections of early tricycles, ordinaries ('Penny Farthings'), racing machines, etc.
Sturmey Archer Archive
Tom Norton Collection of machines
Paper Archive held at Warwick University as part of the National Cycling Archive (NCA)
Catalogues:
Catalogue for library is in-house only. Catalogue for all of the collections is available in-house and part is on-line.
Printed publications:
Friends of the Museum (magazine, quarterly, for members)

Internet home pages:
http://www.cyclemuseum.org.uk
Collection details, 30 pages of information together with some photographs, opening times, activities.

1981
NATIONAL FOOTBALL MUSEUM
Sir Tom Finney Way, Deepdale, Preston, Lancashire, PR1 6RU

Tel: 01772 908442
Fax: 01772 908433
Email: enquiries@nationalfootballmuseum.com

Organisation type and purpose: Independently owned, registered charity (charity number 1050792), museum, suitable for ages: 5+.

Enquiries to: Public Relations Manager
Direct tel: 01772 908403
Direct fax: 01772 908444
Direct email: markb @nationalfootballmuseum.com
Access:
Access to staff: By letter, by email, visitors by prior appointment
Access to building, collections or gallery: No prior appointment required
Hours: Tue to Sat, 1000 to 1700; Sun, 1100 to 1700
Other restrictions: Closed Mon except Bank Holidays; closed Christmas Day.
Access for disabled people: Parking provided, ramped entry, access to all public areas, toilet facilities

General description:
Football, history of football in England.
Information services:
Special visitor services: Materials and/or activities for children.
Education services: Group education facilities, resources for Key Stages 2, 3 and 4.
Services for disabled people: Displays and/or information at wheelchair height.
Collections:
FIFA Museum Collection: Football equipment, artwork, ceramics, metalware, ephemera, toys, particularly strong 1870-1950, collected by Harry Langton
FA Collection: FA archives, international match gifts, art, books
Football League Collection: league archives, books
People's Collection: Mixed collection of memorabilia from players, fans and officials
Wembley Collection: Wembley Stadium artefacts and ephemera
Printed publications:
Museum Guide Book (available for purchase, direct)
Eyewitness Football (pub Dorling Kindersley; illustrated guide based on the Museum's collections)

Internet home pages:
http://www.nationalfootballmuseum.com

1982
NATIONAL GALLERIES OF SCOTLAND
Press & Information Department, Belford Road, Edinburgh, EH4 3DR

Tel: 0131 624 6200
Fax: 0131 343 3250
Email: enquiries@natgalscot.ac.uk

Organisation type and purpose: Art gallery.
Other sites:
Duff house
Banff, Banffshire, AB45 2SX, tel: 01261 818181
National Gallery of Scotland
The Mound, Edinburgh, EH2 2EL, tel: 0131 624 6200, fax: 0131 220 0917, email/website: enquiries@nationalgalleries.org
NGS Picture Library
The Dean Gallery, Belford Road, Edinburgh, EH4 3DS, tel: 0131 624 6258, fax: 0131 623 7135, email/website: picture.library@natgatscot.ac.uk
Paxton House
Berwick-upon-Tweed, Berwickshire, TD15 1SZ, tel: 01289 386291
Scottish National Gallery of Modern Art
Belford Road, Edinburgh, EH4 3DR
Scottish National Portrait Gallery
1 Queen Street, Edinburgh, EH2 1JD, tel: 0131 624 6200, fax: 0131 558 3691, email/website: enquiries@nationalgalleries.org
The Dean Gallery
Belford Road, Edinburgh, EH4 3DS

Enquiries to: Press & Information Assistant
Direct tel: 0131 624 6332
Direct fax: 0131 343 3250
Direct email: lindsay.isaacs@natgalscot.ac.uk
Access:
Access to staff: By letter, by telephone, by email
Hours: Mon to Sat 1000 to 1700; Sun, 1400 to 1700
Access to building, collections or gallery: No prior appointment required
Hours: Mon to Sat, 1000 to 1700, Sun, 1200 to 1700
Access for disabled people: access to all public areas, toilet facilities

General description:
Provision of information on the National Gallery of Scotland, Scottish National Gallery of Modern Art, Scottish National Portrait Gallery and Dean Gallery.
Publications list:
is available in hard copy and online.
Printed publications:
Andrew Geddes 1783-1844:'A Man of Pure Taste'(Smailes H, Black P and Stevenson L 2001)

Portrait Miniatures from the Clarke Collection (Lloyd S 2001)
Rachel Whiteread (Corrin L, Elliott P and Schlieker A 2001)
Rembrandt's Women (Lloyd Williams J et al 2001)
The King Over the Water: Portraits of the Stuarts in Exile after 1689 (Corp E 2001)
The Surrealist and the Photographer: Roland Penrose and Lee Miller (Burke C and Hartley K 2001)
Companion Guide to the National Gallery of Scotland (Clarke M 2000)
Companion Guide to Photography in the National Galleries of Scotland (Stevenson S and Forbes D 2001)
Companion Guide to the Scottish National Gallery of Modern Art (Elliott P 1999)
Companion Guide to the Scottish National Portrait Gallery (Holloway J et al 1999)
Concise Catalogue of Paintings in the National Gallery of Scotland (Clarke M et al)
Concise Catalogue of the Scottish National Gallery of Modern Art (Elliott P)
Concise Catalogue of the Scottish National Portrait Gallery (Smails H)
A selection of titles based on works in the permanent collections and exhibition catalogues are also available.

Address for ordering publications:
Printed publications:
Publications Department, National Galleries of Scotland
Dean Gallery, Belford Road, Edinburgh, EH4 3DS, tel: 0131 624 6256/6259/6261, fax: 0131 315 2963, email: publications@nationalgalleries.org

Internet home pages:
http://www.natgalscot.ac.uk

See also - Dean Gallery; Duff House Country Gallery; National Gallery of Scotland; NGS Picture Library; Paxton House; Scottish National Gallery of Modern Art; Scottish National Portrait Gallery

1983
NATIONAL GALLERY
Trafalgar Square, London, WC2N 5DN

Tel: 020 7747 2885, Information (including TYPETALK)
Fax: 020 7747 2423, Information
Email: information@ng-london.org.uk
Acronym or abbreviation: NG
Formed: 1824

Organisation type and purpose: Museum, art gallery.
Governed by a board of trustees.

Enquiries to: Head of Information
Direct tel: 020 7747 2513
Direct fax: 020 7747 2423
Direct email: miranda.carroll@ng-london.org.uk
Other contacts: Front of House Manager, tel no: 020 7747 2871
Access:
Access to staff: By letter, by telephone, by fax, by email, in person, Internet web pages
Hours: Mon, Tue and Thu to Sun, 1000 to 1800; Wed, 1000 to 2100
Other restrictions: Archives by letter or appointment only; in library the above applies to visitors to Information Desks.
Access for disabled people: level entry, access to all public areas, toilet facilities
Other restrictions: 1 bookable parking space at rear, tel: 020 7747 2854.

General description:
Western European painting from *c.*1250 to *c.* 1900 (oil and tempera, not watercolours); Italian, French, German, early Netherlandish, Flemish, Dutch and Spanish Schools, some British; for the main British School of painting, refer to Tate Britain.
Information services:
CD-ROM based services. Helpline available, tel no: 020 7747 2885.
Micro gallery, 2000 works of art with interactive CD-ROM, handouts available; information desks service, information e-mail, recorded information.
Education Department, exists to help schools and others.
Special visitor services: Guided tours, tape recorded guides, materials and/or activities for children.
Education services: Group education facilities.
Services for disabled people: For the visually impaired; for the hearing impaired; displays and/or information at wheelchair height.
Collections:
Archives of the history of the building and the collection (contact 020 7747 2831)
Catalogues:
Catalogue for library is in-house only. Catalogue for all of the collections is on-line.
Publications list:
is available in hard copy and online.
Printed publications:
Catalogues of the Collection and of Exhibitions
Guide to the National Gallery (some in several languages)
Monthly Lecture List and Season Guides (free at gallery or by subscription)
National Gallery Report (annually)
National Gallery Technical Bulletin (annually)
Electronic and video products:
Large number of videos (list available)
CD-ROMs on selected paintings
Complete Illustrated Catalogue on CD-ROM
Microsoft Art Gallery CD-ROM (Micro gallery on CD-ROM)
Soundguide - CD-ROM of gallery, available for hire
Micro Gallery, computer information room

Address for ordering publications:
Printed publications:
National Gallery Company
St Vincent House, 30 Orange Street, London, WC2H 7HH, tel: 020 7281 9080, fax: 020 7747 5951

Internet home pages:
http://www.nationalgallery.org.uk
Outline of collection; monthly calendar of events; current and forthcoming exhibitions, complete collection online, details of all services provided.

1984
NATIONAL GALLERY
Technical Library, Scientific Department, Trafalgar Square, London, WC2N 5DN

Tel: 020 7747 2400 ext 2829
Fax: 020 7839 3897
Formed: 1950

Organisation type and purpose: National government body, museum, art gallery, research organisation.
Art museum departmental library. Non-Governmental Departmental Body.

Enquiries to: Technical Librarian
Direct tel: 020 7747 2829
Access:
Access to staff: By letter, by telephone, by fax
Hours: Mon to Fri, 0900 to 1730
Other restrictions: No enquiries in person.

General description:
Materials, techniques and history of painting, particularly of European easel painting from *c.* 1300 to 1900, scientific examination of works of art, climate control for works of art, safe exhibition and storage conditions.
Collections:
Eastlake Collection of early books and manuscripts on materials and techniques of painting, and other arts and crafts (part)
Publications list:
is available in hard copy.
Printed publications:
National Gallery Technical Bulletin (£19.95, published by the National Gallery with contributions from the Scientific and Conservation Departments, annually)

Address for ordering publications:
Printed publications:
National Gallery Company Limited
St Vincent House, 30 Orange Street, London, WC2H 7HH, tel: 020 7281 9080

1985
NATIONAL GALLERY OF SCOTLAND
The Mound, Edinburgh, EH2 2EL

Tel: 0131 624 6200
Fax: 0131 220 0917
Email: enquiries@nationalgalleries.org
Formed: 1850

Organisation type and purpose: National government body, national organisation, art gallery, suitable for ages: all ages.
See individual entries.
Parent body:
National Galleries of Scotland
Belford Road, Edinburgh, EH4 3DR, tel: 0131 624 6200, fax: 0131 343 3250, email: enquiries@natgalscot.ac.uk

Enquiries to: Curator
Other contacts: (1) Press and Information Department (2) Curatorial Department for (1) general public enquiries (2) academic enquiries.
Access:
Access to staff: By letter, by telephone, by fax, by email, Internet web pages
Access to building, collections or gallery: No prior appointment required
Hours: Mon to Sat, 1000 to 1700; Sun, 1200 to 1700
Access for disabled people: Parking provided, level entry, access to all public areas, toilet facilities
Other restrictions: Access to all areas except Room A1.

General description:
Widely regarded as one of the finest smaller galleries in the world, the National Gallery of Scotland contains an outstanding collection of paintings, drawings, prints and sculpture by the greatest artists from the Renaissance to Post-Impressionism. The Gallery occupies a handsome Neo-Classical building designed by William Playfair. It contains notable collections of works by Old Masters, Impressionists and Scottish artists. Among them are the Bridgewater Madonna by Raphael, Constable's Dedham Vale and works by Titian, Velazquez, Van Gogh and Gaugin. The Gallery also contains the most comprehensive collection of Scottish art from the 17th to 19th century with masterpieces by such well-known figures as Ramsay, Raeburn and Wilkie. Snap up an Old Master for less than you might think at the Gallery's shop - a twist on the traditional, with surprises round every corner. Temporary exhibitions change on a regular basis, details of which can be found on the website.
Information services:
Library available for reference (for conditions see Access above)
Access to NGS Library catalogues; NGS Libraries are members of UCABLIS (Union Catalogue of Art Books in libraries in Scotland) which is available on-line at the National Library of Scotland, and thus also available via JANET.
Artlink runs a service enabling people with disabilities to visit arts venues in Edinburgh. Register in advance 0131 229 3555
A free Gallery bus runs between the four galleries in Edinburgh.
The National Galleries of Scotland welcome filming in their buildings and grounds (subject to approval by Directors). Regulations and application forms available from the Picture Library.
Free lunchtime lectures and talks on different aspects of the collections are held in the Galleries. Contact the Education Department for details telephone 0131 624 6200.
Study facilities available at the Galleries.
Special visitor services: Tape recorded guides.
Education services: Group education facilities..

continued overleaf

Collections:
Archival files on works of art in the collection
British and foreign exhibition catalogues not available elsewhere in Scotland
Library of National Gallery of Scotland
NGS records before 1907 have been deposited in the Scottish Record Office
Picture Reference library of photographs of works of art not in the collection (letter of introduction required)
Published works on European art 1300-1900: monographs, catalogues of public and private collections, sales catalogues and periodicals
Uncatalogued archives relating to the history of the Gallery
Catalogues:
Catalogue for library is in-house only. Catalogue for all of the collections is published.
Publications list:
is available in hard copy and online.
Printed publications:
Annual Report
Catalogues of permanent collections
Exhibition catalogues
Guide to the National Galleries of Scotland
National Galleries of Scotland Newsletters (6 times a year, free)
National Gallery of Scotland: An architectural and decorative history
Scottish Masters Series

Address for ordering publications:
Printed publications:
Publications Department, National Galleries of Scotland
Dean Gallery, Belford Road, Edinburgh, EH4 3DS, tel: 0131 624 6256/6259/6261, fax: 0131 315 2963, email: publications@nationalgalleries.org

Internet home pages:
http://www.nationalgalleries.org

1986
NATIONAL GAS MUSEUM TRUST, THE
PO Box 28, 195 Aylestone Road, Leicester, LE2 7QH

Tel: 0116 250 3190
Fax: 0116 250 3190
Email: information@gasmuseum.co.uk
Formed: 1977
Formerly: John Doran Gas Museum, date of change, 1996; The Leicester Gas Museum, date of change, 2000

Organisation type and purpose: Museum, suitable for ages: 5+.
Associated with:
The National Gas Archive
Cross Lane, Partington, Near Manchester, tel: 0161 777 7193

Enquiries to: Curator
Access:
Access to staff: By letter, by telephone, by fax, by email, in person, Internet web pages
Hours: Tue, Wed, Thu, 1200 to 1630
Other restrictions: At other times by prior arrangement.

General description:
Information on gas production (from coal); gas lighting, heating and cooking; plus unusual gas appliances, eg hairdryers, radio, washing machines, dishwasher. Also a display on natural gas. A small library of books on gas manufacture is held; leaflets on many old gas appliances held for dating purposes.
Information services:
Special visitor services: Guided tours, materials and/or activities for children..
Collections:
Small collection of books, journals on gas and gas appliances etc
Special collection of gas cookers and fires and unusual appliances, eg dishwasher, hairdryer, radio
Main gas archive collection at The National Gas Archive, Partington
Catalogues:
Catalogue for library is in-house only. Catalogue for part of the collections is only available in-house.
Printed publications:
No specific museum publications, the following held from others:
Burning to Serve
Gas Lighting (Shire publications)
The History of the Gas Light and Coke Company
The Third Man (Biography of William Murdoch)

Internet home pages:
http://www.gasmuseum.co.uk

1987
NATIONAL HERITAGE (MUSEUMS ACTION MOVEMENT)
9A North Street, London, SW4 0HN

Tel: 020 7720 6789
Fax: 020 7978 1815
Formed: 1971

Organisation type and purpose: Membership association, registered charity (charity number 313057).
To support museums and museum-goers.
Organises Museum of the Year Award.

Enquiries to: Chairman
Direct tel: 020 7435 4403
Direct fax: 020 7435 0778
Direct email: jamesbishop3@compuserve.com
Access:
Access to staff: By letter, by telephone, by fax
Hours: Mon to Fri, 1000 to 1630

General description:
Locations of museums and their collections, and general museum information.
Printed publications:
Historic Houses, Castles and Gardens in Great Britain (on sale or free to some grades of membership)
Judges' Report on Museum of the Year Award (annually)
Museum News (for members; three times a year)
Museums and Galleries in Great Britain and Ireland (free to members)

1988
NATIONAL HORSERACING MUSEUM
99 High Street, Newmarket, Suffolk, CB8 8JL

Tel: 01638 667333
Fax: 01638 665600
Formed: 1983

Organisation type and purpose: Independently owned, registered charity (charity number 283656), museum, art gallery, historic building, house or site, suitable for ages: 5+.
To encourage the preservation of items of historical or scientific interest related to horseracing.

Enquiries to: Curator
Other contacts: Director
Access:
Access to staff: By letter, by telephone, visitors by prior appointment
Access to building, collections or gallery: No prior appointment required
Hours: Museum: 3rd March to 10th Oct: daily except Mon, 1100 to 1700; Bank Holidays and Mon in July and August and at other times by prior appointment
Access for disabled people: Parking provided, ramped entry, access to all public areas, toilet facilities
Other restrictions: One parking space outside the museum

General description:
History of horse racing, development of the thoroughbred, racing people, racehorses, video and computer information. Sporting art, including loans from Tate Gallery, trophies, paintings, mounted hooves etc relating to British racing. Hands-on gallery with retired jockeys.
Archive and library.
Teachers' pack and children's activities related to Key Stages of the National Curriculum.
Information services:
Library available for reference (for conditions see Access above)
Special visitor services: Guided tours, materials and/or activities for children.
Education services: Resources for Key Stages 1 and 2..
Collections:
Racing records, racing calendars, paintings
Skeleton of Eclipse
Scanned collection of glass negatives of racehorses
Library
Archives
Printed publications:
Museum illustrated guide (£1.80)
Concise Guide to British Horeseracing History
The Essential Horses in British History

1989
NATIONAL LIGHTHOUSE CENTRE
See - Trinity House National Lighthouse Centre

1990
NATIONAL MARITIME MUSEUM CORNWALL
Discovery Quay, Falmouth, Cornwall, TR11 3QY

Tel: 01326 313388
Fax: 01326 317878
Email: enquiries@nmmc.co.uk
Acronym or abbreviation: NMMC
Formed: 2002
Formerly: Falmouth Maritime Museum and Trust, date of change, 1990; Cornwall Maritime Museum, date of change, 2002

Organisation type and purpose: Voluntary organisation, registered charity (charity number 1067884), museum, suitable for ages: all ages, research organisation.

Enquiries to: Head of Marketing
Direct email: robinbarker@nmmc.co.uk
Other contacts: Education Manager for educational enquiries.
Access:
Access to staff: By letter, by telephone, by fax, by email, visitors by prior appointment, Internet web pages
Hours: Winter: Daily, 1000 to 1700; Summer: Daily, 1000 to 1800
Other restrictions: Closed 6 to 31 January 2003.
Access to building, collections or gallery: No prior appointment required
Access for disabled people: access to all public areas, toilet facilities

General description:
Falmouth Packet Ship Service, Cornwall maritime history, National Small Boat Collection, boat design and construction, navigation and meteorology.
Information services:
Library available for reference (for conditions see Access above)
Special visitor services: Guided tours, materials and/or activities for children.
Education services: Group education facilities, resources for Key Stages 1 and 2, 3, 4 and Further or Higher Education.
Services for disabled people: Displays and/or information at wheelchair height.
Collections:
Bartlett Library (76,000 books)
Photography

Internet home pages:
http://www.nmmc.co.uk

1991
NATIONAL MARITIME MUSEUM

Romney Road, Greenwich, London, SE10 9NF

Tel: 020 8858 4422
Fax: 020 8312 6632
Email: enquiries@nmm.ac.uk
Formed: 1934

Organisation type and purpose: National government body, museum, art gallery, historic building, house or site, suitable for ages: 5+.
To promote an understanding of the history and future of Britain and the sea.
Other addresses:
National Maritime Museum Cornwall (NMMC) Discovery Quay, Falmouth, Cornwall, TR11 3QY, tel: 01326 313388, fax: 01326 317878, email/website: www.nmmc.co.uk

Enquiries to: Information Officer
Other contacts: Technical information, tel no: 020 8312 6607; visitor information, tel no: 020 8312 6565
Access:
Access to staff: By letter, by email, Internet web pages
Access to building, collections or gallery: No prior appointment required
Hours: Museum: Daily, 1000 to 1700; closed 24 to 26 December
Library: Mon to Sat, 1000 to 1645 booking may be needed for Sat
Other restrictions: For items and records in reserve collections, enquire ahead of visit.
Access for disabled people: Parking provided, access to all public areas, toilet facilities
Other restrictions: Limited access at Royal Observatory.
Information leaflet available.

General description:
Maritime history, trade 17th to 21st centuries, shipping, scientific instruments, astronomy 17th to 21st centuries.
Information services:
Library available for reference (for conditions see Access above)
Education and Visitor Booking Unit, tel: 020 8312 6608; Photographic Sales and Services Section, tel: 020 8312 6600; Library, tel: 020 8312 6528; Press Office, tel: 020 8312 6745.
Special visitor services: Guided tours, materials and/or activities for children.
Education services: Group education facilities, resources for Key Stages 1 and 2, 3, 4 and Further or Higher Education.
Services for disabled people: For the visually impaired; displays and/or information at wheelchair height.
Collections:
Oil paintings 3000
Photographic sources 100,000
Records of ships and shipping activity over several centuries
Ship models
Ship plans
Three historic buildings; The Maritime Museum, The Queen's House and The Royal Observatory
Memorial Index, 2500 entries of church, cemetery and public memorials in the world to British people with a maritime association
Catalogues:
Catalogue for library is on-line. Catalogue for part of the collections is on-line.
Publications list:
is available in hard copy and online.
Printed publications:
Books on maritime subjects
Educational materials
Guides to the museum, house and observatory
Microform products:
See website for information on products
Electronic and video products:
See website for information on products
www.jmr.nmm.ac.uk - for the Journal for Maritime Research (online only)
Address for ordering publications:
Printed publications:
Mail Order section, At the same address

Internet home pages:
http://www.nmm.ac.uk
All museum services and resources.
http://www.port.nmm.ac.uk
Portal site for maritime-related internet information.
http://www.rog.nmm.ac.uk
For astronomy information.
http://www.nmmc.co.uk
Cornwall's new maritime museum.

1992
NATIONAL MARITIME MUSEUM

Caird Library, Greenwich, London, SE10 9NF

Tel: 020 8858 4422
Fax: 020 8312 6632
Email: library@nmm.ac.uk and manuscripts @nmm.ac.uk
Acronym or abbreviation: NMM
Formed: 1934

Organisation type and purpose: National government body, museum, suitable for ages: 18+.

Enquiries to: Librarian
Direct tel: 020 8312 6673
Other contacts: Manuscripts Manager for the reservation items ahead of visit.
Access:
Access to staff: By letter, by telephone, by email, in person
Other restrictions: Charges are made for written research enquiries.
Access for disabled people: level entry, toilet facilities
Other restrictions: Parking provided on application only.

General description:
All facets of the maritime history of Great Britain including Royal Navy, merchant shipping, fishing, sailing, archaeology, piracy, navigation, time-keeping at sea, hydrography, dockyards, ports and harbours, shipwrecks and casualties, emigration, astronomy, World War I, World War II, medals, painting.
Information services:
CD-ROM based services, bibliography compilation
Special visitor services: Materials and/or activities for children.
Education services: Group education facilities, resources for Key Stages 1 and 2, 3, 4 and Further or Higher Education.
Services for disabled people: For the visually impaired.
Collections:
Anderson Collection (general maritime subjects)
Gosse Collection (piracy)
Index to Lloyd's List 1838-1927
Lloyd's Captains' Registers 1851-1947
Lloyd's List 1741 to date
Lloyd's Register 1764-1785 and 1794 to date
Macpherson Collection (atlases and other works)
Manuscripts Collection
Maskelyne Collection (astronomy)
Navy Lists 1814 to date
Rare Books Collection: pre-1850
Charts and Atlases: from 15th century onwards
Catalogues:
Catalogue for library is on-line. Catalogue for part of the collections is on-line.
Publications list:
is available in hard copy.
Printed publications:
Books on Maritime subjects
Educational materials
Globes at Greenwich: A catalogue of the Globes and Armillary spheres in the National Maritime Museum
Guides to the Museum, Queen's House and Royal Observatory
Ship Models: Their purpose and development from 1650 to the present
Sundials: An Illustrated History of Popular Dials (2001)
Time and Space Adventures (2001)
Greenwich Guides to: The Seasons, Day and Night & Measuring Time (Dolan G)
Electronic and video products:
Nelson and his Navy (CD-ROM)
National Maritime Museum Picture Library (CD-ROM)
Adventures At Sea: Key Stage 2 Resource (CD-ROM, free)

Address for ordering publications:
Printed publications:
Publications Department, National Maritime Museum
Tel: 020 8312 6667

Internet home pages:
http://www.nmm.ac.uk/searchstation
Online initiative by the National Maritime Museum to make its collections more accessible to the public.
http://port.nmm.ac.uk
An information gateway which assesses and selects the best maritime resources available on the web and provides easy access to them.
Library catalogue, prints and drawings catalogue, historic photographs catalogue.
http://www.nmm.org.uk
The time and tide shop, for National Maritime Museum publications and items.
http://www.port.nmm.ac.uk/research/guides.html
Selection of research guides produced by staff at the National Maritime Museum to assist general research.

1993
NATIONAL MARITIME MUSEUM, HISTORIC PHOTOGRAPHS & SHIPS PLANS

The Old Brass Foundry, Royal Arsenal West, Warren Lane, Woolwich, London, SE18 6TJ

Acronym or abbreviation: NMM
Formed: 1934

Organisation type and purpose: Museum.
All communications to:
National Maritime Museum
Park Row, Greenwich, London, SE10 9NF, tel: 020 8855 1647, fax: 020 8317 0263

Enquiries to: Curator
Access:
Access to staff: By letter, by telephone, by fax, visitors by prior appointment
Other restrictions: All appointments must be made through the National Maritime Museum, Greenwich.
Access to building, collections or gallery: Prior appointment required
Hours: Mon to Fri, 1000 to 1300, 1400 to 1700
Other restrictions: Appointments must be booked two weeks in advance to ensure that material is available on the day of the visit.

General description:
Historic photographs and ships plans.
Covers all things maritime in the age of the camera (from ca. 1845) including ships (sail and steam, naval and mercantile); boats; ports; people; events; shipbuilding and repair; life on board; and shore facilities.
Contains material on naval architecture and marine engineering.
Collections:
Bedford Lemere Collection of negatives of interior views of large passenger liners at the turn of the century
Glass negatives from Portsmouth dockyard showing capital ships from late 19th and early 20th Centuries in various stages of construction including HMS Dreadnought from keel laying to fitting out in 1905-1906
Paper negatives from 1840s of trading vessels.

continued overleaf

Richard Perkins Collection of warship photographs, British and foreign, from ca.1860 until just beforeWorld War II
Ships plans of the following companies:- John I Thorneycroft and Co Ltd
Vickers Armstrong (Elswick) Ltd.
Vosper and Co Ltd.
Alexander Stephen Collection
Denny Collection. Merchant ships.1850-1960s
Royal Navy technical records and plans.1700to date
Catalogues:
Catalogue for part of the collections is published and part is on-line.

Internet home pages:
http://www.nmm.ac.uk
http://www.nmm.ac.uk/cmr/index.html
Centre for maritime research.

1994
NATIONAL MARITIME MUSEUM, LIBRARY AND INFORMATION SERVICES
Park Row, Greenwich, London, SE10 9NF

Tel: 020 8312 6672
Fax: 020 8312 6632
Email: library@nmm.ac.uk
Acronym or abbreviation: NMM

Organisation type and purpose: Museum, public library.

Enquiries to: Library and Information Resources Manager
Direct tel: 020 8312 6673
Other contacts: Library Assistant for general enquiries and information.
Access:
Access to staff: By letter, by telephone, by email, in person
Hours: Mon to Fri, 1000 to 1645
Other restrictions: Sat, 1000 to 1645 (by appointment only).
Access to building, collections or gallery: No access other than to staff
Hours: Mon to Fri, 1000 to 1645
Other restrictions: Sat, 1000 to 1645 (by appointment only).

General description:
Antarctic; Arctic; astronomy; dockyards; East India Company; emigration; exploration; figureheads; flags; genealogy; harbours; life at sea; marine art; marine engineering; maritime fiction; maritime law; medals; merchant shipping; naval history; navigation; oceanography; piracy; ports; seamanship; ship models; shipbuilding; shipping companies; ship wrecks; uniforms; warships; whaling; World War I; World War II; yachting.
Catalogues:
Catalogue for library is on-line. Catalogue for part of the collections is on-line.

Internet home pages:
http://www.nmm.ac.uk/
For the centre for maritime research.
Library catalogue; prints and drawings catalogue.

1995
NATIONAL MINING MUSEUM OF WALES
See - Big Pit National Mining Museum of Wales

1996
NATIONAL MOTOR MUSEUM
Trust Centre, Beaulieu, Brockenhurst, Hampshire, SO42 7ZN

Tel: 01590 612345
Fax: 01590 612655
Email: nmmt@beaulieu.co.uk
Formed: 1961
Formed from: Beaulieu; Montagu Motor Museum, date of change, 1972

Organisation type and purpose: Registered charity (charity number 261929), museum.

Enquiries to: Librarian
Access:
Access to staff: By letter, by telephone, by fax, by email, in person, charges made to all users, Internet web pages
Hours: Mon to Fri, 1000 to 1300 and 1400 to 1700
Access to building, collections or gallery: No prior appointment required
Hours: Mon to Fri, 1000 to 1300 and 1400 to 1700
Access for disabled people: ramped entry, toilet facilities

General description:
Transport, all motor vehicles, motoring, roads, motor sport.
Collections:
Reference Library:
50,000 sales catalogues, 15,000 handbooks and workshop manuals, 9000 bound journals
Complete runs of major motoring magazines with master index, including Autocar from 1895
Film and sound archive
Photographic material
Catalogues:
Catalogue for library is in-house only. Catalogue for all of the collections is published.

Internet home pages:
http://www.beaulieu.co.uk
General information covering services, opening hours, contact details etc.

1997
NATIONAL MOTORBOAT MUSEUM
See - Motorboat Museum

1998
NATIONAL MOTORCYCLE MUSEUM
Coventry Road, Bickenhill, Solihull, West Midlands, B92 OEJ

Tel: 01675 443311
Fax: 01675 443310
Formed: 1984

Organisation type and purpose: Independently owned (charity number XN 74812), museum, suitable for ages: all ages.
To ensure that over sixty years of British motorcycle design and construction are not lost to future generations.

Enquiries to: Information Officer
Access:
Access to staff: By letter
Access to building, collections or gallery: No prior appointment required
Hours: Daily: 1000 to1800, except Christmas Day, Boxing Day
Access for disabled people: access to all public areas

General description:
Historic British motorcycles.
Catalogues:
Catalogue for all of the collections is available in-house and part is on-line.

Internet home pages:
http://www.nationalmotorcyclemuseum.co.uk

1999
NATIONAL MUSEUM & GALLERY CARDIFF
Library, Cathays Park, Cardiff, CF10 3NP

Tel: 029 2057 3202
Fax: 029 2057 3216
Email: john.kenyon@nmgw.ac.uk
Acronym or abbreviation: NMW/NMGW
Formed: 1907

Organisation type and purpose: National government body, museum, art gallery.
Parent body:
National Museums & Galleries of Wales

Set up by Royal Charter and funded through the:
National Assembly for Wales

Enquiries to: Librarian
Direct tel: 029 2057 3202
Direct fax: 029 2037 3216
Access:
Access to staff: By letter, by telephone, by fax, visitors by prior appointment
Hours: Tue to Fri, 1000 to 1700
Access for disabled people: Parking provided, ramped entry, toilet facilities

General description:
Archaeology; art; botany; geology; industrial archaeology; zoology; museum science; architecture; private press; in particular, the special interests of Wales in those subjects.
Collections:
Library of the Cambrian Archaeological Association
Library of the Cardiff Naturalists Society
Tomlin Collection (conchology)
Vaynor Collection (astronomy, travels)
Willoughby Gardner Collection (early books on natural history)
Catalogues:
Catalogue for library is in-house only.
Publications list:
is available in hard copy.
Printed publications:
What's On (quarterly listing of events)
Annual Report
Publications on Museum collections and related topics

Internet home pages:
http://www.cf.ac.uk/nmgw/
For the museum as a whole.

2000
NATIONAL MUSEUM & GALLERY OF WALES, THE
The Castle Gardens, Cardiff, CF5 6DX

Tel: 029 2057 3481
Acronym or abbreviation: NMG
Formed: 1907

Organisation type and purpose: National government body, registered charity (charity number 525774), museum, art gallery, suitable for ages: 5+.
Library, archives and national collections.
Other sites at:
Museum of Welsh Life
St Fagans, Cardiff, CF5 6XB, tel: 02920 573500, fax: 02920 573490, email/website: postawc@btconnect.com
Museum of Welsh Woollen Industry
Dre-Fach Felindre, Llandysul, Dyfed, SA44 5UP, tel: 01559 370929, fax: 01559 371592
Roman Legionary Museum
High Street, Caerleon, NP6 1AE, tel: 01633 423134, fax: 01633 422869
Segontium Roman Museum
Beddgelert Road, Caernarfon, Gwynedd, LL55 2LN, tel: 01286 675625, fax: 01286 678416

Enquiries to: Director
Other contacts: Site Activities Coordinator for general visitor enquiries.
Access:
Access to staff: By letter, by telephone, by fax, by email
Access to building, collections or gallery: No prior appointment required
Hours: Tue to Sun and Bank Holiday Mondays, 1000 to 1700
Closed Christmas and New Year
Access for disabled people: Parking provided, ramped entry, access to all public areas, toilet facilities

General description:
Art, history, geology, archaeology, biodiversity and systematic biology.
Information services:
Education services: Group education facilities, resources for Key Stages 1 and 2, 3 and 4.

Services for disabled people: For the visually impaired; for the hearing impaired; displays and/or information at wheelchair height.
Collections:
National collections relating to all subject areas
Publications list:
is available in hard copy.
Printed publications:
List of publications available

Address for ordering publications:
Printed publications:
Commercial Operations, National Museum and Galleries of Wales
Cathays Park, Cardiff, CF10 3NP, tel: 02920 573477, email: Post@nmgw.ac.uk

Internet home pages:
http://www.nmgw.ac.uk
Collections, access, education, enquiries and general information

2001
NATIONAL MUSEUM OF ANTIQUITIES OF SCOTLAND
See - National Museums of Scotland

2002
NATIONAL MUSEUM OF LABOUR HISTORY
See - People's History Museum

2003
NATIONAL MUSEUM OF PENNY SLOT MACHINES
c/o 50 St Lukes Road, Brighton, East Sussex, BN2 2ZD

Tel: 01273 608620
Acronym or abbreviation: NMPSM
Formed: 1989
Formerly: Vintage Penny Arcade, Remember When ... (R/W); Mechanical Memories (M/M), date of change, 1996

Organisation type and purpose: Voluntary organisation, museum, historic building, house or site, suitable for ages: all ages, consultancy, research organisation, publishing house. Preservation.
Links with:
Antique Amusements Magazine
Association of Independent Museums
National Fairground Museums
Pinball Owners Association
Sussex Museums Group
Other addresses:
Mechanical Memories (M/M)
250/2 Kings Road Arcades, Brighton

Enquiries to: Administrator
Other contacts: Curator
Access:
Access to staff: By letter, by telephone, visitors by prior appointment
Access to building, collections or gallery: Prior appointment required
Hours: Mon to Fri, 0900 to 1700; also by appointment
Other restrictions: Seafront site times are sometimes limited by the sea/weather conditions.
Access for disabled people: Parking provided, ramped entry, access to all public areas, toilet facilities

General description:
Antique mechanical amusement machines, mechanical music machines, vending machines, penny-in-the-slot machines, restoration of such machines, old money boxes. (Reproduction and parts information).
Information services:
Provide props and locations for the production of film, TV, video and advertisements.
Special visitor services: Guided tours, tape recorded guides.
Services for disabled people: For the visually impaired.
Collections:
Limited amount of early trade material, books, photographs, posters and ancillary objects
Publications list:
is available in hard copy.
Printed publications:
Reproduction trade catalogues of 1918 and 1930

Internet home pages:
http://www.lighthouse.org.uk
Shared website, twenty-four hour museum, Brighton Toy Trail.

2004
NATIONAL MUSEUM OF PHOTOGRAPHY, FILM & TELEVISION
Bradford, West Yorkshire, BD1 1NQ

Tel: 01274 202030
Fax: 01274 723155
Email: talk.nmpft@nmsi.ac.uk
Acronym or abbreviation: NMPFT
Formed: 1983
Formed from: National Museum of Science and Industry

Organisation type and purpose: Museum, suitable for ages: all ages.
Affiliated to:
National Museum of Science and Industry
Exhibition Road, South Kensington, London

Enquiries to: Communications Co-ordinator
Other contacts: Duty Curator, telephone between 1400 and 1600
Access:
Access to staff: By letter, by telephone, by fax, by email, visitors by prior appointment
Hours: Tue to Sun, 1000 to 1800
Access to building, collections or gallery: No prior appointment required
Other restrictions: Appointment required for access to collections.
Access for disabled people: Parking provided, level entry, access to all public areas, toilet facilities

General description:
Photography, film, television and media education.
Information services:
Education services: Group education facilities, resources for Key Stages 1 and 2, 3, 4 and Further or Higher Education.
Services for disabled people: For the visually impaired; for the hearing impaired; displays and/or information at wheelchair height.

Internet home pages:
http://www.nmpft.org.uk

2005
NATIONAL MUSEUM OF SCIENCE AND INDUSTRY

Constituent bodies:
National Museum of Photography, Film and Television
National Railway Museum
Science Museum
Science Museum Library

2006
NATIONAL MUSEUM OF SCIENCE AND TECHNOLOGY
See - Science Museum Library

2007
NATIONAL MUSEUMS & GALLERIES ON MERSEYSIDE
PO Box 33, 127 Dale Street, Liverpool, L69 3LA

Tel: 0151 207 0001
Email: press@nmgm.org

Organisation type and purpose: National organisation.

Enquiries to: Communication Manager
Direct tel: 0151 478 4615
Direct fax: 0151 478 4777
Access:
Access to staff: By letter, by email
Access to building, collections or gallery: No prior appointment required
Hours: Mon to Sat, 1000 to 1700; Sun, 1200 to 1700
Other restrictions: Closed 25 to 27 Dec, 1 Jan.

General description:
Administrative headquarters for the eight National Museums & Galleries on Merseyside.

Internet home pages:
http://www.nmgm.org.uk

See also - Conservation Centre; HM Customs & Excise National Museum; Lady Lever Art Gallery; Liverpool Museum; Merseyside Maritime Museum; Museum of Liverpool Life; Sudley House; Walker Art Gallery

2008
NATIONAL MUSEUMS AND GALLERIES OF WALES
Department of Industry, The Collections Centre, Heol Crochendy, Parc Nantgarw, Cardiff, CF15 7QT

Tel: 02920 573560
Fax: 02920 573561
Email: industry@nmgw.ac.uk
Formerly: Department of Industry; Welsh Industrial and Maritime Museum (WIMM), date of change, 1998

Organisation type and purpose: Museum.

Enquiries to: Administrator
Access:
Access to staff: By letter, by telephone, by fax, by email, visitors by prior appointment
Hours: Mon to Fri, 0930 to 1600
Other restrictions: Researchers by prior appointment.
Access to building, collections or gallery: Prior appointment required
Hours: Mon to Fri, 0930 to 1600
Access for disabled people: Parking provided, level entry, access to all public areas, toilet facilities

General description:
All aspects of the industrial, maritime and transport history of Wales from early modern times to present day, specific subject disciplines, extractive industries, mining and quarrying, smelting and metaliferrous industries, light and modern industries, civil engineering and public utilities, land transport, maritime, social history.
Collections:
Documents: Share certificates, personal papers, plans, maps, technical drawings, posters
Reference library of over 15,000 volumes: including HM Inspectors of Mines reports, Lloyds registers and a large number of extant and dead journals
Photographs: 110,000 images including Hansen (shipping), Tempest (aerial), GWR (transport)
Printed publications:
Annual Report

Address for ordering publications:
Printed publications:
Commercial Manager, National Museums and Galleries of Wales
National Museum and Gallery Cardiff, Cathays Park, Cardiff, CF10 3NP

Internet home pages:
http://www.nmgw.ac.uk/industry
More information on collections held in the department and research facilities at the collections centre.
See - Big Pit National Mining Museum of Wales; Museum of the Welsh Woollen Industry; Museum of Welsh Life; National Museum & Gallery Cardiff; Roman Legionary Museum; Segontium Roman Museum; Turner House Gallery; Welsh Slate Museum Llanberis

2009
NATIONAL MUSEUMS OF SCOTLAND

Chambers Street, Edinburgh, EH1 1JF

Tel: 0131 247 4137, library enquiries; 4219, museum enquiries
Fax: 0131 247 4819, general; 4311, library
Email: info@nms.ac.uk
Acronym or abbreviation: NMS
Formed by the amalgamation of: Shambellie House Museum of Costume, National Museum of Antiquities of Scotland, Royal Scottish Museum, Museum of Flight, date of change, 1984; Scottish Agricultural Museum, date of change, 1984-1999; Scottish United Services Museum, date of change, 1984-2000
Formerly: Museum of Antiquities, date of change, 1997; National War Museum of Scotland, date of change, 2000

Organisation type and purpose: Registered charity (charity number SC 011130), museum. Non-departmental public body - NDPB.
The library also includes the collection of the former:
Museum of Antiquities Library
The library is on two sites:
National War Museum of Scotland
Edinburgh Castle
Royal Museum of Scotland
Chambers Street
Constituent museums:
Museum of Flight
East Fortune Airfield, East Lothian, tel: 01620 880308, fax: 01620 880355, email/website: info@nms.ac.uk
Museum of Scottish Country Life
Wester Kittochside, East Kilbride, G76 9HR, tel: 01355 224181, fax: 01355 571290, email/website: info@nms.ac.uk
National War Museum of Scotland
Edinburgh Castle, Edinburgh, EH1 2NG, tel: 0131 225 7534, fax: 0131 225 3848, email/website: library@nms.ac.uk
Royal Museum & Museum of Scotland
Chambers Street, Edinburgh, EH1 1JF, tel: 0131 247 4219/4422, fax: 0131 220 4819, email/website: info@nms.ac.uk or library@nms.ac.uk
Shambellie House
New Abbey, Dumfriesshire, tel: 01387 850375, fax: 01387 850461, email/website: info@nms.ac.uk

Enquiries to: Librarian
Direct tel: 0131 247 4042
Direct fax: 0131 220 4819
Direct email: info@nms.ac.uk
Other contacts: (1) Librarian (2) PR & Marketing Assistant for (1) specific enquiries.
Access:
Access to staff: By letter, by telephone, by fax, by email, visitors by prior appointment, Internet web pages
Hours: Royal Museum Library: Mon to Fri, 1000 to 1300 and 1400 to 1700
National War Museum of Scotland Library: Mon to Fri, 1000 to 1230 and 1400 to 1700
Access for disabled people: access to all public areas, toilet facilities
Other restrictions: Level entry at the Museum of Scotland

General description:
Decorative arts; archaeology; ethnography; history, especially Scottish; geology; zoology; history of science and technology; museology and museum conservation; military history, especially of the Scottish regiments.

The Museum of Scotland tells for the first time the history of Scotland - its land, its people, and their achievements - through the incomparable national collections. The collections include that started by the Society of Antiquaries in 1781 and continued in the former Museum of Antiquities.
Information services:
Library available for reference (for conditions see Access above), on-line searching, CD-ROM based services, bibliography compilation, selective dissemination services
Special visitor services: Guided tours.
Education services: Group education facilities, resources for Key Stages 1 and 2, 3, 4 and Further or Higher Education.
Services for disabled people: For the visually impaired; for the hearing impaired.
Collections:
J A Harvie-Brown manuscripts, library and reprint collections (natural history)
Society of Antiquaries of Scotland manuscripts and archives
The Duke of Cumberland's Papers (microfilm)
W S Bruce manuscripts (natural history)
William Jardine manuscripts (natural history)
Book stock: 80,000 on arts, 30,000 on science, 800 current periodicals
Catalogues:
Catalogue for library is in-house only. Catalogue for all of the collections is only available in-house.
Publications list:
is available in hard copy and online.
Printed publications:
Guides to permanent and temporary exhibitions
Highlight (leaflet, free)
National Museums of Scotland Annual Reports
Collections in Context (Waterson C D)
Going to Church (MacLean C)
Going on Holiday (Simpson E)
Going to School (Withrington D)
No Ordinary Journey - John Rae, Arctic Explorer 1813-1893 (Bunyan I, Calder J et al)
Robert Burns, Farmer (Sprott G)
Scotland's Weather (ed Martin A)
Scottish Endings: Writings on Death (ed Martin A)
The Scots in Sickness and Health (Burnett J)
The Scottish Home (ed Carruthers A)
The Story of the Scottish Soldier 1600-1914 - Bonny Fighters (Calder J)
The Thistle at War: Scotland's Battles (ed McCorry H)
Treasure Islands - A Robert Louis Stevenson Anthology (ed Calder J)
Photographs Series:
Bairns - Scottish Children in Photographs (McGregor I)
Into the Foreground - Scottish Women in Photographs (Leneman L)
To See Oursels - Rural Scotland in Old Photographs (Kidd D I)
Electronic and video products:
Investigating the Lewis Chess Pieces (CD-ROM)

Address for ordering publications:
Printed publications:
NMS Publishing
Royal Museum, Chambers Street, Edinburgh, EH1 1JF, tel: 0131 247 4026, fax: 0131 247 4012, email: publishing@nms.ac.uk

Internet home pages:
http://www.nms.ac.uk
General site for the National Museums of Scotland, including details of current exhibitions, collections and departments of the constituent museums. Includes details of the library collections, services and access arrangements.

See also - Museum of Flight; National War Museum of Scotland; Scottish Agricultural Museum; Shambellie House Museum of Costume

2010
NATIONAL PORTRAIT GALLERY

Heinz Archive and Library, St Martin's Place, London, WC2H 0HE

Tel: 020 7306 0055
Fax: 020 7306 0056, general; 7306 0058, development/press
Acronym or abbreviation: NPG
Formed: 1856

Organisation type and purpose: National government body, art gallery, suitable for ages: all ages.
Archive and library.
Founded in 1856 to collect the likenesses of famous British men and women, and constitutes a unique record of the men and women who created (and are still creating) the history and culture of the nation.
Collections of the gallery's portraits housed at:
Beningbrough Hall
Bodelwyddan Castle
Gawthorpe Hall
Montacute House

Enquiries to: Head of Archive and Library
Access:
Access to staff: By letter, by telephone, visitors by prior appointment
Access for disabled people: ramped entry, toilet facilities

General description:
British portraits and portrait artists, 1400s to present day.
Information services:
Library available for reference (for conditions see Access above)
Consultation service, Wednesday 1400 to 1700.
Special visitor services: Tape recorded guides.
Education services: Group education facilities.
Services for disabled people: For the visually impaired; for the hearing impaired; displays and/or information at wheelchair height.
Collections:
Collection of artists' sitter books, account books, papers, and research papers relating to portrait artists
Extensive collections of portrait engravings, reference photographs of portraits and portrait photographs
Library (library of last resort)
Catalogues:
Catalogue for library is in-house only. Catalogue for part of the collections is published and part is on-line.
Publications list:
is available in hard copy and online.
Printed publications:
Complete Illustrated Catalogue 1856-1979 (1981, new edition in preparation)
Early Georgian Portraits (HMSO, 1977)
Early Victorian Portraits (HMSO, 1974)
Illustrated Report, triennial report 1987-1990
National Portrait Gallery collection (1988)
Regency Portraits, (1985)
Tudor and Jacobean Portraits (HMSO, 1969)
National Portrait Gallery (1997)
Microform products:
Catalogue of 17 portraits in the NPG
The Scharf notebooks

Internet home pages:
http://www.npg.org.uk
Collection search facility, what's on, about the gallery, visitor information, NPG around the country, education, research publications, picture library, bookshop, membership, sponsorship, venue hire, press.

2011
NATIONAL RAILWAY MUSEUM

Leeman Road, York, YO2 4XJ

Tel: 01904 621261
Fax: 01904 611112
Email: nrm@nmsi.ac.uk/nrm
Acronym or abbreviation: NRM
Formed: 1975

Organisation type and purpose: National government body, museum.
Part of:
National Museum of Science and Industry

Enquiries to: Librarian
Direct tel: 01904 686208
Direct fax: 01904 611112
Direct email: nrmlibra@nmsi.ac.uk
Access:
Access to staff: By letter, by telephone, by fax, visitors by prior appointment
Hours: Mon to Fri, 1030 to 1700

General description:
Railway transport operations in the British Isles, railway shipping and related road transport.
Collections:
R C Bond: Papers and notebooks concerning LMS and BR locomotive design and policy, mid-1920s to *c.* 1965
R D Stephen (and W D M Stephen): Scottish locomotives (especially NBR) 1920-1930
Rugby Locomotive Testing Station: Complete correspondence files, test data, and reports *c.* 1936-1959
S H Pearce Higgins: Very large collection especially devoted to minor locomotive builders, and obscure railways in West Midlands eg Shropshire & Montgomeryshire, and Bishop's Castle. Large quantities of negatives, including many of M&GN locomotives
Some 1,000,000 technical drawings of locomotives and rolling stock of British railways origin
Some 1,500,000 photographs and negatives of all aspects of British railways
Official photograph collections of British railway operating companies, including those of the Caledonian, GER, GNR, LMS, LNER, LNWR, LSWR, Lancashire & Yorkshire, Midland, NER and Southern
Over 180 private photographic collections, including:
Roy Cutler: 104 albums of photographs of British main line and industrial locomotives
Eric Mason: Albums of photographs relating to many aspects of the Lancashire & Yorkshire Railway, and albums of photographs of most British locomotive classes
G H Soole: *c.* 1500 negatives, all 1930s, mainly of GWR trains in the Bristol area, and Canadian Pacific Railway in British Columbia
and those of C C B Herbert, M W Earley, Eric Treacy, G H Soole and P Ransome-Wallis, together with the former LPC and LGRP collections, representing the work of railway enthusiasts from the late 19th century to the present day
Catalogues:
Catalogue for library is in-house only. Catalogue for part of the collections is only available in-house.
Printed publications:
A Royal Progress (Kumar, 1997)
Dropping the Fire (Atkins, 1999)
Duchess of Hamilton, Ultimate in Pacific Power (Blakemore and Rutherford, 1990)
Green Arrow (Rutherford, 1997)
Library leaflet 1991 (free)
Mallard the Record Breaker (Rutherford, 1988)
Museum Guide, 1992
Museum Rail Trails, 1992
Railways in Focus (Bartholomew and Blakemore, 1998)
Right Lines - a guide for teachers, 1992
The Golden Age of Steam Locomotive Building (Atkins, 1999)

Internet home pages:
http://www.nrm.org.uk

2012
NATIONAL REGISTER OF ARCHIVES

Acronym or abbreviation: NRA
See - National Archives

2013
NATIONAL RESOURCE CENTRE FOR DANCE
University of Surrey, Guildford, Surrey, GU2 7XH

Tel: 01483 689316
Fax: 01483 689500 (Attn NRCD)
Email: nrcd@surrey.ac.uk
Acronym or abbreviation: NRCD
Formed: 1982

Organisation type and purpose: University department or institute, suitable for ages: 12+, training organisation, publishing house.
National archive.
A national, non-profit archive and information service for dance. The NRCD preserves the nation's dance heritage and enables, supports and enhances the study, research and teaching of dance.

Enquiries to: Manager
Access:
Access to staff: By letter, by telephone, by fax, by email, visitors by prior appointment, charges made to all users, Internet web pages
Hours: Term time: Mon to Wed, 0930 to 1700
Vacations: Mon to Wed, 0930 to 1630
Access for disabled people: Parking provided, level entry, toilet facilities

General description:
The NRCD houses a substantial collection of materials concerning dance in print form (books, cuttings, dissertations, periodicals, press releases, programmes); in visual form (film, posters, photos, video); and in sound recorded form (interviews, talks); and in digital form (CD-ROMs).
Information services:
Education services: Resources for Key Stages 3, 4 and Further or Higher Education..
Collections:
Large collection of core materials: audio; artwork; books; examination syllabi; newspaper cuttings; notation; papers; periodicals; photographs; posters; programmes; publicity; video and film
Collections from dance companies, organisations and individuals which have been catalogued and are therefore accessible:
Audrey Wethered and Chloë Gardner Collection
Betty Meredith Jones Collection
Dalcroze Society Archive
Dance Advance Archive
Dance and the Child International (daCi) Archive
Educational Dance-Drama Theatre Archive
Extemporary Dance Theatre Archive
International Council for Kinetography Laban (ICKL) Archive
Janet Smith and Dancers Archive
Joan Russell Archive
Kokuma Dance Theatre Archive
Kickstart Dance Company Archive
Rudolf Laban Archive
London City Ballet Archive
Lisa Ullmann Archive
Maedée Duprès Archive
Shobana Jeyasingh Dance Company Archive
South Asian Dance Book Collection
EMMA/Midlands Dance Company Archive
Green Candle Dance Company Archive
V-TOL Dance Company Archive
Catalogues:
Catalogue for part of the collections is available in-house and part is published.
Publications list:
is available in hard copy and online.
Printed publications:
The following publications are available for purchase, direct:
Resource packs include:
Black Dance in the UK: Articles and Interviews
Pulcinella (resource pack, Alston)
'Still Life' at the Penguin Café (resource pack, Bintley)
Dance! Education, Training and Careers
Bibliographies of Set Works
Directory of UK Dance Contacts (Jones C and Roberts H eds, 2000, £10)
Many other publications
Electronic and video products:
Dance Current Awareness Bulletin: An invaluable research tool for dance (CD-ROM)
Various videos

Internet home pages:
http://www.surrey.ac.uk/NRCD
Publications listing; services information; catalogue of archive holdings

2014
NATIONAL SMALL BOAT COLLECTION
See - National Maritime Museum Cornwall

2015
NATIONAL SPACE CENTRE
Exploration Drive, Leicester, LE4 5NS

Tel: 0870 6077223
Fax: 0116 2862100
Email: info@spacecentre.co.uk
Formed: June 2001

Organisation type and purpose: National organisation, registered charity (charity number 1078832), museum, suitable for ages: 8+.
Educational facility and research centre.

Enquiries to: Administrator
Access:
Access to staff: By letter, by fax, by email
Access for disabled people: Parking provided, ramped entry, access to all public areas, toilet facilities

General description:
Space science and astronomy in five different themed galleries.
Information services:
Management training.
Special visitor services: Materials and/or activities for children.
Education services: Group education facilities, resources for Key Stages 1 and 2, 3 and 4.
Services for disabled people: For the visually impaired; for the hearing impaired; displays and/or information at wheelchair height.

Internet home pages:
http://www.spacecentre.co.uk

2016
NATIONAL TRAMWAY MUSEUM, THE
Crich, Matlock, Derbyshire, DE4 5DP

Tel: 01773 852565
Fax: 01773 852326
Email: ntm_library@online.rednet.co.uk
Formed: 1955
Formed from: Tramway Museum Society

Organisation type and purpose: Membership association (membership is by subscription), present number of members: 2500, registered charity (charity number 313615), museum.
Transport museum.
Parent body:
Tramway Museum Society
Member of:
Association of British Transport Museums
Association of Independent Museums
Transport Trust
Registered with the:
Museums and Galleries Commission designated as holding a pre-eminent collection

Enquiries to: Librarian
Direct tel: 01773 853787
Other contacts: Admin & Commercial Services Manager
Access:
Access to staff: By letter, by telephone, by fax, by email, visitors by prior appointment, Internet web pages
Hours: Mon to Fri, 0900 to 1700

General description:
History and operation of trams and tramways worldwide; history of trams and tramway equipment manufacturers; tramway films; tramway personalities; light railway systems; transport social history; vehicles, track, overhead management; rapid transit; bus and trolleybus.
Information services:
Library available for reference (for conditions see Access above), bibliography compilation, selective dissemination services. Helpline available, tel no: 01773 853787.

continued overleaf

Tramway construction consultancy; photograph digitising; photographic archive.
Special visitor services: Materials and/or activities for children.
Education services: Group education facilities, resources for Key Stages 1 and 2.
Services for disabled people: Displays and/or information at wheelchair height.
Collections:
12,000 book tiles on database
World Transport Postcard collection
Archives of Municipal Tramways Associations, Bus and Coach Council, BET
Photographic collections (R B Parr, N Forbes, H B Priestley, D W K Jones, M J O'Connor and H Nicol)
Technical drawings (including Glasgow Corporation, Maley and Taunton)
Transport and electrical journals
Catalogues:
Catalogue for library is on-line.
Printed publications:
School activity packs for Key Stage 1 and 2
Guide Book
Journal to Members
List of Films
Museum Stock Book

Internet home pages:
http://www.tramway.co.uk
Access to selected items of photographic archive and ordering service. Museum site information for schools etc.

2017
NATIONAL TRUST (DEVON & CORNWALL REGIONAL OFFICES)

Lanhydrock, Bodmin, Cornwall, PL30 4DE

Tel: 01208 74281
Fax: 01208 77887
Email: enquiries@thenationaltrust.org.uk
Acronym or abbreviation: NT
Full name: National Trust for Places of Historic Interest or Natural Beauty
Formed: 1895

Organisation type and purpose: National organisation, independently owned, membership association (membership is by subscription), registered charity (charity number 205846), suitable for ages: all ages.
Administration and management of Trust sites in Cornwall.

Enquiries to: Customer Service Manager
Access:
Access to staff: By letter, by telephone, by fax, by email, in person, Internet web pages

General description:
The preservation and upkeep of places of historic interest and natural beauty in Cornwall.

Internet home pages:
http://www.nationaltrust.org.uk
Information about the National Trust properties, opening times and facilities, special events, educational information.

See also - Antony House; Cornish Mines and Engines; Cotehele; Cotehele Mill; Godolphin Estate; Lanhydrock; Lawrence House Museum; Levant Steam Engine; Lizard Wireless Station; Marconi Centre; St Anthony Head; St Michael's Mount; Tintagel Old Post Office; Treasurer's House; Trerice Manor House

2018
NATIONAL TRUST (DEVON & CORNWALL REGIONAL OFFICES)

Killerton House, Broadclyst, Exeter, Devon, EX5 3LE

Tel: 01392 881691
Fax: 01392 881954
Email: enquiries@thenationaltrust.org.uk
Acronym or abbreviation: NT
Full name: National Trust for Places of Historic Interest or Natural Beauty
Formed: 1895

Organisation type and purpose: National organisation, independently owned, membership association (membership is by subscription), registered charity (charity number 205846), historic building, house or site, suitable for ages: all ages.
Administration and management of Trust sites in Devon.

Enquiries to: Customer Service Manager
Access:
Access to staff: By letter, by telephone, by fax, by email, in person, Internet web pages

General description:
The preservation and upkeep of places of historic interest and natural beauty in Devon.

Internet home pages:
http://www.nationaltrust.org.uk
Information about the National Trust properties, opening times and facilities, special events, educational information, and publications.

See also - A La Ronde; Arlington Court; Bradley House; Branscombe - Old Bakery, Manor Mill and Forge; Buckland Abbey; Castle Drogo; Church House; Coleton Fishacre House and Garden; Compton Castle; Finch Foundry; Greenway; Killerton House; Killerton: Budlake Old Post Office Room; Killerton: Clyston Mill; Killerton: Marker's Cottage; Killerton: Newhall Equestrian Centre; Knightshayes Court; Loughwood Meeting House; Lundy; Old Mill; Overbecks Museum and Gardens; Saltram House; Shute Barton; Watersmeet House

2019
NATIONAL TRUST (EAST ANGLIA REGIONAL OFFICE)

The Dairy House, Ickworth, Suffolk, IP29 5QE

Tel: 0870 609 5388
Fax: 01284 736066
Email: enquiries@thenationaltrust.org.uk
Acronym or abbreviation: NT
Full name: National Trust for Places of Historic Interest or Natural Beauty
Formed: 1895

Organisation type and purpose: National organisation, independently owned, membership association (membership is by subscription), registered charity (charity number 205846), suitable for ages: all ages.
Administration and management of Trust sites in East Anglia.

Enquiries to: Customer Service Manager
Access:
Access to staff: By letter, by telephone, by fax, by email, in person, Internet web pages

General description:
The preservation and upkeep of places of historic interest and natural beauty in Bedfordshire, Cambridgeshire, Essex, part of Hertfordshire, Norfolk and Suffolk.
Publications list:
is available in hard copy and online.

Internet home pages:
http://www.nationaltrust.org.uk
Information about the National Trust properties, opening times and facilities, special events, educational information, and publications.

See also - Angel Corner; Anglesey Abbey, Gardens and Lode Mill; Blickling Hall; Bourne Mill; Brancaster; Coggeshall Grange Barn; Elizabethan House Museum; Felbrigg Hall, Garden and Park; Flatford: Bridge Cottage; Guildhall of Corpus Christi; Horsey Windpump; Houghton Mill; Ickworth House, Park & Gardens; Melford Hall; Orford Ness National Nature Reserve; Oxburgh Hall, Garden and Estate; Paycocke's; Peckover House; Ramsey Abbey Gatehouse; Rayleigh Mount; Shaw's Corner; Sutton Hoo; Theatre Royal; Thorington Hall; Willington Dovecote & Stables; Wimpole Hall; Wimpole Home Farm

2020
NATIONAL TRUST (EAST MIDLANDS REGIONAL OFFICE)

Clumber Park Stableyard, Worksop, Nottinghamshire, S80 3BE

Tel: 01909 486411
Fax: 01909 486377
Email: enquiries@thenationaltrust.org.uk
Acronym or abbreviation: NT
Full name: National Trust for Places of Historic Interest or Natural Beauty
Formed: 1895

Organisation type and purpose: National organisation, independently owned, membership association (membership is by subscription), registered charity (charity number 205846), historic building, house or site, suitable for ages: all ages.
Administration and management of Trust sites in the East Midlands.

Enquiries to: Customer Service Manager
Access:
Access to staff: By letter, by telephone, by fax, by email, in person, Internet web pages

General description:
The preservation and upkeep of places of historic interest and natural beauty in Derbyshire, Leicestershire, South Lincolnshire, Northamptonshire, Nottinghamshire and Rutland.
Publications list:
is available in hard copy and online.

Internet home pages:
http://www.nationaltrust.org.uk
Information about the National Trust properties, opening times and facilities, special events, educational information, and publications.

See also - Belton House; Calke Abbey; Canons Ashby House; Clumber Park; Grantham House; Gunby Hall; Gunby Hall Estate: Monksthorpe Chapel; Gunby Hall Estate: Whitegates Cottage; Hardwick Hall; High Peak Estate; Kedleston Hall; Lyveden New Bield; Mr Straw's House; National Trust Museum of Childhood; Old Manor; Priest's House; Stainsby Mill: Hardwick Estate; Staunton Harold Church; Sudbury Hall; Tattershall Castle; Tattershall Castle; Winster Market House; Woolsthorpe Manor; Workhouse

2021
NATIONAL TRUST (NORTH WEST REGIONAL OFFICE)

The Hollens, Grasmere, Cumbria, LA22 9QZ

Tel: 0870 609 5391
Fax: 015394 35353
Email: enquiries@thenationaltrust.org.uk
Acronym or abbreviation: NT
Full name: National Trust for Places of Historic Interest or Natural Beauty
Formed: 1895

Organisation type and purpose: National organisation, independently owned, membership association (membership is by subscription), registered charity (charity number 205846), historic building, house or site, suitable for ages: all ages.
Administration and management of Trust sites in the North West region.

Enquiries to: Customer Service Manager
Access:
Access to staff: By letter, by telephone, by fax, by email, in person, Internet web pages

General description:
The preservation and upkeep of places of historic interest and natural beauty in Cheshire, Cumbria, Greater Manchester and Lancashire, Merseyside.
Publications list:
is available in hard copy and online.

Internet home pages:
http://www.nationaltrust.org.uk
Information about the National Trust properties, opening times and facilities, special events, educational information, and publications.

See also - ***20 Forthlin Road, Allerton; Acorn Bank Garden and Watermill; Alderley Edge; Beatrix Potter Gallery; Borrowdale; Cartmel Priory Gatehouse; Dalton Castle; Derwent Island House; Dunham Massey; Dunham Massey: White Cottage; Gawthorpe Hall; Hawkshead and Claife; Hill Top; Little Moreton Hall; Lyme Park; Nether Alderley Mill; Quarry Bank Mill and Styal Estate; Rufford Old Hall; Sizergh Castle & Garden; Speke Hall, Garden and Estate; Steam Yacht Gondola; Tatton Park; Townend; Wasdale, Eskdale and Duddon; Windermere and Troutbeck (including Bridge House); Wordsworth House***

2022
NATIONAL TRUST (SOUTH EAST REGIONAL OFFICE)

Polesden Lacey, Dorking, Surrey, RH5 6BD

Tel: 01372 453401
Fax: 01372 452023
Email: enquiries@thenationaltrust.org.uk
Acronym or abbreviation: NT
Full name: National Trust for Places of Historic Interest or Natural Beauty
Formed: 1895

Organisation type and purpose: National organisation, independently owned, membership association (membership is by subscription), registered charity (charity number 205846), historic building, house or site, suitable for ages: all ages.
Administration and management of Trust sites in the South East region.

Enquiries to: Customer Service Manager
Access:
Access to staff: By letter, by telephone, by fax, by email, in person, Internet web pages

General description:
The preservation and upkeep of Trust properties of historic interest and natural beauty in East Sussex, Kent, Surrey and West Sussex.
Publications list:
is available in hard copy and online.

Internet home pages:
http://www.nationaltrust.org.uk
Information about the National Trust properties, opening times and facilities, special events, educational information, and publications.

See also - ***Alfriston Clergy House; Bateman's; Bodiam Castle; Box Hill; Chartwell; Clandon Park; Claremont Landscape Garden; Emmetts Garden; Hatchlands Park; Ightham Mote; Knole; Lamb House; Leith Hill; Monk's House; Nymans Garden; Oakhurst Cottage; Old Soar Manor; Petworth House; Polesden Lacey; Quebec House; River Wey & Godalming Navigations and Dapdune Wharf; Scotney Castle Garden and Estate; Shalford Mill; Sheffield Park; Sissinghurst Castle Garden; Smallhythe Place; South Foreland Lighthouse; St John's Jerusalem; Standen; Uppark House; Wakehurst Place***

2023
NATIONAL TRUST (THAMES & SOLENT REGIONAL OFFICE)

Hughenden Manor, High Wycombe, Buckinghamshire, HP14 4LA

Tel: 01494 528051
Fax: 01494 463310
Email: enquiries@thenationaltrust.org.uk
Acronym or abbreviation: NT
Full name: National Trust for Places of Historic Interest or Natural Beauty
Formed: 1895

Organisation type and purpose: National organisation, independently owned, membership association (membership is by subscription), registered charity (charity number 205846), historic building, house or site, suitable for ages: all ages.
Administration and management of Trust sites in the Thames and Solent region.

Enquiries to: Customer Service Manager
Access:
Access to staff: By letter, by telephone, by fax, by email, in person, Internet web pages

General description:
The preservation and upkeep of places of historic interest and natural beauty in Berkshire, Buckinghamshire, Hampshire, part of Hertfordshire, Isle of Wight, Greater London and Oxfordshire.
Publications list:
is available in hard copy and online.

Internet home pages:
http://www.nationaltrust.org.uk
Information about the National Trust properties, opening times and facilities, special events, educational information, and publications.

See also - ***2 Willow Road; Ascott; Ashdown House; Ashridge Estate; Basildon Park; Bembridge Windmill; Blewcoat School Gift Shop; Boarstall Duck Decoy; Boarstall Tower; Bradenham Village; Brighstone Shop and Museum; Buckingham Chantry Chapel; Buscot Old Parsonage; Buscot Park; Carlyle's House; Chastleton House; Claydon House; Cliveden; Dorneywood Garden; Eastbury Manor House; Fenton House; George Inn; Great Coxwell Barn; Greys Court; Ham House; Hinton Ampner; Hughenden Manor Estate; King's Head; Lindsey House; Long Crendon Courthouse; Morden Hall Park; Mottisfont Abbey, Garden, House and Estate; Mottistone Manor; Needles Old Battery; Osterley Park House; Pitstone Windmill; Princes Risborough Manor House; Princes Risborough Manor House; Priory Cottages; Rainham Hall; Roman Bath; Runnymede; Sandham Memorial Chapel; Stowe Landscape Gardens; Sutton House; Vyne; Waddesdon Manor; West Green House Garden; West Wycombe Park; West Wycombe Village and Hill; Winchester City Mill***

2024
NATIONAL TRUST (WESSEX REGIONAL OFFICE)

Bishopstrow, Warminster, Wiltshire, BA12 9HW

Tel: 01985 843600
Fax: 01985 843624
Email: enquiries@thenationaltrust.org.uk
Acronym or abbreviation: NT
Full name: National Trust for Places of Historic Interest or Natural Beauty
Formed: 1895

Organisation type and purpose: National organisation, independently owned, membership association (membership is by subscription), registered charity (charity number 205846), historic building, house or site, suitable for ages: all ages.
Administration and management of Trust sites in the Wessex region.

Enquiries to: Customer Service Manager
Access:
Access to staff: By letter, by telephone, by fax, by email, in person, Internet web pages

General description:
The preservation and upkeep of places of historic interest and natural beauty in Bristol/ Bath, Dorset, Gloucestershire, Somerset and Wiltshire.
Publications list:
is available in hard copy and online.

Internet home pages:
http://www.nationaltrust.org.uk
Information about the National Trust properties, opening times and facilities, special events, educational information, and publications.

See also - ***Ashleworth Tithe Barn; Avebury; Avebury Manor and Garden; Barrington Court; Bath Assembly Rooms; Blaise Hamlet; Brean Down; Bredon Barn; Brownsea Island; Chedworth Roman Villa; Cistercian Museum; Clevedon Court; Clouds Hill; Coleridge Cottage; Corfe Castle; Dunster Castle; Dunster Working Watermill; Dyrham Park; Fyne Court; Glastonbury Tor; Great Chalfield Manor; Hailes Abbey; Hardy Monument; Hardy's Cottage; Hidcote Manor Garden; Holnicote Estate; Horton Court; King John's Hunting Lodge; Kingston Lacy; Lacock Abbey and Fox Talbot Museum and Village; Little Clarendon House; Little Fleece Bookshop; Lodge Park and Sherborne Estate; Lytes Cary Manor; Max Gate; Mompesson House; Montacute House; Newark Park; Philipps House and Dinton Park; Priest's House; Prior Park Landscape Garden; Snowshill Manor; Stembridge Tower Mill; Stoke-sub-Hamdon Priory; Stonehenge Down; Stourhead House; Tintinhull Garden; Tyntesfield; West Pennard Court Barn; Westbury College Gatehouse; Westbury Court Garden; Westwood Manor; White Mill; Woodchester Park***

2025
NATIONAL TRUST (WEST MIDLANDS REGIONAL OFFICE)

Attingham Park, Shrewsbury, Shropshire, SY4 4TP

Tel: 01743 708100
Fax: 01743 708150
Email: enquiries@thenationaltrust.org.uk
Acronym or abbreviation: NT
Full name: National Trust for Places of Historic Interest or Natural Beauty
Formed: 1895

Organisation type and purpose: Independently owned, membership association (membership is by subscription), voluntary organisation, registered charity (charity number 205846), suitable for ages: all ages.
Administration and management of Trust sites in the West Midlands.

Enquiries to: Customer Service Manager
Access:
Access to staff: By letter, by telephone, by fax, by email, in person, Internet web pages

General description:
The preservation and upkeep of Trust properties of historic interest and natural beauty in Birmingham, Herefordshire, Shropshire, Staffordshire, Warwickshire and Worcestershire.
Publications list:
is available in hard copy and online.

Internet home pages:
http://www.nationaltrust.org.uk
Information about the National Trust properties, opening times and facilities, special events, educational information, and publications.

See also - ***Attingham Park; Baddesley Clinton Hall; Benthall Hall; Berrington Hall; Biddulph Grange Garden; Brockhampton House and Estate; Charlecote Park; Coughton Court; Croft Castle; Croome Park; Cwmmau Farmhouse; Dudmaston Hall; Farnborough Hall; Fleece Inn; Greyfriars; Hanbury Hall;***

continued overleaf

Hawford Dovecote; Kinver Edge and Holy Austin Rock Houses; Kinwarton Dovecote; Middle Littleton Tithe Barn; Morville Hall; Moseley Old Hall; Packwood House; Shugborough Estate; Sunnycroft; Town Walls Tower; Upton House; Wall Roman Site (Letocetum) Baths and Museum; Wichenford Dovecote; Wightwick Manor; Wilderhope Manor

2026
NATIONAL TRUST (YORKSHIRE & NORTH EAST REGIONAL OFFICES)

Scots' Gap, Morpeth, Northumberland, NE61 4EG

Tel: 01670 774691
Fax: 01670 774317
Email: enquiries@thenationaltrust.org.uk
Acronym or abbreviation: NT
Full name: National Trust for Places of Historic Interest or Natural Beauty
Formed: 1895

Organisation type and purpose: National organisation, independently owned, membership association (membership is by subscription), registered charity (charity number 205846), historic building, house or site, suitable for ages: all ages.
Administration and management of Trust sites in the North East.

Enquiries to: Customer Service Manager
Access:
Access to staff: By letter, by telephone, by fax, by email, in person, Internet web pages

General description:
Administration and management of Trust sites in the region.
The preservation and upkeep of Trust properties of historic interest and natural beauty in Co Durham, Newcastle and Tyneside, Northumberland.
Publications list:
is available in hard copy and online.

Internet home pages:
http://www.nationaltrust.org.uk
Information about the National Trust properties, opening times and facilities, special events, educational information, and publications.

See also - ***Cherryburn; Cragside House, Gardens and Estate; Dunstanburgh Castle; George Stephenson's Birthplace; Gibside; Hadrian's Wall and Housesteads Roman Fort; Lindisfarne Castle; Ormesby Hall; Souter Lighthouse; Washington Old Hall***

2027
NATIONAL TRUST (YORKSHIRE & NORTH EAST REGIONAL OFFICES)

Goddards, 27 Tadcaster Road, York, YO24 1GG

Tel: 01904 702021
Fax: 01904 771970
Email: enquiries@thenationaltrust.org.uk
Acronym or abbreviation: NT
Full name: National Trust for Places of Historic Interest or Natural Beauty
Formed: 1895

Organisation type and purpose: National organisation, independently owned, membership association (membership is by subscription), registered charity (charity number 205846), historic building, house or site, suitable for ages: all ages.
Administration and management of Trust sites in Yorkshire & the North East.

Enquiries to: Customer Service Manager
Access:
Access to staff: By letter, by telephone, by fax, by email, in person, Internet web pages

General description:
The preservation and upkeep of Trust properties of historic interest and natural beauty in Yorkshire, Teesside and North Lincolnshire.
Publications list:
is available in hard copy and online.

Internet home pages:
http://www.nationaltrust.org.uk
Information about the National Trust properties, opening times and facilities, special events, educational information, and publications.

See also - ***Beningbrough Hall and Gardens; Braithwaite Hall; East Riddlesden Hall; Fountains Abbey & Studley Royal; Maister House; Marsden Moor Estate; Moulton Hall; Mount Grace Priory; Nostell Priory; Nunnington Hall; Rievaulx Terrace and Temples; Treasurer's House; Yorkshire Coast***

2028
NATIONAL TRUST FOR SCOTLAND (NORTH-EAST REGION)

The Stables, Castle Fraser, Sauchen, Inverurie, Aberdeenshire, AB51 7LD

Tel: 01330 833225
Fax: 01330 833666
Acronym or abbreviation: NTS
Formed: 1931

Organisation type and purpose: National organisation, independently owned, membership association (membership is by subscription), registered charity (charity number SCO 07410), suitable for ages: all ages.
Administration and management of Trust sites in Perthshire, Angus, Aberdeen & Grampian.
Parent body:
National Trust for Scotland
28 Charlotte Square, Edinburgh, EH2 4ET, tel: 0131 243 9300, fax: 0131 243 9301, email: information@nts.org.uk
National Trust for Scotland sites:
Angus Folk Museum
Kirkwynd, Glamis, Forfar, Angus, DD8 1RT, tel: 01307 840288
Barry Water Mill
Barry, Carnoustie, Angus, DD7 7RJ, tel: 01241 856761
Castle Fraser
Sauchen, Inverurie, Aberdeenshire, AB51 7LD, tel: 01330 833463, fax: 01330 833819
Craigievar Castle
Alford, Aberdeenshire, AB33 8JF, tel: 013398 83635, fax: 013398 83280
Crathes Castle, Garden & Estate
Banchory, Aberdeenshire, AB31 5QJ, tel: 01330 844525, fax: 01330 844797, email/website: crathes@nts.org.uk
Drum Castle, Garden & Estate
Drumoak, Banchory, Aberdeenshire, AB31 5EY, tel: 01330 811204, fax: 01330 811962, email/website: drum-castle@nts.org.uk
Dunkeld
Ell Shop, The Cross, Dunkeld, Perthshire, PH8 0AN, tel: 01350 727460, email/website: dunkeld@nts.org.uk
Dunkeld and The Hermitage
Dunkeld, Perthshire, tel: 01350 728641 (Ranger Office), fax: tel/fax 01796 473233 (Killiecrankie Visitor Centre)
Finavon Doocot
Finavon, Angus
Fyvie Castle
Fyvie, Turriff, Aberdeenshire, AB53 8JS, tel: 01651 891266, fax: 01651 891107
Haddo House
Ellon, Aberdeenshire, AB41 7EQ, tel: 01651 851440, fax: 01651 851888, email/website: haddo@nts.org.uk
House of Dun
Montrose, Angus, DD10 9LQ, tel: 01674 810264, fax: 01674 810722, email/website: houseofdun@nts.org.uk
J M Barrie's Birthplace
9 Brechin Road, Kirriemuir, Angus, DD8 4BX, tel: 01575 572646
Killiecrankie Visitor Centre
Pitlochry, Perth & Kinross, PH16 5LG, tel: 01796 473233, email/website: killiecrankie@nts.org.uk
Leith Hall, Garden & Estate
Huntly, Aberdeenshire, AB54 4NQ, tel: 01464 831216, fax: 01464 831594, email/website: leithhall@nts.org.uk
Museum of Farming Life
Pitmedden Garden, Ellon, Aberdeenshire, AB41 0PD, tel: 01651 842352, fax: 01651 843 188, email/website: sburgess@nts.org.uk
Pitmedden Garden
Ellon, Aberdeenshire, AB41 7PD, tel: 01651 842352, fax: 01651 843188

Enquiries to: Public Affairs Manager
Direct tel: 01330 833559
Direct email: glovie@nts.org.uk
Access:
Access to staff: By letter, by telephone, by fax
Hours: Mon to Fri, 0900 to 1700

General description:
Heritage, conservation and environmental projects.
Publications list:
is available in hard copy.

Internet home pages:
http://www.nts.org.uk

See also - ***Aberdeen Maritime Museum; Angus Folk Museum; Barry Mill; Castle Fraser; Craigievar Castle; Crathes Castle, Garden & Estate; Drum Castle, Garden & Estate; Dunkeld; Dunkeld and The Hermitage; Finavon Doocot; Fyvie Castle; Haddo House; House of Dun; J M Barrie's Birthplace; Killiecrankie Visitor Centre; Leith Hall, Garden & Estate; Museum of Farming Life; Pitmedden Garden***

2029
NATIONAL TRUST FOR SCOTLAND (SOUTH REGION)

Northgate House, 32 Northgate, Peebles, Borders, EH45 8RS

Tel: 01721 722502
Fax: 01721 726000
Email: information@nts.org.uk
Acronym or abbreviation: NTS
Formed: 1931

Organisation type and purpose: Independently owned, membership association (membership is by subscription), registered charity (charity number SCO 07410), suitable for ages: all ages.
Parent body:
National Trust for Scotland
Wemyss House, 28 Charlotte Square, Edinburgh, EH2 4ET, tel: 0131 243 9300, fax: 0131 243 9301, email: information@nts.org.uk
National Trust for Scotland sites:
Balmerino Abbey
Balmerino, Fife
Broughton House
12 High Street, Kirkcudbright, Dumfries & Galloway, DG6 4JX, tel: 01557 330437, email/website: broughtonhouse@nts.org.uk
Caiy Stane
Caiystane View, Edinburgh
Falkland Palace
Falkland, Cupar, Fife, KY15 7BU, tel: 01337 857397, fax: 01337 857980, email/website: falklandpalace@nts.org.uk
Georgian House
7 Charlotte Square, Edinburgh, EH2 4DR, tel: 0131 226 3318, email/website: thegeorgianhouse@nts.org.uk
Gladstone's Land
477B Lawnmarket, Edinburgh, EH1 2NT, tel: 0131 226 5856, fax: 0131 226 4851
Hill of Tarvit Mansion House & Gardens
Cupar, Fife, KY15 5PB, tel: 01334 653127
House of the Binns
Linlithgow, West Lothian, EH49 7NA, tel: 01506 834255, email/website: houseofthebinns@nts.org.uk
Kellie Castle and Garden

Pittenweem, Anstruther, Fife, KY10 2RF, tel: 01333 720271, fax: 01333 720326
Newhailes
Newhailes Road, Musselburgh, East Lothian, EH21 6RY, tel: 0131 665 1546
No 28 Charlotte Square
Edinburgh, EH2 4ET, tel: 0131 243 9300, fax: 0131 243 9339
Preston Mill and Phantassie Doocot
East Linton, East Lothian, EH40 3DS, tel: 01620 860426
Robert Smail's Printing Works
7/9 High Street, Inverleithen, Borders, EH44 6HA, tel: 01896 830206, email/website: smails@nts.org.uk
Royal Burgh of Culross
Culross, Fife, KY12 8JH, tel: 01383 880359, fax: 01383 882675
Threave
Castle Douglas, Dumfries & Galloway, DG7 1RX, tel: 01556 502575, fax: 01556 502683, email/website: threave@nts.org.uk

Enquiries to: Director
Access:
Access to staff: By letter, by telephone, by fax, by email, visitors by prior appointment
Hours: Mon to Fri 0900 to 1700

General description:
Specific information on its own properties and sites also conservation, environmental issues and heritage.
Administration and management of Trust sites in Dumfries & Galloway, Scottish Borders, Edinburgh & The Lothians, and Fife.
Trade and statistical:
Tourist, visitor attractions, building conservation.

Internet home pages:
http://www.nts.org.uk
Information about the National Trust for Scotland properties, opening times and facilities, special events, educational information, and publications.

See also - Balmerino Abbey; Broughton House; Caiy Stane; Falkland Palace; Georgian House; Gladstone's Land; Glenluce Abbey and Glebe; Hill of Tarvit Mansion House & Gardens; House of the Binns; Kellie Castle and Garden; Newhailes; No 28 Charlotte Square; Preston Mill and Phantassie Doocot; Robert Smail's Printing Works; Royal Burgh of Culross; Threave

2030
NATIONAL TRUST FOR SCOTLAND (WEST REGION)

Greenbank House, Flenders Road, Clarkston, Glasgow, G76 8RB

Tel: 0141 616 2266
Fax: 0141 616 0550
Email: kcarr@nts.org.uk
Acronym or abbreviation: NTS
Formed: 1931

Organisation type and purpose: National organisation, membership association, present number of members: 246,000, voluntary organisation, registered charity (charity number SCO 07410), suitable for ages: all ages.
Parent body:
National Trust for Scotland
Wemyss House, 28 Charlotte Square, Edinburgh, EH2 4ET, tel: 0131 243 9300, fax: 0131 243 9301, email: information@nts.org.uk
National Trust for Scotland sites:
Alloa Tower
Alloa Park, Alloa, FK10 1PP, tel: 01259 211701, fax: 01259 218744
Bannockburn Heritage Centre
Glasgow Road, Bannockburn, Stirling, FK7 0LJ, tel: 01786 812664, fax: 01786 810892
Batchelors' Club
Sandgate Street, Tarbolton, South Ayrshire, KA5 5RB, tel: 01292 541940
Black Hill
Lanark, South Lanarkshire
Brodick Castle Garden and Country Park
Brodick, Isle of Arran, tel: 01770 302202, fax: 01770 302312, email/website: brodick@nts.org.uk
Culzean Castle and Country Park
Maybole, South Ayrshire, KA19 8LE, tel: 01655 884455, fax: 01655 884503, email/website: culzean@nts.org.uk
David Livingstone Centre
165 Station Road, Glasgow, South Lanarkshire, G72 9BT, tel: 01698 8231140, fax: 01698 821424
Holmwood House
61-63 Netherlee Road, Cathcart, Glasgow, G44 3YG, tel: 0141 637 2129, fax: 0141 637 2129, email/website: holmwood@nts.org.uk
Hutchesons' Hall
158 Ingram Street, Glasgow, G1 1EJ, tel: 0141 552 8391, fax: 0141552 7031, email/website: hutchesonshall@nts.org.uk
Menstrie Castle
Castle Street, Menstrie, Clackmannanshire
Moirlanich Longhouse
Near Killin, Stirling
Museum of Scottish Country Life
Wester Kittochside, East Kilbride, G76 9HR, tel: 01355 224181, fax: 01355 571290
Pollok House
Pollok Country Park, 2060 Pollokshaws Road, Glasgow, G43 1AT, tel: 0141 616 6410, fax: 0141 616 6521, email/website: pollokhouse@nts.org.uk
Souter Johnnie's Cottage
Main Road, Kirkoswald, Ayrshire, KA19 8HY, tel: 01655 760603
Tenement House
145 Buccleuch Street, Garnethill, Glasgow, G3 6QN, tel: 0141 333 0183, email/website: tenementhouse@nts.org.uk
The Hill House
Upper Colquhoun Street, Helensburgh, G849AJ, tel: 01436 673900, fax: 01436 674685
The Pineapple
North of Airth, Falkirk, tel: 01324 831137
Weaver's Cottage
Shuttle Street, The Cross, Kilbarchan, Renfrewshire, PA10 2JG, tel: 01505 705588

Enquiries to: Public Relations Officer
Other contacts: Regional Director (for policy)
Access:
Access to staff: By letter, by telephone, by fax, by email, Internet web pages
Hours: Mon to Fri, 0900 to 1700

General description:
Specific information on the properties, also conservation and environmental issues, particularly in this region of Scotland.
Administration and management of Trust sites in Ayrshire & Arran, Greater Glasgow & Clyde Valley and Cental Scotland.
Collections:
Many collections appropriate to individual properties (details on request)
Trade and statistical:
Tourist, visitor attractions, building conservation.
Publications list:
is available in hard copy.
Printed publications:
Full colour guide books to many properties
NTS Annual Report (free)
NTS Guide to Over 100 Properties
NTS Handbook
Publications under the following headings:
Architecture and Interiors
Birthplaces, Industrial and Social History
Garden Books, Guides and leaflets
Maps and Charts
Mountains, Islands and Countryside
Walks and Trails
Electronic and video products:
Wide variety of films, slides and videos for sale and hire, including:
A Sampling of Scotland
Britain: Kingdom of the Sea
Countryside in Trust (slides and notes)
Fair Isle - The Happy Island
Gardens in Trust (slides and notes)
House of Dun ... no more handsome and convenient a house of the bigness in all the ancient Kingdom
Scotland a Heritage
Scotland in Trust (slides and notes)
St Kilda Story
The Tenement House, Glasgow
The Work of the Weavers

Internet home pages:
http://www.nts.org.uk

See also - Alloa Tower; Bannockburn Heritage Centre; Batchelors' Club; Black Hill; Brodick Castle Garden and Country Park; Culzean Castle and Country Park; David Livingstone Centre; Hill House; Holmwood House; Hutchesons' Hall; Menstrie Castle; Moirlanich Longhouse; Museum of Scottish Country Life; Pineapple; Pollok House; Souter Johnnie's Cottage; Tenement House; Weaver's Cottage

2031
NATIONAL TRUST FOR SCOTLAND, THE

28 Charlotte Square, Edinburgh, EH2 4ET

Tel: 0131 243 9300
Fax: 0131 243 9301
Email: information@nts.org.uk
Acronym or abbreviation: NTS
Formed: 1931

Organisation type and purpose: Independently owned, membership association (membership is by subscription), registered charity (charity number SCO07410), suitable for ages: all ages.
Conservation of sites which have significance for the natural or built heritage of Scotland.
Other locations:
National Trust for Scotland (North America)
One Boston Place, Fifth Floor, Boston, MA 02108, USA, tel: 00 1 617 619 3631, email/website: nationaltrustforscotland@mediaone.net
National Trust for Scotland London (Office)
19 Cockspur Street, London, SW1Y 5BL, tel: 020 7321 5765, fax: 020 7389 0758
Regional Offices:
Highlands and Islands Regional Office (North)
Balnain House, 40 Huntly Street, Inverness, IV3 5HR, tel: 01463 232034, fax: 01463 732620
Highlands and Islands Regional Office (South)
Lochvoil House, Dunuraran Road, Oban, PA34 4NE, tel: 01631 570000, fax: 01631 570011
National Trust for Scotland (North-East Region)
The Stables, Castle Fraser, Sauchen, Inverurie, Aberdeenshire, AB51 7LD, tel: 01463 232034, fax: 01463 732620
National Trust for Scotland (South Region)
Northgate House, 32 Northgate, Peebles, EH45 8RS, tel: 01721 722502, fax: 01721 726000
National Trust for Scotland (West Region)
Greenbank House, Flenders Road, Clarkston, Glasgow, G76 8RB, tel: 0141 616 2266, fax: 0141 616 0550

Enquiries to: Archivist
Direct tel: 0131 243 9524
Direct email: cbain@nts.org.uk
Access:
Access to staff: By letter, by telephone, by fax, by email
Hours: Mon to Fri, 0930 to 1630
Other restrictions: Limited disabled access.

General description:
Practical aspects of conserving and making available to the public, with information and visitor services, country houses, small buildings, gardens, battlefields, and countryside and all places of natural beauty or historic or architectural interest
in Scotland.
Collections:
Archives of the National Trust for Scotland (1931- current) and some collections of family papers associated with some of our properties
A small reference library
Catalogues:
Catalogue for library is in-house only. Catalogue for all of the collections is only available in-house.
Publications list:

continued overleaf

is available in hard copy.
Printed publications:
Annual Report
Architecture and Interiors
Corporate Brochure
Corporate Plan
Educational publications relating to the properties
Guidebooks, brochures and leaflets to Trust properties
Heritage Scotland (magazine, quarterly)
Resource packs
Scotland's Gardens Scheme Handbook 1999

Internet home pages:
http://www.nts.org.uk
Information about the National Trust for Scotland properties, opening times and facilities, special events, educational information, and publications.

2032
NATIONAL TRUST FOR SCOTLAND HIGHLANDS AND ISLANDS OFFICE (NORTH)

Balnain House, 40 Huntly Street, Inverness, IV3 5HR

Tel: 01463 232034
Telex: 01463 732620
Email: information@nts.org.uk
Acronym or abbreviation: NTS

Organisation type and purpose: Independently owned, membership association (membership is by subscription), voluntary organisation, registered charity, suitable for ages: all ages.
Parent body:
National Trust for Scotland
National Trust for Scotland sites:
Balmacara Estate
Lochalsh House (NTS), Balmacara, Kyle, Ross-shire, IV40 8DN, tel: 01599 566359, email/website: balmacara@nts.org.uk
Boath Doocot
Auldearn, Nairn, Moray
Brodie Castle
Brodie, Forres, Moray, IV36 2TE, tel: 01309 641371, fax: 01309 641600, email/website: brodiecastle@nts.org.uk
Culloden Moor Visitors Centre
Culloden Moor, Inverness, Highland, IV2 5EU, tel: 01463 790607, fax: 01463 794294, email/website: rmackenzie@nts.org.uk
Strome Castle
Ross-shire

Enquiries to: Director

General description:
Specific information on its own properties and sites also conservation, environmental issues and heritage.
Administration and management of Trust sites in Ross-shire, Inverness, Nairn, Moray & The Black Isle, and Northern Islands.

Internet home pages:
http://www.nts.org.uk

See also - Balmacara Estate; Boath Doocot; Brodie Castle; Culloden Moor Visitors Centre; Hugh Miller's Cottage; Strome Castle

2033
NATIONAL TRUST FOR SCOTLAND HIGHLANDS AND ISLANDS OFFICE (SOUTH)

Lochviol House, Dunaran Road, Oban, Argyll, PA34 4NE

Tel: 01631 570000
Fax: 01631 570011
Email: information@nts.org.uk
Acronym or abbreviation: NTS

Organisation type and purpose: Registered charity (charity number SCO 07410), suitable for ages: all ages.
Administration and management of Trust sites in Argyll & Lochaber and West Coast Islands.
Parent body:
National Trust for Scotland
28 Charlotte Square, Edinburgh, EH2 4ET, tel: 0131 243 9300, fax: 0131 243 9301, email: information@nts.org.uk
National Trust for Scotland sites:
Glencoe and Dalness
The National Trust for Scotland Visitor Centre, Glencoe, Argyll, PH49 4LA, tel: 01855 811729, fax: 01855 811772, email/website: glencoe@nts.org.uk
Glenfinnan Monument
National Trust for Scotland Information Centre, Glenfinnan, Highland, PH37 4LT, tel: 01397 722250, email/website: glenfinnan@nts.org.uk

Enquiries to: Director
Access:
Access to staff: By letter, by telephone, by fax, by email, visitors by prior appointment
Hours: Mon to Fri, 0900 to 1700

General description:
Heritage, conservation and environmental projects.
Administration and management of Trust sites in Argyll & Lochaber, and West Coast Islands.

Internet home pages:
http://www.nts.org.uk
Information about the National Trust for Scotland properties, opening times and facilities, special events, educational information, and publications.

See also - Glencoe and Dalness; Glenfinnan Monument

2034
NATIONAL TRUST FOR SCOTLAND SCHOOL OF PRACTICAL GARDENING

See - Threave

2035
NATIONAL TRUST, THE

36 Queen Anne's Gate, London, SW1H 9AS

Tel: 020 7222 9251
Fax: 020 7222 5097
Email: enquiries@thenationaltrust.org.uk
Acronym or abbreviation: NT
Full name: National Trust for Places of Historic Interest or Natural Beauty
Formed: 1895

Organisation type and purpose: National organisation, membership association (membership is by subscription), present number of members: 2.9 million, voluntary organisation, registered charity (charity number 205846), museum, historic building, house or site, suitable for ages: all ages, research organisation, publishing house.
Membership is the principal means by which the NT is supported, but access to its services is not restricted to members.
The National Trust preserves places of historic interest or natural beauty for all to enjoy, now and forever.
Other addresses:
Learning Community and Volunteering Office
Rowan House, Kembrey Park, Swindon, Wiltshire, SN2 6UG, tel: 0870 609 5383
National Trust Conservation Directorate
33 Sheep Street, Cirencester, Gloucestershire, CL7 1RQ, tel: 0870 609 5382
National Trust Enterprises
The Stable Block, Heywood House, Westbury, Wiltshire, BA13 4NA, tel: 0870 609 5381
National Trust for Scotland
Wemyss House, 28 Charlotte Square, Edinburgh, EH2 4ET, tel: 0131 243 9300
National Trust Office for Northern Ireland
Rowallane House, Saintfield, Ballynahinch, Co Down, BT24 7LH, tel: 028 9751 0721, fax: 028 9751 1242
National Trust Office for Wales
Trinity Square, Llandudno, LL30 2DE, tel: 01492 860123, fax: 01492 860233
National Trust Theatre Projects
The National Trust, Sutton House, 2 & 4 Homerton High Street, Hackney, London, E9 6JQ, tel: 020 8986 0242
The National Trust Membership Department
PO Box 39, Bromley, Kent, BR1 3XL, tel: 020 8466 6824
Regional Offices:
National Trust, Devon & Cornwall
Lanhydrock, Bodmin, Cornwall, PL30 4DE, tel: 01208 74281, fax: 01208 77887
National Trust, Devon & Cornwall
Killerton House, Broadclyst, Exeter, Devon, EX5 3LE, tel: 01392 881691, fax: 01392 881954
National Trust, East Anglia
(Bedfordshire, Cambridgeshire, Essex, part of Hertfordshire, Norfolk & Suffolk)
The Dairy House, Ickworth, Suffolk, IP29 5QE, tel: 0870 609 5388, fax: 01284 736066
National Trust, East Midlands
(Derbyshire, Leicestershire, S Lincolnshire, Northamptonshire, Nottinghamshire & Rutland)
Clumber Park Stableyard, Worksop, Nottinghamshire, S80 3BE, tel: 01909 486411, fax: 01909 486377
National Trust, North West
(Cheshire, Cumbria, Greater Manchester & Lancashire, Merseyside)
The Hollens, Grasmere, LA22 9QZ, tel: 0870 609 5391, fax: 015394 35353
National Trust, South East
(East Sussex, Kent, Surrey & West Sussex)
Polesden Lacey, Dorking, Surrey, RH5 6BD, tel: 01372 453401, fax: 01372 452023
National Trust, Thames & Solent
(Berkshire, Buckinghamshire, Hampshire, part of Hertfordshire, Isle of Wight, Greater London & Oxfordshire)
Hughenden Manor, High Wycombe, Buckinghamshire, HP14 4LA, tel: 01494 528051, fax: 01494 463310
National Trust, Wessex
(Bristol/Bath, Dorset, Gloucestershire, Somerset & Wiltshire)
Eastleigh Court, Bishopstrow, Warminster, Wiltshire, BA12 9HW, tel: 01985 843600, fax: 01985 843624
National Trust, West Midlands
(Birmingham, Hereford, Shropshire, Staffordshire, Warwickshire &Worcestershire)
Attingham Park, Shrewsbury, Shropshire, SY4 4TP, tel: 01743 708100, fax: 01743 708150
National Trust, Yorkshire & North East
(Co Durham, Newcastle & Tyneside, Northumberland)
Scots' Gap, Morpeth, Northumberland, NE61 4EG, tel: 01670 774691, fax: 01670 774317
National Trust, Yorkshire & North East
(Yorkshire, Teesside & N Lincolnshire)
Goddards, 27 Tadcaster Road, York, YO24 1GG, tel: 01904 702021, fax: 01904 771970

Enquiries to: Director General
Other contacts: Customer Care Manager for general enquiries.
Access:
Access to staff: By letter, by telephone, by fax, by email, in person, Internet web pages
Hours: Mon to Fri, 0900 to 1700

General description:
Conservation of buildings and land of historic interest or natural beauty held in perpetuity for the nation, inalienably. History of the National Trust. Visitor management, sustainability, policy issues etc.
Collections:
Details may be found in the Trust's handbook and on the website
Some country houses contain antiquarian libraries for which the central catalogue is still in the development stage. All these collections are managed and accessed by different arrangements, many of which are local to the property itself
Publications list:
is available in hard copy and online.

Printed publications:
Magazine (3 times a year, members)
Properties List (every 5 years)
National Trust Handbook (annually)
Books related to the properties eg architecture and horticulture, and cooking and children's stories (sold in National Trust Shops and good bookshops)
Guide books to practically every property open to the public (available at the properties or from Reception at 36 Queen Anne's Gate)
The Lake District: a resource book for teachers
Books for children include:
The Investigating Series: 12 titles connected to Key Stages 2 and 3 of the National Curriculum
The Mud Pack Series, conservation in England, Wales and Northern Ireland
See website for complete list
Electronic and video products:
National Trust British Countryside (CD-ROM, from Anglia Multimedia, tel 01603 615151, £29.99)
Timeline: Trust houses brought to life

Internet home pages:
http://www.nationaltrust.org.uk
Includes a section dedicated to providing online access to information about their holdings, which include buildings, collections, libraries and archives

2036
NATIONAL TRUST MUSEUM OF CHILDHOOD, THE
Sudbury Hall, Sudbury, Ashbourne, Derbyshire, DE6 5HT

Tel: 01283 585337
Email: museumofchildhood@nationaltrust.org.uk

Organisation type and purpose: National organisation, registered charity (charity number 205846), museum, historic building, house or site, suitable for ages: 5+.
Parent body:
The National Trust (East Midlands Region)
East Midlands Regional Office, tel: 07909 486411

Other contacts: Education Officer (01283 585022)
Access:
Access to staff: By letter, by telephone, by email, in person, Internet web pages
Access to building, collections or gallery: No prior appointment required
Hours: Mid Mar to early Nov, Wed to Sun, 1300 to 1700;
Special Christmas openings first and second weekends of Dec, Sat and Sun, 1100 to 1600, last admission 1530;
Open Bank Holiday Mondays
Other restrictions: Closes at dusk if earlier
Access for disabled people: Parking provided, toilet facilities
Other restrictions: Transfer available. 2 manual wheelchairs available. Level entrance. Ground floor fully accessible. No access to other floors. Level entrance to shop. Level entrance to tea-room. Gravel paths, mainly level, only top terrace accessible.

General description:
Housed in the 19th century service wing of Sudbury Hall, the Museum contains fascinating and innovative displays about children from the 18th century onwards. There are chimney climbs for adventurous 'sweep-sized' youngsters, and Betty Cadbury's fine collection of toys and dolls is on show.
Information services:
Helpline available, tel no: 01283 585305.
Evening and morning tours
Special Christmas openings with family activities and tea with Santa Claus
Touch list and handling collection for the visually impaired
Suitable for school groups. Education room/centre. Live interpretation. Hands-on activities. Children's quiz/trail
Special visitor services: Guided tours, materials and/or activities for children.
Education services: Group education facilities.
Services for disabled people: For the visually impaired.
Collections:
Betty Cadbury Collection of dolls, toys and games, 17th-20th century, c. 800 items

Internet home pages:
http://www.nationaltrust.org.uk

2037
NATIONAL TRUST OF GUERNSEY FOLK MUSEUM
Folk Museum, Saumarez Park, Castel, Guernsey, GY5 7UJ, Channel Islands

Tel: 01481 255384
Fax: 01481 255384
Email: folkmuseumntgsy@gtonline
Formed: 1968

Organisation type and purpose: Museum, suitable for ages: 5+.
Parent body:
National Trust of Guernsey
26 Cornet Street, St Peter Port, Guernsey, GY1 1LF, Channel Islands, tel: 01481 728451

Enquiries to: Curator
Other contacts: Retail Manager for sales of goods or publications, retail point in museum.
Access:
Access to staff: By letter, by telephone, by fax, by email, visitors by prior appointment
Access to building, collections or gallery: No prior appointment required
Hours: 25 Mar to 31 Oct: daily, 1000 to 1700
Access for disabled people: toilet facilities

General description:
A museum set out in an 18th-19th century Guernsey farm house. On view: Victorian agricultural and social history specific to Guernsey farming life
1850 to modern day. Recreated rooms, artefacts and clothed static figures (reproduction and original clothing on display), kitchen, parlour, bedrooms (in tableaux), costume room, carriage room, dairy, wash-house, cider barn, as well as transport and children's displays.
Collections:
Agricultural machinery, agricultural hand tools, horse-drawn vehicles, farm-house kitchen, Victorian farm-house bedroom, cider barn, wash-house, dairy
Town-house parlour, Victorian clothing (social and work), Victorian school-room, children's toys
Pictures (original), photographs (original and copied), books
Catalogues:
Catalogue for library is in-house only. Catalogue for all of the collections is only available in-house.
Printed publications:
Guide Book to the Folk Museum (direct)
Buildings in the Town and Parish of St Peter Port (Brett C, direct)
Small selection of specialist pamphlets (prices on application, check availability)

Internet home pages:
http://www.nationaltrust-gsy.org.gg

2038
NATIONAL TRUST OFFICE FOR NORTHERN IRELAND
Rowallane House, Saintfield, Ballynahinch, Co Down, BT24 7LH

Tel: 020 9751 0721
Fax: 028 9751 1242

Organisation type and purpose: National organisation, membership association (membership is by subscription), registered charity (charity number 205846), suitable for ages: all ages.
The preservation and upkeep of places of historic interest or natural beauty.

Enquiries to: Manager
Access:
Access to staff: By letter, by telephone, by fax, by email

General description:
The conservation of places of historic interest or natural beauty in Northern Ireland.

Internet home pages:
http://www.ntni.org.uk

See also - ***Ardress House; Argory; Castle Coole; Castle Ward; Crown Liquor Saloon; Derrymore House; Downhill Estate; Florence Court; Gray's Printing Press; Hezlett House; Mount Stewart House, Garden and Temple of the Winds; Patterson's Spade Mill; Rowallane Garden; Springhill; Wellbrook Beetling Mill***

2039
NATIONAL TRUST OFFICE FOR WALES
Trinity Square, Llandudno, Gwynedd, LL30 2DE

Tel: 01492 860123
Fax: 01492 860233
Email: ntwales@nt.org.uk
Acronym or abbreviation: NT

Organisation type and purpose: National organisation, membership association (membership is by subscription).
The preservation and upkeep of places of historic interest or natural beauty.

Enquiries to: Marketing Manager

General description:
National Trust Office for Wales.

Internet home pages:
http://www.nt.org.uk

See also - ***Aberconwy House; Aberdeunant; Aberdulais Falls and Turbine House; Bwthyn Llywelyn; Chirk Castle; Cilgerran Castle; Conwy Suspension Bridge; Dinefwr; Dolaucothi Gold Mines; Erddig Hall; Kymin; Llanerchaeron; Penrhyn Castle; Plas Newydd; Plas Yn Rhiw; Powis Castle & Garden; Segontium Roman Museum; Skenfrith Castle; St David's Visitor Centre and Shop; Tudor Merchant's House; Ty Mawr Wybrnant; Ty'n-Y-Coed Uchaf***

2040
NATIONAL WAR MUSEUM OF SCOTLAND
The Castle, Edinburgh, EH1 2NG

Tel: 0131 225 7534
Fax: 0131 225 3848
Email: a.carswell@nms.ac.uk
Acronym or abbreviation: NWMS
Formed: 1930
Formerly, and still known as: Scottish United Services Museum (SUSM), date of change, 2000
Formerly: The Scottish National Naval and Military Museum, date of change, 1948

Organisation type and purpose: National government body, professional body, museum, historic building, house or site, suitable for ages: 5+, research organisation.
The museum also has a reference library and archive collection.
Parent body:
National Museums of Scotland (NMS)
Chambers Street, Edinburgh, EH1 1JF, tel: 0131 225 7534, email: feedback@nms.ac.uk

Enquiries to: Director/Curator
Other contacts: Librarian/Archivist for historical enquiries.
Access:
Access to staff: By letter, by telephone, by email, visitors by prior appointment, Internet web pages

continued overleaf

Hours: Mon to Fri, 0930 to 1300 and 1400 to 1700
Access to building, collections or gallery: No prior appointment required
Hours: Summer: daily, 0945 to 1730
Winter: daily, 0945 to 1630
Access for disabled people: Parking provided, ramped entry, access to all public areas, toilet facilities
Other restrictions: Located in Edinburgh Castle - Historic Scotland courtesy vehicle can be requested to pick up and transport within the castle.

General description:
Military history of Scotland and the Scots. The museum collects, presents and interprets material relating to the Scottish experience of war and military service. The permanent exhibitions deal with different themes of this study.
Information services:
Library available for reference (for conditions see Access above)
Special visitor services: Guided tours, tape recorded guides.
Education services: Group education facilities..
Collections:
Scotland's national collection of artefacts illustrating the Scottish experience of war and military service
It includes weapons, uniforms, medals, badges, prints, paintings, drawings, photographs, objets d'art, archives, books, documents, manuscripts, printed ephemera, flags, banners etc
The library contains Scotland's principal military research source material
Catalogues:
Catalogue for library is in-house only. Catalogue for all of the collections is only available in-house.

Internet home pages:
http://www.nms.ac.uk
Part of the NMS website, basic information on collections, staff, opening times etc.

2041
NATIONAL WATERWAYS MUSEUM
Llanthony Warehouse, Gloucester Docks, Gloucester, GL1 2EH

Tel: 01452 318054
Fax: 01452 318066
Email: info@nwm.org.uk
Acronym or abbreviation: NWM
Formed: 1988

Organisation type and purpose: Registered charity (charity number 1074541), museum, suitable for ages: 5+, consultancy, research organisation.
Part of the Waterways Trust, a designated museum.
To maintain and preserve the national collection for inland waterways.
Parent body:
Waterways Trust (TWT)
Willow Grange, Church Road, Watford, WD13 QA, tel: 01923 226081, fax: 01923 201400
Sister museums:
Archives/Curatorial Departments
Canal Museum
Stoke Bruerne
Rochdale Canal Restoration
The Boat Museum
Ellesmere Port

Enquiries to: Curator
Other contacts: (1) Information/Publicity Officer (2) Education Officer for (1) media information and events (2) schools programmes, educational information.
Access:
Access to staff: By letter, by telephone, by fax, by email, visitors by prior appointment, Internet web pages
Hours: Mon to Fri, 0900 to 1700
Access to building, collections or gallery: No prior appointment required
Hours: Daily 1000 to 1700
Other restrictions: Last entry 1630

General description:
200 years of waterway transport and social history, canals and waterways, history and engineering, boat repairing, machinery restoration and operation.
Collections:
Archive and historical collection
Home of the designated National Collection of Inland Waterways - British Waterways objects
Catalogues:
Catalogue for part of the collections is on-line.
Publications list:
is available in hard copy.
Printed publications:
Activity Guide
Canals - ideas for Teachers
Museum Guide Book
Schools and the National Waterways Museum at Gloucester
Short History of Gloucester Docks
Electronic and video products:
Guide Book (CD-ROM)
Video tapes about waterways

Internet home pages:
http://www.nwm.org.uk

2042
NATURAL HISTORY MUSEUM
High Street, Colchester, Essex, CO1 1DN

Tel: 01206 282941
Minicom no. 01206 500145
Fax: 01206 282925
Email: jerry.bowdrey@colchester.gov.uk

Organisation type and purpose: Local government body, museum, historic building, house or site, suitable for ages: all ages.
Other addresses:
Museum Resource Centre
14 Ryegate Road, Colchester, Essex, CO1 1YG, tel: 01206 282931, fax: 01206 282925

Enquiries to: Secretary
Access:
Access to staff: By letter, by telephone, by fax, by email, visitors by prior appointment
Access for disabled people: level entry, access to all public areas, toilet facilities

General description:
General natural history. Specialises in Stag Beetles and Essex wildlife, natural history and environment.
Information services:
Library available for reference (for conditions see Access above)
Special visitor services: Materials and/or activities for children.
Education services: Group education facilities, resources for Key Stages 1 and 2.
Services for disabled people: Displays and/or information at wheelchair height.
Catalogues:
Catalogue for library is in-house only. Catalogue for part of the collections is on-line.

Internet home pages:
http://www.colchestermuseums.org.uk
Search.

2043
NATURAL HISTORY MUSEUM
Darwin Centre, Cromwell Road, London, SW7 5BD

Tel: 020 7942 5000
Fax: 020 7942 5559
Acronym or abbreviation: NHM

Organisation type and purpose: National government body, national organisation, museum, suitable for ages: 8+, research organisation.

Enquiries to: Information Officer

General description:
Specially built centre to house a permanent collection of precious specimens including some belonging to Charles Darwin.

Internet home pages:
http://www.nhm.ac.uk
Main museum home page.

2044
NATURAL HISTORY MUSEUM
Cromwell Road, London, SW7 5BD

Tel: 020 7942 5000
Fax: 020 7942 5559
Email: library@nhm.ac.uk
Acronym or abbreviation: NHM
Formed: 1881
Formerly: British Museum (Natural History)

Organisation type and purpose: International organisation, national government body, museum, public library, suitable for ages: all ages, training organisation, research organisation.
Other libraries:
Botany Library
Tel: 020 79425685, email/website: botlib@nhm.ac.uk
Earth Sciences Library
Tel: 020 7942 5476, email/website: earthscilib@nhm.ac.uk
Entomology Library
Tel: 020 7942 5751, email/website: entlib@nhm.ac.uk
General and Zoology Libraries
Tel: 020 7942 5460, email/website: genlib@nhm.ac.uk
Ornithological and Rothschild Libraries
Akeman Street, Tring, Hertfordshire, HP23 6AP, tel: 020 7942 6158, fax: 020 7942 6150, email/website: ornlib@nhm.ac.uk
Zoological Museum Library
Tring, Hertfordshire, tel: 020 7942 6159

Enquiries to: Librarian
Other contacts: Specialist Library and Information Services, see below
Access:
Access to staff: By letter, by telephone, by fax, by email, visitors by prior appointment, Internet web pages
Hours: Mon to Fri, 1000 to 1630
Access for disabled people: access to all public areas, toilet facilities

General description:
Botany; biodiversity; entomology; geography, expeditions and travel; mineralogy; museum techniques; oceanography; ornithology; palaeontology; parasitology; physical anthropology; tropical medicine; zoology; environmental studies.
Information services:
Library available for reference (for conditions see Access above), on-line searching, CD-ROM based services, bibliography compilation, selective dissemination services. Helpline available, tel no: 020 7942 5011 information line.
Field study tours
Study days for teachers and museum professionals
Special visitor services: Guided tours, tape recorded guides, materials and/or activities for children.
Education services: Group education facilities, resources for Key Stages 1 and 2, 3 and Further or Higher Education.
Services for disabled people: Displays and/or information at wheelchair height.
Collections:
Albert Gunther (zoology)
Day Library (natural history dealers)
John Murray (oceanography)
Joseph Banks (natural history, note-books etc from Cook's first voyage around the world)
Linnaeus Collection (binomial nomenclature system in classification; works on plants and animals)
Richard Owen (anatomy)

Robert Brown (botany, including material from the Australian expedition 1801-1805)
Sloane (natural history and collection of curiosities and artefacts of *c.* 1753. Sloane's collection was the foundation of the British Museum)
Sowerby (natural history, especially botany; the family were artists and publishers)
Sydney Parkinson (natural history; drawings)
Tweeddale Library (zoology)
Walsingham (entomology)
Walter Rothschild (zoology)
Catalogues:
Catalogue for library is on-line.
Publications list:
is available in hard copy and online.
Printed publications:
A large number of publications on the above subjects including:
Bulletin of the Natural History Museum: Botany series, Entomology series, Geology series, Zoology series
Catalogue of the Books and Manuscripts, Maps and Drawings in the British Museum (Natural History)
Catalogue of the Works of Linnaeus
List of Serials of the Natural History Museum
Monographs, handbooks, guide books including:
Coral Fish (Pitkin L)
Crystals (2nd ed, Cressey G and Mercer I F)
From the Beginning (Edwards K and Rosen B)
Gold (Herrington R J et al)
Lichens (Purvis W et al)
Nature's Connections - An Exploration of Natural History (McGirr N)
Snakes (Stafford P)
The Deep Sea (Rice T)
Volcanoes (2nd ed, van Rose S and Mercer I F)

Internet home pages:
http://www.nhm.ac.uk/info/library/index.html
Description of each library, including the Museum Archives, with contact details: provides access to the library catalogue via telnet; link to main museum home page; lists admissions, opening hours and services provided in the library.
http://www.nhm.ac.uk
Main museum home page.

2045
NATURE IN ART MUSEUM AND ART GALLERY

Wallsworth Hall, Twigworth, Gloucester, GL2 9PA

Tel: 01452 731422
Fax: 01452 730937
Email: ninart@globalnet.co.uk
Formed: 1982

Organisation type and purpose: Registered charity (charity number 1000553), museum, art gallery, suitable for ages: 8+.

Enquiries to: Director
Access:
Access to staff: By letter, by telephone, by fax, by email, visitors by prior appointment, Internet web pages
Access to building, collections or gallery: No prior appointment required
Hours: Tue to Sun and Bank Holidays, 1000 to 1700
Other restrictions: Closed 24 to 26 Dec.
Access for disabled people: Parking provided, ramped entry, access to all public areas, toilet facilities

General description:
Fine, decorative and applied art inspired by nature from any period, any culture and/or country. Permanent collection currently spans 1500 years by over 600 artists from over 60 countries.
Information services:
Guided tours by arrangement.
90% of displays/information at wheelchair height.
Introductory talks for groups, demonstrations by arrangement.
Special visitor services: Guided tours, materials and/or activities for children.
Education services: Group education facilities, resources for Key Stages 1 and 2, 3, 4 and Further or Higher Education.
Services for disabled people: For the visually impaired; displays and/or information at wheelchair height.
Collections:
Paintings, prints by a broad range of artists from: Audubon, Wolf, Scott, Picasso, Porter, Lalique, Sutherland, Tunnicliffe, Moore, Shepherd, Rungius and Galle
Contemporary sculpture and crafts
Early illustrations and ethnic art
Broad range of styles and media
Catalogues:
Catalogue for all of the collections is only available in-house.
Printed publications:
Quarterly Magazine (60p, free to Friends of Nature in Art)

Internet home pages:
http://www.nature-in-art.org.uk
Introduction to collection, regularly updated lists of temporary exhibitions, events, artists in residence, courses etc, history of hall, schools information, general visitor information.

2046
NAVAL TEMPLE AND ROUND HOUSE, THE

See - Kymin

2047
NEATH MUSEUM & ART GALLERY

Gwyn Hall, Orchard Street, Neath, West Glamorgan, SA11 1DT

Tel: 01639 645726
Fax: 01639 645726
Formed: 1984

Organisation type and purpose: Local government body, museum, art gallery, suitable for ages: all ages.

Enquiries to: Curator
Access:
Access to staff: By letter, by telephone, by fax, visitors by prior appointment
Access to building, collections or gallery: No prior appointment required
Hours: Tue to Sat, 1000 to 1600

General description:
Local museum for the Neath area, telling the story of the town from prehistoric to modern times. Also a gallery space with changing art/thematic exhibitions.
Information services:
Special visitor services: Materials and/or activities for children.
Education services: Group education facilities, resources for Key Stages 1 and 2..
Collections:
Objects, photographs, art/photographic displays
Temporary exhibitions

2048
NEEDLES OLD BATTERY, THE

West Highdown, Totland, Isle of Wight, PO39 0JH

Tel: 01983 754772
Fax: 01983 756978

Organisation type and purpose: Registered charity (charity number 205846), historic building, house or site, suitable for ages: 5+.
Parent body:
The National Trust (South and South East Region)
Thames and Solent Regional Office, tel: 01494 528051

Enquiries to: Administrator
Access:
Access to staff: By letter, by telephone, by fax, in person
Access to building, collections or gallery: No prior appointment required
Hours: End Mar to end Jun: Sat to Thu, 1030 to 1700
Jul, Aug: daily, 1030 to 1700
Sep to beg Nov: Sat to Thu, 1030 to 1700
Open Good Friday
Other restrictions: Property closes in bad weather; telephone. on day of visit to check.
Access for disabled people: ramped entry, level entry, toilet facilities
Other restrictions: No vehicular access to Battery (visitors with disabilities by arrangement). Many paths are steep and not suitable for people with walking difficulties. Access to the searchlight is by narrow spiral staircase, with further steps to tea-room and headland beyond the Battery.

General description:
Palmerstonian Fort, 200 feet above sea level overlooking the Solent. Built in 1862, prompted by the threat of a French invasion, it still retains two of its original gun barrels. The laboratory, searchlight position and position-finding cells have all been restored and a 65m tunnel leads to stunning views of the Hampshire and Dorset coastline. Because of its remoteness, the site was used by the MOD for the development of the British Space Programme.
Information services:
Guided educational tours by prior arrangement. Suitable for school groups. Children's activity packs. The children's exhibition tells the story of 'The Needles at War' and cartoon information boards throughout explain how .the Battery functioned.
Special visitor services: Materials and/or activities for children.
Education services: Group education facilities.
Services for disabled people: Displays and/or information at wheelchair height.
Collections:
Collection of articles removed from the lighthouse during automation, includes old foghorns and switchgear
Publications list:
is available in hard copy.
Printed publications:
Guide Book (for purchase)
Electronic and video products:
Video Film (for purchase)

Internet home pages:
http://www.nationaltrust.org.uk

2049
NEIDPATH CASTLE

Peebles, Borders, EH45 8NW

Tel: 01721 720333
Email: keith.roxburgh@eidosnet.co.uk

Organisation type and purpose: Independently owned, historic building, house or site, suitable for ages: 5+.
Tourist attraction.
Members of:
Great British Heritage
Historic House Association

Enquiries to: Curator
Access:
Access to staff: By letter, by telephone, by email
Access for disabled people: Parking provided
Other restrictions: Unable to provide disabled access.

General description:
Historic 14th century Borders stronghold. Family home of Fraser, Hay and Douglas families. Besieged by Cromwell's forces in 1650. Visited by Mary Queen of Scots, James VI, Sir Walter Scott, TC Campbell, William Wordsworth.
Pit prison, medieval well, excellent walks, picnic areas.
Collections:
Fine Batiks depicting life of Mary Queen of Scots

continued overleaf

Collection of items found in castle

Internet home pages:
http://www.scotborders.org.uk

2050
NELSON MUSEUM AND LOCAL HISTORY CENTRE, MONMOUTH, THE

Priory Street, Monmouth, Gwent, NP25 3XA

Tel: 01600 710630
Fax: 01600 775001
Email: nelsonmuseum@monmouthshire.gov.uk
Formed: 1924
Formerly: Monmouth Museum

Organisation type and purpose: Museum.
Parent body:
Monmouthshire County Council
Museums at:
Monmouth, Chepstow, Abergavenny, Caldicot Castle

Enquiries to: Curator
Access:
Access to staff: By letter, by telephone, visitors by prior appointment
Hours: Mon to Sat and Bank Holidays, 1000 to 1300 and 1400 to 1700; Sun, 1400 to 1700
Access to building, collections or gallery: No access other than to staff
Hours: Mon to Sat and Bank Holidays, 1000 to 1300 and 1400 to 1700; Sun, 1400 to 1700
Other restrictions: Small entry charge (£1 in 1999).

General description:
History of Monmouth and the Lower Wye Valley area, naval history, Horatio Nelson, the Hon C S Rolls.
Collections:
Admiral Horatio Lord Nelson manuscript material, letters, log-books
Local history reference collection
Local newspapers, 1827 onwards, (microfiche)
The Hon C S Rolls (of Rolls Royce): photographic archive covering life and family
Catalogues:
Catalogue for library is in-house only. Catalogue for all of the collections is only available in-house.

Internet home pages:
http://www.monmouthshire.gov.uk

2051
NELSON TOWER

Grant Park, Forres, Moray

Tel: 01309 673701
Fax: 01309 675863
Email: museums@moray.gov.uk
Formed: 1806

Organisation type and purpose: Local government body, museum, suitable for ages: all ages.
Parent body:
Moray Council Museums Service
Falconer Museum, Tolbooth Street, Forres
Address for enquiries and correspondence:
The Falconer Museum
(Headquarters of Moray Council Museums Service)
Tolbooth Street, Forres, Moray, IV36 1PH, tel: as main number, fax: as main number

Enquiries to: Senior Museums Officer
Direct tel: 01309 676688

General description:
Various social history items connected with the memory of Admiral Nelson and the Trafalgar Club.
Information services:
Induction loop for the hearing impaired.
Special visitor services: Tape recorded guides.
Education services: Group education facilities.
Services for disabled people: For the hearing impaired.
Collections:
Small collection of memorabilia connected to Lord Nelson
Catalogues:
Catalogue for part of the collections is on-line.
Printed publications:
Custodial service, information sheets and leaflets.

Internet home pages:
http://www.moray.org/museums/
Information on catalogue, internet exhibitions, conservation and photography, displays and exhibitions, visitor centre information, educational services, general enquiries etc.

2052
NENE VALLEY RAILWAY MUSEUM

Wansford Station, Stibbington, Peterborough, Cambridgeshire, PE8 6LR

Tel: 01780 784444
Fax: 01780 784440
Email: nvrorg@aol.com
Acronym or abbreviation: NVR
Formed: 1977

Organisation type and purpose: Registered charity (charity number 263617), museum, suitable for ages: all ages.
Heritage passenger carrying railway.
Member of:
Heritage Railways Association (HRA)
2 Littlestone Road, New Romney, Kent, TN28 8LP, tel: 01654 710344

Enquiries to: Manager
Other contacts: Curator for historical aspects of the railway's activities.
Access:
Access to staff: By letter, by telephone, by fax, by email, in person
Access to building, collections or gallery: No prior appointment required
Hours: Daily, 0900 to 1630
Access for disabled people: Parking provided, ramped entry, access to all public areas, toilet facilities
Other restrictions: Ramped access to all trains.

General description:
Local railway history, travelling post office history, Royal Mail history.
Information services:
Special visitor services: Guided tours, materials and/or activities for children..
Collections:
Plans, track diagrams and documentation from 1843 of the railway and its construction and development
Extensive photographic collection
Archive - under development
Catalogues:
Catalogue for part of the collections is only available in-house.
Publications list:
is available in hard copy.

Internet home pages:
http://www.nvr.org.uk
http://www.northlincs.gov.uk/arts/centre.htm

2053
NENE VALLEY RAILWAY

Wansford Station, Old Great North Road, Stibbington, Peterborough, Cambridgeshire, PE8 6LR

Tel: 01780 784444
Fax: 01780 784440
Acronym or abbreviation: NVR
Formed: 1977
Formerly: Peterborough Locomotive Society, date of change, 1977

Organisation type and purpose: Membership association (membership is by subscription), present number of members: 1200, voluntary organisation, registered charity (charity number 263617), historic building, house or site, suitable for ages: all ages.
Heritage steam/diesel railway with British and European stock.
Has links with:
Heritage Railway Association (HRA)
Tel: 01707 643568, fax: 01707 643568

Enquiries to: Curator
Other contacts: General Manager for financial and corporate matters.
Access:
Access to staff: By letter, by telephone, by fax, by email, in person
Hours: Sun to Sat, 0900 to 1630
Other restrictions: All requests for information to the Curator.
Access for disabled people: Parking provided, ramped entry, access to all public areas, toilet facilities
Other restrictions: Ramped access to all trains.

General description:
Services offered to the passenger, visitors, school or other party visitors. Railway information relating to mechanical (steam and diesel traction). Historical (local railway).
Collections:
Plans, track diagram, maps etc of the Nene Valley line, historically and to date. (This collection is held at Huntingdon Record Office and on Database.)
Photographs and artefacts are in the process of being listed and catalogued
Catalogues:
Catalogue for library is in-house only. Catalogue for all of the collections is only available in-house.
Printed publications:
Guide book (£1.95)
Hold Up At Sears Crossing (£6.95 plus 75p p&p)
Nene Steam (3 times a year, £1.50)
Nene Valley Pictorial (£3.95)
Nene Valley Railway Story Book (£2.95)
Peterborough's First Railway (£3.95)
The Nene Railway (A Nostalgic Trip)(95p)
Electronic and video products:
Nene Valley International (video, £12.95)
The Last de Glenn (video, £9.95)

Internet home pages:
http://www.nvr.org.uk

2054
NENTHEAD MINES HERITAGE CENTRE

Nenthead, Alston, Cumbria, CA9 3PD

Tel: 01434 382037
Fax: 01434 382294
Email: administration.office@virgin.net
Formed: 1996
Formerly: North Pennines Heritage Trust (NPHT)

Organisation type and purpose: Registered charity (charity number 700701), museum, historic building, house or site, suitable for ages: 5+.
Parent body:
North Pennines Heritage Trust (NPHT)
at the same address, tel: 01434 382045, email: npht@virgin.net

Enquiries to: Manager
Access:
Access to staff: By letter, by telephone, by fax, by email, in person
Hours: Daily, 1000 to 1700
Access to building, collections or gallery: No prior appointment required
Hours: Apr to Oct: Mon to Sun, 1030 to 1700
Oct to Apr: Mon to Fri, 1030 to 1700
Other restrictions: At other times by prior appointment.
Access for disabled people: Parking provided, toilet facilities

General description:
History and geology of Nenthead and the North Pennines. Local history and geology of former lead mining and processing site, technology, science of materials.

Information services:
Special visitor services: Guided tours, materials and/or activities for children.
Education services: Group education facilities, resources for Key Stages 1 and 2, 3 and 4..
Publications list:
is available in hard copy and online.
Printed publications:
The Nent Force Level and Brewery Shaft (Wilkinson P)
Limekilns of the North Pennines (Robertson A)
Methodism in the Allen Dales (Charlton E M)
Lambley Viaduct (Forsythe R & Blackett-Ord C)
Through the Ages - The Story of Nenthead (Thain L M)
Electronic and video products:
Nenthead Site (video and DVD)

Internet home pages:
http://www.npht.com
NPHT projects throughout the North Pennines.
http://www.npht.com/nenthead/index.htm
Including Nenthead Mines Heritage Centre.
http://www.npht.com/publicat.htm
Publications.

2055
NEO ART - CONTEMPORARY ART GALLERY

The Watson Fothergill Building, 17 George Street, Nottingham, NG1 3BH

Tel: 0115 955 0086
Fax: 0115 955 0086
Email: gallery@neo-art.co.uk
Formed: 1999

Organisation type and purpose: Independently owned, museum, art gallery, historic building, house or site, suitable for ages: 16+.

Enquiries to: Senior Partner
Access:
Access to staff: By letter, by telephone, by fax, by email, in person, Internet web pages
Access for disabled people: level entry

General description:
Contemporary Art Gallery (unique contemporary collection of original art).
Exhibitions of East Midlands artists. Sculpture, ceramics, glass, jewellery, imagery/art consultants, historic building (Victorian architects Watson Fothergill original offices) soon to become a museum to Watson Fothergill (1841-1928).
Information services:
Helpline available, tel no: 0115 955 0086.
Special visitor services: Guided tours..
Collections:
Artefacts: original features, statue, original safes, original scales, stained glass window
Publications list:
is available in hard copy and online.
Printed publications:
Watson Fothergill Architect (Brand K, Nottingham Civic Society)

Internet home pages:
http://www.neo-art.co.uk
Logo, building (artistic photography), artists' lists and works, corporate and business, links to Fothergill Project, sculpture, ceramics, glass etc, prints, framing service.

2056
NETHER ALDERLEY MILL

Congleton Road, Nether Alderley, Macclesfield, Cheshire, SK10 4TW

Tel: 01625 584412 (Countryside Office)
Fax: 01625 527139
Email: netheralderleymill@nationaltrust.org.uk
Formed: 1970

Organisation type and purpose: National organisation, membership association (membership is by subscription), registered charity (charity number 205846), museum, historic building, house or site, suitable for ages: 5+.
Working watermill.
Parent body:
The National Trust (North West)
North West Regional Office, tel: 0870 609 5391
Other addresses:
Cheshire Countryside Office
Macclesfield Road, Nether Alderley, Cheshire, SK10 4UB

Enquiries to: Property Manager
Other contacts: Administrative Assistant
Access:
Access to staff: By letter only
Access to building, collections or gallery: No prior appointment required
Hours: Apr to Oct, Wed, Thu, Fri, Sun, 1300 to 1700
Open Bank Holiday Mondays
Other restrictions: Prior appointment required for special opening outside above hours, eg group visits.
Access for disabled people: Parking provided
Other restrictions: Ground floor largely inaccessible. No access to other floors.

General description:
A fascinating and unusual watermill dating from the 15th century. It has overshot tandem wheels and is powered by water from the lake, beside which the mill is built. After lying derelict for thirty years, the Victorian machinery was restored in the 1960s and is now in full working order, with regular flour-grinding demonstrations.
Printed publications:
Guide Book (60p)

Internet home pages:
http://www.nationaltrust.org.uk

2057
NETHERBOW ARTS CENTRE/ JOHN KNOX HOUSE

43-45 High Street, Edinburgh, EH1 1SR

Tel: 0131 556 9579 or 2647
Fax: 0131 557 5224
Formed: 1972

Organisation type and purpose: Museum.
Theatre and contemporary arts centre.
Parent body:
Church of Scotland
121 George Street, Edinburgh

Enquiries to: Manager
Access:
Access to staff: By letter, by telephone, by fax
Hours: Mon to Sat, 1000 to 1700; and in Jul, Aug, Sun, 1200 to 1700
Access for disabled people: level entry, toilet facilities

General description:
John Knox and the Scottish Reformation, 16th century Scottish history, contemporary art and theatre in Scotland, cultural events in Edinburgh, general tourist information.
Collections:
16th and 17th century bibles
Electrotypes of coins 1539 to 1572
Written information on John Knox, Reformation and Scottish 16th century history
Printed publications:
History and Drama: a Brief Guide
Netherbow Chapbooks on John Knox House including:

2058
NEW ART CENTRE SCULPTURE PARK & GALLERY

Roche Court, East Winterslow, Salisbury, Wiltshire, SP5 1BG

Tel: 01980 862244
Fax: 01980 862447
Email: nac@globalnet.co.uk
Formed: 1958

Organisation type and purpose: Independently owned, suitable for ages: 8+.
Sculpture park and art gallery.

Enquiries to: Curator
Access:
Access to staff: By letter, by telephone, by email, in person, Internet web pages
Hours: Mon to Fri, 0930 to 1730

General description:
20th century British art, specifically sculpture.
Represents the estate of Barbara Hepworth.
Information services:
Special visitor services: Guided tours.
Education services: Group education facilities, resources for Further or Higher Education..
Collections:
Detailed biographies of each artist displaying work in the park or galleries
At Roche Court there is a survey of 20th century sculpture from all over the world. The exhibition consists of over 100 works by leading sculptors, including Barbara Hepworth, Henry Moore, Barry Flanagan and Antony Gormley in an 18th century garden and park. The new Art Centre also has a connection with a gallery in New York. In the grounds there is a classical orangery where works on paper are shown.

Internet home pages:
http://www.sculpture.uk.com
General information about gallery, including directions, map, opening hours, news of upcoming exhibitions and special events.

2059
NEW ART GALLERY WALSALL, THE

Gallery Square, Walsall, West Midlands, WS2 8LG

Tel: 01922 654400
Minicom no. 01922 653160
Fax: 01922 654401
Email: info@artatwalsall.org.uk
Formed: 2000
Formerly: Walsall Museum & Art Gallery, date of change, 2000

Organisation type and purpose: Local government body, registered charity (charity number 1064056), art gallery, suitable for ages: all ages.
The New Art Gallery Walsall opened in February 2000 in the heart of Walsall town centre. A unique civic building for Walsall, the gallery is also a rare example of a brand-new building for the millennial arts. The £21 million world class gallery was made possible by £15.75 million Arts Lottery funding (the 1000th lottery grant awarded since the lottery began in 1994) and commissioned by Walsall Metropolitan Borough Council, which wanted nothing but the best for this vibrant West Midlands town.
Member of:
The Museums Association
Other addresses:
Walsall Museum
Lichfield Street, Walsall, tel: 01922 653116

Enquiries to: Marketing Assistant
Direct tel: 01922 654416
Direct email: wilkinsonc@walsall.gov.uk
Access:
Access to staff: By letter, by telephone, by fax, by email, in person, visitors by prior appointment
Access to building, collections or gallery: No prior appointment required
Hours: Tue to Sat, 1000 to 1700; Sun, 1200 to 1700
Other restrictions: Library available by prior appointment.
Access for disabled people: Parking provided, level entry, access to all public areas, toilet facilities

General description:
Permanent display of the Garman Ryan Collection, as well as regularly changing programme of exhibitions of contemporary visual arts. A Children's Discovery Gallery is

continued overleaf

available for school and family groups. The gallery also holds archive material relating to the sculptor Jacob Epstein.

Information services:
Library available for reference (for conditions see Access above). Helpline available, tel no: Recorded information line: 01922 637575.
Guided tours by prior arrangement.
Discovery Gallery, at ground floor level, which creates an introduction to a three storey children's house, including an artists studio and activity room.
Recorded information line tel: 01922 637575.
Special visitor services: Guided tours, materials and/or activities for children.
Education services: Group education facilities.
Services for disabled people: For the visually impaired; for the hearing impaired; displays and/or information at wheelchair height.

Collections:
The Garman Ryan Collection
Two remarkable women created this collection: Kathleen Garman, lover and later wife of sculptor Jacob Epstein, and her lifelong friend Sally Ryan, a talented sculptor, together they formed an art collection that is intimate, adventurous and eclectic, reflecting their wide-ranging tastes. It was donated to the people of Walsall by Lady Kathleen Garman, widow of sculptor Sir Jacob Epstein, in 1973.
This unique collection is displayed in a two-storey house consisting of a series of intimate, interconnecting rooms, each with a window, making a house for the collection over the first and second floors of the gallery
Works by well-known European artists, including Monet, Rembrandt, Constable, Van Gogh and Picasso, are displayed alongside beautiful artefacts from many different cultures across the world
The temporary exhibition galleries on the third floor are dedicated to exhibiting the best of contemporary and historic art
The galleries chart the long, productive and often controversial career of Jacob Epstein and serve as a memorial to the Epsteins' extraordinary circle of family and friends, Augustus John, Modigliani, Gaudier-Breska and Epsteins' son-in-law Lucien Freud.

Catalogues:
Catalogue for all of the collections is published and is also on-line.

Publications list:
is available in hard copy and online.

Printed publications:
All products sold through the gallery shop
Brochure

Internet home pages:
http://www.artatwalsall.org.uk
Exhibitions, events, workshops, Garman Ryan Collection, information.

2060
NEW FOREST MUSEUM

High Street, Lyndhurst, Hampshire, SO43 7NY

Tel: 023 8028 3914
Fax: 023 8028 4236
Email: nfmuseum@lineone.net
Formed: 1988
Formerly: New Forest Ninth Centenary Trust

Organisation type and purpose: Registered charity (charity number 279373), museum, suitable for ages: all ages.

Enquiries to: Director

Access:
Access to staff: By letter, by telephone, by fax, by email, visitors by prior appointment
Hours: Mon to Fri, 1000 to 1700
Other restrictions: Reference library closes at 1600.
Access for disabled people: level entry, access to all public areas
Other restrictions: Parking provided nearby, toilets nearby.

General description:
New Forest general; management, history, social.

Information services:
Library available for reference (for conditions see Access above), bibliography compilation, selective dissemination services
Special visitor services: Materials and/or activities for children.
Education services: Group education facilities, resources for Key Stages 1 and 2, 3, 4 and Further or Higher Education..

Collections:
Main collection on computerised database
Large collection of ephemera relevant to the New Forest area
Most comprehensive library of published works on the New Forest, free access to readers and researchers

Catalogues:
Catalogue for library is in-house only. Catalogue for all of the collections is only available in-house.

2061
NEW LANARK CONSERVATION TRUST

New Lanark Mills, Lanark, ML11 9DB

Tel: 01555 661345
Fax: 01555 665738
Email: visit@newlanark.org
Formed: 1973

Organisation type and purpose: Independently owned, registered charity, historic building, house or site, suitable for ages: 5+.
Restoration and revitalisation of New Lanark.

Enquiries to: Director
Other contacts: Educational Tours Officer

Access:
Access to staff: By letter, by telephone, by fax, by email, visitors by prior appointment, Internet web pages
Access to building, collections or gallery: No prior appointment required
Hours: Daily, 1000 to 1700
Access for disabled people: Parking provided, ramped entry, toilet facilities
Other restrictions: Assistance required in some areas for wheelchair users.

General description:
Founded in 1785, New Lanark rose to fame in the early 19th century as a model community under the enlightened management of Robert Owen.
Surrounded by native woodland and close to the famous Falls of Clyde, this beautiful 18th century cotton mill village has been carefully restored as a living community, and is now one of Europe's top visitor attractions, with an award-winning Visitor Centre and Hotel.

Information services:
Library available for reference (for conditions see Access above)
Special visitor services: Guided tours, materials and/or activities for children.
Education services: Group education facilities, resources for Key Stages 1 and 2, 3, 4 and Further or Higher Education.
Services for disabled people: For the hearing impaired; displays and/or information at wheelchair height.

Collections:
Restored school building
1820s and 1930s millworkers' house
Robert Owen's house
Period store
Working textile machinery

Publications list:
is available on-line.

Printed publications:
Guidebook (direct)

Internet home pages:
http://www.newlanark.org
Information on entire site.

2062
NEW MILLS HERITAGE AND INFORMATION CENTRE

Rock Mill Lane, New Mills, High Peak, Derbyshire, SK22 3BN

Tel: 01663 746904
Fax: 01663 746904
Formed: 1988

Organisation type and purpose: Local government body, museum, suitable for ages: 5+.
Information centre.

Education facilities by:
Derbyshire County Council

Owned by:
New Mills Town Council

Enquiries to: Administrator
Other contacts: Schools Secretary for education facilities.

Access:
Access to staff: By letter, by telephone, by fax
Hours: Tue to Fri, 0900 to 1600
Access to building, collections or gallery: No prior appointment required
Hours: Tue to Fri, 1100 to 1600; Sat, Sun, 1030 to 1630 (1600 in winter)
Other restrictions: Closed Mon; open Bank Holiday Mon.
Access for disabled people: ramped entry, level entry, access to all public areas, toilet facilities

General description:
History of New Mills - panels and display cases.

Information services:
Library available for reference (for conditions see Access above)
Special visitor services: Materials and/or activities for children.
Education services: Group education facilities, resources for Key Stage 1..

Collections:
Artefacts, pictures, prints, photographs, books, documents, manuscripts and other materials relating to New Mills

Catalogues:
Catalogue for library is on-line.

Publications list:
is available in hard copy and online.

Printed publications:
Many publications including:
Social Structure in some 'dark peak' hamlets of North West Derbyshire in the 17th and 18th centuries (Offprint from The Local Historian, £3.50, direct)
New Mills Urban District Council Surveyor 1946-1974 (£3.95, direct)
The Toors Riverside Park Bridges Trail (35p)
Geology and transport history in the Goyt Valley (£1.25)
Various Second Edition OS 25 inch Maps at Reduced Scale (All £2.10)

Internet home pages:
http://www.newmills.org.uk

2063
NEWARK AIR MUSEUM

Winthorpe Showground, Newark, Nottinghamshire, NG24 2NY

Tel: 01636 707170
Fax: 01636 707170
Email: newarkair@lineone.net
Full name: Newark (Notts & Lincs) Air Museum
Formed: 1963

Organisation type and purpose: Membership association (membership is by subscription), voluntary organisation, registered charity (charity number 256434), museum, suitable for ages: all ages.

Enquiries to: Secretary

Access:
Access to staff: By letter, by email, charges to non-members
Hours: Mar to Oct, 1000 to 1700, daily
Nov to Feb, 1000 to 1600, daily

Access to building, collections or gallery: No prior appointment required
Access for disabled people: Parking provided, level entry, access to all public areas, toilet facilities

Information services:
Special visitor services: Guided tours..
Catalogues:
Catalogue for library is in-house only.
Publications list:
is available in hard copy and online.
Printed publications:
Newark Air Museum Guide Book (Compiled by Howard Heeley, 1999, pub Newark (Notts & Lincs) Air Museum, £1 plus 40p p&p)
Shackleton WR977 - Dedication to Duty (Compiled by Robert Lindsay, Andy Otter and Howard Heeley, 1999, pub Newark (Notts & Lincs) Air Museum, £5.95 plus £1.05 p&p)
Shackleton WR977 - Duty Carried Out 1957-1971 (Compiled by Robert Lindsay and Howard Heeley, 1999, pub Newark (Notts & Lincs) Air Museum, £5.95 plus £1.05 p&p)

Address for ordering publications:
Printed publications:
Shop Manager, Newark Air Museum Trading Co Ltd
at the above address, tel: 01636 707170

2064
NEWARK MUSEUM
Appleton Gate, Newark, Nottinghamshire, NG24 1JY

Tel: 01636 655740
Fax: 01636 655745
Email: museum@newark.gov.uk
Formed: 1912

Organisation type and purpose: Local government body, museum.

Enquiries to: Museums & Heritage Manager
Direct tel: 01636 605111
Access:
Access to staff: By letter, by telephone, in person, visitors by prior appointment
Hours: Mon, Tue, Wed, Fri, Sat, 1000 to 1300 and 1400 to 1700; Thu closed;
Sun (Apr to Oct only), 1400 to 1700
Access for disabled people: ramped entry

General description:
Archaeology, architecture, communications, geography, local history, trade and industry of Newark district, militaria of the Sherwood Foresters, numismatics.
Collections:
Archive of books, documents and manuscripts and photographs

Internet home pages:
http://www.newark-sherwooddc.gov.uk

2065
NEWARK PARK
Ozleworth, Wotton-under-Edge, Gloucestershire, GL12 7PZ

Tel: 01453 842644
Fax: 01453 842644
Email: michael@newark98.freeserve.co.uk

Organisation type and purpose: Registered charity (charity number 205846), museum, historic building, house or site, suitable for ages: 5+.
Parent body:
The National Trust (South West Region)
Wessex Regional Office, tel: 01985 843600

Enquiries to: Manager
Access:
Access to staff: By letter, by telephone
Access to building, collections or gallery: No prior appointment required
Hours: Feb: Sat and Sun, 1100 to 1700;
Apr and May: Wed and Thu, 1100 to 1700;
Jun to Oct: Wed, Thu, Sat, Sun, 1100 to 1700
Other restrictions: Open Bank Holiday Mondays. Closed Easter Bank Holiday. Closes dusk if earlier.
Access for disabled people: Parking provided, ramped entry
Other restrictions: Access to ground floor of house and parts of garden and park. Drop-off point.

General description:
Tudor hunting lodge built for Sir Nicholas Poyntz, a prominent member of Henry VIII's court, from 1544. It was remodelled in late 1700s by James Wyatt. Located on edge of 40ft cliff with outstanding views. Property is lived in, and has an interesting and warm atmosphere.

Internet home pages:
http://www.nationaltrust.org.uk/regions/wessex

2066
NEWARK TOWN TREASURES & ART GALLERY
Town Hall, Market Place, Newark, Nottinghamshire, NG24 1DU

Tel: 01636 680333
Fax: 01636 680350
Email: post@newark.gov.uk
Formed: Apr 1999

Organisation type and purpose: Local government body, museum, art gallery, historic building, house or site, suitable for ages: 5+.

Enquiries to: Curator
Access:
Access to staff: By telephone, by fax, by email, in person
Access to building, collections or gallery: No prior appointment required
Hours: Mon to Fri, 1030 to 1300 and 1400 to 1630
Apr to Oct: Sat, 1300 to 1600
Other restrictions: Prior appointment required for groups and schools.
Access for disabled people: level entry, access to all public areas, toilet facilities
Other restrictions: Lift.

General description:
With its stone Palladian front, the Grade I listed Georgian Town Hall was designed by John Carr of York in 1776, and has been sympathetically refurbished to its original glory with elegant ballroom and Mayor's Parlour. Sumptuous civic gifts and paintings dating from the 17th century. Fine art includes paintings by William Nicholson, William Dobson and Stanley Spencer.
Information services:
Special visitor services: Guided tours, materials and/or activities for children.
Education services: Group education facilities, resources for Key Stages 1 and 2 and 3..
Collections:
Civic Plate. Collection includes 2 silver quilt maces of the Charles II period, a silver gilt loving cup and cover, a silver Monteith, and various paintings and town treasures. 1687-1689.
Catalogues:
Catalogue for part of the collections is on-line.

Internet home pages:
http://www.newarktowntreasures.co.uk
General information on the collection and forthcoming exhibitions.

2067
NEWARKE HOUSES MUSEUM
The Newarke, Leicester, LE2 7BY

Tel: 0116 247 3222
Formed: 1953

Organisation type and purpose: Local government body, museum, historic building, house or site, suitable for ages: 5+.

Enquiries to: Curator
Access:
Access to staff: By letter, by telephone

General description:
Victorian cobbled street, Saturday Shambles Market exhibition, Deacon clock workshop, old fashioned toys, grocer's and chemist's shops, Daniel Lambert display.
Information services:
Education services: Group education facilities..
Collections:
A good collection of local Longcase Clocks
Mapp, National collection of clocks, tickets and passes, 1920- 1955, 1500 items
Deacon clockmaker's workshop and contents, 18th century
Lace bobbins, 17th-20th century, thousands
Catalogues:
Catalogue for library is in-house only.

2068
NEWBURN HALL MOTOR MUSEUM
35 Townfield Gardens, Newburn, Newcastle upon Tyne, NE15 8PY

Tel: 0191 264 2977
Fax: 0191 264 2977
Formed: 1982

Organisation type and purpose: National organisation, independently owned, museum, historic building, house or site, suitable for ages: 8+.

Enquiries to: Curator
Access:
Access to staff: By telephone
Access to building, collections or gallery: No access other than to staff
Hours: Tue to Sun, 1000 to 2100; closed Mon

General description:
Motor vehicles of a defined period (veteran, vintage and post-vintage), make, manufacture or theme, display changed from time to time in a display area of 4000 sq ft.

2069
NEWBURY MUSEUM
See - West Berkshire Museum

2070
NEWCASTLE BOROUGH MUSEUM & ART GALLERY
Brampton Park, Newcastle-under-Lyme, Staffordshire, ST5 0QP

Tel: 01782 619705

Member of:
North Staffordshire Museums Association

Enquiries to: Curator
Access:
Access for disabled people: Parking provided, access to all public areas, toilet facilities
Other restrictions: Chairlift to first floor.

General description:
A local authority museum and art gallery in a Victorian villa set in 8 acres of parkland. Contains collections of predominantly local social history material including the Romans, industries, civic life, wartime, Victorians and childhood. Borough archives from 14th century onwards. Also contains decorative and fine arts; dolls and toys; and militaria.
Collections:
18th and 19th century paintings given in 1882 by Joseph Mayer of Newcastle (later of Liverpool). 18th and 19th Centuries, c. 70 pictures
Lower Street Pottery (archaeological), known erroneously as 'Pomona Porcelain Collection'.
Excavated material from Samuel Bell's factory and his successors, including earliest attempts at making porcelain in Staffordshire, c. 1722-1754, several hundred sherds
The ceramic collection includes Staffordshire flatbacks and ware from the 18th century Pomona pottery.
Borough Archive

continued overleaf

Internet home pages:
http://www.newcastle-staffs.gov.uk

2071
NEWCASTLE DISCOVERY
See - Discovery Museum, Newcastle upon Tyne

2072
NEWCASTLE MUSEUM
See - Hancock Museum

2073
NEWCASTLE UPON TYNE UNIVERSITY
See - Shefton Museum of Greek Art and Archaeology

2074
NEWHAILES
Newhailes Road, Musselburgh, East Lothian, EH21 6RY

Tel: 0131 665 1546

Organisation type and purpose: Historic building, house or site.
Parent body:
National Trust for Scotland

Enquiries to: Property Manager
Other contacts: Booking line, 0131 653 5599
Access:
Access to staff: By letter, by telephone, in person, charges to non-members
Access to building, collections or gallery: No prior appointment required
Hours: House and Visitor Centre, Jun to Oct, Thu to Mon, 1200 to 1700:
Estate, all year, daily, 1000 to 1800
Other restrictions: Visits to house by guided tour only, from 1300, booking essential
Access for disabled people: toilet facilities
Other restrictions: Principal floor of house and Visitor Centre

General description:
Late seventeenth century house and garden.
Information services:
Special visitor services: Guided tours..

Internet home pages:
http://www.nts.org.uk

2075
NEWHALL EQUESTRIAN CENTRE
See - Killerton: Newhall Equestrian Centre

2076
NEWHAM HERITAGE SERVICES
See - Local History and Archaeological Resource Centre

2077
NEWHAVEN FORT
Fort Road, Newhaven, East Sussex, BN9 9DL

Tel: 01273 517622
Fax: 01273 512059
Email: enquiries@newhavenfort.org.uk
Formed: 1988

Organisation type and purpose: Museum, historic building, house or site, suitable for ages: 8+.
Local visitor attraction.
Parent body:
Lewes District Council

Enquiries to: Manager
Access:
Access to staff: By letter
Access for disabled people: Parking provided, toilet facilities
Other restrictions: Level entry available on request, access to most areas.

General description:
A restored Victorian coastal fort built in the 1860s, housing a general collection of military, civil defence and home front artefacts. A number of the larger items, such as artillery pieces, are exhibited in situ.
Information services:
Education services: Group education facilities, resources for Key Stage 2..
Catalogues:
Catalogue for part of the collections is only available in-house.

Internet home pages:
http://www.newhavenfort.org.uk

2078
NEWHAVEN HERITAGE MUSEUM
Pier Place, Newhaven Harbour, Edinburgh, EH6 4LP

Tel: 0131 551 4165

Organisation type and purpose: Local government body, museum, suitable for ages: all ages.
Part of:
The City of Edinburgh Museums and Galleries Service
Which is a division of:
The City of Edinburgh Council's Recreation Department
Tel: 0131 200 2000 (main Council) 0131 529 7844 (Recreation Department HQ)

Enquiries to: Marketing and Sponsorship Officer
Direct tel: 0131 529 7902
Direct fax: 0131 529 3986
Access:
Access to staff: By letter only
Hours: Mon to Sun, 1200 to 1645

General description:
Small museum dedicated to the distinctive customs, costumes and convictions of the former fishing community of Newhaven.
Publications list:
is available on-line.
Printed publications:
The City of Edinburgh Museums and Galleries Service publishes a wide range of material, a list is available by telephoning 0131 529 3983, from April 2000 a selected list will be available on our website at www.cac.org.uk

Internet home pages:
http://www.cac.org.uk
Website for The City of Edinburgh Museums and Galleries Service, it contains: information on each of our 11 venues and their permanent collections; details of current temporary exhibitions; information on past temporary exhibitions; details of selected publications.

2079
NEWHAVEN LOCAL & MARITIME MUSEUM
Paradise Family Leisure Park, Avis Road, Newhaven, East Sussex, BN9 0DH

Tel: 01273 612530
Formed: 1963

Organisation type and purpose: Independently owned, registered charity (charity number 802506), museum, suitable for ages: 8+.
Parent body:
Newhaven Historical Society
At the same address

Enquiries to: Honorary Secretary
Direct tel: 01273 515404
Other contacts: Curator for information on museum contents.
Access:
Access to staff: By letter only
Access for disabled people: Parking provided, level entry, access to all public areas
Other restrictions: Toilet facilities on park site.

General description:
Unique display of photographs and artefacts, illustrating the long history of the Newhaven-Dieppe Cross-Channel service, and of Newhaven and the surrounding villages.
Continuous play audiovisual cinema facility providing visitors with an insight into the local scene.
Information services:
Services for disabled people: Displays and/or information at wheelchair height.
Collections:
Approximately 11,000 photographs illustrating the history of the Newhaven-Dieppe Cross-Channel Service, Newhaven and the local area
Various original minute books and ledgers relating to the operation of the port under the London, Brighton and South Coast Railway and after nationalisation
Various paintings of Newhaven and the ships of the port
Catalogues:
Catalogue for part of the collections is only available in-house.
Printed publications:
Newhaven Times (4 times a year, 30p per copy)

2080
NEWLYN ART GALLERY
New Road, Penzance, Cornwall, TR18 5PZ

Tel: 01736 363715
Fax: 01736 331578
Email: mail@newlynartgallery.co.uk
Formed: 1895

Organisation type and purpose: (charity number 216214), historic building, house or site, suitable for ages: all ages.

Enquiries to: Director
Access:
Access to staff: By telephone, by email
Access for disabled people: level entry, access to all public areas, toilet facilities
Other restrictions: One parking space; lift.

General description:
Contemporary art.

Internet home pages:
http://www.newlynartgallery.co.uk

2081
NEWPORT MUSEUM AND ART GALLERY
John Frost Square, Newport, Gwent, NP20 1PA

Tel: 01633 840064
Fax: 01633 222615
Email: museum@newport.gov.uk
Formed: 1888

Organisation type and purpose: Local government body, museum.
Parent body:
Newport County Borough Council
Civic Centre, Newport, Gwent, NP9 4UR

Enquiries to: Curator
Access:
Access to staff: By letter
Access to building, collections or gallery: No prior appointment required
Hours: Mon to Thu, 0930 to 1700; Fri, Sat, 0930 to 1630
Access for disabled people: level entry, access to all public areas, toilet facilities

General description:
Natural sciences, archaeology and history of Gwent, art subjects generally, local history of Newport and area.
Collections:
Early English and Welsh watercolours
Material from the site of Romano-British town at Caerwent (Venta Silurum)
Monmouthshire Chartist collection
Catalogues:
Catalogue for all of the collections is only available in-house.

Printed publications:
Catalogue - James Flewitt Mollock
Postcards - various
Temporary exhibition catalogues (various)

2082
NEWPORT PAGNELL HISTORICAL SOCIETY COLLECTION

Chandos Hall, Chandos Court, Silver Street, Newport Pagnell, Buckinghamshire, MK16 8ET

Tel: 01908 612356
Acronym or abbreviation: NPHS
Formed: 1984

Organisation type and purpose: Museum, suitable for ages: 8+, research organisation.
Chairman:
Newport Pagnell Historical Society
68 Silver Street, Newport Pagnell, Buckinghamshire, MK16 0EN, email/website: hurstfamily@breathemail.net

Enquiries to: Chairman
Access:
Access to staff: By email
Access for disabled people: ramped entry, toilet facilities

General description:
Mainly a collection of 18th/19th century domestic articles, together with tools and agricultural implements local to Newport Pagnell.
Collections:
Regalia and documents plus a banner, from defunct branches of local Ancient Order of Foresters and Ancient Order of Oddfellows.19th century.
Publications list:
is available in hard copy.
Printed publications:
Following available direct, local shops, website
Various books on Newport Pagnell and surrounding area
Newport Pagnell - A Pictorial History (£12)
Newport Pagnell in the 1950's (£9.50

Internet home pages:
http://www.mkheritage.co.uk/nphs/index.html

2083
NEWSTEAD ABBEY MUSEUM

Ravenshead, Nottingham, NG15 8NA

Tel: 01623 455900
Fax: 01623 455904

Organisation type and purpose: Local government body, museum, historic building, house or site, suitable for ages: 12+.
Parent body:
Nottingham Corporation

Enquiries to: Administrator
Access:
Access to staff: By letter, by telephone, by fax
Access for disabled people: ramped entry, toilet facilities
Other restrictions: House - ground floor access only. Access Guide available. Mobility car for use in the grounds.

General description:
Founded as a monastic house in the late 12th century, Newstead became the Byron family seat in 1540. The poet Lord Byron sold the property in 1818 and it remained a private country house until 1931 when it was presented to Nottingham Corporation. Substantial formal and informal gardens with lakes, ponds and waterfalls.
Information services:
Special visitor services: Guided tours, tape recorded guides.
Education services: Group education facilities, resources for Further or Higher Education.
Services for disabled people: For the visually impaired.
Collections:
Furniture, books, manuscripts and works of art
Manuscript poems, letters, books and personal mementos
Newstead Priory - archival and archaeological material
Byron Family - archival material, furniture, paintings, memorabilia
6th Lord Byron - furniture, books, correspondence, portraits, personal belongings
Wildman & Webb Families - portraits, books, furniture, armour, pictures, prints, photographs, correspondence
Catalogues:
Catalogue for part of the collections is available in-house and part is published.
Printed publications:
Poems of Newstead (Nottingham City Museums & Galleries)
The Life & Works of Lord Byron (Nottingham City Museums & Galleries)
Lord Byron's Newstead (Coope R)
Newstead Abbey (Nottingham City Museums & Galleries)

Internet home pages:
http://www.newsteadabbey.org.uk

2084
NEWTON HOUSE

See - Dinefwr

2085
NEWTON STEWART MUSEUM

York Road, Newton Stewart, Dumfries & Galloway, DG8 6HH

Tel: 01671 402472
Formed: 1978

Organisation type and purpose: Registered charity (charity number ED770/91/PLB), museum, suitable for ages: 12+.

Enquiries to: Honorary Secretary
Direct email: jmclay@argonet.co.uk
Access:
Access to staff: By letter, by telephone, by email, charges made to all users
Hours: Easter to Sep, 1400 to 1700
Access for disabled people: ramped entry

General description:
The museum, housed in the former St John's Church, contains interesting and nostalgic displays of the social and domestic history of the Galloway district.
Catalogues:
Catalogue for all of the collections is only available in-house.

2086
NGS PICTURE LIBRARY

National Galleries of Scotland, Dean Gallery, 73 Belford Road, Edinburgh, EH4 3DS

Tel: 0131 624 6258
Fax: 0131 623 7135
Email: picture.library@natgalscot.ac.uk
Full name: National Galleries of Scotland Picture Library

Organisation type and purpose: National organisation, art gallery, public library.
Parent body:
National Galleries of Scotland
Belford Road, Edinbrugh, EH4 3DR, tel: 0131 624 6200, fax: 0131 343 3250, email: enquiries@natgalscot.ac.uk
Access:
Access to staff: By letter, by telephone, by fax, by email, in person
Hours: Mon to Fri, 0900 to 1700
Access to building, collections or gallery: No prior appointment required
Hours: Mon to Sat, 1000 to 1700, Sun, 1200 to 1700
Other restrictions: Closed 25th, 26th December, open 1st January, 1200 to 1700
Access for disabled people: access to all public areas, toilet facilities

General description:
Brings together the works in all the collections of the National Galleries of Scotland including photographs and slides. Material depicting the work of artists from the Renaissance to the present day, including the major painters, and a wide variety of subjects, media and styles.

Internet home pages:
http://www.natgalscot.ac.uk

2087
NIDDERDALE MUSEUM

King Street, Pateley Bridge, North Yorkshire, HG3 5LE

Tel: 01423 711225
Formed: 1975

Organisation type and purpose: Membership association (membership is by subscription), present number of members: 249, voluntary organisation, registered charity (charity number 53233), museum.
The museum has a large and imaginative display with extensive collections illustrating all aspects of life in the past in Nidderdale.

Enquiries to: Honorary Secretary
Access:
Access to staff: By letter, by telephone, in person, visitors by prior appointment
Access for disabled people: Parking provided
Other restrictions: Stairlift to first floor, wheelchair available.

General description:
A collection of exhibits, displayed in the original Victorian workhouse, illustrating the life and history of the folk of Nidderdale. All aspects of local history, family history in particular.
Collections:
The cobbler's shop. Complete workshop. 1900-1950. 1,500
The Dale's Reservoirs, the story of the building of Gouthwaite, Angram and Scar Reservoirs, 1890-1936

2088
NO 28 CHARLOTTE SQUARE

Edinburgh, EH2 4ET

Tel: 0131 243 9300
Fax: 0131 243 9339

Organisation type and purpose: Museum, art gallery, historic building, house or site.
Parent body:
National Trust for Scotland (South Region)

Enquiries to: Property Manager
Access:
Access to staff: By letter, by telephone, by fax, in person, charges to non-members
Access to building, collections or gallery: No prior appointment required
Hours: Drawing Room Gallery, Mon to Sat, 1000 to1700, Sun, 1200 to 1700:
Access for disabled people: Parking provided
Other restrictions: All public areas and toilets accessible with assistance

General description:
Georgian town houses, Head Office of National Trust for Scotland.
Collections:
Twentieth century Scottish paintings, including the Scottish colourists

Internet home pages:
http://www.nts.org.uk

2089
NORCHARD RAILWAY CENTRE

See - Dean Forest Railway Museum

2090
NORFOLK & SUFFOLK AVIATION MUSEUM

Buckeroo Way, The Street, Flixton, Bungay, Suffolk, NR35 1NZ

Tel: 01986 896644
Email: curator@aviationmuseum.net
Formed: 1972
Incorporating: 446th Bomb Group USAAF Museum, RAF Air-Sea Rescue & Coastal Command Museum, RAF Bomber Command Museum, Royal Observer Corps Museum (ROC)

Organisation type and purpose: Independently owned, registered charity (charity number 281804), museum, historic building, house or site, suitable for ages: 5+.

Enquiries to: Secretary
Other contacts: (1) IT Manager; (2) Curator; (3) Air-Sea Rescue Museum; (4) Royal Observer Corps Museums; (5) 446th Bomb Group Museum for (1) web queries; (2) curatorial queries; (3) air-sea rescue queries; (4) ROC queries; (5) queries to Curator.
Access:
Access to staff: By letter, by telephone, by email, in person, Internet web pages
Access to building, collections or gallery: No prior appointment required
Hours: Apr to Oct: Sun to Thu, 1000 to 1600
Nov to Mar: Sun, Tue, Wed, 1000 to 1500
Other restrictions: Closed 15 Dec to 15 Jan.
Access for disabled people: Parking provided, ramped entry, level entry, access to all public areas, toilet facilities

General description:
Museum of East Anglia's Aviation heritage.
Information services:
Guided tours by prior arrangement.
Special visitor services: Guided tours..
Collections:
Over 25 aircraft including nose sections
2 aircraft hangers
Artefacts from pre WWI to present day in 7 buildings
Nature Trail - 'Adair Walk'.
Friars to Flyers Heritage Trail
Catalogues:
Catalogue for library is in-house only. Catalogue for all of the collections is only available in-house.
Publications list:
is available on-line.

Internet home pages:
http://www.aviationmuseum.net
Information about various museums' collections and programme.

2091
NORFOLK ARCHAEOLOGY & ENVIRONMENT DIVISION

Union House, Gressenhall, Dereham, Norfolk, NR20 4DR

Tel: 01362 860528
Fax: 01362 860951
Email: archaeology+environment.mus @norfolk.gov.uk
Formed: 1991
Formed from: Norfolk Archaeological Unit (NAU), date of change, 1991
Formerly: Norfolk Field Archaeology Division

Organisation type and purpose: Local government body, museum.
Field archaeology (excavations, surveys), field archaeology (records, information, advice, publications (East Anglian Archaeology), biological recording.
Parent body:
Norfolk Museums & Archaeology Service
Shirehall, Market Avenue, Norwich, NR1 3JQ, tel: 01603 493625, fax: 01603 493623, email: museums@norfolk.gov.uk
Other addresses:
Norfolk Archaeological Unit (NAU)
Spire House, 13-15 Cathedral Street, Norwich, NR1 1LU, tel: 01603 878200, fax: 01603 878209, email/website: jayne.bown.mus@norfolk.gov.uk

Enquiries to: Secretary
Other contacts: (1) Archaeology and Environment Officer; (2) Principal Field Archaeologist; (3) Principal Landscape Archaeologist; for (1) Manager; (2) excavations, surveys; (3) records, information, advice..
Access:
Access to staff: By letter, by telephone, by fax, by email, in person, visitors by prior appointment
Access to building, collections or gallery: Prior appointment required

General description:
Archaeological excavations, surveys, information, advice, records, finds, publications, biological records.
Collections:
Norfolk Sites and Monuments Record
Norfolk Air Photo Library
Norfolk Biological Record
Publications list:
is available on-line.

Address for ordering publications:
Printed publications:
Publications, Essex County Council Archaeology Section
Fairfield Court, Fairfield Road, Braintree, CM7 3YQ, tel: 01376 553934, fax: 01376 553934, email: phil.mcmichael@essexcc.gov.uk

Internet home pages:
http://www.eaareports.org.uk
Full list of publications.

2092
NORFOLK LANDSCAPE ARCHAEOLOGY

Union House, Gressenhall, Dereham, Norfolk, NR20 4DR

Tel: 01362 860528
Fax: 01362 860951
Email: archaeology+environment.mus @norfolk.gov.uk
Acronym or abbreviation: NLA
Formed: 1991
Formed from: Norfolk Archaeological Unit (NAU), date of change, 1991

Organisation type and purpose: Local government body, museum.
Field archaeology records, information, advice and resource management.
Parent body:
Norfolk Museums & Archaeology Service
Shirehall, Market Avenue, Norwich, NR1 3JQ, tel: 01603 493625, fax: 01603 493623, email: museums@norfolk.gov.uk

Enquiries to: Manager
Other contacts: (1) Development Control Officer; (2) Records Officer; (3) Senior Landscape Archaeologist for (1) planning advice; (2) records and aerial photos; (3) archaeological finds.
Access:
Access to staff: By letter, by telephone, by fax, by email, in person, visitors by prior appointment
Access to building, collections or gallery: Prior appointment required

General description:
Archaeological information and advice, aerial photographs, identification and recording of archaeological finds, monuments management.
Collections:
Norfolk Sites and Monuments Record
Norfolk Air Photographic Library

2093
NORFOLK MOTORCYCLE MUSEUM

Station Yard, Norwich Road, North Walsham, Norfolk, NR28 0DS

Tel: 01692 406266
Formed: 1994
Still known as: Harmer Classics, date of change, 1994

Organisation type and purpose: Registered charity, museum, suitable for ages: .
To aid the knowledge of the history of engineering from the early 1900s to 1970.

Enquiries to: Chairman
Access:
Access to staff: By letter, by telephone
Hours: Mon to Fri, 1000 to 1630
Access for disabled people: ramped entry

General description:
Motorcycles.
Information services:
Special visitor services: Guided tours..

2094
NORFOLK MUSEUMS & ARCHAEOLOGY SERVICE

Education and Access Department, Castle Museum, Norwich, Norfolk, NR1 3JU

Tel: 01603 495892
Fax: 01603 493623
Email: katrina.siliprandi.mus@norfolk.gov.uk
Formed: 1917

Organisation type and purpose: Local government body, service industry, museum, art gallery, suitable for ages: all ages, training organisation.
Museum Education Department providing a hands-on service to life-long learners, including handling sessions, worksheets and resources, advice, interpretation of collections.
Parent body:
Norfolk County Council
Affiliated to:
County Museum Service
Tel: 01603 223623, fax: 01603 756561, email/website: val.beaumont.mus.@norfolk.gov.uk
Other addresses:
Ancient House Museum
White Hart Lane, Thetford, Norfolk, IP24 1AA, tel: 01842 752599, fax: Faxphone - ring first, email/website: oliver.bone.mus@norfolk.gov.uk
Bridewell Museum
Bridewell Alley, Norwich, Norfolk, NR2 1AQ, tel: 01603 667228, email/website: david.jones.mus@norfolk.gov.uk
Castle Museum
Norwich, Norfolk, NR1 3JU, tel: 01603 493625, fax: 01603 493623, email/website: val.beaumont.mus.@norfolk.gov.uk
Costume & Textiles
Carrow House, 301 King Street, Norwich, Norfolk, tel: 01603 223870, email/website: cathy.terry.mus.@norfolk.gov.uk
Cromer Museum
Cromer, Norfolk, tel: 01263 513543, fax: 01263 511651, email/website: alistair.murphy.mus.@norfolk.gov.uk
Elizabethan House
4 South Quay, Great Yarmouth, Norfolk, tel: 01493 855746, email/website: colin.stott.mus@norfolk.gov.uk
Great Yarmouth Museum Offices
Central Library, Great Yarmouth, Norfolk, tel: 01493 745526, fax: 01493 745459, email/website: colin.stott.mus@norfolk.gov.uk
Lynn Museum
Market Street, King's Lynn, Norfolk, PE30 1NL, tel: 01553 775001, fax: 01553 775001, email/website: ellie.jones.mus@norfolk.gov.uk
Maritime Museum
Great Yarmouth, Norfolk, tel: 01493 842267, email/website: colin.stott.mus@norfolk.gov.uk
Norfolk Rural Life Museum
Gressenhall, Norfolk, tel: 01362 860294, fax: 01362 860385, email/website: richard.wood.mus.@norfolk.gov.uk
Royal Norfolk Regimental Museum
Shire Hall, Norwich, Norfolk, tel: 01603 493649, email/website: kate.thaxton.mus.@norfolk.gov.uk
Strangers' Hall

Charing Cross, Norwich, Norfolk, tel: 01603 667229, email/website: helen.rowles.mus.@norfolk.gov.uk
Tolhouse Museum and Gaol & Exhibition Gallery
Great Yarmouth, Norfolk, tel: 01493 858900, email/website: colin.stott.mus@norfolk.gov.uk
Townhouse Museum of Lynn Life
46 Queen Street, King's Lynn, Norfolk, PE30 5DQ, tel: 01553 773450, email/website: ellie.jones.mus.@norfolk.gov.uk

Enquiries to: Head of Education Department
Other contacts: Education Officer
Access:
Access to staff: By letter, by telephone, by fax, by email, visitors by prior appointment, Internet web pages
Hours: Mon to Fri, 0900 to 1700
Access to building, collections or gallery: No prior appointment required
Hours: Currently Mon to Sat, 1030 to 1700; Sun, 1400 to 1700
Other restrictions: Telephone to confirm opening hours. Some museums closed during winter months.
Study Centre in adjoining building for access to reserve collections by appointment.
Access for disabled people: Parking provided, level entry, access to all public areas, toilet facilities

General description:
Castle, Egyptians, Victorians, archaeology, crime and punishment, Boudica and the Iceni, Romans, Norwich school of painters, Lowestoft porcelain, GNVQ leisure and tourism, museum facilities for disabled people, museum education, Norfolk history, geology, and natural history.
Information services:
Library available for reference (for conditions see Access above). Helpline available, tel no: 01603 493625.
Enquiries about objects, including metal detector finds. Access to reserve collections at Shirehall Resource Centre.
Special visitor services: Guided tours, materials and/or activities for children.
Education services: Group education facilities, resources for Key Stages 1 and 2, 3, 4 and Further or Higher Education.
Services for disabled people: For the visually impaired; for the hearing impaired; displays and/or information at wheelchair height.
Collections:
Norwich School of Painters
Contemporary art and craft
18th century English and Dutch paintings
Norwich silver
Egyptians
Norfolk archaeology, especially Celtic, Roman, Norman and later medieval
Norfolk and worldwide natural history
Lowestoft porcelain
Catalogues:
Catalogue for part of the collections is available in-house and part is published.
Trade and statistical:
Leisure and tourism information for Norfolk Museums service.
Publications list:
is available in hard copy.
Printed publications:
Some teachers' resources
Pupils' worksheets

Internet home pages:
http://www.norfolk.gov.uk/tourism/museums/museum.htm
Basic visitor information about Norfolk Museums Service, teachers' and pupils' resources, detailed information about some collections.

2095
NORFOLK MUSEUMS & ARCHAEOLOGY SERVICE
Shirehall, Market Avenue, Norwich, Norfolk, NR1 3JQ

Tel: 01603 493625
Fax: 01603 493623

Organisation type and purpose: Local government body.
Parent body:
Norfolk County Council
A joint service of:
Borough Council of King's Lynn and West Norfolk
Breckland Council
Broadland District Council
Great Yarmouth Borough Council
Norfolk County Council
North Norfolk District Council
Norwich City Council
South Norfolk Council

Enquiries to: Information Officer
Access:
Access to staff: By letter, by telephone, by fax

General description:
Administrative body for museums and historical sites in the care of Norfolk County Council.

Internet home pages:
http://www.norfolk.gov.uk/tourism/museums

See also - Ancient House Museum; Ancient House Museum; Bridewell Museum; Costume and Textile Study Centre; Cromer Museum; Elizabethan House Museum; Great Yarmouth Museums; Lynn Museum; Norfolk Archaeology & Environment Division; Norfolk Landscape Archaeology; Norwich Castle Museum & Art Gallery; Norwich Castle Study Centre; Roots of Norfolk at Gressenhall; Royal Norfolk Regimental Museum; Strangers' Hall Museum; Tolhouse Museum; Tower Curing Works Museum; Town House Museum

2096
NORFOLK NELSON MUSEUM, THE
26 South Quay, Great Yarmouth, Norfolk, NR30 2RG

Tel: 01493 850698
Fax: 01493 850698
Email: curator@nelson-museum.co.uk
Formed: 2002

Organisation type and purpose: Independently owned, museum, historic building, house or site, suitable for ages: 5+.

Enquiries to: Curator
Access:
Access to staff: By letter, by telephone, by fax, by email
Access to building, collections or gallery: No prior appointment required
Hours: Apr to end of Oct, Mon to Fri, 1000 to 1700, Sat and Sun, 1400 to 1700
Other restrictions: Research library by appointment
Access for disabled people: access to all public areas, toilet facilities

General description:
The museum is housed in a grade II listed building, formerly the seventeenth century home of Sir George England, chairman of the committee which welcomed Charles II to Yarmouth during the Civil War in 1671.
The museum relates, through room displays and interactive displays, the life and times of Lord Nelson
Information services:
Special events programme
Education and meeting room available
Special visitor services: Materials and/or activities for children.
Education services: Group education facilities, resources for Key Stages 1 and 3..
Catalogues:
Catalogue for library is in-house only. Catalogue for all of the collections is only available in-house.
Internet home pages:
http://www.nelson-museum.co.uk

2097
NORFOLK RURAL LIFE MUSEUM
See - Roots of Norfolk at Gressenhall

2098
NORFOLK MILLS AND PUMPS TRUST
Couinty Hall, Martineau Lane, Norwich, Norfolk, NR1 2SG

Tel: 01603 222705
Acronym or abbreviation: Norfolk Windmills Trust

Organisation type and purpose: Membership association, voluntary organisation, registered charity (charity number 1033274).
Supported in its work by:
Norfolk County Council

Enquiries to: Technical Advisor

General description:
Historic wind and water mills and pumps in Norfolk.

Internet home pages:
http://www.norfolkwindmills.co.uk

2099
NORHAM CASTLE
Norham, Northumberland

Tel: 01289 382329

Organisation type and purpose: Historic building, house or site.
Parent body:
English Heritage (North East Region)
Tel: 0191 269 1227/8, fax: 0191 261 1130

Enquiries to: Manager
Access:
Access to staff: By letter, by telephone, in person
Access to building, collections or gallery: No prior appointment required
Hours: End Mar to end Sep: daily, 1000 to 1800
Other restrictions: Opening times are subject to change, for up-to-date information contact English Heritage by phone or visit the website.

General description:
Ruins of one of the strongest of the border castles, built in 1160. Came under siege on several occasions, and was finally largely destroyed by James IV of Scotland in 1513.
Information services:
Special visitor services: Tape recorded guides.
Services for disabled people: For the visually impaired.

Internet home pages:
http://www.english-heritage.org.uk

2100
NORMANBY HALL
Normanby Hall Country Park, Normanby, Scunthorpe, Lincolnshire, DN15 9HU

Tel: 01724 720588
Fax: 01724 720337
Formed: 1964

Organisation type and purpose: Local government body, museum.
Connections with:
North Lincolnshire Council

Enquiries to: Curator
Access:
Access to staff: By letter, by telephone, by fax, in person, visitors by prior appointment

continued overleaf

Access to building, collections or gallery: No access other than to staff
Hours: Mar 25 to Sep 29: Daily, 1300 to 1700
Other restrictions: By prior appointment at other times.
Access for disabled people: Parking provided, ramped entry, toilet facilities

General description:
Regency house designed by Sir Robert Smirke for the Sheffield Family in the 1820s. Furnished in the regency style. Costume gallery with annually changing exhibitions.
Information services:
Special visitor services: Guided tours.
Education services: Group education facilities, resources for Key Stages 1 and 2, 3, 4 and Further or Higher Education.
Services for disabled people: Displays and/or information at wheelchair height.
Collections:
Collection of Regency Furniture
Large Costume Collection (over 4700 items) dating from 18th century to present
North Lincolnshire Museums Reserve Social History Collection
Catalogues:
Catalogue for part of the collections is only available in-house.

Internet home pages:
http://www.northlincs.gov.uk/museums
Information on the house, collections and events.

2101
NORMANBY PARK FARMING MUSEUM
Normanby Hall Country Park, Normanby, Scunthorpe, Lincolnshire, DN15 9HU

Tel: 01724 720588
Fax: 01724 720337
Formed: 1989

Organisation type and purpose: Local government body, museum.
Connections with:
North Lincolnshire Council

Enquiries to: Curator
Access:
Access to staff: By letter, by telephone, by fax, in person, visitors by prior appointment
Access to building, collections or gallery: No prior appointment required
Hours: Mar 25 to Sep 29: Daily, 1300 to 1700
Other restrictions: By prior appointment at other times.
Access for disabled people: Parking provided, level entry, access to all public areas, toilet facilities

General description:
Contains displays of agricultural machinery and hand tools dating from 1820-1940; rural craft workshop reconstructions; a rural industries gallery; and a transport gallery.
Information services:
Programme of children's activities.
Special visitor services: Guided tours, materials and/or activities for children.
Education services: Group education facilities, resources for Key Stages 1 and 2, 3, 4 and Further or Higher Education.
Services for disabled people: For the visually impaired; for the hearing impaired; displays and/or information at wheelchair height.
Collections:
Agricultural implements and tools 1850 to 1950 and craft tools of a similar period
Collections are mainly from regional producers
Catalogues:
Catalogue for part of the collections is only available in-house.

Internet home pages:
http://www.northlincs.gov.uk/museums
Information on the museum, collections and events.

2102
NORMANTON CHURCH
Normanton, Oakham, Rutland, LE15 8PX

Tel: 01572 653026
Fax: 01572 653027
Formed: 1980

Organisation type and purpose: Museum, suitable for ages: 5+.
Access:
Access to staff: By letter, by telephone, by fax
Access to building, collections or gallery: No prior appointment required
Hours: Daily, 1100 to 1600

General description:
Contains a collection of fossils and Anglo-Saxon artefacts excavated during the construction of a reservoir and the building of a dam; all housed in a sunken church. Also a video of the construction, and history of the area prior to the construction.
Information services:
Special visitor services: Guided tours.
Education services: Group education facilities, resources for Key Stages 1 and 2, 3, 4 and Further or Higher Education..
Collections:
Anglo-Saxon skeleton. 950 AD
Ichthyosaur/Plesiosaur bones. Prehistory.

2103
NORRIS MUSEUM
41 The Broadway, St Ives, Huntingdon, Cambridgeshire, PE27 5BX

Tel: 01480 497314
Email: norris.st-ives-tc@co-net.com
Full name: Norris Library and Museum
Formed: 1933

Organisation type and purpose: Local government body, museum, art gallery, suitable for ages: all ages.

Enquiries to: Curator
Access:
Access to staff: By letter, by telephone, by email, in person, visitors by prior appointment
Access to building, collections or gallery: No prior appointment required
Hours: Mon to Fri, 1000 to 1300 and 1400 to 1600; Sat, 1000 to 1200
Access for disabled people: ramped entry, access to all public areas

General description:
The history of Huntingdonshire, from earliest times to the present day: geology, palaeontology, archaeology and local history; also books, manuscripts, paintings, prints and maps.
Information services:
Library available for reference (for conditions see Access above)
Special visitor services: Guided tours.
Education services: Group education facilities, resources for Further or Higher Education..
Collections:
Archaeology and history of Huntingdonshire including palaeontology, books, manuscripts, prints, watercolours, drawings, easel paintings, photographs
Objects made by French prisoners-of-war at the Napoleonic prison camp at Norman Cross
Ice skates used in the Fens, with related objects, and comparable foreign skates
Saxon coins minted at Huntingdon
Catalogues:
Catalogue for library is in-house only. Catalogue for all of the collections is only available in-house.
Printed publications:
Various books etc

2104
NORTH AYRSHIRE MUSEUM
Manse Street, Saltcoats, Ayrshire, KA21 5AA

Tel: 01294 464174
Fax: 01294 464174
Email: namuseum@globalnet.co.uk
Formed: 1957

Organisation type and purpose: Local government body, museum, suitable for ages: 5+.

Enquiries to: Curator
Access:
Access to staff: By letter, by telephone, by fax, by email, in person, Internet web pages
Access to building, collections or gallery: No prior appointment required
Hours: Mon to Sat, 1000 to 1300 and 1400 to 1700; closed Wed
Access for disabled people: level entry, access to all public areas, toilet facilities

General description:
The North Ayrshire Museum shows the history of North Ayrshire with displays on archaeology, costume, transport and popular culture. The museum also includes a section showing the maritime history of the port of Ardrossan and a reconstruction of an Ayrshire cottage interior. Accompanied children can play in the children's activity area.
Collections:
Material on the local and social history of the North Ayrshire area, with good collection of Ayrshire whitework textiles
Good collection of local photographs, and c. 3000 glass lantern slides

Internet home pages:
http://www.users.globalnet.co.uk/~vennel/nam.html

2105
NORTH BERWICK MUSEUM
School Road, North Berwick, East Lothian, EH39 4JU

Tel: 01620 895457
Email: nbm@elothian-museums.demon.co.uk
Formed: 1957

Organisation type and purpose: Local government body, museum, art gallery, historic building, house or site, suitable for ages: 5+.

Enquiries to: Museums Officer
Direct tel: 01620 828203
Direct fax: 01620 828201
Direct email: pgray@eastlothian.gov.uk
Access:
Access to staff: By letter, by telephone, by fax, by email, in person, visitors by prior appointment, Internet web pages

General description:
Covers local history and natural history including geology; archaeology, including finds from Dirleton and Tantallon castles and from Berwick Law; fishing; paintings, especially local topography; local photographs, golf, seaside holidays, fine art, strong temporary exhibition programme.
Information services:
Education facilities, Scottish Key Stages.
Special visitor services: Materials and/or activities for children.
Education services: Group education facilities..
Collections:
Golf, including clubs by East Lothian makers
Catalogues:
Catalogue for all of the collections is only available in-house.

Internet home pages:
http://www.elothian-museums.demon.co.uk/nbm

2106
NORTH CORNWALL MUSEUM AND GALLERY

The Clease, Camelford, Cornwall, PL32 9PL

Tel: 01840 212954
Fax: 01840 212954
Email: camelfordtic@eurobell.co.uk
Formed: 1972

Organisation type and purpose: Independently owned, museum, art gallery, suitable for ages: 8+.

Enquiries to: Curator
Access:
Access to staff: By letter, by email, visitors by prior appointment
Access to building, collections or gallery: No prior appointment required
Hours: 29 Mar to 30 Sep: Mon to Sat, 1000 to 1700

General description:
Museum in a building originally used for making coaches and wagons. The museum covers many aspects of life in North Cornwall from fifty to a hundred years ago. These include farming, the dairy, cidermaking and wagons. A special feature is the reconstruction of a moorland cottage at the turn of the century. There are sections on the tools of the carpenter, cooper, blacksmith, saddler, cobbler, tailor, printer, doctor, granite and slate quarryman. On the domestic side there is a wide range of exhibits from lace bonnets to early vacuum cleaners, and a collection of Cornish and Devonshire pottery.
Collections:
Tools used in slate quarrying

2107
NORTH DEVON MUSEUM SERVICE

The Square, Barnstaple, Devon, EX32 8LN

Tel: 01271 346747
Fax: 01271 346407
Email: museum@northdevon.gov.uk
Formed: 1989

Organisation type and purpose: Local government body, art gallery, suitable for ages: all ages.

Enquiries to: Administrator
Access:
Access to staff: By letter, by telephone, by email, Internet web pages
Access to building, collections or gallery: No prior appointment required
Hours: Tue to Sat, 1000 to 1630
Other restrictions: Closed Bank Holidays.
Access for disabled people: Parking provided, ramped entry, access to all public areas, toilet facilities

Information services:
Services for disabled people: Displays and/or information at wheelchair height.
Collections:
Archaeology
Geology
North Devon Art Potters
Militaria
Fine Art
Coins

Internet home pages:
http://www.northdevonondisk.co.uk
http://www.devonmuseums.net/barnstaple

2108
NORTH DOWN HERITAGE CENTRE

Town Hall, Bangor, Co Down, BT20 4BT

Tel: 028 9127 0371
Fax: 028 9127 1370
Email: heritage@northdown.gov.uk
Formed: 1984

Organisation type and purpose: Museum, suitable for ages: 12+.
Parent body:
North Down Borough Council
Town Hall, Bangor, BT20 4BT

Enquiries to: Manager
Access:
Access to staff: By letter, by email, Internet web pages
Access to building, collections or gallery: No prior appointment required
Hours: Tue to Sat, 1030 to 1630; Sun, 1400 to 1630
Access for disabled people: Parking provided, level entry, toilet facilities

General description:
Housed in the former outbuildings of Bangor Castle, it contains material covering all aspects of North Down's historical, archaeological and natural heritage. The collections deal especially with early Christian times and seaside holiday nostalgia.
Information services:
Special visitor services: Guided tours.
Education services: Group education facilities, resources for Key Stages 1 and 2, 3 and 4.
Services for disabled people: Displays and/or information at wheelchair height.
Collections:
Percy French Collection: unique archive relating to this Irish painter and songwriter
Catalogues:
Catalogue for part of the collections is only available in-house.

Internet home pages:
http://www.northdown.gov.uk/heritage

2109
NORTH EAST OF SCOTLAND AGRICULTURAL HERITAGE CENTRE

See - Aberdeenshire Farming Museum; Aberdeenshire Heritage

2110
NORTH EAST OF SCOTLAND MUSEUMS SERVICE

See - Aberdeenshire Heritage

2111
NORTH LINCOLNSHIRE MUSEUM

Oswald Road, Scunthorpe, Lincolnshire, DN15 7BD

Tel: 01724 843533
Fax: 01724 270474
Email: joanne.mayall@northlincs.gov.uk
Formed: 1909
Formerly: Scunthorpe Museum and Art Gallery, date of change, 1996

Organisation type and purpose: Local government body, museum, art gallery, suitable for ages: 5+.
Parent body:
North Lincolnshire Council
Pittwood House, Ashby Road, Scunthorpe, tel: 01724 296296

Enquiries to: Principal Keeper
Other contacts: Curator
Access:
Access to staff: By letter, by telephone, by fax, by email, visitors by prior appointment
Access to building, collections or gallery: No prior appointment required
Hours: Tue to Sat, 1000 to 1600; Sun and Bank Holidays, 1300 to 1600

Other restrictions: Closed Mon and 25, 26, Dec and 1 Jan.
Access for disabled people: ramped entry, toilet facilities
Other restrictions: Lift for disabled persons to 2nd floor. Wheelchair access to ground floor only.

General description:
The Museum depicts North Lincolnshire's early and later history, through displays of geology, archaeology, social history, local history and costume.
Information services:
Library available for reference (for conditions see Access above)
Identification and information services.
Special visitor services: Guided tours, materials and/or activities for children.
Education services: Group education facilities, resources for Key Stages 1 and 2 and Further or Higher Education..
Collections:
Archaeological finds from region
Geological finds, mainly Jurassic
Local history and bygones
Local photographs
William Fowler of Winterton printmaker, collection of late 18th and early 19th century antiquarian prints
Catalogues:
Catalogue for library is in-house only.
Publications list:
is available in hard copy.

Internet home pages:
http://www.northlincs.gov.uk/museums
Information about North Lincolnshire Museum Service.

2112
NORTH OF ENGLAND LEAD MINING MUSEUM

See - Killhope, The North of England Lead Mining Museum

2113
NORTH OF ENGLAND OPEN AIR MUSEUM

See - Beamish: The North of England Open Air Museum

2114
NORTH PENNINES HERITAGE TRUST

See - Nenthead Mines Heritage Centre

2115
NORTH SOMERSET MUSEUM

Burlington Street, Weston-Super-Mare, Somerset, BS23 1PR

Tel: 01934 621028
Fax: 01934 612526
Email: museum.service@n-somerset.gov.uk
Formed: 1901
Formerly: Woodspring Museum, date of change, 1996

Organisation type and purpose: Local government body, museum, suitable for ages: all ages.
Museum telling the story of North Somerset.
Parent body:
North Somerset Museum Service
at the same address

Enquiries to: Museum Manager
Direct email: nick.goff@n-somerset.gov.uk
Access:
Access to staff: By letter, by telephone, by fax, by email, visitors by prior appointment
Hours: Mon to Fri, 0900 to 1630
Access to building, collections or gallery: No prior appointment required
Hours: Mon to Sat, 1000 to 1630
Access for disabled people: level entry, toilet facilities

General description:
Collections and related information on the human and natural history of North Somerset, including geology, archaeology, natural history, social history, art, and costume.

continued overleaf

Information services:
Special visitor services: Materials and/or activities for children.
Education services: Group education facilities, resources for Key Stages 1 and 2..
Collections:
Human and natural history material relating to North Somerset
Seaside - souvenirs, ephemera, etc. relating to the seaside holiday, 19th-20th century
Catalogues:
Catalogue for part of the collections is available in-house and part is on-line.
Publications list:
is available on-line.
Electronic and video products:
Publications list on website

Internet home pages:
http://www.n-somerset.gov.uk/museum

2116
NORTH STAFFORDS MUSEUM
See - Staffordshire Regiment Museum

2117
NORTH WALES NARROW GAUGE RAILWAY LTD
See - Fairbourne and Barmouth Railway

2118
NORTH WEST MUSEUMS SERVICE
Griffin Lodge, Cavendish Place, Blackburn, Lancashire, BB2 4BS

Tel: 01254 670211
Fax: 01254 681995
Email: nwms@nwmuseums.co.uk
Acronym or abbreviation: NWMS

Organisation type and purpose: Registered charity (charity number 511412).
Regional organisation, area museum council.

Enquiries to: Administrator
Direct email: rosemary@nwms.demon.co.uk
Access:
Access to staff: By letter, by email, Internet web pages

General description:
Assists museums, and museums in partnership with archives and libraries, to enhance their contribution to the cultural, economic and social life of the North West.

Internet home pages:
http://www.nwmuseums.co.uk

2119
NORTH WEST SOUND ARCHIVE
Old Steward's Office, Clitheroe Castle, Clitheroe, Lancashire, BB7 1AZ

Tel: 01200 427897
Fax: 01200 427897
Email: nwsa@ed.lancscc.gov.uk
Formed: 1979

Organisation type and purpose: Local government body, membership association (membership is by subscription).
Sound Archive.

Enquiries to: Sound Archive Officer
Access:
Access to staff: By letter, by telephone, by fax, by email, in person, visitors by prior appointment, Internet web pages
Access for disabled people: level entry

General description:
The archives' extensive collections of over 110,000 sound recordings covering most aspects of northwest life from the middle of the 19th century to date include: local radio; oral history; dialect; regional music, etc. Collections include: Batton Oral History Project; BBC Radio Manchester; BBC Radio Lancashire; Royal Northern College of Music Records; Manchester Jewish Museum Oral History; Manchester Ship Canal Oral History; dialect collection; children's playsongs; etc.
Collections:
Survey of English dialects, Leeds University survey recordings, 1935-1960s
Solidarity, Granada TV's recordings in Poland, 1960s
Equipment collection, early radio and sound recording equipment relating to the region.
Catalogues:
Catalogue for library is in-house only.
Publications list:
is available in hard copy.
Printed publications:
Resources Packs suitable for all ages of children in conjunction with the National Curriculum. Each pack contains a pre-recorded cassette and full transcript (£9.99) including:
Carbolic, clogs and cockroaches - Life at home in the North West 1900-1930
Duckstones, dobbers and darts - Children's Games and Pastimes of Yesteryear
Liverpool to Manchester - Memories & Sounds of the Liverpool to Manchester Railway
The War to End All Wars - Memories of the Great War 1914-1918
High Days and Holidays - Customs and Celebrations Throughout the Year
Trains, Trams and Trolleys - Transport of the Past
Topic Packs - pre-recorded cassette of extracts from recordings and transcript £8.36 including:
Please God, No More Wars - The Home Front and V E Day 1939-1945
Pretoria Remembered - Memories of the Pretoria Colliery Disaster 1910
Theme Packs (shorter than the resource packs, £5.95), including:
Textiles
Whitsuntide
Christmas
A range of titles covering biographical, dialect dictionaries, textile dictionary and any other subjects

Internet home pages:
http://www.lancashire.gov.uk/education/d_lif/ro/content/sound/nwsound.asp

2120
NORTH WOOLWICH OLD STATION MUSEUM
Pier Road, North Woolwich, London, E16 2JJ

Tel: 020 7474 7244
Fax: 020 7473 6065
Email: heritage@newham.gov.uk
Acronym or abbreviation: NWOSM
Formerly: Passmore Edwards Museums (PEMS), date of change, 1994; Newham Museum Service (now Newham Heritage Service, London Borough of Newham, NWOSM is a branch museum), date of change, 1999

Organisation type and purpose: Local government body, museum, suitable for ages: 5+.

Enquiries to: Site Manager
Other contacts: Heritage Services Manager for overall head of service.
Access:
Access to staff: By letter, by telephone, by fax, by email, in person
Access for disabled people: level entry, access to all public areas, toilet facilities

General description:
History of railway transport, especially the Great Eastern Railway.
Information services:
Education services: Resources for Key Stage 2..
Collections:
Railway locomotives and carriages
Railway artefacts, models, posters, memorabilia relating to Great Eastern Railway
Library on transport subjects
Catalogues:
Catalogue for part of the collections is only available in-house.
Printed publications:
Guide Book
Booklet on the history of Great Eastern Railway

2121
NORTH YORKSHIRE MOORS RAILWAY
Pickering Station, 12 Park Street, Pickering, North Yorkshire, YO18 7AJ

Tel: 01751 472508 (Customer Service)
Fax: 01751 476970
Email: info@northyorkshiremoorsrailway.com
Acronym or abbreviation: NYMR
Full name: North Moors Historic Railway Trust
Formed: 1967
Formerly: North Moors Historic Railway Preservation Society, date of change, 1967-1973

Organisation type and purpose: Membership association (membership is by subscription), present number of members: 6500, registered charity, museum, historic building, house or site, suitable for ages: all ages.
Heritage Railway with preserved buildings, locomotives and carriages.
Parent body:
North Yorkshire Moors Historical Railway Trust
Locomotive sheds at:
North Yorkshire Moors Railway
Grosmont, Whitby, Y22 5HF
Station also at:
Goathland
Grosmont
Levisham

Enquiries to: Administrator
Access:
Access to staff: By letter, by telephone, by fax, by email, Internet web pages
Access to building, collections or gallery: No prior appointment required
Hours: Easter to End Oct, Christmas, New Year: Daily, 1000 to 1900
Other restrictions: Archives and collections are not generally accessible.
Access for disabled people: ramped entry, toilet facilities
Other restrictions: Wheelchair places on most trains, although unable to accommodate on our dining services. Toilet facilties available at Pickering and Grosmont Stations; help from staff available with prior notice

General description:
History of steam travel; the historical importance of railways, their development, impact and social influence.
Passenger trains run through the North Yorkshire Moors National Park, pulled normally by steam engines and a limited service of Heritage Diesel locomotives.
Pickering Station has been restored to its 1937 condition and Grosmont Station restored to the British Railways' style of the 1960s.
Information services:
Helpline available, tel no: Talking Timetable: 01751 473535.
Family tickets available
Group travel and educational visits
Special events throughout the year
Pullman dining services, advance booking essential
Private charter trains
Special visitor services: Materials and/or activities for children..
Collections:
Archives
Collection of steam locomotives and rolling stock
Catalogues:
Catalogue for library is in-house only.
Printed publications:
Stockbook
Timetables and general information leaflet (free)
Moorsline Magazine (quarterly)
Mail order department for publications list

Internet home pages:
http://www.northyorkshiremoorsrailway.com
Timetables, information and collections.

2122
NORTHAMPTON AND LAMPORT RAILWAY

Pitsford Road, Chapel Brampton, Northampton, NN6 8BA

Tel: 01604 820327
Formed: 1 November 1995

Organisation type and purpose: Membership association, voluntary organisation, museum, suitable for ages: 5+.
Heritage railway society, working museum.
Parent body:
Northampton & Lamport Railway Preservation Society
at the same address

Enquiries to: Curator
Other contacts: Advertising Officer for press, publicity, adverts.
Access:
Access to staff: By letter only

General description:
Northampton-Market Harborough Line history, history of LNWR, LMSR and BR(M) in Northamptonshire.
Information services:
Special visitor services: Guided tours, materials and/or activities for children.
Education services: Resources for Key Stages 1 and 2, 3, 4 and Further or Higher Education..
Collections:
20th century steam and diesel locomotives, carriages and wagons
Railwayiana
LNWR and MR signalboxes
Manual signalling operation
Catalogues:
Catalogue for part of the collections is published.
Printed publications:
Magazine (journal, quarterly, free to members, £1.50 others)
Stock Book

Address for ordering publications:
Printed publications:
Northampton and Lamport Railway Station Shop

Internet home pages:
http://www.nlr.org.uk

2123
NORTHAMPTON MUSEUMS AND ART GALLERY

Central Museum and Art Gallery, 4-6 Guildhall Road, Northampton, NN1 1DP

Tel: 01604 238548
Minicom no. 01604 238970
Fax: 01604 238720
Email: museums@northampton.gov.uk
Formed: 1865

Organisation type and purpose: Local government body, museum.
Parent body:
Northampton Borough Council
Tel: 01604 233500

Enquiries to: Head of Museums & Heritage Services
Access:
Access to staff: By letter, by telephone, by fax, by email, in person
Access to building, collections or gallery: No prior appointment required
Hours: Mon to Fri, 1000 to 1700
Access for disabled people: access to all public areas, toilet facilities

General description:
Techniques of production and decoration, footwear, boots and shoes, shoemaking.
Information services:
Special visitor services: Tape recorded guides, materials and/or activities for children.
Education services: Group education facilities, resources for Key Stages 1 and 2, 3, 4 and Further or Higher Education.
Services for disabled people: For the visually impaired; for the hearing impaired.
Collections:
All trade journals, of particular interest to social, economic and industrial historians and early saddlery and luggage trade catalogues
Footware and related material including historic and contemporary footware, social and industrial history relating to shoemaking and fine and decorative arts on the theme of shoes and shoemaking
Archaeological and social history collections from Northampton
Fine and decorative art collections, including Italian works from the 16th to 18th centuries
Publications list:
is available in hard copy and online.

Internet home pages:
http://www.northampton.gov.uk/museums

2124
NORTHERN IRELAND MUSEUMS COUNCIL

66 Donegall Pass, Belfast, BT7 1BU

Tel: 028 9055 0215
Fax: 028 9055 0216
Email: info@nimc.co.uk
Acronym or abbreviation: NIMC
Formed: 1993
Formerly: Northern Ireland Museums Advisory Committee

Organisation type and purpose: Statutory body, membership association.
Non-Departmental Public Body.
Supported by:
Department of Culture, Arts and Leisure, Northern Ireland (DCAL)

Enquiries to: Director
Other contacts: (1) Development Officer (2) Assistant Director for (1) training matters, museum registration, care of collections information (2) policy and planning museum development.
Access:
Access to staff: By letter, by telephone, by fax, by email, visitors by prior appointment
Other restrictions: Full range of services to members only.

General description:
Museums of Northern Ireland, management, setting up a new museum, grants and funding, new developments, advocacy with local council and central government.
Printed publications:
Annual Report
Access For All
Museum Beat newsletter

Internet home pages:
http://www.nimc.co.uk
Information on NIMC and the services it provides.

2125
NORTHLANDS VIKING CENTRE

The Old School House, Auckengill, Wick, Caithness, KW1 4XP

Tel: 01847 805518
Fax: 01847 805508
Full name: Highland Council Cultural & Leisure Services
Formed: 1996

Organisation type and purpose: Local government body, museum, suitable for ages: 5+.
Parent body:
Caithness District Council

Enquiries to: Facilities Manager
Direct email: george.sanders@highland.gov.uk
Access:
Access to staff: By letter, by telephone, by fax, by email
Access for disabled people: toilet facilities
Other restrictions: Parking available if requested.

General description:
The Centre tells the story of the Pre-Viking Kingdom of Catti and follows the progress of settlers from their Scandinavian homes to Shetland, Orkney and Caithness. On display are models of the Viking Settlement at Freswick, a Viking longship and genuine examples of currency at the time.

2126
NORTON PRIORY MUSEUM & GARDENS

Tudor Road, Manor Park, Runcorn, Cheshire, WA7 1SX

Tel: 01928 569895
Email: info@nortonpriory.org
Formed: 1975

Organisation type and purpose: Registered charity (charity number 504870), museum.
Archaeological site and historic gardens.
Governing body:
The Nortion Priory Museum Trust

Enquiries to: Administrator
Other contacts: (1) Senior Keeper (2) Community and Education Officer for (1) enquiries collections (2) schools and Lifelong Learning.
Access:
Access to staff: By letter, by telephone, visitors by prior appointment
Hours: Prior appointment for access to staff

General description:
This is the site archive for 1970-1987 excavations at Norton Priory (records and finds); includes historical records and photographs (mainly copies) relating to Norton Priory, and a site-specific contemporary art collection.
Collections:
Excavation archives for Norton Priory and Halton Castle

Internet home pages:
http://www.nortonpriory.org

2127
NORWICH CASTLE MUSEUM & ART GALLERY

Castle Hill, Norwich, Norfolk, NR1 3JU

Tel: 01603 493624

Organisation type and purpose: Registered charity, museum, historic building, house or site, suitable for ages: all ages.
Parent body
Parent body:
Norfolk Museums & Archaeology Service

Enquiries to: Curator
Access:
Access to staff: By letter, by telephone
Access for disabled people: access to all public areas, toilet facilities
Other restrictions: Lifts and ramps throughout the building, guide dogs and hearing dogs are welcome. Carers are not charged admission.

General description:
The Castle was built by the Normans as a Royal Palace 900 years ago. It is now home to home to some of the most outstanding regional collections of fine art, archaeology and natural history.
It contains the world's largest collection of ceramic teapots.
The art gallery also has displays of modern art, including special exhibitions from The Tate.
Interactive displays, models, computers, sound and video bring history to life.
Information services:
Programme of temporary exhibitions, guided tours of the battlements and dungeons
Special events programme

continued overleaf

Induction loops
Special visitor services: Guided tours.
Education services: Group education facilities.
Services for disabled people: For the visually impaired; for the hearing impaired.
Collections:
Lowestoft porcelain
Norwich Civic Regalia and silver, costume and Snap dragons from mayoral processions
The Colman Collection of Norwich School oils, watercolours, drawings and prints
James Bulwer Collection of watercolours of Norfolk topography
Percy Moore Turner Collection of Rembrandt etchings
Bulwer and Miller teapot collections
Numismatic collection, Iron Age, Roman, Saxon and mediaeval coin-hoards.
Long-established collections of the archaeology of the region of all periods, from prehistory to 18th century
Notable items include: Iron Age hoard of tubular gold torcs from Snettisham
Roman cavalry helmet from Worthing
Anglo-Saxon Spong Man, finds from mediaeval Norwich
Egyptian antiquities, death-masks and phrenology, arms and armour

Internet home pages:
http://www.norfolk.gov.uk/tourism/museums

2128
NORWICH CASTLE STUDY CENTRE
Shirehall, Market Avenue, Norwich, Norfolk, NR1 3JQ

Tel: 01603 493625

Organisation type and purpose: Local government body, museum, historic building, house or site, suitable for ages: 12+.
Parent body:
Norfolk Museums & Archaeology Service

Enquiries to: Curator
Access:
Access to staff: By letter, by telephone
Hours: Mon to Fri 1000 to 1700
Access to building, collections or gallery: Prior appointment required
Hours: Tue to Fri, 1000 to 1300, and 1400 to 1630 on the following days:
Fine Art Study Room (for works on paper) and Archaeology Study Room:Tue and Thu
Decorative Arts Study Room: Wed and Fri
Natural History Study Room: 2 days per week
Other restrictions: Archaeology Study Room: by prior arrangement with the curator.
Minimum notice for appointment to view/book from a departmental library, 24 hours; objects, works on paper, or natural history specimens, two weeks' notice

General description:
The reserve collections from the Castle Museum are stored under appropriate environmental conditions at the Shirehall. Public access to the collections is made available for researchers in study rooms.

Internet home pages:
http://www.norfolk.gov.uk/tourism/museums

2129
NORWICH CATHEDRAL
62 The Close, Norwich, Norfolk, NR1 4EH

Tel: 01603 218321
Fax: 01603 766032
Email: vis-profficer@cathedral.org.uk
Full name: The Cathedral of the Holy and Undivided Trinity, Norwich
Formed: 1097

Organisation type and purpose: Registered charity (charity number Ecclesiastical), museum, art gallery, historic building, house or site, suitable for ages: all ages.
Anglican cathedral, place of worship.
The building remains a place of quiet reflection and prayer, as well as for participation in daily worship or the rich pageantry of church festivals.
Link with:
The Friends of Norwich Cathedral
12 The Close, Norwich, NR1 4DH, tel: 01603 218313, fax: 01603 766032, email/website: friends@cathedral.org.uk

Enquiries to: Visitors' & Publicity Officer
Access:
Access to staff: By letter, by telephone, by fax, by email, in person, Internet web pages
Access to building, collections or gallery: No prior appointment required
Hours: Daily, 0600 to 1800
Other restrictions: Prior appointment required for guided tours
Access for disabled people: Parking provided, ramped entry, toilet facilities
Other restrictions: Disabled access lift provided

General description:
Norman cathedral of outstanding beauty, one of the finest complete Romanesque buildings in Europe set within a fine cathedral close. The second highest spire and the medieval monastic cloisters which are the largest in England.
Roof bosses: an unrivalled collection of over 1000 beautifully carved medieval stone sculptures; a Saxon bishop's throne, Edith Cavell's grave.
Information services:
Special visitor services: Guided tours, materials and/or activities for children.
Education services: Group education facilities, resources for Key Stages 1 and 2, 3, 4 and Further or Higher Education.
Services for disabled people: For the visually impaired; displays and/or information at wheelchair height.
Printed publications:
An Architectural History of Norwich Cathedral (Fernie, OUP)
Stories in Stone - The Medieval Roof Bosses of Norwich Cathedral (Rose and Hedgecoe, Herbert)
The Norwich Apocalypse (Rose, VEA)

Address for ordering publications:
Printed publications:
Norwich Cathedral Shop
62 The Close, Norwich, NR1 4DH, tel: 01603 218323, email: norwichcathedralshop@lineone.net

Internet home pages:
http://www.cathedral.org.uk

2130
NORWICH GALLERY
Norwich School of Art and Design, St Georges Street, Norwich, Norfolk, NR3 1BB

Tel: 01603 610561
Fax: 01603 615728
Email: nor.gal@nsad.ac.uk
Formed: 1970

Organisation type and purpose: Learned society, art gallery, university department or institute, suitable for ages: 7 to 12 and independent study for adults, research organisation, publishing house.
Connections with:
Norwich School of Art and Design (NSAD)
St George's Street

Enquiries to: Curator
Other contacts: Assistant Curator for general queries.
Access:
Access to staff: By letter, by telephone, by fax, by email
Access to building, collections or gallery: No prior appointment required
Hours: Mon to Sat, 1000 to 1700
Other restrictions: prior appointment required for access to the library

General description:
Contemporary art; art post 1950s; East International Exhibition.
Mostly student works retained by Norwich School of Art from the 19th Century onwards. The earliest works dating from the 1860s are South Kensington Examination work.
Collections:
Artists' materials and a collection of plaster casts.
Gifts of work from ex- staff, e.g. Charles Hobbis and Noel Spencer.
Lithographs after Cotman a. 9
Three oil paintings and seven drawings by Sir Alfred Munnings.
The library contains a valuable collection of 19th Century books
Publications list:
is available in hard copy.
Printed publications:
Available for purchase, direct

Internet home pages:
http://www.norwichgallery.co.uk
Current exhibitions and open submission provided by the gallery.

2131
NOSTALGIA TOY MUSEUM
High Street, Godshill, Ventnor, Isle of Wight, PO38 3HZ

Tel: 01983 840181
Fax: 01983 821296
Email: toyman@nostalgiatoys.co.uk
Formed: 1989

Organisation type and purpose: Independently owned, museum, suitable for ages: 5+.

Enquiries to: Owner
Access:
Access to staff: By email
Access to building, collections or gallery: No prior appointment required
Hours: Easter to end Oct: daily, 1000 to 1700
Access for disabled people: ramped entry

General description:
Toys.
Collections:
Collection of mainly post-war diecast toy cars from British manufacturers including Dinky, Corgi and Matchbox

2132
NOSTELL PRIORY
Doncaster Road, Wakefield, West Yorkshire, WF4 1QE

Tel: 01924 863892
Fax: 01924 866846
Email: nostellpriory@nationaltrust.org.uk

Organisation type and purpose: National organisation, registered charity (charity number 205846), museum, historic building, house or site, suitable for ages: 8+.
Parent body:
The National Trust (Yorkshire and North East)
Yorkshire Regional Office, tel: 01904 70202

Enquiries to: Manager
Access:
Access to staff: By letter, by telephone, by fax, by email
Access for disabled people: Parking provided, level entry, access to all public areas, toilet facilities
Other restrictions: Designated parking 100yds. Drop-off point. 3 manual wheelchairs available, booking essential. 1 single-seater powered mobility vehicle, booking essential. Ground floor fully accessible. Access to other floors via lift. Level entrance to shop and to tea-room. Map available for those using the batricar.

General description:
Nostell Priory is an 18th century architectural masterpiece by James Paine, built on the site of a medieval priory for Sir Rowland Winn, 4th baronet, in 1733. Later Robert Adam was

commissioned to complete the state rooms which are among the finest examples of his interiors. The Priory houses one of England's best collections of Chippendale furniture, designed specially for the house by the great cabinetmaker. Nostell Priory's other treasures include an oustanding art collection with works by Pieter Brueghel the Younger and Angelica Kauffmann, and the remarkable 18th century doll's house, complete with its original fittings and Chippendale-style furniture. Another treasure is the John Harrison long case clock with its extremely rare movement made of wood. In the grounds are delightful lakeside walks with a stunning collection of rhododendrons and azaleas in late spring.

Information services:
'Take a Closer Look': a chance to look more closely at an object from the house's important collection (weekdays only). 'Housekeepers' Helpful Hints' tips on cleaning and conservation. Tel. for details.
Craft and country fairs, open-air theatre and jazz and other musical spectaculars, send s.a.e. for details.
Braille guide.
Suitable for school groups. Education room/centre. Children's quiz/trail. Family activity packs.
Special visitor services: Materials and/or activities for children.
Education services: Group education facilities.
Services for disabled people: For the visually impaired.

Internet home pages:
http://www.nationaltrust.org.uk

2133
NOTHE FORT MUSEUM OF COASTAL DEFENCE

The Nothe Fort, Barrack Road, Weymouth, Dorset, DT4 8UF

Tel: 01305 766626
Fax: 01305 766465
Email: fortressweymouth@btconnect.com
Formed: 1980

Organisation type and purpose: Registered charity, museum, historic building, house or site, suitable for ages: 8+.
Tourist attraction.
To restore and maintain the Victorian fort.
Parent body:
Weymouth Civic Society
3 Trinity Street, Weymouth

Enquiries to: Curator
Other contacts: Public Relations Officer
Access:
Access to staff: By letter, by telephone, by fax, by email, in person
Hours: Mon to Thu, 0900 to 1600
Other restrictions: Contact curator or public relations officer.
Access to building, collections or gallery: No prior appointment required
Hours: 1 May to 30 Sep: 1000 to 1700
Autumn half-term and Easter: 1030 to 1730
Access for disabled people: ramped entry
Other restrictions: Limited access for disabled, courtyard level only and ramparts with assistance.

General description:
Garrison life in peace and war.
Information services:
Internal catalogue only.
Materials/activities for schools.
Special visitor services: Guided tours, materials and/or activities for children.
Education services: Group education facilities..
Collections:
Photographs of historical interest covering building and manning coastal fort
Catalogues:
Catalogue for all of the collections is only available in-house.

Internet home pages:
http://www.fortressweymouth.co.uk

2134
NOTTINGHAM CASTLE MUSEUM & ART GALLERY

Castle Road, Nottingham, NG1 6EL

Tel: 0115 915 3700
Fax: 0115 915 3653
Email: castle@ncmg.demon.co.uk
Formed: 1878

Organisation type and purpose: Local government body, museum, art gallery, historic building, house or site, suitable for ages: 5+.
Parent body:
Nottingham City Museums & Galleries

Enquiries to: Site Manager
Direct tel: 0115 915 3700
Direct fax: 0115 915 3653
Direct email: enquiries@notmusbhy.demon.co.uk
Access:
Access to staff: By letter, by telephone, by fax, by email, visitors by prior appointment
Access to building, collections or gallery: No prior appointment required
Hours: Museum: daily, 1000 to 1700
Other restrictions: Access to collections and archives in store by prior appointment.
Access for disabled people: Parking provided, ramped entry, access to all public areas, toilet facilities

General description:
Contains fine art and decorative arts (mainly British ceramics, glass, silver and jewellery). Galleries include The History of Nottingham Gallery; The Circle of Life; and Temporary Exhibition Galleries. Also contains the Sherwood Foresters Regimental Museum and the Nemi Collection.
Collections:
Albert Ball memorabilia, 1915-1917, 20 items
British and European oil paintings, watercolours, drawings and prints including: fine collections of women by Paul Sandby and Richard Parkes Bonington. 17th century to 20th century, 5300 items
Bowden Collection, Japanese arms and armour, mainly 16th century to 1876, ca 200 items
Decorative arts
Ethnographical Collection, mainly 19th to 20th century, c. 3000 items
Felix Joseph Collection, Wedgwood jasperware, 1775 to early 19th century, c. 1500 items
Finds from Creswell Crags, mainly Upper Palaeolithic, 100 items
Fine art
Gibbs Collection, a major collection of English domestic Georgian silver, 18th and early 19th century, c. 300 items
History of Nottingham Castle
Hopewell Spencer Fulton Collection, Georgian domestic silver, 18th and early 19th century, c. 300 items
Important collections of English mediaeval alabaster carvings.
Mediaeval ceramics, 10th-16th century, 200 items
Nottingham coin hoards, Roman and Mediaeval, c. 12 hoards, including over 5000 items
Nottinghamshire coins and medals, 17th-19th century, 300-400 items
Nottingham salt-glazed stoneware, 18th century, 200 items
Prehistoric bronze weapons, Bronze Age, c. 50-100 items
Salt-glaze and contemporary ceramics, silver, Nottingham alabasters
Saville Collection, classical antiquities from The Temple of Diana at Nemi near Rome, mainly 3rd and 4th Centuries BC to 2nd century AD, c. 1200 items
Social history
The Robin Hood Volunteer Rifle Corps Collection, mainly 1859-1908, c. 100 items
The Sherwood Foresters Regimental Collection, 18th century to present, over 1000 items
Venetian glass made by Salviati and Co, 1870s, 200 items
W J Thompson Collection, British, European and non-European locks and keys, Roman to late 19th century, 200 items
Catalogues:
Catalogue for library is in-house only. Catalogue for all of the collections is only available in-house.
Printed publications:
Guide to Nottingham Castle Museum
What's On/Events leaflets

2135
NOTTINGHAM SOCIETY OF MODEL ENGINEERS

See - Great Central Railway (Nottingham) Ltd

2136
NOTTINGHAM TRANSPORT HERITAGE CENTRE

See - Great Central Railway (Nottingham) Ltd

2137
NUNEATON MUSEUM AND ART GALLERY

Riversley Park, Coton Road, Nuneaton, Warwickshire, CV11 5TU

Tel: 024 7635 0720 or 7637 6158
Fax: 024 7634 3559
Formed: 1917

Organisation type and purpose: Local government body, art gallery, museum.
Parent body:
Nuneaton & Bedworth Borough Council
Town Hall, Coton Road, Nuneaton, CV11 5AA

Enquiries to: Curator
Access:
Access to staff: By letter, by telephone, by fax, in person
Hours: Office: Mon to Fri, 0900 to 1700;
Other restrictions: Prior appointment with staff preferred if possible.

General description:
George Eliot, local history, ethnography, fine and applied art, exhibitions.
Collections:
George Eliot memorabilia
Printed publications:
Annual Report
Exhibition Guide (free)
Forward Plan
George Eliot novels postcards and information:
Brief Biography (£1.50)
George Eliot Country (£1.50)
George Eliot's Coventry (£3.50)
Little Sister (£1.00)
Those of us who loved her (£6.50)

Internet home pages:
http://www.nuneatonandbedworth.gov.uk/leisure/museums

2138
NUNNINGTON HALL

Nunnington, York, YO62 5UY

Tel: 01439 748283
Fax: 01439 748284
Email: nunningtonhall@nationaltrust.org.uk

Organisation type and purpose: National organisation, registered charity (charity number 205846), museum, historic building, house or site, suitable for ages: 8+.
Parent body:
The National Trust (Yorkshire and North East)
Yorkshire Regional Office, tel: 01904 70202

Enquiries to: Manager

continued overleaf

Access:
Access to staff: By letter, by telephone, by fax, by email
Access for disabled people: Parking provided, toilet facilities
Other restrictions: Designated parking. Drop-off point. 2 manual wheelchairs available. Steps to entrance. Accessible entrance through rear door, ask for assistance. Ground floor largely accessible. No access to other floors. Photograph album. Steps to shop entrance. Level entrance to tea-room. Garden accessible: ramps, grass and gravel.

General description:
The sheltered walled garden on the bank of the River Rye, with its delightful mixed borders, orchards of traditional fruit varieties and springflowering meadows, complements this mellow 17th century manor house. From the magnificent oak-panelled hall, follow three staircases to discover family rooms, the nursery, the haunted room and the attics, with their fascinating Carlisle collection of miniature rooms fully furnished to reflect different periods.
Information services:
Guided tours by arrangement.
Braille guide. Scented plants. Peacock and duck sounds.
Baby-changing and feeding facilities. Frontcarrying baby slings for loan. Toddler reins available for loan.
Suitable for school groups. Children's guide. Children's quiz/trail.
Special visitor services: Materials and/or activities for children.
Services for disabled people: For the visually impaired.
Collections:
Carlisle Collection of miniature rooms.

Internet home pages:
http://www.nationaltrust.org.uk

2139
NYMANS GARDEN

Handcross, Haywards Heath, West Sussex, RH17 6EB

Tel: 01444 400321
Fax: 01444 400253
Email: nymans@nationaltrust.org.uk
Acronym or abbreviation: NT
Formed: 1953

Organisation type and purpose: Registered charity (charity number 205846), historic building, house or site, suitable for ages: 5+. Nymans came to the National Trust in 1953, historic garden, ruins and historic family rooms.
Parent body:
National Trust

Enquiries to: Administrator
Direct tel: 01444 405250
Direct fax: 01444 405254
Other contacts: Visitor Services Manager for marketing contact.
Access:
Access to staff: By telephone
Access to building, collections or gallery: No prior appointment required
Hours: Garden: Mar to beg Nov, Wed to Sun and Bank Holiday Mon, 1100 to 1800; mid Nov to beg Mar, 1100 to 1600
House: End Mar to beg Nov, 1100 to 1700
Open Bank Holiday Mondays
Other restrictions: Garden closes at dusk if earlier. Access may be restricted if ground very wet; tel for details.
Access for disabled people: Parking provided, level entry, access to all public areas, toilet facilities
Other restrictions: Designated parking 50yds. Drop-off point. 6 manual wheelchairs available. 1 single-seater and 1 2-seater powered mobility vehicles available, booking essential. Steps to entrance. Accessible entrance, enter via exit door. Please ask for assistance at house entrance. Wheelchair booking advisable at busy times of the year. Ground floor largely accessible, some steps, ramps available. Level entrance to shop and to restaurant. Grounds largely accessible. Special wheelchair-friendly route in garden. Strong companion recommended. Recommended route map.

General description:
One of the great gardens of the Sussex Weald, still retaining much of its distinctive family style in the historic collection of plants, shrubs and trees. This is reflected also in the surrounding estate, with its woodland walks and wild garden, and in the many rare and exotic species collected from overseas. The Messel family's creativity is much in evidence in the library, drawing room, dining room and forecourt garden.
Information services:
Braille guide. Handling collection. Scented plants.
Suitable for school groups. Audio guide. Children's quiz/trail. Family activity packs.
Adult study days. Materials/activities for children on special days.
Hip-carrying infant seats for loan.
Special visitor services: Guided tours, materials and/or activities for children.
Education services: Group education facilities.
Services for disabled people: For the visually impaired.
Collections:
Family photographs of the Messel family
Printed publications:
Guide Book
Guides to garden, woods, family rooms
Events
Electronic and video products:
National Trust Gardens (video, available direct, in gift shop)

Internet home pages:
http://www.nationaltrust.org.uk

2140
OAK HOUSE MUSEUM

Oak House, Oak Road, West Bromwich, West Midlands, B70 8HJ

Tel: 0121 553 0759
Fax: 0121 525 5167
Formed: 1898

Organisation type and purpose: Local government body, museum, historic building, house or site, suitable for ages: all ages.
Parent body:
Sandwell Municipal Borough Council
Council House, Oldbury, West Midlands

Enquiries to: Curator
Other contacts: Principal Heritage Officer or Visitor Services Manager
Access:
Access to staff: By letter, by telephone, in person
Access to building, collections or gallery: No prior appointment required
Hours: Oct to Mar; Mon to Wed, Fri; 1000 to 1600; Sat, 1330 to 1600
Apr to Sep; Mon to Wed, Fri; 1000 to 1700; Sat, Sun, 1400 to 1700
Access for disabled people: toilet facilities
Other restrictions: Ground floor access only and parking by prior arrangement

General description:
The Oak House is a Tudor yeoman's house, timber-framed, dating from the 16th century with period furniture.
Information services:
Guided tours if pre-booked.
Tours and living history for schools.
Handling collections for schools.
Special visitor services: Guided tours.
Education services: Group education facilities, resources for Key Stages 3 and 4..
Collections:
Period furniture and some reproductions
Printed publications:
A Black & White Guide Book (25p)
Coloured Guide Book (£1.75)
Events Leaflet (2 month period of events, free)

2141
OAKHAM CASTLE

c/o Rutland County Museum, Catmose Street, Oakham, Rutland, LE15 6HW

Tel: 01572 758440
Fax: 01572 758445
Email: museum@rutland.gov.uk

Organisation type and purpose: Historic building open to the public.
Branch of:
Rutland County Council Libraries and Museums

Enquiries to: Curator, Rutland County Museum
Access:
Access to staff: By letter, by telephone, by fax, in person, visitors by prior appointment
Hours: Hours vary seasonally
Other restrictions: Closed Christmas and Good Friday.
Access for disabled people: Parking provided

General description:
Great Hall built by Walkelin de Ferrers in 1180. Traces of other parts of the fortified manor house.
Collections:
Over 200 horseshoes

Internet home pages:
http://www.rutnet.co.uk/rcc/rutlandmuseums
Opening times and summary description.

2142
OAKHURST COTTAGE

Hambledon, Godalming, Surrey, GU8 4HF

Tel: 01428 684090
Fax: 01428 681050
Email: oakhurstcottage@nationaltrust.org.uk

Organisation type and purpose: National organisation, registered charity (charity number 205846), historic building, house or site.
Parent body:
The National Trust (South and South East Region)
South East Regional Office, tel: 01372 453401

Enquiries to: Manager
Access:
Access to staff: By letter, by telephone, by fax, by email
Access to building, collections or gallery: Prior appointment required
Hours: 22 Mar to end Oct, Wed, Thu, Sat, Sun, 1400 to 1500
Open Bank holiday Mondays
Other restrictions: Admission by guided tour. Admission by appointment only.

General description:
A small 16th century timber-framed cottage, restored and furnished as a simple labourer's dwelling. There is a delightful garden containing typical Victorian plants.
Information services:
Children's quiz/trail. Schools and groups by arrangement any day
or evening
Special visitor services: Guided tours, materials and/or activities for children..

Internet home pages:
http://www.nationaltrust.org.uk

2143
OAKWELL HALL AND COUNTRY PARK

Nova Lane, Birstall, Batley, West Yorkshire, WF17 9LG

Tel: 01924 326240
Fax: 01924 326249
Email: oakwell.hall@kirkleesmc.gov.uk
Formed: 1929

Organisation type and purpose: Local government body, historic building, house or site, suitable for ages: 5+.

Enquiries to: Senior Museum Officer

Access:
Access to staff: By letter, by email
Access to building, collections or gallery: No prior appointment required
Hours: Mon to Fri, 1100 to 1700; Sat, Sun, 1200 to 1700
Access for disabled people: Parking provided, toilet facilities
Other restrictions: Access to Visitor Centre and ground floor of hall.

General description:
Oakwell Hall is a 16th century manor house, furnished as a late 17th century house to look as it would have appeared when owned by the original owners, the Batt Family. Furniture and objects are largely original and locally appropriate.
There is an adjacent visitor centre (including the Discover Oakwell Gallery), café, toilets, gardens and 110 acres of country park.
Information services:
Special visitor services: Guided tours, materials and/or activities for children.
Education services: Group education facilities, resources for Key Stages 1 and 2.
Services for disabled people: For the visually impaired; for the hearing impaired; displays and/or information at wheelchair height.
Collections:
Painted panelling in two rooms
Paintings, with Civil War relevance, of Thomas Fairfax and William Cavendish
Catalogues:
Catalogue for all of the collections is only available in-house.
Printed publications:
Oakwell Hall - A Guide (£3.95)

2144
OBAN MUSEUM

Closed

2145
OCTAVIA HILL BIRTHPLACE MUSEUM

1 South Brink Place, Wisbech, Cambridgeshire, PE13 1JE

Tel: 01945 476358
Fax: 01945 476358
Formed: 1995

Organisation type and purpose: Voluntary organisation, registered charity, museum, historic building, house or site, suitable for ages: 16+.
Links with:
Octavia Hill Society
at the same address

Enquiries to: Chairman
Access:
Access to staff: By letter, by telephone, by fax, visitors by prior appointment
Hours: Mon to Fri, 0900 to 1700
Other restrictions: Answerphone outside office hours.
Access to building, collections or gallery: No prior appointment required
Hours: 3rd Wed Mar to end Oct: Wed, Sat, Sun, Bank Holiday Mondays, 1400 to 1730 (last admission 1700)
Other restrictions: By appointment at other times.

General description:
Housing history, open spaces, John Ruskin, Robert Owen, Pestalozzi, sanitary reform, Kyrle Society, Charity Organisation Society, Octavia Hill Housing Trust, National Trust.
Information services:
Special visitor services: Guided tours.
Education services: Group education facilities, resources for Key Stages 1 and 2, 3, 4 and Further or Higher Education..
Collections:
Brion Papers on women and housing
Octavia Hill Housing Trust core archives
Ouvry Papers (family papers of Octavia Hill)
Publications list:
is available in hard copy and online.

2146
OCTOBER GALLERY, THE

24 Old Gloucester Street, London, WC1N 3AL

Tel: 020 7242 7367
Fax: 020 7405 1851
Email: octobergallery@compuserve.com
Formed: 1979

Organisation type and purpose: Registered charity (charity number 327032), art gallery, suitable for ages: all ages.
The October Gallery is a charitable trust dedicated to the advancement and appreciation of art from all cultures. To this end the Gallery is actively engaged in education and promotion of inter-cultural exchange.

Enquiries to: Administrator
Access:
Access to staff: By letter, by telephone, by fax, by email, in person, Internet web pages
Hours: Mon to Fri, 0930 to 1730
Access to building, collections or gallery: No prior appointment required
Hours: Tue to Sat, 1230 to 1730
Access for disabled people: ramped entry

General description:
Contemporary art from Africa, Asia, the Americas, Europe, the Middle East, Australia and Oceania.
Information services:
Special visitor services: Materials and/or activities for children.
Education services: Group education facilities, resources for Key Stages 1 and 2, 3, 4 and Further or Higher Education..
Collections:
Gerald Wilde and collections in the subject areas
Catalogues:
Catalogue for all of the collections is available in-house, part is published and part is on-line.
Publications list:
is available in hard copy.
Printed publications:
Gerald Wilde (ed. Hawes J A, 1988 Synergetic Press, £11.95)
El Anatsui: A Sculpted History of Africa (1998, Saffron with the October Gallery, £14.95)
Numerous small brochures to accompany major exhibitions (£2 each)
More substantial catalogues on artists (£5) including
Elisabeth Lalouschek
Julieta Rubio
Laila Shawa and Wijdan
Kenji Yoshida and others

Internet home pages:
http://www.theoctobergallery.com
Information on gallery, exhibitions, artists, education programme.

2147
OKEHAMPTON CASTLE

Okehampton, Devon

Tel: 01837 52844

Organisation type and purpose: National organisation, advisory body, historic building, house or site.
Parent body:
English Heritage (South West Region)
Tel: 0117 975 0700, fax: 0117 975 0701

Enquiries to: Manager
Access:
Access to staff: By letter, by telephone
Access to building, collections or gallery: No prior appointment required
Hours: 29 Mar to 30 Sep: daily, 1000 to 1800,1 to 31 Oct: daily, 1000 to 1700
Other restrictions: Opening times are subject to change, for up-to-date information contact English Heritage by phone or visit the website.

General description:
This is the site of the ruins of the largest castle in Devon, which includes the Norman motte and the keep's jagged remains.
Information services:
Audio guides also available for visually impaired visitors and those with learning difficulties.
Special visitor services: Tape recorded guides..

Internet home pages:
http://www.english-heritage.org.uk

2148
OLD BELL MUSEUM

Arthur Street, Montgomery, Powys, SY15 6RH

Tel: 01686 668313
Email: curator@oldbellmuseum.org.uk
Formed: 1981

Organisation type and purpose: Independently owned, registered charity, museum, suitable for ages: 5+.
Parent body:
Montgomery Civic Society

Enquiries to: Curator
Access:
Access to staff: By letter, by telephone, by email

General description:
A mixed collection of artefacts from the old County Town displayed to illustrate its history, in a 16th century building run by Montgomery Civic Society. Included are permanent exhibitions of the unique excavation of the Norman Castle (with reconstruction model), the finds from the mediaeval Castle, the workhouse and Cambrian Railway.
Collections:
Montgomery Castle. Excavation finds.1223-1649
Excavations Hendoren Norman motte and bailey castle
Mixed collection of artefacts from Montgomery relating to social and civic life
Workhouse
Cambrian Railway
Catalogues:
Catalogue for part of the collections is only available in-house.
Publications list:
is available in hard copy and online.
Printed publications:
Montgomery Town Trail (available direct or from local shops, for purchase)
Montgomery Guide Book (available direct or from local shops, for purchase)

Internet home pages:
http://www.oldbellmuseum.org.uk
General

2149
OLD BRIDGE HOUSE MUSEUM, THE

Mill Road, Dumfries, DG2 7BE

Tel: 01387 256904
Fax: 01387 265081
Email: elainek@dumgal.gov.uk

Organisation type and purpose: Local government body, historic building, house or site.
Parent body:
Dumfries and Galloway Museum Service
Tel: 01387 253374

Enquiries to: Curator
Direct tel: 01387 253374
Access:
Access to staff: By letter, by telephone, by fax, by email, visitors by prior appointment
Access to building, collections or gallery: No prior appointment required
Hours: Apr to Sep: Mon to Sat, 1000 to 1700; Sun, 1400 to 1700

continued overleaf

General description:
Built in 1660 into the 15th century sandstone Devorgilla's Bridge, the town's oldest house comprises a series of period room settings. These include kitchens of the 1850s and 1900s; a dentist's surgery; and a Victorian nursery.
Information services:
Special visitor services: Materials and/or activities for children..
Collections:
Victorian home with family kitchen, nursery and bedroom
Vernacular chairs, 18th/19th century, (10 chairs)
An early dentist's surgery
Printed publications:
Foreign language leaflets

Internet home pages:
http://www.dumgal.gov.uk/museums

2150
OLD BUCKENHAM CORNMILL
O.S. TM 062 90, Deopham Green, Norfolk

Tel: 01603 222705

Organisation type and purpose: Historic building, house or site.

General description:
Tower cornmill with the largest diameter in England.

2151
OLD GALA HOUSE
Scott Crescent, Galashiels, Scottish Borders, TD1 3JS

Tel: 01750 20096
Fax: 01750 23282
Email: museums@scotborders.gov.uk

Organisation type and purpose: Local government body, museum, art gallery, historic building, house or site, suitable for ages: 5+.
Parent body:
Scottish Borders Council Museum and Gallery Service
Tel: 01750 20096

Enquiries to: Curator
Access:
Access to staff: By letter, by telephone, by fax
Access to building, collections or gallery: No prior appointment required
Hours: Apr, May, Sep, Tue to Sat, 1000 to 1600;
Jun, Jul, Aug, Mon to Sat, 1000 to 1600, Sun, 1300 to 1600;
Oct, Tue to Sat, 1300 to 1600

General description:
The home of the former Lairds of Galashiels and dating from 1583. Collections relate to the early history of Galashiels. Paintings and sculpture are also displayed.
Information services:
Programme of visual arts exhibitions in the Christopher Boyd Gallery
Special visitor services: Materials and/or activities for children.
Education services: Group education facilities..
Collections:
Artefacts relate to the early history of Galashiels, paintings and sculpture are also displayed.

Internet home pages:
http://www.scotborders.gov.uk
http://www.scotborders.org.uk

2152
OLD GAOL MUSEUM
Market Hill, Buckingham, MK18 1JX

Tel: 01280 823020
Fax: 01280 823020
Email: oldgaol@lineone.net
Formed: 1993

Organisation type and purpose: Independently owned, registered charity (charity number 292807), museum, historic building, house or site, suitable for ages: all ages.
Parent body:
Buckingham Heritage Trust
at the same address

Enquiries to: Manager
Access:
Access to staff: By letter, by telephone, by fax, by email, visitors by prior appointment, Internet web pages
Hours: Mon to Sat, 1000 to 1600
Access for disabled people: level entry, access to all public areas, toilet facilities

General description:
Displays covering the story of Buckingham and its surrounding area. The military history of the county. Temporary exhibitions covering related topics not fully covered in the main displays.
Information services:
Special visitor services: Guided tours, materials and/or activities for children.
Education services: Group education facilities, resources for Key Stages 1 and 2, 3, 4 and Further or Higher Education.
Services for disabled people: Displays and/or information at wheelchair height.
Collections:
Objects, photographs, documents etc, covering history of the area.
Catalogues:
Catalogue for part of the collections is only available in-house.

Internet home pages:
http://www.mkheritage.co.uk/ogb

2153
OLD HAA MUSEUM
Burravoe, Yell, Shetland, ZE2 9AY

Tel: 01957 722339
Formed: 1984

Organisation type and purpose: Independently owned, registered charity (charity number SCO 01356), museum, art gallery, historic building, house or site.

Enquiries to: Manager
Access:
Access to staff: By letter, by telephone, in person
Access to building, collections or gallery: No prior appointment required
Hours: Tue, Wed, Thu, Sat, 1000 to 1600; Sun, 1400 to 1700
Access for disabled people: Parking provided, level entry

General description:
17th century Laird's house with local and natural history exhibitions, art/craft gallery, genealogical records, shop, tea-room, garden, car park.

2154
OLD HOUSE MUSEUM
Cunningham Place, Off North Church Street, Bakewell, Derbyshire, DE45 1DD

Tel: 01629 813165
Formed: 1957

Organisation type and purpose: Independently owned, registered charity, museum, historic building, house or site, suitable for ages: 8+.
Parent body:
Bakewell & District Historical Society

Enquiries to: Chairman
Access:
Access to staff: By letter, by telephone
Access to building, collections or gallery: No prior appointment required
Hours: Apr 1st to Oct 1st, 1330 to 1600; Jul to Sep, 1100 to 1600
Access for disabled people: Parking provided, ramped entry

General description:
The museum building is a rare early Tudor Parsonage house with 17th and 19th century additions, 14 rooms. The collections are varied:- craft workshops (wheelwright's, blacksmith's, cobbler's); a 19th century millworker's kitchen; 16th/17th century pieces of furniture; textiles (costumes, lace, samplers); toys; etc.
Information services:
Introductory video on ground floor
Special visitor services: Guided tours..
Collections:
Lace, English and some European, 18th-20th Centuries, about 50 pieces

2155
OLD KILN LIGHT RAILWAY SOCIETY
See - Rural Life Centre, Old Kiln Museum Trust

2156
OLD KILN MUSEUM
See - Rural Life Centre, Old Kiln Museum Trust

2157
OLD MANOR, THE
Norbury, Ashbourne, Derbyshire, DE6 2ED

Tel: 01909 486411 (Regional Office)

Organisation type and purpose: National organisation, registered charity (charity number 205846), historic building, house or site, suitable for ages: 12+.
Parent body:
The National Trust (East Midlands Region)
East Midlands Regional Office, tel: 01909 486411

Enquiries to: Property Manager
Access:
Access to staff: By letter, by telephone
Other restrictions: All enquiries should be directed to Regional Office.

General description:
A stone-built hall, dating from the 13th to 15th centuries and of specialist architectural interest only. The adjacent church (not NT) is also worth visiting.

Internet home pages:
http://www.nationaltrust.org.uk

2158
OLD MERCHANT'S HOUSE, THE
See - Row III House / Old Merchant's House

2159
OLD MILL, THE
Wembury Beach, Wembury, Devon, PL9 0HP

Tel: 01752 862314

Organisation type and purpose: National organisation, registered charity (charity number 205846), historic building, house or site.
Parent body:
The National Trust (South West Region)
Regional Office for Devon, tel: 01392 881691

Enquiries to: Manager

General description:
A café housed in a former mill house, standing on a small beach near the Yealm estuary.

Internet home pages:
http://www.nationaltrust.org.uk/regions/devon

2160
OLD MUSEUM ARTS CENTRE
7 College Square North, Belfast, BT1 6AR

Tel: 028 9023 5053
Fax: 028 9032 2912
Email: info
@oldmuseumartscentre.freeserve.co.uk
Formed: 1990

Organisation type and purpose: Registered charity (charity number XO 1125/89), suitable for ages: pre-school+.
Arts centre.

Enquiries to: Administrator
Other contacts: (1) Development Officer; (2) Director for (1) programming - live events; (2) programming - visual art.
Access:
Access to staff: By letter
Access to building, collections or gallery: No prior appointment required
Hours: Mon to Sat, 0930 to 1730 and approx 2100 on performance evenings

General description:
Year-round programme of contemporary visual art exhibitions which change on a 4-6 week basis.
Year-round programme of live events performance: theatre, dance, music, comedy.
Printed publications:
Brochure with full list of programmed events and exhibitions (once every 3 months, free)

2161
OLD OPERATING THEATRE, MUSEUM AND HERB GARRET, THE

9A St Thomas' Street, London, SE1 9RY

Tel: 020 7955 4791
Fax: 020 7378 8383
Email: curator@thegarret.org.uk
Formed: 1962

Organisation type and purpose: Independently owned, registered charity (charity number 270044), museum, historic building, house or site, suitable for ages: 8+.
Other address:
Cultural Heritage Resources (CHR)
249 Evering Road, London, E5 8AL, email/ website: kpflude@chr.org.uk

Enquiries to: Curator
Access:
Access to staff: By letter, by telephone, by fax, by email, in person, Internet web pages
Hours: Mon to Fri, 1030 to 1645
Other restrictions: Entrance to museum via 32 step, spiral staircase.
Access to building, collections or gallery: No prior appointment required
Other restrictions: Prior appointment required for groups.

General description:
A medical and herbal museum situated in a church garret (1702) where herbs were stored and used for medicinal compounds by Saint Thomas's Hospital. Part of the garret was converted into an operating theatre in 1821. It remains today as the oldest surviving operating theatre in Britain.
Information services:
Special visitor services: Guided tours.
Education services: Group education facilities, resources for Key Stages 2, 3 and 4.
Services for disabled people: For the hearing impaired.
Collections:
Medical instruments including cupping; trepanning; obstetric; amputation; and specimens, Georgian to Victorian
Evelina Tableau relating to former Evelina Child's Hospital in Southwark. Victorian and early 20th century
Apothecary with herbal containers, pestles and mortars, scales, jars; Georgian to Victorian
Documentation on Guys and St Thomas's Hospital, Mediaeval, Georgian and Victorian
Catalogues:
Catalogue for all of the collections is only available in-house.
Publications list:
is available in hard copy.

Internet home pages:
http://www.thegarret.org.uk
Museum resource, availability, bookings.

2162
OLD PAISLEY SOCIETY

11-17 George Place, Paisley, Renfrewshire, PA1 2HZ

Tel: 0141 889 1708
Fax: 0141 889 1708
Email: smashot@virgin.net
Full name: SMASHOT Cottages Heritage Centre
Formed: 1977

Organisation type and purpose: Independently owned, registered charity (charity number SCO 01908), museum.
Parent body:
Scottish Civil Trust

Enquiries to: Executive Secretary
Access:
Access to staff: By letter, by telephone, by fax, by email, Internet web pages
Access to building, collections or gallery: Prior appointment required
Access for disabled people: ramped entry

General description:
18th century weaver's cottage, 19th century millworkers' houses, exhibition rooms, Paisley shawls, linen, lace, photographs, garden with heritage plants, tea-room and gift shop.
Information services:
Special visitor services: Guided tours.
Education services: Group education facilities..
Collections:
Looms, photographs, Paisley shawls, period costume, shuttles
Catalogues:
Catalogue for library is in-house only. Catalogue for all of the collections is only available in-house.

Internet home pages:
http://www.smashot.com

2163
OLD RECTORY MUSEUM

Steeple Row, Rectory Place, Loughborough, Leicestershire, LE11 1UW

Tel: 01509 232419
Formed: 1988
Formed from: Loughborough Archaeological and Historical Society

Organisation type and purpose: Registered charity (charity number 513032), museum, historic building, house or site, suitable for ages: all ages.
Other addresses:
Curator
Old Rectory Museum
53 Staveley Court, Belton Road, Loughborough, Leicestershire, LE11 1HY, tel: 01509 232419

Enquiries to: Curator
Other contacts: Archivist
Access:
Access to staff: By letter, by telephone
Access to building, collections or gallery: No prior appointment required
Hours: Apr to Oct: Sat, 1000 to 1600
Other restrictions: Guided tours to building and museum at other times by prior appointment.
Access for disabled people: Parking provided, ramped entry
Other restrictions: Ramped entry lower floor only.

General description:
13th century building, local museum.
Information services:
Hands-on artefacts for the visually impaired.
Special visitor services: Guided tours.
Services for disabled people: For the visually impaired.

Collections:
Current displays
Artefacts: 100 Years of Loughborough 1888-1988
Lost Charnwood Forest Canal
Engineering Display
Camera Display
Timber Frame Building Display

2164
OLD SARUM

Salisbury, Wiltshire

Organisation type and purpose: National organisation, historic building, house or site.
Parent body:
English Heritage (South West Region)
Tel: 0117 975 0700, fax: 0117 975 0701

General description:
Built in the Iron Age, Romans, Saxons and Normans have all left their mark on this great earthwork near Salisbury, on the edge of the Wiltshire chalk plains. With its huge banks and deep ditch, it was here at Old Sarum that William the Conqueror built a great palace and the original Salisbury Cathedral. In 1226 with the founding of New Sarum, the city we know as Salisbury, the settlement faded away. Although the old cathedral was dismantled and a magnificent new one built in the valley, the castle at Old Sarum remained in use until Tudor times. Today the remains of the prehistoric fortress, the Norman palace, castle and cathedral evoke powerful memories of the people who have ruled England.

Internet home pages:
http://www.english-heritage.org.uk

2165
OLD SCHOOL GALLERY

See - Bleddfa Centre for the Arts

2166
OLD SOAR MANOR

Plaxtol, Borough Green, Sevenoaks, Kent, TN15 0QX

Tel: 01732 810378

Organisation type and purpose: National organisation, registered charity (charity number 205846), historic building, house or site.
Parent body:
The National Trust (South and South East Region)
South East Regional Office, tel: 01372 453401

Enquiries to: Manager
Access:
Access to staff: By letter, by telephone

General description:
The solar block of a late 13th century knight's dwelling. Exhibition on Manor and surrounding areas.

Internet home pages:
http://www.nationaltrust.org.uk

2167
OLD TOWN HALL, NEWTOWN

The Custodian, Ken Cottage, Upper Lane, Brighstone, Isle of Wight, PO30 4AT

Tel: 01983 531785
Formed: 1933

Organisation type and purpose: National organisation, registered charity (charity number 205846), museum, historic building, house or site, suitable for ages: 8+.
Parent body:
The National Trust (South and South East Region)
Thames and Solent Regional Office, tel: 01494 528051
Other addresses:
I W National Trust Office
Longstone Farmhouse, Strawberry Lane, Mottistone, Isle of Wight

continued overleaf

Enquiries to: The Custodian
Other contacts: The Property Manager for person in overall charge of Isle of Wight NT Property.
Access:
Access to staff: By letter, by telephone, in person

General description:
The small, now tranquil, village of Newtown once sent two members to Parliament and the Town Hall was the setting for often turbulent elections. An exhibition inside depicts the exploits of 'Ferguson's Gang', an anonymous group of Trust benefactors in the 1920s and 1930s.
Information services:
Special visitor services: Guided tours, materials and/or activities for children.
Services for disabled people: For the visually impaired.
Printed publications:
Newtown IW (35p)

Internet home pages:
http://www.nationaltrust.org.uk

2168
OLD WARDOUR CASTLE
Tisbury, Wiltshire

Tel: Tel 01747 870487

Organisation type and purpose: National organisation, advisory body, historic building, house or site.
Parent body:
English Heritage (South West Region)
Tel: 0117 975 0700, fax: 0117 975 0701

Enquiries to: Manager
Access:
Access to staff: By letter, by telephone
Access to building, collections or gallery: No prior appointment required
Hours: 29 Mar to 30 Sep: daily, 1000 to 1800,1 to 31 Oct: daily, 1000 to 1700,1 Nov to 28 Mar: Wed to Sun, 1000 to 1300 and 1400 to 1600
Other restrictions: Closed 24 to 26 Dec and 1 Jan
Opening times are subject to change, for up-to-date information contact English Heritage by phone or visit the website.

General description:
Built in the late 14th century, the six-sided castle with its many rooms for guests was designed in the French style of the period. Not only was it a secure house, but, above all, it was also a luxurious residence intended to impress everyone with its builder's wealth, taste and power. Badly damaged during the English Civil War, the old castle survived and is today one of the most attractive 'romantic ruins' in England.
Information services:
Special visitor services: Tape recorded guides..

Internet home pages:
http://www.english-heritage.org.uk

2169
OLDHAM GALLERY
See - Gallery Oldham

2170
OLDHAM MUSEUM
See - Gallery Oldham

2171
OLIVER CROMWELL'S HOUSE
29 St Mary's Street, Ely, Cambridgeshire, CB7 4HF

Tel: 01353 662062
Fax: 01353 668518
Email: tic@eastcambs.gov.uk
Formed: 1990

Organisation type and purpose: Historic building, house or site, suitable for ages: all ages.
Parent body:
East Cambridgeshire District Council (ECDC)

Enquiries to: Manager
Direct tel: 01353 616349
Direct fax: 01353 616391
Direct email: alison.smith@eastcambs.gov.uk
Access:
Access to staff: By letter, by telephone, by fax, by email
Access to building, collections or gallery: No prior appointment required
Hours: Summer: daily, 1000 to 1730
Winter: Mon to Sat, 1000 to 1700; Sun, 1100 to 1600
Access for disabled people: level entry

General description:
The house of Oliver Cromwell and family for 10 years from 1636 onwards. An audiovisual presentation gives visitors an insight into the domestic, military and political aspects of his life, and another on the drainage of the Fens, shows his influence on the geography of the Fens.
Information services:
Special visitor services: Guided tours, materials and/or activities for children.
Education services: Resources for Key Stages 1 and 2..
Collections:
Material on loan from Cromwell Museum, Huntingdon
Printed publications:
Booklet (£1.50)

Internet home pages:
http://www.elyeastcambs.co.uk

2172
OLLERTON WATERMILL
Market Place, Ollerton, Newark, Nottinghamshire, NG22 9AA

Tel: 01623 822469
Formed: 1993

Organisation type and purpose: Independently owned, historic building, house or site, suitable for ages: 5+.

Enquiries to: Owner
Access:
Access to staff: By letter only

General description:
18th century working watermill and award-winning teashop.
Collections:
18th century working watermill with many original features

2173
OPEN HAND OPEN SPACE
571 Oxford Road, Reading, Berkshire, RG30 1HL

Tel: 0118 959 7752
Fax: 0118 959 7752
Email: info@ohos.org.uk

Organisation type and purpose: Registered charity (charity number 28256R), art gallery. Registered under Industrial and Provident Societies Act.
Artist-led volunteer-run studios and gallery.

Enquiries to: Studio Co-ordinator
Access:
Access to staff: By email, visitors by prior appointment
Access to building, collections or gallery: Prior appointment required

General description:
An artist-led gallery and studio complex housed in a former military keep. Providing studios for 13 contemporary visual artists and running a programme of temporary exhibitions and events.

Internet home pages:
http://www.ohos.org.uk

2174
OPEN MUSEUM
Martyrs' School, Parson Street, Glasgow, G4 0PX

Tel: 0141 552 2356
Fax: 0141 552 2356
Email: morag.macpherson@cls.glasgow.gov.uk

Organisation type and purpose: Local government body, museum, suitable for ages: 5+.
Outreach service.
Parent body:
Glasgow Museums
Access:
Access to staff: By letter, by telephone, by fax, by email, Internet web pages

General description:
Museum artefacts, handling and reminiscence kits.

Internet home pages:
http://www.glasgow.gov.uk

2175
ORDER OF ST JOHN
See - Museum and Library of Order of St John

2176
ORDSALL HALL MUSEUM
55 Ordsall Lane, Salford, Greater Manchester, M5 4RS

Tel: 0161 872 0251
Fax: 0161 872 4951

Organisation type and purpose: Local government body, art gallery, historic building, house or site, suitable for ages: all ages.
Parent body:
Salford City Council
Salford Museums Heritage Service
Access:
Access to staff: By letter, by telephone, by fax
Access to building, collections or gallery: No prior appointment required

General description:
Fine Tudor manor house, with period room displays, furniture collections and art.
Information services:
Temporary exhibitions of art and craft
School services and activities
Special visitor services: Materials and/or activities for children.
Education services: Group education facilities, resources for Key Stages 1 and 2..

Internet home pages:
http://www.ordsallhall.org
General information on services

2177
ORFORD CASTLE
Woodbridge, Orford, Suffolk, IP12 2ND

Tel: 01394 450472
Fax: 01394 450160
Formed: 1984

Organisation type and purpose: National government body, historic building, house or site.
Parent body:
English Heritage (East of England Region)
Tel: 01223 582700
Other addresses:
English Heritage
Regional Office
Brookland Avenue, Cambridge, CB2 2BU, tel: 01223 582700, fax: 01223 582701

Enquiries to: Custodian
Access:
Access to staff: By letter, by telephone, by fax, in person

General description:
Orford Castle, as we see it today, was built by Henry II in the 12th century as a coastal defence and is typical of the Norman Conquest. The

building records are the earliest in the kingdom. The unique polygon keep survives almost intact with three immense towers. From the top of the keep there are splendid views of Orford Ness and the surrounding countryside.
Information services:
CD-ROM unit containing details on English castles.
Free children's activity sheet.
Special visitor services: Tape recorded guides, materials and/or activities for children..

Address for ordering publications:
Printed publications:
Publications Department, English Heritage
23 Savile Row, London, W1X 1AB, tel: 020 7973 3000

2178
ORFORD NESS NATIONAL NATURE RESERVE

Quay Office, Orford Quay, Orford, Woodbridge, Suffolk, IP12 2NU

Tel: 01394 450900 (Property Office)
Fax: 01394 450900
Email: orfordness@nationaltrust.org.uk

Organisation type and purpose: National organisation, registered charity (charity number 205846), historic building, house or site, suitable for ages: 8+.
Parent body:
The National Trust (East of England Region)
East Anglia Regional Office, tel: 0870 609 5388

Enquiries to: Property Manager
Other contacts: Education Officer (01728 648501
Access:
Access to staff: By letter, by telephone, by fax, by email, in person, Internet web pages

General description:
The largest vegetated shingle spit in Europe, containing a variety of habitats including shingle, saltmarsh, mudflat, brackish lagoons and grazing marsh. An important location for breeding and passage birds as well as for the shingle flora, which includes a large number of nationally rare species.
Visitors follow a 5½ mile route, which can be walked in total or in part (the full walk involves walking on shingle). Other walks (approx. 3mls) are open seasonally.
The Ness was a secret military site from 1913 until the mid 1980s.
There are new displays and artefacts relating to the Atomic Weapons Research Establishment and their activities on Orford Ness 1953-1971.
Information services:
Helpline available, tel no: infoline, 01394 450057.
Guided tours on natural history, military history and general interest. Contact warden for details
Suitable for school groups. Education room/centre. Basecamp accommodation
Displays on natural history and history of the site.
Family guide. Children's quiz/trail.
Special visitor services: Guided tours.
Education services: Group education facilities, resources for Key Stages 2, 3, 4 and Further or Higher Education..

Internet home pages:
http://www.nationaltrust.org.uk

2179
ORIEL CERI RICHARDS GALLERY

Taliesin Arts Centre, University of Wales, Singleton Park, Swansea, West Glamorgan, SA2 8PZ

Tel: 01792 295526
Minicom no. 01792 513227
Formed: 1984

Organisation type and purpose: Art gallery, university department or institute, suitable for ages: 12+.

Enquiries to: Manager
Access:
Access to staff: By telephone, in person
Access for disabled people: Parking provided, level entry, toilet facilities

General description:
Temporary exhibitions and retail (cards, crafts).
Publications list:
is available on-line.

Internet home pages:
http://www.taliesinartscentre.co.uk

2180
ORIEL MOSTYN GALLERY

12 Vaughan Street, Llandudno, Gwynedd, LL30 1AB

Tel: 01492 879201
Fax: 01492 878869
Email: post@mostyn.org
Formed: 1978

Organisation type and purpose: Independently owned (charity number 507842), art gallery, suitable for ages: 8+.

Enquiries to: Director
Access:
Access to staff: By letter, by telephone, by fax, by email, visitors by prior appointment
Access to building, collections or gallery: No prior appointment required
Hours: Mon to Sat, 1030 to 1730
Access for disabled people: level entry, toilet facilities

General description:
Contemporary art in all media in a programme of seven temporary exhibitions per year. Includes international artists and a focus on artists from Wales in both one-person and group exhibitions. Craft area is a showcase for makers from around the UK, and is Crafts Council registered. Small collection of works loaned on request.
Information services:
Education services: Group education facilities, resources for Key Stages 1 and 2, 3, 4 and Further or Higher Education.
Services for disabled people: For the visually impaired; for the hearing impaired.
Collections:
Small collection of contemporary art works including works by Welsh artists Tim Davies and Peter Finnemore
Publications list:
is available in hard copy.
Printed publications:
Field for the British Isles (Gormley A, hardback, £12.95)
Artists from Wales Series of Monographs (1 annually, £9.95)
Titles to Date: James Rielly; Craig Wood
Past exhibition catalogues include:
Bethan Huws, Watercolours (£9.95)
Facing The Self (Rhys James S, £9.95)
Peter Prendergast 1994-1998 (£6.95)
From The Interior (Williams L, £9.95)

Address for ordering publications:
Printed publications:
Administrator

Internet home pages:
http://www.mostyn.org
Information on current and past exhibitions.

2181
ORIEL MYRDDIN CRAFT CENTRE AND REGIONAL ART GALLERY

Church Lane, Carmarthen, SA31 1LH

Tel: 01267 222775
Fax: 01267 220599
Email: orielmyrddin@carmarthenshire.gov.uk or orielmyrddin@sirgar.gov.uk
Formed: 1992

Organisation type and purpose: Local government body, registered charity (charity number 10131498), art gallery, suitable for ages: all ages.

Enquiries to: Manager
Direct email: relliot@carmarthenshire.gov.uk
Access:
Access to staff: By letter, by email
Access to building, collections or gallery: No prior appointment required
Hours: Mon to Sat, 1000 to 1700
Access for disabled people: level entry, toilet facilities

General description:
A changing programme of exhibitions and related talks and workshops, featuring fine art and craft from across the UK. Retail area with high quality craft.
Information services:
Special visitor services: Materials and/or activities for children.
Education services: Group education facilities.
Services for disabled people: For the hearing impaired.
Collections:
Very small collection of commissioned work for exhibition publications
Printed publications:
Available from the gallery and distribution points - mainly other arts venues/tourist centres
Exhibition catalogues (available direct)

Internet home pages:
http://www.
Under construction.

2182
ORIEL PENDEITSH GALLERY

Castle Ditch, Caernarfon, Gwynedd, LL55 2AY

Tel: 01286 679 564
Fax: 01286 677 647

Organisation type and purpose: Local government body, art gallery.
Parent body:
Gwynedd Museums Service

Enquiries to: Manager
Access:
Access to staff: By letter, by telephone, by fax

Internet home pages:
http://www.gwynedd.gov.uk/museums/arts

2183
ORIENTAL MUSEUM

See - Durham University

2184
ORKNEY MUSEUM, THE

Tankerness House, Broad Street, Kirkwall, Orkney, KW15 1DH

Tel: 01856 873191
Fax: 01856 871560
Email: museum@orkney.gov.uk
Formed: 1968
Formerly: Tankerness House Museum, date of change, 1999

Organisation type and purpose: Local government body, professional body, museum.
Parent body:
Orkney Islands Council
Includes the:
Corrigall Farm Museum
Corrigall, Harray, Orkney, KW17 2LQ, fax: 01856 871560, email/website: museum@orkney.gov.uk
Kirbuster Museum
Hirsay, Orkney
Scapa Flow Visitor Centre & Museum
Lyness, Hoy, Orkney

Enquiries to: Curator
Access:
Access to staff: By letter, by telephone, by fax, in person, visitors by prior appointment

continued overleaf

Access to building, collections or gallery: No access other than to staff
Hours: May to Oct: Mon to Sat, 1030 to 1700

General description:
Mainly comprises the archaeology of Orkney, from Neolithic times to the Norse period, including Bronze Age and Iron Age. Also covers the social history of Orkney, including farming and wartime Orkney.
Catalogues:
Catalogue for part of the collections is only available in-house.

2185
ORKNEY NATURAL HISTORY SOCIETY
See - Stromness Museum

2186
ORKNEY WIRELESS MUSEUM
Kiln Corner, 1 Junction Road, Kirkwall, Orkney, KW15 1LB

Tel: 01856 874272
Formed: 1983

Organisation type and purpose: Registered charity (charity number SCO 02982), museum.

Enquiries to: Trustee
Access:
Access to staff: By letter
Hours: Apr to Sep: Mon to Sat, 1000 to 1630; Sun, 1430 to 1630
Access to building, collections or gallery: Prior appointment required
Access for disabled people: ramped entry

General description:
A small local museum tracing the history of early domestic radio and wartime communications in Orkney (Scapa Flow was the base for the Home Fleet). Maps, charts, valves, transistors, rare wireless sets 1920 onwards, wartime communications equipment.

2187
ORLEANS HOUSE GALLERY
Riverside, Twickenham, Middlesex, TW1 3DJ

Tel: 020 8892 0221
Fax: 020 8744 0501
Email: galleryinfo@richmond.gov.uk
Acronym or abbreviation: OHG
Formed: 1972

Organisation type and purpose: Local government body, museum, art gallery, historic building, house or site, suitable for ages: all ages.
Parent body:
London Borough of Richmond Council (LBRUT) Education, Arts & Leisure Department, Regal House, London Road, Twickenham, Middlesex, TW1 3QB

Enquiries to: Curator
Direct email: m.denovellis@richmond.gov.uk
Access:
Access to staff: By letter, by email
Access to building, collections or gallery: No prior appointment required
Hours: Tue to Sat, 1300 to 1730; closed 1630 Nov to Mar
Other restrictions: Access to permanent collection by appointment.
Access for disabled people: Parking provided, ramped entry, toilet facilities
Other restrictions: Access to ground floor.

General description:
The original house was built as a retirement retreat for James Johnston, Secretary of State for Scotland (1655-1737). The Octagon Room, constructed in about 1720 to a design by James Gibbs, is one of the finest surviving baroque interiors. Ite most famous resident was Louis Philippe, Duc d'Orleans (1883-1850)
Exhibitions (5 per year main gallery, 7 in the stables gallery). Range of contemporary and historical exhibitions - all media - painting, sculpture, photography, multimedia, craft. Local and national relevance. Permanent collection included in main gallery exhibitions and regular In Focus display. Collections of over 200 works primarily comprises 18th and 19th century. Local topographical views. Also houses Richard Burton's collection.
Information services:
Guided tours by prior appointment.
Special needs/excluded youths welcome for visits, the Gallery also has achieved new guides for education projects in this field.
Special visitor services: Guided tours, materials and/or activities for children.
Education services: Group education facilities, resources for Key Stages 1 and 2, 3, 4 and Further or Higher Education.
Services for disabled people: For the visually impaired.
Collections:
Paintings, watercolours, drawings, photographs, prints, objects
Gill Collection, 60 items
Hon Mrs Nellie Ionides Collection, local and topographical works, 18th-20th century, 475
Borough Art Collection, local and topographical works, 18th-20th century, 2000 plus
Burton Collection, Victorian memorabilia, 19th century, c. 200
Paton Collection, local and topographical works, 18th-20th century, 2000 plus items
Other gifts, bequests (individual) and purchases 1972-2001
Catalogues:
Catalogue for part of the collections is published and part is on-line.
Publications list:
is available in hard copy and online.
Printed publications:
History of the house and octagon (available direct, £2)
Catalogue of the collection (pub May 2002, £6.99)
Electronic and video products:
Catalogue available online

Internet home pages:
http://www.richmond.gov.uk/depts/upps/eal/leisure/arts/orleanshouse
Exhibitions, brief information on collections, highlight catalogue of the collection.

2188
ORMESBY HALL
Ormesby, Middlesbrough, Cleveland, TS7 9AS

Tel: 01642 324188
Fax: 01642 300937
Email: ormesbyhall@nationaltrust.org.uk
Formed: 1962

Organisation type and purpose: Registered charity (charity number 205846), historic building, house or site, suitable for ages: 5+.
Parent body:
The National Trust
36 Queen Anne's Gate, London, SW1H 9AB, tel: 020 7222 9251
Other addresses:
The National Trust Yorkshire Regional Office Goddards, Tadcaster Road, Dringhouses, York, YO24 1GG, tel: 01904 702021

Enquiries to: Estate Manager
Access:
Access to staff: By letter, by telephone, by fax, by email
Access for disabled people: Parking provided, ramped entry, toilet facilities
Other restrictions: Ground floor access only.

General description:
Mid 18th century Palladian mansion, notable for its fine plasterwork and carved wood decoration. Victorian laundry and kitchen with scullery and game larder. Stable block let to Cleveland Mounted Police. Large model railway exhibition, attractive garden.
Information services:
Special visitor services: Guided tours, materials and/or activities for children.
Education services: Group education facilities, resources for Key Stages 1 and 2..

Internet home pages:
http://www.nationaltrust.org.uk

2189
OSBORNE HOUSE
York Avenue, East Cowes, Isle of Wight, PO32 6JY

Tel: 01983 200022
Fax: 01983 281380

Organisation type and purpose: National government body, historic building, house or site, suitable for ages: 8+.
Parent body:
English Heritage (South East Region)
Tel: 01483 252000, fax: 01483 252001

Enquiries to: Curator
Direct tel: 01983 282503
Direct email: michael.hunter@english-heritage.org.uk
Access:
Access to staff: By letter, by telephone, by fax, by email, visitors by prior appointment
Access to building, collections or gallery: No prior appointment required
Hours: House and gardens: 29 Mar to 30 Sep: 1000 to 1800 (last admission 1600, house closes 1700). 1 to 31 Oct: 1000 to 1700 daily (last admission 1600, house closes 1700).
Other restrictions: Access to reserve collection by appointment.
Opening times are subject to change, for up-to-date information contact English Heritage by phone or visit the website.
Access for disabled people: Parking provided, ramped entry, toilet facilities
Other restrictions: Exterior and ground floor only, vehicles with disabled passengers may set them down at the house entrance before returning to the car park.

General description:
The magnificent Italianate island retreat of Queen Victoria and Price Albert. Although essentially a family home, Osborne was also used for state affairs. The recently refurbished Durbar Room is the stunning setting for an interactive exhibition displaying a collection of gifts given to the Queen by the Indian people. The extensive grounds surrounding Osborne include the Victorian walled garden with its contemporary design of triumphal arches of Victorian plums festooned with roses, and hot house of tropical plants. The Swiss Cottage, a miniature house designed for the royal children to play in, is complete with furniture that was specially crafted for them. Surrounded by its own gardens, here the princes and princesses grew vegetables, and would use the working kitchen in the Swiss Cottage to cook meals for their parents.
Information services:
Special visitor services: Guided tours, materials and/or activities for children.
Education services: Group education facilities, resources for Key Stages 2, 3 and 4.
Services for disabled people: Displays and/or information at wheelchair height.
Collections:
Paintings, sculpture, furniture acquired by Queen Victoria and Prince Albert for Osborne House 1846-1901
Portraits of the Victorian royal family
Indian artefacts given to Queen Victoria as Jubillee presents
Portraits of native Indians, 19th century
19th century sculpture collection
Catalogues:
Catalogue for all of the collections is only available in-house.
Printed publications:
Guide Book

Internet home pages:
http://www.english-heritage.org.uk

2190
OSTERLEY PARK HOUSE

Jersey Road, Isleworth, Hounslow, Middlesex, TW7 4RB

Tel: 020 8232 5050 (Visitor Services)
Fax: 020 8232 5080
Email: osterley@nationaltrust.org.uk
Formed: 1895

Organisation type and purpose: National organisation, registered charity (charity number 205846), historic building, house or site, suitable for ages: 8+.
Parent body:
The National Trust (South and South East Region)
Thames and Solent Regional Office, tel: 01494 528051

Enquiries to: Visitor Services Manager
Other contacts: (1) Custodian; (2) Property Assistant for questions (1) relating to collection; (2) relating to visits, generally.
Access:
Access to staff: By letter, by telephone, by email, visitors by prior appointment
Hours: Varied: Mon to Sun, 0900 to 1700
Other restrictions: Meetings with staff by prior appointment.
Access to building, collections or gallery: No prior appointment required
Hours: Mar to Nov: Wed to Sun and Bank Holiday Mondays, 1300 to 1630
Other restrictions: Private views and guided tours by prior appointment.
Access for disabled people: Parking provided, toilet facilities
Other restrictions: Steps to entrance. House entry via stairclimber for wheelchair users. Transfer available. Drop-off point. 2 manual wheelchairs available. 2 single-seater, 1 two-seater powered mobility vehicle available. Ground floor accessible with assistance. No access to other floors. Photograph album. Wheelchair access to ground floor (kitchens and Jersey Galleries) via separate entrance. Principal floor accessed via 20 steps. Stairclimber available for wheelchair users. Inside fully accessible.
Chairs without arms are available in the property for resting. Ramped entrance to shop. Level entrance to tea-room. Grounds largely accessible.
General description:
In 1761 the founders of Child's Bank commissioned Robert Adam to transform a crumbling Tudor mansion into an elegant neoclassical villa. This was their house in the country, created for entertainment and to impress friends and business associates. Today the spectacular interiors contain one of Britain's most complete examples of Adam's work. The magnificent 16th century stables survive largely intact and are still in use. The house is set in over 350 acres of landscaped park and farmland, complete with Adam neo-classical garden buildings, ornamental lakes, and pleasure grounds.
Information services:
Helpline available, tel no: Infoline: 01494 755566.
The Jersey Galleries feature contemporary art in a programme of exhibitions from Apr to Oct, admission free. Artist in residence.
Braille guide. Large-print guide. Sympathetic Hearing Scheme.
Suitable for school groups. Education room/centre. Hands-on activities. Children's guide. Children's quiz/trail. Family activity packs.
Special visitor services: Guided tours, materials and/or activities for children.
Education services: Group education facilities, resources for Key Stages 1 and 2, 3, 4 and Further or Higher Education.
Services for disabled people: For the visually impaired; for the hearing impaired; displays and/or information at wheelchair height.
Collections:
Robert Adam original designs for the house and grounds
Furniture, textiles and plasterwork designed by Robert Adam
Painted wall and ceiling panels by Zucchi and Angelica Kauffmann
Etruscan room painted by Pietro Mario Borgnis
Suite of marquetry library furniture attributed to John Linell's workshops
Complete room of Gobelins tapestries, pink and claret with trompe l'oeil medallion paintings by Boucher
Catalogues:
Catalogue for all of the collections is only available in-house.
Printed publications:
Welcome leaflet, property leaflet, events leaflet, artist-in-residence leaflet (free, direct)
Green Guide (free, direct)
Jersey Galleries Diary (free, direct)
Colour Guide Book (£4.50)
Short House Guide (70p)
Estate Guide (£1)
Children's Guide (£1)
Aspects of Osterley (£4)

Internet home pages:
http://www.nationaltrust.org.uk
Basic property information.

2191
OSWESTRY TRANSPORT MUSEUM

Oswald Road, Oswestry, Shropshire, SY11 1RE

Tel: 01691 671749
Email: hignetts@enterprise.net
Full name: Cambrian Railways Society Limited
Formed: 1976

Organisation type and purpose: Voluntary organisation, registered charity (charity number 701496), museum, historic building, house or site, research organisation.

Enquiries to: Secretary
Access:
Access to staff: By letter, by telephone, in person

General description:
History of the Cambrian Railways Company, history and development of the bicycle.
Collections:
Bicycle, documents, pictures and papers
Cambrian Railways, documents, pictures and papers
Printed publications:
Rolling Stock List (£1)

2192
OTLEY MUSEUM

Civic Centre, Cross Green, Otley, West Yorkshire, LS21 1HD

Tel: 01943 461052
Formed: 1961

Organisation type and purpose: Registered charity (charity number 519264), museum, suitable for ages: 8+.
To exhibit and conserve the social and industrial history of Otley from prehistoric times to 21st century.

Enquiries to: Secretary
Access:
Access to staff: By letter, by telephone, in person
Access for disabled people: toilet facilities
Other restrictions: 6 steps to Museum, step walking wheelchair available, please telephone.
Access - under review.

General description:
A local history collection of objects and archives relating to Otley; includes a large collection of flints, a neolithic skeleton, excavated material from the Archbishop of York's Otley Manor House, artefacts from local industries and trades; archives cover all aspects of Otley's social and industrial history from prehistoric times to the 21st century, from schools to printers' engineers.
Collections:
Specialist Collections include:
A large archive devoted to the history of Otley's printing machine industry
Eric Cowling Flint Collection
Catalogues:
Catalogue for all of the collections is only available in-house.
Publications list:
is available in hard copy.
Printed publications:
Annual Report and Newsletter
The Fawkes Family & Their Estates in Wharfedale 1819-1936 (Sharples M, £15)
The Story of Rebuilding the Congregational Church (£3.50)
Twenty Five Challenging Years. (The continuing story of Bridge St Church, £3.50)
The Chippendale Society (Catalogue of the Collection) (£6)
A Walk Round Otley (Wood P, £0.40)
Otley & District in Old Photographs (Wood P, £5)
Otley in Old Postcards (Wood P, £7)
Otley and the Wharfedale Printing Machine (Wood P, £2)
A Guide to the Landscape of Otley (Wood P, £8.50)
Turner & Natural History - The Farnley Project (Lyles A, £5)

2193
OTTERTON MILL CENTRE AND WORKING MUSEUM

Budleigh Salterton, Devon, EX9 7HG

Tel: 01395 568521
Fax: 01395 568521
Email: ottertonmill@ukonline.co.uk
Formed: 1977

Organisation type and purpose: Museum, art gallery, suitable for ages: 5+.
Independent working museum, gallery and craft workshops.

Enquiries to: Director
Access:
Access to staff: By telephone, by fax, by email, Internet web pages
Access to building, collections or gallery: No prior appointment required
Hours: Mid Mar to end Oct: Mon to Sun, 1030 to 1730;
Nov to mid Mar: Mon to Sun, 1100 to 1600
Access for disabled people: Parking provided, level entry
Other restrictions: Access to some areas.

General description:
The production of flour by water power (carried out on site).
History of 1000 year old water mill.
Production of organic breads and other baked goods in our bakery.
Methods used in various crafts produced on site, especially pottery and several techniques of weaving.
Annual programme of, on average, 12 exhibitions in fields of fine arts and crafts.
Information services:
Helpline available
Special visitor services: Guided tours, materials and/or activities for children.
Education services: Group education facilities, resources for Key Stages 1 and 2 and 3.
Services for disabled people: For the visually impaired.
Collections:
Collection on display of the history of East Devon Lace
Publications list:
is available in hard copy.
Printed publications:
Otterton Mill, the last working mill on the River Otter (Desna Greenhow)

continued overleaf

Internet home pages:
http://www.ukonline.co.uk/ottertonmill
Home page, general information, bakery, Mill Museum, exhibitions, craftspeople.

2194
OUNDLE MUSEUM

The Courthouse, Mill Road, Oundle, Peterborough, Cambridgeshire, PE8 4BW

Tel: 01832 272741
Formed: 1993
Incorporates: the former museum at the Drill Hall Centre, date of change, April 2000

Organisation type and purpose: Registered charity (charity number 1045378), museum, suitable for ages: all ages.
Collection, conservation and display of artefacts depicting the social and industrial history of Oundle and district.

Enquiries to: Secretary
Access:
Access to staff: By letter, by telephone, in person
Hours: Daily
Access to building, collections or gallery: No prior appointment required
Hours: Mon to Fri, 0900 to 1600; Sat, Sun, 1400 to 1700
Other times by appointment
Access for disabled people: Parking provided, ramped entry, access to all public areas, toilet facilities
Other restrictions: Lift to first floor, baby changing facilities.

General description:
Artefacts depicting the social and industrial history of Oundle and district.
The history of Oundle in words and pictures.
Brewing exhibition.
A special exhibition which is changed each year:
2002 A Golden Age for Oundle
2003 Local Archaeology.
Printed publications:
Publications by the Oundle Museum Trust include:
Early Nineteenth Century Oundle and the Improvement Act of 1885 (Thomas A, 1999)
Education in Oundle (Moss J, 2001)
Memories of Childhood in Oundle (Richmond J et al, 1999)
Richard Creed's Journal of the Grand Tour when he accompanied the 5th Earl of Exeter to Rome 1699-1700 (Thomas A, 2002)
The Windows of St Peter's Church, Oundle - an architectural guide (Rowe R, 2002)

2195
OUR DYNAMIC EARTH

Holyrood Road, Edinburgh, EH8 8AS

Tel: 0131 550 7800
Fax: 0131 550 7801
Email: enquiries@dynamicearth.co.uk
Formed: 1999

Organisation type and purpose: Independently owned, suitable for ages: 5+.
Visitor attraction.
Member of:
Edinburgh Capital Group
Explore Edinburgh
Scottish Science Trust
Sponsored by:
Millennium Commission Landmark Project

Enquiries to: Marketing Director
Access:
Access to staff: By letter, by telephone, by fax, visitors by prior appointment
Access to building, collections or gallery: No prior appointment required
Hours: Apr to Oct: daily, 1000 to 1800 (last entry 1650)
Nov to Mar: Wed to Sun, 1000 to 1700 (last entry 1550)
Other restrictions: Pre-booking required for groups.
Closed 24, 25 and 26 Dec.
Access for disabled people: Parking provided, ramped entry, access to all public areas, toilet facilities
Other restrictions: Large type guides.

General description:
Our Dynamic Earth is a fantastic journey of discovery for visitors of all ages. Explore the history of planet Earth, travel back in time and witness the Big Bang from the deck of a spaceship. Stand on an erupting volcano, fly over glaciers and feel the chill of polar ice. You could even get caught in a tropical rainstorm. Whatever happens, you'll have the experience of a lifetime. Watch out for special events and activities throughout the year.
Information services:
Special events and exhibitions programme.
Special visitor services: Materials and/or activities for children.
Education services: Group education facilities, resources for Key Stages 1 and 2, 3 and 4.
Services for disabled people: For the visually impaired; displays and/or information at wheelchair height.
Printed publications:
Guide Books (£4 from ticket desk or gift shop)
Selection of printed postcards

Internet home pages:
http://www.dynamicearth.co.uk
Virtual tour of attraction, group booking information, details of education facilities and services, details of corporate facilities.

2196
OVERBECKS MUSEUM AND GARDENS

Sharpitor, Salcombe, Devon, TQ8 8LW

Tel: 01548 842893
Fax: 01548 845020
Email: overbecks@nationaltrust.org.uk

Organisation type and purpose: National organisation, registered charity (charity number 205846), museum, historic building, house or site, suitable for ages: 5+.
Parent body:
The National Trust (South West Region)
Devon and Cornwall Regional Office, tel: 01392 881691

Enquiries to: Manager
Access:
Access to staff: By letter, by telephone, by fax, by email
Access to building, collections or gallery: No prior appointment required
Hours: Museum: End Mar to end Jul and Sep, Sun to Fri, 1100 to 1730: Aug, daily, 1100 to 1730; Oct to beg Nov, Sun to Thu, 1100 to 1700
Garden: All year, daily, 1000 to 1900
Open Easter Saturday
Other restrictions: Garden closes dusk if earlier than 1900.
Access for disabled people: Parking provided
Other restrictions: Designated parking 20yds. Drop-off point. 1 manual wheelchair available. Accessible entrance different from main entrance. Ground floor fully accessible. No access to other floors. Photograph album. Level entrance to shop and to tea-room. Steep gravel paths, strong companion needed. Recommended route map.

General description:
This elegant Edwardian house contains the eclectic collections of the scientist who lived here from 1928 to 1937, Dr Otto Overbeck. Among the items on show are late 19th century photographs of the area, local shipbuilding tools, model boats, toys, shells, animals, a nautical collection and some of Mr Overbeck's drawings. The beautiful and luxuriant garden, with spectacular views over the Salcombe estuary, enjoys a warm microclimate and so is home to many rare plants, trees and shrubs.
Information services:
Braille guide. Touch list. Handling collection.
Suitable for school groups. Children's guide. Children's quiz/trail. Secret room with dolls, toys and other collections; ghost hunt for children.
Guided tours by arrangement, outside normal opening hours.
Special visitor services: Materials and/or activities for children.
Education services: Group education facilities, resources for Key Stages 2 and 3.
Services for disabled people: For the visually impaired.
Collections:
Butterflies of the British Isles
Catalogues:
Catalogue for part of the collections is only available in-house.

Internet home pages:
http://www.nationaltrust.org.uk

2197
OXBURGH HALL, GARDEN AND ESTATE

Oxborough, King's Lynn, Norfolk, PE33 9PS

Tel: 01366 328258
Fax: 01366 328066
Email: oxburghhall@nationaltrust.org.uk
Formed: 1952

Organisation type and purpose: National organisation, registered charity (charity number 205846), historic building, house or site, suitable for ages: all ages.
Parent body:
The National Trust (East of England)
East Anglia Regional Office, tel: 0870 609 5388

Enquiries to: Property Manager
Other contacts: (1) Property Secretary; (2) House Steward for (1) group bookings, event details; (2) historical information.
Access:
Access to staff: By letter, by telephone, by email, visitors by prior appointment, Internet web pages
Access to building, collections or gallery: No prior appointment required
Hours: House: late Mar to beg Nov, Sat to Wed, 1300 to 1700
Open Bank Holiday Mondays, 1100 to 1700
Other restrictions: At other times by prior appointment.
Access for disabled people: Parking provided, ramped entry, toilet facilities
Other restrictions: Designated parking 200yds. Drop-off point. 4 manual wheelchairs available. Ground floor fully accessible. Series of stairs for remainder of the visitor route, including a steep narrow stone staircase. Level entrance to shop and to restaurant. Care necessary near moat, and Chapel 100yds from Hall, access via ramp. Recommended route map.

General description:
This red brick fortified, moated manor house, with its magnificent Tudor gatehouse, complete with accessible Priest's Hole, was built in 1482 by the Bedingfeld family, who still live here. The rooms show the development from medieval austerity to Victorian comfort, and include an outstanding display of embroidery done by Mary, Queen of Scots and Bess of Hardwick. The attractive gardens include a French parterre and there are delightful woodland walks, as well as an interesting Catholic chapel.
Information services:
Guided tours by prior arrangement only.
Braille guide. Touch list.
Front-carrying baby slings for loan. Hip-carrying infant seats for loan.
Suitable for school groups. Hands-on activities. Children's guide. Children's quiz/trail.
Special visitor services: Guided tours, materials and/or activities for children.
Education services: Group education facilities.
Services for disabled people: For the visually impaired.

Collections:
Original Victorian wallpapers
Marian Hangings (embroidery by Mary, Queen of Scots and Elizabeth Shrewsbury during Mary's imprisonment)
Original medieval and Tudor documents including letters from Mary I, Elizabeth I and Henry VIII
Catalogues:
Catalogue for library is in-house only. Catalogue for all of the collections is only available in-house.
Printed publications:
Guide Book of the house, garden, estate and Marian Hanging (available for purchase, £2.95 plus p&p)
Event leaflet and property leaflet (available free of charge)
Internet home pages:
http://www.nationaltrust.org.uk

2198
OXFORD BUS MUSEUM TRUST LIMITED
Old Station Yard, Main Road, Long Hanborough, Witney, Oxfordshire, OX29 8LA

Tel: 01993 883617
Formed: 1968

Organisation type and purpose: Independently owned, registered charity (charity number 1088389), museum.
To collect, restore vehicles, especially buses relative to the Oxfordshire area.
Other Addresses:
Secretary
The Wilows, School Lane, Stadhampton, Oxford, OX44 7TR, tel: 01865 400002

Enquiries to: Honorary Secretary
Access:
Access to staff: By letter, by telephone, by fax
Access to building, collections or gallery: Prior appointment required
Hours: Sat, 1330 to 1630; Sun, 1130 to 1630
Access for disabled people: Parking provided, ramped entry, level entry, access to all public areas

General description:
Over 35 buses dating from turn of the century; trams.
Information services:
Education services: Group education facilities.
Services for disabled people: Displays and/or information at wheelchair height.

2199
OXFORD STORY, THE
6 Broad Street, Oxford, OX1 3AJ

Tel: 01865 728822
Fax: 01865 791716
Email: info@oxfordstory.org.uk

Organisation type and purpose: Museum, suitable for ages: 5+.

Enquiries to: Manager
Direct tel: 01865 790055
Other contacts: Bookings Officer for Group Bookings Co-ordinator.
Access:
Access for disabled people: level entry, access to all public areas, toilet facilities

General description:
The Oxford Story offers a unique introduction to the City. Relax while you watch our 'student life' film, then take a comfortable journey through the University's 900 year history on one of Europe's longest indoor 'dark' rides.
Information services:
Special visitor services: Materials and/or activities for children..

Internet home pages:
http://www.oxfordstory.co.uk
Opening times, prices etc.

2200
OXFORD UNIVERSITY
Bate Collection of Musical Instruments, Faculty of Music, St Aldate's, Oxford, OX1 1DB

Tel: 01865 276139
Fax: 01865 276128
Email: bate.collection@music.ox.ac.uk
Formed: 1970

Organisation type and purpose: Museum.

Enquiries to: Curator
Direct tel: 01865 274721
Direct fax: 01865 27472
Direct email: pitt@prm.ox.ac.uk
Access:
Access to staff: By letter, by email, visitors by prior appointment, letter of introduction required, Internet web pages
Hours: Term time: Mon to Fri, 1400 to 1700; Sat, 1000 to 1200
Vacations: Mon to Fri, 1400 to 1700
Access for disabled people: ramped entry, toilet facilities

General description:
Historical musical instruments, particularly wind and percussion.
Collections:
R B Chatwin archive and working papers
Reginald Morley-Pegge Library, archive and working papers
Catalogues:
Catalogue for part of the collections is on-line.
Publications list:
is available in hard copy and online.
Printed publications:
Catalogues and Guides
Handbooks, plans and measured drawings of a large number of instruments mainly wind
Making Early Percussion Instruments (Montagu J, £5)
Musical Instrument Collections in the British Isles (Bevan C, £7.95)
Electronic and video products:
Cassettes and CDs of the instruments

Internet home pages:
http://www.ashmol.ox.ac.uk/BCMIPage.html
Collection history, information, events, publications, checklists of items in the collection.

2201
OXFORD UNIVERSITY
Balfour Library Pitt Rivers Museum, School of Anthropology and Museum Ethnography, South Parks Road, Oxford, OX1 3PP

Tel: 01865 270928
Fax: 01865 270943
Email: postmaster@prm.ox.ac.uk
Formed: 1882

Organisation type and purpose: Museum, university library, suitable for ages: 16+.
Close links with:
Institute of Social and Cultural Anthropology
Tylor Library, University of Oxford
Member organisation of the:
Donald Baden Powell Quaternary Research Centre
60 Banbury Road, Oxford

Enquiries to: Librarian
Direct tel: 01865 270939
Direct email: mark.dickerson@prm.ox.ac.uk
Other contacts: Director of the Museum
Access:
Access to staff: By letter, by telephone, by fax, by email, visitors by prior appointment
Hours: Vacation hours, 0900 to 1230 and 1400 to 1600; closed August
For Christmas and Easter hours, please phone
Other restrictions: Reference library only to non-members of the University.
Access for disabled people: Parking provided

General description:
Anthropology, ethnology, prehistoric archaeology, material culture, museum studies, ethnomusicology, visual anthropology (including ethnographic film and photography), ethnographic art.
Collections:
Books owned by Henry Balfour, first curator of the Museum, and General Pitt Rivers (incomplete)
Collection of over 100,000 anthropological photographs from *c.* 1850 onwards
Collections of papers of Henry Balfour, E B Tyler, W Baldwin Spencer and others who have made important contributions to the history of anthropology and archaeology (separate Manuscript and Photographic Archive)
Ellen Ettlinger Bequest of books on folklore
June Bedford collection (as yet, incomplete) of books on ethnographic art
Catalogues:
Catalogue for part of the collections is on-line.
Publications list:
is available in hard copy and online.
Printed publications:
Annual Report
Catalogue of the Australian Collections
Catalogue of the Native American Collection
Monograph series; occasional papers on technology, archaeology, miscellaneous publications
The Origin and Development of the Pitt Museum
Internet home pages:
http://www.lib.ox.ac.uk:/olis/
OLIS, union catalogue. Includes all books received post 1995 for Balfour Library.
http://www.prm.ox.ac.uk

2202
OXFORD UNIVERSITY
Pitt Rivers Museum, South Parks Road, Oxford, OX1 3PP

Tel: 01865 270927
Fax: 01865 270943
Telex: 83147 VIADR G
Email: prm@prm.ox.ac.uk
Formed: 1884
Formed from: University of Oxford Museum of Anthropology and World Archaeology

Organisation type and purpose: Museum, university department or institute, suitable for ages: 5+.
Parent body:
University of Oxford
University Offices, Wellington Square, Oxford
Includes the:
Balfour Library
Also:
School of Anthropology, University of Oxford

Enquiries to: Director
Other contacts: Librarian
Access:
Access to staff: By letter, by telephone, by fax, by email, in person, visitors by prior appointment, Internet web pages
Hours: Staff and library: Mon to Fri, 0900 to 1700
Other restrictions: Staff not always on site, pre-arranged visits are therefore advisable.
Access for disabled people: Parking provided, level entry, toilet facilities
Other restrictions: Currently no access to upper galleries.

General description:
Ethnography and prehistory of the whole world and all periods; cultural anthropology; archaeology; comparative technology of pre-industrial societies.
Information services:
Library available for reference (for conditions see Access above)
Special visitor services: Guided tours, tape recorded guides, materials and/or activities for children.
Education services: Group education facilities, resources for Key Stages 1 and 2, 3, 4 and Further or Higher Education..

continued overleaf

Collections:
Books and manuscripts of early travel and exploration
Photographic archive
Wide-ranging collections of everyday objects from all round the world and all periods of human history, displayed in unique Victorian Displays
Catalogues:
Catalogue for library is on-line. Catalogue for all of the collections is on-line.
Publications list:
is available in hard copy and online.
Printed publications:
Occasional papers or monographs, recent titles:
The Cook Collection at the Pitt Rivers Museum (Coote J, 1996)
The Coming of the Sun: A prologue to Ika Sacred Narrative (Tayler D, 1997)
Glimpses of Kyoto Life (Lowe J, 1996)
The Japanese Collections: An Introduction (Nicholson J, 1996)
A Village in Asturias (Taylet D, 1998)

Internet home pages:
http://www.http://www.prm.ox.ac.uk/databases
Object and photograph databases
http://www.prm.ox.ac.uk
General visitor information and links to all specialist information for researchers and teachers, history, collections, research, exhibitions, teaching, Friends of the Museum, current staff.

2203
OXFORD UNIVERSITY

Museum of Natural History, Parks Road, Oxford, OX1 3PW

Tel: 01865 272950
Acronym or abbreviation: OUMNH
Formed: 1860
Formerly: Oxford University Museum, date of change, 1996/97

Organisation type and purpose: Museum, university department or institute.

Enquiries to: Librarian
Direct tel: 01865 272982
Direct fax: 01865 272970
Direct email: stella.brecknell@oum.ox.ac.uk
Other contacts: The Director for permission to use manuscripts.
Access:
Access to staff: By letter, by telephone, by fax, by email, in person
Hours: Mon to Fri, 0900 to 1300 and 1400 to 1700
Other restrictions: Letter of introduction required for manuscripts. Members of the university and others at the Director's discretion.
Access to building, collections or gallery: No prior appointment required
Hours: Mon to Fri, 0900 to 1300 and 1400 to 1700
Access for disabled people: ramped entry, toilet facilities
Other restrictions: Parking provided by appointment; no access to library but alternative arrangements can usually be made by appointment.

General description:
Natural history, taxonomic entomology, Jurassic and Cretaceous geology and palaeontology.
Collections:
Catalogue of the entomology manuscripts now available online from our website

Internet home pages:
http://www.olis.ox.ac.uk
Union catalogue of Oxford Libraries' books and journals and other published media. Certain catalogues for prints and manuscripts are still available in house only, catalogue of entomology manuscripts available online.

2204
OXFORD UNIVERSITY, ETHNOLOGY AND PREHISTORY LIBRARY

See - Oxford University, Balfour Library Pitt Rivers Museum

2205
OXFORDSHIRE MUSEUM, THE

Fletchers House, Park Street, Woodstock, Oxfordshire, OX20 1SN

Tel: 01993 811456
Fax: 01993 813239
Email: oxon.museum@oxfordshire.gov.uk
Formed: 1965
Formerly: Oxfordshire County Museum (also often referred to as the Woodstock Museum), date of change, 1998

Organisation type and purpose: Local government body, museum, art gallery, historic building, house or site, suitable for ages: all ages.
Parent body:
Oxfordshire County Council
Culture Services Department
County Hall, Oxford, OX1 1ND, tel: 01865 810191, fax: 01865 810187

Enquiries to: Curator
Direct tel: 01993 814104
Direct email: carol.anderson@oxfordshire.gov.uk
Access:
Access to staff: By letter, by telephone, by fax, by email, visitors by prior appointment, charges to non-members
Hours: Mon to Fri, 0900 to 1700
Access to building, collections or gallery: No prior appointment required
Hours: Tue to Sat, 1000 to 1700; Sun, 1400 to 1700; Closed Mon
Last admission 1630
Other restrictions: Telephone for details of Bank Holiday opening times.
Access for disabled people: level entry, access to all public areas, toilet facilities
Other restrictions: Designated parking for cars in front of museum.

General description:
A celebration of Oxfordshire life with collections and displays of local history, art, social history of Oxfordshire, Oxfordshire archaeology, natural history of Oxfordshire, industry, landscape and wildlife.
Information services:
Library available for reference (for conditions see Access above)
Lectures, gallery talks and object handling sessions by arrangement
Special visitor services: Guided tours, materials and/or activities for children.
Education services: Group education facilities, resources for Key Stages 1 and 2, 3, 4 and Further or Higher Education.
Services for disabled people: Displays and/or information at wheelchair height.
Collections:
Collections held represent the archaeology, social history and environment of Oxfordshire
Small collection of topographical paintings
Catalogues:
Catalogue for library is in-house only. Catalogue for all of the collections is only available in-house.
Publications list:
is available in hard copy and online.

Internet home pages:
http://www.oxfordshire.gov.uk/things-to-do
http://www.oxfordshire-collections.org.uk
http://www.oxfordshire.gov.uk

2206
OXFORDSHIRE MUSEUMS STORE, THE

Cotswold Dene, Standlake, Oxfordshire, OX29 7QG

Tel: 01865 300972
Fax: 01865 300519
Email: lauren.gilmour@oxfordshire.gov.uk

Organisation type and purpose: Local government body, museum.
A resource centre for museum collections, exhibitions and outreach activities in Oxfordshire.
To collect, conserve and interpret Oxfordshire's County Museum Collections.

Enquiries to: Archaeology Curator and Outreach Officer
Direct tel: 01865 300716
Other contacts: (1) Social History Curator; (2) Natural Sciences Curator for (1) History Collections; (2) Natural Science Collections and Biological Database.
Access:
Access to staff: By letter, by telephone, by fax, by email, visitors by prior appointment
Hours: Mon to Thu, 0830 to 1700; Fri, 0830 to 1630
Access to building, collections or gallery: Prior appointment required
Hours: Please ring for dates and times of Open Days
Access for disabled people: Parking provided, ramped entry, access to all public areas, toilet facilities

General description:
Collections representing the human and natural history of Oxfordshire, with particular strengths in agricultural history and archaeology, and the history of wheelwrighting.
Information services:
Special visitor services: Guided tours..
Collections:
Church Street, Oxford. Mediaeval material from 1970s excavations, mediaeval, c. 3000 items
Dew collection. Social history and archaeology collected in the Heyford area, Roman-19th century, c. 2000 items
Packer collection, local photographs, 1850-1960, 100,000 items
Taunt collection, local photographs, 1850-1920, 100,000 items
Shuffrey Collection - Topographical watercolours and drawings by Oxford artist, James Allen Shuffrey, c. 1900-1930
Catalogues:
Catalogue for part of the collections is only available in-house.

Internet home pages:
http://www.oxfordshire-collections.org.uk

2207
PACKWOOD HOUSE

Lapworth, Solihull, Warwickshire, B94 6AT

Tel: 01564 783294
Fax: 01564 782706
Email: packwood@nationaltrust.org.uk

Organisation type and purpose: National organisation, registered charity (charity number 205846), historic building, house or site, suitable for ages: 8+.
Parent body:
The National Trust (West Midlands)
West Midlands Regional Office, tel: 01743 708100

Enquiries to: Manager
Access:
Access to staff: By letter, by telephone, by fax, by email
Access for disabled people: toilet facilities
Other restrictions: Drop-off point. 2 manual wheelchairs available. Accessible entrance through garden door. Ground floor largely accessible. Great Hall can be viewed from the

Long Gallery doorway. No access to other floors. Steps to shop entrance.

General description:
The house, originally 16th century, is a fascinating 20th century evocation of domestic Tudor architecture. Created by Graham Baron Ash, its interiors were restored during the period between the world wars and contain a fine collection of 16th century textiles and furniture. The gardens have renowned herbaceous borders and a famous collection of yews.

Information services:
Braille guide. Touch list.
Front-carrying baby slings for loan.
Suitable for school groups. Children's guide. Children's quiz/trail.
Special visitor services: Materials and/or activities for children.
Services for disabled people: For the visually impaired.

Internet home pages:
http://www.nationaltrust.org.uk

2208
PAIGNTON AND DARTMOUTH STEAM RAILWAY
Queens Park Station, Torbay Road, Paignton, Devon, TQ4 6AF

Tel: 01803 553760
Fax: 01803 664313
Email: pdsr@talk21.com
Formed: 1973
Formerly: Dart Valley Railway plc (company name)

Organisation type and purpose: Museum. Tourist attraction.

Enquiries to: Information Officer
Access:
Access to staff: By letter, by telephone, by fax, Internet web pages
Hours: Selected dates Mar, Apr, May, Oct, Dec; Daily Jun to Sep
Access for disabled people: ramped entry, level entry
Other restrictions: Toilet facilities at station

General description:
The preservation and operation of a steam railway on the seven miles of track from Paignton to Kingswear.

Internet home pages:
http://www.paignton-steamrailway.co.uk

2209
PAINSHILL PARK
Painshill Park Trust, Portsmouth Road, Cobham, Surrey, KT11 1JE

Tel: 01932 868113
Fax: 01932 868001
Email: info@painshill.co.uk
Formed: 1981

Organisation type and purpose: Local government body, registered charity (charity number 284944), historic building, house or site. 18th century landscape garden.

Enquiries to: Marketing Manager
Access:
Access to staff: By letter, by telephone, by fax, by email, visitors by prior appointment
Access for disabled people: Parking provided, ramped entry, toilet facilities
Other restrictions: Access to restricted areas.

General description:
The garden was created by the Hon. Charles Hamilton, between 1738 and 1773. Since 1981 it has undergone faithful restoration by the Trust. It features a series of scenes and vistas set around a 14 acre meandering lake, including a Gothic temple, ruined abbey, Chinese bridge, Turkish tent, Gothic tower, and crystal grotto. Nothing has been planted which would not have been available to Charles Hamilton. Buildings have been restored using only traditional techniques. The Europa Nostra Medal was awarded for 'Exemplary Restoration'.

Information services:
Helpline available, tel no: 01932 864674.
Special visitor services: Guided tours, materials and/or activities for children.
Education services: Group education facilities, resources for Key Stages 1 and 2..

Collections:
Mausoleum (ruined triumphal arch), Sabine Statue - after Giambologna 1583, sculpture by Ivor Abrahams 1991
Cast iron water wheel and pumping mechanism c. 1830

2210
PAISLEY MUSEUM AND ART GALLERIES
High Street, Paisley, Renfrewshire, PA1 2BA

Tel: 0141 889 3151
Fax: 0141 889 9240
Email: museums.els@renfrewshire.gov.uk
Formed: 1871

Organisation type and purpose: Local government body, museum, art gallery.

Other addresses:
Coats Observatory
49 Oakshaw Street, Paisley, PA1 2DR, tel: 0141 889 2013
Renfrew Museum
Brown Institute, 41 Canal Street, Renfrew, tel: 0141 886 3149, fax: 0141 886 2300

Enquiries to: Principal Officer
Other contacts: Keepers of: Textiles, Social History, Art, Natural History
Access:
Access to staff: By letter, by telephone, by fax, by email, in person, Internet web pages
Hours: Tue to Sat, 1000 to 1700; Sun, 1400 to 1700
Closed Mon except public holidays
Access for disabled people: ramped entry, toilet facilities
Other restrictions: Access restricted to some parts of the building

General description:
The general collection illustrates the local industrial and natural history of Paisley and Renfrew district. The art collection includes a large number of studio ceramics, and also 19th and 20th century Scottish paintings. Features a world famous collection of Paisley shawls.

Collections:
Social history. Ethnography, c. 200 items
Social history. Egyptology, c. 300 items
Social history. Coats collection. 19th and 20th century
Art. 20th century Scottish paintings, contemporary Scottish drawings, 19th century French, c. 3000 items
Historical photographs. Photographic prints, lantern slides and glass negatives, mostly of local interest. Some significant Scottish and foreign ethnography from late 19th century. ca. 1860 onwards, c. 10,000 items
Shawl pattern books

Printed publications:
The Illustrated History of the Paisley Shawl (Reilly V, £14.99 plus p&p)

Internet home pages:
http://www.renfrewshire.gov.uk

2211
PAKENHAM WATERMILL
Pakenham, Suffolk

Tel: 01359 270570

Organisation type and purpose: Historic building, house or site.
Access:
Access to staff: By telephone

General description:
18th century working mill off the A143.

Information services:
Pond dipping for school parties.
Special visitor services: Guided tours..

2212
PAKENHAM WINDMILL
Pakenham, Suffolk

Tel: 01359 230277

Organisation type and purpose: Historic building, house or site.

General description:
19th century tower mill recently restored to full working order.

2213
PALACE STABLES HERITAGE CENTRE
The Palace, Palace Demesne, Armagh, BT60 4EN

Tel: 028 3752 9629
Fax: 028 3752 9630
Formed: 1992

Organisation type and purpose: Historic building, house or site, suitable for ages: all ages.

Enquiries to: Administrator
Other contacts: Manager
Access:
Access to staff: By letter
Access to building, collections or gallery: No prior appointment required
Access for disabled people: Parking provided, level entry, access to all public areas, toilet facilities

General description:
The Palace Stables is a picturesque Georgian building which encloses a cobbled courtyard set in the undulating parkland of the palace demesne. The 'Day in the Life' exhibition portrays a typical day in the stables and palace on the 23rd of July 1776. The exhibition is portrayed via life-like models, an audio commentary and spectacular colourful murals.

Information services:
Special visitor services: Guided tours, tape recorded guides, materials and/or activities for children.
Education services: Group education facilities, resources for Key Stages 1 and 2, 3, 4 and Further or Higher Education.
Services for disabled people: For the visually impaired; for the hearing impaired; displays and/or information at wheelchair height.

Collections:
Archbishop Robinson, Georgian artefacts

2214
PALACERIGG HOUSE MUSEUM

Closed, date of change, 2001

2215
PALLANT HOUSE GALLERY
9 North Pallant, Chichester, West Sussex, PO19 1TJ

Tel: 01243 774557
Fax: 01243 536038
Email: pallant@pallant.co.uk
Formed: 1982

Organisation type and purpose: Registered charity (charity number 293093), art gallery. Historic house.

Links with:
Friends of Pallant House
9 North Pallant, Chichester, PO19 1TJ, tel: 01243 538524, fax: 01243 536038

Enquiries to: Public Relations Manager
Direct email: publicity@pallant.co.uk
Access:
Access to staff: By letter, by fax, by email, visitors by prior appointment

continued overleaf

General description:
20th century British art, includes work by Piper, Sutherland, Nicholson, Sickert.
Also work by Hans Feibusch and a recreation of his London studio.
Paintings in collection and temporary exhibitions displayed in an historic Queen Anne town house, each room reflects a period and the domestic history of the house which also has a Georgian walled garden.
Collections:
Hussey bequest, 20th century British art, 1910-1960, 60 plus items
Art Library, mainly 20th century art, plus some 18th century architecture, 10,000 plus items
Geoffrey Freeman collection, world's largest collection of porcelain from the Bow factory, 1749-1775
Kearley bequest, 20th century British art with some international artists, 1910-1960, 70 plus items
Catalogues:
Catalogue for library is in-house only. Catalogue for all of the collections is only available in-house.
Publications list:
is available in hard copy.

Internet home pages:
http://www.pallanthousegallery.com

2216
PAPPLEWICK PUMPING STATION
Longdale Lane, Ravenshead, Nottinghamshire, NG15 9AJ

Tel: 0115 963 2938
Fax: 0115 955 7172
Email: secretary @papplewickpumpingstation.co.uk
Formed: 1974

Organisation type and purpose: Registered charity (charity number 503462), museum.
Preservation and operation of late Victorian waterworks.
Supported by:
Papplewick Association
5 Ranskill Gardens, Top Valley, Nottingham, NG5 9DX, tel: 0115 955 7172, fax: 0115 955 7172, email/website: secretary@papplewickpumpingstation.co.uk

Enquiries to: Secretary
Access:
Access to staff: By letter, by telephone, by fax, by email, in person, charges made to all users, Internet web pages
Hours: Bank Holidays, Sundays and other times by appointment
Access for disabled people: Parking provided, toilet facilities

General description:
One of Britain's finest Victorian waterworks, complete and in working order. Includes two 1884 James Watt beam engines; six Lancashire boilers. Displayed in an ornate engine house, and set in formal Victorian grounds. This represents a unique example of industrial archaeology. Beam pumping engines in steam, original forge and colliery winding engine, model boats, steam railway.
Information services:
Special visitor services: Guided tours..
Collections:
Complete set of original tools, and maintenance equipment in a steam-powered workshop
Printed publications:
Guide books and leaflets

Internet home pages:
http://www.papplewickpumpingstation.co.uk
Information on museum.

2217
PARADISE MILL
Park Lane, Macclesfield, Cheshire, SK11 6JY

Tel: 01625 618228
Email: silkmuseum@tiscali.co.uk

Organisation type and purpose: Registered charity (charity number 519521), museum, historic building, house or site, suitable for ages: 5+.
Parent body:
Macclesfield Museums Trust

Enquiries to: Director

General description:
Exhibition and displays illustrate a typical family business specialising in silk hand-woven tie cloths on Jacquards with ancillary silk machinery. Room settings are as they were in the 1930s.
Collections:
26 Jacquard handlooms in original location 1860.

Internet home pages:
http://www.silk-macclesfield.org
Information, access to museums, calender of events, education, publications, and news of the Friends of Macclesfield Silk Heritage.

2218
PARC GLYNLLIFON
Clynnog Road, Caernarfon, Gwynedd, LL54 5DY

Tel: 01286 830222
Fax: 01286 830222
Email: gwawrr@gwynedd.gov.uk
Full name: Oriel Parc Glynllifon
Formed: 1987

Organisation type and purpose: Local government body, art gallery, suitable for ages: 5+.

Enquiries to: Secretary
Access:
Access to staff: By letter, by telephone, by fax, by email, in person, visitors by prior appointment
Access to building, collections or gallery: No prior appointment required
Hours: Daily, 1000 to 1800
Access for disabled people: Parking provided, ramped entry, level entry, access to all public areas, toilet facilities

General description:
The mansion and the land surrounding the park are owned by Glynllifon College and are not open to the public. The estate has its origins in the military activities of Thomas Wynne who built Fort Williamsburg in 1776. He formed the Caernarvonshire Militia and the Loyal Newborough Volunteer Infantry, and George III bestowed upon him the title of Lord Newborough in 1776. The Fort can be visited in a tour of the park starting with the workshops built for the 3rd Lord Newborough in the mid 19th century. The workshops are now occupied by local craftspeople and visitors may enjoy a visit, and watch contemporary artists and craftsmen at work. A craft shop and gallery which concentrate on craftwork produced in Wales. A historical exhibition is also available free of charge to visitors.
Information services:
Special visitor services: Guided tours, tape recorded guides.
Education services: Group education facilities..
Collections:
A historical exhibition which includes information on Glynllifon Estate, its Grade I Victorian Gardens, Newborough Family and old craft workshops
Printed publications:
Promotional leaflet (available direct)

Internet home pages:
http://www.gwynedd.gov.uk/arts

2219
PARC HOWARD MUSEUM
Parc Howard, Fienfoel Road, Llanelli, Carmarthenshire, SA15 3AS

Tel: 01554 772029
Full name: Parc Howard Museum and Gallery
Formed: 1911

Organisation type and purpose: Local government body, museum, art gallery.
Collect and display artefacts from Llanelli area.
Parent body:
Carmarthenshire Museum Service
Carmarthenshire County Museum, Abergwili, Carmarthen, SA31 2JG, tel: 01267 231691, fax: 01267 223830, email/website: cdelaney@carmarthenshire.gov.uk

Enquiries to: Heritage Manager
Direct tel: 01267 231691
Direct fax: 01267 223830
Direct email: cdelaney@carmarthenshire.gov.uk
Other contacts: (1) Parks Manager (2) Senior Curator for (1) gardens.
Access:
Access to staff: By letter, by telephone, by fax, by email, visitors by prior appointment, Internet web pages
Access to building, collections or gallery: No prior appointment required
Hours: Oct to Mar: Mon to Fri, 1100 to 1300 and 1400 to 1600; Sat, Sun, 1400 to 1600
Apr to Sep: Mon to Fri, 1100 to 1300 and 1400 to 1800; Sat, Sun, 1400 to 1800

General description:
A collection of industrial, civic and social artefacts with a strong collection of Llanelli pottery and various ceramics, local artists including J D Innes, local history.
Information services:
Group education services by appointment.
Special visitor services: Materials and/or activities for children.
Education services: Group education facilities, resources for Key Stages 1 and 2..
Collections:
Llanelli pottery, local ceramics, 1840-1920, 600 items

2220
PARK GALLERY, THE
Callender Park, Falkirk, Strathclyde, FK1 1YR

Tel: 01324 503770
Fax: 01324 503771
Email: callendar.house@falkirk.gov.uk

Organisation type and purpose: Local government body, art gallery, suitable for ages: all ages.
Parent body:
Falkirk Council

Enquiries to: Visual Arts and Crafts Development Officer
Direct tel: 01324 503788
Access:
Access to staff: By letter, by telephone, by fax, by email, in person
Hours: Mon to Fri, 1000 to 1700
Other restrictions: Professional staff available Mon to Fri; Gallery staff, Mon to Sat.
Access to building, collections or gallery: No prior appointment required
Hours: Mon to Sat, 1000 to 1700
Access for disabled people: Parking provided, ramped entry, access to all public areas, toilet facilities

General description:
Contemporary art exhibitions.
Information services:
Education services: Group education facilities, resources for Key Stages 1 and 2, 3 and Further or Higher Education.
Services for disabled people: For the visually impaired.
Collections:
Contemporary visual arts and documentary art

Internet home pages:
http://www.falkirkmuseums.demon.co.uk/museums/museums.htm
http://www.falkirkmuseums.demon.co.uk/park/park.html
Site location and what's on information.

2221
PASSMORE EDWARDS MUSEUM
See - North Woolwich Old Station Museum

2222
PATTERSON HERITAGE MUSEUM AND FAMILY HISTORY CENTRE, THE
2-6 Station Approach, Birchington-on-Sea, Kent, CT7 9RD

Tel: 01843 841649
Formed: 1994
Formed from: Pembroke Lodge Museum & Family History Centre

Organisation type and purpose: Independently owned, museum, research organisation. Educational, cultural.

Enquiries to: Curator
Access:
Access to staff: By letter, by telephone, in person
Hours: Tue to Sat, 1000 to 1200 and 1400 to 1600
Access to building, collections or gallery: No prior appointment required
Hours: Tue to Sat, 1000 to 1200 and 1400 to 1600

General description:
Paintings, family history.
Information services:
Consultations and guidance for research (family history) service available.
Special visitor services: Tape recorded guides..

2223
PATTERSON'S SPADE MILL
751 Antrim Road, Templepatrick, Co Antrim, BT39 0AP

Tel: 028 9443 3619
Fax: 028 9443 3619
Formed: 1994

Organisation type and purpose: National organisation, registered charity (charity number 205846), museum, historic building, house or site.
Parent body:
National Trust Office for Northern Ireland
Rowallane House, Saintfield, Ballynahinch, Co Down, BT24 7LH, tel: 020 9751 0721, fax: 028 9751 1242
Other addresses:
The National Trust
Rowallane House, Saintfield, Ballynahinch, County Down, BT24 7LH

Enquiries to: Manager
Access:
Access to staff: By letter, by telephone, by fax
Access for disabled people: Parking provided, ramped entry, level entry, access to all public areas, toilet facilities
Other restrictions: Viewing platform: ramped access, wheelchair.

General description:
Last surviving and working water-driven spade mill in Ireland. An historic 19th century workshop setting. Guided tour of traditional spade-making, including history and culture of the humble turf and garden spade. Working demonstrations and hand-made Patterson's Spades for sale.
Information services:
Machinery sounds, some items and raw materials may be touched.
Booked school groups welcome.
Special visitor services: Guided tours, tape recorded guides, materials and/or activities for children.
Education services: Group education facilities, resources for Key Stages 1 and 2, 3, 4 and Further or Higher Education.
Services for disabled people: For the visually impaired; for the hearing impaired; displays and/or information at wheelchair height.
Catalogues:
Catalogue for library is published and is on-line. Catalogue for all of the collections is published and is also on-line.
Publications list:
is available in hard copy and online.

2224
PAXTON HOUSE
The Paxton Trust, Berwick-upon-Tweed, Northumberland, TD15 1SZ

Tel: 01289 386291
Fax: 01289 386660
Email: info@paxtonhouse.com
Formed: 1992

Organisation type and purpose: Registered charity, museum, art gallery, historic building, house or site.
Parent body:
National Galleries of Scotland
Dean Gallery, Belford Road, Edinburgh, EH4 3DS, tel: 0131 624 6200, fax: 0131 3433250, email: enquiries@natgalscot.ac.uk

Enquiries to: Director
Other contacts: Administrator
Access:
Access to staff: By letter, by telephone, by fax, by email, in person, visitors by prior appointment, Internet web pages
Access to building, collections or gallery: No prior appointment required
Hours: Easter to 31 Oct: daily, 1000 to 1730
Access for disabled people: Parking provided, toilet facilities
Other restrictions: Level entry to facilities; lift available to exhibition rooms and 1st floor house.

General description:
18th century Palladian Country Mansion which is fully furnished. It has a gallery where more than 70 paintings from the collection of the National Galleries of Scotland are displayed.
Collections:
18th century Chippendale Furniture, 50 items
19th century Trotter Furniture, 20 items
Paintings, Out-station of National Galleries of Scotland. 17th-19th century
Catalogues:
Catalogue for all of the collections is only available in-house.

Internet home pages:
http://www.paxtonhouse.com/
http://www.scotsborders.org.uk

2225
PAYCOCKE'S
West Street, Coggeshall, Colchester, Essex, CO6 1NS

Tel: 01376 561305
Fax: 01376 561305

Organisation type and purpose: National organisation, registered charity (charity number 205846), historic building, house or site.
Parent body:
The National Trust (East of England)
East Anglia Regional Office, tel: 0870 609 5388

Enquiries to: Manager
Access:
Access to staff: By letter, by telephone, by fax

General description:
A merchant's house, dating from c.1500 and containing unusually rich panelling and wood carving. Coggeshall was famous for its lace, examples of which are displayed inside the house, and there is also a very attractive cottage garden.
Information services:
Services for disabled people: For the visually impaired.

Internet home pages:
http://www.nationaltrust.org.uk

2226
PEACE MUSEUM
10 Piece Hall Yard, Bradford, West Yorkshire, BD1 1PJ

Tel: 01274 780241 or 754009
Fax: 01274 752618
Email: peacemuseum@bradford.gov.uk
Formed: 1998

Organisation type and purpose: Independently owned, registered charity (charity number 1061102), museum, suitable for ages: 8+.
Newsletter Distribution:
Friends of The Peace Museum
Address for correspondence:
Peace Museum Office
Jacobs Well, Manchester Road, Bradford, BD1 5RW, tel: 01274 754009, fax: 01274 752618, email/website: peacemuseum@bradford.gov.uk

Enquiries to: Development Officer
Access:
Access to staff: By letter, by telephone, by fax, by email, Internet web pages
Access to building, collections or gallery: Prior appointment required
Hours: Wed, Fri, 1100 to 1500
Other restrictions: Other times by appointment on 01274 754009.
Free entrance.

General description:
Unique in the UK, covering peace history, non-violence and conflict resolution, it is worth ascending the sixty stairs from a narrow Bradford centre street. It displays personal, community, national and international peacemaking; Peace Movements of 20th century, Nobel Peace Prize Centenary, Women & Pacifism in WWI, Anti-Nuclear Issues. Its educational outreach work includes four free travelling exhibitions and educational programme and an A-V website. Collection contributions very welcome.
Information services:
Special visitor services: Guided tours, materials and/or activities for children.
Education services: Group education facilities, resources for Key Stages 1 and 2, 3, 4 and Further or Higher Education..
Collections:
Peace movement artefacts, banners, posters, art works, photos
Catalogues:
Catalogue for all of the collections is available in-house and part is on-line.
Publications list:
is available in hard copy.
Printed publications:
Nobel Peace Prize Centenary - Exhibition and Education booklets
Women & Pacifism in WWI - Exhibition and booklet
Newsletter (3 times a year, direct, £10 per annum)

Internet home pages:
http://www.peacemuseum.org.uk
Part of collection; travelling exhibition; educational worksheets; general information; virtual tour of gallery.

2227
PEAK DISTRICT MINING MUSEUM AND TEMPLE MINE

The Pavilion, Matlock Bath, Derbyshire, DE4 3NR

Tel: 01629 583834
Email: mail@peakmines.co.uk
Acronym or abbreviation: PDMHS
Formed: 1978

Organisation type and purpose: Independently owned, registered charity (charity number 504662), museum, suitable for ages: 5+.
Parent body:
Peak District Mines Historical Society Limited
Peak District Mining Museum, Matlock Bath, Derbyshire, DE4 3NR

Enquiries to: Project Leader
Access:
Access to staff: By letter, by telephone, by email
Hours: Mon to Fri; 1000 to 1600
Other restrictions: Open daily except for Christmas Day.
Access for disabled people: level entry, access to all public areas

General description:
Lead mining.
Publications list:
is available in hard copy.
Printed publications:
Bulletin (for purchase)
A Glossary of Derbyshire Lead Mining Terms (Rieuwerts J H, £14)
Derbyshire Black Marble (Tomlinson J M, £9.95)
Laws and Customs of the Derbyshire Lead Mines - a summary of this ancient legal system (Rieuwerts J H, £2)
Lead and Lead Mining in Derbyshire - The 1881-2 survey (Stokes A H, new reprint edition, £5.95)
Minerals of the Peak District - comprehensive catalogue of nearly a hundred minerals (Ford T D, et al, £12)

2228
PEAK RAIL

Matlock Station, Matlock, Derbyshire, DE4 3NA

Tel: 01629 580381
Fax: 01629 760645
Email: peakrail@peakrail.co.uk

Organisation type and purpose: Membership association (membership is by subscription), voluntary organisation.

Enquiries to: Managing Director
Other contacts: Joint Managing Director
Access:
Access to staff: By letter, by fax, by email
Access for disabled people: Parking provided, ramped entry, toilet facilities

General description:
Preserved steam railway.

Internet home pages:
http://www.peakrail.co.uk
History, development, details of rolling stock, services and special events.

2229
PECKOVER HOUSE

North Brink, Wisbech, Cambridgeshire, PE13 1JR

Tel: 01945 583463
Fax: 01945 583463
Email: peckover@nationaltrust.org.uk

Organisation type and purpose: National organisation, registered charity (charity number 205846), historic building, house or site, suitable for ages: 8+.
Parent body:
The National Trust (East of England)
East Anglia Regional Office

Enquiries to: Manager
Access:
Access to staff: By letter, by telephone, by fax, by email
Access for disabled people: toilet facilities
Other restrictions: Designated parking. 1 manual wheelchair available, booking essential. 1 single-seater powered mobility vehicle, booking essential. Steps to entrance. Ground floor largely inaccessible. No access to other floors. Steps to shop entrance. Ramped entrance to restaurant. Grounds largely accessible. Recommended route map.

General description:
This outstanding 0.8ha (2 acre) Victorian garden includes an orangery, summer houses, roses, herbaceous borders, fernery, croquet lawn and 17th century thatched barn, which is available for weddings and functions. The town house, built c. 1722, is renowned for its very fine plaster and wood rococo decoration. Displays on the Peckover family.
Information services:
Full events programme.
Handling collection. Scented plants.
Front-carrying baby slings for loan.
Suitable for school groups. Hands-on activities. Family guide.
Booked groups welcome when house open and at other times by appointment.
Special visitor services: Materials and/or activities for children.
Education services: Group education facilities.
Services for disabled people: For the visually impaired.

Internet home pages:
http://www.nationaltrust.org.uk

2230
PEMBROKE CASTLE TRUST

Castle Terrace, Pembroke, Pembrokeshire, SA71 4LA

Tel: 01646 681510
Fax: 01646 622260
Email: pembroke.castle@talk21.com
Formed: 1959

Organisation type and purpose: Independently owned, registered charity (charity number 257729), historic building, house or site, suitable for ages: 5+.

Enquiries to: Manager
Access:
Access to staff: By telephone
Access to building, collections or gallery: No prior appointment required
Access for disabled people: ramped entry
Other restrictions: Parking: dropping off point at castle entrance, parking close by, flat gravelled paths around the grounds.

General description:
A 12th century Norman Castle which has been sympathetically restored, and houses a number of tableaux and displays illustrating the development of the castle, life in the Middle Ages. Pembroke Castle is the birthplace of Henry VII and an account of the Rise of the Tudor Dynasty is vividly told.
General information may be accessed on the website, more specialised information from the Guide Book or specialist books sold in the gift shop.
Information services:
Education services: Resources for Key Stages 1 and 2 and 3..
Printed publications:
Pembroke Castle Guide Book (Ludlow N, £2)
William Marshal (Crouch D, £17.99)
Henry VII (Lockyer R and Thrush A, £17.99)
The Making of the Tudor Dynasty (Griffiths R A and Thomas R S, £10.99)
Wales Castles & Historic Places (CADW, £5.95)
A Company of Forts (Davis P, £9.95)
Pembrokeshire Castles and Strongholds (Fitzgerald M, £4.95)

Internet home pages:
http://www.pembrokecastle.co.uk
General information

2231
PEMBROKE LODGE MUSEUM & FAMILY HISTORY CENTRE

See - Patterson Heritage Museum and Family History Centre

2232
PENDEEN COMMUNITY HERITAGE

See - Geevor Tin Mine Heritage Centre

2233
PENDEEN LIGHTHOUSE

Pendeen Watch, Pendeen, Penzance, Cornwall, TR19 7ED

Tel: 01736 788418

Managed by:
The Trevithick Trust
Tel: 01209 210900
Owned by:
Trinity House

Enquiries to: Manager
Access:
Access to staff: By letter, by telephone
Access to building, collections or gallery: No prior appointment required
Hours: Easter, May and Spring Bank Holidays, Sun to Sat 1000 to 1700;
July and Aug, Sun to Sat, 1100 to 1700

General description:
Built in 1900, this dramatically positioned lighthouse is open with its engine room containing the last surviving 12 inch siren in England.
A grade II listed building, in an area of outstanding natural beauty, Heritage coast, area of great scientific value, area of great historic value, and environmentally sensitve area.
Information services:
Special visitor services: Guided tours..

Internet home pages:
http://www.trevithicktrust.com

2234
PENDENNIS CASTLE

Falmouth, Cornwall, TR11 4LP

Tel: 01326 316594
Fax: 01326 319911
Email: customers@english-heritage.org.uk
Formed: 1954

Organisation type and purpose: National organisation, historic building, house or site, suitable for ages: 5+.
Parent body:
English Heritage (South West Region)
Tel: 0117 975 0700, fax: 0117 975 0701
Other addresses:
English Heritage
23 Savile Row, London, W1S 2ET, tel: 020 7973 3000

Enquiries to: Custodian
Access:
Access to staff: By letter, by fax, by email
Hours: Mon to Fri, 1000 to 1600
Access to building, collections or gallery: No prior appointment required
Hours: 29 Mar to 30 Sep: daily, 1000 to 1800,1 to 31 Oct: daily, 1000 to 1700,1 Nov to 28 Mar: daily, 1000 to 1600
Other restrictions: Closed 24 to 26 Dec and 1 Jan
Opening times are subject to change, for up-

to-date information contact English Heritage by phone or visit the website.
Access for disabled people: Parking provided
Other restrictions: Access to grounds and parts of keep only.

General description:
Pendennis and its sister, St Mawes Castle, are the Cornish end of a chain of castles built by Henry VIII along the south coast. Few of the castles have seen active service, but Pendennis was continually adapted over the following 400 years to meet new enemies. Strengthened prior to the Civil War, Pendennis was host to the future Charles II in 1646, who sailed from there to the Isles of Scilly. It withstood five months of siege before becoming the penultimate Royalist garrison to surrender on the mainland.
Pendennis was re-armed during the late 19th and early 20th centuries, seeing action during the Second World War.
Information services:
Education services: Group education facilities..
Collections:
Coastal defence artillery and related equipment from 1540 to 1940
Historic artillery, mainly 1780-1945
Small arms and militaria, 1840-1945, 400 items
Period Tudor and late Victorian interiors and some WWII rooms

Internet home pages:
http://www.english-heritage.org.uk

2235
PENDLE HERITAGE CENTRE

Colne Road, Barrowford, Nelson, Lancashire, BB9 6JQ

Tel: 01282 661704
Fax: 01282 611718
Email: john.miller@htnw.co.uk
Formed: 1978

Organisation type and purpose: Registered charity (charity number 508300), art gallery.

Enquiries to: Chief Executive
Access:
Access to staff: By letter, by telephone, by fax, by email, letter of introduction required, charges made to all users
Access to building, collections or gallery: Prior appointment required
Hours: Daily, 1000 to 1700
Other restrictions: Closed 25 Dec.
Access for disabled people: Parking provided, ramped entry, toilet facilities

General description:
Local architecture and history.
Information services:
Special visitor services: Guided tours, tape recorded guides..

2236
PENDON MUSEUM TRUST LIMITED

Long Wittenham, Abingdon, Oxfordshire, OX14 4QD

Tel: 01865 408143 and 01865 407365 (answer phone)
Formed: 1954
Formerly: Pendon Museum of Miniature Landscape and Transport

Organisation type and purpose: Membership association (membership is by election or invitation), voluntary organisation, registered charity (charity number 313614), museum, suitable for ages: 8+.

Enquiries to: Public Relations Manager
Other contacts: Marketing Convenor for information on special activities.
Access:
Access to staff: By letter, by telephone
Hours: Staffed and administered by volunteers; most weekday mornings from 1000
Access to building, collections or gallery: No prior appointment required
Hours: Sat, Sun, 1400 to 1700 (except Dec); Wed in Jul and Aug;
Bank Holidays/Easter Weekends: 1100 to 1700

General description:
Vale of White Horse (Berkshire, Oxon, Wiltshire) especially 1920s to 1930s; vernacular architecture; farming; railways, especially the GWR.
Information services:
Library available for reference (for conditions see Access above)
Library usually available to Friends of the Museum; written requests for information.
Special visitor services: Guided tours, tape recorded guides, materials and/or activities for children.
Education services: Group education facilities..
Collections:
General library on railways, especially GWR; architecture and farming
Wide collection of photographs of buildings in Vale of White Horse in 1920s and 1930s and GWR, especially those of Founder, Roye England
Catalogues:
Catalogue for library is in-house only. Catalogue for part of the collections is only available in-house.
Printed publications:
Publications available direct or from Wild Swan
Colour Guide (£1)
Individual members have produced books on various modelling topics
Building and Layout (Williams S)
Coaches (Williams S)
Cottages (Pilton C)
In Search of a Dream (Williams S)
Locos (Williams G)
Electronic and video products:
Video (for sale, direct)

Address for ordering publications:
Printed publications:
Wild Swan Publications
Hagbourne Road, Didcot

Internet home pages:
http://www.pendonmuseum.com
A general survey of the museum; events; opening hours etc.

2237
PENRHYN CASTLE

Bangor, Gwynedd, LL57 4HN

Tel: 01248 353084
Fax: 01248 371281
Email: penrhyncastle@nationaltrust.org.uk
Formed: 1951

Organisation type and purpose: National organisation, registered charity (charity number 205846), museum, suitable for ages: all ages.
Heritage conservation.
Parent body:
The National Trust Office for Wales
Trinity Square, Llandudno, LL30 2DE, tel: 01492 860123, fax: 01492 860233

Enquiries to: Property Manager
Access:
Access to staff: By letter, by telephone, by fax, visitors by prior appointment
Access to building, collections or gallery: No prior appointment required
Hours: Castle: Apr to Jun, Sep and Oct, Wed to Mon, 1200 to 1700; Jul and Aug, Wed to Mon, 1100 to 1700
Grounds: Apr to Jun, Sep and Oct, Wed to Mon, 1100 to 1700; Jul and Aug, Wed to Mon, 1000 to 1700;
Other restrictions: Victorian Kitchen entry as castle, but last admission 1645. Last audio tour 1600.
Access for disabled people: ramped entry, toilet facilities
Other restrictions: Parking 200m from castle, alternative arrangements can be made on request. Dropoff point. 3 manual wheelchairs available. 1 two-seater powered mobility vehicle, booking essential. Ground floor fully accessible. Photograph album. Lift to first floor stable block gallery and museums. Ramped entrance to shop. Level entrance to tea-room.

General description:
This dramatic neo-Norman fantasy castle sits between Snowdonia and the Menai Strait. Built by Thomas Hopper between 1820 and 1845 for the wealthy Pennant family, who made their fortune from Jamaican sugar and Welsh slate, the castle is crammed with fascinating things such as a one-ton slate bed made for Queen Victoria. Hopper also designed its interior with elaborate carvings, plasterwork and mock-Norman furniture. The castle contains an outstanding collection of paintings. The Victorian kitchen and other servants' rooms including scullery, larders and chef's sitting room have been restored to reveal the preparations for the banquet for the Prince of Wales' visit in 1894. The stable block houses an industrial railway museum, a countryside exhibition, a model railway museum and a superb dolls' museum displaying a large collection of 19th- and 20th century dolls. The 18.2ha (45 acres) of grounds include parkland, an extensive exotic tree and shrub collection, and a Victorian walled garden.
Information services:
Specialist guided tours by arrangement
Braille guide. Audio guide. Touch list. Sympathetic Hearing Scheme.
Frontcarrying baby slings for loan. Model railway museum and dolls
museum.
Suitable for school groups. Education room/centre. Audio guide. Hands-on activities. Children's guide. Children's quiz/trail. Adult study days.
Special visitor services: Guided tours, tape recorded guides.
Education services: Group education facilities.
Services for disabled people: For the visually impaired; for the hearing impaired.
Collections:
Carvings, stained glass windows, handmade William Morris wallpapers
One of the best collections of paintings in Wales including Dutch and Italian masters
One ton slate bed, made for Queen Victoria
Egyptology
Historic railway tracks and nameplates
Textiles

Internet home pages:
http://www.nationaltrust.org.uk

2238
PENRHYN CASTLE INDUSTRIAL RAILWAY MUSEUM

Penrhyn Castle, Bangor, Gwynedd, LL57 4HN

Tel: 01248 353084 ext 254
Fax: 01248 371281

Organisation type and purpose: Museum, suitable for ages: all ages.
Heritage conservation.
Parent body:
The National Trust
Trinity Square, Llandudno, LL30 2DE, tel: 01492 860123, fax: 01492 860233

Enquiries to: Railway Museum Engineer
Access:
Access to staff: By letter, by telephone, by fax, in person

General description:
The stable block of Penrhyn Castle houses an industrial railway museum, a countryside exhibition, and a model railway museum.

Internet home pages:
http://www.nationaltrust.org.uk

2239
PENRITH MUSEUM
Robinson's School, Middlegate, Penrith, Cumbria, CA11 7PT

Tel: 01768 212228
Fax: 01768 891759
Email: museum@eden.gov.uk
Formed: 1990

Organisation type and purpose: Local government body, museum.
Explores history and culture of Penrith & Eden Valley through permanent and temporary displays including some contemporary arts interest.
Parent body:
Eden District Council
Email: www.eden.gov.uk
Supported by:
Friends of Penrith Museum

Enquiries to: Curator
Direct tel: 01768 212228
Access:
Access to staff: By letter, by telephone, by email, Internet web pages

General description:
The museum displays artefacts pertaining to the history of the Penrith and Eden district, and its geology, archaeology, social and industrial history. Domestic bygones illustrate the everyday life of the area. The markets and trades are described, and illustrated by exhibits. Early education in Penrith is featured in a building which was a school for 300 years.
Collections:
Archaeology, prints and drawings, photographs, documents of local interest
Geological collection of specimens including many from Cumbria
Catalogues:
Catalogue for all of the collections is only available in-house.
Printed publications:
Penrith: An Historical Record in Photographs

Internet home pages:
http://www.eden.gov.uk

2240
PENSHURST PLACE AND GARDENS
Penshurst, Tonbridge, Kent, TN11 8DG

Tel: 01892 870307
Fax: 01892 870866
Email: enquiries@penshurstplace.com
Formed: 1341

Organisation type and purpose: Independently owned, historic building, house or site, suitable for ages: 5+.

Enquiries to: Public Relations Manager
Access:
Access to staff: By letter, by telephone, by fax, by email, Internet web pages
Access to building, collections or gallery: No prior appointment required
Hours: Weekends; from 28th Feb, and daily from 28th Mar, until 1 Nov
House: 1200 to 1700
Gardens: 1100 to 1800
Access for disabled people: toilet facilities
Other restrictions: Access to some areas

General description:
The ancestral home and gardens of the Sidney family for over 450 years, it features staterooms containing the family collections of fine furniture; portraits; tapestries; armour; and porcelain from 15th, 16th, 17th and 18th Centuries; also includes a toy museum.
Information services:
Guided tours for groups only, room guides in Braille.
Special visitor services: Materials and/or activities for children.
Services for disabled people: For the visually impaired.

Internet home pages:
http://www.penshurstplace.com

2241
PENWITH GALLERY
Back Road West, St Ives, Cornwall, TR26 1NL

Tel: 01736 795579
Full name: Penwith Society of Arts and Penwith Galleries Limited
Formed: 1949

Organisation type and purpose: Membership association (membership is by subscription, election or invitation), present number of members: 50 full members, unlimited associate members, registered charity (charity number 264162), art gallery.
Furtherance of the arts in Cornwall.

Enquiries to: Curator/Company Secretary
Access:
Access to staff: By letter
Hours: Tue to Sat, 1000 to 1300 and 1430 to 1700
Access to building, collections or gallery: No prior appointment required

General description:
Features a programme of changing exhibitions - most works on loan.
Collections:
Barbara Hepworth, sculpture (marble) - Magic Stone

2242
PEOPLE'S HISTORY MUSEUM, THE
The Pump House, Bridge Street, Manchester, M3 3ER

Tel: 0161 839 6061
Fax: 0161 839 6027
Email: info@peopleshistorymuseum.org.uk
Formed: 1990
Formerly known as: National Museum of Labour History
Registered as: National Museum of Labour History (NMLH), date of change, 2002

Organisation type and purpose: Independently owned, registered charity (charity number 295260), museum, suitable for ages: 5+.
Social history museum, archive and study centre.
Head Office:
People's History Museum
103 Princess Street, Manchester, M1 6DD, tel: 0161 228 7212, fax: 0161 237 5965

Enquiries to: Public Relations Manager
Direct email: duncanc @peopleshistorymuseum.org.uk
Other contacts: Development Officer
Access:
Access to staff: By letter, by telephone, by fax, by email, visitors by prior appointment
Access for disabled people: Parking provided, ramped entry, access to all public areas, toilet facilities
Other restrictions: Parking by prior telephone arrangement.

General description:
History of the Labour Movement.
Information services:
Special visitor services: Guided tours, tape recorded guides, materials and/or activities for children.
Education services: Group education facilities, resources for Key Stages 1 and 2, 3, 4 and Further or Higher Education.
Services for disabled people: Displays and/or information at wheelchair height.
Collections:
Variety of artefacts, pictures, prints, photographs, books, documents, manuscripts
Subject and Collections:
Labour Party Archive
Communist Party Archive
Various other subject matter all relating to social history
Houses a major political banner collection
Catalogues:
Catalogue for all of the collections is on-line.

Internet home pages:
http://www.peopleshistorymuseum.org.uk

2243
PEOPLES MUSEUM OF MEMORABILIA
Newcastle upon Tyne

Closed, date of change, 2002

2244
PEOPLE'S PALACE
Glasgow Green, Glasgow, G40 1AT

Tel: 0141 554 0223
Fax: 0141 550 0892
Formed: 1898

Organisation type and purpose: Local government body, museum, art gallery, historic building, house or site, suitable for ages: all ages.
Parent body:
Glasgow Museums

Enquiries to: Curator
Access:
Access to staff: By letter, by telephone, by fax, in person
Access to building, collections or gallery: No prior appointment required
Hours: Mon to Thu, Sat 1000 to 1700; Fri, Sat 1100 to 1700
Other restrictions: 25, 26 Dec and 1, 2 Jan

General description:
The story of the past hundred years of Glasgow and its people; the Glaswegian pride, the entrepreneurial spirit, the work ethic, the language of the streets, the celebrations, the political and social aspirations, are presented in thematic interactive displays.
Collections:
The collection features memorabilia from 1175 to the present, and is used to tell Glasgow's own story

Internet home pages:
http://www.glasgow.gov.uk

2245
PEOPLE'S STORY, THE
Canongate Tolbooth, 163 Canongate, Royal Mile, Edinburgh, EH8 8BN

Tel: 0131 529 4057
Fax: 0131 556 3439
Formed: 1989

Organisation type and purpose: Local government body, museum.
Social history museum.
Part of:
The City of Edinburgh Museums and Galleries Service
Which is a division of:
The City of Edinburgh Council's Culture & Leisure Department
Tel: 0131 200 2000 (Main council) 0131 529 7844 (Culture & Leisure Department HQ)

Enquiries to: Curator
Other contacts: Marketing and Sponsorship Officer
Access:
Access to staff: By letter, by telephone, by fax, in person, visitors by prior appointment
Hours: Mon to Sat, 1000 to 1700
During Edinburgh Festival: Sun, 1400 to 1700

General description:
The history of the ordinary people of Edinburgh over the last 200 years, with an emphasis on the period within living memory.

Catalogues:
Catalogue for all of the collections is published.
Publications list:
is available in hard copy and online.
Printed publications:
The City of Edinburgh Museums and Galleries Service publishes a wide range of material, a list is available by telephoning 0131 529 3983, and on our website

Address for ordering publications:
Printed publications:
Publishing Department, The City of Edinburgh Museums and Galleries Service
Tel: 0131 529 3983

Internet home pages:
http://www.cac.org.uk
Website for The City of Edinburgh Museums and Galleries Service, it contains: information on each of our 11 venues and their permanent collections; details of current temporary exhibitions; information on past temporary exhibitions; details of selected publications.

2246
PERCIVAL DAVID FOUNDATION OF CHINESE ART
53 Gordon Square, London, WC1H 0PD

Tel: 020 7387 3909
Fax: 020 7383 5163
Acronym or abbreviation: PDF
Formed: 1952

Organisation type and purpose: Museum, university department or institute.
Parent body:
School of Oriental and African Studies
University of London

Enquiries to: Museums Administrator
Access:
Access to staff: Members only, charges to non-members
Hours: Gallery: Mon to Fri, 1030 to 1700
Library: Mon to Fri, 1030 to 1300 and 1400 to 1645
Other restrictions: Students and other suitably qualified persons may use the library, but permission must be sought in advance by writing to the Curator stating the purpose for which a reader's ticket is required.

General description:
Art and culture of China especially ceramics.
Catalogues:
Catalogue for part of the collections is published.
Publications list:
is available in hard copy.
Printed publications:
Exhibition Catalogues
Rare Marks on Chinese Ceramics (Pierson S, 1998)
Designs as Signs: Decoration and Chinese Ceramics (Pierson S, 2001)
Guide to the Collection (Scott R E)
Illustrated Catalogues
Monographs
Proceedings of Colloquies on Art and Archaeology in Asia
Microform products:
Slides of ceramics in the collection

Address for ordering publications:
Printed publications:
The Publications Officer, School of Oriental and African Studies
Thornhaugh Street, Russell Square, London, WC1H 0XG, tel: 020 7898 4065, fax: 020 7436 3844, email: ao1@soas.ac.uk

2247
PERCY PILCHER MUSEUM
Stanford Hall, Lutterworth, Leicestershire, LE17 6DH

Tel: 01788 860250
Fax: 01788 860870
Email: enquiries@stanfordhall.co.uk
Formed: 1958

Organisation type and purpose: Independently owned, museum, historic building, house or site, suitable for ages: 12+.

Enquiries to: Administrator
Access:
Access to staff: By letter, by telephone, by fax, by email, Internet web pages
Hours: Mon to Fri, 1000 to 1700
Access to building, collections or gallery: No prior appointment required
Hours: Easter Sat to end Sep: Sat, Sun and Bank Holiday Mon, 1330 to 1700
Access for disabled people: Parking provided, level entry, toilet facilities
Other restrictions: Access to ground floor of the house is by two flights of stone steps which are 2.25m wide. First flight of nine steps has a large flat platform at the top which can act as a resting-place before going on up the 2nd flight of eleven steps to the Front Door. These steps are not very steep and wheelchairs can be got up them if helpers are available, once at entrance to the house the whole of the ground floor - the 5 principal rooms, the Flying Staircase and the Marble Passage can be seen. Access to the tearooms is impossible for wheelchairs, but tea may be brought out. However, on Open Days, trays of tea can be brought down to the Courtyard. For any disabled people who are part of a pre-booked party it may be possible to set up tables in a downstairs room or in the Rose Garden, weather permitting.
The Grounds, Motorcycle Museum, Flying Machine, Craft Centre (most Sundays), Souvenir Shop and Rose Garden are all accessible to wheelchair users.

General description:
A museum dedicated to Lt Percy Sinclair Pilcher RN who is recognised as England's pioneer aviator and who successfully made and flew four different flying machines. Pilcher was killed in 1899 whilst flying his fourth (1898) machine, 'The Hawk', at Stanford. The main exhibit is a full-size replica of the Hawk.
Collections:
Full-size replica of an 1898 Flying Machine
Pictures and photographs relating to the above
Three other flying machines designed and flown by Percy Pilcher

Internet home pages:
http://www.stanfordhall.co.uk

2248
PERCY TENANTRY VOLUNTEER MUSEUM
See - Alnwick Castle

2249
PERRANZABULOE FOLK MUSEUM
Oddfellows Hall, Ponsmere Road, Perranporth, Cornwall

Organisation type and purpose: Museum.

Enquiries to: Honorary Secretary
Access:
Access to staff: By letter

General description:
A small museum showing the history of the parish through photographs and artefacts. Includes a replica of a Cornish kitchen and several costumes.
Catalogues:
Catalogue for part of the collections is only available in-house.

2250
PERTH MUSEUM & ART GALLERY
78 George Street, Perth, Tayside, PH1 5LB

Tel: 01738 632488
Fax: 01738 443505
Email: museum@pkc.gov.uk
Formed: 1935

Organisation type and purpose: Local government body, museum, art gallery, suitable for ages: 5+.

Enquiries to: Curator
Direct email: mataylor@pkc.gov.uk
Access:
Access to staff: By letter, by telephone, by fax, by email, in person
Hours: Mon to Fri, 1000 to 1700
Access to building, collections or gallery: No prior appointment required
Hours: Mon to Sat, 1000 to 1700
Other restrictions: Closed Christmas to New Year.
Access for disabled people: ramped entry, toilet facilities

General description:
Important collections in the fields of natural science, local history, archaeology and art. Changing exhibition programme.
Collections:
Fergusson Art Collection. Single largest and most important collection in existence of the works of the leading Post- Impressionist painter and Scottish colourist John Duncan Fergusson 1874-1961, includes oil and watercolour paintings, drawings, sketchbooks and sculpture, c. 1890-1961, 2-3000 items
Fergusson Archive. Single largest and most important archive relating to the above including photographs, press cuttings, exhibition catalogues, correspondence, library, etc. c. 1905- 1961, c. 5-10,000 items
Fine art (drawings, prints and paintings). Oil and watercolour paintings, drawings and prints including Italian, Spanish, Dutch, English but principally Scottish artists. Strong emphasis on works by local or locally associated artists, local portraits and local topographical works, 16th-20th century, 2-3000 items
Fine art (sculpture). Small collection of British and European sculpture including works by Lawrence Macdonald, John Gibson and an important group by Sir Alfred Gilbert, 19th-20th century, c. 100 items
Applied art (silver). Best single and largest public collection of Perth made silver or silver decorated or otherwise associated with the locality. Includes Flatware and Holloware, c. 17th-20th century, c. 200 items
Applied art (glass). Best single and largest public collection of Perth-made industrial, chemical and studio art glass; also paperweights (Moncrieff, Monart, Vasart, Strathearn, Caithness, Perthshire paperweights), c. 19th-20th century, c. 200 items
Applied art (ceramics). Best single and largest public collection of contemporary locally produced ceramics, contemporary, c. 200 items
Applied art (ceramics). Best single and largest Scottish public collection of Martinware Studio Art pottery mainly from the collection of Sir D Y Cameron, 1874-1930s, 46 items
Archaeology. Based on finds from Perth and Kinross District. Notably finds from mediaeval sites in the Burgh of Perth including textiles, leather, pottery stone, wood, bone and environmental material, c. 12th-16th century, a large number
Costume and Textiles. Associated with Perth and Kinross District. Notably 17th century tablecloth, banner and dance costume associated with the Glover Inc. of Perth, c. 17th century-present day, 2500
Photography. Associated with Perth and Kinross District, around 250,000 negatives
Prints and postcards, 1860- present day, c. 260,000
Numismatics. Notably a collection of Communion tokens with Scottish, British and International provenances, c. 18th-19th century, 5500 items
Ethnography. Collection of material from Oceania, America and Africa. Notably a Tahitian mourner's costume, a headdress from

continued overleaf

the Austral Islands, a Maori Kakapo feather cloak and NW Coast Indian objects including a Salish cloak, horn bracelets and ivory combs, late 18th century-1950s, 1100 items
Social history associated with the history of Perth and Kinross District; includes objects from local industries and trades, 18th century-present day, 5500 items
Natural Sciences. F B White Salix Collection. Unique specimens forming the basis of the 1890 'Revision' of the British Willows, 1860-1890, 2000 items
Perthshire Herbarium. Plants from vice-counties 87, 88 and 89, 1860-to date, 11,500 items
Millais Bird Skins. Specimens collected and used by ornithologist/writer/artist and traveller John Guille Millais d. 1931 and used to illustrate his published works on British ducks, etc. 1840-1920, 1273 items
Local natural history/geology. Outstanding local collections of vertebrates, most insect orders, rocks, fossils and minerals, 18th century-to date, 200,000 items
Catalogues:
Catalogue for part of the collections is available in-house, part is published and part is on-line.

Internet home pages:
http://www.pkc.gov.uk/ah/perth_museum.htm
Information on facilities, access, services, publications and contacts.

2251
PETER ANSON GALLERY
Town House West, Cluny Place, Buckie, Moray, AB56 1HB

Tel: 01309 673701
Fax: 01309 675863
Email: alasdair.joyce@techleis.moray.gov.uk
Formed: 1975

Organisation type and purpose: Art gallery.
Parent body:
Moray Council Museum Service
Falconer Museum, Tolbooth Street, Forres, IV36 1PH, email/website: museums@moray.gov.uk

Enquiries to: Senior Museums Officer
Access:
Access to staff: By letter, by telephone, by fax, by email, in person, Internet web pages
Hours: Mon to Fri, 1000 to 2000; Sat, 1000 to 1200
Access for disabled people: Parking provided, ramped entry

General description:
Contains watercolour paintings by Peter Anson, featuring maritime views mainly in Scotland and the North East.
Collections:
Peter Anson collection of paintings and archival material, 20th century, 1000 items

Internet home pages:
http://www.moray.gov.uk/museums

2252
PETERBOROUGH CATHEDRAL
The Chapter Office, Little Priors Gate, Minster Precinct, Peterborough, Cambridgeshire, PE1 1XS

Tel: 01733 343342
Fax: 01733 552465
Email: a.watson@peterborough-cathedral.org.uk
Formed: 655

Organisation type and purpose: Registered charity (charity number Ecclesiastical), historic building, house or site, suitable for ages: 5+ and all adult groups.
Anglican cathedral.
To promote the glory of God and be a sign of his kingdom in the world.

Enquiries to: Education and Visitor Services Officer
Access:
Access to staff: By letter, by telephone, by fax, by email, in person
Access to building, collections or gallery: No prior appointment required
Hours: Mon to Fri, 0900 to 1715
Sat, 0900 to 1700
Sun, services from 0800, visitors 1200 to 1700
Other restrictions: Prior appointment is required for group visits
Access for disabled people: ramped entry, access to all public areas
Other restrictions: Access to restaurant with toilet, and gift shop

Information services:
Library available for reference (for conditions see Access above)
Special visitor services: Guided tours, materials and/or activities for children.
Education services: Group education facilities, resources for Key Stages 1 and 2, 3, 4 and Further or Higher Education.
Services for disabled people: For the visually impaired; displays and/or information at wheelchair height.
Catalogues:
Catalogue for part of the collections is only available in-house.
Printed publications:
Peterborough Cathedral (the Pitkin Cathedral Guide, new ed 2001, £2.95)
The Geometric Skeleton of Peterborough Cathedral (Stallard F and Bush P, £2.50)
The Bells of Peterborough Cathedral (Lee M, £5.50)
Peterborough (Tebbs H E, £10.95)
Electronic and video products:
Cathedral in Peril (Cathedral Choir, CD)
The Joys of Christmas (Cathedral Choir, CD)
Peterborough Cathedral (video, 40 mins, £14.99)

Address for ordering publications:
Printed publications:
Peterborough Cathedral Shop
Minster Precincts, Peterborough, PE1 1XS

2253
PETERBOROUGH LOCOMOTIVE SOCIETY
See - Nene Valley Railway

2254
PETERBOROUGH MUSEUM & ART GALLERY
Priestgate, Peterborough, Cambridgeshire, PE1 1LF

Tel: 01733 343329
Fax: 01733 341928
Email: museum@peterborough.gov.uk

Organisation type and purpose: Local government body, registered charity (charity number 311798), museum, art gallery, suitable for ages: all ages.

Enquiries to: Visitor Services Manager
Access:
Access to staff: By letter, by telephone, by fax, by email
Access for disabled people: Parking provided, ramped entry, level entry, access to all public areas, toilet facilities

General description:
Natural and social history, archaeology.
Information services:
Temporary exhibitions of contemporary art.
Varied exhibition and events programme.
Special visitor services: Guided tours, materials and/or activities for children.
Education services: Group education facilities, resources for Key Stages 1 and 2..
Collections:
Norman Cross Collection, artefacts made by Napoleonic prisoners of war
Jurassic reptile fossil collection

Internet home pages:
http://www.peterboroughheritage.org.uk

2255
PETERSFIELD GALLERY
See - Flora Twort Gallery

2256
PETRIE MUSEUM OF EGYPTIAN ARCHAEOLOGY
University College London, Malet Place, London, WC1E 6BT

Tel: 020 7679 2884
Fax: 020 7679 2886
Email: petrie.museum@ucl.ac.uk
Acronym or abbreviation: UCL
Formed: 1912

Organisation type and purpose: Museum, university department or institute, suitable for ages: all ages, research organisation.
Teaching and research collection.
Parent body:
University College London

Enquiries to: Administrator
Direct tel: 020 7679 2883
Direct fax: 020 7679 2886
Direct email: h.kilminster@ucl.ac.uk
Access:
Access to staff: By letter, by telephone, by fax, by email, in person, Internet web pages
Access to building, collections or gallery: No prior appointment required
Hours: Tue to Fri, 1300 to 1700; Sat, 1000 to 1300
Other restrictions: Mon: open to researchers - appointments necessary
Access for disabled people: ramped entry, toilet facilities

General description:
Specialised information on the College collection of Egyptian artefacts; culture from Palaeolithic to Coptic periods.
Information services:
Library available for reference (for conditions see Access above)
Special visitor services: Guided tours, tape recorded guides, materials and/or activities for children.
Education services: Group education facilities, resources for Key Stages 2, 3, 4 and Further or Higher Education..
Collections:
Artefacts from Egypt from Predynastic times through to the Islamic period
Catalogues:
Catalogue for all of the collections is on-line.
Printed publications:
Sales list of books for adults and children, jewellery, posters, postcards, slide sets, replicas, etc
Microform products:
Petrie's field notebooks and selected tomb cards
Electronic and video products:
Petrie Archive (CD-ROM)

Internet home pages:
http://www.petrie.ucl.ac.uk
Full description pages of the collection, staff, opening hours, resources and collections database with digital images.

2257
PETWORTH COTTAGE MUSEUM
346 High Street, Petworth, West Sussex, GU28 0AU

Tel: 01798 342100
Fax: 01798 343467
Formed: 1995

Organisation type and purpose: Registered charity (charity number 1044840), museum, suitable for ages: 5+.
Owned by:
The Petworth Cottage Trust
at the same address

Enquiries to: Curator
Direct tel: 01798 324320

Access:
Access to staff: By letter, by fax, visitors by prior appointment

General description:
Domestic interior of an estate worker's cottage c1910.

Collections:
A typical example of the kind of cottage provided for his workers by the great Petworth landowner, Lord Leaconfield. It is furnished as it was around 1910 when it was occupied by Mrs Mary Cummings, a seamstress at Petworth House.

Internet home pages:
http://www.sussexlive.com

2258
PETWORTH HOUSE

Church Street, Petworth, West Sussex, GU28 0AE

Tel: 01798 342207
Fax: 01798 342963
Email: petworth@nationaltrust.org.uk
Formed: 1947

Organisation type and purpose: Registered charity (charity number 205846).
Historic house and park.

Parent body:
The National Trust (South and South East Region)
South East Regional Office, tel: 01372 453401

Enquiries to: Administrative Assistant
Direct tel: 01798 344972

Access:
Access to staff: By letter, by telephone, by fax, by email
Access for disabled people: Parking provided, ramped entry, toilet facilities
Other restrictions: Designated parking 700yds. Transfer available. 5 manual wheelchairs available. Ground floor largely accessible. No access to other floors. Photograph album. Chapel not accessible (stairs). Level entrance to shop. Lift to restaurant. Partly accessible.

General description:
History of the house and deer park, art collection. A magnificent late 17th century mansion set in a beautiful park, landscaped by 'Capability' Brown and immortalised in Turner's paintings. The house contains the Trust's finest and largest collection of pictures, with numerous works by Turner, Van Dyck, Reynolds and Blake, as well as ancient and neo-classical sculpture, fine furniture and carvings by Grinling Gibbons. The Servants' Quarters contain interesting kitchens (including a splendid copper batterie de cuisine of over 1,000 pieces) and other service rooms. On weekdays additional rooms are open to visitors by kind permission of Lord and Lady Egremont. The first phase of 'Capability' Brown's north lawn planting scheme and serpentine paths is now completed.

Information services:
Helpline available, tel no: 01798 342929.
Braille guide. Large-print guide. Touch list. Touch tours by arrangement with Administration Officer.
Suitable for school groups. Education room/centre. Audio guide. Hands-on activities. Children's quiz/trail. Family activity packs.
For specialist tours and school groups contact the administration office.
Open-air concerts in June. Family events throughout the season. Lecture lunches, behind-the-scenes tours and Christmas events. For details send s.a.e.
Special visitor services: Guided tours, materials and/or activities for children.
Education services: Group education facilities.
Services for disabled people: For the visually impaired.

Collections:
Over 300 paintings on display including works by Turner, Van Dyck, Titian, Claude, Gainsborough, Bosch, Reynolds and William Blake
Collection of carvings by Grinling Gibbons

Printed publications:
Children's Guide (80p)
Guide Book (£4.50)
Park leaflet (60p)
Servants' Quarters Guide (£2.50)
Short Guide (75p)

Address for ordering publications:
Printed publications:
National Trust Enterprises Limited
at the same address, tel: 01798 344975, fax: 01798 342963

Internet home pages:
http://www.nationaltrust.org.uk

2259
PEVENSEY CASTLE

Pevensey, East Sussex

Tel: 01323 762604

Organisation type and purpose: Historic building, house or site.

Parent body:
English Heritage (South East Region)
Tel: 01483 252000, fax: 01483 252001

Enquiries to: Curator

General description:
Pevensey is one of Britain's oldest and most important strongholds and the fortifications that survive come from three distinct periods: Roman, Medieval and Second World War. Although besieged several times over the centuries, it was never captured by force. The ruins were refortified in1940, for use in the Second World War. An observation and command post was set up, machine gun pillboxes built, and a blockhouse for anti-tank weapons constructed at the mouth of the Roman West Gate.

Information services:
Audio tour available for the visually impaired and those with learning difficulties.
Special visitor services: Tape recorded guides..

Internet home pages:
http://www.english-heritage.org.uk

2260
PEVERIL CASTLE

Market Place, Castleton, Hope Valley, Derbyshire, S33 8WQ

Tel: 01422 620613

Organisation type and purpose: Historic building, house or site, suitable for ages: all ages.

Parent body:
English Heritage (East Midlands Region)
44 Derngate, Northampton, NN1 1UH, tel: 01604 735400, fax: 01604 735401

Enquiries to: House Manager

Access:
Access to building, collections or gallery: No prior appointment required
Hours: Apr to Sep: daily, 1000 to 1800
Oct: daily, 1000 to 1700
Nov to Mar: Wed to Sun, 1000 to 1600
Other restrictions: Closed 24 to 26 Dec and 1 Jan
Opening times are subject to change, for up-to-date information contact English Heritage by phone or visit the website.

General description:
Built soon after the Norman Conquest of 1066 by William Peveril, the castle played a key role in guarding the Peak Forest area. It was added to in 1176. Henry II made additions, most notably the great square tower, built in 1176, which today stands almost to its original height. The castle offers breathtaking views of the Peak District.

Information services:
Special visitor services: Materials and/or activities for children..

Internet home pages:
http://www.english-heritage.org.uk

2261
PHILIPPS HOUSE AND DINTON PARK

Dinton, Salisbury, Wiltshire, SP3 5HH

Tel: 01985 843600 (Regional Office)

Organisation type and purpose: National organisation, registered charity (charity number 205846), historic building, house or site.

Parent body:
The National Trust (South West Region)
Regional Office for Wessex, tel: 01985 843600

Enquiries to: Manager

Access:
Access to staff: By letter, by telephone
Access to building, collections or gallery: No prior appointment required
Hours: 5 Apr to 27 Oct, Mon, 1300 to 1700;
5 Apr to 27 Oct, Sun, 1000 to 1300
Access for disabled people: ramped entry
Other restrictions: Ground floor accessible with assistance. Park: access limited, but good views of the lake from main access point from St Mary's Road car park

General description:
A neo-Grecian house designed by Jeffry Wyatville for William Wyndham, completed in 1820 and recently restored. The principal rooms on the ground floor are open to visitors and possess fine Regency furniture. The surrounding landscaped park has recently been restored and offers many attractive walks.

Internet home pages:
http://www.nationaltrust.org.uk/regions/wessex

2262
PICKERING CASTLE

Pickering, North Yorkshire, YO18 7AX

Tel: 01751 474989

Organisation type and purpose: National organisation, advisory body, historic building, house or site.

Parent body:
English Heritage (Yorkshire Region)
Tel: 01904 601901

Enquiries to: Manager

Access:
Access to staff: By letter, by telephone
Access to building, collections or gallery: No prior appointment required
Hours: 29 Mar to 30 Sep: daily, 1000 to 1800,1 to 31 Oct: daily, 1000 to 1300 and 1400 to 1700,1 Nov to 31 Mar: Wed to Sun, 1000 to 1300 and 1400 to 1600
Other restrictions: Closed 24 to 26 Dec and 1 Jan.
Opening times are subject to change, for up-to-date information contact English Heritage by phone or visit the website.

General description:
A splendid motte and bailey castle. It is well preserved with much of the original walls, towers and keep remaining, with spectacular views over the surrounding countryside.

Information services:
Education services: Group education facilities..

Internet home pages:
http://www.english-heritage.org.uk

2263
PICKFORD'S HOUSE MUSEUM

41 Friargate, Derby, DE1 1DA

Tel: 01332 255363
Fax: 01332 255277
Formed: 1988

Organisation type and purpose: Local government body, museum, historic building,

continued overleaf

house or site, suitable for ages: 12+.
A family museum.
Owned and financed by:
Derby City Council

Enquiries to: Keeper
Access:
Access to staff: By letter, by telephone, in person
Hours: Mon, 1100 to 1700; Tue to Sat, 1000 to 1700; Sun and Bank Holidays, 1400 to 1700
Access for disabled people: Parking provided, ramped entry
Other restrictions: Access only to ground and lower ground floors.
Video about the museum with signed interpretation.

General description:
Costume history, history of toys and toy theatres, social history: 18th century to present including 1920s/30s haute couture items made for Lady Curzon of Kedleston Hall by such houses as Chanel, Worth, Vionnet, Callot Soeurs. Displays concentrate on Georgian life and the work of architect Joseph Pickford who built the house in the late 1760s as his home and workplace; changing temporary exhibitions.
Information services:
Services for disabled people: For the hearing impaired.
Collections:
Costume and related material (photographs, magazines, patterns)
Curzon Collection of haute couture clothing, 1920s-1930s, 30-40 items
Stanton Collection of costume, 18th-20th century, 65 items
Frank Bradley Toy Theatre collection, historic toy theatres, playbooks, etc. 19th-20th century over 500 items
Catalogues:
Catalogue for part of the collections is only available in-house.

Internet home pages:
http://www.derby.gov.uk/museums

2264
PIECE HALL ART GALLERY & ARTS RESOURCE CENTRE
Piece Hall, Halifax, West Yorkshire, HX1 1RE

Tel: 01422 358087
Fax: 01422 349310
Email: karen.belshaw@calderdale.gov.uk

Organisation type and purpose: Local government body, art gallery, historic building, house or site, suitable for ages: all ages.

Enquiries to: Exhibitions/Marketing Officer
Other contacts: Education Officer
Access:
Access to staff: By letter, by telephone, by fax, by email, visitors by prior appointment
Access to building, collections or gallery: No prior appointment required
Hours: Tue to Sun, 1000 to 1700
Access for disabled people: access to all public areas

General description:
Housed in the historic Piece Hall, originally the trading centre for the local wool weavers.
Contemporary and historical exhibitions of art and craft. All exhibitions are temporary and rotate on a 6-10 week rota.
Information services:
Special visitor services: Materials and/or activities for children.
Education services: Group education facilities, resources for Key Stages 1 and 2, 3, 4 and Further or Higher Education..
Collections:
Art, craft, prints, photographs, industrial machinery, social history, local history
(Duke of Wellington's Regiment Museum based at Bankfield Museum, one of Calderdale Museum and Arts sites)
Catalogues:
Catalogue for part of the collections is only available in-house.
Publications list:
is available in hard copy.
Printed publications:
Range of postcards (25p)

Internet home pages:
http://www.calderdale.gov.uk
Exhibitions, events, details of sites.

2265
PILKINGTON GLASS MUSEUM
See - World of Glass Limited

2266
PINEAPPLE, THE
North of Airth, Falkirk, Strathclyde

Tel: 01324 831137

Organisation type and purpose: Historic building, house or site.
Parent body:
National Trust for Scotland
Building leased to:
Landmark Trust
Shottesbrooke, Maidenhead, Berkshire, tel: 01628 825925

Enquiries to: Groundsman

General description:
Bizarre structure in the shape of a pineapple built as a garden retreat in 1761. The National Trust for Scotland maintains the gardens and policies (car park, pond and woodland); the building is leased to the Landmark Trust who restored the building and walls, creating a holiday home.

2267
PITMEDDEN GARDEN
Ellon, Aberdeenshire, AB41 7PD

Tel: 01651 842352
Fax: 01651 843188

Organisation type and purpose: Historic building, house or site.
Parent body:
National Trust for Scotland (North-East Region)

Enquiries to: Property Manager
Access:
Access to staff: By letter, by telephone, by fax, in person
Access to building, collections or gallery: No prior appointment required
Hours: Beg May to beg Sep, daily 1000 to 1700
Access for disabled people: toilet facilities
Other restrictions: Access to upper garden, museum, Visitor Centre and tearoom, wheelchairs available

General description:
Centrepiece of the property is the Great Garden, originally laid out in 1675. In the 1950s three of the formal parterres were re-created in elaborate floral designs possibly used in the gardens at the Palace of Holyroodhouse in 1647.

See also - Museum of Farming Life

2268
PITSTONE GREEN MUSEUM
Pitstone Green Farm, Vicarage Road, Leighton Buzzard, Bedfordshire, LU7 9EY

Tel: 01582 605464
Email: norman.groom@lineone.net
Formed: 1991

Organisation type and purpose: Registered charity (charity number 273931), museum, suitable for ages: 8+.

Enquiries to: Manager
Access:
Access to staff: By telephone, by email
Access to building, collections or gallery: Prior appointment required
Access for disabled people: Parking provided, ramped entry, toilet facilities

General description:
A rural museum housed in the buildings of an 1831 farm.
The museum contains a wealth of fascinating exhibits including those relating to rural life, local trades and professions, engines and farm machinery, a large Crossley gas engine, a science and vintage radio room, a model railway and a full-size section of a WWII Lancaster Bomber.
Additional entertainment is available on our Family Fun & Craft Days with tractor rides, craft fair and country dancing. The 'Wheels in Motion Day' is devoted to a 'Hartop' stationary engine rally, working farm machinery, together with models and model engineering exhibits.
Information services:
Library available for reference (for conditions see Access above)
Special visitor services: Materials and/or activities for children..
Collections:
Collection of rural rife artefacts including:
Farm machinery and equipment
Local trade and business collections
Scientific items
Domestic items
Photographic collection
Catalogues:
Catalogue for all of the collections is only available in-house.
Publications list:
is available in hard copy.

Internet home pages:
http://website.lineone.net/~pitstonemus
Detailed site plan, details of exhibits, opening times and location details.

2269
PITSTONE WINDMILL
Ivinghoe, Buckinghamshire

Tel: 01494 52805 (Regional Office)

Organisation type and purpose: National organisation, registered charity (charity number 205846), historic building, house or site.
Parent body:
The National Trust (South and South East Region)
Thames and Solent Regional Office, tel: 01494 528051

Enquiries to: Manager
Access:
Access to staff: By letter, by telephone
Access to building, collections or gallery: No prior appointment required
Hours: Jun, Jul, Aug, Sun, 1430 to 1800
Open Bank Holidays

General description:
One of the oldest post-mills in Britain, dating from 1627 and restored entirely by volunteers.

Internet home pages:
http://www.nationaltrust.org.uk

2270
PITT RIVERS MUSEUM
See - Oxford University, Pitt Rivers Museum

2271
PITTENCRIEFF HOUSE MUSEUM
Pittencrieff Park, Dunfermline, Fife, KY12 8QH

Tel: 01383 722935

Parent body:
Fife Council
Museum headquarters:
Fife Council Museums West
Dunfermline Museum, Viewfield Terrace, Dunfermline, KY12 7HY, tel: 01383 313838, fax: 01383 313837, email/website: lesley.botten@fife.gov.uk

Other branch museum:
Inverkeithing Museum
The Friary, Queen Street, Inverkeithing, tel: 01383 313838, fax: 01383 313837, email/ website: lesley.botten@fife.gov.uk
St Margaret's Cave
Tel: 01383 313838, fax: 01383 313837, email/ website: lesley.botten@fife.gov.uk
Access:
Access to staff: By letter, by telephone, by fax, by email, visitors by prior appointment
Other restrictions: All communication to staff should be made through Dunfermline Museum only.
Access to building, collections or gallery: No prior appointment required
Hours: Summer 1100 to 1700, Winter 1100 to 1600, closed Dec, 25th and 26th, Jan, 1st and 2nd
Access for disabled people: Parking provided, ramped entry, level entry, toilet facilities
Other restrictions: Wheelchair access to lower gallery only

General description:
Pittencrieff Park and House is a 17th century estate gifted to the town by Andrew Carnegie.
Collections:
Costume collection of Scottish, mainly local, material from the early 18th century to today. However, it is mostly late 19th to early 20th century

2272
PITTVILLE PUMP ROOM
East Approach Drive, Cheltenham, Gloucestershire, GL52 3JE

Tel: 01242 523852

Organisation type and purpose: Historic building, house or site.
Parent body:
Cheltenham Borough Council

General description:
No longer a museum but open as a building of historic interest.

2273
PLAS MAWR
See - Royal Cambrian Academy of Art

2274
PLAS NEWYDD
Llanfairpwll, Anglesey, Gwynedd, LL61 6DQ

Tel: 01248 714795
Fax: 01248 713673
Email: plasnewydd@nationaltrust.org.uk
Formed: 1895

Organisation type and purpose: National organisation, registered charity (charity number 205846), museum, art gallery, historic building, house or site, suitable for ages: all ages.
Given to The National Trust 1976.
Parent body:
The National Trust Office for Wales
Trinity Square, Llandudno, LL30 2DE, tel: 01492 860123, fax: 01492 860233
Address for Head Office:
The National Trust
36 Queen Anne's Gate, London, SW1H 9AS, tel: 020 7222 9251, fax: 020 7222 5097, email/ website: enquiries@nationaltrust.org.uk

Enquiries to: Manager
Other contacts: House Manager for all enquiries regarding the house and collection.
Access:
Access to staff: By letter, by email, visitors by prior appointment, charges made to all users, charges to non-members
Other restrictions: Charges made to all users - out of hours.
Access for disabled people: Parking provided, ramped entry, toilet facilities
Other restrictions: Designated parking 400yds. Transfer available. Drop-off point. 2 manual wheelchairs available, booking essential. Ground floor fully accessible. Photograph album. No access to first floor. Steps to shop entrance. Lipped and low stepped entrance to tea-room. Grounds largely accessible.

General description:
Set amidst breathtaking scenery, with spectacular views of Snowdonia, this elegant 18th century house was built by James Wyatt and is an interesting mixture of classical and Gothic. The comfortable interior, restyled in the 1930s, is famous for its association with Rex Whistler, whose largest painting is here. There is also an exhibition about his work. A military museum contains campaign relics of the 1st Marquess of Anglesey, who commanded the cavalry at the Battle of Waterloo. There is a fine spring garden and Australasian arboretum with an understorey of shrubs and wildflowers, as well as a summer terrace and, later, massed hydrangeas and autumn colour. A woodland walk gives access to a marine walk on the Menai Strait.
Information services:
Helpline available, tel no: Infoline: 01248 715272.
Connoisseurs' and garden tours by arrangement.
Historical cruises (boat trips on the Menai Strait) operate from the property, weather and tide permitting, tel for details.
Braille guide.
Frontcarrying baby slings for loan.
Suitable for school groups. Family guide. Children's quiz/trail.
Special visitor services: Guided tours, tape recorded guides, materials and/or activities for children.
Services for disabled people: For the visually impaired; displays and/or information at wheelchair height.
Collections:
Family Collection of 16th-19th century paintings, watercolours, sketches etc
Country House Furniture Collection - all periods
Rex Whistler's largest painting on canvas 58 feet long in Dining Room
Rex Whistler Art Exhibition
Cavalry Museum:
Exhibition of relics and paintings of the 1st Marquess of Anglesey and his part in the Battle of Waterloo - Houses the Anglesey leg
Ryan Museum:
Collection of Uniforms given by Lt Col E N Ryan - Colonel Ryan of the Royal Army Medical Corps
Printed publications:
House Guide
Whistler Guide
Short Guides (Welsh, English, German, Dutch, French)
Teachers Resource Pack
Garden Leaflet
Marine Walk

Internet home pages:
http://www.nationaltrust.org.uk

2275
PLAS NEWYDD MUSEUM
High Street, Llangollen, Denbighshire, LL20 8AW

Tel: 01978 861314

Organisation type and purpose: Local government body, museum, historic building, house or site, suitable for ages: 16+.

Enquiries to: Curator
Direct tel: 01824 708223
Direct fax: 01824 708258
Direct email: rose.mcmahon @denbighshire.gov.uk
Access:
Access to staff: By email
Access for disabled people: Parking provided, level entry, toilet facilities
Other restrictions: Designated parking 400yds. Transfer available. Drop-off point. 2 manual wheelchairs available, booking essential. Ground floor fully accessible. Photograph album. No access to first floor. Steps to shop entrance. Lipped and low stepped entrance to tea-room. Grounds largely accessible.

General description:
Plas Newydd was the home of Lady Eleanor Butler and Miss Sarah Ponsonby from 1780-1831. They became famous as The Ladies of Llangollen after leaving unhappy home lives in Ireland, and setting up their gothicised retreat close to the route of the London-Holyhead road that passed through Llangollen. The house is furnished in keeping with its time in the 1780s and early 1800s. Oak furniture reflects the abundance of oak carving that the ladies installed into the very fabric of the house.
Information services:
Helpline available, tel no: Infoline: 01248 715272.
Special visitor services: Guided tours, tape recorded guides, materials and/or activities for children.
Education services: Group education facilities, resources for Key Stage 3.
Services for disabled people: For the visually impaired.
Catalogues:
Catalogue for all of the collections is only available in-house.
Printed publications:
Guide Book
Teachers' Pack

2276
PLAS YN RHIW
Rhiw, Pwllheli, Gwynedd, LL53 8AB

Tel: 01758 780219
Fax: 01758 780219

Organisation type and purpose: National organisation, registered charity (charity number 205846), historic building, house or site.
Parent body:
The National Trust Office for Wales
Trinity Square, Llandudno, LL30 2DE, tel: 01492 860123, fax: 01492 860233

Enquiries to: Manager
Access:
Access to staff: By letter, by telephone, by email
Access to building, collections or gallery: No prior appointment required
Hours: Easter to mid May: Mon, Thur to Sun, 1200 to 1700
Mid May to end of Sep: Mon, Wed to Sun, 1200 to 1700
Oct: Sat and Sun only, but daily during half-term break.
Access for disabled people: level entry, toilet facilities
Other restrictions: Drop-off point. Ground floor largely accessible. No access to other floors. Photograph album. Level entrance to shop.

General description:
This small medieval manor house was rescued from neglect and lovingly restored by the three Keating sisters, who bought it in 1938. The views from the delightful grounds and gardens across Cardigan Bay are among the most spectacular in Britain. The house is 16th century with Georgian additions, and the ornamental gardens contain many interesting flowering trees and shrubs, with beds framed by box hedges and grass paths. Brilliant displays of snowdrops and bluebells can be found in the wood above at the appropriate season.
Information services:
Services for disabled people: For the visually impaired.

Internet home pages:
http://www.nationaltrust.org.uk

2277
PLATT HALL
See - Gallery of Costume

2278
PLUMSTEAD MUSEUM
See - Greenwich Borough Museum

2279
PLYMOUTH ARTS CENTRE

38 Looe Street, Plymouth, Devon, PL4 0EB

Tel: 01752 206114
Fax: 01752 206118
Email: arts@plymouthac.org.uk
Acronym or abbreviation: PAC

Organisation type and purpose: Art gallery, historic building, house or site, suitable for ages: 5+.
Art gallery, cinema, vegetarian restaurant.

Enquiries to: House Manager
Access:
Access to staff: By letter, by telephone, by fax, by email, Internet web pages
Access to building, collections or gallery: No prior appointment required
Hours: Mon to Sat, 1000 to 2030; Sun, 1800 to 2000
Access for disabled people: toilet facilities

General description:
The centre is housed in two grade II listed 18th century town houses, and remains home to three gallery spaces as well as a thriving independent cinema showing a selection of foreign, arthouse and independent films.
The galleries host an ever changing exhibition programme of national and international contemporary artists and their work.
Printed publications:
Guide to exhibitions, films and events (once every other month)

Internet home pages:
http://www.plymouthac.org.uk

2280
PLYMOUTH CITY MUSEUMS AND ART GALLERY

Drake Circus, Plymouth, Devon, PL4 8AJ

Tel: 01752 304774
Fax: 01752 304775
Email: plymouth.museum@plymouth.gov.uk
Acronym or abbreviation: PLYMG
Formed: 1897

Organisation type and purpose: Local government body, museum, art gallery, historic building, house or site, suitable for ages: 5+, consultancy, research organisation.
Historic building, records office, heritage centre.
Parent body:
Plymouth City Council
Other addresses:
Elizabethan House
Merchants House
Mount Edgcumbe House
Tel: 01752 822236, fax: 01752 822199
Plymouth and West Devon Record Office
Tel: 01752 305940, fax: 01752 223939, email/website: pwdro@plymouth.gov.uk
Plymouth Dome
Tel: 01752 603300, fax: 01752 256361, email/website: plymouthdome@plymouth.gov.uk
Smeatons Tower

Enquiries to: Curator
Access:
Access to staff: By letter, by telephone, by fax, by email, visitors by prior appointment
Other restrictions: Access to study collections by appointment.
Access to building, collections or gallery: No prior appointment required
Hours: Tue to Fri, 1000 to 1730, Sat and Bank Holiday Mon, 1000 to 1700
Access for disabled people: level entry, toilet facilities
Other restrictions: Access to 95% of the museum and art gallery.

General description:
Archaeology, social history, ethnography, numismatics, photography, fine art, applied art, decorative art, geology, zoology, botany and archives. Mainly local/regional collections with some nationally important ones.
Information services:
Library available for reference (for conditions see Access above). Helpline available, tel no: 01752 304774.
Special visitor services: Materials and/or activities for children.
Education services: Group education facilities, resources for Key Stages 1 and 2, 3, 4 and Further or Higher Education.
Services for disabled people: For the hearing impaired.
Collections:
Archaeological Collections from Dartmoor and Mount Batten
Astor photographic collection
Benham ethnographic collection
Bignell Lepidoptera collection
City Engineers photographic collection
Cottonian Collection of old master paintings and drawings, including 3000 books mostly 18th century
Dauncey Oceanic Collection
Devonshire 17th/18th century token collection
Drake Relics etc including portraits (Buckland Abbey Museum)
Fielden Skillet Collection
Fosterjohn Paraguayan Collection
Harmsworth ship and prisoner of war model collection
Hooper collection of 17th century halfpennies and farthings
Keys coleoptera collection
Late medieval and post-medieval imported pottery from Plymouth waterfront excavations
Mineral collections of St Aubyn, Serjeant, Gallant and Barstow
Paintings by Newlyn School, Camden Town Group and 20th century Westcountry artists
Plymouth and British Porcelain
Rugg Monk photographic collection
The Flower herbarium
St Aubyn herbarium
Tripe photographic collection
Catalogues:
Catalogue for part of the collections is available in-house and part is published.
Publications list:
is available in hard copy.
Printed publications:
Art, local and natural history, archaeology and other catalogues and guides

Internet home pages:
http://www.plymouthmuseum.gov.uk
Basic information about the collections, exhibitions, events, education, outreach, conservation and other services.
http://www.cottoniancollection.org.uk
Explores this special designated collection and provides educational ideas and content for schools.

2281
POLESDEN LACEY

Great Bookham, Dorking, Surrey, RH5 6BD

Tel: 01372 452048
Fax: 01372 452023
Email: polesdenlacey@nationaltrust.org.uk
Formed: 1895

Organisation type and purpose: National organisation, registered charity, historic building, house or site, suitable for ages: 5+.
Parent body:
The National Trust (South and South East Region)
South East Regional Office, tel: 01372 453401

Enquiries to: Administrator
Other contacts: Administration Assistant for general enquiries.
Access:
Access to staff: By letter, by telephone, by fax, by email, in person, visitors by prior appointment, Internet web pages
Access to building, collections or gallery: No prior appointment required
Hours: House: late Mar to early Nov, Wed to Sun, 1100 to 1700
Garden: all year, daily, 1100 to 1800
Open Bank Holiday Mondays
Other restrictions: Garden closes dusk, if earlier.
Access for disabled people: Parking provided, ramped entry, level entry, access to all public areas, toilet facilities
Other restrictions: Designated parking 100yds. 3 manual wheelchairs available, booking essential. 1 single-seater powered mobility vehicle available, booking essential. Ground floor fully accessible. No access to other floors. Level entrance to shop. Ramped entrance to tea-room. Some gravel and paved surfaces in grounds. Recommended route map.

General description:
In an exceptional setting on the North Downs this originally Regency house was extensively remodelled in 1906-09 by the Hon. Mrs Ronald Greville, a well-known Edwardian hostess. Her collection of fine paintings, furniture, porcelain and silver is displayed in the reception rooms and galleries, as it was at the time of her celebrated house parties. There are extensive grounds, the Edwardian garden extends to 30 acres to include a walled rose garden, 10 acres of lawn and grass, and terraces and landscape walks. King George VI and Queen Elizabeth The Queen Mother spent part of their honeymoon here in 1923.
Information services:
Helpline available, tel no: Infoline 01372 458203.
Front-carrying baby slings for loan. Hip-carrying infant seats for loan.
Children's quiz/trail.
Special visitor services: Materials and/or activities for children.
Services for disabled people: For the visually impaired; displays and/or information at wheelchair height.
Collections:
Mrs Greville's Collection was compiled by advisers instructed to buy whatever was fashionable regardless of price. The eclectic mixture of objects, from Dutch Old Masters to Fabergé trinkets, from the arts of Byzantium to those of French 18th century, was typical of contemporary taste

Internet home pages:
http://www.nationaltrust.org.uk

2282
POLLOCK'S TOY MUSEUM

1 Scala Street, London, W1T 2HL

Tel: 020 7636 3452
Email: toytheatres@pollocksweb.co.uk
Formed: 1968

Organisation type and purpose: Registered charity (charity number 313622), museum, suitable for ages: 3 +.

Enquiries to: Curator
Other contacts: Chairman for Trustee.
Access:
Access to staff: By letter, by telephone, by email, Internet web pages
Hours: Mon to Fri, 1000 to 1700
Access to building, collections or gallery: No prior appointment required

General description:
Toys from 1800 onwards, specialises in toy theatre; tin toys; dolls; puppets; optical toys.
Collections:
Collections of books, documents, manuscripts, pictures and photographs
Brunius Collection: optical toys
Fawdry Collection: toy theatres
Publications list:
is available in hard copy.

Internet home pages:
http://www.pollocksweb.co.uk

2283
POLLOK HOUSE
Pollok Country Park, 2060 Pollokshaws Road, Glasgow, G43 1AT

Tel: 0141 616 6410
Fax: 0141 616 6521
Email: pollokhouse@nts.org.uk
Formed: 1931
Formerly: Glasgow Museums Pollok House, date of change, 1998

Organisation type and purpose: Membership association, voluntary organisation, registered charity (charity number SCO 07410), historic building, house or site, suitable for ages: 5+.
Parent body:
Glasgow City Council
At the same address is:
The Burrell Collection
Managed in partnership by:
Glasgow Museums
National Trust for Scotland (NTS)
Other addresses:
National Trust for Scotland (NTS)
Wemyss House, 28 Charlotte Square, Edinburgh, EH2 4ET, tel: 0131 243 9300, fax: 0131 243 9301, email/website: development@nts.org.uk

Enquiries to: Manager
Other contacts: Functions Co-ordinator for external functions.
Access:
Access to staff: By letter, by telephone, by fax, by email, in person, visitors by prior appointment
Access to building, collections or gallery: No prior appointment required
Hours: Daily, 1000 to 1700
Other restrictions: Closed 25 and 26 Dec; 1 and 2 Jan.
Access for disabled people: Parking provided, ramped entry, level entry, toilet facilities
Other restrictions: Access to main floor and basement, shop, restaurant and servants' quarters, wheelchair lift to principal floor

General description:
Mid eighteenth century house and country park. Furnishings of a major Edwardian country house, major servants' quarters (extending to 42 rooms), restricted library access - art and design library.
Information services:
Costumed tours in summer; programme of temporary exhibitions; explanatory text in French, German, Italian, Spanish.
Special visitor services: Guided tours, tape recorded guides, materials and/or activities for children.
Education services: Group education facilities, resources for Key Stages 1 and 2 and Further or Higher Education.
Services for disabled people: For the visually impaired; displays and/or information at wheelchair height.
Collections:
Stirling Maxwell Collection - Paintings, Spanish art from 16th to early 19th century, William Blake, Silver, Library
Other material held by Glasgow Museums
Publications list:
is available in hard copy.
Printed publications:
Guide Book (available for purchase)
Functions Brochure (free)

2284
PONTEFRACT MUSEUM
5 Salter Row, Pontefract, West Yorkshire, WF8 1BA

Tel: 01977 722740

Organisation type and purpose: Museum, suitable for ages: 5+.

Enquiries to: Curator
Access:
Access to staff: By letter, by telephone
Access for disabled people: level entry, toilet facilities

General description:
A local history museum in an art nouveau library building. Contains important 17th century paintings of the castle and town, and mediaeval finds from St John's Priory, and local collections of pressed glass; liquorice growing and sweet making; printing ephemera; and architectural drawings.
Information services:
Services for disabled people: Displays and/or information at wheelchair height.
Collections:
Artefacts, pictures, prints, photographs, books, documents, manuscripts relating to liquorice and town history
St John's Priory finds, Mediaeval, 900 items
Holmes printing ephemera, 1919-1969, 10,000 items
Pennington architectural drawings (on deposit with West Yorkshire Record Office), 1890-1930, 3000 items
Bagley's pressed glass, 1890-1960, 700 items

2285
PONTYPOOL AND BLAENAVON RAILWAY COMPANY
Council Offices, 101 High Street, Blaenavon, Gwent, NP4 9PT

Tel: 01495 792263
Fax: 01495 792263
Email: railway @pontypoolandblaenavon.freeserve.co.uk
Acronym or abbreviation: P&BR
Formed: 1980

Organisation type and purpose: Membership association (membership is by subscription), present number of members: 200, voluntary organisation, registered charity (charity number 514809).
Member group is the:
Pontypool and Blaenavon Locomotive Group
Pontypool and Blaenavon Railway Society

Enquiries to: Secretary
Access:
Access to staff: By letter, by email, Internet web pages
Hours: Normally open Sun, Bank Holidays, Mon and 1st Sat Apr to Aug (Easter to Sept)

General description:
Preservation, restoration and operation of historic railway items.
Collections:
Steam and diesel rolling stock
Coaches, including two catering vehicles, freight and brake vans
Printed publications:
Guidebook
Members magazine issued periodically

Internet home pages:
http://www.pontypool-and-blaenavon.co.uk

2286
POOLE MUSEUM SERVICE
See - Scaplen's Court; Waterfront Museum

2287
POOR TRAVELLERS HOUSE
97 High Street, Rochester, Kent, ME1 1LX

Tel: 01634 845609
Formed: 1579

Organisation type and purpose: Registered charity, museum, historic building, house or site, suitable for ages: all ages.
Other offices:
Richard Watts Charity
Administration Offices
Maidstone Road, Rochester, Kent, tel: 01634 842194

Enquiries to: Curator - Guide
Direct tel: 01634 842194
Other contacts: Clerk to Trustees
Access:
Access to staff: By letter, by telephone
Access to building, collections or gallery: No prior appointment required
Hours: Mar to Oct: Tue to Sat, 1400 to 1700
Other restrictions: Closed on Bank Holidays. Prior appointment required for groups of 20.

General description:
Provision to provide 1 night's sustenance for Travelling Tradesmen in Tudor period, providing free supper and individual bedroom, each with own fireplace. Each traveller given 4 pennies when leaving in morning, as they continue their search for work.
Information services:
Special visitor services: Guided tours..
Collections:
Pictures, prints, documents, manuscripts, artefacts
6 bedrooms added to house in 1586 for use of Travellers from 1586-1940 (available for viewing)
Catalogues:
Catalogue for library is in-house only. Catalogue for all of the collections is only available in-house.
Printed publications:
Directly on display:
Leaflets (free)
Booklets (25p)
History of Richard Watts Charity (softback, £3) (hardback, £10 - limited edition, 200 copies)

2288
PORT OF LONDON AUTHORITY
See - Museum in Docklands; Museum of London

2289
PORTCHESTER CASTLE
Portchester, Fareham, Hampshire

Tel: 02392 378291

Organisation type and purpose: Historic building, house or site, suitable for ages: 5+.
Parent body:
English Heritage (South East Region)
Tel: 01483 252000, fax: 01483 252001

Enquiries to: Manager
Access:
Access to staff: By letter, by telephone
Access to building, collections or gallery: No prior appointment required
Hours: Apr to Sep: daily, 1000 to 1800
Oct: daily, 1000 to 1700
Nov to Mar, daily, 1000 to 1600
Other restrictions: Closed 24 to 26 Dec and 1 Jan
Opening times are subject to change, for up-to-date information contact English Heritage by phone or visit the website.
Access for disabled people: Parking provided
Other restrictions: Wheelchair access to grounds and lower levels only.

General description:
Porchester Castle has defended Portsmouth Harbour for 2000 years. Many kings have resided there over the centuries, from the time of the Romans to Napoleon. 4000 French prisoners were 'sardined' in the keep during the Napoleonic Wars. The castle has the most complete Roman walls in Europe, and features wall paintings as well as a fabulous view across the Solent.
Information services:
Interactive audio tour.
Castle exhibition.
Special visitor services: Tape recorded guides, materials and/or activities for children.
Education services: Group education facilities..

Internet home pages:
http://www.english-heritage.org.uk

2290
PORTHCAWL MUSEUM AND HISTORICAL SOCIETY
Old Police Station, John Street, Porthcawl, Mid Glamorgan, CF36 3BD

Tel: 01656 782211
Formed: 1977

Organisation type and purpose: Museum, suitable for ages: all ages.
Connections with:
Council of Museums in Wales (CMW)

Enquiries to: General Secretary
Direct tel: 01656 784863
Access:
Access to staff: By letter, by telephone
Access for disabled people: level entry, access to all public areas, toilet facilities
Other restrictions: Parking at rear.

General description:
A small museum housed in a Victorian police station containing collections of local interest relating to the maritime and industrial past of this seaside town on the heritage coast. Regimental memorabilia of 49th Rocce Regiment founded in Porthcawl 1942. Regimental collection of Welsh Guards.
Collections:
Costume. Mid-Victorian onwards
Archives, printed material, slides, photographs
Local history and artefacts. Maps, photographs, and memorabilia relating to the foundation and development of this once prosperous coal and iron exporting harbour.
Catalogues:
Catalogue for library is in-house only.

2291
PORTHCURNO MUSEUM OF SUBMARINE TELEGRAPHY
Porthcurno, Penzance, Cornwall, TR19 6JX

Tel: 01736 810966
Fax: 01736 810966
Email: tunnels@tunnels.demon.co.uk
Formed: 1998
Formed from: Cable & Wireless Porthcurno and Collections Trust, PK Trust

Organisation type and purpose: Registered charity (charity number 1062233), museum, historic building, house or site, suitable for ages: 8+.
Parent body:
The Trevithick Trust
Tel: 01209 210900

Enquiries to: Manager
Other contacts: Curator for research or historical information.
Access:
Access to staff: By letter, by fax, by email, visitors by prior appointment
Access to building, collections or gallery: No prior appointment required
Hours: Nov to Mar; Sun, Mon, 1000 to 1600
Mar to Nov; Sun to Fri and Bank Holiday Sat, 100 to 1700
Other restrictions: Closed Christmas /New Year (phone to check opening dates)
Access for disabled people: Parking provided, level entry, toilet facilities
Other restrictions: Access to all areas except for 1st floor gallery.

General description:
A museum housed in secret Second World War underground communications tunnels, tracing the development of submarine telegraphy from 1850-1970. Archive of telegraph and local history.
Information services:
Library available for reference (for conditions see Access above)
Special visitor services: Guided tours, materials and/or activities for children.
Education services: Resources for Key Stages 2 and 3.
Services for disabled people: Displays and/or information at wheelchair height.
Collections:
Cable and Wireless collection, submarine telegraphy, 1850-1970, 2000 items
The Flying Telegraph, the story of homing pigeons from 1870 through WWII. The Dickin medal, the Victoria Cross for pigeons.
Catalogues:
Catalogue for library is in-house only. Catalogue for all of the collections is available in-house, part is published and part is on-line.
Publications list:
is available in hard copy.

Internet home pages:
http://www.porthcurno.org.uk
Extensive information on the museum and telegraph history.

2292
PORTHLEVEN HARBOUR AND DOCK COMPANY
The Harbour, Porthleven, Helston, Cornwall, TR13 9JN

Tel: 01326 574270
Fax: 01326 574225
Email: kathy@porthlevenharbouranddock.fsnet.co.uk
Formed: 1869

Organisation type and purpose: Independently owned, historic building, house or site, suitable for ages: all ages.
Historic harbour.
Other addresses:
Porthleven Harbour and Dock Company
Celtic House, Harbour Head, Porthleven

Enquiries to: Office Manager
Access:
Access to staff: By letter, by telephone, by fax, by email, in person, visitors by prior appointment
Access for disabled people: access to all public areas

General description:
Historic harbour and buildings.

2293
PORTHMADOG MARITIME MUSEUM
Oakley Wharf, The Harbour, Porthmadog, Gwynedd, LL49 9LU

Tel: 01766 513736
Formed: 1982

Organisation type and purpose: Membership association (membership is by election or invitation), voluntary organisation, registered charity (charity number 514041), museum, suitable for ages: 8+.
Member of the:
Gwyndd and Anglesey Federation of Maritime Museums

Enquiries to: Honorary Secretary
Direct tel: 01766 512864
Other contacts: Curator
Access:
Access to staff: By letter, by telephone, in person, visitors by prior appointment, charges to non-members
Hours: Mon to Sun, 1100 to 1700
Other restrictions: Any other time by appointment.
Access to building, collections or gallery: No prior appointment required
Access for disabled people: access to all public areas, toilet facilities

General description:
Housed in an old slate shed on the Wharf. Local history, the maritime involvement of Porthmadog during the 19th and early 20th century, ie shipbuilding, export of slate and salt trade in the North Atlantic; the three masted topsail schooners built at Porthmadog known as Western Ocean Yachts and other vessels.
Information services:
Gwynedd Archives, telephone: 01286 679095
Special visitor services: Guided tours.
Services for disabled people: Displays and/or information at wheelchair height.
Collections:
Porthmadog Collection
Pictures, photographs, models, various tools specific to shipbuilding and repairs
Catalogues:
Catalogue for all of the collections is only available in-house.
Printed publications:
Leaflets (free, direct)

2294
PORTICO LIBRARY AND GALLERY
57 Mosley Street, Manchester, M2 3HY

Tel: 0161 236 6785
Fax: 0161 236 6803
Formed: 1806

Organisation type and purpose: Membership association (membership is by subscription).
Houses publications of the:
Lancashire and Cheshire Antiquarian Society

Enquiries to: Librarian
Access:
Access to staff: By letter, by telephone, by fax
Hours: Mon to Fri, 0930 to 1630
Other restrictions: Subscription library, open to bona fide researchers.

General description:
19th and early 20th century fiction; travel and topography; 19th century biography; the art gallery's exhibitions are biased towards Northern artists' and craft work.
Printed publications:
In-house monographs on topics related to Manchester and the Library

2295
PORTLAND BASIN MUSEUM
1 Portland Place, Portland Street South, Ashton-under-Lyne, Lancashire, OL7 0QH

Tel: 0161 343 2878
Fax: 0161 343 2869
Email: portland.basin@mail.tameside.gov.uk

Organisation type and purpose: Local government body, museum, suitable for ages: 5+.

Enquiries to: Manager
Access:
Access to staff: By letter, by telephone, by fax, by email, in person
Access for disabled people: Parking provided, level entry, access to all public areas, toilet facilities

General description:
Items concerned with Tameside's social and industrial history, also the natural and archaeological history of the area.
Information services:
Special visitor services: Guided tours, materials and/or activities for children.
Education services: Group education facilities.
Services for disabled people: For the visually impaired; for the hearing impaired; displays and/or information at wheelchair height.
Collections:
Haughton Green Glass. 12,000 glass pieces from a 17th century glassworks, 1650-1680
Catalogues:
Catalogue for part of the collections is only available in-house.

Internet home pages:
http://www.tameside.gov.uk

See also - Wooden Canal Boat Society Limited

2296
PORTLAND CASTLE
Castelton, Portland, Dorset, DT5 1BD

Tel: 01305 820539

Parent body:
English Heritage (South West Region)
Tel: 0117 975 0700, fax: 0117 975 0701

Enquiries to: Manager
Access:
Access to staff: By letter, by telephone
Access to building, collections or gallery: No prior appointment required
Hours: 29 Mar to 30 Sep: daily, 1000 to 1800,1 to 31 Oct: daily, 1000 to 1700,1 Nov to 31 Mar, Fri to Sun, 1000 to 1600
Other restrictions: Closed 24 to 26 Dec and 1 Jan.
Restricted opening in Oct.
Opening times are subject to change, for up-to-date information contact English Heritage by phone or visit the website.

General description:
This coastal fortress was built to defend Weymouth Harbour against potential invasion, and survives largely unaltered to this day. Its appearance is typical of the castles built by Henry VIII in the early 1540s.
Information services:
Special visitor services: Tape recorded guides..

Internet home pages:
http://www.english-heritage.org.uk

2297
PORTSMOUTH HISTORIC DOCKYARD

Porters Lodge, College Road, Portsmouth, Hampshire, PO1 3LJ

Tel: 023 9287 0999 / 023 9286 1533 (Enquiries)
Email: mail@historicdockyard.co.uk
Formerly: Flagship Portsmouth Trust, date of change, 2000

Organisation type and purpose: Registered charity, historic building, house or site, suitable for ages: all ages.

Enquiries to: Public Relations Manager
Direct email: patricia@historicdockyard.co.uk
Access:
Access to staff: By telephone, by email
Access to building, collections or gallery: Prior appointment required
Hours: Daily, 0900 to 1700
Access for disabled people: Parking provided, ramped entry, access to all public areas, toilet facilities

General description:
Historic ships, interactive gallery, museums and exhibitions.
Information services:
Helpline available, tel no: 023 9286 1533.
Special visitor services: Guided tours, tape recorded guides.
Education services: Group education facilities, resources for Key Stages 1 and 2, 3 and 4.
Services for disabled people: For the visually impaired; for the hearing impaired.

Internet home pages:
http://www.historicdockyard.co.uk

2298
PORTSMOUTH MUSEUMS AND RECORDS SERVICE

City Museum and Records Office, Museum Road, Portsmouth, Hampshire, PO1 2LJ

Tel: 023 9282 7261
Minicom no. 023 9287 6550
Fax: 023 9287 5276
Email: cspendlove@portsmouthcc.gov.uk
Formed: 1895

Organisation type and purpose: Local government body, museum.
Record office.
Administered by:
Portsmouth City Council
Tel: 023 9282 2251

Comprises the seven museums:
Charles Dickens Birth Place Museum
contact for all at the same tel, fax and email, tel: 023 9282 7261, fax: 023 9287 5276, email/website: cspendlove@portsmouthcc.gov.uk
City Museum & Record Office
D-Day Museum
Eastney Beam Engine House
Natural History Museum
Southsea Castle
Square Tower

Enquiries to: Manager
Other contacts: (1) Archivist (2) Visitor Services Officer for (1) archives and records (2) group visits.
Access:
Access to staff: By letter, by telephone, by fax, in person
Hours: Mon to Fri, 1000 to 1700
Access for disabled people: Parking provided, ramped entry, access to all public areas, toilet facilities
Other restrictions: Access for City Museum and Records Office - Main Administration Building.

General description:
British fine and decorative art; archaeology; local & social history of Portsmouth; military history; museum administration; museum education services; record office for local businesses; families and church records.
Collections:
Collections of photographs, maps and postcards
Extensive holdings of Anglican, Nonconformist and Roman Catholic church records, many in microform
IGI (Hampshire and surrounding areas)
Official Records of the City of Portsmouth from the 14th century
Records of local businesses, families and organisations
Catalogues:
Catalogue for all of the collections is only available in-house.
Printed publications:
Exhibition catalogues (frequency varies according to programme)
Information Sheets
Microform products:
Parish Registers, Wills (Hampshire)

Internet home pages:
http://www.portsmouthmuseums.co.uk
Overview of sites, holdings, opening hours, contact telephone numbers and email addresses.

2299
POTTERIES MUSEUM & ART GALLERY, THE

Bethesda Street, Hanley, Stoke-on-Trent, Staffordshire, ST1 3DW

Tel: 01782 232323
Minicom no. 01782 232515
Fax: 01782 232500
Email: museums@stoke.gov.uk
Acronym or abbreviation: PM & AG
Formed: 1846
Formerly: Stoke-on-Trent City Museum and Art Gallery, date of change, 1998

Organisation type and purpose: Local government body, museum, art gallery, suitable for ages: 5+.
Parent body:
Stoke-on-Trent City Council
Tel: 01782 236925, fax: 01782 232544
Affiliated to:
North Staffordshire Museums Association
Tel: 01782 236000
West Midlands Arts
Tel: 0121 631 3121, fax: 0121 643 7239
West Midlands Regional Museums Council
Tel: 01527 872258, fax: 01527 576960, email/website: wmrmc@btinternet.com
Divisions at:
Etruria Industrial Museum
Lower Bedford Street, Etruria, tel: 01782 233144, fax: 01782 233145
Ford Green Hall
Ford Green Road, Smallthorne, tel: 01782 233195, fax: 01782 233194, email/website: Ford.Green.Hall@stoke.gov.uk
Gladstone Working Pottery Museum
Uttoxeter Road, Longton, tel: 01782 319232, fax: 01782 598640, email/website: gladstone@stoke.gov.uk

Enquiries to: Manager
Other contacts: Head of Museums
Access:
Access to staff: By letter, by telephone, by fax, by email, in person, visitors by prior appointment, Internet web pages
Hours: Mar to Oct: Mon to Sat, 0900 to 1700; Sun, 1400 to 1700
Nov to Feb: Mon to Sat, 0900 to 1700; Sun, 1300 to 1600
Access to building, collections or gallery: Prior appointment required
Hours: Mar to Oct: Mon to Sat, 1000 to 1700; Sun, 1400 to 1700
Nov to Feb: Mon to Sat, 1000 to 1600; Sun, 1300 to 1600
Access for disabled people: level entry, access to all public areas, toilet facilities
Other restrictions: Limited parking.
Winner of the 1999 Railtrack Adapt Award for excellence in access.

General description:
Ceramics: world class ceramics collection curated by acknowledged experts, collections of archaeology, natural history, decorative arts and community history relating to the local area; Spitfire aircraft in the Reginald Mitchell Gallery; fine art.
Collections:
Local photographic archive of local life, approx 13,000 negatives
Spitfire Gallery
Wide-ranging collections particularly strong on English ceramics and the history of the ceramics industry in Staffordshire
Catalogues:
Catalogue for part of the collections is published and part is on-line.
Publications list:
is available in hard copy and online.
Printed publications:
Books on ceramics
General Museum leaflet
On Show (leaflet about exhibitions and events, 3 times a year)
Potteries Pots - the best in the world - Souvenir Guidebook
Electronic and video products:
Stoke-on-Film 1910-30/40s/50s/60s/70s
Six Towns on Film (one for each town)
Local football teams (3 videos)
Stoke-on-Trent Picture House (video)
Stoke-on-Trent Railways (3 videos)
The Titanic (Captain Smith) (2 videos)
Spitfire Aircraft (3 videos)

Address for ordering publications:
Printed publications:
Visitor Services Assistant - Sales
Tel: 01782 232323

Internet home pages:
http://www.stoke.gov.uk/museums
General information on the museums of the Potteries, collections information, museum publications, exhibitions and events update.

2300
POTTERS BAR MUSEUM

Darkes Lane, Potters Bar, Hertfordshire, EN6 2HN

Tel: 01707 645005
Formed: 1990
Formerly: Potters Bar & District Historical Society, Wyllyotts Museum

Organisation type and purpose: Membership association (membership is by subscription), present number of members: 200, voluntary

continued overleaf

organisation, registered charity (charity number 299475), museum.

Enquiries to: Curator
Direct tel: 01707 654179
Direct fax: 01707 651302
Access:
Access to staff: By letter, visitors by prior appointment
Access for disabled people: ramped entry, toilet facilities

General description:
Local history of Potters Bar and District.
Printed publications:
Monographs on various aspects of local history: railway systems, village histories, bus networks, personal autobiographies

Address for ordering publications:
Printed publications:
Potters Bar & District Historical Society
23 Osborne Road, Potters Bar, Hertfordshire, EN6, tel: 01707 656833

2301
POTTER'S MUSEUM
Jamaica Inn, Bolventor, Launceston, Cornwall, PL15 7TS

Tel: 01566 86838
Fax: 01566 86838
Formed: 1861 in Sussex

Organisation type and purpose: Independently owned, museum, suitable for ages: all ages.

Enquiries to: Manager
Access:
Access to staff: By letter, by telephone, by fax
Access for disabled people: Parking provided, ramped entry, toilet facilities
Other restrictions: Partial entry - ground floor only.

General description:
Potter's Museum of Curiosity contains the lifetime's work of Victorian naturalist/taxidermist, Walter Potter (1835-1918), the founder of the museum who lived all his life in Bramber, Sussex. Many more items have been added since his death. Set out in true Victorian fashion, it contains some 10,000 objects of curiosity from around the world.
Publications list:
is available in hard copy.
Printed publications:
Brochure available by post, for purchase, on request
Mr Potter's Museum of Curiosities (Morris P A)

2302
POWDERHAM CASTLE
Kenton, Exeter, Devon, EX6 8JQ

Tel: 01626 890243
Fax: 01626 890729
Email: castle@powderham.co.uk
Formed: 1391

Organisation type and purpose: Historic building, house or site, suitable for ages: all ages.
Member of:
Historic Houses Association (HHA)

Enquiries to: Manager
Other contacts: The Archivist for historical or genealogical information.
Access:
Access to staff: By letter, by telephone, by fax, by email, visitors by prior appointment, charges made to all users
Hours: Mon to Fri, 0900 to 1730
Access for disabled people: Parking provided, ramped entry, toilet facilities

General description:
Courtenay family history, Devon local history, art and antiques.
Information services:
Special visitor services: Guided tours, materials and/or activities for children.
Education services: Group education facilities, resources for Key Stages 1 and 2.
Services for disabled people: For the visually impaired; for the hearing impaired.
Collections:
Historic family home containing private collection from the last 600 years
Printed publications:
Guide Books
Painters
Architects
Electronic and video products:
Information video or DVD available direct

Internet home pages:
http://www.powderham.co.uk

2303
POWELL-COTTON MUSEUM
Quex Park, Birchington-on-Sea, Kent, CT7 0BH

Tel: 01843 842168
Fax: 01843 846661
Email: powell-cotton.museum@virgin.net
Formed: 1904
Formerly: Quex Park Museum

Organisation type and purpose: Independently owned, registered charity (charity number 307757), museum, art gallery, suitable for ages: all ages.

Enquiries to: Curator
Access:
Access to staff: By letter, by telephone, by fax, by email, visitors by prior appointment
Hours: Mon to Fri, 0900 to 1700
Access to building, collections or gallery: Prior appointment required
Access for disabled people: level entry, toilet facilities

General description:
House built by Major Powell-Cotton to house his collections of African and Asian zoology and ethnography, European and Asian weaponry and decorative arts.
Information services:
Library available for reference (for conditions see Access above)
Special visitor services: Guided tours, materials and/or activities for children.
Education services: Resources for Key Stages 1 and 2..
Collections:
African zoology collections including a primate study collection
African ethnography
Asian zoology
Cannon collection
Chinese export porcelain
Chinese Imperial porcelain
Cutting weapons
European porcelain
Firearms
General decorative arts
Local archaeology collection
Oriental fine arts
Victorian walled kitchen garden with teak glass houses under restoration: collections of old gardening equipment, tools and library

2304
POWIS CASTLE & GARDEN
Welshpool, Powys, SY21 8RF

Tel: 01938 551920
Fax: 01938 554336
Email: powiscastle@nationaltrust.org.uk

Organisation type and purpose: National organisation, registered charity (charity number 205846), historic building, house or site, suitable for ages: 8+.
Parent body:
The National Trust Office for Wales
Trinity Square, Llandudno, LL30 2DE, tel: 01492 860123, fax: 01492 860233

Enquiries to: Manager
Access:
Access to staff: By letter, by telephone, by email
Access to building, collections or gallery: No prior appointment required
Hours: Castle and museum: Easter to end of June, September to November, Wed to Sun, 1300 to 1700; July and August, Tue to Sun, 1300 to 1700
Garden: 1100 to 1800 (dates as for Castle)
Open Bank Holiday Mondays
Access for disabled people: Parking provided, toilet facilities
Other restrictions: Elderly visitors and those with mobility difficulties, heart conditions etc. should call for advice before visiting, as very steep site. Designated parking. Steps to entrance. No wheelchair access to Castle. No access to other floors. Photograph album. Level entrance to shop and to restaurant. Limited tables and chairs seating. Rest bench seating. No access for power mobility vehicles in garden due to steep terraces. Recommended route map.

General description:
Medieval castle originally built by the Welsh Princes and then became the ancestral home of the Herberts and Clives. The Clive Museum contains a beautiful collection of treasures from India. The garden is of the highest horticultural and historical importance.
Information services:
Helpline available, tel no: Infoline 01938 551944.
Guided tours of the castle and/or garden by prior arrangement (additional charge).
Braille guide. Scented plants. Touch tour of castle, must be booked in advance.
Frontcarrying baby slings for loan.
Suitable for school groups. Children's guide. Children's quiz/trail.
Special visitor services: Guided tours, materials and/or activities for children.
Services for disabled people: For the visually impaired.
Collections:
Fine collection of paintings and furniture
Collection brought from India by Clive

Internet home pages:
http://www.nationaltrust.org.uk

2305
POWYS COUNTY OBSERVATORY
See - Spaceguard Centre

2306
POWYSLAND MUSEUM AND MONTGOMERY CANAL CENTRE
Canal Yard, Welshpool, Powys, SY21 7AQ

Tel: 01938 554656
Fax: 01938 554656
Email: powysland@powys.gov.uk
Formed: 1874

Organisation type and purpose: Local government body, museum.

Enquiries to: Curator
Access:
Access to staff: By letter, by telephone, visitors by prior appointment
Access to building, collections or gallery: No prior appointment required
Hours: All Year: Mon, Tue, Thu, Fri, 1100 to 1300 and 1400 to 1700
May to Sep: Sat, Sun, 1000 to 1300 and 1400 to 1700
Oct to Apr: Sat, 1400 to 1700
Access for disabled people: Parking provided, level entry, access to all public areas, toilet facilities

General description:
A local museum focusing on the archaeology and social history of Montgomeryshire. There is a small collection of local geology. Also includes the collection of Montgomeryshire Yeomanry Cavalry memorabilia.
Information services:
Special visitor services: Materials and/or activities for children.

Education services: Group education facilities, resources for Key Stages 1 and 2, 3 and 4..
Catalogues:
Catalogue for part of the collections is only available in-house.

2307
PRESTEIGNE AND DISTRICT MUSEUM
See - Judge's Lodging

2308
PRESTON MANOR
Preston Drove, Brighton, East Sussex, BN1 6SD

Tel: 01273 292770
Fax: 01273 292771
Formed: 1933

Organisation type and purpose: Local government body, registered charity (charity number 266956), museum, historic building, house or site, suitable for ages: 8+.
Parent body:
Royal Pavilion, Libraries & Museums
Brighton & Hove Council, tel: 01273 290000

Enquiries to: Keeper of Preston Manor
Direct tel: 01273 292772
Direct email: david.beevers@brighton-hove.gov.uk
Access:
Access to staff: By letter, by telephone, by fax, by email, visitors by prior appointment
Hours: Mon, 1300 to 1700; Tue to Sat, 1000 to 1700; Sun, 1400 to 1700
Other restrictions: Other times by appointment only.
Access to building, collections or gallery: No prior appointment required
Hours: Mon, 1300 to 1700; Tue to Sat, 1000 to 1700; Sun, 1400 to 1700
Other restrictions: Prior appointment for the library.
General description:
Preston Manor dates in part from c. 1600. It was rebuilt in 1738 and substantially added to in 1905. Today the house and its contents give a rare insight into life during the early years of the twentieth century. The history of an Edwardian gentry home, including servants' quarters and day nursery. Contains pictures, silver, ceramics, social history and family memorabilia. Percy Macquoid and his collection; furniture and silver at Preston Manor.
Information services:
Library available for reference (for conditions see Access above)
Special visitor services: Guided tours, materials and/or activities for children.
Education services: Group education facilities.
Services for disabled people: For the visually impaired.
Collections:
Macquoid Bequest of furniture, silver, pictures and porcelain
Thomas-Stanford Bequest of pictures, furniture, silver and memorabilia
Collection of books and archives connected with Sussex
Catalogues:
Catalogue for library is in-house only. Catalogue for all of the collections is only available in-house.
Printed publications:
Guide Book (£2.95)

Internet home pages:
http://www.museums.brighton-hove.gov.uk
http://www.prestonmanor.virtualmuseum.info

2309
PRESTON MILL AND PHANTASSIE DOOCOT
East Linton, East Lothian, EH40 3DS

Tel: 01620 860426

Organisation type and purpose: Museum, historic building, house or site.
Parent body:
National Trust for Scotland

Enquiries to: Property Manager
Access:
Access to staff: By letter, by telephone, charges to non-members
Hours: End Mar to end Oct, Thu to Mon, 1200 to 1700, Sun, 1300 to 1700
Other restrictions: Key for Phantassie Doocot from the Mill.
Access for disabled people: toilet facilities

General description:
Eighteenth century mill and doocot.

Internet home pages:
http://www.nts.org.uk

2310
PRESTONGRANGE MUSEUM
Morison's Haven, Prestonpans, East Lothian, EH32 9RX

Tel: 0131 653 2904
Email: elms@historyshelf.org
Formed: 1993

Organisation type and purpose: Local government body, museum, historic building, house or site, suitable for ages: 5+.

Enquiries to: Museums Officer
Access:
Access to staff: By letter, by telephone, by fax, by email, in person, Internet web pages
Access for disabled people: Parking provided, level entry, access to all public areas, toilet facilities

General description:
Industrial and social history of East Lothian, particularly of the Prestonpans area. Covers coal-mining and related industries including brickmaking, salt-panning, brewing and pottery.
Information services:
Special visitor services: Guided tours, materials and/or activities for children.
Education services: Group education facilities..
Collections:
Cornish Beam Pumping Engine, unique in Scotland
Steam crane and colliery pugs (one of which is regularly steamed)
Catalogues:
Catalogue for all of the collections is only available in-house.

Internet home pages:
http://www.prestongrangemuseum.org
http://www.elothian-museums.demon.co.uk/pgm

2311
PRIEST HOUSE (SUSSEX PAST), THE
North Lane, West Hoathly, East Grinstead, West Sussex, RH19 4PP

Tel: 01342 810479
Email: priest@sussexpast.co.uk
Formed: 1908 as museum

Organisation type and purpose: Registered charity (charity number 207037), historic building, house or site, suitable for ages: 5+.
Parent body:
Sussex Archaeological Society
Bull House, 92 High Street, Lewes, East Sussex, BN7 1XH, tel: 01273 486260, fax: 01273 486990, email: admin@sussexpast.co.uk website www.sussexpast.co.uk

Enquiries to: Marketing & Publicity Officer
Direct tel: 01273 487188
Direct fax: 01273 486990
Direct email: pro@sussexpast.co.uk

General description:
A collection of vernacular furniture, domestic ironwork, agricultural implements, clocks, embroidery, toys and local photographs, displayed in a 15th century timber-framed house.
Information services:
Helpline available, tel no: 01273 487188.
Special visitor services: Guided tours..
Publications list:
is available in hard copy.
Printed publications:
The Priest House (guide book)

Internet home pages:
http://www.sussexpast.co.uk

2312
PRIEST'S HOUSE
Muchelney, Langport, Somerset, TA10 0DQ

Tel: 01985 843600 (Regional Office)

Organisation type and purpose: National organisation, registered charity (charity number 205846), historic building, house or site.
Parent body:
The National Trust (South West Region)
Regional Office for Wessex, tel: 01985 843100

Enquiries to: Manager
Access:
Access to staff: By letter, by telephone

General description:
A late-medieval hall house built by Muchelney Abbey in 1308 for the parish priest and little altered since the hall was divided in the early 17th century. Interesting features include the Gothic doorway, beautiful double-height tracery windows and a massive 15th century stone fireplace. The house is occupied and furnished by tenants.

2313
PRIEST'S HOUSE MUSEUM AND GARDEN, THE
23-27 High Street, Wimborne Minster, Dorset, BH21 1HR

Tel: 01202 882533
Formed: 1961
Formerly: Wimborne Historical Society; The Museum of East Dorset Life, date of change, 1997

Organisation type and purpose: Registered charity (charity number 1068540; 1068563), museum.

Enquiries to: Curator
Access:
Access to staff: By letter, by telephone, by fax, in person, visitors by prior appointment

General description:
Historic town house, with displays representing the people and businesses housed here over the centuries: 17th century Hall, Georgian Parlour, Victorian Kitchen, Victorian Ironmongers and Stationer's Shops. Childhood, archaeology, and East Dorset Village galleries, special exhibitions gallery, forge, many hands-on elements in displays.
Local history and archaeology, social history, domestic equipment, toys and dolls, printed ephemera, agricultural and rural industries, photographs.
Collections:
Tallant Hinton Roman Villa
Victorian Valentines
Local photographs

Internet home pages:
http://www.visitdorset.com
Opening hours; changes; forthcoming exhibitions and events.

2314
PRIEST'S HOUSE
Easton on the Hill, Stamford, Northamptonshire, PE9 3LL

Tel: 01909 486411 (Regional Office)

Organisation type and purpose: National organisation, registered charity (charity number

continued overleaf

205846), museum, historic building, house or site, suitable for ages: 5+.
Parent body:
The National Trust (East Midlands Region)
East Midlands Regional Office, tel: 01909 486411
Access:
Access to staff: By letter, by telephone
Other restrictions: General enquiries should be made to Regional Office.
Appointments for groups may be made through local representative, at 39 Church St, Easton on the Hill, Stamford PE9 3LL.
Access for disabled people: level entry
Other restrictions: Ground floor fully accessible, no access to other floors

General description:
A pre-Reformation priest's lodge, of specialist architectural interest only, and containing a small museum of village bygones.

Internet home pages:
http://www.nationaltrust.org.uk

2315
PRINCE OF WALES'S OWN REGIMENT OF YORKSHIRE MUSEUM, THE

3 Tower Street, York, YO1 9SB

Tel: 01904 662790
Fax: 01904 658824
Formed: 1925

Organisation type and purpose: National government body, registered charity, museum, suitable for ages: 12+.
Parent body:
Ministry of Defence

Enquiries to: Curator
Access:
Access to staff: By letter, by telephone, by fax
Hours: Mon to Sat, 0930 to 1630
Access to building, collections or gallery: No prior appointment required
Hours: Mon to Sat, 0930 to 1630

General description:
Covers the history of two famous Yorkshire Regiments, The West Yorkshire Regiment (14th Foot) and The East Yorkshire Regiment (15th Foot) from their formation in 1685 to their amalgamation in 1958 to form The Prince of Wales's Own Regiment of Yorkshire, and on to the present day.
Collections:
The Collection includes weapons, medals, uniforms, Regimental Colours, drums, silver, paintings and photographs covering over 300 years of history. This history covers the British Empire and battles and campaigns fought in Scotland, Ireland, on the continent of Europe, America, the West Indies, India, New Zealand, West Africa, South Africa, North Africa and Burma

2316
PRINCES RISBOROUGH MANOR HOUSE

Princes Risborough, Buckinghamshire, HP17 9AW

Tel: 01494 528051 (Regional Office)

Organisation type and purpose: National organisation, registered charity (charity number 205846), historic building, house or site.
Parent body:
The National Trust (South and South East Region)
Thames and Solent Regional Office, tel: 01494 528051

Enquiries to: Manager
Access:
Access to staff: By letter, by telephone
Access to building, collections or gallery: Prior appointment required
Hours: Apr to Oct, Wed, !430 to 1630
Other restrictions: House (hall, drawing room and staircase) and front garden, only by written appointment with the owner.

General description:
A 17th century red-brick house with Jacobean staircase and many original features.

Internet home pages:
http://www.nationaltrust.org.uk

2317
PRIOR PARK LANDSCAPE GARDEN

Ralph Allen Drive, Bath, BA2 5AH

Tel: 01225 833422 (Visitor kiosk)
Email: priorpark@nationaltrust.org.uk

Organisation type and purpose: National organisation, registered charity (charity number 205846), historic building, house or site, suitable for ages: all ages.
Parent body:
The National Trust (South West Region)
Regional Office for Wessex, tel: 01985 843600

Enquiries to: Warden
Access:
Access to staff: By letter, by telephone, by email
Access for disabled people: toilet facilities
Other restrictions: Designated parking. 3 parking bays for disabled visitors only, booking essential.
Wheelchair access limited to top of garden, level path to viewpoint over Bath. Elsewhere very steep.

General description:
A beautiful and intimate 18th century landscape garden, created by local entrepreneur Ralph Allen with advice from the poet Alexander Pope and 'Capability' Brown, and set in a sweeping valley with magnificent views of the City of Bath.
The many interesting features include a Palladian bridge and three lakes. The restoration of the garden is continuing. Prior Park College, a co-educational school, operates from the mansion (not NT). A five-minute walk from the garden leads on to the Bath Skyline, comprising woodlands, meadows and historical landscapes.
Information services:
Helpline available, tel no: 09001 335242.
Suitable for school groups: live interpretation, children's quiz/trail
Braille guide, and large-print guide.
Special visitor services: Materials and/or activities for children.
Services for disabled people: For the visually impaired.

Internet home pages:
http://www.nationaltrust.org.uk/regions/wessex

2318
PRIORY COTTAGES

1 Mill Street, Steventon, Abingdon, Oxfordshire, OX13 6SP

Tel: 01793 762209 (Coleshill Estate Office)

Organisation type and purpose: National organisation, registered charity (charity number 205846), historic building, house or site.
Parent body:
The National Trust (South and South East Region)
Thames and Solent Regional Office, tel: 01494 528051

Enquiries to: Manager
Access:
Access to staff: By letter, by telephone

General description:
Former monastic buildings, now converted into two houses. South Cottage contains the Great Hall of the original priory.

Internet home pages:
http://www.nationaltrust.org.uk

2319
PRIORY OF ST MARY AND ST CUTHBERT, THE

Bolton Abbey, Skipton, North Yorkshire, BD23 6AL

Tel: 01756 710238
Email: office@boltonpriory.org.uk
Acronym or abbreviation: The Priory Church
Formed: 1154

Organisation type and purpose: Historic building, house or site, suitable for ages: 5+. Church.

Enquiries to: Administrator
Access:
Access to staff: By letter, by telephone, by fax, by email
Hours: Mon, Tue, Thu, Fri, 0900 to 1500; Wed, 0900 to 1230
Access for disabled people: level entry

General description:
Historic living Church and ruins in beautiful surroundings.
Information services:
Special visitor services: Guided tours..
Collections:
Pugin stained glass windows

Internet home pages:
http://pages.britishlibrary.net/bolton.priory/

2320
PRITTLEWELL PRIORY MUSEUM

Priory Park, Victoria Avenue, Southend-on-Sea, Essex, SS2 6NB

Tel: 01702 342878
Fax: 01702 349806
Email: southendmuseum@hotmail.com
Formed: 1927

Organisation type and purpose: Museum.
Parent body:
Southend-on-Sea Borough Council
Victoria Avenue, Southend-on-Sea, Essex, S22 6EW
Address for Headquarters:
Southend Central Museum
Victoria Avenue, Southend-on-Sea, SS2 6EW, tel: 01702 434449, fax: 01702 349806, email/website: southendmuseum@hotmail.com

Enquiries to: Manager
Direct tel: 01702 434449
Access:
Access to staff: By letter, by telephone, by fax, in person
Access to building, collections or gallery: No prior appointment required
Hours: Tue to Sat, 1000 to 1300 and 1400 to 1700
Access for disabled people: Parking provided
Other restrictions: Ramped entry downstairs only accessible for wheelchairs.

General description:
The remains of a 12th century Cluniac Priory with later additions. Houses displays of mediaeval religious life and the history of Prittlewell Priory as a private house. A natural history gallery shows the wildlife of South East Essex. There is also an important communications collection, including printing presses, books, radio and television, especially by the local firm ECKO.
Information services:
Education services: Group education facilities..
Collections:
The Caten Collection of Radios
EKCO Collection of radio and television, c. 300 items

Internet home pages:
http://www.southendmuseums.co.uk
General information, links to other museums in Southend.

2321
PROVAND'S LORDSHIP
3 Castle Street, Glasgow, G4 0RB

Tel: 0141 552 8819
Fax: 0141 332 9957

Organisation type and purpose: Local government body, museum, historic building, house or site, suitable for ages: all ages.
Parent body:
Glasgow Museums

Enquiries to: Curator
Access:
Access to staff: By letter, by telephone, by fax
Access to building, collections or gallery: No prior appointment required
Hours: Mon to Thu, Sat 1000 to 1700: Fri and Sun 1100 to 1500
Other restrictions: Closed 25, 26 Dec and 1, 2 Jan

General description:
A rare example of 15th century Scottish domestic architecture. It is the oldest house in Glasgow (1471), it contains a collection of period furniture.
Much work has had to be undertaken on this Grade A listed ancient monument, and following over two years of extensive conservation and restoration work it was reopened to the public in November 2000. The displays recreate home life in the Middle Ages.
Collections:
Machinery for sweet making, used by the Mortan family business which occupied the ground floor of the house in the early 20th century
Scottish domestic furniture and fittings
Catalogues:
Catalogue for part of the collections is only available in-house.

2322
PROVOST ROSS'S HOUSE
See - Aberdeen Maritime Museum

2323
PROVOST SKENE'S HOUSE
Guestrow, Aberdeen, AB10 1AS

Tel: 01224 641086
Acronym or abbreviation: PSH
Formed: 1953

Organisation type and purpose: Local government body, historic building, house or site, suitable for ages: 12+.
Parent body:
Aberdeen Art Gallery & Museums (AAG+M)
School Hill, Aberdeen, AB10 1FQ, tel: 01224 523700, fax: 01224 632133, email/website: info@aagm.co.uk

Enquiries to: Curator
Direct tel: 01224 523702
Direct fax: 01224 632133
Direct email: chrisr@arts-rec.aberdeen.net.uk
Access:
Access to staff: By letter, by telephone, by fax, by email
Access to building, collections or gallery: No prior appointment required
Hours: Mon to Sat, 1000 to 1700; Sun, 1300 to 1600
Other restrictions: Closed 25, 26 Dec, 1, 2 Jan.
Access for disabled people: ramped entry

General description:
Historic house dating from 1545 with period room settings. Unique painted 17th century walls and plaster ceilings. Furnished room settings of 17th, 18th and early 19th centuries, costume gallery with changing exhibitions of historical dress, exhibitions of archaeology and coins.
Information services:
Events programme runs throughout the year.
The Cellar at Provost Skene's House serves light lunches and snacks.
Special visitor services: Guided tours, materials and/or activities for children..
Collections:
All held on computerised records:
Archaeological artefacts
Coins
Decorative Art
Furniture
Paintings (where relevant to the property)
Toys and Dolls
Catalogues:
Catalogue for all of the collections is available in-house and part is on-line.
Printed publications:
House Guide (£2.95)
Free Guide to building for visitors
Other products linked to special exhibitions may be available

Address for ordering publications:
Printed publications:
Shop Manager, Aberdeen Art Gallery
School Hill, Aberdeen, AB10 1FQ, tel: 01224 523670, fax: 01224 632133

Internet home pages:
http://aberdeencity.gov.uk
Comprehensive website for Aberdeen City Council which owns the property.
http://www.aagm.co.uk
Information about Provost Skene's House and parent body, exhibition details and some collection details.

2324
PRUDHOE CASTLE
Prudhoe, Northumberland, NE42 6NA

Tel: 01661 833459

Organisation type and purpose: Historic building, house or site.
Parent body:
English Heritage (North East Region)
Tel: 0191 269 1227/8, fax: 0191 261 1130

Enquiries to: Manager
Access:
Access to staff: By letter, by telephone, in person
Access to building, collections or gallery: No prior appointment required
Hours: End Mar to end Sep: daily, 1000 to 1800
Oct: daily, 1000 to1700
Other restrictions: Opening times are subject to change, for up-to-date information contact English Heritage by phone or visit the website.

General description:
Remains of a once formidable 13th century fortress. Archaeological evidence reveals that a defended enclosure existed on the site as early as the mid-11th century. Inside defensive ditches and ramparts is the Georgian Manor House, gatehouse, chapel, battlements and towers. Small exhibition and video presentation.

Internet home pages:
http://www.english-heritage.org.uk

2325
PUBLIC RECORD OFFICE, THE

Acronym or abbreviation: PRO
To be formed from: Public Record Office (PRO), Historical Manuscripts Commission (HMC), date of change, April 2003
See - National Archives

2326
PUBLIC RECORD OFFICE MUSEUM
See - National Archives

2327
PUMP HOUSE THE PEOPLES HISTORY MUSEUM
See - People's History Museum

2328
PUMPHOUSE EDUCATIONAL MUSEUM, THE
Lavender Pond and Nature Park, Lavender Road, Rotherhithe, London, SE16 1DZ

Tel: 020 7231 2976
Fax: 020 7231 2976
Email: cmarais@ukonline.co.uk
Full name: The Pumphouse Educational Museum & Rotherhithe Heritage Museum
Formed: 1989
Formerly: Rotherhithe Heritage Museum

Organisation type and purpose: Voluntary organisation, registered charity (charity number 802967), museum, historic building, house or site, suitable for ages: 5+.
Environmental study centre.
Education, reminiscence and communication.

Enquiries to: Head of Centre
Access:
Access to staff: By letter, by telephone, by fax, in person
Hours: Mon to Fri, 1000 to 1500
Access for disabled people: Parking provided, ramped entry, level entry, access to all public areas, toilet facilities

General description:
Housed on the ground floor of the Pumphouse built in 1929 to regulate the water level in the Dock System, the museum tells the story of Rotherhithe through artefacts found on the foreshore of the River Thames dating from Roman times to the present day.
The first floor has a permanent hands-on exhibition of artefacts from the Victorian era to the present day showing the differences between then and now. Incorporated in a unique environmental study centre. Used by children to understand the past and by visitors simply to recall those childhood memories, the exhibition allows different generations to recall and compare everyday objects.
A Blitz Room is another permanent display to show life during the war years.
The second floor houses the six foot replica of Queen Elizabeth's wedding cake, designed and iced at Peek Freans, Drummond Road, once the employer of many Rotherhithe residents.
Here also are the classroom facilities for schools, the office, the library and the lunch area, as well as the exit to the 1 hectare nature park and tranquil pond visited by herons, and with a resident pair of swans, tufted ducks and mallards.
Information services:
Inset and advisory service to teachers and universities with teacher training.
Special visitor services: Guided tours, materials and/or activities for children.
Education services: Group education facilities, resources for Key Stages 1 and 2 and Further or Higher Education..
Collections:
Rotherhithe Heritage Museum
Artefacts from the foreshore of the River Thames dating from Roman times
Peek Freans Memorabilia including 6 foot replica of iced wedding cake of Queen Elizabeth II
Exhibitions:
1950s artefacts and memorabilia
The Blitz Room artefacts and memorabilia
Artefacts from the 20th century home - hands-on exhibition
Catalogues:
Catalogue for library is in-house only. Catalogue for all of the collections is only available in-house.

Internet home pages:
http://www.se16.btinternet.co.uk/pumphouse.htm
Description of site and services

2329
QARANC MUSEUM

Full name: Queen Alexandra's Royal Army Nursing Corps Museum
See - Army Medical Services Museum

2330
QUAINTON RAILWAY SOCIETY LIMITED

See - Buckinghamshire Railway Centre

2331
QUAKER HERITAGE CENTRE

Ty Meirion, Sgwar Eldon Square, Dolgellau, Gwynedd

Tel: 01341 424442

Organisation type and purpose: Local government body, museum.
Parent body:
Gwynedd Museums Service
Access:
Access to staff: By letter, by telephone
Access to building, collections or gallery: No prior appointment required
Hours: Apr to Sep, daily, 1000 to 1800
Oct to Mar, daily, 1000 to 1700

General description:
Discover the story of a Quaker community that once lived in the old house, and the persecution that forced them to emigrate to Pennsylvania.

2332
QUAKER TAPESTRY, THE

Friends Meeting House, Stramongate, Kendal, Cumbria, LA9 4BH

Tel: 01539 722975
Fax: 01539 722975
Email: info@quaker-tapestry.co.uk
Full name: Quaker Tapestry Exhibition Centre At Kendal
Formed: 1994

Organisation type and purpose: Independently owned, registered charity (charity number 1035077), museum, suitable for ages: all ages.

Enquiries to: Exhibition Manager
Access:
Access to staff: By letter, by telephone, by email
Hours: Mon to Fri, 0930 to 1700
Access to building, collections or gallery: No prior appointment required
Hours: Apr to Oct: Mon to Sat, 1000 to 1700
Nov and Dec: Mon to Fri, 1000 to 1700
Access for disabled people: Parking provided, level entry, access to all public areas, toilet facilities

General description:
77 panels of 'narrative crewel embroidery' made by 4000 people from 15 countries during the 15 years 1981-1996.
The Tapestry illustrates 350 years of social history from 1652 to the present day. A delightful visual chronicle of Quaker Life through the centuries.
Large screen video, 19th century Quaker costume, gift shop, tea rooms.
Information services:
Special visitor services: Guided tours, materials and/or activities for children.
Education services: Group education facilities, resources for Key Stage 2 and Further or Higher Education.
Services for disabled people: For the visually impaired; for the hearing impaired; displays and/or information at wheelchair height.
Collections:
Quaker costume, 77 panels of embroidery, and artefacts
Catalogues:
Catalogue for all of the collections is published and is also on-line.
Publications list:
is available in hard copy and online.
Printed publications:
Leaflets (available, free)
Publications (for purchase)

Internet home pages:
http://www.quaker-tapestry.co.uk/
Comprehensive site with illustrations of all 77 panels, mail order including publications.

2333
QUARRY BANK MILL AND STYAL ESTATE

Quarry Bank Road, Styal, Wilmslow, Cheshire, SK9 4LA

Tel: 01625 527468
Fax: 01625 539267
Email: enquiries@quarrybankmill.org.uk
Acronym or abbreviation: QBM
Formed: 1976
Formerly: S Greg & Co Ltd, date of change, 1830s; R H Greg & Co Ltd, date of change, 1959; Quarry Bank Mill Trust Limited (QBMT), date of change, 2000
Incorrect but still used: Greg's Mill or Styal Mill

Organisation type and purpose: National organisation, registered charity (charity number 205846), museum, historic building, house or site, suitable for ages: all ages.
Formed as an independent charitable trust in 1976, in 2000 the National Trust undertook the management.
Parent body:
The National Trust (North West)
North West Regional Office, tel: 0870 609 5391

Enquiries to: Curator
Direct email: curator@quarrybankmill.org.uk
Other contacts: Museum Manager
Access:
Access to staff: By letter, by telephone, by fax, by email, visitors by prior appointment
Hours: Mon to Fri, 0900 to 1700
Access to building, collections or gallery: No prior appointment required
Hours: Mill: Oct to late Mar: Tue to Sun, 1030 to 1730 (last admission 1600); late Mar to Sep: daily, 1030 to 1730 (last admission 1600)
Other restrictions: Apprentice House open 1400 to1630 weekdays, 1100 to1630 weekendsand school holidays
(Mar to Sep); 1400 to1530 weekdays, 1100 to 1530 weekends and school holidays (Oct to Mar). Admission to Apprentice House by timed ticket only, available from Mill on arrival. Mill: last admission 1½hrs before closing. Phone or access website for times/prices. Archive/library by prior appointment.
Access for disabled people: Parking provided, toilet facilities
Other restrictions: Access to Curatorial Department difficult, limited access to museum buildings. Designated parking 200yds. Drop-off point. 2 manual wheelchairs available. Ground floor accessible with assistance. Access to other floors via lift. Ground floor of Apprentice House accessible for wheelchairs. Information available for those who cannot go upstairs. Level entrance to restaurant.

General description:
Museum of the Cotton Industries, focussing upon the experiences of the mill-owning family and their workforce, the factory colony, cotton manufacturing processes and power systems. Human interpretation, machine and power demonstrations, displays enlivened through interactive exhibits.
Social history, textile history, local history, technology of textile machinery, technology of power (watermill and steam engines) as applied at Quarry Bank Mill.
Information services:
Library available for reference (for conditions see Access above), bibliography compilation, selective dissemination services
Guided tours available for booked groups from 1030 except Bank Holiday Mondays. Guided tours of Mill at weekends Apr to Sep 1130 to 1400, Oct to March at 1400. No charge for ticket holders. Events throughout the year, leaflet available on request or see website.
Braille guide. Large-print guide. Sympathetic Hearing Scheme.
Front-carrying baby slings for loan. Geese and hens at Apprentice House.
Suitable for school groups. Education room/centre. Live interpretation. Hands-on activities. Children's quiz/trail. Adult study days.
Special visitor services: Materials and/or activities for children.
Education services: Group education facilities, resources for Key Stages 1 and 2, 3, 4 and Further or Higher Education.
Services for disabled people: For the visually impaired; for the hearing impaired; displays and/or information at wheelchair height.
Collections:
Major Collections include Greg Papers and Bleachers' Association Archive
Collections of printed material, manuscript sources, photographic material, textile fabrics, business and personal papers, textile pattern books
Hough collection of textiles
Logan Muckeldt and Stead McAlpine pattern books
Manchester Technical School glass plate slides (of textile machinery)
Working Cotton Machinery - powered, hand, spinning, weaving and preparation
Working waterwheel, beam engine and horizontal engine
Greg archive, mill ledgers, apprentice indentures, personal records, litter books, etc. 1784-1960, c. 600 items
Bleachers Association archive, inventory valuations, business details of c. 50 members, c. 1830-1920, c. 600 items
Catalogues:
Catalogue for library is in-house only. Catalogue for part of the collections is only available in-house.
Publications list:
is available in hard copy and online.
Printed publications:
The following are available directly, personal visits, mail order subject to stock, contact Mill Shop for current details:
Victorian Britain and Quarry Bank Mill (resource book for teachers KS2, £8.50)
A selection of pamphlets, fact sheets, guides, leisure and tourism pack, full colour postcards
Cottoning on to literacy at Quarry Bank Mill (£7.50)
Esther Price: The life story of an apprentice at Quarry Bank Mill (£1.50)
Evidence: Investigate Quarry Bank Mill, the Gregs and their workforce (£10)
Mill Life at Styal (£3.95)
Souvenir Guidebook (£2.50)
The Apprentice House Garden at Quarry Bank Mill, Styal (£1.50)
What became of the Quarry Bank Mill Apprentices? (A5 booklet, £1.75)
Electronic and video products:
The following are available directly, personal visits, mail order subject to stock, contact Mill Shop for current details:
Quarry Bank Mill at Styal, video available directly, personal visits, mail order (£15)
CD-ROM, tape and disk by special arrangement subject to clearance

Address for ordering publications:
Printed publications:
Mill Shop
Tel: 01825 537529

Internet home pages:
http://www.quarrybankmill.org.uk
Taster to museum site; education packages; corporate functions; history, events, links to other sites, eg National Trust.

2334
QUAY ART
43 High Street, Hull, East Yorkshire, HU1 1PT

Tel: 01482 221589
Fax: 01482 609911
Email: admin-quay-art@pop3.poptel.org.uk
Formed: 1996

Organisation type and purpose: Art gallery, suitable for ages: all ages.
Increasing access to the contemporary visual arts.
other branch:
Opt for ART
88 Shannon Road, Longhill, tel: 01482 718300

Enquiries to: Project Leader
Other contacts: Education Officer for community work, schools programmes, educational events.
Access:
Access to staff: By letter, by fax, by email
Hours: Mon to Fri, 1000 to 1730
Access to building, collections or gallery: No prior appointment required
Hours: Hours depends on the exhibition, sometimes the gallery shuts for a period, therefore it is advisable to ring prior to visit
Access for disabled people: ramped entry

General description:
Quay Art runs a programme of contemporary visual art exhibitions and also provides an advisory service for artists and educators. There is a small shop selling original pieces by local artists. Quay Art also runs a range of educational projects outside the gallery, including work in schools, community groups and training programmes for artists.
It is imperative to ring Quay Art before visiting as the gallery space is sometimes shut to the public.
Information services:
Educational facilities not based at the gallery.
Special visitor services: Materials and/or activities for children.
Education services: Group education facilities, resources for Key Stages 1 and 2, 3, 4 and Further or Higher Education..
Catalogues:
Catalogue for library is on-line. Catalogue for all of the collections is on-line.

Internet home pages:
http://www.quay-art.org
Archive of exhibitions, residencies and educational work. Up-to-date information about current projects and discussion essays.

2335
QUEBEC HOUSE
Quebec Square, Westerham, Kent, TN16 1TD

Tel: 01372 453401 (Regional Office)
Formed: 1918

Organisation type and purpose: National organisation, registered charity (charity number 205846), historic building, house or site, suitable for ages: 8+.
Parent body:
The National Trust (South and South East Region)
South East Regional Office, tel: 01372 453401
Administered and maintained by a:
Tenant

Enquiries to: Honorary Curator
Access:
Access to staff: By letter only
Other restrictions: General enquiries (eg admission charges) to Regional Office.
Access to building, collections or gallery: No prior appointment required
Hours: Apr to Oct: Tue and Sun, 1400 to 1800 (last admission 1730)
Access for disabled people: ramped entry, level entry, toilet facilities
Other restrictions: Designated parking 150yds. Ground floor accessible with assistance, booking advisable. The entrance hall is separated from the parlour by a 5in step and another 5in step leads to the inner hall. No access to other floors. Portable ramps on request. One bench on side-lawn. Level gravel paths lead visitors to back of house and to the coach house. Recommended route map.

General description:
General James Wolfe spent his early years in this gabled, red-brick house of 16th century origin, extended in the 17th century. The low ceilinged, panelled rooms contain memorabilia relating to his family and career, and the Tudor stable block houses an exhibition about the Battle of Quebec (1759).
Information services:
Guided tours available for groups by writing well in advance.
Braille guide. Touch list.
Suitable for school groups.
Special visitor services: Guided tours.
Services for disabled people: For the visually impaired.
Collections:
The story of General James Wolfe (1727-1759) who spent his childhood years in the house (then called Spiers) is illustrated through collections of paintings, engravings and memorabilia
There is an exhibition about The Conquest of Quebec in 1759 in the adjoining Coach House
A complete photocopy is available for visitors of the posthumously published 'General Wolfe's Instructions for Young Officers' on display with other 18th century volumes relating to his career
Catalogues:
Catalogue for library is in-house only. Catalogue for all of the collections is only available in-house.
Printed publications:
Quebec House Guide Book (£2 plus p&p)
Quebec House Broadsheet
Quebec House Capture of Quebec (£1 plus p&p)
Electronic and video products:
Tape-recording of House's 18th century Broadwood Square Piano (£6 plus p&p)

Internet home pages:
http://www.nationaltrust.org.uk

2336
QUEEN ALEXANDRA'S ROYAL ARMY NURSING CORPS MUSEUM
See - Army Medical Services Museum

2337
QUEEN ELIZABETH'S HUNTING LODGE
6 Ranger's Road, Chingford, London, E4 7QH

Tel: 020 8529 6681
Formed: 1890
Formerly: Epping Forest Museum

Organisation type and purpose: Local government body, museum, historic building, house or site, suitable for ages: 5+.
Parent body:
Corporation of London
The Warren, Loughton, Essex, IG10 4RW, tel: 020 8532 1010

Enquiries to: Education Officer
Access:
Access to staff: By letter, by telephone
Access for disabled people: toilet facilities
Other restrictions: Limited parking; access ground floor only.

General description:
The Hunting Lodge was built for Henry VIII in 1543. It is a three-storey timber-framed building. Visitors can learn about building techniques, hunting in Tudor Times and associated social history, history of Epping Forest. Contains items illustrating the natural history, social history, archaeology and ecology of Epping Forest. The major part of the collection relates to the natural history of Epping Forest. The rest covers the Forest's social history and archaeology.
The fabric of the building is very visible. The kitchen is furnished with appropriate objects, and replica costumes are on show.
Information services:
Special visitor services: Guided tours, materials and/or activities for children.
Education services: Group education facilities, resources for Key Stages 1 and 2, 3, 4 and Further or Higher Education..
Collections:
Collections now on show include:
Natural history, archaeology, some social history, documents and images relating to history of Epping Forest
Most collections originally from Essex Field Club

2338
QUEEN STREET MILL
Queen Street, Harle Syke, Burnley, Lancashire, BB10 2HX

Tel: 01282 412555
Fax: 01282 430220
Email: queenstreet@museumoflancs.org.uk
Formed: 1984
Formerly: Pennine Heritage, date of change, 1988; Burnley Borough Council, date of change, 1997

Organisation type and purpose: Local government body, museum, historic building, house or site, suitable for ages: 5+.
Parent body:
Lancashire County Museum Service (LCMS)
Stanley Street, Preston, PR1 4YP, tel: 01772 264061
Connections with:
Museum of the Lancashire Textile Industry (MLTI)
Holcombe Road, Helmshore, Lancashire, BB4 4NP

Enquiries to: Assistant Keeper
Other contacts: Visitor Services Officer for liaison with visitors, and bookings.
Access:
Access to staff: By letter, by telephone, by fax, in person, visitors by prior appointment, Internet web pages
Hours: Mon to Fri, 0900 to 1700, Sat and Sun 9000-1700
Access to building, collections or gallery: No prior appointment required
Hours: Apr to Oct: Tue to Fri, 1230 to 1700
May to Sep: Tue to Sat, 1030 to 1700
Mar and Nov: Tue to Thu, 1300 to 1600
Weekends and Bank Holidays, during season
At other times by prior appointment
Access for disabled people: Parking provided, level entry, toilet facilities

General description:
Machinery relating to the Lancashire textile industry. Housed in two adjacent mill buildings - one a fulling mill built in 1789; the other an 1820s-built mill used since the 1920s for cotton spinning. Both include original working environments.
Information services:
Special visitor services: Guided tours.
Education services: Group education facilities..
Collections:
Textile industry related objects including books, manufacturers catalogues, photographs, documents, manuscripts
The last remaining steam-powered weaving shed in Britain with 300 Lancashire looms run by 'Peace', the 500hp steam engine.
The Platt collection of early textile machinery. Includes an 'improved Jenny' and the only complete Arkwright 'Water Frame'.
Library of textile industry and related books
Collection of c. 27,000 photographic negatives
Catalogues:
Catalogue for library is in-house only. Catalogue for part of the collections is only available in-house.

continued overleaf

Printed publications:
Comprehensive teacher's pack (to purchase, direct)

Internet home pages:
http://www.lancashire.com/lcc/museums

2339
QUEEN'S DRAGOON GUARDS REGIMENTAL MUSEUM
See - Cardiff Castle Museum

2340
QUEEN'S LANCASHIRE REGIMENTAL MUSEUM
Regimental Headquarters, Fulwood, Preston, Lancashire, PR2 8AA

Tel: 01772 260362
Fax: 01772 260583
Acronym or abbreviation: QLR Museum
Formed: 1929
Formed from: East Lancashire Regiment, South Lancashire Regiment, Lancashire Regiment and related Militia, Volunteer, Territorial Army, Home Guard and Cadet Units, Loyal Regiment (North Lancashire)
Formerly: South Lancashire Regiment and the Loyal Regiment (North Lancashire) Museum, date of change, 1997

Organisation type and purpose: Membership association (membership is by subscription), registered charity, museum, suitable for ages: all ages.
The mission of the Museum of the Queen's Lancashire Regiment is to collect, document, exhibit, interpret and preserve the Regimental Collection in perpetuity, in order that it may be used to educate both the Regimental family and the general public.

Enquiries to: Curator

General description:
History, uniforms, arms, accoutrements, medals, records and archives of the Regiment, from 1688 to the present day.
Collections:
Collection of the 30th, 40th, 47th, 59th, 81st and 82nd Regiments of Foot
Collection of the East Lancashire Regiment, Loyal Regiment (North Lancashire), Lancashire Regiment, Queen's Lancashire Regiment and South Lancashire Regiment (PWV)
Original manuscript regimental records, books, diaries, letters, photographs, pamphlets and maps
Uniforms, weapons, accoutrements and memorabilia

2341
QUEEN'S OWN HIGHLANDERS (SEAFORTH AND CAMERONS)
Regimental Museum, Cameron Barracks, Inverness, IV2 3XD

Tel: 01463 224380
Formed: 1966

Organisation type and purpose: Independently owned, registered charity (charity number SCO 018068), museum, suitable for ages: 12+.
Regimental museum situated at Fort George, Ardersier.
Parent body:
The Highlanders
Regimental Headquarters

Enquiries to: Curator
Access:
Access to staff: By letter, by telephone, by fax, visitors by prior appointment
Hours: Mon to Fri, 0900 to 1700

General description:
Regimental history, records of regiment, awards, music, colours, uniforms, arms, medals, paintings, prints, ceramics, relating to the Seaforth Highlanders, The Queen's Own Cameron Highlanders, the Queen's Own Highlanders, The Lovat Scouts.
Collections:
Documents
Personal accounts
Photographs
Published histories
Printed publications:
Queen's Own Highlanders - Seaforth and Camerons, An Illustrated History
Regimental Magazine (2 times a year, for subscribers)
The Piper's Day - Regimental Duty Tunes of the Queen's Own Highlanders
Electronic and video products:
Audiotapes of bagpipe music

2342
QUEEN'S PARK ART STUDIO
Rochdale Road, Harpurhey, Manchester, M9 5SH

Tel: 0161 205 2645
Fax: 0161 205 6164

Organisation type and purpose: Local government body.
Parent body:
Manchester City Galleries
Tel: 0161 235 8888
Access:
Access to building, collections or gallery: No access other than to staff
Hours: Not open to the public

General description:
Manchester City Galleries conservation studio workshop for the restoration of artworks.

2343
QUEEN'S ROYAL LANCERS REGIMENTAL MUSEUM, THE
Belvoir Castle, Belvoir, Grantham, Lincolnshire, NG33 7TJ

Tel: 0115 957 3295
Fax: 0115 957 3195
Email: hhqandmuseumqrl@ukonline.co.uk
Formed: 1993
Formed from: 16th/5th The Queen's Royal Lancers, 17th/21st Lancers, date of change, 1993

Organisation type and purpose: Registered charity (charity number 1037202), museum, research organisation.

Enquiries to: Curator
Access:
Access to staff: By letter, by telephone, by fax, by email, Internet web pages
Access for disabled people: Parking provided, toilet facilities

General description:
The Museum tells the story of four famous cavalry regiments - The 5th, 16th, 17th and 21st Lancers - now amalgamated to form The Queen's Royal Lancers. A series of over twenty display cases feature arms, uniform, medals, silver, paintings and personal artefacts.
Information services:
Library available for reference (for conditions see Access above)
Special visitor services: Tape recorded guides.
Services for disabled people: Displays and/or information at wheelchair height.

Internet home pages:
http://www.qrl.uk.com
Information on museum, research, history of regiments, Regiment Association, sales.

2344
QUEEN'S ROYAL SURREY REGIMENT MUSEUM, THE
Clandon Park, West Clandon, Guildford, Surrey, GU4 7RQ

Tel: 01483 223419
Fax: 01483 224636
Formed: 1979
Formerly: East Surrey Regiment Museum, Queen's Royal Regiment Museum, date of change, 1959/60

Organisation type and purpose: Registered charity (charity number 275470), museum.

Enquiries to: Curator
Other contacts: Chairman of Trustees for all matters relating to charitable status; trust matters; legal matters etc.
Access:
Access to staff: By letter, by telephone, by fax, in person
Access to building, collections or gallery: No prior appointment required
Hours: Apr to Oct, Tue to Thu, Sun and Bank Holiday Mon, 1200 to 1700
Other restrictions: Museum closed for viewing from Oct to Apr, prior appointment required between Oct and Apr for research visits.
Access for disabled people: Parking provided, access to all public areas, toilet facilities

General description:
General historical information about The Queen's Royal Surrey, The Queen's Royal and The East Surrey Regiment and their forebears from 1661 to 1959. Movements and engagements of WWI battalions. Uniforms, medals, insignia (but not personal or service records) of the regiments.
Information services:
Services for disabled people: Displays and/or information at wheelchair height.
Collections:
Histories of the Infantry Regiments of Surrey; rolls of honour; WWI war diaries; some original documents; journals; battalion histories; some nominal rolls; photograph albums
Catalogues:
Catalogue for library is in-house only. Catalogue for all of the collections is only available in-house.
Publications list:
is available in hard copy.
Printed publications:
The Territorial Battalions of the Regiments of Surrey and Their Successors (£1.80 inc p&p)
The Surreys in Italy (Italy 1943-1945) (£1.95 inc p&p)
The Final Years 1938-1959 - The East Surrey Regiment (£2.90 inc p&p)
Algiers to Tunis - North Africa 1942-1943 (£2.05 inc p&p)
History of The 2/7th Battalion The Queen's Royal Regiment 1939-1946 (Bullen R E, £3.90 inc p&p)
Salerno Remembered (Curtis G, £4.25 inc p&p)
Background and Guide to the Museum (57p inc p&p)
More than Twice a Hero - Sgt McCabe, 31st Regt (42p inc p&p)
History of The Queen's Royal Surrey Regiment (Riley J P, £1.92 inc p&p)
The Queen's in The Middle East and North Africa 1939-1943 (Major Johnson R B, £2.90 inc p&p)
Malaya 1941-1942 - 2nd Surreys (£2.40 inc p&p)
Toil, Tribulation, Triumph (Atkins T, £5.76 inc p&p)
1661-1966 Summary of Regimental History (£1.58 inc p&p)
Rupert's Progress (Cornwell P, £5.50 inc p&p)

Address for ordering publications:
Printed publications:
The Museum Shop

Internet home pages:
http://www.surrey-online.co.uk/queenssurreys
General description of museum collections with images and layout of galleries.
Access information for visitors and researchers.
Shop price list and purchasing instructions.

2345
QUEENSFERRY MUSEUM
53 High Street, South Queensferry, West Lothian, EH30 9HP

Tel: 0131 331 5545
Fax: 0131 557 3346

Organisation type and purpose: Local government body, museum.
Part of:
The City of Edinburgh Museums and Galleries Service
Which is a division of:
The City of Edinburgh Council's Culture and Leisure Department
Tel: 0131 200 2000 (Main council) 0131 529 7844 (Culture & Leisure Department HQ)
Access:
Access to staff: By letter, by telephone, by fax
Other restrictions: Closed Tue and Wed.
Access to building, collections or gallery: No prior appointment required
Hours: Mon, Thu, Fri, Sat, 1000 to 1300 and 1415 to 1700; Sun, 1200 to 1700
Other restrictions: Access to the permanent collection for research purposes etc, strictly by appointment.

General description:
Commanding magnificent views of the two bridges spanning The Forth, the museum tells the story of the life, work and leisure of Queensferry people, including displays on the Burry Man and the Ferry Fair, the historic ferry crossing to Fife, and the building of the rail and road bridges.
Collections:
Forth Bridge Collection, material includes objects, photographs and documents relating to the construction and subsequent history of the bridge, 1880s to present, c. 60 items
VAT 69 blending and bottling plant, material includes objects, photographs, slides and documents, 1950s-1985, c. 210 items
Catalogues:
Catalogue for all of the collections is published.
Publications list:
is available on-line.
Printed publications:
The City of Edinburgh Museums and Galleries Service publishes a wide range of material, a list is available by telephoning 0131 529 3983, from April 2000 a selected list will be available on our website at www.cac.org.uk

Address for ordering publications:
Printed publications:
Publishing Department, The City of Edinburgh Museums and Galleries Service
Tel: 0131 529 3983, email: Website: www.cac.org.uk

Internet home pages:
http://www.cac.org.uk
Website for The City of Edinburgh Museums and Galleries Service, it contains: information on each of our 11 venues and their permanent collections; details of current temporary exhibitions; information on past temporary exhibitions; details of selected publications.

2346
QUEX HOUSE
See - Powell-Cotton Museum

2347
QUILTERS' GUILD OF THE BRITISH ISLES, THE
Room 190, Dean Clough, Halifax, West Yorkshire, HX3 5AX

Tel: 01422 347669
Fax: 01422 345017
Email: administrator@quiltersguild.org.uk
Formed: 1979
Formerly: Quilters' Guild, date of change, 1998

Organisation type and purpose: International organisation, national organisation, membership association (membership is by subscription), present number of members: 7000, voluntary organisation, registered charity (charity number 1067361), museum, suitable for ages: all ages, research organisation.
To promote and maintain the crafts of quilting, patchwork and appliqué from an educational base and historical perspective.

Enquiries to: Administrator
Access:
Access to staff: By letter, by telephone, by fax, by email, visitors by prior appointment, charges to non-members, Internet web pages
Hours: Mon to Thu, 0930 to 1700; Fri, 0900 to 1430
Other restrictions: Resource Centre: Mon, Tue, Wed, 0930 to 1230; Thu, 1000 to 1600 (with curator).
Access to building, collections or gallery: Prior appointment required
Hours: Mon to Fri, 0930 to 1700
Access for disabled people: access to all public areas, toilet facilities

General description:
History of quilting, how to quilt, contemporary quilting, patchwork and appliqué.
Collections:
Book library, slide library, study packs, videos
Heritage Quilt Collection
Quilt collection historical and contemporary
Catalogues:
Catalogue for library is in-house only.
Printed publications:
Quilt Studies (£10)
Quilt Treasures (1995)
Nineties Catalogue (£10)
The Quilter (quarterly magazine, free to members, £7 to non-members)

Internet home pages:
http://www.quiltersguild.org.uk

2348
R J MITCHELL MEMORIAL MUSEUM
See - Southampton Hall of Aviation

2349
RADNORSHIRE MUSEUM
Temple Street, Llandrindod Wells, Powys, LD1 5DL

Tel: 01597 824513
Fax: 01597 825781
Email: radnorshiremuseum@powys.gov.uk
Formed: 1929

Organisation type and purpose: Local government body, museum, suitable for ages: 5+.

Enquiries to: Curator
Access:
Access to staff: By letter, by telephone, by email, in person, visitors by prior appointment
Access to building, collections or gallery: No prior appointment required
Hours: Tue to Thu, 1000 to 1700; Fri, 1000 to 1630

General description:
Collections covering the old mid-Wales county of Radnorshire and the rise of Llandrindod Wells as a Victorian/Edwardian spa. Collections include fine art; archaeology; costume; and social history.
Information services:
Special visitor services: Materials and/or activities for children.
Education services: Group education facilities, resources for Key Stages 1 and 2, 3 and 4..
Collections:
Roberts Photographic Collection, 1900-1940, 15,000 images
Bronze Age, Iron Age, Roman, Early Christian, Medieval artefacts
Castell Collen, Roman Fort, 5000 items
Victorian/Spa related material
Patterson, doll collection, 1850-1960, 100 items
Thomas Jones watercolour paintings
Lyons collection of early 19th century watercolours, 1835, 120 pictures

Internet home pages:
http://www.powysmuseums.gov.uk

2350
RADSTOCK MUSEUM
Waterloo Road, Radstock, Bath, BA3 3ER

Tel: 01761 437722
Fax: 01761 420470
Formed: 1989

Organisation type and purpose: Independently owned, registered charity, museum, suitable for ages: all ages.
Local history museum.
Parent body:
Radstock-Midsomer Norton & District Museum Society
at the same address

Enquiries to: Administrator
Other contacts: Education Officer
Access:
Access to staff: By letter, by telephone, by fax, visitors by prior appointment
Access to building, collections or gallery: No prior appointment required
Hours: Tue to Fri, Sun, 1400 to 1700; Sat, 1100 to 1700
Other restrictions: Other times for groups by prior appointment.
Closed Dec and Jan.
Access for disabled people: Parking provided, level entry, access to all public areas, toilet facilities

General description:
Displays cover all aspects of the industrial and social life of those who worked in the former North Somerset Coalfield.
Mining and railway artefacts, miner's cottage kitchen, Co-op Store, Victorian school room, carpenter and forge, Wesley & Nelson connections within the area.
Information services:
Special visitor services: Guided tours, materials and/or activities for children.
Education services: Group education facilities, resources for Key Stages 1 and 2, 3 and 4.
Services for disabled people: For the visually impaired; displays and/or information at wheelchair height.
Collections:
Photographic archive, books and documents relating to the North Somerset Coalfield
Catalogues:
Catalogue for all of the collections is only available in-house.
Printed publications:
Publications (for purchase, direct)
Five Arches (Radstock-Midsomer Norton & District Museum Society, journal, 3 times a year)
Electronic and video products:
Videos (for purchase, direct)

Internet home pages:
http://www.radstockmuseum.co.uk

2351
RAGGED SCHOOL MUSEUM
46-50 Copperfield Road, London, E3 4RR

Tel: 020 8980 6405
Fax: 020 8983 3481
Email: enquiries@raggedschoolmuseum.org.uk
Formed: 1990

Organisation type and purpose: Membership association (membership is by subscription, election or invitation), present number of members: 230, registered charity (charity number 800538), museum, historic building, house or site, suitable for ages: all ages.

Enquiries to: Director

continued overleaf

Other contacts: Curator for information about collection or exhibitions.
Access:
Access to staff: By letter, by telephone, by fax
Access to building, collections or gallery: No access other than to staff
Hours: Wed & Thu 1000 to 1700; 1st Sun in month 1400 to 1700
Other restrictions: Wheelchair access to ground floor only.
Access for disabled people: ramped entry, toilet facilities
Other restrictions: Access to ground floor only, at present.

General description:
The museum collects the ordinary things of life, work and leisure, with special interest in work of Dr Barnardo and the development of education in the East End. The collections are small. The museum building, an 1812 canalside warehouse, is a significant feature in itself.
Information services:
Special education needs programme.
Special visitor services: Guided tours, materials and/or activities for children.
Education services: Group education facilities, resources for Key Stages 1 and 2..
Collections:
Social history collection relating to life and work in the East End
Publications list:
is available in hard copy and online.
Printed publications:
Dr Barnardo and the Copperfield Road Ragged Schools (T S Ridge, £3 plus 60p p&p)
Ben's Limehouse (Ben Thomas, £4.75 plus £1 p&p)
Common Ground. Portraits of Tower Hamlets (Photographed by Rehan Jamil, £3 plus 85p p&p)
Domest Life Resource Pack for KS1 and KS2 teachers (£8 inc p&p)
Ocean Views - Portrait of the Ocean Estate in Stepney (photographs by Jamil R, £3 plus £1 p&p)
Ragged Schools, Ragged Children (Claire Seymour, £4 plus 75p p&p)

Address for ordering publications:
Printed publications:
The Adminstrator, Ragged School Museum at the same address

Internet home pages:
http://www.raggedschoolmuseum.org.uk

2352
RAILWAY HERITAGE TRUST
PO Box 686, Melton House, 65/67 Clarendon Road, Watford, Hertfordshire, WD17 1XZ

Tel: 01923 240250
Fax: 01923 207079
Email: rht.railtrack@ems.rail.co.uk
Formed: 1985

Organisation type and purpose: Advisory body.
Independent company, sponsored by Railtrack and Rail Property Ltd, which offers grant aid for the conservation of listed buildings and structures owned by those sponsors.
Heritage funding agency.

Enquiries to: Executive Director
Access:
Access to staff: By letter, by telephone, by fax, visitors by prior appointment
Hours: Mon to Fri, 0900 to 1700

General description:
Repair, restoration and conservation of listed and historic railway buildings and structures owned by Railtrack and Rail Property Ltd, grant aid for this purpose.
Printed publications:
Annual Report

2353
RAILWAY PRESERVATION SOCIETY OF IRELAND
Whitehead Excursion Station, Castleview Road, Whitehead, Carrickfergus, Co Antrim, BT38 9NA

Tel: 028 2826 0803
Fax: 028 2826 0803
Email: rpsitrains@hotmail.com
Acronym or abbreviation: RPSI
Formed: 1964

Organisation type and purpose: Membership association (membership is by subscription), present number of members: 1000, voluntary organisation, registered charity.
We aim to restore, maintain and operate preserved steam locomotives and historic carriages on the main line railways of Ireland.
Member of:
Heritage Railway Association (HRA)

Enquiries to: Honorary Secretary
Other contacts: Chairman
Access:
Access to staff: By letter, by email, visitors by prior appointment, Internet web pages
Hours: Mon to Fri, 0900 to 1700
Access to building, collections or gallery: Prior appointment required
Access for disabled people: Parking provided, ramped entry

General description:
Irish railway preservation, steam locomotives, vintage rolling stock.
Collections:
Irish steam engines and rolling stock
Printed publications:
Journal (to members)
Newsletters (to members)

Internet home pages:
http://www.rpsi-online.org

2354
RAILWORLD
Oundle Road, Peterborough, Cambridgeshire, PE2 9NR

Tel: 01733 344240
Fax: 01733 344240
Formed: 1985
Formerly: Museum of World Railways, date of change, 1992

Organisation type and purpose: Learned society (membership is by election or invitation), present number of members: 10, voluntary organisation, registered charity (charity number 291515), suitable for ages: all ages.
Exhibition Centre & Museum.
Formal objective is public education with the aim to create a permanent public exhibition centre on the rail industry and sustainable integrated transport.
Links with:
Friends of Railworld
Tel: 01733 344240

Enquiries to: Chairman
Other contacts: Vice-Chairman for shared responsibilities.
Access:
Access to staff: By letter, by telephone, by fax, visitors by prior appointment, charges made to all users
Access for disabled people: Parking provided, ramped entry
Other restrictions: Access to most areas.

General description:
The site is located next to the Nene Valley Railway, Town Station. Integrated transport with a focus on railways; environmental issues which relate to transport; Peterborough's local railway history.
Information services:
Special visitor services: Guided tours, materials and/or activities for children.
Education services: Group education facilities, resources for Key Stages 1 and 2, 3, 4 and Further or Higher Education..
Collections:
Modern and future train travel, integrated transport and environmental challenges
Principal displays and video films are on global rail practice
Model railway, Age of Steam and local railway history displays, two large locomotives, two British Hover-trains, hands-on exhibits and flowerbeds
Small library may be accessed at the Trustees' discretion
Printed publications:
Newsletter (produced by Friends of Railworld)

2355
RAINHAM HALL
The Broadway, Rainham, Havering, Essex, RM13 9YN

Tel: 01494 528051 (Regional Office), 01708 555360 (Rainham Hall)

Organisation type and purpose: National organisation, registered charity (charity number 205846), historic building, house or site.
Parent body:
The National Trust (South and South East Region)
Thames and Solent Regional Office, tel: 01494 528051

Enquiries to: Manager
Access:
Access to staff: By letter, by telephone

General description:
An elegant Georgian house, built in 1729 to a symmetrical plan, and with fine wrought-iron gates, carved porch and interior panelling and plasterwork.

Internet home pages:
http://www.nationaltrust.org.uk

2356
RAMSEY ABBEY GATEHOUSE
Abbey School, Ramsey, Huntingdon, Cambridgeshire, PE17 1DH

Tel: 0870 609 5388 (Regional Office)

Organisation type and purpose: Local government body, registered charity (charity number 205846), historic building, house or site.
Parent body:
The National Trust (East of England)
East Anglia Regional Office, tel: 0870 609 5388

Enquiries to: Curator
Access:
Access to staff: By letter, by telephone

General description:
The remnants of a former Benedictine monastery, built on an island in the Fens. The late 15th century gatehouse is richly carved and contains an ornate oriel window.

Internet home pages:
http://www.nationaltrust.org.uk

2357
RAMSEY RURAL MUSEUM
Wood Lane, Huntingdon, Cambridgeshire, PE26 2XD

Tel: 01487 815715
Email: d.yardley@talk21.com
Formed: 1977

Organisation type and purpose: Registered charity (charity number 290110), museum, suitable for ages: 5+.

Enquiries to: Chairman
Direct tel: 01487 814304
Access:
Access to staff: By telephone, by email

Access for disabled people: Parking provided, ramped entry, access to all public areas, toilet facilities

General description:
Housed in 18th century farm buildings, set in open countryside.
Collections include: a wide variety of agricultural implements and tools used by local craftsmen, with examples of well-restored farm machinery, an old village store, chemist's shop, cobbler's shop, Victorian kitchen, living room and bedroom, Victorian schoolroom, display of the history of Ramsey Abbey, AD 969 to the present day, local history centre.
Information services:
Special visitor services: Guided tours..

Internet home pages:
http://www.rural-museum.org.uk
Details of museum.

2358
RAMSGATE MUSEUM
Ramsgate Library, Guildford Lawn, Ramsgate, Kent, CT11 9AY

Tel: 01843 593532
Fax: 01843 852692
Formed: 1904

Organisation type and purpose: Museum, suitable for ages: 5+.

Enquiries to: Librarian
Direct tel: 01843 223626
Direct email: beth.thomson@kent.gov.uk
Access:
Access to staff: By letter, by telephone, by fax, in person
Hours: Mon to Thu, 0930 to 1800; Fri, 0930 to 1900; Sat, 0930 to 1700
Access to building, collections or gallery: No access other than to staff
Hours: Mon to Thu, 0930 to 1800; Fri, 0930 to 1900; Sat, 0930 to 1700
Other restrictions: Museum is open only when public library is open. Appointment required for group visits needing tour.
Access for disabled people: level entry

General description:
The collection is on the ground floor of a grade II listed building. It illustrates the social, municipal and industrial history of the town of Ramsgate from prehistory to World War II, with special emphasis on its growth from fishing village to a Victorian seaside resort and a 20th century port.
Collections:
Collection of 19th and 20th century ceramic souvenirs
Fine Art Collection
Small Maritime Collection
Catalogues:
Catalogue for library is in-house only. Catalogue for all of the collections is only available in-house.

2359
RAVENGLASS AND ESKDALE RAILWAY COMPANY LIMITED
Ravenglass, Cumbria, CA18 1SW

Tel: 01229 717171
Fax: 01229 717011
Email: rer@netcomuk.co.uk
Formed: 1875

Organisation type and purpose: Service industry.

Enquiries to: Information Officer
Access:
Access to staff: By letter, by telephone, by fax, in person, visitors by prior appointment
Access for disabled people: Parking provided, ramped entry, toilet facilities

General description:
Steam railway preservation.
Publications list:
is available in hard copy.

2360
RAYLEIGH MOUNT
Rayleigh, Southend-on-Sea, Essex

Tel: 0870 609 5388 (Regional Office)

Organisation type and purpose: National organisation, registered charity (charity number 205846), historic building, house or site.
Parent body:
The National Trust (East of England)
East Anglia Regional Office, tel: 0870 609 5388

Enquiries to: Manager
Access:
Access to staff: By telephone

General description:
The former site of the Domesday castle erected by Sweyn of Essex.

Internet home pages:
http://www.nationaltrust.org.uk

2361
READING MUSEUM AND ART GALLERY
See - Museum of Reading

2362
READING UNIVERSITY, THE
See - Ure Museum of Greek Archaeology

2363
REALART GALLERY, THE
Meadow Place, Shrewsbury, Shropshire, SY1 1PD

Tel: 01743 270123
Fax: 01743 270123
Email: realartgallery@lineone.net
Formed: 2000

Organisation type and purpose: Independently owned, art gallery, suitable for ages: all ages.
Commercial art gallery.

Enquiries to: Owner
Direct email: deborahnorthwood@lineone.net
Access:
Access to staff: By telephone, by email
Hours: Mon to Sat, 0930 to 1730
Access to building, collections or gallery: No prior appointment required
Hours: Mon to Sat, 1000 to 1730
Access for disabled people: level entry, toilet facilities
Other restrictions: Lift to basement restaurant and gallery and first floor gallery area only.

Collections:
Contemporary living artists: paintings, sculpture, prints, glass, ceramics, textiles, photography, furniture and designer jewellery

2364
RED CAP MUSEUM
See - Royal Military Police Museum

2365
RED HOUSE
Oxford Road, Gomersal, Cleckheaton, West Yorkshire, BD19 4JP

Tel: 01274 335100
Fax: 01274 335105
Formed: 1973

Organisation type and purpose: Local government body, historic building, house or site, suitable for ages: 5+.

Enquiries to: Museum Officer
Access:
Access to staff: By letter, by telephone, by fax, visitors by prior appointment
Access to building, collections or gallery: No prior appointment required
Hours: Mon to Fri, 1100 to 1700; Sat, Sun, 1200 to 1700
Access for disabled people: Parking provided, toilet facilities

General description:
Period house displayed as 1830s home of woollen cloth merchant Joshua Taylor and family. House and family often visited by Charlotte Brontë, and featured in her novel 'Shirley'. Includes period rooms; exhibitions; shop; and period gardens. Brontë gallery with 19th century and Brontë-related collections. 20th century local history gallery. Brontë/Taylor/Shirley country information.
Information services:
Education services: Group education facilities, resources for Key Stages 1 and 2.
Services for disabled people: For the hearing impaired.
Collections:
Furniture and Decorative Arts
Domestic (19th century)
Brontë related/Taylor personalia
Victorian domestic artefacts
20th century domestic, retail, local history
Catalogues:
Catalogue for part of the collections is only available in-house.
Printed publications:
The Taylors of Red House (£1)
Charlotte Brontë's Shirley Country Guide (free)
Red House Room Guide (leaflet, free)

2366
RED HOUSE MUSEUM AND GARDENS
Quay Road, Christchurch, Dorset, BH23 1BU

Tel: 01202 482860
Fax: 01202 481924
Formed: 1951
Formerly: Christchurch Museum

Organisation type and purpose: Local government body, museum, art gallery, historic building, house or site, suitable for ages: all ages.
A Georgian house with attractive grounds, fine roses and a herb garden.
Parent body:
Hampshire County Council Museums Service (HCCMS)
Chilcomb House, Chilcomb Lane, Winchester, SO23 8RD, tel: 01962 846304, fax: 01962 869836

Enquiries to: Curator
Access:
Access to staff: By letter, by telephone, by fax, in person

General description:
Local history and museum of Christchurch and area including Hengistbury Head and Stanpit Marsh, toys, domestic bygones, local industries, costume, archaeology, geology, natural history, Georgian house with aquarium, grounds, rose garden and herb garden, family history, local industry and photographs.
Information services:
Resources for Key Stage 2 for Social History Gallery only.
Guided tours by appointment only.
Loop hearing system at reception
Special visitor services: Materials and/or activities for children.
Education services: Group education facilities, resources for Key Stage 2.
Services for disabled people: For the hearing impaired.
Collections:
Allen White collection of photographs

continued overleaf

Archaeology, natural history and geology galleries relating to Christchurch Area
Arthur Romney Green 1930s room-setting
Collections of photographs and books relating to Christchurch and surrounding area
General Social History Items - kitchen display, toys, costume, personal and hand-held bygones
Catalogues:
Catalogue for all of the collections is on-line.
Printed publications:
Publications list is available from the Librarian, Hampshire County Council Museums Service Headquarters, Chilcomb House, Winchester, SO23 8RD

Address for ordering publications:
Printed publications:
Registrar, Hampshire County Council Museums Service HQ
Tel: 01962 846304, fax: 01962 869836

Internet home pages:
http://www.hants.gov.uk/museum/redhouse
Photographs and description of building and collection.
http://www.hants.gov.uk/museums/
HMCMS web catalogue, whole collection, 100,000 plus web pages.

2367
RED HOUSE STABLES WORKING CARRIAGE MUSEUM
Old Road, Darley Dale, Matlock, Derbyshire, DE4 2ER

Tel: 01629 733583
Fax: 01629 733583
Formed: 1946

Organisation type and purpose: Independently owned, museum, suitable for ages: 5+.
Carriage driving commercial centre.

Enquiries to: Secretary
Other contacts: Proprietor
Access:
Access to staff: By letter, by telephone, by fax, in person
Hours: Mon to Fri, 0900 to 1700
Access to building, collections or gallery: No access other than to staff
Hours: Daily, 1000 to 1700
Access for disabled people: level entry, toilet facilities

General description:
Contains original horse-drawn vehicles and equipment. A collection of over 30 carriages is on display. The vehicles are regularly out on the roads, being used with harness horses, coachman, footman and grooms.
Collections:
Domi-mail Phaura. By Hooper of Derby and London. ca. 1900.
Hansom Cab. Designer Mr John Hansom.1834
Park Drag. Known as private coach. ca. 1860
Road Coach. Ran from Edinburgh-London.1832-1864
Sefton Landau. Known as Canoe Landau. ca. 1800
Spider Phaeton. Used for town and park driving. ca. 1900
Travelling Chariot. Made for Wright family in ca. 1790

2368
RED LODGE, THE
Park Row, Bristol, BS1 5LJ

Tel: 0117 921 1360

Organisation type and purpose: Local government body, museum, historic building, house or site, suitable for ages: 8+.
Parent body:
Bristol City Museums Service

Enquiries to: Curator

General description:
A Tudor Lodge containing fine oak-panelled rooms.

Internet home pages:
http://www.bristol-city.gov.uk/museums

2369
REDCAR AND CLEVELAND BOROUGH COUNCIL
Redcar and Cleveland Museums Service, Margrove Heritage Centre, Boosbeck, Saltburn-by-the-Sea, Cleveland, TS12 3BZ

Tel: 01287 610368 (Apr to Sep) 479500 (all year)
Fax: 01287 610368 (Apr to Sep) 474199 (all year)
Email: museum_services@redcar-cleveland.gov.uk
Acronym or abbreviation: RCMS / MHC
Formed: 1990
Formerly: Cleveland County Council, date of change, 1996

Organisation type and purpose: Local government body, museum, art gallery.
Other addresses:
Kirkleatham Museum
Kirkleatham, Redcar, TS10 5NW, tel: 01642 479500, fax: 01642 474199, email/website: museum_services@redcar-cleveland.gov.uk

Enquiries to: Museums Curator
Other contacts: Education/Outreach Officer
Access:
Access to staff: By letter, by telephone, by fax, in person, visitors by prior appointment
Hours: Sun to Thu, 1000 to 1630; closed Fri and Sat
Access to building, collections or gallery: Prior appointment required
Hours: Sun to Thu, 1000 to 1630; closed Fri and Sat
Access for disabled people: Parking provided, level entry, access to all public areas, toilet facilities

General description:
Local history and archaeology, local wildlife and environment.
Printed publications:
Books on local history and industry
Leaflets on centres history, local history, industry, local wildlife, environment

2370
REDCOATS IN THE WARDROBE
See - Royal Gloucestershire, Berkshire & Wiltshire Regiment Museum

2371
REDHOUSE GLASS CONE
Stuart Crystal, Redhouse Glassworks, Wordsley, Stourbridge, West Midlands, DY8 4AZ

Tel: 01384 812750
Fax: 01384 812751
Email: redhousecone@dudley.gov.uk
Formed: Mar 2002

Organisation type and purpose: Local government body, historic building, house or site, suitable for ages: 8+.
Parent body:
Dudley Metropolitan Borough Council

Enquiries to: Manager
Direct tel: 01384 812752
Direct email: sarahchapman@dudley.gov.uk
Access:
Access to staff: By letter, by telephone, by fax, by email, visitors by prior appointment
Access for disabled people: Parking provided, ramped entry, toilet facilities

General description:
Opened March 2002 after £1.7 million restoration. A 100 ft high glass cone with audio guide and audiovisual interpretation. A range of studios on site, and a glass-making studio.

Information services:
Helpline available, tel no: 01384 812750.
Special visitor services: Guided tours, tape recorded guides.
Services for disabled people: For the hearing impaired.
Collections:
A collection of Stuart Glassware and a display of glass-making equipment -
This includes pieces from Art Deco period, commemorative pieces and modern Stuart Ware
Catalogues:
Catalogue for library is on-line.
Printed publications:
Site Leaflet

Internet home pages:
http://www.redhousecone.co.uk
Layout of site, studios, equipment, opening times and events.

2372
REGIMENTAL MUSEUM 1ST THE QUEEN'S DRAGOON GUARDS
Cardiff Castle, Castle Street, Cardiff, CF1 2RB

Tel: 029 2022 2253
Fax: 029 2087 1384
Email: curator@qdg.org.uk

Organisation type and purpose: Registered charity (charity number 273874), museum.

Enquiries to: Curator
Access:
Access to staff: By letter, by telephone, by fax, by email, visitors by prior appointment

General description:
Laid out in chronological order, the museum tells the history of the 1st King's Dragoon Guards, The Queen's Bays (2nd Dragoon Guards) and 1st the Queen's Dragoon Guards from 1685 to the present day.
Collections:
Archives and artefacts relating to all three regiments
Items held include uniforms; guidons; flags; weapons (from flintlocks to automatic); hundreds of campaign medals, plus orders and decorations; silverware; documents, pictures, photographs, etc, explaining the story of a Cavalry Regiment
Czarevitch Punch Bowl, Romanov, 19th century
Major R W Read KDG MC DFC AFC (2 Bars), medal group representing bravery displayed during the Great War, 1914-1918
Catalogues:
Catalogue for library is in-house only. Catalogue for all of the collections is on-line.

Internet home pages:
http://www.qdg.org.uk

2373
REGIMENTAL MUSEUM OF THE ARGYLL AND SUTHERLAND HIGHLANDERS
The Castle, Stirling, FK8 1EJ

Tel: 01786 475165
Fax: 01786 446038
Email: museum@argylls.co.uk

Organisation type and purpose: Independently owned, museum, suitable for ages: 5+.

Enquiries to: Curator
Access:
Access to staff: By letter, by fax, by email, visitors by prior appointment, charges made to all users

General description:
The story of the 91st (Argyllshire) and 93rd (Sutherland) Highlanders is told up to 1881 when the regiments combined and formed the Argyll and Sutherland Highlanders. The story of the modern Regiment too is told, using personal artefacts, uniforms, weapons, pictures, medals, colours and pipe banners and silver. We also

have a fascinating depiction of a World War I Trench.

Internet home pages:
http://www.argylls.co.uk

2374
REME MUSEUM OF TECHNOLOGY

Isaac Newton Road, Arborfield, Reading, Berkshire, RG2 9NN

Tel: 0118 976 3375
Fax: 0118 976 3375
Email: reme-museum@gtnet.gov.uk
Full name: Royal Electrical and Mechanical Engineers Museum of Technology
Formed: 1958
Formerly: REME Museum, date of change, 1997

Organisation type and purpose: Museum.
Parent body:
The Corps of Electrical and Mechanical Engineers
RH2 REME, Isaac Newton Road, Arborfield, Berkshire, RG2 9NJ

Enquiries to: Director
Other contacts: Senior Curatorial Officer
Access:
Access to staff: By letter, by telephone, by fax, by email, in person
Access for disabled people: Parking provided, level entry, toilet facilities

General description:
The museum displays illustrate the role of the Corps of Royal Electrical and Mechanical Engineers, the Army's main equipment repair force (REME), in the British Army from its inception in 1942. There are displays of trades, training, equipments and technology set in locations around the world where REME has been posted. There is a Medal Room with a memorial to all members of the Corps who have fallen in conflict.
Included in the museums' collections are the Corps Archives, documentary, technical and pictorial. The Archives offer research facilities and access to source material. The Archives are registered as an authorised 'Place of Deposit' for the Public Record Office.
The museum's new Prince Philip Vehicle Hall houses 20 of the museum's historic vehicle fleet together with a scout helicopter.
Information services:
Special visitor services: Guided tours, materials and/or activities for children.
Education services: Group education facilities, resources for Key Stages 1 and 2 and 3.
Services for disabled people: Displays and/or information at wheelchair height.
Collections:
The Documentary Archive containing Corps history, military history and local history
Also reports, research documents and unit histories, personal papers and diaries, newspapers, publications and ephemera
The Technical Archive reflecting the support of developing technology in parts lists, REME repair instruction handbooks, technical hand books and technical drawings
The Pictorial Archive with unit and personal albums, photographic prints, negatives, transparencies, film and video, maps, charts, paintings, cartoons and etchings
The Historic Vehicle collection of over 100 specialist repair and recovery vehicles, mostly housed in Bordon
The Small Arms collection of over 600 weapons spanning developing technology and repair techniques from a 16th century flintlock to a modern SA80 combat rifle - this collection is housed in an armoury
The Electronic and Aeronautical collections, showing the development of communications, RADAR, control equipment and Army aviation
The REME Medal Collection on display in the medal room
The Reserve Collection of items of Corps history and memorabilia

Internet home pages:
http://www.rememuseum.org.uk
Directions, parking and entry, displays and buildings, family events programme, education and schools, Corps Archives, collections, REME Association, shop, band, fund, magazine, FAQs.

2375
RENFREW MUSEUM

Brown Institute, 41 Canal Street, Renfrew, Strathclyde

Tel: 0141 886 3149
Fax: 0141 886 2300

Organisation type and purpose: Local government body, museum, suitable for ages: 5+.
Parent body:
Renfrewshire Council

Enquiries to: Curator
Access:
Access to staff: By letter, by telephone, by fax, in person
Hours: Tue to Sat, 0900 to 1700
Access to building, collections or gallery: No prior appointment required
Hours: Tue to Sat, 1000 to 1300, 1400 to 1700
Access for disabled people: access to all public areas, toilet facilities
Other restrictions: Two shallow steps

General description:
Local history of Renfrew.

2376
RENFREWSHIRE ASTRONOMICAL SOCIETY

See - Coats Observatory

2377
RENISHAW HALL GARDENS, MUSEUM AND ART GALLERY

Renishaw Park, Sheffield, South Yorkshire, S31 9WB

Tel: 01246 432310
Fax: 01246 430760
Email: info@renishaw-hall.co.uk
Formed: 1995
Formed from: The Sitwell Estates

Organisation type and purpose: Independently owned, museum, art gallery, historic building, house or site, suitable for ages: 5+, publishing house.

Enquiries to: Public Relations Manager
Other contacts: Administrator
Access:
Access to staff: By letter, by telephone, by fax, by email, in person, Internet web pages
Access to building, collections or gallery: No prior appointment required
Hours: Museum and Galleries: Fri, Sat, Sun, 0900 to 1700
Bank Holiday Monday
Other restrictions: At other times by prior appointment.
Access for disabled people: Parking provided, ramped entry, toilet facilities

General description:
Paintings by the artists John Piper.
Sitwell Family Museum and Costume Gallery.
Performing Arts Gallery, gowns, paintings, photographs of the stars of the silver screen and stage
National collection of Yuccas.
Sculpture Park.
Information services:
Special visitor services: Guided tours..
Collections:
A collection of items, personal artefacts belonging to the Sitwell family, family items, glassware, lace, copies of the many books they wrote
Collection of gowns and uniforms the Sitwell family wore
Collection of paintings by the war-time artist John Piper
Gertrude Lawrence Exhibition
Maria Callas Exhibition
and much more in the Performing Arts Gallery
Publications list:
is available in hard copy.
Printed publications:
Assorted leaflets on exhibitions and sculpture park (free)
John Piper: A Brief Biography (Sitwell R)
Renishaw Hall and the Sitwells and Events (Sitwell R)
Renishaw Hall Gardens (booklet, £3)

Address for ordering publications:
Printed publications:
Estate Office, Renishaw Hall
Renishaw, Sheffield, S21 3WB

Internet home pages:
http://www.sitwell.co.uk

2378
RESTORMEL CASTLE

Lostwithiel, Cornwall

Tel: 01208 872687

Organisation type and purpose: National organisation, historic building, house or site.
Parent body:
English Heritage (South West Region)
Tel: 0117 975 0700, fax: 0117 975 0701

Enquiries to: Manager
Access:
Access to staff: By letter, by telephone
Access to building, collections or gallery: No prior appointment required
Hours: 29 Mar to 30 Sep: daily, 1000 to 1800,1 to 31 Oct: daily, 1000 to 1700
Other restrictions: Closed 24 to 26 Dec and 1 Jan
Opening times are subject to change, for up-to-date information contact English Heritage by phone or visit the website.

General description:
Surrounded by a deep moat and perched on a high mound, the huge circular keep of this Norman castle survives in remarkably good condition. Built as a symbol of wealth and status, and once home to Edward, the Black Prince, it offers splendid views over the surrounding countryside.

Internet home pages:
http://www.english-heritage.org.uk

2379
REVOLUTION HOUSE MUSEUM

High Street, Chesterfield, Derbyshire, S41 9LA

Tel: 01246 345727
Email: museum@chesterfieldbc.gov.uk
Formed: 1938

Organisation type and purpose: Local government body, historic building, house or site, suitable for ages: 5+.
Governing body:
Chesterfield Borough Council
Town Hall, Rose Hill, Chesterfield, S40 1LP
Address for Correspondence:
Chesterfield Museum & Art Gallery
St Mary's Gate, Chesterfield, S41 7TD, tel: 01246 345727

Enquiries to: Curator
Access:
Access to staff: By letter only

continued overleaf

Access to building, collections or gallery: No prior appointment required
Hours: Good Fri to 31 Aug: Daily, 1000 to 1600
Access for disabled people: level entry
Other restrictions: Access to ground floor only.

General description:
The Revolution House in the Derbyshire village of Old Whittington. Takes its name from the revolution of 1688. Three hundred years ago the cottage was an ale house, and three local noblemen met here to begin planning their part in the events leading to the overthrow of James II.
The ground floor has a display of 17th century furniture, and upstairs there is a changing programme of exhibitions on local themes. Also available is a video presentation of the Story of the Revolution.
Information services:
Special visitor services: Guided tours..
Collections:
Collection of 17th century country furniture
Printed publications:
Advertising leaflet (free)

Internet home pages:
http://www.chesterfieldbc.gov.uk
Basic information on opening hours and location.

2380
RHAYADER FOLK MUSEUM
See - CARAD Chronicles Community Museum

2381
RHEGED
The Village in the Hill, Redhills, Penrith, Cumbria, CA11 0DQ

Tel: 01768 868000
Fax: 01768 868002
Email: enquiries@rheged.com
Formed: 2000
Formerly: Upland Kingdom Discovery Centre, date of change, 2000

Organisation type and purpose: Independently owned, suitable for ages: 5+.
Visitor attraction.

Enquiries to: Marketing & Sales Manager
Access:
Access to staff: By telephone, by email, in person, Internet web pages
Hours: Everyday except Christmas Day, 1000 to 1730
Access to building, collections or gallery: No prior appointment required
Access for disabled people: Parking provided, ramped entry, level entry, access to all public areas, toilet facilities
Other restrictions: Induction loop in cinema, Braille on toilet doors

General description:
Information on Cumbria and the North Pennines, and on British mountaineering history.
Information services:
Special visitor services: Materials and/or activities for children.
Education services: Group education facilities, resources for Key Stages 1 and 2, 3, 4 and Further or Higher Education..
Collections:
Mallory and Irving exhibition
Abraham Brothers Photograph Collection
Mountaineering memorabilia

Internet home pages:
http://www.rheged.com

2382
RHONDDA HERITAGE PARK
Lewis Merthyr Colliery, Coed Cae Road, Trehafod, Pontypridd, Rhondda Cynon Taff, CF37 7NP

Tel: 01443 682036
Fax: 01443 687420
Email: reception@rhonddaheritagepark.com
Formed: 1989

Organisation type and purpose: Local government body, museum, art gallery, historic building, house or site, suitable for ages: all ages.
Tourist attraction.
Parent body:
Rhondda Cynon Taff County Borough Council
The Pavilions, Clydach Vale, CF40 2XX, tel: 01443 424000

Enquiries to: Director
Direct email: john@rhonddaheritagepark.com
Other contacts: Marketing Officer for promotion/public relations.
Access:
Access to staff: By letter only, by email, visitors by prior appointment
Hours: Mon to Fri, 0900 to 1700
Access to building, collections or gallery: No prior appointment required
Hours: Daily 1000 to 1800
Other restrictions: Closed Dec 25, 26; Mondays Oct to Apr
Access for disabled people: Parking provided, ramped entry, level entry, toilet facilities
Other restrictions: Access to most areas.

General description:
Heritage, mining.
Black Gold includes 3 audiovisual shows telling the history of the Rhondda Valleys and mining. A guided tour with an ex-miner includes a visit to the Grade II listed pit head buildings and a trip to 'pit bottom' to experience life as a miner in the 1950s. A reconstructed village street and art gallery at the visitor centre.
Information services:
Children's play park, shop, restaurant
Conference facilities available.
Special visitor services: Guided tours, materials and/or activities for children.
Education services: Group education facilities, resources for Key Stages 1 and 2, 3 and 4.
Services for disabled people: For the hearing impaired.
Collections:
Books, photographs, domestic artefacts, shop artefacts
Variety of mining machinery including:
Hand tools, colliers' tools, 1850-1950
Mine rescue, breathing apparatus, smoke helmets
Mining instruments, methonometers, hygrometers, dust sampling equipment, etc
Large colliery machinery and engines, Lewis Merthyr winding engine, ventilation fans preserved in situ, 1880/1890
Catalogues:
Catalogue for library is in-house only. Catalogue for part of the collections is only available in-house.
Electronic and video products:
Promotional video available for intending group visitors

Internet home pages:
http://wwwhttp://
www.rhonddaheritagepark.com
General information about the attraction.

2383
RHYL LIBRARY, MUSEUM AND ARTS CENTRE
Church Street, Rhyl, Clwyd, LL18 3AA

Tel: 01745 353814
Fax: 01745 331438
Formed: 1986

Organisation type and purpose: Local government body, museum, art gallery, public library, suitable for ages: all ages.
Parent body:
Denbighshire Heritage Service
46 Clwyd Street, Ruthin, Denbighshire, LL15 1HP, tel: 01824 708223, fax: 01824 708258

Enquiries to: Curator
Direct tel: 01824 708223
Direct fax: 01824 708258
Direct email: rose.mcmahon@denbighshire.gov.uk
Access:
Access to staff: By letter, by email
Hours: Mon to Wed, 0930 to 1900; Fri, 0930 to 1900; Thu, 0930 to 1730; Sat, 0930 to 1230
Access to building, collections or gallery: No prior appointment required
Hours: As office hours
Access for disabled people: Parking provided, ramped entry, level entry, access to all public areas, toilet facilities

General description:
The collection reflects the town's role, firstly as a fishing village and later as a seaside resort. The majority of the collection relates to the maritime and social history of Rhyl.
Collections:
Rhyl local history
Catalogues:
Catalogue for part of the collections is only available in-house.

Internet home pages:
http://www.denbighshire.gov.uk

2384
RIBCHESTER ROMAN MUSEUM
Riverside, Ribchester, Preston, Lancashire, PR3 3XS

Tel: 01254 878261
Formed: 1914
Formerly: Ribchester Museum of Roman Antiquities

Organisation type and purpose: Registered charity (charity number 510490), museum.
Parent body:
Ribchester Museum Trust

Enquiries to: Curator
Access:
Access to staff: By letter, by telephone, in person, visitors by prior appointment
Access to building, collections or gallery: No prior appointment required
Hours: Mon to Fri, 0900 to 1700; Sat, Sun, 1200 to 1700
Access for disabled people: Parking provided, ramped entry, level entry, access to all public areas, toilet facilities

General description:
The collection contains material from the Roman fort and civilian site at Ribchester and the surrounding area. The displays include many objects of which the cavalryman tombstone and the replica of the parade helmet particularly stand out. The displays are complemented by models.
Information services:
Special visitor services: Guided tours.
Education services: Group education facilities, resources for Key Stages 2, 3, 4 and Further or Higher Education.
Services for disabled people: Displays and/or information at wheelchair height.
Publications list:
is available in hard copy.

2385
RICHARD III MUSEUM
Monk Bar, Monkgate, York, YO1 7LQ

Tel: 01904 634191
Email: info@richardiiimuseum.co.uk
Formed: 1992
Formerly: Monkbar Museum

Organisation type and purpose: Museum, historic building, house or site, suitable for ages: all ages.

Enquiries to: Manager
Access:
Access to staff: By letter, by telephone, by email
Access to building, collections or gallery: No prior appointment required
Hours: Mar to Oct: daily, 0900 to 1700 (late

opening during peak season)
Nov to Feb: daily, 0930 to 1600

General description:
Monk Bar - York's tallest and most impressive Medieval Gatehouse was built in the 14th century. Originally a guardhouse, it has been both a prison and a police house, and was lived in until 1914.
The Bar boasts a rare example of a working portcullis, last lowered in 1953. Largely original, the ancient mechanism still works, and can be operated by visitors.
There are 3 rooms in all, the uppermost being added by King Richard III, in 1484. Despite his reputation as a deformed, hunchbacked villain, Richard was a popular King in York, known affectionately as 'The Lord of the North'.
In 1992 it was decided to convert Monk Bar into the Richard III Museum, in honour of the king many feel has been unjustly maligned by historians. The exhibition puts Richard on trial, charged with the crime for which history condemns him, the murder of The Princes in the Tower. Visitors are invited to give their own verdict.
Collections:
Various about King Richard III
Catalogues:
Catalogue for part of the collections is on-line.
Publications list:
is available in hard copy and online.
Printed publications:
Various scrolls, books, booklets about Richard III and English history
Various publications about Richard III and War of the Roses
Electronic and video products:
$13\frac{1}{2}$ minute tape 'The Trial of Richard III'
Various Medieval Music (CD-ROM, cassette tape)
Various Shakespeare Richard III (video/audio)

Internet home pages:
http://www.Richard3museum.co.uk
http://www.richardiiimuseum.co.uk
About Richard III, museum, teacher's notes, Summer Theatre events, museum publications etc.

2386
RICHBOROUGH ROMAN FORT

Richborough, Sandwich, Kent

Tel: 01304 612013

Organisation type and purpose: Museum, historic building, house or site, suitable for ages: 8+.
Parent body:
English Heritage (South East Region)
Tel: 01483 252000, fax: 01483 252001

Enquiries to: Curator
Access:
Access to staff: By letter, by telephone
Access to building, collections or gallery: No prior appointment required
Hours: Apr to Sep: daily, 1000 to 1800
Oct: 1000 to 1700
Nov to Feb: Sat and Sun, 1000 to 1600
Mar, Wed to Sun, 1000 to 1600
Other restrictions: Closed 24 to 26 Dec and 1 Jan
Opening times are subject to change, for up-to-date information contact English Heritage by phone or visit the website.

General description:
This fort and township date back to the Roman landing in AD43. The fortified walls and the massive foundations of a triumphal arch, which stood 25 metres (80 feet) high, still survive. The museum shows aspects of Roman life and artefacts from this busy Roman township.
Information services:
Special visitor services: Tape recorded guides..

Internet home pages:
http://www.english-heritage.org.uk

2387
RICHMOND CASTLE

Castle Hill, Richmond, North Yorkshire

Tel: 01748 822493

Organisation type and purpose: National organisation, advisory body, museum, historic building, house or site.
Parent body:
English Heritage (Yorkshire Region)
Tel: 01904 601901

Enquiries to: Manager
Access:
Access to staff: By letter, by telephone, in person
Access to building, collections or gallery: No prior appointment required
Hours: 29 Mar to 30 Sep: daily, 1000 to 1800 (mid Jul to 31 Aug: daily, 0930 to 1900)
1 to 31 Oct: daily, 1000 to 1700,1 Nov to 28 Mar: daily, 1000 to 1600
Other restrictions: Closed 24 to 26 Dec and 1 Jan.
Opening times are subject to change, for up-to-date information contact English Heritage by phone or visit the website.
Access for disabled people: toilet facilities
Other restrictions: Toilets in town centre.

General description:
Dramatically situated on a rocky promontory high up above the River Swale, Richmond Castle occupies a triangular site set within the busy market town of Richmond. Largely unscathed by military conflict, Richmond Castle was the centre of a bustling community for over 500 years. The splendid keep was added in the 12th century as part of the defensive fortifications. By the early 16th century, the castle had ceased to have any military or domestic value, but its neglected appearance appealed to the romantic artists of the 18th century.
Information services:
Free Chiidlen's Activity Sheet
Exhibition, 'Castle, Commerce and Conscience'.
Special visitor services: Materials and/or activities for children..

Internet home pages:
http://www.english-heritage.org.uk

2388
RICHMOND LOCAL STUDIES LIBRARY

Old Town Hall, Whittaker Avenue, Richmond-upon-Thames, Surrey, TW9 1TP

Tel: 020 8332 6820
Email: localstudies@richmond.gov.uk
Formed: c1893

Organisation type and purpose: Local government body, public library, suitable for ages: 8+.
Parent body:
London Borough of Richmond upon Thames

Enquiries to: Librarian
Access:
Access to staff: By letter, by telephone, by email, in person

General description:
The history and development of the London Borough of Richmond upon Thames. The collection is made up of books, pamphlets, news cuttings, local newspapers on microfilm, archives, maps, slides, photographs, prints and drawings.
Collections:
Sladen Collection, over 70 scrapbooks of his correspondence, bills, reviews, etc. compiled by Douglas Sladen
Material relating to George Vancouver
Books by and about Horace Walpole
Books by and about Alexander Pope
Playbill Collection, about 1000 playbills mainly relating to the Theatre Royal (1765-1884)
Catalogues:
Catalogue for library is in-house only.

Internet home pages:
http://www.richmond.gov.uk/depts/opps/eal/leisure/libraries/default.htm

2389
RICHMONDSHIRE MUSEUM

Ryders Wynd, Richmond, North Yorkshire, DL10 4JA

Tel: 01748 825611
Formed: 1978

Organisation type and purpose: Voluntary organisation, registered charity (charity number 505917), museum, suitable for ages: 5+.
Run by a mangement committee.

Enquiries to: Information Officer
Direct tel: 01748 822271
Direct email: angus.goodfellow@btinternet.com
Access:
Access to staff: By letter, by telephone, visitors by prior appointment, charges to non-members
Access for disabled people: level entry, access to all public areas, toilet facilities

General description:
A social history museum relating to Richmondshire and its development from prehistoric times to the 1950s. The collections cover local industry, local history; leadmining, railways, transport; domestic life; veterinary equipment, James Herriot's Vets Surgery; chemist; Post Office; and photographs and prints of Richmond and the surrounding Dales.
Collections:
Domestic bygones; leadmining artefacts; archaeology; legal history items

2390
RIEVAULX ABBEY

Rievaulx, Helmsley, North Yorkshire, YO62 5LB

Tel: 01439 798228
Fax: 01439 798450
Formed: 1132

Organisation type and purpose: National government body, historic building, house or site, suitable for ages: 5+.
Parent body:
English Heritage (Yorkshire Region)
Tel: 01904 601901
Regional Office:
English Heritage (EH)
Tanner Row, York, tel: 01904 601901

Enquiries to: Head Custodian
Access:
Access to staff: By letter, by telephone, by fax, charges to non-members
Access for disabled people: Parking provided, ramped entry, level entry, toilet facilities
Other restrictions: Ramped entry to museum, access to part of site only.

General description:
Although much of what was built by the monks is in ruins, most of the spectacular presbytery stands virtually to its full height. Built during the 13th century, its soaring beauty conveys the splendour that Rievaulx once possessed. Just 12 monks came to Rievaulx in 1132, and yet from these modest beginnings grew one of the wealthiest monasteries of medieval England, and Rievaulx was still a vibrant community when Henry VIII dissolved it in 1538.
Information services:
Digital Audio Tours also available for visually impaired vistors, those with learning difficulties and in French and German.
Exhibition, 'The Works of God and Man'.
Special visitor services: Tape recorded guides.
Education services: Group education facilities.
Services for disabled people: For the visually impaired.
Catalogues:
Catalogue for part of the collections is on-line.

Internet home pages:
http://www.english-heritage.org.uk/

2391
RIEVAULX TERRACE AND TEMPLES

Rievaulx, Helmsley, York, YO62 5LJ

Tel: 01439 798340/748283
Fax: 01439 748284
Email: nunningtonhall@nationaltrust.org.uk

Organisation type and purpose: National organisation, registered charity (charity number 205846), historic building, house or site, suitable for ages: 8+.
Parent body:
The National Trust (Yorkshire and North East Region)
Tel: 01904 702021

Enquiries to: Manager
Access:
Access to staff: By letter, by telephone, by fax, by email
Access for disabled people: Parking provided, level entry
Other restrictions: Designated parking 5yds. Drop-off point. 1 single-seater powered mobility vehicle, booking essential. Accessible entrance via side passage. Reception and temples have steps. Outdoor access excellent. Steps to shop entrance.

General description:
A ½ml-long grass terrace and adjoining woodland, with vistas over Rievaulx Abbey (English Heritage) to Ryedale and the Hambleton Hills. There is an abundance of spring flowers and two mid-18th century temples. The Ionic Temple, intended as a banqueting house, has elaborate ceiling paintings and fine 18th century furniture.
Information services:
Services for disabled people: For the visually impaired.

Internet home pages:
http://www.nationaltrust.org.uk

2392
RIVER & ROWING MUSEUM

Mill Meadows, Henley-on-Thames, Oxfordshire, RG9 1BF

Tel: 01491 415600
Fax: 01491 415601
Email: museum@rrm.co.uk
Formed: 1998

Organisation type and purpose: Independently owned, registered charity (charity number 1001051), museum, suitable for ages: all ages.

Enquiries to: Chief Executive
Other contacts: Collections Manager for collections/library information and access.
Access:
Access to staff: By letter, by telephone, by fax, by email
Access for disabled people: Parking provided, ramped entry, access to all public areas, toilet facilities

General description:
The River & Rowing Museum was designed by David Chipperfield, Architects, to a brief which set out to establish an astonishing Museum. The building is raised on columns above water meadows beside the Thames, and is built of exposed concrete and glass with a terne-coated steel roof, clad in green oak.
The Museum has won numerous awards for its architectural design and innovative galleries, including The Royal Fine Arts Commission Building of the Year 1999 and National Heritage/NPI Museum of the Year 1999.
The Museum has 3 main galleries devoted to the River Thames, the international sport of rowing and the town of Henley. There are also 3 special exhibition galleries, the Riverside Café, shop, Education Centre, library and function rooms.
Information services:
Library available for reference (for conditions see Access above). Helpline available, tel no: 01491 415600.
Special visitor services: Materials and/or activities for children.
Education services: Group education facilities, resources for Key Stages 1 and 2, 3, 4 and Further or Higher Education.
Services for disabled people: For the visually impaired; for the hearing impaired; displays and/or information at wheelchair height.
Collections:
The collections held by the Museum include artefacts, archival material, photographs, library books, paintings and drawings, relating to the Museum's three main themes of the River Thames, rowing and the town of Henley
If people would like to offer items for donation to the Museum please contact the relevant Curator or the Collections Manager and arrange for an appointment for the items to be viewed
Catalogues:
Catalogue for library is in-house only. Catalogue for all of the collections is only available in-house.

Internet home pages:
http://www.rrm.co.uk

2393
RIVER LEA INDUSTRIAL ARCHAEOLOGICAL SOCIETY

c/o Nine Elms, Therfield, Royston, Hertfordshire, SG8 9QE

Tel: 01763 287331
Acronym or abbreviation: RLIAS
Formed: 1970

Organisation type and purpose: Independently owned, research organisation.
Connections with:
(MBEAM)
Markfield Beam Engine & Museum

Enquiries to: Secretary
Access:
Access to staff: By letter
Access to building, collections or gallery: Prior appointment required

General description:
The aim of the Society is to study the industrial archaeology of the Lea Valley from Hertford to the Thames; to record and publish research findings; to assist in the preservation of surviving artefacts (the most notable, so far, is the restoration of Markfield Beam Engine by members).
Collections:
Markfield Beam Engine.
Industrial Artefacts. A modest collection awaiting suitable display on loan in a museum. Over 100 items
Catalogues:
Catalogue for part of the collections is only available in-house.

See also - Markfield Beam Engine & Museum

2394
RIVER WEY & GODALMING NAVIGATIONS AND DAPDUNE WHARF

Navigations Office and Dapdune Wharf, Wharf Road, Guildford, Surrey, GU1 4RR

Tel: 01483 561389
Fax: 01483 531667
Email: riverwey@nationaltrust.org.uk
Formed: 1964

Organisation type and purpose: National organisation, registered charity (charity number 205846), museum, historic building, house or site, suitable for ages: 5+.
Parent body:
The National Trust (South and South East Region)
South East Regional Office, tel: 01372 453401
Other addresses:
The National Trust
Regional Office
Polesden Lacey, Great Bookham, Surrey, RH5 6BD, tel: 01372 453401, fax: 01372 452023

Enquiries to: Manager
Access:
Access to staff: By letter, by telephone, by fax, by email, in person
Access to building, collections or gallery: No prior appointment required
Hours: Dapdune Wharf: late Mar to beg Nov, Thu to Mon, 1100 to 1700
Access for disabled people: Parking provided, ramped entry, level entry, access to all public areas, toilet facilities
Other restrictions: Ramped entrance at Dapdune Wharf. Computer. Ramped entrance to shop and to tea-room.

General description:
Industrial archaeology of the waterway. The Wey Navigation opened in 1653, making it one of the earliest rivers in Britain to be made navigable. In the later 19th century Dapdune Wharf also became the barge-building centre on the waterway.
Information services:
Booked guided tours of Dapdune Wharf for groups, also guided walks along the towpath.
Braille guide. Large-print guide. Touch list. Handling collection.
Suitable for school groups. Education room/centre. Hands-on activities. Children's quiz/trail.
2003 marks the 350th anniversary of the opening of the Wey Navigation, and a variety of special events and activities will take place throughout the year to mark the occasion.
Please contact property for events programme.
Special visitor services: Guided tours, materials and/or activities for children.
Education services: Group education facilities, resources for Key Stages 1 and 2 and 3.
Services for disabled people: For the visually impaired; displays and/or information at wheelchair height.
Collections:
Artefacts connected with the barge-building industry and management of the waterway, including one of the last surviving Wey barges
A photographic archive of over 2000 images of the Godalming & Wey Navigations
Catalogues:
Catalogue for library is in-house only. Catalogue for all of the collections is only available in-house.
Printed publications:
Family Trails (free)
Guide Book (for purchase)
Map (for purchase)
Circular Walks Book (for purchase)
Information sheets
Leaflet Map (free)

Internet home pages:
http://www.nationaltrust.org.uk
General information about the property and special events.

2395
RIVERSIDE MUSEUM

See - Thurrock Museum

2396
ROALD DAHL CHILDREN'S GALLERY, THE

Church Street, Aylesbury, Buckinghamshire, HP20 2QP

Tel: 01296 331441
Fax: 01296 334884
Email: museum@buckscc.gov.uk
Formed from: Buckinghamshire County Museum (BCM)

Organisation type and purpose: Museum, suitable for ages: 3+.

Enquiries to: Marketing & Development Team
Access:
Access to staff: By letter, by telephone, by fax, by email, Internet web pages
Hours: Information Service: Wed 1230 to 1700
Access to building, collections or gallery: No prior appointment required
Hours: Mon to Sat, 1000 to 1700; Sun, 1400 to 1700
Other restrictions: Dahl Gallery is closed to public between 1000 to 1500 on Buckinghamshire School Days.
Access for disabled people: ramped entry, access to all public areas, toilet facilities

General description:
The Roald Dahl Children's Gallery bring science, nature and history to life through the stories of Roald Dahl. Rooms specific to lace, fossils, woodland, clay, jewellery, villages, farming, and Romans and Celts have displays supported by computers, games and hands-on exhibits. Buckinghamshire County Museum houses exhibitions on Buckinghamshire, and runs a rolling-programme of changing exhibitions.
Information services:
Special visitor services: Materials and/or activities for children.
Education services: Group education facilities, resources for Key Stages 1 and 2 and 3.
Services for disabled people: Displays and/or information at wheelchair height.
Collections:
Archaeology, art, ceramics, natural history, social history, textiles
The Ceramics Collection is one of the best in the country

Internet home pages:
http://www.buckscc.gov.uk/museum
BCM homepage.
http://www.buckscc.gov.uk/museum/dahl/index.stm
Dahl Gallery homepage.

2397
ROBERT BURNS CENTRE, THE
Mill Road, Dumfries, DG2 7BE

Tel: 01387 264808
Fax: 01387 264808
Email: Elainek@dumgal.gov.uk
Formed: 1986

Organisation type and purpose: Local government body, museum, historic building, house or site, suitable for ages: 5+.
Parent body:
Dumfries & Galloway Museum Service
Tel: 01387 253374

Enquiries to: Curator
Access:
Access to staff: By letter, by telephone, by fax
Access to building, collections or gallery: No prior appointment required
Hours: Apr to Sep: Mon to Sat, 1000 to 2000; Sun, 1400 to 1700
Oct to Mar: Tue to Sat, 1000 to 1300 and 1400 to 1700
Access for disabled people: Parking provided, ramped entry, access to all public areas, toilet facilities

General description:
Situated in the town's 18th century watermill on the west bank of the River Nith, the Robert Burns Centre tells the story of Robert Burns' last years, spent in the bustling streets and lively atmosphere of Dumfries in the late 18th century. The exhibition is illuminated by many original manuscripts and belongings of the poet. There is a fascinating scale model of Dumfries in the 1790s and a haunting audiovisual presentation. There are museum trails and fun activities, and visitor information to help you explore Dumfries and Galloway's Burns' connections. Browse around the shop with its wide selection of Scottish books, gifts and keepsakes, local craft work and foods. Lively exhibition programme of work by local artists and award-winning café/restaurant.
Information services:
Special visitor services: Tape recorded guides..
Catalogues:
Catalogue for part of the collections is only available in-house.

Internet home pages:
http://www.dumgal.gov.uk/museums

2398
ROBERT BURNS HOUSE, THE
Burns Street, Dumfries, DG1 2PS

Tel: 01387 255297
Fax: 01387 265081
Email: dumfriesmuseum@dumgal.gov.uk
Formerly: Burns House

Organisation type and purpose: National organisation, historic building, house or site, suitable for ages: 8+.
Parent body:
Dumfries & Gallowy Museum Service
Tel: 01387 253374

Enquiries to: Museums Officer
Direct tel: 01387 253374
Access:
Access to staff: By letter, by telephone, by fax, by email, visitors by prior appointment, Internet web pages

General description:
A sandstone house in which the poet Robert Burns spent the last years of his life. The house contains many relics of the poet, including the chair in which he wrote his last poems, original letters and manuscripts, and the famous Kilmarnock and Edinburgh editions.

Internet home pages:
http://www.dumgal.gov.uk/museum

2399
ROBERT CLAPPERTON'S DAYLIGHT PHOTOGRAPHIC STUDIO
The Studio, 28 Scott's Place, Selkirk, Borders, TD7 4DR

Tel: 01750 20523
Email: ian.w.mitchell@lineone.net

Organisation type and purpose: Historic building, house or site, suitable for ages: 8+.
Access:
Access to staff: By letter, by telephone
Access to building, collections or gallery: No prior appointment required
Hours: May, Jun, Jul, Aug, Fri to Sun, 1400 to 1600
Other restrictions: Alternative times by appointment

General description:
The original daylight studio used by Robert Clapperton in the 1860s is a working museum of photography.
Collections:
Photographic archives

Internet home pages:
http://website.lineone.net/~ian.w.mitchell

2400
ROBERT OPIE COLLECTION
See - Museum of Advertising & Packaging

2401
ROBERT OWEN MUSEUM
The Cross, Broad Street, Newtown, Powys, SY16 2BB

Tel: 01686 626345
Email: johnd@robert-owen.midwales.com
Full name: The Robert Owen Memorial Museum
Formed: 1929

Organisation type and purpose: Independently owned, registered charity (charity number 513821), museum, suitable for ages: 8+.

Enquiries to: Curator
Access:
Access to staff: By letter, by email, visitors by prior appointment
Other restrictions: Access for students at mutually convenient time.
Access to building, collections or gallery: No prior appointment required
Hours: Mon to Fri, 0930 to 1200 and 1400 to 1530; Sat, 0930 to 1130
Other restrictions: Closed Christmas Week and Good Friday.
Access for disabled people: access to all public areas, toilet facilities
Other restrictions: Stair climber available: prior notification is advised.

General description:
Contains letters and belongings of Robert Owen (1771-1858); items from New Lanark and the Labour Exchanges; portraits and busts of Robert Owen and his associates; prints and photographs of New Lanark, etc.; contemporary press cuttings and accounts of Robert Owen; pamphlets by Owenites and their opponents; books and pamphlets by Robert Owen; and books about Robert Owen, Owenites and co- operation.
Information services:
Library available for reference (for conditions see Access above)
Special visitor services: Guided tours, materials and/or activities for children..
Catalogues:
Catalogue for all of the collections is only available in-house.
Publications list:
is available in hard copy.
Printed publications:
Various booklets, resource packs, postcards and scroll (available direct, for purchase plus p&p)
Electronic and video products:
The Life of Robert Owen (1771-1858) Part I (Video - 25 minutes)

Internet home pages:
http://robert-owen.midwales.com/index.html

2402
ROBERT SMAIL'S PRINTING WORKS
7/9 High Street, Inverleithen, Borders, EH44 6HA

Tel: 01896 830206
Email: smails@nts.org.uk

Organisation type and purpose: Museum, historic building, house or site.
Parent body:
National Trust for Scotland (South Region)

Enquiries to: Property Manager
Access:
Access to staff: By letter, by telephone, by email, in person, charges to non-members
Access to building, collections or gallery: No prior appointment required
Hours: Apr to Jun and Sep to Oct, Thu to Mon, 1200 to 1700, Sun 1300 to 1700;
Jul and Aug, Thu to Mon, 1000 to 1800, Sun, 1300 to 1700

General description:
Early twentieth century printing works with Victorian office.

Internet home pages:
http://www.nts.org.uk

2403
ROBERTSON MUSEUM AND AQUARIUM
University of London, Marine Biological Station, Millport, Isle of Cumbrae, Ayrshire, KA28 0EG

Tel: 01475 530581
Fax: 01475 530601
Email: dmurphy@udcf.gla.ac.uk

continued overleaf

Acronym or abbreviation: UMBS
Formed: 1886
Formerly: The Marine Biological Association

Organisation type and purpose: Museum, suitable for ages: 5+.
Aquarium.

Enquiries to: Administrator
Access:
Access to staff: By email
Access to building, collections or gallery: No prior appointment required
Hours: Jun to Sep: Sat
Access for disabled people: Parking provided, access to all public areas, toilet facilities

General description:
Houses exhibits on the marine environment of the Clyde sea area; the Robertson collection of marine fauna (mostly invertebrates and fossils) is only accessible to bona fide researchers.
Collections:
Robertson Collection. Shells, ostracods, foraminifera, fossils, Victorian

Internet home pages:
http://www.gla.ac.uk/Acad/Marine

2404
ROBIN HOOD'S BAY AND FYLINGDALES MUSEUM
Fisherhead, Robin Hood's Bay, North Yorkshire

Organisation type and purpose: Museum.

Enquiries to: Chairman

General description:
A small local museum of local history. Contains material on geology and shipping.

2405
ROBSON GALLERY
See - Halliwell's House Museum & Robson Gallery

2406
ROCHDALE ARTS & HERITAGE CENTRE
The Esplanade, Rochdale, Lancashire, OL16 1AQ

Tel: 01706 342154
Fax: 01706 712723
Email: artgallery@rochdale.gov.uk or museum @rochdale.gov.uk
Formed: 1903
Formerly: Rochdale Art Gallery

Organisation type and purpose: Museum, art gallery, suitable for ages: 5+.
Parent body:
Rochdale Metropolitan Borough Council

Enquiries to: Principal Arts & Heritage Officer
Direct email: andy.pearce@rochdale.gov.uk
Access:
Access to staff: By letter, by telephone, by fax, by email, in person
Hours: Mon to Fri, 0900 to 1700
Access for disabled people: access to all public areas, toilet facilities

General description:
Permanent collection of paintings, drawings, prints and sculpture: 18th and 19th century watercolours, Victorian genre, landscape and portraits, 20th century modernist works, local topographical paintings, small collection of Old Master paintings, local social history objects and archives.
Information services:
Library available for reference (for conditions see Access above)
Special visitor services: Guided tours, materials and/or activities for children.
Education services: Group education facilities, resources for Key Stages 1 and 2, 3 and 4.
Services for disabled people: Displays and/or information at wheelchair height.
Collections:
Archive of Rochdale born artist Edward Stott
Small art library; files on artists in the collection
Extensive local history archive
Catalogues:
Catalogue for library is in-house only. Catalogue for all of the collections is only available in-house.
Publications list:
is available in hard copy.
Printed publications:
Many catalogues and publications

See also - Touchstones Rochdale

2407
ROCHDALE MUSEUM SERVICE
The Arts & Heritage Centre, The Esplanade, Rochdale, Lancashire, OL16 1AQ

Tel: 01706 641085
Fax: 01706 712723
Email: museum@rochdale.gov.uk
Formed: 1903

Organisation type and purpose: Local government body, museum, suitable for ages: all ages.

Enquiries to: Curator
Access:
Access to staff: By letter, by telephone, by email
Access for disabled people: level entry, access to all public areas, toilet facilities

General description:
Local, social and natural history, geology.
Collections:
Gracie Fields, large collection of objects, photographic material, audio and video material, on the life of this popular entertainer, 1898-1979, c. 1000 items
John Bright, objects and printed ephemera from the family of this international statesman. 1811-1889, c. 150 items

2408
ROCHDALE PIONEERS MUSEUM
31 Toad Lane, Rochdale, Lancashire, OL12 0NU

Tel: 01706 524920
Fax: 0161 246 2946
Email: museum@co-op.ac.uk
Formed: 1931

Organisation type and purpose: Museum.
Parent body and Archive:
Co-operative College
Holyoake House, Hanover Street, Manchester, M60 0AS, tel: 0161 246 2902, fax: 0161 246 2946, email: enquiries@co-op.ac.uk

Enquiries to: Archivist
Direct tel: 0161 246 2925
Direct email: archive@co-op.ac.uk
Access:
Access to staff: By letter, by telephone, by fax, by email, in person

General description:
Co-operative movement (UK and International); social history; history of retailing; packaging.
Publications list:
is available in hard copy.
Printed publications:
Archive produces lists for various collections
Commemorative Plateware
Co-operative Party
Co-operative Productive Federation
Co-operative Women's Guild
Co-operative Youth
Dividend and Check Systems
Education
Edward Owen Greening Correspondence Collection
George Jacob Holyoake Correspondence Collection
Historical periodicals
Plays and Sketches
Robert Owen Correspondence Collection
Rochdale Pioneers

Internet home pages:
http://www.co-op.ac.uk/toad_lane.htm
Guide to museum.
http://www.co-op.ac.uk/archive.htm
Archive.

2409
ROCHE ABBEY
Maltby, South Yorkshire

Tel: 01709 812739

Organisation type and purpose: National organisation, advisory body, historic building, house or site.
Parent body:
English Heritage (Yorkshire Region)
Tel: 01904 601901

Enquiries to: Manager
Access:
Access to staff: By letter, by telephone
Access to building, collections or gallery: No prior appointment required
Hours: 29 Mar to 30 Sep: daily, 1000 to 1800,1 to 31 Oct: daily, 1000 to 1700
Other restrictions: Opening times are subject to change, for up-to-date information contact English Heritage by phone or visit the website.

General description:
A Cistercian monastery, founded in 1147, set in an enchanting valley landscaped by Capability Brown. Excavation has revealed the complete layout of the abbey.

Internet home pages:
http://www.english-heritage.org.uk

2410
ROCHESTER CASTLE
The Keep, Boley Hill, Rochester, Kent, ME1 1SW

Tel: 01634 402276

Organisation type and purpose: Historic building, house or site.
Parent body:
English Heritage (South East Region)
Eastgate Court, 195-205 High Street, Guildford, Surrey, GU1 3EH, tel: 01483 252000, fax: 01483 252001, email: www.english-heritage.org.uk
Managed by:
Medway City Council

Enquiries to: Curator

General description:
Norman Bishop's Castle built on the Roman city wall. The keep, dungeon and battlements are well-preserved.
Information services:
Exhibition, models and interactive displays
Special visitor services: Tape recorded guides..

Internet home pages:
http://www.english-heritage.org.uk

2411
ROCHESTER CATHEDRAL
Garth House, The Precinct, Rochester, Kent, ME1 1SX

Tel: 01634 401301
Fax: 01634 401410
Email: rochester_cathedral@yahoo.co.uk
Formed: 604 AD

Organisation type and purpose: Voluntary organisation, suitable for ages: all ages.
Cathedral and religious building.
Other addresses:
The Chapter Clerk
Rochester Cathedral Office, Garth House, The Precinct, Rochester, Kent, ME1 1SX, tel: 01634 843366, fax: 01634 401301

Enquiries to: Visits Officer

Access:
Access to staff: By letter, by telephone, by fax, by email, Internet web pages
Hours: Mon to Fri, 1000 to 1800; Sat 1000 to 1700; Sun 1000 to 1800
Access for disabled people: level entry, toilet facilities

General description:
Christianity, Church of England.

Internet home pages:
http://www.rochester.anglican.org/cathedral

2412
ROCKBOURNE ROMAN VILLA
Rockbourne, Fordingbridge, Hampshire, SP6 3PG

Tel: 01725 518541
Email: musmjh@hants.gov.uk
Full name: West Park Roman Villa at Rockbourne
Formed: 1972
Formerly: West Park Roman Villa, Morley Hewitt Memorial Museum

Organisation type and purpose: Local government body, museum, historic building, house or site.
Preservation of archaeological sites.
Parent body:
Hampshire County Council Museums Service
Chilcomb House, Winchester, SO23 8RD, tel: 01962 846304, fax: 01962 869836
Affiliated with:
Red House Museum
Quay Road, Christchurch, Dorset, BH23 1BU, tel: 01202 482860, fax: 01202 481924

Enquiries to: Curator
Access:
Access to staff: By letter, by telephone, by fax, by email, in person, charges made to all users
Access for disabled people: Parking provided, ramped entry, toilet facilities
Other restrictions: Villa site grassed and can be uneven with no paths but accessible by wheelchairs with care.

General description:
Roman villa with dining room, mosaic and hypocaust, exhibition of finds in the site museum, Roman archaeology.
Collections:
Roman artefacts
Catalogues:
Catalogue for all of the collections is on-line.
Publications list:
is available in hard copy.
Printed publications:
Publications list is available from the Librarian, Hampshire County Council Museums Service Headquarters, Chilcomb House, Winchester, SO23 8RD

Address for ordering publications:
Printed publications:
Registrar, Hampshire County Council Museums Service HQ

Internet home pages:
http://www.hants.gov.uk/museums/
HMCMS web catalogue, whole collection, 100,000 plus web pages.

2413
ROMAN ARMY MUSEUM
Greenhead, Carlisle, Cumbria, CA6 7JB

Tel: 016977 47485
Email: info@vindolanda.com

Organisation type and purpose: Independently owned, registered charity (charity number 500210), museum, suitable for ages: 5+.
Parent Body:
The Vindolanda Trust
Chesterholm Museum
Bardon Mill, Hexham, Northumberland
Access:
Access to staff: By letter, by telephone, by fax, by email, Internet web pages
Access for disabled people: ramped entry, level entry, access to all public areas, toilet facilities

General description:
Next to the superb Walltoun Crags Section of Hadrian's Wall, the museum provides an insight into the daily lives of Roman soldiers. The museum has reconstructions, life-sized figures, Roman objects, films, audio commentaries and much more.
Information services:
Special visitor services: Materials and/or activities for children.
Education services: Group education facilities, resources for Key Stages 1 and 2, 3, 4 and Further or Higher Education..
Publications list:
is available in hard copy and online.

Address for ordering publications:
Printed publications:
The Vindolanda Trust, Chesterholm Museum
Bardon Mill, Hexham, Northumberland, NE47 7JN, tel: 01434 344277, fax: 01434 344060, email: info@vindolanda.com

Internet home pages:
http://www.vindolanda.com

2414
ROMAN BATH HOUSE
Castle Hill, Lancaster

Email: museum@lamcaster.gov.uk

Organisation type and purpose: Historic building, house or site, suitable for ages: 5+.
Parent body and address for correspondence:
Lancaster City Museums
Market Square, Lancaster, LA1 1HT, tel: 01524 64637, fax: 01524 841692

Enquiries to: Head of Museums
Access:
Access to staff: By letter, by telephone, by email
Access to building, collections or gallery: No prior appointment required
Hours: Daylight hours

General description:
Remains of a Roman bath house.

2415
ROMAN BATH
5 Strand Lane, London, WC2

Tel: 01494 528051(Regional Office)

Organisation type and purpose: National organisation, registered charity (charity number 205846), historic building, house or site, suitable for ages: 5+.
Parent body:
The National Trust (South & South East Region)
Thames & Solent Regional Office, tel: 01494 528051

Enquiries to: Manager
Access:
Access to staff: By letter, by telephone, by fax
Other restrictions: All enquiries should be directed to Regional Office.
Access to building, collections or gallery: Prior appointment required
Hours: May to Sep, Wed, 1300 to 1700
Other restrictions: 24 hours' notice required for appointment. Bath visible through window from pathway all year.
The Bath is administered and maintained by Westminster City Council. Please note that extensive building work is being carried out to the adjacent building and the approach to the Baths is via a covered pavement.

General description:
The remains of a bath, restored in the 17th century and believed by some to be Roman.

Internet home pages:
http://www.nationaltrust.org.uk

2416
ROMAN BATHS MUSEUM
Stall Street, Bath, BA1 1LZ

Tel: 01225 477773
Fax: 01225 477243
Email: stephen_clews@bathnes.gov.uk
Formed: 1897

Organisation type and purpose: Local government body, museum, historic building, house or site, suitable for ages: all ages.
Internationally known archaeological site and museum.
Part of:
Heritage Services Division
Pump Room, Stall Street, Bath, BA1 1LZ, tel: 01225 477779

Enquiries to: Curator
Direct tel: 01225 477779
Direct email: susan_fox@bathnes.gov.uk
Other contacts: Keeper of Collections
Access:
Access to staff: By letter, by fax, by email, visitors by prior appointment, Internet web pages
Hours: Mon to Fri, 0900 to 1700
Other restrictions: Access restricted for wheelchair users.
Access for disabled people: level entry, toilet facilities
Other restrictions: Wheelchair access to ground floor only.

General description:
Local history and archaeology; Romano-British archaeology.
Information services:
Special visitor services: Guided tours.
Education services: Group education facilities, resources for Key Stages 1 and 2 and 3.
Services for disabled people: For the hearing impaired; displays and/or information at wheelchair height.
Printed publications:
Stanton Drew, Parish Resource Pack 1997 (C Nodder, £3 plus £1 p&p)
Wellow and Shoscombe, Parish Resource Book 1997 (Nodder C, £3 plus £1 p&p)

Internet home pages:
http://www.romanbaths.co.uk
Extensively revised site packed with information.

2417
ROMAN LEGIONARY MUSEUM
High Street, Caerleon, Gwent, NP18 1AE

Tel: 01633 423134
Fax: 01633 422869
Email: rlm@nmgw.ac.uk
Acronym or abbreviation: RLM

Organisation type and purpose: National government body, registered charity (charity number 525774), museum, historic building, house or site, suitable for ages: 5+.
Parent body:
National Museum & Galleries Wales
Tel: 02920 397951

Enquiries to: Manager
Access:
Access to staff: By letter, by telephone, by fax, by email, Internet web pages
Access for disabled people: ramped entry, toilet facilities

General description:
Roman Archaeology.
Information services:
Education services: Group education facilities.
Services for disabled people: For the visually impaired; for the hearing impaired; displays and/or information at wheelchair height.
Collections:
Roman Artefacts
Documentation and Library
Publications list:
is available in hard copy.

continued overleaf

Address for ordering publications:
Printed publications:
Commercial Operations, National Museum and Galleries of Wales
Cathays Park, Cardiff, CF10 3NP, tel: 02920 573477, email: Post@nmgw.ac.uk

Internet home pages:
http://www.nmgw.ac.uk
Collections, access, enquiries, general information, what's on.

2418
ROMAN PAINTED HOUSE TRUST

New Street, Dover, Kent, CT17 9AJ

Tel: 01304 203279
Full name: Dover Roman Painted House Trust
Formed: 1971

Organisation type and purpose: Registered charity (charity number 270499), historic building, house or site, suitable for ages: 5+, research organisation.
Visitor and education centre.
Other addresses:
Kent Archaeological Rescue Unit
5 Harvest Bank Road, West Wickham, Kent, BR4 9DL, tel: 020 8462 4737

Enquiries to: Honorary Manager
Access:
Access to staff: By letter, by telephone
Access to building, collections or gallery: No prior appointment required
Hours: Apr to Sep: Daily, 1000 to 1700
Access for disabled people: Parking provided, level entry

General description:
Major Roman building (Mansio) with five main rooms substantially intact. Complete under floor heating systems, unique wall-paintings (AD 200), adjacent fort wall and bastion. Numerous information panels.
Information services:
Schools special workshops.
Special visitor services: Guided tours, tape recorded guides, materials and/or activities for children.
Education services: Group education facilities, resources for Key Stages 1 and 2 and Further or Higher Education.
Services for disabled people: Displays and/or information at wheelchair height.
Collections:
Objects, pictures, photographs incidental to main monument
Publications list:
is available in hard copy.
Printed publications:
Various publications (direct)

2419
ROMAN THEATRE

Bluehouse Hill, St Albans, Hertfordshire, AL3 6AE

Tel: 01727 835035
Formed: Excavated 1935

Organisation type and purpose: Historic building, house or site.
Postal address:
Roman Theatre
Gorhambury House, St Albans, Hertfordshire, AL3 6AH

Enquiries to: Curator
Access:
Access to staff: By letter, by telephone
Access for disabled people: Parking provided, ramped entry

General description:
Roman theatre.
Printed publications:
Guide Books
Post Cards

2420
ROMAN VILLA

Avondale Road, Newport, Isle of Wight, PO30 1HE

Tel: 01983 529720
Fax: 01983 823841
Email: tony.butler@iow.gov.uk
Formed: 1960

Organisation type and purpose: Local government body, museum, historic building, house or site, suitable for ages: 5+.
Scheduled ancient monument.
Parent body:
Isle of Wight Museums
The Guildhall, High Street, Newport, PO30 1HE, tel: 01983 529720 or 823847, fax: 01983 823841, email/website: tony.butler@iow.gov.uk

Enquiries to: Curator
Direct tel: 01983 823433
Access:
Access to staff: By letter, by telephone, by fax, by email, in person
Hours: Apr to Oct: 1000 to 1630
Other restrictions: No parking.
Access to building, collections or gallery: Prior appointment required
Hours: Apr to Oct: 1000 to 1630
Other restrictions: Group booking off season accepted by arrangement.
Access for disabled people: level entry

General description:
Remains of a 3rd century farm house, with exceptionally well preserved bath suite and hypocaust. Reconstructed dining room and kitchen.
Exhibition area re-telling the story of the Roman Occupation of the Isle of Wight.
Information services:
Special visitor services: Guided tours, tape recorded guides, materials and/or activities for children.
Education services: Group education facilities, resources for Key Stages 1 and 2.
Services for disabled people: For the visually impaired.
Collections:
Extensive archaeological collection of human occupation of the Isle of Wight, 3000 BC to 400 AD, including handling collection
Catalogues:
Catalogue for library is in-house only. Catalogue for all of the collections is only available in-house.
Publications list:
is available in hard copy and online.
Printed publications:
Newport Roman Villa (teachers resource book)
Romans on the Wight

Address for ordering publications:
Printed publications:
Curator of Human History, Isle of Wight Museums
The Guildhall, High Street, Newport, Isle of Wight, PO30 1TY, tel: 01983 823433, fax: 01983 823841, email: tony.butler@iow.gov.uk

2421
ROMANO-BRITISH BATHHOUSE

Poverest Road, St Mary Cray, Kent

Tel: 01689 873826 (Bromly Museum)

Organisation type and purpose: Local government body, historic building, house or site, suitable for ages: 8+.
Parent body:
Bromley Museum
Tel: 01689 873826

Enquiries to: Curator
Access:
Access to building, collections or gallery: Prior appointment required
Hours: Viewing by arrangement with Bromley Museum

General description:
A small Roman bathhouse, thought to have been constructed around AD 270. Nearby lies an Anglo-Saxon cemetery.

2422
ROMNEY, HYTHE AND DYMCHURCH RAILWAY

New Romney Station, Littlestone Road, New Romney, Kent, TN28 8PL

Tel: 01797 362353
Fax: 01797 363591
Email: rhdr@dels.demon.co.uk
Acronym or abbreviation: RH&DR
Formed: 1927

Organisation type and purpose: Historic building, house or site.
Tourist railway.

Enquiries to: Public Relations Manager
Other contacts: Marketing Manager
Access:
Access to staff: By letter, by telephone, by fax, by email, in person, Internet web pages
Hours: Mon to Fri, 0900 to 1700
Access for disabled people: Parking provided, ramped entry, toilet facilities

General description:
Construction and operation of narrow gauge and miniature railways for both the leisure and business market.
Publications list:
is available in hard copy.
Printed publications:
A Visitor's Guide to the Romney, Hythe and Dymchurch Railway (£2.99)
Electronic and video products:
Driver's Eye View of the Romney, Hythe and Dymchurch Railway (video, £13.99)
The Romney, Hythe and Dymchurch Railway (video £13.99)

Internet home pages:
http://www.rhdr.demon.co.uk
Information about core business.

2423
ROOTS OF NORFOLK AT GRESSENHALL

Norfolk Rural Life Museum, Gressenhall, Dereham, Norfolk, NR20 4DR

Tel: 01362 860563
Fax: 01362 860385
Email: gressenhall.museum@norfolk.gov.uk
Formed: 1975
Formerly: Norfolk Rural Life Museum (NRLM), date of change, 2001

Organisation type and purpose: Local government body, museum, suitable for ages: 5+.
Parent body:
Norfolk Museum and Archaeology Service (NMAS)
Shire Hall, Market Avenue, Norwich, tel: 01603 493625

Enquiries to: Manager
Other contacts: Collections Officer
Access:
Access to staff: By letter, by telephone, by fax, by email, visitors by prior appointment
Hours: Tue to Fri, 1030 to 1730
Other restrictions: Not available weekends.
Access to building, collections or gallery: No prior appointment required
Hours: Tue to Sun, 1030 to 1730
Other restrictions: Library available for research by prior appointment with Collections Officer.
Access for disabled people: Parking provided, ramped entry, level entry, access to all public areas, toilet facilities
Other restrictions: Guide dogs welcome

General description:
Displays relating to the history of the Mitford and Launditch Union workhouse, Norfolk, displays relating to farming and rural life in

Norfolk since 1850, working farm and agriculture displays, extensive library containing historic photographs, printed ephemera and books on rural life, Norfolk history and farming, available for research.
Information services:
Library available for reference (for conditions see Access above)
Demonstrations and costumed enactments
Education events for schools,
Early Years Centre for and pre-school groups
Study centre, Education Team 01362 869256
Exhibition Gallery and costume gallery
Special visitor services: Guided tours, tape recorded guides, materials and/or activities for children.
Education services: Group education facilities, resources for Key Stages 1 and 2, 3, 4 and Further or Higher Education.
Services for disabled people: For the hearing impaired; displays and/or information at wheelchair height.
Collections:
Farm tools and agricultural machinery
Rural trades and crafts
Steam engines; internal combustion engines
Historic photographs, printed ephemera and reference books
Carts, wagons, rural transportation
Village life, friendly societies and trades unions
All collections are on computerised database
Catalogues:
Catalogue for library is in-house only. Catalogue for all of the collections is only available in-house.

Internet home pages:
http://www.norfolk.gov.uk/tourism/museums

2424
ROSE THEATRE EXHIBITION
56 Park Street, London, SE1 9AR

Tel: 020 7261 9565
Fax: 020 7633 0367
Email: info@rosetheatre.org.uk
Formed: 1999

Organisation type and purpose: Registered charity (charity number 1003008), historic building, house or site, suitable for ages: 12+.
Site discovered and partially excavated 1989.
Temporary exhibition on the archaeological site of the Rose Theatre, to forward its full excavation, conservation and permanent public display.
Marketing and Operations of the Rose Theatre Exhibition carried out by:
Exhibitions Department (ISGC)
International Shakespeare's Globe Centre, 21 New Globe Walk, London, SE1 9DT, tel: 020 7902 1500
Address for Company Office:
Rose Theatre Trust
21 New Globe Walk, London, SE1 9DT

Enquiries to: Project Co-ordinator
Access:
Access to staff: By letter, by email
Other restrictions: Contact ISGC.
Access for disabled people: level entry, access to all public areas

General description:
Archaeological site of the Rose, Bankside's first theatre, built 1587 and rediscovered in 1989. The Rose was home to the plays of Shakespeare, Marlowe and Kyd and is the only complete site of its kind to survive. The current exhibition tells its history, reveals what was discovered here in 1989, and explains what needs to happen before it can be fully excavated and put on permanent public display.
Information services:
Services for disabled people: Displays and/or information at wheelchair height.

Internet home pages:
http://www.rosetheatre.org.uk
History of the site, information about the exhibition, and the Rose Theatre Trust and Company.

2425
ROSSENDALE MUSEUM
Whitaker Park, Haslingden Road, Rossendale, Lancashire, BB4 6RE

Tel: 01706 217777 or 244682
Minicom no. 01706 226590 (Leisure Dept - Minicom)
Fax: 01706 250037
Formed: 1902

Organisation type and purpose: Local government body, museum, art gallery, suitable for ages: 5+.

Enquiries to: Curator
Access:
Access to staff: By letter, by telephone, by fax, in person
Hours: Mon to Fri, 0900 to 1700: staff available for information
Other restrictions: Wheelchair access, ground floor only.
Access for disabled people: Parking provided, ramped entry
Other restrictions: Access to ground floor only; toilet facilities in park, at kiosk.

General description:
Local history; social history.
Displays include: fine and decorative arts; furniture; ceramics; natural history (no specialised staff); costume and textiles; Victorian drawing room; display of 19th century wallpapers.
Museum is housed in 19th century mill owner's house.
Information services:
Library available for reference (for conditions see Access above)
Special visitor services: Guided tours, tape recorded guides.
Education services: Group education facilities, resources for Key Stages 1 and 2.
Services for disabled people: For the visually impaired; for the hearing impaired.
Collections:
Letters, conveyances, industrial and business archives, ephemera
19th century tune books
Local photographs and slide collection
Textile pattern books
Magazines of local companies and unions
Catalogues:
Catalogue for all of the collections is only available in-house.
Publications list:
is available in hard copy and online.
Printed publications:
The following museum publications, available direct:
Museum Guide Book(£1.25)
Diary of an Edwardian Childhood (£2.95)
Diary of James Melia (£2.95)
Rawtenstall Perspectives (£2.95)
Recipes from Edwardian Haslingden (50p)

2426
ROSSLYN CHAPEL
Rosslyn, Edinburgh, EH25 9PU

Tel: 0131 440 2159
Fax: 0131 440 1979
Email: rosslynch@aol.com
Full name: Rosslyn Chapel Trust
Formed: 1995

Organisation type and purpose: Independently owned, registered charity (charity number SCO 24324), historic building, house or site, suitable for ages: 16+.

Enquiries to: Director
Access:
Access to staff: By email, Internet web pages
Access to building, collections or gallery: No prior appointment required
Hours: Mon to Sat, 1000 to 1700; Sun, 1200 to 1645
Other restrictions: Prior appointment required for groups.
Access for disabled people: Parking provided, level entry, toilet facilities

General description:
Rosslyn Chapel is unique and famed world-wide for the beauty of its carvings and for the aura of mystery and magic that surrounds it.
Built in 1446 by William St Clair, third and last Prince of Orkney, Rosslyn Chapel conforms neither to contemporary architecture nor to any fashion. Rich in ornament, its exact place in the creation of mankind still remains difficult to estimate.
Information services:
Special visitor services: Guided tours, tape recorded guides.
Services for disabled people: Displays and/or information at wheelchair height.
Collections:
The largest number of 'Green Men' found in any medieval building
Carvings of plants from the New World that predate the journeys of Columbus
Printed publications:
Guide Book
Electronic and video products:
Video
Audio Guide

Internet home pages:
http://www.rosslynchapel.org.uk

2427
ROTHERHAM MUSEUM
See - Clifton Park Museum

2428
ROTHERHITHE HERITAGE MUSEUM
See - Pumphouse Educational Museum

2429
ROTHSCHILD COLLECTION
Waddesdon Manor, Waddesdon, Aylesbury, Buckinghamshire, HP18 0JH

Tel: 01296 653203
Fax: 01296 653212
Email: waddesconmanor@nationaltrust.org.uk
Formed: 1957

Organisation type and purpose: Registered charity (charity number 205846), historic building, house or site, suitable for ages: 5+.
Parent body:
The National Trust

Enquiries to: Head of Collections
Access:
Access to staff: By letter, by telephone, by fax, by email, in person, visitors by prior appointment
Access for disabled people: Parking provided, ramped entry, toilet facilities

General description:
A house built by Gabrielle-Hippolyte Destailleur for Baron Ferdinand de Rothschild 1874-1889. It was furnished by Baron Ferdinand and his successors with French 18th century royal furniture; Savonnerie carpets; Sèvres porcelain; gilt bronzes; gold boxes; as well as portraits by Gainsborough and Reynolds, and paintings by Dutch 17th century Masters, all set against a background of French 18th century carved panelling.
Information services:
Helpline available, tel no: 01296 653212.
Special visitor services: Tape recorded guides, materials and/or activities for children.
Services for disabled people: Displays and/or information at wheelchair height.
Collections:
18th century French decorative arts including furniture, gold boxes, carpets, Sèvres porcelain

continued overleaf

English portraits by Reynolds and Gainsborough, and Dutch old masters; drawings and illuminated manuscripts; arms and armour
Catalogues:
Catalogue for part of the collections is published.
Printed publications:
Guidebooks
Waddesdon Manor 'Heritage of a Rothschild House'
Catalogues

Internet home pages:
http://www.waddesdon.org.uk

2430
ROTUNDA MUSEUM
Vernon Road, Scarborough, North Yorkshire, YO11 2NN

Tel: 01723 374839

Organisation type and purpose: Museum, suitable for ages: 5+.

Enquiries to: Curator
Access:
Access to staff: By letter, by telephone, by fax, visitors by prior appointment

General description:
A fine example of a Georgian purpose-built museum which opened in 1829. It was designed by William Smith, 'The Father of English Geology'. The upper galleries are lined with the original curved display cabinets, a T Platform and a painted frieze of the geological section of the Yorkshire Coast. The exhibitions are mainly from the extensive collection of the Scarborough Philosophical and Archaeological Society.
Information services:
Special visitor services: Materials and/or activities for children..
Collections:
Star Carr, finds excavated from the lakeside campsite, including a flint tool assemblage, antler barbed points, flora and faunal evidence, Mesolithic
Clarke Collection of folklore and charms with contemporary records of their use, international, 19th/20th century, 500 charms and 4 MSS volumes

2431
ROUTE 66 CAR MUSEUM
Newcastle

Closed

2432
ROW III HOUSE / OLD MERCHANT'S HOUSE
South Quay, Great Yarmouth, Norfolk, NR30 2RW

Tel: 01493 857900

Organisation type and purpose: Historic building, house or site, suitable for ages: all ages.
Parent body:
English Heritage (East of England Region) Brooklands, 24 Brooklands Avenue, Cambridge, CB2 2BU, tel: 01223 582700, fax: 01223 582701

Enquiries to: Custodian
Access:
Access to staff: By telephone
Other restrictions: Letters should be addressed to English Heritage Regional Office.

General description:
Fine surviving examples of Row Houses, unique to Great Yarmouth. Nearby are the remains of a Franciscan friary with early wall paintings discovered during bomb damage repairs. Row Houses are the result of the peculiar development of Great Yarmouth. The Romans had abandoned the settlement but, thanks to a flourishing herring trade, a new settlement developed in the 13th century, and a pattern of main streets linked by closely spaced parallel alleys evolved. The existing houses date back to a period of great prosperity when the town was rebuilt in brick, flint and tile.

Internet home pages:
http://www.english-heritage.org.uk

2433
ROWALLANE GARDEN
Saintfield, Ballynahinch, Co Down, BT24 7LH

Tel: 028 9751 0131
Fax: 028 9751 1242
Email: rowallane@nationaltrust.org.uk
Formed: 1955

Organisation type and purpose: National organisation, registered charity (charity number 205846), historic building, house or site, suitable for ages: 8+.
Historic garden.
Parent body:
National Trust Office for Northern Ireland Rowallane House, Saintfield, Ballynahinch, Co Down, BT24 7LH, tel: 028 9751 0721, fax: 028 9751 1242

Enquiries to: Property Manager
Access:
Access to staff: By letter, by telephone, by fax, by email
Access for disabled people: Parking provided, level entry, toilet facilities
Other restrictions: Designated parking. 2 manual wheelchairs available. Level entrance to tea-room. Garden is natural and undulating, some parts are inaccessible.

General description:
Historic garden - varied and important plant collection.
Information services:
Scented plants, tours with Head Gardener: tel for details, Sympathetic Hearing Scheme.
Booked school groups welcome.
Year-round programme of garden workshops, fairs and musical events.
Special visitor services: Guided tours, materials and/or activities for children.
Services for disabled people: For the visually impaired; for the hearing impaired.
Printed publications:
Welcome Leaflet
Regional Guide
Children's Trail Leaflet (late 2002)
Events Leaflet

Internet home pages:
http://www.nationaltrust.org.uk

2434
ROWLEY'S HOUSE
See - Shrewsbury Museums Service

2435
RAF AIR-SEA RESCUE & COASTAL COMMAND MUSEUM
See - Norfolk & Suffolk Aviation Museum

2436
RAF BOMBER COMMAND MUSEUM
See - Norfolk & Suffolk Aviation Museum

2437
ROYAL AIR FORCE MUSEUM
Grahame Park Way, Hendon, London, NW9 5LL

Tel: 020 8205 2266
Fax: 020 8200 1751
Email: info@rafmuseum.com
Formed: 1965
Incorporates the former: Battle of Britain Museum, Bomber Command Museum

Organisation type and purpose: National government body, registered charity (charity number 244708), museum.
Subsidiary body:
Royal Air Force Museum Cosford
Tel: 01902 376200, fax: 01902 736211, email/website: cosford@rafmuseum.com

Enquiries to: Keeper of Research & Information Services
Access:
Access to staff: By letter, by fax, by email, visitors by prior appointment
Hours: Mon, Wed, Thu, 1000 to 1700

General description:
Aeronautics, military history, aviation history from the earliest times to date, with particular emphasis on British military aviation; all aspects of the history of the Royal Air Force; technical information on British military aircraft since 1912, (except aerodynamics).
Collections:
Aircrew flying log books
Airfield site plans
Large collection of technical manuals for aircraft, engines, instruments etc
Numerous named archive collections
Supermarine, Fairey and Bristol company drawings
Catalogues:
Catalogue for part of the collections is only available in-house.
Printed publications:
Museum Guidebook
Information sheets:
No 1 - Personnel Records First World War: RFC, RNAS, RAF, WRAF
No 2 - Personnel Records: RAF, RAFVR, RAuxAF, WRAF, WAAF
No 3 - RAF Unit Records
No 4 - RAF Stations: Information Sources
No 5 - RAF Aircraft: Service Histories
No 6 - Record Agents
No 7 - Photocopying and Microform Reproduction Charges

Internet home pages:
http://www.rafmuseum.com
General museum information.

See also - Hawkinge Battle of Britain Museum

2438
ROYAL AIR FORCE MUSEUM
Cosford, Shifnal, Shropshire, TF11 8UP

Tel: 01902 376200
Fax: 01902 376211
Email: cosford@rafmuseum.org
Acronym or abbreviation: RAF Museum
Formed: May 1979
Formerly: Aerospace Museum

Organisation type and purpose: International organisation, national government body, national organisation, registered charity (charity number 244708), museum, suitable for ages: 5+.
Aviation heritage.

Enquiries to: General Manager RAF Museum Cosford
Direct tel: 01902 376202
Direct fax: 01902 376203
Direct email: johnfrancis@rafmuseum.com
Other contacts: Public Relations Manager
Access:
Access to staff: By letter, by telephone, by fax, by email, Internet web pages
Access to building, collections or gallery: No prior appointment required
Hours: Open daily, 1000 to 1800 (last admissions 1600)
Closed 24 to 26 Dec and 1 Jan
Access for disabled people: Parking provided, ramped entry, level entry, access to all public areas, toilet facilities

General description:
One of the largest aviation collections in the United Kingdom. The collection spans over 90 years of aviation history from the first flight across the channel in 1909 and the first civil transport flight in 1919 to the present day.

Information services:
Library available for reference (for conditions see Access above). Helpline available, tel no: 0870 606 2027.
Interactive, hands-on Fun n Flight gallery
Special visitor services: Guided tours.
Education services: Group education facilities, resources for Key Stages 1 and 2, 3, 4 and Further or Higher Education.
Services for disabled people: For the visually impaired.
Collections:
Over 80 historic aircraft
Printed publications:
Guidebook (£3.50)

Internet home pages:
http://www.cosfordairshow.co.uk
http://www.rafmuseum.org.uk/cosford/index.cfm

2439
ROYAL ANGLIAN REGIMENT MUSEUM

Land Warfare Hall, The Imperial War Museum, Duxford Airfield, Duxford, Cambridgeshire, CB2 4QR

Tel: 01223 835000
Formed: 1996

Organisation type and purpose: Museum, suitable for ages: 8+.

Enquiries to: Curator
Direct tel: 01223 835000 ext 298
Direct fax: 01223 835120
Access:
Access to staff: By letter, by telephone, by fax, in person, visitors by prior appointment
Access to building, collections or gallery: Prior appointment required
Hours: Summer: daily, 1000 to 1800
Winter: daily, 1000 to 1600
Access for disabled people: Parking provided, ramped entry, level entry, access to all public areas, toilet facilities

General description:
Material covering the history, since the amalgamations of County Regiments 1958-1960, of the East Anglian and Royal Anglian Regiments. Features a historical family tree; traditions; customs; music; uniforms; overseas deployments and operations; honours and awards; and a roll of honour.
Catalogues:
Catalogue for part of the collections is only available in-house.

2440
ROYAL ANTHROPOLOGICAL INSTITUTE

Information services:
Special visitor services: Guided tours.
Education services: Group education facilities..
See - Anthropology Library

2441
ROYAL ARMOURIES MUSEUM

Armouries Drive, Leeds, West Yorkshire, LS10 1LT

Tel: 0113 220 1999
Fax: 0113 220 1934
Email: enquiries@armouries.org.uk
Formed: Museum 1996

Organisation type and purpose: National government body, registered charity, museum, suitable for ages: 12+.
National museum of Arms and Armour.
Royal Armouries dates from the late 15th century.
Other addresses:
Royal Armouries, Fort Nelson
Down End Road, Fareham, Hampshire, PO17 6AN, tel: 01329 233734, email/website: fnenquiries@armouries.org.uk
Royal Armouries, HM Tower of London
Tower of London, London, EC3A 4AA, tel: 020 7480 6358, email/website: enquiries@armouries.org.uk

Enquiries to: Public Relations Manager
Direct tel: 0113 220 1948
Direct fax: 0113 220 1955
Direct email: nboole@armouries.org.uk
Other contacts: Master of the Armouries for overall responsibility for the Museum in Leeds, The Tower, Fort Nelson.
Access:
Access to staff: By letter, by telephone, by email, visitors by prior appointment
Access to building, collections or gallery: No prior appointment required
Hours: Daily, 1000 to 1700
Other restrictions: Closed 24 and 25 Dec.
Access for disabled people: Parking provided, level entry, access to all public areas, toilet facilities
Other restrictions: Hearing loop installed, wheelchairs available.

General description:
The National Museum of Arms and Armour with material ranging from 4th century, Greek Helmed and Oriental armours, to armours of King Henry VIII and and Indian elephant. live displays, including jousting and storytelling bring the subject to life. Alongside films, music and computer programmes.
Information services:
Library available for reference (for conditions see Access above)
Special visitor services: Materials and/or activities for children.
Education services: Group education facilities, resources for Key Stages 1 and 2, 3, 4 and Further or Higher Education.
Services for disabled people: For the hearing impaired; displays and/or information at wheelchair height.
Collections:
Arms and Armour
Library
Photographic Library
Parker Room
Satic Library
Publications list:
is available in hard copy.
Printed publications:
See Royal Armouries, HM Tower of London

Internet home pages:
http://www.armouries.org.uk/

2442
ROYAL ARMOURIES MUSEUM OF ARTILLERY

Fort Nelson, Down End Road, Fareham, Hampshire, PO17 6AN

Tel: 01329 233734
Fax: 01329 822092
Email: fnenquiries@armouries.org.uk
Formed: 1988
Formerly: Fort Nelson Museum; Tower Armouries (now Royal Armouries HM Tower of London), date of change, 1984

Organisation type and purpose: National government body, statutory body, registered charity (charity number 803617), museum, suitable for ages: 5+.
National Museum (under DCMS), charge to acquire, preserve, display and interpret arms and armour.
Parent body:
Royal Armouries
Armouries Drive, Leeds, LS10 1LT, tel: 0113 220 1852, fax: 0113 220 1934, email: Philip.Abbott@armouries.org.uk

Enquiries to: Keeper
Other contacts: Marketing Manager for daily operational procedures and visitor services.
Access:
Access to staff: By letter, by telephone, by fax, by email, visitors by prior appointment
Access to building, collections or gallery: No prior appointment required
Hours: Apr to Oct, daily, 1000 to 1700
Nov to Mar, daily, 1030 to 1600
Other restrictions: Closed 25 and 26 Dec.
Library by prior arrangement.
Access for disabled people: Parking provided, toilet facilities
Other restrictions: Full access guide available, please request.

General description:
The history and development of artillery and fortification including specialist manuals dating back to 16th century.
Information services:
Library available for reference (for conditions see Access above)
Some picture research facilities for artillery material only.
Special visitor services: Guided tours, tape recorded guides, materials and/or activities for children.
Education services: Group education facilities, resources for Key Stages 2, 3 and Further or Higher Education.
Services for disabled people: For the visually impaired; for the hearing impaired; displays and/or information at wheelchair height.
Collections:
A small reference collection of books and pamphlets on arms and armour
Early books on artillery, handbooks, and drill manuals
Major collection of artillery from 15th century to present day
Publications list:
is available in hard copy.
Printed publications:
Yearbook containing list of acquisitions and specialist monographs on arms and armour

Address for ordering publications:
Printed publications:
Head of Publications, Royal Armouries
Armouries Drive, Leeds, LS10 1LT, tel: 0113 220 1852, fax: 0113 220 1934, email: Paula.Turner@armouries.org.uk

Internet home pages:
http://www.armouries.org.uk
Basic information on collections and programmes at the three sites.

2443
ROYAL ARMY DENTAL CORPS MUSEUM

Acronym or abbreviation: RADC Museum
See - Army Medical Services Museum

2444
ROYAL ARMY MEDICAL CORPS HISTORICAL MUSEUM

Acronym or abbreviation: RAMC
See - Army Medical Services Museum

2445
ROYAL ARMY ORDNANCE CORPS MUSEUM

See - Royal Logistic Corps Museum

2446
ROYAL ARTILLERY HISTORICAL TRUST

Firepower Royal Artillery Museum, Royal Arsenal (West), Warren Lane, Woolwich, London, SE18 6ST

Tel: 020 8855 7755
Fax: 020 8855 7100
Email: research@firepower.org.uk

Organisation type and purpose: Advisory body.
Responsible for:
Firepower
The Royal Artillery Museum
Royal Arsenal (West), Warren Lane, Woolwich, London, SE18 6ST, tel: 020 8855

continued overleaf

7755, fax: 020 8855 7100, email/website: research@firepower.org.uk website: www.firepower.org.uk
Reserve Collection
Rotunda Museum, Woolwich, London, SE18 4BQ
Royal Artillery Library and Archives
James Clavell Library
Firepower, Royal Arsenal (West), Warren Lane, Woolwich, London, SE18 6ST, tel: 020 8855 7755, email/website: research@firepower.org.uk website: www.firepower.org.uk

Enquiries to: Honorary Secretary
Access:
Access to staff: By letter, by email, visitors by prior appointment
Hours: Mon to Fri, 0900 to 1700

General description:
Administration and control of the museum, library, artefacts and archives.

Internet home pages:
http://www.firepower.org.uk

See also - Firepower; Museum of Artillery in the Rotunda; Royal Artillery Institution Library

2447
ROYAL ARTILLERY INSTITUTION LIBRARY

James Clavell Library, Royal Arsenal (West), Warren Lane, Woolwich, London, SE18 6ST

Tel: 020 8312 7125
Email: research@firepower.org.uk

Organisation type and purpose: Independently owned, registered charity.
Part of the Firepower Museum Complex with access to the History Gallery, Gunnery Hall, Medal Gallery and the Field of Fire audiovisual experience.
To record and promote research into the history of the Royal Artillery and related subjects.
Parent body:
Royal Artillery Institution
Academy Road, Woolwich, London, SE18 4DN, tel: 020 8781 5623
Linked organisation:
Firepower Museum
Royal Regiment of Artillery

Enquiries to: Librarian
Access:
Access to building, collections or gallery: Prior appointment required
Hours: David Evans Reading Room, open for readers Wed and Thu, 1000 to 1600

General description:
Materials on Royal Artillery Regimental History; artillery equipments, armed forces, warfare, tactics, training, fortification, military history, military geography and biography.
Collections:
Books, journals, pamphlets, manuscripts, diaries, maps, plans, drawings, photographs, film and microfiche
Printed publications:
History of the Royal Regiment of Artillery (Vols I -VI available, VII in production)

Internet home pages:
http://www.firepower.org.uk

2448
ROYAL BIRMINGHAM SOCIETY OF ARTISTS

4 Brook Street, Birmingham, B3 1SA

Tel: 0121 236 4353
Fax: 0121 236 4555
Acronym or abbreviation: RBSA
Formed: 1812
Formerly: Royal Birmingham Society of Arts (RBSA)

Organisation type and purpose: Independently owned, professional body (membership is by subscription, qualification, election or invitation), present number of members: 700 friends, 30 associates, 76 members, registered charity (charity number 528894), museum, suitable for ages: all ages.
To actively encourage practice and appreciation of fine arts and allied crafts. Fulfilment of a vital community purpose by showcasing local and national professionals plus dedicated amateurs.

Enquiries to: Honorary Secretary
Other contacts: Honorary Curator for gallery hire.
Access:
Access to staff: By letter, by telephone, by fax, charges to non-members
Hours: Mon to Fri, 0900 to 1700
Access to building, collections or gallery: No prior appointment required
Hours: Mon to Wed, Fri, 1030 to 1730; Thu, 1030 to 1900; Sat, 1030 to 1700
Other restrictions: Archive which houses the RBSA Collection by prior appointment.
For exhibitions see programme, or phone gallery for dates.
Access for disabled people: level entry, access to all public areas, toilet facilities

General description:
Practical fine art and allied crafts, history of the Royal Birmingham Society of Arts.
Rotating exhibitions on a yearly basis, 2 galleries and craft gallery, archive. All media is represented in our exhibitions from contemporary to more traditional tastes.
Collections:
Paintings, prints, sculptures etc donated by artists when elected as full members
Bound Exhibition Catalogues continuous from the early years of the Society
Documentation, membership register, diploma works and more from the early years onwards
Printed publications:
Exhibition Catalogues
The History of the RBSA to 1928 (Hill J and Midgeley W, pub Society and Cornish Brothers Ltd, via Kynoch Press, Birmingham)
Pre-Raphaelite Birmingham (Hartnell R, pub Studley Brewin Books 1996
RBSA Members and Friends Newsletter (3 times a year)

Internet home pages:
http://www.rbsa.org.uk
About gallery and current exhibitions

2449
ROYAL BOROUGH MUSEUM COLLECTION

Royal Borough of Windsor & Maidenhead, Tinkers Lane, Windsor, Berkshire, SL4 4LR

Tel: 01628 796829
Fax: 01628 796859
Email: museum.collections@rbwm.gov.uk
Formed: 1951
Incorporates the former: Maidenhead Museum, Guildhall Exhibition

Organisation type and purpose: Local government body, museum.
Parent body:
Royal Borough of Windsor & Maidenhead
Tel: 01628 798888
Links with:
Friends of the Royal Borough Museum Collection
Tel: 01753 869871

Enquiries to: Heritage Development Officer
Access:
Access to staff: By letter, by telephone, by email, visitors by prior appointment
Hours: Mon to Fri, 0900 to 1700 by telephone Wed, 0930 to 1600 in person
Other restrictions: Other days by appointment.
Access for disabled people: Parking provided, level entry, toilet facilities

General description:
History of Windsor and the towns and villages of the Royal Borough of Windsor and Maidenhead.
Collections:
A Y Nutt Collection of paintings
Artefacts, archaeological finds, books, directories, paintings, prints, photographs, maps etc covering the whole Borough, but more for Windsor than other areas
Catalogues:
Catalogue for library is in-house only. Catalogue for all of the collections is only available in-house.
Printed publications:
Historical publications published by the Royal Borough of Windsor and Maidenhead, and those published by the Windsor Local History Publication Group are available through the Honorary Curator
Heritage (newsletter, 3 times a year, free)

Internet home pages:
http://www.rbwm.gov.uk

2450
ROYAL BOTANIC GARDENS

Economic Botany Collections, Centre for Economic Botany, Kew, Richmond-upon-Thames, Surrey, TW9 3AE

Tel: 020 8332 5706
Fax: 020 8332 5768
Email: h.prendergast@rbgkew.org.uk
Formed: 1857
Formerly: Economic Botany Collections, Sir Joseph Bank Centre for Economic Botany

Organisation type and purpose: Local government body, suitable for ages: 8+.
Botanic garden.

Enquiries to: Curator
Access:
Access to staff: By letter, by telephone, by fax, by email, visitors by prior appointment, Internet web pages

General description:
In Museum No.1 an exhibition Plants and People, displays of some 500 objects showing the many ways in which we depend on plants - for medicine, clothing, food, music and much else.
Most collections - the Economic Botany Collections - are stored elsewhere and can be visited by appointment only.
Information services:
Special visitor services: Guided tours, materials and/or activities for children.
Education services: Group education facilities..
Collections:
Some collections are on view in Kew's Museum No. 1 in its Plants and People Exhibition
J Quin, Japanese lacquer and tools, 19th century, c. 150 items
R Spruce, plant and ethnological material from the Amazon, 19th century
H Parkes, Japanese paper and associated artefacts, 19th century
Timber, worldwide - various sizes, 19th-20th century, c. 30,000 items
Royal Pharmaceutical Society of Great Britain, materia medica, 19th-20th century, c. 8000 items
Archaeology, plant materials - Howard Carter, Flinders Petrie, Schweinfurth
See internet pages for full information
Publications list:
is available on-line.

Internet home pages:
http://www.rbgkew.org.uk

2451
ROYAL BURGH OF CULROSS, THE

Culross, Fife, KY12 8JH

Tel: 01383 880359
Fax: 01383 882675
Formed: 1931

Organisation type and purpose: Membership association, voluntary organisation, registered

charity (charity number SCO 07410), historic building, house or site, suitable for ages: 8+.
Parent body:
National Trust for Scotland (South Region)

Enquiries to: Manager
Access:
Access to staff: By letter, by telephone, by fax, visitors by prior appointment, charges to non-members
Access to building, collections or gallery: Prior appointment required
Hours: Apr to Jun and Sep to Oct: daily, 1200 to 1700
Jul and Aug: daily, 1000 to 1800
Access for disabled people: toilet facilities
Other restrictions: Limited access; most of exhibition, ground floor of palace and tea-room

General description:
Small Royal Burgh on the north shore of the Forth which provides a striking introduction to Scottish domestic life in the 16th and 17th centuries. Culross Palace was built between 1597 and 1611 and features 16th and 17th century painted ceilings, decorative painted woodwork and original interiors, 17th and 18th century furniture and decorative items, and a fine collection of Staffordshire and Scottish pottery. A model 17th century garden has been built in the grounds.
The Town House and The Study are open to the public, and The Ark, Bishop Leighton's House, The Nunnery and other restored houses may be viewed from the outside only.
The Town House has a display of the history of the ancient Royal Burgh. The study is furnished as a 17th century merchant's house.
Information services:
Guidebooks in French and German, video in French and German for groups.
Explanatory text in Dutch, French, German, Hebrew, Italian, Japanese, Spanish.
Braille guidebook, induction loop in Town House and Bessie Bar Hall.
Special visitor services: Tape recorded guides.
Education services: Group education facilities, resources for Key Stages 1 and 2.
Services for disabled people: For the visually impaired; for the hearing impaired.
Collections:
Unique range of painted walls and ceilings of 16th and 17th centuries which may be viewed by visitors
Steele bequest of Staffordshire pottery
The Town House has the old burgh weights on display
Printed publications:
Guide books (£2.95 each)
A range of postcards (15p each)
NTS Culross Trail Booklist (50p)
Microform products:
Video and Walkman tapes (available to visitors only)

Address for ordering publications:
Printed publications:
Merchandise Department, National Trust for Scotland
28 Charlotte Square, Edinburgh, EH2 4ET, tel: 0131 243 9300, fax: 0131 243 9301

Internet home pages:
http://www.nts.org.uk

2452
ROYAL CAMBRIAN ACADEMY OF ART

Crown Lane, Conwy, Gwynedd, LL32 8AN

Tel: 01492 593413
Fax: 01492 593413
Email: rca@rcaconwy.org
Acronym or abbreviation: RCA
Formed: 1882
Formerly situated at: Plas Mawr

Organisation type and purpose: Membership association (membership is by election or invitation), present number of members: 100, registered charity (charity number 219648), art gallery.

Enquiries to: Curator
Access:
Access to staff: By letter, by telephone, by fax, by email, Internet web pages
Hours: Tue to Sat, 1100 to 1700; Sun, 1300 to 1630
Other restrictions: No lift to upstairs gallery.

General description:
Past and present members of the Academy since 1882, artists working in Wales.
Collections:
Catalogues of every RCA exhibition since 1882
Printed publications:
Centenary Year (1982) Reference Catalogue (giving history of the Academy)
Exhibition catalogues
Pembrokeshire (Knapp-Fisher J)
Portraits (Williams K)
The Land and the Sea (Williams K)

Internet home pages:
http://www.rcaconwy.org

2453
ROYAL CEREMONIAL DRESS COLLECTION

Kensington Palace, London, W8 4PX

Tel: 020 7937 9561
Fax: 020 7376 0198
Formed: 1984

Organisation type and purpose: National organisation, registered charity, museum, historic building, house or site.
Parent body:
Historic Royal Palace Trust (HRPT)
Hampton Court Palace, Surrey, KT8 9AG

Enquiries to: Director
Direct tel: 020 7937 8799
Other contacts: Curator
Access:
Access to staff: By letter
Access for disabled people: Parking provided, ramped entry, toilet facilities
Other restrictions: Prior notice required.

General description:
Collection of Royal & Ceremonial Dress including uniforms, ceremonial robes and royal dress.
Archive pertaining to these collections.

Internet home pages:
http://www.hrp.org.uk

2454
ROYAL COLLEGE OF DEFENCE STUDIES

37 Belgrave Square, London, SW1X 8NS

Tel: 020 7915 4814
Fax: 020 7915 4800
Acronym or abbreviation: RCDS
Formed: 1970
Also known as: Seaford House
Formerly: Imperial Defence College (IDC), date of change, 1922-1970

Organisation type and purpose: National government body, learned society (membership is by election or invitation), present number of members: 85 current (on site), historic building, house or site.
Government department.
The house originally known as Sefton House was built in 1842 by the Marquess of Westminster. It may be visited on an Open Day.
Connections with:
Ministry of Defence, London (MOD)

Enquiries to: Librarian
Access:
Access to staff: Members only
Hours: Mon to Fri, 0900 to 1700
Other restrictions: Members and OGDs.
Access to building, collections or gallery: No access other than to staff

General description:
Defence, international relations, politics, economics, history.
Catalogues:
Catalogue for library is in-house only.
Publications list:
is available in hard copy.
Printed publications:
Reading Lists
Journal Holdings
New Books Lists
Seaford House Papers (restricted distribution)

Internet home pages:
http://www.mod.uk.rcds/index.html

2455
ROYAL COMMISSION ON HISTORICAL MANUSCRIPTS

See - National Archives

2456
ROYAL CORNWALL MUSEUM

The Royal Institution of Cornwall, River Street, Truro, Cornwall, TR1 2SJ

Tel: 01872 272205
Fax: 01872 40514
Email: enquiries@royal-cornwall-museum.freeserve.co.uk
Formed: 1818

Organisation type and purpose: Registered charity (charity number 221958), museum, art gallery, suitable for ages: 5+.
Parent body:
Royal Institution of Cornwall (RIC)
at the same address

Enquiries to: Director
Other contacts: Office Manager for visit/events bookings.
Access:
Access to staff: By letter, by telephone, by fax, by email, in person, visitors by prior appointment, charges to non-members
Hours: Mon to Fri, 1000 to 1700
Access to building, collections or gallery: No prior appointment required
Hours: Mon to Sat, 1000 to 1700
Other restrictions: Library closed between 1300 and 1400.
Closed Bank Holidays.
Access for disabled people: ramped entry, access to all public areas, toilet facilities
Other restrictions: Lifts.

General description:
General collections, local archaeology and history, British ceramics, Cornish fine art and natural history, including Cornish minerals.
Information services:
Library available for reference (for conditions see Access above)
Special visitor services: Guided tours, tape recorded guides, materials and/or activities for children.
Education services: Group education facilities, resources for Key Stages 1 and 2, 3, 4 and Further or Higher Education.
Services for disabled people: For the hearing impaired.
Collections:
Alfred de Pass Collection of drawings 15th to 20th century
Cornish photographs c 30,000 from 1850
Rashleigh Collection (18th century) Cornish and other minerals
Some parts of all collections viewably via www.chain.org.uk
Catalogues:
Catalogue for library is in-house only. Catalogue for all of the collections is available in-house and part is on-line.
Publications list:
is available on-line.

continued overleaf

Internet home pages:
http://www.royalcornwallmuseum.org.uk
General information re museum and library.
http://www.chain.org.uk
Link to Royal Cornwall Museum online database.

2457
ROYAL CORPS OF TRANSPORT MUSEUM
See - Royal Logistic Corps Museum

2458
ROYAL COURTS OF JUSTICE
Strand, London, WC2A 2LL

Tel: 020 7947 6000
Fax: 020 7947 6622
Acronym or abbreviation: RCJ
Formed: 1882

Organisation type and purpose: National government body, historic building, house or site, suitable for ages: 12+.

Enquiries to: Accommodation Manager
Direct tel: 020 7947 7326
Direct email: lucinda.webb@courtservice.gsi.gov.uk
Access:
Access to staff: By letter, by fax, by email, visitors by prior appointment
Access to building, collections or gallery: No prior appointment required
Other restrictions: No cameras allowed in the building.
Access for disabled people: ramped entry, level entry, toilet facilities
Other restrictions: Access to most areas can be arranged - contact 020 7947 6506 for access arrangements.

General description:
The Royal Courts of Justice is a working court building and the home of the High Court and The Court of Appeal. The building itself is a fine example of Victorian, Gothic architecture and houses a collection of legal costumes and prints and many other works of art.
Information services:
Guided tours on certain dates.
Access for the disabled by prior arrangement.
Special visitor services: Guided tours..
Collections:
Exhibition of legal costumes
Exhibition of legal prints and other works of art
General information on the history of the building.
Electronic and video products:
The Royal Courts of Justice, Past & Present (video)

2459
ROYAL CROWN DERBY VISITOR CENTRE
194 Osmaston Road, Derby, DE23 8JZ

Tel: 01332 712800
Fax: 01332 712863
Email: eparr@royal-crown-derby.co.uk
Formed: 1750
Formerly: Royal Crown Derby Museum, date of change, 1998

Organisation type and purpose: Manufacturing industry, museum.
Tourist attraction and factory shop.
The home and show case of Royal Crown Derby Porcelain.
Parent Company:
Royal Doulton
Minton House, Stoke-on-Trent

Enquiries to: Manager
Other contacts: Tours Organiser
Access:
Access to staff: By letter, by telephone, by fax, by email, visitors by prior appointment
Hours: Mon to Fri, 0930 to 1615
Access to building, collections or gallery: No prior appointment required
Hours: Daily, 0930 to 1700 (last admission 1600)
Other restrictions: Tour available Mon to Fri only

General description:
History of Royal Crown Derby.
The collection shows the comprehensive production of china in the city from 1750 to the present day.
Collections:
A wide collection of Royal Crown Derby porcelain from over past 250 years
Watercolour designs and drawings by Royal Crown Derby artists.
Catalogues:
Catalogue for library is in-house only. Catalogue for all of the collections is only available in-house but part is published.
Publications list:
is available in hard copy and online.
Printed publications:
Imari
Royal Crown Derby Paperweights
Electronic and video products:
Video

Internet home pages:
http://www.royal-crown-derby.co.uk

2460
ROYAL DOULTON VISITOR CENTRE & SIR HENRY DOULTON GALLERY
Nile Street, Burslem, Stoke-on-Trent, Staffordshire, ST6 4AJ

Tel: 01782 292434/292292
Fax: 01782 292424
Email: visitor@royal-doulton.com

Organisation type and purpose: Museum, historic building, house or site.
Member of:
North Staffordshire Museums Association

Enquiries to: Manager

General description:
The Visitor Centre house over a thousand Royal Doulton figures including many rare models.
The Gallery traces Royal Doulton's history from 1815 to the present through exhibits including bone china, Lambeth Art wares, table and nursery wares, and commemoratives.
Collections:
Lambeth art and functional pottery, 1815-1956, c. 40 items
Burslem, ornamental porcelain, 1877-1930, c. 200 items

2461
ROYAL ENGINEERS MUSEUM
Ravelin Building, Prince Arthur Road, Brompton Barracks, Chatham, Kent, ME4 4UG

Tel: 01634 406397
Fax: 01634 822371
Email: remuseum.rhqre@gtnet.gov.uk or museum@royalengineers.com
Acronym or abbreviation: RE Museum
Formed: 1912

Organisation type and purpose: Registered charity (charity number 295173), museum.
Collection owned by:
Institution of Royal Engineers
Brompton Barracks, Chatham
Fund-raising body:
Royal Engineers Museum Foundation

Enquiries to: Curator
Direct fax: 01634 822261
Other contacts: Director for marketing.
Access:
Access to staff: By letter, by telephone, by fax, visitors by prior appointment
Hours: Mon to Thu, 1000 to 1700; Sat, Sun, 1130 to 1700

General description:
Military engineering in general; history of war and role of engineers in it; history of the Corps of Royal Engineers and Royal Sappers and Miners; East India Company and Corps of Indian Engineers; Biographical research: members, former members of Corps of Royal Engineers, limited information on soldiers or company officers, TA, TAVR officers; medals; chemical warfare, military tunnelling, bomb disposal, submarine mining.
Collections:
Gordon of Khartoum manuscripts
F M Burgoyne Papers (Napoleonic Wars, Occupation of France, Crimean War etc)
Dumford Papers (Zulu War)
Boer War, WWI, some WWII, Royal Engineer Unit War Diaries
Royal Engineers training manuals, equipment manuals late 19th century to present, photographs from 1860s
Catalogues:
Catalogue for library is in-house only. Catalogue for all of the collections is only available in-house.
Publications list:
is available in hard copy.
Printed publications:
Publications are by the Institution of Royal Engineers

Address for ordering publications:
Printed publications:
Secretary to the Institution of Royal Engineers
Brompton Barracks, Chatham, ME4 4UG, tel: 01634 822298, fax: 01634 822397

Internet home pages:
http://www.royalengineers.org.uk

2462
ROYAL GLOUCESTERSHIRE, BERKSHIRE & WILTSHIRE REGIMENT MUSEUM
The Wardrobe, 58 The Close, Salisbury, Wiltshire, SP1 2EX

Tel: 01722 414536
Also known as: Redcoats in the Wardrobe

Organisation type and purpose: Museum, historic building, house or site, suitable for ages: 8+.

Enquiries to: Curator
Access:
Access to staff: By letter, by telephone
Access for disabled people: access to all public areas
Other restrictions: Toilets are not wheelchair accessible

General description:
Regimental museum housed in a building dating from the 13th century. Displays tell of a soldier's life and how ot has changed over the past 250 years.

Internet home pages:
http://www.thewardbrobe.org.uk

2463
ROYAL GREEN JACKETS MUSEUM
Peninsula Barracks, Romsey Road, Winchester, Hampshire, SO23 8TS

Tel: 01962 828549
Fax: 01962 828500
Email: museum@royalgreenjackets.co.uk
Acronym or abbreviation: RGJ
Formed: 1926
Formerly: Oxford and Buckinghamshire Light Infantry (Ox&Bucks), The Rifle Brigade (RB), Kings Royal Rifle Corps (KRRC), date of change, 1958

Organisation type and purpose: Professional body, museum, suitable for ages: 8+.

Enquiries to: Curator

Access:
Access to staff: By letter only
Hours: Mon to Fri, 1000 to 1300 and 1400 to 1700; Sat, Sun, 1200 to 1600
Access to building, collections or gallery: No prior appointment required
Access for disabled people: level entry, access to all public areas, toilet facilities

General description:
Displays of Campaigns over 5 continents, including a magnificent Diorama of The Battle of Waterloo. Uniforms, medals, badges and equipment. The library includes war diaries for both world wars.
Catalogues:
Catalogue for library is in-house only.

2464
ROYAL GUNPOWDER MILLS, THE
Beaulieu Drive, Waltham Abbey, Essex, EN9 1JY

Tel: 01992 707370
Fax: 01992 710341
Email: info@royalgunpowdermills.com
Full name: Waltham Abbey Royal Gunpowder Mills Company Limited
Formed: 2001

Organisation type and purpose: Registered charity (charity number 1062968/0), historic building, house or site, suitable for ages: 5+.

Enquiries to: Curator
Access:
Access to staff: By letter, by telephone, by fax, by email, Internet web pages
Access to building, collections or gallery: No prior appointment required
Hours: Mid-Mar to end Oct
Access for disabled people: Parking provided, ramped entry, level entry, toilet facilities

General description:
The Royal Gunpowder Mills is an historic site where gunpowder and explosives have been made for over 300 years. In 175 acres there are over 300 structures, 21 listed buildings and 5 miles of waterways. The artefact collection includes material associated with the manufacture of explosives at Waltham Abbey. The collections are being developed to cover military and civil uses of explosives, including fireworks.
Information services:
Special visitor services: Materials and/or activities for children.
Education services: Group education facilities, resources for Key Stages 1 and 2.
Services for disabled people: For the visually impaired; for the hearing impaired; displays and/or information at wheelchair height.
Collections:
The Artefact Collection includes material associated with the history and manufacture of explosives and fireworks. It includes material recovered from an archaeological excavation of the site. There is a large collection of photographs of the work carried out at Waltham Abbey, and architectural plans (other documents related to the site are held at the Public Records Office)
A library covering the history of explosives is being developed
Printed publications:
Guide to Site (£1)

Internet home pages:
http://www.royalgunpowdermills.com
General guide to history and facilities of the site.

2465
ROYAL HAMPSHIRE REGIMENT MUSEUM
Serles House, Southgate Street, Winchester, Hampshire, SO23 9EG

Tel: 01962 863658
Fax: 01962 888302
Formed: 1933

Organisation type and purpose: Registered charity, museum, suitable for ages: all ages. Regimental museum.

Enquiries to: Curator
Access:
Access to staff: By letter, by telephone, by fax
Hours: Mon to Fri, 0830 to 1700

General description:
History of Royal Hampshire Regiment (37th/67th) 1702-1992, its Regulars, Volunteers, Militia and Territorials. Queries in history of the regiment and those who served are welcomed.
Information services:
Special visitor services: Guided tours.
Services for disabled people: Displays and/or information at wheelchair height.
Catalogues:
Catalogue for library is in-house only. Catalogue for all of the collections is only available in-house.
Printed publications:
A Soldier's Diary (Jackson, M C, Boer War)
The Hampshire Tigers - The Story of the Royal Hampshire Regiment 1945-1992

2466
ROYAL HIGHLAND FUSILIERS REGIMENTAL HEADQUARTERS AND MUSEUM
518 Sauchiehall Street, Glasgow, G2 3LW

Tel: 0141 332 0961
Fax: 0141 353 1493
Email: info.assregsec@rhf.org.uk
Acronym or abbreviation: RHF
Formed: 1960
Formerly: Royal Scots Fusiliers, Highland Light Infantry, date of change, 1959

Organisation type and purpose: Independently owned, membership association, registered charity, museum, public library, suitable for ages: 8+, research organisation.
Regimental headquarters and military museum; the Regiment is Princess Margaret's Own Glasgow and Ayrshire Regiment.

Enquiries to: Curator
Access:
Access to staff: By letter, by telephone, by fax, by email, in person, visitors by prior appointment, Internet web pages
Hours: Mon to Fri, 0830 to 1630
Access to building, collections or gallery: No prior appointment required
Access for disabled people: level entry, access to all public areas, toilet facilities

General description:
Regimental history of the Royal Scots Fusiliers (21st Foot) and the Highland Light Infantry (71st and 74th Foot) who amalgamated to form the Royal Highland Fusiliers in 1959.
Information services:
Library available for reference (for conditions see Access above)
Special visitor services: Guided tours.
Education services: Group education facilities.
Services for disabled people: For the hearing impaired; displays and/or information at wheelchair height.
Collections:
Regimental and War diaries 1914-1918, medal rolls, regimental histories etc
Catalogues:
Catalogue for library is in-house only. Catalogue for all of the collections is only available in-house.

Internet home pages:
http://www.rhf.org.uk

2467
ROYAL INSTITUTION OF GREAT BRITAIN
21 Albemarle Street, London, W1S 4BS

Tel: 020 7409 2992
Fax: 020 7629 3569
Email: ril@ri.ac.uk
Acronym or abbreviation: RI
Formed: 1799

Organisation type and purpose: Learned society (membership is by election or invitation), present number of members: c. 2500.
Scientific body.
Includes the:
Davy-Faraday Research Laboratory
Library and Archives
Michael Faraday Museum
Royal Institution Centre for the History of Science and Technology

Enquiries to: Librarian
Direct tel: 020 7670 2924
Direct email: fjames@ri.ac.uk
Access:
Access to staff: Visitors by prior appointment
Hours: Mon to Fri, 0900 to 1700
Access to building, collections or gallery: No prior appointment required
Access for disabled people: level entry, toilet facilities

General description:
Science for the layman, history and philosophy of science, scientific biography, the social relations of science, solid state and surface chemistry and physics, catalysis, computer molecular modelling.
Collections:
Historic apparatus
Manuscripts of famous scientists connected with The Royal Institution eg H Davy, M Faraday, J Tyndall, J Dewar, W H and W L Bragg, G Porter
Pre-1900 scientific books and periodicals
The Royal Institution Administrative Archives
Catalogues:
Catalogue for library is in-house only. Catalogue for part of the collections is only available in-house.
Publications list:
is available in hard copy.
Printed publications:
Annual Record
Faraday Rediscovered (Gooding D and James F, 1985)
Humphry Davy (King R, 1978)
Historical Guides
Michael Faraday of the Royal Institution (King R, 1973)
Other books and proceedings available
Proceedings of RI
Selections and Reflections: the Legacy of Lawrence Bragg (Thomas J M and Phillips D C eds, 1991, Science Reviews)
The Royal Institution: an informal history (Caroe G)
Microform products:
J Dewar, 1842-1923, catalogue of papers (1991, pub Chadwyck-Healey)
Journals of T A Hirst (Brock W H *et al* eds, pub Mansell, 1980)
J Tyndall, 1820-1893 (catalogue of papers, Friday J R ed. pub Mansell, 1974)
Electronic and video products:
Masterclass format education videotapes (via Public Affairs Officer)
RI Christmas Lectures videotapes (via BBC)

Internet home pages:
http://www.ri.ac.uk

2468
ROYAL INSTITUTION OF SOUTH WALES

c/o Swansea Museum, Victoria Road, Maritime Quarter, Swansea, West Glamorgan, SA1 1SN

Tel: 01792 653763
Fax: 01792 652585
Email: swansea.museum@swansea.gov.uk
Acronym or abbreviation: RISW
Formed: 1835

Organisation type and purpose: Learned society (membership is by subscription), voluntary organisation, registered charity. Friends of Swansea Museum.

Enquiries to: Honorary Secretary
Direct tel: 01792 874143
Other contacts: Curator for museum/local history.
Access:
Access to staff: By letter, by telephone, by email, visitors by prior appointment
Hours: Mon to Fri, 0900 to 1700
Access to building, collections or gallery: Prior appointment required
Access for disabled people: Parking provided

General description:
Local history and studies of Swansea and surrounding area, including natural history, biography, culture, early photography, archaeology, ceramics (Swansea and District) and local topography.
Publications list:
is available in hard copy.
Printed publications:
Available for purchase directly
Minerva: The Journal of Swansea History (annually, Vol 9, 2001, back numbers available)
History of Swansea Vol 2 (Jones W H)
John Humphrey, God's Own Architect (Farmer D)

Internet home pages:
http://www.swansea.gov.uk

2469
ROYAL IRISH FUSILIERS REGIMENTAL MUSEUM

Sovereign's House, The Mall, Armagh, BT61 9DL

Tel: 028 3752 2911
Fax: 028 3752 2911
Email: amanda@rirfus-museum.freeserve.co.uk
Formed: 1962

Organisation type and purpose: Registered charity, museum.

Enquiries to: Curator
Access:
Access to staff: By letter, by telephone, by fax, by email, in person, charges to non-members
Hours: Mon to Fri, 1000 to 1230 and 1330 to 1600

General description:
History of all military campaigns from 1790 to date. History of The Royal Irish Fusiliers (including the Armagh, Cavan, Monaghan Militia Battalions); uniforms, medals, badges and equipment (but not personal records) of the Regiment.
Collections:
The Library covers all campaigns of the Regiment since 1793 including original manuscripts and war diaries for both World Wars

2470
ROYAL LINCOLNSHIRE REGIMENTAL MUSEUM

Museum of Lincolnshire Life, Old Barracks, Burton Road, Lincoln, LN1 3LY

Tel: 01522 528448
Fax: 01522 521264
Email: janetedmond@lincolnshire.gov.uk
Formed: 1969

Organisation type and purpose: Museum.
Displayed as part of the:
Museum of Lincolnshire Life
Other addresses:
The Royal Lincolnshire Regiment
Regimental Secretary, The Keep, Sobraon Barracks, Lincoln, LN1 3PY

Enquiries to: Principal Keeper
Access:
Access to staff: By letter, by telephone, by fax, by email, visitors by prior appointment
Hours: Mon to Fri, 1000 to 1730

General description:
History of the 10th Foot, the Lincolnshire and the Royal Lincolnshire Regiment; war diaries, digests of service, photograph albums, relating to the Regiment; 300 years of history - formation, Indian campaigns, Sudan and Boer Wars, 1st and 2nd World Wars, uniforms, medals, artefact displays.
Information services:
Library available for reference (for conditions see Access above)
Special visitor services: Materials and/or activities for children.
Education services: Group education facilities, resources for Key Stages 1 and 2.
Services for disabled people: Displays and/or information at wheelchair height.
Printed publications:
Grimsby's Own, The Story of The Chums (P Chapman)

2471
ROYAL LOGISTIC CORPS MUSEUM

Princess Royal Barracks, Deepcut, Camberley, Surrey, GU16 6RW

Tel: 01252 833371
Fax: 01252 833484
Email: RHQ@army-rlc.co.uk
Acronym or abbreviation: RLC Museum
Formed: 1993
Formerly: Royal Corps of Transport Museum (RCT Museum), Royal Army Ordnance Corps Museum (RAOC Museum), Army Catering Corps Museum (ACC Museum), Royal Pioneer Corps Museum (RPC Museum), date of change, 1993

Organisation type and purpose: Independently owned (charity number 1047018), museum, suitable for ages: 12+.
Connections with:
Army Catering Corps (ACC)
Royal Army Ordnance Corps (RAOL)
Royal Army Service Corps (RASC)
Royal Corps of Transport (RCT)
Royal Pioneer Corps (RPL)

Enquiries to: Director
Direct tel: 01252 833484
Direct email: query@rlcmuseum.freeserve.co.uk
Other contacts: Curator for The Collection.
Access:
Access to staff: By letter, by telephone, by fax, by email, in person, Internet web pages
Hours: Tue to Fri, 1000 to 1600
Jun to Sep: 1st and 3rd Sat, 1200 to 1600
Access to building, collections or gallery: No prior appointment required
Hours: Tue to Fri, 1000 to 1600
Jun to Sep: 1st and 3rd Sat, 1200 to 1600
Access for disabled people: Parking provided, level entry, access to all public areas, toilet facilities

General description:
History of military logistics, including transport, ordnance, labour, catering and postal services in the British Army and its predecessors, since the 14th century.
Information services:
Special visitor services: Guided tours, materials and/or activities for children.
Education services: Group education facilities.
Services for disabled people: Displays and/or information at wheelchair height.
Collections:
Approximately 20,000 artefacts, 106,000 archive items and 1200 specialist books relating to the Royal Logistic Corps, the Royal Army Service Corps, the Royal Corps of Transport, the Royal Army Ordance Corps, the Royal Pioneer Corps and the Army Catering Corps
Catalogues:
Catalogue for library is in-house only. Catalogue for part of the collections is only available in-house.

Internet home pages:
http://www.army-rlc.co.uk
Museum website is within the Royal Logistic Corps website.

2472
ROYAL LONDON HOSPITAL ARCHIVES AND MUSEUM

The Royal London Hospital, Whitechapel, London, E1 1BB

Tel: 020 7377 7608
Fax: 020 7377 7413
Email: r.j.evans@qmul.ac.uk

Organisation type and purpose: National government body, museum, university department or institute, suitable for ages: 12+. Archive.
Parent body:
Barts and The London Hospital NHS Trust
Headquarters, Royal London Hospital, London, E1 1BB
Affiliated to:
Queen Mary University of London

Enquiries to: Archivist
Access:
Access to staff: By letter, by telephone, by fax, by email, in person
Hours: Mon to Fri, 100 to 1630

General description:
Hospitals, medical and nursing history, dentistry, orthodontics, forensic medicine, health records.
Collections:
Archives of the Royal London Hospital
Archives of the London Chest Hospital
Archives of the Queen Elizabeth Hospital for Children
Archives of the London Hospital Medical College
Collections of the British Orthodontic Society
Edith Cavell Collection: Nursing history, artefacts and archives 1800s-1915
Eva Luckes Collection
London Hospital Surgical Instruments 18th-20th century
Medical and surgical films
Princess Alexandra School of Nursing: Nursing history, uniforms, equipment etc.1880-1993
Publications list:
is available in hard copy.
Printed publications:
The Royal London Hospital: A Brief History (Collins S M, 1995)
London Pride: The Story of a Voluntary Hospital (Clark-Kennedy A E, 1979)
Emblems, Tokens and Tickets of The London Hospital and the London Hospital Medical College (Gibbs D, 1985)
L.H.M.C. 1785-1985 The Story of England's first Medical School (Ellis J)
The Dental School of The London Hospital Medical College 1911-1991 (Fish S F, 1991)
Learning to care: A history of nursing and midwifery education at the Royal London Hospital, 1740-1983 (Parker E R and Collins S M, 1998)
A History of Radiotherapy at The London Hospital 1896-1996 (Hope-Stone H F, 1999)
Patients are People - Memories of Nursing at 'The London' 1939-1958 (Broadley M E, 1995)
Patients Come First. Nursing at 'The London' between the two World Wars (Broadley M E, 1980)
Edith Cavell: Her Life And Her Art - Sa Vie Et Son Art (Daunton C H G, 1990)

Internet home pages:
http://www.brlcf.org.uk
General guide to archives and museum
http://www.bartsandthelondon.org.uk
History of the hospital
http://www.aim25.ac.uk
Detailed guide to archival holdings

2473
ROYAL MARINES MUSEUM
Eastney Esplanade, Southsea, Hampshire, PO4 9PX

Tel: 023 9281 9385
Fax: 023 9283 8420
Email: info@royalmarinesmuseum.co.uk
Formed: 1958

Organisation type and purpose: Registered charity (charity number 272246), museum.

Enquiries to: Curator
Other contacts: Archivist, Marketing Officer
Access:
Access to staff: By letter, by telephone, by fax, in person, visitors by prior appointment
Hours: Mon to Fri, 0900 to 1700
Other restrictions: Library visitors by appointment.

General description:
Royal Marine history 1664 to present, Royal Marine uniform, medals, photographs; documents; books; artefacts. Royal Navy history 1850 to present.
Collections:
Archive diaries, official reports, maps, letters, plans
Books of Royal Marine and Royal Navy interest
Photographs 1850 to present of campaigns and Royal Marine units and individuals
Royal Marine sport
Ships, landing craft
Uniforms (RM), weapons, medals, equipment, flags
Printed publications:
Eastney Barracks: A Pictorial History (£19.95 plus p&p)
Guide Book

Internet home pages:
http://www.royalmarinesmuseum.co.uk
Galleries guide; shop and mail order; corporate facilities; education; libraries.

2474
ROYAL MILITARY POLICE MUSEUM
Roussillon Barracks, Broyle Road, Chichester, West Sussex, PO19 4BN

Tel: 01243 534225
Fax: 01243 534288
Email: museum@rhqrmp.freeserve.co.uk
Formed: 1979
Formerly: Red Cap Museum (RMP Museum)

Organisation type and purpose: Museum. Military museum.

Enquiries to: Curator
Access:
Access to staff: By letter, by telephone, by fax, by email, in person, charges made to all users, Internet web pages
Access for disabled people: Parking provided, ramped entry, access to all public areas, toilet facilities

General description:
History of the military police worldwide, is traced from Tudor times to the present day by means of documents, photographs, medals, artefacts and videos.
Catalogues:
Catalogue for part of the collections is only available in-house.
Printed publications:
RMP Journal (3 times a year, £5.50 subscriptions)

Internet home pages:
http://www.rhqrmp.freeserve.co.uk

2475
ROYAL MILITARY SCHOOL OF MUSIC MUSEUM
Kneller Hall, Whitton, Twickenham, Middlesex, TW2 7DU

Tel: 020 8898 5533

Organisation type and purpose: Museum, suitable for ages: 16+.

Enquiries to: Manager
Direct tel: 020 8744 8652
Direct fax: 020 8744 8668
Direct email: armymusichq@aol.com
Access:
Access to staff: By letter only
Access to building, collections or gallery: Prior appointment required
Access for disabled people: Parking provided, ramped entry, toilet facilities

General description:
A museum of musical instruments; manuscripts; photographs; paintings; and uniforms, mostly of a military nature.

2476
ROYAL MUSEUM AND MUSEUM OF SCOTLAND
Chambers Street, Edinburgh, EH1 1JF

Tel: 0131 225 7534
Fax: 0131 220 4819
Email: info@nms.ac.uk
Acronym or abbreviation: NMS
Formed: 1981
Still known as: Royal Museum of Scotland, date of change, 1998

Organisation type and purpose: National government body, museum.
Houses the:
Council for Scottish Archaeology
Tel: 0131 247 4119, fax: 0131 247 4126
European Ethnological Research Centre
Tel: 0131 247 4086, fax: 0131 220 4819, email/website: a.fenton@nms.ac.uk
Society of Antiquaries of Scotland
Tel: 0131 247 4115, fax: 0131 247 4163, email/website: f.ashmore@nms.ac.uk
Part of:
National Museums of Scotland
Tel: 0131 225 7534, fax: 0131 220 4819, email/website: info@nms.ac.uk
Other museums which are part of The National Museums of Scotland (NMS):
Granton Centre
Tel: 0131 551 4106, fax: 0131 551 4106
Museum of Flight
Tel: 01620 880308, fax: 01620 880355
Museum of Scottish Country Life
Tel: 01355 224181, fax: 01355 571290
National War Museum of Scotland
Tel: 0131 225 7534, fax: 0131 225 3848
Shambellie House Museum of Costume
Tel: 01387 850375, fax: 01387 850461

Enquiries to: Information Desk
Direct tel: 0131 247 4219
Access:
Access to staff: By letter, by telephone, by fax, in person, Internet web pages
Access for disabled people: level entry, access to all public areas, toilet facilities

General description:
The Royal Museum houses the National Museums of Scotlands' international collections relating to archaeology, ethnography, science and industry, the natural world and the decorative arts. The Museum of Scotland displays the national collections of Scottish material from earliest times to the present day.
Information services:
Library available for reference (for conditions see Access above)
Personal access Guides available, book two weeks before your visit, tel: 0131 247 4206
Special visitor services: Tape recorded guides, materials and/or activities for children.
Education services: Group education facilities.
Services for disabled people: For the hearing impaired.
Collections:
Scottish Life Archive of documentary and illustrative evidence of Scotland's material culture and social history
Catalogues:
Catalogue for library is in-house only. Catalogue for all of the collections is only available in-house.
Publications list:
is available in hard copy.
Printed publications:
Annual Report and supplement
Highlight (leaflet, free)
Museum data appears in the Proceedings of the Society of Antiquaries of Scotland
Scottish Material Culture Bibliography
Many books on a wide range of subjects contact NMS Publishing Ltd for an up-to-date list
Electronic and video products:
Various products available contact The Multimedia Team Ltd

Address for ordering publications:
Electronic publications:
The Multimedia Team Limited
Tel: 0131 247 4437, email: e.clark@nms.ac.uk
Printed publications:
NMS Publishing
Royal Museum, Chambers Street, Edinburgh, EH1 1JF, tel: 0131 247 4026, fax: 0131 247 4012, email: c.shanley@nms.ac.uk

Internet home pages:
http://www.nms.ac.uk

2477
ROYAL NATIONAL LIFEBOAT INSTITUTION
Lifeboat Museum, King Edward Parade, Eastbourne, East Sussex, BN21 4BY

Tel: 01323 730717
Formed: 1935
Formerly: Life Boat Museum

Organisation type and purpose: Voluntary organisation, registered charity, museum.
Parent body:
Royal National Lifeboat Institution
West Quay Road, Poole, Dorset

Enquiries to: Honorary Curator
Access:
Access to staff: By letter only
Hours: Jan to Easter, closed
Easter to May and Oct to Dec, 1000 to 1400
Jun to Sep, 1000 to 1700

General description:
History of Eastbourne lifeboats from 1822 onwards including notable rescuers, and photographs. Small collection of lifeboat models, well-stocked souvenir shop.
Collections:
Artefacts from sailing lifeboats
Gallantry medals
Photographs of lifeboats, crews, coxswains, damaged ships to which lifeboats have attended and rescued crews
Scale models of types of old lifeboats
Printed publications:
Brochure detailing history of the lifeboat station (£2.00)

2478
ROYAL NAVAL MUSEUM
HM Naval Base (PP66), Portsmouth, Hampshire, PO1 3NH

Tel: 023 9272 7562
Fax: 023 9272 7575
Email: rnm@royalnavalmuseum.org

Organisation type and purpose: Museum.

continued overleaf

Enquiries to: Librarian and Head of Information Services
Direct tel: 023 9272 3795
Direct fax: 023 9272 3942
Direct email: library@royalnavalmuseum.org
Other contacts: Head of Access for public relations/general intellectual access to collections/media.
Access:
Access to staff: Visitors by prior appointment
Hours: Mon to Fri, 1000 to 1600
Other restrictions: Library is on a secure naval base. Please ensure you contact the library prior to your visit.

General description:
The general history, customs and traditions of the Royal Navy and the Women's Royal Naval Service; specialisation in naval biography, the Nelsonian and Victorian periods, and in naval medals.
Collections:
London Gazettes 1776-1986
Navy lists 1797 to present
Admiralty Library (Portsmouth)
Catalogues:
Catalogue for library is in-house only. Catalogue for all of the collections is only available in-house.
Printed publications:
Catalogue of the Oral History collection
Guide to the Manuscripts of the Royal Naval Museum

Internet home pages:
http://www.royalnavalmuseum.org
General information on services; collections; exhibitions; research facilities and development plan.

2479
ROYAL NAVY SUBMARINE MUSEUM

Haslar Jetty Road, Gosport, Hampshire, PO12 2AS

Tel: 023 9251 0354
Fax: 023 9251 1349
Email: rnsubs@rnsubmus.co.uk
Acronym or abbreviation: RNSMM
Formed: 1979
Formerly: Submarine World, date of change, 1997

Organisation type and purpose: Registered charity (charity number 1054865), museum, research organisation.
Affiliated to:
Submarine Officers Life Members Association
Submariners Association
Links with:
other submarine museums and associations

Enquiries to: Business Services Manager
Other contacts: Director/Curator
Access:
Access to staff: By letter, by telephone, by fax, by email, in person, visitors by prior appointment, Internet web pages
Hours: Mon to Fri, 0900 to 1700
Access to building, collections or gallery: No prior appointment required

General description:
Royal Navy and foreign submarine and submarines' histories.
Collections:
2000 books, 50,000 manuscripts, 100,000 photographs, 5000 artefacts and several submarines, torpedoes and guns
Printed publications:
Information Pack

Internet home pages:
http://www.rnsubmus.co.uk

2480
ROYAL NORFOLK REGIMENTAL MUSEUM

Shirehall, Market Avenue, Norwich, Norfolk, NR1 3JQ

Tel: 01603 493649
Fax: 01603 765651
Email: museums@norfolk.gov.uk
Formed: 1990
Formerly: Royal Norfolk Regiment Museum, Britannia Barracks, Britannia Road, Norwich, date of change, 1990

Organisation type and purpose: Local government body, museum, historic building, house or site, suitable for ages: 8+.
Parent body:
Norfolk Museums and Archaeology Service (NMAS)
Shirehall, Market Avenue, Norwich, NR1 3JQ, tel: 01603 493625, fax: 01603 493623
Royal Norfolk Regiment Association
Britannia House, TA Centre, Aylsham Road, Norwich, NR3 2AD, tel: 01603 400290

Enquiries to: Curator
Access:
Access to staff: By letter, by email, in person
Hours: Mon to Fri, 1000 to 1700

General description:
History of the Royal Norfolk Regiment from 1685.
The displays tell the story of the regiment, its place in world, and in Norfolk history.
Information services:
Library available for reference (for conditions see Access above)
Special visitor services: Guided tours, materials and/or activities for children.
Education services: Group education facilities, resources for Key Stages 2 and 3..
Collections:
Army Lists
A good collection of regimental photographs now catalogued and scanned into a computer database
Medal collection
Small Regimental archive
Catalogues:
Catalogue for library is in-house only. Catalogue for part of the collections is only available in-house.
Electronic and video products:
The Royal Norfolk Regiment in India (video)

Address for ordering publications:
Printed publications:
Visitor Services Officer, Norfolk Museums & Archaeology Service
Shirehall, Market Avenue, Norwich, NR1 3JQ, tel: 01603 493628

Internet home pages:
http://www.norfolk.gov.uk/tourism/museums

2481
ROYAL OBSERVATORY

See - National Maritime Museum

2482
ROYAL OBSERVATORY GREENWICH

Park Row, London, SE10 9NF

Tel: 020 8858 4422 or 020 8312 6771
Fax: 020 8312 6734
Email: astroline@nmm.ac.uk
Acronym or abbreviation: ROG
Formed: 1675
Formerly: Greenwich Observatory, Flamsteed House Museum; Old Royal Observatory, date of change, 1998

Organisation type and purpose: National government body, museum, suitable for ages: 7 to adult.
Astronomy information.
Site location:
Royal Observatory Greenwich (ROG)
Greenwich Park, London, SE10 8XJ, fax: 020 8312 6734, email/website: astroline@nmm.ac.uk

Enquiries to: Information Officer
Direct tel: 020 8312 6553
Other contacts: Education Officer for education enquiries.
Access:
Access to staff: By letter, by telephone, by fax, by email, visitors by prior appointment, Internet web pages
Hours: Mon to Fri, 0900 to 1700
Access to building, collections or gallery: Prior appointment required
Hours: Mon to Fri, 1000 to 1645, last admission 1630
Other restrictions: Prior appointment required for reserve collections.

General description:
Modern astronomy.
Publications list:
is available in hard copy and online.
Printed publications:
Astronomy information leaflets (available free either through website or direct)

Address for ordering publications:
Printed publications:
Astronomy Information Officer

Internet home pages:
http://www.rog.nmm.ac.uk

2483
ROYAL OBSERVER CORPS MUSEUM

See - Norfolk & Suffolk Aviation Museum

2484
ROYAL PAVILION, THE

Libraries and Museums, 4-5 Pavilion Buildings, Brighton, East Sussex, BN1 1EE

Tel: 01273 290900
Fax: 01273 292871
Email: visitor.services@brighton-hove.gov.uk
Formed: 1851
Formerly: Royal Pavilion, Art Gallery & Museum, Brighton Council, date of change, 1997

Organisation type and purpose: Local government body, museum, historic building, house or site.
Parent body:
Brighton & Hove City Council

Enquiries to: Marketing Manager
Access:
Access to staff: By letter, by telephone, by fax, by email, visitors by prior appointment, Internet web pages
Hours: Mon to Fri, 0900 to 1730
Other restrictions: Closed Christmas and Boxing Day.
No office staff at weekends.
Access to building, collections or gallery: No prior appointment required
Hours: Oct to Mar: Daily, 1000 to 1715
Apr to Sep: Daily, 0930 to 1745
Other restrictions: Prior appointment required for guided tours etc.
Access for disabled people: level entry, toilet facilities
Other restrictions: Wheelchair access to ground floor only.
1st floor is NOT wheelchair accessible.

General description:
History and conservation of the Royal Pavilion, including interior decorations and Regency gardens.
Collections:
Photographic library
Typescript of the accounts of the Crace Firm of decorators during their time spent in the Pavilion, 1802-1804, 1815-1819, 1820-23
Inventory of the Royal Pavilion, 1828
Abstract of accounts of the various firms working in the Royal Pavilion

Letters
Quantities of letters from or about George, Prince of Wales, Mrs Fitzherbert, or concerning Brighton and the Royal Pavilion, but also including letters by Byron
Also 'Esher' letters, volume containing 56 letters to or concerning the Prince of Wales and Mrs Fitzherbert
Plan Registry - Approximately 800 plans of the Pavilion and the Pavilion Estate
Proceedings of the Pavilion Committee, 1850-1923
Proceedings of the Pavilion and Library Committee, 1924-1974
Proceedings of the Fine Art Sub-Committee, 1901-1941
Catalogues:
Catalogue for library is in-house only. Catalogue for all of the collections is only available in-house.
Printed publications:
Guide Book (£3.95)
Electronic and video products:
Video (for purchase through Pavilion shops or Heritage Video)

Address for ordering publications:
Printed publications:
Commercial Services, Royal Pavilion at the same address

Internet home pages:
http://www.royalpavilion.org.uk
General information on the Pavilion, prices etc.

2485
ROYAL PHARMACEUTICAL SOCIETY OF GREAT BRITAIN
See - Royal Botanic Gardens

2486
ROYAL PIONEER CORPS MUSEUM

Information services:
Special visitor services: Tape recorded guides.
Services for disabled people: Displays and/or information at wheelchair height.
See - Royal Logistic Corps Museum

2487
ROYAL PUMP ROOM MUSEUM
Crown Place, Harrogate, North Yorkshire, HG1 2RY

Tel: 01423 556188
Fax: 01423 556130
Email: lg12@harrogate.gov.uk
Formed: 1953

Organisation type and purpose: Local government body, museum, historic building, house or site, suitable for ages: all ages.
Parent body:
Harrogate Borough Council
Links with:
Friends of Harrogate District Museums

Enquiries to: Administrator
Other contacts: Curator of Human History for specific enquiries.
Access:
Access to staff: By letter, by telephone, by fax, by email, visitors by prior appointment, Internet web pages
Access to building, collections or gallery: No prior appointment required
Hours: Apr to Oct: Mon to Sat, 1000 to 1700; Sun, 1400 to 1700
Nov to Mar: Mon to Sat, 1000 to 1600
Other restrictions: Appointment required for collections not on display. Not open 24, 25, 26 Dec & 1 Jan.
Access for disabled people: level entry, access to all public areas, toilet facilities

General description:
Housed in the splendid Royal Pump Room, the site of Europe's strongest sulphur well, the museum tells the intriguing story of how Harrogate became a Spa Town.
A general collection including art; local and social history; jewellery; ceramics; costume; toys; bicycles. Also features antiquities and archaeology.
Information services:
Object indentification.
Guided tours on request.
Events for families, children and over 50s.
Special visitor services: Guided tours.
Education services: Group education facilities, resources for Key Stages 1 and 2..
Collections:
Archaeological Collections including the Kent & Ogden Bequests of antiquities, including Egyptology, Greek and Roman material
Social History Collections
Collection of bicycles on loan from Cyclists Touring Club
Costume Collection
Decorative Arts - including Holland-Child Collection of Creamware and Pearlware
Harrogate Borough Council's art collection.
Jewellery - Hull-Grundy Bequest
Not all items are on display, temporary exhibition changes annually
Catalogues:
Catalogue for part of the collections is only available in-house.
Printed publications:
Guide to the Royal Pump Room Museum
Posters, prints and postcards

Internet home pages:
http://www.harrogate.gov.uk/museums

2488
ROYAL PUMP ROOMS ART GALLERY AND MUSEUM
See - Leamington Spa Art Gallery and Museum

2489
ROYAL REGIMENT OF FUSILIERS ASSOCIATION LONDON AREA
H M Tower of London, London, EC3N 4AB

Tel: 020 7488 5611
Fax: 020 7481 1093
Acronym or abbreviation: RRF Museum (London)
Formed: 1685
Formerly: Royal Fusiliers, date of change, 1968

Organisation type and purpose: Membership association (membership is by subscription, qualification), present number of members: 1000, registered charity (charity number 255042), museum.
Regimental Museum.

Enquiries to: Curator
Other contacts: Archivist for research enquiries.
Access:
Access to staff: By letter, visitors by prior appointment
Hours: Archivist only: 0900 to 1500
Other restrictions: Subject to HM Tower of London.

General description:
Military and social history.
Collections:
Regimental Archives 1685 to 1968
Catalogues:
Catalogue for library is in-house only. Catalogue for all of the collections is only available in-house.
Printed publications:
Museum Guide (£1.50)
Royal Fusiliers in the Great War (£35)
Royal Fusiliers Victoria Crosses (£2.50)

2490
ROYAL REGIMENT OF FUSILIERS MUSEUM (ROYAL WARWICKSHIRE)
St Johns House, Warwick, CV34 4NF

Tel: 01926 491653
Fax: 01869 257633
Formed: 1928
Formed from: 6th Foot, Royal Warwickshire Fusiliers, Royal Warwickshire Regiment

Organisation type and purpose: Museum, suitable for ages: 5+.

Enquiries to: Curator
Other contacts: Regimental Secretary
Access:
Access to staff: By letter, by telephone, by fax, visitors by prior appointment
Access to building, collections or gallery: Prior appointment required
Hours: May to Sep: Tue to Sat, 0900 to 1700; Sun, 1430 to 1700

General description:
Military history, British Army, Royal Warwickshire Regiment 1674 to present.
Information services:
Library available for reference (for conditions see Access above)
Special visitor services: Guided tours, materials and/or activities for children.
Education services: Group education facilities, resources for Key Stage 1 and Further or Higher Education.
Services for disabled people: For the visually impaired.
Collections:
Weapons, equipment, uniforms, flags, paintings, silver, musical instruments, documents, photographs, badges and medals, ceramics, ethnography
Catalogues:
Catalogue for part of the collections is only available in-house.

2491
ROYAL REGIMENT OF WALES
See - South Wales Borderers & Monmouthshire Regimental Museum

2492
ROYAL RESEARCH SHIP DISCOVERY
Discovery Point, Discovery Quay, Dundee, DD1 4XA

Tel: 01382 201245
Fax: 01382 225891
Email: info@dundeeheritage.sol.co.uk
Formed: 1993

Organisation type and purpose: Independently owned, registered charity (charity number ED/343/85PLB), museum, historic building, house or site, suitable for ages: 5+.
Historic Ship.
Parent body:
Dundee Heritage Trust
Verdant Works, West Henderson's Wynd, Dundee, DD1 5BT, tel: 01382 225282, fax: 01382 221612, email: info@dundeeheritage.so.co.uk
Branch museum:
Verdant Works
West Henderson's Wynd, Dundee, DD1 5BT, tel: 01382 225282, fax: 01382 221612, email/website: info@dundeeheritage.sol.co.uk

Enquiries to: Curator
Direct tel: 01382 225282
Direct fax: 01382 221612
Other contacts: Operations Manager
Access:
Access to staff: By letter, by telephone, by fax, by email, visitors by prior appointment
Access to building, collections or gallery: No prior appointment required
Hours: Apr to Oct: Mon to Sat, 1000 to 1700;

continued overleaf

Sun, 1100 to 1700
Nov to Mar: Mon to Sat, 1000 to 1600; Sun, 1100 to 1600
Access for disabled people: Parking provided, level entry, access to all public areas, toilet facilities

General description:
The Royal Research Ship Discovery; Antarctic exploration and science; polar explorers eg Scott, Shackleton, Wilson; shipbuilding.
Information services:
Library available for reference (for conditions see Access above)
Education: Scotland, primary, secondary and FE, focus on 5 to 14 curriculum.
Interactive video.
Special visitor services: Guided tours, materials and/or activities for children.
Education services: Group education facilities, resources for Further or Higher Education.
Services for disabled people: For the visually impaired; for the hearing impaired; displays and/or information at wheelchair height.
Collections:
The ship and associated collections of objects, photographs and archives related to the history of the ship and the heroic age of polar explorations
Discovery collections (loan from the Maritime Trust), costume, personalia relating to Capt Scott and other crew members; ship's fitments, eg. bell, harmonium and crockery, 1901-1910
Printed publications:
Dundee Heritage Trust, The Beginning (editors Lythe, Walker, Edwards and Ross, Dundee 1997, ISBN 1870349 09 1)
The Story of Discovery (publ Pilgrim Press Limited, Derby 1996, ISBN 1 874670 28 5)

Internet home pages:
http://www.rrsdiscovery.com

2493
ROYAL SCOTS DRAGOON GUARDS MUSEUM
Edinburgh Castle, Edinburgh, EH1 2YT

Tel: 0131 220 4387
Acronym or abbreviation: Scots DG Museum
Formed: 1963

Organisation type and purpose: Independently owned, registered charity, museum, suitable for ages: 8+.
Regimental museum.
To promote wide interest in the Regiment and to provide education opportunity.

Enquiries to: Regimental Secretary
Direct tel: 0131 310 5100
Direct fax: 0131 310 5101
Other contacts: Museum & Shop Manager for routine opening hours and general enquiries.
Access:
Access to staff: By letter, by fax
Access to building, collections or gallery: No prior appointment required
Other restrictions: Prior appointment required for archives.
Entry free (via Edinburgh Castle ticket).

General description:
By arrangement enquirers may request information from Regimental Archives and on aspects of Regimental history.
Collections:
Range of items depicting the history of 3 Cavalry Regiments:-
The Royal Scots Greys
3rd Dragoon Guards
6th Dragoon Guards
and successors 3rd Carabiniers then The Royal Scots Dragoon Guards
Printed publications:
Publications restricted to Regimental History, availability depends on subject matter

Internet home pages:
http://www.scotsdg.com
Under development but see above website address.

2494
ROYAL SCOTS FUSILIERS
See - Royal Highland Fusiliers Regimental Headquarters and Museum

2495
ROYAL SCOTS REGIMENTAL MUSEUM
The Castle, Edinburgh, EH1 2YT

Tel: 0131 310 5016
Fax: 0131 310 5019
Email: enquiries@theroyalscots.co.uk
Formed: 1949

Organisation type and purpose: Independently owned, registered charity (charity number CR 38685), museum, suitable for ages: 12+.
Regimental charitable trust housed in MOD building.

Enquiries to: Regimental Secretary
Access:
Access to staff: By letter, by fax, by email, visitors by prior appointment
Hours: Mon to Fri, 0930 to 1600
Access to building, collections or gallery: No prior appointment required
Hours: Apr to Sep: daily, 0930 to 1730
Oct to Apr: Mon to Fri, 0930 to 1600
Access for disabled people: level entry, access to all public areas, toilet facilities
Other restrictions: Parking available.

General description:
The history of the Regiment from its formation in 1633 to the present day.
Collections:
Uniforms, weapons, silver, pictures, medals, photographs
Regimentalia relating to The Royal Scots
Catalogues:
Catalogue for library is in-house only. Catalogue for all of the collections is only available in-house.
Printed publications:
Pontius Pilate's Bodyguard - 2 volume history of the Regiment
Museum Brochure
Range of postcards

Internet home pages:
http://www.theroyalscots.co.uk

2496
ROYAL SCOTTISH ACADEMY
17 Waterloo Place, Edinburgh, EH1 3BG

Tel: 0131 558 7097
Fax: 0131 557 6417
Email: info@royalscottishacademy.org
Acronym or abbreviation: RSA
Full name: Royal Scottish Academy of Painting, Sculpture, Architecture and Printmaking
Formed: 1826

Organisation type and purpose: Learned society, professional body (membership is by election or invitation), present number of members: 113, registered charity (charity number SC 004198), art gallery.
Society of elected and nominated Scottish painters, sculptors, architects and printmakers.
The promotion and furtherance of the visual arts in Scotland.
Collections and library (only) now located at:
Royal Scottish Academy
The Dean Gallery, 73 Bedford Road, Edinburgh, EH4 3DS, tel: 0131 624 6277

Enquiries to: Assistant Librarian/Keeper
Direct tel: 0131 624 6277
Direct fax: 0131 557 6417
Access:
Access to staff: By letter, by telephone, by fax, by email, visitors by prior appointment
Hours: Mon to Fri, 1000 to 1300 and 1400 to 1630

General description:
Painting, drawing, sculpture, printmaking, architecture and some decorative arts in Scotland.
Collections:
RSA's own archives (minute books, letter collection, photograph collection, etc.) from 1825 onwards
W G Gillies, RSA Bequest (estate of this artist including letters, pictures, catalogues, etc.)
Catalogues:
Catalogue for library is in-house only. Catalogue for part of the collections is only available in-house.
Printed publications:
The Making of The Royal Scottish Academy (Gordon E, £4.95)

Internet home pages:
http://www.royalscottishacademy.org
General information, current membership, present and forthcoming exhibitions.

2497
ROYAL SCOTTISH MUSEUM
See - National Museums of Scotland

2498
ROYAL SHAKESPEARE THEATRE
See - RSC Collection

2499
ROYAL SIGNALS MUSEUM
Blandford Camp, Blandford, Dorset, DT11 8RH

Tel: 01258 482248
Fax: 01258 482084
Email: RoyalSignalsMuseum@army.mod.uk
Formed: 1938

Organisation type and purpose: Registered charity (charity number 1070420), museum, suitable for ages: all ages.
Run by:
Royal Signals
Regimental Headquarters, 56 Regency Street, London, SW1P 4AD, tel: 020 7414 8432

Enquiries to: Director
Direct tel: 01258 482267
Other contacts: Assistant Archivist for research enquiries.
Access:
Access to staff: By letter, by telephone, by email, visitors by prior appointment
Hours: Mon to Fri 0900 to 1700
Access to building, collections or gallery: No prior appointment required
Hours: Open to the general public Apr to Oct, Sat and Sun, 1000 to 1600
Other restrictions: Closed for 10 days at Christmas and New Year.
Access for disabled people: Parking provided, ramped entry, access to all public areas, toilet facilities

General description:
History of army communications from the Crimean War onwards and the history of the Royal Corps of Signals and its antecedents.
Information services:
Library available for reference (for conditions see Access above). Helpline available, tel no: 01258 482248.
Special visitor services: Guided tours, materials and/or activities for children.
Education services: Group education facilities, resources for Key Stages 2 and 3.
Services for disabled people: Displays and/or information at wheelchair height.
Collections:
Medals, sets of RE and Royal Signals soldiers' medals with personal details 1870-1994, 400 sets
Clandestine radios, SOE and military spy radios of WWII, 1939-1945, 18 sets
Military radios; an almost complete range of military radios of the British Army, 1914-2000, over 90 items

Catalogues:
Catalogue for part of the collections is only available in-house.

Internet home pages:
http://www.royalsignals.army.org.uk/museum

2500
ROYAL SOCIETY OF PAINTERS IN WATERCOLOURS
See - Royal Watercolour Society

2501
ROYAL ULSTER RIFLES REGIMENTAL MUSEUM
5 Waring Street, Belfast, BT1 2EW

Tel: 028 9023 2086
Fax: 028 9023 2086
Email: rurmuseum@yahoo.co.uk
Acronym or abbreviation: RUR Museum
Formed: 1963

Organisation type and purpose: Museum, suitable for ages: 12+.

Enquiries to: Curator
Access:
Access to staff: By letter, by telephone, by email

General description:
History of the Royal Ulster Rifles, the Royal Irish Rifles, the 83rd and 86th Regiments of Foot and associated volunteer and militia regiments. Campaigns; uniforms; medals; arms; badges and equipment from 1793 to 1968. The library contains war diaries, casualty rolls, medal rolls and a few personal records and books of general military interest.
Collections:
Artefacts and papers connected with the Royal Ulster Rifles, the Royal Irish Rifles, the 83rd and 86th Regiments of Foot and associated units. Holdings include personal papers, war diaries, record books, medal rolls, casualty lists, photograph albums and histories. (A computerised list is in progress)
Catalogues:
Catalogue for library is in-house only. Catalogue for all of the collections is only available in-house.

Internet home pages:
http://members.tripod.co.uk/rurmuseum/museum
History, library, resources, locations, museums, FAQ, email.

2502
ROYAL WATERCOLOUR SOCIETY
Bankside Gallery, 48 Hopton Street, London, SE1 9JH

Tel: 020 7928 7521
Fax: 020 7928 2820
Email: rws@banksidegallery.com
Acronym or abbreviation: RWS
Formed: 1804
Formerly: Royal Society of Painters in Watercolours

Organisation type and purpose: Learned society (membership is by election or invitation), present number of members: 90, registered charity (charity number 258348), art gallery.
Connected with:
Bankside Gallery, home of the RWS

Enquiries to: Gallery Director
Access:
Access to staff: By letter, by telephone, by fax, by email, Internet web pages
Hours: Tue, 1000 to 2000; Wed to Fri, 1000 to 1700; Sat, Sun, 1100 to 1700; Mon, closed
Access to building, collections or gallery: No prior appointment required

General description:
Watercolour painting and its history, contemporary work by members of the Society, gallery activities.
Collections:
The RWS Diploma collection (1 work from each member of the society, RWS Archive since its inception 200 years ago)
Catalogues:
Catalogue for library is published.
Printed publications:
Bankside Bulletin (journal of the Royal Watercolour Society and the Royal Society of Painter-Printmakers, quarterly, free to members and friends, £2 to the public)

Internet home pages:
http://www.banksidegallery.com

2503
ROYAL WILTSHIRE YEOMANRY MUSEUM
Church Place, Swindon, Wiltshire, SN1 5EH

Tel: 01793 523865
Fax: 01793 529350
Formed: 1973

Organisation type and purpose: Museum. Small museum, collection owned by charitable trust in Territorial Army building.
Associate member of:
The South West Museums Council

Enquiries to: Administrator
Access:
Access to staff: By letter, by telephone, by fax
Hours: Mon to Fri, 0930 to 1600

General description:
Contains material covering all aspects of The Royal Wiltshire Yeomanry from their formation in 1794. Includes several items of interest from a variety of periods.
Collections:
Letters from the Prime Minister. 1944. 5 items
Collection of Royal Wiltshire Yeomanry uniforms, pictures, silver and equipment
Personal records and RWY papers are held at the Wiltshire County Records Office, Trowbridge
Citation from the King.

2504
RSC COLLECTION
Royal Shakespeare Theatre, Stratford-upon-Avon, Warwickshire, CV37 6BB

Tel: 01789 296655
Full name: RSC Collection Royal Shakespeare Theatre
Formed: 1881

Organisation type and purpose: Registered charity, art gallery, suitable for ages: 8+.
A collection of paintings, theatre costumes and theatre memorabilia.
Parent body:
Royal Shakespeare Theatre
Stratford on Avon, CV37 6BB

Enquiries to: Curator
Access:
Access to staff: By letter, by telephone
Access for disabled people: level entry, toilet facilities

General description:
A collection of over 350 oil paintings, watercolours and prints associated with Shakespeare, his plays and the theatre by predominantly British artists from the 17th century onwards. Also contains portraits, miniatures and sculptures of leading 19th and 20th century Shakespearean actors, actresses and directors, mainly associated with the theatre in Stratford upon Avon. The RSC Collection's costume archive comprises more than 1000 items, dating from the late 18th century. Exhibitions change and relate to the productions in the Royal Shakespeare Theatre.
Information services:
Special visitor services: Guided tours..
Collections:
Pictures, photographs, theatre costumes, RSC and other theatre memorabilia spanning some 100 years
The RSC Collection owns the largest known group of oil paintings - 16 in all - originally commissioned or purchased by Alderman John Boydell for his famous Shakespeare Gallery, Pall Mall (1789-1805). In addition, the Collection has over 50 Boydell engravings

Internet home pages:
http://www.rsc.org.uk/collection/jsp/index.jsp

2505
RUBBISH DUMP WASTE NOT RECYCLING
See - ecoACTIVE Education Centre

2506
RUDDINGTON FRAMEWORK KNITTERS' MUSEUM
Chapel Street, Ruddington, Nottingham, NG11 6HE

Tel: 0115 984 6914
Fax: 0115 984 1174
Email: jack@smirfitt.demon.co.uk
Formed: 1972
Formerly: Ruddington Framework Knitters' Shops Preservation Trust

Organisation type and purpose: Registered charity (charity number 500799), museum, historic building, house or site, suitable for ages: 5+.

Enquiries to: Curator
Access:
Access to staff: By letter, by telephone, by fax, by email, visitors by prior appointment
Hours: Apr to Dec: Wed to Sun, 1030 to 1600
Access for disabled people: ramped entry

General description:
Framework knitting; hosiery; textiles; social and industrial history.
Information services:
Library available for reference (for conditions see Access above), bibliography compilation, selective dissemination services
Documented museum collection.
Special visitor services: Guided tours, tape recorded guides, materials and/or activities for children.
Education services: Group education facilities, resources for Key Stage 2 and Further or Higher Education..
Collections:
Collection of photographs, trade pamphlets, books, patents and other ephemera relating to knitting industry
Catalogues:
Catalogue for library is in-house only.
Publications list:
is available in hard copy and online.
Printed publications:
Cricket and the framework knitters
Newsletter (quarterly)
Ruddington: A framework knitting village
Sermons and stocking frames: the history of Methodism in Ruddington and its links with the framework knitters
The Parkers of Rantergate
Ruddington Framework Knitters' Museum: Resources for schools - Teachers notes and outline worksheets for Key Stage 2
Ruddington Framework Knitters' Trail - An illustrated guided walk through the village including all major locations connected
Poor as a stockinger: framework knitting and the Luddites in Nottinghamshire
Electronic and video products:
Knitting Bibliography (floppy disk)
Sanctuary and cell (VHS video, 10 minutes)

continued overleaf

The Workings of a 19th century Circular Knitting Machine: Griswold (VHS video, 13 minutes)

Internet home pages:
http://www.rfkm.org

2507
RUDYARD LAKE STEAM RAILWAY
Rudyard Station, Rudyard, Leek, Staffordshire, ST13 8PE

Tel: 01995 672280
Fax: 01995 672280
Email: hanson.mike@virgin.net

Organisation type and purpose: Independently owned, historic building, house or site, suitable for ages: 5+.
Tourist railway.
Supported by:
Friends of the Rudyard Lake Steam Railway

Enquiries to: Director
Access:
Access to staff: By letter, by fax, by email, visitors by prior appointment
Access for disabled people: Parking provided, level entry

General description:
History of Rudyard Lake, history of railways at Rudyard, miniature railways.
Collections:
Steam and Internal Combustion Locomotives, carriages, wagons, 1½ mile railway adjacent to historic lake
Railwayana
Printed publications:
Posters

Internet home pages:
http://www.rlsr.org
History of lake and railways, timetables, rolling stock, driver experience courses, news of developments.
http://www.rudyardlakerailway.co.uk
History of lake and railways, timetables, rolling stock, driver experience courses, news of developments.

2508
RUFFORD COUNTRY PARK
Ollerton, Newark, Nottinghamshire, NG22 9DF

Tel: 01623 822944
Fax: 01623 824840
Email: contact form on website

Organisation type and purpose: Historic building, house or site, suitable for ages: all ages.

Enquiries to: Manager
Access:
Access to staff: By letter, by telephone, by fax, by email, in person, Internet web pages
Access to building, collections or gallery: No access other than to staff
Access for disabled people: Parking provided, toilet facilities

General description:
Country park with remains of 12th century abbey; and craft centre.

Internet home pages:
http://www.nottinghamshiretourism.co.uk
http://www.ruffordcraftcentre.org.uk

2509
RUFFORD OLD HALL
Rufford, Ormskirk, Lancashire, L40 1SG

Tel: 01704 821254
Fax: 01704 821254
Email: ruffordoldhall@nationaltrust.org.uk
Formed: 1895

Organisation type and purpose: National government body, registered charity (charity number 205846), museum, historic building, house or site, suitable for ages: 5+.

Parent body:
The National Trust (North West)
North West Regional Office, tel: 0870 609 5391

Enquiries to: Property Manager
Other contacts: House Manager
Access:
Access to staff: By letter, by telephone, by fax, by email
Hours: All week.
Access for disabled people: level entry, toilet facilities
Other restrictions: Limited parking, access to Great Hall only. 2 manual wheelchairs available. Wheelchairs limited to Great Hall because of steps. Ground floor accessible with assistance. No access to other floors. Photograph album. Level entrance to shop and to restaurant. Grounds largely accessible.

General description:
One of Lancashire's finest 16th century buildings, famed for its spectacular Great Hall with an intricately carved 'moveable' wooden screen and dramatic hammerbeam roof. It is rumoured that Shakespeare performed in this hall for the owner, Sir Thomas Hesketh, to whose family Rufford belonged for over 400 years. The house contains fine collections of 16th and 17th century oak furniture, arms, armour and tapestries. There is also an interesting collection of watercolour studies of flowering plants by Ellen Stevens.
Information services:
Braille guide. Large-print guide. Audio guide. Touch list. Sympathetic Hearing Scheme Frontcarrying baby slings for loan.
Suitable for school groups. Education room/centre. Audio guide. Children's guide.
Children's quiz/trail.
Special visitor services: Guided tours, tape recorded guides, materials and/or activities for children.
Education services: Group education facilities, resources for Key Stages 1 and 2, 3 and 4.
Services for disabled people: For the visually impaired; for the hearing impaired.
Collections:
Guide Book
Short Guide
Information Leaflets (free)
Printed publications:
Guide Book
Short Guide
Information leaflets (free)

Internet home pages:
http://www.nationaltrust.org.uk

2510
RUNNYMEDE
North Lodge, Windsor Road, Old Windsor, Berkshire, SL42JL

Tel: 01784 432891
Fax: 01784 479007
Email: runnymede@nationaltrust.org.uk

Organisation type and purpose: National organisation, registered charity (charity number 205846), historic building, house or site, suitable for ages: 5+.
Parent body:
National Trust (South and South East Region)
Thames & Solent Regional Office, tel: 01491 528051

Enquiries to: Manager
Access:
Access to staff: By letter, by telephone, by fax, by email
Access for disabled people: Parking provided, toilet facilities
Other restrictions: Steps to tea-room

General description:
Runnymede is an attractive area of riverside meadows, grassland and broadleaved woodland, rich in flora and fauna, and part-designated a Site of Special Scientific Interest. It was on this site, in 1215, that King John sealed Magna Carta, an event commemorated by the American Bar Association Memorial and John F. Kennedy Memorial. Also here are the Fairhaven Lodges, designed by Lutyens. On the opposite bank of the Thames from Runnymede lies the important archaeological site of Ankerwycke, an area of parkland acquired by the National Trust in 1998 and containing the remains of the 12th century St Mary's Priory and the Ankerwycke Yew, a magnificent tree believed to be over 2000 years old.
Information services:
Hand-held self-guided audio 'wand' tour for hire. Leaflet available.
Programme of guided walks throughout the year.
Cycling permitted on Thames Path.
Special visitor services: Tape recorded guides..

Internet home pages:
http://www.nationaltrust.org.uk

2511
RUPERT BROOKE SOCIETY & MUSEUM, THE
The Orchard, Grantchester, Cambridgeshire, CB3 9ND

Tel: 01223 845788
Fax: 01223 845862
Email: rbs@calan.co.uk
Formed: 1999

Organisation type and purpose: International organisation, membership association (membership is by subscription), museum, historic building, house or site.
The Museum covers the life history of Rupert Brooke.
Aims to: foster an interest in the work of Rupert Brooke, increase knowledge and appreciation of Rupert Brooke and of the village of Grantchester, help to preserve places associated with Rupert Brooke.

Enquiries to: Curator
Other contacts: Secretary for the RB Society information.
Access:
Access to staff: By letter, by telephone, by fax, by email, Internet web pages
Hours: Mon to Fri, 0900 to 1700
Access to building, collections or gallery: No prior appointment required
Hours: Summer opening usually Mon to Sun, 1000-1600 (phone to confirm opening)
Access for disabled people: Parking provided
Other restrictions: ramped entry to tea pavilion, steps into museum.

General description:
The life and works of Rupert Brooke.
Publications list:
is available in hard copy.
Printed publications:
A selection of books including:
Forever England, the Life of Rupert Brooke (Read M)
Old Grantchester, A Sketch book (Willmer E N)
Rupert Brooke & Wilfred Owen (selected and ed Walter G)
Electronic and video products:
Rupert Brooke - His Life and Poetry (audiotape, Hodge D, Read M)

Address for ordering publications:
Printed publications:
The Rupert Brooke Society

Internet home pages:
http://www.rupert-brooke-society.com

2512
RURAL CRAFTS PRESERVATION SOCIETY
See - Usk Rural Life Museum

2513
RURAL LIFE CENTRE, OLD KILN MUSEUM TRUST

Reeds Road, Tilford, Farnham, Surrey, GU10 2DL

Tel: 01252 795571
Fax: 01252 795571
Email: rural.life@lineone.net
Formed: 1973
Still known as: Old Kiln Museum, date of change, 1990

Organisation type and purpose: Independently owned, registered charity (charity number 289150), museum, suitable for ages: all ages.
Museum of country life 1750-1960.
Parent body:
Old Kiln Museum Trust
Affiliated with:
Old Kiln Light Railway Society
Tel: 01252 713026
Surrey Industrial History Group
Tel: 01483 565375
Support Group (Friends) known as:
Rustics

Enquiries to: General Manager
Access:
Access to staff: By letter, by telephone, by fax, by email, in person, visitors by prior appointment, Internet web pages
Hours: Wed to Sun, 1100 to 1600 when museum is open
Other restrictions: Otherwise by appointment.
Access to building, collections or gallery: No prior appointment required
Hours: Apr to Sep: Wed to Sun and Bank Holidays, 1100 to 1800
Winter: Only Wed, 1100 to 1600
Access for disabled people: Parking provided, ramped entry, toilet facilities
Other restrictions: Access to most areas.

General description:
The Rural Life Centre is a museum of past village life covering the years from 1750 to 1960, domestic, social, agricultural, craft and industry. It was founded in 1973 and has been collecting items from all over the area ever since.
The museum is set in over ten acres of garden and woodland and housed in purpose-built and reconstructed buildings including a 30 seated chapel from Eashing dating back to 1857, a village hall and a recently rescued 1883 cricket pavilion from Godalming which now contains the museum's sporting exhibits.
Displays show village crafts and trades, literally from the butcher and the baker right through to the wheelwright. The latter collection is probably the finest in the country. All manner of old farm implements are also preserved, and visitors are introduced to the country scene by a typically furnished country home set up in a 1940s prefab, which coincidentally was the first building on the site when Madge and Henry Jackson first opened their museum.
Information services:
Library available for reference (for conditions see Access above)
Handling collection under development.
Loan boxes, school demonstrations.
Special visitor services: Materials and/or activities for children.
Education services: Group education facilities, resources for Key Stages 2 and 3..
Collections:
Domestic, social, agricultural, industrial and craft artefacts
Anne Mallinson's Selborne Village Collection
Gibbs Family horticultural equipment
Horse-drawn Transport Reserve Collection from the Museum of English Rural Life at Reading
Pohorely Collection of carpentry tools
Various documents and archives relating to the artefact collections
George Sturt, author and wheelwright, books and tools, 1843-1927
Catalogues:
Catalogue for library is in-house only. Catalogue for part of the collections is only available in-house.
Printed publications:
Guide to the Rural Life Centre (direct)
Colour Leaflet (direct)
Annual Diary of Events (direct)
Rustic (newsletter, direct)
Tree List for Arboretum (direct)
Electronic and video products:
The following subjects: Wheelwright, Blacksmith, Waggons and Ploughs, Arboretum (videos, available direct)

Internet home pages:
http://www.rural-life.org.uk
General introduction to the museum; educational facilities (downloadable resources); diary of events, guide to the museum.

2514
RUSHMOOR LOCAL HISTORY GALLERY

c/o Aldershot Military Museum, Queens Avenue, Aldershot, Hampshire, GU11 2LG

Tel: 01252 314598
Fax: 01252 342942
Email: musmim@hants.gov.uk
Also known as: Aldershot Museum

Parent body:
Hampshire County Council Museums Service
Chilcomb House, Chilcomb Lane, Winchester, Hampshire, SO23 8RD, tel: 01962 846304, fax: 01962 869836

Enquiries to: Curator
Access:
Access to staff: By letter, by telephone, by fax, by email, in person
Access to building, collections or gallery: No prior appointment required

General description:
Local history for Rushmoor area, Hampshire 1500 to present day, also includes archaeological material from Farnborough Hill and Cove potteries.
Collections:
Archeological material from Farnborough Hill
Pottery from Cove Potteries
Catalogues:
Catalogue for all of the collections is on-line.
Printed publications:
Publications list is available from the Librarian, Hampshire County Council Museums Service Headquarters, Chilcomb House, Winchester, SO23 8RD

Internet home pages:
http://www.hants.gov.uk/museums/
HMCMS web catalogue, whole collection, 100,000 plus web pages

See also - Aldershot Military Museum

2515
RUSHMORE LOCAL HISTORY MUSEUM

See - Aldershot Military Museum

2516
RUSHTON TRIANGULAR LODGE

Rushton, Kettering, Northamptonshire, NN14 1RP

Tel: 01536 710761

Parent body:
English Heritage (East Midlands Region)
44 Derngate, Northampton, NN1 1UH, tel: 01604 735400, fax: 01604 735401

Enquiries to: House Manager
Access:
Access to staff: By letter, by telephone
Other restrictions: When closed contact Regional Office on 01604 735400.
Access to building, collections or gallery: No prior appointment required
Hours: Apr to Sep, Daily, 1000 to 1800; Oct, Daily, 1000 to 1700.

General description:
Elizabethan folly built in 1597, designed to symbolise the Holy Trinity, with its three sides, three floors, trefoil windows and three triangular gables on each side.

Internet home pages:
http://www.english-heritage.org.uk

2517
RUSKIN GALLERY & RUSKIN CRAFT GALLERY

See - Millenium Galleries

2518
RUSKIN LIBRARY

Lancaster University, Lancaster, LA1 4YH

Tel: 01524 593587
Fax: 01524 593580
Email: ruskin.library@lancaster.ac.uk
Formed: 1998
Formerly: Ruskin Galleries, Bembridge School, Isle of Wight, date of change, Closed 1996

Organisation type and purpose: Art gallery, university library.

Enquiries to: Curator
Direct tel: 01524 593589
Direct fax: 01524 593580
Direct email: s.wildman@lancaster.ac.uk
Other contacts: Deputy Curator tel no: 01524 593588 e-mail r.finnerty@lancaster.ac.uk for appointments for Reading Room.
Access:
Access to staff: By letter, by telephone, by fax, by email, visitors by prior appointment
Hours: Reading Room: Mon to Fri, 1000 to 1630
Access to building, collections or gallery: No access other than to staff
Hours: Public Gallery: Mon to Sat, 1100 to 1600; Sun, 1300 to 1600
Access for disabled people: ramped entry, access to all public areas, toilet facilities

General description:
Art and architecture, history and literature.
Collections:
Whitehouse Collection of manuscripts, books, photographs and pictures relating to John Ruskin (1819-1900) and his associates
Catalogues:
Catalogue for library is on-line. Catalogue for part of the collections is on-line.
Publications list:
is available on-line.

Internet home pages:
http://www.lancs.ac.uk/users/ruskinlib/
Information for visitors, catalogue of collections, etc.

2519
RUSKIN MUSEUM

Coniston Institute, Yewdale Road, Coniston, Cumbria, LA21 8DU

Tel: 01539 441164
Fax: 015394 41132
Email: vmj@ruskinmuseum.com
Formed: 1901
Formerly: Coniston Mechanics Institute & Literary Society from pre 1850 to 1901

Organisation type and purpose: Learned society, registered charity (charity number 222234), museum, art gallery, suitable for ages: 5+.
The Ruskin Museum exists to celebrate and

continued overleaf

promote the life, work and philosophy of John Ruskin, 1819 to 1900, Britain's greatest critic of art and society; to interpret the history of the Coniston area; to preserve the collections gifted to the village, and to display them for the benefit of local residents, visiting tourists and students, in posterity.
Parent body:
The Coniston Institute and Ruskin Museum Charitable Trust
at the same address

Enquiries to: Curator
Direct fax: 01539 441164
Other contacts: Honorary Secretary for constitutional issues.
Access:
Access to staff: By letter, by telephone, by fax, by email, in person, charges made to all users, Internet web pages
Hours: Easter or 1 Apr (which ever earlier) to Mid Nov: Mon to Sun, 1000 to 1730; reduced winter access
Other restrictions: Reference or letter of introduction required for researchers, and access to research library by prior appointment.
Access for disabled people: Parking provided, level entry, access to all public areas, toilet facilities

General description:
John Ruskin; W G Collingwood; Arthur Ransome (Swallows and Amazons); Coniston geology; copper mines; slate quarries; Lakeland sheep farming; husbandry; Herdwicks; Coniston Water as highway and fishery; Donald Campbell (Bluebird).
Information services:
Library available for reference (for conditions see Access above)
Will answer specific written enquiries or advise the enquirer of a suitable source of information or expert.
Guided tours and guided walks, audio guides.
Sessions for disabled people arranged for groups.
Special visitor services: Guided tours, materials and/or activities for children.
Education services: Group education facilities, resources for Key Stages 1 and 2, 3, 4 and Further or Higher Education.
Services for disabled people: Displays and/or information at wheelchair height.
Collections:
Ruskin MSS and letters
Ruskin portraits
Watercolours; drawings; sketchbooks; engravings by or after John Ruskin
Sketchbooks available, page by page, on computer displays (not available on sale)
Local history objects and photographs
78 historic photographs available on computer displays
Interactive CD-ROM provides above-and-under-ground tour of Coniston Copper Mines (copies available for sale)
Photographs of Donald Campbell and Bluebird
Press cuttings re Sir Malcolm Campbell, Donald Campbell, Bluebird
Catalogues:
Catalogue for library is in-house only. Catalogue for all of the collections is only available in-house.
Printed publications:
Stock selection of second-hand books by John Ruskin, copies of contemporary publications about him
Local history, geology books
Electronic and video products:
Coniston Coppermines (CD-ROM, Cumbria Amenity Trust)
Ruskin's Journey (video, Lancaster University, £14.99 plus p&p)

Internet home pages:
http://www.ruskinmuseum.com
History of the museum and its development, pages on aspects of the collections, education provision.

2520
RUSSELL-COTES ART GALLERY AND MUSEUM
East Cliff, Bournemouth, Hampshire, BH1 3AA

Tel: 01202 451800
Fax: 01202 451851
Formed: 1922

Organisation type and purpose: Local government body, museum, art gallery.
Parent body:
Bournemouth Borough Council
Leisure and Tourism Directorate, Arts, Libraries and Museum Division

Enquiries to: Senior Arts and Museum Officer
Access:
Access to staff: Visitors by prior appointment
Hours: Mon to Fri, 0900 to 1700

General description:
Victorian paintings, local history, numismatics, theatre, oriental art and antiquities, archaeology, marine history, ethnography, arms and armour, lepidoptera, furniture, sculpture, Japanese art, Victorian bygones, art and architecture.
Information services:
Special visitor services: Guided tours, tape recorded guides.
Services for disabled people: For the visually impaired; for the hearing impaired.
Collections:
20th century painting
Casa Magni Shelley Collection
Contemporary craft commissions
Italian Maiolica
Lucas Collection (ceramic, furniture, painting, metalwork)
Meader Collection (Victoriana)
Russell-Cotes collection
Sherrin Collection
Victorian paintings
World-wide collections
Publications list:
is available on-line.
Printed publications:
So Fair a House

Internet home pages:
http://www.russell-cotes.bournemouth.gov.uk
Information page.
http://www.russell-cotes.bournemouth.gov.uk/shop
Publications information.

2521
RUSTINGTON HERITAGE ASSOCIATION EXHIBITION CENTRE
34 Woodlands Avenue, Rustington, West Sussex, BN16 2HB

Tel: 01903 784792
Acronym or abbreviation: RHA
Formed: 1983

Organisation type and purpose: Voluntary organisation, registered charity (charity number 1017526), museum.

Enquiries to: Chairman
Access:
Access to staff: By letter, by telephone, visitors by prior appointment
Other restrictions: Closed Oct to Apr. Personal contact with the Chairman at any time.
Access to building, collections or gallery: No prior appointment required
Hours: May to Sep: Wed & Thu, 1430 to 1630; Sat, 1030 to 1230

General description:
Rustington - comprehensive knowledge about the history and people of the village. Social history collection.

2522
RUTHIN GAOL
46 Clwyd Street, Ruthin, Denbighshire, LL15 1HP

Tel: 01824 708281
Fax: 01824 708258
Email: sophie.fowler@denbighshire.gov.uk

Organisation type and purpose: Local government body, museum, suitable for ages: all ages.
Parent body:
Denbighshire County Council

Enquiries to: Manager
Access:
Access to staff: By letter, by telephone, by fax, by email, Internet web pages
Access to building, collections or gallery: No prior appointment required
Hours: Apr to Oct: daily, 1000 to 1700, Thu 1000 to 1900
Nov to Mar: Tue to Sun, 1000 to 1700, closed Mon

General description:
'The Gruelling Experience' is your chance to explore one of North Wales' most fascinating buildings. From 1654 to 1916, thousands of prisoners - men, women and children, innocent and guilty, passed through its gates. See how the prisoners lived their daily lives; what they ate, how they worked and the punishments they suffered. Can you turn the dreaded hand-crank? Explore the cells, including the dark and condemned cells. Visit the Pentonville block with its ingenious Victorian heating, ventilation and communication systems. Then bring yourself up to date with the building's use as a wartime munitions factory.
Information services:
Education services: Group education facilities..
Collections:
Small collection of crime and punishment material

Internet home pages:
http://www.ruthingaol.co.uk

2523
RUTLAND COUNTY MUSEUM
Catmos Street, Oakham, Rutland, LE15 6HW

Tel: 01572 758440
Fax: 01572 758445
Email: museum@rutland.gov.uk
Acronym or abbreviation: RCM
Formed: 1969

Organisation type and purpose: Museum. Museum of Rutland rural life.

Enquiries to: Curator
Access:
Access to staff: By letter, by telephone, by fax, in person, visitors by prior appointment
Hours: Mon to Sat, 1000 to 1700; Sun, 1400 to 1600/1700
Other restrictions: Closed Christmas and Good Friday.
Access for disabled people: level entry, toilet facilities
Other restrictions: Parking in adjacent public car park.

General description:
The museum is housed in the indoor riding school built for the Rutland Fencible Cavalry in 1794.
History and archaeology of the county of Rutland from prehistoric times to the present day. Rutland Yeomanry Cavalry, Leicestershire Yeomanry, Rifle Volunteers, their history, uniforms and equipment. The history of the Leicestershire Yeomanry formed in the mid 19th century extends through the Boer War and two world wars up to the present day.
Collections:
Archaeological material of prehistoric, Roman and Anglo-Saxon date
Domestic materials

Rural life material including rural tradesmen's tools
Books, photographs, ephemera, all relating to Rutland

Internet home pages:
http://www.rutnet.co.uk/rcc/rutlandmuseums
Opening times and collection summary.

2524
RUTLAND RAILWAY MUSEUM

Cottesmore Iron Ore Mines Sidings, Ashwell Road, Cottesmore, Oakham, Rutland, LE15 7BX

Tel: 01572 813203
Formed: 1976
Formed from: Market Overton Industrial Railway Association, date of change, 1980

Organisation type and purpose: Voluntary organisation.
Preservation of railway locomotives, rolling stock and other railway artefacts.

Enquiries to: Honorary Secretary
Access:
Access to staff: By letter, by telephone

General description:
Open-air museum of industrial railways with particular emphasis on local ironstone quarry railways. Steam-hauled railway passenger coach demonstration line.
Printed publications:
Roperunner (3 times a year, members)
The Sundew Story (£3 plus p&p)

Internet home pages:
http://www.emms.org.uk/rutland

2525
RYCOTE CHAPEL

Thame, Oxfordshire

Organisation type and purpose: Historic building, house or site.
Parent body:
English Heritage (South East Region)
Tel: 01483 252000, fax: 01483 252001

Enquiries to: Manager
Access:
Access to staff: By letter, by telephone
Access to building, collections or gallery: No prior appointment required
Hours: 29 Mar to 30 Sep: Fri to Sun, and Bank Holidays, 1400 to 1800
Other restrictions: Opening times are subject to change, for up-to-date information contact English Heritage by phone or visit the website.

General description:
A 15th century chapel with exquisitely carved and painted woodwork and many intriguing features, such as two roofed pews and a musicians' gallery.

Internet home pages:
http://www.english-heritage.org.uk

2526
RYE CASTLE MUSEUM

East Street, Rye, East Sussex, TN31 7JY

Tel: 01797 226728
Formed: 1928
Formerly: Rye Museum, date of change, 1994

Organisation type and purpose: Independently owned, membership association (membership is by subscription), present number of members: 200, registered charity, museum 8+.
To collect and display material in its collection that relates to Rye and the surrounding villages.
Parent body:
Rye Museum Association
at the same address

Enquiries to: Curator
Other contacts: Chairman for Curator on leave.

Access:
Access to staff: By letter, by telephone, visitors by prior appointment, charges to non-members
Hours: Apr to Oct: Thu to Mon, 1030 to 1700; Nov to Mar: Weekends only
Other restrictions: By appointment when not open.
Access for disabled people: ramped entry, access to all public areas, toilet facilities
Other restrictions: Above access and facilities at East Street only.

General description:
Local history, costume, Cinque Ports regalia, 18th century fire engine, Rye art, pottery, paintings, shipbuilding, uniforms and photographs.
Information services:
Library available for reference (for conditions see Access above)
Special visitor services: Guided tours.
Education services: Group education facilities, resources for Key Stages 2 and 3..
Collections:
Jeakes Papers
Meryon and Holloway Papers
Pottery, Mediaeval, 12th-14th century, 19th and 20th centuries - Rye Kilns
Shipbuilding, tools, models, plans, 19th-20th century
Militaria, uniforms, weapons, etc 18th-20th century
Topographical, prints, drawings, watercolours showing geographical changes, 16th-20th century
Catalogues:
Catalogue for library is in-house only. Catalogue for all of the collections is only available in-house.
Printed publications:
Guide Book
Smuggling in Rye
Murder of Allen Orebel
Introduction to Rye Castle Museum (for purchase)
Rye in WWII (for purchase)

2527
RYEDALE FOLK MUSEUM

Hutton le Hole, North Yorkshire, YO6 6UA

Tel: 01751 417367
Fax: 01751 417367
Email: info@ryedalefolkmuseum.co.uk
Formed: 1968
Formerly: Crosland Foundation c/o Ryedale Folk Museum

Organisation type and purpose: Registered charity (charity number 523368), museum, suitable for ages: all ages.
Parent body:
Crosland Foundation
at the same address

Enquiries to: Curator
Access:
Access to staff: By letter, by telephone
Hours: Mon to Fri, 0900 to 1700; in addition, Mar to Oct, Sat, Sun, 0900 to 1700

General description:
Contains 17 rescued and restored historic buildings from the North Yorkshire Moors area; agricultural equipment; and tools from 1750 to 1950, all from North Yorkshire. Features social and domestic history from North Yorkshire, 1650 to 1953. Also contains an Elizabethan glass furnace; craft tools; and transport items.
Collections:
Agriculture
Vernacular buildings
Historic gardens
Industrial archaeology
Crafts
Shops
Trades
Hayes collection of archaeology, 2000 BC-1750, several thousand items
Hayes photography collection, 1900-1960, 2500 items
Catalogues:
Catalogue for library is in-house only. Catalogue for all of the collections is only available in-house.
Printed publications:
History of Merrills
Museum Guide Book

Internet home pages:
http://www.ryedalefolkmuseum.co.uk

2528
RYHOPE ENGINES TRUST

Pumping Station, Ryhope Road, Ryhope, Sunderland, Tyne and Wear, SR2 0ND

Tel: 0191 521 0235
Email: keith-bell@beeb.net
Formed: 1973

Organisation type and purpose: Registered charity (charity number 502448), museum, suitable for ages: 5+.

Enquiries to: Chairman
Access:
Access to staff: By letter, by email, in person
Hours: Sun, 1400 to 1700; Wed, 1800 to 2200
Access to building, collections or gallery: No prior appointment required
Hours: Sun, 1400 to 1700; Bank Holidays, 1000 to 1600
Access for disabled people: Parking provided

General description:
A Victorian waterworks built by Hawksley in 1868. Contains beam engines by Hawthorn, and displays relating to the history of water supply. Engines operate under steam on bank holiday weekends and other times.
Catalogues:
Catalogue for part of the collections is only available in-house.

Internet home pages:
http://www.g3wte.demon.co.uk
General description of museum and regular updated information.
http://ris.niaa.org.uk/museums/ryhope.htm
AMC website with links.

2529
SAATCHI GALLERY, THE

top Floor, 30 Underwood Street, London, N1 7XJ

Tel: 020 7336 7362
Fax: 020 7336 7364
Formed: 1985
Formerly: Saatchi Collection

Organisation type and purpose: Art gallery, suitable for ages: 5+.

Enquiries to: Administrator
Access:
Access to staff: By letter, by fax
Hours: Thu to Sun, 1200 to 1800

General description:
The Saatchi collection is owned by Mr Charles Saatchi. Its aim is to introduce new art or art largely unseen to a UK audience. It has been the first museum in Britain to present a major showing of works by many contemporary British and American artists. The Saatchi collection comprises hundreds of paintings, sculpture and installations displayed at the Saatchi Gallery and frequently on loan to museums around the world.
Collections:
Young British artists; painting, sculpture and installation
Publications list:
is available in hard copy.
Printed publications:
Books, Postcards, Posters, T-shirts

2530
SACREWELL FARM AND COUNTRY CENTRE, THE

Sacrewell Farm, Thornhaugh, Peterborough, Cambridgeshire, PE8 6HJ

Tel: 01780 782254
Fax: 01780 782254
Email: wsatrust@supanet.com
Acronym or abbreviation: WSAT
Formed: 1964

Organisation type and purpose: Registered charity (charity number 233603), historic building, house or site, suitable for ages: all ages, research organisation.
Commercial farm, open farm, crop research station, collections.
Sound farming practice, education, research.
Parent body:
The William Scott Abbott Trust

Enquiries to: Manager
Access:
Access to staff: By letter, by telephone, by fax

General description:
A restored, operating watermill (pitchback) with related bygones exhibition forms part of a larger collection of agricultural and social bygones displayed in stone-built barns and structures dating from around 1760.
Accounts and performance of a commercial farm; agricultural heritage collections; extensive farm archives; research findings from crop station (agronomy based).

Internet home pages:
http://www.peterborough.org.uk

2531
SADDLEWORTH MUSEUM & ART GALLERY

High Street, Uppermill, Oldham, Lancashire, OL3 6HS

Tel: 01457 874093
Fax: 01457 870336
Email: museum-curator@saddleworth.net
Formed: 1962

Organisation type and purpose: Registered charity (charity number 528225), museum, art gallery, suitable for ages: all ages, research organisation.
Affiliated to:
Saddleworth Historical Society (SHS)
at the same address
Links with:
Friends of Saddleworth Museum
at the same address

Enquiries to: Curator
Other contacts: Honorary Archivist for detailed enquiries regarding local history.
Access:
Access to staff: By letter, by telephone, by fax, by email, visitors by prior appointment
Hours: Access to staff is by prior arrangement
Access for disabled people: ramped entry, toilet facilities
Other restrictions: Entry to art gallery by stairlift; access to ground floor by ramp.

General description:
Local textile industry; local history in general, local landscape and buildings; local family history, births, deaths, marriages; local military history.
Collections:
Library of textile related works
Papers relating to local textile firms and mill-owning families running to many thousands of documents and photographs
Edna Lumb, paintings, 1970-1990
Catalogues:
Catalogue for library is in-house only. Catalogue for part of the collections is only available in-house.

2532
SAFFRON WALDEN MUSEUM

Museum Street, Saffron Walden, Essex, CB10 1JL

Tel: 01799 510333
Fax: 01799 510333
Email: museum@uttlesford.gov.uk
Formed: 1835

Organisation type and purpose: Local government body, registered charity, museum, suitable for ages: all ages.
Second oldest (after British Museum) purpose-built museum in the country, Museum of the Year Award 1997.
Parent body:
Saffron Walden Museum Society
Administered by:
Uttlesford District Council
London Road, Saffron Walden, Essex, CB11 4ER

Enquiries to: Curator
Other contacts: (1) Documentation Officer, (2) Natural Sciences Officer for (1) most research enquiries; (2) natural history enquiries, historic collection and data.
Access:
Access to staff: By letter, by telephone, by email, in person, visitors by prior appointment
Hours: Mar to Oct; Mon to Sat 1000 to 1700; Sun and Bank Holidays Mar to Oct, 1400 to 1700
Nov to Feb; Mon to Sat, 1000 to 1630; Sun and Bank Holidays but excluding Christmas Eve, Christmas Day, 1400 to 1630
Other restrictions: Access to reserve collections by appointment only, academic references may be required.
Access to building, collections or gallery: No prior appointment required
Other restrictions: Limited staff cover at weekends, weekdays easier.
Access for disabled people: Parking provided, ramped entry, toilet facilities
Other restrictions: Access to 90% of all areas.

General description:
Social history, ethnography, local archaeology, small ancient Egyptian collection, natural history, geology, local history, decorative arts, ceramics, glass, costume, furniture, dolls and toys.
Information services:
Adult lecture series eg archaeology.
Special visitor services: Materials and/or activities for children.
Education services: Group education facilities, resources for Key Stages 1 and 2, 3, 4 and Further or Higher Education.
Services for disabled people: For the visually impaired; for the hearing impaired; displays and/or information at wheelchair height.
Collections:
Gabriel Harvey marginalia
John Player Documents
Large collection of autograph letters
Southey manuscript
Catalogues:
Catalogue for library is in-house only.
Printed publications:
Saffron Crocus: History and Cookery (1997, £1.50)
Saffron Walden, Local History Activity Guide (1997, £2.50)
Walden Castle (rev 1997, £1)
Worlds of Man (abridged catalogue of ethnography collections, £2.50)

2533
SAINSBURY CENTRE FOR VISUAL ARTS

University of East Anglia, Norwich, Norfolk, NR4 7TJ

Tel: 01603 593199
Fax: 01603 259401
Email: scva@uea.ac.uk
Formed: 1978

Organisation type and purpose: Registered charity, museum, art gallery, university department or institute, suitable for ages: all.

Enquiries to: Receptionist
Other contacts: Administrator for hire of space and services.
Access:
Access to staff: By letter, by telephone, by fax, by email, in person
Hours: Tue to Sun, 1100 to 1700; closed Mon and for two weeks at Christmas

General description:
A Norman Foster designed building, housing:- the Sainsbury collection ; the Anderson Collection; and the University of East Anglia Collection; art and architecture.
Collections:
Robert and Lisa Sainsbury Collection spanning 6000 years and many cultures:-
Modern European sculpture and painting including Bacon, Moore, Picasso, Giacometti
Non-Western art and 20th Century studio ceramics
Anderson Collection of Art Nouveau furniture and jewellery 1900-1910 c. 150
UEA Collection of abstract and constructionist art and design 1916 to present c. 150.
Catalogues:
Catalogue for part of the collections is published.
Publications list:
is available in hard copy.

Internet home pages:
http://www.uea.ac.uk/scva

2534
ST AGATHA'S CHURCH MUSEUM

Cascades Way, Portsmouth, Hampshire, PO1 4AB

Tel: 01329 230330
Fax: 01329 230330
Acronym or abbreviation: St Agatha's Trust
Formed: 1994

Organisation type and purpose: Registered charity (charity number 297920), museum, art gallery, historic building, house or site, suitable for ages: 8+.
To maintain historic church Grade II (star).
Other addresses:
St Agatha's Trust
9 East Street, Fareham, Hampshire, PO16 0BW, tel: 01329 230330

Enquiries to: Chairman
Access:
Access to staff: By letter, by telephone, by fax
Access for disabled people: Parking provided

Collections:
Rescued church furnishings
Textiles, vestments

2535
ST ALBANS MUSEUM

See - Museum of St Albans

2536
ST ALBANS ORGAN MUSEUM

320 Camp Road, St Albans, Hertfordshire, AL1 5PB

Tel: 01727 869693
Fax: 01727 851557
Email: info@stalbansorganmuseum.org.uk
Acronym or abbreviation: SAMMS
Full name: St Albans Musical Museum Society
Formed: 1978
Formed from: St Albans Musical Museum Society

Organisation type and purpose: Registered charity (charity number 276072), museum, suitable for ages: 5+.
To advance the general public's appreciation and knowledge of the art, science and technology relating to the manufacture, operation and

performance of mechanical musical instruments, theatre and cinema organs, and similar instruments.

Enquiries to: Chairman
Direct tel: 01727 851557
Direct email: billorganmuseum@lineone.net
Other contacts: Secretary
Access:
Access to staff: By letter, by telephone, by fax, by email, in person, visitors by prior appointment
Hours: Tue, 0700 to 2200; Sun, 1400 to 1630
Access to building, collections or gallery: Prior appointment required
Hours: Sun, 1400 to 1630
Access for disabled people: Parking provided, ramped entry
Other restrictions: No toilets for wheelchair users

General description:
Advice and technical information relating to mechanical organs, mechanical musical instruments and theatre pipe organs available.
Information services:
Live performances on instruments in the collection, Sundays 1400 to 1630. Concerts at other times, for details request a programme.
Organised groups at other times by arrangement.
Special visitor services: Guided tours..
Collections:
Large collection of piano rolls.
Contains the Charles Hart collection of mechanical musical instruments and theatre pipe organs.
A Wurlitzer organ formerly of the Granada Cinema in Edmonton
The Rutt Theatre Organ
A Mills Violano-Virtuoso
Musical boxes dating from the 1880s
The Bursens Café Organ
Catalogues:
Catalogue for part of the collections is only available in-house.
Publications list:
is available in hard copy.
Printed publications:
A large number of publications
Electronic and video products:
CD-ROMs and Tapes for sale direct on Mechanical Organs and Theatre Organs - Continental and UK

Address for ordering publications:
Electronic publications:
SAMMS
PO Box 59, St Albans, AL2 2BF

Internet home pages:
http://www.stalbansorganmuseum.org.uk

2537
ST ANDREWS MUSEUM

Kinburn House, Kinburn, St Andrews, Fife, KY16 9DP

Tel: 01334 412933
Fax: 01334 413214
Email: museums.east@fife.gov.uk

Organisation type and purpose: Local government body, museum, suitable for ages: 5+.
Parent body:
Fife Council Museums East
County Buildings, St Catherine Street, Cupar, Fife, KY15 4TA, tel: 01334 412933

Enquiries to: Museums Access Co-ordinator
Access:
Access to staff: By letter, by telephone, by fax, by email
Hours: Fife Council Museums East: Mon to Fri, 0900 to 1700
Access to building, collections or gallery: No prior appointment required
Hours: Apr to Sep: Daily, 1000 to 1700
Oct to Mar: Daily, 1030 to 1600
Other restrictions: Prior appointment is required to research collections etc.
Access for disabled people: Parking provided, ramped entry, access to all public areas, toilet facilities

General description:
History of St Andrews and surrounding area depicted in permanent displays and regular temporary exhibitions.
Information services:
Special visitor services: Guided tours, materials and/or activities for children.
Education services: Group education facilities, resources for Key Stages 1 and 2, 3, 4 and Further or Higher Education..
Collections:
Local history, social and industrial history, archaeology, photographs, archives

2538
ST ANDREWS PRESERVATION TRUST MUSEUM

12 North Street, St Andrews, Fife, KY16 9QW

Tel: 01334 477629
Formed: 1981

Organisation type and purpose: Registered charity (charity number SCO 11782), museum, historic building, house or site.

Enquiries to: Curator
Access:
Access to staff: By letter, by telephone

General description:
Housed in an early 1930s conservation conversion from four fishermen's dwellings, the building is of considerable interest. It houses collections begun in the early 1930s and reflects life and work in St Andrews - local history; scrapbooks; shops; crafts; tools; furniture; paintings; costume; and early historic photographs.
Collections:
Artefacts and records which reflect life in St Andrews
Photographic Collection
includes some very early photographs and important historic records of St Andrews, 19th and 20th century
Chemist's Shop, c. 1900: almost complete, including medical books, all green jars, wooden drug drawers, spectacles and cameras, 1900-.
Grocer's Shop, furniture and many items from shop, 1900-.
Local Artists, mainly historic, local interest but very good record

Internet home pages:
http://www.standrewspreservationtrust.co.uk

2539
ST ANDREWS UNIVERSITY MUSEUM COLLECTIONS

St Andrews, Fife, KY16 9AL

Tel: 01334 462417
Fax: 01334 462401
Email: iac@st-andrews.ac.uk

Organisation type and purpose: Museum, university department or institute.

Enquiries to: Curator
Access:
Access to staff: By letter, by telephone, by fax, by email, in person, visitors by prior appointment

General description:
Fine and applied art, furniture, silver, coins, medals and communion tokens, ethnography, history of science, scientific instruments, chemistry, psychology, natural history (geology and zoology), anatomy and pathology (restricted access to latter collection).
Catalogues:
Catalogue for all of the collections is only available in-house.

Internet home pages:
http://www.st-andrews.ac.uk/services/muscoll/museum.html
Information on collections, how to contact staff etc.

2540
ST ANTHONY HEAD

Falmouth, Cornwall

Tel: 01872 862945 (Fal Countryside Office)
Fax: 01872 865619
Email: stanthonyhead@nationaltrust.org.uk

Organisation type and purpose: National organisation, registered charity (charity number 205846), historic building, house or site, suitable for ages: all ages.
Parent body:
The National Trust (South West Region)
Regional Office for Cornwall, tel: 01208 74281

Enquiries to: Area Warden
Direct tel: 01972 580509
Access:
Access to staff: By telephone, by fax, by email
Access for disabled people: ramped entry
Other restrictions: Adapted WC adjacent to main car park

General description:
At the southernmost tip of the Roseland peninsula, St Anthony Head overlooks the spectacular entrance to one of the world's largest natural harbours - Carrick Roads - and the Fal estuary. The starting point for a number of excellent coastal and sheltered creekside walks, the Head also bears newly revealed remains of a century of defensive fortifications.
Printed publications:
NT Coast of Cornwall leaflet no. 18/19 includes maps and details of circular walks in area, as well as information about local history, geology and wildlife.

Internet home pages:
http://www.nationaltrust.org.uk/regions/cornwall

2541
ST AUGUSTINE'S ABBEY AND MUSEUM

St Augustine's Abbey, Longport, Canterbury, Kent, CT1 1TF

Tel: 01227 767345
Fax: 01227 767345
Formed: 598

Organisation type and purpose: National organisation, museum, historic building, house or site, suitable for ages: 8+.
Parent body:
English Heritage (South East Region)
Tel: 01483 252000, fax: 01483 252001
Links with:
Canterbury Archaeological Trust
Canterbury Cathedral Archives
English Heritage Archaeological Stores

Enquiries to: Head Custodian
Direct email: dan.dennis@english-heritage.org.uk
Access:
Access to staff: By letter, by telephone, by fax, by email, in person, charges to non-members
Access to building, collections or gallery: No prior appointment required
Hours: Apr to Sep: daily, 1000 to 1800
Oct: daily, 1000 to 1700
Nov to 31 Mar: daily, 1000 to 1600
Other restrictions: Closed 24 to 26 Dec and 1 Jan
Access for disabled people: Parking provided, ramped entry, level entry, access to all public areas, toilet facilities
Other restrictions: Parking is situated 20 metres from entrance or set down at entrance. There are some steps.

continued overleaf

General description:
This great abbey, founded by St Augustine in 597, marks the rebirth of Christianity in southern England, and St Augustine himself is buried here. Along with the Cathedral, the Abbey is part of the Canterbury World Heritage Site - Christian monuments representing the most important change in English life since Roman times.
Information services:
Interactive audio tour.
Special visitor services: Tape recorded guides.
Education services: Group education facilities, resources for Key Stages 1 and 2, 3 and Further or Higher Education.
Services for disabled people: For the visually impaired; for the hearing impaired.
Collections:
250 artefacts, from domestic Saxon to Medieval stone carvings
Printed publications:
Abbey Guide Book

Internet home pages:
http://www.english-heritage.org.uk

2542
ST AUSTELL CHINA CLAY MUSEUM LIMITED
See - Wheal Martyn China Clay Museum

2543
ST BARBE MUSEUM & ART GALLERY
New Street, Lymington, Hampshire, SO41 9BH

Tel: 01590 676969
Fax: 01590 679997
Email: office@stbarbe-museum.org.uk
Formed: 1992
Also known as: Lymington Museum

Organisation type and purpose: Registered charity (charity number 1018779), museum, art gallery, suitable for ages: 5+.
Parent body:
Hampshire County Council Museums Service
Chilcomb House, Chilcomb Lane, Winchester, SO23 8RD, tel: 01962 846304, fax: 01962 869836

Enquiries to: Curator
Access:
Access to staff: By letter, by telephone, by email
Access for disabled people: ramped entry, access to all public areas, toilet facilities

General description:
The local history relating to the south costal strip, Lymington, Pennington, Hordle, Milford-on-Sea, New Milton and Sway. Material relevant to the natural and human history of Lymington and District.
Information services:
Special visitor services: Materials and/or activities for children.
Services for disabled people: Displays and/or information at wheelchair height.
Collections:
Barton Fossils, internationally important Bartonian fossils, 1000 items
Printed books and ephemera from Kings, a local printing firm, 18th-20th century
Wellsworthy collection, photographs, objects and archive publicity material relating to this engineering firm that made piston rings for Spitfires, Chieftain tanks, 1914-1989, 2500 items
Catalogues:
Catalogue for part of the collections is on-line.
Publications list:
is available in hard copy.
Printed publications:
Publications list is available from the Librarian, Hampshire County Council Museums Service Headquarters, Chilcomb House, Winchester, SO23 8RD
Heywood Summer & The New Forest 1904-1940 (exhibition catalogue, 2000)
Lucy Kemp-Welch 1869-1958 (exhibition catalogue, 1999)
The Golden Age of Sail: Charles Brooking & The British Marine Painters of the 18th Century (exhibition catalogue, 2001)

Address for ordering publications:
Printed publications:

Internet home pages:
http://www.hants.gov.uk/museums/collections
Catalogue.
http://www.st.barbe-museum.org.uk
General information, exhibitions.

2544
ST CATHERINE'S QUAY
See - Blackgang Sawmill and St Catherine's Quay

2545
ST DAVID'S VISITOR CENTRE AND SHOP
Captain's House, High Street, St David's, Haverfordwest, Pembrokeshire, SA62 6SD

Tel: 01437 720385
Fax: 01437 720385

Organisation type and purpose: National organisation, registered charity (charity number 205846), historic building, house or site, suitable for ages: 8+.
Parent body:
The National Trust Office for Wales
Tel: 01492 860123

Enquiries to: Manager
Access:
Access to staff: By letter, by telephone, by fax

General description:
The National Trust owns and protects much of the picturesque and historic St David's Head and surrounding coastline. The Visitor Centre is conveniently situated in the centre of the city of St David's opposite The Cross (owned by the NT). Recently refurbished, the Centre offers a complete guide to the National Trust in Pembrokeshire, its properties, beaches and walks.

Internet home pages:
http://www.nationaltrust.org.uk

2546
ST DAY OLD CHURCH
St Day, Redruth, Cornwall

Tel: 01209 215185
Fax: 01209 215185

Organisation type and purpose: Historic building, house or site.
Parent body:
The Trevithick Trust
Tel: 01209 210900

Enquiries to: Curator
Access:
Access to staff: By letter, by telephone, by fax
Access to building, collections or gallery: No prior appointment required
Hours: Easter to Oct, Sun to Sat, 1000 to 1700

General description:
A church allowed to fall into disrepair as the mining fortunes slipped away, a major programme of stabilisation and repair has been undertaken in order to open the ruins to the public.

Internet home pages:
http://www.trevithicktrust.com

2547
ST EDMUNDSBURY CATHEDRAL
Abbey House, Angel Hill, Bury St Edmunds, Suffolk, IP33 1LS

Tel: 01284 754933
Fax: 01284 768655
Email: cathedral@burycathedral.fsnet.co.uk
Formed: 850

Organisation type and purpose: Registered charity (charity number 268540), historic building, house or site.
Anglican cathedral.
Part of the:
Church of England
Diocese of St Edmundsbury and Ipswich, Churchgates House, Cutler Street, Ipswich, IP1 1UQ, tel: 01473 298500, fax: 01473 298501, email/website: dbf@stedmundsbury.anglican.org

Enquiries to: Visitors' Officer
Direct tel: 01284 748726
Direct email: sarahfriswell@burycathedral.fsnet.co.uk
Access:
Access to staff: By letter, by telephone, by fax, by email, in person, Internet web pages
Access to building, collections or gallery: No prior appointment required
Hours: Daily, 0730 to 1800
Access for disabled people: ramped entry, toilet facilities

Information services:
Special visitor services: Guided tours, materials and/or activities for children.
Education services: Group education facilities, resources for Key Stages 1 and 2, 3 and 4..

Internet home pages:
http://www.stedscathedral.co.uk

2548
ST EDMUNDSBURY MUSEUMS
West Stow Anglo-Saxon Centre, West Stow Country Park, Icklingham Road, West Stow, Bury St Edmunds, Suffolk, IP28 6HG

Tel: 01284 728718
Fax: 01284 728277
Email: weststow@stedsbc.gov.uk
Formed: 1999
Formed from: St Edmundsbury Borough Council
Formerly: West Stow Country Park & Anglo-Saxon Village

Organisation type and purpose: Local government body, professional body, museum, historic building, house or site, suitable for ages: 5+.
Independent Advisory body:
West Stow Anglo-Saxon Village Trust

Enquiries to: Manager
Access:
Access to staff: By letter, by telephone, by fax, by email, in person, visitors by prior appointment
Access to building, collections or gallery: No prior appointment required
Hours: Daily, 1000 to 1600
Other restrictions: Except Christmas Holiday.
Access for disabled people: Parking provided, ramped entry, toilet facilities

General description:
Reconstructed Anglo-Saxon village on original site, display of finds from this and other early Anglo-Saxon sites (settlement and cemetery material), replicas of costume, objects and other items, events with costumed Anglo-Saxons - list on request.
Information services:
Catalogue for collections - published as archaeological site reports.
Special events to help interpret the site.
Special visitor services: Materials and/or activities for children.
Education services: Group education facilities, resources for Key Stage 2 and Further or Higher Education.
Services for disabled people: Displays and/or information at wheelchair height.
Collections:
Archaeology of the site - mainly early Anglo-Saxon (420-650 AD)
Objects from settlement, cemetery at West Stow and other local cemeteries
Experimental archaeology - seven experimental building reconstructions

Catalogues:
Catalogue for all of the collections is published.
Publications list:
is available in hard copy.
Printed publications:
West Stow Revisited - 25 Years of Reconstruction
Understanding West Stow - The Story of the Site
Village Guide - An Introduction to West Stow

2549
ST EDMUNDSBURY MUSEUMS

Manor House Museum, Honey Hill, Bury St Edmunds, Suffolk, IP33 1DT

Tel: 01284 757072
Fax: 01284 747231
Email: manor.house@stedsbc.gov.uk
Full name: The Manor House Museum
Formed: Jan 1993

Organisation type and purpose: Local government body, museum.
Parent body:
St Edmundsbury Borough Council

Enquiries to: Manager
Direct tel: 01284 757074
Other contacts: (1) Assistant Manager (2) Keeper of Costume (3) Collections Manager for (1)venue hire, weddings, guided tours, groups.
Access:
Access to staff: By letter, by telephone, by fax, by email, in person, visitors by prior appointment
Access to building, collections or gallery: Prior appointment required
Hours: Wed to Sun, 1100 to 1600
Access for disabled people: Parking provided, ramped entry, access to all public areas, toilet facilities

General description:
The collections feature: horology; timekeeping in Britain, Europe and America from early origins to the present day: fine and decorative art; artistic tastes and achievements of the local people from early origins to present day: archaeology; local life from early origins to historic times: local history; local life and industry from historic times to recent times; natural history; geological origins and natural environment of the area; textiles, costumes.
Information services:
Helpline available, tel no: 01284 757072.
Special visitor services: Guided tours, materials and/or activities for children.
Education services: Group education facilities, resources for Key Stages 1 and 2, 3, 4 and Further or Higher Education.
Services for disabled people: For the visually impaired; displays and/or information at wheelchair height.
Collections:
English Watches, 17th-20th century; South German (Augburg) Clocks, 16th-17th century; American Clocks, 19th-20th century
Irene Barnes Collection of Costume 1920-1940
Archaeology, West Stow Anglo-Saxon material
Catalogues:
Catalogue for library is in-house only. Catalogue for all of the collections is only available in-house.

Internet home pages:
http://www.stedmundsbury.gov.uk/manorhse.htm

2550
ST GEORGE'S GUILDHALL

27-29 King Street, King's Lynn, Norfolk, PE30 1HA

Tel: 01553 765565
Fax: 01553 762141

Organisation type and purpose: National organisation, registered charity (charity number 205846), art gallery, historic building, house or site, suitable for ages: all ages.
Parent body:
National Trust (East of England Region)
East Anglia Regional Office, tel: 0870 609 5388

Enquiries to: Manager
Other contacts: Education Officer: 01553 779095
Access:
Access to staff: By letter, by telephone, by fax

General description:
The largest surviving English medieval guildhall and now converted into an arts centre, but with many interesting surviving features.

Internet home pages:
http://www.nationaltrust.org.uk

2551
ST GEORGE'S HALL

William Brown Street, Liverpool, L1 1JJ

Tel: 0151 707 2391
Fax: 0151 707 2252
Email: steve.neill@liverpool.gov.uk

Organisation type and purpose: Local government body, historic building, house or site, suitable for ages: 8+.
Corporate and civic events, conference facilities, educational activities, exhibitions, performances.
Parent body:
Liverpool City Council
Affiliated to:
St George's Hall Charitable Trust
at the same address
Supported by:
Friends of St George's Hall
at the same address

Enquiries to: Manager
Other contacts: Administration Officer for bookings.
Access:
Access to staff: By letter, by telephone, by fax, by email, visitors by prior appointment
Other restrictions: No access if an event is on in main hall.
Access to building, collections or gallery: Prior appointment required
Access for disabled people: Parking provided, ramped entry, toilet facilities

General description:
Cultural heritage/performing arts venue. Guided tour for visitors of this neo-classical building, designed by Harvey Lonsdale Elmes (1814-47) and built in 1854.
A Father Willis Organ built between 1851 and 1855, the 3rd largest in the UK with 7737 pipes.
Information services:
Special visitor services: Guided tours.
Services for disabled people: For the hearing impaired.
Publications list:
is available in hard copy.
Printed publications:
Guide Book (£2, direct or Libraries)
Events Leaflet (free, direct or Libraries)

Internet home pages:
http://www.stgeorgeshall.co.uk

2552
ST HELENS MUSEUM AND ART GALLERY

See - World of Glass Limited

2553
ST IVES MUSEUM

Wheal Dream, St Ives, Cornwall, TR26 1PR

Tel: 01736 796005
Formed: 1951

Organisation type and purpose: Museum, suitable for ages: all ages.
Independently administered.

Enquiries to: Honorary Secretary
Access:
Access to staff: By letter only
Other restrictions: By letter only enclosing sae.
Access to building, collections or gallery: Prior appointment required
Hours: Mon before Easter to end Oct (autumn half-term), Mon to Fri 1000 to 1700, Sat 1000 to 1600
Other restrictions: Last admission 30 mins before closing.
Closed Good Friday.

General description:
Art, blacksmithing, boat-building, Cornish kitchen, farming, fire brigade, fishing, flags, geology, Hain Steamship Company, lifeboat, lighthouses, mining, models, photographs, police, railway, shipwrecks, toys, Victorian clothes, wartime memorabilia and much more.

2554
ST IVES SOCIETY OF ARTISTS

Norway Square, St Ives, Cornwall, TR26 1NA

Tel: 01736 795582
Email: gallery@stivessocietyofartists.com
Formed: 1927

Organisation type and purpose: Independently owned, art gallery, historic building, house or site, suitable for ages: 16+.
To promote and present figurative work of the highest standard.

Enquiries to: Curator
Access:
Access to staff: By letter, by telephone, by email, in person, Internet web pages

General description:
The society has two galleries the Norway Gallery and Mariners Gallery situated in the crypt of the former Mariners Church. There is a programme of temporary exhibitions of contemprary artists.

Internet home pages:
http://www.stivessocietyofartists.com

2555
ST JOHN AMBULANCE

See - Museum and Library of Order of St John

2556
ST JOHN'S JERUSALEM

Sutton-at-Hone, Dartford, Kent, DA4 9HQ

Tel: 01732 453401(Regional Office)

Organisation type and purpose: National organisation, registered charity (charity number 205846), historic building, house or site, suitable for ages: 5+.
Parent body:
National Trust (South and South East Region)
South East Regional Office, tel: 01372 453401

Enquiries to: Manager
Access:
Access to staff: By letter, by telephone
Other restrictions: All enquiries should be directed to Regional Office.
Access to building, collections or gallery: No prior appointment required
Hours: Apr to end of Oct, Wed, 1400 to 1800
Other restrictions: The property is occupied as a private residence and is maintained and managed by a tenant on the Trust's behalf. Only the former chapel and garden are open

General description:
A large garden, moated by the River Darent. The chapel was once the east end of a Knights Hospitaller Commandery church built in the 13th century, of which the remainder was converted into a private residence. Access to the chapel only. The tranquil garden contains some magnificent trees and herbaceous borders.

Internet home pages:
http://www.nationaltrust.org.uk

2557
ST JUST MINING SERVICES MUSEUM

See - Geevor Tin Mine Heritage Centre

2558
ST MARGARET'S CAVE

Chalmers Street, Dunfermline, Fife

Tel: 01383 313838
Fax: 01383 313837
Email: lesley.botten@fife.gov.uk

Organisation type and purpose: Local government body, historic building, house or site, suitable for ages: 5+.
Parent body:
Fife Council
Associated with:
Fife Council Museums West
Dunfermline Museum, Viewfield, Dunfermline, KY12 7HY

Enquiries to: Museums Co-ordinator
Access:
Access to staff: By letter, by telephone, by fax, by email
Other restrictions: Access via Dunfermline Museum only as there is no postal address.
Access to building, collections or gallery: No prior appointment required
Hours: Daily Good Friday to end of Sep, 1100 to 1600

General description:
Historic underground cave where St Margaret (Margaret Queen of Scotland) was said to have come for personal prayer.

2559
ST MAWES CASTLE

St Mawes, Truro, Cornwall, TR2 5AA

Tel: 01326 270526

Organisation type and purpose: National organisation, advisory body, historic building, house or site.
Parent body:
English Heritage (South West Region)
Tel: 0117 975 0700, fax: 0117 975 0701

Enquiries to: Manager
Access:
Access to staff: By letter, by telephone
Access to building, collections or gallery: No prior appointment required
Hours: 29 Mar to 30 Sep: daily, 1000 to 1800,1 to 31 Oct; daily 1000 to 1700
1 Nov to 31 Mar; Wed to Sun, 1000 to 1300, 1400 to 1600
Other restrictions: Opening times are subject to change, for up-to-date information contact English Heritage by phone or visit the website.

General description:
St Mawes Castle is the most perfectly preserved of Henry VIII's coastal fortresses. It was built to counter the invasion threat from Europe, working in partnership with its twin castle, Pendennis, across the other side of the Fal Estuary. It quickly fell to landward attack from Parliamentarian forces in 1646 and was not properly refortified until the late 19th and 20th century.
Information services:
Guided tours on Wednesdays in summer.
Special visitor services: Guided tours, tape recorded guides..

Internet home pages:
http://www.english-heritage.org.uk

2560
ST MICHAEL'S MOUNT

Marazion, Penzance, Cornwall, TR17 0EF

Tel: 01736 710507/710233
Fax: 01736 711544
Email: godolphin@manor-office.co.uk
Formed: 1954

Organisation type and purpose: National organisation, registered charity (charity number 205846), historic building, house or site, suitable for ages: 8+.
Parent body:
The National Trust (South West Region)
Cornwall Regional Office, Lanhydrock, Bodmin, Cornwall, PL30 4DE, tel: 01208 74281, fax: 01208 77887
Other addresses:
Manor Office
Marazion, Cornwall, tel: 01736 711544, email/website: godolphin@manor-office.co.uk

Enquiries to: Managing Director
Direct tel: 01736 710507 (office); 01736 710265 (island telephone)
Access:
Access to staff: By letter, by telephone, by fax, by email, visitors by prior appointment
Hours: Manor Office Marazion: Mon to Fri, 0900 to 1700
Office on Island: Mon to Fri, 0930 to 1645
Access to building, collections or gallery: No prior appointment required
Hours: End Mar to end Oct, Mon to Fri, 1030 to 1730
Other restrictions: Subject to weather for boating; causeway opening times given by telephone. Sensible shoes advisable.
Last admission 1645 on the island.
Access for disabled people: toilet facilities
Other restrictions: Access over uneven causeway or by ferry. Climb to Castle steep and uneven. Many surfaces cobbled or unsuitable for wheelchairs. Can be driven to restaurant door. Gardens steeply terraced. Level entry in village.

General description:
Originally the site of a Benedictine priory, the dramatic castle perched on the top of a rocky island dates from the 12th century. It was converted to a private house in the 17th century and contains early rooms, an armoury, a rococo Gothic drawing room and a 14th century church.
Information services:
Village: restaurant, café, introductory video in cinema, two shops.
Special visitor services: Guided tours, materials and/or activities for children.
Education services: Group education facilities.
Services for disabled people: For the visually impaired.
Collections:
18th to 20th century paintings
18th century furniture
Weapons in Armoury
Maps
Silver Collection
Snuff Boxes
18th century costumes
15th century alabasters
Catalogues:
Catalogue for library is in-house only.
Printed publications:
Illustrated History and Guide
Foreign Language Guides
Children's Quiz
Electronic and video products:
Cinema: 10 minute film

Address for ordering publications:
Printed publications:
Manager, Manor Office
Marazion, Cornwall

Internet home pages:
http://www.nationaltrust.org.uk/regions/cornwall
http://www.stmichaelsmount.co.uk

2561
ST MUNGO MUSEUM OF RELIGIOUS LIFE AND ART

2 Castle Street, Glasgow, G4 0RH

Tel: 0141 553 2557
Fax: 0141 552 4744
Formed: 1993

Organisation type and purpose: Local government body, museum, art gallery, suitable for ages: all ages.
Aims to promote mutual understanding and respect between people of different faiths, and of none.
Parent body:
Glasgow Museums
Tel: 0141 287 2699

Enquiries to: Manager
Access:
Access to staff: By letter, by telephone, by fax, in person
Access to building, collections or gallery: No prior appointment required
Hours: Mon to Thu and Sat, 1000 to 1700; Fri and Sun, 1100 to 1700
Other restrictions: Closed 25, 26 Dec and 1, 2 Jan
Access for disabled people: access to all public areas, toilet facilities
Other restrictions: Easy access for wheelchair users, lift to all floors, induction loop in AVA area

General description:
The museum explores the importance of religion in people's lives across the world and across time. It has a number of themed galleries, including the Gallery of Religious Art, Gallery of Religious Life, associated with the world's six main religions, Scottish Gallery and Zen Garden.
Information services:
Audio and video presentations
Exhibitions and events programme
Education room with handling boxes and activity sheets available for schools and community groups.
Function suite for private and corporate hire.
Special visitor services: Materials and/or activities for children.
Education services: Group education facilities..
Printed publications:
Wide selection of publications available from the bookshop

Internet home pages:
http://www.glasgow.gov.uk

2562
ST PETER'S BUNKER MUSEUM

Closed, date of change, 31 December 1996

2563
ST RONAN'S WELL INTERPRETATION CENTRE

Wells Brae, High Street, Innerleithen, Peeblesshire, EH44 6JE

Tel: 01721 724820
Fax: 01721 724424
Email: rhannay@scotborders.gov.uk
Formed: 1990

Organisation type and purpose: Local government body, historic building, house or site, suitable for ages: 5+.
Parent body:
Scottish Borders Council Museum and Gallery Service
Tel: 01750 20096
Other addresses:
Museums Section
North Lanarkshire Council
Buchanan Business Park, Stepps, Glasgow, G33 6HR, tel: 0141 304 1975, fax: 0141 304 1902
Tweedale Museum
High Street, Peebles, tel: 01721 724820, fax: 01721 724424

Enquiries to: Curator
Access:
Access to staff: By letter, by telephone, by fax, by email, in person, visitors by prior appointment
Access to building, collections or gallery: No prior appointment required
Hours: Easter to Oct: daily, 1400 to 1700
Access for disabled people: Parking provided, level entry, toilet facilities

General description:
The exhibition is housed in the original Spa overlooking Innerleithen. The exhibition tells the story of the Wells and their connection with the Cleikum Ceremony, St Ronan's Border Games, Walter Scott, George Hope Tait and James Hogg.
Information services:
Special visitor services: Guided tours..
Collections:
Collections: photographs, documents and artefacts linked to:
The Cleikum Ceremony
St Ronan's Border Games
Walter Scott
James Hogg
George Hope Tait

Internet home pages:
http://www.scotborders.gov.uk

2564
SALFORD ART GALLERY & MUSEUM

Peel Park Avenue, Salford, Greater Manchester, M5 4WU

Tel: 0161 736 2649
Fax: 0161 745 9490
Email: salford.museum@salford.gov.uk
Formed: 1850

Organisation type and purpose: Local government body, museum, art gallery, suitable for ages: all ages.
Parent body:
Salford City Council
Salford Museums Heritage Service

Enquiries to: Heritage Services Manager
Direct email: nicola.power@salford.gov.uk
Access:
Access to staff: By letter, by telephone, by fax, visitors by prior appointment
Hours: Mon to Fri, 0900 to 1645
Access to building, collections or gallery: No prior appointment required
Hours: Mon to Fri, 0900 to 1645; Sat, Sun, 1300 to 1700
Access for disabled people: Parking provided, ramped entry, access to all public areas, toilet facilities
Other restrictions: Information in large print, braille, some audio guides.

General description:
Local and social history, Victorian period street, permanent Victorian art gallery, 20th century art collection, decorative arts collection. Ordsall Hall, a Tudor period building with furnishings and collections.
Information services:
Special visitor services: Tape recorded guides, materials and/or activities for children.
Education services: Group education facilities, resources for Key Stages 1 and 2, 3 and 4.
Services for disabled people: For the visually impaired; displays and/or information at wheelchair height.
Collections:
Royal Lancastrian Pottery
Social History Collection (including oral history, objects, photographs, documents etc, database and CD-ROMs available)
Twentieth century Art Collection
Victorian Art Collection
Printed publications:
Various L S Lowry Publications (for purchase)
Various other publications (for purchase)

Internet home pages:
http://www.salfordmuseum.org
General information on service.
http://www.lifetimes.org.uk
Information on social and local history.

2565
SALFORD MUSEUMS HERITAGE SERVICE

Peel Park, Salford, Greater Manchester, M5 4WU

Tel: 0161 736 2649
Fax: 0161 745 9490
Email: salford.museum@salford.gov.uk
Formed: 1850

Organisation type and purpose: Local government body, museum, art gallery, historic building, house or site, suitable for ages: 5+.
Administrative body for the local government museums.
Parent body:
Salford City Council
Museums and historical sources:
Ordsall Hall Museum
55 Ordsall Lane, Salford, Greater Manchester, M5 4RS, tel: 0161 872 0251, fax: 0161 872 4951
Salford Art Gallery & Museum
Peel Park Avenue, Salford, Greater Manchester, M5 4WU, tel: 0161 736 2649, fax: 0161 745 9490, email/website: salford.museum@salford.gov.uk
Salford Local History Library
Peel Park Avenue, Salford, Greater Manchester, M5 4WU, tel: 0161 736 2649
Working Class Movement Library
Jubilee House, 51 The Crescent, Salford, M5 4WX, tel: 0161 736 3601, fax: 0161 737 4115

Enquiries to: Heritage Services Manager
Direct email: nicola.power@salford.gov.uk
Access:
Access to staff: By letter, by telephone, by fax, by email, visitors by prior appointment, Internet web pages
Hours: Mon to Fri, 0900 to 1700
Access to building, collections or gallery: No prior appointment required
Hours: Mon to Fri, 1000 to 1700; Sat, Sun, 1300 to 1700
Access for disabled people: Parking provided, ramped entry, access to all public areas, toilet facilities

General description:
The subjects covered by the museums of the Heritage Service include: local and social history, Victorian period street, period houses (medieval, Tudor, Stuart) at Ordsall Hall, ceramics, fine art and art at Salford Gallery.
Lancashire Mining Museum covers the history of coalmining with special reference to the former Lancashire coalfield, using traditional museum displays, recreations and temporary exhibitions.
Information services:
Bibliography compilation
Special visitor services: Materials and/or activities for children.
Education services: Group education facilities, resources for Key Stages 1 and 2.
Services for disabled people: For the visually impaired; displays and/or information at wheelchair height.
Collections:
Royal Lancastrian Pottery
Social History collection
Twentieth century art collection
Victorian art collection
Salford Local History Library - Collections of photographs, documents and maps chronicling the history of Salford City
Mining art collection. Works in various media by professional and amateur artists, including coalminers. 1750-1994. ca. 150 items
Mine Plan collection. Mineworking plans. 1800-1994. ca. 2000 items
Library Reference Reserve collection. Rare mining books from various European companies, including England. 1548-1850. ca. 200 items
Printed publications:
Guidebooks
L S Lowry (1987)
L S Lowry: His Life and Work (1990)
Various other L S Lowry publications

Internet home pages:
http://www.salfordmuseum.org

See also - Ordsall Hall Museum; Salford Art Gallery & Museum

2566
SALFORD QUAYS HERITAGE OFFICE

Closed, date of change, December 1999

2567
SALISBURY AND SOUTH WILTSHIRE MUSEUM

The King's House, 65 The Close, Salisbury, Wiltshire, SP1 2EN

Tel: 01722 332151
Fax: 01722 325611
Email: museum@salisburymuseum.org.uk
Acronym or abbreviation: Salisbury Museum
Formed: 1860
Formerly: Salisbury, South Wiltshire and Blackmore Museum, date of change, 1968

Organisation type and purpose: Registered charity (charity number 289850), museum.

Enquiries to: Director
Access:
Access to staff: By letter, by telephone, by fax, by email, visitors by prior appointment
Hours: Mon to Fri, 0900 to 1700
Access for disabled people: Parking provided, level entry

General description:
Archaeology, especially of Wessex, local history, ceramics, costume.
Collections:
Clarendon Palace Collection
Old Sarum Collection
Pitt Rivers Wessex Collection
Stonehenge Collection
Publications list:
is available in hard copy.
Printed publications:
Annual Report
A Walk Through the Cathedral Close
Bronze Age Metalwork in Salisbury Museum
Channels to the Past: the Salisbury Drainage Collection
Clarendon: Medieval Royal Palace
Downton Lace: a history of lace making in Salisbury
Father and Son: Engraved Glass by Laurence and Simon Whistler
General Pitt Rivers: Father of Scientific Archaeology
Salisbury Museum Medieval Catalogue parts 1 & 2 & 3
Salisbury Museum Souvenir Guide
The Brixie Jarvis Collection of Wedgwood
The Giant and Hob Nob
The King's House, Salisbury: short history

Internet home pages:
http://www.salisburymuseum.org.uk

2568
SALISBURY CATHEDRAL

33 The Close, Salisbury, Wiltshire, SP1 2EJ

Tel: 01722 555120
Fax: 01722 555116
Email: visitors@salcath.co.uk
Full name: Dean & Chapter Salisbury Cathedral
Formed: 1220

Organisation type and purpose: Registered charity, historic building, house or site, suitable for ages: 8+.
Anglican Cathedral Church. Charity established by Parliamentary Statute.

Enquiries to: Head of Visitor Services
Access:
Access to staff: By letter, by telephone, by fax, by email, Internet web pages

continued overleaf

Access to building, collections or gallery: No prior appointment required
Hours: 1 Sep to 8 June, Sun to Sat, 0715 to 1815,9 June to 31 Aug, Mon to Sat, 0715 to 2015; Sun, 0715 to 1815
Other restrictions: Access to library by prior appointment
Access for disabled people: Parking provided, ramped entry, toilet facilities

General description:
Medieval cathedral architecture, religious services, choral music.
Information services:
Library available for reference (for conditions see Access above)
Special visitor services: Guided tours, materials and/or activities for children.
Education services: Group education facilities, resources for Key Stages 1 and 2.
Services for disabled people: For the visually impaired.
Catalogues:
Catalogue for library is in-house only. Catalogue for all of the collections is only available in-house.

Internet home pages:
http://www.salisburycathedral.org.uk

2569
SALISBURY LIBRARY
See - Wiltshire Education & Libraries

2570
SALT MUSEUM
162 London Road, Northwich, Cheshire, CW9 8AB

Tel: 01606 41331/40394
Fax: 01606 350420
Email: cheshiremuseum@cheshire.gov.uk
Formed: 1981

Organisation type and purpose: Museum.
Formed in 1981 in current building, but there has been a salt museum in Northwich for over 100 years.
Devoted to the history of the salt industry over 2000 years.
Parent body:
Cheshire County Council Museums Service

Enquiries to: Curator
Access:
Access to staff: By letter, by telephone, by email, visitors by prior appointment
Access to building, collections or gallery: No prior appointment required
Hours: Tue to Fri, 1000 to 1700; Sat, Sun, 1400 to 1700
August, Sat, Sun, 1200 to 1700
Closed Christmas Day, Boxing Day and New Years Day
Access for disabled people: Parking provided, ramped entry, toilet facilities
Other restrictions: Induction loop for introductory film

General description:
Archaeology of the salt industry, industrial, social and economic history of the salt industry in Cheshire, geological and chemical background, existing physical remains of the salt industry. Comparative information on the salt industry outside Britain.
Information services:
Education services: Group education facilities, resources for Key Stages 1 and 2, 3, 4 and Further or Higher Education.
Services for disabled people: For the hearing impaired.
Publications list:
is available in hard copy.
Printed publications:
26 information leaflets on the history of salt, its extraction, processing, use and the people (available separately or £8 the set plus p&p)
A Brief History of Cheshire Salt (book, £1.95 plus 50p p&p)
Exploring Marbury Park (£2.50 plus 60p p&p)
Investigating Salt (document pack, £3.50 plus 60p p&p)
Stretton Watermill (£4.75 plus £1.20 p&p)
Worcestershire Salt (£7.50 plus 70p p&p)
Electronic and video products:
Cheshire Born: Songs and tunes of Old Cheshire (£10 plus 70p p&p)

Internet home pages:
http://www.saltmuseum.org.uk

2571
SALTRAM HOUSE
Plympton, Plymouth, Devon, PL7 1UH

Tel: 01752 333500
Fax: 01752 336474
Email: saltram@nationaltrust.org.uk
Formed: 1967

Organisation type and purpose: Registered charity (charity number 205846), museum, art gallery, historic building, house or site, suitable for ages: 5+.
Historic house, garden and park.
Parent body:
The National Trust (South West Region)
Devon Regional Office, tel: 01392 881691

Enquiries to: House Manager
Other contacts: Office Assistant for group bookings.
Access:
Access to staff: By letter, by email
Access to building, collections or gallery: No prior appointment required
Hours: Open Mon to Thu, Sat and Sun
House: end Mar to end Sep, 1200 to 1630; Oct, Mon to Thu, Sat and Sun, 1130 to 1530
Garden: end Mar to end Oct, 1100 to 1700; beg Nov to end Mar, 1100 to 1600
Gallery: end Mar to end Oct, 1100 to 1700
Other restrictions: Closed Fridays. Open Good Friday. Prior appointment required for groups.
Access for disabled people: Parking provided, ramped entry, toilet facilities
Other restrictions: Ground floor largely accessible. No access to Dining Room, Great Kitchen or children's activity room. Lift to first floor for those who can transfer to chair in lift. 3 manual wheelchairs, pre-booking essential. Recommended route map. Grounds largely accessible.

General description:
George II mansion complete with its original contents. Georgian paintings, Adam interiors, extensive library, period furniture, china, paintings, paintings by Reynolds and Angelica Kauffmann, 4 rooms decorated with 18th century Chinese wallpapers. Superb 18th century gardens contain an orangery, the Chapel Art Gallery and several follies, as well as a newly restored border originally designed by Graham Stuart Thomas.
Information services:
Children's guide, quiz/trail. Family activity packs. Hands-on activities.
Special visitor services: Tape recorded guides, materials and/or activities for children.
Education services: Group education facilities, resources for Key Stages 1 and 2 and Further or Higher Education.
Services for disabled people: For the visually impaired; for the hearing impaired.
Collections:
Parker Family Collection - Reynolds Paintings
Printed publications:
Guide Book
House Guide
Garden Trail
Children's Guide to House
Children's Trail of Garden
Events/property leaflets (free of charge)
Electronic and video products:
Tour Guide of House (audio tape)

Internet home pages:
http://www.nationaltrust.org.uk/regions/devon

2572
SAMUEL JOHNSON BIRTHPLACE MUSEUM
Breadmarket Street, Lichfield, Staffordshire, WS13 6LG

Tel: 01543 264972
Fax: 01534 414779
Email: sjmuseum@lichfield.gov.uk
Formed: 1901

Organisation type and purpose: Local government body, museum, suitable for ages: 5+.
Links with:
Friends of the Johnson Birthplace Museum
Johnson Society
Member of:
North Staffordshire Museums Association
Museum Trustees:
Lichfield City Council
The Guildhall, Bone Street, Lichfield, Staffordshire, tel: 01543 250011, fax: 01543 258441

Enquiries to: Curator
Access:
Access to staff: By letter, by telephone, by email, Internet web pages
Hours: Mon to Fri, 0900 to 1700
Access to building, collections or gallery: Prior appointment required
Hours: 1 Apr to 30 Sep: Daily, 1030 to 1630,1 Oct to 31 Mar: Daily, 1200 to 1630

General description:
Life and work of Samuel Johnson, literary history of the 18th century, local history of Lichfield.
Information services:
Library available for reference (for conditions see Access above)
Special visitor services: Guided tours, materials and/or activities for children.
Education services: Resources for Further or Higher Education.
Services for disabled people: For the visually impaired.
Collections:
Johnsoniana; books, MSS, personal items
Catalogues:
Catalogue for part of the collections is only available in-house.
Printed publications:
Guide book to the house

Internet home pages:
http://www.lichfield.gov.uk/sjmuseum
Opening times, house description, brief biography of Johnson.

2573
SANDAL CASTLE
Manygates Lane, Sandal, Wakefield, West Yorkshire, WF2

Tel: 01924 295352

Organisation type and purpose: Historic building, house or site, suitable for ages: 5+.

Enquiries to: Heritage Officer
Access:
Access to staff: By letter

General description:
The ruins of a mediaeval motte-and-bailey castle which was demolished after the English Civil War, extensively excavated and conserved 1964-1973. Castle history, Wars of the Roses, Civil War.
Collections:
Finds from Castle excavation

2574
SANDFORD ORCAS MANOR HOUSE
The Manor House, Sandford Orcas, Sherborne, Dorset, DT9 4SB

Tel: 01963 220206

Organisation type and purpose: Historic building, house or site, suitable for ages: 8+.

Enquiries to: Administrator
Access:
Access to staff: By letter only
Access for disabled people: Parking provided

General description:
A Tudor period stone-built manor house with gatehouse built in the 1550s; Newel staircases; Jacobean panelling; and with period furnishings, particularly Jacobean, Queen Anne and Chippendale furniture. Also contains 17th century Dutch and 18th century English pictures; Elizabethan and Georgian needlework; and a large collection of 14th-17th century English, German, Netherlandish and Swiss stained glass.
Information services:
Special visitor services: Guided tours..
Catalogues:
Catalogue for part of the collections is only available in-house.
Publications list:
is available in hard copy.

2575
SANDHAM MEMORIAL CHAPEL

Harts Lane, Burghclere, Newbury, Hampshire, RG20 9JT

Tel: 01635 278394 (Custodian)
Fax: 01635 278394
Email: sandham@nationaltrust.org.uk

Organisation type and purpose: Registered charity (charity number 205846), art gallery, suitable for ages: 8+.
Parent body:
The National Trust (South and South East Region)
Thames and Solent Regional Office, tel: 01494 528051

Enquiries to: Manager
Other contacts: Custodian
Access:
Access to staff: By letter, by telephone, by fax, by email

General description:
This red-brick chapel was built in the 1920s for the artist Stanley Spencer to fill with murals inspired by his experiences in World War I. Influenced by Giotto's Arena Chapel in Padua, Spencer took five years to complete what is arguably his finest achievement. The chapel is set amidst lawns and orchards with views across Watership Down.
Information services:
Braille guide. Large-print guide.
Suitable for school groups. Children's quiz/trail.
Special visitor services: Materials and/or activities for children.
Education services: Group education facilities.
Services for disabled people: For the visually impaired.
Collections:
A cycle of 19 paintings by Sir Stanley Spencer based on his WWI experiences
Printed publications:
Stanley Spencer at Burghclere (guide book, £2.50)

Internet home pages:
http://www.nationaltrust.org.uk
National Trust website, information on opening times etc.

2576
SANDHAVEN MEAL MILL

Sandhaven, Fraserburgh, Aberdeenshire, AB43 4EP

Tel: 01771 622906
Fax: 01771 622884
Formed: 1990

Organisation type and purpose: Local government body, museum, historic building, house or site, suitable for ages: 5+.

Parent body:
Aberdeenshire Heritage
Tel: 01771 622906, fax: 01771 622884

Enquiries to: Curator
Access:
Access to staff: By letter, by telephone, by fax
Access to building, collections or gallery: No prior appointment required
Other restrictions: May to Sep, Sat, Sun, 1400 to 1630
Access for disabled people: Parking provided
Other restrictions: Disabled access only to exhibition area

General description:
19th century meal mill and building, working demonstration model.
Collections:
Equipment necessary for, and associated with, the milling of oatmeal
Catalogues:
Catalogue for part of the collections is only available in-house.

2577
SANDTOFT TRANSPORT CENTRE STC

See - Trolleybus Museum at Sandtoft

2578
SANDWELL MUSEUM SERVICE

See - Haden Hill House Museum; Oak House Museum; Wednesbury Museum & Art Gallery

2579
SANDWICH WHITE MILL

on the A257, west of, Sandwich, Kent

Tel: 01304 612076
Email: whitemill_sandwich@hotmail.com

Organisation type and purpose: Museum, historic building, house or site.
Member of:
Kent Windmills

General description:
White corn mill built 1760s. Retains original wooden machinery, outbuildings and miller's cottage. Museum of domestic craft and farming items, photographs of Victorian life.

Internet home pages:
http://www.whitemill-sandwich.co.uk
http://www.kent-museums.org.uk/whitemil/home.html

2580
SANQUHAR TOLBOOTH MUSEUM

High Street, Sanquhar, Dumfries & Galloway, DG4 6BN

Tel: 01659 50186
Fax: 01387 265081
Formed: 1990

Organisation type and purpose: National organisation, registered charity, historic building, house or site.
Parent body:
Dumfries & Galloway Museum Service
Tel: 01387 253374

Enquiries to: Manager
Direct fax: elainek@dumgal.gov.uk
Access:
Access to staff: By letter, by telephone
Hours: Mon closed; Tue to Sat, 1000 to 1300 and 1400 to 1700; Sun, 1400 to 1700

General description:
Social and economic history of Upper Nithsdale, Sanquhar and Kirkconnel from Roman times, mining, knitting, costumes and local literature.

Internet home pages:
http://www.dumgal.gov.uk/museums

2581
SAREHOLE MILL MUSEUM

Cole Bank Road, Hall Green, Birmingham, B13 0BD

Tel: 0121 777 6612
Formed: 1960's

Organisation type and purpose: Local government body, registered charity, historic building, house or site, suitable for ages: 5+. Educational, leisure venue.

Enquiries to: Curatorial Manager
Direct tel: 0121 464 0364
Direct fax: 0121 464 0400
Access:
Access to staff: By letter, by telephone
Hours: Tue to Fri, 0900 to 1700
Access to building, collections or gallery: Prior appointment required
Hours: Apr to Oct: Tue to Fri, 1300 to 1600; Sat, Sun, 1200 to 1600

General description:
Birmingham's last surviving watermill. Features 18th century buildings, restored in the 1960s, containing displays about milling; waterpower; farming; and the site itself. Corn-grinding on Sundays in August and Bank Holiday Mondays. The mill was home to Matthew Boulton from 1756-1761, and was an inspiration to J R R Tolkein, author of 'The Hobbit' and 'The Lord of the Rings'.
Information services:
Helpline available, tel no: Schools Liaison: 0121 303 3890.
Special visitor services: Guided tours, materials and/or activities for children.
Education services: Group education facilities, resources for Key Stages 1 and 2..
Collections:
Agricultural tools and machinery
Catalogues:
Catalogue for all of the collections is only available in-house.
Printed publications:
Guide

Internet home pages:
http://www.bmag.org.uk
General introduction to site.

2582
SARRE WINDMILL

off the A253, Sarre, Kent

Tel: 01843 847573

Organisation type and purpose: Museum, historic building, house or site.
Privately owned.
Member of:
Kent Windmills

Enquiries to: Owner

General description:
Built in 1820, the mill is fully restored and grinds corn. There is a gas engine in the basement. Museum of animals and birds.
Catalogues:
Catalogue for all of the collections is only available in-house.

2583
SASSOON GALLERY

See - Folkestone Museum

2584
SATROSPHERE

The Tramsheds, 179 Constitution Street, Aberdeen, AB24 5TU

Tel: 01224 640340
Fax: 01224 622211
Email: info@satrosphere.net
Formed: 1990

Organisation type and purpose: Registered charity (charity number SCO 14922), museum,

continued overleaf

suitable for ages: 5+.
Hands-on science centre.
Access:
Access to staff: By telephone, by email
Access for disabled people: Parking provided, level entry, access to all public areas, toilet facilities

General description:
Hands-on science/technology exhibits explore heat, light and sound.
Information services:
Education services: Resources for Key Stages 1 and 2 and 3.
Services for disabled people: Displays and/or information at wheelchair height.

Internet home pages:
http://www.satrosphere.net
General information on Satrosphere and details of special events.

2585
SAVINGS BANKS MUSEUM

Ruthwell, Dumfries, DG1 4NN

Tel: 01387 870640
Email: savingsbanksmuseum@btinternet.com
Formed: 1974
Formed from: Duncan Savings Bank Museum, date of change, c.1990

Organisation type and purpose: Independently owned, museum, suitable for ages: 12+.
Parent body:
Lloyds TSB Scotland
Henry Duncan House, PO Box 177, 120 George Street, Edinburgh, EH2 4TS, tel: 0131 225 4555

Enquiries to: Curator
Access:
Access to staff: By letter, by telephone, by email, in person, Internet web pages
Access for disabled people: Parking provided, level entry

General description:
History of savings banks; collection relating to the remarkable life of the Reverend Henry Duncan DD (1774-1846), his founding in 1810 of Savings Banks and their expansion worldwide; his work as antiquarian, geologist, author, artist and publisher.
Also information on medieval Ruthwell Cross, social and family records.
Information services:
Special visitor services: Guided tours..
Collections:
Home safes, savings bank memorabilia, notes and coins
19th century manuscripts on savings banks, social and economic conditions etc
Contains original papers, ledgers and letters relating to the founding of Savings Banks - 1810-1875, similar items relating to the Friendly Society from 1795-1890
Books and other information on the medieval Ruthwell Cross, dated 680
Fossil footprints first identified by Dr Duncan
Catalogues:
Catalogue for library is in-house only. Catalogue for all of the collections is only available in-house.
Printed publications:
Leaflets (50p)

Internet home pages:
http://www.lloydstsb.com/savingsbanksmuseum
History of Dr Duncan and his savings bank.

2586
SAXTEAD GREEN POST MILL

Framlingham, Woodbridge, Suffolk

Tel: 01728 685789

Organisation type and purpose: Museum, historic building, house or site, suitable for ages: 5+.
Parent body:
English Heritage (East of England Region)
Brooklands, 24 Brooklands Avenue, Cambridge, CB2 2BU, tel: 01223 582700, fax: 01223 582701
Access:
Access to staff: By letter, by telephone
Access to building, collections or gallery: No prior appointment required
Hours: Apr to Sep: Mon to Sat, 1000 to 1300 and 1300 to 1800
Oct: Mon to Sat, 1000 to 1300 and 1400 to 1700
Other restrictions: Opening times are subject to change, for up-to-date information contact English Heritage by phone or visit the website.

General description:
18th century post mill with roundhouse. This corn mill, the whole body of which revolves on its base, produced flour and was one of many built in Suffolk from the late 13th century. Although it ceased production in 1947, it is still in working order and you can climb the wooden stairs to the various floors, which are full of fascinating mill machinery.
Information services:
Special visitor services: Tape recorded guides..

Internet home pages:
http://www.english-heritage.org.uk

2587
SCAPA FLOW VISITOR CENTRE & MUSEUM

See - Orkney Museum

2588
SCAPLEN'S COURT

Sarum Street, Poole, Dorset, BH15 1JW

Tel: 01202 262600
Fax: 01202 262622
Email: museums@poole.gov.uk
Formed: 1974

Organisation type and purpose: Local government body, museum, suitable for ages: all ages.
Parent body:
Poole Museums Service
Tel: 01202 262600
Other addresses:
Waterfront Museum
4 High Street, Poole, BH15 1BW, tel: 01202 262600

Enquiries to: Manager
Access:
Access to staff: By letter, by telephone, by fax, by email, in person
Access to building, collections or gallery: Prior appointment required
Hours: The building is used from September to July as an educational resource for local schools. It is only open to the public in August, and at other times as advertised via the local press.

General description:
Local history.
Information services:
Special visitor services: Guided tours, materials and/or activities for children.
Education services: Group education facilities, resources for Key Stages 1 and 2, 3, 4 and Further or Higher Education..

2589
SCARBOROUGH CASTLE

Castle Road, Scarborough, North Yorkshire

Tel: 01723 372451

Parent body:
English Heritage (Yorkshire Region)
Tel: 01904 601901

Enquiries to: Manager
Access:
Access to staff: By letter, by telephone
Access to building, collections or gallery: No prior appointment required
Hours: 29 Mar to 30 Sep: daily, 1000 to 1800 (mid Jul to 31 Aug: daily, 0930 to 1800)
1 to 31 Oct: daily, 1000 to 1700,1 Nov to 31 Mar: daily, 1000 to 1600
Other restrictions: Closed 24 to 26 Dec and 1 Jan.
Opening times are subject to change, for up-to-date information contact English Heritage by phone or visit the website.
Access for disabled people: Parking provided, toilet facilities

General description:
Dominating the skyline high on the clifftops, this dramatic 12th century castle commands spectacular views of the rugged Yorkshire coastline and seaside town of Scarborough. For more than 2500 years, the defensive prominence of the castle's dramatic headland location has attracted attention. The castle features a great rectangular stone keep, the remains of which still stand over three storeys high. It witnessed two prolonged sieges in the Civil War, and was used as a prison and barracks from the 1650s. Today, the Castle's defensive superiority is illustrated by new viewing platforms, which offer a king's-eye panorama.
Information services:
Special visitor services: Tape recorded guides..

Internet home pages:
http://www.english-heritage.org.uk

2590
SCARBOROUGH ART GALLERY

The Crescent, Scarborough, North Yorkshire, YO11 2PW

Tel: 01723 374753

Parent body:
Scarborough Museums & Gallery
Department of Tourism and Leisure Service, tel: 01723 232323
Access:
Access to staff: By letter, by telephone

General description:
Housed in an Italianate villa built in the 1840s, is a collection of seascapes, and views of Scarboprough, including works by Grimshaw, H B Carter, Frank Mason and Ernest Dade. There are also works by Leighton, Ivon Hitchens, Matthew Smith, E Bawden and Eric Ravilious. Scarborough's Family Album is a hands-on display for families, telling the story of Scarborough from fishing village to resort through painters and paintings. It includes costumes and masks to try on, a giant jigsaw and feely painting to make.

2591
SCARBOROUGH MUSEUMS & GALLERY

Department of Tourism and Leisure Services, Londesborough Lodge, The Crescent, Scarborough, North Yorkshire, YO11 2PW

Tel: 01723 232323
Fax: 01723 376941
Formed: 1828

Organisation type and purpose: Local government body, museum, art gallery, suitable for ages: All ages.
Administrative offices responsible for the Scarborough museums and art gallery.
To collect, care for and interpret objects and specimens relevant to the Borough of Scarborough.
Associated body:
Friends of Scarborough Art Gallery
Other addresses:
Rotunda Museum
Vernon Road, Scarborough, North Yorkshire, YO11 2NN, tel: 01723 374839

Scarborough Art Gallery
The Crescent, Scarborough, North Yorkshire, YO11 2PW, tel: 01723 374753
Wood End Museum
The Crescent, Scarborough, North Yorkshire, YO11 2PW, tel: 01723 367326

Enquiries to: Museums & Gallery Officer
Access:
Access to staff: By letter, by telephone, by fax, visitors by prior appointment
Hours: Mon to Fri, 0900 to 1700
Other restrictions: Appointment necessary to see curators or consult collections.
Access to building, collections or gallery: No access other than to staff
Hours: Summer (Spring Bank Holiday to mid-Oct): Tue to Sun, 1000 to 1700
Winter (mid-Oct to Spring Bank Holiday): public opening hours reduced, pelase telephone first

General description:
Collections pertaining to the Borough of Scarborough and adjacent areas, notably social history, archaeology, natural history, geology, fine art, plus associated archival material.
Collections:
Historic and contemporary art (Scarborough Art Gallery)
Collection of first editions of Edith, Osbert and Sacheverell Sitwell and their father Sir George Sitwell
Natural history (Wood End Museum)
Tunny (tuna) Fishing Archive (Wood End Museum)
Yorkshire jurassic rocks and fossils (The Rotunda Museum)
Catalogues:
Catalogue for part of the collections is only available in-house.
Printed publications:
General information, exhibitions programmes etc

Internet home pages:
http://www.scarborough.gov.uk

See also - Rotunda Museum; Scarborough Art Gallery; Wood End Museum of Natural History

2592
SCHOOL OF ART GALLERY AND MUSEUM
University of Wales, Buarth Mawr, Aberystwyth, Ceredigion, SY23 1NG

Tel: 01970 622460
Fax: 01970 622461
Email: neh@aber.ac.uk
Acronym or abbreviation: UWA
Formed: 1876
Formerly: Catherine Lewis Gallery and Print Room, date of change, 1997

Organisation type and purpose: Museum, art gallery, university department or institute, suitable for ages: 12+.
Parent body:
University of Wales
King Street, Aberystwyth, Ceredigion, SY23 2AX
Branch:
School of Art Gallery and Museum: Ceramics Gallery
Aberystwyth Arts Centre, Penglais, Aberystwyth, SY23 3DE, tel: 01970 622460
Other addresses:
Ceramic Gallery
Aberystwyth Arts Centre, University of Wales, Penglais, Aberystwyth, tel: 01970 622460, fax: 01970 622461, email/website: neh@aber.ac.uk

Enquiries to: Senior Lecturer & Keeper of Art
Direct email: rtm@aber.ac.uk
Other contacts: (1) Assistant Curator, (2) Curator of Ceramics for (1) collections & exhibitions, (2) ceramics collection only.
Access:
Access to staff: By letter, by telephone, by email, visitors by prior appointment, Internet web pages
Hours: Mon to Fri, 1000 to 1730
Access to building, collections or gallery: No prior appointment required
Hours: Mon to Fri, 1000 to 1730
Other restrictions: Closed weekends, Easter and Christmas.
Access for disabled people: Parking provided, level entry

General description:
Specialist information in those areas covered by the collection including: fine and decorative art; European prints from 15th century to present; etching Revival; Art in Wales since 1945 and contemporary printmaking etc; 20th century Studio Ceramics.
Collections:
Collections include:
18th & 19th century Welsh and English slipware
5000 wood engravings for periodicals of the 1860s
Art in Wales since 1945
Contemporary British, European, American and Japanese studio pottery
Contemporary Welsh photography
European prints from 15th century to contemporary
George Powell of Nanteos Collection of pictures, bronzes and works on paper by Turner, Burne-Jones, Rossetti, Poynter, Rebecca and Simeon Solomon
Post-war Italian photography
Catalogues:
Catalogue for all of the collections is on-line.
Publications list:
is available in hard copy and online.
Printed publications:
Exhibition catalogues and a small number of postcards/greetings cards

Address for ordering publications:
Printed publications:
School of Art Gallery and Museum
at same address, tel: 01970 622460, fax: 01970 622461, email: bjm@aber.ac.uk

Internet home pages:
http://www.aber.ac.uk/museum
School of Art: the department, galleries and collections. Exhibition programme. Introduction to the Collection.
http://www.aber.ac.uk/art
School of Art: the department, galleries and collections. Exhibition programme. Introduction to the Collection.

2593
SCIENCE MUSEUM LIBRARY
Imperial College Road, South Kensington, London, SW7 5NH

Tel: 020 7942 4242
Fax: 020 7942 4243
Email: smlinfo@nmsi.ac.uk
Formed: 1883

Organisation type and purpose: Museum, public library.
National reference library.
Governing body:
Trustees of the Science Museum
Part of:
National Museum of Science and Industry
Shares building, collections, services and catalogue with:
Central Library of Imperial College of Science, Technology and Medicine

Enquiries to: Information Service
Other contacts: Archivist
Access:
Access to staff: By letter, by telephone, by fax, by email, in person

General description:
History of science and technology (including medicine, engineering and transport) in all periods and countries, biography, science communication, relations of science with other aspects of society.
Collections:
19th and 20th century trade literature
19th and early 20th century scientific and technical books and serials
Archival material, with special relevance to the Museum's collections in the physical sciences and industry
Archive for the history of quantum physics (microfilm)
Comben Collection of historic books on veterinary science and animal husbandry
Rare, mainly pre-1800, printed books and serials on scientific and technical subjects
Catalogues:
Catalogue for part of the collections is on-line.
Printed publications:
Brief guide to the Library

Internet home pages:
http://www.sciencemuseum.org.uk/library/

2594
SCIENCE MUSEUM WROUGHTON
Wroughton Airfield, Swindon, Wiltshire, SN4 9NS

Tel: 01793 814466
Fax: 01793 813569
Email: m.atkinson@nmsi.ac.uk
Formed: 1979

Organisation type and purpose: National organisation, museum.
Reserve collection of large objects of the Science Museum.
Part of:
National Museum of Science and Technology
Science Museum, Exhibition Road, London, SW7 2DD, tel: 020 7938 8000, fax: 020 7938 8118, email/website: http://www.nmsi.ac.uk

Enquiries to: Head of Museum
Direct tel: ext 22
Direct email: s.gillett@nmsi.ac.uk
Access:
Access to staff: By letter, by telephone, by fax, by email, visitors by prior appointment, Internet web pages
Access to building, collections or gallery: Prior appointment required
Hours: 1st and 3rd Wed morning each month
Public open weekends as advertised
Access for disabled people: Parking provided, level entry, toilet facilities

General description:
Air transport/aviation, road transport, agricultural engineering, fire-fighting equipment, space technology, engineering and technology.
Information services:
Special visitor services: Guided tours, materials and/or activities for children.
Education services: Group education facilities, resources for Key Stages 1 and 2 and 3..

Internet home pages:
http://www.sciencemuseum.org.uk/wroughton
Science Museum's pages on access, general information, events, exhibitions, galleries and education facilities.
http://www.nmsi.ac.uk

2595
SCOLTON VISITOR CENTRE
Museum and Country Park, Spittal, Haverfordwest, Pembrokeshire, SA62 5QL

Tel: 01437 731328
Formed: 1979
Formerly: Scolton Country Park; Scolton Manor, date of change, 1999

Organisation type and purpose: Local government body, museum, art gallery, suitable for ages: 4 plus.
Run by:
Pembrokeshire Museum Service
Castle Gallery, Haverfordwest Castle, Haverfordwest, Pembrokeshire, SA61 2EF, tel: 01437 760460

continued overleaf

Enquiries to: Manager
Direct tel: 01437 760460
Access:
Access to staff: By letter, by telephone, visitors by prior appointment

General description:
Scolton House was built in 1842. It now contains refurbished period rooms to illustrate life around 1900. There are good art and social history collections, with some fine furniture including some Higgon items. The museum houses collections on dairying; agriculture; and other local industries. There are also collections on transport; archaeology; and natural history.
Collections:
Llewellin, items from Haverfordwest churn works, 19th/20th century
'Margaret', locomotive, 0-6-OT, 19th century
Owen, W and J, furniture (they were also the architects of Scolton House)
19th century
Catalogues:
Catalogue for library is in-house only. Catalogue for all of the collections is only available in-house.
Printed publications:
Scolton: A Pembrokeshire Country House

Internet home pages:
http://www.pembrokeshire.gov.uk

2596
SCONE PALACE
Scone, Perth, Tayside, PH2 6BD

Tel: 01738 552300
Fax: 01738 552588
Email: visits@scone-palace.co.uk

Organisation type and purpose: Independently owned, historic building, house or site, suitable for ages: all ages.

Enquiries to: Administrator
Access:
Access to staff: By letter, by telephone, by fax, by email, in person, visitors by prior appointment, Internet web pages
Access for disabled people: Parking provided, toilet facilities
Other restrictions: All State Rooms are on one level.

General description:
The home of the Earls of Mansfield, crowning place of The Kings of Scots.
Information services:
Special visitor services: Guided tours, materials and/or activities for children.
Education services: Group education facilities..
Collections:
Famous collection of porcelain and the unique 'Vernis Martin' - papier-mâché.
Extensive collection of paintings, furniture and objets d'art
Murray Star Maze
Mature Pinetum
Douglas Fir and The David Douglas Trail
Catalogues:
Catalogue for part of the collections is on-line.
Printed publications:
Guide Books, a range of postcards and Children's Guide Book (available for purchase)
Property leaflet, publicity material (free)
Education pack available to schools (Sandford Education Award 2001)

Internet home pages:
http://www.scone-palace.co.uk
An introduction to the Palace and its many treasures.

2597
SCOTCH WHISKY HERITAGE CENTRE
354 Castlehill, Edinburgh, EH1 2NE

Tel: 0131 220 0441
Formed: 1987

Organisation type and purpose: Independently owned, suitable for ages: all ages.
Visitor attraction.

Enquiries to: Manager
Direct fax: 0131 220 6288
Direct email: info@whisky-heritage.co.uk
Access:
Access to staff: By letter, by telephone, by fax, by email, in person, Internet web pages
Access for disabled people: access to all public areas, toilet facilities

General description:
Provides an explanation of whisky-making processes through an audiovisual show of the production regions. There is a presentation on blending, and a 'barrel-ride' through the sights, sounds and smells of the history of Scotland's national drink.

Internet home pages:
http://www.whisky-heritage.co.uk

2598
SCOTIA ARCHAEOLOGY
Marda, Ferntower Place, Crieff, Perthshire, PH7 3DD

Tel: 01764 655773
Fax: 01764 655773

Enquiries to: Director
Access:
Access to staff: By letter
Access to building, collections or gallery: No access other than to staff

General description:
Archaeological contracting unit and consultancy, undertaking fieldwork (excavations, surveys etc) throughout Scotland.

2599
SCOTLAND STREET SCHOOL MUSEUM
225 Scotland Street, Glasgow, G5 8QB

Tel: 0141 429 1202
Fax: 0141 420 3292
Formerly: Museum of Education

Organisation type and purpose: Local government body, museum, suitable for ages: 5+.
Parent body:
Glasgow Museums

Enquiries to: Administrator

General description:
Recently restored building designed by Charles Rennie Mackintosh between 1903-1906.
Covers the history of education in Scotland from 1872 to the present day. There are 8000 books, mainly textbooks but also children's literature. Also contains photographs of school children and school buildings, and examples of children's work; school furniture and equipment (covering the major periods and philosophies, including Montessori and Froebel); costume; and some social history.
Information services:
Education services: Group education facilities..

Internet home pages:
http://www.glasgow.gov.uk

2600
SCOTLAND'S SECRET BUNKER
Crown Buildings, St Andrews, Fife, KY16 8QH

Tel: 01333 310301
Fax: 01333 312090
Email: mod@secretbunker.co.uk
Acronym or abbreviation: ADEPT
Full name: Anstruther Defence Establishment Preservation Trust
Formed: 1993

Organisation type and purpose: Independently owned, museum, historic building, house or site, suitable for ages: 5+.

Enquiries to: Managing Director
Access:
Access to staff: By email
Access to building, collections or gallery: Prior appointment required
Access for disabled people: Parking provided

General description:
The former Central Government bunker from where the country's senior leaders and military commanders would have run operations in the event of a nuclear strike against the UK. Set 100 ft. below ground this is a fascinating insight into the hitherto untold period of the Cold War. The centre is filled with authentic artefacts of the period, and the entire history is covered from 1951 to 1993. There are video presentations and display galleries along with all the various operations rooms fully reconstructed.
Information services:
Special visitor services: Guided tours, tape recorded guides.
Education services: Group education facilities..
Collections:
BT museum and history of the telephone collection, 1938-1993
Civil defence exhibition, 1958-1968
Telephone exchange/communications centres, 1951-1993
War telephone system on display, 1993
Catalogues:
Catalogue for library is in-house only. Catalogue for all of the collections is only available in-house.
Publications list:
is available in hard copy and online.

Internet home pages:
http://www.secretbunker.co.uk

2601
SCOTNEY CASTLE GARDEN AND ESTATE
Lamberhurst, Tunbridge Wells, Kent, TN3 8JN

Tel: 01892 891081
Fax: 01892 890110
Email: scotneycastle@nationaltrust.org.uk

Organisation type and purpose: National organisation, registered charity (charity number 205846), historic building, house or site.
Parent Body:
The National Trust (South and South East Region)
South East Regional Office, tel: 01372 453401

Enquiries to: Manager
Access:
Access to staff: By letter, by telephone, by fax, by email
Access to building, collections or gallery: No prior appointment required
Hours: Garden: Late Mar to early Nov, Wed to Sun, 1100 to1800
Old Castle: May to late Sep, Wed to Sun, 1100 to 1800
Estate walks: All year daily
Open Bank Holiday Mondays
Other restrictions: Closed Good Fri.
Last admission 1 hr before closing.
Garden closes 1800 or dusk if earlier.
Access for disabled people: Parking provided, toilet facilities
Other restrictions: Designated parking 75yds. Drop-off point. 3 manual wheelchairs available. Ground floor accessible with assistance. No access to other floors. Level entrance to shop. Grounds largely accessible. Very steep in places. Wheelchair users need strong companion. Recommended route map. Adapted WC outside garden

General description:
One of England's most romantic gardens, designed in the picturesque style around the ruins of a 14th century moated castle. There are rhododendrons and azaleas in profusion, with wisteria and roses rambling over the old ruins. Wonderful vistas and viewpoints abound, and there are beautiful woodland and estate walks.

Information services:
Braille guide. Large-print guide. Audio guide. Children's quiz/trail.
Special visitor services: Materials and/or activities for children.
Services for disabled people: For the visually impaired.

Internet home pages:
http://www.nationaltrust.org.uk

2602
SCOTT GALLERY
See - Hawick Museum & Scott Gallery

2603
SCOTT POLAR RESEARCH INSTITUTE MUSEUM
Lensfield Road, Cambridge, CB2 1ER

Tel: 01223 336540
Fax: 01223 336549
Telex: 81240 CAMSPL G
Email: archives@spri.cam.ac.uk
Acronym or abbreviation: SPRI
Formed: 1920

Organisation type and purpose: Museum, university department or institute, suitable for ages: 12+, research organisation, publishing house.
Connections with:
University of Cambridge

Enquiries to: Curator
Direct tel: 01223 336555
Access:
Access to staff: By letter, visitors by prior appointment
Hours: Mon to Fri, 0900 to 1300 and 1400 to 1730
Access for disabled people: ramped entry

General description:
A small private museum featuring the Arctic and Antarctic, and biography of those involved. Displays cover historical and modern exploration, Arctic indigenes, scientific research, mapping, etc. A special exhibition is arranged annually.
Collections:
Franklin Search expeditions
1845-1860
Captain Scott's expeditions
1901-1913
Catalogues:
Catalogue for library is published. Catalogue for all of the collections is only available in-house but part is published.
Publications list:
is available in hard copy.
Printed publications:
Polar Record (journal, quarterly)

2604
SCOTTISH AGRICULTURAL MUSEUM
RHAS Showground, Ingliston, Newbridge, Midlothian, EH28 8NB

Tel: 0131 333 2674
Fax: 0131 333 2674

Organisation type and purpose: Museum. National body.
Part of:
National Museums of Scotland

Enquiries to: Curator
Access:
Access to staff: By letter, by telephone, by fax, in person
Hours: Mon to Fri, 1000 to 1700

General description:
History of rural life in Scotland and the progress from hand skills to mechanisation in farming and crofting communities, the Agricultural Revolution, the social and economic life of the countryside, traditional use of materials in the countryside, the changing relationship between people and animals.
Catalogues:
Catalogue for library is in-house only. Catalogue for all of the collections is only available in-house.

Internet home pages:
http://www.nms.ac.uk/agriculture

See also - Museum of Scottish Country Life

2605
SCOTTISH BORDERS COUNCIL MUSEUM AND GALLERY SERVICE
Municipal Buildings, High Street, Selkirk, Borders, TD7 4JX

Tel: 01750 20096
Fax: 01750 23282
Email: museums@scotborders.gov.uk
Formed: 1996
Formerly: Berwickshire District Museum Service, Ettrick and Lauderdale Museum Service, Roxburgh District Museum Service, Tweeddale District Museum Service, date of change, 1996

Organisation type and purpose: Local government body, museum, art gallery, suitable for ages: all ages.
Museum service.
Parent body:
Scottish Borders Council (SBC)

Enquiries to: Curator
Access:
Access to staff: By letter, by telephone, by fax, by email, visitors by prior appointment
Access to building, collections or gallery: No prior appointment required

General description:
This is the museum service headquarters and can give general information on all of our 11 museums, their collections and opening times. Specialist themes relate to local history and culture.
Collections:
Walter Mason Archive: Civic and legal archive relating to Selkirk and Scottish Borders from early 16th century to early 19th century
Catalogues:
Catalogue for part of the collections is only available in-house.
Publications list:
is available in hard copy.
Printed publications:
Local history material
Electronic and video products:
Millennium Memories - a selection of memories relating to 20th century experiences in the Scottish Borders (CD-ROM)

Internet home pages:
http://www.scotborders.gov.uk

See also - Coldstream Museum; Drumlanrigs Tower Visitor Centre; Duns Exhibition Room; Eyemouth Museum; Halliwell's House Museum & Robson Gallery; Harestones Countryside Visitor Centre; Hawick Museum & Scott Gallery; Hawick Museum & Scott Gallery; Jim Clark Room; Mary Queen of Scot's House & Visitor Centre; Old Gala House; Sir Walter Scott's Courtroom; St Ronan's Well Interpretation Centre; Tweeddale Museum

2606
SCOTTISH FISHERIES MUSEUM
Harbourhead, Anstruther, Fife, KY10 3AB

Tel: 01333 310628
Fax: 01333 310628
Formed: 1969

Organisation type and purpose: National organisation, registered charity (charity number SC 006185), museum, suitable for ages: 8+.
Library pertaining to Scottish fishing from earliest times.

Enquiries to: Manager
Direct email: andrew@scottish-fisheries-museum.org
Access:
Access to staff: By letter, by telephone, by fax, visitors by prior appointment
Access for disabled people: Parking provided, ramped entry, access to all public areas, toilet facilities

General description:
Fishing vessel records - approximately 1900, general information on Scottish fishing industry.
Information services:
Library available for reference (for conditions see Access above)
Special visitor services: Guided tours, materials and/or activities for children.
Education services: Group education facilities..
Collections:
12,000 photographs
350 paintings
16 actual vessels
The museum has a total of 65,000 items
Catalogues:
Catalogue for library is in-house only. Catalogue for all of the collections is only available in-house.
Trade and statistical:
Government reports and statistics from mid-19th century on Scottish fishing industry.
Publications list:
is available in hard copy.

Internet home pages:
http://www.scottish-fisheries-museum.org

2607
SCOTTISH GALLERY, THE
16 Dundas Street, Edinburgh, EH3 6HZ

Tel: 0131 558 1200
Fax: 0131 558 3900
Email: mail@scottish-gallery.co.uk
Formed: 1842
Formerly: Aitken Dott Limited, date of change, 1896

Organisation type and purpose: Independently owned, art gallery, suitable for ages: 5+, consultancy, publishing house.

Enquiries to: Director
Access:
Access to staff: By letter, by telephone, by fax, by email, Internet web pages

General description:
Contemporary Scottish paintings, contemporary international applied art, publications.
Publications list:
is available on-line.

Internet home pages:
http://www.scottish-gallery.co.uk
Information on current and forthcoming exhibitions, history of the gallery, publications list.

2608
SCOTTISH MARITIME MUSEUM, THE
Kings Inch Road, Glasgow, G51 4BN

Tel: 0141 886 1013
Fax: 0141 886 1015
Email: clydebuilt@tinyworld.co.uk
Formed: 1999

Organisation type and purpose: Museum, suitable for ages: 5+.

Enquiries to: Manager
Access:
Access to staff: By letter, by telephone, by fax, by email, in person
Hours: Mon to Thu, Sat, 1000 to 1800; Sun, 1100 to 1700
Access to building, collections or gallery: No prior appointment required
Hours: Mon to Thu, Sat, 1000 to 1800; Sun, 1100 to 1700

continued overleaf

Access for disabled people: level entry, access to all public areas, toilet facilities

General description:
Maritime history.
Information services:
Special visitor services: Guided tours.
Education services: Group education facilities.
Services for disabled people: Displays and/or information at wheelchair height.

2609
SCOTTISH MARITIME MUSEUM

6 Gottries Road, Irvine, Ayrshire, KA12 8QE

Tel: 01294 278283
Fax: 01294 313211
Formed: 1984

Organisation type and purpose: Registered charity, museum, suitable for ages: 5+, research organisation.
Also at:
Scottish Maritime Museum
Denny Ship Model Tank, Castle Street, Dumbarton, G82 1GS
Scottish Maritime Museum
12 Castle Terrace, Dumbarton, G82 1QY

Enquiries to: Curator
Other contacts: Customer Service Manager for marketing and promotional duties.
Access:
Access to staff: By letter, by telephone, by fax, by email, in person, visitors by prior appointment
Hours: Mon to Fri, 0900 to 1700
Access to building, collections or gallery: Prior appointment required
Hours: Daily, 0900 to 1700
Access for disabled people: Parking provided, level entry, toilet facilities
Other restrictions: Access to all areas with the exception to boarding boats.

General description:
All aspects of Scottish maritime history and activity, including inland waterways, with special interest in shipbuilding.
Information services:
Special visitor services: Guided tours, tape recorded guides, materials and/or activities for children.
Education services: Group education facilities..
Collections:
Wm Fife & Sons, Fairlie Yacht Slip Company: business records 1915-1985
RNVR club (Glasgow): business records 1947-1991
Sir John I Thorneycroft, Vosper Thorneycroft: miscellaneous records and test models from Fort Steyne hydrodynamics test tank
Specialist library, archives and photo-archives
Vessels and machinery
Catalogues:
Catalogue for library is in-house only. Catalogue for all of the collections is only available in-house.

See also - Denny Ship Model Experimental Tank

2610
SCOTTISH MINING MUSEUM

Lady Victoria Colliery, Newtongrange, Dalkeith, Midlothian, EH22 4QN

Tel: 0131 663 7519
Fax: 0131 654 1618
Email: enquiries@scottishminingmuseum.org
Formed: 1982

Organisation type and purpose: Registered charity, museum, suitable for ages: all ages.
Member of:
Edinburgh and Lothians Tourist Board
4 Rothesay Terrace, Edinburgh, tel: 0131 226 6800
Scottish Museums Council
County House, Torphichen Street, Edinburgh, tel: 0131 229 7465

Enquiries to: Director
Other contacts: Keeper for research using archive, library or collections.
Access:
Access to staff: By letter, by telephone, by fax, by email, in person, visitors by prior appointment
Hours: Mon to Fri, 0900 to 1700
Access to building, collections or gallery: No prior appointment required
Hours: Mon to Sun, 1000 to 1700
Access for disabled people: Parking provided, ramped entry, access to all public areas, toilet facilities

General description:
Coal mining.
Information services:
Library available for reference (for conditions see Access above)
Special visitor services: Tape recorded guides.
Education services: Group education facilities..
Collections:
Scotland's national coal mining collection, archive and library: large and small objects, documents, photographs, maps and plans, memorabilia
Catalogues:
Catalogue for part of the collections is only available in-house.
Trade and statistical:
Statistics of UK coal output and manpower from c 1855 onwards.
Printed publications:
Scotland's Black Diamonds
Teachers' Source List on the Scottish Coal Industry

Internet home pages:
http://www.scottishminingmuseum.com

2611
SCOTTISH MOTOR MUSEUM TRUST

See - Motoring Heritage Centre

2612
SCOTTISH MUSEUMS COUNCIL

County House, 20-22 Torphichen Street, Edinburgh, EH3 8JB

Tel: 0131 229 7465
Fax: 0131 229 2728
Email: inform@scottishmuseums.org.uk
Acronym or abbreviation: SMC
Formed: 1964
Formerly: Council for Museums and Galleries in Scotland

Organisation type and purpose: National organisation, membership association, present number of members: 200, registered charity (charity number SCO 15593).
SMC is the membership organisation for local museums and galleries in Scotland. SMC's mission is 'to achieve the best possible museum and gallery provision in Scotland for the public benefit'.
Affiliated to:
Scottish Arts Council
Scottish Executive Education Department (Government sponsoring body)
Scottish Library and Information Council

Enquiries to: Information Officer
Direct tel: 0131 538 7435
Direct fax: 0131 229 2728
Access:
Access to staff: By letter, by telephone, by fax, by email, Internet web pages
Hours: Mon to Fri, 0900 to 1700
Other restrictions: Prior appointment is required.
Limited service for non-members.

General description:
Museums; museology; museography; heritage studies; leisure; tourism; all especially as applied to Scotland.
Collections:
General information on Scottish museums
Catalogues:
Catalogue for library is in-house only.
Trade and statistical:
Data on the number and nature of museums in Scotland.
Publications list:
is available on-line.

Internet home pages:
http://www.scottishmuseums.org.uk
Information about the Scottish Museums Council and museums in Scotland.

2613
SCOTTISH NATIONAL GALLERY OF MODERN ART, THE

Belford Road, Edinburgh, EH4 3DR

Tel: 0131 624 6200
Fax: 0131 343 2802
Email: enquiries@nationalgalleries.org
Acronym or abbreviation: SNGMA
Formed: 1960

Organisation type and purpose: National organisation, art gallery, suitable for ages: 5+.
Parent body:
National Galleries of Scotland
Belford Road, Edinburgh, EH4 3DR, tel: 0131 624 6200, fax: 0131 343 3250, email: enquiries@natgalscot.ac.uk

Enquiries to: Curatorial Department (academic enquiries)
Other contacts: Press & Information Department for general public enquiries.
Access:
Access to staff: By letter, by telephone, by fax, by email, Internet web pages
Access for disabled people: Parking provided, ramped entry, access to all public areas, toilet facilities

General description:
The Scottish National Gallery of Modern Art houses Scotland's finest collection of twentieth and twenty-first century paintings, sculpture and graphic art. The collection is specifically of western art, with works by artists such as Matisse, Picasso and Dali. The gallery also holds an unrivalled collection of twentieth century Scottish art including paintings by Bellany, Gillies, Peploe, Davie and Redpath. The Gallery is situated in extensive parkland, providing the perfect setting for sculptures by Henry Moore, Barbara Hepworth, Anthony Caro and others. The light and airy café has a pleasant buzz all year round, but really comes into its own in the summer when seating extends onto the terrace and lawn to the rear of the Gallery. The shop is the place to go for unusual gifts, and a great range of books and catalogues. Temporary exhibitions change on a regular basis, details of which can be found on the website.
Information services:
Education services: Group education facilities..
Collections:
British and foreign exhibition catalogues not available elsewhere in Scotland
Catalogues:
Catalogue for library is in-house only. Catalogue for all of the collections is published.
Publications list:
is available in hard copy and online.
Printed publications:
Variety of leaflets available on request

Address for ordering publications:
Printed publications:
Publications Department, National Galleries of Scotland
Dean Gallery, Belford Road, Edinburgh, EH4 3DS, tel: 0131 624 6257/6259/6261, fax: 0131 315 2963, email: publications@nationalgalleries.org

Internet home pages:
http://www.nationalgalleries.org

2614
SCOTTISH NATIONAL NAVAL AND MILITARY MUSEUM

See - National War Museum of Scotland

2615
SCOTTISH NATIONAL PORTRAIT GALLERY

1 Queen Street, Edinburgh, EH2 1JD

Tel: 0131 624 6200
Fax: 0131 558 3691
Email: enquiries@nationalgalleries.org
Acronym or abbreviation: SNPG
Formed: 1889

Organisation type and purpose: National government body, national organisation, art gallery, suitable for ages: 5+.
Holds portraits in all media of people who have played a significant role in Scottish history from the 16th century to the present day. Also the National Photography Collection with regular photography exhibitions.
Parent body:
National Galleries of Scotland
Belford Road, Edinburgh, EH4 3DS, tel: 0131 624 6200, fax: 0131 343 3250, email: enquiries@natgalscot.ac.uk

Enquiries to: Press & Information Department
Direct tel: 0131 624 6420
Direct fax: 0131 558 3691
Direct email: helen.watson@natgalscot.ac.uk
Other contacts: Curatorial Dept for academic enquiries.
Access:
Access to staff: By letter, by telephone, by fax, by email, visitors by prior appointment, Internet web pages
Hours: Mon to Fri, 1000 to 1230 and 1400 to 1630
Other restrictions: Reference only.
Access to building, collections or gallery: No prior appointment required
Hours: Mon to Sat, 1000 to 1700; Sun, 1200 to 1700
Access for disabled people: Parking provided, ramped entry, access to all public areas, toilet facilities
Other restrictions: Access to all public areas.

General description:
The Scottish National Portrait Gallery provides a unique visual history of Scotland, told through portraits of the figures who shaped it: royals and rebels, poets and philosophers, heroes and villains. All the portraits are of Scots, but not all are by Scots. The collection also contains works by great English, European and American masters such as Van Dyck, Gainsborough, Rodin and Kokoschka, as well as, of course, works by Ramsay, Raeburn and other Scottish artists. In addition to paintings, it displays sculptures, miniatures, coins, medallions, drawings and watercolours. The gallery also houses the National Photography Collection. The shop, famous for its jewellery, sells a range of gifts that take their inspiration from anything from the Picts to Lulu whilst the café is a hidden island of calm amidst the bustle of the city centre. Temporary exhibitions change on a regular basis, details of which can be found on the website.
Information services:
Education services: Group education facilities..
Collections:
Archive of books, documents
Blaikie Collection (Jacobite engravings), on loan from the National Library of Scotland
Collection of portrait medallions by James and William Tassie
Hill and Adamson Collection (5000 calotypes)
James Drummond Collection (drawings of Edinburgh), on loan from the National Museums of Scotland
Materials relating to works in the collections, artists and sitters
Paintings
Scottish Photography Archive
Sculpture
Catalogues:
Catalogue for library is in-house only. Catalogue for all of the collections is published.
Publications list:
is available in hard copy and online.
Printed publications:
Complete catalogue of the Hill and Adamson Collection
Concise catalogue of the Collection
Exhibition catalogues
Variety of leaflets on request
Electronic and video products:
The Royal House of Stewart (CD-ROM)

Address for ordering publications:
Printed publications:
Publications Department, National Galleries of Scotland
Dean Gallery, Belford Road, Edinburgh, EH4 3DS, tel: 0131 624 6257/6259/6261, fax: 0131 315 2963, email: publications@nationalgalleries.org

Internet home pages:
http://www.nationalgalleries.org
Opening hours, exhibitions etc.

2616
SCOTTISH NATIONAL WAR MEMORIAL

The Castle, Edinburgh, EH1 2YT

Tel: 0131 226 7393
Fax: 0131 225 8920
Email: info@snwm.org
Acronym or abbreviation: SNWM
Formed: July 1927

Organisation type and purpose: Registered charity (charity number SCO 009869), suitable for ages: 5+.
War memorial.
To maintain Rolls of Honour of Scotsmen and women killed in the service of the Crown in the World Wars 1914 to 1918 and 1939 to 1945 and all campaigns since 1945.

Enquiries to: Secretary to the Trustees
Access:
Access to staff: By letter
Hours: Mon, Tue, Thu, Fri, 0900 to 1230
Access to building, collections or gallery: No prior appointment required
Hours: As for Edinburgh Castle
Access for disabled people: ramped entry

General description:
An 18th century barrack block converted 1923-1927 into a War Memorial by Sir Robert Lorima. It contains a number of individual memorials to different regiments along with some fifty regimental colours. On display are the Rolls of Honour to which the public have access. The memorial includes the work of a number of eminent Scottish artists of the 1920s worked in stone, bronze, glass and wood.
Printed publications:
Official Guide
Their Name Liveth (The Story of the Scottish National War Memorial, I Hay)
Microform products:
Six sets of 35mm colour transparencies

Internet home pages:
http://www.snwm.org
Brief history of the memorial and a tour of the interior.

2617
SCOTTISH RAILWAY PRESERVATION SOCIETY

The Station, Union Street, Bo'ness, West Lothian, EH51 9AQ

Tel: 01506 822298
Fax: 01506 828766
Acronym or abbreviation: SRPS
Formed: 1963

Organisation type and purpose: Membership association (membership is by subscription), present number of members: 1300, voluntary organisation, registered charity (charity number SCO02375), museum.
Railway preservation and operation.
Links with:
Heritage Railway Association (HRA)
Tel: 01707 643568, fax: 01707 643568

Enquiries to: Honorary Secretary
Direct tel: 01506 843207
Access:
Access to staff: By letter, by telephone, by fax, by email, visitors by prior appointment
Hours: Mon to Fri, 1000 to 1600
Access for disabled people: Parking provided, ramped entry, toilet facilities

General description:
Railway preservation, restoration of steam locomotives and rolling stock, and their operation; Scottish railways and their historical development; Bo'ness and Kinneil Railway; locations for filming of steam-hauled trains of appropriate vintage; the preservation and display, in work if appropriate, of artefacts pertaining to Scottish railways.
Collections:
Builders plates for study
Railway artefacts ranging from railway buildings to locomotive (etc)
Small collection of books on practical aspects of railways and rolling stock, also photographs
Printed publications:
Blastpipe (magazine, quarterly, free to members or on subscription)
Bo'ness & Kinneil Railway Guide
Other publications as needed

Internet home pages:
http://www.srps.org.uk
Activities of the organisation.

See also - Bo'ness and Kinneil Railway

2618
SCOTTISH RUGBY UNION LIBRARY & MUSEUM

Murrayfield, Edinburgh, EH12 5JP

Tel: 0131 346 5073
Fax: 0131 346 5001
Email: library@sru.org.uk
Acronym or abbreviation: SRU
Formed: 1996
Formerly: Scottish Football Union (SFU), date of change, 1924

Organisation type and purpose: Independently owned, suitable for ages: 5+, research organisation.
Library.

Enquiries to: Library Services Manager
Direct email: fiona.white@sru.org.uk
Access:
Access to staff: By letter, by telephone, by fax, by email, in person, Internet web pages
Access for disabled people: Parking provided, access to all public areas, toilet facilities

General description:
Scottish rugby history. Records of all players and international matches from 1871. Photographs, books, magazines, newspaper articles, and many artefacts relating to the game of rugby football in Scotland and throughout the world.
Information services:
Education services: Group education facilities..
Catalogues:
Catalogue for library is in-house only. Catalogue for all of the collections is only available in-house.
Printed publications:
Non-Sine-Gloria (Library bulletin, free of charge)
Electronic and video products:
Catalogue currently being compiled on computer

Internet home pages:
http://www.sru.org.uk/library

2619
SCOTTISH UNITED SERVICES MUSEUM
See - National War Museum of Scotland

2620
SCOTTISH VINTAGE BUS MUSEUM
M90 Commerce Park, Lathalmond, Dunfermline, Fife, KY12 0SJ

Tel: 01383 623380
Fax: 01383 623375
Acronym or abbreviation: SVBM
Formed: 1985

Organisation type and purpose: Membership association (membership is by subscription), present number of members: 200, registered charity, museum.
To collect and restore vintage buses and create a working museum together with other bus memorabilia.

Enquiries to: Membership Secretary
Direct tel: 01383 720241
Direct email: eddie@17thimblehall.freeserve.co.uk
Access:
Access to staff: By letter
Access for disabled people: Parking provided, ramped entry, toilet facilities

General description:
History of the Scottish Bus Industry.
Collections:
Various books, publications, pictures etc relating to the Scottish Bus Industry
Catalogues:
Catalogue for all of the collections is on-line.

Internet home pages:
http://www.busweb.co.uk/svbm
Museum information on vehicles, events, news etc.

2621
SIR WALTER SCOTT'S COURTROOM
Market Place, Selkirk, Borders, TD7 4BT

Tel: 01750 20096/20761
Fax: 01750 23282
Email: museums@scotborders.gov.uk

Organisation type and purpose: Local government body, museum, historic building, house or site, suitable for ages: 5+.
Parent body:
Scottish Borders Council Museum and Gallery Service
Tel: 01750 20096

Enquiries to: Curator
Access:
Access to staff: By letter, by telephone, by fax, in person
Access to building, collections or gallery: No prior appointment required
Hours: End of Mar to Sep, Mon to Sat, 1000 to 1600; Jun to Aug, Sun, 1400 to 1600;
Oct, Mon to Sat, 1300 to 1600

General description:
Built in 1803 as the Town House and Sheriff Court where Sir Walter Scott presided for almost thirty years. The building has recently been restored. In the former robing room displays tell the story of the building and the civic history of Selkirk.
Collections:
Personalia relating to James Hogg and Mungo Park
Watercolours by Tom Scott

Internet home pages:
http://www.scotborders.gov.uk
http://www.scotborders.org.uk

2622
SCUNTHORPE MUSEUM AND ART GALLERY
See - North Lincolnshire Museum

2623
SEAFORD HOUSE
See - Royal College of Defence Studies

2624
SEAFORD MUSEUM AND HERITAGE SOCIETY
Martello Tower, The Esplanade, Seaford, East Sussex, BN25 1JH

Tel: 01323 898222
Email: museumseaford@tinyonline.co.uk
Acronym or abbreviation: Seaford Museum
Formed: 1971
Formerly: Seaford Museum of Local History, date of change, 2000

Organisation type and purpose: Membership association (membership is by subscription), voluntary organisation, registered charity (charity number 272864), museum.
Postal address:
c/o Tourist Information Centre
25 Clinton Place, Seaford, East Sussex, BN25 1NP

Enquiries to: Public Liaison Officer
Access:
Access to staff: By letter, by email, in person
Hours: Summer: Sun & Bank Holidays, 1100 to 1300, 1430 to 1630; Wed & Sat, 1430 to 1630
Winter: Sun & Bank Holidays, 1100 to 1300 & 1430 to 1630
Access to building, collections or gallery: Prior appointment required
Hours: Tue, Thu, 0930 to 1200

General description:
Seaford and its social history.
Collections:
Seaford Pictorial and Information Archive
Seaford Housing Register - record of history of houses/buildings
Museum of household and other artefacts

Internet home pages:
http://www.seafordmuseum.org
General tour of the museum and building.

2625
SEAFORTH CAMERON MUSEUM
See - Queen's Own Highlanders (Seaforth and Camerons)

2626
SEARCH
50 Clarence Road, Gosport, Hampshire, PO12 1BU

Tel: 023 9250 1957
Fax: 023 9250 1957
Email: musmjw@hants.gov.uk (no attachments please)
Full name: SEARCH, Hampshire Museums' Hands-on Centre for History and Natural History
Formed: 1995
Also known as: Museum Education Service
Formed from: Hampshire County Council Museums Service

Organisation type and purpose: Local government body, museum, suitable for ages: 4+.
Hands-on education centre.
Parent body:
Hampshire County Council Museums Service
Chilcomb House, Chilcomb Lane, Winchester, SO23 8RD, tel: 01962 846304, fax: 01962 869836

Enquiries to: Manager
Access:
Access to staff: By letter, by telephone, by fax, by email, visitors by prior appointment, Internet web pages
Access to building, collections or gallery: Prior appointment required
Hours: Aug, Tue to Fri, Summer Holiday Workshops for children and families. Is sometimes open at other times to coincide with local or national initiatives.
Access for disabled people: Parking provided, level entry, access to all public areas, toilet facilities

General description:
SEARCH is the hands-on education centre for history and science for Hampshire County Council Museum Service, in Gosport, Hampshire. All activities are hands-on and use real museum collections and state of the art equipment.
Information services:
Key Stage and special education.
Reminiscence workshops for older visitors.
Workshops for schools on a range of history and natural science themes.
Occasional family open weekends and holiday workshops.
Contact SEARCH for current programmes.
Special visitor services: Materials and/or activities for children.
Education services: Group education facilities, resources for Key Stages 1 and 2 and Further or Higher Education.
Services for disabled people: For the visually impaired; for the hearing impaired; displays and/or information at wheelchair height.
Collections:
Social history/domestic items 1880-1950s
Roman archaeological material
Natural history specimens - taxidermy, skeletal material, entomological specimens, geology
Catalogues:
Catalogue for all of the collections is only available in-house.
Publications list:
is available in hard copy.
Printed publications:
Going Interactive - training manual for museum professionals (available direct, £40)
Publications list is available from the Librarian, Hampshire County Council Museums Service Headquarters, Chilcomb House, Winchester, SO23 8RD

Address for ordering publications:
Printed publications:
Registrar, Hampshire County Council Museums Service HQ

Internet home pages:
http://www.hants.gov.uk/museum/search
Basic visitor services information.
HMCMS web catalogue, whole collection, 100,000 plus web pages.

2627
SEATON TRAMWAY
Riverside Depot, Harbour Road, Seaton, Devon, EX12 4AA

Tel: 01297 20375
Fax: 01297 625626
Email: info@tram.co.uk
Full name: Modern Electric Tramways Limited
Formed: 1953

Organisation type and purpose: Independently owned, suitable for ages: 5+.
Tramway.
Heritage tramway.

Enquiries to: Managing Director
Other contacts: Commercial Director for retail enquiries.
Access:
Access to staff: By letter, by telephone, by fax, by email, visitors by prior appointment
Access to building, collections or gallery: No prior appointment required
Hours: Easter to Oct: daily, 1000 to 1700
Access for disabled people: Parking provided, level entry, toilet facilities
Other restrictions: Special Tramcar for wheelchair users.

General description:
Tramway from Colyton Station to Seaton Terminus.
Collections:
Trams of various ages.
Printed publications:
Guide Book (for purchase)
Promotional leaflets (free)
Various books (for purchase)
Electronic and video products:
Documentary (video, for purchase)

Internet home pages:
http://www.tram.co.uk
General and archive information.

2628
SECRET BUNKER MUSEUM
See - Bunker Preservation Trust

2629
SEGEDUNUM ROMAN FORT, BATHS AND MUSEUM
Buddle Street, Wallsend, Tyne and Wear, NE28 6HR

Tel: 0191 295 5757
Minicom no. 0191 236 9350
Fax: 0191 295 5858
Email: segedunum@twmuseums.org.uk
Acronym or abbreviation: Segedunum
Formed: 2000
Formerly: Wallsend Heritage Centre, date of change, 2000

Organisation type and purpose: Local government body, registered charity, museum, historic building, house or site, suitable for ages: 5+.
Archaeological site.
Parent body:
Tyne & Wear Museums (TWM)
Discovery Museum, Blandford Square, Newcastle, tel: 0191 232 6789, fax: 0191 230 2614

Enquiries to: Curator
Other contacts: (1) Education Officer (2) Visitor Services Officer for (1) school bookings and activities (2) general services..
Access:
Access to staff: By letter, by telephone, by fax, by email, in person
Other restrictions: By appointment only.
Access to building, collections or gallery: No prior appointment required
Hours: 1 Apr to 31 Aug: daily, 1000 to 1700,1 Sep to 31 Mar: daily, 1000 to 1530
Access for disabled people: Parking provided, level entry, access to all public areas, toilet facilities

General description:
Large interactive museum - Roman galleries, industrial history (coalmining to shipbuilding).
Discover what life was like on Hadrian's Wall, with fascinating displays combining finds unearthed at the Fort with exciting computer interactives.
Explore the Fort's buildings, including the Commanding Officer's House and Headquarters, the Hospital and Soldiers Barracks.
See a complete plan of a Roman Fort, Hadrian's Wall with reconstructed section and reconstructed Roman Bath House.
Temporary exhibition gallery, viewing tower provides extensive views.
Information services:
Special visitor services: Materials and/or activities for children.
Education services: Group education facilities, resources for Key Stage 2.
Services for disabled people: For the visually impaired; for the hearing impaired; displays and/or information at wheelchair height.
Collections:
Archaeological finds
Industrial history memorabilia
The Roman Collections at Segedunum relate to the more recent excavations of the 1970s, 80s and 90s and are constantly being augmented by fresh archaeological fieldwork in the Wallsend area
Items which deserve a special mention are:
The only stone toilet seat from Roman Britain
A collection of rounded stones - defensive missiles for the Fort
Industry Gallery - artefacts associated with local coalmining and shipbuilding

Internet home pages:
http://www.twmuseums.org.uk

2630
SEGONTIUM ROMAN MUSEUM
Beddgelent Road, Caernarfon, Gwynedd, LL55 2LN

Tel: 01286 675625
Fax: 01286 678416
Formed: AD 77

Organisation type and purpose: National organisation, registered charity (charity number 205846), museum, historic building, house or site.
Parent body:
The National Trust Office for Wales
Tel: 01492 860123
In the guardianship of:
Cadw: Welsh Historic Monuments
Managed by:
National Museums & Galleries of Wales
Sponsored by:
Welsh Assembly
Other addresses:
National Museums & Galleries of Wales

Enquiries to: Curator
Access:
Access to staff: By letter, by telephone, by fax, by email, in person

General description:
The remains of a Roman fort, built to defend the Roman Empire against rebellious tribes and later plundered to provide stone for Edward I's castle at Caernarfon. This well preserved Roman fort established about AD77 is the only site in Wales where it is possible to see something of the internal layout of a Roman auxiliary fort. There is a museum containing relics found on-site.
Information services:
Special visitor services: Materials and/or activities for children..
Printed publications:
Education Packs (free of charge)

Internet home pages:
http://www.nationaltrust.org.uk
http://www.cadw.wales.gov.uk

2631
SEIONT II MARITIME TRUST (CAERNARFON MARITIME MUSEUM)
Victoria Dock, Caernarfon, Gwynedd, LL55

Tel: c/o 01248 752083
Formed: 1981

Organisation type and purpose: Registered charity, museum.
Member of the:
Gwynedd and Anglesey Federation of Maritime Museums

Enquiries to: Committee Member
Access:
Access to staff: By letter, by telephone, in person, charges to non-members
Access to building, collections or gallery: No prior appointment required
Hours: Spring Bank Holiday to mid Sep: Sun to Fri, 1100 to 1600
Access for disabled people: level entry, access to all public areas
Other restrictions: Parking areas and toilet facilities nearby.

General description:
Documents, photographs, and artefacts relating to the maritime and industrial heritage of the Caernarfon and Menai Straits area, including those associated with local people.
Information services:
Special visitor services: Guided tours..
Collections:
Interpretation of the engine room and bridge of steam dredger Seiont II
HMS Conway
Catalogues:
Catalogue for all of the collections is only available in-house.
Printed publications:
Port of Caernarfon (Dr Lewis Lloyd)
Seafarers of Caernarfon (Eames A)

2632
SELLY MANOR MUSEUM
Maple Road, Bournville, Birmingham, B30 2AE

Tel: 0121 472 0199
Fax: 0121 471 4101
Email: sellymanor@bvt.org.uk
Formed: 1917

Organisation type and purpose: Independently owned, registered charity (charity number 219260), historic building, house or site, suitable for ages: 5+.
Parent body and correspondence address:
Bournville Village Trust
(The housing association created by George Cadbury in 1900) (BVT)
Oak Tree Lane, Bournville, Birmingham, B30 1UB

Enquiries to: Curator
Access:
Access to staff: By letter, by telephone, by email, in person
Access to building, collections or gallery: No prior appointment required
Hours: Mon to Fri, 1000 to 1700
Access for disabled people: toilet facilities

General description:
Two half-timbered houses from the late Medieval and Tudor periods. Relocated onto their present site in the village by George Cadbury. Excellent oak furniture collection, Tudor Garden, gift shop, regular events.
Information services:
Special visitor services: Guided tours, materials and/or activities for children.
Education services: Group education facilities, resources for Key Stages 1 and 2..
Collections:
The Laurence Cadbury Collection of Furniture, Tudor and Stuart, mostly oak, furniture and household items, c. 1480-c. 1750, 350-400 items
Domestic utensils
Catalogues:
Catalogue for all of the collections is only available in-house.
Printed publications:
Guidebook
Educational material for schools

Internet home pages:
http://www.bvt.org.uk/sellymanor
Visitor information.

2633
SENHOUSE ROMAN MUSEUM
The Battery, Sea Brows, Maryport, Cumbria, CA15 6JD

Tel: 01900 816168
Fax: 01900 816168
Email: romans@senhouse.freeserve.co.uk
Formed: 1991

Organisation type and purpose: Registered charity, museum, historic building, house or site, suitable for ages: 8+.

Enquiries to: Manager
Access:
Access to staff: By letter, by telephone, by fax, by email, in person, visitors by prior appointment

continued overleaf

Access to building, collections or gallery: Prior appointment required
Hours: Mon to Fri, 1000 to 1700
Access for disabled people: Parking provided, level entry, access to all public areas, toilet facilities

General description:
The museum is housed in a building constructed in 1855 for training gunners of the Royal Naval Volunteer Reserve. It is situated next to the site of the Roman Fort of Alavna, from which vicinity much of the display derives. The fort was built to accommodate approximately 1000 infantry and cavalry soldiers of the First Cohort of Spaniards under the command of Marcus Maenius Agrippa. The collection, begun as early as the 1570s, may be the oldest antiquarian collection in the country, and is of international significance.
Information services:
Library available for reference (for conditions see Access above)
Special visitor services: Guided tours, materials and/or activities for children.
Education services: Group education facilities, resources for Key Stages 3, 4 and Further or Higher Education.
Services for disabled people: For the hearing impaired; displays and/or information at wheelchair height.
Collections:
The largest grouping of Roman military altar stones from a single site in this country, c. 120 to c. 190 AD
Serpent stone, a Celtic religious monument in phallic form
The Netherhall Collection of Romano-British artefacts
Catalogues:
Catalogue for library is in-house only.

Internet home pages:
http://www.senhousemuseum.co.uk

2634
SEVENOAKS MUSEUM AND LIBRARY

Buckhurst Lane, Sevenoaks, Kent, TN13 1LQ

Tel: 01732 453118
Fax: 01732 457468
Formed: 1986

Organisation type and purpose: Local government body, museum, art gallery, public library.
Parent body:
Kent County Council (KCC)
County Hall, Maidstone, Kent

Enquiries to: Education Officer
Direct email: gavin.lambert@kent.gov.uk
Other contacts: Arts Officer for gallery enquiries.
Access:
Access to staff: By letter, by telephone
Hours: Mon, Tue, Wed, Fri, 0930 to 1730; Thu, 0930 to 1900; Sat, 0900 to 1700
Other restrictions: May be refurbished in late 2004 so telephone prior to visit.
Access to building, collections or gallery: No access other than to staff

General description:
The collection includes local geology; archaeology; and photographs which tell the story of Sevenoaks. Displays include war; domestic life; artefacts from the St Nicholas' Church excavation (Sevenoaks); and a display on Vincent New, the local printer and artist.
Information services:
Special visitor services: Materials and/or activities for children.
Education services: Group education facilities..
Catalogues:
Catalogue for library is in-house only.

2635
SEVERN VALLEY RAILWAY

The Station, Bewdley, Worcestershire, DY12 1BG

Tel: 01299 403816
Fax: 01299 400839
Acronym or abbreviation: SVR
Formed: 1965

Organisation type and purpose: Voluntary organisation, museum.

Enquiries to: Public Relations Manager
Other contacts: General Manager for seniority.
Access:
Access to staff: By letter, by telephone, by fax, visitors by prior appointment
Access for disabled people: level entry, toilet facilities

General description:
Standard guage steam and diesel railway from Kidderminster to Bridgnorth (16 miles).

Internet home pages:
http://www.svr.co.uk

2636
SEWERBY HALL

Church Lane, Sewerby, Bridlington, East Yorkshire, YO15 1EA

Tel: 01262 677874
Fax: 01262 674265
Email: sewerbyhall@yahoo.com
Formed: 1934

Organisation type and purpose: Local government body, museum, art gallery.
Parent body:
East Riding of Yorkshire Council

Enquiries to: Administrator
Access:
Access to staff: By letter, by telephone, by fax, by email, visitors by prior appointment
Hours: Apr to Oct, Daily, 1030 to 1730
Access for disabled people: Parking provided, ramped entry, toilet facilities

General description:
Local East Yorkshire history and archaeology, maritime history.
Collections:
Amy Johnson Memorabilia Room
Bridlington Coastguard Collection

Internet home pages:
http://www.bridlington.net/sewerby

2637
SHAFTESBURY ABBEY MUSEUM & GARDEN

Abbey Lodge, Park Walk, Shaftesbury, Dorset, SP7 8JR

Tel: 01747 852910
Fax: 01747 852910
Email: user@shaftesburyabbey.fsnet.co.uk
Full name: Shaftesbury Abbey Museum Preservation Trust Company Limited
Formed: 1986

Organisation type and purpose: Independently owned, registered charity (charity number 293260), museum, suitable for ages: 8+.
Supported by:
Friends of Shaftesbury Abbey

Enquiries to: Chairman
Other contacts: Public Relations Manager
Access:
Access to staff: By letter, by email, visitors by prior appointment
Other restrictions: By prior appointment only.
Access to building, collections or gallery: No prior appointment required
Hours: Apr to Oct: daily, 1000 to 1700
Other restrictions: Reference Library by prior appointment only.
Access for disabled people: level entry, access to all public areas, toilet facilities
Other restrictions: Some areas in the garden are not wheelchair accessible.

General description:
The following aspects may be seen and information elaborated by wall panels, audio-tour and (by appointment) the on-site Reference Library.
Museum and ruins on site of wealthy Benedictine Abbey, founded as a nunnery by King Alfred in 888 - dissolved 1537.
Collections of fine-carved stone and other artefacts from Saxon period to mid-16th century and medieval decorated floor tiles. The casket in which the supposed bones of the murdered King Edward the Martyr were found.
Well-kept site contains a medieval herb garden with information on the types and uses of plants grown there.
Information services:
Library available for reference (for conditions see Access above)
Guided tours by prior appointment.
Special visitor services: Tape recorded guides.
Services for disabled people: For the visually impaired; displays and/or information at wheelchair height.
Collections:
The Library contains books and articles on relevant and comparative subjects as follows:
Archaeology, architecture, Abbey Estates
Benedictine and general monastic life and history
Artefacts/Collections
Edward the Martyr
History (context)
Illustrations of artefacts and events
Relevant literature (fiction)
Press cuttings
Much of the Benedictine and associated collection donated by Father Seanneau
Catalogues:
Catalogue for library is in-house only.

2638
SHAFTESBURY AND DISTRICT HISTORICAL SOCIETY

1 Gold Hill, Shaftesbury, Dorset, SP7 8JW

Tel: 01747 852157
Acronym or abbreviation: SDHS
Formed: 1946

Organisation type and purpose: Membership association, voluntary organisation, registered charity (charity number 229883), museum.
Local history society and museum.
Member of:
Area Museum Council for the South West
Dorset Museums Association

Enquiries to: Honorary Secretary
Direct tel: 01747 851950 (Chairman)
Access:
Access to staff: By letter, by telephone, visitors by prior appointment

General description:
Dorset crafts and industries, local history of North Dorset, Victorian objects, Shaftesbury Abbey, archaeology, agriculture.
Collections:
Coins, costume, maps, prints, weights and measures, local customs, 1744 fire engine
Dorset buttons
Valentine cards
Victorian farming equipment
Printed publications:
History of The Dorset Button
Museum leaflet
Shaftesbury Guide
Visitors Guide in French, German, English
Where to Go by Car Around the Shaftesbury Area

2639
SHAFTESBURY LOCAL HISTORY MUSEUM
Sun & Moon Cottage, Gold Hill, Shaftesbury, Dorset, SP7 8JW

Tel: 01747 852157

Organisation type and purpose: Registered charity, museum.
Owned by:
Shaftesbury Historical Society

Enquiries to: Chairman
Access:
Access to staff: By letter, by telephone, in person
Other restrictions: No resident curator, run totally by volunteers.

General description:
Local history of town.
Collections:
Exhibition of finds from 18 month old dig in centre of town, finds include complete 17th century jug
Catalogues:
Catalogue for library is in-house only.

2640
SHALFORD MILL
Shalford, Guildford, Surrey, GU4 8BS

Tel: 01483 561389

Organisation type and purpose: National organisation, registered charity (charity number 205846), historic building, house or site.
Parent body:
The National Trust (South and South East Region)
South East Regional Office, tel: 01372 453401

Enquiries to: Manager
Access:
Access to staff: By letter, by telephone
Access for disabled people: level entry
Other restrictions: Ground floor fully accessible. No access to other floors.

General description:
A large 18th century watermill on the River Tillingbourne, given in 1932 by a group of anonymous National Trust benefactors calling themselves 'Ferguson's Gang'.

Internet home pages:
http://www.nationaltrust.org.uk

2641
SHAMBELLIE HOUSE MUSEUM OF COSTUME
New Abbey, Dumfries & Galloway, DG2 8HQ

Tel: 01387 850 375
Fax: 01387 850 461
Email: nt@nms.ac.uk
Formed: 1982

Organisation type and purpose: National organisation, museum, historic building, house or site.
Parent body:
National Museums of Scotland (NMS)
Chambers Street, Edinburgh, EH1 1JF, tel: 0131 225 7534, fax: 0131 220 4819

Enquiries to: Manager
Access:
Access to staff: By letter, by telephone, by fax, visitors by prior appointment
Hours: Mon to Fri; 1100 to 1700

General description:
Shambellie House, built in 1856 by David Bryce, houses a costume collection relevant to the social functions of a Scottish country house during the period 1860 to 1930.
Information services:
Special visitor services: Guided tours, materials and/or activities for children.
Education services: Group education facilities..
Collections:
Charles Stewart Costume Collection
Internet home pages:
http://www.nms.ac.uk

2642
SHANDY HALL
See - Laurence Sterne Trust

2643
SHARDLOW HERITAGE CENTRE
London Wharf, London Road, Shardlow, Derby, DE72 2GE

Tel: 01332 792489
Email: shardlow.heritage@which.net
Formed: 1996
Formerly: Shardlow Conservation Group, date of change, 1996
Official Title of Company: Shardlow Heritage Trust

Organisation type and purpose: Registered charity (charity number 1052390), museum, historic building, house or site, suitable for ages: 5+, research organisation.

Enquiries to: Information Officer
Access:
Access to staff: By letter, by telephone, by email, in person, Internet web pages
Access to building, collections or gallery: No prior appointment required
Hours: Sat, Sun, Bank Holidays, 1200 to 1700
Other restrictions: Other times by prior appointment.
Access for disabled people: Parking provided, ramped entry, access to all public areas
Other restrictions: Toilet facilities adjacent public house.

General description:
Story of transhipment port between the Trent and Mersey Canal and River Trent. Village history from Roman times to the present day. Audiovisual presentation, full scale narrowboat cabin, canal clothes for children to try, guided walks available.
Information services:
Library available for reference (for conditions see Access above)
Help with research (even family history).
Special visitor services: Guided tours, materials and/or activities for children.
Services for disabled people: For the visually impaired; displays and/or information at wheelchair height.
Collections:
Blacksmiths' tools
Carpenters' tools
Canal-related items
Social history of Shardlow material
Full-sized mock-up of Narrowboat Cabin
Photographs, documents, maps relating to all aspects of the history of Shardlow (copies in exhibition)
Databases in progress:
a) people index
b) places index
c) subject index
d) photographic collection
Printed publications:
Reproduction Edwardian postcards (25p)
Village Trail (25p)
Information Pack for Schools (£10)

Internet home pages:
http://homepages.which.net/~shardlow.heritage/
Homepage, practical information, programme of activities, brief history of village, virtual walk through village, working port 1770-1948, Shardlow name.

2644
SHAW'S CORNER
Ayot St Lawrence, Welwyn Garden City, Hertfordshire, AL6 9BX

Tel: 01438 820307
Fax: 01438 820307
Email: shawscorner@nationaltrust.org.uk
Formed: 1950

Organisation type and purpose: National organisation, registered charity (charity number 205846), historic building, house or site, suitable for ages: 5+.
Parent body:
The National Trust (East of England)
East Anglia Regional Office, tel: 0870 609 5388

Enquiries to: Custodian
Access:
Access to staff: By letter, by telephone, by fax, by email, Internet web pages
Access for disabled people: ramped entry
Other restrictions: 1 manual wheelchair available. Ramped entrance. No access to other floors. Garden accessible via grass slope. Recommended route map.

General description:
Shaw's Corner, an Edwardian villa, in the tranquil village of Ayot St Lawrence, was the home of George Bernard Shaw from 1906 until his death in 1950. The atmospheric rooms remain much as he left them, with many literary and personal effects on display. The garden has richly planted borders with views over the Hertfordshire countryside. At the bottom of the garden stands Shaw's revolving writing hut where many of his works were written.
Information services:
Helpline available, tel no: 01438 820307.
Braille guide. Large-print guide. Touch list. Handling collection. Scented plants. Monocular.
Front-carrying baby slings for loan. Hipcarrying infant seats for loan.
Suitable for school groups. Family activity packs.
Introductory talks for booked groups.
Major events programme.
Special visitor services: Materials and/or activities for children.
Education services: Resources for Further or Higher Education.
Services for disabled people: For the visually impaired; displays and/or information at wheelchair height.
Collections:
The house is furnished with Shaw's personal possessions including his literary works, documents, photographs, pictures, and everyday objects including his spectacles, typewriter, cameras, walking sticks, radio and an Oscar which Shaw won for best screenplay in 1938
Other objects of note are:
Rodin's bust of Shaw
Shaw's writing desk
A marble of Shaw's hand by Sigismund de Strobl
A wardrobe full of Shaw's clothes
Scrapbooks on life of George Bernard Shaw
Printed publications:
House Guide
Children's Trail
Rhyming Guide
Shaw Sayings
Shaw Card
Property Leaflet (free)
Plays: St Joan; Unpleasant; Major Barbara; Pygmalion; Androcles; Man and Superman; Heartbreak House

Internet home pages:
http://www.nationaltrust.org.uk/shawscorner

2645
SHEERNESS HERITAGE CENTRE
10 Rose Street, Sheerness, Kent, ME12 1AJ

Tel: 0179 5663317
Formed: 1989

continued overleaf

Organisation type and purpose: Local government body, museum, historic building, house or site.

Enquiries to: Chairman
Direct tel: 01795 875047
Direct email: pdummott@supanet.com
Access:
Access to staff: By letter, by telephone, by email, in person, charges made to all users
Access to building, collections or gallery: No prior appointment required
Hours: Daily, 1000 to 1530
Other restrictions: Other hours by prior arrangement.
Prior appointment required for large groups.
Access for disabled people: Parking provided, toilet facilities
Other restrictions: Parking in council car park. Public toilets next door.

General description:
Victorian life, WWII, dockyard history, Swale tourist information.
Information services:
Special visitor services: Guided tours, tape recorded guides..
Collections:
Room settings (Victorian)
Pictures of dockyard and Old Sheerness
Richard Montgomery (sunk off Sheppey)
Various articles on subject

2646
SHEFFIELD ARTS DEPARTMENT

See - Graves Art Gallery; Millennium Galleries

2647
SHEFFIELD BUS MUSEUM TRUST

Tinsley Tram Sheds, Sheffield Road, Tinsley, Sheffield, South Yorkshire, S9 2FY

Tel: 0114 255 3010
Email: webmaster@sheffieldbusmuseum.com
Formed: 1987

Organisation type and purpose: Independently owned, registered charity (charity number 1049895), museum, suitable for ages: all ages.
A museum of Public Transport in Sheffield and South Yorkshire provides an educational background to the public of the history of public transport.

Enquiries to: Company Secretary
Access:
Access to staff: By letter, by telephone, by email, Internet web pages
Access for disabled people: ramped entry

General description:
The museum houses a varied collection of double and single deck buses, ranging from pre-1940 exhibits through to the mid-1970s. A working model railway, plus a Sheffield tram are also part of the collection.
Catalogues:
Catalogue for all of the collections is only available in-house.
Publications list:
is available in hard copy and online.

Internet home pages:
http://www.sheffieldbusmuseum.com

2648
SHEFFIELD CITY MUSEUM AND MAPPIN ART GALLERY

Weston Park, Sheffield, South Yorkshire, S10 2TP

Tel: 0114 278 2600
Fax: 0114 275 0957
Email: info@sheffieldgalleries.org.uk
Formerly: Weston Park Museum, Mappin Art Gallery

Organisation type and purpose: Registered charity (charity number 1068850), museum, art gallery.

Parent body:
Sheffield Galleries & Museums Trust
Links with:
IOCM Council
Museums Association
Yorkshire and Humberside Area Museums Council

Enquiries to: Press and Publicity Officer
Direct tel: 0114 278 2612
Direct fax: 0114 278 2604
Direct email: stephanie.potts@sheffieldgalleries.org.uk
Access:
Access to staff: By letter, by telephone, by fax, by email, visitors by prior appointment, Internet web pages
Hours: Tue to Sat, 1000 to 1700; Sun, 1100 to 1700
Access to building, collections or gallery: No prior appointment required
Hours: Tue to Sat, 1000 to 1700; Sun, 1100 to 1700;
Other restrictions: Mon, closed, except Bank Holidays
The Gallery will close in March 2003 for major refurbishment. For informationon regarding date of reopening contact the Sheffield Galleries & Museums Trust.
Access for disabled people: ramped entry, toilet facilities
Other restrictions: Access to all exhibition areas.

General description:
British paintings, Old Masters to the latest in contemporary art, permanent and temporary exhibitions.
Information services:
Academic and general enquiries are dealt with by specific curators.
Programme of family activities
Adult workshops
Education programme
Special visitor services: Materials and/or activities for children.
Education services: Group education facilities, resources for Key Stages 1 and 2, 3, 4 and Further or Higher Education..
Collections:
Victorian art; contemporary art; applied arts
Publications list:
is available in hard copy.
Electronic and video products:
Colour slides (40 titles)

Internet home pages:
http://www.sheffieldgalleries.org.uk

2649
SHEFFIELD CITY MUSEUM

Weston Park, Sheffield, South Yorkshire, S10 2TP

Tel: 0114 278 2600
Fax: 0114 275 0957
Email: info@sheffieldgalleries.org.uk

Organisation type and purpose: Local government body, registered charity (charity number 1068850), museum, art gallery, suitable for ages: 5+.
Parent body:
Sheffield Galleries and Museums Trust

Enquiries to: Press and Publicity Officer
Direct tel: 0114 278 2612
Direct fax: 0114 278 2604
Access:
Access to staff: By letter, by telephone, by fax, by email, in person
Access to building, collections or gallery: No prior appointment required
Hours: Tue to Sat and Bank Holiday Mondays, 1000 to 1700; Sun 1100 to 1700
Other restrictions: Closed Mondays
The Gallery will close in March 2003 for major refurbishment. For information regarding collections and date of reopening contact the Sheffield Galleries & Museums Trust.
Access for disabled people: ramped entry
Other restrictions: Lift to the café and shop.

General description:
Natural history, decorative arts, archaeology and social history.
Information services:
Programme of family activities, museum trails
Adult workshops
Education programme
Special visitor services: Materials and/or activities for children.
Education services: Group education facilities..
Collections:
Archaeology and Ethnography
Bateman Collection (artefacts, manuscripts)
Bradbury Collection (Old Sheffield Plate)
Gatty Collection (antiquities, marine botany)
Heathcote Collection (antiquities)
Natural history collection
Page Collection (cutlery)
Salt Herbarium
Social history collection

Internet home pages:
http://www.sheffieldgalleries.org.uk
Home page, information on all galleries opening times, collections etc.

2650
SHEFFIELD GALLERIES & MUSEUMS TRUST

Leader House, Surrey Street, Sheffield, South Yorkshire, S1 2LH

Tel: 0114 278 2600
Fax: 0114 278 2604
Email: info@sheffieldgalleries.org.uk
Formed: 1998

Organisation type and purpose: Local government body, registered charity (charity number 1068850).
Administrative body.
Jointly funded by:
Sheffield City Council and the Arts Council of England
Trust sites:
Bishops' House
Meersbrook Park, Norton Lees Lane, Sheffield, South Yorkshire, S8 9BE, tel: 0114 278 2600, fax: 0114 278 2604
Graves Art Gallery
Surrey Street, Sheffield, South Yorkshire, S1 1XZ, tel: 0114 273 5158, fax: 0114 273 4705
Mappin Art Gallery
Weston Park, Sheffield, South Yorkshire, S10 2TP, tel: 0114 278 2600, fax: 0114 275 0957
Millennium Galleries
Arundel Gate, Sheffield, South Yorkshire, S1 2PP, tel: 0114 278 2600, fax: 0114 278 2604
Sheffield City Museum
Weston Park, Sheffield, South Yorkshire, S10 2TP, tel: 0114 278 2600, fax: 0114 275 0957
Access:
Access to staff: By letter, by telephone, by fax, by email, visitors by prior appointment, Internet web pages
Hours: Mon to Fri, 0900 to 1730
Access for disabled people: toilet facilities
Other restrictions: Parking in Surrey Street, one step at door, phone prior to visit if assistance required.

General description:
Galleries and Museums Trust has management responsibility for five musems and galleries in Sheffield, including responsibility for policies, forward planning and performance.

Internet home pages:
http://www.sheffieldgalleries.org.uk

See also - Bishops' House; Graves Art Gallery; Millennium Galleries; Sheffield City Museum; Sheffield City Museum and Mappin Art Gallery

2651
SHEFFIELD PARK
Uckfield, East Sussex, TN22 3QX

Tel: 01825 790321 (Property Office)
Fax: 01825 791264
Email: sheffieldpark@nationaltrust.org.uk

Organisation type and purpose: National organisation, registered charity (charity number 205846), historic building, house or site, suitable for ages: 5+.
Parent body:
National Trust (South and South East Region)
South East Region, tel: 01372 453401

Enquiries to: Manager
Access:
Access to staff: By letter, by telephone, by fax, by email

General description:
A magnificent landscape garden, laid out in the 18th century by 'Capability' Brown and further developed in the early years of the 20th century by its owner, Arthur G. Soames. The original four lakes form the centrepiece. There are dramatic shows of daffodils and bluebells in spring, and the rhododendrons, azaleas and stream garden are spectacular in early summer. Autumn brings stunning colours from the many rare trees and shrubs. Enjoy winter walks in this garden for all seasons.
Restored Grand Water Cascades.

Internet home pages:
http://www.nationaltrust.org.uk

2652
SHEFFIELD UNIVERSITY
See - Turner Museum of Glass

2653
SHEFTON MUSEUM OF GREEK ART AND ARCHAEOLOGY
University of Newcastle upon Tyne, Newcastle upon Tyne, NE1 7RU

Tel: 0191 222 8996
Formed: 1956

Organisation type and purpose: Museum, university department or institute, suitable for ages: 8+.
Parent body:
University of Newcastle Upon Tyne
Newcastle Upon Tyne, NE1 7RU, tel: 0191 222 6000

Enquiries to: Director
Direct tel: 0191 222 7846
Direct fax: 0191 222 8561
Direct email: l.allason-jones@ncl.ac.uk
Other contacts: Education Officer for educational visits.
Access:
Access to staff: By letter, by telephone, by fax, by email, visitors by prior appointment
Access to building, collections or gallery: No prior appointment required
Hours: Mon to Fri, 1000 to 1600
Access for disabled people: Parking provided, ramped entry, access to all public areas, toilet facilities

General description:
Archaeological material from Greek and Etruscan civilization, particularly ceramics, terracottas and metalwork. Roman and Greek sculptures from the Wellcome Institute. Museum is particularly famous for its Attic black and red figure vases and for its bronze vessel handles.
Information services:
Education services: Group education facilities, resources for Key Stages 2, 3, 4 and Further or Higher Education..
Collections:
Wellcome Collection of Greek and Roman sculpture
Shefton Collection of Greek and Etruscan pottery and metalwork
Jacobson Collection of Greek pottery and terracottas
Catalogues:
Catalogue for library is in-house only. Catalogue for all of the collections is only available in-house.

Internet home pages:
http://www.ncl.ac.uk/shefton-museum
Arms and armour collection, general information, education pages.

2654
SHEPPY'S CIDER AND RURAL LIFE MUSEUM
Three Bridges, Bradford-on-Tone, Taunton, Somerset, TA4 1ER

Tel: 01823 461233
Fax: 01823 461712
Email: info@sheppyscider.com
Acronym or abbreviation: Sheppys Cider Farm Centre

Organisation type and purpose: Manufacturing industry, museum.
Farmers and cider makers with museum on site.
Parent body:
R J Sheppy and Son

Enquiries to: Manager
Access:
Access to staff: By letter, by telephone, by fax, by email, visitors by prior appointment
Access to building, collections or gallery: No prior appointment required
Hours: Mon to Sat, 0830 to 1800; Sun, 1200 to 1400 (Easter to Christmas only)
Access for disabled people: Parking provided, access to all public areas, toilet facilities

General description:
A privately owned collection of cider-making and agricultural equipment dating from 1700 to 1924. A video show illustrates the year in the life of a farmer cidermaker, from pruning the trees to pressing the apples.
Collections:
Artefacts relating to rural life, agriculture and cider-making
Cider press, 1700
Edwardian/Georgian farmhouse kitchen
Cooper's tools, 1900s
Bottling equipment, 1920s
Apple picking equipment, 1940-.
Printed publications:
Visitor Leaflet

2655
SHERBORNE MUSEUM
Abbey Gate House, Church Lane, Sherborne, Dorset, DT9 3BP

Tel: 01935 812252
Email: admin@shermus.fsnet.co.uk
Formed: 1966

Organisation type and purpose: Independently owned, museum, suitable for ages: all ages.

Enquiries to: Hon Curator
Access:
Access to staff: By letter, by telephone, by email, in person, visitors by prior appointment, Internet web pages
Hours: Easter to end Oct: Tue to Sat, 1030 to 1630, Sun and bank holidays, 1430 to 1630
Other restrictions: By arrangement at other times.
Access to building, collections or gallery: Prior appointment required
Hours: Easter to end Oct: Tue to Sat, 1030 to 1630, Sun & bank holidays, 1430 to 1630
Access for disabled people: level entry, toilet facilities
Other restrictions: Large print size, stairs marked, ground floor video display of upper floors

General description:
The museum concentrates on exhibits directly connected with Sherborne and its immediate neighbourhood. The exhibits consist of a wide selection of paintings, prints and photographs; a model of Sherborne Old Castle; maps; record books; archaeological specimens; a fine Victorian doll's house; costumes; a display covering the history of the silk industry in the town; and agricultural implements, plus an ecclesiastical wall painting, c. 1500.
Information services:
Library available for reference (for conditions see Access above), CD-ROM based services
Loop system installed.
Special visitor services: Guided tours.
Education services: Group education facilities, resources for Key Stages 1 and 2, 3, 4 and Further or Higher Education.
Services for disabled people: For the visually impaired; for the hearing impaired; displays and/or information at wheelchair height.
Catalogues:
Catalogue for part of the collections is only available in-house.

Internet home pages:
http://www.aboutbritain.com/SherborneMuseum.htm
http://www.Sherbornetown.com

2656
SHERBORNE OLD CASTLE
Cheap Street, Sherborne, Dorset, DT9 3YP0

Organisation type and purpose: National organisation, historic building, house or site.
Parent body:
English Heritage (South West Region)
Tel: 0117 975 0700, fax: 0117 975 0701

Enquiries to: Manager
Access:
Access to staff: By letter, by telephone
Access to building, collections or gallery: No prior appointment required
Hours: 29 Mar to 30 Sep: daily, 1000 to 1800,1 to 31 Oct: daily, 1000 to 1300 and 1400 to 1700,1 Nov to 31 Mar: Wed to Sun, 1000 to 1300 and 1400 to 1600
Other restrictions: Closed 24 to 26 Dec and 1 Jan
Opening times are subject to change, for up-to-date information contact English Heritage by phone or visit the website.

General description:
Cromwell said of Sherborne that it was a 'malicious and mischievous castle'. But he would, because it had taken him 16 days to capture this early 12th century castle during the Civil War. It was then abandoned.

Internet home pages:
http://www.english-heritage.org.uk

2657
SHERINGHAM MUSEUM
Station Road, Sheringham, Norfolk, NR26 8RE

Tel: 01263 821871
Fax: 01263 825741
Formed: 1991

Organisation type and purpose: Independently owned, voluntary organisation, registered charity, museum, art gallery.
To educate and inform residents, visitors and organised groups on the history, development and culture of Sheringham.

Enquiries to: Vice Chairman
Direct tel: 01263 822895
Direct fax: 01263 825741
Other contacts: Chairman for matters relating to policies.
Access:
Access to staff: By letter, by telephone

continued overleaf

General description:
Information generally on Sheringham and its immediate area; all information on computer; photographic library; recent finds of 1.5 million year old elephant from cliffs to West of Sheringham; displays on lifeboats, boat building and local fishing industry.
Information services:
Education services: Resources for Key Stages 1 and 2, 3 and 4..
Collections:
All archival material is currently being computerised
Hewitt collection, (slides and negatives showing family life/ costumes of the era), 1920s-1930s
Upcher collection, 1800s
Printed publications:
Victorian Sheringham (educational school pack, £4, no restriction on photocopying)
Sheringham and District in Old Photographs (£3.99)
The Beach, Formation and Change (local studies book, £2.95 plus p&p)
Processes Affecting North Norfolk's Cliffs and Coastal Defences (local studies book, £2.95 plus p&p)
Reprints of vintage postcards (10p to 25p)
Electronic and video products:
Sheringham - East Anglian Film Archive, University of East Anglia (video, £13.50 inc p&p)
Sheringham In Days Gone By (video, £11 inc p&p)

Internet home pages:
http://www.sheringhammuseum.co.uk

2658
SHERWOOD FOREST COUNTRY PARK & VISITOR CENTRE
Edwinstowe, Mansfield, Nottinghamshire, NG21 9HN

Tel: 01623 823202
Fax: 01623 823202
Email: sherwoodforest@nottscc.gov.uk

Organisation type and purpose: Historic building, house or site, suitable for ages: all ages.

Enquiries to: Manager
Access:
Access to staff: By letter, by telephone, by fax, by email, in person, Internet web pages
Access to building, collections or gallery: No prior appointment required
Access for disabled people: Parking provided, toilet facilities

General description:
SSSI site, ancient oak woodland.

Internet home pages:
http://www.sherwood-forest.org.uk
http://www.robinhood.co.uk

2659
SHETLAND CROFTHOUSE MUSEUM
Voe, Boddam, Dunrossness, Lerwick, Shetland, ZE2 9JG

Tel: 01950 460557
Formed: 1972

Organisation type and purpose: Local government body, museum, suitable for ages: 12+.
Connections with:
Shetland Museum
Lower Hillhead, Lerwick, Shetland

Enquiries to: Curator
Direct tel: 01595 695057
Direct fax: 01595 696729
Direct email: tommy.watt@s.c.shetland.gov.uk
Access:
Access to staff: By letter, by telephone, by fax, by email, in person
Access to building, collections or gallery: Prior appointment required
Hours: 1 May to 30 Sep: daily, 1000 to 1300 and 1400 to 1700
Access for disabled people: Parking provided
Other restrictions: Access difficult.

General description:
Agriculture, local furniture.
Publications list:
is available in hard copy.
Printed publications:
Rural Life in Shetland & Guidebook to the Croft House Museum (Tait I, £6)

Address for ordering publications:
Printed publications:
Shetland Museum
Lower Hillhead, Lerwick, Shetland

Internet home pages:
http://www.shetland-museum.org.uk

2660
SHETLAND MUSEUM
Lower Hillhead, Lerwick, Shetland, ZE1 0EL

Tel: 01595 695057
Fax: 01595 696729
Email: museum@sic.shetland.gov.uk
Formed: 1966

Organisation type and purpose: Local government body, museum, suitable for ages: 5+.
Associated with:
Böd of Gremista Museum
Shetland Croft House Museum

Enquiries to: Curator
Access:
Access to staff: By letter, by telephone, by fax, by email
Hours: Mon, Wed, Fri, 1000 to 1900; Tue, Thu, Sat, 1000 to 1700
Access for disabled people: access to all public areas, toilet facilities

General description:
Shetland archaeology, social history, folk life, maritime history, textiles etc at the Croft House Museum, a typical croft home, steading and water mill of *c.* 1870.
Collections:
Historic photographic collection
Catalogues:
Catalogue for library is in-house only.

Internet home pages:
http://www.shetland-museum.org.uk

2661
SHIBDEN HALL
Lister Road, Halifax, West Yorkshire, HX3 6XG

Tel: 01422 352246
Fax: 01422 348440
Email: shibden.hall@calderdale.gov.uk

Organisation type and purpose: Local government body, museum, historic building, house or site, suitable for ages: 5+.

Enquiries to: Manager
Access:
Access to staff: By letter, by telephone, by fax, by email, in person, Internet web pages
Access for disabled people: Parking provided, toilet facilities
Other restrictions: Disabled bell for assistance.

General description:
Shibden Hall, first bulit in about 1420
was the home of the Lister family for over 300 years. The rooms and displays show life as it was lived over the years.
Information services:
Education services: Group education facilities, resources for Key Stages 1 and 2, 3 and Further or Higher Education.
Services for disabled people: For the visually impaired.
Collections:
Furniture, furnishings and artefacts in rooms showing their normal setting
Publications list:
is available on-line.

Internet home pages:
http://www.calderdale.gov.uk

2662
SHIPLEY ART GALLERY
Prince Consort Road, Gateshead, Tyne and Wear, NE8 4JB

Tel: 0191 477 1495
Minicom no. 0191 477 1495
Fax: 0191 478 7917
Formed: 1917

Organisation type and purpose: Local government body, registered charity, museum, art gallery, suitable for ages: 5+.
Parent body:
Tyne & Wear Museums (TWM)
Discovery Museum, Blandford Square, Newcastle upon Tyne, NE1 4JA, tel: 0191 232 6789, fax: 0191 230 2614

Enquiries to: Curator
Other contacts: Education Officer for school visits and activities.
Access:
Access to staff: By letter, by telephone, by fax, in person
Other restrictions: By appointment only.
Access to building, collections or gallery: No prior appointment required
Hours: Mon to Sat, 1000 to 1700; Sun, 1400 to 1700
Access for disabled people: ramped entry, level entry, access to all public areas, toilet facilities

General description:
Contains Old Master and Victorian paintings; prints and watercolours; local decorative arts, especially glass; a wide ranging contemporary craft collection combining a dazzling display of glass, jewellery, ceramics, textiles and furniture alongside stunning historical artworks; and a local and industrial history display.
Information services:
Special visitor services: Materials and/or activities for children.
Education services: Group education facilities.
Services for disabled people: For the visually impaired; for the hearing impaired; displays and/or information at wheelchair height.
Collections:
The gallery houses a fine collection of oil paintings, watercolours, contemporary craft, applied art and local Gateshead history
Shipley bequest, Joseph Shipley's collection of Old Master and British paintings which created the Gallery, 1520-1880, 483 items
The Shipley is also home to the Craft Council's regional computer terminal 'photostore' - the only Gallery in the North East to have this facility
Press-moulded glass by the Gateshead factories of Sowerby's and Davidson's, 1850-1980, c. 300 items
Catalogues:
Catalogue for part of the collections is only available in-house.

Internet home pages:
http://www.twmuseums.org.uk/shipley/index.html
Gallery history, contacts, what's here, facilities, collections, education, directions.

2663
SHIPWRECK & HERITAGE CENTRE
Quay Road, St Austell, Cornwall, PL25 3NJ

Tel: 01726 69897
Fax: 01726 69897
Email: admin@shipwreckcharlestown.com
Formed: 1978

Organisation type and purpose: Independently owned, museum, suitable for ages: 5+.
Visitor centre.

Enquiries to: Administrator

Access:
Access to staff: By letter, by telephone, by fax, by email, visitors by prior appointment
Access to building, collections or gallery: No prior appointment required
Hours: 1 Mar to 31 Oct: daily, 1000 to 1700 (1800 in high season)

General description:
Shipwreck artefacts, history of diving, steam liners, Titanic.
Information services:
Special visitor services: Guided tours.
Education services: Group education facilities, resources for Key Stages 1 and 2, 3, 4 and Further or Higher Education..

Internet home pages:
http://www.shipwreckcharlestown.com
Brief introduction to the Centre.

2664
SHIRE HALL GALLERY, THE
Market Square, Stafford, ST16 2LD

Tel: 01785 278345
Email: shirehallgallery@staffordshire.gov.uk

Parent body:
Staffordshire County Council
Member of:
North Staffordshire Museums Association

General description:
Situated in the Shire Hall formerly used as the Crown Court. The Gallery has fine art historical collections of Staffordshire and topography or works by artists associated with the county. Contemporary fine art and craft collections by British artists. Open access to Court One, refitted in 1845.
Collections:
Contemporary jewellery by many British makers available as a study collection
Designs and documentation relating to Staffordshire County Council's Public Art commissions.

Internet home pages:
http://www.staffordshire.gov.uk/shirehallgallery

2665
SHIRE HALL MUSEUM
Common Place, Walsingham, Norfolk, NR22 6BP

Tel: 01328 820510
Fax: 01328 820098
Email: walsingham.museum@farmline.com
Formed: 1971

Organisation type and purpose: Independently owned, museum, historic building, house or site, suitable for ages: 8+.
Owned by:
Walsingham Estate Company

Enquiries to: Manager
Access:
Access to staff: By letter, by telephone, by fax, visitors by prior appointment
Other restrictions: Telephone for details.
Access for disabled people: ramped entry
Other restrictions: Restricted access in museum.

General description:
Displays on the history of Walsingham and the story of pilgrimage in this fascinating village. The museum is housed in the former Magistrate's Court and part of the museum contains the original Georgian Courtroom, as it was when last used in 1971.
Information services:
Special visitor services: Guided tours.
Education services: Group education facilities..
Collections:
Photographs and artefacts relating to village life in Walsingham and North Norfolk
Information, photographs and artefacts on Walsingham as a religious and legal centre
Publications list:
is available in hard copy.

Printed publications:
Publication list available on request

2666
SHIRE HORSE FARM & CARRIAGE MUSEUM
Lower Gryllis Farm, Treskillard, Camborne, Cornwall, TR16 6LA

Tel: 01209 713606
Formed: 1972

Organisation type and purpose: Independently owned, museum, suitable for ages: 5+.

Enquiries to: Owners
Access:
Access to staff: By letter, by telephone
Access for disabled people: Parking provided, level entry, access to all public areas, toilet facilities

General description:
Horse-drawn vehicles of 19th and 20th century. Commercial, pleasure and farming. 20 Heavy Horses, Suffolk Punch, Clydesdale and Shire.
Information services:
Special visitor services: Tape recorded guides..
Collections:
Horse drawn, dleasure, dommercial vehicles and farm machinery
Working Heavy Horses, Shire, Clydesdale and Suffolk Punch

2667
SHIRLEY'S BONE AND FLINT MILL
See - Etruria Industrial Museum

2668
SHOE MUSEUM, THE
40 High Street, Street, Somerset, BA16 0YA

Tel: 01458 842169

Organisation type and purpose: Independently owned, museum, suitable for ages: 12+.
Parent body:
Clark's Shoes

Enquiries to: Administrator
Access:
Access to staff: By letter, by telephone
Hours: Mon to Fri, 1000 to 1645; Sat, 1000 to 1700; Sun, 1100 to 1700
Other restrictions: Admission free.

General description:
The evolution of footwear from 300 AD but mainly from 18th century to the present day.
Information services:
Guided tours by prior arrangement.
Special visitor services: Guided tours..
Collections:
1200 shoes in the museum
6000 historic shoes held off-site

2669
SHOREHAM AIRCRAFT MUSEUM
13 High Street, Shoreham, Sevenoaks, Kent, TN14 7TB

Tel: 01959 524416
Fax: 01959 524416
Acronym or abbreviation: SAM
Formed: 1978
Formerly: Shoreham Aircraft Preservation Society 1940-45, date of change, 1988

Organisation type and purpose: Independently owned, voluntary organisation, museum, suitable for ages: 8+, research organisation.

Enquiries to: Curator
Access:
Access to staff: By letter, by telephone, by fax
Hours: May to end Sep: Sun only, 1000 to 1700

General description:
Exhibitions of aviation relics recovered and donated from the air battles fought over southern England in 1940, RAF and Luftwaffe, Home Front memorabilia. Aviation Art Gallery.
Publications list:
is available in hard copy.
Printed publications:
Museum colour leaflet (free)
Aviation prints

Internet home pages:
http://www.s-a-m.freeserve.co.uk

2670
SHOREHAM AIRPORT ARCHIVE
Visitor Centre, Shoreham Airport, Shoreham-by-Sea, West Sussex, BN43 5FF

Tel: 01273 441061 and 07885 707425
Fax: 01273 296899
Formed: 1990

Organisation type and purpose: Service industry, voluntary organisation, suitable for ages: all ages, research organisation.
An archive with historical exhibition, similar to small museum.

Enquiries to: Archivist
Access:
Access to staff: By letter, by telephone, by fax, visitors by prior appointment

General description:
Archive relates purely to Shoreham Airport and those who have served there; exhibition and history display.

Internet home pages:
http://www.thearchiveshorham.co.uk

2671
SHOTTS HERITAGE CENTRE
Benhar Road, Shotts, North Lanarkshire, ML7 5EN

Tel: 01501 821556
Formed: 1994

Organisation type and purpose: Local government body, museum, suitable for ages: 12+.
Parent body:
Museums Section
North Lanarkshire Council
Buchanan Business Park, Stepps, Glasgow, G33 6HR, tel: 0141 304 1975, fax: 0141 304 1902

Enquiries to: Curator
Direct tel: 01698 251000
Direct fax: 01698 268867
Access:
Access to staff: By letter, by telephone, by fax
Access for disabled people: Parking provided, ramped entry, access to all public areas, toilet facilities

General description:
A small section within Shotts Library has displays on the area's covenanting history, the local iron industry, social and economic conditions 19th to 21st centuries.
Information services:
Education services: Resources for Key Stages 2 and 4..
Collections:
General displays of industrial and commercial artefacts from the days of the areas heavy industries
Graphic panels and display cases tell the story of the parish during the covenanting uprising of the 17th century
Catalogues:
Catalogue for all of the collections is published.

2672
SHREWSBURY CASTLE AND SHROPSHIRE REGIMENTAL MUSEUM

Castle Street, Shrewsbury, Shropshire, SY1 2AT

Tel: 01743 358516 or 262292
Fax: 01743 270023
Email: shropsrm@zoom.co.uk

Organisation type and purpose: Registered charity (charity number 294260), museum, historic building, house or site, suitable for ages: 5+, research organisation.
Castle: Local government body.
Museum: Independently owned.

Enquiries to: Curator
Access:
Access to staff: By letter, by telephone, by fax, by email, in person, visitors by prior appointment, Internet web pages
Access to building, collections or gallery: No prior appointment required
Hours: Summer: daily, 1000 to 1700
Variable hours outside main Easter to Oct period (phone for details).
Access for disabled people: Parking provided, ramped entry, access to all public areas, toilet facilities
Other restrictions: Parking by prior arrangement; access to all areas except one small display.

General description:
The castle houses the local regimental museum on 3 floors - specialised collections of arms, uniform, medals, badges and related materials (china, silverware, embroideries etc) covering 53rd Regiment, 85th Light Infantry, KSLI, Shrops. Yeomanry and Shrops. Artillery and associated militia, volunteer and territorial units from 1755-1970. Modern army display, castle history display, Lord Lieutenancy display; military history; family history with military connections.
Information services:
Library available for reference (for conditions see Access above)
Guided tours on request by prior arrangement.
Special visitor services: Guided tours, materials and/or activities for children.
Education services: Group education facilities, resources for Key Stages 1 and 2, 3, 4 and Further or Higher Education..
Collections:
British military antiquities of all kinds, post 1755 up to c. 1970
Military Collection - uniform, medals, weapons, badges, trophies, colours, silverware, personal effects
Limited archive and photographic collections covering Shropshire military units 1755-1970
Other displays: Castle history, modern army, Lords Lieutenant
Catalogues:
Catalogue for library is in-house only. Catalogue for all of the collections is only available in-house.
Publications list:
is available in hard copy.
Printed publications:
Works on regimental history and related topics (direct from shop)
Electronic and video products:
CD-ROMs, cassette tapes (for purchase via shop)

Internet home pages:
http://www.shropshireregimental.co.uk
Brief description of regimental history and castle details. Outline history of various local units represented in Museum, basic customer details, hours, fees etc.

2673
SHREWSBURY MUSEUMS SERVICE

Shrewsbury Museum and Art Gallery (Rowley's House), Barker Street, Shrewsbury, Shropshire, SY1 1QH

Tel: 01743 361196
Fax: 01743 358411
Email: museums@shrewsbury-atcham.gov.uk
Formed: 1835

Organisation type and purpose: Local government body, museum, art gallery, historic building, house or site, suitable for ages: all ages.
Parent body:
Shrewsbury and Atcham Borough Council
Tel: 01743 281000, fax: 01743 271594
Affiliated to:
West Midlands Regional Museums Council
Tel: 01527 872258, fax: 01527 576960, email/website: wmrmc@btinternet.com
Member of:
Group for Education in Museums
Tel: 020 7243 4456, email/website: http://www.gen.org.uk
Midlands Federation of Museums and Art Galleries
Tel: 01952 433522, fax: 01952 432204, email/website: igmt@aol.com
Museums Association
Tel: 020 7608 2933, fax: 020 7250 1929
Registered with the:
Resource: The Council for Museums, Archives and Libraries
Tel: 020 7273 1444, fax: 020 7273 1404, email/website: info@resource.gov.uk
Other branch museums:
Coleham Pumping Station
Longden Coleham, Shrewsbury, Shropshire, SY3 7DN, tel: 01743 362947, fax: 01743 358411, email/website: museums@shrewsbury-atcham.gov.uk
Shrewsbury Castle
Castle Street, Shrewsbury, Shropshire, SY1 2AT, tel: 01743 358516, fax: 01743 358411, email/website: museums@shrewsbury-atcham.gov.uk

Enquiries to: Operations Manager
Other contacts: Collections Manager for all enquiries about the collections held by the museums.
Access:
Access to staff: By letter, by telephone, by fax, by email, visitors by prior appointment
Hours: Mon to Fri, 0900 to 1700
Other restrictions: Appointments always advisable.
Access for disabled people: ramped entry
Other restrictions: Stair lift to special exhibitions gallery, all other parts accessible by stairs only.

General description:
Roman and medieval archaeology of Shrewsbury and Shropshire, local history and prehistory, local social and domestic history, Shropshire ceramics (Caughley, Coalport, Jackfield, Benthall, Craven Dunnill, Wrockwardine, Maw), fine art, drawings and watercolours, 18th to 20th century costumes, Shropshire herbarium, flora and fauna, Shropshire geology.
Collections:
Database of large areas of collections
Hazel Bailey costume collection
Kay Kohler embroidery collection
Lily F Chitty collections of archaeology and geology
Local 17th, 18th, 19th century tokens
Morley Tonkin collection of watercolours
Reference books on all areas of museums' collections
Roman material from Viroconium (plus excavation reports)
Shropshire herbarium
Shropshire porcelains and ceramics, including catalogues of Coalport and Caughley porcelains
Shropshire prehistory
Catalogues:
Catalogue for part of the collections is only available in-house.
Printed publications:
Battle of Shrewsbury, 1403 (1979)
Coinage of Wroxeter (1995)
Illustrated History of Shrewsbury (1982) (to be revised 2002)
Old Shrewsbury Show (1980)
Red Data Book of Vascular Plants (1995)
Electronic and video products:
Barrels, Bales and Business (video, 1994 for purchase)

Internet home pages:
http://www.shrewsburymuseums.com
Visitor information, events, contacts, services, special exhibitions, collections, general information.
Approximately 3000 images and information of items from the collections of Shrewsbury Museums Service, The Ironbridge Gorge Museum Trust and The Wedgwood Museum.

2674
SHROPSHIRE COUNTY MUSEUM SERVICE

Ludlow Museum Office, 47 Old Street, Ludlow, Shropshire, SY8 1NW

Tel: 01584 873857
Fax: 01584 872019
Email: ludlow.musem@shropshire_cc.gov.uk
Acronym or abbreviation: SCC
Formed: 1833
Formerly: Buttercross Museum

Organisation type and purpose: Local government body, museum, suitable for ages: all ages.
Parent body:
Shropshire County Museum Service (SHRCM)
Acton Scott Historic Working Farm, Wenlock Lodge, Church Stretton, Shropshire, SY6
Other address:
Ludlow Museum
16-18 Castle Square, Ludlow, Shropshire, tel: 01584 875384

Enquiries to: Curator
Other contacts: Museum Assistant for general enquiries.
Access:
Access to staff: By letter, by telephone, by fax, by email, in person, visitors by prior appointment
Hours: Mon to Fri, 0900 to 1300 and 1400 to 1700
Access to building, collections or gallery: No access other than to staff
Hours: Apr to Oct: Tue to Fri, 1030 to 1300 and 1400 to 1700
Jun to Aug: Mon to Sun, 1030 to 1300 and 1400 to 1700
Access for disabled people: ramped entry, level entry, access to all public areas, toilet facilities

General description:
Palaeontology, mineralogy, petrology, entomology, mollusca, botany, osteology, mammals, birds, social history, local history and art.
Information services:
Library available for reference (for conditions see Access above)
Special visitor services: Materials and/or activities for children.
Education services: Resources for Key Stages 1 and 2.
Services for disabled people: Displays and/or information at wheelchair height.
Collections:
Local photographs, journals, ephemera

Catalogues:
Catalogue for part of the collections is only available in-house.

Internet home pages:
http://www.shropshire-cc.gov.uk/museum.nsf
Information on the county museum service.

See also - Biological Records Centre & Ludlow Museum; Ludlow Museum

2675
SHROPSHIRE REGIMENTAL MUSEUM
See - Shrewsbury Castle and Shropshire Regimental Museum

2676
SHUGBOROUGH ESTATE
Milford, Nr Stafford, Staffordshire, ST17 0XB

Tel: 01889 881388
Fax: 01889 881323
Email: shugborough.promotions@staffordshire.gov.uk

Organisation type and purpose: National organisation, registered charity (charity number 205846), museum, historic building, house or site, suitable for ages: 5+.
Parent body:
The National Trust (West Midlands Region)
West Midlands Regional Office, tel: 01743 708100
Financed and administered by:
Staffordshire County Council

Enquiries to: Property Manager
Access:
Access to staff: By letter, by telephone, by fax, by email, in person, Internet web pages
Access to building, collections or gallery: No prior appointment required
Hours: House and Farm: end of Mar to end of Sep, Tue to Sun, 1100 to 1700
Other restrictions: Open Bank Holiday Mons. House, county museum, farm & gardens open Oct first 3 Suns. Last admission 1615. Opening times vary; tel. to check
Access for disabled people: Parking provided, toilet facilities
Other restrictions: Drop-off point. 6 manual wheelchairs available. Powered mobility vehicles: 2 single-seater. Steps to entrance. Stairclimber available. No access to other floors. Grounds largely accessible. Recommended route map.

General description:
Shugborough is the seat of the Earls of Lichfield. The late 17th century house was enlarged c.1750 and again at the turn of the 19th century, and contains interesting collections of china, silver, paintings and furniture. The stable block houses the original servants' quarters.
There is a rare breeds farmstead.
Information services:
Wide range of guided tours for booked groups daily from 1030, inc. garden tours, connoisseur tours for special-interest groups. Evening tours also available.
Tel. for details
Special events programme includes open-air concerts and themed activities, Christmas evenings and craft festivals
Braille guide. Large-print guide. Audio guide
Suitable for school groups. Education room/centre.
Hands-on activities. Children's guide. Children's quiz/trail
Special visitor services: Guided tours, tape recorded guides, materials and/or activities for children.
Education services: Group education facilities.
Services for disabled people: For the visually impaired.

Internet home pages:
http://www.nationaltrust.org.uk

2677
SHUTE BARTON
Shute, Axminster, Devon, EX13 7PT

Tel: 01297 34692 (NT tenant)

Organisation type and purpose: National organisation, registered charity, historic building, house or site, suitable for ages: all ages.
Parent body:
The National Trust (South West Region)
Devon Regional Office, tel: 01392 881691

Enquiries to: Manager
Access:
Access to staff: By letter, by telephone

General description:
One of the most important surviving nonfortified manor houses of the Middle Ages.
Begun in 1380 and completed in the late 16th century, then partly demolished in the late 18th century, the house has battlemented turrets, late Gothic windows and a Tudor gatehouse.

Internet home pages:
http://www.nationaltrust.org.uk/regions/devon

2678
SIBSEY TRADER WINDMILL
Sibsey, Boston, Lincolnshire

Tel: 01205 460647

Organisation type and purpose: Historic building, house or site.
Parent body:
English Heritage (East Midlands Region)
44 Derngate, Northampton, NN1 1UH, tel: 01604 735400, fax: 01604 735401

Enquiries to: Site Manager
Access:
Access to building, collections or gallery: No prior appointment required
Hours: Apr to Sep, Sat and Bank Holiday 1000 to 1800, Sun, 1100 to 1800.

General description:
A six-story tower windmill built in 1877 containing the original machinery for grinding corn. The mill has recently been restored.

Internet home pages:
http://www.english-heritage.org.uk

2679
SID VALE HERITAGE CENTRE
Church Street, Sidmouth, Devon, EX10 8LZ

Tel: 01395 516139
Email: sidmouth@devonmuseums.net
Acronym or abbreviation: SVHC
Formed: 1951

Organisation type and purpose: Registered charity (charity number 262514), museum.
Parent body:
Sid Vale Association (SVA)
c/o SVHC

Enquiries to: Administrator
Access:
Access to staff: By letter
Other restrictions: Operated entirely by volunteers.
Access to building, collections or gallery: Prior appointment required
Hours: Easter to Oct: Mon, 1400 to 1630; Tue to Sat, 1000 to 1230 and 1400 to 1630

General description:
Local antiquities, Victoriana, costumes and lace, old prints and photographs, world heritage coast information.
Printed publications:
A number of publications on local subjects

2680
SILK MUSEUM
Macclesfield School of Art, Park Lane, Macclesfield, Cheshire, SK11 6JY

Tel: 01625 612045
Fax: 01625 612048
Email: silkmuseum@tiscali.co.uk
Formed: 2002
Formerly: Macclesfield School of Art and Science, date of change, 1879-1950s; Macclesfield College of Further Education, date of change, 1950s-1990s

Organisation type and purpose: Registered charity (charity number 519521), museum, historic building, house or site, suitable for ages: 5+.
Parent body:
Macclesfield Museums Trust
Tel: 01265 613210

Enquiries to: Director
Access:
Access to staff: By letter, by telephone, by fax, by email
Access to building, collections or gallery: No prior appointment required
Hours: Mon to Sat, 1100 to 1700; Sun 1300 to 1700
Other restrictions: Closed Christmas Day, Boxing Day, and New Year's Day
Access for disabled people: ramped entry, toilet facilities
Other restrictions: Wheelchair access is through the garden, right of main entrance. A ramp links the first two galleries, assistance may be required to access the third gallery. Wheelchair lift to first floor.

General description:
The history of the School of Art, displays of sericulture, the properties of silk, dyeing and weaving, design, printing, knitting, embroidery and machinery.
Information services:
Library available for reference (for conditions see Access above)
Computer catalogue available, providing digital access to over 2000 items in the reserve collection
Research facilities are available by appointment through the director 01625 613210.
Special visitor services: Materials and/or activities for children.
Education services: Group education facilities.
Services for disabled people: Displays and/or information at wheelchair height.
Collections:
Artefacts associated with the industry: machines, samples etc.
Catalogues:
Catalogue for all of the collections is only available in-house.

Internet home pages:
http://www.silk-macclesfield.org
Information, access to museums, calender of events, education, publications, and news of the Friends of Macclesfield Silk Heritage.

2681
SILVER STUDIO COLLECTION
See - Museum of Domestic Design & Architecture

2682
SION HILL HALL
Kirby Wiske, Thirsk, North Yorkshire, YO7 4EU

Tel: 01845 587206
Fax: 01845 587486
Email: sionhill.hall@virgin.net
Formed: 1972

Organisation type and purpose: Historic building, house or site.
Charitable trust.
Links with:
H W Mawer Trust

continued overleaf

Tel: 01845 587206, fax: 01845 587486, email/website: sionhill.hall@virgin.net

Enquiries to: Secretary
Other contacts: Resident Trustee
Access:
Access to staff: By letter, by telephone, by fax, by email, Internet web pages
Access to building, collections or gallery: Prior appointment required
Access for disabled people: Parking provided, ramped entry, toilet facilities
Other restrictions: Access to gound floor only

Collections:
Mawer collection of furniture; porcelain; paintings; clocks; and bygones covering the period from 1650 to 1930.
Additions since acquired, comprising period costume from 1850-1930.

Internet home pages:
http://www.sionhillhall.co.uk

2683
SISSINGHURST CASTLE GARDEN
Sissinghurst, Cranbrook, Kent, TN17 2AB

Tel: 01580 710700
Fax: 01580 710702
Email: sissinghurst@nationaltrust.org.uk

Organisation type and purpose: National organisation, registered charity (charity number 205846), historic building, house or site.
Parent body:
The National Trust (South and South East Region)
South East Regional Office, tel: 01494 528051

Enquiries to: Manager
Access:
Access to staff: By letter, by telephone, by fax, by email
Access to building, collections or gallery: No prior appointment required
Hours: Late Mar to early Nov, Mon, Tue, Fri, 1100 to 1830, Sat and Sun, 1000 to 1830
Open Bank Holidays, 1000 to 1830
Other restrictions: Last admission 1 hour before closing or before dusk if earlier.
The library and Vita Sackville-West's study close each day at 1730. Tower and library opening may be restricted early and late season. Please tel. to check details. No tripods or easels in the garden.
Access for disabled people: Parking provided
Other restrictions: Designated parking 115yds. Drop-off point. 4 manual wheelchairs available, booking essential. Level entrance to shopand to restaurant. Paths narrow and uneven so admission restricted to 2 wheelchair users at a time. Unsuitable for large powered vehicles, if transfer to a manual wheelchair is impossible tel. in advance. Trained companions for visually impaired visitors may be available; tel. in advance. Recommended route map.

General description:
One of the world's most celebrated gardens, the creation of Vita Sackville-West and her husband, Sir Harold Nicolson. Developed around the surviving parts of an Elizabethan mansion with a central red-brick prospect tower, a series of small, enclosed compartments, intimate in scale and romantic in atmosphere, provide outstanding design and colour through the season. The study, where Vita worked, and library are also open to visitors.
Information services:
Helpline available, tel no: Infoline 01580 710701.
Braille guide. Large-print guide. Scented plants.
Front-carrying baby slings for loan. Back-carriers for loan. Not ideal for children.
Children's quiz/trail.
Painting in the garden, artists with easels Wed and Thur. Please tel. for details.
Special visitor services: Materials and/or activities for children.
Services for disabled people: For the visually impaired.

Internet home pages:
http://www.nationaltrust.org.uk

2684
SITE GALLERY
1 Brown Street, Sheffield, South Yorkshire, S1 2BS

Tel: 0114 281 2077
Fax: 0114 281 2078
Email: info@sitegallery.org

Organisation type and purpose: Registered charity (charity number 510322), art gallery.

Enquiries to: Director
Access:
Access to staff: By letter, by telephone, by fax, by email

General description:
Contemporary art.
Information services:
Education services: Group education facilities..

Internet home pages:
http://www.sitegallery.org/

2685
SITTINGBOURNE AND KEMSLEY LIGHT RAILWAY
PO Box 300, Sittingbourne, Kent, ME10 2DZ

Tel: 0871 871 4606
Fax: 01795 410952
Email: info@sklr.net
Acronym or abbreviation: SKLR
Formed: 1969
Formed from membership of: Locomotive Club of Great Britain

Organisation type and purpose: Membership association (membership is by subscription), present number of members: 230, registered charity (charity number 1057079), museum, suitable for ages: all ages.
Light railway.
Preservation and operation of South East England's only preserved narrow gauge former industrial railway.

Enquiries to: Director
Direct tel: 07946 717217
Direct email: zdaunt-jones@sklr.net
Access:
Access to staff: By letter, by telephone, by fax, by email, in person, visitors by prior appointment
Hours: Mon to Sun 0900 to 1700
Other restrictions: Access only by steam train; see website for timetable.

General description:
Preservation of historic steam locomotives, rolling stock and freight vehicles, with associated track, signalling etc. Trains run from Sittingbourne Viaduct to Kemsley Down along the preserved southern half of the former Bowater's Industrial Railway, which, until 1969, was used to convey both raw materials and finished paper products between the mills at Sittingbourne and Kemsley, and the dock at Ridham. The museum expalins the full history of the railway, from building the line at the turn of the century, through preservation in 1969, right up to the present day.
Printed publications:
Stock Books, Historical (for purchase, direct)
Guide Books, Historical (for purchase, direct)
SKLR: Timetable and Brochure (free, direct)
Electronic and video products:
SKLR (Video, for purchase, direct)

Internet home pages:
http://www.sklr.net
Full details of railway and operation.

2686
SITWELL ESTATES
See - Renishaw Hall Gardens, Museum and Art Gallery

2687
SIZERGH CASTLE & GARDEN
Sizergh, Kendal, Cumbria, LA8 8AE

Tel: 015395 60070 (House Manager
Fax: 015395 61621
Email: ntrust@sizerghcastle.fsnet.co.uk

Organisation type and purpose: National organisation, registered charity (charity number 205846), museum, historic building, house or site, suitable for ages: 5+.
Parent body:
The National Trust (North West)
North West Regional Office, tel: 0870 609 5391

Enquiries to: House Manager
Access:
Access to staff: By letter, by telephone, by fax, by email
Access for disabled people: Parking provided, level entry, toilet facilities
Other restrictions: Designated parking 250yds. Drop-off point. 2 manual wheelchairs available. 2 single-seater powered mobility vehicles. Ground floor fully accessible, but only limited contents. No access to other floors. Photograph album. Reproduction of Inlaid Chamber panelling in entrance hall. Ramped entrance to shop. Steps to tea-room entrance. Portable ramp available. Grounds largely accessible. Recommended route map.

General description:
The home of the Strickland family for over 760 years, the medieval castle was extended in Elizabethan times and has an exceptional series of oak-panelled interiors with intricately carved chimneypieces and early oak furniture, culminating in the magnificent Inlaid Chamber. The castle is surrounded by handsome gardens which include a particularly imposing and beautiful rock garden. The estate has flower-rich limestone pasture and ancient woodland supporting numerous species of butterfly.
Information services:
Braille guide.
Hip-carrying infant seats for loan.
Suitable for school groups. Children's guide. Children's quiz/trail. Adult study days.
Special visitor services: Materials and/or activities for children.
Services for disabled people: For the visually impaired.

Internet home pages:
http://www.nationaltrust.org.uk

2688
SKENFRITH CASTLE
Skenfrith, Abergavenny, Monmouthshire

Tel: 01874 625515

Organisation type and purpose: National organisation, registered charity (charity number 205846), historic building, house or site.
Parent body:
The National Trust Office for Wales
Tel: 01492 860123
In the Guardianship of:
Cadw: Welsh Historic Monuments

Enquiries to: Manager
Access:
Access to staff: By letter, by telephone

General description:
A Norman castle, built to command one of the main routes between England and Wales. A keep stands on the remains of the motte, and the 13th century curtain wall with towers has also survived.

Internet home pages:
http://www.nationaltrust.org.uk

2689
SKYE MUSEUM OF ISLAND LIFE
Upper Duntulm, Kilmuir, Isle of Skye, Inverness-shire, IV51 9UE

Tel: 01470 552 206
Fax: 01470 552 206
Formed: 1965

Organisation type and purpose: Independently owned, museum.

Enquiries to: Curator
Access:
Access to staff: By letter, by telephone, by fax
Access for disabled people: Parking provided, level entry, toilet facilities

General description:
A group of seven thatched cottages, depicting crofting life in the Highlands a century or so ago. The village includes an original crofter's cottage over 200 years old.
Printed publications:
Museum Guide (£1.50)
Discovering Skye (£2)

2690
SLOUGH MUSEUM
278 High Street, Slough, Berkshire, SL1 1NB

Tel: 01753 526422
Fax: 01753 526422
Email: sloughmuseum@slosm.freeserve.co.uk or info@sloughmuseum.co.uk
Formed: 1986

Organisation type and purpose: Independently owned, registered charity (charity number 285211), museum, suitable for ages: all ages.

Enquiries to: Curator
Access:
Access to staff: By letter, by telephone, by fax, by email
Hours: Mon to Fri, 0930 to 1630
Access to building, collections or gallery: No access other than to staff
Hours: Wed to Sat, 1130 to 1600
Other restrictions: Prior appointment required at all other times.
Access for disabled people: access to all public areas, toilet facilities

General description:
A social history museum about the people and town of Slough, with a small collection of local and social history objects and photographs relating to Slough; Victorians; World War II.
Information services:
Education facilities for Slough Schools only.
Special visitor services: Materials and/or activities for children.
Education services: Group education facilities, resources for Key Stages 2 and 3..
Collections:
Model of 40 ft telescope built in Slough by the world famous astronomer Sir William Herschel plus other family memorabilia, 18th century
Elliman, memorabilia from a family business which created an embrocation to cure aches and pains of horses and humans, 19th century
Printed publications:
The Museum produces various leaflets on the History of Slough

Internet home pages:
http://www.sloughmuseum.co.uk
Events, exhibitions, services, newsletter, '1000' Club, directions, photographs etc.

2691
SMALLHYTHE PLACE
Smallhythe Place, Tenterden, Kent, TN30 7NG

Tel: 01580 762334
Fax: 01580 761960
Email: smallhytheplace@nationaltrust.org.uk
Formed: 1929

Organisation type and purpose: Registered charity (charity number 205846), museum, historic building, house or site, suitable for ages: 5+.
Parent body:
The National Trust (South and South East Region)
South East Regional Office, tel: 01372 453401

Enquiries to: Custodian
Access:
Access to staff: By letter, by telephone, by email, in person
Access to building, collections or gallery: No prior appointment required
Hours: Late Mar to early Nov: Sat to Wed, 1100 to 1700
Open Good Friday
Other restrictions: Last admission 1630 or dusk if earlier. Note: The Barn Theatre may be closed some days at short notice.

General description:
Half-timbered home of Dame Ellen Terry 1899 to 1928. Collection related to Edith Craig, Edward Gordon Craig and Sir Henry Irving.
Information services:
Braille guide. Large-print guide. Touch list. Children's quiz/trail.
Special visitor services: Materials and/or activities for children.
Services for disabled people: For the visually impaired; displays and/or information at wheelchair height.
Collections:
Artefacts, pictures, prints, photographs, books, documents, manuscripts and theatrical costumes
Catalogues:
Catalogue for library is published.
Printed publications:
Guide Book (available for purchase, direct)
Library Catalogue (available for purchase, direct)
Story of the Barn Theatre (available for purchase, direct)

Internet home pages:
http://www.nationaltrust.org.uk

2692
SMITH ART GALLERY AND MUSEUM
40 Albert Place, Dumbarton Road, Stirling, FK8 2RQ

Tel: 01786 471917
Fax: 01786 449523
Email: museum@smithartgallery.demon.co.uk
Formed: 1874
Formerly: Smith Institute, date of change, 1979

Organisation type and purpose: Service industry, registered charity (charity number SC016162), museum, art gallery.
Museum service for Stirling Council area.

Enquiries to: Director
Other contacts: (1) Collections Manager (2) Exhibitions Officer (3) Administrator for (1) collections enquiries (2) enquiries regarding exhibitions and art/collections enquiries (3) room bookings.
Access:
Access to staff: By letter, by telephone, by fax, by email, visitors by prior appointment
Hours: Mon to Fri, 0900 to 1700
Access to building, collections or gallery: No prior appointment required
Hours: Museum: Tue to Sat, 1030 to 1700; Sun, 1400 to 1700; closed all day Monday
Access for disabled people: Parking provided, ramped entry, toilet facilities

General description:
Local and social history of the Stirling area, Scottish art, archaeology, natural history, botany, militaria and numismatics.
Information services:
Reproduction of prints/postcards - small charge levied, by prior arrangement.
Special visitor services: Guided tours, materials and/or activities for children.
Education services: Group education facilities, resources for Further or Higher Education.
Services for disabled people: Displays and/or information at wheelchair height.
Collections:
Harvey oil sketches (major collection in Britain - 82 works)
Exclusive collection of works of Thomas Stuart Smith (1814-1869)
Collection relating to story of William Wallace (300 images digitised for SCRAN)
Collection relating to R B Cunnighame Graham (1882-1936), Laird of Gartmag, founder of the Scottish Labour Party and the National Party of Scotland, 1928
Kidston-Stirling Plant Collection (Stirling Flora 1919)
Collection of domestic and church pewter recognised by the British Pewterers' Society as one of the collections of significance in Scotland
Catalogues:
Catalogue for part of the collections is only available in-house.
Publications list:
is available in hard copy and online.
Printed publications:
Blind Harry's Wallace by William Hamilton of Gilbertfield (King E, 1998, £7.50/£15)
Bright Lights and Sombre Shadows Exhibition catalogue (Victorian paintings)
Joseph Donovan Adam Catalogue (1880-1900)
Newsletter (3 times a year)
Postcards of paintings from collections
Sir George Harvey Exhibition catalogue (Victorian painter)
Introducing Scotland's Liberator - Wm Wallace (King E, 1997, £3.99)
Mountain, Meadow, Moss and Moor - Joseph Denovan Adam (Devaney M, 1996, £2.50)
The Bruce (Barbour J, £9.99)
Wallace (Reese P, £5.99)

Internet home pages:
http://www.smithartgallery.demon.co.uk

2693
SNIBSTON DISCOVERY PARK
Ashby Road, Coalville, Leicestershire, LE67 3LN

Tel: 01530 278444
Fax: 01530 813301
Email: snibston@leics.gov.uk
Formed: 1992

Organisation type and purpose: Local government body, museum, historic building, house or site, suitable for ages: 5+.
Science and discovery park.
Parent body:
Leicestershire Museums, Arts & Records Service (LMARS)
Tel: 01162 656799/656783
Other addresses:
Leicestershire Museums, Arts & Records Service (LMARS)
Tel: 01162 656783

Enquiries to: Curator
Other contacts: Marketing Officer for advertising, marketing, promotions.
Access:
Access to staff: By telephone, by fax, by email, Internet web pages
Hours: Mon to Fri, 1000 to 1700
Access for disabled people: Parking provided, level entry, access to all public areas, toilet facilities

General description:
The museum is located on the site of Snibston Colliery, sunk in 1832/1834 by George Stephenson.
Mining in Leicestershire, extractive industries, brick-making in Leicestershire, transport, rail transport in Leicestershire, working life, costume and textiles (including foundation garments), 20th century designer clothing, domestic and family life, toys and dolls, Palitoy - makers of 'Action Man' and 'Tiny Tears'.
Collections:
Collections mentioned in subjects and including working life collection, transport, Symington Collection, foundation wear

continued overleaf

Next Plc Collection - 20th century clothes
Collection of knitting machines, many built in Leicestershire, both industrial and domestic, 1750s to 1970s
About 100 industrial and about 25 domestic road vehicles, collection of horse-drawn vehicles, motor and electric vehicles and bicycles, 1730 to 1984, horse-drawn about 25; motor and electric about 25; bicycles about 30
Extensive collection of modern coal-mining machinery, 1940s to 1980s
Collection of Leicester made typewriters, other makes are also represented in the collection. 1880s to 1960s, in total about 200
The country's only surviving Brush Falcon Works (of Loughborough) standard gauge steam locomotive, 1906
Collection of Leicester made optics including lenses for still and movie cameras, 1890s to 1970s, c. 200 items
Collection of Leicestershire built aircraft including the unique Reid and Sigrist 'Desford Bobsleigh' and collection of Austers, 1930s to 1960s
Collection of locally built stationary steam engines, including the 1891 Gimson Woolf Compound Beam Engine at the Abbey Pumping, the largest surviving engine of its kind in the country, 1840s to 1940s, fifteen engines, nine are in working condition by steam

Internet home pages:
http://www.leics.gov.uk/museums

2694
SNOWSHILL MANOR

Snowshill, Broadway, Gloucestershire, WR12 7JU

Tel: 01386 852410
Fax: 01386 852410
Email: snowshillmanor@nationaltrust.org.uk

Organisation type and purpose: National organisation, registered charity (charity number 205846), museum, historic building, house or site, suitable for ages: 5+.
Parent body:
The National Trust (South West Region)
Wessex Regional Office, tel: 01985 843600

Enquiries to: Manager
Access:
Access to staff: By letter, by telephone, by fax, by email, Internet web pages
Access for disabled people: toilet facilities
Other restrictions: Transfer available. Drop-off point. Two manual wheelchairs available. Steps to entrance. Accessible entrance different from main entrance. Visitor Centre accessible. Ground floor accessible with assistance, steps to rooms. No access to other floors. Photograph album.

General description:
A Cotswold manor house containing Charles Paget Wade's extraordinary collection of craftsmanship and design, including musical instruments, clocks, toys, bicycles, weavers' and spinners' tools and Japanese armour. Mr Wade's cottage can also be visited.
Information services:
Braille guide. Audio guide. Touch list.
Front-carrying baby slings for loan.
Suitable for school groups.
Special visitor services: Tape recorded guides, materials and/or activities for children.
Education services: Group education facilities.
Services for disabled people: For the visually impaired.

Internet home pages:
http://www.nationaltrust.org.uk/regions/wessex

2695
SIR JOHN SOANE'S MUSEUM

13 Lincoln's Inn Fields, London, WC2A 3BP

Tel: 020 7405 2107
Fax: 020 7831 3957
Email: library@soane.org.uk
Acronym or abbreviation: SJSM
Formed: 1837

Organisation type and purpose: National government body, registered charity (charity number 313609), museum, art gallery, historic building, house or site, suitable for ages: 8+.

Enquiries to: Archivist
Direct tel: 020 7440 4245
Other contacts: Secretary, tel: 020 7440 4263 for group bookings, order publications, disabled access.
Access:
Access to staff: By letter, by telephone, by fax, by email, in person, Internet web pages
Hours: Mon to Sat, 0930 to 1730
Museum open to public: Tue to Sat, 1000 to 1700
Other restrictions: Visitors to research library by prior appointment.

General description:
House and art treasures of Sir John Soane, architect 1753-1837, architectural history, interior design and furniture history.
Information services:
Library available for reference (for conditions see Access above)
Special visitor services: Materials and/or activities for children.
Education services: Group education facilities, resources for Key Stages 1 and 2 and Further or Higher Education.
Services for disabled people: For the visually impaired.
Collections:
Antique Roman fragments
Architectural drawings, 30,000 16th century to 1837 (including Wren, Chambers, R and J Adam, G Dance, Sir J Soane); architectural and arts library
Archive relating to Soane and his circle (his private and architectural papers)
Archive relating to the Museum's history
Books on art and architecture up to 1837
Egyptian sarcophagus
Hogarth paintings
Catalogues:
Catalogue for library is in-house only. Catalogue for all of the collections is available in-house and part is on-line.
Publications list:
is available in hard copy and online.
Printed publications:
A Miscellany of Objects from Sir John Soane's Museum
New Description of SJSM (10th edn, 1998)
Robert Adam: The Creative Mind (exhibition catalogue)
Short Description of SJSM (1997)
Sir John Soane & Enlightenment Thought - Annual Soane Lecture 1996
Soane Connoisseur & Collector (exhibition catalogue)
Soane Revisited (exhibition catalogue)
The Soanes at Home: Domestic Life at Lincolns Inn Fields
The Soane Hogarths (1991)
Microform products:
Microfilms of the drawings collection are available for purchase from Chadwyck-Healey

Address for ordering publications:
Printed publications:
The Secretary

Internet home pages:
http://www.soane.org
General description of Museum, current activities and exhibitions.

2696
SOCIAL HISTORY MUSEUM

Colchester
See - Hollytrees Museum

2697
SOCIETY FOR NAUTICAL RESEARCH

See - National Maritime Museum

2698
SOCIETY OF ANTIQUARIES OF SCOTLAND

See - National Museums of Scotland

2699
SOCIETY OF CHRIST THE SOWER

See - Little Gidding Trust

2700
SOHO HOUSE MUSEUM

Soho Avenue, Handsworth, Birmingham, B18 5LB

Tel: 0121 554 9122
Fax: 0121 554 5929
Formed: 1995

Organisation type and purpose: Local government body, historic building, house or site.
Parent body:
Birmingham Museums and Art Gallery
Chamberlain Square, Birmingham, B3 3DH, tel: 0121 303 2834, fax: 0121 303 1394

Enquiries to: Curator
Access:
Access to staff: By letter
Access to building, collections or gallery: No prior appointment required
Hours: Tue to Sat, 1000 to 1700; Sun, 1200 to 1700
Access for disabled people: ramped entry, toilet facilities
Other restrictions: Access to all public areas.

General description:
Restored 18th century home of Matthew Boulton. Period rooms including the dining room where the Lunar Society met, the cellars and a warm air heating system. Set in an attractive garden.
Field of expertise: silverware, ormolu, clocks, manufacturing, coins, 18th century fine and decorative arts, furniture, Birmingham history, science, engineering, community histories.
Information services:
Special visitor services: Materials and/or activities for children..
Collections:
Fine and decorative art
Furniture of James Newton, George Bullock
Silver, ormolu and toys by Matthew Boulton
Coins from BMAG designated collections
Archive from Birmingham Central Library
Catalogues:
Catalogue for part of the collections is on-line.
Printed publications:
Short guide to house and garden (50p)
Guide Book (available from Autumn 2002, direct)

2701
SOLWAY AVIATION MUSEUM

Aviation House, Carlisle Airport, Crosby-on-Eden, Carlisle, Cumbria, CA6 4NW

Tel: 01228 573823
Fax: 01228 573823
Email: info@solway-aviation-museum.org.uk
Formed: 1961

Organisation type and purpose: Registered charity (charity number 1034715), museum, suitable for ages: 12+.
The preservation of our aviation heritage.

Enquiries to: Managing Director
Direct email: md@solway-aviation-museum.org.uk
Access:
Access to staff: By letter, by telephone, by fax, by email, in person, visitors by prior appointment, Internet web pages
Access for disabled people: Parking provided, ramped entry, access to all public areas, toilet facilities

General description:
Aviation history, local airfields, crash sites, WWII station staff, British jet aircraft.
Edward Haughey Aviation Heritage Centre.
Information services:
Special visitor services: Guided tours, tape recorded guides.
Services for disabled people: Displays and/or information at wheelchair height.
Collections:
A collection of five British jet aircraft held in an open air museum, with displays of aircraft; engines; etc.
Vulcan, B2 British jet bomber, 1949-1981
Blue Streak, British rocket programme, 1900-1965
Canberra, Meteor, Vampire, Phantom, Sikorsky, Lightning, Sea Prince, and Nimrod nose section
Catalogues:
Catalogue for library is in-house only. Catalogue for all of the collections is only available in-house.
Publications list:
is available on-line.

Internet home pages:
http://www.solway-aviation-museum.org.uk

2702
SOMERSET & DORSET RAILWAY TRUST MUSEUM
Washpool Station (West Somerset Railway), Washpool, Watchet, Somerset, TA23 0PP

Tel: 01984 640869
Email: info@sdrt.org
Acronym or abbreviation: SDRT
Full name: Somerset & Dorset Railway Trust
Formed: 1966
Formerly: Somerset & Dorset Railway Circle, date of change, 1979

Organisation type and purpose: Independently owned, registered charity (charity number 265098), museum, suitable for ages: 5+.
The Museum is part of the Somerset & Dorset Railway Trust, a body devoted to studying the history of the Somerset & Dorset Joint Railway.
Parent body:
Somerset & Dorset Railway Trust
Chairman, 5B High Lane, Shalford & Bridgwater, Somerset, TA7 9NB
Honorary Secretary:
Somerset & Dorset Railway Trust Museum
Tel: 01252 429337, fax: 01278 683574

Enquiries to: Curator
Direct tel: 01275 372676
Other contacts: Chairman; Press contact tel no: 01823 323106
Access:
Access to staff: By letter, by telephone, by email, Internet web pages
Other restrictions: Telephone: 01984 640869 or 01643 704996 in advance to check opening.
Access for disabled people: level entry, access to all public areas

General description:
History of the Somerset & Dorset Railway. Museum contains archive paperwork, photographs, station signs, tickets, signalling equipment and other railwayana. Also present are 3 steam locomotives, one diesel shunter, a steam crane, three SDJR coaches and numerous goods vehicles, including a SDJR goods brake van body. Also a 2' gauge diesel locomotive and wagons from a peat works adjacent to the railway.

Information services:
Library available for reference (for conditions see Access above)
Party visits, Station Master tel: 01278 683574
Children's Quiz.
Special visitor services: Materials and/or activities for children..
Collections:
Archives relating to the Somerset & Dorset Railway
Catalogues:
Catalogue for part of the collections is only available in-house.
Publications list:
is available in hard copy and online.
Printed publications:
New museum brochure in preparation
The Trust has published a number of books, generally available from the Museum or the Trust Printed Sales Officer, rarely anywhere else
Electronic and video products:
2 videos published by the Trust (and many others about the Railway published by other people)
Bulletin Index (disk or printed)
Photographs for main collection should be available in the future
Oral History of the Railway (staff memories) (cassette tapes)

Address for ordering publications:
Printed publications:
Postal Sales, Somerset & Dorset Railway Trust 7 Fourth Avenue, Dursley, Gloucestershire, GL11 4NX, tel: 01453 546616
The Curator, Somerset & Dorset Railway Trust 40 Beechwood Road, Easter in Gardens, Bristol, BS20 0NA, tel: 01275 372176

Internet home pages:
http://www.sdrt.org.uk
Information about the Trust, Museum and the former railway.

2703
SOMERSET BRICK AND TILE MUSEUM
East Quay, Bridgwater, Somerset

Tel: 01278 426088

Organisation type and purpose: Museum, historic building, house or site, suitable for ages: all ages.
Parent body and jointly managed by:
Sedgemoor District Council
Somerset County Museum Service
Tel: 01823 320200

Enquiries to: Manager
Access:
Access to staff: By telephone, by letter
Other restrictions: Contact the County Museums Service for information when closed.
Access for disabled people: Parking provided, access to all public areas, toilet facilities

General description:
The only remaining tile kiln in Bridgewater, displayed are the methods and processes involved in the production of bricks, tiles and terracotta artefacts.

Internet home pages:
http://www.somerset.gov.uk/museums

2704
SOMERSET COUNTY MUSEUMS SERVICE
Taunton Castle, Castle Green, Taunton, Somerset, TA1 4AA

Tel: 01823 320201
Fax: 01823 320229
Email: county-museums@somerset.gov.uk
Formed: c.1850
Formerly: Somerset Archaeological and Natural History Society

Organisation type and purpose: Local government body, museum, historic building, house or site, suitable for ages: 5+.
Administrative body for the museums under the care of Somerset County Council.
Parent body:
Somerset County Council

Enquiries to: The County Museums Officer
Direct tel: 01823 320200
Other contacts: Education Officer for activities, enquiries relating to use by schools and colleges.
Access:
Access to staff: By letter, by telephone, by fax, by email, visitors by prior appointment, Internet web pages
Hours: Mon to Fri, 0830 to 1700
Access to building, collections or gallery: No prior appointment required
Hours: Apr to Oct, Tue to Sat and Bank Holiday Mondays, 1000 to 1700;
Nov to Mar, Tue to Sat, 1000 to 1500
Prior appointment required for Collections: Mon to Thu, 0830 to 1700; Fri, 0830 to 1630
Other restrictions: Closed Good Friday

General description:
Material culture relating to the archaeology, social history and natural history of the County of Somerset. Of particular importance are the finds from the Somerset Levels: prehistory to Iron Age; Roman items and the Low Ham Roman Mosaic. Collections of pleistocene mammal bones and the costume collection including early examples of quilts, as well as items from the Somerset Light Infantry Regiment.
Catalogues:
Catalogue for part of the collections is available in-house and part is published.
Printed publications:
To purchase, direct

Internet home pages:
http://www.somerset.gov.uk/museums/musweb3.htm
http://www.somerset.gov.uk/museums
Brief description of the service with staff lists, lists of museums in Somerset, some collection information.
*See - **Glastonbury Lake Village Museum; Somerset Brick and Tile Museum; Somerset Military Museum; Somerset Rural Life Museum***

2705
SOMERSET CRICKET MUSEUM
7 Priory Avenue, Taunton, Somerset, TA1 1XX

Tel: 01823 275893
Formed: 1989

Organisation type and purpose: Independently owned, registered charity (charity number 291525), museum, historic building, house or site.

Enquiries to: Curator
Other contacts: Secretary
Access:
Access to staff: By letter, by telephone, in person
Access for disabled people: Parking provided, ramped entry

General description:
A collection of cricket memorabilia housed in an ancient priory barn. Includes a cricket library and reference library.
Catalogues:
Catalogue for library is in-house only. Catalogue for part of the collections is only available in-house.

2706
SOMERSET HOUSE
*See - **Courtauld Institute Gallery***

2707
SOMERSET MILITARY MUSEUM

Somerset County Museum, The Castle, Castle Green, Taunton, Somerset, TA1 4AA

Tel: 01823 320201
Fax: 01823 320229
Email: info@sommilmuseum.org.uk
Formed: 1974
Formed from: Regimental Museum of The Somerset Light Infantry (Prince Albert's), date of change, 1974

Organisation type and purpose: Registered charity (charity number 1064932), museum, suitable for ages: 8+, research organisation.
Museum is jointly managed by:
The Somerset County Museum Service
Tel: 01823 320200
The Somerset Military Museum Trust

Enquiries to: Curator
Direct tel: 01823 333434
Direct fax: 01823 351639
Access:
Access to staff: By letter, by email, visitors by prior appointment
Hours: Curator contactable Mon to Fri
Access to building, collections or gallery: No prior appointment required
Hours: Apr to Oct: Tue to Sat, 1000 to 1700
Nov to Mar: Tue to Sat, 1000 to 1500
Other restrictions: Curator contactable Mon to Fri
Access for disabled people: toilet facilities

General description:
The Museum features the county regiments of Somerset: The Somerset Light Infantry (13th of Foot), The Somerset and Cornwall Light Infantry, The West Somerset Yeomanry, The North Somerset Yeomanry, The Somerset Militia and the Rifle Volunteers. The Museum also explains the link between these former regiments and the modern regiment - The Light Infantry.
Collections:
The museum records, in cases around the inside walls, the history of the Somerset Light Infantry since its formation in 1685, the Somerset Militia, the Rifle Volunteer Corps and the Territorial Army
Lady Butler's painting, Remnants of an Army, forms the centrepiece of the coverage of the First Afghan War of 1838-42. On 7th April 1842 the 13th Light Infantry (as the Regiment was then titled) defeated the besieging Afghan force at Jellalabad earning national acclaim and the title 'Prince Albert's'.
The centre island cases display the collection of the North and West Somerset Yeomanry Regiments recording their history from the late 18th century
The medal gallery exhibits the medals of some 600 men of the three County Regiments, which include five VCs and two GCs
Archives including photographs and a library are housed elsewhere - access is by prior appointment with the curator
Catalogues:
Catalogue for library is in-house only. Catalogue for all of the collections is only available in-house.

Internet home pages:
http://www.sommilmuseum.org.uk
Museum home page, brief history of the county regiments, research information, items for sale, reader's list, contact details.

2708
SOMERSET RURAL LIFE MUSEUM

Abbey Farm, Chilkwell Street, Glastonbury, Somerset, BA6 8DB

Tel: 01458 831197
Fax: 01458 834684
Email: county-museums@somerset.gov.uk
Formed: 1976

Organisation type and purpose: Museum.
Parent body:
Somerset County Museums Service
Tel: 01823 320200

Enquiries to: Keeper
Access:
Access to staff: By letter, by telephone, by fax, by email, in person, Internet web pages
Access for disabled people: Parking provided, level entry, toilet facilities

General description:
Social history of Somerset, identification of social history objects, costume and fashion, cider making, agricultural equipment and manufacturers.
Information services:
Special visitor services: Materials and/or activities for children.
Education services: Resources for Key Stages 2 and 3.
Services for disabled people: Displays and/or information at wheelchair height.
Collections:
Documents, photographs, pictures and objects relating to the social history of Somerset
Publications list:
is available in hard copy.
Printed publications:
Museum guide (£1)
Many booklets, museum guides and leaflets including:
Information for teachers (free)
Mudhorse fishing in Bridgwater Bay (15p)
Museum trail guides with teachers' notes
Old Glastonbury in Photographs (£3)
Cidermaking in Somerset (£3)
Victorian Somerset: John Hodges - A Farm Labourer (£3)
Victorian Somerset: Farming (£3)
Resource packs and worksheets with teachers' notes
Information for Teachers. A handbook designed for teachers preparing to bring a class to the Museum, including useful details about the galleries and facilities

Internet home pages:
http://www.somerset.gov.uk/museums
Somerset County Museums Service details.

2709
SOMME HERITAGE CENTRE, THE

233 Bangor Road, Newtownards, Co Down, BT23 7PH

Tel: 028 9182 3202
Fax: 028 9182 3214
Email: sommeassociation@dnet.co.uk
Formed: 1994

Organisation type and purpose: Registered charity (charity number XO 252/90), museum, suitable for ages: 10+.
Heritage centre.
Parent body:
Somme Association
at the same address
Connections with:
Friends of the Somme
at the same address

Enquiries to: Curator
Access:
Access to staff: By letter, by telephone, by fax, visitors by prior appointment, Internet web pages
Hours: Apr to Jun: Mon to Thu, 1000 to 1600; Sat, Sun, 1200 to 1600
Jul and Aug: Mon to Fri, 1000 to 1700; Sat, Sun, 1200 to 1700
Sep: Mon to Thu, 1000 to 1600; Sat, Sun, 1200 to 1600
Oct to Mar: Mon to Thu, 1000 to 1600
Access for disabled people: Parking provided, level entry, access to all public areas, toilet facilities

General description:
The collection relates to the Irish home rule crisis 1912-1914 and to Ireland's involvement in World War I. There is an exhibition area showing officers' and other rank's uniforms and equipment, and Ulster Volunteer Force artefacts. Includes a wide range of personal artefacts, e.g. postcards and correspondence; medals; weapons; and items recovered from battlefields.
Information services:
CD-ROM based service, charges apply.
Research into individual soldiers, charges apply.
Special visitor services: Guided tours.
Education services: Group education facilities, resources for Key Stages 1 and 2, 3 and 4..
Collections:
General collection about Irish participation in WWI and Home Rule period
Small WWII collection
Artefacts re, Lt. J V Holland VC (Leinster Regiment), 1914-1918, 10 items
Artefacts and related archives re, Captain J W Charlton OBE, MC and Bar, Croix de Guerre (Royal Inniskilling Fusiliers), 1914-1918, 41 items
Trade and statistical:
General information regarding WWI.
Printed publications:
Battlelines (two times a year, £1.50)
The Incinerator (free, to friends of the Somme)

Internet home pages:
http://www.irishsoldier.org

2710
SOUTER JOHNNIE'S COTTAGE

Main Road, Kirkoswald, Ayrshire, KA19 8HY

Tel: 01655 760603
Minicom no. '

Organisation type and purpose: Museum, historic building, house or site.
Parent body:
National Trust for Scotland (West Region)

Enquiries to: Property Manager
Access:
Access to staff: By letter, by telephone
Access to building, collections or gallery: No prior appointment required
Hours: End Mar to end Oct, daily, 1130 to 1700

General description:
Thatched cottage, home of John Davidson, village shoemaker, who was original Souter Johnnie of Robert Burns' 'Tam o'Shanter'.

Internet home pages:
http://www.nts.org.uk

2711
SOUTER LIGHTHOUSE

Coast Road, Whitburn, Sunderland, Tyne and Wear, SR6 7NH

Tel: 0191 529 3161
Fax: 0191 529 0902
Email: souter@nationaltrust.org.uk
Formed: 1990

Organisation type and purpose: National organisation, registered charity (charity number 205846), historic building, house or site, suitable for ages: 8+.
Parent body:
The National Trust (Yorkshire and North East)
North East Regional Office, Scots Gap, Morpeth, Northumberland, tel: 01670 774691
Other addresses:
National Trust Regional Office
Scots Gap, Morpeth, tel: 01670 774691

Enquiries to: Property Manager
Other contacts: Marketing and Communications Manager for corporate and co-ordinated publicity, marketing, communications.
Access:
Access to staff: By letter, by telephone
Access to building, collections or gallery: No prior appointment required
Hours: Apr to beg Nov, Sat to Thu, 1100 to 1700 (last admission, 1630)
Open Good Friday
Week of Feb half-term, open every day

Access for disabled people: ramped entry, toilet facilities
Other restrictions: Drop-off point. Ground floor largely accessible, 1 step to Victorian keeper's cottage on ground floor. No access to other floors. CCTV enables those unable to climb the tower to see the views from the top. Induction loops at reception and video room. Level entrance to shop. Ramped entrance to tea-room. Coastal path runs to north and south of property, easily accessible. Interpretation panels at regular stages, describing the Leas and Whitburn Coastal Park.

General description:
Boldly painted in red and white hoops, Souter lighthouse opened in 1871 and was the first to use alternating electric current, the most advanced lighthouse technology of its day. The engine room, light tower and keeper's living quarters are all on view, and there is a video, model and information display. See the view from the Tower - 76 steps to a stunning panorama, and see the $4\frac{1}{2}$ ton optic . A ground-floor closed-circuit TV shows the views from the top for those unable to climb. In the Engine Room see the machinery that worked the foghorn and light. The Compass Room contains hands-on exhibits for all visitors, covering storms at sea, communication from ship to shore, pirates and smugglers, lighthouse life, lighting the seas and shipwreck. Immediately to the north is The Leas, $2\frac{1}{2}$ miles of beach, cliff and grassland with spectacular views, flora and fauna.
Information services:
Helpline available, tel no: Infoline: 01670 773966.
CCTV provides view from top of tower at ground floor level.
Braille guide. Touch list. Sympathetic Hearing Scheme.
Suitable for school groups. Education room/centre. Hands-on activities.
Special visitor services: Guided tours, materials and/or activities for children.
Education services: Group education facilities.
Services for disabled people: For the visually impaired; for the hearing impaired; displays and/or information at wheelchair height.
Collections:
Compressors, generators, air storage tanks, battery banks, copies of maritime and lighthouse ephemera, recreation of period keeper's Victorian Cottage
Catalogues:
Catalogue for library is in-house only. Catalogue for all of the collections is only available in-house.
Publications list:
is available in hard copy.
Printed publications:
Souter Lighthouse Guide Book (£2.25)

Internet home pages:
http://www.nationaltrust.org.uk

2712
SOUTH EAST MUSEUM, LIBRARY & ARCHIVE COUNCIL
Headquarters, 15 City Business Centre, Hyde Street, Winchester, Hampshire, SO23 7TA

Tel: 01926 858844
Fax: 01962 878439
Email: info@semlac.org.uk
Acronym or abbreviation: SEMLAC
Formerly: South East Museums Service (SEMS), date of change, 2001; South East Museums Agency (SEMA), date of change, 2002

Organisation type and purpose: Registered charity.
Regional development agency for museums, libraries and archives.
Other location:
SEMLAC (Chatham Office)
The Garden Room, Historic Dockyard, Chatham, Kent, ME4 4TE, tel: 01634 405031
SEMLAC (Reading Office)
Reading Central Library, Abbey Square, Reading, Berkshire, RG1 3BQ, tel: 0118 958 9197
SEMLAC (Suusex Office)
Univercity of Sussex Library, Falmer, Brighton, BN1 9QL, tel: 01273 873494

Enquiries to: Chief Executive
Direct email: helenj@semlac.org.uk
Access:
Access to staff: By letter, by telephone, by fax, by email, Internet web pages
Access to building, collections or gallery: Prior appointment required
Access for disabled people: level entry, toilet facilities
General description:
A regional development agency for the museum, library and archive sector in the South East.
Catalogues:
Catalogue for library is in-house only.
Publications list:
is available on-line.

Address for ordering publications:
Printed publications:
Administrator, SEMLAC
Email: info@semlac.org.uk

Internet home pages:
http://www.semlac.org.uk
Information on SEMLAC services and regional museum, library and archive information.

2713
SOUTH FORELAND LIGHTHOUSE
The Front, St Margaret's Bay, Dover, Kent, CT15 6HP

Tel: 01304 852463
Fax: 01304 205295
Email: southforeland@nationaltrust.org.uk
Formed: 1843

Organisation type and purpose: National organisation, registered charity (charity number 205846), historic building, house or site, suitable for ages: all ages, if physically fit enough.
Site - formed 1635, current building 1843.
Parent body:
The National Trust (South and South East Region)
South East Regional Office, tel: 01372 453401

Enquiries to: Volunteer Co-ordinator
Access:
Access to staff: By letter, by telephone, in person, charges to non-members
Access to building, collections or gallery: No prior appointment required
Hours: Mar to Oct: Thu to Mon, 1100 to 1730
Open Good Friday
Open every day during school holidays between Mar and Oct, 1100 to 1730.
Nov to Feb, open by arrangement for booked groups.
Other restrictions: Admission by guided tour.
Access for disabled people: Parking provided
Other restrictions: Tel. for parking instructions. Ground floor accessible with assistance, ground floor is only reception, shop and public WC. No access to other floors. Please tel. For instructions on how to get to property. Steps to shop entrance.

General description:
A distinctive landmark on the White Cliffs of Dover, this historic building was the site of Faraday's work in pioneering the use of electricity in lighthouses, and was the first to display an electrically powered signal. South Foreland was also used by Marconi for his successful wireless telegraphy experiments. Original 3500-watt lamp on display.
Information services:
Education groups welcomed. Children's quiz/trail.
Braille guide. Large-print guide. Sympathetic Hearing Scheme.
Guided tours for all visitors. Out-of-hours tours for booked groups only.
Special visitor services: Guided tours.
Services for disabled people: For the visually impaired.
Printed publications:
Site Leaflet (free)
Walk Leaflet (£1)
Tour Guide (50p)
Souvenir Guide (£2.50)

Internet home pages:
http://www.nationaltrust.org.uk

2714
SOUTH HATCH RACING CLUB MUSEUM
46 Burgh Heath Road, Epsom, Surrey, KT17 4LX

Tel: 01372 723204
Fax: 01372 742210
Email: info@southhatch.co.uk
Formed: 1985

Organisation type and purpose: Independently owned, museum, suitable for ages: 16+.

Enquiries to: Secretary
Access:
Access to staff: By letter, by telephone
Access to building, collections or gallery: No prior appointment required
Access for disabled people: Parking provided, ramped entry, toilet facilities
General description:
South Hatch is a Victorian House set on the edge of Epsom Downs. It is a privately owned restaurant. The museum runs all through the house showing everything to do with horse-racing, racing in Epsom, and the house itself which was built by a racing family. There is no entry fee but visitors are advised that parts of the museum may be closed due to private functions being held.

2715
SOUTH KENSINGTON MUSEUM
See - Victoria and Albert Museum

2716
SOUTH LANARKSHIRE COUNCIL MUSEUMS
See - Hunter House Museum; John Hastie Museum

2717
SOUTH LANCASHIRE REGIMENT AND THE LOYAL REGIMENT (NORTH LANCASHIRE) MUSEUM
See - Queen's Lancashire Regimental Museum

2718
SOUTH MOLTON & DISTRICT MUSEUM
Town Hall, The Square, South Molton, Devon, EX36 3AB

Tel: 01769 572951
Email: curatorsouthmolton@lineone.net
Formed: 1951

Organisation type and purpose: Local government body, museum, suitable for ages: all ages.
Parent body:
South Molton Council
1 East Street, South Molton

Enquiries to: Curator
Access:
Access to staff: By letter, by telephone, by email, in person, Internet web pages
Access for disabled people: ramped entry

continued overleaf

General description:
Local history including mining on Exmoor; trades of the area past and present; family histories.
Collections:
Fire Engines (2)
Local Long Case Clocks
Photographs, information and artefacts relating to South Molton and surrounding villages
Royal Charters: Town Market Charters
Ore samples from Exmoor Mines
The Rottenbury Collection of rocks and minerals
Catalogues:
Catalogue for all of the collections is only available in-house.

Internet home pages:
http://www.northdevonmuseums.net/southmolton
Main areas of the collections on display, list of temporary exhibitions, contact details.

2719
SOUTH RIBBLE MUSEUM AND EXHIBITION

The Old Grammar School, Church Road, Leyland, Lancashire, PR25 3FJ

Tel: 01772 422041
Fax: 01772 625365
Formed: 1978

Organisation type and purpose: Local government body, museum, art gallery, suitable for ages: 5+.
Parent body:
South Ribble Borough Council
West Paddock, Leyland, tel: 01772 421491

Enquiries to: Curator
Access:
Access to staff: By letter, by telephone, by fax, in person, visitors by prior appointment
Access for disabled people: Parking provided
Other restrictions: Access currently restricted.

General description:
A small borough collection of artefacts relating to the local history of the district. Includes archaeology and industrial history.
Information services:
Visually impaired guide in course of preparation.
Special visitor services: Guided tours..
Collections:
Walton-le-Dale collection of finds from Roman settlement, excavations 1956-1963, 1st-4th century, c. 500 items
Catalogues:
Catalogue for library is in-house only.
Printed publications:
Local history books

2720
SOUTH SHIELDS MUSEUM AND ART GALLERY

Ocean Road, South Shields, Tyne and Wear, NE33 2JA

Tel: 0191 456 8740
Minicom no. 0191 456 8740
Fax: 0191 456 7850
Formed: 1876

Organisation type and purpose: Local government body, registered charity, museum, art gallery, suitable for ages: all ages.
Parent body:
Tyne & Wear Museums (TWM)
c/o Discovery Museum, Blandford Square, Newscastle, NE1 4JA, tel: 0191 232 6789, fax: 0191 230 2614

Enquiries to: Curator
Direct email: alisdair.wilson@tyne-wear-museums.org.uk
Other contacts: (1) Education Officer; (2) Principal Keeper Art; (3) Marketing Officer for (1) information of events/activities etc; (2) enquiries re art collections; (3) press, advertising.
Access:
Access to staff: By letter, by telephone, by fax, by email, visitors by prior appointment
Access to building, collections or gallery: No prior appointment required
Hours: Closed until February 2004
Access for disabled people: level entry, access to all public areas, toilet facilities

General description:
South Shields Museum and Art Gallery takes a look at the local and social history of this proud area, and the influences that have helped to form its individual characteristics.
The Catherine Cookson Gallery tells the story of South Tyneside, land, river and sea, and the history and development of the area.
Local fine and applied art.
Information services:
Temporary exhidbitions.
Special visitor services: Materials and/or activities for children.
Education services: Group education facilities, resources for Key Stages 1 and 2, 3, 4 and Further or Higher Education.
Services for disabled people: For the visually impaired; for the hearing impaired; displays and/or information at wheelchair height.
Collections:
Collections held at the Museum relate to the natural, social, industrial and maritime history of South Shields
Thomas Reed Bequest (paintings)
Extensive collections of local art portraying the area by local artists
Catherine Cookson memorabilia (artefacts, pictures, photographs etc)

Address for ordering publications:
Printed publications:
Commercial Officer, c/o Discovery Museum
Blandford Square, Newcastle Upon Tyne, NE1 4JA, tel: 0191 232 6789

Internet home pages:
http://www.twmuseums.org.uk

2721
SOUTH STAFFORDS MUSEUM

See - Staffordshire Regiment Museum

2722
SOUTH WALES BORDERERS & MONMOUTHSHIRE REGIMENTAL MUSEUM

The Royal Regiment of Wales (24th/41st Foot), The Watton, Brecon, Powys, LD3 7EB

Tel: 01874 613310
Fax: 01874 613275
Email: swb@rrw.org.uk
Acronym or abbreviation: SWB Museum
Formed: 1935
Formerly: 24th Regiment of Foot; South Wales Borderers, date of change, 1881; Royal Regiment of Wales (24th/41st Foot), date of change, 1969

Organisation type and purpose: Registered charity (charity number 273858), museum.
Regimental Headquarters:
The Royal Regiment of Wales (24th/41st Foot)
Maindy Barracks, Cardiff, CF14 3YE, tel: 029 2078 1202, fax: 029 2064 1281, email/website: rhq@rrw.org.uk

Enquiries to: Curator
Direct tel: 01874 613906
Direct fax: 01874 613275
Direct email: martin.everett@rrw.org.uk
Other contacts: Archivist for research.
Access:
Access to staff: By letter, by telephone, by fax, by email, in person
Hours: Apr to Sep: Mon to Sun, 0900 to 1300 and 1400 to 1700
Oct to Mar: weekdays only
Access to building, collections or gallery: No prior appointment required
Hours: Mon to Fri, 0900 to 1700 only
Access for disabled people: ramped entry, access to all public areas, toilet facilities

General description:
300 years of regimental history of the South Wales Borderers and the militia and volunteer units of Brecknock and Monmouthshire including the Royal Regiment of Wales and the 24th/41st Foot; leading authority in the UK on the Zulu Wars of 1877-1879; guns, uniforms, equipment, paintings and war mementoes; large medal collection including 16 VCs.
Information services:
Special visitor services: Guided tours, materials and/or activities for children.
Education services: Group education facilities, resources for Key Stage 2..
Collections:
Original documents, papers, journals etc from the Anglo-Zulu War of 1879
Regimental War diaries of the South Wales Borderers
Publications list:
is available in hard copy.
Printed publications:
History of the Regiment of Wales (24th/41st Foot) 1689-1989 (£35 plus p&p)
South Wales Borderers in the Great War (£38 plus p&p)
The Noble 24th (£35 plus p&p)
Electronic and video products:
Online shop, see website

Address for ordering publications:
Printed publications:
Online shop
Email: www.rrw.org.uk

Internet home pages:
http://www.rrw.org.uk

2723
SOUTH WALES POLICE MUSEUM

Police Headquarters, Cowbridge Road, Bridgend, Mid Glamorgan, CF31 3SU

Tel: 01656 303207
Formed: 1950

Organisation type and purpose: Museum, suitable for ages: 5+.

Enquiries to: Curator
Access:
Access to staff: By letter, by telephone
Other restrictions: Outside visitor hours can be accommodated by prior appointment.
Access to building, collections or gallery: Prior appointment required

General description:
The museum tells the story of policing in South Wales from the Celts right through to the present day, covering the South Wales Constabulary and its ancestral forces - the Glamorgan Constabulary, Cardiff City, Swansea, Neath and Merthyr Tydfil borough police.
Highlights from the Galleries include a reconstruction of a Victorian cell (complete with resident prisoner), an Edwardian charge rooom, a WWII diorama showing a scene from The Blitz, rare gas masks and a Tipstave belonging to the policeman who arrested DIC Penderyn during The Merthyr Rising.
Information services:
Education services: Resources for Key Stage 2..
Collections:
Very extensive archives belonging to South Wales Police are kept at the Glamorgan Record Office, Glamorgan Building, King Edward VII Avenue, Cathays Park, Cardiff, CF10 3NE, tel: 029 2078 0282; fax: 029 2078 0284
Catalogues:
Catalogue for part of the collections is on-line.

2724
SOUTH YORKSHIRE AVIATION MUSEUM

Aeroventure, Sandy Lane, Doncaster, South Yorkshire, DN4 5EP

Tel: 01302 761616
Email: syam@freehosting.net
Acronym or abbreviation: SYAM
Formed: 1984
Known as: Doncaster Aeroventure

Organisation type and purpose: Independently owned, registered charity (charity number 1051994), museum, suitable for ages: 5+.
Aircraft preservation charity and museum.
Member of:
Association of Independent Museums (AIM)
39 Liverpool Road, Chester, CH2 1AB
British Aircraft Preservation Council (BAPC)
Stonewharf, 2 Dale Road, Coalbrooke Dale, Telford, Shropshire, TE8 7DT
Yorkshire Tourist Board
312 Tadcaster Road, York, YO24 1GS

Enquiries to: Curator
Access:
Access to staff: By letter, by telephone
Access for disabled people: Parking provided, ramped entry, level entry, toilet facilities

General description:
Local aviation history, restoration advice ie techniques used, spare parts for projects, aircraft display methods. Displays in an aircraft hanger built in 1940 on the last part of the former Doncaster airfield. The site includes other wartime buildings in the process of being restored. The first air display in Britain was held on Doncaster Racecourse in 1909.
Information services:
Special visitor services: Guided tours, tape recorded guides, materials and/or activities for children.
Education services: Resources for Key Stages 1 and 2, 3, 4 and Further or Higher Education..
Collections:
The Aircraft Collection:
14 aircraft and helicopters from the 1950s and 1960s
Home Front & Royal Observer Corps Exhibitions
Local aviation photograph collection
Local airfield histories
Catalogues:
Catalogue for library is in-house only.

Internet home pages:
http://www.syam.freehosting.net
General information about the Museum's collection and activities, aeroventure, SYAM, aircraft museum.

2725
SOUTHAMPTON CITY ART GALLERY

Civic Centre, Commercial Road, Southampton, SO14 7LP

Tel: 023 8083 2277
Fax: 023 8083 2153
Email: art.gallery@southampton.gov.uk
Formed: 1939

Organisation type and purpose: Local government body, art gallery, suitable for ages: 5+.
Parent body:
Southampton City Council
Tel: 023 8022 3855

Enquiries to: Gallery Director
Other contacts: Exhibitions and Marketing Co-ordinator for exhibition enquiries.
Access:
Access to staff: By letter, by telephone, by fax, by email
Access to building, collections or gallery: No prior appointment required
Hours: Tue to Sat, 1000 to 1700; Sun, 1300 to 1600; Mon, closed
Other restrictions: Admission free.
Access for disabled people: access to all public areas, toilet facilities

General description:
Six centuries of European art including particular collection of contemporary British work.
Information services:
Library available for reference (for conditions see Access above)
Educational services, by arrangement.
Special visitor services: Guided tours.
Education services: Resources for Key Stages 1 and 2, 3, 4 and Further or Higher Education.
Services for disabled people: For the hearing impaired.
Catalogues:
Catalogue for part of the collections is published.
Publications list:
is available in hard copy.
Printed publications:
Martin Creed
Catalogues:
Accelerator
Beverly Semmes
Boudin to Dufy: Impressionist and Other Masters from Le Havre
Chris Ofili: exhibition catalogue
Co-Operators
Frank Griffith: exhibition catalogue
Sir John Everett Millais: exhibition catalogue
Southampton City Art Gallery - Inventory
Tradition and Modernity in Basque Painting 1880-1939
William Shayer
Chloroplast (Morrison P)
A Clean and Solid Mosaic (Gilman H and Ratcliffe W)
The Stuart Portrait: Status & Legacy

Address for ordering publications:
Printed publications:
Gallery Shop Manager, Gallery Shop
Civic Centre, Commercial Road, Southampton, Hampshire, tel: 023 8083 2705

Internet home pages:
http://www.southampton.gov.uk/leisure/arts/index
History of the gallery, current exhibitions listing, some images.

2726
SOUTHAMPTON CITY COUNCIL

Heritage Arts and Entertainment Management

Museums and Galleries:
God's House Tower Archaeology Museum
Hawthorns Urban Wildlife Centre
John Hamsard Gallery
The University, Southampton, SO9 5NH
Southampton City Art Gallery
Southampton Hall of Aviation
Southampton Maritime Museum
Tudor House Museum

2727
SOUTHAMPTON HALL OF AVIATION

Albert Road South, Southampton, SO14 3FR

Tel: 023 8063 5830
Fax: 023 8022 3383
Email: info@spitfireonline.co.uk
Formed: 1982
Formerly: R J Mitchell Memorial Museum

Organisation type and purpose: Registered charity (charity number 262995), museum, suitable for ages: 5+.
Governing body:
R J Mitchell Memorial Museum Co Ltd

Enquiries to: Director
Access:
Access to staff: By letter, by telephone, by fax, by email, visitors by prior appointment, Internet web pages
Hours: Mon, only during school holidays; Tue to Sat, 1000 to 1700; Sun, 1200 to 1700
Access to building, collections or gallery: No prior appointment required
Hours: Mon, only during school holidays; Tue to Sat, 1000 to 1700; Sun, 1200 to 1700
Access for disabled people: level entry, access to all public areas

General description:
History of aviation and aircraft production in and around the Solent, especially the Schneider Trophy, the Spitfire and the Empire flying boats.
Collections:
S6 Schneider winning aircraft, Spitfire MK24, Sandringham 4 engined flying boat

Internet home pages:
http://www.spitfireonline.co.uk

2728
SOUTHAMPTON MARITIME MUSEUM

Wool House, Town Quay Road, Southampton, SO14 2AR

Tel: 023 8063 5904
Fax: 023 8033 9601
Email: historic.sites@southampton.gov.uk
Formed: 1964

Organisation type and purpose: Local government body, museum.
Parent body:
Southampton City Council
Civic Centre, Southampton, SO14 7LP, tel: 023 8083 3333, fax: 023 8083 3381
Branch of:
Cultural Services
Civic Centre, Southampton, SO14 7LP, tel: 023 8063 5904, fax: 023 8033 9601, email/website: historic.sites@southampton.gov.uk

Enquiries to: Historic Sites Manager
Direct tel: 023 8063 5904
Direct fax: 023 8033 9601
Other contacts: Cultural Services Manager for head of service covering museums.
Access:
Access to staff: By letter, by telephone, by fax, by email, in person, visitors by prior appointment

General description:
Southampton maritime history, especially the liners, and the men and women employed on the ships and in the port-based trades.
Exhibitions on the Titanic and the Cunard Line.
Information services:
Education services: Group education facilities, resources for Key Stages 1 and 2 and 3..

Internet home pages:
http://www.southampton.gov.uk/leisure/heritage
Information about the building and current exhibition, extra information about the Titanic.

2729
SOUTHEND CENTRAL MUSEUM AND PLANETARIUM

Victoria Avenue, Southend-on-Sea, Essex, SS2 6EW

Tel: 01702 434449
Fax: 01702 349806
Email: southendmuseum@hotmail.com
Formed: 1981

Organisation type and purpose: Local government body, museum, suitable for ages: 8+.
Parent body:
Southend-on-Sea Borough Council
Civic Centre, Victoria Avenue, Southend-on-Sea, Essex, SS2 6EW, tel: 01702 215000

Enquiries to: Manager
Access:
Access to staff: By letter, by telephone, by fax, by email, in person, visitors by prior appointment
Hours: Mon to Sat, 1000 to 1700
Access to building, collections or gallery: No prior appointment required

continued overleaf

Hours: Mon to Sat, 1000 to 1700
Other restrictions: Closed Bank Holidays.
Access for disabled people: Parking provided, ramped entry

General description:
Displays relating to the human and natural history of South East Essex.
Information services:
Special visitor services: Materials and/or activities for children.
Education services: Group education facilities, resources for Key Stages 1 and 2.
Services for disabled people: Displays and/or information at wheelchair height.
Collections:
Natural history: Minerals, fossils, insects, molluscs, birds, mammals, mainly British material
Human history:
Archaeology, especially stone implements
Social history, especially Victorian
EKCO Collection (radio, television and plastic products of the local firm)
Padgett collection of photographic negatives of South-East Essex
Catalogues:
Catalogue for library is in-house only. Catalogue for all of the collections is only available in-house but part is published.

Internet home pages:
http://www.southendmuseums.co.uk
General, news, courses and events.

2730
SOUTHEND PIER MUSEUM
Under the Pier Station (Shore End), Marine Parade, Southend-on-Sea, Essex, SS1 2EL

Tel: 01702 611214 or 614553
Formed: 1989
Formerly: Southend Pier Museum Foundation

Organisation type and purpose: Independently owned, voluntary organisation, registered charity (charity number 802105), museum, suitable for ages: 5+.
Fully registered with Resource.
Education and entertainment. Preservation of the history of the world's longest pleasure pier.
Maintain and manage a museum for public benefit.
Governing Body:
Southend Pier Museum Trust Limited
Civic Centre, Victoria Avenue, Southend-on-Sea, Essex, SS2 6ER, tel: 01702 215108, fax: 01702 215720 (Secretary)
Other address:
Southend Pier Museum Foundation (SPMF)
36 Shaftesbury Avenue, Thorpe Bay, Essex, SS1 2YS, tel: 01702 614553

Enquiries to: Director
Direct tel: 01702 614553
Other contacts: Secretary for administration.
Access:
Access to staff: By letter, by telephone, by fax, in person
Access to building, collections or gallery: No prior appointment required
Hours: May to Oct: Tue, Wed, Sat, Sun, Bank Holidays, 1100 to 1700 (1730 school holidays)

General description:
The Pier Museum provides extensive information on the subject of Southend Pier. Its history is vast, spanning from 1830 to the present day. The museum specialises in the pier's structure, how it was built and why, extensions and improvements, pleasure boats' use, entertainment, the pier's role in wartime, many disasters which have occurred over the years and repair of the same, the pier's famous railway and various forms of transport used. Staff positions and titles; costume changes throughout the pier's existence; the growth of the fore-shore and Southend town due to the introduction of the pier. The pier's future.
Information services:
Disabled services to be supplied by 2004.
Special visitor services: Guided tours, materials and/or activities for children..
Collections:
Restored toast rack tram, 1890-1949
Signal box, operational with levers, 1929-1978
Restored 1949 pier rolling stock, 1949-1978
RNLI service boards and associated items, 1879-1972
Catalogues:
Catalogue for library is in-house only. Catalogue for all of the collections is only available in-house.
Publications list:
is available in hard copy and online.
Printed publications:
Purchase direct May to Oct or from the Director telephone 01702 614553 any time
Electronic and video products:
Videos

Address for ordering publications:
Printed publications:
The Chairman, Southend Pier Museum Foundation
36 Shaftesbury Avenue, Thorpe Bay, Essex, SS1 2YS, tel: 01702 614553

2731
SOUTHSEA CASTLE MUSEUM
Clarence Esplanade, Southsea, Hampshire, PO5 3PA

Tel: 023 9282 7261
Minicom no. 023 9287 6550
Fax: 023 9287 5276
Email: cspendlove@portsmouthcc.gov.uk
Formed: 1967

Organisation type and purpose: Local government body, historic building, house or site, suitable for ages: 5+.
Parent body:
Portsmouth Museums and Records Service
City Museum and Records Office, Museum Road, Portsmouth, PO1 2LJ, tel: 023 9282 7261, fax: 023 9287 5276, email: cspendlove@portsmouth.cc.gov.uk

Enquiries to: Curator
Direct email: awhitmarsh@portsmouthcc.gov.uk
Access:
Access to staff: By letter, by telephone, visitors by prior appointment
Access for disabled people: Parking provided, level entry

General description:
Henry VIII built Southsea Castle in 1544 to defend Portsmouth Harbour. It was from here that he reputedly witnessed the sinking of the Mary Rose. In 1814 the Castle was enlarged to hold a garrison of 200 men, and additional gun platforms, and the underground Counterscarp Gallery were added. It was an active fortress for over 400 years.
The Castle has displays on Tudor, Civil War and Victorian history, eg Time Tunnel Experience, and Life in the Castle, artillery audiovisual presentation, underground passages, and the military history of Portsmouth.
Information services:
Special visitor services: Guided tours.
Education services: Group education facilities, resources for Key Stages 1 and 2.
Services for disabled people: For the visually impaired.
Collections:
A variety of ordnance, some on carriages, some unmounted, 16th to 19th century, about 30 items

Internet home pages:
http://www.portsmouthmuseums.co.uk

2732
SOUTHWICK HALL
Southwick, Peterborough, Cambridgeshire, PE8 5BL

Tel: 01832 274064
Formed: 1974

Organisation type and purpose: Independently owned, historic building, house or site, suitable for ages: 16+.
Member of:
Historic Houses Association (HHA)

Enquiries to: Manager
Access:
Access to staff: By letter, by telephone
Access for disabled people: toilet facilities
Other restrictions: Access to ground floor only.

General description:
A manor house dating from 1300, open on a limited basis from Easter to August, showing the development of a country house over a 700 year period. Containing special exhibitions of Victorian and Edwardian clothes and artefacts, and local village and farm life.
Collections:
Agricultural and domestic bygones
Collection of carpentry tools
Edwardian/Victorian clothes and artefacts worn by Capron family
Small collection of named bricks. 300 items
Catalogues:
Catalogue for part of the collections is only available in-house.

2733
SOUVENIRS OF BRESSINGHAM LIMITED
See - Bressingham Steam Museum and Gardens

2734
SPACEGUARD CENTRE, THE
Llanshay Lane, Knighton, Powys, LD7 1LW

Tel: 01547 520247
Fax: 01547 520247
Email: spaceguard@spaceguard.com
Formed: 2001
Formerly: Powys County Observatory, date of change, 2001
Now known as: Spaceguard UK

Organisation type and purpose: International organisation, national organisation, independently owned, museum, suitable for ages: 8+.
Public understanding of science (astronomy).
Parent body:
The Spaceguard Foundation

Enquiries to: Director
Access:
Access to staff: By letter, by telephone, by email, in person, Internet web pages
Access to building, collections or gallery: No prior appointment required
Hours: Wed to Sun and Bank Holiday
Guided tours at 1030, 1400, 1600
Access for disabled people: Parking provided, ramped entry, toilet facilities
Other restrictions: Access to all areas except telescope dome.

General description:
General astronomy, earth science, special interest in Near Earth Objects. The hub of the Comet and Asteroid Information Network (CAIN).
Information services:
Special visitor services: Guided tours, materials and/or activities for children.
Education services: Group education facilities, resources for Key Stages 1 and 2, 3 and 4..
Collections:
Telescopes, camera obscura, planetarium, meteorites, satellite downlink (met), seismograph

Internet home pages:
http://www.spaceguarduk.com
Details and information on the Spaceguard Centre and NEO's.

2735
SPEKE HALL, GARDEN AND ESTATE
The Walk, Liverpool, L24 1XD

Tel: 0151 427 7231
Fax: 0151 427 9860
Email: spekehall@ntrust.org.uk
Formed: 1895

Organisation type and purpose: National organisation, registered charity (charity number 205846), museum, historic building, house or site, suitable for ages: 5+.
Parent body:
The National Trust (North West)
North West Regional Office, tel: 0870 609 5391
Grant-aided through:
National Museums and Galleries on Merseyside

Enquiries to: Property Manager
Other contacts: Education & Interpretation Officer: 0151 728 5847 for school visits.
Access:
Access to staff: By letter, by telephone
Access to building, collections or gallery: No prior appointment required
Hours: House: Mar to Oct: Wed to Sun, 1300 to 1730; Nov to early Dec, Sat and Sun, 1300 to 1630
Home Farm: Late Mar to late Jul and beg Sep to late Oct, Wed to Sun, 1100 to 1730; mid Jul to beg Sep, Tue to Sun, 1100 to1730, Nov to early Dec, Sat and Sun
Other restrictions: Garden and Estate are open all year, daily, 1100 to 1730, closing at 1630 in winter.
Access for disabled people: Parking provided, level entry, toilet facilities
Other restrictions: Designated parking. Close to garden entrance. Transfer available. Drop-off point. 4 manual wheelchairs available, booking essential. Ground floor fully accessible. No access to other floors. Photograph album. Courtesy buggy available for elderly and visitors with disabilities. Level entrance to shop and to restaurant. Grounds largely accessible. Recommended route map.

General description:
One of the most famous half-timbered houses in the country, dating from 1530. The unique and atmospheric interior spans many periods: the Great Hall and priest hole evoke Tudor times, while the Oak Parlour and smaller rooms, some with William Morris wallpapers, show the Victorian desire for privacy and comfort. There is also fine Jacobean plasterwork and intricately carved furniture. A fully equipped Victorian kitchen and servants' hall enable visitors to see 'behind the scenes'. The restored garden has spring bulbs, a rose garden, summer border and stream garden, and there are woodland walks and magnificent views of the Mersey basin from The Bund, a high bank. Home Farm, a 5-minute walk from Speke Hall, is a model Victorian farm building, restored and part-adapted to provide a new restaurant, shop, visitor reception and WCs, and offers estate walks, children's play area and orchard.
Information services:
Helpline available, tel no: Infoline: 08457 585702.
Group tours of gardens and estate by arrangement. Large range of events, many for families, during season. Majority are provided free with admission ticket.
Braille guide. Handling collection. Sympathetic Hearing Scheme.
Front-carrying baby slings for loan.
Suitable for school groups. Education room/centre. Live interpretation. Hands-on activities. Children's guide. Children's quiz/trail.
Horse-drawn carriage rides on most Sundays.
Special visitor services: Materials and/or activities for children.
Education services: Group education facilities, resources for Key Stage 2.
Services for disabled people: For the visually impaired; displays and/or information at wheelchair height.
Collections:
Working farm engine at Home Farm Engine House
William Morris wallpapers
Catalogues:
Catalogue for library is in-house only. Catalogue for all of the collections is only available in-house.
Printed publications:
Guide Book (£3)
Children's Guide Book (£1.50, can be purchased direct)
Short Guide (70p)

Internet home pages:
http://www.spekehall.org.uk

2736
SPELTHORNE MUSEUM
Old Fire Station, Market Square, Staines, Middlesex, TW18 4RH

Tel: 01784 461804
Email: staff@spelthorne.free-online.co.uk
Formed: 1980

Organisation type and purpose: Registered charity, museum, suitable for ages: all ages.
Connections with:
Spelthorne Archaeological Field Group (SAFG)
As for museum
Supported by:
Friends of Spelthorne Museum (FOSM)

Enquiries to: Curator
Other contacts: Education Officer for school visits.
Access:
Access to staff: By letter, by telephone, by email, in person
Hours: Wed, Fri, 1400 to 1600; Sat 1330 to 1630
Access for disabled people: Parking provided, ramped entry, level entry

General description:
Local history and archaeology of Borough of Spelthorne (Staines, Ashford, Sunbury, Shepperton, Stanwell, Laleham).
Information services:
Library available for reference (for conditions see Access above)
Special visitor services: Materials and/or activities for children.
Education services: Group education facilities..
Collections:
Bound copies of Middlesex Chronicle 1865 to present date
Records of Staines Linoleum Company
Records of artefacts from former Staines Local History Society, 19th and 20th century
Archaeological archives and artefacts from excavations in Spelthorne 1969 to present
Extensive collection of Roman artefacts excavated in Staines area, 1st-5th century AD, c. 2000 items
Entwhistle collection of records and artefacts relating to history of Staines, early 20th century
Catalogues:
Catalogue for all of the collections is only available in-house.
Publications list:
is available in hard copy.
Printed publications:
Brewing & Bottling (in Spelthorne) (£2)
Up Pontes! Roman Staines (£4)
Fire! - Fire fighting in Spelthorne (£3.50)
Houses of God - Churches in Spelthorne (£4)
Child of the 1890s (£2.50)
Child of Today Looks Back At Victorian Age (£1)
Child of 2000 Meets Child of 200 (£1)

Internet home pages:
http://www.semuseums.org.uk/spelthorne

2737
SPIKE ISLAND
See - Artspace

2738
SPITBANK FORT
The Solent, PO Box 129, Gosport, Hampshire, PO12 2XY

Tel: 023 9250 4207
Fax: 023 9243 9832
Email: enquiries@spitbankfort.co.uk
Formed: 1990

Organisation type and purpose: Independently owned, historic building, house or site.

Enquiries to: Owner
Direct tel: Mobile 07771 66 6289
Access:
Access to staff: By telephone, by email
Access to building, collections or gallery: Prior appointment required

General description:
Victorian man-made island built one mile outside Portsmouth Harbour - virtually unchanged since 1870.
Information services:
Special visitor services: Guided tours..
Publications list:
is available in hard copy and online.

2739
SPITFIRE MUSEUM
See - Potteries Museum & Art Gallery

2740
SPITZ GALLERY - ELEMENT 3, THE
109 Commercial Street, Old Spitalfields Market, London, E1 6BG

Tel: 020 7392 9032
Fax: 020 7377 8915
Email: mail@spitz.co.uk
Formed: 1995
Formed from: The Spitz - Spitalfields Arts Project (SAP)
Formerly: Commercial Gallery, date of change, 1997

Organisation type and purpose: Registered charity (charity number 328159), art gallery, suitable for ages: 5+.
Photojournalism gallery.

Enquiries to: Curator
Direct tel: 020 7392 9034
Direct email: tris@spitz.co.uk
Access:
Access to staff: By letter, by telephone, by fax, by email, in person, Internet web pages
Access for disabled people: ramped entry, toilet facilities

General description:
Mainly photojournalist work.

Internet home pages:
http://www.spitz.co.uk

2741
SPODE MUSEUM TRUST
Spode, Church Street, Stoke-on-Trent, Staffordshire, ST4 1BX

Tel: 01782 744011
Email: spodemuseum@spode.co.uk
Formed: 1987

Organisation type and purpose: Independently owned, registered charity (charity number 519597), museum, historic building, house or site, suitable for ages: 5+.
Connected with:
Keele University Library
Spode Archive, access by permission only, tel: 01782 583232, email/website: h.burton@keele.ac.uk
Spode Customer Services
(for enquiries about current product), tel: 01782 744011 ext 2255, email/website: customer-service@spode10.freeserve.co.uk
Member of:
North Staffordshire Museums Association

continued overleaf

Enquiries to: Curator
Access:
Access to staff: By letter, by email, visitors by prior appointment
Hours: Mon to Thu, 0830 to 1630
Access to building, collections or gallery: No prior appointment required
Hours: Museum: Mon to Sat, 0900 to 1700; Sun, 1000 to 1600
Other restrictions: Keele Archive by permission of museum and appointment only (ticket holders). Blue Room by appointment only.
Access for disabled people: ramped entry, toilet facilities

General description:
Museum: history of ceramics produced at the Spode site since late 18th century including transfer printed earthenware, bone china and Parian statuary, Spode, 'Copeland and Garrett' and Copeland Wares.
Keele Archive: MSS relating to history of Spode and Copeland factories.
Collections:
Archive of patterns from c 1800 to present day, catalogues, advertising material
Reserve Collection (limited access)
Archive of MSS relating to Spode and Copeland at Keele University
Catalogues:
Catalogue for part of the collections is only available in-house.

Internet home pages:
http://www.spode.co.uk
Information on the Spode company history; information on current product, and brief outline on some historical products.

2742
SPRINGHILL
20 Springhill Road, Moneymore, Magherafelt, Co Londonderry, BT45 7NQ

Tel: 028 8674 8210
Fax: 028 8674 8210

Organisation type and purpose: National organisation, registered charity (charity number 205846), museum, historic building, house or site, suitable for ages: 5+.
Parent body:
National Trust Office for Northern Ireland
Rowallane House, Saintfield, Ballynahinch, Co Down, BT24 7LH, tel: 028 9751 0721, fax: 028 9751 1242

Enquiries to: Manager
Other contacts: Education Officer: 028 8674 8215
Access:
Access to staff: By letter, by telephone, by fax, by email
Access to building, collections or gallery: No prior appointment required
Hours: Mid Mar to end Jun and Sep, Sat, Sun and Bank Holiday Mondays, 1200 to 1800
Jul and Aug, daily, 1200 to 1800
Open Bank Holiday Mondays and Good Friday; also open Bank Holidays in Northern Ireland
Other restrictions: Access to house by guided tour only.
Access for disabled people: Parking provided, toilet facilities
Other restrictions: Drop-off point. 1 manual wheelchair available. Steps to entrance. Accessible entrance at rear
of the property. Ground floor fully accessible. No access to other floors. Steps to shop and to tea-room entrances.

General description:
Described as 'one of the prettiest houses in Ulster', Springhill dates from the 1600s. The house tour takes in the exceptional library, Conyngham family furniture, gun room, nursery, resident ghost, and the unusual and colourful costume exhibition which has some fine 17th century Irish pieces.

Information services:
Handling collection. Scented plants. Handling collection is in Costume Museum.
Sympathetic Hearing Scheme.
Suitable for school groups. Education room/centre. Live interpretation. Hands-on activities. Children's guide. Children's quiz/trail. Children's costumes and activities available on request.
Programme of special tours and family days.
Special visitor services: Guided tours, materials and/or activities for children.
Education services: Group education facilities, resources for Key Stages 1 and 2.
Services for disabled people: For the visually impaired; for the hearing impaired.
Collections:
The collection includes c. 2500 items of clothing and accessories from the late 17th century to the present day, the main emphasis is on women's apparel, mainly Victorian but with good 18th century examples

Internet home pages:
http://www.ntni.org.uk

2743
SQUERRYES COURT
Westerham, Kent, TN16 1SJ

Tel: 01959 562345/563118
Fax: 01959 565949
Email: squerryes.court@squerryes.co.uk
Full name: Squerryes Court Manor House and Garden
Formed: 1956

Organisation type and purpose: Independently owned, historic building, house or site, suitable for ages: 16+.

Enquiries to: Administrator
Access:
Access to staff: By letter, by telephone, by fax, by email
Access to building, collections or gallery: No prior appointment required
Hours: 30 Mar to 29 Sep: Wed, Sat, Sun, Bank Holidays, Garden: 1200 to 1730; House: 1330 to 1730
Other restrictions: Prior booking for guided tours, which can be any day.
Access for disabled people: toilet facilities

General description:
17th century manor house lived in by the descendants of John Warde who purchased it in 1731 from the Earl of Jersey. Fine collection of Old Master paintings from Italy, 17th century Dutch and 18th century English schools, furniture, porcelain and tapestries all acquired or commissioned by the family in the 18th century.
Information services:
Guided tours must be pre-booked, and education facilities pre-arranged.
Printed guide to the garden for general visitors, printed garden trail for children.
Special visitor services: Guided tours, materials and/or activities for children.
Education services: Resources for Key Stage 2..
Collections:
17th century Dutch & Flemish Painters
18th century English Paintings
Set of 18th century English Soho Tapestries
Furniture and porcelain collected in the 18th century by the Warde Family
A collection of paintings purchased or commissioned by John Warde between 1747 and 1774, including 17th century and 18th century Italian, Dutch and English schools
Items connected with General James Wolfe of Quebec.
Printed publications:
Guidebook (£2)
Leaflet, garden guide (free)
Squerryes Garden Trail for Children (50p)

Internet home pages:
http://www.squerryes.co.uk
House opening times, admission prices, location, special events.

2744
SS 'GREAT BRITAIN' PROJECT LIMITED
Great Western Dock, Gas Ferry Road, Bristol, BS1 6TY

Tel: 0117 926 0680
Email: enquiries@ss-great-britain.com
Formed: 1970

Organisation type and purpose: Independently owned, registered charity (charity number 262158), museum.

Enquiries to: Director
Access:
Access to staff: By letter, by telephone, by fax, by email, charges to non-members
Hours: Daily, 0900 to 1700
Other restrictions: Closed 24, 25 Dec.
Access for disabled people: Parking provided

General description:
A 320 foot long Victorian steamship designed by Brunel, preserved in its original building dock.
Information services:
Special visitor services: Guided tours, tape recorded guides..
Collections:
The SS Great Britain and her associated objects, passenger diaries connected with the ship, furniture, paintings, photographs
Catalogues:
Catalogue for library is in-house only. Catalogue for all of the collections is only available in-house.
Printed publications:
Guide Book
The Iron Ship - a comprehensive guide to the ship
Range of maritime and Bristol related books

Internet home pages:
http://www.ss-great-britain.com
Summary history, proposed developments, shop & café details, guide map and opening hours.

2745
ST OLAVES' DRAINAGE MILL
East bank of the River Waveney, Below St Olaves' Bridge, On A143, O.S. TM 457 997, Fritton, Norfolk

Organisation type and purpose: Historic building, house or site.

General description:
A tiny, timber boarded trestle drainage mill with a scoopwheel. Major works of repair are in progress.

2746
STAFFORD CASTLE AND VISITOR CENTRE
Newport Road, Stafford, ST16 1DJ

Tel: 01785 257698
Fax: 01785 257698
Email: castlebc@btconnect.com
Formed: 1991

Organisation type and purpose: Local government body, historic building, house or site, suitable for ages: 5+.
Parent body:
Stafford Borough Council (SBC)
Development Department (Leisure and Culture), Civic Offices, Riverside, Stafford, tel: 01785 619000, fax: 01785 619159

Enquiries to: Manager
Access:
Access to staff: By letter
Access to building, collections or gallery: No prior appointment required
Hours: Apr to Oct: Tue to Sun, 1000 to 1700
Nov to Mar: Tue to Sun, 1000 to 1600
Access for disabled people: Parking provided, ramped entry, toilet facilities
Other restrictions: Stone castle, Keep has narrow doors and steps.

General description:
A visitor centre designed as the guardroom of a Norman Motte and Bailey Castle. Includes an audiovisual display and collections for hands-on experience.
Information services:
Special visitor services: Guided tours, materials and/or activities for children.
Education services: Group education facilities, resources for Key Stages 1 and 2 and 3.
Services for disabled people: For the visually impaired; displays and/or information at wheelchair height.
Collections:
Artefacts from archaeological excavations
Collection of reproduction arms and armour
Printed publications:
Basic leaflet only via Visitor Centre

2747 STAFFORDSHIRE ARCHAEOLOGICAL AND HISTORICAL SOCIETY

6 Lawson Close, Aldridge, Walsall, West Midlands, WS9 0RX

Tel: 01922 452230
Formed: 1959
Formerly: South Staffordshire Archaeological and Historical Society (SAHS), date of change, 1995

Organisation type and purpose: Learned society (membership is by subscription), present number of members: 203, registered charity (charity number 500586), suitable for ages: 16+, publishing house.
Undertaking archaeological digs, mainly at Wall, Staffs.
Links with:
Birmingham and District Local History Association
Council for British Archaeology

Enquiries to: Membership Secretary
Access:
Access to staff: By letter, by telephone
Hours: Any time up to 2200

General description:
Local history of Staffordshire, in particular South Staffordshire, archaeology of Staffordshire, concentrating on Lichfield and Tamworth areas.
Collections:
Transactions of 17 similar societies UK and abroad held at Lichfield Joint Record Office
Catalogues:
Catalogue for library is in-house only.
Publications list:
is available in hard copy.
Printed publications:
Contents of Transactions Volumes I-XXXVII (85p inc p&p)
Index to Transactions Volumes I-XXXIV (£3 inc p&p)
Newsletter (3 or 4 times a year)
Transactions (annually, free to members, back numbers at various prices, apply to Membership Secretary)
Electronic and video products:
Index can be supplied on a disc, but only in its published form, not as a database

Internet home pages:
http://pages.britishlibrary.net/sahs
General aims of the Society, list of meetings for current season, membership secretary's name and address.

2748 STAFFORDSHIRE COUNTY COUNCIL

See - Shugborough Estate

2749 STAFFORDSHIRE COUNTY MUSEUM

Shugborough, Milford, Stafford, ST17 0XB

Tel: 01889 881388
Email: ros.shipsides@staffordshire.gov.uk

Parent body:
Staffordshire County Council
Member of:
North Staffordshire Museums Association

Enquiries to: Curator

General description:
Housed in the old stable block of the Shugborough Estate, displays feature the restored laundry, kitchen and brewhouse, together with exhibitions and galleries illustrating life in the county over the past 200 years.
Collections:
Horse-drawn carriages

Internet home pages:
http://www.staffordshire.gov.uk

2750 STAFFORDSHIRE POLICE MUSEUM

Police Headquarters, Cannock Road, Stafford, ST17 0QG

Tel: 01785 232285
Formed: 1992

Organisation type and purpose: Independently owned, museum, suitable for ages: 12+, research organisation.
Member of:
North Staffordshire Museums Association
Police History Society (PHS)

Enquiries to: Curator
Access:
Access to staff: By letter, visitors by prior appointment
Access to building, collections or gallery: Prior appointment required
Hours: Telephone for times.
Access for disabled people: Parking provided, level entry, access to all public areas, toilet facilities

General description:
All objects relate to the history of police in Staffordshire. 3 rooms of display material, library with personnel books, details of SMFF since 1842 to present day, 50 year rule for some information. Forces covered are, Hanley Borough Police, Lichfield City Police, Newcastle Borough Police, Staffordshire and Stoke on Trent Police, Staffordshire County Police, and Stoke on Trent Borough Police.
Information services:
Library available for reference (for conditions see Access above)
Special visitor services: Guided tours.
Education services: Group education facilities, resources for Further or Higher Education..
Collections:
Edalji papers. Case of horse maiming in 1903 which led to the Court of Criminal Appeal in 1909, 1885-1903
Personnel records, details of employees, 1842- six volumes
Collection of photographs of cases, incidents and police officers

Internet home pages:
http://www.staffordshire.police.uk
Description of material held and service provided.

2751 STAFFORDSHIRE REGIMENT MUSEUM

Whittington Barracks, Lichfield, Staffordshire, WS14 9PY

Tel: 0121 311 3229
Fax: 0121 311 3205
Email: museum@rhqstaffords.fsnet.co.uk
Acronym or abbreviation: Staffords
Formed: 1964
Formed by the amalgamation of: South Staffords Museum, North Staffords Museum

Organisation type and purpose: Registered charity (charity number 272602), museum, suitable for ages: all ages.
Regimental museum.
To collect, preserve, document and interpret material evidence of the Regiment and its forebears.
Parent body:
Trustees
Affiliated to:
Association of Independent Museums
Group for Education in Museums
Midlands Federation of Museums and Art Galleries
Museums Association
West Midlands Regional Museums Council
Registered with the:
Museums and Galleries Commission

Enquiries to: Curator
Other contacts: Regimental Secretary (works full time) for Regimental HQ is co-located with the Museum.
Access:
Access to staff: By letter, by telephone, by fax, by email, visitors by prior appointment
Other restrictions: Researchers by appointment Mon to Fri, 1000 to 1600.
Access to building, collections or gallery: No prior appointment required
Hours: Tue to Fri, 0900 to 1630; weekends Apr to Sep, 1230 to 1630
Access for disabled people: Parking provided, ramped entry, access to all public areas, toilet facilities

General description:
History of the South Staffordshire, the North Staffordshire, and the Staffordshire Regiments, and of their predecessors, the 38th, 64th, 80th and 98th Foot, including associated Militia and Volunteers from 1705 onwards.
Information services:
Library available for reference (for conditions see Access above)
Special visitor services: Guided tours, materials and/or activities for children.
Education services: Group education facilities, resources for Key Stages 1 and 2, 3 and 4.
Services for disabled people: Displays and/or information at wheelchair height.
Collections:
A substantial library of records of the regiment is available for research by members of the public, by appointment
Catalogues:
Catalogue for library is in-house only. Catalogue for all of the collections is only available in-house.
Printed publications:
Leaflets
Gulf Knot (£2)
Rats' Tails (Gulf War, £13.50)
Regimental Handbook (£2)
Stafford Knot (journal, annually £3.50)
The Zulu War and the 80th Regiment of Foot (£12.95)
Worth Saving (Campaign Against Amalgamation 1991-93, £14.99)
Staffords in the Great War (£2.50)

Internet home pages:
http://www.armymuseums.org.uk

2752
STAINED GLASS MUSEUM, THE

Ely Cathedral, Ely, Cambridgeshire, CB7 4DN

Tel: 01353 667735
Fax: 01353 665025
Email: admin@stainedglassmuseum.com
Formed: 1972

Organisation type and purpose: Museum.
A national collection of British Stained Glass from 1240 to present day.
Parent body:
The Stained Glass Museum Trust
Tel: 01353 660347

Enquiries to: Curator
Direct tel: 01353 660347
Access:
Access to staff: By letter, by telephone, by fax, by email, in person, Internet web pages
Access to building, collections or gallery: No prior appointment required
Hours: Mon to Sat, 1030 to 1630; Sun, 1200 to 1630
Other restrictions: Notice is required for guided visits and lecture.

General description:
An exhibition of 100 stained glass panels on permanent exhibition covering over 7 centuries from 1240 to present, mainly British. Guided tours by appointment, lectures, stained glass painting and glazing workshops throughout the year, reference library and website.
Information services:
Library available for reference (for conditions see Access above)
Special visitor services: Guided tours, tape recorded guides, materials and/or activities for children.
Education services: Group education facilities, resources for Further or Higher Education.
Services for disabled people: For the visually impaired; displays and/or information at wheelchair height.
Collections:
Stained Glass Panels
Coloured Designs
Workshop Models
Byfield Roundels, English roundels, 15th century
Examples of different Victorian studios, 19th century, c. 30 items
V and A collection, Swiss enamelled panels, 16th century
George III, enamelled portrait, 18th century
Catalogues:
Catalogue for library is on-line. Catalogue for part of the collections is only available in-house.
Printed publications:
Gallery Guide in English and French (£3)
Postcards and A4 prints of exhibits available for purchase
Electronic and video products:
Images in digital form of the main collection for purchase

Internet home pages:
http://www.stainedglassmuseum.com
Images and descriptions of collection, calendar of events.

2753
STAINSBY MILL: HARDWICK ESTATE

c/o Hardwick Hall, Doe Lea, Chesterfield, Derbyshire, S44 5QJ

Tel: 01246 850430 (Hardwick Hall)
Fax: 01246 854200
Email: stainsbymill@nationaltrust.org.uk

Organisation type and purpose: National organisation, registered charity (charity number 205846), historic building, house or site, suitable for ages: 5+.
Parent body:
The National Trust (East Midlands Region)
East Midlands Regional Office, Clumber Park, Worksop, Nottinghamshire, S80 3BE, tel: 01909 486411, fax: 01909 486377

Enquiries to: Property Manager
Other contacts: Mill Steward for the Mill Operator.
Access:
Access to staff: By letter, by telephone, by fax, by email, Internet web pages

General description:
The tranquil workplace of a 19th century miller. A mill has stood on the site since the 13th century, providing flour for the local villages and later for the Hardwick Estate until 1952. Following restoration work, it is in working order with a 17 ft enclosed waterwheel. Flour milling on Thursdays.
Information services:
Suitable for school groups. Children's quiz/trail
Tours on request at the mill, for private out-of-hours tours contact Property Manager at Hardwick Hall
Special event - National Mills Day
Special visitor services: Guided tours.
Education services: Group education facilities, resources for Further or Higher Education..
Collections:
Working machinery
Printed publications:
Mill Booklet (£1.95)

Internet home pages:
http://www.nationaltrust.org.uk

See also - ***Hardwick Hall***

2754
STAMFORD MUSEUM

Broad Street, Stamford, Lincolnshire, PE9 1PJ

Tel: 01780 766317
Fax: 01780 480363
Email: stamford_museum@lincolnshire.gov.uk
Formed: 1961

Organisation type and purpose: Local government body, museum, suitable for ages: 5+.
Parent body:
Lincolnshire County Council Heritage Service
County Offices, Newland, Lincoln, LN1 1YQ, tel: 01552 552222

Enquiries to: Principal Keeper
Access:
Access to staff: By letter, by telephone, by fax, by email, visitors by prior appointment, letter of introduction required
Hours: Mon to Sat, 1000 to 1700
Access to building, collections or gallery: No prior appointment required
Hours: Mon to Sat, 1000 to 1700;
Apr to Sep: Sun, 1400 to 1700; Mon to Sat, 1000 to 1700;
Other restrictions: Closed 24 to 26 Dec, 31 Dec, 1 Jan.
Access for disabled people: Parking provided, ramped entry

General description:
Local history, including family and company information.
Information services:
Special visitor services: Guided tours, materials and/or activities for children.
Education services: Group education facilities, resources for Key Stages 1 and 2, 3, 4 and Further or Higher Education..
Collections:
Local history, information files on local people, places, events
Local history artefacts
Local history photographs
Local topographical pictures
Material relating to Stamford's architectural history
Catalogues:
Catalogue for part of the collections is only available in-house.

Printed publications:
Blackstone Engine Register (£1)
Catalogue of 'Blackstone 160' Exhibition (£2.50)
Children's Trail of Town (15p)
Education packs (£3 to £4.50)
Information leaflets (Malcolm Sargent, Daniel Lambert, Pick Car, Stamford Spitfire and Filming of Middlemarch; 40p)
Leaflet of Siege of Burghley House (£1.50)
Museum Leaflet (free)
Stamford (Clifton-Taylor A, £3.75)
Town Trails, 1 to 7 (architectural: Towntrail, Town Centre, Victorian, Georgian, chimney, stone trail, Churches 75p)

Internet home pages:
http://www.lincolnshire.gov.uk/lccconnect/culturalservices/Heritage/StamfordMus.htm
http://www.yell.co.uk/sites/stamford-museum/
Brief 'Yellow Pages' overview with contact numbers etc.

2755
STANDEN

West Hoathly Road, East Grinstead, West Sussex, RH19 4NE

Tel: 01342 323029
Fax: 01342 316424
Email: standen@nationaltrust.org.uk

Organisation type and purpose: National organisation, registered charity (charity number 205846), historic building, house or site, suitable for ages: 5+.
Parent body:
The National Trust (South and South East Region)
South East Regional Office, tel: 10372 453401

Enquiries to: Administrative Assistant
Access:
Access to staff: By letter, by telephone, by fax, by email
Access to building, collections or gallery: No prior appointment required
Hours: House: Apr to Oct, Wed to Sun and Bank Holidays, 1100 to 1700
Open Bank Holiday Mondays
Other restrictions: Property may close for short periods on Bank Holidays to avoid overcrowding.
Access for disabled people: Parking provided, ramped entry, toilet facilities
Other restrictions: Designated parking 100yds. Drop-off point. 3 manual wheelchairs available. Steps to entrance. Ground floor accessible with assistance, ramps available for the porch and conservatory. No access to other floors. Photograph album. Accessible exit through a side door is different from main exit through the shop. Level entrance to restaurant. The garden is on a hillside with many steps. However, much of the garden is accessible with assistance.

General description:
A family house built in th 1890s, designed by Philip Webb, friend of William Morris, and a show piece of the Arts and Crafts Movement. It is decorated throughout with Morris & Co carpets, fabrics and wallpapers, complemented by contemporary paintings, tapestries and furniture. The house retains many of its original electrical fittings. The beautiful hillside garden gives fine views over the Sussex countryside, and there are delightful woodland walks.
Information services:
Braille guide. Large-print guide. Touch list. Scented plants.
Suitable for school groups. Education room/centre. Hands-on activities. Children's quiz/trail. Adult study days.
Special visitor services: Materials and/or activities for children.
Education services: Group education facilities, resources for Key Stage 2 and Further or Higher Education.
Services for disabled people: For the visually impaired.

Collections:
Arts & Crafts wallpapers, textiles, furniture, metal work and ceramics
Printed publications:
Guide Book (£4.50)
Short House Guide (80p)
Short Garden Guide (70p)

Internet home pages:
http://www.nationaltrust.org.uk

2756
STANFORD HALL MOTORCYCLE MUSEUM

Lutterworth, Leicestershire, LE17 6DH

Tel: 01788 860250
Fax: 01788 860870
Email: enquiries@stanfordhall.co.uk
Formed: 1962

Organisation type and purpose: Independently owned, museum, historic building, house or site, suitable for ages: 16+.

Enquiries to: Administrator
Access:
Access to staff: By letter, by telephone, by fax, by email, Internet web pages
Hours: Mon to Fri, 1000 to 1700
Access to building, collections or gallery: No prior appointment required
Hours: Easter Sat to end Sep: Sat, Sun and Bank Holiday Mon, 1330 to 1700
Access for disabled people: Parking provided, level entry, access to all public areas, toilet facilities
Other restrictions: Access to ground floor of the house is by two flights of stone steps which are 2.25m wide. First flight of nine steps has a large flat platform at the top which can act as a resting-place before going on up the 2nd flight of eleven steps to the Front Door. These steps are not very steep and wheelchairs can be got up them if helpers are available, once at entrance to the house the whole of the ground floor - the 5 principal rooms, the Flying Staircase and the Marble Passage can be seen. Access to the tearooms is impossible for wheelchairs, but tea may be brought out. However, on Open Days, trays of tea can be brought down to the Courtyard. For any disabled people who are part of a pre-booked party it may be possible to set up tables in a downstairs room or in the Rose Garden, weather permitting.
The Grounds, Motorcycle Museum, Flying Machine, Craft Centre (most Sundays), Souvenir Shop and Rose Garden are all accessible to wheelchair users.

General description:
Stanford Hall, built in the 1690s for Sir Roger Cave, is still home to his descendants and is one of the most exquisite examples of architecture of the period.
Historic and racing British motorcycles dating from 1914. Most exhibits are in running order and many are frequently used for rallies.
Collections:
Library contains over 5000 books and many manuscripts, the oldest dating from 1150
Collection of Royal Stuart portraits, previously belonging to the Cardinal Duke of York, the last of the male Royal Stuarts
Also family portraits, examples of furniture and objects collected over the centuries, throughout the house
Motorcycle Museum includes 65 motorcycles, one cycle car and 15 bicycles, ranging from 1912 to the present day. The models include Norton, BSA, Triumph, James, Vincent, Rudge, Sunbeam, Scott, Velocette, Douglas, Ariel, Harley Davidson, Wilkinson and Francis Barnett
A full-size replica of Percy Pilcher's 1898 flying machine, 'The Hawk', with photographs of two of his other three machines

Internet home pages:
http://www.stanfordhall.co.uk

2757
STANLEY SPENCER GALLERY

High Street, Cookham-on-Thames, Berkshire, SL6 9SJ

Tel: 01628 471885
Formed: 1962

Organisation type and purpose: Registered charity (charity number 307989), art gallery.

Enquiries to: Chairman
Other contacts: Group Organiser for groups, talks and walks.
Access:
Access to staff: By letter, by telephone
Access for disabled people: ramped entry, access to all public areas
Other restrictions: Bell and wheelchair ramp.

General description:
The Stanley Spencer Gallery is unique as the only gallery in Britain devoted to an artist in the village where he was born and spent most of his working life. It contains a permanent collection of Sir Stanley Spencer's work together with letters, documents and memorabilia. The Gallery mounts a winter and summer exhibition each year.
Information services:
Library available for reference (for conditions see Access above)
Special visitor services: Guided tours, materials and/or activities for children.
Education services: Group education facilities, resources for Key Stages 1 and 2 and 3.
Services for disabled people: For the visually impaired; displays and/or information at wheelchair height.
Collections:
Landscapes and portraits; religious paintings such as 'The Betrayal' 1914, 'The Last Supper' 1920, 'Christ Preaching at Cookham Regatta' 1959.
Barbara Karmel Bequest includes Sara Tubb and the Heavenly Visitors 1933
A self-portrait 1923, 'Neighbours' 1936, and a landscape 'Beacon Hill' 1927
Viscount Astor collection of scrapbook drawings (1920-1960)
Printed publications:
Stanley Spencer - Catalogue raisonée (Bell K, 1999 Phaidon, direct)
Stanley Spencer - Tate Britain retrospective (2001, Tate Publishing, direct)
Stanley Spencer: An English Vision (McCarthy F, 1997 Yale University Press, direct)
Stanley Spencer (Hawser K, 2001, Tate Publishing, direct)
Stanley Spencer: Letters & Writings (Colew A, 2001, Tate Publishing, direct)
The Barbara Karmel Bequest (direct, £1.50)
The Religious Paintings of Sir Stanley Spencer (direct, £1)
A guided walk around Stanley Spencer's Cookham (direct, £2.95)
Leaflets (free)

Internet home pages:
http://www.stanleyspencer.org
Background on Spencer and Cookham, details of current exhibition.

2758
STANTON WINDMILL

Stanton, Suffolk

Tel: 01359 250622

Organisation type and purpose: Historic building, house or site.
Access:
Access to staff: By telephone

General description:
Post mill dating from 1751 which is remarkably complete and in working order.

2759
STAUNTON HALL

See - Ferrers Gallery

2760
STAUNTON HAROLD CHURCH

Staunton Harold, Ashby-de-la-Zouch, Leicestershire

Tel: 01332 863822 (Calk Abbey)
Fax: 01332 865272
Email: stauntonharold@nationaltrust.org.uk

Organisation type and purpose: National organisation, registered charity (charity number 205846), historic building, house or site, suitable for ages: 8+.
Parent body:
The National Trust (East Midlands Region)
East Midlands Regional Office, tel: 01909 486411

Enquiries to: Property Manager
Access:
Access to staff: By letter, by telephone, by fax, by email, in person, Internet web pages
Access to building, collections or gallery: No prior appointment required
Hours: Apr to Sep, Wed to Sun, 1300 to 1700; Oct, Sat and Sun, 1300 to 1700
Other restrictions: Closes at dusk if earlier
Access for disabled people: ramped entry
Other restrictions: Ground floor fully accessible

General description:
One of the very few churches built during the Commonwealth, set in attractive parkland. The interior retains its original 17th century cushions and has fine panelling and painted ceilings.

Internet home pages:
http://www.nationaltrust.org.uk

2761
STEAM MUSEUM

Rue de Bechet, Trinity, Jersey, JE3 5BE, Channel Islands

Tel: 01534 865307
Fax: 01534 864248
Email: pallotsteammuseum@jerseymail.co.uk
Formed: 1990

Organisation type and purpose: Independently owned, museum, suitable for ages: all ages.

Enquiries to: Trustee
Access:
Access to staff: By letter, by telephone, by fax
Access to building, collections or gallery: No prior appointment required
Hours: Mon to Sat, 1000 to 1700
Access for disabled people: Parking provided, level entry, access to all public areas, toilet facilities

General description:
A fascinating private collection of steam engines, agricultural implements and other machinery, vintage bicycles and a variety of organs, together with numerous items of memorabilia. A display on the Jersey Railways. Steam train rides on certain days from the Victorian station.
Collections:
Merlin/Portable Steam Engine.1925
Compton Cinema Organ (ex Odeon - Guernsey).1937
Ransome Sims and Geoffrey Traction Engine.1904
Litho Printer 1920.
Catalogues:
Catalogue for part of the collections is only available in-house.

2762
STEAM YACHT GONDOLA

NT Gondola Booking Office, The Hollens, Grasmere, Cumbria, LA22 9QZ

Tel: 015394 41288 (Gondola Pier)
Fax: 015394 35353
Email: gondola@nationaltrust.org.uk

Parent body:
National Trust (North West Region)
National Trust (North West Regional Office), tel: 0870 609 5391

continued overleaf

Enquiries to: Manager
Access:
Access to staff: By letter, by telephone, by fax, by email
Access to building, collections or gallery: Prior appointment required
Hours: Apr to end of Oct, daily
Other restrictions: Steam yacht, Gondola, sails from Coniston Pier daily, weather permitting. The National Trust
reserves the right to cancel sailings in the event of high winds. Piers at Coniston and Brantwood (not NT)
Access for disabled people: ramped entry
Other restrictions: Designated parking 50yds, steps to entrance. Not suitable for wheelchairs. Adapted WC at Coniston Boating Centre.

General description:
The steam yacht
Gondola, was first launched in 1859 and now, completely rebuilt by the Trust, provides a steam-powered passenger service in its opulently upholstered saloons. This is the perfect way to view Coniston's spectacular scenery.

Internet home pages:
http://www.nationaltrust.org.uk

2763
STEAM, COAL & CANAL
See - Bridgewater Canal Linear Industrial Heritage Park

2764
STEAM: MUSEUM OF THE GREAT WESTERN RAILWAY
Kemble Drive, Swindon, Wiltshire, SN2 2TA

Tel: 01793 466466
Fax: 01793 466415
Formed: 1962/2000
Formerly: Great Western Railway Museum, date of change, 2000

Organisation type and purpose: Local government body, museum, suitable for ages: all ages.
Parent body:
Swindon Borough Council
Premier House, Swindon, Wiltshire, SN1 1TL

Enquiries to: Curator
Access:
Access to staff: By letter, by telephone, by fax, visitors by prior appointment
Hours: Mon to Fri, 0900 to 1700
Access for disabled people: Parking provided, access to all public areas, toilet facilities
Other restrictions: Disabled parking provided.

General description:
Railway history, Brunel, Great Western railway, social history.
Information services:
Special visitor services: Tape recorded guides.
Education services: Group education facilities, resources for Key Stages 1 and 2 and 3.
Services for disabled people: For the visually impaired; for the hearing impaired; displays and/or information at wheelchair height.
Collections:
Photographs
Books, periodicals and paperwork related to Great Western Railway
Full set on Great Western Railway Parliamentary Acts
Catalogues:
Catalogue for part of the collections is only available in-house.

Internet home pages:
http://www.steam-museum.org.uk
Visitor information, news, events, corporate hire facilities, education.

2765
STEMBRIDGE TOWER MILL
High Ham, Langport, Somerset, TA10 9DJ

Tel: 01458 250818

Organisation type and purpose: National organisation, registered charity (charity number 205846), museum, historic building, house or site, suitable for ages: all ages.
Parent body:
The National Trust (South West Region)
Regional Office for Wessex, tel: 01985 843600
Access:
Access to staff: By letter, by telephone

General description:
The last thatched windmill in England, dating from 1822 and in use until 1910.

Internet home pages:
http://www..nationaltrust.org.uk/regions/wessex

2766
STEPHEN G BEAUMONT MUSEUM
Fieldhead Hospital, Ouchthorpe Lane, Wakefield, West Yorkshire, WF1 3SP

Tel: 01924 327000
Fax: 01924 327340
Formed: 1973

Organisation type and purpose: Museum.
Access:
Access to staff: By letter, by telephone, in person, visitors by prior appointment
Hours: Wed only, 1000 to 1600
Other restrictions: Parking limited.

General description:
The West Riding pauper lunatic asylum, its tools, artefacts and documents.
Collections:
Scale model of the 1818 building
A padded cell, c. 1880
Medical and surgical instruments, 1818-1930s, c. 30 items
Admitting and discharging documents (some with royal signatures), 1818
Tools used in departments, 1818
Restraining appliances and security precautions, 1818
Electrical treatment appliances, 1880s
Catalogues:
Catalogue for part of the collections is only available in-house.

2767
STEPHENSON RAILWAY MUSEUM
Middle Engine Lane, West Chirton, North Shields, Tyne and Wear, NE29 8DX

Tel: 0191 200 7146
Fax: 0191 200 7146
Email: stephenson@twmuseums.org.uk
Formed: 1986

Organisation type and purpose: Local government body, registered charity, museum, suitable for ages: 5+.
Parent body:
Tyne & Wear Museums (TWM)
Discovery Museum, Blandford Square, Newcastle Upon Tyne, NE1 4JA, tel: 0191 232 6789, fax: 0191 230 2614
Associated Group:
The North Tyneside Steam Railway Association (NTSRA)
At same address

Enquiries to: Curator
Other contacts: Education Officer for school visits.
Access:
Access to staff: By letter, by telephone, by fax, by email, visitors by prior appointment, Internet web pages
Access to building, collections or gallery: No prior appointment required
Hours: May to Sep: Sat, Sun and Bank Holidays, 1100 to 1600; Tue to Thu, 1100 to 1500
Other restrictions: Closed Oct to Apr.
Access for disabled people: Parking provided, level entry, access to all public areas, toilet facilities

General description:
The Museum celebrates the pioneering work of George and Robert Stephenson, who lived and worked locally, and traces the history of the railway from horse-drawn waggonway to the present day. Steam-hauled passenger trains operate on the associated North Tyneside Railway.
The museum is home to George Stephenson's 'Billy', a forerunner of the world-famous Rocket, and many other engines from the Great Age of Steam.
A ride on a real steam train can be taken, and the story of coal and electricity is also told. Wall panels describe the regional growth of railways, virtually from birth to their acme.
Information services:
Special visitor services: Materials and/or activities for children.
Education services: Group education facilities, resources for Key Stages 1 and 2.
Services for disabled people: For the visually impaired; displays and/or information at wheelchair height.
Collections:
Displays include an early locomotive 'Billy' of about 1826 and forerunner of The Rocket, built at the Stephenson Works in Newcastle
Two pioneering electrically powered vehicles - a Parcels Van of 1904 and a locomotive of 1909 for a colliery line - illustrate the development of electric traction at the start of the 20th century, while a display 'The Electric century' places the advent of electricity in a broader context
A fleet of three operating steam locomotives provide train services with a set of three period 1950s coaches
Steam and diesel locomotives from 1880 to 1980s
Killingworth Loco, early steam locomotive with tender, c. 1825
A No. 5, working steam locomotive, c. 1840-1880
Peckett ACC5, working steam locomotive, 1939
Bagnall 2994, working steam locomotive, 1950
Consett No. 10, working diesel locomotive, 1958,03 078 working diesel locomotive, c. 1960
Catalogues:
Catalogue for library is in-house only. Catalogue for all of the collections is only available in-house.
Printed publications:
Annual Leaflet: gives details of exhibitions, events, activities, steam train timetable (available April onwards, free)

Internet home pages:
http://www.twmuseums.org.uk/stephenson/index.html
For general information about the museum and its collection and facilities.
http://www.twmuseums.org.uk

2768
STEWARTRY MUSEUM
St Mary Street, Kirkcudbright, Dumfries & Galloway, DG6 4AQ

Tel: 01557 331643
Fax: 01557 331643
Email: davidd@dumgal.gov.uk
Full name: The Stewartry of Kirkcudbright Museum
Formed: 1893

Organisation type and purpose: Local government body, museum, suitable for ages: all ages.
Parent body:
Dumfries & Galloway Museum Service
Tel: 01387 253374

Enquiries to: Curator
Access:
Access to staff: By letter, by telephone, by fax, by email, in person
Access to building, collections or gallery: No prior appointment required

Hours: Variable, but core hours all year: Mon to Sat, 1100 to 1600
Access for disabled people: ramped entry

General description:
A wide-ranging collection illustrating the human and natural history of the Stewartry (the former county area). Significant social history collections.
Information services:
Library available for reference (for conditions see Access above)
Special visitor services: Materials and/or activities for children.
Education services: Group education facilities.
Services for disabled people: Displays and/or information at wheelchair height.
Collections:
Archive and photographic collections for the Stewartry Area of Galloway, as well as general reference local history library
Illustrated books and other work by the artist, Jessie M King, 1900-1949
First World War posters, recruitment posters - an extensive set in good condition, 1914-1918
Catalogues:
Catalogue for library is in-house only. Catalogue for all of the collections is only available in-house.
Publications list:
is available in hard copy.
Printed publications:
Local history booklets eg:
John Faed - The Gatehouse Years (Steel D, 2001)

Internet home pages:
http://www.dumgal.gov.uk/museums

2769
STEYNING MUSEUM TRUST, THE
The Museum, Church Street, Steyning, West Sussex, BN44 3YB

Tel: 01903 813333
Formed: 1983

Organisation type and purpose: Independently owned, membership association (membership is by subscription), present number of members: 350, voluntary organisation, registered charity (charity number 288562), museum, suitable for ages: 5+.
Steyning Museum exists to collect, display, interpret and make accessible material evidence from the past of Steyning and its surrounding area for the delight, education, interest and research purposes of the local community and the general public providing a focus for the interest of the community in its past.

Enquiries to: Curator
Access:
Access to staff: By letter, by telephone, in person
Hours: Summer: Tue, Wed, Fri, Sat, 1030 to 1230, 1400 to 1630; Sun, 1400 to 1630
Winter: Tue, Wed, Fri, Sat, 1030 to 1230, 1400 to 1600; Sun, 1400 to 1600
Access to building, collections or gallery: No prior appointment required
Hours: Summer: Tue, Wed, Fri, Sat, 1030 to 1230, 1400 to 1630; Sun, 1400 to 1630
Winter: Tue, Wed, Fri, Sat, 1030 to 1230, 1400 to 1600; Sun, 1400 to 1600
Other restrictions: Free access, appointments required outside hours.
Access for disabled people: Parking provided, level entry, access to all public areas, toilet facilities

General description:
Local history of Steyning and its surroundings from its time as an important Saxon Town to the present. Its people (at work and at play), its many timber-frame buildings, its 400 year old school, its lost railway are all celebrated, local family history and archaeology.
Information services:
Library available for reference (for conditions see Access above). Helpline available, tel no: 01903 813333.
Special visitor services: Materials and/or activities for children.
Education services: Group education facilities, resources for Key Stages 1 and 2.
Services for disabled people: Displays and/or information at wheelchair height.
Collections:
All the collections illustrate the local history of Steyning and its surrounding parishes
Of wider significance are:
Steyning Market Account Books, 1908-1960
Elsie and Doris Waters (Gert & Daisy) - Archive of records, sheet music etc
Printed publications:
Steyning History Walks (4 vols)
St Cuthman of Steyning (75p)
Steyning Memories (£3.95)
Steyning in Wartime (£2.50)
Schooldays Remembered
Food for Thought (£4.10)

2770
STIRLING UNIVERSITY ART COLLECTION
University of Stirling, Stirling, FK9 4LA

Tel: 01786 473171
Formed: 1967

Organisation type and purpose: Art gallery, university department or institute.

Enquiries to: Curator
Direct tel: 01786 466050
Direct fax: 01786 466866
Direct email: v.a.m.fairweather@stir.ac.uk
Access:
Access to staff: By letter, by telephone, by email, visitors by prior appointment
Other restrictions: Curator available Thu and Fri only.
Access to building, collections or gallery: No prior appointment required
Hours: Pathfoot Concourse Gallery: daily, 0900 to 2200
Other restrictions: Closed between Christmas and New Year.
Access for disabled people: access to all public areas, toilet facilities
Other restrictions: Wheelchair access from back entrance to Pathfoot Building.

General description:
Collection comprises over 350 works including paintings, prints, sketches, tapestries, sculpture and silver. Currently, most of the works, including sculptures are concentrated in the Pathfoot Building with its light, airy courtyards and multi-level concourse gallery. Our collecting area is modern Scottish Art.
Special Collections on display are the J D Fergusson Memorial Collection and the Scottish Arts Council Bequest.
Collections:
J D Fergusson (1874-1961) Memorial Collection presented to the University by the artist's widow, Margaret Morris Fergusson
Scottish Arts Council Bequest
Printed publications:
University of Stirling Art Collection (leaflet, free)
J D Fergusson at Stirling (Pamphlet/catalogue, £3)

Internet home pages:
http://www.stir.ac.uk/artcol

2771
STITCHES & LACE, LACE MUSEUM
Alby Craft Centre, Norwich

Closed, date of change, July 2000

2772
STOCKPORT ART GALLERY
War Memorial Building, Wellington Road South, Stockport, Cheshire, SK3 8AB

Tel: 0161 474 4453
Fax: 0161 480 4960
Email: stockport.art.gallery@stockport.gov.uk
Formed: 1925

Organisation type and purpose: Art gallery, suitable for ages: 5+.

Enquiries to: Manager
Other contacts: (1) Exhibitions Officer; (2) Visual Arts Outreach Officer for (1) exhibition-related queries; (2) education-related queries.
Access:
Access to staff: By letter, by telephone, by fax, by email, in person, Internet web pages
Hours: Mon to Fri, 0830 to 1700; Sat, 0930 to 1700
Access to building, collections or gallery: No prior appointment required
Hours: Mon, Tue, Thu, Fri, 1100 to 1700; Sat, 1000 to 1700
Access for disabled people: Parking provided, ramped entry, toilet facilities
Other restrictions: No disabled access to first floor.

General description:
A magnificent Greco-Roman art gallery and war memorial in the heart of Stockport. It provides a changing contemporary exhibitions programme of local, regional and national significance. There are selected displays from Stockport's small permanent collection of 19th and 20th century British painting. Plus Artlink, a unique picture loan service for individuals and organisations.
Information services:
Special visitor services: Materials and/or activities for children.
Education services: Group education facilities..
Collections:
Stockport Permanent Collection
Small collection of British painting and sculpture: includes 3 L S Lowry local street scenes and a Jacob Epstein bust
19th and 20th century. 800-1000 items
Catalogues:
Catalogue for all of the collections is only available in-house.

Internet home pages:
http://www.stockport.gov.uk/Tourism/artgallery/default.htm

2773
STOCKWOOD CRAFT MUSEUM AND MOSSMAN COLLECTION
Stockwood Country Park, Farley Hill, Luton, Bedfordshire, LU1 4BH

Tel: 01582 738714
Fax: 01582 546763
Email: burgessl@luton.gov.uk
Formed: 1986

Organisation type and purpose: Local government body, museum, suitable for ages: all ages.
Gardens.
Other address:
Luton Museum and Art Gallery
Wardown Park, Luton, LU2 7HA, tel: 01582 546739, fax: 01582 546763, email/website: burgessl@luton.gov.uk

Enquiries to: Public Relations Manager
Direct tel: 01582 546739
Other contacts: (1) Site Manager (2) Education Officer for (1) site information (2) educational visits.
Access:
Access to staff: By letter, by telephone, by fax, by email
Other restrictions: Groups, schools by prior appointment.
Access to building, collections or gallery: No prior appointment required
Hours: April to Oct, Tue to Sun, and Bank

continued overleaf

Holidays 1000 to 1700;
Nov to Mar: Sat, Sun only, 1000 to 1600
Other restrictions: Telephone for details.

General description:
A collection covering Bedfordshire crafts, trades, transport and rural life; period gardens include an Elizabethan Knot Garden and a sculpture garden.
Collections:
Mossman Collection of horse-drawn vehicles, 18th-20th centuries
The Hamilton Finlay Sulpture Garden
Publications list:
is available in hard copy.

Internet home pages:
http://www.luton.gov.uk/enjoying/museums

2774
STOKENCHURCH GALLERY
Wycombe Road, Stokenchurch, Buckinghamshire, HP14 3RQ

Tel: 01494 483416
Fax: 01494 485251
Formed: 1982

Organisation type and purpose: Independently owned, art gallery, suitable for ages: 16+, consultancy.
Picture framing service and art gallery.

Enquiries to: Proprietor
Direct tel: 01491 638730
Access:
Access to staff: By letter, by telephone
Access to building, collections or gallery: No prior appointment required
Hours: Mon to Fri, 1000 to 1730
Access for disabled people: Parking provided, toilet facilities

Collections:
Original paintings, prints and photographs

Internet home pages:
http://www.stokenchurchgallery.co.uk

2775
STOKE-ON-TRENT CHIMNEY POT MUSEUM
34 Station Street, Longport, Burslem, Stoke-on-Trent, Staffordshire, ST6 4NA

Tel: 01782 825801
Formed: 1995
Formerly: Cherished Chimneys, Chimney Pot Museum

Organisation type and purpose: Independently owned, museum, suitable for ages: 5+.

Enquiries to: Curator
Direct email: lancebates@hotmail.com
Access:
Access to staff: By letter, by telephone
Access for disabled people: Parking provided, level entry, toilet facilities

General description:
A collection of chimney pots and artefacts, detailing the manufacturing history and development of the chimney pot. Linked with the social history of climbing boys and chimney sweeps. The museum is housed on two levels with over 1000 chimney pots exhibited (rotating). Reading room - historical research and data available.
Information services:
Special visitor services: Guided tours, tape recorded guides, materials and/or activities for children..
Catalogues:
Catalogue for library is in-house only.

Internet home pages:
http://www.cherishedchimneys.co.uk

2776
STOKE-ON-TRENT CITY MUSEUM AND ART GALLERY
See - Potteries Museum & Art Gallery

2777
STOKESAY CASTLE
Stokesay, Craven Arms, Shropshire, SY7 9AH

Organisation type and purpose: National government body, advisory body, historic building, house or site.
Parent body:
English Heritage (West Midlands Region)
Tel: 0121 625 6820

Enquiries to: Custodian
Access:
Access to staff: By letter
Access to building, collections or gallery: No prior appointment required
Hours: 29 Mar to 30 Sep: daily, 1000 to 1800,1 to 31 Oct: daily, 1000 to 1700,1 Nov to 28 Mar: We to Sun, 1000 to 1300 and 1400 to 1600 Sun
Other restrictions: Closed 24 to 26 Dec and 1 Jan.
Opening times are subject to change, for up-to-date information contact English Heritage by phone or visit the website.

General description:
Stokesay Castle is the finest and best preserved 13th century fortified manor house in England, and gives a rare glimpse into a bygone age. Stokesay retains its magnificent Great Hall, almost untouched since medieval times, as well as its original staircase, an open octagonal hearth and an innovative and fine cruck-built timber roof. A successful combination of impressive fortification and comfortable residence, the grounds include tranquil cottage-style gardens that visitors can stroll through.
Information services:
Special visitor services: Tape recorded guides..

Internet home pages:
http://www.english-heritage.org.uk

2778
STOKE-SUB-HAMDON PRIORY
North Street, Stoke Sub Hamdon, Montacute, Somerset, TA4 6QP

Tel: 01985 843600 (Regional office)

Organisation type and purpose: National organisation, registered charity (charity number 205846), historic building, house or site, suitable for ages: all ages.
Parent body:
The National Trust (South West Region)
Regional Office for Wessex, tel: 01985 843600

Enquiries to: Manager

General description:
A complex of buildings begun in the 14th century for the priests of the chantry chapel of St Nicholas (now destroyed).

Internet home pages:
http://www.nationaltrust.org.uk/regions/wessex

2779
STONDON MUSEUM
Station Road, Lower Stondon, Henlow, Bedfordshire, SG16 6JN

Tel: 01462 850339
Fax: 01462 850824
Email: info@transportmuseum.co.uk
Formed: 1994
Formerly: Stondon Garden Centre & Museum, date of change, 2002

Organisation type and purpose: Museum, suitable for ages: all ages.

Enquiries to: Curator
Other contacts: Secretary
Access:
Access to staff: By letter, by telephone, by fax, by email, in person, Internet web pages
Hours: Daily, 1000 to 1700
Access for disabled people: Parking provided, access to all public areas, toilet facilities

General description:
Largest private collection of transport covering 100 years of motoring 1890 to 1990. Over 400 transport-related exhibits including a full-size replica of Captain Cook's Ship, 'The Endeavour'.
Information services:
Special visitor services: Guided tours.
Education services: Group education facilities.
Services for disabled people: Displays and/or information at wheelchair height.

Internet home pages:
http://www.transportmuseum.co.uk
Full list of exhibits.

2780
STONE CIRCLE, THE
High Street, Avebury, Marlborough, Wiltshire, SN8 1RF

Tel: 01672 539250
Fax: 01672 539388
Email: avebury@nationaltrust.org.uk

Organisation type and purpose: Registered charity (charity number 205846), historic building, house or site.
Megalithic monument.

Enquiries to: Visitor Services Manager
Access:
Access to staff: By letter, by telephone, by fax, by email
Access for disabled people: Parking provided, toilet facilities

General description:
One of the most important Megalithic monuments in Europe.

2781
STONEACRE
Otham, Maidstone, Kent, ME15 8RS

Tel: 01622 862157
Fax: 01622 862157
Email: stoneacrent@aol.com

Organisation type and purpose: National organisation, registered charity (charity number 205846), historic building, house or site, suitable for ages: 5+.
Parent body:
National Trust (South and South East Region)
South East Regional Office, tel: 01372 453401

Enquiries to: Manager
Access:
Access to staff: By letter, by telephone, by fax, by email
Access for disabled people: Parking provided
Other restrictions: Ground floor accessible with assistance. No access to other floors. Grounds largely accessible

General description:
A half-timbered yeoman's house with a great hall and crownpost, dating from the late 15th century and surrounded by a beautiful garden and wild meadows.
Replanting of the garden borders with many unusual and interesting plants for 2003.
Information services:
Services for disabled people: For the visually impaired.

Internet home pages:
http://www.nationaltrust.org.uk

2782
STONEHENGE DOWN
Amesbury, Salisbury, Wiltshire, SP4 7DE

Tel: 01985 843600 (Regional Office)

Organisation type and purpose: National organisation, registered charity (charity number 205846), historic building, house or site, suitable for ages: all ages.
Parent body:
The National Trust (South West Region)
Regional Office for Wessex, tel: 01985 843600

Links with:
English Heritage (owns and administers monument)
Tel: 01980 623108 (Visitor Centre)

Enquiries to: Warden
Access:
Access to staff: By letter, by telephone
Other restrictions: For information consult Regional Office.

General description:
The Trust owns 758ha (1873 acres) of downland surrounding the famous monument, including some fine Bronze Age barrow groups and the Cursus, variously interpreted as an ancient racecourse or processional way. There are recommended walks and an archaeological leaflet.

Internet home pages:
http://www.nationaltrust.org.uk/regions/wessex

2783
STONEHENGE

Amesbury, Salisbury, Wiltshire, SP4 7DE

Tel: 01980 624715 (information line)

Organisation type and purpose: Historic building, house or site.
Links with:
National Trust
Owned and managed by:
English Heritage (South West Region)
Tel: 0117 975 0700, fax: 0117 975 0701

Enquiries to: Manager
Access:
Access to staff: By telephone
Access to building, collections or gallery: No prior appointment required
Hours: 16 Mar to 31 May: daily, 0930 to 1800,1 Jun-31 Aug: daily, 0900 to 1900,1 Sep to 15 Oct: daily, 0930 to 1800,16 to 23 Oct: daily, 0930 to 1700,24 Oct to 15 Mar: daily, 0930 to 1600
Other restrictions: Closed 24 to 26 Dec and 1 Jan
Opening times are subject to change, for up-to-date information contact English Heritage by phone or visit the website.

General description:
The great and ancient stone circle of Stonehenge is one of the wonders of the world. The first 'Stonehenge' consisted of a circular bank and ditch with a ring of 56 wooden posts, now known as Aubrey Holes. The final phase comprised an outer circle of huge standing stones, topped by lintels making a continuous ring. Inside this stood a horseshoe of still larger stones, five pairs of uprights with a lintel across each pair. A huge effort and organisation was needed to carry the stones tens, sometimes hundreds of miles, by land and water, and then to shape and raise them.
Now a World Heritage Site, Stonehenge and all its surroundings remain powerful witnesses to the once great civilization of the Stone and Bronze Ages, between 5000 and 3000 years ago.
Information services:
Guidebooks also available in French, German and Japanese.
Braille guides in English only.
Subject to availability, complementary audio tapes are available in nine languages.
Hearing loop.
Special visitor services: Tape recorded guides..

Internet home pages:
http://www.english-heritage.org.uk

2784
STOTT PARK BOBBIN MILL

Low Stott Park, Newby Bridge, Ulverston, Cumbria, LA12 8AX

Tel: 01539 531087

Organisation type and purpose: Museum, historic building, house or site.

Parent body:
English Heritage (North West Region)
Canada House, 3 Chepstow Street, Manchester, M1 5FW, tel: 0161 242 1400

Enquiries to: Manager
Access:
Access to staff: By letter, by telephone
Hours: Daily, Apr 1 to Oct 31, 1000 to 1800
Other restrictions: Free to English Heritage members and educational groups.

General description:
Victorian bobbin factory, timber coppicing, steam power, Victorian machinery, the industrial Lake District. Watch bobbins made as they were 200 years ago.
Information services:
Special visitor services: Guided tours..

Internet home pages:
http://www.english-heritage.org.uk

2785
STOURHEAD HOUSE

Stourhead Estate Office, Stourton, Warminster, Wiltshire, BA12 6QD

Tel: 01747 841152
Fax: 01747 842005
Email: stourhead@nationaltrust.org.uk
Formed: 1946

Organisation type and purpose: Registered charity (charity number 205846), historic building, house or site, suitable for ages: 5+.
Parent body:
The National Trust (South West Region)
Regional Office for Wessex, tel: 01985 843600

Enquiries to: Administrator
Other contacts: House Manager
Access:
Access to staff: By letter, by telephone, by email
Access to building, collections or gallery: No prior appointment required
Hours: End Mar to end of Oct, Fri to Tue 0100 to 1700; Oct, 1100 to 1600; last admission 30 minutes before closing
Other restrictions: Garden, house and tower close dusk if earlier. In Oct last admission to house and tower 1600

otherwise 30 mins before closing.
Access for disabled people: Parking provided, toilet facilities
Other restrictions: Entrance to house via 13 steps. All showrooms on one floor. Transfer available in main season to house and garden entrances. 6 manual wheelchairs available. 2 two-seater powered mobility vehicles. Ground floor fully accessible. Level entrance to shop and to restaurant. Recommended route map.

General description:
An outstanding example of the English landscape style, this splendid garden was designed by Henry Hoare II and laid out between 1741 and 1780. Classical temples, including the Pantheon and Temple of Apollo, are set around the central lake at the end of a series of vistas, which change as the visitor moves around the paths and through the magnificent mature woodland with its extensive collection of exotic trees. Built in the 1720s, the Palladian mansion was home to the Hoare family, owners of Britain's only independent private bank surviving to the present. The magnificent interior includes an outstanding Regency library, an extensive picture collection, and furniture by Chippendale the Younger. King Alfred's Tower, an intriguing red-brick folly built in 1772 by Henry Flitcroft, is almost 50m high and gives breathtaking views over the estate. Much of the estate woodland and downland is managed for nature conservation, and there are two interesting Iron Age hill-forts, Whitesheet Hill and Park Hill Camp. Leaflet of estate walks available from visitor reception, shop and NT
Wessex office

Information services:
Suitable for school groups. Education room/centre. Hands-on activities. Children's guide. Children's quiz/trail. Family activity packs. Adult study days. For education facilities contact Education Coordinator, telephone 01747 842012.
Braille guide. Large-print guide. Touch tour guide for house available by prior arrangement, telephone 01747 842020.
Sympathetic Hearing Scheme.
Group tours of house and garden by arrangement, tel. for Group Information leaflet.
Special visitor services: Materials and/or activities for children.
Education services: Group education facilities.
Services for disabled people: For the visually impaired; for the hearing impaired.
Collections:
Collection of furniture by Thomas Chippendale the younger
Nearly 500 paintings on display including works by Canaletto, Reynolds, Poussin, Murillo, Panini, Dughet, Largrenee and Woodforde
Catalogues:
Catalogue for part of the collections is only available in-house.
Printed publications:
Colour Guide
Short Guide
Picture List

Internet home pages:
http://www.nationaltrust.org.uk/regions/wessex

2786
STOWE LANDSCAPE GARDENS

Stowe, Buckingham, MK18 5EH

Tel: 01280 822850
Fax: 01280 822437
Email: stowegarden@nationaltrust.org.uk

Organisation type and purpose: National organisation, registered charity (charity number 205846), historic building, house or site.
Parent body:
The National Trust (South and South East Region)
Thames and Solent Regional Office, tel: 01494 528051

Enquiries to: Manager
Access:
Access to staff: By letter, by telephone, by fax, by email
Access for disabled people: Parking provided, level entry
Other restrictions: Designated parking 200yds. Limited numbers of self-drive, two-seater battery-powered vehicles available. Booking essential. Gardens unsuitable for manual wheelchairs and private battery-powered vehicles.

General description:
One of the finest Georgian landscape gardens, made up of valleys and vistas, narrow lakes and rivers with more than 30 temples and monuments designed by many of the leading architects of the 18th century. At the centre is Stowe House (not National Trust), occupied by Stowe School, and all around is Stowe Park. The creation of the Temple family, Stowe has been described as 'a work to wonder at' in its size, splendour and variety. Many of the garden buildings have now been restored, and thousands of new trees and shrubs have been planted in recent years. Work continues on this as well as on the house itself. Six newly restored monuments: the Fane of Pastoral Poetry, Lord Cobham's Monument, the Doric Arch and the George I Equestrian Statue in the garden, and the Conduit House and Wolfe's Obelisk in the park. Restoration of the Queen's Temple, the Corinthian Arch and the South Front and Colonnades of the house.

continued overleaf

Internet home pages:
http://www.nationaltrust.org.uk

2787
STRACEY ARMS DRAINAGE MILL

On the A47, O.S. TG 442 090, Damgate, Norfolk

Organisation type and purpose: Historic building, house or site.

General description:
Tower drainage mill.

2788
STRANGERS' HALL MUSEUM

Charing Cross, Norwich, Norfolk, NR2 4AL

Tel: 01603 667229
Email: museums@norfolk.gov.uk
Formed: 1922

Organisation type and purpose: Local government body, museum, historic building, house or site, suitable for ages: 8+.
Parent body:
Norfolk Museums and Archaeology Service
Tel: 01603 493625, fax: 01603 493623, email: museums@norfolk.gov.uk
Connected with:
Norwich Castle Museum
Castle Hill, Norwich, NR1 3JU, tel: 01603 493625, fax: 01603 493623, email/website: museums@norfolk.gov.uk

Enquiries to: Curator
Direct email: helen.rowles.mus@norfolk.gov.uk
Access:
Access to staff: By letter, by telephone, visitors by prior appointment
Hours: By arrangement
Other restrictions: Open for groups by appointment.
Access to building, collections or gallery: Prior appointment required
Hours: Public tours Wed and Sat, 1030, 1200 and 1400, assemble at Strangers' Hall at least 5 minutes prior to start of tour
Privately organised tours, Mon, Tue Thu or Fri
Other restrictions: Tours limited to 15 people, book tickets in advance from Norwich Castle until 15 minutes prior to start of tour. Booking line 01603 493636

General description:
One of the oldest buildings in Norwich. It is typical of a house occupied by the wealthy mediaeval merchants of Norwich during the city's heyday.
It has a stone vaulted undercroft dating to 1320; the Tudor Great Hall with stone mullioned window and screen; and a Georgian Dining Room; a warren of passages and interlinked rooms; and a formal seventeenth century style garden.
Period room displays show how people lived from the Tudor to the Victorian times.
Information services:
Organised group tours, tel 01603 629127
Education enquiries, tel 01603 495891
Special visitor services: Guided tours.
Education services: Group education facilities, resources for Key Stages 1 and 2..
Catalogues:
Catalogue for all of the collections is only available in-house.

Internet home pages:
http://www.norfolk.gov.uk/tourism/museums

2789
STRANRAER MUSEUM

The Old Town Hall, 55 George Street, Stranraer, Wigtownshire, DG9 7JP

Tel: 01776 705088
Fax: 01776 705835
Email: johnpic@dumgal.gov.uk
Formed: 1939

Organisation type and purpose: Local government body, museum.
Parent body:
Dumfries and Galloway Museum Service
Tel: 01387 253374

Enquiries to: Curator
Access:
Access to staff: By letter, by telephone, by fax, by email
Hours: Mon to Fri, 1000 to 1700; Sat, 1000 to 1300, 1400 to 1700
Access to building, collections or gallery: No prior appointment required
Hours: Mon to Fri, 1000 to 1700; Sat, 1000 to 1300, 1400 to 1700
Other restrictions: Admission free, accessible for wheelchairs.
Access for disabled people: level entry, access to all public areas, toilet facilities

General description:
A general museum devoted to the Wigtownshire area of South West Scotland. Collections include local history; archaeology; natural history; numismatics; geology; fine art; and historic photographs. Also contains local archives, including county records.
Collections:
John Ross. Memorabilia relating to Ross' Arctic explorations. 18th century.
Whithorn Excavation. Finds archive of 1984-1991 archaeological excavation at Whithorn. Medieval over 5000 items

Internet home pages:
http://www.dumgal.gov.uk/museums

2790
STRATFIELD SAYE HOUSE

See - Wellington Exhibition

2791
STRATHCLYDE UNIVERSITY

See - Collins Gallery

2792
STRATHNAVER MUSEUM

Bettyhill, Thurso, Caithness, KW14 7SS

Tel: 01641 521418
Email: strathnavermus@ukonline.co.uk
Formed: 1976

Organisation type and purpose: Museum, suitable for ages: 8+.

Enquiries to: Chairman
Access:
Access to staff: By letter, by telephone, by email

General description:
A collection of local social history with particular reference to the 'Strathnaver Clearances'. There is also a collection of 'Clan Mackay' memorabilia.

2793
STRATHSPEY STEAM RAILWAY

Aviemore Station, Dalfaber Road, Aviemore, Inverness-shire, PH22 1PY

Tel: 01479 810725
Fax: 01479 812220
Email: information@strathspeyrailway.co.uk
Formed: 1978

Organisation type and purpose: (membership is by subscription), present number of members: 800, voluntary organisation, historic building, house or site, suitable for ages: all ages.
Not-for-profit company.
Parent body:
Strathspey Railway Association
Operating company:
Strathspey Railway Company Limited (SRC)
Address for publicity and marketing:
Strathspey Steam Railway
37 Castle Avenue, Balloch, Alexandria, G83 8HW, tel: 01389 752214, email/website: marketing@strathspeyrailway.co.uk

Enquiries to: Superintendent of the Line
Other contacts: Director, Publicity & Marketing for publicity and marketing matters.
Access:
Access to staff: By letter, by telephone, by email
Hours: Mon to Fri, 0900 to 1700
Access to building, collections or gallery: No prior appointment required
Hours: Stations: Daily, 0900 to 1700
Other restrictions: Closed 3 Jan to 29 Mar. Restricted opening Apr, May, Oct to Dec.
Access for disabled people: Parking provided, ramped entry, toilet facilities
Other restrictions: Access to trains for wheelchairs by ramp to coach.

General description:
Operation of a steam railway between Aviemore and Grantown-on-Spey (section Aviemore-Boat of Garten open at present).
Printed publications:
Guide Book
Strathspey Express (journal)
Electronic and video products:
5 Miles of Magic (video, £11 inc p&p)

Internet home pages:
http://www.strathspeyrailway.co.uk
General description of the line, access to the stations, timetable, details of Strathspey Railway Association.

2794
MR STRAW'S HOUSE

7 Blyth Grove, Worksop, Nottinghamshire, S81 0JG

Tel: 01909 482380
Email: mrstrawshouse@nationaltrust.org.uk

Organisation type and purpose: National organisation, registered charity (charity number 205846), historic building, house or site, suitable for ages: 5+.
Parent body:
National Trust (East Midlands Region)
East Midlands Regional Office
East Midlands Regional Office, tel: 07909 486411

Enquiries to: Custodian
Access:
Access to staff: By letter, by telephone, by email, visitors by prior appointment, Internet web pages
Access to building, collections or gallery: Prior appointment required
Hours: Apr to Oct: Tue to Sat, 1100 to 1630
Other restrictions: Closed Good Fri. Admission for all visitors (inc. NT members) is by timed ticket, which must be booked in advance. All bookings by tel. or letter (with s.a.e.) to Property Manager. On quiet days a same-day tel. call is often sufficient

General description:
This modest semi-detached Edwardian house provides a fascinating insight into everyday life in the early part of the 20th century. The interior has remained unaltered since the 1930s and features contemporary wallpaper, Victorian furniture and household objects.
There are also displays of family costume and memorabilia, and a typical suburban garden.
Information services:
Special events programme;
Braille guide, handling collection;
Suitable for school groups; children's quiz/trail
Special visitor services: Guided tours, materials and/or activities for children.
Education services: Group education facilities, resources for Key Stages 1 and 2 and Further or Higher Education.
Services for disabled people: For the visually impaired.
Collections:
Good selection of archives (letters etc) all belonging to one family
Catalogues:
Catalogue for all of the collections is only available in-house.

Printed publications:
Guide Book

Internet home pages:
http://www.nationaltrust.org.uk

2795
STRETTON WATERMILL
162 London Road, Northwich, Cheshire, CW6 8AB

Tel: 01606 41331
Access:
Access to staff: By letter, by telephone
Access for disabled people: Parking provided, ramped entry, toilet facilities

General description:
Working water-driven corn mill.
Collections:
Historical displays, working models

2796
STROME CASTLE
Strome Ferry, Ross-shire

Organisation type and purpose: Historic building, house or site.
Parent body:
National Trust for Scotland Highlands and Islands Office (North)

Other contacts: Enquiries to Iain Turnbull, Lochalsh House (NTS), Balmacara, Kyle, Ross-shire, IV40 8DN; tel 01599 566325, fax 01599 566359
Access:
Access to staff: By letter, by telephone, by fax
Access to building, collections or gallery: No prior appointment required
Hours: All year, daily

General description:
Ruined castle, first recorded in 1472 when it was the stronghold of the Lords of the Isles.

Internet home pages:
http://www.nts.org.uk

2797
STROMNESS MUSEUM
52 Alfred Street, Stromness, Orkney, KW16 3DF

Tel: 01856 850025
Fax: 01856 871560
Acronym or abbreviation: ONHSM
Full name: Orkney Natural History Society Museum
Formed: 1837
Formed from: Orkney Natural History Society

Organisation type and purpose: Membership association, registered charity (charity number SCO 21455), museum, suitable for ages: all ages.
To preserve Orkney's Natural and Maritime History.
Member of:
Council for Museums and Galleries, Scotland

Enquiries to: Curator
Direct tel: 01856 873191
Direct fax: 01856 871560
Other contacts: Hon Secretary
Access:
Access to staff: By letter, by telephone, by fax, visitors by prior appointment
Access to building, collections or gallery: No prior appointment required
Hours: Apr to Sep: Daily, 1000 to 1700
Oct to Mar: Mon to Sat, 1100 to 1530
Access for disabled people: level entry, toilet facilities
Other restrictions: Access to most areas.

General description:
Orkney birds, eggs, butterflies and moths, shells and fossils, fish and mammals, seaweeds, archaeology, bygones and ethnography in a restored Victorian gallery. Shipping, fishing, whaling, Hudson's Bay Company, Scapa Flow and the German Fleet, John Rae, life in Northern Canada, shipwrecks, lifeboats, Orkney lighthouses and the social history of Stromness, Orkney.
Collections:
Scuttling and salvaging of German fleet 1919
Printed publications:
Lighthouses of Orkney (£1.10, plus p&p)
Orkney Croft (65p, plus p&p)
Sail and Steam (£1.10p, plus p&p)
The Ice Bound Whalers (£6.95, hardback; £4.95 softback plus p&p)
The Salvaging of the German Fleet (£1.10, plus p&p)

2798
STROUD DISTRICT MUSEUM SERVICE
See - Museum in the Park

2799
STRUMPSHAW HALL STEAM MUSEUM
Strumpshaw, Norwich, Norfolk, NR13 4HR

Tel: 01603 713392

Organisation type and purpose: Independently owned, museum, suitable for ages: all ages.

Enquiries to: Curator
Access:
Access to staff: By letter
Access for disabled people: Parking provided, ramped entry, access to all public areas

General description:
Steam museum and farm machinery collection.
Collections:
Steam engines and lorries
Working beam engines
Working mechanical organs
Narrow gauge railway, three-quarter mile track
1930s fairground carousel
Tractors and farm machinery
Electronic and video products:
Steam Rally (video)

2800
STUDLEY ROYAL
See - Fountains Abbey & Studley Royal

2801
STYAL MILL
See - Quarry Bank Mill and Styal Estate

2802
SUBMARINE WORLD
See - Royal Navy Submarine Museum

2803
SUDBURY HALL
Sudbury, Ashbourne, Derbyshire, DE6 5HT

Tel: 01283 585305
Fax: 01283 585139
Email: sudburyhall@nationaltrust.org.uk

Organisation type and purpose: National organisation, registered charity (charity number 205846), historic building, house or site, suitable for ages: 5+.
Parent body:
The National Trust (East Midlands Region)
East Midlands Regional Office, tel: 07909 486411

Enquiries to: Property Manager
Other contacts: Education Officer (01283 585022)
Access:
Access to staff: By letter, by telephone, by fax, by email, in person, Internet web pages
Access to building, collections or gallery: No prior appointment required
Hours: Hall: Apr to Oct, Wed to Sun, 1300 to 1700: Open Bank Holiday Mondays
Grounds: mid Mar to Oct, Wed to Sun, 1100 to 1800
Other restrictions: Closes dusk if earlier
Access for disabled people: Parking provided, toilet facilities
Other restrictions: Transfer available from designated parking, dropoff point. 2 manual wheelchairs available.
Steps to entrance. Ground floor largely inaccessible, 11 steps to entry, only one throughout the ground floor. No access to other floors. Level entrance to tea-room. Gravel paths, mainly level, only top terrace accessible.

General description:
One of the most individual of late 17th century houses, with rich interior decoration including wood carving by Gibbons, superb plasterwork, and decorative painted murals and ceilings by Laguerre. The Great Staircase is one of the finest of its kind in an English house.
Information services:
Helpline available, tel no: 01283 585305.
Guided and specialist tours of Hall; 'Behind the Scenes' tours; evening and morning tours by prior arrangement; for details contact Property Manager.
Braille guide; large-print guide, touch list
Suitable for school groups. Live interpretation, hands-on activities.
Children's guide, children's quiz/trail.
Adult study days
Special events programme
Special visitor services: Guided tours, materials and/or activities for children.
Education services: Group education facilities.
Services for disabled people: For the visually impaired.

Internet home pages:
http://www.nationaltrust.org.uk

See also - National Trust Museum of Childhood

2804
SUDLEY HOUSE
Mossley Hill Road, Aigburth, Liverpool, L18 8BX

Tel: 0151 724 3245
Fax: 0151 729 0531
Formed: 1986

Organisation type and purpose: Art gallery, historic building, house or site, suitable for ages: all ages.
Parent body:
National Museums & Galleries on Merseyside (NMGM)

Enquiries to: Director
Other contacts: Marketing Manager for advertising.
Access:
Access to staff: By letter only
Access to building, collections or gallery: No prior appointment required
Hours: Mon to Sat, 1000 to 1700; Sun, 1200 to 1700
Access for disabled people: Parking provided, ramped entry, level entry, toilet facilities

General description:
Contains the collection of 18th and 19th century paintings once owned by Victorian shipowner George Holt, whose family bequeathed them and the family home, Sudley, to the City of Liverpool.
Catalogues:
Catalogue for library is on-line.
Publications list:
is available in hard copy.

Internet home pages:
http://www.nmgm.org.uk

2805
SUFFOLK REGIMENTAL MUSEUM
The Keep, Gibraltar Barracks, Bury St Edmunds, Suffolk, IP33 3RN

Tel: 01284 752394
Closed pending relocation in 2001

continued overleaf

Access:
Access to building, collections or gallery: Prior appointment required

General description:
The main collection is now at Moyse's Hall Museum, only the reserve collection is housed at Gibraltar Barracks.

See also - Moyse's Hall Museum

2806
SULGRAVE MANOR

Manor Road, Sulgrave, Banbury, Oxfordshire, OX17 2SD

Tel: 01295 760205
Fax: 01295 768056
Email: sulgrave-manor@talk21.com
Full name: Sulgrave Manor Board
Formed: 1921

Organisation type and purpose: Registered charity (charity number 1003839), museum, historic building, house or site, suitable for ages: all ages.

Enquiries to: Administrator
Other contacts: Function & Marketing Manager
Access:
Access to staff: By letter, by telephone, by fax, by email, in person, visitors by prior appointment
Hours: Sun to Sat, 0900 to 1700
Access to building, collections or gallery: No prior appointment required
Hours: Mar 29 to Oct 31: Sun, Tue to Thur, Sat, 1400 to 1730 to general public
Open Mon and Fri bank holidays and special event days
Other restrictions: Access is by guided tour only, so visitors must arrive at least one hour before closing.
Visits at other times by prior appointment.
Access for disabled people: toilet facilities

General description:
Tudor period manor house and gardens designed by Sir Reginald Blomfield; 18th century; American Colonial history; home of George Washington's ancestors; the Washington Family in Britain.
Information services:
Library available for reference (for conditions see Access above)
Special visitor services: Guided tours.
Education services: Group education facilities, resources for Key Stages 2 and 3..
Collections:
Exhibition showing the life of George Washington, first President of the United States of America
Elizabethan knot garden
Catalogues:
Catalogue for library is in-house only. Catalogue for all of the collections is only available in-house.
Printed publications:
Guide Book on Sulgrave Manor House, Sulgrave Village, the Washington Family in Britain and George Washington
Electronic and video products:
The British Heritage of George Washington (video)

Internet home pages:
http://www.stratford.co.uk/sulgrave
http://www.sulgravemanor.org.uk

2807
SUNDERLAND MUSEUM & WINTER GARDENS

Mowbray Gardens, Burdon Road, Sunderland, Tyne and Wear, SR1 1PP

Tel: 0191 553 2323
Fax: 0191 553 7828
Formed: 1846

Organisation type and purpose: Local government body, registered charity, museum, art gallery, suitable for ages: 5+.

Parent body:
Tyne and Wear Museums (TWM)
Discovery Museum, Blandford Square, Newcastle, tel: 0191 232 6789, fax: 0191 233 1088

Enquiries to: Curator
Other contacts: Education Officer for school bookings.
Access:
Access to staff: By letter, by telephone, by fax
Other restrictions: By appointment only.
Access to building, collections or gallery: No prior appointment required
Hours: Mon, 1000 to 1600; Tue to Sat, 1000 to 1700; Sun, 1400 to 1700
Access for disabled people: level entry, access to all public areas, toilet facilities

General description:
Time Machine - The first Nissan Car built in Sunderland and treasures from an Egyptian Tomb.
World's Alive - polar bears and penguins, lions and tigers.
Secrets of the Past - unearth what life was like through the ages.
Lost Worlds - Prehistoric swamps and strange creatures that lived millions of years ago.
Largest collection of Sunderland Pottery.
Lifestyle, fashion, politics, crafts, industry of 100 years in Sunderland.
Over 1000 of the world's most exotic flowers, plants and trees.
Information services:
Special visitor services: Materials and/or activities for children.
Education services: Group education facilities, resources for Key Stages 1 and 2, 3, 4 and Further or Higher Education.
Services for disabled people: For the visually impaired; for the hearing impaired; displays and/or information at wheelchair height.
Collections:
First Nissan Car built in Sunderland
Natural History - animal and plantlife
Archaeological finds
Geology - fossils, rocks and minerals
Arts and crafts, paintings, glassware, ceramics, textiles (including work by L S Lowry)
Shipbuilding memorabilia, ship models
Ethnography

Internet home pages:
http://www.twmuseums.org.uk

2808
SUNDERLAND VOLUNTEER LIFE BRIGADE

The Watch House, Pier View, Roker, Sunderland, Tyne and Wear, SR6 0PR

Tel: 0191 5672579
Fax: 0191 5292651
Email: sunderland.vlb@tiscali.co.uk
Acronym or abbreviation: SVLB
Formed: 1877

Organisation type and purpose: Professional body, present number of members: 15 active members, voluntary organisation, registered charity (charity number 1041849), museum, historic building, house or site, suitable for ages: all ages, training organisation.
Coastal search and cliff rescue.
Links with:
RNLI Coastguard

Enquiries to: Secretary
Direct tel: 07754 461728
Direct email: sonia_spence@hotmail.com
Other contacts: Treasurer
Access:
Access to staff: By letter, by telephone, by fax, by email, in person, visitors by prior appointment, Internet web pages
Hours: Mon to Fri, 0900 to 1700

General description:
Volunteer Life Brigade Search and Rescue Unit and its history, a 100 years of Life Saving on the Coast of Sunderland.

Collections:
Model ships and historical photographs
Publications list:
is available in hard copy and online.
Printed publications:
Include leaflets and postcards

Internet home pages:
http://www.communigate.co.uk/ne/svlb/index.phtml
The history of the brigade, other information and publications.

2809
SUNNYCROFT

200 Holyhead Road, Wellington, Telford, Shropshire, TF1 2DR

Tel: 01952 242884
Formed: July 1999

Organisation type and purpose: National organisation, registered charity (charity number 205846), historic building, house or site, suitable for ages: 5+.
Parent body:
The National Trust (West Midlands)
West Midlands Regional Office, tel: 01743 708100
Other addresses:
The National Trust
West Midlands Regional Office
Attingham Park, Shrewsbury, Shropshire, tel: 01743 709343

Enquiries to: Custodian
Access:
Access to staff: By letter, by telephone, visitors by prior appointment, charges to non-members
Hours: Apr to Oct: Wed, 0900 to 1700; Sun, Mon, 1400 to 1800
Other restrictions: Answermachine for messages at other times.
Access to building, collections or gallery: Prior appointment required
Hours: Apr to Oct: Sun, Mon, 1300 to 1700
Open Bank Holiday Mondays
Other restrictions: Admission by timed ticket. Advance booking not possible. Access by guided tour only, except Bank Holiday Mondays. Last admission 1 hr before closing.
Access for disabled people: Parking provided, toilet facilities
Other restrictions: Car parking is for disabled visitors only and booking is essential because of limited space. Drop-off point. Steps to entrance. Ground floor largely inaccessible. Back door to yard has 2 and then 4 steps. Grounds largely accessible. Recommended route map.

General description:
A late-Victorian gentleman's suburban villa, typical of the many thousands of such houses that were built for prosperous business and professional people on the fringes of Victorian towns and cities. Sunnycroft is one of the very few, perhaps the only one, to have survived largely unaltered and complete with its contents, of which a remarkable range remains. The grounds amount to a 'mini-estate', with pigsties, stables, kitchen garden, orchards, conservatory, flower garden and superb Wellingtonia avenue.
Information services:
Out-of-hours tours are available for group visits on Tues; must be booked.
Special visitor services: Guided tours..
Collections:
Collection of everyday furniture and furnishings accumulated by the family over 3 generations
Fine examples of Joan Lander's needlework
Printed publications:
Guide Book
Property Leaflet (free)

Internet home pages:
http://www.nationaltrust.org.uk

2810
SUNNYSIDE MUSEUM
Montrose
See - Montrose Museum and Art Gallery

2811
SURREY HEATH ARCHAEOLOGICAL & HERITAGE TRUST
Archaeology Centre, 4-10 London Road, Bagshot, Surrey, GU19 5HN

Tel: 01276 451181
Acronym or abbreviation: SHAHT
Formed: 1988

Organisation type and purpose: Learned society (membership is by subscription), present number of members: 200, voluntary organisation, registered charity (charity number 299409), museum, suitable for ages: 9 to 75, training organisation, research organisation.
Access:
Access to staff: By letter, by telephone
Hours: By appointment
Access to building, collections or gallery: No prior appointment required

General description:
Archaeology of Borough of Surrey Heath; mesolithic to post-industrial revolution.
Catalogues:
Catalogue for library is in-house only. Catalogue for all of the collections is only available in-house.

2812
SURREY HEATH MUSEUM
Knoll Road, Camberley, Surrey, GU15 3HD

Tel: 01276 707284
Fax: 01276 707183

Organisation type and purpose: Museum.

Enquiries to: Curator
Access:
Access to staff: By letter, by telephone, by fax, in person
Hours: Tue to Sat, 1100 to 1700
Access to building, collections or gallery: No prior appointment required

General description:
A general collection dealing with local and social history and the environment of the Surrey Heath area.
Collections:
Local photographs of rural views and agricultural subjects by artist/photographer Robert Tucker Pain, 1860-1880, c. 70 items
Poulter Drawings, early 20th Century local architectural drawings and plans, 1900-1930, 25 drawings and c. 25 plans
Catalogues:
Catalogue for part of the collections is only available in-house.

Internet home pages:
http://www.surreyheath.gov.uk

2813
SUSSEX ARCHAEOLOGICAL SOCIETY
See - Sussex Past

2814
SUSSEX COMBINED SERVICES MUSEUM
Redoubt Fortress, Royal Parade, Eastbourne, East Sussex, BN21 7AQ

Tel: 01323 410300
Fax: 01323 732240
Email: eastbournemuseum@breathmail
Formed: 1977

Organisation type and purpose: Local government body, museum.

Enquiries to: Curator
Access:
Access to staff: By letter, by telephone, by fax, in person
Hours: Mon to Fri, 0900 to 1700

General description:
A military museum showing the history of the Army, Navy and RAF in Sussex, and Sussex units serving worldwide; particularly of the Royal Sussex Regiment, The Queen's Royal Irish Hussars and service organisations in Sussex.
Collections:
50,000 items including:
The Royal Sussex Regiment and the Queen's Royal Irish Hussars collections
National Collection of the British Model Soldier Society
Rommel's staff car
Catalogues:
Catalogue for part of the collections is only available in-house.

Internet home pages:
http://www.eastbournemuseums.co.uk

2815
SUSSEX FARM MUSEUM
Horam Manor Farm, Heathfield, East Sussex, TN21 0JB

Tel: 01435 813688 and 812597
Fax: 01435 813716
Full name: Farm Museum and Nature Trails
Formed: 1987

Organisation type and purpose: Registered charity (charity number 1062631/0), museum, historic building, house or site.
Craft workers and nature trails. Sussex historical ironworking centre.

Enquiries to: Owner
Access:
Access to staff: By letter, by telephone
Access for disabled people: level entry, toilet facilities

General description:
Farming and country life 1900 to 1950. Sussex Iron Industry 1250-1750.

2816
SUSSEX PAST
Bull House, 92 High Street, Lewes, East Sussex, BN7 1XH

Tel: 01273 486260
Fax: 01273 486990
Email: admin@sussexpast.co.uk
Full name: Sussex Archaeological Society
Formed: 1846

Organisation type and purpose: Learned society, registered charity, museum.
Affiliated to:
Council for British Archaeology
Sussex Past sites:
Anne of Cleves House Museum
52 Southover High Street, Lewes, East Sussex, BN7 1JA, tel: 01273 474610
Fishbourne Roman Palace and Museum
Salthill Road, Fishbourne, Chichester, West Sussex, PO19 3QR, tel: 01243 785859, fax: 01243 539266, email/website: adminfish@sussexpast.co.uk
Lewes Castle & Museums
169 High Street, Lewes, East Sussex, BN7 1YE, tel: 01273 486290, email/website: castle@sussexpast.co.uk
Marlpins Museum
High Street, Shoreham-by-Sea, West Sussex, BN43 5NN, tel: 01273 462994
Michelham Priory
Upper Dicker, Hailsham, East Sussex, BN27 3QS, tel: 01323 844224
The Priest House
North Lane, West Hoathly, East Grinstead, West Sussex, RH19 4PP, tel: 01342 810479, email/website: priest@sussexpast.co.uk

Enquiries to: Public Relations Manager
Direct tel: 01273 487188
Direct fax: 01273 486990
Direct email: pro@sussexpast.co.uk
Access:
Access to building, collections or gallery: Prior appointment required
Hours: Mon to Sat, 1000 to 1700; Sun, 1100 to 1700
Other restrictions: Library: 01273 405738
Museum: 01273 405739

General description:
Sussex archaeology, local history and historic properties.
Information services:
Special visitor services: Guided tours.
Education services: Group education facilities..
Collections:
Artefacts relating to archaeology and history
Collection of prints, pictures, books related to Sussex
Manuscripts
Printed publications:
Sussex Past & Present (magazine, 3 times a year)
Sussex Archaeological Collections (annually, to members or on subscription)

Internet home pages:
http://www.sussexpast.co.uk
Properties open to the public, research, details of organisation and membership.

See also - Anne of Cleves House Museum; Fishbourne Roman Palace Museum; Lewes Castle & Museums; Marlipins Museum; Michelham Priory; Priest House (Sussex Past)

2817
SUSSEX TOY AND MODEL MUSEUM
See - Brighton Toy and Model Museum

2818
SUTCLIFFE GALLERY
1 Flowergate, Whitby, North Yorkshire, YO21 3BA

Tel: 01947 602239
Fax: 01947 820287
Email: photographs@sutcliffe-gallery.fsnet.co.uk
Formed: 1959

Organisation type and purpose: Photographic gallery.

Enquiries to: Managing Director
Access:
Access to staff: By letter, by telephone, by fax, by email, Internet web pages
Hours: Mon to Fri, 0900 to 1700; Sat, 0900 to 1700; Sun, 1400 to 1700
Access to building, collections or gallery: No prior appointment required

General description:
The work of Frank Meadow Sutcliffe Hon FRPS (1853-1941), pioneer of naturalistic photography; 19th century photographs of fishing communities and farm labourers, rural landscapes.
Printed publications:
Reproduction of Sutcliffe's work
Books
Leaflet
Electronic and video products:
A video and a CD-ROM available for purchase by contacting Sutcliffe Gallery direct

Internet home pages:
http://www.sutcliffe-gallery.co.uk
Biographical details and approximately 83 images.

2819
SUTTON HERITAGE CENTRE
See - Honeywood Heritage Centre

2820
SUTTON HOO
Woodbridge, Suffolk, IP12 3DJ

Tel: 01394 389700
Fax: 01394 389702

continued overleaf

Organisation type and purpose: National organisation, registered charity (charity number 205846), historic building, house or site, suitable for ages: 5+.
Parent body:
The National Trust (East of England)
East Anglia Regional Office, tel: 0870 609 5388

Enquiries to: Manager
Other contacts: 01394 389727 (Learning)
Access:
Access to staff: By letter, by telephone, by fax
Access for disabled people: Parking provided, level entry, toilet facilities
Other restrictions: Drop-off point. 6 manual wheelchairs available. 2 single-seater powered mobility vehicles. Ground floor fully accessible. Level entrance to shop and to restaurant. Grounds largely accessible. Recommended route map.

General description:
The Anglo-Saxon royal burial site where the priceless Sutton Hoo treasure was discovered in a huge ship grave in 1939. The exhibition hall houses a full-size reconstruction of the burial chamber from the ship grave, and tells the story of the site, which is described as 'page one of English history'. The burial site (500yds from visitor facilities) forms part of the 99ha (245 acre) estate given to the National Trust by the Annie Tranmer Charitable Trust in 1998.
Information services:
Guided tours available at set times at weekends and some weekdays, additional charge. Tel. to confirm times.
Suitable for school groups. Education room/centre. Children's quiz/trail. Adult study days. Dressing-up box in exhibition. Children's activities during the summer holidays .
Special visitor services: Materials and/or activities for children.
Education services: Group education facilities..

Internet home pages:
http://www.nationaltrust.org.uk

2821
SUTTON HOUSE

2 & 4 Homerton High Street, Hackney, London, E9 6JQ

Tel: 020 8986 2264
Email: suttonhouse@nationaltrust.org.uk

Organisation type and purpose: National organisation, registered charity (charity number 205846), historic building, house or site, suitable for ages: 5+.
Parent body:
The National Trust (South and South East Region)
Thames and Solent Regional Office, tel: 01494 528051
Other addresses:
The National Trust
36 Queen Anne's Gate, London, SW1H 9AB, tel: 020 7222 9251

Enquiries to: Administration Assistant
Direct tel: 020 8525 9055
Direct fax: 020 8525 9051
Access:
Access to staff: By letter, by telephone, by email, charges to non-members
Access to building, collections or gallery: No prior appointment required
Hours: Historic Rooms: beg Feb to 21 Dec, Fri, Sat, 1300 to 1730; Sun, 1130 to 1730 (last admission 1700)
Art Gallery: beg Jan to 21 Dec, Wed to Sun, 1130 to 1700
Open Bank Holiday Mondays 1130 to 1700
Access for disabled people: ramped entry, toilet facilities
Other restrictions: Drop-off point. Level entrance. Ground floor fully accessible. No access to other floors. Level entrance to shop and to tea-room.

General description:
A unique survival in Hackney, Sutton House was built in 1535 by Ralph Sadleir, a rising star at the court of Henry VIII. Home to merchants, Huguenot silk-weavers, schoolmistresses and Edwardian clergy, Sutton House has been altered over the years but remains essentially a Tudor house. Oak-panelled rooms and carved fireplaces survive intact, and there is some outstanding 'Linenfold' panelling dating from the mid-sixteenth century as well as a seventeenth century painted staircase.
Information services:
Braille guide.
Suitable for school groups. Education room/centre. Children's quiz/trail. Adult study days.
Special visitor services: Guided tours, materials and/or activities for children.
Education services: Group education facilities, resources for Key Stages 1 and 2 and Further or Higher Education.
Services for disabled people: For the visually impaired.

Internet home pages:
http://www.nationaltrust.org.uk/regions/thameschilterns

2822
SUTTON PARK

Sutton-on-the-Forest, York, YO61 1DP

Tel: 01347 810249 or 811239
Fax: 01347 811251
Email: info@statelyhome.co.uk

Organisation type and purpose: Independently owned, historic building, house or site, suitable for ages: 16+.

Enquiries to: Administrator
Access:
Access to staff: By letter, by telephone, by fax, by email, visitors by prior appointment, Internet web pages
Hours: Mon to Thu, 0900 to 1300
Access to building, collections or gallery: No prior appointment required
Hours: Gardens, Apr to end Sep, 1100 to 1700
House, open to general public, Apr to end Sep, Wed and Sun, 1330 to 1700
Other restrictions: Prior appointment is required for private parties

General description:
The house is fine example of early Georgian architecture built in 1730 by Thomas Atkinson, and set in magnificent gardens and parkland. In the gardens is a Georgian Icehouse.
Information services:
Special visitor services: Tape recorded guides..
Collections:
18th century furniture and paintings
Collection of porcelain

Internet home pages:
http://www.statelyhome.co.uk

2823
SUTTON POYNTZ PUMPING STATION

See - Water Supply Museum

2824
SWAFFHAM MUSEUM

London Street, Swaffham, Norfolk, PE37 7DQ

Tel: 01760 721230
Fax: 01760 720469
Email: swaffhammuseum@ic24.net
Formed: 1987

Organisation type and purpose: Museum. Independently run - in the process of being run by Company Limited by Guarantee.
Connected with:
Friends of Swaffham Museum
At the same address

Enquiries to: General Secretary
Other contacts: Museum Assistant for education visits.
Access:
Access to staff: By letter, by telephone, by fax, by email, in person
Hours: Apr to Nov: Tue to Sat
1000 to1300
Dec to Mar: Tue to Fri, 1000 to 1300
Access for disabled people: level entry
Other restrictions: Access to exhibition rooms.

General description:
Social history of Swaffham and surrounding area, Stone Age to present day.
Contains fossils, and Roman and Victorian specialities. Home of Howard Carter, Admiral Sir Knyvet-Wilson, and Captain Johns (who wrote the Biggles stories) The Swaffham Pedlar.
Collections:
Photographs: Howard Carter and Admiral Knyvet Wilson
Symonds. Hand-crafted figures from literature, Dickens, Tolkien, Shakespeare, and Commedia Dellarte
Printed publications:
Various publications available

2825
SWALCLIFFE BARN

Main Road, Swalcliffe, Banbury, Oxfordshire

Tel: 01295 788278
Email: swalcliffe.society@virgin.net

Organisation type and purpose: Museum, historic building, house or site, suitable for ages: all ages.
Other addresses:
The Swalcliffe Society
c/o The Old Grange, Swalcliffe, OX15 5EY, email/website: swalcliffe.society@virgin.net

Enquiries to: Chairman
Other contacts: Secretary for Society information.
Access:
Access to staff: By letter, by telephone, by email, visitors by prior appointment
Access for disabled people: Parking provided, ramped entry, access to all public areas, toilet facilities

General description:
The barn, built between 1400 and 1409 by New College, Oxford, is one of the finest in the country, with its mediaeval half-cruck timber roof intact. It houses some of the county's agricultural and trade vehicles.
Catalogues:
Catalogue for part of the collections is only available in-house.

2826
SWALEDALE FOLK MUSEUM

Reeth Green, Reeth, Richmond, North Yorkshire, DL1 6QT

Tel: 01748 884373
Formed: 1974

Organisation type and purpose: Independently owned, museum, suitable for ages: all ages, especially the elderly.
Collection of items, mainly related to Lead Mining and Sheep Farming which was the local form of employment, especially in the 19th century.

Enquiries to: Curator
Access:
Access to staff: Visitors by prior appointment
Access for disabled people: ramped entry

General description:
The collection illustrates how sheep farming and lead mining shaped the lives of people in this remote and beautiful Yorkshire Dale. Exhibits include schools; horseback doctor; clogs; Methodism; brass bands; roads; handknitting; pastimes; Poor Law, etc.
Information services:
Services for disabled people: Displays and/or information at wheelchair height.

Collections:
Objects, pictures, photographs, other materials, books, documents, manuscripts
Catalogues:
Catalogue for part of the collections is only available in-house.

2827
SWANAGE RAILWAY
Station House, Swanage, Dorset, BH19 1HB

Tel: 01929 425800
Fax: 01929 426680
Email: general@swanrail.freeserve.co.uk
Formed: 1976
Formerly: Southern Steam Trust; Swanage Railway Trust, date of change, January 2002

Organisation type and purpose: Service industry, voluntary organisation, registered charity, museum.
Restoring the rail link between Swanage and Wareham, and re-establishing a daily service to connect with the main line. Creating a comprehensive historical record of steam railways and steam technology in Southern England.

Enquiries to: Passenger Services Manager
Direct tel: 07876 427527
Direct email: davidagreen@care4free.net
Access:
Access to staff: By letter, by telephone, by fax, by email, in person
Hours: Daily 0900 to 1700
Other restrictions: Closed Christmas Day.

General description:
Steam railway preservation and running the line from Norden to Swanage.
Printed publications:
Swanage Railway Millennium Souvenir (£3.99)
Swanage Railway News (quarterly)

Internet home pages:
http://www.swanagerailway.co.uk

2828
SWANSEA MUSEUM
Victoria Road, Maritime Quarter, Swansea, West Glamorgan, SA1 1SN

Tel: 01792 653763
Fax: 01792 652585
Email: swansea.museum@swansea.gov.uk
Formed: 1841
Formerly: Royal Institution of South Wales, date of change, 1991

Organisation type and purpose: Local government body, museum, suitable for ages: 5+.
Parent body:
City and County of Swansea
County Hall, Swansea, tel: 01792 636000

Enquiries to: Curator
Access:
Access to staff: By letter, by telephone, by fax, in person
Hours: Closed to the public on Mondays
Other restrictions: Researchers by appointment only.
Access for disabled people: Parking provided

General description:
Local history and studies of Swansea and surrounding area, including natural history, biography, culture, early photography, archaeology, ceramics (Swansea and District) and local topography.
Collections:
Archaeological artefacts and Egyptian Mummy
Local ceramics, local paintings, drawings, prints and photographs, natural history collections
Local history library
Publications list:
is available in hard copy.
Printed publications:
Available for purchase directly
Minerva: The Journal of Swansea History (annually, Vol 9 2001, back numbers available)
History of Swansea Vol 2 (Jones W H)
John Humphrey, God's Own Architect (Farmer D)

Internet home pages:
http://www.swansea.museum.org.uk

See also - Royal Institution of South Wales

2829
SWINDON AND CRICKLADE RAILWAY
Blunsdon Station, Tadpole Lane, Blunsdon, Swindon, Wiltshire, SN25 2DA

Tel: 01793 771615
Email: randallchri@netscape.net
Formed: 1978

Organisation type and purpose: Membership association (membership is by subscription), present number of members: 400, voluntary organisation, registered charity (charity number 1067447), museum.

Enquiries to: Secretary
Direct tel: 01367 536570
Other contacts: Chief Engineer for future planning.
Access:
Access to staff: By letter, by telephone, by email, in person, Internet web pages
Hours: Weekends and Bank holidays only
Access for disabled people: Parking provided, ramped entry, access to all public areas, toilet facilities

General description:
Railway preservation and all trades concerned with this.
Collections:
Steam and diesel locomotives
Historic carriages and waggons
Catalogues:
Catalogue for library is on-line. Catalogue for part of the collections is on-line.
Printed publications:
Guide Book
Magazine (quarterly, members)
Stock List

Internet home pages:
http://www.swindon-cricklade-railway.org

2830
SWINFORD MUSEUM TRUST
Filkins, Lechlade, Gloucestershire, GL7 3JQ

Tel: 01367 860 209
Formed: 1931

Organisation type and purpose: Museum.

Enquiries to: Chairman
Access:
Access to staff: By letter, by telephone
Access for disabled people: level entry

General description:
A collection of objects in domestic use, and craftmen's tools in use in former times, in the parishes of Filkins and Broughton Poggs; and other items of local interest.
Catalogues:
Catalogue for part of the collections is only available in-house.

2831
SWISS GARDEN
Old Warden, Biggleswade, Bedfordshire, SG18 9EA

Tel: 01767 627666
Email: enquire@shuttleworth.org
Formed: 1820

Organisation type and purpose: Historic garden.
Connected with:
Bedfordshire County Council
Cauldwell Street, Bedford, MK40 9AP

Enquiries to: Garden Guardian
Other contacts: Head Gardener
Access:
Access to staff: By telephone, by email, Internet web pages
Hours: Mar to Sep; Sun and Bank Holidays, 1000 to 1800, all other days, 1300 to 1800
Access to building, collections or gallery: No prior appointment required
Hours: Mar to Sep: Sun and Bank Holidays, 1000 to 1800, all other days, 1300 to 1800
Access for disabled people: Parking provided, ramped entry, toilet facilities

General description:
An historic landscaped garden dating from the early 19th century showing influences from its adaptation in the latter half of the century. Two important periods in garden design.
Information services:
Guided tours and party visits at discounted rates any time by appointment, tel 01767 626203
Special visitor services: Guided tours..
Collections:
Unusual and well-restored buildings and features
Restored ironwork features. Hump-backed bridges, arbours
Unusual and rare plants. Trees and shrubs in particular
Minton Peacock in adjoining site, originally in garden.

Internet home pages:
http://www.shuttleworth.org

2832
SYGUN COPPER MINE
Beddgelert, Gwynedd, LL55 4NE

Tel: 01766 510100
Fax: 01766 510102
Email: sygunmine@aol.com
Formed: 1983

Organisation type and purpose: Independently owned, museum, suitable for ages: 5+, consultancy.

Enquiries to: Managing Director
Access:
Access to staff: By email, Internet web pages
Access to building, collections or gallery: No prior appointment required
Hours: Mon to Fri, 1000 to 1700
Access for disabled people: Parking provided, toilet facilities

General description:
Features audiovisual underground tours of 18th and 19th century copper mines, illustrating the life and conditions of the miners. Also features the methods of ore extraction, and geology.
Information services:
Helpline available, tel no: 01766 510101.
Special visitor services: Guided tours..
Collections:
Flotation plant and old mine workings, in the heart of Snowdonia, 15th-19th century

Internet home pages:
http://www.syguncoppermine.co.uk

2833
SYON HOUSE
Syon Park, London Road, Brentford, Middlesex, TW8 8JF

Tel: 020 8560 0883
Fax: 020 8568 0936
Email: info@syonpark.co.uk

Organisation type and purpose: Historic building, house or site, suitable for ages: 16+.

Enquiries to: Administrator
Access:
Access to staff: By letter, by telephone, by email
Access for disabled people: Parking provided, toilet facilities
Other restrictions: Restricted access to house.

General description:
History of the house, gardens and parkland.

continued overleaf

Information services:
Special visitor services: Guided tours, tape recorded guides..
Collections:
Furniture
Pictures by Lely and Van Dyck
Interiors by Robert Adam
Printed publications:
Guide Book (for purchase, direct, £4 plus p&p)

Internet home pages:
http://www.syonpark.co.uk

2834
TABERNACLE CULTURAL CENTRE, THE

Penrallt Street, Machynlleth, Powys, SY20 8AJ

Tel: 01654 703355
Fax: 01654 702160
Email: momawales@tabernac.dircon.co.uk
Formed: 1986
Formerly: Museum of Modern Art, Wales (MOMA Wales), date of change, 1991

Organisation type and purpose: Registered charity, art gallery, suitable for ages: 5+.

Enquiries to: Administrator
Access:
Access to staff: By letter, by telephone, by fax, by email, Internet web pages
Access to building, collections or gallery: No prior appointment required
Hours: Mon to Sat, 1000 to 1600
Access for disabled people: ramped entry, access to all public areas, toilet facilities
Other restrictions: Lift to auditorium and first floor galleries.

General description:
Art in Wales since 1900.
Information services:
Services for disabled people: For the hearing impaired; displays and/or information at wheelchair height.
Collections:
Pictures by artists living or working in Wales since 1900
Pictures by The Brotherhood of Ruralists
Catalogues:
Catalogue for all of the collections is on-line.

Internet home pages:
http://www.tabernac.dircon.co.uk
History of the centre, exhibitions, festival, friends.

2835
TABLEY HOUSE COLLECTION

Tabley House, Tabley Lane, Chester Road, Tabley, Knutsford, Cheshire, WA16 0HB

Tel: 01565 750151
Fax: 01565 653230
Email: inquiries@tableyhouse.co.uk
Formed: 1990

Organisation type and purpose: Registered charity (charity number 1047299), museum, art gallery, historic building, house or site, university department or institute, suitable for ages: all ages.
Parent body:
The Victoria University of Manchester
Oxford Road, Manchester, M13 9PL

Enquiries to: Administrator
Access:
Access to staff: By letter, by telephone, by fax, by email, visitors by prior appointment
Hours: Apr to end Oct, Thu to Sun and Bank Holidays, 1400 to 1700
Other restrictions: Other times and group bookings by appointment.
Access to building, collections or gallery: No prior appointment required
Access for disabled people: Parking provided, ramped entry, toilet facilities
Other restrictions: Please telephone the Administrator prior to visit.

General description:
History of art and social (Leicester family, Lord de Tabley) history. A fine Regency picture collection assembled by Sir John F. Leicester, Bt. (1st Lord de Tabley) with the aim of establishing a National Gallery of British Art.
Information services:
Helpline available, tel no: 01565 750151.
Library available for reference at John Rylands Library, Manchester, by special appointment only.
Guided tours if pre-booked.
Free child quiz.
Special visitor services: Guided tours, materials and/or activities for children.
Services for disabled people: For the visually impaired; for the hearing impaired; displays and/or information at wheelchair height.
Collections:
Finest Palladian mansion in the North West designed by John Carr, completed 1769
First collection of English paintings ever made
Furniture by Chippendale, Bullock and Gillow of Lancaster
Memorabilia from 17th to 20th century
Paintings by J M W Turner, Henry Thompson, James Ward, Dobson, Lely, Reynolds, Cotes, Northcote, Callcott, Fuseli, Lawrence and Martin
Library of the antiquarian collector Sir Peter Leicester, Bt
Series of Regency embroidered waistcoats made for Sir John F Leicester, Bt

Internet home pages:
http://www.tableyhouse.co.uk

2836
TAIN THROUGH TIME

Tower Street, Tain, Ross-shire, IV19 1DY

Tel: 01862 894089
Fax: 01862 894089
Email: info@tainmuseum.demon.co.uk
Formed: 1966
Formerly: Tain and District Museum, The Pilgrimage, St Duthus Collegiate Church, date of change, 1995

Organisation type and purpose: Registered charity (charity number SCO 13145), museum.

Enquiries to: Curator
Direct email: eq@tainmuseum.demon.co.uk
Access:
Access to staff: By letter, by telephone, by email, visitors by prior appointment
Hours: Mid Mar to Oct: Mon to Sun, 1000 to 1800
Other restrictions: Otherwise by arrangement.

General description:
A general collection covering the history and social history of Tain and Ester Ross from the 17th century onwards. There is a substantial photographic archive. Includes the Clan Ross centre with family papers and genealogical records.
Collections:
Archaeology, church, domestic life, Burgh life, Clan Ross, militaria, photographs, archives, reference library
Tain silver, traditional local craft, 18th-20th century, 30 items
Catalogues:
Catalogue for all of the collections is only available in-house.
Publications list:
is available in hard copy.
Printed publications:
A Ballance of Silver - The history of the silversmiths of Tain (1997, £3.50)
Tain Tolbooth (1998, £2.75)
The Pictish stones of Easter Ross (1999, £2.75)
The Collegiate Kirk of St Duthac and The Abbey of Fearn (2000, £4)

Internet home pages:
http://www.cali.co.uk/highexp/ttt

2837
TALES OF THE OLD GAOL HOUSE

Saturday Market Place, King's Lynn, Norfolk, PE30 5DQ

Tel: 01553 774297
Fax: 01553 772361
Email: gaolhouse@west-norfolk.gov.uk
Formed: 1993

Organisation type and purpose: Local government body, museum, historic building, house or site, suitable for ages: 8+.
Visitor attraction.
Parent body:
Borough Council of Kings Lynn and West Norfolk (BCKL and WN)

Enquiries to: Heritage Officer
Direct email: tim.hall@west-norfolk.gov.uk
Access:
Access to staff: By letter, by telephone, by fax, by email, visitors by prior appointment
Access for disabled people: level entry, toilet facilities
Other restrictions: Access to most areas.

General description:
The town's old police station, the collection deals with crime and punishment in King's Lynn, see the18th and 19th century cells in which smugglers and highwaymen were inprisoned; see also a King John Cup and Sword; Town Charters; civic and church plate; and the 'Red Register'.
Collections:
King John Cup. Mediaeval gilt/enamel cup
Catalogues:
Catalogue for part of the collections is only available in-house.

Internet home pages:
http://www.gaolhouses.com

2838
TALIESIN ARTS CENTRE

See - Oriel Ceri Richards Gallery

2839
TALYLLYN RAILWAY

Wharf Station, Tywyn, Gwynedd, LL36 9EY

Tel: 01654 710472
Fax: 01654 711755
Formed: 1865

Organisation type and purpose: Voluntary organisation, museum.
Preservation Society.

Enquiries to: Traffic Manager
Other contacts: Managing Director
Access:
Access to staff: By letter, by telephone, by fax, in person
Hours: Mon to Fri, 0900 to 1700

General description:
Narrow gauge railways; Welsh slate industry history; narrow gauge railway modelling; maintenance of narrow gauge railways, steam and diesel. The Talyllyn runs from Tywyn Wharf to Nant Gwernol and was opened in 1865. The Narrow Gauge Railway Museum is at Tywyn.
Collections:
Archives in conjunction with Gwynedd County Council
6 steam locomotives
A large collection of items from British and Irish narrow gauge lines.
Printed publications:
Timetable, guide, handbook, group travel organisers' guide
Microform products:
16mm film (for hire)
Electronic and video products:
Videos (for purchase)

Internet home pages:
http://www.tallyn.co.uk
Timetables, special events, routes, locomotives.

2840
TAMWORTH CASTLE

The Holloway, Ladybank, Tamworth, Staffordshire, B79 7NA

Tel: 01827 709629
Fax: 01827 709630
Email: heritage@tamworth.gov.uk
Acronym or abbreviation: TAMCM
Full name: Tamworth Castle Museum
Formed: 1899

Organisation type and purpose: Local government body, museum, historic building, house or site, suitable for ages: 5+.
Education and tourism.
Parent body:
Tamworth Borough Council
Marmion House, Lichfield Street, Tamworth, Staffordshire, B79 7BZ, tel: 01827 709709, fax: 01827 709229
Friends Support Society:
Friends of Tamworth Castle and Museum
Member of:
North Staffordshire Museums Association

Enquiries to: Heritage Services Manager
Direct tel: 01827 709633
Direct email: frank-caldwell@tamworth.gov.uk
Other contacts: Museum Manager for events' programme, retail (including publications).
Access:
Access to staff: By letter, by telephone, by email, in person
Other restrictions: Prior appointment necessary for access to Museum collections in storage and the archives.
Access to building, collections or gallery: No prior appointment required
Hours: Tue to Sun, 1200 to 1730; last admission 1630
Other restrictions: Check opening times Autumn/Winter.
Under 5s admitted free.

General description:
Tamworth Castle is a typical Norman motte and bailey castle set in the south-west corner of what was a Saxon burgh. It was first held by the Marmion family, then the de Freville's and the Ferrers, and the Earls of Northampton. Parts are believed to date from the 1180s. The rooms on three floors and the dungeon display the history and aspects of the several owner's lives.
Social history collections displayed in period room settings from Tudor to Victorian eras.
Furniture on loan from the Victoria and Albert Museum, London. Introductory Norman Exhibition. The 'Tamworth Society' exhibition traces the town's history from Roman times to the present day. Great Hall displays arms and armour. Haunted bedroom has replica furniture.
Information services:
Library available for reference (for conditions see Access above). Helpline available, tel no: 01827 709626.
Taped reminiscences in The Tamworth Story exhibition.
Reminiscence boxes for loan.
Replica clothes for young visitors to try on.
2 free quizzes for children plus 'Find Frightened Freda' trail.
Special visitor services: Materials and/or activities for children.
Education services: Group education facilities, resources for Key Stages 1 and 2, 3 and Further or Higher Education.
Services for disabled people: For the visually impaired.
Collections:
Fine and decorative arts, rural and urban social history, archaelogy, militaria, archives and photographs
Period furniture on loan from the Victoria and Albert Museum
Sir Robert Peel (d. 1850) and descendants. Personal items and artefacts from his home, Drayton Manor, including Peel crested tablewares, 19th century
Tamworth coins, silver pennies, 10th-12th century
Catalogues:
Catalogue for part of the collections is only available in-house.
Printed publications:
Tamworth Castle Guidebook (direct, £1.20 plus p&p)
Children's Activity Guide (direct, £2.20 plus p&p)
Borough by Prescription - A History of the Municipality of Tamworth (direct, £5.99 plus p&p)
An Anglo-Saxon Watermill at Tamworth (direct, £28 plus p&p)

Internet home pages:
http://www.tamworth.gov.uk
Tamworth Castle brochure details.
http://www.tamworthcastle.co.uk
Friends of Tamworth Castle and Museum site.
http://www.aboutbritain.com

2841
TANGMERE MILITARY AVIATION MUSEUM

Tangmere, Chichester, West Sussex, PO20 6ES

Tel: 01243 775223 or 789490
Fax: 01243 789490
Email: admin@tangmere-museum.org.uk
Formed: 1982

Organisation type and purpose: Registered charity (charity number 299327), museum, suitable for ages: 8+.

Enquiries to: Marketing Manager
Direct tel: 01243 789490
Direct fax: 01243 789490
Other contacts: Curator for exhibits, artefacts.
Access:
Access to staff: By letter, by telephone, by fax, by email, visitors by prior appointment
Hours: Mon to Fri, 1000 to 1730
Other restrictions: Closed Dec and Jan.
Access to building, collections or gallery: No prior appointment required
Hours: Mar to Oct: daily, 1000 to 1730
Feb and Nov: daily, 1000 to 1630
Access for disabled people: Parking provided, ramped entry, access to all public areas, toilet facilities

General description:
Military aviation, aircraft, Battle of Britain, Royal Flying Corps, Women's Auxiliary Air Force, World War II.
Information services:
Library available for reference (for conditions see Access above). Helpline available, tel no: 01243 775223.
Special visitor services: Guided tours, materials and/or activities for children.
Education services: Group education facilities, resources for Key Stages 3, 4 and Further or Higher Education.
Services for disabled people: Displays and/or information at wheelchair height.
Collections:
Library of RAF related history
Memorabilia
Catalogues:
Catalogue for library is in-house only. Catalogue for all of the collections is only available in-house.
Publications list:
is available in hard copy.
Printed publications:
Guide Book (purchase)
Leaflet (free)
Electronic and video products:
Video of Museum (available from museum shop)

Internet home pages:
http://www.tangmere-museum.org.uk
Origins of museum, description of departments and associated artefacts.

2842
TANK MUSEUM

Bovington, Wareham, Dorset, BH20 6JG

Tel: 01929 405096
Fax: 01929 405360
Email: admin@tankmuseum.co.uk
Full name: Tank Museum and Regimental Museum of the Royal Armoured Corps and Royal Tank Regiment
Formed: 1923

Organisation type and purpose: Registered charity (charity number 274640), museum, suitable for ages: 5+.
Military museum with archive and library.
Member of:
Area Museum Federation of the South West
Association of Independent Museums
Dorset Chamber of Commerce
Museum Association
Under the auspices of the:
Ministry of Defence

Enquiries to: Curator
Direct tel: 01929 405070
Direct email: curator@tankmuseum.co.uk
Other contacts: (1) Librarian, (2) Registrar for (1) archive and library enquiries; (2) collection enquiries.
Access:
Access to staff: By letter, by telephone, by fax, by email, in person, visitors by prior appointment, Internet web pages
Access for disabled people: Parking provided, ramped entry, level entry, access to all public areas, toilet facilities

General description:
Armoured fighting vehicles of the UK and 16 other countries; history and technology; armoured warfare since 1915, tank warfare, history and practice, regimental history, military vehicle technology, weapons technology, twentieth century warfare.
Information services:
Library available for reference (for conditions see Access above)
Guided tours for education, advance booking required.
Acoustiguide available for listening.
Hearing Loop available.
Special visitor services: Guided tours, tape recorded guides.
Education services: Group education facilities.
Services for disabled people: For the hearing impaired.
Collections:
Comprehensive archive and reference library with a fine collection of photographs and films
Minutes of Royal Commission on awards to inventors, reference invention of the tank
Papers of Generals G M Lindsay, J F C Fuller; Colonel R E B Crompton
Records of the British Tank Board, British Tank Mission to Washington
Scale drawings and stowage diagrams
War diaries: Tank Corps, World War I and Royal Armoured Corps, World War II
Designated museum containing the world's finest international collection of armoured fighting vehicles, displays of medals, uniforms, weapons
Catalogues:
Catalogue for library is in-house only. Catalogue for all of the collections is only available in-house.
Printed publications:
Museum Guide (available for purchase)

Address for ordering publications:
Printed publications:
Shop Manager, Tank Museum
Tel: 01929 405141, fax: 01929 405360, email: shop@tankmuseum.co.uk

continued overleaf

Internet home pages:
http://www.tiger-tank.com
Information on the Tank Museum's Tiger Tank.
http://www.tank_museum.org.uk
General museum information, virtual tour.
http://www.tankmuseum.co.uk
General museum information, virtual tour.

2843
TANKERNESS HOUSE MUSEUM
See - Orkney Museum

2844
TAR TUNNEL
Ironbridge Gorge Museum Trust, Coach Road, Coalbrookdale, Telford, Shropshire, TF8 7DQ

Organisation type and purpose: Registered charity (charity number 503717-R), museum, historic building, house or site, suitable for ages: 5+.
Parent body:
Ironbridge Gorge Museum Trust
Tel: 01952 433522
Access:
Access to staff: By letter

General description:
Walk underground in the Tar Tunnel, where an amazing source of bitumen was discovered two hundred years ago.

Internet home pages:
http://www.ironbridge.org.uk

2845
TARBAT DISCOVERY CENTRE
Tarbatness Road, Portmahomack, Tain, Ross-shire, IV20 1YA

Tel: 01862 871351
Fax: 01862 871361
Email: info@tarbat-discovery.co.uk
Formerly: Tarbat Historic Trust

Organisation type and purpose: Independently owned, registered charity (charity number SCO 024422), museum, suitable for ages: 5+.
Archaeological excavation.

Enquiries to: Manager
Access:
Access to staff: By letter, by telephone, by fax, by email, in person
Access for disabled people: Parking provided, access to all public areas, toilet facilities
Other restrictions: No disabled access to crypt.

General description:
Housed in a restored 18th century Grade A listed church, the centre displays the history of the area from a wealthy 8th century Pictish community, through an early medieval trading settlement, to more recent times, and the changes brought about by modern industry.
Collections:
Pictish carvings
Viking silver hoard

Internet home pages:
http://www.tarbat-discovery.co.uk

2846
TATE BRITAIN
Millbank, London, SW1P 4RG

Tel: 020 7887 8000
Fax: 020 7887 8007
Email: information@tate.org.uk
Formed: 1897
Formerly: Tate Gallery

Organisation type and purpose: National government body, art gallery.
Other addresses:
Tate Liverpool
Albert Dock, Liverpool, L3 4BB, tel: 0151 709 3223
Tate Modern
Bankside, Southwark, London, SE1 9TG, tel: 020 7887 8000
Tate St Ives and Barbara Hepworth Museum
Porthmear Beach, St Ives, Cornwall, TR26 1JY, tel: 01736 796226

Enquiries to: Information Officer
Direct tel: 020 7887 8734
Direct fax: 020 7887 8725
Access:
Access to staff: By letter, by telephone, by fax, by email, in person, Internet web pages
Hours: Mon to Fri, 1000 to 1750
Access to building, collections or gallery: Prior appointment required
Hours: Gallery hours: Mon to Sun, 1000 to 1750; closed Dec, 24, 25, 26
Other restrictions: Access to archive and library by appointment only.
Prints and Drawings Room by appointment only.
Access for disabled people: Parking provided, ramped entry, access to all public areas, toilet facilities

General description:
British painting from the 16th century to the present day, modern art (painting, sculpture, prints etc) from about 1900 to the present day and the works of art in the Gallery's collections.
Collections:
The National Collections of British Art from the Tudors to the present day. Displays from the permanent collection rotate to explore the wealth and variety of the Tate's collection
Archive relating to 20th century art and artists
British Collection (16th century to *c.* 1900)
Library of books on art and catalogues of art exhibitions
International Modern Collection (*c.* 1900 to present day)
Drawing Collection
Print Collection
Turner Collection in the Clore Gallery
Publications list:
is available in hard copy and online.
Printed publications:
Medieval Sculpture (Deacon R, & Lindley P, 2001)
Surrealism: Desire Unbound (2001)
Catalogue of colour prints (available for sale)
Exhibitions and Events (leaflets)
Friends of the Tate Gallery (leaflet)
Tate Plan
Tate Britain: The Handbook (Humphreys R, 2001)
Tate Britain: The Guide (Myrone M, 2001)
The Tate Gallery: an illustrated companion (annually)
Electronic and video products:
A selection of videos (Art documentaries) available from the shop

Address for ordering publications:
Printed publications:
Tate Publications Ltd
at the same address, tel: 020 7887 8869, fax: 020 7887 8878, email: tgpl@tate.org.uk

Internet home pages:
http://www.tate.org.uk
Separate sections for each gallery, lists of displays, room lists, events, catalogue of complete collection, with over 8000 images (being added to).

2847
TATE IN EAST ANGLIA FOUNDATION
The Shirehall, Market Street, Norwich, Norfolk, NR1 3JQ

Tel: 01603 493668
Acronym or abbreviation: EAAF
Still known as: Tate in East Anglia

Organisation type and purpose: Registered charity.
To bring art to East Anglia.

Enquiries to: Director
Access:
Access to staff: By letter, by telephone

General description:
A display of works from the Tate Collection.

Internet home pages:
http://www.tate.org.uk

2848
TATE LIVERPOOL
Albert Dock, Liverpool, L3 4BB

Tel: 0151 702 7400
Minicom no. 0151 702 7400 (please use announcement button)
Fax: 0151 702 7401
Email: liverpoolinfo@tate.org.uk
Formed: 1988
Formerly: Tate Gallery Liverpool, date of change, 1999

Organisation type and purpose: National organisation, art gallery.
Parent body:
Tate Britain
Millbank, London, SW1P 4RG, tel: 020 7887 8000, fax: 020 7887 8007
Affiliated to:
Tate St Ives
Porthmeor Beach, St Ives, Cornwall, TR26 1TG, tel: 01736 796226, fax: 01736 794480

Enquiries to: Press and Marketing Officer
Direct tel: 0151 702 7444
Direct email: catherine.oreilly@tate.org.uk
Access:
Access to staff: By letter, by telephone, by fax, by email, Internet web pages
Hours: Tue to Sun, 1000 to 1750; closed Mon, except Bank Holidays
Other restrictions: Closed Good Friday, 25, 26 Dec, 31 Dec, 1 Jan.
Access to building, collections or gallery: No access other than to staff
Hours: Tue to Sun, 1000 to 1750; closed Mon, except Bank Holidays
Access for disabled people: level entry, access to all public areas, toilet facilities
Other restrictions: Wheelchairs avaliable on request.

General description:
Modern and contemporary international art; displays from the Tate Collection; regularly changing temporary exhibitions.
Information services:
Library available for reference (for conditions see Access above). Helpline available, tel no: 0151 702 7402.
Each exhibition has an 'Information Room' with books and other literature relating to the exhibition. Members of the public may use this facility during the Gallery opening hours only. Books may not be borrowed.
Courses run in association with the University of Liverpool.
Introductory talks with British Signed Language interpretation.
Information rooms on each floor, accompanying each display or exhibition.
Information Assistants in the galleries are happy to answer questions about particular exhibits or the Gallery.
Special visitor services: Guided tours, tape recorded guides.
Services for disabled people: For the visually impaired; for the hearing impaired.
Collections:
The national collection of modern art in the north of England.
Publications list:
is available in hard copy.
Printed publications:
Over 140 books, and other printed material related to modern and contemporary art
Exhibition catalogues
Information leaflets

Address for ordering publications:
Printed publications:
Tate Publishing
Millbank, London, SW1P 4RG, tel: 020 7887 8869, email: tgpl@tate.org.uk

Internet home pages:
http://www.tate.org.uk
Catalogue of the Tate Collection; information on exhibitions at all the Tate Galleries.
http://www.tate.org.uk/liverpool/
Information on Tate Liverpool
http://www.tate.org.uk/collections/
Information on the Tate Collection

2849
TATE ST IVES

Porthmeor Beach, St Ives, Cornwall, TR26 1TG

Tel: 01736 796226
Fax: 01736 794480
Formed: 1993
Formerly: Tate Gallery St Ives and Barbara Hepworth Museum

Organisation type and purpose: National organisation, art gallery, suitable for ages: all ages.

Enquiries to: Information Officer
Other contacts: (1) Curator; (2) Administrator; (3) Manager for (1) art matters; (2) general; (3) building matters.
Access:
Access to staff: By letter, by telephone, by fax, by email
Access to building, collections or gallery: No prior appointment required
Hours: Nov to Feb: Tue to Sun, 1000 to 1630
Mar to Oct: Daily, 1000 to 1730
Access for disabled people: Parking provided, ramped entry, level entry, access to all public areas, toilet facilities

General description:
Tate St Ives presents changing displays of work from the Tate Collection, focussing on the post-war modern movement associated with the town. Represented artists include Barbara Hepworth, Ben Nicholson, Navu Gabo, Roger Hilton, Peter Lanyon, John Wells, Patrick Heron, Terry Frost, Wilhelmina Barns-Graham. There are also major exhibitions of work by national and international contemporary artists. Tate St Ives manages the Barbara Hepworth Museum and Sculpture Garden.
Information services:
Special visitor services: Guided tours, materials and/or activities for children.
Education services: Group education facilities.
Services for disabled people: For the visually impaired; displays and/or information at wheelchair height.
Collections:
Paintings, sculpture, ceramics, installation, photography, digital

Internet home pages:
http://www.tate.org.uk
Information on all Tate sites.

2850
TATTERSHALL CASTLE

Tattershall, Lincoln, LN4 4LR

Tel: 01526 342543
Email: tattershallcastle@nationaltrust.org.uk
Formed: 1914

Organisation type and purpose: National organisation, registered charity (charity number 205846), museum, historic building, house or site, suitable for ages: all ages.
Parent body:
The National Trust (East Midlands Region)
East Midlands Regional Office, tel: 07909 486411

Enquiries to: Manager
Access:
Access to staff: By letter only
Hours: Sat to Wed, 0900 to 1700
Access to building, collections or gallery: No prior appointment required
Hours: Mar, Sat and Sun, 1200 to 1600;
Apr to Sep, Sat to Wed, 1100 to 1730;
Oct, Sat to Wed, 1100 to 1600;
Nov to mid Dec, Sat and Sun, 1200 to 1600
Access for disabled people: Parking provided, ramped entry, toilet facilities
Other restrictions: No access other than to ground floor. Audiovisual/video. Steep ramped access to ground floor, requires strong companion. Level entrance to shop.

General description:
A vast fortified and moated red-brick tower, built in medieval times for Ralph Cromwell, Lord Treasurer of England. The building was restored by Lord Curzon (1911-14) and contains four great chambers with enormous Gothic fireplaces, tapestries and brick vaulting. There are spectacular views from the battlements and a guardhouse with museum room.
Information services:
Walk around Tattershall village leaflet available from shop
Brass-rubbing sessions on selected days.
Braille guide
Suitable for school groups. Education room/centre.
Audio guide. Live interpretation. Hands-on activities. Children's guide. Children's quiz/trail
Special visitor services: Tape recorded guides, materials and/or activities for children.
Education services: Group education facilities, resources for Key Stages 1 and 2.
Services for disabled people: For the visually impaired; displays and/or information at wheelchair height.
Publications list:
is available in hard copy.

Internet home pages:
http://www.nationaltrust.org.uk

2851
TATTON PARK

Knutsford, Cheshire, WA16 6QN

Tel: 01625 534400
Fax: 01625 534403
Email: tatton@cheshire.gov.uk
Formed: 1960

Organisation type and purpose: Local government body, national organisation, registered charity (charity number 205846), museum, historic building, house or site, suitable for ages: 5+.
Tatton Park is owned by the National Trust but is managed, maintained and licensed by Cheshire County Council.
Parent body:
The National Trust (North West)
North West Regional Office, tel: 0870 609 5391
Administered and maintained by:
Cheshire County Council

Enquiries to: General Manager
Access:
Access to staff: By letter, by fax, by email, Internet web pages
Access to building, collections or gallery: Prior appointment required
Hours: House: Apr to Sep: Tue to Sun, 1200 to 1600
Tudor Old Hall: Apr to Sep: Sat and Sun, 1200 to 1600
Farm: Apr to Sep: Tue to Sun, 1200 to 1700
Other restrictions: Open Bank Holidays; last entry 1 hour before closing.
House: special opening Oct half-term and Christmas events in Dec. Guided tours Tue to Sun 1200 and 1215 by timed ticket
Tudor Old Hall: Guided tours only Tue to Fri 1500 and 1600 and hourly Sat and Sun.
Access for disabled people: Parking provided, ramped entry, toilet facilities
Other restrictions: Designated parking. Limited spaces. Drop-off point. 3 manual wheelchairs available. 4 single-seater powered mobility vehicles. Ground floor largely accessible, house and Tudor Old Hall. No access to other floors. Photograph album. Level entrance to shop and to restaurant. Grounds largely accessible. Recommended route map.

General description:
This is one of the most complete historic estates open to visitors. The early 19th century Wyatt house sits amid a landscaped deer park and is opulently decorated, providing a fine setting for the Egerton family's collections of pictures, books, china, glass, silver and specially commissioned Gillow furniture. The theme of Victorian grandeur extends into the garden, with fernery, orangery, rose garden, pinetum and Italian and Japanese gardens. There are also the Tudor Old Hall, a working farm, a children's play area and many walks, including 'Wartime Tatton'. The trail around the lake offers the chance to see many varieties of waterfowl.
Information services:
Helpline available, tel no: Infoline: 01625 534435.
Guided tours of house and Tudor Old Hall.
Braille guide. Large-print guide. Sign language interpreters and lip-speakers by arrangement.
Suitable for school groups. Education room/centre. Children's quiz/trail. Living history.
Special visitor services: Guided tours, materials and/or activities for children.
Education services: Group education facilities, resources for Further or Higher Education.
Services for disabled people: For the visually impaired; for the hearing impaired.
Collections:
Over 200 paintings on display including works by Canaletto, Van Dyck, Guercino and Chordin
Over 12,000 books in library and other rooms
Egerton of Tatton - Cheshire Record Office, Chester
Egerton of Tatton Muniments - John Rylands University Library of Manchester
A collection of furniture manufactured by Gillows of Lancaster; of particular importance are the pieces dated to 1811/1812
Wyatt drawings, architectural drawings and plans for the Tatton estate by Samuel, Lewis and Jeffry Wyatt, 1780-1825, c. 180 items
Catalogues:
Catalogue for library is published.
Printed publications:
Guide Book (£3.50)
Picture List (£1)
Garden Guide (£2.50)
Library Catalogue (£25)

Internet home pages:
http://www.tattonpark.org.uk

2852
TECHNIQUEST

Stuart Street, Inner Harbour, Cardiff, CF10 5BW

Tel: 02920 475475
Fax: 02920 482517
Email: paulo@techniquest.org
Acronym or abbreviation: TQ
Formed: 1986

Organisation type and purpose: Registered charity (charity number 517722), suitable for ages: 5+.
Science Discovery centre.

Enquiries to: Marketing Assistant
Access:
Access to staff: By letter, by telephone, by fax, by email
Hours: Mon to Fri, 0900 to 1700; Sat, Sun, 1030 to 1700
Access to building, collections or gallery: No prior appointment required
Hours: Mon to Fri, 0930 to 1630; Sat, Sun, 1030 to 1700
Access for disabled people: Parking provided, level entry, access to all public areas, toilet facilities
Other restrictions: Lift.

continued overleaf

General description:
Techniquest is one of the UK's fastest growing science centres. Facilities include 160 hands-on exhibits; a science theatre; discovery room; planetarium; multi-purpose laboratory; science information centre; and a science shop. Subjects; science, physics, chemistry, biology, geology, astronomy, maths, music.
Information services:
Education services: Group education facilities, resources for Key Stages 1 and 2, 3, 4 and Further or Higher Education.
Services for disabled people: For the hearing impaired; displays and/or information at wheelchair height.

Internet home pages:
http://www.techniquest.org
Details of exhibits, science theatre and planetarium shows.

2853
TEDDY BEAR HOUSE
See - Dorset Teddy Bear House

2854
TEDDY BEAR MUSEUM, THE
19 Greenhill Street, Stratford-upon-Avon, Warwickshire, CV37 6LF

Tel: 01789 293160
Email: info@theteddybearmuseum.com
Formed: 1988

Organisation type and purpose: Independently owned, museum, suitable for ages: 5+ and small children if accompanied.

Enquiries to: Manager
Access:
Access to staff: By letter, by telephone

General description:
Hundreds of teddy bears displayed in a 16th century building once owned by Henry VIII. Chronologically displayed in room settings with rarest bears including the earliest Steiff Bears, in the Hall of Fame.
Information services:
Quiz for children.
Special visitor services: Materials and/or activities for children.
Education services: Resources for Key Stage 1..
Collections:
Rare and unusual teddy bears, mainly German, British and American, including some of the earliest teddy bears from the beginning of the 20th century
Teddy bear literature and memorabilia
Pauline Grattan Bequest of late 20th century limited edition Hermann Bears
Brandreth Collection of early German and American Bears
Printed publications:
The Little History of the Teddy Bear (Brown M, 2000, publ Sutton Publishing, £9.99)
The Teddy Bear Hall of Fame (Brown M, 1996, publ Headline, £9.99)
Museum Brochure (£1.50)

Internet home pages:
http://www.theteddybearmuseum.com
General information on the location and the collection.

2855
TEDDY MELROSE
The Wynd, Melrose, Roxburghshire, TD6 9PA

Tel: 01896 823854

Organisation type and purpose: Museum, suitable for ages: 5+.

Enquiries to: Curator
Access:
Access to staff: By letter, by telephone
Access to building, collections or gallery: No prior appointment required
Hours: Summer months 1000 to 1700, Sun 1200 to 1700;
Off-season weekends only
Access for disabled people: access to all public areas, toilet facilities

General description:
Scotland's Teddy Bear Museum with bears from the early 19th century to the present day.

2856
TEIGNMOUTH AND SHALDON MUSEUM
29 French Street, Teignmouth, Devon, TQ14 8ST

Tel: 01626 777041
Email: teign24@freeserve.co.uk
Formed: 1978
Formerly: Teignmouth Museum

Organisation type and purpose: Independently owned, learned society, registered charity (charity number 275290), museum, suitable for ages: all ages.

Enquiries to: Curator
Access:
Access to building, collections or gallery: Prior appointment required
Hours: Daily, 1000 to 1630
Other restrictions: And by appointment.

General description:
Teignmouth and Shaldon Museum contains primarily local collections. There is a collection of artefacts from a 400 year old wreck including a minion and a swivel gun, also displays of Haldon aerodrome and the atmospheric railway.
Information services:
Library available for reference (for conditions see Access above)
Guided tours for the blind.
Special visitor services: Materials and/or activities for children.
Education services: Group education facilities, resources for Key Stages 1 and 2.
Services for disabled people: For the visually impaired.
Collections:
Documentation dealing with aspects of Teignmouth and Shaldon including the bridge between the 2 towns
Church Rocks Wreck, Spanish Armada 1580, 100 items
Admiral Pellew
Elias Parash Alvars
Donal Crowhurst
Atmospheric Railway
Morgan Giles Boatyard
Printed publications:
Monographs of:
Elias Parash Alvars
The Railway in Teignmouth
Potted History of Teignmouth
Admiral Pellew
Haldon Aerodrome
Donald Crowhurst
Electronic and video products:
Over 100 oral history tapes for research purposes are kept in the Museum

Internet home pages:
http://website.lineone.net/~teignmuseum/index.htm

2857
TELFORD STEAM RAILWAY
The Old Locoshed, Horsehay, Telford, Shropshire

Tel: 07765 858348
Full name: Telford Horsehay Steam Trust Limited
Formed: 1976

Organisation type and purpose: Membership association (membership is by subscription), present number of members: 170, voluntary organisation, registered charity (charity number 1003150), museum, suitable for ages: 18+.
Preserved Railway.

Enquiries to: Marketing Director
Other contacts: Sales Director for bookings/Sales.
Access:
Access to staff: By letter, by telephone, in person
Hours: Railway Open Easter to end September Sun, 1100 to 1600; Bank Holidays, 1100 to 1700
Other restrictions: Note, all staff are volunteers with full-time jobs.
All messages will be returned.

General description:
Restoration of old railway articles including locomotives, carriages, track and buildings.
Catalogues:
Catalogue for part of the collections is published and part is on-line.
Printed publications:
Stock Book and History of TSR

Address for ordering publications:
Printed publications:
The Secretary, Telford Steam Railway

Internet home pages:
http://www.thad.demon.co.uk/tsr

2858
TEMPLE MANOR
Strood, Rochester, Kent

Tel: 01634 827980

Organisation type and purpose: Historic building, house or site.
Parent body:
English Heritage (South East Region)
Eastgate Court, 195-205 High Street, Guildford, Surrey, GU1 3EH, tel: 01483 252000, fax: 01483 252001, email: www.english-heritage.org.uk
Managed by:
Medway City Council

Enquiries to: Curator
Access:
Access to building, collections or gallery: No prior appointment required
Hours: Apr to Sep: Sat, Sun and Bank Holidays, 1000 to 1800
Oct: Sat, Sun and Bank Holidays, 1000 to 1600

General description:
13th century manor house, home of the Knights Templar.

Internet home pages:
http://www.english-heritage.org.uk

2859
TEMPLE NEWSAM ESTATE
Home Farm, Leeds, West Yorkshire, LS15 0AD

Tel: 0113 264 5535
Minicom no. 0113 232 8738
Fax: 0113 232 6485
Formed: 1979
Formerly: Home Farm Rare Breeds Centre

Organisation type and purpose: Local government body, museum, historic building, house or site, suitable for ages: 5+.
Open farm specialising in rare breeds.
Working farm and agricultural museum.
Member of:
Rare Breeds Survival Trust (RBST)

Enquiries to: Visitor Reception
Other contacts: Farm Manager for livestock sales, specialised livestock information.
Access:
Access to staff: By letter, by telephone, by fax, in person
Hours: Daily, 0900 to 1700
Access for disabled people: Parking provided, level entry, toilet facilities

General description:
Collections of local agricultural artefacts mainly early to mid 20th century. Collection of Yorkshire carts and wagons. Very large working farm using rare and traditional breeds of British farm animals. All based in buildings dating from 1693 onwards.

Information services:
Special visitor services: Materials and/or activities for children.
Education services: Group education facilities, resources for Key Stages 1 and 2.
Services for disabled people: For the visually impaired; for the hearing impaired.
Collections:
Ferguson TE20 Petrol Tractor and implements, late 1940s- early 1950s
Hand and petrol lawnmowers made by Thomas Green of Leeds early 20th century
Horse-drawn vehicles, pertaining to Yorkshire and the adjoining area
Horse brasses (on loan)
Seeddrills, pertaining to Yorkshire and adjoining area
Sawbenches, pertaining to Yorkshire
Rare horse-drawn hedgecutters
Catalogues:
Catalogue for all of the collections is only available in-house.
Trade and statistical:
Livestock breeding information. Herd books.
Printed publications:
Schools Packs
I Spy Checklist Challenge leaflet
Farm Trail leaflet
Quizzes and fact sheets on animals and the farm

Internet home pages:
http://www.leeds.gov.uk

2860
TEMPLE NEWSAM HOUSE
Leeds, West Yorkshire, LS15 0AE

Tel: 0113 264 7321
Fax: 0113 260 2285
Formed: 1923

Organisation type and purpose: Art gallery.
Links with:
Leeds Museums and Galleries
Town Hall, Leeds, LS1 3AD

Enquiries to: Curator
Access:
Access to staff: By letter
Access to building, collections or gallery: No prior appointment required
Hours: Mon to Fri, 1000 to 1700
Other restrictions: Closed until Summer 2003 for major repairs.

General description:
A large Tudor-Jacobean mansion with fine interiors, 16th-20th Centuries, used as a museum of fine and decorative arts; contains Old Master and British paintings, pre-1840; furniture; ceramics; silver; wallpapers; and works of art.
Collections:
Chippendale Society collection: documented furniture by Thomas Chippendale, 1760-1779, 12 items
Halifax collection: Old Master and British paintings, 1600- 1840, 200 items
Leeds Creamware, 1780-1820, 1,500 items
Oxley collection: continental metalwork and works of art, 1600-1920, 100 items
Ramsden collection. Peruvian furniture, 1800-1850, 30 items
Catalogues:
Catalogue for all of the collections is published.
Publications list:
is available in hard copy.
Printed publications:
Temple Newsam House Guide Book
Temple Newsam Inventory 1808
Leeds Museum and Galleries Review
An extensive range of titles on various subjects including:
Ceramics
Furniture
Silver
Paintings
History
Architecture
Fashion
Leeds Creamware and Other English Pottery (booklet)

Internet home pages:
http://www.leeds.gov.uk
Guide book, family history.

2861
TENBURY AND DISTRICT MUSEUM
Goff's School, Cross Street, Tenbury Wells, Worcestershire, WR15 8EF

Tel: 01299 832143
Formed: 1977

Organisation type and purpose: Independently owned, registered charity, museum, suitable for ages: all ages.

Enquiries to: Chairman
Access:
Access to staff: By letter, by telephone
Access for disabled people: level entry, access to all public areas

General description:
A folk museum containing artefacts from Tenbury's history. Includes copies of 'Tenbury Advertiser', 1871-1992; an ex spa fountain and bath; farming tools and apparatus; a Hopcrib and tools.
Collections:
Henry Hill Hickman, family mementos (the discovery of anaesthesia)
Late 19th century Newspapers
Tenbury Advertiser, 1871-1992, some dates missing
Catalogues:
Catalogue for part of the collections is only available in-house.

2862
TENBY MUSEUM AND ART GALLERY
Castle Hill, Tenby, Pembrokeshire, SA70 7BP

Tel: 01834 842809
Fax: 01834 842809
Email: tenbymuseum@hotmail.com
Formed: 1878

Organisation type and purpose: Registered charity (charity number 529673), museum, art gallery, suitable for ages: 5+, research organisation, publishing house.

Enquiries to: Curator
Access:
Access to staff: By letter, by telephone, by fax, by email, visitors by prior appointment, Internet web pages
Hours: Research days: Tue to Fri, 1000 to 1230 and 1400 to 1630
Access to building, collections or gallery: No prior appointment required
Hours: Easter to end Oct: daily, 1000 to 1700
Nov to Easter: Mon to Fri, 1000 to 1700
Access for disabled people: Parking provided, ramped entry, level entry, access to all public areas, toilet facilities
Other restrictions: Lifts/disabled lifts.

General description:
The museum is situated in part of the medieval castle. It contains local collections (Tenby and South Pembrokeshire): archaeology, geology, natural history, maritime history, social history. Two art galleries exhibiting works by local artists such as Gwen John and Augustus John.
Information services:
Library available for reference (for conditions see Access above). Helpline available, tel no: 01834 842809 (answerphone).
Temporary exhibitions each year on specific topics.
Special visitor services: Guided tours, materials and/or activities for children.
Education services: Group education facilities, resources for Key Stages 1 and 2, 3, 4 and Further or Higher Education.
Services for disabled people: For the hearing impaired; displays and/or information at wheelchair height.
Catalogues:
Catalogue for library is in-house only. Catalogue for all of the collections is only available in-house.
Printed publications:
Local history booklets and factsheets

Internet home pages:
http://www.tenbymuseum.free-online.co.uk

2863
TENEMENT HOUSE
145 Buccleuch Street, Garnethill, Glasgow, G3 6QN

Tel: 0141 333 0183
Email: tenementhouse@nts.org.uk

Organisation type and purpose: Museum, historic building, house or site.
Parent body:
National Trust for Scotland (West Region)

Enquiries to: Property Manager
Access:
Access to staff: By letter, by telephone, by email
Access to building, collections or gallery: No prior appointment required
Hours: Mar to Oct, daily, 1400 to 1700
Weekday morning visits available for pre-booked educational and other groups

General description:
A typical lower middle class Glasgow tenement flat of the turn of the century, with its original furniture, furnishings, personal possessions and fittings. The ground floor contains an exhibition on tenement living and the history of tenements in Glasgow.
Information services:
Audio tour, guidebook in French, German, Italian, explanatory text in French, German, Braille guidebook.
Special visitor services: Guided tours, tape recorded guides, materials and/or activities for children.
Education services: Group education facilities.
Services for disabled people: For the visually impaired.

Internet home pages:
http://www.nts.org.uk

2864
TENTERDEN MUSEUM
Station Road, Tenterden, Kent, TN30 6HN

Tel: 01580 764310
Formed: 1976

Organisation type and purpose: Registered charity (charity number 271353), museum, suitable for ages: all ages.

Enquiries to: Administrator
Direct fax: 01580 766648
Other contacts: President for genealogy.
Access:
Access to staff: By letter, by telephone, by fax, in person, charges made to all users
Access to building, collections or gallery: No prior appointment required
Hours: Apr to Jun, Oct: daily, 1330 to 1630
Jul to Sep: daily, 1100 to 1630
Access for disabled people: ramped entry

General description:
A local museum containing 1000 years of local history. Features the Cinque Ports; a Victorian market town; hop-growing; local agriculture; Wealden architecture; and the light railways of Col. Stephens; genealogy.

continued overleaf

Information services:
Special visitor services: Guided tours.
Education services: Group education facilities, resources for Key Stages 1 and 2..
Collections:
Cinque Ports - Medieval Shipbuilding
Catalogues:
Catalogue for library is in-house only. Catalogue for all of the collections is only available in-house.

2865
TETBURY POLICE MUSEUM
Old Court House, 63 Long Street, Tetbury, Gloucestershire, GL8 8AA

Tel: 01666 504670
Fax: 01666 504670
Email: tetburypolicmuseum@btinternet.com
Formed: 1983

Organisation type and purpose: Local government body, museum.

Enquiries to: Curator
Other contacts: Town Administrator as Curator is not on site at all times.
Access:
Access to staff: By letter, by telephone, by fax
Hours: Mon to Fri, 1000 to 1500

General description:
Specialist museum based on history of Gloucestershire Constabulary, housed in building containing the former magistrates' court, police office and cells. Gloucestershire is the second oldest police force in the country.
Information services:
Other opening hours, tours etc by special arrangement.
Special visitor services: Guided tours..
Collections:
A wide range of photographs
Clocks, lamps, batons, handcuffs, uniforms, signs, gas masks and helmets
Catalogues:
Catalogue for all of the collections is only available in-house.
Publications list:
is available in hard copy.

2866
TEWKESBURY BOROUGH MUSEUM
64 Barton Street, Tewkesbury, Gloucestershire, GL20 5PX

Tel: 01684 292901
Fax: 01684 292277
Email: museum@tewkgl20.fsnet.co.uk
Formed: 1962

Organisation type and purpose: Local government body, registered charity (charity number 203157), museum, suitable for ages: 5+.

Enquiries to: Curator
Access:
Access to staff: By letter, by telephone, by email, visitors by prior appointment, Internet web pages
Hours: Mon to Sat, 100 to 1700
Access to building, collections or gallery: No prior appointment required
Hours: Mon to Sat, 100 to 1700

General description:
Local history of Tewkesbury and the surrounding borough.
Information services:
Special visitor services: Materials and/or activities for children.
Education services: Group education facilities, resources for Key Stages 2 and 3..
Collections:
Battle of Tewkesbury 1471; diorama and written history
Walker fairground collection.

Internet home pages:
http://www.tewkesburybc.gov.uk

2867
THACKRAY MEDICAL MUSEUM
Beckett Street, Leeds, West Yorkshire, LS9 7LN

Tel: 0113 244 4343
Minicom no. 0113 245 7082
Fax: 0113 247 0219
Email: info@thackraymuseum
Formed: 1997
Formerly: Medical Museum, date of change, 1997

Organisation type and purpose: Independently owned, registered charity (charity number 1016169), museum, suitable for ages: 7+.

Enquiries to: Chief Executive
Other contacts: Librarian for research enquiries.
Access:
Access to staff: By letter, by telephone, by fax, by email, visitors by prior appointment, Internet web pages
Hours: Tue to Sun, 1000 to 1700; Mon, pre-booked groups only
Other restrictions: Library and collection weekdays only.
Access to building, collections or gallery: Prior appointment required
Hours: Tue to Sun, 1000 to 1700; Mon, pre-booked groups only
Access for disabled people: Parking provided, level entry, access to all public areas, toilet facilities

General description:
History of medicine and health care; surgical instruments and medical equipment; history of the international medical supply trades.
Information services:
Library available for reference (for conditions see Access above)
Special visitor services: Guided tours, tape recorded guides, materials and/or activities for children.
Education services: Group education facilities, resources for Key Stages 1 and 2, 3, 4 and Further or Higher Education.
Services for disabled people: For the visually impaired; for the hearing impaired; displays and/or information at wheelchair height.
Collections:
J F Wilkinson collection of 17th and 18th century pharmaceutical ceramics
Surgical Textbooks
Wide-ranging collection of literature and catalogues relating to medical supply trades
Surgical instruments and equipment
Catalogues:
Catalogue for library is in-house only. Catalogue for all of the collections is only available in-house.
Publications list:
is available in hard copy.
Printed publications:
Handlist of Medical Supply Trade Catalogues to 1970 (Humphries A, Medical Museum Publishing, 2000)
Obstetric Forceps: Its History & Evolution (Das K, Medical Museum Publishing, 1993)
Opposite the Infirmary, A History of the Thackray Company 1902 to 1990 (Wainwright P, Medical Museum Publishing, 1997)
Various schools resource packs on the history of medicine and related topics
Microform products:
Grooss KS (ed), Medical Instrument Catalogues: A microfiche collection of sales catalogues of medical instrument makers who have been advertising in printed matter since the 18th century (Inter Documentation Company bv, Leiden, 1994)

Internet home pages:
http://www.thackraymedical.org
http://www.thackraymedicalmuseum.org
http://www.thackraymuseum.org

2868
THAMES BARRIER INFORMATION AND LEARNING CENTRE
1 Unity Way, Woolwich, London, SE18 5NJ

Tel: 020 8305 4188
Fax: 020 8855 2146
Formed: 1984
Formerly: National Rivers Authority (NRA), date of change, 1996

Organisation type and purpose: Historic building, house or site, suitable for ages: 5+.
Head Office:
Environment Agency
Kings Meadow House, Kings Meadow, Reading, RG1 8DQ, tel: 0845 933 3111

Enquiries to: Manager
Direct tel: 020 8305 4161
Direct email: jane.finch@environment-agency.gov.uk
Other contacts: Technical Tour Officer, tel 020 8305 4134 (Mon to Fri) for bookings for technical tours of Barrier.
Access:
Access to staff: By letter, by telephone, by fax, by email
Hours: Mon to Fri, 0900 to 1630; Sat, Sun, 1000 to 1630
Access to building, collections or gallery: No prior appointment required
Hours: 1 Apr to 29 Sep: daily, 1030 to 1630,30 Sep to 31 Mar: daily, 1100 to 1530
Access for disabled people: Parking provided, level entry, toilet facilities
Other restrictions: Lift.

General description:
Information Centre has a working model of the Barrier, an eight minute video on the construction of the Barrier. Information on Barrier, flooding and wildlife plus CD-ROMs on London's River Thames.
Information services:
Special visitor services: Materials and/or activities for children.
Education services: Group education facilities, resources for Key Stages 2 and 3..
Printed publications:
Selection of Environmental Agency Publications (free)
Some publications are available direct
Electronic and video products:
CD-ROM and Video (for purchase, direct)

Address for ordering publications:
Printed publications:
Customer Services, The Environment Agency Head Office

2869
THAMES POLICE MUSEUM
98 Wapping High Street, London, E1V 9NE

Tel: 020 7275 4421
Fax: 020 7275 4490
Email: bob.jeffries@met.police.uk

Organisation type and purpose: Museum, historic building, house or site.

Enquiries to: Curator
Access:
Access to staff: By letter, by telephone, by email, visitors by prior appointment
Hours: By appointment
Access to building, collections or gallery: Prior appointment required

General description:
Marine and Thames Police history.
Collections:
Letters, books, etc. written by founders
Uniforms and items of equipment in use since 1798.

2870
THEATRE COLLECTION
See - Bristol University, Theatre Collection

2871
THEATRE MUSEUM

Russell Street, Covent Garden, London, WC2E 7PR

Tel: 020 7943 4700
Fax: 020 7943 4777
Email: tmenquiries@vam.ac.uk
Full name: National Museum of the Performing Arts
Formed: 1974

Organisation type and purpose: National government body, museum.
Parent body:
Victoria and Albert Museum
UK headquarters of:
SIBMAS
Theatre Information Group
Postal address:
Theatre Museum
1e Tavistock Street, London, WC2E 7PA, tel: 020 7943 4700, fax: 020 7943 4777, email/website: tmenquiries@vam.ac.uk

Enquiries to: Librarian
Access:
Access to staff: By letter, by fax, by email, visitors by prior appointment
Hours: Tue to Sun, 1030 to 1800
Other restrictions: Please telephone for appointments.

General description:
Performing arts, including theatre, opera, dance and popular entertainment.
Information services:
Education services: Group education facilities, resources for Key Stages 3 and 4..
Collections:
270 Special Collections including:
Anthony Crickmay Photograph Collection (dance)
Arnold Rood Collection of Edward Gordon Craig material
British Theatre Association/British Drama League Library
British Puppet and Model Theatre Guild Collection
Cambridge Arts Theatre Archive
C B Cochran Collection of Newscuttings Albums
Claire H de Robilant Collection (dance in South America)
Costume Collection (including many Ballets Russes costumes)
Cyril Beaumont Collection of dance material
Dame Bridget D'Oyly Carte Collection (Gilbert and Sullivan)
English Shakespeare Company Archive
Gabrielle Enthoven Theatre Collection
Gordon Anthony Photograph Collection (dance)
Guy Little Theatrical Photograph Collection
H M Tennent Archive
Harry R Beard Collection (18th and 19th century theatre)
Hippisley Coxe Circus Collection
Houston Rogers Photographic Collection
Hugh (Binkie) Beaumont Photographic Albums
London Archives of the Dance
National Video Archive of Stage Performance
Royal Court Theatre/English Stage Company Archive
Scene and Costume Design Collection
Stone and Hinkins Toy Theatre Collections
Unity Theatre Archive

Internet home pages:
http://theatremuseum.vam.ac.uk
Theatre Museum website.

2872
THEATRE ROYAL

Westgate Street, Bury St Edmunds, Suffolk, IP33 1QR

Tel: 01284 769505(Box Office)
Fax: 01284 706035
Email: admin@theatreroyal.org

Organisation type and purpose: National organisation, registered charity (charity number 205846), historic building, house or site.
Parent body:
The National Trust (East of England)
East Anglia Regional Office, tel: 0870 609 5388

Enquiries to: Manager
Access:
Access to staff: By letter, by telephone, by fax, by email
Access for disabled people: ramped entry, toilet facilities
Other restrictions: Drop-off point. Ground floor largely accessible. No access to other floors.

General description:
A rare and outstanding example of a late-Georgian playhouse, built in 1819 and still in use, presenting a year-round programme of professional drama, comedy, dance, mime, pantomime and amateur works. It boasts a national reputation, and attracts the best touring companies in the country.

Internet home pages:
http://www.nationaltrust.org.uk

2873
THELNETHAM WINDMILL

Thelnetham, Suffolk

Tel: 01473 727853

Organisation type and purpose: Historic building, house or site.
Access:
Access to staff: By telephone

General description:
19th century tower mill, occasionally milling by windpower.

2874
THINKTANK - BIRMINGHAM MUSEUM OF SCIENCE AND DISCOVERY

Millennium Point, Curzon Street, Birmingham, B4 7XG

Tel: 0121 202 2222
Fax: 0121 202 2280
Email: findout@thinktank.ac.uk
Acronym or abbreviation: Thinktank
Formed: 2001
Formerly: Birmingham Museum of Science and Discovery; Discovery Centre Museum of Science and Industry, date of change, 2001

Organisation type and purpose: Registered charity (charity number 1061898), museum, suitable for ages: 5+.

Enquiries to: Marketing Manager
Direct tel: 0121 202 2263
Direct fax: 0121 202 2290
Direct email: joseph.hocking@thinktank.ac.uk
Access:
Access to staff: By letter, by telephone, by fax, by email, in person, Internet web pages
Access to building, collections or gallery: No prior appointment required
Hours: Mon to Thu, 1000 to 1700; Sat, Sun, 1000 to 1700
Other restrictions: Closed Fri except during Birmingham School Holidays.
Access for disabled people: Parking provided, level entry, access to all public areas, toilet facilities

General description:
Birmingham industry and products from pen nibs to James Watt's Smethwick Beam Engine. It features world class historic transport and steam engine collections, including the City of Birmingham Loco, the history of steam power, early industrial machines, and the Railton Land-Speed Record car. There are galleries with displays of human biology, medicine, food and health care, natural history, forensic science, crimes and historic mysteries. The museum is divided into 10 themed galleries on four floors:
Power Up - steam power
Making Things - manufacture
Move It - transport
City Stories - history of Birmingham
The Street - science in everyday life
Kids in the City - under 7s science
Wild Life - conservation and nature
Medicine Matters - Wellcome Trust Gallery.
Thinktank is interactive, informative, and above all, lots of fun with over 200 hands-on games and activities, characters form the past, and real examples of cutting edge innovations - it's a family day out with something for everyone.
Information services:
Education services: Group education facilities, resources for Key Stages 1 and 2, 3, 4 and Further or Higher Education.
Services for disabled people: Displays and/or information at wheelchair height.
Collections:
Charles Thomas collection of writing equipment
City of Birmingham Locomotive
Industrial, scientific and transport collections
Liddel collection of mechanical musical instruments
Railton Mobil Special
Smethwick Beam Engine
Catalogues:
Catalogue for part of the collections is only available in-house.
Printed publications:
Thinktank

Internet home pages:
http://www.thinktank.ac.uk
Full visitor website.

2875
THIRLESTANE CASTLE

Thirlestane Castle Trust, Lauder, Borders, TD2 6RU

Tel: 01578 722430
Fax: 01578 722761
Email: thirlestane@great-houses-scotland.co.uk

Organisation type and purpose: Independently owned, historic building, house or site, suitable for ages: 8+.

Enquiries to: Manager
Access:
Access to staff: By letter, by telephone
Access to building, collections or gallery: No prior appointment required
Hours: Easter from Good Fri for one week; May to Oct, Sun to Fri, 1100 to 1630

General description:
16th century castle, seat of the Earls of Lauderdale with displays of Border country life, pictures, fine art and furniture.

Internet home pages:
http://www.great-houses-scotland.co.uk/thirlestane

2876
THIRSK & DISTRICT MUSEUM SOCIETY

14/16 Kirkgate, Thirsk, North Yorkshire, YO7 1PQ

Tel: 01845 527707
Email: thirskmuseum@supanet.com
Acronym or abbreviation: Thirsk Museum
Formed: 1977

Organisation type and purpose: (membership is by subscription), present number of members: 95, museum.

Enquiries to: Curator
Direct tel: 01845 524510
Access:
Access to staff: By letter, by telephone, by email
Hours: Volunteer staff, availability not guaranteed
Access to building, collections or gallery: No prior appointment required
Hours: Easter to end Oct: Mon, Tue, Wed, Fri, Sat, 1000 to 1600

continued overleaf

Other restrictions: Closed to the public Nov to Easter.
Access for disabled people: ramped entry

General description:
Local history; family history; local topography; photographic archive; cricketing memorabilia; advice on local archives.
Information services:
Special visitor services: Guided tours, materials and/or activities for children..
Collections:
Cricketing memorabilia in the birthplace of Thomas Lord
Veterinary instruments and equipment from 'James Herriot's surgery'.
Catalogues:
Catalogue for all of the collections is available in-house and part is on-line.

Internet home pages:
http://www.thirskmuseum.org
General introduction to museum and collection.
Some archive photographs - selection changed periodically.

2877
THOMAS CARLYLE'S BIRTHPLACE
The Arched House, Ecclefechan, Lockerbie, Dumfries & Galloway, DG11 3DG

Tel: 01576 300666
Formed: 1881

Organisation type and purpose: National organisation, historic building, house or site, suitable for ages: 5+.
Parent body:
National Trust for Scotland
28 Charlotte Square, Edinburgh, tel: 0131 243 9300, fax: 0131 243 9301

Enquiries to: Curator
Access:
Access to staff: By telephone, charges to non-members
Access for disabled people: Parking provided
Other restrictions: Not very suitable for disabled - steps and stairs.

General description:
The Arched House, in which Thomas Carlyle was born on 4 December 1795, was built by his father and uncle (who were both master masons) in 1791. Carlyle was a great writer and historian and one of the most powerful influences on 19th century British thought. The interior of the house is furnished to reflect domestic life at Carlyle's time, and also on show is a notable collection of portraits and his belongings. House opened since 1881 and was handed over to the NTS in 1936 by the Trustees of Carlyle's House Memorial Fund.
Information services:
Special visitor services: Guided tours..
Publications list:
is available in hard copy.
Printed publications:
Brochure (50p)

Internet home pages:
http://www.nts.org.uk

2878
THOMAS NEWCOMEN ENGINE
The Engine House, Mayors Avenue, Dartmouth, Devon, TQ6 9YY

Tel: 01803 834224
Fax: 01803 835631
Email: enquire@dartmouth-information.fsnet.co.uk
Formed: 1993

Organisation type and purpose: Museum, suitable for ages: 12+.
Access:
Access to staff: By letter, by telephone, by fax, by email, in person
Hours: Apr to Oct: Mon to Sat, 0900 to 1700; Sun, 1000 to 1600
Nov to Mar: Mon to Sat, 0900 to 1600
Access to building, collections or gallery: No prior appointment required
Hours: Apr to Oct: Mon to Sat, 0900 to 1700; Sun, 1000 to 1600
Nov to Mar: Mon to Sat, 0900 to 1600
Access for disabled people: level entry, access to all public areas

General description:
The Engine House features the Newcomen Atmospheric Engine, a preserved working steam atmospheric engine which was re-erected here in Thomas Newcomen's home town in 1963 to mark the 300th anniversary of his birth.

2879
THORBURN MUSEUM & GALLERY
See - John Southern Gallery

2880
THORINGTON HALL
Stoke by Nayland, Colchester, Essex, CO6 4SS

Tel: 0870 5388 (Regional Office)

Organisation type and purpose: National organisation, registered charity (charity number 205846), historic building, house or site, suitable for ages: 8+.
Parent body:
The National Trust (East of England Region)
East Anglia Regional Office, tel: 0870 609 5388

Enquiries to: Property Tenant
Access:
Access to staff: By letter only

General description:
An oak-framed, plastered and gabled house, built c.1600 and later extended.

Internet home pages:
http://www.nationaltrust.org.uk

2881
THORNEY HERITAGE MUSEUM
The Tankyard, Station Road, Thorney, Peterborough, Cambridgeshire, PE6 0QE

Tel: 01733 270908
Email: Dot.Thorney@tesco.net
Formed: 1987
Formerly: Thorney Heritage Centre, date of change, 1995

Organisation type and purpose: Registered charity (charity number 298235), museum, suitable for ages: 16+.
Some models for younger people to look at.
Run by:
The Thorney Society

Enquiries to: Secretary
Access:
Access to staff: By letter, by email, in person
Access for disabled people: Parking provided, ramped entry, access to all public areas
Other restrictions: Toilet facilities by arrangement with adjoining building.

General description:
Contains material relating to the history of this parish from the earliest times to the present day, especially from the mid-19th century onwards. Largely a photographic record of the parish interpreted through maps and models. Subjects covered relate specifically to this area, explaining its origin through the formation and drainage of the Fens; the Huguenots; and the Bedford Estate.
Information services:
Guided tours by prior arrangement.
Special visitor services: Guided tours..
Collections:
Transcriptions of family history records for the village
Some 3000 photographs of the people, buildings, events and agriculture, mainly 20th century
Printed publications:
Thorney Abbey: A Brief History (Husband D)
Victorian Thorney (Teulon A)

Internet home pages:
http://www.thorney-museum.org.uk
Introduction to the museum and village.

2882
THORPENESS WINDMILL
Thorpeness, Suffolk

Tel: 01394 384948

Organisation type and purpose: Historic building, house or site.
Access:
Access to staff: By telephone

General description:
19th century working post mill and visitor centre.

2883
THREAVE
Castle Douglas, Dumfries & Galloway, DG7 1RX

Tel: 01556 502575
Fax: 01556 502683
Email: threave@nts.org.uk

Organisation type and purpose: Historic building, house or site.
Parent body:
National Trust for Scotland (NTS)
Wemyss House, 28 Charlotte Square, Edinburgh, EH2 4ET
Under guardianship of:
Historic Scotland

Enquiries to: Property Manager
Other contacts: for Castle, tel: 07711 223101
Access:
Access to staff: By letter, by telephone, by fax, by email, in person, charges to non-members
Access to building, collections or gallery: No prior appointment required
Hours: Estate and garden, all year, daily, 0930 to sunset;
Walled garden and glasshouses, all year, daily, 0930 to 1700;
House, Mar to Oct, Wed, Thu, Fri, Sun, 1100 to 1600
Castle, beg Apr to end Sep, daily, 0930 to 1830
Other restrictions: Guided tours only to house, maximum ten people, two per hour, admission by timed ticket
Access for disabled people: Parking provided, toilet facilities
Other restrictions: Access to most of garden, Visitor Centre, restaurant and shop. Wheelchairs and battery car available

General description:
Victorian house and garden. Nearby Threave Castle, a 14th century Douglas stronghold, stands on Threave Island in the River Dee, and is owned by the Trust under the guardianship of Historic Scotland.
Information services:
Induction loop in Visitor Centre; explanatory text in French, German, Italian and Spanish.
Special visitor services: Guided tours.
Services for disabled people: For the hearing impaired.

Internet home pages:
http://www.nts.org.uk

2884
THREE RIVERS MUSEUM OF LOCAL HISTORY (THREE RIVERS MUSEUM TRUST)
Basing House, Rickmansworth, Hertfordshire, WD3 1HP

Formed: 1988

Organisation type and purpose: Museum, historic building, house or site, suitable for ages: 5+.

Enquiries to: Honorary Secretary
Direct tel: 01923 775882
Direct email: ann@elgar.org

Access:
Access to staff: By letter, by telephone, by email
Access to building, collections or gallery: No prior appointment required
Hours: Mon to Fri, 1400 to 1600; Sat, 1000 to 1600
Other restrictions: Closed Sun and Bank Holidays.

General description:
A collection of artefacts dating from prehistoric times; documents and photographs relating to the Three Rivers area.
Collections:
Artefacts from prehistoric times to the 20th century
Historical documents, pictures, prints and photographs
Chronology of Rickmansworth
Catalogues:
Catalogue for part of the collections is only available in-house.
Printed publications:
A Pocket History of Rickmansworth
Scotsbridge Mill: A Brief History
Down Memory Lane
The Rickmansworth Society & Ricky Week
Rickmansworth's Lion and Eagle
Yesterday-Today (journal)
Postcards of local scenes

See also - Basing House Historic Ruin

2885
THRELKELD QUARRY & MINING MUSEUM
Threlkeld, Keswick, Cumbria, CA12 4TT

Tel: 017687 79747

Organisation type and purpose: Independently owned, museum, historic building, house or site, suitable for ages: 5+, research organisation, publishing house.

Enquiries to: Managing Director
Access:
Access to staff: By letter, by telephone, in person
Access for disabled people: Parking provided, level entry

General description:
The interpretation of the mining and quarrying heritage of the Lake District.
Information services:
Special visitor services: Guided tours.
Education services: Group education facilities.
Services for disabled people: Displays and/or information at wheelchair height.
Collections:
Important collection of vintage excavators looked after by the Vintage Excavator Trust, now 27 in number and growing
Two working demonstration weekends a year in May and September
Working narrow gauge quarry railway
Large collection of mining artefacts, maps, photographs, geology section and minerals
Publications list:
is available in hard copy.

Address for ordering publications:
Printed publications:
Blue Rock Publications
Threlkeld Quarry and Mining Museum

2886
THURNE DYKE DRAINAGE MILL
O.S. TG 401 159, Thurne, Norfolk

Organisation type and purpose: Historic building, house or site.

General description:
Tower drainage mill.

2887
THURROCK MUSEUM
Thameside Complex, Orsett Road, Grays, Essex, RM17 5DX

Tel: 01375 382555
Fax: 01375 392666
Email: jcatton@thurrock.gov.uk
Formed: 1956
Formerly: Thurrock Local History Museum, date of change, 1991

Organisation type and purpose: Local government body, museum, suitable for ages: 8+.
Parent body:
Thurrock Borough Council
Civic Offices, New Road, Grays, Essex
Member of:
Museums Association
Museums in Essex
South Eastern Museums Service
South Midlands Museums Federation

Enquiries to: Heritage & Museums Officer
Access:
Access to staff: By letter, by telephone, by fax, by email, in person, visitors by prior appointment
Hours: Mon to Fri, 0900 to 1700
Access for disabled people: ramped entry, access to all public areas, toilet facilities

General description:
Local archaeology and history of Thurrock, Lower Thames and riverside parishes.
Information services:
Education services: Group education facilities, resources for Key Stages 2, 3, 4 and Further or Higher Education..
Collections:
Archaeological excavation archive material (some on microfiche)
Diaries of Col E A Loftus
Maps
Parish and subject files
Photographic collection
Small quantity of historic manuscripts
Borough Archives (non-public records)
Publications list:
is available in hard copy.
Printed publications:
Boldly from the Marshes (a history of Little Thurrock)
The Downstream Dock (history of Tilbury, 1986)
Panorama: journal of the Thurrock Local History Society (annually)
Thurrock at War (WWI)
Thurrock Goes to War (WWII)
Thurrocks Past: Echoes from a Place (anthology of quotes about Thurrock)
Electronic and video products:
The Story of Belhus (a local country house) (VHS video)
Thurrock's Military History (VHS video)

Address for ordering publications:
Electronic publications:
Thameside Theatre Box Office
Thameside Complex, Orsett Road, Grays, Essex, RM17 5DX

Internet home pages:
http://www.thurrock.gov.uk/museum

2888
THURSFORD COLLECTION
Thursford, Fakenham, Norfolk, NR21 0AS

Tel: 01328 878477
Fax: 01328 878415
Email: geraldine@thursfordcollection.co.uk
Formed: 1976

Organisation type and purpose: Registered charity, museum, suitable for ages: 5+.

Enquiries to: Manager
Access:
Access to staff: By letter only
Access to building, collections or gallery: No prior appointment required
Hours: Easter to mid Oct: daily, 1200 to 1700
Access for disabled people: Parking provided, level entry, access to all public areas, toilet facilities

General description:
Nine mechanical organs, Wurlitzer Organ, Savages Venetian Gondola Switchback Ride, Junior Gallopers Ride, fairground engines, traction engines, ploughing engines, barn engines.
Information services:
All mechanical organs and Wurlitzer Organ are played each opening day.
Special visitor services: Guided tours, materials and/or activities for children.
Services for disabled people: For the visually impaired; for the hearing impaired.

2889
THWAITE MILLS WATERMILL, THE
Thwaite Lane, Stourton, Leeds, West Yorkshire, LS10 1RP

Tel: 0113 249 6453
Fax: 0113 277 6737
Email: armleymills.indmuseum@virgin.net
Formed: 1990
Formerly: Leeds City Council, Leeds Leisure Services, Leeds Museums and Galleries

Organisation type and purpose: Local government body, museum, historic building, house or site, suitable for ages: 8+.

Enquiries to: Curator
Direct tel: 0113 263 7861
Direct fax: 0113 263 7861
Access:
Access to staff: By letter, by telephone, by fax, in person, visitors by prior appointment
Hours: Tue to Sat, 1000 to 1700; Sun, 1300 to 1700
Access for disabled people: Parking provided
Other restrictions: Lift to house and all mill houses, some uneven surfaces.

General description:
Working historic water powered stone-crushing mill; educational facilities; technology of water power.
Information services:
Special visitor services: Guided tours.
Education services: Group education facilities, resources for Key Stages 1 and 2..

2890
TICKENHILL MANOR
See - Hartlebury Castle

2891
TILBURY FORT
Fort Road, Tilbury, Essex, RM18 7NR

Tel: 01375 858489

Organisation type and purpose: Museum, historic building, house or site, suitable for ages: all ages.
Parent body:
English Heritage (East of England Region)
Brooklands, 24 Brooklands Avenue, Cambridge, CB2 2BU, tel: 01223 582700, fax: 01223 582701
Access:
Access to staff: By letter, by telephone
Access to building, collections or gallery: No prior appointment required
Hours: Mar to Sep: daily, 1000 to 1800
Oct: daily, 1000 to 1700
Nov to Mar: Wed to Sun, 1000 to 1300 and 1400 to 1600
Other restrictions: Closed 24 to 26 Dec and 1 Jan
Opening times are subject to change, for up-to-date information contact English Heritage by phone or visit the website.

General description:
The history of the fort from Tudor times to the second World War, exhibition of memorabilia from the two world wars. Tilbury Fort is the

continued overleaf

finest example of 17th century military engineering in England. It is largely unaltered even after the latest reconstructions carried out in the 1860s. Designed by Charles II's chief engineer, it was built as a low-lying and largely earthen construction, designed to withstand bombardment at a time when artillery was the dominant weapon. Today, exhibitions, the powder magazine and bunker-like 'casemates' demonstrate how the fort protected the City. You can even fire an anti-aircraft gun.
Information services:
School's base.
Special visitor services: Tape recorded guides, materials and/or activities for children.
Education services: Group education facilities..

Internet home pages:
http://www.english-heritage.org.uk

2892
TIMESPAN HERITAGE CENTRE & ART GALLERY

Dunrobin Street, Helmsdale, Sutherland, KW8 6JX

Tel: 01431 821327
Fax: 01431 821058
Email: admin@timespan.org.uk
Formed: 1987

Organisation type and purpose: Independently owned, registered charity (charity number SCO 09796), museum, art gallery, suitable for ages: all ages.
Management Committee:
Helmsdale Heritage Society

Enquiries to: Manager
Access:
Access to staff: By letter, by telephone, by fax, by email, in person, visitors by prior appointment
Access to building, collections or gallery: No prior appointment required
Hours: Apr to Oct: Mon to Sat, 0930 to 1700; Sun, 1400 to 1700
Nov to Mar: by prior appointment
Other restrictions: Prior appointment is required for access to objects not on display.
Access for disabled people: Parking provided, level entry, access to all public areas, toilet facilities

General description:
History of Helmsdale and area - natural and social including geology, Kildonan Gold Rush, fishing, folk history, Highland Clearances. Museum is a mixture of artefacts and dramatic settings. Also shows an audiovisual film. Local knowledge and limited genealogy.
Gallery hosts temporary exhibitions by professional artists and craftspeople.
Accompanied by programme of events and children's workshops.
Collections:
Geology specimens, Kildonan Gold Rush artefacts, fishing artefacts, recreated blacksmith's forge, byre, croft house and village shop
Scenes of shooting party, last wolf, last witch-burning, murder in Helmsdale Castle, Vikings, Highland Clearances, Loth Kirk
Local photographs and temporary displays in Helmsdale Room
Herb Garden containing over 100 traditional herbs and plants
Printed publications:
Some Helmsdale Memories (Campbell J D R, paperback, £5.99 plus p&p)

Internet home pages:
http://www.timespan.org.uk

2893
TIMOTHY HACKWORTH VICTORIAN AND RAILWAY MUSEUM

Soho Cottages, Hackworth Close, Shildon, Co Durham, DL4 1PQ

Tel: 01388 777999
Fax: 01388 777999
Formed: 1975

Organisation type and purpose: Local government body, museum, suitable for ages: 5+.
Parent body:
Sedgefield Borough Council

Enquiries to: Manager
Access:
Access to staff: By letter
Access for disabled people: Parking provided

General description:
Items and artefacts relating to early railways with particular emphasis on the pioneering importance of Timothy Hackworth and his role in the development of reliable steam power.
Steam trains from Darlington along the route of the original Stockton & Darlington Railway first opened 27 September 1825. The track now links the Museum to the North Road Railway Museum in Darlington.
Information services:
Some displays/information at wheelchair height.
Special visitor services: Guided tours, materials and/or activities for children.
Education services: Group education facilities, resources for Key Stages 1 and 2.
Services for disabled people: Displays and/or information at wheelchair height.
Collections:
c. 1840 Hackworth Locomotive Braddyll
c. 1830 Beam Engine - possibly by Hackworth
c. 1865 Stockton & Darlington Railway Passenger Coach
Manuscripts and artefacts relating to Hackworth
Hand tools etc from 19th century
Operating 1939 built steam locomotive (built Pockosts of Bristol)
Many and various other times from early railway period including furniture and household items laid out in 'Period Rooms'.
Catalogues:
Catalogue for all of the collections is only available in-house.
Printed publications:
Timothy Hackworth and the Locomotive (book, Young R, 1923, reprinted 2000, £17)
Timothy Hackworth 1786-1850 (booklet, Milburn G, B, 2000, £2.95)
Electronic and video products:
Virtual Reality CD-ROM on Opening of Stockton & Darlington Railway (April, 2002, poa)

Internet home pages:
http://www.hackworthmuseum.co.uk
General museum information.

2894
TINTAGEL CASTLE

Tintagel, Cornwall

Tel: 01840 770328

Organisation type and purpose: National government body, historic building, house or site.
Parent body:
English Heritage (South West Region)
Tel: 0117 975 0700, fax: 0117 975 0701

Enquiries to: Manager
Access:
Access to staff: By letter, by telephone
Access to building, collections or gallery: No prior appointment required
Hours: 24 Mar to 13 Jul: daily, 1000 to 1800,14 Jul to 27 Aug: daily, 1000 to 1900 (later on Wed event evenings)
28 Aug to 30 Sep: daily, 1000 to 1800,1 to 31 Oct: daily, 1000 to 1700,1 Nov to 31 Mar: daily, 1000 to 1600
Other restrictions: Closed 24-26 Dec and 1 Jan 2003
Opening times are subject to change, for up-to-date information contact English Heritage by phone or visit the website.

General description:
With its spectacular location on one of England's most dramatic coastlines, Tintagel is one of the most awe-inspiring and romantic spots in Britain. It is also where the legend of King Arthur was born. The magical remains of the 13th century castle are breathtaking, where Atlantic breakers crash against the cliffs and through Merlin's Cave. Recent excavations indicate links with the 'Dark Age' rulers of Cornwall and have fuelled speculation about the Arthurian legends.

Internet home pages:
http://www.english-heritage.org.uk

2895
TINTAGEL OLD POST OFFICE

Fore Street, Tintagel, Cornwall, PL34 0DB

Tel: 01840 770024
Email: tintageloldpo@nationaltrust.org.uk

Organisation type and purpose: Registered charity (charity number 205846), museum, historic building, house or site, suitable for ages: all ages.
Parent body:
The National Trust (South West Region)
Cornwall Regional Office, Lanhydrock, Bodmin, PL30 4DE, tel: 01208 74281, fax: 01208 77887

Enquiries to: Custodian
Access:
Access to staff: By letter, by telephone, in person, visitors by prior appointment

General description:
14th century manor house that was also used as a letter receiving office during Victorian times. It is well furnished with local oak pieces.
General history of the building and contents.
Information services:
Suitable for school groups. Hip-carrying infant seats for loan.
Special visitor services: Materials and/or activities for children..
Collections:
Collections and samplers
Some telegraph equipment
Everyday items used in Victorian times when it was a manor house/Letter Receiving Office

Internet home pages:
http://www.nationaltrust.org.uk/regions/cornwall

2896
TINTINHULL GARDEN

Farm Street, Tintinhull, Yeovil, Somerset, BA22 9PZ

Tel: 01935 822545
Email: tintinhull@nationaltrust.org.uk

Organisation type and purpose: Membership association (membership is by subscription), registered charity, museum.
Parent body:
The National Trust (South West Region)
The Regional Office for Wessex, tel: 01985 843600

Enquiries to: Head Gardener
Other contacts: Visitor Reception (01935 826357)

General description:
A delightful formal garden, created last century around a 17th century manor house. Small pools, varied borders and secluded lawns are all neatly enclosed within walls and clipped hedges, and there is also an attractive kitchen garden.
Information services:
Services for disabled people: For the visually impaired.

Internet home pages:
http://www.nationaltrust.org.uk/regions/wessex

2897
TIVERTON CASTLE

Park Hill, Tiverton, Devon, EX16 6RP

Tel: 01884 253200 or 255200
Fax: 01884 254200
Email: tiverton.castle@ukf.net
Formed: 1106

Organisation type and purpose: Independently owned, historic building, house or site, suitable for ages: 5+.
Privately owned medieval castle open to public. 4 Star holiday apartments, licensed for civil weddings.

Enquiries to: Owner
Access:
Access to staff: By letter, by telephone, by fax, by email, visitors by prior appointment
Access to building, collections or gallery: Prior appointment required
Hours: Easter to end Jun and Sep: Sun, Thu, Bank Holiday Mon, 1430 to 1730
July to Aug: Sun to Thu, 1430 to 1730
Access for disabled people: Parking provided, level entry, toilet facilities

General description:
Originally built in 1106 by command of Henry I, historic Tiverton Castle was the home of the mediaeval Earls of Devon. In 1645 it was besieged by, and fell to, Fairfax, and it now contains a fine Civil War Armoury. Today it is a peaceful private house open to the public.
Information services:
Special visitor services: Guided tours..
Collections:
Civil War Armoury, a very fine comprehensive collection, which is a valuable reference source, 1630-1688, c. 200 items
Printed publications:
The Taking of Tiverton

Internet home pages:
http://www.tivertoncastle.com

2898
TIVERTON MUSEUM OF MID DEVON LIFE

Beck's Square, Tiverton, Devon, EX16 6PJ

Tel: 01884 256295
Email: curator@tivertonmuseum.org.uk
Formed: 1960
Formerly: Tiverton Society

Organisation type and purpose: Independently owned, registered charity (charity number 239531), museum.
Parent body:
Tiverton and Mid Devon Museum Trust
at the same address

Enquiries to: Curator
Other contacts: Vice Chairman, Trustees
Access:
Access to staff: By letter, by telephone, by email, in person, charges to non-members, Internet web pages
Access to building, collections or gallery: No prior appointment required
Hours: Mon to Fri, 1030 to 1630; Sat, 1000 to 1300
Other restrictions: Closed from Christmas to the beginning of February.
Prior appointment required for library/archives.
Access for disabled people: level entry, access to all public areas, toilet facilities
Other restrictions: Lift.

General description:
Mid Devon social history, industry, agriculture, transport, commerce.
Information services:
Library available for reference (for conditions see Access above), on-line searching
Service point for Devon Records Office, local history and genealogical information, collection indexes.
Some Braille panels for the visually impaired.
Special visitor services: Guided tours, materials and/or activities for children.
Education services: Group education facilities, resources for Key Stages 1 and 2, 3, 4 and Further or Higher Education.
Services for disabled people: For the visually impaired; displays and/or information at wheelchair height.
Collections:
Apportionment lists
Census returns 1851
International genealogical index
John Heathercoat and Company - books, documents and records
Mid Devon artefacts
Newspapers from 1858
Non-Conformist records
Parish registers
Photographic collection (approx. 4000)
Tithe Maps
Printed publications:
Experiences & Reminiscences of Village Life in the Nineteen Fifties (Waller J, 30p)
Knightshayes Court from Knightenhaie to National Trust (Keene B and Butler D, £2)
Land transport educational pack
People of West-Exe - The personal reflections and opinions of Mid-Devonians (Waller T & J, £2)
The Dictionary of Wool (Sampson M, £1.50)
Tiverton Beer and Mineral Water Bottles (Fouracre R, 50p)
Wealth from Wool (Sampson M, £1)
Window on Westexe (Keene B, £1.50)
Electronic and video products:
The Exe Valley Line (railway video, £15 plus £1 p&p)

Internet home pages:
http://www.tivertonmuseum.org.uk
Visitors information, contents of galleries, 'Virtual Victorians' online learning resource, educational programme, museum's services.

2899
TODMORDEN TOY & MODEL MUSEUM

13 Rochdale Road, Todmorden, Lancashire, OL14 5AA

Tel: 01706 818365

Organisation type and purpose: Independently owned, museum, suitable for ages: all ages.

Enquiries to: Curator
Access:
Access to staff: By letter, by telephone, in person
Access to building, collections or gallery: No prior appointment required
Hours: Wed to Sat, 1000 to 1700; Sun, 1100 to 1600

General description:
Toys and models on display and for sale.
Information services:
Special visitor services: Guided tours..

2900
TOLBOOTH ART CENTRE

High Street, Kirkcudbright, Kirkcudbrightshire, DG6 4JL

Tel: 01557 331556
Fax: 01557 331643
Email: davidd@dumgal.gov.uk
Formed: 1993

Organisation type and purpose: Local government body, art gallery, historic building, house or site, suitable for ages: 8+.
Art Centre.
Parent body:
Dumfries & Galloway Museum Service
Tel: 01387 253374
Other address:
The Stewartry Museum
St Mary Street, Kirkcudbright, DG6 4AQ, tel: 01557 331643, fax: 01557 331643

Enquiries to: Curator
Access:
Access to staff: By letter, by telephone, by fax, by email, in person
Access to building, collections or gallery: No prior appointment required
Hours: Mon to Sat, 1100 to 1600, all year
Access for disabled people: level entry, access to all public areas, toilet facilities

General description:
An interpretive centre for the Kirkcudbright artists' colony (flourishing from 1890) with permanent displays of paintings by Kirkcudbright artists.
Collections:
Paintings by Kirkcudbright artists on permanent display
Catalogues:
Catalogue for part of the collections is only available in-house.

Internet home pages:
http://www.dumgal.gov.uk/museums
Site description under museums and services.

2901
TOLBOOTH MUSEUM STONEHAVEN

The Old Pier, Stonehaven, Aberdeenshire, AB39 2JU

Tel: 01771 622906
Fax: 01771 622884
Formed: 1963

Organisation type and purpose: Local government body, museum, historic building, house or site, suitable for ages: 5+.
Parent body:
Aberdeenshire Heritage
Tel: 01771 622906, fax: 01771 622884

Enquiries to: Curator
Access:
Access to staff: By letter, by telephone, by fax

General description:
Local memorabilia, fishing, civic regalia.
Collections:
Social history, photographs
Catalogues:
Catalogue for part of the collections is only available in-house.

2902
TOLGUS TIN

c/o Cornish Gold Site, Portreath Road, Portreath, Redruth, Cornwall, TR6 4HN

Tel: 01209 215185
Fax: 01209 219786 (Goldcentre)

Organisation type and purpose: Historic building, house or site, suitable for ages: 8+.
Parent body:
The Trevithick Trust
Tel: 01209 210900

Enquiries to: Manager
Access:
Access to staff: By letter, by telephone
Access to building, collections or gallery: No prior appointment required
Hours: Jan to Mar, Mon to Wed, 0930 to 1700, Sun, 1030 to 1630;
Apr to Oct, Mon to Fri, 0930 to1700, Sun and Bank Holiday Sats, 1030 to 1630;
Nov to Mar, Sun to Wed 1000 to 1600
Other restrictions: Closed for period over Christmas and New Year (phone to check dates)

General description:
One of two tin streaming works in Cornwall, contains Cornish stamps driven by waterwheel and one of the last round frames.
Information services:
Special visitor services: Guided tours..

Internet home pages:
http://www.trevithicktrust.com

2903
TOLHOUSE MUSEUM
Tolhouse Street, Great Yarmouth, Norfolk, NR30 2SH

Tel: 01493 745526
Fax: 01493 745459

Organisation type and purpose: Local government body, museum, historic building, house or site, suitable for ages: all ages.
Parent body:
Norfolk Museums & Archaeological Service
Managed by:
Great Yarmouth Museums
Tel: 01493 745526

Enquiries to: Custodian
Access:
Access to staff: By letter, by telephone

General description:
One of the oldest houses in East Anglia. A mediaeval merchant's house with local history and archaeology displays. Includes 19th century cells surviving from when it was used as the town jail.
Displays tell the story of crime and punishment from the medieval period to the present.
Information services:
Special visitor services: Tape recorded guides..
Collections:
Great Yarmouth holiday industry, holiday souvenirs, photographs and ephemera, late 18th century to the present
The only surviving Yarmouth Troll cart

2904
TOLPUDDLE MARTYRS MUSEUM
TUC Memorial Cottages, Tolpuddle, Dorchester, Dorset, DT2 7EH

Tel: 01305 848237
Fax: 01305 848237
Email: jpickering@tuc.org.uk

Organisation type and purpose: Museum.
The museum is administered by the TUC in London.
Parent body:
Head of Management Services and Administration Department
Trades Union Congress (TUC)
Congress House, Great Russell Street, London, London, WC1B 3LS

Enquiries to: Warden/Curator
Access:
Access to staff: By letter, by telephone, by fax, in person
Hours: Apr to Oct: Tue to Sat, 1000 to 1730; Sun, 1100 to 1730
Nov to Mar: Tue to Sat, 1000 to 1600; Sun, 1100 to 1600
Open Bank Holidays except Christmas and New Year
Access for disabled people: ramped entry, access to all public areas, toilet facilities

General description:
The Tolpuddle Martyrs and the start of the trade union movement.
Information services:
Education services: Resources for Key Stages 2, 3 and Further or Higher Education.
Services for disabled people: Displays and/or information at wheelchair height.
Publications list:
is available in hard copy and online.
Printed publications:
Pidela: an account of the village of Tolpuddle, Dorset from early times (Wirdnam A, available from museum only, £3.95)
The Story of the Tolpuddle Martyrs and TUC Guide to the Old Crown Court in Dorchester and Tolpuddle Village (50p)
Tolpuddle: an historical account through the eyes of George Loveless (£3)
We'll All Be Union Men: the story of Joseph Arch and his union (Scarth B, £4.95)
The Tolpuddle Martyrs (full colour booklet, £6.99)
Electronic and video products:
Tolpuddle Martyrs (CD-ROM, £12.99)
TUC: The First 125 Years (tape, £2.50)

Address for ordering publications:
Printed publications:
The Shop, TUC National Education Centre
77 Crouch End Hill, London, N8 8DG
TUC Publications, Congress House
Great Russell Street, London, W1B 3LS

Internet home pages:
http://www.tolpuddlemartyrs.org.uk
Pages on the museum; the Martyrs' story; news and events; contacts.

2905
TOLQUHON GALLERY
Tolquhon, Ellon, Aberdeenshire, AB41 7LP

Tel: 0165 1842343
Email: art@tolquhon-gallery.co.uk
Formed: 1987

Organisation type and purpose: Art gallery, suitable for ages: 16+.

Enquiries to: Partner
Access:
Access to staff: By letter, by telephone, by email, in person, Internet web pages
Access to building, collections or gallery: No prior appointment required
Hours: Mon to Sat, 1100 to 1700; Sun, 1400 to 1700
Other restrictions: Closed Thu.
Access for disabled people: access to all public areas

General description:
Contemporary Scottish Art.

Internet home pages:
http://www.tolquhon-gallery.co.uk
Information about the gallery, artists and exhibitions.

2906
TOM BROWN'S SCHOOL MUSEUM
Broad Street, Uffington, Faringdon, Oxfordshire, SN7 7RA

Tel: 01367 820259
Email: museum@uffington.net
Formed: 1984

Organisation type and purpose: Registered charity, museum, historic building, house or site. Preservation of local history. Information on the famous White Horse Hill at Uffington.

Enquiries to: Curator
Access:
Access to staff: By letter, by telephone, by email, Internet web pages

General description:
A 17th century village schoolroom converted to house village artefacts from the White Horse Hill area. Items include prehistoric and Roman artefacts; farm implements; photographs and memorabilia, local history of the area; collection of works by Thomas Hughes.
Collections:
Over 100 editions of Tom Brown's Schooldays by Thomas Hughes

Internet home pages:
http://www.uffington.net/museum

2907
TOM LEONARD MINING MUSEUM
See - Cleveland Ironstone Mining Museum

2908
TOMINTOUL MUSEUM
The Square, Tomintoul, Moray, AB39 9ET

Tel: 01309 673701
Fax: 01309 675863
Email: alasdair.joyce@techleis.moray.gov.uk
Full name: Tomintoul Museum and Visitor Centre
Formed: 1979

Organisation type and purpose: Museum.
Parent body:
Moray Council Museum Service
Tolbooth Street, Forres, Moray, IV36 1PH

Enquiries to: Senior Museums Officer
Direct tel: 01309 676688
Access:
Access to staff: By letter, by telephone, by fax, by email, in person
Hours: Apr to May: Mon to Fri, 0930 to 1200 and 1400 to 1600
Jun to Aug: Mon to Sat, 0930 to1200 and 1400 to 1630
Sep: Mon to Sat, 0930 to 1200 and 1400 to 1600
Oct: Mon to Fri, 0930 to 1200 and 1400 to 1600
Access to building, collections or gallery: No access other than to staff

General description:
Collection covering local, social, and natural history.
Catalogues:
Catalogue for all of the collections is on-line.

Internet home pages:
http://www.moray.gov.uk
On-line catalogue of objects.

2909
TOOLS AND TRADES HISTORY SOCIETY
See - Amberley Working Museum

2910
TOPSHAM MUSEUM
25 The Strand, Topsham, Exeter, Devon, EX3 0AX

Tel: 01392 873244
Email: museum@topsham.org
Formed: 1985

Organisation type and purpose: Voluntary organisation, registered charity, museum.
Run by:
Topsham Museum Society
Tel: 01392 873244, email/website: museum@topsham.org

Enquiries to: Honorary Secretary
Access:
Access to staff: By letter, by telephone, by email, visitors by prior appointment
Hours: Staff available: Mon, 0930 to 1230 or by arrangement. Museum: Easter Sat to end Oct: Mon, Wed, Sat & Sun, 1400 to 1700
Access to building, collections or gallery: No prior appointment required
Hours: Museum: Easter Sat to end Oct: Mon, Wed, Sat & Sun, 1400 to 1700 or by arrangement (closed Nov to Good Friday inclusive)
Access for disabled people: level entry, toilet facilities

General description:
Housed in a late 17th century merchant's house overlooking the Exe; furnished period rooms; 1930s kitchen; displays of local and maritime history; exhibitions on the natural history and wildlife of the Exe estuary; memorabilia of Vivien Leigh, the film star.
Information services:
Multimedia touch screen displays.
Special visitor services: Materials and/or activities for children.
Education services: Group education facilities, resources for Key Stages 1 and 2..

Collections:
Collection of half models from the Holman Shipbuilding Yard
Sail-loft devoted to the history of Topsham, including ship-building and ship-owning
Catalogues:
Catalogue for all of the collections is only available in-house.

2911
TORQUAY MUSEUM
529 Babbacombe Road, Torquay, Devon, TQ1 1HG

Tel: 01803 293975
Fax: 01803 294186
Acronym or abbreviation: TNHS
Full name: Torquay Natural History Society
Formed: 1844

Organisation type and purpose: Independently owned, learned society (membership is by subscription), registered charity (charity number 1025390), museum, suitable for ages: 5+.

Enquiries to: Curator
Other contacts: Honorary Librarian for library enquiries.
Access:
Access to staff: By letter, by telephone, by fax, visitors by prior appointment
Hours: Mon to Fri, 1000 to 1645
Access to building, collections or gallery: No prior appointment required
Hours: Easter to Oct: Mon to Sat, 1000 to 1700; Sun, 1330 to 1700
Access for disabled people: ramped entry, toilet facilities

General description:
Archaeology, palaeontology, geology, botany, zoology, ethnography, social history, Agatha Christie.
Information services:
Library available for reference (for conditions see Access above)
Special visitor services: Materials and/or activities for children.
Education services: Group education facilities, resources for Key Stage 2.
Services for disabled people: For the visually impaired; displays and/or information at wheelchair height.
Collections:
Hester Pengelly Collection: over 2000 autographs and letters, computerised database
William Pengelly's Diaries: excavation records of eminent local archaeologist
Pictorial Records Collection: 40,000 photographs of the local area (semi-computerised database)
Robert Rook Collection: over 4000 items of ephemera, Torquay-related computerised database
Catalogues:
Catalogue for library is in-house only. Catalogue for part of the collections is only available in-house.
Publications list:
is available in hard copy.
Printed publications:
Torquay Natural History Society Transactions & Proceedings (annually, £2.50)
An Introduction to the Geology of the Torquay District (1987, Scrivener M F, £1.25)
Beatrix Potter: Artist, Storyteller and Scientist (1989, Clegg J, £1.95)
Dartmoor Granite and its Uses (1988, Perigal S, £1.25)
The Brunels in Torbay (1989, Tudor G, £1.25)
The Old Devon Farmhouse (1998, Brears P, £19.95)
Torquay Museum Souvenir Guide (ed Chandler B, £1)
Torquay Natural History Society: The First 125 years (1969, Walker H H, 25p)
Torre Abbey's Story Began 770 Years Ago (1966, Walker H H, 20p)
William Pengelly's Techniques of Archaeological Excavation (1994, Warren C N and Rose S, £1.50)

2912
TORRE ABBEY HISTORIC HOUSE & GALLERY
The Kings Drive, Torquay, Devon, TQ2 5JE

Tel: 01803 293593
Email: torre-abbey@torbay.gov.uk
Acronym or abbreviation: Torre Abbey
Formed: 1196

Organisation type and purpose: Local government body, art gallery, historic building, house or site, suitable for ages: 8+.
Parent body:
Torbay Council, Directorate of Education Services
Oldway Mansion, Torquay Road, Paignton, TQ3 2TE, tel: 01803 208208

Enquiries to: Head of Museum Services, Torbay Council
Access:
Access to staff: By letter, by telephone, by email, visitors by prior appointment
Access to building, collections or gallery: No prior appointment required
Hours: Easter to 1 Nov: daily, 0930 to 1800
Other restrictions: Winter opening by prior booking for groups only.
Access for disabled people: Parking provided
Other restrictions: No wheelchair access to any part of the building.

General description:
Founded as a monastery in 1196, Torre Abbey incorporates the most extensive medieval monastic site in the whole of Devon and Cornwall. After the dissolution of the monasteries, Torre Abbey was adapted as a country house. Its present Georgian appearance is the result of modernisations undertaken by the catholic Cary family, who owned Torre Abbey from 1662 to 1930, when it was purchased by the local council. The Council converted it for use as an art gallery and Mayor's parlour. Today's visitors can see the Abbey ruins, the palm house and gardens, and twenty historic rooms, including the dining room and chapel, all of which are filled with fine paintings and antiques. Teas are served in the Victorian kitchen.
Information services:
Library available for reference (for conditions see Access above)
Exhibitions by people with disabilities held from time to time.
Special visitor services: Guided tours, materials and/or activities for children.
Education services: Group education facilities, resources for Key Stages 2 and 3.
Services for disabled people: For the visually impaired.
Collections:
Strong in Victorian art (including Holman Hunt and Burne-Jones)
Torre Abbey specialises in maritime paintings, landscapes, genre and work by local artists
Also holds important collections of Devon miniatures, antiques, Torquay Terracotta and sculpture
The Agatha Christie memorial room contains mementoes of the famous crime writer
Catalogues:
Catalogue for library is in-house only. Catalogue for all of the collections is on-line and part is published.
Publications list:
is available on-line.
Printed publications:
Souvenir Guide (full colour A4)
Short Guides in English, German, Dutch and Italian
Guides to various aspects of the collections, including the Thrupp collection of sculpture, pewter, glass etc

Internet home pages:
http://www.torre-abbey.org.uk
Information for visitors, descriptions of the house and collections, descriptions of educational and other services provided, downloads of colour guide, catalogue of art collections, and of collecting policy.

2913
TORRINGTON MUSEUM
High Street, Torrington, Devon, EX38 8HN

Tel: 01805 624324
Formed: 1976

Organisation type and purpose: Museum.

Enquiries to: Chairman
Other contacts: Hon Archivist for local historical research.
Access:
Access to staff: By letter, by telephone
Hours: May to end Sep: Mon to Fri, 1100 to 1600; Sat, 1100 to 1300
Other restrictions: On first floor of building, no ramp or elevator available.
Telephone only when open.

General description:
Major exhibit on Thomas Fowler, inventor of the thermosiphon (an essential element of heating systems), and of a calculating machine using a ternary system of calculation, enthusiastically reviewed by John Babbage (often considered the father of modern computing systems) from May 2000.
Collections:
Clinton Collection - 17th to 18th century family portraits (part)
Old postcards of Torrington and District
Catalogues:
Catalogue for part of the collections is only available in-house.

2914
TOTNES CASTLE
Castle Street, Totnes, Devon, TQ9 5NU

Tel: 01803 864406

Organisation type and purpose: Historic building, house or site.
Parent body:
English Heritage (South West Region)
Tel: 0117 975 0700, fax: 0117 975 0701

Enquiries to: Manager
Access:
Access to staff: By letter, by telephone
Access to building, collections or gallery: No prior appointment required
Hours: 29 Mar to 30 Sep: daily, 1000 to 1800,1 to 31 Oct: daily, 1000 to 1700
Other restrictions: Opening times are subject to change, for up-to-date information contact English Heritage by phone or visit the website.

General description:
A well-preserved Norman shell keep, in a motte and bailey castle with splendid views down to the River Dart. Built at the heart of a Saxon town, the once great surrounding ditch is today filled with cottages and gardens.

Internet home pages:
http://www.english-heritage.org.uk

2915
TOTNES COSTUME MUSEUM
Bogan House, 43 High Street, Totnes, Devon, TQ9 5NP

Full name: The Devonshire Collection of Period Costume
Formed: 1967

Organisation type and purpose: Registered charity (charity number 277327), museum, historic building, house or site, suitable for ages: 8+.
To collect and exhibit dress, to care and conserve same, to promote research and understanding of dress and its social significance.

Enquiries to: Curator
Direct tel: 01863 862857 (home) 07968 154225

continued overleaf

Other contacts: Chairman of Trust for matters relating to Trust formation etc.
Access:
Access to staff: By letter, by telephone, in person, visitors by prior appointment, charges to non-members
Access to building, collections or gallery: No prior appointment required
Hours: May 27 to end Sep: Mon to Fri, 1100 to 1700
Other restrictions: Or by appointment.

General description:
Museum of dress and textiles in 16th century merchant's town house.
Collection contains male, female and children's clothing and accessories from 18th, 19th and 20th century.
An annual themed exhibition is mounted each year and open in summer, also guided tours and lectures. Individual research using the collection is encouraged, arrangements should be made with the curators. A written guide is available to all visitors to the summer exhibition.
Information services:
Helpline available, tel no: 01863 862857.
Education facilities by arrangement.
Large format printed guide.
Small group guided tours by appointment.
Special visitor services: Guided tours, materials and/or activities for children.
Education services: Group education facilities.
Services for disabled people: For the visually impaired.
Collections:
A pair of silver bullion embroidered gloves (17th century)
Small collection of male and female dress (2nd half 18th century)
Large collection of male and female dress, some children and babies dress from throughout 19th century
Male, female and children's dress (20th century)
In particular, small collection of important items from Liberty's of London
Collection of early 20th century textiles eg Barrow & Larcher, and woven Elizabeth Peacock
Also early 19th century printed cottons
Catalogues:
Catalogue for part of the collections is only available in-house.
Printed publications:
Colour postcards made from photographs of items in the collection (for purchase, direct)

2916
TOTNES ELIZABETHAN MUSEUM
70 Fore Street, Totnes, Devon, TQ9 5RU

Tel: 01803 863821
Fax: 01803 863821
Email: totnes.museum@virgin.net
Formed: 1950

Organisation type and purpose: Local government body, independently owned, registered charity (charity number 296684), museum, historic building, house or site, suitable for ages: 5+.
Parent body:
Totnes Museum Trust
at the same address
Totnes Town Council
Links with:
Totnes Museum Society

Enquiries to: Curator
Access:
Access to staff: By letter, by telephone, by fax, by email, in person, visitors by prior appointment
Hours: Mon to Fri, 0900 to 1700

General description:
Grade I listed building 1575, Elizabethan garden in courtyard, room dedicated to Charles Babbage, inventor and pioneer of the computer, Victorian nursery, Tudor bedroom, Victorian pharmacy and general shop, archaeology exhibition, horology displays, exhibition of wills and Burke Expedition across Australia, study centre with local history and newspaper archives. Totnes times 1860 to present day, tithe maps, visual and literary material on Totnes history, plaster ceiling survey of Totnes.
Collections:
1851 and 1861 Census
Archive photographs
Charters and documents
Chaster diary
Microfiche of parish records for Totnes and surrounding villages
Oral tapes
Peter Clear diary
Rutter Library (on Devon and general history; for reference only)
Vivians Visitations of Devon
Windeat Collection of documents
Archaeology and local history study centre with archives
Printed publications:
Museums Group leaflet (annually)
Microform products:
Baptist Records (microfiche and microfilm)

Internet home pages:
http://www.devonmuseums.net

2917
TOTNES MOTOR MUSEUM

Closed: Collection sold and dispersed

Catalogues:
Catalogue for all of the collections is only available in-house.

2918
TOUCHSTONES ROCHDALE
The Esplanade, Rochdale, Lancashire, OL16 1AQ

Tel: 01706 641085
Email: touchstones@rochdale.gov.uk
Formed: 2002
Formerly: Rochdale Arts & Heritage Centre, date of change, 2002

Organisation type and purpose: Local government body, museum, art gallery, suitable for ages: 5+.
Arts and heritage centre.
Parent body:
Rochdale Metropolitan Borough Council
Municipal Offices, Smith Street, Rochdale

Enquiries to: Principal Arts & Heritage Officer
Direct fax: 01706 712723
Access:
Access to staff: By letter, by telephone, by fax, by email
Access to building, collections or gallery: No prior appointment required
Hours: Telephone for times
Access for disabled people: access to all public areas

General description:
Museum - local history, four art galleries, one permanent collection, local artists, two changing exhibitions, local studies centre and archive, performance venue.
Information services:
Library available for reference (for conditions see Access above)
Special visitor services: Guided tours, materials and/or activities for children.
Education services: Group education facilities, resources for Key Stages 1 and 2, 3, 4 and Further or Higher Education.
Services for disabled people: Displays and/or information at wheelchair height.

2919
TOWER BRIDGE
See - Tower Bridge Experience

2920
TOWER BRIDGE EXPERIENCE, THE
Tower Bridge, London, SE1 2UP

Tel: 020 7403 3761
Fax: 020 7357 7935
Email: enquiries@towerbridge.org.uk
Formed: 1982
Formed from: Corporation of London
Formerly: Tower Bridge

Organisation type and purpose: Museum. Tourist attraction.
Parent body:
Corporation of London
PO Box 270, Guildhall, London, EC2P 2EJ, tel: 020 7606 3030

Enquiries to: Administrator
Direct tel: 020 7403 3761
Direct fax: 020 7357 7935
Other contacts: Marketing Executive for press and publicity.
Access:
Access to staff: By letter, by telephone, by fax
Hours: Mon to Fri, 0915 to 1700
Access for disabled people: access to all public areas, toilet facilities

General description:
Situated inside Tower Bridge, an exciting and interactive exhibition brings to life more than 100 years of the bridge's amazing history. Visitors can discover how and why the bridge was built, and see spectacular London views from the walkways.

2921
TOWER CURING WORKS MUSEUM
Blackfriar's Road, Great Yarmouth, Norfolk

Formed: 2004

Organisation type and purpose: Local government body, museum, historic building, house or site, suitable for ages: all ages.
Parent body:
Norfolk Museums & Archaeology Service
Tel: 01603 493625
Managed by:
Great Yarmouth Museums
Tel: 01493 745526

Enquiries to: Curator

General description:
A new Yarmouth museum, opening in 2004, will replace the Maritime Museum which closed in September 2002.
It will tell the story of Great Yarmouth from its beginnings to the present day, and celebrate the town's maritime and fishing heritage.
Information services:
Temporary exhibition galleries
Special visitor services: Materials and/or activities for children.
Education services: Group education facilities..
Collections:
The following collections were formally at the Maritime Museum
Delf collection. Small marine engines. 20th century
Herring fishery. Models, photographs, equipment, etc. 19th/20th century
Maritime library. Books, journals, photographs, shipbuilding, plans and marine charts.
Pierhead paintings. Mediterranean and local ship portraits. 1840s-1950s

Internet home pages:
http://www.norfolk.gov.uk/tourism/museums/museums.htm
http://www.great-yarmouth.co.uk

2922
TOWER HILL PAGEANT
London

Closed

2923
TOWER MUSEUM, THE
Union Hall Place, Londonderry, BT48 6LU

Tel: 028 7137 2411
Formed: 1992

Organisation type and purpose: Local government body, museum, suitable for ages: 8+.

Enquiries to: Manager
Access:
Access to staff: By letter, by telephone
Access to building, collections or gallery: No prior appointment required
Hours: Tue to Sat, 1000 to 1700
Access for disabled people: level entry, access to all public areas, toilet facilities

General description:
Londonderry's complicated heritage is presented in the ultra modern, hi-tech exhibition, 'The Story of Derry'. The exhibition recounts the history of the City from its original geological formation through to present day using local archaeological, historical and art collections.
Information services:
Group education services.
Special visitor services: Guided tours..
Catalogues:
Catalogue for part of the collections is only available in-house.
Publications list:
is available in hard copy.

See also - Harbour Museum

2924
TOWN DOCKS MUSEUM
See - Hull Maritime Museum

2925
TOWN HALL PLATE ROOM - THE CRYPT
Town Hall, St Aldate's, Oxford, OX1 1BX

Tel: 01865 249811
Fax: 01865 252388
Email: dclark@oxford.gov.uk
Formed: 1897
Formed from: Oxford City Council

Organisation type and purpose: Local government body, historic building, house or site, suitable for ages: 16+.
Parent body:
Oxford City Council

Enquiries to: Manager
Direct tel: 01865 252559
Access:
Access to staff: By letter, by email
Hours: Mon to Fri, 0930 to 1600
Access to building, collections or gallery: Prior appointment required
Hours: Mon to Fri, 0930 to 1600

General description:
The display of historic civic plate includes a large silver gilt mace, two sergeant's maces, a gold porringer and cover from 1680, together with coronation cups and covers from 1665 and 1821.
Catalogues:
Catalogue for part of the collections is only available in-house.

2926
TOWN HOUSE MUSEUM
46 Queen Street, King's Lynn, Norfolk, PE30 1HT

Tel: 01553 773450

Organisation type and purpose: Local government body, museum, suitable for ages: 5+.
Parent body:
Norfolk Museums & Archaeological Service
Tel: 01603 493625

Enquiries to: Curator
Access:
Access to staff: By letter, by telephone
Access to building, collections or gallery: No prior appointment required
Hours: May to Sep, Mon to Sat, 1000 to 1700, Sun 1400 to 1700;
Oct to April, Mon to Sat, 1000 to 1600
Other restrictions: Closed Bank Holidays, Christmas Day, Boxing Day and New Year's Day

General description:
The merchants, tradesmen and families of King's Lynn are remembered in historic room displays. Displays show life in Mediaeval Lynn; Tudor, Stuart and Georgian life; and Victorian times. There is also a range of 20th century history through to the 1950s.

Internet home pages:
http://www.norfolk.gov.uk/tourism/museums
http://www.visitwestnorfolk.com

2927
TOWN WALLS TOWER
Shrewsbury, Shropshire

Tel: 01743 708162 (Attingham Park)
Fax: 01743 708175 (Attingham Park)

Organisation type and purpose: National organisation, registered charity (charity number 205846), historic building, house or site, suitable for ages: 8+.
Parent body:
The National Trust (West Midlands Region)
West Midlands Regional Office, tel: 01743 708100

General description:
Shrewsbury's last remaining watchtower, built in the 14th century and overlooking the River Severn.

Internet home pages:
http://www.nationaltrust.org.uk

2928
TOWNELEY HALL ART GALLERY & MUSEUMS
Museum, Towneley Park, Burnley, Lancashire, BB11 3RQ

Tel: 01282 424213 and 01282 664666
Fax: 01282 436138
Email: towneleyhall@burnley.gov.uk
Formed: 1903

Organisation type and purpose: Membership association, service industry, museum, art gallery, historic building, house or site, suitable for ages: all ages.
Registered Museum.
Parent body:
Burnley Borough Council
Email: www.burnley.gov.uk

Enquiries to: Administrator
Other contacts: Curator
Access:
Access to staff: By letter, by telephone, by fax, by email, in person, visitors by prior appointment, Internet web pages
Hours: Mon to Fri, 1000 to 1700
Other restrictions: Closed Sat and Christmas.
Access for disabled people: Parking provided, level entry, access to all public areas, toilet facilities

General description:
Local history of Burnley and district, Royal Lancastrian Pilkington Pottery, 17th century oak furniture, ivories, archeaology and the history and artefacts of the East Lancashire Regiment.
Information services:
Special visitor services: Guided tours.
Education services: Group education facilities, resources for Key Stage 2..
Collections:
Hardcastle Collection, book illustrations, English and French, 1800-1920, 510 items
Nuttall Bequest, Pilkingtons Royal Lancastrian pottery, 1903-1950, 200 items
Catalogues:
Catalogue for part of the collections is only available in-house.

Internet home pages:
http://www.burnley.gov.uk

2929
TOWNELEY HALL ART GALLERY AND MUSEUMS
Natural History Centre, Towneley Park, Burnley, Lancashire, BB11 3RQ

Tel: 01282 424213
Fax: 01282 36138
Email: towneleyhall@burnley.gov.uk
Acronym or abbreviation: NHC
Formed: 1989
Formed from: Towneley Hall Art Gallery and Museums

Organisation type and purpose: Local government body, professional body, suitable for ages: 5+.
Environmental Studies Centre, designated a Centre for Environmental Excellence by the Lancashire Environmental Action Programme.
Parent body:
Burnley Borough Council
Email: www.burnley.gov.uk

Enquiries to: Secretary
Access:
Access to staff: By letter, by telephone, by fax, by email, in person, visitors by prior appointment
Hours: Mon to Fri, 1000 to 1700
Other restrictions: No Curatorial staff available Sun.
Access for disabled people: Parking provided, level entry

General description:
Biology.
Information services:
Library available for reference (for conditions see Access above)
A classroom, displays and live exhibits.
Special visitor services: Materials and/or activities for children.
Education services: Resources for Key Stage 2.
Services for disabled people: Displays and/or information at wheelchair height.
Printed publications:
A variety of natural science workpacks.

Internet home pages:
http://www.towneleyhall.org.uk

2930
TOWNELEY HALL ART GALLERY & MUSEUMS
Art Gallery, Towneley Park, Burnley, Lancashire, BB11 3RQ

Tel: 01282 424213
Fax: 01282 436138
Formed: 1903

Organisation type and purpose: Professional body, museum, art gallery, historic building, house or site, suitable for ages: 5+.
Parent body:
Burnley Borough Council

Enquiries to: Curator
Other contacts: (1) Keeper of Art; (2) Secretary for (1) art enquiries.
Access:
Access to staff: By letter, by telephone, by email, in person, visitors by prior appointment
Hours: Mon to Fri, 1000 to 1700
Access to building, collections or gallery: No prior appointment required
Hours: Mon to Fri, 1000 to 1700; Sun, 1200 to 1700
Access for disabled people: Parking provided, level entry, toilet facilities
Other restrictions: Access to all areas via virtual tour from late 2002.

continued overleaf

General description:
18th and 19th century British Masters, water colours and oil paintings.
Information services:
Special visitor services: Guided tours, materials and/or activities for children.
Education services: Group education facilities..
Collections:
17th century Lancashire oak furniture
Period rooms
Victorian kitchen
18th & 19th century paintings
Nutall Bequest, Royal Lancastrian Pilkington pots
Catalogues:
Catalogue for part of the collections is available in-house, part is published and part is on-line.
Printed publications:
Towneley Hall Guide (£1)
Towneley Hall leaflet (free)

Internet home pages:
http://www.burnley.gov.uk

2931
TOWNEND

Troutbeck, Windermere, Cumbria, LA23 1LB

Tel: 015394 32628
Email: townend@nationaltrust.org.uk

Organisation type and purpose: National organisation, registered charity (charity number 205846), museum, historic building, house or site, suitable for ages: 5+.
Parent body:
The National Trust (North West)
North West Regional Office, tel: 0870 609 5391

Enquiries to: Manager
Access:
Access to staff: By letter, by telephone, by email

General description:
A very fine example of Lake District vernacular architecture and an exceptional survival. Largely 17th century, the solid stone and slate house belonged to a wealthy yeoman farming family and contains carved woodwork, books, papers, furniture and fascinating domestic implements from the past, largely accumulated by the Browne family who lived here from 1626 to 1943.
Information services:
Children's quiz/trail. Living history - meet George Browne, most Thursdays.
Special visitor services: Materials and/or activities for children..

Internet home pages:
http://www.nationaltrust.org.uk

2932
TOWNER ART GALLERY & LOCAL MUSEUM

High Street, Old Town, Eastbourne, East Sussex, BN20 8BB

Tel: 01323 417961 (admin); 01323 411688 (visitor information)
Minicom no. 01323 415111
Fax: 01323 648182
Email: townergallery@eastbourne.gov.uk
Acronym or abbreviation: The Towner
Formed: 1923
Art Gallery formed 1923
Local Museum formed 1983

Organisation type and purpose: Local government body, museum, art gallery, suitable for ages: all ages.

Enquiries to: Art Administrator
Other contacts: Curator (visual arts)
Access:
Access to staff: By letter, by telephone, by fax, by email, visitors by prior appointment
Access for disabled people: level entry
Other restrictions: Part access to ground floor galleries, attendants' assistance always available.

General description:
Housed in an elegant 18th century building, the Towner is set in Manor Gardens in Eastbourne's Old Town. It has a collection of mainly 19th and 20th century British art, including a gallery devoted to Eric Ravilious and a sculpture by David Nash in the gardens. It also houses the South East Arts Collection of Contemporary Art. A lively and innovative programme of exhibitions and events ensures there is always something new to see and do.
The local museum covers the history of Eastbourne from prehistory. Artefacts range from local archaeological finds to the original station clock, and items from Eastbourne's Roman Villa to an original Victorian kitchen range.
Information services:
Library available for reference (for conditions see Access above). Helpline available, tel no: 01323 417961 for enquiries regarding the Art Collection; tel: 01323 410300 re local history.
Guided tours and education facilities both by arrangement.
Special visitor services: Guided tours, materials and/or activities for children.
Education services: Group education facilities, resources for Key Stages 1 and 2, 3, 4 and Further or Higher Education.
Services for disabled people: Displays and/or information at wheelchair height.
Collections:
Works by Eastbourne artist Eric Ravilious, c. 1930-1942, 400 plus
The Towner Bequest - 21 Victorian genre paintings
The Lucy Carrington Wertheim Bequest - 50 20th century British paintings including Christopher Wood, Frances Hodgkins, Alfred Wallis
The Irene Law Bequest - 23 Old Masters, mainly European, these are part of Towner Collection of mainly 19th and 20th century British art (entire collection computerised, though not accessible for public, yet)
Photographs and postcards of Eastbourne 19th and 20th century, c. 1860-1867, 3000 plus
Local archaeology
Local ephemeral objects etc
Catalogues:
Catalogue for library is in-house only. Catalogue for all of the collections is only available in-house.
Printed publications:
Small selection available from Towner's shop

Internet home pages:
http://www.eastbourne.gov.uk
Local authority website, information about gallery and museum and exhibits programme.

2933
TOY & TEDDY BEAR MUSEUM

373 Clifton Drive North, Lytham St Annes, Lancashire, FY8 2PA

Tel: 01253 713705
Formed: 1989

Organisation type and purpose: Independently owned, museum, suitable for ages: most age groups.

Enquiries to: Owner
Access:
Access to staff: By letter, by telephone
Access for disabled people: Parking provided

General description:
An interesting display of old toys dating back to Victorian times. Arranged on two floors in five large rooms are many old bears along with displays showing the history of the teddy bear. There is also a collection of old dolls, and over 25 dolls' houses, P cars, tin plate, Dinky toys and much more.

2934
TOY MUSEUM

Holmisdale House, Glendale, Isle of Skye, IV55 8WS

Tel: 01470 511240
Email: skye.toy.museum@ukf.net
Formed: 1986

Organisation type and purpose: Independently owned, museum, suitable for ages: 4 to 16+. Award-winning visitor attraction.

Enquiries to: Owner
Access:
Access to staff: By letter, by telephone, by email, in person, Internet web pages
Access to building, collections or gallery: No prior appointment required
Hours: Mon to Sat, 1000 to 1800
Access for disabled people: Parking provided, ramped entry

General description:
Toys, games, dolls - Bisque to Barbie, Victorian to Star Wars.
Guided tours, demonstrations plus 'Hands-On' experience.
Information services:
Victorian/Edwardian packs available comprising:
Original Codd & Stone ink bottles, dip pen, Diabolo, Wizzer, whip & top, coup & ball, slate and pencil, jacks, skipping rope, flower press, explanation leaflet and toy museum colouring book (boxed), reproduction Victorian scraps.
Special visitor services: Guided tours.
Education services: Group education facilities.
Services for disabled people: For the visually impaired; for the hearing impaired.
Collections:
Early Pinball machine, slot machines, teddies, rare Bisque dolls, large Meccano and Star Wars display, Pelhams Puppet Theatre, Hornby, Frog, Jetex, Bayko, early Subbuteo, rare Sasha dolls, Dionne Quintuplets, Brick Player, jigsaws, books

Internet home pages:
http://www.craftsonskye.org.uk
Local information.
http://www.glendale-skye.org.uk
Local information.
http://www.toy-museum.co.uk/
History of museum, museum and pictures, entry rates, the area, our products, how to find us, contact details.

2935
TRADITIONAL HERITAGE MUSEUM

605 Ecclesall Road, Sheffield, South Yorkshire, S11 8PR

Tel: 0114 222 6296
Formed: 1964

Organisation type and purpose: Museum, university department or institute, suitable for ages: 5+.
Parent body:
The National Centre for English Cultural Tradition (NATCECT)
The University of Sheffield, Sheffield, S10 2TN, tel: 0114 222 6296

Enquiries to: Curator
Direct email: j.widdowson@sheffield.ac.uk
Access:
Access to staff: By letter, visitors by prior appointment, charges made to all users
Access to building, collections or gallery: Prior appointment required
Other restrictions: By arrangement outside regular open days and outreach events.
Access for disabled people: Parking provided, ramped entry

General description:
The Museum houses a collection of social and industrial history artefacts illustrating life and work in the Sheffield region, 1850-1950. The

majority of the displays comprise original domestic, workshop and industrial interiors, reconstructed in their local context. Sheffield's cutlery, handtool and silversmithing trades are particularly well represented, along with horn scalepressing, basketmaking, filemaking, shoemaking and clogmaking. Other exhibits include a Victorian cutlery works office, a chemist's, an optician's, a pawnbroker's and a silversmith's retail shop, an early twentieth century kitchen and parlour, a provision merchant's and a high class grocer's and coffee shop, plus displays of English folklore and traditions.

Information services:
Special visitor services: Guided tours, materials and/or activities for children.
Education services: Group education facilities, resources for Key Stages 1 and 2, 3, 4 and Further or Higher Education..

Collections:
Extensive collections of artefacts representative of local domestic life and the handcrafted trades
Working machinery in the Knifegrinder's Workshop and the Horn Scalepressing Workshop
Documents and photographs relevant to the collections are housed in the Archives of the Museum's Parent Body: The National Centre for English Cultural Tradition at The University of Sheffield
The Museum also houses the James Muir Smith Puppet Collection

Catalogues:
Catalogue for all of the collections is only available in-house.

Printed publications:
Parent Body publications (available direct from NATCELT, for purchase) include:
Lore and Language Vols 1-14
NATCECT Occasional Publications, Research Guides, Facsimiles, Bibliographical and Special Series, Conference Papers
Traditional Drama Studies Vols 1, 3, 4
Museum Guide

Address for ordering publications:
Printed publications:
The Secretary, The National Centre for English Cultural Tradition
The University of Sheffield, Sheffield, S10 2TN, tel: 0114 222 6296

Internet home pages:
http://www.shef.ac.uk/english/natcect/thm.html

2936
TRAMWAY MUSEUM
See - National Tramway Museum

2937
TRAMWAY MUSEUM SOCIETY
See - National Tramway Museum

2938
TRAQUAIR HOUSE
Innerleithen, Peeblesshire, EH44 6PW

Tel: 01896 830323
Fax: 01896 830639
Email: enquiries@traquair.co.uk

Organisation type and purpose: Historic home - visitor attraction.

Enquiries to: Administrator

Access:
Access to staff: By letter, by telephone, by fax, by email, in person, visitors by prior appointment

General description:
Former Royal Hunting Lodge, over 1000 years old, close associations with Mary Queen of Scots and the Jacobites, the oldest continually inhabited house in Scotland. 18th century working brewery, gift shop, brewery shop and museum, antique shop, craft workshops and tearoom.

Collections:
18th century library - unique family collection, 17th-18th century, 3500 volumes.

Printed publications:
Traquair Guidebook

2939
TREADGOLD INDUSTRIAL HERITAGE MUSEUM
Bishop Street, Portsmouth, Hampshire, PO1 3DA

Tel: 023 9282 4745
Formed: 1809
Also known as: Treadgolds of Portsea
Formerly: Wm Treadgold & Co (Ironmongers of Portsea), date of change, 1988

Organisation type and purpose: Local government body, museum, historic building, house or site, suitable for ages: 5+.

Parent body:
Hampshire County Council Museums Service (HCCMS)
Chilcomb House, Chilcomb Lane, Winchester, SO23 8RD, tel: 01962 846304

Enquiries to: Curator

Access:
Access to staff: By letter, by telephone, visitors by prior appointment
Access for disabled people: level entry, access to all public areas
Other restrictions: Floors level but uneven

General description:
Opened in 1995, the Treadgold Industrial Heritage Museum comprises the buildings and contents of an iron and steel merchant and manufacturing ironmongers' business which traded on the same site from 1809 to 1988.
Begun in 1809 in one building on the site, it spread into the surrounding houses altering some and replacing others as it grew. The site contains evidence of at least 22 separate buildings built between 1706 and 1870, and is listed Grade II, both for its internal and external structures.
Kept much as it was when it closed in 1988, the workshop with its forges and machinery, the office with its high sloping desks and correspondence, the shop and stores with their stock, and the stable with its tack, the site still carries echoes of the heyday of the business in the 1860s and 70s.
The interpretative area details: the business and family histories, shop and workshop systems and techniques, the building styles and techniques in evidence on the site.

Information services:
Education services: Group education facilities, resources for Key Stage 2 and Further or Higher Education.
Services for disabled people: Displays and/or information at wheelchair height.

Collections:
Stock, machinery, photographs and documents pertaining to the Treadgold ironmongers' business trading on the site between 1809 and business closure in 1988

Catalogues:
Catalogue for all of the collections is on-line.

Printed publications:
Publications list is available from the Librarian, Hampshire County Council Museums Service Headquarters, Chilcomb House, Winchester, SO23 8RD
Treadgolds: The development & decline of a Portsea ironmongers 1800-1988 (Day A, ISBN 0 90155994 6)

Internet home pages:
http://www.hants.gov.uk/museum/treadgold/
HMCMS web catalogue, whole collection, 100,000 plus, web pages.

See also - Monitor 33

2940
TREASURER'S HOUSE
Martock, Somerset, TA12 6JL

Tel: 01935 825801

Organisation type and purpose: National organisation, registered charity (charity number 205846), historic building, house or site, suitable for ages: all ages.

Parent body:
The National Trust (South West Region)
The Regional Office for Wessex, tel: 01985 843600

Enquiries to: Manager

Access:
Access to staff: By letter, by telephone
Access to building, collections or gallery: No prior appointment required
Hours: End of Mar to end Sep, Sun to Tue, 1400 to1700
Other restrictions: Only medieval hall, wall painting and kitchen are shown.
The property may be closed at some stage during 2003 for essential repair work. No WC

General description:
A small medieval house. The Great Hall was completed in 1293 and the solar block, with an interesting wall painting, is even earlier. There is also a kitchen added in the 15th century.

Internet home pages:
http://www.nationaltrust.org.uk/regions/wessex

2941
TREASURER'S HOUSE
Minster Yard, Chapter House Street, York, YO1 7JL

Tel: 01904 624247
Fax: 01904 647372
Email: treasurershouse@nationaltrust.org.uk

Organisation type and purpose: National organisation, registered charity (charity number 205846), museum, historic building, house or site, suitable for ages: 8+.

Parent body:
The National Trust (Yorkshire and North East)
Yorkshire Regional Office, tel: 01904 70202

Enquiries to: Manager

Access:
Access to staff: By letter, by telephone, by fax, by email
Access for disabled people: toilet facilities
Other restrictions: Drop-off point. Steps to entrance. Ground floor accessible with assistance. No access to other floors. Audio-visual/video. Steps to tea-room entrance. Refreshments can be brought to ground floor or garden. Grounds largely accessible.

General description:
This beautiful town house was originally the home of the Treasurers of York Minster and is built over a Roman road. It was acquired by wealthy Yorkshire industrialist Frank Green in 1897 and given into the care of the National Trust in 1930, complete with carefully restored and presented 16th- and 20th century decoration, furniture, china and glass.

Information services:
Audio guide.
Braille guide. Large-print guide. Scented plants. Sympathetic Hearing Scheme.
Suitable for school groups. Audio guide. Children's guide. Children's quiz/trail.
Special visitor services: Tape recorded guides, materials and/or activities for children.
Services for disabled people: For the visually impaired; for the hearing impaired.

Catalogues:
Catalogue for all of the collections is only available in-house.

Internet home pages:
http://www.nationaltrust.org.uk

2942
TREFECCA COLLEGE
See - Howell Harris Museum

2943
TRELISSICK GARDEN
Feock
As shop Gallery, Nr Truro, Cornwall, TR3 6QL

Tel: 01872 864084 (Gallery)
Fax: 01872 865808
Email: trelissick@nationaltrust.org.uk

Organisation type and purpose: National organisation, registered charity (charity number 205846), art gallery, historic building, house or site, suitable for ages: all ages.
Parent body:
The National Trust (South West Region)
Regional Office for Cornwall, tel: 01208 74281

Enquiries to: Manager
Access:
Access to staff: By letter, by telephone, by fax, by email
Access for disabled people: toilet facilities
Other restrictions: Designated parking 30yds. Level entrance to shop and to restaurant. Courtyard
tea-room access up 16 stairs, fitted with hand rail. Grounds largely accessible, recommended route map.

General description:
Beautifully positioned at the head of the Fal estuary, the estate commands panoramic views over the area and has extensive park and woodland walks beside the river. At its heart is the tranquil garden, set on many levels and containing a superb collection of tender and exotic plants which bring colour throughout the year. The display of spring blossom is particularly delightful.
The house is not open, but there is an art and craft gallery, and a fine Georgian stable block.
Copeland China collection, by courtesy of Mrs Spencer Copeland.
Information services:
Programme of theatrical and musical events, winter and spring programmes.
Suitable for school groups.
Special visitor services: Materials and/or activities for children.
Education services: Group education facilities.
Services for disabled people: For the visually impaired.

Internet home pages:
http://www.nationaltrust.org.uk/regions/cornwall

2944
TRERICE MANOR HOUSE
Kestle Mill, Newquay, Cornwall, TR8 4PG

Tel: 01637 875404
Fax: 01637 879300
Email: trerice@nationaltrust.org.uk

Organisation type and purpose: National organisation, registered charity (charity number 205846), museum, historic building, house or site, suitable for ages: 5+.
Parent body:
The National Trust (South West Region)
Regional Office for Devon and Cornwall, tel: 01208 74281

Enquiries to: Manager
Access:
Access to staff: By letter, by telephone, by fax, by email
Access to building, collections or gallery: No prior appointment required
Hours: End Mar to mid Jul, Mon, Wed, Thu, Fri, Sun, 1100 to 1730;
Mid Jul to mid Sep, Mon to Fri and Sun, 1100 to 1730;
Mid Sep to end Sep, Mon, Wed, Thu, Fri, Sun, 1100 to 1730;
Oct to beg Nov, Mon, Wed, Thu, Fri, Sun, 1100 to 1700
Access for disabled people: Parking provided, toilet facilities
Other restrictions: Drop-off point. 2 manual wheelchairs available, booking essential. Level entrance. Ground floor accessible with assistance, ramp available for wheelchairs, otherwise 2 steps down. Wheelchair access to first floor, via side door on to terrace. Level entrance to shop. Ramped entrance to restaurant. Grounds largely accessible.

General description:
This delightful small Elizabethan manor house enjoys a secluded setting and contains fine fireplaces, plaster ceilings, oak and walnut furniture, interesting clocks, needlework and Stuart portraits. The highlight of the interior is the magnificent great chamber with its splendid barrel ceiling. The attractive garden has some unusual plants and an orchard with old varieties of fruit trees, and in the barn there is an exhibition on the history of the lawnmower.
Information services:
Braille guide. Audio guide. Touch list. Handling collection.
Front-carrying baby slings for loan. Hipcarrying infant seats for loan.
Suitable for school groups. Education room/centre. Hands-on activities. Children's quiz/trail.
Special visitor services: Materials and/or activities for children.
Education services: Group education facilities.
Services for disabled people: For the visually impaired.

2945
TREVITHICK COTTAGE
Penponds, Camborne, Cornwall, TR14 0QG

Tel: 01209 612154
Fax: 01209 210900 (Trevithick Trust Tel/fax)
Email: info@trevithicktrust.com

Organisation type and purpose: Independently owned, museum, historic building, house or site, suitable for ages: all ages.
Administered by:
The Trevithick Trust
Owned by:
The National Trust

Enquiries to: Curator

General description:
Local history.

Internet home pages:
http://www.trevithicktrust.com

2946
TREVITHICK TRUST LIMITED
Trevithick Road, Pool, Redruth, Cornwall, TR15 3NP

Tel: 01209 210900
Fax: 01209 210900
Email: info@trevithicktrust.com
Formed: 1993

Organisation type and purpose: (membership is by subscription), present number of members: 300, registered charity (charity number 1041752), museum, historic building, house or site, suitable for ages: 8+.
Administrative body.

Enquiries to: General Manager
Access:
Access to staff: By letter, by telephone, by fax, by email, visitors by prior appointment, Internet web pages
Other restrictions: Not all staff at main office.

General description:
The identification, preservation, protection, management and interpretation of the historical, architectural and engineering heritage in the form of buildings, artefacts, documents, records and land associated with Cornish mining and engineering, and related industries and activities.

Printed publications:
Newsletter

Internet home pages:
http://www.trevithicktrust.com
Site Information.

See also - Cornish Mines and Engines; Industrial Discovery Centre; King Edward Mine; Lizard Lighthouse; Lizard Wireless Station; Pendeen Lighthouse; Porthcurno Museum of Submarine Telegraphy; St Day Old Church; Tolgus Tin; Trevithick Cottage

2947
TRIMONTIUM EXHIBITION
Ormiston Institute, The Square, Melrose, Roxburghshire

Organisation type and purpose: Museum, suitable for ages: 8+.

General description:
Trimontium, the Romans' most northerly military amphitheatre. The fort, together with townships, covers over 350 acres.
The exhibition relates the history including the most up-to-date excavations.
Information services:
Guided walk around the site on Thursday afternoon (takes 3 hours)
Special visitor services: Materials and/or activities for children.
Education services: Group education facilities..

2948
TRINITY GALLERY
Trinity Theatre and Arts Centre, Church Road, Tunbridge Wells, Kent, TN1 1JP

Tel: 01892 678670
Fax: 01892 678680
Acronym or abbreviation: Trinity
Full name: Trinity Theatre and Arts Centre
Formed: 1982

Organisation type and purpose: Registered charity (charity number 3179063), art gallery, suitable for ages: 12+.
Theatre, arts and education centre.

Enquiries to: Managing Director
Access:
Access to staff: By letter, by fax
Access to building, collections or gallery: No prior appointment required
Hours: Mon to Fri, 0900 to 1700; Sat, 1000 to 1500
Access for disabled people: Parking provided, ramped entry, access to all public areas, toilet facilities

General description:
A converted church. The church was saved by the civic society in 1979, and the proposal to turn it into an Arts centre saved it from being knocked to the ground. Since 1982 it has had many re-fits and improvements made to it, mostly supported by members and volunteers. Trinity Theatre and Arts Centre has been, and always will be, at the heart of the community.
Auditorium with continuously changing performances, two galleries exhibiting various artists, café, education suite, cinema.
Information services:
Library available for reference (for conditions see Access above)
Special visitor services: Materials and/or activities for children.
Education services: Group education facilities, resources for Key Stages 1 and 2, 3 and 4.
Services for disabled people: For the hearing impaired; displays and/or information at wheelchair height.
Publications list:
is available in hard copy.
Printed publications:
Brochure (quarterly)
Monthly membership and friends letters

2949
TRINITY HOUSE NATIONAL LIGHTHOUSE CENTRE

Wharf Road, Penzance, Cornwall, TR18 4BN

Tel: 01736 360077
Acronym or abbreviation: THNLC
Formed: 1990
Formerly: National Lighthouse Centre

Organisation type and purpose: Registered charity (charity number 900127), museum, suitable for ages: all ages.
Preservation and presentation of lighthouse equipment in the context of maritime safety.
Registered Office:
Trinity House National Lighthouse Centre
Penwith Council Offices, St Clare, Penzance, Cornwall, TR18 3QW, tel: 01736 362341

Enquiries to: Manager
Other contacts: (1) Company Secretary (2) Company Treasurer for (1) legal and contractual (2) financial.
Access:
Access to staff: By letter, by telephone, visitors by prior appointment, charges made to all users
Hours: Mon to Fri, 1030 to 1600
Other restrictions: Very limited access Nov to Apr.
Access to building, collections or gallery: No prior appointment required
Hours: Easter to 31 Oct: Daily, 1030 to 1630
Other restrictions: No unaccompanied children; admission charges.
Access for disabled people: level entry
Other restrictions: Access to 80% areas.

General description:
Lighthouses, maritime navigational aids and safety, optical apparatus, social history/ Lighthouse Keepers.
Information services:
Library available for reference (for conditions see Access above)
Special visitor services: Guided tours.
Education services: Group education facilities..
Collections:
Comprehensive collection of items demonstrating technological developments in aids to navigation and the life of the Lighthouse Keeper.
Bishop Rock, thought to be the only complete hyper-radial lens in any museum
St Mary's, $3\frac{1}{2}$ ton, 1st order optic, complete with mercury bearing
Coquet, fine example of a fresnel lens and occulting mechanism
Spurn Head, early automatic, fully gas-operated, optic
Three different types of 20th century light vessel optics with gimballed fixing and balance pendulum, plus one late 19th century oil lit lantern system
Catalogues:
Catalogue for all of the collections is only available in-house.
Trade and statistical:
Trade data contact: Trinity House Lighthouse Service, Tower Hill, London EC3N 2DH.
Publications list:
is available in hard copy.
Printed publications:
Books, postcards, etc can be obtained directly, or by mail order, from the Museum. No in-house publications
Electronic and video products:
Encyclopaedia of Lighthouses (disk £8, CD-ROM £25 direct)

2950
TRINITY MARITIME MUSEUM

Newcastle upon Tyne

Close, date of change, 30 April 2002

2951
TROLLEYBUS MUSEUM AT SANDTOFT, THE

Belton Road, Sandtoft, Doncaster, Lincolnshire, DN8 5SX

Tel: 01724 711391
Email: enquiries@sandtoft.org.uk
Full name: The Museum of the Trolleybus
Formed: 1969
Formerly: Home of the Trolleybus, Sandtoft Transport Museum, date of change, 2001

Organisation type and purpose: Membership association (membership is by subscription), voluntary organisation, registered charity (charity number 514382), museum, suitable for ages: 5+, publishing house.
To promote interest in the trolleybus by display and operation of preserved examples of this mode of transport. Operation of a miniature steam railway.
Parent body:
Sandtoft Transport Centre Limited
Affiliated to:
Transport Trust
Supported by:
Bradford Trolleybus Association
Tel: 01274 492026
British Trolleybus Society
Tel: 0118 958 3974
Doncaster Omnibus & Light Railway
Tel: 01302 887664

Enquiries to: Information Officer
Access:
Access to staff: By letter, by email, visitors by prior appointment, Internet web pages
Hours: Open to visitors Bank Holidays Sun, Mon from Easter to end of October 1200 to 1700
telephone for other special days
Access for disabled people: Parking provided, level entry, access to all public areas, toilet facilities
Other restrictions: There maybe wheelchair access problems for trolleybus rides

General description:
History, preservation and operation of British and European trolleybuses; motorbuses and other items of transport interest.
Collections:
Retail shop windows of the 1950s/60s.
Trolleybus related artefacts
Catalogues:
Catalogue for all of the collections is available in-house and part is on-line.
Printed publications:
Annual Programme of events (free with sae)
Gathering Programme (usually £1.50)
Sandtoft Guide
Sandtoft Scene (journal, 3 times a year for members)

Internet home pages:
http://www.sandtoft.org.uk

2952
TROWBRIDGE MUSEUM

The Shires, Court Street, Trowbridge, Wiltshire, BA14 8AT

Tel: 01225 751339
Fax: 01225 754608
Email: clyall@trowbridge.museum.co.uk
Formed: 1990

Organisation type and purpose: Local government body, museum.
Parent body:
The Trowbridge Town Council
10-12 Fore Street, Trowbridge, Wiltshire, tel: 01225 765072, fax: 01225 775460

Enquiries to: Curator
Access:
Access to staff: By letter, by telephone, by fax, visitors by prior appointment
Hours: Tue to Sat, 0900 to 1700
Other restrictions: Building access by appointment after 1600 as museum closed to public after 1600.
Access to building, collections or gallery: No access other than to staff
Hours: Tue to Fri, 1000 to 1600; Sat, 1000 to 1700
Access for disabled people: Parking provided, access to all public areas, toilet facilities

General description:
Wool/cloth production, industrial history, Isaac Pitman, social history, Tudor food, Victorian schoolroom, Victorian mill.
Information services:
Helpline available, tel no: 01225 751339.
Special visitor services: Materials and/or activities for children.
Education services: Group education facilities, resources for Key Stages 1 and 2 and 3..
Catalogues:
Catalogue for all of the collections is available in-house and part is on-line.

2953
TRUE'S YARD FISHING MUSEUM

True's Yard, North Street, King's Lynn, Norfolk, PE30 1QW

Tel: 01553 770479
Fax: 01553 765100
Email: trues.yard@virgin.net
Formed: 1991

Organisation type and purpose: Independently owned, registered charity (charity number 801974), museum, historic building, house or site, suitable for ages: 4 to 80.

Enquiries to: Curator
Access:
Access to staff: By letter, by telephone, by fax, by email, in person, Internet web pages
Access for disabled people: level entry, access to all public areas, toilet facilities

General description:
The Wash fishery; The Wash; West Norfolk history; King's Lynn history; North End history; fisheries history; genealogical resources for King's Lynn; history of Ouse Navigation and Fen Drainage.
Information services:
Library available for reference (for conditions see Access above)
Records Search Service on receipt of postal request.
Special visitor services: Guided tours, tape recorded guides, materials and/or activities for children.
Education services: Group education facilities, resources for Key Stages 1 and 2 and Further or Higher Education.
Services for disabled people: For the hearing impaired.
Collections:
Collection of photographs of historic Lynn; Lynn fishery
Collection of objects relating to the historic fishing quarter of Lynn
Computerised data of shipping information of Wash Ports.18th and 19th century
Census records, Indexed for 1841, 1891 and 1861
Parish records, computerised and indexed births/marriages/ burials of King's Lynn, mainly 19th century
Catalogues:
Catalogue for library is in-house only. Catalogue for all of the collections is only available in-house.
Publications list:
is available in hard copy.
Printed publications:
Privately printed booklets relating to Lynn town and maritime history

Internet home pages:
http://welcome.to/truesyard
Information on North End and True's Yard.

2954
TRURO CATHEDRAL

Truro, Cornwall

Formed: 1880

Organisation type and purpose: Historic building, house or site, suitable for ages: all ages. Anglican cathedral, the Cathedral of Cornwall.
Cathedral Office:
Truro Cathedral
14 St Mary's Street, Truro, Cornwall, TR1 2AF, tel: 01872 276782, email/website: colin@trurocathedral.org.uk

Enquiries to: Visitor Officer
Direct tel: 01872 276782
Direct email: colin@trurocathedral.org.uk
Access:
Access to staff: By letter, by telephone, by email, Internet web pages
Access to building, collections or gallery: No prior appointment required
Hours: Daily, 0730 to 1800

General description:
The Diocese of Truro was created in 1876 and the building of the Cathedral, designed by John Pearson, was commenced in 1880 on the site of the parish church of St Mary, itself consecrated in 1259. The south aisle of the church was incorporated into the Cathedral and the building, consecrated in 1887, was completed, as far as finances would allow, in 1920.
The stained glass, crafted by Clayton and Bell, is considered to be the finest collection of Victorian stained glass in England. The Pieta and the statue of St Nicholas are of the 14th century from Brittany, and were given to the Bishop in 1929.
The organ built by 'Father' Willis, was an integral part of the whole design, and so in this setting is one of the finest examples of his work.
Information services:
Groups tours by appointment.
Tours of the Treasury led by the Canon Treasurer, by appointment.
Visiting bell ringers always very welcome.
The Chapter House also functions as a restaurant.
Special visitor services: Guided tours..

Internet home pages:
http://www.trurocathedral.org.uk

2955
TUDOR HOUSE MUSEUM

See - Museum of Local Life

2956
TUDOR HOUSE MUSEUM

Bugle Street, Southampton, SO14 2AD

Tel: 023 8063 5904
Fax: 023 8033 9601
Email: historic.sites@southampton.gov.uk
Full name: Tudor House Museum and Garden
Formed: 1912

Organisation type and purpose: Local government body, museum.
Parent body:
Southampton City Council
Tel: 023 8083 3333, fax: 023 8083 3381
Branch of the:
Civic Centre Cultural Services
Southampton, SO14 7LP, tel: 023 8063 5904, fax: 023 8033 9601, email/website: historic.sites@southampton.gov.uk
Branch of:
Cultural Services
Civic Centre, Southampton, SO14 7LP, tel: 023 8063 5904, fax: 023 8033 9601, email/website: historic.sites@southampton.gov.uk

Enquiries to: Historic Sites Manager
Direct tel: 023 8063 5904
Direct fax: 023 8033 9601
Other contacts: Cultural Services Manager for head of service covering museums.
Access:
Access to staff: By letter, by telephone, by fax, by email, visitors by prior appointment

General description:
Local history, social and domestic history, Tudor hall and unique Tudor garden.

Internet home pages:
http://www.southampton.gov.uk/leisure/heritage
Information about the building and garden, and current exhibitions.

2957
TUDOR MERCHANT'S HOUSE

Quay Hill, Tenby, Pembrokeshire, SA70 7BX

Tel: 01834 842279
Fax: 01834 842279

Organisation type and purpose: National organisation, registered charity (charity number 205846), historic building, house or site, suitable for ages: 8+.
Parent body:
The National Trust Office for Wales
Trinity Square, Llandudno, LL30 2DE, tel: 01492 860123, fax: 01492 860233

Enquiries to: Manager
Access:
Access to staff: By letter, by telephone
Access to building, collections or gallery: No prior appointment required
Hours: Easter to end Sep: Mon, Tue, Thu to Sat, 1000 to 1700; Sun, 1300 1700
Oct to Nov: Mon, Tues, Thu and Fri, 1000 to 1500; Sun 1200 to 1500

General description:
This late 15th century town house is characteristic of the area and of the time when Tenby was a thriving trading port. The groundfloor chimney at the rear of the house is a fine vernacular example, and the original scarfed roof-trusses survive. The remains of early frescos can be seen on three interior walls and the house is furnished to recreate family life from the Tudor period onwards. There is access to the small herb garden, weather permitting.
Information services:
Suitable for school groups. Hands-on activities. Children's quiz/trail.
Special visitor services: Materials and/or activities for children..

Internet home pages:
http://www.nationaltrust.org.uk

2958
TULLIE HOUSE MUSEUM & ART GALLERY

Castle Street, Carlisle, Cumbria, CA3 8TP

Tel: 01228 34781

Organisation type and purpose: Museum, art gallery.

Enquiries to: Manager
Access:
Access to staff: By letter, by telephone, in person
Access to building, collections or gallery: No prior appointment required
Hours: Apr to Oct, Mon to Sat, 1000 to 1700, Sun, 1200 to 1700; Nov to Mar, Mon to Sat, 1000 to 1600, Sun, 1200 to 1600
Other restrictions: Closed 25-26 Dec, 1 Jan

General description:
Hadrian's Wall, life of Luguvalium and Border history. Covers the archaeology of Cumbria from prehistoric times; Roman artefacts - Hadrian's Wall and other Cumbrian sites; Viking artefacts; mediaeval artefacts; social history; natural history; geology; paintings; ceramics.

2959
TUNBRIDGE WELLS MUSEUM AND ART GALLERY

Civic Centre, Mount Pleasant, Tunbridge Wells, Kent, TN1 1JN

Tel: 01892 554171
Minicom no. 01892 545449
Fax: 01892 534227
Formed: 1885

Organisation type and purpose: Museum, art gallery, suitable for ages: 5+.
Parent body:
Tunbridge Wells Borough Council (TWBC)
Town Hall, Tunbridge Wells, TN1 1JN

Enquiries to: Manager
Access:
Access to staff: By letter, by telephone
Access for disabled people: Parking provided, level entry, access to all public areas

General description:
From Tunbridge ware caskets to Victorian oil paintings and archaeology, and Minnie the LuLu terrier to historic fashions and dolls, there are displays to fascinate everyone at Tunbridge Wells Museum. The Museum displays include local history, Tunbridge ware, toys, dolls, games, historic costume, bygones, natural history and archaeology. The Gallery has frequently changing exhibitions of art and craft, including the Ashton Bequest of Victorian oil paintings and other works from the permanent collections, the work of contemporary artists, and touring shows.
Information services:
Special visitor services: Materials and/or activities for children.
Education services: Group education facilities, resources for Key Stages 1 and 2, 3, 4 and Further or Higher Education..
Collections:
The collections include local history, Tunbridge ware, toys, dolls, games, historic costume, bygones, natural history, fine art and archaeology
Catalogues:
Catalogue for all of the collections is only available in-house.
Printed publications:
A small range of books relating to Tunbridge Wells history and natural history

Internet home pages:
http://www.tunbridgewells.gov.uk/museum
General information, forthcoming exhibitions and events.

2960
TURNER HOUSE GALLERY

Plymouth Road, Penarth, Vale of Glamorgan, CF64 3DM

Tel: 029 2070 8870
Acronym or abbreviation: NMGW

Organisation type and purpose: Registered charity (charity number 525774), museum, art gallery, suitable for ages: 16+.
Parent body:
National Museums and Galleries of Wales
National Museum and Gallery Cardiff, Cathays Park, Cardiff, CF1 3NP, tel: 02920 397951, fax: 02920 373219
Other addresses:
National Museums & Galleries of Wales (NMGW)
Cathays Park, Cardiff, tel: 02920 397951

Enquiries to: Information Officer
Access:
Access to staff: By letter, by telephone, by fax

General description:
Art.
Collections:
Please contact the library at publications address
Printed publications:
Free publicity leaflet and various publications for purchase

Address for ordering publications:
Printed publications:
Shop Supervisor, National Museum and Gallery Cardiff
Cathays Park, Cardiff, CF10 3NP, tel: 029 2039 7951

Internet home pages:
http://www.nmgw.ac.uk
Admission prices, opening times, general information.

2961
TURNER MUSEUM OF GLASS
Sheffield University, Department of Engineering Materials, Sir Robert Hadfield Building, Mappin Street, Sheffield, South Yorkshire, S1 4DU

Tel: 0114 2825491

Organisation type and purpose: Museum, university department or institute, suitable for ages: 12+, consultancy, research organisation. University education and research.

Enquiries to: Manager
Direct tel: 0114 2225500
Direct fax: 0114 2225943
Direct email: j.w.smedley@sheffield.ac.uk
Access:
Access to staff: By letter, by telephone, by fax, by email, visitors by prior appointment
Access for disabled people: ramped entry

General description:
A collection of contemporary studio glass mainly from UK, Europe and USA. Also c. 500 items of glass ranging from Egyptian fragments; Roman and Syrian ware; 18th century English drinking glasses; Victorian pieces; and glass made in Europe and the USA between the wars 1920-1940.
Collections:
Albert Harland. 18th century English drinking glasses. 18th century. ca. 120
W E S Turner Collection, 20th century glass from Sweden, England, Czechoslovakia, USA, Germany, France, Italy, etc. c. 200 items

Internet home pages:
http://www.shef.ac.uk/turnermuseum

2962
TURNPIKE GALLERY
Leigh Library, Civic Square, Leigh, Lancashire, WN7 1EB

Tel: 01942 404469
Fax: 01942 404447
Email: turnpikegallery@wiganmbc.gov.uk
Formed: 1971

Organisation type and purpose: Local government body, art gallery, suitable for ages: all ages.

Enquiries to: Gallery Officer
Direct tel: 01942 404558
Direct email: k.meagan@wiganmbc.gov.uk
Other contacts: Visual Arts Outreach Officer for community-related projects.
Access:
Access to staff: By letter, by telephone, by fax, by email, in person, Internet web pages
Access for disabled people: ramped entry, access to all public areas, toilet facilities

General description:
A contemporary art gallery, staging 6-7 exhibitions per year, covering all areas of practising arts and crafts. All exhibitions are temporary, staging the work of professional artists.
Information services:
Special visitor services: Materials and/or activities for children.
Education services: Group education facilities.
Services for disabled people: For the visually impaired; for the hearing impaired.
Catalogues:
Catalogue for all of the collections is only available in-house.
Publications list:
is available in hard copy and online.

Internet home pages:
http://www.wiganmbc.gov.uk

2963
TURTON TOWER
Chapeltown Road, Turton, Bolton, Lancashire, BL7 0HG

Tel: 01204 852203
Fax: 01204 852203
Email: turtontower.lcc@btinternet.com
Full name: Lancashire County Museum Service, Turton Tower
Formed: 1987
Formerly: Turton Tower Museum

Organisation type and purpose: Local government body, registered charity, museum, art gallery, historic building, house or site, suitable for ages: 8+.
Parent body:
Lancashire County Museum Service (LCMS)
Stanley Street, Preston, PR1 4YP, tel: 01772 264061, fax: 01772 264079, email: information@mus.lancscc.gov.uk
Trustees of:
Turton Tower
Other address:
Lancashire County Museums
Stanley Street, Preston, PR1 4YP, tel: 01722 264061, fax: 01772 264079, email/website: information@mus.lancscc.gov.uk

Enquiries to: Curator
Other contacts: Curator (Applied Art)
Access:
Access to staff: By letter, by telephone, by fax, by email, in person, visitors by prior appointment
Access for disabled people: Parking provided

General description:
Turton Tower was originally built over five centuries ago by the Orrell family to defend their land, and later became a luxurious home. The house was lavishly furnished and extended both in Tudor and early Stuart periods. It contains furniture history, wood crafts (contemporary), English domestic furniture history, Lancashire country house history, general art history.
Collections:
Furniture, 10th-19th century
Holt bequest, ceramics, mainly porcelain, 19th century, 100 items
Bradshaw and Ashworth collections, domestic metalwork, 18th-19th century, 150 items
Portraits, 17th century
Catalogues:
Catalogue for library is in-house only. Catalogue for part of the collections is only available in-house.
Publications list:
is available in hard copy.
Printed publications:
Events leaflet
Leaflet

2964
TUTANKHAMUN EXHIBITION
High West Street, Dorchester, Dorset, DT1 1UW

Tel: 01305 269571
Fax: 01305 268885
Email: info@tutankhamun-exhibition.co.uk
Formed: 1987

Organisation type and purpose: Museum.
Parent body:
World Heritage
25 High West Street, Dorchester, Dorset, tel: 01305 269741, fax: 01305 268885, email: info@world-heritage.org.uk

Enquiries to: Manager
Direct tel: 01305 269741
Direct fax: 01305 268885
Direct email: tutom@aol.com
Access:
Access to staff: By letter, by telephone, by fax, visitors by prior appointment, Internet web pages
Hours: Mon to Fri, 0930 to 1730
Access to building, collections or gallery: No prior appointment required
Hours: Daily, 0930 to 1730; closed Dec, 24 to 26

General description:
Tutankhamun, his history and the discovery of the tomb; ancient Egypt, archaeology and Egyptology, mummification.
Information services:
Education services: Group education facilities, resources for Key Stage 2.
Services for disabled people: Displays and/or information at wheelchair height.
Collections:
Reconstruction of Tutankhamun's tomb including the discovery, antechamber and burial chamber, recreation of Tutankhamun's mummy, facsimiles of many of the major artefacts from Tutankhamun's tomb including the golden funerary mask and the harpooner
Publications list:
is available in hard copy.
Printed publications:
A wide selection of Egyptological books by other publishers availabe from the Exhibition Shop or via mailorder
The Tutankhamun Exhibition Souvenir Guide (£1.50)

Internet home pages:
http://www.tutankhamun-exhibition.co.uk
Information on the exhibition and its contents

2965
TUTBURY MUSEUM TRUST
Charity House, Duke Street, Tutbury, Burton-on-Trent, Staffordshire, DE13 9NE

Tel: 01283 815920

Organisation type and purpose: Museum. Maintained by volunteers.
Member of:
North Staffordshire Museums Association
Access:
Access to staff: By letter, by telephone

General description:
Collection of artefacts bequeathed to the village by Mr Aubrey Bailey, with additional donated items. Comprehensive details of the Fauld Explosion, the largest explosion in WWII with the exception of the atomic bomb.
Printed publications:
Leaflets

2966
TWEEDDALE MUSEUM
The Chambers Institute, High Street, Peebles, Borders, EH45 8AG

Tel: 01721 724820
Fax: 01721 724424
Email: rhannay@scotborders.gov.uk
Formed: 1859

Organisation type and purpose: Local government body, museum, art gallery, suitable for ages: 5+.
Parent body:
Scottish Borders Council Museum and Gallery Service
Tel: 01750 20096
Other addresses:
St Ronans Wells
Wells Brae, Innerleithen, EH44 6JE, tel: 01721 729820

Enquiries to: Curator
Access:
Access to staff: By letter only

General description:
The museum and picture gallery are housed in the Chambers Institution, which was given to the townspeople by Dr William Chambers, the publisher, in 1859. Three galleries display local history, and contemporary art.

continued overleaf

The Picture Gallery is an original Victorian gallery.
Information services:
Library available for reference (for conditions see Access above)
Wide selection of temporary exhibitions
Workshops
Suitable for school visits
Available for corporate events
80% of collection on computerised database
Special visitor services: Materials and/or activities for children.
Education services: Group education facilities, resources for Key Stages 1 and 2, 3 and 4..
Collections:
William Chambers' collection
Local history collections
Geology
Ethnography
Archaeology
Arms
Paintings
Catalogues:
Catalogue for library is in-house only. Catalogue for all of the collections is only available in-house.

Internet home pages:
http://www.scotborders.gov.uk

2967
TWENTY TWENTY APPLIED ARTS

3 High Street, Much Wenlock, Shropshire, TF13 6AA

Tel: 01952 727952
Formed: 1997

Organisation type and purpose: Art gallery, suitable for ages: 16+.

Enquiries to: Managing Director
Access:
Access to staff: By letter, by telephone, in person

General description:
A collection of contemporary craft for sale, precious and non-precious jewellery, studio ceramics and glass, carved wood, some textiles.

2968
TY MAWR WYBRNANT

Penmachno, Betws-y-Coed, Conwy, LL25 0HJ

Tel: 01690 760213
Formed: 1988

Organisation type and purpose: National organisation, registered charity (charity number 205846), historic building, house or site, suitable for ages: 5+.
Parent body:
The National Trust Office for Wales
Trinity Square, Llandudno, LL30 2DE, tel: 01492 860123, fax: 01492 860233
Other Addresses:
The National Trust
Dinar, Betws-y-Coed, tel: 01690 710636

Enquiries to: Curator
Direct tel: 07773 481473
Access:
Access to staff: By letter, by telephone
Access for disabled people: Parking provided, level entry, toilet facilities
Other restrictions: Ground floor accessible with assistance. No access to other floors.

General description:
Situated in the beautiful and secluded Wybrnant Valley, Ty Mawr was the birthplace of Bishop William Morgan (1545-1604), first translator of the entire Bible into Welsh. The house has been restored to its probable 16th to 17th century appearance, and houses a display of Welsh bibles. A footpath leads from the house through woodland and the surrounding fields, which are traditionally managed.
Information services:
Helpline available, tel no: 01690 760213.
Suitable for school groups. Children's guide. Children's quiz/trail.
Special visitor services: Guided tours..
Collections:
Collection of books
Publications list:
is available in hard copy.
Printed publications:
Publications available for purchase

Internet home pages:
http://www.nationaltrust.org.uk

2969
TYMPERLEYS CLOCK MUSEUM

Trinity Street, Colchester, Essex, CO1 1JN

Tel: 01206 282943
Minicom no. 01206 500145
Fax: 01206 282925
Email: tom.hodgson@colchester.gov.uk

Organisation type and purpose: Local government body, museum, historic building, house or site, suitable for ages: all ages.
Other addresses:
Museum Resource Centre
14 Ryegate Road, Colchester, Essex, tel: 01206 282931, fax: 01206 282925

Enquiries to: Secretary
Access:
Access to staff: By letter, by telephone, by fax, by email, visitors by prior appointment
Access for disabled people: ramped entry, access to all public areas, toilet facilities

General description:
Horology, Colchester-made clocks and watches.
Information services:
Special visitor services: Materials and/or activities for children.
Services for disabled people: Displays and/or information at wheelchair height.
Collections:
Clocks, watches, time-pieces
Catalogues:
Catalogue for library is in-house only. Catalogue for all of the collections is available in-house and part is on-line.

Internet home pages:
http://www.colchestermuseums.org.uk
Tymperleys.

2970
TYNEDALE COUNCIL MUSEUMS SERVICE

Dept of Leisure and Tourism, Prospect House, Hexham, Northumberland, NE46 3NH

Tel: 01434 652351
Fax: 01434 652425
Email: museum@tynedale.gov.uk
Formed: 1980

Organisation type and purpose: Local government body, museum, historic building, house or site, suitable for ages: 8+.

Enquiries to: Museums Officer
Access:
Access to staff: By letter, by telephone, by fax, by email, in person, visitors by prior appointment, Internet web pages
Access to building, collections or gallery: No prior appointment required
Hours: Easter to end Oct: daily, 1000 to 1630
Nov to Feb to Easter: Sat, Mon, Tue, 1000 to 1630
Other restrictions: Closed Dec, Jan.

General description:
The history of the Border Reivers; military history, including arms and armour; social history; family history; and the history of the Old Gaol, Moothall and the House of Correction.
Information services:
Library available for reference (for conditions see Access above)
Special visitor services: Guided tours, materials and/or activities for children.
Education services: Group education facilities, resources for Key Stages 2 and 3.
Services for disabled people: For the visually impaired; for the hearing impaired.
Collections:
Border library. Music, history and culture of the area.
Catalogues:
Catalogue for library is in-house only. Catalogue for part of the collections is only available in-house.

Internet home pages:
http://www.tynedale.gov.uk

2971
TYNEMOUTH CASTLE AND PRIORY

North Shields, Tyne and Wear, NE30 4BZ

Tel: 0191 257 1090

Organisation type and purpose: Historic building, house or site.
Parent body:
English Heritage (North East Region)
Tel: 0191 269 1227/8, fax: 0191 261 1130

Enquiries to: Manager
Access:
Access to staff: By letter, by telephone, in person
Access to building, collections or gallery: No prior appointment required
Hours: End Mar to end Sep: daily, 1000 to 1800
Oct: daily, 1000 to 1700
Beg Nov to end Mar: Wed to Sun, 1000 to 1600
Other restrictions: Closed 1300 to 1400 in winter.
Closed 24 to 26 Dec, 1 Jan.
Opening times are subject to change, for up-to-date information contact English Heritage by phone or visit the website.

General description:
It has been a Saxon monastery, a Benedictine priory, founded in 1090, a medieval castle and a World War I gun battery. Castle wall and gatehouse enclose the substantial remains of the priory. The ornate eastern parts of the Benedictine Priory church are only just short of their original height of over twenty-two metres. Beneath them is the small 15th century Percy chapel, restored in the mid-19th century, with its elaborately vaulted ceiling still intact. You can also explore the restored magazines of a coastal defence gun battery.

Internet home pages:
http://www.english-heritage.org.uk

2972
TYNTESFIELD

Wraxall, North Somerset, BS48 1NT

Tel: 0870 458 4500 (information)

Organisation type and purpose: National organisation, registered charity (charity number 205846), historic building, house or site, suitable for ages: all ages.
Parent body:
The National Trust (South West Region)
Regional Office for Wessex, tel: 01985 843600

Enquiries to: Manager

General description:
Tyntesfield is a spectacular Victorian country house and estate, situated on a ridge overlooking the beautiful Yeo Valley, inspired and remodelled by John Norton in 1864, for William Gibbs, a successful merchant. The mansion, an extraordinary Gothic Revival extravaganza, bristling with towers and turrets, survives with its original Victorian interior intact, an unrivalled collection of Victorian decorative arts, an insight into life below stairs and a sumptuously decorated private Chapel. It is surrounded by 200ha (500 acres) of landscaped gardens, kitchen gardens, park,

farmland and estate buildings which include a home farm and sawmill.

Internet home pages:
http://www.nationaltrust.org.uk/tyntesfield

2973
TY'N-Y-COED UCHAF

Penmachno, Betws-y-Coed, Conwy, LL24 0PS

Tel: 01690 760229

Organisation type and purpose: National organisation, registered charity (charity number 205846), historic building, house or site, suitable for ages: 8+.
Parent body:
The National Trust Office for Wales
Trinity Square, Llandudno, LL30 2DE, tel: 01492 860123, fax: 01492 860233

Enquiries to: Manager
Access:
Access to staff: By letter, by telephone

General description:
A traditional smallholding with 19th century farmhouse and outbuildings, providing a fascinating record of an almost-vanished way of life. The house is approached by an interesting walk along the River Machno through fields of nature and conservation interest.

Internet home pages:
http://www.nationaltrust.org.uk

2974
TYRWHITT-DRAKE MUSEUM OF CARRIAGES, THE

Archbishops' Stables, Mill Street, Maidstone, Kent, ME15 6YE

Tel: 01622 754497
Fax: 01622 685022
Acronym or abbreviation: Carriage Museum
Formed: 1946

Organisation type and purpose: Local government body, museum.
Parent body:
Maidstone Borough Council (MBC)
13 Tonbridge Road, Maidstone, Kent, tel: 01622 602000
Other address:
Maidstone Museum & Bentlif Art Gallery
St Faiths Street, Maidstone, ME14 1LH, tel: 01622 754497, fax: 01622 685022

Enquiries to: Collections Manager
Other contacts: (1) Marketing Manager (2) Cultural & Tourism Development Manager for (1) publicity etc (2) overall responsibility.
Access:
Access to staff: By letter, by telephone, by fax, in person, visitors by prior appointment
Hours: Mon to Fri, 0900 to 1700
Access to building, collections or gallery: No prior appointment required
Hours: Mon to Fri, 1030 to 1700
Other restrictions: No prior appointment required from 1 Mar to 31 Oct; prior appointment required for groups only from 1 Nov to 28 Feb.

General description:
Carriages, transport.
Collections:
Broom Collection of glass plate negatives of Royal Mews
Carriage and coaching library
Carriage designs
Carriage making Companies' papers
Catalogues:
Catalogue for library is in-house only. Catalogue for all of the collections is only available in-house.
Publications list:
is available in hard copy.
Printed publications:
Guide (£1.50 plus p&p)

2975
ULLAPOOL MUSEUM & VISITOR CENTRE

7 & 8 West Argyle Street, Ullapool, Ross-shire, IV26 2TY

Tel: 01854 612987
Fax: 01854 612987
Email: ulmuseum@waverider.co.uk
Formed: 1988

Organisation type and purpose: Membership association (membership is by subscription, qualification), present number of members: 340, registered charity (charity number SCO 18225), museum.

Enquiries to: Manager
Access:
Access to staff: By letter, by telephone, by fax, by email, in person
Access to building, collections or gallery: No access other than to staff
Hours: Apr to Oct: Mon to Sat, 0930 to 1730
Nov to Feb: Wed, Thu, Sat, 1100 to 1500
Mar: Mon to Sat, 1100 to 1500
Other restrictions: No Sun opening.
Access for disabled people: level entry, toilet facilities
Other restrictions: All displays upstairs, duplicated downstairs, disabled access to upstairs area restricted due to building's listed status.

General description:
Parish of Lochbroom: social history; natural history; education; emigration; fishing; church history; genealogy; general reference material; photographic archive.
Information services:
Library available for reference (for conditions see Access above)
Group educational facilities by appointment.
Special visitor services: Tape recorded guides, materials and/or activities for children.
Education services: Group education facilities, resources for Key Stages 1 and 2, 3, 4 and Further or Higher Education.
Services for disabled people: For the visually impaired; for the hearing impaired; displays and/or information at wheelchair height.
Catalogues:
Catalogue for part of the collections is only available in-house.
Printed publications:
Museum Leaflet (free available direct)
A Walk around Old Ullapool (leaflet, 20p, available direct)
Postcard of Village Bicentential Tapestries (50p, available direct)
Postcard of Bicentential Quilt (20p, available direct)
Electronic and video products:
Around About Ullapool - An historical tour (tape, £1.95, with photo album, £3.50, available direct)

2976
ULSTER FOLK AND TRANSPORT MUSEUM

Cultra, Holywood, Co Down, BT18 0EU

Tel: 028 9042 8428
Fax: 028 9042 8728

Organisation type and purpose: National government body, registered charity, museum, historic building, house or site, suitable for ages: 5+.
Parent body:
Museums and Galleries of Northern Ireland (MAGNI)

Enquiries to: Managing Director
Access:
Access to staff: By letter, by fax
Hours: Mon to Fri, 0900 to 1700
Access for disabled people: Parking provided, ramped entry, access to all public areas, toilet facilities

General description:
Transport and history of Ulster.
Information services:
Library available for reference (for conditions see Access above)
Special visitor services: Guided tours, materials and/or activities for children.
Education services: Group education facilities, resources for Key Stages 1 and 2, 3, 4 and Further or Higher Education..

Internet home pages:
http://www.nidex.com/uftm
General information site, photographic archive.

2977
ULSTER HISTORY PARK

Cullion, Lislap, Omagh, Co Tyrone, BT79 7SU

Tel: 028 8164 8188
Fax: 028 8164 8011
Email: uhp@omagh.gov.uk
Formed: 1990

Organisation type and purpose: Local government body, museum, suitable for ages: all ages.
Parent body:
Omagh District Council
The Grange, Mountjoy Road, Omagh, Co Tyrone, BT78, tel: 028 8224 5321, fax: 028 8224 3888, email: info@omagh.gov.uk

Enquiries to: Manager
Access:
Access to staff: By letter, by telephone, by email, in person
Access to building, collections or gallery: No prior appointment required
Access for disabled people: Parking provided, level entry, toilet facilities

General description:
Illustrates the settlement history of Ireland from the Mesolithic Period to the 17th century. The emphasis is on full-scale models of houses and other buildings set in a 35-acre site.
Information services:
Special visitor services: Guided tours, materials and/or activities for children.
Education services: Resources for Key Stages 1 and 2, 3 and Further or Higher Education.
Services for disabled people: Displays and/or information at wheelchair height.

Internet home pages:
http://www.omagh.gov.uk/historypark.htm

2978
ULSTER MUSEUM

Botanic Gardens, Belfast, BT9 5AB

Tel: 028 9038 3000
Minicom no. 028 9038 3008
Fax: 028 9038 3003/383103
Email: john.wilson.um@nics.gov.uk
Formed: 1929

Organisation type and purpose: National government body, registered charity (charity number XR 29838), museum, art gallery, suitable for ages: all ages.
Parent body:
Museums and Galleries of Northern Ireland (MAGNI)
at the same address
Branch site is the:
Armagh County Museum
Tel: 01861 523070, fax: 01861 522631, email/website: catherine.mccullough.um@nics.gov.uk
Subsidiary body:
Centre for Environmental Data and Recording (CEDaR)
Tel: 01232 383154, fax: 01232 383003, email/website: damien.mcterran.um@nics.gov.uk

Enquiries to: Managing Director
Other contacts: Marketing Officer 028 9038 3110
Access:
Access to staff: By letter, by telephone, by fax, by email, in person, visitors by prior appointment, Internet web pages

continued overleaf

Other restrictions: Specialist staff contacts available online.
Access to building, collections or gallery: No prior appointment required
Hours: Mon to Fri, 1000 to 1700; Sat, 1300 to 1700; Sun, 1400 to 1700
Access for disabled people: Parking provided, ramped entry, access to all public areas, toilet facilities
Other restrictions: Parking - advance notice preferred, particularly at weekends.

General description:
Archaeology, ethnography, N Ireland local history, militaria, photography, topographic prints and maps, fine art, applied art (incl. glass, silver, ceramics, costume, jewellery), mineralogy, petrology, stratigraphy, palaeontology, vascular plants, algae, mollusca, entomology, vertebrate zoology, marine biology, biological and geological site records.
Information services:
Library available for reference (for conditions see Access above), on-line searching, selective dissemination services
Reproduction of photographic images from the collections; identification of objects.
Special visitor services: Materials and/or activities for children.
Education services: Group education facilities..
Collections:
A R Hogg Collection (historical photographs, *c.* 1900-1939
Belfast Natural History and Philosophical Collection (general)
Belfast Naturalist's Field Club Collection (natural history)
Davis Collection (mineralogy)
Geological Survey of Ireland (geology, NI counties)
Grainger Collection (general)
Hanna Collection (mineralogy)
Historic Irish glass and silver; contemporary studio glass and ceramics
Historic & topographical photographs; militaria
Industrial machinery
Irish Art 17th-20th century
Langham Collection (zoology)
Patterson Collection (fine art)
Prehistoric to Medieval Irish artefacts
Preserved animals and plants
Queen's University Belfast Herbarium (botany) and many other smaller named collections
R J Welch Collection (historical photographs, *c.* 1885-1936)
Robert Lloyd Patterson Collection (fine art)
Rocks, fossils, minerals and gemstones; rare geological maps and early books
Spanish Armada Collection; South Pacific and Native American material
Welch Collection (mollusca, zoology)
Welcome Collection (prehistory)
Wright Collection (palaeontology and zoology)
Catalogues:
Catalogue for part of the collections is published.
Trade and statistical:
Environmental data for Northern Ireland via CEDaR.
Publications list:
is available in hard copy.
Printed publications:
Various publications on Art, Archaeology and Ethnography, Local History and Natural Sciences
Annual Report
Catalogues of the Collections (irregular)
Electronic and video products:
Timescapes (CD-ROM, CDi)

Internet home pages:
http://www.ulstermuseum.org.uk
Opening hours, services, exhibitions, general information.

2979
ULSTER-AMERICAN FOLK PARK
2 Mellon Road, Castletown, Omagh, Co Tyrone, BT78 5QY

Tel: 028 8224 3292
Fax: 028 8224 2241
Email: uafp@iol.ic
Acronym or abbreviation: UAFP
Formed: 1976

Organisation type and purpose: Museum, research organisation.
Parent body:
National Museums & Galleries NI (MAGNI)
Botanic Gardens, Belfast, tel: 028 9038 3000
Affiliated to:
Scotch-Irish Trust of Ulster

Enquiries to: Director
Access:
Access to staff: By letter, by telephone, by fax, by email, in person, visitors by prior appointment, Internet web pages
Hours: Mon to Fri, 0900 to 1700
Access for disabled people: Parking provided, ramped entry, level entry, access to all public areas, toilet facilities
Other restrictions: Some disabled adapted bedrooms in the museum residential centre

General description:
Emigration history, interpretation of 18th and 19th century life in Ireland and America, vernacular architecture of the period.
Information services:
Library available for reference (for conditions see Access above), on-line searching, bibliography compilation
Reminisence Groups working with community and disadvantaged groups.
Special visitor services: Guided tours, materials and/or activities for children.
Education services: Resources for Key Stages 1 and 2, 3, 4 and Further or Higher Education.
Services for disabled people: For the hearing impaired; displays and/or information at wheelchair height.
Collections:
Specialist research library
Emigration Database, contains 30,000+ documents
Artefacts, prints, furniture, documants, manuscripts
Catalogues:
Catalogue for library is in-house only. Catalogue for all of the collections is only available in-house.
Publications list:
is available in hard copy.

Internet home pages:
http://www.folkpark.com
Background information on museums, exhibitions etc, forthcoming events.

2980
UNIVERSITY COLLEGE LONDON
College Art Collections, The Strang Print Room, Wilkins Building, Gower Street, London, WC1E 6BT

Tel: 020 7679 2540
Fax: 020 7813 2803
Email: college.art@ucl.ac.uk
Formed: 1847

Organisation type and purpose: Museum.
Parent body:
University College London (UCL)
Gower Street, London, WC1E 6BT

Enquiries to: Curator
Direct email: e.chambers@ucl.ac.uk
Access:
Access to staff: By letter, by telephone, by fax, by email
Hours: Curators available to answer enquiries, Mon to Fri, 1000 to 1700

General description:
Drawings and sculpture models by John Flaxman; 16th century German drawings; European and British prints c1490-1950; Slade School of Fine Art Prize Collection of paintings, drawings and prints c1890 to present day.
Collections:
Flaxman drawings and sculpture
Grote Collection of 16c German drawings and prints
Slade Prize Collection of paintings, drawings and prints, 1890 to present day
Henry Vaughan Bequest of English watercolours and British and Old Master prints
Catalogues:
Catalogue for all of the collections is only available in-house but part is published.
Publications list:
is available in hard copy.
Printed publications:
Recent publications include:
After Delaroche: Art and its Reproductions in Mid-Nineteenth Century France (Bann S, 1998)
History of Art Department, C J Grant's Political Drama: A Radical Satirist Rediscovered (1998)
The Old Radical: Representations of Jeremy Bentham (Fuller C ed, 1998)
Etching in England (Chambers E, 1999)
History of Art Department, Prints as Propaganda: The German Reformation (1999)
The Wood-Engraving Revival and the Slade, 1921-1950 (Owens S, 1999)

Internet home pages:
http://collections.ucl.ac.uk

2981
UNIVERSITY COLLEGE LONDON
Department of Earth Sciences, Gower Street, London, WC1E 6BT

Tel: 020 7679 7900
Email: w.kirk@ucl.ac.uk or earthsci@ucl.ac.uk
Formed: c1841
Formerly: Department of Geological Sciences, date of change, 2002

Organisation type and purpose: Museum, university department or institute.

Enquiries to: Curator
Access:
Access to staff: By letter, by telephone, by email, visitors by prior appointment
Access for disabled people: access to all public areas, toilet facilities

General description:
Geology.
Information services:
Education services: Resources for Key Stages 2 and 3..
Collections:
Reference and teaching collections of rocks, minerals and fossils
Special Collection: Johnston-Lavis Collection of rocks and minerals, especially Italian volcanics c. 1900, 1500 minerals and 2500 rocks
Rare books held in Manuscrips and Rare Books Room in library
Electronic and video products:
Maps in the Classroom Teachers Resource Pack

Internet home pages:
http://www.earthsciences.ucl.ac.uk/

2982
UNIVERSITY GALLERY
University of Northumbria, Sandyford Road, Newcastle upon Tyne, NE1 8ST

Tel: 0191 227 4424
Fax: 0191 227 4718
Email: mara-helen.wood@northumbria.ac.uk
Formed: 1977

Organisation type and purpose: Art gallery.

Enquiries to: Director
Access:
Access to staff: By letter, by telephone, by fax, by email

Access to building, collections or gallery: No prior appointment required
Hours: Mon to Thu, 1000 to 1700; Fri, Sat, 1000 to 1600

General description:
Contemporary art.

Internet home pages:
http://www.northumbria.ac.uk/universitygallery

2983
UNIVERSITY MUSEUM

Archaeology Department, Nottingham University, University Park, Nottingham, NG7 2RD

Tel: 0115 951 4820
Fax: 0115 951 4812
Email: roger.wilson@nottingham.ac.uk
Formed: 1960s

Organisation type and purpose: Museum, university department or institute, suitable for ages: 16+.

Enquiries to: Director
Direct tel: 0115 951 4813
Other contacts: Secretary
Access:
Access to staff: By letter, by email, visitors by prior appointment
Other restrictions: At present no full-time staff attached to the museum.
Access to building, collections or gallery: Prior appointment required
Access for disabled people: ramped entry, toilet facilities

General description:
Archaeology of the East Midlands (prehistoric, Romano-British, Anglo-Saxon, medieval, post-medieval). Some archaeological material from Mediterranean (Cypriot Bronze Age material, Athenian red figure pottery, Etruscan cinerary urn).
Collections:
The Felix Oswald Collection of Roman artefacts, and his papers and files are deposited with the Museum
Samian pottery (best collection of Samian in Britain)
Romano-British material from a Nottinghamshire site

Internet home pages:
http://www.
Under construction.

2984
UNIVERSITY OF SURREY

See - National Resource Centre for Dance

2985
UNIVERSITY OF SUSSEX

See - Gardner Arts Centre Limited

2986
UNIVERSITY OF WALES

See - School of Art Gallery and Museum

2987
UPLAND KINGDOM DISCOVERY CENTRE

See - Rheged

2988
UPNOR CASTLE

Upnor, Wainscott, Rochester, Kent

Tel: 01634 718742

Organisation type and purpose: Historic building, house or site.
Parent body:
English Heritage (South East Region)
Eastgate Court, 195-205 High Street, Guildford, Surrey, GU1 3EH, tel: 01483 252000, fax: 01483 252001, email: www.english-heritage.org.uk
Managed by:
Medway City Council

Enquiries to: Curator
Access:
Access to building, collections or gallery: No prior appointment required
Hours: April to 30th September, daily, 1000 to 1800, 1st to 31st October, daily 1000 to 1600.
Other restrictions: When Castle is closed call 01634 827980 for entry details.

General description:
16th century gun fort, built to protect Queen Elizabeth I warships.
Information services:
Special visitor services: Tape recorded guides..

Internet home pages:
http://www.english-heritage.org.uk

2989
UPPARK HOUSE

South Harting, Petersfield, Hampshire, GU31 5QR

Tel: 01730 825415
Fax: 01730 825873
Email: uppark@nationaltrust.org.uk
Formed: 1956

Organisation type and purpose: National organisation, registered charity (charity number 205846), historic building, house or site.
Parent body:
The National Trust (South and South East Region)
South East Regional Office, tel: 01372 453401

Enquiries to: Property Manager
Other contacts: House Manager
Access:
Access to staff: By letter, by email
Access for disabled people: Parking provided, ramped entry, access to all public areas, toilet facilities
Other restrictions: Designated parking. Drop-off point. 6 manual wheelchairs available. Ground floor fully accessible. Level entrance to shop. Ramped entrance to restaurant. Grounds largely accessible. Recommended route map. Exhibition building, also in basement of house

General description:
A fine late 17th century house set high on the South Downs with magnificent sweeping views to the sea. The drama of the 1989 fire and restoration adds to the magic of this romantic house. The elegant Georgian interior houses a famous Grand Tour collection that includes paintings, furniture and ceramics. An 18th century dolls' house with original contents is one of the star items in the collection. The complete servants' quarters in the basement are shown as they were in Victorian days when H. G. Wells' mother was housekeeper. The beautiful and peaceful garden is now fully restored in the early 19th century 'picturesque' style, in a downland and woodland setting.
Information services:
Booked group guided tours (mornings) by arrangement.
Braille guide. Large-print guide. Scented garden.
Suitable for school groups. Hands-on activities. Children's guide. Children's quiz/trail only in school holidays.
Front-carrying baby slings for loan.
Special visitor services: Guided tours, materials and/or activities for children.
Education services: Resources for Further or Higher Education.
Services for disabled people: For the visually impaired.
Collections:
An 18th century 'Grand Tour' collection
Paintings by L Giordana, Vernet, Battoni, Davis
18th century furniture
Printed publications:
Guide Book (£4.50)
Children's Guide (£1.80)
Short Guide (80p)
Uppark Restored (£12.99)

Internet home pages:
http://www.nationaltrust.org.uk

2990
UPPER HAMBLE COUNTRY PARK

See - Manor Farm Country Park

2991
UPTON HOUSE

Nr Banbury, Oxfordshire, OX15 6HT

Tel: 01295 670266
Fax: 01295 670266
Email: uptonhouse@nationaltrust.org.uk
Formed: 1895

Organisation type and purpose: Registered charity (charity number 205846), historic building, house or site, suitable for ages: 5+.
Parent body:
The National Trust (West Midlands)
West Midlands Regional Office, tel: 01743 708100
Other addresses:
The National Trust
Head Office
36 Queen Anne's Gate, London, SW1H 9AS, tel: 0870 609 5380, fax: 020 7222 5097

Enquiries to: Property Manager
Access:
Access to staff: By letter, by telephone, by fax, by email, visitors by prior appointment
Access for disabled people: Parking provided, ramped entry
Other restrictions: Designated parking 30yds. Transfer available. Drop-off point. Steps to entrance. Accessible
entrance signed side entrance via ramps. Ground floor fully accessible. No access to other floors. Photograph album. Level entrance to shop. Level entrance to restaurant. Garden partially accessible: lawn on same level as house. Terraces descending steeply into valley. One volunteer-driven buggy provides access to lower part of garden.

General description:
The house, built in 1695 of mellow local stone, was purchased and remodelled 1927-29 by Walter Samuel, 2nd Viscount Bearsted, Chairman of Shell 1921- 46 and son of the founder of that company. Upton contains his outstanding collection of English and continental Old Master paintings including works by Hogarth, Stubbs, Guardi, Canaletto, Brueghel and El Greco; tapestries; French porcelain; Chelsea figures and 18th century furniture. There is also an exhibition of paintings and publicity posters commissioned by Shell during Viscount Bearsted's chairmanship; also Lady Bearsted's restored Art Deco bathroom. The garden is very fine, with terraces

herbaceous borders, kitchen garden, ornamental pools and an interesting 1930s water-garden together with the National Collection of Asters.
Information services:
Helpline available, tel no: 01684 855365.
Guided tours outside normal opening hours by written arrangement. Refreshments can be included. Fine arts study tours, jazz concert, garden tours and other events: please contact the property for details.
Touch list.
Children's quiz/trail. Adult study days.
Special visitor services: Guided tours, materials and/or activities for children.
Services for disabled people: For the visually impaired; displays and/or information at wheelchair height.
Collections:
Spectacular garden, including NCCPG National Collection of Asters

continued overleaf

The Bearsted Collection of paintings and porcelain including paintings by Hogarth, Stubbs, Guardi, Canaletto, Bruegel, Bosch and El Greco
18th century Chelsea Figures, The Dudley Vases (Chelsea, Gold Anchor Period), Vincennes and Sèvres 18th century French porcelain
Catalogues:
Catalogue for part of the collections is published.
Printed publications:
Picture List (free, plus p&p)
Guide Book (£2.25 plus p&p)
Garden Leaflet (10p plus p&p)
Countrylife Article about the House (50p plus p&p)
Porcelain Catalogues (£3 plus p&p)

Internet home pages:
http://www.nationaltrust.org.uk

2992
URE MUSEUM OF GREEK ARCHAEOLOGY

Department of Classics, The University, Whiteknights, Reading, Berkshire, RG6 6AA

Tel: 0118 931 6599
Fax: 0118 931 6661
Email: ure@reading.ac.uk
Formed: 1922

Organisation type and purpose: Museum, university department or institute, suitable for ages: 8+.
Private museum.
Parent body:
University of Reading

Enquiries to: Curator
Other contacts: Assistant Curator for availability for group bookings/education.
Access:
Access to staff: By letter, by telephone, by fax, by email, in person, Internet web pages
Hours: Open to the public most days, phone for details
Other restrictions: School children by prior appointment.
Access for disabled people: Parking provided, access to all public areas, toilet facilities

General description:
Greek painted pottery, research notes relating to it, excavation records, Egyptian antiquities, Cypriot antiquities.
Information services:
Special visitor services: Guided tours, materials and/or activities for children.
Education services: Group education facilities, resources for Key Stage 2 and Further or Higher Education..
Collections:
Rhitson excavation records
Printed publications:
Part of the collection was published in Corpus Vasorum Antiquorum

Internet home pages:
http://www.rdg.ac.uk/Ure/Schools
Museum tour for schools.
http://www.rdg.ac.uk/Ure
Brief description of museum.

2993
USHER GALLERY

Lindum Road, Lincoln, LN2 1NN

Tel: 01522 527980
Fax: 01522 560165
Email: usher.gallery@lincolnshire.gov.uk
Formed: 1927

Organisation type and purpose: Local government body, art gallery.
Parent body:
Lincolnshire County Council
County Offices, Newland, Lincoln, LN1 1YL, tel: 01522 552222, fax: 01522 552243

Enquiries to: Principal Keeper
Access:
Access to staff: By letter, by telephone, by fax, by email, visitors by prior appointment
Access to building, collections or gallery: No prior appointment required
Hours: Tue to Sat, 1000 to 1730; Sun, 1430 to 1700
Access for disabled people: Parking provided, access to all public areas

General description:
This regional gallery houses collections of fine and decorative arts including watches, miniatures, ceramics and silver. Important collections of works by Peter De Wint (1784-1849), and topographical paintings of Lincolnshire. There is an inspiring programme of temporary exhibitions.
Information services:
CD-ROM based services
Collections database being established.
Runs education programmes for schools, art workshops for children 5-11, Saturdays during term-time, and weekdays during half-term. Also workshops for children and adults with special needs, a collection of artefacts available for both school and special needs groups. A junior guide is available for 7 -12 year olds.
Art Loan Scheme, works can be hired for 12 months by people living in Lincolnshire.
Artist in residence, artists are invited to work within the gallery, to display recent work, hold workshops and meet visitors.
Special visitor services: Materials and/or activities for children.
Education services: Group education facilities, resources for Key Stages 1 and 2, 3 and 4..
Collections:
Tennyson Collection: a collection of portraits, photographs and personal items associated with the Linconshire born Poet Laureate Lord Alfred Tennyson (1809-1892) is currently on long-term loan from the Tennyson Research Centre. Various items are on display including the poet's distinctive cloak, hat and walking sticks, and a drawing of the Tennyson Family home by Edward Lear.
Peter De Wint (1784-1849) largest public collection of his works, c. 1802-1849, 160 items
Benjamin West, portrait of Sir Joseph Banks (1743-1820)
Torksey porcelain from the Brampton factory, 200 items
Social history: a diverse collection of objects with a social history context, many have been donated by local people.
Catalogues:
Catalogue for part of the collections is published.
Publications list:
is available in hard copy.

2994
USK CASTLE 2001 LIMITED

Castle House, Monmouth Road, Usk, Monmouthshire, NP15 1SD

Tel: 01291 672563
Formed: 2001

Organisation type and purpose: Registered charity (charity number 1089856), historic building, house or site, suitable for ages: 5+.
Supported by:
Usk Castle Friends

Enquiries to: Manager
Access:
Access to staff: By letter, by telephone, in person
Access to building, collections or gallery: No prior appointment required
Access for disabled people: Parking provided
Other restrictions: Partial access.

General description:
The castle originates from shortly after 1066, but mainly from the medieval period about 1170. The activities of the Marcher Lords, their families and the medieval town of Usk.
Information services:
Special visitor services: Materials and/or activities for children.
Education services: Group education facilities..

Internet home pages:
http://www.uskcastle.com
http://www.castlesofwales.com

2995
USK RURAL LIFE MUSEUM

The Malt Barn, New Market Street, Usk, Gwent, NP15 1AU

Tel: 01291 673777
Formed: 1966
Formerly: Gwent Rural Life Museum, date of change, 2000

Organisation type and purpose: Registered charity (charity number 502130), museum, suitable for ages: all ages.
Founded as an educational charity, and still gives priority to work with children and young people.
Parent body:
Rural Crafts Preservation Society
At the same address

Enquiries to: Chairman
Other contacts: Honorary Secretary
Access:
Access to staff: By letter, by telephone, by email, in person, visitors by prior appointment
Access to building, collections or gallery: No prior appointment required
Hours: Mon to Sat, 1000 to 1600; Sun, 1400 to 1600
Access for disabled people: level entry, toilet facilities
Other restrictions: Parking nearby, internal ramps, access to most areas.

General description:
Rural life from 1800s up to today, vintage tools, tractors, machinery.
Information services:
Special visitor services: Guided tours, materials and/or activities for children.
Education services: Group education facilities, resources for Key Stages 1 and 2, 3, 4 and Further or Higher Education.
Services for disabled people: Displays and/or information at wheelchair height.
Collections:
Computerised catalogue completed 2001,2002/3 archive, and web access to archive will be set up
Catalogues:
Catalogue for all of the collections is only available in-house.

2996
UTTOXETER HERITAGE CENTRE

Carter Street, Uttoxeter, Staffordshire, ST14 8EU

Tel: 01889 567176
Fax: 01889 568426
Formed: 1985

Organisation type and purpose: Local government body, museum, historic building, house or site, suitable for ages: 8+.
Collection and display of the history of the town of Uttoxeter.
Parent body:
Uttoxeter Town Council
Town Hall, High Street, Uttoxeter, Staffordshire, tel: 01889 564085, fax: 01889 568426
Member of:
North Staffordshire Museums Association

Enquiries to: Administrator
Access:
Access to staff: By letter, by telephone, by fax, in person
Other restrictions: Limited number of staff.

General description:
The Heritage Centre is located in a small part timber-framed 17th century building. Our collections are aimed at assisting in putting over to the public elements of the history of the town. We have permanent displays on 17th century

Uttoxeter and a Victorian bedroom, and changing displays on varying themes. Our collections are fairly limited, but we have a fair-sized photographic collection.
Information services:
Special visitor services: Guided tours..
Collections:
Photographic Collections - Uttoxeter and Environs
Staffordshire Trade Tokens - Orme Collection
Small but varied general collection of display items and records
Catalogues:
Catalogue for all of the collections is only available in-house.
Printed publications:
A limited number of publications which include:
A Guide to the Building (basic photocopied format)
Uttoxeter in 1658 (basic photocopied format)
Railways Around Uttoxeter (basic photocopied format)

2997
VALE AND DOWNLAND MUSEUM
Church Street, Wantage, Oxfordshire, OX12 8BL

Tel: 01235 771447
Fax: 01235 764316
Email: museum@wantage.com
Formed: 1975

Organisation type and purpose: Independently owned, museum, historic building, house or site, suitable for ages: all ages.
Registered charity trust.
Owned by the Trust:
Lains Barn

Enquiries to: Curator
Access:
Access to staff: By letter, by email
Access for disabled people: ramped entry, toilet facilities
Other restrictions: Access to nearly all areas.

General description:
A community museum which presents the geology, archaeology and history of the Vale of the White Horse and Downland area of Oxfordshire. Interpretation is shown via a range of interactive media to ensure a good mix of entertainment and education; objects relating to the Wantage Tramway; collection of photographs of the local area.
Information services:
Special visitor services: Guided tours, materials and/or activities for children.
Education services: Group education facilities, resources for Key Stages 1 and 2 and 3.
Services for disabled people: Displays and/or information at wheelchair height.
Collections:
Social History
Archaeology
Photographic
Printed publications:
Brochure (free)
Electronic and video products:
The White Horse of Uffington (CD-ROM, £6.99)
The Vale in Pictures (CD-ROM, £9.99)
The Tanners of Wantage (CD-ROM, £9.95)
The Altered Earth/Taming The White Horse (video, £9.99)

Internet home pages:
http://www.wantage.com/museum

2998
VALE OF GLAMORGAN RAILWAY COMPANY LIMITED
Barry Island Station, Romanwell Road, Barry Island, Vale of Glamorgan, CF62 5TH

Tel: 01446 748816
Fax: 01446 749018
Email: info@valeglamrail.co.uk
Acronym or abbreviation: VOGR
Formed: 1997

Organisation type and purpose: Museum, historic building, house or site, suitable for ages: all ages.
Steam Heritage Centre for pleasure and educational purposes.
Affiliated to the:
Council for Museums in Wales

Enquiries to: Librarian and Archivist
Access:
Access to staff: By letter, by telephone, by fax, by email, in person, Internet web pages
Access for disabled people: Parking provided, level entry, access to all public areas, toilet facilities
Other restrictions: Ramped entry to coaches

General description:
General railway history (especially South Wales railways), history and information on the Woodham Locomotive Scrapyard.
Information services:
Library available for reference (for conditions see Access above)
Special visitor services: Guided tours, materials and/or activities for children.
Education services: Group education facilities, resources for Key Stages 1 and 2.
Services for disabled people: Displays and/or information at wheelchair height.
Collections:
Reference library
Railwayiana
Victorian Station Building
Steam and diesel locomotives
Coaches, including a Taff Vale Railway one of 1874 being restored
Cranes, steam and hand operated
Woodham collection (photos and scrapbooks)
Catalogues:
Catalogue for library is in-house only.
Printed publications:
Barry Island Steam Railway and Heritage Centre Handbook (£4.99)
Barry Island Steam Railway and Heritage Centre Colouring Book (99p)
Steam Heritage Centre, Barry Island Station, Timetable and Information 2002/2003 Events (free)

Internet home pages:
http://www.valeglamrail.co.uk
Information on Barry Island Steam Railway and Heritage Centre

2999
VALENCE HOUSE MUSEUM
Becontree Avenue, Dagenham, Essex, RM8 3HT

Tel: 020 8227 5293
Fax: 020 8227 5293
Email: valancehousemuseum@hotmail.com
Full name: Valence House Museum and Art Gallery
Formed: 1938

Organisation type and purpose: Local government body, museum, art gallery.
Library (reference only).
Parent body:
London Borough of Barking and Dagenham
Connections with:
Friends of Valence House

Enquiries to: Heritage Services Manager
Access:
Access to staff: By letter, by telephone, visitors by prior appointment
Access to building, collections or gallery: No prior appointment required
Hours: Mon to Fri, 0900 to 1630, Sat, 1000 to 1600;
Other restrictions: Closed Easter Saturday

General description:
Local history and archaeology of Barking and Dagenham and the Fanshawe family.
Collections:
Archive collection, Borough and the Fanshawe family
Fanshawe family and other portraits
Maps of the locality and County of Essex
Photographic collection, *c.* 5000 black and white negatives
Works of art by Lely, Dobson, Kneller, Glindoni, A B Bamford
Catalogues:
Catalogue for library is published.
Publications list:
is available in hard copy.
Printed publications:
A Brief History of Barking and Dagenham
Barking and Dagenham Buildings Past and Present
Barking and Ilford: An Extract from the Victoria History of the County of Essex
Barking Pubs Past and Present
Dagenham: An Extract from the Victoria History of the County of Essex
Dagenham Pubs Past and Present
One Hundred Years of Libraries in Barking
Views of Old Barking and Dagenham
The Papers of Sir Richard Fanshawe, Bart (Roger M Walker & W H Liddell, 1999, Manley Publishing, £28)
Other local history publications, all for sale

Internet home pages:
http://www.barking-dagenham.gov.uk

3000
VALLEY HERITAGE CENTRE
See - Museum of Cannock Chase

3001
VENNEL GALLERY, THE
10 Glasgow Vennel, Irvine, Ayrshire, KA12 0BD

Tel: 01294 275059
Fax: 01294 275059
Email: vennel@globalnet.co.uk
Formed: 1983

Organisation type and purpose: Local government body, art gallery, suitable for ages: 5+.

Enquiries to: Curator
Access:
Access to staff: By letter, by telephone, by fax, by email, in person, Internet web pages
Access for disabled people: level entry

General description:
The Vennel Gallery in Irvine has a programme of changing exhibitions of contemporary arts and crafts. The gallery includes the Heckling Shop where Robert Burns worked and the Lodging House where he lived in 1781.

Internet home pages:
http://www.users.globalnet.co.uk/~vennel/vennel.html

3002
VENTNOR HERITAGE MUSEUM
11 Spring Hill, Ventnor, Isle of Wight, PO38 1PE

Tel: 01983 855407
Formed: 1987
Formerly: Ventnor Heritage Centre, date of change, 1996

Organisation type and purpose: Membership association (membership is by subscription), present number of members: 130, voluntary organisation, registered charity (charity number 286848), museum, research organisation.
Parent body:
Ventnor and District Local History Society c/o Ventnor Heritage Museum

Enquiries to: Curator
Access:
Access to staff: By letter, by telephone, in person
Hours: Summer: Mon to Sat, 1000 to 1230 and 1400 to 1630
Winter: Mon to Sat, 1000 to 1200
Access to building, collections or gallery: No access other than to staff

continued overleaf

General description:
Local history for the area of Luccombe to Blackgang, photographs, postcards, artefacts etc. Contains ephemera and artefacts associated with Ventnor and district within a five mile radius of the town. Also a large collection of photographs, prints, and documents.
Collections:
Books, documents, pictures, photographs and other materials
Publications list:
is available in hard copy.
Printed publications:
Here Layeth (booklet, £1.95 plus 50p p&p)
Inns and Ale: Bonchurch to Chale (£1.50 plus 50p p&p)
Old Men Remember (£2.50 plus 50p p&p)
Kaleidoscope of Memories (Howe R, £2)
While I breath I hope (£2)
Various photocopied pamphlets

3003
VERDANT WORKS
27 West Henderson's Wynd, Dundee, DD1 5BT

Tel: 01382 225282
Fax: 01382 221612
Email: info@dundeeheritage.sol.co.uk
Formed: 1996

Organisation type and purpose: Independently owned, registered charity (charity number ED/343/85PLB), museum, historic building, house or site, suitable for ages: 5+.
Parent body:
Dundee Heritage Trust
At the same address
Branch museum:
Discovery Point
Discovery Quay, Dundee, DD1 4XA, tel: 01382 201245, fax: 01382 225891, email/website: info@dundeeheritage.sol.co.uk

Enquiries to: Curator
Access:
Access to staff: By letter, by telephone, by fax, by email, visitors by prior appointment
Access to building, collections or gallery: No prior appointment required
Hours: Apr to Oct: Mon to Sat, 1000 to 1700; Sun, 1100 to 1700
Nov to Mar: Wed to Sat, 1030 to 1600; Sun, 1100 to 1600
Access for disabled people: Parking provided, ramped entry, access to all public areas, toilet facilities

General description:
Verdant Works, an 'A' listed textile mill, has been converted to a museum of Dundee's jute industry. It features a collection of jute processing machinery (ex-Dundee College of Technology). Linen production, jute production, mill architecture, rope-making, polypropylene production, social history.
Information services:
Library available for reference (for conditions see Access above)
Education: Scotland, primary, secondary and FE, focus on 5 to 14 curriculum.
Special visitor services: Guided tours.
Education services: Group education facilities, resources for Further or Higher Education.
Services for disabled people: For the visually impaired; for the hearing impaired; displays and/or information at wheelchair height.
Collections:
Working Jute processing machinery
Archives, photographs and objects related to Dundee's Linen and Jute industries
Printing equipment from the caseroom of D C Thomson the publisher; local newspapers and comics (Beano, etc), c. 1900-1975
Printed publications:
Dundee Heritage Trust, The Beginning (editors Lythe, Walker, Edwards and Ross, Dundee 1997, ISBN 1870349 09 1)
Verdant Works, The Story of Dundee & Jute (publ, Pilgrim Press Limited, ISBN 1 874670 31 5)

Internet home pages:
http://www.verdantworks.com

3004
VERULAMIUM MUSEUM
St Michaels, St Albans, Hertfordshire, AL3 4SW

Tel: 01727 751810
Fax: 01727 859919
Email: a.coles@stalbans.gov.uk
Formed: 1938

Organisation type and purpose: Museum, suitable for ages: all ages.

Enquiries to: Secretary
Direct tel: 01727 751811
Direct email: j.brian@stalbans.gov.uk
Other contacts: Assistant Keeper of Archaeology for library and public enquiries.
Access:
Access to staff: By letter, by telephone, by fax, by email, visitors by prior appointment, Internet web pages
Hours: Mon to Fri, 1000 to 1700
Access for disabled people: Parking provided, ramped entry, access to all public areas, toilet facilities

General description:
Local archaeology: including the material excavated from the Roman town of Verulamium and prehistoric Belgic, Saxon, Iron Age and medieval material.
Information services:
Library available for reference (for conditions see Access above)
Computerised catalogue of collections.
Special visitor services: Materials and/or activities for children.
Education services: Group education facilities, resources for Key Stages 1 and 2, 3 and 4..
Collections:
Definitive collection on Verulamium
Wheeler and Frere collections
Catalogues:
Catalogue for part of the collections is only available in-house.
Printed publications:
Excavation Reports

Internet home pages:
http://www.stalbansmuseums.org.uk

3005
VESTRY HOUSE MUSEUM
Vestry Road, Walthamstow, London, E17 9NH

Tel: 020 8509 1917
Email: vestry.house@al.lbwf.gov.uk
Formed: 1930
Formerly: Walthamstow Museum

Organisation type and purpose: Local government body, museum, historic building, house or site, suitable for ages: all ages.
Also the home to the Local Studies Library and the Waltham Forest Archives.
Parent body:
London Borough of Waltham Forest

Enquiries to: Curator
Other contacts: Clerical Officer for person who deals with upkeep of records.
Access:
Access to staff: By letter, by email
Hours: Mon to Fri, 1000 to 1300 & 1400 to 1730; Sat 1000 to 1300 & 1400 to 1700
Access to building, collections or gallery: No prior appointment required
Hours: Tue, Wed & Fri, 1000 to 1300 & 1400 to 1730; Sat 1000 to 1300 & 1400 to 1700
Closed Sun, Mon & Thu
Other restrictions: Prior appointment required for Local Studies Library and Waltham Forest Archives..
Access for disabled people: ramped entry, toilet facilities
Other restrictions: Limited parking provided; wheelchair access for ground floor only.

General description:
Vestry House Museum is housed in Walthamstow's original workhouse, built in 1730. In the 19th century the building was used as a police station, and the old police cells can still be visited today. The collection celebrates the past and present lives of the people of Waltham Forest, it includes the Bremer Car, the first petrol driven car to be made in England, a look at Victorian life, and a costume gallery. Our temporary exhibition, events and activity programmes make Vestry House a great place to visit.
Information services:
Library available for reference (for conditions see Access above)
Special visitor services: Guided tours, tape recorded guides, materials and/or activities for children.
Education services: Group education facilities.
Services for disabled people: For the visually impaired; for the hearing impaired.
Collections:
The Museum holds a large social history collection, including the nationally significant Bremer Car the first car built in London, and one of the first British cars 1894/1895
The Library holds the Borough's local studies collection
The Archive holds the Borough's archives
Walthamstow tea service with illustrations of local houses
manufactured 1820s, 55 items
Catalogues:
Catalogue for library is in-house only.
Publications list:
is available in hard copy and online.
Printed publications:
Vestry House History
A series of archive photo publications of the local area
World War Two publications and information packs
Walthamstow Historical Society publications
Waltham Forest Oral History Society publications
Chingford Historical Society publications
The Story of the Bremer Car
Alfred Hitchcock From Leytonstone to Hollywood
Waltham Forest in Old Photos

Internet home pages:
http://www.lbwf.gov.uk/leisure/intro/vestry_intro.stm
Detailed information on museum, library and archive.

3006
VICTORIA AND ALBERT MUSEUM
Study Room, Department of Prints, Drawings and Paintings, South Kensington, London, SW7 2RL

Tel: 020 7942 2000
Fax: 020 7942 2266
Email: pdp@vam.ac.uk
Acronym or abbreviation: V&A
Formed: 1852
Formerly: South Kensington Museum (SKM), date of change, 1899

Organisation type and purpose: Museum, suitable for ages: all ages.

Enquiries to: Keeper
Direct tel: 020 7942 2563
Direct fax: 020 7942 2561
Other contacts: Print Room Curator for information about how the Print Room is run and access to the Print Room.
Access:
Access to staff: By letter, by telephone, by fax, by email, in person, visitors by prior appointment, Internet web pages
Access to building, collections or gallery: No prior appointment required

Hours: Tue to Fri, 1000 to 1630; Sat, 1000 to 1300 and 1400 to 1630; last requests for objects 1545
Other restrictions: Free entry to the Museum and to the Study Room of the Department of Prints, Drawings and Paintings
Access for disabled people: ramped entry, toilet facilities

General description:
Architecture, fine and applied art, design, photography, prints, (fine prints, graphic, ephemera) posters, oil paintings, portrait miniatures, drawings and illustration, wallpapers, Constable, Raphael cartoons.
Collections:
Alexander Dyce Bequest - British paintings
Ellison gift - watercolours
Evans Bequest - portrait miniatures
Forster Bequest - British paintings
Ionides Bequest - Old Master drawings, British and foreign paintings
Isabel Constable gift - Constable paintings and drawings
John Sheepshanks Gift - British paintings and watercolours
Jones Bequest - British and foreign paintings
Salting Bequest - Prints and Miniatures
Searight Collection - Images of Near East and Orient
Spiers Collection - Architectural drawings
Townshend bequest - Paintings, drawings, prints and photographs
Henry Vaughan Bequest - full-size oil sketches for John Constable's Leaping Horse and Hay Wain
Publications list:
is available in hard copy and online.
Printed publications:
A Guide to Early Photographic Processes (Coe B and Haworth-Booth M, 1983, £12.95)
A teachers guide to using the Print Room (V&A 1995, £5.95)
Hand lists/leaflets for Prints, Drawings and Paintings Department temporary displays (free)
An Independent Art, Photographs from the Victoria and Albert Museum 1839-1996 (Haworth-Booth M, £30)
Aubrey Beardsley (Calloway S, £25)
British Watercolours at the V&A (Parkinson R, 1998, £25)
Carl and Karin Larsson, Creators of the Swedish Style (Snodin M and Hidemark E eds, £35)
Catalogue of 16th century Italian Ornament Prints in the Victoria and Albert Museum (Miller E, 1998, £50)
Catalogue of Foreign Paintings I, Before 1800 (Kauffmann C M, 1973, £20)
Catalogue of Foreign Paintings II, 1800 to 1900 (Kauffmann C M, 1988, £25)
Catalogue of Paintings at the Theatre Museum, London (Ashton G, 1992, £40)
Catalogue of the Constable Collection (Reynolds G, 1990, £48)
Constable: Information and ideas for teachers (V&A 1996, free)
John Constable (Parkinson R, £25)
The Portrait Miniature in England (Coombs K, £25)
The Power of the Poster (Timmers M ed, £30)
A large number of books on the range of subjects covered by the museum
Prints: Art and Techniques (Lambert S, £9.95)
Impressions of the 20th Century (Timmers M ed, £30)
The Art of the Book (Bettley J ed, £30)
Brand New (Pavitt J ed, £30)
Imperfect Beauty (Cotton C, £24.95)
Benjamin Brechnell Turner (Barnes M, £30)
Lady Howarden, Studies from Life (Dodier V, £30)
16th Century Italian Ornament Prints in the V & A (Miller E, £60)
Microform products:
Local & Traditional Costumes in the V&A (1987)
Paquin Worth Fashion Drawings (1982)
Summary Catalogue of British Posters to 1988 (1990)
Textile Designs 1840-1985 in the V&A Museum (1985)
The National Collection of Watercolours in the V&A Museum (1982)
The Muslim World (1989/90)
Theatre Set Designs in the V&A (1985)
Visual Catalogue of Fashion & Costume in the V&A (1987)
Visual Catalogue of Miniature Paintings in the V&A Museum (1981)
Women Artists in the Victoria & Albert Museum (1994)

Address for ordering publications:
Printed publications:
All stock available from, A & C Black Limited
PO Box 19, Huntingdon, Cambridgeshire, PE19 3SF, tel: 01480 212666, fax: 01480 405014
Mail Order, V&A Enterprises
Mail Order, V&A Museum, South Kensington, London, SW7 2RL, tel: 020 7938 8438
Other Enquiries to, Victoria and Albert Museum Publications
160 Brompton Road, London, SW3 1HW, tel: 020 7938 9663, fax: 020 7938 8370

Internet home pages:
http://www.vam.ac.uk
About the Print Room opening hours, access, type of collections, information about Victoria and Albert as a whole and temporary exhibitions and displays.

3007
VICTORIA AND ALBERT MUSEUM
Cromwell Road, South Kensington, London, SW7 2RL

Tel: 020 7942 2000
Acronym or abbreviation: V&A
Formed: 1852

Organisation type and purpose: National organisation, registered charity, museum, suitable for ages: all ages.
Other addresses:
Bethnal Green Museum
Cambridge Heath Road, London, E2 9PA
Theatre Museum
34 Henrietta Street, London, WC2E 8NA
Wellington Museum
Apsley House, London, W1V 9FA

Enquiries to: Director of Learning and Visitor Services
Direct tel: 020 7942 2188
Direct fax: 020 7942 2193
Direct email: d.anderson@vam.ac.uk
Access:
Access to staff: By letter, by telephone, by email, visitors by prior appointment
Hours: Mon to Fri, 0900 to 1700
Access to building, collections or gallery: No prior appointment required
Hours: Sun to Tue, Thu to Sat, 1000 to 1745; Wed, 1000 to 21.45
Other restrictions: Access to National Art Library for pass holders only (passes on application)
Access for disabled people: Parking provided, ramped entry, toilet facilities
Other restrictions: Access to almost all areas

General description:
Art, craft and design in Europe, North America, Middle East, Far East, South and South East Asia as well as the UK.
Information services:
Special visitor services: Guided tours, materials and/or activities for children.
Education services: Group education facilities, resources for Key Stages 1 and 2, 3, 4 and Further or Higher Education.
Services for disabled people: For the visually impaired; for the hearing impaired; displays and/or information at wheelchair height.
Collections:
Prints, drawings and paintings
Ceramics and glass
Textiles and dress
Sculpture
Furniture and woodwork
Metalwork and jewellery
National Art Library
Catalogues:
Catalogue for library is on-line. Catalogue for all of the collections is available in-house, part is published and part is on-line.
Publications list:
is available in hard copy and online.

Address for ordering publications:
Printed publications:
A & C Black Limited
PO Box 19, Huntingdon, Cambridgeshire, PE19 8SF
V&A Enterprises
Cromwell Road, London, SW7 2RL, email: http://www.vandashop.co.uk

Internet home pages:
http://www.vam.ac.uk
What's on at the museum, about the museum, special exhibitions, branch museums, facilities and resources, Gallery descriptions, courses available, volunteers, Patrons & Friends Membership, fundraising, The Shop

See also - Apsley House, The Wellington Museum

3008
VICTORIANA MUSEUM
Deal

Closed

3009
VINA COOKE MUSEUM OF DOLLS AND BYGONE CHILDHOOD
The Old Rectory, Great North Road, Cromwell, Newark, Nottinghamshire, NG23 6JE

Tel: 01636 821364
Formed: 1984

Organisation type and purpose: Independently owned, museum, historic building, house or site.

Enquiries to: Curator
Access:
Access to staff: By letter, by telephone
Access to building, collections or gallery: No prior appointment required
Hours: Mon to Thu, 1030 to 1200 and 1400 to 1700; Sat, Sun, 1030 to 1700,1 Nov to end Feb: Open but appointment advisable
Other restrictions: Fri by prior appointment only.
Access for disabled people: Parking provided
Other restrictions: Disabled access limited - ring for advice details.

General description:
Dolls and toys 1800 to present day, prams, dolls' houses, books, games, costume and domestic artefacts.
Information services:
Special visitor services: Guided tours.
Education services: Group education facilities, resources for Key Stage 1..

3010
VINDOLANDA ROMAN FORT AND MUSEUM, THE
Bardon Mill, Hexham, Northumberland, NE47 7JN

Tel: 01434 344277

Organisation type and purpose: Museum, historic building, house or site.
Parent body:
Vindolanda Charitable Trust

General description:
Roman fort and town with excavation in progress. Superb museum displaying finds set in gardens and Roman Temple, shop and house.

Internet home pages:
http://www.vindolanda.com

3011
VINTAGE CARRIAGES TRUST

Ingrow Railway Centre, c/o Haworth Railway Station, Keighley, West Yorkshire, BD22 8NJ

Tel: 01535 680425
Fax: 01535 610796
Email: admin@vintagecarriagestrust.org
Acronym or abbreviation: VCT
Formed: 1968

Organisation type and purpose: Registered charity (charity number 510776), museum, suitable for ages: 5+.
Preservation of railway carriages, locomotives and artefacts through display and occasional use. Operation of museum at Ingrow Railway Centre.
Members of:
Association of British Transport & Engineering Museum
Association of Independent Museums
Heritage Railway Association
Servicemark Yorkshire & Humber
Transport Trust
Yorkshire Museums Council
Yorkshire Tourist Board
Branch also at:
The Railway Station
Haworth, Keighley, West Yorkshire, tel: 01535 680425, fax: 01535 610796, email/website: admin@vintagecarriagestrust.org

Enquiries to: Curator
Access:
Access to staff: By letter, by telephone, by email, visitors by prior appointment
Access to building, collections or gallery: No prior appointment required
Hours: Daily, 1100 to 1630 except 25 and 26 Dec
Other restrictions: No unaccompanied children. Prior appointment required for library.
Access for disabled people: Parking provided, level entry, toilet facilities
Other restrictions: Access to all areas except library, wheelchair stairlift to viewing platform, courtesy wheelchair available for loan, Braille guidebook available for loan.

General description:
Purpose-built museum with carriages, a steam locomotive, numerous small exhibits, sound and video presentations bring the collection to life, and, unlike many museums, you are encouraged to sit in the carriage compartments and climb on the footplate of the locomotive.
Our carriages have been used in over 50 cinema/television productions.
Information services:
Library available for reference (for conditions see Access above), on-line searching
Group education services
Special visitor services: Tape recorded guides.
Education services: Resources for Key Stage 2.
Services for disabled people: For the visually impaired; for the hearing impaired; displays and/or information at wheelchair height.
Collections:
9 Railway Carriages, built 1876 to 1951,3 Steam Locomotives
Cast Iron Signs etc
Railway Poster collection
Reference Library
Catalogues:
Catalogue for library is in-house only. Catalogue for all of the collections is available in-house, part is published and part is on-line.
Trade and statistical:
Lead body holding data.
Railway Heritage Register Carriage Survey Project.
Publications list:
is available on-line.
Printed publications:
Books and articles regarding railways
Bellerophon - Haydock to Haworth (the story of an historic steam locomotive)
In Trust - A Guide to the Collection of the Vintage Carriages Trust
Midland Railway Locomotives Album 1880-1910 (photographic studies with descriptive texts, Leeds/Bradford area)
Newsletter (4 times a year, free to members)
Sir Berkeley and Friends (the story of the Manning Wardle railway engines)
Electronic and video products:
Railway Heritage Carriage Survey Project (CD-ROM)
Slow Train Coming - Heritage Railways in the 21st Century (CD-ROM)

Internet home pages:
http://www.vintagecarriagestrust.org
Includes database of over 3800 preserved railway carriages with over 3000 images as well as VCT's own collection. What, where and how of Trust's museum at Ingrow, with opening times and current events. Railway Heritage Register Carriage Survey Project.

*See also - **Keighley and Worth Valley Railway Preservation Society***

3012
VINTAGE GLIDER CLUB

Arewa, Shootersway Lane, Berkhamsted, Hertfordshire, HP4 3NP

Tel: 01442 873258
Fax: 01442 873258
Email: geoffmoore@madasafish.com
Acronym or abbreviation: VGC
Formed: 1972

Organisation type and purpose: International organisation, membership association (membership is by subscription), present number of members: 800 internationally, museum.
Museum - flying, restoration.
and various:
Overseas Gliding Vintage Associations
Associated with:
British Gliding Association

Enquiries to: Membership Secretary
Access:
Access to staff: By letter, by fax, by email, Internet web pages
Hours: 24 hour answerphone and fax

General description:
History of gliding since the early 1920s, plans of vintage gliders, whereabouts of vintage gliders, gliding museums, dates of rallies and similar events.
Collections:
Collection of photographs
Construction plans of gliders especially Slingsby drawings held at Lasham Airfield and microfilm covering a wider range including Slingsby
Printed publications:
Technical Articles
Vintage (Glider) News (3 times a year)

Internet home pages:
http://www.vintagegliderclub.org.uk

3013
VIRTUALLY THE NATIONAL VALVE MUSEUM

75 Millbrook Road, Crowborough, East Sussex, TN6 2SB

Email: allan@r-type.org
Formed: 2000

Organisation type and purpose: Independently owned, museum, suitable for ages: 12+.
Virtual museum.
To preserve and record vintage thermionic valves and related information.

Enquiries to: Curator
Direct tel: 01892 662561
Access:
Access to staff: By letter, by email, Internet web pages
Access to building, collections or gallery: Prior appointment required
Hours: Access is via www.valve-museum.org
Other restrictions: The collection is only accessible via the Internet.

General description:
An extensive collection of vintage radio, television, radar and audio valves, indexed by name, manufacturer, size, shape, base, pins, use etc and additional information. Online table of equivalents covering 4200 valve type designations, including CV numbers and pre-WW2 service types. A collection of publications, datasheets and articles on valves, radio, television and related subjects (this is to be catalogued in the near future).
Collections:
Thermonic valves
Valve, radio, television and related publications, data sheets etc dating back to the 1930s (as yet to be catalogued)
Small collection of radio related artefacts dating from the 1940s
Catalogues:
Catalogue for part of the collections is on-line.
Electronic and video products:
Virtually The National Valve Museum (CD-ROM, £25 incl p&p)

Address for ordering publications:
Printed publications:
Millbrook Computing
at the same address, email: millbrook.computing@btinternet.com

Internet home pages:
http://www.valve-museum.org
Access to 1200 valves with high quality photography and extensive data.

3014
VYNE, THE

Sherborne St John, Basingstoke, Hampshire, RG24 9HL

Tel: 01256 883858
Fax: 01256 881720
Email: thevyne@nationaltrust.org.uk

Organisation type and purpose: National organisation, registered charity (charity number 205846), historic building, house or site, suitable for ages: 8+.
Parent body:
The National Trust (South and South East Region)
Thames and Solent Regional Office, tel: 01949 528051

Enquiries to: Manager
Access:
Access to staff: By letter, by telephone, by fax, by email
Access to building, collections or gallery: No prior appointment required
Hours: House: Late Mar to early Nov, Sat and Sun, 1100 to 1,700, late Mar to early Nov, Sat to Wed, 1100 to 1700
Open Bank Holidays and Good Friday 1100 to 1700 (including house)
Other restrictions: Special opening for groups, by appointment only.
Access for disabled people: Parking provided, ramped entry, toilet facilities
Other restrictions: Transfer available. 6 manual wheelchairs available. Ground floor fully accessible. No access to other floors. Photograph album. Level entrance to shop and to restaurant. Grounds largely accessible.

General description:
Built in the early 16th century for Lord Sandys, Henry VIII's Lord Chamberlain, the house acquired a classical portico in the mid-17th century (the first of its kind in England) and contains a fascinating Tudor chapel with Renaissance glass, a Palladian staircase and a wealth of old panelling and fine furniture. The attractive grounds feature herbaceous borders and a wild garden, with lawns, lakes and woodland walks.

Information services:
Helpline available, tel no: Infoline: 01256 881337.
Braille guide. Large-print guide. Touch list. Scented plants.
Front-carrying baby slings for loan.
Suitable for school groups. Live interpretation. Children's quiz/trail.
Special visitor services: Materials and/or activities for children.
Services for disabled people: For the visually impaired.
Collections:
Glass, early 16th century
Furniture
18th century
Ceramics, early 16th-18th century
Carved panelling, early 16th century
Textiles (wall coverings), 18th century

Internet home pages:
http://www.nationaltrust.org.uk

3015
WADDESDON MANOR
Aylesbury, Buckinghamshire, HP18 0JH

Tel: 01296 653203
Fax: 01296 653208
Email: waddesdonmanor@nationaltrust.org.uk
Formed: 1870

Organisation type and purpose: National organisation, registered charity (charity number 205846), historic building, house or site, suitable for ages: 5+.
Parent body:
The National Trust (NT)
Regional Office for Thames & Solent, tel: 01494 528051, fax: 01494 463310

Enquiries to: Information Officer
Access:
Access to staff: By letter, by fax, visitors by prior appointment
Access for disabled people: Parking provided, ramped entry, toilet facilities
Other restrictions: Designated parking. Drop-off point. 4 manual wheelchairs available. Ground floor fully accessible. Access to other floors via lift. Audiovisual/video. No access to Bachelors' Wing, Prints and Drawings Rooms or Wine Cellars. For safety reasons only 2 wheelchairs allowed on each floor at a time. Level entrance to shop and to restaurant. Grounds largely accessible. Stables approached via steep incline. Recommended route map.

General description:
Waddesdon Manor was built between 1874 and 1889, in the style of a 16th century French château, for Baron Ferdinand de Rothschild to entertain his guests and display his vast collection of art treasures. It houses an extraordinary assemblage of French 18th century decorative arts. The furniture, Savonnerie carpets and Sèvres porcelain rank in importance with the Metropolitan Museum in New York and the Louvre in Paris. Outstanding are the portraits by Gainsborough and Reynolds, and works by Dutch and Flemish Masters of the 17th century. Waddesdon has one of the finest Victorian gardens in Britain, renowned for its seasonal displays, colourful shrubs, mature trees and parterre. Carpet bedding displays are newly created each year, and there is a rose garden and children's garden to visit. The Rococo-style aviary houses a splendid collection of exotic birds, and thousands of bottles of vintage Rothschild wines are found in the wine cellars.
Information services:
Helpline available, tel no: Infoline: 01296 653211.
Braille and audio guides (English and French) for house. Large-print guide. Sympathetic Hearing Scheme.
Frontcarrying baby slings for loan. Children's play area. Children's garden, aviary.
Suitable for school groups. Audio guide. Live interpretation. Children's quiz/trail. Adult study days. Guidebooks in French and German.
Special events throughout the year including: children and family activities days, study days, wine-tasting, phone 01296 653226 for details.
Special visitor services: Tape recorded guides, materials and/or activities for children.
Services for disabled people: For the visually impaired; displays and/or information at wheelchair height.
Collections:
A fine collection of important portraits by Gainsborough and Reynolds, and works by Dutch and Flemish Masters of the 17th century.
Buttons, English and Continental, 18th and 19th century
Fans, French 18th century
Glass, enamels and majolica
Illuminated manuscripts 14th-16th Century
16th and 17th century European arms
Catalogues:
Catalogue for part of the collections is available in-house, part is published and part is on-line.
Publications list:
is available in hard copy and online.
Printed publications:
Guide Books
Catalogues
The Rothschilds at Waddesdon Manor
A Hundred Years at Waddesdon
Waddesdon Manor - The Garden

Internet home pages:
http://www.nationaltrust.org.uk
http://www.waddesdon.org.uk

3016
WAKEFIELD ART GALLERY
Wentworth Terrace, Wakefield, West Yorkshire, WF1 3QW

Tel: 01924 305900
Fax: 01924 305770
Formed: 1934

Organisation type and purpose: Art gallery, suitable for ages: 5+.

Enquiries to: Curator
Direct tel: 01924 305904
Direct email: avella@wakefield.gov.uk
Access:
Access to staff: By letter, by telephone, by fax
Hours: Tue to Fri, 1030 to 1630

General description:
Contains an important 20th century British Fine Art Collection including major work by the locally born sculptors, Barbara Hepworth and Henry Moore. Also contains paintings from earlier periods and other European schools, as well as decorative arts including contemporary craft.
Collections:
Pictures, prints, sculptures
Gott Collection, topographical images of the Yorkshire region (prints, sketches and watercolours), some unique, c. 1700 to c. 1850, c. 1000 items

3017
WAKEFIELD MUSEUM
Wood Street, Wakefield, West Yorkshire, WF1 2EW

Tel: 01924 305351
Minicom no. 01924 305796
Fax: 01924 305353
Email: internet@wakefield.gov.uk
Acronym or abbreviation: WM
Formed: 19th Century

Organisation type and purpose: Local government body, museum, suitable for ages: 5+.
Museum service, education and resource facilities.
Parent body:
Wakefield MDC Museums and Arts

Enquiries to: Curator
Direct tel: 01924 305350
Direct email: cjohnstone@wakefield.gov.uk
Other contacts: Education and Outreach Officer for educational visits and workshops.
Access:
Access to staff: By letter, by telephone, by fax, by email
Access to building, collections or gallery: No access other than to staff
Hours: Mon to Sat, 1030 to 1630; Sun, 1400 to 1630
Other restrictions: Educational classes may be in progress.
Access for disabled people: ramped entry, access to all public areas, toilet facilities

General description:
Covers the history of Wakefield District and its people, from the earliest populations to the present day. Concentrates on social history and archaeology, but also has a significant 19th century natural history collection. Key Stage 1 and 2; social history; wartime Wakefield; miners' strike; Victorians.
Collections:
Charles Waterton Collection (local conservationist), natural history, environment and satire, 1800-1850, 500 items
Sandal Castle, excavation archive, 1964-1973, Medieval and post-medieval, 2000 items
Castleford, excavation archive, 1974-1983, Roman. 6000 items
Castleford pottery, ceramics made in Castleford and Ferrybridge, 1790-1960, 300 items
Mrs Bird, 1940s women's clothes, 1940-1949, 200 items
Plastics, household objects, 1930-1970, 300 items
Photographs, Wakefield District, portraits, civic and topographical, 1880-1975, 1000 items
Catalogues:
Catalogue for library is in-house only. Catalogue for part of the collections is only available in-house.

Internet home pages:
http://www.wakefield.gov.uk

3018
WAKEHURST PLACE
Ardingly, Haywards Heath, West Sussex, RH17 6TN

Tel: 01444 894066
Fax: 01444 894069
Email: wakehurst@kew.org

Organisation type and purpose: National organisation, registered charity (charity number 205846), historic building, house or site, suitable for ages: 5+.
Parent body:
The National Trust (South and South East Region)
South East Regional Office, tel: 01372 453401
Administered and maintained by the:
Royal Botanic Gardens, Kew

Enquiries to: Manager
Access:
Access to staff: By letter, by telephone, by fax, by email
Access to building, collections or gallery: No prior appointment required
Hours: Daily, Feb and Oct, 1000 to 1700, Mar, 1000 to 1800, Apr to Sep 1000 to1900, Nov to Jan, 1000 to 1600
Other restrictions: Closed 25 Dec and 1 Jan. Mansion, Seed Bank and restaurant close 1 hr before gardens.
Access for disabled people: Parking provided, ramped entry, toilet facilities
Other restrictions: Drop-off point. 12 manual wheelchairs available. Level entrance. Steps to shop entrance. Grounds largely accessible. Recommended route map.

General description:
Often described as Kew's country garden, Wakehurst Place contains a series of ornamental features with many plants from across the world

continued overleaf

providing year-round colour and interest. Extensive woodlands, including an informal arboretum and secluded valley, offer delightful walks. Information about the garden and its many interesting features is available within the Elizabethan mansion. The Loder Valley nature reserve may also be visited by permit.
The Wellcome Trust Millennium Building, adjacent to Wakehurst Place, aims to house seeds from ten per cent of the world's flora by 2009, to save species from extinction in the wild. Enjoy the Millennium Seed Bank interactive public exhibition in the Orange Room, and follow the journey of a seed from identification and collection, through to drying and cold storage in the massive underground vaults.
Information services:
Guided tours available Mon, Tues, Thur, Sat, Sun and Bank Holidays: tel. booking office for times and availability. Booked tours on request; write to Administrator.
Scented plants.
Suitable for school groups. Education room/centre. Family guide. Children's quiz/trail. Adult study days.
Special visitor services: Materials and/or activities for children.
Education services: Group education facilities.
Services for disabled people: For the visually impaired.

Internet home pages:
http://www.kew.org

3019
WALKER ART GALLERY, THE

National Museums & Galleries on Merseyside, William Brown Street, Liverpool, L3 8EL

Tel: 0151 478 4199
Fax: 0151 478 4190
Acronym or abbreviation: NMGM
Formed: 1877

Organisation type and purpose: Local government body, art gallery, historic building, house or site, suitable for ages: all ages.
Parent body:
National Museums & Galleries on Merseyside
Controlling also:
Sudley and Lady Lever Art Gallery
The Oratory

Enquiries to: Director
Other contacts: Marketing Manager for advertising.
Access:
Access to staff: By letter only
Other restrictions: Prior appointment necessary for visitors requesting to see staff.
Access to building, collections or gallery: No prior appointment required
Hours: Mon to Sat, 1000 to 1700; Sun, 1200 to 1700

General description:
One of the best-known galleries in the UK. An internationally important collection of paintings dating from the 14th-20th Centuries. It is especially rich in Old Masters, outstanding Victorian and Pre-Raphaelite pictures and modern British works.
Information services:
Helpline available, tel no: 0151 207 0001.
Children and family activity events
Special visitor services: Materials and/or activities for children..
Collections:
Catalogue library related to European art 1300 to the present
Wide-ranging collection of prints, drawings and photographs
Italian and Netherland paintings 1350 -1550,1550 - 1900 includes, Rembrandt, Rubens, Poussin and Degas
Victorian paintings and Pre-Raphaelite art
20th century paintings include works by Lucian Freud, Gilbert & George and Michael Readecker
18th and 19th century watercolours by Turner and Peter deWint
George Romney cartoons
20th century works by Paul Nash, Edward Wandsworth and Eric Ravilious
Publications list:
is available in hard copy.
Printed publications:
Guides, catalogues and monographs

Internet home pages:
http://www.nmgm.org.uk

3020
WALL ROMAN SITE (LETOCETUM) BATHS AND MUSEUM

Watling Street, Wall, Near Lichfield, Staffordshire, WS14 0AW

Tel: 01543 480768

Organisation type and purpose: National organisation, registered charity (charity number 205846), museum, historic building, house or site, suitable for ages: 8+.
Parent body:
The National Trust (West Midlands)
West Midlands Regional Office, tel: 01743 708100
Maintained and managed by:
English Heritage (West Midlands Region)
Tel: 0121 625 6820
Member of:
North Staffordshire Museums Association

Enquiries to: Manager
Access:
Access to staff: By letter, by telephone
Access to building, collections or gallery: No prior appointment required
Hours: Apr to Oct, daily, 1000 to1800
Other restrictions: Opening times are subject to change, for up-to-date information contact English Heritage by phone or visit the website.

General description:
Wall was an important staging post on Watling Street, the Roman military road to North Wales. It provided overnight accommodation and a change of horse for travelling Roman officials and imperial messengers. Foundations of an inn and bath house can be seen, and many of the excavated finds are displayed in the museum on site.
Information services:
English Heritage special events days.
Audio Guide.
Suitable for school groups. Audio guide.
Special visitor services: Tape recorded guides, materials and/or activities for children.
Education services: Group education facilities.
Services for disabled people: For the visually impaired.

Internet home pages:
http://www.english-heritage.org.uk

3021
WALLACE COLLECTION

Hertford House, Manchester Square, London, W1M 6BN

Tel: 020 7563 9500
Fax: 020 7224 2155
Email: admin@the-wallace-collection.org.uk
Formed: 1900

Organisation type and purpose: Museum. Art collection and museum, financed by central government and by self-generated income.

Enquiries to: Head of Finance and Administration
Other contacts: Librarian
Access:
Access to staff: By letter, by telephone, by fax, by email, visitors by prior appointment, Internet web pages
Hours: Mon to Sat, 1000 to 1700; Sun, 1200 to 1700
Access for disabled people: ramped entry, access to all public areas, toilet facilities

General description:
Paintings of the British, Dutch, Flemish, French, Italian and Spanish Schools, miniatures, sculptures, French furniture, European and oriental arms and armour, goldsmiths' work and ceramics.
Collections:
19th century French and English sale catalogues and archival material relevant to the Wallace Collection
Catalogues:
Catalogue for library is in-house only. Catalogue for all of the collections is published.
Publications list:
is available in hard copy and online.
Printed publications:
Catalogue of Furniture, 1996
Catalogue of Pictures vol. 1 (British, German, Italian, Spanish) 1985
Catalogue of Pictures, vol. 2 (French Nineteenth century 1986)
Catalogue of Pictures, vol. 3 (French, before 1815), 1990
Catalogue of Pictures, vol. 4 (Dutch and Flemish), 1992
Catalogue of Sèvres Porcelain, 1989
Ceramics vol. 1 (Pottery, Maiolica, Faience and Stoneware) 1976
European Arms and Armour (2 vols), 1962 (Reprint 1985)
European Arms and Armour Supplement 1986
Illuminated Manuscript Cuttings, 1980
Miniatures, 1980
Oriental Arms and Armour 1913 (reprint 1978)
Sculpture, 1931 (with supplement 1982)
Summary Illustrated Catalogue of Pictures 1979
Other publications include Picture Books, Monographs, Guides and Histories of the Collection

Address for ordering publications:
Printed publications:
Wallace Collection, Hertford House Marketing Limited
As main address

Internet home pages:
http://www.the-wallace-collection.org.uk

3022
WALLPAPER HISTORY SOCIETY

c/o Victoria and Albert Museum, South Kensington, London, SW7 2RL

Tel: 020 7942 2560
Acronym or abbreviation: WHS
Formed: 1986

Organisation type and purpose: Research organisation.

Enquiries to: Secretary
Direct tel: 020 8977 4978
Access:
Access to staff: By letter, by telephone
Hours: Mon to Fri, 0900 to 1700

General description:
History of wallpaper, bibliography, specialist conservation sources, manufacturers specialising in the production of reproduction historic papers, details of museums and archives holding wallpapers.
Collections:
Please note that the Society itself holds no collections, though it has members and contacts in institutions which do have collections of wallpaper
Printed publications:
Wallpaper History Review

3023
WALLSEND HERITAGE CENTRE

See - Segedunum Roman Fort, Baths and Museum

3024
WALMER CASTLE & GARDENS
Kingsdown Road, Walmer, Deal, Kent, CT14 7LJ

Tel: 01304 364288
Fax: 01304 364826

Organisation type and purpose: National organisation, advisory body, suitable for ages: 8+.
Parent body:
English Heritage (South East Region)
Tel: 01483 252000, fax: 01483 252001

Enquiries to: Head Custodian
Direct email: sally.mewton-lynds@english-heritage.org.uk
Access:
Access to staff: By letter, by telephone, by fax, by email, in person
Access to building, collections or gallery: No prior appointment required
Hours: Apr to Sep: daily, 1000 to 1800
Oct: daily, 1000 to 1700
Nov to Dec & Mar: Wed to Sun, 1000 to 1600
Jan to Feb: Sat, Sun, 1000 to 1600
Other restrictions: Closed 24 to 26 Dec, 1 Jan and when the Lord Warden is in residence Opening times are subject to change, for up-to-date information contact English Heritage by phone or visit the website.
Access for disabled people: Parking provided, ramped entry, level entry, toilet facilities
Other restrictions: Easy access to courtyard and garden, easy stairs with handrail to upper floor of castle.

General description:
Walmer Castle was built to withstand the wrath of the French and Spanish following Henry VIII's break with the Roman Catholic Church, but its defences have never, in fact, been put to the test. It does, however, serve as the official residence of the Lord Wardens of the Cinque Ports, a title held by William Pitt the Younger, Winston Churchill and the first Duke of Wellington, who died at Walmer 150 years ago. His room today looks much as it did on 14 September 1852 when he died in his armchair at 3.25pm. The previous Lord Warden, Her Majesty Queen Elizabeth the Queen Mother, used to visit Walmer and some of the rooms used by her are open to visitors, as well as the magnificent Queen Mother's Garden.
Information services:
Special visitor services: Tape recorded guides.
Education services: Group education facilities, resources for Key Stages 1 and 2 and 3.
Services for disabled people: For the visually impaired; for the hearing impaired; displays and/or information at wheelchair height.
Collections:
Duke of Wellington memorabilia, including his famous Wellington boots
Furniture and artefacts of other famous Lord Wardens including William Pitt, WH Smith, Sir Winston Churchill and HM Queen Elizabeth the Queen Mother.
Printed publications:
Walmer Castle & Gardens Guide Book £2.50

Internet home pages:
http://www.english-heritage.org.uk/

3025
WALSALL LEATHER MUSEUM
Littleton Street West, Walsall, West Midlands, WS2 8EQ

Tel: 01922 721153
Fax: 01922 725827
Email: leathermuseum@walsall.gov.uk
Formed: 1988

Organisation type and purpose: Local government body, museum.

Enquiries to: Curator
Access:
Access to staff: By letter, by telephone, by fax, by email, visitors by prior appointment
Hours: Mon to Fri, 0900 to 1700
Access to building, collections or gallery: No prior appointment required
Hours: Tue to Sat, 1000 to 1700, Sun, 1200 to 1700
Nov to Mar, closes 1600
Access for disabled people: Parking provided, level entry, access to all public areas, toilet facilities

General description:
Techniques and history of tanning, saddlery, leather goods, book binding, gloving.
Contemporary design in leather.
Local history of Walsall; history of leather industry, especially working life.
Information services:
Library available for reference (for conditions see Access above)
Special visitor services: Guided tours, materials and/or activities for children.
Education services: Group education facilities, resources for Key Stages 1 and 2 and 3.
Services for disabled people: For the visually impaired; for the hearing impaired; displays and/or information at wheelchair height.
Collections:
Trade Catalogue collection (about 400 volumes, 1870 to present day)
Photographic Archive (approximately 1500 images)
Oral history collection, memories of Walsall Leatherworks including saddlers, tanners, glovers, casemakers etc
Livery Companies' library collection (about 1200 volumes) covering all aspects of leatherworking
Catalogues:
Catalogue for library is published.
Trade and statistical:
Data on local saddlery trade, eg numbers of firms, size of workforce etc.
Publications list:
is available in hard copy.
Printed publications:
The following are available direct from the Leather Museum, include 30p per item for p&p:
Bibliography supplement updated to 1999 (free)
Fact Sheet Number 1 - The Walsall Leather Industry Today (25p)
Fact Sheet Number 2 - Two Hundred Years of Walsall Leather (75p)
Horse Brasses and Decorations (Keegan T, pamphlet 50p)
In the Leather: Walsall Leatherworkers Remember (£1.50)
Leather Bibliography (£1)
Leather Museum Souvenir Guidebook (£1.20)
Leatherworking by Paul Hasluck (Facsimile reprint of manual first published in 1904, £4.95)
Origins and Early History of the Walsall Leather Trades (£1)
Stitching and Skiving: Walsall's Women Leatherworkers (95p)
The Harness Makers' Guide (Facsimile reprint, giving measurements for harness, originally published in 1921, £5.50)
Walsall Leather Museum Teacher's Pack (£5.50)

3026
WALSALL MUSEUM & ART GALLERY
See - New Art Gallery Walsall

3027
WALTHAM ABBEY ROYAL GUNPOWDER MILLS CO LIMITED
See - Royal Gunpowder Mills

3028
WALTHAMSTOW MUSEUM
See - Vestry House Museum

3029
WALTON HALL MUSEUM
Walton Hall Road, Linford, Stanford-le-Hope, Essex, SS17 0RH

Tel: 01375 671874
Fax: 01375 641268
Formed: 1992

Organisation type and purpose: Museum.

Enquiries to: Curator
Access:
Access to staff: By letter, by telephone, by fax
Access for disabled people: Parking provided, level entry

General description:
14th century farmhouse and 17th century barn with other farm buildings, farm machinery and tools, household artefacts, crafts including blacksmith, wheelwright and saddlemaker.
Collections:
Collection of motor rollers
Domestic equipment and children's nurseries and toys
Farm machinery and tools
Military items from both world wars
Village bakery (baking on occasions)
Publications list:
is available in hard copy.

3030
WALTON MARITIME MUSEUM
The Old Lifeboat House, East Terrace, Walton-on-the-Naze, Essex, CO14 8PY

Tel: 01255 678259
Formed: 1984
Formerly: Frinton and Walton Heritage Trust, date of change, 1997

Enquiries to: Vice-President

General description:
The permanent collection consists of artefacts connected with local fishing and yachting, i.e. boats, nets, trawls, models, etc. Includes pictures of the backwaters and the sea shore; steamers arriving at the pier; etc. There is also a collection of fossil shells from the Naze cliffs, and information about the local lifeboat since 1900.

3031
WANDSWORTH MUSEUM
The Court House, 11 Garratt Lane, Wandsworth, London, SW18 4AQ

Tel: 020 8871 7074
Fax: 020 8871 4602
Email: wandsworthmuseum@wandsworth.gov.uk
Formed: 1986

Organisation type and purpose: Local government body, museum, suitable for ages: all ages.

Enquiries to: Curator
Other contacts: Education & Outreach Officer for school and outreach service tel 020 8871 7075.
Access:
Access to staff: By letter, by telephone, by fax, by email, in person
Hours: Mon to Sat, 0900 to 1700; Sun, 1400 to 1700
Other restrictions: Visiting staff by appointment only outside opening times for the Museum.
Access to building, collections or gallery: No prior appointment required
Hours: Tue to Sat, 1000 to 1700; Sun, 1400 to 1700
Access for disabled people: level entry, access to all public areas, toilet facilities

General description:
A local history museum for the London Borough of Wandsworth. The main elements of the collection are archaeology, social history and fine art (i.e. topographical watercolours and engravings).

continued overleaf

Information services:
Displays and information are at present at various heights, some wheelchair height and some higher. There are hearing loops in the shop, information desk and meeting room, and large print labels for exhibitions.
Special visitor services: Materials and/or activities for children.
Education services: Group education facilities, resources for Key Stages 1 and 2..
Collections:
Collections relating to the London Borough of Wandsworth:
Archaeological material
Social history artefacts
Topographical watercolours and prints
Special collections:
Ashenden. Works by, and terms relating to, Wandsworth artist Edward Ashenden. ca. 1910-1950. 586 items
De Montmorency. Works by, and items relating to Putney artists Sir Miles de Montmorency and Rachel Tancock. ca. 1920- 1960. 655 items
Catalogues:
Catalogue for part of the collections is only available in-house.
Printed publications:
Books and postcards relating to the London Borough of Wandsworth

3032
WAR ROOM AND MOTOR HOUSE COLLECTION
30 Park Parade, Harrogate, North Yorkshire, HG1 5AG

Tel: 01423 500704
Formed: 1986

Organisation type and purpose: Independently owned, museum, suitable for ages: 16+, consultancy, research organisation, publishing house.

Enquiries to: Manager
Access:
Access to staff: By letter, by telephone, visitors by prior appointment

General description:
Collections of First and Second World War material: arms, uniform, equipment and printed matter (official publications and posters). Also a collection of die-cast motor vehicle and aircraft models, and architectural cut-outs, including many prototype and pre-production items.
Collections:
Broadwater collection of die-cast model vehicles 1930s-1990s, c. 9000
Library of books covering military history (all periods), and aspects of transport and industry in general, c. 1200 books
Printed publications:
Overlord: the War Room handbook guide to the greatest military amphibious operation of all time (Jewell B, £8.50, post free)

3033
WAREHAM TOWN MUSEUM
Town Hall, East Street, Wareham, Dorset, BH20 4NS

Tel: 01929 553448
Formed: 1983

Organisation type and purpose: Museum.

Enquiries to: Curator
Access:
Access to staff: By letter, by telephone, visitors by prior appointment
Hours: Mon to Sat, 1000 to 1600
Access for disabled people: level entry, access to all public areas, toilet facilities

General description:
Local history of Wareham.
Catalogues:
Catalogue for part of the collections is only available in-house.

3034
WARKWORTH CASTLE AND HERMITAGE
Warkworth, Northumberland, NE65 0UJ

Tel: 01665 711423

Organisation type and purpose: Historic building, house or site.
Parent body:
English Heritage (North East Region)
Tel: 0191 269 1227/8, fax: 0191 261 1130

Enquiries to: Manager
Access:
Access to staff: By letter, by telephone, in person
Access to building, collections or gallery: No prior appointment required
Hours: End Mar to end Sep: daily, 1000 to 1800
Oct; daily, 1000 to 1700
Beg Nov to end Mar: daily, 1000 to 1600
Other restrictions: Closed 1300 to 1400 in winter.
Closed 24 to 26 Dec, 1 Jan.
Opening times are subject to change, for up-to-date information contact English Heritage by phone or visit the website.

General description:
Magnificent eight-towered keep was the large, complex and impressive stronghold of the powerful Percy family. There are many chambers, passageways and dark staircases to explore. Just upstream from the castle, and still much as a medieval hermit would remember, is a curious chapel cut deep into the rock of the river cliff. The ferryman will row you across the river to Warkworth Hermitage.
Information services:
Audio tour also available for children, free children's activity sheets.
Special visitor services: Tape recorded guides, materials and/or activities for children.
Services for disabled people: For the visually impaired.

Internet home pages:
http://www.english-heritage.org.uk

3035
WARNER ARCHIVE
Tilbrook Distribution Limited, Bradbourne Drive, Tilbrook, Milton Keynes, Buckinghamshire, MK7 8BE

Tel: 01908 658021
Fax: 01908 658020
Email: sue_kerry@zoffany.uk.com
Formed: 1870

Organisation type and purpose: Independently owned, manufacturing industry, service industry.
Furnishings and wallcoverings.
Parent body:
Walker Greenbank
4 Brunel Court, Cornerhall, Hemel Hempstead, Hertfordshire, HP3 9XX

Enquiries to: Archivist
Access:
Access to staff: By letter, by telephone, by fax, by email, visitors by prior appointment
Access to building, collections or gallery: Prior appointment required
Hours: Mon to Fri, 1000 to 1600
Access for disabled people: access to all public areas

General description:
Information on Company's history; silk weaving samples; chintz and printed fabric; company information; designer information.
Collections:
Marianne Straub, woven textile designer, 1950-1970
Owen Jones, architect and designer (fabric samples), 1870- 1874
Alex Hunter, woven textile designer, 1932-1958
Coronation fabrics produced for Royal Weddings and Coronations, etc 1893-1995
Catalogues:
Catalogue for library is in-house only. Catalogue for all of the collections is only available in-house.

3036
WARRINGTON MUSEUM AND ART GALLERY
Bold Street, Warrington, Cheshire, WA1 1JG

Tel: 01925 442392
Fax: 01925 442399
Email: museum@warrington.gov.uk
Formed: 1848

Organisation type and purpose: Local government body, museum, art gallery, historic building, house or site, suitable for ages: 5+.

Enquiries to: Heritage and Archives Manager
Access:
Access to staff: By letter, by telephone, by fax, by email, Internet web pages
Hours: Mon to Fri, 1000 to 1730; Sat, 1000 to 1700
Last entry 1630
Other restrictions: Enquiries by appointment.
Access to building, collections or gallery: No prior appointment required
Hours: Mon to Fri, 1000 to 1730; Sat, 1000 to 1700
Last entry 1630
Access for disabled people: ramped entry, access to all public areas, toilet facilities
Other restrictions: Full wheelchair access, passenger lift.

General description:
Birds; insects; reptiles; amphibia and fish; molluscs; botany; fossils; and minerals.
Particularly strong in prehistory, Roman and Mediaeval collections. Also covers ethnography; Egyptology; numismatics; firearms and horology.
The art collections include watercolours, oils and ceramics.
Local industry displays. Recently refurbished Earth's History Gallery with study drawers and computer interactive displays.
Information services:
Full wheelchair access, passenger lift.
Special visitor services: Materials and/or activities for children.
Education services: Group education facilities, resources for Key Stages 1 and 2, 3, 4 and Further or Higher Education.
Services for disabled people: For the visually impaired; displays and/or information at wheelchair height.
Collections:
William Wilson FLS, herbarium of higher plants and British mosses, 1850-1870, c. 2500 items
Linnaeus Greening, spirit collection of British spiders, 1893- 1928, c. 3300 items
Linnaeus Greening, spirit collection of foreign spiders, 1893- 1928, 889 from 21 countries
Linnaeus Greening, world-wide spirit collection of reptiles, amphibia and snakes, 1893-1928, 800 items
Lancashire Tokens, 17th century, 130 items
Virginal by Thomas Bolton, 1684 (not on permanent display, can be viewed by appointment)
Welsh Cruesh, 1760-1765 (not on permanent display, can be viewed by appointment)
Glass, Warrington (made in), 1871-1933, 370 items
Watercolours, mainly 19th century (English), 18th-19th century, 495 items
Catalogues:
Catalogue for part of the collections is only available in-house.

Internet home pages:
http://www.warrington.gov.uk/museum
Information on cross-section of collections, education department and temporary exhibitions.

3037
WARWICK CASTLE
Warwick, CV34 4QU

Tel: 0870 442 2000
Fax: 01926 406611
Email: customer.information@warwick-castle.com

Organisation type and purpose: Historic building, house or site, suitable for ages: all ages.
Parent body:
The Tussaud's Group
Tel: 0870 429 2300, fax: 0870 429 5500

Enquiries to: PR Marketing Assistant
Direct tel: 01926 406633
Access:
Access to staff: By letter, by fax, by email
Access for disabled people: Parking provided, toilet facilities
Other restrictions: Limited access to Castle.

General description:
Founded in the 10th century as a fortified earth work to protect the people of Warwick against the Danes the castle continued to grow in strength and magnificence over the centuries. It was used as a residence until the 20th century and bought by the Tussaud Group in 1978. A number of tourist attractions have been created to retell parts of the castle's history, including the 'Kingmaker', the 'Royal Weekend Party' and 'Death and Glory' as well as the refurbishment of the armoury and the castle mill and engine house.

Internet home pages:
http://www.warwick-castle.co.uk

3038
WARWICK DISTRICT COUNCIL ART GALLERY AND MUSEUM
See - Leamington Spa Art Gallery and Museum

3039
WARWICK DOLL AND TOY MUSEUM
Oken's House, Castle Street, Warwick, CV34 4BP

Tel: 01926 495546
Formed: 1988

Organisation type and purpose: Local government body, museum.
Other address:
St John's Museum
St John's, Warwick, tel: 01926 412132
Other addresses:
Warwickshire Museum
Market Place, Warwick, tel: 01926 41250

Enquiries to: Principal Musseums Officer
Direct tel: 01926 412500
Direct fax: 01926 419840
Direct email: museum@warwickshire.gov.uk
Access:
Access to staff: By letter, by telephone, by fax, by email, visitors by prior appointment

General description:
Dolls, puzzles and toys, dolls houses, social history of childhood.
Collections:
Joy Robinson Collection of Dolls and Toys
Electronic and video products:
Video of working Automata from the collections available directly from the museum (for sale)

Internet home pages:
http://www.warwickshire.go.uk/museums

3040
WARWICK UNIVERSITY
See - Mead Gallery

3041
WARWICKSHIRE MUSEUM OF RURAL LIFE
Closed

3042
WARWICKSHIRE MUSEUM
Market Place, Warwick, CV34 4SA

Tel: 01926 412500
Fax: 01926 419840
Email: museum@warwickshire.gov.uk
Formed: 1932

Organisation type and purpose: Local government body, museum, suitable for ages: 5+.
Parent body:
Warwickshire County Council
Branch museums include:
Market Hall Museum
Tel: 01926 412500, fax: 01926 419840, email/website: museum@warwickshire.gov.uk
St Johns House
Tel: 01926 412132, fax: 01926 419840, email/website: museum@warwickshire.gov.uk
Warwick Doll Museum
Tel: 01926 495546, fax: 01926 419840, email/website: museum@warwickshire.gov.uk

Enquiries to: Administrator
Direct tel: 01926 412827
Direct email: maggiesmith@warwickshire.gov.uk
Access:
Access to staff: By letter, by telephone, by fax, by email, visitors by prior appointment
Access to building, collections or gallery: No prior appointment required
Hours: Mon to Sat, 1000 to 1730
May to Sept, Mon to Sat, 1000 to 1730; Sun, 1100 to 1700
Other restrictions: Groups need to enquire beforehand.

General description:
Geology; archaeology; biology; social history including costume, household items, craft and trade tools, dolls and toys, agricultural implements (all connected with Warwickshire); information is also held on biological, geological and archaeological sites and on plant and animal records for the county.
Collections:
Warwickshire plants and insects, type and figured fossil material of triassic vertebrates, local palaeolithic artefacts, Anglo-Saxon jewellery
Troth and Hillson plough moulds
Warwick woodcarvings
Extensive reserve collections including:
Printed publications:
Booklets and leaflets on local history etc
Drawings notes and photographs of musical instruments
Information sheets

Internet home pages:
http://www.warwickshire.gov.uk/museum

3043
WARWICKSHIRE REGIMENTAL MUSEUM
See - Royal Regiment of Fusiliers Museum (Royal Warwickshire)

3044
WASDALE, ESKDALE AND DUDDON
The Lodge, Wasdale Hall, Wasdale, Cumbria, CA20 1ET

Tel: 01946 726064 (Property Office)
Fax: 01946 726115
Email: wasdale@nationaltrust.org.uk

Organisation type and purpose: National organisation, registered charity (charity number 205846), historic building, house or site, suitable for ages: 8+.
Parent body:
The National Trust (North West Region)
North West Regional Office, tel: 0870 609 5391

Enquiries to: Warden, Wasdale
Direct tel: 019467 26110
Other contacts: Warden, Duddon & Eskdale (01229 716552)
Access:
Access to staff: By letter, by telephone, by fax, by email, in person, Internet web pages

General description:
Here the Trust owns England's highest mountain, Scafell Pike, and deepest lake, Wastwater. Almost the whole of the head of Wasdale is NT-owned, including Great Gable and the famous historic wall patterns at the valley head. Lower down, there is the wooded and tranquil Nether Wasdale Estate. Over 7000ha and eleven farms are covered.
In neighbouring Eskdale, Trust protection covers extensive areas of fell, six farms and Hardknott Roman Fort. In the beautiful and tranquil Duddon valley the National Trust cares for almost 3000ha and nine farms.

Internet home pages:
http://www.nationaltrust.org.uk

3045
WASHINGTON OLD HALL
The Avenue, District 4, Washington Village, Tyne and Wear, NE38 7LE

Tel: 0191 416 6879
Fax: 0191 416 2065
Email: washingtonoldhall@nationaltrust.org.uk

Organisation type and purpose: National organisation, registered charity (charity number 205846), museum, historic building, house or site, suitable for ages: 8+.
Parent body:
The National Trust (Yorkshire and North East)
North East Regional Office, tel: 01670 774691

Enquiries to: Manager
Access:
Access to staff: By letter, by telephone, by fax, by email
Access for disabled people: Parking provided, ramped entry, toilet facilities
Other restrictions: Designated parking. Accessible entrance, please contact property in advance. Ground floor fully accessible. No access to other floors. Steps to tea-room entrance. Refreshments can also be served on ground floor.

General description:
Washington Old Hall is a delightful stone-built 17th century manor house, which incorporates parts of the original medieval home of George Washington's direct ancestors from 1183-1288, remaining in the family until 1613. Substantially rebuilt in the 17th century. It is from here that the family surname of Washington was derived. There are displays on George Washington, and the recent history of the Hall. There is also a fine collection of oil paintings, Delftware and heavily carved oak furniture, giving an authentic impression of gentry life following the turbulence of the English Civil War.
The tranquil Jacobean garden leads to the Nuttery.
Information services:
Introductory talks for group visits.
Braille guide. Tactile opportunities in house and garden.
Suitable for school groups. Children's quiz/trail.
Special visitor services: Materials and/or activities for children.
Services for disabled people: For the visually impaired.

Internet home pages:
http://www.nationaltrust.org.uk

3046
WATCHET MUSEUM
The Market House, Market Street, Watchet, Somerset, TA23 0AN

Tel: 01984 631345
Full name: Watchet Market House Museum
Formed: 1979

continued overleaf

Organisation type and purpose: Registered charity (charity number 275645), museum, historic building, house or site, suitable for ages: 5+.

Enquiries to: Curator
Other contacts: Secretary; tel: 01643 707132 for general correspondence.
Access:
Access to staff: By letter only
Access to building, collections or gallery: No prior appointment required
Hours: Easter to 31 Sep: Daily, 1030 to 1230 and 1430 to 1630
Also Jul and Aug: Daily, 1900 to 2100
Other restrictions: Prior appointment required for group visits.

General description:
Exhibition of the history of the ancient seaport of Watchet. Fossils, Stone Age implements, Romano-British remains, Saxon Mint, maritime history, railways, iron-ore mines, Victoriana, paintings, photographs, models.
Sales counter for local books.
Information services:
Guided tours on prior request.
School visits on request to Curator.
Special visitor services: Guided tours.
Education services: Group education facilities..
Collections:
In addition to the material on display (under subject), the Museum holds records useful for family history research
Iron-ore mining and its railway
1850-1910

3047
WATER SUPPLY MUSEUM
Sutton Poyntz Pumping Station, Sutton Poyntz, Weymouth, Dorset, DT3 6LT

Tel: 01305 832634
Fax: 01305 834287
Email: museum@wessexwater.co.uk
Formed: 1989
Formerly: Wessex Water Museum, Weymouth's Working Museum; The Museum of Water Supply, date of change, 1995

Organisation type and purpose: Museum, historic building, house or site, suitable for ages: 8+.
Commercial company.
Water undertaking.
Head Office Address:
Wessex Water
Public Relations
Claverton Down Road, Claverton Down, Bath, BA2 7WW, tel: 01225 526326, fax: 01225 528955, email/website: museum@wessexwater.co.uk

Enquiries to: Curator
Other contacts: Education Adviser, tel: 01225 524324 for school visits.
Access:
Access to staff: By letter, by telephone, by fax, by email, in person, visitors by prior appointment
Hours: Mon to Fri, 0900 to 1630
Access to building, collections or gallery: Prior appointment required
Hours: Mon to Sat, 0900 to 2100
Other restrictions: All visits by appointment.
Access for disabled people: Parking provided, level entry, toilet facilities
Other restrictions: Specify special needs when booking.

General description:
Operational pumping station still supplying water to Weymouth.
Portland stone buildings dating from 1856, built to accommodate water, steam and electric power.
The Turbine House is a Scheduled Ancient Monument and contains a water turbine driven ram pump (1857).
Pumps, tools and equipment used in the water industry, including sections of wooden water main.
Workshop containing lineshaft and belt-driven machines.
Wessex Water's historical archive, contains Weymouth Waterworks Company (est. 1797) documents and plans.
Interpretation of spring source, which supplies pumping station and is part of SSSI.
Information services:
Library available for reference (for conditions see Access above)
Visits are generally guided, assistance is therefore available for disabled people.
Special visitor services: Guided tours, materials and/or activities for children.
Education services: Resources for Key Stages 2, 3, 4 and Further or Higher Education.
Services for disabled people: Displays and/or information at wheelchair height.
Collections:
Funnel from Brunel's Great Eastern. Once formed part of the 1859 filter system
Spring basin contains funnel from Brunel's Great Eastern. Obtained and installed as a crude filter, it is not generally accessible due to being in an operational area
'Scotch' water turbine driven ram pump made by D Cook & Company Glasgow in 1857, is designated a Scheduled Ancient Monument
1934 vertical triple expansion steam engine by Hathorn Davey, outside and being restored
Sections of wooden water main from the c. 1797 public water supply
Workshop containing belt-driven lathes and drilling machines, the limeshaft equipment dates from 1912
Archive contains architects plans and colour wash drawing by Thomas Hawksley and G R Crickmay from 1854
Catalogues:
Catalogue for library is in-house only. Catalogue for all of the collections is only available in-house.

Internet home pages:
http://www.wessexwater.co.uk
This is a Company website, however a dedicated museum site is being formatted at the moment.

3048
WATER TOWER
City Walls, Chester, Cheshire

Tel: 01244 321616

General description:
Mediaeval Towers on the City Wall, built to protect the harbour. The displays feature the river, city walls and surrounding area.

3049
WATERCRESS LINE
See - Mid-Hants Railway (Watercress Line)

3050
WATERFRONT MUSEUM
4 High Street, Poole, Dorset, BH15 1BW

Tel: 01202 262600
Fax: 01202 262622
Email: museums@poole.gov.uk
Formed: 1974

Organisation type and purpose: Local government body, museum, suitable for ages: all ages.
Parent body:
Poole Borough Council

Enquiries to: Manager
Access:
Access to staff: By letter, by telephone, by fax, by email, in person
Access for disabled people: level entry, access to all public areas, toilet facilities

General description:
Social history of Poole.
Information services:
Special visitor services: Guided tours, materials and/or activities for children.
Education services: Group education facilities, resources for Key Stages 1 and 2, 3, 4 and Further or Higher Education.
Services for disabled people: Displays and/or information at wheelchair height.
Collections:
Social history
Local History Centre
Maritime portraits
Poole Pottery
Dorset Crown Pottery

3051
WATERSIDE GALLERY
2 Marine Terrace, Bideford, Devon, EX39 4HZ

Tel: 01271 860786
Fax: 01271 860786
Email: judy@watersideart.co.uk
Formed: 1990

Organisation type and purpose: Art gallery, suitable for ages: 16+.

Enquiries to: Proprietor
Access:
Access to staff: By letter only
Access for disabled people: access to all public areas
Other restrictions: Entry by 1 shallow step.

General description:
Contemporary paintings and pottery, mostly by local artists from Devon. Imported artefacts and gifts. Local crafts, picture framing. Occasional one-man exhibitions of work by the best local artists. Photographs.

Internet home pages:
http://www.watersideart.co.uk
Illustrations of work for sale, directions to location.

3052
WATERSMEET HOUSE
Watersmeet Road, Lynmouth, Devon, EX35 6NT

Tel: 01598 753348

Organisation type and purpose: National organisation, registered charity (charity number 205846), historic building, house or site.
Parent body:
The National Trust (South West Region)
Regional Office for Devon and Cornwall, tel: 01392 881691

Enquiries to: Manager
Access:
Access to staff: By letter, by telephone
Access to building, collections or gallery: No prior appointment required
Hours: End Mar to end Sep, daily, 1030 to 1730; Oct to beg Nov, daily, 1030 to 1630

General description:
A fishing lodge, built c.1832 in a picturesque valley at the confluence of the East Lyn and Hoar Oak Water, and now a National Trust shop, with refreshments and information. The site has been a tea-garden since 1901 and is the focal point for several beautiful walks.
Information services:
Special visitor services: Materials and/or activities for children..

Internet home pages:
http://www.nationaltrust.org.uk/regions/devon

3053
WATERWAYS TRUST
See - Canal Museum

3054
WATERWORKS MUSEUM
Broomy Hill, Hereford, HR4 0LQ

Tel: 01432 344062
Fax: 01600 890009
Full name: Waterworks Museum - Hereford
Formed: 1974
Formerly: Herefordshire Waterworks Museum, date of change, 1997

Organisation type and purpose: Independently owned, registered charity (charity number 515866), museum, suitable for ages: 5+.
Industrial heritage centre concerned with the supply of drinking water.
Address for Correspondence:
Chairman
Waterworks Museum
Llancraugh Cottage, Marstow, Ross-on-Wye, Herefordshire, HR9 6EH, tel: 01600 890118, fax: 01600 890009

Enquiries to: Chairman
Direct tel: 01600 890118
Other contacts: Education Officer for all education contacts and school visits.
Access:
Access to staff: By letter, by telephone, by fax, visitors by prior appointment
Access for disabled people: Parking provided, level entry, toilet facilities
Other restrictions: Access to all Museum except Well Area.

General description:
A century of industrial heritage brought to life through working engines housed in historic buildings by the River Wye telling the story of drinking water.
Information services:
Also educational facilities and resources for Special Needs.
Special visitor services: Guided tours, materials and/or activities for children.
Education services: Group education facilities, resources for Key Stages 1 and 2, 3, 4 and Further or Higher Education.
Services for disabled people: For the visually impaired; displays and/or information at wheelchair height.
Collections:
Horse-drawn fire engine, 1805
Easton, Anderson & Goolden horizontal turbine and triple-throw pumps, 1850
Water-level instrumentation (various), 1850-1860
Simpson beam engine, 1851
Thorneycroft reversing three-cylinder steam engine, 1880
Gilbert, Gilkes & Gordon double-vortex turbine, 1880s
Joseph Evans double-acting reciprocating pumps, 1888
Warner hydraulic ram (plus other rams and hydrostat), 1889
Hayward-Tyler hot air engine, 1890
Lancashire boiler, 1895
Worth-McKenzie triple expansion steam engine, 1895
Campbell gas engine with hot-tube ignition, 1900
Worth McKenzie twin duplex steam engine, 1906
Overshot 14-foot diameter waterwheel made by the Eagle Foundry of Aberystwyth, 1907
Hindley Alcazar steam donkey engine, 1911
National Gas producer-gas engine, 1912
Worthington Simpson boiler feed pumps (several), 1920s
Tangye 97-litre single-cylinder horizontal diesel engine and triple-throw pumps, 1932
Allen twin-cylinder vertial diesel engine, 1932
Gilbert, Gilkes & Gorden 'Francis-type' turbine, 1937
Crompton-Parkinson motor and Pulsometer spindle-driven centrifugal pump, 1950
Lister diesel locomotive and trucks working on 2 foot gauge track, 1962
Pleuger centrifugal borehole pump and motor, 1970
Hayward-Tyler centrifugal borehole pumps and motors, 1980-1990
Catalogues:
Catalogue for all of the collections is only available in-house.
Printed publications:
Publicity leaflet (free)
Children's leaflet (free)
Guide Book (£1)
Children's Guide Book 9-12 years (50p)
Museum Newsletter (3 times a year, free to members)
Primary Education Pack (free to schools)
Secondary Schools Workbooks on various topics (free to schools)

Address for ordering publications:
Printed publications:
Education Officer, Waterworks Museum - Hereford
7 Vaga Close, Hereford, HR2 7BH, tel: 01432 344062

3055
WATFORD MUSEUM

194 High Street, Watford, Hertfordshire, WD17 2DT

Tel: 01923 232297
Fax: 01923 224772
Email: sarahjo@watford.gov.uk
Formed: 1981

Organisation type and purpose: Local government body, museum, suitable for ages: all ages.
Parent body:
Watford Council

Enquiries to: Museum Manager
Direct email: museum@artsteam-watford.co.uk
Other contacts: Heritage Officer for education and outreach.
Access:
Access to staff: By letter, by telephone, by fax, visitors by prior appointment
Hours: Mon to Fri, 1000 to 1700; Sat, 1000 to 1300 and 1400 to 1700
Access for disabled people: Parking provided, ramped entry, toilet facilities

General description:
Local history, printing (in Watford), brewing (in Watford), wartime Watford, Victorian Watford, art in Hertfordshire, the Earls of Essex and Cassiobury House.
Information services:
Enquiry service - local history.
Special visitor services: Materials and/or activities for children.
Education services: Group education facilities, resources for Key Stages 1 and 2, 3 and 4..
Collections:
Fine art and sculpture collection: 17th and 18th century North European Centre and 19th century English landscape
Includes: Burr bequest, Blackley bequest and Thompson bequest
Local history collections:
Printing, brewing, wartime and Victorian Watford
Prints, drawings, maps, documents relating to Watford, the Earls of Essex and Cassiobury House
Watford Football Club, photographs
Catalogues:
Catalogue for part of the collections is only available in-house.
Publications list:
is available in hard copy.
Printed publications:
Information Sheets
Maps of Watford (£2.20)
Watford and the Civil War (£2.20)
Watford High Street Revisited (£2.20)

Internet home pages:
http://www.hertsmuseums.org.uk/watford

3056
WATTS GALLERY

Down Lane, Compton, Guildford, Surrey, GU3 1DQ

Tel: 01483 810235
Email: admin@wattsgallery.org.uk
Formed: 1904

Organisation type and purpose: Registered charity, art gallery, suitable for ages: all ages.
To promote works of G F Watts.

Enquiries to: Assistant Curator
Other contacts: Curator for matters of legal, financial, business nature.
Access:
Access to staff: By letter, by telephone, by email, in person, visitors by prior appointment, Internet web pages
Access for disabled people: Parking provided, level entry
Other restrictions: Gallery will be totally accessible in 2005 following refurbishment.

General description:
Work by Victorian artist George Frederick Watts OM, RA (1817-1904) - paintings and sculpture, some paintings by other Victorian artists.
Housed in a purpose-built arts and crafts picture gallery. Archive available by appointment, including letters, photographs, newspaper cuttings on G F Watts and Victorian art in general, examples of Compton Pottery from Mary Watts' Compton Potters Arts Guild (run until 1950s on site here), information on Mary Watts and Watts Chapel.
Information services:
Library available for reference (for conditions see Access above)
Special visitor services: Guided tours, materials and/or activities for children..
Collections:
Sir Brinsley Ford Bequest of drawings
Cecil French Bequest of pictures
Paintings, drawings, sculpture, photographs
Books (exhibition catalogues included)
Newspaper cuttings
Letters - microfiche
Notebooks
Pottery
Sales catalogues
Catalogues:
Catalogue for part of the collections is only available in-house.
Publications list:
is available on-line.
Printed publications:
G F Watts and The Watts Gallery (gallery guide, £2.50, available direct)
The Watts Chapel (Franklin Gould V, £4.95, available direct)

Internet home pages:
http://www.wattsgallery.org.uk
Visitor information and pages on other relevant aspects.

3057
WEALD & DOWNLAND OPEN AIR MUSEUM

Singleton, Chichester, West Sussex, PO18 0EU

Tel: 01243 811348
Fax: 01243 811475
Email: office@wealddown.co.uk
Formed: 1969

Organisation type and purpose: Registered charity, museum, suitable for ages: all ages, training organisation, research organisation.
Purpose to encourage interest in traditional buildings, building crafts and technology, rural life and landscapes in South East England through collections, education and recreation.

Enquiries to: Administrator
Direct tel: 01243 811363
Other contacts: Curator
Access:
Access to staff: By letter, by telephone, by fax, by email, in person, Internet web pages
Hours: Office, Mon to Fri, 0900 to 1700
Access for disabled people: Parking provided, toilet facilities

General description:
Building construction, historic timber building, traditional rural crafts and skills, traditional agriculture.
Information services:
Library available for reference (for conditions see Access above)

continued overleaf

Special visitor services: Tape recorded guides, materials and/or activities for children.
Education services: Group education facilities, resources for Further or Higher Education..
Collections:
Library of interest to building conservation architects, historic building exhibits
Building materials displays
Publications list:
is available in hard copy and online.

Internet home pages:
http://www.wealddown.co.uk

3058
WEARDALE MUSEUM

Ireshopeburn, Bishop Auckland, Co Durham, DL13 1EY

Tel: 01388 537417
Email: dtheatherington@argonet.co.uk
Formed: 1984

Organisation type and purpose: Independently owned, museum, historic building, house or site, suitable for ages: all ages.

Enquiries to: Honorary Secretary
Direct tel: 01388 517433
Access:
Access to staff: By letter, by telephone, by email, visitors by prior appointment
Access for disabled people: Parking provided, level entry, access to all public areas, toilet facilities

General description:
Housed in an old manse adjoining High House Chapel (1760), it features a kitchen reflecting the domestic life of a Weardale working family of around 1890, with local period furniture; a display of period costume; Durham quilts and prodded mats; and a 'Children in Weardale a Hundred Years Ago' display. The life of leadmining and farming families over 100 years ago. The oldest MethodistChapel in the world still in continuous weekly use.
Information services:
Special visitor services: Guided tours..
Collections:
Railways of Weardale, Railwayana form the Upper Weardale line
Rocks, mines and minerals, crystallised minerals, rocks and fossils, and a display of lead mining and stone quarrying
Wesley Room, illustrates the story of John Wesley and Methodism
Water and industry, photographs of waterwheels and the construction of Burnhope Reservoir
Catalogues:
Catalogue for library is in-house only. Catalogue for all of the collections is only available in-house.

Internet home pages:
http://www.weardale.co.uk

3059
WEAVER'S COTTAGE

Shuttle Street, The Cross, Kilbarchan, Renfrewshire, PA10 2JG

Tel: 01505 705588

Organisation type and purpose: Museum, historic building, house or site.
Parent body:
National Trust for Scotland (West Region)

Enquiries to: Property Manager
Access:
Access to staff: By letter, by telephone
Access to building, collections or gallery: No prior appointment required
Hours: Mar to Oct, daily, 1300 to 1700

Morning visits available for pe-booked groups

General description:
Typical handloom weaver's cottage built in 1723. Hands-on activities in weaving, prim winding, spinning and carding.

Information services:
Explanatory text in French, German, Italian, Japanese and Spanish, Braille guidebook.
Special visitor services: Materials and/or activities for children.
Education services: Group education facilities.
Services for disabled people: For the visually impaired; for the hearing impaired.

Internet home pages:
http://www.nts.org.uk

3060
WEAVERS' TRIANGLE VISITOR CENTRE

85 Manchester Road, Burnley, Lancashire, BB11 1JZ

Tel: 01282 452403
Formed: 1980

Organisation type and purpose: Voluntary organisation, registered charity (charity number 1024635), museum, suitable for ages: all ages.

Enquiries to: Curator
Access:
Access to staff: By letter, by telephone, in person
Hours: Easter to Sep: Sat to Tue, 1400 to 1600; Sun in Oct; any time by letter
Access to building, collections or gallery: No access other than to staff
Hours: Easter to Sep: Sat to Tue, 1400 to 1600; Sun in Oct; other times by appointment

General description:
Burnley's 19th and 20 century industrial and social history.
Information services:
Education services: Group education facilities, resources for Key Stages 1 and 2, 3, 4 and Further or Higher Education.
Services for disabled people: For the visually impaired.
Collections:
Industrial (mainly cotton manufacture) and domestic artefacts
Small collection of books, photographs and documents relevant to above collection
Steam engine in engine house at Oak Mount Mill

3061
WEDGWOOD MUSEUM

Barlaston, Stoke-on-Trent, Staffordshire, ST12 9ES

Tel: 01782 282818
Fax: 01782 223315
Email: info@wedgwoodmuseum.org.uk
Formed: 1906

Organisation type and purpose: Independently owned, registered charity (charity number 1072442), museum.

Enquiries to: Information Officer
Other contacts: Museum Secretary
Access:
Access to staff: By letter, by telephone, by fax, by email, in person, visitors by prior appointment, Internet web pages
Access for disabled people: Parking provided, level entry, toilet facilities

General description:
Museum galleries closed for rebuilding until 2004 (the factory tour is still open).
Publications list:
is available in hard copy and online.

Internet home pages:
http://www.wedgwoodmuseum.com

3062
WEDNESBURY MUSEUM & ART GALLERY

Holyhead Road, Wednesbury, West Midlands, WS10 7DF

Tel: 0121 556 0683
Formed: 1891

Organisation type and purpose: Local government body, museum, art gallery, suitable for ages: all ages.
Local authority museum.
Parent body:
Sandwell Museum Service
Other addresses:
Haden Hill House
Halesowen Road, Cradley Heath, B64 7SU, tel: 01384 569444
Oak House Museum
Oak Lane, West Bromwich, B70 8HJ, tel: 0121 553 0759

Enquiries to: Visitor Services Manager
Other contacts: Principal Heritage Officer for head of Service.
Access:
Access to staff: By letter, by telephone
Other restrictions: Enquiries regarding collections and objects by letter only - Curator not always on site.
Access to building, collections or gallery: Prior appointment required
Hours: Mon, Tue, Wed, Fri, 1000 to 1700 (last admission 1630); Thu, Sat, 1000 to 1300 (last admission, 1230)
Access for disabled people: Parking provided, ramped entry, level entry
Other restrictions: No access to first floor for wheelchair users.

General description:
A purpose-built gallery (1891), built to house the art collection of Edwin Richards (industrialist, d. 1885). Now also holds and displays ethnography; geology; social history; archaeology; and decorative arts collections. These are supplemented by temporary exhibitions of local history, photography, craft-work and fine art. Ruskin pottery, history of Sandwell Borough, social history of Wednesbury.
Information services:
Education services: Group education facilities, resources for Key Stages 1 and 2..
Collections:
Large collection of Ruskin pottery, produced by W Howson-Taylor's factory in Smethwick 1898-1933, permanent display from the collection
Edwin Richards. Paintings collection of a local industrialist (d. 1885); Mary Richards Bequest of 19th century oils and watercolours, mostly British landscapes; artists include Webb, Syer, Vickers, Leader, Baker, c. 1790-1880, 130 items
Helen Caddick, ethnography. Collection of a local woman, gathered on her extensive travels, 1889-1914, c. 1100 items
George Robbins, geology: fossils, rocks and minerals, collected systematically, pre-1898, c. 4000 items

Internet home pages:
http://www.sandwellmbc.gov.uk
Information regarding Sandwell Museum Service.

3063
WELCH REGIMENT MUSEUM (41ST/69TH FOOT) RRW

The Black & Barbican Towers, Cardiff Castle, Cardiff, CF1 2RB

Tel: 029 2022 9367
Acronym or abbreviation: WRM/RRW
Formed: 1927

Organisation type and purpose: Registered charity (charity number 273195), museum.
Parent body:
Royal Regiment of Wales 24th/41st Foot
Tel: 029 20 781202, fax: 029 20 641281, email: rhq@rrw.org.uk
Connections with:
Museum of the South Wales Borderers & Monmouthshire Regiment
The Barracks, Brecon, Powys, tel: 01874 613310, fax: 01874 613275, email/website: rrw@ukonline.co.uk
Ontario Regiment RCAS
Royal New South Wales Regiment

Also at:
Chairman, Welch Regiment Museum (41st/69th Foot) RRW
Pepers Farm, Burton Lazars, Melton Mowbray, Leicestershire, LE14 2UP

Enquiries to: Curator
Other contacts: Chairman, Board of Trustees
Access:
Access to staff: By letter, by telephone, visitors by prior appointment, charges made to all users
Access to building, collections or gallery: No prior appointment required
Hours: Mon and Wed to Sun, 1000 to 1730
Closed Tuesdays, Christmas Day, Boxing Day and New Year's Day

General description:
History of the Welsh Regiments from early 18th century, the home defence auxiliaries including Home Guard and Army Cadet Force, the expansion of the British Empire and withdrawal directly associated with the regiment.
Collections:
An extensive photographic archive relating to the records of the regiment, they include non military material with reference to the ethnic groups, geography, architecture etc. of the foreign stations where the regiment saw service
Archive of material relating to the expansion of the British Empire and withdrawal, which is directly connected to the services of the regiment
Personal accounts and diaries written by soldiers including:
Cochrane's Account of the War of the Anglo-American War of 1812-1814
Diary of Colour Sergeant Haslock 1824-1848
The Sparke's Diaries of Egypt and Sudan (late 19th century)
Records of Home Defence Auxiliaries including Home Guard and Army Cadet Force 1914-1945 which were affiliated to the regiment
Records of the Services of the 1st and 2nd Battalions, The Welch Regiment 1881-1969
Records of the Services of the 41st 69th Regiments of Foot 1719-1881
Records of the Services of the Home Service/ Reserve Battalions of the regiment 1939-1946
Records of the Services of the Royal Glamorgan Militia and the Militia regiments of Carmarthenshire and Cardiganshire 1797-1908
Records of the Services of the Service Battalions of the regiment 1914-1919
Records of the Services of the Territorial Force Battalions of the Welch Regiment 1908-1920 and the Territorial Force Battalions of the regiment 1920-1969
Records of the Services of the Yeomanry and Volunteers of South Wales 1794-1908
Catalogues:
Catalogue for library is in-house only. Catalogue for all of the collections is only available in-house.
Publications list:
is available in hard copy.
Printed publications:
Owen Roscomyl & The Welsh Horse (1990)
The History of the Welsh Militia and Volunteer Corps - The Glamorgan Regiments of Militia (1990)
The History of the Welsh Militia and Volunteer Corps - The Glamorgan Volunteers, Local Militia & Yeomanry 1796-1831 (1994)
The History of the Welsh Militia and Volunteer Corps - The Militia Regiments of Carmarthenshire, Pembrokeshire and Cardiganshire (1995)

Internet home pages:
http://www.rrw.org.uk

3064
WELFARE STATE INTERNATIONAL
Lanternhouse, The Ellers, Ulverston, Cumbria, LA12 0AA

Tel: 01229 581127
Minicom no. 01229 587146
Fax: 01229 581232
Email: info@welfare-state.com
Formed: 1968

Organisation type and purpose: International organisation, registered charity (charity number 265461), art gallery, suitable for ages: all ages, consultancy, research organisation, publishing house.
Artist-led company pioneering the arts of celebration and ceremony.

Enquiries to: Centre Manager
Direct email: alec@welfare-state.com
Other contacts: Artistic Director
Access:
Access to staff: By letter, by telephone, by fax, by email, visitors by prior appointment, Internet web pages
Hours: Mon to Fri, 0900 to 1700
Access for disabled people: Parking provided, level entry, access to all public areas, toilet facilities

General description:
Arts of celebration.
Information services:
Special visitor services: Guided tours.
Education services: Group education facilities..
Printed publications:
The Dead Good Funerals Book (£9.50 plus p&p)
The Dead Good Guide to Namings & Baby Welcoming Ceremonies (£7.50 plus p&p)
The Dead Good Time Capsule Book (£6.95 plus p&p)
Engineers of the Imagination (£12.99 plus p&p)
Eyes on Stalks (£14.99 plus p&p)

Internet home pages:
http://www.welfare-state.org

3065
WELHOLME GALLERIES
Welholme Road, Grimsby, Lincolnshire, DN32 9LP

Tel: 01472 323576
Fax: 01472 323577
Email: andrew.tulloch@nelincs.gov.uk
Formerly: Great Grimsby Museum and Heritage Service

Organisation type and purpose: Local government body, museum.
Parent body:
North East Lincolnshire Council
Municipal Offices, Town Hall Square, Great Grimsby

Enquiries to: Documentation Officer
Access:
Access to staff: By letter, by telephone, by fax, by email, visitors by prior appointment
Hours: Mon to Thu, 0900 to 1700; Fri, 0900 to 1630

General description:
Lincolnshire history, history of the fishing industry, ships and ship models, archaeology, photography, costume and textiles, ceramics, applied art, decorative art, natural history, social history, agricultural history and geology.
Collections:
Archive material deposited by the Great Central Railway Society
Burton Collection (mid-20th century Grimsby photographs)
Doughty Collection (ship models and marine paintings)
Plans and other documents relating to the shipbuilding and fishing industry
W E R Hallgarth Collection (Lincolnshire photographs)
Printed publications:
Catalogue of Ship Models
Catalogue of Windmill Photographs: Lincolnshire and Nottinghamshire
Guide to the Museum Collections
Information sheets

Internet home pages:
http://www.nelincs.gov.uk

3066
WELLBROOK BEETLING MILL
20 Wellbrook Street, Corkhill, Cookstown, Co Tyrone, BT80 9RY

Tel: 028 8674 8210/8675 1735
Fax: 028 8675 1735
Email: wellbrook@nationaltrust.org.uk
Formed: 1967

Organisation type and purpose: Registered charity, historic building, house or site.
Parent body:
National Trust Office for Northern Ireland
Rowallane House, Saintfield, Ballynahinch, Co Down, BT24 7LH, tel: 028 9751 0721, fax: 028 9751 1242
Other addresses:
Wellbrook Beetling Mill
20 Springhill Road, Maneyware, County Londonderry

Enquiries to: Administrator
Other contacts: Custodian
Access:
Access to staff: By letter, by telephone, by fax, by email
Access to building, collections or gallery: No prior appointment required
Hours: Mid Mar to end Jun, Sep: Sat, Sun and Bank Holiday Mon, 1200 to 1800
Jul and Aug, daily, 1200 to 1800
Other restrictions: Access to mill by guided tour only.
Access for disabled people: Parking provided, access to all public areas
Other restrictions: Access leaflet. Close parking. Access to ground floor of mill only. Shop and picnic areas accessible.

General description:
Linen finishing mill. A hammer mill powered by water for beetling - the final process in linen manufacturing. Original machinery in working order and 'hands-on' demonstration of how linen was manufactured in the 19th century.
Information services:
Helpline available, tel no: 028 8675 1735.
Cottage Industry Exhibition on Linen.
Tel for details of flax sowing and pulling days.
'Touch and Sound' tours for visually impaired visitors by arrangement.
Special visitor services: Guided tours, materials and/or activities for children.
Education services: Group education facilities, resources for Key Stage 2.
Services for disabled people: For the visually impaired.
Printed publications:
NT Guide Book
Wellbrook Schools Resource Book

3067
WELLCOME MUSEUM
See - Egypt Centre

3068
WELLINGTON ARCH
Hyde Park Corner, London, W1J 7JZ

Tel: 020 7930 2726
Fax: 020 7925 1019
Formed from: Office of the Banking Ombudsman

Organisation type and purpose: Historic building, house or site.
Parent body:
English Heritage (London Region)
23 Savile Row, London, W1X 1AB, tel: 020 7973 3000, fax: 020 7937 3001

Enquiries to: House Manager

continued overleaf

Access:
Access to staff: By letter, by telephone, by fax
Access to building, collections or gallery: No prior appointment required
Hours: 1 Apr to 30 Sep, Wed to Sun and Bank Holidays, 1000 to 1800; Oct, Wed to Sun, 1000 to 1700; 1 Nov to 31 March, Wes to Sun 1000 to 1600.
Other restrictions: Closed 24,25,26 Dec and 1 Jan.
Access for disabled people: access to all public areas

General description:
One of the most splendid landmarks in London, Wellington Arch is now open to the public for the first time in history. Originally designed in 1825 as a grand entrance to Buckingham Palace, the Arch has had a fascinating history of both attention and neglect, praise and ridicule, and was last home to London's smallest police station. It offers spectacular views of the London skyline and surrounding Royal Parks, and houses an exhibition on London's statues and monuments.
Catalogues:
Catalogue for library is in-house only.

Internet home pages:
http://www.english-heritage.org.uk

3069
WELLINGTON AVIATION

British School House, Bourton Road, Moreton-in-Marsh, Gloucestershire, GL56 0BG

Tel: 01608 650323
Fax: 01608 650323
Formed: 1990

Organisation type and purpose: Independently owned, museum, suitable for ages: 12+.
Memorial to local Royal Air Force Station.

Enquiries to: Principal
Access:
Access to staff: By letter, by telephone
Access to building, collections or gallery: No prior appointment required
Hours: Tue to Sun, 1000 to 1230 and 1400 to 1730 (last admissions 1200 and 1700)
Access for disabled people: Parking provided, toilet facilities

General description:
Sectioned radial aircraft engines, sections of geodetic aircraft construction, radio/navigational/bomb aiming equipment, RAF/WAAF headgear through the years; Chaplains equipment; purpose made collection of aircraft models.
Collections:
Sectioned Bristol and Armstrong Siddely radial engines
Pictures, photographs of aviation and local military history
Aircraft and engine technical library (in house)
Collection of Royal Air Force treasures not normally found in the larger aircraft museums
Catalogues:
Catalogue for part of the collections is only available in-house.
Printed publications:
Royal Air Force, History of Moreton-in-Marsh (Hamlyn J and Tyack, G V, available for purchase, direct)
Electronic and video products:
The Corporal - Story of Gerry V Tyack 1939-2001, his efforts to record the memory and history of the local Royal Air Force Station (video, for purchase, direct)

Internet home pages:
http://www.wellingtonaviation.org

3070
WELLINGTON EXHIBITION

Stratfield Saye House, Stratfield Saye, Reading, Berkshire, RG7 2BZ

Tel: 01256 882882
Fax: 01256 882115
Formed: 1974

Formerly: Stratfield Saye Preservation Trust

Organisation type and purpose: Independently owned, registered charity (charity number 289822), historic building, house or site.
Heritage site.
The home of the 1st Duke of Wellington with exhibition of his life.

Enquiries to: Administrator
Other contacts: Registrar for enquires about the collection.
Access:
Access to staff: By letter, by telephone
Hours: Mon to Fri, 0900 to 1300 and 1400 to 1700
Access to building, collections or gallery: No access other than to staff
Hours: Jun, Jul and Aug: Wed to Sun
Other restrictions: Pre-booked groups only, Jun, Jul and Aug: Mon and Tue; weekdays in Sep.
Access for disabled people: Parking provided, level entry, toilet facilities

General description:
An exhibition portraying the life and times of Arthur Wellesley, 1st Duke of Wellington. The collection includes many personal possessions, including uniforms and items of interest during the Iron Duke's long life as a soldier and politician. Within the exhibition is the 18 ton funeral hearse, made in 1852 from French cannon captured at Waterloo, only used at the 1st Duke's funeral. The collection also contains furniture and pictures given to the Iron Duke and bought by him in Paris after the Battle of Waterloo in 1815
Information services:
Special visitor services: Guided tours..
Collections:
1st Duke of Wellington's military and political papers housed in Southampton University Library
Printed publications:
Guide Book (available direct, £2.50 plus p&p)

Internet home pages:
http://www.stratfield-saye-house.co.uk
Opening times; history of 1st Duke of Wellington.

3071
WELLINGTON MUSEUM, THE

See - Apsley House, The Wellington Museum

3072
WELLS CATHEDRAL

Cathedral Green, Wells, Somerset, BA5 2UE

Tel: 01749 674483
Fax: 01749 832210
Email: visits@wellscathedral.uk.net

Organisation type and purpose: Historic building, house or site, suitable for ages: 5+.
Anglican cathedral.

Enquiries to: Administrator
Other contacts: Archivist, Librarian, Visits Department
Access:
Access to staff: By letter, by telephone, by fax, by email, visitors by prior appointment, Internet web pages
Access to building, collections or gallery: No prior appointment required
Hours: Apr to Sep, 0700 to 1900
Oct to Mar, 0700 to 1815
Other restrictions: There are restrictions due to services and events
Access for disabled people: ramped entry, toilet facilities
Other restrictions: Parking adjacent to the cathedral

General description:
Religious, historical, architectural, archaeological, archival.
Information services:
A Braille plan and a hearing loop system is available.
Special visitor services: Guided tours.
Education services: Group education facilities.
Services for disabled people: For the hearing impaired.

Internet home pages:
http://www.wellscathedral.org.uk

3073
WELLS MUSEUM DEVELOPMENT TRUST

Cathedral Garden, Wells, Somerset, BA5 2UE

Tel: 01749 675337
Fax: 01749 675337
Formed: 1898

Organisation type and purpose: Independently owned, registered charity (charity number 200738), museum, suitable for ages: 8+.

Enquiries to: Administrator
Other contacts: Curator of Collections for all enquiries relating to collections.
Access:
Access to staff: By letter, by telephone, visitors by prior appointment, charges made to all users
Access for disabled people: level entry, toilet facilities

3074
WELLS MUSEUM

8 Cathedral Green, Wells, Somerset, BA5 2UE

Tel: 01749 673477
Email: wellsmuseum@ukonline.co.uk
Formed: 1894

Organisation type and purpose: Independently owned, registered charity (charity number 200738), museum, research organisation.

Enquiries to: Curator
Access:
Access to staff: By letter, by telephone, by fax, by email, visitors by prior appointment, letter of introduction required
Other restrictions: Curator and Administrator work part time, contact mornings only.
Access to building, collections or gallery: No prior appointment required
Hours: 3 Apr to 30 Oct: Mon to Sun, 1000 to 1730,30 Oct to 2 Apr 2001: Mon to Sun, 1100 to 1600 (closed Tue).
Access for disabled people: level entry, toilet facilities

General description:
Archaeology and geology of the area including the Mendips; local and social history of Wells.
Information services:
Library available for reference (for conditions see Access above)
Special visitor services: Guided tours.
Education services: Group education facilities..
Collections:
18th and 19th century needlework samplers
Phillips Collection (1200 glass plate photographs of Wells)
Catalogues:
Catalogue for library is in-house only. Catalogue for part of the collections is only available in-house.

Internet home pages:
http://www.somerset.gov.uk/museums

3075
WELSH FOLK MUSEUM

See - Museum of Welsh Life

3076
WELSH HIGHLAND RAILWAY LIMITED

Gelerts Farm, Madoc Street West, Porthmadog, Gwynedd, LL49 9DY

Tel: 01766 513402 or 0151 608 1950 (out of season)
Fax: 01766 530774
Acronym or abbreviation: WHR Porthmadog
Formed: 1964

Formerly: Welsh Highland Light Railway (1964) Limited, date of change, 1996

Organisation type and purpose: Statutory body, membership association (membership is by subscription), present number of members: 1200, voluntary organisation, registered charity, museum, consultancy.
To support the rebuilding of the Welsh Highland Railway, to run a tourist train service on the line using heritage stock.
Subsidiary and at the same address is:
Cwmni Rheilffordd Beddgelert Cyf (CRB)

Enquiries to: Chairman
Direct tel: 0151 608 1950
Direct fax: 0151 608 2696
Direct email: dw@allan89.fsnet.co.uk
Other contacts: Commercial Manager 0151 608 1950 for sales etc.
Access:
Access to staff: By letter, by telephone, by fax, by email, visitors by prior appointment, Internet web pages
Hours: Mon to Fri, 0900 to 1700
Other restrictions: Out of season access by prior appointment.
Access for disabled people: Parking provided, level entry, toilet facilities

General description:
General information appertaining to 'two foot' gauge railways, civil and mechanical engineering for 'two foot' gauge railway, repairs, maintenance and spares, steam and diesel engines relevant to the above. Museum and archive material slowly becoming available.
Collections:
Original and copies of works manuals and instruction books
Steam and diesel locomotives
Original archive plate collection of line in use 1890 to 1937
Trade and statistical:
Overseas contacts for importing narrow gauge railway materials into the UK.
Printed publications:
Large stock of books available direct from WHR House (magazine, quarterly, for members)
Quarterly newsletter dealing with WHR heritage topics
Electronic and video products:
Videos

Internet home pages:
http://www.whr.co.uk

3077
WELSH INDUSTRIAL AND MARITIME MUSEUM
See - National Museums and Galleries of Wales

3078
WELSH SLATE MUSEUM LLANBERIS
Padarn Country Park, Llanberis, Gwynedd, LL55 4TY

Tel: 01286 870630
Fax: 01286 871906
Email: slate@nmgw.ac.uk
Formed: 1972

Organisation type and purpose: National government body, national organisation, registered charity (charity number 525774), museum, suitable for ages: 5+.
Welsh Assembly sponsored body.
Parent body:
National Museums & Galleries of Wales (NMGW)
Tel: 02920 397951, email: info@nmgw.ac.uk

Enquiries to: Marketing Officer
Other contacts: Education Officer for education queries.
Access:
Access to staff: By letter, by telephone, by fax, by email, visitors by prior appointment, Internet web pages
Hours: Mon to Fri, 0900 to 1600
Access for disabled people: Parking provided, level entry, toilet facilities

General description:
The museum is housed in the workshops that once serviced the Dinorwig slate quarry. The Chief Engineer's House refurbished as it would have been between 1910 and 1920. Welsh slate industry: history, geology, social.
Information services:
Education services: Group education facilities, resources for Key Stages 1 and 2, 3, 4 and Further or Higher Education..
Collections:
Original workshops for Dinorwig Slate Quarry
Large collections of industrial items/documents relating to the industry
Publications list:
is available in hard copy and online.

Internet home pages:
http://www.nmgw.ac.uk/wsm

3079
WENLOCK PRIORY
Much Wenlock, Shropshire, TF13 6HS

Tel: 01952 727466
Formed: 680

Organisation type and purpose: National organisation, historic building, house or site, suitable for ages: 5+.
Parent body:
English Heritage (West Midlands Region)
Tel: 0121 625 6820

Enquiries to: Curator
Access:
Access to staff: By letter, by telephone
Access to building, collections or gallery: No prior appointment required
Hours: 29 Mar to 30 Sep: 1000 to 1800
Oct: daily, 1000 to 1700,1 Nov to 31 Mar: Wed to Sun, 1000 to 1300 and 1400 to 1600
Other restrictions: Closed 24 to 26 Dec and 1 Jan
Opening times are subject to change, for up-to-date information contact English Heritage by phone or visit the website.
Access for disabled people: Parking provided, ramped entry, access to all public areas, toilet facilities

General description:
The ruins of a large Cluniac property, set in an attractive garden featuring delightful topiary.
Information services:
Special visitor services: Tape recorded guides.
Services for disabled people: For the visually impaired; for the hearing impaired.
Printed publications:
Guide Book

Internet home pages:
http://www.english-heritage.org.uk

3080
WEOLEY CASTLE
Birmingham

Closed until further notice

3081
WERNHER COLLECTION AT RANGER'S HOUSE, THE
Chesterfield Walk, Blackheath, London, SE10 8QX

Tel: 020 8853 0035
Fax: 020 8853 0090

Parent body:
English Heritage (London Region)
23 Savile Row, London, W1X 1AB, tel: 020 7973 3000, fax: 020 7937 3001

Enquiries to: House Manager
Access:
Access to staff: By letter, by telephone, by fax
Access to building, collections or gallery: No prior appointment required
Hours: Apr to Sep: Wed to Sun and Bank Holidays, 1000 to 1800
Oct: Wed to Sun, 1000 to 1700
Nov to Mar: Wed to Sun 1000 to 1600
Other restrictions: Closed 24 to 26 Dec and 1 Jan.
Opening times are subject to change, for up-to-date information contact English Heritage by phone or visit the website.
Access for disabled people: access to all public areas

General description:
A red-brick villa built c.1700 is the new home to the fabulous 'Wernher Collection'. Over 650 works of art with a N. European flavour, amassed by self-made millionaire Julius Wernher at the turn of the 20th century.
Information services:
Special visitor services: Tape recorded guides..
Collections:
Sevres porcelain, the largest private collection of Renaissance jewellery in the UK, limoges, enamels and more

Internet home pages:
http://www.english-heritage.org.uk

3082
WESLEY'S CHAPEL, MUSEUM OF METHODISM AND WESLEY'S HOUSE
49 City Road, London, EC1Y 1AU

Tel: 020 7253 2262
Fax: 020 7608 3825
Formed: 1778

Organisation type and purpose: Independently owned, museum, historic building, house or site, suitable for ages: all ages.
Historic Methodist chapel and period house (John Wesley's house).

Enquiries to: Curator
Other contacts: Office Manager for group bookings, room and hall hire.
Access:
Access to staff: By letter, by telephone, by fax, in person
Hours: Mon to Sat 1000 to 1600; Sun, 1200 to 1400
Access for disabled people: ramped entry, toilet facilities
Other restrictions: Access to most areas (but not Wesley's House).

General description:
History of John Wesley (1703-1791) and the Wesley Family. History of Methodism from 1739 to present. The management of historic houses (18th century town houses). Wesley's work and theology. The Chapel, designed by George Dance the Younger, was built in 1778 by Samuel Tooth. Wesley's house was built in 1779.
Information services:
Library available for reference (for conditions see Access above)
Special visitor services: Guided tours, tape recorded guides, materials and/or activities for children.
Education services: Group education facilities, resources for Key Stages 1 and 2 and Further or Higher Education..
Collections:
Large colletion of Wesley ceramics
Methodist paintings
Wesley's electrical machine and his study chair
Charles Wesley's organ
John Wesley's tomb and pulpit
Catalogues:
Catalogue for library is in-house only. Catalogue for part of the collections is only available in-house.
Publications list:
is available in hard copy.
Printed publications:
Titles by John Wesley
An extensive range of publications about John Wesley, Methodism and related subjects
Electronic and video products:
Wesley's Chapel - Past and Present (video, £10)

continued overleaf

Cassettes and CDs of Charles Wesley's Hymns and Music are available

Address for ordering publications:
Printed publications:
Shop Manageress, Museum of Methodism
Wesley's Chapel, 49 City Road, London, EC1Y 1AU

3083
WESSEX WATER MUSEUM

See - Water Supply Museum

3084
WEST BERKSHIRE MUSEUM

The Wharf, Newbury, Berkshire, RG14 5AS

Tel: 01635 30511
Fax: 01635 38535
Email: heritage@westberks.gov.uk
Formed: 1904
Formed from: Newbury Borough Museum, date of change, 1974; Newbury District Museum, date of change, 1998

Organisation type and purpose: Local government body, museum.

Enquiries to: Administrator
Access:
Access to staff: By letter, by telephone, by fax, by email, visitors by prior appointment

General description:
Kennet & Avon Canal; Greenham Common; Civil War battles; Newbury Wharf; Newbury Coat; archaeological finds, rural industries, fabulous fashions.

3085
WEST COUNTRY ART

Clifton Arcade, Boyces Avenue, Clifton, Bristol, BS8 4AA

Tel: 0117 973 8331
Formed: 1993

Organisation type and purpose: Independently owned, art gallery, historic building, house or site, suitable for ages: 18+.

Enquiries to: Curator
Access:
Access to staff: By letter, by telephone, in person, visitors by prior appointment
Access to building, collections or gallery: No prior appointment required
Hours: Mon to Sat, 1000 to 1730

General description:
Period 19th/early 20th century British and Continental pictures.
Catalogues:
Catalogue for part of the collections is available in-house and part is published.
Publications list:
is available in hard copy.

Address for ordering publications:
Printed publications:
Gallery Director

Internet home pages:
http://freespace.virgin.net/clifton.arcade/Shop2.htm

3086
WEST GREEN HOUSE GARDEN

West Green, Hartley Witney, Hampshire, RG27 8JB

Tel: 01252 844611
Fax: 01252 844611

Organisation type and purpose: National organisation, registered charity (charity number 205846), historic building, house or site, suitable for ages: 5+.
Parent body:
The National Trust (South & South East Region)
Thames & Solent Regional Office, tel: 01494 528051

Enquiries to: Manager
Access:
Access to staff: By letter, by telephone, by fax

General description:
A delightful series of walled gardens surrounding a charming 18th century house. The largest features herbaceous beds with wonderful colour combinations and a superb ornamental kitchen garden. The Nymphaeum is fully restored with water steps and Italianate planting. Also the Lake Field and its Follies and Lake are now open but may, from time to time, be closed due to dampness. Restoration work is ongoing and, at the discretion of the lessee, restrictions are frequently necessary for the development and protection of the garden.

Internet home pages:
http://www.nationaltrust.org.uk

3087
WEST HIGHLAND MUSEUM

8 Cameron Square, Fort William, Inverness-shire, PH33 6AJ

Tel: 01397 702169
Fax: 01397 710927
Formed: 1922

Organisation type and purpose: Museum, suitable for ages: all ages.

Enquiries to: Curator
Access:
Access to staff: By letter, by telephone, visitors by prior appointment
Hours: By appointment only
Access to building, collections or gallery: No prior appointment required
Hours: Mon to Sat, 1000 to 1600;
Jun to Sep: Mon to Sat, 1000 to 1700;
Jul and Aug: Sun also, 1400 to 1700
Other restrictions: Closed Sun except Jul and Aug.
Access for disabled people: level entry, toilet facilities
Other restrictions: Access to ground floor, ambulent for upper floor.

General description:
A local history museum. Contains significant Jacobite collections and important collections to do with the West Highlands, particularly tartans, the 1745 Rising, archaeology; local, social and natural history; and geology.
Information services:
Guided tours if booked.
Resources particularly for primary school age.
Special visitor services: Guided tours.
Education services: Group education facilities..
Collections:
Alexander Carmichael social history collection from many periods
Jacobite collections/Bonny Prince Charlie, mid 18th century
Catalogues:
Catalogue for library is in-house only. Catalogue for all of the collections is only available in-house.

3088
WEST KINGSDOWN WINDMILL

Off A20, between, Wrotham, and, Framlingham, Kent

Tel: 01474 852357

Organisation type and purpose: Historic building, house or site.
Member of:
Kent Windmills
Owned by:
Kent County Council (KCC)

General description:
Windmill has undergone a period of restoration.

3089
WEST LANCASHIRE LIGHT RAILWAY

Station Road, Hesketh Bank, Preston, Lancashire, PR4 6SP

Tel: 01772 815881
Fax: 0870 444 3245
Email: sec@westlancs.org
Formed: 1967

Organisation type and purpose: Membership association (membership is by subscription), present number of members: 85, voluntary organisation, museum.
Narrow gauge steam railway.
Honorary Secretary:
West Lancashire Light Railway
8 Croft Avenue, Orrell, Wigan, Lancashire, WN5 8TW, tel: 01695 622654, email/website: neil_mcmurdy@msn.com or neil@westlancs.org

Enquiries to: Honorary Secretary
Direct tel: 01695 622654 evenings
Access:
Access to staff: By letter, by telephone, in person, Internet web pages
Hours: Sundays and Bank Holidays, 1130 to 1730
Other restrictions: Steam trains run from Easter to the end of October.
Access for disabled people: level entry

General description:
A 2ft gauge line built in 1967 to conserve some of the mainly industrial equipment that was fast disappearing. It serves as a working museum for a variety of historic locomotives and other railway equipment from industrial sites in Britain and overseas. Narrow gauge railway, preservation, restoration, steam locomotives.
Collections:
Six steam locomotives
Petrol, diesel and battery powered locomotives
Railway equipment
Trade and statistical:
Data and exhibits on UK industrial narrow gauge railways.
Publications list:
is available in hard copy.
Printed publications:
Guide/Handbook (£1)
Drive a Steam Loco (leaflet free)
General Information (leaflet free)
Hire a Train (leaflet free)
Membership (leaflet free)
Special Events (leaflet free)

Internet home pages:
http://www.westlancs.org
Guide to Railway, details of all locomotives at Railway and Brief History.

3090
WEST MERCIA CONSTABULARY HERITAGE CENTRE

Closed
See - West Midlands Police Museum

3091
WEST MIDLANDS POLICE MUSEUM

Sparkhill Police Station, 639 Stratford Road, Sparkhill, Birmingham, B11 4EA

Tel: 0121 626 7181
Formed: 1991

Organisation type and purpose: Independently owned, museum.
Part of:
West Midlands Police

Enquiries to: Curator
Direct email: d.a.cross@west-midlands.police.uk
Access:
Access to staff: By letter only, visitors by prior appointment

Access to building, collections or gallery: Prior appointment required
Hours: Part time variable hours
Other restrictions: No access if school is present.

General description:
Historical police items.
Information services:
Education services: Group education facilities, resources for Key Stages 2, 3 and 4..
Collections:
Prisoners' photographs, 1860, 18 items
Prisoners' photographs, 1880-1884, 750 items
Catalogues:
Catalogue for library is in-house only. Catalogue for all of the collections is only available in-house.
Printed publications:
Birmingham - The Sinister Side (£7.99 plus p&p £1.50)

3092
WEST MIDLANDS REGIONAL MUSEUMS COUNCIL

Harris Industrial Estate, Hanbury Road, Stoke Prior, Bromsgrove, Worcestershire, B60 4AD

Tel: 01527 872258
Fax: 01527 576960
Email: wmrmc@wm-museums.co.uk
Acronym or abbreviation: WMRMC
Formed: 1982
Formerly: West Midlands Area Museums Service (WMAMS), date of change, 1997

Organisation type and purpose: National government body, advisory body, membership association (membership is by subscription, qualification), present number of members: 93, registered charity (charity number 513708).
Provision of advice, support, advocacy to museums in the region.

Enquiries to: Chief Executive
Access:
Access to staff: By letter, by telephone, by fax, by email, Internet web pages
Hours: Mon to Fri, 0900 to 1700
Access to building, collections or gallery: Prior appointment required
Access for disabled people: Parking provided, access to all public areas, toilet facilities

General description:
Museum practice and philosophy; library.
Catalogues:
Catalogue for library is in-house only.
Publications list:
is available on-line.

Internet home pages:
http://www.wm-museum.co.uk
Information for museums in the West Midlands.
http://www.wm-museums.co.uk/pub/

3093
WEST OXFORDSHIRE MUSEUM CENTRE

See - Witney & District Museum

3094
WEST PARK MUSEUM

Prestbury Road, Macclesfield, Cheshire, SK10 3BJ

Tel: 01625 619831
Email: silkmuseum@tiscali.co.uk

Organisation type and purpose: Museum, art gallery, historic building, house or site, suitable for ages: all ages.
Parent body:
Macclesfield Borough Council
Managed by:
Macclesfield Museums Trust

Enquiries to: Curator
Other contacts: Education Officer
Access:
Access to staff: By letter, by telephone
Access to building, collections or gallery: No prior appointment required
Hours: Easter to Oct, Tue to Sun and Bank Holidays, 1330 to 1630
Winter opening 1300 to 1600
Other restrictions: Closed Mon and Good Friday
Access for disabled people: ramped entry, access to all public areas
Other restrictions: Wheelchair access

General description:
Purpose-built in 1898, the museum houses Egyptian material; mainly Victorian watercolours and oils, specialising in early work of Charles Tunnicliffe R.A. and other local artists; ethnography; and medals.
Local history artefacts include a wide range of fine and decorative art material and objects.
Displays include Life in Ancient Egypt, Law & Order and the life of Charles Roe.
Information services:
Education services: Group education facilities..
Collections:
Marianne Brocklehurst Egyptian collection. Artefacts collected in the 1870s during trips to Egypt.

Internet home pages:
http://www.silk-macclesfield.org

3095
WEST PARK ROMAN VILLA

See - Rockbourne Roman Villa

3096
WEST PENNARD COURT BARN

West Pennard, Glastonbury, Somerset

Tel: 01985 843600 (Regional Office), 01458 850212 (Keyholder)

Organisation type and purpose: National organisation, registered charity (charity number 205846), historic building, house or site.
Parent body:
The National Trust (South West Region)
Regional Office for Wessex, tel: 01985 843600

Enquiries to: Manager
Access:
Access to staff: By letter, by telephone
Access to building, collections or gallery: Prior appointment required
Hours: Admission by appointment only.
Access by key, to be collected by arrangement with Mr P H Green, Court Barn Farm, West Bradley, Somerset, tel. 01458 850212.

General description:
A 15th century barn of five bays with a roof of interesting construction. Repaired and given to the Trust by the Society for the Protection of Ancient Buildings in 1938.

Internet home pages:
http://www.nationaltrust.org.uk/regions/wessex

3097
WEST SOMERSET RAILWAY

The Railway Station, Minehead, Somerset, TA24 5BG

Tel: 01643 704996
Fax: 01643 706349
Email: info@west-somerset-railway.co.uk
Formed: 1976

Organisation type and purpose: Service industry.
Private railway.
Subsidiary body:
West Somerset Railway Association
The Railway Station, Bishops Lydeard, Somerset, TA4 3BX, tel: 01823 432125, fax: 01823 433959, email/website: wsr@btinternet.com

Enquiries to: Managing Director
Access:
Access to staff: By telephone, by email, in person, visitors by prior appointment
Hours: Mar to Dec, for tourist and local use
Access for disabled people: ramped entry, toilet facilities

General description:
Operation of longest British preserved railway, using steam and diesel power.
Collections:
Archive data on history of Taunton area railways available from West Somerset Railway Association
Publications list:
is available in hard copy and online.
Printed publications:
Information packs
Group Travel Packs
Local accommodation lists
Steam Footplate Experience Details
Timetable brochures

Internet home pages:
http://www.West-Somerset-Railway.co.uk
Timetables, special events, fares, booking details.

3098
WEST SOMERSET RURAL LIFE MUSEUM

The Old School, Allerford, Near Minehead, Somerset, TA24 8HN

Tel: 01643 862529
Formed: 1983
Formerly: Allerford Museum

Organisation type and purpose: Registered charity (charity number 1065071), museum.

Enquiries to: Honorary Secretary
Direct tel: 01398 371284
Access:
Access to staff: By letter, by telephone, in person
Hours: Mon to Fri, 1030 to 1230 and 1400 to 1630
Access to building, collections or gallery: No prior appointment required
Hours: Easter to end Oct: Mon to Fri, 1030 to 1300 and 1400 to 1630
Access for disabled people: level entry
Other restrictions: Toilet facilities adjacent.

General description:
Museum of rural life.
Information services:
Special visitor services: Materials and/or activities for children.
Education services: Group education facilities..
Collections:
Domestic, farm and local industry equipment of the past
A photographic archive of West Somerset
A fully equipped Victorian Schoolroom with 'dressing-up facilities' for children

3099
WEST STOW COUNTRY PARK & ANGLO-SAXON VILLAGE

See - St Edmundsbury Museums

3100
WEST WALES MARITIME HERITAGE SOCIETY

44 Westhaven, Cosheston, Pembroke Dock, Dyfed, SA72 4UL

Tel: 01646 683764
Acronym or abbreviation: WWMHS
Formed: 1984

Organisation type and purpose: Learned society, registered charity (charity number 1042428), suitable for ages: 16+, research organisation.
Vintage boat research and restoration.
Promote research into local maritime heritage.

Enquiries to: Secretary
Access:
Access to staff: By letter, by telephone

continued overleaf

General description:
A collection of maritime artefacts, including a 52 foot harbour service launch; a 27 foot Flambourough Coble; an 18 foot Pembroke one; an 18 foot lightship lifeboat; various smaller craft; a small maritime library; and a vintage dockside steam crane. Scale models of local relevance, eg RY Victoria & Albert 1843, IJN Warship Hiei, RY Enchantress 1862, 74 Gun Ship 1760.
Information services:
Education services: Group education facilities..
Catalogues:
Catalogue for library is in-house only.
Printed publications:
Secret Waterway (available for purchase, locally)
Microform products:
Being prepared
Electronic and video products:
Being prepared

3101
WEST WYCOMBE PARK
West Wycombe, Buckinghamshire, HP14 3AJ

Tel: 01494 513569
Formed: 1750

Organisation type and purpose: National organisation, registered charity, historic building, house or site, suitable for ages: 12+.
Parent body:
The National Trust (South and South East Region)
Thames and Solent Regional Office, tel: 01494 528051

Enquiries to: Curator
Access:
Access to staff: By letter
Access for disabled people: Parking provided, ramped entry, toilet facilities
Other restrictions: Designated parking 150yds. 1 manual wheelchair available, booking essential. Steps to entrance. Accessible entrance with 1 step. Ground floor largely accessible. No access to other floors.

General description:
A perfectly preserved rococo landscape garden, created in the mid-18th century by Sir Francis Dashwood, founder of the Dilettanti Society and the Hellfire Club. The house is among the most theatrical and Italianate in England, its façades formed as classical temples. The interior has Palmyrene ceilings and decoration, with pictures, furniture and sculpture dating from the time of Sir Francis.
Information services:
Tours of house on weekdays. Tours of grounds by written arrangement.
Braille guide.
Special visitor services: Guided tours.
Services for disabled people: For the visually impaired.

Internet home pages:
http://www.nationaltrust.org.uk

3102
WEST WYCOMBE VILLAGE AND HILL
West Wycombe, Buckinghamshire

Tel: 01494 755573 (Regional Office)
Fax: 01494 463310 (Regional Office)

Organisation type and purpose: National organisation, registered charity (charity number 205846), historic building, house or site, suitable for ages: 5+.
Parent body:
The National Trust (South & South East Region)
Thames & Solent Regional Office, tel: 01494 528051, fax: 01494 463310

Enquiries to: Manager
Access:
Access to staff: By letter, by telephone, by fax, by email
Other restrictions: All enquiries should be directed to Regional Office.

General description:
This Chilterns village comprises buildings spanning several hundred years, with particularly fine examples from the 16th to 18th centuries. The hill, with its fine views, is surmounted by an Iron Age hill-fort and is part of the original landscape design of West Wycombe Park. It is now the site of a church and the Dashwood Mausoleum.

Internet home pages:
http://www.nationaltrust.org.uk

3103
WESTBURY COLLEGE GATEHOUSE
College Road, Westbury-on-Trym, Bristol

Tel: 01985 843600 (Regional Office)

Organisation type and purpose: National organisation, registered charity (charity number 205846), historic building, house or site, suitable for ages: all ages.
Parent body:
The National Trust (South West Region)
Regional Office for Wessex, tel: 01985 843600

Enquiries to: Manager
Access:
Access to building, collections or gallery: Prior appointment required
Other restrictions: Access by key, to be collected by written appointment with the vicar, The Vicarage, 44 Eastfield Road, Westbury-on-Trym, Bristol BS9 4AG, tel. 0117 962 1536/0117 950 8644

General description:
The 15th century gatehouse of the College of Priests (founded in the 13th century), of which John Wyclif was prebend. There is an interesting church (not NT) nearby.

Internet home pages:
http://www.nationaltrust.org.uk/regions/wessex

3104
WESTBURY COURT GARDEN
Westbury-on-Severn, Gloucestershire, GL14 1PD

Tel: 01452 760461
Fax: 01452 760461
Email: westburycourt@nationaltrust.org.uk

Organisation type and purpose: National organisation, registered charity (charity number 205846), historic building, house or site, suitable for ages: all ages.
Parent body:
The National Trust (South West Region)
Regional Office for Wessex, tel: 01985 843600

Enquiries to: Manager
Access:
Access to staff: By letter, by telephone, by fax, by email
Access for disabled people: toilet facilities
Other restrictions: Drop-off point, grounds largely accessible.

General description:
A rare and beautiful survival: the only restored Dutch water garden in the country, laid out 1696-1705. The National Trust's first garden restoration, it was restored in 1971 and is planted with species dating from before 1700. Replica 17th century panelling installed in the pavilion. Parterre returned to 17th century style. Small exhibition of 'Kip' engravings on display in summer house.
Information services:
Family guide; children's quiz/trail
Braille guide, scented plants.
Special events: Easter egg trail; Apple Day
Special visitor services: Guided tours, materials and/or activities for children.
Services for disabled people: For the visually impaired.

Internet home pages:
http://www.nationaltrust.org.uk/regions/wessex

3105
WESTBURY MANOR MUSEUM
84 West Street, Fareham, Hampshire, PO16 0JJ

Tel: 01329 824895
Fax: 01329 825917
Email: musmop@hants.gov.uk
Formed: 1990
Formerly: Fareham Museum

Organisation type and purpose: Local government body, museum, historic building, house or site, suitable for ages: all ages.
Restored Westbury Manor.
Parent body:
Hampshire County Council Museums Service
Chilcomb House, Chilcombe Lane, Winchester, SO23 8RD, tel: 01962 846304, fax: 01962 869836

Enquiries to: Curator
Access:
Access to staff: By letter, by telephone, by fax, by email, in person
Access for disabled people: toilet facilities
Other restrictions: Access to level ground floor, but no wheelchair access to first floor.

General description:
Local history and museum of the Borough of Fareham, archaeology, agriculture, natural science, education old and new, strawberry industry, local churches, the making of bricks, chimney pots and tiles; the poor etc.
Collections:
Items relating to local history of Fareham and District
Catalogues:
Catalogue for all of the collections is on-line.
Trade and statistical:
Brickmaking in Hampshire.
Publications list:
is available in hard copy.
Printed publications:
Publications list is available from the Librarian, Hampshire County Council Museums Service Headquarters, Chilcomb House, Winchester, SO23 8RD

Internet home pages:
http://www.hants.gov.uk/museums/
HMCMS web catalogue, whole collection, 100,000 plus web pages.

3106
WESTGATE MUSEUM
High Street, Winchester, Hampshire, SO23 9JX

Tel: 01962 869864
Fax: 01962 848299
Email: museums@winchester.gov.uk
Formed: 1898

Organisation type and purpose: Local government body, museum, historic building, house or site.
Linked to:
Winchester Museums Service
Tel: 01962 848269, fax: 01962 841365, email/website: museums@winchester.gov.uk
Address for Correspondence:
Historic Resource Centre
75 Hyde Street, Winchester, SO23 7DW, tel: 01962 848269

Enquiries to: Curator
Direct tel: 01962 848269
Direct email: gdenford@winchester.gov.uk
Other contacts: Head of Museums Service
Access:
Access to staff: By letter, by telephone, by fax, by email, in person, visitors by prior appointment
Access to building, collections or gallery: No prior appointment required
Hours: Apr to Oct: Mon to Sat, 1000 to 1700; Sun, 1200 to 1700
Feb to Mar: Tue to Sat, 1000 to 1600; Sun, 1200 to 1600

General description:
One of two surviving medieval gateways in the city walls, the Westgate houses a unique collection of historic weights and measures. The painted ceiling of 1554 commemorates the marriage in Winchester of Queen Mary I to Philip II of Spain. Fine views from the roof.
Information services:
Education services: Group education facilities, resources for Key Stages 2, 3, 4 and Further or Higher Education..
Catalogues:
Catalogue for part of the collections is only available in-house.

Internet home pages:
http://www.winchester.gov.uk/heritage

3107
WESTMINSTER ABBEY

Library and Muniment Room, London, SW1P 3PA

Tel: 020 7222 5152 ext 228
Fax: 020 7654 4827
Email: library@westminster-abbey.org
Formed: 1623

Organisation type and purpose: Abbey church library and archives collection.

Enquiries to: Librarian
Direct tel: 020 7654 4826
Other contacts: Keeper of the Muniments for muniments.
Access:
Access to staff: By letter, by telephone, by fax, by email, visitors by prior appointment, Internet web pages
Hours: Mon to Fri, 1000 to 1300 and 1400 to 1645

General description:
History of Westminster Abbey and its precincts, coronations, St Margaret's Westminster.
Collections:
c. 14,000 early printed books
c. 70,000 documents relating to the Abbey since 1066
Collection of books on the history of Westminster Abbey
Collection of illuminated and other medieval manuscripts
Collection of Pamphlets belonging to William Camden (1551-1623)
K H Oldaker Collection of English Bookbindings, 1655-1920
Langley collection of prints and drawings
Large photographic collection
Music Collection (mainly late 16th and 17th centuries)
Catalogues:
Catalogue for library is in-house only. Catalogue for part of the collections is published.
Printed publications:
Westminster Abbey Record Series Vol 1 (1997) - In progress, 2 volumes published to date
Microform products:
Early music and manuscript collections available from World Microfilms, 2-6 Foscote Mews, W9 2HH

Internet home pages:
http://www.westminster-abbey.org/library
For general information on Westminster Abbey and virtual tour, library pages.

3108
WESTMINSTER ABBEY

Broad Sancturary, Westminster, London, SW1P 3PA

Tel: 020 7222 5152
Fax: 020 7233 2072
Email: info@westminster-abbey.org
Formed: 1065

Organisation type and purpose: Museum, historic building, house or site, suitable for ages: all ages.
Abbey church in daily use since its foundation. Worship as well as a tourist attraction.

Enquiries to: Press & Communications Officer
Direct tel: 020 7654 4890
Direct fax: 020 7654 4891
Direct email: press@westminster-abbey.org
Access:
Access to staff: By letter, by email, Internet web pages
Access to building, collections or gallery: No prior appointment required
Hours: Mon to Fri, 0930 to 1545; Sat, 0930 to 1345
Other restrictions: No tourist visiting on Sundays

Information services:
Helpline available, tel no: Information desk tel 020 7654 4900.
Special visitor services: Guided tours, tape recorded guides.
Services for disabled people: For the hearing impaired.
Collections:
The Royal Tombs including Edward the Confessor, Elizabeth I, Mary Queen of Scots, Henry VII
The Coronation Chair
Poets' Corner including memorials and/or tombs to Chaucer, Shakespeare, Dickens, Handel
The Tomb of the Unknown Warrior
Cloisters and much more
Printed publications:
Books and guides can be purchased from the Abbey's shop
Electronic and video products:
CDs, videos and tapes

Internet home pages:
http://www.westminster-abbey.org
History of Westminster Abbey, visitor and services information, special events information

3109
WESTMINSTER ABBEY, CHAPTER HOUSE

East Cloisters, London, SW1P 3PE

Tel: 020 7222 5897
Fax: 020 7222 0960

Organisation type and purpose: Historic building, house or site, suitable for ages: all ages.
Parent body:
English Heritage (London Region)
23 Savile Row, London, W1X 1AB, tel: 020 7973 3000, fax: 020 7937 3001

Enquiries to: Curator
Direct tel: 020 7973 3493
Access:
Access to staff: By letter, by telephone, by fax
Access to building, collections or gallery: No prior appointment required
Hours: Apr to Sep: daily, 0930 to 1700
Oct: daily 1000 to 1700
Nov to Mar: daily, 1000 to 1600.
Other restrictions: Closed 24 to 26 Dec and 1 Jan, may also be closed on state or holy occasions.
Opening times are subject to change, for up-to-date information contact English Heritage by phone or visit the website.

General description:
Built by the Royal Masons in 1250, Westminster Abbey's Chapter House was used in the 14th century by the Benedictine monks for their daily meetings, and subsequently as the meeting place of the King's Great Council and the Commons, predecessors of today's Parliament. A beautiful octagonal building with vaulted ceiling and a delicate central column, it possesses rarely seen examples of medieval sculpture, its original floor of glazed tiles and spectacular wall paintings.
Information services:
Special visitor services: Tape recorded guides..

Internet home pages:
http://www.english-heritage.org.uk

See also - Westminster Abbey Museum

3110
WESTON PARK MUSEUM

See - Sheffield City Museum and Mappin Art Gallery

3111
WESTON PARK

Weston-under-Lizard, Shifnal, Shropshire, TF11 8LE

Tel: 01952 852100
Fax: 01952 850430
Email: enquiries@weston-park.com
Formed: 1986

Organisation type and purpose: Registered charity (charity number 518325), historic building, house or site, suitable for ages: 5+. Educational charity.
Member of:
Historic House Association

Enquiries to: Public Relations Manager
Access:
Access to staff: By email
Access for disabled people: Parking provided, toilet facilities

General description:
Weston Park is a magnificent stately home set in 1000 acres of parkland situated on the Staffordshire/Shropshire border.
Built in 1671 the house boasts a superb collection of paintings, furniture and objets d'art. Outside, visitors can explore the glorious parkland, meander through the formal gardens, take a variety of woodland walks before relaxing for lunch in The Stables Restaurant.
Children will find lots to do with the renowned Woodland Adventure Playground, Pets Corner, Museum, Deer Park and Miniature Railway.
Information services:
Special visitor services: Guided tours.
Education services: Group education facilities, resources for Key Stages 1 and 2..
Collections:
Collections of fine art including: Van Dyck, Constable, Stubbs, Lely, Holbein, Lutyens, Kneller and Gainsborough
Tapestries from the Gobelin factory in Paris
Porcelain

Internet home pages:
http://www.weston-park.com

3112
WESTON'S CIDER

The Bounds, Much Marcle, Ledbury, Herefordshire, HR8 2NQ

Tel: 01531 660233
Fax: 01531 660619
Formed: 1880

Organisation type and purpose: Independently owned, suitable for ages: 16+.

Enquiries to: Managing Director
Access:
Access to staff: By letter, by telephone, by fax

General description:
Cider-making.
Information services:
Special visitor services: Guided tours, tape recorded guides..

3113
WESTONZOYLAND PUMPING STATION

Museum of Steam Power and Land Drainage, Hoopers Lane, Westonzoyland, Bridgwater, Somerset

Email: webmaster@wzlet.org
Formed: 1980

Organisation type and purpose: Independently owned, registered charity (charity number 279765), museum, suitable for ages: 5+.
Honorary Secretary:
Westonzoyland Pumping Station

continued overleaf

23B Parmin Close, Taunton, TAI 2JY, tel: 01823 257516

Enquiries to: Honorary Secretary
Direct tel: 01823 257516
Access:
Access to staff: By letter, by telephone, by email, in person, Internet web pages
Other restrictions: Visits to staff in person only during opening hours.
Access to building, collections or gallery: No prior appointment required
Hours: Sun, 1400 to 1700
Access for disabled people: level entry, access to all public areas

General description:
Covers all aspects of the land drainage of Somerset, and steam power in the county of Somerset. The pumping station buildings date from the 1830s.
Information services:
Special visitor services: Guided tours, materials and/or activities for children.
Education services: Group education facilities.
Services for disabled people: For the visually impaired; displays and/or information at wheelchair height.
Collections:
Land drainage - engines to pipes! 1861 to date. Numerous items including a restored 1861 Easton & Amos machine
Steam. Examples of various types of engine, including some unique engines - run in steam on certain dates of year. Numerous items
Publications list:
is available in hard copy.
Printed publications:
Bogs and Inundations (Miles I, £3.45)
Easton & Amos - A history of the engineering company (Eaton D, £2.95)
Technical Leaflets Nos 1-15 written by members of the Trust, single fold A4 sheet, 20p each)
Newsletter (quarterly, free to members)

Address for ordering publications:
Printed publications:
Honorary Secretary, WET
38 Holway Hill, Taunton, TA1 2HB

Internet home pages:
http://www.wzlet.org

3114
WESTWOOD MANOR
Westwood, Bradford on Avon, Wiltshire, BA15 2AF

Tel: 01225 863374
Fax: 01225 867316

Organisation type and purpose: National organisation, registered charity (charity number 205846), historic building, house or site.
Parent body:
The National Trust (South West Region)
Regional Office for Wessex, tel: 01985 843600

Enquiries to: Manager
Access:
Access for disabled people: level entry
Other restrictions: Steps to garden then level access into house. Ground floor largely accessible.

General description:
A 15th century stone manor house, altered in the early 17th century, with late Gothic and Jacobean windows and fine plasterwork. There is a modern topiary garden. Westwood Manor is administered for the National Trust by the tenant.
Information services:
Children's quiz/trail.
Special visitor services: Materials and/or activities for children.
Services for disabled people: For the visually impaired.

Internet home pages:
http://www.nationaltrust.org.uk/regions/wessex

3115
WETHERIGGS COUNTY POTTERY LIMITED
Clifton Dykes, Penrith, Cumbria, CA10 2DH

Tel: 01768 892733
Fax: 01768 892722
Email: info@wetheriggs-pottery.co.uk

Organisation type and purpose: Independently owned, historic building, house or site, suitable for ages: all ages.

Enquiries to: Managing Director
Other contacts: Personal Assistant for bookings/booking information.
Access:
Access to staff: By letter, by telephone, by email
Access to building, collections or gallery: No prior appointment required
Hours: Easter to end Sep: Wed to Mon, 1000 to 1730
Oct to Easter: Thu to Mon, 1000 to 1700
Aug: daily, 1000 to 1730
All Cumbrian school holidays
Other restrictions: Groups by prior appointment.
Access for disabled people: Parking provided, access to all public areas, toilet facilities

General description:
The last working steam-powered pottery in the UK. Biggest interactive craft experience in Cumbria. Historic museum, playground, tea-room, animals, newt pond and birds of prey.
Information services:
Groups must book prior to visiting.
Special visitor services: Guided tours, materials and/or activities for children..

Internet home pages:
http://www.wetheriggs-pottery.co.uk

3116
WEYBRIDGE MUSEUM
See - Elmbridge Museum

3117
WEYMOUTH MUSEUM
at Brewers Quay, Hope Square, Weymouth, Dorset, DT4 8TR

Tel: 01305 777622
Fax: 01305 761680

Organisation type and purpose: Museum.

Enquiries to: Curator
Access:
Access to staff: By letter, by telephone, by fax, visitors by prior appointment

General description:
Local and social history, including prints and paintings of the area. Local industries which are featured include brewing and the Weymouth Whitehead torpedo works.
Collections:
Bussell collection of prints and paintings of the Weymouth area.

3118
WHEAL MARTYN CHINA CLAY MUSEUM
Carthew, St Austell, Cornwall, PL26 8XG

Tel: 01726 850362
Fax: 01726 850362
Email: info@wheal-martyn.com
Formed: 1975
Formerly: St Austell China Clay Museum Limited

Organisation type and purpose: Independently owned, registered charity (charity number 1001838), museum.

Enquiries to: Manager
Access:
Access to staff: By letter, by telephone, by fax, by email, visitors by prior appointment
Hours: Mon to Fri, 0900 to 1600
Access to building, collections or gallery: No access other than to staff
Hours: Easter to end Oct: Daily, 1000 to 1700
Winter: Tue, Wed, Thu, 1100 to 1600
Other restrictions: Research by appointment.
Access for disabled people: Parking provided, ramped entry, toilet facilities
Other restrictions: Some limited wheelchair access to other areas.

General description:
A collection covering the china clay industry and its tools and equipment, history and technology. The museum is open-air and incorporates two 19th century china clay works and modern pit views; there is a photograph and archive collection, and material covering the local history of the mid-Cornwall area.
Information services:
Some visually impaired services.
Special visitor services: Guided tours, materials and/or activities for children.
Education services: Group education facilities, resources for Key Stages 2, 3, 4 and Further or Higher Education.
Services for disabled people: For the visually impaired.
Collections:
Photograph collection
Tools, including Rosevear bootmakers' collection
Catalogues:
Catalogue for all of the collections is only available in-house.

Internet home pages:
http://www.wheal-martyn.com
History of site museum; opening hours etc.

3119
WHERNSIDE MANOR
Cave and Fell Centre, Dent, Sedburgh, Cumbria, LA10 5RE

Tel: 01539 625213
Email: whernsidemanor@aol.com
Full name: Whernside Manor Bunkhouses
Formed: 2000
Changed ownership, date of change, 2000

Organisation type and purpose: Historic building, house or site.

Enquiries to: Manager
Access:
Access to staff: By letter, visitors by prior appointment
Hours: Mon to Fri, 0900 to 1700
Access to building, collections or gallery: Prior appointment required

General description:
Caving, walking.
Printed publications:
Leaflets available on request

Internet home pages:
http://www.whernsidemanor.com

3120
WHIMPLE DOLLS HOUSE & TOY MUSEUM
Exeter

Closed

3121
WHIPPLE MUSEUM OF THE HISTORY OF SCIENCE
See - Cambridge University, Whipple Museum of the History of Science

3122
WHISKY MUSEUM, THE
24 Fife Street, Dufftown, Moray, AB55 4AL

Tel: 01309 673701
Formed: 2001
Formerly: Dufftown Museum

Organisation type and purpose: Independently owned, registered charity, museum.

Enquiries to: Public Relations Manager
Direct tel: 01340 821097
Direct fax: 01340 821097
Direct email: whiskyshop.dufftown@virgin.net
Access:
Access to staff: By letter, by telephone, by fax, by email, in person
Access for disabled people: Parking provided, level entry, access to all public areas, toilet facilities

General description:
Whisky making and its close connection to the local community, particularly the 9 distilleries of Dufftown, (museum in the process of development).
Information services:
Education services: Group education facilities..
Collections:
Distillery artefacts, old photographs and prints, illicit stills, whisky books

3123
WHITBY ABBEY
Whitby, North Yorkshire

Tel: 01947 603568

Organisation type and purpose: National organisation, advisory body, museum, historic building, house or site.
Parent body:
English Heritage (Yorkshire Region)
Tel: 01904 601901

Enquiries to: Manager
Access:
Access to staff: By letter, by telephone, in person
Access to building, collections or gallery: No prior appointment required
Hours: 29 Mar to 30 Sep: daily, 1000 to 1800 (17 Jul to 31 Aug: daily, 0930 to 1800)
1 to 31 Oct: daily, 1000 to 1700,1 Nov to 31 Mar: daily, 1000 to 1600 (15 to 23 Feb: daily, 1000 to 1700)
Other restrictions: Closed 24 to 26 Dec and 1 Jan.
Opening times are subject to change, for up-to-date information contact English Heritage by phone or visit the website.
Access for disabled people: Parking provided, toilet facilities
Other restrictions: Parking at south entrance, charged.

General description:
Set high on a clifftop, the Abbey remains overlook a picturesque town and harbour with associations as diverse as Victorian jewellery, whaling and Count Dracula. The Abbey today is a gaunt and moving ruin. St Hilda, the abbey's founder, brought monks and nuns to the religious house on the headland in 657. The Synod of 664 was held there where representatives of the Celtic and Roman churches were summoned to decide the date of Easter.
After its dissolution in 1538, Whitby passed to the Cholmley family who built a mansion largely out of materials plundered from the monastery. As part of a major project, begun in 1998, encompassing the whole of the headland, a new visitor centre has been built within the walls of the old mansion. Spectacular audiovisual displays recreate the medieval abbey in all its splendour, and the 17th century house and its interiors and gardens.

Internet home pages:
http://www.english-heritage.org.uk

3124
WHITBY LIFEBOAT MUSEUM
Pier Road, Whitby, North Yorkshire, YO21 3PU

Tel: 01947 602001
Fax: 01947 602001
Formed: 1957

Organisation type and purpose: National organisation, registered charity (charity number 209603), museum, suitable for ages: 5+.

Enquiries to: Curator
Other contacts: Shop Supervisor for information on opening times; products on offer/availability.
Access:
Access to staff: By letter, by telephone, in person, visitors by prior appointment
Access for disabled people: level entry

General description:
The museum is housed in a double boathouse used by the RNLI from 1895 to 1957. The displays cover models; service boards; and the history of Whitby lifeboat from the first one in service up to the present day. Includes photographs of more recent lifeboat services; and a model of the famous hospital ship 'Rohilla' which sank off Whitby in 1914. Various artefacts from the ship are on show.
Catalogues:
Catalogue for part of the collections is only available in-house.

3125
WHITBY MUSEUM AND ART GALLERY
Pannett Park, Whitby, North Yorkshire, YO21 1RE

Tel: 01947 602908
Formed: 1823

Organisation type and purpose: Independently owned, learned society, registered charity, museum, art gallery, suitable for ages: 5+.
Run by:
Whitby Literary and Philosophical Society

Enquiries to: Information Officer
Other contacts: The Society for library and archives.
Access:
Access for disabled people: Parking provided, level entry, access to all public areas, toilet facilities

General description:
Whitby Museum is an independent museum with a unique collection built up over more than 170 years. There is a large marine section, and Captain Cook and Scoresby sections. Fossils are also exhibited, as are artefacts from Whitby's past. Archaeological artefacts; natural history; costumes; weapons; militaria; and coins and medals are also on display.
Information services:
Education services: Group education facilities..
Collections:
The skeletons of marine reptiles on display are of national, if not international, importance, Jurassic
Whitby's jet industry is reflected in a famous collection of jet jewellery and carvings, mostly Victorian
The Museum Library has notable collections
Publications list:
is available in hard copy.
Printed publications:
Whitby Museum Guide (£1.50)
Whitby Museum Teachers' Pack (£5)
Streets of Whitby and Their Associations (Kendall H P, £1.50)
Prints of Old Whitby (Humble A F, £1.50)
Whitby Museum Factsheets eg Fossils, Ammonites, Jet, Shipping, Scoresbys, Hand of Glor, Tempest Prognosticator (10p each)

Internet home pages:
http://www.whitbymuseum.org.uk

3126
WHITBY PICTORIAL ARCHIVES HERITAGE CENTRE
Flowergate, Whitby, North Yorkshire, YO21 3BA

Tel: 01947 821364
Fax: 01947 821436
Email: info@whitbyarchives.freeserve.co.uk
Formed: 1985

Organisation type and purpose: Membership association (membership is by subscription), museum, suitable for ages: all ages, research organisation.
Charitable Trust, tourist facility.
Parent body:
Whitby Pictorial Archives Trust (WPAT)

Enquiries to: Director
Other contacts: Manager
Access:
Access to staff: By letter, by telephone, by fax, by email, in person, charges made to all users, Internet web pages
Hours: Summer: Mon to Fri; 1030 to 1600; Sat, Sun, 1100 to 1500
Winter: Mon to Sun, 1100 to 1500
Other restrictions: Research facilities restricted at weekends.
Access to building, collections or gallery: No prior appointment required
Hours: Apr to Oct: Mon to Fri, 1000 to 1600
Nov to Mar: Mon to Fri, 1100 to 1500
Other restrictions: Appointment advised for research using collections. Collection and file room may be closed some Sat, Sun.
Access for disabled people: level entry, toilet facilities
Other restrictions: Access to all areas except café. Disabled chairlift to lower floor.

General description:
Local, general, family history of Whitby and North Yorkshire, directories, birth, marriage and death records, extensive photographic collection, documents, local records and ephemera.
Growing collection of artefacts and historic objects, maps. New exhibition: The Warring 40s Team, authentic 1940s, educational and entertaining. Rohilla Exhibition.
A full range of photographic and 'on paper' general history files, all filed by subject. These include many census records, parish registers, lists of trades and professional people, monumental inscriptions, ships and school records and many more. Resource material may be consulted in person or by mail order.
Information services:
Archives available for reference.
Local and family history research service either by the enquirer, or on their behalf. Local history advice given.
Special visitor services: Guided tours, materials and/or activities for children.
Education services: Group education facilities, resources for Key Stages 1 and 2, 3 and 4..
Collections:
Photographs, memorabilia and artefacts collected mainly from local sources to mark Whitby's long and distinguished history
Documentary collection, includes photos, maps, documents and oral history tapes
Family history department with collection of North Yorkshire family trees and related material
Genealogical information and lists
Historic photograph collection of Whitby in particular and North Yorkshire in general
The Warring 40s Team
Catalogues:
Catalogue for part of the collections is published.
Trade and statistical:
Local population data and statistics, related information regarding the history of the area, genealogical and photographic records, maps.
Publications list:
is available in hard copy and online.
Printed publications:
Whitby Directory 1781,1784 & 1798 (£4.50)
Whitby Directory 1834 (£4.50)
Whitby Directory 1840 (£4.50)
Whitby Directory 1849 (£4.50)
Local history series of booklets (photographic copies available)
Oral history tapes - interviews with old residents (copies may be ordered)
Whitby Archives
Electronic and video products:
1899 list of Whitby residents (disc)
Other genealogical diskettes available
Videos for sale

Internet home pages:
http://www.freeserve.co.uk/whitbyarchives
Details of archives services, list of items for sale or research, links to other sites.

3127
WHITE MILL
Sturminster Marshall, Wimborne, Dorset, BH21 4BX

Tel: 01258 858051
Fax: 01258 858389
Formed: 1994

Organisation type and purpose: National organisation, registered charity (charity number 205846), historic building, house or site, suitable for ages: 5+.
Parent body:
The National Trust (South West Region)
Regional Office for Wessex, tel: 01985 843600

Enquiries to: Curator
Direct tel: 01258 857184
Direct email: colin.cope@btopenworld.com
Access:
Access to staff: By letter, by telephone, by fax, by email, visitors by prior appointment, charges to non-members
Hours: Curator: Mon to Fri, 0900 to 1700
Access for disabled people: Parking provided, ramped entry
Other restrictions: Ground floor largely accessible. Ramped access to most of ground floor. No access to other floors.
Viewing platform and internal mirrors enable visitors to see most of upper floors.

General description:
Rebuilt in 1776 on a site marked in the Domesday Book, this cornmill was extensively repaired in 1994 and still retains its original elm and applewood machinery (now too fragile to be used). Mill history, country life.
Information services:
Large-print guide. Audio guide.
Special visitor services: Guided tours.
Education services: Group education facilities, resources for Key Stages 1 and 2, 3 and 4.
Services for disabled people: For the visually impaired; displays and/or information at wheelchair height.
Collections:
Hands-on books, pictures
Tapes for visually impaired
Publications list:
is available in hard copy.
Printed publications:
Guide (50p)

Internet home pages:
http://www.nationaltrust.org.uk/regions/wessex

3128
WHITE WELLS SPA COTTAGE
Wells Road, Ilkley Moor, Ilkley, West Yorkshire, LS29 9RF

Tel: 01943 608035
Formed: 1703

Organisation type and purpose: Museum, historic building, house or site, suitable for ages: 5+.
Parent body:
City of Bradford Metropolitan District Council
Countryside Services Department, 8th Floor, Britannia House, Bradford, West Yorkshire, tel: 01274 752666

Enquiries to: Manager
Access:
Access to staff: By letter, by telephone
Access for disabled people: Parking provided
Other restrictions: Limited amount of disabled parking space for visitors at rear of premises.

General description:
18th century cold water plunge bath, built 1791 to replace older bath of 1703 (of which no trace remains).
Bath House has wall displays giving general history of the development of hydrotherapy in the Ilkley Area. (Ilkley flourished as a 'Spa Town' throughout the 19th century, with the development of larger hydros in the 1840s/1850s). Bath can still be used by visitors, free of charge, on New Year's Day, Yorkshire Day (1st August), and at other times when White Wells is open, by arrangement. However, as there are steep narrow steps down in to the bath, it is not recommended for disabled people or people with mobility problems.
Drinks and snacks etc are available from the White Wells Tea Room (for consumption inside or at one of the tables outside) these can be paid for in sterling or euros, no smoking and no alcohol.

3129
WHITEGATES COTTAGE
See - Gunby Hall Estate: Whitegates Cottage

3130
WHITEHALL
1 Malden Road, Cheam, Surrey, SM3 8QD

Tel: 020 8643 1236
Minicom no. 020 8770 4779
Fax: 020 8770 4777
Email: curators@whitehallcheam.fsnet.co.uk
Formed: 1978

Organisation type and purpose: Local government body, museum, art gallery, historic building, house or site, suitable for ages: all ages.
Parent body:
Sutton Council
London Borough of Sutton Heritage Service, Central Library, St Nicholas Way, Sutton, SM1 1EA, tel: 020 8770 4782, fax: 020 8770 4777
Other address:
London Borough of Sutton Heritage Service
Central Library, St Nicholas Way, Sutton, Surrey, SM1 1EA, tel: 020 8770 4781/2, fax: 020 8770 4777, email/website: local.studies@sutton.gov.uk

Enquiries to: Curator
Other contacts: Museum and Historic Houses Officer for all correspondence, contacts concerning museum objects, ethics, loans, etc.
Access:
Access to staff: By letter, by telephone, by email, in person
Access for disabled people: ramped entry

General description:
Local history; Cheam (medieval) pottery; Nonsuch Palace; information on William Gilpin (artist, art critic and headmaster of Cheam School 1752 to 1777) and Cheam School; Tudor Cheam; Victorian Cheam.
Information services:
All information is available through the Sutton Archive and Local Studies Service, telephone 020 8770 4747.
Special visitor services: Guided tours, materials and/or activities for children.
Education services: Group education facilities..
Collections:
Killick Bequest: items formerly owned by members of family of former occupant
Catalogues:
Catalogue for part of the collections is only available in-house.
Publications list:
is available in hard copy.
Printed publications:
Whitehall and Cheam Village: A History and Guide (Jackson P, £2.95)

Address for ordering publications:
Printed publications:
Leisure Stop, Sutton Central Library
St Nicholas Way, Sutton, SM1 1EA, tel: 020 8770 4444, fax: 020 8770 4655, email: sue.butler@sutton.gov.uk

Internet home pages:
http://www.sutton.gov.uk/lfl/heritage/whitehall/index.htm

3131
WHITEHAVEN MUSEUM AND ART GALLERY
See - Beacon

3132
WHITHORN TRUST
45/47 George Street, Whithorn, Newton Stewart, Dumfries & Galloway, DG8 8NS

Tel: 01988 500508
Fax: 01988 500700
Email: enquiries@whithorn.com
Full name: Whithorn, Cradle of Christianity
Formed: 1986

Organisation type and purpose: Independently owned, registered charity (charity number SCO 12178), museum, historic building, house or site, suitable for ages: 5+, research organisation.
To research the evolution of the Christian community and to encourage the understanding and appreciation of these elements in relation to the development of Scottish life and culture.
To research the history of the site using archaeology, and interpret these results in relation to the development of Galloway, Scotland and Europe.

Enquiries to: Business Manager
Access:
Access to staff: By letter, by telephone, by email, in person, Internet web pages
Hours: Mon to Fri, 1030 to 1700
Access to building, collections or gallery: No prior appointment required
Hours: Apr to Oct: daily, 1030 to 1700
Other restrictions: Nov to Mar by prior appointment.
Access for disabled people: Parking provided, level entry, toilet facilities
Other restrictions: The Trust is enhancing disabled access using information technology on site.

General description:
The exhibition details the development of the ecclesiastical settlement at Whithorn. Periods covered include Early Christian, Northumbrian, Hiberno-Norse, Lords of Galloway, Medieval, Reformation, Georgian, Modern. The site is a scheduled monument which has had substantial archaeological investigation. Information available on excavations at Whithorn.
Information services:
Special visitor services: Guided tours, tape recorded guides, materials and/or activities for children.
Education services: Group education facilities, resources for Key Stages 1 and 2, 3, 4 and Further or Higher Education.
Services for disabled people: For the hearing impaired; displays and/or information at wheelchair height.
Collections:
The collection is held by Stranraer Museum (artefacts) with the paper archive held by Royal Commission
The Collections on loan for the exhibition include artefacts from the Whithorn Trust Excavations loaned by Stranraer Museum
Collection of early Christian trade and technology fragments, Northumbrian coins, Hiberno-Norse trade goods including decorated antler work, building materials from Cathedral (Medieval), also collection from Barhobble excavation
On loan from National Museums of Scotland - Bishops' graves goods including 12th century crozier
Catalogues:
Catalogue for part of the collections is published.
Publications list:
is available in hard copy.
Printed publications:
Lecture Series, currently 1-9 available (£3)
Whithorn and St Ninian - The Excavation of a Monastic Town (£30)

Internet home pages:
http://www.whithorn.com
Activities undertaken by the Trust.

3133
WHITTLESEY MUSEUM
Town Hall, Market Street, Whittlesey, Peterborough, Cambridgeshire, PE7 1BD

Tel: 01733 840968
Formed: 1976

Organisation type and purpose: Registered charity (charity number 274486), museum, suitable for ages: 5+.
Connected with:
Whittlesea Society
Town Hall, Market Street, Whittlesey, PE7 1BD

Enquiries to: Curator
Access:
Access to staff: By letter, by telephone

General description:
Social history; costume; agriculture; Sir Harry Smith; brickworks; non-working forge, wheelwrights; scene of education in early 20th century.
Information services:
Special visitor services: Guided tours.
Education services: Group education facilities, resources for Key Stages 1 and 2, 3 and 4..
Printed publications:
Millennium Memories of Whittlesey (book of 44 photographs, £3)
Millennium Memories of Whittlesey No 2 (£3)
Millennium Memories of Whittlesey No 3 (£3)

3134
WHITWORTH ART GALLERY
University of Manchester, Oxford Road, Manchester, M15 6ER

Tel: 0161 275 7450
Fax: 0161 275 7451
Email: whitworth@man.ac.uk
Formed: 1889

Organisation type and purpose: Art gallery, university department or institute.
Parent body:
University of Manchester

Enquiries to: Marketing Officer
Access:
Access to staff: By letter, by telephone, by fax, by email
Access to building, collections or gallery: No prior appointment required
Hours: Mon to Sat, 1000 to 1700; Sun, 1400 to 1700
Access for disabled people: Parking provided, ramped entry, access to all public areas, toilet facilities

General description:
British watercolours and drawings; historic and modern textiles; historic and modern wallpapers; Old Master prints and drawings; Japanese prints; modern paintings, drawings, prints and sculpture.
Information services:
Special visitor services: Guided tours, materials and/or activities for children.
Education services: Resources for Key Stages 1 and 2, 3 and Further or Higher Education..
Collections:
British watercolours
Collections in the subject categories
Coptic textile collection
Finely illustrated printed books collection
Wallpaper collection
William Nicholson Letters
Catalogues:
Catalogue for library is in-house only. Catalogue for part of the collections is on-line.
Publications list:
is available on-line.
Printed publications:
Catalogues of temporary exhibitions
Newsletters (3 times a year)
Publications on the permanent collections

Internet home pages:
http://www.whitworth.man.ac.uk/

3135
WICHENFORD DOVECOTE
Wichenford, Worcestershire

Tel: 01743 708100 (Regional Office)
Email: wichenforddovecote@nationaltrust.org.uk

Organisation type and purpose: National organisation, registered charity (charity number 205846), historic building, house or site, suitable for ages: 12+.
Parent body:
The National Trust (West Midlands Region)
West Midlands Regional Office, tel: 01743 708100

Enquiries to: Property Manager
Access:
Access to staff: By letter, by telephone, by email, Internet web pages
Other restrictions: All enquiries should be directed to Regional Office.

General description:
A 17th century half-timbered black-and-white dovecote.

Internet home pages:
http://www.nationaltrust.org.uk

3136
WICKLEWOOD CORNMILL
O.S. TG 076 026, Near B1135, Wicklewood, Norfolk

Tel: 01603 222705

Organisation type and purpose: Historic building, house or site.
Access:
Access to staff: By telephone

General description:
Tower mill, major repairs under way.

3137
WIGAN HERITAGE SERVICE
The History Shop, Rodney Street, Wigan, Lancashire, WN1 1DG

Tel: 01942 828128
Fax: 01942 827645
Email: heritage@wiganmbc.gov.uk
Formed: 1992

Organisation type and purpose: Local government body, museum, suitable for ages: 12+.

Enquiries to: Manager
Other contacts: Collection Department Manager for collections.
Access:
Access to staff: By letter, by telephone, by fax, by email, in person
Access to building, collections or gallery: No prior appointment required
Hours: Mon, 1000 to 1900; Tue to Fri, 1000 to 1700; Sat, 1000 to 1300
Access for disabled people: ramped entry, toilet facilities
Other restrictions: Access to ground floor only.

General description:
Local history - all types, genealogy.
Information services:
Services for disabled people: Displays and/or information at wheelchair height.
Collections:
Social and industrial history
Family history, parish records, census material

3138
WIGAN PIER EXPERIENCE, THE
Trencherfield Mill, Wigan, Lancashire, WN3 4EF

Tel: 01942 323666
Fax: 01942 701927
Email: wiganpier@wiganmbc.gov.uk
Formed: 1985

Organisation type and purpose: Local government body, museum, suitable for ages: 5+.

Enquiries to: Bookings Officers
Access:
Access to staff: By letter, by telephone, by email
Access for disabled people: Parking provided, access to all public areas, toilet facilities

General description:
At the Wigan Pier Experience you will take a journey through yesteryear. Set in an $8\frac{1}{2}$ acre site beside the redeveloped Leeds-Liverpool Canal. Take a step back in time at 'The Way We Were' Heritage Centre, visit Trencherfield Mill and the Machinery Hall, then visit the newest attraction - Opie's Museum of Memories. Additional on-site attractions include walks, talks, boat trips, events and much more.
Information services:
Special visitor services: Materials and/or activities for children.
Education services: Group education facilities, resources for Key Stages 1 and 2, 3 and Further or Higher Education.
Services for disabled people: For the visually impaired; for the hearing impaired; displays and/or information at wheelchair height.
Publications list:
is available in hard copy.

Internet home pages:
http://www.wiganpier.net

3139
WIGHTWICK MANOR
Wightwick Bank, Wolverhampton, West Midlands, WV6 8EE

Tel: 01902 761400
Fax: 01902 764663
Email: wightwickmanor@nationaltrust.org.uk

Organisation type and purpose: Registered charity (charity number 205846), museum, historic building, house or site, suitable for ages: 8+.
Parent body:
The National Trust (West Midlands)
West Midlands Regional Office, tel: 01743 708100

Enquiries to: Manager
Access:
Access to staff: By letter, by telephone, by fax, by email
Access for disabled people: Parking provided, level entry
Other restrictions: Ground floor accessible with assistance, 2 steps in hall. No access to other floors. Steps to shop entrance. Level entrance to tea-room. Space restricted. Strong companion required for wheelchair users.

General description:
One of only a few surviving examples of a house built and furnished under the influence of the Arts & Crafts Movement. The many original William Morris wallpapers and fabrics, Pre-Raphaelite paintings, Kempe glass and de Morgan ware help conjure up the spirit of the time. An attractive garden reflects the style and character of the house.
Information services:
Guided tours for booked groups Wed, Thur & Sat, and evenings (except Bank Holidays).
Garden tours.
Braille guide.

continued overleaf

Suitable for school groups. Education room/ centre. Hands-on activities. Children's quiz/ trail. Family activity packs during holidays.
Special visitor services: Guided tours, materials and/or activities for children.
Education services: Group education facilities.
Services for disabled people: For the visually impaired.

Internet home pages:
http://www.nationaltrust.org.uk

3140
WILBERFORCE HOUSE
23 High Street, Hull, East Yorkshire, HU1 1NE

Tel: 01482 613902
Fax: 01482 613710
Email: museums@hullcc.gov.uk
Formed: 1906

Organisation type and purpose: Local government body, museum, suitable for ages: 5+.
Parent body:
Kingston Upon Hull City Council
The Guildhall, Lowgate, Kingston Upon Hull, HU1 2AA, tel: 01482 300300
Other addresses:
Kingston Upon Hull City Museums and Art Gallery
Monument Buildings, Ferens Art Gallery, Queen Victoria Square, Kingston Upon Hull, HU1 3RA

Enquiries to: Curator
Access:
Access to staff: By letter, by telephone, by fax, by email
Access to building, collections or gallery: No prior appointment required
Hours: Mon to Sat, 1000 to 1700; Sun, 1330 to 1630

General description:
Social history of Hull, William Wilberforce, the history of slavery, decorative arts of Hull.
Information services:
Special visitor services: Materials and/or activities for children.
Education services: Group education facilities..

3141
WILDERHOPE MANOR
Longville, Much Wenlock, Shropshire, TF13 6EG

Tel: 0870 7706090

Organisation type and purpose: National organisation, registered charity (charity number 205846), historic building, house or site.
Parent body:
The National Trust (West Midlands)
West Midlands Regional Office, tel: 01743 708100

Enquiries to: Manager
Access:
Access to staff: By letter, by telephone

General description:
A gabled and unspoilt manor house, dating from 1586 and with fine views. Although unfurnished, the interior is of interest for its remarkable wooden spiral staircase and fine plaster ceilings. The Manor is used as a Youth Hostel.

Internet home pages:
http://www.nationaltrust.org.uk

3142
WILLESBOROUGH MILL
on A292, Ashford, Kent

Tel: 01233 661866

Organisation type and purpose: Historic building, house or site.
Member of:
Kent Windmills

General description:
Built in 1869, restored in 1991 by Ashford Borough Council.
Collections:
Industrial history

Internet home pages:
http://www.moulin.org.uk

3143
WILLIAM BOOTH BIRTHPLACE MUSEUM
12 Notintone Place, Sneinton, Nottingham, NG2 4QG

Tel: 0115 950 3927
Fax: 0115 959 8604

Organisation type and purpose: International organisation, historic building, house or site.

Enquiries to: Director
Access:
Access to staff: By letter, by telephone, by fax, in person, visitors by prior appointment
Access for disabled people: Parking provided, toilet facilities

General description:
The museum is intended to give visitors a general outline of the life of William Booth and the development of the Salvation Army.

3144
WILLIAM CAREY MUSEUM
Central Baptist Church, Charles Street, Leicester, LE1 1LA

Tel: 0116 276 6862

Organisation type and purpose: Independently owned, suitable for ages: all ages.
Church.

Enquiries to: Archivist
Direct tel: 0116 287 3864
Direct email: keithw.harrison@virgin.net
Access:
Access to staff: By letter, by telephone, by email, visitors by prior appointment
Access to building, collections or gallery: Prior appointment required
Access for disabled people: level entry, access to all public areas, toilet facilities
Other restrictions: Limited parking provided.

General description:
Life of William Carey (1761-1834), English missionary and orientalist, who joined the Baptist Church in 1783 and spent much time in India.
Information services:
Special visitor services: Guided tours.
Services for disabled people: Displays and/or information at wheelchair height.
Collections:
Pictures, manuscripts, tableau
Catalogues:
Catalogue for library is in-house only. Catalogue for all of the collections is only available in-house.
Printed publications:
William Carey

3145
WILLIAM HERSCHEL MUSEUM
19 New King Street, Bath, BA1 2BL

Tel: 01225 311342
Fax: 01225 446865
Formed: 1981

Organisation type and purpose: Museum, historic building, house or site, suitable for ages: 5+.

Enquiries to: Curator
Direct tel: 01225 446865
Access:
Access to staff: By letter, by telephone, by fax, in person, visitors by prior appointment, charges made to all users
Access for disabled people: Parking provided
Other restrictions: Audio tour, raised pictures and plans.

General description:
Astronomy, music, Star Vault Astronomy Show, Georgian town-house.
Publications list:
is available in hard copy.
Electronic and video products:
Herschel's Music (CD-ROMs)

Internet home pages:
http://www.bath-preservation-trust.org.uk

3146
WILLIAM LAMB MEMORIAL STUDIO
See - Lamb Sculpture Studio

3147
WILLIAM MORRIS GALLERY
Water House, Lloyd Park, Forest Road, London, E17 4PP

Tel: 020 8527 3782
Fax: 020 8527 7070
Full name: William Morris Gallery and Brangwyn Gift
Formed: 1950

Organisation type and purpose: Local government body, museum, art gallery, suitable for ages: all ages.
Parent body:
London Borough of Waltham Forest

Enquiries to: Curator
Other contacts: Deputy Curator
Access:
Access to staff: By letter, by telephone, by fax, visitors by prior appointment
Hours: Tue to Sat 1000 to 1300 and 1400 to 1700
Other restrictions: Visits to staff in person by prior appointment only.
Access to building, collections or gallery: No prior appointment required
Hours: Tue to Sat and the first Sunday of each month, 1000 to 1300 and 1400 to 1700
Other restrictions: The use of the library is by prior appointment.
Access for disabled people: ramped entry
Other restrictions: Access for wheelchairs to ground floor only.

General description:
All aspects of life and work of William Morris, textiles, wallpapers, furniture, stained glass, ceramics, designs etc; De Morganware and Martinware ceramic collections; collections of designs and applied art by other members of the arts and crafts movement; Pre-Raphaelite drawings and watercolours; paintings, drawings and etchings, furniture and ceramics by Sir Frank Brangwyn, Rodin sculpture, and applied art 1860-1920.
Information services:
Library available for reference (for conditions see Access above)
Guided tours by prior appointment.
Special visitor services: Guided tours.
Education services: Group education facilities, resources for Key Stages 1 and 2, 3, 4 and Further or Higher Education..
Collections:
Kelmscott Press books (complete set)
Other private press books
William Morris letters
Catalogues:
Catalogue for library is in-house only. Catalogue for all of the collections is only available in-house.
Publications list:
is available in hard copy.
Printed publications:
Postcards and posters
Printed catalogues of the collections:
Henry Holiday (1869-1927) (£4.50)

Karl Parsons: Stained Glass Artist (1884-1934) (£4.50)
May Morris (1862-1938) (£4.50)
Sir Frank Brangwyn (£3.50)
Leaflets and books:
Morris at Merton (£5.50)
Red House Guide (£4.25)
Teachers' Resource Pack (£3.50 inc. p&p)
The Arts and Craft Movement (£7.50)
William de Morgan tiles (£10.50)
William Morris: An Illustrated Life (£3.75 inc. p&p)
William Morris Decor & Design (out of print)
William Morris Textiles (out of print)
Electronic and video products:
Topsy: The Life and Work of William Morris (video, out of print)

Internet home pages:
http://www.lbwf.gov.uk/wmg
General data on gallery and its collections, colour illustrations of items in collection, news and events, acquisitions and exhibitions.

3148
WILLINGTON DOVECOTE & STABLES
21 Chapel Lane, Willington, Bedford, MK44 3QG

Tel: 0870 609 5388 (Regional Office)

Organisation type and purpose: National organisation, registered charity (charity number 205846), historic building, house or site.

Enquiries to: Manager
Access:
Access to staff: By letter, by telephone
Access to building, collections or gallery: Prior appointment required
Hours: Apr to Sep, daily
Other restrictions: By appointment with Mrs J. Endersby, 21 Chapel Lane, Willington MK44 3QG, tel. 01234 838278.

General description:
A distinctive 16th century stable and stone dovecote, lined internally with nesting boxes for 1500 pigeons. They are the remains of a historic manorial complex and a reminder of the part played by the manor and its owner during the dissolution of the monasteries.

3149
WILLIS MUSEUM OF BASINGSTOKE TOWN AND COUNTRY LIFE
Old Town Hall, Market Place
Market Place, Basingstoke, Hampshire, RG21 7QD

Tel: 01256 465902
Fax: 01256 471455
Email: musmst@hants.gov.uk
Formed: 1931
Formerly: Basingstoke Museum

Organisation type and purpose: Local government body, museum, suitable for ages: 5+.
Also has a temporary exhibition gallery.
Parent body:
Hampshire County Council Museums Service
Tel: 01962 846304 (HQ), fax: 01962 869836 (HQ fax)

Enquiries to: Curator
Access:
Access to staff: By letter, by telephone, by fax, by email, in person
Access to building, collections or gallery: No prior appointment required
Hours: Mon to Fri, 1000 to 1700; Sat, 1000 to 1600
Access for disabled people: ramped entry
Other restrictions: Chair lift to 1st and 2nd floors.

General description:
Local history of Basingstoke and district, archaeology, natural science, domestic craft, needlework, society, education, decorative art.
Information services:
Education services: Group education facilities, resources for Key Stages 1 and 2..
Collections:
George Willis Collection of clocks and watches
Local archaeology; natural science, local history
Catalogues:
Catalogue for all of the collections is on-line.
Publications list:
is available in hard copy.
Printed publications:
Publications list is available from the Librarian, Hampshire County Council Museums Service Headquarters, Chilcomb House, Winchester, SO23 8RD
Local history books available for purchase from the Museum Shop

Address for ordering publications:
Printed publications:
Registrar, Hampshire County Council Museums Service HQ

Internet home pages:
http://www.hants.gov.uk/museum/willis
HMCMS web catalogue, whole collection, 100,000 plus web pages.

3150
WILLMER HOUSE MUSEUM
See - Museum of Farnham

3151
WILSON MUSEUM OF NARBERTH
Market Square, Narberth, Dyfed, SA67 7AU

Tel: 01834 861719

Organisation type and purpose: Registered charity (charity number 519783), museum, suitable for ages: all ages.

Enquiries to: Curator
Access:
Access to staff: By letter, by telephone, in person
Access to building, collections or gallery: No prior appointment required
Hours: Mon to Fri, 1030 to 1630; Sat, 1030 to 1230
Access for disabled people: Parking provided, ramped entry

General description:
The collection illustrates the social history of Narberth, a typical Welsh market town, in the 19th and 20th centuries. A well-stocked bookshop offers local and national history, children's books in Welsh and English, poetry etc. Research facilities for local and family historians.
Collections:
Mainly Victorian costume, china, household, fans, commercial, agriculture and transport including rare 'Geared Facile' bicycle
Military - First and Second World Wars
Photographic - cameras and large collection of original photographs
Newspapers - Pembrokeshire County Guardian 1898-1970s
Local history books

3152
WILTON HOUSE
Wilton, Salisbury, Wiltshire, SP2 0BJ

Tel: 01722 746720
Fax: 01722 744447
Email: tourism@wiltonhouse.com

Organisation type and purpose: Independently owned, registered charity (charity number 287144), historic building, house or site, suitable for ages: 5+.
Wilton House Trust.
Member of:
Classic Sights
Historic Houses Association
Treasure Houses of England
Wessex Top Ten

Enquiries to: Tourism Administrator
Access:
Access to staff: By letter, by telephone, by fax, by email, in person
Access to building, collections or gallery: No prior appointment required
Hours: 27 Mar to 27 Oct: daily, 1030 to 1730 (last admission 1630)
Access for disabled people: Parking provided, ramped entry, access to all public areas, toilet facilities

General description:
450 year old home to the Earl of Pembroke. The Inigo Jones designed Double Cube Room houses and an important collection of Van Dycks. Extensive grounds include several small formal gardens with large area of parkland bordered by the River Nadder.
Information services:
Special visitor services: Guided tours, materials and/or activities for children.
Education services: Group education facilities, resources for Key Stages 1 and 2.
Services for disabled people: For the hearing impaired; displays and/or information at wheelchair height.
Collections:
World famous collection of paintings by Van Dyck, and works by Rembrandt, Reynolds and Brueghel
Roman, Greek and 17th century sculpture
Printed publications:
Souvenir Guide Book

3153
WILTSHIRE COLLEGE
See - Lackham Museum of Agriculture and Rural Life

3154
WILTSHIRE EDUCATION & LIBRARIES
Salisbury Library and Galleries, Market Place, Salisbury, Wiltshire, SP1 1BL

Tel: 01722 324145
Fax: 01722 413214
Formerly: Wiltshire Library and Museum Service

Organisation type and purpose: Local government body, art gallery, public library.
Parent body:
Wiltshire County Council
Member of:
WILCO

Enquiries to: District Librarian
Direct tel: 01722 330606
Direct email: chrisharling@wiltshire.gov.uk
Other contacts: Art Curator, tel: 01722 410614; Reference and Local Studies Library, tel: 01722 411098
Access:
Access to staff: By letter, by telephone, by fax, in person, Internet web pages
Hours: Mon to Fri, 0900 to 1700
Access to building, collections or gallery: No access other than to staff
Hours: Mon, 1000 to 1900; Tue, Wed, Fri, 0900 to 1900; Thu, 0900 to 1700; Sat, 0900 to 1700
Access for disabled people: level entry
Other restrictions: Level entry via side entrance.

General description:
History of Salisbury and Wiltshire; arts; general subjects.
Collections:
Edwin Young Watercolour collection - Victorian watercolours of Salisbury
Creasey Collection of contemporary art

continued overleaf

Robin Tonner Collection - 1930s Children's Art
Edgar Barclay Collection - Victorian paintings of Stonehenge
Jerram Collection of Bellringing Books (Guild of Campanologists Collection of books and documents, many hand-annotated, formerly in the Sowter Clerical Library)
John Creasey Literary Museum
Catalogues:
Catalogue for library is on-line.
Printed publications:
Business Key leaflet, and many others
Under 5's: What's On and Education Fact Sheets (free)

Internet home pages:
http://www.wiltshire.gov.uk
Full county website.
http://www.wiltshire.gov.uk/library
Online catalogue, renewals, reservations and information.

3155
WILTSHIRE FIRE DEFENCE AND BRIGADES MUSEUM

Fire Brigade HQ, Manor House, Potterne, Devizes, Wiltshire, SN10 5PP

Tel: 01380 723601
Fax: 01380 727000
Email: andrew.hargreaves@wfb.org.uk
Full name: Wiltshire Fire Defence Collection
Formerly: Wiltshire Fire Defence Collection

Organisation type and purpose: Local government body, museum, historic building, house or site, suitable for ages: 8+.
Combined fire authority (Swindon & Wiltshire).

Enquiries to: Curator
Direct tel: 01380 731188
Access:
Access to staff: By letter, by telephone, by fax, visitors by prior appointment
Hours: By arrangement
Access to building, collections or gallery: Prior appointment required
Access for disabled people: Parking provided, level entry
Other restrictions: Access limited to the ground floor only; the museum is not suitable for disabled access.

General description:
A collection of old manual fire engines; firefighting equipment; documents; and photographs showing and relating to the history of firefighting in Wiltshire since the 17th/18th century.
Information services:
School parties welcome.
Special visitor services: Guided tours..
Catalogues:
Catalogue for all of the collections is only available in-house.

Internet home pages:
http://www.wiltshirefirebrigade.com

3156
WILTSHIRE HERITAGE MUSEUM, ART GALLERY AND LIBRARY

41 Long Street, Devizes, Wiltshire, SN10 1NS

Tel: 01380 727369
Fax: 01380 722150
Email: wanhs@wiltshireheritage.org.uk
Formed: 1853
Formerly: Devizes Museum, date of change, 2000

Organisation type and purpose: Independently owned, registered charity (charity number 1080096), museum, art gallery, suitable for ages: 5+.
Library.
Parent body:
Wiltshire Archaeological and Natural History Society (WANHS)
41 Long Street, Devizes, Wiltshire, SN10 1NS, tel: 01380 727369, fax: 01380 722150, email: wanhs@wiltshireheritage.org.uk

Enquiries to: Curator
Access:
Access to staff: By email
Access to building, collections or gallery: No prior appointment required
Hours: Mon to Sat, 1000 to 1700; Sun, 1200 to 1600
Access for disabled people: level entry

General description:
Natural history, geology, social history of the Kennet region, archaeology of Wiltshire particularly Bronze Age and through to the mediaeval period, local history.
Information services:
Special visitor services: Guided tours, materials and/or activities for children.
Education services: Group education facilities, resources for Further or Higher Education..
Collections:
Buckler Collection of watercolours of Wiltshire houses and churches by John Buckler (1770-1851)
Stourhead Collection from excavations of Bronze Age barrows
Tanner Collection of etchings by Robin Tanner (1930-1985)
Catalogues:
Catalogue for library is in-house only. Catalogue for all of the collections is only available in-house.
Publications list:
is available in hard copy.

Internet home pages:
http://www.wiltshireheritage.org.uk
Full details of museum and library collections, activities and publications

3157
WILTSHIRE LIBRARIES AND HERITAGE

Libraries and Heritage Branch, Education and Libraries Department, Bythesea Road, Trowbridge, Wiltshire, BA14 8BS

Tel: 01225 713700
Fax: 01225 713993
Email: libraryenquiries@wiltshire.gov.uk

Organisation type and purpose: Local government body.
Museums Service.
Parent body:
Wiltshire County Council

Enquiries to: Head of Libraries and Heritage Branch
Access:
Access to staff: By letter, by telephone, by fax, by email
Hours: Mon to Fri, 0900 to 1700
Access to building, collections or gallery: No prior appointment required
Hours: Mon, Thu, Fri, 0900 to 1900; Tue, 0900 to 1700; Wed, 1000 to 1700; Sat, 0900 to 1600
Access for disabled people: Parking provided, level entry, access to all public areas, toilet facilities

General description:
Wiltshire County Historic Photograph Collection.
Collections:
Wiltshire County Historic Photograph Collection, 35,000 records
Museum Objects Database, 155,000 records
Catalogues:
Catalogue for all of the collections is only available in-house.
Electronic and video products:
Museum Objects Database, 155,000 records
Historic Photograph Database, 35,000 records

3158
WILTSHIRE LIBRARY AND MUSEUM SERVICE

See - Wiltshire Education & Libraries

3159
WIMBLEDON LAWN TENNIS MUSEUM

All England Lawn Tennis Club, Church Road, Wimbledon, London, SW19 5AE

Tel: 020 8946 6131
Fax: 020 8944 6497
Formed: 1977

Organisation type and purpose: Independently owned, museum, art gallery, suitable for ages: 5+.
Library.

Enquiries to: Curator
Access:
Access to staff: Charges made to all users
Hours: Mon to Sun, 1030 to 1700
Other restrictions: Facilities for disabled visitors. Pre-booked groups of 15 plus receive a discount. Visitors to the library by appointment.
Access for disabled people: Parking provided, access to all public areas

General description:
History of lawn tennis.
Information services:
Special visitor services: Guided tours, materials and/or activities for children.
Education services: Group education facilities..
Collections:
Collections of exhibits held as gifts or on loan
Rare books on tennis
Printed publications:
The Wimbledon Compendium (annually)
Tennis Fashions over 100 years of costume change

3160
WIMBLEDON MUSEUM OF LOCAL HISTORY

26 Lingfield Road, Wimbledon, London, SW19 4QD

Tel: 020 8296 9914
Formed: 1916

Organisation type and purpose: Registered charity, museum, suitable for ages: 8+.
Parent body:
Wimbledon Society
At the same address

Enquiries to: Chairman
Other contacts: Publications Manager for the supply of publications.
Access:
Access to staff: By letter, by telephone, in person, visitors by prior appointment
Access to building, collections or gallery: Prior appointment required
Hours: Sat, Sun, 1430 to 1700

General description:
Archaeology; artefacts; books; ephemera; maps; manuscripts; natural history; photographs; portraits; press-cuttings; prints; drawings.

3161
WIMBLEDON WINDMILL MUSEUM

Windmill Road, Wimbledon Common, London, SW19 5NR

Tel: 020 8947 2825
Formed: 1976

Organisation type and purpose: Voluntary organisation, registered charity (charity number 1015265), museum, historic building, house or site, suitable for ages: 5+.
A museum of windmills housed in a listed windmill.

Enquiries to: Curator
Access:
Access to staff: By letter, by telephone, visitors by prior appointment
Hours: Mon to Sun, 0900 to 1700

Access for disabled people: Parking provided, level entry, toilet facilities
Other restrictions: Access to ground floor only.

General description:
The history of windmills and milling. Pictures, working models, and the machinery and tools of the trade.

Information services:
Special visitor services: Guided tours, materials and/or activities for children.
Education services: Group education facilities, resources for Key Stages 1 and 2, 3, 4 and Further or Higher Education.
Services for disabled people: Displays and/or information at wheelchair height.

Collections:
Collection of working models of British windmills
Collection of windmill machinery and equipment
The Follen Collection of woodworking tools

Catalogues:
Catalogue for all of the collections is only available in-house.

Publications list:
is available in hard copy.

Printed publications:
The following add p&p:
History of the Commons (book, £2)
Mill Corner Nature Trail (book, £1)
My Side of the Common (book, £1.50)
Wimbledon 1939-45 (book, £4.50)
Windmill Guide Book (£1)
Wimbledon Common Natural History (£25)
Windmills, How They Work (£3.25)
Windmills of England (£29.95)
Mills Open (£4)
An assortment of postcards, maps and posters

3162
WIMPOLE HALL

Arrington, Royston, Cambridgeshire, SG8 0BW

Tel: 01223 207257
Fax: 01223 207383
Email: wimpolehall@nationaltrust.org.uk

Organisation type and purpose: National organisation, registered charity (charity number 205846), historic building, house or site, suitable for ages: 8+.

Parent body:
The National Trust (East of England)
East Anglia Regional Office, tel: 0870 609 5388

Enquiries to: Manager

Access:
Access to staff: By letter, by telephone, by fax, by email
Access for disabled people: Parking provided, toilet facilities
Other restrictions: Designated parking 200yds. Drop-off point. 3 manual wheelchairs available, booking essential. 2 single-seater powered mobility vehicles, booking essential. Steps to entrance. Ground floor accessible with assistance. No access to other floors. Level entrance to shop. Ramped entrance to restaurant.

General description:
This magnificent 18th century house, the largest in Cambridgeshire and set in grand style in an extensive wooded park, has an extraordinary pedigree. The interior features work by Gibbs, Flitcroft and Soane, and the park - complete with folly, Chinese bridge and lakes - was landscaped by Bridgeman, Brown and Repton. There is a series of spectacular avenues and extensive walks through the delightful grounds. The garden has thousands of daffodils in April and colourful parterres in July and August. Walled garden restored to a working vegetable garden, best seen from June to August.

Information services:
Braille guide. Large-print guide. Handling collection.
Front-carrying baby slings for loan.
Suitable for school groups. Education room/centre. Live interpretation. Hands-on activities. Children's guide. Children's quiz/trail.
Special visitor services: Materials and/or activities for children.
Education services: Group education facilities.
Services for disabled people: For the visually impaired.

Internet home pages:
http://www.nationaltrust.org.uk

3163
WIMPOLE HOME FARM

Arrington, Royston, Cambridgeshire, SG8 0BW

Tel: 01223 207257
Fax: 01223 207838
Email: wimpolefarm@nationaltrust.org.uk

Organisation type and purpose: National organisation, registered charity (charity number 205846), museum, historic building, house or site, suitable for ages: 5+.

Parent body:
The National Trust (East of England Region)
East Anglia Regional Office, tel: 0870 609 5388

Enquiries to: Property Manager
Other contacts: Education Officer (01223 207801/206004)

Access:
Access to staff: By letter, by telephone, by fax, by email, in person, Internet web pages
Access to building, collections or gallery: Prior appointment required
Hours: Late Mar to Jun, Sep to early Nov, Tue to Thu, Sat and Sun, daily, 1030 to 1700
Nov to Mar, Sat and Sun, 1100 to 1600
Open Bank Holiday Mondays
Open daily during local school Spring half-term, and Easter holidays.
Access for disabled people: Parking provided, ramped entry, toilet facilities
Other restrictions: Drop-off point. 3 manual wheelchairs available, booking essential. Powered mobility vehicles: 2 singleseater, booking essential. Touch and feed animals. Some gravel areas, concrete and grass pathways. Ramped entrance to shop. Ramped entrance to tearoom.

General description:
A model farm, built by Soane in 1794 and now home to a fascinating range of rare animal breeds, including sheep, goats, cattle, pigs and horses. The Great Barn has a collection of farm implements dating back 200 years and interpretive displays.

Information services:
Special events throughout year.
Special events for children April, May and Aug.
Spring lambing in April.
Tours by arrangement
Suitable for school groups. Education room/centre.
Live interpretation. Hands-on activities. Children's guide. Children's quiz/trail
Children's play area. Special children's corner; touch and feed animals
Special visitor services: Guided tours, materials and/or activities for children.
Education services: Group education facilities..

Collections:
Farm implements

Internet home pages:
http://www.nationaltrust.org.uk

3164
WINCHCOMBE FOLK & POLICE MUSEUM

The Town Hall, High Street, Winchcombe, Cheltenham, Gloucestershire, GL54 5LJ

Tel: 01242 609151
Formed: 1992

Organisation type and purpose: Independently owned, registered charity (charity number 234732), museum, suitable for ages: all ages.
Owned by Winchcombe Town Trust, founded in 1891.
The Museum is run by its own committee, a sub-group of the Town Trust.

Parent body:
Winchcombe Town Trust

Enquiries to: Honorary Curator

Access:
Access to staff: By letter, by telephone
Hours: Mon to Fri, 1000 to 1630
Access to building, collections or gallery: No prior appointment required
Hours: Mon to Sat, 1000 to 1700 (last entry 1630)
Other restrictions: Closed Nov to Mar.

General description:
Folk Museum Collection - illustrates with local artefacts the history of the ancient Cotswold town of Winchcome and its people. Historic items, documents, pictures and memorabilia, family and local history information.
Police Museum Collection - illustrates police history with British and International uniforms both recent and historic and displays of badges, truncheons and other police equipment.

Information services:
Special visitor services: Materials and/or activities for children..

Collections:
Family history information (surnames index)
Local history information and material on display
Local material from 19th and early 20th century cottages, houses and farms illustrating Winchcombe life and work

Printed publications:
Copy of 1815 Winchcombe Enclosure Map, Greet & Sudeley Tenements and Owners (for purchase, direct)
Facsimile of 1813 Felony Poster (for purchase, direct)
Mercian Kings & Mercia (for purchase, direct)
Children's Activity Sheets (free)

Internet home pages:
http://www.winchcombemuseum.org.uk
Location, parking, cost, list of main contents of collections, description of Town Hall etc.

3165
WINCHELSEA MUSEUM

Court Hall, High Street, Winchelsea, East Sussex, TN36 4EN

Tel: 01797 226382
Formed: 1950

Organisation type and purpose: Local government body, museum, historic building, house or site.

Enquiries to: Honorary Curator

Access:
Access to staff: By letter
Hours: Answerphone

General description:
Covers the local history and archaeology of Winchelsea and surrounding area.

3166
WINCHESTER CITY MILL

Bridge Street, Winchester, Hampshire, SO23 8EJ

Tel: 01962 870057
Email: winchestercitymill@nationaltrust.org.uk

Organisation type and purpose: National organisation, registered charity (charity number 205846), historic building, house or site, university department or institute, suitable for ages: 8+.

Parent body:
The National Trust (South and South East Region)
Thames and Solent Regional Office, tel: 01494 528051

National Trust sites:
Winchester City Mill

continued overleaf

Bridge Street, Winchester, Hampshire, SO23 8EJ, tel: 01962 870057

Enquiries to: Manager
Access:
Access to staff: By letter, by telephone, by email

General description:
Spanning the River Itchen, this water-powered corn mill has had a chequered past. First built in medieval times, and restored in 1743, it remained a working watermill until the turn of the last century and has recently been restored to full working order. Milling demonstrations take place throughout the season, and there is something to delight everyone, including exhibition display, working models, impressive mill-races and pretty island garden.
Information services:
Group guided tours by arrangement.
Suitable for school groups. Education room/ centre. Hands-on activities. Children's quiz/ trail.
Special visitor services: Materials and/or activities for children.
Education services: Group education facilities..

3167
WINCHESTER CITY MUSEUM
The Square, Winchester, Hampshire, SO23 9ES

Tel: 01962 863064
Fax: 01962 848299
Email: museums@winchester.gov.uk
Formed: 1903

Organisation type and purpose: Local government body, museum.
Linked to:
Winchester Museums Service
Tel: 01962 848269, fax: 01962 841365, email/ website: museums@winchester.gov.uk
Correspondence address:
Historic Resources Centre
75 Hyde Street, Winchester, SO23 7DW, tel: 01962 848269

Enquiries to: Curator
Direct tel: 01962 848396
Direct email: gdenford@winchester.gov.uk
Other contacts: (1) Head of Museums Service; (2) Visitor Services Officer
Access:
Access to staff: By letter, by telephone, by fax, by email, in person, visitors by prior appointment
Access to building, collections or gallery: No prior appointment required
Hours: Apr to Oct: Mon to Sat, 1000 to 1700; Sun, 1200 to 1700
Nov to Mar: Tue to Sat, 1000 to 1600; Sun, 1200 to 1600
Access for disabled people: level entry, access to all public areas, toilet facilities

General description:
The museum tells the story of Winchester from its Roman origins to the present day. Archaeological discoveries provide the raw material for understanding the City's development and its rise to prominence as the capital of Alfred The Great, and one of the principal centres of the Anglo-Norman Kingdom. More recent history is represented by exhibits on Jane Austen, Winchester's first hospital and the growth of tourism. Reconstructed shops.
Information services:
Special visitor services: Guided tours, materials and/or activities for children.
Education services: Group education facilities, resources for Key Stages 1 and 2, 3 and Further or Higher Education.
Services for disabled people: For the visually impaired; for the hearing impaired; displays and/or information at wheelchair height.
Catalogues:
Catalogue for part of the collections is only available in-house.
Printed publications:
3-part Souvenir Guide to the story of the City from its beginnings to the present day (available in sleeve, £6.99 or each part separately at £2.50)
Venta Belgarum - The Roman Town
Winchester - Saxon and Medieval Winchester
Winchester - In the Modern Age

Internet home pages:
http://www.winchester.gov.uk/heritage

3168
WINCHESTER GALLERY, THE
Park Avenue, Winchester, Hampshire, SO23 8DL

Tel: 01962 852500

Organisation type and purpose: Art gallery, university department or institute, suitable for ages: 5+.

Enquiries to: Director
Access:
Access to building, collections or gallery: No prior appointment required
Hours: Tue to Fri, 1000 to 1630
Access for disabled people: Parking provided, level entry, access to all public areas, toilet facilities

General description:
Contemporary fine art, contemporary craft. Winchester School of Art, Degree Show exhibition.

3169
WINCHESTER MUSEUMS SERVICE
Historic Resources Centre, 75 Hyde Street, Winchester, Hampshire, SO23 7DW

Tel: 01962 848269
Fax: 01962 848299
Email: museums@winchester.gov.uk
Formed: 1847
Formerly: South Eastern Museums Service

Organisation type and purpose: Local government body, museum, art gallery, historic building, house or site, suitable for ages: all ages.
Other museums or galleries:
Guildhall Gallery
The City Museum
Westgate Museum

Enquiries to: Curator
Direct tel: 01962 848396
Direct email: gdenford@winchester.gov.uk
Other contacts: Head of Museums Service
Access:
Access to staff: By letter, by telephone, by fax, by email, in person, visitors by prior appointment, Internet web pages
Hours: Mon to Fri, 0900 to 1700
Access for disabled people: Parking provided, level entry, toilet facilities
Other restrictions: Level entry to ground floor areas.

General description:
The Historic Resources Centre, is the headquarters of Winchester Museums Service. It houses reserve collections of archaeology, topographical art and photographs. The Museums Service education and finds identification services are based at the Historic Resource Centre as is the archaeology fieldwork team and the Sites and Monuments Record for the area. There is small display area for the temporary exhibitions programme.
Information services:
Special visitor services: Materials and/or activities for children.
Education services: Group education facilities, resources for Key Stages 1 and 2 and Further or Higher Education..
Collections:
Archaeology and local history of Winchester and District including topographical prints, photographs and numismatics
Books relating to the history of Winchester and its district
Catalogues:
Catalogue for library is in-house only. Catalogue for part of the collections is only available in-house.
Publications list:
is available in hard copy and online.
Printed publications:
Winchester Museums Service Newsletter
Various books, booklets and leaflets, maps, prints and posters
Winchester Museums Service Information for Teachers (1 copy free per school, additional copies £1, available from Keeper of Education, HRC)
Electronic and video products:
Bygone Winchester (video, £12.99)

Internet home pages:
http://www.winchester.gov.uk/heritage

3170
WINCHESTER PALACE
Clink Street, Southwark, London, SE1

Organisation type and purpose: National organisation, historic building, house or site.
Parent body:
English Heritage (London Region)
Tel: 020 7973 3000
Access:
Access to building, collections or gallery: No prior appointment required
Hours: Any reasonable time

General description:
The west gable end, with its unusual rose window, is the prominent feature of the remains of the Great Hall of this 13th century town house of the Bishops' of Winchester, damaged by fire in 1814.

3171
WINDERMERE AND TROUTBECK (INCLUDING BRIDGE HOUSE)
St Catherine's, Patterdale Road, Windermere, Cumbria, LA23 1NH

Tel: 015394 46027 (Office)
Fax: 015394 46027
Email: windermere@nationaltrust.org.uk

Organisation type and purpose: National organisation, registered charity (charity number 205846), historic building, house or site, suitable for ages: 8+.
Parent body:
The National Trust (North West Region)
North West Regional Office, tel: 0870 609 5391

Enquiries to: Property Manager
Access:
Access to staff: By letter, by telephone, by fax, by email, in person, Internet web pages

General description:
This property includes the beautiful and secluded head of the Troutbeck valley, as well as several sites next to Lake Windermere and six farms. One of these, Troutbeck Park, was once farmed by Beatrix Potter and was her largest farm. Ambleside Roman Fort, tiny Bridge House in Ambleside, and Cockshott Point on the lake at Bowness-on-Windermere are all popular places to visit. Footpaths lead from Ambleside over Wansfell to the Troutbeck Valley and offer high-level views and contrasting valley landscapes.
Information services:
Education services: Group education facilities..

Internet home pages:
http://www.nationaltrust.org.uk

3172
WINDERMERE STEAMBOAT MUSEUM
Rayrigg Road, Windermere, Cumbria, LA23 1BN

Tel: 01539 445565
Fax: 015394 48769
Email: diana.matthews@talk21.com

Formed: 1977

Organisation type and purpose: Registered charity, museum, suitable for ages: 5+.
Affiliated to:
Windermere Nautical Trust Ltd
Beresford Road, Windermere, Cumbria, LA23 2JG, tel: 01593 442117, fax: 01539 445847, email/website: diana.matthews@talk21.com

Enquiries to: Manager
Access:
Access to staff: By letter, by fax, by email
Hours: Apr to Oct: Daily, 0900 to 1700
Nov to Mar: Mon to Fri, 1000 to 1700
Access for disabled people: Parking provided, level entry, access to all public areas, toilet facilities

General description:
Steam launches and steam craft related to Windermere, local history.
Information services:
Special visitor services: Guided tours.
Services for disabled people: Displays and/or information at wheelchair height.
Collections:
Library, steam, engineering and marine
Photographic collection of steamboats, Windermere, old Bowness photographs and postcards from 1860 onwards
Catalogues:
Catalogue for library is in-house only.
Publications list:
is available in hard copy.
Printed publications:
Arthur Ransome books (hardback from £12)
Boat plans of various vessels (from £20)
Books about Arthur Ransome (from £9)
Great Age of Steam on Windermere (George H Pattison, £9.95)
H W Schneider of Barrow & Bowness (Banks A G, £9)
Lake Windermere Festivals (£1.75)
Museum Guidebook (£1.75)
Postcard Collection (20 postcards, £1)
Salvage of S L Dolly (£1.75)
Windermere's Golden Jubilee (£1.75)
White Lady II - The salvage and restoration of a 1930 hydroplane speedboat (£1.75)
Windermere Motor Boat Racing Club - 50 Years of Motor Boat Racing History (£17)
Electronic and video products:
Various Arthur Ransome titles (audio tapes, £17)

Internet home pages:
http://www.steamboat.co.uk

3173
WINDSOR ARTS CENTRE
St Leonards Road, Windsor, Berkshire, SL4 3BL

Tel: 01753 859421
Fax: 01753 621527
Email: admin@windsorartscentre.org
Formed: 1981

Organisation type and purpose: Arts centre. Exhibitions, music and theatre performances, films, classes.

Enquiries to: Director
Direct email: dstubbs@windsorartscentre.org
Access:
Access to staff: By email
Access to building, collections or gallery: No prior appointment required
Hours: Tue to Sat, 1000 to 2300
Access for disabled people: ramped entry, toilet facilities

General description:
Theatre, dance, music, film, workshops, classes and exhibitions for all ages.

3174
WINDSOR ROYAL BOROUGH COLLECTION
See - Royal Borough Museum Collection

3175
WINGFIELD MANOR
Garner Lane, South Wingfield, Alfreton, Derbyshire, DE5 7NH

Tel: 01773 832060

Organisation type and purpose: Historic building, house or site, suitable for ages: all ages.
Parent body:
English Heritage (East Midlands Region)
44 Derngate, Northampton, NN1 1UH, tel: 01604 735400, fax: 01604 735401

Enquiries to: House Manager
Access:
Access to staff: By letter, by telephone
Access to building, collections or gallery: No prior appointment required
Hours: Apr to Sep: Wed to Sun, 1000 to 1800
Oct: Wed to Sun, 1000 to 1700
Nov to Mar: Sat, Sun, 1000 to 1300 and 1400 to 1600
Other restrictions: Closed 24 to 26 Dec and 1 Jan
Opening hours may change, please check with regional office 01604 735400. The manor incorporates a private working farm. Please do not visit outside official opening hours.

General description:
A huge, ruined defensive country mansion built in the mid-15th century. Mary Queen of Scots was imprisoned here in 1569, 1584 and 1585. Unoccupied since the 1770s, the manor's late Gothic Great Hall and the 'High Tower' are testaments to Wingfield Manor in its heyday.
Information services:
Special visitor services: Tape recorded guides..

Internet home pages:
http://www.english-heritage.org.uk

3176
WINSTER MARKET HOUSE, THE
Winster, Matlock, Derbyshire

Tel: 01335 350245

Organisation type and purpose: National organisation, registered charity (charity number 205846), historic building, house or site, suitable for ages: 8+.
Parent body:
The National Trust (East Midlands Region)
East Midlands Regional Office, tel: 01909 486411

Enquiries to: Property Manager
Access:
Access to staff: By letter, by telephone

General description:
A market house of the late 17th or early 18th century, now restored and housing an NT information room.
New interpretation panels and a scale model of Winster Village, built by the local history group.

Internet home pages:
http://www.nationaltrust.org.uk

3177
WINSTON CHURCHILL'S BRITAIN AT WAR MUSEUM
64-66 Tooley Street, London, SE1 2TF

Tel: 020 7403 3171
Fax: 020 7403 5104
Email: britainatwar@dial.pipex.com
Acronym or abbreviation: BAW
Full name: Britain At War Charitable Trust
Formed: 1992

Organisation type and purpose: Registered charity (charity number 1077168), museum, suitable for ages: 5+.

Enquiries to: Manager
Access:
Access to staff: By telephone, by email
Access for disabled people: ramped entry, access to all public areas, toilet facilities
Other restrictions: 1 room not accessible.

General description:
The Britain At War Experience takes you on an unforgettable journey back into wartime Britain. Experience the sights, sounds and smells of the London Blitz, with amazing realistic effects.
Information services:
Special visitor services: Materials and/or activities for children.
Education services: Resources for Key Stages 2 and 3..
Collections:
Information held in the Exhibit on:
Women At War
Evacuation
Bomb Disposal

Internet home pages:
http://www.britainatwar.co.uk
General information regarding the museum, information for school bookings.

3178
WIRELESS MUSEUM, THE
Puckpool Park, Puckpool Hill, Seaview, Isle of Wight, PO34 5AR

Tel: 01983 567665
Fax: 01983 563730
Acronym or abbreviation: GB3WM
Full name: National Wireless Museum (Wireless Preservation Society)
Formed: 1972
Formed from: Wireless Preservation Society

Organisation type and purpose: Registered charity (charity number 1070100), museum, suitable for ages: 12+.

Enquiries to: Curator
Access:
Access to staff: By telephone
Access to building, collections or gallery: Prior appointment required
Access for disabled people: Parking provided, toilet facilities

General description:
Wireless.
Information services:
Special visitor services: Guided tours.
Education services: Group education facilities.
Services for disabled people: Displays and/or information at wheelchair height.

3179
WIRKSWORTH HERITAGE CENTRE
Crown Yard, Market Place, Wirksworth, Derbyshire, DE4 4ET

Tel: 01629 825225
Email: heritage@gilkin.demon.co.uk
Formed: 1984

Organisation type and purpose: Independently owned, registered charity (charity number 515399), museum, historic building, house or site, suitable for ages: all ages.
To tell 'The Wirksworth Story', historical, sociological and industrial background to the town of Wirksworth.
Parent body:
Wirksworth Civic Society
c/o Heritage Centre

Enquiries to: Administrator
Access:
Access to staff: By letter, by telephone, visitors by prior appointment
Hours: Tue and Thu, 1000 to 1200
Answerphone at all other times
Other restrictions: Voluntary staff at counter, leave message to be returned by a Director.

General description:
The Heritage Centre was an old Silk Mill and small signs of its past are still evident. We aim to tell the story of Wirksworth from Roman

continued overleaf

times to the present day. Information available includes, transport, communications, limestone quarrying, lead mining and its ancient customs, including Well Dressing and its relation to the Great Plague. There is a mock cave for children, also information about the Georgian period, recent regeneration of the town and local customs.
Information services:
Special visitor services: Guided tours, materials and/or activities for children.
Education services: Group education facilities, resources for Key Stages 1 and 2 and 3..
Catalogues:
Catalogue for part of the collections is only available in-house.
Printed publications:
Town Trail (pub Wirksworth Civic Society, £1.50)
George Eliot, Adam Bede & Wirksworth (brochure, 50p)
Picture Postcards (pub Wirksworth Civic Society)
Electronic and video products:
The Quarryman's Story (audio tape, pub Wirksworth Heritage Centre)
Wirksworth - Life & Times (video, pub. Alpha Audio Visual, Allestree, Derby)
Internet home pages:
http://www.gilkin.demon.co.uk

3180
WIRRAL ARCHIVES SERVICE
Wirral Museum, Hamilton Square, Birkenhead, Wirral, CH41 5FN

Tel: 0151 666 3903
Email: archives@wirral-libraries.net
Formed: 1974

Organisation type and purpose: Public library.

Enquiries to: Archivist
Other contacts: Information Services Librarian
Access:
Access to staff: By letter, by fax
Hours: Thu, Fri, 1000 to 1700; Sat, 1000 to 1300
Access for disabled people: ramped entry, access to all public areas

General description:
Deposit for public records: schools, hospitals, local government and Poor Law. Business and private records. Antiquarian collections.
Collections:
Archives of local hospitals
Cammell Laird Shipbuilders archive
Local government records
Macclesfield Collection
Poor Law Records
School records
Unichema Chemicals Limited (Price's Patent Candle Company)
Catalogues:
Catalogue for library is in-house only. Catalogue for all of the collections is only available in-house.

3181
WITHERNSEA LIGHTHOUSE MUSEUM
Hull Road, Withernsea, East Yorkshire, HU19 2DY

Tel: 01964 614834
Formed: 1989
Formerly: Withernsea Lighthouse Trust, date of change, 1989

Organisation type and purpose: Registered charity, museum, suitable for ages: all ages.

Enquiries to: Administrator
Other contacts: Board of Trustees for financial arrangements.
Access:
Access to staff: By letter, by telephone, visitors by prior appointment
Hours: End Mar to end Oct: Sat, Sun, 1300 to 1700
Mid Jun to mid Sep: Mon to Fri, 1100 to 1700
Access for disabled people: ramped entry, access to all public areas, toilet facilities
Other restrictions: Parking down driveway, no disabled access to top of lighthouse.

General description:
Local history; maritime, RNLI and HM Coastguard; erosion; The Kay Kendall Memoriam; films 1950.
Information services:
Special visitor services: Guided tours.
Education services: Group education facilities..
Collections:
Artefacts and memorabilia
Printed publications:
Leaflets
Beneath The Guiding Light (book)

3182
WITLEY COURT
Great Witley, Worcestershire

Tel: 01299 896636

Organisation type and purpose: National organisation, advisory body, museum, historic building, house or site.
Parent body:
English Heritage (West Midlands Region)

Enquiries to: Manager
Access:
Access to staff: By letter, by telephone, in person
Access to building, collections or gallery: No prior appointment required
Hours: 29 Mar to 30 Sep: daily, 1000 to 1800,1 to 31 Oct: daily, 1000 to 1700,1 Nov to 28 Mar: Wed to Sun, 1000 to 1600
Other restrictions: Closed 24 to 26 Dec and 1 Jan
Opening times are subject to change, for up-to-date information contact English Heritage by phone or visit the website.

General description:
An early Jacobean manor house, Witley Court was converted in the 19th century into a vast Italianate mansion.The spectacular ruins of this once great house are surrounded by magnificent landscaped gardens - the 'Monster Work' of William Nesfield - and still contain huge stone fountains. The largest, representing Perseus and Andromeda, once shot water 120 feet upwards, with 'the noise of an express train'. The Jerwood Sculpture Park, consisting of modern British sculptures is situated in the grounds.
Information services:
Special visitor services: Tape recorded guides..

Internet home pages:
http://www.english-heritage.org.uk

See also - Jerwood Sculpture Park

3183
WITNEY & DISTRICT MUSEUM
Gloucester Court Mews, 75 High Street, Witney, Oxfordshire, OX8 6LR

Tel: 01993 775915
Formed: 1996
Formerly: West Oxfordshire Museum Centre, date of change, 1996

Organisation type and purpose: Registered charity (charity number 1006722), museum, art gallery, suitable for ages: 8+.
Parent body:
Witney & District Historical & Archaeological Society
Eastways, 2 The Leys, Witney, Oxfordshire, OX8 7AW, tel: 01993 773451

Enquiries to: Curator
Access:
Access to staff: By letter, by telephone, in person
Access for disabled people: level entry, toilet facilities
Other restrictions: Access to downstairs areas only.

General description:
Photographs and artefacts relating to the social, economic and military history of Witney and the contiguous parishes.
Information services:
Special visitor services: Materials and/or activities for children.
Education services: Resources for Key Stages 2, 3, 4 and Further or Higher Education..
Collections:
Photographs, books, documents, tools, domestic items, paintings and prints
Catalogues:
Catalogue for library is in-house only. Catalogue for all of the collections is only available in-house.
Printed publications:
Walk Round Witney (Witney & District Historical & Archaeological Society, £2)
Record of Witney (Witney & District Historical & Archaeological Society Journal, £1.50)

3184
WITTERSHAM STOCKS MILL
On B2082, between, Tenterden, and, Rye, Kent

Tel: 01797 270295

Organisation type and purpose: Historic building, house or site.

General description:
Stocks mill is the tallest post mill in Kent. It was moved to this site in 1781, and acquired and restored by Kent County Council in 1980.
Collections:
Exhibition of old maps and photographs.

3185
WOLLASTON MUSEUM
102 High Street, Wollaston, Wellingborough, Northamptonshire, NN9 7RJ

Tel: 01933 664468 or 625776
Formed: 1970
Formed from: Wollaston Historical Society

Organisation type and purpose: Independently owned, museum, suitable for ages: all ages.

Enquiries to: Executive Secretary
Other contacts: Assistant Secretary
Access:
Access to staff: By letter only
Other restrictions: No staff - all volunteers.

General description:
Village museum reflecting history of the village from earliest times to present day.

3186
WOLVERHAMPTON ART GALLERY
Lichfield Street, Wolverhampton, West Midlands, WV1 1DU

Tel: 01902 552055
Fax: 01902 552053
Email: info.wag@dial.pipex.com
Formed: 1884
Formerly: Municipal Art Gallery & Museum

Organisation type and purpose: Local government body, art gallery, suitable for ages: 5+.

Enquiries to: Marketing Officer
Direct tel: 01902 552040
Direct email: marketing.wag@dial.pipex.com
Access:
Access to staff: By letter, by telephone, by fax, by email
Access for disabled people: level entry, access to all public areas, toilet facilities

General description:
Exciting programme of temporary exhibitions, collection of contemporary art, British and American pop art, 18th and 19th century paintings.

Information services:
Special visitor services: Materials and/or activities for children.
Education services: Group education facilities..
Collections:
Contemporary art
Pop art (British and American)
18th and 19th century paintings
Printed publications:
Leaflet of exhibitions and events (quarterly, free of charge)

Internet home pages:
http://www.wolverhamptonart.org.uk
Information on the gallery and its collections and exhibitions.

3187
WOLVESEY CASTLE (OLD BISHOP'S PALACE)
College Street, Winchester, Hampshire

Tel: 01962 854766

Organisation type and purpose: Historic building, house or site, suitable for ages: 5+.
Parent body:
English Heritage (South East Region)
Tel: 01483 252000, fax: 01483 252001

Enquiries to: Curator
Access:
Access to building, collections or gallery: No prior appointment required
Hours: Apr to Sep: daily, 1000 to 1800
Oct: daily, 1000 to 1700
Other restrictions: Closed Nov to Mar
Opening times are subject to change, for up-to-date information contact English Heritage by phone or visit the website.

General description:
One of the greatest medieval buildings in England, the palace was the chief residence of the Bishops of Winchester. Its extensive ruins still reflect their importance and wealth. The last great occasion at Wolvesey was on 25 July 1554 when Queen Mary and Philip of Spain held their wedding breakfast in the East Hall.

Internet home pages:
http://www.english-heritage.org.uk

3188
WOOD END MUSEUM OF NATURAL HISTORY
The Crescent, Scarborough, North Yorkshire, YO11 2PW

Tel: 01723 367326

Organisation type and purpose: Museum, suitable for ages: 5+.
Parent body:
Scarborough Museums and Gallery
Department of Tourism and Leisure Service, tel: 01723 232323

Enquiries to: Curator
Direct tel: 01723 374839
Access:
Access to staff: By letter, by telephone, by fax
Access for disabled people: Parking provided, ramped entry
Other restrictions: Limited access for people with disabilities.

General description:
The former home of the Sitwell family (Edith Sitwell was born there) now houses the museum of natural history. The displays introduce the local wildlife, rocks and fossils of the heritage caost and North York Moors National Park. What's In Store illustrates the diversity of the Borough's collections and ther si a scale model of medieval Scarborough.
Information services:
Special visitor services: Materials and/or activities for children..

3189
WOODBRIDGE MUSEUM
5 Market Hill, Woodbridge, Suffolk, IP12 4LP

Tel: 01394 380502
Formed: 20 May 1982

Organisation type and purpose: Registered charity (charity number 276373), museum.

Enquiries to: Public Relations Manager
Direct tel: 01394 387644
Access:
Access to staff: By letter, by telephone

General description:
History of Woodbridge, archaeological findings of Anglo-Saxon remains, audio visual of old photographs, places and events, free activity sheets for children, souvenirs.

3190
WOODBRIDGE TIDE MILL
Woodbridge, Suffolk

Tel: 01473 626618

Organisation type and purpose: Historic building, house or site.
Access:
Access to staff: By telephone

General description:
19th century mill, a rare example of its type. Restored to full working order. Watrerwheel turns most days, time depending on tides.

Internet home pages:
http://www.tidemill.org.uk

3191
WOODCHESTER PARK
Old Ebworth Centre, Ebworth Estate, The Camp, Stroud, Gloucestershire, GL6 7ES

Tel: 01452 814213 (Warden)
Fax: 01452 810055
Email: woodchesterpark@nationaltrust.org.uk

Organisation type and purpose: National organisation, registered charity (charity number 205846), historic building, house or site, suitable for ages: all ages.
Parent body:
The National Trust (South West Region)
Regional Office for Wessex, tel: 01985 843600
Parent body for mansion:
Woodchester Mansion Trust
Tel: 01453 750455

Enquiries to: Warden
Other contacts: 01453 750455 for access to house.

General description:
A beautiful secluded valley near Stroud, in the Cotswolds. The valley contains the remains of an 18th- and 19th century landscape park, a chain of five lakes, fringed by woodland pasture and an unfinished Victorian mansion (not NT), which is open to the public on specified days from Easter to October. There are also waymarked trails (steep and strenuous in places) through delightful scenery.

Internet home pages:
http://www.nationaltrust.org.uk/regions/wessex

3192
WOODCHURCH WINDMILL
Woodchurch, Ashford, Kent

Tel: 01233 860043

Organisation type and purpose: Historic building, house or site.
Member of:
Kent Windmills

General description:
White smock mill 1820s restored to full working order.

Collections:
Photographs showing the mill's history and restoration.
Exhibition of memorabilia on loan from Woodchurch Museum

3193
WOODEN CANAL BOAT SOCIETY LIMITED, THE
5 Oaken Clough Terrace, Ashton-under-Lyne, Lancashire, OL7 9NY

Tel: 0161 330 2315
Email: wooden_canal_boat_society@yahoo.co.uk
Acronym or abbreviation: WCBS
Formed: 1996
Formerly: Wooden Boat Craft Trust (WBCT), date of change, 1997

Organisation type and purpose: Registered charity (charity number 1069820), museum, suitable for ages: 16+.
Collection located at:
Portland Basin Museum
Portland Place, Ashton-under-Lyne, OL7 0QA

Enquiries to: Secretary
Direct tel: 07855 601589
Direct email: chris@widdershins.fsnet.co.uk
Access:
Access to staff: By letter, by telephone, by email, Internet web pages
Access to building, collections or gallery: No prior appointment required
Hours: Tue to Sun, 1000 to 1700
Access for disabled people: Parking provided, level entry, toilet facilities

General description:
Collect, maintain and restore wooden canal boats, then put them to work serving today's community.
Information services:
Speaker available.
Special visitor services: Guided tours..
Collections:
6 historic wooden narrow boats, mostly located at Portland Basin Museum

Internet home pages:
http://www.wcbs.org.uk
Overview of society activities and projects.

See also - Portland Basin Museum

3194
WOODHALL SPA COTTAGE MUSEUM TRUST
See - Cottage Museum

3195
WOODHAM LOCOMOTIVE SCRAPYARD
See - Vale of Glamorgan Railway Company Limited

3196
WOODHORN CHURCH
Woodhorn Village, Ashington, Northumberland, NE63 9YA

Tel: 01670 856968 (contact Woodhorn Colliery Museum)

Organisation type and purpose: Local government body, historic building, house or site, suitable for ages: 16+.
Other addresses:
Woodhorn Colliery Museum
Queen Elizabeth II Country Park, Ashington, Northumberland, NE63 9YF, tel: 01670 856968, fax: 01670 810958
Access:
Access to staff: By letter, by telephone, by fax, in person, visitors by prior appointment
Access for disabled people: level entry, access to all public areas

continued overleaf

General description:
A Grade I listed church, heavily restored in the 1840s but still contains many medieval architectural features.

3197 WOODHORN COLLIERY MUSEUM

QEII Country Park, Ashington, Northumberland, NE63 9YF

Tel: 01670 856968
Fax: 01670 810958
Formed: 1989

Organisation type and purpose: Museum, art gallery, historic building, house or site.
Parent body:
Wansbeck District Council (WDC)

Enquiries to: Museums Officer
Access:
Access to staff: By letter, by telephone, by fax, visitors by prior appointment
Access to building, collections or gallery: No prior appointment required
Hours: May to Aug, Wed to Sun, 1000 to 1700
Sep to Apr, Wed to Sun, 1000 to 1600
Access for disabled people: Parking provided, toilet facilities
Other restrictions: Wheelchair available.

General description:
Coal mining history of SE Northumberland. Collections include Miners' Banners and works by the Ashington Group of Painters (the Pitmen Painters).
Information services:
Special visitor services: Guided tours, materials and/or activities for children.
Education services: Group education facilities, resources for Key Stages 2 and 3..
Collections:
Paintings by the Ashington Group (The Pitmen Painters)
Most of Northumberland's Miners' Banners

Internet home pages:
http://www.wansbeck.gov.uk

3198 WOODLAND HERITAGE CENTRE

Brokerswood Country Park, Westbury, Wiltshire, BA13 4EH

Tel: 01373 822238
Fax: 01373 858474
Formed: 1971
Formerly: Phillip's Countryside Museum; Woodland Heritage Museum, date of change, 1997

Organisation type and purpose: Registered charity (charity number L246167), museum, suitable for ages: all, but primarily 5 to 11.

Enquiries to: Education Officer
Direct email: woodland.park@virgin.net
Access:
Access to staff: By letter, by fax, by email
Hours: Mon to Fri, 0900 to 1700
Other restrictions: Opening dependent on season, please phone in advance.
Access to building, collections or gallery: Prior appointment required
Hours: Mon to Fri, 1000 to 1600; Sat, Sun, 1100 to 1600
Winter: Mon to Fri, 1000 to 1600; Sat, Sun, 1200 to 1600

General description:
Forestry and forest management, forests for leisure and recreation, public participation in forestry, natural history, botany, flora, fauna, ornithology, ecology and conservation of woodland.
Collections:
Barber Collection of Birds' Eggs of the World (approximately 2000 species)
Printed publications:
Details of educational facilities (on request)

3199 WOODLANDS MUSEUM & ART GALLERY

See - Greenwich Local History Library

3200 WOODSPRING MUSEUM

See - North Somerset Museum

3201 WOODSTOCK MUSEUM

Catalogues:
Catalogue for library is on-line. Catalogue for all of the collections is on-line.
See - Oxfordshire Museum

3202 WOOLPIT & DISTRICT MUSEUM

c/o Walnut Tree Cottage, Woolpit, Bury St Edmunds, Suffolk, IP30 9RF

Tel: 01359 240822
Formed: 1985
Formerly: Woolpit Bygones Museum, date of change, 1998

Organisation type and purpose: Independently owned, museum.
Parent body:
Woolpit & District Museum Trust

Enquiries to: Curator
Direct tel: 07771 963709
Access:
Access to staff: By letter only
Access for disabled people: Parking provided, level entry
Other restrictions: Chairlift.

General description:
A collection of artefacts including items that allow the museum to show life as it was in a Suffolk village.
Information services:
Helpline available, tel no: 07771 963709.
Special visitor services: Guided tours.
Education services: Group education facilities..
Collections:
Woolpit brick-making
Victorian kitchen
Catalogues:
Catalogue for library is in-house only. Catalogue for all of the collections is only available in-house.
Printed publications:
Woolpit in a Nutshell
Story of the Green Children
Woolpit Church Guide

3203 WOOLSTHORPE MANOR

23 Newton Way, Woolsthorp-by-Colsterworth, Grantham, Lincolnshire, NG33 5NR

Tel: 01476 860338
Fax: 01476 860338
Email: woolsthorpemanor@nationaltrust.org.uk
Formed: 1895

Organisation type and purpose: National organisation, registered charity (charity number 205846), historic building, house or site, suitable for ages: 5+.
Parent body:
The National Trust (East Midlands Region)
East Midlands Regional Office, tel: 01909 486411
Other addresses:
The National Trust
East Midlands Regional Office
Clumber Park, Worksop, S80 3BE

Enquiries to: Property Manager
Access:
Access to staff: By letter, by telephone, by fax, by email, in person, Internet web pages
Access for disabled people: Parking provided, ramped entry, toilet facilities
Other restrictions: Tel. for parking arrangements. Drop-off point. 1 manual wheelchair available, booking essential. Ramped entrance. Ground floor fully accessible, Ramps available to overcome one step. No access to other floors. Photograph album. Level entrance to coffee facility.

General description:
A small 17th century manor house, the birthplace and family home of Sir Isaac Newton, who formulated some of his major works here during the Plague years, 1665-67). An early edition of his Principia is on display. The orchard includes a descendant of the famous apple tree. Science Discovery Centre and exhibition. A recently opened wet kitchen and exhibition exploring life on the farmstead.
Information services:
Tours of house and Science Discovery Centre for booked groups by arrangement with Property Manager throughout year
Special events include: The Science of Christmas' in Dec and 'Seventeenth-Century Christmas'; contact property for full information
Village walk from property. Leaflets available at ticket desk
Braille guide
Suitable for school groups, education room/centre
Hands-on activities. Family guide
Special visitor services: Guided tours, materials and/or activities for children.
Education services: Group education facilities, resources for Key Stage 2.
Services for disabled people: For the visually impaired.

Internet home pages:
http://www.nationaltrust.org.uk

3204 WORCESTER CATHEDRAL

Chapter Office, 10a College Green, Worcester, WR1 2LH

Tel: 01905 28854
Fax: 01905 611139
Email: info@worcestercathedral.org.uk
Formed: 1084

Organisation type and purpose: International organisation, historic building, house or site, suitable for ages: 5+.
Cathedral.

Enquiries to: Visitor Officer
Access:
Access to staff: By letter, by telephone, by fax, by email, visitors by prior appointment, Internet web pages
Access to building, collections or gallery: No prior appointment required
Hours: Daily, 0730 to 1800
Access for disabled people: Parking provided, ramped entry, level entry, toilet facilities

Information services:
Library available for reference (for conditions see Access above)
Specialist, family and school tours available by prior appointment.
Special visitor services: Guided tours, materials and/or activities for children.
Education services: Group education facilities, resources for Key Stages 1 and 2, 3, 4 and Further or Higher Education.
Services for disabled people: For the visually impaired; for the hearing impaired.
Collections:
Library of medieval books, manuscripts and music available by prior appointment
Catalogues:
Catalogue for library is published.
Printed publications:
Brochures
Guidebooks (for purchase)

Internet home pages:
http://www.cofe-worcester.org.uk
Services, facilities, programme, index.

3205
WORCESTER CITY MUSEUM & ART GALLERY
Foregate Street, Worcester, WR1 1DT

Tel: 01905 25371
Fax: 01905 25371
Email: artgalleryandmuseum @cityofworcester.gov.uk

Organisation type and purpose: Local government body, museum, art gallery, suitable for ages: pre-school and 5+.
Parent body:
Worcester City Council

Enquiries to: Curator
Other contacts: Gallery & Exhibitions Officer
Access:
Access to staff: By letter, by telephone, by fax, visitors by prior appointment
Hours: Mon to Fri, 0930 to 1730; Sat, 0930 to 1700
Access to building, collections or gallery: No access other than to staff
Hours: Mon to Fri, 0930 to 1730; Sat, 0930 to 1700
Other restrictions: Closed Sun.
Access for disabled people: access to all public areas, toilet facilities

General description:
Collections relating to: social history, natural history, archaeology, fine and decorative arts. Worcestershire Regiment and Worcestershire Yeomanry Cavalry. A changing programme of temporary exhibitions.
Information services:
Education services: Group education facilities, resources for Key Stages 1 and 2 and Further or Higher Education.
Services for disabled people: For the hearing impaired; displays and/or information at wheelchair height.
Catalogues:
Catalogue for part of the collections is available in-house and part is on-line.
Printed publications:
Free leaflets available

Internet home pages:
http://www.worcestercitymuseums.org.uk

3206
WORCESTERSHIRE COUNTY MUSEUM
Hartlebury Castle, Hartlebury, Kidderminster, Worcestershire, DY11 7XZ

Tel: 01299 250416
Fax: 01299 251890
Email: museum@worcestershire.gov.uk
Formed: 1966
Formerly: Hereford and Worcester County Museum, date of change, 1998

Organisation type and purpose: Local government body, museum.

Enquiries to: County Museums Officer
Access:
Access to staff: By letter, by email, visitors by prior appointment
Hours: Mon to Thu, 0900 to 1700; Fri, 0900 to 1630
Access to building, collections or gallery: No prior appointment required
Hours: Mon to Thu, 1000 to 1700; Fri, Sun, 1400 to 1700
Access for disabled people: Parking provided, level entry, toilet facilities

General description:
Social history; costume, 18th to 20th century; domestic life; county trades and crafts; horse-drawn vehicles; gypsy caravans; bicycles; toys; children's books; archaeological archive for Worcestershire (finds and paper archive from excavated sites).
Information services:
Library available for reference (for conditions see Access above)
Social history index.
Special visitor services: Guided tours.
Education services: Group education facilities, resources for Key Stages 1 and 2..
Collections:
Bromsgrove Guild Archive
The Tickenhall Collection (Folk Life)
Catalogues:
Catalogue for part of the collections is only available in-house.
Printed publications:
Children's Copy Books
Costume Catalogue Parts I & II
Education books
Information sheets (list on application)
May Day and its Customs
Museum Guide
Smock Frocks

See also - Hartlebury Castle

3207
WORCESTERSHIRE REGIMENT MUSEUM
Worcester City Museum and Art Gallery, Foregate Street, Worcester, WR1 1DT

Tel: 01905 25371
Formed: 1923

Organisation type and purpose: Registered charity (charity number 276510), museum.
Office:
The Curator
Worcestershire Regiment Museum, RHQ Norton, Worcester, WR5 2PA, tel: 01905 354359, fax: 01905 353871

Enquiries to: Curator
Direct tel: 01905 354359
Direct fax: 01905 353871
Direct email: rhq_wfr@lineone.net
Access:
Access to staff: By letter, by fax, by email, visitors by prior appointment
Hours: Mon to Fri, 0830 to 1600
Access to building, collections or gallery: No prior appointment required
Hours: Sun to Fri, 0930 to 1730; Sat, 0930 to 1700;
Access for disabled people: access to all public areas, toilet facilities

General description:
History of the Worcestershire Regiment 1694 to 1970 including Militia and Volunteers, and of the Worcestershire and Sherwood Foresters Regiment from 1970 to date.
Collections:
Archives and photographs, reference library and some personal records

3208
WORDSWORTH HOUSE
Main Street, Cockermouth, Cumbria, CA13 9RX

Tel: 01900 824805
Fax: 01900 824805
Email: wordsworthhouse@nationaltrust.org.uk
Formed: 1939

Organisation type and purpose: National organisation, registered charity (charity number 205846), museum, historic building, house or site, suitable for ages: 8+.
Parent body:
The National Trust (North West)
North West Regional Office, tel: 0870 609 5391

Enquiries to: Custodian
Access:
Access to staff: By letter, by telephone, by fax, by email, in person

General description:
The Georgian town house where William Wordsworth was born in 1770. Several rooms contain some of the poet's personal effects. His childhood garden with terraced walk, attractively restored, has views over the River Derwent, referred to in 'The Prelude'.
Information services:
Guided tours on request.
Braille guide. Touch list. Herbs and aromatic plants.
Sound link for video.
Frontcarrying baby slings for loan. Hip-carrying infant seats for loan.
Suitable for school groups. Children's quiz/trail. Live interpretation (special events only).
Special visitor services: Guided tours, materials and/or activities for children.
Services for disabled people: For the visually impaired; for the hearing impaired.
Collections:
Landscape by J W M Turner
Broadwood square piano
Paintings, furniture, panelling and decorations of the period
Printed publications:
Leaflet (direct, free)
Guide Book (direct, 50p)

Internet home pages:
http://www.nationaltrust.org.uk

3209
WORDSWORTH TRUST, THE
See - Dove Cottage and the Wordsworth Museum

3210
WORKHOUSE LIBRARY MUSEUM
Waterside Centre, Glendermott Road, Londonderry, BT47 1AU

Tel: 028 7131 8328

Organisation type and purpose: Local government body, museum, suitable for ages: 5+.
Parent body:
Derry City Council
Heritage & Museum Service
Harbour Museum, Harbour Square, Derry, BT48 6AF, tel: 02871 377331, fax: 02871 377633, email/website: museums@derrycity.gov.uk

Enquiries to: Curator
Other contacts: Curator of Museums for the building.
Access:
Access to staff: By letter, by telephone, by fax
Access for disabled people: Parking provided, access to all public areas, toilet facilities

General description:
World War II, The Famine.
Information services:
Special visitor services: Guided tours, tape recorded guides..
Printed publications:
Atlantic Memorial (booklet, £2.50)

3211
WORKHOUSE, THE
Upton Road, Southwell, Nottinghamshire, NG25 0PT

Tel: 01636 817250
Fax: 01636 817251
Email: theworkhouse@nationaltrust.org.uk

Organisation type and purpose: National organisation, registered charity (charity number 205846), historic building, house or site, suitable for ages: 5+.
Parent body:
The National Trust (East Midlands Region)
East Midlands Regional Office, tel: 01909 486411

Enquiries to: Property Manager
Access:
Access to staff: By letter, by telephone, by fax, by email, in person, Internet web pages
Access to building, collections or gallery: No prior appointment required
Hours: End Mar to Jul and Sep to early Nov, Thu to Mon, 1200 to 1700; Aug, Thu to Mon, 1100 to 1700

continued overleaf

Other restrictions: Last admission 1 hr before closing. Summer half term open daily. Autumn half term open daily except Wednesday
Access for disabled people: Parking provided, ramped entry, toilet facilities
Other restrictions: Drop-off point. 5 manual wheelchairs available. Ground floor fully accessible (except for motorised wheelchairs). Stair access only to other floors. Manual wheelchairs available on other floors. Audiovisual/video. Photograph album. Please ring for details and to book wheelchairs.

General description:
Enter this 19th century brick institution and discover the thought-provoking story of the 'welfare' system of the New Poor Law. The least altered workhouse in existence today, it survives from hundreds that once covered the country. Explore the segregated stairs and rooms. Interactive displays explore poverty through the years and across the country.
Information services:
Braille guide. Large-print guide. Audio guide. Handling collection
Sympathetic Hearing Scheme. Film subtitles on request. Printed script of audio guide.
Hearing loop for audio guide.
Suitable for school groups. Education room/ centre. Audio guide. Hands-on activities. Children's quiz/trail
Special visitor services: Tape recorded guides, materials and/or activities for children.
Education services: Group education facilities.
Services for disabled people: For the visually impaired; for the hearing impaired.
Collections:
Archive records

Internet home pages:
http://www.nationaltrust.org.uk

3212
WORKING SILK MUSEUM, THE
Braintree

Closed, date of change, 2001

3213
WORKSHOP WALES GALLERY
Maworowen, Fishguard, Pembrokeshire, SA65 9QA

Tel: 01348 891619
Formed: 1970

Organisation type and purpose: Independently owned, art gallery, suitable for ages: 16+.

Enquiries to: Manager
Access:
Access to staff: By letter, by telephone, in person
Access to building, collections or gallery: No prior appointment required
Hours: Mar to Oct only
Access for disabled people: Parking provided, ramped entry, access to all public areas

General description:
Collection of contemporary paintings and sculptures by British artists. Specialising in sculpture for outdoor display.
Information services:
Services for disabled people: Displays and/or information at wheelchair height.

3214
WORLD HERITAGE
Heritage House, 25 High West Street, Dorchester, Dorset, DT1 1UW

Tel: 01305 269741
Fax: 01305 268885
Email: info@worldheritage.org.uk
Formed: 1989

Organisation type and purpose: Museum.
A consortium of independent museums and exhibitions. Also operates a literature distribution service, and tourism and Teddy Bear fairs.
Subsidiaries:
The Dinosaur Museum
Tel: 01305 269880, fax: 01305 268885, email/ website: info@dinosaur-museum.org.uk
The Dorset Teddy Bear Museum
Tel: 01305 263200, fax: 01305 268885, email/ website: info@teddybearhouse.co.uk
The Tutankhamun Exhibition
Tel: 01305 269571, fax: 01305 268885, email/ website: info@tutankhamun-exhibition.co.uk

Enquiries to: Manager
Access:
Access to staff: By letter, by telephone, by fax, by email, visitors by prior appointment, Internet web pages
Hours: Mon to Fri, 0900 to 1700

General description:
Egyptology, dinosaurs, fossils, geology, teddy bears, tourism, museum management, terracotta warriors, photography.
Printed publications:
Wide selection of books produced by other publishers, available mail-order or direct from one of the museum shops
Main themes of books: Egyptology, dinosaurs, teddy bears, price lists available

Internet home pages:
http://www.world-heritage.co.uk
http://www.tutankhamun-exhibition.co.uk
http://www.dinosaur-museum.org.uk
http://www.teddybearmuseum.co.uk

3215
WORLD IN MINATURE
Oban

Exhibition closed

3216
WORLD OF COUNTRY LIFE
Sandy Bay, Exmouth, Devon, EX8 5BU

Tel: 01395 274533
Fax: 01395 273457
Email: info@worldofcountrylife.co.uk
Formed: 1979

Organisation type and purpose: Independently owned, museum, suitable for ages: 5+.
Private collection, tourist attraction.

Enquiries to: Manager
Access:
Access to staff: By letter, by telephone, by fax, by email
Access for disabled people: Parking provided, level entry, access to all public areas, toilet facilities

General description:
Steam showmans' engines; steam traction engines; vintage cars and motorcycles; farm machinery and tractors; Thorneycroft Char-a-banc.

Internet home pages:
http://www.worldofcountrylife.co.uk

3217
WORLD OF GLASS LIMITED, THE
Chalon Way East, St Helens, Merseyside, WA10 1BX

Tel: 01744 22766
Fax: 01744 616966
Email: info@worldofglass.com
Formed: 1964
Formed from: Pilkington Glass Museum, date of change, 1964-2000; St Helens Museum and Art Gallery, date of change, 2000

Organisation type and purpose: Independently owned, registered charity, museum, historic building, house or site, suitable for ages: all ages.
Parent body:
Pilkington plc
Corporate Affairs, St Helens, Merseyside, WA10 3TT
Member of:
Museums Association

Enquiries to: Director
Other contacts: Curator for specific collections questions.
Access:
Access to staff: By letter only
Access to building, collections or gallery: No prior appointment required
Hours: Tue to Sun, 1000 to 1700
Other restrictions: Closed Mon except for Bank Holidays.
Access for disabled people: Parking provided, ramped entry, level entry, toilet facilities

General description:
History of glassmaking over the past 4000 years, evolution of glassmaking techniques, historical development of glassmaking processes and use since Phoenician times, modern glassmaking processes and techniques, modern applications of all types of glass, live glass-blowing demonstrations, local history.
Information services:
Helpline available, tel no: 08707 444 777.
Audiovisual show showing history and modern glass.
Identification of antique glass
Special visitor services: Materials and/or activities for children.
Education services: Group education facilities, resources for Key Stages 1 and 2, 3 and Further or Higher Education.
Services for disabled people: Displays and/or information at wheelchair height.
Collections:
Pilkington Glass Collection:
Charting 4000 years of the history of glassmaking along with modern techniques of glass production and usage
St Helens Borough Collection: Local history collection
Catalogues:
Catalogue for library is in-house only. Catalogue for all of the collections is only available in-house but part is published.
Printed publications:
Newsletter (quarterly)

Internet home pages:
http://www.worldofglass.com

3218
WORLD OF THE HONEY BEE
Hebden Bridge

Closed, date of change, 2000

3219
WORSHIPFUL COMPANY OF MERCERS, THE
Mercers' Hall, Ironmonger Lane, London, EC2V 8HE

Tel: 020 7726 4991
Fax: 020 7600 1158
Email: mail@mercers.co.uk
Acronym or abbreviation: Mercers' Company
Formed: 1394

Organisation type and purpose: Membership association (membership is by election or invitation), present number of members: 260.
City of London Livery Company.
Fraternity, corporate body and charitable foundation.

Enquiries to: Archivist and Curator
Direct tel: 020 7776 7244
Direct email: ursulac@mercers.co.uk
Access:
Access to staff: By letter, by telephone, by fax, by email, visitors by prior appointment
Hours: Mon to Fri, 0930 to 1700
Access to building, collections or gallery: No access other than to staff, prior appointment required
Access for disabled people: level entry, toilet facilities

General description:
Access to the company's historic archives and art collection, information regarding the history of the Company and its charitable activities.
Collections:
Mercers' Company archives 1347 to present and records of numerous charitable trusts of which the company is trustee
Catalogues:
Catalogue for library is in-house only. Catalogue for all of the collections is only available in-house.
Publications list:
is available in hard copy.
Printed publications:
General information booklets and bibliographies available free of charge

Internet home pages:
http://www.mercers.co.uk

3220
WORSHIPFUL COMPANY OF PAINTER-STAINERS

Painters' Hall, 9 Little Trinity Lane, London, EC4V 2AD

Tel: 020 7236 6258
Fax: 020 7236 0500
Email: beadle@painters-hall.co.uk
Acronym or abbreviation: Painter-Stainers' Company
Formed: 1268
Formed by the amalgamation of: Worshipful Company of Stainers, date of change, 1268-1502; Worshipful Company of Painters, date of change, 1283-1502

Organisation type and purpose: Membership association (membership is by election or invitation), present number of members: 542, registered charity (charity number 200001), museum, historic building, house or site, suitable for ages: 16+.
Livery company.

Enquiries to: Clerk
Direct tel: 020 7236 7070
Direct fax: 020 7236 7074
Direct email: clerk@painters-hall.co.uk
Access:
Access to staff: By telephone, by fax, by email, visitors by prior appointment
Hours: Mon to Fri, 0900 to 1700
Access to building, collections or gallery: Prior appointment required
Access for disabled people: access to all public areas, toilet facilities

General description:
Historical details of the Company and its membership.
Collections:
Assorted paintings and silver of varying degrees of interest
Charters and other documents of historical interest
Catalogues:
Catalogue for all of the collections is only available in-house.

Internet home pages:
http://www.painters-hall.co.uk
Brief history and details of Painters' Hall. Basic listing and details of the various rooms available for hire at Painters' Hall.

3221
WORTHING MUSEUM AND ART GALLERY

Chapel Road, Worthing, West Sussex, BN11 1HP

Tel: 01903 239999 ext 1140 (Saturday 2221150)
Fax: 01903 236277
Email: museum@worthing.gov.uk
Formed: 1908

Organisation type and purpose: Local government body, museum, art gallery, suitable for ages: all ages.

Postal address for:
Friends of Worthing Museum & Art Gallery
Worthing Archaeological Society

Enquiries to: Curator
Direct tel: 01903 239999 ext 1137
Other contacts: (1) Assistant Curator (Costume); (2) Assistant Curator (Art & Exhibitions) for (1) Costume Collection; (2) Art Collection.
Access:
Access to staff: By letter, by telephone, by fax, by email, in person, visitors by prior appointment
Hours: Mon to Fri, 1000 to 1700
Access for disabled people: Parking provided, ramped entry, access to all public areas, toilet facilities

General description:
Regional archaeology, local history, geology, costume, juvenilia (including dolls), fine and applied art, South Downs folk life, children's books, textiles.
Information services:
Special visitor services: Guided tours.
Education services: Group education facilities, resources for Key Stages 1 and 2, 3, 4 and Further or Higher Education.
Services for disabled people: For the visually impaired; for the hearing impaired; displays and/or information at wheelchair height.
Collections:
19th century watercolours
Costume and Textile Collection
Colin Mears Bequest of children's books and juvenilia
Juvenilia Collection
English drinking glasses collection
Local history ephemera and photographs
Local excavation archives
Catalogues:
Catalogue for part of the collections is published.
Publications list:
is available in hard copy.
Printed publications:
Archaeology around Worthing (1989)
Catalogue of Paintings and Drawings 1988
Costume in Worthing Museum (1981)
Geology Around Worthing (1985)
Highdown and its Saxon Cemetery (1976)
Salvington Mill (1976)
Shepherd of the Downs (song book with music) (1979)
The Dolls at Worthing Museum (1990)
A wide range of leaflets covering everyday life

Internet home pages:
http://www.worthing.gov.uk
Basic information about Museum's collections and services.

3222
WOTTON-UNDER-EDGE HISTORICAL SOCIETY

Wotton-under-Edge Heritage Centre, The Chipping, Wotton-under-Edge, Gloucestershire, GL12 7AD

Tel: 01453 521541
Formed: 1945

Organisation type and purpose: Membership association, present number of members: 70, voluntary organisation, registered charity (charity number 291936), museum, suitable for ages: all ages.

Enquiries to: Honorary Curator & Librarian
Access:
Access to staff: By letter, by telephone, in person
Access to building, collections or gallery: No prior appointment required
Hours: Tue to Fri, 1000 to 1300 and 1400 to 1700 (1600 in winter); Sat, 1000 to 1300
Some Sun in summer, 1430 to 1700
Other restrictions: Charges made for the use of research facilities.
Access for disabled people: Parking provided, level entry, access to all public areas, toilet facilities

General description:
Local history of Wotton-under-Edge and adjoining parishes, local family history, Wotton-under-Edge and adjoining parishes, tourist information point.
Information services:
Services for disabled people: Displays and/or information at wheelchair height.
Collections:
Books, documents, manuscripts, pictures, photographs and artefacts, all in our computerised database
Parish registers and 1891 census on microfiche and 1881 census on CD-ROM
Catalogues:
Catalogue for all of the collections is only available in-house.
Microform products:
Parish registers and 1891 census (microfiche)
Electronic and video products:
1881 census (CD-ROM)

Internet home pages:
http://www.conygres.co.uk

3223
WREST PARK GARDENS

Silsoe, Bedford

Tel: 01525 860152 (weekends only)

Organisation type and purpose: Historic building, house or site.
Parent body:
English Heritage (East of England Region)
Brooklands, 24 Brooklands Avenue, Cambridge, CB2 2BU, tel: 01223 582700, fax: 01223 582701
Access:
Access to staff: By letter, by telephone
Other restrictions: Contact English Heritage (East of England Region) for information.
Access to building, collections or gallery: No prior appointment required
Hours: Apr to Sep: Sat, Sun and Bank Holidays only, 1000 to 1800.
Oct: Sat, Sun, 1000 to 1700
Last admission one hour before closing time
Other restrictions: Opening times are subject to change, for up-to-date information contact English Heritage by phone or visit the website.

General description:
These historic gardens are a rare survival of the formal garden style so common in England in the 18th century, and were inspired by the great gardens of Versailles and the Loire Valley. The history of gardening styles, garden buildings, follies including the baroque Archer Pavilion, Orangery and Bath House, can be seen. Now the gardens are overlooked by a house built in the 1830s, again in the French style, inspired as it was by the great châteaux of 18th century France. The visitor can catch a glimpse of the great library, the grand staircase, and the drawing room.
Information services:
Special visitor services: Tape recorded guides..

Internet home pages:
http://www.english-heritage.org.uk

3224
WREXHAM ARTS CENTRE

Rhosddu Road, Wrexham, Clwyd, LL11 1AU

Tel: 01978 292093
Fax: 01978 292611
Email: arts.centre@wrexham.gov.uk
Formed: 1973

Organisation type and purpose: Local government body, professional body, art gallery, suitable for ages: 5+.
Parent body:
Wrexham County Borough Council (WCBC)
The Guildhall, Wrexham, LL13 8AZ
Supported by the:
Arts Council of Wales

Enquiries to: Curator

continued overleaf

Direct tel: 01978 292640
Direct email: tracy.simpson@wrexham.gov.uk
Other contacts: (1) Visual Arts Officer (2) Education Officer for (1) past catalogues, touring exhibitions; (2) educational workshops.
Access:
Access to staff: By letter, by telephone, by fax, by email, in person
Access to building, collections or gallery: No prior appointment required
Hours: Mon to Fri, 0930 to 1845; Sat, 0930 to 1700
Other restrictions: Closed Sun and Bank Holidays.
Access for disabled people: Parking provided, level entry, access to all public areas, toilet facilities
Other restrictions: Hearing loop, automtic doors.

General description:
A variety of important exhibitions of contemporary art. Main gallery has a programme of 8-9 exhibitions per year. Major exhibitions offered for tour; craft and print displays in Foyer Space. Gallery Two offers a programme of local artists and groups shows.
Information services:
Guided tours on request.
Materials/activities by prior appointment.
Group education services on request by prior appointment.
Education programme includes talks, workshops and projects.
Special visitor services: Guided tours, materials and/or activities for children.
Education services: Group education facilities, resources for Key Stages 1 and 2, 3, 4 and Further or Higher Education.
Services for disabled people: For the hearing impaired.
Catalogues:
Catalogue for part of the collections is published.
Publications list:
is available in hard copy.
Printed publications:
Brochure of exhibitions and events (2 times a year: April to September and October to March)
Previous Catalogues available

Internet home pages:
http://www.wrexham.gov.uk

3225
WRITERS' MUSEUM, THE
Lady Stair's House, Lady Stair's Close, Lawnmarket, Edinburgh, EH1 2PA

Tel: 0131 529 4901
Fax: 0131 220 5057
Email: enquiries@writersmuseum.demon.co.uk
Formed: 1907

Organisation type and purpose: Local government body, museum.
Parent body:
The City of Edinburgh Council's Recreation Department
Museums and Galleries Service Division, tel: 0131 200 2000 (Main council) 0131 529 7844 (Recreation Department HQ)

Enquiries to: Curator
Direct tel: 0131 529 4064
Direct email: elaine @writersmuseum.demon.co.uk
Other contacts: Marketing & Sponsorship Officer
Access:
Access to staff: By letter, by telephone, by fax, by email, in person, visitors by prior appointment
Hours: Mon to Sat, 1000 to 1700; Sun during Edinburgh Festival 1400 to 1700
Access to building, collections or gallery: No prior appointment required
Hours: Mon to Sat, 1000 to 1700; Sun during Edinburgh Festival 1400 to 1700
Other restrictions: Access to the permanent collection for research purposes etc, strictly by appointment.

General description:
Permanent collections relating to the work of Scotland's great literary trio: Robert Burns, Sir Walter Scott and Robert Louis Stevenson. Other Scottish writers are featured in the temporary exhibition programme. The adjacent courtyard has been designated as 'Makars Court', Maker being the Scots word for a writer. It includes commemorative flagstones dedicated to a range of Scottish writers who have worked in the four literary languages of Scotland: Scots, Gaelic, Latin and English.
Catalogues:
Catalogue for all of the collections is published.
Publications list:
is available on-line.
Printed publications:
The City of Edinburgh Museums and Galleries Service publishes a wide range of material, a list is available by telephoning 0131 529 3983, a selected list is available at www.cac.org.uk

Internet home pages:
http://www.writersmuseum.demon.co.uk

3226
WROXETER ROMAN CITY
Wroxeter, Shrewsbury, Shropshire, SY5 6PH

Tel: 01743 761330

Organisation type and purpose: National organisation, advisory body, museum, historic building, house or site.
Parent body:
English Heritage (West Midlands Region)
Tel: 0121 625 6820

Enquiries to: Manager
Access:
Access to staff: By letter, by telephone, in person
Access to building, collections or gallery: No prior appointment required
Hours: 1 to 31 Oct: daily, 1000 to 1700,1 Nov to 28 Mar: daily, 1000 to 1300 and 1400 to 1600
Other restrictions: Closed 24 to 26 Dec and 1 Jan
Opening times are subject to change, for up-to-date information contact English Heritage by phone or visit the website

General description:
The largest excavated Roman British city to have escaped development, it was originally home to 6000 people. The most impressive ruins are the 2nd century municipal baths and the remains of a huge dividing wall. There is a museum for the finds.
Information services:
'Virtual Reality' Wroxeter visit.
Free children's activity sheet.
Special visitor services: Materials and/or activities for children..

Internet home pages:
http://www.english-heritage.org.uk/

3227
WYCOMBE MUSEUM
Castle Hill House, Priory Avenue, High Wycombe, Buckinghamshire, HP13 6PX

Tel: 01494 421895
Fax: 01494 421897
Email: enquiries @wycombemuseum.demon.co.uk
Full name: Wycombe District Museum Service
Formed: 1932
Formerly: The Chair Museum; High Wycombe Local History and Chair Museum, date of change, 1999

Organisation type and purpose: Local government body, museum, historic building, house or site, suitable for ages: all ages.
To provide a comprehensive local museum service enabling our collections, buildings and gardens to be enjoyed, to encourage interest, excite curiosity and promote understanding of the past, present and future of the people in the Wycombe district.

Parent body:
Wycombe District Council (WDC)
Queen Victoria Road, High Wycombe, Buckinghamshire, HP11 1BB, tel: 01494 461000, fax: 01494 461292, email: www.wycombe.gov.uk

Enquiries to: Museums Officer
Direct tel: 01434 421896
Direct email: jrattue @wycombemuseum.demon.co.uk
Other contacts: Museum Assistant for administration.
Access:
Access to staff: By letter, by telephone, by fax, by email, in person, Internet web pages
Access to building, collections or gallery: No prior appointment required
Hours: Mon to Sat, 1000 to 1700; Sun, 1400 to 1700
Other restrictions: Closed Bank Holidays
Access for disabled people: Parking provided, ramped entry, level entry, toilet facilities
Other restrictions: First floor of the museum is accessible only via steep staircase - at present.

General description:
History of the Wycombe district and of its furniture industry, especially Windsor Chairs, general local history and activities for children, also temporary exhibition on other historical subjects and visual arts.
Information services:
Library available for reference (for conditions see Access above)
Special visitor services: Materials and/or activities for children.
Education services: Group education facilities, resources for Key Stages 1 and 2, 3, 4 and Further or Higher Education.
Services for disabled people: Displays and/or information at wheelchair height.
Collections:
Displays and collections relating to the history of the Wycombe area and its people, including the famous collection of Windsor Chairs; collections include:
Wycombe Furniture Industry: catalogues, design books, apprentice indentures etc
Locally and nationally important collection of chairs and other furniture
Examples of Buckinghamshire lace
Trade practices and tools of furniture industry
Local photographs, art
Local history
Catalogues:
Catalogue for library is in-house only. Catalogue for all of the collections is only available in-house.
Printed publications:
Museum bookshop stocks specialist publications on chairs and chairmaking
Books and Articles in Periodicals on rural chairs, the Windsor chair and chairmaking

Internet home pages:
http://www.wycombe.gov.uk/museum
Information on the museum and its services.

3228
WYE COLLEGE MUSEUM OF AGRICULTURE
See - Agricultural Museum, Brook

3229
WYGSTON'S HOUSE MUSEUM OF COSTUME
Leicester

Closed, date of change, 2001

3230
WYMONDHAM HERITAGE MUSEUM, THE
10 The Bridewell, Norwich Road, Wymondham, Norfolk, NR18 0NS

Tel: 01953 600205
Formed: 1984

Formed from: Wymondham Heritage Society

Organisation type and purpose: Independently owned, voluntary organisation, registered charity (charity number 299548), museum, suitable for ages: all ages.
To preserve the heritage and history of Wymondham and the surrounding area for future generations.
Links with:
Wymondham Heritage Society

Enquiries to: Chairman
Direct tel: 01953 607494
Other contacts: Accessions Officer
Access:
Access to staff: By letter, by telephone, in person, visitors by prior appointment, charges made to all users
Access to building, collections or gallery: No prior appointment required
Hours: Mar to Nov: Mon to Sat, 1000 to 1600; Sun, 1400 to 1600
Other restrictions: Prior appointments required for group visits.
Access for disabled people: Parking provided, level entry, toilet facilities
Other restrictions: Access to all areas, except dungeon.

General description:
Local history, various displays chart the history of the building which has served as a prison, a police station and a court house; the story of Wymondham and its people from prehistoric times to the present day, includes farming bygones, brush making, Ketts Rebellion 1549, churches, shopping, Victorians, World War II etc.
Information services:
Some visually impaired services, very limited.
Special visitor services: Guided tours, tape recorded guides, materials and/or activities for children.
Services for disabled people: Displays and/or information at wheelchair height.
Catalogues:
Catalogue for library is in-house only. Catalogue for all of the collections is only available in-house.
Publications list:
is available in hard copy.
Printed publications:
The following publications are available for purchase, in writing, prices range from £1.50 to £3.50:
Wymondham Bridewell
On the Trail of Robert Kett
Wymondham's Old Inns
A Walk Around Old Wymondham
Geology on your Doorstep
Wymondham Market Cross
The Hidden Past
Methodism in Wymondham
Magistrates and their Court
Wymondham Footpath Map, Parish Map and cardboard map holders
Electronic and video products:
Wymondham (video)

Address for ordering publications:
Printed publications:
Manager, Museum Shop, Wymondham Heritage Museum

Internet home pages:
http://www.wymondham-norfolk.co.uk

3231
WYNDHAM MUSEUM OF SOUTH SOMERSET
See - Museum of South Somerset

3232
WYTHENSHAWE HALL
Wythenshawe Park, Northenden, Manchester, M23 0AB

Tel: 0161 998 2331
Fax: 0161 235 8899

Organisation type and purpose: Local government body, historic building, house or site, suitable for ages: all ages.
Parent body:
Manchester City Galleries
Tel: 0161 235 8888

Enquiries to: Manager
Access:
Access to staff: By letter, by telephone, by fax, in person

General description:
Tudor half-timbered house, home of the Tatton family for nearly four centuries. The original house was built around 1540, with alterations and additions through to the 19th century, thus creating a mixture of styles.
During the English Civil War 1642-49 the house was under siege for three months by Cromwell's troops.
The house and what remained of the estate was donated to the city in 1939 and has been open to the public ever since.
The park attractions include the Community Farm and the Horticulture Centre.

Internet home pages:
http://www.manchestergalleries.org
Information, opening times, special events, exhibitions and educational programmes and services.

3233
YARD GALLERY, THE
Courtyard Building, Wollaton Hall, Wollaton Hall Drive, Nottingham, NG8 2AE

Tel: 0115 915 3910

Organisation type and purpose: Local government body, art gallery.

Enquiries to: Exhibitions Officer
Direct tel: 0115 915 3677
Access:
Access to staff: By letter, by telephone, by fax
Access for disabled people: Parking provided, level entry, access to all public areas, toilet facilities

General description:
Art Gallery specialising in exhibitions relating to science.

3234
YARMOUTH CASTLE
Quay Street, Yarmouth, Isle of Wight, PO41 0PB

Tel: 01983 760678
Formed: 1547

Organisation type and purpose: Art gallery, historic building, house or site.
Parent body:
English Heritage (South East Region)
Tel: 01483 252000, fax: 01483 252001

Enquiries to: Curator
Access:
Access to building, collections or gallery: No prior appointment required
Hours: Apr to Sep: daily, 1000 to 1800
Oct: daily, 1000 to 1700
Closed Nov to Mar.
Access for disabled people: Parking provided
Other restrictions: Wheelchair access to ground floor only

General description:
Tudor castle, this last addition to Henry VIII's coastal defences was completed in 1547 to protect the mouth of the Solent. It houses exhibitions of paintings of the Isle of Wight and photographs of old Yarmouth.

Internet home pages:
http://www.english-heritage.org.uk

3235
YELDE HALL MUSEUM
See - Chippenham Museum & Heritage Centre

3236
YEOVIL COMMUNITY ARTS CENTRE
80 South Street, Yeovil, Somerset, BA20 1QH

Tel: 01935 432123
Formed: 1988

Organisation type and purpose: Registered charity (charity number 299372), art gallery, suitable for ages: 12+.
Arts centre.

Enquiries to: Manager
Access:
Access to staff: By letter, by telephone, in person, visitors by prior appointment
Access to building, collections or gallery: No prior appointment required
Hours: Mon to Fri, 1000 to 1630; Sat, 1000 to 1330
Other restrictions: Closed Sun and Bank Holidays.

General description:
A varied programme of exhibitions changing each month. Local, national and international artists exhibiting paintings, drawings, prints, sculpture, ceramics, textiles, photography and jewellery; mainly by contemporary artists.

3237
YESTERDAY'S WORLD
89-90 High Street, Battle, East Sussex, TN33 0AQ

Tel: 01424 774269; 24hr answer/information: 01424 775378
Fax: 01424 775174
Email: info@yesterdaysworld.co.uk
Acronym or abbreviation: BYW
Formed: 1983
Formerly: Buckleys Museum of Shops, date of change, 1986

Organisation type and purpose: Independently owned, museum, historic building, house or site, suitable for ages: all ages.
Visitor attraction.
Shop and social history; golf course (mini); play areas; refreshments. Voted No. 1 Visitor Attraction in South East England 2002 (under 100,000 visitors Excellence for England Awards).

Enquiries to: Office & Marketing Administrator
Access:
Access to staff: By letter, by telephone, by fax, by email, in person, visitors by prior appointment, Internet web pages
Hours: Office: Mon to Fri, 0930 to 1700
Access to building, collections or gallery: No prior appointment required
Hours: Mon to Sun, 0930 to 1800 (last admission 1645)
Other restrictions: Winter: closes 1 hour earlier.
Access for disabled people: toilet facilities
Other restrictions: Limited access to gardens and ground floor available.

General description:
Social history; shops; Victorians; Edwardians; nostalgia. Royal rarities ie personal effects, letters.
Information services:
Special visitor services: Materials and/or activities for children.
Education services: Group education facilities, resources for Key Stages 1 and 2, 3 and 4.
Services for disabled people: For the visually impaired; for the hearing impaired.
Collections:
One of the most extensive collections of artefacts from 1850s-1950s in the country
Printed publications:
Yesterday's World Guide Book
Worksheets
Teachers' Packs
Children's Quiz
Electronic and video products:
Yesterday's World (video)

Internet home pages:
http://www.yesterdaysworld.co.uk
Everything you would need to know about Yesterday's World; directions; prices; opening times; group booking information; collection tour.

3238
YNYSFACH IRON HERITAGE CENTRE
Merthyr Tydfil

Ceased to function

3239
YORK & LANCASTER REGIMENTAL MUSEUM
Central Library and Arts Centre, Walker Place, Rotherham, South Yorkshire, S65 1JH

Tel: 01709 823624
Fax: 01709 823631

Organisation type and purpose: Local government body, museum.
Collection in the care of:
Rotherham Borough Council

Enquiries to: Museums Manager
Direct email: guy.kilminster@rotherham.gov.uk
Access:
Access to staff: By letter, by telephone, by fax, by email, visitors by prior appointment, Internet web pages
Hours: Mon to Sat, 0900 to 1630
Other restrictions: Prior appointment required to access the archive.
Letters should be addressed to the Museums Manager, Clifton Park Museum, Clifton Park, Rotherham, South Yorkshire S65 2AA.

General description:
History of the York and Lancaster Regiment and its predecessors, the 65th and 84th Regiments of Foot, from 1758 up to its disbandment in 1968.
Collections:
The York and Lancaster Regimental Museum and Archive

Internet home pages:
http://www.rotherham.gov.uk

3240
YORK CASTLE MUSEUM
The Eye of York, York, YO1 1RY

Tel: 01904 650333
Fax: 01904 671078
Email: castlemuseum@york.gov.uk
Formed: 1938

Organisation type and purpose: Local government body, museum.
Parent bodies:
City of York Council
The Guildhall, York
York Museums
18 Back Swinegate, York

Enquiries to: Curator
Access:
Access to staff: By letter, by telephone, by fax, by email
Hours: Mon to Fri, 0900 to 1700
Access to building, collections or gallery: No prior appointment required
Hours: Daily, 0930 to 1700
Closed 25, 26 Dec and 1 Jan

General description:
English folk life, costume, textiles, arms and armour; Yorkshire crafts and general social and military history of the county (mainly 19th and 20th century).
Publications list:
is available in hard copy.
Printed publications:
York Castle Museum Guidebook
York Castle Museum Numeracy Trail
Catalogues

Internet home pages:
http://www.york.gov.uk
General information.
http://www.yorkcastlemuseum.org.uk

3241
YORK CITY ART GALLERY
Exhibition Square, York, YO1 2EW

Tel: 01904 551861
Fax: 01904 551866
Email: art.gallery@york.gov.uk

Organisation type and purpose: Local government body.
Links with:
York Castle Museum
Yorkshire Museum

Enquiries to: Curator
Access:
Access to building, collections or gallery: No prior appointment required
Hours: Daily, 1000 to 1700

General description:
European and British paintings from *c.* 1350 to the present, York artists, British water-colours, drawings and prints, particularly related to the topography of York; modern stoneware pottery, visual arts in general (mostly the Western, post-medieval tradition).
Collections:
Eric Milner-White Collection of 20th century British paintings and modern stoneware pottery
Evelyn Collection of York topography
John Burton Bequest of Victorian genre paintings
Lycett Green Collection of Old Masters
Printed publications:
Catalogue of Oil Paintings (3 vols and supplement)
Exhibition catalogues (6 titles)
Gallery News (2 or 3 times a year, free)
York City Art Gallery: An Illustrated Guide

Internet home pages:
http://www.york.art.museum.co.uk

3242
YORK DUNGEON
12 Clifford Street, York, YO1 1RD

Tel: 01904 632599
Fax: 01904 612602
Email: yorkdungeon@merlin-entertainments.com
Formed: 1986
Formed from: Vardon Attractions, date of change, 1997
Formerly: Cannons Ltd, date of change, 1998

Organisation type and purpose: Service industry, museum.
Horror museum.
Links with:
London Dungeon
National Seal Sanctuaries
Sea Life Centres
Part of:
Merlin Entertainments Group Ltd
Other address:
Merlin Entertainments Group Ltd
3 Market Close, Poole, Dorset, BH15 1NQ, tel: 01202 666900, fax: 01202 666655

Enquiries to: Manager
Other contacts: Marketing Assistant
Access:
Access to staff: By letter, by telephone, by fax, by email
Hours: Apr to Sep, 1000 to 1730; Oct to Mar, 1030 to 1630
Access for disabled people: toilet facilities
Other restrictions: Stairlift available

General description:
Deep in the heart of historic York, buried beneath its very paving stones, lies the North's most chillingly famous Museum of Horror, the York Dungeon brings more than 2000 years of gruesomely authentic history vividly back to life and death.

Internet home pages:
http://www.yorkshirenet.co.uk/yorkdungeon
http://www.thedungeons.com

3243
YORK MINSTER
Church House, 10-14 Ogleforth, York, YO1 7JN

Tel: 01904 557200
Fax: 01904 557201
Email: info@yorkminster.org
Full name: The Cathedral & Metropolitan Church of St Peter in York
Formed: 627

Organisation type and purpose: Independently owned, historic building, house or site, suitable for ages: 5+.
The worship of God, Cathedral of the Church of England.

Enquiries to: Chapter Steward
Direct tel: 01904 557210
Other contacts: (1) Collections Manager; (2) Visitors Services Manager for (1) historic enquiries, use of images for commercial purposes; (2) group bookings, tourism etc.
Access:
Access to staff: By letter, by telephone, by email, in person, Internet web pages
Other restrictions: Specialist enquiries may need to book in advance.
Access for disabled people: ramped entry, toilet facilities
Other restrictions: Hearing Loop, model for visually impaired, wheelchairs available.

General description:
Church art and architecture, stained glass, silver, historic church textiles, manuscripts, archives, prints of York and Yorkshire.
Information services:
Library available for reference (for conditions see Access above)
Special visitor services: Guided tours, tape recorded guides.
Education services: Group education facilities, resources for Key Stages 1 and 2, 3, 4 and Further or Higher Education.
Services for disabled people: For the hearing impaired; displays and/or information at wheelchair height.
Collections:
Books and manuscripts related to the history of The Minster and Yorkshire
Archives of: The Dean and Chapter (c1200 to present); Vicar's Choral (c12th century to 19th century)
102 Medieval manuscripts
The Hailstone Collection (books and archives) Yorkshire history 12th to 19th century
Parish silver held on deposit
Lee Collection of Secular York Silver
Evelyn & Green Photographic Collections (c1850-1970s)
Catalogues:
Catalogue for library is on-line. Catalogue for all of the collections is only available in-house.
Publications list:
is available on-line.
Printed publications:
Full list of publications available on website and online shop
York Minster Guide Book (Pitkin Guide)
York Minster (Willey A)
The Stained and Painted Glass of York Minster
The Organs of York Minster
Electronic and video products:
CD-ROMs of Music only

Address for ordering publications:
Printed publications:
York Minster Enterprises
at the same address, tel: 01904 557215, fax: 01904 557220, email: shop@yorkminster.org

Internet home pages:
http://www.yorkminster.org
http://www.york.ac.uk/library
Library access is via University of York website.

3244
YORK RACING MUSEUM
The Knavesmire, York, YO2 1EX

Tel: 01904 620911
Formed: 1965

Organisation type and purpose: Independently owned, museum, suitable for ages: 16+, research organisation.

Enquiries to: Librarian
Other contacts: Curator
Access:
Access to staff: By letter
Access to building, collections or gallery: Prior appointment required
Hours: By appointment or on Race days only

General description:
Material covering racecourses from 1731-present, of racehorses, local racecourses, silks, trophies from English racing.
Catalogues:
Catalogue for library is in-house only. Catalogue for all of the collections is only available in-house.
Publications list:
is available in hard copy.

3245
YORKSHIRE AIR MUSEUM
Halifax Way, Elvington, York, YO41 4AU

Tel: 01904 608595
Fax: 01904 608246
Email: museum@yorkshireairmuseum.co.uk
Acronym or abbreviation: YAM
Formed: 1985

Organisation type and purpose: Registered charity (charity number 516766), museum, historic building, house or site.

Enquiries to: Public Relations Manager
Access:
Access to staff: By letter, by telephone, by fax, by email, in person, charges made to all users
Access to building, collections or gallery: Prior appointment required
Hours: Daily, 1030 to 1600; week-ends and Bank Holidays 1030 to 1700
Winter times vary so telephone first
Access for disabled people: access to all public areas, toilet facilities
Other restrictions: Access, excludes top of Control Tower.

General description:
Aviation (general) - history; Royal Air Force in WW2; Wartime airfields; squadrons and associations (RAF).
Collections:
The Wallis Collection (Barnes Wallis, 1887-1979)
Over 40 historic aircraft
Printed publications:
Magazine, 3 times a year, members

Internet home pages:
http://www.yorkshireairmuseum.co.uk

3246
YORKSHIRE ART SPACE SOCIETY
Persistence Works, 21 Brown Street, Sheffield, South Yorkshire, S1 2BS

Tel: 0114 276 1769
Fax: 0114 276 1769
Email: office@artspace.demon.co.uk
Acronym or abbreviation: YASS
Formed: 1977

Organisation type and purpose: Registered charity (charity number 1049370), suitable for ages: 16+.
Provides affordable workspace for artists and craftspeople. In addition to providing a place for visual artists to work, the Society offers them business support and training, and a wide range of community outreach programmes.

Enquiries to: Director
Access:
Access to staff: By letter, by telephone, by fax, by email, visitors by prior appointment
Access to building, collections or gallery: Prior appointment required
Hours: Mon to Sat, 1100 to 1600
Access for disabled people: Parking provided, level entry, access to all public areas, toilet facilities

General description:
The Society offers membership to the general public, and two open days a year to visit the building. Business support, training, community projects, cheap rent, comfortable studio space, starter studio programme (9 people) for artists/craftspeople in the building.
Information services:
Members work with a wide range of local community groups, people with special needs, young adults, over 60s, schools, colleges and libraries
Special visitor services: Guided tours..
Collections:
Photographs for in-house only
Printed publications:
Available free, direct

Internet home pages:
http://www.artspace.org.uk/

3247
YORKSHIRE COAST
Ravenscar Coastal Centre, Peakside, Ravenscar, Scarborough, North Yorkshire, YO13 0NE

Tel: 01723 870423 (Office) 01947 885900 (Old Costguard Station) 01723 870138 (Coastal Centre)
Fax: 01723 870423
Email: yorkshirecoast@nationaltrust.org.uk

Organisation type and purpose: National organisation, registered charity (charity number 205846), historic building, house or site, suitable for ages: all ages.
Parent body:
The National Trust (Yorkshire and North East Region)
Yorkshire Regional Office, tel: 01904 702021

Enquiries to: Warden
Access:
Access to staff: By letter, by telephone, by fax, by email
Access to building, collections or gallery: No prior appointment required
Hours: Coastguard Station: Mar to May: Sat, Sun, 1000 to 1700
Jun to Sep: daily, 1000 to 1700
Oct: Sat, Sun, 1000 to 1700
Nov to Feb: 1100 to 1600
Ravenscar: Apr to May: 1030 to 1700
End of May to Sep: daily, 1030 to 1700
Other restrictions: Old Coastguard Station and Ravenscar Coastal
Centre also open daily in local school holidays
Access for disabled people: toilet facilities
Other restrictions: Old Coastguard Station: steps to entrance. Ground floor fully accessible. Access to other
floors via lift. Ravenscar Coastal Centre: steps to shop entrance. Adapted WC

General description:
A group of coastal properties extending for 40ml from Saltburn in the north to Filey in the south, and centred around Robin Hood's Bay. The Cleveland Way National Trail follows the clifftop and gives splendid views. A wide range of habitats, including meadow, woodland, coastal heath and cliff grassland, provide sanctuary to many forms of wildlife, from orchids to nesting birds. The area is rich in industrial archaeology and the remains of the alum industry and jet and ironstone mining can be seen. The Old Coastguard Station in Robin Hood's Bay, an exciting exhibition and education centre, is run in partnership with the North York Moor National Park Authority. It shows how the elements have shaped this part of the coastline.
Information services:
Guided walks
Suitable for school groups, hands-on activities
Special visitor services: Materials and/or activities for children.
Education services: Group education facilities..

Internet home pages:
http://www.nationaltrust.org.uk

3248
YORKSHIRE DALES RAILWAY

Acronym or abbreviation: YDRMT
See - Embsay & Bolton Abbey Steam Railway

3249
YORKSHIRE MINING MUSEUM
See - National Coal Mining Museum for England

3250
YORKSHIRE MUSEUM OF FARMING
Murton Lane, Murton, York, YO19 5UF

Tel: 01904 489966
Fax: 01904 489159
Email: info@murtonpark.co.uk
Formed: 1982

Organisation type and purpose: Independently owned, registered charity (charity number 510900), museum, suitable for ages: all ages.

Enquiries to: Curatorial Assistant
Access:
Access to staff: By letter, by telephone, by fax, visitors by prior appointment
Access to building, collections or gallery: No prior appointment required
Hours: March to end Oct: Mon to Sun, 1000 to 1700;
Nov to Feb: Mon to Sun, 1000 to 1600
Other restrictions: Closed Christmas Eve to New Year.
Prior appointment required for Research Library.
Dogs must be on leads - farm animals and poultry on site.
Access for disabled people: Parking provided, ramped entry, level entry, toilet facilities

General description:
Farm equipment from past 200 years. Two museum buildings and outside exhibits. Bee pavilion, grass maze, steam railway (most Sundays from Easter to September and Bank Holidays).
Replica Dark Age village, Celtic settlement and Roman fort used for education purposes - restricted access weekdays, access at weekends. Rare breeds farm animals and poultry.
Information services:
Library available for reference (for conditions see Access above)
Guided tours.
Special visitor services: Guided tours, materials and/or activities for children.
Education services: Resources for Key Stages 1 and 2, 3, 4 and Further or Higher Education.
Services for disabled people: For the visually impaired.
Collections:
Tools
Farm Machinery
Large reference library of books, manuals, photographs, archives - by appointment only
Catalogues:
Catalogue for library is in-house only. Catalogue for all of the collections is only available in-house.
Publications list:
is available in hard copy.
Printed publications:
Educational projects

3251
YORKSHIRE MUSEUM

Museum Gardens, York, YO1 7FR

Tel: 01904 551800
Fax: 01904 551802
Email: yorkshire.museum@york.gov.uk
Formed: c. 1828

Organisation type and purpose: Local government body, museum, suitable for ages: 8+.

Enquiries to: Secretary
Access:
Access to staff: By letter, by telephone, by email
Access to building, collections or gallery: Prior appointment required
Hours: Daily, 1000 to 1700
Access for disabled people: ramped entry, access to all public areas, toilet facilities

General description:
Collections including: archaeology, geology, decorative arts and natural sciences.
Information services:
Guided tours and materials/activities for children - occasionally.
Special visitor services: Guided tours, materials and/or activities for children.
Education services: Group education facilities, resources for Key Stages 1 and 2..
Printed publications:
Alcuin & Charlemagne - The Golden Age of York (£3.95)

Internet home pages:
http://www.york.gov.uk/

3252
YORKSHIRE MUSEUMS COUNCIL

Farnley Hall, Hall Lane, Leeds, West Yorkshire, LS12 5HA

Tel: 0113 263 8909
Fax: 0113 279 1479
Email: info@yhmc.org.uk
Formerly: Yorkshire & Humberside Museums Council

Enquiries to: Information Officer

General description:
The provision of a co-operative service for associated museums, including local authority, universitiy and independent charitable trust museums.

Internet home pages:
http://www.yorkshiremuseums.org.uk

3253
YORKSHIRE SCULPTURE PARK

Bretton Hall, West Bretton, Wakefield, West Yorkshire, WF4 4LG

Tel: 01924 830302
Fax: 01924 830044
Acronym or abbreviation: YSP
Formed: 1977

Organisation type and purpose: Registered charity (charity number 1067908).
Sculpture park.

Enquiries to: Curator
Other contacts: Curator: Archive for YSP archival material.
Access:
Access to staff: By letter, by fax, visitors by prior appointment
Access to building, collections or gallery: No prior appointment required
Hours: Grounds: Winter, daily, 1100 to 1600; Summer, daily, 1000 to 1800
Galleries and Café: Winter, daily, 1100 to 1600; Summer, daily, 1100 to 1700
Other restrictions: Admission free; car parking charge £1.50 per day.
Access for disabled people: Parking provided, toilet facilities
Other restrictions: Free electric scooters for those with mobility difficulties: ask at the information centre or call 01924 830302 to book; access Sculpture Trail - accessible to all.

General description:
Yorkshire Sculpture Park is one of Europe's leading open-air galleries, established to support and promote the practice and understanding of sculpture through exhibitions, projects and residencies. Exhibitions of modern and contemporary art are organised in over 500 acres of 18th century designed landscape, together with three indoor galleries, providing a changing programme of exhibitions, displays and projects.
Information services:
Education services: Group education facilities, resources for Key Stages 1 and 2, 3, 4 and Further or Higher Education.
Services for disabled people: For the visually impaired; displays and/or information at wheelchair height.
Collections:
Sculpture and works on paper, relating to sculptural practice
YSP Archive contains images and written information on YSP Activities
Publications list:
is available in hard copy.

Internet home pages:
http://www.ysp.co.uk

3254
ZETLAND LIFEBOAT MUSEUM

5 King Street, Redcar, Cleveland, TS10 3DT

Tel: 01642 486052
Formed: 1981

Organisation type and purpose: Registered charity, museum, suitable for ages: children under 16 must be accompanied by an adult. Redcar & Cleveland Council own the building, the museum is independently managed.
To preserve and display to the public the world's oldest lifeboat - 'The Zetland'.
Branch of the:
Royal National Lifeboat Institution (RNLI) Poole, Dorset

Enquiries to: Secretary (on rota)
Direct tel: 01642 485370
Access:
Access to staff: By letter, by telephone, in person
Access to building, collections or gallery: No prior appointment required
Hours: 1 May to 30 Sep: Mon to Fri, 1100 to 1600; Sat, Sun, 1200 to 1600
Other restrictions: 1 Oct to 30 Apr: Prior appointment required
Access for disabled people: level entry
Other restrictions: Level entry to Boathouse only.

General description:
The Museum houses the world's oldest lifeboat, 'The Zetland', built in 1802 - it has saved over 500 lives.
Other points of interest are the replica fisherman's cottage. 'Laurie Picknett Gallery' and displays of local maritime history and Redcar memorabilia.
Information services:
Special visitor services: Guided tours..
Collections:
The Zetland Lifeboat (owners - Redcar & Cleveland Council)
Collection of Redcar crested china (owned by Mrs V Robinson)
Breachers buoy and exhibit (donated by Mr H Hurst)
Replica fishermans cottage
Large display of maritime photographs
Large collection of model ships/boats
Zetland Museum Friends Book (donated by Mrs V Robinson)
Catalogues:
Catalogue for all of the collections is only available in-house.
Printed publications:
Printed leaflet (available direct at museum shop, for purchase)

3255
ZILLAH BELL GALLERY

15 Kirkgate, Thirsk, North Yorkshire, YO7 1PQ

Tel: 01845 522479
Full name: Zillah Bell Contemporary Art
Formed: 1987

Organisation type and purpose: Independently owned, art gallery, suitable for ages: 16+.
To exhibit and sell contemporary art.

Enquiries to: Manager
Access:
Access to staff: By letter, by telephone, in person
Hours: Mon to Sat, 1000 to 1700
Access to building, collections or gallery: No prior appointment required
Hours: Mon to Sat, 1000 to 1700
Access for disabled people: level entry
Other restrictions: Partial access to whole gallery.

General description:
An everchanging exhibition of contemporary art - paintings, etchings, sculpture by invited artists from throughout the UK. Most exhibits are for sale.

Abbreviations and Acronyms

The abbreviations and acronyms listed here provide the full names of organisations. Those names preceded by two stars have full entries in the body of the Directory, those with one star are cross-references, and those without a star are to be found within the full entries.

ABBREVIATIONS AND ACRONYMS

A and SH Museum	** Argyll and Sutherland Highlanders Regimental Museum
AAG+M	Aberdeen Art Gallery & Museums
ACC	Army Catering Corps
ACC	** Arts Council Collection
ACC Museum	Army Catering Corps Museum
ACE	Arts Council of England
ACGB	Arts Council of Great Britain
ACW	** Arts Council of Wales
ADBPS	** Aycliffe and District Bus Preservation Society
ADEPT	** Scotland's Secret Bunker
AGA	** Art Galleries Association
AIA	** Association for Industrial Archaeology
AIM	** Association of Independent Museums
AIR	Association of Independent Railways
AIRPS	* Association of Independent Railways and Preservation Societies
Alderney Museum	** Alderney Society Museum
ALMS	** Andrew Logan Museum of Sculpture
ALPHA	Association of London Pumping Heritage Attractions
AMIB	** American Museum in Britain
AMS	** Ancient Monuments Society
AMS Museum	** Army Medical Services Museum
APTC Museum	** Army Physical Training Corps Museum
ARMMS	University of Dundee Archive, Records Management & Museum Services
ARPS	Association of Railway Preservation Societies Limited
ASVA	Association of Scottish Visitor Attractions
B&WLR	** Bredgar and Wormshill Light Railway
BACUP 'NAT'	** Bacup Natural History Society
BAFM	** British Association of Friends of Museums
BAG	** Billingham Art Gallery
BaMMOT	** Birmingham and Midland Museum of Transport
BAMT	** Brenzett Aeronautical Museum Trust
BAPC	British Aircraft Preservation Council
BAW	** Winston Churchill's Britain at War Museum
BBM&L	** British Balloon Museum and Library
BBMF	** Battle of Britain Memorial Flight Visitor Centre
BCAA	Bristol Centre for the Advancement of Architecture
BCG	** Biology Curators Group
BCHM	** Blaise Castle House Museum
BCKL and WN	Borough Council of Kings Lynn and West Norfolk
BCM	Buckinghamshire County Museum
BCRA	British Cave Research Association
BCVM	** British Commercial Vehicle Museum
BDA	British Dental Association
BDAM	** British Dental Association Museum
BDC	Basildon District Council
BDT	** Bo'ness Development Trust
Beamish	** Beamish: The North of England Open Air Museum
Bexhill Costume Museum	** Bexhill Museum of Costume & Social History
BHESS	** Barrow Hill Engine Shed Society Limited
BHI	** British Horological Institute
BHRU	** Bradford Heritage Recording Unit
BHT	** Bowhill House
BHY	** Brewhouse Yard Museum
BITOA	British Incoming Tour Operators Association
BM	** British Museum
BM&AG	** Birmingham Museums and Art Gallery
BMF	** British Museum Friends
BMIHT	** British Motor Industry Heritage Trust
BMS	British Museum Society
BMT	** Biggar Museum Trust
BP	** Big Pit National Mining Museum of Wales
BPM	** Bath Postal Museum
BPT	** Bath Preservation Trust
BPT	** Bunker Preservation Trust
Bramah Museum	** Bramah Tea & Coffee Museum
BRCS	** British Red Cross Museum and Archives
BRM	British Rotorcraft Museum
BRPS	** Bluebell Railway Preservation Society
BTA/ETB	British Tourist Authority/English Tourist Board
BVT	Bournville Village Trust (The housing association created by George Cadbury in 1900)
BW Museum	** Black Watch Regimental Museum
BYW	** Yesterday's World
C&R	County and Regimental Museum
CADVAT	Colchester and District Visual Arts Trust
CADW	Welsh Historic Monuments
Calanais Visitor Centre	** Calanais Standing Stones and Visitor Centre
CARAD	** CARAD Chronicles Community Museum
Carriage Museum	** Tyrwhitt-Drake Museum of Carriages
CAS	** Contemporary Art Society
CBA Scotland	The Council for British Archaeology Scotland
CBHGT	** Castle Bromwich Hall Gardens Trust
CCA	** Centre for Contemporary Arts
CCLR	** Cleethorpes Coast Light Railway
CCLRSA	Cleethorpes Coast Light Railway Supporters Association
CDHS	Chatham Dockyard Historical Society
CDT	Carnegie Dunfermline Trust
CEBB	** Barra Heritage & Cultural Centre
CEDaR	** Centre for Environmental Data and Recording
CHNTO	** Cultural Heritage National Training Organisation
CHR	Cultural Heritage Resources
CHT	** Cornwall Heritage Trust
CKC	** Classic Kawasaki Club
Clearwell Caves	** Clearwell Caves Ancient Iron Mines
CMHL	** Clan Munro Heritage Limited
CMT	** Cody Museum Trust (1993)
CMW	** Council of Museums in Wales
CNHSS	** Croydon Natural History and Scientific Society Museum
COL	Corporation of London
CPT	* Confederation of British Road Passenger Transport
CRA	** Caledonian Railway Association
CRB	Cwmni Rheilffordd Beddgelert Cyf
CRM Society	** Charles Rennie Mackintosh Society
CSA	** Council for Scottish Archaeology
CWCA	** Chillingham Wild Cattle Association
DCAL	Department of Culture, Arts and Leisure, Northern Ireland
DCC	Derry City Council
DCLI Museum	** Duke of Cornwall's Light Infantry Regimental Museum
DCMS	Department for Culture, Media and Sport
DDCT	Dalmellington & District Conservation Trust
DFRS	** Dean Forest Railway Society
DGC	Dumfries & Galloway Council Community Resources
DHT	** Dacorum Heritage Trust Limited
DHT	Dunfermline Heritage Trust
DLOY	Duke of Lancasters Own Yeomanry Museum
DNH&AS	Dorset Natural History and Archaeological Society
DQE	* Discovery Quay Enterprises Limited
DRM	** Downpatrick Railway Museum
EAAF	** Tate in East Anglia Foundation

EATM ** East Anglia Transport Museum
ECDC East Cambridgeshire District Council
EH ** English Heritage
ELMS ** East Lothian Council Museums Service Headquarters
EM&HT ** Emsworth Museum
EmmS ** East Midlands Museums Service
ETC/BTA ** English Tourist Council/British Tourist Authority
FAAM ** Fleet Air Arm Museum
FAST Farnborough Air Sciences Trust
FBSR ** Fairbourne and Barmouth Railway
FCMW ** Fife Council Museums West
FCT ** Faringdon Collection Trust
FEDECRAIL European Federation of Museum and Tourist Railways
FGCHM ** First Garden City Heritage Museum
FHMS ** Felixstowe Museum
FIPT ** Foxton Inclined Plane Trust
FNM ** Florence Nightingale Museum
FOL Friends of Lydd
FOSM Friends of Spelthorne Museum
GAC ** Government Art Collection
GAT ** Gwynedd Archaeological Trust Limited
GB3WM ** Wireless Museum
GCR ** Great Central Railway (Nottingham) Ltd
GLAHM ** Glasgow University, Hunterian Museum
GMTS ** Museum of Transport
GMZ, UCL ** Grant Museum of Zoology and Comparative Anatomy
GN Sikh Museum ** Garu Nanak Sikh Museum
GofHT ** Guild of Handicraft Trust
GoMA ** Gallery of Modern Art
GPM ** Gunnersbury Park Museum
Green's Mill ** Green's Mill & Science Museum
GSC ** Glasgow Science Centre
GTM ** Grampian Transport Museum
GWRL Gloucestershire Warwickshire Railway Limited by guarantee
GWS ** Great Western Society Limited
GWSRPLC ** Gloucestershire Warwickshire Steam Railway
HAC Harrow Arts Council
HAG ** Glasgow University, Hunterian Art Gallery
HAGM ** Herbert Art Gallery and Museum
HAT ** Hertfordshire Archaeological Trust
HCCMS ** Hampshire County Council Museums Service
HCT Hackney Community Transport
HEM ** Haslemere Educational Museum
HFBG ** Historic Farm Buildings Group
HG ** Hatton Gallery
HHA Heysham Heritage Association (voluntary organisation)
HHA Historic Houses Association
HMC Historical Manuscripts Commission
HMPS T&DG HM Prison Service
HMPSM ** HM Prison Service Museum
HMSW ** Heatherbank Museum
HRA ** Heritage Railway Association
HRP ** Hampton Court Palace
HRPT Historic Royal Palace Trust
HS Historic Scotland
HTNW Heritage Trust for the North West (also mount exhibitions)
HVM ** Horsforth Village Museum
IATM International Association of Transport and Communication Museums
ICA ** Institute of Contemporary Arts
ICGA Independent Craft Galleries Association
IDC Imperial Defence College
IHM International Helicopter Museum
IHPS Iron Horse Preservation Society
ISGC International Shakespear's Globe Centre
IWC Isle of Wight Council
IWM ** Imperial War Museum
IWMFVA ** Imperial War Museum, Film and Video Archive

JAMES Joint Area Museums Education Service
JAMT ** Jane Austen's House
JDHT ** Jaguar Daimler Heritage Trust
JII John Innes Institute
JMBT ** John Muir Birthplace
JMC Trust ** Julia Margaret Cameron Trust
KARU Kent Archaeological Rescue Unit
KBC Kettering Borough Council
KBMT ** Keighley Bus Museum Trust Limited
KCC Kent County Council
Killhope ** Killhope, The North of England Lead Mining Museum
KOSB ** King's Own Scottish Borderers Regimental Museum
KRRC Kings Royal Rifle Corps
KSY Museum ** Kent and Sharpshooters Yeomanry Museum
KWVR ** Keighley and Worth Valley Railway Preservation Society
LACF Leeds Art Collections Fund
LALHS Lowestoft Archaeological and Local History Society
LBB London Borough of Bromley
LBNGRS Ltd ** Leighton Buzzard Railway Limited
LBPT ** Cobham Bus Museum
LBPT London Bus Preservation Trust
LBRC ** London Brass Rubbing Centre
LBRUT London Borough of Richmond Council
LCC Lincolnshire County Council
LCMS Lancashire County Museum Service
LDLHS Leatherhead & District Local History Society
LDNPA Lake District National Park Authority
LFB Museum ** London Fire Brigade Museum
LHG ** Lytham Heritage Group
LI Museum ** Light Infantry Museum
LIRA * Lambeg Industrial Research Association
LMA London Museums Agency
LMARS Leicester Museums, Arts & Records Service
LMARS ** Leicestershire Museums, Arts and Records Service
LMRC ** Leeds Museum Resource Centre
LNALS ** Louth Museum
LPLS ** Leeds Philosophical & Literary Society
LTB ** London Tourist Board Limited
LUCS ** Linlithgow Union Canal Society
LYMPH ** Lyme Regis Philpot Museum
M/M Mechanical Memories
MA ** Museums Association
MAGNI ** Museums and Galleries of Northern Ireland
Maidstone Museum ** Maidstone Museum & Bentlif Art Gallery
Making It! ** Making It Discovery Centre
MAMS ** Montrose Air Station Museum
MBC Maidstone Borough Council
MBEAM ** Markfield Beam Engine & Museum
MBR ** Department of the Environment for Northern Ireland
MBRT ** Museum of British Road Transport
Mda Museum Documentation Association
MDMA ** Maldon District Museum
MEG ** Museum Ethnographers Group
Mercers' Company ** Worshipful Company of Mercers
MGC Museums & Galleries Commission
MHC Margrove Heritage Centre
MJM ** Manchester Jewish Museum
Mk G ** Milton Keynes Gallery
MKHA Milton Keynes Heritage Association
MKTGC Milton Keynes Theatre & Gallery Company
MLTI Museum of the Lancashire Textile Industry
MM ** Mechanical Memories Amusement Museum
MOD Ministry of Defence, London
MoDA ** Museum of Domestic Design & Architecture
MOI ** Museum of Installation

MOL ** Museum of London
MOMA Museum of Modern Art, Oxford
MOMA Wales Museum of Modern Art, Wales
MOMI ** Museum of the Moving Image
MOSS ** Ironbridge Open Air Museum of Steel Sculpture
MOSTA ** Museum of St Albans
MPA Mounted Police Association
MRT ** Middleton Railway Trust
MSIM ** Museum of Science and Industry
MTA * Municipal Tramways Association
MTI Museum Training Institute
Mull Rail ** Mull and West Highland Narrow Gauge Railway
MWL ** Museum of Welsh Life
MWWI ** Museum of the Welsh Woollen Industry
NA ** National Archives
NAFW / CADW National Assembly for Wales
NAMHO National Association of Mining History Organisations
NATCECT National Centre for English Cultural Tradition
NAU Norfolk Archaeological Unit
NCA National Caving Association
NCMME ** National Coal Mining Museum for England
NEMLAC North East Museums, Libraries & Archive Council
NESAHC North East of Scotland Agricultural Heritage Centre
NESMS North East of Scotland Museums Service
NG ** National Gallery
NGS National Galleries of Scotland
NHC ** Towneley Hall Art Gallery and Museums
NHDC North Hertfordshire District Council
NHM ** Natural History Museum
NIMC ** Northern Ireland Museums Council
NLA ** Norfolk Landscape Archaeology
NMAS Norfolk Museums and Archaeology Service
NMG ** National Museum & Gallery of Wales
NMGM National Museums & Galleries on Merseyside
NMGNI National Museums and Galleries of Northern Ireland
NMGW National Museums & Galleries of Wales
NMLH National Museum of Labour History
NMM ** National Maritime Museum
NMMC ** National Maritime Museum Cornwall
NMPFT ** National Museum of Photography, Film & Television
NMPSM ** National Museum of Penny Slot Machines
NMS ** National Museums of Scotland
NMW/NMGW ** National Museum & Gallery Cardiff
NPG ** National Portrait Gallery
NPHS ** Newport Pagnell Historical Society Collection
NPHT North Pennines Heritage Trust
NRA * National Register of Archives
NRA National Rivers Authority
NRCD ** National Resource Centre for Dance
NRLM Norfolk Rural Life Museum
NRM ** National Railway Museum
NSAD Norwich School of Art and Design
NSMEE Nottingham Society of Model Engineers
NT ** National Trust
NTS ** National Trust for Scotland
NTSRA North Tyneside Steam Railway Association
NTU Nottingham Trent University
NVR ** Nene Valley Railway
NWM ** National Waterways Museum
NWMS ** National War Museum of Scotland
NWMS ** North West Museums Service
NWOSM ** North Woolwich Old Station Museum
NYMR ** North Yorkshire Moors Railway
OHG ** Orleans House Gallery
OLNCN ** Cowper and Newton Museum
OMBC Oldham Metropolitan Borough, Education & Cultural Services
ONHSM ** Stromness Museum
OUMNH ** Oxford University
Ox&Bucks Oxford and Buckinghamshire Light Infantry
P&BR ** Pontypool and Blaenavon Railway Company
PAC ** Plymouth Arts Centre
Painter-Stainers' Company ** Worshipful Company of Painter-Stainers
PCH Pendeen Community Heritage
PCW EBC Presbyterian Church of Wales
PDF ** Percival David Foundation of Chinese Art
PDMHS ** Peak District Mining Museum and Temple Mine
PEMS Passmore Edwards Museums
PHS Police History Society
PLYMG ** Plymouth City Museums and Art Gallery
PM & AG ** Potteries Museum & Art Gallery
PRO ** National Archives
PRO * Public Record Office
PSGB Pharmaceutical Society of Great Britain
PSH ** Provost Skene's House
QBM ** Quarry Bank Mill and Styal Estate
QBMT Quarry Bank Mill Trust Limited
QLR Museum ** Queen's Lancashire Regimental Museum
R/W Remember When . . .
RADC Museum * Royal Army Dental Corps Museum
RAF Museum ** Royal Air Force Museum
RAMC * Royal Army Medical Corps Historical Museum
RAOC Museum Royal Army Ordnance Corps Museum
RASC Royal Army Service Corps
RB Rifle Brigade
RBK&C Royal Borough of Kensington & Chelsea
RBKC ** Kensington and Chelsea (Royal Borough) Libraries and Arts Services
RBSA ** Royal Birmingham Society of Artists
RBSA Royal Birmingham Society of Arts
RBST Rare Breeds Survival Trust
RCA ** Royal Cambrian Academy of Art
RCDS ** Royal College of Defence Studies
RCHM Royal Commission on Historical Manuscripts
RCJ ** Royal Courts of Justice
RCM ** Rutland County Museum
RCMS / MHC ** Redcar and Cleveland Borough Council
RCMS/KM ** Kirkleatham Museum
RCS ** Museums of the Royal College of Surgeons
RCT Museum Royal Corps of Transport Museum
RE Museum ** Royal Engineers Museum
Resource ** Council for Museums, Libraries and Archives
RFDFMA Royal Forest of Dean Free Miner's Association
RGJ ** Royal Green Jackets Museum
RH&DR ** Romney, Hythe and Dymchurch Railway
RHA ** Rustington Heritage Association Exhibition Centre
RHF ** Royal Highland Fusiliers Regimental Headquarters and Museum
RI ** Royal Institution of Great Britain
RIC Royal Institution of Cornwall
RISW ** Royal Institution of South Wales
RITC Railway Industry Training Council
RLC Museum ** Royal Logistic Corps Museum
RLIAS ** River Lea Industrial Archaeological Society
RLM ** Roman Legionary Museum
RMBC Rotherham Metropolitan Borough Council
RMP Museum Red Cap Museum
RNLI Royal National Lifeboat Institution
RNSMM ** Royal Navy Submarine Museum
ROC Royal Observer Corps Museum
ROG ** Royal Observatory Greenwich
RPC Museum Royal Pioneer Corps Museum

RPSGB	** Museum of the Royal Pharmaceutical Society of Great Britain
RPSI	** Railway Preservation Society of Ireland
RRF Museum (London)	** Royal Regiment of Fusiliers Association London Area
RSA	** Royal Scottish Academy
RUR Museum	** Royal Ulster Rifles Regimental Museum
RVBC	Ribble Valley Borough Council
RWS	** Royal Watercolour Society
SAFG	Spelthorne Archaeological Field Group
SAHS	South Staffordshire Archaeological and Historical Society
Salisbury Museum	** Salisbury and South Wiltshire Museum
SAM	** Shoreham Aircraft Museum
SAMMS	** St Albans Organ Museum
SAP	The Spitz - Spitalfields Arts Project
SBC	Scottish Borders Council
SBC	Stafford Borough Council
SBPT	Suffolk Building Preservation Trust Limited
SBRC	** Biological Records Centre & Ludlow Museum
SCC	** Shropshire County Museum Service
Scots DG Museum	** Royal Scots Dragoon Guards Museum
SDHS	** Shaftesbury and District Historical Society
SDRT	** Somerset & Dorset Railway Trust Museum
Seaford Museum	** Seaford Museum and Heritage Society
SEAL	South East Area Libraries Information Service
Segedunum	** Segedunum Roman Fort, Baths and Museum
SEMA	South East Museums Agency
SEMLAC	** South East Museum, Library & Archive Council
SEMS	South East Museums Service
SFU	Scottish Football Union
SHAHT	** Surrey Heath Archaeological & Heritage Trust
SHDC	South Holland District Council
Sheppys Cider Farm Centre	** Sheppy's Cider and Rural Life Museum
SHRCM	Shropshire County Museum Service
SHS	Saddleworth Historical Society
SIMT	Sheffield Industrial Museums Trust
SJSM	** Sir John Soane's Museum
SKLR	** Sittingbourne and Kemsley Light Railway
SKM	South Kensington Museum
SMBC	Sandwell MBC
SMC	** Scottish Museums Council
SMG	Sussex Museums Group
SNGMA	** Scottish National Gallery of Modern Art
SNPG	** Scottish National Portrait Gallery
SNWM	** Scottish National War Memorial
SPACE	SPACE Foundation (Society for the Promotion of Artistic and Creative Enterprise)
SPMF	Southend Pier Museum Foundation
SPRI	** Scott Polar Research Institute Museum
SRC	Strathspey Railway Company Limited
SRPS	** Scottish Railway Preservation Society
SRU	** Scottish Rugby Union Library & Museum
St Agatha's Trust	** St Agatha's Church Museum
St Eds BC	St Edmundsbury Borough Council
Staffords	** Staffordshire Regiment Museum
SUSM	Scottish United Services Museum
SVA	Sid Vale Association
SVBM	** Scottish Vintage Bus Museum
SVHC	** Sid Vale Heritage Centre
SVLB	** Sunderland Volunteer Life Brigade

SVR	** Severn Valley Railway
SWB Museum	** South Wales Borderers & Monmouthshire Regimental Museum
SWMC	Dawlish Local History Group
SYAM	** South Yorkshire Aviation Museum
TAMCM	** Tamworth Castle
The Great Dunmow Maltings	** Great Dunmow Maltings Preservation Trust Limited
The Order of St John	** Museum and Library of Order of St John
The Priory Church	** Priory of St Mary and St Cuthbert
The Spitz	Spitalfields Arts Project
The Towner	** Towner Art Gallery & Local Museum
Thinktank	** Thinktank - Birmingham Museum of Science and Discovery
Thirsk Museum	** Thirsk & District Museum Society
THNLC	** Trinity House National Lighthouse Centre
THS or Hovercraft Museum	** Hovercraft Museum Trust & Society
TMT Limited	** The Multimedia Team Limited
TNHS	** Torquay Museum
Torre Abbey	** Torre Abbey Historic House & Gallery
TQ	** Techniquest
Trinity	** Trinity Gallery
TTC	Totnes Town Council
TUC	Trades Union Congress
TWBC	Tunbridge Wells Borough Council
TWM	Tyne and Wear Museums
TWT	Waterways Trust
UAFP	** Ulster-American Folk Park
UCL	University College London
UKNIWM	** Imperial War Museum, UK National Inventory of War Memorials
UMBS	** Robertson Museum and Aquarium
UMIS	University Museums in Scotland
UWA	** University of Wales Aberystwyth, School of Art Gallery and Museum
V&A	** Victoria and Albert Museum
VCT	** Vintage Carriages Trust
VGC	** Vintage Glider Club
VOGR	** Vale of Glamorgan Railway Company Limited
WANHS	Wiltshire Archaeological and Natural History Society
Watercress Line	** Mid-Hants Railway (Watercress Line)
WBCT	Wooden Boat Craft Trust
WCBC	Wrexham County Borough Council
WCBS	** Wooden Canal Boat Society Limited
WCHC Ltd	** Llangollen Canal Museum
WDC	Wansbeck District Council
WDC	Warwick District Council
WDC	Wycombe District Council
WHR Porthmadog	** Welsh Highland Railway Limited
WHS	** Wallpaper History Society
WIMM	Welsh Industrial and Maritime Museum
WM	** Wakefield Museum
WMAMS	West Midlands Area Museums Service
WMRMC	** West Midlands Regional Museums Council
WPAT	Whitby Pictorial Archives Trust
WPT	** HMS Warrior (1860) Museum
WRM/RRW	** Welch Regiment Museum (41st/69th Foot) RRW
WSAT	** Sacrewell Farm and Country Centre
WWMHS	** West Wales Maritime Heritage Society
YAM	** Yorkshire Air Museum
YASS	** Yorkshire Art Space Society
YDRMT	* Yorkshire Dales Railway
YSP	** Yorkshire Sculpture Park

Geographical Index

This index has been provided for the convenience of users wishing, either to find what is near to them, or, to plan a trip further afield and more readily find several places to visit.

The first level of index is by country and the second level of indentation is by county or area and is intended to be helpful rather than a rigorous use of the latest local government organisation. The third level is by town, either the actual place or in some cases the nearest location. Finally, the name of the site is followed by the number of the entry in the body of the Directory.

It is particularly important when planning visits to check the times of opening as for several reasons these may sometimes differ from those given in the entry.

England

North Yorkshire

Northamptonshire

Northumberland

Northern Ireland

Scotland

Wales

Channel Islands

Isle of Man

Subject Index

The indexing is based solely on the information provided by the organisations and for this reason in particular the depth of indexing varies considerably. It is nevertheless reasonable to be brief with organisations such as the British Museum or the National Gallery, and more extensive with less well known places with very individual or special collections relevant to local surroundings, history or individuals.

As in the Aslib Directory of Information Sources in the United Kingdom the geographical location of an organisation is shown in the index by the three-letter code in brackets after the name of the organisation. These codes, based on the well-established Chapman Codes for the counties, provide a guide as to where the organisation is located. Thus, if there are many organisations listed under an index term, the user may select one from a particular area. Alternatively it may help the user to eliminate some organisations from the search.

The codes are not intended to be used as part of the address and were felt to be more meaningful and easier to use, for this particular purpose, than the first part of the post code.

Code	County or Area
ABD	Aberdeenshire
BDF	Bedfordshire
BKM	Buckinghamshire
BOR	Borders
BRK	Berkshire
CAM	Cambridgeshire
CEN	Central Region
CHI	Channel Islands
CHS	Cheshire
CLV	Cleveland
CMA	Cumbria
CON	Cornwall
DBY	Derbyshire
DEV	Devon
DGY	Dumfries & Galloway
DOR	Dorset
DUR	Durham
ESS	Essex
EYK	East Yorkshire
FIF	Fifeshire
GLS	Gloucestershire
GMP	Grampian
HAM	Hampshire
HEF	Herefordshire
HLD	Highland
HRT	Hertfordshire
IOM	Isle of Man
KEN	Kent
LAN	Lancashire
LEI	Leicestershire
LIN	Lincolnshire
LND	London

Code	County or Area
LTN	Lothian
MDX	Middlesex
MSY	Merseyside
NBL	Northumberland
NFK	Norfolk
NIR	Northern Ireland
NTH	Northamptonshire
NTT	Nottinghamshire
NBI	Not British Isles
NWS	North Wales
NYK	North Yorkshire
OXF	Oxfordshire
RIR	Republic of Ireland
RUT	Rutland
SAL	Shropshire
SFK	Suffolk
SOM	Somerset
SRY	Surrey
SSX	Sussex
STD	Strathclyde
STS	Staffordshire
SWS	South Wales
SYK	South Yorkshire
TAY	Tayside
TWR	Tyne & Wear
WAR	Warwickshire
WDM	West Midlands
WIL	Wiltshire
WIS	Western Isles
WOR	Worcestershire
WYK	West Yorkshire